2009 Gun Digest®

Edited by
Ken Ramage

Published by

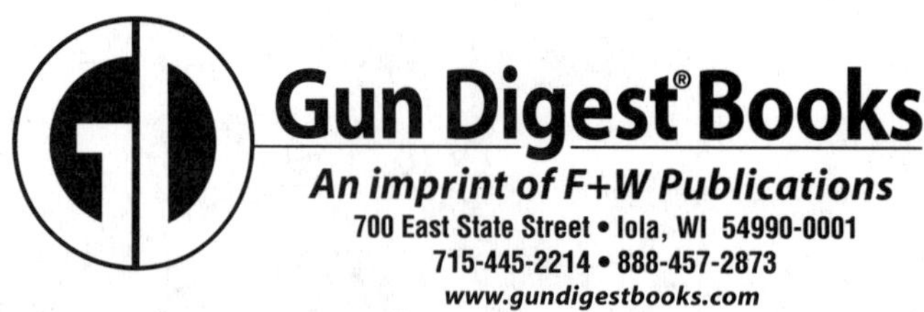

Our toll-free number to place an order or obtain a free catalog is (800) 258-0929.

Manuscripts, contributions and inquiries, including first class return postage, should be sent to the GUN DIGEST Editorial Offices, Gun Digest Books, 700 E. State Street, Iola, WI 54990-0001. All materials recieved will receive reasonable care, but we will not be responsible for their safe return. Material accepted is subject to our requirements for editing and revisions. Author payment covers all rights and title to the accepted material, including photos, drawings and other illustrations. Payment is at our current rates.

CAUTION: Technical data presented here, particularly technical data on handloading and on firearms adjustment and alteration, inevitably reflects individual experience with particular equipment and components under specific circumstances the reader cannot duplicate exactly. Such data presentations therefore should be used for guidance only and with caution. Gun Digest Books accepts no responsibility for results obtained using these data.

ISSN 0072-9043

ISBN 13: 978-0-89689-647-5
ISBN 10: 0-89689-647-1

Designed by Patsy Howell & Tom Nelsen

Edited by Ken Ramage

Printed in the United States of America

TWENTY-SEVENTH ANNUAL

JOHN T. AMBER LITERARY AWARD

Jim Foral

Jim Foral with his favorite rifle, a sporterized Krag that shoots cast bullets extremely well.

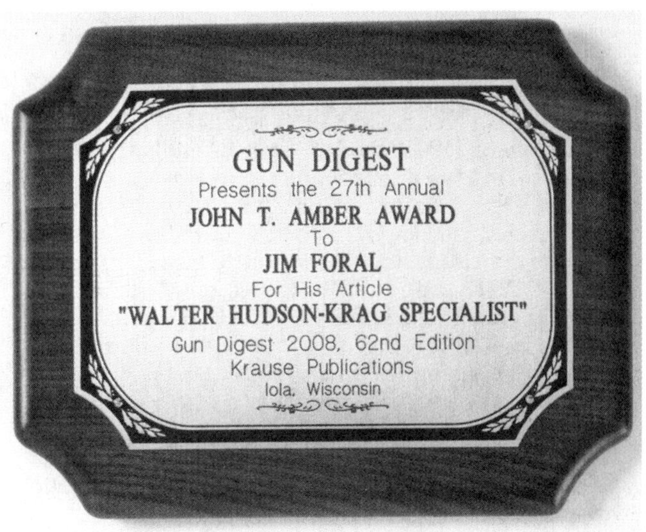

Jim Foral is the winner of this 27th annual John T. Amber Award for his article "Walter Hudson – Krag Specialist", which appeared in GUN DIGEST 2008. This is his second award, his first being for "Lever vs. Bolt" that appeared in GUN DIGEST 2005.

"With fourteen GUN DIGESTS now under my belt, one might conclude that the publisher and I enjoy a good relationship. Over this run, it has been gratifying to mine the pages of the early sporting periodicals and to excavate the forgotten events, trends, and personalities in the rifleman's history. That my stuff continues to be printed demonstrates the abiding public interest in the nostalgic.

"My bride Kathy and I live in Lincoln, Nebraska where I divide my time between shooting, writing and bowfishing."

The only juried literary award in the firearms field, the John T. Amber Award replaced the Townsend Whelen Award originated by the late John T. Amber and later re-named in his honor. Now, a $1000 prize and an engraved brass plaque (new this year) go to the winner of this prestigious annual award.

Nominations for the competition are made by GUN DIGEST editor Ken Ramage and are judged by a distinguished panel of editors experienced in the firearms field. Entries are evaluated for felicity of expression and illustration, originality and scholarship, and subject importance to the firearms field.

This year's Amber Award nominees, in addition to Foral, were:

George Creed, "A Veteran's Story"
Don Findley, "Robert L. Hillberg: Profile of a Firearms Designer"
Hollis M. Flint, "Winchester 22-Caliber Rifles Produced Post-WWII to 1963"
Steve Gash, "The Remington Model 700 Limited Edition Classic, Production History & Cartridge Chronology"
Jesse "Wolf" Hardin, "22 Dreamin': Kids, Rimfire Rifles & the Wild West"
Charles W. Karwan, "You, Me and the CMP"
John Malloy, "Fifty Years in Boy Scout Shooting"
Terry Wieland, "Restored to Life"
Wayne van Zwoll, "Fill Your Hand! …The Best of The Biggest Revolvers"
James E. & Kathleen House, Rimfires From CZ USA – Performance, Looks and Value

Serving as judges for this year's competition were John D. Acquilino, editor of *Inside Gun News*; Bob Bell, former editor-in-chief of *Pennsylvania Game News*; James W. Bequette, v.p., group editorial director of InterMedia Outdoors; David Brennan, editor of *Precision Shooting*; Sharon Cunningham, former director of Pioneer Press; Pete Dickey, former technical editor of *American Rifleman*; Jack Lewis, former editor and publisher of *Gun World; Mark A. Keefe IV*, editor of *American Rifleman* magazine, and Dave Petzal, deputy editor of *Field & Stream*.

INTRODUCTION

We've had another eventful year in the shooting sports. A substantial number of new products were introduced at the 2008 SHOT Show, and more were introduced at the recent NRA Show in Louisville, Ky. Overall, business has been good and the shooting sports has had a good year.

There have been more changes in ownership. The private equity investment firm of Cerberus Capital Management continued its acquisition of firearms companies, to include Marlin Firearms/H&R 1871, Cobb Manufacturing, DPMS and the Iron Brigade Armory.

Two well-known optics brands – Redfield and Weaver – are now under new ownership. In April of this year, owner Meade Instruments sold both to well-known industry companies. Redfield was purchased by Leupold & Stevens. ATK acquired Weaver Optics, which joins (and completes) the existing line of ATK-owned Weaver rings and bases. ATK has only recently introduced a line of shooting sports optics under the Nitrex brand. Earlier, Bushnell was acquired by the private equity firm Mid Ocean Partners.

Industry icon Sturm, Ruger & Company has had two well-known executives move to new endeavors. Bob Stutler retired early this year, following the introduction of Ruger's new LCP 380 ACP pistol at this year's SHOT Show.

Ruger president Steve Sanetti left the company in late spring after many years, to become the new President and CEO of the National Shooting Sports Foundation (NSSF), the organization that owns the annual SHOT Show. Sanetti is an excellent choice for the position, given his many years of high-level industry business exposure and personal shooting experience.

Those of us who are computerized and connected to the Internet now have a couple of additional websites to visit. From the folks at outdoorwire.com (and others), we now have womensoutdoorwire.com and tacticalwire.com. From InterMedia Outdoors we have the new tacticalgunfan.com website. Harris Publications has recently launched a new site called tactical-life.com. Be sure to visit our updated Web Directory towards the back of this edition – check the Contents for the page number.

Like everything else in the economy, prices have gone up for arms and ammunition. The weak dollar makes imported products and raw materials more expensive, and our importers and manufacturers have little choice but to increase prices. As a result, we'll probably see more polymer-frame pistols and long guns wearing synthetic stocks as manufacturers strive to keep their products affordable.

The cost of factory ammunition is up, as are the costs of components. As a result, handloading tools and accessories are selling well, and this traditional shooting sports activity is seeing a nice resurgence.

Hornady and Ruger have combined their resources to introduce two new cartridges – the 300 and 338 Ruger Compact Magnum – and the rifles chambered for them. Also, Ruger teamed with Federal Cartridge to develop the promising new Ruger 327 cartridge – and then delivered the revolver chambered for it. The new, more powerful cartridge was created by simply lengthening the 32 H&R Magnum case. The resulting chamber permits the use of shorter centerfire 32 cartridges if desired, while the new, longer case won't fit into guns chambered for the shorter, earlier 32s.

After many years of contributing the annual report on muzzleloading arms and accessories, J.W. "Doc" Carlson decided to withdraw from the *Gun Digest* staff of contributing editors. We greatly appreciate Doc's efforts and contributions over the years, and wish him and his family all the best.

Our new contributing editor for muzzleloading, Wm. Hovey Smith, is a retired professional geologist who combined his childhood interest in blackpowder guns with his profession to hunt with his favorite muzzleloaders. He started writing outdoor articles in the early 1970s and contributed many articles to national publications, including *Gun Digest*. His interests have always been technology- and hunting-driven, and each year will find him shooting everything from matchlocks to in-lines. Now returned to his native Georgia, he has taken his muzzleloaders throughout North America and also to Africa and Europe. He has several books to his credit and several more in progress, relating to muzzleloading hunting and hunting knives.

We have a somewhat different look this edition, and more articles for you. The article topics are diverse, authoritative and relevant.

Early in the book is the article "Nitro Express!" by Terry Wieland. This article appeared in only a very small portion of the *Gun Digest 2007* print run due to an unusual circumstance — but went on to win the juried 26th annual John T. Amber Award as announced in *Gun Digest 2008*.

Pistol shooters should enjoy Paul Scarlata's article on gunsmithing the new S&W M&P autoloading pistol for USPSA competition. Long-time author Jerry Ahern discusses the revolver for concealed carry and J.M. Ramos installs tactical dress on his Ruger 10/22s.

One of the most eagerly anticipated books that we publish is Flayderman's Guide to Antique American Firearms…and their Values. The brand-new 9th Edition is just out and author Flayderman kindly allowed the publication of an abridged version of his chapter on dueling and dueling pistols. This is probably the most thoroughly researched discussion of dueling and dueling arms to see print.

There are many more articles, of course, and a thoroughly updated and refreshed catalog of currently manufactured firearms and major accessories. The Directory of the Arms Trade has been researched and revised as needed. I hope you enjoy this new edition.

In closing…

This is my final edition as Editor of the *Gun Digest*. Nine editions ago, I succeeded long-time Editor Ken Warner. Nine years–almost a decade–have passed quickly. My retirement begins as this edition, completed, goes to press. I wish you all well; perhaps someday we may share a range day or hunting camp. I'll look forward to that possibility.

Yours truly,

Ken Ramage, Editor
GUN DIGEST

About The Covers

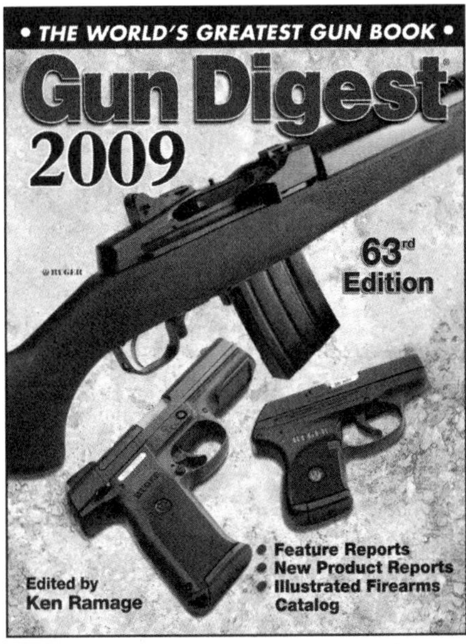

FRONT COVER

(Top) This is the Special Edition Mini-14 Rifle To Benefit NRA-ILA.It features a blued finish and is fitted with a 16 1/8-inch barrel and a patented black Hogue OverMolded stock. The grip cap of the stock features an NRA metal gold-tone logo. This special rifle is chambered for the 223 Remington cartridge and ships with two 20-round magazines. This special edition Mini-14 rifle will only be produced in 2008 and will raise money for the NRA Institute for Legislative Action. Ruger and Hogue partnered on the project. The Mini-14 series of rifles has been extremely popular since the model was first introduced in 1974.

(Lower Left) The 17 + 1-capacity 9mm Ruger SR9 pistol, the first striker-fired pistol from Ruger, is the first model in a new line of high-performance pistols. The SR9 has a short reach from the backstrap to the trigger, slim grip and a narrow slide, creating a comfortable fit for all shooters. The glass-filled nylon frame features a unique reversible backstrap that allows owners to quickly customize the size and feel of the grip, without using separate inserts or special tools. It features an ambidextrous manual safety and magazine latch, and the glass-filled nylon frame and stainless steel slide combine to create a durable, low-maintenance handgun. The rear sight, part of the low profile, high-visibility three-dot sight system, is click-adjustable for elevation. Both front and rear sights are drift-adjustable for windage. A Picatinny rail below the muzzle accepts standard tactical accessories.

(Lower Right) The Ruger LCP (Lightweight Compact Pistol) is an autoloading pistol, chambered for the 380 ACP, that offers typical Ruger reliability and quality in an ultra-light, compact carry pistol form. The 9.4-ounce LCP pistol has a capacity of 6 + 1 rounds of 380 ACP. Only 3.6 inches tall and 0.82-inch wide, the small, lightweight LCP pistol is a reliable back-up or carry pistol.

BACK COVER

The Ruger 22 Charger Pistol is based on the the time-tested Ruger 10/22 rifle action. The 22 Charger, featuring a 10-inch barrel, is mounted in an ergonomically designed, warp-proof laminated stock. The adjustable bipod that ships with every 22 Charger pistol provides added control and stability on the range or in the field. A new extended magazine release facilitates easy removal of the reliable Ruger 10-shot rotary magazine. A combination Weaver-style and "tip-off" sight mount will accommodate your choice of sighting equipment, whether electronic or optical. Sighted either way, this is a nice pistol for long-range target shooting. The 22 Charger pistol has an overall length of 19-1/4 inches and weighs 3-1/2 pounds, without the supplied bipod. The matte black finish compliments the black laminate stock. It comes with a gun rug bearing the Ruger logo.

CONTENTS

ONE GOOD GUN:

REPORTS FROM THE FIELD:

CATALOG OF ARMS AND ACCESSORIES

SMITH & WESSON'S M&P PISTOL FOR USPSA

Practical Plastic for Production

by Paul Scarlata
Photos by Nathan Reynolds

As I finished the stage, the RO instructed me to "Show clear... slide forward...hammer down... and holster." He then, somewhat grudgingly, added, "That's the best run I've seen on this stage so far today." By exerting supreme self-control I was able to keep a straight face while I muttered "thanks," although as I walked back to join my squad, to everyone's delight, I did a little victory dance!

Readers familiar with my crude efforts at journalism are aware that I am an avid (note, I said "avid" not "skillful") action pistol shooter. I first became involved in the sport about thirty years ago when it bore the politically incorrect moniker of "Combat Shooting." My enthusiasm for it grew until, nowadays, most weekends will find me wasting ammunition at various USPSA, IDPA, steel plate and bowling pin matches.

Of the various action pistol disciplines, the one I find most enjoyable are those matches held under the auspices of the USPSA (United States Practical Shooting Association), the U.S. affiliate of the International Practical Shooting Confederation (IPSC).

Over the years two forces have led to both IPSC and USPSA creating new divisions. First we had the so-called "Technology Race" that saw the development of recoil reducing devices (compensators, ported barrels, etc.), electronic dot sights, and high capacity pistols. Shooters who did not wish to, or could not afford to, utilize these mechanical marvels became disenchanted when they had to compete against those who did. The result was the creation of Open and Limited (IPSC - Standard) divisions. The former permitted just about any modification to your handgun that the shooter's bank account could handle while the latter sought to encourage the use of "practical" pistols by forbidding recoil reducing devices, electronic sights, and imposing caliber restrictions. This two tiered system worked well for several years, until......

As competitors are wont to do, Limited shooters began trying to gain an edge and it wasn't long before they were modifying their pistols to the point where they barely – and I mean just barely! – stayed within the limits set down for the division. Once again the hardcore "practical" crowd began crying foul.

The second influence on the sport were firearms laws such as the *Clintonista* high-capacity magazine ban in the United States – and similar laws in other countries – which restricted shooters to 10-round cartridge containers. It was feared that new shooters would be turned off if they had to use an 11-round pistol when competing against

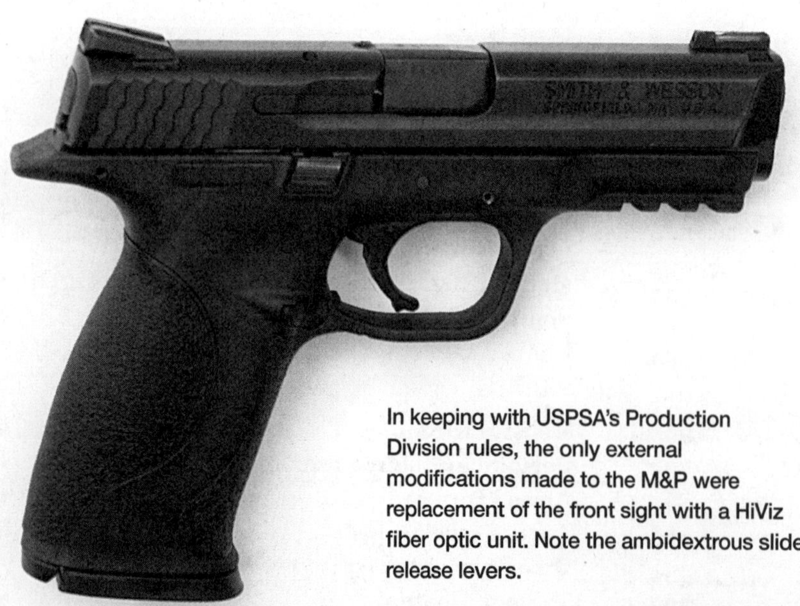

In keeping with USPSA's Production Division rules, the only external modifications made to the M&P were replacement of the front sight with a HiViz fiber optic unit. Note the ambidextrous slide release levers.

1. Power factors are figured by multiplying the bullet weight by velocity and then dividing by 1000. USPSA's Major P.F. is 165 while Minor P.F. is 125.

those Limited shooter who were lucky enough to possess a stockpile of (very expensive) hi-cap magazines. Accordingly, USPSA instituted Limited 10 Division which restricted the shooter to ten rounds loaded in the pistol's magazine, but otherwise the rules are identical the Limited. It proved most popular with owners of single-stack 1911 pistols.

OK, so much for background. As I said at the beginning of this report, I am an avid USPSA shooter. I was turned off by the technology race and began shooting Limited – and ended up spending a lot of money building Limited pistols! In recent years, such mundane matters as putting my daughter through college and graduate school, needing a new car and – *groan!* – buying a house, have put a severe crimp in my "fun funds." Because of this I began looking for a less expensive means of pursuing my favorite sport. Enter Production Division.........

USPSA created Production Division for those persons who wanted to compete with basically factory, stock (read, "inexpensive") pistols. Besides restricting magazine capacity to 10 rounds, there are strict limitations as to what modifications can be made to the pistol (e.g.: internal polishing and detailing of parts, changing the sights, etc.) and the rules mandated that only pistols using DA/SA, DAO or Safe Action type triggers were permitted.

Unlike Open, Limited and Limited Ten divisions, Production did away with the Major/Minor power factor (P.F.) controversy for ammunition by specifying that only Minor P.F. was needed to compete.[1] This had the result of making the readily available, and inexpensive, 9mm Parabellum cartridge the overwhelming choice among Production shooters.

Over the past few years I have used several different pistols in Production division and, while all have proven suitable for the sport, most lacked that "something" that I considered necessary for competition. Last year I obtained a 9mm Smith & Wesson M&P pistol which, until recently, spent most of its time as my "night stand" gun.

The M&P is Smith's newest addition to their extensive line of semi-auto pistols and, IMHO, possibly the best one they have produced so far. Since its introduction, the M&P has been examined extensively in gun magazines and I don't feel it is necessary to repeat the technical nitty-gritty here. Suffice it to say that the M&P is a polymer-framed pistol that uses integral steel rails to strengthen the frame and provide rigidity that improves accuracy and functional reliability. It features a double-action-only (DAO) type trigger, multiple internal safety devices, accepts high-capacity magazines and features an ergonomically-shaped grip with interchangeable inserts (S&W calls them "palm swells") that allow the shooter to fit the pistol to their particular hand size.[2] It is available in 9mm Para, 357 SIG, 40 S&W and 45 ACP, in both standard and compact versions.

I found my M&P a very shootable pistol and, as these things tend to happen, began ruminating upon the idea of using it in competition. With this I mind, I approached my good friend, fellow action pistol shooter, and part-time gunsmith, Lin Webb. Lin has built several competition pistols for me and when I asked him if he could work his magic on the M&P he responded rather guardedly "Well…I haven't done a trigger job on one of them before and, as far as I know, neither has anyone else. I guess someone has to be the first? Leave it with me." I did.

ABOVE: Team S&W shooter Julie Golowski using a 9mm M&P at the 2006 Production Nationals. (Photo courtesy of S&W)

My gunsmith, Lin Webb, used my M&P to compete in several matches before I ever had a chance to try it!

2. I use the medium-sized palm swell which, I guess, means I'm an "average" shooter?

After some time had passed, Lin called and told me *"I think I've figured out how to smooth out the trigger and get the let-off a bit lighter."* The following month, a rather cryptic e-mail arrived from my erstwhile 'smith informing me that *"....I believe it will work. I'm almost done."* A few weeks later a follow-up message arrived *"Yup, it works. I've taken first place Production with it in two matches so far. You're not going to believe the trigger!"* Needless to say, my anxiety level was steadily rising and I could not wait to get my hands on my M&P.

I asked Lin if he would tell the readers in his own words how he accomplished this. No one has ever been able to accuse him of being the taciturn type, so he elaborated thus:

1 Make sure the pistol is unloaded and remove any and all ammo from the same area as the pistol you are working on.

1.1 Make dad-gum sure the gun is unloaded, with no ammo in the same area you are working in.

2 The M&P, like any other semi-auto on the market today, has 'way too much take-up and over-travel as it comes from the factory. Remove the slide, and pull the trigger to the rear and note where the trigger bar engages the sear. If your pistol has the magazine safety, you must hold the mag safety lever up to see this function, so you may as well insert an empty magazine so you'll only need two hands instead of three. If your gun does not have the mag safety lever, you must pull the sear deactivation lever back up in order to see the trigger bar move in its normal operating position. Just be sure to return the deactivation lever to the 'down' position before reassembly.

3 Once you've got it in your head where and how the trigger bar contacts the sear, proceed to remove the sear housing block. Use the correct size pin punch or roll pin punch and remove the pin from the frame. Be sure to support the frame from the bottom so the pin can clear the frame as it is driven out. The pin can be removed from either direction. Then lift the sear housing out of the frame. You can use the same punch you used to remove the pin to pry the sear housing block out of the frame. When you get the sear housing about half-way up, pull the trigger to the rear to take tension off the trigger bar. Continue to lift up on the sear housing, and then it will slide right off the rear of the trigger bar. On older model M&Ps, the ejector will practically fall off the side of the sear housing. This is OK, but on newer models, it will be staked on pretty tightly, so don't bother to remove it.

4 Locate the sear pin, and push it out. It will come out easily and from either direction. Be sure to keep the sear housing in the upright

My newest Production pistol is a customized Smith & Wesson M&P in 9mm. While a number of internal modifications were made, except for one spring all factory parts were used.

The M&P features interchangeable "palm swells" that allow the shooter to fit the pistol to his particular hand size.

position as you remove the pin, and then remove the sear itself. Again, be sure to keep the housing upright so the sear spring and plunger stay in place because if they fall out, they are a pain in the ass to get back in. Use a small piece of leather or wood to clamp the sear in a small vise. Make sure the contact point with the trigger bar is facing up. Using a small fine cut mill file, start cutting the rounded portion of the sear where the trigger bar makes contact. Cut SLOWLY at a 45-degree angle, and remove about 20 percent of this contact point. Finish with a fine cut stone to polish the surface, and then finish by slightly rounding the edges for a smooth "compound" type finish. Then polish the trigger bar where it contacts the sear to a fine mirror-like finish. Remember to go slowly, and don't remove any metal from the trigger bar, just polish only. You might want to put the gun back together at this point to test it out to see where you are. Just this little bit of work will greatly improve the pull.

5 For a further reduced trigger pull weight, remove the sear again and look at the rear of the sear. You'll see a hump where the sear engages the striker and pulls it to the rear during trigger pull. Polish the rear of the sear with a polishing wheel, and also the top flat portion of the sear where the tang of the striker rides across during re-set. Be sure to keep the two surfaces at right angles to each other. In other words, don't round off this edge. Keep it at 90 degrees to each other. Polishing with an aggressive jeweler's polishing compound works quite well. You can also use a Dremel polishing wheel to speed this process, but go slowly. This will remove metal faster than you.think. You can remove the striker now and polish the tang of the striker where it makes contact with the sear. Polish only here, DO NOT remove any metal. To remove the striker, push down on the striker sleeve, just like brand "G" and push the end cap off, while holding your thumb over the striker to keep it from flying into the next room, and remove the striker.

6 To remove the "crunchiness" from the trigger pull, now is the time to do this while the striker is removed. Wrap the slide in several wraps of cloth or use a large piece of leather, and clamp it in a vise with just the rear sight area clear of the vise jaws. Loosen the set screw in the rear sight. Using a brass drift punch, tap the rear sight out from left to right. Don't be afraid to whack it, as some rear sights are tough to remove. Nylon punches give too much, and steel punches will mar the sight. Use a brass punch with nice square edges. If yours is not, straighten it up with a file first. When the sight is almost out, look for the firing pin safety block spring cap and spring underneath the rear sight. Hold your finger over this cap as you continue to tap the sight out. Hold onto to the cap to keep it from flying into the next county. Remember, the striker must be OUT of the gun to be able to do this. Remove the firing pin safety block from the frame.

7 Using a 3/32" pin punch, place the firing pin safety block on the end of the punch. Hold the firing pin block at a 45-degree angle to a 3M polishing wheel and polish the head of the safety block until

The HiViz front sight has the fiber optic rod encased in high-impact polymer to protect it from damage. Its brightness greatly enhances fast target acquisition and accuracy.

The only change I made to the rear sight was to use a marker pen to blacken the dual white dots.

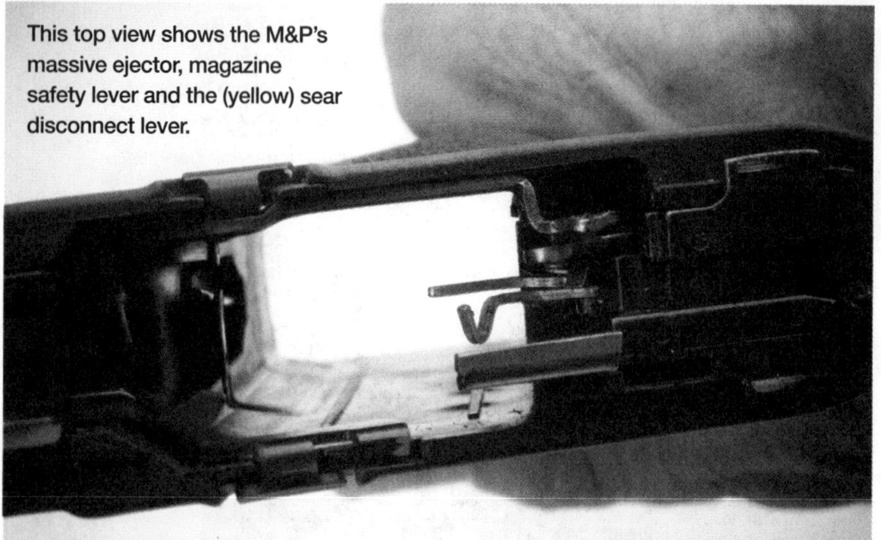

This top view shows the M&P's massive ejector, magazine safety lever and the (yellow) sear disconnect lever.

you have a nice rounded edge all the way around the firing pin block. It will rotate on it's own as you do this. Make sure the polishing wheel rotates downward so as to keep downward pressure on the firing pin block. This will keep it from flying off the pin punch. Do not remove any metal from the top of the firing pin block, just the outer edge only. Be sure to polish the area of the trigger bar that contacts the firing pin block, too. Just polish the trigger bar contact points for the sear and the firing pin safety block contacts to a mirror finish, do not remove any metal from these two areas of the trigger bar. Clean the hole where the firing pin block goes and lube it with a good quality gun lube. Put the firing pin block back in, along with the small spring. Start the rear sight into the dovetail from right to left. Place the spring cap on top of the spring and press it into place. While holding it there, tap the rear sight back over this assembly to hold it in place. Don't let go until the rear sight has almost covered the cap or it will fly out. NOTE: This procedure is very tricky, but go slow and you can do it. Some rear sights are easier to get out and back in than others on the same model gun, so don't be afraid to whack the hell out of it with a brass punch to get it to move. Brass marks can be easily removed with 0000 steel wool.

8 There is one last thing you can do for the ultimate M&P trigger job. Obtain a Glock trigger return spring and replace the stock M&P trigger spring with this spring. Be sure to place the open end of the spring on the trigger bar in the UP position. The end that goes on the trigger pin must be slightly enlarged to fit over the M&P trigger pin, but it can be done. Use a pin punch of the proper size as a guide to align the pin hole and spring as you tap the trigger pin back in. If you have done everything as I have described it, you will have a much improved trigger pull over the stock configuration. If you shoot a lot of USPSA or IDPA matches, your scores will definitely improve. There are several M&P triggers jobs described on the Internet now, and they are very much like I have described it here, however, you must have some familiarity with the M&P to perform these modifications correctly. It isn't as easy as some would have you believe.

I have found out that the 45-caliber M&P differs slightly from the 9mm, 40 S&W, and the 357 SIG calibers. The firing pin is different, the angles on the trigger and sear are different, and pretty much everything as far as a trigger job goes is different, so take your time on the 45s. Again, go slow, and don't remove too much. If you don't feel comfortable doing it yourself, then you will be way ahead of the game to send your gun

For competition I used a Comp-Tac Belt Holster and Beltfeed staggered magazine pouches (opposite page).

Smith & Wesson M&P
Specifications:

Caliber: 9mm, 357 SIG & 40 S&W
OAL: 7.5 inches
Barrel length: 4.25 inches
Height: 5.5 inches
Width: 1.2 inches
Weight (unlocked): 27.45 ounces
Magazine: 17 rounds (9mm)
15 rounds (.357 & .40)
Construction:
frame: Zytel Polymer
slide: Stainless steel with Melonite finish
Sights:
front: Steel Ramp
rear: Novak Lo-Mount

out to some of the shops that advertise M&P trigger jobs on the Internet.

Since working on Paul's pistol, I've done about two dozen M&P trigger jobs without any failure, and no safety parts violations, but they were T&E guns and they were not returned to the general shooting public. Most all of these guns broke the trigger pull gauge at around 3 pounds, and were smooth as silk. If you feel like it, and have the confidence, give it a try. You might want to purchase a spare sear, safety block, and trigger bar from Smith & Wesson just in case you mess something up. That way you can put stock parts back in and get the gun back up and shooting again.

As I make no pretense whatsoever to being technically minded, I will have to take what Lin said at face value. But I can tell you this: once I finally retrieved my M&P from Mr. Webb's clutches, and got a chance to try it, I was most impressed. The trigger take-up was so light and smooth as to be almost unnoticeable; the let-off was a crisp 2.5 pounds while reset distance was less than a half-inch. During rapid fire drills it almost felt as if I was shooting a single-action pistol.

In fact, after getting my M&P back the *only* changes I made to it were to install a HiViz fiber optic front sight and use a marker pen to blacken out the white dots on the rear sight. Aside from the trigger return spring and front sight replacement it remains a100-percent stock pistol and thus abides by USPSA rules to the letter! [3]

Being the M&P has fixed sights I experimented with various brands of factory and handloaded ammo and eventually settled on Cor-Bon's 9mm 147-grain Performance Match ammunition for serious competition shooting. I have used this ammo in several pistols over the years and it has proven to be the most accurate 9mm load I have ever shot. My handload consists of a Berry's 147-grain plated bullet over 3.6 grains of TiteGroup. Both provide 100-percent functioning, shoot close enough to point out to 25 yards to keep me happy, produce low levels of recoil and make Minor P.F. with a bit to spare.

I also experimented with a number of holsters and mag pouches and settled on a Comp-Tac Belt Holster and Belt-feed magazine pouches. The former holds the M&P at just the right height and angle for a fast acquisition and smooth draw while the latter rig holds four spare magazines in a staggered row allowing a fast, secure grip on each to ensure fast and smooth reloads.

Unfortunately, I did not have an opportunity to practice very much with my M&P before the next match but, despite the trepidation I felt at competing with a pistol I had little experience with, I finished 2nd Place overall in Limited Division and 1st Place in B Class. And while I like to think that my personal skill (?) had a little something to do with it, a good measure of the credit must go to Lin's excellent trigger job and the accuracy, reliability and ergonomics that were built into the M&P at the factory.

The M&P has served as my regular Production pistol for several months now and my positive opinion of it continues to grow. As Humphrey Bogart said at the end of his classic film *Casablanca*, "....I think this is the beginning of a beautiful friendship."

Test firing results:	Group Size	Velocity
Cor-Bon 147 gr. Performance Match	1.75"	878 fps
Berry's 147 gr. Plated/3.6 TiteGroup	2"	865 fps

For further information:

Berry's Manufacturing - 401 North 3050 East St. George, Utah 84790. http://www.berrysmfg.com
Cor-Bon Ammunition - 1311 Industry Rd., Sturgis, SC 57785. www.dakotaammo.net
Comp-Tac - P.O. Box 1809 Spring, Texas 77373. http://www.comp-tac.com
Smith & Wesson - 2100 Roosevelt Ave, Springfield, MA 01104. www.smith-wesson.com

3. I inquired of USPSA as to the legality of changing trigger return spring and received the following e-mail: Item 21.4 of the Production rules, allows for action work to enhance reliability, throating, trigger work, etc., this would mean that while doing the action work, springs may be replaced.
John Amidon, VP USPSA, Director NROI

ALL YOU NEED IS A 300 SAVAGE

by Harvey T. Pennington

A hunter's first elk is something to be remembered. Here the author packs out the head of the four-point he took with the 300 Savage.

Sometimes, the inspiration to acquire a particular rifle comes from a most unexpected source. It happened to me once on, of all things, an archery elk hunt in Colorado.

Along with my friends, Glen Buckner and Don Evans, I was enjoying a September elk hunt in the Flattop mountains near Sweetwater Lake in central Colorado, at a location known locally as the Sweetwater Cow Camp. Occasionally, from our tent camp, we would catch a glimpse of a well-known resident of the area. His name was Sam Carr, but he was more commonly referred to by those who lived in the area as "Cowboy" Sam. During the spring, summer and fall, he lived in a small log cabin there at the cow camp and tended to the many cattle, owned by his employer, which grazed in the surrounding hills.

At the time, Sam was probably in his late sixties. He was small in stature, and, by all appearances, arthritic. From our tent we could sometimes see him lead his horse over next to a stump, upon which he would stand so that he could more easily mount.

One mid-day after we had finished our morning's hunt, we decided to pay a call on Cowboy Sam. We walked from our tent over to his cabin and knocked on the door. He opened it and welcomed us in. We had a grand visit with that fine gentleman, during which he shared with us some of his stories about his many years of working as a cowboy, and some of his experiences with the elk in the area. He even showed us an article that had been written about him and published in, I believe, *The American Horseman* magazine.

But, it was when our conversation inevitably got around to elk hunting that I (being more a rifle hunter than a bowhunter) just had to ask his opinion regarding what he considered to be a good rifle for elk. He didn't hesitate in the least before answering, "Aw, all you need is a 300 Savage!"

Well, now, I've got to admit that I was expecting a different answer, one that would have emphasized the need for a more powerful rifle of some type. But, Cowboy Sam had lived and worked much, if not most, of his life in some of the best elk country in the United States, and, it seemed to me, should have had good reason for his opinion.

SAVAGE MODEL 99-EG SOLID FRAME, LEVER ACTION, HIGH POWER REPEATERS

(Top Illustration. Manufacture resumed, Fall 1945.)

Introduced in 1899 in .303 Savage Cal. Action is the same today except for minor improvements. Has 24" tapered, medium weight round barrel. Proof tested. Matted trigger. Rotary box type magazine with numeral indicator. Capacity 5 cartridges plus one in chamber. Light weight, capped, full pistol grip stock and tapered fore-end of selected walnut. Rubbed oil finish, checkered grip and fore-end. Corrugated steel butt plate of shotgun design. Stock dimensions 13" x 1⅞" x 2⅝". Butt plate 1½" x 4⅞". Adjustable semi-buckhorn sporting rear sight and white metal bead front sight on raised ramp base. Case hardened lever. Polished breech bolt. Blued receiver. Receiver tang tapped and drilled for all standard aperture sights. Weight about 7¼ lbs. Calibers: .250/3000 for deer, mountain sheep and goat, etc.; .300 Savage for Alaskan Bear, moose, elk, etc.

SAVAGE MODEL 99-R

(Lower Illustration)

Same as Model 99-EG except larger stock. Dimensions 13½" x 1⅝" x 2⅞", butt plate 1⅝" x 5⅛". Also special large fore-end. Weight about 7½ lbs. Caliber: .300 Savage.

SAVAGE MODEL 99-RS

Same specifications as Model 99-R with following refinements: Redfield No. 70 windage and elevation adjustment rear peep sight and gold bead front sight; ⅞" leather sling strap with quick release swivels and screw studs.

22

This advertisement for the Savage Model 99-EG was reprinted from the 2nd annual edition of Gun Digest (1945). It is to be noted that the Savage Arms Company promoted its 300 Savage cartridge for use in hunting heavier North American game such as moose, elk and "Alaskan Bear." Gunwriters of the time generally agreed that the 300 was perfectly capable of handling such game, in the hands of a good shot.

The Savage Model 99 was a lightweight, easy-to-carry rifle that, because of its trim profile, also carried well in a saddle scabbard. This early (1904) calendar illustration was obviously intended to emphasize that advantage. Indeed, various calibers and styles of the M99 were favored as big-game hunting rifles by many who spent much of their working time on horseback, or others who simply accessed hunting country with the use of horses.

Well, just a few months later, I was browsing in an area gun store back home in Kentucky and saw a Savage Model 99-EG, with a 24-inch barrel. The M99-EG style has a thin forend with a Schnable tip and both the forend and buttstock are checkered; you may already have guessed that it was chambered for the 300 Savage cartridge. The seed that Sam Carr had sown in my mind was about to sprout.

The old M99 (manufactured in the early 1950s) had seen some use, and wouldn't have been a contender in a best-looking-rifle contest. Its buttstock had a significant gouge on its left side, the rear of the forend had a couple of minor cracks and the original blue on the receiver had faded to gray. Otherwise, however, the rifle appeared to be in sound shape. The price was very reasonable, and with Cowboy Sam's recommendation still fresh in my memory, I just couldn't resist. It went home with me.

Even though my friend, Thom Clay, and I had an elk hunt scheduled for Colorado the next October, I wasn't really planning to use the 300 on that hunt. I had at least a couple of other rifles that would do very nicely, and with which I felt quite comfortable. But, as soon as I started working with the old Model 99, the possibility of using it on that year's elk hunt quickly gained momentum.

Of course, I did make some minor modifications to the rifle so that it would better suit my needs. I mounted a Lyman rear aperture sight to the tang of the rifle, and replaced the factory front bead sight with a Redfield "sourdough" front sight. I freshened the original wood finish with Birchwood Casey's Tru-Oil. Also, I added swivels and a carrying sling.

This was my first M99 Savage, and I was impressed when I had time to become acquainted with its unique features. The rotary magazine of the 99 was easy to load, and the cartridges cycled quickly and surely through the action. The magazine's "counter" permitted the shooter to quickly determine (at a glance, through a "window" on the left side of the receiver) the number of cartridges remaining in the magazine. A cocking indicator was conveniently located on the top of the receiver allowing the shooter to know that the rifle was ready to fire, either by glancing at it or simply by feeling it with his thumb. A sliding safety was located just behind the trigger on the right side where it could easily be engaged or disengaged with just a slight movement of the trigger finger. When engaged, the safety not only blocked the trigger from moving, it also locked the lever in place; and, as a bonus to the needs of the hunter, the sliding feature of the safety permitted it to be operated in complete silence.

Being light in weight, and having a flat-sided receiver, the old lever-action rifle was easy to carry and had, well, a friendly, natural feel to it. Its trim dimensions certainly appealed to those who would carry the rifle in a saddle scabbard, an attribute that the Savage company pointed out in sporting illustrations that accompanied some of their advertisements.

Another advantage of the Savage

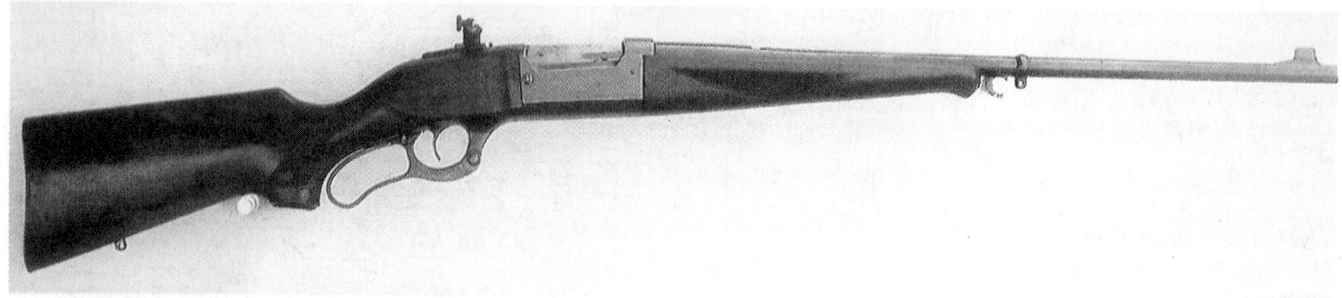

ABOVE: The author's purchase of this Savage Model 99-EG, in the 300 Savage chambering, was inspired by an old cowboy who worked in central Colorado, out of an area known as the Sweetwater Cow Camp. Author's rifle was manufactured in the early 1950s, and far from being in "mint" condition when he bought it. However, the old '99 still functioned flawlessly and shot quite well.

BELOW: The safety of the older Savage 99 was located just to the rear of the trigger, on the right side, where it easily could be manipulated by the shooter's trigger finger. When fully engaged, the safety not only blocked the trigger, it also locked the lever. As a bonus to the hunter, this was a sliding safety, and could be operated silently.

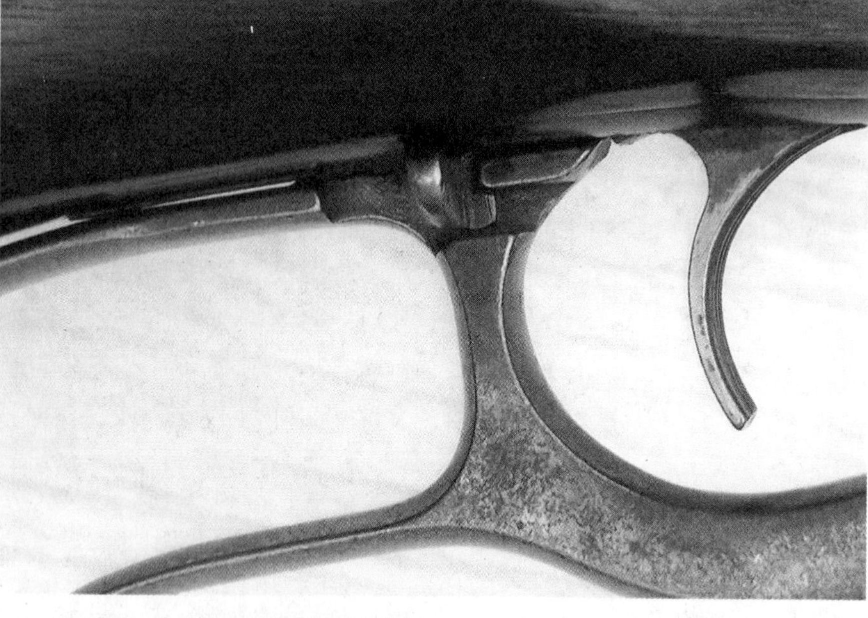

M99 was that it was designed to eject empty cases or unfired cartridges to the right side of the receiver. This feature enabled those who would choose to use a hunting scope to mount it directly on top of the receiver. The top-ejection lever actions, such as the various Winchesters, required a side mount if a scope were to be used, in order to avoid ejection interference. Savage's design was much friendlier to scope-sight users.

When the Savage Model 99 (then the Model 1899) was introduced, it was chambered for the 303 Savage. As originally loaded, that cartridge used a 195-grain softpoint bullet at a velocity of 1,952 fps. Other older chamberings for which the M99 was made available were the 32-40, 38-55, 25-35 and 30-30. The year 1912 saw the introduction of the 22 Savage Hi-Power, an innovative smallbore centerfire cartridge that created quite a stir.

In 1915, the M99 was chambered for the 250-3000 Savage, a stunning new rimless high-velocity cartridge. The 250-3000 proved a very popular cartridge, firing lightweight 87- and 100-grain bullets at 3,000 fps and 2,790 fps, respectively. Although considered suitable for smaller big game, such as deer and antelope, the 250 was seen by most hunters as lacking the requisite power for consistent clean kills on the heavier big game.

Then, in 1920, the Savage Arms Company announced a new cartridge chambered for the M99 that it felt would meet the requirements of those seeking a high-velocity lever-action cartridge for game as heavy as elk, moose and the larger bears. That cartridge was

One of the unique features of the old-style M99s was the port on the left side of the frame allowing the shooter to see the "numeral indicator" which displayed the number of rounds remaining in the rifle's rotary magazine. The author's 300 can hold up to five rounds in the magazine, plus one in the chamber.

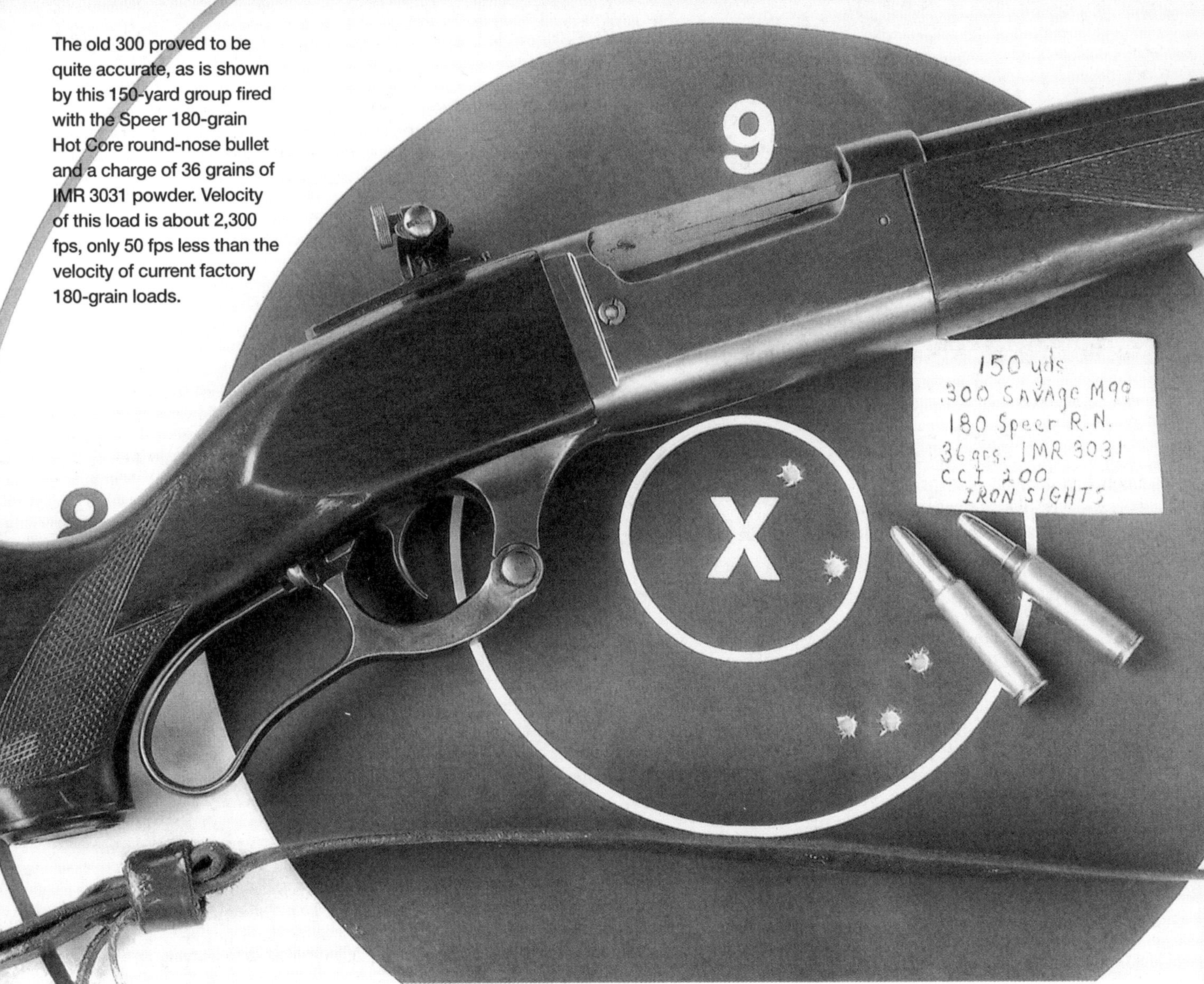

The old 300 proved to be quite accurate, as is shown by this 150-yard group fired with the Speer 180-grain Hot Core round-nose bullet and a charge of 36 grains of IMR 3031 powder. Velocity of this load is about 2,300 fps, only 50 fps less than the velocity of current factory 180-grain loads.

the 300 Savage. The 300 cartridge was originally loaded with 150-grain bullets and was initially listed as having a velocity of 2,700 fps fully the equal of the original loading of the 30 Government 1906 cartridge with its 150-grain loads. Muzzle energy for this loading was 2,426 foot-pounds (fpe), and the mid-range trajectory over 200 yards was just 2.9 inches! About six years later, the Savage company announced the addition of a 180-grain load for the 300 Savage, which had a published velocity of 2,400 fps.

For fans of the lever-action rifle, this new Savage cartridge had to be welcome news. As noted an authority as Col. Townsend Whelen stated that the 300 Savage *"...is one of the few cartridges adapted to lever action rifles that may be said to be powerful enough for any American big game. Reports from the game fields have shown it to kill all game very well. Apparently the cartridge loaded with 180 grain bullets is a little more effective on the larger animals like moose, elk, and large bear, than that loaded with the 150 grain bullet."*

Whelen's opinion was shared by many others, including Jack O'Connor, the long-time Shooting Editor of *Outdoor Life* magazine. O'Connor wrote that *"In 300 Savage caliber, with a 150-grain bullet at approximately 2,700 [fps], and a 180-grain bullet at close to 2,400, the 300 Savage is adequate for any North American big game...."*

Incidentally, one of the most famous users of the 300 Savage was the great Canadian outfitter and guide of the early- to mid-1900s, Bert Riggall (the father-in-law of Canadian writer, Andy Russell), who found the cartridge to be sufficiently powerful for all British Columbia game. Coming from a man of Riggall's experience, that is a compelling recommendation of the 300's power, indeed.

Of course, for the handloader who works with the M99, one dimension that must be kept in mind is that the cartridge must not exceed an overall length of 2.6 inches. And, as with most rear-locking lever actions, the fired cases must be trimmed regularly and checked for any signs of incipient casehead separations.

Since my immediate goal was to develop a load for hunting elk, I decided to forego the 150-grain bullets and concentrate on working up a good 180-grain load. For loading information, I have an extensive library of loading manuals, both current and out-of-print editions. While comparing the information in some of these manuals, it seemed that IMR 3031 was especially compatible with the 180-grain bullet in the

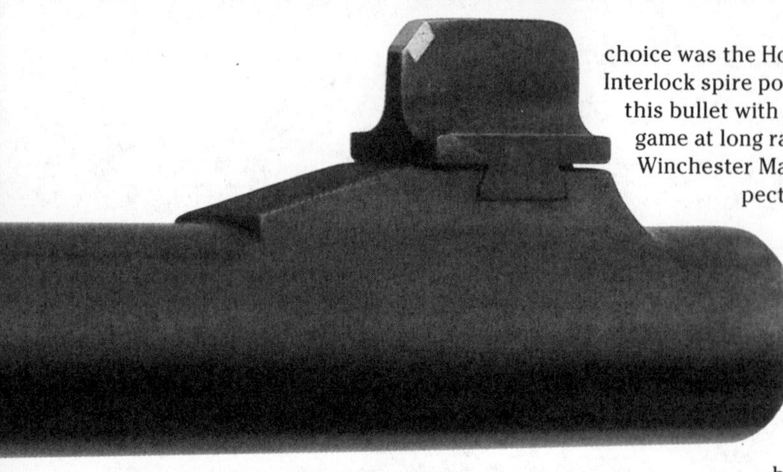

The original factory bead-type front sight of the M99-EG was replaced with an old Redfield "Sourdough" front sight. With its bright brass insert, set on an angle of 45 degrees, this style of front sight is very visible in low-light hunting conditions and is the perfect companion to the Lyman receiver sight.

300 Savage cartridge, and it was with that powder that I started my tests.

As for a bullet, it must be remembered that the rotary magazine of the M99 permits the use of spitzer bullets, so the handloader is not limited in his bullet choice to blunt or flat-nosed bullets as he would be if loading for a rifle having a tubular magazine. My bullet of choice was the Hornady 180-grain Interlock spire point. I had used this bullet with success on game at long range with a 300 Winchester Magnum, and I expected that it would perform as well at shorter, woods-hunting distances in the Savage. Also, this bullet has a flat base, and does not extend as deeply below the neck of the case as would a boat-tail bullet of the same weight. This is critical in considering bullets for use in the M99 Savage, since the maximum overall cartridge length must be kept to only 2.6 inches, and longer bullets simply extend too deeply into the case and unnecessarily limit the powder capacity.

I settled on a load of 36 grains of IMR 3031, and a CCI 200 primer, behind the 180-grain Hornady Spire Point bullet. Velocity ran an average of about 2,300 fps from the 24-inch barrel of my M99. Accuracy was acceptable, with groups averaging around 2 1/2-inches at 100 yards. I sighted the rifle in for 150 yards. With that sighting and load, my bullet would have a drop of only about three inches at 200 yards, which I considered to be the maximum distance at which I should attempt to take an elk with my 300.

So, just over one year later, in October, I was back hunting elk in Colorado's Flattop Mountains near the Sweetwater cow camp. Thom Clay was with me, and the modern rifle season was in. There were several inches of snow on the ground as we left our tent and climbed into the surrounding hills to hunt on the cold opening morning of the season.

We hiked into the black timber above our camp, and, at a certain point, separated, each following a different trail, planning to rendezvous back at our tent around lunch time. The 99 Savage felt just right as I climbed the mountain by way of one of the many game trails in the area.

I was walking slowly, and couldn't have been more than half a mile from where Thom and I had parted company, when I came upon the tracks of several elk in the snow. They were fresh, very fresh. I slipped off my daypack and removed the newly-formed ice from my canteen to eliminate that source of noise.

I took up the trail of the elk, moving slowly. Barely ten minutes had passed when I was surprised to see a large bull elk jump up about 50 yards ahead of me and run to the right, over the side of the hill and out of sight. It had happened so quickly that I hadn't even been able to fully raise my rifle. Just as I was about to curse my bad luck, and apparent lack of attention, another sizeable bull did exactly the same thing. Realizing that a pattern seemed to be developing here, I focused on the spot where they had both appeared, just as a third, smaller bull slowly and deliberately rose from his bed.

This third bull, a four-point, stared in my direction as I slowly raised the 300 to my shoulder. He stood facing me, quartering

The author replaced the 99's factory open rear sight with a Lyman receiver sight, which he greatly prefers for hunting. When hunting, the sight disc insert is removed, and the sight's larger opening is used in the low-light conditions generally encountered when hunting in the timber. Note the position of the M99's cocking indicator, located just in front of the sight base.

This is a lineup of some of the 180-grain bullets suitable for use in the M99 300 Savage. From the left: a Hornady Interlock Spire Point bullet, like the one author used to take his elk; a Hornady round-nose bullet; a Speer Hot Core, author's present favorite; and a Sierra round nose.

slightly to my right. He hesitated too long and the shiny brass insert of the Sourdough front sight found his chest, just in front of the point of his right shoulder. The rifle cracked and the four-point charged off in the same direction that the two larger bulls had taken.

I felt sure of the shot, and, shortly after the bull disappeared from view, the noise he made as he rushed down the hill and through the trees suddenly ceased. Surprisingly, there was no blood trail evident as I followed his tracks down the hill, but the bull had managed to travel only about 60-70 yards before falling, and was dead when I arrived.

After field-dressing the elk, I carried the head and cape back towards camp. Clay, having heard the shot, met me along the way. When we made it back to camp, we gathered our packframes and spent the rest of the day skinning and quartering the elk and packing out the meat.

We were unable to recover the bullet, which had coursed, lengthwise, deeply into the bull's body. Certainly, the bullet had done a good job, except for one thing: there was no blood trail at all. Of course, the lack of a blood trail is not so unusual on an animal the size of an elk, especially when there is no exit wound. With a sharply-pointed 30-caliber bullet, the entrance hole in the hide is usually a very small one. As the animal runs, the hide can shift, blocking the entrance hole and not permitting blood to escape for some time.

That there was no blood trail was not particularly important in this instance, since there had been plenty of tracking snow on the ground. But, it could have been very important if there had been no snow and if the bull had covered more ground before falling. This is one of the reasons I abandoned using spitzer bullets in the 300 for woods hunting and now use round-nose bullets that create a somewhat larger entrance hole, enhancing the chances for a blood trail.

Another advantage of handloading the round-nose 180-grain bullet is that it is quite a bit shorter than a spitzer bullet of the same weight, and intrudes less into the available powder space of the cartridge when each is loaded to the maximum 2.6 inches overall length required by the M99's magazine. After all, the 300 Savage has a very limited powder capacity to begin with. That is probably the reason that Savage's factory-loaded ammunition for the 300 used a "sharp nose" 150-grain bullet, but a "blunt nose" 180-grain bullet.

My favorite round-nose bullet for handloads in the Savage is the 180-grain Speer Hot Core. That bullet does seem to hold together well, and, although I have never had the opportunity to take an elk with it, it shows great power (i.e., great penetration and expansion) on deer. I would not hesitate to use it for elk in the timber, provided a good shot were presented. My favorite load with the Speer round-nose bullet is the same 36-grain load of 3031 that I used with the Hornady spire point to take the elk. The Speer bullet is very accurate, giving 5-shot groups at 150 yards of about 3 inches. Its velocity is about 50 fps slower than the 2,350 fps, which is the current listing for factory 180-grain loads, but its power on game is still very impressive.

As with any rear-locking lever-action rifle, stretching of cases from the use of heavy loads can be an issue. Here, a crack can be seen on a 300 Savage case that had been fired several times; one more shot and this case would have had a complete casehead separation, leaving the "headless" case stuck in the rifle's chamber.

Of course, the 30-caliber bullets of the 300 Savage should not be used for "quartering away" or so-called "raking" shots on elk where the bullet must penetrate much of the length of the animal in order to reach the vital area. As a matter of fact, I don't know of any 30-caliber rifles that I would trust for that job, even with the new "premium" bullets so plentiful today.

One of the old-timers who often relied on such raking shots was the great writer, guide and outdoorsman, Elmer Keith, who hunted elk primarily in the steep, densely timbered wilderness areas of Idaho and Montana. But, as he constantly reminded his readers, for those difficult quartering-away shots he favored larger-caliber rifles and longer, heavier bullets. More than likely, that is the reason that in his description of the 300 Savage, Keith did not specifically refer to it as an elk cartridge, but rather, in his words, as *"...one of the nicest lever action .30 caliber deer and black bear cartridges.... With the 180-grain Soft Point*

Unlike lever rifles with tubular magazines, the Savage 99's rotary magazine permits the use of spitzer (pointed) bullets, but they are much longer than round-nose bullets of the same weight. When seated so that the overall length of the cartridge is kept to 2.6" (as required by the M99's magazine) this 180 Hornady Spire Point intrudes into the already-limited powder space of the comparatively small 300 Savage case. For this reason, author prefers the shorter round- or blunt-nose bullets when 180-grain bullets are to be used.

During the preparation of this article, author chronographed some Winchester and Remington factory 150-grain loads and found their velocities to be virtually identical to the 2,630 fps which is the current published standard for this weight bullet. 300 Savage factory loads are available for both the 150- and 180-grain bullets. Judging from the number of 300s still in use, those factory loads will continue to be manufactured well into the future.

bullet, it is capable of penetrating considerable brush, but owing to its higher velocity is not quite as good a brush cutter as the .33 WCF and .35 Remington, nor does it pack the actual wallop of those two fine loads. It is, however, a more versatile load, in that it can reach out to longer range. Likewise its higher velocity usually kills deer mighty well with lung shots. The 180-grain bullet should always be used in dense heavy timber for close range, but where the timber is more open and that occasional 200-yard shot is offered, the 150-grain load is then better. Effective range is extended out to about 250 yards with the 300 Savage."

Even though the M99 rifle is now out of production, it is still more often used than most would believe. Just before beginning this article, I was talking to my Wyoming friend, Ken Swick, who is a working cowboy. Some years ago, Ken's grandfather, who also had been a cowboy, gave Ken his saddle and rifle. The rifle was a M99 300 Savage. Ken told me that he used his grandfather's rifle (equipped only with factory open sights) this past fall to take a buck mule deer on the ranch where he works. Ken's deer was taken with an old 150-grain Winchester Silvertip factory load at about 175 yards. The deer was hit in the shoulder and died on the spot, without any noticeable movement after hitting the ground.

While on the subject of those 150-grain 300 Savage loads, I did chronograph two different factory loads that had been sitting on my shelves for a number of years. The first was the Western Super X 150-grain Silvertip loading like the one Ken Swick had used to take his deer. It was very accurate and gave an average velocity over my chronograph of 2,618 fps. The second was a box of Remington 150-grain Core-Lokt loads, which chronographed at an average of 2,634 fps, and were also quite accurate. By the way, today's standard velocity for factory 150-grain loads in the 300 Savage is 2,630 fps, virtually identical to my results with both the Super X and Remington loads. At times, I use a slightly lighter handload of 38 grains of IMR 3031, which pushes a 150-grain Hornady Spire Point bullet along at 2,500 fps.

I would be remiss if I did not point out that anyone who handloads for a rear-locking lever-action rifle should always be aware of the possibility of case head separations. That includes those who reload for the M99 Savage. The cartridge case, especially with full-power reloads, does stretch somewhat upon being fired. When it is resized, reloaded and fired again, it stretches again. The stretching is most likely to occur just forward of the extractor groove of the case where the brass thins down to form the inside wall of the case. Eventually, the stretching will work-harden the brass at that point and a crack will appear or, in the worst scenario, a complete casehead separation will occur.

Those who have experienced complete casehead separations know that they should be avoided whenever possible. Obviously, this can be a dangerous situation if some of the gas leaks back into the action. But, even if it does not, I can assure you from first-hand experience that it can be most frustrating trying to remove the headless case from the chamber of the rifle.

While working with my M99 for this

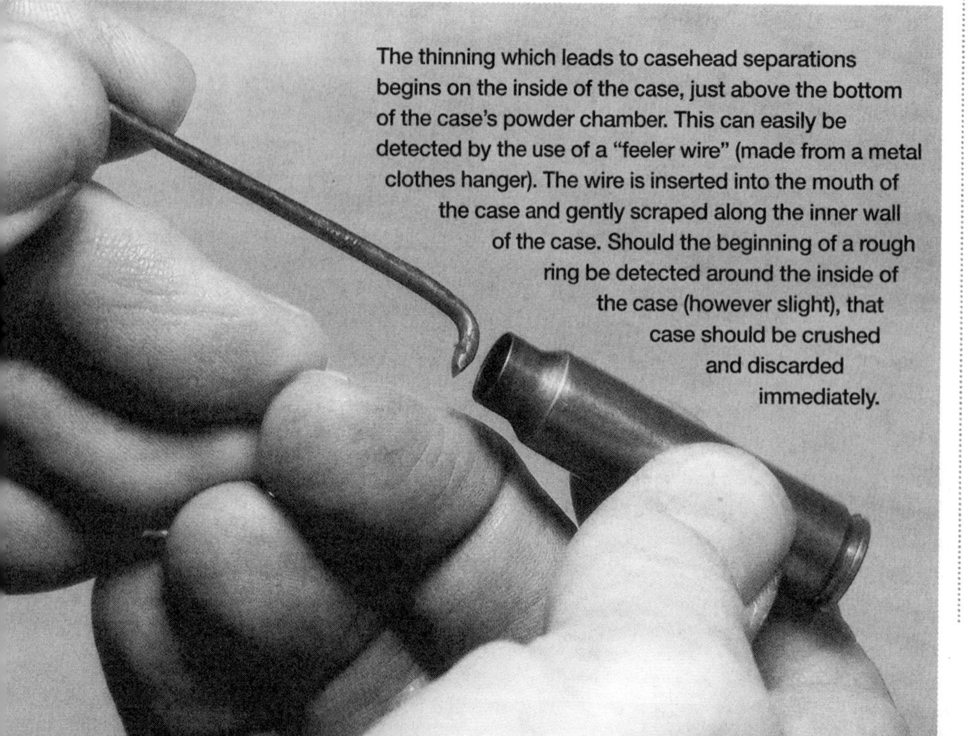

The thinning which leads to casehead separations begins on the inside of the case, just above the bottom of the case's powder chamber. This can easily be detected by the use of a "feeler wire" (made from a metal clothes hanger). The wire is inserted into the mouth of the case and gently scraped along the inner wall of the case. Should the beginning of a rough ring be detected around the inside of the case (however slight), that case should be crushed and discarded immediately.

article, I did have one crack appear (i.e., an "incipient" casehead separation) just forward of the extractor groove on one of my fired 300 cases. I happened to see the crack when I was inserting the case in my case trimmer and, of course, discarded the case. Had I failed to notice the crack and reloaded and fired that case again, there is no doubt that the head of the case would have completely separated, leaving the body of the case stuck in the rifle's chamber.

Several things can be done by the handloader to avoid or minimize this problem. ***First***, the resizing die should be set to resize the fired case the very minimum amount necessary to permit the chambering of the loaded round; if the shoulder of the case is moved back more than necessary during the resizing operation, too much headspace will result, and the case will stretch excessively upon being fired. ***Second***, maximum loads should be avoided; case life can be extended greatly by loading just under the maximum permissible loads. ***Third***, the cases should be visually inspected before each loading, and a "feeler wire" of some kind should be used to detect any thinning on the inside of the lower case wall. My feeler wire is simply a 4-inch piece of clothes-hanger wire, one end of which is sharpened; the last 1/4-inch of the sharpened end is then bent to a 90-degree angle. The sharpened end of this tool is inserted into the case mouth and is used to gently scrape along the lower part of the inner wall of the case to locate any roughened line around the inside of the case, which would indicate that a crack is forming. In the event that such a line is found, that case should be immediately crushed and discarded. ***Finally***, cases should not be expected to last forever, so after, say, four or five firings with heavy handloads (or whatever number your experience tells you), discard those cases and begin using some new ones.

Just because a particular cartridge has declined in popularity certainly doesn't mean that it is no longer a good one. Popularity of the 300 Savage cartridge began to wane after the introduction (in 1952) of the now-famous 308 Winchester, which could produce an additional 200-300 fps over the Savage's ballistics using the same 150- and 180-grain bullet weights. However, Savage continued to produce their 300 in the M99-E Economy Carbine until 1984, when that model (the last rotary-magazine M99) was discontinued.

Once the elk is on the ground, the real work begins. The author and his hunting partner spent the rest of the day skinning, quartering and packing out the elk meat. The four-point was taken in the black timber above the high meadow pictured in the background.

Interestingly, according to D. P. Murray, author of *The Ninety-Nine: A History of the Savage Model 99 Rifle (Revised Third Edition)*, it was the 300 Savage round that was modified by the Army to develop the 7.62 NATO (308) cartridge. The physical similarity of those two rounds is obvious.

Of course, factory ammunition for the 300 Savage (both the 150- and 180-grain loads) continues to be produced and, judging from the number of 300s still in use, it will be available for many, many years to come. The round itself is just as good and just as effective as it ever was. It will continue to take elk, deer and bear for as long as a hunter chooses to use it.

But, Savage has not produced the old Model 99 for many years now. As a matter of fact, the Model 99-EG (like mine) was discontinued in 1960. It received stiff competition after the introduction of two much later lever rifles: first from the Model 88 Winchester and, later, from the Browning Lever Rifle, both of which were chambered for the 308 Winchester and other rounds based upon that case. Even Savage's chambering of its M99 for the 308 (in 1955) and, later, in 243 Win., 358 Win., 284 Win., and 7mm/08 Remington, could do no more than forestall the passing of their fabled lever action.

However, the historical importance of the teaming of the Savage Model 99 and the 300 Savage cartridge is secure. For over sixty years that combination of rifle and cartridge provided lever-action fans with a powerful, fast-handling, relatively flat-shooting package that could be hand-carried or packed in a saddle scabbard with ease. And, during that period of time, it brought down some of the heaviest game on this continent.

By the way, the elk I took with the 300 Savage was my first. "Cowboy" Sam Carr had already finished his work for that year (1985) and had left the Sweetwater Cow Camp by mid-October when my M99 dropped my first elk less than a mile from his old cabin. As it turned out, I never did get to let him know of my success with the 300 Savage, or to thank him for his advice. But, I guess it really doesn't matter. He knew that rifle would do the job, just as long as I did mine.

Yep, Cowboy Sam had been right all along. All I needed was a 300 Savage.

Reference

The Hunting Rifle, by Townsend Whelen. Copyright 1940, by Townsend Whelen. Reprint, 1984, Wolfe Publishing Company, Inc., Prescott, Arizona.

The Big-Game Rifle, by Jack O'Connor. Published by Alfred A. Knopf, New York (1952).

Big Game Hunting, by Elmer Keith (1948). Little, Brown and Company, Boston.

Pet Loads ***(2nd Edition)***, by Ken Waters. Wolfe Publishing Co., Inc., Prescott, Arizona.

The Ninety-Nine ***(Revised Third Edition)***, *A History Of The Savage Model 99 Rifle*. Copyright 1985, by D. P. Murphy, author and publisher.

Gun Digest ***(2nd Annual Edition, 1945)***, Charles R. Jacobs, Editor. Copyright by Klein's Sporting Goods. Published by Paul, Richmond & Company, Chicago, Ill.

SORTING 22 AMMUNITION: –WORTH THE TROUBLE?

by Mike Thomas

ABOVE: While a precision instrument, the all-steel 22 Accuracy Gage from Custom Products is built like a piece of angle iron and should outlast any user.

It seems 22 rimfire accuracy is a far more serious topic today than it was two or three decades ago. One of the reasons has to do with the convenience aspect of the low-noise cartridge. It can be fired many places where centerfire guns and ammunition would be unwelcome. A safe backstop is the major requirement and these can often be found within, or close to heavily-populated cities. The sad fact of gun range closures makes it difficult for many to shoot without traveling long distances.

Often restricted to range use only, rimfire 22s are frequently fired from a benchrest, which leads to a natural interest in accuracy. As an added benefit, perhaps this serves as an impetus to become a better-educated shooter. As kids, many of us used whatever 22 ammunition we could get our hands on with little concern for accuracy. It was all the same, right? We seldom shot at paper targets and had no idea what average group size our particular rifle was capable of with a particular ammunition. If one could consistently hit a can or small game at various unknown distances, what difference did it make?

All becomes more complicated as attitudes toward accuracy change and expectations become more stringent. Serious gun enthusiasts now routinely use serious measuring instruments such as micrometers and dial calipers.

It is a fact, not just a popularly held and reasonable belief that the rim thickness of the 22 rimfire case controls headspace. Supposedly, non-uniform rim thickness that translates to non-uniform headspace can wreak havoc with accuracy. The non-uniformity carries over to the actual ignition (firing) process. As simple minds think, all 22 rims that have the same thickness will be more accurate than those with variance. Oversimplified? Perhaps, but that's the basic concept…

> There are no hard and fast rules here. The greatest benefit should be realized with the cheaper ammunitions

Being at the mercy of the manufacturers, 22 enthusiasts have no control over the production of accurate ammunition. That's not necessarily a bad thing, because the manufacturers do what they do rather well. A person may have to try several different ammunitions before finding the one that shoots most accurately in a given firearm, but the process usually works. Some folks prefer to go beyond that, however. They might do this by purchasing a gage to conveniently measure rim thickness and sort 22 ammunition accordingly. One such gage is the version produced by Neil Jones/Custom Products. I don't know if this was the first commercially manufactured tool for sorting 22 ammunition, but I do know it's been in production for quite some time.

I won't attempt to describe the gage in print; photographs do a much better job. However, it's precise, rugged and made entirely of steel. Like other 22 rimfire enthusiasts, I was curious about whether these things really work. I purchased mine months ago but never used it until recently. Simple instructions come with the gage and suggest indexing the cartridge in the tool's "chamber" *(my word)*, i.e., orienting the headstamp of every cartridge. After an indexed round is dropped into the chamber, a sliding bar is gently moved over the base until it stops. Increments on the bar line up with a mark on the chamber. Numeral 3s go in one group, 4s in another, etc.; 3s and 4s seem to be the most common readings, anyway. Eight incremental marks separate the numbers for those with unlimited time and a penchant for tedium. From a practical standpoint, however, putting every round that falls between the gage's 3-mark and 4-mark in the 3-pile should be sufficient for anyone's use.

My original intent was to use one rifle and one handgun for this project, but quickly realized that, from a true accuracy perspective, two rifles and no handguns would provide results that are more meaningful. I no longer use or possess scoped handguns and a scope sight is essential to the sort of testing that was required. However, there is no reason why handguns, proportionately, would provide markedly different results than those I obtained with rifles.

I selected two reasonably accurate bolt-action rifles that I purchased new some years ago. Both have been fired a good deal with many different ammunitions. A stainless steel Ruger 77/22 with factory wood laminate stock is equipped with an old K-6 Weaver scope. A Winchester Model 52 reproduction from the 1990s with factory walnut stock has a Leupold 4X scope of unknown vintage mounted on the receiver. Neither rifle has been altered or customized in any way.

Five ammunitions, all from the same manufacturers' lots, were chosen for use with the Custom Products gage: CCI Blazer, Federal Lightning, Winchester High Velocity, PMC Scoremaster and Wolf Match Target.

Each is loaded with a 40-grain solid lead bullet and the Winchester round has a copper coating. The first three ammos are considered high velocity, real figures around 1,150 – 1,250 feet per second (fps) at the muzzle. Scoremaster and Wolf Match Target are standard velocity, about 150-200 fps slower. None of the ammunitions are expensive. I purchased the Blazer for less than a dollar a box. The Wolf Match Target was around three dollars per box. The Federal Lightning has been replaced by something called Champion Target, which may be virtually the same stuff, but I have used none of it.

Test parameters: I quickly learned the two standard-velocity ammunitions defied orienting in the Custom Products gage because of the headstamp configurations. One hundred rounds of each were dumped in a plastic container and sorted randomly (non-oriented) using the gage. As with all the ammos, oriented or not, the majority of the rounds fell into two groups, ranging from a low of 69 percent of total (Winchester) to a high of 90 percent of total (Blazer). No significance, if any, should be at-

CCI BLAZER

SORTED

Sort, headstamp oriented 90% of cartridges in groups 3 and 4

#2 – 9
#3 – 46
#4 – 44
#5 – 1

Win. 52B, cartridges from #3
Group size, inches: 1.19, 1.28, 1.085, 648, 2.12, **Average=1.264**

Ruger K77/22, cartridges from #4
Group size, inches: .535, .655, .902, .680, .452, **Average = 0.645**

Sort, headstamp not oriented 86% of cartridges in groups 3 and 4

#1 – 2
#2 – 12
#3 – 60
#4 – 26

Win. 52B, cartridges from #3
Group size, inches: 1.733, .700, .353, .645, .1.16, **Average= .918**

Ruger K77/22, cartridges from #4
Group size, inches: 2.49, .455, 1.33, 1.08, 1.905, **Average = 1.45**

UNSORTED

Win. 52B, Group size, inches: 1.587, .373, .630, .417, .938, **Average= 0.789**

Ruger K77/22, Group size, inches: .768, .575, .675, .335, .958, **Average = 0.662**

Model 52B Winchester, a reproduction 1990's version, was equipped with a 4X Leupold scope. With the right ammunition, this light-barreled sporter is capable of excellent accuracy.

FEDERAL LIGHTNING

SORTED

Sort, headstamp oriented 86% of cartridges in groups 2 and 3
#0 – 1
#1 – 13
#2 – 52
#3 – 34

Win. 52B, cartridges from #2
Group size, inches: .628, 1.358, .864, .656, .713,
Average = .844

Ruger K77/22, cartridges from #3
Group size, inches: .898, .528, .480, .859, 1.452,
Average= .843

Sort, headstamp not oriented 87% of cartridges in groups 2 and 3
#1 – 12
#2 – 49
#3 – 38
#4 – 1

Win. 52B, cartridges from #2
Group size, inches: 1.02, .887, .926, 1.587, .932,
Average= 1.070

Ruger K77/22, cartridges from #3
Group size, inches: 2.39, .402, .952, .651, 1.048,
Average = 1.089

UNSORTED

Win. 52B, Group size, inches: 2.065, .990, 830, .850, 1.638, **Average = 1.275**

Ruger K77/22, Group size, inches: 1.19, .964, .1.093, .855, .882, **Average = .997**

WINCHESTER HIGH VELOCITY

SORTED

Sort, headstamp oriented 78% of cartridges in groups 6 and 7
#5 – 10
#6 – 48
#7 – 30
#8+ – 12

Win. 52B, cartridges from #6
Group size, inches: .590, .495, .525, .690, .690,
Average = .598

Ruger K77/22, cartridges from #7
Group size, inches: .746, .704, 1.186, 1.643, .710,
Average = .998

Sort, headstamp not oriented 78% of cartridges in groups 6 and 7
#4 – 1
#5 – 16
#6 – 45
#7 – 33

Win. 52B, cartridges from #6
Group size, inches: 1.115, .860, 1.044, .999, .620,
Average = .928

Ruger K77/22, cartridges from #7
Group size, inches: .995, .755, 1.041, .819, .905,
Average = .903

UNSORTED

Win. 52B, Group size, inches: 1.653, .747, .755, .766, .780, **Average = .940**

Ruger K77/22, Group size, inches: .974, 1.154, .801, .974, .695, **Average = .920**

PMC SCOREMASTER

SORTED

Sort, headstamp oriented 89% of cartridges in groups 3 and 4
#2 – 9
#3 – 48
#4 – 41
#5 – 2

Win. 52B, cartridges from #3
Group size, inches: 497, .461, .973, .697, .645,
Average = .655

Ruger K77/22, cartridges from #4
Group size, inches: .526, .659, .494, .586, .432,
Average = .539

UNSORTED

Win. 52B, Group size, inches: 1.911, .542, .655, .675, .658, **Average = .888**

Ruger K77/22, Group size, inches: .875, .777, .615, .896, .593, **Average = .751**

WOLF MATCH TARGET

SORTED

Sort, headstamp oriented 78% of cartridges in groups 2 and 3
#1 – 4
#2 – 38
#3 – 45
#4 – 10
#5 – 3

Win. 52B, cartridges from #2
Group size, inches: **.610, .352, .639, .440, .648,**
Average = .538

Ruger K77/22, cartridges from #3
Group size, inches: **.480, .656, .336, .624, 1.257,**
Average = .671

UNSORTED

Win. 52B, Group size, inches: **.540, .559, .662, .876, .764, Average = .680**

Ruger K77/22, Group size, inches: **..628, .548, .588, .390, .760, Average = .583**

tached to these figures until all figures are studied. Only rounds within the two major groups that comprised the percentages were fired for accuracy.

Another hundred rounds of each high-velocity ammo were dumped into the container and sorted with the headstamp oriented in the upright position; a tedious process. Some people claim to do the job while watching TV. The intricate headstamp of the Winchester case required strong illumination to make certain the "Super" was not upside down, but my eyes are not the best.

Five, 5-shot groups were fired at fifty yards using the sorted ammunition. The bore of each rifle was thoroughly cleaned before switching brands, then fouled with several rounds of the ammo to be tested.

After firing the oriented and non-oriented cartridges for group size in each rifle, five additional 5-shot groups were fired from each gun using straight-from-the-box, ungauged ammunition. Testing was performed over several days with ambient temperatures of 90 degrees-plus. Flyers opened several groups considerably. If the flyer was my fault, the group was fired again. If a group

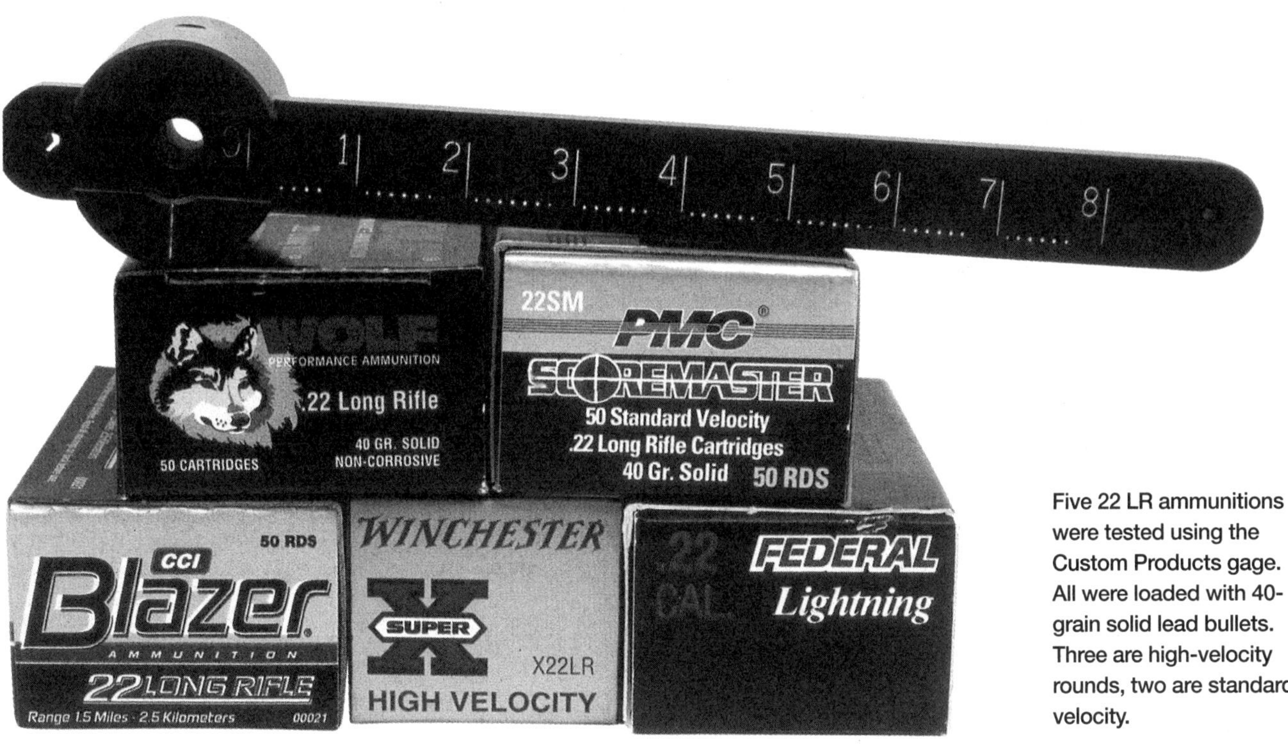

Five 22 LR ammunitions were tested using the Custom Products gage. All were loaded with 40-grain solid lead bullets. Three are high-velocity rounds, two are standard velocity.

Stainless steel Ruger 77/22 has a factory laminate stock, heavy 24-inch barrel, and an old Weaver K6 scope. Like the Winchester, it's accurate with selected ammunition.

contained a flyer that was not shooter-induced, the group was recorded.

A bunch of numbers, true, but there are several invaluable bits of information contained in the tables. Some are blatantly obvious, others subtly hidden – and a few are downright puzzling.

Is sorting 22 ammunition worth the trouble? Review the tables and the clear answer is a not-so-clear "it depends!" The figures speak for themselves, but several aspects merit further discussion. Most groups larger than one inch contained at least one unexplained flyer. It stands to reason that flyers should be more prevalent with unsorted ammunition. Based on my testing, however, that's not always the case. We sort in hopes of getting better accuracy from inexpensive ammunition. To this end, the project showed limited success. While having no background in statistics, I doubt OVERALL results would have been significantly different had I tested fifty ammunitions in twenty rifles. The old rule-of-thumb advice about 22 firearms being particular about the ammunition they shoot most accurately is as true now as it's ever been.

As an example, look at the CCI Blazer figures. The Ruger performed splendidly with ammo that had been sorted by orienting the headstamp, with a group average of 0.645-inch. Yet, unsorted ammunition (for all practical purposes) did about as well with a 0.662-inch. Not bad for stuff that cost $.89 a box. The Winchester rifle did not fare as well, but unsorted ammunition performed best in it.

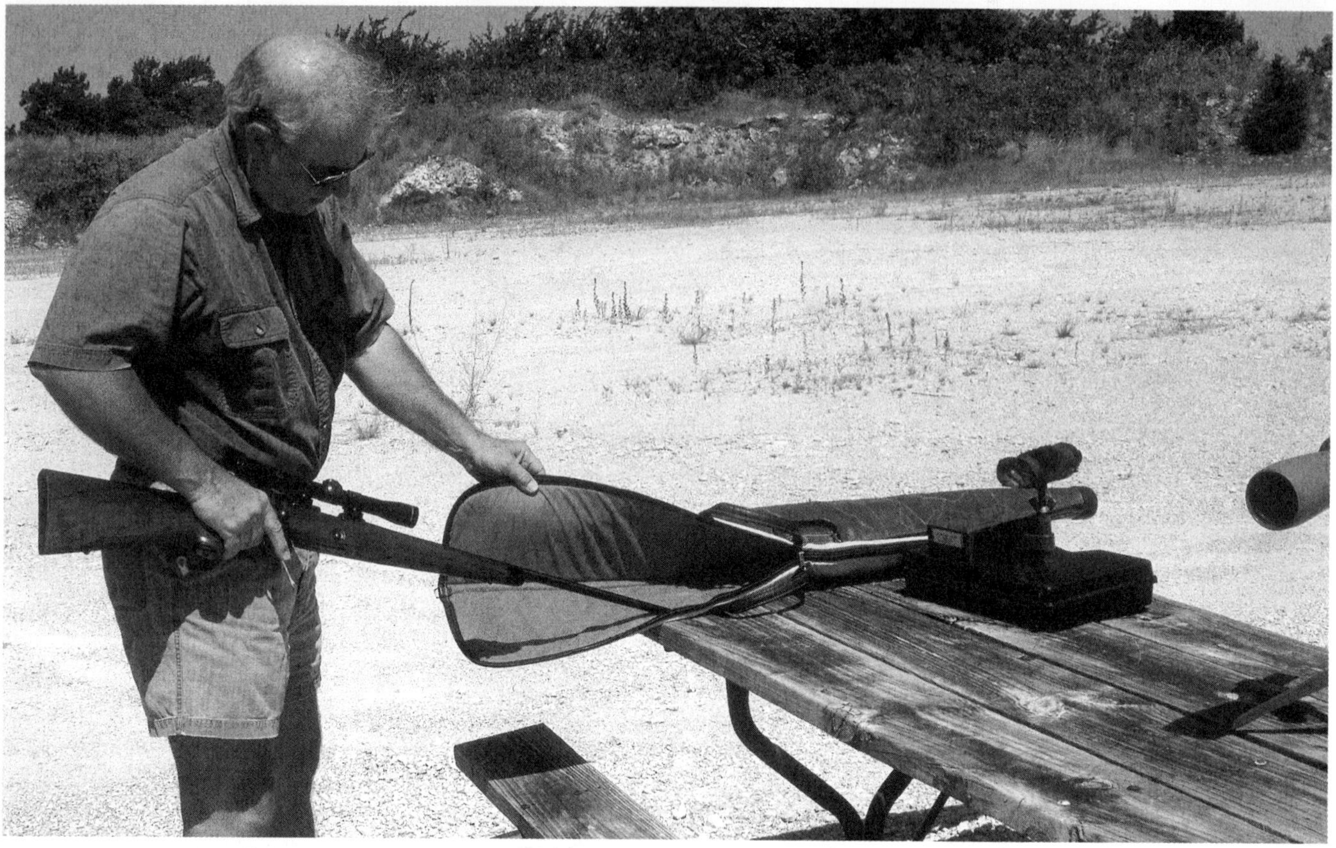

Federal Lightning in the Winchester 52B provided textbook results as to the benefit of ammunition sorting, at least the way many of us visualize the process. An oriented headstamp sort gave an average group size of 0.844-inch. A random sorting increased the average to 1.070 inches. Unsorted ammunition further enlarged it to 1.275 inches.

Winchester High Velocity realized significant benefit, accuracy-wise, from sorting with the headstamp oriented in the Winchester rifle. An average group size of 0.598-inch was recorded. In the Ruger, however, there was almost no difference, with sorted and unsorted ammunition averaging just under an inch.

PMC Scoremaster, not oriented by headstamp because of the logo, shot very well in both rifles. Using random sorting, both rifles averaged under 0.75-inch. Even unsorted ammunition averaged under an inch. There was only one unexplained flyer. Several bricks of Scoremaster were purchased by mail order; cost before shipping was under $1.50 per box.

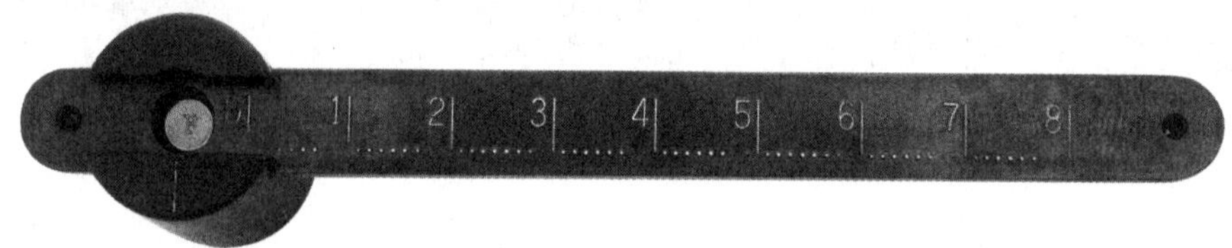

With the calibrated bar pushed all the way to the right, the "chamber" is exposed. For illustration, a cartridge has been placed in the chamber. The next step is the actual gauging process. The bar is GENTLY pushed to the left until resistance is felt. Number indicates group the cartridge is placed in for shooting. Author found the majority of rounds sorted from every box of ammunition fell into two major groups – 3 and 4.

Wolf Match Target has become quite popular with accuracy-oriented shooters. It's easy to see why. Like the Scoremaster, WMT was not oriented by headstamp because of the logo. There was only one unexplained flyer with this ammunition. I recorded one 5-shot group with the Ruger using randomly sorted ammunition that measured 1.257 inches. Even with that thrown in, the five, 5-shot groups averaged 0.671-inch. There was little accuracy difference between sorted and unsorted cartridges with WMT, but it's more expensive and one should expect it to perform well.

Yes, sorting ammunition does work, BUT...not in every situation. There are no hard and fast rules here. The greatest benefit should be realized with the cheaper ammunitions. However, readers who do their own experimentation may be in store for some surprises, just as I was. Some of the cheap ammo really shoots well. It is also important to remember that many self-proclaimed "experts" who are critical of a particular ammunition have not given it an objective fair shake prior to passing judgment. It's up to the individual to make a righteous assessment. Something else to consider is the time and tedium associated with sorting rimfire ammunition. I used to think trimming and turning the case necks of centerfire rifle cartridges was dull work. I've now found something that makes that chore almost exciting!

ORIGINS OF THE 220 SWIFT

by Robert Keen

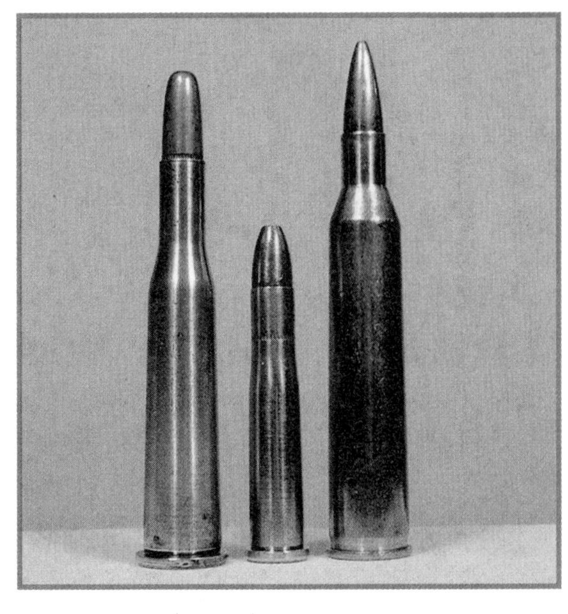

ABOVE: **The line-up of the available commercial 22-caliber cartridges of 1935 after the introduction of the Swift. L-R: 22 Savage Hi-Power or Imp, 22 Hornet, 220 Swift. The Savage and the Hornet pre-date the Swift, of course.**

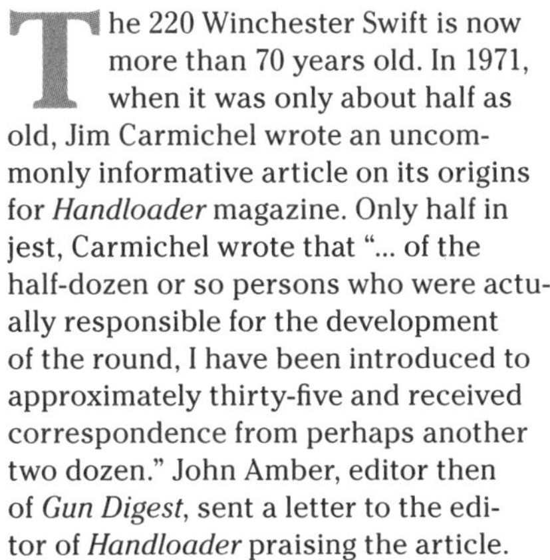

The 220 Winchester Swift is now more than 70 years old. In 1971, when it was only about half as old, Jim Carmichel wrote an uncommonly informative article on its origins for *Handloader* magazine. Only half in jest, Carmichel wrote that "... of the half-dozen or so persons who were actually responsible for the development of the round, I have been introduced to approximately thirty-five and received correspondence from perhaps another two dozen." John Amber, editor then of *Gun Digest*, sent a letter to the editor of *Handloader* praising the article.

All who could reasonably claim to be parents of the Swift are dead now. They cannot help clarify the mystery and confusion that surround the origin of the Swift, but neither can they continue to add to it. The intriguing question raised by Carmichel's article and the focus here is: who was the first person to fire a 220 Swift? Carmichel suggested one answer, but with the perspective of an additional 36 years, a different conclusion is more likely.

The orthodox version of the origin of the Swift, found in most reloading manuals and lists of cartridges, goes something like this: Winchester introduced the cartridge in mid-1935 in their Model 54 rifle. When they brought out the Model 70 a year later, the Swift was one of the original chamberings. With a muzzle velocity of 4,000 feet-per-second (fps), higher than any other commercial cartridge, the Swift generated contention and controversy from its introduction. It was – or it was not – exceptionally accurate; a barrel-burner; an instant killer of big game; and capable of blowing-up rifles even with careful handloading.

THE ANNOUNCEMENT OF THE SWIFT

In pursuing the who-was-first question, an obvious initial step is to examine an original notice of the Swift. *The American Rifleman*, monthly journal of the National Rifle Association, announced the cartridge with only a single paragraph in September 1935:

W. R. A. .220 SWIFT ANNOUNCED

The Winchester M-54 rifle in Super Speed .220-Swift caliber is ready for delivery as is the new ammunition. The muzzle velocity with 48-grain, soft-pointed bullet is 4140 f.-s. The rimmed case is virtually a strengthened revamped 6-mm Lee, but using a head to fit standard actions. The breech pressures are moderate, or no higher than those of the standard .30-'06. The dependable accuracy is 2 inches or smaller at 100 yards. The only change in the special M-54 rifle for this cartridge is a 26-inch length of barrel. The .220 Swift is at its best at 200 to 300 yards, owing to its flat trajectory and short time of flight. It is intended for all game up to, and including, deer.

This appears to be a typical rewrite of a press release, or whatever they called a press release in 1935. Fred Ness, associate editor of the *Rifleman*, probably composed this announcement in a hurry, since he mistakenly included "Super Speed" as part of the name of the cartridge. Super Speed is a Winchester trademark applied only to ammunition. Company literature at the time always identified the cartridge as the 220 Winchester Swift.

In 1935, *American Rifleman* was the only American periodical devoted to firearms, and for a publication of its influence, this short birth announcement seems pretty insignificant. In fact, it was printed on a back page, surrounded by a description of a leather dressing for rifle slings. In the 21st century, manufacturers orchestrate the introduction of a new cartridge so that choirs of gun writers begin to sing its praises on cue in four-part harmony. In 1935, Winchester made no effort to follow-up this bare announcement with an advertising campaign in the magazine. For months before and after the announcement, the Winchester ads in the Rifleman only extolled their rimfire match ammunition and the Model 52 target rifle. Ads by Griffin & Howe and by Sedgley did mention the Swift as an available chambering for custom rifles, but Winchester apparently thought Rifleman readers were exclusively target-shooters. The company, however, did support the Swift with advertising in hunting and outdoors magazines.

Based on the announcement in the *American Rifleman*, the who-was-first question is answered with "a factory

.220 SWIFT

IMAGINE such speed! If maintaining muzzle velocity for 1 minute (impossible, of course), the 48-grain lead-pointed bullet of the new Winchester .220 Swift bolt action rifle would be 7 *miles ahead* of the world's next fastest commercial rifle bullet. It would be *16 miles ahead* of the U. S. Service rifle's .30 Gov't. '06 172-grain boattail bullet. *In just one minute.* Its velocity at the muzzle is 4,140 feet per second.

At 50 yards the 100-yard bullet trajectory or arc with this new Winchester development is 3/10ths of an inch. At 100 yards the 200-yard arc is just 1 inch higher. Here is practically point-blank rifle shooting.

And not only do the Winchester Super Speed .220 Swift hunting bullets (46-, 48- and 56-grain) travel so flat that, in average use, calculations for bullet drop are eliminated. Extended tests with the Winchester .220 Swift Rifle and its Winchester factory-loaded hunting cartridges have revealed remarkable accuracy and astounding power. At 100 yards, average accuracy extreme of under 2 inches has been obtained; consistent bull's-eye accuracy up to 500 yards. And when obtaining vital hits at normal ranges, killing as instantly as a lightning stroke!

A part of the early advertising campaign for the 220 Winchester Swift, this ad appeared in the May 1936 issue of *Sports Afield*.

technician" as the logical conclusion. This is a reasonable response, if one strictly defines the Swift as a rimmed revamp of the 6mm Lee Navy case. As Carmichel pointed out, the path to the introduction of the Winchester Swift certainly went through the Winchester-Western ballistic labs and then on to the marketplace. However, there was a good bit of traffic on that path, including some divergences evident today in the existence of numbers of rifles chambered and marked for the "220 Wotkyns Original Swift," a very different cartridge from the 220 Winchester Swift.

AN ABORTED ANNOUNCEMENT

The Swift's introductory notice in the *Rifleman* was not quite as meager as it first appears. For several years before the September 1935 announcement, the magazine published a continual stream of notices and articles about experimental high-velocity 22 caliber cartridges. This flow peaked in May 1935 with an article by Fred Ness titled "4000 F.-S. With the Hornet Bullet." Written to announce the impending commercial introduction of the Swift, the article "caused quite a sensation among the shooters of the country", as Harvey Donaldson put it. As an announcement it was premature and misleading, but it does hold clues about who might have first fired a Swift.

Ness's title alone is significant. From its reference to Hornet bullets, readers knew that the story involved lightweight 22-caliber bullets. The title also linked the new cartridge to existing widespread interest in the 22 Hornet. About five years earlier, the Hornet had been developed and introduced by Grosvenor L. ("Grove") Wotkyns of Benicia Arsenal in California, and by Townsend Whelen, G. A. Woody, and A. L. Woodworth of Springfield Armory. Articles by Wotkyns, Whelen, and Woody in *American Rifleman* and in *Outdoor Life* generated considerable demand for custom Hornet-chambered rifles. Winchester sold 22 Hornet ammunition several months before they introduced the Hornet-chambered version of their Model 54 rifle. The mention of the Hornet in the title also may have been an allusion to the central role Wotkyns had played in its creation. Ness was to ascribe a similar part for him in the development of the Swift.

Ness's use of triple zeroes to grab attention was surely intentional. In 1915, Savage demonstrated the commercial usefulness of zeroes when they introduced their 250-3000 cartridge. In the May 1934 *Rifleman*, just a year before Ness's article, Hervey Lovell had used the entrancing triple zeros in his article "An Interesting .22-3000 Cartridge." And only five months earlier, in the December 1934 Rifleman, Ned Roberts had given an account of the 22 Niedner Magnum cartridge, which was based on a shortened 25-35 Winchester case necked to 224, and which fired 45-grain Hornet bullets at 3300 fps — not quite three-of-a-kind zeroes, but still pretty nifty with two pairs of numerals.

Aware of the probable impact of his upcoming Swift announcement, Ness had provided a teasing preview of it a month earlier in April 1935. At the end of his own note about the 22 Niedner Magnum, Ness wrote:

> *The .22 Niedner Magnum is, of course, clearly out of the Hornet class. ... The next venture will be the necking down of the .250-Savage, .25-Roberts, 7-mm or even the .30-'06, although a definite limit on practical sizes will be reached, because balance in loading-density must be maintained for efficient combustion. ... However, such rifles have been tried in the past, and are still being used in experiments, and more successfully now with modern components. Before long there are certain to be interesting developments in the realm of ultra-high velocities. It happens I have such a rifle ordered since last November. Watch the next issues of* The American Rifleman.

In the May article the new development was identified, complete with photographs, as the 220 Swift. But (a really big but) the photos clearly showed a 22-250 cartridge, a very different cartridge from the 220 Winchester Swift that was announced in September four months later. The article summarized work that Wotkyns had carried out with the necked-down 250 Savage case, and noted that Wotkyns in January 1935 had released to the press a report specifically mentioning its name as the 220 Swift.

Ness's article was a scrambled assemblage of condensed and abstracted letters from Wotkyns and from John B. Sweany, Wotkyns's coworker in California. The letters related the wonderful accuracy and velocity they had obtained with the 22-250 case and with some 7x57 cases shortened to various lengths and necked to 22-caliber.

Ness used the word "factory" numerous times in describing the Swift; for example, "...the factory .220 Swift cartridge, which is now quite new, is steadily showing improvement, and as ultimately developed will probably exceed anything hitherto imagined." Ness did not actually name the factory, but he was pretty coy in offhandedly mentioning the use of "special brass" developed by Western, and the use of W.R.A. primers by "the factory." He hedged further about the final form of the Swift, writing that "there may

HUNTING & FISHING November, 1930

SHOOTING

BY GROSVENOR L. WOTKYNS

The Search for an All 'Round Rifle

PROBABLY this title is a misnomer, in so far as there is no such thing as an all 'round hunter's rifle. But the point is more particularly: What rifle would you buy if you indulged in many different kinds of hunting and were limited to only one rifle? This means that if there is an ideal rifle, it will be large enough for big game up to including deer, and small enough for small game, down to and including squirrel. Or, phrasing it a little more concisely, not too small for big game, nor too large for small game.

What then, are the possibilities as offered by the manufacturer to the sportsman? There is a range in calibres from .22 up to about .50. Somewhere in between these two extremes is

.44-40—and in most parts of the country—except where long range shooting is the rule—the .44 is large enough for deer. Yet the .44 is too heavy for small game. The .44 has 751 pounds energy, and it tears a big hole. For their model 92, the Winchester people have produced a Special .44 cartridge with an energy in foot pounds at muzzle of nearly eleven hundred pounds—plenty for any kind of deer shooting up to one hundred yards. And, by the same token, too large for small game.

The reader is beginning to see that sacrificing muzzle energy is leave doubt as to efficacy on big game; while increasing calibre or muzzle energy, is taking the arm out of the small game class.

Captain Wotkyns's reputation as a ballistic experimenter is well-known and appreciated. His service as shooting editor of *Hunting and Fishing* in the 1920s and early 1930s has been largely forgotten.

be a change in factory specifications, and no one yet knows the final answer -- which is to be announced later." Ness noted in closing that "the final .220 Swift cartridge as developed in the ballistic laboratory of a great arms manufacturer is certain to be an excellent cartridge."

The evident confusion and disorientation in Ness's article can be explained in part by conflicting and discordant messages that had crossed his desk in early 1935. These are significant in resolving the mystery of the Swift's development.

A PROBABLE SWIFT CHRONOLOGY

From scattered material in *American Rifleman*, from Philip Sharpe's *Complete Guide to Handloading,* and from an article by Richard Simmons in the 1956 *Gun Digest,* there emerges a clear chronology of development of the Wotkyns Swift and the Winchester Swift. Simmons, while preparing to write his 1947 book *Wildcat Cartridges,* had corresponded extensively with Sweany and with Wotkyns before the latter's death in 1945. Sharpe wrote that he knew Wotkyns well and had hunted woodchucks with him. He called Wotkyns "The Archbishop," which was how Wotkyns signed his letters to Sharpe.

In 1929-1930, Wotkyns had been able to persuade three Army colleagues at Springfield Armory to help with developing the 22 Hornet, a cartridge he had devised specifically for use in converted 22 RF rifles. The group had successfully convinced Winchester to produce the cartridge commercially. Hornet rifles and ammunition had enjoyed noteworthy sales, even in the middle of the Great Depression.

In the early 1930s, searching for more velocity in a 22, Wotkyns began to experiment with the 250 Savage case necked to 22-caliber. He was hardly the first to do this. However, Wotkyns was the first to have real success, because he had access to a new Dupont powder, IMR 3031, before it was released for sale to the general public.

In late 1933, before he met Sweany, Wotkyns had asked Adolph Lukes, a well-known California gunsmith and tool-maker, to assemble a rifle for the 22-250 cartridge on a 1903 Springfield action. It's unclear whether Lukes used a barrel from a Springfield 22-caliber M1 or from a W.R.A. 22 Hornet, because Wotkyns reported both to Ness at different times. Using IMR 3031 powder, Wotkyns obtained significantly higher velocity and better accuracy than any previous attempts with a 22 cartridge. Wotkyns also began collaborating with Sweany to develop bullets of improved form for the cartridge.

In late 1933 or early 1934, after achieving velocities approaching 4000 fps with the 22-250, Wotkyns was sufficiently excited to report his results to the Western Cartridge Company. Perhaps because of his productive connection with the Hornet, Western asked him to send the rifle and reloads for their own testing. Wotkyns did so, indicating to Western that his name for the cartridge was "220 Swift." Phil Sharpe would later write that it was unclear whether the Swift was had been christened by Wotkyns or by Winchester-Western. However, in correspondence with Ness published in 1942, Wotkyns makes it clear that he had named the Swift before sending it to Western.

In 1934, while Western ballisticians were working with his rifle and cartridge, Wotkyns teamed with Sweany to investigate several other cartridges necked for the 22 bullet, searching for more velocity, better accuracy, and improved bullets. In late 1934, Ness learned of their work and ordered his rifle as described in the April and May 1935 issues of *The American Rifleman.*

The 1934 communications exchanged among Wotkyns, Western, and Winchester are probably lost permanently. Western reported to Wotkyns that bullets from the 22-250 actually had reached 4000 fps and had caused more damage to the steel backstops of their laboratory chronograph ranges than any other cartridge, including a variety of magnums. Western passed the rifle along to Winchester (a subsidiary of Western Cartridge after 1931), which began its own series of tests. Winchester also apparently, in late 1934, informed Wotkyns that they were going to begin soon to manufacture the cartridge and to chamber rifles for the cartridge.

In January 1935, based on his understanding of Winchester's plans, Wotkyns sent an announcement about the impending introduction of the "220 Swift" to many firearms editors and writers. The cartridge he described was a 22-250, and his communications included photographs of the cartridge and bullets. Judging from Ness's rewrite of this press release, Wotkyns provided some comparative dimensions of his 22-250 case and the 250-3000 Savage; e.g. lengths of 1.910 and 1.914 inches.

Shortly after Wotkyns's announcement had gone out, Winchester tried to put his genie back in the bottle by sending a telegram of vigorous denial to all who had received his communication. Their message stated that the cartridge that Wotkyns had described was *not* the cartridge Winchester was going to release. Winchester asked the writers and editors to hold off publishing information about the 220 Swift until an official corporate announcement was issued, because "changes were being made." This urgent communication from Winchester may largely account for the fractured nature of the article by Ness in the May *Rifleman.*

It's not likely that Wotkyns, with his background in the protocols of military chain of command, would have sent out his announcement in January 1935 unless he had reasonable cause to think that Winchester actually intended soon to release his 22-250 creation. Winchester's abrupt and sudden annulment of his announcement greatly upset Wotkyns. Sharpe records him as being disgusted, disappointed, and "very sour on the subject," but not discouraged.

A best guess is that somebody in Winchester's management read Wotkyns's announcement and decided that Winchester's corporate image would be tarnished if a Savage case were to be used as the basis for the new cartridge. They mandated a switch to a case originated by Winchester. The photo of the necked-down Savage case that appeared with Ness's May article must have caused some heartburn in the Winchester boardroom. They were in fact justified in thinking that the picture would stick with readers, despite the photo caption warning that "further development may result in considerable change in form." This caveat was surely inserted in response to their telegram.

According to Simmons, Winchester told Wotkyns that it would be impossible to use a case from Savage or any other competitor as the basis for their high velocity 22-caliber cartridge. They also asked Wotkyns to suggest a Winchester case that might be feasible, and Wotkyns responded with the suggestion of the 6mm Lee case. The Winchester ballistics lab followed his recommendation and began working with that case. They necked the Lee case to 22-caliber with other slight dimensional changes, strengthened the web, and gave it a semi-rim to fit the common 30-06 bolt face. (Winchester had in fact made a rimmed version of the 6mm Lee case in the early 1900s. Sharpe's *Rifle in America* noted that the rimmed version was used at least in the Blake rifle.)

On April 23, 1935, according to Sharpe, Winchester adopted the final form of the 220 Swift. The date appears on the specification sheet that Winchester submitted to the Sporting Arms and Ammunition Manufacturers Institute (SAAMI). As soon as these specifications were published, Sharpe ordered from Sweany a custom rifle chambered for the cartridge. When factory 220 Winchester Swift ammunition became available later in 1935, Sharpe was able to begin using it immediately.

In the short time between Wotkyns's press announcement in January and the publication of final dimensions in April, Wotkyns and Sweany would have been unable to experiment with the Lee case and to swap results and data with the Winchester lab. About 1940, Wotkyns worked with L. E. Wilson to modify the Winchester Swift to produce the wildcat 22 Wotkyns-Wilson Arrow, which Wotkyns judged to be a significant improvement on the Winchester Swift. When Simmons asked why Winchester did not introduce the 220 Swift with the refinements, Wotkyns replied that "this revision could have been accomplished at the time of the original manufacture, but to demand it at the moment would probably have meant no 220 Swift at all, and half a loaf is better than no loaf."

Disillusioned by Winchester, Wotkyns and Sweany left further work with the 22-250 to others, particularly to Jerry Gebby and to J. Bushnell Smith, who had worked with Sweany for a while in California. The development of the cartridge as the "22 Varminter" and the "22 Wotkyns Original Swift" and its eventual commercial adoption by Remington in 1965 is well documented.

All of this history reinforces the reply of "a Winchester lab technician" as answering the question about the first person to fire a 220 Winchester Swift. However, it is probably safe to assume that a first step on the way to the Swift after Wotkyns' suggestion was a simple necking of the Lee case to 22 caliber in the Winchester lab.

If we provisionally broaden our definition of "220 Swift" to include the 22-6mm Lee stage of development, then the Swift story does not begin with Winchester in early 1935.

W. R. A. .220 SWIFT ANNOUNCED

The Winchester M-54 rifle Super-Speed .220-Swift caliber is ready for delivery as is the new ammunition. The muzzle velocity with 48-grain, soft-point, pointed bullet is 4140 f.-s. The rimmed case is virtually a strengthened revamped 6-mm. Lee, but using a head to fit standard actions. The breech pressures are moderate, or no higher than those of the standard .30-'06. The dependable accuracy is 2 inches or smaller at 100 yards. The only change in the special M-54 rifle for this cartridge is a 26-inch length of barrel. The .220 Swift is at its best at 200 to 300 yards, owing to its flat trajectory and short time of flight. It is intended for all game up to, and including, deer.

Sweany .22-4000 Ready

J. B. Sweany, Winters, California, is ready to fit and chamber .22-caliber barrels for the new W. R. A. .220-Swift factory cartridge, and also for his own rimmed cartridge

The brief announcement of the 220 Swift in *The American Rifleman* of September 1935.

In fact, it begins decades earlier with a different set of experimenters. Before describing their work, however, there are some published loose ends in this account of the 1935 Winchester Swift that need tying up.

THE 22X55

In his May 1935 article, Ness stated that in November 1934 he had sent a barrel blank and Springfield action to Sweany to be chambered for the new 22-250 cartridge. However, between November and the writing of the article (probably February or March), Ness changed his mind and asked for the rifle to be chambered for a cartridge that Sweany called the 22x55. Based on extensive experiments, Sweany had concluded it was superior to "the factory 220 Swift."

The mention of this 22x55 attracted Carmichel's attention, and in the 1971 article he speculated that the 22x55 cartridge was based on the 6mm Lee case. Using a relaxed definition of the Swift to include a 22-6mm Lee, this would make either Wotkyns or Sweany possibly the first to fire a Swift.

In support of this idea, Carmichel wrote that Sweany's letters described the 22x55 as something other than a necked-down 30-06 and 7x57 case. Further, the 6mm Lee case is 2.35 inches or 59.7mm long, while the 220 Winchester Swift is 2.205 inches or 56.0mm long; this put a cartridge of 55mm length really close to the Swift. As added circumstantial evidence, Carmichel noticed that Sweany's 22x55 loads with IMR 3031 powder and 45- and 55-grain bullets were identical with 220 Winchester Swift loads as recommended by the Speer reloading manual.

Neither Sweany nor Ness explicitly identified the parent cartridge of the 22x55. However, it was likely a 7x57 case, not the Lee case, that Sweany shortened and necked to 22 caliber. Two principal points support this.

First, in the May 1935 *Rifleman* article, Ness quotes from a Sweany letter written in late 1934 or early 1935:

The .30-'06 case necked to .22 left a lot of powder space even with a load pretty close to the maximum. So I made a case .470 inch at the base, .420 inch at the shoulder, and with the Springfield slope of 17.5°, to hold just 45 grains of powder. 42 grains of No. 3031 seemed to do the same in this case as 45 grains in the .30-'06 case.

Sweany clearly is describing a 30-06 case shortened and then necked to 22 caliber. Sweany's letter continues:

Then I made a second cartridge of the 7-mm. to its exact dimensions and necked it for the .22 bullet. (The 7-mm. 'as is' can be made to hold just about 42 grains).

Sweany's description here is of a 7x57 case with the exterior dimensions of the reformed 30-06 case above. Immediately after this quote from Sweany's letter, Ness writes:

Though Wotkyns proved that for this work the neck-down [sic] .250 Savage case is more efficient than the necked-down .30-'06 and 7-mm. cases, I am interested in trying these larger shells and am having my rifle chambered for one of them.

Recreation with modern components of Wotkyns's sensation-generating photograph in *The American Rifleman*. L-R: 30-06 M2 ball military round, 22-250 with 50-grain Sierra BlitzKing, 22-250 with Sierra's 45-grain Hornet bullet, three Nosler Ballistic Tip bullets of 55, 50, and 40 grains, and a Sierra 45-grain Hornet bullet.

It is evident that Ness wanted a cartridge that Sweany described as being formed from the 30-06 or 7x57 cases. In the next paragraph, Ness identified the cartridge he ordered as the 22x55.

Second, in the next issue of *American Rifleman,* June 1935, Ness included a brief report entitled "That .22-Sweany Job." A couple of paragraphs and a table in this report bear on the origin of the 22x55:

In the early experiments [Sweany] used I.M.R. powder No. 3031 in the .250-Savage case with Hornet bullets...

After he had experimented with larger cases reshaped from the .30-'06 and 7-mm. caliber, his data showed an average group size under 1-1/2 inches at 100 yards ... He made and used more than a dozen different cases and chambers in these experiments, and these experimental cartridges varied in body length, shoulder diameter and in taper greater and less than the same parts of the straight 7-mm. which was also necked down and tried. In case length, powder capacity and load, some of these different cartridges varied as follows: (based on No. 3031 Powder and W.R.A. 45-grain bullets.)

From this paragraph and table it is clear that Sweany experimentally made 30-06 and 7x57 cases in several conformations. The listed 60mm and 62mm cases were undoubtedly formed from 30-06. The 22x55mm case on the last line of the table may have been formed from either, but it seems certain that the case was not the 6mm Lee Navy. Phil Sharpe photographed fourteen of these different experimental cases from the Wotkyns and Sweany trials that attempted to improve on the 22-250.

DONALDSON'S 1934 220 SWIFT

A second loose end is Harvey Donaldson's claim that he owned and shot a 220 Winchester Swift rifle in 1934 or perhaps earlier. If this date is correct, it effectively subverts the Swift chronology proposed above. His report about his 220 Winchester Swift appeared in the November 1969

.22 Sweany Experimental Loads

Length	Capacity	Max. Load	Drop
48.5 mm	38 grs.	36 grs.	2-3/4"
60.0 mm	45 grs.	42 grs.	3/4"
62.0 mm	42 grs.	40 grs.	2 "
55.0 mm	43 grs.	39 grs.	1-3/8"

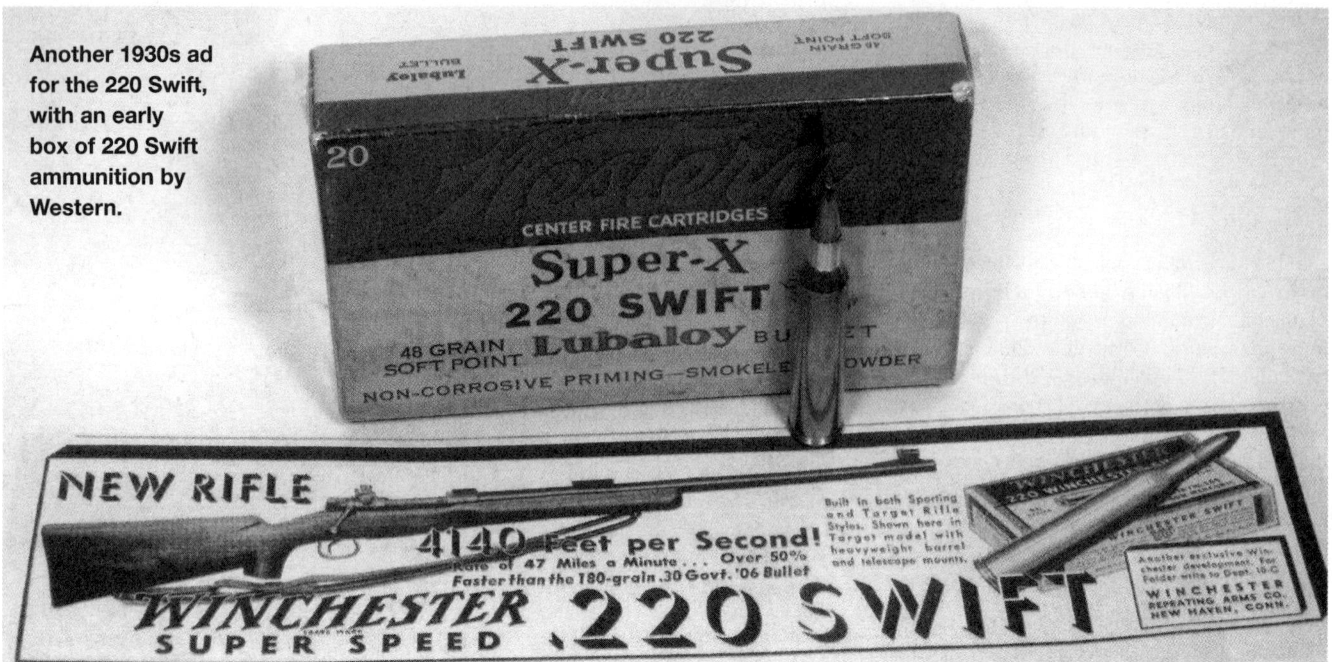

Another 1930s ad for the 220 Swift, with an early box of 220 Swift ammunition by Western.

issue of *Handloader* magazine:

> *A year or two before any .220 Swift rifle was available, and while only a few pilot rifles had been made, Col. Whelen got in touch with Edwin Pugsley, the V-P of Winchester, and suggested that a rifle be sent to me for testing from a bench and in chuck shooting. Very soon this rifle came along, made up on the Model 54 action - for this was before the days of the Model 70. Winchester later gave me this rifle, which I still use in hunting. Whelen said I was the first one outside of the factory to use the new rifle ...*

An accompanying photograph shows a target with a typewritten label: "This five shot group at 100 yards was fired recently, by H. A. Donaldson, with a .220 Win. Swift M/54 rifle that he got from the Winchester Co., in 1934."

Whelen's statement about Donaldson as the first user outside of the factory is almost certainly correct. Whelen undoubtedly was aware that Winchester was working actively with high-velocity cartridges, that they had invited German high-velocity guru Hermann Gerlich to New Haven for consultation in 1934, and that Wotkyns's 22-250 was being tested at Western and at Winchester. Whelen also knew that Donaldson would be interested in the cartridge and could test it intelligently.

In his 1971 article, Carmichel noted that "several .220 Swift rifles were in the hands of shooters before the .220 rifle was formally announced." He describes Winchester's willingness then to chamber rifles for new cartridges before official release to the public. It is quite likely that Donaldson tried out a Model 54 in 220 Winchester Swift before its official announcement in August 1935.

The problem is with the 1934 date that Donaldson attached to Winchester's delivery of his rifle. Some well established dates make a 1934 shipment unlikely. These include (A) the January 1935 date of Wotkyns's premature announcement and Winchester's immediate follow-up, hold-the-presses telegram; (B) Winchester's subsequent request to Wotkyns for a recommendation of a usable Winchester case; and (C) the April 1935 date of finalization of specifications. A delivery date to Donaldson of May 1935 is believable. Winchester conceivably might have produced some Swift rifles and ammunition before writing final SAAMI specifications, making plausible the delivery of one to Donaldson in February or March 1935. When he wrote in 1969 about the 1934 delivery of his rifle, Donaldson was 86 and his wife had died the previous week. If his memory was off by only four months after a lapse of about 35 years, this amounts to an error of less than one percent, which is very respectable under the circumstances.

Wolfe Publishing Company reissued Donaldson's *Handloader* articles along with other correspondence in a 1980 compilation titled *Yours Truly, Harvey Donaldson*. In a 1967 letter, Donaldson wrote (page 66), "I had a Swift sent to me by Mr. Pugsley of Winchester some two years before they were available, for testing purposes..." The correctness of this claim would depend on Donaldson's definition of "available." Winchester first announced the availability of Swift rifles and ammunition in August 1935; it is impossible for Donaldson to have possessed a Winchester Swift rifle two years before that, in August 1933. Perhaps Donaldson meant "readily available in local gun shops."

There also exists confusion about the photo of Donaldson's target with the 1934 label. In the next issue of *Handloader*, January 1970, Donaldson wrote "In a recent letter of mine to the *Handloader* there was shown a recent five-shot 100-yard group from my first .220 Swift, received 35 years ago from Winchester." But just a few paragraphs later Donaldson described his purchase of one of the last pre-64 Winchester Model 70s in 220 Swift, and wrote, "This is the new Swift rifle that made the tiny group of five shots, a print of which was shown in one of my recent letters to the *Handloader*."

Only one illustration was ever published of a five-shot 220 Swift group by Donaldson. Whether Donaldson used his first or his last Swift rifle to make that printed group can not now be determined. Oddly, in the *Yours Truly* collection the sentence about using the new Swift rifle in making the published group was deleted from the reprinted letter of January 1970. The original copies of Donaldson's *Handloader* letters have been lost, so it is impossible to determine whether the deleted sentence was actually written by Donaldson or had been inserted by an editor. Because the editors of the book and magazine are deceased, the confusion will necessarily remain unresolved.

AN UNCLEAR NOTE BY LANDIS

A third loose end is a confusing statement that appears in Charles Landis's 1947 book, *Twenty-Two Caliber Varmint Rifles*. Landis writes on p.184-185:

> *About the year 1934 the author of this work was deluged with a mass of targets, groups, and a number of manuscripts and suggestions on a .22-250 cartridge by the then Capt. Grosvenor Wotkyns, writing from California. Grove, as he was known to his friends, passed away in the spring of 1945.*
>
> *The author visited Captain Wotkyns in his office and at his home and was a guest in his quarters while Grove was stationed at Frankford Arsenal, Bridesburg, Pa., and lived on the arsenal grounds. This was probably about 1925-1928. Wotkyns was quite anxious to have this cartridge put out commercially, at that time, but unfortunately for everyone concerned, including the shooting public, and especially the .22 rifle cranks of the varmint hunting type, it came along at a time when manufacturers were beginning to reduce the number of cartridges rather than to increase them or add better ones.*

The problem here is ambiguity of Landis's phrase, "at that time." It may refer to the 1925-28 dates of the previous sentence, or it may refer to the 1934 date with which Landis introduced the subject of Wotkyns's work on the 22-250. The first possibility is favored for grammatical proximity; the second for its agreement with known history of Wotkyns's work with the 22-250 and his efforts to have it adopted by Winchester-Western.

The clear implication of the first possibility is that Wotkyns had worked with the 22-250 in the mid-1920s in Philadelphia, and that his results were sufficiently rewarding for him to think the cartridge would interest a major arms company. Fred Zeglin not unreasonably accepted this interpretation in his 2005 book, *Wildcat Cartridges*. However, the known chronology of Wotkyns's efforts with the cartridge makes it doubtful that Wotkyns worked with a 22-250 in the 1920s.

Landis probably inserted the remark about his visits in the 1920s in order to establish the credibility of his personal knowledge of Wotkyns's work, and "at that time" refers to Wotkyns's activity in 1934. Some points supporting this conclusion:

(A) Landis clearly indicates (pp. 36, 184) that Wotkyns credited Sweany with the development of the 22-250. Wotkyns did not begin to work with Sweany until late 1933 or early 1934. It is unlikely that Wotkyns would have given Sweany as much credit had Wotkyns been working with the 22-250 in the mid-1920s.

(B) Even if Wotkyns had worked with the 22-250 in the mid-1920s, his results would have been as disappointing as those of other experimenters. Only when IMR-3031 powder became available in the 1930s did the cartridge began to show its potential. Sweany and Wotkyns had a head start over other experimenters with the cartridge because Wotkyns had pre-commercial access to the powder.

(C) In addition to lack of suitable powders, lack of usable bullets would have prevented useful work on the 22-250 in the mid-1920s. Appropriate 224-caliber bullets for high velocity simply did not exist then. Wotkyns, Whelen, and others have described their problems in finding bullets for use with the Hornet in the early 1930s. Had Wotkyns actually worked with the 22-250 in the 1920s, obtaining satisfactory bullets for the Hornet in 1930 would have been easy. Instead, serious work with the high velocities of the 22-250 and the Winchester Swift had to wait until answers to bullet problems had been partially found with the Hornet. These difficulties with bullets explain in part why Ness used the term "Hornet bullet" in the title of his April 1935 article about experiments of Sweany and Wotkyns. It also explains why Ness included descriptions of their efforts in designing bullets.

Wotkyns may have been thinking of working with the necked down 250-3000 case in the mid-20s; he almost surely was not thinking seriously of commercialization. The commercial success of the Hornet probably encouraged Wotkyns to submit his 22-250 rifle and cartridge to Winchester-Western, and was likewise what prompted the corporation to consider seriously his claims for the cartridge.

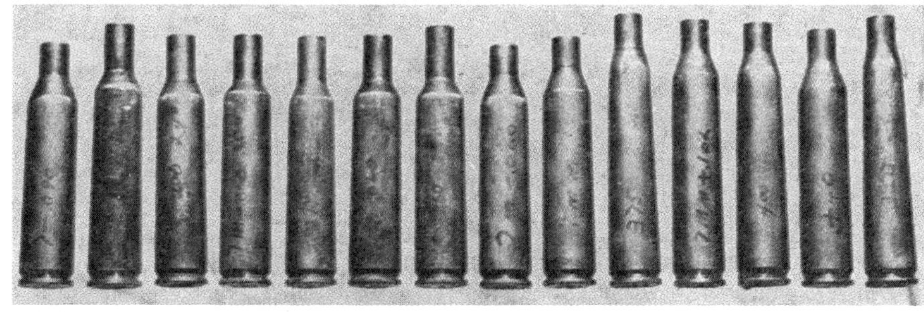

Fourteen cases from experimental work by Sweany and Wotkyns in 1934. Photo is from Sharpe's book, *Complete Guide to Handloading*.

SO WHO DID FIRST SHOOT A SWIFT?

Considering the Swift as a cartridge specified by Winchester in April 1935, the first Swift shooter must have been a Winchester lab technician, with Harvey Donaldson perhaps the first outside of the lab. For a cartridge with the name "220 Swift," Wotkyns would have been the first using his rifle built by Lukes. However, if we use the relaxed Swift definition of a 22 bullet in a necked-down 6mm Lee Navy (236) case, the answer becomes more interesting, and involves a couple of ballistic pioneers who worked a century ago.

Charles Newton, the "Father of High Velocity," is a front-rank contender for the first shooter of a 22-6mm cartridge. *American Rifleman* of January 1942 describes some early correspondence between A. O. Niedner and Ned Roberts. In a letter to Roberts dated November 21, 1910, Niedner wrote that he had just finished making for Newton a 22-caliber chambering tool for the 6mm Lee Navy case. In the March 1913 issue of *Outdoor Life,* Newton himself wrote:

> Immediately following the submission of this cartridge *[the 22 Savage Hi-Power]* the writer, deciding to go the limit in producing a high-power .22, used first the 6mm. Navy shell necked down ...

A photograph of one of Newton's experimental 22-6mm Lee cartridges appears in Simmons's book *Wildcat Cartridges*.

While it's fitting and just that Newton be in contention as the initial shooter of the 22-6mm "Swift," antedating him was an undoubtedly even more appropriate individual, Dr. Franklin W. Mann. In the December 1935 *American Rifleman,* C. G. Williams wrote the following:

> *It was on January 21, 1907, that Dr. F. W. Mann wrote that he was going to purchase a .236 (6-mm.) Winchester rifle and test out that shell for accuracy with various weights of bullets, and then neck down the .236-Navy shell to take .226 bullets for a new high-*

velocity .22 caliber rifle. But it was not until October 1908 that the Doctor obtained his .22 barrel for the action. In a letter written on December 27, 1908, he stated that at 3000 f.-s. the primers were blown out of the pockets and the shells stretched so that they could not be reloaded. The velocity was computed from tests on the revolving-disc chronograph that the Doctor made.

The conclusion is that sometime in late 1908, Dr. Mann became the first person to shoot a Swift, in its guise of a 22-6mm Lee. Although the experience was less than a happy one, it does establish just and good cause for celebrating the Swift's 100th birthday in early December of 2008.

AN ANNOTATED BIBLIOGRAPHY

Here is a chronological list of the principal sources used for this article. Interested individuals may consult them to determine whether the author's interpretations are rational. Literature of the Swift is extensive and frequently contains capsule histories, some notably erroneous; such accounts are not cited here.

Newton, C. "The Designer of the .22 Hi-Power Answers Some Questions," *Outdoor Life*, March 1913. Reprinted on pp.268-269 in B. M. Jennings, Jr., editor. Charles Newton: Father of High Velocity, 1985, 480pp., privately printed by Bruce M. Jennings, Jr., Sheridan, Wyoming. [A description of Newton's early experiments with 22 caliber cartridges, including the necked-down 6mm Lee Navy.]

Ness, F. C. "On Getting a .22 Magnum." *The American Rifleman*, April 1935, p.39. [Information on various 22 high velocity cartridges, with a mention of developments to come.]

Ness, F. C. "4000 F.-S. With the Hornet Bullet." *The American Rifleman*, May 1935, p.5. [The (in)famous preliminary announcement of the Swift.]

Ness, F. C. "That .22-Sweany Job." *The American Rifleman*, June 1935, p.44. [Describes some of Sweany's experimental work on necked-down 30-06 and 7x57 cases.]

Ness, F. C. ".22 High-Velocity News." ." *The American Rifleman*, August 1935, p.49. [Very brief descriptions of experimental work by Sedgley, Donaldson, Wotkyns, Gebby; includes a prediction of a semi-rimless case for the "final .22 high-velocity."]

Donaldson, H. "Forerunners of the Present High-Speed .22's." *The American Rifleman*, September 1935, p.14. [A review of early work on high velocity 22-caliber cartridges by Newton and by Mann.]

Ness, F. C. "W. R. A. .220 Swift Announced." *The American Rifleman*, September 1935, p.45. [Winchester's announcement of the 220 Swift rifle, with the cartridge based on the 6mm Lee case.]

Williams, C. G. "On .22 H. V. Experiments." *The American Rifleman*, December 1935, p.47. [Some notes on early work by Newton, Mann, and Williams.]

Ness, F. C. "Latest Dope on the .220 Swift." *The American Rifleman*, March 1936, p.45. [Some history of Sweany and Wotkyns's work on the Swift, and experimental work by J. B. Smith and Donaldson.]

Sharpe, P. B. *The Rifle in America*, 1938, 641pp., William Morrow and Company, New York. Reprinted 1995 by The National Rifle Association and Odysseus Editions, Inc., Fairfax, Virginia. [Discussion of Swift history on pp.131, 581-582; the rimmed 6mm Lee Navy case is mentioned on p.111.]

Ness, F. C. ".25 Krag Niedner." *The American Rifleman*, January 1942, p.50. [Mentions Niedner's 22-6mm Lee reamer made for Newton in 1910.]

Ness, F. C. "'Swift-Varminter.'" *The American Rifleman*, December 1942, p.45. [Summary of correspondence from Wotkyns about early work with the 22-250 Swift, and recent work with Wilson Arrow.]

Ness, F. C. "'Varminter' is Registered." *The American Rifleman*, October 1944, p.31. [Brief mention of early 22-250 work by Wotkyns, Gebby, and J. B. Smith, and of wartime exigencies of 22-250 case formation.]

Simmons, R. F. *Wildcat Cartridges*, 1947, 333pp, William Morrow and Company, New York. [For Swift history see pp.58-60, 67-68, 73-76, 82-85, 235; some aspects of Swift history given in this book were modified and clarified in Simmons's 1956 article.]

Landis, C. S. *Twenty-two Caliber Varmint Rifles*, 1947, 531pp., Small Arms Technical Publishing Company, Plantersville, South Carolina. [An account of Wotkyns's Swift is found on pp.184-185, including the confusing sentences discussed above.]

Barr, A. H. "Loads for the .220." *The American Rifleman*, March 1950, p.35. [Includes a brief synopsis of Swift history.]

Sharpe, P. B. *Complete Guide to Handoading*, Third edition, Second Revision, with Supplement, 1953, 463pp. and 264pp, Funk & Wagnalls Company, New York. [For history of the Swift, see especially pp. 287, 291, 348-350, and Supplement pp.56-57, 85-86, 191-193.]

Simmons, R. F. "22 High Velocity Cartridges." *Gun Digest*, 1956, p.41. [Detailed recounting of Swift history, based on correspondence with Wotkyns; includes useful brief biographies of Niedner, Newton, Mann, Wotkyns, et al.]

Page, W. "The Passing of the Swift." *Field and Stream*, July 1962, p.62. [Brief, literate history of the origin of the Swift.]

Staff. ".220 Swift." *Handloader*, March-April 1968, p.17. [Notable for three consecutive erroneous sentences on Swift history.]

Donaldson, H. A. "Yours truly, Harvey A. Donaldson." *Handloader*, July-August 1968, p.66. [Mentions Newton's experiments with the 22-6mm Lee.]

Donaldson, H. A. "Yours truly, Harvey A. Donaldson." *Handloader*, November-December 1969, p.66. [Gives a brief history of the Swift, describes his own 228-250 from 1916, mentions receipt of an early pilot rifle in 220 Swift from Winchester. Includes a photo of a 5-shot group from the early Swift.]

Donaldson, H. A. "Yours truly, Harvey A. Donaldson." *Handloader*, January-February 1970, p.66. [Describes extensive experience with the Swift; mentions shooting the 5-shot group with the 1934 and 1963 Swift rifles.]

Carmichel, J. "The Ultramodern/Obsolete .220 Swift." *Handloader*, September-October 1971, p.38. [A fine synopsis of Swift history, with speculation on the 22x55 cartridge.]

Amber, J. T. "Amber on .220 Swift." *Handloader*, January-February 1973, p.9. [Correction and commentary on the 1971 article by Carmichel.]

Wolfe, D. R., editor. *Yours Truly*, Harvey Donaldson, 1980, 271pp., Wolfe Publishing Company, Prescott, Arizona. [Reprints of Donaldson's columns from *Handloader* magazine, with Donaldson's statement deleted about the source of the photo of a target fired with a 220 Swift deleted.]

Carmichel, J. *The Book of the Rifle*, 1985, 564pp., *Outdoor Life* Books, New York. [Pages 278-284 include a rewrite of Carmichel's fine 1971 article on the Swift.]

Zeglin, F. *Wildcat Cartridges*. The Reloader's Guide to Wildcat Cartridge Design, 2005, 287pp., LR Books, Pinedale, Wyoming. [Pages 255-256 are interesting for an interpretation of Landis's 1947 statements about Wotkyns.]

THE OVERLOOKED SAVAGE 99 –IS IT SUITABLE AS A CUSTOM RIFLE?

by David R. Pie
Illustrations by William Kilroy

ABOVE: Gunsmith Doug Wells working on a 99 in his shop.

In 1957, when I was 13 years old, my Dad promised to get me a rifle and take me deer hunting. I wanted a Savage 99-EG 250-3000 in the worst way; and I wanted this rifle equipped with a 4-power Kolmorgen Bear Cub scope. This was my dream rifle.

Sadly, I never got that rifle. Instead, my Dad got me a 1903A3 Springfield. Also, he got me a Bishop semi-inletted stock and a "how-to" magazine article on remodeling the '03A3, which I did with his help. In the years since that first Springfield project I've built many stocks for my own rifles as a hobby. Recently, motivated by my 50-year-old memory of that Model 99 I wanted so badly when I was 13, I undertook a project to build a custom rifle using a worn old Savage 99-EG 250-3000. Dad's gone now, but I can picture him saying to Mom, "That kid never lets go!"

In any case, as I worked through this project, I learned an unexpected lesson: The Savage 99 is a much better rifle than I thought it was. Since 1957 I have owned several factory-original Savage 99s. While I liked these rifles very much, I never thought of a 99 as being anything more than a work-horse rifle. For a number of reasons, I did not think the 99 was a good candidate for a custom rifle. But now my thinking has changed.

SAVAGE 99—PROS & CONS

Only certain rifle actions are widely accepted as suitable for a custom rifle. For an accurate, reliable, and attractive hunting rifle the standard foundation for custom work is a Mauser, a pre-64 Winchester model 70, or one of several single-shot actions. The Savage 99 is conspicuously overlooked as the basis for a fine custom hunting rifle. Since the early 1960s, when gun writer Jack O'Connor first sparked my interest in high-end custom rifles by describing Al Biesen stocks and Tom Burgess metal work, I have seen hundreds of beautiful custom rifles: Mausers, Model 70s and single shots. However, in those many years I can remember seeing only two or three full-custom Savage 99 rifles. Why is this?

With a production run spanning nearly 100 years, the Savage 99 was always popular with hunters. In 1914, Savage Arms Corporation must have dazzled deer and varmint hunters when they offered the Model 99 chambered for the fast flat-shooting 250-3000 Savage cartridge. Because the Savage 99 is a strong action, it was eventually chambered for such high-intensity cartridges as the 308 Winchester, the 284 Winchester, and the 358 Winchester. Another plus of the 99 is that it ejects cases to the side, which permits mounting a scope low on top of the receiver. And, in contrast to Winchester and Marlin lever actions, which use tube magazines, the rotary magazine of the Savage 99 allows the safe use of flat-shooting spitzer bullets.

While the Savage 99 has always been popular with hunters, among shooters contemplating their "ideal" action for a custom rifle the 99 has not been a popular choice. I suspect the 99 may be perceived as exhibiting too many warts compared to a Mauser, Model 70, or an elegant single shot. I believe this view of the 99 may be shared by many professional gunsmiths who know every refinement possible to transform a military Mauser into a custom rifle, but lack this same level of experience with the Savage 99. In my Savage 99 project I learned that common perceptions about inherent Savage 99 shortcomings are largely without merit.

What are these commonly perceived shortcomings of the Savage 99? Here are some examples:

- The Savage 99 has a reputation for having a "springy" action that develops excessive headspace. During the course of my 99 project I learned this is not correct. Some Savage 99s originally left the factory with a marginal fit of their levers and bolt lockup surfaces, which eventually led to excessive headspace. But once these problems are corrected, a Savage 99 is unlikely to ever have a headspace problem again.
- The 99 has a reputation for having a mediocre trigger pull. In fact, many professional gunsmiths have attempted trigger jobs on Savage 99s with mediocre results. Thus, the 99 has a reputation for having a poor trigger pull that cannot be corrected. Compared to the Mauser where a trigger job can be accomplished by simply dropping in an after-market trigger unit, improving the trigger on a 99 is not so easy. However, there are a few gunsmiths who specialize in the Savage 99 and they consistently achieve excellent results with their 99 trigger work. After a properly done trigger job, a 99's trigger pull will be very smooth and predictable with only the slightest movement or creep.

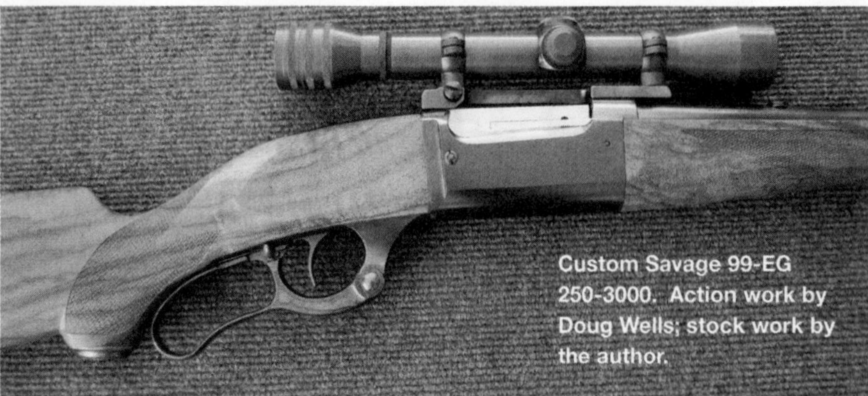
Custom Savage 99-EG 250-3000. Action work by Doug Wells; stock work by the author.

- Today, some staple Savage 99 cartridges such as the 300 Savage may be viewed as being a little boring for a custom rifle. However, there are many useful and exciting cartridge options for the Savage 99, but they are frequently overlooked.
- The 99 has a reputation for being less accurate than a bolt action. Accuracy shortcomings are attributed to the 99's rear bolt lock-up, poor trigger, and two-piece stock. But a tight, tuned Savage 99 action, fitted with a custom barrel and a properly bedded stock, has an accuracy potential that is dramatically under-appreciated by the naysayers. In a way, misconceptions about the accuracy potential of the 99 remind me of how many of us felt about the accuracy potential of semi-automatic rifles. Today phenomenal sub-minute-of-angle accuracy is routinely achieved with custom AR-15 223 rifles and extensively worked-over Ruger 10/22 rimfires. This shattered my long-held perceptions about the limited accuracy potential of semi-automatic rifles.
- Finally, critics say factory Savage 99 stocks have too much drop at the heel, particularly for a scoped rifle, or for a heavy-recoiling cartridge. This problem can also be solved as we will discuss below.

NO MORE RESERVATIONS

I laid to rest my doubts about using a Savage 99 for a custom rifle project after taking a close look at the work of Doug Wells, a gunsmith who specializes in the Savage 99 action. Wells, proprietor of "Lock, Stock, & Barrel," (P.O. Box 46034, Huson, Montana 59846) is a graduate of the gunsmith program at the Colorado School of Trades and has been a full-time working gunsmith for more than 30 years. Along with other gun work, he has made a specialty of the Savage 99. This is quickly evident when you tour his shop. In every corner you see Savage 99 levers, barrels, actions, parts, stocks, and pieces. With his long 99 work experience, there's little about the functioning, problems, refinements, and potential of this rifle that he doesn't know.

When Wells finishes work on a Savage 99, the action feels tight and smooth when you work the lever – noticeably better than a factory-new 99. The trigger pull is excellent. A re-worked, rebarreled, and properly stocked 99 that comes out of Well's shop will usually produce minute-of-angle groups with good loads. Sometimes they produce cloverleaf groups! After handling several Savage 99 actions that Doug had worked over, I could see no unresolved issues that argued against using a 99 for a custom rifle. This is when I committed to the idea of putting together my 99 dream rifle.

To get my 99 project rolling, I cleared my mind of an image of Dad with a disapproving expression on his face. Then, undeterred, I acquired a worn 1936 vintage Savage 99-EG 250-3000 and located a near-mint 4-power Kolmorgen Bear Cub scope. What I wanted to produce from these relics was a rifle that looked similar to the factory Savage 99-EG I coveted when I was 13; only better. For reasons of nostalgia, I wanted to use the original factory barrel for my project. Fortunately, after a good scrubbing, the bore of my 70-year-old 99 barrel looked OK. Then, before starting this project, I took my rifle to the range and discovered that it shot acceptable groups.

Some readers may entertain thoughts of making the same choice I did by selecting a Savage 99 for their own custom rifle project. For these individuals the knowledge I gained working through my project with Doug Wells may be useful.

SELECTING A USED RIFLE

With split oil-soaked stocks, and nearly devoid of blue on their metal surfaces, there are literally thousands of worn old Savage 99s on the used gun market. With some work, most of these can be made into a fine custom rifle. However, Wells offers some advice on selecting a 99 for a custom rifle project:

Some people may be tempted to look for a near-mint condition 99 for an expensive custom rifle project. Don't do it! Destroying a fine vintage rifle is not necessary to obtain a mechanically sound action for a custom rifle. Savage 99s are no longer being made and a growing number of collectors recognize that the best vintage, factory-original 99s are pieces of history that should not be altered. With the action work described below, most of the worn non-collectable 99s sitting in used gun racks can become the foundation for a fine custom rifle. In fact, even a factory-new Savage 99 is likely to have deficiencies in the fit and function of its moving parts. This means that a factory-new 99 will probably require nearly the same amount of custom gunsmith work to tighten, smooth, and correct as an old "beater." This is just another reason why it doesn't pay to use a collectable Savage 99 for your custom rifle project.

An excessively gouged and dinged receiver may be difficult to clean up and finish so that it is suitable for a custom rifle. A lot can be done to clean up a dinged action, but there are limits. Mangled screw heads can be fixed or replaced, but this can be expensive. So, look for a 99 that is not excessively dinged and that has screw heads in decent condition.

In almost all cases, a rifle that has been in a fire should be avoided. The temper may be gone from the springs. Worse yet, the fire may have affected the heat-treatment and strength of critical parts. For a small fee, a competent gunsmith can tell you if the gun got hot enough to cause serious damage.

The condition of the factory barrel is usually not important because a custom rifle project usually includes installing a new barrel. However, if you intend to use the original factory barrel on a fine custom rifle, pay close attention to the bore. Start with a thorough cleaning to remove lead or copper fouling. Then inspect for pits, throat erosion, and various types of mechanical abuse. Enlist the help of a gunsmith if you lack experience to evaluate the bore condition.

Wells advises that takedown models of the Savage 99 are OK for a custom rifle project but they should probably be converted to a fixed-barrel configuration.

Pre-WWII 99s usually exhibit the best workmanship from the factory.

However, post-war lever-safety and tang-safety 99s can be worked over to be suitable for a custom rifle. Very few shooters are likely to consider the box magazine version suitable for a custom project because the 99s excellent rotary magazine is such a signature feature of the classic 99 design.

CARTRIDGE OPTIONS

Savage Arms Corporation chambered the Model 99 in many excellent cartridges, some of which are suitable for a custom rifle. For example, the 22 Savage HP, 243 Winchester, 250-3000 Savage, 38-55 Winchester, 7mm-08 Winchester, 284 Winchester, 308 Winchester or the 358 Winchester are good factory-original options. For those with more exotic taste, how about a 219 Zipper, 22-250 Remington, the 25-284, the 260 Remington, the 270 Titus, the 30-284, the 338-284, or the new 338 Federal? These choices are only some of the options possible.

The specific choice of suitable cartridges for a particular Savage 99 action does vary. For example, actions produced after 1955 were lengthened slightly, and probably strengthened, to allow their use with the 308 Winchester. Only these post-1955 actions should be used for high-intensity cartridges based upon the 308 Winchester or 284 Winchester cases. Also, only specific cartridges are compatible with specific magazine carriers. However, a competent Savage 99 gunsmith can modify or replace specific carriers to allow proper feeding with a range of cartridges. This is a topic to discuss with your gunsmith before purchasing a 99 for a custom project.

I should mention that because of the modest camming force available for chambering and extracting cases with a lever-action rifle, partial full-length resizing is standard procedure when reloading for a 99. Also, because of the 99's rear lockup design, handloaders should avoid overly hot loads with high-intensity cartridges like the 308 or 284 since these can produce bolt compression and case stretch in the Savage 99. The result can be extraction problems or short case-life. However, shooters who use reasonable handloads, or factory ammo, will have no problems with the 99.

A FIX FOR MISALIGNED SCOPE MOUNT HOLES

Before 1957, Savage 99s were not drilled and tapped for a scope mount at the factory. Too often when an owner wanted to mount a scope they recruited an amateur mechanic with a drill press to drill and tap their receiver. Invariably this resulted in holes that were crooked, off-center, and improperly spaced for a standard scope mount.

The 99 I purchased for my project had this problem and Wells suggested this fix: Leupold makes an excellent 1-piece steel base for the Savage 99. A 1-piece base mounts with 3 screws rather than 4 screws used with 2-piece bases; this reduces the number of mounting holes that must line up. To fit the holes in my 99 receiver the spacing between the rear hole and front holes on the Leupold base was too short. So, Doug cut the Leupold base into two pieces, welded in a spacer, and then dressed the base down to look like a new (slightly long) 1-piece base. Another advantage of the Leupold base is that the rear scope ring-mount has an opposed-screw windage adjustment. The holes in my 99 were laterally misaligned and this windage adjustment feature solved the problem. The technique of cutting and welding to lengthen or shorten a Leopold base can be used to solve the problem of many early 99s with non-standard scope mount holes.

ACTION WORK

Both old and new 99s may have mechanical problems. Some of these problems may have existed when the rifle left the factory, some problems can be attributed to the normal wear on moving parts after years of hard use, and some Savage 99 problems were caused by home mechanics trying to fix something. These problems may include a loose drooping lever, a bolt that doesn't reach the full up-and-locked position when the lever is closed, a rough, creepy trigger pull, and excessive headspace. A common problem is a past amateur trigger job where metal was removed inappropriately or angles changed incorrectly.

In the Savage 99 design, headspace, lever lockup, bolt lockup, trigger/sear engagement, and correct functioning of the safety are all interrelated. For this reason, in most cases, it is not possible to fix just one problem with a Savage 99 action. Doug Wells believes the correct way to prepare a Savage 99 action for use in building a fine custom rifle is to start with a complete action job, as follows:*

- To fix a drooping lever, and to correct a condition where the bolt does

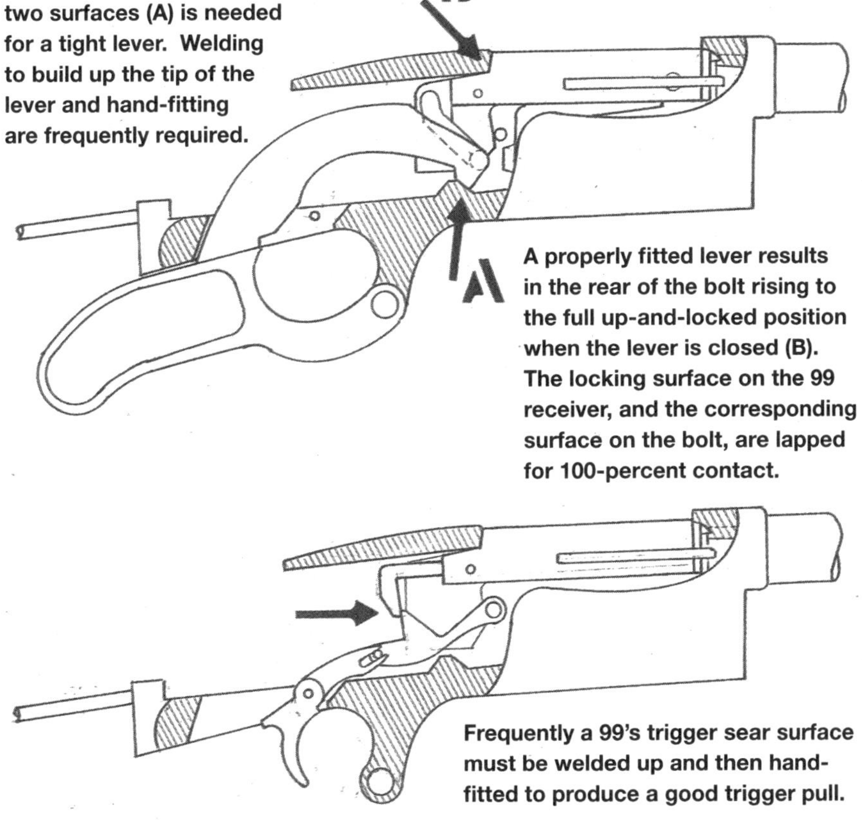

A good fit between these two surfaces (A) is needed for a tight lever. Welding to build up the tip of the lever and hand-fitting are frequently required.

A properly fitted lever results in the rear of the bolt rising to the full up-and-locked position when the lever is closed (B). The locking surface on the 99 receiver, and the corresponding surface on the bolt, are lapped for 100-percent contact.

Frequently a 99's trigger sear surface must be welded up and then hand-fitted to produce a good trigger pull.

not rise completely to the full "up" position at the back of the receiver when the lever is closed, the camming surfaces at the tip of the lever are welded up. By filing and stoning, these new surfaces are hand-fitted. The lever tip is then heat-treated and lapped-in for a final perfect fit. After this work, the lever locks solidly in place when the lever is closed and, simultaneously, the rear of the bolt rises to the full "up" position.

- The locking surfaces at the rear of the bolt, and the corresponding locking surface on the bolt opening in the receiver, are hand-lapped to achieve full contact. Savage 99 headspace problems are sometimes the result of less-than-perfect contact of these locking surfaces when the rifle originally left the factory. Sometimes only a very small point of contact existed; there was just enough contact to indicate correct headspace at the factory, but not enough to keep the bolt from setting back and creating some excess headspace later. Another factory-induced condition that can cause a headspace problem is a lever fitted so tightly that it tried to raise the bolt too high. The bolt can go up only so far, and then it is cammed forward away from the locking surfaces. Again, setback and excess headspace eventually result. But when a 99's lever is properly fitted, when the locking surfaces on the bolt and receiver are lapped-in for 100 percent contact, and with a new barrel fitted and chambered with correct headspace, a 99 is unlikely to have a headspace problem again.

- With the bolt in the full up-and-locked position, the bolt face is lapped so that it is perfectly perpendicular to the bore. This is done using a lapping device that threads into the receiver ring from the front.

- A trigger job is almost always needed for a Savage 99 to be suitable for a custom rifle. If past amateur trigger work needs to be corrected, a Savage 99 trigger job commonly requires welding up the sear surface. Then the new sear surface is cut back, hand-fitted, hardened, and stoned to achieve the correct amount of sear engagement and the correct engagement angle. Thinning the trigger spring is also standard in 99 trigger work.

- After working on the trigger, the safety mechanism will need work to provide correct functioning.

- Finally, bolt raceways and other contact surfaces for moving parts are hand-stoned to smooth the feel of the action.

In addition to the steps listed, each Savage 99 action is likely to have several unique issues that need attention. For example, on my 99 action, the trigger pin was out-of-round and binding. This affected the trigger pull. A new trigger pin fixed the problem. Also, Wells found a rough carrier spindle on the magazine assembly of my action that needed to be smoothed. This roughness existed when the rifle left the factory and it noticeably affected the smoothness of the rotary magazine.

With the action work complete, usually a new barrel is fitted and chambered. Or, if the factory barrel is being used, the barrel will usually need to be set back one turn and re-chambered. This is because lapping the bolt locking surfaces and bolt face will have increased headspace enough that it needs to be corrected.

Finally, accessories such as barrel bands or custom iron sights are fitted and the exterior surfaces of the action and barrel are hand polished so they are ready for engraving or metal finishing.

* **Note:** *I must make it clear that the Savage 99 action work discussed here is not work that can be done by a do-it-yourselfer at home. Savage 99 action work requires high-level skills in welding, heat-treating, stoning, and fine-fitting of various parts. Improperly done, serious safety problems with the functioning of the trigger, the safety, or excessive headspace of the rifle can result. This is work for a master gunsmith who fully understands the Savage 99 action. The information in this article is intended to describe "what is done," not "how it is done."*

STOCK WORK

For a custom rifle stock there are two factors to consider: How it looks and how it functions.

The appearance of a custom stock has always been my first priority. I have always been enamored with the gunny-look of fine early 20th century British rifles and shotguns. With their long grips and elegant lines, those British stockmakers had an eye for what a gun stock should look like. To my eye, the lines of some of the very early Savage 1899 factory stocks match the graceful look of the classic British gunmakers. The semi-pistol grip Model 1899 stock used with the straight grip lever looks particularly good to me.

The trouble is that while these early 1899 stocks look good, they don't function well. This is because they have a very low comb and excessive drop at the heel. This was a problem that started in 1899 and was never properly corrected by the Savage factory; even the last 99s produced in the mid-1980s had this problem. The 1960/mid-70s vintage Savage 99 factory stock with a Monte Carlo comb did raise the top line of the stock; but this stock design still had excessive drop at the heel...and it was ugly!

The problem with a low comb is that the stock can't support your face adequately, particularly when using a scope. Some of the early Model 1899 factory stocks are really too low even for use with iron sights. Excessive drop at the heel becomes a problem when used with a heavy-recoiling cartridge. When fired, the muzzle pivots up and slams the comb of the stock into your face.

The comb of a Savage 99 can be raised when restocking. However, unless the toe-line of the stock is also raised, you will need to use a 6-inch-long buttplate. This would look horrible on a trim Savage 99 that came from the factory with a 4 3/4-inch-long buttplate. Trying to raise both the comb and toe line when restocking a 99 can result in the stock bolt hole exiting the bottom of the stock! Fortunately, many years ago a supplier of semi-finished gunstocks, Reinhart Fajen of Warsaw, Missouri, developed a solution for this problem.

In the old days Reinhart Fajen offered a "high-comb" semi-finished stock for the Savage 99. These stocks incorporated a dog-leg stock bolt hole. Specifically, the receiver end of the stock bolt hole was drilled through the wrist to a point slightly past the grip area in-line with the threaded stock bolt hole in the tang. At the buttplate end of the stock, the start-point for drilling the stock bolt hole was raised about 1 inch above the factory location. The rear portion of the hole was then drilled to intersect the hole drilled from the front. While these two intersecting holes form a slight dog-leg, the angle was not enough that the stock bolt would bind when turning the corner. You could still engage the slot in the bolt head with a screwdriver, engage the threads in the tang, and turn the stock bolt tight. The effect of this dog-leg hole is to allow both the bottom and top lines of the stock to be moved

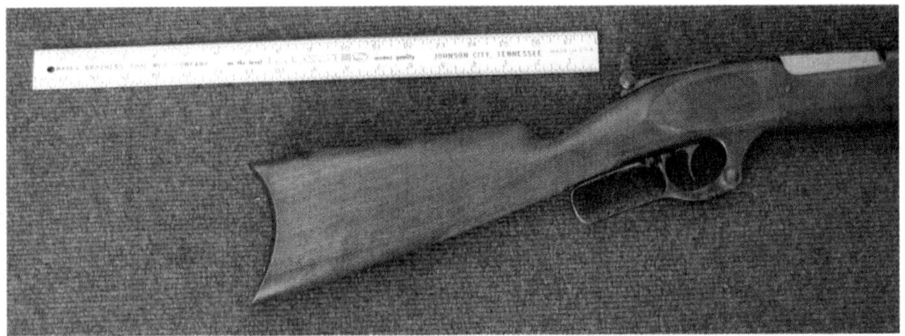

This early Savage 1899 shows the characteristic low comb and excessive drop at the heel.

up without the stock bolt hole exiting the bottom of the stock. This allows about any comb height and any drop-at-the-heel dimension that you might want. There are probably some aesthetic limits in how far the comb and toe line can be raised before the stock starts to look awkward. However, the pictures the 99 stocked by Doug Wells shown here use a dog-leg stock bolt hole to provide a scope-height comb. I think this stock looks pretty good!

Savage 99 buttstocks do have one inherent weakness. The two panels on the stock that sandwich the top and bottom tangs are vulnerable to breaking if the buttstock is subjected to a major side load. I must say that in 50 years of hunting and shooting I have never managed to expose any rifle stock to a side load that would break a 99 buttstock. However, it can happen. For example, if your horse falls down and lands on your 99!

Because the 99 has not been used frequently as the basis for custom rifles, classic custom stock styles for this action are not highly refined like those for the Mauser 98, Winchester Model 70, and Ruger No.1 stocks. The fact is, few top stockmakers have done much work with custom stock styles for the 99. I believe there is an opportunity for some of the very creative professional stockmakers out there to develop and refine the lines of a classic stock style for the Savage 99.

Finally, stock bedding can make the difference between a rifle that is accurate and one that is not. For the Savage 99, good buttstock bedding is routine for any stockmaker. However, forearm bedding is always an issue with a two-piece stock if best accuracy is an objective. Many gun-builders like to use a short steel lug attached to the barrel as part of their forearm bedding system. This lug is drilled, tapped and used to attach the forearm. The forearm is then glass-bedded around this lug so that the front- and rear-facing surfaces of the block keep the forearm from moving fore-and-aft with recoil. The benefit of additional contact points between the forearm and barrel to achieve best accuracy is a topic open for discussion and experimentation.

THE COST OF A SAVAGE 99 CUSTOM RIFLE

There are so many worn, non-collectable Savage 99 rifles available that the price for a basic 99 action is quite reasonable. In fact, compared to other options for building a custom rifle, an old 99 action is one of the best bargains out there.

The time required to complete a 99 action job varies with each rifle, but it generally takes a master gunsmith like Wells 2 1/2 or 3 full days of work. Fitting a new barrel, barrel bands, iron sights, scope mounts, and hand-polishing the barrel and action can extend the work to a week or more. Custom gun work is not cheap, but the cost of a full action job on a Savage 99 probably won't exceed what it costs for a gunsmith to clean up a military Mauser or any other action suitable for a custom rifle. A custom stock for a Savage 99 will not exceed the cost of any other two-piece custom stock.

I realize that some readers aren't interested in a custom rifle. They bought a used Savage 99 rifle 20 years ago for $200 and, at some point, discovered their rifle has mechanical problems. After reading this article they may want to get these problems fixed. Not realizing the work time involved, they can't imagine a need to spend more than about $50 for repairs on their $200 gun. Today a gunsmith can barely afford to disassemble a rifle and evaluate its problems for $50. If an old Savage 99 has sentimental value, the owner may find it worth the cost to hire a specialist to get their 99 functioning properly. But a gunsmith can't afford to spend several days working on your rifle for nothing. It helps me put the cost of gun work in perspective when I consider the hourly rate I pay a dentist, car mechanic, or a plumber!

MY COMPLETED SAVAGE 99

Now finished, I believe my Savage 99-EG 250-3000 conforms to the basic standards for a fine rifle. If Dad was around, I think he might even shrug his shoulders and give me a sideways nod that said, "It's pretty nice."

With Doug Wells' action work, this is a mechanically near-perfect Savage 99.

Beyond the good-looking California English walnut, my stock work probably does not match anybody else's idea of what is needed for a perfect Savage 99…but it satisfies my dream. Remember, this rifle is the product of 50-year-old memories mixed with some aesthetic standards I developed in later years. With its low comb, the stock does not fully support my face when looking through the scope. However, I really don't care because this stock looks like the stock I remember wanting when I was a kid. In fact, with the light-recoil of the 250-3000 Savage cartridge, this stock works fine for me. Some people may think the forearm on my rifle is too long for the short barrel, but Savage Arms used long forearms on the short-barrel EG model – and I like it. I believe that accommodating an individual's personal taste, dreams and desires, rather than conforming to a convention, is a lot of what building a custom rifle is all about. At least for me, this rifle has proven the Savage 99 is suitable for a custom rifle.

FINAL THOUGHTS

That so few full custom Savage 99 rifles are built does not mean that there is something wrong with the 99. I believe the scarcity of custom Savage 99s reflects the fact that very few custom rifle gunsmiths have invested the years of time needed to master this action. I know that many gunsmiths routinely tell drooping-lever Savage 99 owners, "Your rifle cannot be fixed, hang it on the wall." However, a few gunsmiths like Doug Wells have made a specialty of the Savage 99. They know how to correct almost any mechanical problem and can transform a worn old Savage 99 into a real gem, honed and smoothed, suitable for a custom rifle. Tightened, with a good trigger pull, and with a fine barrel, the Savage 99 is ready for the best of the stockmaker's art. Overlooked and underappreciated in the custom gun world, the many non-collectable worn old 99s sitting in used gun racks across the country are excellent candidates to be transformed into fine custom rifles.

THE DOUBLE ACTION REVOLVER FOR CONCEALED CARRY

After 157 Years, Does It Still Measure Up?

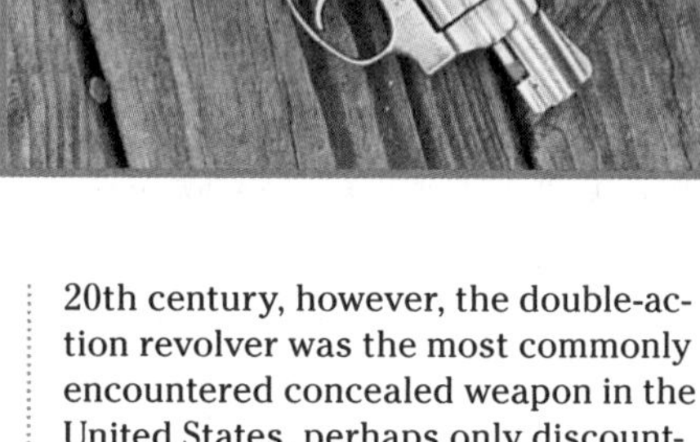

by Jerry Ahern
Photos by Sharon Ahern

In 1851, inventor Robert Adams obtained a British patent for the first successful double-action revolver. Although hardly the epitome of mechanical perfection, the Adams revolver and its subsequent improvements effectively started a revolution in personal defense. The double-action revolver came along slowly in the United States, starting to truly gain ground in America only in the waning years of the 19th century, although some British double actions saw service as private purchase firearms during the American Civil War years. By the turn of the 20th century, however, the double-action revolver had even penetrated the ranks of the American military, despite a rather dubious caliber choice (an underpowered .38) in a swing-out cylinder Colt. The double-action revolver's popularity would not erode until the late 1970s and early 1980s, when the double-action semi-automatic at last came into its own, this flatter, faster loading, higher-capacity handgun — at least temporarily — largely supplanting the double-action revolver as the arm of choice for lawmen and civilians alike. During the first seven and one-half decades of the 20th century, however, the double-action revolver was the most commonly encountered concealed weapon in the United States, perhaps only discounting the ever ubiquitous 25 automatic.

The Colt in 41 Long Colt, a formidable weapon then as now, and not too large for concealed carry. This is an 1895 New Army and Navy, precursor of the Official Police and dates from 1904.

Although the American armed forces returned to the 45 caliber after their unsuccessful flirtation with 38-caliber revolvers and had, for the first time, adopted a semi-automatic pistol, the exigencies of World War I brought double-action revolvers from Smith & Wesson and Colt back into the U.S. military as substitute standard weapons, a situation which would recur during World War II. Privately purchased snub-nosed 38 Special revolvers were in use during the Viet Nam War as "sleeping bag" guns. In actuality, revolvers were still issued in the U.S. military as special purpose weapons well into the end of the 20th century, signed out to plain-clothes military intelligence and law enforcement personnel as well as uniformed security officers, pilots and others, certain of these applications involving concealed carry.

In Europe, the double-action semi-automatic took serious hold in the late 1920s with the success of the Walther PP and PPK, the double-action auto rising to prominence as a military weapon with the Walther P-38. The question of reliability concerning the automatic generally — whether a traditional single-action style such as the 1911A1 or the more modern European double actions — was off-putting to most of American law enforcement, the civilian population following suit. When the Illinois State Police adopted the Smith & Wesson Model 39 in 1967-68, they were all alone among major departments and remained that way for some years to come. One of the reasons for Illinois switching to the Model 39 was the belief that the gun would be carried both on-duty and off-duty, taking snubby off-duty double-action revolvers out of the picture entirely.

The double-action revolver's principal claim to fame was quickness from the holster or pocket. It certainly wasn't accuracy. In appropriate hands, a traditional single-action revolver was much more accurate than even the best double action, a condition largely unchanged despite a century and one-half's strides in double-action lockwork designs. This accuracy question only has merit as regards target accuracy, however, not practical accuracy in combat. Single-action revolvers are vastly simpler affairs, the amount of moving parts required to raise a hammer from full rest and subsequently trip it, all in one double-action cycling of the trigger, considerably more complicated.

The terms "double action" and "single action" are a point of confusion to many people. By double action, what is meant is that two functions are performed with one action: the hammer is raised and released with the operator merely working the trigger. A single action requires two separate actions to be performed by the operator: cock the hammer, thus setting the sear, and pulling the trigger, thus terminating hammer/sear engagement. Two actions are needed to fire a single action, one to fire a double action, unless, of course, one chooses to fire the double action in the more deliberate and usually more accurate single-action mode, which applies to most double-action revolvers, but not all. One can easily grasp the confusion suffered by the tyro!

The first American double-action revolvers were developed by Smith & Wesson. Colt entered the lists later. Smith & Wesson's initial double-action offering premiered in 1880, a top-break, the 38 Double Action. Colt's Lightning, also a 38, but utilizing a loading gate rather than a swing-out cylinder, appeared in 1877. The Thunderer was Colt's Lightning Model produced in the heavier 41 caliber. In 1899, Smith & Wesson introduced what indisputably can be considered the most enduringly popular double-action revolver ever designed, a true benchmark, the Smith & Wesson Military & Police. Original calibers were 38 S&W and 32 Winchester Centerfire. As this is written, this revolver is still available as the Model 10 in blued carbon steel and as the Model 64 in stainless steel, both with four-inch barrels, both for 38 Special +P.

When Teddy Roosevelt was Police Commissioner of New York City, he was sent serial number "1" of the Colt New Police 32. He must have liked the revolver, acquiring over four thousand of them for the New York City police department in 1896. This double-action revolver eventually morphed into the Colt Police Positive, the Hartford version of a benchmark modern double action. Teddy Roosevelt liked his Colts.

The double-action revolver has been associated with some rather interesting people over the years, most of them real, a few fictional, at least two of them having crossed the line from fiction into reality for many. By this latter reference, I could mean no other personages than Dr. John H. Watson and the world's first consulting detective, Mr. Sherlock Holmes, both gentlemen of 221B Baker Street, London.

Although various arms entered into Holmes' exploits — even an extremely lethal airgun — both the Great Detective and his Boswell usually relied on 450-caliber double-action revolvers — it was the British service round, after all — Holmes' Webley Metropolitan Police a snub-nosed model, Watson's Second

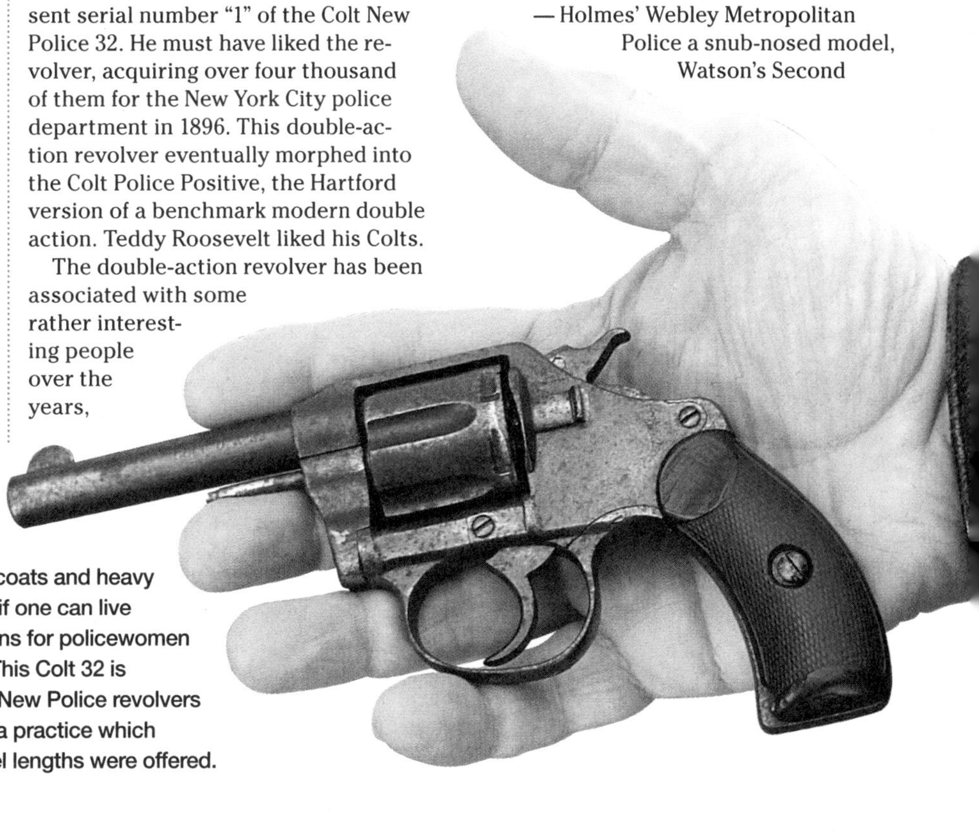

The sights of these service-style revolvers are rudimentary and quite similar, whether a Colt, as is this specimen, or a Smith & Wesson.

The diminutive Colt 32 was an ideal size for concealed carry in the days of woolen sportcoats and heavy outerwear, and it's still quite practical today, if one can live with the caliber. 32s were often the issue guns for policewomen well past the mid-point of the 20th century. This Colt 32 is interesting in that it is one of a batch of Colt New Police revolvers made with frames still marked New Pocket, a practice which continued for about four years. Various barrel lengths were offered. This gun was made in 1905-06.

At top, a heavily customized Smith & Wesson Model 686 by Mahovsky's Metalife, the barrel slab-sided and engraved, custom round butted, fitted with a crane lock and treated to a buttery smooth action job. Only a six-gun! At center a stock 6-inch blue Model 586. At bottom, a Model 681, action tuned and crane lock fitted and round-butted by Mahovsky, this is a fixed sight L-Frame, very early on discontinued. The gun is extremely accurate and durable in the extreme, the Metalife SS Chromium M treatment applied over the stainless steel. The wooden grips on both stainless revolvers are Smith & Wesson Goncalo Alves Combat Stocks, both good looking and functional.

Model Adams, a full-sized weapon. Holmes and Watson count among the first of a long list of detectives — in fiction and reality — to rely on the double-action revolver. But, so did bad guys.

For example, in 1895, John Wesley Hardin got into a crap game in El Paso, Texas, only to discover -- at least to his way of thinking — that the game was rigged! Wes Hardin jerked his 41-caliber double-action Colt Thunderer smokewagon and took back only what he had lost. Later, he was arrested and fined $25 for carrying a concealed weapon, the Colt confiscated. On other occasions, Hardin was also known to carry a shorter barreled Lightning with ivory grips, a gift from his cousin.

Pat Garrett, the inordinately tall (standing well over six feet, he was often referred to as "Long John") lawman who took down Billy The Kid, as history relates, had a Colt 1877 double action engraved on the backstrap as a gift from his friends in El Paso. But, Billy The Kid, not in that most famous of flipped photos where he carried a Colt Single Action Army, was known to use the 41-caliber double-action Colt as well. And, when Emilio Estevez portrayed Billy in "Young Guns II," in some scenes he actually used a genuine Colt Model 1877 Thunderer double action.

Miss Bonnie Parker and Mr. Clyde Barrow were serious Colt users and, among the guns in their car when Texas Ranger Frank Hamer got them, was a 45 Colt New Service. Until the advent of the 500 Smith & Wesson revolver, the New Service was the largest double-action revolver ever produced.

Although some of the Old West lawmen who survived into the modern era of the 20th century — men like Wyatt Earp and Bat Masterson — may have used double actions at times, one of the most famous of 20th century lawmen relied on a double-action revolver. That was Eliot Ness. In the well-respected television series starring the late Robert Stack, Ness carried a four-inch double action. If memory serves, it was a Colt. In the film with Kevin Costner, Ness carries a 45 automatic. In real life, Eliot Ness carried a two-inch barreled Colt Detective Special 38 Special. According to Ness himself in *The Untouchables* and *Four Against The Mob*, both written with Oscar Fraley, he never drew his gun in the line of duty. Sadly, Eliot Ness died before *The Untouchables* was turned into a television series and he was turned into the most storied lawman of the 20th century.

A 20th century lawman who drew his gun quite a lot in the line of duty and survived many gunfights, Bill Jordan was, quite possibly, the most passionate supporter of the double-action revolver one could imagine. When the Smith & Wesson Model 59 came out, Bill Jordan got one, a gift from the factory, if memory serves. He thought the large-capacity 9mm made a nice backup gun, but stuck with his four-inch Model 19 357 Magnum double-action revolver as primary ordnance. Bill Jordan was a gunfighting United States Border Patrol officer back in the days when gunfights with smugglers were so hot and heavy along the Mexican Border that horse-backing officers would carry a flour sack filled with spare ammo lashed to their saddle horns. Jordan authored the classic book on modern gunfighting, *No Second Place Winner*, as well as numerous gun articles.

Bill Jordan was always a very pleasant guy — unless you were a crook — and even appeared on television doing quick draw with a double-action revolver. He could place an aspirin tablet on the back of his gunhand, draw and drill the tablet before it hit the floor. Another trick was to place a cocked single-action revolver in a volunteer's hand, then outdraw the person with his double-action revolver before the single-action's hammer could fall. It is because of Jordan that the Model 19 357 Magnum came to exist.

A fan of fast gunplay when required, Jordan wanted the power of the 357 Magnum cartridge in the handier package of a K-Frame revolver. The 357 S&W Magnum, as introduced on April 8, 1935 (the first example was presented to then-FBI Director J. Edgar Hoover) in what was to become the Model 27 was a truly custom revolver of the first rank. The caliber was indeed handy for law/anti-law encounters as well as being a fine big game-getter. After World War II, production of civilian firearms resumed; Smith & Wesson introduced several new models of double-action revolvers, among these in 1954 the Model 28

Highway Patrolman. This was a plainer, less pricey, law enforcement-oriented version of the Model 27, available with a 4-inch or 6-inch barrel, the shorter barrel more comfortable when the gun was worn behind the wheel of a patrol car.

The revolver that Jordan pushed for — essentially a 38 Special Model 15 Combat Masterpiece, but in 357 Magnum and with more hand-filling stocks — became known as the Model 19 Combat Magnum. Initially offered in two barrel lengths with a choice of blue or nickel finish, the gun debuted on November 15, 1955. Bill Jordan was the recipient of this soon-to-be-legendary revolver. He promptly thereafter appeared on national television as a guest on the popular "You Asked For It" program. He held up his brand new Model 19 and proclaimed, "The answer to a peace officer's dream!"

Originally available in four-inch and six-inch lengths, it was offered not long afterward with skinnier grips and a 2 1/2-inch barrel for concealed carry. All three barrel length options were eventually available on the Model 66, the Stainless Combat Magnum. The first of these guns debuted in 1971, 4-inch versions only, the other two lengths arriving on the scene by the middle of the decade. The Model 66 2-1/2 was possibly the hottest selling double-action revolver on the planet, except, of course, for the double-action revolver worn as a concealed weapon by the movies' favorite cop, "Dirty Harry."

The Model 29 6-1/2 was sought after long before Clint Eastwood first played the role in 1972. Afterward, finding one of these 44 Magnum double-action revolvers sitting unclaimed on a dealer's shelf was almost less likely than finding the proverbial money tree growing in your backyard. The concept for the 44 Magnum cartridge was the brainchild of noted firearms authority and pundit Elmer Keith. Smith & Wesson completed the first Model 29, sending it to Remington for the ammunition-maker to use in load development. Elmer Keith received the third Model 29 made. "The world's most powerful handgun," as Clint Eastwood's character would describe it, premiered in 1956. With the Model 29, prolific screenwriter Harry Julian Fink took an aficionado's double-action hunting handgun and turned it into a full-fledged movie star.

A major problem, of course, with larger handguns of any operating system, double-action revolvers included, is concealment. Despite Bill Jordan's devotion to the Model 19 357 Combat Magnum with 4-inch barrel, the gun that he carried in the muff pocket of his sweats when he went jogging was a J-Frame snub-nose 38 Special; if memory serves, a Bodyguard Airweight.

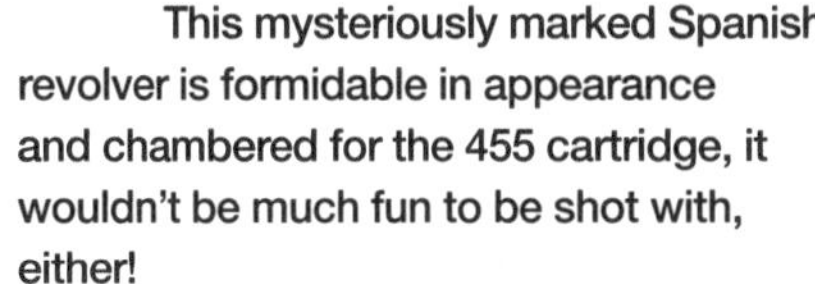

This mysteriously marked Spanish revolver is formidable in appearance and chambered for the 455 cartridge, it wouldn't be much fun to be shot with, either!

The "...peace officer's dream..." of 1955 was about to endure a rude awakening.

On April 11, 1986 the death knell rang on the double-action revolver as an issue weapon for America's most high-profile law enforcement agency, the FBI. It started a trend. For some time, FBI personnel and Metro-Dade police had been in pursuit of a violent two-man crew wanted in association with bank and armored car robberies. It wasn't quite ten in the morning when one of the cars associated with the fugitive duo was spotted. To employ an egregiously overused expression, it was then that "all hell broke loose." The two bad guys were armed with shoulder-holstered 357 Magnum revolvers, only one of these loaded with Magnum rounds. Michael Lee Platt, who would prove to be the most methodically deadly of the duo, had a folding stock semi-auto 223 equipped with 30-round magazines. And, he seemed to enjoy using it, especially with head and groin shots on men already wounded. Platt's partner, William Russell Matix, had a 12-gauge folding-stock shotgun fitted with an 8-round extended length magazine loaded with #6 shot. The FBI Special Agents just had handguns and a shotgun which was only successfully deployed after the shootout was well underway.

Special Agent Edmundo Mireles, badly wounded, revealed himself as an iron-willed hero. He ended the bloody firefight by emptying the six shots from the

The 4-inch Model 686.

cylinder of his Smith & Wesson Model 13 (I have read an account giving the revolver a 4-inch barrel, but the issue weapons had 3-inch barrels), all but one round entering into Platt and Matix. Matix died before medical personnel arrived. Platt died very quickly after their arrival.

Two FBI agents lay dead in the line of duty: Special Agent Jerry Dove and Special Agent Benjamin Grogan.

The shootout eventually led to the FBI switching to 10mm S&W semi-automatics, eschewing revolvers because of limited firepower and the +P 38 Special round they'd used for something with greater penetration. These 10mm autos manifested problems and, while such issues were being addressed, the FBI switched to 9mm autos. The double-action revolver was made the "fall guy" in this excessively bloody gun battle, the most intense in FBI history. Curiously, two FBI personnel in the gunfight had been allowed to carry high-capacity 9mm semi-automatics. Nobody blamed these, although close to 30 shots were fired at the killers from the two pistols. The actual FBI issue load in the 357 Magnum caliber Model 13s was the .38 Special +P 158-grain lead semi-wadcutter hollow point, not a 357 Magnum round. Although the FBI revolvers were given a great deal of the blame, issues ranging from ammunition choice to tactics to planning were of much greater import. In the end, the double-action revolver was out. The 10mm auto the FBI chose in its stead was itself replaced. The "10mm Lite" became the 40 S&W, the caliber of choice for platoons of today's American law enforcement personnel.

A perusal of current Smith & Wesson offerings reveals that only three basic K-Frame Models remain in the line, all 4-inchers, all 38 Specials. The 3-inch Model 13, along with the once highly prized Model 66 2-1/2 and its blued Model 19 counterpart, also 357 Magnums, are no longer made.

The most popular of all double-action revolvers these days are J-Frame-sized, whether from Smith & Wesson itself or from Taurus or Charter Arms. So many of these revolvers, of course, are no longer offered in 38 Special, but instead in 357 Magnum. Compounding the caliber issue in so small a revolver are metallurgical concerns. Only five basic models of J-Frame Smith & Wesson exist in 38 Special, including the original Model 36. Even the Model 60 has been morphed into a 357! If you want a Model 640 in 38 Special, you can't get it. One can, however, obtain a current production "Classic" Model 40 in 38 Special, complete with its original grip safety.

The first handgun I ever purchased was a 2-inch barrel 38 Special S&W J-Frame, a blued Model 36. That was forty years ago, as this is written. One can understand that I have a certain fondness for the things. Be that as it may, the combination of 357 Magnum recoil in guns as light as 12 ounces, rubber grips notwithstanding, will discourage practice. The key to successful service from a small double-action revolver is to shoot it. People used to complain about +P 38 Special rounds from an alloy-framed Smith & Wesson Airweight.

Ahern wearing a Hip-Gripped original Smith & Wesson Model 60 38 Special, the revolver acquired a quarter-century ago.

Can it be that today's shooters are so much tougher and stronger than pistoleros of yesteryear? I think not.

The typical steel-framed J-Frame Smith & Wesson double action of yore weighed 21 ounces. That is over a half-pound difference between the steel gun in 38 and the Scandium/Titanium/Stainless combination found in the 357 Magnum Model 360PD weighing 12 ounces. Twelve and one-half ounces to 13-1/2 ounces was typical weight for the "punishing" 38 Special Airweights. Then, why does anyone want a 12-ounce 357 Magnum? Certainly not to shoot it! My opinion, of course, for what it's worth.

Whatever one's choice in a double-action revolver — whether the firearm is the size of the N-Frame Model 29 or the

RIGHT: The DeSantis fabric Patriot Shoulder Rig works quite well and has the advantage of being ambidextrous and able to function with various versions of K-Frame and L-Frame size revolvers.

LEFT: Galco's Miami Classic for an L-Frame revolver is extremely concealable when properly adjusted and properly worn. And, it is comfortable.

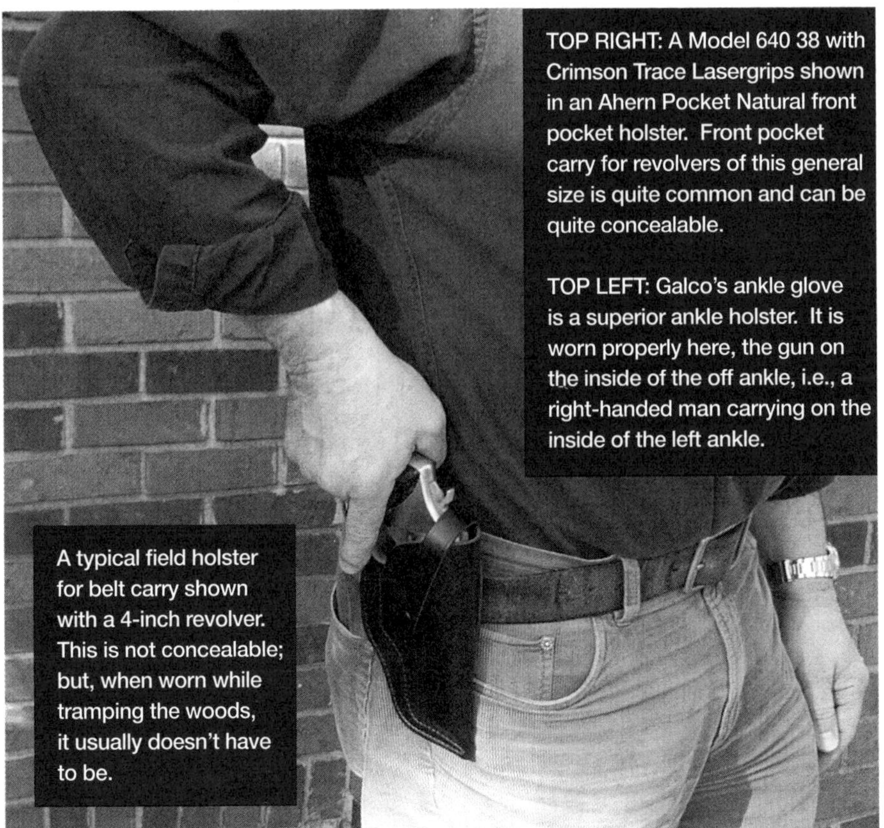

TOP RIGHT: A Model 640 38 with Crimson Trace Lasergrips shown in an Ahern Pocket Natural front pocket holster. Front pocket carry for revolvers of this general size is quite common and can be quite concealable.

TOP LEFT: Galco's ankle glove is a superior ankle holster. It is worn properly here, the gun on the inside of the off ankle, i.e., a right-handed man carrying on the inside of the left ankle.

A typical field holster for belt carry shown with a 4-inch revolver. This is not concealable; but, when worn while tramping the woods, it usually doesn't have to be.

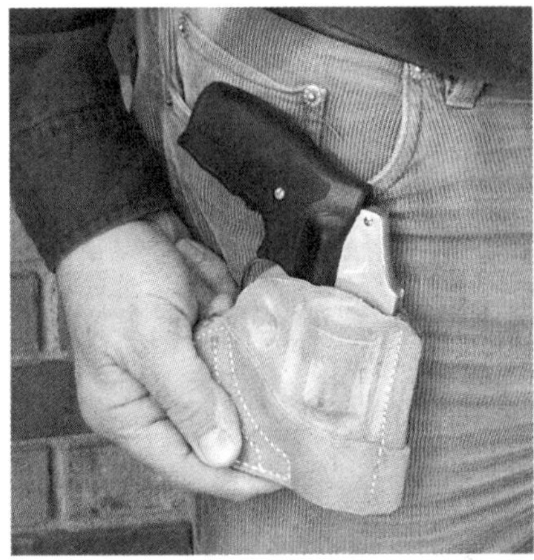

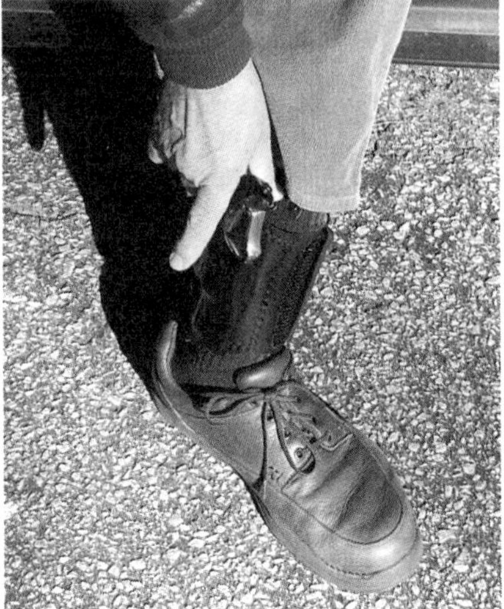

original Model 36, whether a 6-inch Colt Python or a 2-inch Detective Special, Cobra or Agent — the guns can be effectively concealed. What is said here is just as true, of course, for Taurus, Charter Arms and Ruger revolvers. Movies place an inordinate emphasis on shoulder holsters, for example. Almost as well-known as "Dirty Harry's" Model 29 was the shoulder holster in which he carried it in most of the films, the shoulder holster itself marketed as "The Dirty Harry Shoulder Holster." For a double-action revolver that size, a shoulder rig was practical. However, larger guns can be carried at waist level if one knows how. Over the years, when I've done seminars on how to carry and spot concealed weapons, I've taken a 6-inch barrel revolver and positioned it inside the waistband of my trousers, behind my left hip bone, butt forward, the entire weapon positioned so that the muzzle is angled toward the front. This keeps even a 6-inch double-action Colt or Smith & Wesson or Ruger or Taurus within the average man's body plane, thus effectively concealed under a normal covering garment.

Most double-action revolvers that will be carried concealed are not 6-inch barrel models or longer. Most, instead, are a nominal 2-, 3- or 4-inches in barrel length.

With a 4-inch barrel, the most practical on-body carries are with a holster worn inside the waistband, with an actual belt-mounted holster or with a shoulder holster. In most cases, however, the straight up and down vertical shoulder holster is usually the least concealable when serious concealment — rather than just covering up the gun — is at issue.

For a shoulder holster for the double-action revolver with a nominal 4-inch or even 3-inch barrel — or, for that matter one of the no longer produced Smith & Wesson Model 19 2-1/2 or Model 66 2-1/2 or the long-gone Colt 357 Magnum Lawman MK III 2-inch or short-bareled Diamondback or Python — the diagonal/horizontal shoulder holster is usually best. Some people refer to these shoulder systems as "horizontal" and wear them that way. They are most concealable and faster when worn as a "diagonal." Although most full-line and custom holster makers offer such shoulder rigs, three of the best are from Galco (which really pioneered with these rigs and popularized them), DeSantis and custom maker Sam Andrews. The Galco Miami Classic is probably the most well-known shoulder holster in the world because of the "Miami Vice" television series. Similarly, the DeSantis diagonal rig is what is worn by Bruce Willis in the "Die Hard" films. Currently, DeSantis only offers a fabric diagonal rig for double-action revolvers. Galco still offers the Miami Classic for "wheelguns," as double-action revolvers are sometimes called. As a custom maker, Sam Andrews will likely be able to make whatever the customer requires.

In belt holsters, the single tunnel loop variety is to be avoided for strong-side carry except when the gun is worn more or less openly. This style allows the butt of the gun to swing away from the body, thus profiling or outlining under clothing, disallowing any true concealment. Select either a holster utilizing two (or more, for different carry angles) belt slots, sometimes called generically a "pancake" style holster, since this type of slot arrangement was popularized by Roy Baker with his "Pancake" holsters. Or, choose a holster combining a single tunnel loop on the body side of the holster with a belt slot at the rear of the holster. This is a very effective system, one well-known example of this type developed years ago by Bianchi International and dubbed the "Askins

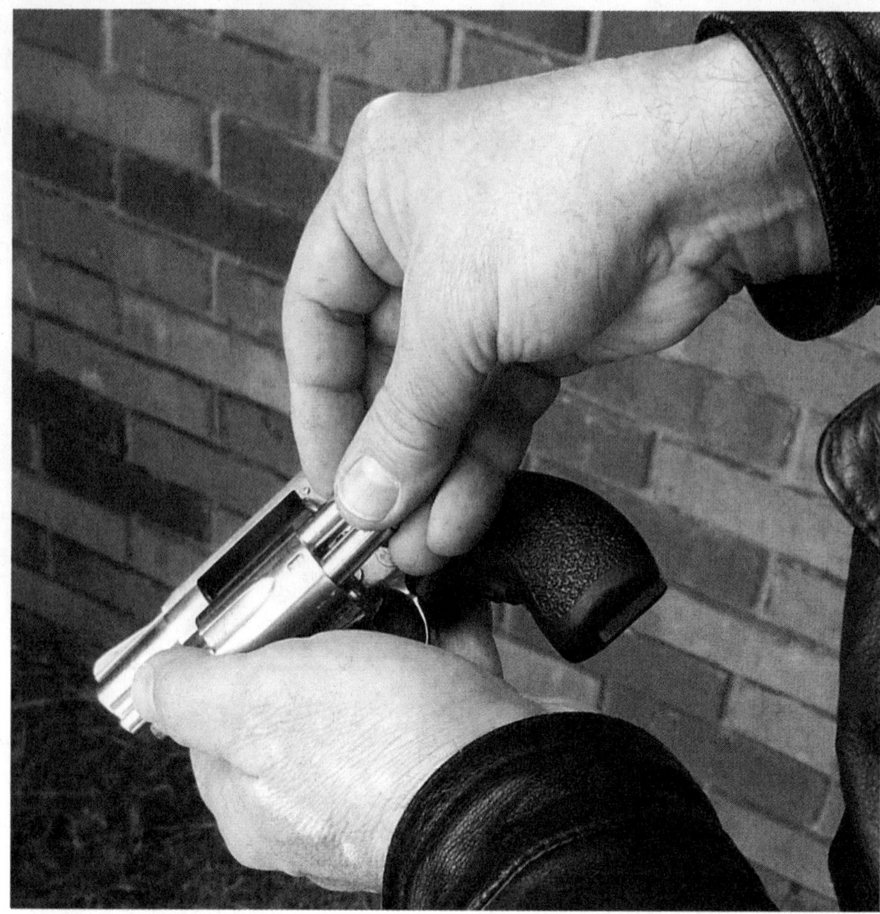

Supposedly, British officers were taught to load their Webley service revolvers this way. Be that as it may, absent speed loaders, this two-at-a-time loading technique is reliable and faster than single loading.

Avenger" after the famous firearms authority and writer Col. Charles Askins.

Double-action revolvers were/are often carried crossdraw, wherein the operator reaches to the opposite side of his body rather than his hip for the weapon, and these types of holsters may indeed be adequate with merely a single tunnel loop.

Whereas a snap closure safety strap is essential to the operation of most diagonal shoulder holsters, and even though all of these waist-level style holsters, of course, can be had with or without various types of safety strap arrangements, in the belt holster and, even more so, with inside-waistband holsters, the safety strap is largely unnecessary.

When it come to the smaller revolvers with their nominal 2-inch barrels and usually fixed sights (meaning less chance of snagging on clothing), concealment options grow. What was said about shoulder- and waist-level holsters for the longer barreled guns certainly applies; but, other factors — useful ones — enter in. For one thing, a great many double-action snubby revolvers are five-shooters. This imparts a narrower cylinder to the gun, aiding somewhat in concealment, closer to the flatness of a semi-automatic pistol.

Aside from all the carries mentioned above, these smaller guns can be worn in ankle holsters and even crotch holsters. The Galco Ankle Glove is an excellent example of the ankle holster and the K.L. Null Holsters crotch holster (Ken Null may be the only source in the U.S.A. still offering such a holster for a snubby revolver) is truly well-designed and well-made. Although Bianchi International and Safariland used to offer upside-down shoulder rigs for these double-action small revolvers, Null alone offers upside-down holsters for this or any revolver, to the best of my knowledge. Null's shoulder holsters of this type are excellent, by the way, whether one chooses the horsehide or plastic version.

For decades, my favorite way to carry a J-Frame snubby 38 double action was with the excellent Barami Hip Grip. These are still available in limited quantity, even more limited for double-action revolvers besides the J-Frame S&Ws, including Taurus, Charter Arms, Colt and Rossi models. The Hip Grip incorporates a shelf extension rising from the upper most portion of the right grip panel from behind the recoil shield. Slip the revolver inside the waistband, sans holster, and the shelf hooks over the waistband or waistband and belt. This keeps the revolver from sliding down into the wearer's pants and out the bottom of the trouser leg. The Hip Grip can work well for women, also. If one finds the comparatively skinny Hip Grip too skinny for comfortable shooting — I never did — you can acquire a Tyler T-Grip which fills in on the grip front strap, enlarging the grip surface.

These smaller double-action revolvers can even be carried in front pocket holsters. Indeed, J. Henry Fitzgerald, Colt's consummate ballistician/shooter/gunsmith/showman during the early decades of the 20th century, carried two Colt New Service double-action revolvers with barrels cut down to 2-inch length, the fronts of the trigger guards removed, the hammer spurs excised and new front sights attached. These 6-shot 45 Colt revolvers would be drawn with lightning speed from his leather-lined trouser pockets. The "Fitz Specials," as they came to be known, were adopted by Captains W.E. Fairbairn and E.A. Sykes as recommended arms in their landmark book *Shooting To Live*, detailing their police training techniques used in the embattled streets of Shanghai. Later, during World War II, these men went on to work with the British special forces and the American OSS. The well-respected Col. Rex Applegate was no stranger to these admittedly odd but quite effective double-action revolvers. After the tragic kidnapping of the Lindbergh baby, America's favorite aviator had Fitz make one of these for him. On his earlier world-famous trans-Atlantic flight, Charles Lindbergh had a Detective Special along.

The modern double-action revolver has other useful accessories beside Hip Grips, Tyler T-Grips and the like. There are speedloaders which, when trained with, can allow terribly rapid reloading of the double-action revolver, one of its principal shortcomings where compared to the speed and ease with which a semi-automatic pistol can be refreshed with an already loaded spare magazine. I have always favored my quite old Safariland loaders, but there are other brands, HKS having a fine reputation.

Quite possibly, the most terrific revolver accessory on the market is the laser grip device from Crimson Trace. Crimson Trace Laser Grips are made for a wide range of semi-autos, of course, but the firm's most popular seller out of all the models it makes for revolvers and semi-autos is for the J-Frame. Actually, there are several different models for the J-Frame Smith & Wessons and, I would hazard a guess that, if Colt had not abandoned its small D-Frame revolvers — the Detective Special, Cobra, Agent and Diamondback — Crimson Trace would be making hot-selling Lasergrips for these as well.

Note to entrepreneurs out there: I would imagine that the Detective Special is totally public domain, by now, all patents likely expired. Just a thought!

The Crimson Trace Laser Grips almost never affect holstering, the batteries are easily and cheaply found, service life for the laser component terrific (the unit our daughter uses on her J-Frame is well over five years old), and, the laser itself not withstanding, the grips are comfortable and concealable. The laser unit is built into the right grip plate and zeroed at fifty feet from the factory. Zero is adjustable, of course, both for windage and elevation. I've been involved with experimenting with lasers since about 1974. I've never seen a better one than Crimson Trace Lasergrips and I use these on several handguns.

The Null "Vam" holster was developed for police and security personnel who needed fast access to an inconspicuous gun while seated behind the wheel. Unlike many such holsters, the Vam is perfectly acceptable when up and moving about. It is also, when practiced with, quite possibly the fastest crossdraw rig Ahern has ever seen or tried. This one is from horsehide, which wears like iron.

Ahern holds a 4-inch revolver in his right hand, a 2-inch snubby in his left, the two extremes of practical double-action revolver concealables, both serious weapons in good hands.

Perhaps, consideration of the laser as a sighting device for a design the first commercially successful example of which debuted in 1851 encourages the right perspective for the double-action revolver. With Smith & Wesson back in good hands, one can actually purchase the updated version of a "modern" revolver which debuted in 1899 from the original manufacturer — the Military & Police Model 10. The J-Frame Smith & Wesson, which first appeared as the Model 36 in 1950, inspired a host of other guns, many from Smith & Wesson itself, but from other fine firms as well, both foreign and domestic. One can still buy a 2-inch blue Model 36 in 38 Special from Smith & Wesson.

My maternal grandfather, Hunting Colfax Morrell, carried a revolver from time to time, one can presume, since he was quite the "gunny" guy, an expert rifleman, yet, the only handgun he owned was a nickel-plated Hopkins & Allen 32 top-break. It cost just a few dollars in the Montgomery Ward catalogue of 1896; but, it still works. The Hopkins & Allen was a short-barreled double action of overall diminutive proportions, even fitted with a quite innovative folding hammer spur to facilitate smoother draws from the trouser or jacket pocket. In those days, the double-action revolver, although mechanically more complicated than single-action revolvers and the new single-action autoloaders, was the simplest defensive arm to operate quickly and reliably from concealment when one's life was on the line.

Some things just never change.

The conclusion which will be drawn is that the double-action revolver, when sensibly considered for its weight and size, is still viable for concealed carry, if one takes the time and effort to do it right.

THE ART OF ENGRAVED & CUSTOM GUNS

by Tom Turpin

This unusual and seldom seen single-shot rifle is from the Montana shop of Lee Helgeland. The rifle project began when Lee acquired the Schmidt–Habermann (sometimes called a Kettner) action quite a number of years ago. Rick Stickley did the barrel work about fifteen years ago. That included milling an integral quarter-rib and front sight ramp, as well as a sling swivel base. He chambered the barrel for the 7x57R cartridge and fitted the barrel to the action. Lee reshaped the action and lever for a better look, as well as fashioning a set of scope rings for the rifle from a set of "gunmaker" rings from Germany. He then crafted the beautiful stock from a stick of Turkish walnut, fitted a genuine horn buttplate, grip cap and forend tip to the stock, checkered it in a borderless pattern 28 LPI, and gold-plated all the internal parts. Photo by Steven Dodd Hughes

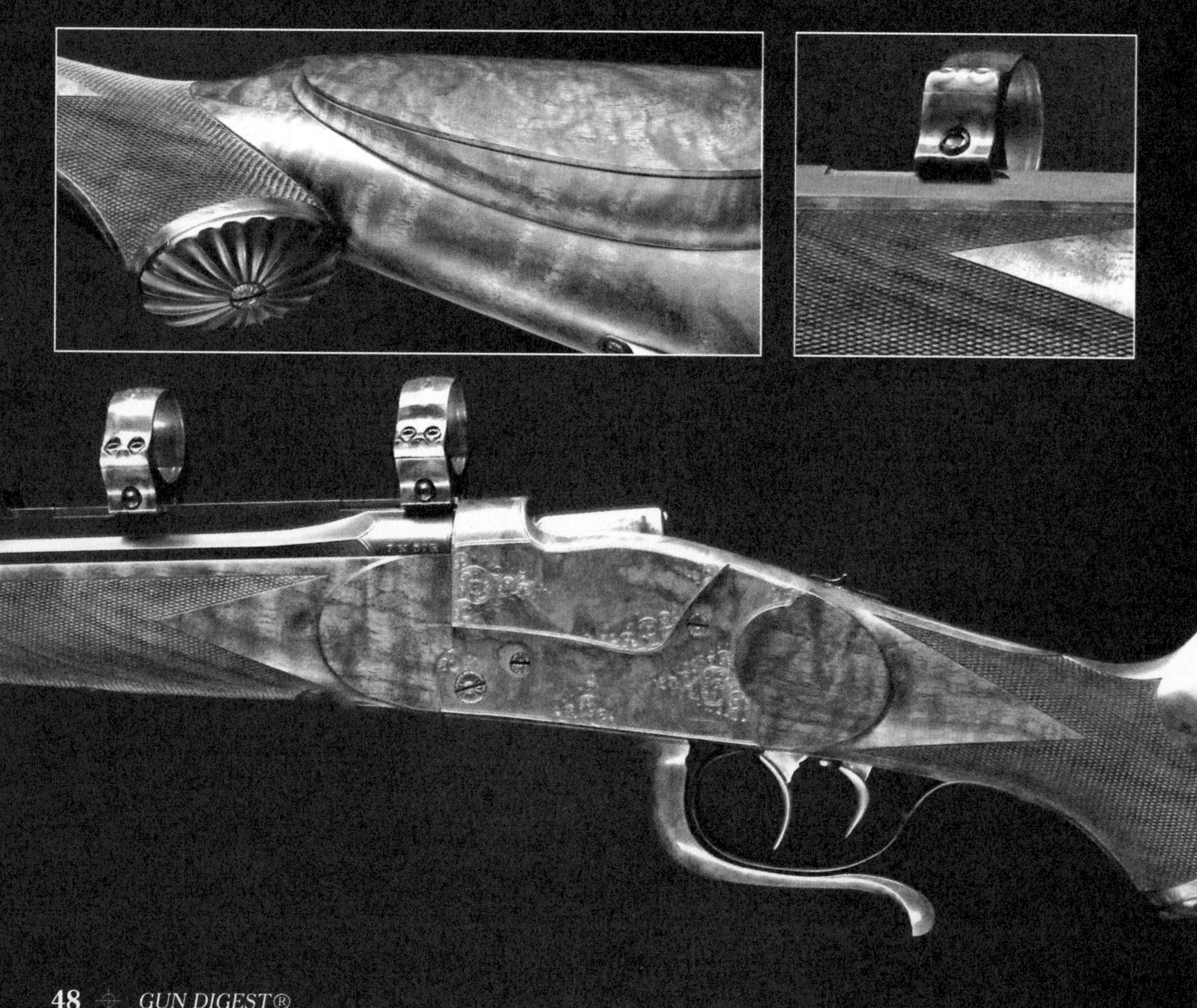

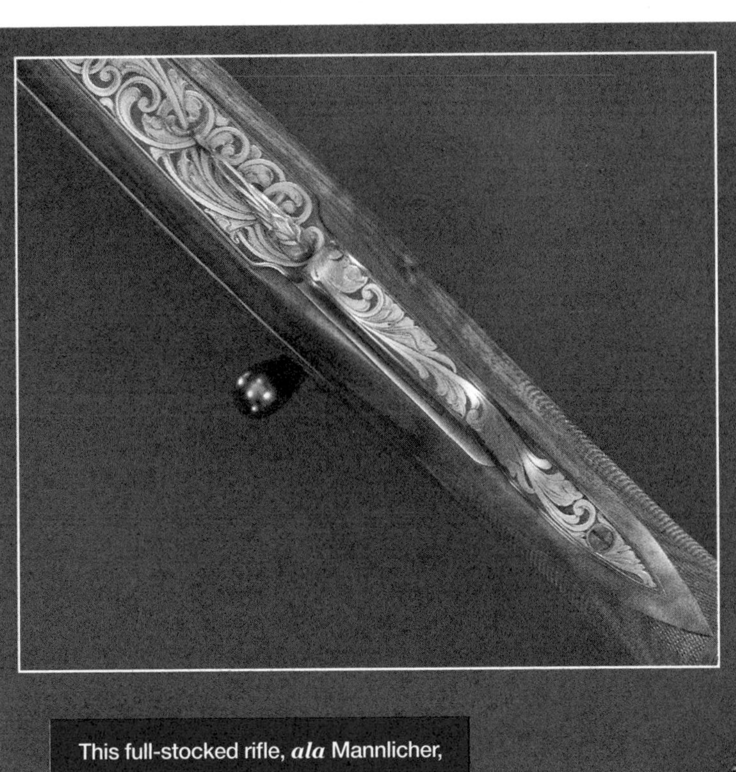

This full-stocked rifle, *ala* Mannlicher, is from the shop of Al Lofgren. Starting with a Swedish Mauser action, custom barreled for the 6.5x55 cartridge, Lofgren turned it into this lovely custom rifle. Very Germanic in styling, to include the double-set trigger and stock carvings, it exemplifies the Teutonic styling. Al did all the stockwork, to include the carving; Dave Norin did most of the metalwork; and Brian Hochstrat did the engraving.

Photo by Tom Alexander Photography

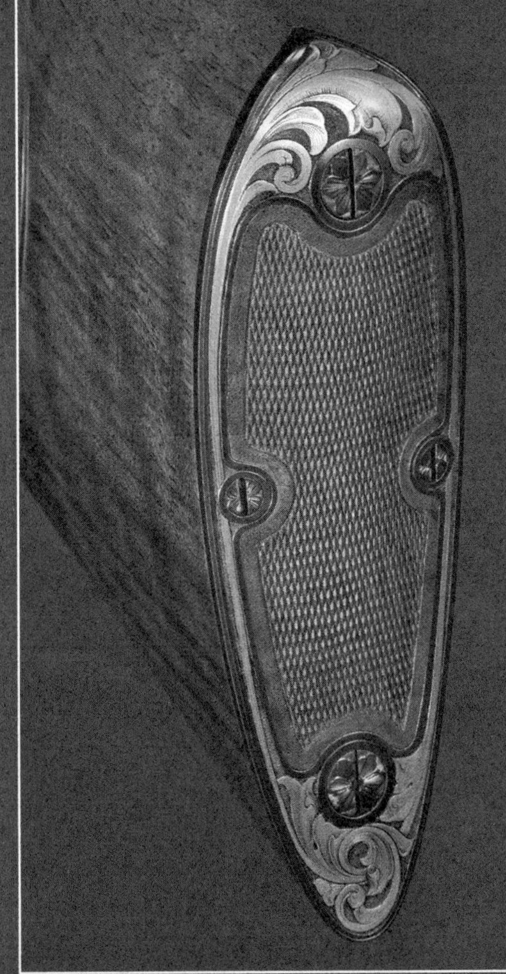

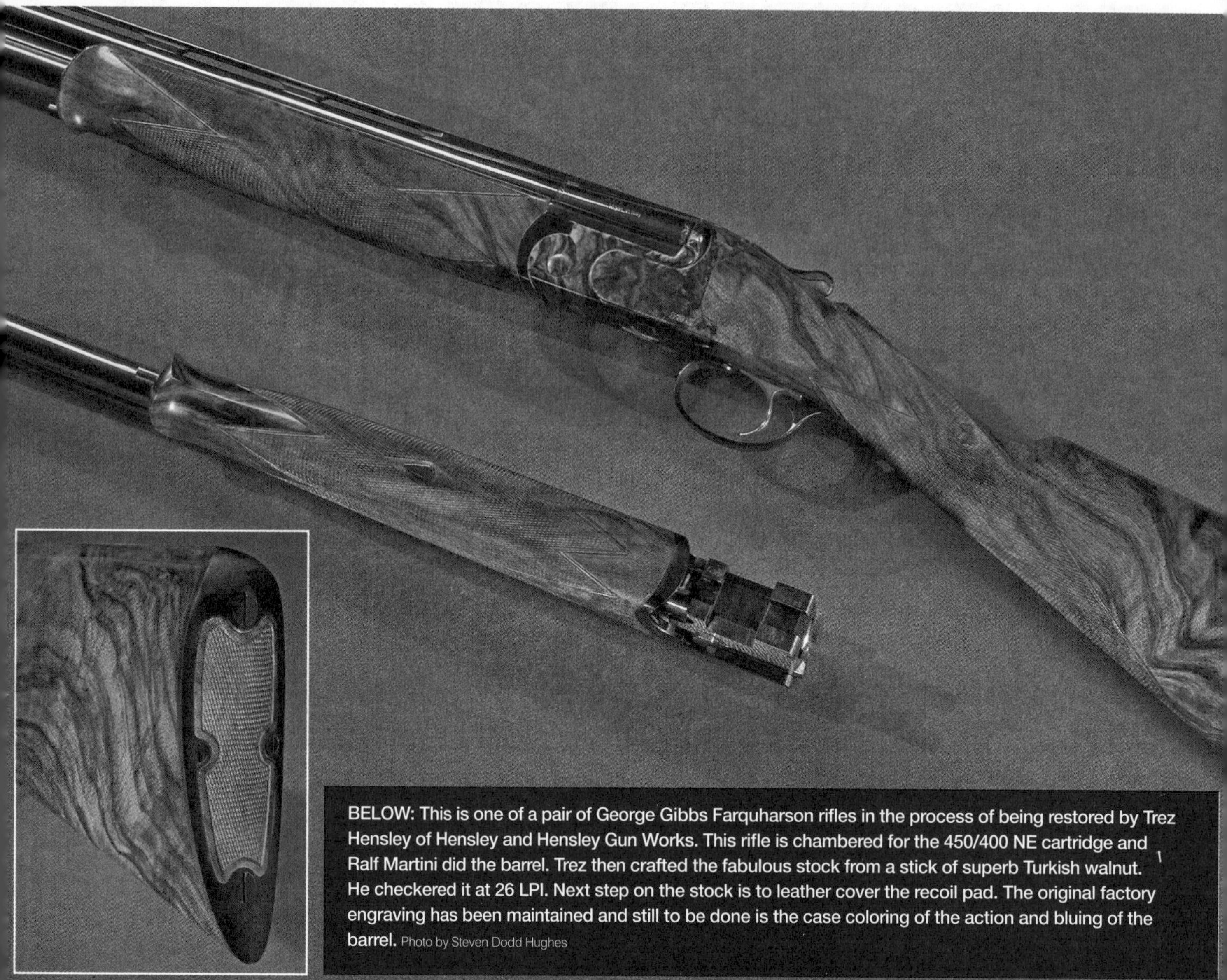

BELOW: This is one of a pair of George Gibbs Farquharson rifles in the process of being restored by Trez Hensley of Hensley and Hensley Gun Works. This rifle is chambered for the 450/400 NE cartridge and Ralf Martini did the barrel. Trez then crafted the fabulous stock from a stick of superb Turkish walnut. He checkered it at 26 LPI. Next step on the stock is to leather cover the recoil pad. The original factory engraving has been maintained and still to be done is the case coloring of the action and bluing of the barrel. Photo by Steven Dodd Hughes

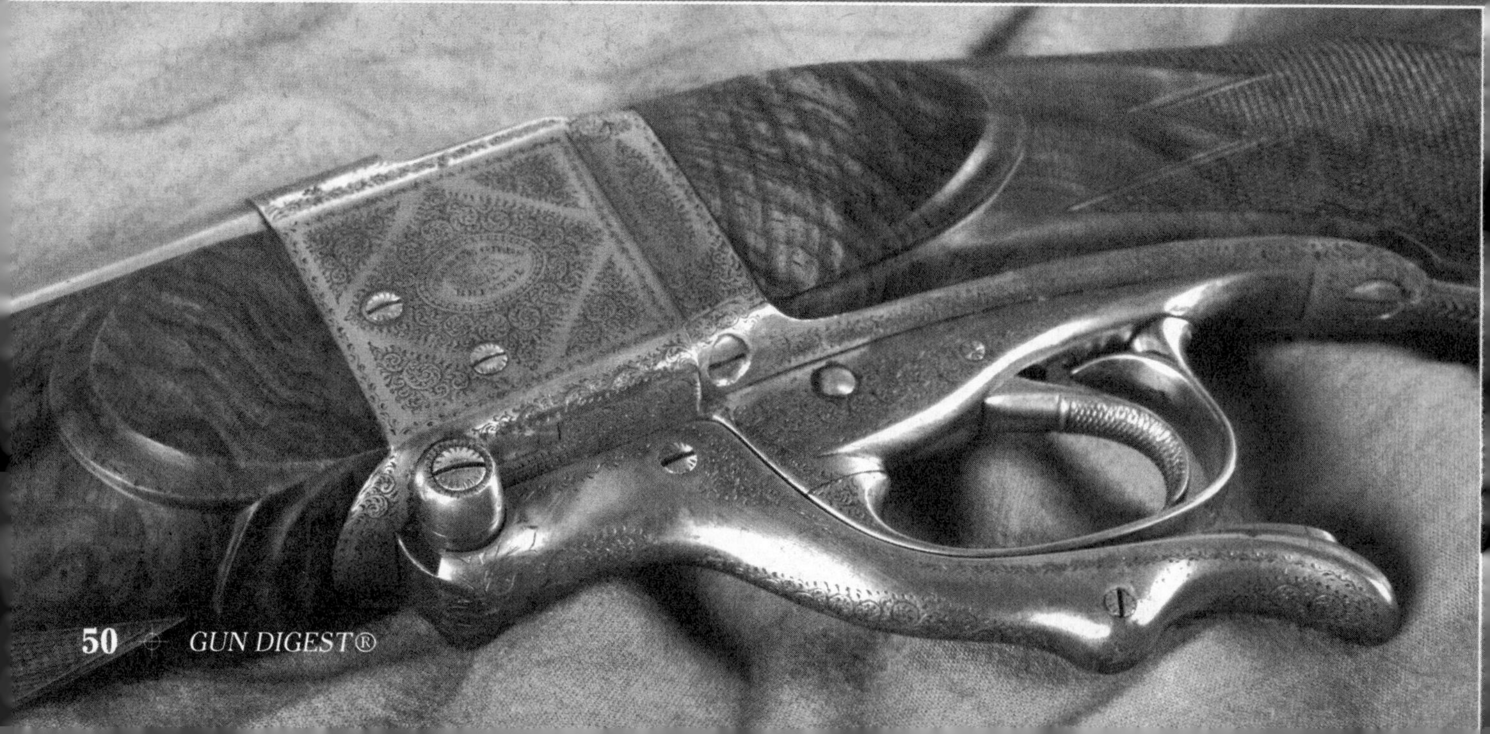

This Caesar Guerini O/U 20-bore shotgun, with an extra set of 28-bore barrels, was delivered to Al Lind for one of his exquisite stock jobs. Bill Dowtin of Old World Walnut supplied the superlative blank of Circassian walnut, and Al whittled it into this lovely stock. He also fitted the stock with an elegant skeleton buttplate. The result is the lovely gun shown here. Photo by Tom Alexander Photography

BELOW: This beautiful big-game rifle started with a Johannsen magnum Mauser action and a Krieger 375 H&H barrel. The action is fitted a Swarovski scope mounted in Joe Smithson quick-detach scope mounts. Lee Helgeland executed the metalwork on the rifle and Barry Lee Hands engraved it. Gary Goudy stocked the rifle in a piece of Thessier French walnut, which he says is the oldest piece of walnut he has ever used. It was cut sometime in the 1920s. He checkered the stock with a fastidious point pattern. The owner of this rifle, by the way, owns a cherry orchard, explaining the unusual inlay on the floorplate. Photos by Gary Bolster Photography

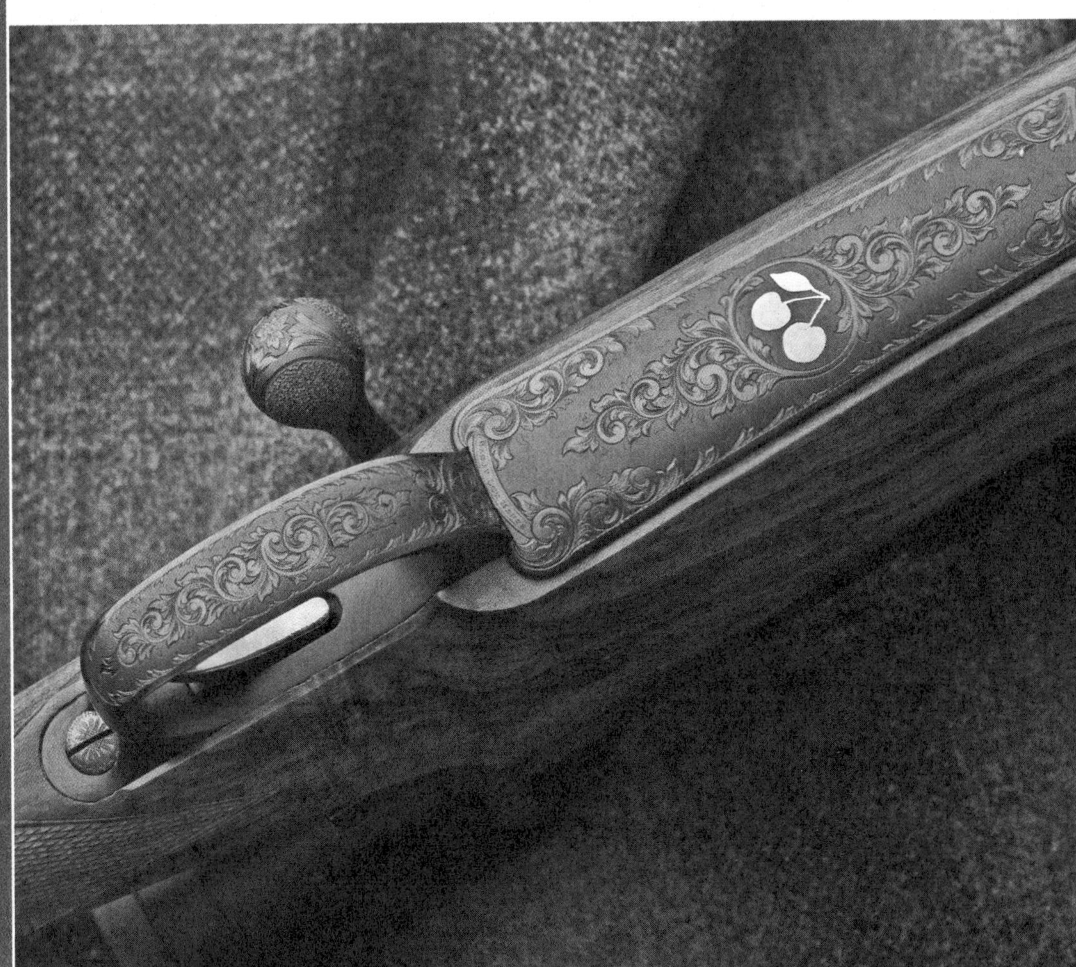

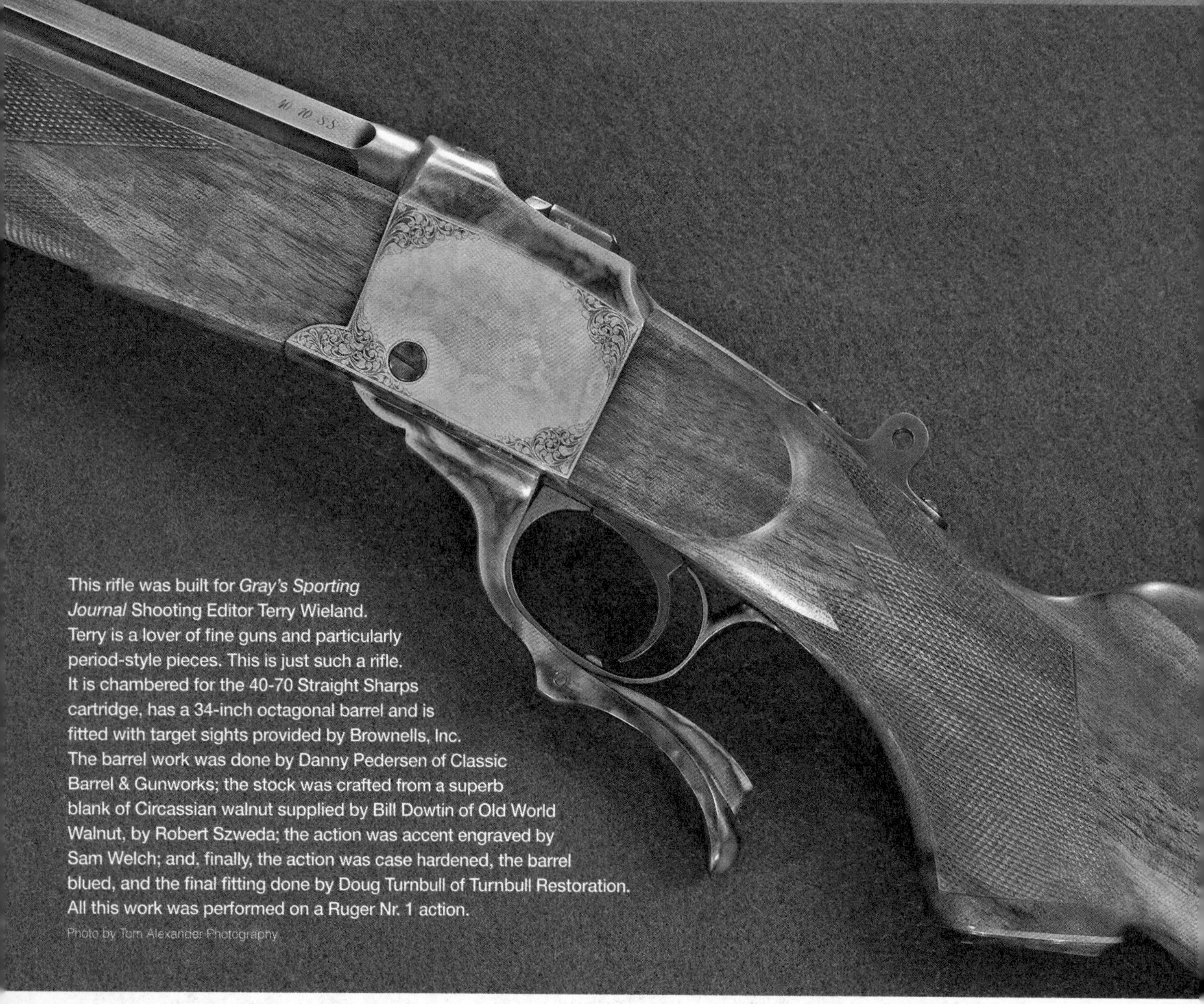

This rifle was built for *Gray's Sporting Journal* Shooting Editor Terry Wieland. Terry is a lover of fine guns and particularly period-style pieces. This is just such a rifle. It is chambered for the 40-70 Straight Sharps cartridge, has a 34-inch octagonal barrel and is fitted with target sights provided by Brownells, Inc. The barrel work was done by Danny Pedersen of Classic Barrel & Gunworks; the stock was crafted from a superb blank of Circassian walnut supplied by Bill Dowtin of Old World Walnut, by Robert Szweda; the action was accent engraved by Sam Welch; and, finally, the action was case hardened, the barrel blued, and the final fitting done by Doug Turnbull of Turnbull Restoration. All this work was performed on a Ruger Nr. 1 action. Photo by Tom Alexander Photography

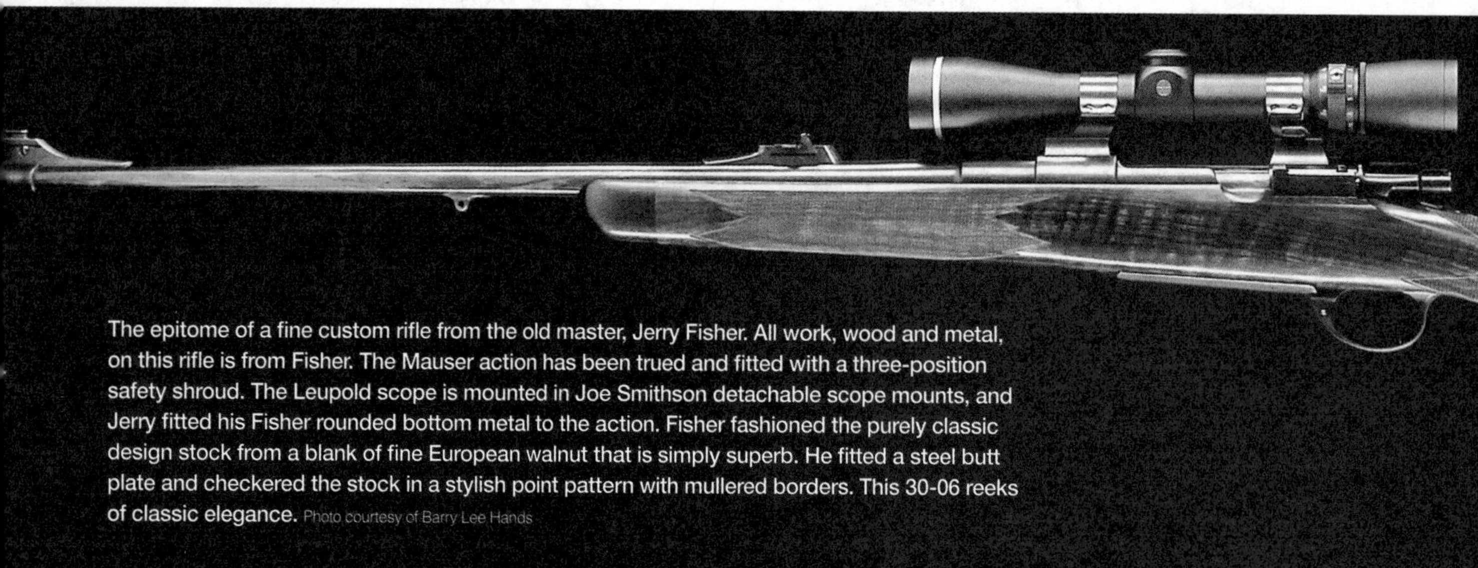

The epitome of a fine custom rifle from the old master, Jerry Fisher. All work, wood and metal, on this rifle is from Fisher. The Mauser action has been trued and fitted with a three-position safety shroud. The Leupold scope is mounted in Joe Smithson detachable scope mounts, and Jerry fitted his Fisher rounded bottom metal to the action. Fisher fashioned the purely classic design stock from a blank of fine European walnut that is simply superb. He fitted a steel butt plate and checkered the stock in a stylish point pattern with mullered borders. This 30-06 reeks of classic elegance. Photo courtesy of Barry Lee Hands

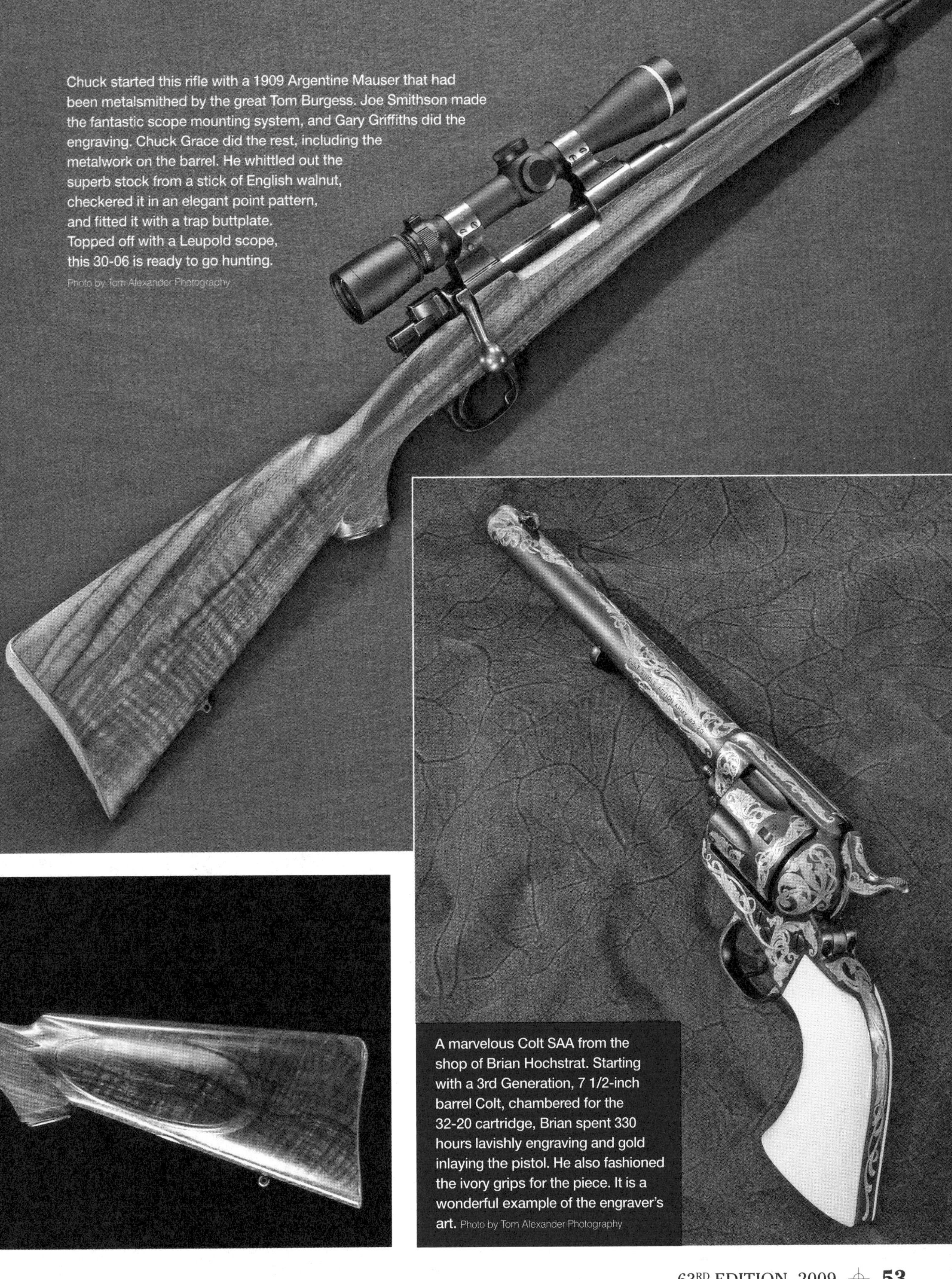

Chuck started this rifle with a 1909 Argentine Mauser that had been metalsmithed by the great Tom Burgess. Joe Smithson made the fantastic scope mounting system, and Gary Griffiths did the engraving. Chuck Grace did the rest, including the metalwork on the barrel. He whittled out the superb stock from a stick of English walnut, checkered it in an elegant point pattern, and fitted it with a trap buttplate. Topped off with a Leupold scope, this 30-06 is ready to go hunting. Photo by Tom Alexander Photography

A marvelous Colt SAA from the shop of Brian Hochstrat. Starting with a 3rd Generation, 7 1/2-inch barrel Colt, chambered for the 32-20 cartridge, Brian spent 330 hours lavishly engraving and gold inlaying the pistol. He also fashioned the ivory grips for the piece. It is a wonderful example of the engraver's art. Photo by Tom Alexander Photography

It would be very difficult for anyone to identify the manufacturer of this rifle. Believe it or not, it is a Kimber. However, Steve Heilmann completely, and I mean completely, remodeled the gun, including fashioning his own bottom metal and adding a tang safety while he was at it. Talley mounts hold the Leupold scope in place. Keith Heppler whittled the stock from a superb piece of English walnut, featuring a Biesen steel buttplate and checkering it in a point pattern, cut 26 LPI. Dennis Reese did the super engraving. Photo by Tom Alexander Photography

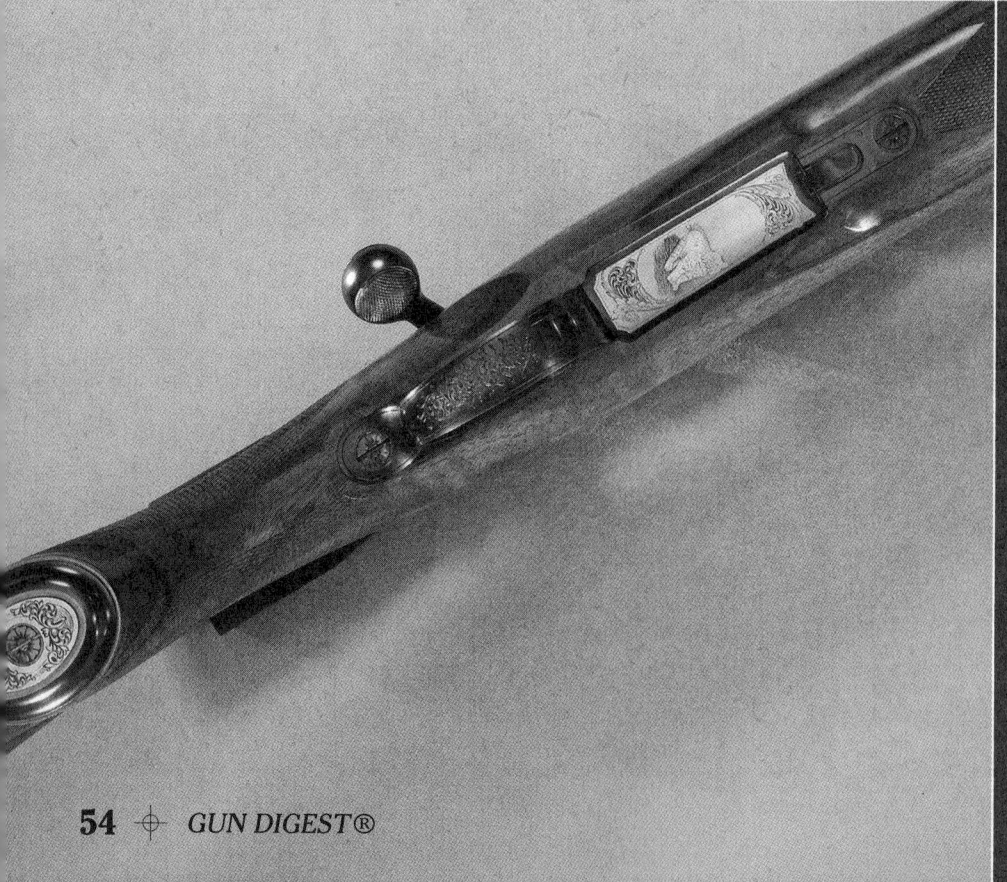

ABOVE: Shane Thompson built this rifle for himself as his hunting rifle. He started with a commercial Mauser action. He fitted and recontoured a Douglas XX barrel and chambered it for the 280 Remington cartridge. He did extensive metalwork to the action including making custom rings and bases, and a custom floorplate. He fashioned a sculpted safety button and checkered it. He did all the finish work, including rust bluing the metalwork and added nitre-blued accents. Shane stocked his rifle with a stick of English walnut, and checkered it in a 24 lines-per-inch point pattern with mullered border. The finished rifle weighs 8 lbs. with scope. To date, it has accounted for an Alaskan moose, two caribou, two black bears and a nice four-point mule deer buck. Photo by Eugene Wright

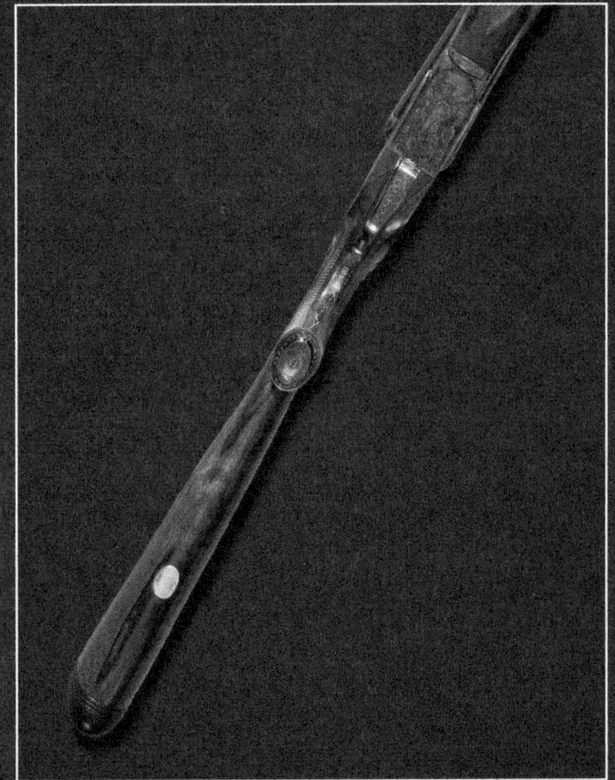

This lovely double shotgun originated as an AYA sidelock barreled action in-the-white. Dale Tate, articled at Purdey as an actioner, rebuilt the gun in the Purdey likeness. Charles Lee, articled at Purdey as an engraver, executed the lovely scroll engraving on the gun. Dennis Earl Smith did all the stockwork, finished it in oil, and checkered it 24 LPI. The client for this fine gun loves it, and uses it in the field. Photo by Tom Alexander Photography

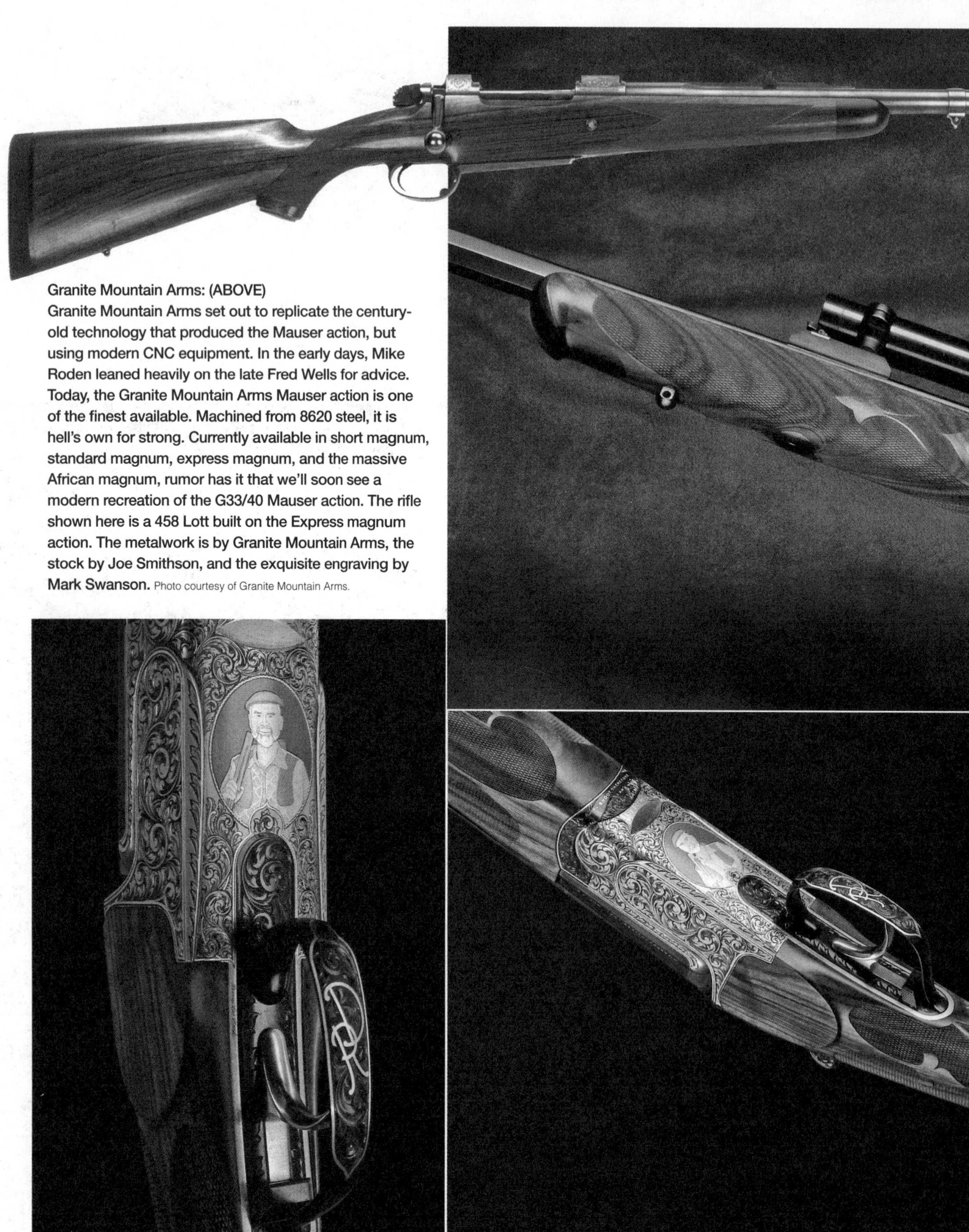

Granite Mountain Arms: (ABOVE)
Granite Mountain Arms set out to replicate the century-old technology that produced the Mauser action, but using modern CNC equipment. In the early days, Mike Roden leaned heavily on the late Fred Wells for advice. Today, the Granite Mountain Arms Mauser action is one of the finest available. Machined from 8620 steel, it is hell's own for strong. Currently available in short magnum, standard magnum, express magnum, and the massive African magnum, rumor has it that we'll soon see a modern recreation of the G33/40 Mauser action. The rifle shown here is a 458 Lott built on the Express magnum action. The metalwork is by Granite Mountain Arms, the stock by Joe Smithson, and the exquisite engraving by Mark Swanson. Photo courtesy of Granite Mountain Arms.

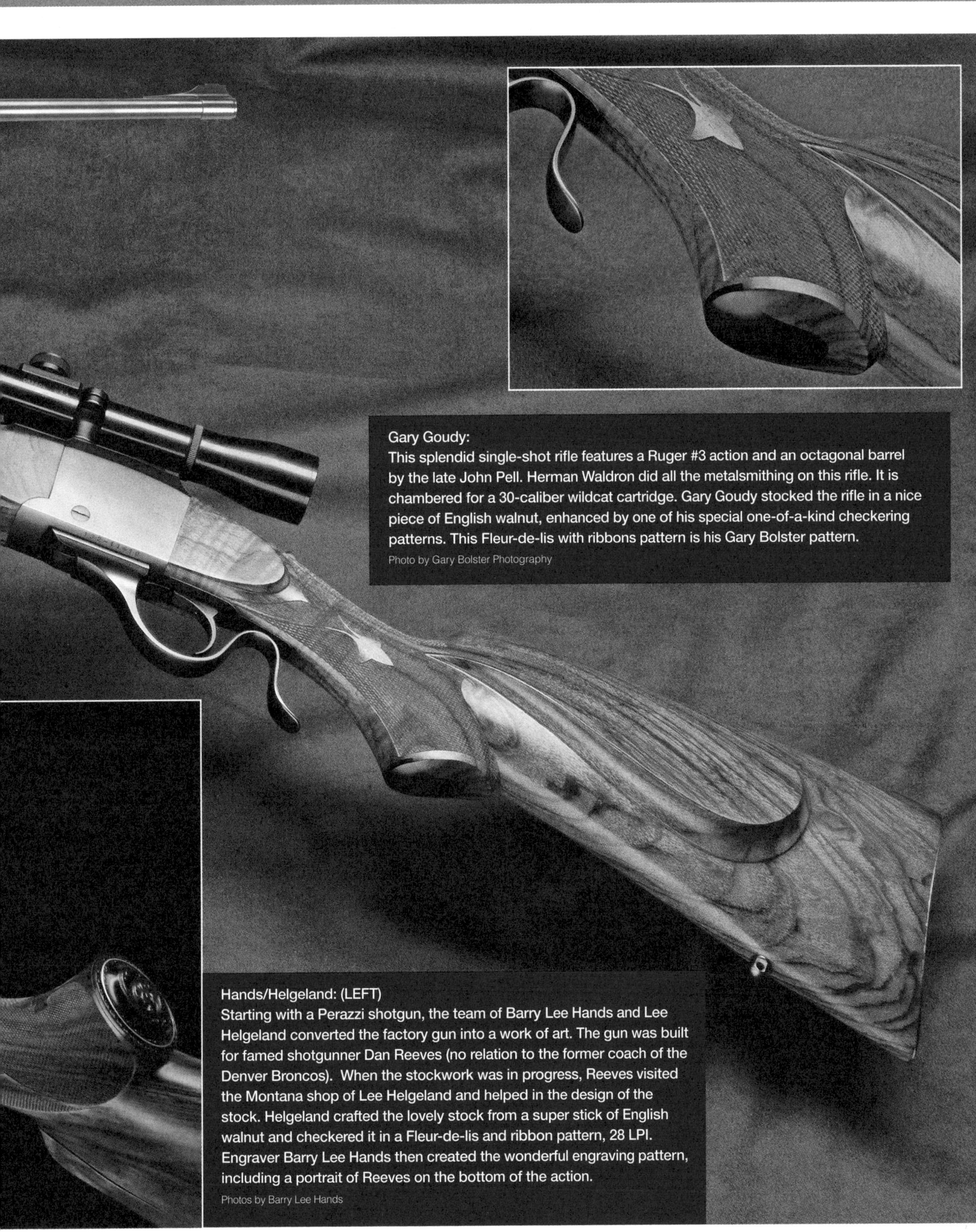

Gary Goudy:
This splendid single-shot rifle features a Ruger #3 action and an octagonal barrel by the late John Pell. Herman Waldron did all the metalsmithing on this rifle. It is chambered for a 30-caliber wildcat cartridge. Gary Goudy stocked the rifle in a nice piece of English walnut, enhanced by one of his special one-of-a-kind checkering patterns. This Fleur-de-lis with ribbons pattern is his Gary Bolster pattern.

Photo by Gary Bolster Photography

Hands/Helgeland: (LEFT)
Starting with a Perazzi shotgun, the team of Barry Lee Hands and Lee Helgeland converted the factory gun into a work of art. The gun was built for famed shotgunner Dan Reeves (no relation to the former coach of the Denver Broncos). When the stockwork was in progress, Reeves visited the Montana shop of Lee Helgeland and helped in the design of the stock. Helgeland crafted the lovely stock from a super stick of English walnut and checkered it in a Fleur-de-lis and ribbon pattern, 28 LPI. Engraver Barry Lee Hands then created the wonderful engraving pattern, including a portrait of Reeves on the bottom of the action.

Photos by Barry Lee Hands

HANDGUN SIGHTS —BETTER THAN EVER!

by Robert K. Campbell

Today we have more powerful and more accurate handguns introduced almost on a monthly basis. Handgun sights are better than ever, although we have the usual small percentage of shooters who wonder why we have handgun sights at all! The first handguns were designed for use just beyond arm's length. A large horse pistol might extend the cavalryman's effectiveness beyond saber range, when steel ruled the battlefield and gunpowder was an adjutant. The edged weapon never jammed or ran out of bullets. The only pieces commonly fitted with good sights were expensive target pistols.

What criteria dictate the choice of handgun sights? It isn't the shooter's personal preference, although this plays a part. The target must dictate the choice of sights. Most personal defense battles occur at conversational range. A coarse but bright and easy-to-pick-up front sight is indicated. Hunting ranges are predictable by experienced hunters and the sights need to be accurate to the longest likely range. Competition requires a mix of ease of acquisition and accuracy. Ranges are clearly defined in competition so this is the easiest of problems to tackle.

ABOVE: This is the XS Big Dot, an increasingly popular option well suited for home defense.

An all-around handgun used by an experienced handgunner for competition such as IDPA, hunting medium game and also for personal defense should feature a good set of sights, along with good power and accuracy. Over the years I have managed to accumulate quite a few handguns that meet this demanding criteria. I have used practically every type of handgun sight available with varying degrees of success. I will relate some of these experiences as we "look over" handgun sights.

Handgun accuracy vastly improved with the introduction of the Colt single-action revolver. For the first time handguns were accurate enough to connect with man-sized targets well past fifty yards. Sights evolved from a simple post near the muzzle to a notch in the top strap and a high profile front sight. Many of these older handguns shoot high at moderate ranges as they were intended to make hits on an Indian war pony at 100 yards—–it is far easier to correct at close range. Period accounts indicate a trooper armed with a 7 1/2-inch Colt revolver could connect with a war pony and, on occasion, a warrior at the 100-yard range or a little beyond. I have confirmed this with my own Hartford Model revolver. However, many of

The author finds the SIG P229 a highly accurate pistol. The factory sights, with white insert, are quite precise when properly lined up.

This young woman is practicing firing around cover. The use of cover is a great way to increase your survival quotient. The good sights of this 44 Magnum revolver are accuracy multipliers.

The sights on this Argentine High Power are typical of military sights of the last century.

the sights found on turn-of-the-century revolvers were poor combat sights, although they had a degree of precision if properly aligned...which took time. The first service automatics were no better.

As a result, techniques of quickly addressing a threat were developed that did not rely upon the sights or which relied upon only the front sight. Wild Bill Hickock, the great 'Fitz' Fitzgerald and Colonel Rex Applegate, among others, discussed such instinctive, or point-shooting, techniques. The Applegate Point pretty much summed up the discipline. The Applegate Point demands that the shooter take a step toward the threat while raising the pistol to eye level. The shooter's eyes remain on the target. As soon as the front sight breaks the plane between the eyes and the target, the pistol is fired. This technique worked well enough at the close ranges usually encountered in combat. Its deficiency is in addressing an adversary at longer range, or one behind cover.

This young shooter finds the Glock accurate enough at moderate range, and controllable.

About 1921 a lawman named Tom Threepersons had a special custom sight added to his 4 3/4-inch barrel 45 Colt revolver. This front sight was square and squat, allowing a much better sight picture than anything I have seen from the period. The next big step was the Smith and Wesson adjustable sight. These sights, with their clear precise adjustments and high visibility blades, were the best of the best for decades.

Adjustable sights are not the most rugged sights and may be knocked out of alignment. Also, these sights are set higher on the frame as a rule and are easier to catch on doorjambs and vehicle doors. Just look at the doorjambs around a police station sometime. The average height of a man dictates the height of the lock and the point-of-hip carry adopted by law officers results in lots of contact between guns and doors!

On one occasion I received a blow from a 2x4 that cleaned both the rear sight and hammer spur off my Smith & Wesson Model 29 44 Magnum. On other occasions, cops have knocked the sights right out of their Combat Magnums. Rugged fixed sights are really best for a service pistol, but there were no fixed-sight big-bore revolvers at the time. Smith and Wesson did give us the heavy-barrel 357 with fixed sights but, with automatics the rage today, revolvers are pretty much a dead issue. Automatic pistols were better but the staked-in front sight of the 1911 sometimes flew off after a few thousand

The Heinie sight was once a custom option but today the sights are found on many Taurus products, including the PT 1911.

rounds. That is really jumping the gun!

Today there are new iterations of older designs. You may find a GI 45 with good sights, and the Navy Arms Deluxe revolver has a larger sight channel than the original Frontier Six-Shooter. If a pistol is acquired for practical use vs. nostalgia, it needs better sights.

I prefer to purchase a pistol with good factory sights. I have not had the best results with revolver add-on sights, and modifying the automatic can be expensive. (An exception is the easy-to-fit Glock pistol.) The little adjustable sights that fit into the original dovetail of the automatic and protrude over the rear of the slide are probably the most breakage-prone sights I have ever seen. The Bomar sight requires custom installation and is vault-tough, well suited to rugged use. Originally developed for target competition, the Bomar has proven to be adaptable for outdoors and defense use. Caspian has introduced a tactical sight that offers fine adjustments. A fine performer in a compact package, this sight has been fitted to one of my custom pistols.

Let's look at a few more types and decide which may fit your needs. If the primary need is personal defense, fixed sights are the top choice. Fixed sights may not be easily regulated for different bullet weights, but can be adjusted, to an extent, for windage and elevation. You simply have less freedom in changing loads. Revolver fixed sights are snag-free and indestructible. Modern automatic pistols may still have small sights on some versions of the 1911 and a few others, but the rest of the sights are superb. Many factory pistols now offer either the Novak or Heinie high-visibility sights. These do not trap shadows, and let the light in for an excellent sight picture. They are rugged and pose little likelihood of damage.

Hunting revolvers are most often fitted with adjustable sights. These revolvers may need to be sighted in for different ranges and for different loads. If, like myself, you are an experimenter then adjustable sights are demanded. At present Taurus revolver sights seem the most rugged adjustable sights. They are compact with a design that rides fairly low but offers a good sight picture.

Personal defense pistols demand sights that may be acquired quickly while giving a good measure of accuracy at moderate range. Often, the need for 24-hour protection demands self-luminous iron sights. I think the

This is a Glock automatic fitted with the Wilson Combat Nite Eyes combination. This makes for fast shooting and a 24-hour capability.

Glock pistol is often modified not only because it is so easy to do, but also because the factory sights tend to be dislodged easily. I have quit counting the number of times I have seen the front sight of a Glock take flight. Often, contact with the holster when making a draw dislodges the sight--bad news.

A good high-visibility front sight is an asset not only to a good sight picture but also to a good crisp draw. When I draw my pistols in practice, I shoot my elbow to the rear and grasp the pistol firmly as I scoop it from the holster. I then bring the pistol to a point just in front of my navel and my hands meet. My eyes on focused on the target but I pick up the front sight in my peripheral vision and move the pistol toward the target. A fine front sight is OK for a hunting pistol but when speed is essential a larger front sight is a good addition to the pistol. I like the new Novak fiber optic sight but also find the XS sight a good option. My experience tends to move me toward choosing a pistol sight that allows excellent accuracy potential, wringing all we can from a pistol. As a result I have fitted my Glock Model 37 with a set of Ameriglo Operator sights. These sights feature a narrower front post than any others I am aware of for the Glock pistol. This makes the Glock a 50-yard rather than a 25-yard pistol if need be. On the other hand, there is probably nothing faster to a first-shot hit than the XS big dot front if home defense is your goal. To each his own; be certain you understand exactly the problem you may be facing. A versatile sight that is effective in a variety of circumstances is always a good choice.

This young lady is practicing fast shooting at close range with the SIG P229. The weak arm is curled to the chest to avoid interfering with the draw and firing at conversational range.

There are several idioms available in combat sights. As an example, the Glock features what I like to call the 1-1-1 type of sight. The front sight blade is thick and the rear sight and front post are of roughly equal width to the eye. However, the 1-2-1 structure is better suited to good accuracy. In this system the front post is much thinner than the rear sight wings, affording the opportunity for great accuracy. Naturally, with such a fine sight the inexperienced shooter may miss by a mile, which says something about the blocky Glock sight. The XS front post is an anomaly, much larger than the rear, which is an inverted V. But these sights are certainly capable at conversational range. Remember, sights really control your speed of fire and a good set of sights that you can keep focused on during a firing string is a great aid to fast, precision work.

Good sights encourage marksmanship. Good work was done with early handgun sights, often in spite of their sights. Today, options are available that our grandfathers only dreamed of. With a little forethought and some experimentation, your prospects of connecting with the target are bright indeed.

This is the excellent Ameriglo Operator sight.

THE 9.3 X 62 – A NEW BUDGET RIFLE FOR AN OLD AFRICAN VETERAN

by Tom Turpin

Have we progressed much in the past century when it comes to firearm and cartridge design? Well, I guess the answer to that question is yes, no, and maybe! For example, the Mauser Model 98, introduced in 1898, is still the basis for just about every successful bolt-action rifle in existence today. Sure, some modifications were made here and there, but the basics are mostly still Peter Paul Mauser's original design. In addition, when some genius does mess with the original design — in the name of progress of course — they usually screw it up, not improve it. Several have tried to improve it, but few, if any, have really succeeded.

When it comes to cartridges, we've seen far more relatively new developments; however, I suspect very few of them are apt to become "classics." Mostly, the new ones simply drive old bullets faster, which, by and large, is unnecessary.

Jack O'Connor perhaps said it best when he wrote, "We live in a magnum age, a time when enthusiastic riflemen go out with 30-caliber super magnums powerful enough to explode an enraged grizzly into a red mist, a cloud

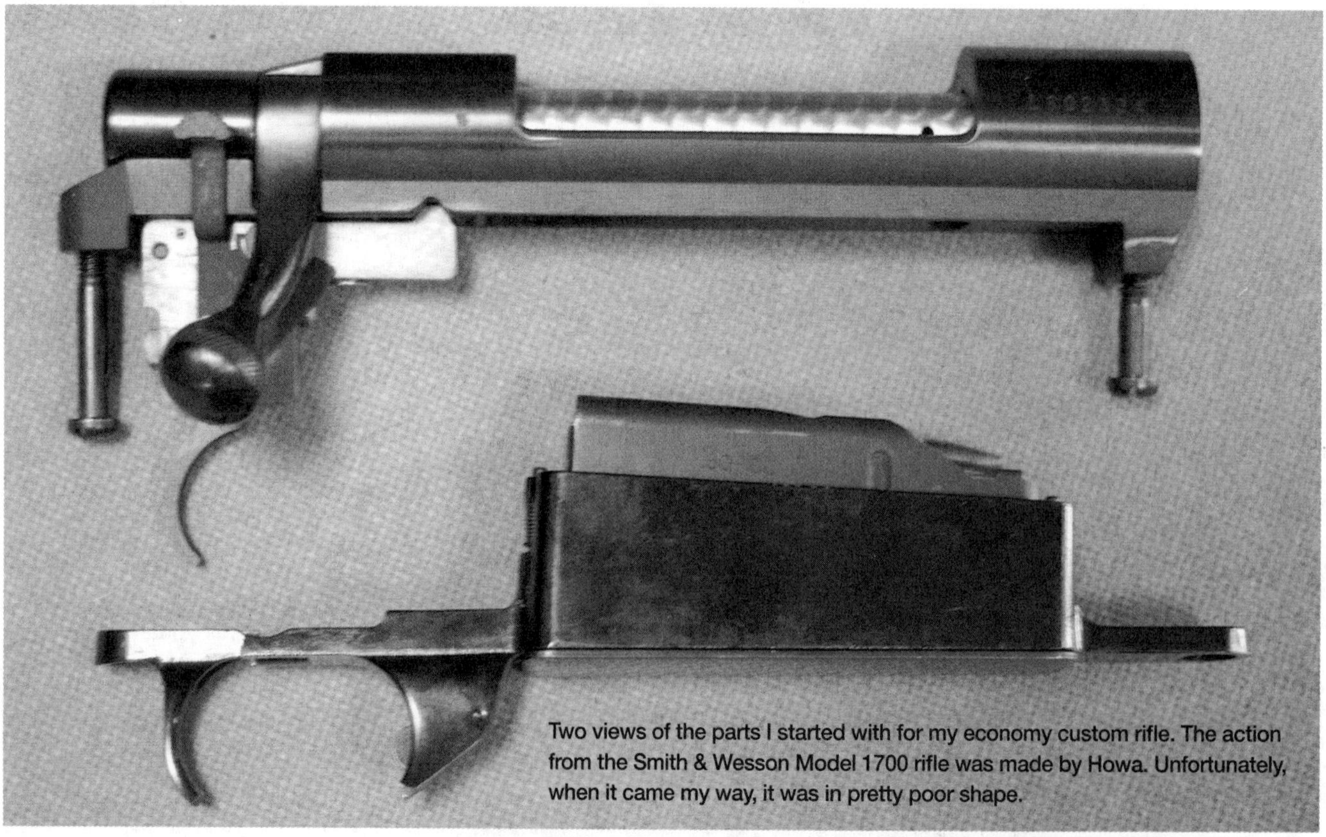

Two views of the parts I started with for my economy custom rifle. The action from the Smith & Wesson Model 1700 rifle was made by Howa. Unfortunately, when it came my way, it was in pretty poor shape.

of hair, and a few scraps of hide – and then return with spike bucks that dress out about 65 pounds." Amen, brother! This pearl of wisdom appeared in the April, 1967 *Outdoor Life* magazine in O'Connor's column, "The Appeal of the Mild Cartridges".

With today's near-mania for large, and overbore magnum cartridges, it seems odd that some of the really old-timers in the cartridge world are, even today, still among the most popular in use in the field. Need I say more than the 30-06, 270 and 7x57? The '06 was introduced in 1906, the 270 in 1925 and the 7x57 before the turn of the century, in 1892. We could add the old standard 375 H&H, which came out in 1912. Isn't it strange that this is so? Today's introductions are expected to lay everything low within fifty yards of the muzzle, from blast alone!

A while back, my pal and colleague Terry Wieland and I were exchanging e-mails. During that exchange, I mentioned a few of the rifle projects that I had, to one degree or the other, in the works. He commented, "You need professional help, and I don't mean a professional gunmaker!" He was pulling my leg only slightly. He has minimally fewer rifles being crafted than I do! Another crony and colleague, John Barsness, calls us (himself included) rifle loonies. It's a pretty accurate description I think, although he caught some flak from a few readers for using that term in print.

Though I have no earthly need for another rifle, I have several in the making. Need doesn't enter into the decision with me - want is the only necessity - other than having the means to pay for my folly. Even this requirement is not always absolutely necessary. I've gotten a few projects going over the years without the foggiest notion how I would pay the bill when it came due! Somehow, with some divine intervention I suspect, a check for an article or some other unexpected windfall just happened along at precisely the right time.

Just a few months ago, I took delivery of my latest addition, a pre-64 Winchester Model 70 action, Krieger barrel, Blackburn bottom metal, fine stick of English walnut, Talley mounts and a Leupold 1.5x5 scope — all put together into a rifle by Kentucky maker, Craig Click. The caliber – a 458 Lott, just in case a rhino invades my Arizona pea patch.

In addition to the Lott, Craig is also working on a Mauser-actioned 338, and is doing some metalwork on a pristine 1909 Argentine Mauser action, and a G-33/40 small ring Mauser action. The 1909 will eventually become my go-to 30-06 with a Danny Pedersen cut-rifled barrel, and a stock made from a stick of English to kill for. I'll probably ask pal Gary Goudy to stock it for me.

The G-33/40 is already barreled with a Pedersen barrel, and is chambered for the 25-06 cartridge. I intend for this rifle to be a very light-weight hunting rifle. For the stock, Bill Dowtin of Old World Walnut found me a stick of very good, and exceptionally light-weight, New Zealand walnut. It isn't a flashy blank, but it's no slouch either. Another friend, Lee Helgeland, has agreed to do the stock for this rifle.

As if that wasn't enough, I recently had Dakota Arms build me one of their Model 76's chambered for the 257 Weatherby cartridge. I provided a beautiful stick of English walnut that I got from David Miller and a Danny Pedersen .257 barrel. Dakota did the rest, except for the checkering. Kathy Forster will take care of that chore.

I also recently picked up a lovely pre-64 Winchester Model 70 action, made in 1949 or '50, which is in wonderful original condition. I'll use it for something one of these days, although I have no plans at the moment. I'll probably send it, a barrel, and a stick of English that has been drying for about twenty years now, to Shane Thompson. Shane crafts a lovely classic-styled rifle. What caliber you ask? Probably a neat little 7x57 Mauser.

Lately I have been toying with the idea of building up yet another rifle chambered for an old-timer, the 9.3x62mm. It is experiencing somewhat of a renaissance in popularity in this country these days. In fact, in the USA, it is probably more admired today than it has ever been. This is not true the

For comparative purposes, shown here are a 30-06 round (L), a 338 Win Mag round (C), and a 9.3x62 round (R). Many believe, this scribe included, that the 9.3x62 will do anything that the 338 Win Mag will do.

EMPIRE RIFLES

This wonderful rifle was made by Empire Rifle Co. and features a modern manufactured Mauser '98 action and a Schmidt & Bender 1.5-6X variable scope. It is, as can be seen, a lovely rifle.

world over however. Outside the USA, it has always been very popular.

This cartridge was introduced in 1905. A German gunmaker, Herr Otto Bock, designed the cartridge as an all-around big game cartridge, adequate for most hunting in the German Colonies in Africa. It was and is very successful there, although, of course, the colonies are long gone.

At least three other versions of the 9.3 are out there: the 9.3x57, 9.3x64 and 9.3x74R, all using the same .366-inch diameter bullet. Somewhere I either heard or read that another European manufacturer, Sako I believe, has developed another 9.3 cartridge, this time a 9.3x66.

Typical of European cartridge designations, the 9.3 is the diameter of the bullet in millimeters, and the 57, 62, 64, or 74, is the length of the cartridge case, also measured in millimeters. In the case of the 9.3x74R, the "R" indicates that it is a rimmed case.

In the past, the only 9.3 chambering that I have had any experience with is the 9.3x74R. I once owned a Heym O/U double rifle chambered for that cartridge. Alas, I never shot anything but paper with it however. Ballistically, the 9.3x62 is a twin of the 9.3x74R. Both propel a 286-grain bullet in factory loads at around 2300-2400 fps or so.

Anemic you say – perhaps so with today's magnum mentality - but it is a performer par excellence. In addition, the chambering seems to be one of a very few cartridges out there, another being the 375 H&H, which appear to be inordinately deadly killers for some reason.

The 9.3x62 is a really good cartridge for an all-around big-game rifle, particularly when hunting in areas inhabited by really big and/or potentially dangerous animals. In North America, I'm thinking primarily of moose, elk and the big bears. In Africa, it should be (and has been for years) superb for use on the larger antelope species and on the big cats, where legal. Many Cape buffalo and even elephant have fallen to the 9.3x62 as well. John Taylor, in his bible *African Rifles and Cartridges*, had this to say about it. "It's a simply splendid general purpose cartridge and its shells could be bought in almost any store throughout the length and breadth of Africa; this being a most definite recommendation for any cartridge."

Still, I had done nothing to start the 9.3 ball rolling. No really suitable action was readily available, and I didn't want to use my hoarded pre-64 Model 70 for this purpose.

Then, as luck would have it, an acquaintance stopped by my house. He told me that on a whim, he had recently bought a rifle, and later regretted doing so. He asked if I would be interested in it. He didn't know who made the rifle. Talk about trolling with really good bait!

Anyway, I told him I'd have a look if he would bring it by the house. Next evening, he did so. My visions of another pre-64 Model 70, or commercial Mauser, or even another G-33/40, were quickly dashed. He pulled a really dilapidated looking rifle from the trunk of his car – neither cased nor blanket-wrapped; actually, with no protective padding of any kind. That should tell you something.

The rifle turned out to be a Smith & Wesson Model 1700 chambered for the 30-06, with an old El Paso Weaver 3-9X variable scope, mounted in Redfield mounts. Of course, S&W didn't make the rifle. It was made for them by Howa in Japan, the same company that made rifles for Weatherby. The action is, in most ways, identical to the currently available Howa Model 1500, imported by Legacy Sports International. The biggest difference is with the bottom metal and magazine box.

The Smith Model 1700 had a detachable magazine whereas the Howa 1500 has a more conventional internal box and button release floorplate. Otherwise, I can tell little, if any differences. This 1700, however, showed all indications of having been run over by an eighteen-wheeler!

The bottom metal was broken in several places, rust was prevalent all over the place, and the barrel showed a small, but noticeable bulge, about half an inch back from the muzzle. The stock was OK with a few dings here and there, but they seemed to be honest use scars, and not the result of mistreatment. The action itself, other than the bottom metal and magazine, appeared to be just fine.

My devious mind wandered all over the place. I could envision this as the basis for building a very useable pickup truck rifle. The only problem with that scenario is that I don't drive a pickup. So, I decided to use the action as the basis for building the 9.3x62 Mauser.

Friend John Barsness has written considerably about the cartridge in recent months, and he obviously likes it a lot. So have other colleagues, and I've been feeling inadequate as a result. Not only have I never shot the cartridge, I'd never even seen one! The unexpected availability of the Howa action moved the project up a notch or two.

An immediate problem to address was replacing the bottom metal and magazine box. I didn't want a single shot 9.3x62! As best I could determine, Howa no longer makes the detachable box magazine and bottom metal. The currently available Howa 1500 bottom metal and box is available from Legacy Sports International, so I ordered a new one from them. Unfortunately, the detachable box magazine is wider than the currently available bottom metal, meaning that the replacement is too narrow to fit properly in the old stock magazine box opening. I could glass it to fit, but it would be noticeable with no way of covering up the repair. Still, for a pickup, knock-around, low budget rifle, it is no big deal.

Nevertheless, in addition to glassing the old stock to fit, I decided to also order a stock from Boyd's Gunstock Industries. Boyd makes a classic styled laminated wood stock designed by friend and fellow outdoor writer, Jon Sundra. I have a couple of them on other rifles and they work and look just fine.

These handloads use Ramshot Big Game powder and Nosler 250-grain Ballistic Tip bullets. They are both accurate, and deadly.

I sent Randy Boyd a letter requesting one of their VIP (Virtual Inlet Part) stocks for the Weatherby Vanguard, which is made by the same manufacturer, and is identical to the Howa action. The stock, which requires minimal fitting and then finishing, costs $65.42 plus shipping. Once I've given the rifle a range workout or three, I'll fit the new stock to the rifle.

Next I called Danny Pedersen and asked if he made barrels for the 9.3 (.366"), and further, if he had chambering reamers for the 9.3x62. The answer in both cases was yes. In fact, he told me the two most popular cartridges he was currently producing barrels for were the 9.3x62 and 9.3x64! He told me to send the action on up and he'd get to it as soon as he could.

Next I did a bit of research on reloading components. I found that Swift, Speer, Nosler, Barnes, Woodleigh, Lapua, A-Square and Norma all make bullets, ranging from 232 grains thru 320 grains, for the 9.3. Most are readily available. Norma, Graf, Lapua, A-Square and RWS all make 9.3x62 cases that are also, in most cases, ready for immediate delivery. I'm sure there are others.

Both Graf and Sons and Midway have 9.3x62 brass in stock. Graf & Sons even have their own line of brass cases made for the 9.3x62, among others. I suspect that one would be hard-pressed to find components in small town gunshops, but through mail order or on-line, there is no problem.

While waiting for the newly barreled action and stock, I contacted Nosler, Norma, Speer, Woodleigh A-Square and Barnes, requesting a small supply of 9.3 (.366") diameter bullets. I also contacted RCBS for a set of dies for the 9.3x62. Redding also has dies available for the cartridge. Additionally, I ordered some Lapua and Graf brass from Graf & Sons, Inc. (4050 S. Clark St., Mexico, MO 65265).

My pal and colleague John Barsness, already noted as a fan of the 9.3x62 and an experienced user of the cartridge, recommended using Ramshot Big Game powder for the cartridge. I hate to admit it, but I had never used any powder from Ramshot. This would be a good opportunity to try it out, but my local shop had none in stock. I contacted Brenda Kneeland of Western Powder and requested a sample of Big Game, which she generously provided in short order.

Pal John also gave me a load to start with that had worked well in his 9.3x62s. According to him, it would drive a 286-grain bullet at somewhere around 2400 fps. If history is any indicator, that should be a very lethal load, suitable for use on about anything that walks, crawls or flies! While at it, I checked my loading manuals and came up with a couple different loads using two different powders, IMR-4895 and IMR-4064, and 250-grain Nosler BT bullets.

Finally, I called Gary Turner of Talley Manufacturing and ordered a set of his wonderful scope mounts to fit the Howa action. When they came in a few days later, I went through my "goodie box" of rifle parts and accessories. There, I found a well-used, but still excellent, Leupold 1.5-5X scope available. Figuring that a scope in this magnification range should be about ideal for a rifle chambered for the 9.3x62, I set it aside for the rifle.

After what seemed like eons, but in reality only a couple months, I received the barreled action from Danny. I took it, the factory stock and the new bottom metal to my pal Curt Crum for some assistance with the stock. He epoxied some matching wood into the magazine well to

LEFT: These two rounds are handloaded with Ramshot Big Game powder and, on the left the Nosler 250-grain Ballistic Tip bullet, and on the right, the Norma 232-grain Oryx bullet. Both shot very well and would handle most any situation.

BELOW: The author managed to get this one group in during a rare lull in the wind. It measures under an inch and I suspect the others would have as well, had it not been for the horrific winds on the range.

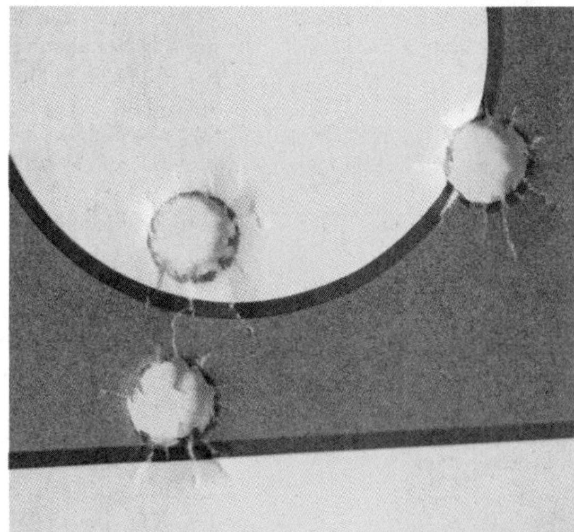

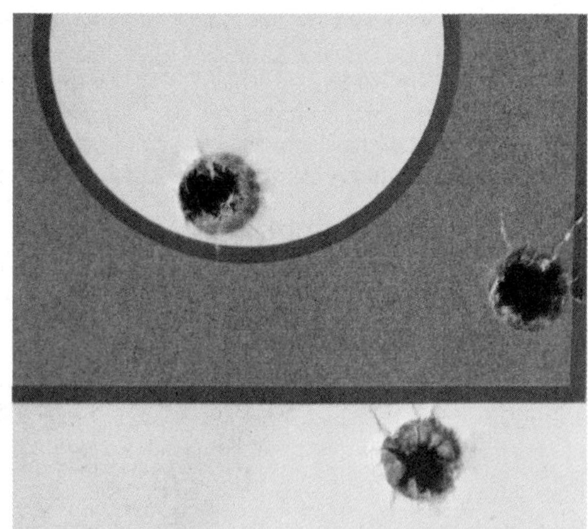

RIGHT: These three-shot groups were shot using both the beautiful Empire rifle and my bargain basement rifle. While the groups are mediocre at best, considering the range conditions at the time they were shot, they are great.

take up the excess space, and then bedded the newly-barreled action and new bottom metal into the old stock. When I got the rifle back a couple weeks later, I could hardly tell that the stock and new bottom metal weren't always together.

I mounted the scope in the Talley mounts on the rifle as soon as I got it home. All that was left to be done was to take the rifle to the range and check it out. While at it, I called friend George Sandmann, the owner of Empire Rifle Co., and requested he loan me one of his fine rifles chambered for the 9.3x62. Since I had no prior experience with a rifle chambered for this cartridge, it seemed prudent to have at least one other for comparison purposes. A few days after our conversation, Big Brown delivered one to my house.

The Empire offering is a beautiful rifle, built on a modern K98 Mauser action with all the refinements custom makers customarily add to a military surplus Mauser. The rifle is stocked in the classic style using a very nice stick of walnut. Topped with a Schmidt &

The author's custom on a budget 9.3x62 that was put together from inexpensively procured components. Obviously, it isn't nearly as nice as the Empire Rifles product, but it shoots almost as well.

Bender 1.5-6X variable scope, it would be adequate for most anything.

When range day dawned, I packed up the two 9.3x62-chambered rifles, along with a few other rifles that needed shooting, and headed out to my local range. When I arrived, I found the conditions not exactly ideal for checking rifle (and shooter) accuracy potential. We had a 90 degree cross-wind gusting between 15 and 25 MPH. The wind, at times, blew so hard that it was blowing the targets off the frames! Even so, I had to get with the program and do the shooting. Editors and deadlines have little respect for terrible weather!

During the session, I fired both rifles with two different bullets, and three different powders. I used both Norma and Lapua brass, but relied on Federal 210M match primers for all loads. I had no time to load several different powder charges with each powder. That would have to wait until later. Instead, I selected what appeared to be an "average" load from several different loading manuals.

I used the first few rounds to get the rifles sighted at 50 yards. Once that was done, I moved the target stand back to 100 yards, and commenced to shoot for groups.

Both rifles shot very well indeed. Both averaged around 1.25 MOA for three-shot groups, in spite of very poor range conditions, weather wise. I am confident that additional load development and calm range conditions, would produce sub-MOA accuracy from both rifles. I doubt if I could have gotten much tighter groups under those conditions, even with my most accurate rifles.

While there is much work remaining to be done with the rifle, it is clear to me that the cartridge is a very good one indeed. In fact, it is so impressive that a rethinking of my planned use of the pre-64 action is in order. I think I'll send it off to Shane with instructions to build up an addition to my permanent battery of rifles. A 9.3x62 would be a very nice addition and, considering the rifles that I already have, more useful to me than the 7x57, as good as it is.

I'm a believer. Try one; you may just like it as much as I do.

THE FORGOTTEN 45

by Ron Terrell

In some categories, octogenarians are considered too old to contribute much to society or their particular world of influence. Outdated and Obsolete are words often associated with items or people in the 80-year-old category.

On the other hand, if that 80-year-old item is a 1920 Ford or Cadillac vehicle, there is suddenly a great deal of value attached to it. An Arthur Rubenstein or Albert Einstein who survives to be an octogenarian is revered for a mastery of music and genius in the scientific world.

The firearms and shooting worlds have their own 80-plus-year-olds that are still able to play vital roles in today's competitive markets. The 1873 Colt Single Action Army, for example, may be used on a much wider front today than it was 135 years ago. Colt's 1911 45 ACP – one of the world's all time great firearms designs – and its clones have several hundred thousand rounds fired through them each year. The 30-06 and 30-30 are other examples of 80-plus-year-old cartridges that see constant use in the game and target fields.

Another cartridge – or, more accurately, a cartridge variation – that deserves modern attention is the 88-year-old 45 Auto Rim. It is generally believed to have been developed by the Peters Cartridge Company in 1920 and was first called the 45 Automatic Rim. That was shortened pretty quickly to the Auto Rim. Winchester listed a load for this cartridge for a brief period of time but Remington has been the primary supplier of loaded ammo and unprimed brass for most of the 45 AR's life. Until about 14-15 years ago, both loaded ammo and unprimed brass could still be obtained through dealers on a special order basis. Remington still produces brass for the 45 Auto Rim but loaded ammo in no longer available. Midway Arms of Columbia, Mo. is one firm that markets Remington's brass through their voluminous catalog.

Another bright spot for handloaders is that Starline of Sedalia, Mo. has added the Auto Rim case to their production line. During a few months' stay in south Texas last winter, I processed and loaded over 1,000 Auto Rims in Starline brass.

The 45 Auto Rim is nothing more than the 45 ACP case with a thicker rim. The obvious reason for the rim goes back to the original purpose and design of the round. Before and during World War I, firearms manufacturers, specifically Colt and others licensed to produce the 1911 45 automatic pistol, were not able to produce enough pistols to supply the needs of the U.S. and her allies' armies. Colt and Smith & Wesson were already producing large frame revolvers and were able to add the 45 ACP chambering to these revolvers quickly enough to get them into the hands of servicemen. The combined production of these two firms exceeded 300,000 1917s.

Since a double-action revolver ejects fired cases via a single push on an ejector rod that lifts all cases out of the cylinder simultaneously the rimless ACP cases had to be pushed out individually with a rod of some kind. To alleviate this problem, half-moon shaped pieces of flat steel designed to hold three cartridges were produced. Two such clips held a cylinder full of six rounds, and all could be ejected with one stroke of the ejector rod.

Shooters who have used this system can swear to (or at) the difficulty in extracting the fired cases from these half-moon clips. More about them later, but this problem was what brought about the introduction of the Auto Rim.

Peters Cartridge Company simply added a thick rim to the ACP case. The rim thickness was determined by the space taken up by the half-moon clips and ACP case combination. This new round could now be ejected in the same manner as other rimmed cartridges in double-action revolvers. The system worked and tens of thousands of military and civilian shooters have used and continue to use these large-framed 45 revolvers.

Referring back to the half-moon clip problems, Ranch Products, Molinto, Ohio, has come up with an easier way to remove fired 45 cases from those clips. In fact, they took it a step further and developed additional clips. They make full clips (holding six rounds) in both stainless and blue finish as well as half-moon clips. Additionally, they make third-moon clips that hold two rounds (sort of like open-ended figure-eights). That still didn't solve the problem of removing fired cases from these clips, however, so they made a handy little tool that pulls the cases out with a minimum of effort. The abundance of 45 ACP ammo on the market offers unlimited choices for users of the big 45 and many competitive shooters have stated that the full-moon clip is one of the fastest reloading systems they have ever used. Jerry Miculek used a Model 625 S&W in setting his speed record of 12 rounds, with a reload, in three seconds! A full-moon clip held those second six.

The best solution to the whole problem, though, came when Peters developed the

Auto Rim case. When Remington took over the Peters line, production and use of the Auto Rim increased dramatically. In consideration of the steel used in some of the older pistols, loaded ammo was kept on the mild side. A 230-grain lead bullet lumbered along at about 750 fps – not a whole lot slower than the ACP round – but not a barn-burner, either.

Like a lot of other cartridges, the 45 Auto Rim's popularity died down after WWI and through the mid-'30s. There was a modest upsurge of interest during the WWII years but it was not until target shooters competing in 45 matches started using the big 45 ACP in revolvers during the 1950s that the double-action 45s (and the Auto Rim case) had a revival.

My own introduction to 45 competition came through the back door during the mid-'60s. A friend in a pistol club in Ft. Collins, Colo. had a slightly-tuned G.I. 1911 45 and an unaltered S&W 1917 that fell within my budget limits so I acquired both. Adding a 6-inch barreled Colt Match Target (oh, how I wish I still had that one!) to my pistol box made me feel a little more comfortable on the firing line next to the more well equipped shooters.

That 1911 was carried as a duty weapon during some law enforcement years and remains unchanged from its original purchase condition except for the addition of Crimson Trace Corporation's laser grip. The 1917 is another story.

In addition to using the '17 in competition (I was never all that good but had a lot of fun anyway), I had the idea of using it for hunting. Handguns were not legal for big-game hunting in Colorado while we lived there but we did a lot of varmint hunting and going after coyote and bobcat – plus jackrabbits, marmot and even prairie dogs – with a handgun added a lot of challenge to the hunts.

A couple of changes had to be made to the '17 to equip it for hunting. First, the G.I. sights did not give a lot of flexibility so I added a "Wonder Sight" (no longer available) to the rear and a custom Keith-style long-range sight to the front. I used that sight combination for about 10 years until another modification was made.

The other change was to bypass factory ammo and work up some handloads. I ended up using Lyman's #452490 gas check hollowpoint semi-wadcutter bullet that weighed 225 grains. A variation on that bullet was to drop a BB in the hole to plug the hollowpoint opening and pour the lead in on that. The cast bullet weighed 248 grains and the BB acted as an expander plug that spread the bullet to about 75-caliber when fired into wet pack.

To find the best loads for hunting, I did some early load development that, perhaps unwisely considering the age of that'17, pushed that 225-grain HP slug to almost 1300 fps. My chosen top load was 10.0 grains of Herco for a velocity of 1241 fps. With 8.0 grains of Unique, a top velocity of 1096 fps was reached. Those loads worked fine but I was concerned that a steady diet of those pressures would have been too much for that WWII vet.

The modification that followed the original sight change came after a visit with Lin Alexiou, head of Trapper Gun. After explaining some thoughts I had on modernizing the '17, Lin suggested I send it to him. He worked his magic and I ended up with a 3 1/2-inch barrel from a 1955 S&W and an adjustable rear sight (also original S&W). He had to mill a groove for the sight and do a little welding to mate the barrel and frame but, for him, not a problem. A trigger job and tune-up with a final treatment of satin stainless capped it off.

That Trapper-altered 17/55 has been used over the years as a hunting and home defense pistol and has also served as one of the big-bore training tools for several grandsons. The only change in recent years has been the addition of Crimson Trace Corporation's excellent laser sight grips for the big S&W N-frame. When carried in a Roy's Leather Goods pancake holster and loaded with the 225-grain HP at 976 fps or the same bullet with BB at 997 fps or with CorBon's excellent 200-grain ACP load at 966 fps, I feel comfortable in dealing with whatever might arise.

Reviewing some of those earlier loading records for this fat powerhouse rekindled an interest in the Auto Rim. Since those first tests, a whole slew of new powders and other components have been introduced. And even some of the older powders like Unique and Herco have had upgraded formulations. That raised questions about the performance of the Auto Rim with some of these new components – and the search was on!

To do the kind of evaluation I had in mind, it was necessary to look at the gun platform. After WWI, S&W brought out a commercial version of the 1917 in 1921. Popularity of, and demand for, these big 45s yo-yoed for about two decades. It stayed in production until 1939 when the outbreak of WWII caused all firearms manufacturers to commit their production capabilities to the war effort. Then, after WWII ended, production of the commercial '17 started up again and continued until 1949. In 1950, a new, revamped pistol with longer barrel, adjustable sights and better grip was introduced. It was named the Model 1950 45 Target. It didn't catch on and only about 1160 were sold during the next 18 months.

Another modification was made by adding a heavy 6 1/2-inch barrel and reintroducing it in March, 1955, as the 45 Hand Ejector Model of 1955 (later

Black Hills and Remington 45 Auto Rim ammo boxes join Smith & Wesson's Model 625 revolver in offering shooters a great choice for pleasure shooting, hunting or self defense.

changed to the Model 25). This model stayed in production until the late '80s until, in 1989, it was released in stainless steel as the Model 625. The current production model is a heavy N-frame but with a K-frame grip. Those of us with smallish hands appreciate that.

Smith & Wesson pretty much holds a monopoly on firearms chambered for the ACP that will also take the Auto Rim. Dan Wesson and Taurus have both brought out 45 ACP revolvers in recent years but neither accommodates the Auto Rim. The 625 I used as the platform for my loading tests has a 5-inch barrel. It is also available with a 4-inch barrel. In 2003, S&W's Performance Center produced a special 625-10 with 2-inch barrel, making it one of the most powerful "belly" guns on the market at that time. Evidently that was a successful move for the S&W folks, for they came out with a new variation of it called the 325PD (Personal Defense) that has a titanium cylinder, Scandium frame, a 2 1/2-inch barrel and weighs 21-1/2 oz. CorBon has done all Auto Rim fans a big favor by recently introducing a great self-defense load featuring a 200-grain JHP bullet at 1,050 fps. Thanks, CorBon!

So, since my intention was to see just how an upgraded 45 Auto Rim could perform, I knew I needed the strongest pistol chambered for this round I could get. My old original 1917 and my customized 17/55 would have some of the loads I planned to develop fired in both of them. The (large) balance of loads would be fired through a new Model 625-8.

A multitude of powder and bullet manufacturers have tested their products in just about every imaginable combination so there was a lot of information to review. My goal was not to try to duplicate their findings but to use their results as guidelines for what I wanted to do.

One area of research was in the realm of new powders. It had been a number of years since I had needed to replenish my pistol powder supply and, during that time, several new powders had been introduced. Chris Hodgdon of Hodgdon Powder Company was extremely helpful in giving me new data and recommending some of their new powders. So was Pete Jackson of Alliant.

For bullets I turned to Oregon Trail for cast bullets in 180-, 200-, 225- and 255-grain weights and to Sierra for jacketed bullets in 185-, 230- and 240-grain weights. A wide assortment of both cast and jacketed bullets from other firms was on hand but this project was already growing much larger than originally intended so I limited my bullet selection to the seven mentioned above.

Some of my favorite powders for 45s from earlier tests were selected. These included the old stand-bys: Unique, Herco, Bullseye, HS-6 and 700X. Even the old, now discontinued, Trap 14 from Hodgdon, was included due to its performance in those earlier tests. New additions included Hodgdon's Universal, Clays and TopMark and Alliant's Red Dot (not a new powder but it had not been used in my earlier tests so it was included here).

Whether or not powder deteriorates or loses some of its effectiveness over the years is an ongoing question. That's not an issue we'll get into here but a later look might be interesting. Just for curiosity's sake, however, I used some of my 30-40 year-old powders alongside new production of those same powders just to see what – if anything – would happen. A couple of the comparisons are shown in the chart.

Most of my supply of original Remington 45 Auto Rim loads had been used up over the years in plinking and training sessions. I had enough on hand to include chronograph and accuracy results here, but all test loads were handloads.

To assemble all loads, my old C-H 444X semi-progressive press and dies were used while working at my home bench. For our Texas trip, lightweight loading tools and carbide dies from Lee Precision, Inc. were used. Since we were going to be limiting our chronograph/accuracy tests to five rounds in half-grain increments, each load was hand-weighed on Lyman's excellent little LE500 electronic scale. CCI standard Large Pistol primers served as the igniter on all except the lead 255 and Sierra jacketed bullets where Federal Large Pistol primers were used.

We're fortunate to own enough land that we can have a fairly extensive range practically out our back door. A covered shooting shed makes it comfortable to shoot even during hot or bad weather. Ken Oehler's M35P chronograph and screens gave both accuracy and velocity readings.

As mentioned, some of the powders used in these tests were new to me so I started low and worked up to more powerful results. Consequently, you will notice in the chart that some of these readings were in the squib category. When those results showed up on the chronograph I would make a note to go back and load another batch, working up in half-grain increments. A few other loads were too warm to start with so some loads were not fired. Those bullets were pulled and powder reduced to safe levels.

My ultimate goal was multiple: First, I wanted to see just how far this octogenarian could be safely pushed with different bullet weights. Then, out of those findings, I wanted to select good hunting loads – again with different weights – for a variety of game.

Actually, I wanted to end up with several loads. I wanted to find mild, moderate and warm loads for each of my 45 ARs. As a general rule, I prefer autos to revolvers but there are some revolvers that just demand to be used. My Colt and Ruger single-action 45s, for example, and my Ruger Bearcat. And, very definitely, my 17/55 S&W 45 Auto Rim. For that one, I wanted a load that was pretty warm, was controllable in repeat shots and offered consistent accuracy. Another load for it would be for the purpose of practice and training newer shooters.

The loading and range tests extended over a period of about a year. Where possible, I tried to choose days at the range that fit into a moderate temperature spread. All targets were set at 25 yards and the first chronograph screen was at a measured ten feet from the muzzle. Each group was measured for accuracy. Noted in the chart comments section is the frequent fact that many groups would have 3- or 4-round clusters that measured extremely small groups. Since the human factor (old eyes and hands) entered into the picture, I was especially impressed with the sizes of many of the groups. While I rate myself as a fair to middlin' shooter, I make no claims at being a marksman. Every effort was made to hold the same sight picture, grip and trigger release but there's no doubt that I didn't always succeed. That's the reason I feel that those tight 3- and 4-shot clusters were more indicative of a load's true accuracy potential than some of those wider groups where flyers were involved.

The charts show some really good combinations. As a general rule, those rounds with very narrow extreme spread readings are among the most accurate. Not always, though. And it is also not a given that the heavier bullets with the same powder charge will give lower velocities. A test of this kind often raises as many questions as it answers. The variety of the loads used here does give a good look at the potential of this old-timer, however. As always, remember that while these loads proved safe in my gun, they may not be safe in yours - back off and work up!

A look in the mirror tells me that the octogenarian years are not too far down the road for me. If I make it that far, my hope is that I can contribute just a little of what the 88-year-old 45 Auto Rim continues to contribute!

LOADING CHART

Firearm: S&W M625-8, 5" bbl.
CCI & Federal LP primers; Starline Brass; Oregon Trail cast and Sierra jacketed bullets
Oehler 35P chronograph & skyscreens
(O) = Old production of currently offered powders; new production may be somewhat reformulated.
(N) = New production of current powders.

Powder	Grs.	Bullet/ Wt.	FPS	ES	Grp.	Comments
Herco (O)	7.0	180	868	120	2.8"	
	7.5	–	951	34	1.5"	Good medium load
	8.0	–	999	30	1.4"	
	8.5	–	1060	40	4.0"	Three = 1.3"
	9.0	–	1117	74	3.7"	Three = 1.9"
	9.5	–	1188	25	4.8"	Three = 1.2"
	7.0	200	913	85	3.3"	Four = 1.6"
	7.5	–	969	54	2.9"	Three =1.2"
	8.0	–	1031	90	3.6"	
	8.5	–	1089	26	1.8"	Four = 0.9" Excellent load!
	9.0	–	1136	21	2.7"	Four = 1.8" Excellent top load!
	9.5	–	1201	39	3.0"	Three = 2.0"
	6.5	225	843	28	3.0"	
	7.0	–	895	39	4.7"	
	7.5	–	961	41	3.5"	Three = 1.5"
Herco (N)	7.0	180	832	138	3.4"	
	7.5	–	896	45	4.0"	
	8.0	–	941	123	2.0"	
	8.5	–	1011	94	2.8"	Four = 2.0"
	9.0	–	1024	55	2.5"	Four = 1.6"
	9.5	–	1134	82	3.1"	Four = 2.5"
	7.0	200	960	47	2.8"	
	7.5	–	1018	151	3.1"	
	8.0	–	1034	92	3.9"	Four = 2.0"
	8.5	–	1049	69	2.7"	
	9.0	–	1090	91	3.1"	Three = 1.3"
	9.5	–	1127	31	4.3"	Three = 2.4"
	6.5	225	825	118	4.2"	Three = 1.9"
	7.0	–	881	36	3.3"	
	7.5	–	992	137	2.2"	
	8.0	–	997	80	1.8"	Four = 1.2"
	8.5	–	1045	71	3.2"	
Unique (O)	6.5	180	781	70	3.2"	
	7.0	–	814	38	1.6"	Good low range load.
	7.5	–	894	85	3.3"	
	8.0	–	909	102	3.1"	
	8.5	–	954	58	3.1"	Three = 1.5"
	9.0	180	983	79	2.6"	Three = 1.4"
	6.5	200	773	55	3.3"	Four = 2.2"
	7.0	–	830	70	3.6"	Three = 0.9"
	7.5	–	879	34	4.1:	Three = 2.0"
	8.0	–	919	85	2.7"	Four = 1.4"
	8.5	–	964	41	2.1"	Three = 1.3" Good warm load.
	9.0	–	1014	59	2.5"	Three = 1.3"
	6.0	225	735	43	3.0"	Duplicates factory load
	6.5	–	784	26	4.1"	
	7.0	–	841	58	3.9"	Four = 1.7"
	8.0	–	937	50	2.5"	Four = 1.5"
	8.5	–	983	94	3.8"	Four = 2.2"
	9.0	–	1026	54	3.4"	Four = 1.8"

Powder	Grs.	Bullet/ Wt.	FPS	ES	Grp.	Comments
Unique (N)	6.5	180	770	45	4.4"	Four = 2.4"
	7.0	–	860	96	2.8"	Four = 1.7"
	7.5	–	922	79	2.0"	
	8.0	–	1001	58	4.1"	Three =1.6"
	8.5	–	1034	94	6.0"	
Unique (N)	9.0	–	1097	90	5.7"	
	6.5	200	860	35	2.4"	Four = 1.1"
	7.0	–	889	64	3.5"	Three = 1.5"
	7.5	–	969	61	4.0"	Four = 2.2"
	8.0	–	1013	62	1.9"	VG; warm load.
	8.5	–	1024	86	3.8"	Three = 1.8"
	9.0	–	1114	81	2.8"	
	6.0	225	782	99	2.3"	
	6.5	–	845	47	2.2"	Four = 1.2
	7.0	–	916	41	2.8"	Three = 1.4
	7.5	–	980	67	3.1"	Four = 2.0
	8.0	–	1018	71	2.5"	
	8.5	–	1073	32	3.0"	
	9.0	–	1124	32	3.7"	Three = 1.4" Exc. top hunting load
Bullseye (O)	5.0	180	862	8	4.8"	
	5.5	–	949	24	2.9"	
	6.0	–	1008	14	2.2"	Four = 1.2"
	6.5	–	1048	24	3.4"	Three = 1.7"
	7.0	–	1110	52	4.0"	Three = 1.7"
	5.0	200	874	38	3.5"	Four = 2.0"
	5.5	–	950	14	2.0"	Four = 0.8"
	6.0	–	1012	35	2.5"	Four = 1.6"
	6.5	–	1066	24	1.9"	Three = 0.4" cluster.
	7.0	–	1081	22	4.0"	Three = 1.7"
	4.5	225	768	39	2.6"	Three = 1.1"
	5.0	–	829	74	2.5"	Three = 1.4"
	5.5	–	904	23	3.0"	Three = 1.4"
	6.0	–	1000	24	2.3"	
	6.5	–	1037	28	3.1"	
	7.0	–	1138	24	.8"	Cluster - One of best top loads!
Bullseye (N)	5.0	180	840	46	2.8"	Four = 1.1"
	5.5	–	912	53	3.8"	Four = 2.0"
	6.0	–	975	85	2.1"	Three = 0.9"
	6.5	–	1056	42	3.4"	Four = 2.6"
	7.0	–	1130	38	3.2"	Three = 1.8"
	5.0	200	864	36	2.0"	Three = 0.65"
	5.5	–	939	14	3.6"	Three = 1.5"
	6.0	–	1002	20	3.8"	Three = 1.8"
	6.5	–	1058	19	3.2"	Three = 1.7
	7.0	–	1118	12	1.7"	Three = 0.75"
	4.5	225	768	39	2.6"	Three =1.1"
	5.0	–	829	74	2.5"	Three =1.4"
	5.5	–	904	23	3.0"	Three = 1.4"
	6.0	–	966	17	3.0"	Three =1.6"
	6.5	–	1017	26	2.8"	Three = 0.6"
	7.0	–	1084	16	2.3"	

Powder	Grs.	Bullet/ Wt.	FPS	ES	Grp.	Comments
Clays	3.5	180	601	50	3.1"	
	4.0	–	743	52	3.7"	Three = 0.6"
	4.5	–	840	70	2.8"	
	5.0	–	907	51	4.9"	
	5.5	–	983	54	4.7"	
	6.0	–	1053	30	3.2"	Three = 1.8"
	3.5	200	677	72	4.1"	Four = 2.7"
	4.0	–	753	60	1.6"	Duplicates factory load..
	4.5	–	866	20	3.2"	
	5.0	–	922	50	3.2"	
	5,5	–	993	23	3.2"	
	6.0	–	1046	56	2.8"	Three = 1.5"
	3.5	225	537	27	1.0"	
	4.0	–	639	31	.9"	Great practice/training load
	4.5	–	758	31	3.0"	Duplicates factory load
	5.0	–	899	23	3.9"	Three = 1.6"
	5.5	–	962	16	3.9"	
	6.0	'	1018	18	2.5"	
Universal	6.0	180	749	71	2.1"	
	6.5	–	801	181	3.0"	
	7.0	–	924	73	2.2"	
	7.5	–	957	101	3.3"	Three =1.8" Good load
	8.0	–	1054	59	2.4"	Four = 1.9"
	8.5	–	1163	59	2.9"	Three =1.4"
	6.0	200	841	98	3.3"	Four = 1.5"
	6.5	–	883	64	2.2"	Four = 0.9" Good med load
	7.0	–	957	101	3.3"	Three = 1.8"
	7.5	–	993	22	1.7"	Good medium load
	8.0	–	1054	59	2.4"	Four =1.9"
	8.5	–	1163	59	2.9"	Three = 1.4"
	5.5	225	713	100	3.7"	
	6.0	–	802	25	4.5"	
	6.5	–	870	69	4.7"	
	7.0	–	935	43	3.3"	
	7.5	–	1036	106	2.2"	Three = 0.4" cluster
	8.0	–	1109	40	4.4"	Three = 1.3"
	8.5	–	1183	29	2.5"	Three = 1.0"
Red Dot	5.0	180	786	41	2.9"	Duplicates factory load
	5.5	–	885	60	3.1"	
	6.0	–	957	54	2.1"	
	6.5	–	1039	36	2.5"	Four = 2.0"
	7.0	–	1099	63	3.2"	Three = 2.3"
	7.5	–	1151	43	2.9"	Four = 1.5"
	5.0	200	827	59	1.9"	Good moderate load
	5.5	–	890	95	3.2"	
	6.0	–	918	92	2.4"	
	6.5	–	1044	77	3.4"	Four = 1.9"
	7.0	–	1097	31	1.9"	Good hunting load
	7.5	–	1161	36	1.8"	–

Powder	Grs.	Bullet/ Wt.	FPS	ES	Grp.	Comments
Red Dot	4.5	225	717	55	2.1"	
	5.0	–	800	40	1.7"	Good practice/training load
	5.5	–	858	14	3.1"	
	6.0	–	927	38	2.8"	
	6.5	–	1012	21	1.9"	Good hunting load
	7.0	–	1070	24	2.2"	–
	7.5	–	1115	22	2.3"	Warm - primer flattening
PB	5.0	180	663	88	3.5"	Four = 2.1"
	5.5	–	729	80	3.0"	Four = 2.2"
	6.0	–	786	95	1.9"	Duplicates factory load
	6.5	180	844	50	3.1"	Three = 1.2"
	7.0	–	898	82	2.3"	
	7.5	–	951	39	1.6"	Three = 0.9"
	5.0	200	663	59	2.1"	
	5.5	–	729	72	4.6"	
	6.0	–	821	69	4.2	Four = 2.1"
	6.5	–	853	45	3.3"	Three = 1.3"
	7.0	–	918	70	4.2"	
	7.5	–	946	47	4.2"	Four = 2.1"
	4.5	225	596	43	3.2"	
	5.0	–	659	55	2.8"	Four = 1.6"
	5.5	–	740	78	3.3"	Four = 2.2"
	6.0	–	805	45	3.4"	
	6.5	–	850	68	1.6"	Three = 0.95"
	7.0	–	915	20	3.6"	Three =1.5"
	7.5	–	968	11	3.4"	Four = 2.0
800X	8.0	180	900	68	3.5"	
	8.5	–	950	32	1.4"	
	9.0	–	1025	28	3.0"	Four = 1.6"
	8.0	200	915	46	3.3"	Four = 2.2"
	8.5	–	971	41	2.0"	Four = 0.95"
	9.0	–	1031	50	1.9"	Three = 0.95"
	8.0	225	863	28	3.7"	
	8.5	–	925	14	2.2"	
	9.0	–	991	46	2.0"	
Win 231	5.0	180	682	57	2.7"	Three = 0.85"
	5.5	–	744	65	4.8"	Duplicates factory load
	6.0	–	835	56	4.3"	Three = 0.75"
	6.5	–	927	39	1.9"	Good medium load
	7.0	–	976	51	2.2"	Four = 1.0"
	7.5	–	1065	22	3.5"	Three = 1.4"
	5.0	200	690	80	3.0"	Three = 0.8"
	5.5	–	757	68	3.1"	Four = 1.5"
	6.0	–	853	39	2.9"	
	6.5	–	940	33	3.1"	
	7.0	–	1005	42	3.2"	Three = 2.2"
	7.5	–	1052	44	2.8"	Three =1.2"
	4.5	225	637	60	3.3"	Four = 1.1"

Powder	Grs.	Bullet/ Wt.	FPS	ES	Grp.	Comments
Win 231	5.0	–	720	13	3.7"	
	5.5	–	787	57	3.4"	Four = 1.9"
	6.0	–	845	24	3.6"	Three = 1.4"
	6.5	–	921	46	3.9"	
	7.0	–	981	30	3.0"	
	7.5	–	1034	28	2.4"	Three = 1.7"
HP38	5.5	180	769	59	3.3"	Three =1.6"
	6.0	–	843	66	3.6"	Four = 1.8"
HP38	6.5	–	918	40	2.6"	Three = 1.3"
	7.0	–	976	19	1.6"	Good medium load
	7.5	–	1046	31	2.2"	
	8.0	–	1115	38	3.8"	Three = 1.5"
	5.5	200	798	71	3.4"	Three = 1.3"
	6.0	–	881	54	2.1"	
	6.5	–	940	37	3.0"	
	7.0	–	1005	31	1.7"	Four = 0.6"
	7.5	–	1061	21	3.8"	Three = 1.0"
	8.0	–	1114	16	2.4"	
	5.0	225	731	18	2.7"	
	5.5	–	798	22	2.4"	
	6.0	–	874	23	3.0"	
	6.5	–	887	49	5.0"	
	7.0	–	976	19	1.6"	Good medium load
	7.5	–	1046	31	2.2"	
	8.0	–	1115	38	3.8"	Three = 1.5"
HS 6	8.0	180	798	71	2.1"	
	8.5	–	865	59	4.3"	Three = 2.1"
	9.0	–	954	139	4.0"	
	9.5	–	978	74	3.8"	
	10.0	–	1011	30	2.3"	
	10.5	1070	99	3.8"		
	8.0	200	802	77	3.9"	
	8.5	–	841	92	1.7"	Three = 0.7"
	9.0	–	903	80	2.2"	Three =1.2"
	9.5	–	983	64	3.6"	
	10.0	–	1044	35	3.2"	
	10.5	–	1101	34	2.9"	
	8.0	225	813	99	3.6"	
	8.5	–	876	72	4.0"	Three =1.3"
	9.0	–	930	27	2.7"	Three =1.5"
	9.5	–	1014	78	4.6"	
	10.0	–	1052	35	4.6"	Four = 2.8"
	10.5	–	1110	31	3.5"	Three =1.6"
Trap 14	8.0	180	934	74	4.2"	
	8.5	–	998	71	4.2"	
	9.0	–	1017	134	3.7"	
	9.5	–	1060	52	3.8"	Three =1.1"
	10.0	–	1083	166	3.6"	Four = 2.0"

Powder	Grs.	Bullet/ Wt.	FPS	ES	Grp.	Comments
Trap 14	8.0	200	1005	112	5.5"	
	8.5	–	1040	99	4.0"	
	9.0	–	1062	109	3.2"	
	9.5	–	1081	82	4.0"	
	10.0	–	1122	51	3.3"	
	7.5	225	961	75	3.4"	Four = 3.2"
	8.0	–	969	60	3.1"	Three = 0.8"
	8.5	–	1011	81	4.5"	Four = 3.0"
	9.0	–	1041	71	3.6"	
	9.5	–	1068	89	2.3"	Three = 0.8"
	4.5	180	571	70	1.6"	
	5.0	–	674	132	4.0"	
	5.5	–	764	72	3.1"	Four = 1.6"
	6.0	–	871	44	3.3"	
	6.5	–	963	117	2.1"	
	7.0	–	999	122	3.0"	Four = 2.1"
TopMark	4.5	200	629	103	2.5"	
	5.0	–	706	41	3.5"	Three =1.6"
	5.5	–	803	52	1.6"	Good practice load
	6.0	–	894	61	3.3"	
	6.5	–	954	33	2.4"	Three = 0.7"
	7.0	–	1025	26	3.8"	
	4.5	225	586	89	4.6"	
	5.0	–	664	102	4.1"	
	5.5	–	792	45	3.7	
	6.0	–	858	41	2.2"	
	6.5	–	949	102	3.4"	Three = 1.3"
	7.0	–	996	26	1.3"	Good medium load
Grey B	3.5	180	624	82	2.4"	Three = 1.0"
	4.0	–	666	26	4.7"	
	4.5	–	754	46	1.6"	Duplicates factory.
	5.0	–	844	40	4.6"	
	5.5	–	909	22	1.5"	Good medium load
	6.0	–	972	30	4.1"	
	3.5	200	611	60	1.6"	
	4.0	–	702	35	1.9"	Three = 0.7"
	4.5	–	773	19	3.5"	
	5.0	–	856	59	3.0"	
	5.5	–	900	18	2.2"	
	6.0	–	962	18	2.4"	
	3.0	225	535	68	5.7"	Three = 1.5"
	3.5	–	604	11	3.1"	Three = 1.7"
	4.0	–	688	15	5.2"	Four = 2.0"
Grey B	4.5	225	740	28	3.3"	
	5.0	–	810	26	2.5"	
	5.5	–	862	20	3.8"	Three = 2.0"
	6.0	–	929	36	3.1"	Three = 2.0"
Titegroup	5.0	180	831	39	4.2"	

Powder	Grs.	Bullet/ Wt.	FPS	ES	Grp.	Comments
Titegroup	5.5	–	914	41	4.2"	
	6.0	–	997	58	5.0"	
	6.5	–	1049	33	3.2"	Three = 1.4"
	7.0	–	1117	27	4.3"	Three =1.3"
	7.5	–	1182	21	2.3"	Good top load
	5.0	200	843	56	1.6"	Good med load
	5.5	–	933	42	2.4"	Three = 1.3"
	6.0	–	1002	34	1.9"	Good mod load
	6.5	–	1049	29	2.7"	Four =1.7"
	7.0	–	1117	13	2.1"	
	7.5	–	1172	21	2.0"	
	4.5	225	772	30	3.0"	Four = 2.1"
	5.0	–	854	54	2.8"	
	5.5	–	921	27	3.8"	Four = 2.0"
	6.0	–	972	22	2.6"	
	6.5	–	1008	13	4.6"	Four = 2.9"
	7.0	–	1083	17	4.0"	
	7.5	–	1147	8	2.2"	Four = 1.0"
SR 4756	7.0	180	712	64	4.8"	Three = 1.5"
	7.5	–	753	62	3.3"	Three = 0.9"
	8.0	–	821	92	3.8"	Four = 1.3"
	8.5	–	879	137	2.4"	Three = 1.3"
	9.0	–	958	109	2.3"	Three = 1.5"
	9.5	–	1018	79	2.6"	Three = 1.6"
	10.0	–	1025	78	1.5"	Good hunt load
	7.0	200	748	83	2.6"	Three = 1.5"
	7.5	–	774	77	3.0"	Three = 1.5"
	8.0	–	820	59	2.8"	Four = 2.0"
	8.5	–	932	143	3.2"	
	9.0	–	971	54	3.3"	Four = 2.4"
	9.5	–	1029	52	4.2"	Four = 2.0"
	10.0	–	1052	93	3.0"	Three = 1.5
	6.5	225	672	72	4.2"	Four = 1.7
	7.0	–	749	57	3.4"	Four = 2.1"
	7.5	–	801	34	2.0"	
	8.0	–	892	56	3.7"	Four = 1.5
	8.5	–	955	50	3.1"	Four = 1.2"
	9.0	–	1007	62	3.3"	Four = 2.1"
	9.5	225	1041	50	3.4"	Four = 2.0"
	10.0	–	1078	25	4.2"	
AL 5	9.0	180	888	59	3.1"	Three = 1.9"
	9.5	–	938	35	1.9"	
	10.0	–	990	65	1.5"	
	9.0	200	905	28	2.6"	
	9.5	–	975	51	4.0"	
	10.0	–	1016	31	2.9"	
	8.5	225	862	46	4.3"	
	9.0	–	913	39	2.5"	

Powder	Grs.	Bullet/ Wt.	FPS	ES	Grp.	Comments
AL 5	9.5	–	948	34	4.1"	
700X	5.5	180	932	42	3.3"	
	6.0	–	982	42	2.4"	Three = 1.1"
	6.5	–	1048	42	4.0"	
	7.0	–	1128	52	2.1"	Four = 1.0"
	7.5	–	1187	50	5.1"	Three = 2.2"
	5.5	200	924	18	3.3"	
	6.0	–	1006	62	3.4"	
	6.5	–	1080	46	4.5"	
	7.0	–	1126	23	2.4"	
	7.5	–	1189	34	2.5"	
	5.0	225	850	18	2.8"	
	5.5	–	924	17	2.5"	Four = 1.9"
	6.0	–	991	32	3.0"	
	6.5	–	1047	23	3.2"	Four = 1.3"
	7.0	–	1099	12	2.8"	Four = 1.5"
OREGON TRAIL 255 Gr.						
Herco	7.0		956	34	2.9"	Burns clean
	7.5		1012	39	1.5"	Good hunting load - accurate
	8.0		1062	15	2.7"	Four = 2.0"
Clays	5.0		900	17	2.5"	Warm - some primer flattening
	5.5		940	18	3.4"	Three = 2.5" - Hot! Sticky extraction!
	6.0		973			HOT! Extraction hard; primer flattened/cratered; only one shot fired
Universal	6.5		990	31	1.5"	Warm; exc. accuracy
	7.0		1040	7	2.0"	Consistent; accurate
	7.5		1076	46	4.1"	Four = 2.1" HOT! Hard extraction; don't use!
Red Dot	6.0		976	15	1.6"	Three = 0.8"; Very acc.; warm; top load
	6.5		1026	20	2.0"	Warm! Back off to 6.0.
	7.0		1080			HOT! Extraction hard! Primer crater/flatten. Only one shot fired
Win 231	6.0		897	27	2.9"	Three = 1.1". Warm but ok for regular use
	6.5		951	25	2.1"	Four = 1.4" VG accuracy
	7.0		995	19	2.9"	Three = 1.2" Warm but good accuracy
	7.5		1047	12	1.9"	Exc. accuracy but HOT; don't use
HP 38	6.5		960	26	2.6"	Good moderate load
	7.0		1018	12	1.2"	Exc. accuracy; top load this powder
	7.5		1055	14	3.1"	Sticky extraction.
700X	5.5		951	20	2.8"	Warm
	6.0		1004	14	2.7"	Warm; consistent; slight primer cratering
	6.5		1042	10	3.5"	Three - 1.3"; hot; cratering; sticky extraction

SIERRA JACKETED BULLETS

Powder	Grs.	Bullet/ Wt.	FPS	ES	Grp.	Comments
Herco	8.0	185	920	54	2.9"	Three = 0.6"
	8.5	972	49	2.4"		
	9.0	1029	62	2.6"		
	9.5	1072	62	1.5"		Good load! Exc. accuracy; Warm; Top load.
	7.0	230	876	32	3.1"	Four = 1.3"
	7.5	230	936	33	2.5"	Four = 1.8"; VG load
	8.0		969	51	2.6"	
	6.5	240	872	48	3.2"	
	7.0		892	39	2.1"	Three = 1.3"; Good load; Accurate
	7.5		929	24	2.3"	Three = 1.3"
Unique	8.0	185	1019	72	2.8"	Three = 0.7"
	8.5		1064	35	2.3"	Three = 0.7"
	9.0		1104	45	1.4"	Exc. accuracy; VG hunting load
	7.0	230	913	35	1.7"	Three = 0.6"; VG mid-range hunting load
	7.5		964	12	2.4"	
	8.0		1004	43	1.3"	Exc. accuracy!
	6.5	240	858	30	2.3"	
	7.0		916	73	3.0"	Three = 1.6"; Good load
	7.5		964	38	2.5"	
Universal	7.0	185	936	115	2.9"	Four = 1.6"
	7.5		1017	84	2.8"	Three =1.5"
	8.0		1102	92	3.0"	Three = 1.8"
	7.0	230	995	7	2.4"	Four = 1.1"; Three = .5"; Accurate; good load.
	7.5		1051	25	2.2"	Three = 0.7"; Accurate; warm.
	8.0		1102	23	3.0"	Three = 0.6"; Warm but ok; top load
	6.5	240	914	38	2.2"	Three = 1.4"
	7.0		989	19	3.6"	Three = 0.8"; Warm but ok
	7.5		1028	14	4.0"	Three = 1.2"; 7.0 grains better load
PB	7.5	185	943	86	3.4"	Three = 1.5"
	8.0		1035	63	3.6"	Three = 0.7"; Good load.
	8.5		1070	28	2.1"	Four = 1.2"
	7.0	230	937	37	2.4"	Three = 1.1"
	7.5		990	29	2.7"	Four = 1.5"; Accurate; good load
	8.0		1055	14	2.3"	Four = 1.4"; Warm but ok; good top load.
	7.0	240	924	27	2.2"	Three = 1.1"; Good load; accurate
	7.5		974	35	2.3"	

Powder	Grs.	Bullet/ Wt.	FPS	ES	Grp.	Comments
PB	8.0		1023	45	1.6"	Four = 0.7"; VG acc; good big game load
800X	8.5	185	953	40	1.7"	Three = 0.7"; Good hunting load.
	9.0		997	26	3.0"	Three = 0.9"
	9.5		1057	22	2.9"	Four = 1.7"; Good top load
800X	8.0	230	919	26	2.1"	Four = 1.0"; Good mid-range load.
	8.5		984	36	2.5"	
	9.0		1027	37	3.2"	Four = 1.9"
	7.5	240	854	41	3.0"	
	8.0		917	32	3.0"	Four = 1.9"
	8.5		968	33	2.9	"

REMINGTON FACTORY 45 AUTO RIM

PISTOL	FPS	ES	Grp.	Comments
625	769	27	3.7"	
17/55	712	37	3.7"	
GI/1917	75	29	3.25"	

AUTHOR'S HANDLOADS – 45 AUTO RIM

PISTOL	FPS	ES	Grp.	Comments
625 - HP	1069	15	2.7"	
625 - BB	1098	26	2.5"	
17/55	976	60	3.0"	
17/55 - BB	997	34	2.2"	

FACTORY 45 ACP - WITH FULL MOON CLIPS

PISTOL	FPS	ES	Grp.	Comments
Federal Premium 230 gr. Hydra Shok JHP:				
625	901	41	3.0"	
17/55	809	27	3.1"	
Winchester 185-gr. Silver Tip HP:				
625	915	62	4.0"	Three = 1.9"
17/55	834	25	3.0"	
Super Vel 190 gr. HP: (Old - discontinued)				
625	969	35	2.9"	
17/55	873	63	3.1"	
Cor-Bon 45ACP +P 200-gr. JHP:				
625	1075	20	3.8"	Four = 1.9"; Great load! Hunting or defense.
17/55	966	45	2.3"	Four = 1.1"; VG accuracy! Use for ACP defense.

THE PUNITIVE EXPEDITION & ITS SMALL ARMS 1916-17

by James W. Hurst

ABOVE: Known as "Black Jack" in reference to his strict discipline and high standards during his service with the all-black 10th Cavalry, General John J. Pershing led a successful campaign against Pancho Villa during the Punitive Expedition of 1916.

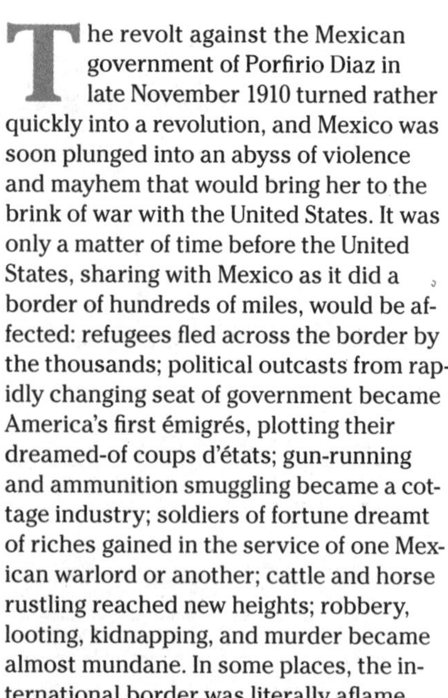

The revolt against the Mexican government of Porfirio Diaz in late November 1910 turned rather quickly into a revolution, and Mexico was soon plunged into an abyss of violence and mayhem that would bring her to the brink of war with the United States. It was only a matter of time before the United States, sharing with Mexico as it did a border of hundreds of miles, would be affected: refugees fled across the border by the thousands; political outcasts from rapidly changing seat of government became America's first émigrés, plotting their dreamed-of coups d'états; gun-running and ammunition smuggling became a cottage industry; soldiers of fortune dreamt of riches gained in the service of one Mexican warlord or another; cattle and horse rustling reached new heights; robbery, looting, kidnapping, and murder became almost mundane. In some places, the international border was literally aflame.

Residents of the border areas of Texas, New Mexico, and Arizona were most vociferous in their appeals to President Wilson's administration to do something in order to bring stability to the border area. Due to other pressing international concerns, the best that could be done was to place small units of the regular army near potential hotspots and simply hope for the best. After all, Congress reasoned, it was not as if the United States were being invaded by hostile foreigners. However, congressional complacency toward the course of events along the border were shaken by Francisco (Pancho) Villa's March 9, 1916, attack on an American border community.

Columbus, New Mexico, was a watering station for the El Paso and Southwestern Railroad that ran from the copper mines near Bisbee, Arizona eastward along the international border to the ASARCO smelter in El Paso, Texas, some seventy-five miles to the east. The Thirteenth was stationed at Columbus as the military force responsible for patrolling the international border from Noria, New Mexico, in the east to Hermanas, New Mexico, in the west, a distance of some sixty-five miles as the crow flies.

To accomplish its mission, the Thirteenth had twenty-one officers and five hundred and thirty-two enlisted men, divided into Headquarters and Machine Gun Troops and four Rifle Troops (12 officers and 321 men, less 79 non-combatants) in camp at Columbus; two troops (7 officers and 151 men) at Gibson's Line Ranch, fourteen miles west of Columbus. One troop of two officers and 65 men were at the Border Gate, three miles south of town.[1] Both day and night, at irregular intervals, patrols were sent east and west along the international border as a precaution against incursions from Mexico by rustlers, arms smugglers, and bandits.

The northern Mexican states of Chihuahua and Sonora were battlegrounds over which the followers of Venustiano Carranza (Carranzistas), Francisco Villa (Villistas) and Álvaro Obregón (Obregonistas) struggled for supremacy. The pre-Revolutionary era of Porfirio Díaz had been friendly to foreign investment; the Revolution unleashed a storm of anti-foreign and especially anti-American sentiment. In the north, Carranza played heavily on anti-Americanism to rally his supporters; Villa was a staunch defender of American interests who on numerous occasions declared his affection for, and loyalty to, the United States. As Carranza and Villa fought for control of Chihuahua State and leadership of the Revolution, President Wilson faced a dilemma: which of the two powerful leaders to recognize as de facto leader of the Revolution? Events during the spring and summer of 1915 were to provide Wilson with the answer.

In April the Villistas were defeated by Carranzista forces at Matamoras, across from Brownsville, Texas, and at Celaya, Guanajuato State. At virtually the same time Villa himself suffered a stunning defeat at León at the hands of General Álvaro Obregón, and his army began to disintegrate. Late summer and early fall witnessed the beginning of the end of the legend of Villa's invincibility, as the unwavering faith in his leadership that had sustained his followers began to fade. In the meantime, on October 19, the American Secretary of State, Robert Lansing, announced the recognition of Carranza as de facto head of the Mexican government. Villa was unaware of Wilson's decision and determined to demonstrate his ability to defeat Carranzista forces as well as seeking much-needed ammunition and supplies, Villa attacked the Sonoran town of Agua Prieta, directly across the border from Douglas, Arizona.

What Villa did not know, however, was that Wilson had given permission to allow six thousand Carranzista troops to be transported on American railroad cars across New Mexico and Arizona to Douglas, where they simply stepped across the border into Agua Prieta, Sonora and took up positions in the barbwire-protected trenches. On November 1, 1915, Villa launched his Division of the North, roughly fifteen thousand men, in a frontal assault on the Carranzista defensive lines. The reinforced firepower of the defenders (Villa believed there were only 1200 soldiers in the small town) simply slaughtered the Villistas, and Villa decided that perhaps his usual tactic of a night attack would succeed. When shortly after midnight he ordered the attack, led by marijuana-stoned Yaqui Indians who slithered through the barbwire, his men were suddenly illuminated by powerful searchlights powered by American electricity. The result was a bloodbath: machinegun fire and rapid-fire artillery mercilessly cut down the Villista attackers. Their panic-driven retreat was brutally harassed by artillery, and the slaughter that followed was exceeded only by Villa's humiliation.

Branded a bandit by Mexico's de facto government, faced daily with desertions from his ranks, trusting only his closest followers (Los Dorados, the "Golden Ones"), and driven by desire for revenge, Villa made his way eastward out of the Sierra Madres and north through Chihuahua State toward the American border. He settled in a remote camp near Boca Grande, near the Casas Grande River, and made his plans for an attack on Columbus, New Mexico. He sent scouts to Palomas with instructions to proceed to Columbus and gather information on troop strength, guard posts, and locations of barracks and stables. The scouts used a sporting house in Palomas as their base of operations and gathered information in the company of prostitutes while posing as shoppers. They produced a rather accurate map but their estimate of fewer than one hundred soldiers present in Columbus proved disastrous. On the basis of their information, however, Villa decided to attack.

On March 8, the Villistas departed Boca Grande and began their march toward the border. At 3:30 a.m. the following day, they counter-marched across the tracks and halted one and one-half miles or so west of Cootes Hill, which was on the west side of Camp Furlong. Villa gave further specific orders for the attack, announced that he would remain in the rear in a "reserve" position with a guard of Dorados, and ordered his men forward.2 The time was close to 4:00 a.m.

When Lieutenant John P. Lucas stepped off the train from a weeks' polo-playing in El Paso, he had no idea that in a matter of hours he would be in a fight for his life. Lucas was the officer in command of the Thirteenth Cavalry's machinegun squad, and after retiring for the night he was awakened by horsemen riding past his adobe. As he arose to investigate, shots were fired and he realized the garrison was under attack. Lucas acted quickly to muster his men and bring the machinegun troopers into action, as it was now obvious to him that the town was swarming with Mexican attackers. The Villistas were already in the commercial part of town and were taken under fire by the duty Officer of the Day, Lieutenant Castleman, and as many riflemen as he had been able to muster. In the darkness there were few targets of opportunity for the troopers, and they were shooting at gun flashes and the shouts of the attacking Villistas.

The fight turned dramatically in favor of the defenders when the Commercial Hotel and other buildings caught fire. The attacking Villistas were then illuminated in spectacular fashion, and the rifle and machinegun fire took a deadly toll. The initial fighting in Columbus lasted perhaps ninety minutes, but with daylight now upon the scene the Thirteenth Cavalry mustered itself for an attack.

As Villa's attackers retreated west-southwest, their movements were observed by Colonel Slocum and several other officers from a vantage point on Cootes Hill. Major Frank Tompkins, the Thirteenth Cavalry's Executive Officer, organized a troop of about thirty men and moved forward and followed the littered trail of the fleeing bandits. Running low on supplies, he decided to abandon pursuit of the bandits and ordered his tired troopers back to Columbus.

When news of the attack and reports of the loss of American lives spread across the United States, the reaction was one of palpable outrage.3 Not since the War of 1812 had foreign invaders attacked the country. Newspaper headlines across the nation cried for revenge, for immediate retribution, and for Villa's head. The morning after the raid, President Wilson's Cabinet met, and the President formulated a call for Villa's capture. Headlines screamed, "Villa Wanted, Dead or Alive." Fortunately calmer heads prevailed and, following a meeting with General Hugh Scott, Secretary of State Newton D. Baker prepared the orders sent to General John J. Pershing, the man chosen to lead the Expedition: the American force was to enter Chihuahua State and capture or destroy the outlaws who were responsible for the attack on Columbus, then return home.

The mission, known as the Punitive Expedition, stands as a fulcrum upon which the older forces of warfare were balanced against the newer ones: cavalry, infantry, and artillery on one side; the aeroplane, the automobile, the truck, the motorcycle, mobile telegraphic communication, well-organized tech-

Calvary gathered around the campfire inside the camp at Columbus, New Mexico.

niques of intelligence-gathering, and the motion picture on the other. And the soldiers were equipped with two new small arms: the Model 1903 Springfield rifle and the Colt 45-caliber pistol.

The 1903 Springfield, the rifle of the Punitive Expedition, was the result of the Army's desire to replace the old Krag, which had come in for so much criticism since the Spanish-American and Philippine Wars, with a more modern rifle and cartridge. In 1901 the Springfield Armory began working with a Mauser-actioned rifle and an experimental 30-caliber cartridge. The Mauser action was modified, and the new 30-caliber rimless cartridge was loaded with the Krag's old 220-grain round-nose bullet. The Springfield-Mauser rifle, chambered for the new 30-caliber cartridge, was officially adopted in 1903 and was popularly known as the 30/'03 Springfield. The rifle was loaded with five rounds through the use of a charger strip carried in a canvas ammunition belt. The infantry belt had ten pouches with one five-round strip each; the cavalry belt had eight cartridge pouches and one pouch that carried two magazines for the Colt 45 ACP pistol. The rear sight was a folding leaf adjustable for both windage and elevation; the front sight was a blade protected by a stamped metal cover.

In subsequent months the new rifle was field-tested, and the ballistic results were called into question. The 30/'03 cartridge propelled its 220-grain bullet from the rifle's 24-inch barrel at a muzzle velocity of 2200 feet per second (fps), and by 1906 the Army was convinced that higher velocities were needed. Ordnance experts, probably influenced by the German example, decided to scrap the old round-nose bullet in favor of the pointed (or spitzer) bullet. They shortened the 30/'03 cartridge case by 0.10-inch, loaded it with a 150-grain spitzer bullet, and the new Model 30/'06 was born. All rifles were recalled to the Springfield Armory and fitted with re-chambered barrels. Production of the rifle was soon extended to the Rock Island Arsenal, and by early January 1905 the arsenal was meeting its production quota of one hundred and twenty-five rifles a day.4

The success of the '03 Springfield was due in no small part to the choice of a proven action, the German Mauser. This action had demonstrated its reliability in the most demanding circumstances of military combat, and when fitted with properly manufactured barrels, its accuracy was second to none. With the development and application of the new 30-caliber cartridge in 1906, the Army was equipped with a rifle as dependable and as accurate as any military rifle in the world. The care expended on the early Springfields, from metal bluing to the quality of walnut chosen for stocks, made them rivals of some of the better civilian hunting rifles. In future years they were used successfully in Olympic and other international competitions. (Minor cosmetic changes would be made to the Springfield subsequent to the Expedition's experience, but it remained what it had been from its inception: a durable, easily maintained, dependable, and deadly accurate rifle.)

A new pistol accompanied the Springfield rifle. In January 1907, the Chief of Ordnance had referred to the Springfield Armory nine handguns for testing and consideration to replace the 38-caliber revolver that was then the military's sidearm. Only pistols that fired a 45-caliber cartridge with a 230-grain bullet were considered. One submission, the 1906 Colt 45, was already commercially available. Among the other submissions, the most notable were the Luger, the Savage automatics, and the Colt and Smith & Wesson double-action revolvers. After lengthy tests in firing, durability, reliability and field maintenance the 1906 Colt was chosen––contingent upon certain modifications as recommended by the Ordinance Board. John M. Browning, the pistol's designer, affected the required changes, and in 1910 the pistol was resubmitted to the Army for further testing. The following year it was accepted and designated as "U.S. Pistol, Caliber .45, Model of 1911."

Browning's pistol proved itself an outstanding choice. The rimless cartridge was loaded with a jacketed bullet of 230 grains, which traveled at 830 fps. The magazine held seven rounds, the barrel was five inches long, and the

Francisco ("Pancho") Villa (1878-1923), whose border activities precipitated the Punitive Expedition.

pistol weighed close to two and one half pounds. Field-stripping and cleaning were relatively easy, and tolerances were such that jamming was rare in all but the harshest physical conditions. It was an admittedly difficult pistol to master: recoil was severe and the loose-fitting slide and barrel that were necessary to keep the gun functioning under adverse conditions meant that accuracy was somewhat less than desirable. At close quarters, however, there was no question that it was a "man-stopper." Indeed, its killing power became legendary, and the angle of the grip in relation to the barrel made it a natural-pointing handgun.

One member of Pershing's Expedition who was not enamored of the Colt 1911 was Lieutenant George S. Patton. In 1915 Patton had narrowly missed serious physical injury when the Colt 1911 pistol he was using fired unexpectedly. No one seems to know exactly what the problem had been, but Patton consequently switched to a Colt 1873 single-action revolver in 45 Colt. He also took the sensible precaution of loading the revolver with five rounds and made certain that the hammer rested on an empty chamber.5

It was service with the Punitive Expedition that proved to be the 1911's testing ground. General Pershing had also recognized that the general proficiency with the new pistol had not been high enough to inspire confidence in its effectiveness. The exceptions to this observation were the positive results that had been shown in the mounted attack with the pistol, even in the hands of average shots. The relatively close quarters in such attacks made the 1911 a formidable weapon indeed. From his headquarters in Dublan, Chihuahua, on November 1, 1916, General Pershing convened a board to conduct experiments that would determine the best methods of using the pistol in combat and of training men for that use.

With a view to developing a scientific method of training men in mounted work with the pistol, a list of questions was sent to all cavalry officers in Mexico. They were directed to give the subject careful thought, with special consideration to the tactical features in the pistol charge. They were required to prepare and submit their written suggestions for consideration by Pershing's appointed board of officers. On the basis of the responses, the board would then design the experiments in methods of instructing both the men and their horses in work with the new pistol. Daily tests in firing were held, both mounted and dismounted. This resulted not only in increased proficiency in marksmanship, but in the development of both a pistol manual and a course of pistol practice.

The board also made a number of recommendations for modifications of the pistol itself: the slide stop lever on the pistol should be lengthened to make it more easily reached by the thumb; the magazine lips which hold the cartridges should be made stronger to preclude allowing the cartridge from springing up too soon, causing a jam; the hammer should be modified to prevent pinching the hand between hammer and grip safety; and the hammer should be configured so that it can be let down from the cocked position without slipping. Further recommendations included 1) procurement of eight 22-caliber pistols of the same weight and configuration as the 1911 for each organization for training purposes, 2) a certain amount of practice with the 45 1911 each month as conditions permitted, and 3) that blank cartridges be supplied for use in accustoming horses to the sound of firing.

The Benét-Mercie Machine Rifle

The "Bennie," as it was often called, was adopted by the Army in 1909 and was officially designated a "machine rifle." Manufactured by both Colt and the Springfield Armory, and chambered in the "30-'06" rifle cartridge, it was intended to be a relatively light automatic weapon for both infantry and cavalry. The gun was loaded with a metal strip that held 30 rounds, and ammunition was transported in wooden boxes, each of which contained ten strips. Assuming no malfunctions, its rate of fire was 400 rounds per minute. The Bennie was often referred to as the "Daylight Gun" because it was so difficult to assemble in the dark, and there was always the possibility of inserting the loading strip upside down, thus assuring a malfunction. A slightly bent loading strip almost guaranteed a jammed gun, and in cold weather the firing pin and extractor proved susceptible to shattering. Only the best-trained and skilled gun crews could assure that the Bennie would function reliably. The earliest production guns were fitted with a telescopic sight used on Springfield '03 sniper rifles, the idea being that the sight would enable the gunner to spot his sights more easily. This practice was, however, soon abandoned as impractical; in use with the Expedition in Mexico, the gun's leaf sight was implemented. A number of problems arose with the gun in Mexico, probably due more to the lack of experienced gun crews rather than with the gun itself, but in several situations the fire-power it provided proved effective.

A major problem in the pursuit of the Columbus attackers was quite simply one of manpower. From among those units available, Pershing chose his combat force of cavalry, infantry, and artillery regiments. In addition to the combat arms were Army engineers, a field hospital and ambulance company staffs, two wagon companies of 27 wagons, 112 mules, and 6 horses, a Signal Corps unit to man field radios, and the 1st Aero Squadron. When this Provisional Division crossed into Mexico on March 15-16, 1916, it had 4,800 men and 4,175 animals. General Funston promised additional men and materiel as they became available, and steps were taken to move more men and supplies to Columbus via the railroads.

The departure for Mexico was taken in two columns, one from Columbus through Palomas and the other from the Culberson's Ranch some fifty miles to the west in the Bootheel. The columns converged and encamped at Casas Grande where the Rio Casas Grande and the Mexican Northwestern Railroad met. From here Pershing's initial strategy against the Columbus raiders took shape. It was essentially that which had been used a generation or so earlier by Generals Crook and Miles against the recalcitrant Apaches of New Mexico and Arizona. Three, later four, small highly mobile cavalry units sought and engaged the Columbus raiders wherever and whenever they could be found. Each unit was to act independently while maintaining communication with each other when necessary. Forage for the horses and food for the men was to be secured locally and paid for in hard currency.

Between March 29 and June 9, Expedition units clashed ten times with Villista bands and once with Carranzista regulars. Two of these conflicts were especially significant: Guerrero on March 29 and Parral on April 12. In his flight after Columbus, Villa had been wounded in the leg in a skirmish with Carranzista forces at Guerrero (March 26-27) and was taken away from the area in a carriage accompanied by his bodyguard of Dorados. The morning of the 29th while most of the nearly 400 Villistas slept, Colonels Dodd and Erwin of the Seventh Cavalry attacked with a force of 370 troopers. The Villistas were taken by surprise and routed. The Seventh suffered five wounded; the loss to the bandit band was 56 killed and more than 30 wounded.

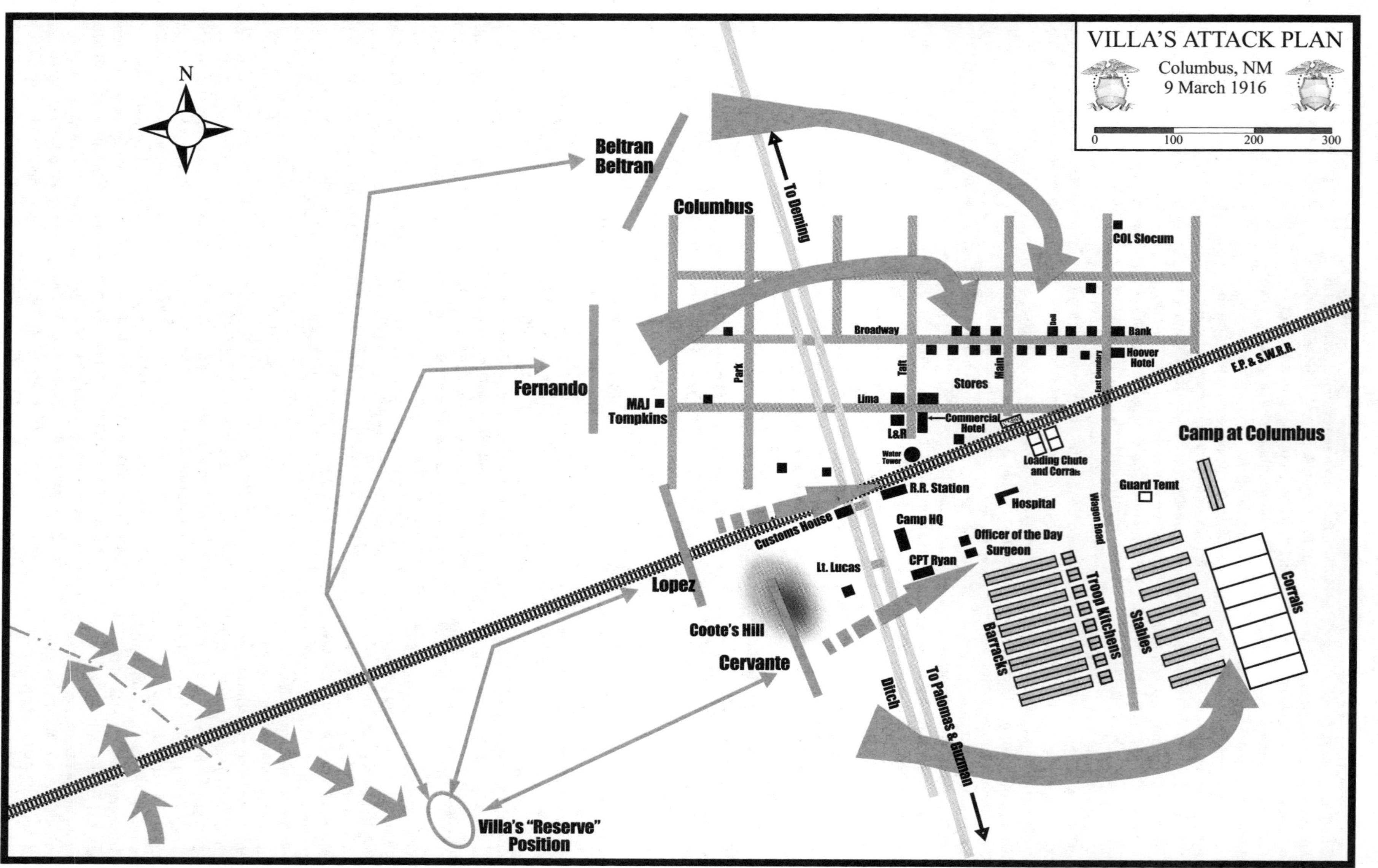
VILLA'S ATTACK PLAN
Columbus, NM
9 March 1916
0
100
200
300
N
Beltran
Beltran
Columbus
To Deming
COL Slocum
Broadway
Bank
Hoover Hotel
East Boundary
Main
Taft
Stores
Park
Lima
Fernando
MAJ Tompkins
Commercial Hotel
L&R
Water Tower
E.P. & S.W.R.R.
Camp at Columbus
Loading Chute and Corrals
Guard Temt
R.R. Station
Hospital
Wagon Road
Customs House
Camp HQ
Officer of the Day
Surgeon
CPT Ryan
Lt. Lucas
Lopez
Troop Kitchens
Stables
Corrals
Barracks
Coote's Hill
Cervante
Ditch
To Palomas & Guzman
Villa's "Reserve" Position

They had no idea that the American pursuers could have arrived so far south into Mexico in such a short time. It was a scenario that would be repeated several more times during the days of the Expedition's active pursuit, and it sent Villa into an apprehensive flight for concealment, a flight quite literally for his life.

The path to Parral began April 2 when General Pershing gave instructions to Major Tompkins of the Thirteenth Cavalry to make a scout south toward Parral, about 400 miles south of Namiquipa, with an eye toward flushing the wounded Villa. He was further ordered to make every attempt to avoid a confrontation with Carranzista forces, as the political situation between President Wilson and First Jefe Carranza had become increasingly strained. Tompkins' command consisted of less than 100 men, 12 pack mules, rations for five days and 500 Mexican pesos. Ten days later he was near Parral where it was rumored that Villa had been seen.

Tompkins entered Parral with a handful of men to seek supplies, information, and perhaps a day's respite from the rigors of life in the field. Instead, he was greeted with a hostile mob bent on causing an incident that would precipitate a confrontation with the Carranzista garrison. Tompkins led his column out of town and almost immediately found his command under fire from armed civilians and Carranzista soldiers. As his men returned fire, the civilians lost their taste for a fight, but cavalry from Parral's garrison followed and attempted to flank the Americans. Tompkins decided to ride for Santa Cruz de Villegas, where he had reason to believe he would find the Tenth Cavalry.

As the Thirteenth made its retreat, it became evident that the trailing Mexican cavalry had formed its ranks for an attack. Captain Frederick Turner's troop of 20 men dismounted and formed a line to oppose the Mexican advance with their Springfield rifles. The Carranzistas launched their attack at a gallop and, when they were within 200 yards, Turner gave the command to fire. The first line of attacking cavalry became a tangle of downed men and horses, and the riflemen of the Thirteenth continued to pour an accurate fire into the Mexicans' ranks. The attackers wavered, halted, and finally retreated; their retreat was harassed by further rifle fire from the American cavalrymen. Forty Carranzistas were killed and an unknown number were wounded; among the dead was a Major, and among the wounded was a Colonel. The Thirteenth suffered two killed and six wounded. After Tompkins and his command arrived at Santa Cruz, he was joined by Major Charles Young and elements of the Tenth Cavalry. The arrival of the rest of the Tenth under Colonel William C. Brown precluded any further trouble from the Carranzista at Parral.

Expedition units clashed with Villistas six more times after Parral; the final clash was June 9 at Santa Clara Canyon where two bandits were killed and several were wounded. In the clashes with Villa's bands, the Expedition had inflicted casualties of 251 killed and 166 wounded. Casualties to Pershing's forces were 15 killed and 31 wounded. Of the total number of Villistas killed, 135 of them were men who had taken part in the raid on Columbus. Villa was in hiding, his force from Columbus was crushed, and his two closest commanders, Cárdenas and Cervantes, were dead. Pershing consolidated his forces at Casas Grande, worried about the effects of inactivity on his troops, sent out daily patrols to gather what information was available, made plans to resume the offensive, and awaited further orders.

As the month of June wore on, reports reached Pershing that Carranzista forces had appeared in large numbers to the south in Chihuahua City, and on his eastern flank near Carrizal at Villa Ahumada, a station on the major north-south railroad to El Paso, Texas. He sent two troops of the Tenth Cavalry to scout the situation at Ahumada, and they arrived, 83 officers and men plus three guides, at the town of Carrizal on June 21. Captain Boyd, senior officer and therefore in command, decided that in order to reach Ahumada his orders directed him to go through Carrizal rather than around it. The officer in charge of the Mexican soldiers in town, General Felix U. Gómez, was under orders to resist any American force attempting to pass through. Boyd met with Gómez and was informed that the garrison would resist any American incursion. The Captain's reply was that his orders were to go through Carrizal and he intended to follow his orders.

The result gave definition to the word "fiasco." Boyd ordered an attack on foot, which meant that he had perhaps sixty men with which to attack an entrenched position defended by well over two hundred riflemen whose fire-power was enhanced by at least one machinegun. The attack would be in the open in broad daylight over a distance of three hundred yards.

When the troopers of the Tenth, led by both Captain Boyd and Lieutenant Adair, got within 250 yards of the Mexican entrenchments, a machinegun opened fire followed quickly by volleys of rifle fire. The Americans returned fire and were soon near the Mexican line when both Boyd and Adair were killed. With loss of their leadership the men of C Troop wavered, and when, ten minutes into the fight, Captain Morey of K Troop was wounded, the situation became hopeless. Within 30 minutes of the initial attack the Americans were in retreat, taking fire from both flanks. The damage they had inflicted on the defenders, however, was enough to discourage immediate pursuit. The "battle" had lasted less than an hour. The Tenth Cavalry's casualties were 12 killed, 11 wounded, and 23 captured; the Carranzistas suffered 42 killed (among whom was General Félix U. Gómez) and 51 wounded.

The ruins of Columbus, New Mexico after being raided by Pancho Villa.

The fight at Carrizal marked both an end and a beginning. It was the end of the active phase of the Expedition; it was the beginning of a period of diplomatic negotiation that moved the United States and Mexico away from the possibility of open warfare. Pershing and his men remained in Mexico until they were ordered home in January 1917. The Expedition arrived at Columbus, New Mexico in February, having carried out its orders successfully.

In just a matter of months these men would be part of the American Expeditionary Force in France, commanded by General Pershing. In the years that followed their participation in the Great War, many of Pershing's men expressed the belief that the hardships they had faced in France were quite small when compared to what they had endured during the fighting phase of the Expedition in Mexico.

Endnotes:

1&2 Since his costly defeats of Agua Prieta and Hermosillo, the Lion of the North's tactics changed to night attacks during which he would be with the "reserve" in the rear.

3 The Army reported seven men killed and seven wounded; ten civilians were killed; by Villa's own reckoning he had lost 100 men (some reports gave a higher number).

4 Bruce Canfield, "Not All 03s Are Springfields," *American Rifleman* (February 2005), 50-1; 69-72.

5 This was the sidearm that Patton used in his famous shoot-out with Villista bandits on May 14, 1916. Patton and several others were in three automobiles on a foraging mission seeking grain for cavalry mounts when they flushed several Villistas who were hiding at the San Miguelito ranch near Rubio, Chihuahua. Three Villistas were killed, one of whom was a close aide to Pancho Villa. Patton gained a degree of notoriety not only for the gunfight, but for returning to Rubio with the dead bandits' bodies strapped across the hoods of the automobiles. Carlo D'Este, *Patton: A Genius for War* (New York: HarperCollins, 1995), 173-76.

THE REBIRTH OF "OLD RELIABLE"– THE SHARPS RIFLE

by Toby Bridges

ABOVE: This early custom Shiloh Model 1874 Sharps, in 50-70 Government, was known as the company's "Gemmer Sharps."

Of the half-million or so *"breech-loading"* rifles and carbines purchased from twenty different arms makers by the U.S. Ordnance Board during the Civil War, nearly 20 percent were produced by the Sharps Rifle Manufacturing Company, of Hartford, Conn. The only other breech-loaded firearms to see greater use were produced by the Spencer Repeating Rifle Company, of Boston, Mass.

Official records of ordnance purchased by the United States government from January 1, 1861 to June 30, 1866 show that a total of 80,512 carbines and 9,141 rifles of Sharps manufacture were delivered. During that same period, Spencer produced a total of 94,196 carbines and 12,471 rifles for the war. Mounted cavalry troops tended to prefer the 7-shot repeating Spencer lever-action carbines and easier loading self-contained cartridges over the slower loading single-shot percussion breech-loaded Sharps with combustible paper or linen cartridges. On the other hand, the rugged construction and longer-range accuracy of the Sharps made it revered among foot soldiers. And it was the outstanding reliability of Sharps-built rifles or carbines during this period that earned them their well-deserved *"Old Reliable"* reputation.

Oddly enough, the man whose name became known around the world, thanks to the quality and accuracy associated with Sharps rifles, had very little to do with the company during this period. And he had no involvement with the production of the later big-bore cartridge rifles that were even better known for their long-range large game taking performance.

Christian Sharps learned the gun-making trade during the 1830s while

The Sharps New Model 1863 carbine, an early Shiloh reproduction carried by this Union cavalry trooper, could pass for an original.

working with the production of the Hall breech-loading Model 1819 flintlock rifle produced at Harpers Ferry Arsenal. While Hall later developed a percussion version, Sharps had conceived a still better *"drop block"* design and received his first patent in September of 1848. Only about 200 each of his percussion Model 1849 and Model 1850 drop-block action rifles were produced by Pennsylvania based manufacturer A.S. Nippes. Both were 44-caliber rifles, built with automatic priming systems.

Production of the 52-caliber Model 1851 and Model 1852 rifles was moved to the Robbins & Lawrence plant in Windsor, Vt. The rifles were built for the newly formed Sharps Rifle Manufacturing Company, headquartered in Hartford, Conn. During the production of the Model 1853 and Model 1855 rifles, both the Robbins & Lawrence and Sharps firms suffered significant losses. The Sharps Rifle Manufacturing Company then moved all manufacturing to Hartford.

The Sharps Rifle Manufacturing Company had been established in 1851 by a group of investors. And Christian Sharps' role in the operation had been relegated to *"Technical Advisor."* His only real tie to the company was that the rifles were being produced under his patents, and Sharps received a $1 royalty for every rifle built. In 1853, Sharps left the company that bore his name, moved to Philadelphia, and opened a new arms-making firm known as C. Sharps & Company, specializing in small pocket pistols and derringers. Other than a small-bore 31- and 38-caliber percussion drop-block rifle built in the late 1850s, the only other *"long guns"* actually produced by Christian Sharps were the Sharps & Hankins 52 rimfire single-shot carbines and rifles produced from 1861 to 1867. Sharps died March 12, 1874 at age 64.

Confederate and Union troops do some swapping in background, while the Civil War-era Sharps and "Sharps-like" breechloaders sit in the foreground. Left to right, New Model 1863 carbine, New Model 1863 rifle, and the Confederate Sharps copy often referred to as the "Richmond Sharps." All guns shown are early Shiloh reproductions.

All of the Sharps rifles produced up through the Model 1855 were of the original *"slant breech"* design. Shooters of the time who had the opportunity to use the Sharps breechloaders acknowledged that they were the best firearms available. Christian Sharps' original design was a definite improvement over other early breech-loading single-shot rifle designs, but did experience considerable gas leakage between the rear of the barrel and face of the breechblock.

The *"straight breech"* block design that first appeared on the New Model 1859 did help alleviate some of the gas leakage. The rifles and carbines built on through the Civil War with New Model 1863 and New Model 1865 markings generally reflect improvements to further reduce the escape of gases from a burning powder charge. Basically, these Sharps guns were all the same design, based on the New Model 1859.

The 115,000 rifles and carbines produced from 1859 to 1866 represented approximately 65 percent of the total number of Sharps breechloaders ever manufactured. No other official military arm of the Civil War went on to remain as popular with civilian shooters and hunters, not even the Remington rolling block rifles. While the latter went on to be produced in far greater numbers, the true rolling block action was not perfected until about 1866.

Dixie Gun Work's line-up of Model 1874 Sharps rifles, by Pedersoli, include (from right) an engraved Silhouette Rifle, a standard version of that rifle, and the Lightweight Target-Hunter rifle. The rifle at far left is a Pedersoli "John Bodine" Remington rolling block rifle.

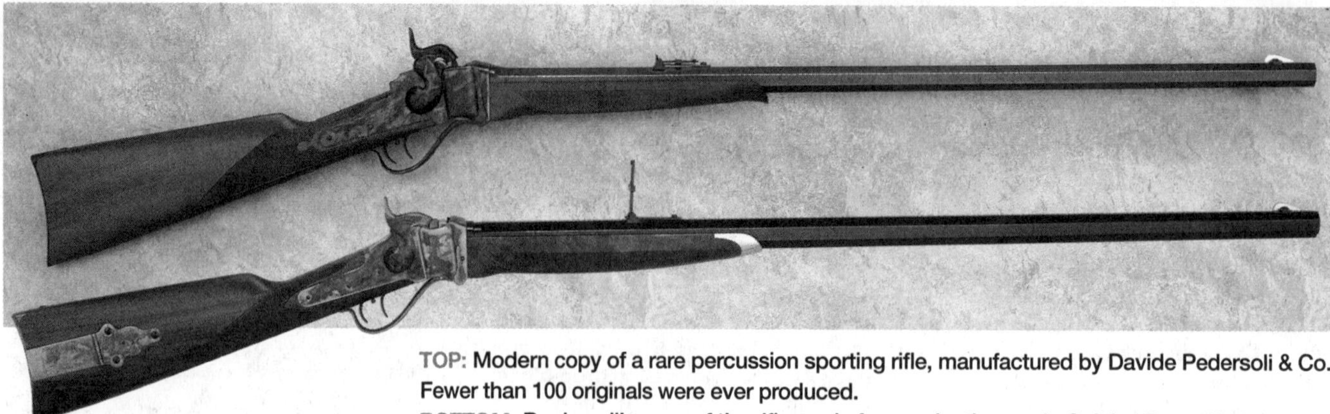

TOP: Modern copy of a rare percussion sporting rifle, manufactured by Davide Pedersoli & Co. Fewer than 100 originals were ever produced.
BOTTOM: Perdersoli's copy of the rifle made famous by the movie Quigley Down Under. Appropriately, it is known as the "Quigley Model."

The Sharps dropping-block action lent itself well to making the transition from percussion ignition to handling the newly developed cartridges that evolved quickly following the end of the war. In fact, in 1867 the U.S. Government decided to convert or have converted a number of percussion military arms into metallic cartridge breechloaders. And the Sharps was one of the designs selected for conversion. In all, the Sharps Rifle Manufacturing Company converted 31,098 carbines and 1,086 rifles to accept one or the other of the experimental 52-70 rimfire, 52-70 centerfire or 50-70 centerfire cartridges. All were fitted with new breechblocks with firing pins and an extractor. Those converted to the 50-70 cartridge also required soldering a new 50-caliber barrel liner in place. In 1870, Springfield Armory additionally converted about 1,300 more Sharps rifles and carbines to the newly designated 50-70 Government cartridge.

From 1869 to 1871, the Sharps Rifle Manufacturing Company produced their first entirely *"new made"* cartridge model – the Sharps New Model 1869. What really set this model apart from the converted percussion military models was the much cleaner looking lockplate, which had been trimmed of the pellet priming system that gave the Civil War-era percussion models a "high hump" contour. The lines of the new lockplate were a lot cleaner. In all, only about 1,000 New Model 1869 carbines and rifles were produced, chambered for early cartridges like the 44-77 Sharps and 50-70 Government. That production also included about 200 sporting rifles that would set the stage for the famous Model 1874 Rifle, which became the favored gun of the professional buffalo hunter.

The rifle that shooters today most recognize as the *"Sharps"* thanks to recent movies like *Quigley Down Under*, is the Model 1874, which actually saw its earliest production in 1871. The feature that probably best helps identify an early Model 1874 from the New Model 1869 is the thickness of the lockplate. The plates of earlier percussion models, built with the pellet priming system, were 3/8-inch thick, as was the plate of the New Model 1869. The thickness of the lockplate found on the newest cartridge model had been thinned to half that thickness. The *"Model 1874"* markings were not used on the rifle until after several years production. Sharps' famous *"Old Reliable"* trademark began to show up on the barrels in 1876, after the company, then known as just Sharps Rifle Company, had moved to Bridgeport, Conn.

The Model 1874 was chambered for a variety of cartridges during the ten years that it was in production, from *"small-bore"* 40-caliber centerfires to *"big-bore"* 50-caliber centerfires. Two favorites of the buffalo hunter were the 50-90 Sharps and 45-100 Sharps. The special order 45-120 Sharps and 50-140 Sharps cartridges were basically introduced too late to have been used extensively during the decimation of the American bison, which by 1880 were so scarce that it was no longer feasible to market-hunt the big animals.

Most Sharps collectors and historians tend to recognize the Model 1877 as the most refined and graceful of the side-hammer single-shot rifles. Only about 100 of the rifles were produced, in 45 caliber, in 1877 and 1878. These were built to comply with the "Creedmoor" match competition rules that required a single trigger and a rifle weighing 10 pounds or less. To get the weight down, Sharps Rifle Company built the Model 1877 with a slim and trim back-action lock and much lighter receiver. The rifle was built with a nicely checkered pistol grip buttstock and Schnable forend. (The company also produced a few Model 1874 Creedmoor rifles chambered for the 44-90 Sharps Bottleneck cartridge.)

The last model ever produced by the Sharps Rifle Company was the Model 1878 Sharps-Borchardt. This was a very modernistic "hammerless" rifle that has only been somewhat duplicated by more recent single-shot designs like the Ruger No. 1. Lighter than the Model 1874, which was still in production, the Borchardt model was most commonly chambered for the easily available 45-70 Government cartridge, as well as other smaller calibers like the 40-50 Sharps. The vast majority of the different variations available weighed in at less than 10 pounds.

Chambered for large .45- and .50-caliber centerfire cartridges like the 45-120 and 50-90, this Pedersoli model has been dubbed the "Boss Sharps."

Other than the hammerless drop-block action, the one other feature that set this model apart from other Sharps rifles was a sliding safety. The company produced about 8,700 of the rifles before ceasing the manufacture of all Sharps rifles.

Along with the demise of the great buffalo herds of the West also came the demise of Sharps rifle production. Shooters and hunters no longer had a need for a rifle that consumed powder and lead in such great quantities. And Sharps Rifle Company found it increasingly difficult to compete with the new repeating lever-action rifle models produced by Winchester. Thus, manufacturing at the Sharps plant in Bridgeport, Conn. ceased in 1880, with the last assembled rifles shipped in 1881. During the 32 years of Sharps rifle production, only about 160,000 rifles were ever built. However, those rifles solidly established a legacy that few other rifles have ever come close to matching.

Enter The Modern Sharps Reproduction

It may or may not be entirely correct to claim that more rifles of Sharps' design have been built in the past 32 years than during the entire 32-year run of original Sharps rifle production – but the modern total wouldn't miss it by much!

In the summer of 1974, two entirely different companies, separated by an ocean, independently set out to make a somewhat faithful modern-manufactured copy of the original Civil War-era percussion Sharps breechloaders. One was a relatively new U.S. firm known as Shiloh Products, Inc., the other a well-established Italian manufacturer of high quality double shotguns known as IAB Arms. And both were successful.

A draftsman and technical illustrator by trade and blackpowder shooter by heart, Len Mule' was the real mastermind behind what would become known as the Shiloh Sharps. Before making the decision to completely manufacture a "reproduction" of the famous breech-loaded rifles and carbines, he was manufacturing extremely high quality bullet moulds for blackpowder shooters. The four-cavity design of Mule's moulds earned them a solid reputation for producing a lot of round balls or Minie' bullets quickly – up to 400 per hour. They were sold as the "Shiloh IV" moulds. The company also offered quality lead furnaces as well, along with a few other bullet casting products.

Through 1973 the 1974, Len Mule' devoted much of his life to researching Sharps breech-loading rifles and carbines. Not only did he read everything he could find in print, he also visited major museums, including the West Point Museum and the Smithsonian, consulted with leading Sharps experts and collectors in this country, and spent hundreds of hours looking over hundreds of original rifles. One of those experts was Frank M. Sellers, the author of the acclaimed book, *Sharps Firearms.*

In late summer 1974, Mule' and his partner, Wolfgang Droege, visited Dixie Gun Works, in Union City, Tennessee. (At that time, the author was working there as an antique arms buyer and Dixie's catalog editor.) When they left, with them they took a huge selection of original Sharps parts to use for making new tooling. And when these two entrepreneurs showed up at the National Sporting Goods Association Show (predecessor to the SHOT Show) in January 1975, they displayed for the very first time a pair of newly assembled percussion ignition Sharps breechloaders – a "New Model 1863 Rifle" and a "New Model 1863 Carbine." In that short period of time, this pair had worked with Pinetree Casting (a division of Ruger) to develop the tooling needed to turn out completely modern manufactured duplicates of the original percussion Sharps breechloaders.

The availability of original parts from Dixie Gun Works' stockpile of Civil War salvage contributed greatly to the authenticity of the early Shiloh reproductions, allowing Shiloh Products Inc. to actually develop tooling based on the dimensions of original parts. Arms authorities immediately praised the percussion rifles and carbines that, at first, slowly trickled out of the Farmingdale, New York plant in early 1976, for their true to the original detail and quality. The only real variation from the originals they copied was that Shiloh elected to make the Lawrence priming system non-functional.

Len Mule' realized that while the percussion models were being well-received by Civil War re-enactors and Sharps buffs in general, it would be the later cartridge models that would be most appealing to shooters in general. And in mid-1976, he purchased an original Model 1874 Hartford-made Sharps sporting rifle, then began researching and working on the blueprints of the cartridge models Shiloh would put into production. Again, he called upon the expertise of author Frank Sellers, plus turned to well-known gun writer Elmer Keith for input on the Model 1874 metallic cartridge rifle models that went into production in late 1977. The company, then widely known as "The Shiloh Rifle Co.", became fully engaged in making both the most widely-used and the best known of the original Sharps rifles, and manufactured the early C. Sharps Arms rifles as well.

Ironically, the start of Sharps reproduction manufacturing in Italy actually began with the destruction of two fine original Model 1874 Sharps rifles. In the spring of 1974, SILE Industries had shipped a variety of original sample rifles to IAB Arms, located in Brescia. These were being sent to the respected manufacturer of high-quality double shotguns for the purpose of making the tooling to build both percussion and cartridge model Sharps breechloaders. Two of the rifles happened to be chambered for the 45-70 Government, and at that time Italy imposed a ban on the importation of *any* arms chambered for military

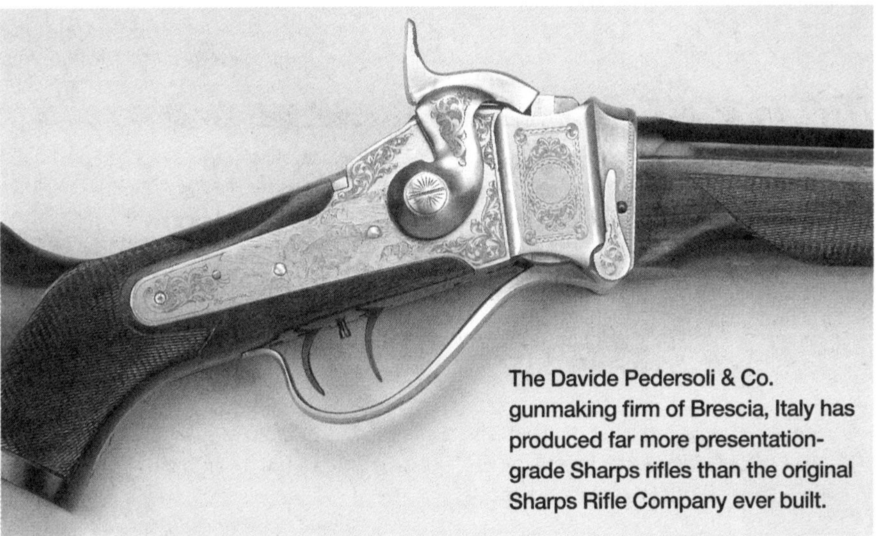

The Davide Pedersoli & Co. gunmaking firm of Brescia, Italy has produced far more presentation-grade Sharps rifles than the original Sharps Rifle Company ever built.

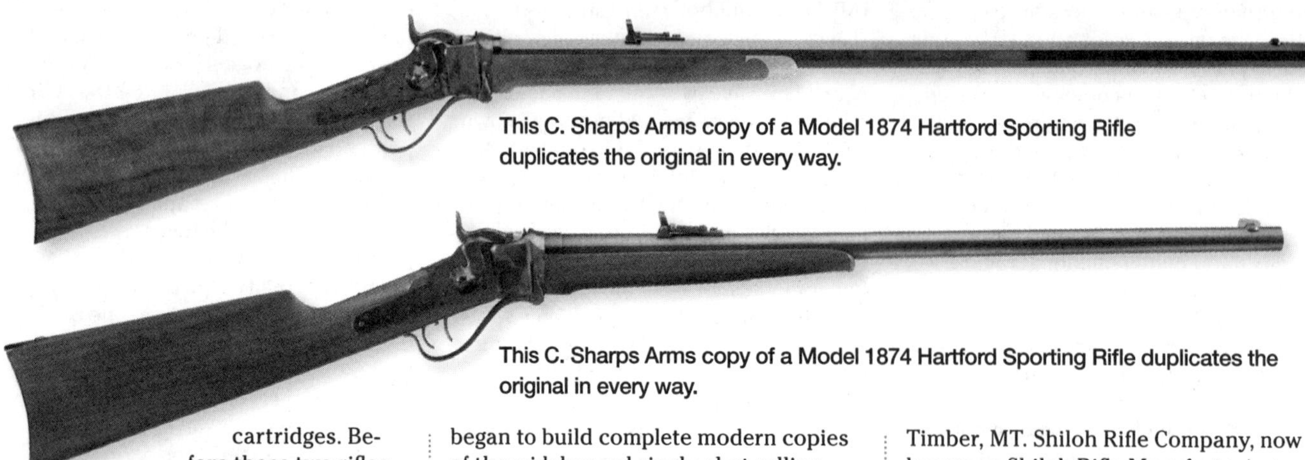

This C. Sharps Arms copy of a Model 1874 Hartford Sporting Rifle duplicates the original in every way.

This C. Sharps Arms copy of a Model 1874 Hartford Sporting Rifle duplicates the original in every way.

cartridges. Before those two rifles could be delivered to IAB Arms, custom officials had cut the barrels – right through the chambers!

IAB's first reproduction Sharps rifles and carbines arrived in the U.S. in late 1975, sold by SILE Distributors. Since then, the company has produced nearly 80,000 Sharps reproductions, which have been sold under a variety of "brand" names, including Dixie Gun Works, Taylor's & Company, Tristar Sporting Arms, Armisport, and E.M.F. & Co. Easily the most authentic copy of the "New Model 1863" percussion Sharps carbine ever shot by the author was imported by a company known as Garrett Arms during the mid-1980s. Built in Italy by IAB Arms, even the Lawrence pellet priming system was functional on this Sharps copy.

Working in collaboration with Navy Arms, in 1970 the firm of Davide Pedersoli & Co., also of Brescia, Italy, began producing *most of* a modern Remington Rolling Block copy. Actually, at that time the Italian manufacturer reproduced everything but the barrel, and the parts were all shipped to Navy Arms' facility in New Jersey, where the actions were fitted with a 45-70 barrel. Then, in 1983, Pedersoli began to build complete modern copies of the widely used single-shot rolling block-action blackpowder cartridge rifles dating from the late 1800s.

Today, Pedersoli is also recognized as one of the more prolific manufacturers of Sharps rifles and carbines. The company produced its first Sharps, a "Sporting Rifle" model in 45-70 Government, back in January, 1993. Today, the company catalogs the most complete selection of Sharps rifle and carbine models available from a single manufacturer. Many of the rifles offered as other "brands" in this country are actually produced in Italy by Davide Pedersoli & Co.

Armi Chiappa, better known in the U.S. as Armi Sport, is another Italian manufacturer of Sharps rifles and carbines. Altogether, the company offers more than a dozen different models or variations, ranging from a percussion New Model 1859 Rifle and Carbine to an elaborately engraved deluxe copy of a Model 1874 Hartford-built Sporting Rifle. Again, like IAB Arms and the Pedersoli company, Armi Sport's Sharps reproductions are offered by a number of importers in the U.S., primarily Cimarron F.A. Co. and Taylor's & Co.

In the U.S., the heart of Sharps rifle manufacturing today is located in Big Timber, MT. Shiloh Rifle Company, now known as Shiloh Rifle Manufacturing Company, moved from their original manufacturing facility located on Long Island, New York to the C. Sharps Arms facility in the small south-central Montana town in 1983. C. Sharps Arms was already operating its custom shop and distribution center there, and the move brought these two companies together under one roof, which was a primary reason for Shiloh's relocation. That relationship ended in 1986, when both companies set out to establish their own Sharps lines. The manufacturing facilities of two companies are still within a block of each other.

When it comes to *production* Sharps copies, many blackpowder cartridge rifle shooters today continue to consider the rifles produced by Shiloh Rifle Manufacturing Company to be the cream of the crop. The fit and finish of the Model 1863 percussion rifle and carbine, along with the many versions of the Model 1874 metallic cartridge rifles produced by this maker, is superb and in no way second to the quality of any other maker. Shiloh manufactured the Sharps rifle that Americans are now most familiar with, thanks to the movie featuring actor Tom Selleck – *Quigley Down Under.* And much

Often referred to as "The English Model," the Sharps Model 1877 is considered by many to be the most graceful American single-shot ever produced. The beautiful rifle shown here was built by C. Sharps Arms.

Today's Sharps fan can go all out with a rifle like this custom Model 1874 "Boss Gun" with Grade III options by C. Sharps Arms – but it can cost three times that of the standard model.

like the rifles produced at the original Sharps plants in Hartford and Bridgeport, Connecticut, it's often hard to recognize one of the Shiloh rifles as one particular version or another due to all of the optional custom features available.

C. Sharps Arms was founded in 1975 by John Schoffstall, and brought its first Sharps New Model 1863 Rifle and Carbine reproductions to market in 1976. At that time, the company relied heavily on the early Shiloh operation in Farmingdale, New York to do their manufacturing. John played an instrumental role in getting Shiloh to make the move to Montana in 1983, where the company continued to produce both Shiloh and C. Sharps Arms rifles. Today, C. Sharps Arms has full manufacturing capability and is noted for the extremely high quality versions of the Model 1874 Hartford- and Bridgeport-produced Sharps originals. The company also offers a beautiful rendition of the Model 1877 Sharps, also known as "The English Model," but if this slim and trim back-action lock Sharps reproduction catches your eye, be ready to hang on to your pocket book. With a few optional upgrades, this great-handling beauty could set you back more than $10,000!

The Sharps manufacturers just covered are the primary makers of today's modern Sharps breech-loading rifles and carbines. Prior to the early reproductions that were successfully brought to market in 1975 by Shiloh Products, Inc., there were several other attempts during the late 1960s and early 1970s, but they simply failed to get off the ground. Those makers featured here are the companies that have worked hard to build and market quality copies of the big and famous drop-block single shots that are so often simply referred to as "Old Reliable."

Additionally, there are a few others now building some really fine custom Sharps-style guns. Axtell Rifle Company, of Sheridan, Mont. currently custom-crafts a copy of the Model 1877 Creedmoor match rifle, of which the Sharps plant in Bridgeport, Conn. produced only about 100 units. And as you might guess, since these are hand-machined and hand-built, prices are pretty much out of the average shooter's price range. But then, these aren't average rifles.

Perhaps the most unique Sharps copy presently manufactured is the "Lil Reliable" currently available from the Little Sharps Rifle Manufacturing Company, of Big Sandy, Mont. As the name suggests, this is a scaled-down version of the Sharps Model 1874. In fact, these slim, trim and lightweight drop-block breechloaders are built with dimensions that are nearly 25 percent smaller than the full-size originals. The scaled-down 7-pound rifle comes in a wide range of chamberings, appropriately smaller than the standard calibers of a standard-scale Model 1874. The Little Sharps Rifle Manufacturing Company chambers the rifle in calibers such as 22 Long Rifle, 22 Hornet, 30-30 Winchester and 38-55 Winchester. One of the light rifles in a low recoiling caliber would be ideal for younger shooters or for the ladies also wanting to get in on some "Sharpshooting."

Many Sharps collectors believe that the tooling for the Model 1875 was modified for the later production of the hammerless Model 1878 Sharps Borchardt rifle. Original shown here with a new-made Leatherwood Hi-Lux Optics "Wm. Malcolm" telescopic rifle sight.

Whose Sharps Is That Anyway?

Sharps rifles earned their reputation for long-range accuracy during the Civil War when they were put into the hands of a volunteer group known as "Berdan's Sharpshooters." Those making up this elite unit were some of the finest marksmen in the country, and most were outfitted with the Sharps New Model 1859 Rifle, some of which had been fitted with early telescopic rifle sights. These shooters' ability to hit an enemy solider at great distances became legendary among Union troops – and feared by Confederate troops. Then, during the heyday of the buffalo hide hunting years, 1870 to 1880, the rifle of choice among professional buffalo hunters was the "Big Fifty" (50-90) Sharps. Not only did the accuracy and knockdown power of the large-bore single-shot ensure clean one-shot kills of an animal that often topped 1,500 pounds, the rifles also delivered the big, heavy and slow-moving lead bullets with amazing accuracy.

With such a reputation, it is no wonder that the Sharps rifle is very likely the most identifiable firearm ever made in the U.S. It is also no wonder that so many historical-minded shooters are now wanting to experience shooting and hunting with the hefty drop-block single-shot breechloaders. One thing is certain, there is now one heck of a selection of new-made Sharps guns to choose from. In fact, there are easily more models in production right now than ever at one time at any of the different original Sharps manufacturing plants. This selection also includes a few models or versions that were never originally built.

The number of variations from each of the different manufacturers or importers is such that it would take more room than we have here to take a detailed look at each model of each brand. So, here we'll look at the standard models currently being produced or imported, and who offers that variation. Then we'll look at a few modernized versions or models based on the Sharps design.

New Model 1859 Rifle and Carbine

Like the originals they copy, the reproductions of the New Model 1859 Rifle come with a 30-inch barrel, and the carbine copies come with a true-to-the-original 22-inch barrel. In reality, the original New Model 1859 and New Model 1863 are the same guns, just with different barrel markings. All 1859 carbines were built with an iron patchbox, while nearly half of the 1863 carbines were made without one. Original guns were produced in 52-caliber, today's reproductions are 54-caliber.

This model is offered by Armi Sport, Dixie Gun Works, Flintlock's, Etc., Taylor's & Company, and Davide Pedersoli & Co. Typical retail prices range from about $925 for the carbine to $1,050 for the rifle. Note: Taylor's & Co. also offer the rifle with double-set target triggers as the "Berdan Sharps," which retails for $1,089.

New Model 1863 Rifle and Carbine

These are the models that Shiloh Products, Inc. first reproduced in 1975, and which the company still offers today. During the late 1970s, Shiloh retailed the rifle model for $375, while the carbine sold for $345. Today, the

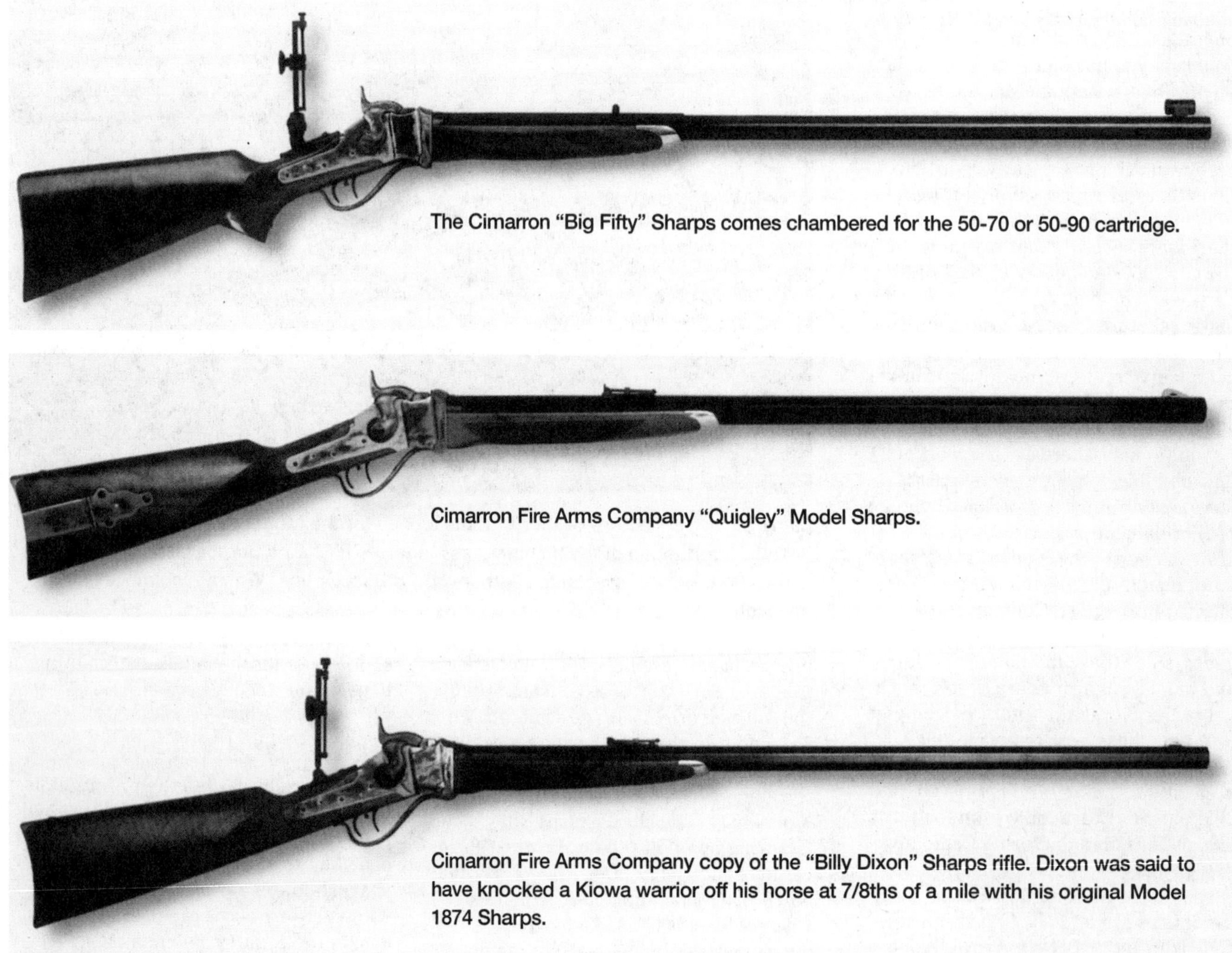

The Cimarron "Big Fifty" Sharps comes chambered for the 50-70 or 50-90 cartridge.

Cimarron Fire Arms Company "Quigley" Model Sharps.

Cimarron Fire Arms Company copy of the "Billy Dixon" Sharps rifle. Dixon was said to have knocked a Kiowa warrior off his horse at 7/8ths of a mile with his original Model 1874 Sharps.

company gets $1,865 for the rifle and $1,609 for the carbine. The rifle features a 30-inch barrel, the carbine a 22-inch barrel. (Again, the New Model 1863 and New Model 1859 are the same guns.)

Other companies offering these models include Armi Sport, Flintlocks, Etc., IAB Arms, Davide Pedersoli & Co., and Tristar Sporting Arms. Retail prices for the Italian made copies range from $900 for the carbine to $1,050 for the rifle.

Model 1874 Hartford Sharps

Today's Sharps rifle manufacturers have taken a lot of liberties with the features of this model, but then so did the original Sharps Rifle Manufacturing Company. One of the typical distinguishing features of an original produced at the Hartford plant from 1871 to early 1874 was the round collar at the base of the barrel. Later Bridgeport models (1874 to 1881) typically did not have this feature. Like the originals, various copies of this metallic cartridge Sharps rifle are available in a wide variety of calibers, including quite a few "obsolete" chamberings.

Companies offering copies of the Hartford cartridge model Sharps include Armi Sport, C. Sharps Arms, Cimarron Firearms Co., Dixie Gun Works, E.M.F. Firearms, Flintlocks, Etc., IAB Arms, IAR Arms, Navy Arms, Davide Pedersoli & Co., Shiloh Rifle Manufacturing Co., Taylor's & Co., Tristar Sporting Arms, and A. Uberti. There are many variations of these rifles, from the standard "Sporting Rifle" models, to copies of the 1874 military rifle and carbine, to "Long Range" and Creedmoor target models, along with some very elaborate "Deluxe" editions. Consequently, prices vary greatly, from around $900 for some standard models to as much as $6,000 or $7,000 for engraved and gold inlayed guns.

ABOVE: Sheri Otto Moore with buffalo she took with one of the "Lil' Reliable" 3/4-scale Model 1874 rifles produced by her father Ron Otto. Note the smaller overall dimensions of this Sharps.
BELOW: The lighter weight and scaled-down size of the Sharps rifle produced by Little Sharps rifle Mfg. makes this copy of the Model 1874 ideal for the ladies and younger shooters.

Model 1874 Bridgeport Sharps

With the move in 1874 from Hartford to Bridgeport, CT, the company shortened its name to just Sharps Rifle Company. Again, a typical feature of the rifles built at this plant was the omission of the relief collar associated with Hartford-built Sharps rifle barrels. In 1876, the company began to mark their barrels with the well-known "Old Reliable" marking on the barrel. Today, "Old Reliable" is a registered trademark of C. Sharps Arms.

Companies now offering Model 1874 Sharps rifles with typical Bridgeport features include C. Sharps Arms, Cimarron Firearms Co., Dixie Gun Works, Flintlocks, Etc., IAB Arms, Davide Pedersoli & Co., Shiloh Rifle Manufacturing Co., and Tristar Sporting Arms. Typical retail prices range about that same as for the Hartford models.

Sharps Model 1877 Rifle

This is one of the rarest of original Sharps rifles, built to meet the single trigger and under 10-pound weight restrictions for competing in the revered "Creedmoor" matches. Today, only C. Sharps Arms and Axtell Rifle Co. reproduce this fine drop-block single-shot rifle. While the original was only built as a long-range competition model, Axtell Rifle Co. is now offering "hunting rifle" versions known as the "Lower Sporter" and "Lower Business" rifles, priced at $2,900. And if you think that sounds a bit high, the company also offers a fancier

Two different 500-grain bullets from Parker Productions.

"Custom Express" version that retails for $5,200. C. Sharps Arms only offers the rifle in its original Creedmoor configuration, with a base price of $7,250.

Percussion Sporters

More than half of all original Sharps rifles and carbines ever produced were built between 1859 and 1866. And of the 100,000-plus percussion ignition guns built during that period, only about 100 were sporting rifles. These also rank among the rarest of rare Sharps rifles. Typically, the guns were built with better-than-average-quality wood, and most often are found with double-set triggers. Some featured a tapered round barrel, others were built with a full octagon barrel. Several companies today offer modern copies of these rare original percussion Sharps.

Available from Armi Sport, Flintlocks, Etc., IAB Arms, Davide Pedersoli & Co., and Shiloh Rifle Manufacturing Co. Retail prices for these can range from around $650 to $1,600 depending on maker.

Produced in smaller calibers, from 22 LR up to 40-50 Sharps, the light Lil' Sharps from Little Sharps Rifle Mfg. is a great hunting rifle. Rusty Sparks used his to take this great mountain lion trophy.

(Note: To determine who actually manufactured a particular "brand" of Sharps rifle, you'll have to contact the company whose name appears on the gun. Some "brands" offer Sharps copies from several different makers.)

Other Sharps-Style Rifles

The 3/4-scale Model 1874 offered by Little Sharps Rifle Manufacturing would be ideal for the hunter looking for a light (7 to 8 pounds) rifle to pack in the field, but no original Sharps of this configuration was ever manufactured. C. Sharps Arms also offers a model you won't find anywhere else – the Model 1875. Sharps Rifle Company produced fewer than 10 of the originals, mostly for displaying at the 1876 Centennial Exposition in Philadelphia. The design, by Nelson King, won several medals. However, King departed Sharps soon after and the Model 1875 was never put into full production. Since some of the parts are identical to those of the Model 1878 Borchardt, Sharps experts feel that the tooling was converted to produce the newer hammerless design. Some also believe that the Model 1875 influenced the design found in Browning's 1878 patent, to later become the 1885 Winchester High Wall. The C. Sharps Arms modern copy of the Model 1875 would make an excellent, high quality hunting and target rifle – with retail prices starting at $1,295.

Jim Leatherwood prepares to touch off a shot with an original Model 1878 Sharps-Borchardt. The rifle sports one of his long Wm. Malcolm scope reproductions.

Original Sharps cartridge rifles were produced in an amazing range of calibers. Most popular then and now tend to be the big .45s and .50s (i.e. 45-90, 50-70, 50-90, etc.). The old 45-70 Government cartridge, introduced in 1873, was by 1875 offered as a standard chambering for the Sharps Model 1874. More original Sharps metallic cartridge rifles were built in 45-70 than in any other caliber. And the same holds true today, thanks to the availability of commercially-loaded ammo and the ease of finding loading components for those who like to roll their own.

It's been 126 years since the original Sharps Rifle Company closed its doors and ceased production of the most famous of all the big single-shot black-powder cartridge rifles. Even so, the Sharps lives on with more followers and more rifle choices than at any other time in history. It must be shooting's version of *deja vu.*

NITRO EXPRESS!

In the heyday of British India, the double was the classic tiger rifle. The hunter is unidentified, but the rifle is a 375 Holland & Holland Royal. Such is fame. (Courtesy Westley Richards)

by Terry Wieland

Sir Samuel White Baker was one of the greatest hunters of the Victorian age.

If Frederick Courteney Selous personified the ethical, thoughtful pursuer of big game, White epitomized the adventurer who would go anywhere and hunt anything. Not that Sir Samuel was any less ethical than Selous, but Baker seemed to find himself in situations that called for fast, accurate shooting first and thoughtful analysis a distant second. Baker went looking for trouble, and he found it.

On one memorable occasion in the Sudan, Baker was facing an enraged bull elephant at close quarters. He loosed off his famous muzzleloader "Baby" and the five-ounce lead ball floored the elephant just as Baby's recoil did the same to Baker. The two regained their senses at about the same time, and as the elephant came again, Sir Sam finished him off with a shot from one of his pair of 10-bore E.M. Reilly doubles that served him as "light" rifles.

This incident occurred around 1871. Such experiences (and he had many) instilled in Baker a deep belief in the killing power of heavy bullets. Although he also wanted all the velocity he could get, he refused to obtain it at the expense of bullet weight, and this put Baker at the center of a controversy that convulsed the big-game hunting world of the late 1800s. It was a controversy that put two great names in British gunmaking – James Purdey and Holland & Holland – on opposite sides of the fence. It also set the stage for the greatest breakthrough in the history of dangerous-game cartridges: the 450 Nitro Express.

The 450 Nitro Express was introduced by John Rigby & Co. in 1897 or '98, although the later is generally quoted as the first year in which actual rifles became available.

The cartridge launched a 480-grain bullet at 2150 feet per second (fps), and generated 4930 foot/pounds of energy (fpe). It eclipsed everything else then available, and was quickly proven to be more than adequate for anything, including elephant, under virtually any conditions. To this day, those numbers are the benchmark for dangerous-game rifles.

Accounts of the 450's birth often suggest that it sprang up out of nowhere, a brilliant invention that elbowed aside a host of inadequate blackpowder cartridges, but such was not the case. As with most signifi cant firearm developments, it was the logical result of evolution and steady progress.

The 450's roots were spelled out in the designation "nitro express." The first part of the name, "nitro," came from the use of nitrocellulose (smokeless) gunpowder—which was in the process of revolutionizing the rifle in almost every way. As for "express," it was a continuation of the express rifles (and later cartridges) that had by that time been around for more than 40 years; the term was introduced in 1856 by James Purdey to describe a new

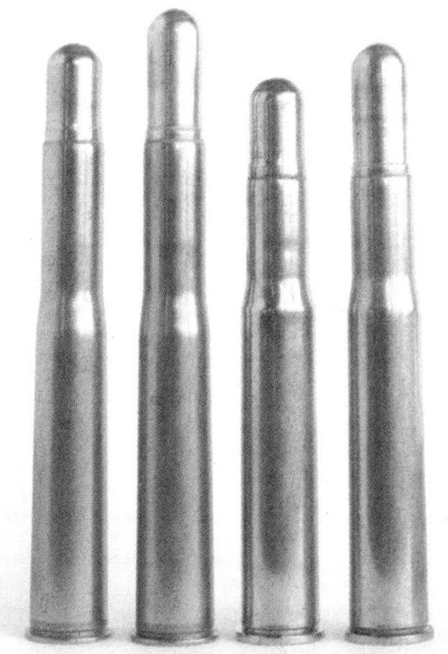

The two 400s, in modern loads by A-Square with Dead Tough soft and Monolithic Solids: Left, the original 450/400 (3 1/4-in.); right, the 450/400 Jeffery (3-in.). This was originally a blackpowder cartridge. The radically different case configuration of the modern-ized Jeffery round was intended to overcome a tendency to case-sticking in the original, with its extremely long neck. Properly loaded, both are fine cartridges in a double rifle.

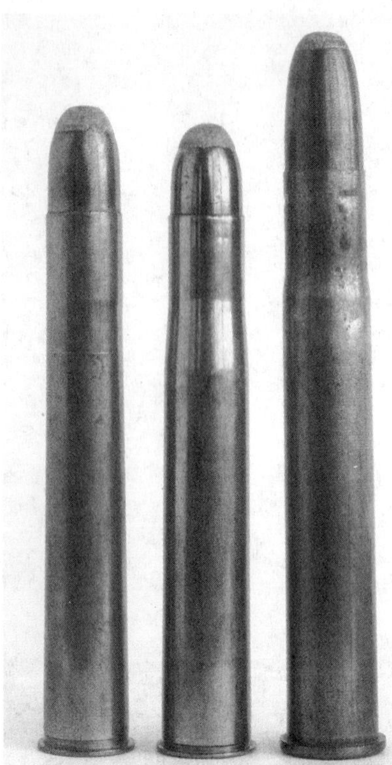

The late, lamented 450s: From left, the original 450 Nitro Express, introduced by John Rigby, which revolutionized hunting. The 500/450 (center) is the 500 NE necked down. This was H&H's standard chambering in 450 to counter Rigby. Finally, a 475 No. 2, shown to indicate the difference in case size; the original 450 No. 2 was simply this cartridge with a smaller bullet.

breed of high-velocity muzzle loader, and the name was taken from the high-speed "express" trains which were then transforming travel in Britain.

Express became synonymous with velocity, but by today's standards it was pretty modest: 1600 fps more or less, given the limitations of black-powder, whether loaded in a cartridge or poured down the barrel.

Today, the 450 Nitro Express is usually seen as a beginning—the birth of the great double rifles, of high-stakes ivory hunting and shooting on control, and of professional hunting in all its aspects. In fact, however, the arrival of the 450 was just as much the end of a different era—an era which saw the proponents of James Purdey's express rifles pitted against Sir Samuel Baker and his friends at Holland & Holland. Baker and Henry Holland were firm believers in heavy bullets for the biggest game, and mightily distrusted light bullets at high speed that expanded quickly—often too quickly.

Any modern rifleman, reading about the controversy, will be struck by the similarities between the arguments back and forth in 1890, and those that occurred throughout the 20th century and now into the 21st in America. The O'Connor-Keith-Weatherby battle over velocity versus bullet weight essentially carried on a feud that began when the first stag-stalker returned from the Highlands of Scotland in 1857 to report spectacular kills with his smallbore Purdey express rifle, and its revolutionary lightweight hollow-point bullets.

The history of rifles resembles a skein of wool, with hundreds of interwoven strands; it is impossible to follow just one without having it overtaken by another. But the roots of the velocity/bullet weight controversy lie far, far back in the transition from round lead balls to elongated projectiles, first in muzzleloaders, then in cartridge rifles. The weight of a round lead ball is constant. Once you switch to a cylindrical bullet, however, everything becomes variable. You can lengthen the bullet and increase the weight, or you can lighten the bullet by a variety of means, and thereby increase velocity with the same charge of gunpowder.

No one knows exactly who first struck upon the idea of a hollow-point bullet, but it was sometime after the virtues of the hollow-base bullet had become apparent. The Minié ball, with its large cavity and thin skirt that expanded to grip the rifling, was a force in riflery for a relatively short period, but it had far-reaching effects. Gunmakers began to explore the relationship between bullet weight and length, and the stabilizing effect of rifling. The concept of sectional density (if not the actual term) began to dictate the direction of bullet development.

By the 1870s, with cartridge rifles displacing muzzleloaders for all but the heaviest uses, gunmakers realized there was a limit to how much black-powder could be stuffed in a case. With a muzzleloader, one can always drop in

The cartridge that changed everything: Rigby's 450 Nitro Express 3-1/4 inch.

The major players in the 470-class of cartridges: From left, Holland's 500/465, Westley Richards's 476 NE, the famous 470 NE, and the 475 No. 2. The 470 was introduced by Joseph Lang, adopted by John Rigby, and chambered by almost everyone; the 475 No. 2 was a "trade" cartridge developed by Eley Brothers to be chambered by anyone. Not shown is the 475 NE, a straight-taper cartridge similar in shape to both the 450 NE and 500 NE.

an extra handful of powder; with a cartridge, that is impossible. The only way to increase velocity was by reducing bullet weight. Some inventive soul hit on the idea of hollowing out the nose of the bullet. It worked in two ways: The reduced weight increased the velocity, and the softer hollowed-out nose increased expansion, which was exacerbated in turn by the higher velocity.

Stag stalkers returned from Scotland with breathless tales of beasts struck down as if by lightning. Spectacular kills became the order of the day, and all based on the barely understood concept that velocity somehow increased killing power out of all proportion. Inevitably, some British hunters took the small-caliber (500 and down) express rifles to India and Africa to tackle tigers, lions, buffalo of various descriptions, and even elephants. Just as inevitably, many of these intrepid souls did not come back, and it rapidly became apparent that, while velocity might kill spectacularly sometimes, spectacular failures were all too common.

Professional hunters especially regarded the small express rifles with distrust. Having one's life on the line tends to breed conservatism and a tendency to cling to that which is known to work, and what worked with elephants, rhinos, and Cape buffalo were huge lead balls launched from small cannons. In fact, Baker's famous "Baby" got its nickname from the Arabic *Jenab al Mootfah*, meaning "child of a cannon."

In Britain, however, competition among rifle makers was intense, and the debate had commercial as well as technical undertones. Purdey, H&H, Rigby, Lang, Jeffery, Greener and Westley Richards were frantically developing new rifle actions and new cartridges to go with them. Westley Richards introduced the Anson & Deeley boxlock in 1875, and transformed the world of both rifles and shotguns. From Scotland came the famous Farquharson single-shot rifle.

Then, as now, companies were looking for an edge, something to set them apart from the competition. For James Purdey, the answer was the express rifle and its descendants with their high velocity and hollow-point bullets. For Holland & Holland, it was an alliance with Sir Samuel Baker and his hard-won experience and belief in rifles with heavier bullets.

Samuel White Baker had one of those lives that defy belief. Even in an era that produced such phenomena as Sir Richard Burton, General Gordon, and Selous, Baker stood out.

Born into money in 1821, he began hunting the moment he leapt from his crib, and never stopped. At the age of 19, he made his first serious contribution to the world of firearms when he persuaded George Gibbs, the Bristol riflesmith, to make him a rifle the likes of which had never been seen before. At the time, it was believed that only small charges of powder could produce accuracy; Baker believed in big bullets, with bigger charges of powder. His Gibbs fired a four-ounce conical bullet, propelled by 16 drams (437 grains) of blackpowder. Its rifling consisted of two grooves; the projectile had corresponding belts and was wrapped in a greased silk patch for smooth passage down the bore. The monster had a 36-inch barrel and weighed 21 pounds.

"An extraordinary success attended this rifle, which became my colossal companion for many years in wild sports with dangerous game," Baker wrote, a half-century later, in his valedictory (and perhaps greatest) book, *Wild Beasts and Their Ways.*

In between, Baker hunted tigers in Ceylon, killed elephants from horseback in Africa (armed only with a saber, if you can imagine), was married, widowed, and, during a hunting trip to the Balkans with an Indian maharajah, purchased a companion in a white slave market. Florence Maria Finnian von Sass became his constant companion and eventually his wife, and together they searched for the source of the Nile, hunted throughout Abyssinia, governed the Sudan, fought the slave trade – well, you get the idea.

Baker never lost his deep interest in rifles and what made them work, especially in terms of dangerous game. He was always looking for a better gun and, equally vital, a better bullet.

He was a highly intelligent man and a fine writer, and his early books were best-sellers in Britain, which gobbled up accounts of exploration and adventure from all over the world. Baker became a national hero, and his

The 500 trio, from left: the original 500 Black Powder Express, an original Kynoch 500 NE 3-inch loaded with a solid, and 500 NE 3-1/4 inch. The blackpowder cartridge fired a 340-grain bullet at about 1950 fps; the nitro-express loadings fire a 570-grain bullet at 2150 fps. In between, there is also a 500 Nitro for Black Powder, a low-pressure load with cordite powder for use in blackpowder rifles.

The 577 NE was derived, more or less directly, from the military 577 Snider (left), by way of a number of blackpowder variations. Although it has existed in several lengths, the 3-inch case is now standard. Shown are an original Kynoch soft-nose, and a new German-made solid.

opinions carried immense weight. In fact, it was his writing that inspired Frederick Courteney Selous to go to Africa. Naturally, with Baker's first-hand experience hunting the world's most dangerous game, anything he had to say about rifles was gospel; since Baker carried guns made by E.M. Reilly, Selous had a Reilly in his luggage when he embarked for Africa.

But Samuel Baker's real alliance came to be with Holland's. In 1837, tobacconist Harris Holland went into the gun business in London, and was soon challenging such established firms as James Purdey and Joseph Lang. Later, a nephew, Henry Holland, was brought into the business and it became Holland & Holland. Henry Holland was still an apprentice when, in 1869, Baker approached them with an order for a rifle that would become famous in itself: "Baby," also known as H&H rifle No. 1526. It was a 3-bore that fired a fi ve-ounce (2187 grain) bullet. The rifle weighed 20 pounds.

In 1871, Baker took the rifle and his lovely Florence and departed for Africa. He hunted across the Sudan and down the Nile to Lake Albert, describing the expedition in *The Nile Tributaries of Abyssinia*. The book, naturally, sold out quickly. Big-game hunting, largely inspired by Baker, was all the rage among the gentlemen of London, as well as those departing for the colonies on business or with the army.

While Purdey's express rifles had gained a good reputation on Scottish stag, the results in India and Africa had been decidedly less stellar. Purdey promoted light bullets at high velocity, but Sir Samuel Baker and his close friend, Henry Holland, espoused large rifles with heavy, solid lead bullets that carried immense punch and penetrated deeply. In the hotly contested commercial world of London, the controversy was carried on in the pages of *The Field*, accompanied by cartoons in *Punch* and letters in the *Times*.

Sir Samuel Baker believed in heavy bullets, especially for elephants, but he hunted all kinds of game – lions, tigers, rhinos, Cape buffalo – and was serious about digging out bullets to see how they performed. As Purdey's "express" rifles gained adherents, Baker became more than a little sceptical. From *Wild Beasts and Their Ways*, published in 1890:

"The Express rifle is a term signifying velocity, and this is generally accompanied by a hollow bullet, which is intended to serve two purposes – to lighten the bullet, and therefore to reduce the work of the powder, and to secure an expansion and smash-up of the lead upon impact with the animal. I contend that this smashing up of the bullet is a mistake...

"If the animal is small and harmless, this should be the desired result. If, on the other hand, the animal should be large and dangerous, there cannot be a greater mistake than the hollow Express projectile.

"I have frequently heard persons of great experience dilate with satisfaction upon the good shots made with their little 450 hollow Express exactly behind the shoulder of a tiger... I have also heard of their failures, which were to themselves sometimes incomprehensible.

"A solid Express .577 never fails if the direction is accurate towards a vital part."

Sir Samuel Baker had a proprietary interest in the 577, since he is credited with its development. He persuaded H&H to take the military 577 Snider cartridge and lengthen it to 2-3/4 inches. This became the 577 Express, which Baker eventually settled on as his favorite all-around rifle. It fired a 650-grain lead bullet at 1650 fps. He believed that a properly directed 577 would handle anything, even including elephant, and he continued to advocate the use of solid lead bullets. For elephant and other large game, the bullets could be hardened; for soft-skinned, smaller game, they could be left as pure, soft lead.

The key, as he said repeatedly, was penetration to the vitals—a bullet that held together, mushroomed, and penetrated.

Henry Holland himself echoed these sentiments in his chapter in *Big Game Shooting* in 1894, the year after Baker's death. He quoted Baker liberally, crediting him with many of the developments that had made H&H one of the pre-eminent riflemakers in the world. And, like Baker, he stressed the importance of the bullet – not just the rifle or the cartridge – and how it performed on impact.

If one must use hollow points, Holland advocated the use of bullets with smaller cavities, which increased the weight, reduced the velocity, and made the bullet tougher, all at the same time.

As these developments were taking place, the world of rifles was changing rapidly. Following France's lead, in 1888 the British war office adopted a smokeless-powder cartridge, the 303 British. Smaller calibers and higher velocities demanded drastic changes in bullet design, and the lead bullet jacketed with copper was displacing the old standby paper-jacketed bullet. The military began with heavy-for-caliber round-nosed bullets, which eventually gave way to the German "spitzer" (pointed) bullet. With velocities at the unheard-of levels of 2500 fps, everything gunmakers believed about terminal ballistics went out the window.

The London gunmakers who catered to the Africa trade were not immediately seduced by small calibers and high velocities, but they recognized that smokeless powder and higher velocities were the way of the future. John Rigby & Co., one of the oldest and best riflemakers, took the existing 450 Express cartridge, which had a straight, tapered case, put a judicious amount of smokeless powder in it, devised a copper-jacketed solid bullet, and called it the 450 Nitro Express.

From that moment, everything that went before was obsolete. To see exactly how profound the change was, one need only compare the ballistic performance of the 450 NE with its blackpowder predecessor.

The 450 Black Powder Express (as it is now known) was one of the best and most popular cartridges ever designed, and the personal favorite of Frederick Selous. There was a wide variety of ammunition and loadings, but the 365-grain bullet at 1700 fps, with energy of 2340 fpe, was typical. It was a tremendous cartridge for deer in the Scottish Highlands, and was widely used as a light-game rifl e in the colonies, but that was it.

The nitro-express version increased bullet weight by 33 percent (480 gr.) and velocity by 25 percent (2150 fps), and more than doubled the muzzle energy to 4930 fpe. An excellent deer cartridge had been turned into the definitive elephant cartridge.

Almost immediately, H&H took Baker's 577 Express and did the same thing. The dates on this are hazy—and it is not even certain that H&H was the first—but the 577 Nitro Express was born within months of the 450. Even by today's inflated standards, its ballistic performance was impressive: 750-grain bullet, 2050 fps, and 7010 fpe. Had he been alive, Samuel Baker would have been in ecstasy.

Very quickly, a number of other nitro-express cartridges followed. Someone – no one knows who – turned the 500 Black Powder Express into the 500 Nitro Express, initially with a 3 1/4-inch case, and then with the more common 3-inch. It was and is a great cartridge, but made in modest numbers throughout most of its existence, and only now really getting the recognition it always deserved. Ballistically, it fell between the 450 and 577 (570-grain bullet, 2150 fps, 5850 fpe).

Logic would tell you that with these three in the lineup, not much else was needed. But logic and commercial reality are often at war.

While the 450 was destined to become the real workhorse of the group, London gunmakers suffered mightily from the "not invented here" syndrome. Holland & Holland wanted a 450 of its own, and created one by necking down the 500 case. The basic cartridge had been around for decades in blackpowder form, but in its nitro express guise, it is associated with H&H.

Because each of these was based on an existing blackpowder case, a few problems surfaced. These cases were made of thin brass and the higher pressures of cordite (the British extruded smokeless powder, packed into the case in long strands), combined with tropical heat, caused some case splitting and sticking in chambers. To solve the problem, the cartridge company Eley Brothers developed a new 450 (called, with deafening logic, the 450 No. 2). The 450 No. 2 was a long, necked case made of heavier brass with a much thicker rim than that required by blackpowder cartridges. It was the last word in case strength, and so roomy that pressures were never a problem.

In fact, with one exception (which we will get to shortly), pressure and extraction problems were never a serious concern with any of the new nitro-express cartridges. Improvements in the quality of the brass solved the problem for most of them, with the dimensions remaining the same. However, Eley Brothers released their 450 No. 2 to the trade and it became a standard chambering for many small gunmakers who did not have the resources to develop their own.

The term "released to the trade" means that any riflemaker was free to chamber the cartridge, and Eley Brothers would manufacture standard ammunition. This was in contrast to the "proprietary" system that was then growing up in Britain, whereby a riflemaker would develop a cartridge and chamber it exclusively; ammunition was then made by Eley, Kynoch, or one of the other cartridge companies, and sold by the riflemaker under his own name. This practice later became widespread, but in 1900 it was just beginning.

The proprietary system was not as iron-clad as a patent or copyright, but it served to deter the widespread adoption of a single great design like the 450 NE. If you owned an H&H rifle, you did not want to go to Rigby to buy your ammunition and vice versa. It was a cozy system that led to some bizarre developments in both cartridges and bullets.

Just as each riflemaker had his own ideas about what constituted a good cartridge, so did they develop their own bullets. These designs—some great, some dreadful—were available only in their own ammunition. Consistent bullet failure gave some cartridges a bad reputation, and by extension the rifles and makers themselves. Conversely, some gained immeasurably by good bullet performance. A few years later, when Rigby introduced its immortal 416, it was loaded with bullets clad in soft steel, and their performance (both softs and solids) became legendary.

Stages of development: Clockwise from top, a 500-caliber 530-grain cast bullet with lubrication grooves packed with lubricant; Woodleigh WeldCore soft, a copper cup with a lead core, and the open end forming the expanding nose; lubricated cast 500 bullet with copper gas-check; cast 458-caliber 500-grain bullet; Woodleigh Solid, the reverse of the soft, with the open end of the copper cup forming the base of the bullet. Center is a light-weight cast hollowpoint; such bullets were the basis of the "express" rifle.

In 1900, however, all of this was still to come. The final great development from that early nitro-express period was the biggest, the most powerful, the most intimidating cartridge to come along for many a long year.

In 1901, W.J. Jeffery unveiled a brand-new cartridge based on a new case design: the 600 Nitro Express. It fired a 900-grain bullet at 2050 fps, for 8400 fpe. There were actually three different loadings for the 600, but this is the most powerful and the one most often quoted. For the next 30 years, the 600 was a Jeffery specialty, and the company built about 60 of them – half doubles, half single-shots. Other gunmakers manufactured a few as well, and H&H estimates that, altogether, about 100 rifles were made. The 600 gained a reputation out of all proportion to the small number in actual use. It became the tool of the professional ivory hunter, saved for only the direst situations, with most day-to-day hunting done with a rifle in the 450 class.

With three different 450s as well as the 500, 577 and 600 NE, every hole appeared to be filled. Then, between 1905 and 1907 (again, the dates are vague) the British government imposed a ban on 450-caliber cartridges in India and the Sudan.

There was unrest in both colonies, and both were awash in old 450 Martini-Henry rifles (the British military arm up until 1888). To cut off ammunition supplies for these rifles, the Colonial Office banned 450s altogether. As a rifle market, the Sudan was not terribly important; most of the hunting that went on there was for slave traders, which the British had been battling since the days of General Gordon and the Mahdi, but India was another matter. It was a major market for all the British gunmakers, from the maharajahs, to army officers going out to join their regiments, to civil servants, to the likes of

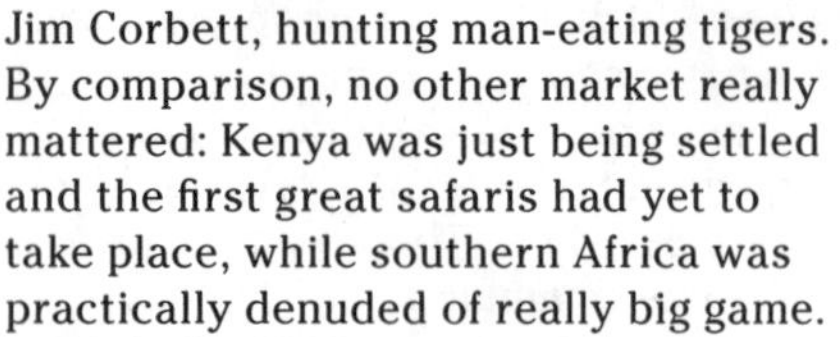

Jim Corbett, hunting man-eating tigers. By comparison, no other market really mattered: Kenya was just being settled and the first great safaris had yet to take place, while southern Africa was practically denuded of really big game.

With the 450 banned in India, there began a scramble to replace it. Eley Brothers necked up their 450 No. 2 to 475; H&H necked up its 500/450 to 465; in Birmingham, Westley Richards took the 500 NE 3-inch and necked it down to 476. The greatest of all, however, was developed by Joseph Lang: The 470 Nitro Express was created by necking down the 500 3-inch. Instead of making it proprietary, Lang released it to the trade. Rather than developing a cartridge of its own, Rigby adopted the 470, as did a host of lesser makers, and its fortune was made.

By the way, there already existed a 475 Nitro Express, essentially the 450 NE case but with slightly less taper and a .475-inch-diameter bullet. It is truly a mystery, with no one having any idea who developed it originally, or when. It just was. But not many were made, and few are seen today. It is, however, a first-rate dangerous-game cartridge.

Ballistically, all these new developments were really echoes of the 450: bullets around 500 grains, velocity of about 2150 fps, energy around 5000 fpe. Gunmakers recognized this as the ideal combination of reliable killing power on elephant (and, of course, anything smaller), which could be built into a rifle of manageable weight (ten pounds, give or take) with recoil that was substantial but not prohibitive. A hundred years later, those numbers have not changed. In 1956, when Winchester entered the fray with its 458, that was the performance they aimed for and claimed (but failed, alas, to deliver).

Because the 450 was the standard, there was little interest in cartridges of lesser power, and only one was developed. The 450/400 had been a popular blackpowder cartridge, formed by necking down the 450 3 1/4-inch. However, this gave the 400 an extraordinarily long neck, and when it was turned into a "nitro express," the long neck and thin brass gave serious extraction diffi ulties in some rifl es.

W.J. Jeffery solved the problem by shortening the case to three inches,

Manton & Co. 470 Nitro Express boxlock (left) and a recent John Rigby (California) 500 Nitro Express sidelock (right). (Courtesy Terry Wieland)

reducing neck length, and giving the cartridge a more pronounced shoulder. The result was the 400 Jeffery Nitro Express. The new development did not eclipse the old, however, and today rifles are found in both chamberings, and ammunition for both is still manufactured. For a few years, the 450/400 was regarded as the best "all-around" cartridge among the nitro-express clan.

Jeffery was also responsible for what may be the weirdest and least explicable development among nitro-express cartridges, the 475 No. 2 (Jeffery) Nitro Express. Jeffery took Eley's 475 No. 2 and loaded it with a slightly larger (.488- versus .483-in.) and heavier (500 grains versus 480) bullet, at lower velocity (2150 fps instead of 2200). To this day, the variant causes problems for those considering buying a 475 No. 2 rifle. A rifle regulated with one will not shoot well with the other, and the difference in bullet diameter can raise pressures to undesirable levels if a Jeffery cartridge is fired in a standard chamber.

Exactly what Jeffery's rationale was is now anyone's guess. The company was one of the all-time great riflemakers, originators of more fine cartridges than H&H, but that one defies understanding.

Major players of the nitro-express era, from left: 450/400 Jeffery (3"), 450 NE, 500/450, 500/465, 476 NE, 470 NE, 475 No. 2, 500 NE 3", 500 NE 3¼", 577 NE, .600 NE.

For an all-too-brief period, the paper patch was king. It provided a gas seal for the bullet as well as preventing lead from fouling the rifling. It was used in both military cartridges (450 Martini-Henry, left) and sporting cartridges such as the 450 No. 1 Express (center) and the 500 Black Powder Express. The paper patch allowed the use of pure lead bullets, which afforded superb terminal performance.

The nitro-express period ended, effectively, in 1907— just ten years after it began. Although the designation has been applied to cartridges since that time, none has had a lasting impact. The originals were all rimmed cartridges intended for double rifles, with a few single-shots. By 1907, however, John Rigby had become the London agent for Mauser, persuaded the Mauserwerke to produce oversized magnum actions, and work was beginning on huge rimless magazine-rifle cartridges. The result was the 416 Rigby, 404 and 500 Jeffery, and the 505 Gibbs, to name the most famous.

In 1912, Holland & Holland unveiled a cartridge which, although intended for magazine rifles, also became one of the most popular double-rifle cartridges of all time: the 375 Belted Rimless Magnum, also known as the 375 H&H.

Although technically not a nitro-express cartridge, the 375 could be considered the last and greatest of them all—the period at the end of the sentence. An entire book could be written about the 375 H&H, which many consider the greatest hunting cartridge ever developed. In African terms, it is certainly the most versatile.

Its revolutionary "rimless belted" design gave positive headspacing without the potential problems of a rim jamming in a magazine rifle; the case has a pronounced taper which ensures reliable feeding from the magazine, and also makes extraction easy in a double or single-shot. Most of all, the 375 has killing power out of all proportion to its size, and this is due entirely to its 300-grain round-nose bullet. This has been the standard loading for the 375 from the beginning, and has proven itself on everything from elephant on down. A 300-grain 375 is a long bullet and heavy for caliber, and gives extraordinary penetration. Had Sir Samuel Baker been alive to see it, he would have heartily approved.

Henry Holland lived until 1930, dying in his 85th year. He oversaw the great H&H cartridge developments of that era, including the 500/450, 500/465, 577 NE and the 375 H&H. In all of these cartridges can be seen the influence of Sir Samuel Baker.

Presumably, Mr. Holland looked back with some satisfaction on the fact that the coming of the nitro-express cartridges had effectively ended the use of hollowpoint bullets for dangerous game. With the higher velocities, the overriding concern was to come up with a jacketed softpoint that would not over-expand, and not one of the successful cartridges used anything like a hollow-point. As well, their great rival, James Purdey & Son, which championed the express rifle and the hollowpoint bullet, never attached their name to a successful cartridge in the new era. While Purdey continued to manufacture a few double rifles, the firm ceased to be a real force in the field.

For Sir Samuel Baker, it was a posthumous victory, but a victory nonetheless.

ACCURATE BLACKPOWDER CARTRIDGES -WHAT WORKS- THE SECRETS REVEALED

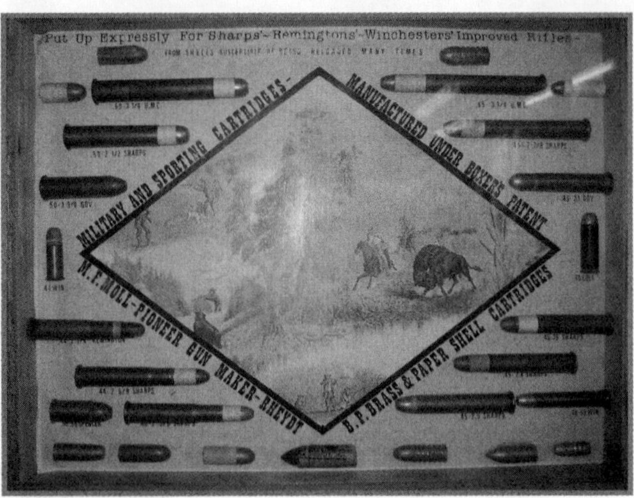

Author Moll's cartridge board bears a striking resemblance to those of 19th-century American makers. Note the various paper-patched cartridges.

by Markus F. Moll and David J. Moses

Markus Moll, born 1959, is a certified Master Gunmaker and recognized expert in restoring, building and loading blackpowder guns from the flintlock pistol to the African double. Re-creation of Sharps target and buffalo rifles is a specialty. In the last 17 years, he has not only recreated some of the most famous accurate rifles of the 19th century but has rediscovered the now long-forgotten science of loading the accurate blackpowder cartridge. He lives and works in his hometown of Rheydt in Westphalia, Germany. These notes are his digest of the essentials required for best accuracy, published here for the first time in any language. Although some of his recommendations may seem controversial and rub against 21st century conventional wisdom, what works, you find here.

COMPONENTS OF THE BLACKPOWDER CARTRIDGE

PROPELLANT/PRIMER

Blackpowder is the *only* propellant to use. This is not just to produce an authentic shooting experience with its characteristic smog and pleasant, hollow report, but because it is still the *best* propellant for the old blackpowder cartridges. At the present time, the following grades of blackpowder are available:

Swiss (CH)– Ch 2, Ch 3, Ch 4, Ch 5
Goex– Fg, FFg, FFFg
Elephant– Fg, FFg, FFFg

Grades or brands not mentioned here are unsuitable for our purposes as are all blackpowder substitutes. Live it or live with it.

Grain size: As a rule, the more powder you need, the larger the grain size must be. For example, if you shoot
45-2.1", load 65 gr. Ch 2 or 3;
45-2.4", load 93 gr. Ch 3 or 4;
45-3¼", load 115 gr. Ch 4 or 5.

The reason for a large grain size in a narrow powder column is to achieve a uniform, controlled combustion of the powder column. The coarser the powder, the more room there is between each powder grain and the easier the priming charge reaches up the column for more complete and uniform ignition. The relative diameter of the powder charge to its length is also a determining factor, i.e. it makes a big difference whether you shoot a .40 or a .50. An amount of powder in a .40 barrel will not stack as tall in a .50, so the .50 can take a finer grain than a .40 might tolerate since the primer flash will have less distance to travel to permeate the entire charge. If you think you need more power, it is wrong to go to a finer grain hoping for a bigger bang. Since the flash cannot travel so high up the column, the back of your charge tries to push the yet unburnt powder forward as if it were part of the projectile. This crushes the top powder kernels, making them burn even faster, if more erratically, and adds unnecessarily to recoil. If you need more power, then you must use a case with a larger powder chamber, same as with smokeless. The bottleneck cases such as the 11.15x60R, 577/450 Martini-Henry, 44-77 Remington, etc. offer advantages in this area, but not for blackpowder since case fouling in the shoulder region makes for problems of its own over the long term.

A shooter, disappointed with the "lame" ballistics of his 45-70-405 might go to a 45-90-550 or 45-110-550 in a 2 7⁄8-inch case. But he might regret it after his first bench session with the suddenly thunderous report and savage recoil of that 10-lb. sporter. A gun with plenty of iron in the barrel not only shoots better but is more fun to shoot, too.

Priming: The primer must also be correctly matched to the expected powder column:

Tall powder column: A long-burning Federal 215 Magnum primer
Short powder column: Any standard Large Rifle primer
Short, wide powder column: A primer with a broad flame front, e.g. Berdan primer with 2 flash holes

In order to widen the primer flame front, some shooters first place a thin piece of tissue paper directly over the flash hole before loading the powder. Despite American prejudice toward the convenience of the Boxer (actually Gardner) priming system, two flash holes are often the better solution for a variety of reasons we cannot go into now.

Cases: Cases should be of good quality. Especially inexpensive cases often show a variance in powder capacity and

Making your own wads is easy using a sharp punch of appropriate diameter and a hammer. Place the wad material on a flat wood board and tap out what you need.

usually have a very short life. You should choose Norma (.45 Basic), Huntington Die Specialties, Ballard and Horneber brands. These cases are dimensionally uniform, correctly heat-treated and possess a long life expectancy. Fired cases are best cleaned in a solution of citric acid and water, strength to suit.

WADDING

When choosing wadding, it is important to take into account for what purpose the load is to be used. If the cartridge is to be used for hunting, it is best to use a 5⁄16-inch thick grease cookie between two card wads cut from waxed paper milk cartons, e.g. Tetra-Pak. Or, you could use a greased felt wad separated from the bullet base by a dry Tetra-Pak card. The grease should keep the barrel fouling soft and thus allow several shots without having to wipe the bore. From a hunting aspect, the expected increase in group size is of no importance. Should the load be for target shooting, the only wad necessary is a dry Tetra-Pak card between the powder and bullet since, for best results, the bore must be wiped after every shot. The use of grease cookies in target cartridges is, as a rule, undesirable since it reduces powder capacity, a prime consideration for long-range shooting where the entire case capacity is required. On the other hand, some individual rifles may shoot well without bore wiping, but none for very long. The reason is that the degree of barrel fouling depends upon the caliber and the amount of powder. It is logical that barrel fouling will be greater in a 45-120-550 than in a 45-55-405.

BULLETS

Before the bullet is chosen, some important barrel dimensions must first be determined: rifling twist rate, groove depth and bore diameter. Also important is the desired purpose of the cartridge. Shall the bullet be used for hunting, target shooting or even long-range shooting?

First, the bullet weight must be matched to the rifling twist. The twist rate for original Sharps rifles in .40 - .45 varies between 1:18" and 1:22". In my experience, a long-range rifle in .45 will need a bullet of 530-550 gr. for a 1:18" or 1:19" twist. For a twist of 1:22", a .45 bullet should weigh no more than 510 gr. and 480 gr. is better. Given equal powder charges, the lighter bullet will always give a higher muzzle velocity (V_0) but rapidly loses velocity at longer distances compared to initially slower, heavier yet *longer* bullets of the same caliber. Remember, it is the length and not the weight of the bullet that determines the correct twist. With lead bullets, weight is merely a convenient indicator of bullet length and is useful for other ballistic calculations as well.

Hunting cartridges are only used at distances up to about 160 yards. Since a high striking velocity is desired for hunting cartridges, a .45 bullet should weigh between 330 and 420 gr. Such light bullets lose velocity very quickly and are unsuitable for greater distances. You can achieve a high V_0 by combining a large powder charge with a light bullet at the expense of sectional density, a trade-off that many hunters still gladly make. In the 1870s and 1880s, these so-called "Express" loads pushing short bullets past 1600 fps were very popular and effective for hunting all but the largest and most dangerous of game. The concept lives on today in the 9.3x72R, .444 Marlin, .45-70-300 and others with bullets less than about 2 ½ calibers long.

Choice of Bullet Style: Blackpowder cartridges use only paper-patched or grooved, lubricated lead bullets. With grooved bullets, we distinguish between *a)* tapered, *b)* nose riding, *c)* Pope-style and *d)* stepped or 2-diameter bullets. With paper-patched bullets, there are *a)* tapered or *b)* cylindrical bullets, with or without a hollow base.

Again, the intended use, the land/groove profile, the groove depth and the expected V_0 determine your bullet choice. Example: If you have a 45-70 rifle with a 1:20" twist and 0.004-inch groove depth, you should choose a 500-530 gr. grooved bullet of form D or B. But if you have a 45-120 rifle with the same twist and groove depth, you must use a paper-patch bullet of the same weight. Reason: The high bullet velocity causes barrel leading with grooved lead bullets and the patch prevents this. The patch also resists the bullet "jumping" the rifling.

As a rule, paper-patch bullets shoot better than grooved bullets due to their ballistically advantageous, smooth sur-

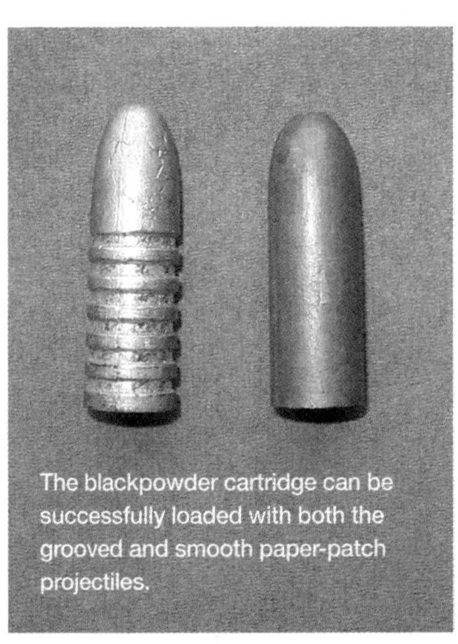

The blackpowder cartridge can be successfully loaded with both the grooved and smooth paper-patch projectiles.

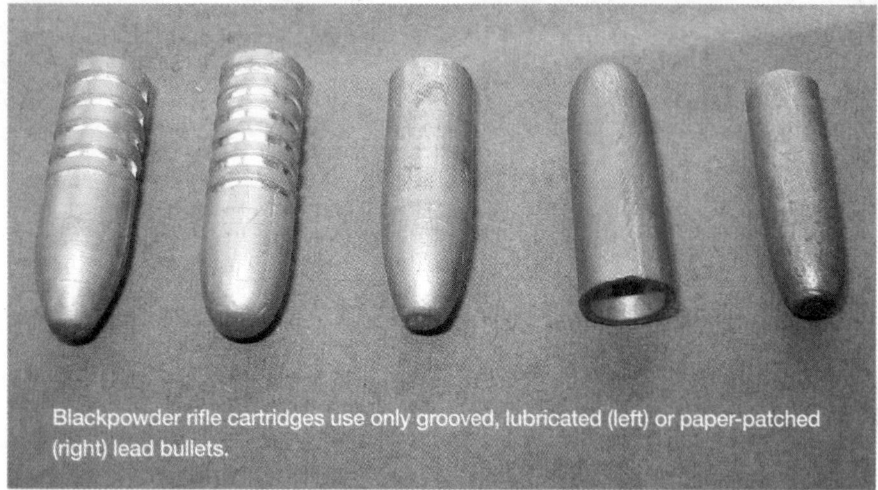
Blackpowder rifle cartridges use only grooved, lubricated (left) or paper-patched (right) lead bullets.

face but only provided that the barrel has shallow rifling, preferably 0.004-inch or less, and an even number of grooves. The bullet diameter and the correct type of patch paper are essential to achieving good groups. The better flight characteristics of the paper-patch bullet first become evident past the 500-yard mark. Naturally, the barrel throat, or leade, must be suitable to your choice of bullet or be modified for it.

LEADE / RIFLING PROFILE

Old original Sharps, Remington or Trapdoor Springfields had no leade (or throat) at all. In those days, bullets were used that were either smaller than bore diameter, had tapered sides or sat deep in the case, e.g. 50-70 Gov't. For hunting, mostly tapered bullets were used since their ogival form allowed bullets to be seated for more than half their length inside the case. This worked fine, even with a fouled barrel.

Target shooters mostly used cylindrical bullets patched to land diameter or just under it. Here, the bullet with its smaller diameter would sit loosely in the chamber. Since the bullet centers itself in the rifling, the loose seat is not a disadvantage. In fact, due to zero bullet pull and no jump to the rifling, cartridges loaded this way shoot very accurately. Prerequisite is that the rifling must be very shallow, under 0.004-inch, so that the bullet cannot slug up too much and deformation is held to a minimum. This way, the rifling cuts into the paper and not the lead and the bullet retains most of its original form as it leaves the barrel for the target.

Make a template pattern and use it to cut your patches.

Original Sharps Long-Range barrels show that the land diameter tapers strongly from the chamber to the muzzle. This means that the bullet in the cartridge neck fits the rifling there loosely but, since the bullet slugs up on ignition, this is no disability.

For those that bring up the justified argument that the bullets in the old Sharps and Remington factory rounds sat firmly in their cases, they are right and it would seem to contradict what we have just written. To understand this apparent contradiction, one must know that the old cartridges were about 0.016-inch smaller in diameter than their modern variants. At the same time, the chambers, especially in target rifles, were cut tighter than today, especially in the head area. Also, cartridge makers did not finally figure out how to keep case necks from loosening around the bullets until the dawn of the 20th Century. So if the round fit well ahead of the rim and the bullet centered itself in the rifling, then bullet pull lost by neck expansion was no disadvantage.

Unfortunately, most current makers of blackpowder breechloaders dispense with the leade in their oversize chambers. As a rule, a leade must then be reamed before they will shoot right. I prefer to use a leade which, by nitro standards, is "incorrect." It is actually just a gentle tapering of the lands. Years of research have shown that this leade offers the possibility of successfully combining new cartridge cases, oversize factory chambers and old and proven loading techniques. All known bullet styles can be used in such a throat, either undersized paper patch bullets or lubed bullets engaging at full or ½ groove depth.

LOADING THE BLACKPOWDER CARTRIDGE

After you have assembled the components for your particular rifle, loading begins.

Seat the primers and measure out each powder charge. The case volume and the intended use determine the amount of powder. Here we will load target cartridges.

A powder scale should be used for measuring each powder charge. There is some controversy over how accurately the charge must be weighed. Some shooters are of the opinion that up to 5 gr. variance in the powder charge makes no difference in accuracy. In my opinion, this is only partially correct. There is a difference between a 45-2.1" whose load varies between 50 and 55 gr. powder and a 45-2" whose load varies from 115 to 120 gr. The larger the powder charge, the less effect charge fluctuations will have on target grouping. But if you want to shoot past 300 yards and still hit something, charges must be meticulously weighed regardless. For those who have to know it all, you should always test your loads over a chronograph.

Finding the right load could be relatively simple. First, we start with original loading data, e.g. a 45-2" was loaded with 110 or even 120 gr. powder. This is the origin of the rumor that the 1874 Sharps fired a 45-120 in the old days. It did, but in a 2" case, not 3 ¼"! Modern cartridge cases have less powder capacity than the originals. A 45-90-2.4" was loaded in the 1800s with 100 gr. powder (see *Sellers*, p. 340). In some modern cases it is a big problem just trying to get 90 gr. into a 2.4" case. Let us ask some questions toward finding the proper type and quantity of blackpowder needed to correctly load a 45-2.4" case:

How much powder do I need?

We read in *Sellers' Sharps Firearms*, p. 331 that the U.S. Long Range Team in 1879 loaded between 106 and 115 grains powder. Comparing this load

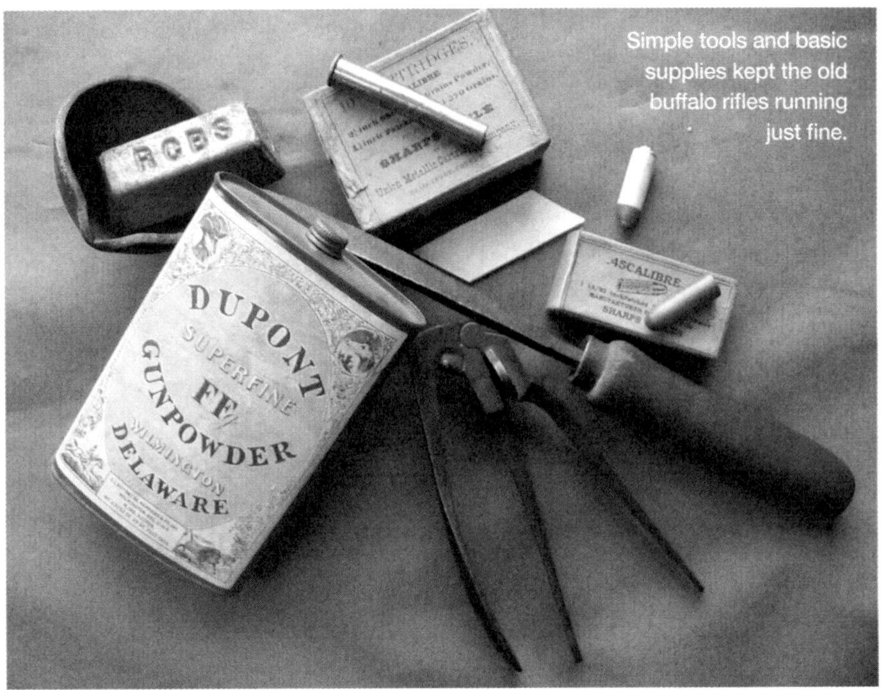

Simple tools and basic supplies kept the old buffalo rifles running just fine.

data to that of the English team, we find that, with the same weight bullet, they loaded only 90 to 100 grains powder. What does this mean? The answer lies in that the American team used Fg grade Laflin & Rand powder and the English used Curtis's & Harvey's "Diamond Grain" No. 5 or 6, which was clearly stronger than the American powder. Many buffalo hunters knew this, too, and, as reported by buffalo-runner Frank Meyer, preferred the significantly more expensive English powder. But how does this relate to blackpowders currently available?

The quality and energy of the currently manufactured Swiss powders corresponds exactly to those of the old Diamond Grain. The American GOEX powders appear to be somewhat stronger than the old Laflin & Rand but they are otherwise similar. Elephant powder is below GOEX in strength but is more hygroscopic, thus making it more suitable

Typical components of a blackpowder rifle cartridge (top to bottom): primed cartridge case; blackpowder charge; wad and paper-patched bullet.

An assembled blackpowder round, ready to fire.

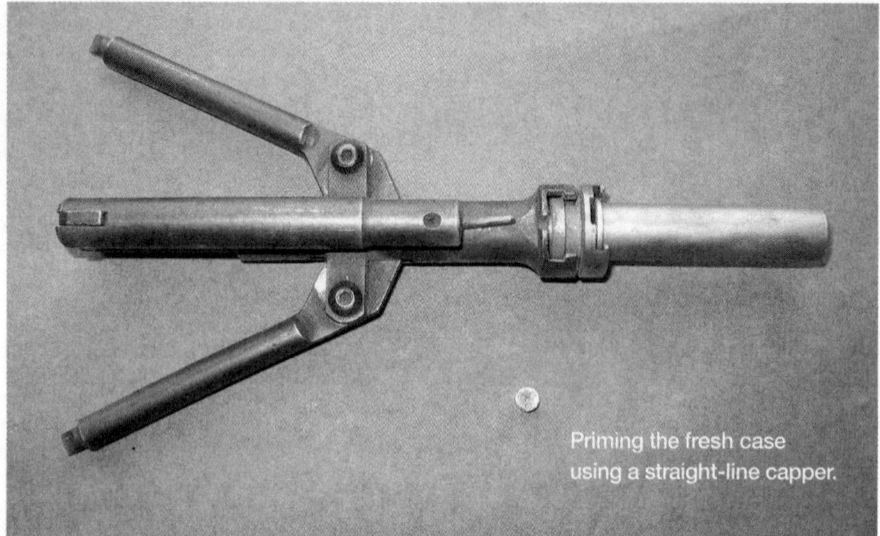
Priming the fresh case using a straight-line capper.

for shooting in an arid climate where keeping the fouling soft is more important than losing a few feet per second.

My opinions on these powders may be easily confirmed for yourself. Load, either by weight or volume, the same amount of each different powder and fire a series of at least 10 rounds per load over the chronograph. Load for load, Swiss powder will always give the highest and most consistent velocities.

What grain size should I use?

Ch 3 or Ch 4 should be used for a .45 load of 90 to 100 grains. In 2000, an experiment in the Swiss Federal Arsenal at Thun (pronounced "toon") revealed that, of all Swiss powders, Ch 4 had the most uniform internal ballistics. Therefore, Ch 4 should be the preferred powder if it fits that application. Tip: Buy several powder cans of the same grade and carefully mix up their contents. This will smooth out any manufacturing differences.

Weigh out 95 gr. Ch 4 and fill the case using a drop tube. The drop tube is nothing more than a 30-inch long copper or brass tube with a funnel at the top, same as used by muzzleloading target shooters. Thanks to the great drop, the powder grains pack more compactly and uniformly in the case. A drop tube MUST be used!

Now check the fill height of your case. There should still be room on top for a card wad with 3⁄16" left to seat the bullet. The loading technique whereby the bullet is separately seated into the rifling before the case is not discussed here. Most new 45-2.4" cases will allow 95 gr. Ch 4 to be loaded with this technique.

Should the powder charge be compressed?

This is a difficult question to answer. My own experience has shown that it is better when the powder is only very lightly compressed. As soon as you feel or hear a "crunching" of the powder grains, stop pressing or else they will be irregularly crushed. Crushing leads to variable ignition and thus velocity fluctuations which lead to flyers. After all cases have been loaded and pressed with a card wad, you can then tend to the bullet.

How is the bullet held in the case?

Lightly! The bullet must be seated by hand and must also be capable of being removed by hand. Do not succumb to the temptation of compressing the charge with the bullet. Also, especially with paper-patch bullets, do not crimp the case! Keep in mind that with hunting, military or magazine-fed rifles, loading techniques will differ from those for target guns.

Which bullet weight should I use?

A .45 rifle suitable for long-range shooting should have a rifling twist of 1:18" or 1:20" and a bullet of 530 to 550 gr. weight. Not coincidentally, this weight bullet has the most favorable exterior ballistics in .45 caliber.

How do I make a paper-patch bullet?

Assuming that you have a proper mould for paper patch bullets, cast some bullets from pure lead which are just under land diameter of the rifle you are loading for. Then cut ca. 0.020-inch thick cotton-content paper into strips. An especially good paper is Southworth's 9-lb. 25-percent cotton fiber onionskin available from your stationer, or online. It is very similar to original patch paper. Other papers may be suitable for patching and if you have a paper that works you should stick with it. Lay the lightly moistened paper on a smooth surface such as a glass plate with a sharp corner pointing to the right. Then wrap the bullet as in the illustration. Allow the bullet to dry nose-down overnight. As you wrap, be careful that the top edge of the paper is above the start of the cylindrical portion of the bullet and that the angled ends of the paper do not overlap. It is important that the patch show no waves or creases and sits tightly. Twist the excess paper at the bullet base and stuff it into the hollow. If it is a solid-base bullet, trim the pigtail as close as you can with fingernail clippers. The knack of wrapping the bullet tight yet without ripping the paper is quickly learned.

HOW TO WRAP THE PATCH

Do I need to lubricate?

Depending upon the individual barrel, it may be advantageous to lightly lubricate the patched bullet. As a rule, the simple and traditional formula of one part salt-free beef tallow to one part beeswax does well although there are no limits to your own experimentation. Never use any petroleum-based oil or grease for bullet lubrication.

IMPORTANT!

Check to make sure that cases are not too long. If the mouth of the case extends beyond the chamber even the least bit, the patch will tear. Keep case length below chamber length at all times. Be sure to de-burr the case mouth; a sharp edge here will tear the patch. In both cases, a leaded barrel and poor shooting will result. Look through the shot or have an assistant observe whether the patch separates just forward of the muzzle. Under no circumstances may the patch remain on the bullet!

In the case of poor shooting, check the bore to make sure there is no leading. If there is, that means that the patch began to separate from the bullet while still in the bore. The cause is usually that cases are too long, they

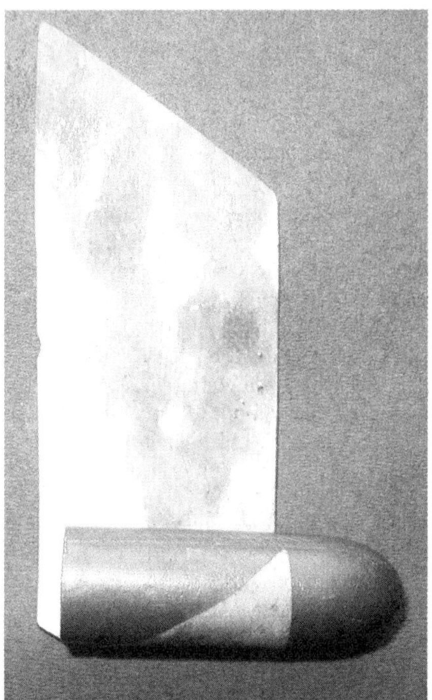

Be sure the top edge of the paper is above the start of the cylindrical portion of the bullet and that the angled ends of the paper do not overlap.

Twist the excess paper at the bullet base and stuff it into the hollow.

have burrs on the mouth or that the bullet sits too tightly in the case.

If the barrel shows no leading, check whether the patch has completely separated from the bullet. As a rule, paper bits are easily seen on the ground 1-3 yards ahead of the muzzle. In case of doubt, attempt to assemble a complete patch from the pieces left over for analysis. If the patch does not separate, then your barrel is unsuitable or the bullet has the wrong diameter and/or hardness.

To Review:

- Seat primer
- Adjust powder charge and grain size to the case length
- Charge powder using a drop tube
- Insert wadding
- Seat the bullet by hand
- Observe paper bits after shooting
- Wipe bore after every shot

INTERPRETING THE TARGET

In order to determine the optimal loads for your rifle, you need to keep records in a scorebook. Entries include weather conditions, group sizes with various loads and, at long ranges, your sight settings. Especially useful are chronograph readings if you have them. A well-loaded blackpowder cartridge will show an average variance of, at most, only about 16 fps from shot to shot.

Now you should look to see if the bullet holes are round or oval. At ranges up to 100 yards, holes are usually round. Slightly oval holes indicate a bullet that may be under-stabilized. Choosing a shorter (lighter) bullet will achieve more toward stability than increasing the powder charge ever can. At very great distances, the hole will also be oval but this is because the bullet is still pointing in the direction you fired it yet is falling down from the great height of its trajectory into the target paper.

Barrel Profile: Whereas military Sharps or T rapdoor rifles make do with 3 lands the same width as grooves, sporting and target rifles by Sharps and Remington used a combination of 6 narrow lands with grooves between 0.003-inch and 0.005-inch deep. For military purposes, the 3-groove barrel was good since there were fewer corners where fouling could build up; it could stay usable for more shots. Shooting tests prove that this principle worked well and 3-groove barrels hardly have problems related to excessive fouling. But it begs the question why everyone doesn't use a 3-groove barrel. The answer is in the interior ballistics:

1. For various reasons, paper-patch bullets do not function in 3-groove barrels.
2. The 3-groove profile only works with moderate loads, e.g. 60 to 70 gr. powder and a bullet weight between 480 and 500 gr. The faster twist needed for heavier (longer) bullets would force the naked bullet to jump the rifling.
3. Due to the high surface friction produced by three wide lands, the barrel overheats quickly and bullets show a lower V0 than a barrel with 6 or more grooves.

Practical tests show that individual marksmen can deliver the best possible groups with a Trapdoor Spring-

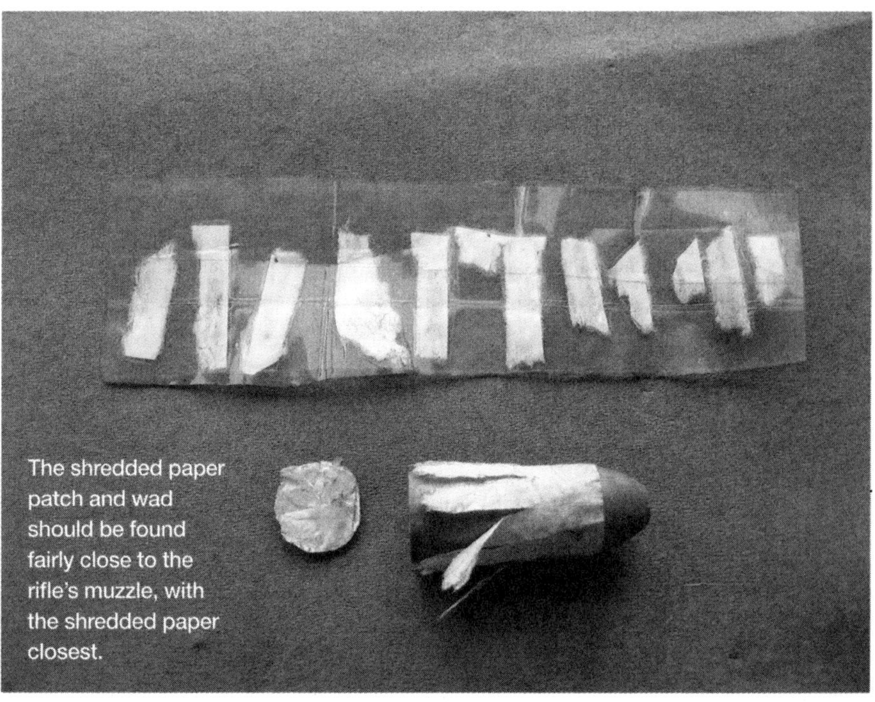

The shredded paper patch and wad should be found fairly close to the rifle's muzzle, with the shredded paper closest.

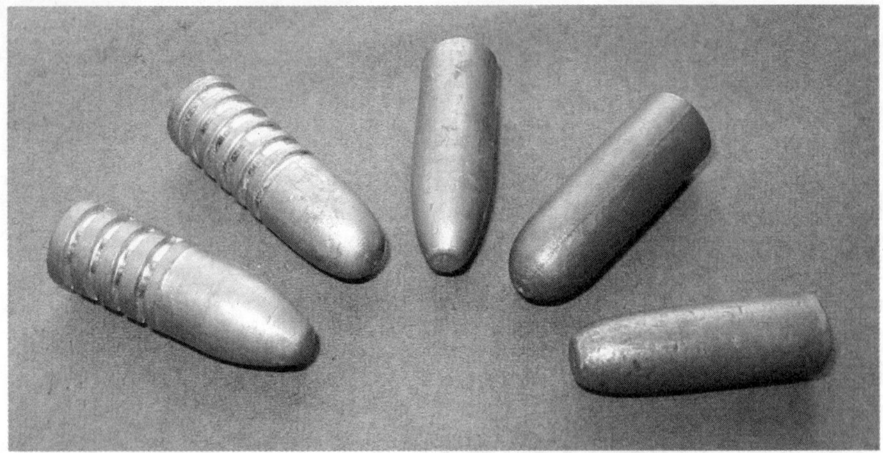

Whether you're shooting lubed or paper-patched bullets, bullet weight and diameter must be closely matched to the rifle's bore size and rifling twist for best results.

field at even the longest ranges (see Freeman R. Bull's tests up to 2000 yards). These shooters are at a disadvantage with a higher sensitivity to crosswind and very high mid-range trajectory of up to 30 feet with their lighter, slower bullets. They must also set their diopter sights very high and suffer an uncomfortable shooting position for it. But for ranges up to 300 yards, 3-groove rifling works just fine.

I would like to say here that all previous points and those that follow have been determined through years of personal experimentation and can be proven to the doubtful at any time. Naturally, as always, "Your mileage may vary."

These observations leave the conclusion that a multi-groove barrel is the best for cartridges with a high bullet weight, large powder charge and the highest possible velocity. The best gunmakers of the past must have thought so, too, since their target and sporting guns used them without exception. Let's look at three of the most successful rifling patterns of the blackpowder era suitable for breechloaders.

William Ellis Metford

Metford's rifling pattern, patented in 1865, features progressive (gain twist) rifling where the twist gradually tightens as the rifling approaches the muzzle. Using a combination of very shallow grooves and a hard-alloy paper patch bullet, Metford reduced bullet deformation as much as possible, the ideal being a perfectly smooth bullet flying downrange. His rifling pattern was used exclusively by George Gibbs, also of Bristol and a disciple of his. The disadvantage is that these barrels only function well with very hard paper-patch bullets.

Alexander Henry

Henry's barrel is based upon Joseph Whitworth's famous hexagonal rifling except Henry added a land in each corner so that shooting cylindrical bullets was no longer a problem. Henry, too, started with bullets made to the negative of the barrel profile. Then patent issues arose with Whitworth so that Henry abandoned the hexagonal profile and went instead to the 7-groove pattern we know today, arguably the most trouble-free rifling of all time for the blackpowder gun. This profile, patented in 1860, was chosen for the British Martini-Henry rifles of the 1870s. In Europe, Henry rifling was extensively used in hunting rifles well into the 20th century and it is still known there as "Express" rifling.

Henry rifling shoots equally well with either paper-patch or grooved bullets. It is important, however, that the bullet not have a hollow base. Depending upon the powder charge, wiping the bore between shots is generally not necessary to give good shooting.

John Rigby

John Rigby may rightly be named as the inventor of the modern rifling profile. His 1867 design is itself based upon Henry's 7-groove system. Rigby recognized that several narrow lands reduce bullet friction, work against fouling and are suitable for lead bullets. After 1868, his rifles dominated all long-range shooting matches. He was a shooting member of the Irish Creedmoor team of 1874 and shot with his own muzzle-loading rifle against the Sharps and Remington breechloaders of the Americans.

Today, Rigby's profile with 8 narrow lands is used unchanged by Badger Barrels. It is also worth mentioning that Harry Pope essentially took Rigby rifling and combined it with a gain twist. Rigby barrels shoot equally well with either grooved or paper patch bullets.

And now a few words about the surface quality of the lands and grooves: They are highly polished! Honed and polished barrels reduce bullet friction, slow wear and give powder fouling no place to stick. This high surface finish is best achieved today with hammer forging even though it has some disadvantages.

Owners of some Shiloh or Pedersoli rifles might note that their barrels have a fairly rough interior or, if they are polished at all, only the lands will have any real shine to them. This is the result of a lack of finish work after the rifling has been cut. Especially sloppy barrels will still show the reamer marks on the lands from when the bore was reamed to size before rifling. Tool marks are acceptable as long as they follow the rifling from breech to muzzle, but if you see scratches or grooving across the lands, then a rework of the barrel profile is unavoidable. The best thing is to just stay away from unpolished barrels if you can.

Not only does the blackpowder fouling set in the scratches but grooved bullets will deposit lead as well. The result is that the shooting deteriorates due to an irregular narrowing of the bore where the scratches are deepest and deposits are heaviest. Such a defect can only be cured by honing or even freshing the barrel. Naturally, paper-patch bullets avoid the leading issue if the bore is not too rough. That's why Shiloh and Pedersoli barrels do better with patched bullets than with greased lead.

It has been discouraging over the past years to see gun magazine test articles written by shooters who attempt to use loading techniques best suited to smokeless revolvers and one-size-fits-all components, with mediocre shooting as a result. Our ancestors could be quite particular about the shooting qualities of their guns and such tests leave the unfair impression that blackpowder guns don't shoot. This is certainly not the case and is proven annually at the international MLAIC and BPCR matches. With quality powder, a proper bullet, correct loading techniques and a good barrel, any shooter willing to proceed scientifically can have a gun that will shoot as well or better than anything Bodine, Farquharson or Rigby ever used.

THE RUGER 10/22 GOES TACTICAL

by J.M. Ramos

Being active in the sport-shooting fraternity has its own reward, especially when competing in various disciplines. In the past twenty-five years, the writer has participated in many IPSC and IDPA action-shooting events, both local and regional. Target shooting and competition is a wonderful stress-reliever, particularly for those who love this sport. It also create a solid bond between parents and their children by educating them early in the safe use of firearms, the tradition of marksmanship -- but most of all, the responsibilities involved in the ownership and safekeeping of firearms as a law-abiding citizen in the free world.

The Clinton administration Crime Bill in effect for about a decade (1994-2004) is clear proof that honest gun owners are not immune to prohibition, restriction and – perhaps eventually – confiscation. When the controversial bill eventually sunset a few years ago, many of the prohibited items such as military-type arms, hi-capacity magazines, folding stocks, muzzle devices, bayonet lugs etc., were revived in production and today are selling hotter than ever. There is no doubt that fear of another politically orchestrated prohibition, possibly more stringent than the previous, is fuelling the current demand for such weaponry and related accessories.

The 1980s can be remembered as the "golden era" of exotic weaponry. The so-called "assault weapons," the main target of the Clinton bill, are in vogue. These firearms are best described as semi-auto versions of various military small arms, like the Russian AK-47, German H&K G3, Swiss SIG AMT, Belgian FAL, U.S. M-16 and M-14 to name a few. Today, these politically incorrect guns are called "Tactical Guns." The new name sounds more civilized but it is highly doubtful the anti-gun forces would really care much for it.

Twenty-first century semi-auto tactical weapons are a far cry from their exotic1980 counterparts. Thirty years ago,

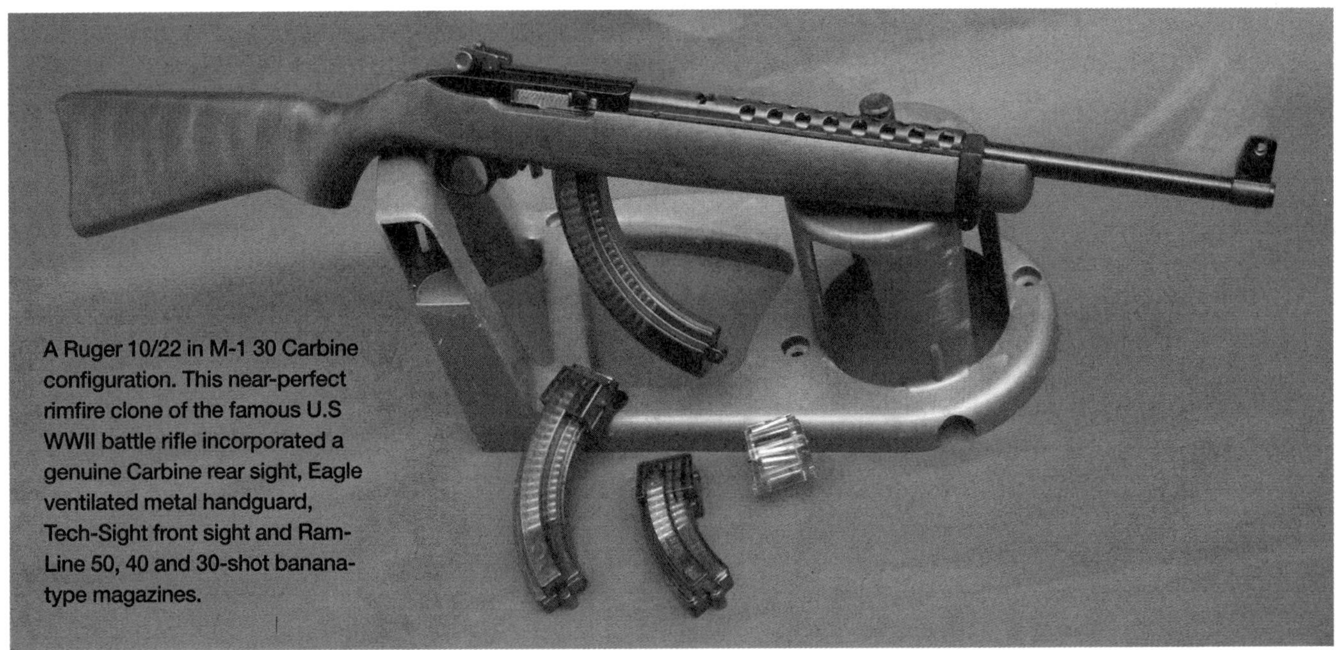

A Ruger 10/22 in M-1 30 Carbine configuration. This near-perfect rimfire clone of the famous U.S WWII battle rifle incorporated a genuine Carbine rear sight, Eagle ventilated metal handguard, Tech-Sight front sight and Ram-Line 50, 40 and 30-shot banana-type magazines.

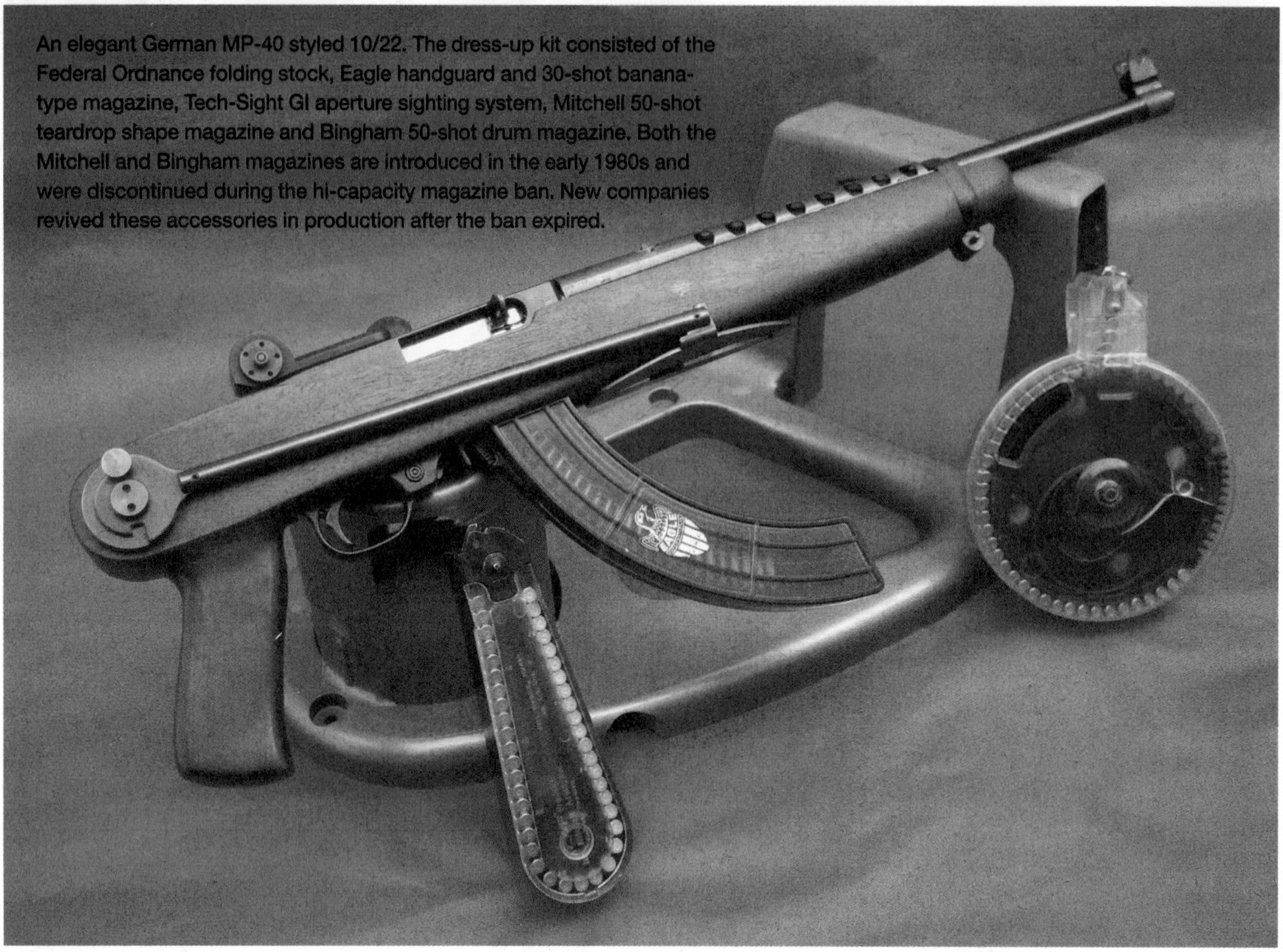

An elegant German MP-40 styled 10/22. The dress-up kit consisted of the Federal Ordnance folding stock, Eagle handguard and 30-shot banana-type magazine, Tech-Sight GI aperture sighting system, Mitchell 50-shot teardrop shape magazine and Bingham 50-shot drum magazine. Both the Mitchell and Bingham magazines are introduced in the early 1980s and were discontinued during the hi-capacity magazine ban. New companies revived these accessories in production after the ban expired.

BELOW: A rear perspective view of the Bushnell Trophy MP red dot scope mounted on the RAM 10/22 accessory mount. The RAM mount served as a front-end extension to Tech-Sight rear sight base seen below the scope with optional hooded aperture peep sight. The Bushnell scope features a red or green reticle with built-in sunshade. The author preferred this scope to the more expensive and more sophisticated EoTech for its finer and clearer reticle that produced better long-range groups.

die-hard military weapon aficionados were quite satisfied with the out-of-the-box configuration of the gun as delivered from the factory. Today, that outlook has changed. The designs of these latest fighting arms are significantly refined and even superior to their vintage Cold War production versions. Infantry rifles today are designed to accept a multitude of accessories: optics, BUIS sights, vertical forward grips, lights, etc. This advantage is made possible by the universal Picatinny rail system. This versatile mounting system is possibly one of the most useful features ever devised for military small arms, and has proven equally suitable with handguns, sporting guns, hunting rifles and shotguns.

Dress-up kits for the ever-popular Ruger 10/22 are also making waves in the tactical gun scene. Such aftermarket bolt-on devices were first introduced in the 1980s by independent accessory producers: Ram-Line, Feather Enterprise, Eagle Industries, Choate Machine & Tool and others. The first generation kits manufactured by these companies consisted primarily of folding stocks, barrel

A standard 10/22 Carbine in hi-tech "SAW"format. This version utilized a Choate Zytel fixed pistol grip format complemented by CAA's vertical forward grip, Tech-Sights, cut-down Masen 10/22 flash hider (modified to muzzle brake format), the Bushnell Trophy scope is mounted to Brownell's AR-15 riser. The magazine system, a 200-round quad format, consisted of four Ram-Line 50-shot banana-type magazines connected together.

shrouds, flash hiders, metal and polymer hand guards, extended magazine catches, assorted clip-on type bipods, replacement military style sights and – most notably – hi-capacity magazines of various capacities and configurations ranging from banana type, tear-drop shape and drum. Most of these after-market magazines are back in production today.

Contrary to the bolt-on accessories of yesteryear, the current generation of 10/22 dress-up kits are much more elaborate, very radical and extremely well made. Some of the kits will transform the standard Ruger 22 carbine to the latest military configurations that are unbelievably realistic. Some of the best dress-up kits available today include an AK-style short barreled Krinkov, (www. Krinker-plinker.com), an elegant H&K G3 style rifle or an ultra-compact MP5K (www.Rhinelandarms.com). If you are a traditionalist, you can check out the futuristic Austrian AUG bullpup rifle style with full wooden furniture or go for the top of the line from this California-based company – the eye-popping 22 clone of the magnificent Walther 2000 tactical sniping rifle (www. Ironwooddesigns.com). These custom kits vary in prices ranging from $350 for the Krinker kit to a whopping $950 for the WA 2000 Ironwood 10/22 clone. The kits are by no means cheap, being more expen-

The Krinker-Plinker rear sight is an excellent design. Its high profile format, however, will obstruct the view through a low mounted scope. Such a setup will require a riser to bring the eyepiece closer to the shooter's eye. A perfect scope for an elevated iron sight is the EoTech seen here with the eyepiece clearing the iron sight's aperture sight.

The 1980s can be considered the "Golden Era" of exotic weaponry. It is also remembered as the decade of the imports and rimfire clones. These high quality European rimfire clones of the French Famas bullpup (top) and Israeli Galil (bottom) battle rifles are best sellers and possibly some of the most sought after by collectors today. During this time, it was the Ruger 10/22 that was considered America's primary import fighter, thanks to many innovations in after-market accessories and hi-capacity magazines produced for this gun.

sive than the actual gun itself, but they sure add sizzle to your 10/22s, with the added bonus of your having the best-looking rimfire self-loader in the clubhouse.

For those who surf the net, basement experimentalists will occasionally exhibit their creations. Some are good, but most are crude and have a long way to go to be considered presentable. Although there are many aftermarket accessories currently available to upgrade the 10/22 to a hi-tech format, it takes careful planning and selection of custom parts to create a high performance tactical type 10/22 that is both attractive and accurate. One of the biggest mistakes made is bolting accessories onto various parts of the gun, simply to have more gadgets on it, without first analyzing their intended function and the overall configuration when completed. Often, the result of a rush job is a complete disaster, with time and money invested, only to end up with a cobbled gun that is totally unattractive, overly decorated, clumsy and heavy.

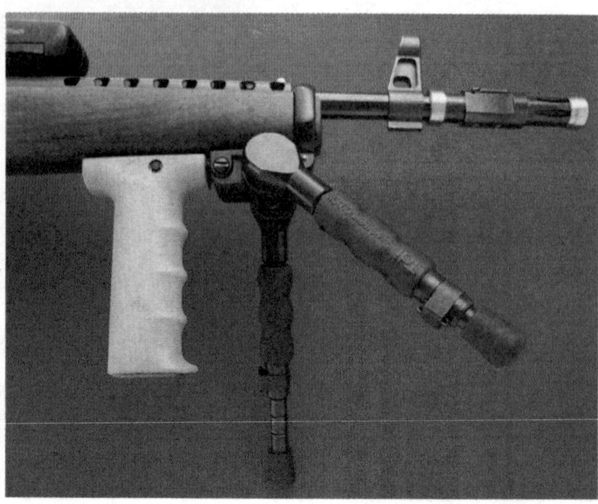

One of the most unique features of the CAA bipod is being able to deploy the legs in the usual 90-degree or 45-degree forward angle to allow an extremely low prone shooting position. The author also found the 45-degree angle a more natural configuration for supporting the arm while engaging targets downhill from the shooting position.

Three of the popular red dot scopes tested on the custom tactical 10/22s. From left to right: Tasco TS red dot, EoTech and Bushnell Trophy MP. The Tasco, the cheapest at under $100, is ideal for starters and provides good accuracy up to 25 yards. The mid-price Bushnell at $250 is the author's top choice, providing excellent accuracy up to 100 yards. At $400 the Eo-Tech 512 is the most sophisticated among the three optics tested and is in use by the military and police. It is best suited for full-bore tactical rifles.

Creating a premier tactical 10/22 is like building a custom 1911 pistol put together from the ground up with carefully selected custom parts to create a one of a kind masterpiece. This same principle can be universally applied to any type of firearm be a single shot or a self-loader. In other words, sky is the limit. Like the 1911, the 10/22 is a perfect candidate for such type of customizing project. Both guns are probably the most accessorized guns in the world today based on the number of after market components available from endless number of independent sources. Among the vast number of rimfire self-loading rifles produced over the past century, it was the 10/22 that truly fired the imaginations of the many acces-

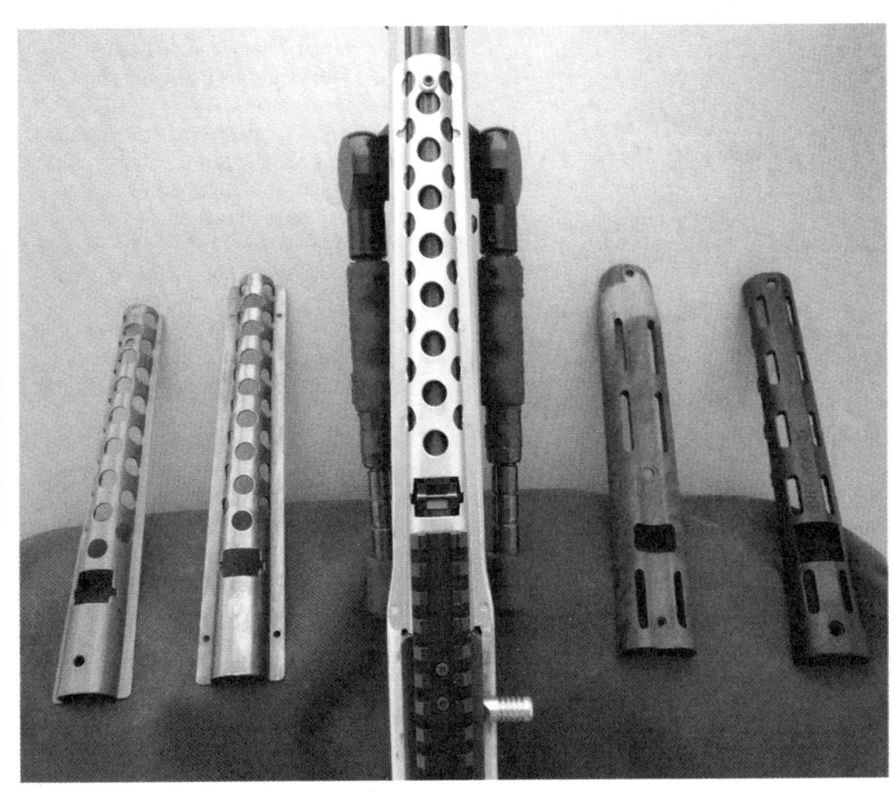

Handguards for rifle serves two purpose (1) to shield the hand from hot barrel after prolonged firing session and (2) cosmetics. The metal hand guards on the right and on the gun are Eagle brands while the two on the left are made by Choate and Ram-Line to complement their 10/22 Zytel and polymer stocks.

A 10/22 with a Krinker-Plinker dress-up kit. This best selling kit transform the Ruger .22 carbine into an authentic looking AK-74 carbine – Russia's current main battle rifle. Additional enhancement accessories include the CAA quick-detach forend storage grip and bipod connected to Volquartsen extended 10/22 Picatinny scope mount, AR-15 flash hider and Eo-Tech 512 scope.

One of the most desirable accessories for a tactical-type firearm is a muzzle attachment ,such as flash hider or muzzle brake. The two 16-inch "Compact" barrels on the left have a turned muzzle to accommodate long flash hiders for that popular "shorty" look. The other two barrels on the right are also 16 inches in length but utilize a typical slip-on type muzzle device.

sory innovators and eventually lead to the creation of endless bolt-on devices and dress-up kits that benefited avid 10/22 fans. The extreme popularity and demand for such gadgets owes much to the 10/22's overall design features that allow it to be transformed into a multitude of configurations using the right parts or accessories. The unrivalled reliability and ruggedness of mechanical components are the primary contributing factors to the gun's continued success in the international market with nearly five million produced to date. Needless to say, the writer can be included in the list of millions of Ruger 10/22 fans.

During the para-military heyday of the Reagan era, most gun writers focused their attention to this popular hardware. The writer is no exception, with number of articles and books on the subject to his credit. In this write-up, three decades after, the writer aims to top it all up with the creation of truly unique and versatile custom tactical 10/22s by selecting some accessories from the past and blending them with the very latest gizmos today's aftermarket accessory industry has to offer. The end result can be best described as "best of both worlds," a sort of custom "baby boomer's pet plinker." Firearms accessories came a long way. Two decades ago, wood and metal were the main ingredients in the dress-up kits. Today, space-age polymers and aircraft-grade alloys replaced the steel. The traditional styling of the past is now superceded by super hi-tech designs of the futuristic Buck Rogers century. As noted earlier, careful selection of after-market accessories to be incorporated to a 10/22 tactical project is crucial. Bear in mind that the mail order industry is currently flooded with these devices so you can virtually transform your favorite 22 carbine to almost any configuration you can imagine. One great thing about today's state-of-the-art accessories (optical sights, vertical front grips, muzzle devices, lights, etc.) that are designed for the U.S. M-16 rifle is that they can also be adapted to the 10/22. This is made possible by the introduction of the versatile Picatinny rail mounting system.

Accessories chosen by the author to be utilized in this 10/22 tactical conversion project are marketed by Command Arms Accessories (CAA), Tech-Sights, Eagle Industries, Brownell's and Ruger Firearms. Various optical sights (Eotech, Bushnell and Tasco) tested in this project are store-bought. The fixed-type stocks used in the project are both factory and Ram-Line production. The classic wood/metal Mini-14 folding stock pattern is of 1980 manufacture by Ram-Line and Federal Ordnance (German MP-40 style). Comple-

The overall design of the 10/22 has stood the test of time. With the popularity of tactical-type long arms, the more popular lever safety is now replacing the classic push button safety. To complement the custom tactical package, a speed lever type safety was designed by the writer to be faster and more efficient to operate. View showing the lever on "Safe" position, blocking the front end of the trigger guard.

menting the dress-up kit for the various stocks used in the project is the Eagle ventilated handguard. Eagle International first introduced this accessory in the mid-1980s and included it with their 10/22 dress-up kit until the company closed its Arvada, CO doors in the early 1990s.

A new Eagle International re-opened its door recently. The new company is now based in Hazen, ND. Once again, Eagle is re-introducing its original product lines of the exotic gun era, as well as new ones.

Also in that same decade, Ram-Line and Choate produced polymer handguards to match their polymer and Zytel stocks. The plastic guards, however, are much thicker and higher than the metal type and will not rest flush underneath the extended front end of the scope-mounting rail without a clearance cut. The extended portion of the rail acts as a depressor for the rear section of the handguard, locking it in place when the stock screw is tightened. The front end of the metal part is connected to the barrel by a small socket head screw with a matching bushing. During regular fieldstripping, the handguard remains connected with the upper receiver group.

The "shorty" look appears to be in vogue in today's latest breed of tactical firearms, whether AR or AK type. In 2006 Ruger introduced the "compact" version of the 10/22 Carbine with 16-inch barrel, which is selling quite well. As a note of interest, it was actually Ram-Line that introduced the first mass-produced 16-inch steel-lined polymer barrel for the 10/22 as far back as the mid-1980s to complement their "Backpacker" dress-up kit, which was designed to compete with the AR-7 Explorer in the survival gun market. The company called it the "Ultralight" barrel. This barrel is surprisingly accurate, very light and truly ahead of its time. Twenty-five years later, many current accessory manufacturers followed the footsteps of Ram-Line, introducing their own steel-lined lightweight barrels for the 10/22 utilizing modern carbon fiber or an aluminum shroud instead of polymer in various diameters and lengths. To make a 16-inch barrel looks even shorter, the muzzle end was turned down for about 5 inches and a new front sight base fabricated and press-fitted at the rear of the turned section. A vintage M-16 Colt Commando long flash hider conceals the turned portion of the muzzle and creates a very attractive "shorty" barrel in the legal 16-inch format. The extra weight of the flash hider at the muzzle also helps stabilize the barrel during rapid fire and results in improved accuracy.

Although red dot sights are rapidly gaining popularity over iron sights in tactical type firearms, the author still prefer the latter. Many iron sights for

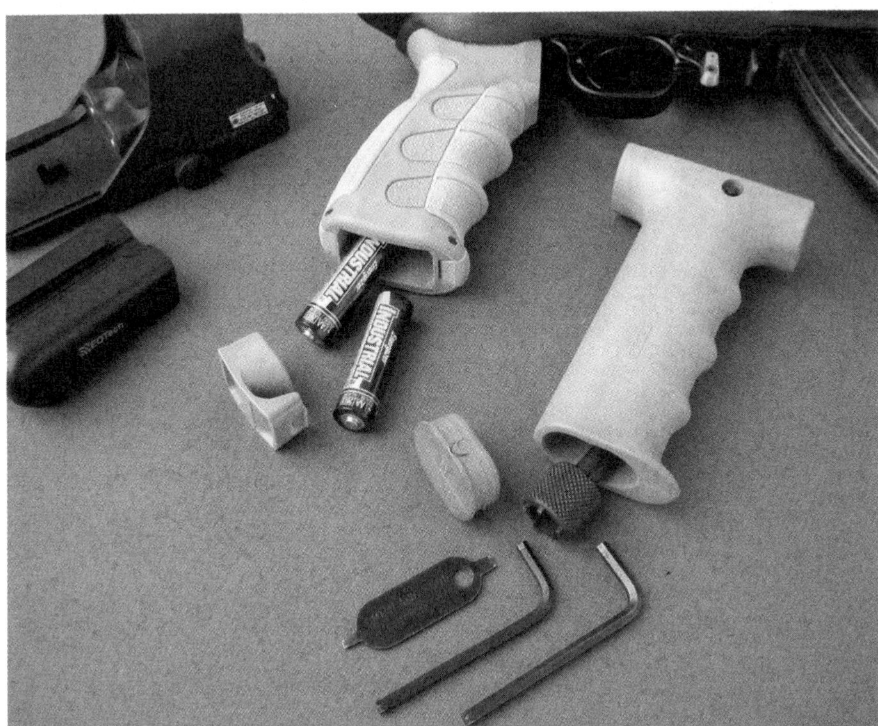

CAA introduced some of the finest tactical accessories in the market today. Their versatile UPG47 with 6-piece interchangeable inserts (left) and VG1 quick detach vertical combat grip (right) are superb examples of user-friendly accessories for serious tactical application. Both accessories have a built-in storage for spare batteries, sight adjustment and disassembly tool for this custom 10/22. (Note: additional inserts for the UPG47 are not shown.)

A 10/22 in tactical configuration utilizing the Ram-Line "Realtree" fixed-type polymer stock complemented by CAA green color VG1 grip. The Harris bipod connects directly to the sling swivel attachment stud in the stock. Beside the gun is Choate's Zytel metal side-folding stock used as a more compact option.

Author's favorite 10/22 combines dress-up kits of the exotic 80s to futuristic tactical weapon accessories of today to create what he calls "best of both worlds" tactical rimfire masterpiece. The classic Ram-Line wood/metal folding stock is complemented by the latest CAA UPG47 pistol grip, VG1 forward combat grip and bipod. Bushnell Trophy and Tech-Sights aided in the accuracy department, while the vintage Colt Commando flash hider, Ranch extended steel magazine catch and lever-type safety all contributed to the unique aesthetics and ergonomics of the hybrid gun. MWG's new improved 50-shot teardrop shape magazine provided reliable firepower.

the 10/22 have been introduced over the years; mostly open sights for hunting and micrometer sights for competition. Eagle International was the first company to market a military-style sight for the 10/22 called the "Zypher" back in the '80s. The Zypher is similar in concept to the M-1 carbine design but rather flimsy in overall construction. Sight adjustment is rudimentary via multiple miniature screws. The peep sight is difficult to set precisely since it is manually adjusted for both elevation and windage without any graduation lines to reference. To date, the best iron sight ever tested by the author for the 10/22 is the GI aperture sighting system by Tech-Sights. Founded in 2004 by Larry Nesseth and his son Erik, the first sight introduced by the company was for the popular SKS rifle. Both Larry and Erik served in the U.S. military and came to prefer the precision and rugged dependability of the "GI" aperture sight. After leaving the service, father and son set out to produce a battle-proven sighting system for the sporting, hunting and law enforcement market. In 2006, they expanded their aperture sighting system to include the 10/22. The new sight is available in two versions: the standard TSR 100 and the top-of-the-line TSR 200. Complementing the sights are optional accessories to include an alternate aperture for the standard version (TS220), a hooded aperture sight (TS156), an adjusting tool (TS155) and a 0.920-inch barrel dovetail adaptor (TS157) for bull-barreled 10/22s. In addition to the excellent sight picture and rugged construction of Tech Sights, both rear and front sights accept any optional sight components made for AR-type rifles. For maximum sight visibility in low light conditions, the front sight post can be replaced with the AR-15 "Sightlink" fiber optic accessory (available from Brownells). Other custom 10/22 accessories acquired from Brownells includes the steel extended magazine release made by Ranch Products, the Volquartsen "extended" charging handle assembly and extra-power recoil spring which proven to work better than the lighter factory spring once the components start fouling after prolonged usage. For optical installation, the RAM accessory mounting rail for the 10/22 was found to be the ideal choice for the tactical conversion. The part is very well made and finished. The Ram accessory is used in conjunction with the Tech-Sight accessory. The rail is used as a front-end extension of the aperture sight base and required drilling two new holes at the rear of the part. Two matching assembly holes (threaded) on top of the receiver will be required to connect the part at the rear. The two original mounting holes at the top front end of the receiver will secure the front end of the RAM rail. The rail front end will extend about an inch and a half past the receiver front end. The extended portion will act as a retainer for the metal handguard at the rear during stock assembly.

When TDI USA, Inc. and First Samco, Inc. teamed up to form the new Command Arms Accessories, the products of their joint venture were designed for the law enforcement, military and civilian competition market. Many of their innovations included Picatinny rail systems, advanced light and laser devices, handgrips, stocks, bipods and adaptors – all carrying a lifetime warranty. CAA's products are first rate in quality and very advanced in concept. They are the leading edge in tactical weapon accessories technology. From their product line, the author selected the new UPG47, a very sophisticated AK-47 type pistol grip with six interchangeable inserts to replace the vintage AR-15 pistol grip in the Ram-Line folding stock. A matching forward vertical grip was also purchased to complement the new pistol

Comparison view of three 10/22 trigger groups. The trigger group mated to the gun has the standard lever safety with serrated cylindrical knob. The trigger group below has the extended-type lever with oblong knob (removed from the lever). The third trigger group has the usual factory push button-type safety.

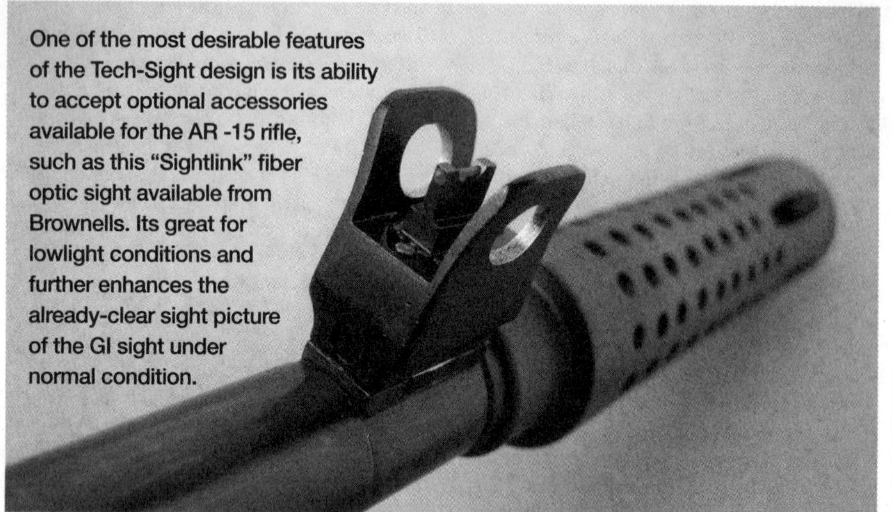
One of the most desirable features of the Tech-Sight design is its ability to accept optional accessories available for the AR -15 rifle, such as this "Sightlink" fiber optic sight available from Brownells. Its great for lowlight conditions and further enhances the already-clear sight picture of the GI sight under normal condition.

grip. Both parts are tan in color, perfectly blending with the classic wooden furniture. Another impressive accessory from CAA is their revolutionary bipod. The Israeli-made accessory is truly unique and innovative and easily makes many similar devices in the market today obsolete. In addition to its ruggedness and simplicity of design, there are no external springs or fragile small stamped parts to get lost or damaged. The locking mechanism of the bipod is concealed inside the legs. Another excellent feature not found on any similar device is the ability to rotate the legs in four graduations. The legs can be folded either to the rear or front when not in use. They can be deployed in the standard 90-degree vertical position or at a 45-degree angle forward for shooting from a very low prone position for minimum exposure to enemy fire. The legs of the bipod can be instantly detached from the base for compact carry; regular bipods do not have this feature. For rapid deployment, the legs can be quickly re-attached. The author found the best application for the 45-degree forward angle is while engaging targets downhill. This set-up appears more natural than the usual 90-degree setting for the bipod. The bipod design features works very well in any given situation. The device attaches directly to the rail offering less bulk than those ones that requires a separate mounting platform. A large screw secures the base to the rail. When not using the bipod, it is best to leave the base attached to the rail and only detach the two legs for storage. The base itself is small, very light and not in the way while using the gun without the legs in place.

A good mounting rail is needed to attach the forward grip and bipod to the fore grip. Most of the rails available for the AR used for this purpose are not compatible with the 10/22 stock simply because the grip seats a bit low under the fore grip. The mounting side of the rail is flat and sticks out of the stock underside when installed. It's outright unattractive and the setup looks very bulky. The most suitable rail for mounting the CAA VG1 vertical grip on the 10/22 stock is Ruger's own Weaver type scope mount (Part #NSBA) available as an optional accessory from the company. The 10/22 Compact model comes with an optional Weaver type tip-off mount and not the usual 3/4-inch scope dovetail mount that is supplied with the Carbine version. The bottom contour of the Weaver type mount is perfectly tailored for the underside radius of the fore grip. The part is also thinner than the standard bottom mounting rails used in the full-bore battle rifles, which results in a flush fit between the underside of the forearm and the top edge of the vertical grip. No gaps, just a perfect fit. The grip is also tight when installed to the mount so everything is solid. The CAA Universal Equipment Mount also fit the Ruger part perfectly since the VG1 grip and bipod mount shares the same size dovetail groove and push-button lock. The CAA accessory allows the use of the Harris bipod when attached to a fore grip rail.

In terms of mechanical improvement, the 10/22 has undoubtedly stood the test of time. However, the author feels the time has come for a much-desired change in its manual safety design. The push button type safety is out of date. To activate the button from SAFE to FIRE, or vice-versa, requires shifting the grip on the gun. When the famous M-1 30 Carbine first entered the service, it originally came with a push button-type safety. Soon, this flaw was realized in combat and the button safety was eventually replaced with the lever type and then did not require shifting the hold on the gun. The trigger finger only has to operate the lever on one side of the trigger housing – all without changing the grip on the gun while keeping an eye on the target. To make the custom tactical package truly complete and modern, the writer designed and perfected a lever-type safety for the 10/22 that replaces the factory push button-type safety. It features a spring-loaded steel ball powered by a strong small spring. The safety operates smoothly and positively. The lever type safety has a small serrated knob that is easy and conveniently operated by the trigger finger. (NOTE: The writer is currently negotiating with an after-market accessory manufacturer to produce his tactical lever safety device for the 10/22. Hopefully, by the time you read this article, the custom safety is in full production.)

If the trend for tactical rimfire guns continues to be strong, the market will be flooded with mass-produced dress-up kits for this little carbine, while interest in bolt-on parts will soon diminish. However, a one-of-a-kind 22 tactical carbine masterpiece will always stand alone, accumulating value and admiring fans over the years – assuming it is done right and professionally. As centerfire ammunition becomes more costly, self –loading rimfire guns like the 10/22 will continue to take the top spot in sales. Hi-tech rimfire beauties will always attract the attention of the most discriminating exotic gun aficionados the world over who just can't get enough of Bill Ruger's magical little 22. With a little help from his friends, the independent accessory innovators, possibilities are endless.

Sources Of Accessories

Command Arms Accessories
76 Vincent Circle
Ivyland, PA 18974
(267) 803-1517
www.Commandarms.com

MB Products, Inc
1000 Hwy. Drive
Hazen, ND 58545-3003
1-888-932-4536
www.Eagleaccessory.com

Tech-Sights
2242 183/4 Avenue,
Rice Lake, WI 54868
(715) 234-1793
www.Tech-Sights.com

Brownell's, Inc.
200 S Front Street
Montezuma, IA 50171-9989
1-800-741-0015
www.Brownell.com

Sturm, Ruger & Co., Inc.
41 Sunapee Street
Newport, NH 03773
(603) 863-3300
www.Ruger.com

A.H. HARDY
LOCAL BOY MAKES GOOD

by Jim Foral

National pride was one reason for America's unprecedented reception to the long-range rifle shooting craze of the mid-1870s. The endless coverage by mainstream journalists had fixed the public's attention on the phenomenon, and had fashioned sharpshooting riflemen into media celebrities and heroes to suddenly gun-struck boys. Great throngs of onlookers collected at the Creedmoor range on Long Island to watch the practice shoots of Cols. Gildersleeve and Bodine, Major Henry Fulton and their illustrious teammates. Initially, their international matches also attracted sizable gatherings. Before long, the people grew weary of watching the backs of the competitor's heads, and pointlessly straining to even see the thousand-yard target. This once trendy pastime had lost its ability to draw and hold the spectator, and public interest waned.

When trapshooting fell into fashion in the 1880s, it quickly developed into a tremendously popular and enduring sport. Each observer had his own reason for braving the crowds. Many came to watch a loved one shoot. Others enjoyed the simple mingling with their fellow man. Almost no one came a second time with the expectation of being entertained. Legions were struck with an insight leading to a nearly universal conclusion: trap shooting was a decidedly less than riveting spectator sport.

At the larger Eastern tournaments, the trap-shooting clubs enlivened their programs with intermission performances by exhibition shooters. Doc Carver, Ira Paine, and Adam H. Bogardus were the standouts in a very small and novel field. In some respects, they became the event's attraction and almost instantly developed into major luminaries. Spectators were able to identify with the performers, and the accompanying audible and visual stimulation satisfied the sensory requirements without the insipid repetition. Their work at the time was groundbreaking, and the crowds went wild over it.

These flamboyant and mercenary showmen shot for themselves and for their benefit. They were shameless self-promoters who contested separately-staged competitions among themselves into a seemingly endless spectacle. The era's sporting tabloids devoted a lot of ink to their antics; it was what the people wanted to see.

Unavoidably, the arms merchant perceived that guns and ammunition could be showcased and sold through the influence of a paid demonstrator, and shooting as a wholesome pastime could be concurrently promoted. The flashy entertainer had unwittingly paved the way and set the standards for the professional shooter that would be along shortly.

Just after the century's turning, the Texas rifle expert Adolph Topperwein began his long association with Winchester, beneficially keeping that firm's name in front of the public. Peters Cartridge Company signed up George Bartlett, a colorful Wild West personality, whose exploits as a U.S. Marshal put some notches on his gun.

Incubating here in Nebraska, meantime, was a simple saddlemaker awaiting greater notice, and a break. A self-taught marksman and self-developed

ABOVE: **Capt. Hardy aims a brace of Colt Officer's Model 38s, 1915.**

showman, Albert Howard Hardy was busily improving his trick-shooting act before small cowtown gatherings.

Hardy was born to homesteaders a few miles north of Schuyler, Nebraska in the Centennial year of 1876. His love for firearms began with bow and arrow lessons from friendly Indians and progressed with the covert ownership of a 22 rifle at the age of seven. The fascination might have taken a different direction when the gun was taken to school, confiscated by a teacher, and returned to the boy's parents. By the time he was ten, young Hardy was afflicted with a full-blown attraction to guns, but his parent's hatred for them was just as fierce. The boy has somehow acquired both a 22 rifle and a pistol. When his mother became aware, the guns were gathered up, buried in a cave, and rusted to uselessness before they were discovered. Moved by his passion and determination, Mrs. Hardy consented to the lad owning a gun in exchange for a life-long pledge to abstain from alcohol and tobacco. The grateful youngster replaced the guns, practiced with the new ones throughout his boyhood, and never forgot the promise to his mother. Later, he would attribute his shooting skills to her wise admonition.

Determined to be a marksman, Hardy possessed a particular leaning towards the impractical, entertaining display of a craft, and away from shooting at stationary scoreable targets. Towards this end, he practiced industriously.

Seventeen-year-old Hardy went to Omaha to learn the saddler's trade in 1893 and worked there for several months before he was smitten by the lure of the frontier West. His wanderings brought him to a cattle ranch outside of Hyannis, Nebraska where he supported himself by hunting the bountied gray wolf and gunning ducks and prairie chickens for the Omaha markets. He then arranged a job in a saddle shop in Alliance, Nebraska.

The journey to that village pivots on an incident that remains a part of the regional lore of the Sandhill cattle country of the west-central part of the state. In 1894, Albert and his older brother Elmer, both shy of train fare, jumped a train bound for Alliance. They were detected at a stop halfway to the destination, and a brakeman tried to knock young Albert from a car with his lantern. Albert fired a pistol shot on either side of the man's head to discourage the assault, and the brakeman retreated. By this time, the train was slowing as it approached Hyannis, and Elmer let go two shots, the pre-arranged signal to leave the train. Quite naturally, the brakeman thought he was being fired upon once more. The elder Hardy was arrested and jailed in Hyannis, but Albert was too young to prosecute.

In the 1890s, Hyannis was a remote wide-open cow town rife with the usual vices. Two hundred souls, most with a hand in the cattle business, called it home. There was gambling to be had and fleshy favors to be bargained for. A cowboy celebrating payday by riding his horse into a saloon was not a fairy tale dreamed up by the B-Western writer: it happened regularly in Hyannis. The last time the stunt was pulled, I am informed, was a short fifteen years ago.

In the spring of 1894, the case came before the court. Burlington Northern had sent their best lawyers to convict the Hardy miscreants of attempted murder while the boys had retained a cut-rate local attorney. On the stand and under oath, Albert testified that his fire had been in self-defense and his brother has fired his gun simply as a signal to get off the train. The boy's lawyer suggested to the jurors that it could be proven that the Hardys intended no harm, and if they had, the railroad man would not be there to testify.

The court adjourned outdoors, whereupon one of the most unorthodox displays in the history of Old West justice unfolded on the dirt streets of Hyannis. In front of a crowd of cowboy witnesses who roared their approval, Albert proceeded to cut playing cards edgewise with revolver bullets. A postage stamp was fixed to an envelope and perforated three times in as many tries. Elmer confidently held small objects in his hand, and little brother just as assuredly shot them out. The court reconvened and within five minutes the jury returned with a not guilty verdict.

While detained awaiting trial, Albert endeared himself to the townspeople. The county judge assisted the young man in setting up a saddle shop, and a juror advanced him a loan. Almost instantly, he became a well-liked and respected member of the small community. Musically gifted, he learned to bow a fiddle and joined the town's cornet band and fiddled the area hoedowns. He courted and married the county schoolmarm. Legend has it that the people of Grant County, by common consent, conferred upon him the honorary title of Captain.

Together with a bunch of cowpunchers, 20-year-old Hardy cross-countried ahorseback 135 miles of Nebraska sandhills – from Hyannis to North Platte – to witness Buffalo Bill Cody's first Wild West Show in Bill's hometown. This was in 1896. From every corner of the state its citizens gathered for the event and filled every available seat.

From the popular press, Albert had absorbed all the glorification of Bill and his supernatural marksmanship, and he was in North Platte to watch the dashing longhaired man he'd read so much about, shoot. The acts of Johnny Baker and Annie Oakley conditioned the assembly for Cody, who opened by shooting glass balls out of the air with a rifle – from the saddle of a horse at full gait.

Young Albert Hardy idolized Buffalo Bill, the hero of his adolescence. Later, the two struck up a warm and lifelong friendship. Bill provided encouragement with career decisions and direction. The need to be close to infant daughters kept Hardy from accepting Bill's invitation to tour the world with the Wild West Show. When the iconic symbol of the Old West died in Denver in 1917, Bill's protégé was selected as a pallbearer.

Hyannis was where Hardy refined his shooting skills and polished up an act, putting on public shows at small fairs and for the amusement of small bands of cowboys, just for the sport and recreation that was in it. Before long, he was in great demand and it became apparent he might have to choose between the saddle shop or his fondness for the rifle. Preparation and drill were constant. One year eleven cases of 22 Shorts - 110,000 rounds - were expended in practice.

In 1904, the Peters Cartridge Company was in the market for additional demonstrators. By then it was no secret to the industry that in the wilds of Nebraska lived a ripe and well-credentialed talent replete with experience and his own following. Capt. Bartlett, still Peters' lone representative, pilgrimaged from Cincinnati to Hyannis to recruit Capt. Hardy. He accepted the position and Peters assigned him a worthwhile mid-western territory, the extent of which was never clearly delineated. Hardy closed the saddle shop, sold his house in Hyannis, and took up residence in Lincoln, Nebraska, the hometown of your correspondent. At the time, Lincoln was home to 50,000 and was one of the more progressive cities on the plains.

A. H. Hardy shooting at the Nebraska State Fairground in December, 1905 and on his way to a record for aerial wooden balls. We Lincolnites no longer spectate from ahead of the firing line.

It was from this home base that he worked the region's county and state fairs, carnivals and other events that Peters felt his representation could benefit them. Hardy safeguarded and advanced the goodwill of the organization and promoted the wholesomeness of shooting generally. He settled into the focus on his new career and the raising of four children. Period city directories list his occupation as "traveling agent". During slack time, and the off-season, he continued to turn out saddles and high quality leatherwork on his own.

While in Capital City, Mr. Hardy was something of a celebrity to those with a sporting bent. People here and everywhere else were ardently caught up in the popular pastime of trapshooting. The Lincoln Gun Club enjoyed their own shooting park, as did the members of the outlying University Place Gun club. This city's highbrows dusted clay pigeons and fraternized at the Capital Beach Gun Club's facility, new in 1907. Very much in demand locally, Captain Hardy made regular professional appearances at the facility of each club. After entertaining his fellows, he then transformed into the competition. A top-flight trap shooter, he was generally regarded as the man to beat. In 1906, he took a team from Lincoln to the great American Handicap held on the campus of the Chicago Gun Club, where they broke a world's record, smashing 494 X 500 rock. The year previously, the strong Lincoln squad brought home fourth place.

In those days, the Nebraska State Fair was an agriculturally focused tradition. The state's farmers and cattlemen came to Lincoln to see for themselves the newest strains of corn and sorghum for the first time. Also on display were the impossibly huge swine and goliath Angus. These organisms flew in the face of genetic mediocrity and showed what could be done.

While on the semi-annual trip to town, the rural people allowed themselves other cultural distractions. More curiosity than attraction, Spray – "The Only Lady High Diver in the World" - dove a reported 90 feet into a water-filled horse tank, and did it twice daily. A distant popping signaled a migration to the edge of the fairgrounds. At the Peters booth, there was A.H. Hardy, dutifully wearing the Circle P armband and flying the company banners and achieving the unachievable with rifle and revolver. He gave Peters and his fans their money's worth; early demonstrations often went into extra innings. A show before a hometown gathering on June 10, 1907 went a full six hours. He was a popular State Fair fixture, a powerful draw, and a star that shined brightly for as long as he was in Star City.

Every community of size boasted a gun club during the glory days of trapshooting. This 1907 congregation, the defunct Capital Beach Gun Club, enjoyed their grounds at the northern edge of your author's hometown. Hardy's show was an occasional attraction.

To a greater or lesser extent, shooting objects out of the air was a staple in the routine of Hardy and his peers. It was while in Lincoln that he added a new facet to this basic feature. "Along about 1907, I decided I would try for some long runs at aerial targets, using a 22", he once reflected. He started with a thousand frozen apples. In front of a sizable assembly, each apple was tossed fifteen feet upwards. Only six hit the ground unshot.

For a period of years "going on the road" for Peters sometimes meant a ten-minute trolley ride. Hardy spent the Christmas of 1905 at the Nebraska State Fairgrounds shooting two and a half-inch wooden balls out of the air. Before he missed, he made a record string of 5,152 straight. But one rifle was used, and it was not cleaned during the entire two-day event. Peters semi-smokeless 22 Shorts had made this possible and the company got their fair share of mileage from this advertiseable point.

In November of 1907, Hardy established another record with the clean-shooting rimfires. His intention to shoot for ten continuous days was upset by a three-day blizzard. Still, he nailed 13,066 balls before the miss. That fall he'd made a run of 992 X 1000 marbles and gained national attention via Peters half-page ads proudly promoting the merits of their wonderful rimfire Shorts.

A proficient thrower, whose consistency and cadence could be relied upon, was instrumental to the success of these aerial endeavors.

Capt. Hardy developed the plinking of airborne targets to a crowd-pleasing specialty. His act was particularly enlivened when a stopwatch was introduced into the mix, and the transfixed fairgoers

Captain Hardy, decked out in the full Peters uniform, cuts a card held edgewise with a S&W 38 about 1908. It's close-range, but not easy and not safe, either.

watched the bullet catch the ball at a pace faster than one per second. Hardy set two records at this game. On one occasion he broke 500 balls in eleven minutes and sixteen seconds, and another a hundred balls in 85 seconds.

A popular number that wrested cheers from the bleachers was actually a mechanized adaptation of one of Buffalo Bill's tricks. Bill liked to gallop into an arena and, from the saddle, shatter glass balls thrown in front of him with a Winchester lever-action 44-40. When Hardy witnessed the feat in 1896, he recognized that shot cartridges were being used, a deduction based entirely on the report of the rifle. He knew too that the caper done with bulleted cartridges was inherently dangerous. At the time, though, the prank was Bill's trade secret.

Later, Captain Hardy was overcome with the bug to modernize Cody's thrill. At the 1910 Hastings, Nebraska Frontier Days, he sped into the local race track, and from the back seat of a motor car doing thirty, proceeded to reduce the balls to shards with one-half ounce of #10 shot - ala Buffalo Bill - in front of 20,000 of his fellow Nebraskans. The exercise went off with a howl, and Hardy included it in his play list whenever space permitted.

In 1909, a sportsman's journal had printed an article critical of Wild Bill Hickok's marksmanship abilities. Allegedly, Bill on occasion had thrown a quart can into the atmosphere, drawn a holstered Colt Single Action with each hand and hit the can three times before it landed - twice with the right gun and once with the left. In the minds of many, this smacked of a spurious dime

Here Mr. & Mrs. Topperwein are in 1910, photographed separately.

novel stunt and was widely challenged. An appeal was broadcast to Hardy to repeat the feat and prove the claim. Hardy strapped on the Colts and rose to Wild Bill's defense. On his second attempt, he was able to duplicate Bill's achievement and silenced his attackers.

When Capt. Hardy and his peers performed, they each dipped into an understandably common and limited bag of tricks, none being beyond the collective capability. The forté or innovation of one demonstrator was never exclusive to himself, but easily mastered and ultimately duplicated by the others. Thus, the individual professionals were essentially equally proficient, and their repertoires were a communal resource. They could all unerringly pluck from the air three or four wooden balls tossed at once. A tin can stayed up long enough to gather five rifle or pistol hits. Pennies or nuts, tossed and hit a few feet forward of the shooter, were actually easy marks and a universal stock in trade. The inerrant descent of iron washers didn't necessarily signify a miss; the hole taped over and still pierced proved the shooter's skill. Figure shooting - tracing the outline of an Indian chief, jackrabbit or whatever with rimfire bullets – was deceptively simple but still thrilled the multitudes. A lucky onlooker always got the holey souvenir. Splitting a business or playing card edgewise, often held between someone's fingers, was Hardy's signature stunt, and it conveyed a faith in Peters ammunition.

Another popular trick was to eject a 22 empty from the rifle, giving it an upward toss and reloading the rifle in one motion. Hitting the ejected shell in mid-air completed the movement.

With a six-shooter in each hand, Capt. Hardy could simultaneously break two bottles ten feet apart and twenty-five feet distant. With either hand he broke small objects with the gun held upside down or sideways. At fifteen yards, he would face two clay targets, one stationary, the other swinging. His twin Colt Officer's Models discharged as one, shattering both targets at the same instant. Not all of his contemporaries were as adept at fancy revolver work.

Some made a splash by contorting themselves into unnatural positions to shoot at difficult targets. Captain Bartlett, in particular, made this a specialty. Most were highly skilled at shooting accurately from the hip and facing away from the target and sighting with mirrors. When there was a miss, however, some of the spectators

Mr. & Mrs. Topperwein toured as a team but each was a standout in their own right.

tended to move on, and it behooved Hardy's fellow demonstrators to practice and remain in top form.

Hardy took offense to the term generally used to describe himself and his brother performers. "Trick Shot" erroneously inferred a deception and its use was discouraged. "Expert Fancy Shooter" was perfectly accurate, he felt, and was his choice of job titles.

Mr. Hardy was known to have used a variety of guns during his long fancy shooting career. Evidently partial to Smith and Wesson revolvers, he was variously pictured with the cataloged gamut. His working 38 Specials were 6 1/2-inch barreled Hand Ejector Target models, and triggers were tuned as necessary. A favorite double-action exhibition 38 was a nickel-finished S&W with an 8-inch barrel rifled by Harry Pope. He was once seen posed with a holstered short-barreled Smith. Small-framed, it was suggestive of a rimfire chambering. The Captain wrote approvingly of a pet Colt Officer's Model 38 that he liked to use as a single action. He owned a pair of these D.A. Officer's Models. Another preferred Colt was the Camp Perry model, a 22 single shot built on the Officer's Model frame. Hardy appreciated the two-pound trigger pull on his gun.

A Lyman-sighted Winchester Model 1890 pump was an early choice of 22 repeaters. Later he was seen with two Marlin lever actions, one of which had its wrist thickened with a rawhide wrapping. Capt. Hardy liked Marlin products. John Marlin was one of many within the industry he called a friend. Centerfire Marlins included a Model 27 slide action in 32-20 and a 30-30 Marlin lever-action Model of 1893. He relied upon a Marlin 12-gauge pump for his serious shotgunning. A poster of the late 1920s vintage shows Mr. Hardy holding a Remington Model '08 semi-automatic high-power rifle.

All sighting requirements for Hardy's fancy shooting were served with the commonest of sights. The simple Lyman #1 or Marble's tang sight - with the peep hole reamed out to a fair-sized eighth-inch – worked better for him than anything else on a rifle. He was the only professional to habitually use the peep sight. Up front was always a simple but oversized gold bead. This proved to be the best combination for shooting in all lights. An ordinary U-notch straight bar rear, with the same gold bead, performed almost as well. With his revolvers, Hardy got along nicely with the factory's target sights, which consisted of an adjustable U-notch rear and Paine gold bead front, an excellent but outmoded system.

Early in 1911, the Peters decision-makers transferred Capt. Hardy to the Western metropolis of Denver, Colorado, assigning him a new territory which included New Mexico, southern Wyoming, and the whole of Colorado. The announcement was made public in the May 1911 number of Outdoor Life magazine. In those days, Denver was a great hotbed of gun crankery and shooting activity. The marksmanship-mad Coloradoans had a city trap club that conducted shoots every Sunday. At the National Guard Armory, the range was abuzz with activity nightly. Just as importantly, the extraordinarily competitive Denver Rifle and Revolver Club near Golden held events each weekend, and truthfully boasted that some of the best rifle shots in the U.S. were among its members. Denver was the natural habitat for a man like A.H. Hardy; it was his kind of town.

The Denver Indoor Rifle and Pistol Club hadn't kept itself up. In 1912, Hardy reorganized the club, revitalized the program and schedules, and was the main force behind its renewed success. This is where he competed against the West's finest indoor shooters with his deluxe scoped Steven's gallery rifle.

Around Denver, Hardy enjoyed dignitary status. He was always on hand wherever mass quantities of Peters ammunition were being consumed, such as the major regional trap tournaments like the Denver Handicap. As he'd been in Nebraska, he was a formidable competitor at these events. Unavoidably, he fell into the elite Denver clique of gun cranks, among them J.A. McGuire, owner and editor of the Denver-based Outdoor Life magazine. The Editor detected in the expert fancy shooter an unusual eloquence and a flair for expression, and encouraged contributions to his periodical.

Hardy wrote of Colt revolvers he'd tried out and an Ithaca side-by-side that had satisfied him. He illustrated how a rimfire firing pin should and shouldn't contact the cartridge rim for best ignition and accuracy. There were short pieces profiling Denver youths who'd shown uncommon promise as crack shots. His typewriter issued a brilliant editorial on the need for rifle practice by both civilian and soldier.

In 1924, Hardy authored a nine-part series in Outdoor Life on the subject of exhibition shooting. The misconception that a person must be a natural-

Capt. Hardy updating Buffalo Bill's trick from the back seat of a roadster doing thirty miles per hour at the 1910 Hastings, Nebraska Frontier Days. Just as Bill had done from a horse, the balls were broken with 44-40 shot cartridges.

Capt. A.H. Hardy, touted by his employer as "One of the World's Greatest Marksmen" in a Peters publicity shot in 1910.

With a Marlin 22 lever action and Peters Shorts, Hardy traces an Indian Chief head on a piece of sheet metal. The best seats in the house were actually saddles.

born shot to become an expert was exposed. "Anyone" with fair health and eyesight, the proper enthusiasm and determination could develop into a championship-level shooter. Stressing the importance of confidence and self-control, he outlined a schedule for practice and volunteered pointers for acquiring skill, and suggested how to coordinate the harmonious working of the eyes, nerves, and muscles.

In 1910, a Kentucky gun club published an unpretentious account in Outdoor Life detailing their unconventional turkey shoots. The firing line was reported to have been a full 300 yards in front of the live turkey targets. These were not customary rifle matches; the shooting was strictly offhand with 38 Special revolvers. One bullet in four or five produced a bleeding turkey, and this was said to be a good average.

Some scoffed and dismissed the story as a fabrication. The editor of a nationally prominent bi-weekly branded them liars in print. Outdoor Life's J. A. McGuire recognized that a vindication was a matter of duplicating the slandered Kentuckian's purported results. On March 6, 1911, McGuire conscripted Hardy, drove him to a farm field outside of town, where a turkey silhouette had been painted on a piece of oilcloth and staked out at a paced 300 yards. Hardy sighted in briefly, and fighting a cold wind, fired fifteen shots for record. Three drew blood on the turkey image, equaling the Kentucky average.

Publicity was the plan and the outcome. The Associated Press wired a dispatch to the daily papers nationwide, and Denver's morning newspaper carried the story the following day. Outdoor Life provided space for detailed coverage just as soon as practicable, nicely putting the imputation to rest. Afterwards, when a safe range was available, Capt. Hardy shot a 300-yard turkey as part of his act, often hitting the bird half the time.

Attracted perhaps by the competitive shooting possibilities, Captain Hardy signed up with the Colorado National Guard in 1913. He was assigned to the local Ordnance Department unit and received a Captain's commission, giving him a dual captaincy of sorts. At the Camp Perry National Matches that summer, Capt. Hardy shot with both the state rifle and pistol teams. Reading between the lines, the impression is that he accepted his issue Springfield with some reluctance. Though certainly no stranger to the rifle, he found the 30-caliber long-range scene a decidedly

Note the absence of eye and ear protection as Mrs. Topperwein plinks spent shotshells from her husband's fingers. Please don't duplicate this stunt with anyone but your current spouse.

Some of Hardy's contemporaries relied upon gymnastic gimmicks to set apart their acts. Gnarled up here is Capt. Jack O'Connell in 1911.

foreign environment. Being trussed up in a shooting jacket, or "football suit" as he considered it, was also new and unnatural. Nonetheless, having faced the thirty-six-inch bull in the thousand-yard Wimbledon Cup Match, our Capt. Hardy with a respectable 94 X 100, finished well ahead of the pack. He tied with standout Capt. K.K.V. Casey, 1908 Olympian and veteran of multiple Palma teams, in the Governor's Cup match and did remarkably well overall but returned to Denver trophyless. His less-than-record-breaking performance puzzled those expecting greater of a professional shooter. When questioned about it, the stock answer was logical and simple, but generally took some time to sink in. One excels in what one practices, he made clear, but only if one practices intelligently. The best pitcher in the league couldn't shortstop successfully, nor should he be expected to. Likewise, a gifted concert violinist couldn't pick up a cello and hope to keep his orchestral end up with that unfamiliar instrument. Moreover, long-range marksmanship was a unique discipline requiring expertness in the evaluation and allowance for wind and the contention with mirage. Mastery was a product of proper coaching and diligent practice, not innate ability.

Precisely directing 38-caliber pistol bullets is where Albert Hardy predominated, and he put this forté on display that summer of 1913 at the Military Revolver Matches. The issue 38 Colt double action with its four-pound pull contrasted strikingly to his tuned exhibition guns but with some acquainting, he made the transition. The five-member Colorado NG pistol squad, including Capt. Hardy, competed for a handily won Perry's crowning pistol competition, the fifty-yard timed and slow fire Championship Match. Second place belonged to the highly skilled New York guardsmen who in the final tally trailed by an astounding 91 points. The previous winter, Hardy and three members of the Perry crew, doing business as the Denver Revolver team, defeated a huge field of opposition in a postal match organized by the esteemed United States Revolver Assn. In this fifty-yard timed fire contest, they finished with a score of 774, bettering the world's record by a full 49 points, and brought home to Denver the coveted Winan's Trophy.

Hardy entertained the idle competitors at Perry with his famous fancy shooting demonstrations. As a non-competitor representing Peters, he returned in 1918 and 1920. Capt. Hardy conceptualized and devised a surprise fire set up to aid in training law enforcement personnel. In a contrived urban setting of fake building fronts, silhouette figures are suddenly presented. The officer instantly sorts good guy from bad, draws his service gun and engages the target while it is still in sight. Running man targets and sidewalk-situated figures fired upon from a moving auto was also part of the course. Dubbed Hogan's Alley, this training arrangement was first instituted at Camp Perry in 1929.

In 1926, Captain Hardy was re-assigned to Beverly Hills, California, where he was kept busy beyond the demands of his Peters representation. Ads in American Rifleman generated a steady demand for the holsters, cartridge belts, custom gun cases ant other leatherwork he became nationally noted for.

He coached pistol marksmanship to the 2,500-man force of the LAPD and started a program of intra-divisional competition. One of the teams developed captured a National Championship at Camp Perry.

The record-setting Denver Revolver Club Team of 1913 and pride of the Mile High City. Seated l/r – A.M. Poindexter, Capt. A.H. Hardy. Standing l/r – Arthur Smith, C. McCutcheon.

Captain Hardy in a 1911 studio portrait.

Hardy's abilities with a gun found another commercial outlet within Hollywood's film industry. Howard Hughes hired him to do all the machinegun work in his 1930s picture Hell's Angels. In the big-screen depiction of Annie Oakley's life, Albert's youngest daughter Kathryn shooting doubled for Barbara Stanwyck while his own marksmanship made the male lead look good.

In 1938, after thirty-four years as a representative and salesman, A.H. Hardy, aged sixty-three years, retired from Peters sponsorship to devote his full attention to his mail-order leather business. After a brief illness, Captain Hardy passed away in a Los Angeles hospital on August 13, 1950.

These days, there is little need or interest, and I daresay little tolerance for a rifle-shooting exhibition shoot. In this modern world of instantly available electronic pseudo-reality, no expert fancy shooter could be showman enough to compete. Almost everywhere, "the edge of town" is not a safe place to shoot, and even in Nebraska, guns and crowds and state fairs do not mix any longer.

After a century's passing, Hyannis still celebrates Capt. Hardy, and even now they claim him as an adopted one of their own. He felt indebted to these people; their backing had been a foothold to his success. In a spirit of reciprocal admiration, the village caretakes a repository of Hardy mementos and artifacts, safeguarding them for themselves and for posterity.

During his few years in Lincoln, he enjoyed a citywide notoriety beyond sporting circles, but his fame faded after he left town. 1911 is now too long ago and far away for citizens of a sizeable city to remember the prime of a minor local celebrity. In Colorado, he was accepted as a native. Denver was his sphere of great accomplishment and influence. Here he is grouped with and remembered along with so many of a fabled era's shooting notables, whose deeds are better recognized and preserved.

In the history of the shooting sports, Albert Hardy's impact is not an especially huge one. As we all aspire to do, he left his mark upon the world. In another century, he dazzled our Mid-Western forebears with feats of seemingly impossible marksmanship. He made a name for himself in each of the places he happened to light and in every vocational pursuit that called to him. As a personality, Hardy's prominence was with an impressive number of circles, unbounded by his Peters territories. For a boy sprouted from humble Nebraska roots, this is not an insignificant legacy.

ABOUT DUELING & DUELING PISTOLS

Throwing Down a Gauntlet

by Norm Flayderman

What constitutes an American dueling pistol…or, for that matter, any "dueling pistol?" How might it differ from a large "holster pistol," "horse pistol," "target pistol" or "officer's pistol?" It's a cloudy subject, at best, and a question that may not be easily resolved to everyone's satisfaction.

The conclusions drawn from the following discussion are likely numbered among the earliest attempts (if not the initial salvo!) to question and provide a logical rationale to understand "dueling" and "dueling pistols." Ostensibly, both subjects have been taken for granted by historians, collectors and the public at large as historical fact. These remarks venture to step into that breach and approach the subjects from a rational and questioning viewpoint. In offering this alternate perception of dueling, it clearly becomes subject to challenge. For an energetic researcher it affords potential for a sensible resolution to what has unmistakably been a long-standing enigma. Resolving that inaccuracy will add substantially to the literature of firearms and American folklore. It's a topic overdue for serious, unemotional inquiry…just waiting to be tapped. Optimistically, these remarks will offer incentive for that investigation.

The Practice of Dueling In America (…and the casual approach to the facts)

A much-abused subject, dueling in 19th century America has spawned a vast treasury of legend and folklore, all too often contradictory and aggrandized. The wide gap between

ABOVE: Pair of large flintlock "dueling pistols" by Middletown, Conn. Maker Simeon North. Stylistically somewhat different (especially shape of handles) from the pair presented by the state of Connecticut to Macdonough. Ten and a half-inch octagon barrels. Fifty two-caliber smoothbore. Checkered walnut stocks; single set triggers (a.k.a. "hair triggers") engraved iron mountings. From the collection of William R. Orbelo.

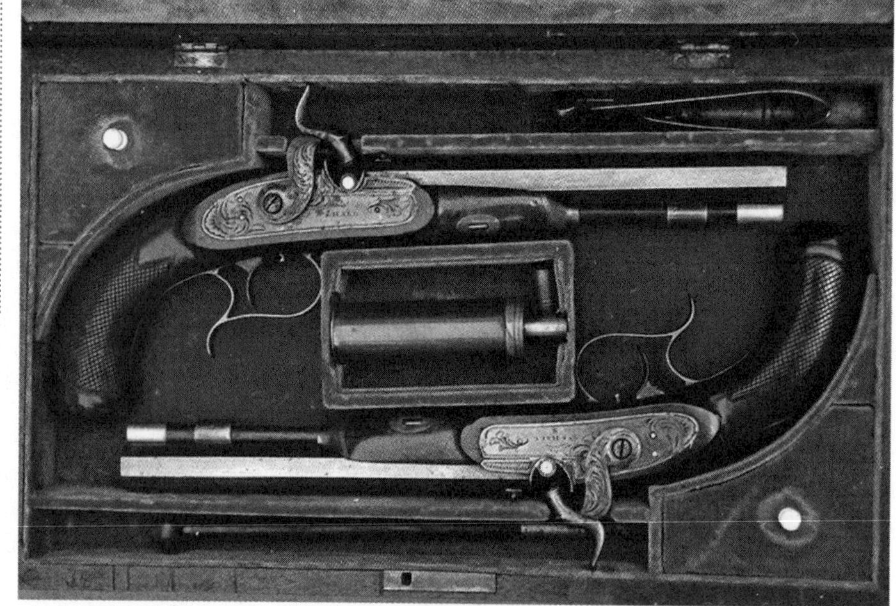

Cased pair of American percussion dueling pistols circa late 1830s – 1850 with their locks and 8-inch octagon barrels marked "S. HALL NEW YORK" .44-caliber with deep rifled bores. Black walnut halfstocks with checkered handles, each gun fitted with single set trigger (a.k.a. "hair triggers").

perception and reality has been further magnified, often altered, by time and re-telling. Dueling is undeniably a subject that fascinates our collective imagination and clamors for attention! Before probing the essentials requisite of "dueling pistols," it is relevant to offer introductory comment about the time-honored "gentlemanly" practice itself.

It is regrettable there has been such a great propensity to accept, unquestioned, most dueling accounts (almost without exception), merely because they appeared in print over a century and half ago. There is an obvious willingness to believe that newspapers and other literature of earlier centuries must be accurate and more honest than any published in more recent eras; the reverse is likely true. The subject is rife with fictitious reports, distortions and spurious quotations. For many who chose to write about dueling, the subject proved too tempting not to embellish...especially so as there was little likelihood of contradiction.

The practice of dueling to defend one's honor or take revenge for a real or imagined slight, was a somber part of the American scene, particularly in the pre-Civil War years. Although observed in all sections of America and by officers of various branches of the military, the vast majority of such contests took place in the South and Southwest and by mid-century, in California. Duels in America, that is, those conducted under a formalized set of rules, were fought almost exclusively with firearms. Handguns were the usual weapon of choice; infrequent encounters are noted with rifles or shotguns, or an occasional motley assortment of less conventional weapons (many of them merely fabrication and magnified by time). Most duels arranged under such precepts were customarily fought between men of equal standing, those who would have considered themselves the upper strata of society.

The most cursory examination of dueling reveals how remarkably widespread was its practice; enough so that laws were almost universally passed against the custom. Many states, as well as the federal

To the Public.

Whereas MARCUS GILLIAM, has by means the most base and false, tryed to destroy my reputation; and would not concede to any efforts that have been made by my friends to have the matter investigated; and at the same time declined to say that he was of opinion that I was guilty of the act, which has according to report, been laid to my charge; he has also refused to give me the satisfaction that an injured person has a right to require. I therefore pronounce him a *liar*, a *base slanderer* and a *coward*.

WM. NOBLE.

Petersburg, March 12, 1825.

To the Public.

The circumstances attending the loss of my Pocket Book were so strong, and so fully warranted my suspicions, as to convince me and every friend with whom I advised, that I could not, with propriety, accept the invitation contained in the note of William Noble. The ground of my refusal was, that I did not believe him to be a gentleman, which was distinctly stated to his friend who handed me the note. A regard to public opinion alone induces me to take this notice of an unprincipled vagabond & scoundrel.

Marius Gilliam.

MARCH 14th, 1825.

Public Challenge to a Duel (popularly referred to as "posting" an individual for a real or imagined slur, misbehavior, or other wrongdoing, etc.). Publicly posting printed broadsides or posters such as these was a conveniently proper and customary manner to challenge a transgressor to a duel. The act of bringing the accusation to public notice could hardly be ignored by the party thus disgraced. In Petersburg, Virginia, on March 12, 1825 William Noble publicly challenged Marius Gilliam to a duel for the reasons so-described here. Two days later Gilliam made public his refusal to the duel (highly unusual) naming, in turn his adversary William Noble "... an unprincipled vagabond and scoundrel." These mementos of that altercation may suggest a duel dodged... or perhaps a more bitter one in the offing?

government, administered oaths to elected and public officials to affirm that they had never engaged in, would not engage in, nor would be party to such contests.

Lorenzo Sabine (1803-1877), a highly regarded American historian, in his ***"Notes on Duels and Duelling...With Preliminary Historical Essay"*** (1855), possibly the very first credible study of dueling and rational examination of the subject, placed it neatly in perspective:

> *"In the United States, as in England, killing in a duel is murder; but here, as there, opinion is superior to law. Bennett,[1] as far as I have been able to ascertain, is the only person who has been executed for taking the life of a fellow-man in single combat since we became a free people. In some States, the parties have seldom been held even to answer; in others the inquiry in the courts has been confined to the single question of "...the fairness of the fight;" and this point determined in favor of the survivor, acquittal has followed as a matter of*

LEFT: A cased pair of American-made flintlock "dueling" pistols by Simeon North of Middletown, Connecticut. Fifty-four-caliber; smoothbores. Their 10-inch barrels each engraved: "VOTED BY THE GENERAL ASSEMBLY OF THE STATE OF CONNECTICUT TO COMMODORE THOMAS MAC DONOUGH." These were presented by the governor and legislature of the State of Connecticut circa 1817 to honor a native son for his capture of an English squadron of vessels on Lake Champlain Sept. 11, 1814. (Photograph courtesy of the Smithsonian Institution's Museum of American History.) A near-identical pair of S. North "duelers" was also presented by the Governor and Legislature of Connecticut to U.S. Naval Commodore Isaac Hull to commemorate his daring escapade while commanding the USS Constitution in the War of 1812.

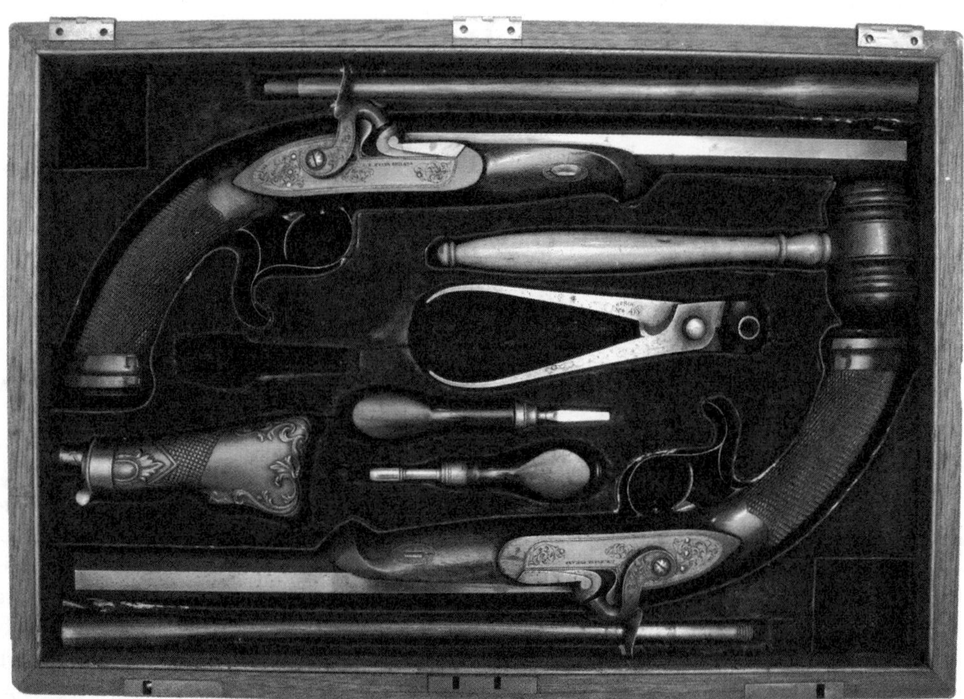

Cased pair of American-made percussion "dueling" pistols made by G.B. Evans of Phila. Caliber .48 smoothbore with 10-inch octagon barrels. Each pistol fitted with a large inscribed silver plate on its left side inscribed: "PRESENTED TO GENERAL EDWARD S. SALOMON. DECLARED BY THE VOTE OF HIS FELLOW CITIZENS AS THE MOST POPULAR SOLDIER OF COOK COUNTY [Illinois] AT THE FAIR OF THE CHICAGO [Military Training League] SEPT. 1867." During the Civil War Salomon led the 82nd Illinois Infantry through many heated battles including Gettysburg. In 1870 he was appointed by President Grant as "Governor" of the Territory of Washington.

1. Sabine refers to a duel fought in Illinois in 1820 in which William Bennett was indicted, tried and convicted of murder for killing his opponent in a duel with firearms and executed by hanging for the infraction.

course. In one State, we find the judge of a court on the dueling ground as a principal; and another, the ex-governor is there as a second; in a third, we read of principals and seconds, attended by an immense concourse in carriages, on horseback, and on foot...on their way to the appointed spot, without hindrance...[in other cases] the judicial records show the mockery of a sentence against the parties who had completed their arrangements for a mortal strike, of a fine of one dollar and an imprisonment of one minute. Yet in these states there are not only statute laws, but constitutional provisions in the book adverse to this relic of the Dark Ages."

Sabine's ***Notes on Duels and Duelling*** should be required reading for any student of the subject. Of the many American duels cited, some were merely named, while others were described in protracted detail. Immediately apparent is the frequency that such recourse was taken by U.S. senators, congressmen and legislators of all states; the very same that passed laws prohibiting dueling!

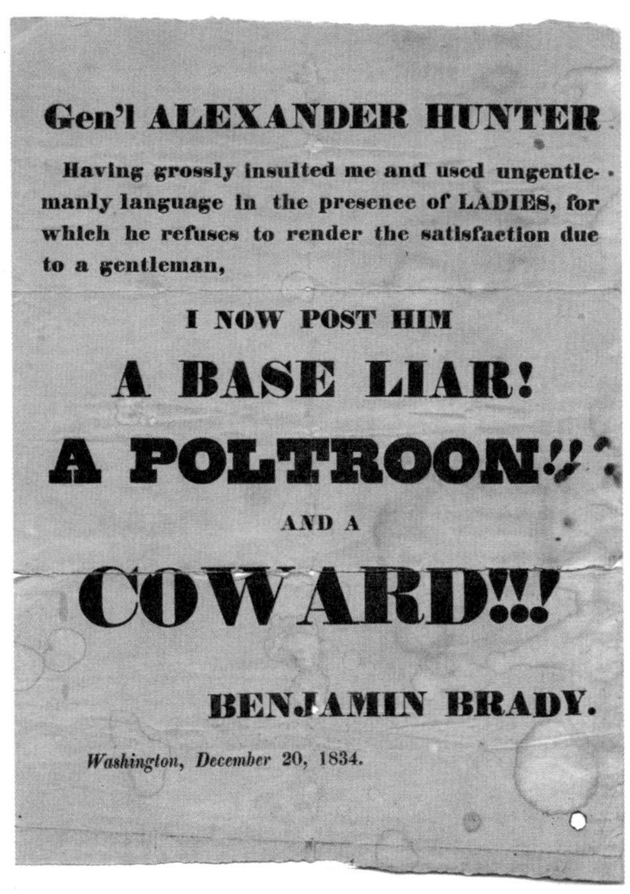
Gen'l ALEXANDER HUNTER

Having grossly insulted me and used ungentlemanly language in the presence of LADIES, for which he refuses to render the satisfaction due to a gentleman,

I NOW POST HIM

A BASE LIAR!

A POLTROON!!

AND A

COWARD!!!

BENJAMIN BRADY.

Washington, December 20, 1834.

PUBLICLY "POSTING" THE GENERAL FOR HIS UNGENTLEMANLY BEHAVIOR. Tantamount to an open challenge to a duel, and to be read by his fellow citizens in Washington D.C. No self-respecting gentleman (or military officer) could ignore this base insult and have his honor remain unblemished.

Defining "Duel" And "Dueling"

It is essential that the term duel be defined and distinguished from merely a fight or encounter between two individuals. Primary definitions of duel: "...a prearranged combat between two persons fought with deadly weapons according to an accepted code of procedure" or "a formal fight between two persons armed with deadly weapons; prearranged and witnessed by two others called seconds, one for each combatant" (from Random House and Webster's dictionaries, respectively).

The secondary definition of duel covers its broadest possible interpretation: "any contest between two persons or parties" or "any contest or encounter suggesting such a fight, usually between two persons." Hence, that might indicate a wide host of contests, such as a "verbal duel...judicial duel...a scholarly duel." It is in its secondary connotation that the terminology is most often employed, and where much illogical and distorted (often fictitious) dueling stories are hatched.

Overworking The Code Duello

Repeatedly encountered in dueling literature is the phrase code duello. It is a generalized or generic term to indicate the adoption of some established or negotiated rules, along general principles, that two duelists and their seconds agree upon to conduct a formalized duel in America. It is noted that on occasion, duels were never fought because the principals or their seconds were unable to agree on the very rules by which they were to be conducted.

Thoroughbreds Only, Please

In Europe, dueling, in its earlier eras, was almost exclusively the practice of the landed gentry. The bourgeoisie and the proletariat were generally not considered qualified (but that was soon to be modified). In the British social system, where (prior to the Industrial Revolution) one's blood counted more than his bank account, rules governing duels were apparently more closely observed. In some of its codes, even the seriousness of the offense and the acceptance of an apology to avert a duel had a ranking and a protocol. Countless breaches of behavior and deportment could precipitate a duel. Physical blows and questioning one's parentage, as serious as they were, did not appear to be as base or amoral as bedding down a lady of high birth.

With the passage of time it is clear that in England and likely much of Europe, the exclusivity of dueling and confining the practice only to the "landed gentry" became subject to considerable modification. The widespread development and advance of the Industrial Revolution, along with a simultaneous growth of an increasingly important and wealthy middle-class, accompanied a corresponding change in attitude towards what constituted the very terminology of "gentleman."

Some writers have maintained that few men participated in a duel seeking satisfaction from the death of their opponent; rather, the duel itself offered the opportunity to risk one's life by proving one's honor and enhanced reputation. That may have had validity in some duels, but could hardly be accurate as a generalization. As D. D. Bruce in ***Violence and Culture in the Antebellum South*** (1979) observed, dueling made men careful, compelling them to be thoughtful and respectful of their choice of words. The duel acted as a strong deterrent to impugning another gentleman's reputation; its mere threat was preventative. A decided distinction was made between authentic duels and common physical violence.

A *"Code Duello"* Custom-Made For Americans

South Carolina Governor John Lyde Wilson's ***Code of Honor; or Rules for the Government of Principals and Seconds***

Photographs of the title pages of the two most often mentioned dueling codes of Great Britain (right) and America (opposite page).

THE BRITISH

CODE OF DUEL:

A REFERENCE TO

THE LAWS OF HONOUR,

AND

THE CHARACTER OF GENTLEMAN.

Honesta mors turpi vita potior. TACITUS.
Ex abusu, non arguiter ad usum. AX. LEG.

AN APPENDIX,

IN WHICH IS STRICTLY EXAMINED,

THE CASE BETWEEN THE TENTH HUSSARS AND MR. BATTIER;
CAPT. CALLA'N, MR. FINCH, &c. NOTED.

LONDON:

KNIGHT AND LACEY, PATERNOSTER ROW,

1824.

in Dueling, first published in 1838 and reissued at various times to 1883 (and possibly later), contrast the American view of dueling to that of Europe. It is significant that it is the most often mentioned of the two American codes yet to surface with even a modicum of frequency.* Invariably it is accorded the status of the American counterpart to the widely known British codes; an importance clearly overemphasized by one and all. Circulation and recognition of American Codes were significantly less than credited. The most telling observation attesting to that fact was made by Sabine in his 1855 landmark reference ***Notes on Duel and Duelling*** where he asserted (italics added):

> *"I am not aware that American duellists have ever adopted a written code or that rules among them are entirely uniform. Certain points, however, are well established. I suppose for example, that in a duel upon a mere question of honor, and exchange of shots, whether with or without effect, is sufficient; while a combat of positive wrong or deep injury may be and ordinarily should be, continued until the aggressor offers satisfactory explanation or apology, or until the fall or disability of one of the parties…it seems well settled that the challenged, in the matters of weapon, time and distance, shall be governed by usage between gentlemen; and that propositions to sit across a cask of powder, to jump from a precipice or a building, to meet at midnight, at a lone or distant spot, without friend or surgeons, may be rejected by the challenger."*

Governor Wilson, a man who had engaged in numerous duels, specifically stated in the preface to his "***Code***": "I believe that nine duels out of ten, if not ninety-nine out of one hundred originate in the want of experience of the seconds." That clearly implied that any ***code duello*** observed for an American duel was most likely improvised at the whim of the participants or their seconds; if followed at all.

*The other code (unknown to Sabine in 1855) was ***"The Code of Honor; or The 39 Articles…Showing the Whole Manner in Which the Duel is to Conducted; with Amusing Anecdotes by a Southron"***[1]

Thus, it becomes apparent that formalized dueling codes, i.e. the ***code duello*** in the United States, were improvised and tailored by the combatants for the individual duel, taking into account some generally understood precepts of "gentlemanly" behavior and conventional, local customs.

And, those improvised, impromptu rules obviously made for an unmitigated miscellany of dueling formats. Their vagueness and ambiguity ceded a virtually bottomless supply of fresh fuel for the creative writing talents of the host of reporters, dueling aficionados, dilettantes and devotees possessing literary talents and a ready pen-in-hand…through the ages.

Pistols "Sanctioned" For Duels

Bearing in mind the foregoing commentary on the American conception of a ***code duello***, it becomes readily understandable that the specifics of firearms that might be chosen for weapons were likely to be generalized, if not dubious… and they were!

Nowhere in the ***"British Code of Duel"*** (1824), that widely known and obviously well-circulated work, are specifics revealed for the firearms that might be used other than alluding to the general type of ignition of the pistol in its instructions for the seconds "…To examine the pistols and see that they are perfect even to the flint, that preclude mis-fire; and then to load them equally in the presence of each other." From practical experience in personally viewing and handling antique English handguns customarily considered as "dueling pistols," they are invariably fitted with long (approximate 8-inch to 10-inch) smoothbore barrels with a wide range of calibers. Rifled bores were not prohibited, although they apparently were occasionally utilized (as was often the case on the continent).

Governor Wilson's 1838 ***Code of Honor or Rules for the Government of Principals and Seconds in Duelling*** specifically dealt with the subject. Its section "Arms

1. Sabine refers to a duel fought in Illinois in 1820 in which William Bennett was indicted, tried and convicted of murder for killing his opponent in a duel with firearms and executed by hanging for the infraction.

and the Manner of Loading and Presenting Them" states: "The arms used should be smooth-bore pistols, not exceeding 9 inches in length with flint and steel. Percussion pistols may be mutually used if agreed on, but to object on that account is lawful." The "***Code***" continued with instructions for loading, the manner of presenting pistols to participants and fighting positions with the pistols. Regardless of the suggestion for the use of "smooth-bore pistols" it is well recorded that many with rifled bores of varying calibers were chosen by a wide cross-section of duelists… as were others with set triggers (often termed "hair triggers").

THE CODE OF HONOR;

OR

RULES FOR THE GOVERNMENT

OF

PRINCIPALS AND SECONDS

IN

DUELLING

BY JOHN LYDE WILSON.

CHARLESTON, S. C.:
PRINTED BY JAMES PHINNEY,
In the rear of 48 Broad-st.
1858.

The American Edition of 1858 shown here was merely a later reprint of the original 1838 Edition…written by the Governor of South Carolina John Lyde Wilson. Although often accorded the status of being well-known and recognized by American duellists (and the myriad of authors, reporters and dueling aficionados/disciples that followed), this American code had but very minor circulation or recognition of its existence!

Defining "Dueling Pistol"

In much the same manner as they embroidered the practice of dueling…a wealth of misconception, myth and unverified vague tradition flourished alongside the characterization and history of the "dueling pistol." It is apparently customary for collectors, historians and authors to believe there is a "hard and fast" authoritative definition of exactly what constitutes a dueling pistol. It became evident upon examining the subject that no such generally sanctioned rendering, contemporary to the era of their usage, or concurrent with modern arms collecting literature, was or has been arrived at by a general consensus. Other than the single, broad qualifying feature of a "smooth-bore barrel" (i.e. without rifling) neither the recorded American code…nor the more widely recognized British code, contained further qualifying features for the pistol. It is obvious that there was, indeed, broad latitude as to the type handgun British or American duelists might choose to employ. Thus, the enigma: Did many well-known American and British gunmakers devote some of their manufacturing and sales energies to the development of a style of handgun whose features were peculiar to and designed specifically for the practice of dueling, as many authors have proclaimed or would have you believe? Or, was the handgun that emerged to be "traditionally" accepted by arms historians and collectors as the "classic" dueling pistol merely the result of normal evolutionary innovations and improvements in all firearms and advances in industrial and manufacturing techniques…the result of numerous influences, dueling merely being one among many? Those questions have apparently never been posed. They are deserving of deeper investigation and resolution. Resorting to the threadbare analogy of "which came first, the chicken or the egg?" reduces the dilemma to its essentials and likely best expresses the quandary.

On reviewing the subjects "dueling pistols" and "dueling" in a generous cross-section of antique arms literature, it becomes apparent that most treatises and discourses describing the development and evolution of "dueling pistols" are ostensibly predicated on theory and assumption, if not outright conjecture. Many writers, including those of the nineteenth century, reached plausible, reasoned conclusions that almost every innovation introduced on a particular style of large, non-military handguns was designed specifically as a result of…and for the sole benefit and use by those engaged in the practice of dueling. However, there does not appear to be solid documentary evidence to substantiate such common and deep-rooted beliefs. Those conclusions and explanations appear to be based more on the allure, imagery and the romanticized aura surrounding dueling, and are often in contention with one another. The assumption that they were designed solely for dueling…and therefore should be made more accurate, possess better balance and be easier to handle than any normal handgun of those respective eras, appears tenuous at best…merely presumptions taken on faith from some earlier writer, news reporter or weapons specialist's article which, by virtue of time, became deep-rooted in arms lore. There is no doubting those same handguns commonly termed "dueling pistols" were used in such contests…or that some innovations popularly attributed to their development may be feasibly and reasonably granted them. Lest I be castigated for demeaning the widely admired, if not awe-inspiring dueling pistol, it cannot remain unsaid (and reiterated here) that the subject of dueling did decidedly play a role in the early development of some of these pistols… and was obviously instrumental in naming the entire genre. Printed and documentary evidence exists that well-known, widely recognized British gunmakers (notably Rigby, Wogdon and Manton) recommended, developed and adopted certain innovations they asserted were designed specifically for dueling pistols.

The actual term "dueling pistol" was apparently in common usage, although used sparingly for an advertisement or printed label of a British gunmaker or merchant in the early 19th century. The same use of those words "dueling pistol" is rarely observed in advertisements by an American firearms merchant or gunmaker. Should a concerted effort be made, it is likely that other indication of use of the terminology will surface. However, the very fact that the practice of dueling was frowned upon by society in general (even though widely practiced) and that it was generally prohibited by legislative statute and a miscellany of (governmental) ordinances, would ostensibly preclude gunmakers from devoting their special talents to fabricating weapons designed expressly for such purpose. Nor would it be thought prudent to be noted for promoting and trafficking in weapons exclusively intended for their clientele to use for unlawful purposes; all the foregoing to the detriment of other "common" handguns (excepting specific target types) that were more likely to be employed in potentially life-threatening situations. And further: it is seemingly inconsistent to infer that a dueling pistol, by virtue of its implied use, required greater accuracy (or as some have implied, less accuracy!) or ease of handling than any other form of large handgun. Improvements, changes and innovations on all types of firearms are more reasonably attributed to normal technical and manufacturing innovations, fashion trends, cost of production and selling price. Thus, the origins and accuracy and very definition of "true dueling weapon" are dubious.

It is justly logical to conclude that there is no fundamental difference to large size, single shot, flintlock or percussion handguns that may have been sold in their day as officer's pistols...holster pistols...target pistols...or dueling pistols! The vagueness of terminology has the earmarks of belonging solely in the eye of the beholder...or the gunmaker...or arms scholar...or just as plausibly, the creative writer of both earlier and current eras. Of all those various named handgun categories, none has aroused as much interest nor bequeathed such a legacy of disputable and uncertain arms lore as those said to have been specifically designed and purchased for...or actually used in a formalized duel. There is an obvious aura and wide range of fascination...from the valorous to the macabre, surrounding the practice of dueling and those handguns generally considered to have been specifically designed for that deliberate intent. With the passage of time and the many early and repeated usages of the terminology in the general literature of America and Britain, (especially firearms treatises) the "dueling pistol" has become a unique, yet indeterminate entity. An examination of firearms literature specifically dealing with dueling pistols clearly reflects a wide disparity among authors as to the attribution and development of innovations, modifications and technical improvements in handguns said to be specifically designed for, and unique to dueling. Risking redundancy: A significant flaw, apparently inherent with such studies is the almost complete lack of documentation in the form of footnotes alluding to valid sources. Also lacking are direct quotations from gunmakers, merchants, duelists or others contemporary to the fabrication of those same dueling firearms. All too often such treatises, laboring under the guise of accuracy, do not include even a sparse bibliography of published references utilized by the writer for their sources.

In view of preliminary rational study and personal experience in handling many of these same pistols, accompanied with an awareness of the diverse personalities that originally owned...or were presented with them, it is reasonably concluded that the term "dueling pistol" is fundamentally generic, to include handguns of varying configurations, designed for a variety of roles and functions...in similar manner to the collective terminology "pepperbox", "deringer", "bootleg pistol" or even the unseemly "Saturday Night Special". It is suitably comparable to other eponymous names embodied early in the formal and informal history of firearms... and subsequently the jargon of firearms collecting. The significant, and most notable, dissimilarity was the mystique and sense of fearlessness, if not chivalry, that accompanied the "dueling" pistol. Its very name carried with it a certain poignancy and aggressive spirit...much as the legendary terminology "Bowie Knife" is all-embracing and entered the language in a similar manner. And that subject, too, has proven equally contentious as to the origins of its name! Thus it becomes evident that this genre of handgun had captured the imagination and fascination (if not morbid curiosity) of the gunmaker, arms merchant and the consumer (who was not necessarily a duelist!) of their day... and the popular writer and collector of present day, allowing the terminology permanent residency in the language.

Further demonstration of the incongruity of the terminology "dueling pistol" and confirmation that the nomenclature was generic and merely a term of convenience is apparent when

Cased set of percussion "dueling pistols" by one of America and Philadelphia's most noted makers HENRY DERINGER. Known almost exclusively for his small, pocket-sized, single-shot percussion pistols (of which there were many imitators during their period of manufacture) he is also known to have produced a few pistols similar to these large "duelers" this pair with 9 1/2-inch barrels and also marked with name of the Louisiana dealer for whom they were made by Deringer: "MAN'D FOR A. MILLSPAUGH / WASHINGTON, LA." Fitted in their original leather-covered wooden case, red velvet lined, accompanied by their original accessories.

viewing the below illustrated cased and matched pair of fine quality American percussion pistols of the type normally considered and classified as "duelers:"

Made by, and fully marked, "G.B. EVANS – PHILADELPHIA" and representative of the best of the American arms maker's craftsmanship, each pistol bears a large, silver plaque inset on its left side engraved with the lengthy inscription: ***"Presented to General Edward S. Salomon. Declared by the vote of his fellow citizens as the most popular Soldier of Cook County*** [Illinois] at the Fair of the Chicago [Military Training League], September, 1867." Each is 17 inches overall with 10-inch octagon barrels; caliber 48 smooth-bores. Breech of barrels, barrel tangs, sidelocks and hammers are profusely scroll engraved. Walnut halfstocks with checkered handles. Guns are fitted with single set triggers (i.e. "hair triggers"). General Salomon had earlier led the 82nd Illinois Infantry Regiment through many heated battles of the Civil War including Gettysburg. In 1870 he was appointed by President Grant as the governor of the Territory of Washington.

Should that fine set not prove the point, this spectacular pair by one of America's best known early arms makers, Simeon North of Connecticut further supports the contention that the terminology "dueling pistol" is merely generic: In the collections of the Smithsonian Institution in Washington D.C. is this historical matched pair of elegantly embellished, gold mounted and engraved flintlock, half-stock 54-caliber smoothbore pistols; locks marked "S.NORTH/MIDDLETOWN/CONN." Their 10-inch barrels each engraved: "VOTED BY THE GENERAL ASSEMBLY OF THE STATE OF CONNECTICUT TO COMMODORE THOMAS MACDONOUGH [sic]". The pistols were presented by the governor and legislature of the state of Connecticut circa 1817 to honor a native son, U.S. Naval Commodore Macdonough's capture of an English squadron on Lake Champlain on Sept. 11th 1814.

Also on record is a near-identical Simeon North set of flintlock pistols, made on order of the General Assembly of Connecticut and presented by the governor to U.S. Naval Commodore Isaac Hull to commemorate the escape of the U.S.S. Constitution from a British squadron while on her passage from Chesapeake Bay to Boston during the War of 1812.

And… if those above misnamed "dueling pistols" do not prove the point that such terminology is generic to include a broad cross-section of other handgun types, here are two more that firmly buttress that contention.

Made by noted Baton Rouge, Louisiana firearms and Bowie knife makers. Large percussion halfstock "dueling pistol" marked "SEARLES & F'PATRICK [sic]" on the back action lock. Nine-inch octagon barrel; large caliber. Daniel Searles and Rees Fitzpatrick were well-known gunsmiths whose shops were located near each other. Although the most of their work was independent, this pistol is evidence of a short-lived partnership. Both makers are also known (and played a role) in the legend of the American Bowie knife.

Well illustrated and described in the often quoted ***"The British Duelling Pistol"*** (by John Atkinson, 1978) are two pairs of classically designed British flintlock "duelling pistols" (styled similarly to the same genre of American manufacture). One set by the noted London maker H. W. Mortimer was made for no less than King George III… a fellow hardly likely to be engaged in single combat! The second pair of fine "saw handle" duelers, circa 1815-1820, were made for and presented to the Duke of Wellington by the East India Co. They are considered by the author to be representative of the classic dueling type.

Other so-called "duelers" are known and recorded having belonged to, being presented to or purchased by citizens and officers with no known record of having engaged in a duel or any proclivity for doing so. Were such pistols as those illustrated and described here (or many others similarly owned and presented), all of which are categorized under the general terminology "dueling pistols," to have been specifically designed (and in the public's concept, uniquely adapted) for dueling, they would hardly have been found suitable for an organizational, governmental (or other) presentation to a public figure, reigning monarch, distinguished personage or national hero! Nor would they have been wielded only incidentally by ordinary citizenry for the more conventional roles of a handgun.

Having ventured into relatively unexamined territory (and possibly belabored the subjects to the dueling devotee's vexation) it is essential to recognize that these large single shot, non-military flintlock and percussion handguns are invariably representative of the best of the American gunmaker's craftsmanship and artistry. The mere fact that "dueling pistol" has been the traditional, generically applied nomenclature to describe and classify a broad range of styles and types…to the detriment of their other, possibly more urgent functions…is imperative to cite and recognize. There is but slightest likelihood (if any) that there were the multitudes of "gentlemen" (English or American) seeking uniquely designed handguns with which to engage in duels, as might appear to have been indicated in dueling (and firearms) literature. Consequently, the marketplace for such narrowly specialized "dueling pistols" was relatively small. Judging from the great many gunmakers on both sides of the Atlantic known to have produced "dueling pistols" and the specimens yet surviving of those same type handguns, it becomes further obvious that the purposes for which they were actually designed were multifold…and their generic name merely being all-embracing. There is no doubting that the inspiration for some innovations or improvements in these handguns was influenced by dueling. However, there is every reason to believe that the trade for which they were sold was generalized and that the great majority of buyers were men who were neither duelists nor preparing for the eventuality of a duel. Thus, the conclusion, that the wide spectrum of uses for which these handguns were designed, purchased and put to use (dueling included) lends them considerably greater significance than the narrowly confined designation "dueling pistol" to which they have been confined.

Perhaps the entire subject and foregoing may have been placed in its clearest perspective by Colonel William Orbelo, well-known arms author and collector of American dueling pistols. When asked what was the difference between a target pistol and a dueling pistol, he candidly answered: "….The target!"

This article is an abridged version of *"Dueling and Dueling Pistols"* that appears as Chapter VII-F of the new edition of *Flayderman's Guide to Antique American Firearms...and their Values, 9th Edition.* The book is available through local bookstores, or from Krause Publications. MSRP: $39.99

RIFLE SCOPES THAT MAKE SENSE

by Wayne van Zwoll

ABOVE: **The fine new Swarovski 1.7-10x42 is truly versatile. Here Wayne uses it on a Remington 700 Ti.**

"Foolproof, streamlined scope with windage and elevation adjustments built into the mount.... Factory sealed with nitrogen, changes in altitude or temperature cannot cause condensation or fogging. Nothing to get out of order ... made to last a lifetime."
– ad for the Leupold Pioneer, circa 1950.

Just big enough

Not long ago I visited a handful of gunshops on assignment to rank their level of customer service. At one I hovered over the optics counter and asked the young clerk for an all-around rifle scope.

"You'll want a 3 to 9 by 50," he told me with the confidence borne of youth. He fished one out.

"What do those numbers mean?"

"The 3 and the 9 show the magnification range: 3 to 9 power. The 50 is the field of view in yards at 100 yards." He was pleased with himself, and it seemed only charitable to leave him that way.

Of course, he was wrong. Field of view in a variable scope changes when you change power and has nothing to do with the third number. That number – here 50 – is the diameter of the front or objective lens in millimeters. Field is independent of lens diameters. Truth is, small scopes usually have bigger fields than scopes with bells the size of oil cans. That's because, as a rule, small scopes are of low magnification, which offers a wide field of view. Increase power in a variable by turning up the dial, and your field shrinks, no matter how big the front lens. High-power variables typically have big objectives because magnification also shrinks the exit pupil, a measure of the light reaching your eye. Big front lenses compensate by hiking exit pupil size (the formula: objective diameter / power = exit pupil). But that magnum glass gives you a brighter sight picture only at high magnification in poor light. The pupil of a healthy human eye dilates to about 6mm in the dimmest of shooting light. The exit pupil in a scope of modest power may exceed 6mm, giving the eye all the light it can use, without big front glass.

The clerk obviously knew nothing of this. But he squandered his credibility earlier by not asking me what I wanted a scope for. A 3-9x50 is indeed versatile, but it's not a sight I'd install on a 308 carbine for use mainly in the Poconos. I'd not fit it to a 25-06 in Utah either. Though both cartridges work well on a variety of game, they're best served by different sights. Besides, a 3-9x50 isn't my first pick for anything.

"Thank you." I handed the scope back. A glance at the stacks of boxes behind this clerk told me he was expecting to sell mostly high-power variables with more magnification than I would ever need. More, I suspect, than you'll ever need too.

If bigger were always better, the affluent among us would be living in gymnasiums and driving cement trucks to work. Oddly enough, many hunters carry the biggest scopes they can fit on their rifles.

A big scope adds weight to your rifle.

A big scope has inertia that can wrest it free of the rings' grip during recoil.

A big scope must be mounted high above the bore, forcing your cheek off the comb to aim.

A big scope doesn't slide easily into saddle scabbards.

A big scope can destroy a rifle's balance, fore and aft, and makes it top-heavy.

A big scope costs more than a small scope of the same quality.

Big scopes are sized to give you a bright picture and high resolution at high magnification, which not only restricts field of view but also affects eye relief, the distance from your eyeball to the ocular lens. It's easier to make a scope with generous, non-critical eye relief if magnification is low.

Too much magnification is a recent plague. The first receiver-mounted scopes were designed for hunting, by and for hunters used to shooting iron sights. They had to deliver a big field of view and plenty of eye relief. Bill Weaver's $19 Model 330 scope, a 3x brought out in 1930 when Bill was only 24, became the most successful short scope of its day. During the 1930s new scopes appeared from myriad companies, many of which vanished after World War II. One of the best sights came from Rudolph Noske's shop. Gun Digest editor John Amber praised it. Available in 2 3/4x or 4x, the Noske "A" featured a 7/8-inch tube 10 inches long – with 6 inches of eye relief! Prices, in 1939: $52 and $54.

Next came the Lyman Alaskan. In the gun-sight business since 1878, Lyman had acquired rights to Winchester's scope line in 1928, to Stevens scopes a year later. The Winchester A5 became the Lyman 5A. The 3x Lyman 438 showed Stevens bloodlines. Both these Lymans wore achromatic lenses by Bausch & Lomb. The 2-3/4x Alaskan, introduced in 1937, is surely Lyman's best-known scope. It had a 7/8-inch tube 10 1/2 inches long, with B&L glass, 5 inches of eye relief and a 40-foot field. During the '40s, when snipers used this scope in WWII, the Alaskan sold to hunters for $50 – and a Winchester Model 70 listed for under $100! Wray Hageman, the Alaskan's designer, followed with the 4x Challenger in 1948, the 6x, 8x and 10x Wolverines in 1953. So Lyman entered an era of ever more powerful sights.

Post-war scope developments came fast. The magnesium fluoride lens coating pioneered by Zeiss engineer A. Smakula in the late 1930s led to even better films to boost brightness. Nitrogen purging made scopes fog-free, and reticles were engineered to stay in their optical center. During the 1960s Leupold built a new factory, variable power wooed hunters and rifles began appearing without iron sights. But even as powerful, complex scopes redefined the market, earlier, more modest designs remained practical.

The 6x Leupold on Wayne's Montana/Serengeti rifle in 257 Roberts is a fine open-country sight.

LEFT: **The fine new Swarovski 1.7-10x42 is truly versatile. Here Wayne uses it on a Remington 700 Ti.**

Modesty is a virtue

Some years ago, nestled behind a spotting scope on a cold, flat rock in the iron grip of a Wyoming dawn, I tried to blow life into my fingers. A ceiling the color of sea ice slowly brightened coulees, then the islands of sage. The buck appeared as expected. He was a big buck but far away. He vanished into a cut.

I hunted him in careful half-loops to the brink of the long gully, as if jump-shooting mallards. At a corner, where the cut yawned, we met eye to eye. Rocketing from his bed, the four-point bounded up the 10-foot bank and raced across the prairie. At 30 feet, I should have piled him up. But I'd left my variable scope set at 10x. The reticle's bounce, and that of the deer, jerked the animal in and out of my tiny field of view. Only the most generous dose of luck gave me the kill – after two ineffective shots.

Later that morning, I watched through a binocular as my partner stalked a deer. It darted off just before I heard the faint report of Jim's rifle. But the buck didn't drop. I grabbed my 300 Dakota, cinched the sling tight and held at backline. The trigger broke as the crippled deer paused at the lip of a deep ravine. Another sprint, then the "whuck" of a strike. My 180-grain Scirocco had shredded the lungs. Though my scope had been set at 4x, this 300-yard shot was not difficult.

Now, 4x is modest magnification indeed. But modesty is a virtue in rifle scopes. Modest power. Modest dimensions. At least, that's my view. For hunting big game, I've seldom wished for magnification of over 6x, and have come to like the low profiles and easy heft of fixed-power models, especially 3x and 2-1/2x sights with tube-diameter noses. They complement trim rifles, slide into scabbards like Peacemakers into gunfighting leather. They can be mounted low so the rifle points like a shotgun.

Modest magnification ensures bright images in dark thickets, and it is astonishingly effective at long range. While increasingly disenchanted with the notion of taking long shots, I've killed two animals at over 400 yards with 4x sights. They could not have been better killed with more powerful glass. As bigger and more complex scopes command a growing share of the market, I find none more appealing – or useful – than the slender fixed-power models whose numbers diminish with each passing year.

Besides giving you fast aim, a low-power, fixed-power scope – or a variable turned to the low end – can help you estimate yardage quickly. I know, for instance, the coverage at 100 yards of the center wire in my 4x Zeiss Conquest. Superimposing the reticle on a distant deer gives me a close read of the range. Of course, that procedure works at any magnification. But with the power turned up, you'll take longer to find the animal in the smaller field. And you may wish to aim with lower magnification, either because the deer is moving or you're too unsteady to control the sight at high power. If you're constantly changing power on a variable, you've another strike against you, because you won't recall how much that second-plane reticle subtends at all settings, if indeed you remember the setting! Aiming should be a simple act. Anything that complicates it or slows you down is bad business.

When guiding other hunters, I caution them to keep variables at low power: "You'll always have time to turn that dial up for a long shot, but a short shot is often urgent." Nonetheless, I forgot one day, and a client who deserved a big bull missed his chance at two that might have made the records book. The elk trotted across a broad opening just 80 yards off. He couldn't find them in his sight, a 2.5-8x variable he'd left at 8x. I felt his pain.

For most big game, you don't need much magnification to make a lethal hit, even if the range is long. A couple of years ago, I hunted into a herd of elk spread across a charred mountain face. Climbing onto a parallel ridge, I got above the cows and slinged up in prone over a rock. When the bull fed into my crosswire, he was 300 yards out. I could have turned up my 3-9x Leupold VX-II, but didn't. Instead, I laid the intersection just under his backline and squeezed. The 250-grain softpoint from my 358 Norma flew true; had the elk been a grapefruit, I'd have hit it. I've measured the chest depth of many elk. Mature bulls routinely tape 27 to 28 inches, back to brisket. A target that big is easy to quarter in a 3x scope as far as you can consistently hold bullets within 3 minutes of angle. Magnification over 4x is superfluous most of the time. Remember that a 4x scope makes a deer at 300 yards appear as big as one looks to the naked eye at 75 – an easy distance for a rifleman using iron sights. And a reticle obscures less rib than does a front bead!

No, you can't aim as precisely with a low-power scope; but under field conditions, you can't aim precisely with any scope. A bigger target image comes with more pronounced reticle movement; you just see more clearly what low magnification won't tell you. It's more than you need to know most of the time.

I have shot one deer with a 20x scope. It was a Coues buck, a dainty creature not much bigger than a collie. It appeared in the purple light of an Arizona dawn, ghosting through desert scrub. I dropped to my belly, snapping the bipod legs forward on the David Miller rifle. The shot alley was narrow at ground level, but a 30-caliber bullet is slender. I guessed the range at 400 yards. The deer stepped into the scope field, I nudged the reticle up what looked like 16 inches and fired. The 168-grain Sierra from the 300 Weatherby hit exactly where I had hoped it would, 410 paces away.

That would have been a tough shot with a 4x scope. David Miller and Curt Crum, who spend a lot of time hunting Coues deer in open country, rely on Leupold 6.5-20x scopes to reach bucks that would be difficult if not impossible to approach. Their 300 Weatherby rifles have the precision to drill vitals at ranges that test their marksmanship. But they practice a great deal on quarter-mile targets, and their hunting style all but precludes close shots. My preference for walking has led me to lighter rifles, more modest optics.

A word on reticles for big game: Choose a reticle bold enough to see easily. Better that a crosswire looks a bit heavy in good light at long range than to lose a fine reticle when you must fire quickly up close. German #4 and #7 reticles rank among my favorites. They're versions of the plex reticles sold Stateside, all of which came from Leupold's Duplex. European renditions have squared-off, not pointed, posts. They're easier to use in determining yardage. I also like their more open center – though Leupold now has a Duplex with shorter posts. I also like a dot – provided it is big enough to stand out in dark places. Remember when specifying a dot that size in minutes is the number of inches subtended at 100 yards, and that a low-power scope needs "more minutes" of dot than a high-power sight.

By the numbers

The bantamweights in optical sights are low-power, fixed-power models with tube-diameter front ends. More popular are variables of similar profile. They're a tad heavier, and the power dial increases the length of the ocular housing. If you crawl the stock like I do, forward scope placement matters. Extra-long oculars can put the scope's rear lens too near your eye for a full sight picture – or to clear your brow during recoil. Special bases or rings are a fix. Herewith specifications for the most compact of low-power scopes:

brand, model, power x objective diameter	length (in.)	weight (oz.)	field (ft.@100 yds.)
Burris Compact 4x20	8.4	8.0	24
Burris Fullfield 1.75-5x20	10.7	10.0	55-20
Burris Fullfield 2.5x20	10.8	10.0	55
Bushnell Banner 4x20	11.5	10.0	27
Kahles 1.1-4x24 (30mm tube)	10.9	14.7	119-35
Leupold Vari-X III 1.5-5x20	9.3	9.5	66-23
Leupold Vari-X II 1-4x20	9.2	9.0	75-28
Leupold 2.5x20	8.0	6.5	40
Pentax Lightseeker 2.5x25	10.0	9.0	55
Pentax Lightseeker 0/Vx27 (0-4x)	8.9	10.3	54-15
Nikon Monarch UCC 1.5-4.5x20	10.0	9.3	50-17
Nikon Monarch UCC 1.5-4.5x20 EER	10.0	9.3	34-11
Schmidt & Bender 1.25-4x20 (30mm)	11.5	14.3	96-30
Sightron 2.5x20	10.3	9.0	41
Simmons 1.5-5x20		9.5	10.8
Simmons 2.5x20	7.4	7.0	24
Swarovski 1.25-4x24 (30mm)	10.6	12.7	98-32
Swift 1.5-4.5x21	10.9	9.6	69-25
Swift 1x20	7.5	9.6	113
Weaver V3 1-3x20	9.1	8.5	87-31
Weaver K2.5 2.5x20	9.6	7.1	37
Zeiss ZM/Z 1.25-4x24 (30mm)	11.4	16.7	96-30
Zeiss VM/V 1.1-4x24 (30mm)	11.8	14.5	108-31

When comparing scopes, remember that eye relief and field of view are coupled to magnification in an "optical triangle." Increase eye relief, and field shrinks. All 2.5x scopes and many 4x models will give you more than the 24 feet in a Leupold M8 4x. That relatively tight field is the price of generous eye relief, a Leupold trademark. Still, a 24-foot window lets you see much more country than a variable cranked to 9x (around 12 feet), 12x (10 feet) or 14x (8 feet). It allows you to lead a pronghorn buck with afterburners on, sort out a string of caribou without losing the middle, keep track of elk sifting in and out of aspens.

The Swift 1x scope delivers a panoramic view, as do other 1x models (also called 0x because they do not magnify). I don't care for them. Some magnification is helpful, and up to 3x or 4x you can aim as quickly as with a wide-open aperture sight. Also, magnification of less than 2.5x shows you the barrel on most rifles. That can be distracting, and it's why I'm not keen on low-power variables. If you must have a variable, make it a 2-7x or 2.5-8x. On the low end, you'll be fast enough to tumble deer that burst from the shintangle a car-length away. Dial it up, and you have the resolution for shots across soybean fields. Most deer hunters buy mid-size variables. My surveys for the Rocky Mountain Elk Foundation show that in elk camps you'll find more 3-9x and 3.5-10x sights than all other variables combined!

Notice that the lightest fixed-power scopes weigh 10 ounces or less. You'll appreciate these sights when toting a rifle all day. Light weight also helps the scope stay put in the rings under stiff recoil. There's no ideal weight for a scope. Good lenses can be heavy, and you want the sight to be durable too. My rule of thumb: a hunting scope and mount should come to no more than 15 percent of the rifle's bare weight. So on a 7-pound rifle, you're allowed 16.8 ounces. Reduce rifle weight to 6 pounds, and your scope ceiling drops to 14.4 ounces. Steel bases and rings look nice but add ounces and are no more effective than the best alloy mounts – like those furnished by Gary Turner at Talley (just an ounce apiece!). A lightweight sight keeps the rifle's center of gravity low between your hands, where it belongs.

Here's a size and weight chart of some popular mid-range variables. Bigger objectives (choosing a 50mm lens instead of 40mm glass) typically adds more weight than does a step up in tube diameter (from 1 inch to 30mm).

If you stick with 4x or 6x fixed-power scopes, you needn't fret about weight.

brand, model, power x objective diameter	length (in.)	weight (oz.)
Bushnell 3-9x50	15.5	19.0
Kahles 2.5-10x50 (30mm tube)	13.0	17.5
Leupold 3.5-10x50	12.0	15.0
Nikon 3-9x40	12.5	12.5
Pentax 3-9x43	12.5	15.0
Schmidt & Bender 3-12x50 (34mm tube)	14.0	28.5
Swarovski 3-10x42	12.5	12.5
Tasco 3-9x50	12.5	16.0
Zeiss 2.5-10x48 (30mm tube)	15.5	24.0

Even a 6x42 can slip under the 12-ounce mark. With it, you should have enough magnification for even open-country hunting in the West. The picture you get with a 6x at 300 yards is essentially what you'd see over open sights at 50. If you prefer a variable of 2 to 3-1/2x on the low end and 7 to 10x on top, you'll have a wider magnification range than you need. An objective of 42mm gives you plenty of brightness at dawn and dusk at the middle powers – those you'll most likely use. For 2-7x and 2 1/2-8x scopes, the 32mm and 36mm front ends make most sense. You'll do well to leave a variable set at the bottom power or at one you expect to use for a shot – certainly no higher than 6x. When toting a variable scope on a deer or elk hunt, I usually keep it at 4x.

While the 3-9x40x is unarguably one of the most versatile big game scopes, I'll choose Leupold's 2 1/2-8x36 or the traditional Swarovski 3-9x36 for their smaller objectives. That is, if I can't have a fixed-power sight.

Popular pipe

Since the 1950s scopes have, like me, added girth. A little, in each case, has proven useful. But as with people, scopes too big around the middle neither look good nor perform well.

During my youth, you could buy scopes with 7/8-inch tubes (the Lyman Alaskan) and with 26mm chassis (Lyman's Challenger and the Stith Bear Cub, plus European models). The 1-inch scope eventually gained enough traction to become the new standard Stateside. By the time 30mm scopes assaulted the U.S. market, they'd already upstaged 26mm sights in Europe. Big has since gotten bigger. Schmidt and Bender now offers 34mm scopes in its tactical line. Shooters support the trend.

Here's how historically common tube sizes compare:

Tube Diameter	inches	millimeters
3/4-inch	.750	19.05mm
7/8-inch	.875	22.23mm
1-inch	1.000	25.40mm
	1.024	26.00mm
	1.181	30.00mm
	1.339	34.00mm

A low-power scope with extended eye relief is ideal for takedown rifles like this Browning 81.

"A 30mm tube is stronger than a 1-inch," an optics engineer told me. Then he shrugged. "That's all the benefit you'll see in a hunting scope, unless the erector assembly is also oversize." He explained that many 30mm tubes feature the erector lenses used in comparable 1-inch scopes, so there's really no optical edge. "You do get increased latitude in windage and elevation adjustments, because the erector assembly has more room to move." That's good news if you must dial up lots of elevation for very long shooting, or correct laterally for a skewed mount. Otherwise, you might as well stay with the 1-inch tube. "Strength is an academic issue," my friend concluded. "Unless you throw your rifle under a road grader, you'll never test the durability of a one-inch alloy scope body."

Neither will you see less light through its lenses. Brightness is a function of exit pupil size, and of the quality of lens coatings. A 4.5-14x40 scope set at 8x has a 5mm exit pupil, whether the tube is 30mm or an inch in diameter, whether the erector assembly is oversize or not. Bigger glass improves resolution, so theoretically 1-inch erectors will play second fiddle to those built specifically for 30mm tubes. But given high-quality lenses throughout both scopes, any difference will be difficult if not impossible to detect.

Kimber's Caprivi is equipped here with a low-power Leupold variable, a "dangerous game" sight.

When you boost diameter, you increase weight, right? Well, not significantly, unless the lenses in the erector assembly grow too. And then you probably won't feel the change. For example, Leupold lists a 30mm "Long Range" version of its 4.5-14x40 VX III, a 1-inch scope in standard form. Both weigh 15.4 ounces. The Leupold 6.5-20x40 EFR Target with 1-inch tube scales 17 ounces, an ounce more than a 6.5-20x40 "Long Range" 30mm scope! The difference: the EFR's front-end adjustable objective, a tad heavier than the turret-mounted AO knob on the LR model. If you make such comparisons, be sure the scopes are equivalent in other ways. It's common, for instance, to see a 30mm illuminated version of a 1-inch scope with standard reticle. The bigger scope typically weighs a quarter-pound more, but the additional weight is in the illumination system, not the tube.

Except on 1,000-yard rifles where adjustment latitude matters, I prefer 1-inch tubes, mainly for cosmetic reasons. Paired with sensibly proportioned front and rear bells, a 1-inch body doesn't appear to burden a featherweight rifle. A bulkier scope on a lightweight rifle looks awkward – like a huge camper on a pickup that strains to carry it. Scopes with big tubes also tend to be heavier than those with 1-inch pipe. Extra bulk mounted high can make a rifle top-heavy. In wind it can also act as a sail.

Leupold now lists more 30mm tubes than 1-inch in its VX-L line. Eight of its 18 VX-IIIs have the big body – plus all VX-7s and Mark 4 Long Range Tactical scopes. Swarovski's latest Z6 stable and more than half the Zeiss line of hunting sights (the top-end Victorys) feature a 30mm tube. In fact, few companies of note in the hunting optics field lack a 30mm sight. Most of these scopes cost more than 1-inch models. The 30mm tube may well become a standard for another generation of shooters, just as the 1-inch scope replaced the Noske and other slender sights of the WWII era. To those of us seduced by Lyman Alaskans slung low on early Winchester 70s and Savage 99s, the new look will take some getting used to.

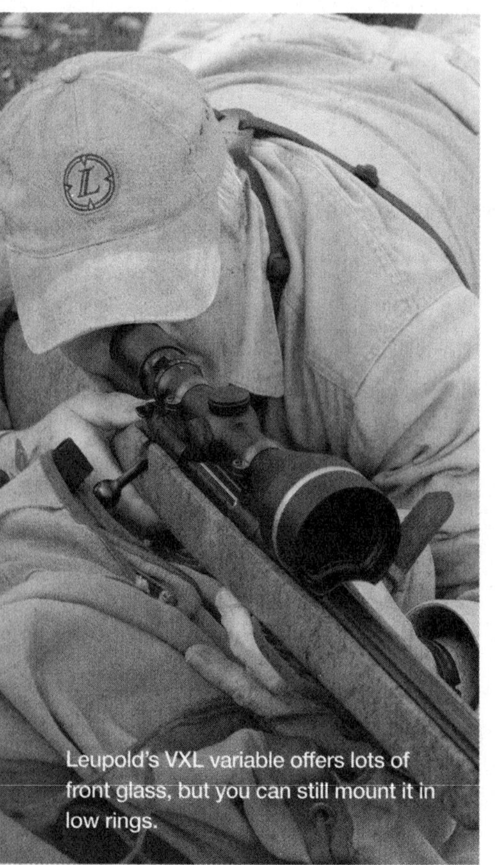
Leupold's VXL variable offers lots of front glass, but you can still mount it in low rings.

The prairie dog exception

Recently, I killed an elk with a Kimber rifle in 260 Remington. The bullet landed right where I'd aimed. Had I superimposed a squirrel-size target on the elk's rib, the Sierra softpoint would have nailed it. But at 275 yards I couldn't have seen such a small target in my hunting scope. No rifle can deliver reliable hits farther than you can see well. And you'll need high magnification to aim at small rodents far away. A prairie dog peeking from its hole presents a target the size of a marble. You'll need lots of magnification, a scope like the 30x Leupold target sight on my H-S Precision. Over a Harris bipod, this heavy-barrel nail-driver can spit 52-grain hollowpoints into a 45 ACP case at 100 yards. Still, when the barrel heats or when mirage grabs the target, that 30x magnification becomes a liability. In a brisk breeze, rifle wobble is as big a handicap as bullet drift. High magnification also trims field of view and reduces brightness.

These factors make variable scopes a smart choice for varmint shooters.

What about illumination?

Besides magnifying the target, rifle scopes have two advantages over iron sights. Scopes put the sight picture on one sharply focused plane. And they brighten target images in poor light. Lenses don't really "gather" light. They can only deliver incident light. Still, rifle scopes can extend shooting hours by concentrating incident rays into a shaft of light the diameter of your scope's exit pupil. When the exit pupil is at least as big as your eye's pupil, you get maximum benefit. In truly dark conditions, even the biggest brightest lenses leave you with a dim sight picture. Eventually you lose not only the target image but the reticle as well. Which you lose first depends on the nature of the target and the design of the reticle.

Just past sunset at the hem of an Oregon meadow 33 years ago, I found myself eye to eye with a six-point bull elk. But when the rifle crawled to my cheek, its Lyman Alaskan showed me only the faint image of the elk. My 3-minute dot had disappeared. Panicked, I thought briefly of centering the animal's shoulder in my field of view and pulling the trigger. But the elk wasn't that close. I tried looking off-center in the scope. No luck. Then I moved the scope's center to a patch of ivory-colored grass. A tiny gray dot appeared. Gluing my eye to it, I swung it up into the ribs just as the dot evaporated.

There's an easier way to kill in dim light. Electronic or illuminated reticles show up even when night has fallen. Battery-powered, most are adjustable for brightness. A rheostat, typically with 10 or 11 settings, allows you to turn down the brightness under dark conditions, and up if you want to see it during daylight. You're smart to use the lowest setting practical. Too much brilliance, and the retcle becomes more prominent than necessary, hiding your target. It also loses its clean-edged profile, and tells your eye's pupil to contract – so you receive less light around the reticle and consequently lose track of your target.

Red dot sights offer a similar view and controls but are of different construction. Aimpoint built the first red dot sight in 1975. Inventor Gunnar Sandberg called it the single-point sight because you looked into it with one eye and around it with the other – you couldn't see through it at all! Since then, Aimpoint has maintained its position as the leader in red dot technology. On current models, a compound front lens corrects for parallax, bringing the dot to your eye in a line parallel with the sight's optical axis. With an Aimpoint, you hit where you see the dot, even when your eye is off-axis and the dot appears off-center in the field. Aimpoint sights with no magnification boast unlimited eye relief, so you can aim fast, with both eyes open. The company's latest circuitry has boosted battery life to 50,000 hours with the brightness set at 7 (in a range of 1 to 10). You get a choice of 2- or 4-minute dot; that's 1- or 2-minute with the 2x converter.

I've killed a couple of moose with an Aimpoint sight. The first, a bull, trotted by in dark timber. He stopped at 90 yards, all but invisible to the naked eye. But the Aimpoint dot found a sliver of shoulder, and a 30-06 bullet was on its way. The second animal, a cow, galloped at twilight through heavy rain in shaded forest ahead of a line of beaters. Iron sights or a black reticle would have been swallowed up by the gloom. With Aimpoint's dot at its low setting, I made the fast shot easily. Aimpoints are popular hunting sights in their native Sweden. In the U.S., you'll find red dot sights mostly on handguns; but riflemen who ply the timber can use them to great advantage.

Trijicon, a company that's successfully marketed its ACOG (Advanced Combat Optical Gunsight) to military units, combines tritium and fiber-optic illumination in its hunting scopes. The AccuPoint line comprises 1.25-4x24, 3-9x40 and 2.5-10x56 models with red or yellow pyramid-on-post reticles. Trijicon's TriPower also relies on a fluorescent collector. I used an AccuPoint on a Colorado elk hunt, sneaking into bedding cover with an 1895 Marlin. When a bull rose from his bed, that bright yellow delta found him right away in the mottled fall foliage – and stayed with him for follow-up shots.

A clever, battery-free solution to fading reticles is Bushnell's FireFly. You simply give this reticle a cople of seconds of flashlight beam before a dawn or late-afternoon hunt. FireFly stays black in daylight, but when the light fades, it automatically starts to glow green. It lasts as long as an evening hunt.

On scopes of high magnification I forego lighted reticles, as powerful optics are best suited to long shooting in open places under good light. They also suggest still targets, deliberate shooting and a requisite for precision. Lastly, I prefer slim, clean-looking sights. Though some battery warts have been supplanted by cleverly tucked compartments in the turret, I'd rather save my batteries for red dot sights. Besides, the reticle is only one part of a dim sight picture. A lighted reticle does not illuminate your target.

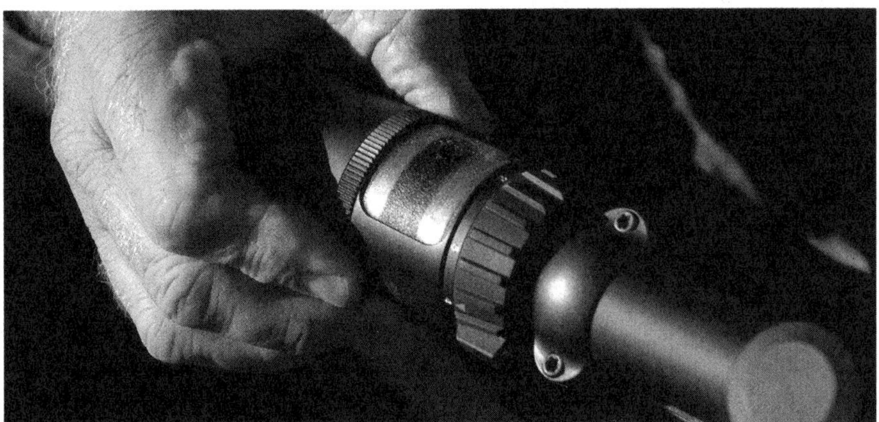

The adjustable fiber-optic window on this Trijicon scope illuminates the reticle without batteries.

Curt Crum aims with a 6 1/2-20x Leupold and the Marksman rifle he builds with David Miller.

Though I'll choose fixed-power scopes for big game, I'm much enamored of high-power variables for small targets – for essentially the same reasons I like a choice of magnification in spotting scopes. With both instruments, you sometimes want all the power on the dial; but circumstance can also dictate lower magnification – to find a sodpoodle quickly, follow a moving coyote or reduce the effect of mirage or wind. In my view 6-1/2 to 20x is a useful power range for heavy varmint rifles. A 6-24x is, of course, as good. The 8x32x now in catalogs costs you little at the low end; on the other hand, you won't find many situations that require 32x magnification.

Because scopes of high magnification are bred to enhance precision, most are now equipped with adjustable objectives. AO scopes wear a calibrated ring on the front bell that lets you "zero out" parallax at any yardage. It also sharpens focus, an advantage above 9x or so. The latest AO innovation is replacement of the front ring with a third turret dial. It's handier and takes weight off the front bell. Target adjustment knobs are another useful option on high-power scopes for heavy-barreled prairie dog rifles. Leupold came up recently with capless knobs of clever design. Adjustments should feel crisp, and must move point of impact reliably if they're to be of any use afield. The best are fashioned to allow a reset to zero.

One of the most important components of any scope is the reticle. Reticles for varmint shooting needn't grab your eye as should a crosswire in a big game scope, but they must not obscure little animals. I favor a fine dot, from 1/2-minute in a 10x scope to 1/4-minute in a 20x.

Trendier are rangefinding reticles, which have also become popular in high-power hunting scopes. The simplest comprise two horizontal stadia wires. The space between them subtends a specified measure at a given range. Variable-power scopes deliver accurate reads only at a single magnification – unless the reticle is in the front focal plane, per European custom. A reticle there changes apparent size as you change magnification, but stays in constant relationship with the target. Redfield once sold a rangefinding reticle designed to read accurately at any power setting. You fit the target between the stadia wires by changing power, then read the range on a vertical scale in the scope field. Shepherd scopes employ two reticles, one in the front focal plane and one in the rear, so you can range with one and aim with the other. Installed so you can still aim quickly, they work on small targets and large. A 6-18x Shepherd is an ideal sight on long-range rifles used for both big game and varmints.

Other reticles with stadia wires include the Burris Ballistic Plex and Swarovski's TDS Tri-Factor reticle. They're similar. The thin wire beneath the intersection of the plex-like reticle has horizontal hash marks. Each space between the marks is incrementally bigger than the one above it, to track the steepening arc of a bullet at long range. If, for example, you zero at 100 yards with a 30-06, you'll likely hit near the first hash mark (3 inches low) at 200 yards, the second mark (13 inches low) at 300 and the third tic (30 inches low) at 400. At 500 yards, your bullet strikes near the top of the bottom post. You can zero faster bullets at 200 yards and use the center wire for all shots to 250. No matter the cartridge, it's imperative to zero with care and shoot at extended yardage to track bullet impact on targets relative to those hash marks. When you've determined the yardages at which bullet arc intersects the marks, record them!

Another rangefinding device is the mil dot reticle. "Mil" refers not to "military" but "milliradian" or the space between 3/4-minute dots strung vertically and horizontally along a crosswire. A mil is 1/6400 of a degree in angular measurement. That amounts to 3.6 inches at 100 yards, or 3 feet at 1,000 yards. To find the range with this reticle, divide target height in mils at 100 yards by the number of spaces subtending it. You come up with the answer in hundreds of yards. For example, a coyote 18 inches at the shoulder (5 mils at 100 yards) appears in your scope to stand two dots high. You divide 2 into 5 and come up with 2.5; so the coyote is 250 yards away. You can also divide target size in yards by the number of mils subtended and multiply by 1,000. Variable scopes with mil dots are usually calibrated at high-end magnification. Whether you use a powerful scope on a big game rifle or on a 220 Swift with a barrel as thick as a truck axle, long shots are difficult. Consistent hits result from solid marksmanship, not sophisticated optics. You must read conditions accurately, hold the rifle still and squeeze the trigger gently. The best scope can only help you aim.

Wayne killed this Utah bull with a 1.5-5x32 Weaver on a Remington Model Seven rifle in 308.

30-30: SHORT MAGNUM FOR THE FRONTIER

by Wayne van Zwoll

ABOVE: **The Savage 99 was chambered to the 30-30 from 1900 to 1940. This one is in 300 Savage.**

Defining "deer rifle"

When a Winchester Model 94 listed for $89 and I could scrounge just $30 for a battle-weary SMLE, deer hunting held more appeal than a date with Annette Funicello. My 303 killed a few whitetails before I made a life on the West Coast with rifles that shot flatter. Not long ago, as a plethora of short magnum cartridges clamored for attention on the covers of shooting magazines, I retreated to the loading room and dusted off a box of 30-30 cartridges.

They looked smaller than they'd seemed in the 1960s. Then I remembered the well-dressed hunter from The City. Every November, he came out to the corn fields, woodlots and swamps. We farm boys liked to see bucks tumble, but it did seem The City Hunter had more than his share of shooting. Once, he looked into a patch of low briars his companions were about to walk by. With his binocular he spied a shiny black thing. It turned out to be the nose of a nine-point buck. He killed it. Another time, he waited by the pickup while Ron, Bill and I pushed through a treed swale. Ron broke cover about 100 yards shy of the truck and unloaded. In short grass a few yards farther on, a buck jumped. He'd been right there, hiding like a rabbit! Helpless, Ron watched as The City Hunter killed that buck too.

The author used this stainless Marlin in 30-30 to kill deer, elk, bear and pronghorn in one year.

We had to admit, he was a good shot. And that he was patient and knew where to look for deer.

The City Hunter could have carried a fancy bolt-action rifle. He looked oddly equipped with his iron-sighted Winchester Model 94. Then again, maybe he knew something we didn't.

Deer rifles have changed a great deal over the last 40 years. But they'd changed even more during the preceding four decades. If you go back 120 years, to the 1880s, you'll have turned another page in time. This period brought the shameful decimation of game on the western frontier. For market and sport and to deny the Plains Indian his subsistence, riflemen mowed down the bison. Rail crews feasted on mountain sheep, deer and elk killed by contract shooters. Conservation had yet to root in the collective conscience. And blackpowder still fueled cartridges. Their lead bullets traveled just a tad faster than sound. But hunters of that era thought themselves well off indeed. Metallic cartridges had not only obviated the need to stuff powder and ball, separately, down the bore; they'd made repeaters practical.

The 30-30 came from Winchester's shop in the mid-1890s. Commonly acknowledged as America's first small-bore smokeless big-game round, it appeared in the Winchester Model 1894 rifle in 1895. The only domestic smokeless cartridge predating it was the 30-40 Krag, developed for the Krag-Jorgensen military rifle. Original 30-30 ammunition featured a 160-grain bullet and 30 grains of smokeless powder. (The cartridge was named, after the fashion of that time, for the bore diameter and the powder charge.) Muzzle velocity: a modest 1,970 fps. Soon other popular rifles chambered the new round. Marlin's 1893, first bored to 32-40 and 38-55, added the 25-36, 30-30 and 32 Special as they became available. Arthur Savage's Model 1899 offered the 30-30 as early as 1900 and into the 1940s. The cartridge even showed up in Remington Rolling Block and Winchester 1885 singleshots. The 30-30 endured competition from the 30-40 Krag and even the 30-06, as the bolt-action magazine rifle redefined warfare on European battlefields. Returning GIs took Krags and Springfields to hunting camp – but whitetail thickets and saddle scabbards gave the edge to leveraction carbines in 30-30. The cartridge gained such momentum that even bolt rifles like Savage Models 40 and 340 and Winchester's 54 were chambered for it.

Few sporting rounds popular today date even to World War II. The 300 Savage and 300 H&H are, alas, almost dead. They and the still-vigorous 270 date to the 1920s. The 375 H&H steamrollers on after nearly 100 years. The 30-06 is ancient, having just passed the century mark. But the 30-30 predates the '06 by a decade. About the only commonly loaded biggame cartridge with a longer history is the 45-70, the government's blackpowder infantry round of 1873. But this number gets most play in the Cowboy Action game, and by shooters toting period rifles on hunts of historical color. Taking a bison with a Sharps or a Winchester 1886 (or an affordable clone) qualifies as sport and a bow to pioneers with fewer choices.

To understand the continued celebrity of the 30-30 among hunters who can now pick from among myriad modern cartridges, you must know something about its past. The lever-action 30-30 came honestly by its reputation as America's deer rifle.

Rocket ball beginnings

The first successful breech-loading rifle Stateside was developed by William Jenks during the 1840s. Jenks worked at the N.P. Ames Company. Remington saw promise in this rifle and its buoyant Welsh designer. It bought the business, plus the services of William Jenks, for $2,581. The rifle benefitted from improvements like Edward Maynard's percussion lock. Meanwhile, Steven Taylor had patented a hollow-base bullet with its own powder charge. A perforated end cap admitted sparks from an outside primer. Inventor Walter Hunt developed a similar bullet, with a cork base seal. This "rocket ball" would change history.

Hunt, then 50, had come up with many good ideas, from the lock-stitch needle to the safety pin. In 1849 he was awarded a patent for a breech-loading "Volitional" repeating rifle. Fellow New Yorker George Arrowsmith helped with cash and business savvy. Gunsmith Lewis Jennings improved it, assigning patent rights to Arrowsmith, who sold *all* rights to the rifle for $100,000 to financier Courtlandt Palmer.

Sales of Hunt-Jennings rifles proved disappointing. Palmer soon stopped production. The project might have died there, but for the talents of Horace Smith and Daniel Wesson and young gun mechanic B. Tyler Henry. The Hunt-Jennings project was bought by a group of New York financiers. Henry was hired by its new president, Oliver F. Winchester.

"... Where is the military genius . . . (to) so modify the science of war as to best develop the capacities of this terrible engine – the exclusive use of which would enable any government. . . to rule the world?" Long ago, this might have been written of the horse, later the atomic bomb. But this was Oliver Winchester's appeal to the U.S. Government for military adoption of the Henry rifle. Besides the advantage of increased firepower, breech-loading repeaters were proving safer in battle. A Navy report showed how, in the heat of battle, muzzle-loading rifles could become dangerous:

"Of the whole number (27,574 guns collected). . . we found at least 24,000 of these loaded; about one half of these contained two loads each, one fourth from three to ten loads each.... In many of these guns, from two to six balls have been found with only one charge of powder. In some, the balls [were] at the bottom of the bore with the charge of powder on top .... Twenty-three loads were found in one Springfield rifle-musket...."

Oliver Winchester was a successful Baltimore shirt-maker with a new and profitable plant in New Haven. In 1855, when he invested in Volcanic Repeating Arms, that one factory was employing more than 1,500 workers and grossing $600,000 annually.

But the gun enterprise soon faltered. In February, 1857, it was declared insolvent. Winchester bought all assets for $40,000 and reorganized the firm into the New Haven Arms Company. He directed

John Browning's Model 1894 followed his short-action Model 1892. He produced both during a 17-year stint designing Winchester's greatest firearms. This '92 is a Legacy reproduction.

shop foreman Henry to improve the Volcanic rifle and its ammunition. Henry earned a patent for a lever-action repeating rifle with a tubular magazine and a two-pronged firing pin. The Henry's main fault was its fragile slotted magazine. Still, with 15 rounds, the rifle had double the fire-power of the Spencer. And one movement of the lever would reload and cock, while the Spencer required a separate cocking motion. War gave Southern troops a belly-full of "that damned Yankee rifle that can be loaded on Sunday and fired all week." Its 44-caliber 216-grain pointed bullet was driven by 26 grains of blackpowder to 1,025 fps

In 1866, after B. Tyler Henry left the firm, successor Nelson King redesigned the rifle's troublesome magazine. The subsequent Model 1866 would anchor a lever-action dynasty for Winchester Repeating Arms.

Much of the company's early growth came from abroad. In 1866, Benito Juarez, the Mexican leader opposing Emperor Maximillian, ordered 1,000 rifles and 500,000 rounds of ammunition. Winchester salesman Thomas Emmett Addis smuggled the arms across the Rio Grande to Monterrey. There he rented an empty store with a cot, so he could guard the guns. When Juarez's people proved unwilling to pay, Addis threatened to sell the guns to Maximillian. He left town in a coach with $57,000 cash, sticking a scarf pin in his thigh periodically during the grueling three-day trip home, so he wouldn't doze off and fall prey to his guards.

Refining the lever-action

Oliver Winchester would not see the lever-action rifle mature. He died December 10, 1880 at age 70. His only son, William Wirt Winchester, succumbed to tuberculosis just a few months later. Thomas G. Bennett, Oliver's son-in-law, would guide the firm through its most rapid growth. Meanwhile, a young gunsmith in Utah was establishing his own shop.

In 1878 John Moses Browning turned 23. In a spartan room with no drafting tools, the unschooled son of a Mormon immigrant sketched a single-shot rifle action. He then hand-forged the parts, shaping them with a file and a chisel and a foot-lathe his father had brought by ox-cart from Missouri. The rifle functioned perfectly. Its massive parts and simple construction suited it to the frontier. With help from brothers Matt, Ed, Sam and George, John built a small factory. A touring English gunmaker, Frank Rushton, helped set up the equipment.

John Browning priced his rifle at $25. Within a week after opening the shop for sales, the entire stock had sold. And a burglar had made off with John's prototype!

Even before he'd received a patent for his first rifle, John had built another dropping-block action. By 1882 he'd built a repeating rifle. The following year Winchester salesman Andrew McAusland delivered a used Browning single-shot to Winchester president Thomas Bennett, who lost no time traveling to Ogden and what was billed as the biggest gun store between Omaha and the Pacific. He found half a dozen youths in a shop no bigger than a livery. But Bennett was no fool. "How much will you take for rights to your rifle?" he asked John.

"Ten thousand dollars," said John coolly. It was an enormous sum in Utah in 1883.

"Eight thousand." Bennett would certainly have paid ten. The rifle became Winchester's Model 1885. John immediately turned to his next project, a lever-action. Bennett bought that gun too. Winchester sold it as the Model 1886, a repeater that could handle cartridges previously used only in single-shots. It cost Winchester $50,000 – "more money than there was in Ogden," according to Browning.

Thomas Bennett kept John busy. During their 20-year association, Winchester bought 44 Browning patents, apparently for asking price but with no royalties. Only 10 were manufactured as Winchesters. Bennett paid for designs he couldn't use, just to keep them from competitors. John Browning developed mechanisms "so simple and fool-proof that he measured in inches, not thousandths." So claimed his shop foreman. When Browning was asked for a lever-action rifle to replace the aging 1873, Bennett offered $10,000 "if you can get a prototype to me in three months. Make it two months and I'll give you $15,000."

John Browning replied. "The price is $20,000 if I can deliver it in 30 days. If I'm late, you get it free."

Incredulous, Bennett agreed. Within two weeks John and his brothers had built a prototype for what would become the Winchester Model 1892. Bennett cut a check for $20,000.

The short-action 1892 spawned the Model 1894, Winchester's multi-million-unit best-seller, a lever gun that brought the company into the 20th century and survived into the 21st. John Browning was granted the patent August 21, 1894. In November the rifle began its long run with this introduction: "We believe that no repeating rifle system ever made will appeal to the eye and understanding of the rifleman as this will and that use will continue to warrant first impressions."

While the Model 1894 was designed with smokeless cartridges in mind, the first chamberings were two blackpowder rounds: the 32-40 and 38-55. That year Winchester listed both 20- and 26-inch barrels. The August, 1895 catalog added the smokeless 25-35 and 30-30, in round 26-inch nickel-steel barrels only. Two years late came the Extra Light Weight Rifle, with 22- and 26-inch barrels. The 32 Winchester Special joined the cartridge roster in 1902. Until 1908 shooters could special-order longer and shorter

This weathered Winchester 94 has lived a rough life in outfitter camps in British Columbia.

Initially, Winchester 1894 rifles were offered with long octagon barrels, as on this fine specimen.

barrels. Muzzle-length magazines became standard on carbines, but you could for a time get full-, half- and 2/3-length tubes. Early on, the company supplied carbine, rifle and shotgun buttstocks, straight wrists and pistol grips. Some options came at no charge. Over the '94's long tenure, options dwindled.

In 1936 Winchester discontinued all Model 1894 rifles (by popular definition those with long barrels) and the 25-35 chambering. The 25-35 reappeared for a decade beginning in 1940, but carbines in 30-30 and 32 Special became, for the World War II generation and its children, the archetypal Model 94. New Haven presented its one-millionth Model 94, appropriately engraved, to President Calvin Coolidge in 1927. President Harry Truman got number 1,500,000 in 1948, President Dwight Eisenhower the two-millionth just five years later. The Model 94 hit the 2.5-million mark in 1961. By 1970, three million had been shipped. Nine years later Winchester auctioned carbine number 3,500,000 in Las Vegas for $18 million, then the highest price ever paid for a Winchester rifle. By that time several new versions of the 94 had debuted, some to commemorate models, people and events of times past. A decade later, after 4.7 million Model 94s had come off the line, the Trapper carbine appeared in 30-30 only, a nod to the compact rifles favored by woodsmen during the 94's adolescence.

Better than the 94?

If, during the middle decades of the 20th century, you owned a 30-30 that wasn't a Winchester, it was likely a Marlin. John Mahlon Marlin was just 18 years old in 1853, when he apprenticed as a machinist in Connecticut. He agreed to work for no wages for six months, after which he'd get paid $1.50 – a week!

Gunmaking followed: deringer-style pistols first, then Ballard rifles. The first successful Marlin lever-action was a side-loading, top-ejecting rifle named the Model 1881 for its year of introduction (but not until 1888). It had a 28-inch octagon barrel in 45-70 or 40-60 and sold initially for $32. A later, lighter version came in 32-40, 38-55 and 45-85 Marlin. Some historians claim the 1881 was the first successful big-bore lever gun – or the first modern deer rifle. The subsequent 1889 had side ejection, a more reliable carrier. It came after the Model 1888, designed by L.L. Hepburn for the short 32-20, 38-40 and 44-40.

Hepburn wasted no time in re-engineering the Model 1889 for longer cartridges. The Model 1893 appeared first in 32-40 and 38-55, later in 25-36, 30-30 and 32 Special. Its lockup and two-piece firing pin differed markedly from the 1889s. When the lever was ajar, the rear piece would fall out of line with the front piece, preventing discharge. A standard 1893 had a 26-inch barrel, though barrels from 20 to 32 inches could be ordered. A lightweight version wore an 18- or 20-inch barrel. In 1905 Marlin listed a Grade B variation, the barrels marked "For Black Powder," only in 32-40 and 38-55. Other barrels were stamped "Special Smokeless Steel."

The Model 1893 became the Model 93 in 1905, though nothing was changed. By the 1920s, it had established itself as a favorite among deer hunters, a rival to Winchester's Model 94. In 1932, the 93 listed for $36. The last of recorded production went to J.F. Galef Company in New York four years later, which offered the rifles at a Depression price of $25. The 93 was a prototype for the Models 1936 and later 336.

Clawing its way clear of the Depression in the 1930s, Marlin reintroduced its Model 93. Changes in sights, stock and forend produced a new name. The Model 1936 replaced the 93 in 1937. Heralded as "a new gun especially for American big game," the 1936 featured a "... solid frame, 20-inch round tapered special smokeless barrel, proof-tested, crown muzzle, Ballard-type rifling, visible hammer, case-hardened receiver, steel butt plate. New design full pistol grip buttstock of genuine American black walnut... New 'Sure-Grip' semi-beavertail forearm, rounded and nicely shaped, Silver bead front sight dovetailed to the barrel and flat top Rocky Mountain rear sight.... Seven shots in caliber 30-30 or 32 Special." That was the Carbine model, with barrel bands. The 1936 Sporting Carbine wore a 2/3 magazine, steel forend cap. All variations had pistol-grip stocks and listed for $32 in 1937. There were known both as the 1936 and Model 36. Model 36 rifles, carbines and sporting carbines stayed in Marlin's line until 1947.

A year later, Marlin's Model 336 replaced the 36. The obvious difference between the two actions is the round bolt of the 336. "In this sturdy locking mechanism the round breech bolt is completely encased in the area of the locking bolt by a solid bridge of steel in the receiver... furnishing a strong, safe breech ... with a newly designed extractor, these high-power repeaters function smoothly with the new bolt." The bolt was chrome-plated and "easily removed for cleaning...." The

Marlin's 1895 in 45-70 looks like a 336 in 30-30, save for bigger loading and ejection ports.

flat mainspring of the 36 gave way to a coil mainspring. The "Marlin bulls-eye" near the stock's toe, deleted for a time on Model 36s, was reinstated.

Some early literature specified Ballard-type rifling for the Model 336, while some told of a "new Micro-Groove barrel." In 1951, Marlin's 336 Carbine was redesignated the 336C. The 336SC and 336A versions followed the Model 36 nomenclature for Sporting Carbine and Rifle. The 336A (and the Deluxe variation) were dropped in 1962. The SC survived one more year. The original 336C prospered until 1983. From 1954 to 1962 there was a Deluxe Sporting Carbine; the straight-grip 336T (for Texan) completed the line from 1954 to 1983. The original 336C was chambered in 30-30 and 32 Special. Marlin added the 35 Remington in 1953. For five years beginning in 1955, hunters could buy the 336SC in 219 Zipper. The 32 Special was dropped in 1964. Subsequently, the firm cataloged a number of variations, some with new and more powerful chamberings like the 356 Winchester and 444 Marlin.

While many small changes have been made in the production of parts for the 336, it is essentially the same rifle now that it was 50 years ago. Marlin is proud that its receivers are forged and machined, that their steel innards give you the smooth, solid feel of rifles built before the intrusion of alloy castings and music wire. Unlike late-model Winchester Model 94s, current Model 336s have all the qualities of their forebears.

A season with the 30-30

Nothing tells you about a rifle or a cartridge like betting your season on it. After hunting with so many modern bolt rifles that I cycled the actions and winced at the recoil in my sleep, I decided to commit a year to a lever gun in 30-30. Tony Aeschliman, then my contact at Marlin, kindly supplied a stainless 336 for the project. Hornady came through with new and ambitious LeverEvolution loads – ammunition with resilient polymer tips that rest safely against primers in tubular magazines. These pointed bullets fly flatter than traditional flat-point and round-nose bullets. Dave Emary, who headed the project, employed a "Light Magnum" powder charge to put this 30-30 load hot on the heels of the 300 Savage ballistically. A 160-grain bullet leaves a 20-inch barrel at 2,300 fps. At 250 yards, the new 30-30 hits half again as hard as traditional loads – without exceeding safe breech pressures. Here's how Hornady's LeverEvolution 30-30 fares against the competition, given a 20-inch barrel zeroed 3 inches high at 100 yards.

	160 Evolution	170 Federal	170 Hornady	170 Remington	170 Winchester
drop at 250 yds. (inches)	-7.4	-13.6	-13.7	-16.1	-14.8
vel./energy at 100 yds. (fps/ft-lbs)	2,056/1,502	1,759/1,168	1,757/1,165	1,674/1,058	1,720/1,117

The new cartridges weren't available when I embarked on my first hunt of the season, for black bears in coastal Alaska. We motored in a 52-foot fishing boat out of Wrangell, 330-horse diesels putting suds on sun-shot chop. As we cleared Prince of Wales Island, a red dusk settled on the Pacific, its reflected light a shimmering aisle to Japan. "Bear Necessity" hugged the island's rocky coast at seven knots.

Mark Galla had the wheel. In spring, he operates Peak 'n' Seas Outfitters mainly from his boat, prowling a small segment of Alaska's 40,000 miles of shore. "That's more than in the entire Lower 48." Circumnavigating Prince of Wales Island alone is a 400-mile trip. We'd topped off our 1,200-gallon diesel reserve, as even in quiet seas this boat gulped a gallon a mile.

Hunting by boat makes sense in southeast Alaska, where some areas get 18 feet of rain each year. Coastal mountains vault from barnacled beaches that hem dense forests. Marine highways beat game trails for ease of travel and for spotting bears seeking new grass on tidal flats.

"I've never had a hunter with a 30-30," admitted Mark over steaks and salad that evening. "To tell you the truth, I'm not thrilled about it. These bears run big, and the cover is so dense we lose blood trails."

After a couple of days, we anchored in a cove ringed by the dilapidated buildings of an abandoned fishing village. I jumped at the chance to don jogging shorts and hie off into the bush. Logging roads took me through conifer forests that showed me more bears than I'd seen from the vessel. Hidden by foliage and bends in the trail, I literally ran right up on several. A huge boar bounded into the brush, then sat down and watched me pass. Perfect cover for the 30-30, I thought.

My chance came one evening, when Mark and I motored into the ocean, then around the reefs toward a stream outlet. We idled into the for-

This Alaskan black bear fell to the author's 30-30. Mark Galla outfitted the island hunt.

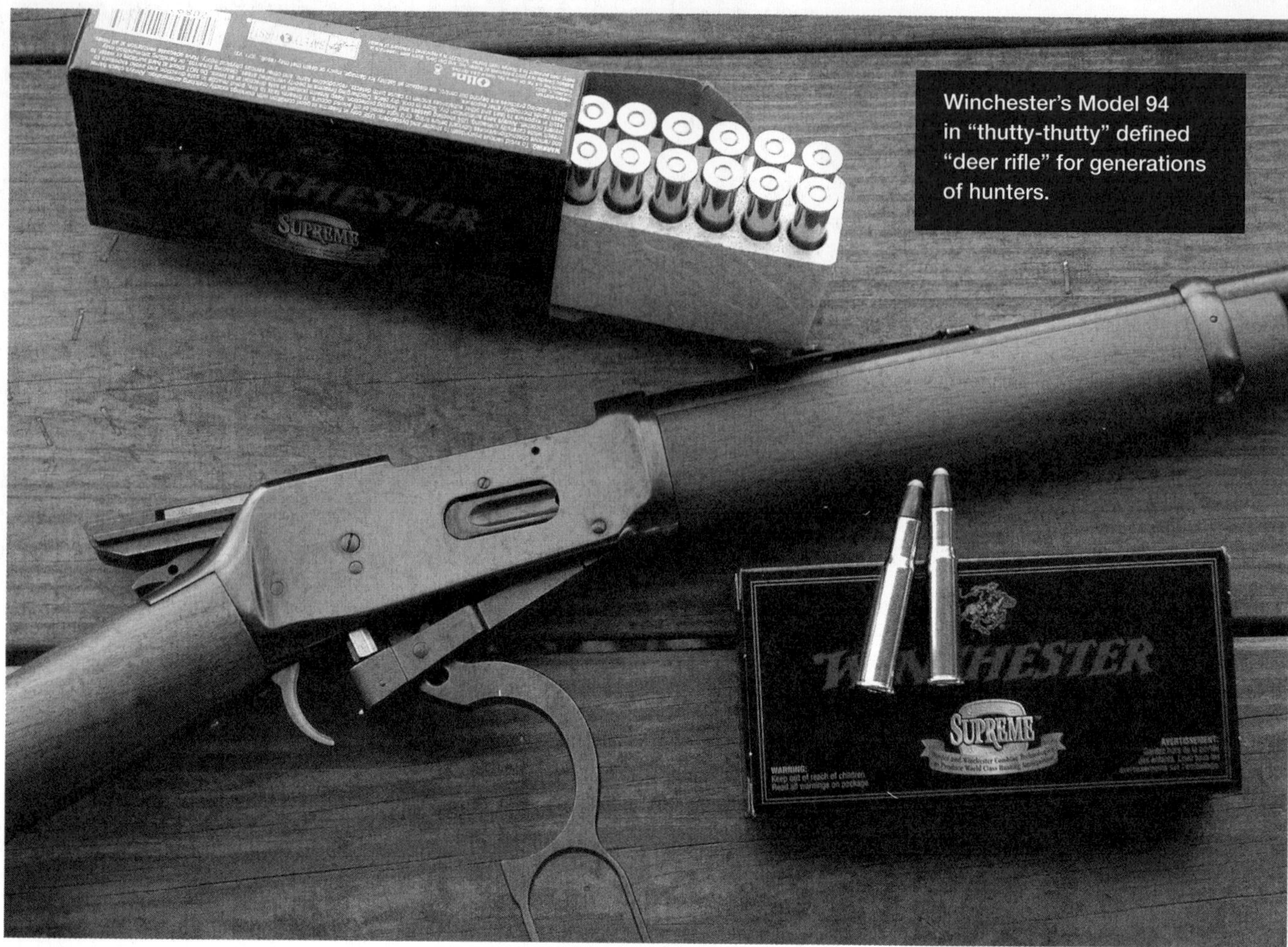

Winchester's Model 94 in "thutty-thutty" defined "deer rifle" for generations of hunters.

est until the stream got too shallow, then tied up with a long line to a rock. Alaska's coastal waters can rise and fall more than 20 feet in six-hour tidal swings, so a thoughtless mooring can leave your boat beached or adrift!

Donning packs, we followed bear trails through tidal grass, then sat beneath a giant Sitka spruce at the edge of a meadow. Half an hour later, Mark nudged my sleeve. Across the meadow, 200 yards away, a pair of bruins had slipped from the timber. We crept on hands and knees toward a spruce small enough for a studio apartment at Christmas. Then the wind shifted.

Instantly, the sow melted into the trees. The boar paused. Rising to clear the long grass, I pegged his elbow and fired. The 170-grain flatnose Hornady struck audibly, and the bear plunged into the forest.

We found no blood for 30 steps; then it painted a trail. In the dense brush I found myself clutching the Marlin. Suddenly, almost close enough to touch, the bear moved. I fired.

"A seven-footer!" Mark grinned. And, he conceded, fine work from the 30-30.

Four months later, I hiked into Utah's Uinta Mountains with the Marlin carbine I'd used in Alaska – but with Hornady's new loads. Though elk were rutting, big antlers proved scarce. On the final morning, I beat dawn to a north slope and followed elk sounds toward a copse of aspens near ridgeline. In thin light I glmpsed a herd of cows, then a young bull. But the herd bull was moving off, beyond them.

Then another bull bellowed. Close by. I eased to an aspen and waited. Movement! With my scent leaking like gasoline fumes into a swirling breeze, further delay was risky. I stepped forward and found a shot alley just as the elk saw me. At 19 yards I centered his throat and fired. He dropped instantly.

Many riflemen say the 30-30 isn't adequate for elk. But a 1939 survey of 2,200 elk hunters in my home state of Washington ranked it and the 30 Remington (essentially a rimless 30-30) most popular. Of course, traditional 30-30 bullets lose their muscle at distance. But I had faith enough in my Marlin for one more elk hunt, in Montana's Bob Marshall Wilderness.

Tough bulls, distant bucks

Watching John Way's linebacker shoulders rock to the rhythm of his horse, I wondered about my decision. John and his Paws Up Outfitters crew were leading Mike Schwiebert and me 14 miles to a tent camp. There'd be no changing rifles. Unloading under white canvas, I fingered the carbine's slim receiver.

The stars vanished by 4 o'clock. Flashlight beams danced in the dark as we wolfed toast. Hooves sucked at the mud and limbs swiped my face as I trailed Darrell along the river, then up into a side canyon. Horses sweating despite the cold drizzle, we swung stiffly from our saddles to prowl the lodgepoles. Ten hours later we rode back to camp, having seen no elk.

Other hunters had done better. We heard the story as we dug into pork chops and mashed potatoes. "... almost rode by him ... a seven-point ... punched him hard with the Weatherby ... 300 yards."

Would my chance at an elk come beyond my carbine's reach?

Stars and heavy frost greeted us the next morning. We tucked into eggs, tightened cinches, tugged at lead ropes and were once again swallowed up in black timber. We rode farther, hiked higher and tackled thicker places but heard not a single elk. Late in the afternoon we agreed to cowboy up for one more go.

The trail switch-backed up a rough east face cloaked in lodgepole. The horses slowed to a grind as the path steepened. We tied them a quarter mile below ridgeline; then Darrell blew mightily into his pipe.

Our first answer of the day quavered faintly from a distant canyon. "We can try there tomorrow," I said. Darrell bugled again. A passionate response rang much closer. He was coming!

Fire in our lungs and lead in our legs, we raced up through the timber. The bull spurred us on with a bray that seemed to shake the trees.

At last we could gulp no more air. Darrell crouched by a pine. I wrung a few more steps from my legs, then threw myself prone. Almost immediately black and tan winked between aspens. Antlers glinted. Then was upon us. I fired into the chest between sternum and shoulder. He spun, trotted off, then stopped, almost hidden in second-growth. I dared not move – but then decided I must. Crawling slowly to the side, I spotted a patch of rib. At the shot the elk stumbled from cover. I fired again and he toppled. An old, heavy bull with thick beams. I was ecstatic!

Elk hunting finished, I turned the carbine to mule deer. The Judith Basin hid its big bucks, but the last evening of a warm week's hunt, I bellied into a swale where deer had traveled in the days previous. As the sun dipped low, antlers appeared on the horizon. They weren't big; I decided they were big enough.

There was no brush to hide me, and the deer quickly spotted my motionless form. Too late, I said softly as the crosswire became still. The "thwuck" of a hit followed the report. The deer turned and trotted from sight. I paced 155 yards to the hoofprints. The buck lay dead 20 yards farther on.

In Wyoming, pronghorns had proven less elusive. But my carbine suffered grievously. I'd traded its 2-1/2x Leupold for a 6x Burris Compact scope. A friend spotted for me in a pasture as I zeroed the rifle from prone. Trotting downrange to replace the target face, I didn't see my amigo jump in his Suburban to set steel targets farther out. And he didn't remember the rifle in front of his tires.... A packet of Super Glue and a roll of duct tape later, the shattered stock was again functional. The first bullet landed an inch from point of aim at 100 yards. At 200, I hit a grapefruit-size bullseye.

Next morning I crawled through cactus and sage to the top of a small hill. A handsome pronghorn buck paused for a last look at 160 yards. The crosswire settled, I pressed the trigger. The pointed Hornady blew through both lungs, and the buck collapsed – by all appearances an instant kill.

I'm pleased to have spent a season with the 30-30. I like this round, as much for its gentle manner and efficiency as for the precision and extra reach of Hornady's LeverEvolution cartridges. The Marlin rifle proved a pleasure to carry as well as to shoot. Something about the feel of an exposed-hammer lever gun, with its tight, slim waist and easy tilt to muzzle, revives images of spurs bobbing under full scabbards and pack mules with antlers atop sawbucks, of red plaid cruisers and stringers of big whitetails bending meat-poles. Marlin has managed to render a solid post-war design using modern methods but without sacrificing this flagship rifle's cachet or its "gunny" looks or handling qualities. Pick up a 336, and you can't help but marvel that the mechanism is older than the automobile! Proven on America's frontier, it has gotten better, incrementally, with age. Toss that rifle to your cheek, and you see a buck streaking through the trees. Flick the lever; it responds eagerly. Snick, snick. This rifle wants to hunt. It shares with Winchester's Model 94 the allegiance of generations of hunters. It is the quintessential deer gun, the best of what rifles used to be when people depended on them for more than sport.

Hornady's LeverEvolution ammo in a Marlin carbine with 2-1/2x Leupold scope helped the author down this big bull elk in Montana's Bob Marshall Wilderness. The 30-30 has a lethal sting!

CAPE BUFFALO –WHY NOT!

by Bill Pace

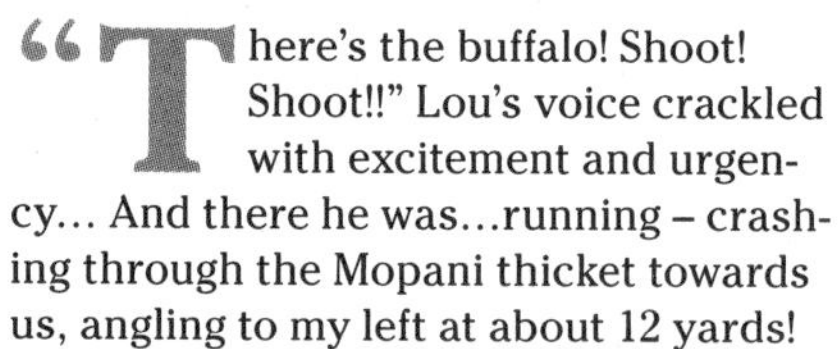

"There's the buffalo! Shoot! Shoot!!" Lou's voice crackled with excitement and urgency... And there he was...running – crashing through the Mopani thicket towards us, angling to my left at about 12 yards!

I later wondered what had brought me to that moment: I had recently married Berit, the widow of Finn Aagaard, well-known Professional Hunter and writer. She frequently told me: "I'd like to show you Africa, it's so beautiful." Despite the powers of Berit's siren persuasion, I know the hunt had really begun years before when a small boy wondered towards Grand Daddy's house through a patch of woods at dusk. He held his trusty Daisy "Golden Eagle" BB gun at the ready, eyes searching. *(What a beauty that BB gun was; gleaming copper barrel and action, a black lacquered stock with a Golden Eagle decal).* A slight movement – yes! A motion that became a cottontail, cautiously emerging. The faithful rifle came up swiftly – *thunk*!! The rabbit jumped, terribly disoriented, thunk! thunk! As fast as he could lever the gun and fire again, the boy poured in the lead. The rabbit lay still; a triumphant hunter stood over his first game animal. There had been many birds, but this was the first "real animal" of many to follow. The boy was me, and as the memory of mingled pride and excitement came stealing back, I knew this was the real beginning of my hunt .... for Cape buffalo.

Author with buffalo bull and rifle.

The clincher was my rifle, a Jeffrey 500 x 3-inch BPE; it had come from Wallis and Wallis Auctioneers in Sussex, England. Engraved on the barrel rib was "W. J. Jeffrey & Co. Queen Victoria Street, London, B.C." On the barrel was "Jeffrey rifles hold the highest record in the world for accuracy of shooting." Nothing bashful about the Jeffreys! A letter to Jeffrey disclosed that it was made in 1893, one of their "Better"-grade guns. With 26-inch steel barrels, top snap, double under bites and Greener cross bolt, it had the last improvements of the hammer doubles. Its back-action "island locks" were smooth and crisp; its bores perfect; it showed little actual use. Over the years I killed a number of whitetails with it, but buffalo kept appearing in my mind every time I shouldered it. Surely it deserved a trip to the Dark Continent.... Cape buffalo? Why not??

The combination of Berit's salesmanship, memories, and "the rifle" led to an inevitable decision ... buffalo it would be!! Phone calls and internet searches for a 2006 hunt proved fruitless until we contacted a friend of Berit and Finn's, Colonel Dennis Behrens of Expedition Adventures. Dennis quickly arranged a 7-day hunt in Zimbabwe for us with HHK Safaris. "It's the only thing available in 2006 that I can find – and Lou Hallamore will be your P.H." We took it. Despite the U.S. State Department's dire warnings we faced no problems in Zimbabwe; they just wanted us to spend money there.

HHK's facilities in the Chirisa area were excellent, beautifully situated on a bluff overlooking a scenic "sand river." Their well-trained, smiling and willing staff, great food and hot showers made our stay a happy one. I would gladly return!

Trip arrangements were easy; a call to Linda Schrader at Falcon Travel in San Antonio, Texas took care of our travel needs. Linda has extensive experience in arranging safari travel and knows all the "hunters welcome" accommodations. Another important "preparation" was arranging rifle permits for South Africa. Edo at Riflepermits.com was the answer for me.

Safari deposit mailed, the next step was practical preparation. Most important was suitable ammo and getting into shape for the "lots of walking" we'd been warned to expect. The physical preparation was the simplest. Regular three-mile walks with fully loaded ammo belt, boots and binoculars, and a five- or ten-pound dumbbell prepared me for the eight- or nine-mile treks we made each of our first two hunting days.

After absorbing the books, DVDs, and articles I had on hand, I realized that the 340-grain Lyman bullet I had been shooting was much too light for buffalo. Kynamco presently loads a 440-grain Woodleigh jacketed softpoint for this caliber in a "Nitro for Black" loading at a published velocity of 1,900 fps which produces around 2,990 foot/pounds of energy. Uncertainty of delivery by their sole importer, Galazan, and their quoted $980 for 50 rounds persuaded me to load my own. Midway stocked Woodleigh bullets, so I ordered the 440-grain BPE slugs.

The Jeffrey was regulated for the standard 500 x 3-inch BPE load of 136 grains of Curtis and Harvey's Diamond Grade #6 blackpowder and a 340-grain copper-tubed bullet (*hollowpoint closed with a copper cup*). Kynoch had also loaded a Nitro for Black 440-grain bullet pushed by 53 to 55 grains of Cordite. To drive the heavier bullets fast enough with current blackpowder to shoot the barrels together was my objective. Due to my aging eyesight, I felt that 50 yards was the most ethical range for a shot, so loads were tested initially at 50 yards.

Berit told me our P.H. would insist that I shoot standing off cross-sticks. The DVDs I'd watched confirmed this practice, so I made a set and loads were developed off sticks. I found that I got a lot of erratic lefts and rights due to the recoil vectors of two barrels; with my skinny frame I shot better offhand.

My starting blackpowder tests with Woodleigh 440s were loaded as follows: Bell brass (500 Nitro); Fed. 215 primer; powder charge; 1 - 0.060-in. Walter's wad; bullet firmly crimped:

140 gr. Swiss 2 Fg – 1,734 fps
110 gr. Swiss 3 Fg – 1,660 fps
136 gr. KIK 2 Fg – 1,808 fps

Frustrations with a new chronograph resulted in many wasted tests until I returned it and bought an Oehler #35. The Oehler cured my confusion and put me back on track. Sadly, none of my blackpowder loads produced consistent groupings with barrels shooting together – usually left and right barrels were 6-10 inches apart at 50 yards. Although each barrel shot separate groups, they did not shoot together into "a minute of buffalo heart."

One factor to address was that my barrels were 0.512-inch groove diameter and the Woodleigh bullets 0.510-inch. My solution was to squeeze a 50-caliber gas check through my .510-inch lubricizer die and insert them up-side down over the powder. This configuration insured complete obturation, but produced no evident increase in velocity or accuracy, and recovered bullets appeared to have slugged up to fill the 0.512-inch groove diameter.

Dave Scovil, editor of Wolfe Publishing's *Handloader, Rifle* and *Successful Hunter* magazines, wrote of his own African hunt using cast bullets and black-

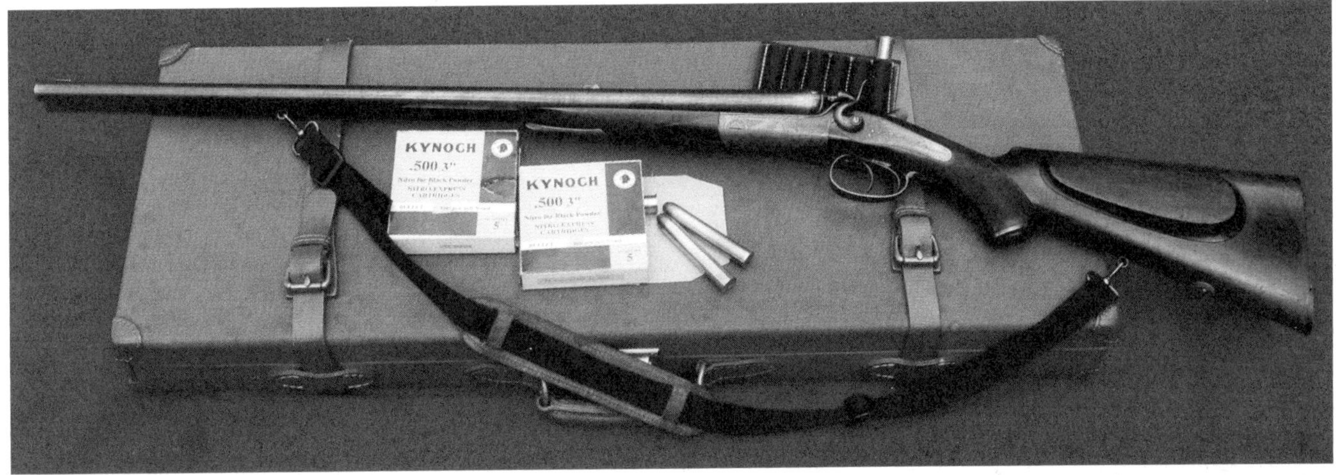

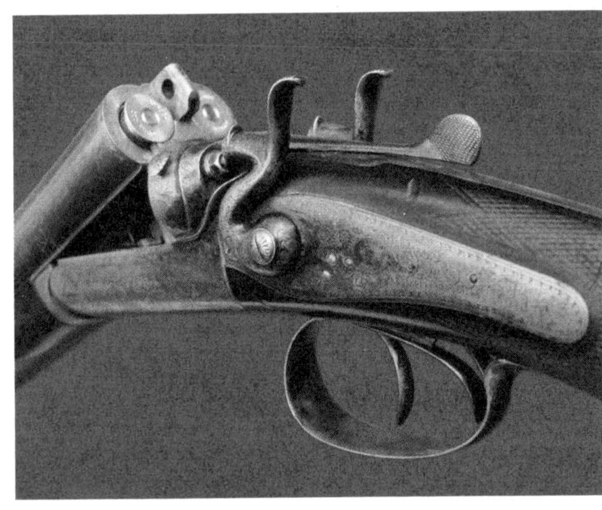

Author's 1893 500 Jeffrey.

Author and hunting buddy Jim, pleased with sight-in target, with our two PHs.

powder in a 50-caliber Winchester. I purchased his DVD of the hunt and subsequently wrote Dave with questions about loads. He graciously shared his loading info and ideas about bullets, weights, velocities, and adequacy of same. Dave reaffirmed the need for bullets heavier than 340 grains and strongly suggested "hard cast bullets" for Cape buffalo.

Ross Seyfried, America's premier "Double Rifle" guru, had written a fine article about loading for the 500 BPE in the October 2002 issue of *Handloader* magazine. I contacted him, and after telling him of my hunt preparations, Ross quickly stated: "I am afraid those Woodleigh bullets will let you down; they are too soft. You need a hard, cast bullet." He explained that "Cape buffalo have extremely tough bones and their ribs overlap; it is not easy to get through them."

I e-mailed Woodleigh Bullets, reporting this conversation and got a friendly, informative response from McDonald, owner of the Woodleigh Bullets. He said that experienced hunters successfully used his 440 SP on many buffalo and that they were suitable for behind-the-shoulder lung shots. With a hard cast bullet one would get better penetration. "Nuff said!" I ordered a mould from NEI – #.512/435 – and cast bullets using Linotype metal found in Finn's old loading area. These, sized to .512-inch, SPG-lubed, and with gas checks installed, weighed 435 grains. Bingo! A good weight match for the Woodleigh; maybe it would be amenable to my barrel twist.

Feeling I needed to boost my BP loads to get the accuracy, velocity, and performance I wanted, I tried duplex loads. It is generally accepted that one grain of smokeless is equal in energy/pressure to three grains of blackpowder. With this in mind I tried the following loads using the same basic load column with a little less powder compression and staying within the range of original BP loading of 136 grains of black with the same brass, primers and wads.

Linotype bullet – 15 grs. #4759; 100 grs. 1Fg Swiss, (equivalent to 145 grs. BP) gave 1,638 fps.

Linotype bullet – 12 grs. #4198; 120 grs. KIK 2Fg, (equivalent to 156 grs. BP) gave 1,738 fps.

Linotype bullet – 6 grs. #4198; 134 grs. KIK 2Fg, (equivalent to 152 grs.) gave 1,809 fps.

Woodleigh bullet – 15 grs. #4759; 115 grs. 1Fg Swiss, (equivalent to 160 grs.) gave 1,570 fps.

Again, I did not get consistent group size or good velocity; I felt I had pushed the blackpowder envelope pretty far. Fortunately a copy of Graeme Wright's *Shooting the British Double Rifle* was located. His pressure information, gleaned from tests he had personally performed at the Birmingham Proof House and Kynamco, was gratefully reviewed! Now I could be confident I would not endanger the old rifle that I enjoyed so. Graeme's data directed me to Hodgdon's Varget powder and also the #4198 that Seyfried had success with.

It was my goal for each bullet to shoot well at or near the original published velocities for that bullet weight. Starting with conservative smokeless loads, I began following Seyfried's recommendations, but quickly switched

Loading front half of buffalo into the safari vehicle.

Winchester's Super Grex for the Dacron filler he used. It was too much trouble to police the Dacron "snow" at the range as it did not disintegrate when shot! I later switched to 20 grains of Midway's "shot buffer" when I ran out of the Grex, with no evidence of pressure change.

Initial smokeless loads were structured as follows:

Bell "500 Nitro" Brass; Win. Large Rifle primers; powder charge; 0.060-in. Walters wad; 20 grains shot buffer (or Grex); 0.060-in. wad and bullet, firmly crimped in my RCBS dies.

Woodleigh Bullets were used in the following loads:

50.0 grains #4198 –
1,670 fps (Rt. barrel)
1,620 fps (L. barrel)

I noticed several times this L-R barrel velocity difference; it is possibly due to greater wear in one barrel. This load actually shot fairly well at 50 yards, into three inches with the 5th shot into 4-3/4 inches. My notes said: "Snappy load," but I felt the velocity was too low for buffalo, so tried the following loads with Woodleigh's bullets:

51 grains #4198 (inverted gas check); 1,630 fps. L&R in 1-1/2 inches at 50 yards; 53.0 grains #4198 (inverted gas check). 1,724 fps. L&R in 2 inches. My notes said: "Opened sticky."

54.5 grains # 4198 (no gas check): 1,781 fps. Acceptable 50 yard accuracy – off-hand.

The same load with Fed. 215 primer – 1809 fps. (215 primer consistently gave faster velocity)

56.0 grains #4198 (no gas check); 1,823 fps. "Wide L – R shots."

These loads were beginning to bring velocity closer to "Buffalo fps." Due to the earlier noted "sticky opening," I went to Federal 215 primers for their sturdier primer cups. This cured all sticky action opening. Why did some lower velocity smokeless loads shoot better than black?

Simultaneously I was testing Varget. After starting with 68 grains of Varget, I tried 72 grains; it shot well enough that I stopped further testing the Woodleighs in the interest of time. This load gave 1, 865 fps and shot about 1-1/2 inches low of point-of-aim at 50 yards. Since Graeme had pressure-tested this load to 76.0 grains, I felt comfortable regarding pressure.

My 435-grain cast bullet tests were also done with both powders. Varget was more bulky and proved consistent in my shooting. My note reads: 72 grains "75 yards, cross sticks, 2 shots in black, L @ 10 o'clock, R @ 2 o'clock, velocity 1,860 fps. Powerful load, same elevation, good load." This was well within my "buffalo heart" group requirement and velocity was OK so I took it to Africa as well.

Hearing that Hawk bullets produced soft copper jacketed bullets that were easy on "old soft steel barrels," I ordered some 350-grain bullets for smaller game and included them in my tests. It quickly became apparent that the 350 Hawk, close to the 340 grains that the rifle was regulated for, was easy to load for. It shot well right from the start with every load configuration: 53 grains #4198 gave 1,854 fps and decent accuracy. Seventy-two grains of Varget was also tried with the 350-grain and consistently gave 1,950 fps. It shot into 1-1/2 inches at 50 yards, and about three inches at 100 yards on one occasion. So, 72 grains of Varget went to Africa with this bullet, too.

Shortly before leaving to hunt, Hawk's website announced a new .510-inch bullet, a 400 RN with 0.050-inch thick copper jacket. This suggested a much stouter bullet than the Woodleigh, so I called Hawk. "Yes, we have them in stock; they were made up in a special run for a bear hunter in Alaska." He added: "They ought to perform well for heavy-boned animals, like buffalo." I ordered a box. They seemed harder than the 350-grain Hawks, so I called to confirm they would be safe in my old barrels. To their credit, Hawk did a microscopic comparison and called back: "Grain structure is the same; I feel they will be OK in your rifle."

With days left until our trip I loaded them ahead of 70 grains of Varget and fired five rounds offhand at an 8-inch steel plate at 50 yards – in front of a bunch of Black Powder Cartridge Rifle Silhouette shooters, (nothing like an audience!) Notes read: "Felt good, hit plate with both barrels, all shots." Seventy-two grains of Varget produced a 4-shot 3 1/2-inch group, at 1,860 fps, but about 1-1/2 inches low. Seventy-two grains of Varget got the nod again! With the usual shooter tendency to shoot high with iron sights when hurried, I felt 1 1/2-inch low would be OK for off-hand shots.

Four shells, all loaded with 72 grains of Varget, seemed redundant, but I felt the Woodleigh, Linotype, and 400 grains were logically usable for buffalo. The 350 would do fine for smaller game. The final test was penetration.

Nothing was wasted: elephant bones used as road signs.

Years earlier, Finn had helped Jack Carter develop Trophy Bonded Bullets. To test bullet performance, he had built a wooden box that held 24 inches of tightly packed wet telephone directories. I set it up with a slick-covered Cabela's catalogue (skin), a one-inch hard pine board, (ribs), an old dry cow femur, then 20 inches of wet phone books and a final pine board. My final load results were as follows:

Linotype 435-grain bullet – 1st shot penetration 18-1/2 inches. It missed the bone, "still shootable;" 2nd and 3rd shot hit bone or fragments, penetration 17 inches. "Held together well."

Woodleigh 440-grain bullet – 1st shot penetrated 10 inches after hitting bone. 2nd shot 13-1/2 inches penetration after hitting bone fragments. They weighed 326 grains and 374 grains, well-expanded.

Hawk 400-grain bullet – 1st missed bone, penetrated 19 inches. 2nd hit bone, shed jacket penetrated 8 inches, core to 10-12 inches. 1st bullet was reusable. Good solid??

Although none of the bullets performed perfectly, the Linotype and 400-grain Hawk seemed to offer the best penetration; I planned to use one of them for a follow-up shot since everyone thought a softpoint should be first.

One final consideration: Brass! My supply of Bell brass was only 20 rounds and by now well used. I felt I needed 40-

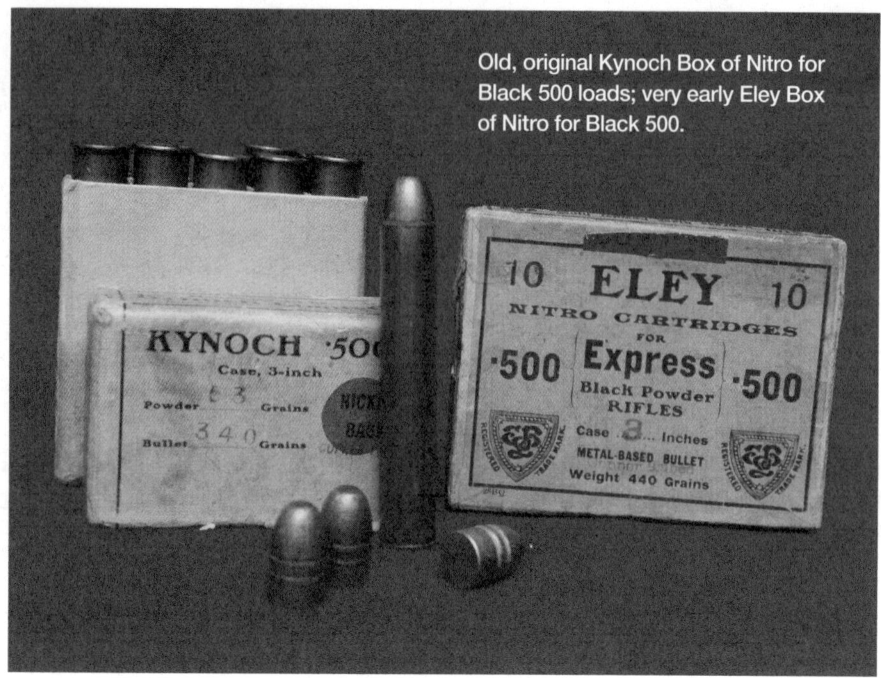

Old, original Kynoch Box of Nitro for Black 500 loads; very early Eley Box of Nitro for Black 500.

50 rounds, so called various suppliers for more. No Bell; no 500s. Forgetting my Scottish ancestry I gritted my teeth and emailed Kynamco. Yes, they could provide 50 rounds of brass with boxes.

The brass arrived; I tested ten rounds to see if it shot the same place as my Bell brass; it did. Loads were carefully assembled with the help of my almost-12-year-old great grandson. After the boxes were assembled and labeled, they looked like factory loads. Hopefully I would have no problems with airline "original manufacturer's container" or South African regulations. Nitro designation on the box would not cause any "black-powder" concerns at the airlines either.

We reviewed our preparations: visas, rifle permits, inoculations, malaria prophylaxis, tickets, lodging, travel insurance, cash security (*pick-pocket protection*) in the form of money belts, and finally a Kalispell gun case. We were ready!

Preparations and long travel behind us, the hunt was almost incidental, anti-climactic – almost, that is! Lots of walking, frustration of a missed shot, then on the third day – explosion! Sudden action!! A shoot-out that started at 12 paces with a buffalo running hard towards 7 o'clock and ended ten shots and two to three minutes later with the bull dead and my heart pounding! The Jeffrey tasted danger and came through with flying colors! The gun and ammo had performed up to expectations, and it all happened so suddenly, so unexpectedly that I did not have time to get nervous, or run. *(With Berit watching, I had to perform!)*

Before and after bullets from buffalo, L/R: 400-grain Hawk – smashed left hip/femur; unfired Hawk; Hawk recovered, .573 – nose expansion; NEI unfired; NEI recovered with shoulder chip.

It began when we first spotted the bull lying in a donga, (gully) asleep. As he departed, he was limping badly. "This is an injured animal; he may charge at any moment. Don't get more than three feet away from me!" was Lou's urgent command. We followed the bull into the Mopani thicket and quickly lost its tracks. Our first sweep through the edge revealed no exiting track, so Alfred the tracker stated: "He is still in there!" We started back deeper into the thicket. Berit and Milani, the required Government Scout, were bringing up the rear while our two trackers and Lou were in the lead. The trackers were studying the ground, when suddenly Lou stopped and shouted: "There's the buffalo! Shoot! Shoot!" The bull erupted from behind a large termite hill, running hard to our left. I don't recall cocking the rifle or shouldering it, just swinging on that left shoulder and an inner voice saying: "Keep swinging through!" Hardly aware of the crack of shot or the thump of recoil, I dimly heard Lou as he hissed "Reload! Reload!" I was automatically reloading the fired right barrel as we trotted in the direction where the bull had disappeared into the thick Mopani. All was very quiet. Lou was crouching, studying the bush with his binoculars. "Can you see that black spot?" he pointed 12-15 yards into the bush, "that is part of the buffalo – hit it!!" The spot was smaller than my hand, but the Jeffrey spoke as fast as I could get on target. The bull disappeared to our left. Running after him, I reloaded just in time to break through the thicket and see his rump; a quick left and right into his left hip as he vanished again, deeper into the brush.

Silence, a very long minute or two, then came a drawn out, melancholy bellow. "Great! He's down; that is the death bellow!" Lou was pulling me in the direction of the sound while I instinctively reloaded. As we rounded the thicket, Lou shouted: "My God! He's still on his feet! Shoot! Shoot!" There he was, at about 12 paces, on his feet behind a screen of Mopani. I fired two shots as fast as I could recover from recoil, and the bull went down! He fell towards us and I made no objection as Lou ordered "put two more into his shoulders!"

Big shouts, handshakes, I even got a bashful hug from Clemens, our #2 tracker as he passed me. Berit gave me the real thing, and a kiss to boot! Lou and I gave each other a back-slapping hug. It had been a very exciting 2-3 minutes for all of us! I dropped to one knee, said my thanks, and we approached the bull cautiously, going around his rear. Suddenly his right rear leg moved and his head swung up! I called to Lou who had not initially noticed the movement. "Shoot him in that white spot behind the shoulder!!" – so I did, and the big head fell still.

Berit examined his left front leg; it was quite swollen, pussy and wet; it appeared to be lacerated; probably injured in a poacher's snare. This had caused him a lot of pain and explained the limp and reluctance to go any distance; he only ran far enough to hide each time I shot. "You did him a favor; the lions would have gotten him in a day or two," Lou stated.

Thanks to Lou and his fine crew, the "after-hunt" carcass care took but a short while. They gutted it, careful to save everything, even the stomach contents and blood which would be used as lion bait. The buffalo was then chopped in two with a very primitive, deadly-looking axe, loaded into the back of the Toyota and taken to the skinning shed.

We examined the messed-up lung tissue, Berit shocked the staff when she dug out the heart, then put her fingers into the bullet hole through both atria. "This was your first shot" she said, "I was watching as you shot. This one actually killed him; he just didn't know he was dead!" Nothing was wasted; the skin would be sold for leather; the meat dried, then sold or traded to the local natives for road work. I got the head, the tail, and – Oh, yes – the scrotum! It will make an excellent bag for my 58-cal. ...rifle balls!

Of special interest was ammo performance. In the confusion at the kill site we did not do a thorough post-mortem. There were no exit holes, but only four bullets were recovered. Two of these were the Hawk 400-grain with 0.050-inch thick jackets. One had performed well as a solid, slightly bulged at the nose to 0.573-inch and weighed 395.0 grains. The second had smashed the left hip femur; fragmented and separated from the jacket. The pieces weighed 273 grains. The third was a Linotype solid which weighed 435 grains with gas check and lube; its recovered weight was 367.6 grains. This solid performed well; it had a chip off its front, but otherwise retained its shape. I feel it was my best penetrator. The 4th bullet was my last shot at about three feet. A Hawk 350-grain SP with a muzzle velocity of 1,950 fps, this bullet expanded to a diameter of 1.070 inches and did not exit the chest cavity. Its retained weight was 343.2 grains; it had lots of "thump at close range!" None of the Woodleigh 440-grain SPs were recovered; I am certain some bullets were lost in the initial gutting, and "lion-bait" gathering.

The realization that I hit this bull 10 times at close range, and none of the bullets exited, was astonishing! All the warnings I was given about their tough bones and muscle really hit home. It's true these were bullets traveling less than 2,000 fps, but even so, I was CLOSE on all shots. Frankly, I was sure some would penetrate and exit on the right side; but, there were no exit holes. Bullets were recovered under the off-side skin.

So, my first trip to Africa ended happily: a nice trophy; new friends; Berit and I shared a special adventure. I found that old saying "If you hunt Africa you will not rest until you go again" or words to that effect to be true. A need to return is already haunting me! If I go again, you know which rifle I will take in my "battery" – my old friend the Jeffrey; it needs to go too.

More Cape buffalo – why not??

PS – As I write this, we are planning another buffalo hunt, this one for both Berit and myself in Australia! According to the experts, the Asian buffalo are bigger and tougher to kill, but not as aggressive. She will take Finn's old 375 and I will have my Jeffrey. Both will speak again – to buffalo!

Reference

Col. Dennis Behrens Kynamco
Expedition Adventures kynamco@aol.com
142 Elsmere Place
San Antonio, TX 78212

Walter's Wads
Tel. 210 735 2373 thetinwadman@cox.net
behrsafari@aol.com Tel. 405-799-0376

Linda Scrader Oehler Research, Inc
Falcon Travel, Inc Post Office Box 9135
3030 Orchard Hill Austin, TX 78766
San Antonio, TX 78230 Tel. 512-327-6900
Tel. 210-479-9895 Toll Free 800-531-5125
lacarroll@earthlink.net Fax 512-327-6903

Edo Braseke
www.riflepermits.com
edo@riflepermits.com

HHK Safaris
www.hhksafaris.co
hhk@mweb.co.zw

Lou Hallamore
hhk@mweb.co.zw

NEI
neihandtools@hotmail.com
Woodleigh Bullets
zedfield@swanhill.net.au

Hawk Bullets
www.hawkbullets.com
Tel. 856-299-2800

Midway
www.midwayusa.com

SPG
spg@blackpowderspg.com
Tel. 307 587 7621

TESTFIRE
SIG SAUER'S P250

by Dave Workman

About midway in 2007, Sig Sauer announced that it was developing a truly modular semiautomatic pistol, one that could be changed to handle 9mm, 357 SIG, 40 S&W or 45 ACP with a change of basic components around a steel frame "fire control unit" that nestles into a polymer grip, and serves as the platform for a steel barrel and slide.

In a legal sense, this steel component is the firearm. It's the one part that bears the serial number. Everything else is interchangeable. This steel frame has "rails" fore and aft on which the slide rides, and rearward slide motion is stopped by solid steel. I only found two small springs on the whole assembly, and a relative handful of parts. By any definition, it is the doggonedest bit of engineering I've seen in years.

Enter the SIG P250, a handgun Sig Sauer has been advertising with slogans such as "Any Mission, Any Shooter, One Solution" and "One Gun, Infinite Possibilities." If this is an answer to someone's prayer, now would be the appropriate time to say "Amen, brother!"

Design work on this pistol actually began back in 2002, I learned, primarily to address law enforcement needs. But why should cops have all the advantages or, for that matter, get all the goodies?

The financial impact of such a handgun on the commercial and law enforcement markets should be immediately obvious. A municipal police or county sheriff's department can purchase one set of pistols, but switch components at will to fit every cop on the street, regardless of hand size and caliber preference. For the private citizen with an adequate bank account, it means he or she can have several guns in one to address various situations. Getting spare parts should also be simpler.

ABOVE: All that ammunition, and the pistol never hiccupped. The selection includes three brands of FMJ "ball" ammo, assorted hollowpoints.

If there is a "pistol for the 21st Century," one would have to look very hard to find a better candidate than the SIG P250. It is lightweight, rugged and reliable, and as accurate as other pistols from this renowned pistol manufacturer.

Let's cut right to the chase and explain what puts this pistol on the leading edge of what will certainly become an engineering technology curve as other gun makers start developing similar shooting "systems."

For openers, according to Sig Sauer, this pistol has 30 to 40 percent fewer parts than traditional semi-auto handguns, depending upon the specific model. It features an ambidextrous slide release and reversible magazine release, allowing it to be used by right- or left-hand shooters.

The size can be changed from full size to compact and sub-compact, and back again, depending upon the task. The "grip shell" — a piece made from a nylon derivative, according to Eric Von Bosse, SIG Sauer's product manager — can be swapped to fit small or larger hands by moving the steel firing mechanism into alternate grip frames in small, medium and large sizes. You can switch from a standard trigger to a short trigger. Barrels and slide assemblies are all interchangeable and they feature full-length recoil spring guide rods. The P250 comes with SIGLITE night sights.

Nylon grip shell weighs next to nothing and Workman was impressed at its durability and ergonomic design.

P250 is not much different in overall dimensions than Workman's Colt Commander.

SIG Sauer builds the P250 with a 3.9-inch barrel. The pistol has a locking breech design. Overall width on the small and medium frame pistols is 1.3 inches and on the large pistol model, 1.4 inches. Overall length is on a full-size model is 7.2 inches and overall height of the gun is 5.1 inches.

Topping all of this off, according to SIG Sauer, with a little practice, a shooter can take this handgun apart in just under one minute and reassemble it in just over a minute for a total dismantling and rebuilding in two minutes. I tried it several times and that's just about the speed I managed without working at it much.

And you thought they only made baseball caps that meet the "one size fits all" standard. In this case, it is "one gun that fits all."

I'll have to admit, when I first set eyes on the prototype, I openly acknowledged to one of the SIG Sauer gang that this was quite possibly the most innovative handgun design I'd ever set eyes on. My hand fit best around the smaller-size grip housing yet the full-size version was hardly awkward.

The synthetic grip is almost weightless, yet it is very strong. It is molded to allow for a firm, comfortable grip, with recesses on both sides for trigger fingers, and there is molded fine line knurling on the front and rear of the grip, while the side "panels" have a textured surface with the SIG Sauer logo molded in the center. The front of this polymer grip base features a molded accessory rail, but since I am no fan of lasers or "tactical" flashlights, if I were to carry this gun, that rail would never be used.

The stainless steel slide features a Nitron finish, and coupled with the synthetic grip frame, that makes the P250 virtually impervious to weather condi-

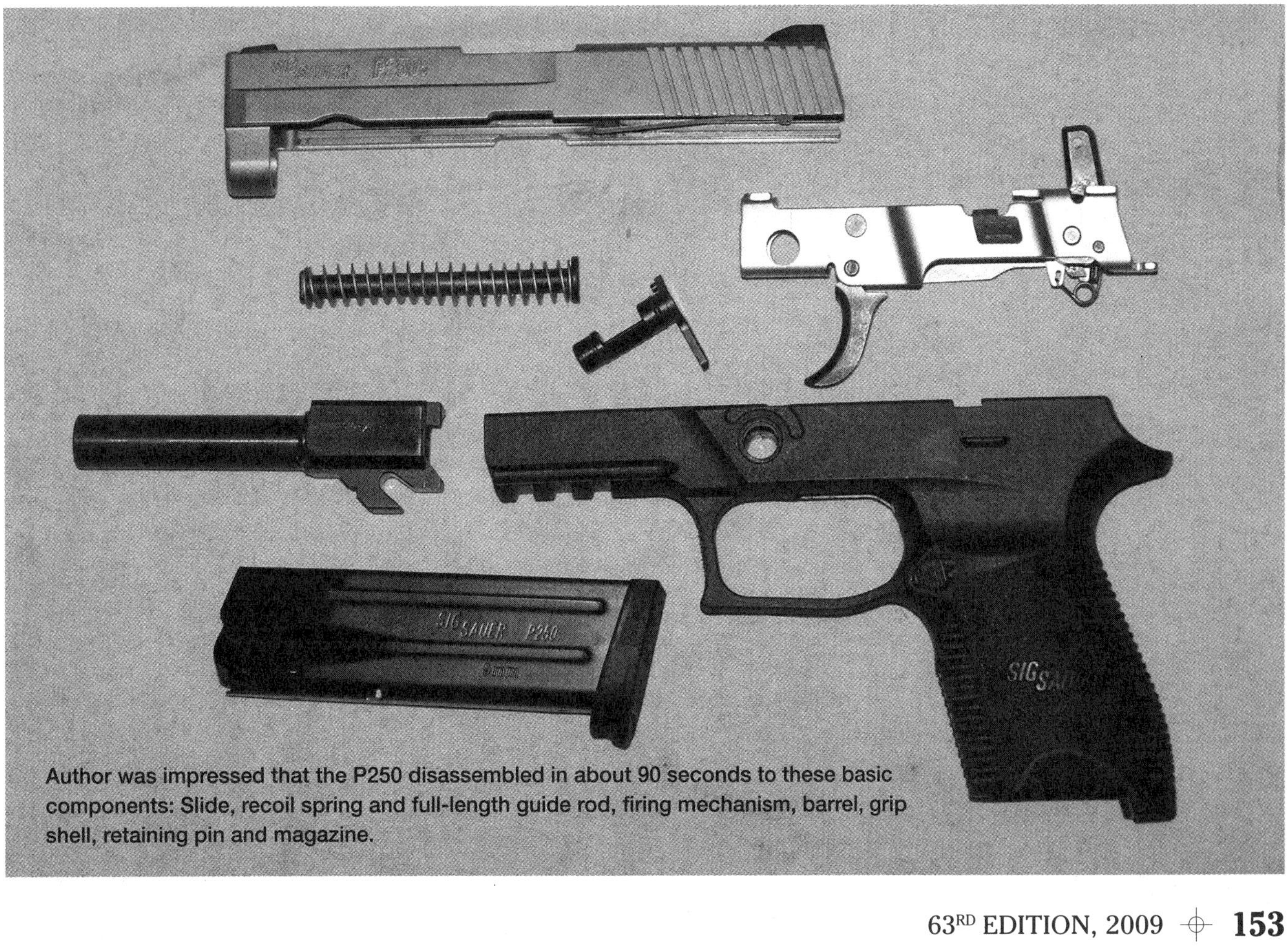

Author was impressed that the P250 disassembled in about 90 seconds to these basic components: Slide, recoil spring and full-length guide rod, firing mechanism, barrel, grip shell, retaining pin and magazine.

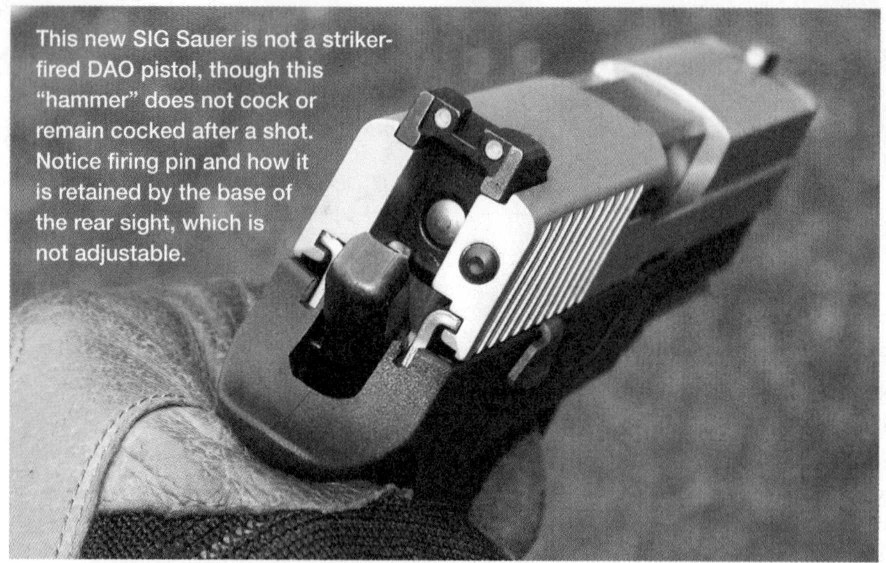

This new SIG Sauer is not a striker-fired DAO pistol, though this "hammer" does not cock or remain cocked after a shot. Notice firing pin and how it is retained by the base of the rear sight, which is not adjustable.

Author Workman gave the SIG Sauer P250 quite a workout on the range, with a variety of ammunition.

tions. Of course, polymer grip frames are hardly new to the handgun scene. This is the first time that they merely serve as an interchangeable housing for the actual pistol firing controls, which pop in and out rather easily.

This double-action only pistol has a hammer of sorts but it cannot be cocked. The hammer comes out of the grip shell, riding on the steel inner firing control framework. It has a smooth trigger pull ranging between 5.5 and 6.5 pounds, and this trigger pull is consistent. The full size version is not so big that one can't adequately conceal it under a cover garment, while the compact and sub-compact presentations easily vanish under some kind of cover for concealed carry. On the other hand, that full-size P250 platform is ample as a duty-size sidearm.

It was with no small amount of anticipation that I took delivery of the test model (Serial No. EAU001555), chambered in 9mm. I rounded up a selection of ammunition from Remington, Federal, Black Hills, CCI, Silver Bear and Golden Bear, along with some of my own 9mm handloads and beat feet for the range.

My test pistol came with only one 15-round magazine, a stout lock, and a padded case with slots for small combination or keyed padlocks. Right out of the box, it shot like gangbusters, with no need to drift the front sight (the rear does not appear to move at all, as it nestles into a recess in the top of the slide and extends downward to retain the firing pin; another design innovation in the parts reduction department!).

My first impression was the trigger stroke was very long, and this will take some getting used to for guys like me who prefer single-action semi-autos on the Model 1911 platform. However, it the same stroke shot after shot, and once you get the hang of it, the P250 rocks. I shot up a couple of tin cans, and a fair share of Birchwood Casey Shoot-N-C targets, and the only significant thing that occurred was that I discovered Remington 9mm ball ammo prints a little higher than Federal 9mm ball ammo, with Golden Bear ball ammo printing somewhere in between. Now, for jacketed hollowpoints, I had a selection of Federal Hydra Shok, Silver Bear and Black Hills, the latter using what appeared to be Hornady XTP bullets.

With but a rare flyer, I'm happy to say this gun put them all right where they belong, with a shift of sight picture to adjust for the different loads, from a dead-center hold to a 6 o'clock hold.

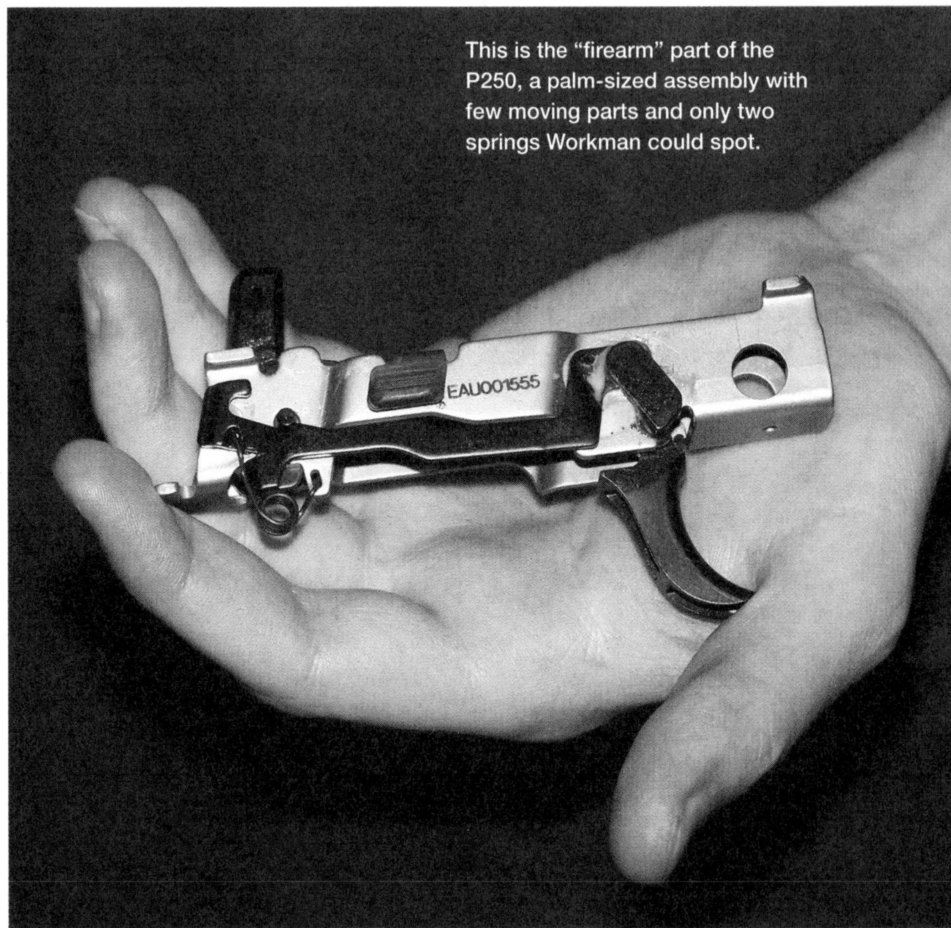

This is the "firearm" part of the P250, a palm-sized assembly with few moving parts and only two springs Workman could spot.

I was shooting off a Caldwell sandbag rest or offhand, as the mood suited me, and under less than ideal conditions. It snowed and rained the night before, leaving the range cold and damp, and muddy. I'll say this for the record: The P250 didn't hiccup, and the Silver Bear 9mm ammunition that had given me fits during an earlier test of the Ruger SR9 semi-auto acquitted itself rather well in the SIG Sauer pistol, and I am at a loss to explain why it worked in one gun and did poorly in the other.

When I test a pistol, the first thing I do at the range is function fire the gun, meaning that I'll load up a magazine and just blip off rounds until it's empty to see how well the gun runs out of the box. My P250 test gun roared to life, and never faltered during the entire evaluation, and that translates to a lot of lead downrange.

Compared to my Colt Commander, the P250 is just about the same length but in terms of slide width, the SIG Sauer is thicker, something of a given on many of today's modern pistols. Frankly, with advances in metallurgy, I am befuddled why so many pistol makers today build their handguns with such thick slides. It is not as though there is any risk of a thinner slide coming apart, but on the other hand, if the weight is added to tame recoil a bit, that makes some sense, though not much.

Target on left is the work of Federal FMJ 124-grainers, while the one on the right was produced with Silver Bear 124-grain JHPs. Range was 15 yards.

Now, if this is simply to make the gun more rugged, I don't happen to think that's necessary because I've never suspected any gun from SIG Sauer to be any less than completely sound. I have personally never heard of a SIG Sauer pistol's slide failing, and I've interviewed some people who have literally tens of thousands of rounds through their guns without a sign of metal fatigue. Oh, well.

The fastest muzzle velocity recorded over the screens of my Chrony Delta was 1,112 fps from the Black Hills 124-grain ammo, followed by the 124-grain Federal FMJ clocking at 1,042 fps. The slowest velocities I got were from the Silver Bear JHP at 982.3 fps and the Golden Bear FMJ at 998.4 fps.

Remington's 124-grain FMJ scooted out at 1,018 fps while the Federal Hydra-Shok moved along at 1,025 fps.

All that said, I would be confident to enter unfriendly neighborhoods, walk down dark alleys or just head to the range with the SIG Sauer P250. It passed the test of crummy Pacific Northwest weather with flying colors, and proved itself to be accurate and reliable.

TESTFIRE
REMINGTON ARMS R 15 VTR

by L.P. Brezny

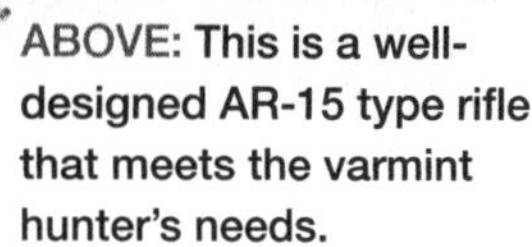

ABOVE: This is a well-designed AR-15 type rifle that meets the varmint hunter's needs.

Remington is not your dad's old company anymore. It has changed and, with new owners, has done some rethinking as to the direction the Big Green machine is going. A major new addition to Remington's product offering for 2008 will be a line of AR-15-type rifles. The AR-15 type fits into the "black gun" family, and is used by military, government agencies and law enforcement around the world. Why then would a sporting arms manufacturer turn to a military rifle as a part of its over-the-counter firearms package? Because the AR -15 design is becoming the most sought-after rifle in current production today.

The R-15 is fitted with a fluted barrel to reduce heat buildup when taking on prairie dogs or other high-volume targets.

Remington, a corporate companion to Bushmaster Firearms, decided to enter the AR market by developing a rifle that was not directly tied to a military application, but rather a rifle with strong identification among varmint hunters – the R-15 VTR.

UTAH: TESTING THE NEW R-15 VTR

I can't say I was surprised that Remington moved into the AR-15 line of firearms. I had been asked by my friend and colleague Eddie Stevenson almost a year earlier to put together some ideas as to just what a varmint-dedicated AR rifle should include. Now, some seven or eight months later, I found myself in Lehi, Utah partnering up with my old friends at CODA Hunts for a three-day evaluation of the new Remington auto-loading rifle that, only a short time before, had been only a design idea on a piece of paper.

After packing a big Dodge 4X4 with everything needed for a three-day mountain coyote hunt, partners Dan Stone, Kendall Johnson and I turned west and didn't look back until we almost reached the Nevada border. This was big-time coyote country, and a perfect place to wring out Remington's new AR-15 class rifle.

I had been offered one of two R-15 rifles, with the first being an M-4 type carbine with a telescoping stock and short 18-inch barrel. The R-15 was also to be built using the standard fixed military style stock, but that version was not available at the time. As another option Remington had built a full-size rifle version of the R-15 that used a longer 22-inch pipe, and a fixed stock system. This would be the rifle I'd take afield for that first R-15 coyote hunting experiences.

As all Remington R-15 rifles make use of a Weaver flattop sight base, scope sights were mounted on my test rifle. Burris varmint-style glass of 3.5 – 14X magnification had been selected by Remington for my field evaluation.

R-15s will be chambered for either the 223 Remington or 204 Ruger cartridge. My rifle was chambered in 204 Ruger, and test ammunition for the coyote hunt was Remington's 40-grain Accutip-V, a good choice for the task at hand.

One nice feature on the R-15 is the use of commercial sling studs. Sometimes the mil-spec sling system on battle rifles can weigh as much as a quarter-pound of solid steel. Not so

Model R-15 VTF
Specifications:

- Semiautomatic, w/Bushmaster receiver (Upper and Lower).
- Free-floating, button-rifled and fluted ChroMoly barrel, 18- or 22-inch.
- Single-stage clean-breaking trigger.
- Forend tube drilled for accessory rails.
- Advantage camo-covered (complete rifle).
- Five-round magazine.
- Fixed or six-position stock (buyer's choice).
- Flattop Weaver upper.
- Accessories to be offered at later date.
- Lockable hard case.

Price: $999

Author shot the new R-15 for three full days while hunting from a cold mountain camp in western Utah.

with the R-15. Remington decided to fit standard hunting rifle sling studs to the buttstock and forend assembly for a hunter-friendly detachable sling setup.

Even the finish of the R-15 is different from many variations of the rifle. Remington decided against the standard "black gun" look and instead uses a camo pattern, the Advantage Max-1 HD pattern, on all rifles. With a free-floating barrel-style handguard, fluted barrel, and fitted pistol grip, this 7 3/4-pound rifle feels good, whether used over shooting sticks or fired offhand.

The trigger is a Remington-designed single-stage system with a crisp, clean let-off. This helped the rifle easily shoot tight groups during the 100-yard zero check prior to going into the field. My rifle shot sub-MOA, which is getting to be almost standard with the better-grade ARs.

The factory magazine shipped with the R-15 holds only 5 rounds. Remington wanted to get away from the military thing and stay within all 50 states' hunting rifle requirements regarding magazine capacity. With the massive aftermarket associated with AR -15 class rifles there is no problem picking up magazines that can hold from 10 to 30 rounds. Also, Remington will be introducing a complete line of accessories for the basic R-15 rifle, all under the Remington brand.

In the field I did find several problems come up. First of all, double-check the magazine latch to ensure a secure magazine. Also, bolt position needs to be visually checked to ensure it is fully closed. A partially closed bolt or a loose magazine will result in a malfunction.

I carried the rifle for three days out of a cold camp at 6000 feet above sea level, in dead-of-winter conditions. No heat for three days, and plenty of snow each day. The rifle took a pounding, to say the least, but fired when I asked it to perform. I think I am credited with the first coyote taken using the new Remington R15. A big male dog was running along some rim rock at just under 300 yards as it came to a Fox-Pro jackrabbit call. One shot using the Remington 40-grain Accutip-V bullet dropped him. Hunting the heavy sage-brush was tough in the snow-covered conditions. We sent many rounds downrange at fast-moving 'yotes, but hit few. The hunt was concluded with six dogs down, plus a called badger that was hungry and real mad at something.

There was heavy expenditure of ammunition during an evening hunt for jackrabbits. Here the R-15 got a wild and fast workout on high-velocity bunnies that turned cold hard snow to fine mist beneath their flying feet. The R-15, in this application, was unquestionably in its glory. The follow-up shot is right there thanks to the auto-feed system, and the gunner's ability stay on the scope without lifting his or her head.

While many models of the AR 15 type rifles sell for around $2000, this rifle will be affordable at $999; in some cases even less. How can Remington do this? Because sister company Bushmaster builds the receiver for the R-15, and the gun has been designed for hunters, without those $300 handguards and $800 combat stocks. Even so, the R-15 is not a cut-down no-frills rifle. Rather, the R-15 is a very nice package for coyote and varmint hunters, and other applications of a similar nature. The rifle, as set up by Remington, can be fitted with current aftermarket accessories like special pistol grips, lights, lasers, battle sights and modular-style stocks. I'd say get in line early because the R-15 is going to sell fast and become a major fixture in the AR autoloader marketplace.

TESTFIRE

RUGER'S CHARMING CHARGER

by Dave Workman

Sooner or later, it had to happen; a handgun built on the legendary 10/22 action.

Perhaps it was inevitable. Eventually, considering the phenomenal popularity of the Ruger 10/22 semiautomatic rimfire rifle, somebody at Ruger was going to take that remarkable action and design a handgun around it.

It has finally happened, and the result is a terrific sporting pistol that seems to have been designed primarily for target shooters, but should have a long career as a small game handgun, provided there is one important addition to the basic design. I'll discuss that momentarily.

Ruger's 10/22 pistol is dubbed the Charger, and it certainly is that. Allow me to guarantee one thing right up front to get it out of the way before moving on the meat of this review: The Charger is a fun gun, and you will not be able to resist the urge to slap in an after-market 25-round Butler Creek banana clip and hose down a target with this new pistol. Get it out of your system right away and then sit down for some serious shooting that could ultimately put high scores on your record at the range, and maybe some tasty meat in the pot.

My younger son, Josh, got involved in this evaluation and he went through two 25-round magazines quicker than I could load up a couple of factory 10-rounders. Before the evaluation was over, he wanted to do it again and again, causing me to conclude that the Charger lives up to the somewhat appropriate observation that one of my shooting buddies once had about the Ruger 10/22: "It's a lead hose." It is nothing to go through a 500-round brick of rimfire ammunition in one sitting with a Ruger semi-auto rifle, and I confess, it's just as easy with the Charger.

Ruger supplies a fully-zippered gun case with each Charger pistol. It's made from rugged nylon, unzips to fold out, and is machine-washable.

The Charger seems to have been well thought out; that is, it's a gun that was a long-time coming, and I have to believe that part of the reason is because Ruger designers wanted to make sure they delivered a pistol that is practical, functional and lives up to a sterling reputation.

With a 10-inch tapered barrel that comes clean (no sights) from the factory, the Charger is fitted with a handsome gray laminate hardwood pistol grip stock that will appear radical to some, and well-designed by others. It has a wide forend with a QD sling swivel stud that was installed only for mounting the telescoping bipod that comes as part of the package. There is a palm swell on both sides of the pistol grip, a rather pronounced "beavertail" at the rear and an ample flare at the base. Perhaps not surprisingly, there is no checkering anywhere on this stock, though one might suggest it for the truly precision shooters to maintain a constant grip. One other thing to note about the laminated stock was that the barrel does not exactly float; instead having contact with the wood for about two inches out from the receiver. After that, the wood falls away from the barrel dramatically.

Empty and without the bipod attached, the Charger weighs 3 ½ pounds and it is 19 ¼ inches overall. It is because of that size and weight that there is literally no recoil when shooting this pistol. Ruger supplies

Siblings: The Ruger 10/22 rifle has been around for many years, and the new Charger is a chip off that old block!

a zippered gun rug/case that can be folded out and used as a shooting pad. This gun rug does not have carrying handles for some inexplicable reason, but it is roomy enough to house the Charger with bipod attached. It's also washable, so if you get it dirty, toss it in the laundry to clean it up.

Because it is built around the 10/22 action, the Charger will accept any rotary magazine made for the popular rifle (in January 2008, Ruger announced that it had shipped the 5 millionth Ruger 10/22). It is quite possibly the most successful rimfire self-loader on the map, and certainly the most successful model with a rotary magazine.

My test gun *(Serial # 490-01057)* has a tough-looking black matte finish on the barrel and receiver, and it came from the factory with a Weaver-type base mounted on top finished to match the receiver. I quickly slapped on a Bushnell Elite 3200 long eye-relief 2-6x32mm pistol scope that is finished in handsome matte silver, and the contrast between scope, black Weaver Lever-Lock rings and the matte finish of the gun was stunning. I have used this scope on other handguns, typically big bores with plenty of recoil and this model has never faltered. If it can handle that kind of punishment, I figured correctly that putting it on the Charger was not going to create a problem.

The only significant difference between the 10/22 rifle action and that found on the Charger is the magazine release. On the pistol, the release is a small lever that projects downward at the rear of the magazine well, while on the rifle (mine, at least) there is a simple button to press. During the shooting sessions, I discovered that inserting the magazine seemed to require pressing this release lever.

As on all 10/22 models I've ever fired, the bolt does not remain open after the last shot, and when one locks the bolt back, it requires that a small lever behind the magazine and situated next to the release be depressed. I was especially impressed with the way the Charger's grip seemed to fit my average-size hand, and the trigger let-off was crisp with no discernible creep.

What disappointed me about the Charger is something that can be remedied in about five minutes: It needs a rear QD sling swivel stud so that it may be carried on a sling for hunting. I don't care that Ruger's initial intent may have been to produce a very accurate pistol for target shooting from a bench, which the Charger surely is, but I do care that the designers of a gun with this one's inherent attributes somehow overlooked the hunting application. I'll give them the benefit of doubt here. It might just be that they were so busy making sure the Charger delivers the goods on all other levels that they simply forgot a lot of characters like myself just might want to bonk a bunny or a bushytail.

Where I live out in the West, this pistol would be considered well-designed for shooting grouse or rabbits in the head. In the Southeast or Midwest, I can see

LEFT: Author liked that hand-filling pistol grip with its flared base and palm swell.

BELOW: A single screw in front of the magazine well holds everything in place.

some enterprising squirrel or raccoon hunter filling his bag with this pistol, too.

I'll toss this out just to be able to say I did it: There is one other temptation that must be resisted like a date with a tax assessor: Under no circumstances should anyone pop the Charger's barreled action out of the stock and stick it into an aftermarket rifle stock, especially one of those with a folding butt. Do that and you are breaking the law.

But on the other hand, at some future date, I can see folks at Ramline or Butler Creek perhaps coming up with an aftermarket stock for the Charger. I would be particularly interested in a synthetic replacement stock if I owned this pistol, because in my native Pacific Northwest, the monsoon climate through the winter would not harm a synthetic stock at all.

The Charger's barrel, cut with a 1:16-inch rifling twist, has a slightly recessed target-style crown, and I suspect this contributes to the pistol's accuracy. Once I got the scope adjusted, the Charger began delivering little tiny groups at 15 and 25 yards that convinced me of the gun's longer-range capabilities. I'd bet a patient shooter will be able to knock over metal rams and chickens, and punch other targets be they paper or live tissue, way out there at 75 and 100 yards, particularly when using something like Federal Match ammo.

With a variety of ammunition, the Charger never skipped a beat. I can say this with some certainty that my gun isn't an anomaly, but a typical sample because I've lost count of the number of rounds that have gone down the tube of my Ruger 10/22 rifle without benefit of a cleaning patch, and I have a pal who has had three of them and burned through thousands of rounds and never cleaned them once.

That kind of service speaks volumes for the durability and reliability of the Ruger Charger's proven 10/22 action. I have never seen one of these actions fail, and that covers a lot of years, and a hell of a lot of ammunition under some awful conditions.

And speaking of ammunition, did I find a perfect cartridge for this pistol? Nope. I have a rather healthy supply of 22 Long Rifle ammunition from Federal, Winchester, Remington and CCI, and nothing malfunctioned. From subsonic to hyper velocity rounds, that faithful Ruger 10/22 action will digest them all.

For a smallbore precision metallic target shooter, the Ruger Charger is top-notch, and it is certainly in he price range of most shooters with an MSRP of $369.50 at this writing. Once I had the crosshairs adjusted in the Elite 3200 scope, it shot very consistent groups. It strikes me that the Charger could give

certain single-shot 22-caliber pistols a real run for their money in a metallic silhouette match, with the advantage of not having to shift position for each subsequent shot, the problem with having to reload every time you press the trigger.

My advice is to get a couple of spare rotary magazines for the Charger and a few bricks of ammunition because you're going to need them!

Charger Pistol
Specifications:

Manufacturer: Sturm, Ruger, Inc., 200 Ruger Road, Dept. GD, Prescott, AZ 86301; (520) 541-8820; www.ruger.com
Action: Semi-automatic
Barrel length: 10 inches, 1:16-inch twist
Magazine Capacity: 10 rounds
OAL: 19-1/4 inches
MSRP: $369.50

ABOVE: It may not seem like the most comfortable rest, but lean against a wide tree trunk, and you can have a very steady rest on a knee with the Ruger Charger. Workman says that target shooters better not get too possessive, because small game hunters are going to want this gun in the field!

Goofy stance or not, the younger Workman demonstrates he's got some marksmanship in his blood.

TESTFIRE WEATHERBY MARK XXII

by Layne Simpson

Remember the Weatherby Mark XXII in 22 LR? It was introduced by Roy Weatherby in 1961 and while production ceased in 1988 the name is again very much alive and this time around the rifle is a bolt action rather than an autoloader. The barreled action of the new Mark XXII (pronounced "Mark 22") is built by Anschutz but it is stocked here in America by Weatherby in American walnut. The action is nothing more or less than the Anschutz Model 64 and you can choose between 22 Long Rifle and 17 HMR. In either caliber it is guaranteed to shoot five bullets inside half an inch at 50 yards with good ammunition, and a target included with the rifle proves that the fellow who shot it before you bought it was also capable of that level of accuracy. As I write this I have shot four different Mark XXII rifles, three in 17 HMR, the other in 22 LR and all lived up to that claim with accurate ammunition.

Like all Weatherby rifles used to have and some still do, the Mark XXII has a high-gloss finish on its stock and a flawless polish job beneath a coat of dark bluing on all of its metal parts. In other words, it looks the way old-fashioned people like me think a Weatherby rifle is supposed to look. It is the perfect small-game companion to a Deluxe grade Mark V rifle or a Vanguard Deluxe and it is the kind of rifle that gets plenty of attention from other shooters at the gun club.

All stocks I have examined had a flawless finish and most had just enough contrasting figure in the walnut to be classified as a cut above others in its price range. The styling of the stock is Roy Weatherby's original Monte Carlo with plenty of 18-line checkering at the wrist and forearm. The person who cut the checkering knew his or her business because it is nicely executed with no runovers at the borders and not a single diamond left begging to be pointed up.

The receiver of the Mark XXII is both grooved and drilled and tapped for scope mounting.

TESTFIRE

ABOVE: Replacing the synthetic bolt knob with one of steel would put the Mark XXII even closer to perfection.

Attachment of a thin rubber butt pad to the stock is so nicely done it appears to have sprouted from the wood. Same goes up front for a rosewood forend tip and its contrasting maple spacer. The forearm tip is fitted to the stock at a 45-degree angle, a touch originated by Roy Weatherby many years ago, back during his pre-Mark V days when he built his custom rifles around the FN Mauser action. The grip of the stock is also capped in rosewood and the stock wears quick-detachable sling swivel posts. Wood-to-metal fit is quite good although I am not exactly excited about the shape of the cutout in the side of the stock for the safety lever. I would also like to see the synthetic knob of the bolt handle replaced by steel.

Everything I said about the finish on the wood applies to the metal finish as well—absolutely flawless. Any blue job is only as good as the polishing job beneath it and those who are responsible for that at the Anschutz factory get gold stars from me. As is customary these days, no sights are on the 23-inch barrel but the receiver is both grooved and drilled and tapped for the mounting of a telescopic sight. The barrel starts with a diameter of .870-inch at the receiver and from there it tapers to .635-inch at the muzzle. Rifling twist rate is 1:16 inches for 22 LR and 1:9 inches for 17 HMR. The barrel is thin enough to make the Mark XXII light enough to carry in the field all day long but heavy enough for accurate shooting. Over-

Dieter Anschutz (left) and Ed Weatherby (right) teamed up to bring us the rifle the author is holding.

all length of the rifle is a hair over 41 inches and while Weatherby says the weight is supposed to be 6-1/2 pounds, the one you see in this report weighed four ounces less. This is no surprise since the densities of walnut stocks can vary enough to change actual rifle weight either way. When wearing a scope of reasonable weight, the Mark XXII will come in at a field-ready weight of less than 7-1/2 pounds, just about right for close-range varminting, for hunting small game, or for a Saturday afternoon at the range with the kids.

Weatherby Mark XXII
Accuracy Results/17HMR:

Loads	Accuracy (in.)	Velocity (fps)
Federal 17-gr. V-Max	0.418	2618
Hornady 17-gr. V-Max	0.566	2537
Remington 17-gr. Accu-Tip	0.588	2587
CCI 20-gr. Gamepoint	0.685	2422
Hornady 20-gr. XTP	0.701	2414
CCI 17-gr. TNT	0.776	2554
Average Accuracy	**0.622**	

Attaching the rosewood tip to the forearm at a 45-degree angle started with Roy Weatherby back in the 1940s.

The 17 HMR magazine holds four rounds, the one in 22 LR holds five.

The Mark XXII has a two-position safety lever at the right-hand side of the receiver bridge and its trigger is fully adjustable. It comes from the factory with about a 40-ounce pull weight but it can be reduced by another 10 ounces or so. The trigger on the rifle I shot broke crisply with a pull-to-pull weight variation of less than two ounces. I could feel no creep, but over-travel was there.

As is commonly seen in 22 rimfires, contact between the root of the bolt handle and a shoulder in the receiver takes care of lockup during firing. Dual-opposed extractors up front snatch fired cases from the chamber with total reliability, even when fouling has accumulated from many shots. The first step in removing the bolt from the receiver is to place the safety in its off position and make sure the rifle is totally unloaded. Then retract the bolt while simultaneously holding down the release button at the left side of the receiver and holding back the trigger. Same procedure applies for installing the bolt–both the trigger and release have to be depressed and the safety has to be in its forward position. I find bolt travel to be exceptionally smooth except for the last bit of rotation to the locked and unlocked positions when the end of the cocking cam jumps from or drops into its indention in the front surface of the cocking piece. This detail is inherent in the design of the Anschutz Model 64 action and is not unique to those built by that company for Weatherby. Keeping the entire cocking cam surface lubricated with a good grease helps but does not entirely eliminate the "click" heard when the bolt is opened and closed.

A couple of slotted-head screws hold the one-piece trigger guard/magazine housing assembly to the action. It is machined from steel and the bottom of the trigger bow is engraved with Weatherby's famous "Flying W", a very nice touch indeed. Capacity of the detachable magazine is five 22 LR or four 17 HMR and while it does extend below the belly of the stock, it is not enough to make the rifle uncomfortable in the one-hand carry. One magazine comes with the package and those of standard or extra capacity (10 rounds in 22 LR) are available at additional cost. The magazine release is located just forward of the trigger bow and while it is easy to reach, it is not likely to be accidentally bumped in the field. Weatherby rifles use the same magazines as Anschutz rifles and while you could buy extras from Anschutz, they would not have the "Flying W" molded into their floorplates.

Anytime I need to accuracy-test a rimfire rifle I can usually count on less than ideal conditions at the range and my luck did not change when the fellow in the brown truck delivered a Mark XXII to my home. As I got settled in at the bench, the wind was gusting up to 20 miles per hour and, on top of that, stiff breezes seemed to switch direction from one trigger squeeze to the next. It takes less than the breath of a fair maiden to push one of those tiny bullets of the 17 HMR off course and it surely showed in the averages I squeezed off. Still, at least one group fired with each load measured less than half an inch and I managed to equal Weatherby's half-inch accuracy guarantee with one of six loads tried and came close to the magic mark with a couple more. I know rifle and shooter could do better under better conditions but at the very least I proved to myself that the Weatherby accuracy guarantee is within reach. My tests also included some rapid-fire shooting for functioning and the rifle never missed a single lick. The top cartridge of a fully loaded magazine did not feed as smoothly as the other three but it never failed to make its way into the chamber.

A lot of things about this joint venture between Weatherby and Anschutz have impressed me, and at the top of the list is overall quality. The little rifle also handles nicely in the field. The Mark XXII is the kind of rifle you buy for yourself today with the thought of someday passing it on to your son who will, in turn, do the same a few decades down the road. In other words, it is the kind of rifle that will outlast several generations of hunters and shooters. Not only that but it does a great job of continuing a tradition of fine rifles that began back in the 1940s with Roy Weatherby and is still carried on by his son Ed today.

TESTFIRE
FIRST STRIKE

Ruger's new SR9 represents the brand's take on a striker-fired semiauto pistol.

by Brad Fitzpatrick

There are many classic debates among handgunners—brand quality, semiauto versus revolver, single versus double action, and other nuances of taste and style that stir shooters to lengthy conversation. One such debate is the merits of striker-fired semi-autos, which ignite the primer with a spring-loaded pin, versus more traditional hammer-fired pistols. Some companies have embraced the striker design–Glock, in particular–while others continue producing hammer-fired guns.

Sturm, Ruger and company is one brand that has always manufactured pistols that were fired via a hammer. Until now. Their recent release of the SR9 9mm semiauto demonstrates to the shooting world how Ruger envisions the ideal striker-fired, polymer-framed semiauto and blends modern technology with the brand's traditional styling touches, function and ergonomic design.

Ruger has a strong reputation among handgun aficionados—from the original Mark I and the Single Six to the more recent Super Redhawk and P345, Ruger has built a loyal following of handgunners who depend on accuracy, reliability and ease of function, particularly in handguns designed for defense. The SR9 does not disappoint. My own SR9 loaded every round and ejected every spent case without a single malfunction—which is dually impressive because it was new out of the box and had no "break-in" period to lose factory burrs or imperfections. Those who purchase handguns for personal defense understandably demand absolute, unfailing reliability, and although no gun can promise that I was impressed with the SR9's lack of squibs, jams and other failures. My only immediate concern was a rough lip on the feed ramp—a worry that proved unsubstantiated. After several hundred rounds the load ramp still fed cartridges with aplomb.

Ruger has designed the SR9 with several features intended specifically for a defense handgun. Like other striker guns it is double-action-only with a cocking indicator that is housed at the rear of the slide and projects farther as the slack is pulled out of the trigger. It has an impressive magazine capacity—17+1 in standard form (a 10+1 version is also available in jurisdictions that limit magazine capacity). To keep those rounds in the 10-ring the SR9 has low-profile, adjustable sights with three white dots. Ruger has obviously heard complaints about higher profile adjustables catching on holsters and clothing. Likewise, they understand that quality defense pistols should have adjustable sights so that the pistol fires on-target for each shooter. The SR9 sports three-dot white sights that allow for rapid target acquisition while focusing your eyes downrange. At the range I was impressed by how quickly the sights aligned and how easy it was to see the large white dots while focusing on the target, allowing for the rapid sustained shooting that is a hallmark of defense pistols. Like most all defense pistols, the SR9 comes with a built-in Picatinny rail for mounting accessories such as flashlights or laser sights.

The ergonomics of the SR9 brought mixed reviews. I wanted several different shooters of varying physical size and experience to give comment on how they

SR9 Pistol
Specifications:

Manufacturer: Sturm, Ruger, Inc., 200 Ruger Road, Dept. GD, Prescott, AZ 86301; (520) 541-8820; www.ruger.com
Caliber: 9mm Luger (9mmx19)
Magazine Capacity: 17+1 and 10-round magazines
Barrel length: 4.4 inches, Stainless Steel
Weight: 26.50 oz.
OAL: 7.55 inches
MSRP: $525.00

thought the SR9 fit and shot. Certain aspects drew praise all around (the sights), while the one complaint from most shooters was trigger pull. Both inexperienced and experienced shooters felt that there was excessive travel. One of the experienced shooters said, "Too much slop." A new shooter added, "I never knew when the dang thing was about to go off!" I'm personally not bothered with the SR9's trigger pull—many striker-fired pistols have long trigger travel, and the SR9's pull feels smoother than many other factory-installed triggers. If you are trying to keep your shots in the 10-ring simply pull out the slack until the trigger tightens and squeeze from there. Ruger claims six-and-a-half pounds of pressure will break the trigger—I measured it at six and a quarter. The reality of defense pistols, though, is that they are not bench-rest or silhouette guns and if you find yourself in a potentially life-threatening situation you don't want a trigger with two pounds of pull that may go off under a trembling finger. The SR9's trigger may take some getting used to for those unaccustomed to the design but after some time on the range all testers found the sweet spot and learned to live with, if not like, the trigger.

Currently all versions of the SR9 include a 4.14 inch barrel, giving the gun an overall length of 7.55 inches, which means it is certainly no compact but still small enough that it can be carried without hassle. Ruger has managed to keep weight down--at just over 26 ounces the SR9 adds little heft while carrying. The light weight means more barrel jump, but not an excessive amount and in the give-and-take of recoil versus gun weight I believe Ruger has played the middle ground quite well. I had no problems with target acquisition due to recoil on follow-up shots. Its slim slide and grip mean that it sits well against the hip and doesn't create a bulge in clothing like many thicker pistols do.

The SR9 has a safety and magazine release that are both ambidextrous, which is a feature sometimes overlooked by the right-handed majority. The single southpaw in our group enjoyed the fact that the Ruger works for lefties and righties equally well. I am a big fan of ambidextrous guns not because I'm left handed but because they make both the safety and magazine release accessible easily from either side of the gun. There were some complaints about the small safety which if far back on the gun—again, a matter of taste. My thumb hit the safety every time I reached for it. The SR9 fit well in most shooters hands—those that didn't like it generally held the gun lower than it was designed to be held and thus felt there was too much swell front-to-back. Ruger includes a reversible backstrap that can be changed by simply removing a pin and inserting the backstrap with the opposite side facing out. The choice of a flat grip or curved one was another matter of taste—and the reason Ruger made it simple to change! What garnered praise all around was how well the narrow grip fit in each shooter's hand and how well it absorbed recoil. Some polymers have grips that are too slick. Not the Ruger. Wrap your hand around the narrow-checkered grip and that is where the gun stays. The reality of a defense handgun is that it may have to be pulled quickly and a shift in grip may mean disaster. Three of us took turns holstering, gripping and drawing the Ruger and by the end of the session we all gave high praise to the grip design, including one shooter who said, "If my life depended on getting a gun clear of a holster and hitting where I wanted that grip would be the one I'd want".

Accuracy was measured at ten and twenty-two feet with each person firing five rounds. For comparison I brought a Walther PPK and a Beretta Tomcat—two small handguns to compare with the beefier SR9. In slow-fire scenarios the Walther and the SR9 were more accurate, with the edge going to the SR9 for overall accuracy while the much smaller Tomcat lagged behind. Without question the improved accuracy was a result of a longer barrel, more heft and much better sights. And the Ruger was better able to deliver follow-up shots that hit where they were supposed to. Those who previously criticized the grip of the SR9 quickly agreed that the larger handle, although somewhat cumbersome to conceal when compared to two true compacts, made the SR9 much easier to shoot.

Finish quality of the SR9 is on par with most competitors. It is available in both blued and stainless versions that retail for $565 and $525, respectively. Ruger offers a variety of additional gear, including Picatinny rail accessories, holsters, clips and locks. The SR9 comes standard with two clips of either 10- or 17-round capacity, depending on the model. Disassembly of the SR9 is simple and straightforward, and anyone familiar with the disassembly procedure for Ruger's current semiautos will quickly recognize that the SR9 breaks down in much the same way. Simply lock the slide and release the magazine, lower the slide release lever inside the chamber (and don't forget to lift it again upon reassembly!), remove the barrel pin and pull the slide forward. The mainspring and barrel simply pop out. Ruger offers detailed instruction in their manual and those should always be carefully followed.

By the end of the day the Ruger had been put through its paces, most of its break-in period was over and every shooter was in agreement that the SR9 was a fine gun. Ruger's first foray into the world of striker-fired semiautos was a success. It handled well, carried well and most importantly fired each time it was asked to without any hesitation or failure. No one ever wants to be put in a defense situation but if that moment arrives your life depends on how well your gun works, and the SR9 works—no debate about it!

ONE GOOD GUN
A SAVAGE MODEL 99

by Jim Romanelli

You don't hear much about the Savage Model 99 or the 300 Savage cartridge anymore, but when I was a youngster in the 1950s farm country of Pennsylvania it was a pretty popular combination.

My first introduction to that outfit was by an uncle who, since the early 1940s, owned a Savage M99G (featherweight take-down) in the 30-caliber chambering and, years later, installed a 4X Weaver scope on its deck. My earliest recollection was seeing that rifle leaning in his closet and always hoping that one day I'd be allowed to give it a try. Every time I asked, the answer was that I was a little too young and had to wait 'til I got a little more meat on my bones.

I was 11 years old when I finally got to fire that rifle. It happened when my Dad and I were at my uncle's farm while he was in the middle of his "sighting-in session", just before the deer season.

Uncle Dick put a piece of plywood with a white circle painted on it (about 10 inches in diameter) out around 100 yards. From a rest on the hood of his old Ford he hit that circle two out of two shots, and my Dad proceeded to do the same. As you can tell, they weren't interested in tack-driving, only in what it took to put venison on the table.

On our way back from the target, Uncle Dick must have seen that sorry-eyed Bassett hound look on my face when I saw him nudge my father and nod towards me. I heard Dad say, "I don't see why not." Then my Uncle asked, "Jim, you want to see if you can hit anything with this?"

Well, I couldn't have been any more surprised than if I had been struck by lightning. I was only about 10 feet behind them, but I know that I broke the sound barrier in closing

While perhaps not a collector's dream, the author's customized Savage is truly a rifleman's pleasure.

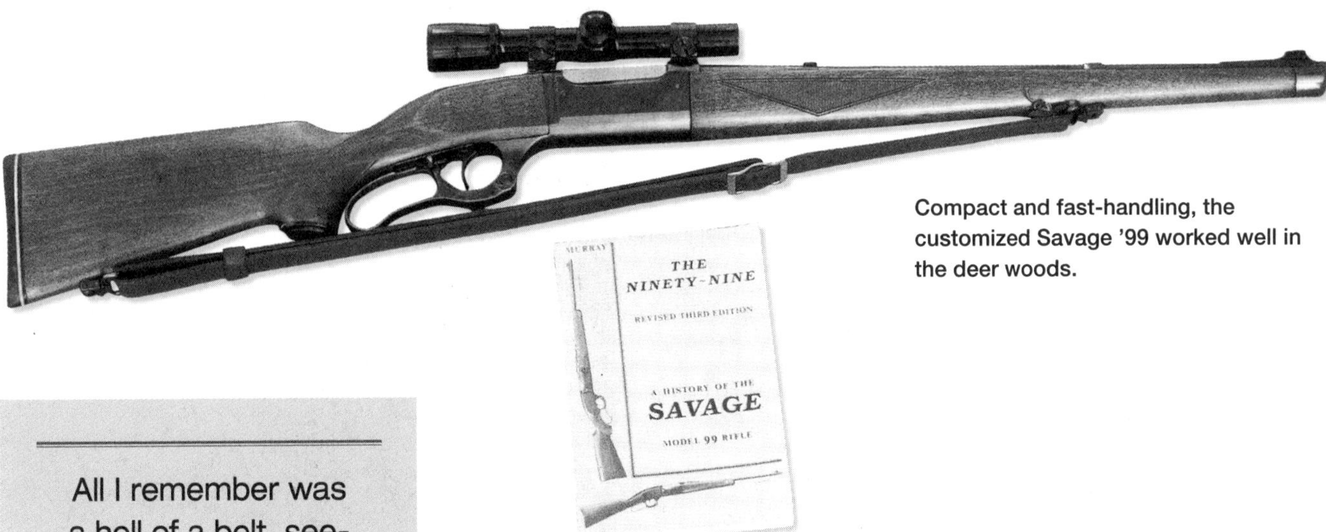

Compact and fast-handling, the customized Savage '99 worked well in the deer woods.

All I remember was a hell of a belt, seeing my uncle holding onto the scope – and the both of them belly-laughing while I was on the ground wondering what happened.

that distance. We were only about 50 yards away from the target when he handed me the Savage. It seemed to weigh a ton compared to the Daisy BB gun and the Remington Model 121 22LR that I was allowed to shoot.

He showed me how to open and close the action, load the magazine and put the safety on. There were some other instructions on breathing, holding steady and sight picture that I barely heard since I couldn't get over the excitement of actually holding the rifle that I was only allowed to look at for the past 11 years.

He handed me a cartridge, I loaded it and thought that I'd go one better than both my Uncle and Dad by trying the shot offhand. I'll never forget seeing the target through the scope and trying to keep those crosshairs from dancing around. Keep in mind that I was only 11 years old and didn't weigh 80 pounds soaking wet...so when I finally pulled the trigger, a little more happened than I expected.

All I remember was a hell of a belt, seeing my uncle holding onto the scope – and the both of them belly-laughing while I was on the ground wondering what happened.

As I recall, Dad said "There's a hole in the corner of the plywood." That was bullseye enough for me and I could feel my chest swell with pride almost as fast as my shoulder did from the pain of that steel buttplate. I can remember my Uncle saying, "Jim, if that had been an elephant, we'd be having tail soup for supper."

Although I was more than game to try another shot, I was lucky to have two adults around with common sense to override my enthusiasm. The rest of the day, my left arm reminded me of my graduation into the centerfires.

As the years passed, I grew a little bigger and become less sensitive to recoil. I got into the fad of faster, flatter-shooting cartridges housed in more modern bolt rifles topped with variable-power range-finding scopes.

Whenever my Uncle saw me with a new rifle and equipment he'd ask, "Where's the safari, Jim?" His opinion was that if a deer couldn't be got with the Savage – along with a little woods savvy – then that deer couldn't be got at all.

He would make that point time and again by harvesting 95 percent of his deer within 50 yards. That other five percent proved that if you have only one rifle and know how to shoot it well, that variable scopes and belted magnum trajectories weren't necessary. I once saw him shoot twice at a doe out past 300 yards and put her down on the spot. A quick post-mortem showed the bullets struck her in the neck and chest.

It wasn't until 1988 that his statement came to haunt me. I was in a little gun shop browsing the racks and spotted a couple of Savage Model 99s in the 300 Savage chambering. One was a Model F in nice condition and the other was customized in the Mannlicher style, with a 20-inch barrel chambered for the 300 Savage cartridge, and wearing a Weaver K2.5X scope. It was love at first sight and the next day I was back at the gun shop, trading in one of my heavy tack-driving bolt guns with its 3-12X variable scope.

The rifle's serial number put the Savage's date of manufacture around 1954, but when it was customized I'll never know. I brought it to my local gunsmith to see what he could tell me and he believed that it was customized at the factory, by the evidence of the matching wood and tell-tale Savage checkering.

I have found this little Savage has never exceeded 1 1/2-inch groups at 100 yards with either 150- or 180-grain bullets and that the K2.5X scope is no hindrance when shooting a practical field ranges (point-blank to 200+yds.). I don't mind saying that its recoil is a lot lighter than what I remember from 30 years earlier. If I need to take a shot beyond 200 yards, then I think I need to learn to hunt a little better.

It is by far the handiest rifle I have ever handled. In the past 10 years it has been my woods companion through many miles, and it looks it with the honest dings and scratches earned from the thick brushy areas I hunt. Every one of those scars is a reminder of a memorable hunt to harvest a little venison for the table.

My Uncle has long since passed into the happy hunting ground, but I tend to agree with him that this little custom Savage M99 Mannlicher is all the rifle I'll ever need.

ONE GOOD GUN
RUGER SINGLE SIX

by Steve Gash

I couldn't wait for high school to be over. I had endured four long, torturous years of lectures, tests, and book reports, but enough was enough, and I was ready to escape. Don't laugh: in May of 1961, I had a calendar on the wall on which I carefully Xed-out each day as matriculation approached.

But finally I was out, and there was an upside to all this folderol: presents! And not just trinkets, either. Oh, to be sure, there were plenty of them, but what quickened my pulse were those unique rectangular envelopes addressed to "Master Steve Gash," and that almost always meant money! A buck here, two there, and as the late Senator Everett M. Dirksen once said, pretty soon you were talking real money. (Of course, the good Senator was referring to government spending, and the units were millions, but the principle's the same.) I had sent out graduation announcements to every living human being that I could possibly call a relative, and they responded nicely. Most cards contained a dollar, sometimes two, but occasionally some flush soul would cough up a fiver. Imagine, five dollars! Eventually I collected a grand total of $47. To a 17-year old kid in 1961, this was indeed "real money."

Even then, there was but one material lust in my life: guns, and the current object of desire was a popular revolver that had been on the market since 1953, the Ruger Single Six.

A local store carried a modest selection of firearms, among which was a brand new Single Six, nestled in its original box. Every chance I had, I hotfooted it the 15 blocks from Pittsburg (Kansas) High to the store to gaze starry-eyed at its lovely countenance. The kindly proprietor wanted $55 for it, and as May dissolved into June, it became possible. After all, I had a whopping $47 in my pocket. I scrounged up the remaining $8, and proudly walked into the store, and bought my very first gun.

ABOVE: A target of opportunity: one of several fat blue grouse taken with the Single Six 22 *(circa 1978)*.

Of course, my parents, relatives, and just about anybody else thought that it was perfectly fine for a 17-year old to waltz into a store, plunk down his money, and walk out with a handgun in its box. (Try that today!) The neat little 22 looked to me like the perfect companion. And for the past 48 years, it has been just that.

After I got my prize home, I examined its every nuance. Fit and finish were impeccable, and its weight and balance were then (and now) perfect. It has a 5 1/2-inch barrel, fixed sights, and the rounded loading gate instituted in 1957. The black, hard rubber grips were sharply checkered. Cocking the hammer elicited those four clicks that told you that this sturdy revolver meant business.

The Single Six and I have hunted many species in many places. Chasing pheasants in western Kansas during the mid- to late-1960s was a tradition, but it was a hit-or-miss deal. One year there would be birds everywhere; the next, we

The Ruger Single Six has been a classic since its introduction in 1953 This revolver, purchased in 1961, has accompanied the author on numerous ventures afield, taken much game, and ventilated countless cans.

Rimfire 22 ammunition comes in all flavors, with power tailored to the need. CCI's CB Longs with their 29-grain bullet loaf along at about 727 fps, perfect for forest grouse. Long Rifle ammo features 40-grain bullets. Standard Velocity (1070 fps) ammo is also great for small game and provides plenty of plinking fun. The High Velocity (1255 fps) and Hyper Velocity (1435 fps) Long Rifle versions pack more punch for larger small game.

were lucky to get one or two. Once we encountered an unexpected bonus near Webster Reservoir. There was a population explosion of black-tailed jackrabbits, and there seemed to be one behind every bunch of grass, so we proceeded to collect quite a few. My companions mostly used 22 rifles or their pheasant guns, but I stuck with the Single Six, and we brought home a couple of coolers full of hares. (Yes, they are good to eat. They make a very fine "jackrabbit stew." Remember, at the time my companions and I were starving college students, and free meat was, well, free meat!)

But it was after I moved to Colorado that the little revolver really came into its own and saw the most use. I found that on big game hunts the 22 was handy in case a fellow ran into a grouse, cottontail, or snowshoe hare. I hunted mule deer and elk every fall, and once in a while, a tasty target of opportunity would present itself. Cottontails and forest grouse were the usual fare, and many a fine camp meal was collected with the Single Six.

In 1977, I drew a coveted once-in-a-lifetime permit for a Colorado Big Horn. Later, while scouting for the hunt, I saw the occasional blue grouse. One fine day after hunting over a very steep mountain with a 7mm Magnum in my hand, and the Single Six on my belt, I stumbled onto a bunch of fat blue grouse. Finding blues if you were actually hunting them was rare, so this chance encounter was a big deal to me. These plump little forest chickens had definitely read the Blue Grouse Manual, especially the part about being "fool hens."

The first grouse was in a small crevice between two granite boulders, and its view was restricted, so it fluttered up onto one of the boulders, to gaze at me with considerable interest. By that time I had slung my 7mm over my shoulder, and unlimbered the Single Six. I took careful aim, and fired. A clean miss. But to my amazement the grouse didn't fly, or even walk off, but continued to observe the festivities with great interest. I shot again. Bullseye! I promptly dressed it and placed it in my daypack. My wife and I consider blues the best tasting game bird in existence, so I was really proud of myself for getting one blue grouse.

I had moved on only a few steps when I saw another grouse, then another, and yet another! Did I have "grouse fever?" What do you think? Sheep were the furthest thing from my mind at that point. The fool hens thoughtfully stood around and patiently waited while I reloaded my six-shooter, and then resumed my fusillade. I bagged three more and had my limit. I used standard velocity 22 Shorts on this foray. They dispatched grouse cleanly, and after all, I didn't want to disturb any wary ovine in the area. (Yes, I eventually got a nice 36-inch, 3/4-curl ram on the last weekend of the season.)

Once while elk hunting near timberline on Dome Peak, I jumped a pair of snowshoe hares. They scampered off about 20 yards, and stopped to look back. That was a fatal mistake for one of them; the other hare took off like a rocket. Snowshoes are high on our taste quotient, too. The Single Six proved itself once again.

In the years I have had the Single Six, I have tested, both on paper and game, many types of ammunition. For the utmost in low noise, Standard Velocity 22 Shorts are fine, if low powered. CCI's CB Long ammo is the modern-day equivalent. Also, Shorts are sometimes hard to find these days. Standard Velocity Long Rifle rounds also work well, and are a bit more accurate at rabbit ranges, and are appropriate for an afternoon of casual plinking. For pests, the current crop of High Velocity Long Rifle ammo with their lightweight bullets does a fine job. I just have to check point of impact with the various shells relative to the Single Six's fixed sights.

When nostalgia takes hold on a casual tromp through the fields or woods, or when on an elk hunt in the mountains, my high school graduation present usually goes along in its scarred leather holster. The little 22 is light, handy, and just fine for fur or feathers.

There are many wonderful handguns available, most of which can cover almost any shooting chore, and I have more than a few. But none evokes as many pleasant memories of another time, of the generosity of friends and relatives, and of countless rewarding moments in the field as does the old Single Six. Every time I see it, it's like meeting an old friend. Heck, it is an old friend.

HANDGUNS TODAY: AUTOLOADERS

by John Malloy

A number of factors influence the world of firearms. Among such factors, autoloading handguns seem disproportionately affected by political considerations. At the time of this writing in 2008, two questions of great importance are still undecided. The Supreme Court of the United States has not handed down a decision on the District of Columbia vs. Heller lawsuit, and the next President of the United States has not been elected. If you are reading this before these decisions have been made, please support any groups trying to bring things to conclusions that will benefit responsible firearms ownership and usage in the United States.

Lawsuits, or the possibility of lawsuits, continue to affect the manufacturers of autoloading handguns. Magazine disconnects, key locks, loaded chamber indicators, padlocks, locking cases—these and more have been added to many autoloading pistols in an effort to acquire protection from anti-gun lawsuits. Some shooters look askance at additional gadgetry that could fail at a critical time. To their credit, some manufacturers have been ingenious in adding unobtrusive safety devices.

We have become used to the major media's irresponsible treatment of firearms issues. Now, there seems to be a glimmer of hope. Here in my home area of North Florida, following the brutal murder of a local woman, the local media reported positively on pistol self-defense courses for women. After a series of multiple killings throughout the country, some in the national press began to question the concept of "gun free" zones. The idea that handguns carried by ordinary citizens could have ended the killings was actually aired. Perhaps reality will continue to influence the media.

Concerning the guns themselves, a big question always stands: What do pistol shooters want? The manufacturers address that question every year.

The 1911 Colt/Browning design is getting close to the century mark. However, it is still king of the hill, and at least three more companies are coming out with new pistols based on the 1911 this year. For some time, companies have strived, and are still striving, to reduce the 1911 to the smallest possible dimensions. This trend became obvious when the demand for personal protection sidearms grew after 1988, when concealed-carry became a national movement. There are still a lot of small 1911s being offered, with new ones this year. However, now, a move to stretch the standard 5-inch barrel by another inch seems to be growing. There are a surprising number of companies now offering 1911 target pistols with 6-inch barrels.

Large-capacity polymer-frame service pistols went on the back burner when the so-called "Assault Weapons Ban" took effect in 1994. However, the 2004 sunset of that law has encouraged more development in that area. Many manufacturers now offer a full-size polymer-frame pistol with a staggered-column magazine, and some new ones were introduced this year. At the same time, thin is in; the polymer-frame pistol has been flattened into a single-column-magazine configuration, to fit it for unobtrusive concealed carry. Not to leave anything out, the very tiny polymer-frame pistols for concealed carry are of interest, and a new one just came out.

It is always interesting to follow trends in autoloading handguns. The creativity of different companies is amazing. As mentioned above, some of the features evolve with time. Some, however, seem to be more like fads. Mercifully, we appear to be nearing the end of the hooked trigger guard era. Now, some of the features that came into being for competition pistols or SWAT team pistols—beavertail tangs, magazine slam pads, extended controls, accessory rails and the like—are being used on small concealed-carry pistols. I have to scratch my head—such things add a bit of extra weight and some extra bulk, and seem to serve little purpose on a carry gun.

Since pistol-caliber carbines seem to get overlooked among the traditional hunting and target rifles, we will once again cover them here. Good thing, too, for development in this previously-neglected niche is booming now. There are a number of semiautomatic pistol-caliber carbines being introduced, and some of them are reproductions of historic firearms that began life as submachine guns. In some cases, the carbines are also offered in the original short barrel length, which makes them "short-barrel rifles" subject to BATF regulation and taxation. Some people, however, just have to have a "lookalike," and there seems to be a market for them.

Related items that are becoming more popular are large pistols that, in some cases, also had their design origin as submachine guns. They have been approved by BATF as pistols, and thus are, technically and legally, pistols, even though of unconventional appearance. For want of a better name, let's just call them "unconventional pistols." The anti-gun forces might want to use another name, but we will not give them the advantage of using their terminology.

Both the unconventional pistols and the pistol-caliber carbines are fun to shoot. I suspect some people may buy them with personal protection in mind, and then wind up using them primarily for recreational shooting.

This is a good year. Both in terms of conventional autoloading handguns and those of more exotic appearance, firearms companies have really been creative recently. Let's take a look at what the companies are offering:

AMERICAN CLASSIC

With the demise of the Spanish Llama pistols a few years ago, we lost a source of affordable 45-caliber 1911-type handguns. Now, S&B Distribution of Wanamassa, NJ, has come up with a replacement. Made by a new manufacturer in the Philippines, the American Classic 1911 is a "mil-spec" 45. Two versions are offered. The Standard pistol has a matte finish and looks very much like a World War II 1911A1. The Deluxe version is polished blue. It has higher sights, a beavertail tang, ventilated trigger and other niceties. The pistols are made of 4140 steel, weigh 36 ounces and come with an 8-round magazine.

ARMALITE

Armalite planned to introduce their new large-frame 45 ACP pistol (tentatively called the AR-26) at the February 2008 SHOT Show, but the prototype didn't arrive in time. Plans were to launch it later in 2008.

ARMSCOR

The Philippine Armscor company has introduced a number of new variants in its Rock Island Armory 1911 pistol line.

One of the new items for 2008 is a longer match target 45 pistol with a 6-inch barrel. Also, some of the 45 ACP and Super 38 variants are now available with nickel finishes.

Last year, a compact tactical 45 with a 3 1/2-inch barrel was introduced. It has entered production, and a limited run was expected early in 2008.

A new variant—a 9mm Commander-size pistol was displayed at the February 2008 SHOT Show, but the magazines did not make it with the guns. Hopes were that complete pistols would be available soon.

BERSA

Bersa celebrates it 50th anniversary this year, and I was expecting to see a commemorative pistol indicating half a century of making Bersa firearms. However, not all companies go in for that sort of thing. Bersa continues to make a line of conventional double-action personal protection pistols in 380, 9mm, 40 S&W and 45 ACP.

BOBERG

A new name in national firearms circles. One of the most interesting new pistols introduced at the 2008 SHOT Show was the Boberg XR9. It is a compact 9mm pistol that can hide under a 4x6 index card. The first thing that catches the eye when looking at the new pistol is how long the barrel is in relation to the gun's compact size. A 4 1/4-inch barrel resides in a handgun that is only 5-3/4 inches long.

Engineer Arne Boberg accomplished this by extending the barrel rearward over the magazine well. As the action operates, a cartridge feeds rearward from the magazine into a special lift ramp. The cartridge is aligned with the bore, and chambered during the forward movement of the slide. The action is locked breech, locked by a rotating barrel.

The system offers a number of advantages. Beside the long barrel in a short pistol, the cartridge doesn't have to try to find its way to the chamber at a sharp angle from the magazine. The feed system more precisely aligns the cartridge with the chamber, allowing more precise chamber dimensions. The chamber doesn't have to be oversized.

The combination of a long barrel and precise dimensions results in increased velocity and accuracy. Boberg has tested his pistol against a number of other companies' 9mm offerings—of different sizes—and has charted velocity and energy. The Boberg came out on top in all cases. The slogan used in company literature touts "full-size power" in a pocket-size pistol.

The most noticeable thing about the Boberg XR9 is how long the barrel is in relation to the pistol's overall length. Tests indicated that the design provides a measurable increase in power.

Loading the magazine (which doesn't even need a follower) is simple. Push the cartridges, bullet first, into the upper rear of the magazine. The sloping noses of the bullets help cam their way in. It is easier than loading a conventional magazine, and no loading device is needed.

The Boberg pistol has a double-action-only trigger, and weighs 19.5 ounces with magazine.

If it sounds interesting, check out BobergEngineering.com.

CENTURY

Century International Arms is offering a new pistol, the X9, which probably falls into the "unconventional pistol" category. The new 9mm, made by Shooters Arms Manufacturers (SAM) in the Philippines, looks a bit like—gasp—a

Century International Arms offers a big long-range pistol, the Draco, in 7.62x39 chambering.

MAC. Previous MAC-type pistols, which were roughly patterned after the MAC-10 submachine gun, are ones the anti-gunners hate so much. Weighing in at a little over three pounds, the X9 has a 3 3/4-inch barrel, and comes with a 14-round magazine. It has a manual safety at the left front of the trigger guard.

Another big long-range pistol offered by Century is the Draco, based on the AK design. Made in Romania, the unconventional-looking 5 ½-pound pistol is chambered for the 7.62x39 cartridge, and comes with one 30-round magazine. Barrel length is 12-1/4 inches.

Century is also offering the Arcus line of 9mm pistols again. Based on the Browning Hi-Power, the Arcus pistols are available in a 4-inch compact version or a 4.7-inch full-size model. Finishes are black or two-tone. Each pistol comes with two magazines.

COBRA

Will different colors make certain pistols more appealing to some shooters? Cobra Enterprises of Utah thinks so. Cobra is offering a variety of tastefully-colored pistols in the metal-frame (not polymer) lines. Colors are Black Chrome, Royal Blue, Ruby Red, Majestic Pink, Imperial Purple and King Cobra Copper. Available on their small-frame and larger-frame 32 and 380 automatics, the colors look amazingly good. Perhaps color will make a difference.

COLT

Colt planned to make limited runs of two semiautomatic pistols in 2008, and introduced a new 45 for personal protection. Let's look at them one by one.

WWI – The WWI Replica is an authentic reproduction of the 1911 U.S. military sidearm, circa 1918. It is based on original blueprints, and features original rollmarks and inspector marks. Each pistol comes with two 7-round magazines, and also with reproductions of the World War I-style screwdriver and instruction manual of the period.

An authentic replica of the 1911 U. S. military sidearm of World War I is back in production by Colt, its original manufacturer.

DELTA ELITE – Also back in the line for a limited run is the 10mm Delta Elite. Chambered for the powerful 10mm Auto cartridge, the stainless-steel Colt has 9+1 capacity. This run of pistols will contain new features such as a bushingless bull barrel and beavertail tang, but has all the original rollmarkings.

NEW AGENT – The Colt Concealed Carry pistol, introduced only last year, is no longer in the line. It has been replaced by a very similar 45-caliber pistol with a different name. Colt apparently watched Smith & Wesson's success in applying old revolver names to autoloaders, and decided to do something in a like vein. The new lightweight pistol is called the New Agent, harking back to the company's Agent revolvers of times past. The New Agent has a 3-inch barrel and weighs 25 ounces. Even with its shortened grip frame, a redesigned magazine gives it 7 + 1 capacity. A deep, squared sight "trench" runs along the top of the slide.

Too new for the catalog, but displayed at the 2008 SHOT Show, was a double-action version of the New Agent. Same general specifications as the single-action New Agent, but with a double-action trigger mechanism. Colt has not had good luck with its double-action autoloaders in the past. Let's hope this one breaks the chain.

CZ

Several new CZ offerings for 2008:

CZ P-06 – Recall that the CZ P-01 was developed several years ago to modify the original 9mm CZ 75 design to NATO service pistol specifications. Such modifications included an aluminum frame, M3 rail, recontoured trigger and rubber grips. Now, a new model, essentially the same pistol, but in 40 S&W chambering, is available as the P-06.

CZ 97 BD – A decocker version of the big 45-caliber CZ 97 B has been added to the CZ line. I like the new decocker—it lowers the hammer in a two-stage, controlled manner, and doesn't let the hammer "slam" down. The 97 BD comes in 45 ACP, and the finish is black polycoat.

CZ-USA also handles the Dan Wesson line of 1911 pistols, and two new variants were introduced. (See DAN WESSON)

DAN WESSON

Well, alphabetically, that worked out to be pretty convenient.

As mentioned, CZ-USA handles Dan Wesson offerings, and two new Dan Wesson 1911 variants were introduced for 2008.

DW VALOR – Said to have "everything you need and nothing you don't," the Valor's most striking feature is the new ceramic-based matte-black finish, which covers the stainless-steel parts. The pistol has adjustable night sights, slim grips and beavertail tang. It is made as a single-column 45.

DW SS CUSTOM – The new SSC is a stainless-steel single-column competition pistol in 40 S&W. It is the only Dan Wesson gun being made in that caliber at this time. Features include beavertail, beveled magazine well, fiber-optic front sight, ambidextrous safety, 8 + 1 capacity and Shark Skin grips.

DOUBLE STAR

Can we ever have too many companies offering 1911 variants? I would hope not. Double Star Corporation, a company known for its AR-style rifles, has entered the 1911 niche. The company proudly states it is the only company headed by a woman to offer a 1911. President/CEO Teresa Starnes decided the venerable 45 would fit in nicely with the company's offerings, and the new 1911 was introduced in prototype at the February 2008 SHOT Show. Unnamed at the time, the prototype pistol simply had "Double Star 45 ACP" on the slide.

About four years previously, the company had started development of a 1911 frame with a rail, to be offered as a frame only. Eventually, a decision was made to offer a complete pistol, based on that new frame. Plans were to sell the frames first, then the completed pistols.

Double Star also offers a number of other things of interest to this report. Long-range 223 pistols of AR type are available with 7.5, 10.5 or 11.5-inch barrel lengths. They can also provide a stocked version of the 10.5 and 11.5-inchers that is considered a BATF "Short Barrel Rifle" and requires the transfer tax. The Star 15 9mm carbine is an AR with a 16-inch barrel. It accepts Colt 9mm magazines or modified Uzi magazines.

DSA

DSA, Inc., in Barrington, IL, is known for their AR- and FAL-type rifles. In early 2008, the company introduced a

DSA Inc. introduced the big Swiss-designed TP-9 pistol chambered for 9mm. The unconventional pistol is light for its size, weighing just 44 ounces.

new pistol, the TP-9. The pistol comes from Brugger & Thomet in Switzerland. That Swiss company acquired an original Steyr design in 2004 and improved it to its present form.

The big pistol is a polymer-frame blowback 9mm. The polymer and steel parts add up to just 44 ounces—less than three pounds, and light for its size. For want of a better name, let's call this an unconventional pistol, approved by BATF as a pistol, but showing a definite submachine gun heritage. It is truly ambidextrous, with safety, operating handle and magazine release usable from either side. 15- and 30-round magazines come as standard, but 10-round magazines are also available. The magazines to be included depend on how much different communities trust their citizens.

For those shooters willing to undergo more paperwork and expense, the TP-9 is also available with a folding polymer stock as a legal Short Barrel Rifle.

A logical question—will the TP-9 pistol be available in other chamberings? Yes, DSA plans to introduce a 45 ACP version, probably within a year or so.

EAA

Four new offerings from European American Armory. Two are Italian, new variants in the Witness series, and were too new to appear in the 2008 catalog. Two are new Serbian-made pistols.

Within the Italian-made Witness offerings, the new Limited Pro is a new competition pistol designed to be competitive in Production Class events. It comes with a 4 3/4-inch barrel.

The Witness Stock 2 pistol is similar to the previous Stock production-class pistol, but has a competition frame—a full-length frame to the end of the slide. Controls are ambidextrous, and it has a 4 1/2-inch cone barrel.

The two Zastava personal-protection pistols from Serbia include a double-action and a single-action model. Mechanically, they are not related.

The Zastava EZ is a double-action large-capacity pistol of modern design, showing a bit of SIG influence. It has ambidextrous controls, and a lightweight frame with an integral accessory rail. It is offered in full-size (4-inch barrel, 33 ounces) and compact (3 1/2-inch barrel, 30 ounces) variants. Chamberings are 9mm, 40 S&W and 45 ACP.

The Zastava M88 is a slim compact steel-frame pistol, catalogued in 9mm and 40 S&W. It is based on the Tokarev design, which is itself based on the colt 1911. Overshadowed by polymer designs, this simple single-action steel pistol represents a type we don't see much of now, and it is good to see this sort of pistol being offered. The slide-mounted manual safety is functional and works well. Previous incarnations of modified Tokarev designs, in order to be imported, incorporated frame-mounted safeties that locked the action, but were not convenient to operate. The safety on the M88 works. Capacity of the single-column pistol is 8+1 in 9, and 6+1 in 40.

The unique "tube chamber" Witness pistol introduced in prototype in the last edition of this publication is still in development, and no definite date has been set for production.

ED BROWN

Ed Brown Products has introduced a special edition commemorative 1911 to honor Col. Jeff Cooper, who died on September 25, 2006. Cooper originated the sport of practical pistol competition in 1958, so the commemorative pistol comes 50 years later. Plans were to offer it only during 2008, ending orders on September 25.

The pistol uses the best of Ed Brown features to make a tribute that is functional as well as decorative. The decorations include Cooper's signature engraved on the right side of the slide, forward of the ejection port. On the other side, the letters DVC are inlayed in gold. These letters represent the Latin words Diligentia, Vis, Celeritas, meaning Accuracy, Power, Speed. Cooper applied these to practical pistol shooting, and they eventually formed the motto of the International Practical Shooting Confederation (IPSC) which he founded in 1976.

With each Jeff Cooper pistol will come a leather-bound copy of Cooper's classic book, *Principles of Personal Defense*. Ed Brown worked with the Cooper family on this project, and a portion of the proceeds of the commemorative will go to the Jeff Cooper Legacy Foundation.

In addition to the Cooper commemorative, the firm introduced two new variants of their Special Forces model, too new to make it into the 2008 catalog. The two new guns are a light-rail variant and a bob-tail version.

FIRESTORM

The Firestorm line of 45-caliber 1911-style pistols faded away several years ago when the manufacturer, Llama-Gabilondo, went out of business. SGS Importers have come up with another supplier, and the Firestorm brand is back with us. The first offerings are military-specification standard "Government Model" pistols in 45 ACP. Scheduled for the future are deluxe variants, high-capacity models, and different calibers.

FNH

A number of items introduced by FNH-USA last year are now in production, along with some not envisioned last year. Let's take them one by one.

FNP-45 – The new 45 ACP FNP-45, introduced last year, is now offered in three new variants. It can be had as a matte black stainless (black polymer frame, black slide), matte silver stain-

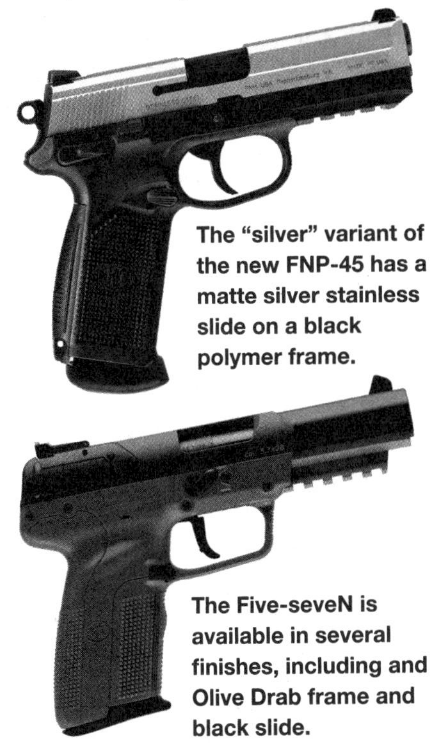

The "silver" variant of the new FNP-45 has a matte silver stainless slide on a black polymer frame.

The Five-seveN is available in several finishes, including and Olive Drab frame and black slide.

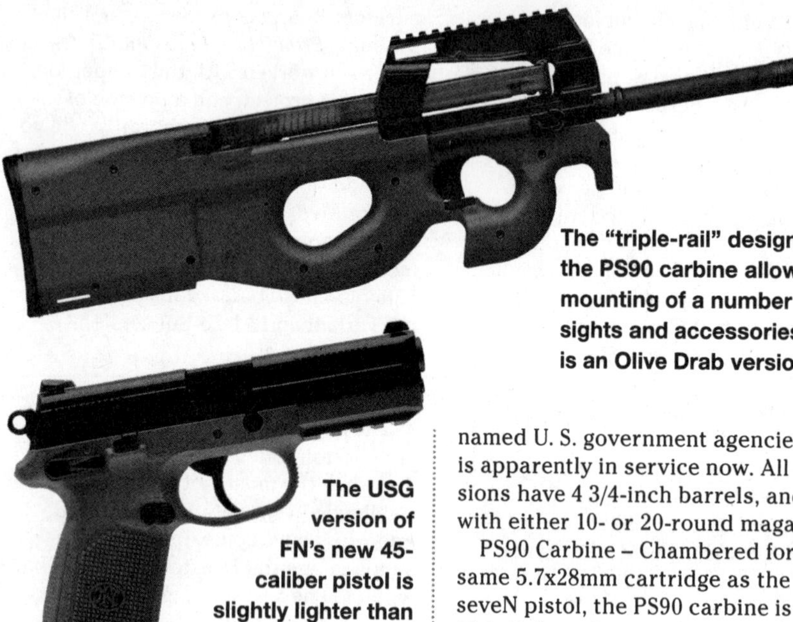

The "triple-rail" design of the PS90 carbine allows mounting of a number of sights and accessories. Here is an Olive Drab version.

The USG version of FN's new 45-caliber pistol is slightly lighter than other variants and has a "flat dark earth" polymer frame.

less (black poly frame, matte stainless slide), or as the USG (possibly standing for United States Government?) model ("flat dark earth" frame, black slide). Barrel length is 4-1/2 inches, and the pistols are furnished with either 10- or 14-round magazines. There are subtle differences in the USG model, and it weighs about an ounce less than the 33-ounce heft of the other two. All variants have interchangeable flat and arched backstrap inserts.

FNP-9, FNP-40 – The 9mm and 40-caliber pistols have new USG variants, distinguished from the earlier versions by their "flat dark earth" frames.

FNP-357 – So new that a specimen was not available to display at the Feb 2008 SHOT Show, the FNP-357 is essentially the same as the FNP-40, but chambered for the 357 SIG cartridge. Two variants, with black and silver slides, are catalogued.

Five-seveN – This 5.7x28 delayed-blowback pistol has been given a facelift, and the grip and trigger guard shapes are more conventional, less exotic than the initial offerings, and the frames can incorporate an improved accessory rail. Three different models are offered, but—pay attention, now—they are not the same as the larger-bore guns. Slides on all are black, but frames can be olive drab, black or "flat dark earth." Yes, there is a USG variant shown in the catalog, but it has a black frame, not flat dark earth. The USG was reportedly developed for several unnamed U. S. government agencies, and is apparently in service now. All versions have 4 3/4-inch barrels, and come with either 10- or 20-round magazines.

PS90 Carbine – Chambered for the same 5.7x28mm cartridge as the Five-seveN pistol, the PS90 carbine is a 16-inch barrel semiautomatic version of the FN P90 submachinegun. The "Triple Rail" version of the carbine was introduced last year, and is apparently the standard model now. A number of sights and accessories can be mounted on the three rails. With a barrel just over 16 inches, the overall length comes to a bit over 26 inches. The PS90 is an exotic-looking firearm, and we will probably see them appearing in motion pictures soon. The carbine is offered with either a 30-round magazine (standard) or a 10-round magazine (for those who can't be trusted by their local government). The 5.7x28 sporting cartridge, which achieves 1700 feet per second (fps) from the pistol gets up to 2100 fps from the longer carbine barrel. Perhaps we'll see them in the varmint field, too.

GIRSAN

Turkey is becoming an increasingly important contributor to the firearms world—in particular, in the production of autoloading handguns. Girsan is a Turkish company, established in 1994. Its principal product line is the Yavuz 16 series of pistols. These are 9mm pistols based on the Beretta 92 mechanism, and are made in both open-top and closed-top variants. The pistols have 15 + 1 capacity, and are available in 9x19 and 9x21 chamberings.

GLOCK

Recall that in early 2007, Glock brought out a new modification of the 45-caliber Glock 21. The new 45 was so new it was not even featured in the Glock catalog of the early part of the year. The model designation was Glock 21 SF, with SF standing for "short frame." A change in the frame reduced the distance from trigger to backstrap, to create a subtly different feel. A number of shooters, especially those with smaller hands or shorter fingers, liked the new variant.

Now, the same treatment has been given to the Model 30, the compact Glock 45. The new Model 30 SF has the reduced girth of the 21 SF grip in a smaller package. The 30 SF has a 3 3/4-inch barrel and weighs 24 ounces. Capacity is 10 +1.

HECKLER & KOCH

Derived from an HK submachine gun, the Heckler & Koch USC model gray-colored utility carbine was offered last year in 45 ACP. For 2008, the color has changed to black. It features reinforced polymer construction, with a rubberized cheekpiece and recoil pad. Operation is simple blowback. With a 16-inch barrel, the overall length is just under 36 inches. Weight is about six pounds. The USC comes with adjustable sights. Advertised magazine capacity is 10 rounds of 45 ACP ammunition, but magazines of greater capacity may become available later.

HI-POINT

Small Hi-Point changes just sort of slip into the line without any notice in the catalog. A few years ago, the pistols came with orange-colored sights, an unusual choice that worked very well. For 2008, the pistols come with orange rear sights and yellow front sights. A small point, without doubt, but in years to come, collectors will want to know these things.

HOGUE

Recall that the Hogue Avenger, introduced in prototype last year, is a pistol design that keeps all the forces in a straight line with its fixed barrel. A development of European designer Peter Spielberger, it is said to reduce recoil and muzzle jump over a conventional tilting-barrel mechanism, as well as promote greater accuracy. As of early 2008, production had been established here in the United States, with a production rate of about 50 to 60 units a month. However, the first few hundred units will go to Austria for proof-house testing. So, availability for U. S. shooters was anticipated to come later, probably around late summer, 2008. Initial sales will be as conversion units for

1911-type pistols; later, the Avenger will be available as a complete pistol.

IVER JOHNSON

The Iver Johnson 45-caliber 1911-style pistols were reported ready for production in early 2008. They will be available in "Raven" configuration (basically military 1911A1 specifications, with fixed sights) and Eagle series (target versions with adjustable sights).

The 22-caliber 1911 pistols were predicted to be ready for production during summer 2008.

Iver Johnson is also producing a limited number of what is generally known as the "Baby Browning" 25 automatic. They are assembling new guns on a small cache of low-number PSA (Precision Small Arms) frames.

KAHR

The new Kahr 45-caliber pistols the company introduced last year are now in full production. Kahr now makes a variety of stainless-steel and polymer-frame pistols in 9mm, 40 S&W and 45 ACP. The company's latest catalog emphasizes how thin their guns are, with slide widths of an inch or less, and overall widths not much more.

Recall that Kahr now produces the Auto-Ordnance and Thompson firearms lines.

For those who don't mind extra money and hassle, the Thompson 1927A1 semiautomatic carbine was offered last year with a 10 1/2-inch barrel, which duplicated the appearance of the original Thompson submachine guns. This barrel length puts it into the "short barrel rifle" (SBR) class with the BATF, and requires extra paperwork and taxation. For some, it seems worth it to get the original "Tommy Gun" look. New for 2008 is another 45-caliber semiautomatic SBR, this one in the style of the World War II model M1 submachine gun. Like the original M1 Thompson, this model will take box magazines only and will not accept drum magazines.

Also appearing for 2008 is the semiautomatic 1927A1 Thompson pistol. The big 45 pistol is essentially the Thompson "short barrel rifle" modified so that it cannot be used with a shoulder stock. As a BATF-legal pistol, this unconventional pistol is not subject to the SBR restrictions. Barrel length is 10-1/2 inches, and overall length is a bit over 23 inches. It comes with a horizontal forearm and a 50-round drum magazine. It can also take the 30-round box magazine, as well as the 100-round and 10-round drums. The absurd 10-round drum is required for localities that restrict magazines of semiautomatic firearms to 10 cartridges or less.

KIMBER

Kimber has introduced fourteen new or upgraded models for 2008. Let's look at them:

SIS – The new SIS pistols are based on the 45-caliber 1911-type pistols provided to the Special Investigation Section of the Los Angeles Police Department. They have a darkened stainless-steel slide, frame and magazine housing. They have stippled grips and a beavertail tang. Night sights are provided, with a special cocking shoulder at the front of the rear sight that allows one-hand cocking in emergencies. Perhaps the most distinctive feature of the SIS pistols is in the design of the retraction grooves on the slide—they are formed of (what else?) the stylized letters SIS. Four variants are available: the Custom (5-inch barrel), Custom/RL (with rail), Pro (4-inch) and Ultra (3-inch barrel).

Raptor – The new Raptor is the Stainless Raptor II, a 45 with a 5-inch barrel. A Custom Shop item, it has distinctive scaled grips, with scaling on the slide and frame gripping surfaces.

Refined Carry Pistol – The Ultra RCP II is a small pistol with an aluminum frame, spurless hammer and short tang. It has a 3-inch barrel and weighs 25 ounces. For compactness, it replaces traditional sights with a trough sight.

Gold Combat – Upgraded features appear on three full-size 5-inch pistols in the Gold Combat line, the Gold Combat II, the Gold Combat/RL II (with rail) and the Gold Combat Stainless II. All come with 5-inch bull barrel, flat-top slide and distinctive herringbone-pattern Micarta grips.

New 9mm variants – The 9mm cartridge still has it advocates. Five Kimber models are now available in 9mm chambering—Stainless Gold Match II, Stainless II, Stainless Pro Carry II, Stainless Ultra Carry II and Stainless CDP II.

Just a reminder to help in breaking Kimber's model codes: Custom guns are 5-inchers, Pro guns are 4 inches and Ultra pistols have 3-inch barrels.

KEL-TEC

Kel-Tec recently introduced its 223 PLR-16 Long Range Pistol, and at the 2008 SHOT Show, introduced a 22 Long Rifle (22 LR) companion to the centerfire pistol. Actually, the new rimfire PLR-22 pistol is almost a look-a-like. It has the same general appearance and the same 18 1/2-inch overall length. Because of the structural differences, the blowback 22 has a slightly-longer 10.1-inch barrel and is a bit lighter, at 45 ounces. It is designed to use a 27-round Kel-Tec magazine, or an Atchison 22 LR magazine designed for M-16 conversions. The PLR-22 uses the same operating mechanism as the also-new Kel-Tec SU-22 rifle, a 4-pound semiautomatic carbine with a 16-inch barrel.

Herringbone Micarta grips set off the upgraded Kimber Gold Combat II pistol, a full-size 45.

The new stainless-steel Raptor II has a scaled-pattern grips, with a similar pattern on the gripping surfaces of the slide and frame.

A more compact version of Kimber's SIS pistol is offered as the SIS Pro, with a 4-inch barrel.

The Refined Carry Pistol is a compact carry pistol by Kimber. It features a 3-inch barrel, spurless hammer, short tang and trough sight.

KRISS / TDI

TDI (Transformational Defense Industries, Inc), founded in 2002, had developed a controlled-recoil 45 ACP Kriss Vector submachinegun design for military and law enforcement use. The submachine gun was introduced in 2007. At the February 2008 SHOT Show, the company introduced a semiautomatic carbine version of the Kriss.

The heart of the Kriss design is a rearward-moving bolt linked to a slotted component called a slider. The slider is forced downward as the bolt moves back, compressing the recoil spring in a downward—rather than rearward—direction. This change in force vectors is claimed to give less felt recoil, and less muzzle climb. The "Vector" name for the gun is thus derived. This type of operation is termed a delayed blowback by the company. I had an all-too-brief opportunity to shoot both the submachine gun version and the new semiautomatic carbine, and can attest that both the felt recoil and muzzle rise seemed subdued.

The Kriss carbine uses a polymer frame, with steel and aluminum parts to handle the stress of firing. The rather exotic appearance of the Kriss is due in part to the trigger mechanism being actually above the line of the bore. Forward of the trigger is the receiver section in which the bolt, slider and recoil spring mechanisms operate. The magazine is positioned at the forward part of this section. The gun can use a standard 13-round Glock 21 magazine, or a 30-rounder can be made from a TDI extension kit. Although they were not tried, the extended Glock-style magazines offered by Scherer would probably also work.

The charging handle is on the left side of the carbine. During operation, it is folded flat against the gun. When it is pivoted out to open the action, the very act of pivoting it opens the bolt about ¼ inch. In this position, it can then be easily determined if a cartridge is in the chamber. The forward portion of the receiver section, just above the barrel, has a recess designed to hold a tactical flashlight. This frees up some of the attached rails for sights, foregrips and other accessories. The carbine has a 16-inch barrel, and weighs six pounds. Overall length is about 35 inches.

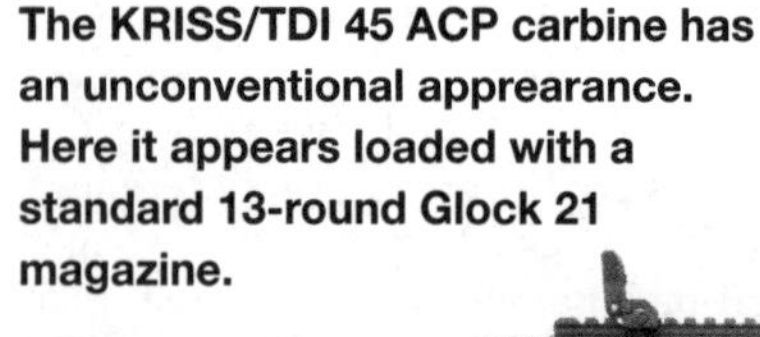

The KRISS/TDI 45 ACP carbine has an unconventional appearance. Here it appears loaded with a standard 13-round Glock 21 magazine.

LES BAER

New from Les Baer custom for 2008 was the Baer H.C. 40, a large-capacity 18+1 pistol made in 40 S&W. The gun is built on the Caspian double-stack frame. It has wood grips and most of the niceties shooters seem to like nowadays. Accuracy guarantee is an impressive 2-1/2 inches at 50 yards.

MAGNUM RESEARCH

A number of new things have sneaked into the Magnum Research line recently. The big Desert Eagle pistol, in 357 and 44 Magnum and 50 Action Express, is available in a dazzling array of finishes, with the magazine base plates finished to match the finish of the pistol. If the black oxide magazine body is not satisfactory, the custom shop can furnish complete magazines to match the pistols, available in 24K gold, chrome, nickel, titanium gold, titanium carbon nitride…well, you get the idea. Also, if you want a nickel body with a gold base plate, that is available also. One of the most striking pistol finishes is the Tiger Stripe variant, with titanium gold embellished with tiger stripes across the entire gun.

The smaller "Baby" Eagle, in 9mm, 40 and 45, is still called the "Baby" in the catalog, but the pistols themselves simply say "Desert Eagle Pistol." They are offered in standard (4 1/2-inch barrel), semi-compact (3.9-inch) and compact (3.6-inch barrel) versions, and in 9mm, 40 S&W and 45 ACP chamberings. New in the line are polymer frame variants in compact and semi-compact sizes. Some steel-frame "Baby" Eagles are also available with a frame accessory rail.

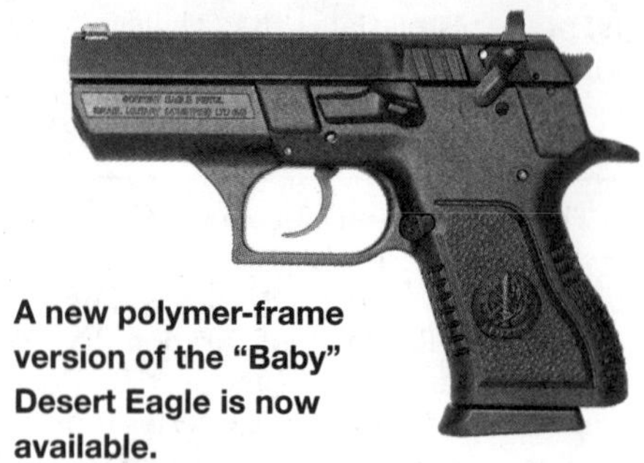

A new polymer-frame version of the "Baby" Desert Eagle is now available.

"Baby" Desert Eagle with the new accessory rail incorporated into the frame.

MILITARY PRECISION

One of the most widely-used and best-known submachine guns of World War II was the German MP-40, often known as the Schmeisser. (Just a quick historical note: Hugo Schmeisser was an early pioneer in German submachine gun development, but there is no evidence that he had any part in the development that led to the MP-40. Still, it is a catchy name.) In the decades following the war, Americans became familiar with the MP-40 through countless motion pictures. Denmark and other countries continued to use the MP-40 as a standard military arm for some time. Now Military Precision, of Springboro, Ohio, offers shooters, collectors and reenactors shootable semiautomatic versions of this historic firearm.

The company is offering several newly-made autoloading variants of the MP-40. The variants fall into both pistol and pistol-caliber carbine categories. The firm actually started out making MP-40 look-alike blank-firing "non-guns," and learned there was a demand for the real thing. Unlike the original open-bolt submachine guns, the new semiauto 9mm guns are hammer-fired, and fire from the closed bolt position. Named the model SSR-40, they have been approved for sale by BATF.

The SSR-40 pistol has the exact outward appearance as the original submachine gun, but the folding stock is permanently folded, and cannot be extended. As a legal semiautomatic pistol, the SSR-40 gives new meaning to the concept of an unconventional pistol.

The SSR-40 semiautomatic carbine has a skeleton stock and a 16-inch barrel.

Military Precision's new semiautomatic new 9mm pistol is a pistol of unconventional appearance.

The carbine uses a 16-inch barrel, and this version can use the folding stock, or have the stock permanently open. For those who like to spend extra money for transfer taxes, a semiauto short barrel rifle (SBR) variant is in the works. It will have the original barrel length of about 10 inches, and will come with a functioning extendable stock. This version may appeal to those who want a shooter with an authentic outward appearance, and who do not mind the extra paperwork and expense.

Military Precision also offers leather slings, magazine pouches and spare magazines. Original German magazines will also work.

Caliber for all variations is, of course, the original 9mm Parabellum (9mm Luger).

MSAR

Microtech Small Arms Research, Inc. (MSAR) brought out a pistol-caliber carbine that has the distinctive look of a Steyr AUG. Introduced in 9mm chambering, the MSC-08 carbine uses 9mm Glock magazines, including aftermarket large-capacity ones, such as the Scherer offerings. This should have some appeal for those already using 9mm Glock pistols. The carbine's barrel is 16-1/2 inches long. It comes with either a 1.5X optical sight, or a 9-inch Picatinny rail for mounting other choices of sighting systems. It is designed so that later potential caliber changes can be readily accomplished. Planned deliveries were scheduled to begin in Summer 2008.

NIGHTHAWK

Too new to make the 2008 catalog, Nighthawk Custom's new 9mm Lady Hawk pistol is sized to fit smaller hands. Based on the 1911 design, the frame is thinned front to back, and it uses thin grips. With a 4 1/4-inch barrel, it has 9+1 capacity. Finish is titanium blue with hard chrome trigger, hammer and grip safety.

OLYMPIC

AR-type long-range pistols and AR-style pistol-caliber carbines are offered by Olympic Arms. A new magazine is in the works for the 45 ACP caliber carbine. In their line of 1911 pistols, Olympic is ahead of the trend to the longer 6-inch barrel length recently becoming more popular. They now offer 6-inch barrels in their Matchmaster, Big Deuce and Trail Boss pistols.

The Whitney 22-caliber pistol offered by Olympic now has the option of adjustable sights. Recall that the Whitney design takedown is by means of a threaded nut at the muzzle. I guess, if you have a threaded barrel, you might as well use it for something. A compensator, threaded to match the barrel threads, is now offered for the Whitney.

PARA

Para USA (that's the official name the company is using now) has introduced a number of 1911 variants of interest to us here.

Super Hawg – The Super Hawg's 6-inch barrel and fiber-optic front sight would seem to offer an aid to precise sighting. The longer barrel also adds velocity, so the new big Hawg may see service in some types of hunting. 45 ACP, and available in both single-column and staggered-column versions.

PDA – Personal Defense Assistant (PDA) is the designation of Para's new small personal protection pistol. Trigger mechanism is light double action (LDA), and the gun is compact and trim. The tang is the minimum needed to house the grip safety, and the hammer is spurless. The striking finish is flat black, but with polished slide flats. Decent sights are provided, and although the barrel length is only 3 inches, a match-grade barrel is used. Because, according to Para, "you need accuracy in a defensive pistol." Two chamberings are offered: 45 ACP, with 6+1 capacity, and 9mm, with 8+1 capacity.

Gun Rights – Two 45-caliber pistols constitute the Para "Gun Rights" selection. For each gun sold, Para will make a donation to the National Rifle Association's Institute for Legislative Action. Para considers this a good way to support our firearms rights, and have a good pistol to boot. Two variants are offered, one a single-column version,

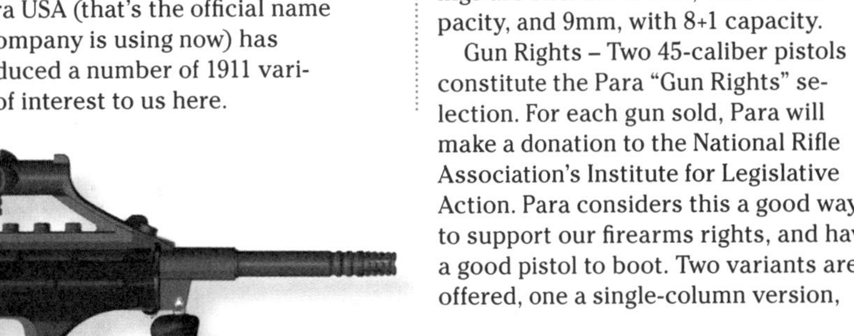

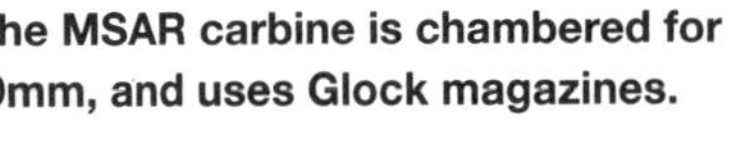

Looking very much like a Steyr AUG, the MSAR carbine is chambered for 9mm, and uses Glock magazines.

and one as a 14+1 staggered-column gun. Both are stainless steel, have 5-inch match-grade barrels, and offer other refinements. The legend GUN RIGHTS appears on the right side of the slide.

We can't leave Para without commenting on Todd Jarrett's setting the speed record for firing 1000 rounds through a 45. Imagine a job during which you can take a 10-minute break to fire a pistol a thousand times. Actually, it took Jarrett 10 minutes and 44 seconds, and the gun was so hot it was difficult to hold, much less to shoot. He used a Para PXT 1911 SSP, which was loaded from a table piled with 10-round magazines. A team of helpers picked up the ejected magazines, reloaded them and put them back on the table for Jarrett to use again. The barrel got so hot it changed color from bright stainless to a deep bronze. After cooling, the pistol continued to be shot (more slowly) until it had reached the 5000-round mark. Jarrett then shot a 10-round 25-yard group that measured 1.92 inches. All this suggests that the Para pistols seem to hold up all right.

PSA

Precision Small Arms manufactures the classic "Baby Browning" 25 ACP pistol under license from FN in Belgium, and has been doing so since 1987. PSA also distributes it in the United States as the PSA-25. Even with the limitation of its 25 ACP cartridge, the company feels that the little pistol (it is small enough to hide under a 3x5 index card) is a viable choice for personal protection. Modern loads for the little 25-caliber round can be more effective than those of the past. The pistol is 4 inches long, 2.88 inches high, 0.88-inch wide, and weighs 9.7 ounces. A 7-ounce aluminum-frame version was planned for Spring 2008.

ROCK ISLAND

The Rock Island Arsenal line of 1911-type pistols has some new variants. (See ARMSCOR)

ROCK RIVER

In their 1911 line, Rock River Arms has caved in to demand, and has added a new pistol to their line, now in 9mm chambering. The RRA Service Auto 9mm is a 5-inch blued pistol with rosewood grips. It has a fixed target rear sight and dovetailed front, in your choice of .125- or .090-inch widths. The new 9 has a beavertail tang, extended thumb safety lever and other niceties. It is guaranteed to shoot 1-inch groups at 25 yards.

Another 9mm is poised to join Rock River's lineup. The RRA Off Duty Carry 9mm pistol is a compact pistol that will use a Kart 3 ½-inch barrel. Again, with beavertail tang, extended safety, and finished in similar fashion to the Service Auto. This short-barrel version will have an accuracy guarantee of 1 1/2-inches at 25 yards.

Rock River also makes 9mm AR-style carbines. A new feature is that the magazine well/feed block is now a part of the lower receiver, and the lower receiver is marked for 9mm.

Waiting in the wings, but not in the catalog or ready for display, are a new carbine and pistol in 40 S&W.

ROHRBAUGH

The 2008 Rohrbaugh catalog lists the little all-metal pistols in 9mm and 380 ACP. Well, almost. By February 2008, the 380 was still being readied for production. Because of the differences in case rims, the 380 needs a different extractor and other changes. Production of the 380 was anticipated by mid-2008.

RUGER

Sturm, Ruger and Company has come out with a trio of new offerings. Let's take them one at a time.

The Ruger SR9 – The polymer-frame full-size large-capacity service pistol was popularized by the Glock 17 in the early 1980s. However, development of that niche went on the back burner after the "Assault Weapon Ban" (AWB) of 1994. The 10-shot magazine capacity limit diverted development toward smaller 10-shot polymer-frame "carry" pistols for personal protection. Then, in 2004, the AWB was allowed to sunset, and larger-capacity pistols became of interest again. A number of companies began to offer such pistols. In early 2008, Ruger introduced their offering, the SR9. The SR9 is a relatively slim pistol with a staggered-column, large capacity magazine (17+1 capacity). It is Ruger's first striker-fired pistol. The trigger mechanism is called by some double-action-only, and by others as Glock-type. The rearward movement of the slide partially sets the action, and the trigger completes it by releasing the striker. Chambered, at least at this time, only for the 9mm cartridge, it comes with a 4.14-inch stainless-steel barrel. An accessory rail is present at the front of the frame.

When multiple interchangeable grip straps were introduced for polymer-frame pistols some years ago, a situation was created akin to that of interchangeable choke tubes for shotguns—one went into the gun, the others got lost. Ruger has solved the problem by supplying only one backstrap unit—flat on one side, curved on the other. Whichever is selected, the other option is always still in the pistol.

Although many new polymer pistols have no manual safety, Ruger has incorporated a thumb safety on the left side of the SR9's frame. It is an up-down bar located in approximately the same position as the safety lever on a 1911 Colt. Ambidextrous, it also appears on the other side for left-hand use.

The Ruger LCP – A relatively few years ago, small light polymer-frame 25-size 32 Automatics were introduced by another company. Then, similar little guns were offered in 380 caliber. Ruger looked at the popularity of such pistols, and decided to enter that niche. The Ruger LCP (Lightweight Compact Pistol) was introduced on February 2, 2008, at a special press conference at the 2008 SHOT Show. The new Ruger 380 has a polymer frame, weighs 9.4 ounces and has 6+1 capacity. Trigger is double-ac-

The Ruger Charger comes with a bipod that can be attached when desired.

The Ruger SR9 has a polymer frame and a stainless-steel barrel. (right view)

The Ruger LCP has a polymer frame and a double-action-only trigger.

tion-only. With a 2.75-inch barrel, the little pistol measures 5.2x3.6 inches, almost able to hide beneath a 3x5 index card.

The 22 Charger – Other companies are using Ruger 10/22-type actions to make long-range rimfire pistols for hunting and silhouette shooting. Why not Ruger? The new Charger makes that question moot—Ruger now offers its own pistol in that niche. In 22 Long Rifle chambering, and with a 10-inch barrel, the pistol weighs about 3-1/2 pounds. If the owner chooses to attach the included bipod, that will up the weight some. The Charger uses the same reliable 10-round rotary magazine of the 10/22. However, a new magazine release has been introduced.

SARSILMAZ

The Turkish Sarsilmaz company uses the CZ 75 as the basis of its pistol designs, and its Kilinc 9mm pistol is the standard sidearm of the Turkish armed forces. Sarsilmaz also manufactures pistols for Bernardelli and Armalite. For 2008, the firm offered a number of new models and variations under the Sarsilmaz name.

K2 – The K2 is a 15+1 9mm based on the CZ 75. It has a slide-mounted decocker and a squared, forward-sloping squared trigger guard. The frame is forged steel, and the barrel length is about 4 ½ inches. A number of finishes are offered. A K2C also exists–a compact with a shorter barrel–but it was not available at the February 2008 SHOT Show, and was not yet in the catalog.

Kilinc 2000 Mega – The full-size Kilinc is a 15+1 pistol available in 9mm. The Mega variant has a shortened tang, vertical squared trigger guard, and has a manual safety mounted on the frame. The rear sight is dovetailed into the slide, but slopes forward to give a no-snag profile. The Mega can be had in black, chrome, gold, gloss blue and matte finishes.

Combat Master / CM9 A polymer-frame 9mm Combat Master is made with a rail moulded into the frame. The 15+1 pistol has a barrel length of about 3.8 inches. The manual safety is mounted on the frame. The CM9 is available in black or two-tone.

Vatos / V8 – The aluminum-frame Vatos 9mm appears to be a simplification of the CZ 75 design. As with most of the other full-size Sarsilmaz pistols, the capacity is 15+1. The barrel is about 4 ½ inches long. The Vatos was introduced in prototype last year, and is now in production. Production guns have an accessory rail on the frame.

The 45 ACP Kilinc pistol that was displayed last year is still in development, and is not ready for production.

The Sarsilmaz Combat Master has a 3.8-inch barrel and features adjustable sights.

The Sarsilmaz K2 Compact has a full-size grip and shorter barrel.

SIG SAUER

As of October 1, 2007, SIGARMS changed its name to SIG SAUER, and that is what we will use. Not as easy as it sounds, though. What letters should we capitalize? SIG is three initials, standing for Schweizerische Industrie Gesellschaft. Sauer, on the other hand, is a German industrial family name, representing J. P. Sauer & Son. However, the 2008 catalog uses all capital letters in every presentation, so we will also.

The big news from SIG SAUER is the P 250, the "modular" pistol. The heart is the modular frame and fire-control assembly. This relatively small component really is the frame--the legal receiver--and contains the serial number. Everything else, in different sizes, shapes and calibers, connects to it.

A shooter can have optional sizes of grip frames and slides, and barrels in four different calibers—9mm, 40 S&W, 357 SIG and 45 ACP. Once a caliber is chosen, the gun can be a full-size, compact or subcompact, with a barrel length of 4.7, 3.9 or 3.1 inches. It can have large, medium or small grips, and standard or short trigger length can be chosen. Weight runs about 22 to 30 ounces, depending on options. In addition, the slides are stainless, but you can choose natural stainless (for a two-tone effect with the black grip frame) or black Nitron finish over the stainless (for an all-black pistol).

To keep the choices at least a bit simpler, the trigger mechanism is always double-action-only. And, you don't have to make a decision about a rail—all the grip frames have one.

And, yes, of course, the company still makes all those other guns. Collectors should note that they will all be marked "SIG SAUER" now. Years from now, someone will ask when the change took place.

SMITH & WESSON

The company must have been apprehensive at first, but it has been wildly successful in applying respected old revolver names to semiautomatic pistols. First, a number of years ago, came the use of "Chief's Special" for several autoloaders. Then, two years ago, the M&P (Military & Police) revolver designation was used for S&W's new polymer-frame service pistol. It apparently sounded right. For 2008, the usage of the M&P name has expanded to an entire M&P "Series," which includes polymer-frame pistols in calibers 45 ACP, 40 S&W, 357 SIG and 9mm, selected revolvers, and AR-type rifles. What, no shotguns? Well, not yet.

The polymer M&P pistols interest us here, for several new items have been introduced. The M&P 45 was introduced last year as a full-size service pistol with a 4 1/2-inch barrel. Now it has been joined by a "mid-size" M&P 45 and an M&P 45 Compact. The mid-size 45 has a 4-inch barrel, weighs about 28 ounces and has 10+1 capacity. The compact version has the same 4-inch barrel, but has a shorter grip frame. It weighs about 26 ounces and has 8+1 capacity.

Two new 9mm M&P polymer-frame pistols have also been introduced. The full-size 9mm, as introduced, uses a 4 1/4-inch barrel. Apparently there was some demand for a longer barrel, and now the M&P 9L is available, with a 5-inch barrel.

There is also a special 9mm M&P, the M&P 9JG, named for championship pistol shooter Julie Goloski. It has a 4.25-inch barrel and has an "awareness ribbon" engraved on the slide. A donation will be made for each pistol sold to a breast cancer awareness charity. How does the company made a flat black poly-frame pistol look like a ladies' gun? Easy. Pink grip inserts are supplied with each M&P 9JG in addition to the standard black ones.

The SteelMaster from STI is a ported 9mm competition pistol.

In the 22-caliber pistol line, a new variant of the S&W Model 22A is now available with a Realtree APG Camo finish. As with the other offerings in the 22A rimfire line, the new camo pistol has a 5.5-inch barrel and 10+1 capacity. The camo pattern looks pretty good. Don't set it down somewhere when you're out in the woods.

The 22-caliber S&W Model 22A is now available with a camo finish.

A shorter mid-size S&W M&P 45 reduces the barrel to 4 inches, but retains the full-size grip.

SPRINGFIELD

Some law enforcement agencies require a manual thumb safety on any autoloading pistol used by their officers. To meet this criterion, Springfield Armory has designed a variant of its XD polymer-frame pistol with an ambidextrous thumb safety arrangement. The XD already was the only polymer-frame pistol that offered a grip safety. The new safety feature appears on the XD Service Model 45 with 4-inch barrel. The new gun uses a 13-round magazine (thus offering 14 round capacity) and weighs about 30 ounces.

The XD line also has some new color variations. The guns can be had as bi-tone (bright slide, black frame) or with dark earth or olive drab frames.

Last year, Springfield added a small new 9mm pistol to its line of 1911 offerings. The Springfield EMP (Enhanced Micro Pistol) was introduced as a small-grip, small-size carry pistol. The frame was re-engineered to decrease the front-to-back dimension. According to a company engineer, that meant redesigning 15 different parts. The result was a 9mm carry pistol that felt much smaller in the grip section. Now, the company offers a new 40-caliber version that has had similar treatment. One difference is that the EMP 40 comes with a steel frame, rather than an aluminum one. This difference bumps the weight up, but that may be appreciated with the 40 S&W cartridge. The EMP 40 has a 3-inch barrel and weighs 33 ounces. It forms an attractive package with a bi-tone finish (bright slide, black frame) and rosewood grips.

STI

For 2008, STI International introduced 5 new handguns. Four are variations of their 1911 line.

The VIP is a compact pistol offered in 9, 40 and 45. It has a 3.9-inch barrel. The frame design is unusual—a steel or aluminum upper frame with a polymer grip frame.

The Rogue is a small 9mm with a 3-inch barrel and an aluminum "officer" frame. The slide is lightened at the front, and the pistol weighs 21 ounces.

Staying with 9mm, but getting much larger, the SteelMaster is a competition pistol with a modular steel frame and polymer grip frame. Barrel length of the ported barrel is 4.15 inches. The flat-top slide is lightened both front and rear. The pistol comes with a C-More Red Dot sight that has a blast shield to protect it from the barrel port gases.

The Sentinel Premier is a steel-frame 45 with a traditional 5-inch barrel. With a matte blue finish, it has tritium night sights and other niceties.

The fifth new handgun is the Texican, which is—whoops—a single-action revolver. This is a real departure for STI, but you'll have to read about it elsewhere.

TAURUS

Taurus has a plethora of new offerings for 2008 in its auto pistol lines. Some are new variants of existing models, with changes in finish, grips, materials used or addition of certain features. Two lines are completely new.

The 800 Series pistols are the first polymer-frame pistols Taurus has offered with an outside hammer. While an industry trend has gone to striker-fired polymer pistols, Taurus learned that a lot of shooters just like an external hammer. The new 800 series pistols have the outside hammer, but retain features previously found on the Taurus 24/7 OSS military pistol. The 800 is conventional double-action, and has second-strike capability—in case of a misfire, it automatically allows a second pull of the trigger. It has ambidextrous safety and decocking levers, allowing safe decocking, or carrying "cocked and locked." Modular backstraps allow fitting to different hand sizes. The new 800s are available, all with 4-inch barrels, as Model 809 (9mm, 17+1), Model 840 (40 S&W, 15+1), or Model 845 (45 ACP, 12+1). I like it when model numbers form some kind of pattern. The full 800 series was scheduled for Summer 2008 availability.

The Taurus 1911 introduced a prototype variant with a frame accessory rail last year. The rail version is now a production item, added to the 1911 series of 45-caliber autos.

New, thin single-column polymer-frame carry pistols comprise the 700 series. The new pistols are another departure for Taurus—single-action triggers with a conventional striker-fired design locked by a manual safety. Nicknamed "Slim," the 700 pistol will be available in two models. The 709B is 9mm, 8+1, with a black polymer frame and blue slide. The 709SS is similar, but has a matte stainless-steel slide for a two-tone appearance.

"World's Foremost Pistol Maker" is how the 2008 catalog describes Taurus. The company does make a lot of pistols, in calibers 22, 25, 32, 380, 9mm, 38 Super, 40 S&W and 45 ACP.

TDI

Transformational Defense Industries has introduced the Kriss 45-caliber carbine. (See KRISS)

TG INTERNATIONAL

Ever see a spy movie in which the tiny "Skorpion" submachine gun was used by the bad guys? The Skorpion was developed in Czechoslovakia and used during the Cold War years. It was used by the Czech communist government, by other restrictive regimes, and by terrorist organizations, generally in clandestine, rather than military, usage. In spite of its low-powered 7.65mm (32 ACP) cartridge, it became one of the most notorious submachine guns of all time.

Now, a legal pistol, based on the Skorpion design, will be available. TG International, of Louisville, TN, will offer the newly-manufactured "Scorpion" pistol. (Note the spelling of the name has been Americanized.) Some years ago, the stock of guns was declared

The 800 series pistols are Taurus" first polymer-frame pistols with an outside hammer. This is the Model PT845, a 45 ACP.

Tisas new 1911 45 was demonstrated by Ozge Kalfa at the February 2008 SHOT Show.

surplus by the Czech Republic. The Czech firm of D-Technik began plans to convert the submachine guns to autoloading pistols. The 2004 sunset of the American "Assault Weapons Ban" made the project feasible: America, still the land with the greatest personal freedom, was the greatest market for personal firearms. In 2005, two prototypes were submitted to the BATF, and were approved. Production began in April, 2007. The display at the February 2008 SHOT Show was the first commercial display of the new Scorpion pistol.

In order to make the conversions, Skorpion guns and repair parts kits were acquired. New frames were manufactured, and changes were made to internal parts, assuring that the guns could not be converted back to full-auto condition. No provision is made in the new frames for the shoulder stock. The new semiautomatic Scorpion pistols are offered in a padded case with a nylon holster, one 10-round magazine and two 20-round magazines. Chambered for the original 32 ACP cartridge, the barrel length is 4 ½ inches. The gun is about 10 ½ inches long and weighs about 2 ½ pounds. Even with a fully-loaded 20 round magazine, the weight only goes up to 3 pounds. Interesting, no? For more information, check sales@tnguns.com.

THOMPSON

A new Thompson 1927 A1 pistol has been introduced, along with a new short-barrel rifle version of the WWII Thompson M1. (See KAHR)

TISAS

The Turkish Tisas company has come out with a couple of new offerings. Let's look at them individually.

ZIG M/1911 – Can we ever have too many companies offering 1911 variants? I would hope not. The Turkish firm Tisas introduced a modern double-action 45 pistol last year, and in February 2008 went back to basics, introducing a new 1911 pistol. The pistol is essentially a basic 1911A1 variant, without the add-ons that many consider superfluous. It does have larger, higher sights. Many considered the small sights the only real disadvantage of the original World War II-style 1911A1 pistol, so the new Tisas should have some appeal. The new 1911 offering is blued, with checkered plastic grips. It should be no surprise that it has a 5-inch barrel and a 7-shot magazine.

ZIGANA C – The unnamed double-action Tisas 45-caliber pistol was introduced in prototype last year, and was announced to the public in the previous edition of this publication. The pistol is now in production as the Zigana C. It is conventional double action, has a 4.75-inch barrel and a 10-shot magazine.

At the time of this writing, a United States importer had not been named, and availability date of the new Tisas pistols in America was not certain.

VLTOR

Do you remember the Bren Ten pistol of the early 1980s? Using the concepts and experiences of Jeff Cooper, and consulting with Cooper himself, Dornaus & Dixon Enterprises of Huntington Beach, CA, attempted to offer a new cartridge and pistol combination. They felt it would prove to be better than the 45 ACP and the Colt 1911. The result was 1) the 10mm Automatic cartridge, a new powerful high-pressure pistol round, and 2) the Bren Ten pistol, a big, strong full-size pistol incorporating features of the CZ 75 and other designs.

Within a few years, the company ran into financial problems and failed. The cartridge was a useful one, and lived on. Colt, S&W and other companies chambered pistols for it. Then, in 1991, it looked as if the pistol would be given another chance. Peregrine Industries was formed, also in Huntington Beach, CA, to bring out a revised Bren Ten, to be called the Peregrine Falcon. Things looked promising for a short time, then that company also failed.

Now the gun design is getting a third chance. Vltor Weapon Systems of Tucson, AZ, is planning to bring back the basic Bren Ten design, as the Fortis pistol. The first announcement was made at the 2008 SHOT Show, at which an original Bren Ten was displayed. The Fortis is planned, in first offering, as a full-size service pistol with a 5-inch barrel. Chambering will be for the original 10mm round, and the pistol will weigh 38 ounces.

Vltor general manager Eric Kincel has a personal interest in this project. As

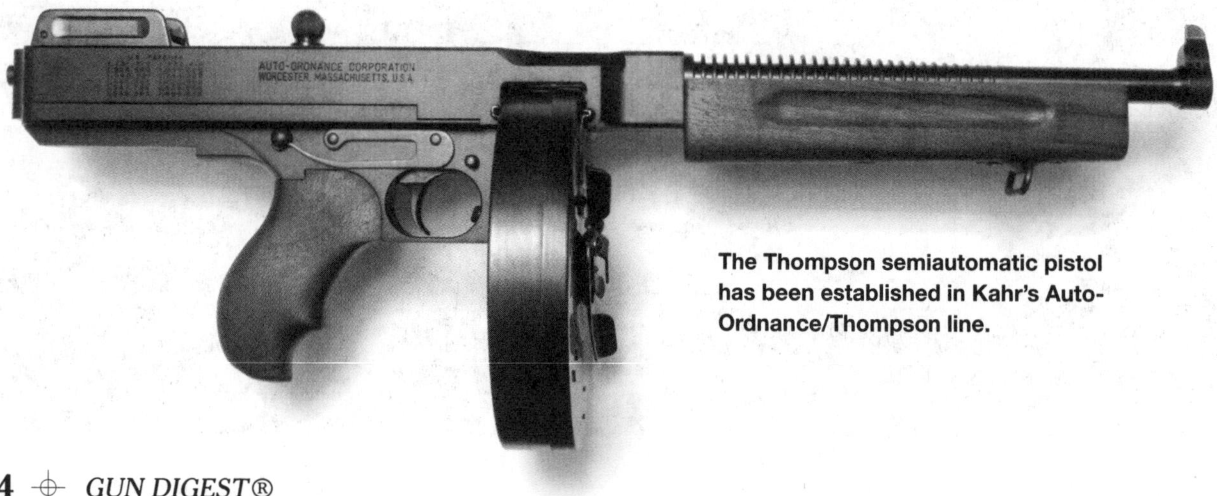

The Thompson semiautomatic pistol has been established in Kahr's Auto-Ordnance/Thompson line.

Vltor general manager Eric Kincel holds an original Bren Ten pistol, which has been out of production for some time. Vltor plans to offer a new version of the innovative pistol.

a young firearms writer for *Gun World* magazine, he wrote an article about the reincarnation of the Bren Ten as the Peregrine Falcon. For those of you who think (as I do) that it is a good thing to save every issue of every magazine, read the July 1991 issue. Also, for more information, check www.vltor.com.

The Bren Ten failed for reasons that had nothing to do with the features of the pistol itself. It is good to see another entity interested in rejuvenating the design. Perhaps the third time will be the charm.

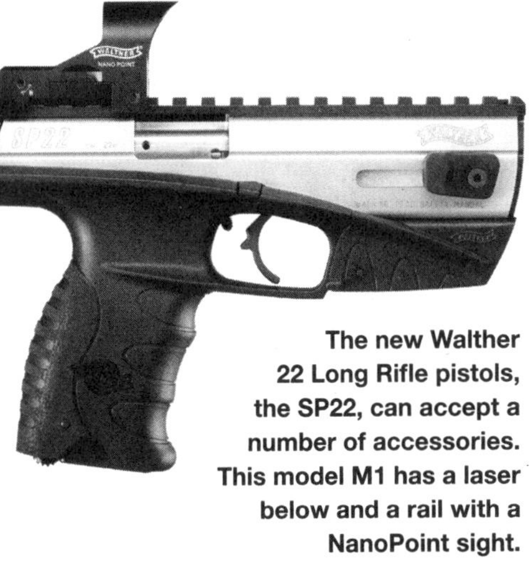

The new Walther 22 Long Rifle pistols, the SP22, can accept a number of accessories. This model M1 has a laser below and a rail with a NanoPoint sight.

The Walther PPS First Edition is a special version with and "anthracite" finish on the polymer frame.

WALTHER

Thin is in! Along with a number of other companies, Walther has come to the conclusion that it would be good to have a thin, flat, polymer-frame concealed-carry pistol in the line. The new Walther PPS (for Police Pistol, Slim—this is straight out of the Walther catalog) is just a tiny bit wider than the magic figure of one inch. Actually, just measuring the width of the slide and frame gives us a little under one inch. The single-column pistol is available in both 9mm and 40 S&W calibers.

What is the capacity of the new pistol? Well, it all depends. For the 9mm, a 6-round magazine is standard, but a 7-shot magazine is also included. The 7-rounder has an extension that lengthens the grip a bit. An 8-shot magazine, with an even longer extension, is also available. For the 40, the figures for the similar options are 5, 6 and 7 cartridges.

Barrel length is about 3 inches, with either caliber. The slides have an interesting angled ejection port—unusual in these days when the straight-across ejection port is used as the barrel-locking surface on many pistols. Rails are incorporated into the frames. Finish is black polymer frame and black slide.

With one exception: there is a special "First Edition" variant that has an "anthracite" polymer frame. This is a metallic effect on the polymer frame, to distinguish it. With the First Edition, the slide is also marked with that designation, and the pistols have their own serial number range. Each First Edition comes with a special aluminum case and all three magazine variations.

The Walther SP22 M2 has a 6-inch barrel and polymer grip frame.

Walther pioneered the interchangeable backstrap concept some years ago, and each PPS comes with large and small backstraps. They have carried the idea further, though. The backstrap also acts as a locking device for the pistol. When the backstrap is removed, the pistol cannot be fired. Walther calls this the "Quicksafe" innovation.

The Walther SP22 line is new. These 22 LR pistols have an internal bolt that is operated by tabs forward of the trigger guard. The tabs are on both sides of the gun, and are pulled rearward together to open the action, somewhat similar to the operation of the Czech Skorpion. Grip frames and other components can be changed to produce a number of different variations. All varieties share the basic operating system, and common 10-round magazines.

Walther offers the SP22 as four distinct variants. The SP22 M1 might be considered a sport model, with a 4-inch barrel and polymer grip frame. The M2 variant is similar, but has a 6-inch barrel. The SP22 M3 is a Target version, with 6-inch match-grade barrel and adjustable trigger. The M4 is the highest Match grade, with a shaped wooden grip. Options such as different grips, rails, laser sights, and barrel weights are available.

POSTSCRIPT

Those of us who enjoy shooting autoloading handguns realize that the years pass on by. In order for the sports that we enjoy to continue, younger shooters must constantly come in to such activities. Unfortunately, today's political climate works to keep young people from shooting pistols or owning pistols. If people do not have the chance to develop an interest when they are young, they are less likely to share our interests later in life. The anti-gun forces count on this. This year, plan to take some young people with you when you go shooting.

HANDGUNS TODAY: SIX-GUNS & OTHERS

by John Taffin

When it comes to firearms these truly are the good old days! No, we can't go into the local gun shop and find a brand-new Bright Blue pinned and recessed Smith & Wesson six-gun, a Royal Blue Colt Python, a Ruger Three-Screw Flat-Top, or a 2nd Generation Colt Single Action Army; nor can we buy anything without jumping through federal, state, and local restrictions and regulations. However, the upside is the firearms market has changed from relatively few choices to an almost endless catalog of great guns. Those offered today may not be as finely finished as the "Old Classics," but they are held to tighter tolerances, made of stronger materials and, in most cases, shoot more accurately than their counterparts from the 1950s.

2009 marks the 50th anniversary of the Ruger Super Blackhawk. In 1959 the retail price of the original 7 1/2-inch Super Blackhawk 44 Magnum was $120. When Ruger could no longer supply the wooden box which originally housed the Super Blackhawks, the price was lowered to $116. Today a blued 7 1/2-inch New Model Super Blackhawk 44 Magnum retails for $631, or about 5.5 times more than it did in 1959. A house built in 1959 now costs about 30 times the original price, cars are at least 20 times what they were in 1959, and that same year I was pumping gas for $.16 a gallon. Yes, when it comes to firearms these really are the good old days! Let's take a look at just a few of today's offerings.

CHARTER ARMS

Charter Arms revolvers have always been an important part of the Taffin family. I've had my original 44 Bulldog for more than 40 years and it has traveled with me more than any other six-gun I own. It has been carried in pockets, boot tops, and stashed in a motor home when we took a vacation trip while the kids were still in high school. It is rarely ever shot, but always loaded, and always ready. This same gun was carried by my wife, Diamond Dot, on her fly fishing trips but she spent so much time in the water we had to switch to a stainless steel version for her.

Both of those 44 Special Bulldogs are now loaded and stashed around the house along with a third puppy, which is the latest version called the Bulldog Pug. A regular inquiry on many of the Internet sites is "How do these guns hold up?" I don't have the slightest idea how they would hold up–even though I've used them for more than 40 years–for the simple reason I do not see these guns as candidates for shooting hundreds upon hundreds of rounds every week. That is not what they were designed for. They are self-defense guns pure and simple and I have had to draw mine in such situations twice. Fortunately, I did not have to fire them, which is exactly what we hope for with every self-defense gun. They are a little larger than the standard 38 Special, and I certainly like the idea of the 44 Special–especially since we now have good self-defense 44 Special ammunition available. Check out a Bulldog Pug 44 Special from Charter Arms if you are looking for an easy-to-pack big bore defensive revolver.

At the other end of the spectrum we have the Charter Arms Pathfinder 22 revolver. They have also been around a long time and, this year, there is a significant improvement in that both the 22 and the 22 Magnum versions are now available with 4-inch barrels and adjustable sights. Adding adjustable sights makes these little revolvers great choices for hikers, campers, backpackers, and they also pack nicely into tackle boxes.

More than 50 years ago High Standard offered a 22 double-action revolver with one of the best-designed grip frames ever produced. That revolver was the Sentinel; a lightweight, dull matte-finish six-gun offered with both 4- and 6-inch

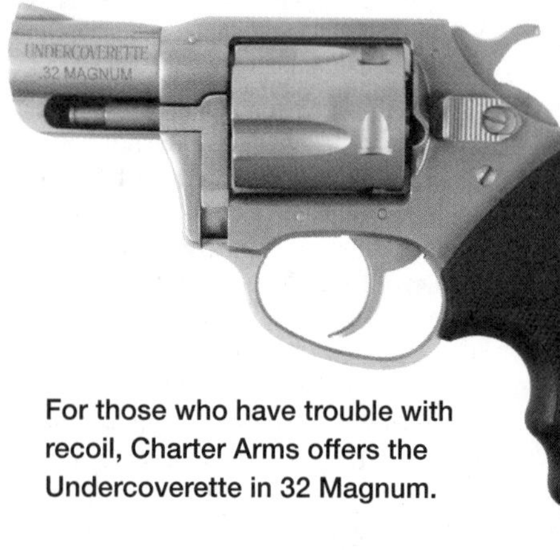

For those who have trouble with recoil, Charter Arms offers the Undercoverette in 32 Magnum.

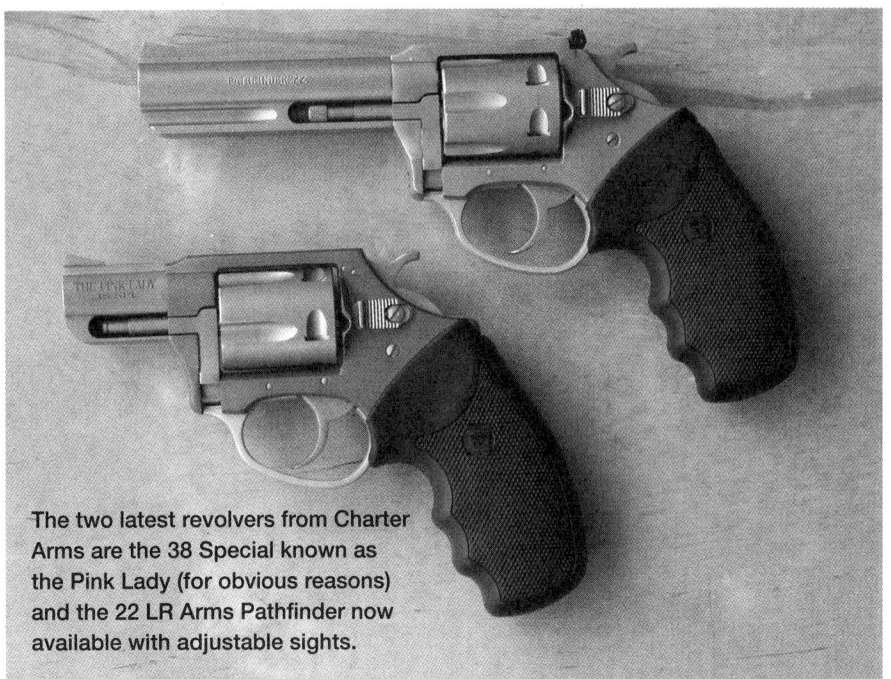

The two latest revolvers from Charter Arms are the 38 Special known as the Pink Lady (for obvious reasons) and the 22 LR Arms Pathfinder now available with adjustable sights.

barrels. Someone at High Standard came up with an excellent idea to appeal to the ladies looking for a purse gun. The barrel of the Sentinel was cut back to just a little over 2 inches, false ivory grips were fitted, the hammer was bobbed off, and the finish was changed drastically: if I recall correctly, it was offered in nickel, gold, blue, and pink finishes. Now, 50 years later, Charter Arms has taken up this same theme somewhat by offering the Pink Lady. This is their basic Undercover 38 Special snub-nosed revolver with a pink frame. Grips are soft finger-grooved rubber for comfortable shooting and I expect this to be a big seller among the ladies. Charter Arms also offers the Undercoverette in 32 Magnum for those who cannot handle the recoil of a lightweight 38 Special.

COLT

Except for three shutdowns totaling less than 20 years, the original Single Action Army by Colt has been in production since 1873. The first run from 1873 to 1941 saw more than 350,000 Single Actions being produced in well over 30 chamberings. When the 2nd Generation arrived in 1956, four chamberings–45 Colt, 357 Magnum, 38 Special, and 44 Special–were offered until the machinery wore out once again and production ceased in 1974. This time the shutdown was only about two years and then the 3rd Generations arrived. The 38 Special disappeared, and the 44-40 chambering was once again offered.

The 3rd Generation Single Actions have been an off-again, on-again proposition, with quality up and down the scale, sometimes a production model, and sometimes a Custom Shop offering. The good news is currently produced Colts have a reputation for excellent quality. Cylinders once again have full length bushings, a feature which was dropped in 1976. The original and genuine Single Action Army is offered in both blue with a case hardened frame and full nickel plating in the three standard barrel lengths of 4-3/4, 5-1/2, and 7-1/2 inches, and chamberings of 45 Colt, 357 Magnum, 38 Special, 44-40, 38-40, and 32-20. I can't for the life of me understand why they don't offer the 44 Special!

FREEDOM ARMS

Dick Casull began experimenting with his "45 Magnum" even before the 44 Magnum arrived. He was quite limited in what revolver he could use for his special loads in that the only one suitable was the Colt Single Action (Ruger's much stronger Super Blackhawk was still several years away). Using 4140 steel, five-shot cylinders were made as large as possible to still fit the frame window of the Colt Single Action. In 1954 using a Colt Single Action 45 with an oversized five-shot cylinder, Casull hit 1550 fps with 250-grain bullets. In 1957, he decided to build his own single-action frame. Thus, using 4140 steel for the frame and 4150 steel for the cylinder, the first "454 Magnum" was created. In the early 1960s, reports of Dick Casull and his 45 Magnum started showing up in gun magazines. At the time, Casull was also converting Ruger Super Blackhawks to five-shot 45s. In March 1979 Wayne Baker and Casull began Freedom Arms, producing 22 Miniguns, and four years later, in October 1983, the first five-shot 454 Casull left the Freedom Arms factory located in Freedom, Wyoming. Since the Freedom Arms 454 six-gun has just celebrated its Silver Anniversary, it would be good to do a mini-review of Freedom Arms' six-guns.

The original Single Action Army dating back to 1873 is still produced by Colt in the both blue/case hardened and nickel-plated versions such as these 7 1/2-inch 45 Colts. Custom stocks are by Paul Persinger.

From the very beginning, the Freedom Arms 454 revolver, now known as the Model 83, has been built to exacting tolerances. Cylinders are line-bored; that is, locked into the frame and then a pilot hole drilled to begin each chamber, which should be in precise alignment with the barrel for top accuracy. They are hand-fitted from the very beginning by mating one particular cylinder to one particular barrel and frame–all for the goal of building the best possible revolver.

In February 1986 Freedom Arms offered their first Model 83 chambered in 45 Colt, followed one month later by the 44 Magnum. In January 1991 the first five-shot 22 Long Rifle Model 83 (originally known as the Model 252) arrived and it quickly became the revolver of choice with the 22 silhouette shooters. The test gun I had was so accurate I hesitated to publish the results, knowing that many would find them hard to believe. One year later, in January 1992, Freedom Arms added the 357 Magnum chambering to the Model 83 line; originally dubbed the "353 Casull" this super-strong 357 Magnum permitted 357 Super-Mag ballistics. In December 1993, Freedom Arms went really big-bore by chambering the Model 83 (it was originally the Model 555) for the 50 Action Express.

Freedom Arms had two more big bores to introduce in the Model 83 before the turn of the century. In December 1997, the Model 83 41 Magnum arrived first as the Model 654; (the most accurate six-gun I have ever encountered is my 10-inch Freedom Arms 41 Magnum). In April of 1999 the 475 Linebaugh arrived in a Model 83. Then Hornady and Ruger teamed up to produce the 480 Ruger, which is nothing more than a slightly shortened 475 Linebaugh.

In 1997, the Model 83 was joined by the Mid-Frame, now known as the Model 97. The Model 1997 is about 90 percent the size of the Freedom Arms standard Model 83, and as expected, is built to the same exacting tolerances and specifications as the original. It is slightly smaller than a Colt Single Action Army and, to me, the grip frame feels much like the old Colt Bisley. The first Model 97 arrived not as the traditional Freedom Arms five-shooter, but rather a true six-gun chambered for six 357 Magnum rounds. Available with both adjustable and fixed sights, the Model 97 is available with standard barrel lengths of 4-1/4, 5-1/2, and 7-1/2 inches. By August 1998, the Model 97 was unveiled as a five-shot 45 Colt; slightly smaller than a Colt Single Action with the strength of the Ruger Blackhawk. To add to its versatility, an extra cylinder is available chambered in 45 ACP. The 41 Magnum arrived as a five-shot Model 97 in April 2000, followed by the Freedom Arms Model 97 Premiere Grade chambered in 22 Long Rifle in July 2002.

Ruger's two newest double-action revolvers, both stainless steel, are the 4-inch 45 Colt Redhawk and the 3-inch SP101 in 327 Federal Magnum.

The arrival of the 21st century also saw the arrival of three more Freedom Arms single actions. The Model 97 32 Magnum with an extra 32-20 cylinder has proven to be an extremely accurate and easy shooting six-gun and my 7-1/2 inch Model 97 has now been joined by a 10-inch dual-cylindered 32 Magnum and the new 327 Federal Magnum. The latest big-bore Model 97 is in 44 Special and is probably the finest factory single-action 44 Special ever produced. Freedom Arms newest chambering in the Model 83 is their very own cartridge, the 500 Wyoming Express. As you read this, a special Silver Anniversary revolver should be available.

RUGER

As we have mentioned 2009 marks the Golden Anniversary of what is probably the number one six-gun selection for many handgun hunters, the 44 Magnum Super Blackhawk. Ruger currently gives sixgunners a choice of 11 Super Blackhawks. The standard 7 1/2-inch blued version is joined by a 10 1/2-inch long-range Ruger as well as two shorter-barreled versions, 4-5/8 and 5-1/2 inches, both of which have standard model grip frames with a rounded trigger guard instead of the square-back Dragoon style; all four are also available in stainless steel. Most shooters find the original Super Blackhawk grip frame to their liking; however, I always get nailed on the knuckle by the square-back trigger guard. For me the Bisley Model was the answer more than 20 years ago, and Ruger still offers the 7 1/2-inch blued Bisley 44 Magnum. Probably the greatest bargains around today for the handgun hunter are the stainless steel Super Blackhawk and Bisley Hunter Models. Both of these have heavy-ribbed 7 1/2-inch barrels scalloped for Ruger scope rings and a long ejector rod and housing for easier removal of fired brass. The Super Blackhawk Hunter has a Super Blackhawk grip frame, but with a rounded trigger guard.

In 1979 Ruger's big-bore single-action Blackhawks were joined by the Redhawk. The 44 Redhawk represented the new wave of 44 Magnums of the'80s—big, tough, able to withstand the recoil of standard 44 Magnums and the new heavyweight bullet loads were soon demanded by handgun hunters. Until the arrival of the Redhawk, it was generally conceded that single actions were stronger than double actions. However, the 44 Magnum Redhawk is actually larger than–and probably stronger than–the Super Blackhawk and soon became a favorite of handgun hunters who used 300-grain hard cast bullets

Ruger's Super Redhawk 480 Ruger now has a five-shot cylinder.

An excellent choice for the outdoorsmen in all kinds of weather is the Colt SAA-sized New Vaquero here shown in polished-stainless with a 4 5/8-inch barrel in 45 Colt.

Ruger's 44 Magnum Super Blackhawk has now turned to gold as it celebrates its 50th Anniversary.

Ruger's SP101 in 32 Magnum, 327 Magnum and 357 Magnum is now offered with Crimson Trace Laser Grips.

Ruger's heavy-duty Packin' Pistol is the 2 1/2-inch Super Redhawk offered in 44 Magnum, 454 Casull, and a five-shot version in 480 Ruger.

over heavy doses of WW296 or H110. The first Redhawk, a 7 1/2-inch stainless six-gun, was soon joined by a 5 1/2-inch stainless model, and blued versions of both barrel lengths; more chamberings were added: 357 Magnum and 41 Magnum (both long gone), and 45 Colt.

It took quite awhile but we finally have 4-inch Redhawks. Ruger first offered it in 44 Magnum last year and now 45 Colt has been added. The 4-inch Redhawk wears totally new grips. Instead of the smallish, smooth wooden stocks found on the other Redhawks, these are newly designed finger-groove, pebble-grained rubber grips from Hogue. The original Redhawk has fully adjustable sights with an interchangeable front sight system. The 4-inch version has the adjustable rear sight and a ramp-style fixed front sight blade with a red insert.

Ruger still offers the excellent and popular Super Redhawk. The Alaskan version, with a 2 1/2-inch barrel and special rubber stocks, makes a powerful yet easy-packin' pistol. The original Super Redhawk is offered in both 7 1/2- and 9 1/2-inch barrel lengths and chambered in 44 Magnum, 454 Casull, and 480 Ruger; the latter has a five-shot cylinder.

Federal announced a new cartridge, the 327 Federal Magnum, in a press release in November 2007. "The 327 Federal Magnum is ideal for personal defense and has the potential for future application in field use. Using a slightly longer 32 H&R Magnum case and our advanced powder and bullet technology, we're able to offer more performance out of a smaller platform. And its recoil is milder than the 357 Magnum." SAAMI specs for the 327 Federal Magnum are set at a maximum of 45,000 psi. To put that into perspective that is more than twice the figure used for the 32 H&R Magnum, and well above the 357 Magnum's 36,000 psi and the 44 Magnum at 35,000 psi. It is easy to see the 327 Federal Magnum is definitely a real magnum. Ruger's SP101, although somewhat regarded as a pocket pistol, is large enough and stout enough to handle the 327 Federal Magnum with ease, and I would like to see Ruger offer a longer-barreled version also. The stainless steel construction of the SP101, along with the comfortable rubber grips, make it perfectly suitable for any type of weather, and it is small enough to be carried quite easily and comfortably. Federal is offering three loads for the 327 Magnum: an 85-grain Hydra-Shok JHP rated at 1,330 fps (The original 32 Magnum with the 85-grain bullet was right at 1,000 fps.); the American Eagle 100-grain SP, 1,300 fps and the Speer 115-grain Gold Dot HP at 1,300 fps. The latter was the only load I had at my disposal for testing and Federal certainly does not fudge on the muzzle velocity as these clock out of my SP101 3 1/16-inch barrel at 1,383 fps. Recoil is snappy but definitely not punishing in any way. The Ruger SP101 rear sight is adjustable for windage only and with the factory front sight this load shoots about 3 inches high for me. Once I settle on an everyday carrying load I will replace the pinned-in front sight blade if necessary.

Ruger's smallest six-gun, the 22 Bearcat celebrated its 50th anniversary in 2008 and a special gold-embellished Anniversary Model is now available. Ruger's other fixed-sighted single-action six-gun, the Vaquero, was replaced several years ago by the smaller-framed New Vaquero. The original Vaquero used the same size frame as the Super Blackhawk, while the New Vaquero utilizes the same size frame as the original 357 Blackhawk of 1955, making it the same basic size as the Colt Single Action. The New Vaquero in 45 Colt is offered in blue or bright polished stainless in 4 5/8-, 5 1/2-, or 7 1/2-inch barrel lengths while the 357 Magnum is cataloged only in the two shorter barrels.

SMITH & WESSON

The newest 22 six-gun from Smith & Wesson is the Model 63-4, a J-Frame stainless steel revolver with a 5-inch heavy barrel. To go with the stainless steel, grips are finger-grooved rubber with molded-in checkering. The heavy ribbed barrel features the enclosed ejector rod first introduced by Smith & Wesson in 1907. The cylinder holds 8 rounds, and the sights are not only screw-adjustable for both windage and elevation, they are square and black, the way sights should be.

Over the years Smith & Wesson has used six frame sizes for their double-action revolvers; these in the order they were first offered are K, N, I, J, L, and X. The J-frame arrived in 1950 when the

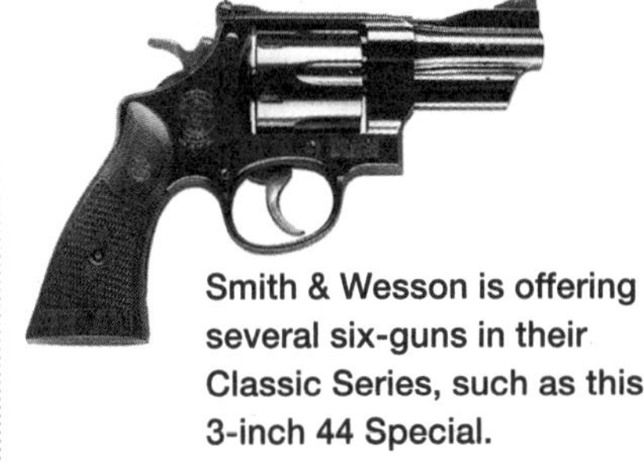

Smith & Wesson is offering several six-guns in their Classic Series, such as this 3-inch 44 Special.

I-frame was enlarged slightly to accommodate a five-shot 38 Special cylinder; the new gun was the Chiefs Special. With the heavier, longer barrel and the cylinder and the tight tolerances held by Smith & Wesson's modern machinery, this little 22 is superbly accurate.

One of the all-time great six-guns was the original Smith & Wesson 44 Magnum. I'd rank it with the Colt Single Action and Government Model as the top three handguns worthy of engraving and custom grips. By the late 1990s the original design was gone and replaced by the full underlug-barrel 44 Magnums. With the arrival of the 50th anniversary of the 44 Magnum in 2006, Smith & Wesson brought out a Golden Anniversary version with the same 6 1/2-inch barrel as the original. It was popular enough to be kept in the catalog and later joined by a nickel-plated version. Now the 4-inch 44 Magnum is available once again. The latter is one of the old S&W models now being offered in their Classic Series. Old-style revolvers, such as the 1917 Classic, have been brought back. New for this year is the 6 1/2-inch Model 24 in 44 Special, 6 1/2-inch Model 25 in 45 Colt, and the 6 1/2-inch Model 27 in 357 Magnum–all in a choice of blue or nickel-plate; the 27 is also available in a 4-inch barrel. The long-standard 6 1/2-inch barrel was dropped in favor of the 6-inch barrel decades ago; it is great to see the correct barrel length return.

All the foregoing Classic Series six-guns are very attractive with their blue or nickel-plated finishes and can be rated at the top for both form and function. The Night Guard Series is low on form but very high on function. This matte-black, scandium-frame 2 1/2-inch revolver has Pachmayr Compac grips, XS 24/7 Standard Dot Tritium front sight matched to a Cylinder and Slide Extreme Duty fixed rear sight, and is offered in several models: Model 325 in 45 ACP; Model 329, 44 Magnum; Model 396, 44 Special; and two versions in 357 Magnum, a seven-shot Model 386 and an eight-shot Model 327. For those who think the 44 Special is dead, notice Smith & Wesson is offering three 44 Specials this year alone as the much sought-after and very popular five-shot Model 396 is also back.

In the 1920s and 1930s two of the most popular Smith & Wessons among law enforcement officers, especially those in rural areas, were the 38/44 Heavy Duty and the 1926 Model 44 Special. Thanks to the urgings of Clint Smith, Smith & Wesson brought back the Heavy Duty-style 4-inch fix-sight revolver and now offers both a 45 ACP and 44 Special version. The 44 Special is the Model 21, while the 45 ACP version is the Model 22 and both are available in blue or nickel-plated finishes. Two very popular 38 Special pocket pistols are also back in the Classic Series. One is the original Chiefs Special Model 36 while the Centennial, with its grip safety, is the Model 40. Both of these are also available blue or nickel-plated.

We would be remiss if we didn't mentioned two of the best six-guns offered by Smith & Wesson in recent times. They are the 329PD, a 26-ounce 44 Magnum, and the 360Sc and its hammerless counterpart, the 340Sc–both chambered in 357 Magnum and weighing only 12 ounces. The original Smith & Wesson 4-inch 44 Magnum, half again as heavy, has always been brutal with full-house 44 Magnum rounds and the 329PD even more so, however this easy-packin' 44 makes a most enjoyable-shooting 44 Special and the power of the 44 Magnum

The Smith & Wesson 6 1/2-inch Model 24 in 44 Special is back in both blue and nickel-plating, and...

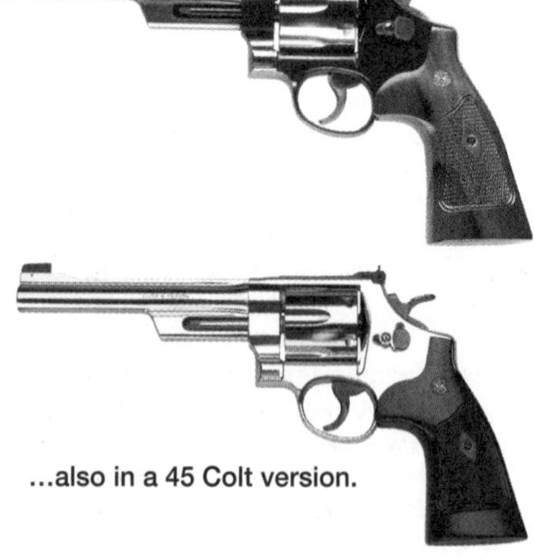

...also in a 45 Colt version.

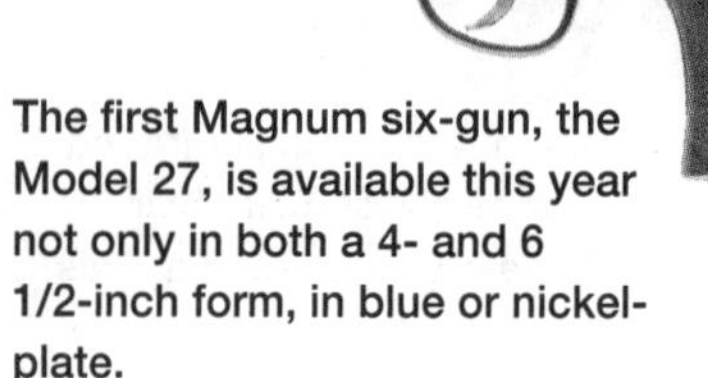

The first Magnum six-gun, the Model 27, is available this year not only in both a 4- and 6 1/2-inch form, in blue or nickel-plate.

Smith & Wesson's latest 22 revolver, the Model 63-4, is shown with an original I-frame 22.

The original Chiefs Special from Smith & Wesson is back as the 38 Special Classic Model 36.

The Heavy Duty of the 1930s has been resurrected by Smith & Wesson in the 45 ACP/45 Auto Rim Classic Model 22, and...

...the 44 Special Classic Model 21.

Smith & Wesson reached all the way back to 1917 to bring back this Classic World War I-era 45 ACP.

is there if needed. It is carried a lot and shot a little with 44 Magnum rounds. The J-frame scandium/titanium 357s carry oh-so-easy in the front pocket. My 340Sc is my everyday concealed-carrying gun and it is the first gun I ever carried that I have to feel to see if it is still there. They are brutal with 357 loads but quite tolerable with 38 Special +P loads, the power of the 357 Magnum is there if needed.

STI

Last year in these pages we said the STI Texican was long on promise and short on delivery; however, it is now reality and it is a dandy! The first run of Texicans, which are manufactured in Connecticut (no, not by Colt or USFA) are 5 1/2-inch 45 Colts. There are no castings in the Texican with all parts either forged or made from aerospace-spec. steel bar stock, 4150 chrome moly. All the internal parts are EDMed. Barrels are made from Green Mountain blanks with a 1-12 twist; the mainframe, loading gate, and hammer are all color case-hardened by Turnbull, and the specially designed pawl rides on a fixed pivot and is expected to have three to four times the life expectancy of other traditional pawl springs.

I found the fitting and polish of the Texican to be exceptional. Giving the frame-to-trigger guard the finger test (running a finger from the bottom of the cylinder down the mainframe to the trigger guard) results in no perceptible feel of where the two parts meet; a sure sign of careful fitting and finishing. Flat surfaces are flat and there are no dished-out screw holes. The action is very smooth with a 2-1/4 pound trigger pull, and the cylinder locks up tight! There is no perceptible play, either side-to-side or front-to-back, when the hammer is cocked or at rest.

The first thing I did to test the precise nature of the tolerances the Texican is held to was to measure the chamber throats. Using a set of plug gauges, I found all six to be perfectly reamed to 0.452-inch. Since the Texican is a tra-

The STI Texican is a traditionally styled single-action six-gun and should only be carried loaded with five rounds and the hammer down an empty chamber.

This 1930 Austin holster by El Paso Saddlery made for the Colt Single Action works just fine for the STI Texican.

New from Taurus this year are two +P rated 22-ounce six-shot 38 Specials Model 856B2, blue and the stainless steel Model 856SS2.

ditionally styled single action, there is no transfer bar safety; to load and unload, the hammer is placed on half cock, the loading gate opened, the ejector rod used to expel cases one at a time as the cylinder is rotated, and the cylinder is then rotated again as fresh cartridges are placed one at a time. Being a traditional single action means although the Texican is a true six-gun with a capacity of six rounds, it MUST be carried with only five rounds and the hammer down on an empty chamber.

The Texican gets an "A" for accuracy. Every factory load and handload tried produced anything from good to exceptional accuracy. The Texican grips are described as unbreakable ABS Polymer. I certainly realize grips are highly subjective and most of my six-guns and semi-automatics are fitted with custom stocks. Sometimes this is for esthetics and other times for practicality. The grips on the Texican are sharply checkered, which is a mistake on this beautiful six-gun. One hundred rounds of 260-grain bullets at 900-1,000 fps from the Texican left me with a red tender spot on the palm of my hand. This situation is easily remedied by a pair of smooth custom stocks, exactly what the Texican deserves.

The Judge from Taurus is an exceptionally versatile revolver that fires standard 45 Colt, or .410 shotshells, slugs or buckshot.

TAURUS

One of the best ideas to come along in a long time is The Judge from Taurus. Taurus has taken their basic five shot big-bore Tracker platform and extended the length of both the frame and cylinder to allow for the use of .410 shotgun shells while chambering this same cylinder to also accept standard 45 Colt rounds. So this one basic revolver actually can be used four ways. Shooters have a choice of filling the cylinder with 45 Colt rounds or .410 shot shells, buckshot, or rifle slugs. This certainly makes The Judge the most versatile revolver available.

The Judge has a cylinder length of 2-1/2 inches, and is offered in two barrel lengths, 3 and 6-1/2 inches, and either all blue or stainless steel. Hammer and trigger are wide target style with the hammer spur checkered and the trigger face smooth as all triggers should be. Both the sights and the grips on the Judges are rated A+. The sights are fixed and consist of a square notch rear sight mated up with an easy-to-see red fiber-optic front sight. The front sight really picks up available light and stands out brightly against a dark background. There is nothing pretty about the grips but they receive their ratings for comfort. They bolt on the grip frame stud from the bottom and are Taurus' Ribbers with soft horizontal lines. They fit my hand very well, are extremely secure as they seem to stick to my palm and they also do an excellent job of minimizing felt recoil with .410 shotgun shells.

I expected poor accuracy using 45 Colt rounds and ineffective performance with shotshells and I was wrong on both counts. Four different 45 Colt loads were fired in the 6 1/2-inch Judge at 50 feet with all loads averaging 1-1/2 inches for five shots. With the long jump the 45 bullets had to make for the length of that 2 1/2-inch cylinder I expected shots scattered all over the paper. Winchester shotshells, loaded with #4, #6, and #9 shot, were fired at distances of both five feet and ten feet. Since I view this six-gun primarily for defense against poisonous snakes there was no reason to test them at any greater distance. At five feet, any one of the shot sizes selected would surely do the job. However, #9 performed superbly, putting at least 98-99 percent of the pellets inside an eight-inch circle on the Caldwell Orange Peel Target.

Using Winchester's three-ball buckshot I fired at half-size silhouette targets at 30 feet. Whether I shot one round or three rounds–all the balls hit the target, making The Judge a candidate for serious home defense. The final test was .410 rifled slugs. I set up a half-size silhouette target at 30 feet and fired the three rounds I had from a standing two-handed position. These lighter slugs printed about three inches low at 30 feet, and all three grouped into two inches. All this means The Judge will perform quite satisfactorily–and then some– with 45 bullets and .410 shotshells, buckshot or slugs. This versatility allows the shooter to load with all of one type or any combination thereof. I think The Judge will be very popular with hikers, backpackers, fishermen–anyone who wanders outdoors–and also serve quite well as a defensive home or car gun.

Taurus never does anything in a small way and their small guns are a perfect example of this. They catalog more than four dozen snub-nosed revolvers designed for concealed carry in 22, 32 Magnum, 38 Special, 357 Magnum–and even

Taurus offers the five-shot Tracker in several options, including this 4-inch 44 Magnum.

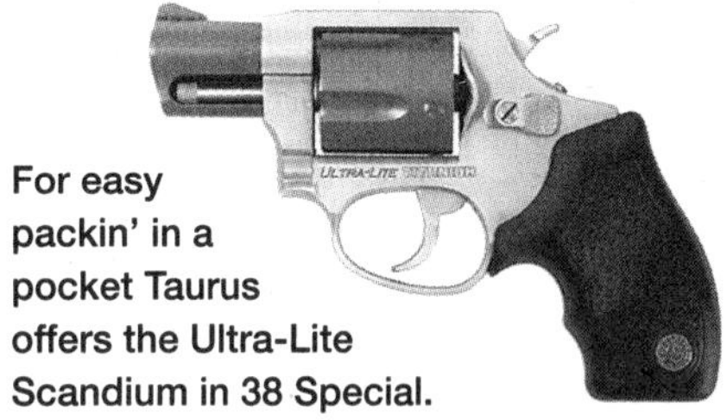

For easy packin' in a pocket Taurus offers the Ultra-Lite Scandium in 38 Special.

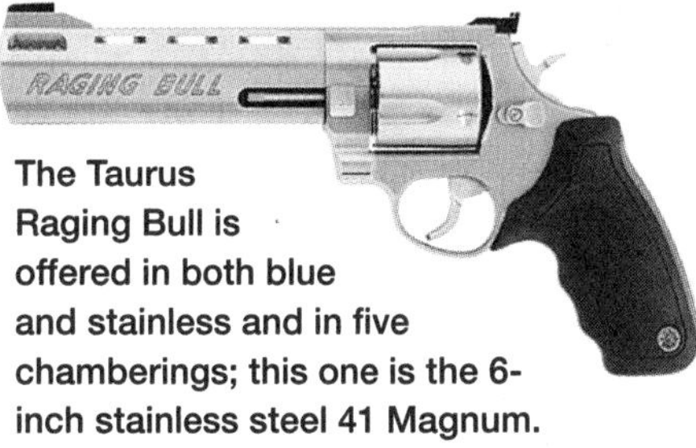

The Taurus Raging Bull is offered in both blue and stainless and in five chamberings; this one is the 6-inch stainless steel 41 Magnum.

17 HMR. Three of their latest versions are six-shot 38 Specials with a blued or stainless steel Model 856 weighting 22 ounces and rated for +P loads, while the Model 856MG has a magnesium frame and weighs in at only 13 ounces; standard 38 Specials only here. Just as with the 44 Bulldogs mentioned in the Charter Arms section, I also have two Taurus 38 Specials always at hand. The Ultra-Light stainless steel with factory Taurus finger-grooved rubber grips is always in reaching distance while I am typing articles, and the Ultra-Light Titanium with bobbed hammer and Crimson Trace Laser grips always rides in my jacket pocket. Both of these are only fired occasionally to keep in practice; however, they are both kept loaded with Speer Gold HP 38 Specials and I would–and do–stake my life on them. That's the highest recommendation I can give any firearm.

At the other end of the Taurus spectrum we have the really big-bore blasters, the Raging Bulls. These are, of course, designed with the big-game hunter in mind and are offered in both blue and stainless versions and chambered in 41 Magnum, 44 Magnum, 454 Casull, 480 Ruger and also a long-cylinder version in 500 S&W. The 444 Multi is one of the best-looking revolvers offered by Taurus; it is a 4-inch Ultra-Lite 44 Magnum made for easy packin'.

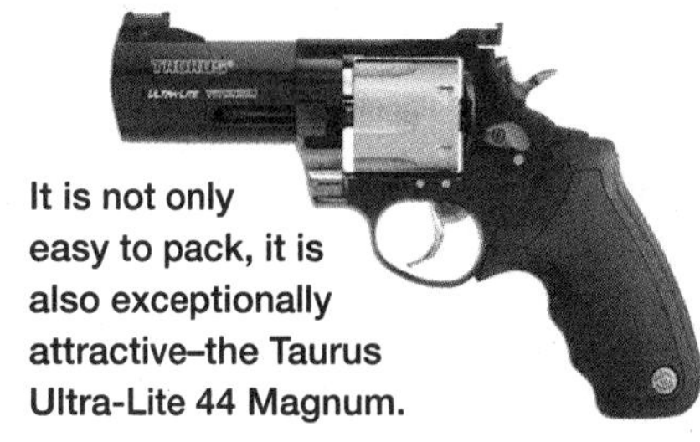

It is not only easy to pack, it is also exceptionally attractive–the Taurus Ultra-Lite 44 Magnum.

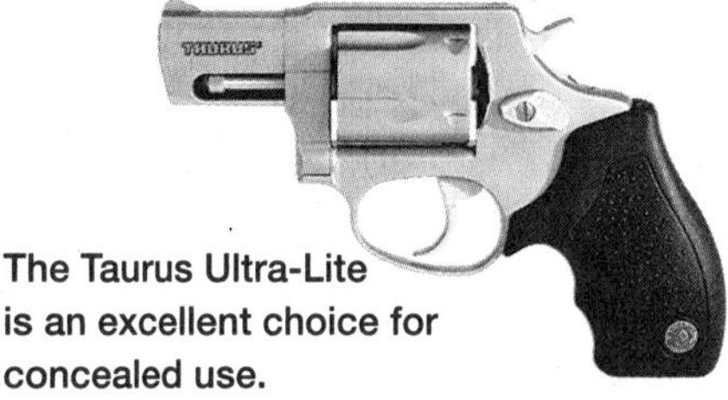

The Taurus Ultra-Lite is an excellent choice for concealed use.

Taurus offers several options in concealed hammer, small-framed revolvers.

THOMPSON/CENTER

Single-shot pistols from Thompson/Center are extremely popular with handgun hunters. Interchangeable barrels systems for both the G2 Contender and the Encore make it possible for the hunter to use the same frame for different barrels suitable for everything from mice to moose. The original Contender was often hard to open. However, this was solved several years ago with the G2 which opens very easily simply by pulling back on the bottom of the trigger guard. The G2 is available in both 12- and 14-inch versions and either blued finish with walnut stock and forearm or stainless steel with a rubber grip and rubber forearm. Calibers for big-game hunters include 30-30, 375 JDJ, and 45-70 while small game and varmint hunters can choose from such smallbore chamberings as 22LR, 22 Hornet, 223 Remington, and 204 Ruger.

The Encore is basically a stronger Contender designed to handle higher-pressure cartridges. Contender and Encore barrels are not interchangeable but are relegated to their specific model actions. The Encore is catalogued in 12- and 15-inch barrels and blue with walnut stock and forearm, stainless steel with rubber stock and forearm, or Hardwoods Camo finish. There is also a Pistol Hunter Package offered with a 15-

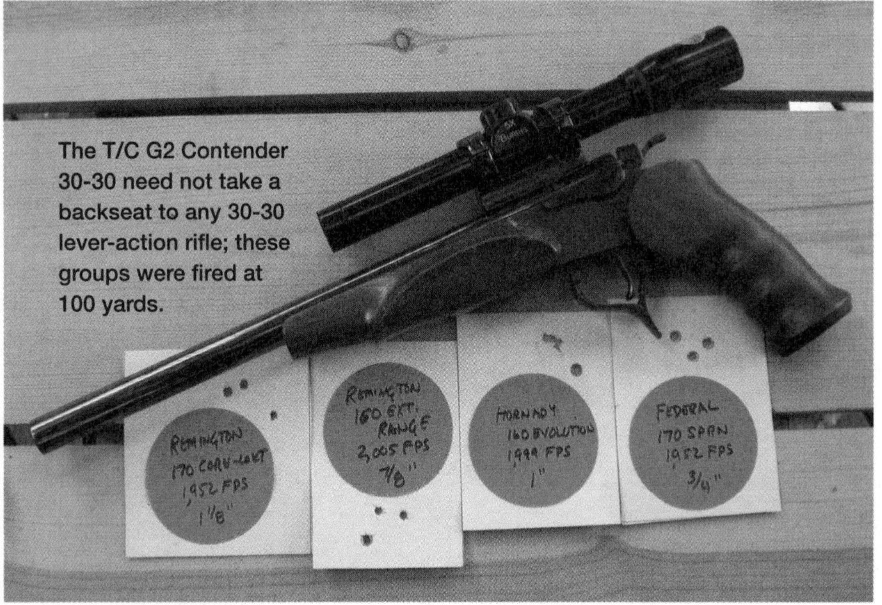

The T/C G2 Contender 30-30 need not take a backseat to any 30-30 lever-action rifle; these groups were fired at 100 yards.

The G2 Contender features an easily and quickly interchangeable barrel system.

USFA's Cowboy is an easy-shooting 45, even with Keith bullets at 900 fps.

inch barrel, rubber stock and forearm, and a 2.5-7X T/C Recoil Proof variable scope and a padded carrying case.

Chamberings for the Encore include some very serious hunting cartridges such as 225 Winchester, 243 Winchester, 25-06, 270, 7-08, 308, 30-06, 375 JDJ, and the two latest six-gun magnum cartridges from Smith & Wesson, the 460 and 500.

UNITED STATES FIREARMS (USFA)

After many years of testing virtually every six-gun offered as well as most semi-automatics and single-shots, I am not easily impressed, and it takes something very special to stir my mind, heart, soul, and spirit. USFA's single-action six-guns definitely stir me in every way. The beautiful finish harkens back to pre-war single actions: the main frame beautifully case-colored in Armory Bone Case and the balance of the six-gun finished in a deep, dark Dome Blue color. Grips furnished as standard are checkered hard rubber with a "US" molded into the top part of the grip. Normally, I prefer to fit favored single-action six-guns with custom grips made of ivory, stag, or some exotic wood. However, in the case of USFA single action six-guns the grips are so perfectly fitted to the frame and feel so good in the hand I am very hesitant to change them, although I usually do. If one looks at the grips on most single-action six-guns, the fitting leaves a lot to be desired–not so here. These grips have been fitted to the grip frame on the factory-built revolver as carefully as a set of custom grips by the master gripmakers.

There are several things to look for as far as fit on any single-action six-guns. One is the radiusing of the lower part of the back of the hammer and the two "ears" formed by the back strap where it screws into the mainframe on both sides of the hammer. A smooth mating of the contours of all three is a real indication of careful fitting, as is the fit of the trigger guard to the bottom of the mainframe and where the back strap meets the mainframe. All of these meeting places should feel totally smooth to the finger; USFA single actions are fitted just about perfectly in all of these areas.

USFA Single Actions are available with a V- or square-notch rear sight and a front sight with a square profile rather than tapering to the top. Sixgunners also have a choice of a cross-pin or screw-in "blackpowder" cylinder pin latch. Chamberings offered in USFA single actions are 45 Colt, 32 WCF (32-20), 41 Long Colt, 38 Special, 38 WCF (38-40), 44 WCF (44-40), 45 ACP, 44 Russian, and 44 Special. The latter can be marked as "RUSSIAN AND S&W SPECIAL 44" as early Colt Single Actions were marked. They could be used with either 44 Russian or the then-relatively new 44 Special.

The basic price for a USFA single action is now $975 for a 4 3/4-, 5 1/2-, or 7 1/2-inch gun finished in Old Armory Bone Case and Dome Blue. Custom touches available include a case-colored hammer, full blue finish, nickel finish, walnut, pearl or ivory stocks; and special engraving from names all the way up to full coverage scroll engraving. Three special models are also offered: the Rodeo, Rodeo II and the Cowboy. The much less expensive Rodeo, $550, is the same basic six-gun as the Single Action and has a subdued matte blue finish instead of the beautiful finish of the standard revolver; Rodeo II is satin nickeled with blued screws, trigger, and basepin, while the stocks are hard brown rubber dubbed Burlwood; the Cowboy is an all-blue six-gun with Burlwood grips; prices for the latter two are $605 and $790 respectively. All three versions are offered in 4 3/4- and 5 1/2-inch lengths and in 45 Colt or 38 Special. The Cowboy is also available with a 7 1/2-inch barrel. USFA also offers an antique version, The Gunslinger, a six-gun made to look as if it has been in service 100+ years, and such special six-guns as the Custer Colt and the highly engraved and ivory-stocked Theodore Roosevelt Single Action.

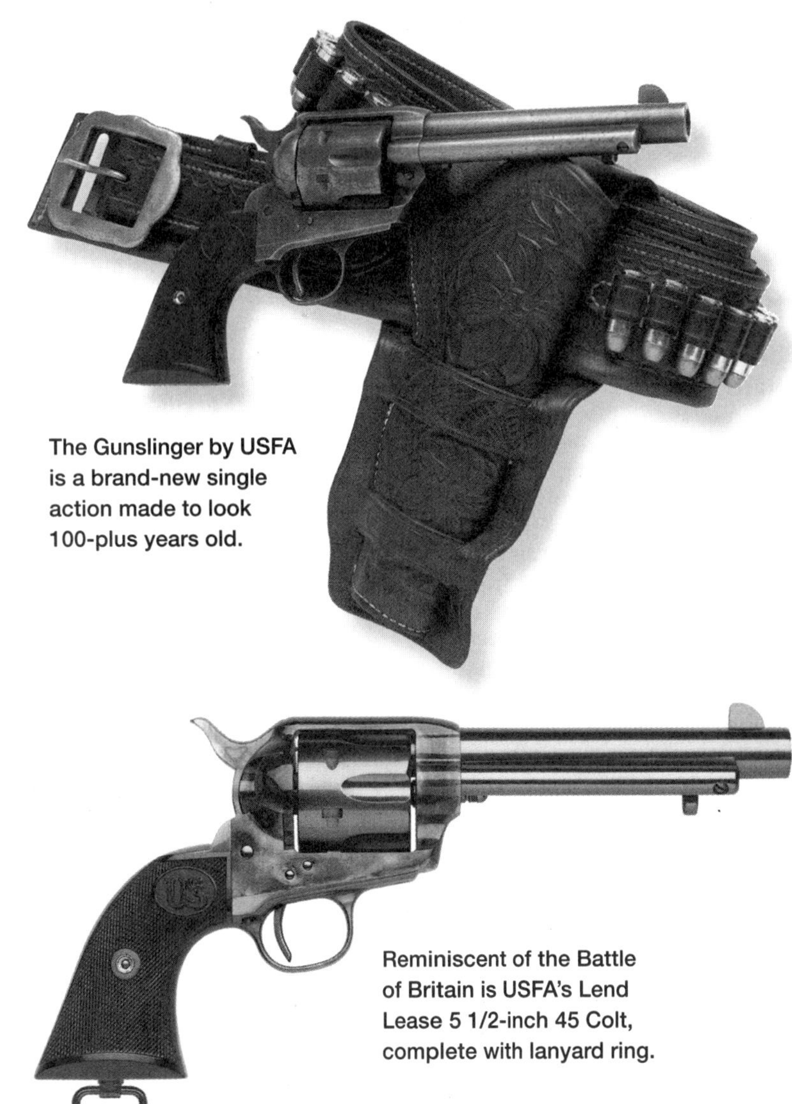

The Gunslinger by USFA is a brand-new single action made to look 100-plus years old.

Reminiscent of the Battle of Britain is USFA's Lend Lease 5 1/2-inch 45 Colt, complete with lanyard ring.

The newest offerings from USFA are the satin-nickeled Rodeo II and the all-blue Cowboy.

Now that USFA is firmly established with their Single Action they are branching out to produce other single-action six-guns. Two new revolvers are being announced this year, the 44 Remington Model 1858 percussion revolver and the Model 1875 Remington; USFA is also exhibiting a prototype of one of the lesser known revolvers from the frontier period, the Forehand & Wadsworth. Forehand & Wadsworth was eventually purchased by Hopkins & Allen who also produced the Merwin, Hulbert. USFA's Forehand & Wadsworth is a solid-frame single-action revolver, chambered in 44-40.

WESSON FIREARMS

Dan Wesson revolvers have a well-deserved reputation for accuracy and for many years ruled the long-range silhouette game. The original Dan Wesson company was started by Dan Wesson himself, was taken over by the family at his death, then lost, then regained—and then shut its doors. It was eventually purchased, moved to New York and is now owned by CZ.

Dan Wesson six-guns were once offered in all of the SuperMag chamberings: 357SM, 375SM and 445SM; as of this writing only the 445 remains. It is offered in the Alaskan Guide Special, a 5-inch barreled, six-shot revolver with a compensator, the DW VH8 with an 8-inch Heavy Vent Rib Barrel and crafted of stainless steel, and the Super Ram Silhouette model with special competition sights.

It appears that Wesson Firearms is reintroducing the small-frame Dan Wesson revolver, stainless steel, with interchangeable barrels, and offered in 22LR, 32 Magnum, 32-20, and 357 Magnum. I have examples of all of these produced by the original Dan Wesson factory and they all can be described as tack-drivers. I expect no less from currently produced Wesson revolvers.

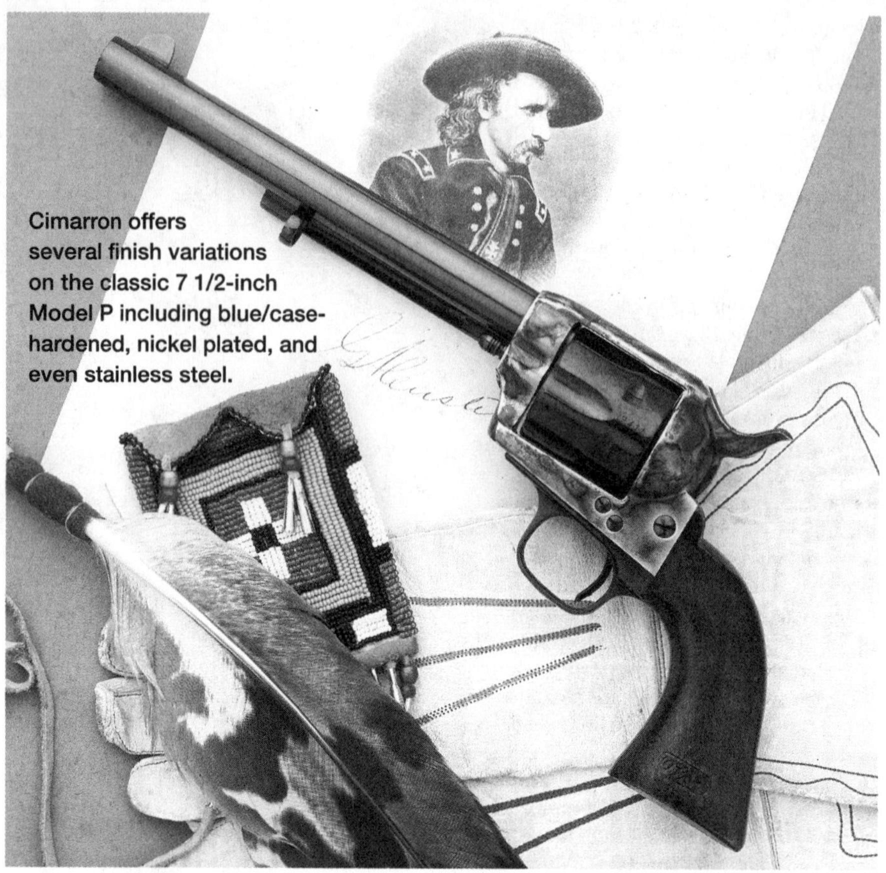

Cimarron offers several finish variations on the classic 7 1/2-inch Model P including blue/case-hardened, nickel plated, and even stainless steel.

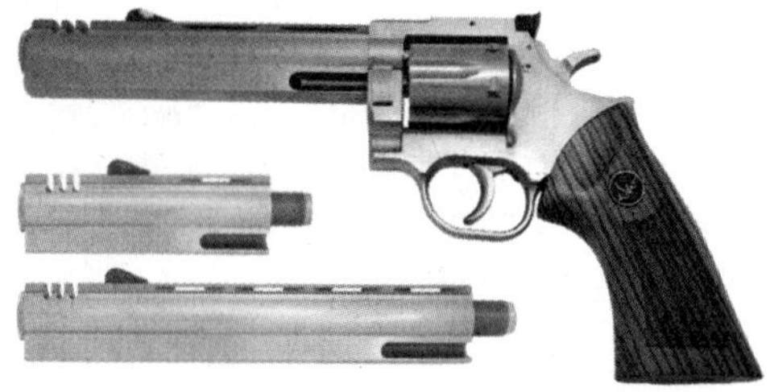

Wesson Firearms once again catalogs their small frame revolver in stainless steel with interchangeable barrels and a choice of 22, 32 Magnum, 32-20 and 357 Magnum.

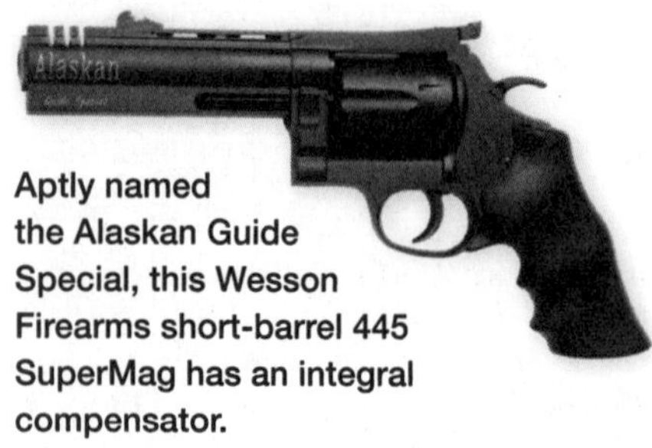

Aptly named the Alaskan Guide Special, this Wesson Firearms short-barrel 445 SuperMag has an integral compensator.

Wesson Firearms offers their stainless steel 445 SuperMag with a heavy barrel and Hogue exotic wood stocks.

REPLICA SIX-GUNS

We now have excellent imported replicas of nearly every six-gun, both percussion and cartridge style, and every lever action and single-shot rifle from the 19th century. Not only are they available in hundreds of versions, they are extremely close to the originals in form and still remain relatively low in price. Various models are available from American Western Arms, Cimarron, Charles Daley, Dixie Gunworks, EMF, Navy Arms, Taylor's & Co, and Uberti. From the late 1950s until well into the 1980s cartridge-firing imported single-action six-guns for the most part had poorly carried out case colors and a brass grip frame; today we have truly authentic looking replica six-guns available and much of the credit for this goes to the great rise of Cowboy Action Shooting in the 1990s and the demand for authentically-styled firearms. Today almost every frontier-era cartridge-firing six-gun is being offered to shooters.

We now have the Colt cartridge conversions: the 1871-72 Open-Top; the Single Action Army, and the Bisley Model. Remington replica six-guns are offered in both the 1875 and 1890 versions; and we can also fill our need for a Smith & Wesson six-gun with variations patterned after the Schofield, Russian Model #3 and the

U.S. Scout Model. The U.S. Cavalry Models were nickel plated and issued to Indian scouts. Nickel plating was needed to give extra protection to the scout guns.

New Model #3. Multiply all these models by the number of calibers, finishes, barrel lengths–then add in variations such as a change in the grip frame–and it is easy to see just how many hundreds of six-guns we are talking about here. Today's replicas are offered, or have been offered, in more than a dozen different chamberings. Shooters can pick from 19th-century cartridges such as the 32-20, 38 Long Colt, 38-40, 44-40, 44 Russian, 44 Colt, 45 S&W, 45 Colt, and even the 41 Long Colt. Twentieth-century cartridges available in replica six-guns include the 32 Magnum, 44 Special, 357 Magnum, and 45 ACP.

There is a virtual supermarket out there of replica Colt SAAs offered in blue, blue/case-color, nickel, and even stainless steel. The four most popular frontier chamberings of 45 Colt, 44-40, 38-40 and 32-20 are readily available, along with 38 Special, 357 Magnum and 44 Special. Cimarron's SAA is the Model

P, EMF has the 1873 Hartford Model and Great Western II, and for Taylor's and Uberti it is the Model 1873. In addition to other versions, Navy Arms also offers the 1873 Gunfighter, mainly designed for Cowboy Action Shooting, as is the Evil Roy version from Cimarron and Taylor's Smoke Wagon. All three are specially tuned and timed for competition.

Beretta and **Taurus** offer slightly different replicas, as both the Stampede and Gaucho have transfer bar safeties but still have the traditional look and half-cock on the hammer for loading and unloading. It appears Taurus has dropped the Gaucho from their line-up; this is unfortunate as the four examples I have handled were excellent six-guns.

AWA does not import finished six-guns, but rather parts which are then assembled and finished in Florida. AWA's replica SAAs consist of the 1873, a more finely-finished and tuned Ultimate 1873, and their top model, the Octagonal Ultimate with an octagon barrel.

Cimarron offers a Wyatt Earp Buntline styled after the one used by Kurt Russell in *Tombstone* and they also offer the short-barreled Sheriff's Model. Cimarron was the first to offer a scaled-down SAA-based Lightning, which has a grip frame patterned after the 1877 Colt DA Lightning. Their full-sized six-gun with the same grip frame is known as the New Thunderer, and the smaller Model P Jr. six-gun is also offered with a standard grip; Beretta and EMF also offer single actions with the Lightning grip frame. Another version of the Single Action offered by Cimarron, EMF and Uberti, is the Bisley Model. Originally this was offered as a Flat-Top Target version of the Colt SAA, with a wide hammer and trigger and a larger target grip frame, but the Bisley Model soon found favor as an everyday packin' pistol with standard sights instead of target sights.

Remington's first cartridge firing six-gun was the Model 1875 chambered in 45 Colt, 44-40 and 44 Remington. At first glance, the Remington Single Action looks much like a Colt but there are several differences. The grip frame of the Remington is part of the main frame, resulting in a more solid and possibly stronger six-gun. The trigger guard is brass, separate from the main frame, and does not form part of the front grip strap as on the Colt. The Remington 1875 achieves its most distinctive appearance from a web under the barrel running from the end of ejector housing to the front of the frame. The cylinder base pin also runs all the way to the end of the ejector tube. In 1890 Remington streamlined their Model of 1875 by removing most of the under-barrel web, cutting the barrel length to 5-3/4 inches, and adding a lanyard ring. Current replica Remingtons are faithful to the original design and are available from Cimarron, EMF and Navy Arms.

Cimarron offers presentation Bisleys that rival the engraved guns of the late 1800s.

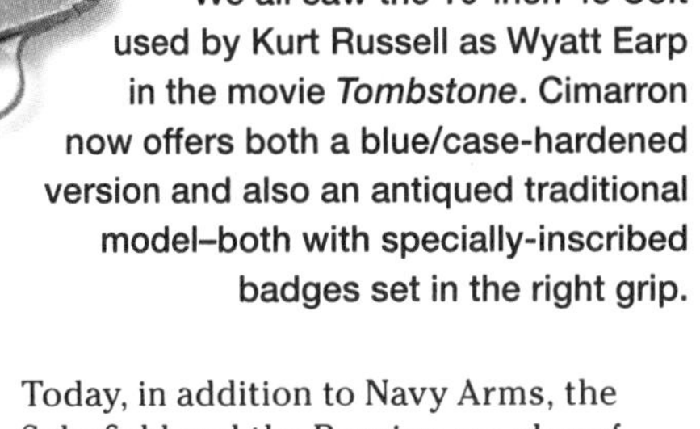

We all saw the 10-inch 45 Colt used by Kurt Russell as Wyatt Earp in the movie *Tombstone*. Cimarron now offers both a blue/case-hardened version and also an antiqued traditional model–both with specially-inscribed badges set in the right grip.

We can thank the late Val Forgett of **Navy Arms** for making the Model 1875 Schofield (manufactured by Uberti) a reality. It is quite faithful to the original Schofield except the cylinder is longer and chambered–not for the 45 Smith & Wesson–for the very much alive and well 45 Colt. The first barrel length offered was 7 inches, soon followed by a 5-incher. Chamberings offered were the 44-40 and 38 Special. Forgett considered the introduction of the Schofield to be enough of a success to justify a second Smith & Wesson replica single action, the New Model Russian chambered for the historic 44 Russian. The Navy Arms New Model Russian or Model 3 Russian is a faithful copy of the original complete with what are probably the tiniest sights ever placed upon a big-bore six-gun. Today, in addition to Navy Arms, the Schofield and the Russian are also offered by Cimarron, Taylor's and Uberti; Beretta's Laramie is patterned after a Target Model New Model #3. However, it is not chambered in the original 44 Russian but rather in 45 Colt and 38 Special with both 5- and 7-inch blued and nickel-plated examples being offered.

There is one great Old West six-gun that has yet to be replicated and that is the Merwin, Hulbert. Available for only a very short time during the last quarter of the 19th century, it was the most sophisticated revolver of that time–or any time. There is no way they could build those guns with the machinery they had, but they did! There is a real ongoing effort to resurrect the Merwin, Hulbert and bring it back into production. Maybe this year?

By the time we turn the calendar to 2009, the Supreme Court will have decided the 2nd Amendment case and we will have a new president and a different congressional make-up. These are the good old days as far as the choices and proliferation of six-guns, however they are not the good old days when it comes to our basic freedoms, which seem to continually shrink. As a wise man once said: "Eternal Vigilance is the price of liberty." This was true more than 200 years ago and is even truer today.

The Elmer Keith Museum is finally reality and nestled in the Cabela's store in Boise Idaho. Many of Keith's great six-guns, such as the Number 5SAA, several other 44 Specials and 44 Magnums, and dozens of other six-guns, rifles and many game trophies are on display. A life-like manikin of Keith complete with his famous hat sits at a desk in his office, turns around and speaks very realistically for seven minutes. The last thing he says is "Join The NRA." Every shooter should heed his advice.

RIFLE REVIEW

by Layne Simpson

ABOVE: The new Browning X-Bolt in 308 worked fine ion this Colorado pronghorn.

One of the most useful of my proud possessions is a collection of Gun Digest. I am missing the 1st edition as well as numbers 3, 4, 6, 9 and 11 but I have all the rest. In addition to being an important part of my reference library, they are also nice to have around anytime I want to hop aboard my imaginary time travel machine and reminisce about guns of the past. The 2nd edition is always interesting because it was published soon after the final shots of World War II were fired and the various manufacturers had yet to come up with prices. In fact, at the time the production of many of the guns described and pictured there had yet to resume. That issue was kicked off with an article by Charles T. Haven entitled "Our Small Arms and Their Makers." It was followed by "The Proper Big Game Rifle" by Elmer Keith and funny thing is, Jack O'Connor is in the lead photo. Then came the rifles.

Winchester was up first in that 2nd edition and the first rifles pictured were Model 70s in Standard, National Match, Target, Bull Gun and Super Grade variations. The standard grade gun was shown in 22 Hornet, 220 Swift, 250-3000 Savage, 257 Roberts, 270 Winchester, 7x57mm Mauser, 30-06, 300 H&H Magnum, 375 H&H Magnum and believe it or not, 35 Remington. Open sights were standard and if the optional Lyman 48WJS or 57W receiver sight was chosen instead, the rifle came with the dovetail slot in its barrel filled with a steel blank. The target rifles were in "30 Gov't '06" and 300 Holland & Holland and a footnote promised 1945 as the year production would resume. I am sure a lot of returning GIs also drooled over the variety of Winchester lever actions. There was the Model 71 with 20- or 24-inch barrel in 348, the Model 64 in 219 Zipper, 30-30 and 32 Winchester Special, the Model 65 in 218 Bee, 25-20 and 32-20 and probably the one most of them ended up buying, the Model 94 in 25-35, 30-30 and 32 Special.

Remington rifles came next with the Model 81 Woodsmaster in 30 Remington, 300 Savage, 32 Remington and 35 Remington on first base. I still have one in 300 Savage and I still love to hunt deer with it. Next was the Model 141 Gamemaster in 30, 32, and 35 Remington. I don't have a Model 141 but I do have the earlier Model 14C in 35 Remington and each time I look at it I am reminded of how rifles used to be made and how they will never again be made. Remington's bolt action at the time was the Model 720 in 257 Roberts, 270 and 30-06 and that rifle would be replaced by the Model 721/721 in 1949.

Marlin was also there with its Model 36, a rifle that would, in 1948, evolve into today's Model 336. There was the Carbine with 20-inch barrel and full-length magazine, the Sporting Carbine with half-magazine and the Rifle with a 24-inch barrel, all in 30-30 and 32 Special (the 219 Zipper and 35 Remington came

A button on the bolt handle of the Browning X-Bolt allows the bolt to be rotated with the safety engaged, a design detail sure to make two groups of hunters happy.

later in the Model 336). Rounding out the centerfire rifles in that 2nd edition were a couple of Savage 99s in 250 and 300 Savage. At the time, Weatherby rifles were still being built on whatever actions Roy could get his hands on and the first GUN DIGEST edition I have that includes them is 1951. In the 1945 issue are opposing views in a two-part article titled "High Velocity vs Heavy Bullets" and I don't have to tell you which side of the argument was written by Roy Weatherby and which was written by Elmer Keith.

That was then and her is a brief look at now.

BROWNING

They tell me the new X-Bolt from Browning is called that because when viewed from just the right angle the four-front and four-rear holes drilled and tapped in the top of the receive appear to be in an "X" pattern. For those with a good imagination that might be true but my guess is the real reason the name was chosen is because X-Bolt is easy to remember and it has a snappy ring to it, same as A-Bolt does. Regardless of why they chose to give it that name, it is to my knowledge the first rifle to provide a total of eight holes up top for scope mounting. Other features include three locking lugs with 60 degrees of bolt rotation, a free-floating barrel and detachable rotary magazine holding, depending on the cartridge, four or five rounds. The one in 308 I used to bag a Colorado pronghorn weighed seven pounds, 10 ounces with a Sightron 3-9X scope and had an excellent trigger. Called the Feather Trigger, it is of three-lever design and fully adjustable with a three to five pound pull weight range. The X-Bolt is slated for availability in a whole bunch of calibers ranging from 243 Winchester to 375 H&H Magnum and initially four variations will be offered, Hunter with walnut stock and satin blued metal finish, Medallion with a fancier walnut stock and shiny blue finish, Composite Stalker with synthetic stock (with Dura Touch Armor Coat finish) and blued barreled action and Stainless Stalker which is the same except for its stainless barreled action.

A couple of years back I used an A-Bolt Mountain Ti in 300 WSM to take my best elk yet and it has become one of my favorite mountain rifles because it is accurate and weighs only 7-1/4 pounds with a Zeiss 3-9X scope. Its chambering options continue to increase in number and now include 243, 7mm-08, 308, and four WSMs in 270, 7mm, 300 and 323 calibers. In fact, the entire A-Bolt family continues to grow like weeds—if you bought one of each variation in every caliber offered you'd own 121 of them in calibers ranging from 22 Hornet (Micro Hunter) to 375 H&H Magnum.

Moving on to rimfires, the T-Bolt with its "double helix" detachable magazine is now available in 22 LR, 22 WMR and 17 HMR. A couple of new variations are also offered, Composite Sporter with synthetic stock and blued metal and Composite Target/Varmint which is the same except for its heavier barrel. Weights are 4-1/2 and 5-1/4 pounds, respectively, and both barrels are 22 inches long.

CHAPPARAL

This company offers very nice reproductions of several Winchester lever guns of the past and my favorite is the Model 1873 with an octagon barrel. Both round and octagon barrels in lengths ranging from 19 to 24 inches are offered and the calibers are 357 Magnum/38 Special, 38-40, 44-40 and 45 Colt. Also quite interesting is the Model 1876 full-stocked saddle ring carbine in 45-75, which I believe was the first cartridge offered by Winchester in this rifle.

CHARLES DALY

It is one of those rifles that I did not want to put down, even after examining it for a very long time and if you ever get your hands on the Little Sharps from Charles Daly, chances are the bug will bite you just as hard. Think of a 1887 Sharps rifle that got put up wet and shrunk down to 80 percent of its original size and you've got the Little Sharps. It comes with an adjustable tang sight and its octagon barrel is drilled and tapped for a reproduction of the old William Malcolm scope that is also available from Charles Daly. The one I want has a 26-inch barrel in 38-55 Winchester but a 24-inch barrel is available, as are 22 LR, 22 WMR, 22 Hornet, 218 Bee, 357 Magnum, 44-40, 44 Magnum and 30-30 Winchester.

COOPER FIREARMS OF MONTANA

Last year I mentioned the coming of Dan Cooper's Model 52 and now that I have my hands on one I can tell you it is more than worth the wait. Before this one came along the Model 57M in various rimfire chamberings and a few Model 38 centerfire rifles built in the early days were the only repeating rifles built by Cooper; even though other models had turnbolt actions they were single shots and this includes the present Model 22. That rifle, by the way, is guaranteed to shoot three bullets inside half an inch and the two I shot in 17 Remington and 6.5-284 did it anytime I pulled my end of the saw. The biggest challenge Cooper had to overcome was to design a magazine-fed rifle capable of delivering the same level of accuracy and in order to accomplish that he basically came up with a repeating version of the Model 22

Bullet (Handloads)	Powder		Velocity	Accuracy
	(Type)	(Grs)	(fps)	(Inches)
Sierra 75-gr.	HP Ramshot BigGame	54.0	3617	0.55
Sierra 100-gr.	MatchKing IMR-4831	53.0	3312	0.47
Berger 110-gr.	HP RL-22	57.0	3188	0.64
Sierra 117-gr.	SBT H4831	52.0	3020	0.44
Swift 120-gr.	A-Frame RL-25	56.0	3011	0.86
Federal (Premium Ammunition)				
Nosler 85-gr.	Ballistic Tip	NA	3468	0.82
Nosler 100-gr.	Ballistic Tip	NA	3231	0.73
Sierra 117-gr.	SBT	NA	3105	0.52
Nosler (Custom Ammunition)				
Nosler 100-gr.	Ballistic Tip	NA	3187	0.71
Nosler 110-gr.	AccuBond	NA	3012	1.07
Nosler 115-gr.	Ballistic Tip	NA	2981	0.58

Cooper's new Model 42 is a magazine-fed bolt gun in the entire family of 30-06 cartridges, plus the 240 Weatherby Magnum and possibly 9.3x62mm Mauser.

Case coloring on the action of the Cooper Model 52 Western Classic is by Doug Turnbull and this one has an octagon barrel in 25-06.

with an improvement or two. The new Model 52 has three locking lugs at the front of its bolt because as Dan recently put it, "the three-lug bolt is the Cooper signature and after having built over 30,000 rifles with a half-inch accuracy guarantee, I am convinced it is more accurate than a two-lug bolt." He obviously has something there since the Model 52 repeater is proving to be every bit as accurate as the single-shot Model 22.

Each Model 52 comes with test groups fired at the factory and the two that came with a 25-06 I managed to get my hands on measured an incredible .050 inch for one and an even more incredible .007 inch for the other, the latter basically three bullets in the same hole. Both were handloads with Reloder 22 powder, the former with the Nosler 85-grain Ballistic Tip, the latter with Speer's 120-grain Grand Slam. Cooper rifles are accuracy-tested on an indoor 50-yard range and even though 100-yard groups fired by most of us are usually more than twice as large as groups fired at half that distance, those test groups measure well under quarter-minute-of-angle any way you look at them. In my hands, the Western Classic in 25-06 you see in this report delivered the following average accuracy for five three-shot groups at 100 yards.

Machined from solid bar stock, the Model 52 receiver bears a strong resemblance to the Model 22 receiver except it is about half an inch longer. The Model 52 has a Sako-style extractor and Model 70-style ejector housed in a slot in the receiver floor, the latter basically the same as on the Pre-64 Winchester Model 70. The trigger can be adjusted down to 16 ounces and a two-position safety located beside the tang blocks the trigger but does not lock bolt rotation. The one-piece trigger guard/magazine housing is an absolute marvel of precision machining and the rifle has the first detachable magazine that I can honestly describe as attractive (capacity is three rounds).

The Model 52 is available in five variations, Classic, Custom Classic, Western Classic, Jackson Game and Jackson Hunter. The Jackson Hunter has a synthetic stock with full-length action bedding block while all the rest wear claro or French walnut in various grades. Several extra-cost options such as skeleton grip cap and buttplate and case-colored scope mounting rings are available. Standard features of the various models are too numerous to mention so I refer you to the Cooper website. The Western Classic I am shooting comes standard with AAA-grade claro walnut with ebony fore-end tip and steel grip cap, a 24-inch octagon barrel and case coloring of its receiver and trigger guard by Doug Turnbull. The stock has 22-line hand-cut checkering at wrist and forearm in Lenard Brownell's borderless pattern. The finish is hand-rubbed oil. The Model 52 is presently available in 25-06, 270 Winchester, 280 Remington, 30-06, 338-06, 35 Whelen and 240 Weatherby Magnum and if you twist Dan's arm hard enough you could probably get one in 9.3x62mm Mauser as well.

CZ USA

The American and Lux variations of the CZ 452 in 22 LR, 22 WMR, 17 HMR and 17 Mach 2 are now available with a left-hand action. I am happy to see this because the sadly neglected 17 Mach 2 is one of my favorite cartridges. Both rifles have a nicely checkered walnut stock and blued steel barreled action and come with typically good CZ accuracy. Also new is the 453 Varmint Fluted which, in case you have not already guessed, has a medium heavy fluted barrel in 17 HMR. Southpaw shooters are not overlooked in bigger cartridges either---the 527 American in 22 Hornet, 221 Fireball, 223 Remington and 204 Ruger now comes with its bolt on either side. The longer CZ makes big-game rifles for the American market the more the 550 American looks the way it should and its new stock for 2008 is the best yet. Caliber choices run from 223 and 6.5x55 to 30-06 and 9.3x62mm. But my favorite CZ of all is the 550 Safari Classic with its handsome walnut stock--I'll take a pair in and 375 H&H and 505 Gibbs.

HARRINGTON & RICHARDSON

A few years back I used an H&R Ultra Hunter single-shot rifle in 308 Winchester

The new Ultra Varmint from H&R is far more accurate than its price tag seems to indicate.

to take a very nice caribou in Canada. Whenever I think about that hunt I also think about the great number of hunters who, like me, enjoy hunting with single shots but tend to overlook H&R while choosing far more expensive rifles from other companies. My Ultra Hunter is not as pretty as some single-shot rifles but it is just as accurate, it kills game just as dead and it costs about half as much as the next more expensive spread. Now you know why I plan to add the new Ultra Varmint with a thumbhole stock in 223 Remington to my battery. And speaking of thumbhole stocks, the equally new Stainless Steel Ultra Hunter has one and is available in everybody's favorite moose-masher, the 45-70 Government.

KIMBER

True to its name, the new Sonora variation of the Model 8400 would be an excellent choice for bumping off a Coues deer at extremely long range. It has the accuracy and with its 25-06, 30-06 and 300 Winchester Magnum chamberings it also has the reach. Its stainless steel barreled action rests in a laminated stock designed to shoot over sandbags or a bipod and barrel lengths are 24 and 26 inches. Nominal weight is 8-3/4 pounds. Also new is the Model 8400 Talkeetna which with its synthetic stock and stainless barreled action is to a brown bear hunter what the Caprivi with its walnut and blued steel is to a Cape buffalo hunter. As one might expect, it is in 375 Holland & Holland.

LEGACY SPORTS INTERNATIONAL

Several new variations of the Howa rifle will be here in plenty of time for 2008 varminting and big-game hunting, including the Ranchland with a "Coyote Sand" finish on its synthetic stock (can you guess what it's intended for?), the Compact Heavy Barrel Varminter and the Youth with short buttstock. Possibly the most interesting rifle offered here is the Howa/Axion which has a recoil-absorbing stock from Knoxx Industries. Not sure why anyone would want it on the 223 but it might make the 375 Ruger more fun to shoot.

LES BAER CUSTOM

The super-accurate AR-15 from Les Baer is now available in 6.5 Grendel and and as might be expected, the company is also offering super-accurate ammo for it. It is loaded in Lapua brass by Black Hills. All LBC rifles are guaranteed to shoot five bullets inside half an inch at 100 yards and the two in 223 I've shot easily lived up to their billing. Who would ever thought a rifle built for war could be so accurate?

MARLIN

Biggest news from Marlin is the company has been purchased by Cerberus Capital Management, the group that also owns Remington and Bushmaster. Next biggest news is a bolt-action centerfire rifle called XL7 and my most sincere congratulations go out to this American company for using American labor to build it here in America at a suggested retail price of less than $350. A Marlin official told me that all but one component part of the rifle is made at the North Haven, CT plant and that part is also made by an American company. Marlin's previous bolt gun, the MR-7, consisted of design details borrowed from commercially successful rifles built by other companies and while the XL7 is quite a bit different from the MR-7, a close look brings similarities with other rifles to mind. At first glance its Pro-Fire trigger appears to be similar to the Accu-Trigger from Savage, its bolt shroud might have been spooked from the bushes by the Weatherby Mark V and the front of the bolt is pure Remington Model 700 with a Sako extractor. The barrel locknut? Savage came up with the idea on the Model 340 rifle back in 1947 and carried it over into the Model 110 when it was introduced in 1958. Available only with a pillar-bedded synthetic stock wearing a black or camo finish, the XL7 weighs 6-1/2 pounds, has a two-position safety and a 22-inch barrel in 25-06, 30-06 or 270 Winchester.

In addition to selling tons of ammunition for Hornady, the LeverEvolution bullet developed by that company and offered in 30-30, 308 Marlin Express, 35 Remington, 444 Marlin and 45-70 has also sold more than a few Model 336 rifles for Marlin. Tube-magazine-friendly pointed bullets loaded in the ammo combined with the excellent accuracy of the Model 336 have extended the deer hunter's reach by enough to notice. And now that Hornady is loading the same type of bullet in 357 Magnum and 44 Magnum ammo, the Marlin 1894 in those calibers should enjoy a boost in popularity as well.

NOSLER CUSTOM

New to the Nosler centerfire rifle line is the John Nosler Limited. It is actually a fancier rifle than the already-fancy Limited Edition. Both have very nice walnut stocks and are available in 280 Remington Improved and 300 WSM. A less expensive synthetic-stocked rifle is called Model 48 is available in more calibers, 260 Remington, 7mm-08, 308 and three WSMs of 270, 300 and 323 caliber. Up in the Yukon I shot some groups with a Model 48 that was being carried on the hunt by John Nosler's grandson, JR. It was in 323 WSM and quite accurate with Nosler ammo

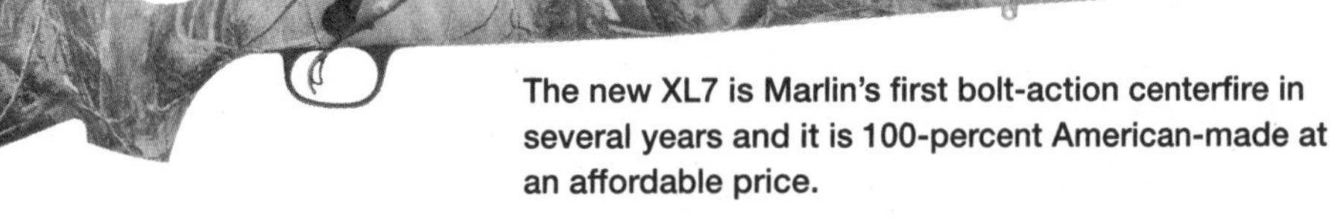

The new XL7 is Marlin's first bolt-action centerfire in several years and it is 100-percent American-made at an affordable price.

Remington's new Model 798 Safari in 375 H&H and 458 Magnum wears what the company calls a Real Wood stock but what the stock's maker, S&K Industries, calls Ultra Wood.

loaded with 200-grain AccuBond bullet. All Nosler rifles are guaranteed to shoot three bullets into half an inch at 100 yards with Nosler ammunition.

REMINGTON

Who would have ever thought?–an AR-15 rifle right there in the Remington catalog. But is makes sense when you consider that Remington is a sister company to Bushmaster, one of the larger manufacturers of AR-15 rifles. If you've seen one rifle of this type you've seen them all so there is nothing out of the ordinary to report here except to say they decided to drop the "A" and call it the R-15 Predator with either 18- or 20-inch barrel. Calibers are the usual 204 Ruger and 223 Remington and one wonders why Remington's 6.8 SPC is not there as well. Nominal weights are said to be 6-3/4 pounds for the carbine and 7-3/4 pounds for the rifle, both clad from butt to muzzle in Advantage Max-1 HD camo. Winchester used to advertise its lever actions as rifles you could load on Sunday and shoot all week. Now Remington has one as well and it shoots faster too.

My vote for the most interesting item from Remington for 2008 goes to the Model 798 Safari on the '98 Mauser action. Available with a 22-inch barrel in 375 H&H Magnum and 458 Winchester Magnum (where's the 416 Mag?), it wears what Remington describes as a nicely figured Real Wood walnut stock but it is called Ultra Wood by its maker (see S&K Industries a bit further on in this report). The only change I'd like to see them make is a full-band sling swivel on the barrel rather than the half-band they chose to use. This rifle looks good enough, feels good enough and is good enough to take on a serious hunt, whether it be coastal grizzly in Alaska or buffalo in Zambia.

Remington's no-nonsense Model 770 is now available with a barreled action of stainless steel resting in a synthetic stock dressed in Realtree AP-HD camo and it comes with a Bushnell 3-9x scope already mounted. Barrel lengths are 22 inches in 270 and 30-06 and 24 inches in 7mm Remington Magnum and 300 Winchester Magnum. The Model 770 is not as inexpensive as it used to be but my guess is a bit of shopping around would turn up this new version at a real-world price of less than $500.

Like all AR-15s, the one now sold by Remington is fun to shoot, especially when some generous person keeps handing you boxes of ammunition.

Exactly 25 years ago Remington took a group of gunwriters to Pincher Creek, British Columbia for an official unveiling of the new Model Seven. I remember it well because only one deer was taken during the entire trip. But I made up for it shortly thereafter by using the first FS version of the Model Seven to be built by the Custom Shop to take a nice blacktail on the Queen Charlotte Islands (I still have that little 7mm-08) To commemorate the 25th birthday of one of America's favorite deer rifles, Remington is offering a limited edition version during 2008. Whereas my old "Seven" has a 18-1/2 inch barrel, this one measures 22 inches and will squeeze a bit more speed from the 7mm-08. It also wears the CDL style of stock which originated with the Model 700 and just might be the best-looking standard production stock ever built by Remington. The grip cap on this one reads "Model Seven" 1983-2008". Like all Model 700s, all Model Sevens now have Remington's great X-Mark Pro trigger. Actually, I'm not done with the Model Seven yet. The new Predator in 17 Fireball, 204 Ruger, 223, 243 and 22-250 has a 22-inch barrel and the entire rig is covered in Mossy Oak Brush camo. It is a great little varmint rig for more walking than sitting.

There are those who, like me, are quite fond of the original Model 700 CDL because of the classical styling of its stock and its satin blued metal finish and there are those who will like a new version with a shiny blue finish on its metal. This is why they now offer two versions. Chambering options for this one are 270, 30-06 and 7mm Remington Magnum. In case you failed to notice, back in 2006 Remington kicked of its Model 700 CDL Stainless Fluted Limited Edition with the 30-06, followed by the 17 Fireball in 2007 and for 2008 the chambering is 260 Remington in a 24-inch barrel. They say the Model 700 CDL/B&C is the first firearm to be licensed by the Boone & Crockett club. It has a brown laminated wood stock and 24 or 26-inch barrel, the length depending on whether it is chambered to 243 Winchester, 7mm-08 Remington, 270, 30-06, 300 WSM, 7mm

Remington Magnum or 300 Winchester Magnum. This year's Rocky Mountain Elk Foundation of the Model 700 XCR has as 26-inch barrel in 7mm Ultra Mag and Remington promises to donate a portion of the dollars you spend on one to the RMEF. Last but not least in new Model 700 variants is the VTR with an integral muzzle brake machined into its 22-inch triangular-shaped barrel. The stock with its vented forearm is green, barrel and action are black and cartridge options are 204 Ruger, 223, 22-250 and 308. Nominal weight is 7-1/2 pounds. When you drill a hole as small as 17-caliber through a heavy barrel you end up with a barrel that's still quite heavy which is what is worn by the Model 700 Varmint Synthetic Stainless Fluted in its newest chambering, the 17 Fireball. Barrel length is 26 inches and nominal rifle weight is 8-1/2 pounds.

Remington is adding several options for those who shoot a rifle from the other side. They include the Model 700 SPS Varmint LH with 26-inch barrel in 17 Fireball, 223, 22-250, 243 and 308, the Model 700 XCR LH in stainless and synthetic with 24-inch barrel in 270, 30-06, 7mm Remington Magnum and 300 Ultra Mag and just for kids, the Model 700 SPS Youth with 20-inch barrel in 243 and 7mm-08.

Who says gun companies don't listen to writers? During Remington's new products seminar last year I mentioned that while the Model 504 is a great little rifle, it would look even better if its rather homely bolt handle were replaced by one that resembled the handle on the Model 700 rifle. In addition to making that modification to the rifle they changed its stock styling to that of the Model 700 CDL, replaced its orange magazine follower with black and renamed it the Model 547. I especially like the looks of the custom shop version; with a price tag of around $1000 it is a lot of rifle for the money and available in 22 LR and 17 HMR. Also new in the rimfire department are colorful versions of the Model 597 autoloader, blaze camo for guys and pink camo for gals (and, okay some guys as well) and a version called Yellow Jacket with its thumbhole-style laminated stock.

ROSSI

Called the Matched Pair, this single-shot comes with two barrels in many useful combinations including a 12- or 20-gauge barrel matched up with a second barrel in 17 HMR, 22 WMR, 223, 243, 270, 308 or 30-06. Or you can get a .410 barrel along with a barrel in 22 LR or 17 HMR. Regardless of which pair

The Savage Model 25 in 204 Ruger and 223 Remington shown here has three locking lugs at the front of its bolt, the primary difference between it and last year's Model 40 in 22 Hornet.

you decide on, the outfit will come in a zippered case. All Rossi long guns of current production have what the company describes as an onboard security system–simply place the key into the side of the hammer and a twist of the wrist makes it inconvenient to use by unauthorized hands.

RUGER

Latest from Ruger is the Compact Magnum version of the Model 77 chambered for the 300 RCM and the 338 RCM. Hornady is loading the ammo on the shortened 375 Ruger case. Barrel length is 20 inches (everybody got their ears on?) and stock options are walnut and black synthetic. Magazine capacity is three rounds and nominal weight is 6-3/4 pounds. Open sights consist of a fully-adjustable Williams at the rear and a ramped brass bead up front.

SAKO

The new A7 from Sako looks like the result of a romance between the Sako 85 and the Tikka T3. And the two just might have sneaked off together since Sako and Tikka rifles are built at the same factory in Rhiihimaki. Missing from its receiver roof is the ever-familiar integral scope mounting base of the original Sako action and in its place is a separate two-piece, Weaver-style base. The single-stack detachable magazine appears to be Tikka T3 all the way. The game plan includes a short action for cartridges ranging from 22-250 to 300 WSM and a medium-length action for the 30-06 family and 300 Winchester Magnum with barrel lengths of 22-1/2 and 24-1/2 inches. If you have priced the least expensive Sako 85 lately you know why they decided to do the A7–it is slated to cost about half as much. Other news from Sako is a high-grade Model 85 Deluxe with a select walnut stock and a price of just under three grand.

SAVAGE

At first glance, this year's new Model 25 in 204 Ruger and 223 Remington looks like last year's Model 40 in 22 Hornet, right down to its tubular receiver. But their actions differ in one important detail. Whereas lockup of the Model 40 is taken care of by the root of its bolt handle bearing on a recess in the receiver, the Model 25 has three locking lugs at the front of its bolt. Its synthetic magazine is detached from the rifle by pressing a lever located at the front of the magazine opening in the synthetic trigger guard assembly. The roof of the receiver is drilled and tapped for scope mounting and a Weaver-style, two-piece base is included with the rifle. The ejector is a spring-loaded, plunger-type and it has a Tikka-style extractor. The bolt is removed by placing the safety in its off position and holding back the trigger while retracting the bolt.

Savage's AccuTrigger is there and the one on the rifle I shot arrived with a pull weight of 36 ounces with a pull-to-pull variation of four ounces and no creep but there was some overtravel. The two-position safety located just behind the bolt handle operated smoothly with positive stops at its two positions–it does not lock the bolt from rotation. The Lightweight Varminter has a laminated wood stock (available in standard and thumbhole styles) and a medium-heavy 24-inch barrel while the Classic wears walnut and has a lighter 22-inch barrel. Assembly is typically Savage. After the barrel is threaded and finish-chambered and with the bolt in its locked position, the barrel is manually screwed into the receiver until a headspace gauge in the chamber makes contact with the face of the bolt. Two steel pins are then installed transversely through the bottom of the receiver ring and barrel shank to hold everything together. The one I shot was in 204 Ruger and it averaged from 1.27 to 1.84 inches for five, five-shot groups at 100 yards with most of the loads I tried. More accurate in that particular rifle was the Hornady 40-grain factory load (0.79-inch) and a handload consisting of Remington case, Remington 7-1/2 primer and 26.0 grains of Benchmark behind the Sierra 39-grain BlitzKing (0.68-inch).

Other good news from Savage is a special edition Model 110 to celebrate the 50th anniversary of that rifle and another limited-production Model 110 in 300 Savage, a chambering not offered by Savage since the Model 99 was dropped from production many years ago.

E.R. SHAW

This is the company that makes rifle barrels and you can now get one already installed on a left- or right-hand Savage action and fitted to a laminated wood stock made by Boyd's. Called the Mark VII, it is available in blue or stainless steel and with various barrel weights ranging from 16 to 26 inches in length. Over 90 standard and wildcat chamberings from 17 Fireball to 458 Lott are available.

S&K INDUSTRIES

Forgive me for straying from the subject of rifles, but I cannot resist devoting a bit of ink to Ultra Walnut stocks from S&K Industries. In addition to offering completely finished drop-in stocks for various rifles and shotguns, the company is presently furnishing stocks to Remington for its Model 788 Safari rifle and the Model 1100 G3 shotgun (Remington refers to the stocks as "Real Wood"). The idea came about due to the fact that walnut blanks in the higher grades that are thick enough to be used in making rifle stocks have become extremely expensive. Thinner blanks of the same quality (commonly used in the furniture industry) are less expensive but too thin to be used in making a one-piece rifle stock.

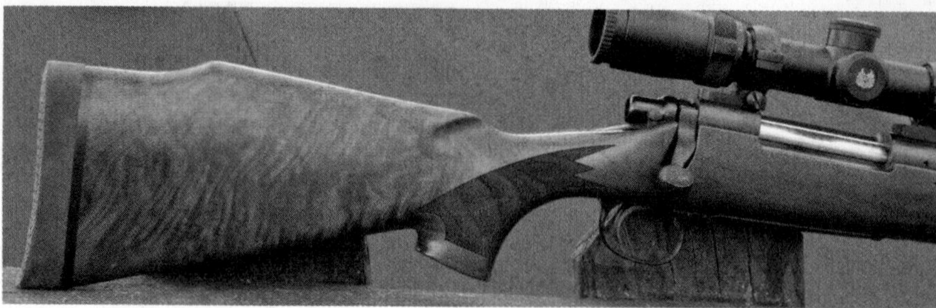
Its unique construction makes this nicely figured Ultra Wood stock from S&K Industries less expensive than it looks.

The solution those clever fellows at S&K came up with is to use a powerful adhesive to bond two blanks of walnut to a thin walnut spacer in order to come up with a blank thick enough to be used in making a stock. Then to make the blank stronger and more resistant to warping, they decided to place thin layers of carbon fiber on both sides of the spacer before bonding the three layers of wood together. In combined thickness the walnut and carbon fiber fillers measure only about a quarter of an inch so only by looking at the top or bottom surface of the stock can you see that it is of laminated construction. The blank is inletted, shaped and finish-sanded and then given six coats of clear polyurethane topped off with DuPont Imron, the same tough skin worn by many automobiles. All surfaces of the stock, including beneath the recoil pad and in the inletting receive the same seven-coat finish.

Bottom line is a stock with the warmth and beauty of fine walnut but one that's stronger and more stable than non-laminated walnut. And as nicely figured walnut stocks go, it costs less than a one-piece stock of the same grade. The one I have on a long-action Model 700 weighs 40-1/2 ounces, about the same as Remington's standard BDL-style wood stock. The folks at S&K say the two thin layers of carbon make the Ultra Walnut stock comparable in strength and warp resistance to a multiple-laminated wood stock but it is much lighter because its construction requires the use of less glue. (S&K Industries Ultra Walnut Stocks, S. Hwy 13, Lexington, MO 64067/660-259-691/www.sandkgunstocks.com)

SPRINGFIELD ARMORY

If you got busy last year and did not get around to buying one of the 500 M1A rifles built by Springfield Armory to commemorate the 100th birthday of the National Matches at Camp Perry, procrastinate no longer because only a few remain for sale. The receiver has several special markings such as "NRA", "1 of 500" and "Camp Perry 1907-2007" and the buttstock is also specially marked. This is but one of many variations of the ever-popular M1A rifle. Some of the others included SOCOM II with enough rails to hang every gadget you can afford to buy, the Scout Squad with its 18-inch barrel, the Loaded M1A which comes with everything you forgot to buy for your SOCOM II, the Super Match which will hold its own in accuracy with any AR-15 and for those just want something fun and simple to shoot, there's the Standard M1A with a nice walnut stock and nothing else.

TAYLOR'S & COMPANY

I never cease to be impressed by the quality of reproduction revolvers and rifles imported by this company. I wouldn't mind taking home the 1860 Henry rifle with brass frame and white barrel, the 1873 Sporting Rifle with checkered pistol grip stock and half-octagon barrel, the Model 92 Takedown with 24-inch octagon barrel and the Lightning pump gun (I'll take all four in 44-40). And what about that 1865 Spencer and all its accessories, including the authentically reproduced leather shoulder sling and Blakeslee Box with six loading tubes. Make mine in 56-50 please.

THOMPSON/CENTER

Introduced last year with a 308-length action, a second version of the Icon rifle with a 30-06-length action is now available. Other calibers are 270, 7mm Remington Magnum and 300 Winchester Magnum. Two variants of both action lengths are now available, Standard with walnut stock and blued steel and Weather Shield in synthetic and stainless steel.

TRISTAR

Known for the importation of shotguns of various types, this company also offers a reproduction of the Model 1874 Sharps in 45-70 with octagon barrel lengths of 28 and 32 inches and a weight of approximately 9-1/2 pounds. It has double-set triggers, a case-colored frame and blued barrel. The rifle comes with blade front and adjustable-ladder rear sights on its barrel but an extra-cost Creedmore set with both short and long adjustable tang sights and a globe-style front sight is available.

TURNBULL RESTORATIONS

Doug Turnbull, who is world renowned for his incredibly beautiful vintage firearms restorations, is so fond of the old Winchester Model 1886 lever gun that he recently used one to take a Cape buffalo in Africa. He has come up with a new cartridge for the '86 and for the Winchester Model 71 called the 475 Turnbull. On the shortened 50-110 Winchester case, it uses bullets of .475-inch diameter designed for the 475 Linebaugh and other handgun cartridges. Muzzle velocity with a 325-grain bullet is said to be 2400 fps for respective energy deliveries of 4150 and 2827 foot-pounds at the muzzle and at 100 yards. Quality Cartridge will offer the ammo and for those who had rather load their own, reloading dies and unprimed brass will be available from Turnbull. Rifles ranging from standard to highly embellished are available and Turnbull also converts customer-furnished rifles.

WEATHERBY

As much as I like the 7mm-08 cartridge and as much as I enjoy the great accuracy of Weatherby's Vanguard rifle, it had not dawned on me that the two had not been matched up until now. Just in time for the upcoming hunting season, several variations of that rifle will be available in that chambering, including the Synthetic, the Sporter, the Sub-MOA and the Synthetic Package which comes with a scope already mounted and a hard carrying case. Other new additions are 223 Remington in the Youth/Compact and 204 Ruger in the Varmint Special. Vanguard upgrade offerings from the custom shop have also increased in number and stock options range from fancy walnut to laminated wood to synthetic with a dozen different colors of finish. And what do I consider to be the ideal four-Vanguard battery for North America? That's an easy one—the Deluxe in 300 Weatherby Magnum for bluebird days, the Stainless in 300 Weatherby Magnum for bluebirdless days, the Sub-MOA in 25-06 for deer and the Varmint in 223 Remington for the wee critters.

The 257 Weatherby Magnum is now the second most popular cartridge at Weatherby, beat out in popularity only by the 30-378 Weatherby Magnum.

I am not sure why they chose to call it the Compact Firing Platform, but think of the Remington XP-100 with a Weatherby Mark V action, a 16-inch barrel and a rear-grip stock and you've got it. The number of caliber options now include 223, 22-250, 243 and 7mm-08. Other features are a composite stock with tan pebble grain finish, bead-blasted blue metal finish and ambidextrous grip.

Roy Weatherby's Mark V is still alive and well and you'd never guess which of its chamberings has been No. 1 and No. 2 in sales for the past three years. If you guessed 30 caliber in first place you are close but it is not the 300 Weatherby Magnum. That one was tied for second place but in 2007 it was edged into third place behind the 257 Magnum which, by the way was Roy's favorite cartridge and one of mine as well. The number one best seller in the Mark V is the 30-378 Weatherby Magnum. In case you don't already know, it was created by Roy for Uncle Sam who needed to test the ability of various top-secret materials to resist the impact of high-speed projectiles. Roy was able to reach 6000 feet per second with special lightweight bullets made by Ray Speer. Sometime later, guys and gals up in Pennsylvania who shoot 1000-yard benchrest matches put the big cartridge on the map among competitive shooters but its big following today is among big-game hunters.

WINCHESTER

The Model 70 is back and it is not being built in Tokyo or Hong Kong or Bangladesh or Ho Chi Minh City as some have wildly speculated it might be. Rather, it is being built right here in America, in Columbia which is the capital city of South Carolina. The company building it is FNH/USA which is owned by the same company that owns Browning and Winchester Repeating Arms. Production of the Model 70 did not begin until May 2008 so the photos you saw in various magazines published prior to then were rifles made up of parts produced by U.S. Repeating Arms before that company closed its doors. My guess is both quality and accuracy of the FN-built rifle will be much better than what we saw during those last few years of USRAC production.

Except for a new trigger, the FNH rifle should be like what we expected a Model 70 to be like prior to the dying days of USRAC. Whether or not its new M.O.A. trigger is a good thing or a bad thing depends on the age of the shooter. Old-timers who hate to see change will yearn for the original trigger while it won't matter either way to everybody else. As for me, I always liked the ruggedness and simplicity of the old one but will have no objection to the new one if it proves to be as good as claimed. Other than that, there's not much else to say about the design of the new Model 70 that hasn't been said about other Model 70s a thousand times in the past. Several of the popular calibers will be there in Super Grade, Featherweight, Sporter and Extreme Weather SS variations. Welcome back old classic.

It still seems odd to thumb through the Winchester catalog and not see several pages full of Model 94s. Perhaps next year? Or the next?

NEW SHOTGUNS

by John Haviland

The escalating price of lead shot has many shotgun shooters looking for ways to reduce their shooting costs. Dave Kern of MEC shotshell reloaders says the high price of lead shot has both hurt and helped MEC. While the soaring price of lead shot has caused some shooters to curtail their shooting and shotshell reloading, the substantially increased the price of what used to be bargain-priced shotshells has prompted other shooters to take up reloading or to start reloading again. Many of these reloaders have started loading 20- and 28-gauge shells to save shot. Barbara Fausti, of Fausti Stefano, of Italy, says there has been somewhat of a shift to smaller gauges, like the 20- and 28-gauge, in response to higher shot prices. "Although, that move may also be because hunters have found these guns are light to carry and lively in your hands," she says.

Let's see what shotgun manufacturers have in store for target shooters and hunters this year.

BERETTA

The Beretta UGB25 Xcel autoloader features a break-open barrel that allows the shooter and bystanders to see the gun is unloaded while the shooter waits his turn during competition. The UGB25 Xcel's barrel is positioned low in the receiver to transmit recoil in line with the shooter's shoulder and minimize felt recoil. The Xcel's short-recoil action cycles all 12-gauge 2 3/4-inch shells from subsonics to 1 1/2-oz. magnum loads.

Beretta calls the SV10 Perennia its third generation over-and-under. The Perennia has reinforced ejectors and hinge pin and a quick-detachable trigger housing. The tang safety/barrel selector has been redesigned and a new lockup maintains a tight fit between the stock and receiver.

BROWNING

Keeping with the idea light is more, Browning's Silver autoloader is now available in a Sporting Micro 12-gauge with an aluminum receiver and a slender barrel with a 2 3/4-inch chamber that's ported at the muzzle to reduce recoil. Its 13 1/2-inch length of pull fits smaller stature shooters. The Silver Micro is similar, but with a three-inch chamber and a 13 7/8-inch length of pull.

The Silver Rifled Deer Stalker 12-gauge has a thick-walled barrel with a three-inch chamber and 1-28 rifling twist for shooting slugs. Its composite stock and forearm are covered with Dura-Touch Armor coating and its metal is covered with a black matte finish. A cantilever scope mount is attached to the barrel and extends back over the receiver. The Silver Rifled Deer is similar, but covered from butt to muzzle in Mossy Oak Break-Up camouflage.

The Silver NWTF is also covered in Mossy Oak Break-Up camouflage. This gun is intended for turkeys and comes with a 3- or 3 1/2-inch chamber, HiViz fiber optic sights and three Invector-Plus choke tubes.

Six new models also lighten up the Cynergy Feather over-and-under. The models share the same size receiver and are available in 20- and 28-gauge and .410-bore with 26 or 28 inch barrels. The

Browning Cynergy Classic Trap Unsingle 12-gauge.

Browning Cynergy Euro Sporting 20-gauge.

Browning Cynergy Feather over-and-under 20- and 28-gauge and .410-bore.

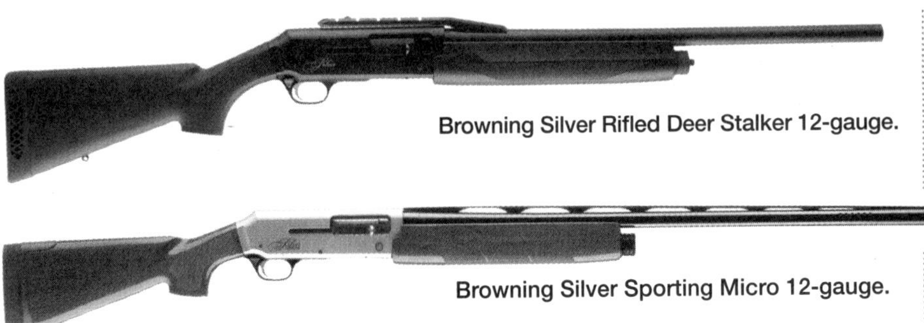
Browning Silver Rifled Deer Stalker 12-gauge.

Browning Silver Sporting Micro 12-gauge.

lightest are the .410 and 20 at 4 lbs., 14 oz. with 26 inch barrels. The heaviest is the 28-gauge with 28 inch barrels at 5 lbs. 3 oz. Compare those weights with the 12-gauge Cynergy at 6 lbs., 13 oz.

The Cynergy Euro Sporting 20 gauge is beefier at 6 ½ lbs. with 28, 30 or 30 inch barrels. The Euro is dressed up with grade III and IV walnut, gold enhanced engraving and a silver nitrate finished metal and HiViz Pro-Comp fiber-optic sights.

The Cynergy Classic Trap Unsingle 12-gauge comes with single and double-barrel sets of either 30 or 32 inches. Both sets weigh the same. The rib on the single barrel is adjustable for sight picture and shot charge point of impact. The stock has an adjustable Monte Carlo comb and a right hand palm swell. The beavertail forearm has a groove running along the top of both sides for a sure grip of the fingers. The gun comes in an aluminum case.

The Citori over-and-under line has also been expanded. The Citori 525 Feather is now chambered in 20- and 28-gauge and .410. These guns have 26 or 28 inch barrels and weigh from 6 lbs. 3 oz. in 20-gauge to 6 lbs. 10 oz. in .410. The Citori 625 Field 12-gauge has a tight radius grip and a Schnabel forearm. The gun also has Browning's new Vector Pro lengthened forcing cones and three Invector-Plus choke tubes. Barrels are 26 or 28 inches. The Citori 625 Field 12-gauge has a tight radius grip and a Schnabel forearm. The gun also has Browning's new Vector Pro lengthened forcing cones and three Invector-Plus choke tubes. Barrels are 26 or 28 inches.

Interest for the 16-gauge seems to build, then wane. Remington chambered the 16 in its Model 870 for a couple years, but has discontinued it. Now Browning is taking up the 16 in its BPS pump Hunter and Upland Special. The BPS Hunter and Upland Special 16s might have some staying power because they are made on the 20-gauge frame. In the Upland Special this makes the 16-gauge gun an ounce or so lighter than the 20-gauge version. The BPS Upland Special 16 weighs 6 lbs. 13 oz. with a 26-inch barrel and an ounce less with a 24-inch barrel. The gun has a straight grip and Browning's signature satin-finished walnut. The BPS Hunter has a curved grip and 26- or 28-inch barrels.

CABELA'S/FAUSTI

The huge mail-order company, Cabela's, is selling Fausti Italian Style side-by-side shotguns. I shot a Style 20-gauge last fall while hunting mallards along hay field creeks. If I do say so myself, I did rather well with the gun and shot quite a few singles and two doubles.

But the Style boxlock 20-gauge is really a thicket gun for ruffed grouse in the alders and quail in the mesquite. With its 28-inch barrels, straight grip stock and splinter forearm the gun weighs 6 lbs. 4 oz. It has double triggers, although a single trigger is available. Five screw-in chokes come with the gun in Cylinder, Improved Cylinder, Improved Modified, Modified and Full.

Patterning the gun showed there was little use for its Full choke except for shooting pheasants at 40-plus yards. The Cylinder and Improved Cylinder chokes would be the most useful for the close shots on grouse and quail. With 7/8 oz. of 7-1/2s the Cylinder choke threw a useable pattern diameter of 25 inches at 20 yards and 38 inches at 30 yards. The Improved Cylinder choke printed a 30-inch usable pattern at 30 yards. While the choke tubes are identified with small hash marks on their rim, it would be nice to have the chokes identified on their sides in big letters, instead of having to squint at the marks while trying to remember how many marks represent each choke.

A number of options are available on the Style. The 20-gauge Style comes with 2 3/4- or 3-inch chambers and a solid rib on barrels from 23.6 to 30 inches. The gun has extractors or extractors and ejectors and a single trigger or double triggers. The Style is also available in 12-, 16-, 20-, 28- and .410.

The receiver and tang are fully covered with engraving. A gold-colored "C" on the trigger guard denotes it's a Cabela's gun.

CZ-USA

The CZ Sporting 12-gauge is designed for sporting clays and is fitted with 30- or 32-inch barrels, an adjustable comb, a curved grip with palm swells on both sides and a full forearm with finger grooves running parallel to the barrels. The Sporting has chrome-lined bores with extended forcing cones and a red fiber optic front bead. The gun weighs 9 pounds.

The side-by-side Partridge and Grouse are chambered in 12-, 20- and 28-gauge and .410-bore. The guns have chrome-plated receivers with scroll engraving and boxlock actions with crossbolts locks. The Grouse has a single trigger and a curved grip with a rounded knob. The Partridge has double triggers and a straight grip. The 12-gauge guns have 28-inch barrels while the others have 26-inch barrels. The Partridge 12-gauge weighs 7 lbs., the 20-gauge 6 lbs. 3 oz., 28-gauge 5 lbs., 10 oz. and the .410 5 lbs. 3 oz. The Grouse guns, in their respective gauges, weigh a few more ounces.

FRANCHI

The 1-12 Upland Hunter 12-gauge weighs a feather under 6 lbs. 5 oz., which is a heavy pound lighter than regular 1-12 autoloaders. The Upland Hunter diet included slimming down the stock, forearm, receiver and barrel. Barrel length is 26 inches, which can weave through ruffed grouse thickets just fine and helps put gun weight toward the butt for point shooting.

The 1-12 Sporting is also a light gun at 6-1/2 lbs. Its 30-inch barrel is ported a few inches back from the muzzle. Extended choke tubes in Cylinder, Improved Cylinder, Modified, Improved Modified and Full.

H&R

The inexpensive 12-gauge Topper Trap Gun is intended to get young shooters interested in clay target shooting. But, after shooting a 23 my first time at trap with the gun, I think novice and seasoned shooters will like the gun. The gun's drop at the comb is 1-3/4 inches and has no further drop over the comb's length to the butt. The gun throws patterns a bit high of aim so clay targets can be floated above the barrel for a good look. The gun's trimmings include walnut stock and beavertail forearm with nice figure and checkering on the grip. A Pachmayr Decelerator recoil pad soaks up recoil. The 30-inch barrel has a ventilated rib with mid- and front beads and an Improved Modified extended choke tube.

After firing a shot with the Trap gun I held the gun with my right hand around the grip and pushed the release button on the back of the receiver with my thumb. The weight of the 30-inch barrel fully opened the action and the empty shell popped out and flew over my shoulder. I dropped a fresh shell into the chamber, snapped the gun shut, cocked the hammer and was ready to shoot again in a second. What a fun gun.

The Ultra Slug Hunter hinge-action now has the option of a laminated thumbhole stock. The Ultra-Lite Slug Hunter weighs almost three pounds less than standard Ultra Slug Hunter guns. The lighter weight is the result of a thin 24-inch barrel in 12- or 20-gauge and removing the regular open sights (a scope base is provided).

Select Slug Hunter guns now have Ultragon rifling that have an oval shape to their six lands. The Ultragon rifling is similar to the parabolic rifling that Charles Newton used in his rifles way back in the 1930s. The Ultragon lands have rounded edges and a dished out tops that do not leave sharp cuts in sabot jackets or lead slugs. H&R states this produces better accuracy and higher velocity and also longer barrel life and easier cleaning.

MOSSBERG

The Reserve series of side-by-sides include the Silver and Onyx models each in 12-, 20- and 28-gauge. The Silver has blued barrels and silver-colored receivers. The metal is all blued on the Onyx models. Both models have chrome-lined bores and five choke tubes. The 28-gauge guns weigh 6 lbs. 6 oz., the 20-gauge 6 lbs. 8 oz. and the 12-gauge 7 lbs. 2 oz.

The Model 500 pump Super Bantam, Turkey and Slugster are 20-gauge guns with 22-inch barrels. The guns have a standard 12-inch length of pull to fit young shooters. A stock spacer and extra rubber recoil pad are included to add an inch to the length of pull. When the shooter has grown enough to use a full-size shotgun, send in the certificate that comes with the guns to receive half off the price of a full-size stock.

Mossberg Onyx SxS, availale in 12-, 20- and 28-gauge.

Mossberg Silver SxS, available in 12-, 20- and 28-gauge.

Mossberg Super Bantam Slugster.

Mossberg Model 500 Super Bantam Turkey 20-gauge pump-action shotgun.

REMINGTON

The 1100 G3 is an improvement to the Remington Model 1110 12- and 20-gauge. It has key internal parts coated with Teflon to make the gun easier to clean and facilitate cycling by reducing the buildup of powder fouling. The G3 also has a walnut stock constructed with Remington's Realwood. The Realwood process starts with a stock sawn in half lengthwise, adding a thin carbon fiber sheet between the wood and then gluing everything together. The result is an extra strong stock that will likely never warp. The new synthetic ShurShot thumbhole stock with a nearly vertical grip is intended for shotgunners who take a definite aim with their guns at turkeys and big game. The ShurShot has a high comb that elevates the eye so the shooter doesn't have to crane his neck to see through an electronic sight or a scope. The ShurShot grip also directs a lot of the recoil from magnum loads into the palm and web of the hand. Recoil is further reduced by adding Remington's new SuperCell recoil pad to the butt of a ShurShot stock. The SuperCell's soft pad absorbs recoil energy and releases it over a longer time to reduce kick. Remington states that a SuperCell pad on a pump-action shotgun produces about half the recoil as an autoloading shotgun without the pad.

The Model 11-87 Sportsman Super Mag Turkey and Cantilever and Model 870 Express Turkey and Cantilever are available with the ShurShot stock and forearm in black or Mossy Oak Break-Up camo.

A vertical grip synthetic stock is also available on the Model 870 12-gauge Desert Recon. The gun has olive drab powder-coated metal that matches the "Digital Tiger" camo pattern on the stock and forearm. The magazine tube holds up to seven shells and a ported choke tube reduces muzzle jump. I loaded the magazine full on a Desert Recon with a 20-inch barrel and banged away at a line of swinging steel plates at 30 yards. The gun's recoil was light and after firing

The Model 870 12-gauge Desert Recon has a "Digital Tiger" camo pattern on the stock and forearm.

and reloading a few times the plates had next to no paint left on them. Actually, the gun would be great for turkeys. Not because of all the shells it holds, but because its 20-inch barrel is so handy to carry and quick to get on target.

Along the line of a more traditional shotgun, the Model 1100 Premier Sporting series feature nickel-plated receivers with scroll engraving. The Premier is chambered in 12-, 20- and 28-gauges with 2 3/4-inch chambers and a 3-inch .410. A hard case protects the gun.

WINCHESTER

After a pause in production, three models of Winchester's 12-gauge pump shotguns are back as Speed Pumps. The Walnut Field wears a glossy finished walnut stock and forearm with point pattern checkering. The Black Shadow Field has a black synthetic stock and forearm and matching matte finish on its metal. Barrels on both models are 26 or 28 inches. The Defender has a synthetic stock and forearm and an 18-inch barrel with a Cylinder bore. All three models have over-sized 0.742-inch diameter chrome-lined bores.

The Super X3 autoloader has two new models in the Classic Field and Turkey. The Classic Field has a grAy Perma-Cote finish applied to external metal for corrosion protection. Its walnut stock and forearm has traditional diamond checkering and the butt wears a Pachmayr Decelerator pad. The Turkey has a 24-inch barrel chambered for 12-gauge 3 1/2-inch shells, and a Pachmayr Decelerator pad helps absorbs some of their fierce recoil. The gun is covered with Mossy oak camo. The gun come with open sights as a TRUGLO red dot scope mounted on a cantilever base attached to the barrel. Of course an Extra Full choke is screwed in the muzzle.

Weatherby Athena D'Italia, Grade IV.

Weatherby Orion D'Italia, Grade I.

Weatherby SA-08 Field autoloading shotgun.

Weatherby Orion D'Italia, Sporting Clays.

Weatherby PA-08 Knoxx Strutter.

Weatherby SA-08 Youth shotgun.

Weatherby PA-08 Upland shotgun.

WEATHERBY

Weatherby has pretty much revamped its entire line of over-and-unders and autoloaders and added a line of pump guns.

The D'Italia over-and-unders are now made by Fausti Stefano of Italy and include three Athena models and four Orion models in 12-, 20- and 28-gauge with 26-, 28-, 30- or 32-inch barrels. The Athena D'Italia comes in V, IV and III grades with differing classes of walnut and sideplates engraved or with gold game bird scenes. The three Orion D'Italia look similar to the Athenas, but cost a few hundred dollars less. All these guns have a vented mid- and top rib, single triggers and tang-mounted safety. The Orion D'Italia 12-gauge Sporting Clays is a heavy gun and has a vertically adjustable comb, a fuller forearm and ported barrels.

The Weatherby PA-08 12-gauge pumps are priced to compete with the Remington 870 Express and Mossberg 500 pumps. The PA-08 models have aluminum receivers, Improved Cylinder, Modified and Full choke tubes and grooves in the top of the receiver to accept Weaver-style bases for mounting scopes and electronic sights.

The Upland has 26- or 28-inch barrels with a ventilated rib and weighs 6-1/2 lbs. Its walnut stock and forearm have point pattern checkering. All external metal has a black matte finish. The three Knoxx PA-08 guns have a Knoxx stock that has a pistol grip handle and a butt adjustable for length of pull. The Knoxx Strutter X Camo and Synthetic have 24-inch barrels with a ventilated rib. They come with Modified, Full and Extra Full chokes. The Knoxx HD has an 18 inch barrel with a fixed Cylinder choke.

The SA-08 gas-operated autoloaders include the 12- and 20-gauge Upland and 20-gauge Youth with walnut stocks and forearms and matte black finish on their metal. The Youth has a 12 1/2-inch length of pull and weighs 5 lbs.12 oz. The Upland 12-gauge weighs a pound more. Both guns come with two caps that screw on the guns' gas valve. One valve is set to bleed off the right amount of gas to reliably cycle the guns with light target loads and the other valve is for magnum loads.

TODAY'S MUZZLELOADING: BLACKPOWDER REVIEW

by Wm. Hovey Smith

With the introduction of new models of traditional guns alongside improvements in in-line guns and technology, the market for muzzleloading guns continues to evolve with a few new companies participating while others have withdrawn or changed their marketing approaches. Because of a lack of demand, Marlin discontinued sales of the latest derivation of the historic H&R Huntsman design. Austin & Halleck also ceased production of their bolt-action and traditionally designed muzzleloaders in 2007.

A traditional Hawken rifle with a walnut or maple stock has been introduced by Davide Pedersoli and is now sold by Dixie Gun Works and Cabela's in 54-caliber. This 10-pound rifle is as pure a derivation of the set-trigger Hawken design as is likely to be seen in a commercially-made gun. It has a 1:65 round-ball twist to its 34 11/16ths browned octagonal barrel with 1-inch flats, and a traditionally adjustable rear sight. The maple-stocked version retails for about $1,000 and the same rifle stocked in walnut is available from Dixie for $725. Both versions weight about 10 pounds. The barrel has a patent breech and is held to the forend by two wedges.

For those who want a 50-caliber version of this classic design, Tradition's new offering is its Mountain Rifle as a single-keyed gun with a 28-inch matte blue octagon barrel with a 1:48-inch twist to shoot both round balls and mid-weight conical bullets. Hunters who want to use a traditional gun will appreciate its lighter 8-pound weight, shorter barrel and more convenient handling characteristics compared to the more traditional Hawken design described above. This rifle is available for $676 in percussion and $735 as a flintlock.

Another new Pedersoli design sold by Dixie is the Howdah Pistol. These massive double-barreled pistols were first made as muzzleloaders and later chambered for cartridges like the 577 Snyder. They were designed to be used as last-ditch defense firearms while tiger hunting from elephants. These were to be discharged at very close range when the tiger or leopard had leapt on the top of the elephant and was endangering the hunter in the howdah, a small shelter carried on the pachyderm's back. The reproduction pistol is 50-caliber and/or 20-gauge. It is available three ways: twin rifled 50-caliber bores; one rifled 50-caliber barrel and the other in 20-gauge smoothbore; with two 20-gauge smoothbore barrels. Because of its intended use at very close range, it only has a bead front sight which is lined up by sighting down the sunken rib between the two barrels. The Howdah lists for $675 for pistols with rifled barrels and $625 for the 20-gauge smoothbore.

Demand of traditionally designed muzzleloaders rises and falls as with any other aspect of popular culture. Interest in these guns reached a peak with the anniversaries of the nation's Revolutionary and Civil wars and should show resurgence with the coming 200th anniversary of the War of 1812. Significant events during this conflict included the burning of the nation's capitol by the British, and climaxed with the Battle of New Orleans.

Muzzleloading hunters have embraced the new in-line designs to the extent that CVA and Thompson/Center Arms have eliminated or largely reduced sidelock rifle production in favor of modern designs. However, many hunters still love the Hawkens and flint long rifles that have brought home game for decades and will continue to use them.

In recognition of the demand for more sophisticated and easy-to-use muzzleloaders, Thompson/Center Arms has introduced a new variety of the Encore called the Endeavor. This gun has a recoil-absorbing stock, SIMS recoil pad, one turn detachable breech plug that may be removed with the fingers and a new frame styling that has an Art Deco look. The new stock design, available in black or a Real Tree AP camo pattern, will reduce felt recoil by 50 percent. The new buttstock is also available as a separate-purchase-item and will fit any Encore muzzleloading or centerfire rifle or shotgun.

The Thompson/Center Triumph, a fixed-barrel muzzleloader with a pivoting breech, may now be purchased with a complete camo wrap in Realtree AP or with blued or stainless Weather Shield barrels.

European makers, such as Davide Pedersoli and Armi Chiappa, continue to make very good replicas of historic American and European guns to meet demands on both sides of the Atlantic. these include muzzleloading designs as well as replicas of historic black-powder cartridge guns. At the SHOT Show It is not unusual to run into a German shooter, enamored with guns of the American West who shoots replica Sharps rifles, and others who own copies of their own country's historic military and civilian arms.

MODERN MUZZLELOADING DESIGN

Although there is still a contingent who shoot traditional guns, the majority of U.S. muzzleloading gun sales are to hunters who prefer the convenience and more accustomed feel of in-line designs. Simple adaptations of bolt-action designs to muzzleloaders were tried by Remington, Ruger and Austin & Halleck. These guns shot well, but the necessity of completely cleaning the bolts after each shooting session was more bother than many shooters were willing to endure.

Looking back to the technologically-simpler designs of single-shot cartridge rifles, muzzleloaders based on pivoting block, falling block, rolling block and swinging block designs were first introduced as more-or-less copies of Ballard, Sharps, Winchester, Remington and Snyder designs. Ultimately, it was realized that the breech plug and barrel contained almost all of the pressures, while the frames and moving breechblocks served mostly to secure the #209 primer and hold a firing pin in the proper firing position. Because of the low pressures exerted behind the breech plug, there was no need for massive steel receivers on muzzleloading guns. A detachable breechblock pivoting on a single pin or light-metal-alloy block with a steel insert was strong enough and less expensive to manufacture than a block with all-steel components.

To varying degrees this approach has been used in new-generation muzzleloaders made by Thompson/Center Arms, Knight, CVA, Remington and Traditions who make one or more models loosely based on old blackpowder cartridge actions. As I happened to own both an original Snyder 577 swinging block action and the new Remington Genesis, it was an interesting experience to hunt with both guns last fall. Unfortunately, no game I was willing to shoot appeared when I was carrying these guns, but it was interesting to compare their shooting qualities.

Hands down, the Genesis with its scope sight, 150-grain powder capacity and modern stocking had the advantages of longer range, better accuracy, lighter weight — and its simplified bolt operating mechanism was easier to clean. The Snyder with its massive external hammer felt like a muzzleloader, shot like one, belched lots of black smoke; but suffered in the accuracy department with the blackpowder loads that I had ordered from Cabela's. The Old West Scrounger now loads the Snyder cartridge with a special variant of Hodgdon's Triple Seven powder and a redesigned coated hollowpoint bullet that promises much better accuracy. This load and gun might be just the ticket for Mississippi where external hammer single-shot cartridge guns of antique designs will be allowed during the state's 2008-2009 muzzleloading season. In every respect, except weather resistance and convenience in reloading, the muzzleloading gun outperformed its cartridge-gun ancestor.

DROP BARREL DESIGNS

The 1973 Gun Digest described Harrington and Richardson's new Huntsman muzzleloading rifle and shotgun as an economically priced gun that should give blackpowder shooters a "field day." Introduced in 12-gauge, 45- and 58-calibers, the gun was based on the company's popular Topper single-shot shotgun action, "but in the center of the barrel breech there's a percussion cap nipple." Complete with a brass ramrod, the gun sold for $59.95.

I suspect the historic shotgun maker thought that the shotgun version would be the most popular, but it was the 45-caliber muzzleloading guns that started killing deer during the increasing number of blackpowder hunting seasons, as they have been doing every since. The original gun had a knockout breech plug, which was later replaced by a stronger screwed-in plug.

The Huntsman was the lowest price really workable muzzleloader available to hunters until the model was discontinued in 1976, and large numbers were sold to those who wanted to give black-powder hunting a try.

With features like "sealed breech ignition" and "in-line action" the guns sound modern today. With these "new" features and an operating mechanism used by hundreds of thousands of owners of the company's single-barreled shotguns, why did the gun have only a two-or-three-year production span?

In a word, litigation. These guns looked like shotguns and some users erroneously assumed that they could disassemble a shotgun shell, pour the powder down the barrel, load a bullet on top and shoot the gun. When so loaded against the manufacturer's recommendations and in spite of "For blackpowder only" imprinted on the barrel, and tens of thousands of words in print saying "Never use any smokeless powder in any muzzleloading gun," people tried smokeless powders, exploded their guns and sued Harrington and Richardson. To remove themselves from this liability, Harrington and Richardson discontinued the gun. According to company sources, there was no evidence than anyone who used blackpowder loads according to the manufacturer's recommendations ever damaged a gun.

Although not made for more than 25 years, the original Huntsman is still used every year by safe and capable

Today's Drop-Barrel Muzzleloaders

Maker	45 cal.	50 cal.	Weight	CF Cartridge	ML Shotgun	Pistol	Price*
CVA Accura	X	X	7.3 lb.				$500
CVA Optima	X	X	8.8 lb.	X			$425
CVA Wolf		X	7.0 lb.				$230
Knight KP 1		X	8.0 lb.	X	X		$550
Knight Shadow		X	7 ¾ lb.				$300
Knight Vision		X	7 ¾ lb.				$425
Lyman Mustang		X	7.5 lb.				$485
Pedersoli Denali		X	8.5 lb.				$380
MDM Buckwacka	X	X	7 ¾ lb.		X	X	$350
Rossi Muzzleloader		X	6.3 lb.	X			$225
Thompson Encore		X	7.0 lb.	X		X**	$700
Thompson Triumph		X	6.4 lb.				$500
Traditions Pursuit	X	X	8¼ lb.		X		$350

* Mid-range prices

** Muzzleloading barrels and forends available from the T/C Custom Shop.

CVA's Optima Pro with a Holosight on a muzzleloading shotgun barrel. Muzzleloading turkey hunters will find this a very effective combination.

hunters to take their deer. The design was sound; it offered unique features to the muzzleloading hunter and was available in an inexpensive, handy gun.

Marlin purchased H&R 1871 / New England Firearms, the successor company to Harrington and Richardson, and re-introduced a modernized version of the Huntsman in 2001 under the New England Firearms brand. The new gun featured a plastic primer holder to ease the loading and extraction of the #209 primer, fiber-optic sights and a detachable, screw-in breech plug. These 45- and 50-caliber muzzleloading barrels could also be retrofitted to recent production guns, and the gun was also offered as a combo set, with either 12-gauge or 243 rifle cartridge barrels. The price of the muzzleloading gun was about $170, making it one of the least expensive American-made muzzleloading rifles. The Huntsman was discontinued in 2008, although some may remain in dealer's inventories.

CVA OPTIMA, WOLF AND ACCURA

With so much interest in dropping-barrel muzzleloaders, CVA introduced a similar design operated by a short spur under the trigger guard. The Optima and Optima Pro are available in either 45- or 50-calibers and offer a choice of 26- or 29-inch barrels with fiber-optic sights. The synthetic stock has a pronounced Monte Carlo comb and is available in camouflage or black. Unlike several of the other break-open designs, the Optima features a solid aluminum ramrod instead of a telescoping version.

For guns with equivalent features, the Optima and Optima Pro sell for starting prices of between $100 and $150 less than Winchester's pivoting-block Apex and bolt-action X-150. After the introduction of the Optima series, CVA introduced the less expensive Wolf dropping-barrel muzzleloader at a price of about $230, and this year the company offers the new Accura which has the best trigger pull of the entire series. This gun also uses a lever to drop the barrel, employs premium Bergara barrels; the increased functionality and value is reflected in its higher price of about $500.

KNIGHT

Knight, the company that pioneered first the striker-fired in-line design and later designed bolt-actions guns specifically for muzzleloaders, now has three drop-barrel designs. Two, the KP1 and Shadow, have external hammers and the Vision is among the new hammerless muzzleloaders.

The KP1 is a versatile platform and is available with a 50-caliber muzzleloading barrel, seven centerfire chamberings, two cartridge shotgun gauges, as a muzzleloading shotgun and in various finishes and combination packages – all of which will interchange on the same frame.

The Shadow is a basic no-frills, but quite capable, muzzleloader available in 50-caliber and priced at about $300. With a drop-barrel hammerless design and removable trigger assembly, the Vision promises to be a gun that will be very easy to maintain and simple to shoot at a mid-range price of about $425.

LYMAN MUSTANG

With the look of a European folding single-barrel hammerless shotgun, the Mustang's barrel pivots around a large knuckle enabling the barrel and buttstock to nearly touch for more compact storage. This gun is only available in 50 caliber, but is outfitted with a premium recoil pad and fiber-optic sights. The

Mounting scopes on drop-barrel muzzleloaders, such this CVA Optima Pro, ensures more accurate shot placement and increases your effective range.

Knight Revolution rolling block rifle with action removed.

stock is clad with an "ultra grain" finish, giving it the appearance of being made of high-grade walnut. Although the design is not as familiar to many Americans as the detachable forend design more commonly used on domestic guns, it is a solid, shootable gun.

DAVIDE PEDERSOLI DENALI

Another muzzleloading design with strong European derivation is Davide Pedersoli's Denali. This gun features an internal hammer with a cocking-indicator pin and uses a long operating lever, part of the trigger guard, to break the action. The Denali is robust, chambered in 50-caliber and its 8-1/2 pound weight will enable it to soak up the recoil from three-pellet loads. This gun is available in a Hardwoods break-up camo pattern, with a Hardwoods finished carbon-fiber stock or with a wooden stock covered with a fancy wood-grain pattern.

MILLENNIUM DESIGNED MUZZLELOADERS (MDM)

Marlin's decision to return the Huntsman to the market may have been partly because a new company, Millennium Designed Muzzleloaders, took a look at the Huntsman and decided to update it by making a gun designed to be a muzzleloader and nothing else. Their Buckwacka preserved the lifter opening mechanism and look of the Topper shotgun. MDM upgraded the gun with a #209-ignition system, removable screw-in breech plug, a "magnum" barrel safe to use with three 50-grain Pyrodex pellets or 150 grains of FFg blackpowder, an action that cannot be opened if the gun is cocked and interchangeable muzzleloading blackpowder rifle and shotgun barrels. In addition MDM also offers a pistol based on this design.

New materials were used such as stainless steel and camo-dipped stocks. New design additions included fiber-optic peep or Patridge-style rear sights, recessed barrel crowns, and rifle and shotgun barrels tapped for scope mounts. MDM decided to offer the gun with fast twist 45- and 50-caliber barrels of from 23 to 25 inches to shoot conical bullets. Other additions included an unbreakable ramrod and interchangeable chokes for the shotgun using the popular Winchester-Browning-Mossberg system of screw-in chokes.

How do the MDM guns compare to the old H&Rs? The MDM's stock is a bit bulkier, which enhances its capabilities for deer and turkey shooting but makes it feel and swing less like a shotgun. In all other respects the Buckwacker is a superior, more versatile muzzleloader than the old or new Huntsman, and this is reflected in MDM's higher prices.

ROSSI

Rossi, the Brazilian gunmaker, makes a slightly different external-hammer design that it sells under its own name. Like both the MDM and H&R, the Rossi uses a thumb-activated drop-barrel design, but the Rossi also has a side safety on the receiver. In addition the Rossi is available as sets that can include a 50-caliber muzzleloading barrel and a choice of 243 cartridge rifle, 20-gauge cartridge shotgun or 22- and 17-caliber rimfire barrels.

Although also available in stainless steel, the typical Rossi features a blued

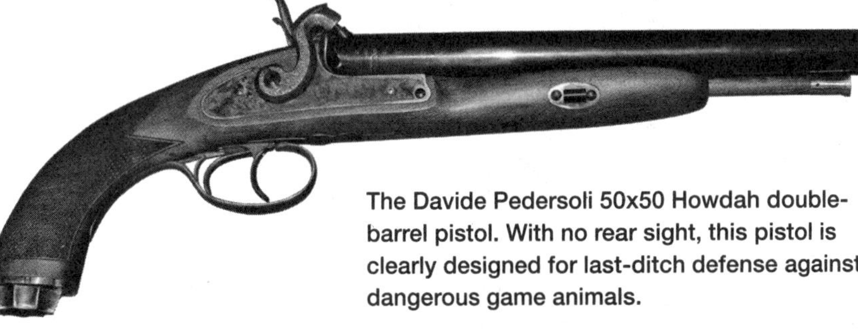
The Davide Pedersoli 50x50 Howdah double-barrel pistol. With no rear sight, this pistol is clearly designed for last-ditch defense against dangerous game animals.

23-inch 50-caliber barrel with fiber optic sights, a walnut-finished hardwood stock and the same type of collapsible brass or stainless ramrods first pioneered by H&R. Although Rossi features a Monte Carlo stock on some of their rifles, Rossi uses a more conventional shotgun stock with a generous recoil pad.

THOMPSON/CENTER ARMS 209X50 ENCORE AND TRIUMPH

A muzzleloading version of Thompson/Center's Encore rifle was introduced in 1998 as the 209x.50. Touted as "The most powerful 50-caliber muzzleloader in the world," the new rifle was designed to use three, 50-grain Pyrodex pellets and a sabot bullet to increase the killing range of muzzleloading rifles. The Encore action is a robust underlever dropping-barrel action with a separate trigger-hammer mechanism. Like the Huntsman and Buckwacker, the external hammer must be cocked for each shot.

The Encore is a rugged, reliable rifle that features easily interchangeable centerfire rifle and shotgun barrels in addition to 45- and 50-caliber muzzleloading rifle barrels. It was initially available with a 12-gauge muzzleloading shotgun tube. Because of the interchangeable nature of components, this gun must be sold, even with the muzzleloading barrel, as a centerfire rifle.

I was an early fan of Thompson/Center Contender pistols and once owned #1618 which I purchased when a lieutenant of engineers in Alaska. I was quickly attracted to the muzzleloading version of the Encore pistol and obtained one as soon as it was available. With this pistol, stoked with my favorite load of 100 grains of Pyrodex (later Triple Seven) pellets and a 370-grain Thompson/Center MaxiBall, I have taken whitetail deer, hogs (up to 350 pounds), an African warthog and employed it to finish off a 700-pound blue wildebeest. This load would consistently penetrate 27 inches of tough game animal. Although now discontinued from regular production, 209x50 muzzleloading barrels and forends are still available from Thompson/Center's Custom Shop.

Traditions Rex 50-caliber over/under double rifle has sufficient weight to soak up large powder charges. Although available in several styles, the Rex features excellent wood and has panels on the receiver featuring a deer on one side and a bighorn sheep on the other.

A new departure for Thompson/Center was the manufacture of an aluminum-framed break-open design with a quick-removable breech plug named the Triumph. This 50-caliber rifle still retains an external hammer, has extensions of the stock extending into the receiver frame and the trigger guard pulls down to break the barrel for easy priming. It is available in either weather-shield or camo-clad finishes. With its lightweight frame and resultant 6-1/4 pound over-all weight, recoil would be stout with three-pellet loads, but it should be fine when stoked with two pellets and a 300-grain bullet. With an average price of about $500, many shooters will probably opt for this gun in preference to the more expensive Encore.

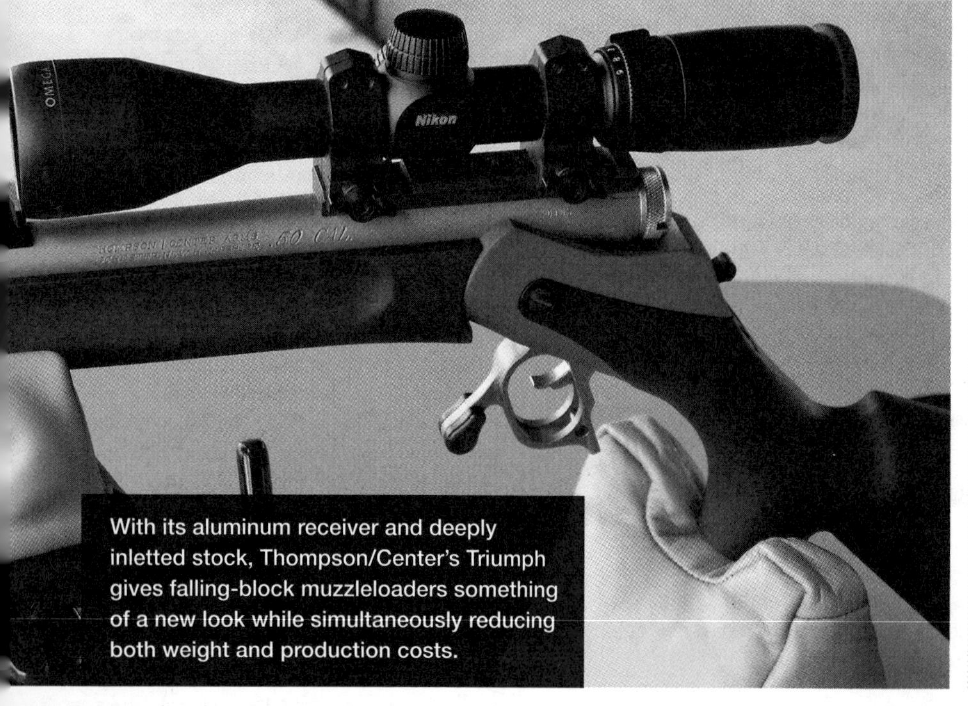

With its aluminum receiver and deeply inletted stock, Thompson/Center's Triumph gives falling-block muzzleloaders something of a new look while simultaneously reducing both weight and production costs.

TRADITIONS' PURSUIT PRO

Available in a variety of finishes in 45 and 50 calibers as well as a 12-gauge muzzleloading shotgun, the 8 1/4-pound Pursuit employs a backwards-moving rectangular slide forward of the trigger guard to open the barrel. With its mid-range pricing of about $350, solid feel and good shooting characteristics the guns have attracted a loyal following. Each year more user-friendly features have been added to the design that now includes a ported barrel, easy breech plug removal, a counter-sunk muzzle for easier loading and, on some models, a recoil-reducing stock. A variety of stocking and finishing options are also available. These guns look much like the external hammer break-barrel single-shot shotguns that many shooters grew up with.

WHAT DROP-BARREL DESIGNS OFFER

Sealed breech ignition, weather resistance, easy loading, short over-all length, accuracy, simplicity and easy cleaning are the chief attributes of falling-barrel muzzleloaders. Even when a scope is mounted, there is no fiddling with a capper trying to coax a #209 primer underneath a low-lying scope.

Some state fish and game departments prohibit these designs because they demand an exposed ignition system or do not allow #209-primed guns on some hunts. Traditions now offer a Westerner version of its Pursuit with a cut-out on the rear of the barrel, so that the ignition is exposed, to make it legal in Colorado and other states. Check the laws and hunt regulations for the states you plan to hunt.

IF ONE BARREL IS GOOD, AREN'T TWO BETTER?

It would seem that this was the question posed by Traditions with their 50-caliber Express Double rifle. Built on a 12-gauge shotgun frame, the twin barrels share a common adjustable fiber-optic sight. The lower, fixed barrel is sighted in with these sights and the strike of bullets from the upper barrel is adjusted by applying pressure with set screws to change the point of aim to correspond with the lower barrel. The gun is available in a walnut-stocked version in blued steel, a camo-finished stock with nickel-plated barrel and as the Rex model with high-gloss walnut and blued steel. Although the Rex that I received has depictions of a whitetail buck on one side of the receiver and a bighorn sheep on the other, it would take a better man than I to go sheep hunting with the 12-pound gun. In brief firing tests, the gun shot reasonably well, carried well and digested 150-grain powder loads without a burp.

If you are hunting from a stand and might have rapid shots at game as it moved nearby, this gun would swing like the shotgun it so closely resembles and make rapid hits on multiple targets at ranges up to 50 yards. With a scope, hits out to 100 yards on deer-sized targets proved to be no problem. Rather than being a deer or boar gun, I suspect the Express Double may more nearly be a "poor man's African double" which, at $1,200 or so, costs an order of magnitude less than a typical 470 side-by-side rifle. While more testing is needed employing heavier bullets, the weight and handling characteristics of the gun are favorable attributes. One not-so-favorable aspect is a very hard trigger pull that does not appear to be easily adjustable.

Swinging-block actions on the Remington Genesis and Snyder rifle. In a strange twist, the muzzleloading Genesis is a flatter-shooting, more powerful hunting tool than the original cartridge Snyder. The only advantage the old warhorse offers is rapidity of fire.

CONVENIENCE FEATURES

Hand-detachable breech plugs are now appearing on some Thompson/Center Arms and Traditions muzzleloaders. Knight is also offering new breech plugs for their guns that eliminate the need for the Full Plastic Jacket primer holders. Recoil reduction is also receiving attention, with Thompson/Center Arms, Traditions and CVA offering new stock designs.

NEW BULLETS AND POWDERS

Hornady has introduced a new streamlined hollow-based copper-plated muzzleloading bullet that promises to be easier to load than saboted projectiles. Called the FPB, this 350-grain bullet is available only in 50-caliber in 2008.

MDM has a new 265-grain Dyno-Core Magnum; a full-caliber pure lead bullet with a large plastic tip driving into an expansion chamber, which promises rapid expansion on deer-size game. MDM has also introduced Dyno-Core Premium 222- and 285-grain saboted bullets made of tungsten alloy (in an apparent move to comply with potential lead-bullet restrictions in California), which are advertised to out-penetrate and out-expand some 30-30 and 308 Winchester bullets.

Hodgdon is now marketing Magnum Triple Seven pellets designed to produce enhanced velocities from muzzleloader barrels. Like the previous formulations, these pellets may be loaded either-end-down and work best with #209-primed guns. Both Winchester and Remington now make special muzzleloader #209 primers to produce optimum results with these pellets.

In an effort to produce powders in

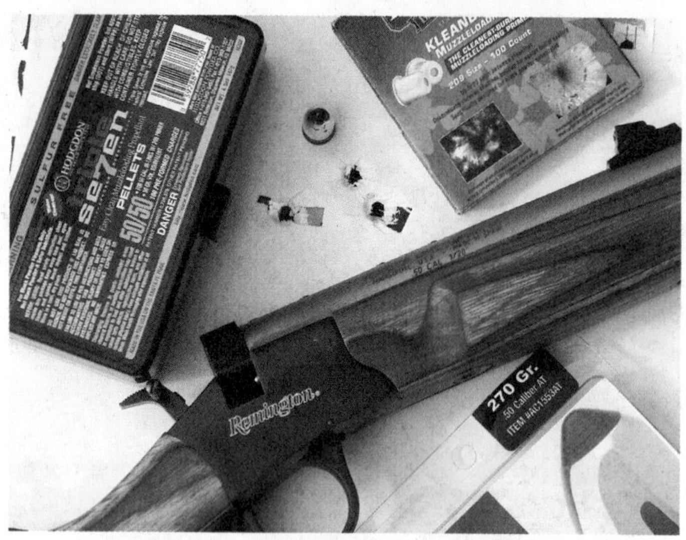

The Remington Genesis with shooting components, including Hodgdon's Triple Seven powder and Remington's #209 primers for muzzleloading guns.

easier-to-use packagings, Hornady has introduced the L-N-L (lock and load) featuring a plastic stem on the bottom of a 0.452-inch saboted bullet that holds two or three powder pellets.

Pioneer Powder's Gold Super Sticks are tapered rectangular columns of powder that are the equivalent of 150-grain charges. To load, it is simply dropped down the bore of the rifle and the bullet seated on top. This removes the need to count pellets while retaining the powder's easy-clean characteristics. MDM also introduced their Thunder Charge consumable cartridges for muzzleloaders where the propellant charge is fixed to the bullet and the assembly is loaded as one unit.

GOEX's bid for the sulfur-free blackpowder substitute market is Pinnacle, which is available in FFg and FFFg granulations. This loose powder may be loaded volume-for-volume for blackpowder and may even be used in flintlocks, according to the manufacturer.

SHOOTING AND HUNTING WITH THE NEW GUNS

Hodgdon's new Magnum Triple Seven pellets were used in both the Remington Genesis and Traditions Express Double. With both guns, the number of shots fired during load development produced sufficient fouling to cause some aggravation in operating the swing block on the Genesis and withdrawing the breech plugs from the Double. Using some saboted Remington muzzleloading bullets that I had on hand, I quickly found that the Genesis demanded that its barrel be very well cleaned between shots to produce consistent accuracy and that this particular bullet-sabot combination only worked best with 100-grain loads. Before range shooting was completed, I had to remove the breechblock, clean it with water and scrub the face of the breech.

Even with 150-grain powder loads and a 338-grain PowerBelt bullet, the Express double was a very mild-recoiling gun to shoot. I quickly found that you needed to adjust the set screws on the free-floating barrel to move the end of the barrel in the direction that you wanted to bullet to go. Before each series of shots it was necessary to insure that all of the adjusting screws were firmly seated without stripping the seats of the screws with the Allen wrench. Ultimately, I achieved 100-yard benchrest groups where both barrels struck within 3 inches of point of aim.

When prepping the Express prior to shooting, heavily lubricate the

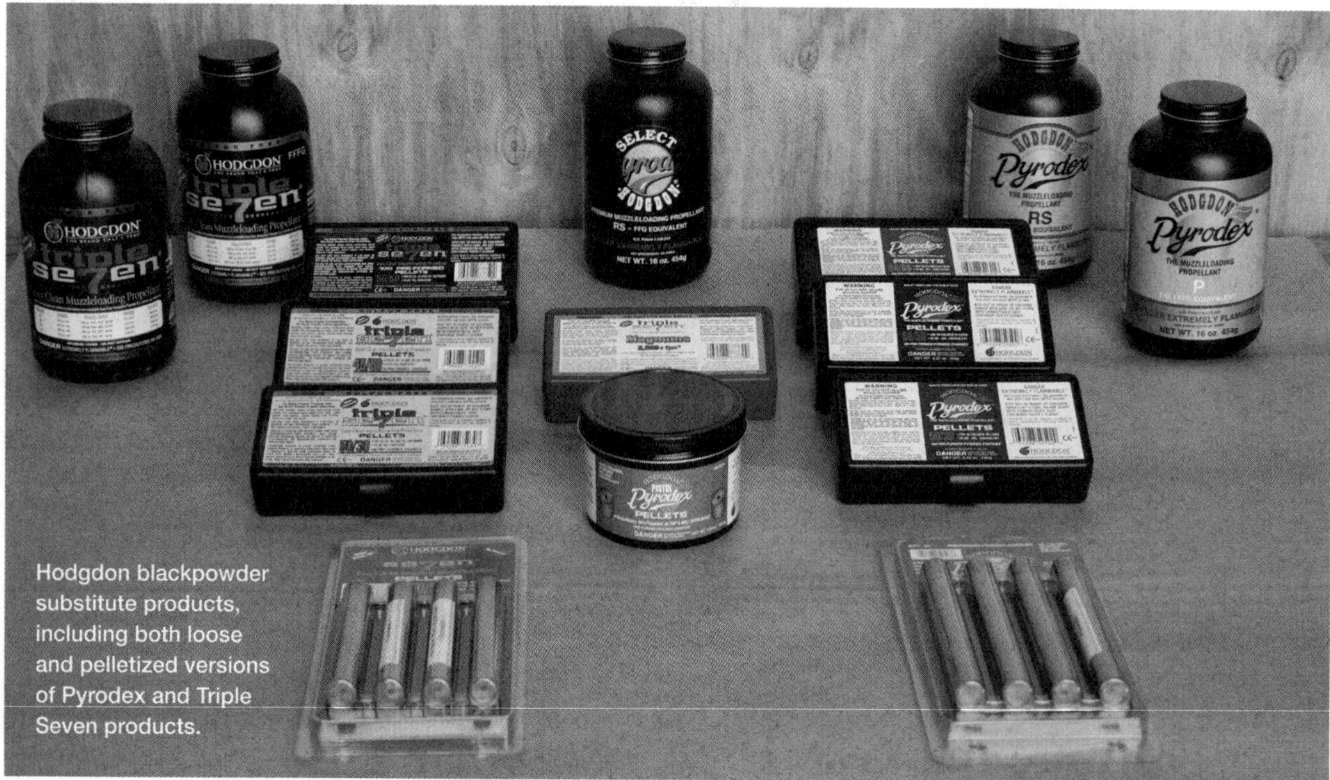

Hodgdon blackpowder substitute products, including both loose and pelletized versions of Pyrodex and Triple Seven products.

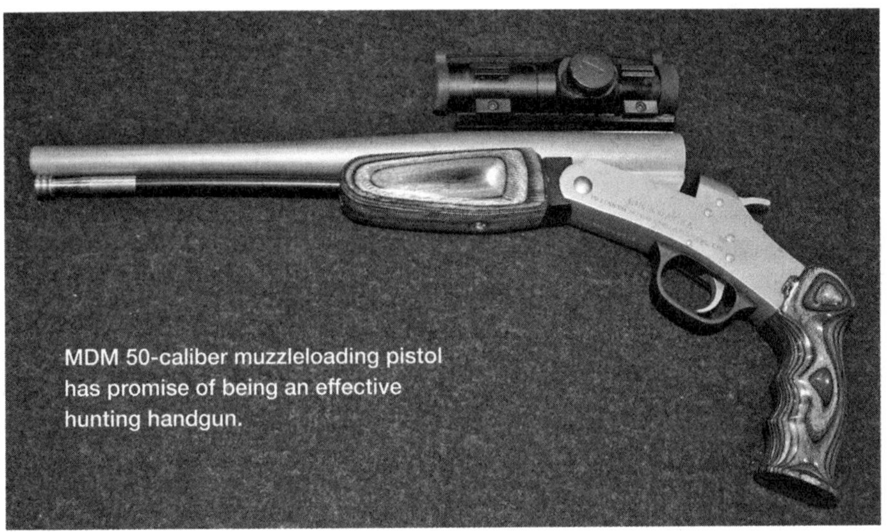
MDM 50-caliber muzzleloading pistol has promise of being an effective hunting handgun.

breech plugs with high-temperature grease and allow the excess to stay in the back part of the barrels to facilitate withdrawing the breech plugs after the shooting session.

When loading the #209 primers in the Express, be sure the barrels are fully opened, lest a primer be fumbled with cold fingers, fall into the deep receiver and tie up the gun. Once, a #209 primer got so badly wedged in the barrel locking mechanism that I had to dig it out with the awl on my pocketknife. (A good reason for carrying a pocketknife with multiple-tool capabilities when hunting.)

A VISIT TO HODGDON

Any company that has the stamina to make 777 attempts to produce a new product deserves a visit, and I was pleased to make a mid-winter trek to Hodgdon Powder's operations in Kansas City, Kansas. Although the mailing address for the company is Shawnee Mission, there is no such town, only a post office. After my two-day trip from Georgia through one of the winter's first snow and sleet storms, I ultimately made connections with Chris Hodgdon, the grandson of the company founder Bruce Hodgdon.

This has historically been, and is, a family-owned company; but one that has had the foresight to bring in exciting new developments that originated from outside the company. This was the case when Dan Pawlak, the inventor of Pyrodex powder, developed the first smokeless powder substitute with Hodgdon and later when Dean Barrett came up with the sulfur-free Triple Seven powder on his 777th attempt. Hodgdon has grown from repackaging surplus military powders to buying out it's largest competitor, Du Pont Powder, and is now manufacturing and marketing the IMR and Winchester-brand powders; a line of more than 50 powders suitable for nearly all civilian applications.

For safety reasons, the manufacturing, packaging and shipment of Hodgdon powders takes place in rural Herington, Kansas, nearly 90 miles from Kansas City. The company headquarters and a smaller testing operation are located in Kansas City. There is a larger testing facility at the Herington factory. All of the operations are automated and remotely monitored. No one is allowed in or near the bunkered buildings when compounding, or drying is taking place. Once the powder has been made, and the pellets formed, automated production equipment packages the final product.

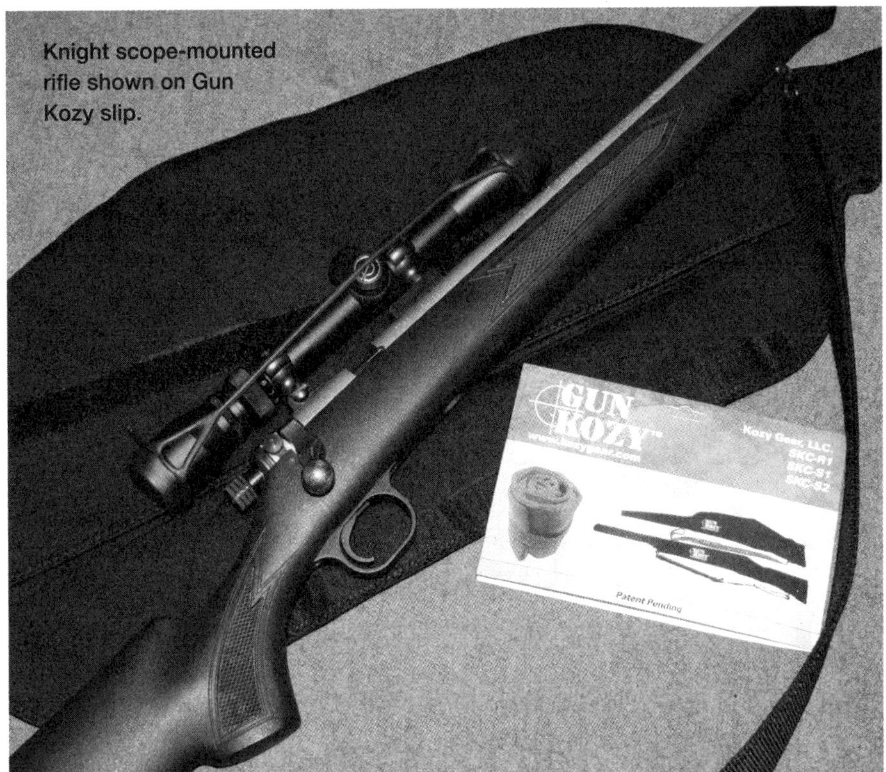

Knight scope-mounted rifle shown on Gun Kozy slip.

USEFUL GADGETS

One common need is a simple slipcase to protect a muzzleloading gun on the way to the deer stand or duck blind. Gun Kosy's Velcro-fastened slips add an extra level of protection against mud and snow. Styles are available for both scope-mounted and plain-barreled in-lines.

Otis Portable Cleaning Kits work well with removable-breech-plug in-line guns, including muzzleloading shotguns, and greatly reduce the bulk of blackpowder cleaning gear. The Otis kits are issued to U.S. combat units in the Middle East.

CONCLUSIONS

Far from being a dying shooting sport, muzzleloading is continuing to evolve, with the line increasingly blurred between the appearance, components used and ballistic efficiencies of muzzleloaders and cartridge guns. Through all of this, the user is benefiting from increased performance and ease of use, whether his inclination is the traditional or modern versions of front-loading guns.

HUNTING & SHOOTING OPTICS

by Wayne van Zwoll

ABOVE: **Remington's John Trull checks the view through a new Swarovski Z6 on a Remington R-15 VTR.**

Keeping track of hunting optics was once a matter of perusing a half-dozen catalogs, each with a half-dozen rifle-scopes. You picked a binocular from fewer sources still. These days, people who've never used a rifle-scope on a hunt are importing or marketing optical sights by the bushel. The frenzy for editorial space compels them to add variations – and frills – to bolster lists of new items. China's enthusiasm for the Japanese practice of contracting optics manufacture has expanded the field. Brands that once defined other products now cover optics too. Columbia Sportswear catalogs a line of rifle-scopes, binoculars and spotting scopes, including a Bonehead binocular. (Some names have become more inscrutable than specifications).

Nor has advertising hype diminished. "Ready, aim…kill!" exhorts the purveyor of a new tactical sight. Another scope is truly fearsome: "It's bold, tough and eats elephants for breakfast!" I couldn't make this up. Other catalogs have so much hardware to showcase that it must rely solely on spec tables. Carson crams 33 binoculars into a few pages. CenterPoint, a relative newcomer, lists 23 rifle-scopes for 2008.

Why the hyperbole? Why so many options? The common answer is competition. While I find a 4x rifle-scope and an 8x32 binocular adequate for my big game hunting, other sportsmen are of different mind. And if they're not, it's in the best interests of importer and manufacturer to convert them. I've never needed a lighted reticle or range-finding device in a rifle-scope, or even variable power. But as power steering, cell phones and home computers were once novelties, we come to need what was once unnecessary.

Higher levels of precision and repeatability in rifle-scope adjustments surely benefit competitive shooters. Red-dot sights have improved the effectiveness of handguns and shotguns. Make no mistake: the relentless drive toward better optics, no matter how incremental the progress, has helped us achieve higher scores, faster aim and more kills afield. Brighter, sharper images have blessed those of us whose once-keen eyesight has diminished with age. More sophisticated scopes have even fueled development of long-range rifles and cartridges.

While price is usually a good measure of optical quality, you may not need the best glass – or be able to detect any advantage over products costing much less. Even modestly priced optics now are vastly superior to the top-end rifle-scopes and binoculars of my youth. Were I shopping, I'd insist on fully multi-coated lenses (to ensure maximum light transmission) and a hydrophobic lens coating that sheds rain. Other options depend on application. On the mountain, durability matters; so does light weight. A binocular that scales more than 24 ounces is too heavy for the single strap I prefer to a harness. Scopes for big-game rifles should, I think, add no more than 12 percent to the rifle's weight. By that measure a 7-pound rifle should carry no more than 13 ounces of sight. My 6-pound rifles wear 4x32 or 6x36 scopes, or 2.5-8x36 or 3-9x36 variables. Big glass has no place in my kit.

But big lenses and high magnification seem popular with increasing numbers of sportsmen. So too sophisticated scope reticles and even computer-generated data fed to electronic range-finding sights to help with holdover at long range. You'll pay accordingly. As compelling to me are more traditional optics with state-of-the art coatings. In this list you'll find the new Leupold rifle-scope that recently helped me shoot a distant bull elk with a 270 Weatherby. You'll also see the 8x32 Pentax binocular that sifted from a lattice of branches the outline of another elk, which dropped to my iron-sighted 32 Special.

Beyond a certain level of quality and integrity, what you choose in hunting optics matters less than how you use them – and the fortunes you meet on the trail.

AIMPOINT

A decade ago, in a dark forest in Sweden, I spied a moose trotting through the shadows nearly 100 yards off. Shouldering the Blaser 30-06, I swung with it and fired as it paused in a narrow alley between the tall conifers. It dashed out of sight, but I was confident the bullet had struck home. We found the moose dead, a bull that might have gotten the better of me had I not carried an Aimpoint sight. The red dot showed up in the gloom as no crosswire could.

One advantage held by the 1x Aimpoint sight is unlimited eye relief. You get a full field of view right away, no matter how close your eye is to the lens. You can easily shoot with both eyes open. Models with magnification have generous eye relief. The newest Aimpoints feature Advanced Circuit Efficiency Technology that reduces power demand, boosting battery life to 50,000 hours with the brightness set on 7 (on a scale of 1 to 11). The 9000 series comprises several models, including compact versions that weigh as little as 6.5 ounces. Windage and elevation adjustments have positive clicks, each moving point of impact 13mm at 100 meters. The small footprint and light weight of Aimpoint sights, with their durability, battery longevity and excellent optics, keep the wind behind this company's sales. Aimpoint.com

ALPEN

A couple of decades ago, no one had heard of Alpen sporting optics. Now the import company has a complete line of rifle-scopes, spotting scopes and binoculars. Some have won industry awards for value. In 2008 top-end Rainier 42mm binoculars are joined by compact versions. At just 25 ounces, the new 8x32 and 10x32 are 20 percent lighter; still, they feature BAK4 lenses and phase-corrected coatings, magnesium frames, locking diopter dial, twist-out eyecups. The affordable Teton 42mm binoculars have bigger siblings in 8x50 and 10x50 glasses. In the AlpenPro Porro prism series, there's a new 8x30 with close interpupillary measure. Existing 8x42s and 10x50s now have twist-up eyecups. Rainier 20-60x80 spotting scopes come with straight or angled eyepieces easily turned by hand for comfortable viewing. Both take Alpen's camera adapter. At a lower price-point, new 20-60x80 scopes have earned "great buy" accolades from the outdoors press. There's a new AR rifle-scope line for air guns, whose double-shuffle recoil can put the skids under scopes that withstand the severe but unidirectional recoil of a 458. Alpenoutdoors.com

ATK

Nitrex once appeared as a Speer ammunition brand. In 2008 it has been adopted by ATK (which owns Speer, Federal and several other industry icons) to describe an optics line. In rifle-scopes, it includes a 1.5-5x32, a 3-9x42, a 3-10x50 and a 6-20x50 AO. The 6-20x's AO dial is the traditional front-end ring. Windage and elevation dials are finger-friendly, with 1/4-minute clicks. The 6-20x has eighth-minute clicks for finer scope tuning, and a range of 240 clicks, predictably higher than the 176-click range of the others. The 6-20 has a finer TrexPlex reticle than its siblings too. As is customary in the American market, ATK kept the reticle in the second focal plane. It doesn't change dimensions as you turn the power dial. Nitrex scopes have fast-focus eyepieces. Eye relief ranges from 3.6 inches (the 1.5-5x) to 3.3 inches (the 6-20x). Weights: 12.7, 14.4, 18.4 and 24 ounces, respectively. Matte black is the standard finish, but you can also specify a black gloss or silver 3-9, a black gloss 3-10, a silver 6-20.

The 3-9x42 I've used accommodates low mounting in Leupold rings. There's plenty of tube for perfect placement, fore-and-aft. The matte finish is as dull as you'll want and seems durable. The eyepiece and power dial move smoothly but with due restraint. Reticle posts crowd the center but allow a clear view of the target. Eye relief does not seem to change from low power to high, but remains generous. Checking windage and elevation dials with the rifle secured in a Caldwell Steady Rest, I found routine return to zero. Images in this Nitrex scope are bright and sharp, with a flat field and little color fringing. The 42mm front lens packs as much glass as fits in a round tube clamped in low rings. Mechanically and optically, this is a better scope than the $300 price suggests. You can buy a 3-10x50 for about $330, a 6-20x50 for $400.

Nitrex binoculars are imported too. The new 8x42 and 10x42 weigh 25 ounces and feature tripod adapters. Rubber armor on these center-focus, roof-prism glasses make them easy to grip in cold and wet weather. Phase-correction coatings enhance image quality. A 10x42 Nitrex binocular I examined delivers bright, razor-edged images. I'm not as keen about eyecups that pull straight out instead of twisting (they're easily compressed), and I'd as soon have smooth barrel contours instead of ribbing and the Nitex label in bold relief. I do like the click-detent diopter dial – and the price: just $290. The 8x42 is $10 less. Compact versions, 8x25 and 10x25, weigh 11 ounces, cost $180 and $190. Nitrexoptics.com

BARRETT

A well-known maker of 50-caliber rifles, Barrett has a vested interest in boosting first-round hit capability at extreme range. Its latest product, BORS (for Barrett Optical Ranging System) does just that. It's an electronic device you can pair with the best optical sights to get both superior resolution and dead-accurate range compensation hundreds of yards from the muzzle. It weighs 13 ounces, which you must add to the weight of your scope, because BORS is a scope attachment, not the sight itself. The heart of BORS is a small ranging computer with factory-installed cartridge tables. It's powered by a CR-123 lithium battery. The other BORS components: an elevation knob, a knob adapter and a set of rings that marry the computer to your sight. The rings mount to any M1913 rail and are secured with the hex

Alpen scopes deliver great value. Wayne finds it here in a 3-9x40 on a Remington 700 BDL.

Tactical knobs are made for frequent field use, with big, finger-adjust dials, precise return to zero.

nuts preferred for affixing heavy sights to hard-kicking rifles. Horizontally split, the beefy ring tops fasten to the ring bottoms with quartets of 8-32 screws. Screws and wrenches are provided.

The BORS computer features a 12x2-character liquid crystal display and a four-button keypad. It can operate through a wide range of temperatures (-4 F to 158 F) and at elevations from below sea level to 20,000 feet. I attached one to a Leupold Mark 4 Long Range/Tactical 4.5-14x50 scope with mil dot reticle. After you install the battery and press the 6-o'clock power button on the BORS unit, you're ready to engineer a shot. The screen shows zero range and indicates any cant. At extended range, you'll want the sight exactly over the bore. Tip the rifle, and the relationship of bore-line to sight-line changes. The BORS unit automatically compensates for vertical shot angle too. You can precisely adjust the scope for up to 90 degrees of inclination and declination, in increments of 2 degrees! At extreme range you'll also need data on temperature and barometric pressure. Both come on-screen when you press the 9-o'clock button.

A "Determine Range" display is one of six alternatives to your "Operator's Screen." Specify target size, then move the horizontal wire of your reticle from top to bottom of the target, or vice versa. The range appears in yards or meters in the window. Now you can return to the Operator's Screen and use the BORS elevation knob to dial the range. The dial brings your horizontal wire to the proper place for a dead-on hold.

Naturally, the BORS unit must "know" the arc of your bullet before it can adjust for yardage. You provide that information by entering cartridge data or bullet characteristics into the "Cartridge Information" screen. The unit stores as many as 100 ballistics tables.

The BORS unit is quite compact, blending nicely into the profile of a 50 BMG rifle with a 30mm tactical scope. It suits traditional heavy-barreled bolt guns as well. While it adds more weight and bulk than you'll want on a hunting rifle, the value of BORS lies not in short shooting where shots come fast and the hills grow steeper by the hour. It's a sniper's unit, a device that can help you hit with Barrett's accurate 50-caliber rifles at extreme distances. BORS gives you the best of optical sight pictures and quick-as-a-wink data on-screen at the same time. If your battery dies, you use the scope as if it wore no electronics. Recoil and blast from my 50-caliber Barrett 107 haven't fazed the instrument. Barrettrifles.com

BRUNTON

Binoculars have built the Brunton brand, but the company "started in the 1890s with an invention for field geologists," according to President John Smithbaker. Now you'll find compasses and GPS units, transits, headlamps, camp cookwear and stoves.

The best Brunton binocular is the Epoch, a full-size roof-prism glass with 43mm objectives and your choice of magnification: 7.5x, 8.5x or 10.5x. They retail for a bit less than $1,300. The 8-15x35 zoom Epoch earned a "Gear of the Year" award from *Outside* magazine. It lists at $1,639 (down from the initial price). Like its fixed-power siblings, it features lockable, twist-out eyecups and accepts a doubler to boost magnification. Eterna and Echo binoculars are less costly but still boast fully multi-coated lenses. Eterna 8x45 and 11x45 full-size models snared a "Best Buy" rating from *Consumer's Digest.* A 15x51 with tripod adapter gives you spotting-scope power, both eyes open. The 8x32 and 10x32 are my picks for the trail.

Eterna Compact 18-38x50 and full-size 20-60x80 spotting scopes offer fully multi-coated lenses with ED (extra-low dispersion) fluorite glass. The Echo Compact, a 12-36x50, weighs only 21 ounces.

Brunton also markets rifle-scopes with the NRA label. They include affordable fixed-power 4x32 and 6x42 scopes ($109 and $119) and a 6-24x50 target scope with adjustable objective ($149 with mil-dot reticle). The 1.5-6x40 and 3.5-9x40 list for about $100. Another series, with fast-focus eyepieces, includes four variables, from 1.5-5x to 3.5-10x, and a 6-24x50. New Echo and Lite-Tech lines range in price from $156 to $330, and $104 to $149, respectively. Brunton.com and nrasportsoptics.com

BURRIS

Among the most useful reticles for long-range shooting, the Burris Ballistic Plex now comes in an alternative form, called the Ballistic Mil-Dot. It has a hash-marked lower wire (with five tics instead of the traditional three); but the other sections inside the plex posts carry standard mil dots. It's available on many Burris scopes, including the laser-ranging Laserscope. New for 2008 are Fullfield II LRS and Fullfield 30 scopes. The LRS's lighted reticle employs a flat battery housing on the turret instead of an eyepiece wart. A new, bargain-priced Timberline series includes a 4x20, a 2-7x26, a 3-9x32 and a 4.5-14x32. You'll notice an olive finish now standard on Fullfield II Tactical scopes and the new Fullfield TAC30 variables (3-9x40, 3.5-10x50 and 4.5-14x42). Burris also offers six-screw rings for tactical sights, as well as a complete list of mounts for standard sights. Its catalog includes handgun scopes, reflex sights, red dot sights spotting scopes and binoculars. Burrisoptics.com

BUSHNELL

The 2008 Bushnell catalog weighs more than some binoculars. It lists new Elite 6500-series rifle-scopes: 2.5-16x42, 2.5-16x50 and 4.5-30x50. The nearly-seven-times magnification range is the broadest in the industry. Also new: an e2 binocular (8x42 or 10x42) that delivers Elite-level optical performance at less cost. Excursion EX binoculars retail for $230 to $320. Fully multi-coated optics include lenses with PC-3 phase correction coating, a lockable focus dial. There's less than an ounce difference between 36mm and 42mm versions (both in 8x and 10x magnification). Hunters should appreciate the compact profile of the Excursion spotting scope, with its folded light path. Choose a 15-45x60 or

Bob Baker of Freedom Arms favors a Bushnell 2-6x EER scope on his 44 Magnum Model 83.

20-60x80. Bushnell's ample line of laser range-finders now includes the Scout 1000, a 5 x, 6.6-ounce, pocket instrument with 1,000-yard capability and ARC technology that takes shot angle into account. A single button makes this Scout a cinch to use with one hand. Bushnell.com

CABELA'S

Like most other firms marketing rifle-scopes and binoculars, Cabela's imports them. Its catalogs feature the Cabela's brand alongside venerated labels like Leupold, Nikon, Swarovski and Zeiss. Cabela's optics cost less but work just fine. Five fixed-power scopes and 11 variables comprise the Alaskan Guide series. There's now a higher-end "premium" AG trio: a 3-9x, a 4-12xAO and a 6.5-20 AO, all with 40mm objectives – and priced at under $360. These and most Alaskan Guide sights fit 1-inch rings, as do the AG Rangefinding 3.5-10x42 and 4.5-13x42 scopes. There's also a stable of a roof-prism binoculars and compact laser range-finders. Cabelas.com

DOCTER

In 1991 Docter began manufacturing sports optics in what was once the Carl Zeiss Jena factory in Thuringia, Germany. Since then, its optics have become well-known world-wide. Last December, Merkel USA became the company's U.S. importer. The line includes 8x42 and 10x42 binoculars, and a big, bright 8x58. Rifle-scopes in Docter's line include 1-inch 6x42 and 8x56 fixed-power Classic models, and 30mm variables in 1-4x24, 1.5-6x42, 2.5-8x48 and 3-12x56 configurations. A fast-focus eyepiece, resettable windage/elevation dials and lighted reticles complement top-drawer optics. The electronically controlled Unipoint dot is of constant size, while the first-plane main reticle varies in dimension with magnification. Docter Sport variables were designed for the U.S. market. These 1-inch scopes (3-9x40, 3-10x40, 4.5-14x40 AO and 8-25x50 AO) have reticles in the rear focal plane. Merkel-usa.com and docter-germany.com

ELCAN

Few sportsmen would have imagined Raytheon in the hunting field. Elcan is the outdoors connection, a subsidiary of Raytheon and an optics firm pioneering a digital rifle-scope. The name is an acronym: Ernst Leitz, Canada – the Leitz optical firm dating to 1849 in Germany. While Elcan has been building infrared scopes for U.S. military units since the 1980s, it is just now tapping the civilian market.

At 28 ounces, DigitalHunter is not lightweight. It is also bulky. The Elcan scope has been out for a couple of years now, and has yet to set the industry afire or inspire copies. Hunters are, by and large, conservative. Tradition matters. Still, DigitalHunter has some features many new hunters will want. And already its price has been trimmed by roughly 25 percent, to less than $1,200. Infrared and laser range-finding capabilities will surely make this bold new scope more newsworthy. And Raytheon won't run out of development money any time soon. Elcansportingoptics.com

KAHLES

Kahles dates way back. In 1898, Karl Robert Kahles merged the Simon Plossl Company and the Opto-Mechanical Workshop of Karl Fritsch to form the Kahles Company in Vienna. Two years later, it was selling Telorar rifle-scopes in five magnifications, plus binoculars and telescopes. The Helia scope series came along in 1926. Though World War II severely damaged the Kahles factory, Friedrich Kahles III had it rebuilt and soon produced one of the first variable-power rifle-scopes. In 1972, the company pioneered the multi-coating of lenses. During the last decade, it has introduced digital controls on illuminated scopes and a clever elevation dial called multizero. Now a subsidiary of Swarovski, Kahles operates independently. Its Helia C line includes 1-inch fixed-power and 30mm variable and fixed versions, with reticles in the first focal plane. The newest rifle-scope series, the KX, includes 3-9x42, 3.5-10x50 and 4-12x50 models with 1-inch tubes. They're designed for the American market, with prices as low as you'll find in the Kahles catalog. As for binoculars, Kahles lists 8x32, 8x42 and 10x42 roof-prism models with click-stop twist-out eyecups, phase-corrected prisms. They're fully submersible, too. Kahlesoptik.com

LANDMARK OUTDOORS

Yukon optics appeared a few years ago in a market already crowded with imports. Now the brand is part of Landmark Outdoors, which also markets tactical rifle-scopes under the SightMark banner. Its new Laser DualShot combines a reflex red dot sight with a laser unit that projects a beam from its 9-o'clock post on the sight's base. Sight and laser unit can be separated. More traditional optics from SightMark include 3-9x40 and 8.5-25x50 tactical scopes. The latter has a lighted mil dot reticle. For

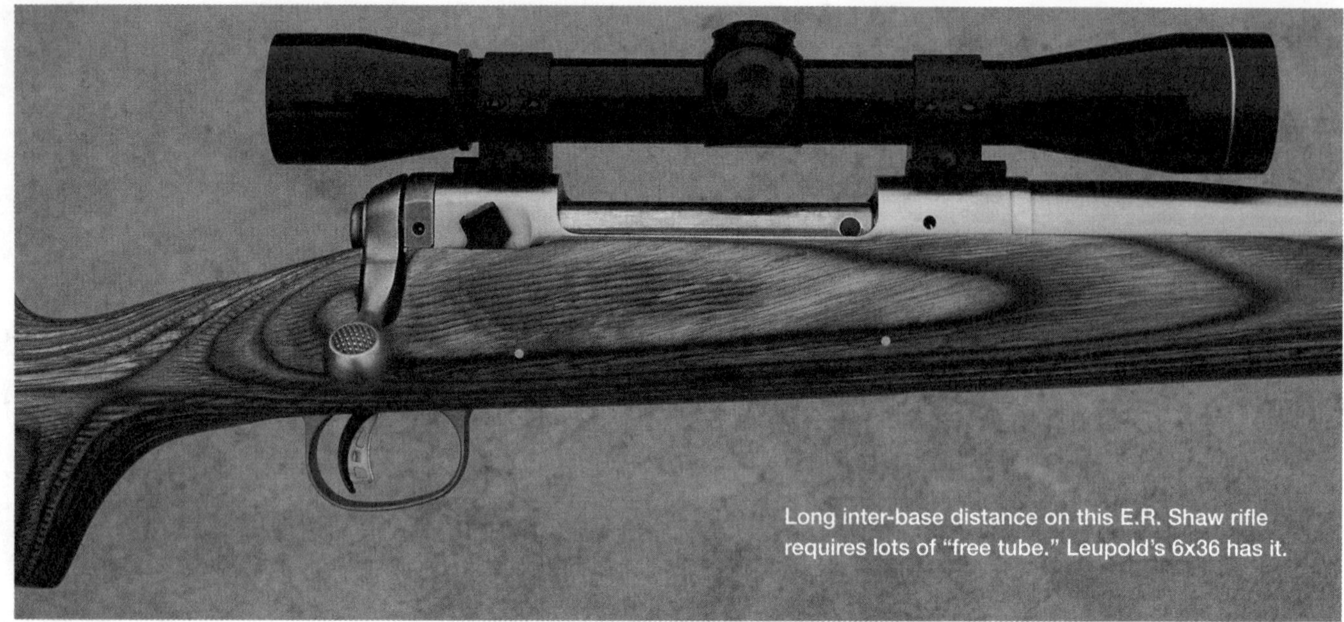

Long inter-base distance on this E.R. Shaw rifle requires lots of "free tube." Leupold's 6x36 has it.

2008 Yukon has announced a rifle-scope series with 1-inch tubes. The flagship: a 3-9x40 with multi-coated optics and oversize windage and elevation knobs. Better known for its binoculars, Yukon has expanded that line with new Rambler and Frontier series. Both are of roof-prism design. The Rambler comes in 8x25, 8x32 and 8x42 configurations, the Frontier in 8x and 10x models with 42mm objectives. Landmarkoutdoors.com

The BORS unit on this Leupold scope enhances the long-range capability of a 50-caliber Barrett.

LEICA

Instead of plumping its catalogs with price-point binoculars, Leica unapologetically improves and refines it best glass. The Geovid laser-ranging binocular, the first of its kind, now comes in a more compact chassis – and a lower price! Duovid 8 + 12x42 and 10 + 15x50 binoculars offer a choice of magnification. The legendary Trinovid binocular gave way not long ago to the Ultravid. This year, the Ultravid has been trumped by the even brighter, sharper Ultravid HDs. These new models feature fluorite glass in every lens. Exposed surfaces wear proprietary AquaDura lens coating, a hydrophobic compound that beads water and makes lens cleaning easier. Leica Ultravid HDs come in eight configurations: 8x32 and 10x32; 7x42, 8x42 and 10x42; 8x50, 10x50 and 12x50. Leica Televid 62 and 77 spotting scopes are unchanged for 2008. They still rank at the top of the field. Leica-camera.com

LEUPOLD & STEVENS

There's much new at Leupold. Following its 100th anniversary, the Oregon optics icon announced a new line of Mark 2 tactical scopes with 1-inch tubes "for police departments and civilian shooters who want features of Mark 4 sights at a lower price," says the company's Pat Mundy. Half-height target knobs feature half-minute clicks for fast run-up to long-range zero. There's a 1.5-4x20, a 3-9x40, plus another 3-9x40 with a standard windage knob for an easy slide into scabbards. The 4-12x40 and 6-18x40 (the latter with quarter-minute clicks) have adjustable objectives. The VX-7L marries the optical excellence of VX-7 glass with the low-profile ("three-quarter-moon") objective of the VX-L series. Choose a 3.5-14x56 or a 4.5-18x56. VX-7 scopes feature European-style eyepieces and "lift and lock" windage and elevation dials. The power selector ring is matched to a "Ballistic Aiming System" so you can tailor the magnification and reticle to target and distance. The matched-lens system delivers extra-sharp images. Argon/Krypton gas has replaced nitrogen in the tube, to better prevent fogging.

Leupold's new FX-III 1x14mm Prismatic Sight has been a hit, not only with riflemen but pistol shooters and shotgunners. Its generous eye relief, wide field and low profile make it ideal for AR-15-style carbines. A magnification module can be added. The FX-III Prismatic has fully multi-coated optics and a bold circle-dot reticle option. Rugged? This sight survived 28,000 blows on a test machine duplicating the recoil of a 375 H&H! It attaches to a Weaver base. Also from Beaverton: Acadia and Mojave binoculars with excellent optics but a modest price tag. The top-end Golden Ring Binocular is shipped now with HD (also ED, extra-low dispersion, fluorite) objective glass in 8x32, 10x32, 8x42 and 10x42 configurations. Phase-corrected prisms ensure true, crisp colors. This year Leupold stepped outside its box to offer a line of innovative flashlights with many features in compact housings. Leupold.com

MEOPTA

European optics have a longstanding reputation for excellence. Meopta's line of binoculars and rifle-scopes is short on gadgets and long on quality. The Meostar binocular series comprises 7x, 8x and 10x center-focus roof-prism models with twist-up eyecups and 42mm objectives. For extra-bright images, pick a 7x50, 10x50 or 8x56. The Meostar 12x50 paired with the company's 2x doubler gives you spotting-scope capability. The company's R1 4-16x44 Long Range Target Scope is the latest in a distinguished line of rifle sights. It features low-profile target knobs and a front-end adjustable objective, with second-plane plex or mil dot reticle and a 30mm tube. At the top of the hunting scope series, the Artemis 3000 3-9x42 also has that big tube and etched rear-plane reticle. It has earned industry plaudits. The 2000 and illuminated 2100 series offer those features in a solid steel 30mm tube. Choose the tank-tough 6x42, or a variable: 1.5-6x42, 2-8x42, 3-9x42, 3-12x50. Meopta offers two range-finding options in its stable of eight reticles. The firm's Meostar S1 spotting scopes, with 75mm objectives, come with standard or APO glass, straight or angled rear tube, 30x wide-angle or 20-60 zoom eyepiece. Meopta.com

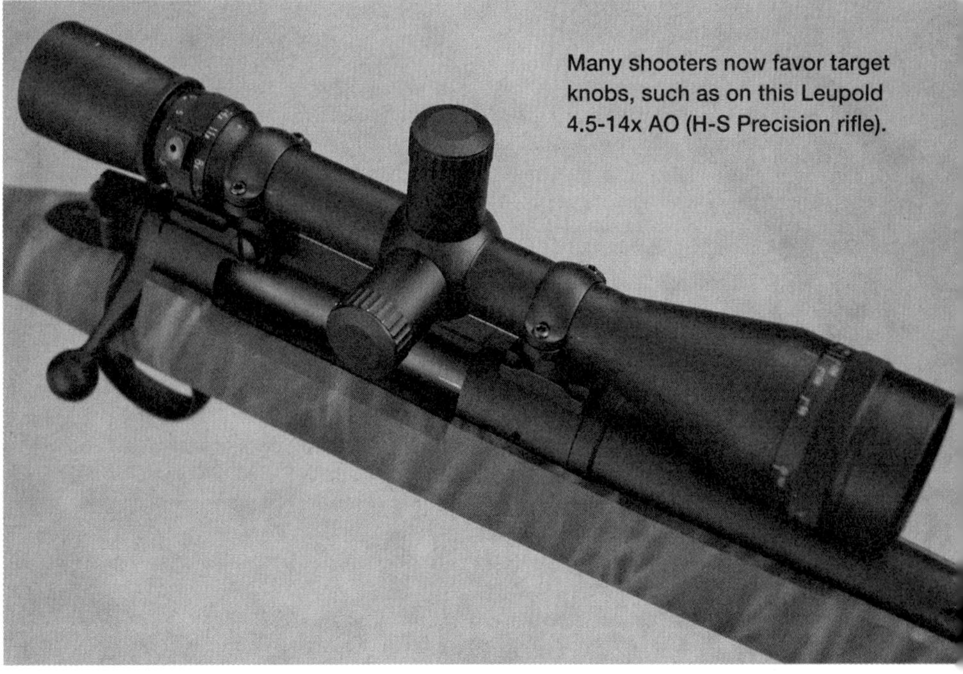

Many shooters now favor target knobs, such as on this Leupold 4.5-14x AO (H-S Precision rifle).

MILLET

Once known only for its scope mounts and a modest selection of hunting scopes, Millet broke the mold last year with Target and Varmint models (4-16x and 6-25x) featuring turret-mounted parallax dials and target knobs. Optional illuminated reticles include a mil dot. The Tactical series, including a 10x and 1-4x and 4-16x variables, have 30mm tubes, a lighted Donut-Dot reticle option. A Zoom Dot red dot sight fits rails on handguns, tactical carbines. Buck Gold hunting scopes cover many applications with 1.5-6x44 to 6-25x56 models. Finger-friendly windage/elevation dials have coil-spring returns. Fast-focus eyepieces come standard. Turret-mounted AO and lighted reticle are available on some models. A "Buck Silver" line offers 3-9x, 4-12x and 6-18x variables and a 2x LEE scope, all with 1-inch tubes. Millet catalogs an SP series of electronic red dot sights, also rails for popular centerfire rifles and a complete line of rings and traditional bases. The company markets a wide variety of iron sights for handguns. Millettsights.com

NIGHTFORCE

NXS rifle-scopes are built to higher standards than necessary, to ensure the best sights possible for sportsmen, soldiers and law enforcement officers. Tests at the north-central Idaho firm include submersion in 100 feet of water

This Savage 112V wears a high-power Meopta variable – a lot of scope for the money!

for 24 hours, freezing in a box cooled to a minus 80 degrees F, and then heating within an hour to 250 degrees F. Every scope is slammed in a recoil device delivering 1,250 Gs – both ways! Durable to a fault, these scopes feature main tubes of lightweight bronze alloy. Dissimilar alloys in the erector tube assembly guarantee repeatable movement. Lens coatings must pass mil-spec abrasion tests. The 3.5-15x50 and 3.5-15x56 NSX are 30mm scopes with Nightforce reticles in the field center. Four-times magnification comes with more powerful sights too: the 5.5-22x50 and 5.5-22x56, the 8-32x56 and 12-42x56. Compact scopes for hunting (a 1-4x24 and a 2.5-10x24) round out the Nightforce line. Turret parallax dials adorn all NSX sights save two benchrest scopes, an 8-32x56 and a 12-42x56 that wear front-sleeve parallax rings. Precision Benchrest scopes feature illuminated reticles and resettable 1/8-minute windage and elevation dials. Because its scopes are popular with competitive and tactical shooters, Nightforce catalogs a line of accessories specific to those applications – from rings in four sizes to mil-radian knobs for NXS scopes so you can click in mils (.1 mil per click, 5 per revolution). Titanium inserts in ring bases, and tapered rails to accommodate long-range shooting are custom touches. New for 2008 is a Zero-stop turret, with an elevation dial that can be set to return reliably to any of the 400 detents in its adjustment range. There's also a rail-mounted device to show shot angle. Nightforce scopes are priced from $1,215. Nightforceoptics.com

NIKON

The Monarch rifle-scope line has three new entries for 2008. The 8-32x50ED SF has 1/8-minute adjustments and a turret dial to refine focus and zero-out parallax – interchangeable turrets too, for a choice of knobs. It should excel in prairie dog towns. The 4-16x50SF is more versatile, a fine scope for long-range shooting at big game. Most practical for mobile hunters is the 2-8x32. It combines light weight (a little over 13 ounces) with a compact profile, practical power range. Besides a new laser range-finder for bowhunters, Nikon starts 2008 with a new top-end binocular. The EDG series (7x4, 8x42, 10x42, 8x32 and 10x32) has ED glass, open-bridge design and a locking diopter you adjust by pulling out the center focus knob. "The EDG is the best glass Nikon has ever offered," says marketing VP Jon LaCorte. Weights: 23 to 29 ounces.

Last year Nikon overhauled its flagship Monarch rifle-scope line, giving each sight a four-times power range and 4 inches of eye relief. From the 2.5-10x42 to the 6-24x50, all scopes have one-piece main tubes. Quarter-minute clicks are standard on the four hunting models, eighth-minute on the 5-20x44 and 6-24x50, which come with sunshades, target-style adjustments and a turret-mounted parallax knob (the latter also standard on 3-12x42 and 4-16x42 versions). The BDC reticle is available on all six. In addition, Nikon unveiled a Monarch X series with 30mm tubes. The 2.5-10x and 4-16x feature Nikoplex or mil dot reticles, both etched. The 2.5-10x is also available with an illuminated mil dot. A turret-mounted parallax knob is standard on Monarch X sights. The new IRT 4-12x42 scope incorporates a laser rangefinder that delivers 1-yard accuracy to 400 steps and registers reflective objects to 800. This 26-ounce scope provides continuous reads on moving game. A BDC reticle helps with holdover. Nikonsportoptics.com

Schmidt & Bender equips many tactical rifles with its superlative P/M sights. Note knobs, level.

PENTAX

Denver-based Pentax imports a useful array of sports optics. The DCF roof prism binoculars come in 8x and 10x magnification, with objectives of 32mm to 50mm (you'll also find a 12.5x50 and 8x25 and 10x25 compacts). DCFs offer phase-corrected prisms in aluminum and polycarbonate shells. PCF Porro prism glasses in 8x40, 10x50, 12x50 and 20x60 offer high-value alternatives, as do the less expensive XCF Porros in 8x40, 10x50, 12x50 and 16x50. New for 2008 is the 9x28 BCF LV roof-prism binocular. At only 13 ounces, it's an easy carry. If, like me, you hike in steep country, the 9x28 BCF LV should make your must-see list.

For the same reasons, I like the Lightseeker SL 3-9x32 rifle-scope. It has plenty of magnification but a low profile and a bigger exit pupil than you can use at 5x. It weighs just 12 ounces! The Gameseeker stable includes eight 1-inch variable models and 4x32 and 6x42 fixed-power sights. The Lightseeker 30 series pairs 30mm tubes with 3-10x40, 4-16x50, 6-24x50 and 8.5-32x50 optics. A Whitetails Unlimited line, 3-9x to 6.5-20x, serves the mid-price market. Pentaxsportoptics.com

SCHMIDT & BENDER

When you make the best, you needn't chase the new. That's my view, apparently shared by people at Schmidt & Bender. The German firm, 50 years old this year, is renowned for rifle-scopes of superlative quality. Rather than focus on SHOT Show announcements, it works constantly to up-grade its scopes with improved optics and innovations like Posicon adjustments that tell you the reticle position in relationship to its range of movement. Optically and cosmetically, a Schmidt & Bender will spoil you. The 6x42 in my rack has no peer as a long-range big game sight – unless it's the new 10x42 PM II. All S&B scopes except special 34mm Police/Marksman models feature 30mm tubes. The 3-12x was recently adopted by the U.S. Marine Corps for its 30- and 50-caliber sniper rifles. For American hunters, S&B is trotting out a new 1-inch variable scope, a 2.5-10x40 with second-plane reticle. Available the last half of 2008, this 16-ounce scope will list for about $1400. After half a century, and this year under new ownership within the family, Schmidt & Bender is growing exactly as fast as it deems consistent with building the very best rifle-scopes. Schmidt-bender.de or (the website of its U.S. importer) scopes@cyberportal.net

SHEPHERD

Shepherd scopes have two reticles, one in the front focal plane and one in the rear. So you get an aiming reticle that doesn't change size with power changes, coupled with a range-finding reticle that varies in dimension as you change power. Superimposed, they appear as one. The range-finding reticle comprises a series of circles. They're of decreasing diameter, top to bottom, to match target size as it diminishes with distance. To determine yardage, match a deer-size target with one of the circles (they subtend 18 inches at the specified ranges). A new 6-8x M556 is specially designed for AR-style rifles and varmint shooting. The Nebraska company also sells binoculars. Shepherdscopes.com

SIGHTRON

Sightron's imported rifle-scope stable includes the Big Sky series with 15 offerings, from fixed-power 4x and 6x glass to variables 16x at the top end. They're fully multi-coated. External lenses wear "Zact-7," a seven-layer coating to transmit the most light possible. They also get a hydrophobic wash to disperse rain. Adjustment dials are finger-friendly and resettable. Eye relief is a generous 3.8 inches. Retail prices start at $420. A recent addition under the Big Sky umbrella is a Dangerous Game 1.25-5x20 sight with over 6 inches of "clear tube" for mounting. The SII Big Sky line now has 4.5-14x40 and 6.5-20x50 listings. I like the dot-reticle option in these and in new 36x42 and 6-24x42 SII Big Sky target scopes. It's also available in the 5-20x42. A SIIISS Long Range 30mm series highlights 2008 offerings. Target knobs and turret-mounted parallax dials complement ExacTrack adjustments. Choose a 3.5-10x44 or 3.5-10x56 (illuminated reticle), a 6-24x50 or 8-32x56. Sightron has come up with a "ballistic" reticle with a couple of simple hash marks on the lower wire. Simple and effective. Called the Hunter Holdover, it's available on 3-9x42, 3-12x42 and 45.5-14x42 SIIs – also on the 3-9x40 SI. I'm pleased to see the Porro Prism design in new Sightron binoculars: 7x, 10x and 12x, all with 50mm objectives. There's also a new spotting scope kit, with a 20-60x63 scope, wide-angle 25x eyepiece and accessories. Sightron.com

SIMMONS

Simmons, Weaver and Redfield, now subsidiaries of telescope-maker Meade, have undergone an overhaul in the last few years. But delivery of the popular Simmons Master Series has been spotty in the face of strong demand. "The scopes are great values," says Sherry Kerr, who handles press relations. "And this year we're filling orders, not just taking them." At the top of the heap is the Aetec, in 2.8-10x44 and 4-14x44, the latter with turret-dial parallax adjustment. HydroShield lens coatings keep rain from ruining the view. ProHunter scopes, from 2-7x32 to 6-18x40, deliver a generous 4 1/4 inches of eye relief, with turret-mounted AO on 4-12x and 6-18x sights. ProDiamond and ProSport lines are modestly priced. Handgunners choose from 2x20, 4x32 and 2-6x32 scopes with up to 20 inches of eye relief. The Simmons Red Dot sight comes in 30mm and 42mm diameters, with five bright reticles. The company also imports binoculars, laser range-finders and spotting scopes (15-45x60 and 65, 20-60x77 and 80, 25-75x90). Simmonsoptics.com

SWAROVSKI

After introducing six-times magnification ranges in a new line of rifle-scopes last year, Swarovski has followed with a Ballistic Turret cleverly designed to hold several zero settings, determined via ballistics tables or by live firing. Once set, the elevation dial can be quickly returned to that color-coded spot on the dial, so you can aim where you want to hit. Ballistic Turret is an option on 1-inch 4-12x50 and 6-18x50 AV scopes. Another development for long-range enthusiasts is Swarovski's Ballistic Reticle, with a ladder of 10 hash marks on the six-o'clock wire. You match impact distances to hash marks on the company website. Tom Hogan, a technical specialist at the firm, tells me the BR reticle will be available in three AV scopes, plus the Z6 1.7-10 and 2-12x50. Other news at Swarovski: an "Easy to Clean" coating to become standard treatment on exterior glass. There's also a "Snap Shot Adapter" that mates almost any pocket-size digital camera with optical zoom to a binocular eyecup. "The adapter turns a binocular barrel into a camera lens," says Swarovski Marketing Manager Caroline McDonald. "You can shoot photos as through any telephoto lens." I'm still much impressed with last year's Z6 rifle-scopes, having used a 1.7-10x42 on a hunt. Bright, flat fields, razor-sharp images. Swarovskioptik.com

Swarovski's Z6 scopes offer six-times magnification. Here: a 1.7-10x42 on a Cooper M52 in .270.

TASCO

Arguably the leader in low-cost sports optics, Tasco has consolidated its lines of rifle-scopes and binoculars. There's a long-range emphasis in rifle-scopes, with four 6-24x variables (40, 42 and 44mm objective lenses). That series includes two 2.5-10x42s and a 10-40x50. All wear front-sleeve adjustable objectives. "World-Class" scopes comprise nine models, from a 1.5-4.5x32 to a 4-16x50 AO. The most affordable "Pronghorn" line offers 2.5x32, 4x32 and two 3-9x sights. Tasco also catalogs a 3-9x32 rimfire scope, a series of red dot sights and a reflex sight. Its binocular line, bigger now with the addition of a top-end 10x42 "Sierra" glass, encompasses full-size and compact models, roof- and Porro-prism profile. The spotting scope section features compact models of folded-beam design, plus 15-45x50 and 20-60x scopes with 60mm and 80mm objectives. Tasco.com

TRIJICON

Well-known in military circles courtesy of its ACOG (Advanced Combat Optical Gunsight), Trijicon now offers hunters more traditional options. AccuPoint scopes are illuminated by tritium and exposed fiber-optic filament – no batteries. This year AccuPoint come with plex and crosswire-and-dot reticles, as well as the super-fast delta. A couple of years ago I used an AccuPoint on a 45-70 Marlin M1895 to kill an elk in a Colorado thicket. The delta shone like a beacon. An adjustable cover lets you trim light from the fiber optic coil. Choose 1.25-4x24, 3-9x40 or 2.5-10x56. Also new this year: the Trijicon RX30, a compact, parallax-free 42mm reflex sight ideal for handguns and shotguns. Fiber optics and a battery-free tritium-phosphorus lamp light the reticle. A new ACOG joins it, a 4x32 for the civilian market, with an adjustable rail mount and a bullet drop compensator (to 800 meters). Trijicon.com

TRUGLO

Better known for its tritium and fiber optic sight inserts, TruGlo also catalogs a series of red-dot sights. They're waterproof, lightweight and compatible with any Weaver-style mount. They boast unlimited eye relief and an 11-station rheostat to control the brightness of the 5-minute dot. Multi-coated lenses and click-stop windage/elevation adjustments are standard; tube diameters range from 1 inch to 45mm. Choose 1x or 2x. New dual-color models feature four reticles, each of which can be illuminated in red or green. A reflex red-dot sight weighs less than 2 ounces and is ideal for handguns. Its 4-minute dot has automatic and manual brightness modes. TruGlo also fields two lines of conventional rifle-scopes. The XLE comes in 1.5-6x44, 3-9x44 and 3.5-10x50 configurations, the Infinity in 4-16x44 and 6-24, both with front-sleeve AO. There's also a 4x32 scope for rimfires and shotguns, and an illuminated series in 4x32, 1.5-5x32, 2-7x32 and 3-9x44. TruGlo continues to grow its list of luminescent iron sights and shotgun beads. Truglo.com

VORTEX

In rifle scopes, the first-rank Viper label covers six variables, 2-7x32 to 6.5-20x50. High-power models wear turret-mounted parallax adjustments and target knobs. Argon gas-filled to prevent fogging, these 1-inch sights have fully multi-coated lenses, fast-focus eyepieces and resettable windage and elevation dials. Less expensive Diamondback sights (1.75-5x32 to 4-12x40) also boast these features. For 2008 Vortex has announced a new entry-level Crossfire scope. It comprises 12 models (three illuminated) with fully multi-coated lenses. Prices start at just $100. Vortexoptics.com

WEAVER

I've long thought Weaver's K-series and Classic variables ranked among the best buys for hunters on a budget. They're rugged and sleek, with bright, sharp optics – more so now than when their forebears came off the line in Texas. Classic Extreme scopes appeared last year. "Take one on a hunt," urged Blake Anderson, who heads Weaver's marketing efforts. He joined me on the tundra, where a 1.5-4.5x helped me kill a black bear and two

The Trijicon AccuPoint has a sliding window that lets you adjust exposure of the fiber optic coil.

caribou. The Classic Extreme series are optically excellent, if not lightweight. The 1.5-4.5x24, 2.5-10x50 and 2.5-10x56 feature 30mm tubes, fast-focus eyepieces, an illuminated dot in plex and German #4 reticles. They have resettable windage and elevation dials, generous eye relief. The 2.5-10x models carry turret-mounted parallax dials. For targets and varmint shooting, Weaver T-series sights match much more expensive scopes. They come with extra oversized adjustment knobs, a sunshade and screw-in steel lens caps. Two T-24s announced a year ago feature 1/2-minute and 1/8-minute dots. Their target-style adjustments allow for fast changes of zero to compensate for wind and range. Dual-spring mechanisms ensure repeatability. The Weaver flagship series these days is the Grand Slam, 1.5-5x32 to 6-20x40. Classic K- and V- sights, and Classic Handgun scopes, complete the line. Bill Weaver's Depression-era 330 scope may seem primitive next to its progeny, but current scopes are made for the same purpose as the original – to provide ordinary shooters with extraordinary value in a dependable hunting scope. Weaveroptics.com

WILLIAMS

Eight decades after it appeared "on the range" in Davison Michigan, Williams Gunsight Company still produces what many hunters consider the best iron sights around. The alloys used in the Fool Proof and 5D receiver sights (alas, they no longer cost $5!) reduce weight without compromising strength. FP sights have micrometer adjustments and internal locks. You can equip them with target knobs. Target versions of the FP are available, with globe front sights, for competitive shooters. WGRS sights fit receiver dovetails and topside factory-tapped holes on many rifles. Williams also makes a variety of open rear sights and front sight beads and ramps. Some have been installed as factory equipment on sporting rifles. My first deer fell to a 303 SMLE with a Williams "African" rear sight I'd installed, with a gold bead on a Williams ramp up front. To accommodate handgunners and shotgunners, the firm now offers a line of fiber-optic sights and beads. Williams sells scope mounts, sling swivels, gun screws and gunsmithing tools – even its own muzzle brake. You'll also find other accessories, plus gunsmithing services, on the range. Williamsgunsight.com

XS SIGHT SYSTEMS

A few weeks ago as I write this, I shared a wild patch of Texas with Ashley Emerson, an avid rifle and pistol enthusiast who more than a decade ago developed a line of iron sights. I thought them among the best I'd ever used: simple, strong, clean-looking and compact. They seemed the perfect complement to slug guns, lever-action carbines and muzzleloaders. Since then, the company has changed its name a couple of times. Glory be, the sights are still available! In fact, the line has grown to include open sights for rifles and pistols. Ashley and I used them in Texas on steel plates and in a quest for big feral hogs. The big shallow V rear notch with white centerline is ideal for quick shots in thickets. Paired with a fat front bead, it's as fast on a revolver as on a Marlin lever gun. Receiver-sight options include ghost-ring models for most popular rifles. Tritium inserts in beads and open rear sights help in dim light. Now XS Sight Systems, the company Ashley Emerson started, fields an impressive line of sights for sporting arms. Xssights.com

ZEISS

Since its introduction a few years ago of the affordable but excellent line of Conquest rifle scopes, Zeiss has successfully courted American hunters. Last spring it unveiled a range-finding rifle-scope, the 3-12x56 Victory Diarange. At the 2008 SHOT Show, Zeiss announced another entry in the top-flight Victory series. New 8x45 and 10x45 T* RF binoculars feature a laser range-finding unit that requires no "third eye" emitter but delivers a more compact beam than the competition, increasing effective range. "We get reads to 1,300 yards on reflective targets," says Shannon Jackson, representing Zeiss. "They're accurate to within a yard out to 660." The ranging device responds to a single touch: press the right-hand button and the LED reticle lights up; release it, and yardage appears within one second. The light-emitting diode makes for an easier read than a liquid crystal display (LCD); and this one self-compensates for brightness. There's a scan mode for moving targets. And you can program this instrument with computer data to show recommended holdover for six standard trajectories. "This is a first-class binocular even without the electronics," declares Zeiss's Rich Moncrief. Also new for 2008: Rapid-Z reticles on selected Conquest and Victory rifle-scopes, Fluorite glass and LotuTec on the big Diavari 6-24x72. Zeiss.com

Weaver's new illuminated Classic Extreme scopes have 30mm tubes, top-flight optics.

HANDLOADING UPDATE

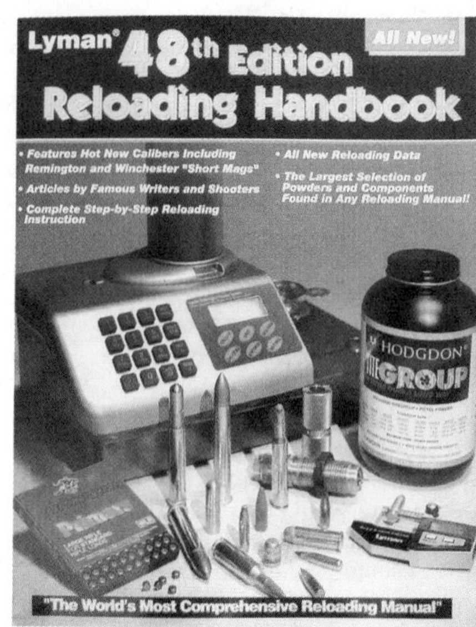

by Larry Sterett

When the current upward-spiraling ammunition prices, it is only natural that an increase in handloading activity would follow, resulting in an increase in new tools and components for handloaders. It has to at least a certain degree, as new calibers require new loading dies and new components, and there have been several new cartridges introduced.

FORSTER PRECISION PRODUCTS

Forster has upgraded their B-2 Co-Ax reloading press to a B-3 by redesigning the yoke to provide 1-1/2 inches more clearance. The B-3 press, which has three times more mechanical advantage than an ordinary "C" press, will now accommodate even the longest 7/8x14 loading dies.

The other new item at Forster Products is their Precision Plus Bump Neck Sizing Die. This die sizes the case neck and headspace length in one step. The result is better neck alignment with the case's center line. Precision Plus neck die sets are available for seventeen different cartridges from the 204 Ruger to the 30-06. Each set comes with three pre-selected bushings, and extra bushings may b e purchased. They're available in 0.001-inch increments, and some 93 bushings are currently available. (For example, Bush-244 has an inside diameter of 0.244-inch, while Bush-333 has an inside diameter of 0.333-inch.) These bushings are cryogenically treated and then cycled through a controlled heating process to improve dimensional stability, prolonged metal life, and increased wear resistance.

DILLON PRECISION PRODUCTS

Owners of a Dillon RL 500B, AT 500, or L 650 press who handload any larger capacity cases should be interested in the Dillon 'Belted Magnum' Powder System. This Powder System features a new, maximum-capacity, steel powder bar which can dispense more than 100 grains of extruded IMR powder. It will not work with standard powder measures, but it based on the Dillon SL 900 Shot Dispenser, meaning you need to purchase the entire system. How3ever, it has an integral drain, so it's easy to empty the hopper when there's a need to change powder types.

RL 550B users who crank out hundred-plus rounds of handgun cartridges (25-20 to 45 Winchester Magnum) can

ABOVE: Lyman Products publishes a number of valuable books for handloaders, such as this Reloading Handbook, 48th Edition.

Left to right: 30-06 Springfield, 308 Marlin Express, 6.8mm Remington SPC, 338 RCM, 300 RCM, Creedmoor, and 223 (5.56x45mm) Remington. Hornday has loading dies for all of these cartridges, including the new 6.5, 300 and 338.

increase their production rate 25 percent or more by adding an automatic case feeder. Available in 110 volt U.S. or 220 volt Euro models, this feeder streamlines the process by reducing hand movement.

Toolhead stands are now available for the RL 550B and XL 650 presses. These stands provide a place for storage of complete caliber conversions units: loading dies, powder measure, shellplate, locator buttons, etc. Powder-coated, these stands are available individually or in packages of three, along with reloading data labels. (Dillon stocks more than seven dozen Caliber Conversion Kits, from 30 Luger/30 Mauser to 45-70 Government, for their XL 650 press, and more than 150 Kits for the RL 550B. The RL 550B range from the 22 Remington Jet to the 460 Weatherby Magnum, and include the 50 Action Express and 500 Smith &Wesson, plus a number of wildcat cartridges.)

A couple of other handy Dillon products include the Toolholders, with or without wrenches, for the RL 550B and XL 1650 presses, and the Bench Wrench. The Toolholders bolt onto the respective presses, and hold all the needed wrenches for that tool in one location. The Bench Wrench fits any 1-inch die lock ring, and rings are available to replace those difficult-to-loosen lock rings found on some reloading dies. The opposite end of the new wrench is a 7/16" box-end for adjusting the powder bar on any Dillon Powder Measure.

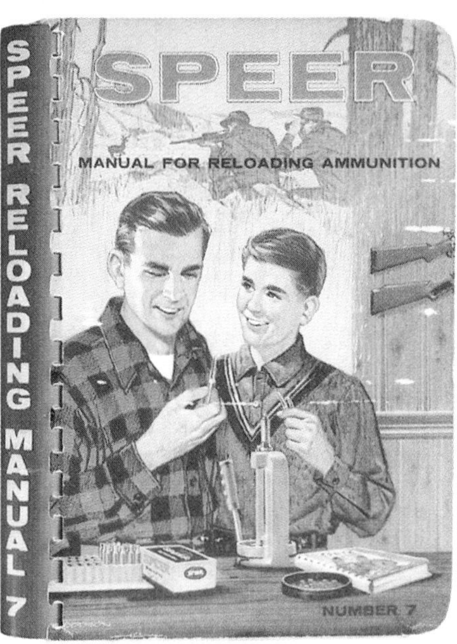

Data from older reloading manuals or handbooks can be useful, especially for cartridges no longer listed in current manuals. However, the data is useable only if the powders suggested are still in production. The *Ideal Handbook No. 34* is from 1942, and features data on such cartridges as the 22-3000 Lovell, 22-3000 2R Lovell, 22 Niedner Magnum, 22-4000 Sedgley, 25 Krag, 275 H & H Magnum, 303 Savage, 401 Winchester, and the 45-90 Winchester. It also features a few shotshell loads and many interesting articles. The Speer *Reloading Manual No.7* dates from 1966. It features more than a dozen articles, plus loading data on such new (in that era) cartridges as the 256 Winchester, 6.5mm and 350 Remington Magnums, and the 221 Remington Fireball. Other information is these older manuals is also useful.

RCBS

RCBS celebrated its 65th anniversary in 2008 and offered customers the option of purchasing some 3000+ RCBS products on-line through the RCBS.com website. Among the new RCBS products is an Auto Index Upgrade Kit for the Pro2000 Manual Progressive Press. The Kit converts any Pro2000 Manual to auto-indexing. The changeover process is quick and simple, and the APS priming system and other features of the Pro2000 are retained.

With the increasing popularity in shooting and reloading the 50 BMG cartridge, has come the need for suitable case trimmers. RCBS has a new High Capacity Case Trimmer Kit which will handle not only the 50 BMG case, but the 416 Barrett, and other big bore cases. It comes with .408, .416, and .500 pilots.

Several cartridges have been added to the RCBS line of reloading dies. In the Gold Medal Match line, which features a micrometer seating die thimble, the 17 Remington Fireball, 6.5x47 Lapua, 260 Remington, and 280 Remington have been added. This brings the number of different cartridges in this particular line to 45. Other new die sets include the 17 Remington Fireball, 308 Marlin Express, and 375 Ruger to Group A of the Standard die sets. The 370 SAKO/9.3x66 has been added to Group D, and four cartridges—40-60 Winchester, 45-60 Winchester, 45-75 Winchester, and 56-50 Spencer—have been added to the Legacy Series of die sets. (The Legacy Series of die sets is now available for fourteen of the old blackpowder cartridges, from the 38-55 Winchester to the 56-50 Spencer. It includes six of the Sharps Straight cartridges, from the 40-70 to the 50-90 Sharps Straight.) For big-bore shooters, full-length die sets, neck sizers and trim dies are now available for the 416 Barrett cartridge. These 416 dies are 1-1/2x12 dies and are designed for use in the AmmoMaster-2 or AmmoMaster Single Stage presses. (For reloaders of the 50 BMG cartridge three separate seating plug assemblies are available to seat the 50 BMG Speer and Hornady A-Max bullets.)

By the time you read this, RCBS will probably have reloading dies available for the three new cartridges, the 300 and 338 Ruger, and the 6.5.mm Creed introduced by Hornady and Sturm, Ruger. They may even have dies for the 450 Bushmaster cartridge by now.

Handloaders churning out large quantities of cartridges, and who do not like to trim cases, should check out the RCBS X-Dies. Trim the case once, then never again. The X-sizer die eliminates the need for repeat trimming, provided the case has initially been trimmed to 0.020-inch off the maximum case length. Once standardized, the special X-Die mandrel and die neck wall prevent the case neck from lengthening beyond the maximum length. (X-Dies are currently available for 39 different bottleneck cartridges, from the 204 Ruger to the 375 Remington Ultra Mag.)

RCBS will no longer produce custom bullet moulds, or one-of-a-kind (wildcat) custom loading dies. The firm still offers approximately 650 special order die sets and 350 case-forming die sets in their special order catalog. Plus, they have more than a thousand other cartridges not listed in the special order catalog for which they can produce reloading dies and/or forming die sets. For information on availability, email rcbs.tech@atk.com or call 1-800-533-5000. Such orders must be paid in advance in U.S. funds, are not subject to cancellation or return, and may take from four to six weeks for delivery.

WILLIAMS GUN SIGHT CO., INC

Williams is not usually thought of as being connected with handloading equipment. Even so, this Michigan firm has one item—Primer Pocket Peener—which can be useful to shotshell reloaders. Modern shotshell hulls can be reloaded four or five time more than could the older paper hulls. However, the primer pocket sometimes enlarges, becoming too loose to retain the new primer. The PPP will correct this condition. Place the peener through the primer pocket of the offending hull, and insert in the resizing block. A light tap on the peener with a hammer will bring the pocket back to the correct size to retain the new primer, and permit further reloading of the hull.

Good equipment and components can produce good reloads, provided the handloader follows the data provided in an up-to-date reloading guide or manual. Most of the powder companies provide 'comp' guides for the more popular cartridges, in addition to the book-size manuals they sell. (The 'comp' guides are usually updated every year or two, while the manuals often appear about every four or five years.) As this is written, the latest *VihtaVuori Reloading Guide* is the 68-page Edition 6. It features data for rifle cartridges from the 22 Hornet to the 50 Browning, and handgun data from the 7mm T/C-U to the 500 Smith & Wesson. (Five each of the cartridges feature revised data from the previous edition.) Data is included for five of the most popular Cowboy Action Shooting cartridges. (Some cartridges for which reloading data may not be available elsewhere include the 6.5mm Grendel, 300 Lapua Magnum, 9.3x66 SAKO, 9x21, and 38 Super Lapua. Another feature of this guide is the Burning Rate Chart located inside the front cover. This handy chart lists the approximate burning rate, from fast burning to slow burning, for eleven brands of current canister powders.

The 296-page hardbound 4th edition of the regular *VihtaVuori Reloading Manual* is now available. Divided into ten sections, it has pages at the end for recording personal reloading data. As with all such manuals, it covers the products of the said company–in this instance, VihtaVuori powder–along with a bit of history, a thorough discussion of handloading components: cases, primers, powders, and bullets–and the handloading process. Chapters seven and eight are devoted to loading data for rifle and handgun cartridges, while the final two cover ballistics and conversion units. The 53 rifle cartridges for which data is provided range from the 22 Hornet tp the 50 Browning, and include a few for which data is not always readily available, such as the 6.5x47 Lapua, 7.5x55 Swiss, 300 Lapua Magnum, and the 9.3x66 SAKO. (None of the factory and/or wildcat cartridges, such as the 6.5x53R, 8.2x53R or 9.5x53R, are included.) Each cartridge covered includes a dimensioned drawing, brief specs, such as the country of origin, year of introduction, maximum case and cartridge lengths, and a brief history. (A warning appears under the 22 PPC-USA data stating: Never chamber a 22 PPC-USA cartridge in a 22 PPC rifle. The outside neck diameter of the 22 PPC-USA case is considerably larger than that of the 22 PPC. This can prevent easy bullet release on firing leading to excessive chamber pressures that may in turn lead to…injury.")

The handgun data section provides loading information for 26 cartridges, from the 7mm T/C-U to the 500 S & W Magnum. Format is the same as for the rifle cartridges. A couple of lesser-known handgun cartridges for which data is provided include the 7mm GJW and the 38 Super Lapua. The 7mm GJW is based on the 5.6x50mm Magnum case, while the 38 Super Lapua is a rimless 38 Super with a slightly modified head. This cartridge was designed for IPSC "race gun" competition, and is not CIP- or SAAMI-supported. (Loads for the 38 Super Lapua do not exceed 43,500 psi (250 Mpa), while loads for the 38 Super do not exceed 33,350 psi (230 Mpa).

Chapter 2 features reports on big-game hunting, Cowboy Action Shooting, and NRA competition shooting. The big-game article dealt mainly with the 7.62x53R and 9.3.x62mm cartridges for hunting moose. When loaded with a Lapua E314 jacketed 174-grain flat nose bullet the 7.62x53R cartridge is apparently a decent short range moose cartridge, if 180 dead moose is an indication. Even more interesting was the custom-built bullpup rifle based on an old M91 Mosin-Nagant.

Handloaders need to make their measurements—powder, case length, overall cartridge length, bullet diameter, flash-hole size, etc.—with care. This requires good measuring equipment, and the L.S. Starrett Company is a source for such. Ask your Starrett dealer (or go to www.starrett.com) for a copy of the Starrett booklet, *Precision Measuring Tools for Ammunition Reloading and Gunsmiths*.

BARNES BULLETS

Barnes has several new bullets in their line this year, plus the fourth edition of the *Barnes Reloading Manual* is now

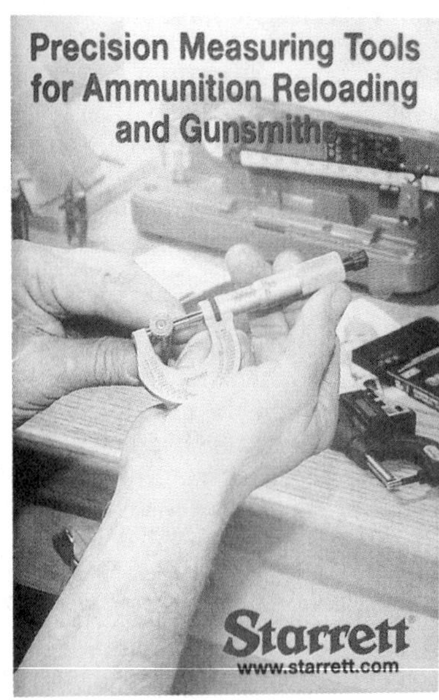

Reliable reloading data, such as this *VihtaVuori Reloading Guide No. 6*, and precision measuring tools, such as the L. S. Starrett calipers and micrometers, help contribute to the production of more accurate handloads.

available. This latest manual features extensive loading data for the Barnes TSX (Triple-Shock X) and Maximum-Range X (MRX) bullets, along with data for some of the "big bore" rifles, including the 470, 500, and 577 Nitro Express, and the 505 Gibbs. (Barnes naturally produces bullets for these cartridges.) Loading data for most rifle cartridges has been expanded, along with data for many handgun cartridges, such as the 45 GAP, and even recommended loads for Barnes Expander MZ, long-range Spit-Fire MZ and TMZ muzzleloader bullets.

U.S. handloaders and shooters can obtain a free copy of the new ($15.99 value) Barnes "Bullet Myths Busted" DVD by visiting www.barnesbullets.com and requesting one. (There's a $7.50 shipping and handling fee for those residing outside the U.S.) This DVD explains why some hunting bullets are more deadly than others, and tackles popular misconceptions about bullet performance.

NEWLON PRECISION

Designed a wildcat cartridge? If you have the equipment and ability to chamber your own barrel and loading dies, a source for die blanks is Newlon Precision (2465 Coachman Rd., Dept. GD, Mariposa, CA 95338, or newlon@sti.net). Newlon has 17-4PH stainless steel die blanks with pilot hole sizes from 17 to 338-caliber. The dies use standard 3/8x12 Hornady, Redding, or Wilson bushings.

K & M SERVICES

Anyone handloading for a number of different rifle cartridges is going to have to do some case neck turning eventually. K & M Services (5430 Salmon Run Rd., Dept. GD, Dover, PA) has a Micro Adjustable Neck Turner which will accept a dial indicator, and a separate part called a 'pilot jack' is available. (The K&M cutter adjustment is a fine .0022-in. per turn.) Standard tool steel pilots are available in 17, 19, 20, 22, 6mm, 25, 6.5mm, 270, 7mm, 30, 338, and 50 BMG calibers. Fluted carbide pilots are available in the same, except for the 19 caliber. K & M has a number of other products available.

HARRELL'S PRECISION

Harrell's Precision (5756 Hickory Drive, Dept. GD, Salem VA 24153 or www.harrellsprec.com) produces a couple of portable loading presses for those handloaders with a desire to load at the range. The Compact Press has a built-in C-clamp, and can be used to resize. Three sizes--PPC, 308, and Mag--of this simple, rugged press are available. A second press is the Combo, which can be used to resize up to 30-06 length cases, plus the short magnums. It comes with a removable heavy-duty C-clamp, and features two rams—one for resizing and one for seating bullets using Wilson Straight Line dies.

LYMAN PRODUCTS CORPORATION

Lyman has several new items for handloaders, including an updated E-Zee Case Length Gauge II. This latest gauge provides an easy (E-Zee) way to check the case length of more than 70 popular handgun and rifle cases. Among the newest cartridges featured are the 204 Ruger, 45 GAP, Winchester's short magnums, and the 500 Smith & Wesson. Even the 416 Rigby is featured.

Owners of one of the original Lyman Digital Powder Systems, either the DPS I or DPS II, can now upgrade to the high-speed performance of the DPS 3. The DPS Speed Upgrade Kit retails for less than three sawbucks, and installs in seconds without tools. For few cents more there's also a 1200 DPS Digital Reloaders Log and PC Interface, which allows a handloader to transfer memory directly from a computer to a DPS system. It stores thousands of loads in standard reloading manual format, with sections provided for comments.

Not exactly new, the Lyman 4500 Lube Sizer for cast lead bullets is one of the few such tools available for handloaders. It features a solid cast frame, with or without built-in heating element (115v or 230v). A new, longer ball knob handle provides increased leverage for sizing and lubing larger bullets, and the 4500 comes with a gascheck seater and a complimentary tube of bullet lube. (Lyman has additional lube available in five varieties, including Alox, Super Moly, and Orange Magic Premium.) Currently, there are sixty sizing dies available for the 4500 in sizes from 0.224- to 0.512-inch, while the top punches depend on the cast bullet mould number to fit the bullet nose shape correctly.

Shotshell reloaders have not been forgotten. The 230-page softbound 5th edition of the *Shotshell Reloading Handbook* is the most up-to-date volume on the subject available. It provides loading data for all shotshells from the .410-bore to the 10 gauge, and for most of the popular brands of hulls, along with lots of other pertinent information. Lyman has four other vol-

Lyman's 1200 DPS Speed Upgrade Kit makes the original DPS (Digital Powder System) even better, and faster.

umes useful to handloaders, *Cast Bullet Handbook, 3rd Edition, Guide to Big Game Cartridges & Rifles, Pistol & Revolver Handbook, 3rd Edition*, and the *Reloading Handbook, 48th Edition*. These large softbound volumes have a great deal of useful information, and while the first mentioned does not have much loading data, it does provide dimensioned drawings of rifle cartridges from the 243 Winchester to the 500 A-Square, including the 470 Nitro Express and the 475 No.2.

WESTERN POWDERS

Western Powders has two new slim load guides: a 16-page 3.2.2 edition for Accurate Powders, and a 12-page 4.2 edition for Ramshot Powders. Both guides feature data for eight new cartridges, including the 5.7x28mm FN, 20 Tactical, 20 Vartarg, 20 Vartarg Turbo, 20 PPC, 20 BR, 6.5mm Grendel and the 338 Federal. Not all the same cartridges are covered in both guides. The Ramshot guide features Cowboy Action loads for four cartridges, while the Accurate guide does not. The Accurate guide has a couple of loads for the 458 Lott, a cartridge that isn't listed in the Ramshot guide. The Accurate guide includes more shotshell loads than does the Ramshot guide. See your dealer for copies of both guides.

QUALITY CARTRIDGE

Handloaders, if they reload for a number of different calibers, always seem to be looking for a source of brass for an obsolete or wildcat cartridge. (Brass for wildcats is often easier to locate than brass for obsolete cartridges.) A firm which can supply full box quantities of empty brass, or loaded ammunition, for nearly 250 different cartridges of the non-factory variety is Quality Cartridge (P.O. Box 445, Dept. GD, Hollywood, MD 20636). The firm has been in business for more than a decade, and has cartridges ranging from the 17 OTTR to the 550 Magnum, in boxes of 20 or 50, depending on the case. Currently, a box of 20 empty cases ranges in price from around $32.00 to $86.00, with the average being around $40.00+, plus shipping. Loaded ammunition costs more. (The firm will also produce custom headstamped cases, and design and develop wildcats if anyone is interested.)

Quality Cartridge doesn't have brass for every cartridge ever manufactured, just many.

For example, brass is available for the 240 and 244 Holland & Holland Magnums, 242 Vickers, 275 Holland & Holland Magnum, and the 333 Jeffery cartridges. They do not currently have brass for the 26 BSA, 280 Jeffery 280 Ross, 33 BSA or 400 BSA. They have brass for the 256 Newton, but not for the 30 or 35 Newton cartridges. Still, 250 cartridges cover a lot of calibers if you need new brass.

REDDING RELOADING EQUIPMENT

Redding has a host of new products for handloaders, including loading die sets for the 300 RCM, 338 RCM and 327 Federal Magnum. (Redding will still produce custom dies. However, if they have not produced the die in the past, there's a "one-time engineering and set-up charge" of $50 to cover the cost of researching the tooling, making shop drawings, etc. If the required dies can be produced with existing tooling, there will be no tooling charge. If some tooling must be done, there will be a tooling fee, which may be as little as $50.00, or as much as $300 if new reamers are required.)

Primer pockets, flashholes, and case necks are all essential features of a cartridge case, particularly if the shooter is interested in producing the most accurate handloads possible. Redding has new flash hole deburring tools, primer pocket uniformers, and a new case neck gauge. There are two deburrers, a Universal Tool that will handle all cases from .22 to .338, with standard 0.080-inch flash holes, and the Small, which is for 17- and 20-caliber cases, with .060-inch flashholes. Both tools use pilot stops, one of which is supplied with each tool, with other pilots being available in sizes from 17 to 338 caliber. The primer pocket uniformers are available in two sizes, one for larger primer pockets and one for small primer pockets. The depth of the cut is to SAAMI specs, and is controlled by a ground shoulder which will not change. The large primer pocket uniformer is for large primer pockets on rifle cases only, and should *NOT* be used on Large Pistol primer pockets. The Small Rifle primer pocket uniformer is dimensionally correct for Small Rifle and Small Pistol primer pockets.

The Redding Case Neck Gage comes with a dial indicator accurate to 0.001-inch, two mandrels to permit measurements of all case sizes from 22 to 338 caliber, plus two pilots, 22 and 30 caliber. It can be mounted directly onto the loading bench, or clamped in place.

Two other useful items from Redding for handloaders include a DVD, *Advanced Reloading – Beyond the Basics*, and Imperial Application Media. The Media consists of small ceramic spheres charged with Imperial Dry Neck Lube. It's housed in a small canister into which the case necks, from 17 caliber up, can be dipped. Redding still carries the Imperial Dry Neck Lube and Sizing Die Was, plus an Action Wax.

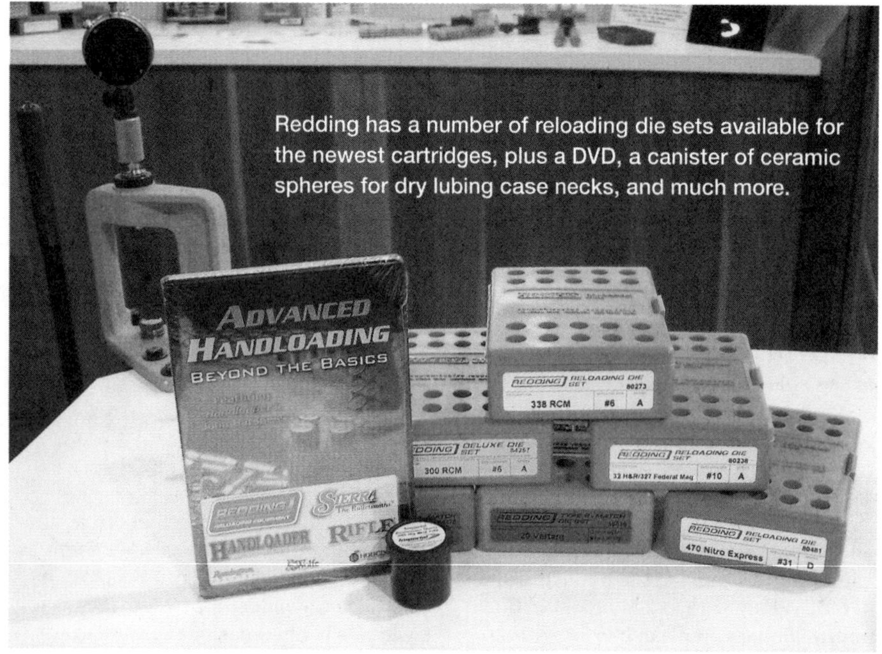

Redding has a number of reloading die sets available for the newest cartridges, plus a DVD, a canister of ceramic spheres for dry lubing case necks, and much more.

SINCLAIR INTERNATIONAL

Sinclair International has a great new Custom Press. Machined from a solid billet of aluminum, it features no sharp corners, a 1-inch ram with snap-in shellholder slot, and a 2 1/2-inch throat opening to accept up to 308-size cases for resizing. The linkage is covered—no bolts, nuts, or clips exposed—the primer exit is out the bottom, and there's an optional mounting plate available for the shooter with a preference for quick take-down and storage, or who likes to take the press to the range.

Sinclair handles a wide array of handloading equipment, in addition to the items they manufacture. For those benchrest shooters with a yen for straight-line hand dies there's an Arbor Press available separately, or as part of a kit featuring stainless steel Wilson micrometer bullet seaters and neck sizing dies. The press is constructed with a stainless steel post and handle, and utilizes a ratchet height adjustment. The Wilson neck sizing dies are available in nine calibers from the 22 PPC to the 308 Winchester, with the seating dies corresponding.

UNIQUE TEC, INC.

The Arizona firm of Unique Tec, Inc. (www.uniquetek.com) has a high-strength 14-inch clear polycarbonate powder measure tube that will double the capacity of a Dillon Powder Measure. It comes with a powder baffle, but uses the original Dillon Powder Measure lid. If you own a Dillon measure, this Unique Tec tube will just replace the original powder tube.

HUNTINGTON RELOADING SUPPLIES

Huntington (www.huntingtons.com) in Oroville, CA, not only has reloading dies for thousands of different cartridges, but is another source for hard-to-find brass, such as cases for the 22 Remington Jet, 7x61mm Sharpe & Hart, and 303 Savage. The firm stocks at least ten different brands of empty brass cases, from BELL to Winchester.

Handloaders purchasing a Hornady Lock-n-Load AP press outfit could be eligible for a 'free' 500 bullets, the number of loaded rounds the AP is capable of churning out per hour.

HORNADY MFG. CO.

Hornady Mfg. Co., in Grand Island, NE has a host of new bullets, brass cases, and cartridges, plus loading equipment, including a One Shot Case Sizing Wax. (This wax is like the hair cream of yesteryear, "A little dab will do 'ya.") New Dimension die sets are available for five new cartridges, including the 17 Remington Fireball, 6.5mm Creedmoor, 30 T/C, and 300 and 338 RCM. (Hornady now loads ammunition for the 450 Nitro Express 3 1/4-inch, and loading dies may be available by the time you read this.)

Hornady will produce custom-made dies for any cartridge—any time! These are available in Custom-Grade or Match-Grade New Dimension configurations. All that's needed, besides money, is a chamber cast, three fired cases, or a chamber reamer drawing. Delivery time is six to eight weeks, and payment is due at the time of order. A Custom-Grade 2-die set for a case length of 2.5 inches or less will cost $120, while a 3-die set will cost $145, and Match-Grade dies go for $161, while a 4-die set for handgun cartridges is $200 as this is written. Radius shoulder dies cost more, as do dies for longer cases, and beyond 3.6 inches the cost is on a quote basis. Cases with a diameter over 0.585-inch are also on a quote basis, as there's a $50 per die charge for non-standard bullet diameters. All prices are based on standard 7/8x14 die stock.

Hornady will also produce forming dies and, in addition, has a hydraulic forming die kit. Prices depend on the case length, etc.

Handloading the 50 BMG cartridge requires a hefty amount of powder and regular measures empty in a hurry. Hornady has a special L-N-L measure for the big 50, which features an oversized hopper tube, and a metering capacity of up to 265 grains at a time. There is also a High Capacity Conversion Kit for regular L-N-L measures. It includes an extended hopper tube, a clear drop tube, and two metering units.

The 7th edition of the *Hornady Handbook of Cartridge Reloading* is one of the largest currently available to handloaders. Well over three-quarters of the *Handbook's* 992 pages are filled with loading data for 74 handgun and 142 rifle cartridges. The handgun cartridges range from the 22 Remington Jet to the 500 Smith & Wesson, but do not include the 5.7x28mm, 45 GAP, or the new 327 Federal cartridges. As with all such handbooks, it's impossible to keep up with the latest, as it takes time to develop loads after a new cartridge is introduced. The rifle section features loads for cartridges from the 17 Mach I to the 50 BMG, with a few wildcats and some oldies included. If a handloader requires data for the 5.6x50mm Magnum, the 219 Zipper, 5.6x57mm RWS, 5.6x52R (22 Savage High Power), 6.5x52mm Carcano, 7x61mm Sharpe & Hart, or 376 Steyr, it's here. Data for Hornady's newest cartridges, the 300 and 338 RCM and 6.5mm Creedmoor, is not included, as the cartridges were introduced after the handbook was published.

Each cartridge for which data is provided includes a dimensioned drawing, along with specs such as the bullet diameter, maximum case and cartridge length, etc., and a short history. An illustration is provided of each of the Hornady bullets for which loading data is listed, along the ballistic coefficient, sectional density, length of loaded cartridge, powders and charge, with the maximum loads shown in red-colored boxes. In addition to such features as a history of the Hornady firm, the step-by-step basics of reloading, ballistics elements, and special tips, this handbook has an excellent illustrated glossary, followed by a baker's dozen pages for notes.

LEE PRECISION, INC.

Lee Precision, Inc. is celebrating 50 years in the business with a new Breech Lock Challenger loading press featuring a super strong "O" style frame design, all steel linkage, and an adjustable-length lever with hardwood ball grip. It has the Breech Lock Quick Change Die System that permits changing dies with a twist of the wrist. The press comes with three Breech Lock bushings, and extra bushings are available in pairs for less than a sawbuck. For new handloaders, Lee has a 50th Anniversary Kit and a Breech Lock Challenger Kit, both of which feature one of the new presses, a powder measure, safety scale, and lots of other goodies. (Lee still manufactures the Classic Lee Loader, but it's packaged in plastic, not cardboard. Available for 14 rifle cartridges from the

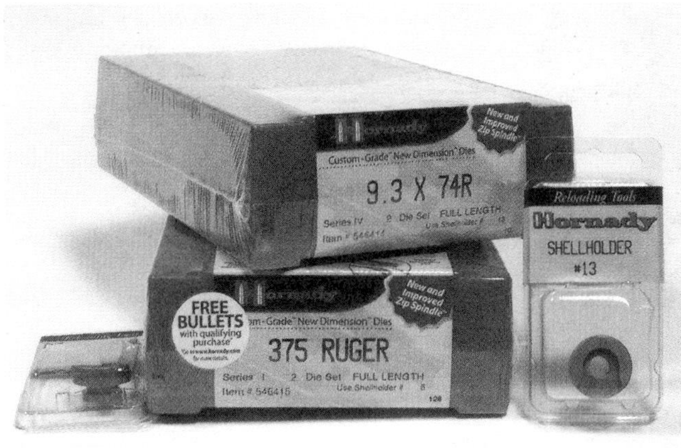

Purchasers of Hornady reloading dies should check with their dealer. They may receive some free bullets for a startup.

Hodgdon's annual *Reloading Manual* is as up-to-date as any such manual can be. It doesn't have the drawings the larger book-size manuals have, but the actual loading data is current. The latest manual has loads for the 17 Remington Fireball, 308 Marlin Express, and the 375 Ruger cartridges, plus loads for more than 140 rifle cartridges and 80-plus handgun cartridges.

22 Hornet to the 45-70 Government, and six handgun cartridges from the 9mm Luger to the 45 Colt, plus two limited production sizes, 44 Special and 225 Winchester, it may be a bit slow, but it produces excellent ammunition.)

Lee Precision has had factory crimp dies for rifle and straight-wall handgun cartridges for years, and taper crimp dies for similar handgun cartridges. Now there's a factory crimp die for five bottleneck pistol cartridges, 30 Luger, 30 Mauser/7.62 Tokarov, 357 SIG, and 400 Cor-Bon.

One of the handiest data manuals available for handloaders, and one of the most up-to-date, is *Hodgdon's Annual Manual.* The latest edition of this 178-page magazine-size manual contains several feature articles, plus loading data for more than 80 handgun cartridges from the 17 Bumble Bee to the 500 Smith & Wesson Magnum. There's data for more than 140 rifle cartridges from the 17 Ackley Hornet to the 50 BMG, and including the 17 Remington Fireball, 30 Marlin Express, and 375 Ruger. If you load for a 470 Nitro Express, or a 500 Cyrus, you'll find a few suggested loads for them also.

The Auto-Mate from MEC can turn a manually-operated MEC 8567 Grabber or 9000 Series progressive shotshell pressd into an electrically-opreated loading machine, and it's easy to convert.

MAYVILLE ENGINEERING (MEC)

When it comes to reloading shotshells, there are probably more MEC loaders being used than any other brand. Mayville Engineering has just made it easier and faster to use your MEC progressive with the introduction of the Auto-Mate. With your progressive MED 8567 Grabber, or 9000 Series press bolted onto the top of the Auto-Mate, the operating arm connected, the hoppers filled, and wads at hand, you're about ready. Plus in the Auto-Mate, check everything, turn it on, and start loading. It should have happed years ago, although there is a hydraulic conversion unit for the Grabber (NOT for 600, 650, or 900G presses).

AMERICAN PIONEER POWDER

Not exactly handloading in the usual sense of the term, muzzleloading is the original handloading, and American Pioneer Powder (www.americanpioneerpowder.com) has a new product, the Gold Super Sticks. These Super Sticks provide 150-grain performance in .50-caliber muzzleloader rifles. Using 250- and 300-grain bullets, Jim Shockey was able to obtain muzzle velocities in the 1,900-2,000 fps+ range. The sticks burn cleanly and consistently, and are definitely handier to load than loose powder.

OLD WESTERN SCROUNGER

The Old Western Scrounger has celebrated 30 years in the business, and is another source for obsolete ammunition and cases. The firm did, and may still, have a loading press and dies for loading 50 BMG and 20mm cartridges with ease.

Handloading equipment and components continue to be introduced each year. New cartridges require new loading dies, new load development and manuls, new components, and possibly new shell holders, trim dies, etc. The products mentioned in this report do not cover everything available, but hopefully the major and newest products to make handloading fun, and worthwhile.

The Guns of Europe
THE NEW WALTHER PPS
Flat, Neat & Attractive

by Raymond Caranta

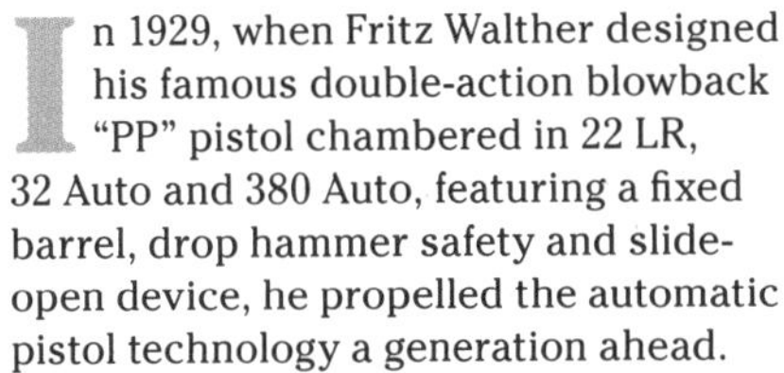

In 1929, when Fritz Walther designed his famous double-action blowback "PP" pistol chambered in 22 LR, 32 Auto and 380 Auto, featuring a fixed barrel, drop hammer safety and slide-open device, he propelled the automatic pistol technology a generation ahead.

So much so, that by 1974 there was a suddenly perceived lack of innovative design in Europe when the German police shifted to the 9mm Luger cartridge.

Ten years later (1984), when the 9mm Luger seemed a universal proposition, and many American police agencies adopted it up until 1990, when their national industry developed the 40 SW cartridge, with its heavier bullet and higher terminal energy.

THE WALTHER PPK

Two years after the introduction of the original "PP" (for *Polizeï Pistole*), it was completed by a more compact version with similar improvements in the same popular chamberings, the seven-shot "PPK" (*Polizeï Pistole Kriminal*), specifically intended for plainclothes use (6.18 inches long, 4.21 inches high and 1 inch thick – 22.9-oz loaded weight).

This sophisticated pistol readily competed on the international market with the Belgian Browning 1910 and soon achieved worldwide success, which since 1938, created strong competition from Mauser and J.P. Sauer, in Germany.

ABOVE: The Walther PPS (6-shot) with a 7-shot Manurhin PPK, left view.

After World War II, similar designs were developed in Italy, Argentina, China, Hungary, Czech Republic and Spain. However, even if the new-style German 9mm Luger police models designed in accordance with the latest technical specifications, progressively superseded the older Walther PPs in service, the smaller PPK remained without any equivalent on the market, until the introduction of the Glock 26 in 1995.

THE MODERN PPK COMPETITORS

This compact 10-shot 9mm Glock pistol (6.4 inches long, 4.17 inches high and 1.21 inches thick; empty weight – 22.1 oz. / loaded – 26.4 oz.) was scarcely bigger than the slim "PPK", but it could deliver – without reloading – three more 9mm rounds, the new international standard ammunition (9mm muzzle energy: 360 foot-pounds vs. 144 foot-pounds in 32 ACP) at an additional weight of 3.5 ounces.

Other mini-9mm Luger automatics followed, such as the Kel-Tec P11 (1995), Truvelo ADP (1997 - now "Wilson" since 2006), Taurus Millennium (1998), Smith & Wesson CS9 (1999), Standard (1999), Kahr PM9 and Rohrbaugh (2002), Springfield Armory XD Sub-Compact (2003), CZ 2075 Rami (2004) and, more recently, in 2007, Smith & Wesson M&P9 Compact, Kel-Tec PF9 and Beretta PX4 Storm Sub-Compact.

LEFT: Field-stripping of Walther PPS.

The Walther "PPS First Edition" in its case, with the two 7- and 8-shot spare magazines.

The first Walther reaction came in 2001, with their 10-shot 9mm P99 Compact (6.61 inches long, 4.33 inches high and 1.26 inches thick; empty weight - 21oz. / loaded - 25.35 oz.), made in the U.S.A. under license and, since 2004, in Germany.

However, if we carefully compare all these PPK competitors, two classes of them can be identified:

1. Those heavier (than the PPK) when loaded, such as the ADP (24.7 oz.), Smith & Wesson CS9 (23.7-oz.; a trifle), Standard (25.57-oz.), Springfield Armory XD Sub-Compact (24.78-oz.), Walther P99 Compact (25.35-oz.), Glock 26 (26.4-oz.), Smith & Wesson M&P9 Compact (30.8-oz.), CZ Rami (29-oz.) and Beretta PX4 Storm Sub-Compact, all having a 10-round (or more) magazine capacity, with the exception of the Smith & Wesson CS9 and Taurus Millennium (7-shot, like the 32 Auto PPK). Also, the ADP, Smith & Wesson CS9 and M&P9 Compact, Glock 26, Walther P99 Compact, Beretta PX4 Storm Sub-Compact and CZ Rami are more or less thicker than the old PPK.
2. Those lighter than the all-steel 32 Auto PPK, such as the Kel-Tec P11 (21.42-oz. with 10 shots) and PF-9 (17.83-oz. with 7 shots), Kahr PM9 (18.46-oz. with 6 shots) and Rohrbaugh R-9 (16-oz. with 6 shots). In this connection, note that some rare 32 Auto PPK's were available with light alloy receivers, weighing only 18.64-oz. loaded, and that the Kel-Tec P11 and PF-9, Kahr PM9 and Rohrbaugh R-9 are all smaller than the PPK.

THE NEW WALTHER PPS

Therefore, recognizing the gap in their line of compact 9mm police pistols, Walther introduced at the March, 2007 IWA Show a new PPS (for *Police Pistol Slim*) having a 1-inch thickness, like the original PPK, and weighing only 0.71-oz. more empty, with the same dimensions, but chambered in 9mm Luger with single-stack magazines having 6-shot (4.37-inch pistol height), 7-shot (4.88-inch height) and 8-shot (5. 27-inch height) capacities.

Our sample bears the serial number "048" in the limited "First Edition" production batch, released in October 2007.

DESCRIPTION

The Walther PPS is a hammerless short recoil tilting barrel automatic, featuring a very flat gray-veined polymer receiver and a square-shaped dull black slide. The striker mechanism is of the short stroke DAO type with automatic trigger safety. The trigger guard opening is quite long, to allow fast shooting with gloves.

The hold-open device is external, on the left side, and the tilting ambidextrous magazine catch matches the trigger guard contour. When operated, it ejects the magazine.

While the short 6-shot magazine is flush with the grip base, the longer 7- and 8-shot magazines are shaped so as to efficiently accomodate wide hands.

The modern pivoting extractor is located on the right side, while the asymmetrical ejection port is chamfered at the rear and cleared toward the left, to facilitate extraction.

A low rib provides a fast alignment between the front and rear removable sights.

Transverse serrations are moulded at the front and rear of the grip, while the removable backstrap instantly uncocks and neutralizes the gun when slipped off.

In front of the trigger guard, there is a short Picatinny rail for fitting a small laser sight or tactical light.

When the trigger is pulled, the red rear end of the striker protrudes, meaning that the action is pre-cocked.

The square and sober lines of the upper part of the gun, matching the scarcely curved ones of the grip, confer to this PPS a modern and highly personalized silhouette, typical of the current Walther styling.

SHOOTING THE WALTHER PPS

The grip is slightly thinner and wider than that of the PPK, but similarly canted.

As a matter of fact, its perimeter measures 5.31" under the trigger guard, instead of 5" for the PPK. At the bottom of the grip, the 5.43- inch height is the same.

The 1.57-inch distance between the

On this upside-down view, the backstrap latch is shown behind the lower grip opening.

Walther PPS versus PPK

Feature	PPS 2007	PPK 1931
Caliber	9 mm Luger	32 Auto
Magazine capacity	6 – 7 – 8 shots	7 shots
Overall length	6.3 inches	6.18 inches
Height	4.37 inches	4.21 inches
Thickness	1.02 inches	1-inch
Empty weight	21.78-oz.	21-oz.
Loaded weight	24.35-oz. (6 shots)	22.9-oz. (7 shots)
Barrel length	3.19 inches	3.26 inches
Sight radius	5.85 inches	4.33 inches
Trigger pull	5.5 lbs. (DAO) with 0.47-inch stroke for test specimen	S.A. = 4.4 lbs. D.A. = 12.6 lbs.
Hold-open device	External	Internal
Safety devices	Double action Trigger (disconnect) Hammerless Removable backstrap Striker (automatic) Loading indicator Cocking indicator Magazine disconnector (optional)	Double action Drop hammer Rebounding hammer Inertia firing pin Loading indicator External hammer
Receiver material	Polymer	Steel
Operation	Short recoil and short stroke DAO	Blowback, fixed barrel, selective double action with drop hammer

trigger guard and the base of the front strap, is the same with the 6-shot magazine (2.24 inches for the 7-shot and 2.4 inches for the 8-shot one). With the basic 6-shot magazine, the balance point is located above the rear end of the trigger.

In shooting configuration, the distance between the middle of the trigger and the rear of the grip is 2.71 inches for the PPS, against 2.68 inches for the PPK in double action and 2.44 inches in single action at the second pull. The PPS trigger travel is about 0.47-inch.

The top of the PPS rear sight is 1.48 inches above the hand, like that of the PPK. The sights are well proportioned for fast aiming, with three white reference points. Windage is set by driving the rear sight, and elevation, by fitting front sights of different heights.

The trigger pull is set at 6 pounds, according to the manual. It starts at about 2 pounds, reaching its let-off point at the last 0.12-inch of travel.

THE WALTHER "PPS" ACCURACY

At first, it must be said that the small Walther "PPS" is obviously a close defense powerful handgun (360 fpe, with a simplified recoil velocity of 12.7/14.1 fps, while a conventional 9mm service pistol weighing two pounds, scores approximately 10 fps and the 32 Auto PPK, with 144 fpe, recoils at 6.6/7.5 fps).

This characteristic is demonstrated by the fact that the manufacturer's test target is shot from a rest at 10 meters (5 shots in H - 0.7 in. x W - 1.3-in).

However, Jean-Pierre Vignes, my shooting pal, decided to perform our standard test at the ISU slow-fire target with a 2-inch ten-ring and an 8-inch bullseye, at 25 meters, single-hand, using Brazilian Magtech ammunition with 124-grain jacketed bullets. His first ten-shot grouping measuring 3.58 inches x 2.32 inches was centered 1.37-inch left of center, aiming at 6 o'clock.

Correcting, his next grouping, properly centered, scored 90/100 for 2.79 x 3.19 inches.

Next, in a computer-controlled rapid fire session at five rotating and falling military half-silhouettes at 10 meters with random factor involved, I obtained a 100 percent result (56/56 hits) with my old PPK and 96 percent (54/56 hits) with the new PPS, the recoil velocity of which is twice that of the 32 Auto model.

On this view, the right forefinger of the operator is actuating the magazine catch for ejecting the magazine.

RELIABILITY

During two weeks of testing involving the firing of 300 rounds of Magtech and Fiocchi jacketed ammunition (expanding bullets are prohibited in Europe) without any cleaning or lubrication, no malfunction was experienced with our Walther PPS (s/n 048).

CONCLUSION

The 9mm Luger Walther PPS is a compact and extra-flat high-power design consisting of only 24 major components, with the same dimensions and weight as the vintage PPK model, but delivering for each shot *twice the PPK's muzzle energy* with an acceptable felt recoil.

Its simple and short DAO trigger mechanism avoids, in case of emergency, the critical transition between the first and second shots typical of the conventional selective double-action models, while providing a similar accuracy level. How will it compare to smaller and lighter American competitors such as the Kel-Tec P11 and PF9, Kahr PM9 and Rohrbaugh R9?

It seems a matter of compromise between the desired accuracy level and the product being available at the right time. Only the future will tell!

AMMUNITION, BALLISTICS & COMPONENTS

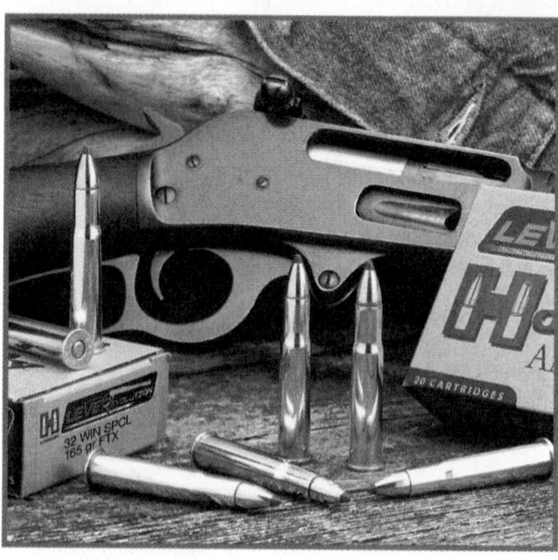

ABOVE: As a limited run, the sedate 32 Win. Special received a boost of a 165-grain FlexTip at 2,410 fps.

by Holt Bodinson

A falling dollar, soaring commodity prices for metals and a war have driven ammunition prices through the ceiling this year and even created some short term supply problems in calibers like 223 and 9mm. Then, the endangered California Condor came soaring into view, supposedly getting a bit of lead poisoning on the way in from big game gut piles. Spurred on by the Peregrine Fund, the game and fish agencies of California and Arizona climbed onboard the "get the lead out" bandwagon. California even banned 22 rimfire in the "historic" range of the Condor. Yet, overall it's been a vibrant year for the ammunition and component companies, and there've been some pleasant surprises.

Responding to the lead issue, the industry is fielding an array of non-toxic projectiles and loads. Barnes added a polymer tip to their Triple-Shock X bullet. Winchester and Nosler teamed up to introduce the "E-Tip;" Remington decided to load Lapua's all copper "Naturalis" bullet and Federal unveiled the "Speer TNT Green." Oh, yes, and all the majors and minors have introduced upland steel shotshell loads.

Who would have expected the 5mm Remington Rimfire Magnum to be revived? Loaded by Aguila under the Centurion label, the feisty little 20-caliber is back. Hornady and Ruger are also back in the news with their introduction of the 300 and 338 Ruger Compact Magnums while Federal and Ruger teamed up to give us the ultimate 32-caliber magnum handgun cartridge, the Ruger 327.

There are lots of new components, including two, new, magnum rifle powders from Hodgdon and a new black powder replacement powder from Western Powders.

Remington and Winchester tied this year for the longest, jaw-breaking, branding of ammunition: Remington: the "Premier AccuTip Bonded Sabot Slug."

Winchester: the "Supreme Elite XP3 Sabot Slug." Putting on a straight face, be sure to ask for them by name from your local dealer.

It's been a busy but challenging year.

A-SQUARE

As a member of SAAMI, A-Square has been in the forefront of standardizing such familiar cartridges as the 6.5-06 A-Square, 7mm STW, 338-06 A-Square, 405 Win. and the 458 Lott. This year A-Square is SAAMI standardizing the ever efficient 416 Taylor–the 458 Winchester Magnum case necked down to 40-caliber and generating approximately 2,400 fps with a 400-grain bullet. A-Square has moved their operations to South Dakota. See all the news at www.asquarecompany.com.

AMERICAN PIONEER POWDER

Here comes the "Super Stick"–a 150-grain equivalent, single stick of American Pioneer Powder's Jim Shockey's Gold. As a general replacement for blackpowder, the American Pioneer Powder line is clean burning, non-corrosive, and consistent. Jim Shockey's Gold is just a little bit better. Think of it as a premium powder. www.americanpioneerpowder.com

BARNES BULLETS

It's nice when a plan comes together. Barnes aggressive and innovative pursuit of lead-free bullets has resulted in one of the most accurate bullets ever developed and has positioned the company as a major industry leader. This year Barnes took their successful Triple-Shock design, streamlined it and gave it a sharp polymer tip. Named the Tipped TSX, the new bullet offers improved downrange ballistics, a bit faster expansion than the Triple-Shock and will be available in a range of bullet weights in 270, 7mm, 30 and 338 calibers. Another new design is their Multi-Purpose Green (MPG) bullet that shares the same basic design as the Varmint Grenade. Both bullets incorporate a powdered-metal, copper-tin core inside a gilding metal jacket. It's a highly frangible design but it's tough enough to withstand the rig-

Barnes Varmint Grenade and Multi-Purpose Green bullets incorporate a non-toxic, powdered copper-tin core.

Add a polymer tip to Barnes Triple-Shock X bullet and you get a "Tipped TSX."

ors of autoloading rifles and fast twist barrels. The MPG bullet, available in 5.56mm and 30-caliber, was designed specifically for the military and law enforcement while the Varmint Grenade is available in 204 and 6mm calibers as well. The Triple-Shock X bullet is still a Barnes stalwart, and there are a number of new offerings this year including Triple-Shocks for the 7.62x39, 303/7.7mm, 325 WSM/8mm, 405 Win., 416, 50BMG and 300- and 350-grain Shocks in 458-caliber. If you own a 500 Jeffrey, and everyone should, Barnes has added a 535-grain Banded Solid to its impressive line of copper-zinc, flat-nosed, dangerous game solids. Finally, Barnes *Number 4 Reloading Manual* is fresh off the press with more than 600 pages of interesting good data. www.barnesbullets.com

BERGER BULLETS

While they say, "They're just trying to catch up," Berger has added a number of new bullets to their match lines including a 35-grain/.204 flat base, 108-grain/6mm BT, and three 270 VLD's in 130, 140 and 150-grains. Berger Bullets is now promoting their Match VLD's as effective big game bullets and offer a free 30 minute DVD to prove it. www.bergerbullets.com

BLACK HILLS AMMUNITION

Where quality spells demand, Black Hills is now back-ordered for millions of rounds of ammunition, largely due to the expanding war on terrorists, special operations requirements for highly accurate ammunition and the constant needs of the civilian market. Owners Jeff and Kristi Hoffman run the company almost on a family basis but this year, they have purchased a new plant consisting of 65,000 square feet of operating space on 10 acres to play catch-up. Their story is a remarkable story of a husband and wife team who built a quality custom ammunition business from scratch and is now a major league player. New this year is a 142-grain Sierra MatchKing loading at 2,950 fps for the 6.5-284 Norma that is being chambered by Savage and Barnes Varmint Grenade loadings for the 22-250 Rem. and 243 Win. www.black-hills.com

Black Hills has added the Barnes Varmint Grenade bullet to its 243 Winchester loadings.

BRENNEKE

Coat it red for Special Forces and law enforcement deployment and green for us deer hunters; Brenneke is fielding a new 12-gauge/2 3/4" slug load featuring a 1 1/4 ounce slug at 1,476 fps. Using FBI-spec ballistic gelatin, the new slug produced exceptional penetration and an average accuracy of 2.95" at 100 yards. There's a new 20-gauge K.O. slug load for those who like the mild recoil of a 20-gauge featuring 3/4-ounce slug at 1,606 fps. Zeroed at 94 yards, it drops only 1.6 inches between 25 and 100 yards. See them at www.brennekeusa.com.

CENTURION

The 5mm Remington Rimfire Magnum is back. Remington discontinued their little 20-caliber sparkplug in 1981 and left the owners of 52,000 Remington 5mm rifles and 30,000 T/C Contender barrels starved for ammunition. Loaded by Aguila under the Centurion label, the fresh stock of 5mm RRM features a 30-grain JHP at 2,300 fps. Testing the new Centurion ammunition in a Remington Model 591, I recorded an average velocity of 2,318 fps and five-shot groups at 100 yards ranging from 15/16" to 1 1/4".

ABOVE: Brenneke's 20-gauge 3/4 oz. K.O. slug load at 1,606 fps is potent and easy on the shoulder.

LEFT: Loaded by Aguila under the Centurion label, the 5mm Rem. Rimfire Magnum is back.

Look for a variety of new rifles and handguns chambered for the hot 5mm RRM. It was a great cartridge when it was introduced, and it's even better now with Eley priming and modern rimfire powders. www.centurionammo.com.

CENTURY INTERNATIONAL ARMS

A great and economical source for military surplus and hard-to-find commercial loads. The latest listing includes items like 5.45x39 Bulgarian steel core, 7.62 x 25, even an odd prototype cartridge by H&K, the 4.3x45. Under CIA's "HotShot" label is a fresh stock of 7.62 Nagant, and in their Hirtenberger hunting line are 5.6x50 Magnum, 6.5x57R and 7x57R. Lots more at www.centuryarms.com.

CORBON/GLASER

Now celebrating their 25th Anniversary, CorBon is rolling out an impressive array of new offerings in their hunting and defense lines including the 300 Whisper, 458 Socom, 338 Lapua, 416 Rigby, 6.5x284 Norma and 6.8 SPC. Teaming up with the Thunder Ranch Training Center, CorBon is now offering a new line of Thunder Ranch Defensive Ammunition in 9mm Luger, 40 S&W and 45 Auto featuring their deep penetrating Barnes X bullet. CorBon continues to load a full range of Glaser Safety Slugs that ramp up the effectiveness of handgun rounds like the 25 Auto, 32 Auto, 32 NAA, 9mm Makrov, 357 SIG and even the venerable 30-'06. If you are looking for premium and hard-to-find ammunition, turn to www.corbon.com and www.safetyslug.com.

DKG TRADING

In addition to their complete lines of NobelSport shotgun ammunition and components and Silver, Brown and Gold Bear, Russian sporting and military ammunition, DKG Trading has had a unique relationship with the Centurion brand loaded by Aguila. The exciting news is that DKG is distributing Centurion's new 5mm Remington Rimfire Magnum ammunition. For their full catalog, turn to www.dkgtrading.com.

EXTREME SHOCK

Featuring their highly frangible bullets, often with cores of powdered Tungsten, Extreme Shock produces an extensive line of exotic military, law enforcement and sporting ammunition. They offer everything from a "NyTrilium Air Freedom Round," designed as a handgun cartridge that will not penetrate the skin of an airliner, to a 50 BMG round that will penetrate one inch of mild steel but fragments so quickly that it will not exit a soft target. www.extremeshockusa.com

FEDERAL

Teaming with Ruger, Federal has taken the 32 H&R Magnum case, lengthened it a bit to increase powder capacity and christened it the 327 Federal Magnum. Introduced initially in Ruger's compact SP101, the 327 Federal Magnum, loaded with a 100-grain SP at 1,500 fps, is designed to deliver 357 Magnum ballistics with 20 percent less recoil. Firearms chambered for the 327 Federal will also digest the good old 32 S&W and the later 32 H&R Magnum cartridges. There's another totally new Federal cartridge. Partnering with Sako, Federal is introducing the 370 Sako Magnum that looks like an improved 30-'06 case necked up to accept 9.3mm (.366-inch) diameter bullets. The advantages of the new, non-belted cartridge are that it functions through a normal length action and allows more rounds to be stuffed into a normal depth magazine. Initial loadings feature 286-grain bullets at 2,550 fps. CCI and Speer have gone green. Under the "Speer TNT Green" label, CCI and Speer have developed non-toxic, lead-free, jacketed bullets for the rimfire and centerfire lines. Speer TNT Green will be offered initially as a 30-grain bullet in the 22 WMR and later as a 43-grain bullet in the 222, 223, and 22-250. Maybe the Triple Deuce is due for a comeback! Speaking of bullets, Federal's highly successful Trophy Bonded Bear Claw has been given a facelift with the additional of a sharp polymer tip, a streamlined body and a boat-tail. Look for this premium, bonded-core, nickel-plated bullet across the centerfire line. Trading bullet weight for velocity, Federal has turned to Barnes Tipped Triple-Shock X bullet to develop some screaming big game loads like the 110-grain Barnes in the 270 Win. at 3,400 fps and the 130-grain in the 300 Win. Mag. at 3,500 fps. Over in the shotshell stable, the Wing-Shok Pheasants Forever line sports two, new, non-toxic steel loads featuring #3 and #5 shot in the 3-inch/20 and 12-gauge at 1,350 fps and 1,450 fps respectfully. Catch Federal's entire extensive 2009 lineup at www.federalpremium.com.

Federal's WingShok upland bird loads now feature non-toxic steel shot.

HODGDON

Now the supplier of Hodgdon, IMR, Winchester and Vihtouvori powders, Hodgdon is not sitting on its laurels. This year they are bringing two new powders to the handloading bench: Winchester Supreme 780 and Hodgdon Hybrid 100V.

Winchester Supreme 780 is the same magnum level, ball powder that Winchester loads in its Supreme line of high performance hunting cartridges. Supreme 780 has a burn speed comparable to H4831. Hodgdon Hybrid 100V is an innovative, small grain powder that shares its chemistry with ball powder but its shape with extruded powders. While its burn speed is close to that of H4350, Hodgdon's data indicates it's capable of delivering hyper-velocities in some cases. The company has issued three new reloading manuals for this year. Their large, 5,000+

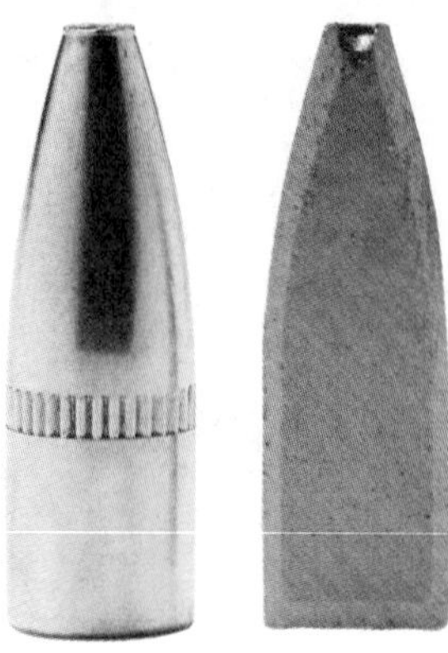

Speer's TNT Green bullet will be offered initially in the 22 WMR and later in the 222, 223 and 22-250.

load manual, a basic reloading manual, and a muzzleloading manual. You need all three. The full-blown manual covers both standard and a host of wildcat cartridges, the muzzleloading manual, Pyrodex and Triple Seven, while the basic manual, released at a later date, contains data on Hodgdon's new powders. Better, yet, go to one of three reloading web sites maintained by Hodgdon to obtain the most up-to-date data. www.hodgdon.com www.imrpowder.com www.wwpowder.com

HORNADY

Hornady receives the blue ribbon this year for the bringing to the shooting world the most extensive selection of new cartridges and components. Taking the parent 375 Ruger case, Hornady has necked it down to 338 and 300-caliber to create a new line of short, rimless magnums, the Ruger Compact Magnums (RCM). All three members of the RCM family match the velocities of the traditional factory belted magnums and do it in the compact 20-inch barrel of the Ruger M77 Hawkeye. High power and 3-gun match shooters have been given a radical, new cartridge this year, the 6.5 Creedmoor. Designed to function through a 308 Win. length magazine when loaded with those long, efficient 6.5 match bullets, the new cartridge delivers 3,020 fps with Hornady's new 120-grain A-MAX and 2,820 fps with the 140-grain A-MAX. Velocities were derived from a 28-inch match barrel. Even the nearly obsolete 32 Special gets some octane this year. Hornady is loading a 165-grain Flex Tip bullet to an impressive velocity of 2,410 fps. It's a one-time run so stock up. Hornady is rolling out a new 22 WMR loading this year featuring a 30-grain V-Max bullet at 2,200 fps. The big game hunting community received a big boost this year with the reintroduction of 450 Nitro Express 3 1/4" and Hornady's new copper clad, steel jacketed Dangerous Game Solid and Dangerous

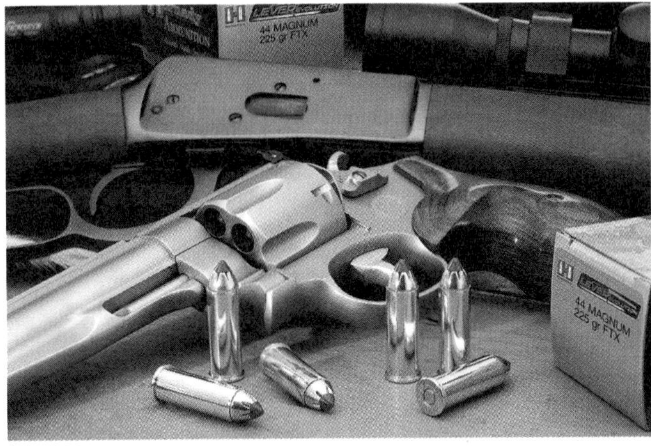

Hornady added spitzer FlexTip bullets to its 357 and 44 Magnum loadings for both rifles and revolvers.

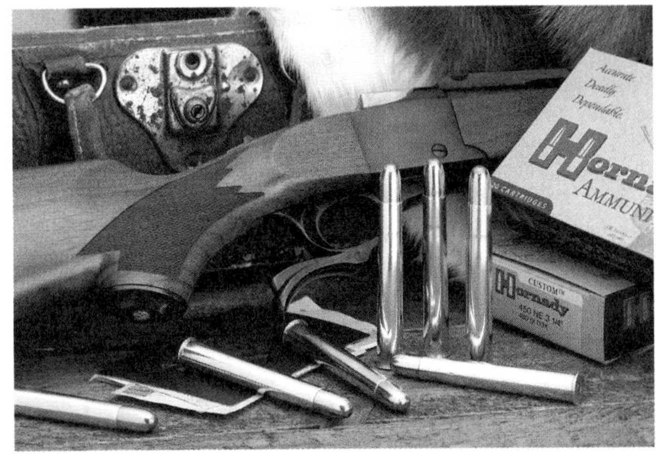

Classic big game hunters will appreciate Hornady's revival of the 450 N.E.

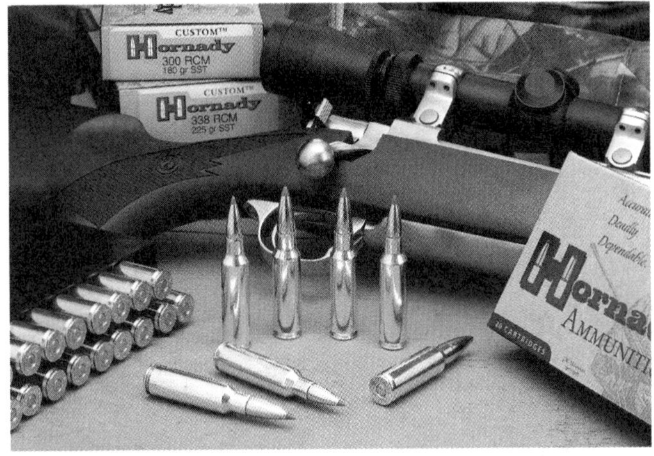

LEFT & BELOW: Teamed with Ruger, Hornady necked the 375 RCM down to create the 300 and 338 Ruger Compact Magnums.

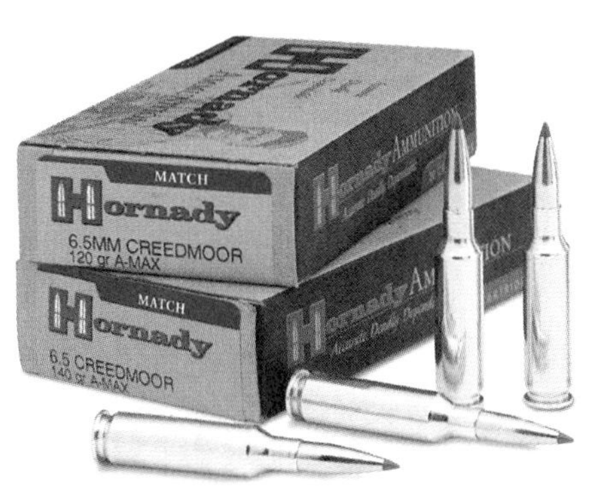

Hornady's 6.5 Creedmoor should be a smoking success in match circles.

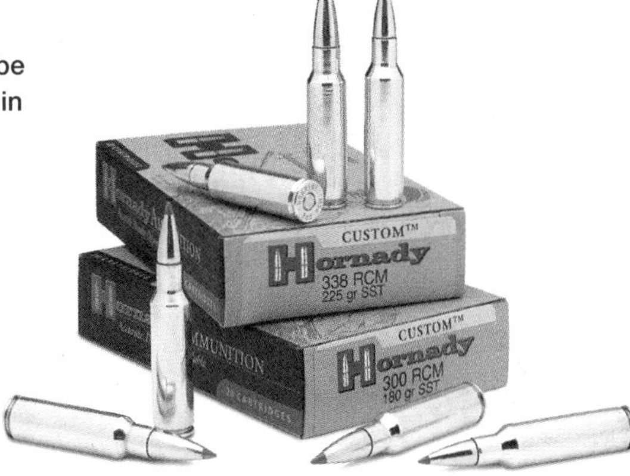

Game Expanding bullets. Bringing their Flex Tip technology to the handgunning world, Hornady is loading Flex-Tip bullets in both the 357 and the 44 Magnum. The advantage of the Flex Tip bullet is that the polymer tip prevents the hollow point from clogging and not expanding while increasing the expanding qualities of the bullet over a wide range of terminal velocities. Hornady has fielded some great products for the muzzleloader. This year it's the 50-caliber, SST-ML High Speed Low Drag sabot loaded with either a 250- or 300-grain SST Flex Tip bullet. The new sabot is said to reduce loading effort by more than 50 percent. Even more interesting is the new 350-grain, 50-caliber FPB bullet. It's a full-bodied, hollow base, jacketed projectile with a Flex Tip that does away with the need for a sabot. The FPB loads with only 25 pounds of pressure and eliminates bullet and plastic sabot fouling. Accuracy is said to be "surgical." See all their new products at www.hornady.com.

KENT CARTRIDGE

Home of non-toxic Tungsten Matrix shot and degradable "Bio-Wad" components, Kent offers a full selection of GAMEBORE shotshells in those hard-to-find 2" and 2 1/2" case lengths for 12, 16, 20 and 28 gauges. The line even includes a 2 1/2" /12-gauge blackpowder loading of #6 and a 2 1/2"/12-gauge shotshell featuring 1 1/16 oz. of Tungsten Matrix in #5 and #6. Lots of interesting shotshells at www.kentgamebore.com.

MDM

Will the black powder replacement, Black Mag'3, ever be successfully marketed? It keeps appearing and then disappearing. MDM now controls it and promises to put it on your dealer's shelves this year. MDM has been successful with their own line of muzzleloading rifles and projectiles like the Dyno-Core Magnum and the Dyno-Core Premium. Black Mag'3? We're hoping. www.MDM-muzzleloaders.com and www.magkor.com.

NAVY ARMS/OLD WESTERN SCROUNGER

Get your 32 long rimfire ammunition here. There are always interesting and new products available from the Old Western Scrounger, now owned by Navy Arms. www.navyarms.com

NORMA

More belt-less magnum introductions are on the way. Norma promises a new family of modern magnums in 300, 338 and 375 calibers based on the 416 Rigby case. Stay tuned. In the meantime, Norma's African PH series of premium big game cartridges loaded with Woodleigh bullets continues to grow and now includes some of the real classics, the 375 Flanged Magnum, 404 Jeffery, 416 Rigby, 500/416 Nitro Express, 450 Rigby Rimless, 458 Lott, 470 Nitro Express, 500 Jeffery, 500 Nitro Express 3" and 505 Gibbs. www.norma.cc.

Norma is highly focused on their premium African PH line of big game cartridges.

Nosler's new "Reloading Guide" is full of new loads and data.

BELOW: Teamed with Winchester, Nosler has developed the non-toxic E-Tip bullet.

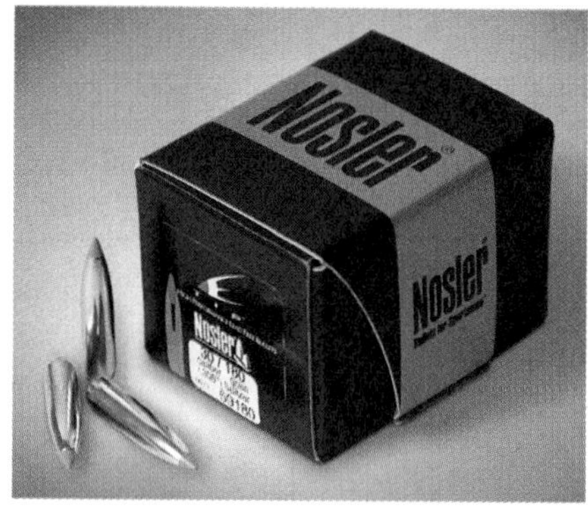

NOSLER

It's a race for the green--green as in "get the lead out." Nosler's new E-Tip bullet does it. Featuring a solid copper alloy, boat tail body pierced by a deep cavity capped off with a polymer tip, the 30-caliber E-Tips in 150 and 180-grain weights are the first but not the last of the Nosler E-Tip introductions. Along the Nosler green line, there is also a new assortment of lead-free, homogeneous solids in 375, 416 and 458-caliber. There are 270/110-grain, 338/250-grain and 375/300-grain additions to the successful AccuBond design and a new 224/60-grain Ballistic Tip Varmint bullet. The Nosler Custom Brass line is constantly expanding. This year the 264 Win. Mag., 7mm STW and 338 Win. Mag. have been added to the catalog. Finally, fresh off the press is an updated "Nosler Reloading Guide No. 6." It's a great company at www.nosler.com.

POLYWAD

It's neither square nor round, and that's why it's named a "Squound." Polywad is loading a completely radical looking steel shot that reminds me of a tiny Foster slug. The Squound sports a dome-shaped nose, straight sides and a deep dished cavity in the base. Flying nose first, some Squounds will tumble upon impact and cut large cavities, others will sail on nose first and create deep wound cavities. The typical pattern thrown by Squounds is slightly more open than that of conventional non-toxic loads. Just the load for waterfowl over decoys. The second new item in Polywad's inventory is the Gram Crak-R shell in 28 and .410 gauges. The Gram Crak-R is a buffered shot, bio-wad design that makes the smaller gauges perform like a bit bigger gun. The secret to the shell design is the use of a poly-buffer combined with a Kraft paper shot cup. I used the 28-gauge Gram Crak-R's this past dove season, and they were reaching out there and tagging doves at 45-50 yards. See the whole product line at www.polywad.com.

PMC AMMUNITION/POONGSAN

Utilizing a new ball powder, PMC is introducing the PMC223A loading. The new 223 round exhibits minimal shot-to-shot deviation, resulting in exceptional accuracy, while muzzle flash has virtually been eliminated. www.poongsan.co.kr.

QUALITY CARTRIDGE

This is a remarkable company that manufactures over 200 obscure, obsolete and wildcat brass cases. How about the 6mm Ozark, 7mm Gibbs, 300 ICL Grizzly or the 40-82 Winchester? Don't miss their complete inventory at www.qual-cart.com.

REMINGTON

Looking ever so much like a intercontinental missile with a vented, green nose cone, Remington's new Premier AccuTip Bonded Sabot Slug is said to be an exceptionally accurate 58 caliber, 385-grain brass-jacketed slug that expands to 1" whether the distance is 50 yards or 200. It's available in 12 gauge with a 2 3/4" load at 1,850 fps and a 3" shell at 1,900 fps. The 7mm Remington Ultra Mag is now available in 3 power levels beginning with full power and then stair stepping down to 7mm Remington Magnum and 280 Remington performance levels. Extending the concept even further, there are new "managed-recoil" softy loads for the 260 Rem., 7mm-08 Rem. and 300 Rem. Ultra Mag. The successful, pee wee 17 Remington Fireball has been upgraded with a heavier and much needed 25-grain JHP at 3,850 fps plus unprimed component brass will now be available. Loading the Lapua "Naturalis" non-toxic, copper bullet in the 243 Win., 7mm Rem. Mag., 30-'06 and 308 Win., Remington has created a new Premier Green Centerfire Rifle Ammunition line. Green for Big Green. It was a "Naturalis." If you are looking for a 223 game bullet, there's a 62-grain bonded PSP load available this year. Just the thing for those little Texas whitetails. The 10 and 20 gauges have been added to the high density shot, Wingmaster HD line that has been so popular with turkey hunters and waterfowlers. Even the diminutive 2 1/2"/.410 shell has been upgraded with 1/2 oz. of magnum grade #8 shot at 1,300 fps for the sporting clays and dove fields. www.remington.com.

RWS

Fiocchiusa will be marketing the RWS line this year. See it at www.fiocchiusa.com.

SCHROEDER BULLETS

Steve Schroeder is THE source for odd sized jacketed bullets and difficult to find component brass. The last time I spoke with him he was producing both brass and bullets for the Russian 5.45x18 PSM assassin pistol. While 5mm Rem. Rimfire Magnum ammunition is now available, Schroeder has kept the obsolete 5mm Remington rifles shooting with his centerfire conversion kits for years. I've used them, and they are easy to install and produce sensational events. He doesn't have a web site. Reach him in San Diego, CA at (619)423-8124

SIERRA

The MatchKing line has been expanded with the addition of a 6mm 95-grain HPBT, a 30-caliber 135-grain HPBT and a 22-caliber 77-grain HPBT with a cannelure. www.sierrabullets.com

New in the Sierra MatchKing line is a 30-caliber, 135-grain HPBT.

Sierra has added a cannelure to its popular 22-caliber, 77-grain HPBT MatchKing.

TEN-X AMMUNITION

When I saw Richard Pumerantz, President of Ten-X Ammunition, unveil loaded 50-95 Winchester blackpowder ammunition at the recent SHOT Show, I knew I was in heaven. Ten-X Ammunition now loads over 100 cartridges, ranging from the 25-20 Win. to the 577 Snider, for cowboy action shooting, hunting and simply for the enjoyment of putting old guns back into action. The company offers both smokeless and black powder loads as well as a well thought out selection of different bullet diameters. Their latest product is a complete reloading kit for the 38mm and 40mm shells used by law enforcement. www.tenxammo.com.

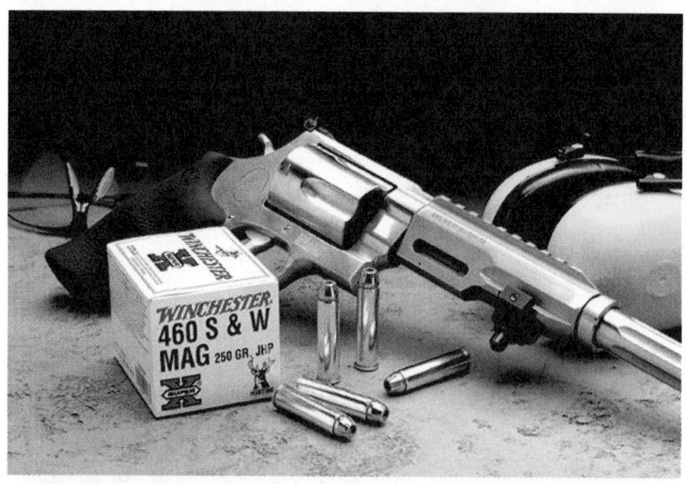

Winchester's new load for the 460 S&W reduces recoil up to 49 percent.

WESTERN POWDERS

There's a new blackpowder replacement powder in the market. It's Western Powder's Blackhorn 209. The new propellant is designed specifically for 209-primed in-lines. It is non-corrosive, non-hygroscopic, temperature insensitive and upon combustion, leaves a minimal amount of residue. Western Powder President, Doug Phair, claims you can "Load 5, 10, 20 or more tight-fitting bullet sabot projectiles as easily as the first" and "There is no rush to clean your muzzleloader after use." Data on Blackhorn 209 as well as Western Powder's Ramshot and Accurate brands can be found at www.westernpowders.com.

Winchester is greening up with the non-toxic E-Tip in their rifle cartridge lines.

WINCHESTER

Big Red has gone green with the introduction of their new lead-free E-Tip bullet. Developed jointly with Nosler, the E-Tip is 95 percent copper, 5 percent zinc and sports a sharp polymer tip and a boattail. Claiming the E-Tip exhibits almost 100 percent weight retention, Winchester will initially load it in the Supreme line in 180-grains for the 308 Win, 30-'06, 300 WSM and 300 Win. Mag. The 325 WSM is getting a mild facelift this year with the addition of a 200-grain XP3 bullet loading. Hunting African big game has gone mainstream so Winchester is coming out with their own "Safari" line of cartridges which includes both Nosler Partition and Nosler solids in the 375 H&H, 416 Rem. Mag. and 458 Win. Mag. The 460 S&W has been known to dish out a bit of unpleasant recoil so Winchester is addressing the problem with a reduced loading featuring a 250-grain JHP at a mild 1,450 fps. Winchester claims there is a 49 percent reduction in recoil compared to their 260-grain Partition Gold at 2,000 fps. The three-inch, 12-gauge slug load is receiving two new slugs, the non-toxic, polymer tipped Supreme Elite XP2 sabot slug and the Supreme Rackmaster slug that performs well in both smooth and rifled bores. Hitting 1,435 fps with a 40-grain LHP bullet, this new Super-X loading is the fastest Long Rifle in Winchester's rimfire stable. Yet, there are also two, new, slow loads, the Super-X Sub-Sonic that moves a 40-grain LHP along at 1,065 fps and a Super-X CB Match cartridge, featuring a 29-grain LRN at a sedate 770 fps. The 22 Winchester Magnum gets a dose of rocket fuel with a new 30-grain JHP at 2,250 fps. In response to many of the states adopting non-toxic shot regulations of their own, Winchester is fielding two steel dove loads for the 12 and 20-gauge 2 3/4-inch shells, featuring #7 shot at 1,300 fps. Finally, to give upland bird hunters a slight edge on those tough and wily late season pheasants, there's a new 12-gauge 3" Super Pheasant shell featuring 1 5/8 oz. of #4 and #5 shot at 1,350 fps. www.winchester.com

Western Powder's Blackhorn 209 is a non-corrosive, low ash, replacement for blackpowder.

WOLF PERFORMANCE AMMUNITION

There's a market for it. Wolf is introducing three new loads for Alexander Arms' 6.5 Grendel including a 110-grain FMG, a 123-grain SP and a 120-grain "Multi-Purpose Tactical" bullet. www.wolfammo.com

Average Centerfire Rifle Cartridge Ballistics & Prices

Many manufacturers do not supply suggested retail prices. Others did not get their pricing to us before press time. All pricing can vary dependent on the exact brand and style of ammo selected and/or the retail outlet from which you make your purchase. Pricing has been rounded to the nearest dollar and represents our best estimate of average pricing. An * after the cartridge means these loads are available with Nosler Partition or Swift A-Frame bullets. Listed pricing may or may not reflect this bullet type. ** = these are packed 50 to box, all others are 20 to box. Wea. Mag.= Weatherby Magnum. Spfd. = Springfield. A-Sq. = A-Square. N.E.=Nitro Express.

Cartridge	Bullet Wgt. Grs.	VELOCITY (fps)					ENERGY (ft. lbs.)					TRAJ. (in.)				Est. Price/ box
		Muzzle	100 yds.	200 yds.	300 yds.	400 yds.	Muzzle	100 yds.	200 yds.	300 yds.	400 yds.	100 yds.	200 yds.	300 yds.	400 yds.	
17, 22																
17 Remington Fireball	20	4000	3380	2840	2360	1930	710	507	358	247	165	1.6	1.5	-2.8	-13.5	NA
17 Remington Fireball	25	3850	3280	2780	2330	1925	823	597	429	301	206	0.9	0.0	-5.4	NA	NA
17 Remington	25	4040	3284	2644	2086	1606	906	599	388	242	143	+2.0	+1.7	-4.0	-17.0	$17
204 Ruger	32	4225	3632	3114	2652	2234	1268	937	689	500	355	.6	0.0	-4.2	-13.4	NA
204 Ruger	40	3900	3451	3046	2677	2336	1351	1058	824	636	485	.7	0.0	-4.5	-13.9	NA
204 Ruger	45	3625	3188	2792	2428	2093	1313	1015	778	589	438	1.00	0.0	-5.5	-16.9	NA
221 Fireball	50	2800	2137	1580	1180	988	870	507	277	155	109	+0.0	-7.0	-28.0	0.0	$14
22 Hornet	34	3050	2132	1415	1017	852	700	343	151	78	55	+0.0	-6.6	-15.5	-29.9	NA
22 Hornet	35	3100	2278	1601	1135	929	747	403	199	100	67	+2.75	0.0	-16.9	-60.4	NA
22 Hornet	45	2690	2042	1502	1128	948	723	417	225	127	90	+0.0	-7.7	-31.0	0.0	$27**
218 Bee	46	2760	2102	1550	1155	961	788	451	245	136	94	+0.0	-7.2	-29.0	0.0	$46**
222 Remington	40	3600	3117	2673	2269	1911	1151	863	634	457	324	+1.07	0.0	-6.13	-18.9	NA
222 Remington	50	3140	2602	2123	1700	1350	1094	752	500	321	202	+2.0	-0.4	-11.0	-33.0	$11
222 Remington	55	3020	2562	2147	1773	1451	1114	801	563	384	257	+2.0	-0.4	-11.0	-33.0	$12
22 PPC	52	3400	2930	2510	2130	NA	1335	990	730	525	NA	+2.0	1.4	-5.0	0.0	NA
223 Remington	40	3650	3010	2450	1950	1530	1185	805	535	340	265	+2.0	+1.0	-6.0	-22.0	$14
223 Remington	40	3800	3305	2845	2424	2044	1282	970	719	522	371	0.84	0.0	-5.34	-16.6	NA
223 Remington	50	3300	2874	2484	2130	1809	1209	917	685	504	363	1.37	0.0	-7.05	-21.8	NA
223 Remington	52/53	3330	2882	2477	2106	1770	1305	978	722	522	369	+2.0	+0.6	-6.5	-21.5	$14
223 Remington	55	3240	2748	2305	1906	1556	1282	922	649	444	296	+2.0	-0.2	-9.0	-27.0	$12
223 Remington	60	3100	2712	2355	2026	1726	1280	979	739	547	397	+2.0	+0.2	-8.0	-24.7	$16
223 Remington	64	3020	2621	2256	1920	1619	1296	977	723	524	373	+2.0	-0.2	-9.3	-23.0	$14
223 Remington	69	3000	2720	2460	2210	1980	1380	1135	925	750	600	+2.0	+0.8	-5.8	-17.5	$15
223 Remington	75	2790	2554	2330	2119	1926	1296	1086	904	747	617	2.37	0.0	-8.75	-25.1	NA
223 Remington	77	2750	2584	2354	2169	1992	1293	1110	948	804	679	1.93	0.0	-8.2	-23.8	NA
223 WSSM	55	3850	3438	3064	2721	2402	1810	1444	1147	904	704	0.7	0.0	-4.4	-13.6	NA
223 WSSM	64	3600	3144	2732	2356	2011	1841	1404	1061	789	574	1.0	0.0	-5.7	-17.7	NA
222 Rem. Mag.	55	3240	2748	2305	1906	1556	1282	922	649	444	296	+2.0	-0.2	-9.0	-27.0	$14
225 Winchester	55	3570	3066	2616	2208	1838	1556	1148	836	595	412	+2.0	+1.0	-5.0	-20.0	$19
224 Wea. Mag.	55	3650	3192	2780	2403	2057	1627	1244	943	705	516	+2.0	+1.2	-4.0	-17.0	$32
22-250 Rem.	40	4000	3320	2720	2200	1740	1420	980	660	430	265	+2.0	+1.8	-3.0	-16.0	$14
22-250 Rem.	50	3725	3264	2641	2455	2103	1540	1183	896	669	491	0.89	0.0	-5.23	-16.3	NA
22-250 Rem.	52/55	3680	3137	2656	2222	1832	1654	1201	861	603	410	+2.0	+1.3	-4.0	-17.0	$13
22-250 Rem.	60	3600	3195	2826	2485	2169	1727	1360	1064	823	627	+2.0	+2.0	-2.4	-12.3	$19
220 Swift	40	4200	3678	3190	2739	2329	1566	1201	904	666	482	+0.51	0.0	-4.0	-12.9	NA
220 Swift	50	3780	3158	2617	2135	1710	1586	1107	760	506	325	+2.0	+1.4	-4.4	-17.9	$20
220 Swift	50	3850	3396	2970	2576	2215	1645	1280	979	736	545	0.74	0.0	-4.84	-15.1	NA
220 Swift	55	3800	3370	2990	2630	2310	1765	1390	1090	850	650	0.8	0.0	-4.7	-14.4	NA
220 Swift	55	3650	3194	2772	2384	2035	1627	1246	939	694	506	+2.0	+2.0	-2.6	-13.4	$19
220 Swift	60	3600	3199	2824	2475	2156	1727	1364	1063	816	619	+2.0	+1.6	-4.1	-13.1	$19
22 Savage H.P.	71	2790	2340	1930	1570	1280	1225	860	585	390	190	+2.0	-1.0	-10.4	-35.7	NA
6mm (24)																
6mm BR Rem.	100	2550	2310	2083	1870	1671	1444	1185	963	776	620	+2.5	-0.6	-11.8	0.0	$22
6mm Norma BR	107	2822	2667	2517	2372	2229	1893	1690	1506	1337	1181	+1.73	0.0	-7.24	-20.6	NA
6mm PPC	70	3140	2750	2400	2070	NA	1535	1175	895	665	NA	+2.0	+1.4	-5.0	0.0	NA
243 Winchester	55	4025	3597	3209	2853	2525	1978	1579	1257	994	779	+0.6	0.0	-4.0	-12.2	NA
243 Winchester	60	3600	3110	2660	2260	1890	1725	1285	945	680	475	+2.0	+1.8	-3.3	-15.5	$17
243 Winchester	70	3400	3040	2700	2390	2100	1795	1435	1135	890	685	1.1	0.0	-5.9	-18.0	NA
243 Winchester	75/80	3350	2955	2593	2259	1951	1993	1551	1194	906	676	+2.0	+0.9	-5.0	-19.0	$16
243 Winchester	85	3320	3070	2830	2600	2380	2080	1770	1510	1280	1070	+2.0	+1.2	-4.0	-14.0	$18
243 Winchester	90	3120	2871	2635	2411	2199	1946	1647	1388	1162	966	1.4	0.0	-6.4	-18.8	NA
243 Winchester*	100	2960	2697	2449	2215	1993	1945	1615	1332	1089	882	+2.5	+1.2	-6.0	-20.0	$16
243 Winchester	105	2920	2689	2470	2261	2062	1988	1686	1422	1192	992	+2.5	+1.6	-5.0	-18.4	$21
243 Light Mag.	100	3100	2839	2592	2358	2138	2133	1790	1491	1235	1014	+1.5	0.0	-6.8	-19.8	NA
243 WSSM	55	4060	3628	3237	2880	2550	2013	1607	1280	1013	794	0.6	0.0	-3.9	-12.0	NA
243 WSSM	95	3250	3000	2763	2538	2325	2258	1898	1610	1359	1140	1.2	0.0	-5.7	-16.9	NA
243 WSSM	100	3110	2838	2583	2341	2112	2147	1789	1481	1217	991	1.4	0.0	-6.6	-19.7	NA
6mm Remington	80	3470	3064	2694	2352	2036	2139	1667	1289	982	736	+2.0	+1.1	-5.0	-17.0	$16
6mm Remington	100	3100	2829	2573	2332	2104	2133	1777	1470	1207	983	+2.5	+1.6	-5.0	-17.0	$16
6mm Remington	105	3060	2822	2596	2381	2177	2105	1788	1512	1270	1059	+2.5	+1.1	-3.3	-15.0	$21
6mm Rem. Light Mag.	100	3250	2997	2756	2528	2311	2345	1995	1687	1418	1186	1.59	0.0	-6.33	-18.3	NA
6.17(.243) Spitfire	100	3350	3122	2905	2698	2501	2493	2164	1874	1617	1389	2.4	3.20	0.0	-8.0	NA
240 Wea. Mag.	87	3500	3202	2924	2663	2416	2366	1980	1651	1370	1127	+2.0	+2.0	-2.0	-12.0	$32
240 Wea. Mag.	100	3395	3106	2835	2581	2339	2559	2142	1785	1478	1215	+2.5	+2.8	-2.0	-11.0	$43
25																
25-20 Win.	86	1460	1194	1030	931	858	407	272	203	165	141	0.0	-23.5	0.0	0.0	$32**
25-35 Win.	117	2230	1866	1545	1282	1097	1292	904	620	427	313	+2.5	-4.2	-26.0	0.0	$24
250 Savage	100	2820	2504	2210	1936	1684	1765	1392	1084	832	630	+2.5	+0.4	-9.0	-28.0	$17
257 Roberts	100	2980	2661	2363	2085	1827	1972	1572	1240	965	741	+2.5	-0.8	-5.2	-21.6	$20
257 Roberts+P	117	2780	2411	2071	1761	1488	2009	1511	1115	806	576	+2.5	-0.2	-10.2	-32.6	$18
257 Roberts+P	120	2780	2560	2360	2160	1970	2060	1750	1480	1240	1030	+2.5	+1.2	-6.4	-23.6	$22

Many manufacturers do not supply suggested retail prices. Others did not get their pricing to us before press time. All pricing can vary dependent on the exact brand and style of ammo selected and/or the retail outlet from which you make your purchase. Pricing has been rounded to the nearest dollar and represents our best estimate of average pricing. An * after the cartridge means these loads are available with Nosler Partition or Swift A-Frame bullets. Listed pricing may or may not reflect this bullet type. ** = these are packed 50 to box, all others are 20 to box. Wea. Mag.= Weatherby Magnum. Spfd. = Springfield. A-Sq. = A-Square. N.E.=Nitro Express.

Cartridge	Bullet Wgt. Grs.	VELOCITY (fps)					ENERGY (ft. lbs.)					TRAJ. (in.)				Est. Price/ box
		Muzzle	100 yds.	200 yds.	300 yds.	400 yds.	Muzzle	100 yds.	200 yds.	300 yds.	400 yds.	100 yds.	200 yds.	300 yds.	400 yds.	
257 Roberts	122	2600	2331	2078	1842	1625	1831	1472	1169	919	715	+2.5	0.0	-10.6	-31.4	**$21**
257 Light Mag.	117	2940	2694	2460	2240	2031	2245	1885	1572	1303	1071	+1.7	0.0	-7.6	-21.8	**NA**
25-06 Rem.	87	3440	2995	2591	2222	1884	2286	1733	1297	954	686	+2.0	+1.1	-2.5	-14.4	**$17**
25-06 Rem.	90	3440	3043	2680	2344	2034	2364	1850	1435	1098	827	+2.0	+1.8	-3.3	-15.6	**$17**
25-06 Rem.	100	3230	2893	2580	2287	2014	2316	1858	1478	1161	901	+2.0	+0.8	-5.7	-18.9	**$17**
25-06 Rem.	117	2990	2770	2570	2370	2190	2320	2000	1715	1465	1246	+2.5	+1.0	-7.9	-26.6	**$19**
25-06 Rem.*	120	2990	2730	2484	2252	2032	2382	1985	1644	1351	1100	+2.5	+1.2	-5.3	-19.6	**$17**
25-06 Rem.	122	2930	2706	2492	2289	2095	2325	1983	1683	1419	1189	+2.5	+1.8	-4.5	-17.5	**$23**
25 WSSM	85	3470	3156	2863	2589	2331	2273	1880	1548	1266	1026	1.0	0.0	-5.2	-15.7	**NA**
25 WSSM	115	3060	284	2639	2442	2254	2392	2066	1778	1523	1398	1.4	0.0	-6.4	-18.6	**NA**
25 WSSM	120	2990	2717	2459	2216	1987	2383	1967	1612	1309	1053	1.6	0.0	-7.4	-21.8	**NA**
257 Wea. Mag.	87	3825	3456	3118	2805	2513	2826	2308	1870	1520	1220	+2.0	+2.7	-0.3	-7.6	**$32**
257 Wea. Mag.	100	3555	3237	2941	2665	2404	2806	2326	1920	1576	1283	+2.5	+3.2	0.0	-8.0	**$32**
257 Scramjet	100	3745	3450	3173	2912	2666	3114	2643	2235	1883	1578	+2.1	+2.77	0.0	-6.93	**NA**
6.5																
6.5x47 Lapua	123	2887	NA	2554	NA	2244	2285	NA	1788	NA	1380	NA	4.53	0.00	-10.7	**NA**
6.5x50mm Jap.	139	2360	2160	1970	1790	1620	1720	1440	1195	985	810	+2.5	-1.0	-13.5	0.0	**NA**
6.5x50mm Jap.	156	2070	1830	1610	1430	1260	1475	1155	900	695	550	+2.5	-4.0	-23.8	0.0	**NA**
6.5x52mm Car.	139	2580	2360	2160	1970	1790	2045	1725	1440	1195	985	+2.5	0.0	-9.9	-29.0	**NA**
6.5x52mm Car.	156	2430	2170	1930	1700	1500	2045	1630	1285	1005	780	+2.5	-1.0	-13.9	0.0	**NA**
6.5x52mm Carcano	160	2250	1963	1700	1467	1271	1798	1369	1027	764	574	+3.8	0.0	-15.9	-48.1	**NA**
6.5x55mm Light Mag.	129	2750	2549	2355	2171	1994	2166	1860	1589	1350	1139	+2.0	0.0	-8.2	-23.9	**NA**
6.5x55mm Swe.	140	2550	NA	NA	NA	NA	2020	NA	NA	NA	NA	0.0	0.0	0.0	0.0	**$18**
6.5x55mm Swe.*	139/140	2850	2640	2440	2250	2070	2525	2170	1855	1575	1330	+2.5	+1.6	-5.4	-18.9	**$18**
6.5x55mm Swe.	156	2650	2370	2110	1870	1650	2425	1950	1550	1215	945	+2.5	0.0	-10.3	-30.6	**NA**
260 Remington	125	2875	2669	2473	2285	2105	2294	1977	1697	1449	1230	1.71	0.0	-7.4	-21.4	**NA**
260 Remington	140	2750	2544	2347	2158	1979	2351	2011	1712	1448	1217	+2.2	0.0	-8.6	-24.6	**NA**
6.5 Creedmoor	120	3020	2815	2619	2430	2251	2430	2111	1827	1574	1350	1.4	0.0	-6.5	-18.9	**NA**
6.5 Creedmoor	140	2820	2654	2494	2339	2190	2472	2179	1915	1679	1467	1.7	0.0	-7.2	-20.6	**NA**
6.5-284 Norma	142	3025	2890	2758	2631	2507	2886	2634	2400	2183	1982	1.13	0.0	-5.7	-16.4	**NA**
6.71 (264) Phantom	120	3150	2929	2718	2517	2325	2645	2286	1969	1698	1440	+1.3	0.0	-6.0	-17.5	**NA**
6.5 Rem. Mag.	120	3210	2905	2621	2353	2102	2745	2248	1830	1475	1177	+2.5	+1.7	-4.1	-16.3	**Disc.**
264 Win. Mag.	140	3030	2782	2548	2326	2114	2854	2406	2018	1682	1389	+2.5	+1.4	-5.1	-18.0	**$24**
6.71 (264) Blackbird	140	3480	3261	3053	2855	2665	3766	3307	2899	2534	2208	+2.4	+3.1	0.0	-7.4	**NA**
6.8mm Rem.	115	2775	2472	2190	1926	1683	1966	1561	1224	947	723	+2.1	0.0	-3.7	-9.4	**NA**
27																
270 Winchester	100	3430	3021	2649	2305	1988	2612	2027	1557	1179	877	+2.0	+1.0	-4.9	-17.5	**$17**
270 Win. (Rem.)	115	2710	2482	2265	2059	NA	1875	1485	1161	896	NA	0.0	4.8	-17.3	0.0	**NA**
270 Winchester	130	3060	2776	2510	2259	2022	2702	2225	1818	1472	1180	+2.5	+1.4	-5.3	-18.2	**$17**
270 Win. Supreme	130	3150	2881	2628	2388	2161	2865	2396	1993	1646	1348	1.3	0.0	-6.4	-18.9	**NA**
270 Winchester	135	3000	2780	2570	2369	2178	2697	2315	1979	1682	1421	+2.5	+1.4	-6.0	-17.6	**$23**
270 Winchester*	140	2940	2700	2480	2260	2060	2685	2270	1905	1590	1315	+2.5	+1.8	-4.6	-17.9	**$20**
270 Win. Light Magnum	130	3215	2998	2790	2590	2400	2983	2594	2246	1936	1662	1.21	0.0	-5.83	-17.0	**NA**
270 Winchester*	150	2850	2585	2336	2100	1879	2705	2226	1817	1468	1175	+2.5	+1.2	-6.5	-22.0	**$17**
270 Win. Supreme	150	2930	2693	2468	2254	2051	2860	2416	2030	1693	1402	1.7	0.0	-7.4	-21.6	**NA**
270 WSM	130	3275	3041	2820	2609	2408	3096	2669	2295	1564	1673	1.1	0.0	-5.5	-16.1	**NA**
270 WSM	140	3125	2865	2619	2386	2165	3035	2559	2132	1769	1457	1.4	0.0	-6.5	-19.0	**NA**
270 WSM	150	3120	2923	2734	2554	2380	3242	2845	2490	2172	1886	1.3	0.0	-5.9	-17.2	**NA**
270 Wea. Mag.	100	3760	3380	3033	2712	2412	3139	2537	2042	1633	1292	+2.0	+2.4	-1.2	-10.1	**$32**
270 Wea. Mag.	130	3375	3119	2878	2649	2432	3287	2808	2390	2026	1707	+2.5	-2.9	-0.9	-9.9	**$32**
270 Wea. Mag.*	150	3245	3036	2837	2647	2465	3507	3070	2681	2334	2023	+2.5	+2.6	-1.8	-11.4	**$47**
7mm																
7mm BR	140	2216	2012	1821	1643	1481	1525	1259	1031	839	681	+2.0	-3.7	-20.0	0.0	**$23**
7mm Mauser*	139/140	2660	2435	2221	2018	1827	2199	1843	1533	1266	1037	+2.5	0.0	-9.6	-27.7	**$17**
7mm Mauser	145	2690	2442	2206	1985	1777	2334	1920	1568	1268	1017	+2.5	+0.1	-9.6	-28.3	**$18**
7mm Mauser	154	2690	2490	2300	2120	1940	2475	2120	1810	1530	1285	+2.5	+0.8	-7.5	-23.5	**$17**
7mm Mauser	175	2440	2137	1857	1603	1382	2313	1774	1340	998	742	+2.5	-1.7	-16.1	0.0	**$17**
7x57 Light Mag.	139	2970	2730	2503	2287	2082	2722	2301	1933	1614	1337	+1.6	0.0	-7.2	-21.0	**NA**
7x30 Waters	120	2700	2300	1930	1600	1330	1940	1405	990	685	470	+2.5	-0.2	-12.3	0.0	**$18**
7mm-08 Rem.	120	3000	2725	2467	2223	1992	2398	1979	1621	1316	1058	+2.0	0.0	-7.6	-22.3	**$18**
7mm-08 Rem.*	140	2860	2625	2402	2189	1988	2542	2142	1793	1490	1228	+2.5	+0.8	-6.9	-21.9	**$18**
7mm-08 Rem.	154	2715	2510	2315	2128	1950	2520	2155	1832	1548	1300	+2.5	+1.0	-7.0	-22.7	**$23**
7mm-08 Light Mag.	139	3000	2790	2590	2399	2216	2777	2403	2071	1776	1515	+1.5	0.0	-6.7	-19.4	**NA**
7x64mm Bren.	140	Not Yet Announced														**$17**
7x64mm Bren.	154	2820	2610	2420	2230	2050	2720	2335	1995	1695	1430	+2.5	+1.4	-5.7	-19.9	**NA**
7x64mm Bren.*	160	2850	2669	2495	2327	2166	2885	2530	2211	1924	1667	+2.5	+1.6	-4.8	-17.8	**$24**
7x64mm Bren.	175	Not Yet Announced														**$17**
284 Winchester	150	2860	2595	2344	2108	1886	2724	2243	1830	1480	1185	+2.5	+0.8	-7.3	-23.2	**$24**
280 Remington	120	3150	2866	2599	2348	2110	2643	2188	1800	1468	1186	+2.0	+0.6	-6.0	-17.9	**$17**
280 Remington	140	3000	2758	2528	2309	2102	2797	2363	1986	1657	1373	+2.5	+1.4	-5.2	-18.3	**$17**
280 Remington*	150	2890	2624	2373	2135	1912	2781	2293	1875	1518	1217	+2.5	+0.8	-7.1	-22.6	**$17**
280 Remington	160	2840	2637	2442	2556	2078	2866	2471	2120	1809	1535	+2.5	+0.8	-6.7	-21.0	**$20**
280 Remington	165	2820	2510	2220	1950	1701	2913	2308	1805	1393	1060	+2.5	+0.4	-8.8	-26.5	**$17**

Many manufacturers do not supply suggested retail prices. Others did not get their pricing to us before press time. All pricing can vary dependent on the exact brand and style of ammo selected and/or the retail outlet from which you make your purchase. Pricing has been rounded to the nearest dollar and represents our best estimate of average pricing. An * after the cartridge means these loads are available with Nosler Partition or Swift A-Frame bullets. Listed pricing may or may not reflect this bullet type. ** = these are packed 50 to box, all others are 20 to box. Wea. Mag.= Weatherby Magnum. Spfd. = Springfield. A-Sq. = A-Square. N.E.=Nitro Express.

Cartridge	Bullet Wgt. Grs.	VELOCITY (fps)					ENERGY (ft. lbs.)					TRAJ. (in.)				Est. Price/ box
		Muzzle	100 yds.	200 yds.	300 yds.	400 yds.	Muzzle	100 yds.	200 yds.	300 yds.	400 yds.	100 yds.	200 yds.	300 yds.	400 yds.	
7x61mm S&H Sup.	154	3060	2720	2400	2100	1820	3200	2520	1965	1505	1135	+2.5	+1.8	-5.0	-19.8	NA
7mm Dakota	160	3200	3001	2811	2630	2455	3637	3200	2808	2456	2140	+2.1	+1.9	-2.8	-12.5	NA
7mm Rem. Mag. (Rem.)	140	2710	2482	2265	2059	NA	2283	1915	1595	1318	NA	0.0	-4.5	-1.57	0.0	NA
7mm Rem. Mag.*	139/140	3150	2930	2710	2510	2320	3085	2660	2290	1960	1670	+2.5	+2.4	-2.4	-12.7	$21
7mm Rem. Hvy Mag	139	3250	3044	2847	2657	2475	3259	2860	2501	2178	1890	1.1	0.0	-5.5	-16.2	NA
7mm Rem. Mag.	150/154	3110	2830	2568	2320	2085	3221	2667	2196	1792	1448	+2.5	+1.6	-4.6	-16.5	$21
7mm Rem. Mag.*	160/162	2950	2730	2520	2320	2120	3090	2650	2250	1910	1600	+2.5	+1.8	-4.4	-17.8	$34
7mm Rem. Mag.	165	2900	2699	2507	2324	2147	3081	2669	2303	1978	1689	+2.5	+1.2	-5.9	-19.0	$28
7mm Rem Mag.	175	2860	2645	2440	2244	2057	3178	2718	2313	1956	1644	+2.5	+1.0	-6.5	-20.7	$21
7mm Rem. SA ULTRA MAG	140	3175	2934	2707	2490	2283	3033	2676	2277	1927	1620	1.3	0.0	-6	-17.7	NA
7mm Rem. SA ULTRA MAG	150	3110	2828	2563	2313	2077	3221	2663	2188	1782	1437	2.5	2.1	-3.6	-15.8	NA
7mm Rem. SA ULTRA MAG	160	2960	2762	2572	2390	2215	3112	2709	2350	2029	1743	2.6	2.2	-3.6	-15.4	NA
7mm Rem. WSM	140	3225	3008	2801	2603	2414	3233	2812	2438	2106	1812	1.2	0.0	-5.6	-16.4	NA
7mm Rem. WSM	160	2990	2744	2512	2081	1883	3176	2675	2241	1864	1538	1.6	0.0	-7.1	-20.8	NA
7mm Wea. Mag.	140	3225	2970	2729	2501	2283	3233	2741	2315	1943	1621	+2.5	+2.0	-3.2	-14.0	$35
7mm Wea. Mag.	154	3260	3023	2799	2586	2382	3539	3044	2609	2227	1890	+2.5	+2.8	-1.5	-10.8	$32
7mm Wea. Mag.*	160	3200	3004	2816	2637	2464	3637	3205	2817	2469	2156	+2.5	+2.7	-1.5	-10.6	$47
7mm Wea. Mag.	165	2950	2747	2553	2367	2189	3188	2765	2388	2053	1756	+2.5	+1.8	-4.2	-16.4	$43
7mm Wea. Mag.	175	2910	2693	2486	2288	2098	3293	2818	2401	2033	1711	+2.5	+1.2	-5.9	-19.4	$35
7.21(.284) Tomahawk	140	3300	3118	2943	2774	2612	3386	3022	2693	2393	2122	2.3	3.20	0.0	-7.7	NA
7mm STW	140	3325	3064	2818	2585	2364	3436	2918	2468	2077	1737	+2.3	+1.8	-3.0	-13.1	NA
7mm STW Supreme	160	3150	2894	2652	2422	2204	3526	2976	2499	2085	1727	1.3	0.0	-6.3	-18.5	NA
7mm Rem. Ultra Mag.	140	3425	3184	2956	2740	2534	3646	3151	2715	2333	1995	1.7	1.60	-2.6	-11.4	NA
7mm Firehawk	140	3625	3373	3135	2909	2695	4084	3536	3054	2631	2258	+2.2	+2.9	0.0	-7.03	NA
30																
7.21 (.284) Firebird	140	3750	3522	3306	3101	2905	4372	3857	3399	2990	2625	1.6	2.4	0.0	-6.0	NA
30 Carbine	110	1990	1567	1236	1035	923	977	600	373	262	208	0.0	-13.5	0.0	0.0	$28**
303 Savage	190	1890	1612	1327	1183	1055	1507	1096	794	591	469	+2.5	-7.6	0.0	0.0	$24
30 Remington	170	2120	1822	1555	1328	1153	1696	1253	913	666	502	+2.5	-4.7	-26.3	0.0	$20
7.62x39mm Rus.	123/125	2300	2030	1780	1550	1350	1445	1125	860	655	500	+2.5	-2.0	-17.5	0.0	$13
30-30 Win.	55	3400	2693	2085	1570	1187	1412	886	521	301	172	+2.0	0.0	-10.2	-35.0	$18
30-30 Win.	125	2570	2090	1660	1320	1080	1830	1210	770	480	320	-2.0	-2.6	-19.9	0.0	$13
30-30 Win.	150	2390	2040	1723	1447	1225	1902	1386	989	697	499	0.0	-7.5	-27.0	-63.0	NA
30-30 Win. Supreme	150	2480	2095	1747	1446	1209	2049	1462	1017	697	487	0.0	-6.5	-24.5	0.0	NA
30-30 Win.	160	2300	1997	1719	1473	1268	1879	1416	1050	771	571	+2.5	-2.9	-20.2	0.0	$18
30-30 Win. Lever Evolution	160	2400	2150	1916	1699	NA	2046	1643	1304	1025	NA	3.00	0.20	-12.1	NA	NA
30-30 PMC Cowboy	170	1300	1198	1121			638	474				0.0	-27.0	0.0	0.0	NA
30-30 Win.*	170	2200	1895	1619	1381	1191	1827	1355	989	720	535	+2.5	-5.8	-23.6	0.0	$13
300 Savage	150	2630	2354	2094	1853	1631	2303	1845	1462	1143	886	+2.5	-0.4	-10.1	-30.7	$17
300 Savage	180	2350	2137	1935	1754	1570	2207	1825	1496	1217	985	+2.5	-1.6	-15.2	0.0	$17
30-40 Krag	180	2430	2213	2007	1813	1632	2360	1957	1610	1314	1064	+2.5	-1.4	-13.8	0.0	$18
7.65x53mm Arg.	180	2590	2390	2200	2010	1830	2685	2280	1925	1615	1345	+2.5	0.0	-27.6	0.0	NA
7.5x53mm Argentine	150	2785	2519	2269	2032	1814	2583	2113	1714	1376	1096	+2.0	0.0	-8.8	-25.5	NA
308 Marlin Express	160	2660	2430	2226	2026	1836	2513	2111	1761	1457	1197	3.0	1.7	-6.7	-23.5	NA
307 Winchester	150	2760	2321	1924	1575	1289	2530	1795	1233	826	554	+2.5	-1.5	-13.6	0.0	Disc.
307 Winchester	180	2510	2179	1874	1599	1362	2519	1898	1404	1022	742	+2.5	-1.6	-15.6	0.0	$20
7.5x55 Swiss	180	2650	2450	2250	2060	1880	2805	2390	2020	1700	1415	+2.5	+0.6	-8.1	-24.9	NA
7.5x55mm Swiss	165	2720	2515	2319	2132	1954	2710	2317	1970	1665	1398	+2.0	0.0	-8.5	-24.6	NA
308 Winchester	55	3770	3215	2726	2286	1888	1735	1262	907	638	435	-2.0	+1.4	-3.8	-15.8	$22
308 Winchester	150	2820	2533	2263	2009	1774	2648	2137	1705	1344	1048	+2.5	+0.4	-8.5	-26.1	$17
308 Winchester	165	2700	2440	2194	1963	1748	2670	2180	1763	1411	1199	+2.5	0.0	-9.7	-28.5	$20
308 Winchester	168	2680	2493	2314	2143	1979	2678	2318	1998	1713	1460	+2.5	0.0	-8.9	-25.3	$18
308 Win. (Fed.)	170	2000	1740	1510	NA	NA	1510	1145	860	NA	NA	0.0	0.0	0.0	0.0	NA
308 Winchester	178	2620	2415	2220	2034	1857	2713	2306	1948	1635	1363	+2.5	0.0	-9.6	-27.6	$23
308 Winchester*	180	2620	2393	2178	1974	1782	2743	2288	1896	1557	1269	+2.5	-0.2	-10.2	-28.5	$17
308 Light Mag.*	150	2980	2703	2442	2195	1964	2959	2433	1986	1606	1285	+1.6	0.0	-7.5	-22.2	NA
308 Light Mag.	165	2870	2658	2456	2263	2078	3019	2589	2211	1877	1583	+1.7	0.0	-7.5	-21.8	NA
308 High Energy	165	2870	2600	2350	2120	1890	3020	2485	2030	1640	1310	+1.8	0.0	-8.2	-24.0	NA
308 Light Mag.	168	2870	2658	2456	2263	2078	3019	2589	2211	1877	1583	+1.7	0.0	-7.5	-21.8	NA
308 High Energy	180	2740	2550	2370	2200	2030	3000	2600	2245	1925	1645	+1.9	0.0	-8.2	-23.5	NA
30-06 Spfd.	55	4080	3485	2965	2502	2083	2033	1483	1074	764	530	+2.0	+1.9	-2.1	-11.7	$22
30-06 Spfd. (Rem.)	125	2660	2335	2034	1757	NA	1964	1513	1148	856	NA	0.0	-5.2	-18.9	0.0	NA
30-06 Spfd.	125	3140	2780	2447	2138	1853	2736	2145	1662	1279	953	+2.0	+1.0	-6.2	-21.0	$17
30-06 Spfd.	150	2910	2617	2342	2083	1853	2820	2281	1827	1445	1135	+2.5	+0.8	-7.2	-23.4	$17
30-06 Spfd.	152	2910	2654	2413	2184	1968	2858	2378	1965	1610	1307	+2.5	+1.0	-6.6	-21.3	$23
30-06 Spfd.*	165	2800	2534	2283	2047	1825	2872	2352	1909	1534	1220	+2.5	+0.4	-8.4	-25.5	$17
30-06 Spfd.	168	2710	2522	2346	2169	2003	2739	2372	2045	1754	1497	+2.5	+0.4	-8.0	-23.5	$18
30-06 Spfd. (Fed.)	170	2000	1740	1510	NA	NA	1510	1145	860	NA	NA	0.0	0.0	0.0	0.0	NA
30-06 Spfd.	178	2720	2511	2311	2121	1939	2924	2491	2111	1777	1486	+2.5	+0.4	-8.2	-24.6	$23
30-06 Spfd.*	180	2700	2469	2250	2042	1846	2913	2436	2023	1666	1362	-2.5	0.0	-9.3	-27.0	$17
30-06 Spfd.	220	2410	2130	1870	1632	1422	2837	2216	1708	1301	988	+2.5	-1.7	-18.0	0.0	$17
30 Mag.																
30-06 Light Mag.	150	3100	2815	2548	2295	2058	3200	2639	2161	1755	1410	+1.4	0.0	-6.8	-20.3	NA

AVERAGE CENTERFIRE RIFLE CARTRIDGE BALLISTICS & PRICES (CONT.)

Many manufacturers do not supply suggested retail prices. Others did not get their pricing to us before press time. All pricing can vary dependent on the exact brand and style of ammo selected and/or the retail outlet from which you make your purchase. Pricing has been rounded to the nearest dollar and represents our best estimate of average pricing. An * after the cartridge means these loads are available with Nosler Partition or Swift A-Frame bullets. Listed pricing may or may not reflect this bullet type. ** = these are packed 50 to box, all others are 20 to box. Wea. Mag.= Weatherby Magnum. Spfd. = Springfield. A-Sq. = A-Square. N.E.=Nitro Express.

Cartridge	Bullet Wgt. Grs.	VELOCITY (fps)					ENERGY (ft. lbs.)					TRAJ. (in.)				Est. Price/ box
		Muzzle	100 yds.	200 yds.	300 yds.	400 yds.	Muzzle	100 yds.	200 yds.	300 yds.	400 yds.	100 yds.	200 yds.	300 yds.	400 yds.	
30-06 Light Mag.	180	2880	2676	2480	2293	2114	3316	2862	2459	2102	1786	+1.7	0.0	-7.3	-21.3	**NA**
30-06 High Energy	180	2880	2690	2500	2320	2150	3315	2880	2495	2150	1845	+1.7	0.0	-7.2	-21.0	**NA**
30 T/C	150	3000	2772	2555	2348	2151	2997	2558	2173	1836	1540	1.5	0.0	-6.9	-20.0	**NA**
30 T/C	165	2850	2644	2447	2258	2078	2975	2560	2193	1868	1582	1.7	0.0	-7.6	-22.0	**NA**
300 REM SA ULTRA MAG	150	3200	2901	2622	2359	2112	3410	2803	2290	1854	1485	1.3	0.0	-6.4	-19.1	**NA**
300 REM SA ULTRA MAG	165	3075	2792	2527	2276	2040	3464	2856	2339	1898	1525	1.5	0.0	-7	-20.7	**NA**
300 REM SA ULTRA MAG	180	2960	2761	2571	2389	2214	3501	3047	2642	2280	1959	2.6	2.2	-3.6	-15.4	**NA**
7.82 (308) Patriot	150	3250	2999	2762	2537	2323	3519	2997	2542	2145	1798	+1.2	0.0	-5.8	-16.9	**NA**
300 RCM	150	3300	3056	2825	2606	2397	3627	3110	2658	2262	1914	1.1	0.0	-5.4	-16.0	**NA**
300 RCM	165	3140	2921	2713	2514	2324	3612	3126	2697	2316	1979	1.3	0.0	-6.0	-17.5	**NA**
300 RCM	180	3000	2802	2613	2432	2258	3597	3139	2729	2363	2037	1.5	0.0	-6.5	-18.9	**NA**
300 WSM	150	3300	3061	2834	2619	2414	3628	3121	2676	2285	1941	1.1	0.0	-5.4	-15.9	**NA**
300 WSM	180	2970	2741	2524	2317	2120	3526	3005	2547	2147	1797	1.6	0.0	-7.0	-20.5	**NA**
300 WSM	180	3010	2923	2734	2554	2380	3242	2845	2490	2172	1886	1.3	0	-5.9	-17.2	**NA**
308 Norma Mag.	180	3020	2820	2630	2440	2270	3645	3175	2755	2385	2050	+2.5	+2.0	-3.5	-14.8	**NA**
300 Dakota	200	3000	2824	2656	2493	2336	3996	3542	3131	2760	2423	+2.2	+1.5	-4.0	-15.2	**NA**
300 H&H Magnum*	180	2880	2640	2412	2196	1990	3315	2785	2325	1927	1583	+2.5	+0.8	-6.8	-21.7	**$24**
300 H&H Magnum	220	2550	2267	2002	1757	NA	3167	2510	1958	1508	NA	-2.5	-0.4	-12.0	0.0	**NA**
300 Win. Mag.	150	3290	2951	2636	2342	2068	3605	2900	2314	1827	1424	+2.5	+1.9	-3.8	-15.8	**$22**
300 Win. Mag.	165	3100	2877	2665	2462	2269	3522	3033	2603	2221	1897	+2.5	+2.4	-3.0	-16.9	**$24**
300 Win. Mag.	178	2900	2760	2568	2375	2191	3509	3030	2606	2230	1897	+2.5	+1.4	-5.0	-17.6	**$29**
300 Win. Mag.*	180	2960	2745	2540	2344	2157	3501	3011	2578	2196	1859	+2.5	+1.2	-5.5	-18.5	**$22**
300 W.M. High Energy	180	3100	2830	2580	2340	2110	3840	3205	2660	2190	1790	+1.4	0.0	-6.6	-19.7	**NA**
300 W.M. Light Mag.	180	3100	2879	2668	2467	2275	3840	3313	2845	2431	2068	+1.39	0.0	-6.45	-18.7	**NA**
300 Win. Mag.	190	2885	1691	2506	2327	2156	3511	3055	2648	2285	1961	+2.5	+1.2	-5.7	-19.0	**$26**
300 W.M. High Energy	200	2930	2740	2550	2370	2200	3810	3325	2885	2495	2145	+1.6	0.0	-6.9	-20.1	**NA**
300 Win. Mag.*	200	2825	2595	2376	2167	1970	3545	2991	2508	2086	1742	-2.5	+1.6	-4.7	-17.2	**$36**
300 Win. Mag.	220	2680	2448	2228	2020	1823	3508	2927	2424	1993	1623	+2.5	0.0	-9.5	-27.5	**$23**
300 Rem. Ultra Mag.	150	3450	3208	2980	2762	2556	3964	3427	2956	2541	2175	1.7	1.5	-2.6	-11.2	**NA**
300 Rem. Ultra Mag.	150	2910	2686	2473	2279	2077	2820	2403	2037	1716	1436	1.7	0.0	-7.4	-21.5	**NA**
300 Rem. Ultra Mag.	180	3250	3037	2834	2640	2454	4221	3686	3201	2786	2407	2.4	0.0	-3.0	-12.7	**NA**
300 Rem. Ultra Mag.	180	2960	2774	2505	2294	2093	3501	2971	2508	2103	1751	2.7	2.2	-3.8	-16.4	**NA**
300 Rem. Ultra Mag.	200	3032	2791	2562	2345	2138	4083	3459	2916	2442	2030	1.5	0.0	-6.8	-19.9	**NA**
300 Wea. Mag.	100	3900	3441	3038	2652	2305	3714	2891	2239	1717	1297	+2.0	+2.6	-0.6	-8.7	**$32**
300 Wea. Mag.	150	3600	3307	3033	2776	2533	4316	3642	3064	2566	2137	+2.5	+3.2	0.0	-8.1	**$32**
300 Wea. Mag.	165	3450	3210	3000	2792	2593	4360	3796	3297	2855	2464	+2.5	+3.2	0.0	-7.8	**NA**
300 Wea. Mag.	178	3120	2902	2695	2497	2308	3847	3329	2870	2464	2104	+2.5	-1.7	-3.6	-14.7	**$43**
300 Wea. Mag.	180	3330	3110	2910	2710	2520	4430	3875	3375	2935	2540	+1.0	0.0	-5.2	-15.1	**NA**
300 Wea. Mag.	190	3030	2830	2638	2455	2279	3873	3378	2936	2542	2190	+2.5	+1.6	-4.3	-16.0	**$38**
300 Wea. Mag.	220	2850	2541	2283	1964	1736	3967	3155	2480	1922	1471	+2.5	+0.4	-8.5	-26.4	**$35**
300 Warbird	180	3400	3180	2971	2772	2582	4620	4042	3528	3071	2664	+2.59	+3.25	0.0	-7.95	**NA**
300 Pegasus	180	3500	3319	3145	2978	2817	4896	4401	3953	3544	3172	+2.28	+2.89	0.0	-6.79	**NA**
31																
32-20 Win.	100	1210	1021	913	834	769	325	231	185	154	131	0.0	-32.3	0.0	0.0	**$23****
303 British	150	2685	2441	2210	1992	1787	2401	1984	1627	1321	1064	+2.5	+0.6	-8.4	-26.2	**$18**
303 British	180	2460	2124	1817	1542	1311	2418	1803	1319	950	687	+2.5	-1.8	-16.8	0.0	**$18**
303 Light Mag.	150	2830	2570	2325	2094	1884	2667	2199	1800	1461	1185	+2.0	0.0	-8.4	-24.6	**NA**
7.62x54mm Rus.	146	2950	2730	2520	2320	NA	2820	2415	2055	1740	NA	+2.5	+2.0	-4.4	-17.7	**NA**
7.62x54mm Rus.	180	2580	2370	2180	2000	1820	2650	2250	1900	1590	1100	+2.5	0.0	-9.8	-28.5	**NA**
7.7x58mm Jap.	150	2640	2399	2170	1954	1752	2321	1916	1568	1271	1022	+2.3	0.0	-9.7	-28.5	**NA**
7.7x58mm Jap.	180	2500	2300	2100	1920	1750	2490	2105	1770	1475	1225	+2.5	0.0	-10.4	-30.2	**NA**
8x56 R	205	2400	2188	1987	1797	1621	2621	2178	1796	1470	1196	+2.9	0.0	-11.7	-34.3	**NA**
8mm																
8x57mm JS Mau.	165	2850	2520	2210	1930	1670	2965	2330	1795	1360	1015	+2.5	+1.0	-7.7	0.0	**NA**
32 Win. Special	165	2410	2145	1897	1669	NA	2128	1685	1318	1020	NA	2.0	0.0	-13.0	-19.9	**NA**
32 Win. Special	170	2250	1921	1626	1372	1175	1911	1393	998	710	521	+2.5	-3.5	-22.9	0.0	**$14**
8mm Mauser	170	2360	1969	1622	1333	1123	2102	1464	993	671	476	+2.5	-3.1	-22.2	0.0	**$18**
325 WSM	180	3060	2841	2632	2432	2242	3743	3226	2769	2365	2009	+1.4	0.0	-6.4	-18.7	**NA**
325 WSM	200	2950	2753	2565	2384	2210	3866	3367	2922	2524	2170	+1.5	0.0	-6.8	-19.8	**NA**
325 WSM	220	2840	2605	2382	2169	1968	3941	3316	2772	2300	1893	+1.8	0.0	-8.0	-23.3	**NA**
8mm Rem. Mag.	185	3080	2761	2464	2186	1927	3896	3131	2494	1963	1525	+2.5	+1.4	-5.5	-19.7	**$30**
8mm Rem. Mag.	220	2830	2581	2346	2123	1913	3912	3254	2688	2201	1787	+2.5	+0.6	-7.6	-23.5	**Disc.**
33																
338 Federal	180	2830	2590	2350	2130	1930	3200	2670	2215	1820	1480	1.80	0.00	-8.2	-23.9	**NA**
338 Federal	185	2750	2550	2350	2160	1980	3105	2660	2265	1920	1615	1.90	0.00	-8.3	-24.1	**NA**
338 Federal	210	2630	2410	2200	2010	1820	3225	2710	2265	1880	1545	2.30	0.00	-9.4	-27.3	**NA**
338-06	200	2750	2553	2364	2184	2011	3358	2894	2482	2118	1796	+1.9	0.0	-8.22	-23.6	**NA**
330 Dakota	250	2900	2719	2545	2378	2217	4668	4103	3595	3138	2727	+2.3	+1.3	-5.0	-17.5	**NA**
338 Lapua	250	2963	2795	2640	2493	NA	4842	4341	3881	3458	NA	+1.9	0.0	-7.9	0.0	**NA**
338 RCM	200	2950	2744	2547	2359	2179	3865	3344	2881	2471	2108	1.6	0.0	-6.9	-20.0	**NA**
338 RCM	225	2775	2598	2427	2264	2106	3847	3372	2944	2560	2216	1.8	0.0	-7.7	-22.2	**NA**

Many manufacturers do not supply suggested retail prices. Others did not get their pricing to us before press time. All pricing can vary dependent on the exact brand and style of ammo selected and/or the retail outlet from which you make your purchase. Pricing has been rounded to the nearest dollar and represents our best estimate of average pricing. An * after the cartridge means these loads are available with Nosler Partition or Swift A-Frame bullets. Listed pricing may or may not reflect this bullet type. ** = these are packed 50 to box, all others are 20 to box. Wea. Mag.= Weatherby Magnum. Spfd. = Springfield. A-Sq. = A-Square. N.E.=Nitro Express.

Cartridge	Bullet Wgt. Grs.	VELOCITY (fps)					ENERGY (ft. lbs.)					TRAJ. (in.)				Est. Price/ box
		Muzzle	100 yds.	200 yds.	300 yds.	400 yds.	Muzzle	100 yds.	200 yds.	300 yds.	400 yds.	100 yds.	200 yds.	300 yds.	400 yds.	
338 Win. Mag.	200	2960	2658	2375	2110	1862	3890	3137	2505	1977	1539	+2.5	+1.0	-6.7	-22.3	**$27**
338 Win. Mag.*	210	2830	2590	2370	2150	1940	3735	3130	2610	2155	1760	+2.5	+1.4	-6.0	-20.9	**$33**
338 Win. Mag.*	225	2785	2517	2266	2029	1808	3871	3165	2565	2057	1633	+2.5	+0.4	-8.5	-25.9	**$27**
338 W.M. Heavy Mag.	225	2920	2678	2449	2232	2027	4259	3583	2996	2489	2053	+1.75	0.0	-7.65	-22.0	**NA**
338 W.M. High Energy	225	2940	2690	2450	2230	2010	4320	3610	3000	2475	2025	+1.7	0.0	-7.5	-22.0	**NA**
338 Win. Mag.	230	2780	2573	2375	2186	2005	3948	3382	2881	2441	2054	+2.5	+1.2	-6.3	-21.0	**$40**
338 Win. Mag.*	250	2660	2456	2261	2075	1898	3927	3348	2837	2389	1999	+2.5	+0.2	-9.0	-26.2	**$27**
338 W.M. High Energy	250	2800	2610	2420	2250	2080	4350	3775	3260	2805	2395	+1.8	0.0	-7.8	-22.5	**NA**
338 Ultra Mag.	250	2860	2645	2440	2244	2057	4540	3882	3303	2794	2347	1.7	0.0	-7.6	-22.1	**NA**
8.59(.338) Galaxy	200	3100	2899	2707	2524	2347	4269	3734	3256	2829	2446	3	3.80	0.0	-9.3	**NA**
340 Wea. Mag.*	210	3250	2991	2746	2515	2295	4924	4170	3516	2948	2455	+2.5	+1.9	-1.8	-11.8	**$56**
340 Wea. Mag.*	250	3000	2806	2621	2443	2272	4995	4371	3812	3311	2864	+2.5	+2.0	-3.5	-14.8	**$56**
338 A-Square	250	3120	2799	2500	2220	1958	5403	4348	3469	2736	2128	+2.5	+2.7	-1.5	-10.5	**NA**
338-378 Wea. Mag.	225	3180	2974	2778	2591	2410	5052	4420	3856	3353	2902	3.1	3.80	0.0	-8.9	**NA**
338 Titan	225	3230	3010	2800	2600	2409	5211	4524	3916	3377	2898	+3.07	+3.80	0.0	-8.95	**NA**
338 Excalibur	200	3600	3361	3134	2920	2715	5755	5015	4363	3785	3274	+2.23	+2.87	0.0	-6.99	**NA**
338 Excalibur	250	3250	2922	2618	2333	2066	5863	4740	3804	3021	2370	+1.3	0.0	-6.35	-19.2	**NA**
34, 35																
348 Winchester	200	2520	2215	1931	1672	1443	2820	2178	1656	1241	925	+2.5	-1.4	-14.7	0.0	**$42**
357 Magnum	158	1830	1427	1138	980	883	1175	715	454	337	274	0.0	-16.2	-33.1	0.0	**$25****
35 Remington	150	2300	1874	1506	1218	1039	1762	1169	755	494	359	+2.5	-4.1	-26.3	0.0	**$16**
35 Remington	200	2080	1698	1376	1140	1001	1921	1280	841	577	445	+2.5	-6.3	-17.1	-33.6	**$16**
35 Rem. Lever Evolution	200	2225	1963	1721	1503	NA	2198	1711	1315	1003	NA	3.00	-1.30	-17.5	NA	**NA**
356 Winchester	200	2460	2114	1797	1517	1284	2688	1985	1434	1022	732	+2.5	-1.8	-15.1	0.0	**$31**
356 Winchester	250	2160	1911	1682	1476	1299	2591	2028	1571	1210	937	+2.5	-3.7	-22.2	0.0	**$31**
358 Winchester	200	2490	2171	1876	1619	1379	2753	2093	1563	1151	844	+2.5	-1.6	-15.6	0.0	**$31**
358 STA	275	2850	2562	2292	2039	NA	4958	4009	3208	2539	NA	+1.9	0.0	-8.6	0.0	**NA**
350 Rem. Mag.	200	2710	2410	2130	1870	1631	3261	2579	2014	1553	1181	+2.5	-0.2	-10.0	-30.1	**$33**
35 Whelen	200	2675	2378	2100	1842	1606	3177	2510	1958	1506	1145	+2.5	-0.2	-10.3	-31.1	**$20**
35 Whelen	225	2500	2300	2110	1930	1770	3120	2650	2235	1870	1560	+2.6	0.0	-10.2	-29.9	**NA**
35 Whelen	250	2400	2197	2005	1823	1652	3197	2680	2230	1844	1515	+2.5	-1.2	-13.7	0.0	**$20**
358 Norma Mag.	250	2800	2510	2230	1970	1730	4350	3480	2750	2145	1655	+2.5	+1.0	-7.6	-25.2	**NA**
358 STA	275	2850	2562	229*2	2039	1764	4959	4009	3208	2539	1899	+1.9	0.0	-8.58	-26.1	**NA**
9.3mm																
9.3x57mm Mau.	286	2070	1810	1590	1390	1110	2710	2090	1600	1220	955	+2.5	-2.6	-22.5	0.0	**NA**
9.3x62mm Mau.	286	2360	2089	1844	1623	NA	3538	2771	2157	1670	1260	+2.5	-1.6	-21.0	0.0	**NA**
370 Sako Mag.	286	3550	2370	2200	2040	2880	4130	3570	3075	2630	2240	2.4	0.0	-9.5	-27.2	**NA**
9.3x64mm	286	2700	2505	2318	2139	1968	4629	3984	3411	2906	2460	+2.5	+2.7	-4.5	-19.2	**NA**
9.3x74Rmm	286	2360	2136	1924	1727	1545	3536	2896	2351	1893	1516	0.0	-6.1	-21.7	-49.0	**NA**
375																
38-55 Win.	255	1320	1190	1091	1018	963	987	802	674	587	525	0.0	-23.4	0.0	0.0	**$25**
375 Winchester	200	2200	1841	1526	1268	1089	2150	1506	1034	714	527	+2.5	-4.0	-26.2	0.0	**$27**
375 Winchester	250	1900	1647	1424	1239	1103	2005	1506	1126	852	676	+2.5	-6.9	-33.3	0.0	**$27**
376 Steyr	225	2600	2331	2078	1842	1625	3377	2714	2157	1694	1319	2.5	0.0	-10.6	-31.4	**NA**
376 Steyr	270	2600	2372	2156	1951	1759	4052	3373	2787	2283	1855	2.3	0.0	-9.9	-28.9	**NA**
375 Dakota	300	2600	2316	2051	1804	1579	4502	3573	2800	2167	1661	+2.4	0.0	-11.0	-32.7	**NA**
375 N.E. 2-1/2"	270	2000	1740	1507	1310	NA	2398	1815	1362	1026	NA	+2.5	-6.0	-30.0	0.0	**NA**
375 Flanged	300	2450	2150	1886	1640	NA	3998	3102	2369	1790	NA	+2.5	-2.4	-17.0	0.0	**NA**
375 Ruger	270	2840	2600	2372	2156	1951	4835	4052	3373	2786	2283	1.8	0.0	-8.0	-23.6	**NA**
375 Ruger	300	2660	2344	2050	1780	1536	4713	3660	2800	2110	1572	2.4	0.0	-10.8	-32.6	**NA**
375 H&H Magnum	250	2670	2450	2240	2040	1850	3955	3335	2790	2315	1905	+2.5	-0.4	-10.2	-28.4	**NA**
375 H&H Magnum	270	2690	2420	2166	1928	1707	4337	3510	2812	2228	1747	+2.5	0.0	-10.0	-29.4	**$28**
375 H&H Magnum*	300	2530	2245	1979	1733	1512	4263	3357	2608	2001	1523	+2.5	-1.0	-10.5	-33.6	**$28**
375 H&H Hvy. Mag.	270	2870	2628	2399	2182	1976	4937	4141	3451	2150	1845	+1.7	0.0	-7.2	-21.0	**NA**
375 H&H Hvy. Mag.	300	2705	2386	2090	1816	1568	4873	3793	2908	2195	1637	+2.3	0.0	-10.4	-31.4	**NA**
375 Rem. Ultra Mag.	270	2900	2558	2241	1947	1678	5041	3922	3010	2272	1689	1.9	2.7	-8.9	-27.0	**NA**
375 Rem. Ultra Mag.	300	2760	2505	2263	2035	1822	5073	4178	3412	2759	2210	2.0	0.0	-8.8	-26.1	**NA**
375 Wea. Mag.	300	2700	2420	2157	1911	1685	4856	3901	3100	2432	1891	+2.5	-.04	-10.7	0.0	**NA**
378 Wea. Mag.	270	3180	2976	2781	2594	2415	6062	5308	4635	4034	3495	+2.5	+2.6	-1.8	-11.3	**$71**
378 Wea. Mag.	300	2929	2576	2252	1952	1680	5698	4419	3379	2538	1881	+2.5	+1.2	-7.0	-24.5	**$77**
375 A-Square	300	2920	2626	2351	2093	1850	5679	4594	3681	2917	2281	+2.5	+1.4	-6.0	-21.0	**NA**
38-40 Win.	180	1160	999	901	827	764	538	399	324	273	233	0.0	-33.9	0.0	0.0	**$42****
40, 41																
400 A-Square DPM	400	2400	2146	1909	1689	NA	5116	2092	3236	2533	NA	2.98	0.00	-10.0	NA	**NA**
400 A-Square DPM	170	2980	2463	2001	1598	NA	3352	2289	1512	964	NA	2.16	0.00	-11.1	NA	**NA**
408 CheyTac	419	2850	2752	2657	2562	2470	7551	7048	6565	6108	5675	-1.02	0.00	1.9	4.2	**NA**
405 Win.	300	2200	1851	1545	1296		3224	2282	1589	1119		4.6	0.0	-19.5	0.0	**NA**
450/400-3"	400	2050	1815	1595	1402	NA	3732	2924	2259	1746	NA	0.0	NA	-33.4	NA	**NA**

Average Centerfire Rifle Cartridge Ballistics & Prices (cont.)

Many manufacturers do not supply suggested retail prices. Others did not get their pricing to us before press time. All pricing can vary dependent on the exact brand and style of ammo selected and/or the retail outlet from which you make your purchase. Pricing has been rounded to the nearest dollar and represents our best estimate of average pricing. An * after the cartridge means these loads are available with Nosler Partition or Swift A-Frame bullets. Listed pricing may or may not reflect this bullet type. ** = these are packed 50 to box, all others are 20 to box. Wea. Mag.= Weatherby Magnum. Spfd. = Springfield. A-Sq. = A-Square. N.E.=Nitro Express.

Cartridge	Bullet Wgt. Grs.	VELOCITY (fps)					ENERGY (ft. lbs.)					TRAJ. (in.)				Est. Price/ box
		Muzzle	100 yds.	200 yds.	300 yds.	400 yds.	Muzzle	100 yds.	200 yds.	300 yds.	400 yds.	100 yds.	200 yds.	300 yds.	400 yds.	
416 Dakota	400	2450	2294	2143	1998	1859	5330	4671	4077	3544	3068	+2.5	-0.2	-10.5	-29.4	NA
416 Taylor	400	2350	2117	1896	1693	NA	4905	3980	3194	2547	NA	+2.5	-1.2	15.0	0.0	NA
416 Hoffman	400	2380	2145	1923	1718	1529	5031	4087	3285	2620	2077	+2.5	-1.0	-14.1	0.0	NA
416 Rigby	350	2600	2449	2303	2162	2026	5253	4661	4122	3632	3189	+2.5	-1.8	-10.2	-26.0	NA
416 Rigby	400	2370	2210	2050	1900	NA	4990	4315	3720	3185	NA	+2.5	-0.7	-12.1	0.0	NA
416 Rigby	410	2370	2110	1870	1640	NA	5115	4050	3165	2455	NA	+2.5	-2.4	-17.3	0.0	$110
416 Rem. Mag.*	350	2520	2270	2034	1814	1611	4935	4004	3216	2557	2017	+2.5	-0.8	-12.6	-35.0	$82
416 Rem. Mag.*	400	2400	2175	1962	1763	1579	5115	4201	3419	2760	2214	+2.5	-1.5	-14.6	0.0	$80
416 Wea. Mag.*	400	2700	2397	2115	1852	1613	6474	5104	3971	3047	2310	+2.5	0.0	-10.1	-30.4	$96
10.57 (416) Meteor	400	2730	2532	2342	2161	1987	6621	5695	4874	4147	3508	+1.9	0.0	-8.3	-24.0	NA
404 Jeffrey	400	2150	1924	1716	1525	NA	4105	3289	2614	2064	NA	+2.5	-4.0	-22.1	0.0	NA
425, 44																
425 Express	400	2400	2160	1934	1725	NA	5115	4145	3322	2641	NA	+2.5	-1.0	-14.0	0.0	NA
44-40 Win.	200	1190	1006	900	822	756	629	449	360	300	254	0.0	-33.3	0.0	0.0	$36**
44 Rem. Mag.	210	1920	1477	1155	982	880	1719	1017	622	450	361	0.0	-17.6	0.0	0.0	$14
44 Rem. Mag.	240	1760	1380	1114	970	878	1650	1015	661	501	411	0.0	-17.6	0.0	0.0	$13
444 Marlin	240	2350	1815	1377	1087	941	2942	1753	1001	630	472	+2.5	-15.1	-31.0	0.0	$22
444 Marlin	265	2120	1733	1405	1160	1012	2644	1768	1162	791	603	+2.5	-6.0	-32.2	0.0	Disc.
444 Marlin Light Mag	265	2335	1913	1551	1266		3208	2153	1415	943		2.0	-4.90	-26.5	0.0	NA
444 Mar. Lever Evolution	265	2325	1971	1652	1380	NA	3180	2285	1606	1120	NA	3.00	-1.40	-18.6	NA	NA
45																
45-70 Govt.	300	1810	1497	1244	1073	969	2182	1492	1031	767	625	0.0	-14.8	0.0	0.0	$21
45-70 Govt. Supreme	300	1880	1558	1292	1103	988	2355	1616	1112	811	651	0.0	-12.9	-46.0	-105.0	NA
45-70 Lever Evolution	325	2050	1729	1450	1225	NA	3032	2158	1516	1083	NA	3.00	-4.10	-27.8	NA	NA
45-70 Govt. CorBon	350	1800	1526	1296			2519	1810	1307			0.0	-14.6	0.0	0.0	NA
45-70 Govt.	405	1330	1168	1055	977	918	1590	1227	1001	858	758	0.0	-24.6	0.0	0.0	$21
45-70 Govt. PMC Cowboy	405	1550	1193				1639	1280				0.0	-23.9	0.0	0.0	NA
45-70 Govt. Garrett	415	1850					3150					3.0	-7.0	0.0	0.0	NA
45-70 Govt. Garrett	530	1550	1343	1178	1062	982	2828	2123	1633	1327	1135	0.0	-17.8	0.0	0.0	NA
450 Marlin	350	2100	1774	1488	1254	1089	3427	2446	1720	1222	922	0.0	-9.7	-35.2	0.0	NA
450 Mar. Lever Evolution	325	2225	1887	1585	1331	NA	3572	2569	1813	1278	NA	3.00	-2.20	-21.3	NA	NA
458 Win. Magnum	350	2470	1990	1570	1250	1060	4740	3065	1915	1205	870	+2.5	-2.5	-21.6	0.0	$43
458 Win. Magnum	400	2380	2170	1960	1770	NA	5030	4165	3415	2785	NA	+2.5	-0.4	-13.4	0.0	$73
458 Win. Magnum	465	2220	1999	1791	1601	NA	5088	4127	3312	2646	NA	+2.5	-2.0	-17.7	0.0	NA
458 Win. Magnum	500	2040	1823	1623	1442	1237	4620	3689	2924	2308	1839	+2.5	-3.5	-22.0	0.0	$61
458 Win. Magnum	510	2040	1770	1527	1319	1157	4712	3547	2640	1970	1516	+2.5	-4.1	-25.0	0.0	$41
450 Dakota	500	2450	2235	2030	1838	1658	6663	5544	4576	3748	3051	+2.5	-0.6	-12.0	-33.8	NA
450 N.E. 3-1/4"	465	2190	1970	1765	1577	NA	4952	4009	3216	2567	NA	+2.5	-3.0	-20.0	0.0	NA
450 N.E. 3-1/4"	500	2150	1920	1708	1514	NA	5132	4093	3238	2544	NA	+2.5	-4.0	-22.9	0.0	NA
450 No. 2	465	2190	1970	1765	1577	NA	4952	4009	3216	2567	NA	+2.5	-3.0	-20.0	0.0	NA
450 No. 2	500	2150	1920	1708	1514	NA	5132	4093	3238	2544	NA	+2.5	-4.0	-22.9	0.0	NA
458 Lott	465	2380	2150	1932	1730	NA	5848	4773	3855	3091	NA	+2.5	-1.0	-14.0	0.0	NA
458 Lott	500	2300	2062	1838	1633	NA	5873	4719	3748	2960	NA	+2.5	-1.6	-16.4	0.0	NA
450 Ackley Mag.	465	2400	2169	1950	1747	NA	5947	4857	3927	3150	NA	+2.5	-1.0	-13.7	0.0	NA
450 Ackley Mag.	500	2320	2081	1855	1649	NA	5975	4085	3820	3018	NA	+2.5	-1.2	-15.0	0.0	NA
460 Short A-Sq.	500	2420	2175	1943	1729	NA	6501	5250	4193	3319	NA	+2.5	-0.8	-12.8	0.0	NA
460 Wea. Mag.	500	2700	2404	2128	1869	1635	8092	6416	5026	3878	2969	+2.5	+0.6	-8.9	-28.0	$72
475																
500/465 N.E.	480	2150	1917	1703	1507	NA	4926	3917	3089	2419	NA	+2.5	-4.0	-22.2	0.0	NA
470 Rigby	500	2150	1940	1740	1560	NA	5130	4170	3360	2695	NA	+2.5	-2.8	-19.4	0.0	NA
470 Nitro Ex.	480	2190	1954	1735	1536	NA	5111	4070	3210	2515	NA	+2.5	-3.5	-20.8	0.0	NA
470 Nitro Ex.	500	2150	1890	1650	1440	1270	5130	3965	3040	2310	1790	+2.5	-4.3	-24.0	0.0	$177
475 No. 2	500	2200	1955	1728	1522	NA	5375	4243	3316	2573	NA	+2.5	-3.2	-20.9	0.0	NA
50, 58																
505 Gibbs	525	2300	2063	1840	1637	NA	6166	4922	3948	3122	NA	+2.5	-3.0	-18.0	0.0	NA
500 N.E.-3"	570	2150	1928	1722	1533	NA	5850	4703	3752	2975	NA	+2.5	-3.7	-22.0	0.0	NA
500 N.E.-3"	600	2150	1927	1721	1531	NA	6158	4947	3944	3124	NA	+2.5	-4.0	-22.0	0.0	NA
495 A-Square	570	2350	2117	1896	1693	NA	5850	4703	3752	2975	NA	+2.5	-1.0	-14.5	0.0	NA
495 A-Square	600	2280	2050	1833	1635	NA	6925	5598	4478	3562	NA	+2.5	-2.0	-17.0	0.0	NA
500 A-Square	600	2380	2144	1922	1766	NA	7546	6126	4920	3922	NA	+2.5	-3.0	-17.0	0.0	NA
500 A-Square	707	2250	2040	1841	1567	NA	7947	6530	5318	4311	NA	+2.5	-2.0	-17.0	0.0	NA
500 BMG PMC	660	3080	2854	2639	2444	2248	13688		500 yd. zero			+3.1	+3.9	+4.7	+2.8	NA
577 Nitro Ex.	750	2050	1793	1562	1360	NA	6990	5356	4065	3079	NA	+2.5	-5.0	-26.0	0.0	NA
577 Tyrannosaur	750	2400	2141	1898	1675	NA	9591	7633	5996	4671	NA	+3.0	0.0	-12.9	0.0	NA
600, 700																
600 N.E.	900	1950	1680	1452	NA	NA	7596	5634	4212	NA	NA	+5.6	0.0	0.0	0.0	NA
700 N.E.	1200	1900	1676	1472	NA	NA	9618	7480	5774	NA	NA	+5.7	0.0	0.0	0.0	NA

Notes: Blanks are available in 32 S&W, 38 S&W and 38 Special. "V" after barrel length indicates test barrel was vented to produce ballistics similar to a revolver with a normal barrel-to-cylinder gap. Ammo prices are per 50 rounds except when marked with an ** which signifies a 20 round box; *** signifies a 25-round box. Not all loads are available from all ammo manufacturers. Listed loads are those made by Remington, Winchester, Federal, and others. DISC. is a discontinued load. Prices are rounded to the nearest whole dollar and will vary with brand and retail outlet. † = new bullet weight this year; "c" indicates a change in data.

Cartridge	Bullet Wgt. Grs.	VELOCITY (fps)			ENERGY (ft. lbs.)			Mid-Range Traj. (in.)		Bbl. Lgth. (in).	Est. Price/ box
		Muzzle	50 yds.	100 yds.	Muzzle	50 yds.	100 yds.	50 yds.	100 yds.		
22, 25											
221 Rem. Fireball	50	2650	2380	2130	780	630	505	0.2	0.8	10.5"	**$15**
25 Automatic	35	900	813	742	63	51	43	NA	NA	2"	**$18**
25 Automatic	45	815	730	655	65	55	40	1.8	7.7	2"	**$21**
25 Automatic	50	760	705	660	65	55	50	2.0	8.7	2"	**$17**
30											
7.5mm Swiss	107	1010	NA	NA	240	NA	NA	NA	NA	NA	**NEW**
7.62mmTokarev	87	1390	NA	NA	365	NA	NA	0.6	NA	4.5"	**NA**
7.62 Nagant	97	790	NA	NA	134	NA	NA	NA	NA	NA	**NEW**
7.63 Mauser	88	1440	NA	NA	405	NA	NA	NA	NA	NA	**NEW**
30 Luger	93†	1220	1110	1040	305	255	225	0.9	3.5	4.5"	**$34**
30 Carbine	110	1790	1600	1430	785	625	500	0.4	1.7	10"	**$28**
30-357 AeT	123	1992	NA	NA	1084	NA	NA	NA	NA	10"	**NA**
32											
32 S&W	88	680	645	610	90	80	75	2.5	10.5	3"	**$17**
32 S&W Long	98	705	670	635	115	100	90	2.3	10.5	4"	**$17**
32 Short Colt	80	745	665	590	100	80	60	2.2	9.9	4"	**$19**
32 H&R Magnum	85	1100	1020	930	230	195	165	1.0	4.3	4.5"	**$21**
32 H&R Magnum	95	1030	940	900	225	190	170	1.1	4.7	4.5"	**$19**
327 Federal Magnum	100	1500	1320	1180	500	390	310	-0.2	-4.50	4-V	**NA**
32 Automatic	60	970	895	835	125	105	95	1.3	5.4	4"	**$22**
32 Automatic	60	1000	917	849	133	112	96			4"	**NA**
32 Automatic	65	950	890	830	130	115	100	1.3	5.6	NA	**NA**
32 Automatic	71	905	855	810	130	115	95	1.4	5.8	4"	**$19**
8mm Lebel Pistol	111	850	NA	NA	180	NA	NA	NA	NA	NA	**NEW**
8mm Steyr	112	1080	NA	NA	290	NA	NA	NA	NA	NA	**NEW**
8mm Gasser	126	850	NA	NA	200	NA	NA	NA	NA	NA	**NEW**
9mm, 38											
380 Automatic	60	1130	960	NA	170	120	NA	1.0	NA	NA	**NA**
380 Automatic	85/88	990	920	870	190	165	145	1.2	5.1	4"	**$20**
380 Automatic	90	1000	890	800	200	160	130	1.2	5.5	3.75"	**$10**
380 Automatic	95/100	955	865	785	190	160	130	1.4	5.9	4"	**$20**
38 Super Auto +P	115	1300	1145	1040	430	335	275	0.7	3.3	5"	**$26**
38 Super Auto +P	125/130	1215	1100	1015	425	350	300	0.8	3.6	5"	**$26**
38 Super Auto +P	147	1100	1050	1000	395	355	325	0.9	4.0	5"	**NA**
9x18mm Makarov	95	1000	NA	NA	NA	NA	NA	NA	NA	NA	**NEW**
9x18mm Ultra	100	1050	NA	NA	240	NA	NA	NA	NA	NA	**NEW**
9x23mm Largo	124	1190	1055	966	390	306	257	0.7	3.7	4"	**NA**
9x23mm Win.	125	1450	1249	1103	583	433	338	0.6	2.8	NA	**NA**
9mm Steyr	115	1180	NA	NA	350	NA	NA	NA	NA	NA	**NEW**
9mm Luger	88	1500	1190	1010	440	275	200	0.6	3.1	4"	**$24**
9mm Luger	90	1360	1112	978	370	247	191	NA	NA	4"	**$26**
9mm Luger	95	1300	1140	1010	350	275	215	0.8	3.4	4"	**NA**
9mm Luger	100	1180	1080	NA	305	255	NA	0.9	NA	4"	**NA**
9mm Luger	115	1155	1045	970	340	280	240	0.9	3.9	4"	**$21**
9mm Luger	123/125	1110	1030	970	340	290	260	1.0	4.0	4"	**$23**
9mm Luger	140	935	890	850	270	245	225	1.3	5.5	4"	**$23**
9mm Luger	147	990	940	900	320	290	265	1.1	4.9	4"	**$26**
9mm Luger +P	90	1475	NA	NA	437	NA	NA	NA	NA	NA	**NA**
9mm Luger +P	115	1250	1113	1019	399	316	265	0.8	3.5	4"	**$27**
9mm Federal	115	1280	1130	1040	420	330	280	0.7	3.3	4"V	**$24**
9mm Luger Vector	115	1155	1047	971	341	280	241	NA	NA	4"	**NA**
9mm Luger +P	124	1180	1089	1021	384	327	287	0.8	3.8	4"	**NA**
38											
38 S&W	146	685	650	620	150	135	125	2.4	10.0	4"	**$19**
38 Short Colt	125	730	685	645	150	130	115	2.2	9.4	6"	**$19**
39 Special	100	950	900	NA	200	180	NA	1.3	NA	4"V	**NA**
38 Special	110	945	895	850	220	195	175	1.3	5.4	4"V	**$23**
38 Special	110	945	895	850	220	195	175	1.3	5.4	4"V	**$23**
38 Special	130	775	745	710	175	160	120	1.9	7.9	4"V	**$22**
38 Special Cowboy	140	800	767	735	199	183	168			7.5" V	**NA**
38 (Multi-Ball)	140	830	730	505	215	130	80	2.0	10.6	4"V	**$10****

Notes: Blanks are available in 32 S&W, 38 S&W and 38 Special. "V" after barrel length indicates test barrel was vented to produce ballistics similar to a revolver with a normal barrel-to-cylinder gap. Ammo prices are per 50 rounds except when marked with an ** which signifies a 20 round box; *** signifies a 25-round box. Not all loads are available from all ammo manufacturers. Listed loads are those made by Remington, Winchester, Federal, and others. DISC. is a discontinued load. Prices are rounded to the nearest whole dollar and will vary with brand and retail outlet. † = new bullet weight this year; "c" indicates a change in data.

Cartridge	Bullet Wgt. Grs.	VELOCITY (fps)			ENERGY (ft. lbs.)			Mid-Range Traj. (in.)		Bbl. Lgth. (in).	Est. Price/ box
		Muzzle	50 yds.	100 yds.	Muzzle	50 yds.	100 yds.	50 yds.	100 yds.		
38 Special	148	710	635	565	165	130	105	2.4	10.6	4"V	**$17**
38 Special	158	755	725	690	200	185	170	2.0	8.3	4"V	**$18**
38 Special +P	95	1175	1045	960	290	230	195	0.9	3.9	4"V	**$23**
38 Special +P	110	995	925	870	240	210	185	1.2	5.1	4"V	**$23**
38 Special +P	125	975	929	885	264	238	218	1	5.2	4"	**NA**
38 Special +P	125	945	900	860	250	225	205	1.3	5.4	4"V	**#23**
38 Special +P	129	945	910	870	255	235	215	1.3	5.3	4"V	**$11**
38 Special +P	130	925	887	852	247	227	210	1.3	5.50	4"V	**NA**
38 Special +P	147/150(c)	884	NA	NA	264	NA	NA	NA	NA	4"V	**$27**
38 Special +P	158	890	855	825	280	255	240	1.4	6.0	4"V	**$20**
357											
357 SIG	115	1520	NA	NA	593	NA	NA	NA	NA	NA	**NA**
357 SIG	124	1450	NA	NA	578	NA	NA	NA	NA	NA	**NA**
357 SIG	125	1350	1190	1080	510	395	325	0.7	3.1	4"	**NA**
357 SIG	150	1130	1030	970	420	355	310	0.9	4.0	NA	**NA**
356 TSW	115	1520	NA	NA	593	NA	NA	NA	NA	NA	**NA**
356 TSW	124	1450	NA	NA	578	NA	NA	NA	NA	NA	**NA**
356 TSW	135	1280	1120	1010	490	375	310	0.8	3.5	NA	**NA**
356 TSW	147	1220	1120	1040	485	410	355	0.8	3.5	5"	**NA**
357 Mag., Super Clean	105	1650									**NA**
357 Magnum	110	1295	1095	975	410	290	230	0.8	3.5	4"V	**$25**
357 (Med.Vel.)	125	1220	1075	985	415	315	270	0.8	3.7	4"V	**$25**
357 Magnum	125	1450	1240	1090	585	425	330	0.6	2.8	4"V	**$25**
357 (Multi-Ball)	140	1155	830	665	420	215	135	1.2	6.4	4"V	**$11****
357 Magnum	140	1360	1195	1075	575	445	360	0.7	3.0	4"V	**$25**
357 Magnum FlexTip	140	1440	1274	1143	644	504	406	NA	NA	NA	**NA**
357 Magnum	145	1290	1155	1060	535	430	360	0.8	3.5	4"V	**$26**
357 Magnum	150/158	1235	1105	1015	535	430	360	0.8	3.5	4"V	**$25**
357 Mag. Cowboy	158	800	761	725	225	203	185				**NA**
357 Magnum	165	1290	1189	1108	610	518	450	0.7	3.1	8-3/8"	**NA**
357 Magnum	180	1145	1055	985	525	445	390	0.9	3.9	4"V	**$25**
357 Magnum	180	1180	1088	1020	557	473	416	0.8	3.6	8"V	**NA**
357 Mag. CorBon F.A.	180	1650	1512	1386	1088	913	767	1.66	0.0		**NA**
357 Mag. CorBon	200	1200	1123	1061	640	560	500	3.19	0.0		**NA**
357 Rem. Maximum	158	1825	1590	1380	1170	885	670	0.4	1.7	10.5"	**$14****
40, 10mm											
40 S&W	135	1140	1070	NA	390	345	NA	0.9	NA	4"	**NA**
40 S&W	155	1140	1026	958	447	362	309	0.9	4.1	4"	**$14*****
40 S&W	165	1150	NA	NA	485	NA	NA	NA	NA	4"	**$18*****
40 S&W	180	985	936	893	388	350	319	1.4	5.0	4"	**$14*****
40 S&W	180	1015	960	914	412	368	334	1.3	4.5	4"	**NA**
400 Cor-Bon	135	1450	NA	NA	630	NA	NA	NA	NA	5"	**NA**
10mm Automatic	155	1125	1046	986	436	377	335	0.9	3.9	5"	**$26**
10mm Automatic	170	1340	1165	1145	680	510	415	0.7	3.2	5"	**$31**
10mm Automatic	175	1290	1140	1035	650	505	420	0.7	3.3	5.5"	**$11****
10mm Auto. (FBI)	180	950	905	865	361	327	299	1.5	5.4	4"	**$16****
10mm Automatic	180	1030	970	920	425	375	340	1.1	4.7	5"	**$16****
10mm Auto H.V.	180†	1240	1124	1037	618	504	430	0.8	3.4	5"	**$27**
10mm Automatic	200	1160	1070	1010	495	510	430	0.9	3.8	5"	**$14****
10.4mm Italian	177	950	NA	NA	360	NA	NA	NA	NA	NA	**NEW**
41 Action Exp.	180	1000	947	903	400	359	326	0.5	4.2	5"	**$13****
41 Rem. Magnum	170	1420	1165	1015	760	515	390	0.7	3.2	4"V	**$33**
41 Rem. Magnum	175	1250	1120	1030	605	490	410	0.8	3.4	4"V	**$14****
41 (Med. Vel.)	210	965	900	840	435	375	330	1.3	5.4	4"V	**$30**
41 Rem. Magnum	210	1300	1160	1060	790	630	535	0.7	3.2	4"V	**$33**
41 Rem. Magnum	240	1250	1151	1075	833	706	616	0.8	3.3	6.5V	**NA**
44											
44 S&W Russian	247	780	NA	NA	335	NA	NA	NA	NA	NA	**NA**
44 S&W Special	180	980	NA	NA	383	NA	NA	NA	NA	6.5"	**NA**
44 S&W Special	180	1000	935	882	400	350	311	NA	NA	7.5"V	**NA**
44 S&W Special	200†	875	825	780	340	302	270	1.2	6.0	6"	**$13****
44 S&W Special	200	1035	940	865	475	390	335	1.1	4.9	6.5"	**$13****
44 S&W Special	240/246	755	725	695	310	285	265	2.0	8.3	6.5"	**$26**
44-40 Win. Cowboy	225	750	723	695	281	261	242				**NA**

Notes: Blanks are available in 32 S&W, 38 S&W and 38 Special. "V" after barrel length indicates test barrel was vented to produce ballistics similar to a revolver with a normal barrel-to-cylinder gap. Ammo prices are per 50 rounds except when marked with an ** which signifies a 20 round box; *** signifies a 25-round box. Not all loads are available from all ammo manufacturers. Listed loads are those made by Remington, Winchester, Federal, and others. DISC. is a discontinued load. Prices are rounded to the nearest whole dollar and will vary with brand and retail outlet. † = new bullet weight this year; "c" indicates a change in data.

Cartridge	Bullet Wgt. Grs.	VELOCITY (fps)			ENERGY (ft. lbs.)			Mid-Range Traj. (in.)		Bbl. Lgth. (in).	Est. Price/ box
		Muzzle	50 yds.	100 yds.	Muzzle	50 yds.	100 yds.	50 yds.	100 yds.		
44 Rem. Magnum	180	1610	1365	1175	1035	745	550	0.5	2.3	4"V	$18**
44 Rem. Magnum	200	1400	1192	1053	870	630	492	0.6	NA	6.5"	$20
44 Rem. Magnum	210	1495	1310	1165	1040	805	635	0.6	2.5	6.5"	$18**
44 Rem. Mag. FlexTip	225	1410	1240	1111	993	768	617	NA	NA	NA	NA
44 (Med. Vel.)	240	1000	945	900	535	475	435	1.1	4.8	6.5"	$17
44 R.M. (Jacketed)	240	1180	1080	1010	740	625	545	0.9	3.7	4"V	$18**
44 R.M. (Lead)	240	1350	1185	1070	970	750	610	0.7	3.1	4"V	$29
44 Rem. Magnum	250	1180	1100	1040	775	670	600	0.8	3.6	6.5"V	$21
44 Rem. Magnum	250	1250	1148	1070	867	732	635	0.8	3.3	6.5"V	NA
44 Rem. Magnum	275	1235	1142	1070	931	797	699	0.8	3.3	6.5"	NA
44 Rem. Magnum	300	1200	1100	1026	959	806	702	NA	NA	7.5"	$17
44 Rem. Magnum	330	1385	1297	1220	1406	1234	1090	1.83	0.00	NA	NA
440 CorBon	260	1700	1544	1403	1669	1377	1136	1.58	NA	10"	NA
45, 50											
450 Short Colt/450 Revolver	226	830	NA	NA	350	NA	NA	NA	NA	NA	NEW
45 S&W Schofield	180	730	NA	NA	213	NA	NA	NA	NA	NA	NA
45 S&W Schofield	230	730	NA	NA	272	NA	NA	NA	NA	NA	NA
45 G.A.P.	185	1090	970	890	490	385	320	1.0	4.7	5"	NA
45 G.A.P.	230	880	842	NA	396	363	NA	NA	NA	NA	NA
45 Automatic	165	1030	930	NA	385	315	NA	1.2	NA	5"	NA
45 Automatic	185	1000	940	890	410	360	325	1.1	4.9	5"	$28
45 Auto. (Match)	185	770	705	650	245	204	175	2.0	8.7	5"	$28
45 Auto. (Match)	200	940	890	840	392	352	312	2.0	8.6	5"	$20
45 Automatic	200	975	917	860	421	372	328	1.4	5.0	5"	$18
45 Automatic	230	830	800	675	355	325	300	1.6	6.8	5"	$27
45 Automatic	230	880	846	816	396	366	340	1.5	6.1	5"	NA
45 Automatic +P	165	1250	NA	NA	573	NA	NA	NA	NA	NA	NA
45 Automatic +P	185	1140	1040	970	535	445	385	0.9	4.0	5"	$31
45 Automatic +P	200	1055	982	925	494	428	380	NA	NA	5"	NA
45 Super	185	1300	1190	1108	694	582	504	NA	NA	5"	NA
45 Win. Magnum	230	1400	1230	1105	1000	775	635	0.6	2.8	5"	$14**
45 Win. Magnum	260	1250	1137	1053	902	746	640	0.8	3.3	5"	$16**
45 Win. Mag. CorBon	320	1150	1080	1025	940	830	747	3.47			NA
455 Webley MKII	262	850	NA	NA	420	NA	NA	NA	NA	NA	NA
45 Colt	200	1000	938	889	444	391	351	1.3	4.8	5.5"	$21
45 Colt	225	960	890	830	460	395	345	1.3	5.5	5.5"	$22
45 Colt + P CorBon	265	1350	1225	1126	1073	884	746	2.65	0.0		NA
45 Colt + P CorBon	300	1300	1197	1114	1126	956	827	2.78	0.0		NA
45 Colt	250/255	860	820	780	410	375	340	1.6	6.6	5.5"	$27
454 Casull	250	1300	1151	1047	938	735	608	0.7	3.2	7.5"V	NA
454 Casull	260	1800	1577	1381	1871	1436	1101	0.4	1.8	7.5"V	NA
454 Casull	300	1625	1451	1308	1759	1413	1141	0.5	2.0	7.5"V	NA
454 Casull CorBon	360	1500	1387	1286	1800	1640	1323	2.01	0.0		NA
460 S&W	200	2300	2042	1801	2350	1851	1441	0	-1.60	NA	NA
460 S&W	260	2000	1788	1592	2309	1845	1464	NA	NA	7.5"V	NA
460 S&W	250	1450	1267	1127	1167	891	705	NA	NA	8.375-V	NA
460 S&W	250	1900	1640	1412	2004	1494	1106	0	-2.75	NA	NA
460 S&W	395	1550	1389	1249	2108	1691	1369	0	-4.00	NA	NA
475 Linebaugh	400	1350	1217	1119	1618	1315	1112	NA	NA	NA	NA
480 Ruger	325	1350	1191	1076	1315	1023	835	2.6	0.0	7.5"	NA
50 Action Exp.	325	1400	1209	1075	1414	1055	835	0.2	2.3	6"	$24**
500 S&W	275	1665	1392	1183	1693	1184	854	1.5	NA	8.375	NA
500 S&W	350	1400	1231	1106	1523	1178	951	NA	NA	10"	NA
500 S&W	400	1675	1472	1299	2493	1926	1499	1.3	NA	8.375	NA
500 S&W	440	1625	1367	1169	2581	1825	1337	1.6	NA	8.375	NA
500 S&W	500	1425	1281	1164	2254	1823	1505	NA	NA	10"	NA

RIMFIRE AMMUNITION—BALLISTICS & PRICES

Note: The actual ballistics obtained with your firearm can vary considerably from the advertised ballistics. Also, ballistics can vary from lot to lot with the same brand and type load.

Cartridge	Bullet Wt. Grs.	Velocity (fps) 22-1/2" Bbl.		Energy (ft. lbs.) 22-1/2" Bbl.		Mid-Range Traj. (in.)	Muzzle Velocity
		Muzzle	100 yds.	Muzzle	100 yds.	100 yds.	6" Bbl.
17 Aguila	20	1850	1267	NA	NA	NA	NA
17 Hornady Mach 2	17	2100	1530	166	88	0.7	NA
17 HMR	17	2550	1902	245	136	NA	NA
17 HMR	20	2375	1776	250	140	NA	NA
5mm Rem. Rimfire Mag.	30	2300	1669	352	186	NA	24
22 Short Blank	—	—	—	—	—	—	—
22 Short CB	29	727	610	33	24	NA	706
22 Short Target	29	830	695	44	31	6.8	786
22 Short HP	27	1164	920	81	50	4.3	1077
22 Colibri	20	375	183	6	1	NA	NA
22 Super Colibri	20	500	441	11	9	NA	NA
22 Long CB	29	727	610	33	24	NA	706
22 Long HV	29	1180	946	90	57	4.1	1031
22 LR Pistol Match	40	1070	890	100	70	4.6	940
22 LR Sub Sonic HP	38	1050	901	93	69	4.7	NA
22 LR Standard Velocity	40	1070	890	100	70	4.6	940
22 LR AutoMatch	40	1200	990	130	85	NA	NA
22 LR HV	40	1255	1016	140	92	3.6	1060
22 LR Silhoutte	42	1220	1003	139	94	3.6	1025
22 SSS	60	950	802	120	86	NA	NA
22 LR HV HP	40	1280	1001	146	89	3.5	1085
22 Velocitor GDHP	40	1435	0	0	0	NA	NA
22 LR Hyper HP	32/33/34	1500	1075	165	85	2.8	NA
22 LR Stinger HP	32	1640	1132	191	91	2.6	1395
22 LR Hyper Vel	30	1750	1191	204	93	NA	NA
22 LR Shot #12	31	950	NA	NA	NA	NA	NA
22 WRF LFN	45	1300	1015	169	103	3	NA
22 Win. Mag.	30	2200	1373	322	127	1.4	1610
22 Win. Mag. V-Max BT	33	2000	1495	293	164	0.60	NA
22 Win. Mag. JHP	34	2120	1435	338	155	1.4	NA
22 Win. Mag. JHP	40	1910	1326	324	156	1.7	1480
22 Win. Mag. FMJ	40	1910	1326	324	156	1.7	1480
22 Win. Mag. Dyna Point	45	1550	1147	240	131	2.60	NA
22 Win. Mag. JHP	50	1650	1280	300	180	1.3	NA
22 Win. Mag. Shot #11	52	1000	—	NA	—	—	NA

Shotshell Loads & Prices

NOTES: * = 10 rounds per box. ** = 5 rounds per box. Pricing variations and number of rounds per box can occur with type and brand of ammunition. Listed pricing is the average nominal cost for load style and box quantity shown. Not every brand is available in all shot size variations. Some manufacturers do not provide suggested list prices. All prices rounded to nearest whole dollar. The price you pay will vary dependent upon outlet of purchase. # = new load spec this year; "C" indicates a change in data.

Dram Equiv.	Shot Ozs.	Load Style	Shot Sizes	Brands	Avg. Price/ box	Velocity (fps)
10 Gauge 3-1/2" Magnum						
4-1/2	2-1/4	premium	BB, 2, 4, 5, 6	Win., Fed., Rem.	$33	1205
Max	2	premium	4, 5, 6	Fed., Win.	NA	1300
4-1/4	2	high velocity	BB, 2, 4	Rem.	$22	1210
Max	18 pellets	premium	00 buck	Fed., Win.	$7**	1100
Max	1-7/8	Bismuth	BB, 2, 4	Bis.	NA	1225
Max	1-3/4	high density	BB, 2	Rem.	NA	1300
4-1/4	1-3/4	steel	TT, T, BBB, BB, 1, 2, 3	Win., Rem.	$27	1260
Mag	1-5/8	steel	T, BBB, BB, 2	Win.	$27	1285
Max	1-5/8	Bismuth	BB, 2, 4	Bismuth	NA	1375
Max	1-1/2	steel	T, BBB, BB, 1, 2, 3	Fed.	NA	1450
Max	1-3/8	steel	T, BBB, BB, 1, 2, 3	Fed., Rem.	NA	1500
Max	1-3/8	steel	T, BBB, BB, 2	Fed., Win.	NA	1450
Max	1-3/4	slug, rifled	slug	Fed.	NA	1280
Max	24 pellets	Buckshot	1 Buck	Fed.	NA	1100
Max	54 pellets	Super-X	4 Buck	Win.	NA	1150
12 Gauge 3-1/2" Magnum						
Max	2-1/4	premium	4, 5, 6	Fed., Rem., Win.	$13*	1150
Max	2	Lead	4, 5, 6	Fed.	NA	1300
Max	2	Copper plated turkey	4, 5	Rem.	NA	1300
Max	18 pellets	premium	00 buck	Fed., Win., Rem.	$7**	1100
Max	1-7/8	Wingmaster HD	4, 6	Rem.	NA	1225
Max	1-7/8	heavyweight	5, 6	Fed.	NA	1300
Max	1-3/4	high density	BB, 2, 4, 6	Rem.		1300
Max	1-7/8	Bismuth	BB, 2, 4	Bis.	NA	1225
Max	1-5/8	Hevi-shot	T	Hevi-shot	NA	1350
Max	1-5/8	Wingmaster HD	T	Rem.	NA	1350
Max	1-5/8	high density	BB, 2	Fed.	NA	1450
Max	1-3/8	Heavyweight	2, 4, 6	Fed.	NA	1450
Max	1-3/8	steel	T, BBB, BB, 2, 4	Fed., Win., Rem.	NA	1450
Max	1-1/2	FS steel	BBB, BB, 2	Fed.	NA	1500
Max	1-1/2	Supreme H-V	BBB, BB, 2, 3	Win.	NA	1475
Max	1-3/8	H-speed steel	BB, 2	Rem.	NA	1550
Max	1-1/4	Steel	BB, 2	Win.	NA	1625
Max	24 pellets	Premium	1 Buck	Fed.	NA	1100
Max	54 pellets	Super-X	4 Buck	Win.	NA	1050
12 Gauge 3" Magnum						
4	2	premium	BB, 2, 4, 5, 6	Win., Fed., Rem.	$9*	1175
4	1-7/8	premium	BB, 2, 4, 6	Win., Fed., Rem.	$19	1210
4	1-7/8	duplex	4x6	Rem.	$9*	1210
Max	1-3/4	turkey	4, 5, 6	Fed., Fio., Win., Rem.	NA	1300
Max	1-3/4	high density	BB, 2, 4	Rem.	NA	1450
Max	1-5/8	high density	BB, 2	Fed.	NA	1450
Max	1-5/8	Wingmaster HD	4, 6	Rem.	NA	1227
Max	1-5/8	high velocity	4, 5, 6	Fed.	NA	1350
4	1-5/8	premium	2, 4, 5, 6	Win., Fed., Rem.	$18	1290
Max	1-1/2	Wingmaster HD	T	Rem.	NA	1300
Max	1-1/2	Hevi-shot	T	Hevi-shot	NA	1300
Max	1-1/2	high density	BB, 2, 4	Rem.	NA	1300
Max	1-5/8	Bismuth	BB, 2, 4, 5, 6	Bis.	NA	1250
4	24 pellets	buffered	1 buck	Win., Fed., Rem.	$5**	1040
4	15 pellets	buffered	00 buck	Win., Fed., Rem.	$6**	1210
4	10 pellets	buffered	000 buck	Win., Fed., Rem.	$6**	1225
4	41 pellets	buffered	4 buck	Win., Fed., Rem.	$6**	1210
Max	1-3/8	heavyweight	5, 6	Fed.	NA	1300
Max	1-3/8	high density	B, 2, 4, 6	Rem. Win.	NA	1450
12 Gauge 3" Magnum *(cont.)*						
Max	1-3/8	slug	slug	Bren.	NA	1476
Max	1-1/4	slug, rifled	slug	Fed.	NA	1600
Max	1-3/16	saboted slug	copper slug	Rem.	NA	1500
Max	7/8	slug, rifled	slug	Rem.	NA	1875
Max	1-1/8	low recoil	BB	Fed.	NA	850
Max	1-1/8	steel	BB, 2, 3, 4	Fed., Win., Rem.	NA	1550
Max	1-1/16	high density	2, 4	Win.	NA	1400
Max	1	steel	4, 6	Fed.	NA	1330
Max	1-3/8	buckhammer	slug	Rem.	NA	1500
Max	1	slug, rifled	slug, magnum	Win., Rem.	$5**	1760
Max	1	saboted slug	slug	Rem., Win., Fed.	$10**	1550
Max	385 grs.	partition gold	slug	Win.	NA	2000
Max	1-1/8	Rackmaster	slug	Win.	NA	1700
Max	300 grs.	XP3	slug	Win.	NA	2100
3-5/8	1-3/8	steel	BBB, BB, 1, 2, 3, 4	Win., Fed., Rem.	$19	1275
Max	1-1/8	steel	BB, 2, 4	Rem.	NA	1500
Max	1-1/8	steel	T, BBB, BB, 2, 4, 5, 6	Fed., Win.	NA	1450
Max	1-1/8	steel	BB, 2	Fed.	NA	1400
4	1-1/4	steel	T, BBB, BB, 1, 2, 3, 4, 6	Win., Fed., Rem.	$18	1400
Max	1-1/4	FS steel	BBB, BB, 2	Fed.	NA	1450
12 Gauge 2-3/4"						
Max	1-5/8	magnum	4, 5, 6	Win., Fed.	$8*	1250
Max	1-3/8	lead	4, 5, 6	Fiocchi	NA	1485
Max	1-3/8	turkey	4, 5, 6	Fio.	NA	1250
Max	1-3/8	steel	4, 5, 6	Fed.	NA	1400
Max	1-3/8	Bismuth	BB, 2, 4, 5, 6	Bis.	NA	1300
3-3/4	1-1/2	magnum	BB, 2, 4, 5, 6	Win., Fed., Rem.	$16	1260
Max	1-1/4	Supreme H-V	4, 5, 6, 7-1/2	Win. Rem.	NA	1400
3-3/4	1-1/4	high velocity	BB, 2, 4, 5, 6, 7-1/2, 8, 9	Win., Fed., Rem., Fio.	$13	1330
Max	1-1/4	high density	B, 2, 4	Win.	NA	1450
Max	1-1/4	high density	4, 6	Rem.	NA	1325
3-1/4	1-1/4	standard velocity	6, 7-1/2, 8, 9	Win., Fed., Rem., Fio.	$11	1220
Max	1-1/8	Hevi-shot	5	Hevi-shot	NA	1350
3-1/4	1-1/8	standard velocity	4, 6, 7-1/2, 8, 9	Win., Fed., Rem., Fio.	$9	1255
Max	1-1/8	steel	2, 4	Rem.	NA	1390
Max	1	steel	BB, 2	Fed.	NA	1450
3-1/4	1	standard velocity	6, 7-1/2, 8	Rem., Fed., Fio., Win.	$6	1290
3-1/4	1-1/4	target	7-1/2, 8, 9	Win., Fed., Rem.	$10	1220
3	1-1/8	spreader	7-1/2, 8, 8-1/2, 9	Fio.	NA	1200
3	1-1/8	target	7-1/2, 8, 9, 7-1/2x8	Win., Fed., Rem., Fio.	$7	1200
2-3/4	1-1/8	target	7-1/2, 8, 8-1/2, 9, 7-1/2x8	Win., Fed., Rem., Fio.	$7	1145
2-3/4	1-1/8	low recoil	7-1/2, 8	Rem.	NA	1145
2-1/2	26 grams	low recoil	8	Win.	NA	980
2-1/4	1-1/8	target	7-1/2, 8, 8-1/2, 9	Rem., Fed.	$7	1080
Max	1	spreader	7-1/2, 8, 8-1/2, 9	Fio.	NA	1300
3-1/4	28 grams (1 oz)	target	7-1/2, 8, 9	Win., Fed., Rem., Fio.	$8	1290
3	1	target	7-1/2, 8, 8-1/2, 9	Win., Fio.	NA	1235
2-3/4	1	target	7-1/2, 8, 8-1/2, 9	Fed., Rem., Fio.	NA	1180
3-1/4	24 grams	target	7-1/2, 8, 9	Fed., Win., Fio.	NA	1325
3	7/8	light	8	Fio.	NA	1200
3-3/4	8 pellets	buffered	000 buck	Win., Fed., Rem.	$4**	1325

SHOTSHELL LOADS & PRICES (CONT.)

NOTES: * = 10 rounds per box. ** = 5 rounds per box. Pricing variations and number of rounds per box can occur with type and brand of ammunition. Listed pricing is the average nominal cost for load style and box quantity shown. Not every brand is available in all shot size variations. Some manufacturers do not provide suggested list prices. All prices rounded to nearest whole dollar. The price you pay will vary dependent upon outlet of purchase. # = new load spec this year; "C" indicates a change in data.

Dram Equiv.	Shot Ozs.	Load Style	Shot Sizes	Brands	Avg. Price/ box	Velocity (fps)
12 Gauge 2-3/4" *(cont.)*						
4	12 pellets	premium	00 buck	Win., Fed., Rem.	$5**	1290
3-3/4	9 pellets	buffered	00 buck	Win., Fed., Rem., Fio.	$19	1325
3-3/4	12 pellets	buffered	0 buck	Win., Fed., Rem.	$4**	1275
4	20 pellets	buffered	1 buck	Win., Fed., Rem.	$4**	1075
3-3/4	16 pellets	buffered	1 buck	Win., Fed., Rem.	$4**	1250
4	34 pellets	premium	4 buck	Fed., Rem.	$5**	1250
3-3/4	27 pellets	buffered	4 buck	Win., Fed., Rem., Fio.	$4**	1325
Max	1	saboted slug	slug	Win., Fed., Rem.	$10**	1450
Max	1-1/4	slug, rifled	slug	Fed.	NA	1520
Max	1-1/4	slug	slug	Lightfield		1440
Max	1-1/4	saboted slug	attached sabot	Rem.	NA	1550
Max	1	slug, rifled	slug, magnum	Rem., Fio.	$5**	1680
Max	1	slug, rifled	slug	Win., Fed., Rem.	$4**	1610
Max	1	sabot slug	slug	Sauvestre		1640
Max	7/8	slug, rifled	slug	Rem.	NA	1800
Max	400	plat. tip	sabot slug	Win.	NA	1700
Max	385 grains	Partition Gold Slug	slug	Win.	NA	1900
Max	385 grains	Core-Lokt bonded	sabot slug	Rem.	NA	1900
Max	325 grains	Barnes Sabot	slug	Fed.	NA	1900
Max	300 grains	SST Slug	sabot slug	Hornady	NA	2050
3	1-1/8	steel target	6-1/2, 7	Rem.	NA	1200
2-3/4	1-1/8	steel target	7	Rem.	NA	1145
3	1#	steel	7	Win.	$11	1235
3-1/2	1-1/4	steel	T, BBB, BB, 1, 2, 3, 4, 5, 6	Win., Fed., Rem.	$18	1275
3-3/4	1-1/8	steel	BB, 1, 2, 3, 4, 5, 6	Win., Fed., Rem., Fio.	$16	1365
3-3/4	1	steel	2, 3, 4, 5, 6, 7	Win., Fed., Rem., Fio.	$13	1390
Max	7/8	steel	7	Fio.	NA	1440
16 Gauge 2-3/4"						
3-1/4	1-1/4	magnum	2, 4, 6	Fed., Rem.	$16	1260
3-1/4	1-1/8	high velocity	4, 6, 7-1/2	Win., Fed., Rem., Fio.	$12	1295
Max	1-1/8	Bismuth	4, 5	Bis.	NA	1200
2-3/4	1-1/8	standard velocity	6, 7-1/2, 8	Fed., Rem., Fio.	$9	1185
2-1/2	1	dove	6, 7-1/2, 8, 9	Fio., Win.	NA	1165
2-3/4	1		6, 7-1/2, 8	Fio.	NA	1200
Max	15/16	steel	2, 4	Fed., Rem.	NA	1300
Max	7/8	steel	2, 4	Win.	$16	1300
3	12 pellets	buffered	1 buck	Win., Fed., Rem.	$4**	1225
Max	4/5	slug, rifled	slug	Win., Fed., Rem.	$4**	1570
Max	.92	sabot slug	slug	Sauvestre	NA	1560
20 Gauge 3" Magnum						
3	1-1/4	premium	2, 4, 5, 6, 7-1/2	Win., Fed., Rem.	$15	1185
Max	1-1/4	Wingmaster HD	4, 6	Rem.	NA	1185
3	1-1/4	turkey	4, 6	Fio.	NA	1200
Max	1-1/4	Hevi-shot	2, 4, 6	Hevi-shot	NA	1250
Max	1-1/8	high density	4, 6	Rem.	NA	1300
Max	18 pellets	buck shot	2 buck	Fed.	NA	1200
Max	24 pellets	buffered	3 buck	Win.	$5**	1150
2-3/4	20 pellets	buck	3 buck	Rem.	$4**	1200

Dram Equiv.	Shot Ozs.	Load Style	Shot Sizes	Brands	Avg. Price/ box	Velocity (fps)
20 Gauge 3" Magnum *(cont.)*						
3-1/4	1	steel	1, 2, 3, 4, 5, 6	Win., Fed., Rem.	$15	1330
Max	7/8	steel	2, 4	Win.	NA	1300
Max	1-1/16	high density	2, 4	Win.	NA	1400
Max	1-1/16	Bismuth	2, 4, 5, 6	Bismuth	NA	1250
Mag	5/8	saboted slug	275 gr.	Fed.	NA	1900
20 Gauge 2-3/4"						
2-3/4	1-1/8	magnum	4, 6, 7-1/2	Win., Fed., Rem.	$14	1175
2-3/4	1	high velocity	4, 5, 6, 7-1/2, 8, 9	Win., Fed., Rem., Fio.	$12	1220
Max	1	Bismuth	4, 6	Bis.	NA	1200
Max	1	Hevi-shot	5	Hevi-shot	NA	1250
Max	1	Supreme H-V	4, 6, 7-1/2	Win. Rem.	NA	1300
Max	7/8	Steel	2, 3, 4	Fio.	NA	1500
2-1/2	1	standard velocity	6, 7-1/2, 8	Win., Rem., Fed., Fio.	$6	1165
2-1/2	7/8	clays	8	Rem.	NA	1200
2-1/2	7/8	promotional	6, 7-1/2, 8	Win., Rem., Fio.	$6	1210
2-1/2	1	target	8, 9	Win., Rem.	$8	1165
Max	7/8	clays	7-1/2, 8	Win.	NA	1275
2-1/2	7/8	target	8, 9	Win., Fed., Rem.	$8	1200
Max	3/4	steel	2, 4	Rem.	NA	1425
2-1/2	7/8	steel - target	7	Rem.	NA	1200
Max	1	buckhammer	slug	Rem.	NA	1500
Max	5/8	Saboted Slug	Copper Slug	Rem.	NA	1500
Max	20 pellets	buffered	3 buck	Win., Fed.	$4	1200
Max	5/8	slug, saboted	slug	Win.,	$9**	1400
2-3/4	5/8	slug, rifled	slug	Rem.	$4**	1580
Max	3/4	saboted slug	copper slug	Fed., Rem.	NA	1450
Max	3/4	slug, rifled	slug	Win., Fed., Rem., Fio.	$4**	1570
Max	.9	sabot slug	slug	Sauvestre		1480
Max	260 grains	Partition Gold Slug	slug	Win.	NA	1900
Max	260 grains	Core-Lokt Ultra	slug	Rem.	NA	1900
Max	260 grains	saboted slug	platinum tip	Win.	NA	1700
Max	3/4	steel	2, 3, 4, 6	Win., Fed., Rem.	$14	1425
Max	250 grains	SST slug	slug	Hornady	NA	1800
Max	1/2	rifled, slug	slug	Rem.	NA	1800
28 Gauge 2-3/4"						
2	1	high velocity	6, 7-1/2, 8	Win.	$12	1125
2-1/4	3/4	high velocity	6, 7-1/2, 8, 9	Win., Fed., Rem., Fio.	$11	1295
2	3/4	target	8, 9	Win., Fed., Rem.	$9	1200
Max	3/4	sporting clays	7-1/2, 8-1/2	Win.	NA	1300
Max	5/8	Bismuth	4, 6	Bis.	NA	1250
410 Bore 3"						
Max	11/16	high velocity	4, 5, 6, 7-1/2, 8, 9	Win., Fed., Rem., Fio.	$10	1135
Max	9/16	Bismuth	4	Bis.	NA	1175
410 Bore 2-1/2"						
Max	1/2	high velocity	4, 6, 7-1/2	Win., Fed., Rem.	$9	1245
Max	1/5	slug, rifled	slug	Win., Fed., Rem.	$4**	1815
1-1/2	1/2	target	8, 8-1/2, 9	Win., Fed., Rem., Fio.	$8	1200
Max	1/2	sporting clays	7-1/2, 8, 8-1/2	Win.	NA	1300
Max		Buckshot	5-000 Buck	Win.	NA	1135

NYLON COATED GUN CLEANING RODS

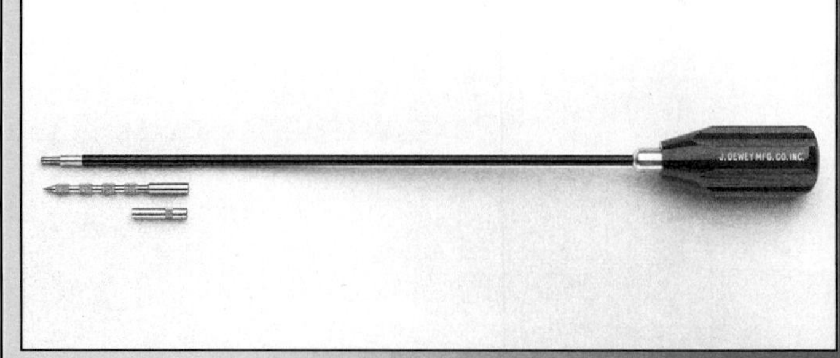

J. Dewey cleaning rods have been used by the U.S. Olympic shooting team and the benchrest community for over 20 years. These one-piece, spring-tempered, steel-base rods will not gall delicate rifling or damage the muzzle area of front-cleaned firearms. The nylon coating elmininates the problem of abrasives adhering to the rod during the cleaning operation. Each rod comes with a hard non-breakable plastic handle supported by ball bearings, top and bottom, for ease of cleaning.

The brass cleaning jags are designed to pierce the center of the cleaning patch or wrap around the knurled end to keep the patch centered in the bore.

Coated rods are available from 17-caliber to shotgun bore size in several lengths to meet the needs of any shooter. Write for more information.

J. DEWEY MFG. CO., INC.
P.O. Box 2014, Southbury, CT 06488
Phone: 203-264-3064 • Fax: 203-262-6907
Web: www.deweyrods.com

BLACK HILLS GOLD AMMUNITION

Black Hills Ammunition has introduced a new line of premium performance rifle ammunition. Calibers available in the Black Hills Gold Line are .243, .270, .308, .30-06, and .300 Win Mag. This line is designed for top performance in a wide range of hunting situations. Bullets used in this ammunition are the Barnes X-Bullet with XLC coating and the highly accurate Nosler Ballistic-Tip™.

Black Hills Ammunition is sold dealer direct. The Gold line is packaged in 20 rounds per box, 10 boxes per case. Black Hills pays all freight to dealers in the continental United States. Minimum dealer order is only one case.

BLACK HILLS AMMUNITION
P.O. Box 3090, Rapid City, SD 57709
Phone: 1-605-348-5150 • Fax: 1-605-348-9827
Web: www.black-hills.com

La Porte County Historical Society Museum

La Porte, Indiana

Featuring the W. A. Jones Antique Firearms Collection of over 850 guns, this museum has what has been called the "best-kept secret in the firearms collecting community." The Kesling Automobile Collection includes a Duesenberg, Auburns, Cords, a Tucker, and 30 other rare cars from around the world. With over 80,000 items, the museum showcases many displays, including a Log Cabin, Victorian rooms, a recreated block of Main Street, a barn, and more.

Hours: Tue. – Sat. 10:00 a.m. – 4:30 p.m.
Mention this Ad and get $1 off regular admission.
2405 Indiana Ave., La Porte, Indiana 219-324-6767
www.laportecountyhistory.org

2009 GUN DIGEST Complete Compact CATALOG

A

B

C

D

E

F

S

T

U

V

W

Z

NUMBERS

Includes models suitable for several forms of competition and other sporting purposes.

Accu-Tek AT-380 II 380 ACP
Auto-Ordnance 1911A1 Standard
Auto-Ordnance 1911PKZSEW
Baer Custom Carry
Auto-Ordnance Deluxe
Baer Premium II

ACCU-TEK AT-380 II 380 ACP PISTOL

Caliber: 380 ACP, 6-shot magazine. **Barrel:** 2.8". **Weight:** 23.5 oz. **Length:** 6.125" overall. **Grips:** Textured black composition. **Sights:** Blade front, rear adjustable for windage. **Features:** Made from 17-4 stainless steel, has an exposed hammer, manual firing-pin safety block and trigger disconnect. Magazine release located on the bottom of the grip. American made, lifetime warranty. Comes with two 6-round stainless steel magazines and a California-approved cable lock. Introduced 2006. Made in U.S.A. by Excel Industries.

Price: Satin stainless **$249.00**

ARMALITE AR-24 PISTOL

Caliber: 9mm Para., 10- or 15-shot magazine. **Barrel:** 4.671", 6 groove, right-hand cut rifling. **Weight:** 34.9 oz. **Length:** 8.27" overall. **Grips:** Black polymer. **Sights:** Dovetail front, fixed rear, 3-dot luminous design. **Features:** Machined slide, frame and barrel. Serrations on forestrap and backstrap, external thumb safety and internal firing pin box, half cock. Two 15-round magazines, pistol case, pistol lock, manual and cleaning brushes. Manganese phosphate finish. Compact comes with two 13-round magazines, 3.89" barrel, weighs 33.4 oz. Made in U.S.A. by ArmaLite.

Price: AR-24 Full Size.............................. **$550.00**
Price: AR-24 Compact **$550.00**

AUTO-ORDNANCE 1911A1 AUTOMATIC PISTOL

Caliber: 45 ACP, 7-shot magazine. **Barrel:** 5". **Weight:** 39 oz. **Length:** 8.5" overall. **Grips:** Brown checkered plastic with medallion. **Sights:** Blade front, rear drift-adjustable for windage. **Features:** Same specs as 1911A1 military guns-parts interchangeable. Frame and slide blued; each radius has non-glare finish. Introduced 2002. Made in U.S.A. by Kahr Arms.

Price: 1911PKZSE Parkerized, plastic grips **$627.00**
Price: 1911PKZSEW Parkerized **$662.00**
Price: 1911PKZMA Parkerized, Mass. Compliant (2008)..... **$627.00**

BAER H.C. 40 AUTO PISTOL

Caliber: 40 S&W, 18-shot magazine. **Barrel:** 5". **Weight:** 37 oz. **Length:** 8.5" overall. **Grips:** Wood. **Sights:** Low-mount adjustable rear sight with hidden rear leaf, dovetail front sight. **Features:** Double-stack Caspian frame, beavertail grip safety, ambidextrous thumb safety, 40 S&W match barrel with supported chamber, match stainless steel barrel bushing, lowered and flared ejection port, extended ejector, match trigger fitted, integral mag well, bead blast blue finish on lower, polished sides on slide. Introduced 2008. Made in U.S.A. by Les Baer Custom, Inc.

Price: **$2,960.00**

BAER 1911 CUSTOM CARRY AUTO PISTOL

Caliber: 45 ACP, 7- or 10-shot magazine. **Barrel:** 5". **Weight:** 37 oz. **Length:** 8.5" overall. **Grips:** Checkered walnut. **Sights:** Baer improved ramp-style dovetailed front, Novak low-mount rear. **Features:** Baer forged NM frame, slide and barrel with stainless bushing. Baer speed trigger with 4-lb. pull. Partial listing shown. Made in U.S.A. by Les Baer Custom, Inc.

Price: Custom Carry 5", blued **$1,995.00**
Price: Custom Carry 5", stainless **$2,120.00**
Price: Custom Carry 4" Commanche length, blued **$1,995.00**
Price: Custom Carry 4" Commanche length, stainless **$2,120.00**

BAER 1911 ULTIMATE RECON PISTOL

Caliber: 45 ACP, 7- or 10-shot magazine. **Barrel:** 5". **Weight:** 37 oz. **Length:** 8.5" overall. **Grips:** Checkered cocobolo. **Sights:** Baer improved ramp-style dovetailed front, Novak low-mount rear. **Features:** NM Caspian frame, slide and barrel with stainless bushing. Baer speed trigger with 4-lb. pull. Includes integral Picatinny rail and Sure-Fire X-200 light. Made in U.S.A. by Les Baer Custom, Inc. Introduced 2006.

Price: Bead blast blued **$3,070.00**
Price: Bead blast chrome **$3,390.00**

BAER 1911 PREMIER II AUTO PISTOL

Caliber: 38 Super, 400 Cor-Bon, 45 ACP, 7- or 10-shot magazine. **Barrel:** 5". Weight: 37 oz. **Length:** 8.5" overall. **Grips:** Checkered rosewood, double diamond pattern. **Sights:** Baer dovetailed front, low-mount Bo-Mar rear with hidden leaf. **Features:** Baer NM forged steel frame and barrel with stainless bushing, deluxe Commander hammer and sear, beavertail grip safety with pad, extended ambidextrous safety; flat mainspring housing; 30 lpi checkered front strap. Made in U.S.A. by Les Baer Custom, Inc.

Price: 5" 45 ACP **$1,790.00**
Price: 5" 400 Cor-Bon **$1,890.00**
Price: 5" 38 Super **$2,070.00**
Price: 6" 45 ACP, 400 Cor-Bon, 38 Super, from.......... **$1,990.00**
Price: Super-Tac, 45 ACP, 400 Cor-Bon, 38 Super, from .. **$2,280.00**

Baer 1911 Stinger

Beretta 92FS

Beretta Bobcat

Beretta PX4 Storm

Beretta Tomcat

Beretta U22 Neos

Beretta Model M9

BAER 1911 S.R.P. PISTOL

Caliber: 45 ACP. **Barrel:** 5". **Weight:** 37 oz. **Length:** 8.5" overall. **Grips:** Checkered walnut. **Sights:** Trijicon night sights. **Features:** Similar to the F.B.I. contract gun except uses Baer forged steel frame. Has Baer match barrel with supported chamber, complete tactical action. Has Baer Ultra Coat finish. Introduced 1996. Made in U.S.A. by Les Baer Custom, Inc.

Price: Government or Commanche length **$2,590.00**

BAER 1911 STINGER PISTOL

Caliber: 45 ACP, 7-round magazine. **Barrel:** 5". **Weight:** 34 oz. **Length:** 8.5" overall. **Grips:** Checkered cocobolo. **Sights:** Baer dovetailed front, low-mount Bo-Mar rear with hidden leaf. **Features:** Baer NM frame. Baer Commanche slide, Officer's style grip frame, beveled mag well. Made in U.S.A. by Les Baer Custom, Inc.

Price: Blued **$1,890.00**
Price: Stainless **$1,970.00**

BAER 1911 PROWLER III PISTOL

Caliber: 45 ACP, 8-round magazine. **Barrel:** 5". **Weight:** 34 oz. **Length:** 8.5" overall. **Grips:** Checkered cocobolo. **Sights:** Baer dovetailed front, low-mount Bo-Mar rear with hidden leaf. **Features:** Similar to Premier II with tapered cone stub weight, rounded corners. Made in U.S.A. by Les Baer Custom, Inc.

Price: Blued **$2,590.00**

BERETTA MODEL 92FS PISTOL

Caliber: 9mm Para., 10-shot magazine. **Barrel:** 4.9". **Weight:** 34 oz. **Length:** 8.5" overall. **Grips:** Checkered black plastic. **Sights:** Blade front, rear adjustable for windage. Tritium night sights available. **Features:** Double action. Extractor acts as chamber loaded indicator, squared trigger guard, grooved front and backstraps, inertia firing pin. Matte or blued finish. Introduced 1977. Made in U.S.A.

Price: With plastic grips **$600.00**

BERETTA MODEL 80 CHEETAH SERIES DA PISTOLS

Caliber: 380 ACP, 10-shot magazine (M84); 8-shot (M85); 22 LR, 7-shot (M87). **Barrel:** 3.82". **Weight:** About 23 oz. (M84/85); 20.8 oz. (M87). **Length:** 6.8" overall. **Grips:** Glossy black plastic (wood optional at extra cost). **Sights:** Fixed front, drift-adjustable rear. **Features:** Double action, quick takedown, convenient magazine release. Introduced 1977. Made in U.S.A.

Price: Model 84 Cheetah, plastic grips **$650.00**

BERETTA MODEL 21 BOBCAT PISTOL

Caliber: 22 LR or 25 ACP. Both double action. **Barrel:** 2.4". **Weight:** 11.5 oz.; 11.8 oz. **Length:** 4.9" overall. **Grips:** Plastic. **Features:** Available in nickel, matte, engraved or blue finish. Introduced in 1985.

Price: Bobcat, 22 or 25, blue **$300.00**
Price: Bobcat, 22, stainless **$375.00**
Price: Bobcat, 22 or 25, matte **$300.00**

BERETTA MODEL 3032 TOMCAT PISTOL

Caliber: 32 ACP, 7-shot magazine. **Barrel:** 2.45". **Weight:** 14.5 oz. **Length:** 5" overall. **Grips:** Checkered black plastic. **Sights:** Blade front, drift-adjustable rear. **Features:** Double action with exposed hammer; tip-up barrel for direct loading/unloading; thumb safety; polished or matte blue finish. Made in U.S.A. Introduced 1996.

Price: Matte **$400.00**
Price: Inox **$500.00**

BERETTA MODEL U22 NEOS

Caliber: 22 LR, 10-shot magazine. **Barrel:** 4.5"; 6". **Weight:** 32 oz.; 36 oz. **Length:** 8.8"; 10.3". **Sights:** Target. **Features:** Integral rail for standard scope mounts, light, perfectly weighted, 100 percent American made by Beretta.

Price: **$250.00**
Price: Inox **$350.00**

BERETTA MODEL PX4 STORM

Caliber: 9mm Para., 40 S&W. Capacity: 17 (9mm Para.); 14 (40 S&W). **Barrel:** 4". **Weight:** 27.5 oz. **Grips:** Black checkered w/3 interchangeable backstraps. **Sights:** 3-dot system coated in Superluminova; removable front and rear sights. **Features:** DA/SA, manual safety/hammer decocking lever (ambi) and automatic firing pin block safety. Picatinny rail. Comes with two magazines (17/10 in 9mm Para. and 14/10 in 40 S&W). Removable hammer unit. American made by Beretta. Introduced 2005.

Price: **$575.00**
Price: 45 ACP **$625.00**

BERETTA MODEL M9

Caliber: 9mm Para. Capacity: 15. **Barrel:** 4.9". **Weight:** 32.2-35.3 oz. **Grips:** Plastic. **Sights:** Dot and post, low profile, windage adjustable rear. **Features:** DA/SA, forged aluminum alloy frame, delayed locking-

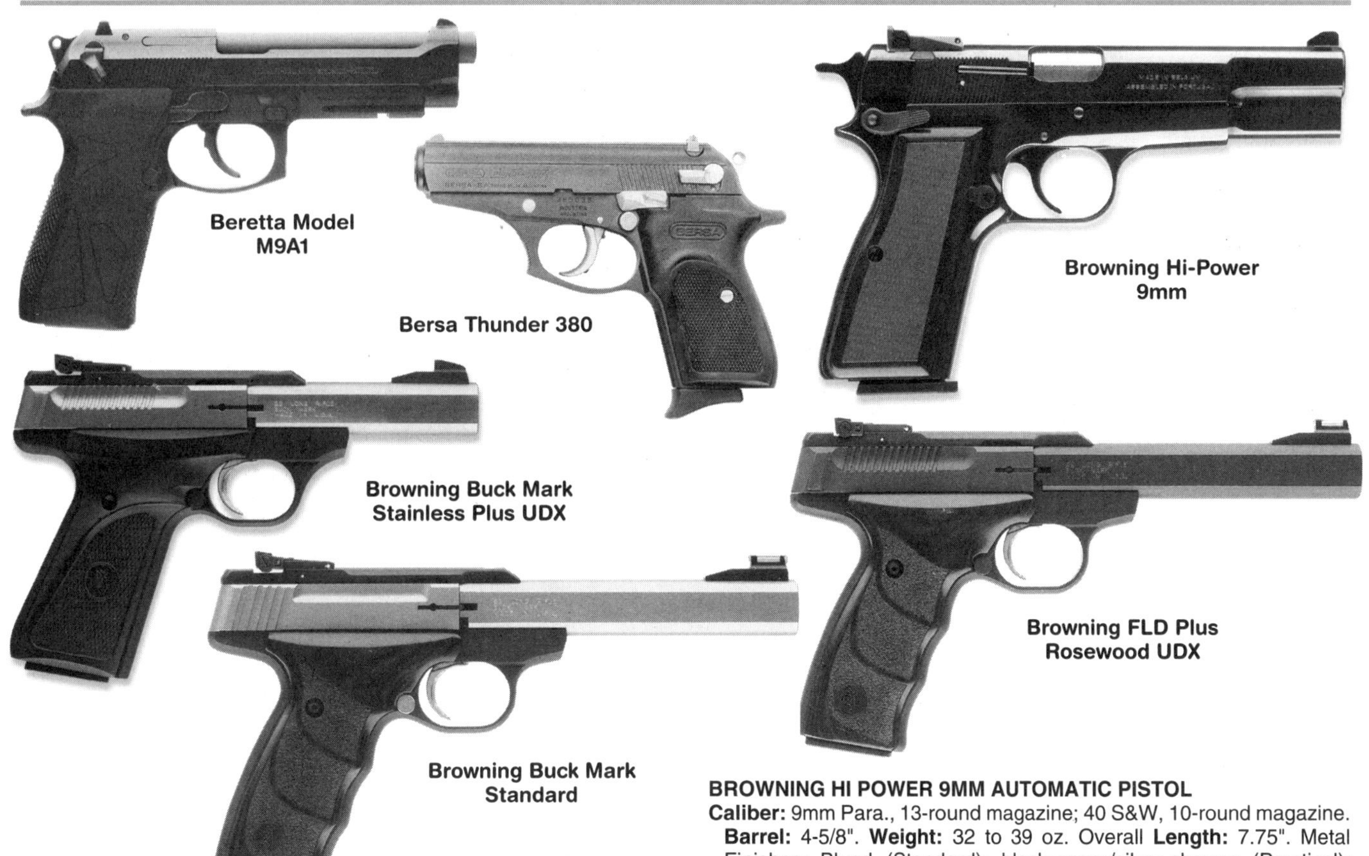
Beretta Model M9A1

Bersa Thunder 380

Browning Hi-Power 9mm

Browning Buck Mark Stainless Plus UDX

Browning FLD Plus Rosewood UDX

Browning Buck Mark Standard

bolt system, manual safety doubles as decocking lever, combat-style trigger guard, loaded chamber indicator. Comes with two magazines (15/10). American made by Beretta. Introduced 2005.

Price: **$600.00**

BERETTA MODEL M9A1

Caliber: 9mm Para. Capacity: 15. **Barrel:** 4.9". **Weight:** 32.2-35.3 oz. **Grips:** Plastic. **Sights:** Dot and post, low profile, windage adjustable rear. **Features:** Same as M9, but also includes integral Mil-Std-1913 Picatinny rail, has checkered frontstrap and backstrap. Comes with two magazines (15/10). American made by Beretta. Introduced 2005.

Price: **$700.00**

BERSA THUNDER 45 ULTRA COMPACT PISTOL

Caliber: 45 ACP. **Barrel:** 3.6". **Weight:** 27 oz. **Length:** 6.7" overall. **Grips:** Anatomically designed polymer. **Sights:** White outline rear. **Features:** Double action; firing pin safeties, integral locking system. Available in matte, satin nickel, gold, or duo-tone. Introduced 2003. Imported from Argentina by Eagle Imports, Inc.

Price: Thunder 45, matte blue **$402.00**
Price: Thunder 45, stainless **$480.00**
Price: Thunder 45, satin nickel **$445.00**

BERSA THUNDER 380 SERIES PISTOLS

Caliber: 380 ACP, 7 rounds **Barrel:** 3.5". **Weight:** 23 oz. **Length:** 6.6" overall. **Features:** Otherwise similar to Thunder 45 Ultra Compact. 380 DLX has 9-round capacity. 380 Concealed Carry has 8 round capacity. Imported from Argentina by Eagle Imports, Inc.

Price: Thunder 380 Matte **$310.00**
Price: Thunder 380 Satin Nickel **$336.00**
Price: Thunder 380 Blue DLX **$332.00**
Price: Thunder 380 Matte CC (2006) **$315.00**

BERSA THUNDER 9 ULTRA COMPACT/40 SERIES PISTOLS

Caliber: 9mm Para., 40 S&W. **Barrel:** 3.5". **Weight:** 24.5 oz. **Length:** 6.6" overall. **Features:** Otherwise similar to Thunder 45 Ultra Compact. 9mm Para. High Capacity model has 17-round capacity. 40 High Capacity model has 13-round capacity. Imported from Argentina by Eagle Imports, Inc.

Price: Thunder 9mm Para. Matte **$402.00**
Price: Thunder 40 High Capacity Satin Nickel **$419.00**

BROWNING HI POWER 9MM AUTOMATIC PISTOL

Caliber: 9mm Para., 13-round magazine; 40 S&W, 10-round magazine. **Barrel:** 4-5/8". **Weight:** 32 to 39 oz. Overall **Length:** 7.75". Metal Finishes: Blued (Standard); black-epoxy/silver-chrome (Practical); black-epoxy (Mark III). **Grips:** Molded (Mark III); wraparound Pachmayr (Practical); or walnut grips (Standard). **Sights:** Fixed (Practical, Mark III, Standard); low-mount adjustable rear (Standard). Cable lock supplied. **Features:** External hammer with half-cock and thumb safeties. Fixed rear sight model available. Commander-style (Practical) or spur-type hammer, single action. Includes gun lock. Imported from Belgium by Browning.

Price: Mark III **$897.00**
Price: Standard, fixed sights. **$922.00**
Price: Standard, adjustable sights **$988.00**

BROWNING BUCK MARK PISTOLS

Common Features: Caliber: 22 LR, 10-shot magazine. Action: Blowback semi-auto. Trigger: Wide grooved style. **Sights:** Ramp front, Browning Pro-Target rear adjustable for windage and elevation. **Features:** Machined aluminum frame. Includes gun lock. Introduced 1985. Hunter, Camper Stainless, STD Stainless, 5.5 Target, 5.5 Field all introduced 2005. Multiple variations, as noted below. **Grips:** Cocobolo, target-style (Hunter, 5.5 Target, 5.5 Field); polymer (Camper, Camper Stainless, Micro Nickel, Standard, STD Stainless); checkered walnut (Challenge); laminated (Plus and Plus Nickel); laminated rosewood (Bullseye Target, FLD Plus); rubber (Bullseye Standard). Metal finishes: Matte blue (Hunter, Camper, Challenge, Plus, Bullseye Target, Bullseye Standard, 5.5 Target, 5.5 Field, FLD Plus); matte stainless (Camper Stainless, STD Stainless, Micro Standard); nickel-plated (Micro Nickel, Plus Nickel, and Nickel). Made in U.S.A. From Browning.

Price: Hunter, 7.25" heavy barrel, 38 oz., Truglo sight **$360.00**
Price: Camper, 5.5" heavy barrel, 34 oz. **$315.00**
Price: FLD Camper Stainless URX, 5.5" tapered bull barrel, 34 oz. **$355.00**
Price: Standard URX, 5.5" flat-side bull barrel, 34 oz. **$380.00**
Price: Standard Stainless URX, 5.5" flat-side bull barrel, 34 oz. **$419.00**
Price: Micro Standard URX, 4" flat-side bull barrel, 32 oz. . . . **$380.00**
Price: Micro Standard Stainless URX, 4" flat-side bull barrel, 32 oz. **$419.00**
Price: Challenge, 5.5" lightweight taper barrel, 25 oz. **$381.00**
Price: Bullseye URX, 7.25" fluted bull barrel, 36 oz. **$522.00**
Price: Bullseye Target Stainless, 7.25" fluted bull barrel, 36 oz. **$689.00**

Browning Stainless Camper

Browning Pro-9

Charles Daly Empire EFS

Cobra Patriot 45

Charles Daly M-5 Government

Colt XSE Government

Cobra Patriot 380

BROWNING BUCK MARK PISTOLS *(cont.)*

Price: 5.5 Target, 5.5" round bull barrel, target sights, 35.5 oz. **$547.00**
Price: 5.5 Field, 5.5" round bull barrel, 35 oz. **$547.00**
Price: Plus Stainless UDX (2007). **$484.00**
Price: Plus UDX (2007). **$446.00**
Price: FLD Plus Rosewood UDX (2007). **$446.00**
Price: Stainless Camper, 5.5" tapered bull barrel (2008) **$355.00**

BROWNING PRO-9, PRO-40 PISTOLS

Caliber: 9mm, 16-round magazine; 40 S&W, 14-round magazine. **Barrel:** 4". **Weight:** 30-33 oz. **Overall Length:** 7.25". **Features:** Polymer frame, stainless-steel frames and barrels, double-action, ambidextrous decocker and safety. Fixed, 3-dot-style sights, 6" sight radius. Molded composite grips with interchangeable backstrap inserts. Cable lock supplied.
Price: **$641.00**

CHARLES DALY ENHANCED 1911 PISTOLS

Caliber: 45 ACP. **Barrel:** 5". **Weight:** 38 oz. **Length:** 8.75" overall. **Grips:** Checkered double diamond hardwood. **Sights:** Dovetailed front and dovetailed snag-free low profile rear sights, 3-dot system. **Features:** Extended high-rise beavertail grip safety, combat trigger, combat hammer, beveled magazine well, flared and lowered ejection port. Field Grade models are satin-finished blued steel. EMS series includes an ambidextrous safety, 4" barrel, 8-shot magazine. ECS series has a contoured left hand safety, 3.5" barrel, 6-shot magazine Two magazines, lockable carrying case. Introduced 1998. Empire series are stainless versions. Imported from the Philippines by K.B.I., Inc.
Price: EFS, blued, 39.5 oz., 5" barrel **$649.00**
Price: EMS, blued, 37 oz., 4" barrel **$649.00**
Price: ECS, blued, 34.5 oz., 3.5" barrel **$649.00**

CHARLES DALY M-5 POLYMER-FRAMED HI-CAP 1911 PISTOL

Caliber: 9mm Para., 12-round magazine; 40 S&W 17-round magazine; 45 ACP, 13-round magazine. **Barrel:** 5". **Weight:** 33.5 oz. **Length:** 8.5" overall. **Grips:** Checkered polymer. **Sights:** Blade front, adjustable low-profile rear. **Features:** Stainless steel beaver-tail grip safety, rounded trigger-guard, tapered bull barrel, full-length guide rod, matte blue finish on frame and slide. 40 S&W models in M-5 Govt. 1911, M-5 Commander, and M-5 IPSC introduced 2006; M-5 Ultra X Compact in 9mm Para. and 45 ACP introduced 2006; M-5 IPSC .45 ACP introduced 2006. Made in Israel by BUL, imported by K.B.I., Inc.
Price: M-5 Govt. 1911, 40 S&W/45 ACP, matte blue . . **$749.00**
Price: M-5 Commander, 40 S&W/45 ACP, matte blue . . **$749.00**
Price: M-5 Ultra X Compact, 9mm Para., 3.1" barrel, 7" OAL, 28 oz. **$749.00**
Price: M-5 Ultra X Compact, 45 ACP, 3.1" barrel, 7" OAL, 28 oz. **$749.00**

COBRA ENTERPRISES FS32, FS380 AUTO PISTOL

Caliber: 32 ACP, 380 ACP, 7-shot magazine. **Barrel:** 3.5". **Weight:** 2.1 lbs. **Length:** 6-3/8" overall. **Grips:** Black composition. **Sights:** Fixed. **Features:** Choice of bright chrome, satin nickel or black finish. Introduced 2002. Made in U.S.A. by Cobra Enterprises of Utah, Inc.
Price: **$165.00**

COBRA ENTERPRISES PATRIOT 45 PISTOL

Caliber: 45 ACP ACP, 6, 7, or 10-shot magazine. **Barrel:** 3.3". **Weight:** 20 oz. **Length:** 6" overall. **Grips:** Black polymer. **Sights:** Rear adjustable. **Features:** Stainless steel or black melonite slide with load indicator; Semiauto locked breech, DAO. Made in U.S.A. by Cobra Enterprises of Utah, Inc.
Price: **$380.00**

COBRA ENTERPRISES CA32, CA380 PISTOL

Caliber: 32 ACP, 380 ACP. **Barrel:** 2.8". **Weight:** 22 oz. **Length:** 5.4". **Grips:** Black molded synthetic. **Sights:** Fixed. **Features:** Choice of black, satin nickel, or chrome finish. Made in U.S.A. by Cobra Enterprises of Utah, Inc.
Price: **$157.00**

COLT MODEL 1991 MODEL O AUTO PISTOL

Caliber: 45 ACP, 7-shot magazine. **Barrel:** 5". **Weight:** 38 oz. **Length:** 8.5" overall. **Grips:** Checkered black composition. **Sights:** Ramped blade front, fixed square notch rear, high profile. **Features:** Matte finish. Continuation of serial number range used on original G.I. 1911A1 guns. Comes with one magazine and molded carrying case. Introduced 1991.
Price: Blue **$786.00**
Price: Stainless **$839.00**

COLT XSE SERIES MODEL O AUTO PISTOLS

Caliber: 45 ACP, 8-shot magazine. **Barrel:** 4.25", 5". **Grips:** Checkered, double diamond rosewood. **Sights:** Drift-adjustable 3-dot combat. **Features:** Brushed stainless finish; adjustable, two-cut aluminum trigger; extended ambidextrous thumb safety; upswept beavertail with palm swell; elongated slot hammer. Introduced 1999. From Colt's Mfg. Co., Inc.
Price: XSE Government (5" bbl.) **$944.00**
Price: XSE Government (4.25" bbl.) **$944.00**
Price: XSE Delta Elite 10mm, 5" bbl, 9+1 (2008) **$983.00**

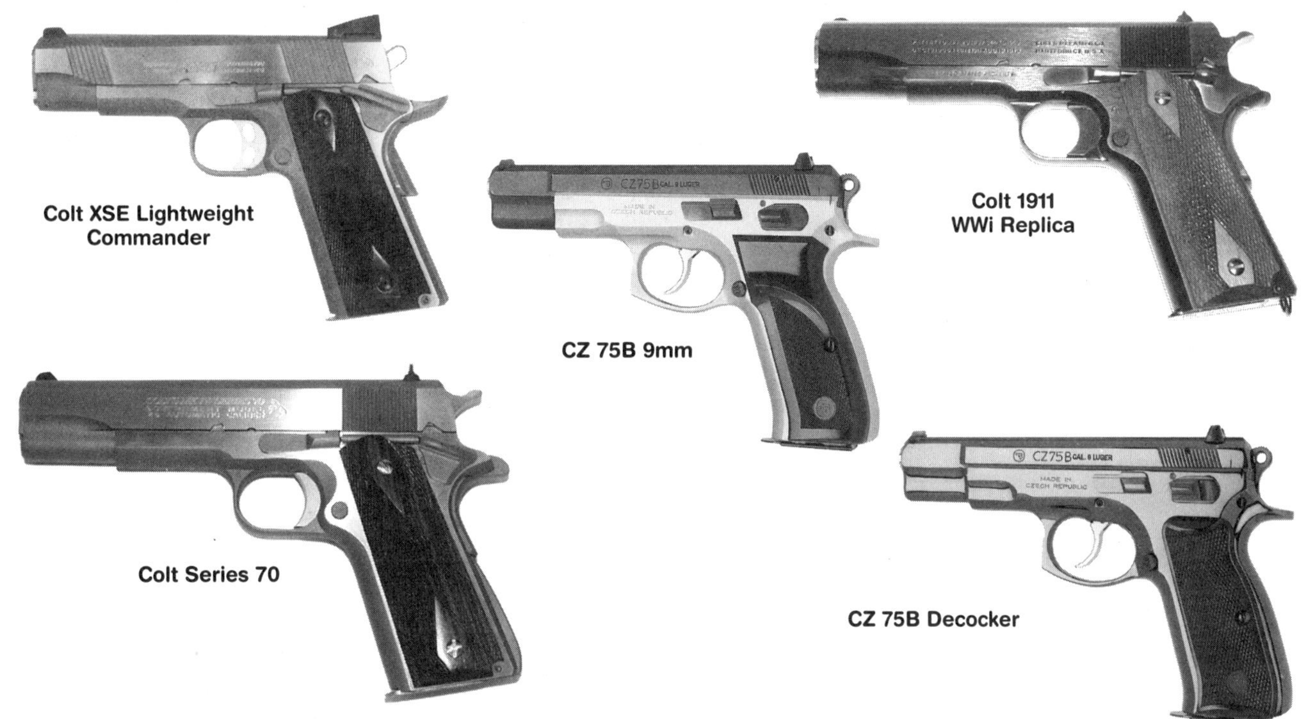
Colt XSE Lightweight Commander

CZ 75B 9mm

Colt 1911 WWi Replica

Colt Series 70

CZ 75B Decocker

COLT XSE LIGHTWEIGHT COMMANDER AUTO PISTOL

Caliber: 45 ACP, 8-shot. **Barrel:** 4.25". **Weight:** 26 oz. **Length:** 7.75" overall. **Grips:** Double diamond checkered rosewood. **Sights:** Fixed, glare-proofed blade front, square notch rear; 3-dot system. **Features:** Brushed stainless slide, nickeled aluminum frame; McCormick elongated slot enhanced hammer, McCormick two-cut adjustable aluminum hammer. Made in U.S.A. by Colt's Mfg. Co., Inc.

Price: Stainless **$944.00**

COLT DEFENDER

Caliber: 45 ACP, 7-shot magazine. **Barrel:** 3". **Weight:** 22-1/2 oz. **Length:** 6.75" overall. **Grips:** Pebble-finish rubber wraparound with finger grooves. **Sights:** White dot front, snag-free Colt competition rear. **Features:** Stainless finish; aluminum frame; combat-style hammer; Hi Ride grip safety, extended manual safety, disconnect safety. Introduced 1998. Made in U.S.A. by Colt's Mfg. Co., Inc.

Price: 07000D, stainless. **$885.00**
Price: 07810D New Agent, blued, trench sights (2008) **$885.00**

COLT SERIES 70

Caliber: 45 ACP. **Barrel:** 5". **Weight:** NA. **Length:** NA. **Grips:** Rosewood with double diamond checkering pattern. **Sights:** Fixed. **Features:** Custom replica of the Original Series 70 pistol with a Series 70 firing system, original rollmarks. Introduced 2002. Made in U.S.A. by Colt's Mfg. Co., Inc.

Price: Blued **$919.00**
Price: Stainless **$950.00**

COLT 38 SUPER

Caliber: 38 Super. **Barrel:** 5". **Weight:** NA. **Length:** 8.5" **Grips:** Checkered rubber (stainless and blue models); wood with double diamond checkering pattern (bright stainless model). **Sights:** 3-dot. **Features:** Beveled magazine well, standard thumb safety and service-style grip safety. Introduced 2003. Made in U.S.A. by Colt's Mfg. Co., Inc.

Price: Blued **$837.00**
Price: Stainless **$866.00**
Price: Bright Stainless **$1,090.00**

COLT 1918 WWI REPLICA

Caliber: 45 ACP, 2 7-round magazines. **Barrel:** 5". **Weight:** 38 oz. **Length:** 8.5". **Grips:** Checkered walnut with double diamond checkering pattern. **Sights:** Tapered blade front sight, U-shaped rear notch. **Features:** Reproduction based on original 1911 blueprints. Original rollmarks and inspector marks. Smooth mainspring housing with lanyard loop, WWI-style manual thumb and grip safety, black oxide finish. Introduced 2007. Made in U.S.A. by Colt's Mfg. Co., Inc.

Price: Blued **$990.00**

CZ 75B AUTO PISTOL

Caliber: 9mm Para., 40 S&W, 10-shot magazine. **Barrel:** 4.7". **Weight:** 34.3 oz. **Length:** 8.1" overall. **Grips:** High impact checkered plastic. **Sights:** Square post front, rear adjustable for windage; 3-dot system. **Features:** Single action/double action design; firing pin block safety; choice of black polymer, matte or high-polish blue finishes. All-steel frame. B-SA is a single action with a drop-free magazine. Imported from the Czech Republic by CZ-USA.

Price: 75B, black polymer, 16-shot magazine **$544.00**
Price: 75B, glossy blue, dual-tone or satin nickel **$560.00**
Price: 40 S&W, black polymer, 12-shot magazine **$560.00**
Price: 75B SA, 9mm Para./40 S&W, single action **$554.00**
Price: 75 Stainless 9mm Para. (2006), 16-shot magazine . . . **$687.00**

CZ 75BD Decocker

Similar to the CZ 75B except has a decocking lever in place of the safety lever. All other specifications are the same. Introduced 1999. Imported from the Czech Republic by CZ-USA.

Price: 9mm Para., black polymer **$554.00**

CZ 75B Compact Auto Pistol

Similar to the CZ 75 except has 14-shot magazine in 9mm Para., 3.9" barrel and weighs 32 oz. Has removable front sight, non-glare ribbed slide top. Trigger guard is squared and serrated; combat hammer. Introduced 1993. Imported from the Czech Republic by CZ-USA.

Price: 9mm Para., black polymer **$575.00**
Price: 9mm Para., dual tone or satin nickel **$593.00**
Price: 9mm Para. D PCR Compact, alloy frame **$593.00**

CZ 75 Champion Pistol

Similar to the CZ 75B except has a longer frame and slide, rubber grip to accommodate new heavy-duty magazine. Ambidextrous thumb safety, extended magazine release; three-port compensator. Blued slide and stain nickel frame finish. Introduced 2005. Imported from the Czech Republic by CZ-USA.

Price: 9mm Para., 16-shot mag. **$1,691.00**
Price: 40 S&W, 12-shot mag. **$1,741.00**

CZ 75 Tactical Sport

Similar to the CZ 75B except the CZ 75 TS is a competition ready pistol designed for IPSC standard division (USPSA limited division). Fixed target sights, tuned single-action operation, lightweight polymer match trigger with adjustments for take-up and overtravel, competition hammer, extended magazine catch, ambidextrous manual safety, checkered walnut grips, polymer magazine well, two tone finish. Introduced 2005. Imported from the Czech Republic by CZ-USA.

Price: 9mm Para., 20-shot mag. **$1,219.00**
Price: 40 S&W, 16-shot mag. **$1,219.00**

CZ 85
CZ 97B
CZ 75/85 Kadet
CZ 100
Dan Wesson Pointman

CZ 75 SP-01 Pistol

Similar to NATO-approved CZ 75 Compact P-01 model. Features an integral 1913 accessory rail on the dust cover, rubber grip panels, black polycoat finish, extended beavertail, new grip geometry with checkering on front and back straps, and double or single action operation. Introduced 2005. The Shadow variant designed as an IPSC "production" division competition firearm. Includes competition hammer, competition rear sight and fiber-optic front sight, modified slide release, lighter recoil and main spring for use with "minor power factor" competition ammunition. Includes polycoat finish and slim walnut grips. Finished by CZ Custom Shop. Imported from the Czech Republic by CZ-USA.

Price: SP-01 9mm Para., black polymer, 19+1 . . . . **$635.00**

CZ 85B/85 Combat Auto Pistol

Same gun as the CZ 75 except has ambidextrous slide release and safety levers; non-glare, ribbed slide top; squared, serrated trigger guard; trigger stop to prevent overtravel. Introduced 1986. The CZ 85 Combat features a fully adjustable rear sight, extended magazine release, ambidextrous slide stop and safety catch, drop free magazine and overtravel adjustment. Imported from the Czech Republic by CZ-USA.

Price: 9mm Para., Black polymer **$572.00**
Price: Combat, black polymer **$639.00**
Price: Combat, dual-tone, glossy blue, satin nickel **$623.00**

CZ 83B DOUBLE-ACTION PISTOL

Caliber: 32 ACP, 380 ACP, 12-shot magazine. **Barrel:** 3.8". **Weight:** 26.2 oz. **Length:** 6.8" overall. **Grips:** High impact checkered plastic. **Sights:** Removable square post front, rear adjustable for windage; 3-dot system. **Features:** Single action/double action; ambidextrous magazine release and safety. Blue finish; non-glare ribbed slide top. Imported from the Czech Republic by CZ-USA.

Price: Glossy blue, 32 ACP or 380 ACP **$451.00**
Price: Satin Nickel **$476.00**

CZ 97B AUTO PISTOL

Caliber: 45 ACP, 10-shot magazine. **Barrel:** 4.85". **Weight:** 40 oz. **Length:** 8.34" overall. **Grips:** Checkered walnut. **Sights:** Fixed. **Features:** Single action/double action; full-length slide rails; screw-in barrel bushing; linkless barrel; all-steel construction; chamber loaded indicator; dual transfer bars. Introduced 1999. Imported from the Czech Republic by CZ-USA.

Price: Black polymer **$709.00**
Price: Glossy blue **$727.00**

CZ 75 KADET AUTO PISTOL

Caliber: 22 LR, 10-shot magazine. **Barrel:** 4.88". **Weight:** 36 oz. **Grips:** High impact checkered plastic. **Sights:** Blade front, fully adjustable rear. **Features:** Single action/double action mechanism; all-steel construction. Introduced 1999. Kadet conversion kit consists of barrel, slide, adjustable sights, and magazine to convert the centerfire 75 to rimfire. Imported from the Czech Republic by CZ-USA.

Price: Black polymer **$605.00**
Price: Kadet conversion kit **$335.00**

CZ 100 B AUTO PISTOL

Caliber: 9mm Para., 40 S&W. **Barrel:** 3.7". **Weight:** 24 oz. **Length:** 6.9" overall. **Grips:** Grooved polymer. **Sights:** Blade front with dot, white outline rear drift adjustable for windage. **Features:** Double action only with firing pin block; polymer frame, steel slide; has laser sight mount. Introduced 1996. Imported from the Czech Republic by CZ-USA.

Price: 9mm Para, 12-shot magazine **$458.00**
Price: 40 S&W, 10-shot magazine **$458.00**

CZ 2075 RAMI/RAMI P AUTO PISTOL

Caliber: 9mm Para., 40 S&W. **Barrel:** 3". **Weight:** 25 oz. **Length:** 6.5" overall. **Grips:** Rubber. **Sights:** Blade front with dot, white outline rear drift adjustable for windage. **Features:** Single-action/double-action; alloy or polymer frame, steel slide; has laser sight mount. Imported from the Czech Republic by CZ-USA.

Price: 9mm Para., alloy frame, 10 and 14-shot magazines . . . **$611.00**
Price: 40 S&W, alloy frame, 8-shot magazine **$611.00**
Price: RAMI P, polymer frame, 9mm Para., 40 S&W **$557.00**

CZ P-01 AUTO PISTOL

Caliber: 9mm Para., 14-shot magazine. **Barrel:** 3.85". **Weight:** 27 oz. **Length:** 7.2" overall. **Grips:** Checkered rubber. **Sights:** Blade front with dot, white outline rear drift adjustable for windage. **Features:** Based on the CZ 75, except with forged aircraft-grade aluminum alloy frame. Hammer forged barrel, de-cocker, firing-pin block, M3 rail, dual slide serrations, squared trigger guard, re-contoured trigger, lanyard loop on butt. Serrated front and back strap. Introduced 2006. Imported from the Czech Republic by CZ-USA.

Price: CZ P01 . . . . **$612.00**
Price: CZ P01 with Crimson Trace Laser Grips **$795.00**

DAN WESSON FIREARMS POINTMAN SEVEN AUTO PISTOL

Caliber: 10mm, 45 ACP. **Barrel:** 5". **Grips:** Diamond checkered cocobolo. **Sights:** Bo-Mar style adjustable target sight. **Weight:** 38 oz. **Features:** Stainless-steel frame and serrated slide. Series 70-style 1911, stainless-steel frame, forged stainless-steel slide. One-piece match-grade barrel and bushing. 20-LPI checkered mainspring housing, front and rear slide cocking serrations, beveled magwell, dehorned by hand. Lowered and flared ejection port, Ed Brown slide stop and memory groove grip safety, tactical extended thumb safety. Commander-style match hammer, match grade sear, aluminum trigger with stainless bow, Wolff springs. Introduced 2000. Made in U.S.A. by Dan Wesson Firearms, distributed by CZ-USA.

Price: 45 ACP, 7+1 . . . . **$1,096.00**
Price: 10mm, 8+1 . . . . **$1,128.00**

Dan Wesson DW RZ-10

Desert Baby Eagle

EAA Witness

Desert Eagle Mark XIX

EAA Zastava EZ

Ed Brown Classic Custom

Dan Wesson Commander Classic Bobtail Auto Pistols
Similar to Pointman Seven, a Commander-sized frame with 4.25" barrel. Available with stainless finish, fixed night sights. Introduced 2005. Made in U.S.A. by Dan Wesson Firearms, distributed by CZ-USA.
Price: 45 ACP, 7+1, 34 oz. **$1,128.00**
Price: 10mm, 8+1, 34 oz. **$1,159.00**

DAN WESSON DW RZ-10 AUTO PISTOL
Caliber: 10mm. **Barrel:** 5". **Grips:** Diamond checkered cocobolo. **Sights:** Bo-Mar style adjustable target sight. **Weight:** 38.3 oz. **Features:** Stainless-steel frame and serrated slide. Series 70-style 1911, stainless-steel frame, forged stainless-steel slide. Commander-style match hammer. Reintroduced 2005. Made in U.S.A. by Dan Wesson Firearms, distributed by CZ-USA.
Price: 10mm, 8+1 . . . . **$1,128.00**

DESERT EAGLE MARK XIX PISTOL
Caliber: 357 Mag., 9-shot; 44 Mag., 8-shot; 50 AE, 7-shot. **Barrel:** 6", 10", interchangeable. **Weight:** 357 Mag.-62 oz.; 44 Mag.-69 oz.; 50 AE-72 oz. **Length:** 10.25" overall (6" bbl.). **Grips:** Polymer; rubber available. **Sights:** Blade on ramp front, combat-style rear. Adjustable available. **Features:** Interchangeable barrels; rotating three-lug bolt; ambidextrous safety; adjustable trigger. Military epoxy finish. Satin, bright nickel, chrome, brushed, matte or black-oxide finishes available. 10" barrel extra. Imported from Israel by Magnum Research, Inc.
Price: Black-6, 6" barrel **$1,440.00**
Price: Black-10, 10" barrel **$1,540.00**
Price: Component System Package, 3 barrels, carrying case **$2,766.00**

DESERT BABY EAGLE PISTOLS
Caliber: 9mm Para., 40 S&W, 45 ACP, 10- or 15-round magazines. **Barrel:** 3.64", 3.93", 4.52". **Weight:** 26.8 to 39.8 oz. **Length:** 7.25" to 8.25" overall. **Grips:** Polymer. **Sights:** Drift-adjustable rear, blade front. **Features:** Steel frame and slide; slide safety; decocker. Reintroduced in 1999. Imported from Israel by Magnum Research, Inc.
Price: **$569.00**

EAA WITNESS FULL SIZE AUTO PISTOL
Caliber: 9mm Para., 38 Super, 18-shot magazine; 40 S&W, 10mm, 15-shot magazine; 45 ACP, 10-shot magazine. **Barrel:** 4.50". **Weight:** 35.33 oz. **Length:** 8.10" overall. **Grips:** Checkered rubber. **Sights:** Undercut blade front, open rear adjustable for windage. **Features:** Double-action/single-action trigger system; round trigger guard; frame-mounted safety. Introduced 1991. Polymer frame introduced 2005. Imported from Italy by European American Armory.
Price: 9mm Para., 38 Super, 10mm, 40 S&W, 45 ACP, full-size steel frame, Wonder finish **$514.00**
Price: 45/22 22 LR, full-size steel frame, blued **$472.00**
Price: 9mm Para., 40 S&W, 45 ACP, full-size polymer frame . **$472.00**

EAA WITNESS COMPACT AUTO PISTOL
Caliber: 9mm Para., 40 S&W, 10mm, 12-shot magazine; 45 ACP, 8-shot magazine. **Barrel:** 3.6". **Weight:** 30 oz. Length: 7.3" overall. Otherwise similar to Full Size Witness. Polymer frame introduced 2005. Imported from Italy by European American Armory.
Price: 9mm Para., 10mm, 40 S&W, 45 ACP, steel frame, Wonder finish **$514.00**
Price: 9mm Para., 40 S&W, 45 ACP, polymer frame **$472.00**

EAA WITNESS-P CARRY AUTO PISTOL
Caliber: 10mm, 15-shot magazine; 45 ACP, 10-shot magazine. **Barrel:** 3.6". **Weight:** 27 oz. **Length:** 7.5" overall. Otherwise similar to Full Size Witness. Polymer frame introduced 2005. Imported from Italy by European American Armory.
Price: 10mm, 45 ACP, polymer frame, from **$545.00**

EAA ZASTAVA EZ PISTOL
Caliber: 9mm Para., 15-shot magazine; 40 S&W, 11-shot magazine; 45 ACP, 10-shot magazine. **Barrel:** 3.5" or 4." **Weight:** 30-33 oz. **Length:** 7.25" to 7.5" overall. Features include ambidextrous decocker, slide release and magazine release; three dot sight system, aluminum frame, steel slide, accessory rail, full-length claw extractor, loaded chamber indicator. M88 compact has 3.6" barrel, weighs 28 oz. Introduced 2008. Imported by European American Armory.
Price: 9mm Para. or 40 S&W, blued **$499.00**
Price: 9mm Para. or 40 S&W, chromed **$539.00**
Price: 45 ACP, chromed **$539.00**
Price: M88, from **$499.00**

ED BROWN CLASSIC CUSTOM
Caliber: 45 ACP, 7 shot. **Barrel:** 5". **Weight:** 40 oz. Stocks: Cocobolo wood. **Sights:** Bo-Mar adjustable rear, dovetail front. **Features:** Single-action, M1911 style, custom made to order, stainless frame and slide available. Special mirror-finished slide.
Price: Model CC-BB, blued **$2,895.00**
Price: Model CC-SB, blued and stainless **$2,995.00**
Price: Model CC-SS, stainless **$3,095.00**

ED BROWN KOBRA AND KOBRA CARRY
Caliber: 45 ACP, 7-shot magazine. **Barrel:** 5" (Kobra); 4.25" (Kobra Carry). **Weight:** 39 oz. (Kobra); 34 oz. (Kobra Carry). **Grips:** Hogue exotic wood. **Sights:** Ramp, front; fixed Novak low-mount night sights, rear. **Features:** Has snakeskin pattern serrations on forestrap and mainspring housing, dehorned edges, beavertail grip safety.

Ed Brown Kobra KC-SB

Ed Brown Kobra

Ed Brown Kobra Carry

Ed Brown Executive

Ed Brown Special Forces

Firestorm 45 Gov't

Excel Arms Accelerator MP-22

Firestorm Mini

ED BROWN KOBRA AND KOBRA CARRY *(cont.)*

Price: Kobra K-BB, blued **$1,995.00**
Price: Kobra K-SB, stainless and blued **$2,095.00**
Price: Kobra K-SS, stainless **$2,195.00**
Price: Kobra Carry blued, blued/stainless, or stainless from **$2,095.00**

Ed Brown Executive Pistols

Similar to other Ed Brown products, but with 25-lpi checkered frame and mainspring housing.

Price: Elite blued, blued/stainless, or stainless, from **$2,195.00**
Price: Carry blued, blued/stainless, or stainless, from **$2,295.00**
Price: Target blued, blued/stainless, or stainless (2006) from **$2,470.00**

Ed Brown Special Forces Pistol

Similar to other Ed Brown products, but with ChainLink treatment on forestrap and mainspring housing. Entire gun coated with Gen III finish. "Square cut" serrations on rear of slide only. Dehorned. Introduced 2006.

Price: SF-BB blued **$1,995.00**

EXCEL ARMS ACCELERATOR MP-17/MP-22 PISTOLS

Caliber: 17 HMR, 22 WMR, 9-shot magazine. **Barrel:** 8.5" bull barrel. **Weight:** 54 oz. **Length:** 12.875" overall. **Grips:** Textured black composition. **Sights:** Fully adjustable target sights. **Features:** Made from 17-4 stainless steel, comes with aluminum rib, integral Weaver base, internal hammer, firing-pin block. American made, lifetime warranty. Comes with two 9-round stainless steel magazines and a California-approved cable lock. 22 WMR Introduced 2006. Made in U.S.A. by Excel Arms.

Price: **$412.00**
Price: Camo finishes (2008) **$491.00**

FIRESTORM AUTO PISTOLS

Caliber: 22 LR, 32 ACP, 10-shot magazine; 380 ACP, 7-shot magazine; 9mm Para., 40 S&W, 10-shot magazine; 45 ACP, 7-shot magazine. **Barrel:** 3.5". **Weight:** From 23 oz. **Length:** From 6.6" overall. **Grips:** Rubber. **Sights:** 3-dot. **Features:** Double action. Distributed by SGS Importers International.

Price: 22 LR, matte or duotone, from **$274.95**
Price: 380, matte or duotone, from **$274.95**
Price: Mini Firestorm 9mm Para., matte, duotone, nickel, from **$408.95**
Price: Mini Firestorm 40 S&W, matte, duotone, nickel, from . . **$399.95**
Price: Mini Firestorm 45 ACP, matte, duotone, chrome, from . **$416.95**

GLOCK 17/17C AUTO PISTOL

Caliber: 9mm Para., 17/19/33-shot magazines. **Barrel:** 4.49". **Weight:** 22.04 oz. (without magazine). Length: 7.32" overall. **Grips:** Black polymer. **Sights:** Dot on front blade, white outline rear adjustable for windage. **Features:** Polymer frame, steel slide; double-action trigger with "Safe Action" system; mechanical firing pin safety, drop safety; simple takedown without tools; locked breech, recoil operated action. ILS designation refers to Internal Locking System. Adopted by Austrian armed forces 1983. NATO approved 1984. Imported from Austria by Glock, Inc.

Price: Fixed sight **$690.00**

GLOCK 19/19C AUTO PISTOL

Caliber: 9mm Para., 15/17/19/33-shot magazines. **Barrel:** 4.02". **Weight:** 20.99 oz. (without magazine). **Length:** 6.85" overall. Compact version of Glock 17. Pricing the same as Model 17. Imported from Austria by Glock, Inc.

Price: Fixed sight **$699.00**
Price: 19C Compensated (fixed sight) **$675.00**

Glock 17C

Glock 22

Glock 26

Glock 35

Glock 30

Glock 31

GLOCK 20/20C 10MM AUTO PISTOL

Caliber: 10mm, 15-shot magazines. **Barrel:** 4.6". **Weight:** 27.68 oz. (without magazine). **Length:** 7.59" overall. **Features:** Otherwise similar to Model 17. Imported from Austria by Glock, Inc. Introduced 1990.

Price: Fixed sight, from **$700.00**

GLOCK 21/21C AUTO PISTOL

Caliber: 45 ACP, 13-shot magazines. **Barrel:** 4.6". **Weight:** 26.28 oz. (without magazine). **Length:** 7.59" overall. **Features:** Otherwise similar to Model 17. Imported from Austria by Glock, Inc. Introduced 1991. SF version has tactical rail, smaller diameter grip, 10-round magazine capacity. Introduced 2007.

Price: Fixed sight, from **$700.00**

GLOCK 22/22C AUTO PISTOL

Caliber: 40 S&W, 15/17-shot magazines. **Barrel:** 4.49". **Weight:** 22.92 oz. (without magazine). **Length:** 7.32" overall. **Features:** Otherwise similar to Model 17, including pricing. Imported from Austria by Glock, Inc. Introduced 1990.

Price: Fixed sight, from **$641.00**

GLOCK 23/23C AUTO PISTOL

Caliber: 40 S&W, 13/15/17-shot magazines. **Barrel:** 4.02". **Weight:** 21.16 oz. (without magazine). **Length:** 6.85" overall. **Features:** Otherwise similar to Model 22, including pricing. Compact version of Glock 22. Imported from Austria by Glock, Inc. Introduced 1990.

Price: Fixed sight **$641.00**

Price: 23C Compensated (fixed sight) **$694.00**

GLOCK 26 AUTO PISTOL

Caliber: 9mm Para. 10/12/15/17/19/33-shot magazines. **Barrel:** 3.46". **Weight:** 19.75 oz. **Length:** 6.29" overall. Subcompact version of Glock 17. Pricing the same as Model 17. Imported from Austria by Glock, Inc.

Price: Fixed sight **$690.00**

GLOCK 27 AUTO PISTOL

Caliber: 40 S&W, 9/11/13/15/17-shot magazines. **Barrel:** 3.46". **Weight:** 19.75 oz. (without magazine). **Length:** 6.29" overall. **Features:** Otherwise similar to Model 22, including pricing. Subcompact version of Glock 22. Imported from Austria by Glock, Inc. Introduced 1996.

Price: Fixed sight **$750.00**

GLOCK 29 AUTO PISTOL

Caliber: 10mm, 10/15-shot magazines. **Barrel:** 3.78". **Weight:** 24.69 oz. (without magazine). **Length:** 6.77" overall. **Features:** Otherwise similar to Model 20, including pricing. Subcompact version of Glock 20. Imported from Austria by Glock, Inc. Introduced 1997.

Price: Fixed sight **$672.00**

GLOCK 30 AUTO PISTOL

Caliber: 45 ACP, 9/10/13-shot magazines. **Barrel:** 3.78". **Weight:** 23.99 oz. (without magazine). **Length:** 6.77" overall. **Features:** Otherwise similar to Model 21, including pricing. Subcompact version of Glock 21. Imported from Austria by Glock, Inc. Introduced 1997. SF version has tactical rail, octagonal rifled barrel with a 1:15.75 rate of twist, smaller diameter grip, 10-round magazine capacity. Introduced 2008

Price: Fixed sight **$700.00**

GLOCK 31/31C AUTO PISTOL

Caliber: 357 Auto, 15/17-shot magazines. **Barrel:** 4.49". **Weight:** 23.28 oz. (without magazine). **Length:** 7.32" overall. **Features:** Otherwise similar to Model 17. Imported from Austria by Glock, Inc.

Price: Fixed sight, from **$641.00**

GLOCK 32/32C AUTO PISTOL

Caliber: 357 Auto, 13/15/17-shot magazines. **Barrel:** 4.02". **Weight:** 21.52 oz. (without magazine). **Length:** 6.85" overall. **Features:** Otherwise similar to Model 31. Compact. Imported from Austria by Glock, Inc.

Price: Fixed sight **$669.00**

GLOCK 33 AUTO PISTOL

Caliber: 357 Auto, 9/11/13/15/17-shot magazines. **Barrel:** 3.46". **Weight:** 19.75 oz. (without magazine). **Length:** 6.29" overall. **Features:** Otherwise similar to Model 31. Subcompact. Imported from Austria by Glock, Inc.

Price: Fixed sight, from **$641.00**

GLOCK 34 AUTO PISTOL

Caliber: 9mm Para. 17/19/33-shot magazines. **Barrel:** 5.32". **Weight:** 22.9 oz. **Length:** 8.15" overall. Competition version of Glock 17 with extended barrel, slide, and sight radius dimensions. Imported from Austria by Glock, Inc.

Price: Adjustable sight, from **$648.00**

GLOCK 35 AUTO PISTOL

Caliber: 40 S&W, 15/17-shot magazines. **Barrel:** 5.32". **Weight:** 24.52 oz. (without magazine). **Length:** 8.15" overall. **Features:** Otherwise similar to Model 22. Competition version of Glock 22 with extended barrel, slide, and sight radius dimensions. Imported from Austria by Glock, Inc. Introduced 1996.

Price: Adjustable sight **$648.00**

GLOCK 36 AUTO PISTOL

Caliber: 45 ACP, 6-shot magazines. **Barrel:** 3.78". **Weight:** 20.11 oz. (without magazine). **Length:** 6.77" overall. **Features:** Single-stack magazine, slimmer grip than Glock 21/30. Subcompact. Imported from Austria by Glock, Inc. Introduced 1997.

Price: Adjustable sight **$616.00**

Heckler & Koch USP45

Heckler & Koch USP Compact

Heckler & Koch USP45 Tactical

Heckler & Koch Mark 23 Special Operations

Hi-Point 9mm Comp

Heckler & Koch USP45 Compact

GLOCK 37 AUTO PISTOL

Caliber: 45 GAP, 10-shot magazines. **Barrel:** 4.49". **Weight:** 25.95 oz. (without magazine). **Length:** 7.32" overall. **Features:** Otherwise similar to Model 17. Imported from Austria by Glock, Inc. Introduced 2005.

Price: Fixed sight, from **$562.00**

GLOCK 38 AUTO PISTOL

Caliber: 45 GAP, 8/10-shot magazines. **Barrel:** 4.02". **Weight:** 24.16 oz. (without magazine). **Length:** 6.85" overall. **Features:** Otherwise similar to Model 37. Compact. Imported from Austria by Glock, Inc.

Price: Fixed sight **$614.00**

GLOCK 39 AUTO PISTOL

Caliber: 45 GAP, 6/8/10-shot magazines. **Barrel:** 3.46". **Weight:** 19.33 oz. (without magazine). **Length:** 6.3" overall. **Features:** Otherwise similar to Model 37. Subcompact. Imported from Austria by Glock, Inc.

Price: Fixed sight **$614.00**

HECKLER & KOCH USP AUTO PISTOL

Caliber: 9mm Para., 15-shot magazine; 40 S&W, 13-shot magazine; 45 ACP, 12-shot magazine. **Barrel:** 4.25-4.41". **Weight:** 1.65 lbs. **Length:** 7.64-7.87" overall. **Grips:** Non-slip stippled black polymer. **Sights:** Blade front, rear adjustable for windage. **Features:** New HK design with polymer frame, modified Browning action with recoil reduction system, single control lever. Special "hostile environment" finish on all metal parts. Available in SA/DA, DAO, left- and right-hand versions. Introduced 1993. 45 ACP Introduced 1995. Imported from Germany by Heckler & Koch, Inc.

Price: USP 45 .... **$919.00**
Price: USP 40 and USP 9mm **$859.00**

HECKLER & KOCH USP COMPACT AUTO PISTOL

Caliber: 9mm Para., 13-shot magazine; 40 S&W and .357 SIG, 12-shot magazine; 45 ACP, 8-shot magazine. Similar to the USP except the 9mm Para., 357 SIG, and 40 S&W have 3.58" barrels, measure 6.81" overall, and weigh 1.47 lbs. (9mm Para.). Introduced 1996. 45 ACP measures 7.09" overall. Introduced 1998. Imported from Germany by Heckler & Koch, Inc.

Price: USP Compact 45 .... **$959.00**
Price: USP Compact 9mm Para., 40 S&W **$879.00**

HECKLER & KOCH USP45 TACTICAL PISTOL

Caliber: 40 S&W, 13-shot magazine; 45 ACP, 12-shot magazine. **Barrel:** 4.90-5.09". **Weight:** 1.9 lbs. **Length:** 8.64" overall. **Grips:** Non-slip stippled polymer. **Sights:** Blade front, fully adjustable target rear. **Features:** Has extended threaded barrel with rubber O-ring; adjustable trigger; extended magazine floorplate; adjustable trigger stop; polymer frame. Introduced 1998. Imported from Germany by Heckler & Koch, Inc.

Price: USP Tactical 45 .... **$1,239.00**
Price: USP Tactical 40 .... **$1,179.00**

HECKLER & KOCH USP COMPACT TACTICAL PISTOL

Caliber: 45 ACP, 8-shot magazine. Similar to the USP Tactical except measures 7.72" overall, weighs 1.72 lbs. Introduced 2006. Imported from Germany by Heckler & Koch, Inc.

Price: USP Compact Tactical **$1,179.00**

HECKLER & KOCH MARK 23 SPECIAL OPERATIONS PISTOL

Caliber: 45 ACP, 12-shot magazine. **Barrel:** 5.87". **Weight:** 2.42 lbs. **Length:** 9.65" overall. **Grips:** Integral with frame; black polymer. **Sights:** Blade front, rear drift adjustable for windage; 3-dot. **Features:** Civilian version of the SOCOM pistol. Polymer frame; double action; exposed hammer; short recoil, modified Browning action. Introduced 1996. Imported from Germany by Heckler & Koch, Inc.

Price: **$2,139.00**

HECKLER & KOCH P2000 AUTO PISTOL

Caliber: 9mm Para., 13-shot magazine; 40 S&W and .357 SIG, 12-shot magazine. **Barrel:** 3.62". **Weight:** 1.5 lbs. **Length:** 7" overall. **Grips:** Interchangeable panels. **Sights:** Fixed Patridge style, drift adjustable for windage, standard 3-dot. Incorporates features of HK USP Compact pistol, including Law Enforcement Modification (LEM) trigger, double-action hammer system, ambidextrous magazine release, dual slide-release levers, accessory mounting rails, recurved, hook trigger guard, fiber-reinforced polymer frame, modular grip with exchangeable back straps, nitro-carburized finish, lock-out safety device. Introduced 2003. Imported from Germany by Heckler & Koch, Inc.

Price: **$879.00**
Price: P2000 LEM DAO, 357 SIG, intr. 2006 .... **$879.00**
Price: P2000 SA/DA, 357 SIG, intr. 2006 .... **$879.00**

HECKLER & KOCH P2000 SK AUTO PISTOL

Caliber: 9mm Para., 10-shot magazine; 40 S&W and .357 SIG, 9-shot magazine. **Barrel:** 3.27". **Weight:** 1.3 lbs. **Length:** 6.42" overall. **Sights:** Fixed Patridge style, drift adjustable. **Features:** Standard accessory rails, ambidextrous slide release, polymer frame, polygonal bore profile. Smaller version of P2000. Introduced 2005. Imported from Germany by Heckler & Koch, Inc.

Price: **$919.00**

Hi-Point C-9

Kahr K9

Kahr PM45

HI-POINT FIREARMS MODEL 9MM COMPACT PISTOL

Caliber: 9mm Para., 8-shot magazine. **Barrel:** 3.5". **Weight:** 25 oz. **Length:** 6.75" overall. **Grips:** Textured plastic. **Sights:** Combat-style adjustable 3-dot system; low profile. **Features:** Single-action design; frame-mounted magazine release; polymer frame. Scratch-resistant matte finish. Introduced 1993. Comps are similar except they have a 4" barrel with muzzle brake/compensator. Compensator is slotted for laser or flashlight mounting. Introduced 1998. Made in U.S.A. by MKS Supply, Inc.

Price: C-9 9mm **$140.00**
Price: C-9 Comp **$169.00**
Price: C-9 Comp-L w/laser sight **$219.00**

Hi-Point Firearms Model 380 Polymer Pistol

Similar to the 9mm Compact model except chambered for 380 ACP, 8-shot magazine, adjustable 3-dot sights. Weighs 25 oz. Polymer frame. Action locks open after last shot. Includes 10-shot and 8-shot magazine; trigger lock. Introduced 1998. Comps are similar except they have a 4" barrel with muzzle compensator. Introduced 2001. Made in U.S.A. by MKS Supply, Inc.

Price: CF-380 . . . . **$120.00**
Price: 380 Comp **$120.00**
Price: 380 Comp-L w/laser sight **$190.00**

HI-POINT FIREARMS 40SW/POLY AND 45 AUTO PISTOLS

Caliber: 40 S&W, 8-shot magazine; 45 ACP (9-shot). **Barrel:** 4.5". **Weight:** 32 oz. **Length:** 7.72" overall. **Sights:** Adjustable 3-dot. **Features:** Polymer frames, last round lock-open, grip mounted magazine release, magazine disconnect safety, integrated accessory rail, trigger lock. Introduced 2002. Made in U.S.A. by MKS Supply, Inc.

Price: 40SW Poly **$179.00**
Price: 40SW Poly w/laser **$239.00**
Price: 45 ACP **$179.00**
Price: 45 ACP w/laser **$239.00**

KAHR K SERIES AUTO PISTOLS

Caliber: K9: 9mm Para., 7-shot; K40: 40 S&W, 6-shot magazine. **Barrel:** 3.5". **Weight:** 25 oz. **Length:** 6" overall. **Grips:** Wraparound textured soft polymer. **Sights:** Blade front, rear drift adjustable for windage; bar-dot combat style. **Features:** Trigger-cocking double-action mechanism with passive firing pin block. Made of 4140 ordnance steel with matte black finish. Contact maker for complete price list. Introduced 1994. Made in U.S.A. by Kahr Arms.

Price: K9093C K9, matte stainless steel **$855.00**
Price: K9093CN K9, matte stainless steel w/tritium night sights **$985.00**
Price: K9094C K9 matte blackened stainless steel **$891.00**
Price: K9098 K9 Elite 2003, stainless steel **$932.00**
Price: K4043 K40, matte stainless steel **$855.00**
Price: K4043N K40, matte stainless steel w/tritium night sights **$985.00**
Price: K4044 K40, matte blackened stainless steel **$891.00**
Price: K4048 K40 Elite 2003, stainless steel **$932.00**

Kahr MK Series Micro Pistols

Similar to the K9/K40 except is 5.35" overall, 4" high, with a 3.08" barrel. Weighs 23.1 oz. Has snag-free bar-dot sights, polished feed ramp, dual recoil spring system, DA-only trigger. Comes with 5-round flush baseplate and 6-shot grip extension magazine. Introduced 1998. Made in U.S.A. by Kahr Arms.

Price: M9093 MK9, matte stainless steel **$855.00**
Price: M9093N MK9, matte stainless steel, tritium night sights **$958.00**
Price: M9098 MK9 Elite 2003, stainless steel **$932.00**

Kahr TP45

Price: M4043 MK40, matte stainless steel **$855.00**
Price: M4043N MK40, matte stainless steel, tritium night sights **$958.00**
Price: M4048 MK40 Elite 2003, stainless steel **$932.00**

KAHR P SERIES PISTOLS

Caliber: 380 ACP, 9x19, 40 S&W, 45 ACP. Similar to K9/K40 steel frame pistol except has polymer frame, matte stainless steel slide. Barrel length 3.5"; overall length 5.8"; weighs 17 oz. Includes two 7-shot magazines, hard polymer case, trigger lock. Introduced 2000. Made in U.S.A. by Kahr Arms.

Price: KP9093 9mm Para. **$739.00**
Price: KP4043 40 S&W **$739.00**
Price: KP4543 45 ACP **$805.00**
Price: KP3833 380 ACP (2008) **$649.00**

KAHR PM SERIES PISTOLS

Caliber: 9x19, 40 S&W, 45 ACP. Similar to P-Series pistols except has smaller polymer frame (Polymer Micro). Barrel length 3.08"; overall length 5.35"; weighs 17 oz. Includes two 7-shot magazines, hard polymer case, trigger lock. Introduced 2000. Made in U.S.A. by Kahr Arms.

Price: PM9093 PM9 . . . . **$771.00**
Price: PM4043 PM40 . . . . **$771.00**
Price: PM45 (2007) **$838.00**

KAHR T SERIES PISTOLS

Caliber: T9: 9mm Para., 8-shot magazine; T40: 40 S&W, 7-shot magazine. **Barrel:** 4". **Weight:** 28.1-29.1 oz. **Length:** 6.5" overall. **Grips:** Checkered Hogue Pau Ferro wood grips. **Sights:** Rear: Novak low profile 2-dot tritium night sight, front tritium night sight. **Features:** Similar to other Kahr makes, but with longer slide and barrel upper, longer butt. Trigger cocking DAO; lock breech; "Browning-type" recoil lug; passive striker block; no magazine disconnect. Comes with two magazines. Introduced 2004. Made in U.S.A. by Kahr Arms.

Price: KT9093 T9 matte stainless steel **$831.00**
Price: KT9093-NOVAK T9, "Tactical 9," Novak night sight . . . **$968.00**
Price: KT4033 40 S&W. **$831.00**

KAHR TP SERIES PISTOLS

Caliber: TP9: 9mm Para., 7-shot magazine; TP40: 40 S&W, 6-shot magazine. Barrel: 4". **Weight:** 19.1-20.1 oz. **Length:** 6.5-6.7" overall. **Grips:** Textured polymer. Similar to T-series guns, but with polymer frame, matte stainless slide. Comes with two magazines. TP40s introduced 2006. Made in U.S.A. by Kahr Arms.

Price: TP9093 TP9 . . . . **$697.00**
Price: TP9093-Novak TP9 . . . . **$838.00**
Price: TP4043 TP40 . . . . **$697.00**
Price: TP4543 (2007) **$697.00**

Kel-Tec P-3AT

Kel-Tec P-32

Kimber Pro Carry II

Kimber Ultra Carry II

Kimber Gold Match II

Kimber CDP II

KAHR CW SERIES PISTOL

Caliber: 9mm Para., 7-shot magazine; 40 S&W and 45 ACP, 6-shot magazine. **Barrel:** 3.5-3.64". **Weight:** 17.7-18.7 oz. **Length:** 5.9-6.36" overall. **Grips:** Textured polymer. Similar to P-Series, but CW Series have conventional rifling, metal-injection-molded slide stop lever, no front dovetail cut, one magazine. CW40 introduced 2006. Made in U.S.A. by Kahr Arms.

Price: CW9093 CW9 . . . . **$533.00**
Price: CW4043 CW40 . . . . **$533.00**
Price: CW4543 45 ACP (2008) **$566.00**

KEL-TEC P-11 AUTO PISTOL

Caliber: 9mm Para., 10-shot magazine. **Barrel:** 3.1". **Weight:** 14 oz. **Length:** 5.6" overall. **Grips:** Checkered black polymer. **Sights:** Blade front, rear adjustable for windage. **Features:** Ordnance steel slide, aluminum frame. Double-action-only trigger mechanism. Introduced 1995. Made in U.S.A. by Kel-Tec CNC Industries, Inc.

Price: From **$333.00**

KEL-TEC PF-9 PISTOL

Caliber: 9mm Para.; 7 rounds. **Weight:** 12.7 oz. **Sights:** Rear sight adjustable for windage and elevation. **Barrel Length:** 3.1". **Length:** 5.85". **Features:** Barrel, locking system, slide stop, assembly pin, front sight, recoil springs and guide rod adapted from P-11. Trigger system with integral hammer block and the extraction system adapted from P-3AT. MIL-STD-1913 Picatinny rail. Made in U.S.A. by Kel-Tec CNC Industries, Inc.

Price: From **$333.00**

KEL-TEC P-32 AUTO PISTOL

Caliber: 32 ACP, 7-shot magazine. **Barrel:** 2.68". **Weight:** 6.6 oz. **Length:** 5.07" overall. **Grips:** Checkered composite. **Sights:** Fixed. **Features:** Double-action-only mechanism with 6-lb. pull; internal slide stop. Textured composite grip/frame. Now available in 380 ACP. Made in U.S.A. by Kel-Tec CNC Industries, Inc.

Price: From **$318.00**

KEL-TEC P-3AT PISTOL

Caliber: 380 ACP; 7-rounds. **Weight:** 7.2 oz. **Length:** 5.2". **Features:** Lightest 380 ACP made; aluminum frame, steel barrel.

Price: From **$324.00**

KEL-TEC PLR-16 PISTOL

Caliber: 5.56mm NATO; 10-round magazine. **Weight:** 51 oz. **Sights:** Rear sight adjustable for windage, front sight is M-16 blade. **Barrel Length:** 9.2". **Length:** 18.5". **Features:** Muzzle is threaded 1/2"-28 to accept standard attachments such as a muzzle brake. Except for the barrel, bolt, sights, and mechanism, the PLR-16 pistol is made of high-impact glass fiber reinforced polymer. Gas-operated semi-auto. Conventional gas-piston operation with M-16 breech locking system. MIL-STD-1913 Picatinny rail. Made in U.S.A. by Kel-Tec CNC Industries, Inc.

Price: Blued **$665.00**

Kel-Tec PLR-22 Pistol

Similar to PLR-16, except chambered for .22 LR, 27-round magazine. **Weight:** 45 oz. **Barrel length:** 10.1". **Length:** 18.5". Made in U.S.A. by Kel-Tec CNC Industries, Inc.

Price: Blued . . . . **NA**

KIMBER CUSTOM II AUTO PISTOL

Caliber: 45 ACP. **Barrel:** 5". **Weight:** 38 oz. **Length:** 8.7" overall. **Grips:** Checkered black rubber, walnut, rosewood. **Sights:** Dovetailed front and rear, Kimber low profile adj. or fixed sights. **Features:** Slide, frame and barrel machined from steel or stainless steel. Match grade barrel, chamber and trigger group. Extended thumb safety, beveled magazine well, beveled front and rear slide serrations, high ride beavertail grip safety, checkered flat mainspring housing, kidney cut under trigger guard, high cut grip, match grade stainless steel barrel bushing, polished breech face, Commander-style hammer, lowered and flared ejection port, Wolff springs, bead blasted black oxide or matte stainless finish. Introduced in 1996. Made in U.S.A. by Kimber Mfg., Inc.

Price: Custom II **$795.00**
Price: Custom II Walnut (double-diamond walnut grips) **$819.00**

Kimber Stainless II Auto Pistols

Similar to Custom II except has stainless steel frame. 9mm Para. chambering and 45 ACP with night sights introduced 2008. Also chambered in 38 Super. Target version also chambered in 10mm.

Price: Stainless II 45 ACP **$913.00**
Price: Stainless II 38 Super, polished **$1,086.00**
Price: Stainless II 9mm Para. (2008) **$923.00**
Price: Stainless II 45 ACP w/night sights (2008) **$1,066.00**
Price: Stainless II Target 45 ACP (stainless, adj. sight) . . . **$1,025.00**
Price: Stainless II Target 10mm **$1,113.00**

Kimber Pro Carry II Auto Pistol

Similar to Custom II, has aluminum frame, 4" bull barrel fitted directly to the slide without bushing. HD with stainless steel frame. Introduced 1998. Made in U.S.A. by Kimber Mfg., Inc.

Price: Pro Carry II **$834.00**
Price: Pro Carry II w/night sights **$942.00**
Price: Stainless Pro Carry II w/night sights **$1,028.00**
Price: Pro Carry HD II, from **$947.00**

Kimber Compact Stainless II Auto Pistol

Similar to Pro Carry II except has stainless steel frame, 4-inch bbl., grip is .400" shorter than standard, no front serrations. Weighs 34 oz. 45 ACP only. Introduced in 1998. Made in U.S.A. by Kimber Mfg., Inc.

Price: **$947.00**

Kimber Ultra Carry II Auto Pistol

Lightweight aluminum frame, 3" match grade bull barrel fitted to slide without bushing. Grips .4" shorter. Low effort recoil. Weighs 25 oz. Introduced in 1999. Made in U.S.A. by Kimber Mfg., Inc.

Price: Stainless Ultra Carry II 45 ACP **$916.00**
Price: Stainless Ultra Carry II 9mm Para. (2008) **$960.00**
Price: Stainless Ultra Carry II 45 ACP with night sights (2008) **$1,024.00**

Kimber CDP II

North American Arms Guardian

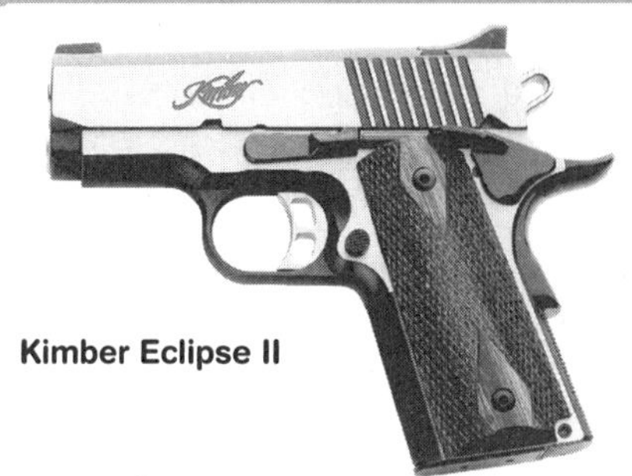

Kimber Eclipse II

Kimber Eclipse Pro II

Korth Auto Pistol

Kimber Gold Match II Auto Pistol

Similar to Custom II models. Includes stainless steel barrel with match grade chamber and barrel bushing, ambidextrous thumb safety, adjustable sight, premium aluminum trigger, hand-checkered double diamond rosewood grips. Barrel hand-fitted for target accuracy. Made in U.S.A. by Kimber Mfg., Inc.

Price: Gold Match II **$1,256.00**
Price: Gold Match Stainless II 45 ACP **$1,427.00**
Price: Gold Match Stainless II 9mm Para. (2008) **$1,458.00**

Kimber Team Match II Auto Pistol

Similar to Gold Match II. Identical to pistol used by U.S.A. Shooting Rapid Fire Pistol Team, available in 45 ACP and 38 Super. Standard features include 30 lines-per-inch front strap extended and beveled magazine well, red, white and blue Team logo grips. Introduced 2008.

Price: **$1,451.00**

Kimber CDP II Series Auto Pistol

Similar to Custom II, but designed for concealed carry. Aluminum frame. Standard features include stainless steel slide, fixed Meprolight tritium 3-dot (green) dovetail-mounted night sights, match grade barrel and chamber, 30 LPI front strap checkering, two-tone finish, ambidextrous thumb safety, hand-checkered double diamond rosewood grips. Introduced in 2000. Made in U.S.A. by Kimber Mfg., Inc.

Price: Ultra CDP II 9mm Para. (2008) **$1,295.00**
Price: Compact CDP II 45 ACP **$1,255.00**
Price: Pro CDP II 45 ACP. **$1,255.00**
Price: Custom CDP II (5" barrel, full length grip) **$1,255.00**

Kimber Eclipse II Series Auto Pistol

Similar to Custom II and other stainless Kimber pistols. Stainless slide and frame, black oxide, two-tone finish. Gray/black laminated grips. 30 lpi front strap checkering. All models have night sights; Target versions have Meprolight adjustable Bar/Dot version. Made in U.S.A. by Kimber Mfg., Inc.

Price: Eclipse Ultra II (3" barrel, short grip) **$1,152.00**
Price: Eclipse Pro II (4" barrel, full length grip) **$1,152.00**
Price: Eclipse Pro Target II (4" barrel, full length grip, adjustable sight) **$1,261.00**
Price: Eclipse Custom II 10mm **$1,209.00**
Price: Eclipse Target II (5" barrel, full length grip, adjustable sight) **$1,261.00**

KIMBER SIS AUTO PISTOL

Caliber: 45 ACP, 7-round magazine. **Barrel:** 3", ramped match grade. **Weight:** 31 oz. **Grips:** Stippled black laminate logo grips. **Sights:** SIS fixed tritium Night Sight with cocking shoulder. **Features:** Named for LAPD Special Investigation Section. Stainless-steel slides, frames and serrated mainspring housings. Flat top slide, solid trigger, SIS-pattern slide serrations, gray KimPro II finish, black small parts. Bumped and grooved beavertail grip safety, Kimber Service Melt on slide and frame edges, ambidextrous thumb safety, stainless steel KimPro Tac-Mag magazine. Rounded mainspring housing and frame on Ultra version. Introduced 2007. Made in U.S.A. by Kimber Mfg., Inc.

Price: SIS Ultra (2008) **$1,316.00**
Price: SIS Pro (2008) **$1,316.00**

Olympic Arms Matchmaster 5

KORTH USA PISTOL SEMI-AUTO

Caliber: 9mm Para., 9x21. **Barrel:** 4", 4.5". **Weight:** 39.9 oz. **Grips:** Walnut, Palisander, Amboinia, Ivory. **Sights:** Fully adjustable. **Features:** DA/SA, 2 models available with either rounded or combat-style trigger guard, recoil-operated, locking block system, forged steel. Available finishes: High polish blue plasma, high polish or matted silver plasma, gray pickled finish, or high polish blue. "Schalldampfer Modell" has special threaded 4.5" barrel and thread protector for a suppressor, many deluxe options available, 10-shot mag. From Korth USA.

Price: From. **$15,000.00**

NORTH AMERICAN ARMS GUARDIAN DAO PISTOL

Caliber: 25 NAA, 32 ACP, 380 ACP, 32 NAA, 6-shot magazine. **Barrel:** 2.49". **Weight:** 20.8 oz. **Length:** 4.75" overall. **Grips:** Black polymer. **Sights:** Low profile fixed. **Features:** Double-action only mechanism. All stainless steel construction. Introduced 1998. Made in U.S.A. by North American Arms.

Price: From. **$402.00**

OLYMPIC ARMS MATCHMASTER 5 1911 PISTOL

Caliber: 45 ACP, 7-shot magazine. **Barrel:** 5" stainless steel. **Weight:** 40 oz. **Length:** 8.75" overall. **Grips:** Smooth walnut with laser-etched scorpion icon. **Sights:** Ramped blade, LPA adjustable rear. **Features:** Matched frame and slide, fitted and head-spaced barrel, complete ramp and throat jobs, lowered and widened ejection port, beveled mag well, hand-stoned-to-match hammer and sear, lightweight long-shoe over-travel adjusted trigger, shaped and tensioned extractor, extended thumb safety, wide beavertail grip safety and full-length guide rod. Made in U.S.A. by Olympic Arms, Inc.

Price: **$899.00**

Olympic Arms Matchmaster 6

Olympic Arms Enforcer

Olympic Arms Cohort

Olympic Arms Big Deuce

Olympic Arms Westerner

Olympic Arms Constable

OLYMPIC ARMS MATCHMASTER 6 1911 PISTOL

Caliber: 45 ACP, 7-shot magazine. **Barrel:** 6" stainless steel. **Weight:** 44 oz. **Length:** 9.75" overall. **Grips:** Smooth walnut with laser-etched scorpion icon. **Sights:** Ramped blade, LPA adjustable rear. **Features:** Matched frame and slide, fitted and head-spaced barrel, complete ramp and throat jobs, lowered and widened ejection port, beveled mag well, hand-stoned-to-match hammer and sear, lightweight long-shoe over-travel adjusted trigger, shaped and tensioned extractor, extended thumb safety, wide beavertail grip safety and full length guide rod. Made in U.S.A. by Olympic Arms, Inc.

Price: $995.00

OLYMPIC ARMS ENFORCER 1911 PISTOL

Caliber: 45 ACP, 6-shot magazine. **Barrel:** 4" bull stainless steel. **Weight:** 35 oz. **Length:** 7.75" overall. **Grips:** Smooth walnut with etched black widow spider icon. **Sights:** Ramped blade front, LPA adjustable rear. **Features:** Compact Enforcer frame. Bushingless bull barrel with triplex counter-wound self-contained recoil system. Matched frame and slide, fitted and head-spaced barrel, complete ramp and throat jobs, lowered and widened ejection port, beveled mag well, hand-stoned-to-match hammer and sear, lightweight longshoe over-travel adjusted trigger, shaped and tensioned extractor, extended thumb safety, wide beavertail grip safety and full length guide rod. Made in U.S.A. by Olympic Arms.

Price: $1,039.00

OLYMPIC ARMS COHORT PISTOL

Caliber: 45 ACP, 7-shot magazine. **Barrel:** 4" bull stainless steel. **Weight:** 36 oz. **Length:** 7.75" overall. **Grips:** Fully checkered walnut. **Sights:** Ramped blade front, LPA adjustable rear. **Features:** Full size 1911 frame. Bushingless bull barrel with triplex counter-wound self-contained recoil system. Matched frame and slide, fitted and head-spaced barrel, complete ramp and throat jobs, lowered and widened ejection port, beveled mag well, hand-stoned-to-match hammer and sear, lightweight long-shoe over-travel adjusted trigger, shaped and tensioned extractor, extended thumb safety, wide beavertail grip safety and full length guide rod. Made in U.S.A. by Olympic Arms.

Price: $975.00

OLYMPIC ARMS BIG DEUCE PISTOL

Caliber: 45 ACP, 7-shot magazine. **Barrel:** 6" stainless steel. **Weight:** 44 oz. **Length:** 9.75" overall. **Grips:** Double diamond checkered exotic cocobolo wood. **Sights:** Ramped blade front, LPA adjustable rear. **Features:** Carbon steel parkerized slide with satin bead blast finish full size frame. Matched frame and slide, fitted and head-spaced barrel, complete ramp and throat jobs, lowered and widened ejection port, beveled mag well, hand-stoned-to-match hammer and sear, lightweight long-shoe over-travel adjusted trigger, shaped and tensioned extractor, extended thumb safety, wide beavertail grip safety and full length guide rod. Made in U.S.A. by Olympic Arms.

Price: $1,039.00

OLYMPIC ARMS WESTERNER SERIES 1911 PISTOLS

Caliber: 45 ACP, 7-shot magazine. **Barrel:** 4", 5", 6" stainless steel. **Weight:** 35-43 oz. **Length:** 7.75-9.75" overall. **Grips:** Smooth ivory laser-etched Westerner icon. **Sights:** Ramped blade, LPA adjustable rear. **Features:** Matched frame and slide, fitted and head-spaced barrel, complete ramp and throat jobs, lowered and widened ejection port, beveled mag well, hand-stoned-to-match hammer and sear, lightweight long-shoe over-travel adjusted trigger, shaped and tensioned extractor, extended thumb safety, wide beavertail grip safety and full length guide rod. Entire pistol is fitted and assembled, then disassembled and subjected to the color case hardening process. Made in U.S.A. by Olympic Arms, Inc.

Price: Constable, 4" barrel, 35 oz. **$1,159.00**
Price: Westerner, 5" barrel, 39 oz. **$1,039.00**
Price: Trail Boss, 6" barrel, 43 oz. **$1,099.00**

OLYMPIC ARMS SCHUETZEN PISTOL WORKS 1911 PISTOLS

Caliber: 45 ACP, 7-shot magazine. **Barrel:** 4", 5.2", bull stainless steel. **Weight:** 35-38 oz. **Length:** 7.75-8.75" overall. **Grips:** Double diamond checkered exotic cocobolo wood. **Sights:** Ramped blade, LPA adjustable rear. **Features:** Carbon steel parkerized slide with satin bead blast finish full size frame. Matched frame and slide, fitted and head-spaced barrel, complete ramp and throat jobs, lowered and widened ejection port, beveled mag well, hand-stoned-to-match hammer and sear, lightweight long-shoe over-travel adjusted trigger, shaped and tensioned extractor, extended thumb safety, wide beavertail grip safety and full length guide rod. Custom made by Olympic Arms Schuetzen Pistol Works. Parts are hand selected and fitted by expert pistolsmiths. Several no-cost options to choose from. Made in U.S.A. by Olympic Arms Schuetzen Pistol Works.

Price: Journeyman, 4" bull barrel, 35 oz. **$1,299.00**
Price: Street Deuce, 5.2" bull barrel, 38 oz. **$1,299.00**

OLYMPIC ARMS OA-93 AR PISTOL

Caliber: 5.56 NATO. **Barrel:** 6.5" button-rifled stainless steel. **Weight:** 4.46 lbs. **Length:** 17" overall. **Sights:** None. **Features:** Olympic Arms integrated recoil system on the upper receiver eliminates the buttstock, flat top upper, free floating tubular match handguard, threaded muzzle with flash suppressor. Made in U.S.A. by Olympic Arms, Inc.

Price: $1,080.00

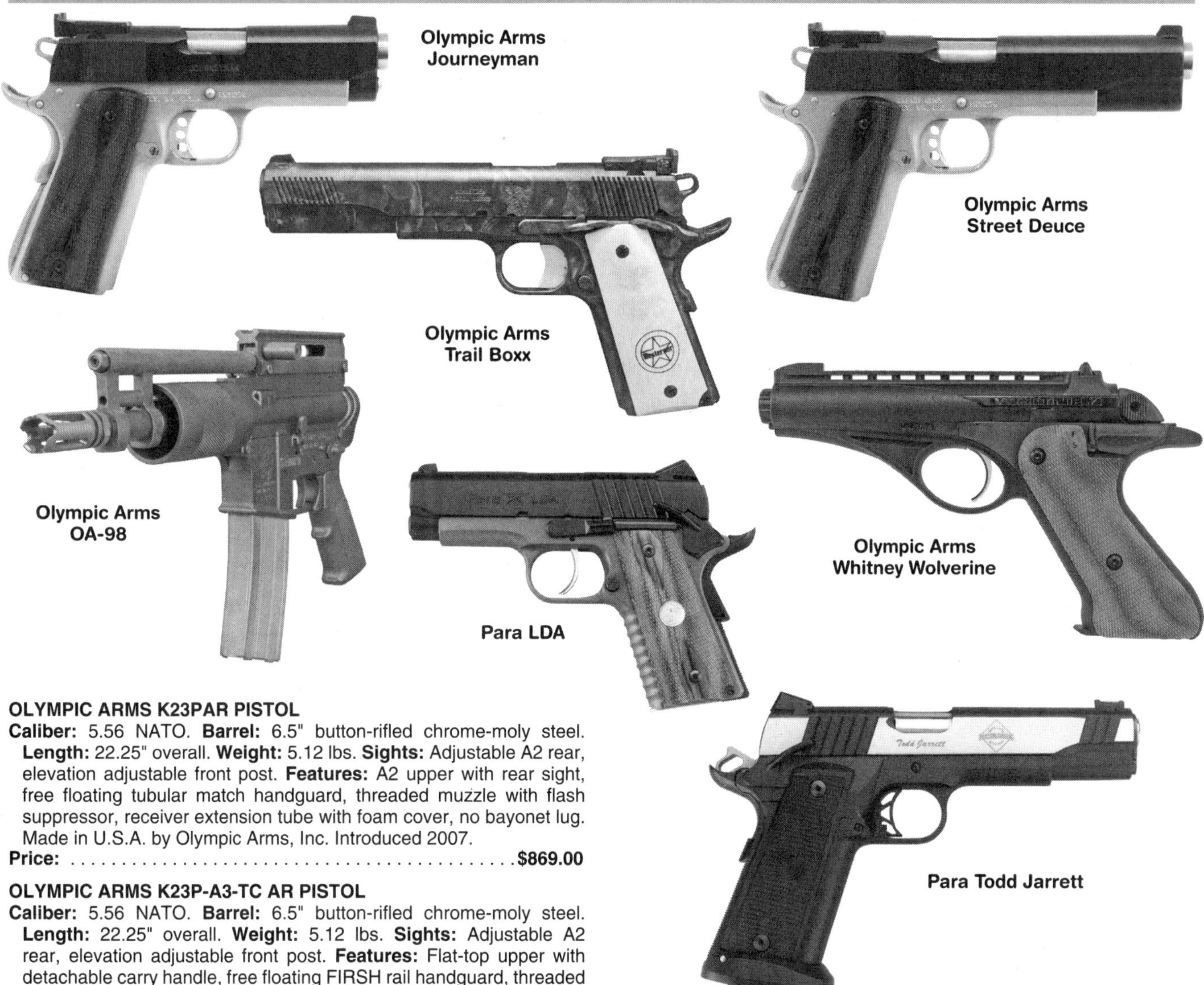
Olympic Arms Journeyman

Olympic Arms Street Deuce

Olympic Arms Trail Boxx

Olympic Arms OA-98

Olympic Arms Whitney Wolverine

Para LDA

Para Todd Jarrett

OLYMPIC ARMS K23PAR PISTOL

Caliber: 5.56 NATO. **Barrel:** 6.5" button-rifled chrome-moly steel. **Length:** 22.25" overall. **Weight:** 5.12 lbs. **Sights:** Adjustable A2 rear, elevation adjustable front post. **Features:** A2 upper with rear sight, free floating tubular match handguard, threaded muzzle with flash suppressor, receiver extension tube with foam cover, no bayonet lug. Made in U.S.A. by Olympic Arms, Inc. Introduced 2007.

Price: **$869.00**

OLYMPIC ARMS K23P-A3-TC AR PISTOL

Caliber: 5.56 NATO. **Barrel:** 6.5" button-rifled chrome-moly steel. **Length:** 22.25" overall. **Weight:** 5.12 lbs. **Sights:** Adjustable A2 rear, elevation adjustable front post. **Features:** Flat-top upper with detachable carry handle, free floating FIRSH rail handguard, threaded muzzle with flash suppressor, receiver extension tube with foam cover, no bayonet lug. Made in U.S.A. by Olympic Arms, Inc. Introduced 2007.

Price: **$1,018.00**

OLYMPIC ARMS WHITNEY WOLVERINE PISTOL

Caliber: 22 LR, 10-shot magazine. **Barrel:** 4.625" stainless steel. **Weight:** 19.2 oz. **Length:** 9" overall. **Grips:** Black checkered with fire/safe markings. **Sights:** Ramped blade front, dovetail rear. **Features:** Polymer frame with natural ergonomics and ventilated rib. Barrel with 6-groove 1x16 twist rate. All metal magazine shell. Made in U.S.A. by Olympic Arms.

Price: **$294.00**

PARA USA PXT 1911 SINGLE-ACTION SINGLE-STACK AUTO PISTOLS

Caliber: 38 Super, 9mm Para., 45 ACP. **Barrel:** 3.5", 4.25", 5". **Weight:** 28-40 oz. **Length:** 7.1-8.5" overall. **Grips:** Checkered cocobolo, textured composition, Mother of Pearl synthetic. **Sights:** Blade front, low-profile Novak Extreme Duty adjustable rear. High visibility 3-dot system. **Features:** Available with alloy, steel or stainless steel frames. Skeletonized trigger, spurred hammer. Manual thumb, grip and firing pin lock safeties. Full-length guide rod. PXT designates new Para Power Extractor throughout the line. Introduced 2004. Made in U.S.A. by Para USA.

Price: 1911 SSP 9mm Para. (2008) **$929.00**

Price: 1911 SSP 45 ACP (2008) **$899.00**

PARA USA PXT 1911 SINGLE-ACTION HIGH-CAPACITY AUTO PISTOLS

Caliber: 9mm Para., 45 ACP, 10//14/18-shot magazines. **Barrel:** 3", 5". **Weight:** 34-40 oz. **Length:** 7.1-8.5" overall. **Grips:** Textured composition. **Sights:** Blade front, low-profile Novak Extreme Duty adjustable rear or fixed sights. High visibility 3-dot system. **Features:** Available with alloy, steel or stainless steel frames. Skeletonized match trigger, spurred hammer, flared ejection port. Manual thumb, grip and firing pin lock safeties. Full-length guide rod. Introduced 2004. Made in U.S.A. by Para USA.

Price: PXT P14-45 Gun Rights (2008), 14+1, 5" barrel **$1,129.00**

Price: P14-45 (2008), 14+1, 5" barrel **$899.00**

Para USA PXT Limited Pistols

Similar to the PXT-Series pistols except with full-length recoil guide system; fully adjustable rear sight; tuned trigger with over-travel stop; beavertail grip safety; competition hammer; front and rear slide serrations; ambidextrous safety; lowered ejection port; ramped match-grade barrel; dove-tailed front sight. Introduced 2004. Made in U.S.A. by Para USA.

Price: Todd Jarrett 40 S&W, 16+1, stainless **$1,729.00**

Para USA LDA Single-Stack Auto Pistols

Similar to LDA-series with double-action trigger mechanism. Cocobolo and polymer grips. Available in 45 ACP. Introduced 1999. Made in U.S.A. by Para USA.

Price: Black Watch Companion, 7+1, 3.5" barrel **$1,049.00**

Price: SSP, 8+1, 5" barrel **$1,079.00**

Para USA LDA Hi-Capacity Auto Pistols

Similar to LDA-series with double-action trigger mechanism. Polymer grips. Available in 9mm Para., 40 S&W, 45 ACP. Introduced 1999. Made in U.S.A. by Para USA.

Price: High-Cap 45, 14+1 . . . . **$1,099.00**

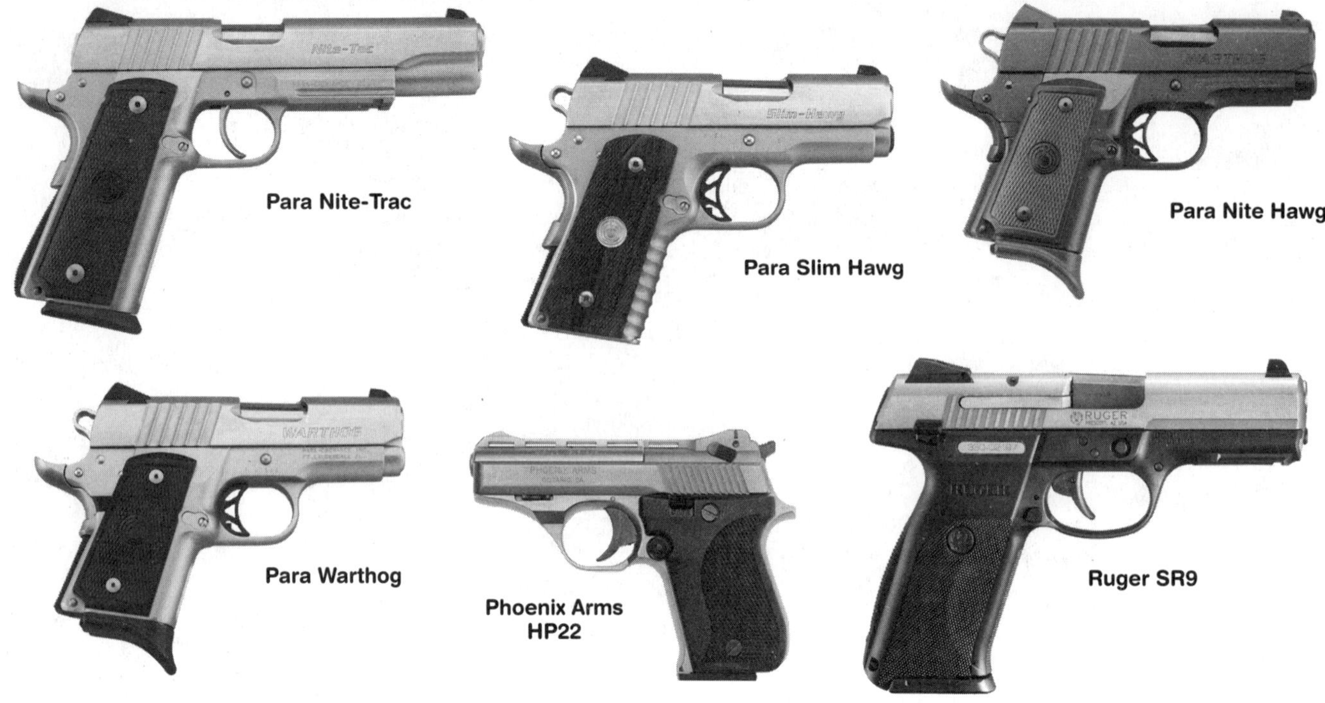
Para Nite-Trac

Para Slim Hawg

Para Nite Hawg

Para Warthog

Phoenix Arms HP22

Ruger SR9

Para USA LDA Light Rail Pistols
Similar to PXT and LDA-series above, with built-in light rail. Polymer grips. Available in 45 ACP. Made in U.S.A. by Para USA.
Price: Nite-Tac 45, stainless **$1,199.00**

PARA USA WARTHOG
Caliber: 9mm Para., 45 ACP, 6, 10, or 12-shot magazines. **Barrel:** 3". **Weight:** 24 to 31.5 oz. **Length:** 6.5". **Grips:** Varies by model. **Features:** Single action. Big Hawg (2008) is full-size .45 ACP on lightweight alloy frame, 14+1, match grade ramped barrel, Power extractor, three white-dot fixed sights. Made in U.S.A. by Para USA.
Price: Slim Hawg (2006) single stack .45 ACP, stainless, 6+1 . . . . **$1,099.00**
Price: Nite Hawg .45 ACP, black finish, 10+1 . . . . **$1,059.00**
Price: Warthog .45 ACP, Regal finish, 10+1 . . . .**$929.00**
Price: Big Hawg (2008). **$929.00**

PHOENIX ARMS HP22, HP25 AUTO PISTOLS
Caliber: 22 LR, 10-shot (HP22), 25 ACP, 10-shot (HP25). **Barrel:** 3". **Weight:** 20 oz. **Length:** 5.5" overall. **Grips:** Checkered composition. **Sights:** Blade front, adjustable rear. **Features:** Single action, exposed hammer; manual hold-open; button magazine release. Available in satin nickel, matte blue finish. Introduced 1993. Made in U.S.A. by Phoenix Arms.
Price: With gun lock **$130.00**
Price: HP Range kit with 5" bbl., locking case and accessories (1 Mag) **$171.00**
Price: HP Deluxe Range kit with 3" and 5" bbls., 2 mags, case **$210.00**

PICUDA .17 MACH-2 GRAPHITE PISTOL
Caliber: 17 HM2, 22 LR, 10-shot magazine. **Barrel:** 10" graphite barrel, "French grey" anodizing. **Weight:** 3.2 pounds. **Length:** 20.5" overall. **Grips:** Barracuda nutmeg laminated pistol stock. **Sights:** None, integral scope base. **Features:** MLP-1722 receiver, target trigger, match bolt kit. Introduced 2008. Made in U.S.A. by Magnum Research, Inc.
Price: **$699.00**

ROCK RIVER ARMS BASIC CARRY AUTO PISTOL
Caliber: 45 ACP. **Barrel:** NA. **Weight:** NA. **Length:** NA. **Grips:** Rosewood, checkered. **Sights:** dovetail front sight, Heinie rear sight. **Features:** NM frame with 20-, 25- or 30-LPI checkered front strap, 5-inch slide with double serrations, lowered and flared ejection port, throated NM Kart barrel with NM bushing, match Commander hammer and match sear, aluminum speed trigger, dehorned, Parkerized finish, one magazine, accuracy guarantee. 3.5 lb. Trigger pull. Introduced 2006. RRA Service Auto 9mm has forged NM frame with beveled mag well, fixed target rear sight and dovetail front sight, KKM match 1:32 twist 9mm Para. barrel with supported ramp. Guaranteed to shoot 1-inch groups at 25 yards with quality 9mm Para. 115-124 grain match ammunition. Intr. 2008. Made in U.S.A. From Rock River Arms.
Price: Basic Carry PS2700 . . . . **$1,600.00**
Price: Limited Match PS2400 . . . . **$2,185.00**
Price: RRA Service Auto 9mm Para. PS2715 . . . . **$1,790.00**

Ruger LCP

ROCK RIVER ARMS LAR-15/LAR-9 PISTOLS
Caliber: .223/5.56mm NATO chamber 4-shot magazine. **Barrel:** 7", 10.5" Wilson chrome moly, 1:9 twist, A2 flash hider, 1/2-28 thread. **Weight:** 5.1 lbs. (7" barrel), 5.5 lbs. (10.5" barrel). **Length:** 23" overall. Stock: Hogue rubber grip. **Sights:** A2 front. **Features:** Forged A2 or A4 upper, single stage trigger, aluminum free-float tube, one magazine. Similar 9mm Para. LAR-9 also available. From Rock River Arms, Inc.
Price: LAR-15 7" A2 AR2115 . . . .**$920.00**
Price: LAR-15 10.5" A4 AR2120. . . . .**$910.00**
Price: LAR-9 7" A2 9MM2115. . . . . **$1,090.00**

RUGER SR9 AUTOLOADING PISTOL
Caliber: 9mm Para. **Barrel:** 4.14". **Weight:** 26.25, 26.5 oz. **Grips:** Glass-filled nylon in two color options—black or OD Green, w/flat or arched reversible backstrap. **Sights:** Adjustable 3-dot, built-in Picatinny-style rail. **Features:** Semi-DA, 6 configurations, striker-fired, through-hardened stainless steel slide, brushed or blackened stainless slide with black grip frame or blackened stainless slide with OD Green grip frame, ambi manual 1911-style safety, ambi mag release, mag disconnect, loaded chamber indicator, Ruger camblock design to absorb recoil, two 10 or 17-shot mags. Intr. 2008. Made in U.S.A. by Sturm, Ruger & Co.
Price: SR9 (17-Round), SR9-10 (SS). **$525.00**
Price: KBSR9 (17-Round), KBSR9-10 (Blackened SS) **$565.00**
Price: KODBSR9 (17-Round), KODBSR9-10 (OD Green Grip) **$565.00**

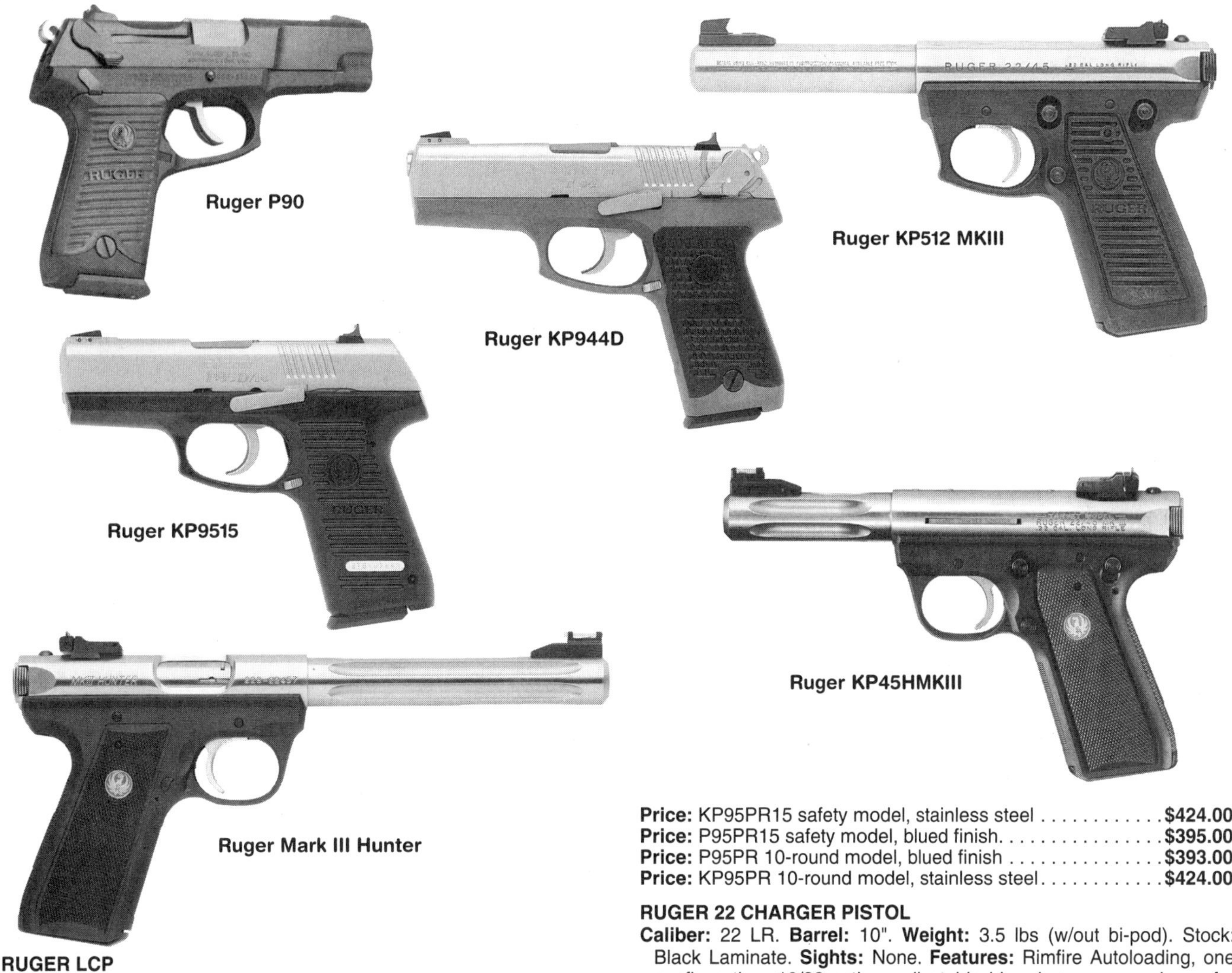
Ruger P90
Ruger KP944D
Ruger KP512 MKIII
Ruger KP9515
Ruger KP45HMKIII
Ruger Mark III Hunter

RUGER LCP

Caliber: 380 ACP. **Barrel:** 2.75" **Weight:** 9.4 oz. **Grips:** Glass-filled nylon. **Sights:** Fixed. **Features:** SA, one configuration, ultra-light compact carry pistol in Ruger's smallest pistol frame, through-hardened stainless steel slide, blued finish, lock breach design, 6-shot mag. Intr. 2008. Made in U.S.A. by Sturm, Ruger & Co.

Price: LCP. **$330.00**

RUGER P90 MANUAL SAFETY MODEL AUTOLOADING PISTOL

Caliber: 45 ACP, 8-shot magazine. **Barrel:** 4.50". **Weight:** 33.5 oz. **Length:** 7.75" overall. **Grips:** Grooved black synthetic composition. **Sights:** Square post front, square notch rear adjustable for windage, both with white dot. **Features:** Double action; ambidextrous slide-mounted safety-levers. Stainless steel only. Introduced 1991.

Price: KP90 with extra mag, loader, case and gunlock **$599.00**
Price: P90 (blue) **$557.00**

Ruger KP94 Autoloading Pistol

Sized midway between full-size P-Series and compact KP94. 4.2" barrel, 7.5" overall length, weighs about 34 oz. KP94 manual safety model. Slide gripping grooves roll over top of slide. KP94 has ambidextrous safety-levers; Stainless slide, barrel, alloy frame. Also blue. Includes hard case and lock, spare magazine. Introduced 1994. Made in U.S.A. by Sturm, Ruger & Co.

Price: P944, blue, manual safety, .40 cal. **$525.00**
Price: KP944 (40-caliber) (manual safety-stainless) **$610.00**

RUGER P95 AUTOLOADING PISTOL

Caliber: 9mm, 15-shot magazine. **Barrel:** 3.9". **Weight:** 30 oz. **Length:** 7.25" overall. **Grips:** Grooved; integral with frame. **Sights:** Blade front, rear drift adjustable for windage; 3-dot system. **Features:** Molded polymer grip frame, stainless steel or chrome-moly slide. Suitable for +P+ ammunition. Safety model, decocker. Introduced 1996. Made in U.S.A. by Sturm, Ruger & Co. Comes with lockable plastic case, spare magazine, loader and lock, Picatinny rails.

Price: KP95PR15 safety model, stainless steel **$424.00**
Price: P95PR15 safety model, blued finish. **$395.00**
Price: P95PR 10-round model, blued finish **$393.00**
Price: KP95PR 10-round model, stainless steel. **$424.00**

RUGER 22 CHARGER PISTOL

Caliber: 22 LR. **Barrel:** 10". **Weight:** 3.5 lbs (w/out bi-pod). Stock: Black Laminate. **Sights:** None. **Features:** Rimfire Autoloading, one configuration, 10/22 action, adjustable bi-pod, new mag release for easier removal, precision-rifled barrel, black matte finish, combination Weaver-style and tip-off scope mount, 10-shot mag. Intr. 2008. Made in U.S.A. by Sturm, Ruger & Co.

Price: CHR22-10. . . . . **$369.50**

RUGER MARK III STANDARD AUTOLOADING PISTOL

Caliber: 22 LR, 10-shot magazine. **Barrel:** 4.5", 4.75", 5.5", 6", or 6-7/8". **Weight:** 33 oz. (4.75" bbl.). **Length:** 9" (4.75" bbl.). **Grips:** Checkered composition grip panels. **Sights:** Fixed, fiber-optic front, fixed rear. **Features:** Updated design of original Standard Auto and Mark II series. Hunter models have lighter barrels. Target models have cocobolo grips; bull, target, competition, and hunter barrels; and adjustable sights. Introduced 2005.

Price: MKIII4, MKIII6 (blued) **$342.00**
Price: MKIII512 (blued bull barrel) **$405.00**
Price: KMKIII512 (stainless bull barrel) **$512.00**
Price: MKIII678 (blued) **$405.00**
Price: KMKIII678GC (stainless slabside barrel) **$589.00**
Price: KMKIII678H (stainless fluted barrel) **$602.00**
Price: KMKIII45HCL (Crimson Trace Laser Grips, intr. 2008) . **$764.00**

Ruger 22/45 Mark III Pistol

Similar to other 22 Mark III autos except has Zytel grip frame that matches angle and magazine latch of Model 1911 45 ACP pistol. Available in 4" standard, 4.5", 5.5", 6-7/8" bull barrels. Comes with extra magazine, plastic case, lock. Introduced 1992. Hunter introduced 2006.

Price: P4MKIII, 4" bull barrel, adjustable sights **$316.00**
Price: P45GCMKIII, 4.5" bull barrel, fixed sights **$314.00**
Price: P512MKIII (5.5" bull blued barrel, adj. sights) **$316.00**
Price: KP512MKIII (5.5" stainless bull barrel, adj. sights **$422.00**
Price: Hunter KP45HMKIII 4.5" barrel (2007), KP678HMKIII, 6-7/8" stainless fluted bull barrel, adj. sights **$517.00**

Sabre Defence Sphinx 9mm

Sabre Defence Sphinx 45 ACP

SIG-Sauer P220

SIG-Sauer P229 Sport

SIG-Sauer P232

SABRE DEFENCE SPHINX PISTOLS

Caliber: 9mm Para., 45 ACP., 10-shot magazine. **Barrel:** 4.43". **Weight:** 39.15 oz. **Length:** 8.27" overall. **Grips:** Textured polymer. **Sights:** Fixed Trijicon Night Sights. **Features:** CNC engineered from stainless steel billet; grip frame in stainless steel, titanium or high-strength aluminum. Integrated accessory rail, high-cut beavertail, decocking lever. Made in Switzerland. Imported by Sabre Defence Industries.

Price: 45 ACP (2007) **$2,990.00**
Price: 9mm Para. Standard, titanium w/decocker **$2,700.00**

SEECAMP LWS 32 STAINLESS DA AUTO

Caliber: 32 ACP Win. Silvertip, 6-shot magazine. **Barrel:** 2", integral with frame. **Weight:** 10.5 oz. **Length:** 4-1/8" overall. **Grips:** Glass-filled nylon. **Sights:** Smooth, no-snag, contoured slide and barrel top. **Features:** Aircraft quality 17-4 PH stainless steel. Inertia-operated firing pin. Hammer fired double-action-only. Hammer automatically follows slide down to safety rest position after each shot, no manual safety needed. Magazine safety disconnector. Polished stainless. Introduced 1985. From L.W. Seecamp.

Price: **$425.00**

SIG SAUER 250 COMPACT AUTO PISTOL

Caliber: 9mm Para. (16-round magazine), 357 SIG, 40 S&W and 45 ACP. **Barrel:** NA. **Weight:** 24.6 oz. **Length:** 7.2" overall. **Grips:** Interchangeable polymer. **Sights:** Siglite night sights. **Features:** Modular design allows for immediate change in caliber and size; subcompact, compact and full. Six different grip combinations for each size. Introduced 2008. From Sig Sauer, Inc.

Price: P250 . . . . **$699.00**

SIG SAUER 1911 PISTOLS

Caliber: 45 ACP, 8-shot magazine. **Barrel:** 5". **Weight:** 40.3 oz. **Length:** 8.65" overall. **Grips:** Checkered wood grips. **Sights:** Novak night sights. Blade front, drift adjustable rear for windage. **Features:** Single-action 1911. Hand-fitted dehorned stainless-steel frame and slide; match-grade barrel, hammer/sear set and trigger; 25-lpi front strap checkering, 20-lpi mainspring housing checkering. Beavertail grip safety with speed bump, extended thumb safety, firing pin safety and hammer intercept notch. Introduced 2005. XO series has contrast sights, Ergo Grip XT textured polymer grips. Target line features adjustable target night sights, match barrel, custom wood grips, non-railed frame in stainless or Nitron finishes. TTT series is two-tone 1911 with Nitron slide and black controls on stainless frame. Includes burled maple grips, adjustable combat night sights. STX line available from Sig Sauer Custom Shop; two-tone 1911, non-railed, Nitron slide, stainless frame, burled maple grips. Polished cocking serrations, flat-top slide, magwell. Carry line has Novak night sights, lanyard attachment point, gray diamondwood or rosewood grips, 8+1 capacity. Compact series has 6+1 capacity, 7.7" OAL, 4.25" barrel, slim-profile wood grips, weighs 30.3 oz. RCS line (Compact SAS) is Customs Shop version with anti-snag dehorning. Stainless or Nitron finish, Novak night sights, slim-profile gray diamondwood or rosewood grips. 6+1 capacity. 1911 C3 (2008) is a 6+1 compact .45 ACP, rosewood custom wood grips, two-tone and Nitron finishes. **Weight:** About 30 ounces unloaded, lightweight alloy frame. **Length:** 7.7". From Sig Sauer, Inc.

Price: Nitron **$1,143.00**
Price: Stainless. **$1,115.00**
Price: XO Black **$958.00**
Price: Target Nitron (2006) **$1,172.00**
Price: TTT (2006) **$1,229.00**
Price: STX (2006) **$1,386.00**
Price: Carry Nitron (2006). **$1,143.00**
Price: Compact Nitron. **$1,143.00**
Price: RCS Nitron **$1,243.00**
Price: C3 (2008) **$1,243.00**

SIG SAUER P220 AUTO PISTOLS

Caliber: 45 ACP, (7- or 8-shot magazine). **Barrel:** 4.4". **Weight:** 27.8 oz. **Length:** 7.8" overall. **Grips:** Checkered black plastic. **Sights:** Blade front, drift adjustable rear for windage. Optional Siglite night sights. **Features:** Double action. Stainless-steel slide, Nitron finish, alloy frame, M1913 Picatinny rail; safety system of decocking lever, automatic firing pin safety block, safety intercept notch, and trigger bar disconnector. Squared combat-type trigger guard. Slide stays open after last shot. Introduced 1976. P220 SAS Anti-Snag has dehorned stainless steel slide, front Siglite Night Sight, rounded trigger guard, dust cover, Custom Shop wood grips. Equinox line is Custom Shop product with Nitron stainless-steel slide with a black hard-anodized alloy frame, brush-polished flats and nickel accents. Truglo tritium fiber-optic front sight, rear Siglite night sight, gray laminated wood grips with checkering and stippling. From Sig Sauer, Inc.

Price: P220R **$929.00**
Price: P220R Two-Tone, matte-stainless slide, black alloy frame. **$1,058.00**
Price: P220 Elite Stainless (2008) **$1,286.00**
Price: P220 Crimson Trace, w/lasergrips **$1,159.00**
Price: P220 Two-Tone SAO, single action (2006), from . . . **$1,086.00**
Price: P220R DAK (2006) **$853.00**
Price: P220R Equinox (2006) **$1,143.00**

SIG SAUER P220 CARRY AUTO PISTOLS

Caliber: 45 ACP, 8-shot magazine. **Barrel:** 3.9". **Weight:** NA. **Length:** 7.1" overall. **Grips:** Checkered black plastic. **Sights:** Blade front, drift adjustable rear for windage. Optional Siglite night sights. **Features:** Similar to full-size P220, except is "Commander" size. Single stack, DA/SA operation, Nitron finish, Picatinny rail, and either post and dot contrast or 3-dot Siglite night sights. Introduced 2005. From Sig Sauer, Inc.

Price: P220 Carry, from **$929.00**
Price: P220 Carry Elite Stainless (2008) **$1,286.00**

SIG-Sauer Mosquito

Smith & Wesson M&P

Smith & Wesson 457 TDA

Smith & Wesson M&P Compact

Smith & Wesson 908

Smith & Wesson M&P 45 Bi-Tone

Sig Sauer P229 DA Auto Pistol

Similar to the P228 except chambered for 9mm Para. (10- or 15-round magazines), 40 S&W, 357 SIG (10- or 12-round magazines). Has 3.86" barrel, 7.1" overall length and 3.35" height. Weight is 32.4 oz. Introduced 1991. Frame made in Germany, stainless steel slide assembly made in U.S.; pistol assembled in U.S. From Sig Sauer, Inc.

Price: P229, from **$929.00**
Price: P229 Platinum Elite (2008). **$1,215.00**

SIG SAUER SP2022 PISTOLS

Caliber: 9mm Para., 357 SIG, 40 S&W, 10-, 12-, or 15-shot magazines. **Barrel:** 3.9". **Weight:** 30.2 oz. **Length:** 7.4" overall. **Grips:** Composite and rubberized one-piece. **Sights:** Blade front, rear adjustable for windage. Optional Siglite night sights. **Features:** Polymer frame, stainless steel slide; integral frame accessory rail; replaceable steel frame rails; left- or right-handed magazine release, two interchangeable grips. From Sig Sauer, Inc.

Price: SP2009, Nitron finish **$613.00**

Sig Sauer P226 Pistols

Similar to the P220 pistol except has 4.4" barrel, measures 7.7" overall, weighs 34 oz. Chambered in 9mm, 357 SIG, or 40 S&W. X-Five series has factory tuned single-action trigger, 5" slide and barrel, ergonomic wood grips with beavertail, ambidextrous thumb safety and stainless slide and frame with magwell, low-profile adjustable target sights, front cocking serrations and a 25-meter factory test target. From Sig Sauer, Inc.

Price: P226R, from **$929.00**

SIG SAUER P232 PERSONAL SIZE PISTOL

Caliber: 380 ACP, 7-shot. **Barrel:** 3.6". **Weight:** 17.6-22.4 oz. **Length:** 6.6" overall. **Grips:** Checkered black composite. **Sights:** Blade front, rear adjustable for windage. **Features:** Double action/single action or DAO. Blow-back operation, stationary barrel. Introduced 1997. From Sig Sauer, Inc.

Price: P232, from **$629.00**

SIG SAUER P239 PISTOL

Caliber: 9mm Para., 8-shot, 357 SIG 40 S&W, 7-shot magazine. **Barrel:** 3.6". **Weight:** 25.2 oz. **Length:** 6.6" overall. **Grips:** Checkered black composite. **Sights:** Blade front, rear adjustable for windage. Optional Siglite night sights. **Features:** SA/DA or DAO; blackened stainless steel slide, aluminum alloy frame. Introduced 1996. Made in U.S.A. by Sig Sauer, Inc.

Price: P239, from **$800.00**

SIG SAUER MOSQUITO PISTOL

Caliber: 22 LR, 10-shot magazine. **Barrel:** 3.9". **Weight:** 24.6 oz. **Length:** 7.2" overall. **Grips:** Checkered black composite. **Sights:** Blade front, rear adjustable for windage. **Features:** Blowback operated, fixed barrel, polymer frame, slide-mounted ambidextrous safety. Introduced 2005. Made in U.S.A. by Sig Sauer, Inc.

Price: Mosquito, from **$343.00**

SMITH & WESSON M&P AUTO PISTOLS

Caliber: 9mm Para., 40 S&W, 357 Auto. **Barrel:** 4.25". **Weight:** 24.25 oz. **Length:** 7.5" overall. **Grips:** One-piece Xenoy, wraparound with straight backstrap. **Sights:** Ramp dovetail mount front; tritium sights optional; Novak Lo-mount Carry rear. **Features:** Zytel polymer frame, embedded stainless steel chassis; stainless steel slide and barrel, stainless steel structural components, black Melonite finish, reversible magazine catch, 3 interchangeable palmswell grip sizes, universal rail, sear deactivation lever, internal lock system, magazine disconnect. Ships with 2 magazines. Internal lock models available. Overall height: 5.5"; width: 1.2"; sight radius: 6.4". Introduced November 2005. 45 ACP version introduced 2007, 10+1 or 14+1 capacity. **Barrel:** 4.5". **Length:** 8.05". **Weight:** 29.6 ounces. **Features:** Picatinny-style equipment rail; black or bi-tone, dark-earth-brown frame. Bi-tone M&P45 includes ambidextrous, frame-mounted thumb safety, take down tool with lanyard attachment. Compact 9mm Para./357 SIG/40 S&W versions introduced 2007. Compacts have 3.5" barrel, OAL 6.7". 10+1 or 12+1 capacity. **Weight:** 21.7 ounces. **Features:** Picatinny-style equipment rail. Made in U.S.A. by Smith & Wesson.

Price: Full Size, from. **$656.00**
Price: Compacts, from **$656.00**
Price: Midsize, from **$695.00**
Price: Crimson Trace Lasergrip models, from **$908.00**
Price: Thumb-safety M&P models, from **$719.00**

SMITH & WESSON MODEL 457 TDA AUTO PISTOL

Caliber: 45 ACP, 7-shot magazine. **Barrel:** 3.75". **Weight:** 29 oz. **Length:** 7.25" overall. **Grips:** One-piece Xenoy, wraparound with straight backstrap. **Sights:** Post front, fixed rear, 3-dot system. **Features:** Aluminum alloy frame, matte blue carbon steel slide; bobbed hammer; smooth trigger. Introduced 1996. Made in U.S.A. by Smith & Wesson.

Price: Model 457, black matte finish **$711.00**

SMITH & WESSON MODEL 908 AUTO PISTOL

Caliber: 9mm Para., 8-shot magazine. **Barrel:** 3.5". **Weight:** 24 oz. **Length:** 6-13/16". **Grips:** One-piece Xenoy, wraparound with straight backstrap. **Sights:** Post front, fixed rear, 3-dot system. **Features:** Aluminum alloy frame, matte blue carbon steel slide; bobbed hammer; smooth trigger. Introduced 1996. Made in U.S.A. by Smith & Wesson.

Price: Model 908, black matte finish **$679.00**
Price: Model 908S, stainless matte finish **$679.00**
Price: Model 908S Carry Combo, with holster **$703.00**

Smith & Wesson 4013 TSW

Smith & Wesson 910 DA

Smith & Wesson 3913 LadySmith

Smith & Wesson SW1911

Springfield Armory EMP

SMITH & WESSON MODEL 4013 TSW AUTO

Caliber: 40 S&W, 9-shot magazine. **Barrel:** 3.5". **Weight:** 26.8 oz. **Length:** 6 3/4" overall. **Grips:** Xenoy one-piece wraparound. **Sights:** Novak 3-dot system. **Features:** Traditional double-action system; stainless slide, alloy frame; fixed barrel bushing; ambidextrous decocker; reversible magazine catch, equipment rail. Introduced 1997. Made in U.S.A. by Smith & Wesson.

Price: Model 4013 TSW **$1,027.00**

SMITH & WESSON MODEL 910 DA AUTO PISTOL

Caliber: 9mm Para., 10-shot magazine. **Barrel:** 4". **Weight:** 28 oz. **Length:** 7-3/8" overall. **Grips:** One-piece Xenoy, wraparound with straight backstrap. **Sights:** Post front with white dot, fixed 2-dot rear. **Features:** Alloy frame, blue carbon steel slide. Slide-mounted decocking lever. Introduced 1995.

Price: **$648.00**

SMITH & WESSON MODEL 3913 TRADITIONAL DOUBLE ACTIONS

Caliber: 9mm Para., 8-shot magazine. **Barrel:** 3.5". **Weight:** 24.8 oz. **Length:** 6.75" overall. **Grips:** One-piece Delrin wraparound, textured surface. **Sights:** Post front with white dot, Novak LoMount Carry with two dots. **Features:** TSW has aluminum alloy frame, stainless slide. Bobbed hammer with no half-cock notch; smooth .304" trigger with rounded edges. Straight backstrap. Equipment rail. Extra magazine included. Introduced 1989. The 3913-LS Ladysmith has frame that is upswept at the front, rounded trigger guard. Comes in frosted stainless steel with matching gray grips. Grips are ergonomically correct for a woman's hand. Novak LoMount Carry rear sight adjustable for windage. Extra magazine included. Introduced 1990.

Price: 3913TSW **$924.00**
Price: 3913-LS **$909.00**

SMITH & WESSON MODEL SW1911 PISTOLS

Caliber: 45 ACP, 8 rounds. **Barrel:** 5". **Weight:** 39 oz. **Length:** 8.7". **Grips:** Wood or rubber. **Sights:** Novak Lo-Mount Carry, white dot front. **Features:** Large stainless frame and slide with matte finish, single-side external safety. No. 108284 has adjustable target rear sight, ambidextrous safety levers, 20-lpi checkered front strap, comes with two 8-round magazines. DK model (Doug Koenig) also has oversized magazine well, Doug Koenig speed hammer, flat competition speed trigger with overtravel stop, rosewood grips with Smith & Wesson silver medallions, oversized magazine well, special serial number run. No. 108295 has olive drab Crimson Trace lasergrips. No. 108299 has carbon-steel frame and slide with polished flats on slide, standard GI recoil guide, laminated double-diamond walnut grips with silver Smith & Wesson medallions, adjustable target sights. Tactical Rail No. 108293 has a Picatinny rail, black Melonite finish, Novak Lo-Mount Carry Sights, scandium alloy frame. Tactical Rail Stainless introduced 2006. SW1911PD gun is Commander size, scandium-alloy frame, 4.25" barrel, 8" OAL, 28.0 oz., non-reflective black matte finish. Gunsite edition has scandium alloy frame, beveled edges, solid match aluminum trigger, Herrett's logoed tactical oval walnut stocks, special serial number run, brass bead Novak front sight. SC model has 4.25" barrel, scandium alloy frame, stainless-steel slide, non-reflective matte finish.

Price: From **$1,051.00**
Price: Crimson Trace Laser Grips **$1,367.00**

SMITH & WESSON ENHANCED SIGMA SERIES DAO PISTOLS

Caliber: 9mm Para., 40 S&W; 10-, 16-shot magazine. **Barrel:** 4". **Weight:** 24.7 oz. **Length:** 7.25" overall. **Grips:** Integral. **Sights:** White dot front, fixed rear; 3-dot system. Tritium night sights available. **Features:** Ergonomic polymer frame; low barrel centerline; internal striker firing system; corrosion-resistant slide; Teflon-filled, electroless-nickel coated magazine, equipment rail. Introduced 1994. Made in U.S.A. by Smith & Wesson.

Price: From **$450.00**

SMITH & WESSON MODEL CS9 CHIEF'S SPECIAL AUTO

Caliber: 9mm Para., 7-shot magazine. **Barrel:** 3". **Weight:** 20.8 oz. **Length:** 6.25" overall. **Grips:** Hogue wraparound rubber. **Sights:** White dot front, fixed 2-dot rear. **Features:** Traditional double-action trigger mechanism. Alloy frame, stainless slide. Ambidextrous safety. Introduced 1999. Made in U.S.A. by Smith & Wesson.

Price: Stainless **$782.00**

SMITH & WESSON MODEL CS45 CHIEF'S SPECIAL AUTO

Caliber: 45 ACP, 6-shot magazine. **Weight:** 23.9 oz. **Features:** Introduced 1999. Made in U.S.A. by Smith & Wesson.

Price: from **$787.00**

SPRINGFIELD ARMORY EMP ENHANCED MICRO PISTOL

Caliber: 9mm Para., 40 S&W; 9-round magazine. **Barrel:** 3" stainless steel match grade, fully supported ramp, bull. **Weight:** 26 oz. **Length:** 6.5" overall. **Grips:** Thinline cocobolo hardwood. **Sights:** Fixed low profile combat rear, dovetail front, 3-dot tritium. **Features:** Two 9-round stainless steel magazines with slam pads, long aluminum match-grade trigger adjusted to 5 to 6 lbs., forged aluminum alloy frame, black hardcoat anodized; dual spring full-length guide rod, forged satin-finish stainless steel slide. Introduced 2007. From Springfield Armory.

Price: 9mm Para. Compact Bi-Tone **$1,329.00**
Price: 40 S&W Compact Bi-Tone (2008) **$1,329.00**

Springfield Armory XD

Springfield Armory XD

Springfield Armory XD 45 ACP Extended

Springfield Armory XD 45 ACP

Springfield Armory 1911A1 Standard

Springfield Armory Full-Size 1911A1

Springfield Armory TRP

SPRINGFIELD ARMORY XD POLYMER AUTO PISTOLS

Caliber: 9mm Para., 40 S&W, 45 ACP. **Barrel:** 3", 4", 5". **Weight:** 20.5-31 oz. **Length:** 6.26-8" overall. **Grips:** Textured polymer. **Sights:** Varies by model; Fixed sights are dovetail front and rear steel 3-dot units. **Features:** Three sizes in X-Treme Duty (XD) line: Sub-Compact (3" barrel), Service (4" barrel), Tactical (5" barrel). Three ported models available. Ergonomic polymer frame, hammer-forged barrel, no-tool disassembly, ambidextrous magazine release, visual/tactile loaded chamber indicator, visual/tactile striker status indicator, grip safety, XD gear system included. Introduced 2004. XD 45 introduced 2006. Compact line introduced 2007. Compacts ship with one extended magazine (13) and one compact magazine (10). From Springfield Armory.

Price: Sub-Compact OD Green 9mm Para./40 S&W, fixed sights **$543.00**
Price: Compact 45 ACP, 4" barrel, Bi-Tone finish (2008) **$589.00**
Price: Compact 45 ACP, 4" barrel, OD green frame, stainless slide (2008) **$653.00**
Price: Service Black 9mm Para./40 S&W, fixed sights **$543.00**
Price: Service Dark Earth 45 ACP, fixed sights **$571.00**
Price: Service Black 45 ACP, external thumb safety (2008)... **$571.00**
Price: V-10 Ported Black 9mm Para./40 S&W **$573.00**
Price: Tactical Black 45 ACP, fixed sights **$616.00**
Price: Service Bi-Tone 40 S&W, Trijicon night sights (2008) .. **$695.00**

SPRINGFIELD ARMORY GI 45 1911A1 AUTO PISTOLS

Caliber: 45 ACP; 6-, 7-, 13-shot magazines. **Barrel:** 3", 4", 5". **Weight:** 28-36 oz. **Length:** 5.5-8.5" overall. **Grips:** Checkered double-diamond walnut, "U.S" logo. **Sights:** Fixed GI style. **Features:** Similar to WWII GI-issue 45s at hammer, beavertail, mainspring housing. From Springfield Armory.

Price: GI .45 4" Champion Lightweight, 7+1, 28 oz. **$619.00**
Price: GI .45 5" High Capacity, 13+1, 36 oz. **$676.00**
Price: GI .45 5" OD Green, 7+1, 36 oz. **$619.00**
Price: GI .45 3" Micro Compact, 6+1, 32 oz. **$667.00**

SPRINGFIELD ARMORY MIL-SPEC 1911A1 AUTO PISTOLS

Caliber: 38 Super, 9-shot magazines; 45 ACP, 7-shot magazines. **Barrel:** 5". **Weight:** 35.6-39 oz. **Length:** 8.5-8.625" overall. **Features:** Similar to GI 45s. From Springfield Armory.

Price: Mil-Spec Parkerized, 7+1, 35.6 oz. **$715.00**
Price: Mil-Spec Stainless Steel, 7+1, 36 oz. **$784.00**
Price: Mil-Spec 38 Super, 9+1, 39 oz. **$775.00**

Springfield Armory Custom Loaded Champion 1911A1 Pistol

Similar to standard 1911A1, slide and barrel are 4". 7.5" OAL. Available in 45 ACP only. Novak Night Sights. Delta hammer and cocobolo grips. Parkerized or stainless. Introduced 1989.

Price: Stainless, 34 oz. **$1,031.00**
Price: Lightweight, 28 oz. **$989.00**

Springfield Armory Custom Loaded Ultra Compact Pistol

Similar to 1911A1 Compact, shorter slide, 3.5" barrel, 6+1, 7" OAL. Beavertail grip safety, beveled magazine well, fixed sights. Videki speed trigger, flared ejection port, stainless steel frame, blued slide, match grade barrel, rubber grips. Introduced 1996. From Springfield Armory.

Price: Stainless Steel **$1,031.00**

SPRINGFIELD ARMORY CUSTOM LOADED MICRO-COMPACT 1911A1 PISTOL

Caliber: 45 ACP, 6+1 capacity. **Barrel:** 3" 1:16 LH. **Weight:** 24-32 oz. **Length:** 4.7". **Grips:** Slimline cocobolo. **Sights:** Novak LoMount tritium. Dovetail front. **Features:** Aluminum hard-coat anodized alloy frame, forged steel slide, forged barrel, ambi-thumb safety, Extreme Carry Bevel dehorning. Lockable plastic case, 2 magazines.

Price: Lightweight Bi-Tone **$992.00**

SPRINGFIELD ARMORY CUSTOM LOADED LONG SLIDE 1911A1 PISTOL

Caliber: 45 ACP, 7+1 capacity. **Barrel:** 6" 1:16 LH. **Weight:** 41 oz. **Length:** 9.5". **Grips:** Slimline cocobolo. **Sights:** Dovetail front; fully adjustable target rear. **Features:** Longer sight radius, 7.9".

Price: Bi-Tone Operator w/light rail **$1,189.00**

Springfield Armory Tactical Response Loaded Pistols

Similar to 1911A1 except 45 ACP only, checkered front strap and main-spring housing, Novak Night Sight combat rear sight and matching dove-tailed front sight, tuned, polished extractor, oversize barrel link; lightweight speed trigger and combat action job, match barrel and bushing, extended ambidextrous thumb safety and fitted beavertail grip safety. Checkered cocobolo wood grips, comes with two Wilson 7-shot magazines. Frame is engraved "Tactical" both sides of frame with "TRP." Introduced 1998. TRP-Pro Model meets FBI specifications for SWAT Hostage Rescue Team. From Springfield Armory.

Price: 45 TRP Service Model, black Armory Kote finish, fixed Trijicon night sights **$1,741.00**

Taurus 22

Taurus 1911B-1

Taurus 24-7 OSS

Taurus 92

Taurus 24

Taurus 99SS

Taurus 100

Taurus 132 Millennium Pro

TAURUS MODEL 800 SERIES
Caliber: 9mm Para., 40 S&W, 45 ACP. **Barrel:** 4". **Weight:** 32 oz. **Length:** 8.25". **Grips:** Checkered. **Sights:** Novak. **Features:** DA/SA. Blue and Stainless Steel finish. Introduced in 2007. Imported from Brazil by Taurus International.
Price: 809B, 9mm Para., Blue, 17+1 .... **$623.00**

TAURUS MODEL 1911
Caliber: 45 ACP, 8+1 capacity. **Barrel:** 5". **Weight:** 33 oz. **Length:** 8.5". **Grips:** Checkered Black. **Sights:** Heinie Straight 8. **Features:** SA. Blue, Stainless Steel, Duotone Blue, and Blue/Gray finish. Standard/ Picatinny Rail, Standard Frame, Alloy Frame, and Alloy/Picatinny Rail. Introduced in 2007. Imported from Brazil by Taurus International.
Price: 1911B, Blue **$719.00**
Price: 1911SS, Stainless Steel **$816.00**
Price: 1911SS-1, Stainless Steel **$847.00**
Price: 1911 DT, Duotone Blue **$795.00**

TAURUS MODEL 917
Caliber: 9mm Para., 19+1 capacity. **Barrel:** 4.3". **Weight:** 32.2 oz. **Length:** 8.5". **Grips:** Checkered Rubber. **Sights:** Fixed. **Features:** SA/DA. Blue and Stainless Steel finish. Medium Frame. Introduced in 2007. Imported from Brazil by Taurus International.
Price: 917B-20, Blue **$542.00**
Price: 917SS-20, Stainless Steel **$559.00**

TAURUS MODEL 22/25 AUTO PISTOLS
Caliber: 22 LR, 8-shot (PT 22); 25 ACP, 9-shot (PT 25). **Barrel:** 2.75". **Weight:** 12.3 oz. **Length:** 5.25" overall. **Grips:** Smooth rosewood or mother-of-pearl. **Sights:** Fixed. **Features:** Double action. Tip-up barrel for loading, cleaning. Blue, nickel, duo-tone or blue with gold accents. Introduced 1992. Made in U.S.A. by Taurus International.
Price: 22B or 25B, checkered wood grips................ **$248.00**

TAURUS MODEL 24/7
Caliber: 9mm Para., 40 S&W, 45 ACP. **Barrel:** 4". **Weight:** 27.2 oz. **Length:** 7-1/8". **Grips:** "Ribber" rubber-finned overlay on polymer. **Sights:** Adjustable. **Features:** SA/DA; accessory rail, four safeties, blue or stainless finish. One-piece guide rod, flush-fit magazine, flared bushingless barrel, Picatinny accessory rail, manual safety, user changeable sights, loaded chamber indicator, tuned ejector and lowered port, one piece guide rod and flat wound captive spring. Introduced 2003. Long Slide models have 5" barrels, measure 8-1/8" overall, weigh 27.2 oz. Imported from Brazil by Taurus International.
Price: 40BP, 40 S&W, blued, 10+1 or 15+1 .... **$452.00**

TAURUS MODEL 92 AUTO PISTOL
Caliber: 9mm Para., 10- or 17-shot mags. **Barrel:** 5". **Weight:** 34 oz. **Length:** 8.5" overall. **Grips:** Checkered rubber, rosewood, mother-of-pearl. **Sights:** Fixed notch rear. 3-dot sight system. Also offered with micrometer-click adjustable night sights. **Features:** Double action, ambidextrous 3-way hammer drop safety, allows cocked & locked carry. Blue, stainless steel, blue with gold highlights, stainless steel with gold highlights, forged aluminum frame, integral key-lock. .22 LR conversion kit available. Imported from Brazil by Taurus International.
Price: Blued or Stainless, from **$542.00**

Taurus Model 99 Auto Pistol
Similar to 92, fully adjustable rear sight.
Price: From **$559.00**

TAURUS MODEL 100/101 AUTO PISTOL
Caliber: 40 S&W, 10- or 11-shot mags. **Barrel:** 5". **Weight:** 34 oz. **Length:** 8.5". **Grips:** Checkered rubber, rosewood, mother-of-pearl. **Sights:** 3-dot fixed or adjustable; night sights available. **Features:** Single/double action with three-position safety/decocker. Reintroduced in 2001. Imported by Taurus International.
Price: From **$542.00**

TAURUS MODEL 111 MILLENNIUM PRO AUTO PISTOL
Caliber: 9mm Para., 10- or 12-shot mags. **Barrel:** 3.25". **Weight:** 18.7 oz. **Length:** 6-1/8" overall. **Grips:** Checkered polymer. **Sights:** 3-dot fixed; night sights available. Low profile, 3-dot combat. **Features:** Double action only, polymer frame, matte stainless or blue steel slide, manual safety, integral key-lock. Deluxe models with wood grip inserts.
Price: From....................................... **$419.00**
Price: 111Pti titanium slide **$592.00**

TAURUS 132 MILLENNIUM PRO AUTO PISTOL
Caliber: 32 ACP, 10-shot mag. **Barrel:** 3.25". **Weight:** 18.7 oz. **Grips:** Polymer. **Sights:** 3-dot fixed; night sights available. **Features:** Double-action-only, polymer frame, matte stainless or blue steel slide, manual safety, integral key-lock action. Introduced 2001.
Price: From....................................... **$419.00**

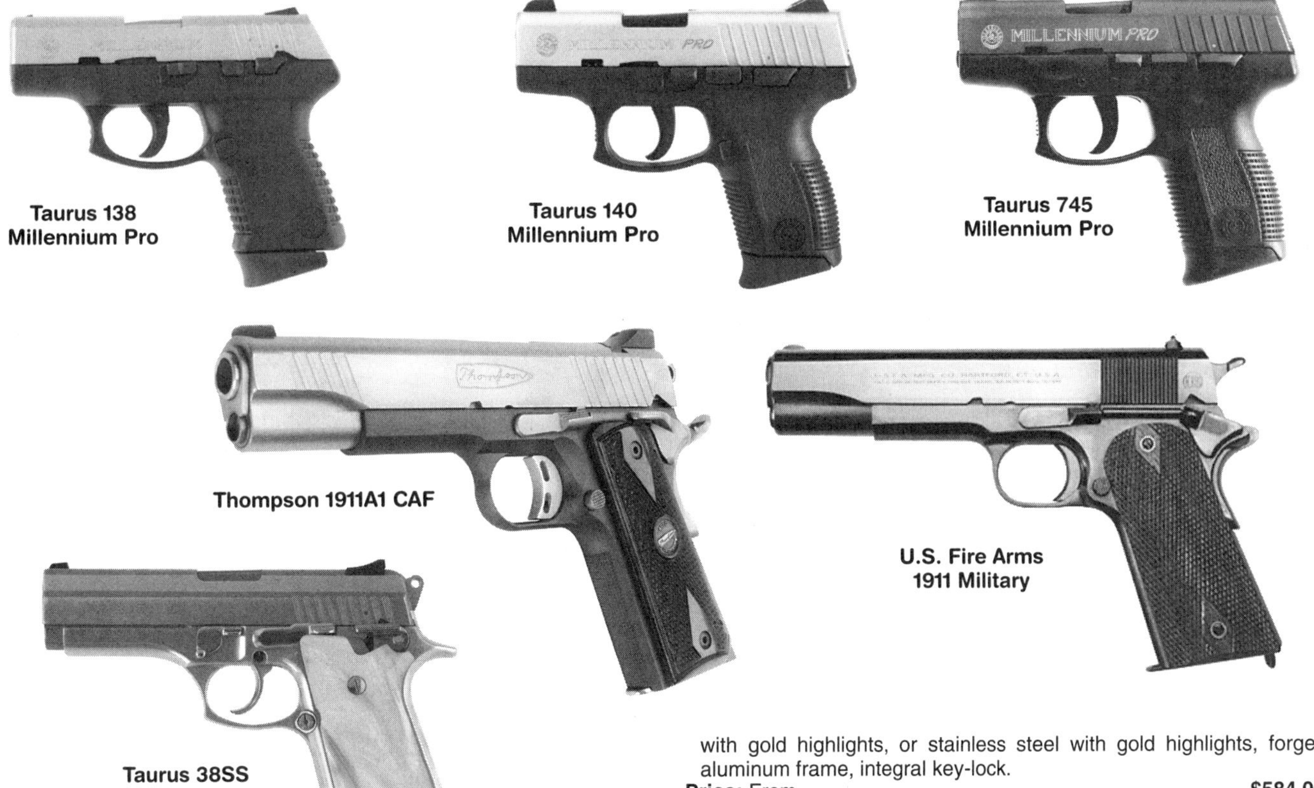
Taurus 138 Millennium Pro

Taurus 140 Millennium Pro

Taurus 745 Millennium Pro

Thompson 1911A1 CAF

U.S. Fire Arms 1911 Military

Taurus 38SS

TAURUS 138 MILLENNIUM PRO SERIES

Caliber: 380 ACP, 10- or 12-shot mags. **Barrel:** 3.25". **Weight:** 18.7 oz. **Grips:** Polymer. **Sights:** Fixed 3-dot fixed. **Features:** Double-action-only, polymer frame, matte stainless or blue steel slide, manual safety, integral key-lock.

Price: From **$419.00**

TAURUS 140 MILLENNIUM PRO AUTO PISTOL

Caliber: 40 S&W, 10-shot mag. **Barrel:** 3.25". **Weight:** 18.7 oz. **Grips:** Checkered polymer. **Sights:** 3-dot fixed; night sights available. **Features:** Double action only; matte stainless or blue steel slide, black polymer frame, manual safety, integral key-lock action. From Taurus International.

Price: From **$436.00**

TAURUS 145 MILLENNIUM AUTO PISTOL

Caliber: 45 ACP, 10-shot mag. **Barrel:** 3.27". **Weight:** 23 oz. Stock: Checkered polymer. **Sights:** 3-dot fixed; night sights available. **Features:** Double-action only, matte stainless or blue steel slide, black polymer frame, manual safety, integral key-lock. Compact model is 6+1 with a 3.25" barrel, weighs 20.8 oz. From Taurus International.

Price: 145BP, blued **$436.00**
Price: 145SSP, stainless, ... **$453.00**

TAURUS MODEL 911 AUTO PISTOL

Caliber: 9mm Para., 10-shot mag. **Barrel:** 4". **Weight:** 28.2 oz. **Length:** 7" overall. **Grips:** Checkered rubber, rosewood, mother-of-pearl. **Sights:** Fixed, 3-dot blue or stainless; night sights optional. **Features:** Double action, semi-auto ambidextrous 3-way hammer drop safety, allows cocked & locked carry. Blue, stainless steel, blue with gold highlights, or stainless steel with gold highlights, forged aluminum frame, integral key-lock.

Price: From **$584.00**

TAURUS MODEL 940 AUTO PISTOL

Caliber: 40 S&W, 10-shot mag. **Barrel:** 3-5/8". **Weight:** 28.2 oz. **Length:** 7" overall. **Grips:** Checkered rubber, rosewood or mother-of-pearl. **Sights:** Fixed, 3-dot blue or stainless; night sights optional. **Features:** Double action, semi-auto ambidextrous 3-way hammer drop safety, allows cocked & locked carry. Blue, stainless steel, blue with gold highlights, or stainless steel with gold highlights, forged aluminum frame, integral key-lock.

Price: From **$584.00**

TAURUS MODEL 945/38S SERIES

Caliber: 45 ACP, 8-shot mag. **Barrel:** 4.25". **Weight:** 28.2/29.5 oz. **Length:** 7.48" overall. **Grips:** Checkered rubber, rosewood or mother-of-pearl. **Sights:** Fixed, 3-dot; night sights optional. **Features:** Double-action with ambidextrous 3-way hammer drop safety allows cocked & locked carry. Forged aluminum frame, 945C has ported barrel/slide. Blue, stainless, blue with gold highlights, stainless with gold highlights, integral key-lock. Introduced 1995. 38 Super line based on 945 frame introduced 2005. 38S series is 10+1, 30 oz., 7.5" overall. Imported by Taurus International.

Price: From **$625.00**

THOMPSON CUSTOM 1911A1 AUTOMATIC PISTOL

Caliber: 45 ACP, 7-shot magazine. **Barrel:** 4.3". **Weight:** 34 oz. **Length:** 8" overall. **Grips:** Checkered laminate grips with a Thompson bullet logo inlay. **Sights:** Front and rear sights are black with serrations and are dovetailed into the slide. **Features:** Machined from 420 stainless steel, matte finish. Thompson bullet logo on slide. Flared ejection port, angled front and rear serrations on slide, 20-lpi checkered mainspring housing and frontstrap. Adjustable trigger, combat hammer, stainless steel full-length recoil guide rod, extended beavertail grip safety; extended magazine release; checkered slide-stop lever. Made in U.S.A. by Kahr Arms.

Price: 1911TC, 5", 39 oz., 8.5" overall, stainless frame **$813.00**

THOMPSON TA5 1927A-1 LIGHTWEIGHT DELUXE PISTOL

Caliber: 45 ACP, 50-round drum magazine. **Barrel:** 10.5" 1:16 right-hand twist. **Weight:** 94.5 oz. **Length:** 23.3" overall. **Grips:** Walnut, horizontal foregrip **Sights:** Blade front, open rear adjustable. **Features:** Based on Thompson machine gun design. Introduced 2008. Made in U.S.A. by Kahr Arms.

Price: TA5 (2008) **$1,117.00**

U.S. FIRE ARMS 1910 COMMERCIAL MODEL AUTOMATIC PISTOL

Caliber: 45 ACP, 7-shot magazine. **Barrel:** 5". **Weight:** NA. **Length:** NA. **Grips:** Browning original wide design, full checkered diamond walnut grips. **Sights:** Fixed. **Features:** High polish Armory Blue, fire blue appointments, 1905 patent dates, grip safety, small contoured checkered thumb safety and round 1905 fire blue hammer with hand cut checkering. Introduced 2006. Made in U.S.A. by United States Fire Arms Mfg. Co.

Price: **$1,895.00**

Walther PPK/S
U.S. Fire Arms Super 38
Walther PPK
Walther P99
Walther P22

U.S. FIRE ARMS 1911 MILITARY MODEL AUTOMATIC PISTOL
Caliber: 45 ACP, 7-shot magazine. **Barrel:** 5". **Weight:** NA. **Length:** NA. **Grips:** Browning original wide design, full checkered diamond walnut grips. **Sights:** Fixed. **Features:** Military polish Armory Blue, fire blue appointments, 1905 patent dates, grip safety, small contoured checkered thumb safety and round 1905 fire blue hammer with hand cut checkering. Introduced 2006. Made in U.S.A. by United States Fire Arms Mfg. Co.
Price: **$1,895.00**

U.S. FIRE ARMS SUPER 38 AUTOMATIC PISTOL
Caliber: 38 Auto, 9-shot magazine. **Barrel:** 5". **Weight:** NA. **Length:** NA. **Grips:** Browning original wide design, full checkered diamond walnut grips. **Sights:** Fixed. **Features:** Armory blue, fire blue appointments, 1913 patent date, grip safety, small contoured checkered thumb safety and spur 1911 hammer with hand cut checkering. Supplied with two Super 38 Auto. mags. Super .38 roll mark on base. Introduced 2006. Made in U.S.A. by United States Fire Arms Mfg. Co.
Price: **$1,995.00**

U.S. FIRE ARMS ACE 22 LONG RIFLE AUTOMATIC PISTOL
Caliber: 22 LR, 10-shot magazine. **Barrel:** 5". **Weight:** NA. **Length:** NA. **Grips:** Browning original wide design, full checkered diamond walnut grips. **Sights:** Fixed. **Features:** Armory blue commercial finish, fire blue appointments, 1913 patent date, grip safety, small contoured checkered thumb safety and spur 1911 hammer with hand cut checkering. Supplied with two magazines. Ace roll mark on base. Introduced 2006. Made in U.S.A. by United States Fire Arms Mfg. Co.
Price: **$1,995.00**

WALTHER PPS PISTOL
Caliber: 9mm Para., 40 S&W. 6-, 7-, 8-shot magazines for 9mm Para.; 5-, 6-, 7-shot magazines for 40 S&W. **Barrel:** 3.2". **Weight:** 19.4 oz. **Length:** 6.3" overall. Stocks: Stippled black polymer. **Sights:** Picatinny-style accessory rail, 3-dot low-profile contoured sight. **Features:** PPS-"Polizeipistole Schmal," or Police Pistol Slim. Measures 1.04 inches wide. Ships with 6- and 7-round magazines. Striker-fired action, flat slide stop lever, alternate backstrap sizes. QuickSafe feature decocks striker assembly when backstrap is removed. Loaded chamber indicator. First Edition model, limited to 1,000 units, has anthracite grey finish, aluminum gun case. Introduced 2008. Made in U.S.A. by Smith & Wesson.
Price: **$665.00**
Price: First Edition. **$665.00**

WALTHER PPK/S AMERICAN AUTO PISTOL
Caliber: 32 ACP, 380 ACP, 7-shot magazine. **Barrel:** 3.27". **Weight:** 23-1/2 oz. Length: 6.1" overall. Stocks: Checkered plastic. **Sights:** Fixed, white markings. **Features:** Double action; manual safety blocks firing pin and drops hammer; chamber loaded indicator on 32 and 380; extra finger rest magazine provided. Made in the United States. Introduced 1980. Made in U.S.A. by Smith & Wesson.
Price: **$573.00**

Walther PPK American Auto Pistol
Similar to Walther PPK/S except weighs 21 oz., has 6-shot capacity. Made in the U.S. Introduced 1986. Made in U.S.A. by Smith & Wesson.
Price: Stainless, 32 ACP or 380 ACP **$573.00**

WALTHER P99 AUTO PISTOL
Caliber: 9mm Para., 9x21, 40 S&W, 10-shot magazine. **Barrel:** 4". **Weight:** 25 oz. Length: 7" overall. **Grips:** Textured polymer. **Sights:** Blade front (comes with three interchangeable blades for elevation adjustment), micrometer rear adjustable for windage. **Features:** Double-action mechanism with trigger safety, decock safety, internal striker safety; chamber loaded indicator; ambidextrous magazine release levers; polymer frame with interchangeable backstrap inserts. Comes with two magazines. Introduced 1997. Made in U.S.A. by Smith & Wesson.
Price: From **$740.00**

WALTHER P22 PISTOL
Caliber: 22 LR. **Barrel:** 3.4", 5". **Weight:** 19.6 oz. (3.4"), 20.3 oz. (5"). **Length:** 6.26", 7.83". **Grips:** NA. **Sights:** Interchangeable white dot, front, 2-dot adjustable, rear. **Features:** A rimfire version of the Walther P99 pistol, available in nickel slide with black frame, or green frame with black slide versions. Made in U.S.A. by Smith & Wesson.
Price: From **$335.00**

WILSON COMBAT ELITE PROFESSIONAL
Caliber: 9mm Para., 38 Super, 40 S&W; 45 ACP, 8-shot magazine. **Barrel:** Compensated 4.1" hand-fit, heavy flanged cone match grade. **Weight:** 36.2 oz. Length: 7.7" overall. **Grips:** Cocobolo. **Sights:** Combat Tactical yellow rear tritium inserts, brighter green tritium front insert. **Features:** High-cut front strap, 30-lpi checkering on front strap and flat mainspring housing, High-Ride Beavertail grip safety. Dehorned, ambidextrous thumb safety, extended ejector, skeletonized ultralight hammer, ultralight trigger, Armor-Tuff finish on frame and slide. Introduced 1997. Made in U.S.A. by Wilson Combat.
Price: **$3,050.00**

Includes models suitable for several forms of competition and other sporting purposes.

Baer 1911 Ultimate Master

Baer 1911 Bullseye Wadcutter

Colt Gold Cup Model O

Colt Special Combat Government

Competitor Single Shot

BAER 1911 ULTIMATE MASTER COMBAT PISTOL
Caliber: 38 Super, 400 Cor-Bon 45 ACP (others available), 10-shot magazine. **Barrel:** 5", 6"; Baer NM. **Weight:** 37 oz. **Length:** 8.5" overall. **Grips:** Checkered cocobolo. **Sights:** Baer dovetail front, low-mount Bo-Mar rear with hidden leaf. **Features:** Full-house competition gun. Baer forged NM blued steel frame and double serrated slide; Baer triple port, tapered cone compensator; fitted slide to frame; lowered, flared ejection port; Baer reverse recoil plug; full-length guide rod; recoil buff; beveled magazine well; Baer Commander hammer, sear; Baer extended ambidextrous safety, extended ejector, checkered slide stop, beavertail grip safety with pad, extended magazine release button; Baer speed trigger. Made in U.S.A. by Les Baer Custom, Inc.
Price: 45 ACP Compensated **$2,790.00**
Price: 38 Super Compensated **$2,940.00**

BAER 1911 NATIONAL MATCH HARDBALL PISTOL
Caliber: 45 ACP, 7-shot magazine. **Barrel:** 5". **Weight:** 37 oz. Length: 8.5" overall. **Grips:** Checkered walnut. **Sights:** Baer dovetail front with under-cut post, low-mount Bo-Mar rear with hidden leaf. **Features:** Baer NM forged steel frame, double serrated slide and barrel with stainless bushing; slide fitted to frame; Baer match trigger with 4-lb. pull; polished feed ramp, throated barrel; checkered front strap, arched mainspring housing; Baer beveled magazine well; lowered, flared ejection port; tuned extractor; Baer extended ejector, checkered slide stop; recoil buff. Made in U.S.A. by Les Baer Custom, Inc.
Price: **$1,890.00**

Baer 1911 Bullseye Wadcutter Pistol
Similar to National Match Hardball except designed for wadcutter loads only. Polished feed ramp and barrel throat; Bo-Mar rib on slide; full length recoil rod; Baer speed trigger with 3-1/2-lb. pull; Baer deluxe hammer and sear; Baer beavertail grip safety with pad; flat mainspring housing checkered 20 lpi. Blue finish; checkered walnut grips. Made in U.S.A. by Les Baer Custom, Inc.
Price: From **$1,890.00**

BF CLASSIC PISTOL
Caliber: Customer orders chamberings. **Barrel:** 8-15" Heavy Match Grade with 11-degree target crown. **Weight:** Approx 3.9 lbs. **Length:** From 16" overall. **Grips:** Thumbrest target style. **Sights:** Bo-Mar/Bond ScopeRib I Combo with hooded post front adjustable for height and width, rear notch available in .032", .062", .080" and .100" widths; 1/2-MOA clicks. **Features:** Hand fitted and headspaced, drilled and tapped for scope mount. Etched receiver; gold-colored trigger. Introduced 1988. Made in U.S.A. by E. Arthur Brown Co. Inc.
Price: **$699.00**

COLT GOLD CUP MODEL O PISTOL
Caliber: 45 ACP, 8-shot magazine. **Barrel:** 5", with new design bushing. **Weight:** 39 oz. **Length:** 8.5". **Grips:** Checkered rubber composite with silver-plated medallion. **Sights:** Patridge-style front, Bo-Mar-style rear adjustable for windage and elevation, sight radius 6.75". **Features:** Arched or flat housing; wide, grooved trigger with adjustable stop; ribbed-top slide, hand fitted, with improved ejection port.
Price: Blue **$1,022.00**
Price: Stainless **$1,071.00**

COLT SPECIAL COMBAT GOVERNMENT
Caliber: 45 ACP, 38 Super. **Barrel:** 5". **Weight:** 39 oz. Length: 8.5". **Grips:** Rosewood w/double diamond checkering pattern. **Sights:** Clark dovetail, front; Bo-Mar adjustable, rear. **Features:** A competition-ready pistol with enhancements such as skeletonized trigger, upswept grip safety, custom tuned action, polished feed ramp. Blue or satin nickel finish. Introduced 2003. Made in U.S.A. by Colt's Mfg. Co.
Price: **$1,676.00**

COMPETITOR SINGLE-SHOT PISTOL
Caliber: 22 LR through 50 Action Express, including belted magnums. **Barrel:** 14" standard; 10.5" silhouette; 16" optional. **Weight:** About 59 oz. (14" bbl.). **Length:** 15.12" overall. **Grips:** Ambidextrous; synthetic (standard) or laminated or natural wood. **Sights:** Ramp front, adjustable rear. **Features:** Rotary cannon-type action cocks on opening; cammed ejector; interchangeable barrels, ejectors. Adjustable single stage trigger, sliding thumb safety and trigger safety. Matte blue finish. Introduced 1988. From Competitor Corp., Inc.
Price: 14", standard calibers, synthetic grip **$575.00**

CZ 75 CHAMPION COMPETITION PISTOL
Caliber: 9mm Para., 40 S&W, 16-shot mag. **Barrel:** 4.4". **Weight:** 2.5 lbs. **Length:** 9.4" overall. **Grips:** Black rubber. **Sights:** Blade front, fully adjustable rear. **Features:** Single-action trigger mechanism; three-port compensator (40 S&W, 9mm Para. have two port) full-length guide rod; extended magazine release; ambidextrous safety; flared magazine well; fully adjustable match trigger. Introduced 1999. Imported from the Czech Republic by CZ-USA.
Price: Dual-tone finish **$1,691.00**

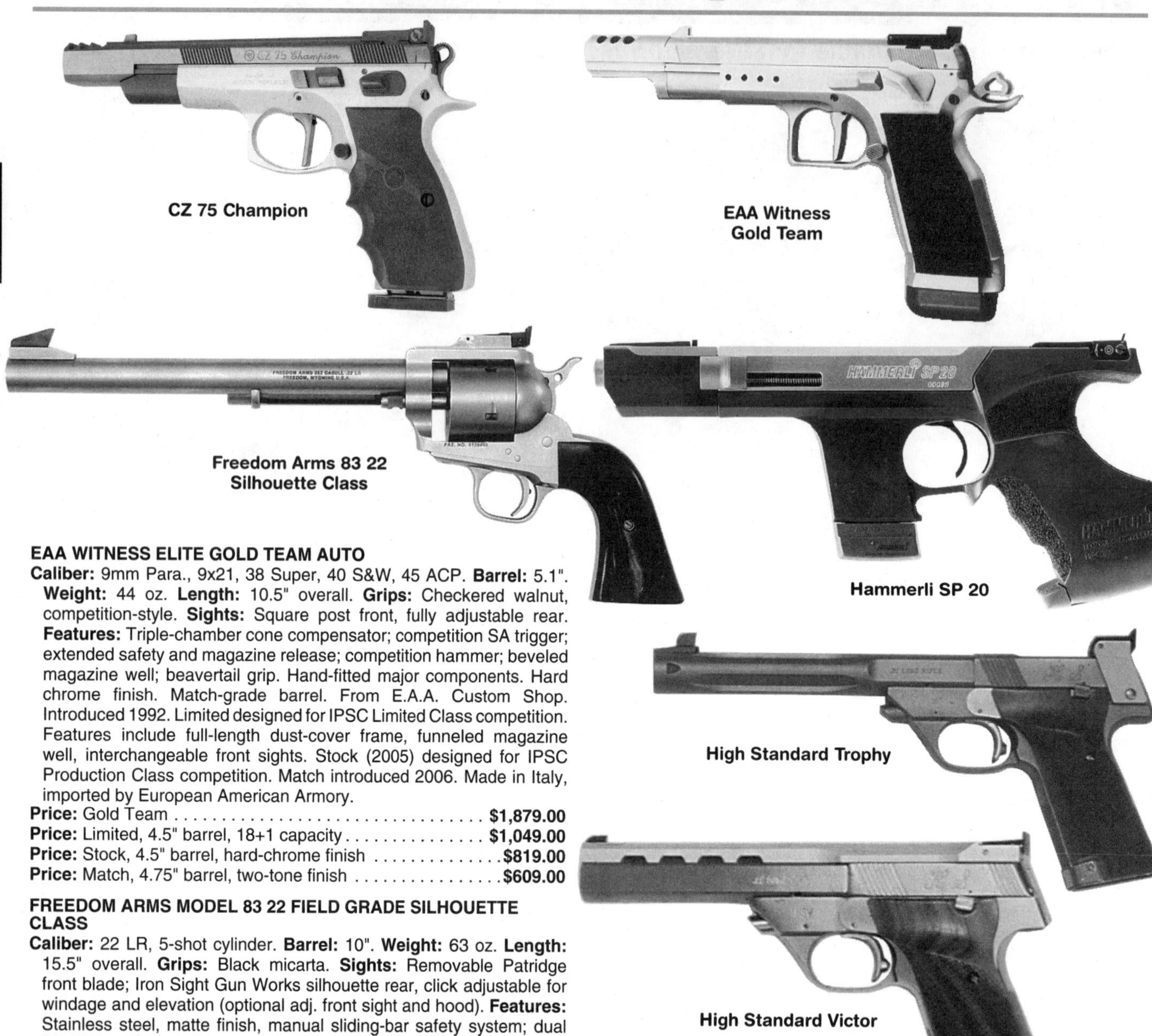

CZ 75 Champion

EAA Witness Gold Team

Freedom Arms 83 22 Silhouette Class

Hammerli SP 20

High Standard Trophy

High Standard Victor

EAA WITNESS ELITE GOLD TEAM AUTO

Caliber: 9mm Para., 9x21, 38 Super, 40 S&W, 45 ACP. **Barrel:** 5.1". **Weight:** 44 oz. **Length:** 10.5" overall. **Grips:** Checkered walnut, competition-style. **Sights:** Square post front, fully adjustable rear. **Features:** Triple-chamber cone compensator; competition SA trigger; extended safety and magazine release; competition hammer; beveled magazine well; beavertail grip. Hand-fitted major components. Hard chrome finish. Match-grade barrel. From E.A.A. Custom Shop. Introduced 1992. Limited designed for IPSC Limited Class competition. Features include full-length dust-cover frame, funneled magazine well, interchangeable front sights. Stock (2005) designed for IPSC Production Class competition. Match introduced 2006. Made in Italy, imported by European American Armory.

Price: Gold Team **$1,879.00**
Price: Limited, 4.5" barrel, 18+1 capacity **$1,049.00**
Price: Stock, 4.5" barrel, hard-chrome finish **$819.00**
Price: Match, 4.75" barrel, two-tone finish **$609.00**

FREEDOM ARMS MODEL 83 22 FIELD GRADE SILHOUETTE CLASS

Caliber: 22 LR, 5-shot cylinder. **Barrel:** 10". **Weight:** 63 oz. **Length:** 15.5" overall. **Grips:** Black micarta. **Sights:** Removable Patridge front blade; Iron Sight Gun Works silhouette rear, click adjustable for windage and elevation (optional adj. front sight and hood). **Features:** Stainless steel, matte finish, manual sliding-bar safety system; dual firing pins, lightened hammer for fast lock time, pre-set trigger stop. Introduced 1991. Made in U.S.A. by Freedom Arms.

Price: Silhouette Class **$1,860.00**

FREEDOM ARMS MODEL 83 CENTERFIRE SILHOUETTE MODELS

Caliber: 357 Mag., 41 Mag., 44 Mag.; 5-shot cylinder. **Barrel:** 10", 9" (357 Mag. only). **Weight:** 63 oz. (41 Mag.). **Length:** 15.5", 14.5" (357 only). **Grips:** Pachmayr Presentation. **Sights:** Iron Sight Gun Works silhouette rear sight, replaceable adjustable front sight blade with hood. **Features:** Stainless steel, matte finish, manual sliding-bar safety system. Made in U.S.A. by Freedom Arms.

Price: Silhouette Models, from **$1,623.00**

HAMMERLI SP 20 TARGET PISTOL

Caliber: 22 LR, 32 S&W. **Barrel:** 4.6". **Weight:** 34.6-41.8 oz. **Length:** 11.8" overall. **Grips:** Anatomically shaped synthetic Hi-Grip available in five sizes. **Sights:** Integral front in three widths, adjustable rear with changeable notch widths. **Features:** Extremely low-level sight line; anatomically shaped trigger; adjustable JPS buffer system for different recoil characteristics. Receiver available in red, blue, gold, violet or black. Introduced 1998. Imported from Switzerland by Larry's Guns of Maine.

Price: Hammerli 22 LR **$1,539.00**

HIGH STANDARD SUPERMATIC TROPHY TARGET PISTOL

Caliber: 22 LR, 9-shot mag. **Barrel:** 5.5" bull or 7.25" fluted. **Weight:** 44-46 oz. **Length:** 9.5-11.25" overall. Stock: Checkered hardwood with thumbrest. **Sights:** Undercut ramp front, frame-mounted micro-click rear adjustable for windage and elevation; drilled and tapped for scope mounting. **Features:** Gold-plated trigger, slide lock, safety-lever and magazine release; stippled front grip and backstrap; adjustable trigger and sear. Barrel weights optional. From High Standard Manufacturing Co., Inc.

Price: 5.5" barrel, adjustable sights **$795.00**
Price: 7.25", adjustable sights **$845.00**

HIGH STANDARD VICTOR TARGET PISTOL

Caliber: 22 LR, 10-shot magazine. **Barrel:** 4.5" or 5.5" polished blue; push-button takedown. **Weight:** 46 oz. **Length:** 9.5" overall. Stock: Checkered walnut with thumbrest. **Sights:** Undercut ramp front, micro-click rear adjustable for windage and elevation. Also available with scope mount, rings, no sights. **Features:** Stainless steel frame. Full-length vent rib. Gold-plated trigger, slide lock, safety-lever and magazine release; stippled front grip and backstrap; polished blue slide; adjustable trigger and sear. Comes with barrel weight. From High Standard Manufacturing Co., Inc.

Price: 4.5" or 5.5" barrel, vented sight rib, universal scope base **$795.00**

Kimber Super Match II

Smith & Wesson Model 22A

Ruger MKIII512

Springfield Armory 1911A1 Trophy Match

STI Executive

KIMBER SUPER MATCH II

Caliber: 45 ACP, 8-shot magazine. **Barrel:** 5". **Weight:** 38 oz. **Length:** 8.7" overall. **Grips:** Rosewood double diamond. **Sights:** Blade front, Kimber fully adjustable rear. **Features:** Guaranteed shoot 1" group at 25 yards. Stainless steel frame, black KimPro slide; two-piece magazine well; premium aluminum match-grade trigger; 30 lpi front strap checkering; stainless match-grade barrel; ambidextrous safety; special Custom Shop markings. Introduced 1999. Made in U.S.A. by Kimber Mfg., Inc.

Price: **$2,089.00**

KIMBER RIMFIRE TARGET

Caliber: 22 LR, 10-shot magazine. **Barrel:** 5". **Weight:** 23 oz. **Length:** 8.7" overall. **Grips:** Rosewood, Kimber logo, double diamond checkering, or black synthetic double diamond. **Sights:** Blade front, Kimber fully adjustable rear. **Features:** Bumped beavertail grip safety, extended thumb safety, extended magazine release button. Serrated flat top slide with flutes, machined aluminum slide and frame, matte black or satin silver finishes, 30 lines-per-inch checkering on frontstrap and under trigger guard; aluminum trigger, test target, accuracy guarantee. No slide lock-open after firing the last round in the magazine. Introduced 1999. Made in U.S.A. by Kimber Mfg., Inc.

Price: **$782.00**

RUGER MARK III TARGET MODEL AUTOLOADING PISTOL

Caliber: 22 LR, 10-shot magazine. **Barrel:** 5.5" to 6-7/8". **Weight:** 41 to 45 oz. **Length:** 9.75" to 11-1/8" overall. **Grips:** Checkered cocobolo/laminate. **Sights:** .125" blade front, micro-click rear, adjustable for windage and elevation, loaded chamber indicator; integral lock, magazine disconnect. Plastic case with lock included. Mark II series introduced 1982, discontinued 2004. Mark III introduced 2005.

Price: MKIII512 (bull barrel, blued) **$405.00**
Price: KMKIII512 (bull barrel, stainless) **$512.00**
Price: MKIII678 (blued Target barrel, 6-7/8") **$405.00**
Price: KMKIII678GC (stainless slabside barrel) **$589.00**
Price: KMKIII678H (stainless fluted barrel) **$602.00**
Price: KMKIII45HCL (Crimson Trace Laser Grips, intr. 2008) . **$764.00**

SMITH & WESSON MODEL 41 TARGET

Caliber: 22 LR, 10-shot clip. **Barrel:** 5.5", 7". **Weight:** 41 oz. (5.5" barrel). **Length:** 10.5" overall (5.5" barrel). **Grips:** Checkered walnut with modified thumbrest, usable with either hand. **Sights:** 1/8" Patridge on ramp base; micro-click rear adjustable for windage and elevation. **Features:** 3/8" wide, grooved trigger; adjustable trigger stop drilled and tapped.

Price: S&W Bright Blue, either barrel **$1,209.00**

SMITH & WESSON MODEL 22A PISTOLS

Caliber: 22 LR, 10-shot magazine. **Barrel:** 4", 5.5" bull. **Weight:** 28-39 oz. **Length:** 9.5" overall. **Grips:** Dymondwood with ambidextrous thumbrests and flared bottom or rubber soft touch with thumbrest. **Sights:** Patridge front, fully adjustable rear. **Features:** Sight bridge with Weaver-style integral optics mount; alloy frame, stainless barrel and slide; blue/black finish. Introduced 1997. The 22S is similar to the Model 22A except has stainless steel frame. Introduced 1997. Made in U.S.A. by Smith & Wesson.

Price: from **$284.00**
Price: Realtree APG camo finish (2008). **$332.00**

SPRINGFIELD ARMORY LEATHAM LEGEND TGO SERIES PISTOLS

Three models of 5" barrel, 45 ACP 1911 pistols built for serious competition. TGO 1 has deluxe low mount Bo-Mar rear sight, Dawson fiber optics front sight, 3.5 lb. trigger pull.

Price: TGO 1 . . . . **$3,095.00**

Springfield Armory Trophy Match Pistol

Similar to Springfield Armory's Full Size model, but designed for bullseye and action shooting competition. Available with a Service Model 5" frame with matching slide and barrel in 5" and 6" lengths. Fully adjustable sights, checkered frame front strap, match barrel and bushing. In 45 ACP only. From Springfield Inc.

Price: **$1,573.00**

STI EAGLE 5.0, 6.0 PISTOL

Caliber: 9mm Para., 9x21, 38 & 40 Super, 40 S&W, 10mm, 45 ACP, 10-shot magazine. **Barrel:** 5", 6" bull. **Weight:** 34.5 oz. **Length:** 8.62" overall. **Grips:** Checkered polymer. **Sights:** STI front, Novak or Heinie rear. **Features:** Standard frames plus 7 others; adjustable match trigger; skeletonized hammer; extended grip safety with locator pad. Introduced 1994. Made in U.S.A. by STI International.

Price: . . . . (5.0 Eagle) **$1,794.00,** (6.0 Eagle), $1,894.00

STI EXECUTIVE PISTOL

Caliber: 40 S&W. **Barrel:** 5" bull. **Weight:** 39 oz. **Length:** 8-5/8". **Grips:** Gray polymer. **Sights:** Dawson fiber optic, front; STI adjustable rear. **Features:** Stainless mag. well, front and rear serrations on slide. Made in U.S.A. by STI.

Price: **$2,464.00**

STI TROJAN

Caliber: 9mm Para., 38 Super, 40 S&W, 45 ACP. **Barrel:** 5", 6". **Weight:** 36 oz. **Length:** 8.5". **Grips:** Rosewood. **Sights:** STI front with STI adjustable rear. **Features:** Stippled front strap, flat top slide, one-piece steel guide rod.

Price: (Trojan 5") **$1,024.00**
Price: (Trojan 6", not available in 38 Super) **$1,344.00**

Includes models suitable for hunting and competitive courses of fire, both police and international.

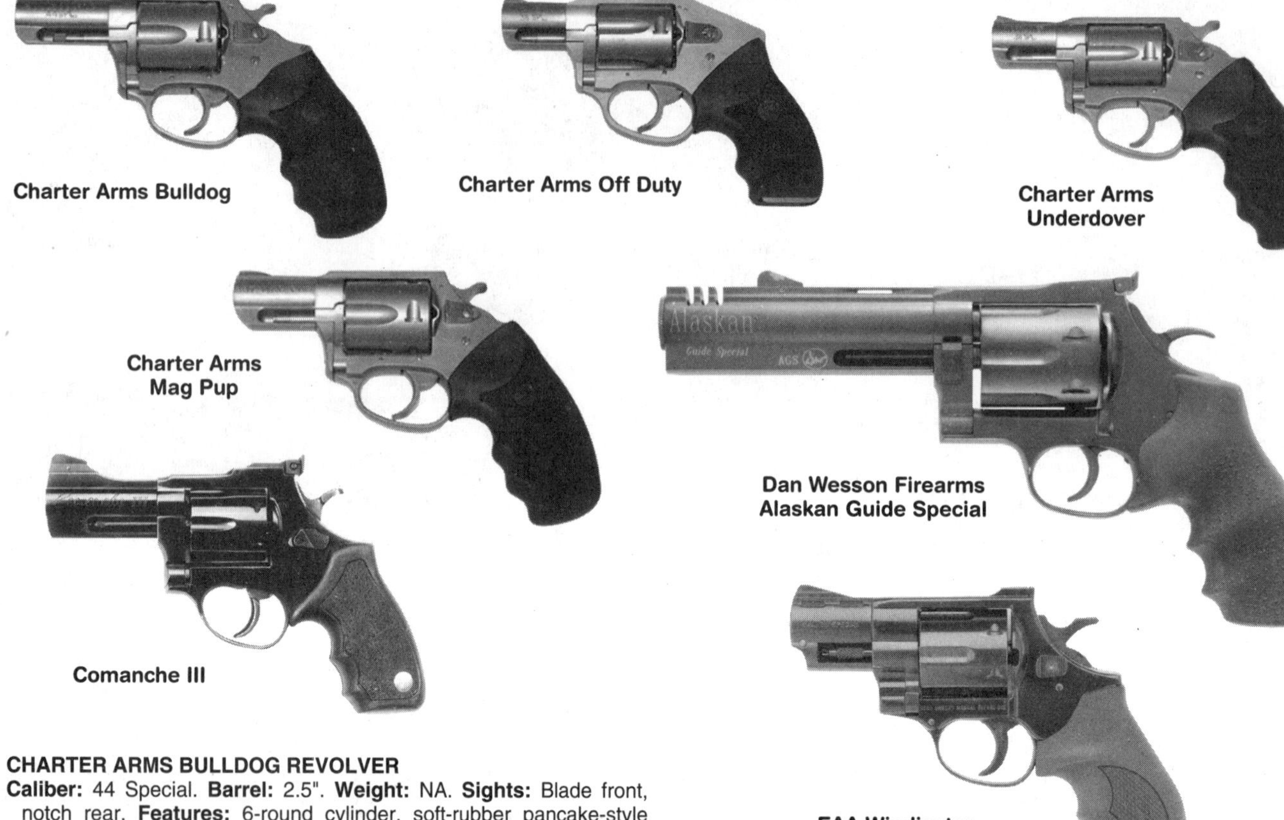

Charter Arms Bulldog

Charter Arms Off Duty

Charter Arms Underdover

Charter Arms Mag Pup

Dan Wesson Firearms Alaskan Guide Special

Comanche III

EAA Windicator

CHARTER ARMS BULLDOG REVOLVER

Caliber: 44 Special. **Barrel:** 2.5". **Weight:** NA. **Sights:** Blade front, notch rear. **Features:** 6-round cylinder, soft-rubber pancake-style grips, shrouded ejector rod, wide trigger and hammer spur. American made by Charter Arms, distributed by MKS Supply.

Price: Blued **$324.00**
Price: Stainless **$347.00**
Price: Police Bulldog, .38 Spec., 4" barrel, 24 oz. **$299.00**

CHARTER ARMS OFF DUTY REVOLVER

Caliber: 38 Spec. **Barrel:** 2". **Weight:** 12.5 oz. **Sights:** Blade front, notch rear. **Features:** 5-round cylinder, aluminum casting, DAO. American made by Charter Arms, distributed by MKS Supply.

Price: Aluminum **$353.00**

CHARTER ARMS UNDERCOVER REVOLVER

Caliber: Barrel: 2". **Weight:** 16 oz. **Sights:** Blade front, notch rear. **Features:** 6-round cylinder. American made by Charter Arms, distributed by MKS Supply.

Price: Blued **$359.00**

CHARTER ARMS UNDERCOVER SOUTHPAW REVOLVER

Caliber: 38 Spec. +P. **Barrel:** 2". **Weight:** 12 oz. **Sights:** NA. **Features:** Cylinder release is on the right side and the cylinder opens to the right side. Exposed hammer for both single and double-action firing. 5-round cylinder. American made by Charter Arms, distributed by MKS Supply.

Price: Blued **$375.00**

CHARTER ARMS MAG PUG REVOLVER

Caliber: 357 Mag. **Barrel:** 2.2". **Weight:** 23 oz. **Sights:** Blade front, notch rear. **Features:** 5-round cylinder. American made by Charter Arms, distributed by MKS Supply.

Price: Blued **$325.00**
Price: Stainless **$335.00**

COMANCHE I, II, III DA REVOLVERS

Caliber: 22 LR, 9 shot. 38 Spec., 6 shot. 357 Mag, 6 shot. **Barrel:** 6", 22 LR; 2" and 4", 38 Spec.; 2" and 3", 357 Mag. **Weight:** 39 oz. **Length:** 10.8" overall. **Grips:** Rubber. **Sights:** Adjustable rear. **Features:** Blued or stainless. Distributed by SGS Importers.

Price: I Blue **$236.95**
Price: I Alloy **$258.95**
Price: II 38 Spec., 3" bbl., 6-shot, stainless, intr. 2006 . . . . . . **$236.95**
Price: II 38 Spec., 4" bbl., 6-shot, stainless **$219.95**
Price: III 357 Mag, 3" bbl., 6-shot, blue **$253.95**
Price: III 357 Mag. 4" bbl., 6-shot, blue **$274.95**

DAN WESSON FIREARMS ALASKAN GUIDE SPECIAL

Caliber: 445 SuperMag; also chambers and fires 44 Magnum, 44 Special, 6 shots. **Sights:** Blade front, adjustable rear. **Barrel:** Compensated 4" vent heavy barrel assembly. **Weight:** 54.4 oz. **Length:** 11.7". **Features:** Stainless steel with baked on, non-glare, matte black coating, special laser engraving. Made in U.S.A. by Dan Wesson Firearms, distributed by CZ-USA.

Price: **$1,295.00**

DAN WESSON FIREARMS VH8 445 SUPERMAG

Caliber: 445 SuperMag; also chambers and fires 44 Magnum, 44 Special, 6 shots. **Sights:** Blade front, adjustable rear. **Barrel:** 8" full-length underlug. **Weight:** 54.4 oz. **Length:** 14.6". **Features:** Stainless-steel frame and barrel. Interchangeable barrels. Made in U.S.A. by Dan Wesson Firearms, distributed by CZ-USA.

Price: **$1,070.00**

EAA WINDICATOR REVOLVERS

Caliber: 38 Spec., 6-shot; 357 Mag., 6-shot. **Barrel:** 2", 4". **Weight:** 30 oz. (4"). **Length:** 8.5" overall (4" bbl.). **Grips:** Rubber with finger grooves. **Sights:** Blade front, fixed or adjustable on rimfires; fixed only on 32, 38. **Features:** Swing-out cylinder; hammer block safety; blue finish. Introduced 1991. Imported from Germany by European American Armory.

Price: 38 Spec. 2" barrel, alloy frame **$285.00**
Price: 38 Spec. 4" barrel, alloy frame **$295.00**
Price: 357 Mag, 2" barrel, steel frame **$295.00**
Price: 357 Mag, 4" barrel, steel frame **$315.00**

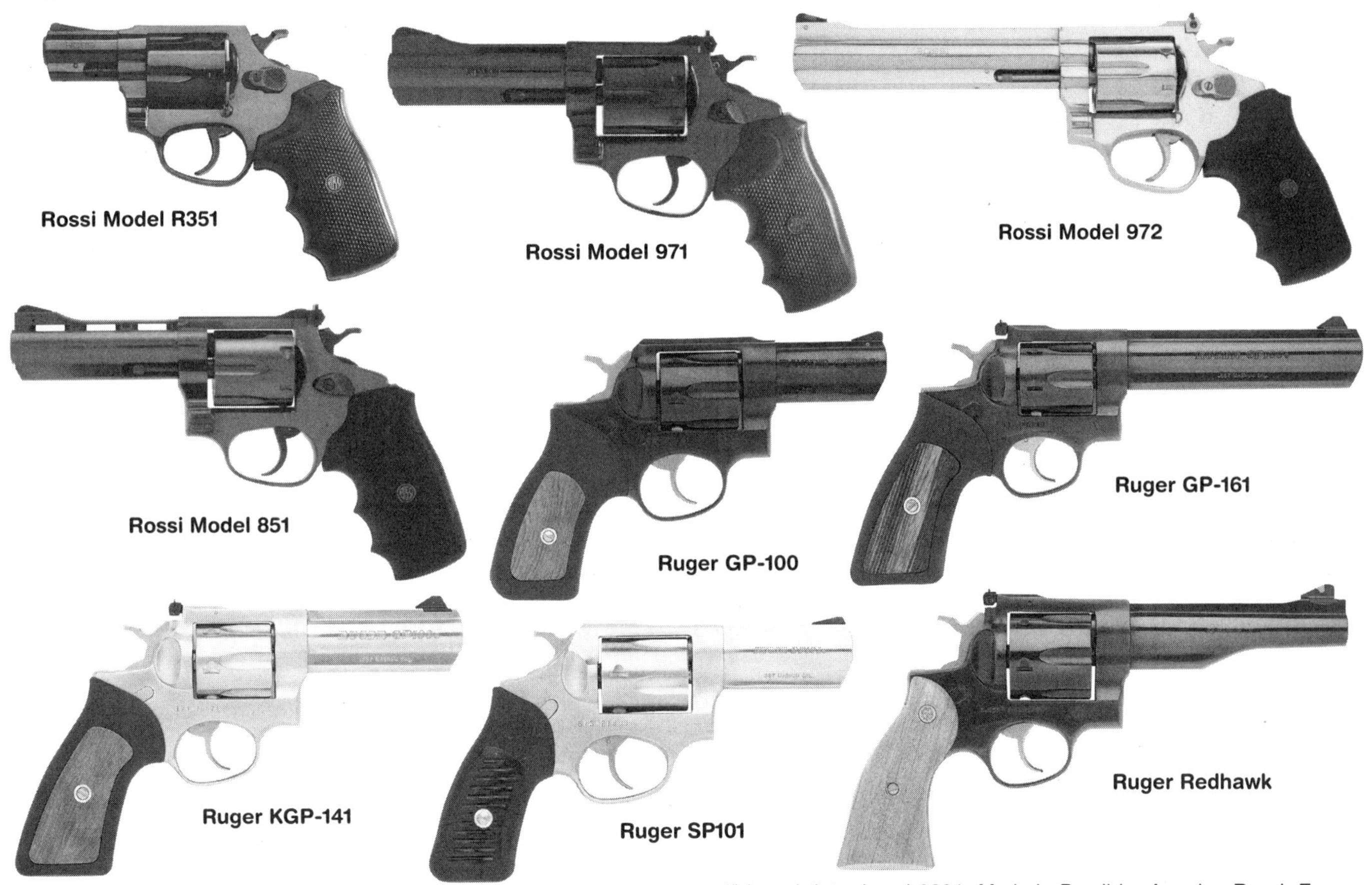
Rossi Model R351
Rossi Model 971
Rossi Model 972
Rossi Model 851
Ruger GP-100
Ruger GP-161
Ruger KGP-141
Ruger SP101
Ruger Redhawk

KORTH USA REVOLVERS

Caliber: 22 LR, 22 WMR, 32 S&W Long, 38 Spec., 357 Mag., 9mm Para. **Barrel:** 3", 4", 5.25", 6". **Weight:** 36-52 oz. Grips, Combat, Sport: Walnut, Palisander, Amboinia, Ivory. Grips, Target: German Walnut, matte with oil finish, adjustable ergonomic competition style. **Sights:** Adjustable Patridge (Sport) or Baughman (Combat), interchangeable and adjustable rear w/Patridge front (Target) in blue and matte. **Features:** DA/SA, 3 models, over 50 configurations, externally adjustable trigger stop and weight, interchangeable cylinder, removable wide-milled trigger shoe on Target model. Deluxe models are highly engraved editions. Available finishes include high polish blue finish, plasma coated in high polish or matted silver, gold, blue, or charcoal. Many deluxe options available. 6-shot. From Korth USA.

Price: from **$8,000.00**
Price: Deluxe Editions, from **$12,000.00**

ROSSI R461/R462/R971/R972

Caliber: .357 Mag. **Barrel:** 2" (R46), 4" (R971), 6" (R972). **Weight:** 26-35 oz. **Grips:** Rubber. **Sights:** Fixed (R46), Fully Adjustable (R97). **Features:** DA/SA, 4 models available, +P rated frame, blue carbon or high polish stainless steel, patented Taurus Security System, 6-shot.

Price: From **$352.00**

ROSSI MODEL R351/R352/R851 REVOLVERS

Caliber: .38 Spec. **Barrel:** 2" (R35), 4" (R85). **Weight:** 24-32 oz. **Grips:** Rubber. **Sights:** Fixed (R35), Fully Adjustable (R85). **Features:** DA/SA, 3 models available, +P rated frame, blue carbon or high polish stainless steel, patented Taurus Security System, 5-shot (R35) 6-shot (R85).

Price: From **$352.00**

ROSSI MODEL 971/972 REVOLVERS

Caliber: 357 Mag. +P, 6-shot. **Barrel:** 4", 6". **Weight:** 32 oz. **Length:** 8.5" or 10.5" overall. **Grips:** Rubber. **Sights:** Blade front, adjustable rear. **Features:** Single/double action. Patented key-lock Taurus Security System; forged steel frame. Introduced 2001. Made in Brazil by Amadeo Rossi. Imported by BrazTech/Taurus.

Price: Model 971 (blued finish, 4" bbl.) **$406.00**
Price: Model 972 (stainless steel finish, 6" bbl.) **$460.00**

Rossi Model 851

Similar to Model 971/972, chambered for 38 Spec. +P. Blued finish, 4" barrel. Introduced 2001. Made in Brazil by Amadeo Rossi. From BrazTech/Taurus.

Price: **$364.00**

RUGER GP-100 REVOLVERS

Caliber: 38 Spec. +P, 357 Mag., 6-shot. **Barrel:** 3" full shroud, 4" full shroud, 6" full shroud. **Weight:** 3" full shroud-36 oz., 4" full shroud-38 oz. **Sights:** Fixed; adjustable on 4" full shroud, all 6" barrels. **Grips:** Ruger Santoprene Cushioned Grip with Goncalo Alves inserts. **Features:** Uses action, frame features of both the Security-Six and Redhawk revolvers. Full length, short ejector shroud. Satin blue and stainless steel.

Price: GPF-141 (357, 4" full shroud, adj. sights, blue) **$598.00**
Price: GP-161 (357, 6" full shroud, adj. sights, blue), 46 oz. . . **$598.00**
Price: KGP-141 (357, 4" full shroud, adj. sights, stainless) . . . **$660.00**
Price: KGP-161 (357, 6" full shroud, adj. sights, stainless) 46 oz. **$660.00**
Price: KGPF-331 (357, 3" full shroud, stainless) **$640.00**

RUGER SP101 REVOLVERS

Caliber: 327 Federal, 6-shot; 38 Spec. +P, 357 Mag., 5-shot. **Barrel:** 2.25", 3-1/16". **Weight:** (38 & 357 mag models) 2.25"-25 oz.; 3-1/16"-27 oz. **Sights:** Adjustable on 327, fixed on others. **Grips:** Ruger Cushioned Grip with inserts. **Features:** Compact, small frame, double-action revolver. Full-length ejector shroud. Stainless steel only. Introduced 1988.

Price: KSP-321X (2.25", 357 Mag.) **$572.00**
Price: KSP-331X (3-1/16", 357 Mag.) **$572.00**
Price: KSP-821X (2.25", 38 Spec.) **$572.00**
Price: KSP-327331X (3-1/16", 327 Federal, intr. 2008) **$527.00**
Price: KSP-331X-LG (Crimson Trace Laser Grips, intr. 2008) . **$814.00**

Ruger SP101 Double-Action-Only Revolver

Similar to standard SP101 except double-action-only with no single-action sear notch. Spurless hammer, floating firing pin and transfer bar safety system. Available with 2.25" barrel in 357 Mag. Weighs 25 oz., overall length 7". Natural brushed satin, high-polish stainless steel. Introduced 1993.

Price: KSP321XL (357 Mag.) **$572.00**
Price: KSP321XL-LG (357 Mag., Crimson Trace Laser Grips, intr. 2008) **$814.00**

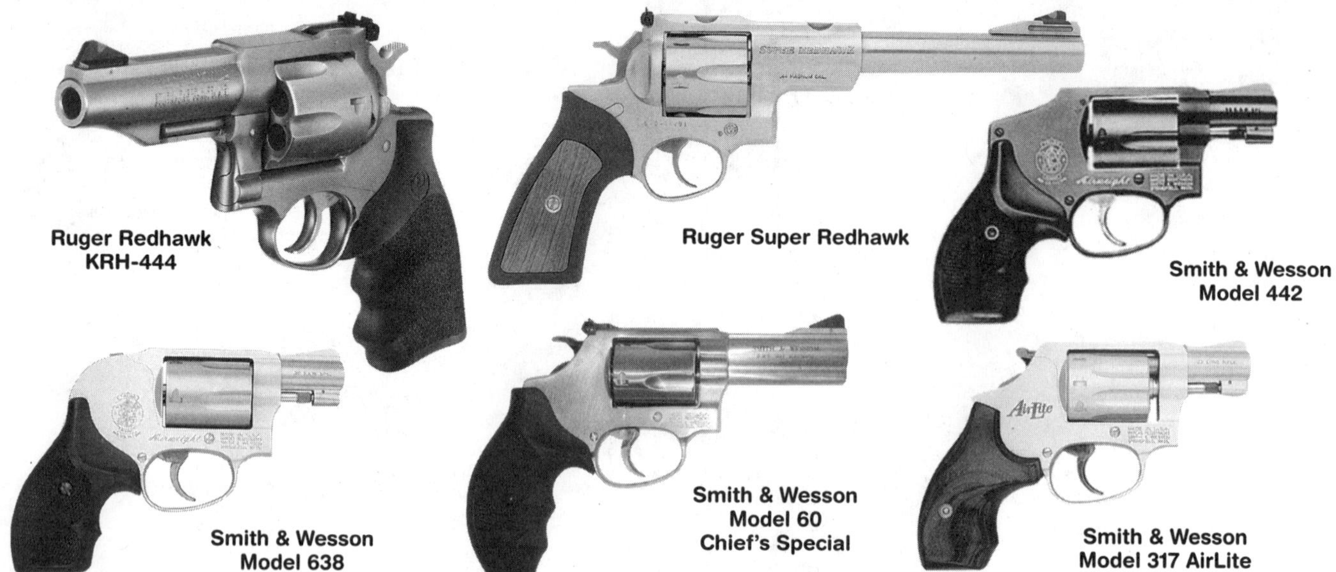

Ruger Redhawk KRH-444

Ruger Super Redhawk

Smith & Wesson Model 442

Smith & Wesson Model 638

Smith & Wesson Model 60 Chief's Special

Smith & Wesson Model 317 AirLite

RUGER REDHAWK

Caliber: 44 Rem. Mag., 45 Colt, 6-shot. **Barrel:** 4", 5.5", 7.5". **Weight:** About 54 oz. (7.5" bbl.). **Length:** 13" overall (7.5" barrel). **Grips:** Square butt cushioned grip panels. **Sights:** Interchangeable Patridge-type front, rear adjustable for windage and elevation. **Features:** Stainless steel, brushed satin finish, blued ordnance steel. 9.5" sight radius. Introduced 1979.

Price: KRH-44, stainless, 7.5" barrel **$836.00**
Price: KRH-44R, stainless 7.5" barrel w/scope mount **$888.00**
Price: KRH-445, stainless 5.5" barrel **$836.00**
Price: RH-445, blued 5.5" barrel **$766.00**
Price: KRH-444, stainless 4" barrel (2007) **$836.00**
Price: KRH-45-4, Hogue Monogrip, 45 Colt (2008) **$836.00**

RUGER SUPER REDHAWK REVOLVER

Caliber: 44 Rem. Mag., 45 Colt, 454 Casull, 480 Ruger, 5 or 6-shot. **Barrel:** 2.5", 5.5", 7.5", 9.5". **Weight:** About 54 oz. (7.5" bbl.). **Length:** 13" overall (7.5" barrel). **Grips:** Hogue Tamer Monogrip. **Features:** Similar to standard Redhawk except has heavy extended frame with Ruger Integral Scope Mounting System on wide topstrap. Wide hammer spur lowered for better scope clearance. Incorporates mechanical design features and improvements of GP-100. Ramp front sight base has Redhawk-style Interchangeable Insert sight blades, adjustable rear sight. Satin stainless steel and low-glare stainless finishes. Introduced 1987.

Price: KSRH-2454, 2.5" 454 Casull/45 Colt, Hogue Tamer Monogrip, Alaskan Model **$963.00**
Price: KSRH-2480-5, 2.5" 480 Ruger, Hogue Tamer Monogrip (2008) **$963.00**
Price: KSRH-7, 7.5" 44 Mag, Ruger grip **$888.00**
Price: KSRH-7454, 7.5" 45 Colt/454 Casull **$963.00**
Price: KSRH-7480-5, 7.5" 480 Ruger **$963.00**
Price: KSRH-9, 9" 44 Mag, Ruger grip **$888.00**
Price: KSRH-9480-5, 9.5", 480 Ruger, intr. 2008 .... **$963.00**
Price: KSRH-2, 2.5" 44 Mag, Alaskan Model, intr. 2008 ..... **$963.00**

SMITH & WESSON M&P REVOLVERS

Caliber: 38 Spec., 357 Mag., 5 rounds (Centennial), 8 rounds (large frame). **Barrel:** 1.87" (Centennial), 5" (large frame). **Weight:** 13.3 oz. (Centennial), 36.3 oz. (large frame). **Length:** 6.31" overall (small frame), 10.5" (large frame). **Grips:** Synthetic. **Sights:** Integral U-Notch rear, XS Sights 24/7 Tritium Night. **Features:** Scandium alloy frame, stainless steel cylinder, matte black finish. Made in U.S.A. by Smith & Wesson.

Price: M&P 340, double action **$869.00**
Price: M&P 340CT, Crimson Trace Lasergrips **$1,122.00**
Price: M&P R8 large frame **$1,311.00**

SMITH & WESSON NIGHT GUARD REVOLVERS

Caliber: 357 Mag., 38 Spec. +P, 5-, 6-, 7-, 8-shot. **Barrel:** 2.5 or 2.75" (45 ACP). **Weight:** 24.2 oz. (2.5" barrel). **Length:** 7.325" overall (2.5" barrel). **Grips:** Pachmayr Compac Custom. **Sights:** XS Sight 24/7 Standard Dot Tritium front, Cylinder & Slide Extreme Duty fixed rear. **Features:** Scandium alloy frame, stainless PVD cylinder, matte black finish. Introduced 2008. Made in U.S.A. by Smith & Wesson.

Price: Model 325 45 ACP, 2.75" barrel **$1,044.00**
Price: Model 327 38/357, 2.5" barrel **$1,044.00**
Price: Model 396 44 Special, 2.5" barrel **$980.00**

SMITH & WESSON J-FRAME REVOLVERS

The smallest S&W wheelguns come in a variety of chamberings, barrel lengths, and materials, as noted in the individual model listings below.

SMITH & WESSON 60LS/642LS LADYSMITH REVOLVERS

Caliber: .38 Spec. +P, 357 Mag., 5-shot. **Barrel:** 1-7/8" (642LS); 2-1/8" (60LS) **Weight:** 14.5 oz. (642LS); 21.5 oz. (60LS); **Length:** 6.6" overall (60LS); . **Grips:** Wood. **Sights:** Black blade, serrated ramp front, fixed notch rear. **Features:** 60LS model has a Chiefs Special-style frame. 642LS has Centennial-style frame, frosted matte finish, smooth combat wood grips. Introduced 1996. Comes in a fitted carry/storage case. Introduced 1989. Made in U.S.A. by Smith & Wesson.

Price: From **$711.00**

SMITH & WESSON MODEL 442/637/638/642 AIRWEIGHT REVOLVERS

Caliber: 38 Spec. +P, 5-shot. **Barrel:** 1-7/8". **Weight:** 15 oz. (37, 442); 20 oz. (3); 21.5 oz.; **Length:** 6-3/8" overall. **Grips:** Soft rubber. **Sights:** Fixed, serrated ramp front, square notch rear. **Features:** Aluminum-alloy frames. Models 37, 637; Chiefs Special-style frame with exposed hammer. Introduced 1996. Models 442, 642; Centennial-style frame, enclosed hammer. Model 638, Bodyguard style, shrouded hammer. Comes in a fitted carry/storage case. Introduced 1989. Made in U.S.A. by Smith & Wesson.

Price: From **$545.00**

SMITH & WESSON MODEL 60 CHIEF'S SPECIAL

Caliber: 357 Mag., 38 Spec. +P, 5-shot. **Barrel:** 2-1/8", 3" or 5". **Weight:** 22.5 oz. (2-1/8" barrel). **Length:** 6-5/8 overall (2-1/8" barrel). **Grips:** Rounded butt synthetic grips. **Sights:** Fixed, serrated ramp front, square notch rear. **Features:** Stainless steel construction, satin finish, internal lock. Introduced 1965. The 5-inch-barrel model has target semi-lug barrel, rosewood grip, red ramp front sight, adjustable rear sight. Made in U.S.A. by Smith & Wesson.

Price: 2-1/8" barrel, intr. 2005 .... **$727.00**
Price: 3" barrel, 7.5" OAL, 24 oz. **$758.00**
Price: 5" semi-lug barrel, 9-3/8" OAL, 30.5 oz. **$798.00**

SMITH & WESSON MODEL 317 AIRLITE REVOLVERS

Caliber: 22 LR, 8-shot. **Barrel:** 1-7/8", 3". **Weight:** 10.5 oz. **Length:** 6.25" overall (1-7/8" barrel). **Grips:** Rubber. **Sights:** Serrated ramp front, fixed notch rear. **Features:** Aluminum alloy, carbon and stainless steels, Chiefs Special-style frame with exposed hammer. Smooth combat trigger. Clear Cote finish. Introduced 1997. Made in U.S.A. by Smith & Wesson.

Price: Model 317, 1-7/8" barrel **$695.00**
Price: Model 317 w/HiViz front sight, 3" barrel, 7.25 OAL **$758.00**

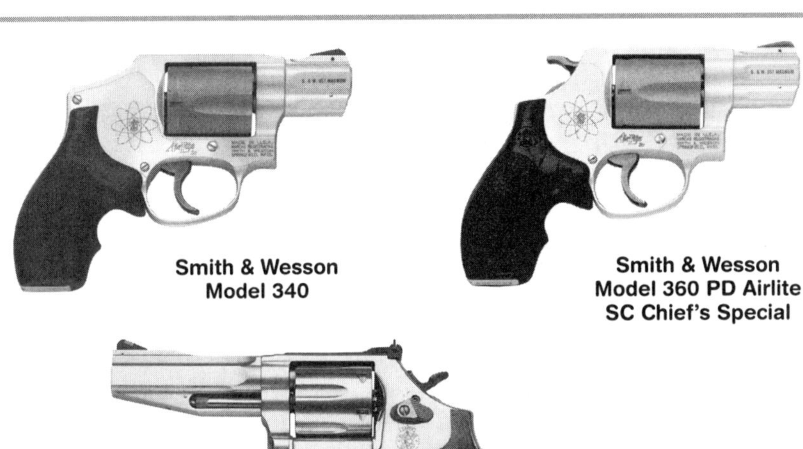

Smith & Wesson Model 340

Smith & Wesson Model 360 PD Airlite SC Chief's Special

Smith & Wesson Model 686 SSR

Smith & Wesson Model 10

Smith & Wesson Model 21

SMITH & WESSON MODEL 340/340PD AIRLITE SC CENTENNIAL

Caliber: 357 Mag., 38 Spec. +P, 5-shot. **Barrel:** 1-7/8". **Weight:** 12 oz. **Length:** 6-3/8" overall (1-7/8" barrel). **Grips:** Rounded butt rubber. **Sights:** Black blade front, rear notch **Features:** Centennial-style frame, enclosed hammer. Internal lock. Matte silver finish. Scandium alloy frame, titanium cylinder, stainless steel barrel liner. Made in U.S.A. by Smith & Wesson.

Price: Model 340 . . . . **$1,019.00**
Price: Model 340PD **$1,019.00**

SMITH & WESSON MODEL 351PD REVOLVER

Caliber: 22 Mag., 7-shot. **Barrel:** 1-7/8". **Weight:** 10.6 oz. **Length:** 6.25" overall (1-7/8" barrel). **Sights:** HiViz front sight, rear notch. **Grips:** Wood. **Features:** Seven-shot, aluminum-alloy frame. Chiefs Special-style frame with exposed hammer. Nonreflective matte-black finish. Internal lock. Made in U.S.A. by Smith & Wesson.

Price: **$758.00**

SMITH & WESSON MODEL 360/360PD AIRLITE CHIEF'S SPECIAL

Caliber: 357 Mag., 38 Spec. +P, 5-shot. **Barrel:** 1-7/8". **Weight:** 12 oz. **Length:** 6-3/8" overall (1-7/8" barrel). **Grips:** Rounded butt rubber. **Sights:** Black blade front, fixed rear notch. **Features:** Chiefs Special-style frame with exposed hammer. Internal lock. Scandium alloy frame, titanium cylinder, stainless steel barrel. Made in U.S.A. by Smith & Wesson.

Price: From **$988.00**

SMITH & WESSON MODEL 640 CENTENNIAL DA ONLY

Caliber: 357 Mag., 38 Spec. +P, 5-shot. **Barrel:** 2-1/8". **Weight:** 23 oz. **Length:** 6.75" overall. **Grips:** Uncle Mike's Boot grip. **Sights:** Serrated ramp front, fixed notch rear. **Features:** Stainless steel. Fully concealed hammer, snag-proof smooth edges. Internal lock. Introduced 1995 in 357 Mag.

Price: **$727.00**

SMITH & WESSON MODEL 649 BODYGUARD REVOLVER

Caliber: 357 Mag., 38 Spec. +P, 5-shot. **Barrel:** 2-1/8". **Weight:** 23 oz. **Length:** 6-5/8" overall. **Grips:** Uncle Mike's Combat. **Sights:** Black pinned ramp front, fixed notch rear. **Features:** Stainless steel construction, satin finish. Internal lock. Bodyguard style, shrouded hammer. Made in U.S.A. by Smith & Wesson.

Price: **$727.00**

SMITH & WESSON K-FRAME/L-FRAME REVOLVERS

These mid-size S&W wheelguns come in a variety of chamberings, barrel lengths, and materials, as noted in the individual model listings below. 17 variations for 2006.

SMITH & WESSON MODEL 10 REVOLVER

Caliber: 38 Spec. +P, 6-shot. **Barrel:** 4". **Weight:** 36 oz. **Length:** 8-7/8" overall. **Grips:** Soft rubber; square butt. **Sights:** Fixed; black blade front, square notch rear. Blued carbon steel frame.

Price: Blue **$687.00**

SMITH & WESSON MODEL 64/67 REVOLVERS

Caliber: 38 Spec. +P, 6-shot. **Barrel:** 3". **Weight:** 33 oz. **Length:** 8-7/8" overall. **Grips:** Soft rubber. **Sights:** Fixed, 1/8" serrated ramp front, square notch rear. Model 67 (**Weight:** 36 oz. **Length:** 8-7/8") similar to Model 64 except for adjustable sights. **Features:** Satin finished stainless steel, square butt.

Price: From **$632.00**

SMITH & WESSON MODEL 617 REVOLVERS

Caliber: 22 LR, 6- or 10-shot. **Barrel:** 4". **Weight:** 41 oz. (4" barrel). **Length:** 9-1/8" (4" barrel). **Grips:** Soft rubber. **Sights:** Patridge front, adjustable rear. Drilled and tapped for scope mount. **Features:** Stainless steel with satin finish; 4" has .312" smooth trigger, .375" semi-target hammer; 6" has either .312" combat or .400" serrated trigger, .375" semi-target or .500" target hammer; 8-3/8" with .400" serrated trigger, .500" target hammer. Introduced 1990.

Price: From **$837.00**

SMITH & WESSON MODELS 619/620 REVOLVERS

Caliber: 38 Spec. +P; 357 Mag., 7 rounds. **Barrel:** 4". **Weight:** 37.5 oz. **Length:** 9.5". **Grips:** Rubber. **Sights:** Integral front blade, fixed rear notch on the 619; adjustable white-outline target style rear, red ramp front on 620. **Features:** Replaces Models 65 and 66. Two-piece semi-lug barrel. Satin stainless frame and cylinder. Made in U.S.A. by Smith & Wesson.

Price: **$711.00**

SMITH & WESSON MODEL 686/686 PLUS REVOLVERS

Caliber: 357 Mag., 38 S&W Special; 6 rounds. **Barrel:** 2.5", 4", 6". **Weight:** 35 oz. (2.5" barrel). **Length:** 7.5", (2.5" barrel). **Grips:** Rubber. **Sights:** White outline adjustable rear, red ramp front. **Features:** Satin stainless frame and cylinder. Plus series guns have 7-shot cylinders. Introduced 1996. Powerport (PP) has Patridge front, adjustable rear sight. Introduced early 1980s. Stock Service Revolver (SSR) intr. 2007. Capacity: 6. **Barrel:** 4". Sight: Interchangeable front, adjustable rear. Grip: Wood Finish: Satin stainless frame and cylinder. **Weight:** 38.3 oz. **Features:** Chamfered charge holes, custom barrel w/recessed crown, bossed mainspring. High-hold ergonomic grip. Made in U.S.A. by Smith & Wesson.

Price: 686 . . . . **$830.00**
Price: Plus, 7 rounds **$853.00**
Price: PP, 6" barrel, 6 rounds, 11-3/8" OAL **$853.00**
Price: SSR **$964.00**

SMITH & WESSON N-FRAME REVOLVERS

These large-frame S&W wheelguns come in a variety of chamberings, barrel lengths, and materials, as noted in the individual model listings below.

SMITH & WESSON MODEL 21

Caliber: 44 Special, 6-round. Barrel: 4" tapered. **Weight:** NA. **Length:** NA. **Grips:** Smooth wood. **Sights:** Pinned half-moon service front; service rear. **Features:** Carbon steel frame, blued finish.

Price: **$924.00**

Smith & Wesson Model 325PD

Smith & Wesson Model 625

Smith & Wesson Model 657

Smith & Wesson Model 460V

Smith & Wesson Model 500

SMITH & WESSON MODEL 29 50TH ANNIVERSARY REVOLVER
Caliber: 44 Mag, 6-round. **Barrel:** 6.5". **Weight:** 48.5 oz. **Length:** 12". **Grips:** Cocobolo. **Sights:** Adjustable white-outline rear, red ramp front. **Features:** Carbon steel frame, polished-blued finish. Introduced 2005. Includes 24 carat gold-plated anniversary logo on frame, cleaning kit with screwdriver, mahogany presentation case, square-butt frame, serrated trigger. Original Model 29 made famous by "Dirty Harry" character created in 1971 by Clint Eastwood.
Price: **$5,000.00**

SMITH & WESSON MODEL 329PD/357PD AIRLITE REVOLVERS
Caliber: 41 Mag. (357PD); 44 Spec., 44 Mag. (329PD); 45 ACP (325PD); 6-round. **Barrel:** 2.75" (325PD). **Weight:** 21.5 oz. (325PD, 2.75" barrel). **Length:** 7.25" (325PD, 2.75" barrel). **Grips:** Wood. **Sights:** Adj. rear, HiViz orange-dot front. **Features:** Scandium alloy frame, titanium cylinder. 4" model has HiViz green front sight and Ahrends finger-groove wood grips. Weighs 26.5 oz.
Price: From **$1,153.00**

SMITH & WESSON MODEL 625/625JM REVOLVERS
Caliber: 45 ACP, 6-shot. **Barrel:** 4", 5". **Weight:** 43 oz. (4" barrel). **Length:** 9-3/8" overall (4" barrel). **Grips:** Soft rubber; wood optional. **Sights:** Patridge front on ramp, S&W micrometer click rear adjustable for windage and elevation. **Features:** Stainless steel construction with .400" semi-target hammer, .312" smooth combat trigger; full lug barrel. Glass beaded finish. Introduced 1989. "Jerry Miculek" Professional (JM) Series has .265"-wide grooved trigger, special wooden Miculek Grip, five full moon clips, gold bead Patridge front sight on interchangeable front sight base, bead blast finish. Unique serial number run. Mountain Gun has 4" tapered barrel, drilled and tapped, Hogue Rubber Monogrip, pinned black ramp front sight, micrometer click-adjustable rear sight, satin stainless frame and barrel, weighs 39.5 oz.
Price: 625JM **$988.00**

SMITH & WESSON MODEL 629 REVOLVERS
Caliber: 44 Magnum, 44 S&W Special, 6-shot. **Barrel:** 4", 5", 6.5". **Weight:** 41.5 oz. (4" bbl.). **Length:** 9-5/8" overall (4" bbl.). **Grips:** Soft rubber; wood optional. **Sights:** 1/8" red ramp front, white outline rear, internal lock, adjustable for windage and elevation. Classic similar to standard Model 629, except Classic has full-lug 5" barrel, chamfered front of cylinder, interchangeable red ramp front sight with adjustable white outline rear, Hogue grips with S&W monogram, drilled and tapped for scope mounting. Factory accurizing and endurance packages. Introduced 1990. Classic Power Port has Patridge front sight and adjustable rear sight. Model 629CT has 5" barrel, Crimson Trace Hoghunter Lasergrips, 10.5" OAL, 45.5 oz. weight. Introduced 2006.
Price: From **$948.00**

SMITH & WESSON MODEL 657 REVOLVER
Caliber: 41 Mag., 6-shot. **Barrel:** 7.5" full lug. **Weight:** 52 oz. **Grips:** Soft rubber. **Sights:** Pinned 1/8" red ramp front, micro-click rear adjustable for windage and elevation. Target hammer, drilled and tapped, unfluted cylinder. **Features:** Stainless steel construction.
Price: **$869.00**

SMITH & WESSON X-FRAME REVOLVERS
These extra-large X-frame S&W wheelguns come in a variety of chamberings, barrel lengths, and materials, as noted in the individual model listings below. 7 variations for 2006.

SMITH & WESSON MODEL 460V REVOLVERS
Caliber: 460 S&W Mag., 5-shot. Also chambers 454 Casull, 45 Colt. **Barrel:** 8-3/8" gain-twist rifling. **Weight:** 62.5 oz. **Length:** 11.25". **Grips:** Rubber. **Sights:** Adj. rear, red ramp front. **Features:** Satin stainless steel frame and cylinder, interchangeable compensator. 460XVR (X-treme Velocity Revolver) has black blade front sight with interchangeable green Hi-Viz tubes, adjustable rear sight. 7.5"-barrel version has Lothar-Walther barrel, 360-degree recoil compensator, tuned Performance Center action, pinned sear, integral Weaver base, non-glare surfaces, scope mount accessory kit for mounting full-size scopes, flashed-chromed hammer and trigger, Performance Center gun rug and shoulder sling. Interchangeable Hi-Viz green dot front sight, adjustable black rear sight, Hogue Dual Density Monogrip, matte-black frame and shroud finish with glass-bead cylinder finish, 72 oz. Compensated Hunter has tear drop chrome hammer, .312 chrome trigger, Hogue Dual Density Monogrip, satin/matte stainless finish, HiViz interchangeable front sight, adjustable black rear sight. XVR introduced 2006.
Price: 460V **$1,319.00**
Price: 460XVR, from **$1,319.00**

SMITH & WESSON MODEL 500 REVOLVERS
Caliber: 500 S&W Mag., 5 rounds. Barrel: 4", 8-3/8". **Weight:** 72.5 oz. **Length:** 15" (8-3/8" barrel). **Grips:** Hogue Sorbothane Rubber. **Sights:** Interchangeable blade, front, adjustable rear. **Features:** Recoil compensator, ball detent cylinder latch, internal lock. 6.5"-barrel model has orange-ramp dovetail Millett front sight, adjustable black rear sight, Hogue Dual Density Monogrip, .312" chrome trigger with over-travel stop, chrome tear-drop hammer, glassbead finish. 10.5"-barrel model has red ramp front sight, adjustable rear sight, .312 chrome trigger with overtravel stop, chrome tear drop hammer with pinned sear, hunting sling. Compensated Hunter has .400 orange ramp dovetail front sight, adjustable black blade rear sight, Hogue Dual Density Monogrip, glassbead finish w/black clear coat. Made in U.S.A. by Smith & Wesson.
Price: From **$1,319.00**

Taurus Model 17 Tracker

Taurus Model 66

Taurus Model 44

Taurus Model 65

Taurus Model 82

Taurus Model 85

Taurus Model 94

Taurus Judge

Taurus Model 444 Raging Bull

TAURUS MODEL 17 "TRACKER"
Caliber: 17 HMR, 7-shot. **Barrel:** 6.5". **Weight:** 45.8 oz. **Grips:** Rubber. **Sights:** Adjustable. **Features:** Double action, matte stainless, integral key-lock.
Price: From **$390.00**

TAURUS MODEL 44 REVOLVER
Caliber: 44 Mag., 6-shot. **Barrel:** 4", 6.5", 8-3/8". **Weight:** 44-3/4 oz. **Grips:** Rubber. **Sights:** Adjustable. **Features:** Double-action. Integral key-lock. Introduced 1994. New Model 44S12 has 12" vent rib barrel. Imported from Brazil by Taurus International Manufacturing, Inc.
Price: From....................................... **$617.00**

TAURUS MODEL 65 REVOLVER
Caliber: 357 Mag., 6-shot. **Barrel:** 4". **Weight:** 38 oz. **Length:** 10.5" overall. **Grips:** Soft rubber. **Sights:** Fixed. **Features:** Double action, integral key-lock. Seven models for 2006 Imported by Taurus International.
Price: From **$419.00**

Taurus Model 66 Revolver
Similar to Model 65, 4" or 6" barrel, 7-shot cylinder, adjustable rear sight. Integral key-lock action. Imported by Taurus International.
Price: From **$469.00**

TAURUS MODEL 82 HEAVY BARREL REVOLVER
Caliber: 38 Spec., 6-shot. **Barrel:** 4", heavy. **Weight:** 36.5 oz. **Length:** 9-1/4" overall (4" bbl.). **Grips:** Soft black rubber. **Sights:** Serrated ramp front, square notch rear. **Features:** Double action, solid rib, integral key-lock. Imported by Taurus International.
Price: From **$403.00**

TAURUS MODEL 85 REVOLVER
Caliber: 38 Spec., 5-shot. **Barrel:** 2". **Weight:** 17-24.5 oz., titanium 13.5-15.4 oz. **Grips:** Rubber, rosewood or mother-of-pearl. **Sights:** Ramp front, square notch rear. **Features:** Blue, matte stainless, blue with gold accents, stainless with gold accents; rated for +P ammo. Integral keylock. Some models have titantium frame. Introduced 1980. Imported by Taurus International.
Price: From **$403.00**

TAURUS MODEL 94 REVOLVER
Caliber: 22 LR, 9-shot cylinder; 22 Mag, 8-shot cylinder **Barrel:** 2", 4", 5". **Weight:** 18.5-27.5 oz. **Grips:** Soft black rubber. **Sights:** Serrated ramp front, click-adjustable rear. **Features:** Double action, integral key-lock. Introduced 1989. Imported by Taurus International.
Price: From **$369.00**

TAURUS MODEL 4510 JUDGE
Caliber: 3" .410/45 LC, 2.5" .410/45 LC. **Barrel:** 3". **Weight:** 35.2 oz., 22.4 oz. **Length:** 7.5". **Grips:** Ribber. **Sights:** Fiber Optic. **Features:** DA/SA. Matte Stainless and Ultra-Lite Stainless finish. Introduced in 2007. Imported from Brazil by Taurus International.
Price: 4510T TRACKERSS Matte Stainless **$569.00**
Price: 4510TKR-3B Judge **$519.00**

TAURUS RAGING BULL MODEL 416
Caliber: 41 Magnum, 6-shot. **Barrel:** 6.5". **Weight:** 61.9 oz. **Grips:** Rubber. **Sights:** Adjustable. **Features:** Double-action, ported, ventilated rib, matte stainless, integral key-lock.
Price: **$706.00**

TAURUS MODEL 425 TRACKER REVOLVERS
Caliber: 357 Mag., 7-shot; 41 Mag., 5-shot. **Barrel:** 4" and 6". **Weight:** 28.8-40 oz. (titanium) 24.3-28. (6"). **Grips:** Rubber. **Sights:** Fixed front, adjustable rear. **Features:** Double-action stainless steel, Shadow Gray or Total Titanium; vent rib (steel models only); integral key-lock action. Imported by Taurus International.
Price: From....................................... **$569.00**

TAURUS MODEL 444 ULTRALIGHT
Caliber: 44 Mag, 5-shot. **Barrel:** 4". **Weight:** 28.3 oz. **Length:** 9.8"overall. **Grips:** Cushioned inset rubber. **Sights:** Fixed red-fiber optic front, adjustable rear. **Features:** UltraLite titanium blue finish, titanium/alloy frame built on Raging Bull design. Smooth trigger shoe, 1.760" wide, 6.280" tall. Barrel rate of twist 1:16", 6 grooves. Introduced 2005. Imported by Taurus International.
Price: **$681.00**

TAURUS MODEL 444/454/480 RAGING BULL REVOLVERS
Caliber: 44 Mag., 45 LC, 454 Casull, 480 Ruger, 5-shot. **Barrel:** 5", 6.5", 8-3/8". **Weight:** 53-63 oz. **Length:** 12" overall (6.5" barrel). **Grips:** Soft black rubber. **Sights:** Patridge front, adjustable rear. **Features:** Double-action, ventilated rib, ported, integral key-lock. Introduced 1997. Imported by Taurus International.
Price: From **$641.00**

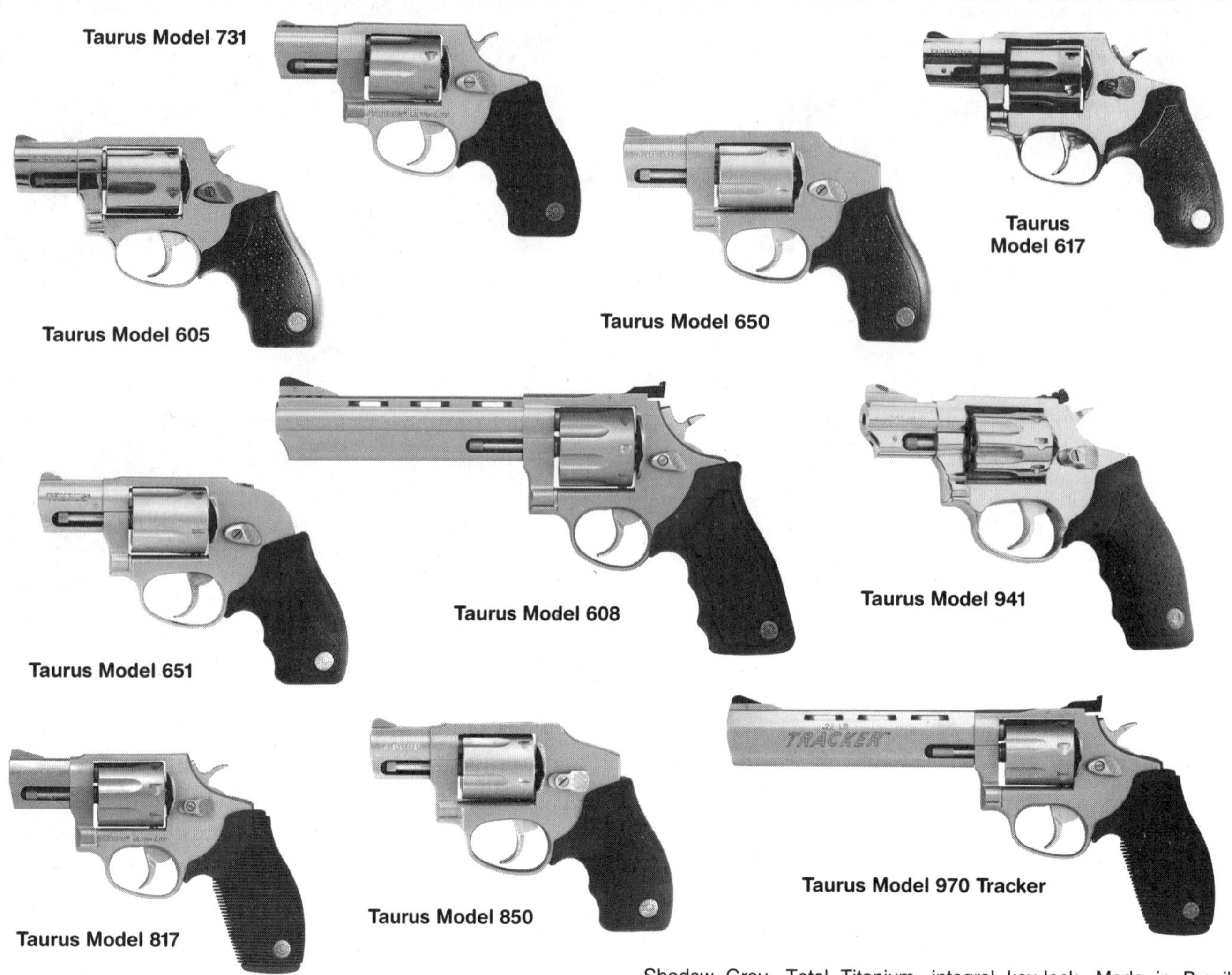

Taurus Model 731

Taurus Model 605

Taurus Model 650

Taurus Model 617

Taurus Model 608

Taurus Model 941

Taurus Model 651

Taurus Model 817

Taurus Model 850

Taurus Model 970 Tracker

TAURUS MODEL 605 REVOLVER

Caliber: 357 Mag., 5-shot. **Barrel:** 2". **Weight:** 24 oz. **Grips:** Rubber. **Sights:** Fixed. **Features:** Double-action, blue or stainless or titanium, concealed hammer models DAO, porting optional, integral key-lock. Introduced 1995. Imported by Taurus International.

Price: From **$403.00**

TAURUS MODEL 608 REVOLVER

Caliber: 357 Mag. 38 Spec., 8-shot. **Barrel:** 4", 6.5", 8-3/8". **Weight:** 44-57 oz. **Length:** 9-3/8" overall. **Grips:** Soft black rubber. **Sights:** Adjustable. **Features:** Double-action, integral key-lock action. Available in blue or stainless. Introduced 1995. Imported by Taurus International.

Price: From.. **$584.00**

TAURUS MODEL 617 REVOLVER

Caliber: 357 Mag., 7-shot. **Barrel:** 2". **Weight:** 28.3 oz. **Length:** 6.75" overall. **Grips:** Soft black rubber. **Sights:** Fixed. **Features:** Double-action, blue, Shadow Gray, bright spectrum blue or matte stainless steel, integral key-lock. Available with porting, concealed hammer. Introduced 1998. Imported by Taurus International.

Price: **$436.00**

TAURUS MODEL 650CIA REVOLVER

Caliber: 357 Mag., 5-shot. **Barrel:** 2". **Weight:** 24.5 oz. **Grips:** Rubber. **Sights:** Ramp front, square notch rear. **Features:** Double-action only, blue or matte stainless steel, integral key-lock, internal hammer. Introduced 2001. From Taurus International.

Price: From **$411.00**

TAURUS MODEL 651 PROTECTOR REVOLVER

Caliber: 357 Mag., 5-shot. **Barrel:** 2". **Weight:** 17-24.5 oz. **Grips:** Rubber. **Sights:** Fixed. **Features:** Concealed single-action/double-action design. Shrouded cockable hammer, blue, matte stainless, Shadow Gray, Total Titanium, integral key-lock. Made in Brazil. Imported by Taurus International Manufacturing, Inc.

Price: From **$411.00**

Taurus Model 731 Revolver

Similar to the Taurus Model 605, except in .32 Magnum.

Price: **$469.00**

TAURUS MODEL 817 ULTRA-LITE REVOLVER

Caliber: 38 Spec., 7-shot. **Barrel:** 2". **Weight:** 21 oz. **Length:** 6.5" overall. **Grips:** Soft rubber. **Sights:** Fixed. **Features:** Double-action, integral key-lock. Rated for +P ammo. Introduced 1999. Imported from Brazil by Taurus International.

Price: From **$436.00**

TAURUS MODEL 850 CIA REVOLVER

Caliber: 38 Spec., 5-shot. **Barrel:** 2". **Weight:** 17-24.5 oz. **Grips:** Rubber, mother-of-pearl. **Sights:** Ramp front, square notch rear. **Features:** Double-action only, blue or matte stainless steel, rated for +P ammo, integral key-lock, internal hammer. Introduced 2001. From Taurus International.

Price: From **$398.00**

TAURUS MODEL 941 REVOLVER

Caliber: 22 LR (Mod. 94), 22 WMR (Mod. 941), 8-shot. **Barrel:** 2", 4", 5". **Weight:** 27.5 oz. (4" barrel). **Grips:** Soft black rubber. **Sights:** Serrated ramp front, rear adjustable. **Features:** Double-action, integral key-lock. Introduced 1992. Imported by Taurus International.

Price: From **$386.00**

TAURUS MODEL 970/971 TRACKER REVOLVERS

Caliber: 22 LR (Model 970), 22 Magnum (Model 971); 7-shot. **Barrel:** 6". **Weight:** 53.6 oz. **Grips:** Rubber. **Sights:** Adjustable. **Features:** Double barrel, heavy barrel with ventilated rib; matte stainless finish, integral key-lock. Introduced 2001. From Taurus International.

Price: From **$453.00**

Both classic six-shooters and modern adaptations for hunting and sport.

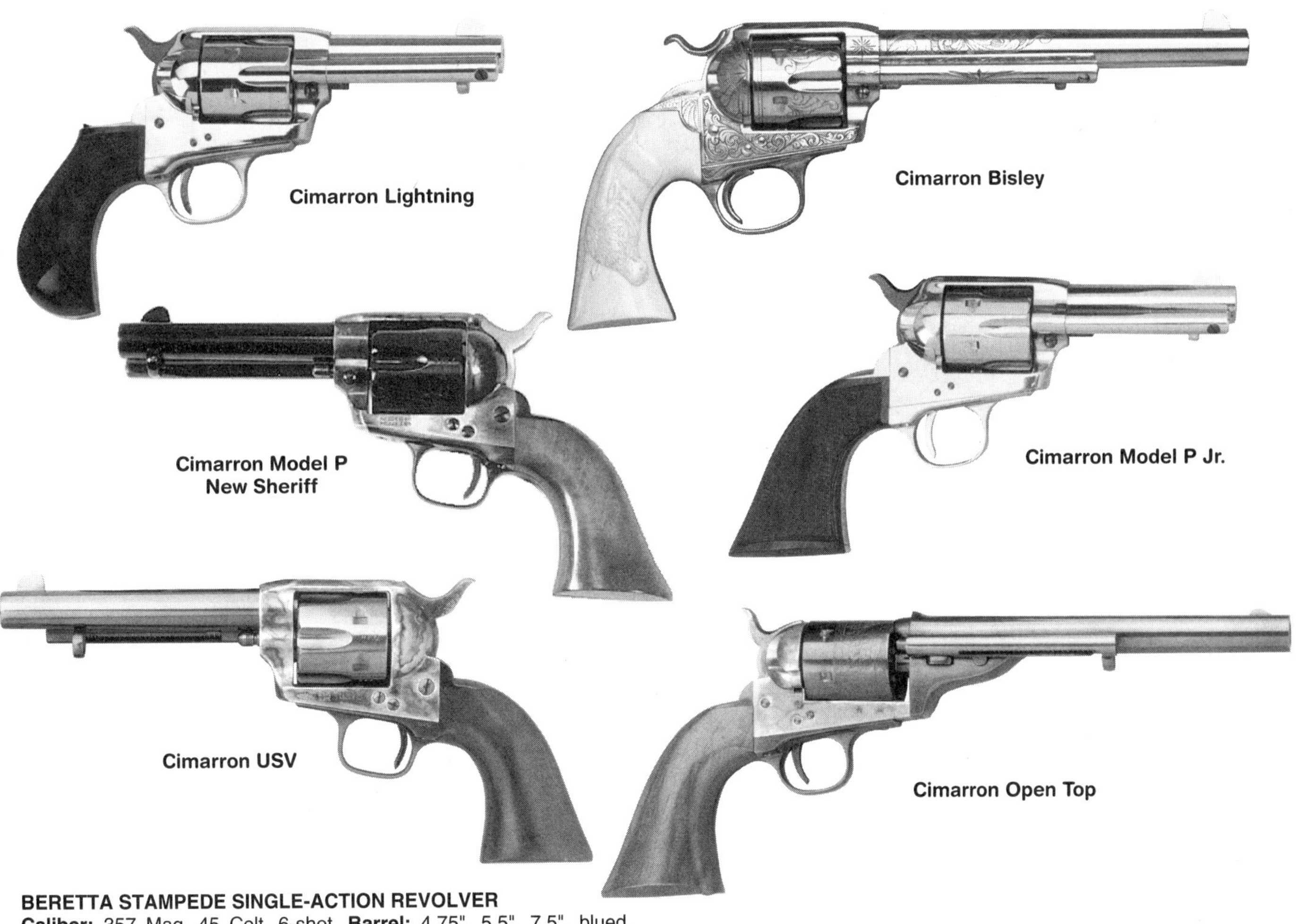

Cimarron Lightning

Cimarron Bisley

Cimarron Model P New Sheriff

Cimarron Model P Jr.

Cimarron USV

Cimarron Open Top

BERETTA STAMPEDE SINGLE-ACTION REVOLVER

Caliber: 357 Mag, 45 Colt, 6-shot. **Barrel:** 4.75", 5.5", 7.5", blued. **Weight:** 36.8 oz. (4.75" barrel). **Length:** 9.5" overall (4.75" barrel). **Grips:** Wood, walnut, black polymer. **Sights:** Blade front, notch rear. **Features:** Transfer-bar safety. Introduced 2003. Stampede Inox (2004) is stainless steel with black polymer grips. Compact Stampede Marshall (2004) has birdshead-style walnut grips, 3.5" barrel, color-case-hardened frame, blued barrel and cylinder. Manufactured for Beretta by Uberti.

Price: Blued, color-case-hardened frame **$600.00**
Price: Old West, wood grips **$675.00**
Price: Old West Marshall, birds-head wood grips. **$700.00**
Price: Inox. **$750.00**

CIMARRON LIGHTNING SA

Caliber: 22 LR, 32-20, 32 H&R, 38 Colt, **Barrel:** 3.5", 4.75", 5.5". **Grips:** Smooth or checkered walnut. **Sights:** Blade front. **Features:** Replica of the Colt 1877 Lightning DA. Similar to Cimarron Thunderer, except smaller grip frame to fit smaller hands. Standard blue, charcoal blue or nickel finish with forged, old model, or color case hardened frame. Introduced 2001. From Cimarron F.A. Co.

Price: From **$441.00**

CIMARRON MODEL P

Caliber: 32 WCF, 38 WCF, 357 Mag., 44 WCF, 44 Spec., 45 Colt, 45 LC and 45 ACP. **Barrel:** 4.75", 5.5", 7.5". **Weight:** 39 oz. **Length:** 10" overall (4" barrel). **Grips:** Walnut. **Sights:** Blade front, fixed or adjustable rear. **Features:** Uses "old model" black powder frame with "Bullseye" ejector or New Model frame. Imported by Cimarron F.A. Co.

Price: from **$480.00**
Price: Laser Engraved, from **$879.00**
Price: New Sheriff, from **$480.00**

Cimarron Bisley Model Single-Action Revolvers

Similar to 1873 Model P, special grip frame and trigger guard, knurled wide-spur hammer, curved trigger. Available in 357 Mag., 44 WCF, 44 Spl., 45 Colt. Introduced 1999. Imported by Cimarron F.A. Co.

Price: From **$519.00**

CIMARRON MODEL "P" JR.

Caliber: 32-20, 32 H&R, **Barrel:** 3.5", 4.75", 5.5". **Grips:** Checkered walnut. **Sights:** Blade front. **Features:** Styled after 1873 Colt Peacemaker, except 20 percent smaller. Blue finish with color case-hardened frame; Cowboy action. Introduced 2001. From Cimarron F.A. Co.

Price: **$397.00**

CIMARRON U. S. VOLUNTEER ARTILLERY MODEL SINGLE-ACTION

Caliber: 45 Colt. **Barrel:** 5.5". **Weight:** 39 oz. **Length:** 11.5" overall. **Grips:** Walnut. **Sights:** Fixed. **Features:** U.S. markings and cartouche, case-hardened frame and hammer; 45 Colt only. Imported by Cimarron F.A. Co.

Price: **$519.00**

CIMARRON 1872 OPEN TOP REVOLVER

Caliber: 38, 44 Special, 44 Colt, 44 Russian, 45 LC, 45 S&W Schofield. **Barrel:** 5.5" and 7.5". **Grips:** Walnut. **Sights:** Blade front, fixed rear. **Features:** Replica of first cartridge-firing revolver. Blue, charcoal blue, nickel or Original finish; Navy-style brass or steel Army-style frame. Introduced 2001 by Cimarron F.A. Co.

Price: **$480.00**

CIMARRON THUNDERER REVOLVER

Caliber: 357 Mag., 44 WCF, 45 Colt, 6-shot. **Barrel:** 3.5", 4.75", with ejector. **Weight:** 38 oz. (3.5" barrel). **Grips:** Smooth or checkered walnut. **Sights:** Blade front, notch rear. **Features:** Thunderer grip. Introduced 1993. Imported by Cimarron F.A. Co.

Price: Stainless. **$629.00**

Cimarron Thunderer

Colt Single-Action Army

EAA Bounty Hunter

EMF 1875 Outlaw

EMF 1890 Police

COLT SINGLE-ACTION ARMY REVOLVER

Caliber: 357 Mag., 38 Spec., .32/20, 44-40, 45 Colt, 6-shot. **Barrel:** 4.75", 5.5", 7.5". **Weight:** 40 oz. (4.75" barrel). **Length:** 10.25" overall (4.75" barrel). **Grips:** Black Eagle composite. **Sights:** Blade front, notch rear. **Features:** Available in full nickel finish with nickel grip medallions, or Royal Blue with color case-hardened frame. Reintroduced 1992. Sheriff's Model and Frontier Six introduced 2008.

Price: P1540, 32-20, 4.75" barrel, color case-hardened/blued finish **$1,290.00**
Price: P1656, 357 Mag., 5.5" barrel, nickel finish **$1,490.00**
Price: P1876, 45 LC, 7.5" barrel, nickel finish **$1,490.00**
Price: P2830S SAA Sheriff's, 3" barrel, 45 LC (2008) **$1,290.00**
Price: P2950FSS Frontier Six Shooter, 5.5" barrel, 44-40 (2008) **$1,350.00**

EAA BOUNTY HUNTER SA REVOLVERS

Caliber: 22 LR/22 WMR, 357 Mag., 44 Mag., 45 Colt, 6-shot. **Barrel:** 4.5", 7.5". **Weight:** 2.5 lbs. Length: 11" overall (4-5/8" barrel). **Grips:** Smooth walnut. **Sights:** Blade front, grooved topstrap rear. **Features:** Transfer bar safety; 3-position hammer; hammer forged barrel. Introduced 1992. Imported by European American Armory.

Price: Blue or case-hardened, from **$420.00**
Price: Nickel **$440.00**
Price: 22 LR/22 WMR, blue **$305.00**
Price: As above, nickel **$335.00**

EMF MODEL 1873 FRONTIER MARSHAL

Caliber: 357 Mag., 45 Colt. **Barrel:** 4.75", 5-1/2", 7.5". **Weight:** 39 oz. **Length:** 10.5" overall. **Grips:** One-piece walnut. **Sights:** Blade front, notch rear. Features: Bright brass trigger guard and backstrap, color case-hardened frame, blued barrel and cylinder. Introduced 1998. Imported from Italy.

Price: **$450.00**

EMF HARTFORD SINGLE-ACTION REVOLVERS

Caliber: 357 Mag., 32-20, 38-40, 44-40, 44 Spec., 45 Colt. **Barrel:** 4.75", 5.5", 7.5". **Weight:** 45 oz. **Length:** 13" overall (7.5" barrel). **Grips:** Smooth walnut. **Sights:** Blade front, fixed rear. **Features:** Identical to the original Colts. All major parts serial numbered using original Colt-style lettering, numbering. Bullseye ejector head and color case-hardening on old model frame and hammer. Introduced 1990. Imported by E.M.F. Co.

Price: Old Model **$490.00**
Price: Cavalry or Artillery **$505.00**
Price: Nickel plated, add **$220.00**
Price: Case-hardened New Model frame **$490.00**

EMF 1893 Buntline Revolver

Similar to the Hartford single-action revolver except has 12-inch barrel; available in 45 Colt. Imported by E.M.F. Co.

Price: Case-hardened/blue **$461.00**

EMF Great Western II Express Single-Action Revolver

Same as the regular model except uses grip of the Colt Lightning revolver. Barrel lengths of 4.75". Introduced 2006. Imported by E.M.F. Co.

Price: Stainless, Ultra Ivory grips **$715.00**
Price: Walnut grips **$690.00**

EMF 1875 OUTLAW REVOLVER

Caliber: 357 Mag., 44-40, 45 Colt. **Barrel:** 7.5", 9.5". **Weight:** 46 oz. **Length:** 13.5" overall. **Grips:** Smooth walnut. **Sights:** Blade front, fixed groove rear. **Features:** Authentic copy of 1875 Remington with firing pin in hammer; color case-hardened frame, blue cylinder, barrel, steel backstrap and trigger guard. Also available in nickel, factory engraved. Imported by E.M.F. Co.

Price: All calibers **$480.00**
Price: Nickel, add **$220.00**
Price: Laser Engraved **$685.00**

EMF 1890 Police Revolver

Similar to the 1875 Outlaw except has 5.5" barrel, weighs 40 oz., with 12.5" overall length. Has lanyard ring in butt. No web under barrel. Calibers: 45 Colt. Imported by E.M.F. Co.

Price: **$450.00**
Price: Nickel **$675.00**

EMF 1873 GREAT WESTERN II

Caliber: .357, 45 LC, 44/40. **Barrel:** 4 3/4", 5.5", 7.5". **Weight:** 36 oz. **Length:** 11" (5.5"). **Grips:** Walnut. **Sights:** Blade front, notch rear. **Features:** Authentic reproduction of the original 2nd generation Colt single-action revolver. Standard and bone case hardening. Coil hammer spring. Hammer-forged barrel.

Price: 1873 Californian **$510.00**
Price: 1873 Custom series, bone or nickel, ivory-like grips . . **$690.00**
Price: 1873 Stainless steel, ivory-like grips **$715.00**

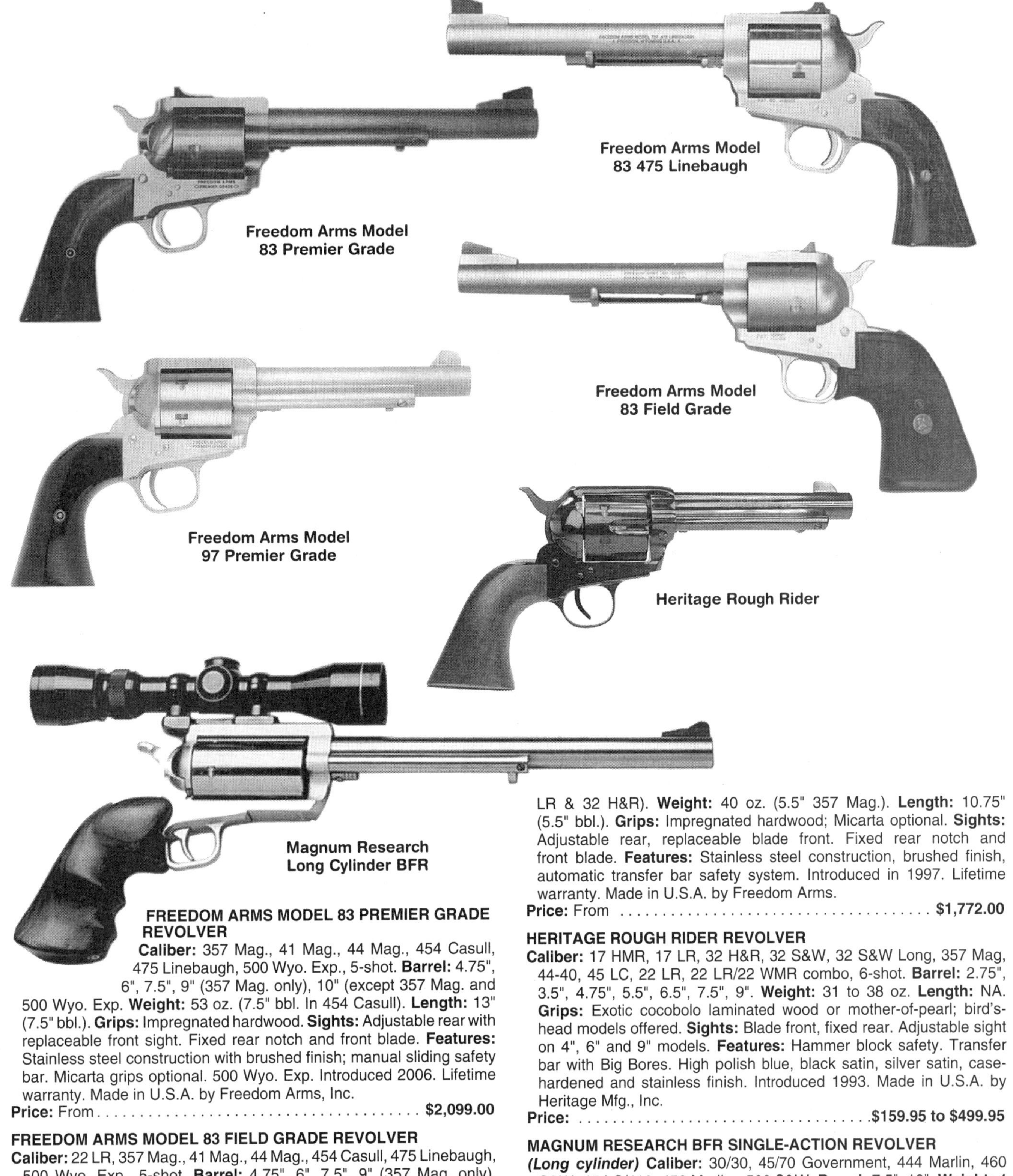

Freedom Arms Model 83 475 Linebaugh

Freedom Arms Model 83 Premier Grade

Freedom Arms Model 83 Field Grade

Freedom Arms Model 97 Premier Grade

Heritage Rough Rider

Magnum Research Long Cylinder BFR

FREEDOM ARMS MODEL 83 PREMIER GRADE REVOLVER

Caliber: 357 Mag., 41 Mag., 44 Mag., 454 Casull, 475 Linebaugh, 500 Wyo. Exp., 5-shot. **Barrel:** 4.75", 6", 7.5", 9" (357 Mag. only), 10" (except 357 Mag. and 500 Wyo. Exp. **Weight:** 53 oz. (7.5" bbl. In 454 Casull). **Length:** 13" (7.5" bbl.). **Grips:** Impregnated hardwood. **Sights:** Adjustable rear with replaceable front sight. Fixed rear notch and front blade. **Features:** Stainless steel construction with brushed finish; manual sliding safety bar. Micarta grips optional. 500 Wyo. Exp. Introduced 2006. Lifetime warranty. Made in U.S.A. by Freedom Arms, Inc.

Price: From **$2,099.00**

FREEDOM ARMS MODEL 83 FIELD GRADE REVOLVER

Caliber: 22 LR, 357 Mag., 41 Mag., 44 Mag., 454 Casull, 475 Linebaugh, 500 Wyo. Exp., 5-shot. **Barrel:** 4.75", 6", 7.5", 9" (357 Mag. only), 10" (except 357 Mag. and 500 Wyo. Exp.) **Weight:** 56 oz. (7.5" bbl. In 454 Casull). **Length:** 13.1" (7.5" bbl.). **Grips:** Pachmayr standard, impregnated hardwood or Micarta optional. **Sights:** Adjustable rear with replaceable front sight. Model 83 frame. All stainless steel. Introduced 1988. Made in U.S.A. by Freedom Arms Inc.

Price: From **$1,623.00**

FREEDOM ARMS MODEL 97 PREMIER GRADE REVOLVER

Caliber: 17 HMR, 22 LR, 32 H&R, 357 Mag., 6-shot; 41 Mag., 44 Special, 45 Colt, 5-shot. **Barrel:** 4.25", 5.5", 7.5", 10" (17 HMR, 22 LR & 32 H&R). **Weight:** 40 oz. (5.5" 357 Mag.). **Length:** 10.75" (5.5" bbl.). **Grips:** Impregnated hardwood; Micarta optional. **Sights:** Adjustable rear, replaceable blade front. Fixed rear notch and front blade. **Features:** Stainless steel construction, brushed finish, automatic transfer bar safety system. Introduced in 1997. Lifetime warranty. Made in U.S.A. by Freedom Arms.

Price: From **$1,772.00**

HERITAGE ROUGH RIDER REVOLVER

Caliber: 17 HMR, 17 LR, 32 H&R, 32 S&W, 32 S&W Long, 357 Mag, 44-40, 45 LC, 22 LR, 22 LR/22 WMR combo, 6-shot. **Barrel:** 2.75", 3.5", 4.75", 5.5", 6.5", 7.5", 9". **Weight:** 31 to 38 oz. **Length:** NA. **Grips:** Exotic cocobolo laminated wood or mother-of-pearl; bird's-head models offered. **Sights:** Blade front, fixed rear. Adjustable sight on 4", 6" and 9" models. **Features:** Hammer block safety. Transfer bar with Big Bores. High polish blue, black satin, silver satin, case-hardened and stainless finish. Introduced 1993. Made in U.S.A. by Heritage Mfg., Inc.

Price: . . . . **$159.95 to $499.95**

MAGNUM RESEARCH BFR SINGLE-ACTION REVOLVER

(Long cylinder) **Caliber:** 30/30, 45/70 Government, 444 Marlin, 460 S&W, 45 LC/410, 450 Marlin, .500 S&W. **Barrel:** 7.5", 10". **Weight:** 4 lbs., 4.36 lbs. **Length:** 15", 17.5".

(Short cylinder) **Caliber:** 50 AE, 454 Casull, 22 Hornet, BFR 480/475. **Barrel:** 6.5", 7.5", 10". **Weight:** 3.2 lbs, 3.5 lbs., 4.36 lbs. (10"). **Length:** 12.75 (6"), 13.75", 16.25".

Sights: All have fully adjustable rear, black blade ramp front. **Features:** Stainless steel construction, rubber grips, all 5-shot capacity. Barrels are stress-relieved and cut rifled. Made in U.S.A. From Magnum Research, Inc.

Price: From **$899.00**

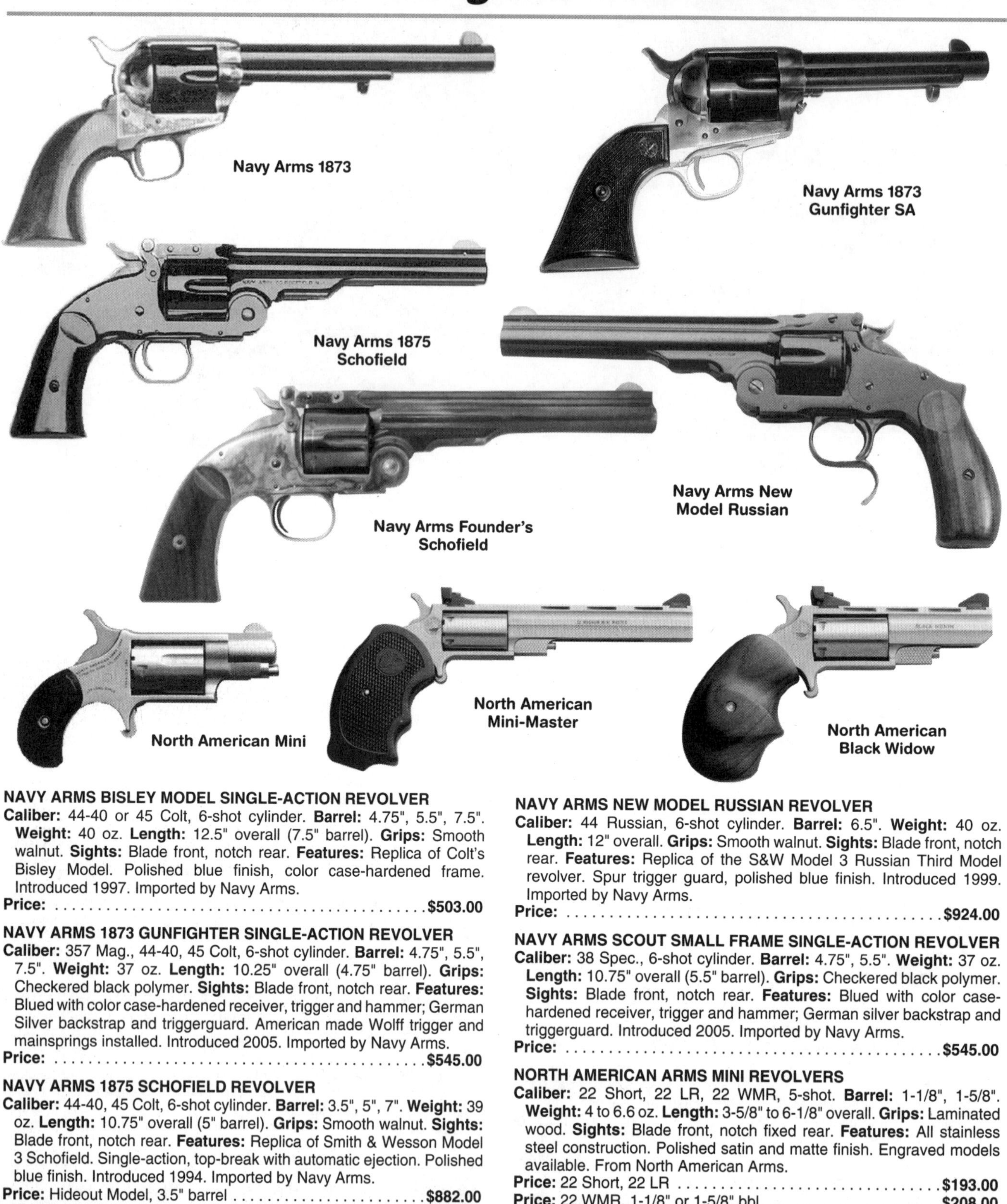

Navy Arms 1873

Navy Arms 1873 Gunfighter SA

Navy Arms 1875 Schofield

Navy Arms New Model Russian

Navy Arms Founder's Schofield

North American Mini

North American Mini-Master

North American Black Widow

NAVY ARMS BISLEY MODEL SINGLE-ACTION REVOLVER

Caliber: 44-40 or 45 Colt, 6-shot cylinder. **Barrel:** 4.75", 5.5", 7.5". **Weight:** 40 oz. **Length:** 12.5" overall (7.5" barrel). **Grips:** Smooth walnut. **Sights:** Blade front, notch rear. **Features:** Replica of Colt's Bisley Model. Polished blue finish, color case-hardened frame. Introduced 1997. Imported by Navy Arms.

Price: **$503.00**

NAVY ARMS 1873 GUNFIGHTER SINGLE-ACTION REVOLVER

Caliber: 357 Mag., 44-40, 45 Colt, 6-shot cylinder. **Barrel:** 4.75", 5.5", 7.5". **Weight:** 37 oz. **Length:** 10.25" overall (4.75" barrel). **Grips:** Checkered black polymer. **Sights:** Blade front, notch rear. **Features:** Blued with color case-hardened receiver, trigger and hammer; German Silver backstrap and triggerguard. American made Wolff trigger and mainsprings installed. Introduced 2005. Imported by Navy Arms.

Price: **$545.00**

NAVY ARMS 1875 SCHOFIELD REVOLVER

Caliber: 44-40, 45 Colt, 6-shot cylinder. **Barrel:** 3.5", 5", 7". **Weight:** 39 oz. **Length:** 10.75" overall (5" barrel). **Grips:** Smooth walnut. **Sights:** Blade front, notch rear. **Features:** Replica of Smith & Wesson Model 3 Schofield. Single-action, top-break with automatic ejection. Polished blue finish. Introduced 1994. Imported by Navy Arms.

Price: Hideout Model, 3.5" barrel **$882.00**
Price: Wells Fargo, 5" barrel **$882.00**
Price: U.S. Cavalry model, 7" barrel, military markings **$882.00**

NAVY ARMS FOUNDER'S MODEL SCHOFIELD REVOLVER

Caliber: 45 Colt, 38 Spl., 6-shot cylinder. **Barrel:** 7.5". **Weight:** 41 oz. **Length:** 13.75". **Grips:** Deluxe hand-rubbed walnut with cartouching. **Sights:** Blade front, notch rear. **Features:** Charcoal blued with bone color case-hardened receiver, trigger, hammer and backstrap. Limited production "VF" serial number prefix. Introduced 2005. Imported by Navy Arms.

Price: **$924.00**

NAVY ARMS NEW MODEL RUSSIAN REVOLVER

Caliber: 44 Russian, 6-shot cylinder. **Barrel:** 6.5". **Weight:** 40 oz. **Length:** 12" overall. **Grips:** Smooth walnut. **Sights:** Blade front, notch rear. **Features:** Replica of the S&W Model 3 Russian Third Model revolver. Spur trigger guard, polished blue finish. Introduced 1999. Imported by Navy Arms.

Price: **$924.00**

NAVY ARMS SCOUT SMALL FRAME SINGLE-ACTION REVOLVER

Caliber: 38 Spec., 6-shot cylinder. **Barrel:** 4.75", 5.5". **Weight:** 37 oz. **Length:** 10.75" overall (5.5" barrel). **Grips:** Checkered black polymer. **Sights:** Blade front, notch rear. **Features:** Blued with color case-hardened receiver, trigger and hammer; German silver backstrap and triggerguard. Introduced 2005. Imported by Navy Arms.

Price: **$545.00**

NORTH AMERICAN ARMS MINI REVOLVERS

Caliber: 22 Short, 22 LR, 22 WMR, 5-shot. **Barrel:** 1-1/8", 1-5/8". **Weight:** 4 to 6.6 oz. **Length:** 3-5/8" to 6-1/8" overall. **Grips:** Laminated wood. **Sights:** Blade front, notch fixed rear. **Features:** All stainless steel construction. Polished satin and matte finish. Engraved models available. From North American Arms.

Price: 22 Short, 22 LR **$193.00**
Price: 22 WMR, 1-1/8" or 1-5/8" bbl. **$208.00**
Price: 22 WMR, 1-1/8" or 1-5/8" bbl. with extra 22 LR cylinder **$236.00**

NORTH AMERICAN ARMS MINI-MASTER

Caliber: 22 LR, 22 WMR, 5-shot cylinder. **Barrel:** 4". **Weight:** 10.7 oz. **Length:** 7.75" overall. **Grips:** Checkered hard black rubber. **Sights:** Blade front, white outline rear adjustable for elevation, or fixed. **Features:** Heavy vented barrel; full-size grips. Non-fluted cylinder. Introduced 1989.

Price: Fixed sight **$272.00**
Price: Adjustable sight **$301.00**
Price: Adjustable sight, with extra WMR/LR cylinder **$330.00**

Ruger New Model Blackhawk 50th Anniversary

Ruger Bisley Single-Action

Ruge Super Blackhawk Hunter

Ruger New Model Blackhawk

Ruger New Vaquero

Ruger New Bearcat

North American Arms Black Widow Revolver

Similar to Mini-Master, 2" heavy vent barrel. Built on 22 WMR frame. Non-fluted cylinder, black rubber grips. Available with Millett Low Profile fixed sights or Millett sight adjustable for elevation only. Overall length 5-7/8", weighs 8.8 oz. From North American Arms.

Price: Adjustable sight, 22 LR or 22 WMR **$287.00**
Price: As above with extra WMR/LR cylinder **$316.00**
Price: Fixed sight, 22 LR or 22 WMR **$258.00**
Price: As above with extra WMR/LR cylinder **$287.00**

RUGER NEW MODEL SINGLE SIX & NEW MODEL .32 H&R SINGLE SIX REVOLVERS

Caliber: 17 HMR, 22 LR, 22 Mag. **Barrel:** 4-5/8", 5.5", 6.5", 7.5", 9.5". 6-shot. **Grips:** Rosewood, black laminate. **Sights:** Adjustable or fixed. **Features:** Blued or stainless metalwork, short grips available, convertible models available. Introduced 2003 in 17 HMR .

Price: 17 HMR (blued) **$503.00**
Price: 22 LR/22 Mag., from **$492.00**

RUGER NEW MODEL BLACKHAWK/BLACKHAWK CONVERTIBLE

Caliber: 30 Carbine, 357 Mag./38 Spec., 41 Mag., 45 Colt, 6-shot. **Barrel:** 4-5/8", 5.5", 6.5", 7.5" (30 carbine and 45 Colt). **Weight:** 36 to 45 oz. Lengths: 10-3/8" to 13.5". **Grips:** Rosewood or black checkered. **Sights:** 1/8" ramp front, micro-click rear adjustable for windage and elevation. **Features:** Rosewood grips, Ruger transfer bar safety system, independent firing pin, hardened chrome-moly steel frame, music wire springs through-out. Case and lock included. Convertibles come with extra cylinder.

Price: 30 Carbine, 7.5" (BN31, blued) **$525.00**
Price: 357 Mag. (blued or satin stainless), from **$525.00**
Price: 41 Mag. (blued) **$525.00**
Price: 45 Colt (blued or satin stainless), from **$525.00**
Price: 357 Mag./9mm Para. Convertible (BN34X, BN36X) . . . **$599.00**
Price: 45 Colt/45 ACP Convertible (BN44X, BN455X) **$599.00**
Price: 50th Anniversary 44 Mag match set **$1,350.00**

Ruger Bisley Single-Action Revolver

Similar to standard Blackhawk, hammer is lower with smoothly curved, deeply checkered wide spur. The trigger is strongly curved with wide smooth surface. Longer grip frame. Adjustable rear sight, ramp-style front. Unfluted cylinder and roll engraving, adjustable sights. Chambered for 44 Mag. and 45 Colt; 7.5" barrel; overall length 13.5"; weighs 48-51 oz. Plastic lockable case. Orig. fluted cylinder introduced 1985; discontinued 1991. Unfluted cylinder introduced 1986.

Price: RB-44W (44 Mag), RB45W (45 Colt) **$663.00**

RUGER NEW MODEL SUPER BLACKHAWK

Caliber: 44 Mag., 6-shot. Also fires 44 Spec. **Barrel:** 4-5/8", 5.5", 7.5", 10.5" bull. **Weight:** 45-55 oz. **Length:** 10.5" to 16.5" overall. **Grips:** Rosewood. **Sights:** 1/8" ramp front, micro-click rear adjustable for windage and elevation. **Features:** Ruger transfer bar safety system, fluted or unfluted cylinder, steel grip and cylinder frame, round or square back trigger guard, wide serrated trigger, wide spur hammer. With case and lock.

Price: Blue, 4-5/8", 5.5", 7.5" (S458N, S45N, S47N) **$631.00**
Price: Blue, 10.5" bull barrel (S411N) **$642.00**
Price: Stainless, 4-5/8", 5.5", 7.5" (KS458N, KS45N, KS47N) **$647.00**
Price: Stainless, 10.5" bull barrel (KS411N) **$674.00**

RUGER NEW MODEL SUPER BLACKHAWK HUNTER

Caliber: 44 Mag., 6-shot. **Barrel:** 7.5", full-length solid rib, unfluted cylinder. **Weight:** 52 oz. **Length:** 13-5/8". **Grips:** Black laminated wood. **Sights:** Adjustable rear, replaceable front blade. **Features:** Reintroduced Ultimate SA revolver. Includes instruction manual, high-impact case, set 1" medium scope rings, gun lock, ejector rod as standard.

Price: Hunter model, satin stainless, 7.5" (KS47NHNN) **$759.00**
Price: Hunter model, Bisley frame, satin stainless 7.5" (KS47NHB) **$759.00**

RUGER NEW VAQUERO SINGLE-ACTION REVOLVER

Caliber: 357 Mag., 45 Colt, 6-shot. **Barrel:** 4-5/8", 5.5", 7.5". **Weight:** 39-45 oz. **Length:** 10.5" overall (4-5/8" barrel). **Grips:** Rubber with Ruger medallion. **Sights:** Fixed blade front, fixed notch rear. **Features:** Transfer bar safety system and loading gate interlock. Blued model color case-hardened finish on frame, rest polished and blued. Engraved model available. Gloss stainless. Introduced 2005.

Price: 357 Mag., blued or stainless **$640.00**
Price: 45 Colt, blued or stainless **$640.00**

RUGER NEW BEARCAT SINGLE-ACTION

Caliber: 22 LR, 6-shot. **Barrel:** 4". **Weight:** 24 oz. **Length:** 9" overall. **Grips:** Smooth rosewood with Ruger medallion. **Sights:** Blade front, fixed notch rear. **Features:** Reintroduction of the Ruger Bearcat with slightly lengthened frame, Ruger transfer bar safety system. Available in blue only. Rosewood grips. Introduced 1996 (blued), 2003 (stainless). With case and lock.

Price: SBC4, blued **$486.00**
Price: KSBC-4, satin stainless **$524.00**
Price: SBC-4-50, blued 50th Anniversary Bearcat **$758.00**

Taurus Gaucho 357

Taurus Gaucho 45

Uberti 1873 Cattleman

Uberti Bisley

Uberti 1875 Outlaw

STI TEXICAN SINGLE-ACTION REVOLVER

Caliber: 45 Colt, 6-shot. **Barrel:** 5.5", 4140 chrome-moly steel by Green Mountain Barrels. 1:16 twist, air gauged to .0002". Chamber to bore alignment less than .001". Forcing cone angle, 3 degrees. **Weight:** 36 oz. **Length:** 11". **Grips:** "No crack" polymer. **Sights:** Blade front, fixed notch rear. **Features:** Parts made by ultra-high speed or electron discharge machined processes from chrome-moly steel forgings or bar stock. Competition sights, springs, triggers and hammers. Frames, loading gates, and hammers are color case hardened by Turnbull Restoration. Frame, back strap, loading gate, trigger guard, cylinders made of 4140 re-sulphurized Maxell 3.5 steel. Hammer firing pin (no transfer bar). S.A.S.S. approved. Introduced 2008. Made in U.S.A. by STI International.

Price: 5.5" barrel **$1,260.00**

TAURUS SINGLE-ACTION GAUCHO REVOLVERS

Caliber: 38 Spl, 357 Mag, 44-40, 45 Colt, 6-shot. **Barrel:** 4.75", 5.5", 7.5", 12". **Weight:** 36.7-37.7 oz. **Length:** 13". **Grips:** Checkered black polymer. **Sights:** Blade front, fixed notch rear. **Features:** Integral transfer bar; blue, blue with case hardened frame, matte stainless and the hand polished "Sundance" stainless finish. Removable cylinder, half-cock notch. Introduced 2005. Imported from Brazil by Taurus International.

Price: S/A-357-B, 357 Mag., Sundance blue finish, 5.5" barrel **$520.00**
Price: S/A-357-S/S7, 357 Mag., polished stainless, 7.5" barrel **$536.00**
Price: S/A-45-B **$520.00**

UBERTI 1851-1860 CONVERSION REVOLVERS

Caliber: 38 Spec., 45 Colt, 6-shot engraved cylinder. **Barrel:** 4.75", 5.5", 7.5", 8" **Weight:** 2.6 lbs. (5.5" bbl.). **Length:** 13" overall (5.5" bbl.). **Grips:** Walnut. **Features:** Brass backstrap, trigger guard; color case-hardened frame, blued barrel, cylinder. Introduced 2007. Imported from Italy by Stoeger Industries.

Price: 1851 Navy **$519.00**
Price: 1860 Army **$549.00**

UBERTI 1871-1872 OPEN TOP REVOLVERS

Caliber: 38 Spec., 45 Colt, 6-shot engraved cylinder. **Barrel:** 4.75", 5.5", 7.5". **Weight:** 2.6 lbs. (5.5" bbl.). **Length:** 13" overall (5.5" bbl.). **Grips:** Walnut. **Features:** Blued backstrap, trigger guard; color case-hardened frame, blued barrel, cylinder. Introduced 2007. Imported from Italy by Stoeger Industries.

Price: **$499.00**

UBERTI 1873 CATTLEMAN SINGLE-ACTION

Caliber: 45 Colt; 6-shot fluted cylinder. **Barrel:** 4.75", 5.5", 7.5". **Weight:** 2.3 lbs. (5.5" bbl.). **Length:** 11" overall (5.5" bbl.). **Grips:** Styles: Frisco (pearl styled); Desperado (buffalo horn styled); Chisholm (checkered walnut); Gunfighter (black checkered), Cody (ivory styled), one-piece walnut. **Sights:** Blade front, groove rear. **Features:** Steel or brass backstrap, trigger guard; color case-hardened frame, blued barrel, cylinder. NM designates New Model plunger style frame; OM designates Old Model screw cylinder pin retainer. Imported from Italy by Stoeger Industries.

Price: 1873 Cattleman Frisco **$789.00**
Price: 1873 Cattleman Desperado (2006) **$789.00**
Price: 1873 Cattleman Chisholm (2006) **$539.00**
Price: 1873 Cattleman NM, blued 4.75" barrel **$400.00**
Price: 1873 Cattleman NM, Nickel finish, 7.5" barrel **$609.00**

UBERTI 1873 CATTLEMAN BIRD'S HEAD SINGLE ACTION

Caliber: 357 Mag., 45 Colt; 6-shot fluted cylinder **Barrel:** 3.5", 4", 4.75", 5.5". **Weight:** 2.3 lbs. (5.5" bbl.). **Length:** 10.9" overall (5.5" bbl.). **Grips:** One-piece walnut. **Sights:** Blade front, groove rear. **Features:** Steel or brass backstrap, trigger guard; color case-hardened frame, blued barrel, cylinder. Imported from Italy by Stoeger Industries.

Price: 1873 Cattleman Bird's Head OM 3.5" barrel **$539.00**

UBERTI 1873 BISLEY SINGLE-ACTION REVOLVER

Caliber: 357 Mag., 45 Colt (Bisley); 22 LR and 38 Spec. (Stallion), both with 6-shot fluted cylinder. **Barrel:** 4.75", 5.5", 7.5". **Weight:** 2 to 2.5 lbs. **Length:** 12.7" overall (7.5" barrel). **Grips:** Two-piece walnut. **Sights:** Blade front, notch rear. **Features:** Replica of Colt's Bisley Model. Polished blue finish, color case-hardened frame. Introduced 1997. Imported by Stoeger Industries.

Price: 1873 Bisley, 7.5" barrel **$569.00**

UBERTI 1873 BUNTLINE AND REVOLVER CARBINE SINGLE-ACTION

Caliber: 357 Mag., 44-40, 45 Colt; 6-shot fluted cylinder **Barrel:** 18". **Length:** 22.9" to 34". **Grips:** Walnut pistol grip or rifle stock. **Sights:** Fixed or adjustable. **Features:** Imported from Italy by Stoeger Industries.

Price: 1873 Revolver Carbine, 18" barrel, 34" OAL **$729.00**
Price: 1873 Catttleman Buntline Target, 18" barrel, 22.9" OAL **$639.00**

UBERTI OUTLAW, FRONTIER, AND POLICE REVOLVERS

Caliber: 45 Colt, 6-shot fluted cylinder. **Barrel:** 5.5", 7.5". **Weight:** 2.5 to 2.8 lbs. **Length:** 10.8" to 13.6" overall. **Grips:** Two-piece smooth walnut. **Sights:** Blade front, notch rear. **Features:** Cartridge version of 1858 Remington percussion revolver. Nickel and blued finishes. Imported by Stoeger Industries.

Price: 1875 Outlaw nickel finish **$629.00**
Price: 1875 Frontier, blued finish **$539.00**
Price: 1890 Police, blued finish **$549.00**

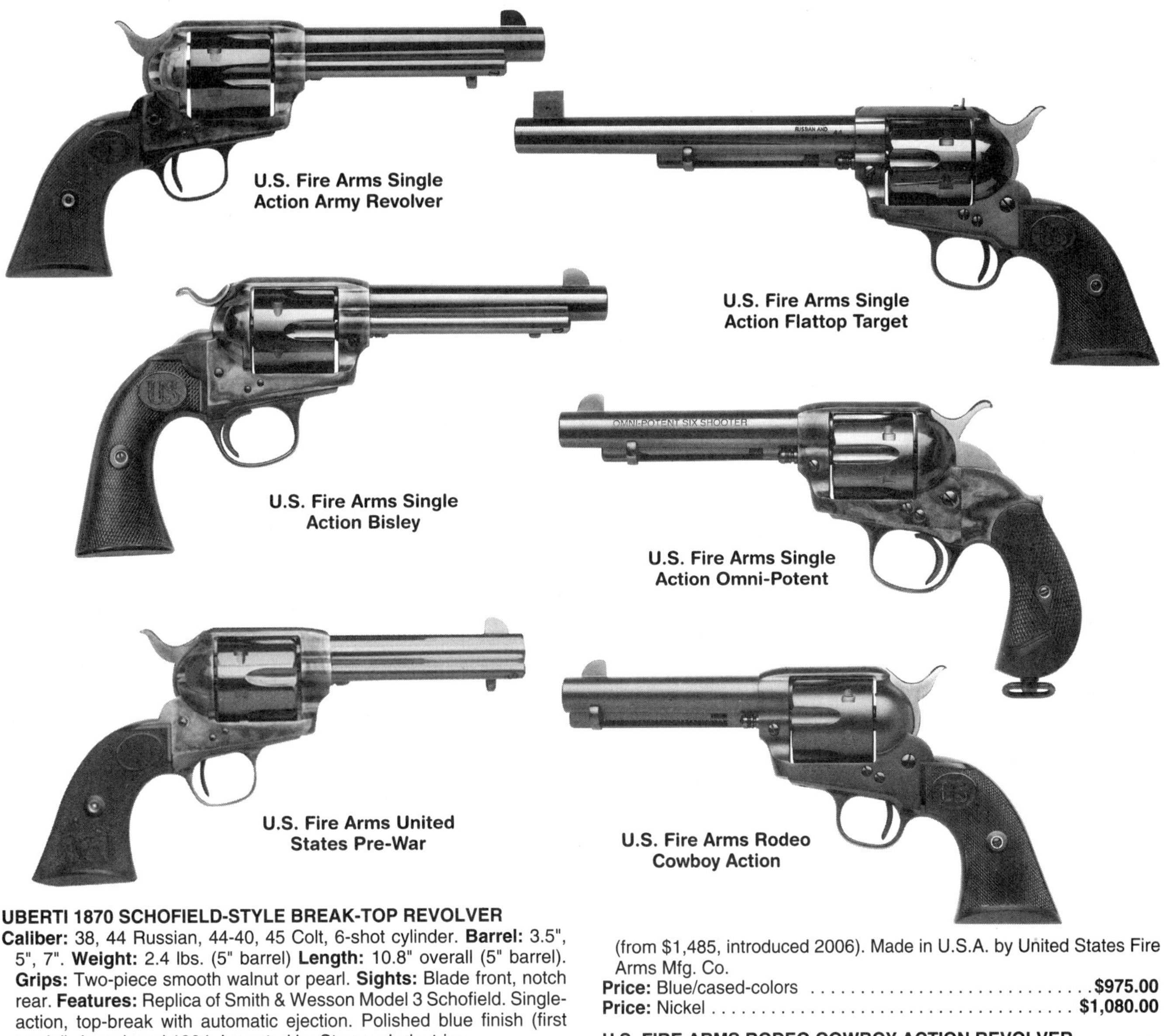

U.S. Fire Arms Single Action Army Revolver

U.S. Fire Arms Single Action Flattop Target

U.S. Fire Arms Single Action Bisley

U.S. Fire Arms Single Action Omni-Potent

U.S. Fire Arms United States Pre-War

U.S. Fire Arms Rodeo Cowboy Action

UBERTI 1870 SCHOFIELD-STYLE BREAK-TOP REVOLVER

Caliber: 38, 44 Russian, 44-40, 45 Colt, 6-shot cylinder. **Barrel:** 3.5", 5", 7". **Weight:** 2.4 lbs. (5" barrel) **Length:** 10.8" overall (5" barrel). **Grips:** Two-piece smooth walnut or pearl. **Sights:** Blade front, notch rear. **Features:** Replica of Smith & Wesson Model 3 Schofield. Single-action, top-break with automatic ejection. Polished blue finish (first model). Introduced 1994. Imported by Stoeger Industries.

Price: No. 3-2nd Model, nickel finish **$1,369.00**

U.S. FIRE ARMS SINGLE-ACTION REVOLVER

Caliber: 45 Colt (standard); 32 WCF, 38 WCF, 38 Spec., 44 WCF, 44 Special, 6-shot cylinder. **Barrel:** 4.75", 5.5", 7.5". **Weight:** 37 oz. **Length:** NA. **Grips:** Hard rubber. **Sights:** Blade front, notch rear. **Features:** Recreation of original guns; 3" and 4" have no ejector. Available with all-blue, blue with color case-hardening, or full nickel-plate finish. Other models include Government Inspector Series ($1,485, walnut grips), Custer Battlefield Gun ($1,485, 7.5" barrel), Patriot Series ($1,280, lanyard loop in 30 Carbine), Flattop Target ($1,495), Sheriff's Model ($1,085, with barrel lengths starting at 2"), Snubnose ($1,295, barrel lengths 2", 3", 4"), Omni-Potent Six-Shooter and Omni-Target Six-Shooter (from $1,485), Bisley and Bisley Target (from $1,485, introduced 2006). Made in U.S.A. by United States Fire Arms Mfg. Co.

Price: Blue/cased-colors **$975.00**

Price: Nickel **$1,080.00**

U.S. FIRE ARMS RODEO COWBOY ACTION REVOLVER

Caliber: 45 Colt, **Barrel:** 4.75", 5.5". **Grips:** Rubber. **Features:** Historically correct Armory bone case hammer, blue satin finish, transfer bar safety system, correct solid firing pin. Entry level basic cowboy SASS gun. Other models include Cowboy ($945) and Gunslinger ($1,045). 2006 version includes brown-rubber stocks.

Price: **$50.00**

U.S. FIRE ARMS U.S. PRE-WAR

Caliber: 45 Colt (standard); 32 WCF, 38 WCF, 38 Spec., 44 WCF, 44 Special. **Barrel:** 4.75", 5.5", 7.5". **Grips:** Hard rubber. **Features:** Armory bone case/Armory blue finish standard, cross-pin or black powder frame. Introduced 2002. Made in U.S.A. by United States Firearms Mfg. Co.

Price: **$1,270.00**

Specially adapted single-shot and multi-barrel arms.

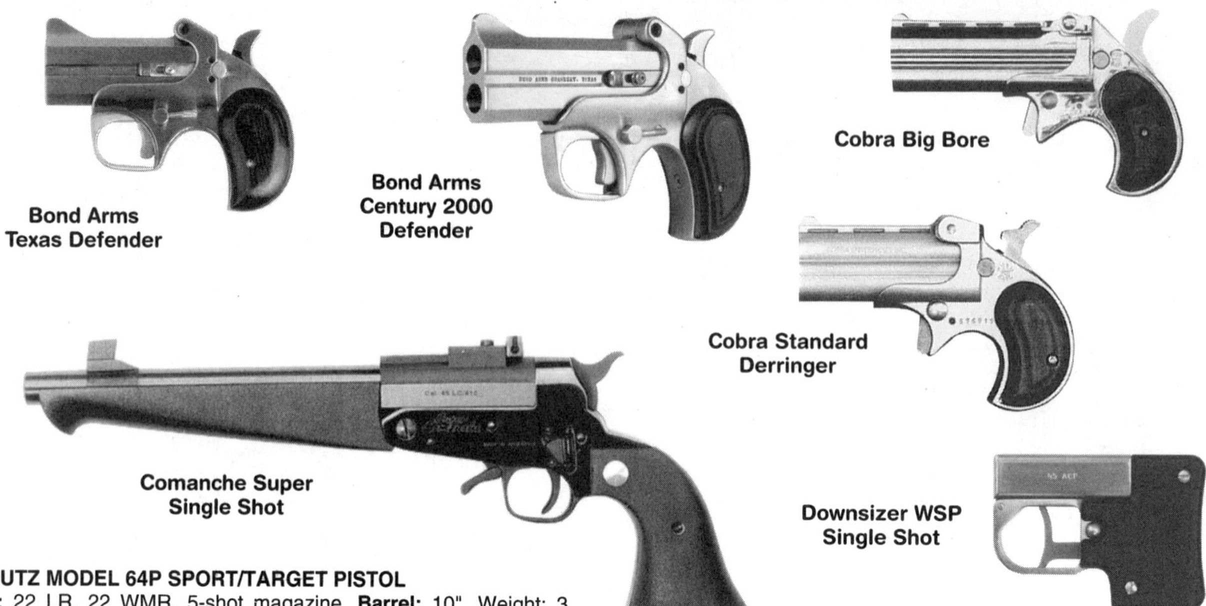
Bond Arms Texas Defender

Bond Arms Century 2000 Defender

Cobra Big Bore

Cobra Standard Derringer

Comanche Super Single Shot

Downsizer WSP Single Shot

ANSCHUTZ MODEL 64P SPORT/TARGET PISTOL
Caliber: 22 LR, 22 WMR, 5-shot magazine. **Barrel:** 10". Weight: 3 lbs. 8 oz. **Length:** 18.5" overall. Stock: Choate Rynite. **Sights:** None furnished; grooved for scope mounting. **Features:** Right-hand bolt; polished blue finish. Introduced 1998. Imported from Germany by AcuSport.
Price: 22 LR **$455.95**
Price: 22 WMR **$479.95**

BOND ARMS TEXAS DEFENDER DERRINGER
Caliber: From 22 LR to 45 LC/410 shotshells. **Barrel:** 3". **Weight:** 20 oz. **Length:** 5". **Grips:** Rosewood. **Sights:** Blade front, fixed rear. **Features:** Interchangeable barrels, stainless steel firing pins, cross-bolt safety, automatic extractor for rimmed calibers. Stainless steel construction, brushed finish. Right or left hand.
Price: **$389.00**
Price: Interchangeable barrels, 22 LR thru 45 LC, 3" **$139.00**
Price: Interchangeable barrels, 45 LC, 3.5" .... **$159.00 to $189.00**

BOND ARMS RANGER
Caliber: 45 LC/.410 shotshells. **Barrel:** 4.25". **Weight:** 23.5 oz. **Length:** 6.25". **Features:** Similar to Snake Slayer except no trigger guard. Intr. 2008. From Bond Arms.
Price: **$599.00**

BOND ARMS CENTURY 2000 DEFENDER
Caliber: 45 LC/.410 shotshells. **Barrel:** 3.5". **Weight:** 21 oz. **Length:** 5.5". **Features:** Similar to Defender series.
Price: **$404.00**

BOND ARMS COWBOY DEFENDER
Caliber: From 22 LR to 45 LC/.410 shotshells. **Barrel:** 3". **Weight:** 19 oz. **Length:** 5.5". **Features:** Similar to Defender series. No trigger guard.
Price: **$389.00**

BOND ARMS SNAKE SLAYER
Caliber: 45 LC/.410 shotshell (2.5" or 3"). **Barrel:** 3.5". **Weight:** 21 oz. **Length:** 5.5". **Grips:** Extended rosewood. **Sights:** Blade front, fixed rear. **Features:** Single-action; interchangeable barrels; stainless steel firing pin. Introduced 2005.
Price: **$455.00**

BOND ARMS SNAKE SLAYER IV
Caliber: 45 LC/410 shotshell (2.5" or 3"). **Barrel:** 4.25". **Weight:** 22 oz. **Length:** 6.25". **Grips:** Extended rosewood. **Sights:** Blade front, fixed rear. **Features:** Single-action; interchangeable barrels; stainless steel firing pin. Introduced 2006.
Price: **$485.00**

BROWN CLASSIC SINGLE-SHOT PISTOL
Caliber: 17 Ackley Hornet through 375x444. **Barrel:** 15" air-gauged match grade. Weight: About 3 lbs. 7 oz. **Grips:** Walnut; thumb rest target-style. **Sights:** None furnished; drilled and tapped for scope mounting. **Features:** Falling block action gives rigid barrel-receiver mating; hand fitted and headspaced. Introduced 1998. Made in U.S.A. by E.A. Brown Mfg.
Price: **$699.00**

CHARTER ARMS DIXIE DERRINGERS
Caliber: 22 LR, 22 WMR. **Barrel:** 1.125". **Weight:** 5-6 oz. **Length:** 4" overall. **Grips:** Black polymer **Sights:** Blade front, fixed notch rear. **Features:** Stainless finish. Introduced 2006. Made in U.S.A. by Charter Arms, distributed by MKS Supply.
Price: **$112.00**

COBRA BIG BORE DERRINGERS
Caliber: 22 WMR, 32 H&R Mag., 38 Spec., 9mm Para., 380 ACP. **Barrel:** 2.75". **Weight:** 14 oz. **Length:** 4.65" overall. **Grips:** Textured black or white synthetic or laminated rosewood. **Sights:** Blade front, fixed notch rear. **Features:** Alloy frame, steel-lined barrels, steel breech block. Plunger-type safety with integral hammer block. Black, chrome or satin finish. Introduced 2002. Made in U.S.A. by Cobra Enterprises of Utah, Inc.
Price: **$165.00**

COBRA LONG-BORE DERRINGERS
Caliber: 22 WMR, 38 Spec., 9mm Para. **Barrel:** 3.5". **Weight:** 16 oz. **Length:** 5.4" overall. **Grips:** Black or white synthetic or rosewood. **Sights:** Fixed. **Features:** Chrome, satin nickel, or black Teflon finish. Introduced 2002. Made in U.S.A. by Cobra Enterprises of Utah, Inc.
Price: **$165.00**

COBRA STANDARD SERIES DERRINGERS
Caliber: 22 LR, 22 WMR, 25 ACP, 32 ACP. **Barrel:** 2.4". **Weight:** 9.5 oz. Length: 4" overall. **Grips:** Laminated wood or pearl. **Sights:** Blade front, fixed notch rear. **Features:** Choice of black powder coat, satin nickel or chrome finish. Introduced 2002. Made in U.S.A. by Cobra Enterprises of Utah, Inc.
Price: **$145.00**

COMANCHE SUPER SINGLE-SHOT PISTOL
Caliber: 45 LC, .410 **Barrel:** 10". **Sights:** Adjustable. **Features:** Blue finish, not available for sale in CA, MA. Distributed by SGS Importers International, Inc.
Price: **$200.00**

DOWNSIZER WSP SINGLE-SHOT PISTOL
Caliber: 357 Mag., 45 ACP, **Barrel:** 2.10". **Weight:** 11 oz. **Length:** 3.25" overall. **Grips:** Black polymer. **Sights:** None. **Features:** Single shot, tip-up barrel. Double action only. Stainless steel construction. Measures .900" thick. Introduced 1997. From Downsizer Corp.
Price: **$499.00**

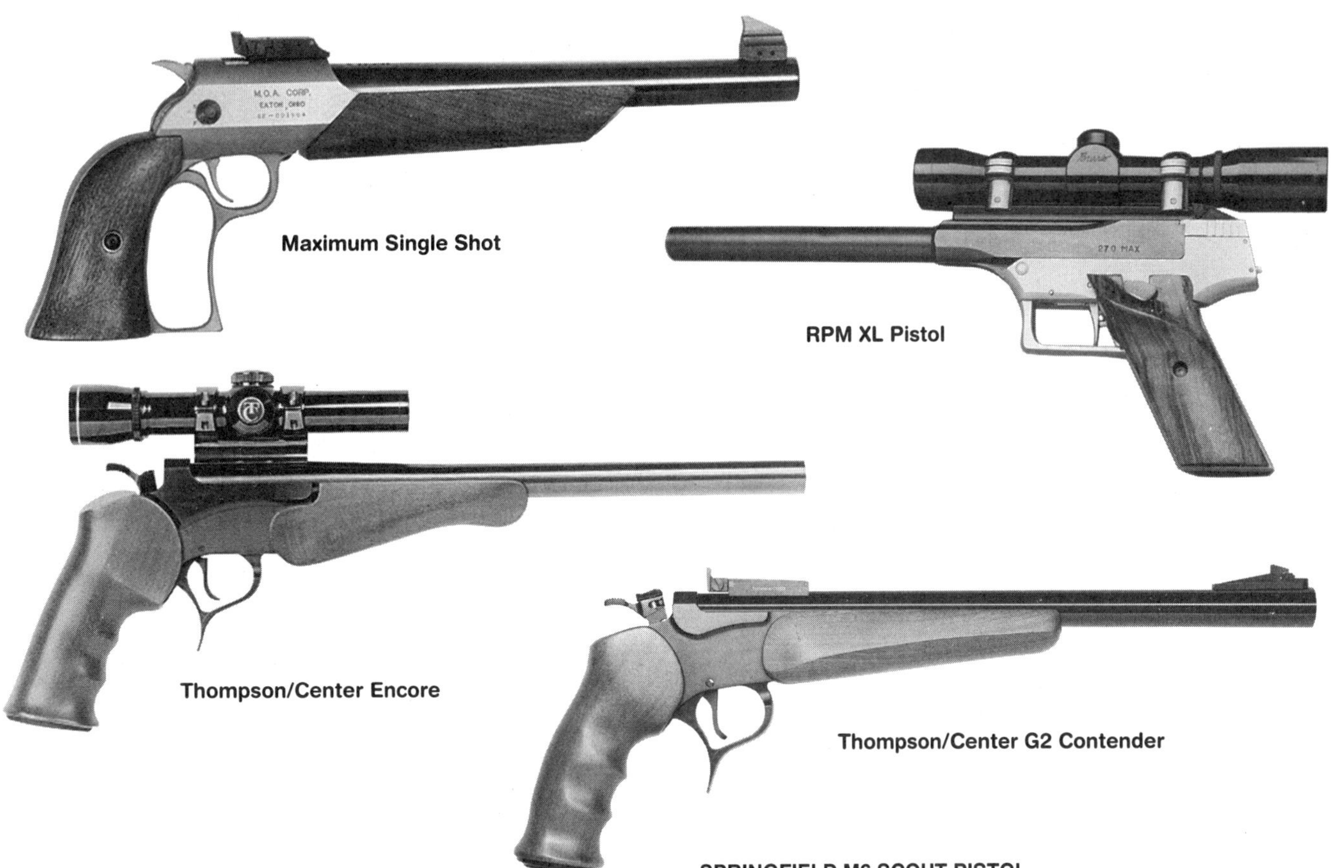

Maximum Single Shot

RPM XL Pistol

Thompson/Center Encore

Thompson/Center G2 Contender

MAXIMUM SINGLE-SHOT PISTOL

Caliber: 22 LR, 22 Hornet, 22 BR, 22 PPC, 223 Rem., 22-250, 6mm BR, 6mm PPC, 243, 250 Savage, 6.5mm-35M, 270 MAX, 270 Win., 7mm TCU, 7mm BR, 7mm-35, 7mm INT-R, 7mm-08, 7mm Rocket, 7mm Super-Mag., 30 Herrett, 30 Carbine, 30-30, 308 Win., 30x39, 32-20, 350 Rem. Mag., 357 Mag., 357 Maximum, 358 Win., 375 H&H, 44 Mag., 454 Casull. **Barrel:** 8.75", 10.5", 14". **Weight:** 61 oz. (10.5" bbl.); 78 oz. (14" bbl.). **Length:** 15", 18.5" overall (with 10.5" and 14" bbl., respectively). **Grips:** Smooth walnut stocks and forend. Also available with 17" finger groove grip. **Sights:** Ramp front, fully adjustable open rear. **Features:** Falling block action; drilled and tapped for M.O.A. scope mounts; integral grip frame/receiver; adjustable trigger; Douglas barrel (interchangeable). Introduced 1983. Made in U.S.A. by M.O.A. Corp.

Price: Stainless receiver, blue barrel **$839.00**

Price: Stainless receiver, stainless barrel **$937.00**

RPM XL SINGLE SHOT PISTOL

Caliber: 22 LR through 45-70. **Barrel:** 8", 10.75", 12", 14". **Weight:** About 60 oz. **Grips:** Smooth Goncalo Alves with thumb and heel rests. **Features:** Barrel drilled and tapped for scope mount. Visible cocking indicator. Spring-loaded barrel lock, positive hammer-block safety. Trigger adjustable for weight of pull and over-travel. Contact maker for complete price list. Made in U.S.A. by RPM.

Price: XL Hunter model (action only) **$945.00**

Price: Extra barrel, ISGW rear sight/hooded front included . . . . **$370.00 to $424.00**

SPRINGFIELD M6 SCOUT PISTOL

Caliber: 22 LR/45 LC/410, 22 Hornet, 45 LC/410. **Barrel:** 10". **Weight:** NA. **Length:** NA. **Grips:** NA. **Sights:** NA. **Features:** Adapted from the U.S. Air Force M6 Survival Rifle, also available as a carbine with 16" barrel.

Price: . . . . **$169.00 to $197.00**

Price: Pistol/Carbine . . . . **$183.00 to $209.00**

THOMPSON/CENTER ENCORE PISTOL

Caliber: 22-250, 223, 204 Ruger, 6.8 Rem., 260 Rem., 7mm-08, 243, 308, 270, 30-06, 375 JDJ, 204 Ruger, 44 Mag., 454 Casull, 480 Ruger, 444 Marlin single shot, 450 Marlin with muzzle tamer, no sights. **Barrel:** 12", 15", tapered round. **Weight:** NA. **Length:** 21" overall with 12" barrel. **Grips:** American walnut with finger grooves, walnut forend. **Sights:** Blade on ramp front, adjustable rear, or none. **Features:** Interchangeable barrels; action opens by squeezing the trigger guard; drilled and tapped for scope mounting; blue finish. Announced 1996. Made in U.S.A. by Thompson/Center Arms.

Price: **$615.00**

Thompson/Center G2 Contender Pistol

A second generation Contender pistol maintaining the same barrel interchangeability with older Contender barrels and their corresponding forends (except Herrett forend). The G2 frame will not accept old-style grips due to the change in grip angle. Incorporates an automatic hammer block safety with built-in interlock. Features include trigger adjustable for overtravel, adjustable rear sight; ramp front sight blade, blued steel finish.

Price: **$600.00**

Both classic arms and recent designs in American-style repeaters for sport and field shooting.

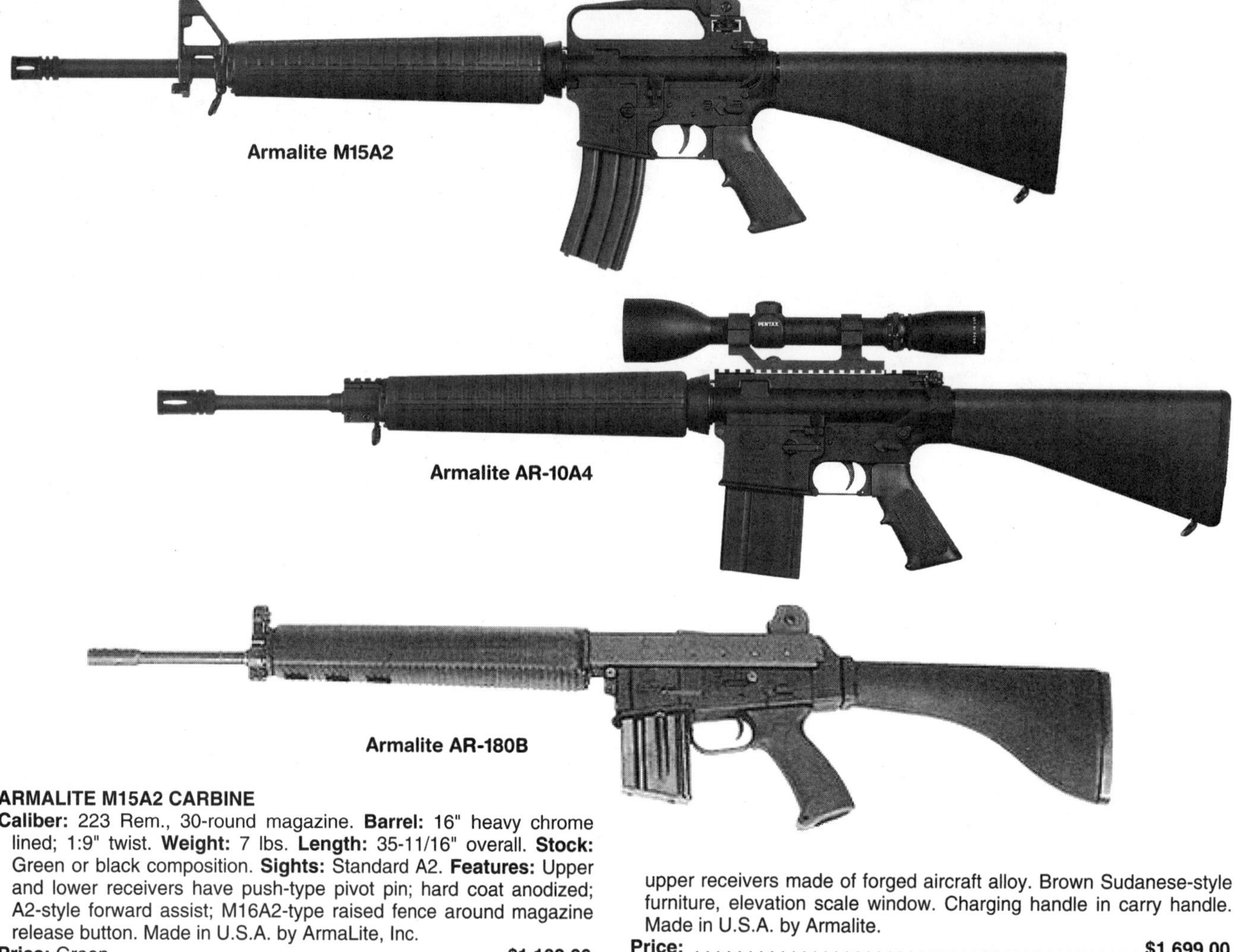

Armalite M15A2

Armalite AR-10A4

Armalite AR-180B

ARMALITE M15A2 CARBINE

Caliber: 223 Rem., 30-round magazine. **Barrel:** 16" heavy chrome lined; 1:9" twist. **Weight:** 7 lbs. **Length:** 35-11/16" overall. **Stock:** Green or black composition. **Sights:** Standard A2. **Features:** Upper and lower receivers have push-type pivot pin; hard coat anodized; A2-style forward assist; M16A2-type raised fence around magazine release button. Made in U.S.A. by ArmaLite, Inc.

Price: Green **$1,103.00**
Price: Black. **$1,103.00**

ARMALITE AR-10A4 SPECIAL PURPOSE RIFLE

Caliber: 308 Win., 10- and 20-round magazine. **Barrel:** 20" chrome-lined, 1:11.25" twist. **Weight:** 9.6 lbs. **Length:** 41" overall. **Stock:** Green or black composition. **Sights:** Detachable handle, front sight, or scope mount available; comes with international style flattop receiver with Picatinny rail. **Features:** Forged upper receiver with case deflector. Receivers are hard-coat anodized. Introduced 1995. Made in U.S.A. by ArmaLite, Inc.

Price: Green **$1,502.00**
Price: Black. **$1,502.00**

ArmaLite AR-10A2

Utilizing the same 20" double-lapped, heavy barrel as the ArmaLite AR10A4 Special Purpose Rifle. Offered in 308 Win. only. Made in U.S.A. by ArmaLite, Inc.

Price: AR-10A2 rifle or carbine **$1,504.00**

ARMALITE AR-180B RIFLE

Caliber: 223 Rem., 10-shot magazine. **Barrel:** 19.8". **Weight:** 6 lbs. **Length:** 38". **Stock:** Synthetic. **Sights:** Rear sight adjustable for windage, small and large apertures. **Features:** Lower receiver made of polymer, upper formed of sheet metal. Uses standard AR-15 magazines. Made in U.S.A. by Armalite.

Price: **$852.00**

ARMALITE AR-10B RIFLE

Caliber: 308 Win. **Barrel:** 20" chrome lined. **Weight:** 9.5 lbs. **Length:** 41". **Stock:** Synthetic. **Sights:** Rear sight adjustable for windage, small and large apertures. **Features:** Early-style AR-10. Lower and upper receivers made of forged aircraft alloy. Brown Sudanese-style furniture, elevation scale window. Charging handle in carry handle. Made in U.S.A. by Armalite.

Price: **$1,699.00**

ARSENAL, INC. SLR-107F

Caliber: 7.62x39mm. **Barrel:** 16.25". **Weight:** 7.3 lbs. **Stock:** Left-side folding polymer stock. **Sights:** Adjustable rear. **Features:** Stamped receiver, 24mm flash hider, bayonet lug, accessory lug, stainless steel heat shield, two-stage trigger. Introduced 2008. Made in U.S.A. by Arsenal, Inc.

Price: SLR-107F **$799.00**
Price: SLR-107FR, includes scope rail **$879.00**

ARSENAL, INC. SLR-107CR

Caliber: 7.62x39mm. **Barrel:** 16.25". **Weight:** 6.9 lbs. **Stock:** Left-side folding polymer stock. **Sights:** Adjustable rear. **Features:** Stamped receiver, front sight block/gas block combination, 500-meter rear sight, cleaning rod, stainless steel heat shield, scope rail, and removable muzzle attachment. Introduced 2007. Made in U.S.A. by Arsenal, Inc.

Price: SLR-107CR **$979.00**

ARSENAL, INC. SLR-106CR

Caliber: 5.56 NATO. **Barrel:** 16.25", Steyr chrome-lined barrel, 1:7 twist rate. **Weight:** 6.9 lbs. **Stock:** Black polymer folding stock with cutout for scope rail. Stainless-steel heatshield handguard. **Sights:** 500-meter rear sight and rear sight block calibrated for 5.56 NATO. Warsaw Pact scope rail. **Features:** Uses Arsenal, Bulgaria, Mil-Spec receiver, two-stage trigger, hammer and disconnector. Polymer magazines in 5- and 10-round capacity in black and green, with Arsenal logo. Others are 30-round black waffles, 20- and 30-round versions in clear/smoke waffle, featuring the "10" in a double-circle logo of Arsenal, Bulgaria. Ships with 5-round magazine, sling, cleaning kit in a tube, 16" cleaning rod, oil bottle. Introduced 2007. Made in U.S.A. by Arsenal, Inc.

Price: SLR-106CR **$979.00**

Auto-Ordnance 1927 A-1 Thompson

Benelli R1

Benelli R1 APG Camo

Barrett Model 82A-1

AUTO-ORDNANCE 1927 A-1 THOMPSON
Caliber: 45 ACP. **Barrel:** 16.5". **Weight:** 13 lbs. **Length:** About 41" overall (Deluxe). **Stock:** Walnut stock and vertical forend. **Sights:** Blade front, open rear adjustable for windage. **Features:** Recreation of Thompson Model 1927. Semi-auto only. Deluxe model has finned barrel, adjustable rear sight and compensator; Standard model has plain barrel and military sight. From Auto-Ordnance Corp.
Price: Deluxe **$1,282.00**
Price: 1927A1C lightweight model (9.5 lbs.). **$1,034.00**

Auto-Ordnance Thompson M1/M1-C
Similar to the 1927 A-1 except is in the M-1 configuration with side cocking knob, horizontal forend, smooth unfinned barrel, sling swivels on butt and forend. Matte-black finish. Introduced 1985.
Price: M1 semi-auto carbine. **$1,205.00**
Price: M1-C lightweight semi-auto **$962.00**

Auto-Ordnance 1927 A-1 Commando
Similar to the 1927 A-1 except has Parkerized finish, black-finish wood butt, pistol grip, horizontal forend. Comes with black nylon sling. Introduced 1998. Made in U.S.A. by Auto-Ordnance Corp.
Price: **$1,205.00**

BARRETT MODEL 82A-1 SEMI-AUTOMATIC RIFLE
Caliber: 50 BMG, 10-shot detachable box magazine. **Barrel:** 29". **Weight:** 28.5 lbs. **Length:** 57" overall. **Stock:** Composition with energy-absorbing recoil pad. **Sights:** Scope optional. **Features:** Semi-automatic, recoil operated with recoiling barrel. Three-lug locking bolt; muzzle brake. Adjustable bipod. Introduced 1985. Made in U.S.A. by Barrett Firearms.
Price: From **$8,050.00**

BENELLI R1 RIFLE
Caliber: 300 Win. Mag., 300 WSM, 270 WSM (24" barrel); 30-06 Spfl., 308 Win. (22" barrel); 300 Win. Mag., 30-06 Spfl., (20" barrel). **Weight:** 7.1 lbs. **Length:** 43.75" to 45.75". **Stock:** Select satin walnut or synthetic. **Sights:** None. **Features:** Auto-regulating gas-operated system, three-lug rotary bolt, interchangeable barrels, optional recoil pads. Introduced 2003. Imported from Italy by Benelli USA.
Price: Synthetic with ComforTech gel recoil pad **$1,465.00**
Price: Satin walnut **$1,290.00**
Price: APG HD camo, 30-06 (2008) **$1,595.00**

BERETTA CX4/PX4 STORM CARBINE
Caliber: 9mm Para., 40 S&W, 45 ACP. **Weight:** 5.75 lbs. Barrel **Length:** 16.6", chrome lined, rate of twist 1:16 (40 S&W) or 1:10 (9mm Para.). **Length:** NA. **Stock:** Black synthetic. **Sights:** NA. **Features:** Introduced 2005. Imported from Italy by Beretta USA.
Price: Cx4 Carbine, 40 S&W, 10+1 . . . . **$800.00**
Price: Cx4 Carbine, 8000 Series, 9mm Para., 10+1 . . . . **$775.00**
Price: Cx4 Carbine, 8045 Series, 45 ACP, 8+1 . . . . **$800.00**
Price: Cx4 Px4 Carbine, 40 S&W, 14+1 . . . . **$698.00**
Price: Cx4 Px4 Carbine, 9mm Para., 17+1 . . . . **$698.00**

Beretta CX4 Carbine

Browning Mark II Safari

Browning Lightweight Stalker

Browning Lightweight Stalker

Bushmaster XM15 E2S Carbine

BROWNING BAR SAFARI AND SAFARI W/BOSS SEMI-AUTO RIFLES

Caliber: Safari: 243 Win., 25-06 Rem., 270 Win., 7mm Rem. Mag.., 30-06 Spfl., 308 Win., 300 Win. Mag., 338 Win. Mag. Safari w/BOSS: 270 Win., 7mm Rem. Mag., 30-06 Spfl., 300 Win. Mag., 338 Win. Mag., plus 270 WSM, 7mm WSM, 300 WSM. **Barrel:** 22-24" round tapered. **Weight:** 7.4-8.2 lbs. **Length:** 43-45" overall. **Stock:** French walnut pistol grip stock and forend, hand checkered. **Sights:** No sights. **Features:** Has new bolt release lever; removable trigger assembly with larger trigger guard; redesigned gas and buffer systems. Detachable 4-round box magazine. Scroll-engraved receiver is tapped for scope mounting. BOSS barrel vibration modulator and muzzle brake system available. Mark II Safari introduced 1993. Imported from Belgium by Browning.

Price: BAR MK II Safari, from **$1,030.00**
Price: BAR Safari w/BOSS, from **$1,145.00**

BROWNING BAR SHORTTRAC/LONGTRAC AUTO RIFLES

Caliber: (ShortTrac models) 270 WSM, 7mm WSM, 300 WSM, 243 Win., 308 Win.; (Long Trac models) 270 Win., 30-06 Spfl., 7mm Rem. Mag., 300 Win. Mag. **Barrel:** 23". **Weight:** 6 lbs. 10 oz. to 7 lbs. 4 oz. **Length:** 41.5" to 44". **Stock:** Satin-finish walnut, pistol-grip, fluted forend. **Sights:** Adj. rear, bead front standard, no sights on BOSS models (optional). **Features:** Designed to handle new WSM chamberings. Gas-operated, blued finish, rotary bolt design (LongTrac models).

Price: BAR ShortTrac, 243 Win., 308 Win. from **$1,026.00**
Price: BAR ShortTrac Left-Hand, intr. 2007, from **$1,066.00**
Price: BAR LongTrac Left Hand, 270 Win., 30-06 Spfl., from **$1,066.00**
Price: BAR LongTrac, from. **$1,026.00**
Price: BAR LongTrac Mossy Oak Break Up, intr. 2007, from **$1,163.00**

BROWNING BAR STALKER AUTO RIFLES

Caliber: 243 Win., 308 Win., 270 Win., 30-06 Spfl., 270 WSM, 7mm WSM, 300 WSM, 300 Win. Mag., 338 Win. Mag. **Barrel:** 20-24". **Weight:** 7.1-7.75 LBS. **Length:** 41-45" overall. **Stock:** Black composite stock and forearm. **Sights:** Hooded front and adjustable rear. **Features:** Gas-operated action with seven-lug rotary bolt; dual action bars; 2-, 3- or 4-shot magazine (depending on cartridge). Introduced 2001. Imported by Browning.

Price: BAR ShortTrac or LongTrac Stalker, from **$1,043.00**
Price: BAR Lightweight Stalker, from **$1,022.00**

BUSHMASTER SUPERLIGHT CARBINES

Caliber: 223 Rem., 30-shot magazine. **Barrel:** 16", heavy; 1:9" twist. **Weight:** 6.25 lbs. **Length:** 31.25-34.5" overall. **Stock:** 6-position telestock or Stubby (7.25" length). **Sights:** Fully adjustable M16A2 sight system. **Features:** Adapted from original G.I. Pencil-barrel profile. Chrome-lined barrel with manganese phosphate finish. "Shorty" handguards. Has forged aluminum receivers with pushpin. Made in U.S.A. by Bushmaster Firearms, Inc.

Price: (A2). **$1130.00**
Price: (A3) **$1,215.00**
Price: (A3) Stubby Stock. **$1,190.00**

Bushmaster XM15 E2S Dissipator Carbine

Similar to the XM15 E2S Shorty carbine except has full-length "Dissipator" handguards. Weighs 7.6 lbs.; 34.75" overall; forged aluminum receivers with push-pin style takedown. Made in U.S.A. by Bushmaster Firearms, Inc.

Price: A2, with TeleStock **$1,215.00**
Price: A3, with Stubby stock **$1,190.00**

Bushmaster Varminter

Century International AES-10 Hi-Cap with bipod

Century International WASR-10 Hi-Cap

Century International WASR-2 Hi-Cap

Bushmaster XM15 E25 AK Shorty Carbine

Similar to the XM15 E2S Shorty except has 14.5" barrel with an AK muzzle brake permanently attached giving 16" barrel length. Weighs 7.3 lbs. Introduced 1999. Made in U.S.A. by Bushmaster Firearms, Inc.

Price: (A2 type) **$1,180.00**
Price: (A3 type) **$1,265.00**

Bushmaster M4/M4A3 Post-Ban Carbine

Similar to the XM15 E2S except has 14.5" barrel with Mini Y compensator, and fixed telestock. MR configuration has fixed carry handle; M4A3 has removable carry handle.

Price: (M4) **$1,180.00**
Price: (M4A3) **$1,265.00**

BUSHMASTER VARMINTER RIFLE

Caliber: 223 Rem., 5-shot. **Barrel:** 24", 1:9" twist, fluted, heavy, stainless. **Weight:** 8.75 lbs. **Length:** 42.25". **Stock:** Rubberized pistol grip. **Sights:** 1/2" scope risers. **Features:** Gas-operated, semi-auto, two-stage trigger, slotted free floater forend, lockable hard case.

Price: **$1,325.00**

CENTURY INTERNATIONAL AES-10 HI-CAP RIFLE

Caliber: 7.62x39mm. 30-shot magazine. **Barrel:** 23.2". **Weight:** NA. **Length:** 41.5" overall. **Stock:** Wood grip, forend. **Sights:** Fixed-notch rear, windage-adjustable post front. **Features:** RPK-style, accepts standard double-stack AK-type mags. Side-mounted scope mount, integral carry handle, bipod. Imported by Century Arms Int'l.

Price: AES-10, from **$450.00**

CENTURY INTERNATIONAL GP WASR-10 HI-CAP RIFLE

Caliber: 7.62x39mm. 30-shot magazine. **Barrel:** 16.25", 1:10 right-hand twist. **Weight:** 7.2 lbs. **Length:** 34.25" overall. **Stock:** Wood laminate or composite, grip, forend. **Sights:** Fixed-notch rear, windage-adjustable post front. **Features:** Two 30-rd. detachable box magazines, cleaning kit, bayonet. Version of AKM rifle; U.S.-parts added for BATFE compliance. Threaded muzzle, folding stock, bayonet lug, compensator, Dragunov stock available. Made in Romania by Cugir Arsenal. Imported by Century Arms Int'l.

Price: GP WASR-10, from **$350.00**

CENTURY INTERNATIONAL WASR-2 HI-CAP RIFLE

Caliber: 5.45x39mm. 30-shot magazine. **Barrel:** 16.25". **Weight:** 7.5 lbs. **Length:** 34.25" overall. Stocks: Wood laminate. **Sights:** Fixed-notch rear, windage-adjustable post front. **Features:** 1 30-rd. detachable box magazine, cleaning kit, sling. WASR-3 HI-CAP chambered in 223 Rem. Imported by Century Arms Int'l.

Price: GP WASR-2/3, from **$250.00**

CENTURY INTERNATIONAL M70AB2 SPORTER RIFLE

Caliber: 7.62x39mm. 30-shot magazine. **Barrel:** 16.25". **Weight:** 7.5 lbs. **Length:** 34.25" overall. Stocks: Metal grip, wood forend. **Sights:** Fixed-notch rear, windage-adjustable post front. **Features:** 2 30-rd. double-stack magazine, cleaning kit, compensator, bayonet lug and bayonet. Paratrooper-style Kalashnikov with under-folding stock. Imported by Century Arms Int'l.

Price: M70AB2, from. **$480.00**

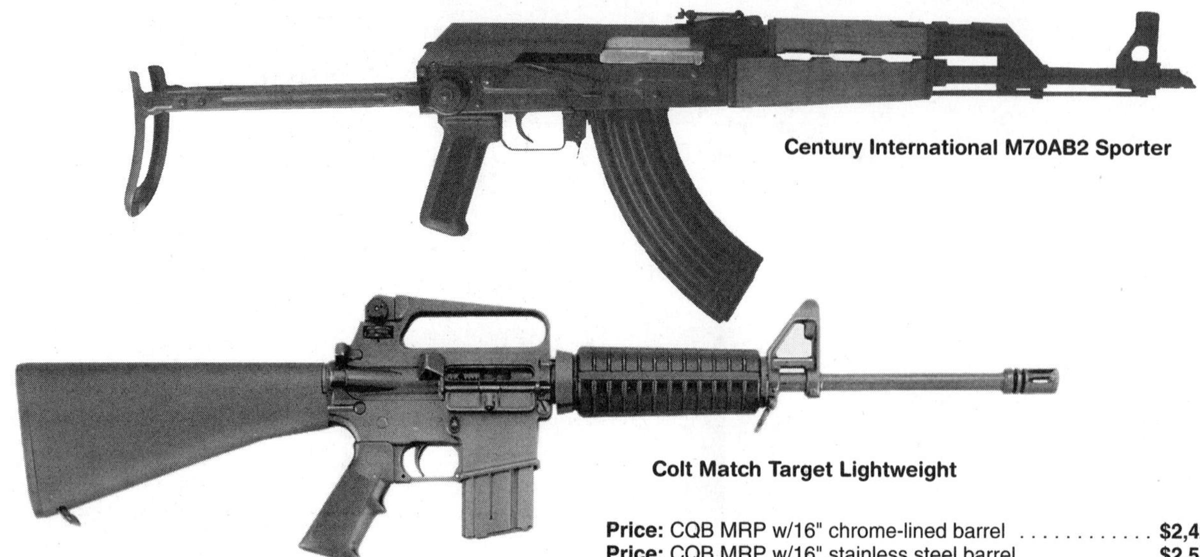
Century International M70AB2 Sporter

Colt Match Target Lightweight

COLT MATCH TARGET MODEL RIFLE

Caliber: 223 Rem., 5-shot magazine. **Barrel:** 16.1" or 20". **Weight:** 7.1 to 8.5 lbs. **Length:** 34.5" to 39" overall. **Stock:** Composition stock, grip, forend. **Sights:** Post front, rear adjustable for windage and elevation. **Features:** 5-round detachable box magazine, flash suppressor, sling swivels. Forward bolt assist included. Introduced 1991. Made in U.S.A. by Colt's Mfg. Co., Inc.

Price: Match Target HBAR MT6601 . . . . **$1,182.00**

DPMS PANTHER ARMS AR-15 RIFLES

Caliber: 223 Rem., 7.62x39. **Barrel:** 16" to 24". **Weight:** 7.75 to 11.75 lbs. **Length:** 34.5" to 42.25" overall. **Stock:** Black Zytel composite. **Sights:** Square front post, adjustable A2 rear. **Features:** Steel or stainless steel heavy or bull barrel; hardcoat anodized receiver; aluminum free-float tube handguard; many options. From DPMS Panther Arms.

Price: Panther Bull Twenty (20" stainless bull bbl.) **$920.00**
Price: Arctic Panther. **$1,099.00**
Price: Panther Classic **$799.00**
Price: Panther Bull Sweet Sixteen (16" stainless bull bbl.) . . . **$885.00**
Price: DCM Panther (20" stainless heavy bbl., n.m. sights) **$1,099.00**
Price: Panther 7.62x39 (20" steel heavy bbl.) **$859.00**

DPMS PANTHER ARMS CLASSIC AUTO RIFLE

Caliber: 5.56x45mm. **Barrel:** Heavy 16" to 20" w/flash hider. **Weight:** 7 to 9 lbs. **Length:** 34-11/16" to 38-7/16". **Sights:** Adj. rear and front. **Stock:** Black Zytel w/trap door assembly. **Features:** Gas operated rotating bolt, mil spec or Teflon black finish.

Price: Panther A2 Tactical 16" **$814.00**
Price: Panther Southpaw **$899.00**
Price: Panther Lite 16 . . . . **$725.00**
Price: Panther Carbine **$799.00**
Price: Panther The Agency Rifle. **$1,999.00**

DSA Z4 GTC CARBINE WITH C.R.O.S.

Caliber: 5.56 NATO **Barrel:** 16" 1:9 twist M4 profile fluted chrome lined heavy barrel with threaded Vortec flash hider. **Weight:** 7.6 lbs. **Stock:** 6 position collapsible M4 stock, Predator P4X free float tactical rail. **Sights:** Chrome lined Picatinny gas block w/removable front sight. **Features:** The Corrosion Resistant Operating System incorporates the new P.O.F. Gas Trap System with removable gas plug eliminates problematic features of standard AR gas system, Forged 7075T6 DSA lower receiver. Introduced 2006. Made in U.S.A. by DSA, Inc.

Price: **$1,800.00**

DSA CQB MRP, STANDARD MRP

Caliber: 5.56 NATO **Barrel:** 16" or 18" 1:7 twist chrome-lined or stainless steel barrel with A2 flash hider **Stock:** 6 position collapsible M4 stock. **Features:** LMT 1/2" MRP upper receiver with 20.5" Standard quad rail or 16.5" CQB quad rail, LMT-enhanced bolt with dual extractor springs, free float barrel, quick change barrel system, forged 7075T6 DSA lower receiver. EOTech and vertical grip additional. Introduced 2006. Made in U.S.A. by DSA, Inc.

Price: CQB MRP w/16" chrome-lined barrel **$2,420.00**
Price: CQB MRP w/16" stainless steel barrel. **$2,540.00**
Price: Standard MRP w/16" chrome-lined barrel **$2,620.00**
Price: Standard MRP w/16" or 18" stainless steel barrel . . . **$2,740.00**

DSA STD CARBINE

Caliber: 5.56 NATO. **Barrel:** 16" 1:9 twist D4 w/A2 flash hider. **Weight:** 6.25 lbs. **Length:** 31". **Stock:** A2 buttstock, D4 handguard w/ heatshield. **Sights:** Forged A2 front sight with lug. **Features:** Forged 7075T6 DSA lower receiver, forged A2 or flattop upper receiver. Introduced 2006. Made in U.S.A. by DSA, Inc.

Price: A2 or Flattop STD Carbine. **$1,025.00**
Price: With LMT SOPMOD stock **$1,267.00**

DSA 1R CARBINE

Caliber: 5.56 NATO. **Barrel:** 16" 1:9 twist D4 w/A2 flash hider. **Weight:** 6.25 lbs. **Length:** Variable. **Stock:** 6 position collapsible M4 stock, D4 handguard w/heatshield. **Sights:** Forged A2 front sight with lug. **Features:** Forged 7075T6 DSA lower receiver, forged A2 or flattop upper receiver. Introduced 2006. Made in U.S.A. by DSA, Inc.

Price: A2 or Flattop 1R Carbine **$1,055.00**
Price: With VLTOR ModStock **$1,175.00**

DSA XM CARBINE

Caliber: 5.56 NATO. **Barrel:** 11.5" 1:9 twist D4 with 5.5" permanently attached flash hider. **Weight:** 6.25 lbs. **Length:** Variable. **Stock:** Collapsible, Handguard w/heatshield. **Sights:** Forged A2 front sight with lug. **Features:** Forged 7075T6 DSA lower receiver, forged A2 upper receiver. Introduced 2006. Made in U.S.A. by DSA, Inc.

Price: **$1,055.00**

DSA STANDARD

Caliber: 5.56 NATO. **Barrel:** 20" 1:9 twist heavy barrel w/A2 flash hider. **Weight:** 6.25 lbs. **Length:** 38-7/16". **Stock:** A2 buttstock, A2 handguard w/heatshield. **Sights:** Forged A2 front sight with lug. **Features:** Forged 7075T6 DSA lower receiver, forged A2 or flattop upper receiver. Introduced 2006. Made in U.S.A. by DSA, Inc.

Price: A2 or Flattop Standard **$1,025.00**

DSA DCM RIFLE

Caliber: 223 Wylde Chamber. **Barrel:** 20" 1:8 twist chrome moly match grade Badger Barrel. **Weight:** 10 lbs. **Length:** 39.5". **Stock:** DCM freefloat handguard system, A2 buttstock. **Sights:** Forged A2 front sight with lug. **Features:** NM two stage trigger, NM rear sight, forged 7075T6 DSA lower receiver, forged A2 upper receiver. Introduced 2006. Made in U.S.A. by DSA, Inc.

Price: **$1,520.00**

DSA S1

Caliber: 223 Rem. Match Chamber. **Barrel:** 16", 20" or 24" 1:8 twist stainless steel bull barrel. **Weight:** 8.0, 9.5 and 10 lbs. **Length:** 34.25", 38.25" and 42.25". **Stock:** A2 buttstock with free float aluminum handguard. **Sights:** Picatinny gas block sight base. **Features:** Forged 7075T6 DSA lower receiver, Match two stage trigger, forged flattop upper receiver, fluted barrel optional. Introduced 2006. Made in U.S.A. by DSA, Inc.

Price: **$1,155.00**

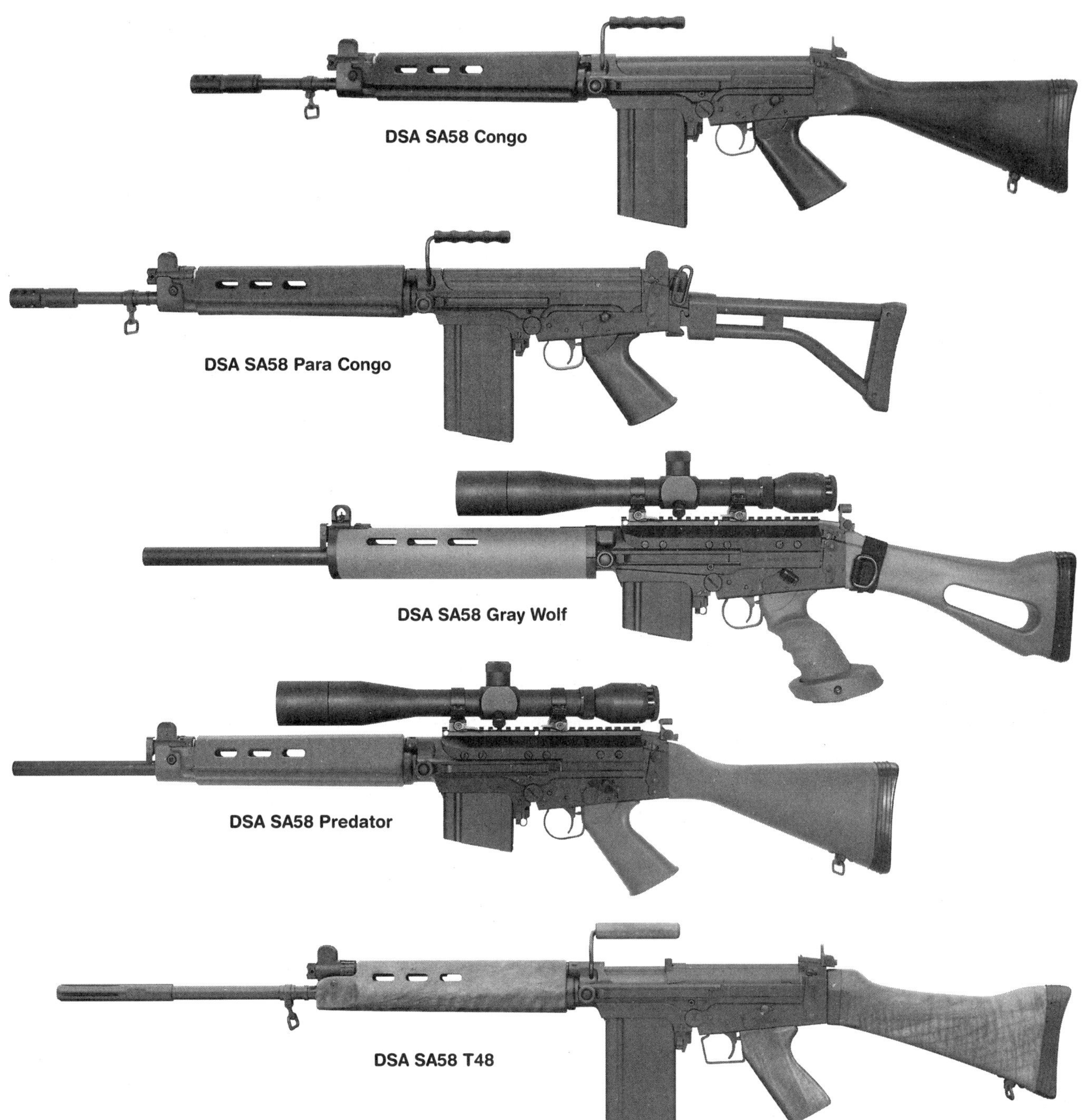

DSA SA58 CONGO, PARA CONGO

Caliber: 308 Win. **Barrel:** 18" w/short Belgian short flash hider. **Weight:** 8.6 lbs. (Congo); 9.85 lbs. (Para Congo). **Length:** 39.75" **Stock:** Synthetic w/military grade furniture (Congo); Synthetic with non-folding steel para stock (Para Congo). **Sights:** Elevation adjustable protected post front sight, windage adjustable rear peep (Congo); Belgian type Para Flip Rear (Para Congo). **Features:** Fully-adjustable gas system, high-grade steel upper receiver with carry handle. Made in U.S.A. by DSA, Inc.

Price: Congo **$1,850.00**

Price: Para Congo **$2,095.00**

DSA SA58 GRAY WOLF

Caliber: 308 Win. **Barrel:** 21" match-grade bull w/target crown. **Weight:** 13 lbs. **Length:** 41.75". **Stock:** Synthetic. **Sights:** Elevation-adjustable post front sight, windage-adjustable match rear peep. **Features:** Fully-adjustable gas system, high-grade steel upper receiver, Picatinny scope mount, DuraCoat finish. Made in U.S.A. by DSA, Inc.

Price: **$2,120.00**

DSA SA58 PREDATOR

Caliber: 243 Win., 260 Rem., 308 Win. **Barrel:** 16" and 19" w/target crown. **Weight:** 9 to 9.3 lbs. **Length:** 36.25" to 39.25". **Stock:** Green synthetic. **Sights:** Elevation-adjustable post front; windage-adjustable match rear peep. **Features:** Fully-adjustable gas system, high-grade steel upper receiver, Picatinny scope mount, DuraCoat solid and camo finishes. Made in U.S.A. by DSA, Inc.

Price: 243 Win., 260 Rem. **$1,695.00**

Price: 308 Win. **$1,640.00**

DSA SA58 T48

Caliber: 308 Win. **Barrel:** 21" with Browning long flash hider. **Weight:** 9.3 lbs. **Length:** 44.5". **Stock:** European walnut. **Sights:** Elevation-adjustable post front, windage adjustable rear peep. **Features:** Gas-operated semi-auto with fully adjustable gas system, high grade steel upper receiver with carry handle. DuraCoat finishes. Made in U.S.A. by DSA, Inc.

Price: **$1,995.00**

DSA SA58 G1

DSA SA58 Standard

DSA SA58 Carbine

DSA SA58 Medium Contour Tactical

DSA SA58 Medium Contour

DSA SA58 G1

Caliber: 308 Win. **Barrel:** 21" with quick-detach flash hider. **Weight:** 10.65 lbs. **Length:** 44". **Stock:** Steel bipod cut handguard with hardwood stock and synthetic pistol grip. **Sights:** Elevation-adjustable post front, windage adjustable rear peep. **Features:** Gas-operated semi-auto with fully adjustable gas system, high grade steel upper receiver with carry handle, original GI steel lower receiver with GI bipod. DuraCoat finishes. Made in U.S.A. by DSA, Inc.

Price: **$1,850.00**

DSA SA58 STANDARD

Caliber: 308 Win. **Barrel:** 21" bipod cut w/threaded flash hider. **Weight:** 8.75 lbs. **Length:** 43". **Stock:** Synthetic, X-Series or optional folding para stock. **Sights:** Elevation-adjustable post front, windage-adjustable rear peep. **Features:** Fully adjustable short gas system, high grade steel or 416 stainless upper receiver. Made in U.S.A. by DSA, Inc.

Price: High-grade steel **$1,595.00**
Price: Folding para stock **$1,845.00**

DSA SA58 CARBINE

Caliber: 308 Win. **Barrel:** 16.25" bipod cut w/threaded flash hider. **Weight:** 8.35 lbs. **Length:** 37.5". **Stock:** Synthetic, X-Series or optional folding para stock. **Sights:** Elevation-adjustable post front, windage-adjustable rear peep. **Features:** Fully adjustable short gas system, high grade steel or 416 stainless upper receiver. Made in U.S.A. by DSA, Inc.

Price: High-grade steel **$1,595.00**
Price: Stainless steel **$1,850.00**

DSA SA58 TACTICAL CARBINE

Caliber: 308 Win. **Barrel:** 16.25" fluted with A2 flash hider. **Weight:** 8.25 lbs. **Length:** 36.5". **Stock:** Synthetic, X-Series or optional folding para stock. **Sights:** Elevation-adjustable post front, windage-adjustable match rear peep. **Features:** Shortened fully adjustable short gas system, high grade steel or 416 stainless upper receiver. Made in U.S.A. by DSA, Inc.

Price: High-grade steel **$1,595.00**
Price: Stainless steel **$1,850.00**

DSA SA58 MEDIUM CONTOUR

Caliber: 308 Win. **Barrel:** 21" w/threaded flash hider. **Weight:** 9.75 lbs. **Length:** 43". **Stock:** Synthetic military grade. **Sights:** Elevation-adjustable post front, windage-adjustable match rear peep. **Features:** Gas-operated semi-auto with fully adjustable gas system, high grade steel receiver. Made in U.S.A. by DSA, Inc.

Price: **$1,595.00**

DSA SA58 Bull

DSA SA58 OSW

Excel Arms Accelerator

Heckler & Koch USC

Hi-Point Carbine

DSA SA58 BULL BARREL RIFLE

Caliber: 308 Win. **Barrel:** 21". **Weight:** 11.1 lbs. **Length:** 41.5". **Stock:** Synthetic, free floating handguard. **Sights:** Elevation-adjustable windage-adjustable post front, match rear peep. **Features:** Gas-operated semi-auto with fully adjustable gas system, high grade steel or stainless upper receiver. Made in U.S.A. by DSA, Inc.

Price: **$1,745.00**
Price: Stainless steel **$1,995.00**

DSA SA58 MINI OSW

Caliber: 308 Win. **Barrel:** 11" or 13" w/A2 flash hider. **Weight:** 9 to 9.35 lbs. **Length:** 32.75" to 35". **Stock:** Fiberglass reinforced short synthetic handguard, para folding stock and synthetic pistol grip. **Sights:** Adjustable post front, para rear sight. **Features:** Semi-auto or select fire with fully adjustable short gas system, optional FAL rail handguard, SureFire Vertical Foregrip System, EOTech HOLOgraphic Sight and ITC cheekrest. Made in U.S.A. by DSA, Inc.

Price: **$1,845.00**

EXCEL ARMS ACCELERATOR RIFLES

Caliber: 17 HMR, 22 WMR, 17M2, 22 LR, 9-shot magazine. **Barrel:** 18" fluted stainless steel bull barrel. **Weight:** 8 lbs. **Length:** 32.5" overall. Grips: Textured black polymer. **Sights:** Fully adjustable target sights. **Features:** Made from 17-4 stainless steel, aluminum shroud w/ Weaver rail, manual safety, firing-pin block, last-round bolt-hold-open feature. Four packages with various equipment available. American made, lifetime warranty. Comes with one 9-round stainless steel magazine and a California-approved cable lock. Introduced 2006. Made in U.S.A. by Excel Arms.

Price: MR-17 17 HMR. **$498.00**
Price: MR-22 22 WMR **$498.00**
Price: SR-17 17 Mach 2 . . . . **$498.00**
Price: SR-22 22 LR **$498.00**

HECKLER & KOCH USC CARBINE

Caliber: 45 ACP, 10-shot magazine. **Barrel:** 16". **Weight:** 8.6 lb. **Length:** 35.4" overall. **Stock:** Skeletonized polymer thumbhole. **Sights:** Blade front with integral hood, fully adjustable diopter. **Features:** Based on German UMP submachine gun. Blowback operation; almost entirely constructed of carbon fiber-reinforced polymer. Free-floating heavy target barrel. Introduced 2000. From H&K.

Price: **$1,249.00**

HI-POINT 9MM CARBINE

Caliber: 9mm Para., 40 S&W, 10-shot magazine. **Barrel:** 16.5" (17.5" for 40 S&W). **Weight:** 4.5 lbs. **Length:** 31.5" overall. **Stock:** Black polymer, camouflage. **Sights:** Protected post front, aperture rear. Integral scope mount. **Features:** Grip-mounted magazine release. Black or chrome finish. Sling swivels. Available with laser or red dot sights. Introduced 1996. Made in U.S.A. by MKS Supply, Inc.

Price: Black, 9mm Para. **$220.00**
Price: Black, 40 S&W **$242.00**
Price: Camo stock **$235.00**

Les Baer Flattop

Les Baer IPSC

Olympic Arms K9 Carbine

Olympic Arms K3B

LES BAER CUSTOM ULTIMATE AR 223 RIFLES

Caliber: 223. **Barrel:** 18", 20", 22", 24". **Weight:** 7.75 to 9.75 lb. **Length:** NA. **Stock:** Black synthetic. **Sights:** None furnished; Picatinny-style flattop rail for scope mounting. **Features:** Forged receiver; Ultra single-stage trigger (Jewell two-stage trigger optional); titanium firing pin; Versa-Pod bipod; chromed National Match carrier; stainless steel, hand-lapped and cryo-treated barrel; guaranteed to shoot 1/2 or 3/4 MOA, depending on model. Made in U.S.A. by Les Baer Custom Inc.

Price: Super Varmint Model $2,150.00
Price: Super Match Model (introduced 2006) $2,290.00
Price: M4 Flattop model $2,240.00
Price: Police Special 16" (2008) $1,690.00

LR 300 SR LIGHT SPORT RIFLE

Caliber: 223. **Barrel:** 16.25"; 1:9" twist. **Weight:** 7.2 lbs. **Length:** 36" overall (extended stock), 26.25" (stock folded). **Stock:** Folding, tubular steel, with thumbhole-type grip. **Sights:** Trijicon post front, Trijicon rear. **Features:** Uses AR-15 type upper and lower receivers; flattop receiver with weaver base. Accepts all AR-15/M-16 magazines. Introduced 1996. Made in U.S.A. from Z-M Weapons.

Price: AXL.................................... $2,139.00

OLYMPIC ARMS K9, K10, K40, K45 PISTOL-CALIBER AR15 CARBINES

Caliber: 9mm Para., 10mm, 40 S&W, 45 ACP; 32/10-shot modified magazines. **Barrel:** 16" button rifled stainless steel, 1x16 twist rate. **Weight:** 6.73 lbs. **Length:** 31.625" overall. **Stock:** A2 grip, M4 6-point collapsible stock. **Features:** A2 upper with adjustable rear sight, elevation adjustable front post, bayonet lug, sling swivel, threaded muzzle, flash suppressor, carbine length handguards. Made in U.S.A. by Olympic Arms, Inc.

Price: K9GL, 9mm Para., Glock lower $959.00
Price: K10, 10mm, modified 10-round Uzi magazine $869.00
Price: K40, 40 S&W, modified 10-round Uzi magazine $869.00
Price: K45, 45 ACP, modified 10-round Uzi magazine....... $869.00

OLYMPIC ARMS K3B SERIES AR15 CARBINES

Caliber: 5.56 NATO, 30-shot magazines. **Barrel:** 16" button rifled chrome-moly steel, 1x9 twist rate. **Weight:** 5-7 lbs. **Length:** 31.75" overall. **Stock:** A2 grip, M4 6-point collapsible buttstock. **Features:** A2 upper with adjustable rear sight, elevation adjustable front post, bayonet lug, sling swivel, threaded muzzle, flash suppressor, carbine length handguards. Made in U.S.A. by Olympic Arms, Inc.

Price: K3B base model, A2 upper...................... $815.00
Price: K3B-M4 M4 contoured barrel & handguards $899.00
Price: K3B-M4-A3-TC A3 upper, M4 barrel, FIRSH rail handguard................................ $1,079.00
Price: K3B-CAR 11.5" barrel with 5.5" permanent flash suppressor $839.00
Price: K3B-FAR 16" featherweight contoured barrel $880.00

Olympic Arms Plinker Plus AR15

Olympic Arms Plinker Plus 20

Ruger Mini-14/5 Ranch

OLYMPIC ARMS PLINKER PLUS AR15 MODELS

Caliber: 5.56 NATO, 30-shot magazine. Barrel 16" or 20" button-rifled chrome-moly steel, 1x9 twist. **Weight:** 7.5-8.5 lbs. **Length:** 35.5"-39.5" overall. **Stock:** A2 grip, A2 buttstock with trapdoor. **Sights:** A1 windage rear, elevation-adjustable front post. **Features:** A1 upper, fiberlite handguards, bayonet lug, threaded muzzle and flash suppressor. Made in U.S.A. by Olympic Arms, Inc.

Price: Plinker Plus. **$629.00**
Price: Plinker Plus 20 . . . .**$779.00**

REMINGTON MODEL 750 WOODSMASTER

Caliber: 243 Win., 270 Win., 308 Win., 30-06 Spfl., 35 Whelen. 4-shot magazine. **Barrel:** 22" round tapered. **Weight:** 7.5 lbs. **Length:** 42.6" overall. **Stock:** Restyled American walnut forend and stock with machine-cut checkering. Satin finish. **Sights:** Gold bead front sight on ramp; step rear sight with windage adjustable. **Features:** Replaces wood-stocked Model 7400 line introduced 1981. Gas action, SuperCell recoil pad. Positive cross-bolt safety. Carbine chambered in 308 Win., 30-06 Spfl., 35 Whelen. Receiver tapped for scope mount. Introduced 2006. Made in U.S.A. by Remington Arms Co.

Price: 750 Woodsmaster **$852.00**
Price: 750 Woodsmaster Carbine (18.5" bbl.) **$852.00**
Price: 750 Synthetic stock (2007). **$751.00**

ROCK RIVER ARMS STANDARD A2 RIFLE

Caliber: 45 ACP. **Barrel:** NA. **Weight:** 8.2 lbs. **Length:** NA. **Stock:** Thermoplastic. **Sights:** Standard AR-15 style sights. **Features:** Two-stage, national match trigger; optional muzzle brake. Pro-Series Government package includes side-mount sling swivel, chrome-lined 1:9 twist barrel, mil-spec forged lower receiver, Hogue rubber grip, NM two-stage trigger, 6-position tactical CAR stock, Surefire M73 quad rail handguard, other features. Made in U.S.A. From Rock River Arms.

Price: Standard A2 AR1280 . . . .**$945.00**
Price: Pro-Series Government Package GOVT1001 (2008) **$2,290.00**
Price: Elite Comp AR1270 (2008). **$1,145.00**

RUGER MINI-14 RANCH RIFLE AUTOLOADING RIFLE

Caliber: 223 Rem., 5-shot detachable box magazine. **Barrel:** 18.5". Rifling twist 1:9". **Weight:** 6.75 to 7 lbs. **Length:** 37.25" overall. **Stock:** American hardwood, steel reinforced, or synthetic. **Sights:** Protected blade front, fully adjustable Ghost Ring rear. **Features:** Fixed piston gas-operated, positive primary extraction. New buffer system, redesigned ejector system. Ruger S100RM scope rings included on Ranch Rifle. Heavier barrels added in 2008.

Price: Mini-14/5, Ranch Rifle, blued, scope rings. **$830.00**
Price: K-Mini-14/5, Ranch Rifle, stainless, scope rings **$894.00**
Price: K-Mini-14/5P, Ranch Rifle, stainless, synthetic stock . .**$894.00**
Price: K-Mini-6.8/5P, All-Weather Ranch Rifle, stainless, synthetic stock (2008) **$894.00**

Ruger NRA Mini-14 Rifle

Similar to the Mini-14 Ranch Rifle except comes with two 20-Round magazines and special Black Hogue OverMolded stock with NRA gold-tone medallion in grip cap. Special serial number sequence (NRA8XXXXX). For 2008 only.

Price: M-14/20C-NRA. **$1035.00**
Price: M-14/5C-NRA (5-round magazines). **$1035.00**

Ruger Mini Thirty Rifle

Similar to the Mini-14 Ranch Rifle except modified to chamber the 7.62x39 Russian service round. **Weight:** 6.75 lbs. Has 6-groove barrel with 1:10" twist, Ruger Integral Scope Mount bases and protected blade front, fully adjustable Ghost Ring rear. Detachable 5-shot staggered box magazine. Stainless w/synthetic stock. Introduced 1987.

Price: Stainless, scope rings **$894.00**

SABRE DEFENCE SABRE RIFLES

Caliber: 5.56 NATO, 6.5 Grendel, 30-shot magazines. **Barrel:** 20" 410 stainless steel, 1x8 twist rate; or 18" vanadium alloy, chrome-lined barrel with Sabre Gill-Brake. **Weight:** 6.77 lbs. **Length:** 31.75" overall. **Stock:** SOCOM 3-position stock with Samson M-EX handguards. **Sights:** Flip-up front and rear sights. **Features:** Fluted barrel, Harris bipod, and two-stage match trigger, Ergo Grips; upper and matched lower CNC machined from 7075-T6 forgings. SOCOM adjustable stock, Samson tactical handguards, M4 contour barrels available in 14.5" and 16" are made of MIL-B-11595 vanadium alloy and chrome lined. Introduced 2002. From Sabre Defence Industries.

Price: 6.5 Grendel (2007) **$1,409.00**
Price: Competition Extreme, 20" barrel **$1,999.00**
Price: Competition Special, 5.56mm, 18" barrel. **$1,799.00**
Price: SPR Carbine. **$2,499.00**
Price: M4 Carbine, 14.5" barrel **$1,349.00**
Price: M4 Flat-top Carbine, 16" barrel **$1,349.00**

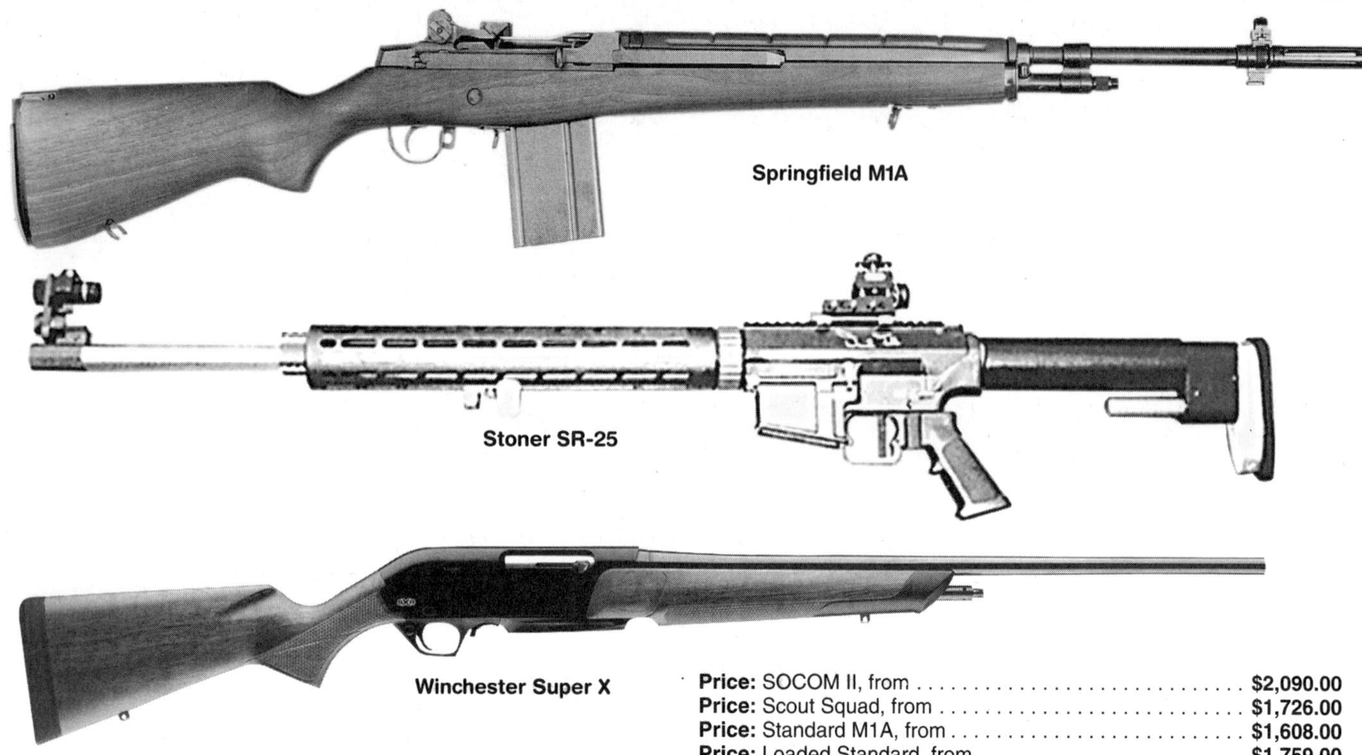
Springfield M1A

Stoner SR-25

Winchester Super X

SIG 556 AUTOLOADING RIFLE

Caliber: 223 Rem., 30-shot detachable box magazine. **Barrel:** 16". Rifling twist 1:9". **Weight:** 6.8 lbs. **Length:** 36.5" overall. **Stock:** Polymer, folding style. **Sights:** Flip-up front combat sight, adjustable for windage and elevation. **Features:** Based on SG 550 series rifle. Two-position adjustable gas piston operating rod system, accepts standard AR magazines. Polymer forearm, three integrated Picatinny rails, forward mount for right- or left-side sling attachment. Aircraft-grade aluminum alloy trigger housing, hard-coat anodized finish; two-stage trigger, ambidextrous safety, 30-round polymer magazine, battery compartments, pistol-grip rubber-padded watertight adjustable butt stock with sling-attachment points. SIG 556 SWAT model has flat-top Picatinny railed receiver, tactical quad rail. SIG 556 HOLO sight options include front combat sight, flip-up rear sight, and red-dot style holographic sighting system with four illuminated reticle patterns. DMR features a 24" military grade cold hammer-forged heavy contour barrel, 5.56mm NATO, target crown. Imported by Sig Sauer, Inc.

Price: SIG 556 .... **$1,565.00**
Price: SIG 556 HOLO (2008) **$1,643.00**
Price: SIG 556 DMR (2008) **$2,286.00**

SMITH & WESSON M&P15 RIFLES

Caliber: 5.56mm NATO/223, 30-shot steel magazine. **Barrel:** 16", 1:9 **Weight:** 6.74 lbs., w/o magazine. **Length:** 32-35" overall. **Stock:** Black synthetic. **Sights:** Adjustable post front sight, adjustable dual aperture rear sight. **Features:** 6-position telescopic stock, thermo-set M4 handguard. 14.75" sight radius. 7-lbs. (approx.) trigger pull. 7075 T6 aluminum upper, 4140 steel barrel. Chromed barrel bore, gas key, bolt carrier. Hard-coat black-anodized receiver and barrel finish. Introduced 2006. Made in U.S.A. by Smith & Wesson.

Price: M&P15 No. 811000 .... **$1,304.00**
Price: M&P15T No. 811001, free float modular rail forend . **$1,754.00**
Price: M&P15A No. 811002, folding battle rear sight **$1,320.00**
Price: M&P15A No. 811013, optics ready compliant (2008). **$1,095.00**

SPRINGFIELD ARMORY M1A RIFLE

Caliber: 7.62mm NATO (308), 5- or 10-shot box magazine. **Barrel:** 25-1/16" with flash suppressor, 22" without suppressor. **Weight:** 9.75 lbs. **Length:** 44.25" overall. **Stock:** American walnut with walnut-colored heat-resistant fiberglass handguard. Matching walnut handguard available. Also available with fiberglass stock. **Sights:** Military, square blade front, full click-adjustable aperture rear. **Features:** Commercial equivalent of the U.S. M-14 service rifle with no provision for automatic firing. From Springfield Armory

Price: SOCOM 16 .... **$1,855.00**
Price: SOCOM II, from **$2,090.00**
Price: Scout Squad, from **$1,726.00**
Price: Standard M1A, from **$1,608.00**
Price: Loaded Standard, from **$1,759.00**
Price: National Match, from **$2,249.00**
Price: Super Match (heavy premium barrel) about **$2,818.00**
Price: Tactical, from **$3,780.00**

STONER SR-15 M-5 RIFLE

Caliber: 223. **Barrel:** 20". **Weight:** 7.6 lbs. **Length:** 38" overall. **Stock:** Black synthetic. **Sights:** Post front, fully adjustable rear (300-meter sight). **Features:** Modular weapon system; two-stage trigger. Black finish. Introduced 1998. Made in U.S.A. by Knight's Mfg.

Price: **$1,695.00**

STONER SR-25 CARBINE

Caliber: 7.62 NATO, 10-shot steel magazine. **Barrel:** 16" free-floating **Weight:** 7.75 lbs. **Length:** 35.75" overall. **Stock:** Black synthetic. **Sights:** Integral Weaver-style rail. Scope rings, iron sights optional. **Features:** Shortened, non-slip handguard; removable carrying handle. Matte black finish. Introduced 1995. Made in U.S.A. by Knight's Mfg. Co.

Price: **$3,345.00**

WILSON COMBAT TACTICAL RIFLES

Caliber: 5.56mm NATO, accepts all M-16/AR-15 Style Magazines, includes one 20-round magazine. **Barrel:** 16.25", 1:9 twist, match-grade fluted. **Weight:** 6.9 lbs. **Length:** 36.25" overall. **Stock:** Fixed or collapsible. **Features:** Free-float ventilated aluminum quad-rail handguard, Mil-Spec parkerized barrel and steel components, anodized receiver, precision CNC-machined upper and lower receivers, 7075 T6 aluminum forgings. Single stage JP Trigger/ Hammer Group, Wilson Combat Tactical Muzzle Brake, nylon tactical rifle case. M-4T version has flat-top receiver for mounting optics, OD green furniture, 16.25" match-grade M-4 style barrel. SS-15 Super Sniper Tactical Rifle has 1-in-8 twist, heavy 20" match-grade fluted stainless steel barrel. Made in U.S.A by Wilson Combat.

Price: UT-15 Tactical Carbine......................... **$1,785.00**
Price: M4-TP Tactical Carbine **$1,575.00**
Price: SS-15P Super Sniper........................... **$1,795.00**

WINCHESTER SUPER X RIFLE

Caliber: 270 WSM, 30-06 Spfl., 300 Win. Mag., 300 WSM, 4-shot steel magazine. **Barrel:** 22", 24", 1:10", blued. **Weight:** 7.25 lbs. **Length:** up to 41-3/8". **Stock:** Walnut, 14-1/8"x 7/8"x 1.25". **Sights:** None. **Features:** Gas operated, removable trigger assembly, detachable box magazine, drilled and tapped, alloy receiver, enlarged trigger guard, crossbolt safety. Reintroduced 2008. Made in U.S.A. by Winchester Repeating Arms.

Price: Super X Rifle, from.............................. **$899.00**

Both classic arms and recent designs in American-style repeaters for sport and field shooting.

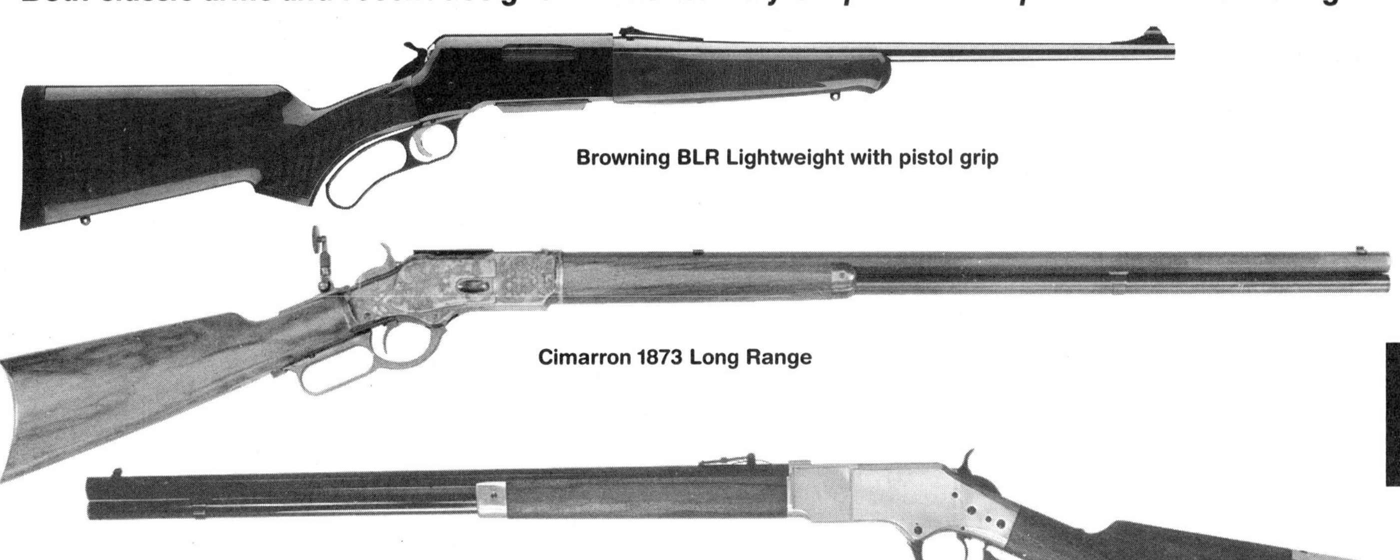

Browning BLR Lightweight with pistol grip

Cimarron 1873 Long Range

Cimarron 1866 Winchester Replica

BROWNING BLR RIFLES

Action: Lever action with rotating bolt head, multiple-lug breech bolt with recessed bolt face, side ejection. Rack-and-pinion lever. Flush-mounted detachable magazines, with 4+1 capacity for magnum cartridges, 5+1 for standard rounds. **Barrel:** Button-rifled chrome-moly steel with crowned muzzle. **Stock:** Buttstocks and forends are American walnut with grip and forend checkering. Recoil pad installed. Trigger: Wide-groove design, trigger travels with lever. Half-cock hammer safety; fold-down hammer. **Sights:** Gold bead on ramp front; low-profile square-notch adjustable rear. **Features:** Blued barrel and receiver, high-gloss wood finish. Receivers are drilled and tapped for scope mounts, swivel studs included. Action lock provided. Introduced 1996. Four model name variations for 2006, as noted below. Imported from Japan by Browning.

BROWNING BLR LIGHTWEIGHT W/PISTOL GRIP, SHORT AND LONG ACTION; LIGHTWEIGHT '81, SHORT AND LONG ACTION

Calibers: Short Action, 20" Barrel: 22-250 Rem., 243 Win., 7mm-08 Rem., 308 Win., 358, 450 Marlin. Calibers: Short Action, 22" Barrel: 270 WSM, 7mm WSM, 300 WSM, 325 WSM. Calibers: Long Action 22" Barrel: 270 Win., 30-06. Calibers: Long Action 24" Barrel: 7mm Rem. Mag., 300 Win. Mag. **Weight:** 6.5-7.75 lbs. **Length:** 40-45" overall. **Stock:** New checkered pistol grip and Schnabel forearm. Lightweight '81 differs from Pistol Grip models with a Western-style straight grip stock and banded forearm. Lightweight w/Pistol Grip Short Action and Long Action introduced 2005. Model '81 Lightning Long Action introduced 1996.

Price: Lightweight w/Pistol Grip Short Action, from **$893.00**
Price: Lightweight w/Pistol Grip Long Action **$940.00**
Price: Lightweight '81 Short Action **$878.00**
Price: Lightweight '81 Long Action **$831.00**
Price: Lightweight '81 Takedown Short Action, intr. 2007, from **$857.00**
Price: Lightweight '81 Takedown Long Action, intr. 2007, from **$904.00**

CHARLES DALY MODEL 1892 LEVER-ACTION RIFLES

Caliber: 45 Colt; 5-shot magazine with removable plug. **Barrel:** 24.25" octagonal. **Weight:** 6.8 lbs. **Length:** 42" overall. **Stock:** Two-piece American walnut, oil finish. **Sights:** Post front, adjustable open rear. **Features:** Color case-hardened receiver, lever, buttplate, forend cap. Introduced 2007. Imported from Italy by K.B.I., Inc.

Price: 1892 Rifle **$1,009.00**
Price: Take Down Rifle **$1,149.00**
Price: Large Loop Carbine **$1,009.00**

CIMARRON 1860 HENRY RIFLE CIVIL WAR MODEL

Caliber: 44 WCF, 45LC; 12-shot magazine. **Barrel:** 24" (rifle). **Weight:** 9.5 lbs. **Length:** 43" overall (rifle). **Stock:** European walnut. **Sights:** Bead front, open adjustable rear. **Features:** Brass receiver and buttplate. Uses original Henry loading system. Copy of the original rifle. Charcoal blue finish optional. Introduced 1991. Imported by Cimarron F.A. Co.

Price: from **$1,363.00**

CIMARRON 1866 WINCHESTER REPLICAS

Caliber: 38 Spec., 357, 45LC, 32 WCF, 38 WCF, 44 WCF. **Barrel:** 24" (rifle), 20" (short rifle), 19" (carbine), 16" (trapper). **Weight:** 9 lbs. **Length:** 43" overall (rifle). **Stock:** European walnut. **Sights:** Bead front, open adjustable rear. **Features:** Solid brass receiver, buttplate, forend cap. Octagonal barrel. Copy of the original Winchester '66 rifle. Introduced 1991. Imported by Cimarron F.A. Co.

Price: 1866 Sporting Rifle, 24" barrel, from **$1,038.00**
Price: 1866 Short Rifle, 20" barrel, from **$1,038.00**
Price: 1866 Carbine, 19" barrel, from **$987.00**
Price: 1866 Trapper, 16" barrel, from **$943.00**

CIMARRON 1873 SHORT RIFLE

Caliber: 357 Mag., 38 Spec., 32 WCF, 38 WCF, 44 Spec., 44 WCF, 45 Colt. **Barrel:** 20" tapered octagon. **Weight:** 7.5 lbs. **Length:** 39" overall. **Stock:** Walnut. **Sights:** Bead front, adjustable semi-buckhorn rear. **Features:** Has half "button" magazine. Original-type markings, including caliber, on barrel and elevator and "Kings" patent. From Cimarron F.A. Co.

Price: **$1,169.00**

Cimarron 1873 Deluxe Sporting Rifle

Similar to the 1873 Short Rifle except has 24" barrel with half-magazine.

Price: **$1,299.00**

CIMARRON 1873 LONG RANGE RIFLE

Caliber: 44 WCF, 45 Colt. **Barrel:** 30", octagonal. **Weight:** 8.5 lbs. **Length:** 48" overall. **Stock:** Walnut. **Sights:** Blade front, semi-buckhorn ramp rear. Tang sight optional. **Features:** Color case-hardened frame; choice of modern blue-black or charcoal blue for other parts. Barrel marked "Kings Improvement." From Cimarron F.A. Co.

Price: **$1,231.00**

DIXIE ENGRAVED 1873 SPORTING RIFLE

Caliber: 44-40, 13-shot magazine. **Barrel:** 24.25", tapered octagon. **Weight:** 8.25 lbs. **Length:** 43.25" overall. **Stock:** Walnut. **Sights:** Blade front, adjustable rear. **Features:** Engraved frame polished bright (casehardened on plain). Replica of Winchester 1873. Made in Italy. From Dixie Gun Works.

Price: CR204A **$1,600.00**
Price: Plain, blued rifle in .44/40, .45 LC, .32/20, .38/40. . . . **$ 1,050.00**
Price: Plain, blued carbine in .44/40 or .45 LC **$895.00**

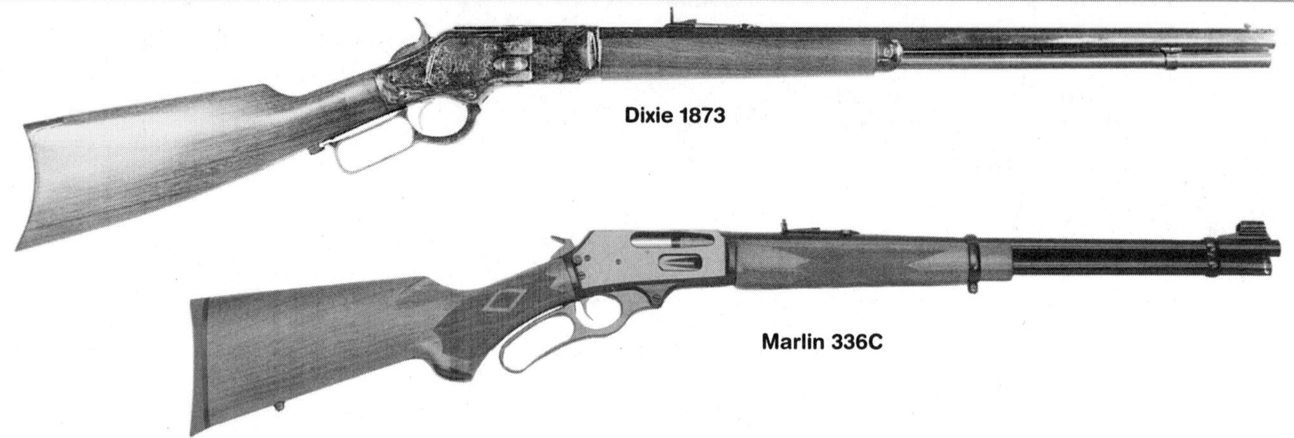
Dixie 1873

Marlin 336C

DIXIE 1873 DELUXE SPORTING RIFLE
Caliber: .44-40, .45 LC, .32-20 and .38-40, 13-shot magazine. **Barrel:** 24.25", tapered octagon. **Weight:** 8.25 lbs. **Length:** 43.25" overall. **Stock:** Walnut. Checkered pistol grip buttstock and forearm. **Sights:** Blade front, adjustable rear. **Features:** Color casehardened frame. Engraved frame polished bright. Replica of Winchester 1873. Made in Italy. From Dixie Gun Works.
Price: ....**$ 1,050.00 to $ 1,100.00**

DIXIE LIGHTNING RIFLE AND CARBINE
Caliber: .44-40 or .45 LC, 10-shot magazine. **Barrel:** 26" round or octagon, 1:16" or 1:36" twist. **Weight:** 7.25 lbs. **Length:** 43" overall. **Stock:** Walnut. **Sights:** Blade front, open adjustable rear. **Features:** Checkered forearm, blued steel furniture. Made by Pedersoli in Italy. Imported by Dixie Gun Works.
Price: ....**.25.00**
Price: Carbine **$1,225.00**

E.M.F. 1860 HENRY RIFLE
Caliber: 44-40 or 45 Colt. **Barrel:** 24". **Weight:** About 9 lbs. **Length:** About 43.75" overall. **Stock:** Oil-stained American walnut. **Sights:** Blade front, rear adjustable for elevation. **Features:** Reproduction of the original Henry rifle with brass frame and buttplate, rest blued. Imported by E.M.F.
Price: Brass frame **$1,129.00**
Price: Casehardened frame **$1,229.00**

E.M.F. 1866 YELLOWBOY LEVER ACTIONS
Caliber: 38 Spec., 44-40, 45 LC. **Barrel:** 19" (carbine), 24" (rifle). **Weight:** 9 lbs. **Length:** 43" overall (rifle). **Stock:** European walnut. **Sights:** Bead front, open adjustable rear. **Features:** Solid brass frame, blued barrel, lever, hammer, buttplate. Imported from Italy by E.M.F.
Price: Rifle **$1,045.00**
Price: Border Rifle, Short **$970.00**

E.M.F. MODEL 1873 LEVER-ACTION RIFLE
Caliber: 32/20, 357 Mag., 38/40, 44-40, 45 Colt. **Barrel:** 18", 20", 24", 30". **Weight:** 8 lbs. **Length:** 43.25" overall. **Stock:** European walnut. **Sights:** Bead front, rear adjustable for windage and elevation. **Features:** Color case-hardened frame (blue on carbine). Imported by E.M.F.
Price: **$1,050.00**

E.M.F. MODEL 1873 REVOLVER CARBINE
Caliber: 357 Mag., 45 Colt. **Barrel:** 18". **Weight:** 4 lbs., 8 oz. **Length:** 3/4" overall. **Stock:** One-piece walnut. **Sights:** Blade front, notch rear. **Features:** Color case-hardened frame, blue barrel, backstrap and trigger guard. Introduced 1998. Imported from Italy by EMF, Inc.
Price: Standard....................................**$580.00**

HENRY BIG BOY LEVER-ACTION CARBINE
Caliber: 357 Magnum, 44 Magnum, 45 Colt, 10-shot tubular magazine. **Barrel:** 20" octagonal, 1:38 right-hand twist. **Weight:** 8.68 lbs. **Length:** 38.5" overall. **Stock:** Straight-grip American walnut, brass buttplate. **Sights:** Marbles full adjustable semi-buckhorn rear, brass bead front. **Features:** Brasslite receiver not tapped for scope mount. Made in U.S.A. by Henry Repeating Arms.
Price: H006 44 Magnum, walnut, blued barrel **$899.00**
Price: H006DD Deluxe 44 Magnum, engraved receiver.... **$1,955.00**

Henry .30/30 Lever-Action Carbine
Same as the Big Boy except has straight grip American walnut, 30-30 only, 6-shot. Receivers are drilled and tapped for scope mount. Made in U.S.A. by Henry Repeating Arms.
Price: H009 Blued receiver, round barrel **$749.00**
Price: H009B Brass receiver, octagonal barrel...............**$969.00**

MARLIN MODEL 336C LEVER-ACTION CARBINE
Caliber: 30-30 or 35 Rem., 6-shot tubular magazine. **Barrel:** 20" Micro-Groove. **Weight:** 7 lbs. **Length:** 38.5" overall. **Stock:** Checkered American black walnut, capped pistol grip. Mar-Shield finish; rubber buttpad; swivel studs. **Sights:** Ramp front with Wide-Scan hood, semi-buckhorn folding rear adjustable for windage and elevation. **Features:** Hammer-block safety. Receiver tapped for scope mount, offset hammer spur; top of receiver sandblasted to prevent glare. Includes safety lock.
Price: **$530.00**

Marlin Model 336SS Lever-Action Carbine
Same as the 336C except receiver, barrel and other major parts are machined from stainless steel. 30-30 only, 6-shot; receiver tapped for scope. Includes safety lock.
Price: **$650.00**

Marlin Model 336W Lever-Action Rifle
Similar to the Model 336C except has walnut-finished, cut-checkered Maine birch stock; blued steel barrel band has integral sling swivel; no front sight hood; comes with padded nylon sling; hard rubber buttplate. Introduced 1998. Includes safety lock. Made in U.S.A. by Marlin.
Price: **$452.00**
Price: With 4x scope and mount **$495.00**

Marlin Model XLR Lever-Action Rifles
Similar to Model 336C except has an 24" stainless barrel with Ballard-type cut rifling, stainless steel receiver and other parts, laminated hardwood stock with pistol grip, nickel-plated swivel studs. Chambered for 30-30 Win. with Hornady spire-pointed Flex-Tip cartridges. Includes safety lock. Introduced 2006. Similar models chambered for 308 Marlin Express introduced in 2007
Price: Model 336XLR **$816.00**
Price: Model 308MXLR, laminated stock, stainless barrel (2007)......................................**$816.00**

MARLIN MODEL 444 LEVER-ACTION SPORTER
Caliber: 444 Marlin, 5-shot tubular magazine. **Barrel:** 22" deep cut Ballard rifling. **Weight:** 7.5 lbs. **Length:** 40.5" overall. **Stock:** Checkered American black walnut, capped pistol grip, rubber rifle buttpad. Mar-Shield finish; swivel studs. **Sights:** Hooded ramp front, folding semi-buckhorn rear adjustable for windage and elevation. **Features:** Hammer-block safety. Receiver tapped for scope mount; offset hammer spur. Includes safety lock.
Price: **$619.00**

Marlin Model 444XLR Lever-Action Rifle
Similar to Model 444 except has an 24" stainless barrel with Ballard-type cut rifling, stainless steel receiver and other parts, laminated hardwood stock with pistol grip, nickel-plated swivel studs. Chambered for 444 Marlin with Hornady Evolution spire-pointed Flex-Tip cartridges. Includes safety lock. Introduced 2006.
Price: (Model 444XLR) **$816.00**

Marlin 1894 Cowboy

Marlin 1895

Marlin 1895M

MARLIN MODEL 1894 LEVER-ACTION CARBINE

Caliber: 44 Spec./44 Mag., 10-shot tubular magazine. **Barrel:** 20" Ballard-type rifling. **Weight:** 6 lbs. **Length:** 37.5" overall. **Stock:** Checkered American black walnut, straight grip and forend. Mar-Shield finish. Rubber rifle buttpad; swivel studs. **Sights:** Wide-Scan hooded ramp front, semi-buckhorn folding rear adjustable for windage and elevation. **Features:** Hammer-block safety. Receiver tapped for scope mount, offset hammer spur, solid top receiver sand blasted to prevent glare. Includes safety lock.

Price: **$576.00**

Marlin Model 1894C Carbine

Similar to the standard Model 1894 except chambered for 38 Spec./357 Mag. with full-length 9-shot magazine, 18.5" barrel, hammer-block safety, hooded front sight. Introduced 1983. Includes safety lock.

Price: **$576.00**

MARLIN MODEL 1894 COWBOY

Caliber: 357 Mag., 44 Mag., 45 Colt, 10-shot magazine. **Barrel:** 20" tapered octagon, deep cut rifling. **Weight:** 7.5 lbs. **Length:** 41.5" overall. **Stock:** Straight grip American black walnut, hard rubber buttplate, Mar-Shield finish. **Sights:** Marble carbine front, adjustable Marble semi-buckhorn rear. **Features:** Squared finger lever; straight grip stock; blued steel forend tip. Designed for Cowboy Shooting events. Introduced 1996. Includes safety lock. Made in U.S.A. by Marlin.

Price: **$822.00**

Marlin Model 1894SS

Similar to Model 1894 except has stainless steel barrel, receiver, lever, guard plate, magazine tube and loading plate. Nickel-plated swivel studs.

Price: **$704.00**

MARLIN MODEL 1895 LEVER-ACTION RIFLE

Caliber: 45-70 Govt., 4-shot tubular magazine. **Barrel:** 22" round. **Weight:** 7.5 lbs. **Length:** 40.5" overall. **Stock:** Checkered American black walnut, full pistol grip. Mar-Shield finish; rubber buttpad; quick detachable swivel studs. **Sights:** Bead front with Wide-Scan hood, semi-buckhorn folding rear adjustable for windage and elevation. **Features:** Hammer-block safety. Solid receiver tapped for scope mounts or receiver sights; offset hammer spur. Includes safety lock.

Price: **$619.00**

Marlin Model 1895G Guide Gun Lever-Action Rifle

Similar to Model 1895 with deep-cut Ballard-type rifling; straight-grip walnut stock. Overall length is 37", weighs 7 lbs. Introduced 1998. Includes safety lock. Made in U.S.A. by Marlin.

Price: **$630.00**

Marlin Model 1895GS Guide Gun

Similar to Model 1895G except receiver, barrel and most metal parts are machined from stainless steel. Chambered for 45-70 Govt., 4-shot, 18.5" barrel. Overall length is 37", weighs 7 lbs. Introduced 2001. Includes safety lock. Made in U.S.A. by Marlin.

Price: **$752.00**

Marlin Model 1895 Cowboy Lever-Action Rifle

Similar to Model 1895 except has 26" tapered octagon barrel with Ballard-type rifling, Marble carbine front sight and Marble adjustable semi-buckhorn rear sight. Receiver tapped for scope or receiver sight. Overall length is 44.5", weighs about 8 lbs. Introduced 2001. Includes safety lock. Made in U.S.A. by Marlin.

Price: **$785.00**

Marlin Model 1895XLR Lever-Action Rifle

Similar to Model 1895 except has an 24" stainless barrel with Ballard-type cut rifling, stainless steel receiver and other parts, laminated hardwood stock with pistol grip, nickel-plated swivel studs. Chambered for 45-70 Govt. Government with Hornady Evolution spire-pointed Flex-Tip cartridges. Includes safety lock. Introduced 2006.

Price: (Model 1895MXLR) **$816.00**

Marlin Model 1895M Lever-Action Rifle

Similar to Model 1895G except has an 18.5" barrel with Ballard-type cut rifling. Chambered for 450 Marlin. Includes safety lock.

Price: (Model 1895M) **$678.00**

Marlin Model 1895MXLR Lever-Action Rifle

Similar to Model 1895M except has an 24" stainless barrel with Ballard-type cut rifling, stainless steel receiver and other parts, laminated hardwood stock with pistol grip, nickel-plated swivel studs. Chambered for 450 Marlin with Hornady Evolution spire-pointed Flex-Tip cartridges. Includes safety lock. Introduced 2006.

Price: (Model 1895MXLR) **$874.00**

MOSSBERG 464 LEVER ACTION RIFLE

Caliber: 30-30 Win., 6-shot tubular magazine. **Barrel:** 20" round. **Weight:** 6.7 lbs. **Length:** 38.5" overall. **Stock:** Hardwood, quick detachable swivel studs. **Sights:** Folding rear sight, adjustable for windage and elevation. **Features:** Blued receiver and barrel, receiver drilled and tapped, two-position top-tang safety. Introduced 2008. From O.F. Mossberg & Sons, Inc.

Price: **$473.00**

NAVY ARMS 1874 SHARPS #2 CREEDMORE RIFLE

Caliber: .45-70 Govt. **Barrel:** 30" octagon. **Weight:** 10 lbs. **Length:** 48" overall. **Sights:** Soule target grade rear tang sight, front globe with 12 inserts. **Features:** Highly polished nickel receiver and action, double-set triggers. From Navy Arms.

Price: Model SCR072 (2008) **$1,816.00**

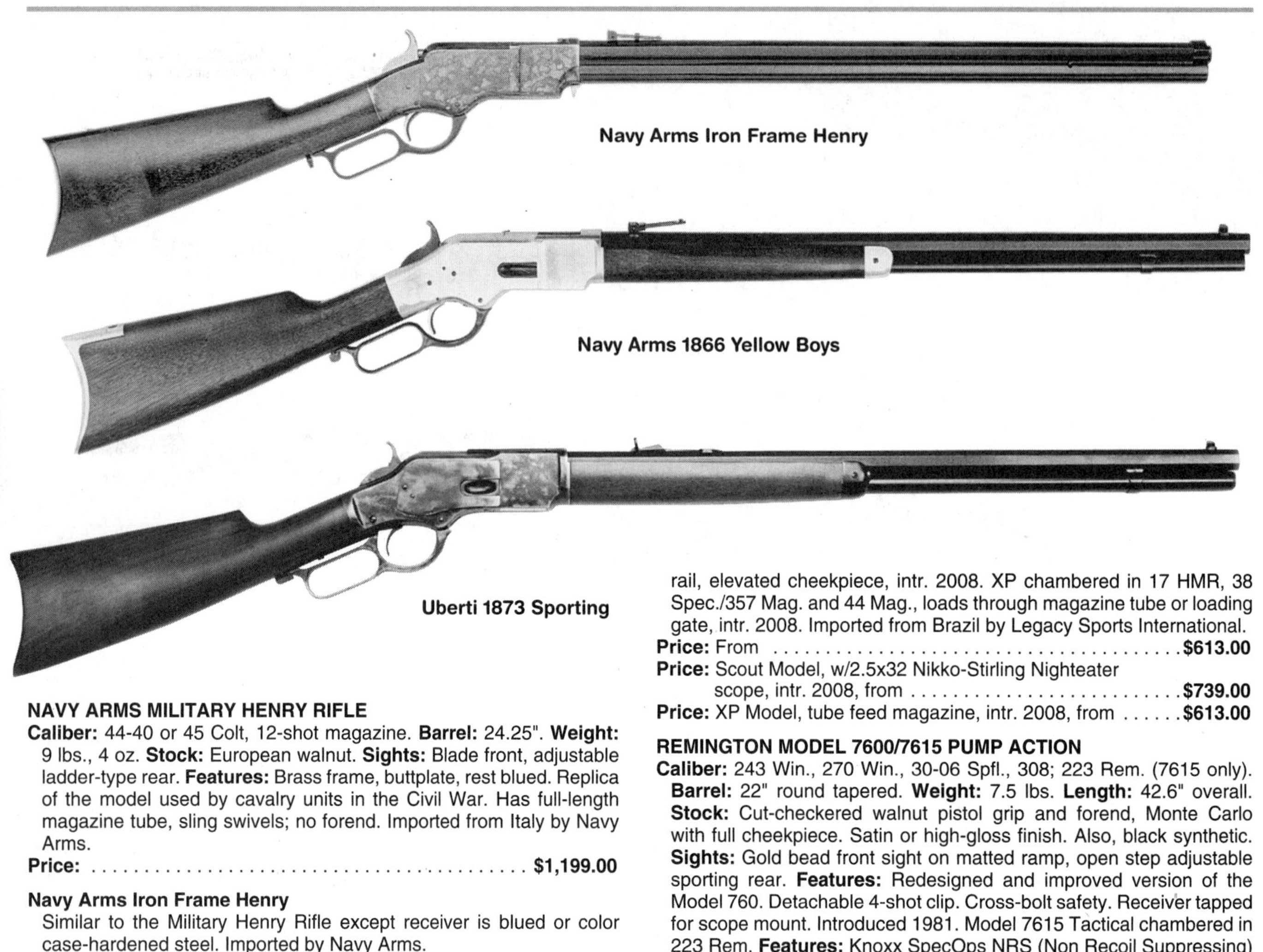
Navy Arms Iron Frame Henry

Navy Arms 1866 Yellow Boys

Uberti 1873 Sporting

NAVY ARMS MILITARY HENRY RIFLE

Caliber: 44-40 or 45 Colt, 12-shot magazine. **Barrel:** 24.25". **Weight:** 9 lbs., 4 oz. **Stock:** European walnut. **Sights:** Blade front, adjustable ladder-type rear. **Features:** Brass frame, buttplate, rest blued. Replica of the model used by cavalry units in the Civil War. Has full-length magazine tube, sling swivels; no forend. Imported from Italy by Navy Arms.

Price: **$1,199.00**

Navy Arms Iron Frame Henry

Similar to the Military Henry Rifle except receiver is blued or color case-hardened steel. Imported by Navy Arms.

Price: Blued **$1,247.00**

NAVY ARMS 1866 YELLOW BOY RIFLE

Caliber: 38 Spec., 44-40, 45 Colt, 12-shot magazine. **Barrel:** 20" or 24", full octagon. **Weight:** 8.5 lbs. **Length:** 42.5" overall. **Stock:** Walnut. **Sights:** Blade front, adjustable ladder-type rear. **Features:** Brass frame, forend tip, buttplate, blued barrel, lever, hammer. Introduced 1991. Imported from Italy by Navy Arms.

Price: Yellow Boy Rifle, 24.25" barrel **$966.00**

Price: Yellow Boy Carbine, 19" barrel **$952.00**

NAVY ARMS 1873 WINCHESTER-STYLE RIFLE

Caliber: 357 Mag., 44-40, 45 Colt, 12-shot magazine. **Barrel:** 24.25". **Weight:** 8.25 lbs. **Length:** 43" overall. **Stock:** European walnut. **Sights:** Blade front, buckhorn rear. **Features:** Color case-hardened frame, rest blued. Full-octagon barrel. Imported by Navy Arms.

Price: **$1,092.00**

Price: 1873 Carbine, 19" barrel **$1,064.00**

Price: 1873 Sporting Rifle (octagonal bbl., checkered walnut stock and forend) **$1,183.00**

Price: 1873 Border Model, 20" octagon barrel **$1,092.00**

Price: 1873 Deluxe Border Model **$1,218.00**

PUMA MODEL 92 RIFLES AND CARBINES

Caliber: 17 HMR (XP and Scout models, only; intr. 2008), 38 Spec./357 Mag., 44 Mag., 45 Colt, 454 Casull, 480 Ruger (.44-40 in 20" octagonal barrel). **Barrel:** 16" and 20" round; 20" and 24" octagonal. 1:30" rate of twist (exc. 17 HMR is 1:9"). **Weight:** 7.7 lbs. **Stock:** Walnut stained hardwood. **Sights:** Blade front, V rear, buckhorn sights sold separately. **Features:** Finishes available in blue/blue, blue/case colored and stainless/stainless with matching crescent butt plates. .454 and .480 calibers have rubber recoil pads. Full-length magazines, thumb safety. Large lever loop or HiViz sights available on select models. Magazine capacity is 12 rounds with 24" bbl.; 10 rounds with 20" barrel; 8 rounds in 16" barrel. Introduced in 2002. Scout includes long-eye-relief scope, rail, elevated cheekpiece, intr. 2008. XP chambered in 17 HMR, 38 Spec./357 Mag. and 44 Mag., loads through magazine tube or loading gate, intr. 2008. Imported from Brazil by Legacy Sports International.

Price: From **$613.00**

Price: Scout Model, w/2.5x32 Nikko-Stirling Nighteater scope, intr. 2008, from **$739.00**

Price: XP Model, tube feed magazine, intr. 2008, from **$613.00**

REMINGTON MODEL 7600/7615 PUMP ACTION

Caliber: 243 Win., 270 Win., 30-06 Spfl., 308; 223 Rem. (7615 only). **Barrel:** 22" round tapered. **Weight:** 7.5 lbs. **Length:** 42.6" overall. **Stock:** Cut-checkered walnut pistol grip and forend, Monte Carlo with full cheekpiece. Satin or high-gloss finish. Also, black synthetic. **Sights:** Gold bead front sight on matted ramp, open step adjustable sporting rear. **Features:** Redesigned and improved version of the Model 760. Detachable 4-shot clip. Cross-bolt safety. Receiver tapped for scope mount. Introduced 1981. Model 7615 Tactical chambered in 223 Rem. **Features:** Knoxx SpecOps NRS (Non Recoil Suppressing) adjustable stock, parkerized finish, 10-round detachable magazine box, sling swivel studs. Introduced 2007.

Price:7600 Wood **$768.00**

Price:7600 Synthetic. **$643.00**

Price: 7615 Ranch Carbine **$955.00**

Price: 7615 Camo Hunter. **$1,009.00**

Price: 7615 Tactical 223 Rem., 16.5" barrel, 10-rd. magazine (2008). **$955.00**

TRISTAR SHARPS 1874 SPORTING RIFLE

Caliber: 45-70 Govt. **Barrel:** 28", 32", 34" octagonal. **Weight:** 9.75 lbs. **Length:** 44.5" overall. **Stock:** Walnut. **Sights:** Dovetail front, adjustable rear. **Features:** Cut checkering, case colored frame finish.

Price: **$959.00**

UBERTI 1873 SPORTING RIFLE

Caliber: 357 Mag., 44-40, 45 Colt. **Barrel:** 19" to 24.25". **Weight:** Up to 8.2 lbs. **Length:** Up to 43.3" overall. **Stock:** Walnut, straight grip and pistol grip. **Sights:** Blade front adjustable for windage, open rear adjustable for elevation. **Features:** Color case-hardened frame, blued barrel, hammer, lever, buttplate, brass elevator. Imported by Stoeger Industries.

Price: 1873 Carbine, 19" round barrel **$1,119.00**

Price: 1873 Short Rifle, 20" octagonal barrel **$1,249.00**

Price: 1873 Special Sporting Rifle, 24.25" octagonal barrel **$1,379.00**

UBERTI 1866 YELLOWBOY CARBINE, SHORT RIFLE, RIFLE

Caliber: 38 Spec., 44-40, 45 Colt. **Barrel:** 24.25", octagonal. **Weight:** 8.2 lbs. **Length:** 43.25" overall. **Stock:** Walnut. **Sights:** Blade front adjustable for windage, rear adjustable for elevation. **Features:** Frame, buttplate, forend cap of polished brass, balance charcoal blued. Imported by Stoeger Industries.

Price: 1866 Yellowboy Carbine, 19" round barrel. **$1,079.00**

Price: 1866 Yellowboy Short Rifle, 20" octagonal barrel . . . **$1,129.00**

Price: 1866 Yellowboy Rifle, 24.25" octagonal barrel **$1,129.00**

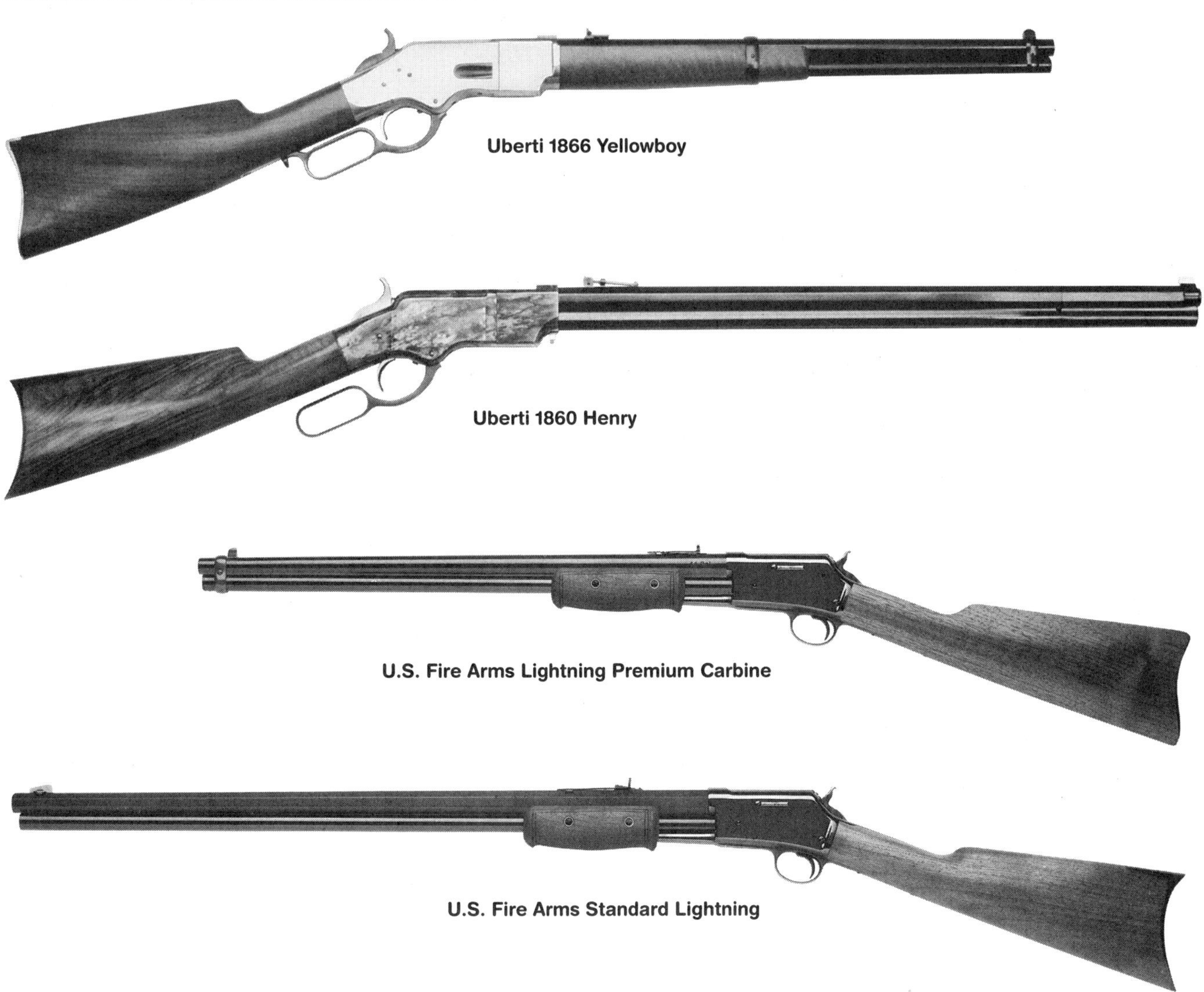

Uberti 1866 Yellowboy

Uberti 1860 Henry

U.S. Fire Arms Lightning Premium Carbine

U.S. Fire Arms Standard Lightning

UBERTI 1860 HENRY RIFLE

Caliber: 44-40, 45 Colt. **Barrel:** 24.25", half-octagon. **Weight:** 9.2 lbs. **Length:** 43.75" overall. **Stock:** American walnut. **Sights:** Blade front, rear adjustable for elevation. Imported by Stoeger Industries.

Price: 1860 Henry Trapper, 18.5" barrel, brass frame **$1,329.00**
Price: 1860 Henry Rifle Iron Frame, 24.25" barrel **$1,419.00**

UBERTI LIGHTNING RIFLE

Caliber: 357 Mag., 45 Colt, 10+1. **Barrel:** 20" to 24.25". **Stock:** Walnut. Finish: Blue or case-hardened. Introduced 2006. Imported by Stoeger Industries.

Price: 1875 Lightning Rifle, 24.25" barrel **$1,259.00**
Price: 1875 Lightning Short Rifle, 20" barrel **$1,259.00**
Price: 1875 Lightning Carbine, 20" barrel **$1,179.00**

UBERTI SPRINGFIELD TRAPDOOR RIFLE

Caliber: 4-70, single shot. **Barrel:** 22" or 32.5". **Stock:** Walnut. Finish: Blue and case-hardened. Introduced 2006. Imported by Stoeger Industries.

Price: Springfield Trapdoor Carbine, 22" barrel **$1,429.00**
Price: Springfield Trapdoor Army, 32.5" barrel **$1,669.00**

U.S. FIRE ARMS STANDARD LIGHTNING MAGAZINE RIFLE

Caliber: 45 Colt, 44 WCF, 44 Spec., 38 WCF, 15-shot. **Barrel:** 26". **Stock:** Oiled walnut. Finish: High polish blue. Nickel finish also available. Introduced 2002. Made in U.S.A. by United States Fire-Arms Manufacturing Co.

Price: Round barrel............................... **$1,480.00**
Price: Octagonal barrel, checkered forend **$1,750.00**
Price: Half-round barrel, checkered forend **$1,999.00**
Price: Premium Carbine, 20" round barrel **$1,480.00**
Price: Baby Carbine, 20" special taper barrel **$1,999.00**
Price: Trapper, 16" special taper barrel **$2,155.00**
Price: Cowboy Action Lightning **$1,345.00**
Price: Cowboy Action Lightning Carbine, 20" round barrel . **$1,345.00**

Includes models for a wide variety of sporting and competitive purposes and uses.

Anchutz 1733D

Barrett Model 95

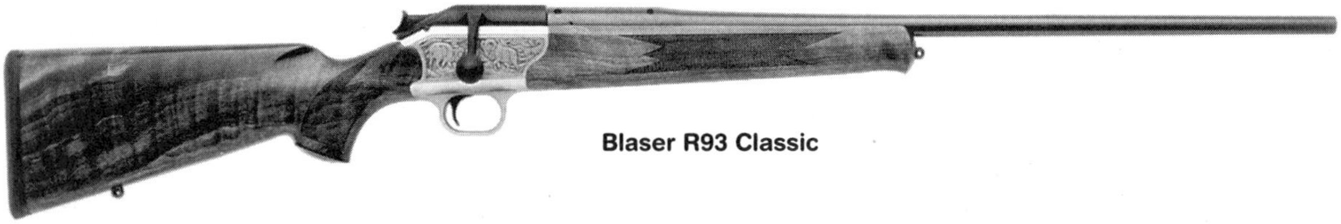

Blaser R93 Classic

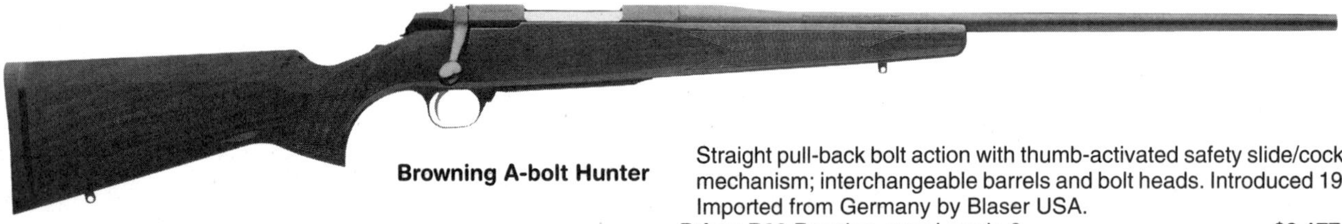

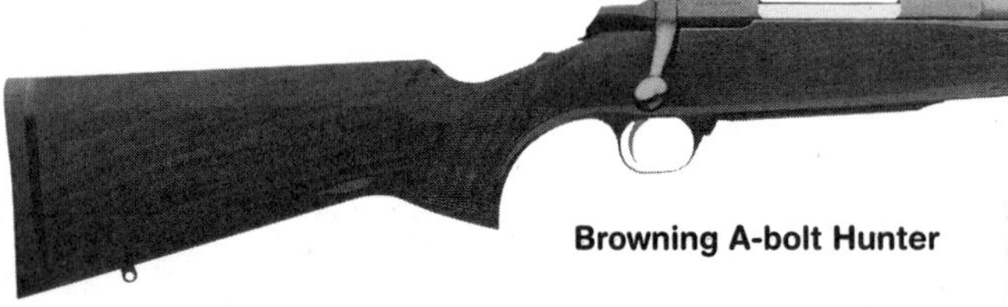

Browning A-bolt Hunter

Anschutz 1733D Rifle

Similar to the 1740 Monte Carlo except has full-length, walnut, Mannlicher-style stock with skip-line checkering, rosewood Schnabel tip, and is chambered for 22 Hornet. Weighs 6.4 lbs., overall length 39", barrel length 19.7". Imported from Germany by Merkel USA.

Price: **$1,899.00**

BARRETT MODEL 95 BOLT-ACTION RIFLE

Caliber: 50 BMG, 5-shot magazine. **Barrel:** 29". **Weight:** 23.5 lbs. **Length:** 45" overall. **Stock:** Energy-absorbing recoil pad. **Sights:** Scope optional. **Features:** Bolt-action, bullpup design. Disassembles without tools; extendable bipod legs; match-grade barrel; muzzle brake. Introduced 1995. Made in U.S.A. by Barrett Firearms Mfg., Inc.

Price: From **$6,360.00**

BLASER R93 BOLT-ACTION RIFLE

Caliber: 22-250 Rem., 243 Win., 6.5x55, 270 Win., 7x57, 7mm-08 Rem., 308 Win., 30-06 Spfl., 257 Wby. Mag., 7mm Rem. Mag., 300 Win. Mag., 300 Wby. Mag., 338 Win. Mag., 375 H&H, 416 Rem. Mag. **Barrel:** 22" (standard calibers), 26" (magnum). **Weight:** 7 lbs. **Length:** 40" overall (22" barrel). **Stock:** Two-piece European walnut. **Sights:** None furnished; drilled and tapped for scope mounting. **Features:** Straight pull-back bolt action with thumb-activated safety slide/cocking mechanism; interchangeable barrels and bolt heads. Introduced 1994. Imported from Germany by Blaser USA.

Price: R93 Prestige, wood grade 3. **$3,177.00**
Price: R93 Luxus **$4,326.00**
Price: R93 Professional **$3,031.00**
Price: R93 Grand Luxe **$7,972.00**
Price: R93 Attache **$5,990.00**

BROWNING A-BOLT RIFLES

Common Features: Short-throw (60") fluted bolt, three locking lugs, plunger-type ejector; adjustable trigger is grooved. Chrome-plated trigger sear. Hinged floorplate, detachable box magazine. Slide tang safety. Receivers are drilled and tapped for scope mounts, swivel studs included. Barrel is free-floating and glass-bedded, recessed muzzle. Safety is top-tang sliding button. Engraving available for bolt sleeve or rifle body. Introduced 1985. 30 model name variations, as noted below. Imported from Japan by Browning.

BROWNING A-BOLT HUNTER

Calibers: 22" Barrel: 223 Rem., 22-250 Rem., 243 Win., 270 Win., 30-06 Spfl., 7mm-08 Rem., 308 Win. **Barrel:** 270 WSM, 7mm WSM, 300 WSM, 325 WSM (intr. 2005). **Calibers:** 24" Barrel: 25-06 Rem. **Calibers:** 26" Barrel: 7mm Rem. Mag., 300 Win. Mag., 338 Win. Mag **Weight:** 6.25-7.2 lbs. **Length:** 41.25-46.5" overall. **Stock:** Sporter-style walnut; checkered grip and forend. **Metal Finish:** Low-luster blueing.

Price: Hunter, left-hand, from **$765.00**

Browning A-Bolt Medallion

Browning A-Bolt White Gold Medallion

Browning A-Bolt Stainless Stalker

Browning A-Bolt Varmint Stalker

BROWNING A-BOLT HUNTER FLD

Caliber: 23" Barrel: 270 WSM, 7mm WSM, 300 WSM, 325 WSM (intr. 2005). **Weight:** 6.6 lbs. **Length:** 42.75" overall. **Features:** FLD has low-luster blueing and select Monte Carlo stock with right-hand palm swell, double-border checkering. Otherwise similar to A-Bolt Hunter.

Price: FLD **$840.00**

BROWNING A-BOLT MOUNTAIN TI

Caliber: 223 WSSM, 243 WSSM, 25 WSSM (all added 2005); 270 WSM, 7mm WSM, 300 WSM. **Barrel:** 22" or 23". **Weight:** 5.25-5.5 lbs. **Length:** 41.25-42.75" overall. **Stock:** Lightweight fiberglass Bell & Carlson model in Mossy-Oak New Break Up camo. Metal Finish: Stainless barrel, titanium receiver. **Features:** Pachmayr Decelerator recoil pad. Introduced 1999.

Price: From **$1,706.00**

Browning A-Bolt Micro Hunter and Micro Hunter Left-Hand

Calibers: 20" Barrel: 22-250 Rem., 243 Win., 308 Win., 7mm-08. Calibers: 22" Barrel: 22 Hornet, 270 WSM, 7mm WSM, 300 WSM, 325 WSM (2005). **Weight:** 6.25-6.4 lbs. **Length:** 39.5-41.5" overall. **Features:** Classic walnut stock with 13.3" LOP. Otherwise similar to A-Bolt Hunter.

Price: Micro Hunter, from **$712.00**

Price: Micro Hunter Left-hand, from **$743.00**

BROWNING A-BOLT MEDALLION

Calibers: 22" Barrel: 223 Rem., 22-250 Rem., 243 Win., 308 Win., 270 Win., 280 Rem., 30-06. Calibers: 23" Barrel: 270 WSM, 7mm WSM, 300 WSM, 325 WSM (intr. 2005). Calibers: 24" Barrel: 25-06 Rem. Calibers: 26" Barrel: 7mm Rem. Mag., 300 Win. Mag., 338 Win. Mag., 375 H&H. **Weight:** 6.25-7.1 lbs. **Length:** 41.25-46.5" overall. **Stock:** Select walnut stock, glossy finish, rosewood grip and forend caps, checkered grip and forend. Metal Finish: Engraved high-polish blued receiver.

Price: Medallion, from **$821.00**

Price: Medallion WSSM in 223/243 Win./25 WSSM **$872.00**

Price: Medallion w/BOSS, intr. 1987, from **$919.00**

Price: Medallion w/Boss, left-hand, from **$871.00**

BROWNING A-BOLT WHITE GOLD MEDALLION, RMEF WHITE GOLD, WHITE GOLD MEDALLION W/BOSS

Calibers: 22" Barrel: 270 Win., 30-06. Calibers: 23" Barrel: 270 WSM, 7mm WSM, 300 WSM, 325 WSM (intr. 2005). Calibers: 26" Barrel: 7mm Rem. Mag., 300 Win. Mag. **Weight:** 6.4-7.7 lbs. **Length:** 42.75-46.5" overall. **Stock:** select walnut stock with brass spacers between rubber recoil pad and between the rosewood gripcap and forend tip; gold-filled barrel inscription; palm-swell pistol grip, Monte Carlo comb, 22 lpi checkering with double borders. **Metal Finish:** Engraved high-polish stainless receiver and barrel. BOSS version chambered in 270 Win. and 30-06 (22" barrel) and 7mm Rem. Mag. and 300 Win. Mag. (26" barrel). Introduced 1988. RMEF version has engraved gripcap, continental cheekpiece; gold engraved, stainless receiver and bbl. Introduced 2004.

Price: White Gold Medallion, from **$1,202.00**

Price: Rocky Mt. Elk Foundation White Gold, 325 WSM, intr. 2007 . . . . **$1,312.00**

BROWNING A-BOLT STAINLESS STALKER, STAINLESS STALKER LEFT-HAND

Calibers: 22" Barrel: 223 Rem., 243 Win., 270 Win., 280 Rem., 7mm-08 Rem., 30-06 Spfl., 308 Win. Calibers: 23" Barrel: 270 WSM, 7mm WSM, 300 WSM, 325 WSM (intr. 2005). Calibers: 24" Barrel: 25-06 Rem. Calibers: 26" Barrel: 7mm Rem. Mag., 300 Win. Mag., 338 Win. Mag., 375 H&H. **Weight:** 6.1-7.2 lbs. **Length:** 40.9-46.5" overall. **Features:** Similar to the A-Bolt Hunter model except receiver and barrel are made of stainless steel; other exposed metal surfaces are finished silver-gray matte. Graphite-fiberglass composite textured stock. No sights are furnished, except on 375 H&H, which comes with open sights. Introduced 1987.

Price: Stainless Stalker left-hand, from **$963.00**

Price: Stainless Stalker w/Boss, from **$1,015.00**

BROWNING A-BOLT VARMINT STALKER, VARMINT STALKER WSSM

Calibers: 24" Barrel: 223 Rem., 223 WSSM, 243 WSSM, 25 WSSM. Calibers: 26" Barrel: 22-250. **Weight:** 7.8-8.2 lbs. **Length:** 42.75-45.75" overall. **Features:** Similar to the A-Bolt Stainless Stalker except has black graphite-fiberglass stock with textured finish and matte blue-finish on all exposed metal surfaces. Medium-heavy varmint barrel. No sights are furnished. Introduced 1987.

Price: Varmint Stalker **$895.00**

Browning A-Bolt Composite Stalker

Browning A-Bolt Eclipse Hunter

Browning A-Bolt M-1000 Eclipse

Cooper Model 21 Bolt

BROWNING A-BOLT COMPOSITE STALKER

Calibers: 22" Barrel: 270 Win., 30-06. Calibers: 23" Barrel: 270 WSM, 7mm WSM, 300 WSM, 325 WSM (intr. 2005). Calibers: 24" Barrel: 25-06 Rem. Calibers: 26" Barrel: 7mm Rem. Mag., 300 Win. Mag., 338 Win. Mag. **Weight:** 6.1-7.2 lbs. **Length:** 40.75-46.5" overall. **Features:** Similar to the A-Bolt Stainless Stalker except has black composite stock with textured finish and matte-blued finish on all exposed metal surfaces except bolt sleeve. No sights are furnished.

Price: Composite Stalker, from **$815.00**

BROWNING A-BOLT ECLIPSE HUNTER W/BOSS, M-1000 ECLIPSE W/BOSS, M-1000 ECLIPSE WSM, STAINLESS M-1000 ECLIPSE WSM

Calibers: 22" Barrel: 270 Win., 30-06. Calibers: 26" Barrel: 7mm Rem. Mag., 300 Win. Mag., 270 WSM, 7mm WSM, 300 WSM. **Weight:** 7.5-9.9 lbs. **Length:** 42.75-46.5" overall. **Features:** All models have gray/black laminated thumbhole stock. Introduced 1996. Two versions have BOSS barrel vibration modulator and muzzle brake. Hunter has sporter-weight barrel. M-1000 Eclipses have long actions and heavy target barrels, adjustable triggers, bench-style forends, 3-shot magazines. Introduced 1997.

Price: Eclipse Hunter w/BOSS, from **$1,180.00**
Price: M-1000 Eclipse, from **$1,100.00**
Price: M-1000 Eclipse w/BOSS, from **$1,181.00**
Price: Stainless M-1000 Eclipse WSM, from **$1,314.00**

BROWNING X-BOLT RIFLES

Calibers: 243 Win., 25-06 Rem., 270 Win., 270 WSM, 280 Rem., 30-06 Spfl., 300 Win. Mag., 300 WSM, 308 Win., 325 WSM, 338 Win. Mag., 375 H&H Mag., 7mm Rem. Mag., 7mm WSM, 7mm-08 Rem. Barrels: 22", 23", 24", 26", varies by model. Matte blued or stainless free-floated barrel, recessed muzzle crown. **Weight:** 6.3-7 lbs. **Stock:** Hunter and Medallion models have wood stocks; Composite Stalker and Stainless Stalker models have composite stocks. Inflex Technology recoil pad. **Sights:** None, drilled and tapped receiver, X-Lock scope mounts. **Features:** Adjustable three-lever Feather Trigger system, polished hard-chromed steel components, factory pre-set at 3.5 lbs., alloy trigger housing. Bolt unlock button, detachable rotary magazine, 60-degree bolt lift, three locking lugs, top-tang safety, sling swivel studs. Medallion has metal engraving, gloss finish walnut stock, rosewood fore-end grip and pistol grip cap. Introduced 2008. From Browning.

Price: X-Bolt Hunter, from. **$799.00**
Price: X-Bolt Medallion, from **$899.00**
Price: X-Bolt Composite Stalker, from **$799.00**
Price: X-Bolt Stainless Stalker, from. **$999.00**

CARBON ONE BOLT-ACTION RIFLE

Caliber: 22-250 to 375 H&H. **Barrel:** Up to 28". **Weight:** 5.5 to 7.25 lbs. **Length:** Varies. **Stock:** Synthetic or wood. **Sights:** None furnished. **Features:** Choice of Remington, Browning or Winchester action with free-floated Christensen graphite/epoxy/steel barrel, trigger pull tuned to 3 to 3.5 lbs. Made in U.S.A. by Christensen Arms.

Price: Carbon One Hunter Rifle, 6.5 to 7 lbs. **$1,775.00**
Price: Carbon One Custom, 5.5 to 6.5 lbs., Shilen trigger . . **$3,900.00**
Price: Carbon Extreme **$2,450.00**

CENTURY INTERNATIONAL M70 SPORTER DOUBLE-TRIGGER BOLT ACTION RIFLE

Caliber: 22-250 Rem., 270 Win., 300 Win. Mag, 308 Win., 24" barrel. **Weight:** 7.95 lbs. **Length:** 44.5". **Sights:** Flip-up U-notch rear sight, hooded blade front sight. **Features:** Mauser M98-type action; 5-rd fixed box magazine. 22-250 has hinged floorplate. Monte Carlo stock, oil finish. Adjustable trigger on double-trigger models. 300 Win. Mag. Has 3-rd. fixed box magazine. 308 Win. holds 5 rounds. 300 and 308 have buttpads. Manufactured by Zastava in Yugoslavia, imported by Century International.

Price: M70 Sporter Double-Trigger. **$500.00**
Price: M70 Sporter Double-Trigger 22-250 . . . . **$475.00**
Price: M70 Sporter Single-Trigger .300 Win. Mag. **$475.00**
Price: M70 Sporter Single/Double Trigger 308 Win. **$500.00**

CHEYTAC M-200

Caliber: 408 CheyTac, 7-round magazine. **Barrel:** 30". **Length:** 55", stock extended. **Weight:** 27 lbs. (steel barrel); 24 lbs. (carbon fiber barrel). **Stock:** Retractable. **Sights:** None, scope rail provided. **Features:** CNC-machined receiver, attachable Picatinny rail M-1913, detachable barrel, integral bipod, 3.5-lb. trigger pull, muzzle brake. Made in U.S. by CheyTac, LLC.

Price: **$13,795.00**

CZ 527 Lux

CZ 527 FS

CZ 527 American

COOPER MODEL 21 BOLT-ACTION RIFLE

Caliber: 17 Rem., 19-223, Tactical 20, .204 Ruger, 222 Rem, 222 Rem. Mag., 223 Rem, 223 Rem A.I., 6x45, 6x47. **Barrel:** 22" or 24" in Classic configurations, 24"-26" in Varminter configurations. **Weight:** 6.5-8.0 lbs., depending on type. **Stock:** AA-AAA select claro walnut, 20 lpi checkering. **Sights:** None furnished. **Features:** Three front locking-lug bolt-action single shot. Action: 7.75" long, Sako extractor. Button ejector. Fully adjustable single-stage trigger. Options include wood upgrades, case-color metalwork, barrel fluting, custom LOP, and many others.

Price: from **$1,345.00**

COOPER MODEL 22 BOLT-ACTION RIFLE

Caliber: 22-250 Rem., 22-250 Rem. AI, 25-06 Rem., 25-06 Rem. AI, 243 Win., 243 Win. AI, 220 Swift, 250/3000 AI, 257 Roberts, 257 Roberts AI, 7mm-08 Rem., 6mm Rem., 260 Rem., 6 x 284, 6.5 x 284, 22 BR, 6mm BR, 308 Win. **Barrel:** 24" or 26" stainless match in Classic configurations. 24" or 26" in Varminter configurations. **Weight:** 7.5 to 8.0 lbs. depending on type. **Stock:** AA-AAA select claro walnut, 20 lpi checkering. **Sights:** None furnished. **Features:** Three front locking-lug bolt-action single shot. Action: 8.25" long, Sako style extractor. Button ejector. Fully adjustable single-stage trigger. Options include wood upgrades, case-color metalwork, barrel fluting, custom LOP, and many others.

Price: from **$1,450.00**

COOPER MODEL 38 BOLT-ACTION RIFLE

Caliber: 17 Squirrel, 17 He Bee, 17 Ackley Hornet, 17 Mach IV, 19 Calhoon, 20 VarTarg, 221 Fireball, 22 Hornet, 22 K-Hornet, 22 Squirrel, 218 Bee, 218 Mashburn Bee. **Barrel:** 22" or 24" in Classic configurations, 24" or 26" in Varminter configurations. **Weight:** 6.5-8.0 lbs. depending on type. **Stock:** AA-AAA select claro walnut, 20 lpi checkering. **Sights:** None furnished. **Features:** Three front locking-lug bolt-action single shot. Action: 7" long, Sako style extractor. Button ejector. Fully adjustable single-stage trigger. Options include wood upgrades, case-color metalwork, barrel fluting, custom LOP, and many others.

Price: from **$1,345.00**

CZ 527 LUX BOLT-ACTION RIFLE

Caliber: 204 Ruger, 22 Hornet, 222 Rem., 223 Rem., detachable 5-shot magazine. **Barrel:** 23.5"; standard or heavy barrel. **Weight:** 6 lbs., 1 oz. **Length:** 42.5" overall. **Stock:** European walnut with Monte Carlo. **Sights:** Hooded front, open adjustable rear. **Features:** Improved mini-Mauser action with non-rotating claw extractor; single set trigger; grooved receiver. Imported from the Czech Republic by CZ-USA.

Price: Brown laminate stock **$654.00**

Price: Model FS, full-length stock, cheekpiece **$730.00**

CZ 527 American Bolt-Action Rifle

Similar to the CZ 527 Lux except has classic-style stock with 18 lpi checkering; free-floating barrel; recessed target crown on barrel. No sights furnished. Introduced 1999. Imported from the Czech Republic by CZUSA.

Price: from **$671.00**

CZ 550 AMERICAN CLASSIC BOLT-ACTION RIFLE

Caliber: 22-250 Rem., 243 Win., 6.5x55, 7x57, 7x64, 308 Win., 9.3x62, 270 Win., 30-06. **Barrel:** free-floating barrel; recessed target crown. **Weight:** 7.48 lbs. **Length:** 44.68" overall. **Stock:** American classic-style stock with 18 lpi checkering or FS (Mannlicher). **Sights:** No sights furnished. **Features:** Improved Mauser-style action with claw extractor, fixed ejector, square bridge dovetailed receiver; single set trigger. Introduced 1999. Imported from the Czech Republic by CZ-USA.

Price: FS (full stock) **$706.00**

Price: American, from **$712.00**

CZ 550 American Safari Magnum Bolt-Action Rifle

Similar to CZ 550 American Classic. Chambered for 375 H&H Mag., 416 Rigby, 458 Win. Mag., 458 Lott. American pattern stock in 3 different laminate color combinations, as well as field and fancy grade American black walnut. Overall length is 46.5"; barrel length 25"; weighs 9.9 lbs. Hooded front sight, express rear with one standing, two folding leaves. Imported from the Czech Republic by CZ-USA.

Price: **$1,073.00**

CZ 750 SNIPER RIFLE

Caliber: 308 Winchester, 10-shot magazine. **Barrel:** 26". **Weight:** 11.9 lbs. **Length:** 48" overall. **Stock:** Polymer thumbhole. **Sights:** None furnished; permanently attached Weaver rail for scope mounting. **Features:** 60-degree bolt throw; oversized trigger guard and bolt handle for use with gloves; full-length equipment rail on forend; fully adjustable trigger. Introduced 2001. Imported from the Czech Republic by CZ-USA.

Price: **$1,999.00**

Dakota 76 Traveler

Dakota 76 Classic

Dakota Longbow

DSA DS-MP1

DAKOTA 76 TRAVELER TAKEDOWN RIFLE

Caliber: 257 Roberts, 25-06 Rem., 7x57, 270 Win., 280 Rem., 30-06 Spfl., 338-06, 35 Whelen (standard length); 7mm Rem. Mag., 300 Win. Mag., 338 Win. Mag., 416 Taylor, 458 Win. Mag. (short magnums); 7mm, 300, 330, 375 Dakota Magnums. **Barrel:** 23". **Weight:** 7.5 lbs. **Length:** 43.5" overall. **Stock:** Medium fancy-grade walnut in classic style. Checkered grip and forend; solid buttpad. **Sights:** None furnished; drilled and tapped for scope mounts. **Features:** Threadless disassembly. Uses modified Model 76 design with many features of the Model 70 Winchester. Left-hand model also available. Introduced 1989. African chambered for 338 Lapua Mag., 404 Jeffery, 416 Rigby, 416 Dakota, 450 Dakota, 4-round magazine, select wood, two stock cross-bolts. 24" barrel, weighs 9-10 lbs. Ramp front sight, standing leaf rear. Introduced 1989.Made in U.S.A. by Dakota Arms, Inc.

Price: Classic **$6,095.00**
Price: Safari **$7,895.00**
Price: African **$9,495.00**

DAKOTA 76 CLASSIC BOLT-ACTION RIFLE

Caliber: 257 Roberts, 270 Win., 280 Rem., 30-06 Spfl., 7mm Rem. Mag., 338 Win. Mag., 300 Win. Mag., 375 H&H, 458 Win. Mag. **Barrel:** 23". **Weight:** 7.5 lbs. **Length:** 43.5" overall. **Stock:** Medium fancy grade walnut in classic style. Checkered pistol grip and forend; solid buttpad. **Sights:** None furnished; drilled and tapped for scope mounts. **Features:** Has many features of the original Winchester Model 70. One-piece rail trigger guard assembly; steel gripcap. Model 70-style trigger. Many options available. Left-hand rifle available at same price. Introduced 1988. From Dakota Arms, Inc.

Price: From **$4,595.00**

DAKOTA LONGBOW T-76 TACTICAL RIFLE

Caliber: 300 Dakota Magnum, 330 Dakota Magnum, 338 Lapua Magnum. **Barrel:** 28", .950" at muzzle **Weight:** 13.7 lbs. **Length:** 50" to 52" overall. **Stock:** Ambidextrous McMillan A-2 fiberglass, black or olive green color; adjustable cheekpiece and buttplate. **Sights:** None furnished. Comes with Picatinny one-piece optical rail. **Features:** Uses the Dakota 76 action with controlled-round feed; three-position firing pin block safety, claw extractor; Model 70-style trigger. Comes with bipod, case tool kit. Introduced 1997. Made in U.S.A. by Dakota Arms, Inc.

Price: **$4,795.00**

DAKOTA MODEL 97 BOLT-ACTION RIFLE

Caliber: 22-250 to 330. **Barrel:** 22" to 24". **Weight:** 6.1 to 6.5 lbs. **Length:** 43" overall. **Stock:** Fiberglass. **Sights:** Optional. **Features:** Matte blue finish, black stock. Right-hand action only. Introduced 1998. Made in U.S.A. by Dakota Arms, Inc.

Price: From **$3,095.00**

DAKOTA PREDATOR RIFLE

Caliber: 17 VarTarg, 17 Rem., 17 Tactical, 20 VarTarg, 20 Tactical, .20 PPC, 204 Ruger, 221 Rem Fireball, 222 Remington, 22 PPC, 223 Rem., 6mm PPC, 6.5 Grendel. **Barrel:** 22" match grade stainless;. **Weight:** NA. **Length:** NA. **Stock:** Special select walnut, sporter-style stock, 23 lpi checkering on forend and grip. **Sights:** None furnished. Drilled and tapped for scope mounting. **Features:** 13-5/8" LOP, 1/2" black presentation pad, 11" recessed target crown. Serious Predator includes XXX walnut varmint style stock w/semi-beavertail forend, stainless receiver. All-Weather Predator includes varmint style composite stock w/semi-beavertail forend, stainless receiver. Introduced 2007. Made in U.S.A. by Dakota Arms, Inc.

Price: Classic **$4,295.00**
Price: Serious **$3,295.00**
Price: All-Weather. **$1,995.00**

DSA DS-MP1

Caliber: 308 Win. match chamber. **Barrel:** 22", 1:10 twist, hand-lapped stainless-steel match-grade Badger Barrel with recessed target crown. **Weight:** 11.5 lbs. **Length:** 41.75". **Stock:** Black McMillan A5 pillar bedded in Marine-Tex with 13.5" length of pull. **Sights:** Tactical Picatinny rail. **Features:** Action, action threads and action bolt locking shoulder completely trued, Badger Ordnance precision ground heavy recoil lug, machined steel Picatinny rail sight mount, trued action threads, action bolt locking shoulder, bolt face and lugs, 2.5-lb. trigger pull, barrel and action finished in Black DuraCoat, guaranteed to shoot 1/2 MOA at 100 yards with match-grade ammo. Introduced 2006. Made in U.S.A. by DSA, Inc.

Price: **$2,800.00**

Ed Brown 702 Savanna

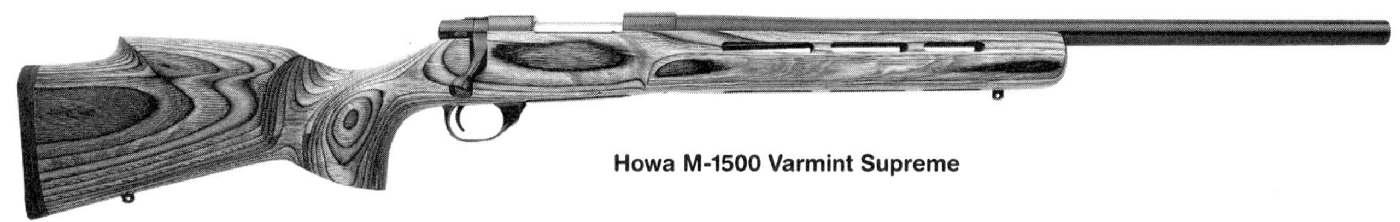

Howa M-1500 Varmint Supreme

EAA/ZASTAVA M-93 BLACK ARROW RIFLE

Caliber: 50 BMG. **Barrel:** 36". **Weight:** 7 to 8.5 lbs. **Length:** 60". **Stock:** Synthetic. **Sights:** Scope rail and iron sights. **Features: Features:** Mauser action, developed in early 1990s by Zastava Arms Factory. Fluted heavy barrel with recoil reducing muzzle brake, self-leveling and adjustable folding integral bipod, back up iron sights, heavy duty carry handle, detachable 5 round box magazine, and quick detachable scope mount. Imported by EAA. Imported from Russia by EAA Corp.

Price: **$7,035.00**

ED BROWN SAVANNA RIFLE

Caliber: Many calibers available. **Barrel:** 24". **Weight:** 8 to 8.5 lbs. **Stock:** Fully glass-bedded McMillan fiberglass sporter. **Sights:** None furnished. Talley scope mounts utilizing heavy-duty 8-40 screws. **Features:** Custom action with machined steel trigger guard and hinged floor plate.

Price: **$3,195.00**

ED BROWN MODEL 704 BUSHVELD

Caliber: 338 Win. Mag., 375 H&H, 416 Rem. Mag., 458 Win. Mag., 458 Lott and all Ed Brown Savanna long action calibers. **Barrel:** 24" medium or heavy weight. **Weight:** 8.25 lbs. **Stock:** Fully bedded McMillan fiberglass with Monte Carlo style cheekpiece, Pachmayr Decelerator recoil pad. **Sights:** None furnished. Talley scope mounts utilizing heavy-duty 8-40 screws. **Features:** Stainless steel barrel, additional Calibers: iron sights.

Price: From **$2,995.00**

ED BROWN MODEL 704 EXPRESS

Caliber: 375 H&H, 416 Rem, 458 Lott, other calibers available. **Barrel:** 24" #4 Stainless barrel with black Gen III coating for superior rust protection. **Weight:** 9 lbs. Stocks: Hand-bedded McMillan fiberglass stock. Monte Carlo style with cheek piece and full 1" thick Pachmayr Decel recoil pad. **Sights:** Adjustable iron sights. **Features:** Ed Brown controlled feed action. A special dropped box magazine ensures feeding and allows a full four-round capacity in the magazine, plus one in the chamber. Barrel band is standard for lower profile when carrying the rifle through heavy brush.

Price: From **$3,695.00**

HOWA M-1500 RANCHLAND COMPACT

Caliber: 223 Rem., 22-250 Rem., 243 Win., 308 Win. and 7mm-08. **Barrel:** 20" #1 contour, blued finish. **Weight:** 7 lbs. **Stock:** Hogue Overmolded in black, OD green, Coyote Sand colors. 13.87" LOP. **Sights:** None furnished; drilled and tapped for scope mounting. **Features:** Three-position safety, hinged floor plate, adjustable trigger, forged one-piece bolt, M-16 style extractor, forged flat-bottom receiver. Also available with Nikko-Stirling Nighteater 3-9x42 riflescope. Introduced in 2008. Imported from Japan by Legacy Sports International.

Price: Rifle Only, (2008) **$499.00**
Price: Rifle with 3-9x42 Nighteater scope (2008) **$599.00**

HOWA M-1500 THUMBHOLE SPORTER

Caliber: 204, 223 Rem., 22-250 Rem., 243 Win., 6.5x55 (2008) 25-06 Rem., 270 Win., 7mm Rem. Mag., 308 Win., 30-06 Spfl., 300 Win. Mag., 338 Win. Mag., 375 Ruger. Similar to Camo Lightning except stock. **Weight:** 7.6 to 7.7 lbs. **Stock:** S&K laminated wood in nutmeg (brown/black) or pepper (grey/black) colors, raised comb with forward taper, flared pistol grip and scalloped thumbhole. **Sights:** None furnished; drilled and tapped for scope mounting. **Features:** Three-position safety, hinged floor plate, adjustable trigger, forged one-piece bolt, M-16 style extractor, forged flat-bottom receiver. Introduced in 2001. Imported from Japan by Legacy Sports International.

Price: Blue/Nutmeg, standard calibers . . . .**$699.00 to $721.00**
Price: Stainless/Pepper, standard calibers . . . .**$799.00 to $886.00**

HOWA M-1500 VARMINTER SUPREME AND THUMBHOLE VARMINTER SUPREME

Caliber: 204, 223 Rem., 22-250 Rem., 243 Win., 308 Win. **Stock:** Varminter Supreme: Laminated wood in nutmeg (brown), pepper (grey) colors, raised comb and rollover cheekpiece, full pistol grip with palm-filling swell and broad beavertail forend with six vents for barrel cooling. Thumbhole Varminter Supreme similar, adds a high, straight comb, more vertical pistol grip. **Sights:** None furnished; drilled and tapped for scope mounting. **Features:** Three-position safety, hinged floor plate, adjustable trigger, forged one-piece bolt, M-16 style extractor, forged flat-bottom receiver, hammer forged bull barrel and recessed muzzle crown; overall length, 43.75", 9.7 lbs. Introduced 2001. Barreled actions imported by Legacy Sports International; stocks by S&K Gunstocks.

Price: Varminter Supreme, Blue/Nutmeg **$816.00**
Price: Varminter Supreme, Stainless/Pepper **$925.00**
Price: Thumbhole Varminter Supreme, Blue/Nutmeg. **$816.00**
Price: Thumbhole Varminter Supreme, Stainless/Pepper **$925.00**

HOWA CAMO LIGHTNING M-1500

Caliber: 204, 223 Rem., 22-250 Rem., 243 Win., 25-06 Rem., 270 Win., 308 Win., 30-06 Spfl., 300 Win. Mag., 338 Win. Mag., 7mm Rem. Mag. **Barrel:** 22" standard calibers; 24" magnum calibers; #2 and #6 contour; blue and stainless. **Weight:** 7.6 to 9.3 lbs. **Length:** 42" to 44.5" overall. **Stock:** Synthetic with molded cheek piece, checkered grip and forend. **Sights:** None furnished; drilled and tapped for scope mounting. **Features:** Three-position safety, hinged floor plate, adjustable trigger, forged one-piece bolt, M-16 style extractor, forged flat bottom receiver. Introduced in 1993. Barreled actions imported by Legacy Sports International.

Price: Blue, #2 barrel, standard calibers. **$583.00**
Price: Stainless, #2 barrel, standard calibers **$693.00**
Price: Blue, #2 barrel, magnum calibers. **$605.00**
Price: Stainless, #2 barrel, magnum calibers **$716.00**
Price: Blue, #6 barrel, standard calibers. **$599.00**
Price: Stainless, #6 barrel, standard calibers **$729.00**

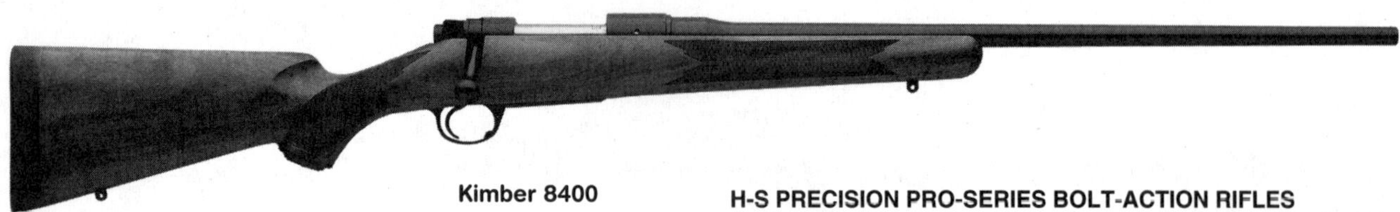

Kimber 8400

HOWA/HOGUE M-1500

Caliber: 204, 223 Rem., 22-250 Rem., 243 Win., 6.5x5 (2008), 25-06 Rem., 270 Win., 308 Win., 30-06 Spfl., 300 Win. Mag., 338 Win. Mag., 7mm Rem. Mag., 375 Ruger (2008). **Barrel:** Howa barreled action; stainless or blued, 22" #2 contour. **Weight:** 7.4 to 7.6 lbs. **Stock:** Hogue Overmolded, black, or OD green; ambidextrous palm swells. **Sights:** None furnished; drilled and tapped for scope mounting. **Length:** 42" to 44.5" overall. **Features:** Three-position safety, hinged floor plate, adjustable trigger, forged one-piece bolt, M-16 style extractor, forged flat bottom receiver, aluminum pillar bedding and free-floated barrels. Introduced in 2006. Available w/3-10x42 Nikko-Stirling Nighteater scope, rings, bases (2008). from Imported from Japan by Legacy Sports International.

Price: Blued, rifle only . . . . **$499.00 to $589.00**
Price: Blue, rifle with scope package (2008) . . . . . . **$599.00 to $687.00**
Price: Stainless, rifle only . . . . **$625.00 to $749.00**

HOWA/HOGUE M-1500 COMPACT HEAVY BARREL VARMINTER

Chambered in 223 Rem., 308 Win., has 20" #6 contour heavy barrel, recessed muzzle crown. **Stock:** Hogue Overmolded, black, or OD green; ambidextrous palm swells. **Sights:** None furnished; drilled and tapped for scope mounting. **Length:** 44.0" overall. **Features:** Three-position safety, hinged floor plate, adjustable trigger, forged one-piece bolt, M-16 style extractor, forged flat bottom receiver, aluminum pillar bedding and free-floated barrels. **Weight:** 9.3 lbs. Introduced 2008. Imported from Japan by Legacy Sports International.

Price: Blued, rifle only . . . . **$499.00 to $589.00**
Price: Blue, rifle with scope package (2008) . . . . . . **$599.00 to $687.00**
Price: Stainless, rifle only . . . . **$625.00 to $749.00**
Price: Compact Heavy Barrel (2008) **$599.00**

HOWA/AXIOM M-1500

Caliber: 204, 223 Rem., 22-250 Rem., 243 Win., 6.5x55 (2008), 25-06 Rem. (2008), 270 Win., 308 Win., 30-06 Spfl., 7mm Rem, 300 Win. Mag., 338 Win. Mag., 375 Ruger standard barrel; 204, 223 Rem., 243 Win. and 308 Win. heavy barrel. **Barrel:** Howa barreled action, 22" contour standard barrel, 20" #6 contour heavy barrel, and 24" #6 contour heavy barrel. **Weight:** 8.6-10 lbs. **Stock:** Knoxx Industries Axiom V/S synthetic, black or camo. Adjustable length of pull from 11.5" to 15.5". **Sights:** None furnished; drilled and tapped for scope mounting. **Features:** Three-position safety, adjustable trigger, hinged floor plate, forged receiver with large recoil lug, forged one-piece bolt with dual locking lugs Introduced in 2007. Standard-barrel scope packages come with 3-10x42 Nikko-Stirling Nighteater scope, rings, bases (2008). Heavy barrels come with 4-16x44 Nikko-Stirling scope. Imported from Japan by Legacy Sports International.

Price: Axiom Standard Barrel, black stock, ... **$799.00 to $859.00**
Price: Axiom 20" and 24" Varminter, black or camo stock, from **$850.00**
Price: Axiom 20" and 24" Varminter, camo stock w/scope (2008) **$1,050.00**

HOWA M-1500 ULTRALIGHT 2-N-1 YOUTH

Caliber: 223 Rem., 22-250 Rem., 243 Win., 308 Win., 7mm-08. **Barrel:** 20" #1 contour, blued. **Weight:** 6.8 lbs. **Length:** 39.25" overall. **Stock:** Hogue Overmolded in black, 12.5" LOP. Also includes adult-size Hogue Overmolded in OD green. **Sights:** None furnished; drilled and tapped for scope mounting. **Features:** Bolt and receiver milled to reduce weight, three-position safety, hinged floor plate, adjustable trigger, forged one-piece bolt, M-16 style extractor, forged flat-bottom receiver. Scope package includes 3-9x42 Nikko-Stirling riflescope with bases and rings. Imported from Japan by Legacy Sports International.

Price: Blue, Youth Rifle **$599.00**
Price: w/Scope package (2008) **$625.00**

H-S PRECISION PRO-SERIES BOLT-ACTION RIFLES

Caliber: 30 chamberings, 3- or 4-round magazine. **Barrel:** 20", 22", 24" or 26", sporter contour Pro-Series 10X match-grade stainless steel barrel. Optional muzzle brake on 30 cal. or smaller. **Weight:** 7.5 lbs. **Length:** NA. **Stock:** Pro-Series synthetic stock with full-length bedding block chassis system, sporter style. **Sights:** None; drilled and tapped for bases. **Features:** Accuracy guarantee: up to 30 caliber, 1/2 minute of angle (3 shots at 100 yards), test target supplied. Stainless steel action, stainless steel floorplate with detachable magazine, matte black Teflon finish. Made in U.S.A. by H-S Precision, Inc.

Price: SPR **$2,680.00**
Price: SPL Lightweight (2008) **$2,825.00**

KENNY JARRETT BOLT-ACTION RIFLE

Caliber: 223 Rem., 243 Improved, 243 Catbird, 7mm-08 Improved, 280 Remington, .280 Ackley Improved, 7mm Rem. Mag., 284 Jarrett, 30-06 Springfield, 300 Win. Mag., .300 Jarrett, 323 Jarrett, 338 Jarrett, 375 H&H, 416 Rem., 450 Rigby., other modern cartridges. **Barrel:** NA. **Weight:** NA. **Length:** NA. **Stock:** NA. **Features:** Tri-Lock receiver. Talley rings and bases. Accuracy guarantees and custom loaded ammunition.

Price: Signature Series **$7,640.00**
Price: Wind Walker **$7,380.00**
Price: Original Beanfield (customer's receiver) **$5,380.00**
Price: Professional Hunter **$10,400.00**
Price: SA/Custom **$6,630.00**

KIMBER MODEL 8400 BOLT-ACTION RIFLE

Caliber: 25-06 Rem., 270 Win., 7mm, 30-06 Spfl., 300 Win. Mag., 338 Win. Mag., or 325 WSM, 4 shot. **Barrel:** 24". **Weight:** 6 lbs. 3 oz. to 6 lbs 10 oz. **Length:** 43.25". **Stock:** Claro walnut or Kevlar-reinforced fiberglass. **Sights:** None; drilled and tapped for bases. **Features:** Mauser claw extractor, two-position wing safety, action bedded on aluminum pillars and fiberglass, free-floated barrel, match grade adjustable trigger set at 4 lbs., matte or polished blue or matte stainless finish. Introduced 2003. Sonora model (2008) has brown laminated stock, hand-rubbed oil finish, chambered in 25-06 Rem., 30-06 Spfl., and 300 Win. Mag. Weighs 8.5 lbs., measures 44.50" overall length. Front swivel stud only for bipod. Stainless steel bull barrel, 24" satin stainless steel finish. Made in U.S.A. by Kimber Mfg. Inc.

Price: Classic **$1,172.00**
Price: Classic Select Grade, French walnut stock (2008) . . . **$1,359.00**
Price: SuperAmerica, AAA walnut stock **$2,240.00**
Price: Sonora **$1,359.00**

Kimber Model 8400 Caprivi Bolt-Action Rifle

Similar to 8400 bolt rifle, but chambered for .375 H&H and 458 Lott, 4-shot magazine. **Stock:** Claro walnut or Kevlar-reinforced fiberglass. **Features:** Twin steel crossbolts in stock, AA French walnut, pancake cheekpiece, 24 lines-per-inch wrap-around checkering, ebony forend tip, hand-rubbed oil finish, barrel-mounted sling swivel stud, 3-leaf express sights, Howell-type rear sling swivel stud and a Pachmayr Decelerator recoil pad in traditional orange color. Introduced 2008. Made in U.S.A. by Kimber Mfg. Inc.

Price: **$3,196.00**

KIMBER MODEL 84M BOLT-ACTION RIFLE

Caliber: 22-250 Rem., 204 Ruger, 223 Rem., 243 Win., 260 Rem., 7mm-08 Rem., 308 Win., 5-shot. **Barrel:** 22", 24", 26". **Weight:** 5 lbs., 10 oz. to 10 lbs. **Length:** 41" to 45". **Stock:** Claro walnut, checkered with steel gripcap; synthetic or gray laminate. **Sights:** None; drilled and tapped for bases. **Features:** Mauser claw extractor, three-position wing safety, action bedded on aluminum pillars, free-floated barrel, match-grade trigger set at 4 lbs., matte blue finish. Includes cable lock. Introduced 2001. Montana (2008) has synthetic stock, Pachmayr Decelerator recoil pad, stainless steel 22" sporter barrel. Made in U.S.A. by Kimber Mfg. Inc.

Price: Classic (243 Win., 260, 7mm-08 Rem., 308) **$1,114.00**
Price: Varmint (22-250) **$1,224.00**
Price: Montana **$1,276.00**

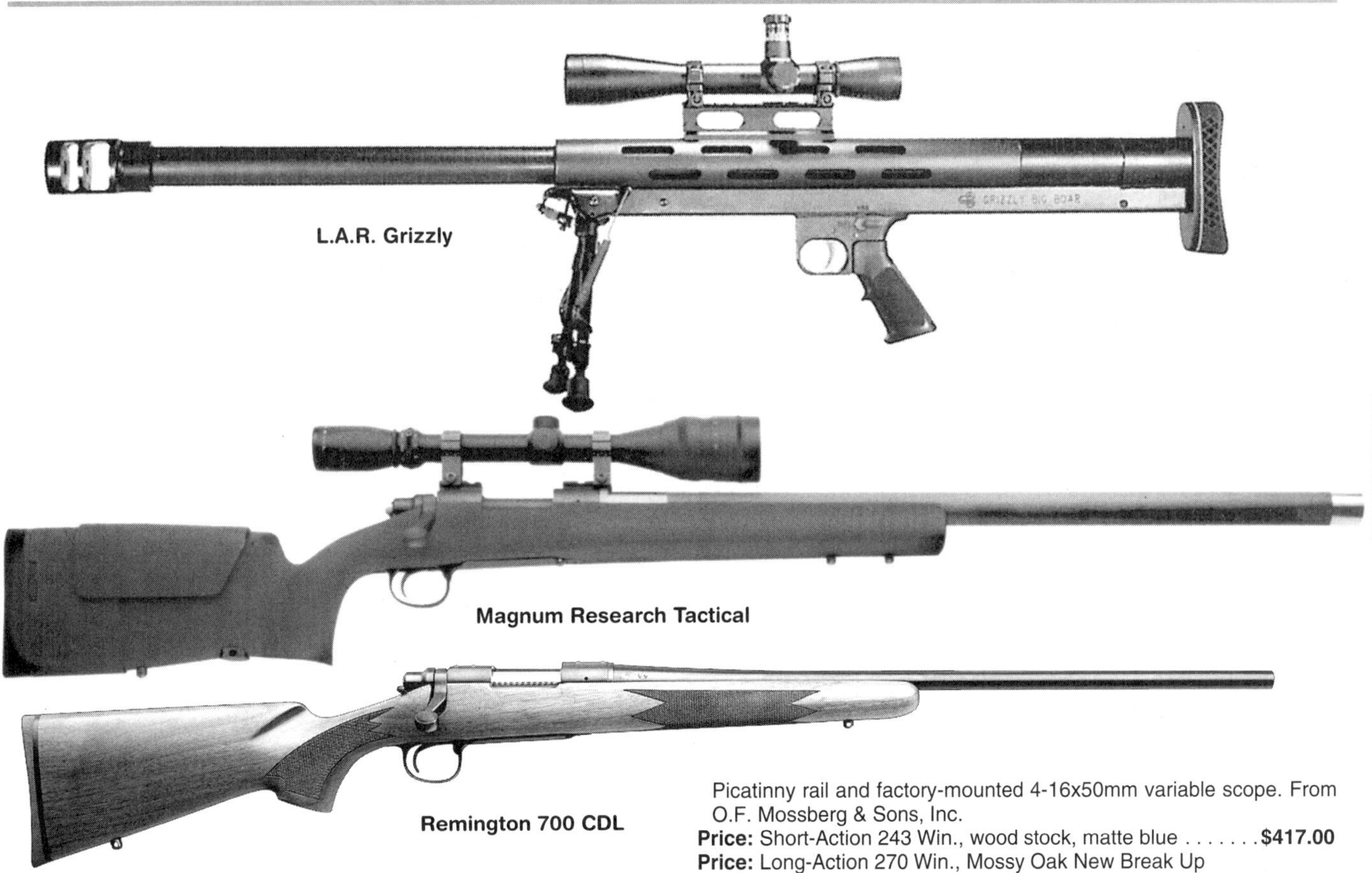

L.A.R. Grizzly

Magnum Research Tactical

Remington 700 CDL

L.A.R. GRIZZLY 50 BIG BOAR RIFLE

Caliber: 50 BMG, single shot. **Barrel:** 36". **Weight:** 30.4 lbs. **Length:** 45.5" overall. **Stock:** Integral. Ventilated rubber recoil pad. **Sights:** None furnished; scope mount. **Features:** Bolt-action bullpup design, thumb and bolt stop safety. All-steel construction. Introduced 1994. Made in U.S.A. by L.A.R. Mfg., Inc.

Price: $1,903.00

MAGNUM RESEARCH MOUNTAIN EAGLE MAGNUMLITE RIFLES

Caliber: 22-250 Rem., 223 Rem., 280 Rem., 7mm WSM, 30-06 Spfl., 308 Win., 300 WSM, 300 Win. Mag., 3-shot magazine. **Barrel:** 24" sport taper graphite; 26" bull barrel graphite. **Weight:** 7.1-9.2 lbs. **Length:** 44.5-48.25" overall (adjustable on Tactical model). **Stock:** Hogue OverMolded synthetic, H-S Precision Tactical synthetic, H-S Precision Varmint synthetic. **Sights:** None. **Features:** Remington Model 700 receiver. Introduced: 2001. From Magnum Research, Inc.

Price: MLR3006B26 H-S Tactical stock $2,295.00
Price: MLR7MMBST24 Hogue stock $2,295.00
Price: MLRT22250 H-S Tactical stock, 26" bull barrel $2,400.00

MARLIN XL7 BOLT ACTION RIFLE

Caliber: 25-06 Rem. 270 Win., 30-06 Spfl., 4-shot magazine. **Barrel:** 22" 1:10" right-hand twist, recessed barrel crown. **Weight:** 6.5 lbs. **Length:** 42.5" overall. **Stock:** Black synthetic or Realtree APG-HD camo, Soft-Tech recoil pad, pillar bedded. **Sights:** None. **Features:** Pro-Fire trigger is user adjustable down to 2.5 lbs. Fluted bolt, steel sling swivel studs, high polished blued steel, checkered bolt handle, molded checkering, one-piece scope base. Introduced: 2008. From Marlin Firearms, Inc.

Price: Black Synthetic. $326.00
Price: Camouflaged $356.00

MOSSBERG 100 ATR BOLT-ACTION RIFLE

Caliber: 243 Win. (2006), 270 Win., 308 Win. (2006), 30-06 Spfl., 4-round magazine. **Barrel:** 22", 1:10 twist, free-floating, button-rifled, recessed muzzle crown. **Weight:** 6.7 to 7.75 lbs. **Length:** 42"-42.75" overall. **Stock:** Black synthetic, walnut, Mossy Oak New Break Up camo, Realtree AP camo. **Sights:** Factory-installed Weaver-style scope bases; scoped combos include 3x9 factory-mounted, bore-sighted scopes. **Features:** Marinecote and matte blue metal finishes, free gun lock, side lever safety. Introduced 2005. Night Train (2008)comes with Picatinny rail and factory-mounted 4-16x50mm variable scope. From O.F. Mossberg & Sons, Inc.

Price: Short-Action 243 Win., wood stock, matte blue $417.00
Price: Long-Action 270 Win., Mossy Oak New Break Up camo, matte blue $409.00
Price: Scoped Combo 30-06 Spfl., Walnut-Dura-Wood stock, Marinecote finish. $509.00
Price: Bantam Short Action 308 Win., 20" barrel $417.00
Price: Night Train Short-Action Scoped Combo (2008) $510.00

MOSSBERG 4X4 BOLT-ACTION RIFLE

Caliber: 25-06 Rem, 270 Win., 30-06 Spfl., 7mm Rem. Mag., .300 Win. Mag., .338 Win. Mag., detachable box magazine, 4 rounds standard, 3 rounds magnum. **Barrel:** 24", 1:10 twist, free-floating, button-rifled, recessed muzzle crown. **Weight:** 7+ lbs. **Length:** 42" overall. **Stock:** Skeletonized synthetic laminate (2008); black synthetic, laminated, select American black walnut. **Sights:** Factory-installed Weaver-style scope bases. **Features:** Marinecote and matte blue metal finishes, free gun lock, side lever safety. Scoped combos include factory-mounted, bore-sighted 3-9x40mm variable. Introduced 2007. From O.F. Mossberg & Sons, Inc.

Price: 25-06 Rem., walnut stock, matte blue $591.00
Price: Scope Combo, 270 Win., black synthetic. $504.00
Price: 300 Win. Mag., synthetic laminate stock (2008). $516.00

REMINGTON MODEL 700 CDL CLASSIC DELUXE RIFLE

Caliber: 223 Rem., 243 Win., 25-06 Rem., 270 Win., 7mm-08 Rem., 7mm Rem. Mag., 7mm Rem. Ultra Mag., 30-06 Spfl., 300 Rem. Ultra Mag., 300 Win. Mag., 35 Whelen. **Barrel:** 24" or 26" round tapered. **Weight:** 7.4 to 7.6 lbs. **Length:** 43.6" to 46.5" overall. **Stock:** Straight-comb American walnut stock, satin finish, checkering, right-handed cheek piece, black fore-end tip and grip cap, sling swivel studs. **Sights:** None. **Features:** Satin blued finish, jeweled bolt body, drilled and tapped for scope mounts. Hinged-floorplate magazine capacity: 4, standard calibers; 3, magnum calibers. SuperCell recoil pad, cylindrical receiver, integral extractor. Introduced 2004. CDL SF (stainless fluted) chambered for 260 Rem., 257 Wby. Mag., 270 Win., 270 WSM, 7mm-08 Rem., 7mm Rem. Mag., 30-06 Spfl., 300 WSM. Left-hand versions introduced 2008 in six calibers. Made in U.S. by Remington Arms Co., Inc.

Price: Standard Calibers: 24" barrel $931.00
Price: Magnum Calibers: 26" barrel $957.00
Price: CDL SF (2007), from $1,065.00
Price: CDL LH (2008), from $957.00
Price: CDL High Polish Blued (2008), from $931.00

Remington 700 BDL
Remington 700 SPS Varmint
Remington Model 700 LSS
Remington 700 Alaskan Ti
Remington 700 VLS

REMINGTON MODEL 700 BDL RIFLE

Caliber: 243 Win., 270 Win., 7mm Rem. Mag. 30-06 Spfl., 300 Rem Ultra Mag. **Barrel:** 22, 24, 26" round tapered. **Weight:** 7.25-7.4 lbs. **Length:** 41.6-46.5" overall. **Stock:** Walnut. Gloss-finish pistol grip stock with skip-line checkering, black forend tip and gripcap with white line spacers. Quick-release floorplate. **Sights:** Gold bead ramp front; hooded ramp, removable step-adjustable rear with windage screw. **Features:** Side safety, receiver tapped for scope mounts, matte receiver top, quick detachable swivels.

Price: 243 Win., 270 Win., 30-06 . . . . **$900.00**
Price: 7mm Rem. Mag. 300 Rem Ultra Mag. **$927.00**

REMINGTON MODEL 700 SPS RIFLES

Caliber: 17 Rem. Fireball, 204 Ruger, 22-250 Rem., 6.8 Rem SPC, 223 Rem., 243 Win., 270 Win. 270 WSM, 7mm-08 Rem., 7mm Rem. Mag., 7mm Rem. Ultra Mag., 30-06 Spfl., 308 Win., 300 WSM, 300 Win. Mag., 300 Rem. Ultra Mag. **Barrel:** 20", 24" or 26" carbon steel. **Weight:** 7 to 7.6 lbs. **Length:** 39.6" to 46.5" overall. **Stock:** Black synthetic, sling swivel studs, SuperCell recoil pad. **Sights:** None. Introduced 2005. SPS Stainless replaces Model 700 BDL Stainless Synthetic. **Barrel:** Bead-blasted 416 stainless steel. **Features:** Plated internal fire control component. SPS DM features detachable box magazine. Buckmaster Edition versions feature Realtree Hardwoods HD camouflage and Buckmasters logo engraved on floorplate. SPS Varmint includes X-Mark Pro trigger, 26" heavy contour barrel, vented beavertail forend, dual front sling swivel studs. Made in U.S. by Remington Arms Co., Inc.

Price: SPS, from **$620.00**
Price: SPS DM (2005) **$649.00**
Price: SPS Youth, 20" barrel (2007) 243 Win., 7mm-08. . . . . . **$604.00**
Price: SPS Varmint (2007) **$663.00**
Price: SPS Stainless, (2005), from **$729.00**
Price: SPS Buckmasters Youth (2008), 243 Win. **$687.00**
Price: SPS Youth LH (2008), 243 Win., 7mm-08 . . . . **$620.00**
Price: SPS Varmint LH (2008) **$689.00**

REMINGTON MODEL 700 MOUNTAIN LSS RIFLES

Caliber: 270 Win., 280 Rem., 7mm-08 Rem., 30-06. **Barrel:** 22" satin stainless steel. **Weight:** 6.6 lbs. **Length:** 41.6" to 42.5" overall. **Stock:** Brown laminated, sling swivel studs, SuperCell recoil pad, black forend tip. **Sights:** None. **Barrel:** Bead-blasted 416 stainless steel, lightweight contour. Made in U.S. by Remington Arms Co., Inc.

Price: **$1,040.00**

REMINGTON MODEL 700 ALASKAN TI

Caliber: 25-06 Rem., 270 Win., 270 WSM, 280 Rem., 7mm-08 Rem., 7mm Rem. Mag., 30-06 Spfl., 300 WSM, 300 Win. Mag. **Barrel:** 24" round tapered. **Weight:** 6 lbs. **Length:** 43.6" to 44.5" overall. **Stock:** Bell & Carlson carbon-fiber synthetic, sling swivel studs, SuperCell gel recoil pad. **Sights:** None. **Features:** Formerly Model 700 Titanium, introduced 2001. Titanium receiver, spiral-cut fluted bolt, skeletonized bolt handle, X-Mark Pro trigger, satin stainless finish. Drilled and tapped for scope mounts. Hinged-floorplate magazine capacity: 4, standard calibers; 3, magnum calibers. Introduced 2007. Made in U.S. by Remington Arms Co., Inc.

Price: from **$2,159.00**

REMINGTON MODEL 700 VLS/VLSS TH RIFLES

Caliber: 204 Ruger, 223 Rem., 22-250 Rem., 243 Win., 308 Win. **Barrel:** 26" heavy contour barrel (0.820" muzzle O.D.), concave target-style barrel crown **Weight:** 9.4 lbs. **Length:** 45.75" overall. **Stock:** Brown laminated stock, satin finish, with beavertail forend, gripcap, rubber buttpad. **Sights:** None. **Features:** Introduced 1995. VLSS TH (varmint laminate stock stainless) thumbhole model introduced 2007. Made in U.S. by Remington Arms Co., Inc.

Price: VLS. **$951.00**
Price: VLSS TH. **$1,053.00**

Remington 700 XCR

Remington 770

Remington Seven XCR Camo

REMINGTON MODEL 700 VS SF II/SENDERO SF II RIFLES

Caliber: 17 Rem. Fireball, 204 Ruger, 220 Swift, 223 Rem., 22-250 Rem., 308 Win. **Barrel:** satin blued 26" heavy contour (0.820" muzzle O.D.). VS SF has satin-finish stainless barreled action with 26" fluted barrel. **Weight:** 8.5 lbs. **Length:** 45.75" overall. **Stock:** H.S. Precision composite reinforced with aramid fibers, black (VS SF II) Contoured beavertail fore-end with ambidextrous finger grooves, palm swell, and twin front tactical-style swivel studs. **Sights:** None. **Features:** Aluminum bedding block, drilled and tapped for scope mounts, hinged floorplate magazines. Introduced 1994. Sendero model is similar to VS SF II except chambered for 264 Win. Mag, 7mm Rem. Mag., 7mm Rem. Ultra Mag., 300 Win. Mag., 300 Rem. Ultra Mag. Polished stainless barrel. Introduced 1996. Made in U.S. by Remington Arms Co., Inc.

Price: VS SF II **$1,284.00**
Price: Sendero SF II **$1,311.00**

REMINGTON MODEL 700 XCR RIFLE

Caliber: 25-06 Rem., 270 Win., 270 WSM, 7mm-08 Rem., 7mm Rem. Mag., 7mm Rem Ultra Mag, 30-06 Spfl., 300 WSM, 300 Win. Mag., 300 Rem. Ultra Mag., 338 Rem. Ultra Mag., 338 Win. Mag., 375 H&H Mag., 375 Rem. Ultra Mag. **Barrel:** 24" standard caliber; 26" magnum. **Weight:** 7.4 to 7.6 lbs. **Length:** 43.6" to 46.5" overall. **Stock:** Black synthetic, SuperCell recoil pad, rubber overmolded grip and forend. **Sights:** None. **Features:** XCR (Xtreme Conditions Rifle) includes TriNyte Corrosion Control System; drilled and tapped for scope mounts. 375 H&H Mag., 375 Rem. Ultra Mag. chamberings come with iron sights. Introduced 2005. XCR Tactical model introduced 2007. **Features:** Bell & Carlson OD green tactical stock, beavertail forend, recessed thumbhook behind pistol grip, TriNyte coating over stainless steel barrel, LTR fluting. Chambered in 223 Rem., 300 Win. Mag., 308 Win. 700XCR Left Hand introduced 2008 in 270 Win., 7mm Rem. Mag., 30-06 Spfl., 300 Rem Ultra Mag. Made in U.S. by Remington Arms Co., Inc.

Price: from **$1,065.00**
Price: XCR Tactical (2007) **$1,365.00**
Price: 700XCR Left Hand (2008) **$1,092.00**
Price: XCR Compact Tactical (2008), 223 Rem., 308 Win. . **$1,434.00**

REMINGTON MODEL 770 BOLT-ACTION RIFLE

Caliber: 243 Win., 270 Win., 7mm Rem. Mag., 7mm-08 Rem., 308 Win., 30-06 Spfl., 300 Win. Mag. **Barrel:** 22" or 24", button rifled. **Weight:** 8.5 lbs. **Length:** 42.5" to 44.5" overall. **Stock:** Black synthetic. **Sights:** Bushnell Sharpshooter 3-9x scope mounted and bore-sighted. **Features:** Upgrade of Model 710 introduced 2001. Unique action locks bolt directly into barrel; 60-degree bolt throw; 4-shot dual-stack magazine; all-steel receiver. Introduced 2007. Made in U.S.A. by Remington Arms Co.

Price: **$452.00**
Price: Youth, 243 Win. **$452.00**
Price: Stainless Camo (2008), stainless barrel, nickel-plated bolt, Realtree camo stock **$532.00**

REMINGTON MODEL SEVEN CDL/CDL MAGNUM

Caliber: 17 Rem. Fireball, 243 Win., 260 Rem., 270 WSM, 7mm-08 Rem., 308 Win., 300 WSM, 350 Rem. Mag. **Barrel:** 20"; 22" magnum. **Weight:** 6.5 to 7.4 lbs. **Length:** 39.25" to 41.25" overall. **Stock:** American walnut, SuperCell recoil pad, satin finished. **Sights:** None. **Features:** Satin finished carbon steel barrel and action, 3- or 4-round magazine, hinged magazine floorplate. Furnished with iron sights and sling swivel studs, drilled and tapped for scope mounts. CDL versions introduced 2007. Made in U.S.A. by Remington Arms Co.

Price: CDL **$929.00**
Price: CDL Magnum **$997.00**
Price: Predator (2008) **$799.00**
Price: 25th Anniversary (2008), 7mm-08 . . . . **$969.00**

REMINGTON MODEL 798/799 BOLT-ACTION RIFLES

Caliber: 243 Win., 270 Win., 7mm Rem. Mag., 308 Win., .30-06 Spfl., .300 Win. Mag., .375 H&H Mag., .458 Win. Mag. **Barrel:** 20" to 26". **Weight:** 7.75 lbs. **Length:** 39.5" to 42.5" overall. **Stock:** Brown or green laminated, 1-inch rubber butt pad. **Sights:** None. Receiver drilled and tapped for standard Mauser 98 (long- and short-action) scope mounts. **Features:** Model 98 Mauser action (square-bridge Mauser 98). Claw extractor, sporter style 2-position safety, solid steel hinged floorplate magazine. Introduced 2006. Made in U.S.A. by Remington Arms Co.

Price: Model 798 SPS, black synthetic stock (2008), from **$527.00**
Price: Model 798 Satin Walnut Stock (2008), from. **$648.00**
Price: Model 798 Safari Grade (2008), from. **$1,141.00**

RUGER COMPACT MAGNUMS

Caliber: .338 RCM, .300 RCM; 3-shot magazine. **Barrel:** 20". **Weight:** 6.75 lbs. **Length:** 39.5-40" overall. **Stock:** American walnut and black synthetic; stainless steel and Hawkeye Matte blued finishes. **Sights:** Adjustable Williams "U" notch rear sight and brass bead front sight. **Features:** Based on a shortened .375 Ruger case, the .300 and .338 RCMs match the .300 and .338 Win. Mag. in performance; RCM stock is 1/2 inch shorter than standard M77 Hawkeye stock; LC6 trigger; steel floor plate engraved with Ruger logo and "Ruger Compact Magnum"; Red Eagle recoil pad; Mauser-type controlled feeding; claw extractor; 3-position safety; hammer-forged steel barrels; Ruger scope rings. Walnut stock includes extensive cut-checkering and rounded profiles. Intr. 2008. Made in U.S.A. by Sturm, Ruger & Co.

Price: HM77RCM (walnut/Hawkeye Matte Blued) **$995.00**
Price: HKM77PRCM (synthetic/SS) **$995.00**

Ruger Compact Magnum HM77RCM.jpg

Ruger Magnum

Ruger 77/22 Hornet Varmint

Ruger M77 Hawkeye

Ruger M77 Hawkeye Alaskan

Ruger KM77RLFP MKII

RUGER MAGNUM RIFLE

Caliber: 375 H&H, 416 Rigby, 458 Lott. **Barrel:** 23". **Weight:** 9.5 to 10.25 lbs. **Length:** 44". **Stock:** AAA Premium Grade Circassian walnut with live-rubber recoil pad, metal gripcap, and studs for mounting sling swivels. **Sights:** Blade, front; V-notch rear express sights (one stationary, two folding) drift-adjustable for windage. **Features:** Floorplate latch secures the hinged floorplate against accidental dumping of cartridges; one-piece bolt has a non-rotating Mauser-type controlled-feed extractor; fixed-blade ejector.

Price: M77RSMMKII **$2,334.00**

RUGER 77/22 HORNET BOLT-ACTION RIFLE

Caliber: 22 Hornet, 6-shot rotary magazine. **Barrel:** 20" or 24". **Weight:** About 6.25 to 7.5 lbs. **Length:** 39.5" to 43.5" overall. **Stock:** Checkered American walnut, black rubber buttpad; brown laminate. **Sights:** None. **Features:** Same basic features as rimfire model except slightly lengthened receiver. Uses Ruger rotary magazine. Three-position safety. Comes with 1" Ruger scope rings. Introduced 1994.

Price: 77/22RH (rings only, no sights) **$732.00**

Price: K77/22VHZ Varmint, laminated stock, no sights **$812.00**

RUGER M77 HAWKEYE RIFLES

Caliber: 204 Ruger, 223 Rem., 22-250 Rem., 243 Win., 257 Roberts, 25-06 Rem., 270 Win., 280 Rem., 7mm/08, 7mm Rem. Mag., 308 Win., 30-06 Spfl., 300 Win. Mag., 338 Win. Mag., 338 Federal, 358 Win. Mag.,4-shot magazine, except 3-shot magazine for magnums; 5-shot magazine for 204 Ruger and 223 Rem. **Barrel:** 22", 24". **Weight:** 6.75 to 8.25 lbs. **Length:** 42-44.4" overall. **Stock:** American walnut. **Sights:** None furnished. Receiver has Ruger integral scope mount base, Ruger 1" rings. **Features:** Includes Ruger LC6 trigger, new red rubber recoil pad, Mauser-type controlled feeding, claw extractor, 3-position safety, hammer-forged steel barrels, Ruger scope rings. Walnut stock includes wrap-around cut checkering on the forearm and, more rounded contours on stock and top of pistol grips. Matte stainless version features synthetic stock. Hawkeye Alaskan and African chambered in 375 Ruger. Alaskan features matte-black finish, 20" barrel, Hogue OverMolded synthetic stock. African has 23" blued barrel, checkered walnut stock, left-handed model. 375's have windage-adjustable shallow "V" notch rear sight, white bead front sights. Introduced 2007. Left-hand models available 2008.

Price: HM77R walnut/blued **$779.00**

Price: HKM77RFP synthetic/stainless **$779.00**

Price: Synthetic/Diamondblack Alaskan **$1,139.00**

Price: African walnut/blued **$1,139.00**

Price: Grey/Brown Hogue stock models (2008) **$821.00**

Price: HM77LR left hand (2008) **$779.00**

Ruger M77RSI International Carbine

Same as standard Model 77 except 18" barrel, full-length International-style stock, steel forend cap, loop-type steel sling swivels. Integral base receiver, open sights, Ruger 1" steel rings. Improved front sight. Available in 243 Win., 270 Win., 308 Win., 30-06. Weighs 6.25 to 7 lbs. Length overall is 38.25" to 39".

Price: M77RSIMKII **$911.00**

Ruger M77 Mark II All-Weather and Sporter Model Stainless Rifle

Similar to wood-stock M77 Mark II except all metal parts are stainless steel, has an injection-molded, glass-fiber-reinforced polymer stock. Laminated wood stock. Chambered for 223 Rem., 22/250, 25/06, 260 Rem., 7mm WSM, 7mm/08, 7mm SWM, 280 Rem., 300 WSM, 204 Ruger, 243 Win., 270 Win., 308 Win., 30-06 Spfl., 7mm Rem. Mag., 300 Win. Mag., 325 WSM, 338 Win. Mag. Fixed-blade-type ejector, three-position safety, new trigger guard with patented floorplate latch. Integral Scope Base Receiver, 1" Ruger scope rings, built-in sling swivel loops. Introduced 1990.

Price: K77RLFPMKII Ultra-Light, synthetic stock, rings, no sights **$837.00**

Price: K77LRBBZMKII, left-hand bolt, rings, no sights, laminated stock **$805.00**

Price: K77RBZMKII, no sights, laminated wood stock, 223 Rem., 22/250, 243 Win., 270 Win., 7mm Rem. Mag., 30-06 Spfl., 308 Win., 300 Win. Mag., 338 Win. Mag. **$837.00**

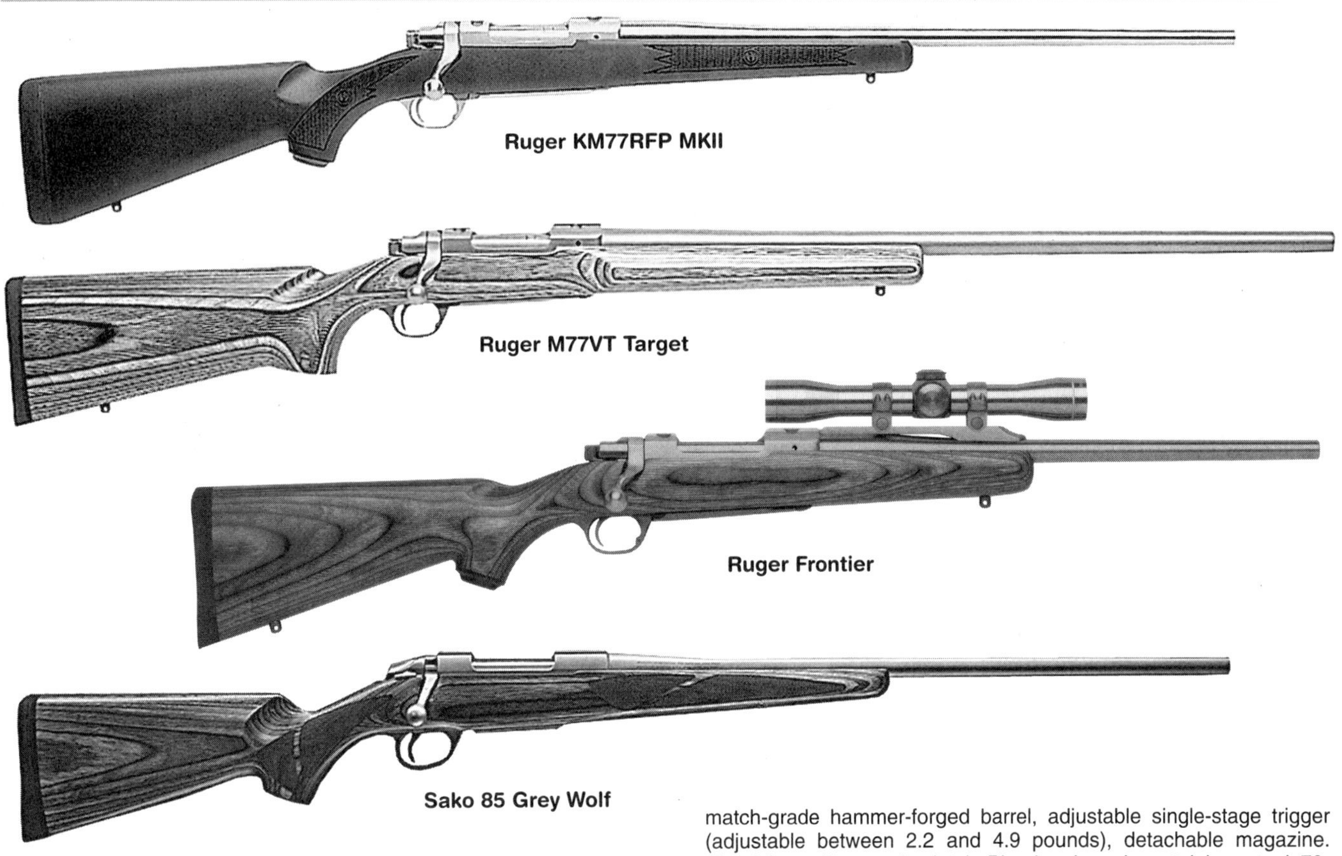
Ruger KM77RFP MKII

Ruger M77VT Target

Ruger Frontier

Sako 85 Grey Wolf

Ruger M77RL Ultra Light

Similar to standard M77 except weighs 6.5 lbs., chambered for 223 Rem., 243 Win., 257 Roberts, 270 Win., 308 Win., 30-06 Spfl., barrel tapped for target scope blocks, 20" Ultra Light barrel. Overall length about 40". Ruger's steel 1" scope rings supplied. Introduced 1983.

Price: M77RLMKII **$837.00**

Ruger M77 Mark II Compact Rifles

Similar to standard M77 except reduced 16.5" barrel, weighs 5 to 6.75 lbs. Chambered for 223 Rem., 243 Win., 260 Rem., 308 Win., and 7mm-08.

Price: M77CR MKII (blued finish, walnut stock) **$779.00**

Price: KM77CRBBZ MKII (stainless finish, black laminated stock) **$837.00**

RUGER M77VT TARGET RIFLE

Caliber: 22-250 Rem., 223 Rem., 204 Ruger, 243 Win., 25-06 Rem., 308 Win. **Barrel:** 26" heavy stainless steel with target grey finish. **Weight:** 9 to 9.75 lbs. **Length:** Approx. 45.75" to 46.75" overall. **Stock:** Laminated American hardwood with beavertail forend, steel swivel studs; no checkering or gripcap. **Sights:** Integral scope mount bases in receiver. **Features:** Ruger diagonal bedding system. Ruger steel 1" scope rings supplied. Fully adjustable trigger. Steel floorplate and trigger guard. New version introduced 1992.

Price: K77VTMKII **$935.00**

RUGER FRONTIER RIFLE

Caliber: 243 Win., 7mm/08, 308 Win., 338 Fed., 358 Win. **Barrel:** 16.5". **Weight:** 6.75 lbs. **Stock:** Black laminate. **Features:** Front scope mounting rib, blued finish; overall length 35.5". Introduced 2005, stainless in 2006.

Price: Blued, walnut **$831.00**

Price: Target Grey, laminate. **$936.00**

SAKO A7 BOLT-ACTION RIFLE

Caliber: 22-250 Rem., 243 Win., 7mm-08 Rem., 308 Win., 338 Federal, 270 WSM, 300 WSM (short actions); 25-06 Rem., 270 Win., 30-06; 7mm Rem. Mag., 300 Win. Mag., Win. Mag., (long actions). **Barrel:** 22-7/16", short-action calibers; 24-3/8", long-action calibers. **Weight:** 6.4 lbs. **Length:** 42 5-16" overall. **Stock:** Synthetic **Sights:** None. **Features:** Based on Sako 75 design. Machined forged-steel bolt, match-grade hammer-forged barrel, adjustable single-stage trigger (adjustable between 2.2 and 4.9 pounds), detachable magazine. "Total Control" magazine latch. Blued and no-glare stainless steel, 70-degree bolt throw. Introduced 2008. Imported from Finland by Beretta USA.

Price: From **$1,700.00**

SAKO TRG-42 BOLT-ACTION RIFLE

Caliber: 338 Lapua Mag. and 300 Win. Mag. **Barrel:** 27-1/8". **Weight:** 11.25 lbs. **Length:** NA. **Stock:** NA. **Sights:** NA. **Features:** 5-shot magazine, fully adjustable stock and competition trigger. Imported from Finland by Beretta USA.

Price: **$2,775.00**

SAKO MODEL 85 BOLT-ACTION RIFLES

Caliber: 22-250 Rem., 243 Win., 25-06 Rem., 260, 6.5x55mm, 270 Win., 270 WSM, 7mm-08 Rem., 308 Win., 30-06; 7mm WSM, 300 WSM, 338 Federal. **Barrel:** 22.4", 22.9", 24.4". **Weight:** 7.75 lbs. **Length:** NA. **Stock:** Polymer, laminated or high-grade walnut, straight comb, shadow-line cheekpiece. **Sights:** None furnished. **Features:** Controlled-round feeding, adjustable trigger, matte stainless or nonreflective satin blue. Quad model is polymer/stainless with four interchangeable barrels in 22 LR, 22 WMR 17 HMR and 17 Mach 2; 50-degree bolt-lift, ambidextrous palm-swell, adjustable butt-pad. Introduced 2006. Imported from Finland by Beretta USA.

Price: Sako 85 Hunter, walnut/blued **$1,700.00**

Price: Sako 85 Grey Wolf, laminated/stainless **$1,575.00**

Price: Sako 85 Quad, polymer/stainless **$925.00**

Price: Sako 85 Quad Combo, four barrels **$2,175.00**

SAKO 75 HUNTER BOLT-ACTION RIFLE

Caliber: 223 Rem., 22-250 Rem., 243 Win., 25-06 Rem., 260, 270 Win., 270 WSM, 280 Rem., 300 Win. Mag., 30-06; 7mm-08 Rem., 308 Win., 270 Wby. Mag., 7mm Rem. Mag., 7mm STW, 7mm Wby. Mag., 300 Wby. Mag., 338 Win. Mag., 340 Wby. Mag., 375 H&H. **Barrel:** 22", standard calibers; 24", 26" magnum calibers. **Weight:** About 6 lbs. **Length:** NA. **Stock:** European walnut with matte lacquer finish. **Sights:** None furnished; dovetail scope mount rails. **Features:** New design with three locking lugs and a mechanical ejector, key locks firing pin and bolt, cold hammer-forged barrel is free-floating, two-position safety, hinged floorplate or detachable magazine that can be loaded from the top, short 70-degree bolt lift. Five action lengths. Introduced 1997. Imported from Finland by Beretta USA.

Price: From **$1,375.00**

Sako 75 Hunter

Sako 75 Deluxe

Sako 75 Varmint

Savage Model 12FV

Sako 75 Deluxe Rifle

Similar to 75 Hunter except select wood rosewood gripcap and forend tip. Available in 17 Rem., 222, 223 Rem., 25-06 Rem., 243 Win., 7mm-08 Rem., 308 Win., 25-06 Rem., 270 Win., 280 Rem., 30-06; 270 Wby. Mag., 7mm Rem. Mag., 7mm STW, 7mm Wby. Mag., 300 Win. Mag., 300 Wby. Mag., 338 Win. Mag., 340 Wby. Mag., 375 H&H, 416 Rem. Mag. Introduced 1997. Imported from Finland by Beretta USA.

Price: from **$2,175.00**

Sako 75 Varmint Rifle

Similar to Model 75 Hunter except chambered only for 17 Rem., 222 Rem., 223 Rem., 22-250 Rem., 22 PPC and 6mm PPC, 24" heavy barrel with recessed crown; set trigger; beavertail forend. Introduced 1998. Imported from Finland by Beretta USA.

Price: **$1,850.00**

SAUER 202 BOLT-ACTION RIFLE

Caliber: Standard 243 Win., 6.5x55, 270 Win., 308 Win., 30-06; magnum 7mm Rem. Mag., 300 Win. Mag., 300 Wby. Mag., 375 H&H. **Barrel:** 23.6" (standard), 26" (magnum). **Weight:** 7.7 lbs. (standard). **Length:** 44.3" overall (23.6" barrel). **Stock:** Select American Claro walnut with high-gloss epoxy finish, rosewood grip and forend caps; 22 lpi checkering. Synthetic also available. **Sights:** None furnished; drilled and tapped for scope mounting. **Features:** Short 60" bolt throw; detachable box magazine; six-lug bolt; quick-change barrel; tapered bore; adjustable two-stage trigger; firing pin cocking indicator. Introduced 1994. Imported from Germany by Sig Sauer, Inc.

Price: Standard Calibers: right-hand.................. **$1,035.00**
Price: Magnum Calibers: right-hand **$1,106.00**
Price: Standard Calibers: synthetic stock **$985.00**
Price: Magnum Calibers: synthetic stock **$1,056.00**

SAVAGE MODEL 25 BOLT ACTION RIFLES

Caliber: 204 Ruger, 223 Rem., 4-shot magazine. **Barrel:** 24", medium-contour fluted barrel with recessed target crown, free-floating sleeved barrel, dual pillar bedding. **Weight:** 8.25 lbs. **Length:** 43.75" overall. **Stock:** Brown laminate with beavertail-style forend. **Sights:** Weaver-style bases installed. **Features:** Diameter-specific action built around the 223 Rem. bolthead dimension. Three locking lugs, 60-degree bolt lift, AccuTrigger adjustable from 2.5 to 3.25 lbs. Model 25 Classic Sporter has satin lacquer American walnut with contrasting forend tip, wraparound checkering, 22" blued barrel. **Weight:** 7.15 lbs. **Length:** 41.75". Introduced 2008. Made in U.S.A. by Savage Arms, Inc.

Price: Model 25 Lightweight Varminter.................. **$588.00**
Price: Model 25 Lightweight Varminter Thumbhole **$635.00**
Price: Model 25 Classic Sporter....................... **$616.00**

SAVAGE CLASSIC SERIES MODEL 14/114 RIFLES

Caliber: 204 Ruger, 223 Rem., 22-250 Rem., 243 Win., 7mm-08 Rem., 308 Win., 270 WSM, 300 WSM (short action Model 14), 2- or 4-shot magazine; 270 Win., 7mm Rem. Mag., 30-06 Spfl., 300 Win. Mag. (long action Model 114), 3- or 4-shot magazine. **Barrel:** 22" or 24". **Weight:** 7 to 7.5 lbs. **Length:** 41.75" to 43.75" overall (Model 14); 43.25" to 45.25" overall (Model 114). **Stock:** Satin lacquer American walnut with ebony forend, wraparound checkering, Monte Carlo Comb and cheekpiece. **Sights:** None furnished. Receiver drilled and tapped for scope mounting. **Features:** AccuTrigger, high luster blued barreled action, hinged floorplate. From Savage Arms, Inc.

Price: Model 14 or 114 Classic, from **$767.00**
Price: Model 14 or 114 American Classic, detachable box magazine, from.............................. **$735.00**
Price: Model 14 or 114 Euro Classic, oil finish, from **$809.00**

SAVAGE MODEL 12 SERIES VARMINT RIFLES

Caliber: 204 Ruger, 223 Rem., 22-250 Rem. 4-shot magazine. **Barrel:** 26" stainless barreled action, heavy fluted, free-floating and button-rifled barrel. **Weight:** 10 lbs. **Length:** 46.25" overall. **Stock:** Dual pillar bedded, low profile, laminated stock with extra-wide beavertail forend. **Sights:** None furnished; drilled and tapped for scope mounting. **Features:** Recessed target-style muzzle. AccuTrigger, oversized bolt handle, detachable box magazine, swivel studs. Model 112BVSS has heavy target-style prone laminated stock with high comb, Wundhammer palm swell, internal box magazine. Model 12FVSS has black synthetic stock, additional chamberings in 308 Win., 270 WSM, 300 WSM. Model 12FV has blued receiver. Model 12BTCSS has brown laminate vented thumbhole stock. Made in U.S.A. by Savage Arms, Inc.

Price: Model 12 Varminter, from....................... **$934.00**
Price: Model 112BVSS................................ **$847.00**
Price: Model 12FVSS, from **$776.00**
Price: Model 12FV **$620.00**
Price: Model 12BTCSS (2008).......................... **$981.00**
Price: Model 12 Long Range (2008).................. **$1,208.00**

Savage Model 116FSAK

Savage Model 111F

Savage Model 111F

Savage Model 11FCNS

Savage Model 11G

SAVAGE MODEL 16/116 WEATHER WARRIORS

Caliber: 204 Ruger, 223 Rem., 22-250 Rem., 243 Win., 7mm-08 Rem., 308 Win., 270 WSM, 7mm WSM, 300 WSM (short action Model 16), 2- or 4-shot magazine; 270 Win., 7mm Rem. Mag., 30-06 Spfl., 300 Win. Mag., 338 Win. Mag. (long action Model 114), 3- or 4-shot magazine. **Barrel:** 22", 24"; stainless steel with matte finish, free-floated barrel. **Weight:** 6.5 to 6.75 lbs. **Length:** 41.75" to 43.75" overall (Model 16); 42.5" to 44.5" overall (Model 116). **Stock:** Graphite/fiberglass filled composite. **Sights:** None furnished; drilled and tapped for scope mounting. **Features:** Quick-detachable swivel studs; laser-etched bolt. Left-hand models available. Model 116FSS introduced 1991; 116FSAK introduced 1994. Made in U.S.A. by Savage Arms, Inc.

Price: Model 16FHSS or 116FHSS, hinged floorplate magazine, from **$676.00**

Price: Model 16FLHSS or 116FLHSS, left hand models, from . **$676.00**

Price: Model 16FSS or 116FSS, internal box magazine, from . **$640.00**

Price: Model 16FCSS or 116FCSS, detachable box magazine, from **$676.00**

Price: Model 16FHSAK or 116FHSAK, adjustable muzzle brake, ... **$739.00**

SAVAGE MODEL 10GXP3, 110GXP3 PACKAGE GUNS

Caliber: 223 Rem., 22-250 Rem., 243 Win., 7mm-08 Rem., 308 Win., 300 WSM (10GXP3). 25-06 Rem., 270 Win., 30-06 Spfl., 7mm Rem. Mag., 300 Win. Mag., 300 Rem. Ultra Mag. (110GXP3). **Barrel:** 22" 24", 26". **Weight:** 7.5 lbs. average. **Length:** 43" to 47". **Stock:** Walnut Monte Carlo with checkering. **Sights:** 3-9x40mm scope, mounted & bore sighted. **Features:** Blued, free floating and button rifled, internal box magazines, swivel studs, leather sling. Left-hand available.

Price: Accu-Trigger, from **$633.00**

SAVAGE MODEL 11FXP3, 111FXP3, 111FCXP3, 11FYXP3 (YOUTH) PACKAGE GUNS

Caliber: 223 Rem., 22-250 Rem., 243 Win., 308 Win., 300 WSM (11FXP3). 270 Win., 30-06 Spfl., 25-06 Rem., 7mm Rem. Mag., 300 Win. Mag., 338 Win. Mag., 300 Rem. Ultra Mag. (11FCXPE & 111FXP3). **Barrel:** 22" to 26". **Weight:** 6.5 lbs. **Length:** 41" to 47". **Stock:** Synthetic checkering, dual pillar bed. **Sights:** 3-9X40mm scope, mounted & bore sighted. **Features:** Blued, free floating and button rifled, Top loading internal box mag (except 111FXCP3 has detachable box magazine.). Nylon sling and swivel studs. Some left-hand available.

Price: Model 11FXP3, from **$601.00**

Price: Model 111FCXP3 . . . . . **$499.00**

Price: Model 11FYXP3, 243 Win., 12.5" pull (youth) **$593.00**

SAVAGE MODEL 16FXP3, 116FXP3 SS ACTION PACKAGE GUNS

Caliber: 223 Rem., 243 Win., 308 Win., 300 WSM, 270 Win., 30-06 Spfl., 7mm Rem. Mag., 300 Win. Mag., 338 Win. Mag., 375 H&H, 7mm S&W, 7mm Rem. Ultra Mag., 300 Rem. Ultra Mag. **Barrel:** 22", 24", 26". **Weight:** 6.75 lbs. average. **Length:** 41" to 46". **Stock:** Synthetic checkering, dual pillar bed. **Sights:** 3-9X40mm scope, mounted & bore sighted. **Features:** Free floating and button rifled. Internal box magazine., nylon sling and swivel studs.

Price: from **$695.00**

SAVAGE MODEL 11/111 HUNTER SERIES BOLT ACTIONS

Caliber: 223 Rem., 22-250 Rem., 243 Win., 7mm-08 Rem., 308 Win., 270 WSM, 7mm WSM, 300 WSM (short action Model 11), 2- or 4-shot magazine; 25-06 Rem., 270 Win., 7mm Rem. Mag., 30-06 Spfl., 300 Win. Mag., (long action Model 111), 3- or 4-shot magazine. **Barrel:** 22" or 24"; blued free-floated barrel. **Weight:** 6.5 to 6.75 lbs. **Length:** 41.75" to 43.75" overall (Model 11); 42.5" to 44.5" overall (Model 111). **Stock:** Graphite/fiberglass filled composite or hardwood. **Sights:** Ramp front, open fully adjustable rear; drilled and tapped for scope mounting. **Features:** Three-position top tang safety, double front locking lugs. Introduced 1994. Made in U.S.A. by Savage Arms, Inc.

Price: Model 11F or 111F **$564.00**

Price: Model 11FL or 111FL, left hand models, from **$564.00**

Price: Model 11FCNS or 111FCNS, detachable box magazine, from **$591.00**

Price: Model 11G or 111G, hardwood stock, from **$582.00**

Price: Model 11BTH or 111BTH, laminate thumbhole stock (2008) **$735.00**

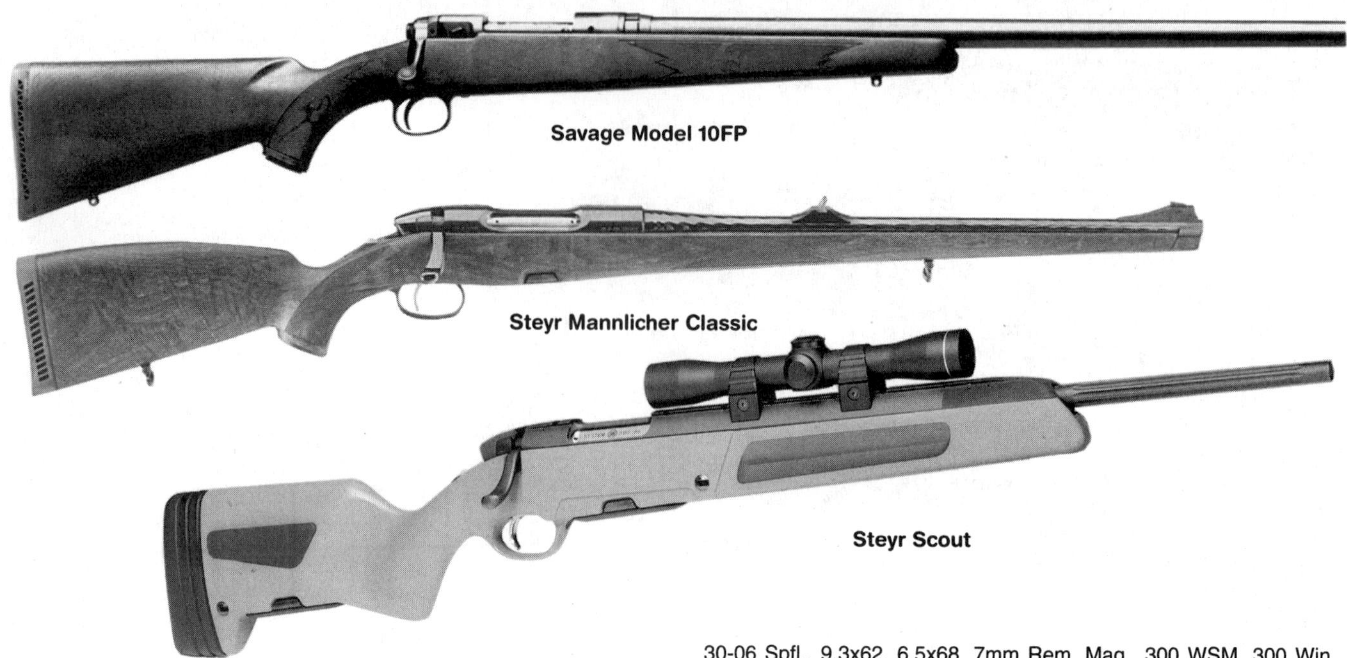
Savage Model 10FP

Steyr Mannlicher Classic

Steyr Scout

SAVAGE MODEL 10FP/110FP LAW ENFORCEMENT SERIES RIFLES

Caliber: 223 Rem., 308 Win. (Model 10), 4-shot magazine; 25-06 Rem., 300 Win. Mag., (Model 110), 3- or 4-shot magazine. **Barrel:** 24";matte blued free-floated heavy barrel and action. **Weight:** 6.5 to 6.75 lbs. **Length:** 41.75" to 43.75" overall (Model 10); 42.5" to 44.5" overall (Model 110). **Stock:** Black graphite/fiberglass composition, pillar-bedded, positive checkering. **Sights:** None furnished. Receiver drilled and tapped for scope mounting. **Features:** Black matte finish on all metal parts. Double swivel studs on the forend for sling and/or bipod mount. Right- or left-hand. Model 110FP introduced 1990. Model 10FP introduced 1998. Model 10FCPXP has HS Precision black synthetic tactical stock with molded alloy bedding system, Leupold 3.5-10x40mm black matte scope with Mil Dot reticle, Farrell Picatinny Rail Base, flip-open lens covers, 1.25" sling with QD swivels, Harris bipod, Storm heavy duty case. Made in U.S.A. by Savage Arms, Inc.

Price: Model 10FP, 10FLP (left hand), 110FP **$649.00**
Price: Model 10FCP folding Choate stock **$896.00**
Price: Model 10FCP McMillan, McMillan fiberglass tactical stock **$1,178.00**
Price: Model 10FCP HS-Precision, HS-Precision tactical stock, ... **$984.00**
Price: Model 10FCPXP **$2,418.00**

Savage Model 110-50th Anniversary Rifle

Same action as 110-series rifles, except offered in 300 Savage, limited edition of 1,000 rifles. Has high-luster blued barrel and action, unique checkering pattern, high-grade hinged floorplate, scroll pattern on receiver, 24-karat gold-plated double barrel bands, 24-karat gold-plated AccuTrigger, embossed recoil pad. Introduced 2008. Made in U.S.A. from Savage Arms, Inc.

Price: Model 110 50th Anniversary. **$1,724.00**

SMITH & WESSON I-BOLT RIFLES

Caliber: 25-06 Rem., 270 Win., 30-06 Win. (4 round magazine), 7mm Rem. Mag., 300 Win. Mag. (3 round magazine). **Barrel:** 23", 1:10" right-hand twist, 1:9" right-hand twist for 7mm Mag. Thompson/Center barrel. Blued and stainless. **Weight:** 6.75 lbs. **Stock:** Black synthetic, Realtree AP camo, walnut. Length of pull, 13-5/8", drop at comb, 7/8". Monte Carlo cheekpiece. **Sights:** Adjustable post front sight, adjustable dual aperture rear sight. **Features:** Adjustable Tru-Set Trigger. Introduced 2008. Made in U.S.A. by Smith & Wesson.

Price: Black synthetic stock **$830.00**
Price: Camo stock. **$901.00**
Price: Walnut stock. **$893.00**

STEYR MANNLICHER CLASSIC RIFLE

Caliber: 222 Rem., 223 Rem., 243 Win., 25-06 Rem., 308 Win., 6.5x55, 6.5x57, 270 Win., 270 WSM, 7x64 Brenneke, 7mm-08 Rem., 7.5x55, 30-06 Spfl., 9.3x62, 6.5x68, 7mm Rem. Mag., 300 WSM, 300 Win. Mag., 8x68S, 4-shot magazine. **Barrel:** 23.6" standard; 26" magnum; 20" full stock standard calibers. **Weight:** 7 lbs. **Length:** 40.1" overall. **Stock:** Hand-checkered fancy European oiled walnut with standard forend. **Sights:** Ramp front adjustable for elevation, V-notch rear adjustable for windage. **Features:** Single adjustable trigger; 3-position roller safety with "safe-bolt" setting; drilled and tapped for Steyr factory scope mounts. Introduced 1997. Imported from Austria by Steyr Arms, Inc.

Price: Half stock, standard calibers **$3,587.00**
Price: Full stock, standard calibers. **$3,969.00**

Steyr Pro Hunter Rifle

Similar to the Classic Rifle except has ABS synthetic stock with adjustable butt spacers, straight comb without cheekpiece, palm swell, Pachmayr 1" swivels. Special 10-round magazine conversion kit available. Introduced 1997. Imported from Austria by Steyr Arms, Inc.

Price: From **$1,561.00**

STEYR SCOUT BOLT-ACTION RIFLE

Caliber: 308 Win., 5-shot magazine. **Barrel:** 19", fluted. **Weight:** NA. **Length:** NA. **Stock:** Gray Zytel. **Sights:** Pop-up front & rear, Leupold M8 2.5x28 IER scope on Picatinny optic rail with Steyr mounts. **Features:** luggage case, scout sling, two stock spacers, two magazines. Introduced 1998. Imported from Austria by Steyr Arms, Inc.

Price: From **$1,951.00**

STEYR SSG 69 PII BOLT-ACTION RIFLE

Caliber: 22-250 Rem., 243 Win., 308 Win., detachable 5-shot rotary magazine. **Barrel:** 26". **Weight:** 8.5 lbs. **Length:** 44.5" overall. **Stock:** Black ABS Cycolac with spacers for length of pull adjustment. **Sights:** Hooded ramp front adjustable for elevation, V-notch rear adjustable for windage. **Features:** Sliding safety; NATO rail for bipod; 1" swivels; Parkerized finish; single or double-set triggers. Imported from Austria by Steyr Arms, Inc.

Price: SSG-PII, heavy barrel, no sights **$1,743.00**
Price: SSG-PIIK, 20" heavy barrel, no sights **$1,743.00**
Price: SSG-PIV, 16.75" threaded heavy barrel with flash hider **$1,777.00**

THOMPSON/CENTER ICON BOLT-ACTION RIFLE

Caliber: 22-250 Rem., 243 Win., 308 Win., 30TC, 3-round box magazine. **Barrel:** 24", button rifled. **Weight:** 7.5 lbs. **Length:** 44.5" overall. **Stock:** Walnut, 20-lpi grip and forend cut checkering with ribbon detail. **Sights:** None; integral Weaver style scope mounts. **Features:** Interchangeable bolt handle, 60-degree bolt lift, Interlok Bedding System, 3-lug bolt with T-Slot extractor, cocking indicator, adjustable trigger, preset to 3 to 3.5 lbs of pull. Introduced 2007. From Thompson/Center Arms.

Price: **$1,025.00**

Thompson/Center Icon

Tikka T-3 Hunter

Weatherby Mark V Lazermark

TIKKA T3 BIG BOAR SYNTHETIC BOLT-ACTION RIFLE

Caliber: 308 Win., 30-06 Spfl., 300 WSM. **Barrel:** 19". **Weight:** 6.1 lbs. **Length:** 39.5" overall. **Stock:** Laminated. **Sights:** None furnished. **Features:** Detachable, 3-round. Receiver dove-tailed for scope mounting. Reintroduced 1996. Imported from Finland by Beretta USA.

Price: **$695.00**

Tikka T3 Super Varmint Rifle

Similar to the standard T-3 rifle except has 23-3/8" heavy stainless barrel. Chambered for 22-250 Rem., 223 Rem., 308 Win. Reintroduced 2005. Made in Finland by Sako. Imported by Beretta USA.

Price: **$1,425.00**

TIKKA T3 HUNTER

Caliber: 223 Rem., 22-250 Rem., 243 Win., 308 Win., 25-06 Rem., 270 Win., 30-06 Spfl., 300 Win. Mag., 338 Win. Mag., 270 WSM, 300 WSM, 6.5x55 Swedish Mauser, 7mm Rem. Mag. **Stock:** Walnut. Sight: None furnished. **Barrel:** 22-7/16", 24-3/8". **Features:** Detachable magazine, aluminum scope rings. Introduced 2005. Imported from Finland by Beretta USA.

Price: **$625.00**

Tikka T3 Stainless Synthetic

Similar to the T-3 Hunter except stainless steel, synthetic stock. Available in 243 Win., 2506, 270 Win., 308 Win., 30-06 Spfl., 270 WSM, 300 WSM, 7mm Rem. Mag., 300 Win. Mag., 338 Win. Mag. Introduced 2005. Imported from Finland by Beretta USA.

Price: **$895.00**

ULTRA LIGHT ARMS BOLT-ACTION RIFLES

Caliber: 17 Rem. to 416 Rigby. **Barrel:** Douglas, length to order. **Weight:** 4.75 to 7.5 lbs. **Length:** Varies. **Stock:** Kevlar graphite composite, variety of finishes. **Sights:** None furnished; drilled and tapped for scope mounts. **Features:** Timney trigger, hand-lapped action, button-rifled barrel, hand-bedded action, recoil pad, sling-swivel studs, optional Jewell trigger. Made in U.S.A. by New Ultra Light Arms.

Price: Model 20 (short action). **$3,100.00**
Price: Model 24 (long action) **$3,200.00**
Price: Model 28 (magnum action) **$3,500.00**
Price: Model 40 (300 Wby. Mag., 416 Rigby) **$3,500.00**
Price: Left-hand models, add **$100.00**

WEATHERBY MARK V BOLT-ACTION RIFLES

Caliber: Deluxe version comes in all Weatherby calibers plus 243 Win., 270 Win., 7mm-08 Rem., 30-06 Spfl., 308 Win. **Barrel:** 24", 26", 28". **Weight:** 6.75 to 10 lbs. **Length:** 44" to 48.75" overall. **Stock:** Walnut, Monte Carlo with cheekpiece; high luster finish; checkered pistol grip and forend; recoil pad. **Sights:** None furnished. **Features:** 4 models with Mark V action and wood stocks; other common elements include cocking indicator; adjustable trigger; hinged floorplate, thumb safety; quick detachable sling swivels. Ultramark has hand-selected exhibition-grade walnut stock, maplewood/ebony spacers, 20-lpi checkering. Chambered for 257 and 300 Wby Mags. Lazermark same as Mark V Deluxe except stock has extensive oak leaf pattern laser carving on pistol grip and forend; chambered in Wby. Magnums—257, 270 Win., 7mm., 300, 340, with 26" barrel. Introduced 1981. Sporter is same as the Mark V Deluxe without the embellishments. Metal has low-luster blue, stock is Claro walnut with matte finish, Monte Carlo comb, recoil pad. Chambered for these Wby. Mags: 257, 270 Win., 7mm, 300, 340. Other chamberings: 7mm Rem. Mag., 300 Win. Introduced 1993. Six Mark V models come with synthetic stocks. Ultra Lightweight rifles weigh 5.75 to 6.75 lbs.; 24", 26" fluted stainless barrels with recessed target crown; Bell & Carlson stock with CNC-machined aluminum bedding plate and tan “spider web” finish, skeletonized handle and sleeve. Available in 243 Win., Wby. Mag., 25-06 Rem., 270 Win., 7mm-08 Rem., 7mm Rem. Mag., 280 Rem, 308 Win., 30-06 Spfl., 300 Win. Mag. Wby. Mag chamberings: 240, 257, 270 Win., 7mm, 300. Introduced 1998. Accumark uses Mark V action with heavy-contour 26" and 28" stainless barrels with black oxidized flutes, muzzle diameter of .705". No sights, drilled and tapped for scope mounting. Stock is composite with matte gel-coat finish, full length aluminum bedding Hasblock. Weighs 8.5 lbs. Chambered for these Wby. Mags: 240 (2007), 257, 270, 7mm, 300, 340, 338-378, 30-378. Other chamberings: 22-250 (2007), 243 Win. (2007), 25-06 Rem. (2007), 270 Win. (2007), 308 Win.(2007), 7mm Rem. Mag., 300 Win. Mag. Introduced 1996. SVM (Super VarmintMaster) has 26" fluted stainless barrel, spiderweb-pattern tan laminated synthetic stock, fully adjustable trigger. Chambered for 223 Rem., 22-250 Rem., 243. Mark V Synthetic has lightweight injection-molded synthetic stock with raised Monte Carlo comb, checkered grip and forend, custom floorplate release. Weighs 6.5-8.5 lbs., 24-28" barrels. Available in 22-250 Rem., 243 Win., 25-06 Rem., 270 Win., 7mm-08 Rem., 7mm Rem., Mag, 280 Rem., 308 Win., 30-06 Spfl., 308 Win., 300 Win. Mag., 375 H&H Mag, and these Wby. Magnums: 240, 257, 270 Win., 7mm, 300, 30-378, 338-378, 340. Introduced 1997. Fibermark composites are similar to other Mark V models except has black Kevlar and fiberglass composite stock and bead-bead-blast blue or stainless finish. Chambered for 9 standard and magnum calibers. Introduced 1983; reintroduced 2001. SVR comes with 22" button-rifled chrome-moly barrel, .739 muzzle diameter. Composite stock w/bedding block, gray spiderweb pattern. Made in U.S.A. From Weatherby.

Price: Mark V Deluxe . . . . **$2,062.00 to $2,939.00**
Price: Mark V Ultramark **$2,780.00**
Price: Mark V Lazermark **$2,313.00**
Price: Mark V Sporter **$1,402.00**
Price: Mark V SVM **$1,825.00**
Price: Mark V Ultra Lightweight . . . . **$1,754.00 to $1,841.00**
Price: Mark V Ultra Lightweight LH. **$1,911.00**
Price: Mark V Accumark. . . . . **$1,750.00 to $1,814.00**
Price: Mark V Accumark w/Accubrake **$2,073.00**
Price: Mark V Accumark LH **$1,884.00**
Price: Mark V Synthetic . . . . **$1,132.00 to $1,411.00**

WEATHERBY MARK V BOLT-ACTION RIFLES *(cont.)*

Price: Mark V Fibermark Composite **$1,350.00**
Price: Mark V Fibermark Composite w/Accubrake **$1,620.00**
Price: Mark V SVR Special Varmint Rifle **$1,176.00**

WEATHERBY VANGUARD BOLT-ACTION RIFLES

Caliber: 257, 300 Wby Mags; 223 Rem., 22-250 Rem., 243 Win., 25-06 Rem. (2007), 270 Win., 270 WSM, 7mm Rem. Mag., 308 Win., 30-06 Spfl., 300 Win. Mag., 300 WSM, 338 Win. Mag. **Barrel:** 24" barreled action, matte black. **Weight:** 7.5 to 8.75 lbs. **Length:** 44" to 46-3/4" overall. **Stock:** Raised comb, Monte Carlo, injection-molded composite stock. **Sights:** None furnished. **Features:** One-piece forged, fluted bolt body with three gas ports, forged and machined receiver, adjustable trigger, factory accuracy guarantee. Vanguard Stainless has 410-Series stainless steel barrel and action, bead blasted matte metal finish. Vanguard Deluxe has raised comb, semi-fancy grade Monte Carlo walnut stock with maplewood spacers, rosewood forend and grip cap, polished action with high-gloss-blued metalwork. Vanguard Synthetic Package includes Vanguard Synthetic rifle with Bushnell Banner 3-9x40mm scope mounted and boresighted, Leupold Rifleman rings and bases, Uncle Mikes nylon sling, and Plano PRO-MAX injection-molded case. Sporter has Monte Carlo walnut stock with satin urethane finish, fineline diamond point checkering, contrasting rosewood forend tip, matte-blued metalwork. Sporter SS metalwork is 410 Series bead-blasted stainless steel. Vanguard Youth/Compact has 20" No. 1 contour barrel, short action, scaled-down non-reflective matte black hardwood stock with 12.5" length of pull and full-size, injection-molded composite stock. Chambered for 223 Rem., 22-250 Rem., 243 Win., 7mm-08 Rem., 308 Win. Weighs 6.75 lbs.; OAL 38.9". Sub-MOA Matte and Sub-MOA Stainless models have pillar-bedded Fiberguard composite stock (Aramid, graphite unidirectional fibers and fiberglass) with 24" barreled action; matte black metalwork, Pachmayr Decelerator recoil pad. Sub-MOA Stainless metalwork is 410 Series bead-blasted stainless steel. Sub-MOA Varmint guaranteed to shoot 3-shot group of .99" or less when used with specified Weatherby factory or premium (non-Weatherby calibers) ammunition. Hand-laminated, tan Monte Carlo composite stock with black spiderwebbing; CNC-machined aluminum bedding block, 22" No. 3 contour barrel, recessed target crown. Varmint Special has tan injection-molded Monte Carlo composite stock, pebble grain finish, black spiderwebbing. 22" No. 3 contour barrel (.740 muzzle dia.), bead blasted matte black finish, recessed target crown. Made in U.S.A. From Weatherby.

Price: Vanguard Synthetic . . . .**$525.00 to $543.00**
Price: Vanguard Stainless . . . .**$656.00 to $678.00**
Price: Vanguard Deluxe, 7mm Rem. Mag., 300 Win. Mag. (2007) **$908.00**
Price: Vanguard Synthetic Package, 25-06 Rem. (2007) **$680.00**
Price: Vanguard Sporter . . . .**$689.00 to $712.00**
Price: Vanguard Sporter SS . . . .**$830.00 to $857.00**
Price: Vanguard Youth/Compact **$620.00**
Price: Vanguard Sub-MOA Matte, 25-06 Rem. (2007) **$877.00**
Price: Vanguard Sub-MOA Stainless, 270 WSM **$1,027.00**
Price: Vanguard Sub-MOA Varmint, 204 Ruger (2007) **$1,003.00**
Price: Vanguard Varmint Special, 204 Ruger (2007) **$671.00**

WINCHESTER MODEL 70 BOLT-ACTION RIFLES

Caliber: varies by model. **Barrel:** Blued, or free-floating, fluted stainless hammer-forged barrel, 22", 24", 26". Recessed target crown. **Weight:** 6.75 to 7.25 lbs. **Length:** 41 to 45.75 " overall. **Stock:** Walnut (three models) or Bell and Carlson composite; textured charcoal-grey matte finish, Pachmayr Decelerator recoil pad. **Sights:** None. **Features:** Claw extractor, three-position safety, M.O.A. three-lever trigger system, factory-set at 3.75 lbs. Super Grade features fancy grade walnut stock, contrasting black fore-end tip and pistol grip cap, and sculpted shadowline cheekpiece. Featherweight Deluxe has angled-comb walnut stock, Schnabel fore-end, satin finish, cut checkering. Sporter Deluxe has satin-finished walnut stock, cut checkering, sculpted cheekpiece. Extreme Weather SS has composite stock, drop @ comb, 0.5"; drop @ heel, 0.5". Introduced 2008. Made in U.S.A. from Winchester Repeating Arms.

Price: Extreme Weather SS, 270 Win., 270 WSM, 30-06 Spfl., 300 Win. Mag., 300 WSM, 308 Win., 325 WSM, from. . . . **$1,149.00**
Price: Super Grade, 30-06 Sprg., 300 Win. Mag., from **$1,499.00**
Price: Featherweight Deluxe, 243 Win., 270 Win., 270 WSM, 30-06 Spfl., 300 Win. Mag., 300 WSM, 308 Win., 325 WSM, 7mm-08 Rem., from **$999.00**
Price: Sporter Deluxe, 270 Win., 270 WSM, 30-06 Spfl., 300 Win. Mag., 300 WSM, 325 WSM, from **$999.00**

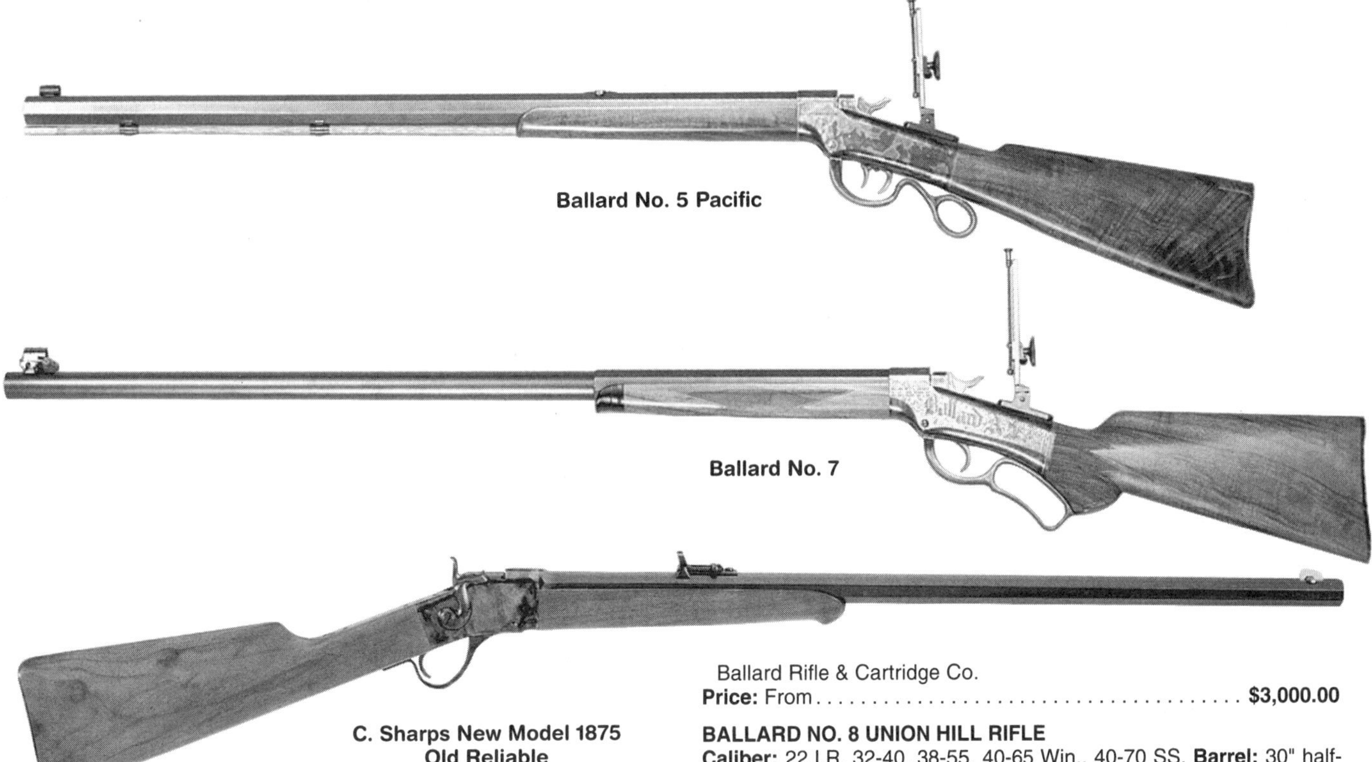

Ballard No. 5 Pacific

Ballard No. 7

C. Sharps New Model 1875 Old Reliable

ARMALITE AR-50 RIFLE

Caliber: 50 BMG **Barrel:** 31". **Weight:** 33.2 lbs. **Length:** 59.5" **Stock:** Synthetic. **Sights:** None furnished. **Features:** A single-shot bolt-action rifle designed for long-range shooting. Available in left-hand model. Made in U.S.A. by Armalite.

Price: **$3,229.00**

BALLARD NO. 1 3/4 FAR WEST RIFLE

Caliber: 22 LR, 32-40, 38-55, 40-65, 40-70, 45-70 Govt., 45-110, 50-70, 50-90. **Barrel:** 30" std. or heavyweight. **Weight:** 10.5 lbs. (std.) or 11.75 lbs. (heavyweight bbl.) **Length:** NA. **Stock:** Walnut. **Sights:** Blade front, Rocky Mountain rear. **Features:** Single- or double-set triggers, S-lever or ring-style lever; color case-hardened finish; hand polished and lapped Badger barrel. Made in U.S.A. by Ballard Rifle & Cartridge Co.

Price: **$3,050.00**

BALLARD NO. 4 PERFECTION RIFLE

Caliber: 22 LR, 32-40, 38-55, 40-65, 40-70, 45-70 Govt., 45-90, 45-110, 50-70, 50-90. **Barrel:** 30" or 32" octagon, standard or heavyweight. **Weight:** 10.5 lbs. (standard) or 11.75 lbs. (heavyweight bbl.). **Length:** NA. **Stock:** Smooth walnut. **Sights:** Blade front, Rocky Mountain rear. **Features:** Rifle or shotgun-style buttstock, straight grip action, single or double-set trigger, "S" or right lever, hand polished and lapped Badger barrel. Made in U.S.A. by Ballard Rifle & Cartridge Co.

Price: **$3,260.00**

BALLARD NO. 5 PACIFIC SINGLE-SHOT RIFLE

Caliber: 32-40, 38-55, 40-65, 40-90, 40-70 SS, 45-70 Govt., 45-110 SS, 50-70 Govt., 50-90 SS. **Barrel:** 30", or 32" octagonal. **Weight:** 10.5 lbs. **Length:** NA. **Stock:** High-grade walnut; rifle or shotgun style. **Sights:** Blade front, Rocky Mountain rear. **Features:** Standard or heavy barrel; double-set triggers; under-barrel wiping rod; ring lever. Introduced 1999. Made in U.S.A. by Ballard Rifle & Cartridge Co.

Price: **$3,350.00**

BALLARD NO. 7 LONG RANGE RIFLE

Caliber: 32-40, 38-55, 40-65, 40-70 SS, 45-70 Govt., 45-90, 45-110. **Barrel:** 32", 34" half-octagon. **Weight:** 11.75 lbs. **Length:** NA. **Stock:** Walnut; checkered pistol grip shotgun butt, ebony forend cap. **Sights:** Globe front. **Features:** Designed for shooting up to 1000 yards. Standard or heavy barrel; single or double-set trigger; hard rubber or steel buttplate. Introduced 1999. Made in U.S.A. by Ballard Rifle & Cartridge Co.

Price: From **$3,000.00**

BALLARD NO. 8 UNION HILL RIFLE

Caliber: 22 LR, 32-40, 38-55, 40-65 Win., 40-70 SS. **Barrel:** 30" half-octagon. **Weight:** About 10.5 lbs. **Length:** NA. **Stock:** Walnut; pistol grip butt with cheekpiece. **Sights:** Globe front. **Features:** Designed for 200-yard offhand shooting. Standard or heavy barrel; double-set triggers; full loop lever; hook Schuetzen buttplate. Introduced 1999. Made in U.S.A. by Ballard Rifle & Cartridge Co.

Price: From **$3,425.00**

BALLARD MODEL 1885 HIGH WALL SINGLE SHOT RIFLE

Caliber: 17 Bee, 22 Hornet, 218 Bee, 219 Don Wasp, 219 Zipper, 22 Hi-Power, 225 Win., 25-20 WCF, 25-35 WCF, 25 Krag, 7mmx57R, 30-30, 30-40 Krag, 303 British, 33 WCF, 348 WCF, 35 WCF, 35-30/30, 9.3x74R, 405 WCF, 50-110 WCF, 500 Express, 577 Express. **Barrel:** Lengths to 34". **Weight:** NA. **Length:** NA. **Stock:** Straight-grain American walnut. **Sights:** buckhorn or flattop rear, blade front. **Features:** Faithful copy of original Model 1885 High Wall; parts interchange with original rifles; variety of options available. Introduced 2000. Made in U.S.A. by Ballard Rifle & Cartridge LLC.

Price: **$2,250.00**

BARRETT MODEL 99 SINGLE SHOT RIFLE

Caliber: 50 BMG. **Barrel:** 33". **Weight:** 25 lbs. **Length:** 50.4" overall. **Stock:** Anodized aluminum with energy-absorbing recoil pad. **Sights:** None furnished; integral M1913 scope rail. **Features:** Bolt action; detachable bipod; match-grade barrel with high-efficiency muzzle brake. Introduced 1999. Made in U.S.A. by Barrett Firearms.

Price: From **$3,930.00**

BROWN MODEL 97D SINGLE SHOT RIFLE

Caliber: 17 Ackley Hornet through 45-70 Govt. **Barrel:** Up to 26", air gauged match grade. **Weight:** About 5 lbs., 11 oz. **Stock:** Sporter style with pistol grip, cheekpiece and Schnabel forend. **Sights:** None furnished; drilled and tapped for scope mounting. **Features:** Falling block action gives rigid barrel-receiver matting; polished blue/black finish. Hand-fitted action. Many options. Made in U.S.A. by E. Arthur Brown Co., Inc.

Price: From **$999.00**

BROWNING MODEL 1885 HIGH WALL SINGLE SHOT RIFLE

Caliber: 22-250 Rem., 30-06 Spfl., 270 Win., 7mm Rem. Mag., 454 Casull, 45-70 Govt. **Barrel:** 28". **Weight:** 8 lbs., 12 oz. **Length:** 43.5" overall. **Stock:** Walnut with straight grip, Schnabel forend. **Sights:** None furnished; drilled and tapped for scope mounting. **Features:** Replica of J.M. Browning's high-wall falling block rifle. Octagon barrel with recessed muzzle. Imported from Japan by Browning. Introduced 1985.

Price: **$1,260.00**

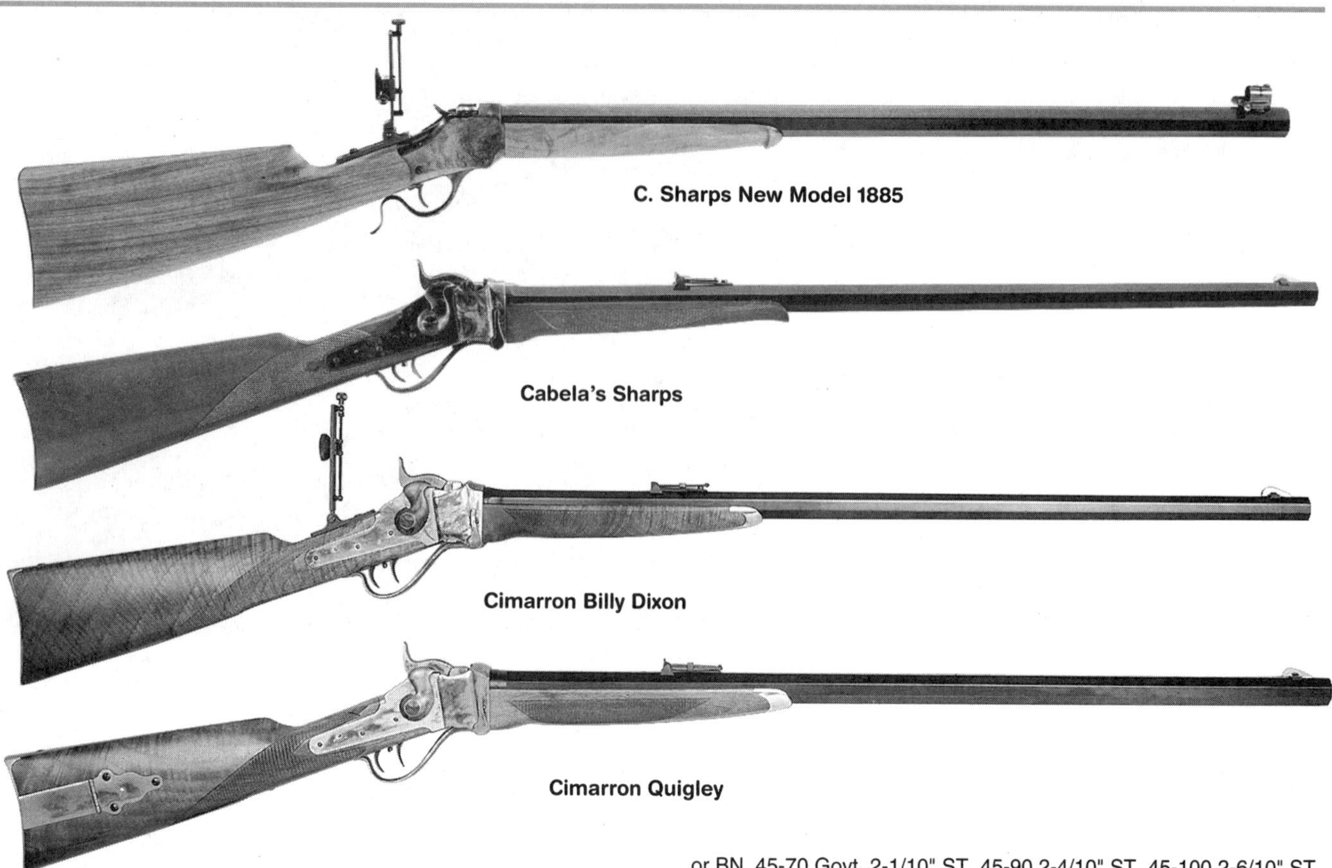

C. Sharps New Model 1885

Cabela's Sharps

Cimarron Billy Dixon

Cimarron Quigley

C. SHARPS ARMS NEW MODEL 1875 OLD RELIABLE RIFLE

Caliber: 22 LR, 32-40 & 38-55 Ballard, 38-56 WCF, 40-65 WCF, 40-90 3-1/4", 40-90 2-5/8", 40-70 2-1/10", 40-70 2-1/4", 40-70 2-1/2", 40-50 1-11/16", 40-50 1-7/8", 45-90, 45-70 Govt., 45-100, 45-110, 45-120. Also available on special order only in 50-70, 50-90, 50-140. **Barrel:** 24", 26", 30" (standard), 32", 34" optional. **Weight:** 8-12 lbs. **Stock:** Walnut, straight grip, shotgun butt with checkered steel buttplate. **Sights:** Silver blade front, Rocky Mountain buckhorn rear. **Features:** Recreation of the 1875 Sharps rifle. Production guns will have case-colored receiver. Available in Custom Sporting and Target versions upon request. Announced 1986. From C. Sharps Arms Co.

Price: 1875 Sporting Rifle (30" tapered octagonal bbl.) **$1,295.00**

C. Sharps Arms 1875 Classic Sharps

Similar to New Model 1875 Sporting Rifle except 26", 28" or 30" full octagon barrel, crescent buttplate with toe plate, Hartford-style forend with cast German silver nose cap. Blade front sight, Rocky Mountain buckhorn rear. Weighs 10 lbs. Introduced 1987. From C. Sharps Arms Co.

Price: **$1,595.00**

C. Sharps Arms Model 1875 Target & Sporting Rifle

Similar to New Model 1875 in all listed calibers except 22 LR; 34" tapered octagon barrel; globe with post front sight, Long Range Vernier tang sight with windage adjustments. Pistol grip stock with cheek rest; checkered steel buttplate. Introduced 1991. From C. Sharps Arms Co.

Price: **$1,250.50**

C. SHARPS ARMS 1874 BRIDGEPORT SPORTING RIFLE

Caliber: 38-55 TO 50-3.25. **Barrel:** 26", 28", 30" tapered octagon. **Weight:** 10.5 lbs. **Length:** 47". **Stock:** American black walnut; shotgun butt with checkered steel buttplate; straight grip, heavy forend with Schnabel tip. **Sights:** Blade front, buckhorn rear. Drilled and tapped for tang sight. **Features:** Double-set triggers. Made in U.S.A. by C. Sharps Arms.

Price: **$1,795.00**

C. SHARPS ARMS NEW MODEL 1885 HIGHWALL RIFLE

Caliber: 22 LR, 22 Hornet, 219 Zipper, 25-35 WCF, 32-40 WCF, 38-55 WCF, 40-65, 30-40 Krag, 40-50 ST or BN, 40-70 ST or BN, 40-90 ST or BN, 45-70 Govt. 2-1/10" ST, 45-90 2-4/10" ST, 45-100 2-6/10" ST, 45-110 2-7/8" ST, 45-120 3-1/4" ST. **Barrel:** 26", 28", 30", tapered full octagon. **Weight:** About 9 lbs., 4 oz. **Length:** 47" overall. **Stock:** Oil-finished American walnut; Schnabel-style forend. **Sights:** Blade front, buckhorn rear. Drilled and tapped for optional tang sight. **Features:** Single trigger; octagonal receiver top; checkered steel buttplate; color case-hardened receiver and buttplate, blued barrel. Many options available. Made in U.S.A. by C. Sharps Arms Co.

Price: From **$1,650.00**

C. SHARPS ARMS CUSTOM NEW MODEL 1877 LONG RANGE TARGET RIFLE

Caliber: 44-90 Sharps/Rem., 45-70 Govt., 45-90, 45-100 Sharps. **Barrel:** 32", 34" tapered round with Rigby flat. **Weight:** About 10 lbs. **Stock:** Walnut checkered. Pistol grip/forend. **Sights:** Classic long range with windage. **Features:** Custom production only.

Price: From **$7,250.00**

CABELA'S SHARPS SPORTING RIFLE

Caliber: 45-70 Govt., 45-120, 45-110. **Barrel:** 32", tapered octagon. **Weight:** 9 lbs. **Length:** 47.25" overall. **Stock:** Checkered walnut. **Sights:** Blade front, open adjustable rear. **Features:** Color case-hardened receiver and hammer, rest blued. Introduced 1995. Imported by Cabela's.

Price: 45-70 Govt., 45-90 .... **$1399.99**

Price: (Heavy Target Sharps, 45-70 Govt., 45-120) .... **$1,499.99 and $1,599.99**

Price: (Quigley Sharps, 45-70 Govt., 45-120, 45-110) **$1,699.99**

CIMARRON BILLY DIXON 1874 SHARPS SPORTING RIFLE

Caliber: 40-40, 50-90, 50-70, 45-70 Govt. **Barrel:** 32" tapered octagonal. **Weight:** NA. **Length:** NA. **Stock:** European walnut. **Sights:** Blade front, Creedmoor rear. **Features:** Color case-hardened frame, blued barrel. Hand-checkered grip and forend; hand-rubbed oil finish. Introduced 1999. Imported by Cimarron F.A. Co.

Price: **$1,988.00**

CIMARRON QUIGLEY MODEL 1874 SHARPS SPORTING RIFLE

Caliber: 45-110, 50-70, 50-40, 45-70 Govt., 45-90, 45-120. **Barrel:** 34" octagonal. **Weight:** NA. **Length:** NA. **Stock:** Checkered walnut. **Sights:** Blade front, adjustable rear. **Features:** Blued finish; double-set triggers. From Cimarron F.A. Co.

Price: **$2,156.00**

CENTERFIRE RIFLES—Single Shot

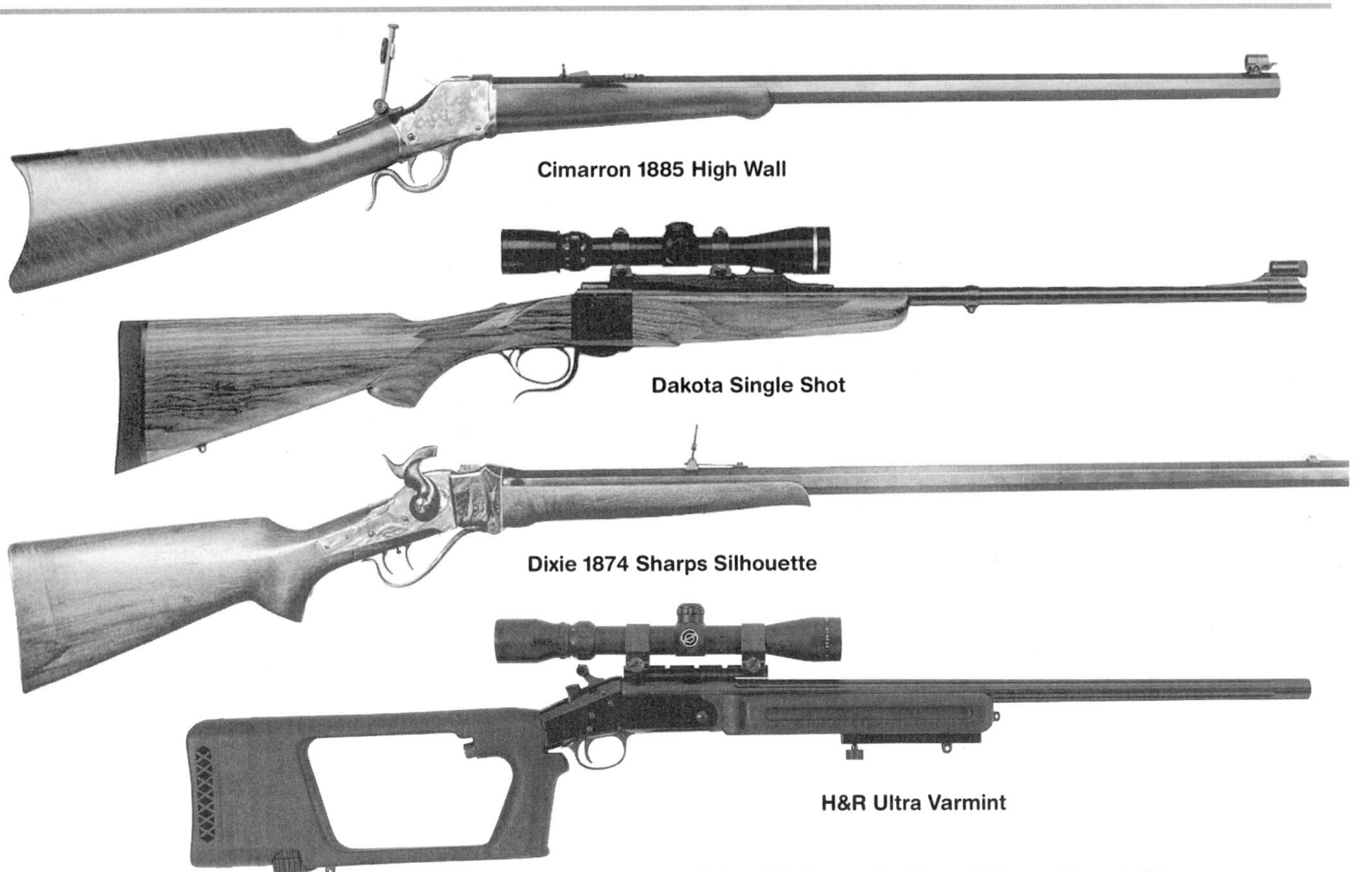

Cimarron 1885 High Wall

Dakota Single Shot

Dixie 1874 Sharps Silhouette

H&R Ultra Varmint

CIMARRON SILHOUETTE MODEL 1874 SHARPS SPORTING RIFLE

Caliber: 45-70 Govt. **Barrel:** 32" octagonal. **Weight:** NA. **Length:** NA. **Stock:** Walnut. **Sights:** Blade front, adjustable rear. **Features:** Pistol-grip stock with shotgun-style buttplate; cut-rifled barrel. From Cimarron F.A. Co.

Price: **$1,585.00**

CIMARRON MODEL 1885 HIGH WALL RIFLE

Caliber: 38-55, 40-65, 45-70 Govt., 45-90, 45-120, 30-40 Krag, 348 Winchester. **Barrel:** 30" octagonal. **Weight:** NA. **Length:** NA. **Stock:** European walnut. **Sights:** Bead front, semi-buckhorn rear. **Features:** Replica of the Winchester 1885 High Wall rifle. Color case-hardened receiver and lever, blued barrel. Curved buttplate. Optional double-set triggers. Introduced 1999. Imported by Cimarron F.A. Co.

Price: **$974.00**
Price: With pistol grip **$1,030.00**

DAKOTA MODEL 10 SINGLE SHOT RIFLE

Caliber: Most rimmed and rimless commercial calibers. **Barrel:** 23". **Weight:** 6 lbs. **Length:** 39.5" overall. **Stock:** Medium fancy grade walnut in classic style. Checkered grip and forend. **Sights:** None furnished. Drilled and tapped for scope mounting. **Features:** Falling block action with underlever. Top tang safety. Removable trigger plate for conversion to single set trigger. Introduced 1990. Made in U.S.A. by Dakota Arms.

Price: From **$4,695.00**
Price: Action only **$1,875.00**
Price: Magnum action only **$1,875.00**

DIXIE 1874 SHARPS BLACK POWDER SILHOUETTE RIFLE

Caliber: 45-70 Govt., 40-65. **Barrel:** 30"; tapered octagon; blued; 1:18" twist. **Weight:** 11.35 lbs. **Length:** 49.25" overall. **Stock:** Oiled walnut. **Sights:** Blade front, ladder-type hunting rear. **Features:** Replica of the Sharps #1 Sporter. Shotgun-style butt with checkered metal buttplate; color case-hardened receiver (bright or engraved model), hammer, lever and buttplate. Tang is drilled and tapped for tang sight. Double-set triggers. Meets standards for NRA blackpowder cartridge matches. Introduced 1995. Imported from Italy by Dixie Gun Works.

Price: Plain **$1,150.00**
Price: Engraved, from **$2,000.00**

Dixie 1874 Sharps Lightweight Hunter/Target Rifle

Same as the Dixie 1874 Sharps Black Powder Silhouette model except has a straight-grip buttstock with military-style buttplate. Based on the 1874 military model. Introduced 1995. Imported from Italy by Dixie Gun Works.

Price: CR0212 . . . . **$1,150.00**

E.M.F. PREMIER 1874 SHARPS RIFLE

Caliber: 45/70, 45/110, 45/120. **Barrel:** 32", 34". **Weight:** 11-13 lbs. **Length:** 49", 51" overall. **Stock:** Pistol grip, European walnut. **Sights:** Blade front, adjustable rear. **Features:** Superb quality reproductions of the 1874 Sharps Sporting Rifles; casehardened locks; double-set triggers; blue barrels. Imported from Pedersoli by E.M.F.

Price: Business Rifle. **$1,130.00**
Price: "Quigley", Patchbox, heavy barrel **$1,800.00**
Price: Silhouette, pistol-grip **$1,500.00**
Price: Super Deluxe Hand Engraved **$3,150.00**

E.M.F. 1885 HIGHWALL RIFLES

Caliber: 38/55, 45/70. **Barrel:** 30". **Weight:** 10 lbs. **Length:** 47". **Stock:** Walnut, straight or pistol grip. **Sights:** Bead front, semi-buckhorn rear. **Features:** Reproduction of the Winchester 1885 Highwall Rifle, curved butt plate. Case-hardened receiver and lever, blue barrel. Imported by E.M.F.

Price: Standard. **$900.00**
Price: Deluxe pistol grip **$1,020.00**

HARRINGTON & RICHARDSON ULTRA VARMINT/ULTRA HUNTER RIFLES

Caliber: 204 Ruger, 22 WMR, 22-250 Rem., 223 Rem., 243 Win., 25-06 Rem., 30-06. **Barrel:** 22" to 26" heavy taper. **Weight:** About 7.5 lbs. **Stock:** Laminated birch with Monte Carlo comb or skeletonized polymer. **Sights:** None furnished. Drilled and tapped for scope mounting. **Features:** Break-open action with side-lever release, positive ejection. Scope mount. Blued receiver and barrel. Swivel studs. Introduced 1993. Ultra Hunter introduced 1995. From H&R 1871, Inc.

Price: Ultra Varmint Fluted, 24" bull barrel, polymer stock **$406.00**
Price: Ultra Hunter Rifle, 26" bull barrel in 25-06 Rem., laminated stock **$357.00**
Price: Ultra Varmint Rifle, 22" bull barrel in 223 Rem., laminated stock **$357.00**

H&R Ultra Hunter

H&R Buffalo

Model 1885 High Wall

Navy Arms #2 Creedmoor

HARRINGTON & RICHARDSON BUFFALO CLASSIC & TARGET RIFLES

Caliber: 45-70 Govt. **Barrel:** 32" heavy. **Weight:** 8 lbs. **Length:** 46" overall. **Stock:** Cut-checkered American black walnut. **Sights:** Williams receiver sight; Lyman target front sight with 8 aperture inserts. **Features:** Color case-hardened Handi-Rifle action with exposed hammer; color case-hardened crescent buttplate; 19th century checkering pattern. Introduced 1995. Target model (introduced 1998) is similar to the Buffalo Classic rifle except chambered for 38-55 Win., has 28" barrel. The barrel, steel trigger guard and forend spacer, are highly polished and blued. Color case-hardened receiver and buttplate. Made in U.S.A. by H&R 1871, LLC.

Price: Buffalo Classic Rifle **$449.00**

Price: Target Model Rifle **$449.00**

HARRIS GUNWORKS ANTIETAM SHARPS RIFLE

Caliber: 40-65, 45-75. **Barrel:** 30", 32", octagon or round, hand-lapped stainless or chrome-moly. **Weight:** 11.25 lbs. **Length:** 47" overall. **Stock:** Choice of straight grip, pistol grip or Creedmoor with Schnabel forend; pewter tip optional. Standard wood is A Fancy; higher grades available. **Sights:** Montana Vintage Arms #111 Low Profile Spirit Level front, #108 mid-range tang rear with windage adjustments. **Features:** Recreation of the 1874 Sharps sidehammer. Action is color case-hardened, barrel satin black. Chrome-moly barrel optionally blued. Optional sights include #112 Spirit Level Globe front with windage, #107 Long Range rear with windage. Introduced 1994. Made in U.S.A. by Harris Gunworks.

Price: **$2,400.00**

KRIEGHOFF HUBERTUS SINGLE-SHOT RIFLE

Caliber: 222, 243 Win., 270 Win., 308 Win., 30-06 Spfl., 5.6x50R Mag., 5.6x52R, 6x62R Freres, 6.5x57R, 6.5x65R, 7x57R, 7x65R, 8x57JRS, 8x75RS, 9.3x74R, 7mm Rem. Mag., 300 Win. Mag. **Barrel:** 23.5". **Weight:** 6.5 lbs. **Length:** 40.5. **Stock:** High-grade walnut. **Sights:** Blade front, open rear. **Features:** Break-open loading with manual cocking lever on top tang; takedown; extractor; Schnabel forearm; many options. Imported from Germany by Krieghoff International Inc.

Price: Hubertus single shot, from **$5,995.00**

Price: Hubertus, magnum calibers **$6,995.00**

MEACHAM HIGHWALL SILHOUETTE OR SCHUETZEN RIFLE

Caliber: any rimmed cartridge. **Barrel:** 26-34". **Weight:** 8-15 lbs. **Sights:** none. Tang drilled for Win. base, 3/8 dovetail slot front. **Stock:** Fancy eastern walnut with cheekpiece; ebony insert in forearm tip. **Features:** Exact copy of 1885 Winchester. With most Winchester factory options available, including double set triggers. Introduced 1994. Made in U.S.A. by Meacham T&H Inc.

Price: From **$3,899.00**

MERKEL K1 MODEL LIGHTWEIGHT STALKING RIFLE

Caliber: 243 Win., 270 Win., 7x57R, 308 Win., 30-06 Spfl., 7mm Rem. Mag., 300 Win. Mag., 9.3x74R. **Barrel:** 23.6". **Weight:** 5.6 lbs. unscoped. **Stock:** Satin-finished walnut, fluted and checkered; sling-swivel studs. **Sights:** None (scope base furnished). **Features:** Franz Jager single-shot break-open action, cocking/uncocking slide-type safety, matte silver receiver, selectable trigger pull weights, integrated, quick detach 1" or 30mm optic mounts (optic not included). Imported from Germany by Merkel USA.

Price: Jagd Stutzen Carbine **$4,195.00**

Price: Jagd, fine engraved hunting scenes **$3,795.00**

MODEL 1885 HIGH WALL RIFLE

Caliber: 30-40 Krag, 32-40, 38-55, 40-65 WCF, 45-70 Govt. **Barrel:** 26" (30-40), 28" to 30" all others. Douglas Premium #3 tapered octagon. **Weight:** 9 lbs, 4 oz. **Length:** 47" overall. **Stock:** Premium American black walnut. **Sights:** Marble's standard ivory bead front, #66 long blade top rear with reversible notch and elevator. **Features:** Receiver with octagon top, thick-wall High Wall with coil spring action. Tang drilled, tapped for High Wall tang sight. Receiver, lever, hammer and breechblock color case-hardened. Available from Montana Armory, Inc.

Price: **$1,350.00**

NAVY ARMS 1874 SHARPS "QUIGLEY" RIFLE

Caliber: .45-70 Govt. **Barrel:** 34" octagon. **Weight:** 10 lbs. **Length:** 50" overall. Grips: Walnut checkered at wrist and forend. **Sights:** High blade front, full buckhorn rear. **Features:** Color case-hardened receiver, trigger, military patchbox, hammer and lever. Double-set triggers, German silver gripcap. Reproduction of rifle from "Quigley Down Under" movie.

Price: Model SQR045 (20087) **$2,026.00**

NAVY ARMS 1874 SHARPS NO. 2 CREEDMOOR RIFLE

Caliber: 45/70. **Barrel:** 30" tapered round. **Stock:** Walnut. **Sights:** Front globe, "soule" tang rear. **Features:** Nickel receiver and action. Lightweight sporting rifle.

Price: **$1,816.00**

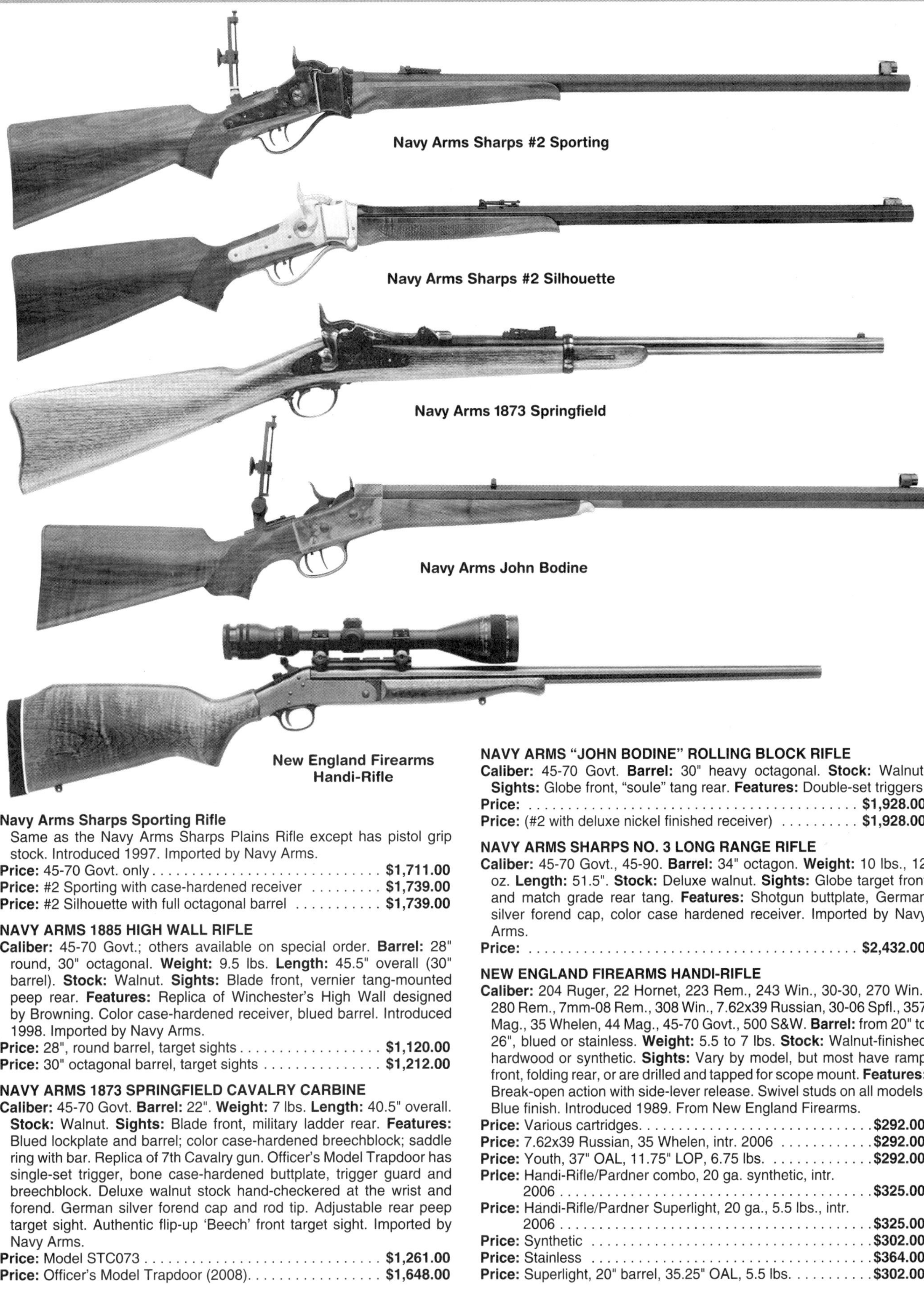
Navy Arms Sharps #2 Sporting

Navy Arms Sharps #2 Silhouette

Navy Arms 1873 Springfield

Navy Arms John Bodine

New England Firearms Handi-Rifle

Navy Arms Sharps Sporting Rifle

Same as the Navy Arms Sharps Plains Rifle except has pistol grip stock. Introduced 1997. Imported by Navy Arms.

Price: 45-70 Govt. only **$1,711.00**
Price: #2 Sporting with case-hardened receiver **$1,739.00**
Price: #2 Silhouette with full octagonal barrel **$1,739.00**

NAVY ARMS 1885 HIGH WALL RIFLE

Caliber: 45-70 Govt.; others available on special order. **Barrel:** 28" round, 30" octagonal. **Weight:** 9.5 lbs. **Length:** 45.5" overall (30" barrel). **Stock:** Walnut. **Sights:** Blade front, vernier tang-mounted peep rear. **Features:** Replica of Winchester's High Wall designed by Browning. Color case-hardened receiver, blued barrel. Introduced 1998. Imported by Navy Arms.

Price: 28", round barrel, target sights **$1,120.00**
Price: 30" octagonal barrel, target sights **$1,212.00**

NAVY ARMS 1873 SPRINGFIELD CAVALRY CARBINE

Caliber: 45-70 Govt. **Barrel:** 22". **Weight:** 7 lbs. **Length:** 40.5" overall. **Stock:** Walnut. **Sights:** Blade front, military ladder rear. **Features:** Blued lockplate and barrel; color case-hardened breechblock; saddle ring with bar. Replica of 7th Cavalry gun. Officer's Model Trapdoor has single-set trigger, bone case-hardened buttplate, trigger guard and breechblock. Deluxe walnut stock hand-checkered at the wrist and forend. German silver forend cap and rod tip. Adjustable rear peep target sight. Authentic flip-up 'Beech' front target sight. Imported by Navy Arms.

Price: Model STC073 . . . . **$1,261.00**
Price: Officer's Model Trapdoor (2008). **$1,648.00**

NAVY ARMS "JOHN BODINE" ROLLING BLOCK RIFLE

Caliber: 45-70 Govt. **Barrel:** 30" heavy octagonal. **Stock:** Walnut. **Sights:** Globe front, "soule" tang rear. **Features:** Double-set triggers.

Price: **$1,928.00**
Price: (#2 with deluxe nickel finished receiver) **$1,928.00**

NAVY ARMS SHARPS NO. 3 LONG RANGE RIFLE

Caliber: 45-70 Govt., 45-90. **Barrel:** 34" octagon. **Weight:** 10 lbs., 12 oz. **Length:** 51.5". **Stock:** Deluxe walnut. **Sights:** Globe target front and match grade rear tang. **Features:** Shotgun buttplate, German silver forend cap, color case hardened receiver. Imported by Navy Arms.

Price: **$2,432.00**

NEW ENGLAND FIREARMS HANDI-RIFLE

Caliber: 204 Ruger, 22 Hornet, 223 Rem., 243 Win., 30-30, 270 Win., 280 Rem., 7mm-08 Rem., 308 Win., 7.62x39 Russian, 30-06 Spfl., 357 Mag., 35 Whelen, 44 Mag., 45-70 Govt., 500 S&W. **Barrel:** from 20" to 26", blued or stainless. **Weight:** 5.5 to 7 lbs. **Stock:** Walnut-finished hardwood or synthetic. **Sights:** Vary by model, but most have ramp front, folding rear, or are drilled and tapped for scope mount. **Features:** Break-open action with side-lever release. Swivel studs on all models. Blue finish. Introduced 1989. From New England Firearms.

Price: Various cartridges. **$292.00**
Price: 7.62x39 Russian, 35 Whelen, intr. 2006 . . . . **$292.00**
Price: Youth, 37" OAL, 11.75" LOP, 6.75 lbs. **$292.00**
Price: Handi-Rifle/Pardner combo, 20 ga. synthetic, intr. 2006 . . . . **$325.00**
Price: Handi-Rifle/Pardner Superlight, 20 ga., 5.5 lbs., intr. 2006 . . . . **$325.00**
Price: Synthetic **$302.00**
Price: Stainless **$364.00**
Price: Superlight, 20" barrel, 35.25" OAL, 5.5 lbs. **$302.00**

New England Firearms Superlight

New England Firearms Survivor

Remington No. 1 Mid-Range

Rossi Single Shot

NEW ENGLAND FIREARMS SURVIVOR RIFLE

Caliber: 223 Rem., 308 Win., .410 shotgun, 45 Colt, single shot. **Barrel:** 20" to 22". **Weight:** 6 lbs. **Length:** 34.5" to 36" overall. **Stock:** Black polymer, thumbhole design. **Sights:** None furnished; scope mount provided. **Features:** Receiver drilled and tapped for scope mounting. Stock and forend have storage compartments for ammo, etc.; comes with integral swivels and black nylon sling. Introduced 1996. Made in U.S.A. by New England Firearms.

Price: Blue or nickel finish. **$304.00**

NEW ENGLAND FIREARMS SPORTSTER/VERSA PACK RIFLE

Caliber: 17M2, 17 HMR, 22 LR, 22 WMR, .410 bore single shot. **Barrel:** 20" to 22". **Weight:** 5.4 to 7 lbs. **Length:** 33" to 38.25" overall. **Stock:** Black polymer. **Sights:** Adjustable rear, ramp front. **Features:** Receiver drilled and tapped for scope mounting. Made in U.S.A. by New England Firearms.

Price: Sportster 17M2, 17 HMR **$193.00**
Price: Sportster **$161.00**
Price: Sportster Youth **$161.00**
Price: Sportster 22/410 Versa Pack **$176.00**

REMINGTON MODEL SPR18 SINGLE SHOT RIFLES

Caliber: 223 Rem., 243 Win., 270 Win., .30-06 Spfl., 308 Win., 7.62x39mm. **Barrel:** 23.5" chrome-lined hammer forged, all steel receiver, spiral-cut fluting. **Weight:** 6.75 lbs. **Stock:** Walnut stock and fore-end, swivel studs. **Sights:** adjustable, with 11mm scope rail. **Length:** 39.75" overall. **Features:** Made in U.S. by Remington Arms Co., Inc.

Price: Blued/walnut (2008) **$277.00**
Price: Nickel/walnut (2008). **$326.00**

REMINGTON NO. 1 ROLLING BLOCK MID-RANGE SPORTER

Caliber: 45-70 Govt. **Barrel:** 30" round. **Weight:** 8.75 lbs. **Length:** 46.5" overall. **Stock:** American walnut with checkered pistol grip and forend. **Sights:** Beaded blade front, adjustable center-notch buckhorn rear. **Features:** Recreation of the original. Polished blue metal finish. Many options available. Introduced 1998. Made in U.S.A. by Remington.

Price: **$2,927.00**
Price: Silhouette model with single-set trigger, heavy barrel **$3,366.00**

ROSSI SINGLE-SHOT RIFLES

Caliber: 17, 223 Rem., 243 Win., 270 Win., .30-06, 308 Win., 7.62x39, 22-250. **Barrel:** 22" (Youth), 23". **Weight:** 6.25-7 lbs. Stocks: Wood, Black Synthetic (Youth). **Sights:** Adjustable sights, drilled and tapped for scope. **Features:** Single-shot break open, 13 models available, positive ejection, internal transfer bar mechanism, manual external safety, trigger block system, Taurus Security System, Matte blue finish, youth models available.

Price: **$263.00**

ROSSI MATCHED PAIRS

Gauge/Caliber: 12, 20, .410, 22 Mag, 22 LR, 17 HMR, 223 Rem, 243 Win., 270 Win., .30-06, 308Win., .50 (black powder). **Barrel:** 23", 28". **Weight:** 5-6.3 lbs. Stocks: Wood or black synthetic. **Sights:** Bead front on shotgun barrel, fully adjustable front and rear on rifle barrel, drilled and tapped for scope, fully adjustable fiber optic sights (black powder). **Features:** Single-shot break open, 27 models available, internal transfer bar mechanism, manual external safety, blue finish, trigger block system, Taurus Security System, youth models available.

Price: Rimfire/Shotgun, from. $178.00
Price: Centerfire/Shotgun $299.00
Price: Black Powder Matched Pair, from $262.00

RUGER NO. 1B SINGLE SHOT

Caliber: 223 Rem., 204 Ruger, 25-06 Rem., 270 Win., 30-06 Spfl., 7mm Rem. Mag., 300 Win. Mag., 308 Win. **Barrel:** 26" round tapered with quarter-rib; with Ruger 1" rings. **Weight:** 8.25 lbs. **Length:** 42.25" overall. **Stock:** Walnut, two-piece, checkered pistol grip and semi-beavertail forend. **Sights:** None, 1" scope rings supplied for integral mounts. **Features:** Under-lever, hammerless falling block design has auto ejector, top tang safety.

Price: 1B $1,093.00
Price: K1-B-BBZ stainless steel, laminated stock 25-06 Rem., 7mm Rem. Mag., 270, 300 Win. Mag., 243 Win., 30-06 . . . . $1,130.00

RUGER NO. 1A LIGHT SPORTER

Caliber: 243 Win., 270 Win., 7x57, 30-06. **Weight:** 7.25 lbs. Similar to the No. 1B Standard Rifle except has lightweight 22" barrel, Alexander Henry-style forend, adjustable folding leaf rear sight on quarter-rib, dovetailed ramp front with gold bead.

Price: No. 1A. $1,093.00

RUGER NO. 1A LIGHT STANDARD

Caliber: 204 Ruger. **Weight:** About 7.25 lbs. **Length:** 38.25" overall. Similar to the No. 1A Light Sporter but doesn't come with sights.

Price: No. 1-AB. $1,093.00

Ruger No. 1V Varminter

Similar to the No. 1B Standard Rifle except has 24" heavy barrel. Semi-beavertail forend, barrel ribbed for target scope block, with 1" Ruger scope rings. Calibers 204 Ruger (26" barrel), 22-250 Rem., 223 Rem., 25-06 Rem. Weight about 9 lbs.

Price: No. 1V. $1,093.00
Price: K1-V-BBZ stainless steel, laminated stock 204 Ruger $1,130.00

Ruger No. 1 RSI International

Similar to the No. 1B Standard Rifle except has lightweight 20" barrel, full-length International-style forend with loop sling swivel, adjustable folding leaf rear sight on quarter-rib, ramp front with gold bead. Calibers 30-06 Spfl., 270 and 7x57. Weight is about 7.25 lbs.

Price: No. 1 RSI $1,130.00

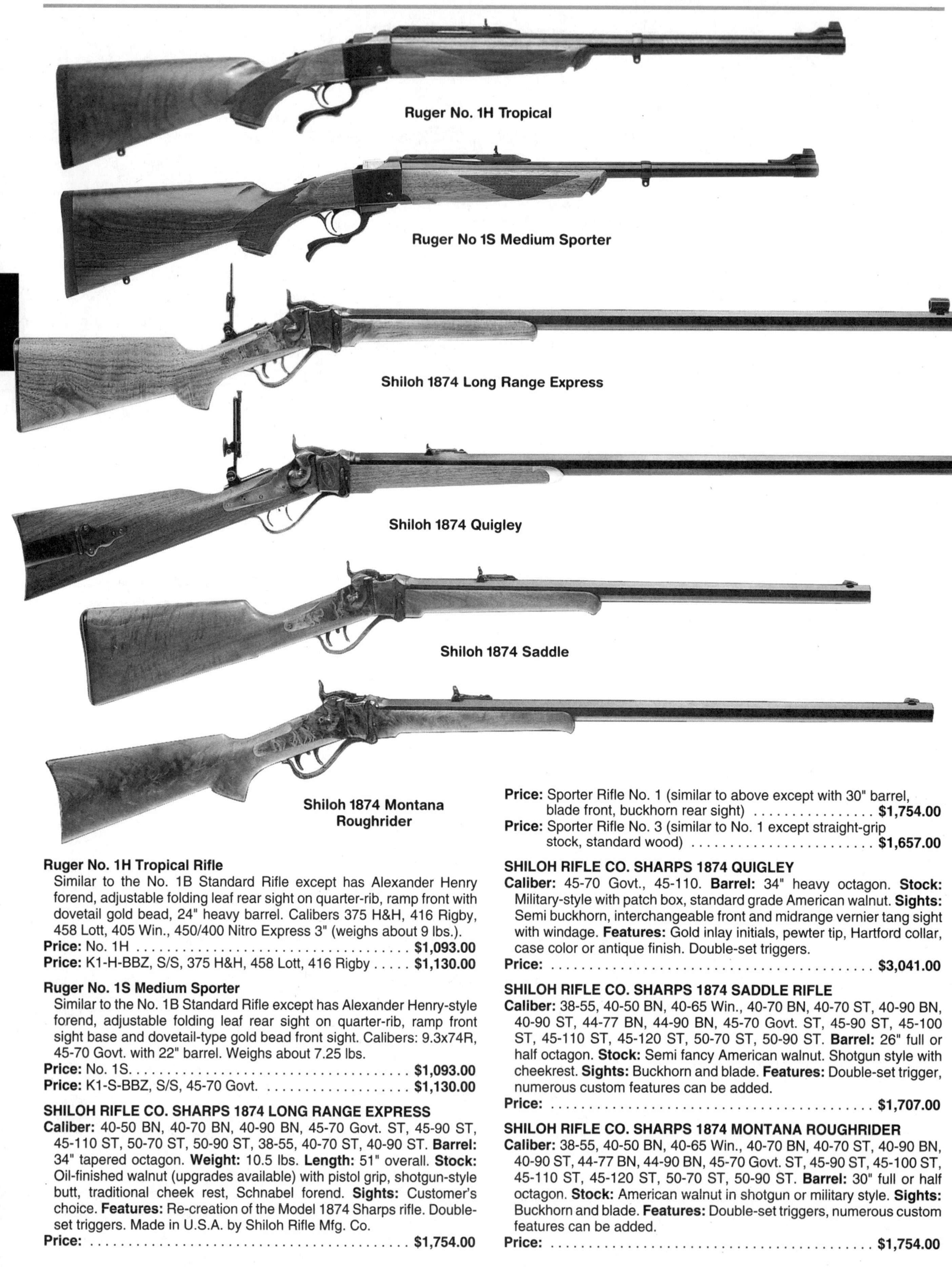

Ruger No. 1H Tropical

Ruger No 1S Medium Sporter

Shiloh 1874 Long Range Express

Shiloh 1874 Quigley

Shiloh 1874 Saddle

Shiloh 1874 Montana Roughrider

Ruger No. 1H Tropical Rifle

Similar to the No. 1B Standard Rifle except has Alexander Henry forend, adjustable folding leaf rear sight on quarter-rib, ramp front with dovetail gold bead, 24" heavy barrel. Calibers 375 H&H, 416 Rigby, 458 Lott, 405 Win., 450/400 Nitro Express 3" (weighs about 9 lbs.).

Price: No. 1H **$1,093.00**

Price: K1-H-BBZ, S/S, 375 H&H, 458 Lott, 416 Rigby **$1,130.00**

Ruger No. 1S Medium Sporter

Similar to the No. 1B Standard Rifle except has Alexander Henry-style forend, adjustable folding leaf rear sight on quarter-rib, ramp front sight base and dovetail-type gold bead front sight. Calibers: 9.3x74R, 45-70 Govt. with 22" barrel. Weighs about 7.25 lbs.

Price: No. 1S. **$1,093.00**

Price: K1-S-BBZ, S/S, 45-70 Govt. **$1,130.00**

SHILOH RIFLE CO. SHARPS 1874 LONG RANGE EXPRESS

Caliber: 40-50 BN, 40-70 BN, 40-90 BN, 45-70 Govt. ST, 45-90 ST, 45-110 ST, 50-70 ST, 50-90 ST, 38-55, 40-70 ST, 40-90 ST. **Barrel:** 34" tapered octagon. **Weight:** 10.5 lbs. **Length:** 51" overall. **Stock:** Oil-finished walnut (upgrades available) with pistol grip, shotgun-style butt, traditional cheek rest, Schnabel forend. **Sights:** Customer's choice. **Features:** Re-creation of the Model 1874 Sharps rifle. Double-set triggers. Made in U.S.A. by Shiloh Rifle Mfg. Co.

Price: **$1,754.00**

Price: Sporter Rifle No. 1 (similar to above except with 30" barrel, blade front, buckhorn rear sight) **$1,754.00**

Price: Sporter Rifle No. 3 (similar to No. 1 except straight-grip stock, standard wood) **$1,657.00**

SHILOH RIFLE CO. SHARPS 1874 QUIGLEY

Caliber: 45-70 Govt., 45-110. **Barrel:** 34" heavy octagon. **Stock:** Military-style with patch box, standard grade American walnut. **Sights:** Semi buckhorn, interchangeable front and midrange vernier tang sight with windage. **Features:** Gold inlay initials, pewter tip, Hartford collar, case color or antique finish. Double-set triggers.

Price: **$3,041.00**

SHILOH RIFLE CO. SHARPS 1874 SADDLE RIFLE

Caliber: 38-55, 40-50 BN, 40-65 Win., 40-70 BN, 40-70 ST, 40-90 BN, 40-90 ST, 44-77 BN, 44-90 BN, 45-70 Govt. ST, 45-90 ST, 45-100 ST, 45-110 ST, 45-120 ST, 50-70 ST, 50-90 ST. **Barrel:** 26" full or half octagon. **Stock:** Semi fancy American walnut. Shotgun style with cheekrest. **Sights:** Buckhorn and blade. **Features:** Double-set trigger, numerous custom features can be added.

Price: **$1,707.00**

SHILOH RIFLE CO. SHARPS 1874 MONTANA ROUGHRIDER

Caliber: 38-55, 40-50 BN, 40-65 Win., 40-70 BN, 40-70 ST, 40-90 BN, 40-90 ST, 44-77 BN, 44-90 BN, 45-70 Govt. ST, 45-90 ST, 45-100 ST, 45-110 ST, 45-120 ST, 50-70 ST, 50-90 ST. **Barrel:** 30" full or half octagon. **Stock:** American walnut in shotgun or military style. **Sights:** Buckhorn and blade. **Features:** Double-set triggers, numerous custom features can be added.

Price: **$1,754.00**

Shiloh 1874 Creedmoor

Thompson/Center Encore

Thompson/Center Encore "Katahdin"

Thompson/Center Contender

Traditions 1874 Sharps Deluxe

SHILOH RIFLE CO. SHARPS CREEDMOOR TARGET
Caliber: 38-55, 40-50 BN, 40-65 Win., 40-70 BN, 40-70 ST, 40-90 BN, 40-90 ST, 44-77 BN, 44-90 BN, 45-70 Govt. ST, 45-90 ST, 45-100 ST, 45-110 ST, 45-120 ST, 50-70 ST, 50-90 ST. **Barrel:** 32", half round-half octagon. **Stock:** Extra fancy American walnut. Shotgun style with pistol grip. **Sights:** Customer's choice. **Features:** Single trigger, AA finish on stock, polished barrel and screws, pewter tip.
Price: **$2,535.00**

THOMPSON/CENTER ENCORE RIFLE
Caliber: 22-250 Rem., 223 Rem., 243 Win., 204 Ruger, 6.8 Rem. Spec., 25-06 Rem., 270 Win., 7mm-08 Rem., 308 Win., 30-06 Spfl., 7mm Rem. Mag., 300 Win. Mag. **Barrel:** 24", 26". **Weight:** 6 lbs., 12 oz. (24" barrel). **Length:** 38.5" (24" barrel). **Stock:** American walnut. Monte Carlo style; Schnabel forend or black composite. **Sights:** Ramp-style white bead front, fully adjustable leaf-type rear. **Features:** Interchangeable barrels; action opens by squeezing trigger guard; drilled and tapped for T/C scope mounts; polished blue finish. Introduced 1996. Made in U.S.A. by Thompson/Center Arms.
Price: . . . . **$604.00 to $663.00**
Price: Extra barrels **$277.00**

Thompson/Center Stainless Encore Rifle
Similar to blued Encore except stainless steel with blued sights, black composite stock and forend. Available in 22-250 Rem., 223 Rem., 7mm-08 Rem., 30-06 Spfl., 308 Win. Introduced 1999. Made in U.S.A. by Thompson/Center Arms.
Price: . . . . **$680.00 to $738.00**

THOMPSON/CENTER ENCORE "KATAHDIN" CARBINE
Caliber: 45-70 Govt., 450 Marlin. **Barrel:** 18" with muzzle tamer. **Stock:** Composite.
Price: **$619.00**

Thompson/Center G2 Contender Rifle
Similar to the G2 Contender pistol, but in a compact rifle format. Weighs 5.5 lbs. Features interchangeable 23" barrels, chambered for 17 HMR, 22 LR, 223 Rem., 30/30 Win. and 45/70 Govt.; plus a 45 Cal. Muzzleloading barrel. All of the 16.25" and 21" barrels made for the old-style Contender will fit. Introduced 2003. Made in U.S.A. by Thompson/Center Arms.
Price: . . . . **$622.00 to $637.00**

TRADITIONS 1874 SHARPS DELUXE RIFLE
Caliber: 45-70 Govt. **Barrel:** 32" octagonal; 1:18" twist. **Weight:** 11.67 lbs. **Length:** 48.8" overall. **Stock:** Checkered walnut with German silver nose cap and steel buttplate. **Sights:** Globe front, adjustable Creedmore rear with 12 inserts. **Features:** Color case-hardened receiver; double-set triggers. Introduced 2001. Imported from Pedersoli by Traditions.
Price: **$999.00**

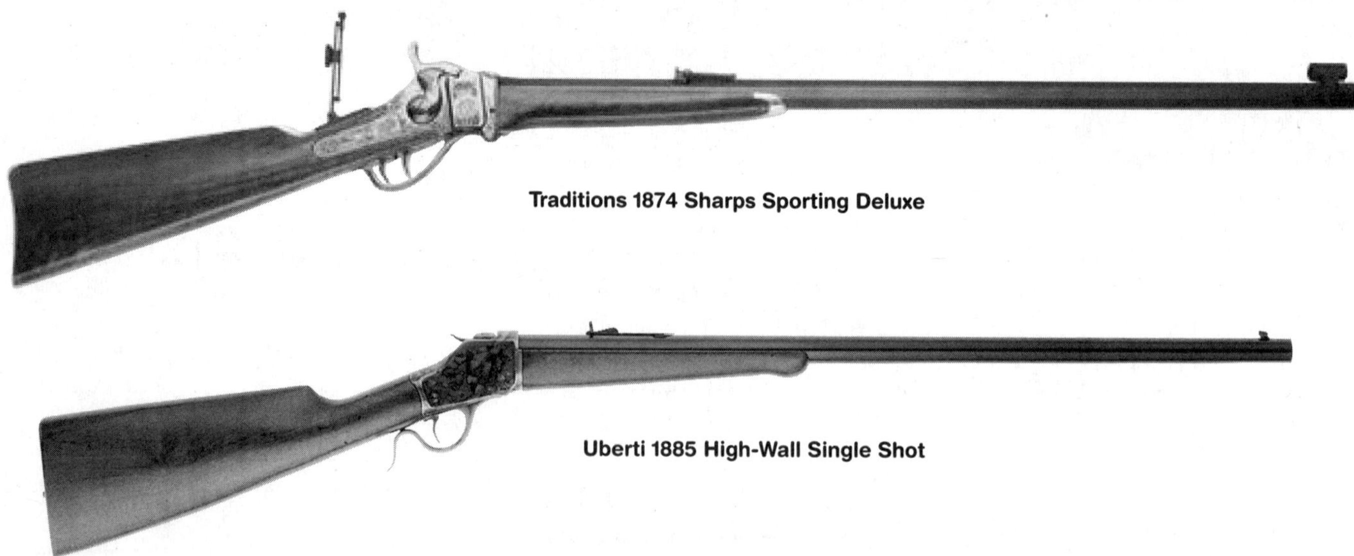

Traditions 1874 Sharps Sporting Deluxe

Uberti 1885 High-Wall Single Shot

Traditions 1874 Sharps Sporting Deluxe Rifle
Similar to Sharps Deluxe but custom silver engraved receiver, European walnut stock and forend, satin finish, set trigger, fully adjustable.
Price: **$1,999.00**

Traditions 1874 Sharps Standard Rifle
Similar to 1874 Sharps Deluxe except has blade front and adjustable buckhorn-style rear sight. Weighs 10.67 pounds. Introduced 2001. Imported from Pedersoli by Traditions.
Price: **$769.00**

TRADITIONS ROLLING BLOCK SPORTING RIFLE
Caliber: 45-70 Govt. **Barrel:** 30" octagonal; 1:18" twist. **Weight:** 11.67 lbs. **Length:** 46.7" overall. **Stock:** Walnut. **Sights:** Blade front, adjustable rear. **Features:** Antique silver, color case-hardened receiver, drilled and tapped for tang/globe sights; brass buttplate and trigger guard. Introduced 2001. Imported from Pedersoli by Traditions.
Price: **$769.00**

TRADITIONS ROLLING BLOCK SPORTING RIFLE IN 30-30 WINCHESTER
Caliber: 30-30. **Barrel:** 28" round, blued. **Weight:** 8.25 lbs. **Stock:** Walnut. **Sights:** Fixed front, adjustable rear. **Features:** Steel buttplate, trigger guard, barrel band.
Price: **$769.00**

UBERTI 1874 SHARPS SPORTING RIFLE
Caliber: 45-70 Govt. **Barrel:** 30", 32", 34" octagonal. **Weight:** 10.57 lbs. with 32" barrel. **Length:** 48.9" with 32" barrel. **Stock:** Walnut. **Sights:** Dovetail front, Vernier tang rear. **Features:** Cut checkering, case-colored finish on frame, buttplate, and lever. Imported by Stoeger Industries.
Price: Standard Sharps (2006), 30" barrel **$1,459.00**
Price: Special Sharps (2006) 32" barrel **$1,729.00**
Price: Deluxe Sharps (2006) 34" barrel **$2,749.00**
Price: Down Under Sharps (2006) 34" barrel **$2,249.00**
Price: Long Range Sharps (2006) 34" barrel **$2,279.00**

UBERTI 1885 HIGH-WALL SINGLE-SHOT RIFLES
Caliber: 45-70 Govt., 45-90, 45-120 single shot. **Barrel:** 28" to 23". **Weight:** 9.3 to 9.9 lbs. **Length:** 44.5" to 47" overall. **Stock:** Walnut stock and forend. **Sights:** Blade front, fully adjustable open rear. **Features:** Based on Winchester High-Wall design by John Browning. Color case-hardened frame and lever, blued barrel and buttplate. Imported by Stoeger Industries.
Price: 1885 High-Wall, 28" round barrel **$969.00**
Price: 1885 High-Wall Sporting, 30" octagonal barrel **$1,029.00**
Price: 1885 High-Wall Special Sporting, 32" octagonal barrel **$1,179.00**

Designs for sporting and utility purposes worldwide.

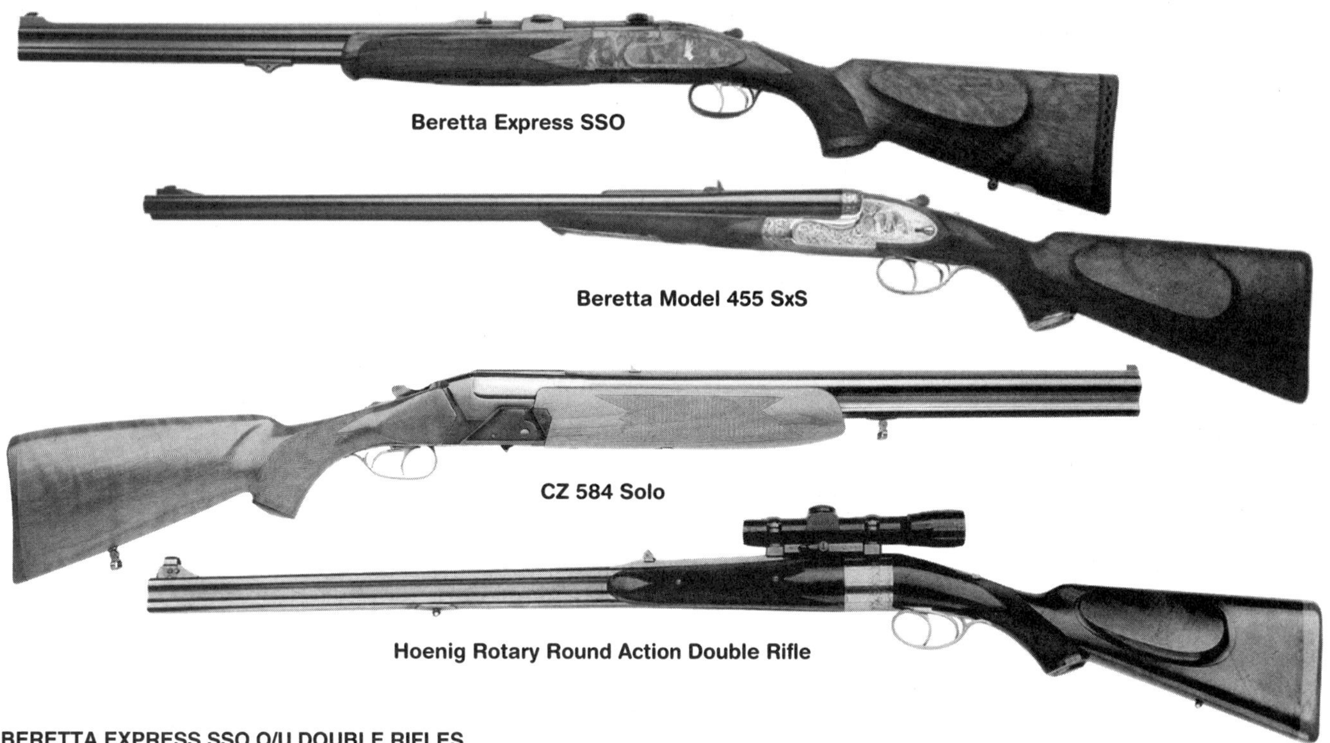

Beretta Express SSO

Beretta Model 455 SxS

CZ 584 Solo

Hoenig Rotary Round Action Double Rifle

BERETTA EXPRESS SSO O/U DOUBLE RIFLES

Caliber: 375 H&H, 458 Win. Mag., 9.3x74R. **Barrel:** 25.5". **Weight:** 11 lbs. **Stock:** European walnut with hand-checkered grip and forend. **Sights:** Blade front on ramp, open V-notch rear. **Features:** Sidelock action with color case-hardened receiver (gold inlays on SSO6 Gold). Ejectors, double triggers, recoil pad. Introduced 1990. Imported from Italy by Beretta U.S.A.

Price: SSO6 . . . . **$21,000.00**
Price: SSO6 Gold **$23,500.00**

BERETTA MODEL 455 SXS EXPRESS RIFLE

Caliber: 375 H&H, 458 Win. Mag., 470 NE, 500 NE 3", 416 Rigby. **Barrel:** 23.5" or 25.5". **Weight:** 11 lbs. **Stock:** European walnut with hand-checkered grip and forend. **Sights:** Blade front, folding leaf V-notch rear. **Features:** Sidelock action with easily removable sideplates; color case-hardened finish (455), custom big game or floral motif engraving (455EELL). Double triggers, recoil pad. Introduced 1990. Imported from Italy by Beretta U.S.A.

Price: Model 455. . . . . **$36,000.00**
Price: Model 455EELL **$47,000.00**

CZ 584 SOLO COMBINATION GUN

Caliber/Gauge: 7x57R; 12, 2-3/4" chamber. **Barrel:** 24.4". **Weight:** 7.37 lbs. **Length:** 45.25" overall. **Stock:** Circassian walnut. **Sights:** Blade front, open rear adjustable for windage. **Features:** Kersten-style double lump locking system; double-trigger Blitz-type mechanism with drop safety and adjustable set trigger for the rifle barrel; auto safety, dual extractors; receiver dovetailed for scope mounting. Imported from the Czech Republic by CZ-USA.

Price: **$851.00**

CZ 589 STOPPER OVER/UNDER GUN

Caliber: 458 Win. Magnum. Barrels: 21.7". **Weight:** 9.3 lbs. **Length:** 37.7" overall. **Stock:** Turkish walnut with sling swivels. **Sights:** Blade front, fixed rear. **Features:** Kersten-style action; Blitz-type double trigger; hammer-forged, blued barrels; satin-nickel, engraved receiver. Introduced 2001. Imported from the Czech Republic by CZ USA.

Price: **$2,999.00**
Price: Fully engraved model **$3,999.00**

DAKOTA DOUBLE RIFLE

Caliber: 470 Nitro Express, 500 Nitro Express. **Barrel:** 25". **Stock:** Exhibition-grade walnut. **Sights:** Express-style. **Features:** Round action; selective ejectors; recoil pad; Americase. From Dakota Arms Inc.

Price: **$25,000.00**

EAA/BAIKAL IZH-94 COMBINATION GUN

Caliber/Gauge: 12, 3" chamber; 222 Rem., 223 Rem., 5.6x50R, 5.6x55E, 7x57R, 7x65R, 7.62x39, 7.62x51, 308 Win., 7.62x53R, 7.62x54R, 30-06. **Barrel:** 24", 26"; imp., mod. and full choke tubes. **Weight:** 7.28 lbs. **Stock:** Walnut; rubber buttpad. **Sights:** Express-style. **Features:** Hammer-forged barrels with chrome-lined bores; machined receiver; single-selective or double triggers. Imported by European American Armory.

Price: Blued finish. **$549.00**
Price: 20 ga./22 LR, 20/22 Mag, 3" **$629.00**

GARBI EXPRESS DOUBLE RIFLE

Caliber: 7x65R, 9.3x74R, 375 H&H. **Barrel:** 24.75". **Weight:** 7.75 to 8.5 lbs. **Length:** 41.5" overall. **Stock:** Turkish walnut. **Sights:** Quarter-rib with express sight. **Features:** Side-by-side double; H&H-pattern sidelock ejector with reinforced action, chopper lump barrels of Boehler steel; double triggers; fine scroll and rosette engraving, or full coverage ornamental; coin-finished action. Introduced 1997. Imported from Spain by Wm. Larkin Moore.

Price: **$19,900.00**

HOENIG ROTARY ROUND ACTION DOUBLE RIFLE

Caliber: Most popular calibers from 225 Win. to 9.3x74R. **Barrel:** 22" to 26". **Stock:** English Walnut; to customer specs. **Sights:** Swivel hood front with button release (extra bead stored in trap door gripcap), express-style rear on quarter-rib adjustable for windage and elevation; scope mount. **Features:** Round action opens by rotating barrels, pulling forward. Inertia extractor system, rotary safety blocks strikers. Single lever quick-detachable scope mount. Simple takedown without removing forend. Introduced 1997. Made in U.S.A. by George Hoenig.

Price: **$25,000.00**

HOENIG ROTARY ROUND ACTION COMBINATION

Caliber: 28 ga. **Barrel:** 26". **Weight:** 7 lbs. **Stock:** English Walnut to customer specs. **Sights:** Front ramp with button release blades. Foldable aperture tang sight windage and elevation adjustable. Quarter-rib with scope mount. **Features:** Round action opens by rotating barrels, pulling forward. Inertia extractor; rotary safety blocks strikers. Simple takedown without removing forend. Made in U.S.A. by George Hoenig.

Price: **$25,000.00**

Hoenig Rotary Round Action Combination

Krieghoff Classic Double Rifle

Merkel 96K Engraved

Savage 24F Combination

Springfield M6 Scout

KRIEGHOFF CLASSIC DOUBLE RIFLE

Caliber: 7x57R, 7x65R, 308 Win., 30-06 Spfl., 8x57 JRS, 8x75RS, 9.3x74R, 375NE, 500/416NE, 470NE, 500NE. **Barrel:** 23.5". **Weight:** 7.3 to 8 lbs; 10-11 lbs. Big 5. **Stock:** High grade European walnut. Standard model has conventional rounded cheekpiece, Bavaria model has Bavarian-style cheekpiece. **Sights:** Bead front with removable, adjustable wedge (375 H&H and below), standing leaf rear on quarter-rib. **Features:** Boxlock action; double triggers; short opening angle for fast loading; quiet extractors; sliding, self-adjusting wedge for secure bolting; Purdey-style barrel extension; horizontal firing pin placement. Many options available. Introduced 1997. Imported from Germany by Krieghoff International.

Price: With small Arabesque engraving **$8,950.00**
Price: With engraved sideplates **$12,300.00**
Price: For extra barrels **$5,450.00**
Price: Extra 20-ga., 28" shotshell barrels **$3,950.00**

Krieghoff Classic Big Five Double Rifle

Similar to the standard Classic except available in 375 Flanged Mag. N.E., 500/416 NE, 470 NE, 500 NE. Has hinged front trigger, non-removable muzzle wedge (models larger than 375 caliber), Universal Trigger System, Combi Cocking Device, steel trigger guard, specially weighted stock bolt for weight and balance. Many options available. Introduced 1997. Imported from Germany by Krieghoff International. Imperial Model introduced 2006.

Price: **$11,450.00**
Price: With engraved sideplates **$14,800.00**

LEBEAU-COURALLY EXPRESS RIFLE SXS

Caliber: 7x65R, 8x57JRS, 9.3x74R, 375 H&H, 470 N.E. **Barrel:** 24" to 26". **Weight:** 7.75 to 10.5 lbs. **Stock:** Fancy French walnut with cheekpiece. **Sights:** Bead on ramp front, standing left express rear on quarter-rib. **Features:** Holland & Holland-type sidelock with automatic ejectors; double triggers. Built to order only. Imported from Belgium by Wm. Larkin Moore.

Price: **$41,000.00**

MERKEL DRILLINGS

Caliber/Gauge: 12, 20, 3" chambers, 16, 2-3/4" chambers; 22 Hornet, 5.6x50R Mag., 5.6x52R, 222 Rem., 243 Win., 6.5x55, 6.5x57R, 7x57R, 7x65R, 308 Win., 30-06 Spfl., 8x57JRS, 9.3x74R, 375 H&H. **Barrel:** 25.6". **Weight:** 7.9 to 8.4 lbs. depending upon caliber. **Stock:** Oil-finished walnut with pistol grip; cheekpiece on 12-, 16-gauge. **Sights:** Blade front, fixed rear. **Features:** Double barrel locking lug with Greener cross bolt; scroll-engraved, case-hardened receiver; automatic trigger safety; Blitz action; double triggers. Imported from Germany by Merkel USA.

Price: Model 96K (manually cocked rifle system), from **$8,095.00**
Price: Model 96K Engraved (hunting series on receiver) . . **$9,295.00**

MERKEL BOXLOCK DOUBLE RIFLES

Caliber: 5.6x52R, 243 Winchester, 6.5x55, 6.5x57R, 7x57R, 7x65R, 308 Win., 30-06 Springfield, 8x57 IRS, 9.3x74R. **Barrel:** 23.6". **Weight:** 7.7 oz. **Length:** NA. **Stock:** Walnut, oil finished, pistol grip. **Sights:** Fixed 100 meter. **Features:** Anson & Deely boxlock action with cocking indicators, double triggers, engraved color case-hardened receiver. Introduced 1995. Imported from Germany by Merkel USA.

Price: Model 140-2, from **$11,495.00**

RIZZINI EXPRESS 90L DOUBLE RIFLE

Caliber: 30-06 Spfl., 7x65R, 9.3x74R. **Barrel:** 24". **Weight:** 7.5 lbs. **Length:** 40" overall. **Stock:** Select European walnut with satin oil finish; English-style cheekpiece. **Sights:** Ramp front, quarter-rib with express sight. **Features:** Color case-hardened boxlock action; automatic ejectors; single selective trigger; polished blue barrels. Extra 20 gauge shotgun barrels available. Imported for Italy by Wm. Larkin Moore.

Price: With case **$3,850.00**

SPRINGFIELD ARMORY M6 SCOUT RIFLE/SHOTGUN

Caliber/Gauge: 22 LR or 22 Hornet over 410 bore. **Barrel:** 18.25". **Weight:** 4 lbs. **Length:** 32" overall. **Stock:** Folding detachable with storage for 15 22 LR, four 410 shells. **Sights:** Blade front, military aperture for 22; V-notch for 410. **Features:** All metal construction. Designed for quick disassembly and minimum maintenance. Folds for compact storage. Introduced 1982; reintroduced 1996. Imported from the Czech Republic by Springfield Armory.

Price: Parkerized **$183.00**

Designs for hunting, utility and sporting purposes, including training for competition.

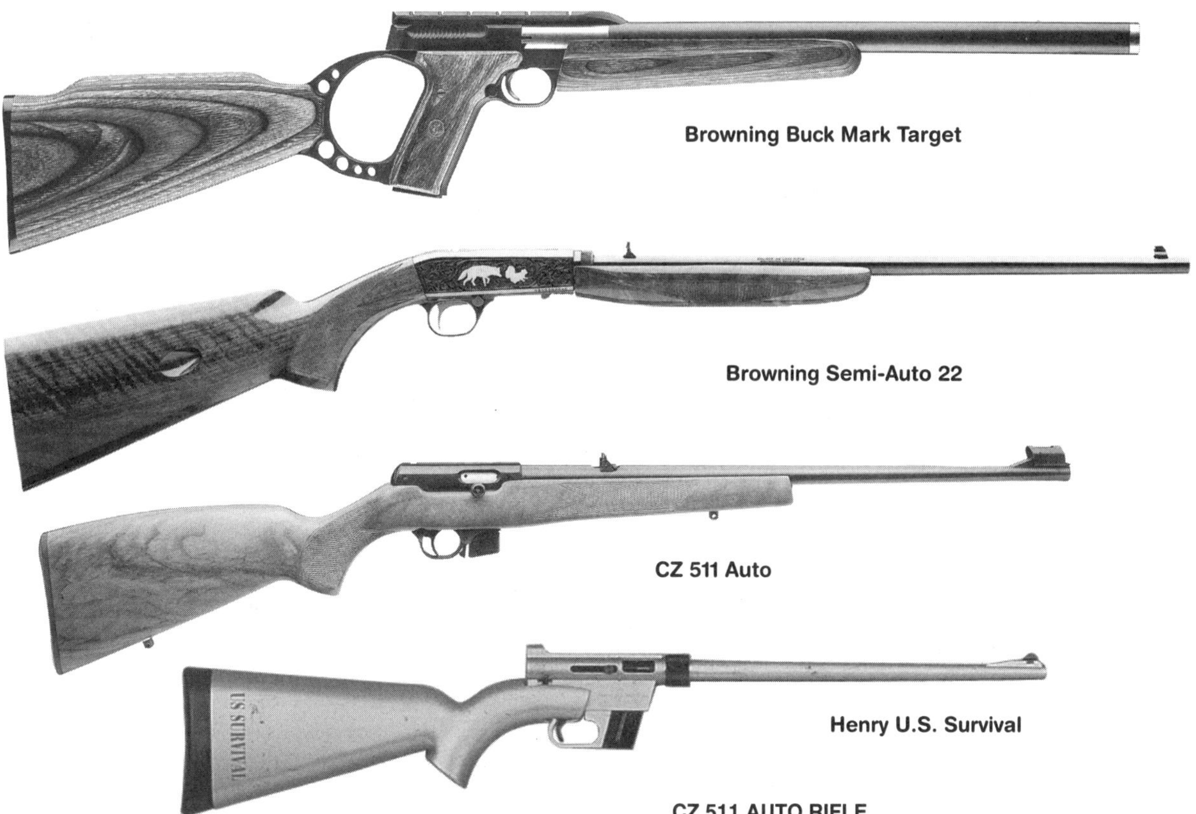

Browning Buck Mark Target

Browning Semi-Auto 22

CZ 511 Auto

Henry U.S. Survival

AR-7 EXPLORER CARBINE

Caliber: 22 LR, 8-shot magazine. **Barrel:** 16". **Weight:** 2.5 lbs. **Length:** 34.5", 16.5" stowed. **Stock:** Molded Cycolac; snap-on rubber buttpad. **Sights:** Square blade front, aperture rear. **Features:** Takedown design stores barrel and action in hollow stock. Light enough to float. Reintroduced 1999. From AR-7 Industries, LLC.

Price: Black matte finish **$150.00**
Price: AR-20 Sporter (tubular stock, barrel shroud) **$200.00**
Price: AR-7 camo- or walnut-finish stock **$164.95**

BROWNING BUCK MARK SEMI-AUTO RIFLES

Caliber: 22 LR, 10+1. Action: A rifle version of the Buck Mark Pistol; straight blowback action; machined aluminum receiver with integral rail scope mount; manual thumb safety. **Barrel:** Recessed crowns. **Stock:** Stock and forearm with full pistol grip. **Features:** Action lock provided. Introduced 2001. Four model name variations for 2006, as noted below. **Sights:** FLD Target, FLD Carbon, and Target models have integrated scope rails. Sporter has Truglo/Marble fiber optic sights. Imported from Japan by Browning.

Price: FLD Target, 5.5 lbs., bull barrel, laminated stock **$631.00**
Price: Target, 5.4 lbs., blued bull barrel, wood stock **$612.00**
Price: Sporter, 4.4 lbs., blued sporter barrel w/sights **$612.00**

BROWNING SA-22 SEMI-AUTO 22 RIFLES

Caliber: 22 LR, 11+1. **Barrel:** 16.25". **Weight:** 5.2 lbs. **Length:** 37" overall. **Stock:** Checkered select walnut with pistol grip and semi-beavertail forend. **Sights:** Gold bead front, folding leaf rear. **Features:** Engraved receiver with polished blue finish; cross-bolt safety; tubular magazine in buttstock; easy takedown for carrying or storage. The Grade VI is available with either grayed or blued receiver with extensive engraving with gold-plated animals: right side pictures a fox and squirrel in a woodland scene; left side shows a beagle chasing a rabbit. On top is a portrait of the beagle. Stock and forend are of high-grade walnut with a double-bordered cut checkering design. Introduced 1987. Imported from Japan by Browning.

Price: Grade I, scroll-engraved blued receiver **$574.00**
Price: Grade VI BL, gold-plated engraved blued receiver . . **$1,251.00**

CZ 511 AUTO RIFLE

Caliber: 22 LR, 8-shot magazine. **Barrel:** 22.2". **Weight:** 5.39 lbs. **Length:** 38.6" overall. **Stock:** Walnut with checkered pistol grip. **Sights:** Hooded front, adjustable rear. **Features:** Polished blue finish; detachable magazine; sling swivel studs. Imported from the Czech Republic by CZUSA.

Price: **$351.00**

HENRY U.S. SURVIVAL RIFLE AR-7 22

Caliber: 22 LR, 8-shot magazine. **Barrel:** 16" steel lined. **Weight:** 2.25 lbs. **Stock:** ABS plastic. **Sights:** Blade front on ramp, aperture rear. **Features:** Takedown design stores barrel and action in hollow stock. Light enough to float. Silver, black or camo finish. Comes with two magazines. Introduced 1998. From Henry Repeating Arms Co.

Price: H002S Silver finish **$236.95**
Price: H002B Black finish **$236.95**
Price: H002C Camo finish **$296.95**

MAGNUM RESEARCH MAGNUMLITE RIFLES

Caliber: 22 WMR, 17 HMR, 22 LR 17M2, 10-shot magazine. **Barrel:** 17" graphite. **Weight:** 4.45 lbs. **Length:** 35.5" overall. **Stock:** Hogue OverMolded synthetic or walnut. **Sights:** Integral scope base. **Features:** Magnum Lite graphite barrel, French grey anodizing, match bolt, target trigger. 22 LR/17M2 rifles use factory Ruger 10/22 magazines. 4-5 lbs. average trigger pull. Graphite carbon-fiber barrel weighs approx. 13.04 ounces in 22 LR, 1:16 twist. Introduced: 2007. From Magnum Research, Inc.

Price: MLR22H 22 LR. **$629.00**

MARLIN MODEL 60 AUTO RIFLE

Caliber: 22 LR, 14-shot tubular magazine. **Barrel:** 19" round tapered. **Weight:** About 5.5 lbs. **Length:** 37.5" overall. **Stock:** Press-checkered, walnut-finished Maine birch with Monte Carlo, full pistol grip; Mar-Shield finish. **Sights:** Ramp front, open adjustable rear. **Features:** Matted receiver is grooved for scope mount. Manual bolt hold-open; automatic last-shot bolt hold-open. Model 60C is similar except has hardwood Monte Carlo stock with Mossy Oak Break-Up camouflage pattern. From Marlin.

Price: **$179.00**
Price: With 4x scope **$186.00**
Price: Model 60C camo **$211.00**

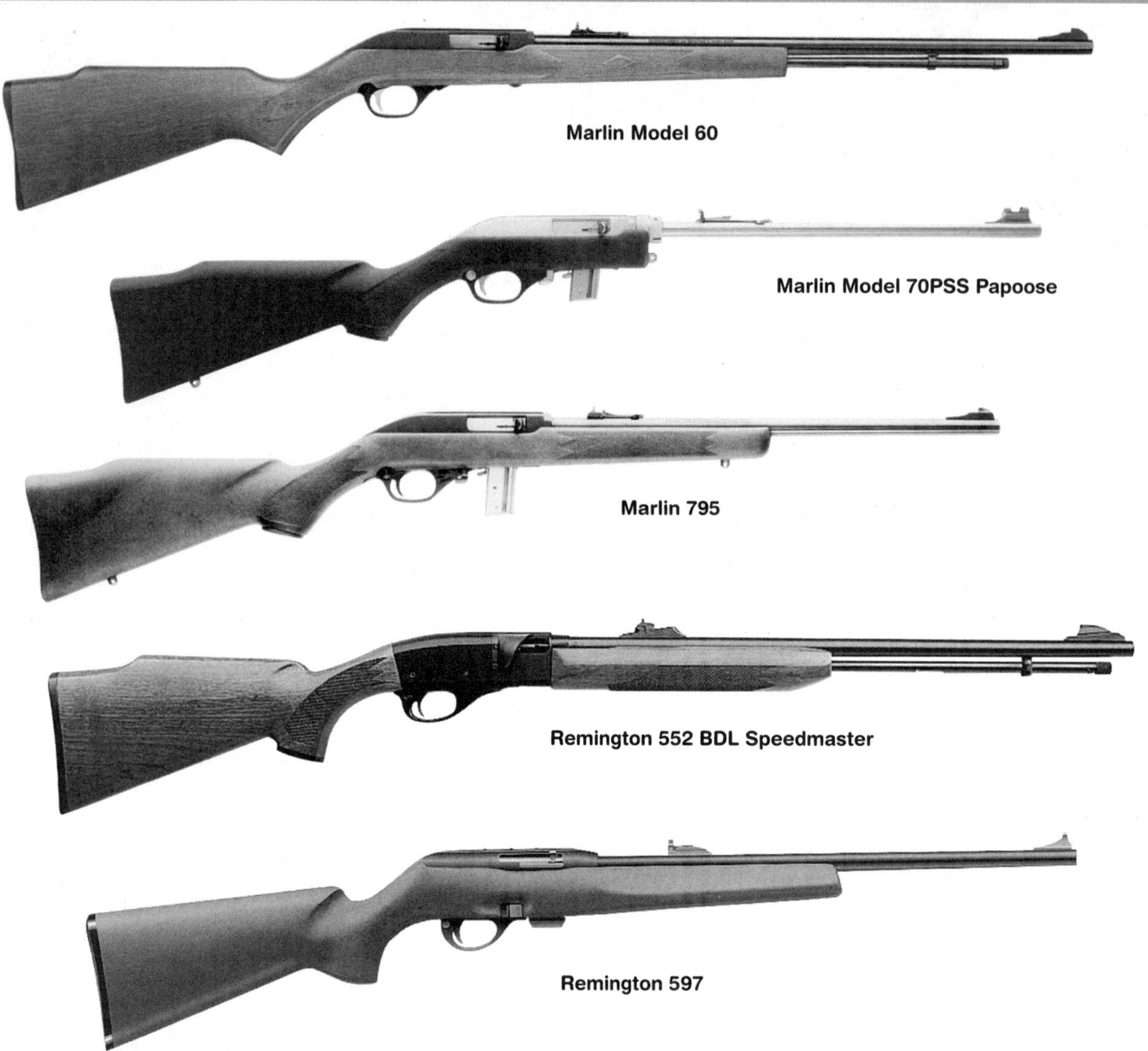

Marlin Model 60

Marlin Model 70PSS Papoose

Marlin 795

Remington 552 BDL Speedmaster

Remington 597

Marlin Model 60SS Self-Loading Rifle

Same as the Model 60 except breech bolt, barrel and outer magazine tube are made of stainless steel; most other parts are either nickel-plated or coated to match the stainless finish. Monte Carlo stock is of black/gray Maine birch laminate, and has nickel-plated swivel studs, rubber buttpad. Introduced 1993. From Marlin.

Price: **$283.00**

MARLIN 70PSS PAPOOSE STAINLESS RIFLE

Caliber: 22 LR, 7-shot magazine. **Barrel:** 16.25" stainless steel, Micro-Groove rifling. **Weight:** 3.25 lbs. **Length:** 35.25" overall. **Stock:** Black fiberglass-filled synthetic with abbreviated forend, nickel-plated swivel studs, molded-in checkering. **Sights:** Ramp front with orange post, cut-away Wide Scan hood; adjustable open rear. Receiver grooved for scope mounting. **Features:** Takedown barrel; cross-bolt safety; manual bolt hold-open; last shot bolt hold-open; comes with padded carrying case. Introduced 1986. Made in U.S.A. by Marlin.

Price: **$284.00**

MARLIN MODEL 795 AUTO RIFLE

Caliber: 22. **Barrel:** 18" with 16-groove Micro-Groove rifling. Ramp front sight, adjustable rear. Receiver grooved for scope mount. **Stock:** Black synthetic. **Features:** 10-round magazine, last shot hold-open feature. Introduced 1997. SS is similar to Model 795 except stainless steel barrel. Most other parts nickel-plated. Adjustable folding semi-buckhorn rear sights, ramp front high-visibility post and removable cutaway wide scan hood. Made in U.S.A. by Marlin Firearms Co.

Price: 795 . . . . **$157.00**
Price: 795SS **$227.00**

MOSSBERG MODEL 702 PLINKSTER AUTO RIFLE

Caliber: 22 LR, 10-round detachable magazine. **Barrel:** 18" free-floating. **Weight:** 4.1 to 4.6 lbs. **Sights:** Adjustable rifle. Receiver grooved for scope mount. **Stock:** Solid pink or pink marble finish synthetic. **Features:** Ergonomically placed magazine release and safety buttons, crossbolt safety, free gun lock. Made in U.S.A. by O.F. Mossberg & Sons, Inc.

Price: Pink Plinkster (2008) **$177.00**

REMINGTON MODEL 552 BDL DELUXE SPEEDMASTER RIFLE

Caliber: 22 S (20), L (17) or LR (15) tubular magazine. **Barrel:** 21" round tapered. **Weight:** 5.75 lbs. **Length:** 40" overall. **Stock:** Walnut. Checkered grip and forend. **Sights:** Big game. **Features:** Positive cross-bolt safety, receiver grooved for tip-off mount.

Price: **$572.00**
Price: Smoothbore model (2007) **$612.00**

REMINGTON 597 AUTO RIFLE

Caliber: 22 LR, 10-shot clip; 22 WMR, 8-shot clip. **Barrel:** 20". **Weight:** 5.5 lbs. **Length:** 40" overall. **Stock:** Black synthetic. **Sights:** Big game. **Features:** Matte black finish, nickel-plated bolt. Receiver is grooved and drilled and tapped for scope mounts. Introduced 1997. Made in U.S.A. by Remington.

Price: Synthetic Scope Combo (2007) **$229.00**
Price: Model 597 Magnum **$476.00**
Price: Model 597 w/Mossy Oak Blaze Pink or Orange, 22 LR (2008) **$252.00**
Price: Model 597 Stainless TVP, 22 LR (2008) **$532.00**
Price: Model 597 Yellow Jacket HB, 22 LR (2008). **$505.00**

Ruger 10/22 Deluxe Sporter

Ruger 10/22 Target

RUGER 10/22 AUTOLOADING CARBINE

Caliber: 22 LR, 10-shot rotary magazine. **Barrel:** 18.5" round tapered. **Weight:** 5 lbs. **Length:** 37.25" overall. **Stock:** American hardwood with pistol grip and barrel band or synthetic. **Sights:** Brass bead front, folding leaf rear adjustable for elevation. **Features:** Detachable rotary magazine fits flush into stock, cross-bolt safety, receiver tapped and grooved for scope blocks or tip-off mount. Scope base adaptor furnished with each rifle.

Price: Model 10/22 RB (black matte) **$261.00**
Price: Model 10/22CRR Compact RB (black matte), 2006.... **$298.00**

Ruger 10/22 Deluxe Sporter

Same as 10/22 Carbine except walnut stock with hand checkered pistol grip and forend; straight buttplate, no barrel band, has sling swivels.

Price: Model 10/22 DSP **$345.00**

Ruger 10/22T Target Rifle

Similar to the 10/22 except has 20" heavy, hammer-forged barrel with tight chamber dimensions, improved trigger pull, laminated hardwood stock dimensioned for optical sights. No iron sights supplied. Introduced 1996. Made in U.S.A. by Sturm, Ruger & Co.

Price: 10/22T **$470.00**
Price: K10/22T, stainless steel **$518.00**

Ruger K10/22RPF All-Weather Rifle

Similar to the stainless K10/22/RB except has black composite stock of thermoplastic polyester resin reinforced with fiberglass; checkered grip and forend. Brushed satin, natural metal finish with clear hardcoat finish. Weighs 5 lbs., measures 37" overall. Introduced 1997. From Sturm, Ruger & Co.

Price: **$308.00**

SAVAGE MODEL 64G AUTO RIFLE

Caliber: 22 LR, 10-shot magazine. **Barrel:** 20", 21". **Weight:** 5.5 lbs. **Length:** 40", 41". **Stock:** Walnut-finished hardwood with Monte Carlo-type comb, checkered grip and forend. **Sights:** Bead front, open adjustable rear. Receiver grooved for scope mounting. **Features:** Thumb-operated rotating safety. Blue finish. Side ejection, bolt hold-open device. Introduced 1990. Made in Canada, from Savage Arms.

Price: From....................................... **$175.00**

THOMPSON/CENTER 22 LR CLASSIC RIFLE

Caliber: 22 LR, 8-shot magazine. **Barrel:** 22" match-grade. **Weight:** 5.5 pounds. **Length:** 39.5" overall. **Stock:** Satin-finished American walnut with Monte Carlo-type comb and pistol gripcap, swivel studs. **Sights:** Ramp-style front and fully adjustable rear, both with fiber optics. **Features:** All-steel receiver drilled and tapped for scope mounting; barrel threaded to receiver; thumb-operated safety; trigger guard safety lock included. New 22 Classic Benchmark TGT target rifle variant has 18" heavy barrel, brown laminated target stock, blued with matte finish, 10-shot magazine and no sights; drilled and tapped.

Price: T/C 22 LR Classic (blue) **$396.00**
Price: T/C 22 LR Classic Benchmark **$505.00**

Classic and modern models for sport and utility, including training.

Browning BL-22

Henry Lever-Action 22

Henry Golden Boy 22

Henry Pump-Action 22

Marlin Model 39A

BROWNING BL-22 RIFLES

Action: Short-throw lever action, side ejection. Rack-and-pinion lever. Tubular magazines, with 15+1 capacity for 22 LR. **Barrel:** Recessed muzzle. **Stock:** Walnut, two-piece straight grip Western style. Trigger: Half-cock hammer safety; fold-down hammer. **Sights:** Bead post front, folding-leaf rear. Steel receiver grooved for scope mount. **Weight:** 5-5.4 lbs. **Length:** 36.75-40.75" overall. **Features:** Action lock provided. Introduced 1996. FLD Grade II Octagon has octagonal 24" barrel, silver nitride receiver with scroll engraving, gold-colored trigger. FLD Grade I has satin-nickel receiver, blued trigger, no stock checkering. FLD Grade II has satin-nickel receivers with scroll engraving; gold-colored trigger, cut checkering. Both introduced 2005. Grade I has blued receiver and trigger, no stock checkering. Grade II has gold-colored trigger, cut checkering, blued receiver with scroll engraving. Imported from Japan by Browning.

Price: BL-22 Grade I/II, from. **$494.00**
Price: BL-22 FLD Grade I/II, from **$529.00**
Price: BL-22 FLD, Grade II Octagon **$786.00**

HENRY LEVER-ACTION RIFLES

Caliber: 22 Long Rifle (15 shot), 22 Magnum (11 shots), 17 HMR (11 shots). **Barrel:** 18.25" round. **Weight:** 5.5 to 5.75 lbs. **Length:** 34" overall (22 LR). **Stock:** Walnut. **Sights:** Hooded blade front, open adjustable rear. **Features:** Polished blue finish; full-length tubular magazine; side ejection; receiver grooved for scope mounting. Introduced 1997. Made in U.S.A. by Henry Repeating Arms Co.

Price: H001 Carbine 22 LR. **$319.95**
Price: H001L Carbine 22 LR, Large Loop Lever. **$329.95**
Price: H001Y Youth model (33" overall, 11-round 22 LR) **$319.95**
Price: H001M 22 Magnum, 19.25" octagonal barrel, deluxe walnut stock **$469.95**
Price: H001V 17 HMR, 20" octagonal barrel, Williams Fire Sights **$539.95**

Henry Lever Octagon Frontier Model

Same as Lever rifles except chambered in 17 HMR, 22 Short/22 Long/22 LR, 22 Magnum; 20" octagonal barrel **Sights:** Marbles full adjustable semi-buckhorn rear, brass bead front. Weighs 6.25 lbs. Made in U.S.A. by Henry Repeating Arms Co.

Price: H001T Lever Octagon **$419.95**
Price: H001TM Lever Octagon 22 Magnum. **$529.95**

HENRY GOLDEN BOY 22 LEVER-ACTION RIFLE

Caliber: 17 HMR, 22 LR (16-shot), 22 Magnum. **Barrel:** 20" octagonal. **Weight:** 6.25 lbs. **Length:** 38" overall. **Stock:** American walnut. **Sights:** Blade front, open rear. **Features:** Brasslite receiver, brass buttplate, blued barrel and lever. Introduced 1998. Made in U.S.A. from Henry Repeating Arms Co.

Price: H004 22 LR **$499.95**
Price: H004M 22 Magnum **$579.00**
Price: H004V 17 HMR **$599.00**
Price: H004DD 22 LR Deluxe, engraved receiver **$1,200.00**

HENRY PUMP-ACTION 22 PUMP RIFLE

Caliber: 22 LR, 15-shot. **Barrel:** 18.25". **Weight:** 5.5 lbs. **Length:** NA. **Stock:** American walnut. **Sights:** Bead on ramp front, open adjustable rear. **Features:** Polished blue finish; receiver grooved for scope mount; grooved slide handle; two barrel bands. Introduced 1998. Made in U.S.A. from Henry Repeating Arms Co.

Price: H003T 22 LR **$499.95**
Price: H003TM 22 Magnum **$579.95**

MARLIN MODEL 39A GOLDEN LEVER-ACTION RIFLE

Caliber: 22, S (26), L (21), LR (19), tubular magazine. **Barrel:** 24" Micro-Groove. **Weight:** 6.5 lbs. **Length:** 40" overall. **Stock:** Checkered American black walnut; Mar-Shield finish. Swivel studs; rubber buttpad. **Sights:** Bead ramp front with detachable Wide-Scan hood, folding rear semi-buckhorn adjustable for windage and elevation. **Features:** Hammer block safety; rebounding hammer. Takedown action, receiver tapped for scope mount (supplied), offset hammer spur, gold-colored steel trigger. From Marlin Firearms.

Price: **$593.00**

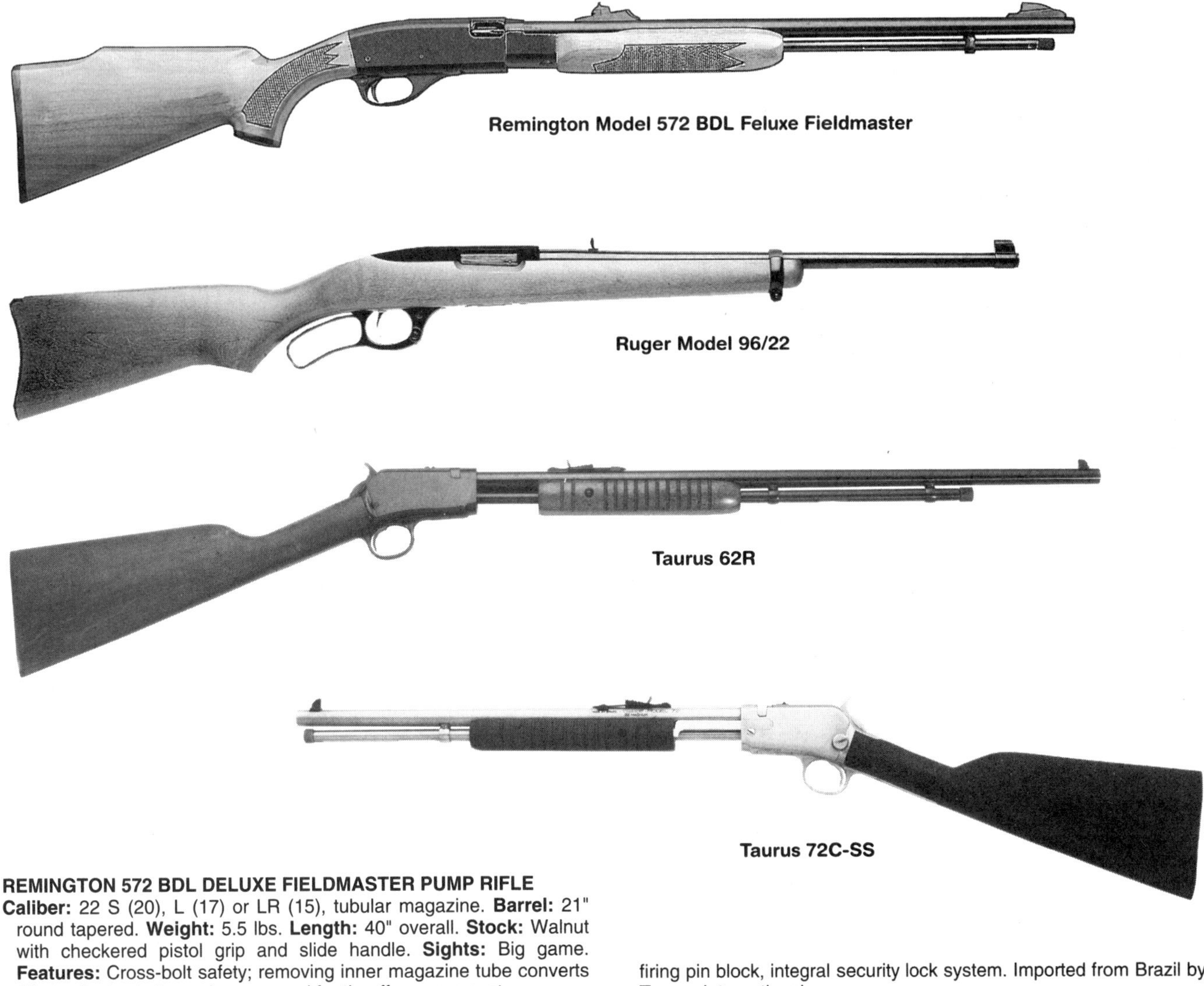

Remington Model 572 BDL Feluxe Fieldmaster

Ruger Model 96/22

Taurus 62R

Taurus 72C-SS

REMINGTON 572 BDL DELUXE FIELDMASTER PUMP RIFLE

Caliber: 22 S (20), L (17) or LR (15), tubular magazine. **Barrel:** 21" round tapered. **Weight:** 5.5 lbs. **Length:** 40" overall. **Stock:** Walnut with checkered pistol grip and slide handle. **Sights:** Big game. **Features:** Cross-bolt safety; removing inner magazine tube converts rifle to single shot; receiver grooved for tip-off scope mount.

Price: **$585.00**

RUGER MODEL 96 LEVER-ACTION RIFLE

Caliber: 22 WMR, 9 rounds; 17 HMR, 9 rounds. **Barrel:** 18.5". **Weight:** 5.25 lbs. **Length:** 37-3/8" overall. **Stock:** Hardwood. **Sights:** Gold bead front, folding leaf rear. **Features:** Sliding cross button safety, visible cocking indicator; short-throw lever action. Introduced 1996. Made in U.S.A. by Sturm, Ruger & Co.

Price: 96/22M, 22 WMR or 17 HMR **$451.00**

TAURUS MODEL 62 PUMP RIFLE

Caliber: 22 LR, 12- or 13-shot. **Barrel:** 16.5" or 23" round. **Weight:** 72 oz. to 80 oz. **Length:** 39" overall. **Stock:** Premium hardwood. **Sights:** Adjustable rear, bead blade front, optional tang. **Features:** Blue, case hardened or stainless, bolt-mounted safety, pump action, manual firing pin block, integral security lock system. Imported from Brazil by Taurus International.

Price: From **$299.00**

Taurus Model 72 Pump Rifle

Same as Model 62 except chambered in 22 Magnum or 17 HMR; 16.5" barrel holds 10-12 shots, 23" barrel holds 11-13 shots. Weighs 72 oz. to 80 oz. Introduced 2001. Imported from Brazil by Taurus International.

Price: From **$329.00**

TAURUS THUNDERBOLT PUMP ACTION

Caliber: 38/.357, 45 Long Colt, 12 or 14 rounds. **Barrel:** 26" blue or polished stainless. **Weight:** 8.1 lbs. **Length:** 43" overall. **Stock:** Hardwood stock and forend. Gloss finish. **Sights:** Longhorn adjustable rear. Introduced 2004. Imported from Brazil by Taurus International.

Price: C45BR **$705.00**

Includes models for a variety of sports, utility and competitive shooting.

Anschutz 1710D

Browning T-Bolt

Cooper Model 57 Classic

Cooper Custom Classic

ANSCHUTZ 1416D/1516D CLASSIC RIFLES

Caliber: 22 LR (1416D), 22 WMR (1516D), 5-shot clip. **Barrel:** 22.5". **Weight:** 6 lbs. **Length:** 41" overall. **Stock:** European hardwood with walnut finish; classic style with straight comb, checkered pistol grip and forend. **Sights:** Hooded ramp front, folding leaf rear. **Features:** Uses Match 64 action. Adjustable single-stage trigger. Receiver grooved for scope mounting. Imported from Germany by Merkel USA.

Price: 1416D KL, 22 LR **$899.00**
Price: 1416D KL Classic left-hand **$949.00**
Price: 1516D KL, 22 WMR **$919.00**

ANSCHUTZ 1710D CUSTOM RIFLE

Caliber: 22 LR, 5-shot clip. **Barrel:** 24.25". **Weight:** 7-3/8 lbs. **Length:** 42.5" overall. **Stock:** Select European walnut. **Sights:** Hooded ramp front, folding leaf rear; drilled and tapped for scope mounting. **Features:** Match 54 action with adjustable single-stage trigger; roll-over Monte Carlo cheekpiece, slim forend with Schnabel tip, Wundhammer palm swell on pistol grip, rosewood gripcap with white diamond insert; skip-line checkering on grip and forend. Introduced 1988. Imported from Germany by Merkel USA.

Price: **$1,649.00**

BROWNING T-BOLT RIMFIRE RIFLE

Caliber: 22 LR, 10-round rotary box Double Helix magazine. **Barrel:** 22", free-floating, semi-match chamber, target muzzle crown. **Weight:** 4.8 lbs. **Length:** 40.1" overall. **Stock:** Walnut, satin finish, cut checkering, synthetic buttplate. **Sights:** None. **Features:** Straight-pull bolt-action, three-lever trigger adjustable for pull weight, dual action screws, sling swivel studs. Crossbolt lockup, enlarged bolt handle, one-piece dual extractor with integral spring and red cocking indicator band, gold-tone trigger. Top-tang, thumb-operated two-position safety, drilled and tapped for scope mounts. Varmint model has raised Monte Carlo comb, heavy barrel, wide forearm. Introduced 2006. Imported from Japan by Browning.

Price: Sporter **$649.00**
Price: Target/Varmint, intr. 2007 . . . . . **$699.00**
Price: Composite Target/Varmint, intr. 2008 . . . . . **$699.00**
Price: Sporter, 17 HMR, 22 Mag., intr. 2008. . . . . **$699.00**
Price: Composite Sporter, 17 HMR, 22 Mag., intr. 2008 . . . . . **$699.00**

DAVEY CRICKETT SINGLE SHOT RIFLE

Caliber: 22 LR, 22 WMR, single shot. **Barrel:** 16-1/8". **Weight:** About 2.5 lbs. **Length:** 30" overall. Stocks: American walnut. **Sights:** Post on ramp front, peep rear adjustable for windage and elevation. **Features:** Drilled and tapped for scope mounting using special Chipmunk base ($13.95). Engraved model also available. Made in U.S.A. Introduced 1982. Formerly, Chipmunk model. From Keystone Sporting Arms.

Price: From **$220.00**

COOPER MODEL 57-M BOLT-ACTION RIFLE

Caliber: 22 LR, 22 WMR, 17 HMR, 17 Mach 2. **Barrel:** 22" or 24" stainless steel or 4140 match grade. **Weight:** 6.5-7.5 lbs. **Stock:** AA-AAA select Claro walnut, 22 lpi hand checkering. **Sights:** None furnished. **Features:** Three rear locking lug, repeating bolt-action with 5-shot magazine. for 22 LR and 17M2; 4-shot magazine for 22 WMR and 17 HMR. Fully adjustable trigger. Left-hand models add $150 to base rifle price. 1/4"-group rimfire accuracy guarantee at 50 yards; 0.5"-group centerfire accuracy guarantee at 100 yards. Options include wood upgrades, case-color metalwork, barrel fluting, custom LOP, and many others.

Price: Classic **$1,349.00**
Price: LVT **$1,459.00**
Price: Custom Classic **$1,995.00**
Price: Western Classic **$2,698.00**
Price: TRP-3 (22 LR only, benchrest style) **$1,295.00**
Price: Jackson Squirrel Rifle **$1,498.00**
Price: Jackson Hunter (synthetic) **$1,298.00**

CZ 452 Lux

CZ 452 Varmint

CZ 452 American Classic

Marlin 917V

Marlin Model 915YN "Little Buckaroo"

CZ 452 LUX BOLT-ACTION RIFLE

Caliber: 22 LR, 22 WMR, 5-shot detachable magazine. **Barrel:** 24.8". **Weight:** 6.6 lbs. **Length:** 42.63" overall. **Stock:** Walnut with checkered pistol grip. **Sights:** Hooded front, fully adjustable tangent rear. **Features:** All-steel construction, adjustable trigger, polished blue finish. Imported from the Czech Republic by CZ-USA.

Price: 22 LR, 22 WMR **$421.00**

CZ 452 Varmint Rifle

Similar to the Lux model except has heavy 20.8" barrel; stock has beavertail forend; weighs 7 lbs.; no sights furnished. Available in 22 LR, 22 WMR, 17HMR, 17M2. Imported from the Czech Republic by CZ-USA.

Price: from **$574.00**

CZ 452 American Bolt-Action Rifle

Similar to the CZ 452 M 2E Lux except has classic-style stock of Circassian walnut; 22.5" free-floating barrel with recessed target crown; receiver dovetail for scope mounting. No open sights furnished. Introduced 1999. Imported from the Czech Republic by CZ-USA.

Price: 22 LR, 22 WMR **$421.00**

HARRINGTON & RICHARDSON ULTRA HEAVY BARREL 22 MAG RIFLE

Caliber: 22 WMR, single shot. **Barrel:** 22" bull. **Stock:** Cinnamon laminated wood with Monte Carlo cheekpiece. **Sights:** None furnished; scope mount rail included. **Features:** Hand-checkered stock and forend; deep-crown rifling; tuned trigger; trigger locking system; hammer extension. Introduced 2001. From H&R 1871 LLC.

Price: **$193.00**

HENRY ACU-BOLT RIFLE

Caliber: 22, 22 Mag., 17 HMR; single shot. **Barrel:** 20". **Weight:** 4.15 lbs. **Length:** 36". **Stock:** One-piece fiberglass synthetic. **Sights:** Scope mount and 4x scope included. **Features:** Stainless barrel and receiver, bolt-action.

Price: H007 22 LR, ... **$399.00**

HENRY "MINI" BOLT ACTION 22 RIFLE

Caliber: 22 LR, single shot youth gun. **Barrel:** 16" stainless, 8-groove rifling. **Weight:** 3.25 lbs. **Length:** 30", LOP 11.5". **Stock:** Synthetic, pistol grip, wraparound checkering and beavertail forearm. **Sights:** William Fire sights. **Features:** One-piece bolt configuration manually operated safety.

Price: H005 22 LR, black fiberglass stock **$239.95**

Price: H005S 22 LR, orange fiberglass stock.............. **$239.95**

MARLIN MODEL 917 BOLT-ACTION RIFLES

Caliber: 17 HMR, 4- and 7-shot clip. **Barrel:** 22". **Weight:** 6 lbs., stainless 7 lbs. **Length:** 41". **Stock:** Checkered walnut Monte Carlo SS, laminated black/grey. **Sights:** No sights but receiver grooved. **Features:** Swivel studs, positive thumb safety, red cocking indicator, safety lock, SS 1" brushed aluminum scope rings.

Price: 917 .... **$240.00**

Price: 917S Stainless steel barrel **$287.00**

Price: 917VT Laminated thumbhole stock (2008), from **$382.00**

MARLIN MODEL 915YN "LITTLE BUCKAROO"

Caliber: 22 S, L, LR, single shot. **Barrel:** 16.25" Micro-Groove. **Weight:** 4.25 lbs. **Length:** 33.25" overall. **Stock:** One-piece walnut-finished, press-checkered Maine birch with Monte Carlo; Mar-Shield finish. **Sights:** Ramp front, adjustable open rear. **Features:** Beginner's rifle with thumb safety, easy-load feed throat, red cocking indicator. Receiver grooved for scope mounting. Introduced 1989.

Price: **$203.00**

Price: 915YS (stainless steel with fire sights) **$227.00**

RIMFIRE RIFLES—Bolt Actions & Single Shot

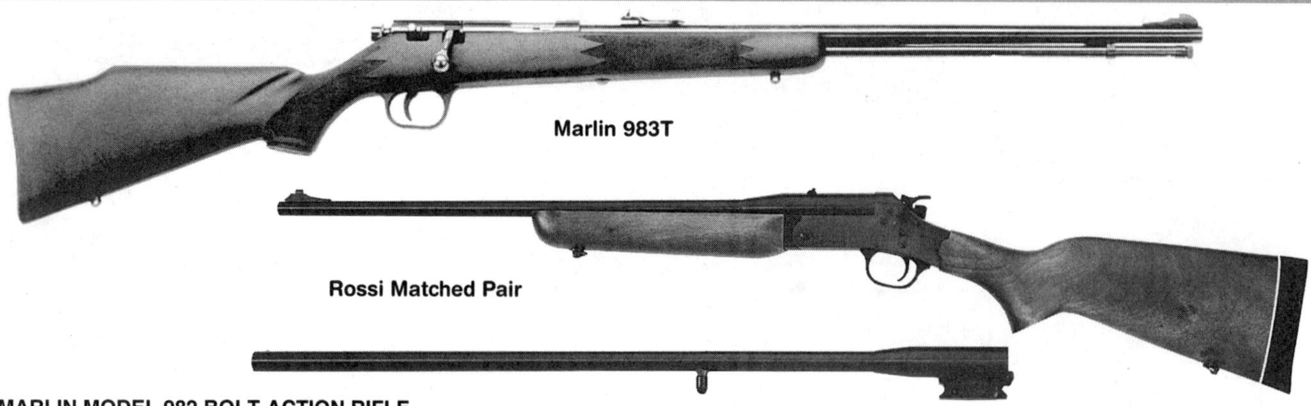
Marlin 983T

Rossi Matched Pair

MARLIN MODEL 982 BOLT-ACTION RIFLE
Caliber: 22 WMR. **Barrel:** 22" Micro-Groove. **Weight:** 6 lbs. **Length:** 41" overall. **Stock:** Walnut Monte Carlo genuine American black walnut with swivel studs; full pistol grip; classic cut checkering; rubber rifle butt pad; tough Mar-Shield finish. **Sights:** Adjustable semi-buckhorn folding rear, ramp front sight with brass bead and Wide-Scan front sight hood. **Features:** 7-shot clip, thumb safety, red cocking indicator, receiver grooved for scope mount. 982S has stainless steel front breech bolt, barrel, receiver and bolt knob. All other parts are either stainless steel or nickel-plated. Has black Monte Carlo stock of fiberglass-filled polycarbonate with molded-in checkering, nickel-plated swivel studs. Introduced 2005. Made in U.S.A. by Marlin Firearms Co.
Price: 982VS (heavy stainless barrel, 7 lbs). **$309.00**
Price: 982VS-CF (carbon fiber stock). **$350.00**

Marlin Model 925M Bolt-Action Rifles
Similar to the Model 982 except chambered for 22 WMR. Has 7-shot clip magazine, 22" Micro-Groove barrel, checkered walnut-finished Maine birch stock. Introduced 1989.
Price: 925M. **$234.00**

MARLIN MODEL 983 BOLT-ACTION RIFLE
Caliber: 22 WMR. **Barrel:** 22"; 1:16" twist. **Weight:** 6 lbs. **Length:** 41" overall. **Stock:** Walnut Monte Carlo with sling swivel studs, rubber buttpad. **Sights:** Ramp front with brass bead, removable hood; adjustable semi-buckhorn folding rear. **Features:** Thumb safety, red cocking indicator, receiver grooved for scope mount. 983S is same as the Model 983 except front breech bolt, striker knob, trigger stud, cartridge lifter stud and outer magazine tube are of stainless steel; other parts are nickel-plated. Introduced 1993. 983T has a black Monte Carlo fiberglass-filled synthetic stock with sling swivel studs. Introduced 2001.Made in U.S.A. by Marlin Firearms Co.
Price: 983 . . . . **$308.00**
Price: 983S (stainless barrel) **$337.00**
Price: 983T (fiberglass stock) **$245.00**

MEACHAM LOW-WALL RIFLE
Caliber: Any rimfire cartridge. **Barrel:** 26-34". **Weight:** 7-15 lbs. **Sights:** none. Tang drilled for Win. base, 3/8" dovetail slot front. **Stock:** Fancy eastern walnut with cheekpiece; ebony insert in forearm tip. Features; Exact copy of 1885 Winchester. With most Winchester factory options available including double set triggers. Introduced 1994. Made in U.S.A. by Meacham T&H Inc.
Price: From **$3,899.00**

MOSSBERG MODEL 817 VARMINT BOLT-ACTION RIFLE
Caliber: 17 HMR, 5-round magazine. **Barrel:** 21"; free-floating bull barrel, recessed muzzle crown. **Weight:** 4.9 lbs. (black synthetic), 5.2 lbs. (wood). **Stock:** Black synthetic or wood; length of pull, 14.25". **Sights:** Factory-installed Weaver-style scope bases. **Features:** Blued or brushed chrome metal finishes, crossbolt safety, gun lock. Introduced 2008. Made in U.S.A. by O.F. Mossberg & Sons, Inc.
Price: Black synthetic stock, chrome finish (2008) **$216.00**

MOSSBERG MODEL 801/802 BOLT RIFLES
Caliber: 22 LR, 10-round detachable magazine. **Barrel:** 18" free-floating. **Weight:** 4.1 to 4.6 lbs. **Sights:** Adjustable rifle. Receiver grooved for scope mount. **Stock:** Solid pink or pink marble finish synthetic. **Features:** Ergonomically placed magazine release and safety buttons, crossbolt safety, free gun lock. 801 Half Pint has 12.25" length of pull, 16" barrel, and weighs 4 lbs. Hardwood stock; removable magazine plug. Made in U.S.A. by O.F. Mossberg & Sons, Inc.
Price: Pink Plinkster (2008) **$177.00**
Price: Half Pint (2008). **$177.00**

NEW ENGLAND FIREARMS SPORTSTER SINGLE-SHOT RIFLES
Caliber: 22 LR, 22 WMR, 17 HMR, single-shot. **Barrel:** 20". **Weight:** 5.5 lbs. **Length:** 36.25" overall. **Stock:** Black polymer. **Sights:** None furnished; scope mount included. **Features:** Break open, side-lever release; automatic ejection; recoil pad; sling swivel studs; trigger locking system. Introduced 2001. Made in U.S.A. by New England Firearms.
Price: **$149.00**
Price: Youth model (20" barrel, 33" overall, weighs 5-1/3 lbs.) **$149.00**
Price: Sportster 17 HMR **$180.00**

NEW ULTRA LIGHT ARMS 20RF BOLT-ACTION RIFLE
Caliber: 22 LR, single shot or repeater. **Barrel:** Douglas, length to order. **Weight:** 5.25 lbs. **Length:** Varies. **Stock:** Kevlar/graphite composite, variety of finishes. **Sights:** None furnished; drilled and tapped for scope mount. **Features:** Timney trigger, hand-lapped action, button-rifled barrel, hand-bedded action, recoil pad, sling-swivel studs, optional Jewell trigger. Made in U.S.A. by New Ultra Light Arms.
Price: 20 RF single shot **$800.00**
Price: 20 RF repeater **$850.00**

ROSSI MATCHED PAIR SINGLE-SHOT RIFLE/SHOTGUN
Caliber: 22 LR or 22 Mag. **Barrel:** 18.5" or 23". **Weight:** 6 lbs. **Stock:** Hardwood (brown or black finish). **Sights:** Fully adjustable front and rear. **Features:** Break-open breech, transfer-bar manual safety, includes matched 410-, 20 or 12 gauge shotgun barrel with bead front sight. Introduced 2001. Imported by BrazTech/Taurus.
Price: Blue **$139.95**
Price: Stainless steel **$169.95**

REMINGTON MODEL FIVE SERIES
Caliber: 17 HMR, 22 LR, 22 WMR. **Barrel:** 16.5" (Youth), 22". **Barrel:** Carbon-steel, hammer-forged barrel, 1:16 twist, polished blue finish. **Weight:** 5.5 to 6.75 lbs. **Stock:** Hardwood, laminate, European Walnut. **Length:** 35.25" to 40.75" overall. **Features:** Detachable, steel magazine box with five-round capacity; steel trigger guard; chrome-plated bolt body; single stage trigger with manual two-position safety; buttplate; sling swivel studs (excluding Youth version); adjustable big game-style rifle sights; and dovetail-style receiver. Introduced 2006. Model Five Youth (22 LR) has 12.4-inch length of pull, 16.5-inch barrel, single-shot adapter. Model Five Laminate has weather-resistant brown laminate stock. Model Five European Walnut has classic satin-finish stock. Made in U.S.A. by Remington.
Price: Model Five Youth, 22 LR (2008). **$237.00**
Price: Model Five Laminate, 17 HMR (2008), 22 LR, 22 WMR **$363.00**
Price: Model Five European Walnut, 22 LR (2008) **$363.00**

RUGER K77/22 VARMINT RIFLE
Caliber: 22 LR, 10-shot, 22 WMR, 9-shot detachable rotary magazine. **Barrel:** 24", heavy. **Weight:** 7.25 lbs. **Length:** 43.25" overall. **Stock:** Laminated hardwood with rubber buttpad, quick-detachable swivel studs. **Sights:** None furnished. Comes with Ruger 1" scope rings. **Features:** Stainless steel or blued finish. Three-position safety, dual extractors. Stock has wide, flat forend. Introduced 1993.
Price: K77/22VBZ, 22 LR **$812.00**
Price: K77/22VMBZ, 22 WMR **$812.00**

Ruger 77/17

Savage Mark I-G

Savage Mark II-BV

Savage Model 93G

RUGER 77/22 RIMFIRE BOLT-ACTION RIFLE

Caliber: 22 LR, 10-shot rotary magazine; 22 WMR, 9-shot rotary magazine. **Barrel:** 20". **Weight:** About 6 lbs. **Length:** 39.25" overall. **Stock:** Checkered American walnut, laminated hardwood, or synthetic stocks, stainless sling swivels. **Sights:** Plain barrel with 1" Ruger rings. **Features:** Mauser-type action uses Ruger's rotary magazine. Three-position safety, simplified bolt stop, patented bolt locking system. Uses the dual-screw barrel attachment system of the 10/22 rifle. Integral scope mounting system with 1" Ruger rings. Blued model introduced 1983. Stainless steel and blued with synthetic stock introduced 1989.

Price: 77/22R (no sights, rings, walnut stock). **$732.00**
Price: K77/22RP (stainless, no sights, rings, synthetic stock) .**$732.00**
Price: 77/22RM (22 WMR, blued, walnut stock) **$732.00**
Price: K77/22RMP (22 WMR, stainless, synthetic stock) **$732.00**

RUGER 77/17 RIMFIRE BOLT-ACTION RIFLE

Caliber: 17 HMR (9-shot rotary magazine. **Barrel:** 22" to 24". **Weight:** 6.5-7.5 lbs. **Length:** 41.25-43.25" overall. **Stock:** Checkered American walnut, laminated hardwood; stainless sling swivels. **Sights:** Plain barrel with 1" Ruger rings. **Features:** Mauser-type action uses Ruger's rotary magazine. Three-position safety, simplified bolt stop, patented bolt locking system. Uses the dual-screw barrel attachment system of the 10/22 rifle. Integral scope mounting system with 1" Ruger rings. Introduced 2002.

Price: 77/17RM (no sights, rings, walnut stock) **$732.00**
Price: K77/17VMBBZ (Target grey bbl, black laminate stock) .**$812.00**

SAVAGE MARK I-G BOLT-ACTION RIFLE

Caliber: 22 LR, single shot. **Barrel:** 20.75". **Weight:** 5.5 lbs. **Length:** 39.5" overall. **Stock:** Walnut-finished hardwood with Monte Carlo-type comb, checkered grip and forend. **Sights:** Bead front, open adjustable rear. Receiver grooved for scope mounting. **Features:** Thumb-operated rotating safety. Blue finish. Rifled or smooth bore. Introduced 1990. Made in Canada, from Savage Arms Inc.

Price: Mark I-G, rifled or smooth bore, right- or left-handed . . .**$209.00**
Price: Mark I-GY (Youth), 19" barrel, 37" overall, 5 lbs. **$209.00**
Price: Mark I-GSB (22 LR shot cartridge) **$209.00**

SAVAGE MARK II BOLT-ACTION RIFLE

Caliber: 22 LR, 10-shot magazine. **Barrel:** 20.5". **Weight:** 5.5 lbs. **Length:** 39.5" overall. **Stock:** Walnut-finished hardwood with Monte Carlo-type comb, checkered grip and forend. **Sights:** Bead front, open adjustable rear. Receiver grooved for scope mounting. **Features:** Thumb-operated rotating safety. Blue finish. Introduced 1990. Made in Canada, from Savage Arms, Inc.

Price: Mark II-BV. **$322.00**
Price: Mark II-GY (youth), 19" barrel, 37" overall, 5 lbs. **$209.00**
Price: Mark II-GL, left-hand **$209.00**
Price: Mark II-F, 17 HM2 . . . .**$236.00**
Price: Mark II XP Camo Scope Package (2008). **$400.00**
Price: Mark II Classic T, thumbhole walnut stock (2008) **$555.00**

Savage Mark II-FSS Stainless Rifle

Similar to the Mark II except has stainless steel barreled action and black synthetic stock with positive checkering, swivel studs, and 20.75" free-floating and button-rifled barrel with detachable magazine. Weighs 5.5 lbs. Introduced 1997. Imported from Canada by Savage Arms, Inc.

Price: **$258.00**

SAVAGE MODEL 93G MAGNUM BOLT-ACTION RIFLE

Caliber: 22 WMR, 5-shot magazine. **Barrel:** 20.75". **Weight:** 5.75 lbs. **Length:** 39.5" overall. **Stock:** Walnut-finished hardwood with Monte Carlo-type comb, checkered grip and forend. **Sights:** Bead front, adjustable open rear. Receiver grooved for scope mount. **Features:** Thumb-operated rotary safety. Blue finish. Introduced 1994. Made in Canada, from Savage Arms.

Price: Model 93G **$241.00**
Price: Model 93F (as above with black graphite/fiberglass stock) **$229.00**
Price: Model 93 Classic, American walnut stock (2008). **$534.00**
Price: Model 93 Classic T, American walnut thumbhole stock (2008) **$569.00**

Savage Model 93FSS

Savage Model 93FVSS

Savage Model 30G Stevens "Favorite"

Savage Cub G Youth

Winchester Wildcat Bolt Action 22

Savage Model 93FSS Magnum Rifle

Similar to Model 93G except stainless steel barreled action and black synthetic stock with positive checkering. Weighs 5.5 lbs. Introduced 1997. Imported from Canada by Savage Arms, Inc.

Price: **$291.00**

Savage Model 93FVSS Magnum Rifle

Similar to Model 93FSS Magnum except 21" heavy barrel with recessed target-style crown, satin-finished stainless barreled action, black graphite/fiberglass stock. Drilled and tapped for scope mounting; comes with Weaver-style bases. Introduced 1998. Imported from Canada by Savage Arms, Inc.

Price: **$331.00**

SAVAGE MODEL 30G STEVENS "FAVORITE"

Caliber: 22 LR, 22 WMR Model 30GM, 17 HMR Model 30R17. **Barrel:** 21". **Weight:** 4.25 lbs. **Length:** 36.75". **Stock:** Walnut, straight grip, Schnabel forend. **Sights:** Adjustable rear, bead post front. **Features:** Lever action falling block, inertia firing pin system, Model 30G half octagonal barrel, Model 30GM full octagonal barrel.

Price: Model 30G **$291.00**
Price: Model 30 Takedown **$316.00**

SAVAGE CUB T MINI YOUTH

Caliber: 22 S, L, LR; 17 Mach 2. **Barrel:** 16". **Weight:** 3.5 lbs. **Length:** 33". **Stock:** Walnut finished hardwood thumbhole stock. **Sights:** Bead post, front; peep, rear. **Features:** Mini single-shot bolt action, free-floating button-rifled barrel, blued finish. From Savage Arms.

Price: Cub T Thumbhole, walnut stained laminated **$248.00**
Price: Cub T Pink Thumbhole (2008) **$248.00**

WINCHESTER WILDCAT BOLT ACTION 22

Caliber: 22 S, L, LR; one 5-round and three 10-round magazines. **Barrel:** 21". **Weight:** 6.5 lbs. **Length:** 38-3/8". **Stock:** Checkered hardwood stock, checkered black synthetic Winchester buttplate, Schnabel fore-end. **Sights:** Bead post, front; buckhorn rear. **Features:** Steel sling swivel studs, blued finish. Wildcat Target/Varmint rifle has .866" diameter bull barrel. Receiver drilled, tapped, and grooved for bases. Adjustable trigger, dual front steel swivel studs. Reintroduced 2008. From Winchester Repeating Arms.

Price: **$230.00**
Price: Wildcat/Varmint **$299.00**

Includes models for classic American and ISU target competition and other sporting and competitive shooting.

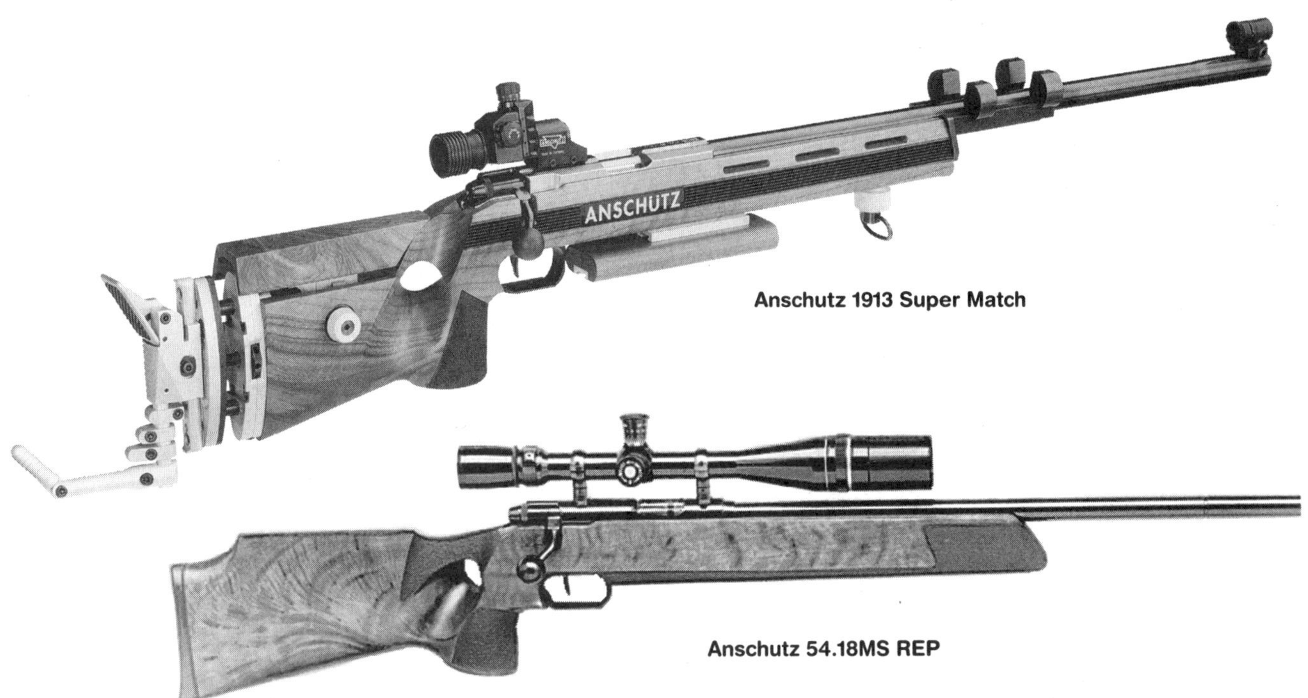
Anschutz 1913 Super Match

Anschutz 54.18MS REP

ANSCHUTZ 1903 MATCH RIFLE

Caliber: 22 LR, single shot. **Barrel:** 21.25". **Weight:** 8 lbs. **Length:** 43.75" overall. **Stock:** Walnut-finished hardwood with adjustable cheekpiece; stippled grip and forend. **Sights:** None furnished. **Features:** Uses Anschutz Match 64 action. A medium weight rifle for intermediate and advanced Junior Match competition. Available from Champion's Choice.

Price: Right-hand **$965.00**

ANSCHUTZ 64-MP R SILHOUETTE RIFLE

Caliber: 22 LR, 5-shot magazine. **Barrel:** 21.5", medium heavy; 7/8" diameter. **Weight:** 8 lbs. **Length:** 39.5" overall. **Stock:** Walnut-finished hardwood, silhouette-type. **Sights:** None furnished. **Features:** Uses Match 64 action. Designed for metallic silhouette competition. Stock has stippled checkering, contoured thumb groove with Wundhammer swell. Two-stage #5098 trigger. Slide safety locks sear and bolt. Introduced 1980. Imported from Germany by Merkel USA.

Price: 64-MP R **$1,029.00**

Price: 64-S BR Benchrest (2008) **$1,349.00**

Anschutz 2007 Match Rifle

Uses same action as the Model 2013, but has a lighter barrel. European walnut stock in right-hand, true left-hand or extra-short models. Sights optional. Available with 19.6" barrel with extension tube, or 26", both in stainless or blue. Introduced 1998. Available from Gunsmithing, Inc.

Price: Right-hand, blue, no sights **$2,410.90**

ANSCHUTZ 1827BT FORTNER BIATHLON RIFLE

Caliber: 22 LR, 5-shot magazine. **Barrel:** 21.7". **Weight:** 8.8 lbs. with sights. **Length:** 40.9" overall. **Stock:** European walnut with cheekpiece, stippled pistol grip and forend. **Sights:** Optional globe front specially designed for Biathlon shooting, micrometer rear with hinged snow cap. **Features:** Uses Super Match 54 action and nine-way adjustable trigger; adjustable wooden buttplate, biathlon butthook, adjustable hand-stop rail. Uses Anschutz/Fortner system straight-pull bolt action, blued or stainless steel barrel. Introduced 1982. Available from Champion's Choice.

Price: Nitride finish with sights, about **$2,895.00**

ANSCHUTZ SUPER MATCH SPECIAL MODEL 2013 RIFLE

Caliber: 22 LR, single shot. **Barrel:** 25.9". **Weight:** 13 lbs. **Length:** 41.7" to 42.9". **Stock:** Adjustable aluminum. **Sights:** None furnished. **Features:** 2313 aluminum-silver/blue stock, 500mm barrel, fast lock time, adjustable cheek piece, heavy action and muzzle tube, w/ handstop and standing riser block. Introduced in 1997. Available from Champion's Choice.

Price: Right-hand **$3,195.00**

ANSCHUTZ 1912 SPORT RIFLE

Caliber: 22 LR. **Barrel:** 26" match. **Weight:** 11.4 lbs. **Length:** 41.7" overall. **Stock:** Non-stained thumbhole stock adjustable in length with adjustable butt plate and cheek piece adjustment. Flat forend raiser block 4856 adjustable in height. Hook butt plate. **Sights:** None furnished. **Features:** "Free rifle" for women. Smallbore model 1907 with 1912 **stock:** Match 54 action. Delivered with: Hand stop 6226, forend raiser block 4856, screw driver, instruction leaflet with test target. Available from Champion's Choice.

Price: **$2,545.00**

Anschutz 1913 Super Match Rifle

Same as the Model 1911 except European walnut International-type stock with adjustable cheekpiece, or color laminate, both available with straight or lowered forend, adjustable aluminum hook buttplate, adjustable hand stop, weighs 13 lbs., 46" overall. Stainless or blue barrel. Available from Champion's Choice.

Price: Right-hand, blue, no sights, walnut stock **$2,695.00**

Anschutz 54.18MS REP Deluxe Silhouette Rifle

Same basic action and trigger specifications as the Anschutz 1913 Super Match but with removable 5-shot clip magazine, 22.4" barrel extendable to 30" using optional extension and weight set. Weight is 8.1 lbs. Receiver drilled and tapped for scope mounting. Stock is thumbhole silhouette version or standard silhouette version, both are European walnut. Introduced 1990. Available from Champion's Choice.

Price: Thumbhole stock **$2,195.00**

Anschutz 1907 Standard Match Rifle

Same action as Model 1913 but with 7/8" diameter 26" barrel (stainless or blue). Length is 44.5" overall, weighs 10.5 lbs. Choice of stock configurations. Vented forend. Designed for prone and position shooting ISU requirements; suitable for NRA matches. Also available with walnut flat-forend stock for benchrest shooting. Available from Champion's Choice.

Price: Right-hand, blue, no sights **$1,655.00**

Anschutz 1907

Armalite AR-10(T)

Bushmaster A2

Bushmaster DCM

ARMALITE AR-10(T) RIFLE

Caliber: 308 Win., 10-shot magazine. **Barrel:** 24" target-weight Rock 5R custom. **Weight:** 10.4 lbs. **Length:** 43.5" overall. **Stock:** Green or black composition; N.M. fiberglass handguard tube. **Sights:** Detachable handle, front sight, or scope mount available. Comes with international-style flattop receiver with Picatinny rail. **Features:** National Match two-stage trigger. Forged upper receiver. Receivers hard-coat anodized. Introduced 1995. Made in U.S.A. by ArmaLite, Inc.

Price: Green **$2,126.00**
Price: Black **$2,126.00**

ARMALITE M15A4(T) EAGLE EYE RIFLE

Caliber: 223 Rem., 10-round magazine. **Barrel:** 24" heavy stainless; 1:8" twist. **Weight:** 9.2 lbs. **Length:** 42-3/8" overall. **Stock:** Green or black butt, N.M. fiberglass handguard tube. **Sights:** One-piece international-style flattop receiver with Weaver-type rail, including case deflector. **Features:** Detachable carry handle, front sight and scope mount (30mm or 1") available. Upper and lower receivers have push-type pivot pin, hard coat anodized. Made in U.S.A. by ArmaLite, Inc.

Price: Green or black furniture **$1,429.00**

BLASER R93 LONG RANGE SPORTER 2 RIFLE

Caliber: 308 Win., 10-shot detachable box magazine. **Barrel:** 24". **Weight:** 10.4 lbs. **Length:** 44" overall. **Stock:** Aluminum with synthetic lining. **Sights:** None furnished; accepts detachable scope mount. **Features:** Straight-pull bolt action with adjustable trigger; fully adjustable stock; quick takedown; corrosion resistant finish. Introduced 1998. Imported from Germany by Blaser USA.

Price: **$3,733.00**

BUSHMASTER A2 RIFLE

Caliber: 308 Win., 5.56mm. **Barrel:** 16", 20". **Weight:** 8.3 lbs. **Length:** 38.25" overall (20" barrel). **Stock:** Black composition; A2 type. **Sights:** Adjustable post front, adjustable aperture rear. **Features:** Patterned after Colt M-16A2. Chrome-lined barrel with manganese phosphate exterior. Forged aluminum receivers with push-pin takedown. Available in stainless barrel and camo stock versions. Made in U.S.A. by Bushmaster Firearms Co.

Price: (A3 type) **$1,240.00**

BUSHMASTER DCM COMPETITION RIFLE

Caliber: 223. **Barrel:** 20" extra-heavy (1" diameter) barrel with 1.8" twist for heavier competition bullets. **Weight:** About 12 lbs. with balance weights. **Length:** NA. **Stock:** NA. **Sights:** A2 rear sight. **Features:** Has special competition rear sight with interchangeable apertures, extra-fine 1/2- or 1/4-MOA windage and elevation adjustments; specially ground front sight post in choice of three widths. Full-length handguards over free-floater barrel tube. Introduced 1998. Made in U.S.A. by Bushmaster Firearms, Inc.

Price: **$1,185.00**

Colt Match Target HBAR

Colt Match Target HBAR II

Colt Accurized Rifle

Ed Brown Marine Sniper

BUSHMASTER VARMINTER RIFLE

Caliber: 5.56mm. **Barrel:** 24", fluted. **Weight:** 8.4 lbs. **Length:** 42.25" overall. **Stock:** Black composition, A2 type. **Sights:** None furnished; upper receiver has integral scope mount base. **Features:** Chrome-lined .950" extra heavy barrel with counter-bored crown, manganese phosphate finish, free-floating aluminum handguard, forged aluminum receivers with push-pin takedown, hard anodized mil-spec finish. Competition trigger optional. Made in U.S.A. by Bushmaster Firearms, Inc.

Price: **$1,360.00**

COLT MATCH TARGET HBAR & M4 RIFLES

Caliber: 223 Rem. **Barrel:** 20". **Weight:** 8 lbs. **Length:** 39" overall. **Stock:** Synthetic. **Sights:** Front: elevation adj. post; rear: 800-meter, aperture adj. for windage and elevation. **Features:** Heavy barrel, rate of rifling twist 1:7. Introduced 1991. Made in U.S.A. by Colt. M4 variant has 16.1" barrel.

Price: Model MT6601, MT6601C **$1,183.00**
Price: Model 6400C **$1,289.00**

Colt Match Target Competition HBAR Rifle

Similar to the Match Target except has removable carry handle for scope mounting, 1:9" rifling twist, 9-round magazine. Weighs 8.5 lbs. Introduced 1991.

Price: Model MT6700C **$1,250.00**

Colt Match Target Competition HBAR II Rifle

Similar to the Match Target Competition HBAR except has 16:1" barrel, overall length 34.5", and weighs 7.1 lbs. Introduced 1995.

Price: Model MT6731 .... **$1,172.00**

Colt Accurized Rifle

Similar to the Match Target Model except has 24" barrel. Features flat-top receiver for scope mounting, stainless steel heavy barrel, tubular handguard, and free-floating barrel. Matte black finish. Weighs 9.25 lbs. Made in U.S.A. by Colt's Mfg. Co., Inc.

Price: Model CR6724 .... **$1,334.00**

EAA/HW 660 MATCH RIFLE

Caliber: 22 LR. **Barrel:** 26". **Weight:** 10.7 lbs. **Length:** 45.3" overall. **Stock:** Match-type walnut with adjustable cheekpiece and buttplate. **Sights:** Globe front, match aperture rear. **Features:** Adjustable match trigger; stippled pistol grip and forend; forend accessory rail. Introduced 1991. Imported from Germany by European American Armory.

Price: About **$999.00**
Price: With laminate stock **$1,159.00**

ED BROWN MODEL 704 TACTICAL

Caliber: 308 Win., 300 Win. Mag. **Barrel:** 26". SS with GEN III Coating. **Weight:** 11.25 lbs. **Stock:** Hand bedded McMillan A-3 fiberglass tactical stock with recoil pad. **Sights:** None furnished. Leupold Mark 4 30mm scope mounts utilizing heavy-duty screws. **Features:** Custom short or long action, steel trigger guard, hinged floor plate, additional calibers available.

Price: From **$2,995.00**

ED BROWN MODEL 704, M40A2 MARINE SNIPER

Caliber: 308 Win., 30-06 Springfield. **Barrel:** Match-grade 24". **Weight:** 9.25 lbs. **Stock:** Hand bedded McMillan GP fiberglass tactical stock with recoil pad in special Woodland Camo molded-in colors. **Sights:** None furnished. Leupold Mark 4 30mm scope mounts with heavy-duty screws. **Features:** Steel trigger guard, hinged floor plate, three position safety.

Price: From **$2,995.00**

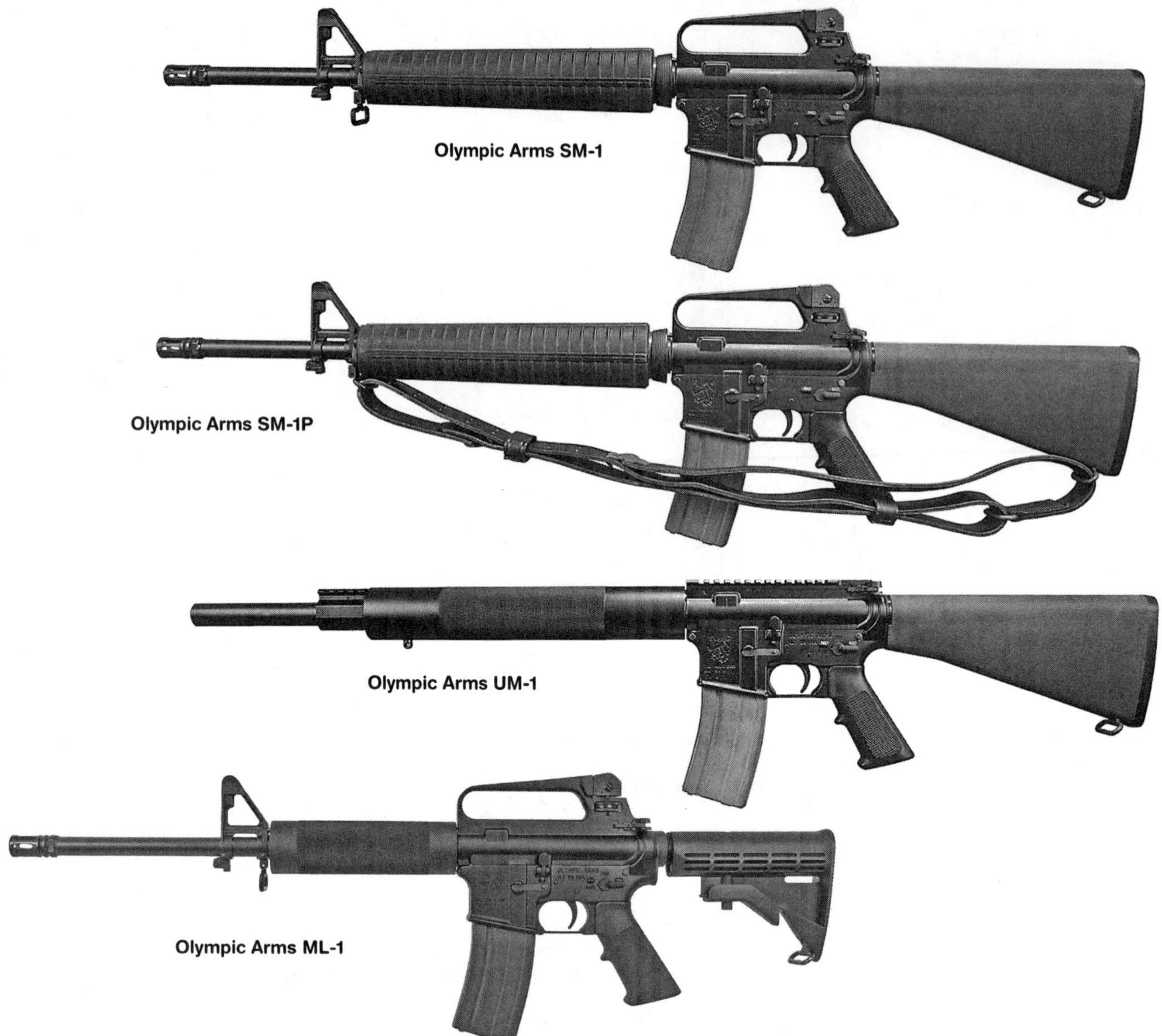
Olympic Arms SM-1

Olympic Arms SM-1P

Olympic Arms UM-1

Olympic Arms ML-1

OLYMPIC ARMS SM SERVICEMATCH AR15 RIFLES

Caliber: 223 Rem. minimum SAAMI spec, 30-shot magazine. **Barrel:** 20" broach-cut Ultramatch stainless steel 1x8 twist rate. **Weight:** 10 lbs. **Length:** 39.5" overall. **Stock:** A2 grip, A2 buttstock with trapdoor. **Sights:** A2 NM rear, elevation adjustable front post. **Features:** DCM-ready AR15, free-floating handguard looks standard, A2 upper, threaded muzzle, flash suppressor. Premium model adds pneumatic recoil buffer, Bob Jones interchangeable sights, two-stage trigger and Turner Saddlery sling. Made in U.S.A. by Olympic Arms, Inc.

Price: SM-1, 20" DCM ready **$1,099.00**
Price: SM-1P, Premium 20" DCM ready. **$1,493.00**

OLYMPIC ARMS UM ULTRAMATCH AR15 RIFLES

Caliber: 223 Rem. minimum SAAMI spec, 30-shot magazine. **Barrel:** 20" or 24" bull broach-cut Ultramatch stainless steel 1x10 twist rate. **Weight:** 8-10 lbs. **Length:** 38.25" overall. **Stock:** A2 grip, A2 buttstock with trapdoor. **Sights:** None, flat-top upper and gas block with rails. **Features:** Flat top upper, free floating tubular match handguard, Picatinny gas block, crowned muzzle, factory trigger job and "Ultramatch" pantograph. Premium model adds pneumatic recoil buffer, Harris S-series bipod, hand selected premium receivers and William Set Trigger. Made in U.S.A. by Olympic Arms, Inc.

Price: UM-1, 20" Ultramatch. **$1,150.00**

OLYMPIC ARMS ML-1/ML-2 MULTIMATCH AR15 CARBINES

Caliber: 223 Rem. minimum SAAMI spec, 30-shot magazine. **Barrel:** 16" broach-cut Ultramatch stainless steel 1x10 twist rate. **Weight:** 7-8 lbs. **Length:** 34-36" overall. **Stock:** A2 grip and varying buttstock. **Sights:** None. **Features:** The ML-1 includes A2 upper with adjustable rear sight, elevation adjustable front post, free floating tubular match handguard, bayonet lug, threaded muzzle, flash suppressor and M4 6-point collapsible buttstock. The ML-2 includes bull diameter barrel, flat top upper, free floating tubular match handguard, Picatinny gas block, crowned muzzle and A2 buttstock with trapdoor. Made in U.S.A. by Olympic Arms, Inc.

Price: ML-1 or ML-2 . . . . **$1,026.00**

OLYMPIC ARMS K8 TARGETMATCH AR15 RIFLES

Caliber: 5.56 NATO, 223 WSSM, 243 WSSM, .25 WSSM 30/7-shot magazine. **Barrel:** 20", 24" bull button-rifled stainless/chrome-moly steel 1x9/1x10 twist rate. **Weight:** 8-10 lbs. **Length:** 38"-42" overall. **Stock:** A2 grip, A2 buttstock with trapdoor. **Sights:** None. **Features:** Barrel has satin bead-blast finish; flat-top upper, free-floating tubular match handguard, Picatinny gas block, crowned muzzle and "Targetmatch" pantograph on lower receiver. K8-MAG model uses Winchester Super Short Magnum cartridges. Includes 24" bull chrome-moly barrel, flat-top upper, free-floating tubular match handguard, Picatinny gas block, crowned muzzle and 7-shot magazine. Made in U.S.A. by Olympic Arms, Inc.

Price: K8 . . . . **$839.00**
Price: K8-MAG **$1,182.00**

Remington 40-XB Rangemaster

Sako TRG-22

Springfield Armory M1A Super Match

Springfield Armory M1A/M-21

REMINGTON 40-XB RANGEMASTER TARGET CENTERFIRE

Caliber: 15 calibers from 220 Swift to 300 Win. Mag. **Barrel:** 27.25". **Weight:** 11.25 lbs. **Length:** 47" overall. **Stock:** American walnut, laminated thumbhole or Kevlar with high comb and beavertail forend stop. Rubber non-slip buttplate. **Sights:** None. Scope blocks installed. **Features:** Adjustable trigger. Stainless barrel and action. Receiver drilled and tapped for sights. Model 40-XB Tactical (2008) chambered in 308 Win., comes with guarantee of 0.75-inch maximum 5-shot groups at 100 yards. **Weight:** 10.25 lbs. Includes Teflon-coated stainless button-rifled barrel, 1:14 twist, 27.25 inch long, three longitudinal flutes. Bolt-action repeater, adjustable 40-X trigger and precision machined aluminum bedding block. Stock is H-S Precision Pro Series synthetic tactical stock, black with green web finish, vertical pistol grip. From Remington Custom Shop.

Price: 40-XB KS, aramid fiber stock, single shot **$2,780.00**
Price: 40-XB KS, aramid fiber stock, repeater **$2,634.00**
Price: 40-XB Tactical 308 Win. (2008) **$2,927.00**
Price: 40-XB Thumbhole Repeater. **$2,927.00**

REMINGTON 40-XBBR KS

Caliber: Five calibers from 22 BR to 308 Win. **Barrel:** 20" (light varmint class), 24" (heavy varmint class). **Weight:** 7.25 lbs. (light varmint class); 12 lbs. (heavy varmint class). **Length:** 38" (20" bbl.), 42" (24"bbl.). **Stock:** Aramid fiber. **Sights:** None. Supplied with scope blocks. **Features:** Unblued benchrest with stainless steel barrel, trigger adjustable from 1-1/2 lbs. to 3.5 lbs. Special two-oz. trigger extra cost. Scope and mounts extra.

Price: Single shot **$3,806.00**

REMINGTON 40-XC KS TARGET RIFLE

Caliber: 7.62 NATO, 5-shot. **Barrel:** 24", stainless steel. **Weight:** 11 lbs. without sights. **Length:** 43.5" overall. **Stock:** Aramid fiber. **Sights:** None furnished. **Features:** Designed to meet the needs of competitive shooters. Stainless steel barrel and action.

Price: **$3,000.00**

REMINGTON 40-XR CUSTOM SPORTER

Caliber: 22 LR, 22 WM. **Features:** Model XR-40 Target rifle action. Many options available in stock, decoration or finish.

Price: Single shot **$4,391.00**
Price: 40-XR BR KS, bench rest 22 LR, ... **$2,927.00**

SAKO TRG-22/TRG-42 BOLT-ACTION RIFLE

Caliber: 308 Win., 10-shot magazine. **Barrel:** 26". **Weight:** 10.25 lbs. **Length:** 45.25" overall. **Stock:** Reinforced polyurethane with fully adjustable cheekpiece and buttplate. **Sights:** None furnished. Optional quick-detachable, one-piece scope mount base, 1" or 30mm rings. **Features:** Resistance-free bolt, free-floating heavy stainless barrel, 60-degree bolt lift. Two-stage trigger is adjustable for length, pull, horizontal or vertical pitch. Introduced 2000. Imported from Finland by Beretta USA.

Price: TRG-22 Green Folding Stock. **$4,000.00**
Price: TRG-22 Green or black stock **$2,775.00**
Price: TRG-42 Green stock **$2,775.00**

SPRINGFIELD ARMORY M1A SUPER MATCH

Caliber: 308 Win. **Barrel:** 22", heavy Douglas Premium. **Weight:** About 11 lbs. **Length:** 44.31" overall. **Stock:** Heavy walnut competition stock with longer pistol grip, contoured area behind the rear sight, thicker butt and forend, glass bedded. **Sights:** National Match front and rear. **Features:** Has figure-eight-style operating rod guide. Introduced 1987. From Springfield Armory.

Price: About **$2,479.00**

Springfield Armory M1A/M-21 Tactical Model Rifle

Similar to M1A Super Match except special sniper stock with adjustable cheekpiece and rubber recoil pad. Weighs 11.6 lbs. From Springfield Armory.

Price: **$2,975.00**

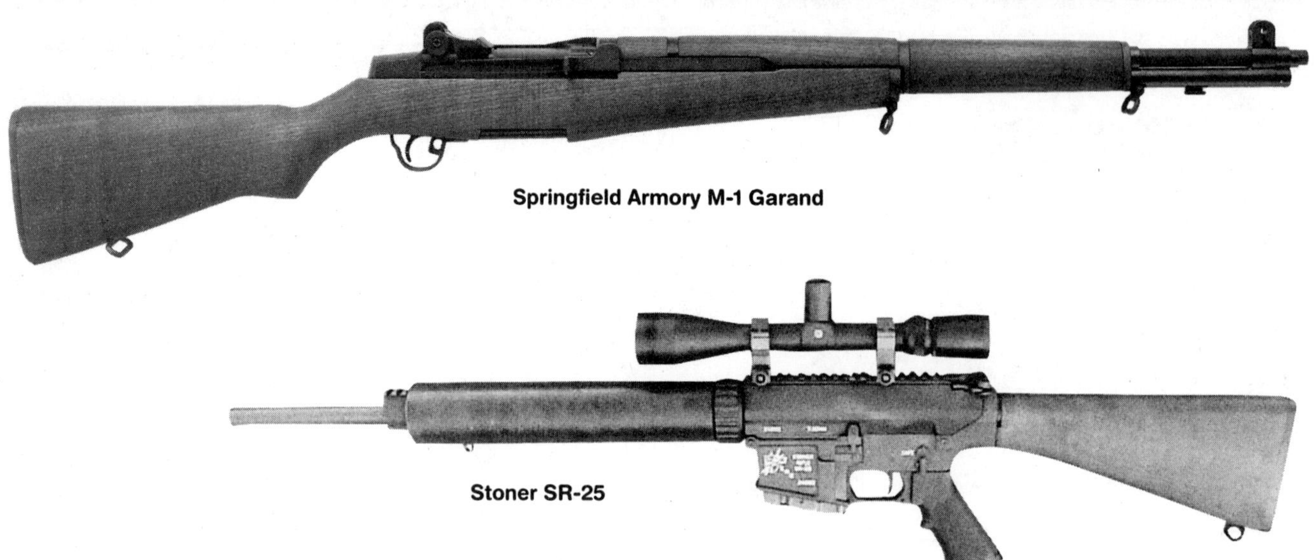
Springfield Armory M-1 Garand

Stoner SR-25

SPRINGFIELD ARMORY M-1 GARAND AMERICAN COMBAT RIFLES

Caliber: 30-06 Spfl., 308 Win., 8-shot. **Barrel:** 24". **Weight:** 9.5 lbs. **Length:** 43.6". **Stock:** American walnut. **Sights:** Military square post front, military aperture, MOA adjustable rear. **Features:** Limited production, certificate of authenticity, all new receiver, barrel and stock with remaining parts USGI mil-spec. Two-stage military trigger.

Price: About **$2,479.00**

STONER SR-15 MATCH RIFLE

Caliber: 223. **Barrel:** 20". **Weight:** 7.9 lbs. **Length:** 38" overall. **Stock:** Black synthetic. **Sights:** None furnished; flattop upper receiver for scope mounting. **Features:** Short Picatinny rail, two-stage match trigger. Introduced 1998. Made in U.S.A. by Knight's Mfg. Co.

Price: **$1,650.00**

STONER SR-25 MATCH RIFLE

Caliber: 7.62 NATO, 10-shot steel magazine, 5-shot optional. **Barrel:** 24" heavy match; 1:11.25" twist. **Weight:** 10.75 lbs. **Length:** 44" overall. **Stock:** Black synthetic AR-15A2 design. Full floating forend of mil-spec synthetic attaches to upper receiver at a single point. **Sights:** None furnished. Has integral Weaver-style rail. Rings and iron sights optional. **Features:** Improved AR-15 trigger, AR-15-style seven-lug rotating bolt. Introduced 1993. Made in U.S.A. by Knight's Mfg. Co.

Price: **$3,345.00**

Price: SR-25 Lightweight Match (20" medium match target contour barrel, 9.5 lbs., 40" overall) **$3,345.00**

TIME PRECISION 22 RF BENCH REST RIFLE

Caliber: 22 LR, single shot. **Barrel:** Shilen match-grade stainless. **Weight:** 10 lbs. with scope. **Length:** NA. **Stock:** Fiberglass. Pillar bedded. **Sights:** None furnished. **Features:** Shilen match trigger removable trigger bracket, full-length steel sleeve, aluminum receiver. Introduced 2008. Made in U.S.A. by Time Precision.

Price: .... **NA**

Includes a wide variety of sporting guns and guns suitable for various competitions.

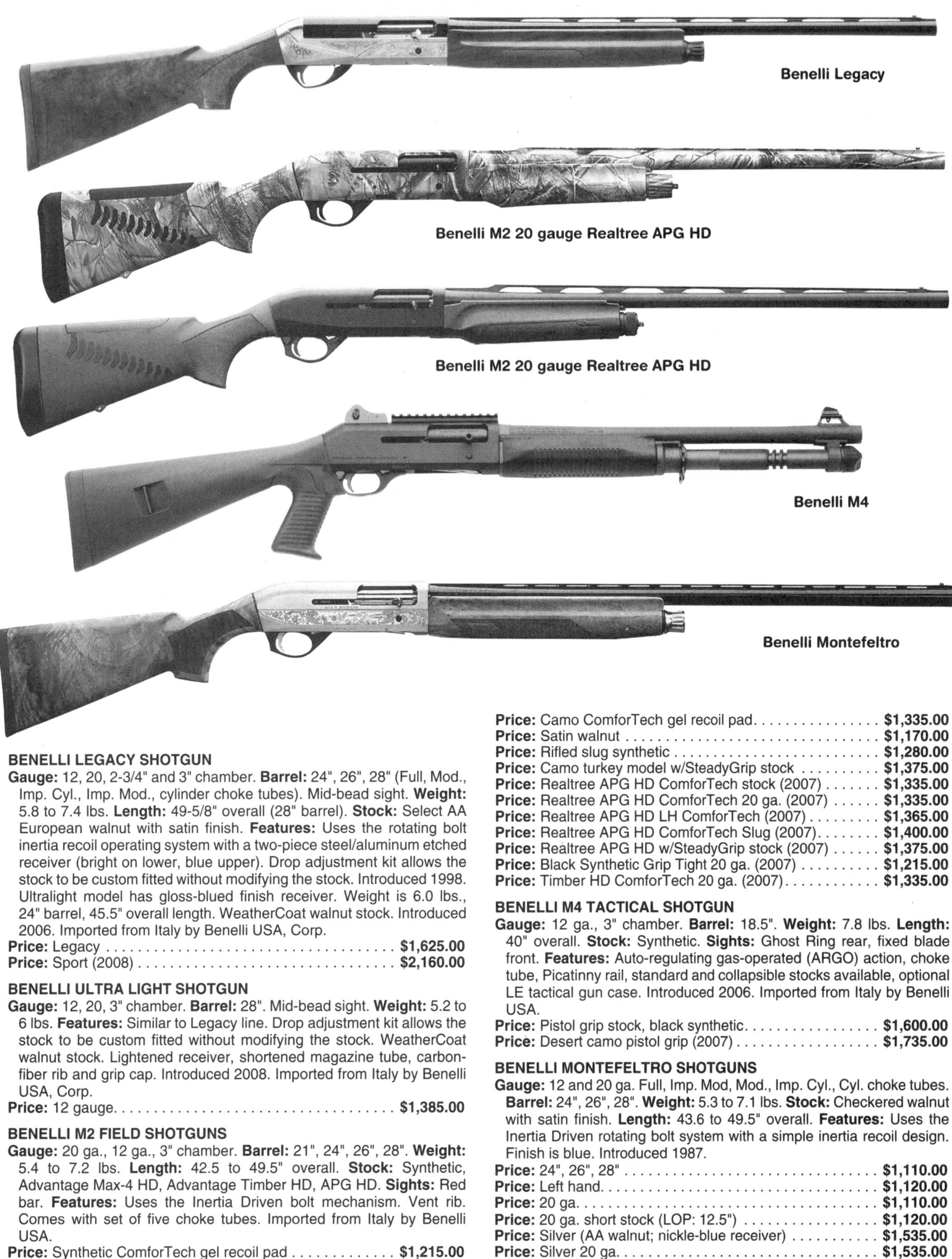

Benelli Legacy

Benelli M2 20 gauge Realtree APG HD

Benelli M2 20 gauge Realtree APG HD

Benelli M4

Benelli Montefeltro

BENELLI LEGACY SHOTGUN

Gauge: 12, 20, 2-3/4" and 3" chamber. **Barrel:** 24", 26", 28" (Full, Mod., Imp. Cyl., Imp. Mod., cylinder choke tubes). Mid-bead sight. **Weight:** 5.8 to 7.4 lbs. **Length:** 49-5/8" overall (28" barrel). **Stock:** Select AA European walnut with satin finish. **Features:** Uses the rotating bolt inertia recoil operating system with a two-piece steel/aluminum etched receiver (bright on lower, blue upper). Drop adjustment kit allows the stock to be custom fitted without modifying the stock. Introduced 1998. Ultralight model has gloss-blued finish receiver. Weight is 6.0 lbs., 24" barrel, 45.5" overall length. WeatherCoat walnut stock. Introduced 2006. Imported from Italy by Benelli USA, Corp.

Price: Legacy **$1,625.00**
Price: Sport (2008) **$2,160.00**

BENELLI ULTRA LIGHT SHOTGUN

Gauge: 12, 20, 3" chamber. **Barrel:** 28". Mid-bead sight. **Weight:** 5.2 to 6 lbs. **Features:** Similar to Legacy line. Drop adjustment kit allows the stock to be custom fitted without modifying the stock. WeatherCoat walnut stock. Lightened receiver, shortened magazine tube, carbon-fiber rib and grip cap. Introduced 2008. Imported from Italy by Benelli USA, Corp.

Price: 12 gauge. **$1,385.00**

BENELLI M2 FIELD SHOTGUNS

Gauge: 20 ga., 12 ga., 3" chamber. **Barrel:** 21", 24", 26", 28". **Weight:** 5.4 to 7.2 lbs. **Length:** 42.5 to 49.5" overall. **Stock:** Synthetic, Advantage Max-4 HD, Advantage Timber HD, APG HD. **Sights:** Red bar. **Features:** Uses the Inertia Driven bolt mechanism. Vent rib. Comes with set of five choke tubes. Imported from Italy by Benelli USA.

Price: Synthetic ComforTech gel recoil pad **$1,215.00**
Price: Camo ComforTech gel recoil pad. **$1,335.00**
Price: Satin walnut **$1,170.00**
Price: Rifled slug synthetic **$1,280.00**
Price: Camo turkey model w/SteadyGrip stock **$1,375.00**
Price: Realtree APG HD ComforTech stock (2007) **$1,335.00**
Price: Realtree APG HD ComforTech 20 ga. (2007) **$1,335.00**
Price: Realtree APG HD LH ComforTech (2007) **$1,365.00**
Price: Realtree APG HD ComforTech Slug (2007). **$1,400.00**
Price: Realtree APG HD w/SteadyGrip stock (2007) **$1,375.00**
Price: Black Synthetic Grip Tight 20 ga. (2007) **$1,215.00**
Price: Timber HD ComforTech 20 ga. (2007). **$1,335.00**

BENELLI M4 TACTICAL SHOTGUN

Gauge: 12 ga., 3" chamber. **Barrel:** 18.5". **Weight:** 7.8 lbs. **Length:** 40" overall. **Stock:** Synthetic. **Sights:** Ghost Ring rear, fixed blade front. **Features:** Auto-regulating gas-operated (ARGO) action, choke tube, Picatinny rail, standard and collapsible stocks available, optional LE tactical gun case. Introduced 2006. Imported from Italy by Benelli USA.

Price: Pistol grip stock, black synthetic. **$1,600.00**
Price: Desert camo pistol grip (2007) **$1,735.00**

BENELLI MONTEFELTRO SHOTGUNS

Gauge: 12 and 20 ga. Full, Imp. Mod, Mod., Imp. Cyl., Cyl. choke tubes. **Barrel:** 24", 26", 28". **Weight:** 5.3 to 7.1 lbs. **Stock:** Checkered walnut with satin finish. **Length:** 43.6 to 49.5" overall. **Features:** Uses the Inertia Driven rotating bolt system with a simple inertia recoil design. Finish is blue. Introduced 1987.

Price: 24", 26", 28" **$1,110.00**
Price: Left hand. **$1,120.00**
Price: 20 ga. **$1,110.00**
Price: 20 ga. short stock (LOP: 12.5") **$1,120.00**
Price: Silver (AA walnut; nickle-blue receiver) **$1,535.00**
Price: Silver 20 ga. **$1,535.00**

Benelli Super Black Eagle II Realtree APG HD Slug

Benelli Super Black Eagle II

Beretta 3901 Citizen

Beretta UGB

BENELLI SUPER BLACK EAGLE II SHOTGUNS

Gauge: 12, 3-1/2" chamber. **Barrel:** 24", 26", 28" (Cyl. Imp. Cyl., Mod., Imp. Mod., Full choke tubes). **Weight:** 7.1 to 7.3 lbs. **Length:** 45.6 to 49.6" overall. **Stock:** European walnut with satin finish, polymer, or camo. Adjustable for drop. **Sights:** Red bar front. **Features:** Uses Benelli inertia recoil bolt system. Vent rib. Advantage Max-4 HD, Advantage Timber HD camo patterns. Features ComforTech stock. Introduced 1991. Left-hand models available. Imported from Italy by Benelli USA.

Price: Satin walnut, non-ComforTech **$1,480.00**
Price: Camo stock, ComforTech gel recoil pad **$1,635.00**
Price: Black Synthetic stock **$1,415.00**
Price: Max-4 or Timber HD Camo stock. **$1,535.00**
Price: Satin walnut Rifled slug **$1,560.00**
Price: Timber HD turkey model w/SteadyGrip stock. **$1,615.00**
Price: Realtree APG HD SteadyGrip stock (2007) **$1,615.00**
Price: Realtree APG HD w/ComforTech stock (2007) **$1,665.00**
Price: Realtree APG HD LH ComforTech stock (2007) **$1,700.00**
Price: Realtree APG HD Slug Gun (2007) **$1,735.00**

BENELLI CORDOBA SHOTGUN

Gauge: 20; 12; 3" chamber. **Barrel:** 28" and 30", ported, 10mm sporting rib. **Weight:** 7.2 to 7.3 lbs. **Length:** 49.6 to 51.6". **Features:** Designed for high-volume sporting clays and Argentina dove shooting. Inertia-driven action, Extended Sport CrioChokes, 4+1 capacity. Ported. Imported from Italy by Benelli USA.

Price: Black synthetic GripTight ComforTech stock **$1,735.00**
Price: Black synthetic GripTight ComforTech stock, 20 ga., **(2007) $1,735.00**
Price: Max-4 HD ComforTech stock (2007) **$1,870.00**

BENELLI SUPERSPORT & SPORT II SHOTGUNS

Gauge: 20; 12; 3" chamber. **Barrel:** 28" and 30", ported, 10mm sporting rib. **Weight:** 7.2 to 7.3 lbs. **Length:** 49.6 to 51.6". **Stock:** Carbon fiber, ComforTech (Supersport) or walnut (Sport II). **Sights:** Red bar front, metal midbead. Sport II is similar to the Legacy model except has nonengraved dual tone blue/silver receiver, ported wide-rib barrel, adjustable buttstock, and functions with all loads. Walnut stock with satin finish. Introduced 1997. **Features:** Designed for high-volume sporting clays. Inertia-driven action, Extended CrioChokes, 4+1 capacity. Ported. Imported from Italy by Benelli USA.

Price: Carbon fiber ComforTech stock **$1,800.00**
Price: Carbon fiber ComforTech stock, 20 ga. (2007) **$1,800.00**
Price: Sport II 20 ga. (2007) **$1,580.00**

BERETTA 3901 SHOTGUNS

Gauge: 12, 20 gauge; 3" chamber, semi-auto. **Barrel:** 26", 28". **Weight:** 6.55 lbs. (20 ga.), 7.2 lbs. (12 ga.). **Length:** NA. **Stock:** Wood, X-tra wood (special process wood enhancement), and polymer. **Features:** Based on A390 shotgun introduced in 1996. Mobilchokes, removable trigger group. 3901 Target RL uses gas operating system; Sporting style flat rib with steel front bead and mid-bead, walnut stock and forearm, satin matte finish, adjustable LOP from 12P13", adjustable for cast on/off, Beretta's Memory System II to adjust the parallel comb. Weighs 7.2 lbs. 3901 Citizen has polymer stock. 3901 Statesman has basic wood and checkering treatment. 3901 Ambassador has X-tra wood stock and fore end; high-polished receiver with engraving, Gel-Tek recoil pad, optional TruGlo fiber-optic front sight. 3901 Rifled Slug Shotgun has black high-impact synthetic stock and fore end, 24" barrel,1:28 twist, Picatinny cantilever rail. Introduced 2006. Made in U.S. by Beretta USA.

Price: 3901 Target RL. **$900.00**
Price: 3901 Citizen, synthetic or wood, from **$750.00**
Price: 3901 Statesman **$900.00**
Price: 3901 Rifled Slug Shotgun. **$800.00**

BERETTA UGB25 XCEL

Gauge: 12, 2-3/4" chambers. **Barrel:** 28", 30", 32"; competition-style interchangeable vent rib; Optima choke tubes. **Weight:** 7.7-9 lbs. **Stock:** High-grade walnut with oil finish; hand-checkered grip and forend, adjustable. **Features:** Break-open semiautomatic. High-resistance fiberglass-reinforced technopolymer trigger plate, self-lubricating firing mechanism. Rounded alloy receiver, polished sides, external cartridge carrier and feeding port, bottom eject. two technopolymer recoil dampers on breech bolt, double recoil dampers located in the receiver, Beretta Recoil Reduction System, recoil-absorbing Beretta Gel Tek recoil pad. Optima-Bore barrel with a lengthened forcing cone, Optimachoke and Extended Optimachoke tubes. Steel-shot capable, interchangeable aluminum alloy top rib. Introduced 2006. Imported from Italy by Beretta USA.

Price: **$3,875.00**

Beretta AL391 Urika Sporting

Beretta AL391 Urika Gold Sporting

Beretta A391 Xtrema2 3.5

BERETTA AL391 TEKNYS SHOTGUNS
Gauge: 12, 20 gauge; 3" chamber, semi-auto. **Barrel:** 26", 28". **Weight:** 5.9 lbs. (20 ga.), 7.3 lbs. (12 ga.). **Length:** NA. **Stock:** X-tra wood (special process wood enhancement). **Features:** Flat 1/4 rib, TruGlo Tru-Bead sight, recoil reducer, stock spacers, overbored bbls., flush choke tubes. Comes with fitted, lined case.
Price: From **$1,425.00**

BERETTA AL391 URIKA AND URIKA 2 AUTO SHOTGUNS
Gauge: 12, 20 gauge; 3" chamber. **Barrel:** 22", 24", 26", 28", 30"; five Mobilchoke choke tubes. **Weight:** 5.95 to 7.28 lbs. **Length:** Varies by model. **Stock:** Walnut, black or camo synthetic; shims, spacers and interchangeable recoil pads allow custom fit. **Features:** Self-compensating gas op-eration handles full range of loads; recoil re-ducer in receiver; enlarged trigger guard; re-duced-weight receiver, barrel and forend; hard-chromed bore. Introduced 2000. AL391 Urika 2 (2007) has self-cleaning action, X-Tra Grain stock finish. AL391 Urika 2 Gold has higher-grade select oil-finished wood stock, upgraded engrav-ing (gold-filled gamebirds on field models, gold-filled laurel leaf on competition version). Kick-Off recoil reduction system available in Syn-thetic, Realtree Advantage Max-4 and AP models. Imported from Italy by Beretta USA.
Price: Urika, from **$998.00**
Price: Urika 2 X-tra Grain, from **$1,300.00**
Price: Urika 2 Gold, from **$1,450.00**
Price: Urika 2 Synthetic **$875.00**
Price: Urika 2 Realtree AP Kick-Off, ... **$1,350.00**

BERETTA A391 XTREMA2 3.5 AUTO SHOTGUNS
Gauge: 12 ga. 3.5" chamber. **Barrel:** 24", 26", 28". **Weight:** 7.8 lbs. **Stock:** Synthetic. **Features:** Semi-auto goes with two-lug rotating bolt and self-compensating gas valve, extended tang, cross bolt safety, self-cleaning, with case.
Price: From **$1,100.00**

BREDA GRIZZLY
Gauge: 12, 3.5" chamber. **Barrel:** 28". **Weight:** 7.2 lbs. **Stock:** Black synthetic or Advantage Timber with matching metal parts. **Features:** Chokes tubes are Mod., IC, Full; inertia-type action, four-round magazine. Imported from Italy by Legacy Sports International.
Price: Blued/black (2008) **$1,826.00**
Price: Advantage Timber Camo (2008) **$2,121.00**

BREDA XANTHOS
Gauge: 12, 3" chamber. **Barrel:** 28". **Weight:** 6.5 lbs. **Stock:** High grade walnut. **Features:** Chokes tubes are Mod., IC, Full; inertia-type action, four-round magazine, spark engraving with hand-engraved details and hand-gilding figures on receiver. Blued, Grey or Chrome finishes. Imported from Italy by Legacy Sports International.
Price: Blued (2007) **$2,309.00**
Price: Grey (2007) **$2,451.00**
Price: Chrome (2007) **$3,406.00**

BREDA ECHO
Gauge: 12, 20. 3" chamber. **Barrel:** 28". **Weight:** 6.0-6.5 lbs. **Stock:** Walnut. **Features:** Chokes tubes are Mod., IC, Full; inertia-type action, four-round magazine, blue, grey or nickel finishes, modern engraving, fully checkered pistol grip. Imported from Italy by Legacy Sports International.
Price: Blued, 12 ga. (2008) **$1,897.00**
Price: Grey, 12 ga. (2008) **$1,969.00**
Price: Nickel, 12 ga. (2008) **$2,214.00**
Price: Nickel, 20 ga. (2008) **$2,214.00**

BREDA ALTAIR
Gauge: 12, 20. 3" chamber. **Barrel:** 28". **Weight:** 5.7-6.1 lbs. **Stock:** Oil-rubbed walnut. **Features:** Chokes tubes are Mod., IC, Full; gas-actuated action, four-round magazine, blued finish, lightweight frame. Imported from Italy by Legacy Sports International.
Price: Blued, 12 ga. (2008) **$1,320.00**
Price: Grey, 20 ga. (2008) **$1,320.00**

BROWNING GOLD AUTO SHOTGUNS
Gauge: 12, 3" or 3-1/2" chamber; 20, 3" chamber. **Barrel:** 12 ga.-26", 28", 30", Invector Plus choke tubes; 20 ga.-26", 30", Invector choke tubes. **Weight:** 7 lbs., 9 oz. (12 ga.), 6 lbs., 12 oz. (20 ga.). **Length:** 46.25" overall (20 ga., 26" barrel). **Stock:** 14"x1.5"x2-1/3"; select walnut with gloss finish; palm swell grip. **Features:** Self-regulating, self-cleaning gas system shoots all loads; lightweight receiver with special non-glare deep black finish; large reversible safety button; large rounded trigger guard, gold trigger. The 20 gauge has slightly smaller dimensions; 12 gauge have back-bored barrels, Invector Plus tube system. Introduced 1994. Gold Evolve shotguns have new rib design, HiViz sights. Imported by Browning.
Price: Gold Evolve Sporting, 12 ga., 2-3/4" chamber **$1,326.00**
Price: Gold Superlite Hunter, 12 or 20 ga., 26" or 28" barrel, 6.6 lbs. **$1,161.00**

BROWNING GOLD NWTF TURKEY SERIES AND MOSSY OAK SHOTGUNS
Gauge: 12, 10, 3-1/2" chamber. Similar to the Gold Hunter except has specialized camouflage patterns, including National Wild Turkey Federation design. Includes extra-full choke tube and HiViz fiber-optic sights on some models and Dura-Touch coating. Camouflage patterns include Mossy Oak New Break-Up (NBU) or Mossy Oak New Shadow Grass (NSG). NWTF models include NWTF logo on stock. Introduced 2001. From Browning.
Price: NWFT Gold Ultimate Turkey, 24" barrel, 12 ga. 3-1/2" chamber **$1,513.00**
Price: NWFT Gold 10 Gauge, 24" barrel, 3-1/2" chamber . . **$1,506.00**

Browning NWTF Mossy Oak® Break-Up™

Browning Gold Light 10 gauge

Charles Daly Field Pump

Charles Daly Maxi-Mag Field Hunter VR-MC

Charles Daly Superior II

Escort Model AS

BROWNING GOLD GOLDEN CLAYS AUTO SHOTGUNS

Gauge: 12, 2-3/4" chamber. **Barrel:** 28", 30", Invector Plus choke tubes. **Weight:** about 7.75 lbs. **Length:** From 47.75 to 50.5". **Stock:** Select walnut with gloss finish; palm swell grip, shim adjustable. **Features:** Ported barrels, "Golden Clays" models feature gold inlays and engraving. Otherwise similar to Gold series guns. Imported by Browning.

Price: Gold "Golden Clays" Sporting Clays, intr. 2005 . . . . . **$1,941.00**
Price: Gold Sporting Clays **$1,184.00**
Price: Gold Ladies Sporting Clays **$1,184.00**

Browning Gold Light 10 Gauge Auto Shotgun

Similar to the Gold Hunter except has an alloy receiver that is 1 lb. lighter than standard model. Offered in 26" or 28" bbls. With Mossy Oak Break-Up or Shadow Grass coverage; 5-shot magazine. Weighs 9 lbs., 10 oz. (28" bbl.). Introduced 2001. Imported by Browning.

Price: Camo model only **$1,390.00**

BROWNING SILVER AUTO SHOTGUNS

Gauge: 12, 3" or 3-1/2" chamber; 20, 3" chamber. **Barrel:** 12 ga.-26", 28", 30", Invector Plus choke tubes. **Weight:** 7 lbs., 9 oz. (12 ga.), 6 lbs., 7 oz. (20 ga.). **Stock:** Satin finish walnut. **Features:** Active Valve gas system, semi-humpback receiver. Invector Plus tube system, three choke tubes. Imported by Browning.

Price: Silver Hunter, 12 ga., 3.5" chamber **$1,128.00**
Price: Silver Hunter, 20 ga., 3" chamber, intr. 2008 . . . . **$979.00**
Price: Silver Micro, 20 ga., 3" chamber, intr. 2008 . . . . **$979.00**
Price: Silver Sporting Micro, 12 ga., 2-3/4" chamber, intr. 2008. . . . . **$1,132.00**
Price: Silver Rifled Deer, Mossy Oak New Break-Up, 12 ga., 3" chamber, intr. 2008 . . . . **$1,199.00**
Price: Silver Rifled Deer Stalker, 12 ga., 3" chamber, intr. 2008. . . . . **$1,199.00**

CHARLES DALY FIELD SEMI-AUTO SHOTGUNS

Gauge: 12, 20, 28. **Barrel:** 22", 24", 26", 28" or 30". **Stock:** Synthetic black, Realtree Hardwoods or Advantage Timber. **Features:** Interchangeable barrels handle all loads including steel shot. Slug model has adjustable sights. Maxi-Mag is 3.5" chamber.

Price: Field Hunter, from. **$419.00**

CHARLES DALY SUPERIOR II SEMI-AUTO SHOTGUNS

Gauge: 12, 20, 28. **Barrel:** 26", 28" or 30". **Stock:** Select Turkish walnut. **Features:** Factory ported interchangeable barrels; wide vent rib on Trap and Sport models; fluorescent red sights.

Price: Superior II Hunter, from **$569.00**
Price: Superior II Sport **$609.00**
Price: Superior II Trap. **$629.00**

ESCORT SEMI-AUTO SHOTGUNS

Gauge: 12, 20; 3" or 3.5" chambers. **Barrel:** 22" (Youth), 26" and 28". **Weight:** 6.7-7.8 lbs. **Stock:** Polymer in black, Shadow Grass® or Obsession® camo finish, Turkish walnut, select walnut. **Sights:** Optional HiViz Spark front. **Features:** Black-chrome or dipped-camo metal parts, top of receiver dovetailed for sight mounts, gold plated trigger, trigger guard safety, magazine cut-off. Three choke tubes (IC, M, F) except the Waterfowl/Turkey Combo, which adds a .665 turkey choke to the standard three. Waterfowl/Turkey combo is two-barrel set, 24"/26" and 26"/28". Several models have Trio recoil pad. Models are: AS, AS Select, AS Youth, AS Youth Select, PS, PS Spark and Waterfowl/Turkey. Introduced 2002. Camo introduced 2003. Youth, Slug and Obsession camo introduced 2005. Imported from Turkey by Legacy Sports International.

Price: . . . . **$499.00 to $650.00**

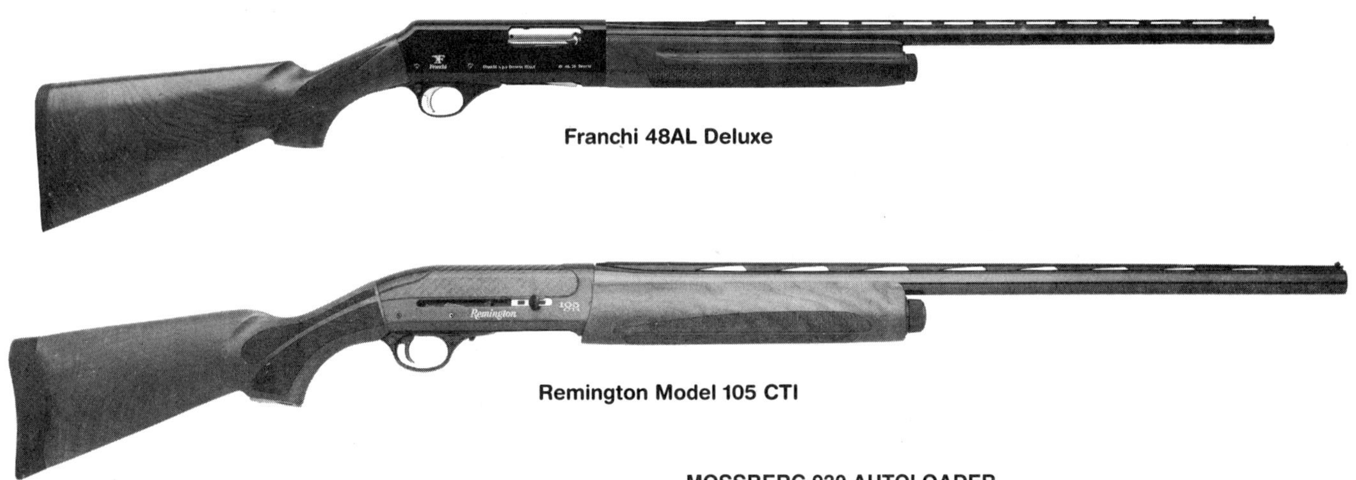

Franchi 48AL Deluxe

Remington Model 105 CTI

FRANCHI INERTIA I-12 SHOTGUN

Gauge: 12, 3" chamber. **Barrel:** 24", 26", 28" (Cyl., IC, Mod., IM, F choke tubes). **Weight:** 7.5 to 7.7. lbs. **Length:** 45" to 49". **Stock:** 14-3.8" LOP, satin walnut with checkered grip and forend, synthetic, Advantage Timber HD or Max-4 camo patterns. **Features:** Inertia-Driven action. AA walnut stock. Red bar front sight, metal mid sight. Imported from Italy by Benelli USA.

Price: Synthetic. **$799.00**
Price: Camo **$889.00**
Price: Satin walnut **$919.00**

FRANCHI MODEL 720 SHOTGUNS

Gauge: 20, 3" chamber. **Barrel:** 24", 26", 28" w/(IC, Mod., F choke tubes). **Weight:** 5.9 to 6.1 lbs. **Length:** 43.25" to 49". **Stock:** WeatherCoat finish walnut, Max-4 and Timber HD camo. **Sights:** Front bead. **Features:** Made in Italy and imported by Benelli USA.

Price: **$949.00**
Price: Walnut, 12.5" LOP, 43.25" OAL **$859.00**

FRANCHI 48AL FIELD AND DELUXE SHOTGUNS

Gauge: 20 or 28, 2-3/4" chamber. **Barrel:** 24", 26", 28" (Full, Cyl., Mod., choke tubes). **Weight:** 5.4 to 5.7 lbs. **Length:** 42.25" to 48". **Stock:** Walnut with checkered grip and forend. **Features:** Long recoil-operated action. Chrome-lined bore; cross-bolt safety. Imported from Italy by Benelli USA.

Price: AL Field 20 ga. **$819.00**
Price: AL Deluxe 20 ga., A grade walnut **$1,029.00**
Price: AL Field 28 ga. **$939.00**

FRANCHI 720 COMPETITION SHOTGUN

Gauge: 20; 4+1. **Barrel:** 28" ported; tapered target rib and bead front sight. **Weight:** 6.2 lbs. **Stock:** Walnut with WeatherCoat. **Features:** Gas-operated, satin nickel receiver.

Price: **$1,069.00**

HARRINGTON & RICHARDSON EXCELL AUTO 5 SHOTGUNS

Gauge: 12, 3" chamber. **Barrel:** 22", 24", 28", four screw-in choke tubes (IC, M, IM, F). **Weight:** About 7 lbs. **Length:** 42.5" to 48.5" overall, depending on barrel length. **Stock:** American walnut with satin finish; cut checkering; ventilated buttpad. Synthetic stock or camo-finish. **Sights:** Metal bead front or fiber-optic front and rear. **Features:** Ventilated rib on all models except slug gun. Imported by H&R 1871, Inc.

Price: Synthetic, black, 28" barrel, 48.5" OAL **$415.00**
Price: Walnut, checkered grip/forend, 28" barrel, 48.5" OAL . . **$461.00**
Price: Waterfowl, camo finish **$521.00**
Price: Turkey, camo finish, 22" barrel, fiber optic sights **$521.00**
Price: Combo, synthetic black stock, with slug barrel. **$583.00**

LANBER SEMI-AUTOMATIC SHOTGUNS

Gauge: 12, 3". **Barrel:** 26", 28", chrome-moly alloy steel, welded, ventilated top and side ribs. **Weight:** 6.8 lbs. **Length:** 48-3/8". **Stock:** Walnut, oiled finish, laser checkering, rubber buttplate. **Sights:** Fiber-optic front. **Features:** Extractors or automatic ejectors, control and unblocking button. Rated for steel shot. Lanber Polichokes. Imported by Lanber USA.

Price: Model 2533. . . . . **$600.00**

MOSSBERG 930 AUTOLOADER

Gauge: 12, 3" chamber, 4-shot magazine. **Barrel:** 24", 26", 28", over-bored to 10-gauge bore dimensions; factory ported, Accu-Choke tubes. **Weight:** 7.5 lbs. **Length:** 44.5" overall (28" barrel). **Stock:** Walnut or synthetic. Adjustable stock drop and cast spacer system. **Sights:** "Turkey Taker" fiber-optic, adjustable windage and elevation. Front bead fiber-optic front on waterfowl models. **Features:** Self-regulating gas system, dual gas-vent system and piston, EZ-Empty magazine button, cocking indicator. Interchangeable Accu-Choke tube set (IC, Mod, Full) for waterfowl and field models. XX-Full turkey Accu-Choke tube included with turkey models. Ambidextrous thumb-operated safety, Uni-line stock and receiver. Receiver drilled and tapped for scope base attachment, free gun lock. Introduced 2008. From O.F. Mossberg & Sons, Inc.

Price: Turkey, from **$518.00**
Price: Waterfowl, from **$518.00**
Price: Combo, from. **$575.00**
Price: Field, from. **$540.00**
Price: Slugster, from **$518.00**

REMINGTON MODEL 105 CTI SHOTGUN

Gauge: 12, 3" chamber, 4-shot magazine. **Barrel:** 26", 28" (IC, Mod., Full ProBore chokes). **Weight:** 7 lbs. **Length:** 46.25" overall (26" barrel). **Stock:** Walnut with satin finish. Checkered grip and forend. **Sights:** Front bead. **Features:** Aircraft-grade titanium receiver body, skeletonized receiver with carbon fiber shell. Bottom feed and eject, target grade trigger, R3 recoil pad, FAA-approved lockable hard case, .735" overbored barrel with lengthened forcing cones. TriNyte coating; carbon/aramid barrel rib. Introduced 2006.

Price: **$1,548.00**

REMINGTON MODEL SPR453 SHOTGUN

Gauge: 12; 3.5" chamber, 4+1 capacity. **Barrel:** 24", 26", 28" vent rib. **Weight:** 8 to 8.25 lbs. **Stock:** Black synthetic. **Features:** Matte finish, dual extractors, four extended screw-in SPR choke tubes (improved cylinder, modified, full and super-full turkey. Introduced 2006. From Remington Arms Co.

Price: Black synthetic **$497.00**

REMINGTON MODEL 11-87 SPORTSMAN SHOTGUNS

Gauge: 12, 20, 3" chamber. **Barrel:** 26", 28", RemChoke tubes. Standard contour, vent rib. **Weight:** About 7.75 to 8.25 lbs. **Length:** 46" to 48" overall. **Stock:** Black synthetic or Mossy Oak Break Up Mossy Oak Duck Blind, and Realtree Hardwoods HD and AP Green HD camo finishes. **Sights:** Single bead front. **Features:** Matte-black metal finish, magazine cap swivel studs. Sportsman Deer gun has 21-inch fully rifled barrel, cantilever scope mount.

Price: Sportsman Camo (2007), 12 or 20 ga.. . . . . **$867.00**
Price: Sportsman black synthetic, 12 or 20 ga. **$757.00**
Price: Sportsman Deer FR Cantilever, 12 or 20 ga.. . . . . **$867.00**
Price: Sportsman FR Cantilever, ShurShot stock, 12 ga.. . . . . **$994.00**
Price: Sportsman Youth Synthetic 20 ga., (2008). **$757.00**
Price: Sportsman Youth Camo 20 ga., (2008) **$818.00**
Price: Sportsman Super Magnum 12 ga., 28" barrel (2008). . . **$846.00**
Price: Sportsman Super Magnum Shurshot Turkey 12 ga., (2008) **$972.00**
Price: Sportsman Super Magnum Waterfowl 12 ga., (2008) . . **$972.00**
Price: Sportsman Super Magnum Waterfowl 12 ga., (2008) . . **$972.00**

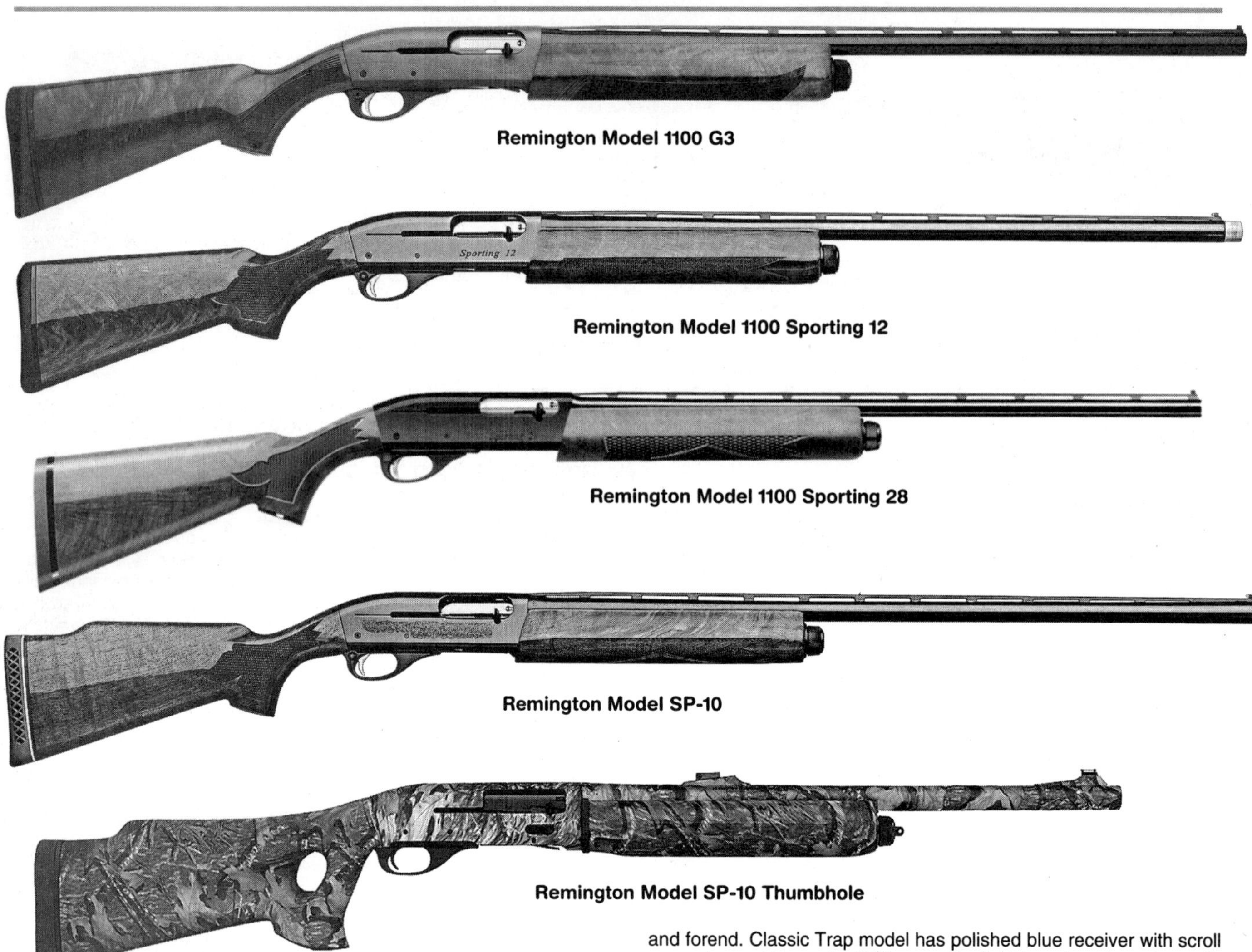

Remington Model 1100 G3

Remington Model 1100 Sporting 12

Remington Model 1100 Sporting 28

Remington Model SP-10

Remington Model SP-10 Thumbhole

REMINGTON MODEL 1100 G3 SHOTGUN

Gauge: 20, 12; 3" chamber. **Barrel:** 26", 28". **Weight:** 6.75-7.6 lbs. **Stock:** Realwood semi-Fancy carbon fiber laminate stock, high gloss finish, machine cut checkering. **Features:** Gas operating system, pressure compensated barrel, solid carbon-steel engraved receiver, titanium coating. Action bars, trigger and extended carrier release, action bar sleeve, action spring, locking block, hammer, sear and magazine tube have nickel-plated, Teflon coating. R3 recoil pad, overbored (.735" dia.) vent rib barrels, ProBore choke tubes. 20 gauge have Rem Chokes. Comes with lockable hard case. Introduced 2006.

Price: G3, 12 or 20 ga. **$1,239.00**
Price: G3 Left Hand, 12 ga. 28" barrel (2008) **$1,329.00**

REMINGTON MODEL 1100 TARGET SHOTGUNS

Gauge: .410 bore, 28, 20, 12. **Barrel:** 26", 27", 28", 30" light target contoured vent rib barrel with twin bead target sights. **Stock:** Semi-fancy American walnut stock and forend, cut checkering, high gloss finish. **Features:** Gold-plated trigger. Four extended choke tubes: Skeet, Improved Cylinder, Light Modified and Modified. 1100 Tournament Skeet (20 and 12 gauge) receiver is roll-marked with "Tournament Skeet." 26" light contour, vent rib barrel has twin bead sights, Extended Target Choke Tubes (Skeet and Improved Cylinder). Model 1100 Premier Sporting (2008) has polished nickel receiver, gold accents, light target contoured vent rib Rem Choke barrels. Wood is semi-fancy American walnut stock and forend, high-gloss finish, cut checkering, sporting clays-style recoil pad. Gold trigger, available in 12, 20, 28 and .410 bore options, Briley extended choke tubes, Premier Sporting hard case. Competition model (12 gauge) has overbored (0.735" bore diameter) 30" barrel. **Weight:** 8 lbs. 10mm target-style rib with twin beads. Extended ProBore choke tubes in Skeet, Improved Cylinder, Light-Modified, Modified and Full. Semi-fancy American walnut stock and forend. Classic Trap model has polished blue receiver with scroll engraving, gold accents, 30" low-profile, light-target contoured vent rib barrel with standard .727" dimensions. Comes with specialized Rem Choke trap tubes: Singles (.027"), Mid Handicap (.034"), and Long Handicap (.041"). Monte Carlo stock of semi-fancy American walnut, deep-cut checkering, high-gloss finish.

Price: Sporting 12, 28" barrel, 8 lbs. **$1,084.00**
Price: Sporting 20, 28" barrel, 7 lbs. **$1,084.00**
Price: Sporting 28, 27" barrel, 6.75 lbs. **$1,129.00**
Price: Sporting 410, 27" barrel, 6.75 lbs. **$1,129.00**
Price: Tournament Skeet, 12 or 20 ga.. . . . . **$1,084.00**
Price: Classic Trap, 12 ga. 30" barrel, ... **$1,084.00**
Price: Premier Sporting (2008), from.. . . . . **$1,129.00**
Price: Competition, standard stock, 12 ga. 30" barrel **$1,529.00**
Price: Competition, adjustable comb **$1,692.00**

REMINGTON MODEL SP-10 MAGNUM SHOTGUN

Gauge: 10, 3-1/2" chamber, 2-shot magazine. **Barrel:** 23", 26", 30" (full and mod. RemChokes). **Weight:** 10.75 to 11 lbs. **Length:** 47.5" overall (26" barrel). **Stock:** Walnut with satin finish (30" barrel) or camo synthetic (26" barrel). Checkered grip and forend. **Sights:** Twin bead. **Features:** Stainless steel gas system with moving cylinder; 3/8" vent rib. Receiver and barrel have matte finish. Brown recoil pad. Comes with padded Cordura nylon sling. Introduced 1989. SP-10 Magnum Camo has buttstock, forend, receiver, barrel and magazine cap covered with Mossy Oak Duck Blind Obsession camo finish; bolt body and trigger guard have matte black finish. RemChoke tube, 26" vent rib barrel with mid-rib bead and Bradley-style front sight, swivel studs and quick-detachable swivels, non-slip Cordura carrying sling. Introduced 1993.

Price: SP-10 Magnum, satin finish walnut stock. **$1,727.00**
Price: SP-10 Magnum Thumbhole Camo,
Mossy Oak Obsession (2007) **$2,001.00**
Price: SP-10 Magnum Full Camo **$1,891.00**
Price: SP-10 Magnum Waterfowl **$1,900.00**

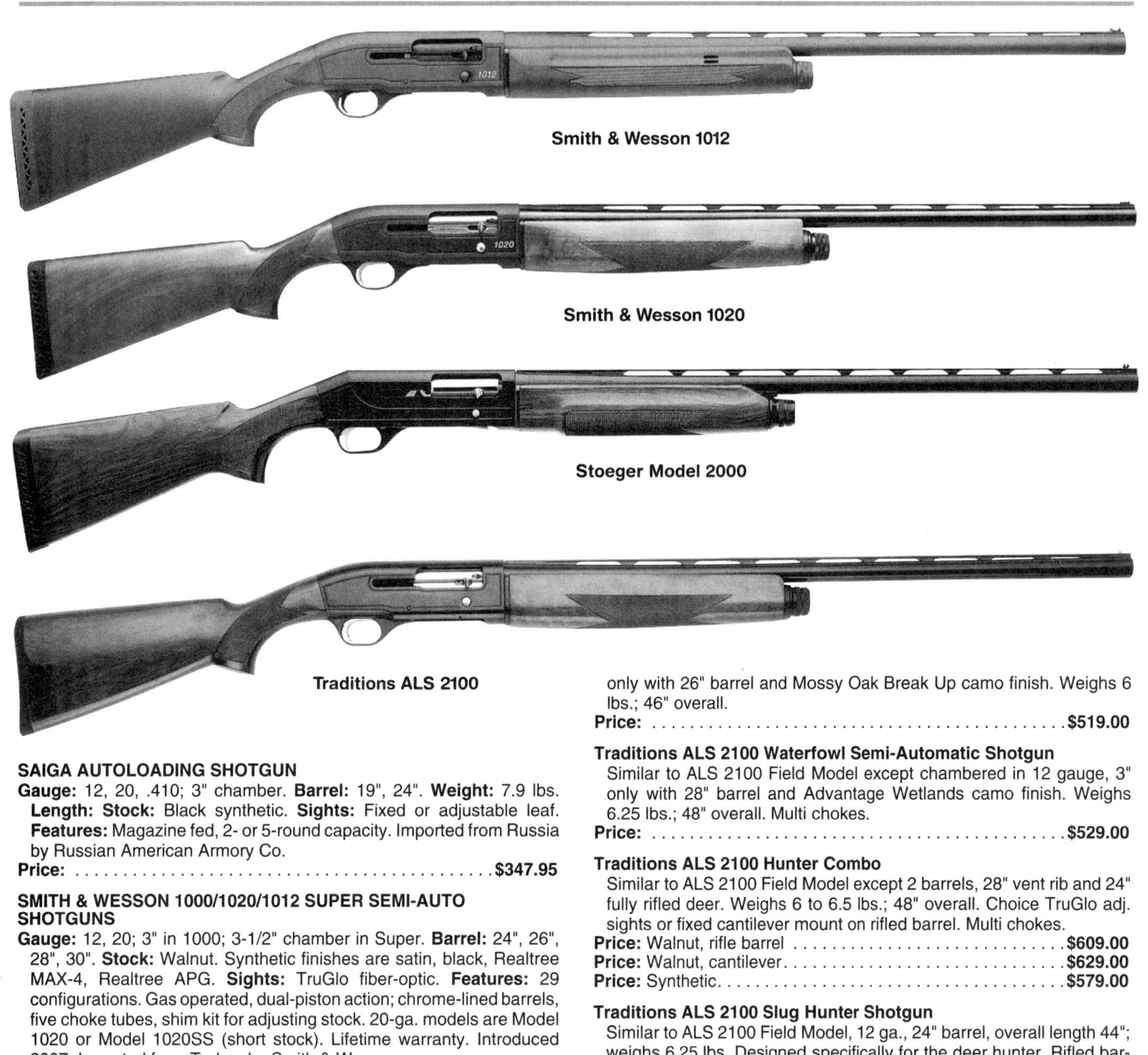

Smith & Wesson 1012

Smith & Wesson 1020

Stoeger Model 2000

Traditions ALS 2100

SAIGA AUTOLOADING SHOTGUN

Gauge: 12, 20, .410; 3" chamber. **Barrel:** 19", 24". **Weight:** 7.9 lbs. **Length: Stock:** Black synthetic. **Sights:** Fixed or adjustable leaf. **Features:** Magazine fed, 2- or 5-round capacity. Imported from Russia by Russian American Armory Co.

Price: **$347.95**

SMITH & WESSON 1000/1020/1012 SUPER SEMI-AUTO SHOTGUNS

Gauge: 12, 20; 3" in 1000; 3-1/2" chamber in Super. **Barrel:** 24", 26", 28", 30". **Stock:** Walnut. Synthetic finishes are satin, black, Realtree MAX-4, Realtree APG. **Sights:** TruGlo fiber-optic. **Features:** 29 configurations. Gas operated, dual-piston action; chrome-lined barrels, five choke tubes, shim kit for adjusting stock. 20-ga. models are Model 1020 or Model 1020SS (short stock). Lifetime warranty. Introduced 2007. Imported from Turkey by Smith & Wesson.

Price: From **$623.00**

STOEGER MODEL 2000 SHOTGUNS

Gauge: 12, 3" chamber, set of five choke tubes (C, IC, M, F, XFT). **Barrel:** 24", 26", 28", 30". **Stock:** Walnut, synthetic, Timber HD, Max-4. **Sights:** Red bar front. **Features:** Inertia-recoil. Minimum recommended load: 3 dram, 1-1/8 oz. Imported by Benelli USA.

Price: Walnut **$499.00**
Price: Synthetic. **$479.00**
Price: Max-4 . . . . **$549.00**
Price: Black synthetic pistol grip (2007) **$479.00**
Price: APG HD camo pistol grip (2007), 18.5" barrel **$535.00**

TRADITIONS ALS 2100 SERIES SEMI-AUTOMATIC SHOTGUNS

Gauge: 12, 3" chamber; 20, 3" chamber. **Barrel:** 24", 26", 28" (Imp. Cyl., Mod. and Full choke tubes). **Weight:** 5 lbs., 10 oz. to 6 lbs., 5 oz. **Length:** 44" to 48" overall. **Stock:** Walnut or black composite. **Features:** Gas-operated; vent rib barrel with Beretta-style threaded muzzle. Introduced 2001 by Traditions.

Price: Field Model (12 or 20 ga., 26" or 28" bbl., walnut stock) **$479.00**
Price: Youth Model (12 or 20 ga., 24" bbl., walnut stock). **$479.00**
Price: (12 or 20 ga., 26" or 28" barrel, composite stock) **$459.00**

Traditions ALS 2100 Turkey Semi-Automatic Shotgun

Similar to ALS 2100 Field Model except chambered in 12 gauge, 3" only with 26" barrel and Mossy Oak Break Up camo finish. Weighs 6 lbs.; 46" overall.

Price: **$519.00**

Traditions ALS 2100 Waterfowl Semi-Automatic Shotgun

Similar to ALS 2100 Field Model except chambered in 12 gauge, 3" only with 28" barrel and Advantage Wetlands camo finish. Weighs 6.25 lbs.; 48" overall. Multi chokes.

Price: **$529.00**

Traditions ALS 2100 Hunter Combo

Similar to ALS 2100 Field Model except 2 barrels, 28" vent rib and 24" fully rifled deer. Weighs 6 to 6.5 lbs.; 48" overall. Choice TruGlo adj. sights or fixed cantilever mount on rifled barrel. Multi chokes.

Price: Walnut, rifle barrel **$609.00**
Price: Walnut, cantilever. **$629.00**
Price: Synthetic. **$579.00**

Traditions ALS 2100 Slug Hunter Shotgun

Similar to ALS 2100 Field Model, 12 ga., 24" barrel, overall length 44"; weighs 6.25 lbs. Designed specifically for the deer hunter. Rifled barrel has 1 in 36" twist. Fully adjustable fiber-optic sights.

Price: Walnut, rifle barrel **$529.00**
Price: Synthetic, rifle barrel. **$499.00**
Price: Walnut, cantilever. **$549.00**
Price: Synthetic, cantilever **$529.00**

Traditions ALS 2100 Home Security Shotgun

Similar to ALS 2100 Field Model, 12 ga., 20" barrel, overall length 40", weighs 6 lbs. Can be reloaded with one hand while shouldered and ontarget. Swivel studs installed in stock.

Price: **$399.00**

TRISTAR VIPER SEMI-AUTOMATIC SHOTGUNS

Gauge: 12, 20; shoots 2-3/4" or 3" interchangeably. **Barrel:** 26", 28" barrels (carbon fiber only of-fered in 12-ga. 28" and 20-ga. 26"). **Stock:** Wood, black synthetic, Mossy Oak Duck Blind camouflage, faux carbon fiber finish (2008) with the new Comfort Touch technology. **Features:** Magazine cut-off, vent rib with matted sight plane, brass front bead (camo models have fiber-optic front sight), five round magazine-shot plug included, and 3 Beretta-style choke tubes (IC, M, F). Viper synthetic, Viper camo have swivel studs. Five-year warranty. Viper Youth models have shortened length of pull and 24" barrel. Imported by Tristar Sporting Arms Ltd.

Price: From **$389.00**
Price: Camo models (2008), from. **$499.00**

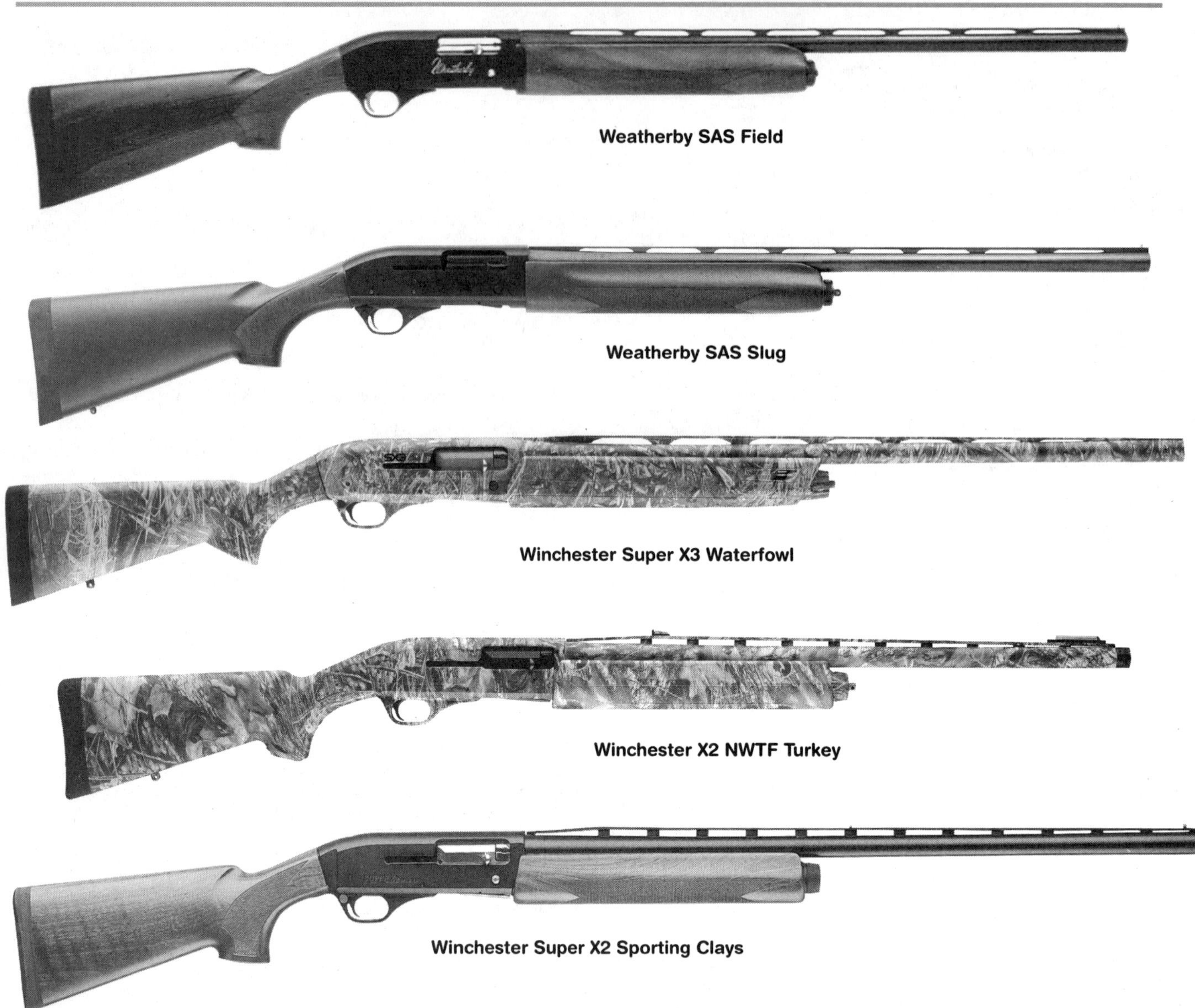

Weatherby SAS Field

Weatherby SAS Slug

Winchester Super X3 Waterfowl

Winchester X2 NWTF Turkey

Winchester Super X2 Sporting Clays

VERONA MODEL SX400 SEMI AUTO SHOTGUNS

Gauge: 12. **Barrel:** 26", 30". **Weight:** 6.5 lbs. **Stock:** Walnut, black composite. **Sights:** Red dot. **Features:** Aluminum receivers, gas-operated, 2-3/4" or 3" Magnum shells without adj. or Mod., 4 screw-in chokes and wrench included. Sling swivels, gold trigger. Blued barrel. Imported from Italy by B.C. Outdoors.

Price: 401S, 12 ga. **$398.40**
Price: 405SDS, 12 ga. **$610.00**
Price: 405L, 12 ga. **$331.20**

WEATHERBY SAS (SEMI-AUTOMATIC SHOTGUNS)

Gauge: 12 ga. **Barrel:** Vent ribbed, 24" to 30". **Weight:** 7 lbs. to 7.75 lbs. **Stock:** SAS field and sporting clays, walnut. SAS Shadow Grass, Break-Up, Synthetic, composite. **Sights:** SAS sporting clays, brass front and mid-point rear. SAS Shadow Grass and Break-Up, HiViz front and brass mid. Synthetic has brass front. **Features:** Easy to shoot, load, clean; lightweight, reduced recoil, IMC system includes 3 chrome-moly screw-in choke tubes. Slug gun has 22" rifled barrel with matte blue finish and cantilever base for scope mounting.Made in Italy. Imported by Weatherby.

Price: Field, Sporting Clays, Fall Flight (2007), Apparition Excel (2007), Synthetic, Slug Gun . . . . **$926.00 to $977.00**

WINCHESTER SUPER X3 SHOTGUNS

Gauge: 12, 3" and 3.5" chambers. **Barrel:** 26", 28", .742" back-bored; Invector Plus choke tubes. **Weight:** 7 to 7.25 lbs. **Stock:** Composite, 14.25"x1.75"x2". Mossy Oak New Break-Up camo with Dura-Touch Armor Coating. Pachmayr Decelerator buttpad with hard heel insert, customizable length of pull. **Features:** Alloy magazine tube, gunmetal grey Perma-Cote UT finish, self-adjusting Active Valve gas action, lightweight recoil spring system. Electroless nickel-plated bolt, three choke tubes, two length-of-pull stock spacers, drop and cast adjustment spacers, sling swivel studs. Introduced 2006. Made in Belgium, assembled in Portugal by U.S. Repeating Arms Co.

Price: From **$945.00**
Price: Cantilever Deer. **$995.00**
Price: Waterfowl w/Mossy Oak Brush camo, intr. 2007 . . . . **$1,216.00**
Price: Field model, walnut stock, intr. 2007 . . . . **$979.00**

WINCHESTER SUPER X2 AUTO SHOTGUNS

Gauge: 12, 3", 3-1/2" chamber. **Barrel:** Belgian, 24", 26", 28"; Invector Plus choke tubes. **Weight:** 7-1/4 to 7.5 lbs. **Stock:** 14.25"x1.75"x2". Walnut or black synthetic. **Features:** Gas-operated action shoots all loads without adjustment; vent rib barrels; 4-shot magazine. Introduced 1999. Assembled in Portugal by U.S. Repeating Arms Co.

Price: Universal Hunter T **$1,252.00**
Price: NWTF Turkey, 3-1/2", Mossy Oak Break-Up camo . . **$1,236.00**
Price: Universal Hunter Model **$1,252.00**

Winchester Super X2 Sporting Clays Auto Shotguns

Similar to the Super X2 except has two gas pistons (one for target loads, one for heavy 3" loads), adjustable comb system and high-post rib. Back-bored barrel with Invector Plus choke tubes. Offered in 28" and 30" barrels. Introduced 2001. From U.S. Repeating Arms Co.

Price: Super X2 sporting clays **$999.00**
Price: Signature red stock. **$1,015.00**
Price: Practical MK I, composite stock, TruGlo sights **$1,116.00**

Includes a wide variety of sporting guns and guns suitable for competitive shooting.

Benelli Nova Pump

Benelli Nova Pump Slug

Browning BPS Trap

Browning BPS 10 gauge Mossy Oak® Shadow Grass

Browning BPS 10 gauge

BENELLI SUPERNOVA PUMP SHOTGUNS

Gauge: 12; 3.5" chamber. **Barrel:** 24", 26", 28". **Length:** 45.5-49.5". **Stock:** Synthetic; Max-4 , Timber, APG HD (2007). **Sights:** Red bar front, metal midbead. **Features:** 2-3/4", 3" chamber (3-1/2" 12 ga. only). Montefeltro rotating bolt design with dual action bars, magazine cut-off, synthetic trigger assembly, adjustable combs, shim kit, choice of buttstocks. 4-shot magazine. Introduced 2006. Imported from Italy by Benelli USA.

Price: Synthetic ComforTech **$455.00**
Price: Camo ComforTech **$545.00**
Price: SteadyGrip . . . . **$465.00 to $560.00**
Price: Tactical, Ghost Ring sight. . . . . **$400.00 to $545.00**
Price: Field & Slug combo (2007) **$655.00**
Price: Rifled Slug ComforTech (2007) **$645.00**
Price: Tactical desert camo pistol grip, 18" barrel (2007) **$545.00**

BENELLI NOVA PUMP SHOTGUNS

Gauge: 12, 20. **Barrel:** 24", 26", 28". **Stock:** Black synthetic, Max-4, Timber and APG HD. **Sights:** Red bar. **Features:** 2-3/ 4", 3" chamber (3-1/2" 12 ga. only). Montefeltro rotating bolt design with dual action bars, magazine cut-off, synthetic trigger assembly, 4-shot magazine. Introduced 1999. Field & Slug Combo has 24" barrel and rifled bore; open rifle sights; synthetic stock; weighs 8.1 lbs. Imported from Italy by Benelli USA.

Price: Black synthetic stock **$360.00**
Price: Timber HD or Max-4 camo stock **$455.00**
Price: H20 model, black synthetic, matte nickel finish **$535.00**
Price: APG HD stock (2007) **$455.00**
Price: Tactical, 18.5" barrel, Ghost Ring sight **$375.00**
Price: Black synthetic stock, 20 ga. **$360.00**
Price: Black synthetic youth stock, 20 ga. **$375.00**
Price: Timber HD stock or APG HD stock (2007), 20 ga.. . . . . **$455.00**
Price: Field & Slug Combo, black synthetic, cantilever mount . **$560.00**

BROWNING BPS PUMP SHOTGUNS

Gauge: 10, 12, 3-1/2" chamber; 12, 16, or 20, 3" chamber (2-3/4" in target guns), 28, 2-3/4" cham-ber, 5-shot magazine, .410, 3" chamber. **Barrel:** 10 ga.-24" Buck Special, 28", 30", 32" Invector; 12, 20 ga.-22", 24", 26", 28", 30", 32" (Imp. Cyl., Mod. or Full), .410-26" barrel. (Imp. Cyl., Mod. and Full choke tubes.) Also available with Invector choke tubes, 12 or 20 ga.; Upland Special has 22" barrel with Invector tubes. BPS 3" and 3-1/2" have back-bored barrel. **Weight:** 7 lbs., 8 oz. (28" barrel). **Length:** 48.75" overall (28" barrel). **Stock:** 14.25"x1.5"x2.5". Select walnut, semi-beavertail forend, full pistol grip stock. **Features:** All 12 gauge 3" guns except Buck Special and game guns have back-bored barrels with Invector Plus choke tubes. Bottom feeding and ejection, receiver top safety, high post vent rib. Double action bars eliminate binding. Vent rib barrels only. All 12 and 20 gauge guns with 3" chamber available with fully engraved receiver flats at no extra cost. Each gauge has its own unique game scene. Introduced 1977. Stalker is same gun as the standard BPS except all exposed metal parts have a matte blued finish and the stock has a black finish with a black recoil pad. Available in 10 ga. (3-1/2") and 12 ga. with 3" or 3-1/2" chamber, 22", 28", 30" barrel with In-vector choke system. Introduced 1987. Rifled Deer Hunter is similar to the standard BPS except has newly designed receiver/ magazine tube/barrel mounting system to eliminate play, heavy 20.5" barrel with rifle-type sights with adjustable rear, solid receiver scope mount, "rifle" stock dimensions for scope or open sights, sling swivel studs. Gloss or matte finished wood with checkering, polished blue metal. Introduced 1992. Imported from Japan by Browning.

Price: Stalker (black syn. stock), 12 ga., from **$512.00**
Price: Rifled Deer Hunter (22" rifled bbl., cantilever mount), intr. 2007. . . . . **$655.00**
Price: Trap, intr. 2007 . . . . **$683.00**
Price: Hunter, 16 ga., intr. 2008 . . . . **$566.00**
Price: Upland Special, 16 ga., intr. 2008 . . . . **$566.00**

Browning BPS 10 Gauge Camo Pump Shotgun

Similar to the standard BPS except completely covered with Mossy Oak Shadow Grass camouflage. Available with 24", 26", 28" barrel. Introduced 1999. Imported by Browning.

Price: **$752.00**

Charles Daly Maxi-Mag Turkey

Escort AimGuard

Escort Field Hunter

Mossberg Model 835 Mossy Oak® Camo

Browning BPS NWTF Turkey Series Pump Shotgun
Similar to the BPS Standard except has full coverage Mossy Oak Break-Up camo finish on synthetic stock, forearm and exposed metal parts. Offered in 10 and 12 gauge, 3" or 3-1/2" chamber; 24" bbl. has extra-full choke tube and HiViz fiber-optic sights. Introduced 2001. From Browning.
Price: 10 ga., 3-1/2" chamber **$775.00**
Price: 12 ga., 3-1/2" chamber **$760.00**
Price: 12 ga., 3" chamber **$636.00**

Browning BPS Micro Pump Shotgun
Similar to the BPS Stalker except 20 ga. only, 22" Invector barrel, stock has pistol grip with recoil pad. Length of pull is 13.25"; weighs 6 lbs., 12 oz. Introduced 1986.
Price: **$529.00**

CHARLES DALY FIELD PUMP SHOTGUNS
Gauge: 12, 20. **Barrel:** Interchangeable 18.5", 24", 26", 28", 30" multi-choked. **Weight:** NA. **Stock:** Synthetic, various finishes, recoil pad. Receiver: Machined aluminum. **Features:** Field Tactical and Slug models come with adustable sights; Youth models may be upgraded to full size. Imported from Turkey by K.B.I., Inc.
Price: Field Tactical **$249.00**
Price: Field Hunter **$269.00**
Price: Field Hunter, Realtree Hardwood **$289.00**
Price: Field Hunter Advantage **$289.00**

CHARLES DALY MAXI-MAG PUMP SHOTGUNS
Gauge: 12 gauge, 3-1/2". **Barrel:** 24", 26", 28"; multi-choke system. **Weight:** NA. **Stock:** Synthetic black, Realtree Hardwoods, or Advantage Timber receiver, aluminum alloy. **Features:** Handles 2-3/4", 3" and 3-1/2" loads. Interchangeable ported barrels; Turkey package includes sling, HiViz sights, XX Full choke. Imported from Turkey by K.B.I., Inc.
Price: Field Hunter **$299.00**
Price: Field Hunter Advantage **$319.00**
Price: Field Hunter Hardwoods **$319.00**
Price: Field Hunter Turkey **$399.00**

DIAMOND 12 GA. PUMP SHOTGUNS
Gauge: 12, 2-3/4" and 3" chambers. **Barrel:** 18"-30". **Weight:** 7 lbs. **Stock:** Walnut, synthetic. **Features:** Aluminum one-piece receiver sculpted for lighter weight. Double locking on fixed bolt. Gold, Elite and Panther series with vented barrels and 3 chokes. All series slug guns available (Gold and Elite with sights). Imported from Istanbul by ADCO Sales.
Price: Gold, 28" vent rib w/3 chokes, walnut **$359.00**
Price: Gold, 28", synthetic **$329.00**
Price: Gold Slug, 24" w/sights, walnut or synthetic. **$329.00 to $359.00**
Price: Silver Mariner 18.5" Slug, synthetic **$399.00**
Price: Silver Mariner 22" vent rib w/3 chokes **$419.00**
Price: Elite, 22" slug w/sights; 24", 28" vent rib w/3 chokes, **walnut** .... **$329.00 to $349.00**
Price: Panther, 28", 30" vent rib w/3 chokes, synthetic **$279.00**
Price: Panther,18.5", 22" Slug, synthetic .... **$209.00 to $265.00**
Price: Imperial 12 ga., 28" vent rib w/3 chokes, 3.5" chamber, **walnut** .... **$$399.00**

E.M.F. OLD WEST PUMP (SLIDE ACTION) SHOTGUN
Gauge: 12. **Barrel:** 20". **Weight:** 7 lbs. **Length:** 39-1/2" overall. **Stock:** Smooth walnut with cushioned pad. **Sights:** Front bead. **Features:** Authentic reproduction of Winchester 1897 pump shotgun; blue receiver and barrel; standard modified choke. Introduced 2006. Imported from China for E.M.F. by TTN.
Price: **$474.90**

ESCORT PUMP SHOTGUNS
Gauge: 12, 20; 3" chamber. **Barrel:** 18" (AimGuard and MarineGuard), 22" (Youth Pump), 26", and 28" lengths. **Weight:** 6.7-7.0 lbs. **Stock:** Polymer in black, Shadow Grass® camo or Obsession® camo finish. Two adjusting spacers included. Youth model has Trio recoil pad. **Sights:** Bead or Spark front sights, depending on model. AimGuard and MarineGuard models have blade front sights. **Features:** Black-chrome or dipped camo metal parts, top of receiver dovetailed for sight mounts, gold plated trigger, trigger guard safety, magazine cut-off. Three choke tubes (IC, M, F) except AimGuard/MarineGuard which are cylinder bore. Models include: FH, FH Youth, AimGuard and Marine Guard. Introduced in 2003. Imported from Turkey by Legacy Sports International.
Price: .... **$269.00 to $399.00**

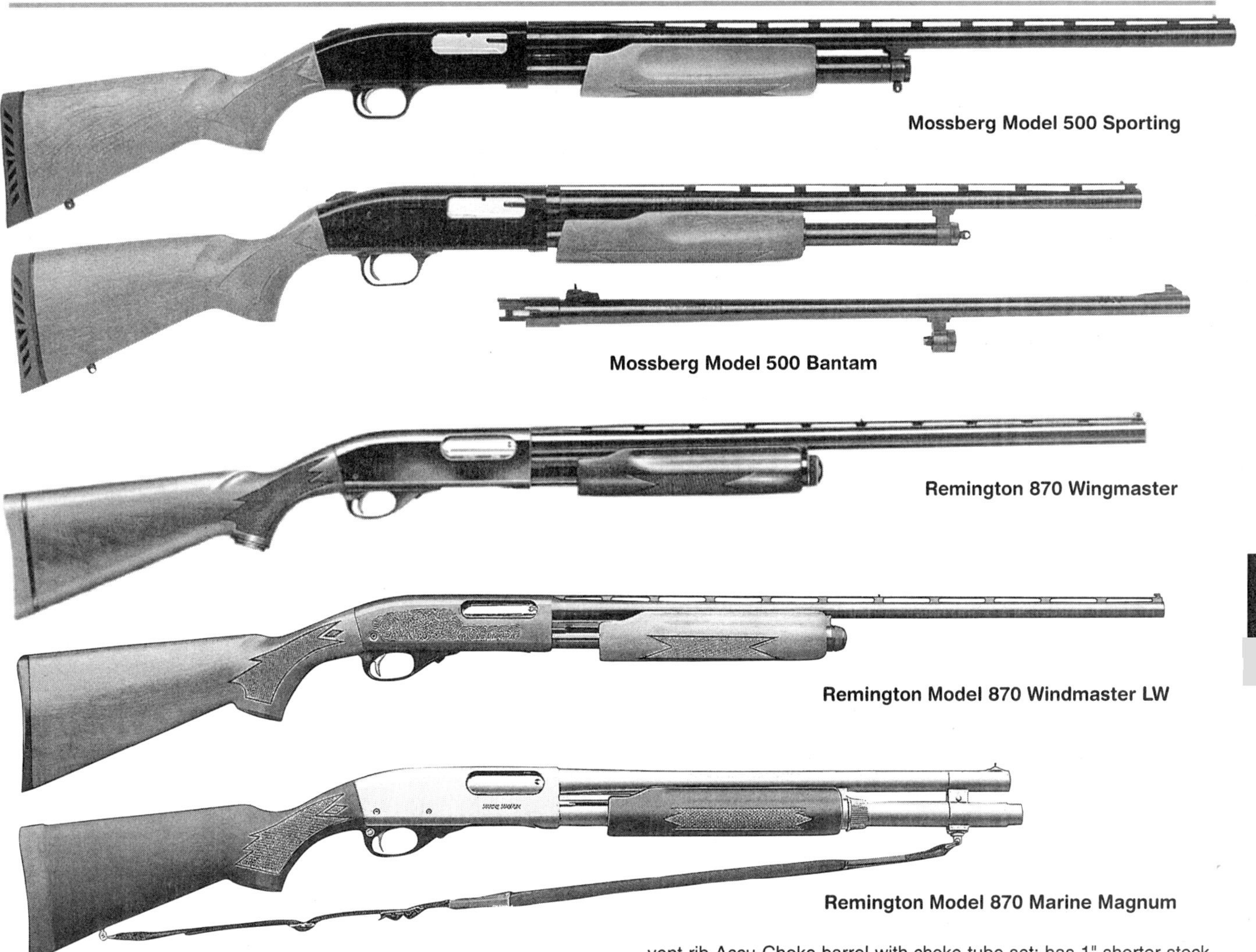

Mossberg Model 500 Sporting

Mossberg Model 500 Bantam

Remington 870 Wingmaster

Remington Model 870 Windmaster LW

Remington Model 870 Marine Magnum

MOSSBERG MODEL 835 ULTI-MAG PUMP SHOTGUNS

Gauge: 12, 3-1/2" chamber. **Barrel:** Ported 24" rifled bore, 24", 28", Accu-Mag choke tubes for steel or lead shot. **Weight:** 7.75 lbs. **Length:** 48.5" overall. **Stock:** 14"x1.5"x2.5". Dual Comb. Cut-checkered hardwood or camo synthetic; both have recoil pad. **Sights:** White bead front, brass mid-bead; fiber-optic rear. **Features:** Shoots 2-3/4", 3" or 3-1/2" shells. Back-bored and ported barrel to reduce recoil, improve patterns. Ambidextrous thumb safety, twin extractors, dual slide bars. Mossberg Cablelock included. Introduced 1988.

Price: Thumbhole Turkey **$648.00**
Price: Tactical Turkey **$606.00**
Price: Synthetic Thumbhole Turkey, from. **$469.00**
Price: Turkey, from **$463.00**
Price: Waterfowl, from **$416.00**
Price: Combo, from. **$532.00**

MOSSBERG MODEL 500 SPORTING PUMP SHOTGUNS

Gauge: 12, 20, .410, 3" chamber. **Barrel:** 18.5" to 28" with fixed or Accu-Choke, plain or vent rib. **Weight:** 6-1/4 lbs. (.410), 7-1/4 lbs. (12). **Length:** 48" overall (28" barrel). **Stock:** 14"x1.5"x2.5". Walnut-stained hardwood, black synthetic, Mossy Oak Advantage camouflage. Cut-checkered grip and forend. **Sights:** White bead front, brass mid-bead; fiber-optic. **Features:** Ambidextrous thumb safety, twin extractors, disconnecting safety, dual action bars. Quiet Carry forend. Many barrels are ported. From Mossberg.

Price: Turkey. **$389.00**
Price: Waterfowl **$389.00**
Price: Combo, from. **$382.00**
Price: Field, from. **$338.00**
Price: Slugster, from **$338.00**

Mossberg Model 500 Bantam Pump Shotgun

Same as the Model 500 Sporting Pump except 12 or 20 gauge, 22" vent rib Accu-Choke barrel with choke tube set; has 1" shorter stock, reduced length from pistol grip to trigger, reduced forend reach. Introduced 1992.

Price: **$382.00**
Price: Super Bantam (2008), from **$338.00**

NEW ENGLAND PARDNER PUMP SHOTGUN

Gauge: 12 ga., 3". **Barrel:** 28" vent rib, screw-in Modified choke tube. **Weight:** 7.5 lbs. **Length:** 48.5". **Stock:** American walnut, grooved forend, ventilated recoil pad. **Sights:** Bead front. **Features:** Machined steel receiver, double action bars, five-shot magazine.

Price: **$200.00**

REMINGTON MODEL 870 WINGMASTER SHOTGUNS

Gauge: 12, 20, 28 ga., .410 bore. **Barrel:** 25", 26", 28", 30" (RemChokes). **Weight:** 7-1/4 lbs. **Length:** 46", 48". **Stock:** Walnut, hardwood. **Sights:** Single bead (Twin bead Wingmaster). **Features:** Light contour barrel. Double action bars, cross-bolt safety, blue finish. LW is 28 gauge and .410-bore only, 25" vent rib barrel with RemChoke tubes, high-gloss wood finish. Limited Edition Model 870 Wingmaster 100th Anniversary Commemorative Edition (2008 only) is 12 gauge with gold centennial logo, "100 Years of Remington Pump Shotguns" banner. Gold-plated trigger, American B Grade walnut stock and forend, high-gloss finish, fleur-de-lis checkering.

Price: Wingmaster, walnut, blued. **$773.00**
Price: LW .410-bore **$788.00**
Price: 100th Anniversary (2008), 12 ga., 28" barrel **$1,035.00**
Price: Wingmaster, claro walnut, 12 or ga. **$955.00**

Remington Model 870 Marine Magnum Shotgun

Similar to 870 Wingmaster except all metal plated with electroless nickel, black synthetic stock and forend. Has 18" plain barrel (cyl.), bead front sight, 7-shot magazine. Introduced 1992. XCS version with TriNyte corrosion control introduced 2007.

Price: **$752.00**

Remington Model 870 Express Deer Gun

Remington Model 870 Express Turkey Gun

Remington Model 870 Express Youth Turkey Gun

Remington Model 870 Express Super Magnum

Remington Model 870 Classic Trap Shotgun

Similar to Model 870 Wingmaster except has 30" vent rib, light contour barrel, singles, mid- and long-handicap choke tubes, semi-fancy American walnut stock, high-polish blued receiver with engraving. Chamber 2.75". From Remington Arms Co.

Price: **$1,015.00**
Price: XCS (2007). **$869.00**

Remington Model 870 Express Shotguns

Similar to Model 870 Wingmaster except laminate, syn-thetic black, or camo stock with solid, black recoil pad and pressed checkering on grip and forend. Out-side metal surfaces have black oxide finish. Comes with 26" or 28" vent rib barrel with mod. RemChoke tube. ShurShot Turkey (2008) has ShurShot synthetic pistol-grip thumbhole design, extended forend, Mossy Oak Obsession camouflage, matte black metal finish, 21" vent rib barrel, twin beads, Turkey Extra Full Rem Choke tube. Receiver drilled and tapped for mounting optics. ShurShot FR CL (Fully Rifled Cantilever, 2008) includes compact 23" fully-rifled barrel with integrated cantilever scope mount.

Price: 12 and 20 ga., laminate or synthetic right-hand stock . .**$373.00**
Price: 12 or 20 ga., laminate or synthetic left-hand stock. **$401.00**
Price: Express Synthetic, 12 ga., 18" barrel (2007) **$359.00**
Price: Express Synthetic, 12 and 20 ga., 7 round capacity, from. **$388.00**
Price: Express Synthetic, 12 and 20 ga., 7 round capacity, from. **$388.00**
Price: Express Synthetic Deer FR 12 ga., rifle sights, ...**$416.00**
Price: Express Laminate Deer FR 12 ga., rifle sights, ...**$416.00**
Price: Express Synthetic or Laminate Turkey 12 ga., 21" barrel **$388.00**
Price: Express Camo Turkey 12 ga., 21" barrel **$445.00**
Price: Express Combo Turkey/Deer Camo 12 ga.,. **$648.00**
Price: Express Synthetic Youth Combo 20 ga.. . . . .**$543.00**
Price: Express Magnum ShurShot Turkey (2008) **$503.00**
Price: Express Magnum ShurShot FR CL (2008). **$547.00**

Remington Model 870 Express Super Magnum Shotgun

Similar to Model 870 Express except 28" vent rib barrel with 3-1/2" chamber, vented recoil pad. Introduced 1998. Model 870 Express Super Magnum Waterfowl (2008) is fully camouflaged with Mossy Oak Duck Blind pattern, 28-inch vent rib Rem Choke barrel, "Over Decoys" Choke tube (.007") fiber-optic HiViz single bead front sight; front and rear sling swivel studs, padded black sling.

Price: **$420.00**
Price: Super Magnum synthetic, 26" **$420.00**
Price: Super Magnum turkey camo (full-coverage RealTree Advantage camo), 23" **$513.00**
Price: Super Magnum combo (26" with Mod. RemChoke and 20" fully rifled deer barrel with 3" chamber and rifle sights; wood stock) **$579.00**
Price: Super Magnum synthetic turkey, 23" (black) . . . .**$$435.00**
Price: Super Magnum Waterfowl (2008). **$572.00**

Remington Model 870 Special Purpose Shotguns (SPS)

Similar to the Model 870 Express synthetic, chambered for 12 ga. 3" and 3-1/2" shells, has Realtree Hardwoods HD or APG HD camo-synthetic stock and metal treatment, TruGlo fiber-optic sights. Intro-duced 2001. SPS Max Gobbler introduced 2007. Knoxx SpecOps adjustable stock, Williams Fire Sights fiber-optic sights, R3 recoil pad, Realtree APG HD camo. Drilled and tapped for Weaver-style rail

Price: SPS 12 ga. 3". **$671.00**
Price: SPS Super Mag Max Gobbler (2007). **$819.00**
Price: SPS Super Mag Max Turkey ShurShot 3-1/2" (2008) . .**$644.00**
Price: SPS Synthetic ShurShot FR Cantilever 3" (2008) **$671.00**

STOEGER MODEL P350 SHOTGUNS

Gauge: 12, 3.5" chamber, set of five choke tubes (C, IC, M, IM, XF). **Barrel:** 18.5",24", 26", 28". **Stock:** Black synthetic, Timber HD, Max-4 HD, APG HD camos. **Sights:** Red bar front. **Features:** Inertia-recoil, mercury recoil reducer, pistol grip stocks. Imported by Benelli USA.

Price: Synthetic. **$319.00**
Price: Max-4, Timber HD **$389.00**
Price: Black synthetic pistol grip (2007) **$319.00**
Price: APG HD camo pistol grip (2007) **$419.00**

Winchester Speed Pump Walnut Field

Winchester Speed Pump Black Shadow Field

Winchester Speed Pump Defender

WINCHESTER SPEED PUMP SHOTGUNS

Gauge: 12, 3" chambers. **Barrel:** 18"; 26" and 28" barrels are .742" back-bored, chrome plated; Invector Plus choke tubes. **Weight:** 7 lbs. **Stock:** Walnut or composite. **Features:** Rotary bolt, four lugs, dual steel action bars. Walnut Field has gloss-finished walnut stock and forearm, cut checkering. Black Shadow Field has composite stock and forearm, non-glare matte finish barrel and receiver. Speed Pump Defender has composite stock and forearm, chromed plated, 18" cylinder choked barrel, non-glare metal surfaces, five-shot magazine, grooved forearm. Weight, 6.5 lbs. Reintro-duced 2008. Made in U.S.A. from Winchester Repeating Arms Co.

Price: Walnut Field **$399.00**
Price: Black Shadow Field **$349.00**
Price: Defender. **$299.00**

Includes a variety of game guns and guns for competitive shooting.

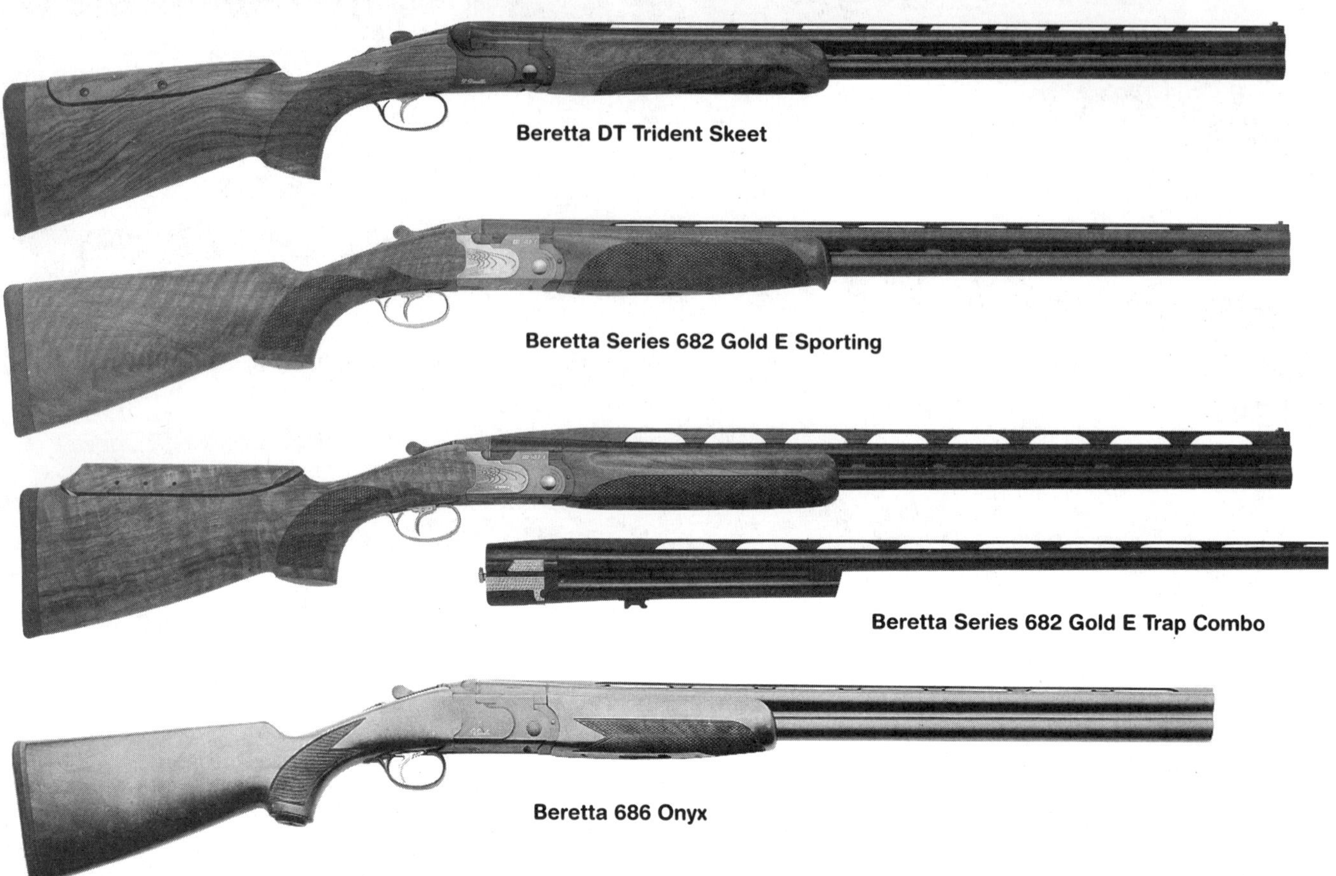

Beretta DT Trident Skeet

Beretta Series 682 Gold E Sporting

Beretta Series 682 Gold E Trap Combo

Beretta 686 Onyx

BERETTA DT10 TRIDENT SHOTGUNS

Gauge: 12, 2-3/4", 3" chambers. **Barrel:** 28", 30", 32", 34"; competition-style vent rib; fixed or Optima choke tubes. **Weight:** 7.9 to 9 lbs. **Stock:** High-grade walnut stock with oil finish; hand-checkered grip and forend, adjustable stocks available. **Features:** Detachable, adjustable trigger group, raised and thickened receiver, forend iron has adjustment nut to guarantee wood-to-metal fit. Introduced 2000. Imported from Italy by Beretta USA.

Price: DT10 Trident Trap, adjustable stock. **$7,400.00**
Price: DT10 Trident Top Single **$10,475.00**
Price: DT10 Trident X Trap Combo **$10,475.00**
Price: DT10 Trident Skeet **$7,400.00**
Price: DT10 Trident Sporting, from. **$6,775.00**
Price: DT10L Sporting **$8,925.00**

BERETTA SV10 PERENNIA O/U SHOTGUN

Gauge: 12, 3" chambers. **Barrel:** 26", 28", 30". Optima-Bore profile, polished blue. Bore diameter 18.6mm (0.73 in.) Self-adjusting dual conical longitudinal locking lugs, oversized monobloc bearing shoulders, replaceable hinge pins. Venti-lated top rib, 6x6mm. Long guided extractors, automatic ejection or mechanical extraction. Optimachoke tubes. **Weight:** 7.3 lbs. **Stock:** Quick take-down stock with pistol grip or English straight stock. Kick-off recoil reduction system available on request on Q-Stock. **Length of pull:** 14.7", drop at comb, 1.5", drop at heel, 2.36" or 1.38"/2.17". Semibeavertail forend with elongated forend lever. New checkering pattern, matte oil finish, rubber pad. **Features:** Floral motifs and game scenes on side panels; nickel-based protective finish, arrowhead-shaped side-plates, solid steel alloy billet. Kick-Off recoil reduction mechanism available on select models. Fixed chokes on request, removable trigger group, titanium single selective trigger. Manual or automatic safety, newly designed safety and selector lever. Gel-Tek recoil pad available on re-quest. Polypropylene case, 5 chokes with spanner, sling swivels, plastic pad, Beretta gun oil. In-troduced 2008. Imported from Italy by Beretta USA.

Price: From **$3,250.00**

BERETTA SERIES 682 GOLD E SKEET, TRAP, SPORTING O/U SHOTGUNS

Gauge: 12, 2-3/4" chambers. **Barrel:** skeet-28"; trap-30" and 32", Imp. Mod. & Full and Mobilchoke; trap mono shotguns-32" and 34" Mobilchoke; trap top single guns-32" and 34" Full and Mobilchoke; trap combo sets-from 30" O/U, to 32" O/U, 34" top single. **Stock:** Close-grained walnut, hand checkered. **Sights:** White Bradley bead front sight and center bead. **Features:** Receiver has Greystone gunmetal gray finish with gold accents. Trap Monte Carlo stock has deluxe trap recoil pad. Various grades available. Imported from Italy by Beretta USA.

Price: 682 Gold E Trap with adjustable stock. **$4,425.00**
Price: 682 Gold E Trap Top Combo **$6,075.00**
Price: 682 Gold E Sporting **$3,975.00**
Price: 682 Gold E Skeet, adjustable stock **$4,425.00**

BERETTA 686 ONYX O/U SHOTGUNS

Gauge: 12, 20, 28; 3", 3.5" chambers. **Barrel:** 26", 28" (Mobilchoke tubes). **Weight:** 6.8-6.9 lbs. **Stock:** Checkered American walnut. **Features:** Intended for the beginning sporting clays shooter. Has wide, vented target rib, radiused recoil pad. Polished black finish on receiver and barrels. Introduced 1993. Imported from Italy by Beretta U.S.A.

Price: White Onyx. **$1,925.00**
Price: Onyx Pro. **$1,875.00**
Price: White Onyx Sporting. **$2,025.00**

BERETTA SILVER PIGEON O/U SHOTGUNS

Gauge: 12, 20, 28, 3" chambers (2-3/4" 28 ga.). .410 bore, 3" chamber. **Barrel:** 26", 28". **Weight:** 6.8 lbs. **Stock:** Checkered walnut. **Features:** Interchangeable barrels (20 and 28 ga.), single selective gold-plated trigger, boxlock action, auto safety, Schnabel forend.

Price: Silver Pigeon S. **$2,350.00**
Price: Silver Pigeon S Combo **$3,175.00**
Price: Silver Pigeon II **$2,750.00**
Price: Silver Pigeon III **$2,975.00**
Price: Silver Pigeon IV **$3,150.00**
Price: Silver Pigeon V. **$3,575.00**

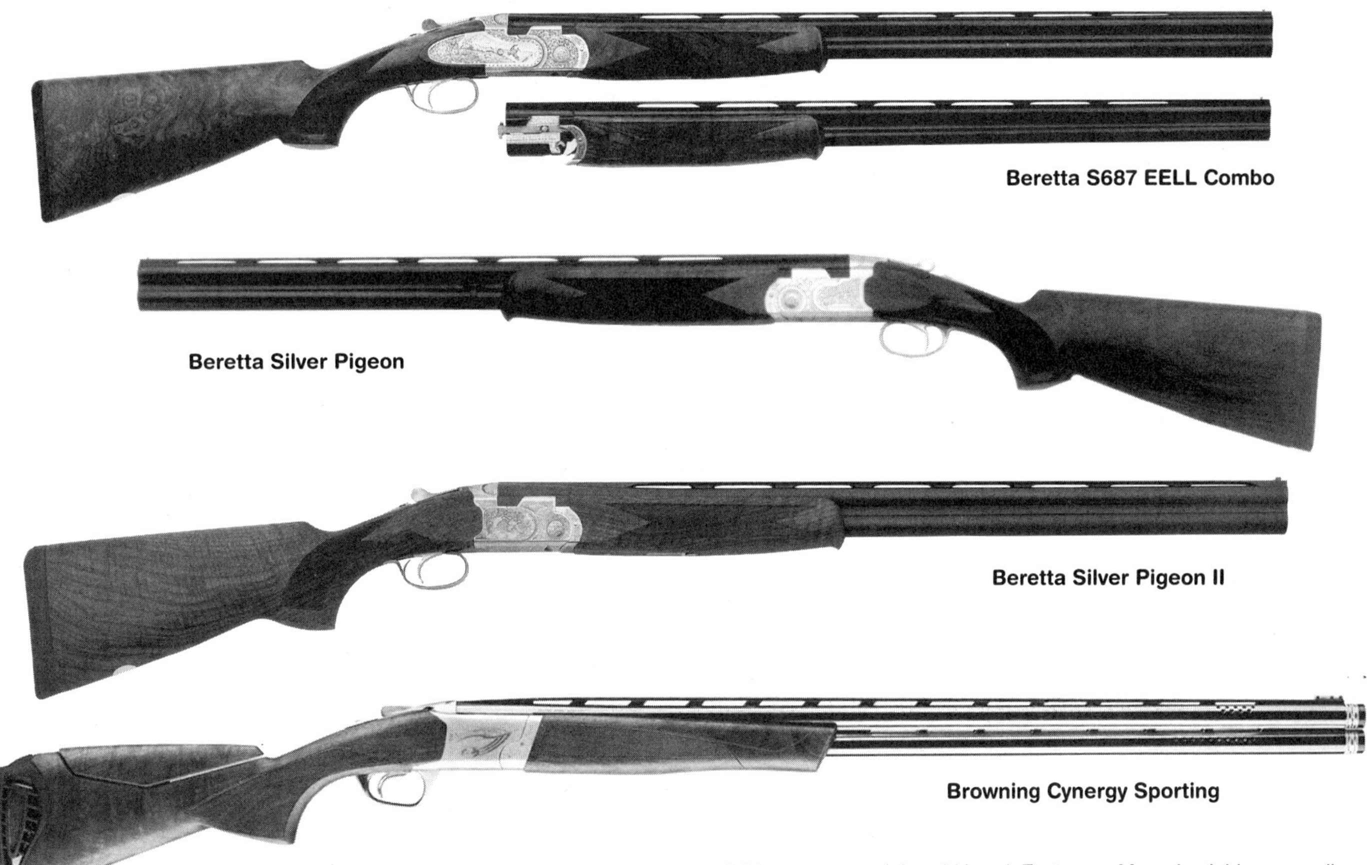

Beretta S687 EELL Combo

Beretta Silver Pigeon

Beretta Silver Pigeon II

Browning Cynergy Sporting

BERETTA ULTRALIGHT O/U SHOTGUNS

Gauge: 12, 2-3/4" chambers. **Barrel:** 26", 28", Mobilchoke tubes. **Weight:** About 5 lbs., 13 oz. **Stock:** Select American walnut with checkered grip and forend. **Features:** Low-profile aluminum alloy receiver with titanium breech face insert. Electroless nickel receiver with game scene engraving. Single selective trigger; automatic safety. Introduced 1992. Ultralight Deluxe except has matte electroless nickel finish receiver with gold game scene engraving; matte oil-finished, select walnut stock and forend. Imported from Italy by Beretta U.S.A.

Price: **$2,075.00**
Price: Ultralight Deluxe **$2,450.00**

BERETTA COMPETITION SHOTGUNS

Gauge: 12, 20, 28, and .410 bore, 2-3/4", 3" and 3-1/2" chambers. **Barrel:** 26" and 28" (Mobilchoke tubes). **Stock:** Close-grained walnut. **Features:** Highly-figured, American walnut stocks and forends, and a unique, weather-resistant finish on barrels. Silver designates standard 686, 687 models with silver receivers; 686 Silver Pigeon has enhanced engraving pattern, Schnabel forend; Gold indicates higher grade 686EL, 687EL models with full sideplates. Imported from Italy by Beretta U.S.A.

Price: S687 EL Gold Pigeon II (deep relief engraving) **$5,495.00**
Price: S687 EL Gold Pigeon II combo, 20/28 or 28/.410 . . . **$5,495.00**
Price: S687 EELL Gold Pigeon Sporting (D.R. engraving) . . **$6,495.00**
Price: Gold Sporting Pigeon **$5,495.00**

BILL HANUS 16-GAUGE BROWNING CITORI M525 FIELD

Gauge: 16. **Barrel:** 26" and 28". **Weight:** 6-3/4 pounds. **Stock:** 1-1/2" x 2-3/8" x 14-1/4" and cast neutral. Adjusting for cast-on for left-handed shooters or cast-off for right-handed shooters, $300 extra. Oil finish. **Features:** Full pistol grip with a graceful Schnable forearm and built on a true 16-gauge frame. Factory supplies three Invector choke tubes: IC-M-F and Bill Hanus models come with two Briley-made skeet chokes for close work over dogs and clay-target games.

Price: **$1,995.00**

BROWNING CYNERGY O/U SHOTGUNS

Gauge: 12, 20, 28. **Barrel:** 26", 28", 30", 32". **Stock:** Walnut or composite. **Sights:** White bead front most models; HiViz Pro-Comp sight on some models; mid bead. **Features:** Mono-Lock hinge, recoil-reducing interchangeable Inflex recoil pad, silver nitride receiver; striker-based trigger, ported barrel option. 12 models cataloged for 2006. Nine new models introduced 2006: Cynergy Sporting, Adjustable Comb; Cynergy Sporting Composite with TopCote; Cynergy Sporting Composite CF; Cynergy Field, Composite; Cynergy Classic Sporting; Cynergy Classic Field; Cynergy Camo Mossy Oak New Shadow Grass; Cynergy Camo Mossy Oak New Break-Up; and Cynergy Camo Mossy Oak Brush. Imported from Japan by Browning.

Price: Cynergy Classic Field, 12 ga., from **$2,252.00**
Price: Cynergy Classic Sporting, from **$3,296.00**
Price: Cynergy Euro Sporting, 12 ga.; 28", 30", or 32" barrels **$3,501.00**
Price: Cynergy Euro Sporting Composite 12 ga. **$3,295.00**
Price: Cynergy Euro Sporting, adjustable comb, intr. 2006 . **$3,843.00**
Price: Cynergy Sporting Composite w/TopCote, intr. 2006 . **$3,295.00**
Price: Cynergy Feather, 12 ga. intr. 2007 . . . . **$2,430.00**
Price: Cynergy Feather, 20, 28 ga., .410, intr. 2008 . . . . **$2,447.00**
Price: Cynergy Euro Sporting 20 ga., intr. 2008 . . . . **$3,465.00**

BROWNING CITORI O/U SHOTGUNS

Gauge: 12, 20, 28 and .410. **Barrel:** 26", 28" in 28 and .410. Offered with Invector choke tubes. All 12 and 20 gauge models have back-bored barrels and Invector Plus choke system. **Weight:** 6 lbs., 8 oz. (26" .410) to 7 lbs., 13 oz. (30" 12 ga.). **Length:** 43" overall (26" bbl.). **Stock:** Dense walnut, hand checkered, full pistol grip, beavertail forend. Field-type recoil pad on 12 ga. field guns and trap and skeet models. **Sights:** Medium raised beads, German nickel silver. **Features:** Barrel selector integral with safety, automatic ejectors, three-piece takedown. 23 models cataloged for 2008. Two limited-run models reintroduced 2006: Citori 4-Barrel Skeet Set, Grade I; Citori 4-Barrel Skeet Set, Grade VII. Citori 625 Field (intr. 2008) includes Vector Pro extended forcing cones, new wood checkering patterns, silver-nitride finish with high-relief engraving, gloss oil finish with Grade II/III walnut with radius pistol grip, Schnabel forearm, 12 gauge, three Invector Plus choke tubes. Citori 625 Sporting (intr. 2008) includes standard and adjustable combs, 32", 30", and 28" barrels, five Diamond Grade extended Invector Plus choke tubes. Triple Trigger System allows adjusting length of pull and choice of wide checkered, narrow smooth, and wide smooth canted trigger shoe. HiViz Pro-Comp fiber-optic front sights. Imported from Japan by Browning.

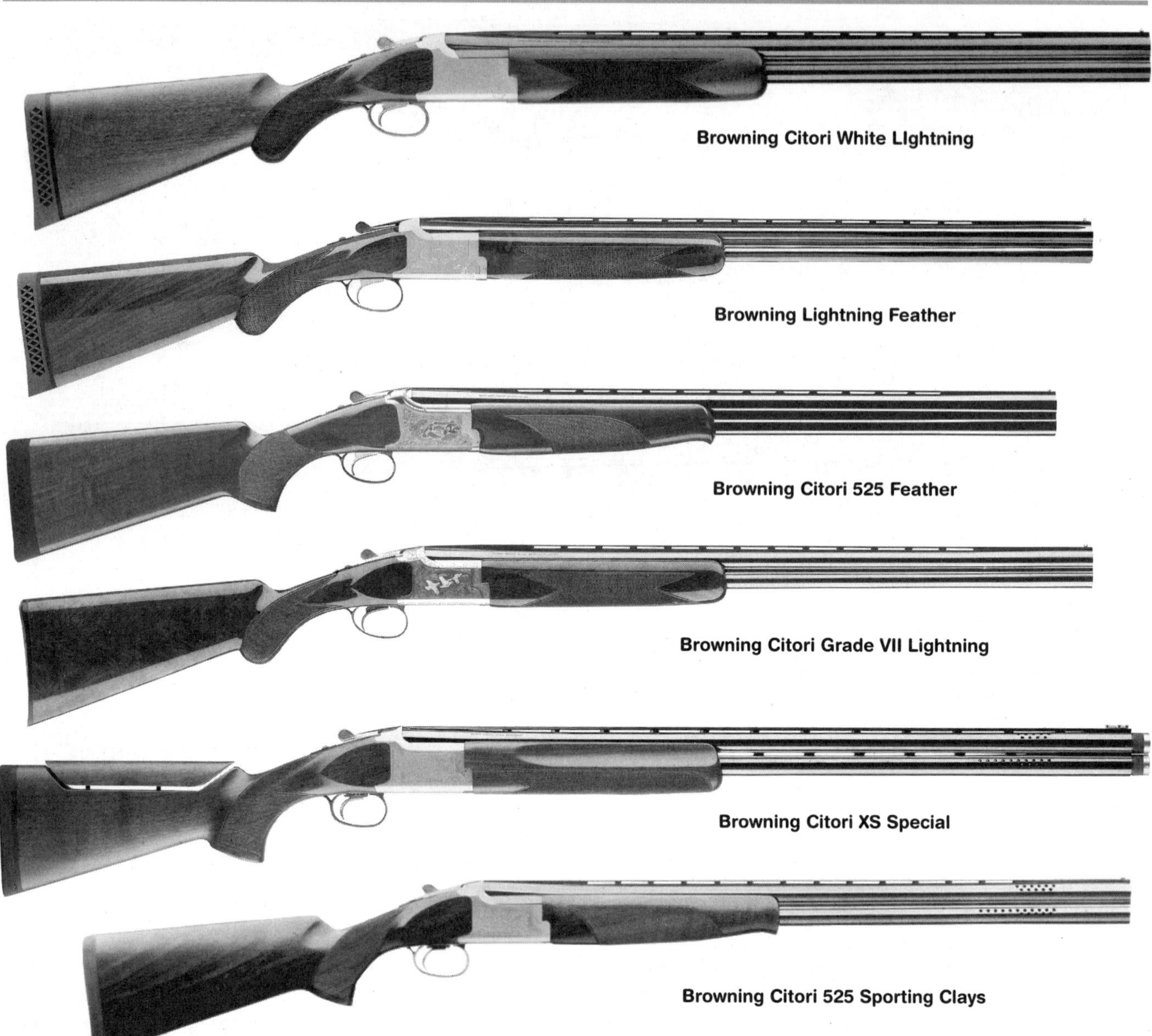

Browning Citori White Lightning

Browning Lightning Feather

Browning Citori 525 Feather

Browning Citori Grade VII Lightning

Browning Citori XS Special

Browning Citori 525 Sporting Clays

BROWNING CITORI O/U SHOTGUNS *(cont.)*

Price: Lightning, from **$1,763.00**
Price: White Lightning, from **$1,836.00**
Price: 525 Field, from **$2,144.00**
Price: Superlight Feather **$2,098.00**
Price: Lightning Feather, 12 and 20 ga.,. **$1,869.00**
Price: Citori 4-Barrel Skeet Set, Grade I, intr. 2006 . . . . **$8,412.00**
Price: 525 Feather, 20 and 28 ga., .410, intr. 2008, from . . . **$2,278.00**
Price: 625 Field, 12 ga. intr. 2008. **$2,299.00**
Price: 625 Sporting, 12 ga., standard comb, intr. 2008 . . . . **$3,299.00**
Price: 625 Sporting, 12 ga., adj. comb, intr. 2008. . . . . **$3,499.00**

Browning Citori High Grade Shotguns

Similar to standard Citori except has engraved hunting scenes and gold inlays, high-grade, hand-oiled walnut stock and forearm. Introduced 2000. From Browning.

Price: Gran Lightning, engraved receiver, from **$2,429.00**
Price: Grade IV Lightning, engraved gray receiver, introduced 2005, from. **$2,608.00**
Price: Grade VII Lightning, engraved gray or blue receiver, introduced 2005, from. **$4,146.00**
Price: GTS High Grade, intr. 2007 . . . . **$4,056.00**

Browning Citori XS Sporting O/U Shotguns

Similar to the standard Citori except available in 12, 20, 28 or .410 with 28", 30", 32" ported barrels with various screw-in choke combinations: S (Skeet), C (Cylinder), IC (Improved Cylinder), M (Modified), and IM (Improved Modified). Has pistol grip stock, rounded or Schnabel forend. Weighs 7.1 lbs. to 8.75 lbs. Introduced 2004. Ultra XS Prestige (intr. 2008) has silver-nitride finish receiver with gold accented, high-relief Ultra XS Special engraving. Also, single selective trigger, hammer ejectors, gloss oil finish walnut stock with right-hand palm swell, adjustable comb, Schnabel forearm. Comes with five Invector-Plus Midas Grade choke tubes.

Price: XS Special, 12 ga.; 30", 32" barrels **$2,727.00**
Price: XS Sporting, 12 or 20 ga. **$2,472.00**
Price: XS Skeet, 12 or 20 ga. **$2,659.00**
Price: 525 Sporting Grade I, 12 ga. intr. 2005 . . . . **$2,319.00**
Price: 525 Golden Clays, 12 or 20 gauge. **$3,058.00**
Price: 525 Golden Clays, 28 or .410. . . . . **$4,653.00**
Price: XS Special High Post Rib, intr. 2007 . . . . **$2,980.00**
Price: Ultra XS Prestige, intr. 2008. **$4,477.00**

Browning Citori XT Trap O/U Shotgun

Similar to the Citori XS Special except has engraved silver nitride receiver with gold highlights, vented side barrel rib. Available in 12 gauge with 30" or 32" barrels, Invector-Plus choke tubes, adjustable comb and buttplate. Introduced 1999. Imported by Browning.

Price: XT Trap. **$2,486.00**
Price: XT Trap w/adjustable comb **$2,785.00**
Price: XT Trap Gold w/adjustable comb, introduced 2005 . . **$4,612.00**

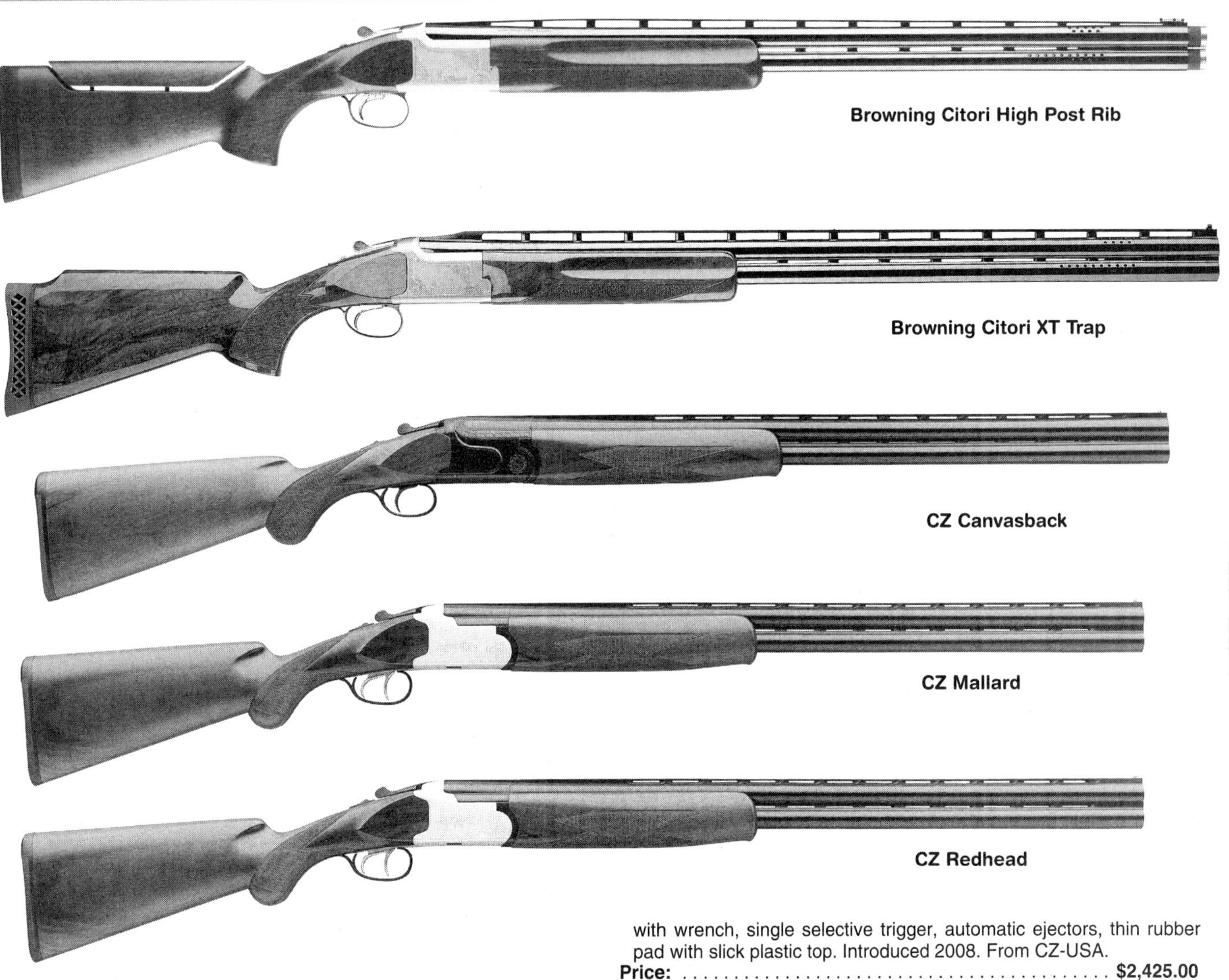

CENTURION O/U SHOTGUN
Gauge: 12, 2-3/4 & 3" chambers, 20, 28, 410. **Barrel:** 28", 5 choke tubes. **Weight:** 7.35 lbs. (12); 6.14 lbs. (20); 5.8 lbs. (28); 5.3 lbs. (410). **Length:** 45". **Stock:** Glossy Turkish walnut. **Features:** Single selective trigger, automatic safety, extractors, ventilated recoil pad, front bead sight. Manufactured by CFS in Turkey. Imported by Century International.
Price: **$470.00**

CHARLES DALY MODEL 206 O/U SHOTGUN
Gauge: 12, 3" chambers. **Barrel:** 26", 28", 30", chrome-moly steel. **Weight:** 8 lbs. **Stock:** Check-ered select Turkish walnut stocks. **Features:** Single selective trigger, extractors or selective automatic ejectors. Sporting model has 10mm ventilated rib and side ventilated ribs. Trap model comes with 10mm top rib and side ventilated ribs and includes a Monte Carlo Trap buttstock. Both competition ribs have mid-brass bead and front fluorescent sights. Five Multi-Choke tubes. In-troduced 2008. Imported from Turkey by K.B.I., Inc.
Price: Field, 26" or 28", extractors **$649.00**
Price: Field, 26" or 28", auto-eject **$759.00**
Price: Sporting, 28" or 30" ported, ... **$799.00**
Price: Trap, 28" or 30" ported, ... **$869.00**

CZ SPORTING OVER/UNDER
Gauge: 12, 3" chambers. **Barrel:** 30", 32" chrome-lined, back-bored with extended forcing cones. **Weight:** 9 lbs. **Length:** NA. **Stock:** Neutral cast stock with an adjustable comb, trap style forend, pistol grip and ambidextrous palm swells. #3 grade Circassian walnut. At lowest position, drop at comb: 1-5/8"; drop at heel: 2-3/8"; length of pull: 14-1/2". **Features:** Designed for Sporting Clays and FITASC competition. Hand engraving, satin black-finished receiver. Tapered rib with center bead and a red fiber-optic front bead, 10 choke tubes with wrench, single selective trigger, automatic ejectors, thin rubber pad with slick plastic top. Introduced 2008. From CZ-USA.
Price: **$2,425.00**

CZ CANVASBACK
Gauge: 12, 20, 3" chambers. **Barrel:** 26", 28". **Weight:** 7.3 lbs. **Length:** NA. **Stock:** Round-knob pistol grip, Schnabel forend, Turkish walnut. **Features:** Single selective trigger, set of 5 screw-in chokes, black chrome finished receiver. From CZ-USA.
Price: **$781.00**

CZ MALLARD
Gauge: 12, 20, 28, .410, 3" chambers. **Barrel:** 26". **Weight:** 7.7 lbs. **Length:** NA. **Stock:** Round-knob pistol grip, Schnabel forend, Turkish walnut. **Features:** Double triggers and extractors, coin finished receiver, multi chokes. From CZ-USA.
Price: **$536.00**

CZ REDHEAD
Gauge: 12, 20, 3" chambers. **Barrel:** 28". **Weight:** 7.4 lbs. **Length:** NA. **Stock:** Round-knob pistol grip, Schnabel forend, Turkish walnut. **Features:** Single selective triggers and extractors (12 & 20 ga.), screw-in chokes (12, 20, 28 ga.) choked IC and Mod (.410), coin finished receiver, multi chokes. From CZ-USA.
Price: **$954.00**

CZ WOODCOCK
Gauge: 12, 20, 28, .410, 3" chambers. **Barrel:** 26". **Weight:** 7.7 lbs. **Length:** NA. **Stock:** Round-knob pistol grip, Schnabel forend, Turkish walnut. **Features:** Single selective triggers and extractors (auto ejectors on 12 & 20 ga.), screw-in chokes (12, 20, 28 ga.) choked IC and Mod (.410), coin finished receiver, multi chokes. The sculptured frame incorporates a side plate, resembling a true side lock, embellished with hand engraving and finished with color casehardening. From CZ-USA.
Price: **$1,270.00**

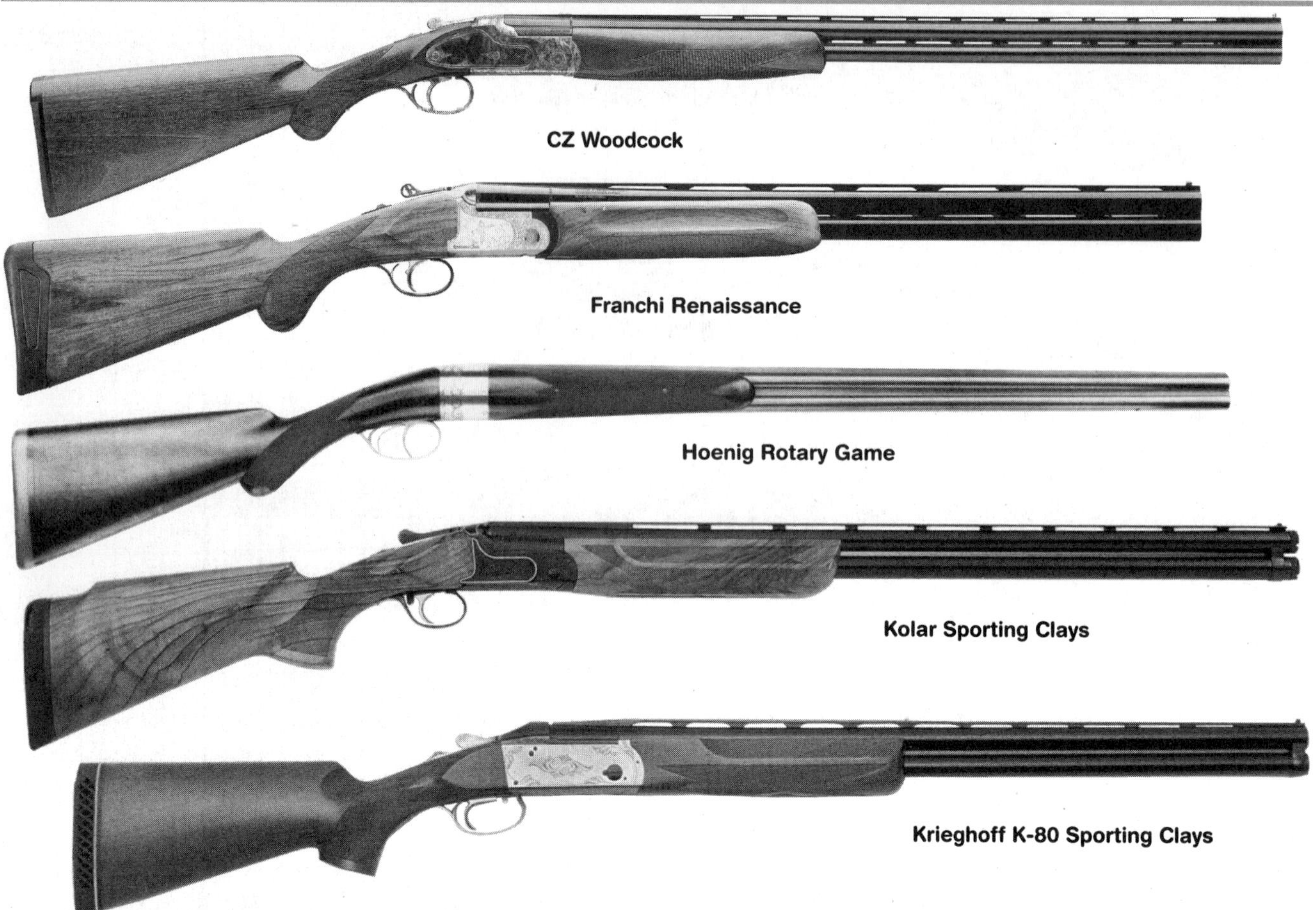

CZ Woodcock

Franchi Renaissance

Hoenig Rotary Game

Kolar Sporting Clays

Krieghoff K-80 Sporting Clays

ESCORT OVER/UNDER SHOTGUNS

Gauge: 12, 3" chamber. **Barrel:** 28". **Weight:** 7.4 lbs. **Stock:** Walnut or select walnut with Trio recoil pad; synthetic stock with adjustable comb. Three adjustment spacers. **Sights:** Bronze front bead. **Features:** Blued barrels, blued or nickel receiver. Trio recoil pad. Five interchangeable chokes (SK, IC, M, IM, F); extractors or ejectors (new, 2008), barrel selector. Hard case available. Introduced 2007. Imported from Turkey by Legacy Sports International.

Price: ....$599.00 to $799.00

FRANCHI RENAISSANCE AND RENAISSANCE SPORTING O/U SHOTGUNS

Gauge: 12, 20, 28, 3" chamber. **Barrel:** 26", 28". **Weight:** 5.0 to 6.0 lbs. **Length:** 42-5/8" to 44-5/8". **Stock:** 14.5" LOP, European oil-finished walnut with standard grade A grade, and AA grade choices. Prince of Wales grip. **Features:** TSA recoil pad, interchangeable chokes, hard case. Introduced 2006. ***Sporting model:*** **Gauge:** 12 , 3". **Barrel:** 30" ported. **Weight:** 7.9 lbs. **Length:** 46 5/8". **Stock:** 14.5" LOP, A-grade European oil-finished walnut. **Features:** TSA recoil pad, adjustable comb, lengthened forcing cones, extended choke tubes (C, IC, M and wrench), hard case. Introduced 2007. Imported from Italy by Benelli USA.

Price: Field **$1,559.00**
Price: Classic **$1,739.00**
Price: Elite.................................... **$2,279.00**
Price: Sporting **$2,139.00**

HOENIG ROTARY ROUND ACTION GAME GUN O/U SHOTGUN

Gauge: 20, 28. **Barrel:** 26", 28", solid tapered rib. **Weight:** 6 lbs. and 6-1/4 lbs. **Stock:** English walnut to customer specifications. **Features:** Round action opens by rotating barrels, pulling forward. Inertia extraction system, rotary wing safety blocks strikers. Simple takedown without removing forend. Introduced 1997. Made in U.S.A. by George Hoenig.

Price: **$20,000.00**

KIMBER MARIAS O/U SHOTGUN

Gauge: 20, 16; 3". **Barrel:** 26", 28", 30". **Weight:** 6.5 lbs. **Length:** NA. **Stock:** Turkish walnut stocks, 24-lpi checkering, oil finish. **LOP:** 14.75". **Features:** Hand-detachable back-action sidelock, bone-charcoal case coloring. Hand-engraving on receiver and locks, Belgian rust blue barrels, chrome lined. Five thinwall choke tubes, automatic ejectors, ventilated rib. Gold line cocking indicators on locks. Grade I has 28" barrels, Prince of Wales stock in grade three Turkish walnut in either 12 or 20 gauge. Grade II shas grade four Turkish walnut stocks, 12 gauge in Prince of Wales and 20 with either Prince of Wales or English profiles. Introduced 2008. Imported from Italy by Kimber Mfg., Inc.

Price: Grade II.................................... **$5,799**

KOLAR SPORTING CLAYS O/U SHOTGUNS

Gauge: 12, 2-3/4" chambers. **Barrel:** 30", 32", 34"; extended choke tubes. **Stock:** 14-5/8"x2.5"x1-7/8"x1-3/8". French walnut. Four stock versions available. **Features:** Single selective trigger, detachable, adjustable for length; overbored barrels with long forcing cones; flat tramline rib; matte blue finish. Made in U.S. by Kolar.

Price: Standard.................................. **$8,995.00**
Price: Elite...................................... **$12,495.00**
Price: Elite Gold **$15,295.00**
Price: Legend **$15,995.00**
Price: Select **$18,995.00**
Price: Custom .... **Price on request**

Kolar AAA Competition Trap O/U Shotgun

Similar to the Sporting Clays gun except has 32" O/U /34" Unsingle or 30" O/U /34" Unsingle barrels as an over/under, unsingle, or combination set. Stock dimensions are 14.5"x2.5"x1.5"; American or French walnut; step parallel rib standard. Contact maker for full listings. Made in U.S.A. by Kolar.

Price: Over/under, choke tubes, standard **$9,595.00**
Price: Unsingle, choke tubes, standard **$10,195.00**
Price: Combo (30"/34", 32"/34"), standard **$12,595.00**

Kolar AAA Competition Skeet O/U Shotgun

Similar to the Sporting Clays gun except has 28" or 30" barrels with Kolarite AAA sub gauge tubes; stock of American or French walnut with matte finish; flat tramline rib; under barrel adjustable for point of impact. Many options available. Contact maker for complete listing. Made in U.S.A. by Ko-lar.

Price: Standard, choke tubes **$10,495.00**
Price: Standard, choke tubes, two-barrel set **$12,995.00**

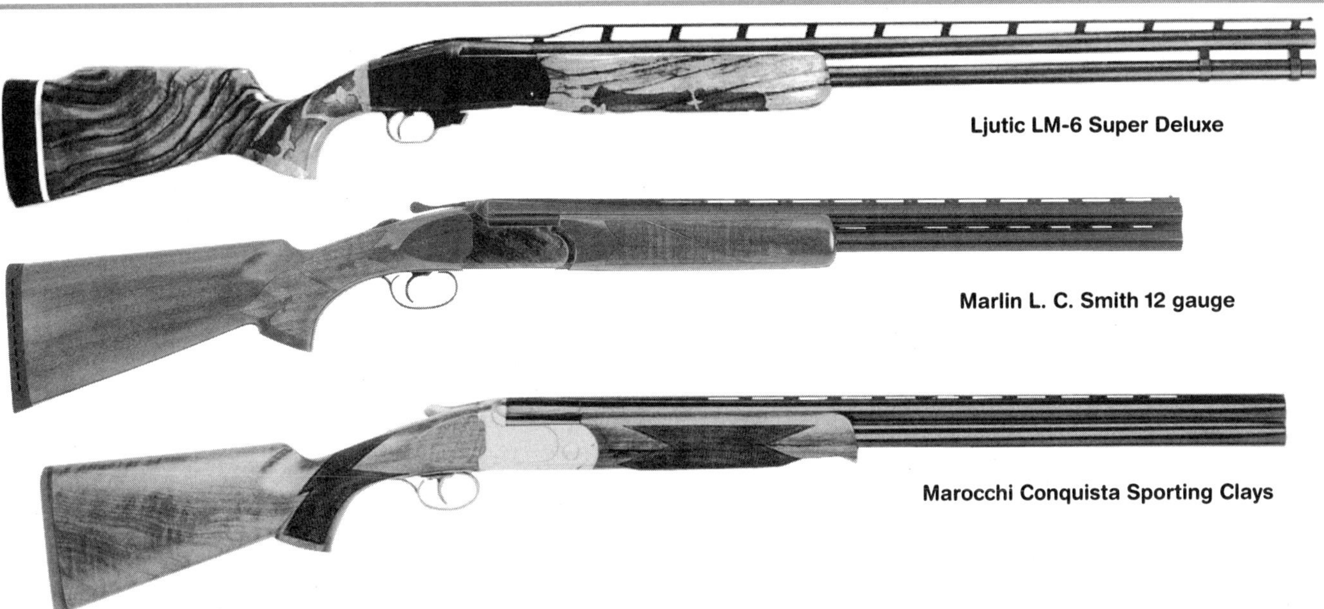

Ljutic LM-6 Super Deluxe

Marlin L. C. Smith 12 gauge

Marocchi Conquista Sporting Clays

KRIEGHOFF K-80 SPORTING CLAYS O/U SHOTGUN

Gauge: 12. **Barrel:** 28", 30", 32", 34" with choke tubes. **Weight:** About 8 lbs. **Stock:** #3 Sporting stock designed for gun-down shooting. **Features:** Standard receiver with satin nickel finish and classic scroll engraving. Selective mechanical trigger adjustable for position. Choice of tapered flat or 8mm parallel flat barrel rib. Free-floating barrels. Aluminum case. Imported from Germany by Krieghoff International, Inc.

Price: Standard grade with five choke tubes, from **$9,395.00**

KRIEGHOFF K-80 SKEET O/U SHOTGUNS

Gauge: 12, 2-3/4" chambers. **Barrel:** 28", 30", 32", (Skeet & Skeet), optional choke tubes). **Weight:** About 7.75 lbs. **Stock:** American skeet or straight skeet stocks, with palm-swell grips. Walnut. **Features:** Satin gray receiver finish. Selective mechanical trigger adjustable for position. Choice of ventilated 8mm parallel flat rib or ventilated 8-12mm tapered flat rib. Introduced 1980. Imported from Germany by Krieghoff International, Inc.

Price: Standard, skeet chokes **$8,375.00**

Price: Skeet Special (28", 30", 32" tapered flat rib, skeet & skeet choke tubes) **$9,100.00**

KRIEGHOFF K-80 TRAP O/U SHOTGUNS

Gauge: 12, 2-3/4" chambers. **Barrel:** 30", 32" (Imp. Mod. & Full or choke tubes). **Weight:** About 8.5 lbs. **Stock:** Four stock dimensions or adjustable stock available; all have palm-swell grips. Checkered European walnut. **Features:** Satin nickel receiver. Selective mechanical trigger, adjustable for position. Ventilated step rib. Introduced 1980. Imported from Germany by Krieghoff International, Inc.

Price: K-80 O/U (30", 32", Imp. Mod. & Full), from **$8,850.00**

Price: K-80 Unsingle (32", 34", Full), standard, from **$10,080.00**

Price: K-80 Combo (two-barrel set), standard, from...... **$13,275.00**

Krieghoff K-20 O/U Shotgun

Similar to the K-80 except built on a 20-gauge frame. Designed for skeet, sporting clays and field use. Offered in 20, 28 and .410; 28", 30" and 32" barrels. Imported from Germany by Krieghoff International Inc.

Price: K-20, 20 gauge, from **$9,575.00**

Price: K-20, 28 gauge, from **$9,725.00**

Price: K-20, .410, from **$9,725.00**

LEBEAU-COURALLY BOSS-VEREES O/U SHOTGUN

Gauge: 12, 20, 2-3/4" chambers. **Barrel:** 25" to 32". **Weight:** To customer specifications. **Stock:** Exhibition-quality French walnut. **Features:** Boss-type sidelock with automatic ejectors; single or double triggers; chopper lump barrels. A custom gun built to customer specifications. Imported from Belgium by Wm. Larkin Moore.

Price: From.................................... **$96,000.00**

LJUTIC LM-6 SUPER DELUXE O/U SHOTGUNS

Gauge: 12. **Barrel:** 28" to 34", choked to customer specs for live birds, trap, international trap. **Weight:** To customer specs. **Stock:** To customer specs. Oil finish, hand checkered. **Features:** Custom-made gun. Hollow-milled rib, pull or release trigger, push-button opener in front of trigger guard. From Ljutic Industries.

Price: Super Deluxe LM-6 O/U **$19,995.00**

Price: Over/Under combo (interchangeable single barrel, two trigger guards, one for single trigger, one for doubles) **$27,995.00**

Price: Extra over/under barrel sets, 29"-32" **$6,995.00**

LUGER CLASSIC O/U SHOTGUNS

Gauge: 12, 3" and 3-1/2" chambers. **Barrel:** 26", 28", 30"; Imp. Cyl. Mod. and Full choke tubes. **Weight:** 7.5 lbs. **Length:** 45" overall (28" barrel) **Stock:** Select-grade European walnut, hand-checkered grip and forend. **Features:** Gold, single selective trigger; automatic ejectors. Introduced 2000.

Price: Classic (26", 28" or 30" barrel; 3-1/2" chambers)......**$919.00**

Price: Classic Sporting (30" barrel; 3" chambers)...........**$964.00**

MARLIN L. C. SMITH O/U SHOTGUNS

Gauge: 12, 20. **Barrel:** 26", 28". **Stock:** Checkered walnut w/recoil pad. **Length:** 45". **Weight:** 7.25 lbs. **Features:** 3" chambers; 3 choke tubes (IC, Mod., Full), single selective trigger, selective automatic ejectors; vent rib; bead front sight. Imported from Italy by Marlin. Introduced 2005.

Price: LC12-OU (12 ga., 28" barrel) **$1,254.00**

Price: LC20-OU (20 ga., 26" barrel, 6.25 lbs., OAL 43") ... **$1,254.00**

MAROCCHI CONQUISTA SPORTING CLAYS O/U SHOTGUNS

Gauge: 12, 2-3/4" chambers. **Barrel:** 28", 30", 32" (ContreChoke tubes); 10mm concave vent rib. **Weight:** About 8 lbs. **Stock:** 14-1/2" to 14-7/8"x2-3/16"x1-7/16"; American walnut with checkered grip and forend; sporting clays butt pad. **Sights:** 16mm luminescent front. **Features:** Lower mono-block and frame profile. Fast lock time. Ergonomically-shaped trigger adjustable for pull length. Automatic selective ejectors. Coin-finished receiver, blued barrels. Five choke tubes, hard case. Available as true left-hand model, opening lever operates from left to right; stock has left-hand cast. Introduced 1994. Imported from Italy by Precision Sales International.

Price: Grade I, right-hand **$1,490.00**

Price: Grade I, left-hand **$1,615.00**

Price: Grade II, right-hand **$1,828.00**

Price: Grade II, left-hand............................ **$2,180.00**

Price: Grade III, right-hand, from **$3,093.00**

Price: Grade III, left-hand, from **$3,093.00**

Marocchi Conquista Trap O/U Shotguns

Similar to Conquista Sporting Clays model except 30" or 32" barrels choked Full & Full, stock dimensions of 14.5" to 14-7/8"x1-11/16"x1-9/32"; weighs about 8-1/4 lbs. Introduced 1994. Imported from Italy by Precision Sales International.

Price: Grade I, right-hand **$1,490.00**

Price: Grade II, right-hand **$1,828.00**

Price: Grade III, right-hand, from **$3,093.00**

Merkel Model 2001EL

Perazzi MX8

Marocchi Conquista Skeet O/U Shotguns

Similar to Conquista Sporting Clays model except 28" (skeet & skeet) barrels, stock dimensions of 14-3/8" to 14.75"x2-3/16"x1.5". Weighs about 7-3/4 lbs. Introduced 1994. Imported from Italy by Precision Sales International.

Price: Grade I, right-hand **$1,490.00**
Price: Grade II, right-hand **$1,828.00**
Price: Grade III, right-hand, from **$3,093.00**

MAROCCHI MODEL 99 SPORTING TRAP AND SKEET O/U SHOTGUNS

Gauge: 12, 2-3/4", 3" chambers. **Barrel:** 28", 30", 32". **Stock:** French walnut. **Features:** Boss Locking system, screw-in chokes, low recoil, lightweight Monoblock barrels and ribs. Imported from Italy by Precision Sales International.

Price: Grade I **$2,350.00**
Price: Grade II. **$2,870.00**
Price: Grade II Gold **$3,025.00**
Price: Grade III **$3,275.00**
Price: Grade III Gold. **$3,450.00**
Price: Blackgold **$4,150.00**
Price: Lodestar **$5,125.00**
Price: Brittania **$5,125.00**
Price: Diana **$6,350.00**

MAROCCHI CONQUISTA USA MODEL 92 SPORTING CLAYS O/U SHOTGUN

Gauge: 12, 3" chambers. **Barrel:** 30"; back-bored, ported (ContreChoke Plus tubes); 10 mm concave ventilated top rib, ventilated middle rib. **Weight:** 8 lbs. 2 oz. **Stock:** 14.25" to 14-5/8"x 2-1/8"x1-3/8"; American walnut with checkered grip and forend; sporting clays butt pad. **Features:** Low profile frame; fast lock time; automatic selective ejectors; blued receiver and barrels. Comes with three choke tubes. Ergonomically shaped trigger adjustable for pull length without tools. Barrels are back-bored and ported. Introduced 1996. Imported from Italy by Precision Sales International.

Price: **$1,490.00**

MERKEL MODEL 2001EL O/U SHOTGUN

Gauge: 12, 20, 3" chambers, 28, 2-3/4" chambers. **Barrel:** 12-28"; 20, 28 ga.-26.75". **Weight:** About 7 lbs. (12 ga.). **Stock:** Oil-finished walnut; English or pistol grip. **Features:** Self-cocking Blitz boxlock action with cocking indicators; Kersten double cross-bolt lock; silver-grayed receiver with engraved hunting scenes; coil spring ejectors; single selective or double triggers. Imported from Germany by Merkel USA.

Price: **$9,395.00**

Merkel Model 2000CL O/U Shotgun

Similar to Model 2001EL except scroll-engraved case-hardened receiver; 12, 20, 28 gauge. Imported from Germany by Merkel USA.

Price: **$7,995.00**

PERAZZI MX8/MX8 SPECIAL TRAP, SKEET O/U SHOTGUNS

Gauge: 12, 2-3/4" chambers. **Barrel:** Trap: 29.5" (Imp. Mod. & Extra Full), 31.5" (Full & Extra Full). Choke tubes optional. Skeet: 27-5/8" (skeet & skeet). **Weight:** About 8.5 lbs. (trap); 7 lbs., 15 oz. (skeet). **Stock:** Interchangeable and custom made to customer specs. **Features:** Has detachable and interchangeable trigger group with flat V springs. Flat 7/16" vent rib. Many options available. Imported from Italy by Perazzi U.S.A., Inc.

Price: MX Trap Single. **$10,934.00**

Perazzi MX8 Special Skeet O/U Shotgun

Similar to the MX8 Skeet except has adjustable four-position trigger, skeet stock dimensions. Imported from Italy by Perazzi U.S.A., Inc.

Price: From **$11,166.00**

PERAZZI MX8 O/U SHOTGUNS

Gauge: 12, 2-3/4" chambers. **Barrel:** 28-3/8" (Imp. Mod. & Extra Full), 29.5" (choke tubes). **Weight:** 7 lbs., 12 oz. **Stock:** Special specifications. **Features:** Has single selective trigger; flat 7/16" x 5/16" vent rib. Many options available. Imported from Italy by Perazzi U.S.A., Inc.

Price: Standard. **$12,532.00**
Price: Sporting **$11,166.00**
Price: Trap Double Trap (removable trigger group) **$15,581.00**
Price: Skeet **$12,756.00**
Price: SC3 grade (variety of engraving patterns) . . . . **$23,000.00+**
Price: SCO grade (more intricate engraving, gold inlays). **$39,199.00+**

Perazzi MX8/20 O/U Shotgun

Similar to the MX8 except has smaller frame and has a removable trigger mechanism. Available in trap, skeet, sporting or game models with fixed chokes or choke tubes. Stock is made to customer specifications. Introduced 1993. Imported from Italy by Perazzi U.S.A., Inc.

Price: From **$11,731.00**

PERAZZI MX12 HUNTING O/U SHOTGUNS

Gauge: 12, 2-3/4" chambers. **Barrel:** 26.75", 27.5", 28-3/8", 29.5" (Mod. & Full); choke tubes available in 27-5/8", 29.5" only (MX12C). **Weight:** 7 lbs., 4 oz. **Stock:** To customer specs; interchangeable. **Features:** Single selective trigger; coil springs used in action; Schnabel forend tip. Imported from Italy by Perazzi U.S.A., Inc.

Price: From. **$11,166.00**
Price: MX12C (with choke tubes). From. **$11,960.00**

Perazzi MX20 Hunting O/U Shotguns

Similar to the MX12 except 20 ga. frame size. Non-removable trigger group. Available in 20, 28, .410 with 2-3/4" or 3" chambers. 26" standard, and choked Mod. & Full. Weight is 6 lbs., 6 oz. Imported from Italy by Perazzi U.S.A., Inc.

Price: From. **$11,166.00**
Price: MX20C (as above, 20 ga. only, choke tubes). From **$11,960.00**

PERAZZI MX10 O/U SHOTGUN

Gauge: 12, 2-3/4" chambers. **Barrel:** 29.5", 31.5" (fixed chokes). **Weight:** NA. **Stock:** Walnut; cheekpiece adjustable for elevation and cast. **Features:** Adjustable rib; vent side rib. Externally selective trigger. Available in single barrel, combo, over/under trap, skeet, pigeon and sporting models. Introduced 1993. Imported from Italy by Perazzi U.S.A., Inc.

Price: MX200410 . . . . **$18,007.00**

Perazzi MX28

Piotti Boss

Remington Premier Field Grade

Remington Premier Upland Grade

Rizzini S790 Emel

PERAZZI MX28, MX410 GAME O/U SHOTGUN
Gauge: 28, 2-3/4" chambers, .410, 3" chambers. **Barrel:** 26" (Imp. Cyl. & Full). **Weight:** NA. **Stock:** To customer specifications. **Features:** Made on scaled-down frames proportioned to the gauge. Introduced 1993. Imported from Italy by Perazzi U.S.A., Inc.
Price: From **$22,332.00**

PIOTTI BOSS O/U SHOTGUN
Gauge: 12, 20. **Barrel:** 26" to 32", chokes as specified. **Weight:** 6.5 to 8 lbs. **Stock:** Dimensions to customer specs. Best quality figured walnut. **Features:** Essentially a custom-made gun with many options. Introduced 1993. Imported from Italy by Wm. Larkin Moore.
Price: From **$48,000.00**

POINTER OVER/UNDER SHOTGUN
Gauge: 12, 20, 28, .410, 3" chambers. **Barrel:** 28", blued. **Weight:** 6.1 to 7.6 lbs. **Stock:** Turkish Walnut. Sight: Fiber-optic front, bronze mid-bead. Choke: IC/M/F. **Features:** Engraved nickel receiver, automatic ejectors, fitted hard plastic case. Clays model has oversized fiber-optic front sight and palm swell pistol grip. Introduced 2007. Imported from Turkey by Legacy Sports International.
Price: .... **$1,299.00 to $1,499.00**

REMINGTON PREMIER OVER/UNDER SHOTGUNS
Gauge: 12, 20, 28, 3" chambers; 28, 2-3/4" chambers. **Barrel:** 26", 28", 30" in 12 gauge; overbored (.735), polished blue; 7mm vent rib. **Sights:** Ivory front bead, steel mid bead. **Weight:** 6.5 to 7.5 lbs. **Stock:** Walnut, cut checkering, Schnabel forends. Checkered pistol grip, checkered forend, satin finish, rubber butt pad. Right-hand palm swell. **Features:** Single selective mechanical trigger, selective automatic ejectors; serrated free-floating vent rib. Five flush mount ProBore choke tubes for 12s and 20s; 28-gauge equipped with 3 flush mount ProBore choke tubes. Hard case included. Introduced 2006. Made in Italy, imported by Remington Arms Co.
Price: Premier Field, nickel-finish receiver, from **$2,086.00**
Price: Premier Upland, case-colored receiver finish, from .. **$2,226.00**
Price: Premier Ruffed Grouse, 20 ga., 26" barrel **$2,380.00**
Price: Premier Competition STS (2007) **$2,540.00**
Price: Premier Competition STS Adj. Comb (2007) **$2,890.00**

REMINGTON SPR310 OVER/UNDER SHOTGUNS
Gauge: 12, 20, 28, .410 bore, 3" chambers; 28, 2-3/4" chambers. **Barrel:** 26", 28", 29.5"; blued chrome-lined. **Weight:** 7.25 to 7.5 lbs. **Stock:** Checkered walnut stock and forend, 14.5" LOP; 1.5" drop at comb; 2.5" drop at heel. **Features:** Nickel finish or blued receiver. Single selective mechanical trigger, selective automatic ejectors; serrated free-floating vent rib. SC-4 choke tube set on most models. Sporting has ported barrels, right-hand palm swell, target forend, wide rib. Introduced 2008. Imported by Remington Arms Co.
Price: SPR310, from **$598.00**
Price: SPR310 Sporting **$770.00**

RIZZINI S790 EMEL O/U SHOTGUN
Gauge: 20, 28, .410. **Barrel:** 26", 27.5" (Imp. Cyl. & Imp. Mod.). **Weight:** About 6 lbs. **Stock:** 14"x1.5"x2-1/8". Extra fancy select walnut. **Features:** Boxlock action with profuse engraving; automatic ejectors; single selective trigger; silvered receiver. Comes with Nizzoli leather case. Introduced 1996. Imported from Italy by Wm. Larkin Moore & Co.
Price: From **$9,725.00**

Rizzini S792 EMEL O/U Shotgun
Similar to S790 EMEL except dummy sideplates with extensive engraving coverage. Nizzoli leather case. Introduced 1996. Imported from Italy by Wm. Larkin Moore & Co.
Price: From **$9,075.00**

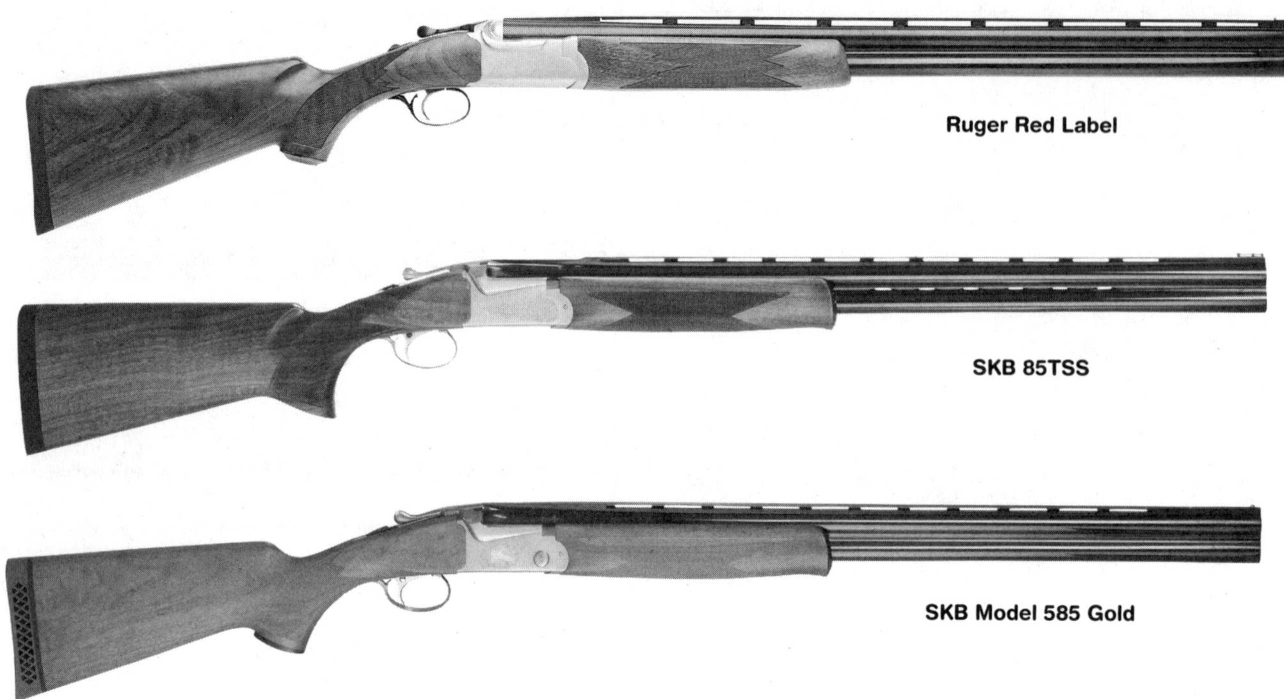

RIZZINI UPLAND EL O/U SHOTGUN

Gauge: 12, 16, 20, 28, .410. **Barrel:** 26", 27.5", Mod. & Full, Imp. Cyl. & Imp. Mod. choke tubes. **Weight:** About 6.6 lbs. **Stock:** 14.5"x1-1/2"x2.25". **Features:** Boxlock action; single selective trigger; ejectors; profuse engraving on silvered receiver. Comes with fitted case. Introduced 1996. Imported from Italy by Wm. Larkin Moore & Co.

Price: From **$3,350.00**

Rizzini Artemis O/U Shotgun

Same as Upland EL model except dummy sideplates with extensive game scene engraving. Fancy European walnut stock. Fitted case. Introduced 1996. Imported from Italy by Wm. Larkin Moore & Co.

Price: From **$2,100.00**

RIZZINI S782 EMEL O/U SHOTGUN

Gauge: 12, 2-3/4" chambers. **Barrel:** 26", 27.5" (Imp. Cyl. & Imp. Mod.). **Weight:** About 6.75 lbs. **Stock:** 14.5"x1.5"x2.25". Extra fancy select walnut. **Features:** Boxlock action with dummy sideplates, extensive engraving with gold inlaid game birds, silvered receiver, automatic ejectors, single selective trigger. Nizzoli leather case. Introduced 1996. Imported from Italy by Wm. Larkin Moore & Co.

Price: From **$11,450.00**

RUGER RED LABEL O/U SHOTGUNS

Gauge: 12, 20, 3" chambers; 28 2-3/4" chambers. **Barrel:** 26", 28", 30" in 12 gauge. **Weight:** About 7 lbs. (20 ga.); 7.5 lbs. (12 ga.). **Length:** 43" overall (26" barrels). **Stock:** 14"x1.5"x2.5". Straight grain American walnut. Checkered pistol grip or straight grip, checkered forend, rubber butt pad. **Features:** Stainless steel receiver. Single selective mechanical trigger, selective automatic ejectors; serrated free-floating vent rib. Comes with two skeet, one Imp. Cyl., one Mod., one Full choke tube and wrench. Made in U.S. by Sturm, Ruger & Co.

Price: Red Label with pistol grip stock **$1,899.00**

Price: English Field with straight-grip stock **$1,899.00**

Price: Sporting clays (30" bbl.) **$1,899.00**

Ruger Engraved Red Label O/U Shotgun

Similar to Red Label except scroll engraved receiver with 24-carat gold game bird (pheasant in 12 gauge, grouse in 20 gauge, woodcock in 28 gauge). Introduced 2000.

Price: Engraved Red Label, pistol grip only **$2,117.00**

SAVAGE MILANO O/U SHOTGUNS

Gauge: 12, 20, 28, and 410, 2-3/4" (28 ga.) and 3" chambers. **Barrel:** 28"; chrome lined, elongated forcing cones, automatic ejectors. 12, 20, and 28 come with 3 Interchokes (F-M-IC); 410 has fixed chokes (M-IC). **Weight:** 12 ga., 7.5 lbs; 20, 28 gauge, .410, 6.25 lbs. **Length:** NA. **Stock:** Satin finish Turkish walnut stock with laser-engraved checkering, solid rubber recoil pad, Schnabel forend. **Features:** Single selective, mechanical set trigger, fiber-optic front sight with brass mid-rib bead. Introduced 2006. Imported from It-aly by Savage Arms, Inc.

Price: **$1,714.00**

SKB MODEL GC7 O/U SHOTGUNS

Gauge: 12 or 20, 3"; 28, 2-3/4"; .410, 3". **Barrel:** 26", 28", Briley internal chokes. **Weight:** NA. **Length:** NA. **Stock:** Grade II and Grade III American black walnut, high-gloss finish, finger-groove forend. **Sights:** Top ventilated rib, sloped with matte surface (Game). **Features:** Low-profile boxlock action; Greener crossbolt locking action, silver-nitride finish; automatic ejec-tors, single selective trigger. Introduced 2008. Imported from Japan by SKB Shotguns, Inc.

Price: GC7 Game Bird Grade 1, from **$1,569.00**

Price: GC7 Clays Grade 1, from **$1,679.00**

SKB MODEL 85TSS O/U SHOTGUNS

Gauge: 12, 20, .410: 3"; 28, 2-3/4". **Barrel:** Chrome lined 26", 28", 30", 32" (w/choke tubes). **Weight:** 7 lbs., 7 oz. to 8 lbs., 14 oz. **Stock:** Hand-checkered American walnut with matte finish, Schnabel or grooved forend. Target stocks available in various styles. **Sights:** HiViz competition sights. **Features:** Low profile boxlock action with Greener-style cross bolt; single selective trigger; manual safety. Back-bored barrels with lengthened forcing cones. Introduced 2004. Imported from Japan by SKB Shotguns, Inc.

Price: Sporting Clays, Skeet, fixed comb, from **$2,199.00**

Price: Sporting clays, Skeet, adjustable comb, from **$2,429.00**

Price: Trap, standard or Monte Carlo **$2,399.00**

Price: Trap adjustable comb **$2,529.00**

Price: Trap Unsingle (2007) **$2,799.00**

SKB MODEL 585 O/U SHOTGUNS

Gauge: 12 or 20, 3"; 28, 2-3/4"; .410, 3". **Barrel:** 12 ga.-26", 28", (InterChoke tubes); 20 ga.-26", 28" (InterChoke tubes); 28-26", 28" (InterChoke tubes); .410-26", 28" (InterChoke tubes). **Weight:** 6.6 to 8.5 lbs. **Length:** 43" to 51-3/8" overall. **Stock:** 14-1/8"x1.5"x2-3/16". Hand checkered walnut with matte finish. **Sights:** Metal bead front (field). **Features:** Boxlock action; silver nitride finish; manual safety, automatic ejectors, single selective trigger. All 12-gauge barrels are back-bored, have lengthened forcing cones and longer choke tube system. Introduced 1992. Imported from Japan SKB Shotguns, Inc.

Price: Field **$1,699.00**

Price: Two-barrel field set, 12 & 20 . . . . . . **$2,749.00**

Price: Two-barrel field set, 20 & 28 or 28 & .410 . . . . . . **$2,829.00**

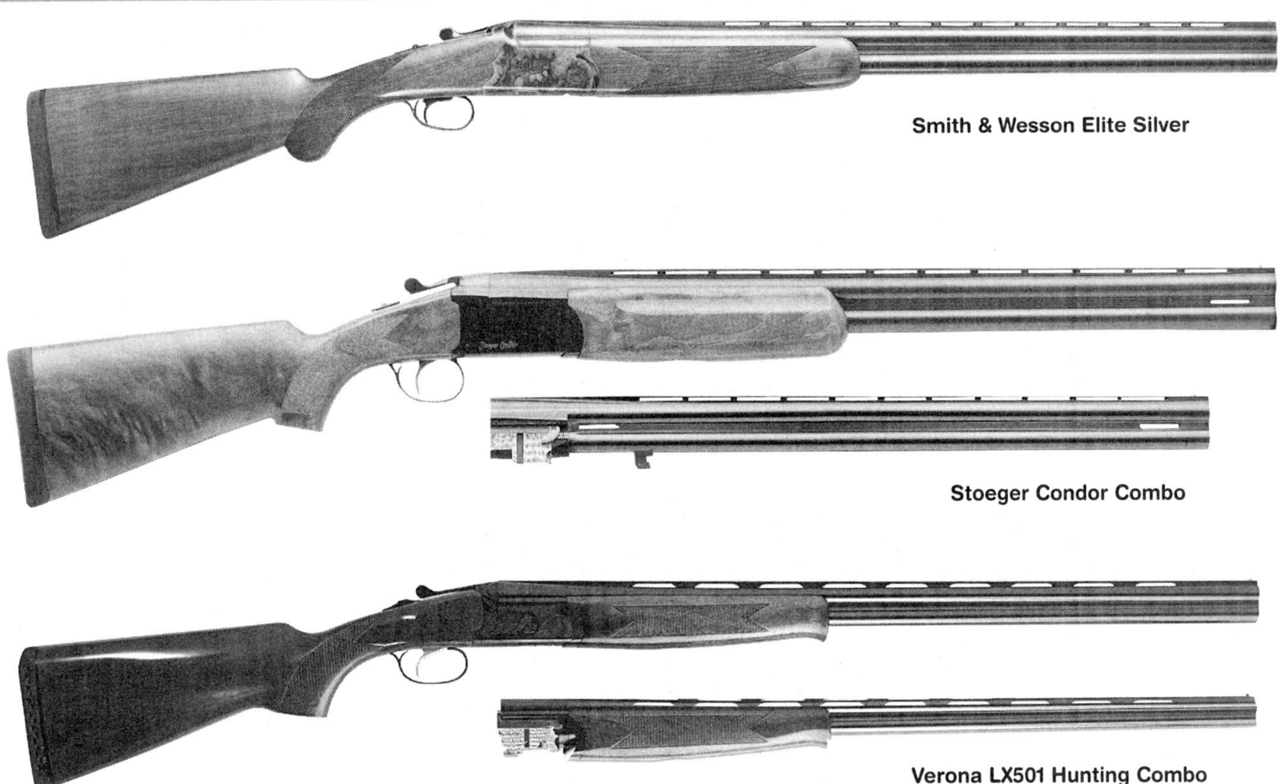

Smith & Wesson Elite Silver

Stoeger Condor Combo

Verona LX501 Hunting Combo

SMITH & WESSON ELITE SILVER SHOTGUNS

Gauge: 12, 3" chambers. **Barrel:** 26", 28", 30", rust-blued chopper-lump. **Weight:** 7.8 lbs. **Length:** 46-48". **Sights:** Ivory front bead, metal mid-bead. **Stock:** AAA (grade III) Turkish walnut stocks, hand-cut checkering, satin finish. **Features:** Smith & Wesson-designed trigger-plate action, hand-engraved receivers, bone-charcoal case hardening, lifetime warranty. Five choke tubes. Introduced 2007. Made in Turkey, imported by Smith & Wesson.

Price: **$2,380.00**

STOEGER CONDOR O/U SHOTGUNS

Gauge: 12, 20, 2-3/4" 3" chambers; 16, .410. **Barrel:** 22", 24", 26", 28", 30". **Weight:** 5.5 to 7.8 lbs. **Sights:** Brass bead. **Features:** IC, M, or F screw-in choke tubes with each gun. Oil finished hardwood with pistol grip and forend. Auto safety, single trigger, automatic extractors.

Price: Condor, 12, 20, 16 ga. or .410 . . . . **$399.00**
Price: Condor Supreme (w/mid bead), 12 or 20 ga. **$599.00**
Price: Condor Combo, 12 and 20 ga. Barrels, from **$549.00**
Price: Condor Youth, 20 ga. or .410 . . . . **$399.00**
Price: Condor Competition, 12 or 20 ga. **$599.00**
Price: Condor Combo, 12/20 ga., RH or LH (2007) **$829.00**
Price: Condor Outback, 12 or 20 ga., 20" barrel. **$369.00**

TRADITIONS CLASSIC SERIES O/U SHOTGUNS

Gauge: 12, 3"; 20, 3"; 16, 2-3/4"; 28, 2-3/4"; .410, 3". **Barrel:** 26" and 28". **Weight:** 6 lbs., 5 oz. to 7 lbs., 6 oz. **Length:** 43" to 45" overall. **Stock:** Walnut. **Features:** Single-selective trigger; chrome-lined barrels with screw-in choke tubes; extractors (Field Hunter and Field I models) or automatic ejectors (Field II and Field III models); rubber butt pad; top tang safety. Imported from Fausti of Italy by Traditions.

Price: Field Hunter: Blued receiver; 12 or 20 ga.; 26" bbl. has IC and Mod. tubes, 28" has mod. and full tubes **$669.00**
Price: Field I: Blued receiver; 12, 20, 28 ga. or .410; fixed chokes (26" has I.C. and mod., 28" has mod. and full). . **$619.00**
Price: Field II: Coin-finish receiver; 12, 16, 20, 28 ga. or .410; gold trigger; choke tubes **$789.00**
Price: Field III: Coin-finish receiver; gold engraving and trigger; 12 ga.; 26" or 28" bbl.; choke tubes **$999.00**
Price: Upland II: Blued receiver; 12 or 20 ga.; English-style straight walnut stock; choke tubes **$839.00**
Price: Upland III: Blued receiver, gold engraving; 20 ga.; high-grade pistol grip walnut stock; choke tubes **$1,059.00**
Price: Upland III: Blued, gold engraved receiver, 12 ga. Round pistol grip stock, choke tubes **$1,059.00**
Price: Sporting Clay II: Silver receiver; 12 ga.; ported barrels with skeet, i.c., mod. and full extended tubes. **$959.00**
Price: Sporting Clay III: Engraved receivers, 12 and 20 ga., walnut stock, vent rib, extended choke tubes. **$1,189.00**

TRADITIONS MAG 350 SERIES O/U SHOTGUNS

Gauge: 12, 3-1/2". **Barrel:** 24", 26" and 28". **Weight:** 7 lbs. to 7 lbs., 4 oz. **Length:** 41" to 45" overall. **Stock:** Walnut or composite with Mossy Oak Break-Up or Advantage Wetlands camouflage. **Features:** Black matte, engraved receiver; vent rib; automatic ejectors; single selective trigger; three screw-in choke tubes; rubber recoil pad; top tang safety. Imported from Fausti of Italy by Traditions.

Price: (Mag Hunter II: 28" black matte barrels, walnut stock, includes I.C., Mod. and Full tubes) **$799.00**
Price: (Turkey II: 24" or 26" camo barrels, Break-Up camo stock, includes Mod., Full and X-Full tubes). **$889.00**
Price: (Waterfowl II: 28" camo barrels, Advantage Wetlands camo stock, includes IC, Mod. and Full tubes). **$899.00**

TRISTAR HUNTER EX O/U SHOTGUN

Gauge: 12, 20, 28, .410. **Barrel:** 26", 28". **Weight:** 5.7 lbs. (.410); 6.0 lbs. (20, 28), 7.2-7.4 lbs. (12). Chrome-lined steel mono-block bar-rel, five Beretta-style choke tubes (SK, IC, M, IM, F). **Length:** NA. **Stock:** Walnut, cut checkering. 14.25"x1.5"x2-3/8". **Sights:** Brass front sight. **Features:** All have extractors, engraved receiver, sealed actions, self-adjusting locking bolts, single selective trigger, ventilated rib. 28 ga. and .410 built on true frames. Five-year warranty. Imported from Italy by Tristar Sporting Arms Ltd.

Price: From **$549.00**

VERONA LX501 HUNTING O/U SHOTGUNS

Gauge: 12, 20, 28, .410 (2-3/4", 3" chambers). **Barrel:** 28"; 12, 20 ga. have Interchoke tubes, 28 ga. and .410 have fixed Full & Mod. **Weight:** 6-7 lbs. **Stock:** Matte-finished walnut with machine-cut checkering. **Features:** Gold-plated single-selective trigger; ejectors; engraved, blued receiver, non-automatic safety; coil spring-operated firing pins. Introduced 1999. Imported from Italy by B.C. Outdoors.

Price: 12 and 20 ga. **$878.08**
Price: 28 ga. and .410. . . . . **$926.72**
Price: .410. . . . . **$907.01**
Price: Combos 20/28, 28/.410 . . . . **$1,459.20**

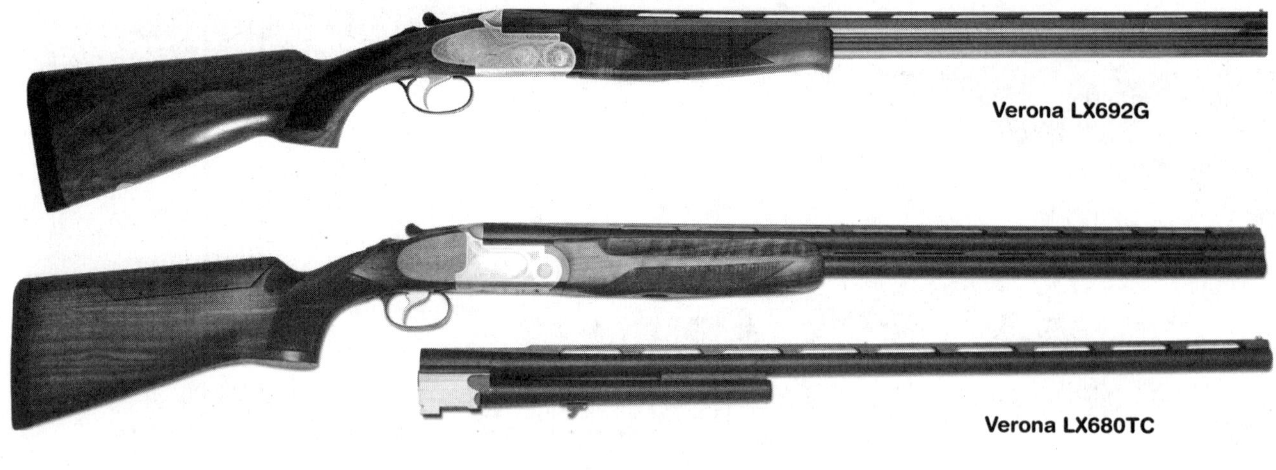

Verona LX692G

Verona LX680TC

Verona LX702 GTC

Weatherby Athena Grade V Classic Field

Verona LX692 Gold Hunting O/U Shotguns

Similar to Verona LX501 except engraved, silvered receiver with false sideplates showing gold inlaid bird hunting scenes on three sides; Schnabel forend tip; hand-cut checkering; black rubber butt pad. Available in 12 and 20 gauge only, five Interchoke tubes. Introduced 1999. Imported from Italy by B.C. Outdoors.

Price: **$1,295.00**
Price: LX692G Combo 28/.410...................... **$2,192.40**

Verona LX680 Sporting O/U Shotgun

Similar to Verona LX501 except engraved, silvered receiver; ventilated middle rib; beavertail forend; hand-cut checkering; available in 12 or 20 gauge only with 2-3/4" chambers. Introduced 1999. Imported from Italy by B.C. Outdoors.

Price: **$1,159.68**

Verona LX680 Skeet/Sporting/Trap O/U Shotgun

Similar to Verona LX501 except skeet or trap stock dimensions; beavertail forend, palm swell on pistol grip; ventilated center barrel rib. Introduced 1999. Imported from Italy by B.C. Outdoors.

Price: **$1,736.96**

Verona LX692 Gold Sporting O/U Shotgun

Similar to Verona LX680 except false sideplates have gold-inlaid bird hunting scenes on three sides; red high-visibility front sight. Introduced 1999. Imported from Italy by B.C. Outdoors.

Price: Skeet/sporting.............................. **$1,765.12**
Price: Trap (32" barrel, 7-7/8 lbs.) **$1,594.80**

VERONA LX680 COMPETITION TRAP O/U SHOTGUNS

Gauge: 12. **Barrel:** 30" O/U, 32" single bbl. **Weight:** 8-3/8 lbs. combo, 7 lbs. single. **Stock:** Walnut. **Sights:** White front, mid-rib bead. **Features:** Interchangeable barrels switch from OU to single configurations. 5 Briley chokes in combo, 4 in single bbl. extended forcing cones, ported barrels 32" with raised rib. By B.C. Outdoors.

Price: Trap Single (LX680TGTSB).................... **$1,736.96**
Price: Trap Combo (LX680TC)....................... **$2,553.60**

VERONA LX702 GOLD TRAP COMBO O/U SHOTGUNS

Gauge: 20/28, 2-3/4" chamber. **Barrel:** 30". **Weight:** 7 lbs. **Stock:** Turkish walnut with beavertail forearm. **Sights:** White front bead. **Features:** 2-barrel competition gun. Color case-hardened side plates and receiver with gold inlaid pheasant. Vent rib between barrels. 5 Interchokes. Imported from Italy by B.C. Outdoors.

Price: Combo **$2,467.84**
Price: 20 ga....................................... **$1,829.12**

Verona LX702 Skeet/Trap O/U Shotguns

Similar to Verona LX702. Both are 12 gauge and 2-3/4" chamber. Skeet has 28" barrel and weighs 7.75 lbs. Trap has 32" barrel and weighs 7-7/8 lbs. By B.C. Outdoors.

Price: Skeet **$1,829.12**
Price: Trap **$1,829.12**

WEATHERBY ATHENA GRADE V AND GRADE III CLASSIC FIELD O/U SHOTGUNS

Gauge: Grade V: 12, 20, 3" chambers. Grade III: 12, 20, 3" chambers; 28, 2-3/4" chambers. **Barrel:** 26", 28" monobloc, IMC multi-choke tubes. Modified Greener crossbolt action. Matte ventilated top rib with brilliant front bead. **Weight:** 12 ga., 7.25 to 8 lbs.; 20 ga. 6.5 to 7.25 lbs. **Length:** 43" to 45". **Stock:** Rounded pistol grip, slender forend, Old English recoil pad. Grade V has oil-finished AAA American Claro walnut with 20-lpi checkering. Grade III has AA Claro walnut with oil finish, fine-line checkering. **Features:** Silver nitride/gray receivers; Grade V has rose and scroll engraving with gold-overlay upland game scenes. Grade III has hunting scene engraving. Top levers engraved with gold Weatherby flying "W". Introduced 1999. Imported from Japan by Weatherby.

Price: Grade V **$2,773.00**
Price: Grade III **$2,510.00**

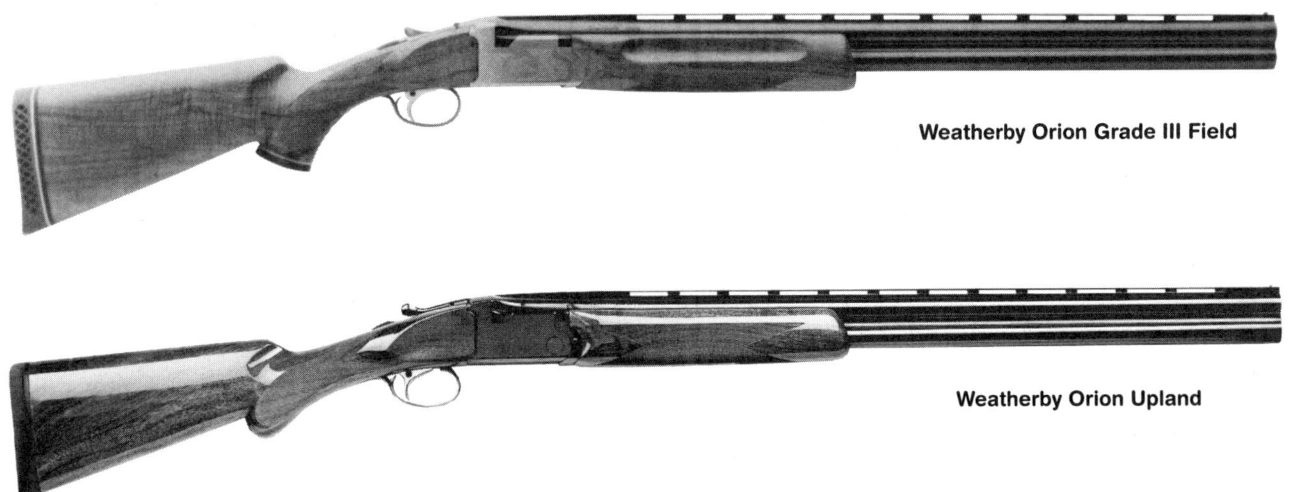

Weatherby Orion Grade III Field

Weatherby Orion Upland

WEATHERBY ORION O/U SHOTGUNS

Gauge: 12, 20, 3" chambers; 28, 2-3/4" chamber. **Barrel:** 26", 28", IMC multi-choke tubes. Matte ventilated top rib with brilliant bead front sight. **Weight:** 6-1/2 to 8 lbs. **Stock:** 14.25"x1.5"x2.5". American walnut, checkered grip and forend. Old English recoil pad. **Features:** Selective automatic ejectors, single selective inertia trigger. Top tang safety, Greener cross bolt. Silver-gray receiver. Grade III has A-grade oil-finished Claro walnut fancy stock with fineline checkering, 24k gold plate overlay. Grade II Field stock has high-gloss finish, and bird on receiver is not gold. Available in 12 gauge, 26", 28", 30" barrels, 20 gauge, 26" 28", both with 3" chambers, 28 gauge, 26", 2-3/4" chambers. All have IMC choke tubes. Orion Upland has plain blued receiver, gold W on trigger guard; rounded pistol grip, slender forend of Claro walnut with high-gloss finish; gold front bead, black butt pad. Available in 12 and 20 gauge with 26" and 28" barrels. Introduced 1999. SSC (Super Sporting Clays) is 12 ga. only, 3" chamber, with 28", 30", 32" barrels and skeet, SC1, Imp. Cyl., SC2, Mod. IMC choke tubes. Weighs about 8 lbs. Stock measures 14-3/4"x2.25"x1.5"; claro walnut with satin oil finish, Schnabel forend tip, sporter-style pistol grip, Pachmayr Decelerator recoil pad. Lengthened forcing cones and back-boring; ported barrels with 12mm grooved rib with mid-bead sight; mechanical trigger is adjustable for length of pull. Stock is cast off from top to bottom of the butt (3 to 6 millimeters). Introduced 1998. Imported from Japan by Weatherby.

Price: Grade III Classic Field **$2,258.00**
Price: Classic Field **$1,873.00**
Price: Upland Classic Field **$1,500.00**
Price: Super Sporting Clays **$2,378.00**

WINCHESTER SELECT MODEL 101 O/U SHOTGUNS

Gauge: 12, 2-3/4", 3" chambers. **Barrel:** 28", 30", 32", ported, Invector Plus choke system. **Weight:** 7 lbs. 6 oz. to 7 lbs. 12. oz. **Stock:** Checkered high-gloss grade II/III walnut stock, Pachmayr Decelerator sporting pad. **Features:** Chrome-plated chambers; back-bored barrels; tang barrel selec-tor/safety; Signature extended choke tubes. Model 101 Field comes with solid brass bead front sight, three tubes, engraved receiver. Model 101 Sporting has adjustable trigger, 10mm runway rib, white mid-bead, Tru-Glo front sight, 30" and 32" barrels. Camo version of Model 101 Field comes with full-coverage Mossy Oak Duck Blind pattern. Model 101 Pigeon Grade Trap has 10mm steel runway rib, mid-bead sight, interchangeable fiber-optic front sight, porting and vented side ribs, adjustable trigger shoe, fixed raised comb or adjustable comb, Grade III/IV walnut, 30" or 32" barrels, molded ABS hard case. Reintroduced 2008. From Winchester Repeating Arms. Co.

Price: Select Model 101 Field **$1,899.00**
Price: Select Model 101 Sporting **$1,999.00**
Price: Select Model 101 Field Mossy Oak **$2,239.00**
Price: Select Model 101 Pigeon Grade Trap, intr. 2008 . . . . **$2,149.00**
Price: Select Model 101 Pigeon Grade Trap w/adj. comb, intr. 2008 . . . . **$2,279.00**

Variety of models for utility and sporting use, including some competitive shooting.

Bill Hanus Birdgun

CZ Bobwhite

CZ Ringneck

CZ Durango

ARRIETA SIDELOCK DOUBLE SHOTGUNS

Gauge: 12, 16, 20, 28, .410. **Barrel:** Length and chokes to customer specs. **Weight:** To customer specs. **Stock:** To customer specs. Straight English with checkered butt (standard), or pistol grip. Select European walnut with oil finish. **Features:** Essentially custom gun with myriad options. H&H pattern hand-detachable sidelocks, selective automatic ejectors, double triggers (hinged front) standard. Some have selfopening action. Finish and engraving to customer specs. Imported from Spain by Quality Arms, Inc.

Price: Model 557 . . . . **$4,500.00**
Price: Model 570 . . . . **$5,350.00**
Price: Model 578 . . . . **$5,880.00**
Price: Model 600 Imperial **$7,995.00**
Price: Model 601 Imperial Tiro **$9,160.00**
Price: Model 801 . . . . **$14,275.00**
Price: Model 802 . . . . **$14,275.00**
Price: Model 803 . . . . **$9,550.00**
Price: Model 871 . . . . **$6,670.00**
Price: Model 872 . . . . **$17,850.00**
Price: Model 873 . . . . **$16,275.00**
Price: Model 874 . . . . **$13,125.00**
Price: Model 875 . . . . **$19,850.00**
Price: Model 931 . . . . **$20,895.00**

AYA MODEL 4/53 SHOTGUNS

Gauge: 12, 16, 20, 28, 410. **Barrel:** 26", 27", 28", 30". **Weight:** To customer specifications. **Length:** To customer specifications. **Features:** Hammerless boxlock action; double triggers; light scroll engraving; automatic safety; straight grip oil finish walnut stock; checkered butt. Made in Spain. Imported by New England Custom Gun Service, Lt.

Price: **$2,999.00**
Price: No. 2 . . . . **$4,799.00**
Price: No. 2 Rounded Action **$5,199.00**

BERETTA 471 SIDE-BY-SIDE SHOTGUNS

Gauge: 12, 20; 3" chamber. **Barrel:** 24", 26", 28"; 6mm rib. **Weight:** 6.5 lbs. **Stock:** English or pistol stock, straight butt for various types of recoil pads. Beavertail forend. English stock with recoil pad in red or black rubber, or in walnut and splinter forend. Select European walnut, checkered, oil finish. **Features:** Optima-Choke Extended Choke Tubes. Automatic ejection or mechanical extraction. Firing-pin block safety, manual or automatic, open top-lever safety. Introduced 2007. Imported from Italy by Beretta U.S.A.

Price: Silver Hawk **$3,750.00**
Price: 471EL **$8,350.00**

BILL HANUS NOBILE III BY FABARM

Gauge: 20. **Barrel:** 28" Tribor® barrels with 3" chambers and extra-long 82mm (3-1/4") internal choke tubes. **Weight:** 5.75 lbs. **Stock:** Upgraded walnut 1-1/2"x2-1/4"x14-3/8", with 1/4" cast-off to a wood butt plate. Altering to 1/4" cast-on for left-handed shooters, $300 extra. **Features:** Tribor® barrels feature extra-long forcing cones along with over-boring, back-boring and extra-long (82mm vs 50mm) choke tubes which put more pellets in the target area. Paradox®-rifled choke tube for wider patterns at short-range targets. Adjustable for automatic ejectors or manual extraction. Adjustable opening tension. Fitted leather case.

Price: **$3,495.00**

CZ BOBWHITE AND RINGNECK SHOTGUNS

Gauge: 12, 20, 28, .410. (5 screw-in chokes in 12 and 20 ga. and fixed chokes in IC and Mod in .410). **Barrel:** 20". **Weight:** 6.5 lbs. **Length:** NA. **Stock:** Sculptured Turkish walnut with straight English-style grip and double triggers (Bobwhite) or conventional American pistol grip with a single trigger (Ringneck). Both are hand checkered 20 lpi. **Features:** Both color case-hardened shotguns are hand engraved.

Price: Bobwhite **$695.00**
Price: Ringneck **$912.00**

CZ DURANGO AND AMARILLO SHOTGUNS

Gauge: 12, 3" chambers. **Barrel:** 20". **Weight:** 6.7 lbs. **Length:** NA. **Stock:** Hand checkered walnut with old style round knob pistol grip. **Features:** The Durango comes with a single trigger, while the Amarillo is a double trigger shotgun The receiver, trigger guard, and forend metal are finished in 19th century color case-hardening.

Price: **$795.00**

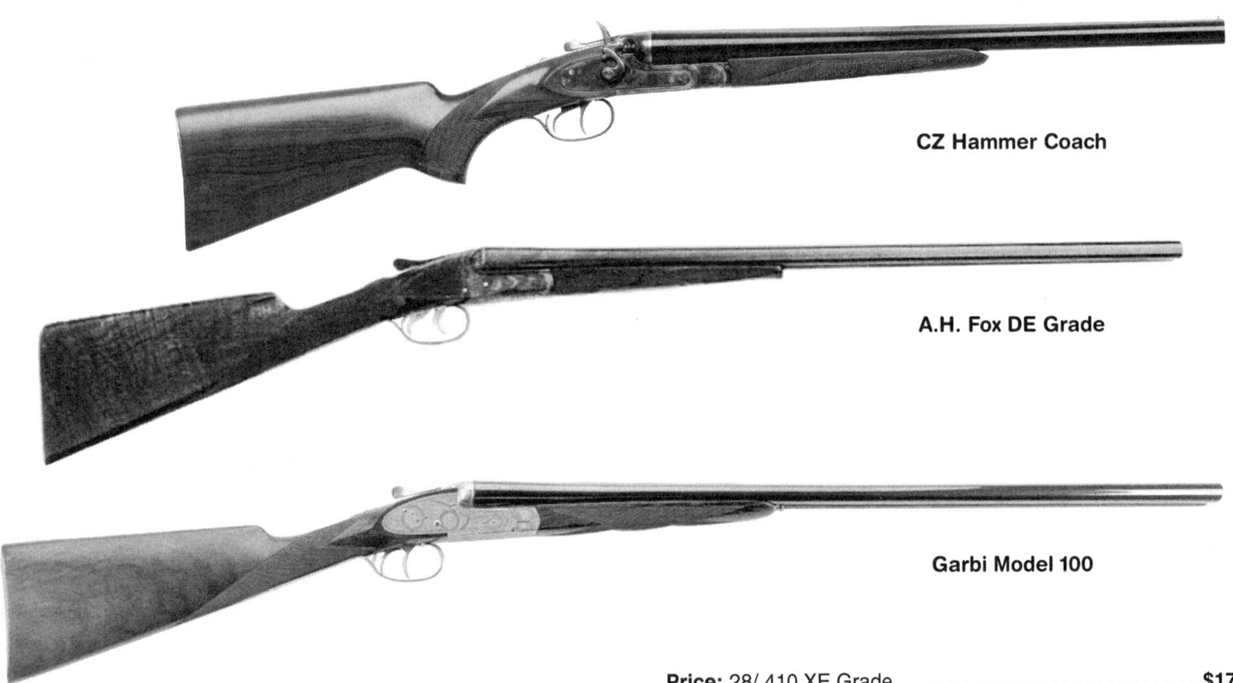

CZ Hammer Coach

A.H. Fox DE Grade

Garbi Model 100

CZ HAMMER COACH SHOTGUNS

Gauge: 12, 3" chambers. **Barrel:** 20". **Weight:** 6.7 lbs. **Length:** NA. **Stock:** NA. **Features:** Following in the tradition of the guns used by the stagecoach guards of the 1880's, this cowboy gun features double triggers, 19th century color case-hardening and fully functional external hammers.

Price: **$795.00**

DAKOTA PREMIER GRADE SHOTGUN

Gauge: 12, 16, 20, 28, .410. **Barrel:** 27". **Weight:** NA. **Length:** NA. **Stock:** Exhibition-grade English walnut, hand-rubbed oil finish with straight grip and splinter forend. **Features:** French grey finish; 50 percent coverage engraving; double triggers; selective ejectors. Finished to customer specifications. Made in U.S. by Dakota Arms.

Price: From **$14,950.00**

Dakota Legend Shotgun

Similar to Premier Grade except has special selection English walnut, full-coverage scroll engraving, oak and leather case. Made in U.S. by Dakota Arms.

Price: From **$19,000.00**

E.M.F. OLD WEST HAMMER SHOTGUN

Gauge: 12. **Barrel:** 20". **Weight:** 8 lbs. **Length:** 37" overall. **Stock:** Smooth walnut with steel butt place. **Sights:** Large brass bead. **Features:** Colt-style exposed hammers rebounding type; blued receiver and barrels; cylinder bore. Introduced 2006. Imported from China for E.M.F. by TTN.

Price: **$449.90**

FOX, A.H., SIDE-BY-SIDE SHOTGUNS

Gauge: 16, 20, 28, .410. **Barrel:** Length and chokes to customer specifications. Rust-blued Chromox or Krupp steel. **Weight:** 5-1/2 to 6.75 lbs. **Stock:** Dimensions to customer specifications. Hand-checkered Turkish Circassian walnut with hand-rubbed oil finish. Straight, semi or full pistol grip; splinter, Schnabel or beavertail forend; traditional pad, hard rubber buttplate or skeleton butt. **Features:** Boxlock action with automatic ejectors; double or Fox single selective trigger. Scalloped, rebated and color case-hardened receiver; hand finished and handengraved. Grades differ in engraving, inlays, grade of wood, amount of hand finishing. Introduced 1993. Made in U.S. by Connecticut Shotgun Mfg.

Price: CE Grade **$13,500.00**
Price: XE Grade **$15,500.00**
Price: DE Grade **$18,000.00**
Price: FE Grade **$23,000.00**
Price: Exhibition Grade **$36,500.00**
Price: 28/.410 CE Grade **$15,500.00**
Price: 28/.410 XE Grade **$17,500.00**
Price: 28/.410 DE Grade **$20,000.00**
Price: 28/.410 FE Grade **$25,000.00**

GARBI MODEL 100 DOUBLE SHOTGUN

Gauge: 12, 16, 20, 28. **Barrel:** 26", 28", choked to customer specs. **Weight:** 5-1/2 to 7.5 lbs. **Stock:** 14.5"x2.25"x1.5". European walnut. Straight grip, checkered butt, classic forend. **Features:** Sidelock action, automatic ejectors, double triggers standard. Color case-hardened action, coin finish optional. Single trigger; beavertail forend, etc. optional. Five additional models available. Imported from Spain by Wm. Larkin Moore.

Price: From **$4,850.00**

Garbi Model 101 Side-by-Side Shotgun

Similar to the Garbi Model 100 except hand engraved with scroll engraving; select walnut stock; better overall quality than the Model 100. Imported from Spain by Wm. Larkin Moore.

Price: From **$6,250.00**

Garbi Model 103 A & B Side-by-Side Shotguns

Similar to the Garbi Model 100 except has Purdey-type fine scroll and rosette engraving. Better overall quality than the Model 101. Model 103B has nickel-chrome steel barrels, H&H-type easy opening mechanism; other mechanical details remain the same. Imported from Spain by Wm. Larkin Moore.

Price: Model 103A. From **$8,000.00**
Price: Model 103B. From **$11,800.00**

Garbi Model 200 Side-by-Side Shotgun

Similar to the Garbi Model 100 except has heavy-duty locks, magnum proofed. Very fine Continen-tal-style floral and scroll engraving, well figured walnut stock. Other mechanical features remain the same. Imported from Spain by Wm. Larkin Moore.

Price: **$11,200.00**

KIMBER VALIER SIDE-BY-SIDE SHOTGUN

Gauge: 20, 16, 3" chambers. Barrels: 26" or 28", IC and M. **Weight:** 6 lbs. 8 oz. **Stock:** Turkish walnut, English style. **Features:** Sidelock design, double triggers, 50-percent engraving; 24 lpi checkering; auto-ejectors (extractors only on Grade I). Color case-hardened sidelocks, rust blue barrels. Imported from Turkey by Kimber Mfg., Inc.

Price: Grade II **$4,999.00**

LEBEAU-COURALLY BOXLOCK SIDE-BY-SIDE SHOTGUN

Gauge: 12, 16, 20, 28, .410-bore. **Barrel:** 25" to 32". **Weight:** To customer specifications. **Stock:** French walnut. **Features:** Anson & Deely-type action with automatic ejectors; single or double triggers. Custom gun built to customer specifications. Imported from Belgium by Wm. Larkin Moore.

Price: From **$25,500.00**

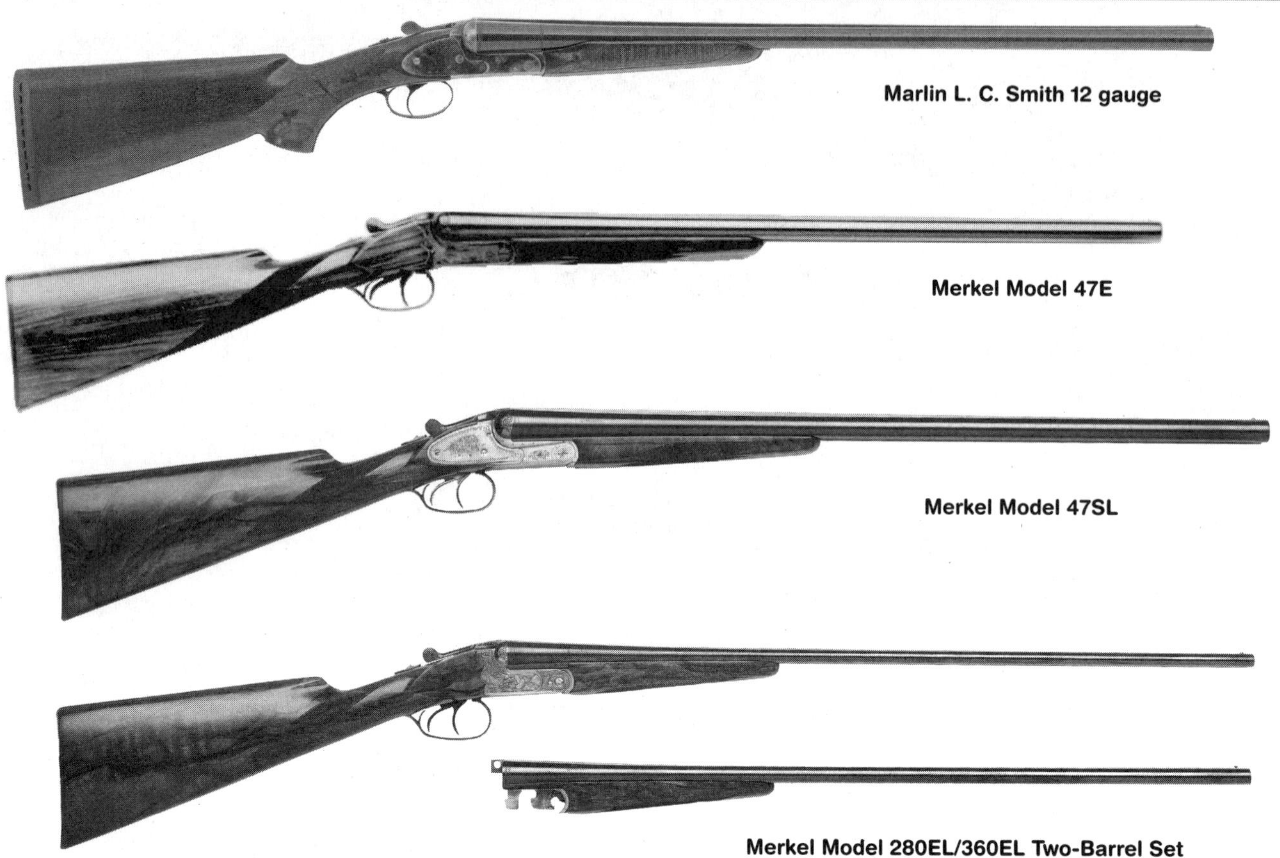

LEBEAU-COURALLY SIDELOCK SIDE-BY-SIDE SHOTGUN

Gauge: 12, 16, 20, 28, .410-bore. **Barrel:** 25" to 32". **Weight:** To customer specifications. **Stock:** Fancy French walnut. **Features:** Holland & Holland-type action with automatic ejectors; single or double triggers. Custom gun built to customer specifications. Imported from Belgium by Wm. Larkin Moore.

Price: From **$56,000.00**

MARLIN L. C. SMITH SIDE-BY-SIDE SHOTGUN

Gauge: 12, 20, 28, .410. **Stock:** Checkered walnut w/recoil pad. **Features:** 3" chambers, single trigger, selective automatic ejectors; 3 choke tubes (IC, Mod., Full); solid rib, bead front sight. Imported from Italy by Marlin. Introduced 2005.

Price: LC12-DB (28" barrel, 43" OAL, 6.25 lbs) **$1,962.00**
Price: LC28-DB (26" barrel, 41" OAL, 6 lbs) **$1,484.00**

MERKEL MODEL 47E, 147E SIDE-BY-SIDE SHOTGUNS

Gauge: 12, 3" chambers, 16, 2.75" chambers, 20, 3" chambers. **Barrel:** 12, 16 ga.-28"; 20 ga.-26.75" (Imp. Cyl. & Mod., Mod. & Full). **Weight:** About 6.75 lbs. (12 ga.). **Stock:** Oil-finished walnut; straight English or pistol grip. **Features:** Anson & Deeley-type boxlock action with single selective or double triggers, automatic safety, cocking indicators. Color case-hardened receiver with standard arabesque engraving. Imported from Germany by GSI.

Price: Model 47E (H&H ejectors) **$4,395.00**
Price: Model 147E (as above with ejectors) **$5,495.00**

Merkel Model 47SL, 147SL Side-by-Side Shotguns

Similar to Model 47E except H&H style sidelock action with cocking indicators, ejectors. Silver-grayed receiver and sideplates have arabesque engraving, engraved border and screws (Model 47S), or fine hunting scene engraving (Model 147S). Imported from Germany by GSI.

Price: Model 47SL **$8,495.00**
Price: Model 147SL **$10,495.00**

Merkel Model 280EL, 360EL Shotguns

Similar to Model 47E except smaller frame. Greener cross bolt with double under-barrel locking lugs, fine engraved hunting scenes on silver-grayed receiver, luxury-grade wood, Anson and Deely boxlock action. H&H ejectors, single-selective or double triggers. Introduced 2000. From Merkel.

Price: Model 280EL (28 gauge, 28" barrel, Imp. Cyl. and Mod. chokes) **$7,295.00**
Price: Model 360EL (.410, 28" barrel, Mod. and Full chokes) **$7,295.00**
Price: Model 280/360EL two-barrel set (28 and .410 gauge as above) **$10,5955.00**

Merkel Model 280SL and 360SL Shotguns

Similar to Model 280EL and 360EL except has sidelock action, double triggers, English-style arabesque engraving. Introduced 2000. From Merkel.

Price: Model 280SL (28 gauge, 28" barrel, Imp. Cyl. and Mod. chokes) **$10,995.00**
Price: Model 360SL (.410, 28" barrel, Mod. and Full chokes) **$10,995.00**

PIOTTI KING NO. 1 SIDE-BY-SIDE SHOTGUN

Gauge: 12, 16, 20, 28, .410. **Barrel:** 25" to 30" (12 ga.), 25" to 28" (16, 20, 28, .410). To customer specs. Chokes as specified. **Weight:** 6.5 lbs. to 8 lbs. (12 ga. to customer specs.). **Stock:** Dimensions to customer specs. Finely figured walnut; straight grip with checkered butt with classic splinter forend and hand-rubbed oil finish standard. Pistol grip, beavertail forend. **Features:** Holland & Holland pattern sidelock action, automatic ejectors. Double trigger; non-selective single trigger optional. Coin finish standard; color case-hardened optional. Top rib; level, file-cut; concave, ventilated optional. Very fine, full coverage scroll engraving with small floral bouquets. Imported from Italy by Wm. Larkin Moore.

Price: From **$29,600.00**

Piotti King Extra Side-by-Side Shotgun

Similar to the Piotti King No. 1 except with upgraded engraving. Choice of any type of engraving, including bulino game scene engraving and game scene engraving with gold inlays. Engraved and signed by a master engraver. Other mechanical specifications remain the same. Imported from Italy by Wm. Larkin Moore.

Price: From **$35,000.00**

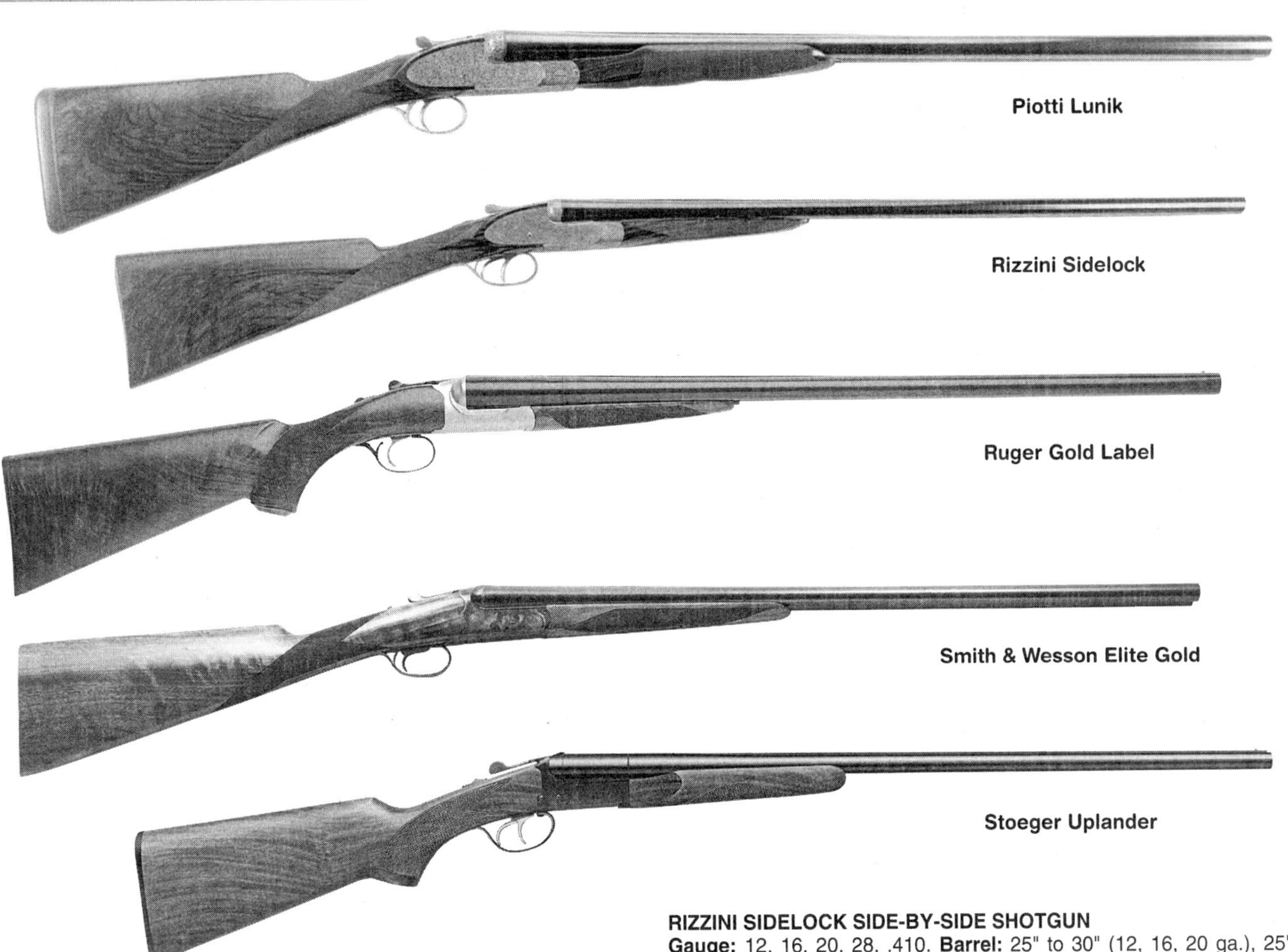

Piotti Lunik Side-by-Side Shotgun

Similar to the Piotti King No. 1 in overall quality. Has Renaissance-style large scroll engraving in relief. Best quality Holland & Holland-pattern sidelock ejector double with chopper lump (demi-bloc) barrels. Other mechanical specifications remain the same. Imported from Italy by Wm. Larkin Moore.

Price: From **$30,900.00**

PIOTTI PIUMA SIDE-BY-SIDE SHOTGUN

Gauge: 12, 16, 20, 28, .410. **Barrel:** 25" to 30" (12 ga.), 25" to 28" (16, 20, 28, .410). **Weight:** 5-1/2 to 6-1/4 lbs. (20 ga.). **Stock:** Dimensions to customer specs. Straight grip stock with walnut checkered butt, classic splinter forend, hand-rubbed oil finish are standard; pistol grip, beavertail forend, satin luster finish optional. **Features:** Anson & Deeley boxlock ejector double with chopper lump barrels. Level, file-cut rib, light scroll and rosette engraving, scalloped frame. Double triggers; single non-selective optional. Coin finish standard, color case-hardened optional. Imported from Italy by Wm. Larkin Moore.

Price: From **$14,800.00**

REMINGTON SPR210 SIDE-BY-SIDE SHOTGUNS

Gauge: 12, 20, 28, .410 bore, 3" chambers; 28, 2-3/4" chambers. **Barrel:** 26", 28", blued chrome-lined. **Weight:** 6.75 to 7.5 lbs. **Stock:** checkered walnut stock and forend, 14.5" LOP; 1.5" drop at comb; 2.5" drop at heel. **Features:** Nickel or blued receiver. Single selective mechanical trigger, selective automatic ejectors; SC-4 choke tube set on most models. Steel receiver/mono block, auto tang safety, rubber recoil pad. Introduced 2008. Imported by Remington Arms Co.

Price: SPR210, from **$479.00**

REMINGTON SPR220 SIDE-BY-SIDE SHOTGUNS

Gauge: 12, 20, 2-3/4" or 3" chambers. **Barrel:** 20", 26", blued chrome-lined. **Weight:** 6.5 to 7 lbs. Otherwise similar to SPR210 except has double trigger/extractors. Introduced 2008. Imported by Remington Arms Co.

Price: SPR220, from **$342.00**

RIZZINI SIDELOCK SIDE-BY-SIDE SHOTGUN

Gauge: 12, 16, 20, 28, .410. **Barrel:** 25" to 30" (12, 16, 20 ga.), 25" to 28" (28, .410). To customer specs. Chokes as specified. **Weight:** 6.5 lbs. to 8 lbs. (12 ga. to customer specs). **Stock:** Dimensions to customer specs. Finely figured walnut; straight grip with checkered butt with classic splinter forend and hand-rubbed oil finish standard. Pistol grip, beavertail forend. **Features:** Sidelock action, auto ejectors. Double triggers or non-selective single trigger standard. Coin finish standard. Imported from Italy by Wm. Larkin Moore.

Price: 12, 20 ga. From **$66,900.00**

Price: 28, .410 bore. From **$75,500.00**

RUGER GOLD LABEL SIDE-BY-SIDE SHOTGUN

Gauge: 12, 3" chambers. **Barrel:** 28" with skeet tubes. **Weight:** 6.5 lbs. **Length:** 45". **Stock:** American walnut straight or pistol grip. **Sights:** Gold bead front, full length rib, serrated top. **Features:** Spring-assisted break-open, SS trigger, auto eject. Five interchangeable screw-in choke tubes, combination safety/barrel selector with auto safety reset.

Price: **$3,226.00**

SMITH & WESSON ELITE GOLD SHOTGUNS

Gauge: 20, 3" chambers. **Barrel:** 26", 28", 30", rust-blued chopper-lump. **Weight:** 6.5 lbs. **Length:** 43.5-45.5". **Sights:** Ivory front bead, metal mid-bead. **Stock:** AAA (grade III) Turkish walnut stocks, hand-cut checkering, satin finish. English grip or pistol grip. **Features:** Smith & Wesson-designed trigger-plate action, hand-engraved receivers, bone-charcoal case hardening,lifetime warranty. Five choke tubes. Introduced 2007. Made in Turkey, imported by Smith & Wesson.

Price: **$2,380.00**

STOEGER UPLANDER SIDE-BY-SIDE SHOTGUNS

Gauge: 16, 28, 2-3/4 chambers. 12, 20, .410, 3" chambers. **Barrel:** 22", 24", 26", 28". **Weight:** 7.3 lbs. **Sights:** Brass bead. **Features:** Double trigger, IC & M fixed choke tubes with gun.

Price: With fixed or screw-in chokes. **$369.00**

Price: Supreme, screw-in chokes, 12 or 20 ga. **$489.00**

Price: Youth, 20 ga. or .410, 22" barrel, double trigger **$369.00**

Price: Combo, 20/28 ga. or 12/20 ga. **$649.00**

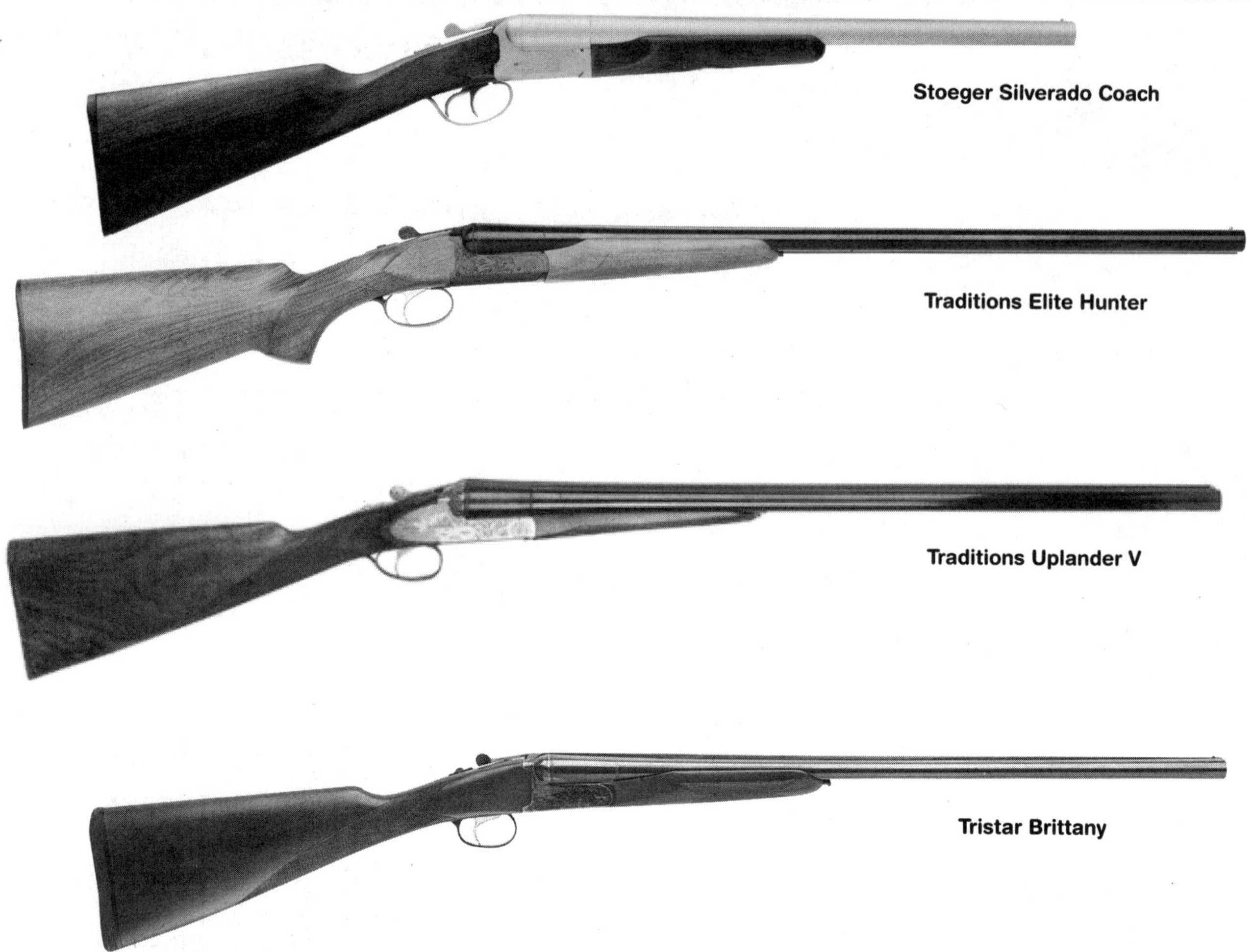

Stoeger Silverado Coach

Traditions Elite Hunter

Traditions Uplander V

Tristar Brittany

STOEGER COACH GUN SIDE-BY-SIDE SHOTGUNS

Gauge: 12, 20, 2-3/4", 3" chambers. **Barrel:** 20". **Weight:** 6.5 lbs. **Stock:** Brown hardwood, classic beavertail forend. **Sights:** Brass bead. **Features:** IC & M fixed chokes, tang auto safety, auto extractors, black plastic buttplate. Imported by Benelli USA.

Price: Supreme blued finish **$469.00**
Price: Supreme blued barrel, stainless receiver **$469.00**
Price: Silverado Coach Gun with English synthetic stock. **$469.00**

TRADITIONS ELITE SERIES SIDE-BY-SIDE SHOTGUNS

Gauge: 12, 3"; 20, 3"; 28, 2-3/4"; .410, 3". **Barrel:** 26". **Weight:** 5 lbs., 12 oz. to 6.5 lbs. **Length:** 43" overall. **Stock:** Walnut. **Features:** Chrome-lined barrels; fixed chokes (Elite Field III ST, Field I DT and Field I ST) or choke tubes (Elite Hunter ST); extractors (Hunter ST and Field I models) or automatic ejectors (Field III ST); top tang safety. Imported from Fausti of Italy by Traditions.

Price: Elite Field I DT C 12, 20, 28 ga. or .410; IC and Mod. fixed chokes (F and F on .410); double triggers . . **$789.00 to $969.00**
Price: Elite Field I ST C 12, 20, 28 ga. or .410; same as DT but with single trigger . . . . **$969.00 to $1,169.00**
Price: Elite Field III ST C 28 ga. or .410; gold-engraved receiver; high-grade walnut stock **$2,099.00**
Price: Elite Hunter ST C 12 or 20 ga.; blued receiver; IC and Mod. choke tubes **$999.00**

TRADITIONS UPLANDER SERIES SIDE-BY-SIDE SHOTGUNS

Gauge: 12, 3"; 20, 3". **Barrel:** 26", 28". **Weight:** 6-1/4 lbs. to 6.5 lbs. **Length:** 43" to 45" overall. **Stock:** Walnut. **Features:** Barrels threaded for choke tubes (Improved Cylinder, Modified and Full); top tang safety, extended trigger guard. Engraved silver receiver with side plates and lavish gold inlays. Imported from Fausti of Italy by Traditions.

Price: Uplander III Silver 12, 20 ga. **$2,699.00**
Price: Uplander V Silver 12, 20 ga. **$3,199.00**

TRISTAR BRITTANY CLASSIC SIDE-BY-SIDE SHOTGUN

Gauge: 12, 16, 20, 28, .410, 3" chambers. **Barrel:** 27", chrome lined, three Beretta-style choke tubes (IC, M, F). **Weight:** 6.3 to 6.7 lbs. **Stock:** Rounded pistol grip, satin oil finish. **Features:** Engraved case-colored one-piece frame, auto se-lective ejectors, single selective trigger, solid raised barrel rib, top tang safety. Imported from Spain by Tristar Sporting Arms Ltd.

Price: From **$1,419.00**

WEATHERBY SBS ATHENA D'ITALIA SIDE-BY-SIDE SHOTGUNS

Gauge: D'Italia: 12, 20, 2-3/4" or 3" chambers, 28, 2-3/4" chambers. **Barrel:** 26" on 20 and 28 gauges; 28" on 12 ga. Chrome-lined, lengthened forcing cones, backbored. **Weight:** 6.75 to 7.25 lbs. **Length:** 42.5" to 44.5". **Stock:** Walnut, 20-lpi laser cut checkering, "New Scottish" pattern. **Features:** All come with foam-lined take-down case. Machined steel receiver, hardened and chromed with coin finish, engraved triggerguard with roll-formed border. D'Italia has double triggers, brass front bead. PG is identical to D'Italia, except for rounded pistol grip and semi-beavertail forearm. Deluxe features sculpted frameheads, Bolino-style engraved game scene with floral engraving. AAA Fancy Turkish walnut, straight grip, 24-lpi hand checkering, hand-rubbed oil finish. Single mechanical trigger; right barrel fires first. Imported from Italy by Weatherby.

Price: SBS Athena D'Italia, 12 or 20 ga.. . . . . **$2,925.00**
Price: SBS Athena D'Italia, 28 ga. **$3,065.00**
Price: SBS Athena D'Italia PG, 12 or 20 ga.. . . . . **$3,599.00**
Price: SBS Athena D'Italia Deluxe, 12 or 20 ga.. . . . . **$7,625.00**
Price: SBS Athena D'Italia Deluxe, 28 ga. **$7,789.00**

Variety of designs for utility and sporting purposes, as well as for competitive shooting.

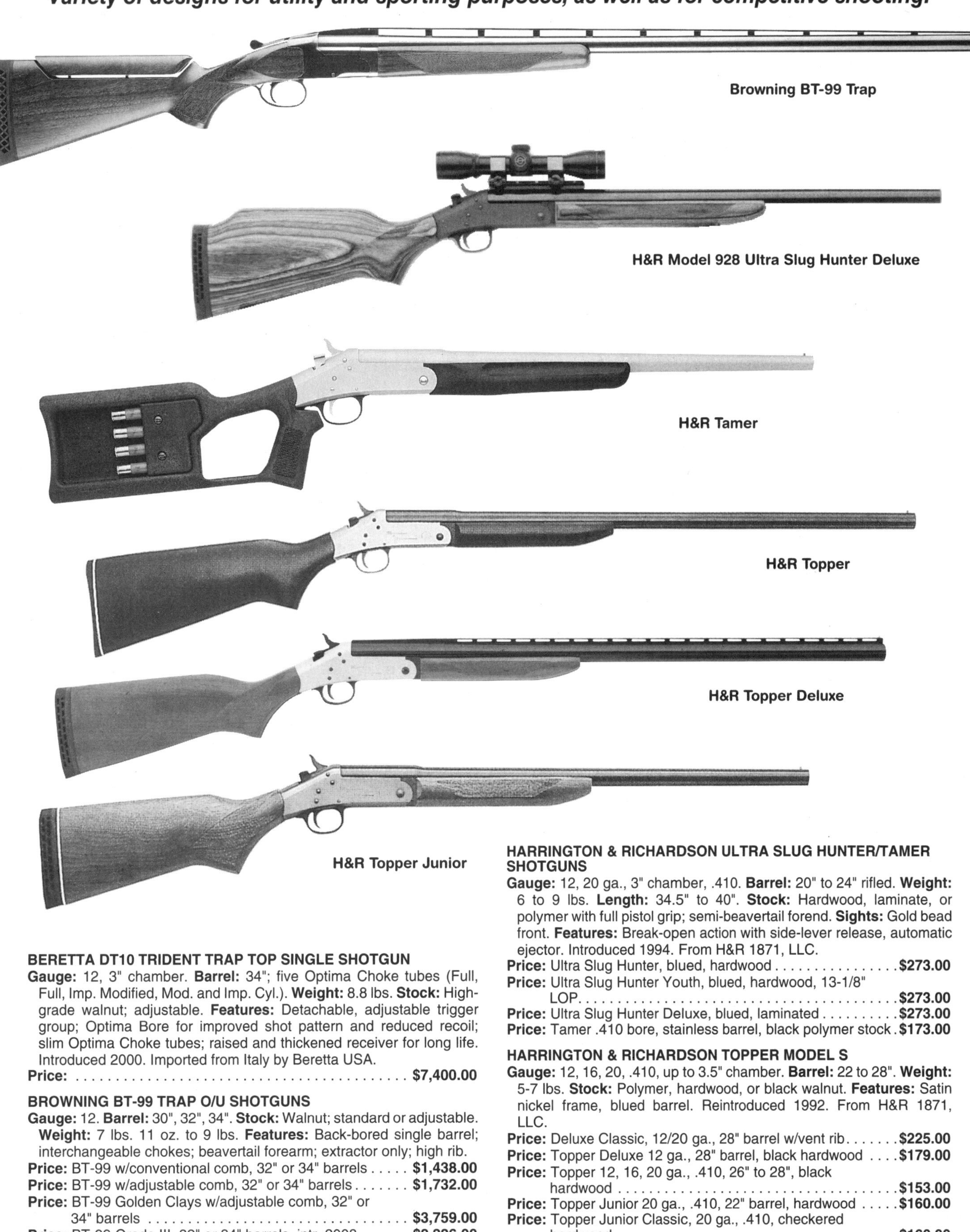

Browning BT-99 Trap

H&R Model 928 Ultra Slug Hunter Deluxe

H&R Tamer

H&R Topper

H&R Topper Deluxe

H&R Topper Junior

BERETTA DT10 TRIDENT TRAP TOP SINGLE SHOTGUN

Gauge: 12, 3" chamber. **Barrel:** 34"; five Optima Choke tubes (Full, Full, Imp. Modified, Mod. and Imp. Cyl.). **Weight:** 8.8 lbs. **Stock:** High-grade walnut; adjustable. **Features:** Detachable, adjustable trigger group; Optima Bore for improved shot pattern and reduced recoil; slim Optima Choke tubes; raised and thickened receiver for long life. Introduced 2000. Imported from Italy by Beretta USA.

Price: **$7,400.00**

BROWNING BT-99 TRAP O/U SHOTGUNS

Gauge: 12. **Barrel:** 30", 32", 34". **Stock:** Walnut; standard or adjustable. **Weight:** 7 lbs. 11 oz. to 9 lbs. **Features:** Back-bored single barrel; interchangeable chokes; beavertail forearm; extractor only; high rib.

Price: BT-99 w/conventional comb, 32" or 34" barrels **$1,438.00**

Price: BT-99 w/adjustable comb, 32" or 34" barrels **$1,732.00**

Price: BT-99 Golden Clays w/adjustable comb, 32" or 34" barrels **$3,759.00**

Price: BT-99 Grade III, 32" or 34" barrels, intr. 2008 . . . . . . **$2,226.00**

HARRINGTON & RICHARDSON ULTRA SLUG HUNTER/TAMER SHOTGUNS

Gauge: 12, 20 ga., 3" chamber, .410. **Barrel:** 20" to 24" rifled. **Weight:** 6 to 9 lbs. **Length:** 34.5" to 40". **Stock:** Hardwood, laminate, or polymer with full pistol grip; semi-beavertail forend. **Sights:** Gold bead front. **Features:** Break-open action with side-lever release, automatic ejector. Introduced 1994. From H&R 1871, LLC.

Price: Ultra Slug Hunter, blued, hardwood **$273.00**

Price: Ultra Slug Hunter Youth, blued, hardwood, 13-1/8" LOP. **$273.00**

Price: Ultra Slug Hunter Deluxe, blued, laminated **$273.00**

Price: Tamer .410 bore, stainless barrel, black polymer stock . **$173.00**

HARRINGTON & RICHARDSON TOPPER MODEL S

Gauge: 12, 16, 20, .410, up to 3.5" chamber. **Barrel:** 22 to 28". **Weight:** 5-7 lbs. **Stock:** Polymer, hardwood, or black walnut. **Features:** Satin nickel frame, blued barrel. Reintroduced 1992. From H&R 1871, LLC.

Price: Deluxe Classic, 12/20 ga., 28" barrel w/vent rib. **$225.00**

Price: Topper Deluxe 12 ga., 28" barrel, black hardwood **$179.00**

Price: Topper 12, 16, 20 ga., .410, 26" to 28", black hardwood **$153.00**

Price: Topper Junior 20 ga., .410, 22" barrel, hardwood **$160.00**

Price: Topper Junior Classic, 20 ga., .410, checkered hardwood **$160.00**

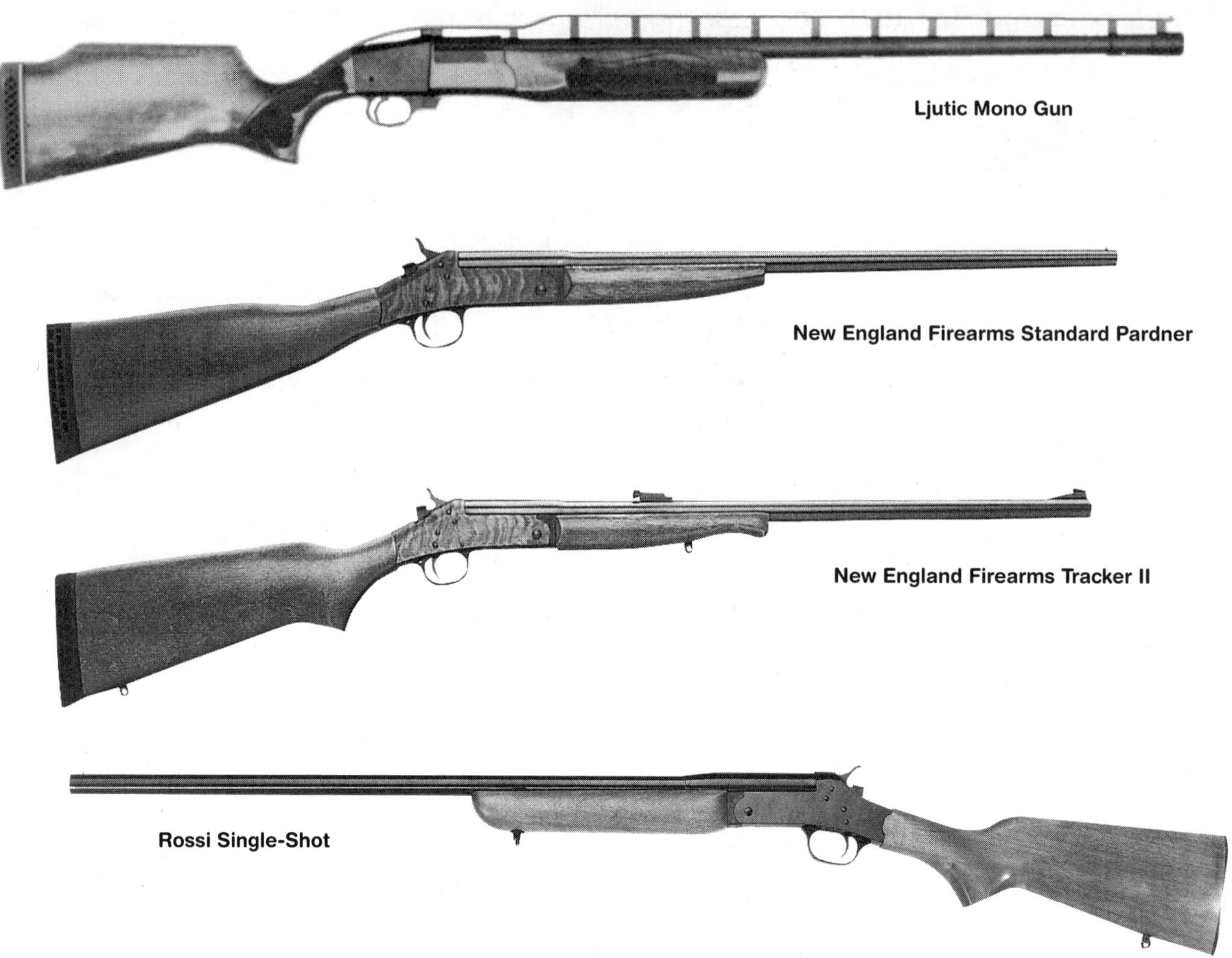

Ljutic Mono Gun

New England Firearms Standard Pardner

New England Firearms Tracker II

Rossi Single-Shot

KRIEGHOFF K-80 SINGLE BARREL TRAP GUN
Gauge: 12, 2-3/4" chamber. **Barrel:** 32" or 34" Unsingle. Fixed Full or choke tubes. **Weight:** About 8-3/4 lbs. **Stock:** Four stock dimensions or adjustable stock available. All hand-checkered European walnut. **Features:** Satin nickel finish. Selective mechanical trigger adjustable for finger position. Tapered step vent rib. Adjustable point of impact.
Price: Standard grade Full Unsingle, from **$10,080.00**

KRIEGHOFF KX-5 TRAP GUN
Gauge: 12, 2-3/4" chamber. **Barrel:** 32", 34"; choke tubes. **Weight:** About 8.5 lbs. **Stock:** Factory adjustable stock. European walnut. **Features:** Ventilated tapered step rib. Adjustable position trigger, optional release trigger. Fully adjustable rib. Satin gray electroless nickel receiver. Fitted aluminum case. Imported from Germany by Krieghoff International, Inc.
Price: **$5,395.00**

LJUTIC MONO GUN SINGLE BARREL SHOTGUN
Gauge: 12 only. **Barrel:** 34", choked to customer specs; hollow-milled rib, 35.5" sight plane. **Weight:** Approx. 9 lbs. **Stock:** To customer specs. Oil finish, hand checkered. **Features:** Custom gun. Pull or release trigger; removable trigger guard contains trigger and hammer mechanism; Ljutic pushbutton opener on front of trigger guard. From Ljutic Industries.
Price: Std., med. or Olympic rib, custom bbls., fixed choke.. **$6,995.00**
Price: As above with screw-in choke barrel **$7,395.00**
Price: Stainless steel mono gun **$7,995.00**

Ljutic LTX Pro 3 Deluxe Mono Gun
Deluxe, lightweight version of the Mono gun with high quality wood, upgrade checkering, special rib height, screw-in chokes, ported and cased.
Price: **$8,995.00**
Price: Stainless steel model **$9,995.00**

NEW ENGLAND FIREARMS PARDNER AND TRACKER II SHOTGUNS
Gauge: 10, 12, 16, 20, 28, .410, up to 3.5" chamber for 10 and 12 ga. 16, 28, 2-3/4" chamber. **Barrel:** 24" to 30". **Weight:** Varies from 5 to 9.5 lbs. **Length:** Varies from 36" to 48". **Stock:** Walnut-finished hardwood with full pistol grip, synthetic, or camo finish. **Sights:** Bead front on most. **Features:** Transfer bar ignition; break-open action with side-lever release. Introduced 1987. From New England Firearms.
Price: Pardner, all gauges, hardwood stock, 26" to 32" blued barrel, Mod. or Full choke **$140.00**
Price: Pardner Youth, hardwood stock, straight grip, 22" blued barrel **$149.00**
Price: Pardner Screw-In Choke model, intr. 2006 .... **$164.00**
Price: Turkey model, 10/12 ga., camo finish or black .... **$192.00 to $259.00**
Price: Youth Turkey, 20 ga., camo finish or black **$192.00**
Price: Waterfowl, 10 ga., camo finish or hardwood **$227.00**
Price: Tracker II slug gun, 12/20 ga., hardwood **$196.00**

REMINGTON SPR100 SINGLE-SHOT SHOTGUNS
Gauge: 12, 20, .410 bore, 3" chambers. **Barrel:** 24", 26", 28", 29.5", blued chrome-lined. **Weight:** 6.75 to 7.5 lbs. **Stock:** Walnut stock and forend. **Features:** Nickel or blued receiver. Cross-bolt safety, cocking indicator, titanium-coated trigger, selectable ejector or extractor. Introduced 2008. Imported by Remington Arms Co.
Price: SPR100, from **$479.00**

ROSSI SINGLE-SHOT SHOTGUNS
Gauge: 12, 20, .410. **Barrel:** 22" (Youth), 28". **Weight:** 3.75-5.25 lbs. **Stocks:** Wood. **Sights:** Bead front sight, fully adjustable fiber optic sight on Slug and Turkey. **Features:** Single-shot break open, 8 models available, positive ejection, internal transfer bar mechanism, trigger block system, Taurus Security System, blued finish, Rifle Slug has ported barrel.
Price: **$131.00**

Rossi Matched Pair

Tar-Hunt RSG-20 Mountaineer

Thompson/Center Encore Rifled Slug

Thompson/Center Encore Turkey

ROSSI MATCHED PAIRS

Gauge/Caliber: 12, 20, .410, .22 Mag, .22LR, .17HMR, .223 Rem, .243 Win, .270 Win, .30-06, .308 Win, .50 (black powder). **Barrel:** 23", 28". **Weight:** 5-6.3 lbs. **Stocks:** Wood or black synthetic. **Sights:** Bead front on shotgun barrel, fully adjustable front and rear on rifle barrel, drilled and tapped for scope, fully adjustable fiber optic sights (black powder). **Features:** Single-shot break open, 27 models available, internal transfer bar mechanism, manual external safety, blue finish, trigger block system, Taurus Security System, youth models available.

Price: Rimfire/Shotgun, from. **$178.00**
Price: Centerfire/Shotgun **$299.00**
Price: Black Powder Matched Pair, from **$262.00**

ROSSI MATCHED SET

Gauge/Caliber: 12, 20, .22 LR, .17 HMR, .243 Win, .270 Win, .50 (black powder). **Barrel:** 33.5". **Weight:** 6.25-6.3 lbs. **Stocks:** Wood. **Sights:** Bead front on shotgun barrel, fully adjustable front and rear on rifle barrel, drilled and tapped for scope, fully adjustable fiber optic sights (black powder). **Features:** Single-shot break open, 4 models available, internal transfer bar mechanism, manual external safety, blue finish, trigger block system, Taurus Security System, youth models available.

Price: From **$374.00**

TAR-HUNT RSG-12 PROFESSIONAL RIFLED SLUG GUN

Gauge: 12, 2-3/4" or 3" chamber, 1-shot magazine. **Barrel:** 23", fully rifled with muzzle brake. **Weight:** 7.75 lbs. **Length:** 41.5" overall. **Stock:** Matte black McMillan fiberglass with Pachmayr Decelerator pad. **Sights:** None furnished; comes with Leupold windage or Weaver bases. **Features:** Uses rifle-style action with two locking lugs; two-position safety; Shaw barrel; single-stage, trigger; muzzle brake. Many options available. All models have area-controlled feed action. Introduced 1991. Made in U.S. by Tar-Hunt Custom Rifles, Inc.

Price: 12 ga. Professional model **$2,800.00**
Price: Left-hand model add. **$125.00**

Tar-Hunt RSG-16 Elite Shotgun

Similar to RSG-12 Professional except 16 gauge; right- or left-hand versions.

Price: **$2,800.00**

Tar-Hunt RSG-20 Mountaineer Slug Gun

Similar to the RSG-12 Professional except chambered for 20 gauge (2-3/4" and 3" shells); 23" Shaw rifled barrel, with muzzle brake; two-lug bolt; one-shot blind magazine; matte black finish; McMillan fiberglass stock with Pachmayr Decelerator pad; receiver drilled and tapped for Rem. 700 bases. Right- or left-hand versions. Weighs 6.5 lbs. Introduced 1997. Made in U.S. by Tar-Hunt Custom Rifles, Inc.

Price: **$2,800.00**

THOMPSON/CENTER ENCORE RIFLED SLUG GUN

Gauge: 20, 3" chamber. **Barrel:** 26", fully rifled. **Weight:** About 7 lbs. **Length:** 40.5" overall. **Stock:** Walnut with walnut forearm. **Sights:** Steel; click-adjustable rear and ramp-style front, both with fiber optics. **Features:** Encore system features a variety of rifle, shotgun and muzzle-loading rifle barrels interchangeable with the same frame. Break-open design operates by pulling up and back on trigger guard spur. Composite stock and forearm available. Introduced 2000.

Price: **$684.00**

THOMPSON/CENTER ENCORE TURKEY GUN

Gauge: 12 ga. **Barrel:** 24". **Features:** All-camo finish, high definition Realtree Hardwoods HD camo.

Price: **$763.00**

Designs for utility, suitable for and adaptable to competitions and other sporting purposes.

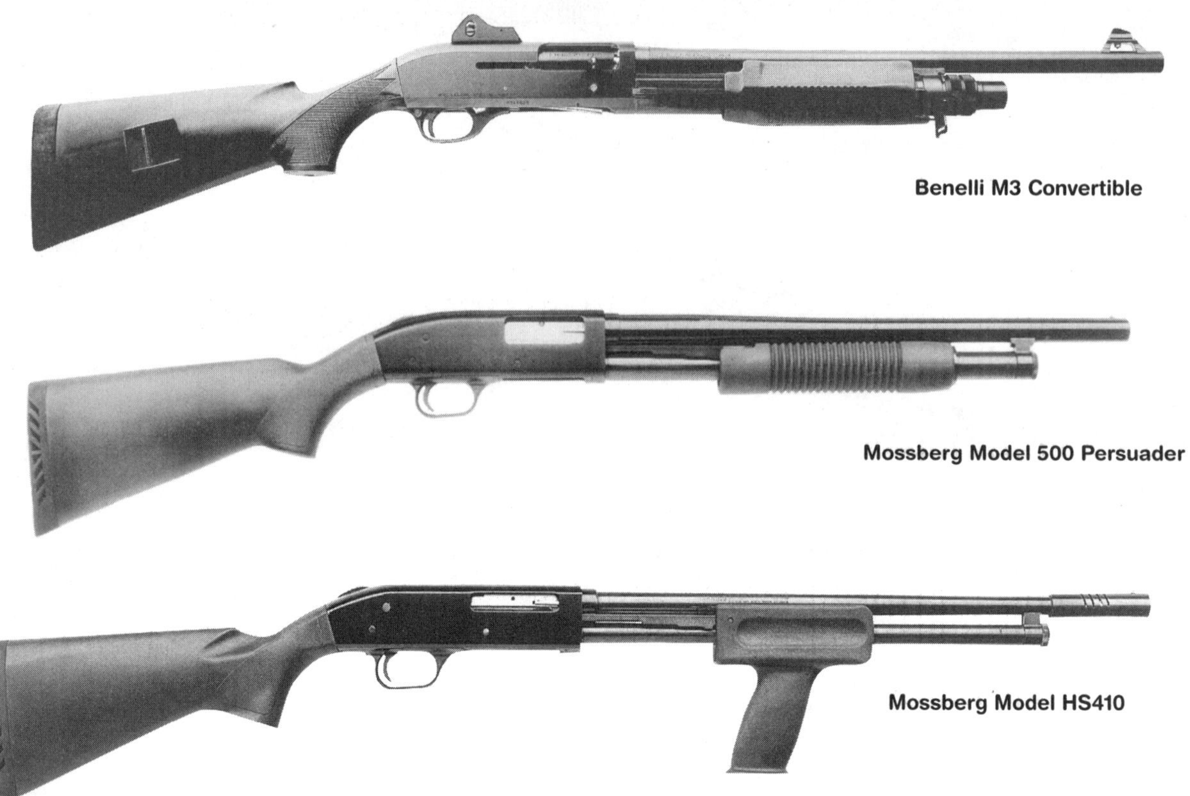

Benelli M3 Convertible

Mossberg Model 500 Persuader

Mossberg Model HS410

BENELLI M3 CONVERTIBLE SHOTGUN

Gauge: 12, 2-3/4", 3" chambers, 5-shot magazine. **Barrel:** 19.75" (Cyl.). **Weight:** 7 lbs., 4oz. **Length:** 41" overall. **Stock:** High-impact polymer with sling loop in side of butt; rubberized pistol grip on stock. **Sights:** Open rifle, fully adjustable. Ghost ring and rifle type. **Features:** Combination pump/auto action. Alloy receiver with inertia recoil rotating locking lug bolt; matte finish; automatic shell release lever. Introduced 1989. Imported by Benelli USA. Price with pistol grip, open rifle sights.

Price: With standard stock, open rifle sights. **$1,255.00**
Price: With ghost ring sight system, standard stock **$1,335.00**
Price: With ghost ring sights, pistol grip stock **$1,335.00**

BENELLI M2 TACTICAL SHOTGUN

Gauge: 12, 2-3/4", 3" chambers, 5-shot magazine. **Barrel:** 18.5" IC, M, F choke tubes. **Weight:** 6.7 lbs. **Length:** 39.75" overall. **Stock:** Black polymer. **Sights:** Rifle type ghost ring system, tritium night sights optional. **Features:** Semi-auto intertia recoil action. Cross-bolt safety; bolt release button; matte-finish metal. Introduced 1993. Imported from Italy by Benelli USA.

Price: With rifle sights **$1,065.00**
Price: With ghost ring sights, standard stock **$1,175.00**
Price: With ghost ring sights, pistol grip stock **$1,175.00**
Price: With rifle sights, pistol grip stock **$1,065.00**
Price: ComforTech stock, rifle sights **$1,175.00**
Price: Comfortech Stock, Ghost Ring. **$1,280.00**

CROSSFIRE SHOTGUN/RIFLE

Gauge/Caliber: 12, 2-3/4". **Chamber:** 4-shot/223 Rem. (5-shot). **Barrel:** 20" (shotgun), 18" (rifle). **Weight:** About 8.6 lbs. **Length:** 40" overall. **Stock:** Composite. **Sights:** Meprolight night sights. Integral Weaver-style scope rail. **Features:** Combination pump-action shotgun, rifle; single selector, single trigger; dual action bars for both upper and lower actions; ambidextrous selector and safety. Introduced 1997. Made in U.S. From Hesco.

Price: About **$1,895.00**
Price: With camo finish **$1,995.00**

FABARM S.A.8. TACTICAL SEMI-AUTOMATIC SHOTGUN

Gauge: 12, 3" chamber, 8-shot magzine. **Barrel:** 20". **Weight:** 6.6 lbs. **Length:** 41.2" overall. **Stock:** Polymer pistol-grip stock. **Sights:** Ghost ring. **Features:** Gas operated; matte receiver; twin forged action bars; over-sized bolt handle and safety button; Picatinny rail; Cylinder bore choke tube with muzzle break. Introduced 2001. Imported from Italy by Tristar Sporting Arms.

Price: **$1,099.00**

MOSSBERG MODEL 500 SPECIAL PURPOSE SHOTGUNS

Gauge: 12, 20, .410, 3" chamber. **Barrel:** 18.5", 20" (Cyl.). **Weight:** 7 lbs. **Stock:** Walnut-finished hardwood or black synthetic. **Sights:** Metal bead front. **Features:** Available in 6- or 8-shot models. Top-mounted safety, double action slide bars, swivel studs, rubber recoil pad. Blue, Parkerized, Marinecote finishes. Mossberg Cablelock included. From Mossberg. The HS410 Home Security model chambered for .410 with 3" chamber; has pistol grip forend, thick recoil pad, muzzle brake and has special spreader choke on the 18.5" barrel. Overall length is 37.5", weight is 6.25 lbs. Blue finish; synthetic field stock. Mossberg Cablelock and video included. Mariner model has Marinecote metal finish to resist rust and corrosion. Synthetic field stock; pistol grip kit included. 500 Tactical 6-shot has black synthetic tactical stock. Introduced 1990.

Price: Rolling Thunder, 6-shot **$450.00**
Price: Tactical Cruiser, 18.5" barrel **$413.00**
Price: Persuader/Cruiser, 6 shot, from **$375.00**
Price: Persuader/Cruiser, 8 shot, from **$375.00**
Price: HS410 Home Security **$385.00**
Price: Mariner 6 or 9 shot, from **$512.00**
Price: Tactical 6 shot, from. **$485.00**

MOSSBERG MODEL 590 SPECIAL PURPOSE SHOTGUN

Gauge: 12, 3" chamber, 9 shot magazine. **Barrel:** 20" (Cyl.). **Weight:** 7.25 lbs. **Stock:** Synthetic field or Speedfeed. **Sights:** Metal bead front or Ghost Ring. **Features:** Top-mounted safety, double slide action bars. Comes with heat shield, bayonet lug, swivel studs, rubber recoil pad. Blue, Parkerized or Marinecote finish. Mossberg Cablelock included. From Mossberg.

Price: Synthetic stock, from **$448.00**
Price: Speed Feed stock, from **$525.00**

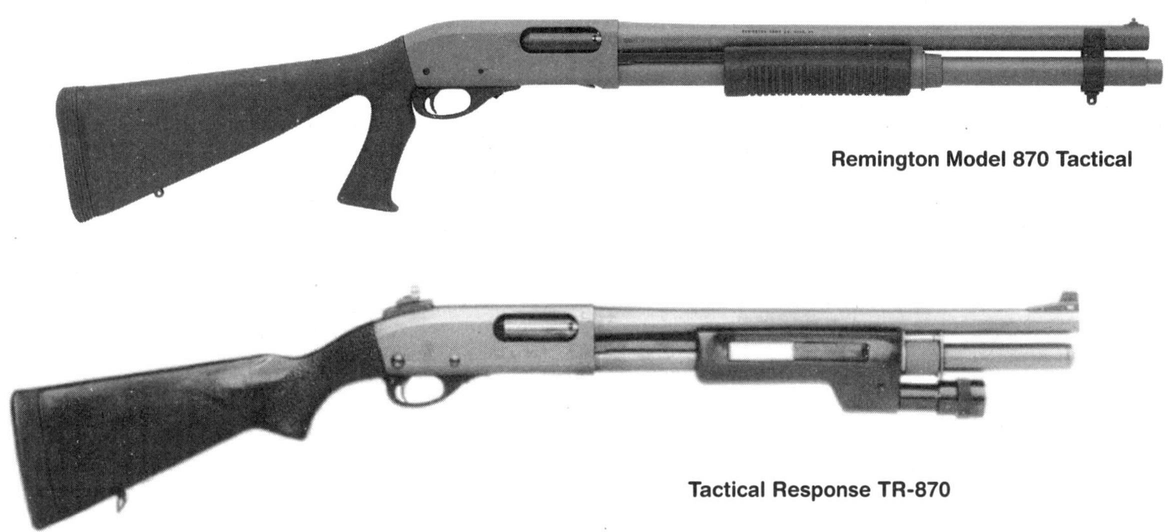

Remington Model 870 Tactical

Tactical Response TR-870

REMINGTON MODEL 870 AND MODEL 1100 TACTICAL SHOTGUNS

Gauge: 870: 12, 2-3/4 or 3" chamber; 1100: 2-3/4". **Barrel:** 18", 20", 22" (Cyl or IC). **Weight:** 7.5-7.75 lbs. **Length:** 38.5-42.5" overall. **Stock:** Black synthetic, synthetic Speedfeed IV full pistol-grip stock, or Knoxx Industries SpecOps stock w/recoil-absorbing spring-loaded cam and adjustable length of pull (12" to 16", 870 only). **Sights:** Front post w/dot only on 870; rib and front dot on 1100. **Features:** R3 recoil pads, LimbSaver technology to reduce felt recoil, 2-, 3- or 4-shot extensions based on barrel length; matte-olive-drab barrels and receivers. Model 1100 Tactical is available with Speedfeed IV pistol grip stock or standard black synthetic stock and forend. Speedfeed IV model has an 18" barrel with two-shot extension. Standard synthetic-stocked version is equipped with 22" barrel and four-shot extension. Introduced 2006. From Remington Arms Co.

Price: 870, Speedfeed IV stock, 3" chamber, 38.5" overall, from . . . **$587.00**
Price: 870, SpecOps stock, 3" chamber, 38.5" overall, from . . **$587.00**
Price: 1100, synthetic stock, 2-3/4" chamber, 42.5" overall . . . **$928.00**
Price: 1100, synthetic stock, 2-3/4" chamber, 42.5" overall . . . **$928.00**
Price: 870 TAC Desert Recon (2008), 18" barrel . . . **$719.00**

TACTICAL RESPONSE TR-870 STANDARD MODEL SHOTGUNS

Gauge: 12, 3" chamber, 7-shot magazine. **Barrel:** 18" (Cyl.). **Weight:** 9 lbs. **Length:** 38" overall. **Stock:** Fiberglass-filled polypropolene with non-snag recoil absorbing butt pad. Nylon tactical forend houses flashlight. **Sights:** Trak-Lock ghost ring sight system. Front sight has Tritium insert. **Features:** Highly modified Remington 870P with Parkerized finish. Comes with nylon three-way adjustable sling, high visibility non-binding follower, high performance magazine spring, Jumbo Head safety, and Side Saddle extended 6-shot shell carrier on left side of receiver. Introduced 1991. From Scattergun Technologies, Inc.

Price: Standard model . . . **$815.00**
Price: FBI model . . . **$770.00**
Price: Patrol model . . . **$595.00**
Price: Border Patrol model . . . **$605.00**
Price: K-9 model (Rem. 11-87 action) . . . **$995.00**
Price: Urban Sniper, Rem. 11-87 action . . . **$1,290.00**
Price: Louis Awerbuck model . . . **$705.00**
Price: Practical Turkey model . . . **$725.00**
Price: Expert model . . . **$1,350.00**
Price: Professional model . . . **$815.00**
Price: Entry model . . . **$840.00**
Price: Compact model . . . **$635.00**
Price: SWAT model . . . **$1,195.00**

TRISTAR COBRA PUMP

Gauge: 12, 3". **Barrel:** 28". **Weight:** 6.7 lbs. Three Beretta-style choke tubes (IC, M, F). **Length:** NA. **Stock:** Matte black synthetic stock and forearm. **Sights:** Vent rib with matted sight plane. **Features:** Five-year warranty. Cobra Tactical Pump Shotgun magazine holds 7, return spring in forearm, 20" barrel, Cylinder choke. Introduced 2008. Imported by Tristar Sporting Arms Ltd.

Price: . . . **$309.00**
Price: Tactical . . . **$309.00**

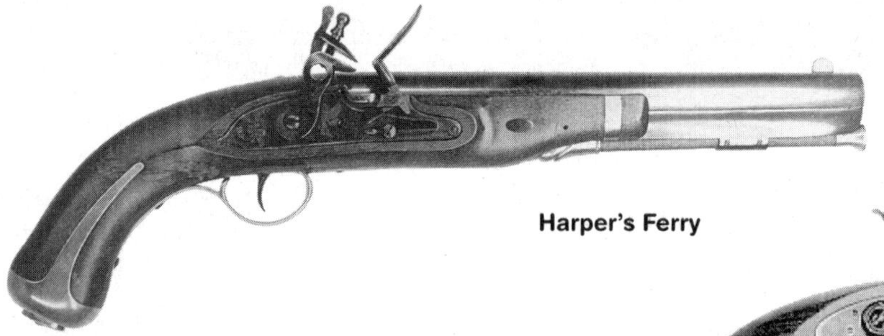

Harper's Ferry

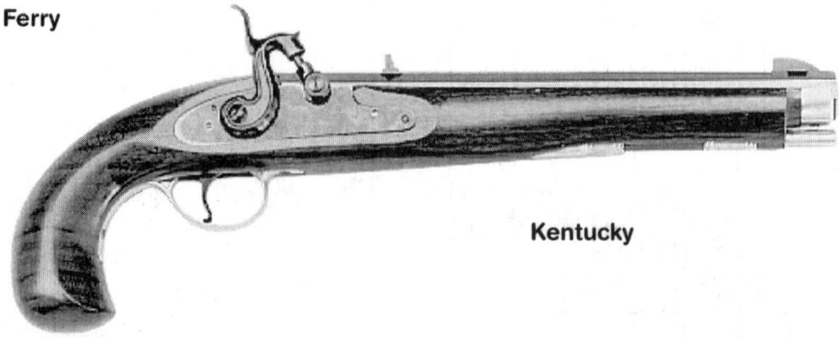

Kentucky

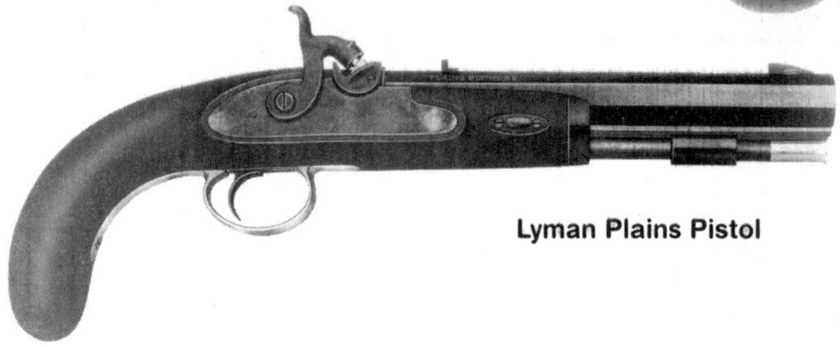

Lyman Plains Pistol

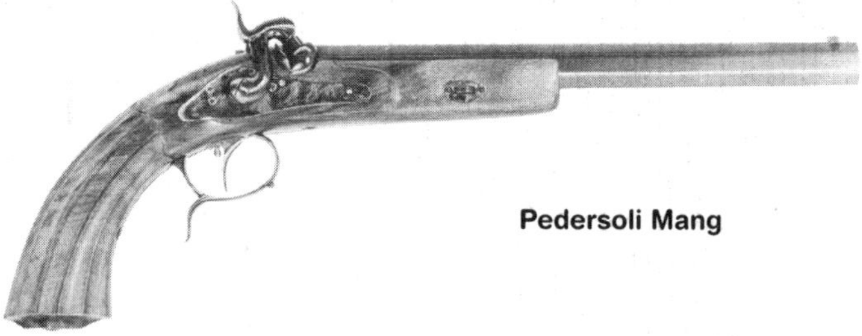

Pedersoli Mang

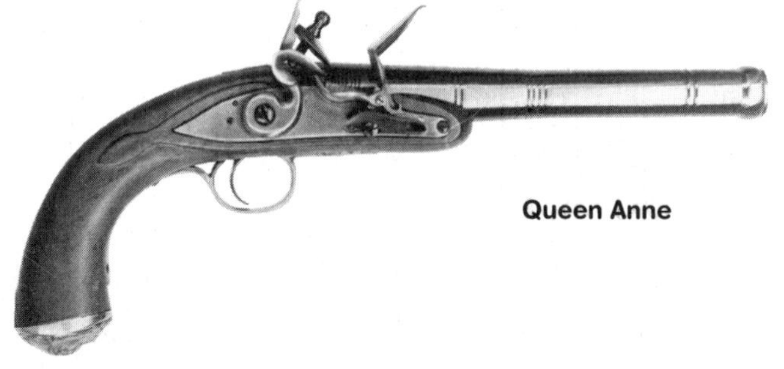
Queen Anne

FRENCH-STYLE DUELING PISTOL
Caliber: 44. **Barrel:** 10". **Weight:** 35 oz. **Length:** 15.75" overall. **Stocks:** Carved walnut. **Sights:** Fixed. **Features:** Comes with velvet-lined case and accessories. Imported by Mandall Shooting Supplies.
Price: **$295.00**

HARPER'S FERRY 1805 PISTOL
Caliber: 58 (.570" round ball). **Barrel:** 10". **Weight:** 40 oz. **Length:** 16.25" overall. **Stocks:** Walnut. **Sights:** Fixed. **Features:** Case-hardened lock, brass-mounted German silver-colored barrel. Replica of the first U.S. gov't.-made flintlock pistol. Imported by Navy Arms, Dixie Gun Works.
Price: Dixie Gun Works RH0225 . . . . **$425.00**
Price: Dixie Kit FH0411. . . . . **$350.00**

KENTUCKY FLINTLOCK PISTOL
Caliber: 44, 45. **Barrel:** 10-1/8". **Weight:** 32 oz. **Length:** 15.5" overall. **Stocks:** Walnut. **Sights:** Fixed. **Features:** Specifications, including caliber, weight and length may vary with importer. Case-hardened lock, blued barrel; available also as brass barrel flintlock Model 1821. Imported by The Armoury.
Price: Single cased set (Navy Arms) **$360.00**
Price: Double cased set (Navy Arms) **$590.00**

KENTUCKY PERCUSSION PISTOL
Similar to Flint version but percussion lock. Imported by The Armoury, Navy Arms, CVA (50-cal.).
Price: . . . . **$129.95 to $225.00**
Price: Steel barrel (Armoury) **$179.00**
Price: Single cased set (Navy Arms) **$355.00**
Price: Double cased set (Navy Arms) **$600.00**

LE PAGE PERCUSSION DUELING PISTOL
Caliber: .45. **Barrel:** 10" octagon, rifled. **Weight:** 40 oz. **Length:** 15.25" overall. **Stocks:** Walnut, fluted butt. **Sights:** Blade front, open style rear. **Features:** Double set trigger. Bright barrel, brass furniture (silver plated). Imported by Dixie Gun Works
Price: PH0310. . . . .**$495.00**

LYMAN PLAINS PISTOL
Caliber: 50 or 54. **Barrel:** 8"; 1:30" twist, both calibers. **Weight:** 50 oz. **Length:** 15" overall. **Stocks:** Walnut half-stock. **Sights:** Blade front, square notch rear adjustable for windage. **Features:** Polished brass trigger guard and ramrod tip, color case-hardened coil spring lock, springloaded trigger, stainless steel nipple, blackened iron furniture. Hooked patent breech, detachable belt hook. Introduced 1981. From Lyman Products.
Price: Finished **$244.95**
Price: Kit **$189.95**

PEDERSOLI MANG TARGET PISTOL
Caliber: 38. **Barrel:** 10.5", octagonal; 1:15" twist, **Weight:** 2.5 lbs. **Length:** 17.25" overall. **Stocks:** Walnut with fluted grip. **Sights:** Blade front, open rear adjustable for windage. **Features:** Browned barrel, polished breech plug, remainder color case-hardened. Imported from Italy by Dixie Gun Works.
Price: PH0503. . . . . **$1,250.00**

QUEEN ANNE FLINTLOCK PISTOL
Caliber: 50 (.490" round ball). **Barrel:** 7.5", smoothbore. **Stocks:** Walnut. **Sights:** None. **Features:** German silver-colored steel barrel, fluted brass trigger guard, brass mask on butt. Lockplate left in the white. Made by Pedersoli in Italy. Introduced 1983. Imported by Dixie Gun Works.
Price: RH0211 . . . . **$300.00**
Price: Kit FH0421 . . . . **$260.00**

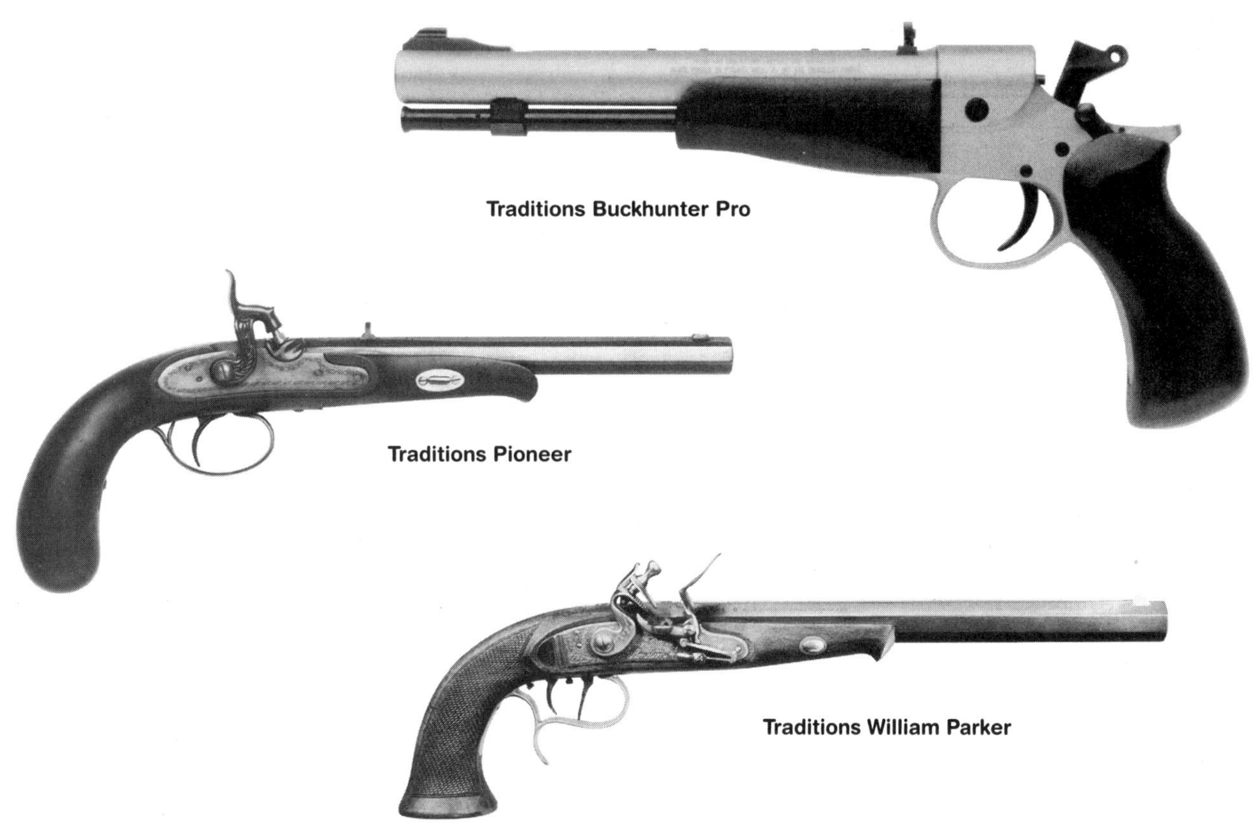
Traditions Buckhunter Pro

Traditions Pioneer

Traditions William Parker

TRADITIONS BUCKHUNTER PRO IN-LINE PISTOL
Caliber: 50. **Barrel:** 9.5", round. **Weight:** 48 oz. **Length:** 14" overall. **Stocks:** Smooth walnut or black epoxy-coated hardwood grip and forend. **Sights:** Beaded blade front, folding adjustable rear. **Features:** Thumb safety; removable stainless steel breech plug; adjustable trigger, barrel drilled and tapped for scope mounting. From Traditions.
Price: With walnut grip **$229.00**
Price: Nickel with black grip **$239.00**
Price: With walnut grip and 12.5" barrel **$239.00**
Price: Nickel with black grip, muzzle brake and 14.75" fluted barrel **$289.00**
Price: 45 cal. nickel w/bl. grip, muzzle brake and 14.75" fluted bbl. **$289.00**

TRADITIONS KENTUCKY PISTOL
Caliber: 50. **Barrel:** 10"; octagon with 7/8" flats; 1:20" twist. **Weight:** 40 oz. **Length:** 15" overall. **Stocks:** Stained beech. **Sights:** Blade front, fixed rear. **Features:** Bird's-head grip; brass thimbles; color case-hardened lock. Percussion only. Introduced 1995. From Traditions.
Price: Finished **$139.00**
Price: Kit **$109.00**

TRADITIONS PIONEER PISTOL
Caliber: 45. **Barrel:** 9-5/8"; 13/16" flats, 1:16" twist. **Weight:** 31 oz. **Length:** 15" overall. **Stocks:** Beech. **Sights:** Blade front, fixed rear. **Features:** V-type mainspring. Single trigger. German silver furniture, blackened hardware. From Traditions.
Price: **$139.00**
Price: Kit **$119.00**

TRADITIONS TRAPPER PISTOL
Caliber: 50. **Barrel:** 9.75"; 7/8" flats; 1:20" twist. **Weight:** 2.75 lbs. **Length:** 16" overall. **Stocks:** Beech. **Sights:** Blade front, adjustable rear. **Features:** Double-set triggers; brass buttcap, trigger guard, wedge plate, forend tip, thimble. From Traditions.
Price: Percussion **$189.00**
Price: Flintlock **$209.00**
Price: Kit **$149.00**

TRADITIONS VEST-POCKET DERRINGER
Caliber: 31. **Barrel:** 2.25"; brass. **Weight:** 8 oz. **Length:** 4.75" overall. **Stocks:** Simulated ivory. **Sights:** Bead front. **Features:** Replica of riverboat gamblers' derringer; authentic spur trigger. From Traditions.
Price: **$109.00**

TRADITIONS WILLIAM PARKER PISTOL
Caliber: 50. **Barrel:** 10-3/8"; 15/16" flats; polished steel. **Weight:** 37 oz. **Length:** 17.5" overall. **Stocks:** Walnut with checkered grip. **Sights:** Brass blade front, fixed rear. **Features:** Replica dueling pistol with 1:20" twist, hooked breech. Brass wedge plate, trigger guard, cap guard; separate ramrod. Double-set triggers. Polished steel barrel, lock. Imported by Traditions.
Price: **$269.00**

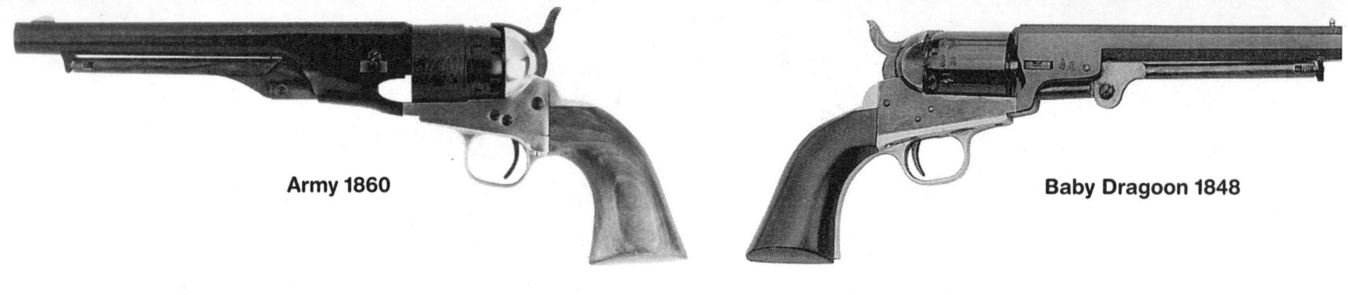

Army 1860

Baby Dragoon 1848

Dixie Wyatt Earp

Le Mat Revolver

New Model 1858 Army Percussion

ARMY 1860 PERCUSSION REVOLVER

Caliber: 44, 6-shot. **Barrel:** 8". **Weight:** 40 oz. **Length:** 13-5/8" overall. **Stocks:** Walnut. **Sights:** Fixed. **Features:** Engraved Navy scene on cylinder; brass trigger guard; case-hardened frame, loading lever and hammer. Some importers supply pistol cut for detachable shoulder stock, have accessory stock available. Imported by Cabela's (1860 Lawman), E.M.F., Navy Arms, The Armoury, Cimarron, Dixie Gun Works (half-fluted cylinder, not roll engraved), Euroarms of America (brass or steel model), Armsport, Traditions (brass or steel), Uberti U.S.A. Inc., United States Patent Fire-Arms.

Price: Dixie Gun Works RH0125 . . . . **$240.00**
Price: Brass frame (E.M.F.) **$215.00**
Price: Single cased set (Navy Arms) **$300.00**
Price: Double cased set (Navy Arms) **$490.00**
Price: 1861 Navy: Same as Army except 36-cal., 7.5" bbl., weighs 41 oz., cut for shoulder stock; round cylinder (fluted available), from Cabela's, CVA (brass frame, 44 cal.), United States Patent Fire-Arms . . . . **$99.95 to $385.00**
Price: Steel frame kit (E.M.F.) **$240.00**
Price: Colt Army Police, fluted cyl., 5.5", 36-cal. (Cabela's) . **$229.99**
Price: With nickeled frame, barrel and backstrap, gold-tone fluted cylinder, trigger and hammer, simulated ivory grips (Traditions) **$199.00**

BABY DRAGOON 1848, 1849 POCKET, WELLS FARGO

Caliber: 31. **Barrel:** 3", 4", 5", 6"; seven-groove; RH twist. **Weight:** About 21 oz. **Stocks:** Varnished walnut. **Sights:** Brass pin front, hammer notch rear. **Features:** No loading lever on Baby Dragoon or Wells Fargo models. Unfluted cylinder with stagecoach holdup scene; cupped cylinder pin; no grease grooves; one safety pin on cylinder and slot in hammer face; straight (flat) mainspring. From Armsport, Cimarron F.A. Co., Dixie Gun Works, E.M.F., Uberti U.S.A. Inc.

Price: 5.5" barrel, 1849 Pocket with loading lever (Dixie). . . . **$250.00**
Price: 4" (Uberti USA Inc.) **$275.00**

DIXIE WYATT EARP REVOLVER

Caliber: 44. **Barrel:** 12", octagon. **Weight:** 46 oz. **Length:** 18" overall. **Stocks:** One-piece hardwood. **Sights:** Fixed. **Features:** Highly polished brass frame, backstrap and trigger guard; blued barrel and cylinder; case-hardened hammer, trigger and loading lever. Navy-size shoulder stock requires minor fitting. From Dixie Gun Works.

Price: RH0130 . . . . **$187.50**

LE MAT REVOLVER

Caliber: 44/20 ga. **Barrel:** 6.75" (revolver); 4-7/8" (single shot). **Weight:** 3 lbs., 7 oz. **Length:** 14" overall. **Stocks:** Hand-checkered walnut. **Sights:** Post front, hammer notch rear. **Features:** Exact reproduction with all-steel construction; 44-cal. 9-shot cylinder, 20-gauge single barrel; color case-hardened hammer with selector; spur trigger guard; ring at butt; lever-type barrel release. From Navy Arms.

Price: Cavalry model (lanyard ring, spur trigger guard) **$750.00**
Price: Army model (round trigger guard, pin-type barrel release). **$750.00**
Price: Naval-style (thumb selector on hammer) **$750.00**

NEW MODEL 1858 ARMY PERCUSSION REVOLVER

Caliber: 36 or 44, 6-shot. **Barrel:** 6.5" or 8". **Weight:** 38 oz. **Length:** 13.5" overall. **Stocks:** Walnut. **Sights:** Blade front, groove-in-frame rear. **Features:** Replica of Remington Model 1858. Also available from some importers as Army Model Belt Revolver in 36-cal., a shortened and lightened version of the 44. Target Model (Uberti U.S.A. Inc., Navy Arms) has fully adjustable target rear sight, target front, 36 or 44. Imported by Cabela's, Cimarron F.A. Co., CVA (as 1858 Army, brass frame, 44 only), Navy Arms, The Armoury, E.M.F., Euroarms of America (engraved, stainless and plain), Armsport, Traditions (44 only), Uberti U.S.A. Inc.

Price: Steel frame, Dixie RH0220. . . . . **$315.00**
Price: Steel frame kit (Euroarms) . . . . **$115.95 to $150.00**
Price: Stainless steel Model 1858 (Euroarms, Uberti U.S.A. Inc., Cabela's, Navy Arms, Armsport, Traditions) . . . . **$169.95 to $380.00**
Price: Target Model, adjustable rear sight (Cabela's, Euroarms, Uberti U.S.A. Inc., Stone Mountain Arms) . . . . **$95.95 to $399.00**
Price: Brass frame (CVA, Cabela's, Traditions, Navy Arms) . . . . **$79.95 to $199.99**
Price: As above, kit (Dixie Gun Works RV0100) **$182.50**
Price: Buffalo model, 44-cal. (Cabela's) **$119.99**
Price: Hartford model, steel frame, cartouche (E.M.F.) **$225.00**
Price: Improved Conversion (Cimarron) **$492.00**

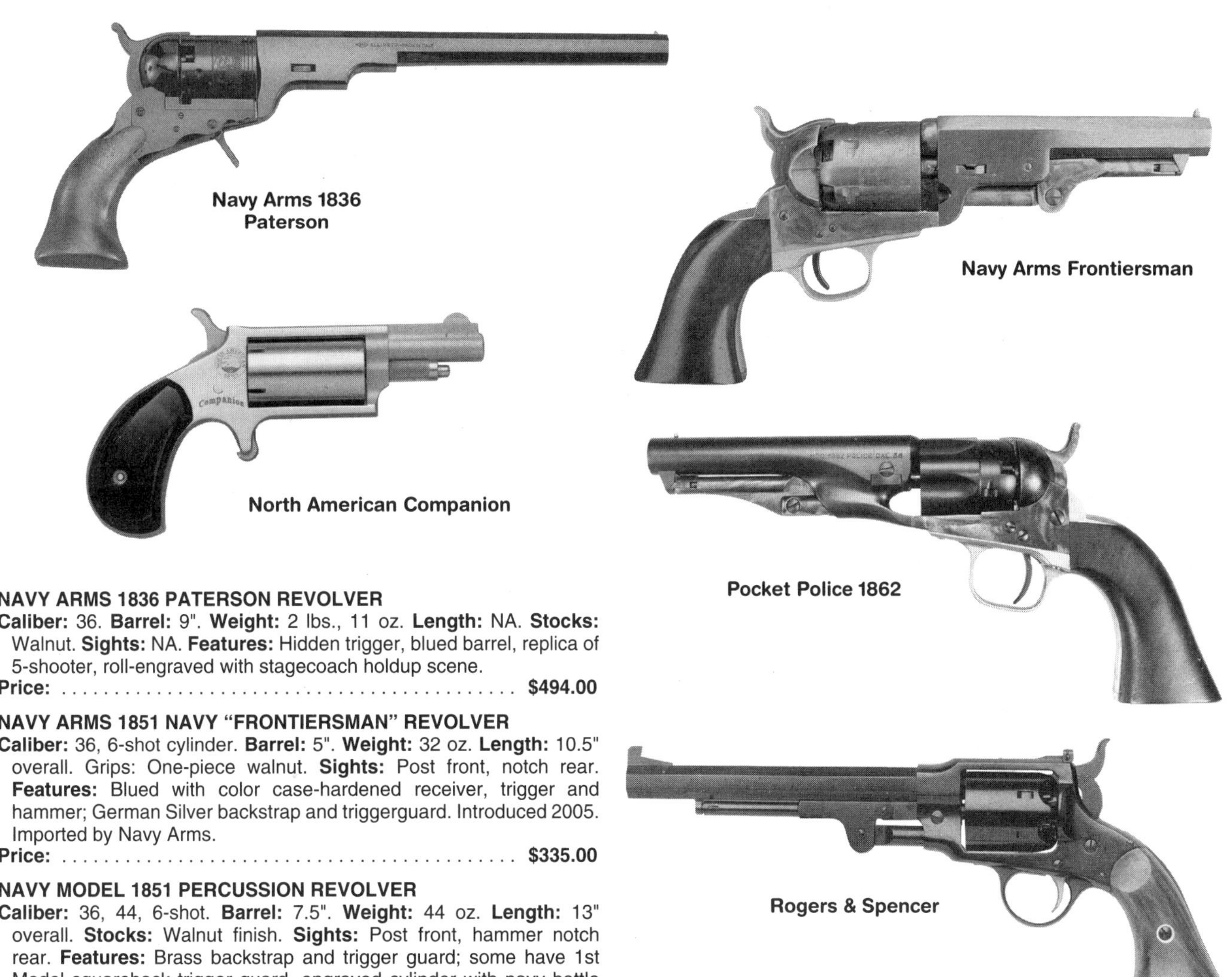
Navy Arms 1836 Paterson

Navy Arms Frontiersman

North American Companion

Pocket Police 1862

Rogers & Spencer

NAVY ARMS 1836 PATERSON REVOLVER
Caliber: 36. **Barrel:** 9". **Weight:** 2 lbs., 11 oz. **Length:** NA. **Stocks:** Walnut. **Sights:** NA. **Features:** Hidden trigger, blued barrel, replica of 5-shooter, roll-engraved with stagecoach holdup scene.
Price: **$494.00**

NAVY ARMS 1851 NAVY "FRONTIERSMAN" REVOLVER
Caliber: 36, 6-shot cylinder. **Barrel:** 5". **Weight:** 32 oz. **Length:** 10.5" overall. Grips: One-piece walnut. **Sights:** Post front, notch rear. **Features:** Blued with color case-hardened receiver, trigger and hammer; German Silver backstrap and triggerguard. Introduced 2005. Imported by Navy Arms.
Price: **$335.00**

NAVY MODEL 1851 PERCUSSION REVOLVER
Caliber: 36, 44, 6-shot. **Barrel:** 7.5". **Weight:** 44 oz. **Length:** 13" overall. **Stocks:** Walnut finish. **Sights:** Post front, hammer notch rear. **Features:** Brass backstrap and trigger guard; some have 1st Model squareback trigger guard, engraved cylinder with navy battle scene; case-hardened frame, hammer, loading lever. Imported by The Armoury, Cabela's, Cimarron F.A. Co., Navy Arms, E.M.F., Dixie Gun Works, Euroarms of America, Armsport, CVA (44-cal. only), Traditions (44 only), Uberti U.S.A. Inc., United States Patent Fire-Arms.
Price: Brass frame (Dixie Gun Works RH0100) **$225.00**
Price: Steel frame (Dixie Gun Works RH0210). **$200.00**
Price: Engraved model (Dixie Gun Works RH0110) **$250.00**
Price: Kit (Dixie Gun Works RV0200) **$157.00**
Price: Confederate Navy (Cabela's) **$139.99**
Price: Hartford model, steel frame, German silver trim, **cartouche (E.M.F.)** **$190.00**
Price: Man With No Name Conversion (Cimarron, 2006) . . . **$480.00**

NORTH AMERICAN COMPANION PERCUSSION REVOLVER
Caliber: 22. **Barrel:** 1-1/8". **Weight:** 5.1 oz. **Length:** 4.5" overall. **Stocks:** Laminated wood. **Sights:** Blade front, notch fixed rear. **Features:** All stainless steel construction. Uses standard #11 percussion caps. Comes with bullets, powder measure, bullet seater, leather clip holster, gun rag. Long Rifle or Magnum frame size. Introduced 1996. Made in U.S. by North American Arms.
Price: Long Rifle frame **$200.00**

North American Magnum Companion Percussion Revolver
Similar to the Companion except has larger frame. Weighs 7.2 oz., has 1-5/8" barrel, measures 5-7/16" overall. Comes with bullets, powder measure, bullet seater, leather clip holster, gun rag. Introduced 1996. Made in U.S. by North American Arms.
Price: **$215.00**

POCKET POLICE 1862 PERCUSSION REVOLVER
Caliber: 36, 5-shot. **Barrel:** 4.5", 5.5", 6.5", 7.5". **Weight:** 26 oz. **Length:** 12" overall (6.5" bbl.). **Stocks:** Walnut. **Sights:** Fixed. **Features:** Round tapered barrel; half-fluted and rebated cylinder; case-hardened frame, loading lever and hammer; silver or brass trigger guard and backstrap. Imported by Dixie Gun Works, Navy Arms (5.5" only), Uberti U.S.A. Inc. (5.5", 6.5" only), United States Patent Fire-Arms and Cimarron F.A. Co.
Price: Dixie Gun Works RH0422 . . . . **$290.00**
Price: Hartford model, steel frame, cartouche (E.M.F.) **$300.00**

ROGERS & SPENCER PERCUSSION REVOLVER
Caliber: 44. **Barrel:** 7.5". **Weight:** 47 oz. **Length:** 13.75" overall. **Stocks:** Walnut. **Sights:** Cone front, integral groove in frame for rear. **Features:** Accurate reproduction of a Civil War design. Solid frame; extra large nipple cut-out on rear of cylinder; loading lever and cylinder easily removed for cleaning. From Dixie Gun Works, Euroarms of America (standard blue, engraved, burnished, target models), Navy Arms.
Price: Dixie Gun Works RH1320 . . . . **$350.00**
Price: Nickel-plated **$215.00**
Price: Engraved (Euroarms) **$430.00**
Price: Kit version RH0920. . . . . **$315.00**
Price: Target version (Euroarms) . . . . **$239.00 to $270.00**
Price: Burnished London Gray (Euroarms) . . . . . **$245.00 to $370.00**

SHERIFF MODEL 1851 PERCUSSION REVOLVER
Caliber: 36, 44, 6-shot. **Barrel:** 5". **Weight:** 40 oz. **Length:** 10.5" overall. **Stocks:** Walnut. **Sights:** Fixed. **Features:** Brass backstrap and trigger guard; engraved navy scene; case-hardened frame, hammer, loading lever. Imported by E.M.F.
Price: Steel frame **$169.95**
Price: Brass frame **$140.00**

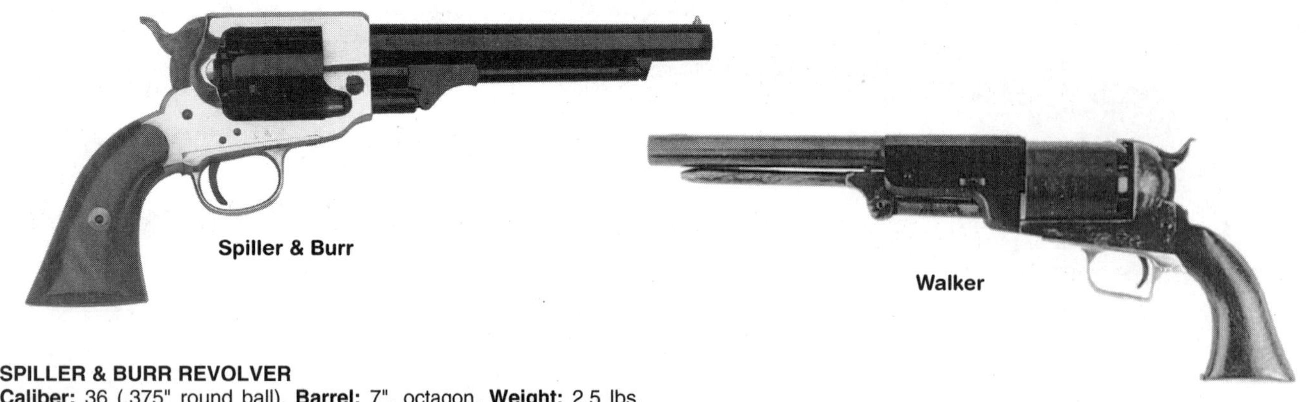
Spiller & Burr

Walker

SPILLER & BURR REVOLVER

Caliber: 36 (.375" round ball). **Barrel:** 7", octagon. **Weight:** 2.5 lbs. **Length:** 12.5" overall. **Stocks:** Two-piece walnut. **Sights:** Fixed. **Features:** Reproduction of the C.S.A. revolver. Brass frame and trigger guard. Also available as a kit. From Dixie Gun Works, Navy Arms.

Price: **$232.50**
Price: Kit form (Dixie) **$175.00**

UBERTI 1847 WALKER REVOLVERS

Caliber: 36 (.375" round ball), 5-shot engraved cylinder. **Barrel:** 7.5" 11 grooves. **Weight:** 2.6 lbs. **Stocks:** One-piece hardwood. **Sights:** Fixed. **Features:** Copy of Sam Colt's first commercially-made revolving pistol, loading lever available, no trigger guard. Case-hardened hammer. Made in Italy by Uberti, imported by Benelli USA.

Price: Walker with loading lever, 9" barrel, 6 shot (E.M.F.) .. **$390.00**
Price: Dixie RH0120 .... **$233.00**
Price: Kit (Dixie RH0300) **$175.50**

UBERTI 1848 DRAGOON AND POCKET REVOLVERS

Caliber: 44 6-shot engraved cylinder. **Barrel:** 7.5" 7 grooves. **Weight:** 4.1 lbs. **Stocks:** One-piece walnut. **Sights:** Fixed. **Features:** Copy of Eli Whitney's design for Colt using Walker parts. Blued barrel, backstrap, and trigger guard. Made in Italy by Uberti, imported by Benelli USA.

Price: 1848 Whitneyville Dragoon, 7.5" barrel **$400.00**
Price: 1848 Dragoon, 1st thru 3rd models, 7.5" barrel **$350.00**
Price: 1848 Baby Dragoon, 4" barrel **$300.00**

UBERTI 1858 NEW ARMY REVOLVERS

Caliber: 44 6-shot engraved cylinder. **Barrel:** 8" 7 grooves. **Weight:** 2.7 lbs. **Length:** 13.6". **Stocks:** Two-piece walnut. **Sights:** Fixed. **Features:** Blued or stainless barrel, backstrap; brass trigger guard. Made in Italy by Uberti, imported by Benelli USA.

Price: 1858 New Army Stainless 8" barrel **$365.00**
Price: 1858 New Army 8" barrel **$300.00**
Price: 1858 Target Carbine 18" barrel **$475.00**
Price: 1862 Pocket Navy 5.5" barrel, 36 caliber **$300.00**
Price: 1862 Police 5.5" barrel, 36 caliber **$300.00**

UBERTI 1861 NAVY PERCUSSION REVOLVER

Caliber: 36, 6-shot. **Barrel:** 7.5", 7-groove, round. **Weight:** 2 lbs., 6 oz. **Length:** 13". **Stocks:** One-piece walnut. **Sights:** German silver blade front sight. **Features:** Rounded trigger guard, "creeping" loading lever, fluted or round cylinder, steel backstrap, trigger guard, cut for stock. Imported by Cimarron F.A. Co., Uberti U.S.A. Inc., Dixie Gun Works.

Price: **$285.00**

1862 POCKET NAVY PERCUSSION REVOLVER

Caliber: 36, 5-shot. **Barrel:** 5.5", 6.5", octagonal, 7-groove, LH twist. **Weight:** 27 oz. (5.5" barrel). **Length:** 10.5" overall (5.5" bbl.). **Stocks:** One-piece varnished walnut. **Sights:** Brass pin front, hammer notch rear. **Features:** Rebated cylinder, hinged loading lever, brass or silver-plated backstrap and trigger guard, color-cased frame, hammer, loading lever, plunger and latch, rest blued. Has original-type markings. From Cimarron F.A. Co., Uberti U.S.A. Inc., Dixie Gun Works.

Price: With brass backstrap, trigger guard **$250.00**

WALKER 1847 PERCUSSION REVOLVER

Caliber: 44, 6-shot. **Barrel:** 9". **Weight:** 84 oz. **Length:** 15.5" overall. **Stocks:** Walnut. **Sights:** Fixed. **Features:** Case-hardened frame, loading lever and hammer; iron backstrap; brass trigger guard; engraved cylinder. Imported by Cabela's, Cimarron F.A. Co., Navy Arms, Uberti U.S.A. Inc., E.M.F., Cimarron, Traditions, United States Patent Fire-Arms.

Price: Dixie RH0200 .... **$360.00**
Price: Dixie Kit RH0400 .... **$250.00**
Price: Hartford model, steel frame, cartouche (E.M.F.) **$350.00**

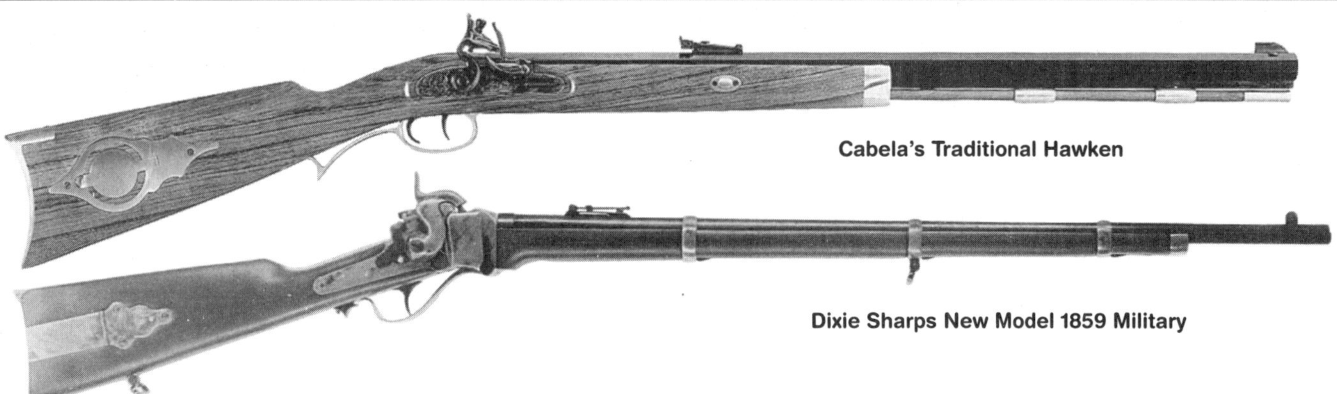

Cabela's Traditional Hawken

Dixie Sharps New Model 1859 Military

ARMOURY R140 HAWKEN RIFLE
Caliber: 45, 50 or 54. **Barrel:** 29". **Weight:** 8.75 to 9 lbs. **Length:** 45.75" overall. **Stock:** Walnut, with cheekpiece. **Sights:** Dovetailed front, fully adjustable rear. **Features:** Octagon barrel, removable breech plug; double set triggers; blued barrel, brass stock fittings, color case-hardened percussion lock. From Armsport, The Armoury.
Price: . . . . **$225.00 to $245.00**

BOSTONIAN PERCUSSION RIFLE
Caliber: 45. **Barrel:** 30", octagonal. **Weight:** 7.25 lbs. **Length:** 46" overall. **Stock:** Walnut. **Sights:** Blade front, fixed notch rear. **Features:** Color case-hardened lock, brass trigger guard, buttplate, patchbox. Imported from Italy by E.M.F.
Price: **$285.00**

CABELA'S BLUE RIDGE RIFLE
Caliber: 32, 36, 45, 50, .54. **Barrel:** 39", octagonal. **Weight:** About 7.75 lbs. **Length:** 55" overall. **Stock:** American black walnut. **Sights:** Blade front, rear drift adjustable for windage. **Features:** Color case-hardened lockplate and cock/hammer, brass trigger guard and buttplate, double set, double-phased triggers. From Cabela's.
Price: Percussion **$569.99**
Price: Flintlock **$599.99**

CABELA'S TRADITIONAL HAWKEN
Caliber: 50, 54. **Barrel:** 29". **Weight:** About 9 lbs. **Stock:** Walnut. **Sights:** Blade front, open adjustable rear. **Features:** Flintlock or percussion. Adjustable double-set triggers. Polished brass furniture, color case-hardened lock. Imported by Cabela's.
Price: Percussion, right-hand or left-hand **$339.99**
Price: Flintlock, right-hand **$399.99**

CABELA'S KODIAK EXPRESS DOUBLE RIFLE
Caliber: 50, 54, 58, 72. **Barrel:** Length NA; 1:48" twist. **Weight:** 9.3 lbs. **Length:** 45.25" overall. **Stock:** European walnut, oil finish. **Sights:** Fully adjustable double folding-leaf rear, ramp front. **Features:** Percussion. Barrels regulated to point of aim at 75 yards; polished and engraved lock, top tang and trigger guard. From Cabela's.
Price: 50, 54, 58 calibers **$929.99**
Price: 72 caliber **$959.99**

COOK & BROTHER CONFEDERATE CARBINE
Caliber: 58. **Barrel:** 24". **Weight:** 7.5 lbs. **Length:** 40.5" overall. **Stock:** Select walnut. **Features:** Re-creation of the 1861 New Orleans-made artillery carbine. Color case-hardened lock, browned barrel. Buttplate, trigger guard, barrel bands, sling swivels and nosecap of polished brass. From Euroarms of America.
Price: **$563.00**
Price: Cook & Brother rifle (33" barrel) **$606.00**

CVA OPTIMA PRO 209 BREAK-ACTION RIFLE
Caliber: 45, 50. **Barrel:** 29" fluted, blue or nickel. **Weight:** 8.8 lbs. **Stock:** Ambidextrous Mossy Oak® Camo or black FiberGrip. **Sights:** Adj. fiber-optic. **Features:** Break-action, stainless No. 209 breech plug, aluminum loading rod, cocking spur, lifetime warranty.
Price: Mossy Oak® Camo **$399.95**
Price: Camo, nickel bbl. **$379.95**
Price: Mossy Oak® Camo/blued **$349.95**
Price: Black/nickel **$329.95**
Price: Black/blued **$299.95**
Price: Blued fluted bbl. **$99.95**
Price: Nickel fluted bbl. **$115.95**

CVA Optima 209 Magnum Break-Action Rifle
Similar to Optima Pro but with 26" bbl., nickel or blue finish, 50 cal.
Price: Mossy Oak® Camo/nickel **$310.00**
Price: Mossy Oak® Camo/blue **$290.00**
Price: Black/blued **$235.00**

CVA Optima Elite
Similar to Optima Pro but chambered for 45, 50 black powder plus 243, 270, 30-06 centerfire car-tridges.
Price: Hardwoods Green HD/blue **$415.00**
Price: Black Fleck/blue **$355.00**

CVA BUCKHORN 209 MAGNUM
Caliber: 50. **Barrel:** 24". **Weight:** 6.3 lbs. **Sights:** Illuminator fiber-optic. **Features:** Grip-dot stock, thumb-actuated safety; drilled and tapped for scope mounts.
Price: Black stock, blue barrel **$145.00**

CVA KODIAK MAGNUM RIFLE
Caliber: 50. No. 209 primer ignition. **Barrel:** 28"; 1:28" twist. **Stock:** Ambidextrous black or Mossy Oak® camo. **Sights:** Fiber-optic. **Features:** Blue or nickel finish, recoil pad, lifetime warranty. From CVA.
Price: Mossy Oak® camo; nickel barrel **$300.00**
Price: Black stock; nickel barrel **$255.00**
Price: Black stock; blued barrel **$225.00**

DIXIE EARLY AMERICAN JAEGER RIFLE
Caliber: 54. **Barrel:** 27.5" octagonal; 1:24" twist. **Weight:** 8.25 lbs. **Length:** 43.5" overall. **Stock:** American walnut; sliding wooden patchbox on butt. **Sights:** Notch rear, blade front. **Features:** Flintlock or percussion. Browned steel furniture. Imported from Italy by Dixie Gun Works.
Price: Flintlock FR0838. . . . . **$850.00**
Price: Percussion PR0835, case-hardened **$850.00**
Price: Kit **$725.00**

DIXIE DELUXE CUB RIFLE
Caliber: .32, .36, .40 & .45. **Barrel:** 28" octa-gon. **Weight:** 6.25 lbs. **Length:** 44" overall. **Stock:** Walnut. **Sights:** Fixed. **Features:** Short ri-fle for small game and beginning shooters. Brass patchbox and furniture. Flint or percussion, fin-ished or kit. From Dixie Gun Works
Price: Finished, from. **$530.00**
Price: Kit, from **$440.00**
Price: Super Cub (.50 cal) **$610.00**
Price: Super Cub Kit (.50 cal) **$510.00**

DIXIE PEDERSOLI 1857 MAUSER RIFLE
Caliber: 54. **Barrel:** 39-3/8". **Weight:** 9.5 lbs. **Length:** 54.75" overall. **Stock:** European walnut with oil finish, sling swivels. **Sights:** Fully adjustable rear, lug front. **Features:** Percussion (musket caps). Armory bright finish with color case-hardened lock and barrel tang, engraved lockplate, steel ramrod. Introduced 2000. Imported from Italy by Dixie Gun Works.
Price: PR1330. . . . . **$1,050.00**

DIXIE SHARPS NEW MODEL 1859 MILITARY RIFLE
Caliber: 54. **Barrel:** 30", 6-groove; 1:48" twist. **Weight:** 9 lbs. **Length:** 45.5" overall. **Stock:** Oiled walnut. **Sights:** Blade front, ladder-style rear. **Features:** Blued barrel, color case-hardened barrel bands, receiver, hammer, nosecap, lever, patchbox cover and buttplate. Introduced 1995. Imported from Italy by Dixie Gun Works.
Price: PR0862. . . . . **$1,050.00**

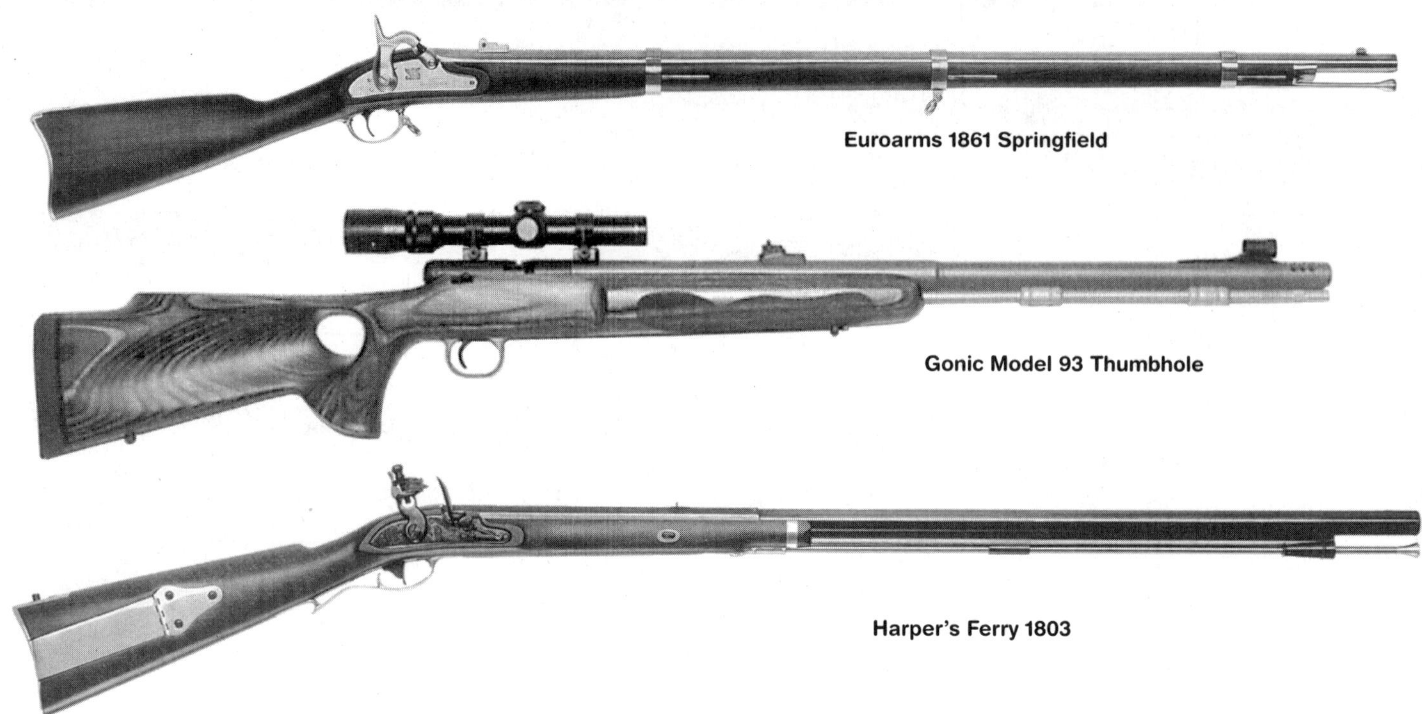

Euroarms 1861 Springfield

Gonic Model 93 Thumbhole

Harper's Ferry 1803

DIXIE U.S. MODEL 1816 FLINTLOCK MUSKET

Caliber: .69. **Barrel:** 42", smoothbore. **Weight:** 9.75 lbs. **Length:** 56 7/8" overall. **Stock:** Walnut w/oil finish. **Sights:** Blade front. **Features:** All metal finished "National Armory Bright," three barrel bands w/ springs, steel ramrod w/button-shaped head. Imported by Dixie Gun Works.

Price: FR0305. . . . . **$1,075.00**
Price: PR0257, Percussion conversion **$975.00**

E.M.F. 1863 SHARPS MILITARY CARBINE

Caliber: 54. **Barrel:** 22", round. **Weight:** 8 lbs. **Length:** 39" overall. **Stock:** Oiled walnut. **Sights:** Blade front, military ladder-type rear. **Features:** Color case-hardened lock, rest blued. Imported by E.M.F.

Price: **$600.00**

EUROARMS VOLUNTEER TARGET RIFLE

Caliber: 451. **Barrel:** 33" (two-band), 36" (three-band). **Weight:** 11 lbs. (two-band). **Length:** 48.75" overall (two-band). **Stock:** European walnut with checkered wrist and forend. **Sights:** Hooded bead front, adjustable rear with interchangeable leaves. **Features:** Alexander Henry-type rifling with 1:20" twist. Color case-hardened hammer and lockplate, brass trigger guard and nosecap, remainder blued. Imported by Euroarms of America, Dixie Gun Works.

Price: PR1031. . . . . **$925.00**

EUROARMS 1861 SPRINGFIELD RIFLE

Caliber: 58. **Barrel:** 40". **Weight:** About 10 lbs. **Length:** 55.5" overall. **Stock:** European walnut. **Sights:** Blade front, three-leaf military rear. **Features:** Reproduction of the original three-band rifle. Lockplate marked "1861" with eagle and "U.S. Springfield." White metal. Imported by Euroarms of America.

Price: **$730.00**

EUROARMS ZOUAVE RIFLE

Caliber: 54, 58 percussion. **Barrel:** 33". **Weight:** 9.5 lbs. Overall **length:** 49". **Features:** One-piece solid barrel and bolster. For 54 caliber, .535 R.B., .540 minnie. For 58 caliber, .575 R.B., .577 minnie. 1863 issue. Made in Italy. Imported by Euroarms of America.

Price: **$469.00**

EUROARMS HARPERS FERRY RIFLE

Caliber: 58 flintlock. **Barrel:** 35". **Weight:** 9 lbs. Overall **length:** 59.5". **Features:** Antique browned barrel. Barrel .575 RB. .577 minnie. 1803 issue. Made in Italy. Imported by Euroarms of America.

Price: **$735.00**

GONIC MODEL 93 M/L RIFLE

Caliber: 45, 50. **Barrel:** 26"; 1:24" twist. **Weight:** 6.5 to 7 lbs. **Length:** 43" overall. **Stock:** American hardwood with black finish. **Sights:** Adjustable or aperture rear, hooded post front. **Features:** Adjustable trigger with side safety; unbreakable ramrod; comes with A. Z. scope bases installed. Introduced 1993. Made in U.S. by Gonic Arms, Inc.

Price: Model 93 Standard (blued barrel). **$720.00**
Price: Model 93 Standard (stainless brl., 50 cal. only) **$782.00**

Gonic Model 93 Deluxe M/L Rifle

Similar to the Model 93 except has classic-style walnut or gray laminated wood stock. Introduced 1998. Made in U.S. by Gonic Arms, Inc.

Price: Blue barrel, sights, scope base, choice of stock. **$902.00**
Price: Stainless barrel, sights, scope base, choice of stock (50 cal. only) **$964.00**

Gonic Model 93 Mountain Thumbhole M/L Rifles

Similar to the Model 93 except has high-grade walnut or gray laminate stock with extensive hand-checkered panels, Monte Carlo cheekpiece and beavertail forend; integral muzzle brake. Introduced 1998. Made in U.S. by Gonic Arms, Inc.

Price: Blued or stainless **$2,700.00**

HARPER'S FERRY 1803 FLINTLOCK RIFLE

Caliber: 54 or 58. **Barrel:** 35". **Weight:** 9 lbs. **Length:** 59.5" overall. **Stock:** Walnut with cheekpiece. **Sights:** Brass blade front, fixed steel rear. **Features:** Brass trigger guard, sideplate, buttplate; steel patchbox. Imported by Euroarms of America, Navy Arms (54-cal. only), Cabela's, and Dixie Gun Works.

Price: . . . . **$495.95 to $995.00**
Price: 54-cal. (Navy Arms) **$625.00**
Price: 54-cal. (Cabela's) **$599.99**
Price: 54-cal. (Dixie Gun Works), FR0171 . . . . **$995.00**
Price: 54-cal. (Euroarms) **$809.00**

HAWKEN RIFLE

Caliber: 45, 50, 54 or 58. **Barrel:** 28", blued, 6-groove rifling. **Weight:** 8.75 lbs. **Length:** 44" overall. **Stock:** Walnut with cheekpiece. **Sights:** Blade front, fully adjustable rear. **Features:** Coil mainspring, double-set triggers, polished brass furniture. From Armsport and E.M.F.

Price: . . . . **$220.00 to $345.00**

J.P. HENRY TRADE RIFLE

Caliber: 54. **Barrel:** 34"; 1" flats. **Weight:** 8.5 lbs. **Length:** 45" overall. **Stock:** Premium curly maple. **Sights:** Silver blade front, fixed buckhorn rear. **Features:** Brass buttplate, side plate, trigger guard and nosecap; browned barrel and lock; L&R Large English percussion lock; single trigger. Made in U.S. by J.P. Gunstocks, Inc.

Price: **$965.50**

J.P. Murray

Kentucky Flintlock

Knight 50 Caliber DISC in-Line

Knight Master Hunter DISC Extreme

Knight American Knight

J.P. MURRAY 1862-1864 CAVALRY CARBINE

Caliber: 58 (.577" Minie). **Barrel:** 23". **Weight:** 7 lbs., 9 oz. **Length:** 39" overall. **Stock:** Walnut. **Sights:** Blade front, rear drift adjustable for windage. **Features:** Blued barrel, color case-hardened lock, blued swivel and band springs, polished brass buttplate, trigger guard, barrel bands. From Euroarms of America.

Price: Dixie Gun Works PR0173. . . . . **$750.00**

KENTUCKY FLINTLOCK RIFLE

Caliber: 44, 45, or 50. **Barrel:** 35". **Weight:** 7 lbs. **Length:** 50" overall. **Stock:** Walnut stained, brass fittings. **Sights:** Fixed. **Features:** Available in carbine model also, 28" bbl. Some variations in detail, finish. Kits also available from some importers. Imported by The Armoury.

Price: About . . . . **$217.95 to $345.00**

Kentucky Percussion Rifle

Similar to Flintlock except percussion lock. Finish and features vary with importer. Imported by The Armoury and CVA.

Price: About **$259.95**
Price: 45 or 50 cal. (Navy Arms) **$425.00**
Price: Kit, 50 cal. (CVA) **$189.95**

KNIGHT 50 CALIBER DISC IN-LINE RIFLE

Caliber: 50. **Barrel:** 24", 26". **Weight:** 7 lbs., 14 oz. **Length:** 43" overall (24" barrel). **Stock:** Checkered synthetic with palm swell grip, rubber recoil pad, swivel studs; black, Advantage or Mossy Oak® Break-Up camouflage. **Sights:** Bead on ramp front, fully adjustable open rear. **Features:** Bolt-action in-line system uses #209 shotshell primer for ignition; primer is held in plastic drop-in Primer Disc. Available in blued or stainless steel. Made in U.S. by Knight Rifles (Modern Muzzleloading).

Price: . . . . **$439.95 to $632.45**

Knight Master Hunter II DISC In-Line Rifle

Similar to Knight 50 caliber DISC rifle except features premium, wood laminated two-tone stock, gold-plated trigger and engraved trigger guard, jeweled bolt and fluted, air-gauged Green Mountain 26" barrel. **Length:** 45" overall, weighs 7 lbs., 7 oz. Includes black composite thumbhole stock. Intro-duced 2000. Made in U.S. by Knight Rifles (Modern Muzzleloading).

Price: **$1,099.95**

KNIGHT MUZZLELOADER DISC EXTREME

Caliber: 45 fluted, 50. **Barrel:** 26". **Stock:** Stainless steel laminate, blued walnut, black composite thumbhole with blued or SS. **Sights:** Fully adjustable metallic. **Features:** New full plastic jacket ignition system.

Price: 50 SS laminate **$703.95**
Price: 45 SS laminate **$769.95**
Price: 50 blue walnut **$626.95**
Price: 45 blue walnut **$703.95**
Price: 50 blue composite **$549.95**
Price: 45 blue composite **$632.45**
Price: 50 SS composite **$632.45**
Price: 45 SS composite **$703.95**

Knight Master Hunter DISC Extreme

Similar to DISC Extreme except fluted barrel, two-tone laminated thumbhole Monte Carlo-style stock, black composite thumbhole field stock included. Jeweled bolt, adjustable premium trigger.

Price: 50 . . . . **$1,044.95**

KNIGHT AMERICAN KNIGHT M/L RIFLE

Caliber: 50. **Barrel:** 22"; 1:28" twist. **Weight:** 6 lbs. **Length:** 41" overall. **Stock:** Black composite. **Sights:** Bead on ramp front, open fully adjustable rear. **Features:** Double safety system; one-piece removable hammer assembly; drilled and tapped for scope mounting. Introduced 1998. Made in U.S. by Knight Rifles.

Price: Blued, black comp **$197.95**
Price: Blued, black comp VP **$225.45**

KNIGHT WOLVERINE 209

Caliber: 50. **Barrel:** 22". **Stock:** HD stock with SS barrel, break-up stock blued, black composite thumbhole with stainless steel, standard black composite with blued or SS. **Sights:** Metallic with fiber-optic. **Features:** Double safety system, adjustable match grade trigger, left-hand model available. Full plastic jacket ignition system.

Price: Starting at **$302.45**

Knight Wolverine 209

London Armory 1861

Lyman Trade Percussion

Lyman Deerslayer

Lyman Great Plains

KNIGHT REVOLUTION

Caliber: 50, 209 primer ignition. **Barrel:** Stainless, 27". **Weight:** 7 lbs., 14 oz. **Stock:** Walnut, laminated, black composite, Mossy Oak® Break-Up™ or Hardwoods Green finish. **Features:** Blued or stainless finish, adjustable trigger and sights.

Price: . . . . **NA**

LONDON ARMORY 1861 ENFIELD MUSKETOON

Caliber: 58, Minie ball. **Barrel:** 24", round. **Weight:** 7 to 7.5 lbs. **Length:** 40.5" overall. **Stock:** Walnut, with sling swivels. **Sights:** Blade front, graduated military-leaf rear. **Features:** Brass trigger guard, nosecap, buttplate; blued barrel, bands, lockplate, swivels. Imported by Euroarms of America, Navy Arms.

Price: . . . . **$300.00 to $521.00**
Price: Kit . . . . **$365.00 to $402.00**

LONDON ARMORY 2-BAND 1858 ENFIELD

Caliber: .577" Minie, .575" round ball. **Barrel:** 33". **Weight:** 10 lbs. **Length:** 49" overall. **Stock:** Walnut. **Sights:** Folding leaf rear adjustable for elevation. **Features:** Blued barrel, color case-hardened lock and hammer, polished brass buttplate, trigger guard, nosecap. From Navy Arms, Euroarms of America, Dixie Gun Works.

Price: PR0330 . . . .**$650.00**

LONDON ARMORY 3-BAND 1853 ENFIELD

Caliber: 58 (.577" Minie, .575" round ball, .580" maxi ball). **Barrel:** 39". **Weight:** 9.5 lbs. **Length:** 54" overall. **Stock:** European walnut. **Sights:** Inverted "V" front, traditional Enfield folding ladder rear. **Features:** Re-creation of the famed London Armory Company Pattern 1853 Enfield Musket. One-piece walnut stock, brass buttplate, trigger guard and nosecap. Lockplate marked "London Armoury Co." and with a British crown. Blued Baddeley barrel bands. From Euroarms of America, Navy Arms.

Price: About . . . . **$350.00 to $606.00**

LYMAN TRADE RIFLE

Caliber: 50, 54. **Barrel:** 28" octagon;1:48" twist. **Weight:** 8.75 lbs. **Length:** 45" overall. **Stock:** European walnut. **Sights:** Blade front, open rear adjustable for windage or optional fixed sights. **Features:** Fast twist rifling for conical bullets. Polished brass furniture with blue steel parts, stainless steel nipple. Hook breech, single trigger, coil spring percussion lock. Steel barrel rib and ramrod ferrules. Introduced 1980. From Lyman.

Price: 50 cal. percussion. **$581.80**
Price: 50 cal. flintlock **$652.80**
Price: 54 cal. percussion **$581.80**
Price: 54 cal. flintlock **$652.80**

LYMAN DEERSTALKER RIFLE

Caliber: 50, 54. **Barrel:** 24", octagonal; 1:48" rifling. **Weight:** 7.5 lbs. **Stock:** Walnut with black rubber buttpad. **Sights:** Lyman #37MA beaded front, fully adjustable fold-down Lyman #16A rear. **Features:** Stock has less drop for quick sighting. All metal parts are blackened, with color case-hardened lock; single trigger. Comes with sling and swivels. Available in flint or percussion. Introduced 1990. From Lyman.

Price: 50 cal. flintlock **$652.80**
Price: 50 or 54 cal., percussion, left-hand, carbine **$695.40**
Price: 50 or 54 cal., flintlock, left-hand **$645.00**
Price: 54 cal. flintlock **$780.50**
Price: 54 cal. percussion **$821.80**
Price: Stainless steel **$959.80**

LYMAN GREAT PLAINS RIFLE

Caliber: 50, 54. **Barrel:** 32"; 1:60" twist. **Weight:** 9 lbs. **Stock:** Walnut. **Sights:** Steel blade front, buckhorn rear adjustable for windage and elevation and fixed notch primitive sight included. **Features:** Blued steel furniture. Stainless steel nipple. Coil spring lock, Hawken-style trigger guard and double-set triggers. Round thimbles recessed and sweated into rib. Steel wedge plates and toe plate. Introduced 1979. From Lyman.

Price: Percussion **$469.95**
Price: Flintlock **$494.95**
Price: Percussion kit **$359.95**
Price: Flintlock kit **$384.95**
Price: Left-hand percussion **$474.95**
Price: Left-hand flintlock **$499.95**

Markesbery KM Colorado

Mississippi 1841

Lyman Great Plains Hunter Model

Similar to Great Plains model except 1:32" twist shallow-groove barrel and comes drilled and tapped for Lyman 57GPR peep sight.

Price: **$959.80**

MARKESBERY KM BLACK BEAR M/L RIFLE

Caliber: 36, 45, 50, 54. **Barrel:** 24"; 1:26" twist. **Weight:** 6.5 lbs. **Length:** 38.5" overall. **Stock:** Two-piece American hardwood, walnut, black laminate, green laminate, black composition, X-Tra or Mossy Oak® Break-Up™ camouflage. **Sights:** Bead front, open fully adjustable rear. **Features:** Interchangeable barrels; exposed hammer; Outer-Line Magnum ignition system uses small rifle primer or standard No. 11 cap and nipple. Blue, black matte, or stainless. Made in U.S. by Markesbery Muzzle Loaders.

Price: American hardwood walnut, blue finish **$536.63**
Price: American hardwood walnut, stainless **$553.09**
Price: Black laminate, blue finish **$539.67**
Price: Black laminate, stainless **$556.27**
Price: Camouflage stock, blue finish **$556.46**
Price: Camouflage stock, stainless **$573.73**
Price: Black composite, blue finish **$532.65**
Price: Black composite, stainless **$549.93**
Price: Green laminate, blue finish **$539.00**
Price: Green laminate, stainless **$556.27**

Markesbery KM Brown Bear Rifle

Similar to KM Black Bear except one-piece thumbhole stock with Monte Carlo comb. Stock in Crotch Walnut composite, green or black laminate, black composite or X-Tra or Mossy Oak® Break-Up™ camouflage. Made in U.S. by Markesbery Muzzle Loaders, Inc.

Price: Black composite, blue finish **$658.83**
Price: Crotch Walnut, blue finish **$658.83**
Price: Camo composite, blue finish **$682.64**
Price: Walnut wood **$662.81**
Price: Black wood **$662.81**
Price: Black laminated wood **$662.81**
Price: Green laminated wood **$662.81**
Price: Camo wood **$684.69**
Price: Black composite, stainless **$676.11**
Price: Crotch Walnut composite, stainless **$676.11**
Price: Camo composite, stainless **$697.69**
Price: Walnut wood, stainless **$680.07**
Price: Black wood, stainless **$680.07**
Price: Black laminated wood, stainless **$680.07**
Price: Green laminate, stainless **$680.07**
Price: Camo wood, stainless **$702.76**

Markesbery KM Grizzly Bear Rifle

Similar to KM Black Bear except thumbhole buttstock with Monte Carlo comb. Stock in Crotch Walnut composite, green or black laminate, black composite or X-Tra or Mossy Oak® Break-Up camouflage. Made in U.S. by Markesbery Muzzle Loaders, Inc.

Price: Black composite, blue finish **$642.96**
Price: Crotch Walnut, blue finish **$642.96**
Price: Camo composite, blue finish **$666.67**
Price: Walnut wood **$646.93**
Price: Black wood **$646.93**
Price: Black laminate wood **$646.93**
Price: Green laminate wood **$646.93**
Price: Camo wood **$670.74**
Price: Black composite, stainless **$660.98**
Price: Crotch Walnut composite, stainless **$660.98**
Price: Black laminate wood, stainless **$664.20**
Price: Green laminate, stainless **$664.20**
Price: Camo wood, stainless **$685.74**
Price: Camo composite, stainless **$684.04**
Price: Walnut wood, stainless **$664.20**
Price: Black wood, stainless **$664.20**

Markesbery KM Polar Bear Rifle

Similar to KM Black Bear except one-piece stock with Monte Carlo comb. Stock in American Hard-wood walnut, green or black laminate, black composite, or X-Tra or Mossy Oak® Break-Up™ cam-ouflage. Interchangeable barrel system, Outer-Line ignition system, cross-bolt double safety. Avail-able in 36, 45, 50, 54 caliber. Made in U.S. by Markesbery Muzzle Loaders, Inc.

Price: American Hardwood walnut, blue finish **$539.01**
Price: Black composite, blue finish **$536.63**
Price: Black laminate, blue finish **$541.17**
Price: Green laminate, blue finish **$541.17**
Price: Camo, blue finish **$560.43**
Price: American Hardwood walnut, stainless **$556.27**
Price: Black composite, stainless **$556.04**
Price: Black laminate, stainless **$570.56**
Price: Green laminate, stainless **$570.56**
Price: Camo, stainless **$573.94**

MARKESBERY KM COLORADO ROCKY MOUNTAIN RIFLE

Caliber: 36, 45, 50, 54. **Barrel:** 24"; 1:26" twist. **Weight:** 6.5 lbs. **Length:** 38.5" overall. **Stock:** American hardwood walnut, green or black laminate. **Sights:** Firesight bead on ramp front, fully adjustable open rear. **Features:** Replicates Reed/Watson rifle of 1851. Straight grip stock with or without two barrel bands, rubber recoil pad, large-spur hammer. Made in U.S. by Markesbery Muzzle Loaders, Inc.

Price: American hardwood walnut, blue finish **$545.92**
Price: Black or green laminate, blue finish **$548.30**
Price: American hardwood walnut, stainless **$563.17**
Price: Black or green laminate, stainless **$566.34**

MDM BUCKWACKA IN-LINE RIFLES

Caliber: 45, 50. **Barrel:** 23", 25". **Weight:** 7 to 7.75 lbs. **Stock:** Black, walnut, laminated and camouflage finishes. **Sights:** Williams Fire Sight blade front, Williams fully adjustable rear with ghost-ring peep aperture. **Features:** Break-open action; Incinerating Ignition System incorporates 209 shotshell primer directly into breech plug; 50-caliber models handle up to 150 grains of Pyrodex; synthetic ramrod; transfer bar safety; stainless or blued finish. Made in U.S. by Millennium Designed Muzzleloaders Ltd.

Price: 50 cal., blued finish **$309.95**
Price: 50 cal., stainless **$339.95**
Price: Camouflage stock .... **$359.95 to $389.95**

MDM M2K In-Line Rifle

Similar to Buckwacka except adjustable trigger and double-safety mechanism designed to prevent misfires. Made in U.S. by Millennium Designed Muzzleloaders Ltd.

Price: .... **$529.00 to $549.00**

MISSISSIPPI 1841 PERCUSSION RIFLE

Caliber: 54, 58. **Barrel:** 33". **Weight:** 9.5 lbs. **Length:** 48-5/8" overall. **Stock:** One-piece European walnut full stock with satin finish. **Sights:** Brass blade front, fixed steel rear. **Features:** Case-hardened lockplate marked "U.S." surmounted by American eagle. Two barrel bands, sling swivels. Steel ramrod with brass end, browned barrel. From Navy Arms, Dixie Gun Works, Cabela's, Euroarms of America.

Price: Dixie Gun Works PR0870. .... **$825.00**

Navy Arms 1763 Charleville

Navy Arms Whitworh

New England Firearms Sidekick

New England Firearms Huntsman

NAVY ARMS 1763 CHARLEVILLE

Caliber: 69. **Barrel:** 44-5/8". **Weight:** 8 lbs., 12 oz. **Length:** 59-3/8" overall. **Stock:** Walnut. **Sights:** Brass blade front. **Features:** Replica of French musket used by American troops during the American Revolution. Imported by Navy Arms.

Price: **$1,425.00**

NAVY ARMS 1861 SPRINGFIELD RIFLE

Caliber: 58. **Barrel:** 40". **Weight:** 10 lbs., 4 oz. **Length:** 56" overall. **Stock:** Walnut. **Sights:** Blade front, military leaf rear. **Features:** Steel barrel, lock and all furniture have polished bright finish. Has 1855-style hammer. Imported by Navy Arms.

Price: **$1,005.00**

NAVY ARMS 1863 C.S. RICHMOND RIFLE

Caliber: 58. **Barrel:** 40". **Weight:** 10 lbs. **Length:** NA. **Stocks:** Walnut. **Sights:** Blade front, adjustable rear. **Features:** Copy of three-band rifle musket made at Richmond Armory for the Confederacy. All steel polished bright. Imported by Navy Arms.

Price: **$1,005.00**

NAVY ARMS 1863 SPRINGFIELD

Caliber: 58, uses .575 Minie. **Barrel:** 40", rifled. **Weight:** 9.5 lbs. **Length:** 56" overall. **Stock:** Walnut. **Sights:** Open rear adjustable for elevation. **Features:** Full-size, three-band musket. Polished bright metal, including lock. From Navy Arms.

Price: Finished rifle **$1,005.00**

NAVY ARMS PARKER-HALE VOLUNTEER RIFLE

Caliber: 451. **Barrel:** 32". **Weight:** 9.5 lbs. **Length:** 49" overall. **Stock:** Walnut, checkered wrist and forend. **Sights:** Globe front, adjustable ladder-type rear. **Features:** Recreation of the type of gun issued to volunteer regiments during the 1860s. Rigby-pattern rifling, patent breech, detented lock. Stock is glass bedded for accuracy. Imported by Navy Arms.

Price: **$1,167.00**

NAVY ARMS PARKER-HALE WHITWORTH MILITARY TARGET RIFLE

Caliber: 45. **Barrel:** 36". **Weight:** 9.25 lbs. **Length:** 52.5" overall. **Stock:** Walnut. Checkered at wrist and forend. **Sights:** Hooded post front, open step-adjustable rear. **Features:** Faithful reproduction of Whitworth rifle. Trigger has detented lock, capable of fine adjustments without risk of the sear nose catching on the half-cock notch and damaging both parts. Introduced 1978. Imported by Navy Arms.

Price: **$1,220.00**

NEW ENGLAND FIREARMS SIDEKICK

Caliber: 50, 209 primer ignition. **Barrel:** 26" (magnum). **Weight:** 6.5 lbs. **Length:** 41.25". **Stock:** Black matte polymer or hardwood. **Sights:** Adjustable fiber-optic open, tapped for scope mounts. **Features:** Single-shot based on H&R break-open action. Uses No. 209 shotgun primer held in place by special primer carrier. Telescoping brass ramrod. Introduced 2004.

Price: Wood stock, blued frame, black-oxide barrel) **$216.00**

Price: Stainless barrel and frame, synthetic stock) **$310.00**

NEW ENGLAND FIREARMS HUNTSMAN

Caliber: 50, 209 primer ignition. **Barrel:** 22" to 26". **Weight:** 5.25 to 6.5 lbs. **Length:** 40" to 43". **Stock:** Black matte polymer or hardwood. **Sights:** Fiber-optic open sights, tapped for scope mounts. **Features:** Break-open action, transfer-bar safety system, breech plug removable for cleaning. Introduced 2004.

Price: Stainless Huntsman **$306.00**

Price: Huntsman **$212.00**

Price: Pardner Combo 12 ga./50 cal muzzleloader **$259.00**

Price: Tracker II Combo 12 ga. rifled slug barrel /50 cal. **$288.00**

Price: Handi-Rifle Combo 243/50 cal. **$405.00**

New England Firearms Stainless Huntsman

Similar to Huntsman, but with matte nickel finish receiver and stainless bbl. Introduced 2003. From New England Firearms.

Price: **$81.00**

PACIFIC RIFLE MODEL 1837 ZEPHYR

Caliber: 62. **Barrel:** 30", tapered octagon. **Weight:** 7.75 lbs. **Length:** NA. **Stock:** Oil-finished fancy walnut. **Sights:** German silver blade front, semi-buckhorn rear. Options available. **Features:** Improved underhammer action. First production rifle to offer Forsyth rifle, with narrow lands and shallow rifling with 1:14" pitch for high-velocity round balls. Metal finish is slow rust brown with nitre blue accents. Optional sights, finishes and integral muzzle brake available. Introduced 1995. Made in U.S. by Pacific Rifle Co.

Price: From **$995.00**

Pacific Rifle Big Bore African Rifles

Similar to the 1837 Zephyr except in 72-caliber and 8-bore. The 72-caliber is available in standard form with 28" barrel, or as the African with flat buttplate, checkered upgraded wood; weight is 9 lbs. The 8-bore African has dual-cap ignition, 24" barrel, weighs 12 lbs., checkered English walnut, engraving, gold inlays. Introduced 1998. Made in U.S. by Pacific Rifle Co.

Price: 72-caliber, from **$1,150.00**

Price: 8-bore, from **$2,500.00**

Peifer TS-93

Prairie River Arms PRA Bullpup

Remington Genesis

C.S. Richmond 1863

Savage 10MLSS-IIXP

PEIFER MODEL TS-93 RIFLE

Caliber: 45, 50. **Barrel:** 24" Douglas premium; 1:20" twist in 45; 1:28" in 50. **Weight:** 7 lbs. **Length:** 43.25" overall. **Stock:** Bell & Carlson solid composite, with recoil pad, swivel studs. **Sights:** Williams bead front on ramp, fully adjustable open rear. Drilled and tapped for Weaver scope mounts with dovetail for rear peep. **Features:** In-line ignition uses #209 shotshell primer; fast lock time; fully enclosed breech; adjustable trigger; automatic safety; removable primer holder. Blue or stainless. Made in U.S. by Peifer Rifle Co. Introduced 1996.

Price: Blue, black stock. **$730.00**
Price: Blue, wood or camouflage composite stock, or stainless with black composite stock **$803.00**
Price: Stainless, wood or camouflage composite stock **$876.00**

PRAIRIE RIVER ARMS PRA BULLPUP RIFLE

Caliber: 50. **Barrel:** 28"; 1:28" twist. **Weight:** 7.5 lbs. **Length:** 31.5" overall. **Stock:** Hardwood or black all-weather. **Sights:** Blade front, open adjustable rear. **Features:** Bullpup design thumbhole stock. Patented internal percussion ignition system. Left-hand model available. Dovetailed for scope mount. Introduced 1995. Made in U.S. by Prairie River Arms, Ltd.

Price: 4140 alloy barrel, hardwood stock **$199.00**
Price: All Weather stock, alloy barrel **$205.00**

REMINGTON GENESIS MUZZLELOADER

Caliber: 50. **Barrel:** 28", 1-in-28" twist, blued, camo, or stainless fluted. **Weight:** 7.75 lbs. **Length:** NA. **Stock:** Black synthetic, Mossy Oak New Break-Up, Realtree Hardwoods HD. **Sights:** Williams fiber-optic sights, drilled and tapped for scope mounts. **Features:** TorchCam action, 209 primer, up to 150-grain charges. Over-travel hammer, crossbolt safety with ambidextrous HammerSpur (right- and left-handed operation). Buckmasters version has stainless fluted barrel with a Realtree Hardwoods HD camo stock, laser-engraved Buckmasters logo. Aluminum anodized ramrod with jag, front and rear swivel studs, removable 7/16" breech plug; optimized for use with Remington Kleanbore 209 Muzzleloading Primers. Introduced 2006. Made in U.S. by Remington Arms Co.

Price: Genesis ML, black synthetic, carbon matte blued **$237.00**
Price: Genesis MLS Overmold synthetic, tainless satin **$307.00**
Price: Genesis ML Camo Mossy Oak Break-Up full camo . . . **$349.00**
Price: Genesis ML SF Synthetic Thumbhole, stainless satin . **$405.00**
Price: Genesis ML SF Buckmasters (2007) **$363.00**
Price: Genesis ML SF laminate thumbhole, stainless satin . . **$538.00**

RICHMOND, C.S., 1863 MUSKET

Caliber: 58. **Barrel:** 40". **Weight:** 11 lbs. **Length:** 56.25" overall. **Stock:** European walnut with oil finish. **Sights:** Blade front, adjustable folding leaf rear. **Features:** Reproduction of the three-band Civil War musket. Sling swivels attached to trigger guard and middle barrel band. Lockplate marked "1863" and "C.S. Richmond." All white metal. Brass buttplate and forend cap. Imported by Euroarms of America, Navy Arms, and Dixie Gun Works.

Price: Euroarms **$730.00**
Price: Dixie Gun Works PR0846 . . . . **$1,050.00**
Price: Navy Arms **$1,005.00**

ROCKY MOUNTAIN HAWKEN

Caliber: NA. **Barrel:** 34-11/16". **Weight:** 10 lbs. **Length:** 52" overall. **Stock:** Walnut or maple. **Sights:** Blade front, drift adjustable rear. Fea-tures: Percussion, double set trigger, casehard-ened furniture, hook breech, brown barrel. Made by Pedersoli in Italy. Imported by Dixie Gun Works.

Price: Maple Stock PR3430 . . . . **$995.00**
Price: Walnut Stock PR3435 . . . . **$725.00**

ROSSI MUZZLELOADERS

Caliber: .50. **Barrel:** 20", 23". **Weight:** 5-6.3 lbs. **Stocks:** Wood. **Sights:** Fully adjustable fiber optic sights. **Features:** Black powder break open, 2 models available, manual external safety, Taurus Security System, blue or stainless finish, youth models available. From Rossi USA.

Price: **$209.00**
Price: Youth Size (2008). **$269.00**

SAVAGE MODEL 10ML MUZZLELOADER RIFLE SERIES

Caliber: 50. **Barrel:** 24", 1:24 twist, blue or stainless. **Weight:** 7.75 lbs. **Stock:** Black synthetic, Realtree Hardwood JD Camo, brown laminate. **Sights:** Green adjustable rear, Red FiberOptic front. **Features:** XP Models scoped, no sights, designed for smokeless powder, #209 primer ignition. Removeable breech plug and vent liner.

Price: Model 10ML-II **$531.00**
Price: Model 10ML-II Camo **$569.00**
Price: Model 10MLSS-II Camo **$628.00**
Price: Model 10MLBSS-II **$667.00**
Price: Model 10ML-IIXP **$569.00**
Price: Model 10MLSS-IIXP **$628.00**

SECOND MODEL BROWN BESS MUSKET

Caliber: 75, uses .735" round ball. **Barrel:** 42", smoothbore. **Weight:** 9.5 lbs. **Length:** 59" overall. **Stock:** Walnut (Navy); walnut-stained hardwood (Dixie). **Sights:** Fixed. **Features:** Polished barrel and lock with brass trigger guard and buttplate. Bayonet and scabbard available. From Navy Arms, Dixie Gun Works, Cabela's.

Price: Finished . . . . **$475.00 to $950.00**
Price: Kit, Dixie Gun Works, FR0825 . . . .**$750.00**
Price: Carbine (Navy Arms) **$835.00**
Price: Dixie Gun Works FR0810 . . . . **$995.00**

THOMPSON/CENTER TRIUMPH MAGNUM MUZZLELOADER

Caliber: 50. **Barrel:** 28" Weather Shield coated. **Weight:** NA. **Length:** NA. **Stock:** Black composite or Realtree AP HD Camo. **Sights:** NA. **Features:** QLA 209 shotshell primer ignition. Introduced 2007. Made in U.S. by Thompson/Center Arms.

Price: . . . . **NA**

THOMPSON/CENTER ENCORE 209X50 MAGNUM

Caliber: 50. **Barrel:** 26"; interchangeable with centerfire calibers. **Weight:** 7 lbs. **Length:** 40.5" overall. **Stock:** American walnut butt and forend, or black composite. **Sights:** TruGlo fiber-optic front and rear. **Features:** Blue or stainless steel. Uses the stock, frame and forend of the Encore centerfire pistol; break-open design using trigger guard spur; stainless steel universal breech plug; uses #209 shotshell primers. Introduced 1998. Made in U.S. by Thompson/Center Arms.

Price: Stainless with camo stock **$772.00**
Price: Blue, walnut stock and forend **$678.00**
Price: Blue, composite stock and forend **$637.00**
Price: Stainless, composite stock and forend **$713.00**
Price: All camo Realtree Hardwoods **$729.00**

THOMPSON/CENTER FIRE STORM RIFLE

Caliber: 50. **Barrel:** 26"; 1:28" twist. **Weight:** 7 lbs. **Length:** 41.75" overall. **Stock:** Black synthetic with rubber recoil pad, swivel studs. **Sights:** Click-adjustable steel rear and ramp-style front, both with fiber-optic inserts. **Features:** Side hammer lock is the first designed for up to three 50-grain Pyrodex pellets; patented Pyrodex Pyramid breech directs ignition fire 360 degrees around base of pellet. Quick Load Accurizor Muzzle System; aluminum ramrod. Flintlock only. Introduced 2000. Made in U.S. by Thompson/ Center Arms.

Price: Blue finish, flintlock model with 1:48" twist for round balls, conicals **$436.00**
Price: SST, flintlock **$488.00**

THOMPSON/CENTER HAWKEN RIFLE

Caliber: 50. **Barrel:** 28" octagon, hooked breech. **Stock:** American walnut. **Sights:** Blade front, rear adjustable for windage and elevation. **Features:** Solid brass furniture, double-set triggers, button rifled barrel, coil-type mainspring. From Thompson/Center Arms.

Price: Percussion model **$590.00**
Price: Flintlock model **$615.00**

TRADITIONS BUCKSKINNER CARBINE

Caliber: 50. **Barrel:** 21"; 15/16" flats, half octagon, half round; 1:20" or 1:66" twist. **Weight:** 6 lbs. **Length:** 37" overall. **Stock:** Beech or black laminated. **Sights:** Beaded blade front, fiber-optic open rear click adjustable for windage and elevation or fiber-optics. **Features:** Uses V-type mainspring, single trigger. Non-glare hardware; sling swivels. From Traditions.

Price: Flintlock **$249.00**
Price: Flintlock, laminated stock **$303.00**

TRADITIONS DEERHUNTER RIFLE SERIES

Caliber: 32, 50 or 54. **Barrel:** 24", octagonal; 15/16" flats; 1:48" or 1:66" twist. **Weight:** 6 lbs. **Length:** 40" overall. **Stock:** Stained hardwood or All-Weather composite with rubber buttpad, sling swivels. **Sights:** Lite Optic blade front, adjustable rear fiber-optics. **Features:** Flint or percussion with color case-hardened lock. Hooked breech, oversized trigger guard, blackened furniture, PVC ramrod. All-Weather has composite stock and C-nickel barrel. Drilled and tapped for scope mounting. Imported by Traditions, Inc.

Price: Percussion, 50; blued barrel; 1:48" twist **$189.00**
Price: Percussion, 54 . . . . **$169.00**
Price: Flintlock, 50 caliber only; 1:48" twist **$179.00**
Price: Flintlock, All-Weather, 50-cal. **$239.00**
Price: Redi-Pak, 50 cal. flintlock **$219.00**
Price: Flintlock, left-handed hardwood, 50 cal. **$209.00**
Price: Percussion, All-Weather, 50 or 54 cal. **$179.00**
Price: Percussion, 32 cal. **$199.00**

Traditions Pursuit

Traditions PA Pellet

Traditions Shenandoah

Traditions Panther Sidelock Rifle

Similar to Deerhunter rifle, but has blade front and windage-adjustable-only rear sights, black com-posite stock.

Price: $129.00

TRADITIONS PURSUIT BREAK-OPEN MUZZLELOADER

Caliber: 45, 54 and 12 gauge. **Barrel:** 28", tapered, fluted; blued, stainless or Hardwoods Green camo. **Weight:** 8.25 lbs. **Length:** 44" overall. **Stock:** Synthetic black or Hardwoods Green. **Sights:** Steel fiber-optic rear, bead front. Introduced 2004 by Traditions, Inc.

Price: Steel, blued, 45 or 50 cal., synthetic stock $279.00
Price: Steel, nickel, 45 or 50 cal., synthetic stock $309.00
Price: Steel, nickel w/Hardwoods Green stock $359.00
Price: Matte blued; 12 ga., synthetic stock $369.00
Price: Matte blued; 12 ga. w/Hardwoods Green stock $439.00
Price: Lightweight model, blued, synthetic stock $199.00
Price: Lightweight model, blued, Mossy Oak® Break-Up™ Camo stock $239.00
Price: Lightweight model, nickel, Mossy Oak® Break-Up™ Camo stock $279.00

TRADITIONS EVOLUTION BOLT-ACTION BLACKPOWDER RIFLE

Caliber: 50 percussion. **Barrel:** 26", fluted with porting. **Sights:** Steel fiber-optic. **Weight:** 7 to 7.25 lbs. **Length:** 45" overall. **Features:** Bolt-action, cocking indicator, thumb safety, aluminum ramrod, sling studs. Wide variety of stocks and metal finishes. Introduced 2004 by Traditions, Inc.

Price: Synthetic stock $279.00
Price: Walnut X-wood $349.00
Price: Brown laminated $469.00
Price: Advantage Timber $369.00
Price: Synthetic, TruGlo sights $249.00
Price: Mossy Oak® Break-up™ $279.00
Price: Nickel finish $309.00
Price: Beech/nickel, Advantage/nickel, Advantage 54 cal. $289.00

TRADITIONS PA PELLET FLINTLOCK

Caliber: 50. **Barrel:** 26", blued, nickel. **Weight:** 7 lbs. **Stock:** Hardwood, synthetic and synthetic break-up. **Sights:** Fiber-optic. **Features:** Removeable breech plug, left-hand model with hardwood stock. 1:48" twist.

Price: Hardwood, blued $259.00
Price: Hardwood left, blued $269.00

TRADITIONS HAWKEN WOODSMAN RIFLE

Caliber: 50 and 54. **Barrel:** 28"; 15/16" flats. **Weight:** 7 lbs., 11 oz. **Length:** 44.5" overall. **Stock:** Walnut-stained hardwood. **Sights:** Beaded blade front, hunting-style open rear adjustable for windage and elevation. **Features:** Percussion only. Brass patchbox and furniture. Double triggers. From Traditions.

Price: 50 or 54 .... $299.00
Price: 50-cal., left-hand $279.00
Price: 50-cal., flintlock $299.00

TRADITIONS KENTUCKY RIFLE

Caliber: 50. **Barrel:** 33.5"; 7/8" flats; 1:66" twist. **Weight:** 7 lbs. **Length:** 49" overall. **Stock:** Beech; inletted toe plate. **Sights:** Blade front, fixed rear. **Features:** Full-length, two-piece stock; brass furniture; color case-hardened lock. From Traditions.

Price: $279.00

TRADITIONS PENNSYLVANIA RIFLE

Caliber: 50. **Barrel:** 40.25"; 7/8" flats; 1:66" twist, octagon. **Weight:** 9 lbs. **Length:** 57.5" overall. **Stock:** Walnut. **Sights:** Blade front, adjustable rear. **Features:** Brass patchbox and ornamentation. Double-set triggers. From Traditions.

Price: Flintlock $529.00
Price: Percussion $519.00

TRADITIONS SHENANDOAH RIFLE

Caliber: 36, 50. **Barrel:** 33.5" octagon; 1:66" twist. **Weight:** 7 lbs., 3 oz. **Length:** 49.5" overall. **Stock:** Walnut. **Sights:** Blade front, buckhorn rear. **Features:** V-type mainspring; double-set trigger; solid brass buttplate, patchbox, nosecap, thimbles, trigger guard. Introduced 1996. From Traditions.

Price: Flintlock $419.00
Price: Percussion $399.00
Price: 36 cal. flintlock, 1:48" twist $419.00
Price: 36 cal. percussion, 1:48" twist $449.00

TRADITIONS TENNESSEE RIFLE

Caliber: 50. **Barrel:** 24", octagon; 15/16" flats; 1:66" twist. **Weight:** 6 lbs. **Length:** 40.5" overall. **Stock:** Stained beech. **Sights:** Blade front, fixed rear. **Features:** One-piece stock has inletted brass furniture, cheekpiece; double-set trigger; V-type mainspring. Flint or percussion. From Traditions.

Price: Flintlock $339.00
Price: Percussion $329.00

TRADITIONS TRACKER 209 IN-LINE RIFLES

Caliber: 45, 50. **Barrel:** 22" blued or C-nickel finish; 1:28" twist, 50 cal. 1:20" 45 cal. **Weight:** 6 lbs., 4 oz. **Length:** 41" overall. **Stock:** Black, Advantage Timber® composite, synthetic. **Sights:** Lite Optic blade front, adjustable rear. **Features:** Thumb safety; adjustable trigger; rubber butt pad and sling swivel studs; takes 150 grains of Pyrodex pellets; one-piece breech system takes 209 shotshell primers. Drilled and tapped for scope. From Traditions.

Price: (Black composite or synthetic stock, 22" blued barrel) $129.00
Price: (Black composite or synthetic stock, 22" C-nickel barrel) $139.00
Price: (Advantage Timber® stock, 22" C-nickel barrel) $189.00
Price: (Redi-Pak, black stock and blued barrel, powder flask, capper, ball starter, other accessories) $179.00
Price: (Redi-Pak, synthetic stock and blued barrel, with scope) $229.00

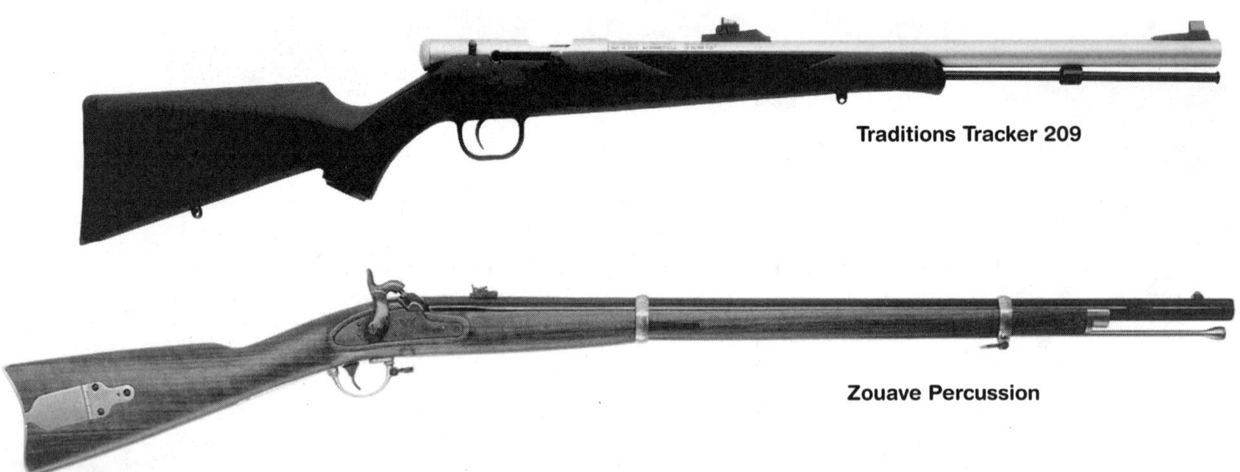
Traditions Tracker 209

Zouave Percussion

ULTRA LIGHT ARMS MODEL 209 MUZZLELOADER
Caliber: 45 or 50. **Barrel:** 24" button rifled; 1:32 twist. **Weight:** Under 5 lbs. **Stock:** Kevlar/Graphite. **Features:** Recoil pad, sling swivels included. Some color options available. Adj. Timney trigger, positive primer extraction.
Price: $1,100.00

WHITE MODEL 97 WHITETAIL HUNTER RIFLE
Caliber: 45, 50. **Barrel:** 22", 1:20" twist (45 cal.); 1:24" twist (50 cal.). **Weight:** 7.7 lbs. **Length:** 40" overall. **Stock:** Black laminated or black composite. **Sights:** Marble TruGlo fully adjustable, steel rear with white diamond, red bead front with high-visibility inserts. **Features:** In-line ignition with FlashFire one-piece nipple and breech plug that uses standard or magnum No. 11 caps, fully adjustable trigger, double safety system, aluminum ramrod; drilled and tapped for scope. Hard case. Made in U.S.A. by Split Fire Sporting Goods.
Price: Whitetail w/laminated or composite stock. $499.95
Price: Adventurer w/26" stainless barrel & thumbhole stock) $699.95
Price: Odyssey w/24" carbon fiber wrapped barrel & thumbhole stock $1,299.95

WHITE MODEL 98 ELITE HUNTER RIFLE
Caliber: 45, 50. **Barrel:** 24", 1:24" twist (50 cal). **Weight:** 8.6 lbs. **Length:** 43.5" overall. **Stock:** Black laminate wtih swivel studs. **Sights:** TruGlo fully adjustable, steel rear with white diamond, red bead front with high-visibility inserts. **Features:** In-line ignition with FlashFire one-piece nipple and breech plug that uses standard or magnum No. 11 caps, fully adjustable trigger, double safety system, aluminum ramrod, drilled and tapped for scope, hard gun case. Made in U.S.A. by Split Fire Sporting Goods.
Price: Composite or laminate wood stock. $499.95

White Thunderbolt Rifle
Similar to the Elite Hunter but is designed to handle 209 shotgun primers only. Has 26" stainless steel barrel, weighs 9.3 lbs. and is 45.5" long. Composite or laminate stock. Made in U.S.A. by Split Fire Sporting Goods.
Price: $599.95

WHITE MODEL 2000 BLACKTAIL HUNTER RIFLE
Caliber: 50. **Barrel:** 22", 1:24" twist (50 cal.). **Weight:** 7.6 lbs. **Length:** 39-7/8" overall. **Stock:** Black laminated with swivel studs with laser engraved deer or elk scene. **Sights:** TruGlo fully adjustable, steel rear with white diamond, red bead front with high-visibility inserts. **Features:** Teflon finished barrel, in-line ignition with FlashFire one-piece nipple and breech plug that uses standard or magnum No. 11 caps, fully adjustable trigger, double safety system, aluminum ramrod, drilled and tapped for scope. Hard gun case. Made in U.S.A. by Split Fire Sporting Goods.
Price: Laminate wood stock, w/laser engraved game scene . $599.95

WHITE LIGHTNING II RIFLE
Caliber: 45 and 50 percussion. **Barrel:** 24", 1:32 twist. **Sights:** Adj. rear. **Stock:** Black polymer. **Weight:** 6 lbs. **Features:** In-line, 209 primer ignition system, blued or nickel-plated bbl., adj. trigger, Delrin ramrod, sling studs, recoil pad. Made in U.S.A. by Split Fire Sporting Goods.
Price: $299.95

WHITE ALPHA RIFLE
Caliber: 45, 50 percussion. **Barrel:** 27" tapered, stainless. **Sights:** Marble TruGlo rear, fiber-optic front. **Stock:** Laminated. **Features:** Lever action rotating block, hammerless; adj. trigger, positive safety. All stainless metal, including trigger. Made in U.S.A. by Split Fire Sporting Goods.
Price: $449.95

WINCHESTER APEX SWING-ACTION MAGNUM RIFLE
Caliber: 45, 50. **Barrel:** 28". **Stock:** Mossy Oak® Camo, Black Fleck. **Sights:** Adj. fiber-optic. **Weight:** 7 lbs., 12 oz. Overall **length:** 42". **Features:** Monte Carlo cheekpiece, swing-action design, external hammer.
Price: Mossy Oak®/stainless $489.95
Price: Black Fleck/stainless $449.95
Price: Full Mossy Oak® $469.95
Price: Black Fleck/blued $364.95

WINCHESTER X-150 BOLT-ACTION MAGNUM RIFLE
Caliber: 45, 50. **Barrel:** 26". **Stock:** Hardwoods or Timber HD, Black Fleck, Break-Up™. **Weight:** 8 lbs., 3 oz. **Sights:** Adj. fiber-optic. **Features:** No. 209 shotgun primer ignition, stainless steel bolt, stainless fluted bbl.
Price: Mossy Oak®, Timber, Hardwoods/stainless. $349.95
Price: Black Fleck/stainless $299.95
Price: Mossy Oak®, Timber, Hardwoods/blued $279.95
Price: Black Fleck/blued $229.95

ZOUAVE PERCUSSION RIFLE
Caliber: 58, 59. **Barrel:** 32.5". **Weight:** 9.5 lbs. **Length:** 48.5" overall. **Stock:** Walnut finish, brass patchbox and buttplate. **Sights:** Fixed front, rear adjustable for elevation. **Features:** Color case-hardened lockplate, blued barrel. From Navy Arms, Dixie Gun Works, E.M.F., Cabela's, Euroarms of America.
Price: Dixie Gun Works PR0853 (58) $648.00

Knight TK2000

CABELA'S BLACKPOWDER SHOTGUNS

Gauge: 10, 12, 20. **Barrel:** 10-ga., 30"; 12-ga., 28.5" (Extra-Full, Mod., Imp. Cyl. choke tubes); 20-ga., 27.5" (Imp. Cyl. & Mod. fixed chokes). **Weight:** 6.5 to 7 lbs. **Length:** 45" overall (28.5" barrel). **Stock:** American walnut with checkered grip; 12- and 20-gauge have straight stock, 10-gauge has pistol grip. **Features:** Blued barrels, engraved, color case-hardened locks and hammers, brass ramrod tip. From Cabela's.

Price: 10-gauge **$849.99**
Price: 12-gauge **$719.99**
Price: 20-gauge **$659.99**

DIXIE MAGNUM PERCUSSION SHOTGUN

Gauge: 10, 12, 20. **Barrel:** 30" (Imp. Cyl. & Mod.) in 10-gauge; 28" in 12-gauge. **Weight:** 6.25 lbs. **Length:** 45" overall. **Stock:** Hand-checkered walnut, 14" pull. **Features:** Double triggers; light hand engraving; case-hardened locks in 12-gauge, polished steel in 10-gauge; sling swivels. From Dixie Gun Works.

Price: 12 ga. PS0930 .... **$825.00**
Price: 12-ga. Kit PS0940 .... **$725.00**
Price: 20-ga. PS0334 .... **$725.00**
Price: 10-ga. PS1030 .... **$825.00**
Price: 10-ga. kit PS1040 .... **$750.00**
Price: Coach Gun, 12 ga. 20" bbl PS0914 .... **$675.00**

KNIGHT TK2000 MUZZLELOADING SHOTGUN (209)

Gauge: 12. **Barrel:** 26", extra-full choke tube. **Weight:** 7 lbs., 9 oz. **Length:** 45" overall. **Stock:** Synthetic black or Advantage Timber HD; recoil pad; swivel studs. **Sights:** Fully adjustable rear, blade front with fiber-optics. **Features:** Receiver drilled and tapped for scope mount; in-line ignition; adjustable trigger; removable breech plug; double safety system; Imp. Cyl. choke tube available. Made in U.S. by Knight Rifles.

Price: .... **$349.95 to $399.95**

KNIGHT VERSATILE TK2002

Gauge: 12. **Stock:** Black composite, blued, Advantage Timber HD finish. Both with sling swivel studs installed. **Sights:** Adjustable metallic TruGlo fiber-optic. **Features:** Full plastic jacket ignition system, screw-on choke tubes, load without removing choke tubes, jug-choked barrel design. Improved cylinder and modified choke tubes available.

Price: .... **$349.95 to $399.95**

WHITE TOMINATOR SHOTGUN

Caliber: 12. **Barrel:** 25" blue, straight, tapered stainless steel. **Weight:** NA. **Length:** NA. **Stock:** Black laminated or black wood. **Sights:** Drilled and tapped for easy scope mounting. **Features:** Internchangeable choke tubes. Custom vent rib with high visibility front bead. Double safeties. Fully adjustable custom trigger. Recoil pad and sling swivel studs. Made in U.S.A. by Split Fire Sporting Goods.

Price: **$349.95**

Benjamin & Sheridan EB17/EB22

ARS HUNTING MASTER AR6 AIR PISTOL
Caliber: 22 (177 +20 special order). **Barrel:** 12" rifled. **Weight:** 3 lbs. **Length:** 18.25 overall. **Power:** NA. **Grips:** Indonesian walnut with checkered grip. **Sights:** Adjustable rear, blade front. **Features:** 6 shot repeater with rotary magazine, single or double action, receiver grooved for scope, hammer block and trigger block safeties.
Price: . . . . **NA**

BEEMAN P1 MAGNUM AIR PISTOL
Caliber: 177, 20. **Barrel:** 8.4". **Weight:** 2.5 lbs. **Length:** 11" overall. **Power:** Top lever cocking; spring-piston. **Grips:** Checkered walnut. **Sights:** Blade front, square notch rear with click micrometer adjustments for windage and elevation. Grooved for scope mounting. **Features:** Dual power for 177 and 20 cal.; low setting gives 350-400 fps; high setting 500-600 fps. All Colt 45 auto grips fit gun. Dry-firing feature for practice. Optional wood shoulder stock. Imported by Beeman.
Price: **$470.00**

BEEMAN P3 PNEUMATIC AIR PISTOL
Caliber: 177. **Barrel:** NA. **Weight:** 1.7 lbs. **Length:** 9.6" overall. **Power:** Single-stroke pneumatic; overlever barrel cocking. **Grips:** Reinforced polymer. **Sights:** Front and rear fiber-optic sights. **Features:** Velocity 410 fps. Polymer frame; automatic safety; two-stage trigger; built-in muzzle brake.
Price: **$220.00**
Price: w/scope **$300.00**

BEEMAN/FEINWERKBAU P44
Caliber: 177, single shot. **Barrel:** 9.17". **Weight:** 2.10 lbs. **Length:** 16.54" overall. **Power:** Pre-charged pneumatic. **Grips:** Walnut grip. **Sights:** front and rear sights. **Features:** 500 fps, sighting line adjustable from 360 to 395mm, adjustable 3-d grip in 3 sizes, adjustable match trigger, delivered in special transport case.
Price: **$2,199.00**

BEEMAN/FEINWERKBAU P56
Caliber: 177, 5-shot magazine. **Barrel:** 8.81". **Weight:** 2.43 lbs. **Length:** 16.54" overall. **Power:** Pre-charged pneumatic. **Grips:** Walnut Morini grip. **Sights:** front and rear sights. **Features:** 500 fps, match-adjustable trigger, adjustable rear sight, front sight accepts interchangeable inserts, delivered in special transport case.
Price: **$2,654.00**

BEEMAN/FWB 103 AIR PISTOL
Caliber: 177. **Barrel:** 10.1", 12-groove rifling. **Weight:** 2.5 lbs. **Length:** 16.5" overall. **Power:** Single-stroke pneumatic, underlever cocking. **Grips:** Stippled walnut with adjustable palm shelf. **Sights:** Blade front, open rear adjustable for windage and elevation. Notch size adjustable for width. Interchangeable front blades. **Features:** Velocity 510 fps. Fully adjustable trigger. Cocking effort 2 lbs. Imported by Beeman.
Price: Right-hand **$2,110.00**
Price: Left-hand **$2,350.00**

BEEMAN HW70A AIR PISTOL
Caliber: 177. **Barrel:** 6-1/4", rifled. **Weight:** 38 oz. **Length:** 12-3/4" overall. **Power:** Spring, barrel cocking. **Grips:** Plastic, with thumbrest. **Sights:** Hooded post front, square notch rear adjustable for windage and elevation. Comes with scope base. **Features:** Adjustable trigger, 31-lb. cocking effort, 440 fps MV; automatic barrel safety. Imported by Beeman.
Price: **$270.00**

BENJAMIN & SHERIDAN CO2 PISTOLS
Caliber: 22, single shot. **Barrel:** 6-3/8", brass. **Weight:** 1 lb. 12 oz. **Length:** 9" overall. **Power:** 12-gram CO2 cylinder. **Grips:** American Hardwood. **Sights:** High ramp front, fully adjustable notched rear. **Features:** Velocity to 500 fps. Turnbolt action with cross-bolt safety. Gives about 40 shots per CO2 cylinder. Black or nickel finish. Made in U.S. by Crosman Corp.
Price: EB22 (22) **$185.00**

BENJAMIN & SHERIDAN PNEUMATIC PELLET PISTOLS
Caliber: 177, 22, single shot. **Barrel:** 9-3/8", rifled brass. **Weight:** 2 lbs., 8 oz. **Length:** 12.25" overall. **Power:** Underlever pnuematic, hand pumped. **Grips:** American Hardwood. **Sights:** High ramp front, fully adjustable notch rear. **Features:** Velocity to 525 fps (variable). Bolt action with cross-bolt safety. Choice of black or nickel finish. Made in U.S. by Crosman Corp.
Price: Black finish, HB17 (177), HB22 (22) **$115.00**

CROSMAN C11
Caliber: .177, 18-shot BB or pellet. **Weight:** 1.4 lbs. **Length:** 8.5". **Power:** 12g CO2. **Sights:** Fixed. **Features:** Compact semi-automatic BB pistol. Velocity up to 480 fps. Under barrel weaver style rail.
Price: **$59.90**

CROSMAN MAGNUM AIR PISTOLS
Caliber: 177, pellets. **Barrel:** Rifled steel. **Weight:** 2 lbs. **Length:** 9.38". **Power:** CO2. **Grips:** NA. **Sights:** Blade front, rear adjustable. **Features:** Single/double action accepts sights and scopes with standard 3/8" dovetail mount. Model 3576W features 6" barrel for increased accuracy. From Crosman.
Price: 3576W **$50.00**

CROSMAN MODEL 1008 REPEAT AIR PISTOL
Caliber: 177, 8-shot pellet clip. **Barrel:** 4.25", rifled steel. **Weight:** 17 oz. **Length:** 8.625" overall. **Power:** CO2 Powerlet. **Grips:** Checkered black plastic. **Sights:** Post front, adjustable rear. **Features:** Velocity about 430 fps. Break-open barrel for easy loading; single or double semi-automatic action; two 8-shot clips included. Optional carrying case available. From Crosman.
Price: **$60.00**

CROSMAN PRO77
Caliber: .177, 17-shot BB. **Weight:** 1.31 lbs. **Length:** 6.75". **Power:** 12g CO2. **Sights:** Fixed. **Features:** Compact pistol with realistic recoil. Under the barrel weaver style rail. Velocity up to 325 fps.
Price: Pro77CS **$114.00**
Price: Pro77KT **$116.00**

CROSMAN T4
Caliber: .177, 8-shot BB or pellet. **Weight:** 1.32 lbs. **Length:** 8.63". **Power:** 12g CO2. **Sights:** Fixed front, windage adjustable rear. **Features:** Shoots BBs or pellets. Easy patent-pending CO2 piercing mechanism. Under the barrel weaver style rail.
Price: T4CS **$136.00**
Price: T4KT **$138.00**

DAISY POWERLINE® MODEL 15XT AIR PISTOL
Caliber: 177 BB, 15-shot built-in magazine. **Barrel:** NA. **Weight:** NA. **Length:** 7.21". **Power:** CO2. **Grips:** NA. **Sights:** NA. **Features:** Velocity 425 fps. Made in the U.S.A. by Daisy Mfg. Co.
Price: **$50.99**
Price: With electronic point sight **$64.99**

DAISY MODEL 717 AIR PISTOL
Caliber: 177, single shot. **Weight:** 2.25 lbs. **Length:** 13-1/2" overall. **Grips:** Molded checkered woodgrain with contoured thumbrest. **Sights:** Blade and ramp front, open rear with windage and elevation adjustments. **Features:** Single pump pneumatic pistol. Rifled steel barrel. Crossbolt trigger block. Muzzle velocity 360 fps. From Daisy Mfg. Co.
Price: **$220.94**

DAISY MODEL 747 TRIUMPH AIR PISTOL
Caliber: 177, single shot. **Weight:** 2.35 lbs. **Length:** 13-1/2" overall. **Grips:** Molded checkered woodgrain with contoured thumbrest. **Sights:** Blade and ramp front, open rear with windage and elevation adjustments. **Features:** Single pump pneumatic pistol. Lothar Walther rifled high-grade steel barrel; crowned 12 lands and grooves, right-hand twist. Precision bore sized for match pellets. Muzzle velocity 360 fps. From Daisy Mfg. Co.
Price: **$264.99**

DAISY POWERLINE® 201

Caliber: 177 BB or pellet. **Weight:** 1 lb. **Length:** 9.25" overall. **Sights:** Blade and ramp front, fixed open rear. **Features:** Spring-air action, trigger-block safety and smooth-bore steel barrel. Muzzle velocity 230 fps. From Daisy Mfg. Co.

Price: **$29.99**

DAISY POWERLINE® 693 AIR PISTOL

Caliber: 177, single shot. **Weight:** 1.10 lbs. **Length:** 7.9" overall. **Grips:** Molded checkered. **Sights:** Blade and ramp front, fixed open rear. **Features:** Semi-automoatic BB pistol with a nickel finish and smooth bore steel barrel. Muzzle veocity 400 fps. From Daisy Mfg. Co.

Price: **$76.99**

DAISY POWERLINE® 5170 CO2 PISTOL

Caliber: 177 BB. **Weight:** 1 lb. **Length:** 9.5" overall. **Sights:** Blade and ramp front, open rear. **Features:** CO2 semi-automatic action, manual trigger-block safety, upper and lower rails for mounting sights and other accessories and a smooth-bore steel barrel. Muzzle velocity 520 fps. From Daisy Mfg. Co.

Price: **$59.99**

DAISY POWERLINE® 5501 CO2 BLOWBACK PISTOL

Caliber: 177 BB. **Weight:** 1 lb. **Length:** 9.5" overall. **Sights:** Blade and ramp front, open rear. **Features:** CO2 semi-automatic blow-back action, manual trigger-block safety, and a smooth-bore steel barrel. Muzzle velocity 430 fps. From Daisy Mfg. Co.

Price: **$99.99**

EAA/BAIKAL IZH-M46 TARGET AIR PISTOL

Caliber: 177, single shot. **Barrel:** 10". **Weight:** 2.4 lbs. **Length:** 16.8" overall. **Power:** Underlever single-stroke pneumatic. **Grips:** Adjustable wooden target. **Sights:** Micrometer fully adjustable rear, blade front. **Features:** Velocity about 440 fps. Hammer-forged, rifled barrel. Imported from Russia by European American Armory.

Price: **$430.00**

GAMO P-23, P-23 LASER PISTOL

Caliber: 177, 12-shot. **Barrel:** 4.25". **Weight:** 1 lb. **Length:** 7.5". **Power:** CO2 cartridge, semi-automatic, 410 fps. **Grips:** Plastic. **Sights:** NA. **Features:** Walther PPK cartridge pistol copy, optional laser sight. Imported from Spain by Gamo.

Price: . . . . **$89.95**, (with laser) **$139.95**

GAMO PT-80, PT-80 LASER PISTOL

Caliber: 177, 8-shot. **Barrel:** 4.25". **Weight:** 1.2 lbs. **Length:** 7.2". **Power:** CO2 cartridge, semi-automatic, 410 fps. **Grips:** Plastic. **Sights:** 3-dot. **Features:** Optional laser sight and walnut grips available. Imported from Spain by Gamo.

Price: . . . . **$108.95**, (with laser) **$159.95**

Price: (with walnut grip) **$119.95**

HAMMERLI AP-40 AIR PISTOL

Caliber: 177. **Barrel:** 10". **Weight:** 2.2 lbs. **Length:** 15.5". **Power:** NA. **Grips:** Adjustable orthopedic. **Sights:** Fully adjustable micrometer. **Features:** Sleek, light, well balanced and accurate.

Price: **$1,400.00**

MAGNUM RESEARCH DESERT EAGLE

Caliber: .177, 8-shot pellet. 5.7" rifled. **Weight:** 2.5 lbs. 11" overall. **Power:** 12g CO2. **Sights:** Fixed front, adjustable rear. Velocity of 425 fps. 8-shot rotary clip. Double or single action. The first .177 caliber air pistol with BLOWBACK action. Big and weighty, designed in the likeness of the real Desert Eagle.

Price: **$172.31**

MAGNUM BABY DESERT

Caliber: .177, 15-shot BB. 4" **Weight:** 1.0 lbs. 8-1/4" overall. **Power:** 12g CO2. **Sights:** Fixed front and rear. Velocity of 420 fps. Double action BB repeater. Comes with bonus Picatinny top rail and built-in bottom rail.

Price: **$41.54**

MORINI CM 162 EL MATCH AIR PISTOLS

Caliber: 177, single shot. **Barrel:** 9.4". **Weight:** 32 oz. **Length:** 16.1" overall. **Power:** Scuba air. **Grips:** Adjustable match type. **Sights:** Interchangeable blade front, fully adjustable match-type rear. **Features:** Power mechanism shuts down when pressure drops to a preset level. Adjustable electronic trigger.

Price: **$1,075.00**

PARDINI K58 MATCH AIR PISTOLS

Caliber: 177, single shot. **Barrel:** 9". **Weight:** 37.7 oz. **Length:** 15.5" overall. **Power:** Precharged compressed air; single-stroke cocking. **Grips:** Adjustable match type; stippled walnut. **Sights:** Interchangeable post front, fully adjustable match rear. **Features:** Fully adjustable trigger. Short version K-2 available. Imported from Italy by Larry's Guns.

Price: **$819.00**

RWS 9B/9N AIR PISTOLS

Caliber: 177, single shot. **Barrel:** 8". **Weight:** 2.38 lbs. **Length:** 10.4". **Power:** 550 fps. **Grips:** Right hand with thumbrest. **Sights:** Adjustable. **Features:** Spring-piston powered. Black or nickel finish.

Price: 9B/9N **$150.00**

SMITH & WESSON 586

Caliber: .177, 10-shot pellet. Rifled. **Power:** 12g CO2. **Sights:** Fixed front, adjustable rear. 10-shot rotary clip. Double or single action. Replica revolvers that duplicate both weight and handling.

Price: 4" barrel, 2.5 lbs, 400 fps **$215.34**

Price: 6" barrel, 2.8 lbs, 425 fps **$231.49**

Price: 8" barrel, 3.0 lbs, 460 fps **$247.65**

Price: S&W 686 Nickel, 6" barrel, 2.8 lbs, 425 fps **$253.03**

STEYR LP10P MATCH AIR PISTOL

Caliber: 177, single shot. **Barrel:** 9". **Weight:** 38.7 oz. **Length:** 15.3" overall. **Power:** Scuba air. **Grips:** Adjustable Morini match, palm shelf, stippled walnut. **Sights:** Interchangeable blade in 4mm, 4.5mm or 5mm widths, adjustable open rear, interchangeable 3.5mm or 4mm leaves. **Features:** Velocity about 500 fps. Adjustable trigger, adjustable sight radius from 12.4" to 13.2". With compensator. Recoil elimination.

Price: **$1,400.00**

TECH FORCE SS2 OLYMPIC COMPETITION AIR PISTOL

Caliber: 177 pellet, single shot. **Barrel:** 7.4". **Weight:** 2.8 lbs. **Length:** 16.5" overall. **Power:** Spring piston, sidelever. **Grips:** Hardwood. **Sights:** Extended adjustable rear, blade front accepts inserts. **Features:** Velocity 520 fps. Recoilless design; adjustments allow duplication of a firearm's feel. Match-grade, adjustable trigger; includes carrying case. Imported from China by Compasseco, Inc.

Price: **$295.00**

TECH FORCE 35 AIR PISTOL

Caliber: 177 pellet, single shot. **Weight:** 2.86 lbs. **Length:** 14.9" overall. **Power:** Spring-piston, underlever. **Grips:** Hardwood. **Sights:** Micrometer adjustable rear, blade front. **Features:** Velocity 400 fps. Grooved for scope mount; trigger safety. Imported from China by Compasseco, Inc.

Price: **$39.95**

Tech Force S2-1 Air Pistol

Similar to Tech Force 8 except basic grips and sights for plinking.

Price: **$29.95**

WALTHER LP300 MATCH PISTOL

Caliber: 177. Barrel: 236mm. Weight: 1.018g. Length: NA. Power: NA. Grips: NA. Sights: Integrated front with three different widths, adjustable rear. Features: Adjustable grip and trigger.

Price: **$1,800.00**

WALTHER PPK/S

Caliber: .177, 15-shot steel BB. 3-1/2". **Weight:** 1.2 lbs. 6-1/4" overall. **Power:** 12g CO2. **Sights:** Fixed front and rear. Velocity of 295 fps. Lookalike of one of the world's most famous pistols. Realistic recoil. Heavyweight steel construction.

Price: **$71.92**

Price: With laser sight **$94.23**

Price: With BiColor pistol, CO2, targets, shooting glasses, BBs **$84.62**

WALTHER CP99 COMPACT

Caliber: .177, 17-shot steel BB semi-auto. 3". **Weight:** 1.7 lbs. 6-1/2" overall. **Power:** 12g CO2. **Sights:** Fixed front and rear. Velocity of 345 fps. Realistic recoil, blowback action. Heavyweight steel construction. Built-in Picatinny mount.

Price: **$83.08**

AIRFORCE CONDOR RIFLE

Caliber: .177, .22 single shot. **Barrel:** 24" rifled. **Weight:** 6.5 lbs. **Length:** 38.75" overall. **Power:** Pre-charged pneumatic. Stock: NA. **Sights:** Intended for scope use, fiber-optic open sights optional. **Features:** Lothar Walther match barrel, adjustable power levels from 600-1,300 fps. 3,000 psi fill pressure. Automatic safety. Air tank volume: 490cc. An integral extended scope rail allows easy mounting of the largest air-gun scopes. Operates on high-pressure air from scuba tank or hand pump. Manufactured in the U.S.A by AirForce Airguns

Price: Gun only (.22 or .177) **$589.95**

AIRFORCE TALON AIR RIFLE

Caliber: .177, .22, single-shot. **Barrel:** 18" rifled. **Weight:** 5.5 lbs. **Length:** 32.6". **Power:** Pre-charged pneumatic. Stock: NA. **Sights:** Intended for scope use, fiber-optic open sights optional. **Features:** Lothar Walther match barrel, adjustable power levels from 400-1,000 fps, 3,000 psi fill pressure. Automatic safety. Air tank volume: 490cc. Operates on high-pressure air from scuba tank or hand pump. Manufactured in the U.S.A. by AirForce Airguns.

Price: Gun only (.22 or .177). **$479.95**

AIRFORCE TALON SS AIR RIFLE

Caliber: .177, .22, single-shot. **Barrel:** 12" rifled. **Weight:** 5.25 lbs. **Length:** 32.75". **Power:** Pre-charged pneumatic. Stock: NA. **Sights:** Intended for scope use, fiber-optic open sights optional. **Features:** Lothar Walther match barrel, adjustable power levels from 400-1,000 fps. 3,000 psi fill pressure. Automatic safety. Chamber in front of barrel strips away air turbulence, protects muzzle and reduces firing report. Air tank volume: 490cc. Operates on high-pressure air from scuba tank or hand pump. Manufactured in the U.S.A. by AirForce Airguns.

Price: Gun only (.22 or .177). **$499.95**

AIRROW MODEL A-8SRB STEALTH AIR RIFLE

Caliber: 177, 22, 25, 9-shot. **Barrel:** 20"; rifled. **Weight:** 6 lbs. **Length:** 34" overall. **Power:** CO2 or compressed air; variable power. Stock: Telescoping CAR-15-type. **Sights:** Variable 3.5-10x scope. **Features:** Velocity 1100 fps in all calibers. Pneumatic air trigger. All aircraft aluminum and stainless steel construction. Mil-spec materials and finishes. From Swivel Machine Works, Inc.

Price: About **$2,299.00**

AIRROW MODEL A-8S1P STEALTH AIR RIFLE

Caliber: #2512 16" arrow. **Barrel:** 16". **Weight:** 4.4 lbs. **Length:** 30.1" overall. **Power:** CO2 or compressed air; variable power. Stock: Telescoping CAR-15-type. **Sights:** Scope rings only. 7 oz. rechargeable cylinder and valve. **Features:** Velocity to 650 fps with 260-grain arrow. Pneumatic air trigger. Broadhead guard. All aircraft aluminum and stainless steel construction. Mil-spec materials and finishes. A-8S Models perform to 2,000 PSIG above or below water levels. Waterproof case. From Swivel Machine Works, Inc.

Price: **$1,699.00**

ANSCHÜTZ 2002 MATCH AIR RIFLES

Caliber: .177, single shot. **Barrel:** 25.2". **Weight:** 10.8 lbs. **Length:** 42.5" overall. Stock: European walnut, blonde hardwood or colored laminated hardwood; stippled grip and forend. Also available with flat-forend walnut stock for benchrest shooting and aluminum. **Sights:** Optional sight set #6834. **Features:** Muzzle velocity 575 fps. Balance, weight match the 1907 ISU smallbore rifle. Uses #5021 match trigger. Recoil and vibration free. Fully adjustable cheekpiece and buttplate; accessory rail under forend. Available in pneumatic and compressed air versions. Imported from Germany by Gunsmithing, Inc., Accuracy International, Champion's Choice.

Price: Right-hand, blonde hardwood stock, with sights **$1,275.00**
Price: Right-hand, walnut stock **$1,275.00**
Price: Right-hand, color laminate stock **$1,300.00**
Price: Right-hand, aluminum stock, butt plate **$1,495.00**
Price: Left-hand, color laminate stock **$1,595.00**
Price: Model 2002D-RT Running Target, right-hand, no sights **$1,248.90**
Price: #6834 Sight Set **$227.10**

ARS HUNTING MASTER AR6 AIR RIFLE

Caliber: .22, 6-shot repeater. **Barrel:** 25-1/2". **Weight:** 7 lbs. **Length:** 41-1/4" overall. **Power:** Precompressed air from 3000 psi diving tank. Stock: Indonesian walnut with checkered grip; rubber buttpad. **Sights:** Blade front, adjustable peep rear. **Features:** Velocity over 1000 fps with 32-grain pellet. Receiver grooved for scope mounting. Has 6-shot rotary magazine. Imported by Air Rifle Specialists.

Price: **$580.00**

BEEMAN HW100

Caliber: .177 or .22, 14-shot magazine. **Barrel:** 21-1/2". **Weight:** 9 lbs. **Length:** 42.13" overall. **Power:** Pre-charged. Stock: Walnut Sporter checkering on the pistol grip & forend; walnut thumbhose with lateral finger grooves on the forend & stippling on the pistol grip. **Sights:** None. Grooved for scope mounting. **Features:** 1140 fps .177 caliber; 945 fps .22 caliber. 14-shot magazine, quick-fill cylinder. Two-stage adjustable match trigger and manual safety.

Price: .177 or .22 caliber Sport Stock **$1,560.00**
Price: .177 or .22 caliber Thumbhole Stock **$1,560.00**

BEEMAN R1 AIR RIFLE

Caliber: .177, .20 or .22, single shot. **Barrel:** 19.6", 12-groove rifling. **Weight:** 8.5 lbs. **Length:** 45.2" overall. **Power:** Spring-piston, barrel cocking. Stock: Walnut-stained beech; cut-checkered pistol grip; Monte Carlo comb and cheekpiece; rubber buttpad. **Sights:** Tunnel front with interchangeable inserts, open rear click-adjustable for windage and elevation. Grooved for scope mounting. **Features:** Velocity 940-1000 fps (177), 860 fps (20), 800 fps (22). Non-drying nylon piston and breech seals. Adjustable metal trigger. Milled steel safety. Right- or left-hand stock. Adjustable cheekpiece and buttplate at extra cost. Custom and Super Laser versions available. Imported by Beeman.

Price: Right-hand **$700.00**
Price: Left-hand **$750.00**

BEEMAN R7 AIR RIFLE

Caliber: .177, .20, single shot. **Barrel:** 17". **Weight:** 6.1 lbs. **Length:** 40.2" overall. **Power:** Spring-piston. Stock: Stained beech. **Sights:** Hooded front, fully adjustable micrometer click open rear. **Features:** Velocity to 700 fps (177), 620 fps (20). Receiver grooved for scope mounting; double-jointed cocking lever; fully adjustable trigger; checkered grip. Imported by Beeman.

Price: **$390.00**

BEEMAN R9 AIR RIFLE

Caliber: .177, .20, single shot. **Barrel:** NA. **Weight:** 7.3 lbs. **Length:** 43" overall. **Power:** Spring-piston, barrel cocking. Stock: Stained hardwood. **Sights:** Tunnel post front, fully adjustable open rear. **Features:** Velocity to 1000 fps (177), 800 fps (20). Adjustable Rekord trigger; automatic safety; receiver dovetailed for scope mounting. Imported from Germany by Beeman Precision Airguns.

Price: **$460.00**

BEEMAN R11 MKII AIR RIFLE

Caliber: .177, single shot. **Barrel:** 19.6". **Weight:** 8.6 lbs. **Length:** 43.5" overall. **Power:** Spring-piston, barrel cocking. Stock: Walnut-stained beech; adjustable buttplate and cheekpiece. **Sights:** None furnished. Has dovetail for scope mounting. **Features:** Velocity 910-940 fps. All-steel barrel sleeve. Imported by Beeman.

Price: **$650.00**

BEEMAN RX-2 GAS-SPRING MAGNUM AIR RIFLE

Caliber: .177, .20, .22, single shot. **Barrel:** 19.6", 12-groove rifling. **Weight:** 8.8 lbs. **Power:** Gas-spring piston air; single stroke barrel cocking. Stock: Laminated wood stock. **Sights:** Tunnel front, click-adjustable rear. **Features:** Velocity adjustable to about 1200 fps. Imported by Beeman.

Price: .177, .20, .22 regular, right-hand **$850.00**

BEEMAN R1 CARBINE

Caliber: .177,. 20, .22 single shot. **Barrel:** 16.1". **Weight:** 8.6 lbs. **Length:** 41.7" overall. **Power:** Spring-piston, barrel cocking. Stock: Stained beech; Monte Carlo comb and checkpiece; cut checkered pistol grip; rubber buttpad. **Sights:** Tunnel front with interchangeable inserts, open adjustable rear; receiver grooved for scope mounting. **Features:** Velocity up to 1000 fps (177). Non-drying nylon piston and breech seals. Adjustable metal trigger. Machined steel receiver end cap and safety. Right- or left-hand stock. Imported by Beeman.

Price: 177, 20, 22, right-hand . . . . **$700.00**; left-hand **$750.00**

BEEMAN/FEINWERKBAU 603 AIR RIFLE

Caliber: .177, single shot. **Barrel:** 16.6". **Weight:** 10.8 lbs. **Length:** 43" overall. **Power:** Single stroke pneumatic. Stock: Special laminated hardwoods and hard rubber for stability. Multi-colored stock also available. **Sights:** Tunnel front sight with interchangeable inserts, click micrometer match aperture rear sight. **Features:** Velocity to 570

Beretta CX4 Storm

fps. Recoilless action; double supported barrel; special, short rifled area frees pellet from barrel faster. Fully adjustable match trigger with separately adjustable trigger and trigger slack weight. Trigger and sights blocked when loading latch is open. Imported by Beeman.

Price: Right-hand **$3,000.00**
Price: Left-hand **$3,250.00**
Price: Junior **$2,670.00**

BEEMAN/FEINWERKBAU 700 P ALUMINUM OR WOOD STOCK

Caliber: .177, single shot. **Barrel:** 16.6". **Weight:** 10.8 lbs. Aluminum; 9.9 lbs. Wood. **Length:** 43.3-46.25" Aluminum; 43.7" Wood. **Power:** Pre-charged pneumatic. Stock: Aluminum stock P laminated hardwood. **Sights:** Tunnel front sight with interchangeable inserts, click micrometer match aperture rear sight. **Features:** Velocity 570 fps. Recoilless action. Anatomical grips can be tilted and pivoted to the barrel axis. Adjustable buttplate and cheekpiece.

Price: Aluminum 700, precharged, right **$3,710.00**
Price: Aluminum 700, precharged, universal **$2,890.00**
Price: Wood Stock 700, precharged, right **$1,970.00**

BEEMAN/FEINWERKBAU P70 FIELD TARGET

Caliber: .177, single shot. **Barrel:** 24.6". **Weight:** 10.6 lbs. **Length:** 43.3" overall. **Power:** Pre-charged pneumatic. Stock: Aluminum stock (red or blue) anatomical grips, buttplate & cheekpiece. **Sights:** None, receiver grooved for scope mounting. **Features:** 870 fps velocity. At 50 yards, this air rifle is capable of achieving 1/2-inch groups. Match adjustable trigger. 2001 US Field Target National Champion.

Price: P70FT, precharged, right (red or blue). **$3,530.00**
Price: P70FT, precharged, left (red or blue). **$3,650.00**

BEEMAN/FEINWERKBAU P700 .177 BASIC AIR RIFLE

Caliber: .177, single shot. **Barrel:** 16.73". **Weight:** 9.04 lbs. **Length:** 43.31" overall. **Power:** Pre-charged pneumatic. Stock: Beech wood stock. **Sights:** Tunnel front sight with interchangeable inserts, click micrometer match aperture rear sight. **Features:** Velocity to 570 fps. Recoilless action; match adjustable trigger. Interior absorber.

Price: P700 Basic, .177 . . . . **$1,150.00**

BEEMAN/HW 97 AIR RIFLE

Caliber: .177, .20, single shot. **Barrel:** 17.75". **Weight:** 9.2 lbs. **Length:** 44.1" overall. **Power:** Spring-piston, underlever cocking. Stock: Walnut-stained beech; rubber buttpad. **Sights:** None. Receiver grooved for scope mounting. **Features:** Velocity 830 fps (177). Fixed barrel with fully opening, direct loading breech. Adjustable trigger. Imported by Beeman Precision Airguns.

Price: Right-hand only **$625.00**

BENJAMIN & SHERIDAN PNEUMATIC (PUMP-UP) AIR RIFLE

Caliber: .177 or .22, single shot. **Barrel:** 19-3/8", rifled brass. **Weight:** 5-1/2 lbs. **Length:** 36-1/4" overall. **Power:** Underlever pneumatic, hand pumped. Stock: American walnut stock and forend. **Sights:** High ramp front, fully adjustable notched rear. **Features:** Variable velocity to 800 fps. Bolt action with ambidextrous push-pull safety. Black or nickel finish. Made in the U.S. by Benjamin Sheridan Co.

Price: 392 or 397 . . . . **$249.40**

BERETTA CX4 STORM

Caliber: .177, 30-shot semi auto. 17-1/2", rifled. **Weight:** 5.25 lbs. 30.75" overall. **Power:** 88g CO2. Stock: Replica style. **Sights:** Adjustable front and rear. Blowback action. Velocity of 600 fps. Accessory rails.

Price: **$276.92**

BSA SUPERTEN MK3 AIR RIFLE

Caliber: .177, .22 10-shot repeater. **Barrel:** 17-1/2". **Weight:** 7 lbs., 8 oz. **Length:** 37" overall. **Power:** Precharged pneumatic via buddy bottle. Stock: Oil-finished hardwood; Monte Carlo with cheekpiece, cut checkered grip; adjustable recoil pad. **Sights:** No sights; intended for scope use. **Features:** Velocity 1000+ fps (177), 1000+ fps (22). Patented 10-shot indexing magazine, bolt-action loading. Left-hand version also available. Imported from U.K.

Price: **$599.95**

BSA SUPERTEN MK3 BULLBARREL

Caliber: .177,. 22, .25, single shot. **Barrel:** 18-1/2". **Weight:** 8 lbs., 8 oz. **Length:** 43" overall. **Power:** Spring-air, underlever cocking. Stock: Oil-finished hardwood; Monte Carlo with cheekpiece, checkered at grip; recoil pad. **Sights:** Ramp front, micrometer adjustable rear. Maxi-Grip scope rail. **Features:** Velocity 950 fps (177), 750 fps (22), 600 fps (25). Patented rotating breech design. Maxi-Grip scope rail protects optics from recoil; automatic anti-beartrap plus manual safety. Imported from U.K.

Price: Rifle, MKII Carbine (14" barrel, 39-1/2" overall) **$349.95**

BSA MAGNUM SUPERSPORTЄ AIR RIFLE, CARBINE

Caliber: .177, .22, .25, single shot. **Barrel:** 18-1/2". **Weight:** 6 lbs., 8 oz. **Length:** 41" overall. **Power:** Spring-air, barrel cocking. Stock: Oil-finished hardwood; Monte Carlo with cheekpiece, recoil pad. **Sights:** Ramp front, micrometer adjustable rear. Maxi-Grip scope rail. **Features:** Velocity 950 fps (177), 750 fps (22), 600 fps (25). Patented Maxi-Grip scope rail protects optics from recoil; automatic anti-beartrap plus manual tang safety. Muzzle brake standard. Imported for U.K.

Price: **$194.95**
Price: Carbine, 14" barrel, muzzle brake **$214.95**

BSA METEOR AIR RIFLE

Caliber: .177, .22, single shot. **Barrel:** 18-1/2". **Weight:** 6 lbs. **Length:** 41" overall. **Power:** Spring-air, barrel cocking. Stock: Oil-finished hardwood. **Sights:** Ramp front, micrometer adjustable rear. **Features:** Velocity 650 fps (177), 500 fps (22). Automatic anti-beartrap; manual tang safety. Receiver grooved for scope mounting. Imported from U.K.

Price: Rifle **$144.95**
Price: Carbine **$164.95**

CROSMAN MODEL POWERMASTER 664SB AIR RIFLES

Caliber: .177 (single shot pellet) or BB, 200-shot reservoir. **Barrel:** 20", rifled steel. **Weight:** 2 lbs. 15 oz. **Length:** 38-1/2" overall. **Power:** Pneumatic; hand-pumped. Stock: Wood-grained ABS plastic; checkered pistol grip and forend. **Sights:** Fiber-optic front, fully adjustable open rear. **Features:** Velocity about 645 fps. Bolt action, cross-bolt safety. From Crosman.

Price: **$105.50**

CROSMAN MODEL PUMPMASTER 760 AIR RIFLES

Caliber: .177 pellets (single shot) or BB (200-shot reservoir). **Barrel:** 19-1/2", rifled steel. **Weight:** 2 lbs., 12 oz. **Length:** 33.5" overall. **Power:** Pneumatic, hand-pump. Stock: Walnut-finished ABS plastic stock and forend. **Features:** Velocity to 590 fps (BBs, 10 pumps). Short stroke, power determined by number of strokes. Fiber-optic front sight and adjustable rear sight. Cross-bolt safety. From Crosman.

Price: Model 760 . . . . **$40.00**

CROSMAN MODEL REPEATAIR 1077 RIFLES

Caliber: .177 pellets, 12-shot clip. **Barrel:** 20.3", rifled steel. **Weight:** 3 lbs., 11 oz. **Length:** 38.8" overall. **Power:** CO2 Powerlet. Stock: Textured synthetic or hardwood. **Sights:** Blade front, fully adjustable rear. **Features:** Velocity 590 fps. Removable 12-shot clip. True semi-automatic action. From Crosman.

Price: **$68.00**

CROSMAN 2260 AIR RIFLE

Caliber: .22, single shot. **Barrel:** 24". **Weight:** 4 lbs., 12 oz. **Length:** 39.75" overall. **Power:** CO2 Powerlet. Stock: Hardwood. **Sights:** Blade front, adjustable rear open or peep. **Features:** About 600 fps. Made in U.S. by Crosman Corp.

Price: **$80.00**

CROSMAN MODEL CLASSIC 2100 AIR RIFLE

Caliber: 177 pellets (single shot), or BB (200-shot BB reservoir). **Barrel:** 21", rifled. **Weight:** 4 lbs., 13 oz. **Length:** 39-3/4" overall. **Power:** Pump-up, pneumatic. Stock: Wood-grained checkered ABS plastic. **Features:** Three pumps give about 450 fps, 10 pumps about 755 fps (BBs). Cross-bolt safety; concealed reservoir holds over 200 BBs. From Crosman.

Price: Model 2100B **$55.00**

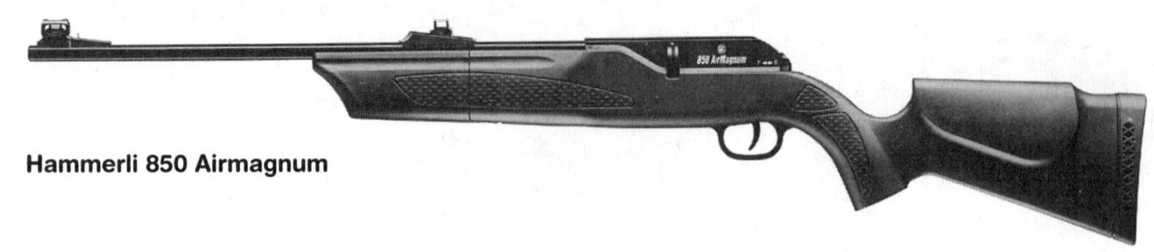

Hammerli 850 Airmagnum

CROSMAN MODEL 2260 AIR RIFLE
Caliber: 22, single shot. **Barrel:** 19", rifled steel. **Weight:** 4 lbs., 12 oz. **Length:** 39.75" overall. Stock: Full-size, American hardwood. **Features:** Variable pump power; three pumps give 395 fps, six pumps 530 fps, 10 pumps 600 fps (average). Full-size adult air rifle. From Crosman.
Price: **$80.00**

DAISY 1938 RED RYDER AIR RIFLE
Caliber: BB, 650-shot repeating action. **Barrel:** Smoothbore steel with shroud. **Weight:** 2.2 lbs. **Length:** 35.4" overall. Stock: Wood stock burned with Red Ryder lariat signature. **Sights:** Post front, adjustable Vslot rear. **Features:** Walnut forend. Saddle ring with leather thong. Lever cocking. Gravity feed. Controlled velocity. From Daisy Mfg. Co.
Price: **$55.95**

DAISY MODEL 840B GRIZZLY AIR RIFLE
Caliber: 177 pellet single shot; or BB 350-shot. **Barrel:** 19", smoothbore, steel. **Weight:** 2.25 lbs. **Length:** 36.8" overall. **Power:** Single pump pneumatic. Stock: Molded wood-grain stock and forend. **Sights:** Ramp front, open, adjustable rear. **Features:** Muzzle velocity 320 fps (BB), 300 fps (pellet). Steel buttplate; straight pull bolt action; cross-bolt safety. Forend forms pump lever. From Daisy Mfg. Co.
Price: **$60.99**
Price: (840C in Mossy Oak Breakup Camo) **$64.99**

DAISY MODEL 105 BUCK AIR RIFLE
Caliber: 177 or BB. **Barrel:** Smoothbore steel. **Weight:** 1.6 lbs. **Length:** 29.8" overall. **Power:** Lever cocking, spring air. Stock: Stained solid wood. **Sights:** TruGlo fiber-optic, open fixed rear. **Features:** Velocity to 275. Cross-bolt trigger block safety. From Daisy Mfg. Co.
Price: **$39.99**

DAISY POWERLINE® TARGET PRO 953 AIR RIFLE
Caliber: 177 pellets, single shot. **Weight:** 6.40 lbs. **Length:** 39.75" overall. **Power:** Pneumatic single-pump cocking lever; straight-pull bolt. Stock: Full-length, match-style black composite. **Sights:** Front and rear fiber optic. **Features:** Rifled high-grade steel barrel with 1:15 twist. Max. Muzzle Velocity of 560 fps. From Daisy Mfg. Co.
Price: **$118.99**

DAISY POWERLINE® 500 BREAK BARREL
Caliber: 177 pellet, single shot. **Barrel:** Rifled steel. **Weight:** 6.6 lbs. **Length:** 45.7" overall. Stock: Stained solid wood. **Sights:** Truglo® fiber-optic front, micro-adjustable open rear, adjustable 4x32 riflescope. **Features:** Auto rear-button safety. Velocity to 490 fps. Made in U.S.A. by Daisy Mfg. Co.
Price: **$120.99**

DAISY POWERLINE® 800 BREAK BARREL
Caliber: 177 pellet, single shot. **Barrel:** Rifled steel. **Weight:** 6.6 lbs. **Length:** 46.7" overall. Stock: Black composite. **Sights:** Truglo® fiber-optic front, micro-adjustable open rear, adjustable 4x32 riflescope. **Features:** Auto rear-button safety. Velocity to 800 fps. Made in U.S.A. by Daisy Mfg. Co.
Price: **$142.99**

DAISY POWERLINE® 880 AIR RIFLE
Caliber: 177 pellet or BB, 50-shot BB magazine, single shot for pellets. **Barrel:** Rifled steel. **Weight:** 3.7 lbs. **Length:** 37.6" overall. **Power:** Multi-pump pneumatic. Stock: Molded wood grain; Monte Carlo comb. **Sights:** Hooded front, adjustable rear. **Features:** Velocity to 685 fps. (BB). Variable power (velocity, range) increase with pump strokes; resin receiver with dovetailed scope mount. Made in U.S.A. by Daisy Mfg. Co.
Price: **$71.99**

DAISY POWERLINE® 901 AIR RIFLE
Caliber: 177. **Barrel:** Rifled steel. **Weight:** 3.7 lbs. **Length:** 37.5" overall. **Power:** Multi-pump pneumatic. Stock: Advanced composite. **Sights:** Fiber-optic front, adjustable rear. **Features:** Velocity to 750 fps. (BB); advanced composite receiver with dovetailed mounts for optics. Made in U.S.A. by Daisy Mfg. Co.
Price: **$104.99**

DAISY POWERLINE® 1000 BREAK BARREL
Caliber: 177 pellet, single shot. **Barrel:** Rifled steel. **Weight:** 6.6 lbs. **Length:** 46.7" overall. Stock: Black composite. **Sights:** Truglo® fiber-optic front, micro-adjustable open rear, adjustable 4x32 riflescope. **Features:** Auto rear-button safety. Velocity to 750 fps (BB). Made in U.S.A. by Daisy Mfg. Co.
Price: **$159.99**

EAA/BAIKAL IZH-61 AIR RIFLE
Caliber: 177 pellet, 5-shot magazine. **Barrel:** 17.8". **Weight:** 6.4 lbs. **Length:** 31" overall. **Power:** Spring-piston, side-cocking lever. Stock: Black plastic. **Sights:** Adjustable rear, fully hooded front. **Features:** Velocity 490 fps. Futuristic design with adjustable stock. Imported from Russia by European American Armory.
Price: **$121.00**

GAMO VIPER AIR RIFLE
Caliber: 177. **Barrel:** NA. **Weight:** 7.25 lbs. **Length:** 43.5". **Power:** Single-stroke pneumatic, 1200 fps. Stock: Synthetic. **Sights:** 3-9x40IR scope. **Features:** 30-pound cocking effort. Imported from Spain by Gamo.
Price: **$299.95**

GAMO HUNTER AIR RIFLES
Caliber: 177. **Barrel:** NA. **Weight:** 6.5-10.5 lbs. **Length:** 43.5-48.5". **Power:** Single-stroke pneumatifc, 850-1,000 fps. Stock: Wood. **Sights:** Varies by model **Features:** Adjustable two-stage trigger, rifled barrel, raised scope ramp on receiver. Realtree camo model available.
Price: Sport. **$219.95**
Price: Pro **$279.95**

HAMMERLI AR 50 AIR RIFLE
Caliber: 177. **Barrel:** 19.8". **Weight:** 10 lbs. **Length:** 43.2" overall. **Power:** Compressed-air. Stock: Anatomically-shaped universal and right-hand; match style; multi-colored laminated wood. **Sights:** Interchangeable element tunnel front, adjustable Hammerli peep rear. **Features:** Vibration-free firing release; adjustable match trigger and trigger stop; stainless air tank, built-in pressure gauge. Gives 270 shots per filling. Imported from Switzerland by Sig Sauer, Inc.
Price: **$1,653.00**

HAMMERLI MODEL 450 MATCH AIR RIFLE
Caliber: 177, single shot. **Barrel:** 19.5". **Weight:** 9.8 lbs. **Length:** 43.3" overall. **Power:** Pneumatic. Stock: Match style with stippled grip, rubber buttpad. Beech or walnut. **Sights:** Match tunnel front, Hammerli diopter rear. **Features:** Velocity about 560 fps. Removable sights; forend sling rail; adjustable trigger; adjustable comb. Imported from Switzerland by Sig Sauer, Inc.
Price: Beech stock **$1,355.00**
Price: Walnut stock. **$1,395.00**

HAMMERLI 850 AIR MAGNUM
Caliber: .177, 22, 8-shot repeater. 23-1/2", rifled. **Weight:** 5.8 lbs. 41" overall. **Power:** 88g CO2. Stock: All-weather polymer, Monte Carlo, textured grip and forearm. **Sights:** Hooded fiber optic front, fiber optic adjustable rear. Velocity of 760 fps (177), 655 (22). Blue finish. Rubber buttpad. Bolt-Action. Scope compatible.
Price: .177, .22 . . . . **$248.08**

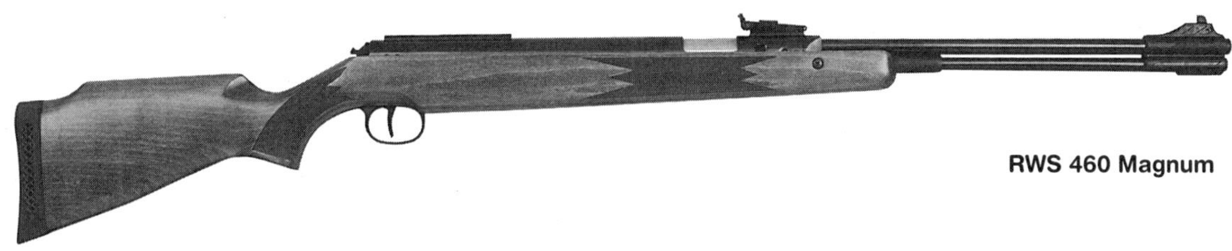

RWS 460 Magnum

HAMMERLI STORM ELITE

Caliber: .177, single shot. 19-1/2", rifled. **Weight:** 6.8 lbs. 45-1/2" overall. **Power:** Spring-air, break-barrel cocking. Stock: Synthetic, burled wood look, checkered grip and forearm, cheekpiece. **Sights:** Hooded fiber optic front, fiber optic adjustable rear. Velocity of 1000 fps. 24 lbs. cocking effort. Nickel finish. Rubber buttpad. Scope compatible.

Price: **$222.31**

HAMMERLI RAZOR

Caliber: 177, 22, single shot. **Barrel:** 19", rifled. **Weight:** 17.5 lbs. **Length:** 45-1/2" overall. **Power:** Spring-air, break-barrel cocking. Stock: Vaporized beech wood, checkered grip and forearm, cheekpiece. Sleek curves. **Sights:** Hooded fiber optic front, fiber optic adjustable rear. **Features:** Velocity of 1000 fps (177), 820 (22). 35 lbs. cocking effort. Blued finish. Rubber buttpad. Scope compatible.

Price: **$309.23**

HAMMERLI NOVA

Caliber: .177, single shot. 18", rifled. **Weight:** 7.8 lbs. 45-1/2" overall. **Power:** Spring-air, under-lever cocking. Stock: Vaporized beech wood competition, checkered grip and forearm, cheekpiece. **Sights:** Hooded fiber optic front, fiber optic adjustable rear. Velocity of 1000 fps. 36 lbs. cocking effort. Blued finish. Rubber buttpad. Scope compatible.

Price: **$341.92**

HAMMERLI QUICK

Caliber: .177, single shot. 18-1/4", rifled. **Weight:** 5.5 lbs. 41" overall. **Power:** Spring-air, break-barrel cocking. Stock: Synthetic impact proof, checkered grip and forearm, cheekpiece. **Sights:** Hooded fiber optic front, fiber optic adjustable rear. Compact, light-weight. Velocity of 620 fps. 18 lbs. cocking effort. Blued finish. Rubber buttpad. Scope compatible. Automatic Safety.

Price: **$102.69**

RWS 460 MAGNUM

Caliber: .177, 22, single shot. 18-7/16", rifled. **Weight:** 8.3 lbs. 45" overall. **Power:** Spring-air, underlever cocking. Stock: American Sporter, checkered grip and forearm. **Sights:** Ramp front, adjustable rear. Velocity of 1350 fps (177), 1150 (22). 36 lbs. cocking effort. Blue finish. Rubber buttpad. Top-side loading port. Scope compatible.

Price: .177, .22 .... **$480.69**

RWS MODEL 34

Caliber: .177, .22, single shot. **Barrel:** 19-1/2", rifled. **Weight:** 7.3 lbs. **Length:** 45" overall. **Power:** Spring-air, break-barrel cocking. Stock: Wood. **Sights:** Hooded front, adjustable rear. **Features:** Velocity of 1000 fps (177), 800 (22). 33 lbs. cocking effort. Blued finish. Scope compatible.

Price: .177, .22 .... **$236.92**

RWS 34 PANTHER

Caliber: .177, .22, single shot. 19-3/4", rifled. **Weight:** 7.7 lbs. 46" overall. **Power:** Spring-air, break-barrel cocking. Stock: Synthetic black. **Sights:** Ramp fiber optic front, adjustable fiber optic rear. Velocity of 1000 fps (177), 800 (22). 33 lbs. cocking effort. Blued finish. Scope compatible. Automatic safety.

Price: .177, .22 .... **$236.92**

RWS 48

Caliber: 177, 22, single shot. 17", rifled, fixed. **Weight:** 9.0 lbs. 42-1/2" overall. **Power:** Spring-air, side-lever cocking. Stock: Wood stock. **Sights:** Adjustable front, adjustable rear. Velocity of 1100 fps (177), 900 (22). 39 lbs. cocking effort. Blued finish. Scope compatible. Automatic safety.

Price: .177, .22 .... **$409.23**

TECH FORCE 6 AIR RIFLE

Caliber: 177 pellet, single shot. **Barrel:** 14". **Weight:** 6 lbs. **Length:** 35.5" overall. **Power:** Spring-piston, sidelever action. Stock: Paratrooper-style folding, full pistol grip. **Sights:** Adjustable rear, hooded front. **Features:** Velocity 800 fps. All-metal construction; grooved for scope mounting. Imported from China by Compasseco, Inc.

Price: **$69.95**

TECH FORCE 25 AIR RIFLE

Caliber: 177, 22 pellet; single shot. **Barrel:** NA. **Weight:** 7.5 lbs. **Length:** 46.2" overall. **Power:** Spring piston, break-action barrel. Stock: Oil-finished wood; Monte Carlo stock with recoil pad. **Sights:** Adjustable rear, hooded front with insert. **Features:** Velocity 1,000 fps (177); grooved receiver and scope stop for scope mounting; adjustable trigger; trigger safety. Imported from China by Compasseco, Inc.

Price:177 or 22 caliber **$125.00**

Price: Includes rifle and Tech Force 96 red dot point sight **$164.95**

WALTHER LEVER ACTION

Caliber: .177, 8-shot lever action. 18.9", rifled. **Weight:** 7.5 lbs. 38.3" overall. **Power:** Two 12g CO2. Stock: Wood. **Sights:** Fixed front, adjustable rear. Classic design. Velocity of 630 fps. Scope compatible.

Price: **$269.18**

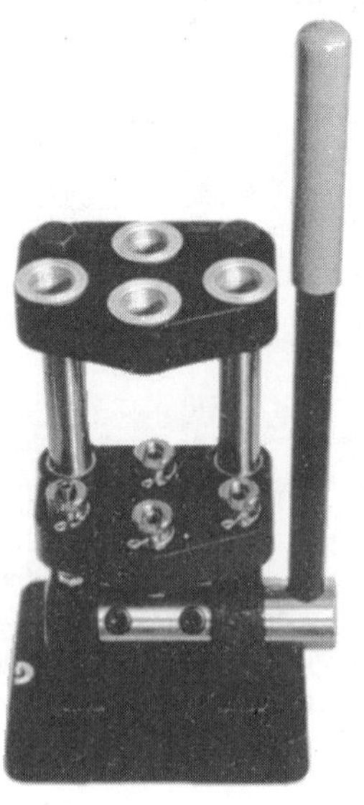
CH4D No. 444

CH4D 444-X Pistol Champ

Corbin CSP-1

Forster Co-Ax

CH4D Heavyduty Champion

Frame: Cast iron
Frame Type: O-frame
Die Thread: 7/8-14 or 1-14
Avg. Rounds Per Hour: NA
Ram Stroke: 3-1/4"
Weight: 26 lbs.
Features: 1.185" diameter ram with 16 square inches of bearing surface; ram drilled to allow passage of spent primers; solid steel handle; toggle that slightly breaks over the top dead center. Includes universal primer arm with large and small punches. From CH Tool & Die/4D Custom Die.
Price: **$261.98**

CH4D No. 444 4-Station "H" Press

Frame: Aluminum alloy
Frame Type: H-frame
Die Thread: 7/8-14
Avg. Rounds Per Hour: 200
Ram Stroke: 3-3/4"
Weight: 21 lbs.
Features: Two 7/8" solid steel shaft "H" supports; platen rides on permanently lubed bronze bushings; loads smallest pistol to largest magnum rifle cases and has strength to full-length resize. Includes four rams, large and small primer arm and primer catcher. From CH Tool & Die/4D Custom Die, Co.
Price: **$235.46**

CH4D No. 444-X Pistol Champ

Frame: Aluminum alloy
Frame Type: H-frame
Die Thread: 7/8-14
Avg. Rounds Per Hour: 200
Ram Stroke: 3-3/4"
Weight: 12 lbs.
Features: Tungsten carbide sizing die; Speed Seater seating die with tapered entrance to automatically align bullet on case mouth; automatic primer feed for large or small primers; push-button powder measure with easily changed bushings for 215 powder/load combinations; taper crimp die. Conversion kit for caliber changeover available. From CH Tool & Die/4D Custom Die, Co.
Price: . . . . **$292.00 to $316.50**

CORBIN CSP-2 Mega Mite

Frame: Steel
Frame Type: H-Frame
Die Thread: 1.5x12
Avg. Rounds Per Hour: NA
Ram Stroke: 6"
Weight: 80 lbs.
Features: Handles 50 BMG and 20mm, smaller calibers with standard reloading adapter kit included. Die adapters for all threads available. Side- roller handle or extra long power handle, left- or right-hand operation. Ram is bearing guided. Uses standard Corbin-H swaging, drawing and jacket-making dies. Cold-forms lead bullets up to 12 gauge. Optional floor stand available.
Price: **$750.00**

CORBIN CSP-1H Hydro Mite Hyrdraulic Drawing/ Swaging Press

Frame: Steel
Frame Type: Cabinet Mtg.
Die Thread: 1.5x12
Avg. Rounds Per Hour: NA
Ram Stroke: NA
Weight: 300 lbs.
Features: Reloads standard calibers, swages bullets up to 458 caliber, draws jackets and extrudes small diameter lead wire. Optional speed and thrust control unit available. Uses Corbin-S swaging and drawing dies. Comes with T-slot ram adapter for standard shell holders. Make free 22 and 6mm jackets from fired 22 cases using optional Corbin kit.
Price: **$2,995.00**

CORBIN Benchrest S-Press

Frame: All steel
Frame Type: O-Frame
Die Thread: 7/8-14 and T-slot adapter
Avg. Rounds Per Hour: NA
Ram Stroke: 4" and 2"
Weight: 22 lbs.
Features: Roller bearing linkage, removeable head, right- or left-hand mount.
Price: **$349.00**

METALLIC CARTRIDGE PRESSES

FORSTER Co-Ax Press B-3

Frame: Cast iron
Frame Type: Modified O-frame
Die Thread: 7/8-14
Avg. Rounds Per Hour: 120
Ram Stroke: 4"
Weight: 18 lbs.
Features: Snap in/snap out die change; spent primer catcher with drop tube threaded into carrier below shellholder; automatic, handle-activated, cammed shellholder with opposing spring-loaded jaws to contact extractor groove; floating guide rods for alignment and reduced friction; no torque on the head due to design of linkage and pivots; shellholder jaws that float with die permitting case to center in the die; right- or left-hand operation; priming device for seating to factory specifications. "S" shellholder jaws included. From Forster Products.
Price: $366.00
Price: Optional LS shellholder jaws $32.00

HOLLYWOOD Senior Press

Frame: Ductile iron
Frame Type: O-frame
Die Thread: 7/8-14
Avg. Rounds Per Hour: 50-100
Ram Stroke: 6-1/2"
Weight: 50 lbs.
Features: Leverage and bearing surfaces ample for reloading cartridges or swaging bullets. Precision ground one-piece 2-1/2" pillar with base; operating handle of 3/4" steel and 15" long; 5/8" steel tie-down rod for added strength when swaging; heavy steel toggle and camming arms held by 1/2" steel pins in reamed holes. The 1-1/2" steel die bushing takes standard threaded dies; removed, it allows use of Hollywood shotshell dies. From Hollywood Engineering.
Price: $900.00

HOLLYWOOD Senior Turret Press

Frame: Ductile iron
Frame Type: H-frame
Die Thread: 7/8-14
Avg. Rounds Per Hour: 50-100
Ram Stroke: 6-1/2"
Weight: 50 lbs.
Features: Same features as Senior press except has three-position turret head; holes in turret may be tapped 1-1/2" or 7/8" or four of each. Height 15". Comes complete with one turret indexing handle; one operating handle and three turret indexing handles; one 5/8" tie down bar for swaging. From Hollywood Engineering.
Price: $1,000.00

HORNADY Lock-N-Load Classic

Frame: Die cast heat-treated aluminum alloy
Frame Type: O-frame
Die Thread: 7/8-14
Avg. Rounds Per Hour: NA
Ram Stroke: 3-5/8"
Weight: 14 lbs.
Features: Features Lock-N-Load bushing system that allows instant die changeovers. Solid steel linkage arms that rotate on steel pins; 30° angled frame design for improved visibility and accessibility; primer arm automatically moves in and out of ram for primer pickup and solid seating; two primer arms for large and small primers; long offset handle for increased leverage and unobstructed reloading; lifetime warranty. Comes as a package with primer catcher, PPS automatic primer feed and three Lock-N-Load die bushings. Dies and shellholder available separately or as a kit with primer catcher, positive priming system, automatic primer feed, three die bushings and reloading accessories. From Hornady Mfg. Co.
Price: Press and Three Die Bushings $129.44
Price: Classic Reloading Kit $347.06

LEE Hand Press

Frame: ASTM 380 aluminum
Frame Type: NA
Die Thread: 7/8-14
Avg. Rounds Per Hour: 100
Ram Stroke: 3-1/4"
Weight: 1 lb. 8 oz.
Features: Small and lightweight for portability; compound linkage for handling up to 375 H&H and case forming. Dies and shellholder not included. From Lee Precision, Inc.
Price: $34.98

Lee Breech Lock Challenger

Frame: ASTM 380 alloy
Frame Type: O-frame
Die Thread: 7/8-14
Avg. Rounds Per Hour: 100
Ram Stroke: 3-21-32"
Weight: 6 lbs. 1 oz.
Features: Features the Breech Lock Quick Change die system. Change dies instantly, no die adjustments. "O" frame press allows for maximum hand clearance. Positive spent primer catcher in Lee Lever Prime System. Steel linkage with adjustable length lever. From Lee Precision, Inc.
Price: $69.00

LEE Classic Cast

Features: Cast iron, O-type. Adjustable handle moves from right to left, start and stop position is adjustable. Large 1-1/8" diameter hollow ram catches primers for disposal. Automatic primer arm with bottom of stroke priming. Two assembled primer arms included. From Lee Precision, Inc.
Price: $120.00

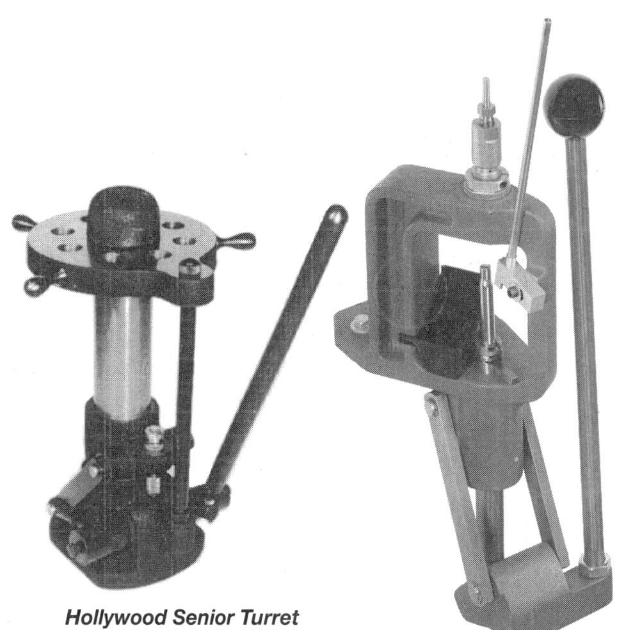

Hollywood Senior Turret

Hornady Lock-N-Load Classic

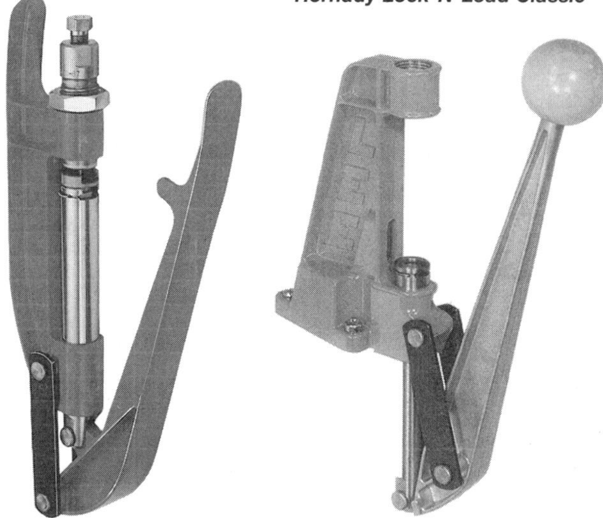

Lee Hand Press

Lee Reloader

METALLIC CARTRIDGE PRESSES

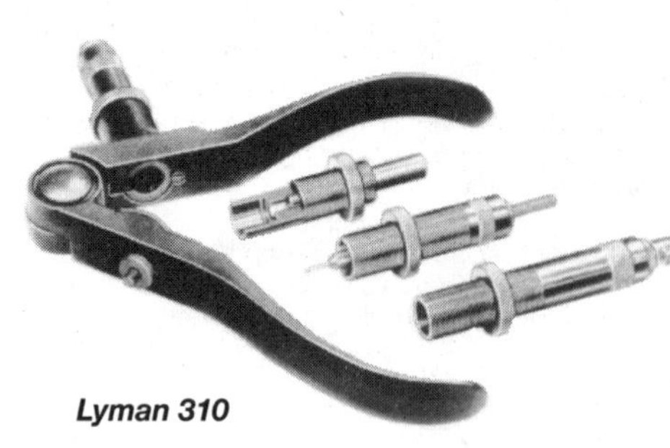

Lyman 310

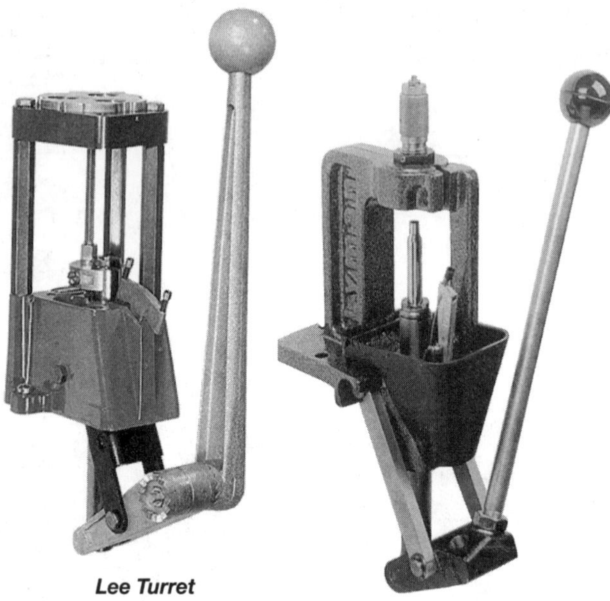

Lee Turret

Lyman Crusher II

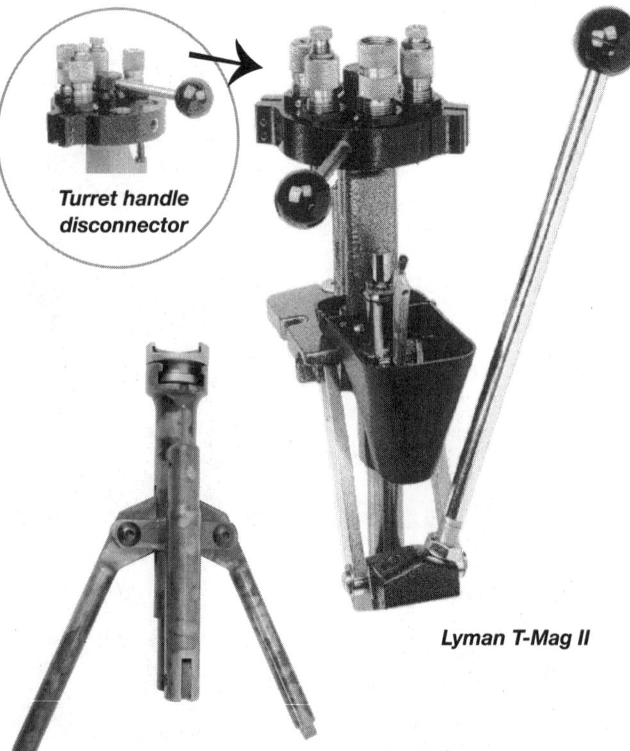

Turret handle disconnector

Lyman T-Mag II

Meacham Re-De-Capper

LEE Reloader Press

Frame: ASTM 380 aluminum
Frame Type: C-frame
Die Thread: 7/8-14
Avg. Rounds Per Hour: 100
Ram Stroke: 3"
Weight: 1 lb., 12 oz.
Features: Balanced lever to prevent pinching fingers; unlimited hand clearance; left- or right-hand use. Dies and shellholders not included. From Lee Precision, Inc.
Price: **$34.98**

LEE Turret Press

Frame: Steel and ASTM 380 aluminum alloy
Frame Type: O-frame
Die Thread: 7/8-14
Avg. Rounds Per Hour: 250
Ram Stroke: 3"
Weight: 7 lbs. 2 oz.
Features: Features Quick change turret. Lee Lever Prime System with large and small primer arms. Built in primer catcher, adjustable handle for right- or left-hand use. Available in 3 hole manual index or 4 hole Auto index. From Lee Precision, Inc.
Price: Three-Hole Turret with Manual-Index. **$89.98**
Price: Four-Hole Turret with Auto-Index **$95.98**

LEE Classic Turret Press

Frame: Steel and cast iron
Frame Type: O-frame
Die Thread: 7/8-14
Avg. Rounds Per Hour: 300
Ram Stroke: 3-15/16"
Weight: 13 lbs. 8 oz.
Features: Features Quick change turret and all steel and cast iron construction. Perimeter turret support assures turret cannot tilt. Long stroke handles the largest cases with ease. Large ram is drilled through to dispose primers in attached PVC tube. Includes Lee Lever Prime system with large and small primer arms. From Lee Precision, Inc.
Price: Lee Classic Turret Press 90064 (2006) **$125.00**
Price: Lee Classic Cast 50 Cal BMG 90859 (2006) **$231.00**

LYMAN 310 Tool

Frame: Stainless steel
Frame Type: NA
Die Thread: .609-30
Avg. Rounds Per Hour: NA
Ram Stroke: NA
Weight: 10 oz.
Features: Compact, portable reloading tool for pistol or rifle cartridges. Adapter allows loading rimmed or rimless cases. Die set includes neck resizing/decapping die, primer seating chamber; neck expanding die; bullet seating die; and case head adapter. From Lyman Products Corp.
Price: Dies **$45.00**
Price: Handles $47.50
Price: Carrying pouch $9.95

LYMAN AccuPress

Frame: Die cast
Frame Type: C-frame
Die Thread: 7/8-14
Avg. Rounds Per Hour: 75
Ram Stroke: 3.4"
Weight: 4 lbs.
Features: Reversible, contoured handle for bench mount or hand-held use; for rifle or pistol; compound leverage; Delta frame design. Accepts all standard powder measures. From Lyman Products Corp.
Price: **$34.95**

LYMAN Crusher II

Frame: Cast iron
Frame Type: O-frame
Die Thread: 7/8-14
Avg. Rounds Per Hour: 75
Ram Stroke: 3-7/8"
Weight: 19 lbs.
Features: Reloads both pistol and rifle cartridges; 1" diameter ram; 4-1/2" press opening for loading magnum cartridges; direct torque design; right- or left-hand use. New base design with 14 square inches of flat mounting surface with three bolt holes. Comes with priming arm and primer catcher. Dies and shellholders not included. From Lyman Products Corp.
Price: **$116.50**

LYMAN T-Mag II

Frame: Cast iron with silver metalflake powder finish
Frame Type: Turret
Die Thread: 7/8-14
Avg. Rounds Per Hour: 125
Ram Stroke: 3-13/16"
Weight: 18 lbs.
Features: Re-engineered and upgraded with new turret system for ease of indexing and tool-free turret removal for caliber changeover; new flat machined base for bench mounting; new nickel-plated non-rust handle and links; and new silver hammertone powder coat finish for durability. Right- or left-hand operation; handles all rifle or pistol dies. Comes with priming arm and primer catcher. Dies and shellholders not included. From Lyman Products Corp.
Price: **$164.95**
Price: Extra turret **$37.50**

MEACHAM Anywhere Portable Reloading Press

Frame: Anodized 6061 T6 aircraft aluminum
Frame Type: Cylindrical
Die Thread: 7/8-14
Avg. Rounds Per Hour: NA
Ram Stroke: 2.7"
Weight: 2 lbs. (hand held); 5 lbs. (with docking kit)
Features: A lightweight portable press that can be used hand-held, or with a docking kit, can be clamped to a table top up to 9.75" thick. Docking kit includes a powder measure mount that clamps to the press body and a holder for the other die. Designed for neck sizing and bullet seating of short-action cartridges, it can be used for long-action cartridges with the addition of an Easy Seater straight line seating die. Dies not included.
Price: **$99.95**
Price: (with docking kit) **$144.95**
Price: Easy Seater **$114.95**
Price: Bushing type Neck Sizer **$74.95**
Price: Pope Style Re-De-capper: **$99.95**

PONSNESS/WARREN Metal-Matic P-200

Frame: Die cast aluminum
Frame Type: Unconventional
Die Thread: 7/8-14
Avg. Rounds Per Hour: 200+
Weight: 18 lbs.
Features: Designed for straight-wall cartridges; die head with 10 tapped holes for holding dies and accessories for two calibers at one time; removable spent primer box; pivoting arm moves case from station to station. Comes with large and small primer tool. Optional accessories include primer feed, extra die head, primer speed feeder, powder measure extension and dust cover. Dies, powder measure and shellholder not included. From Ponsness/Warren.
Price: **$215.00**
Price: Extra die head **$44.95**
Price: Powder measure extension **$29.95**
Price: Primer feed **$44.95**
Price: Primer speed feed **$14.50**
Price: Dust cover **$21.95**

RCBS Partner

Frame: Aluminum
Frame Type: O-frame
Die Thread: 7/8-14
Avg. Rounds Per Hour: 50-60
Ram Stroke: 3-5/8"
Weight: 5 lbs.
Features: Designed for the beginning reloader. Comes with primer arm equipped with interchangeable primer plugs and sleeves for seating large and small primers. Shellholder and dies not included. Available in kit form (see Metallic Presses-Accessories). From RCBS.
Price: **$78.95**

RCBS AmmoMaster-2 Single Stage Press

Frame: Aluminum base; cast iron top plate connected by three steel posts.
Frame Type: NA
Die Thread: 1-1/4"-12 bushing; 7/8"-14 threads
Avg. Rounds Per Hour: 50-60
Ram Stroke: 5-1/4"
Weight: 19 lbs.
Features: Single-stage press convertible to progressive. Will form cases or swage bullets. Case detection system to disengage powder measure when no case is present in powder charging station; five-station shellplate; Uniflow Powder measure with clear powder measure adaptor to make bridged powders visible and correctable. 50-cal. conversion kit allows reloading 50 BMG. Kit includes top plate to accommodate either 1-3/8" x 12 or 1-1/2" x 12 reloading dies. Piggyback die plate for quick caliber change-overs available. Reloading dies not included. From RCBS.
Price: AmmoMaster-2 No. 88703 .... **$292.95**
Price: 50 BMG 1-1/2" **die kit No. 88705** **$417.95**
Price: 50 BMG 1-1/2" **press conversion kit No. 88709** **$137.95**
Price: Piggyback/AmmoMaster die plate **$34.95**
Price: Dust cover **$17.95**

RCBS Reloader Special-5

Frame: Aluminum
Frame Type: 30° offset O-frame
Die Thread: 1-1/4"-12 bushing; 7/8-14 threads
Avg. Rounds Per Hour: 50-60
Ram Stroke: 3-1/16"
Weight: 7.5 lbs.
Features: Single-stage press convertible to progressive with RCBS Piggyback II or 3. Primes cases during resizing operation. Will accept RCBS shotshell dies. From RCBS.
Price: **$139.95**

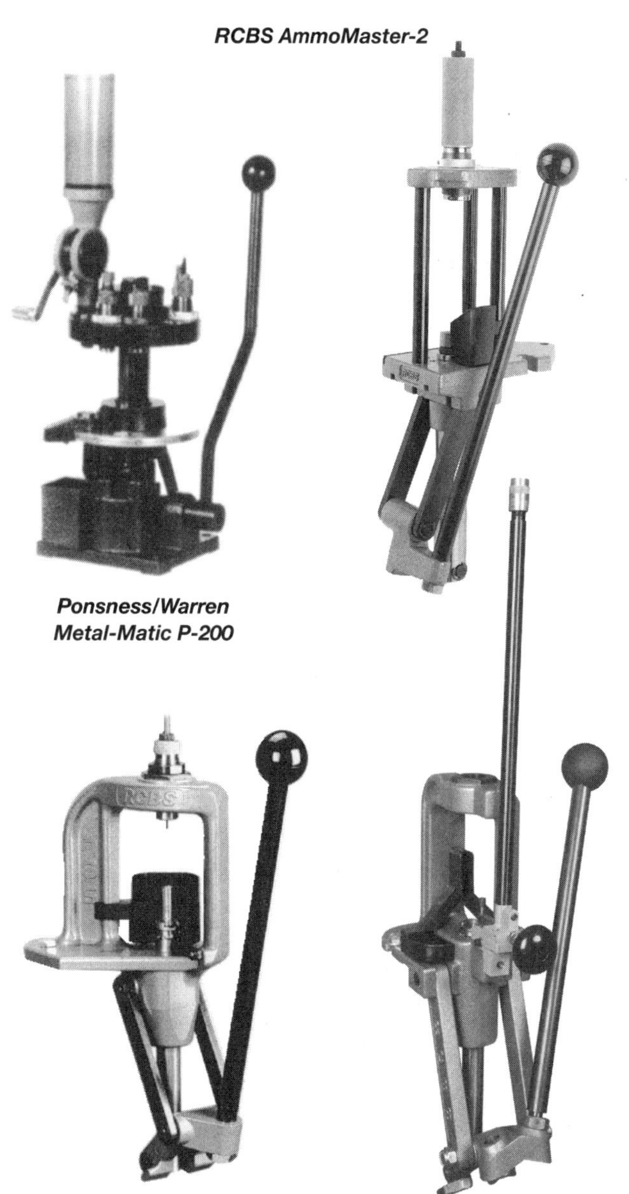

RCBS AmmoMaster-2

Ponsness/Warren Metal-Matic P-200

RCBS Reloader Special-5

RCBS Rock Crusher Supreme

RCBS Rock Chucker Supreme

Frame: Cast iron
Frame Type: O-frame
Die Thread: 1-1/4"-12 bushing; 7/8-14 threads
Avg. Rounds Per Hour: 50-60
Ram Stroke: 4.25"
Weight: 17 lbs.
Features: Redesigned to allow loading of longer cartridge cases. Made for heavy-duty reloading, case forming and bullet swaging. Provides 4" of ram-bearing surface to support 1" ram and ensure alignment; ductile iron toggle blocks; hardened steel pins. Comes standard with Universal Primer Arm and primer catcher. Can be converted from single-stage to progressive with Piggyback II conversion unit. From RCBS.
Price: **$167.95**

REDDING T-7 Turret Press

Frame: Cast iron
Frame Type: Turret
Die Thread: 7/8-14
Avg. Rounds Per Hour: NA
Ram Stroke: 3.4"
Weight: 23 lbs., 2 oz.
Features: Strength to reload pistol and magnum rifle, linkage pins heat-treated, precision ground and in double shear; hollow ram to collect spent primers; removable turret head for caliber changes; progressive linkage for increased power as ram nears die; rear turret support for stability and precise alignment; 7-station turret head; priming arm for both large and small primers. Also available in kit form with shellholder and one die set. From Redding Reloading Equipment.
Price: **$369.00**
Price: Kit **$420.00**

REDDING Boss

Frame: Cast iron
Frame Type: O-frame
Die Thread: 7/8-14
Avg. Rounds Per Hour: NA
Ram Stroke: 3.4"
Weight: 11 lbs., 8 oz.
Features: 36° frame offset for visibility and accessibility; primer arm positioned at bottom ram travel; positive ram travel stop machined to hit exactly top-dead-center. Also available in kit form with shellholder and set of Redding A dies. From Redding Reloading Equipment.
Price: **$168.50**
Price: Kit $222.50
Price: Big Boss Press (heavier frame, longer stroke for mag. cartridges) .... **$213.00 to $264.00**

REDDING Ultramag

Frame: Cast iron
Frame Type: Non-conventional
Die Thread: 7/8-14
Avg. Rounds Per Hour: NA
Ram Stroke: 4-1/8"
Weight: 23 lbs., 6 oz.
Features: Unique compound leverage system connected to top of press for tons of ram pressure for case forming and bullet swaging; large 4-3/4" frame opening for loading oversized cartridges; hollow ram for spent primers. Kit available with shellholder and one set Redding A dies. From Redding Reloading Equipment.
Price: **$384.00**
Price: Kit **$435.00**

ROCK CRUSHER Press

Frame: Cast iron
Frame Type: O-frame
Die Thread: 2-3/4"-12 with bushing reduced to 1-1/2"-12
Avg. Rounds Per Hour: 50
Ram Stroke: 6"
Weight: 67 lbs.
Features: Designed to load and form ammunition from 50 BMG up to 23x115 Soviet. Frame opening of 8-1/2" x 3-1/2"; 1-1/2" x 12"; bushing can be removed and bushings of any size substituted; ram pressure can exceed 10,000 lbs. with normal body weight; 40mm diameter ram. Angle block for bench mounting and reduction bushing for RCBS dies available. Accessories for Rock Crusher include powder measure, dies, shellholder, bullet puller, priming tool, case gauge and others. From The Old Western Scrounger.
Price: **$795.00**
Price: Angle block **$57.95**
Price: Reduction bushing **$21.00**
Price: Shellholder **$47.25**
Price: Priming tool, 50 BMG, 20 Lahti **$65.10**

Progressive Presses

CORBIN Benchrest S-Press

Frame: All steel
Frame Type: O-Frame
Die Thread: 7/8-14 and **T-slot adapter**
Avg. Rounds Per Hour: NA
Ram Stroke: 4" and 2"
Weight: 22 lbs.
Features: Roller bearing linkage, removeable head, right- or left-hand mount.
Price: **$329.00**

Redding Boss

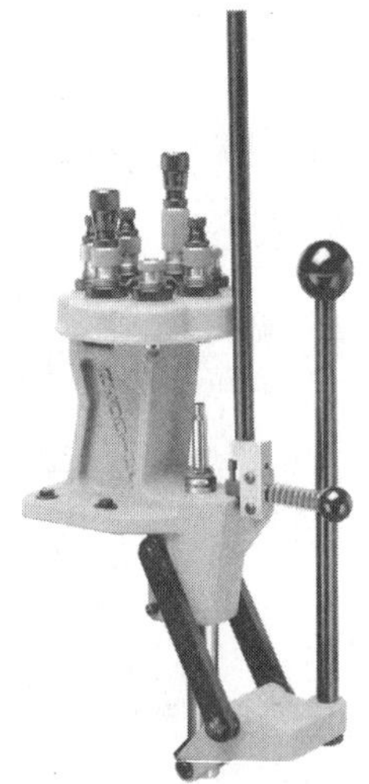

Redding Turret Press

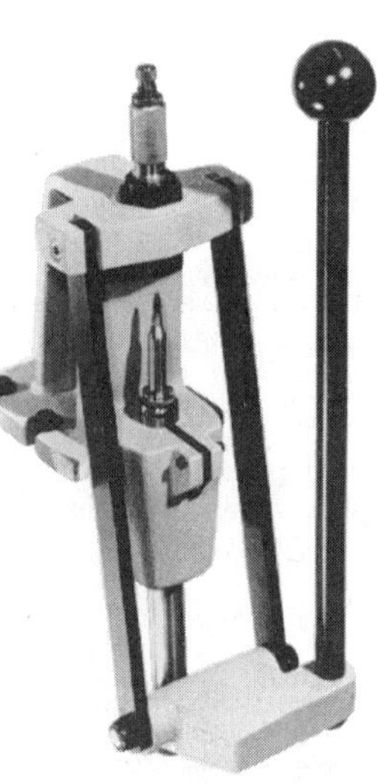

Redding Ultramag

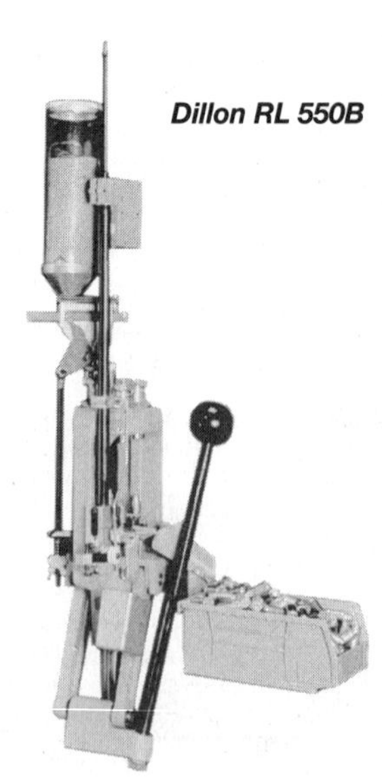

Dillon RL 550B

DILLON RL 550B

Frame: Aluminum alloy
Frame Type: NA
Die Thread: 7/8-14
Avg. Rounds Per Hour: 500-600
Ram Stroke: 3-7/8"
Weight: 25 lbs.
Features: Four stations; removable tool head to hold dies in alignment and allow caliber changes without die adjustment; auto priming system that emits audible warning when primer tube is low; a 100-primer capacity magazine contained in DOM steel tube for protection; new auto powder measure system with simple mechanical connection between measure and loading platform for positive powder bar return; a separate station for crimping with star-indexing system; 220 ejected-round capacity bin; 3/4-lb. capacity powder measure. Height above bench, 35"; requires 3/4" bench overhang. Will reload 120 different rifle and pistol calibers. Comes with one caliber conversion kit. Dies not included. From Dillon Precision Products, Inc.
Price: **$395.95**

DILLON Super 1050

Frame: Ductile iron
Frame Type: Platform type
Die Thread: 7/8-14
Avg. Rounds Per Hour: 1000-1200
Ram Stroke: 2-5/16"
Weight: 62 lbs.
Features: Eight stations; auto case feed; primer pocket swager for military cartridge cases; auto indexing; removable tool head; auto prime system with 100-primer capacity; low primer supply alarm; positive powder bar return; auto powder measure; 515 ejected round bin capacity; 500-600 case feed capacity; 3/4-lb. capacity powder measure. Has lengthened frame and short-stroke crank to accommodate long calibers. Loads all pistol rounds as well as 30 M1 Carbine, 223, and 7.62x39 rifle rounds. Height above the bench, 43". Dies not included. From Dillon Precision Products, Inc.
Price: **$1,539.95**

DILLON Square Deal B

Frame: Zinc alloy
Frame Type: NA
Die Thread: None (unique Dillon design)
Avg. Rounds Per Hour: 400-500
Ram Stroke: 2-5/16"
Weight: 17 lbs.
Features: Four stations; auto indexing; removable tool head; auto prime system with 100-primer capacity; low primer supply alarm; auto powder measure; positive powder bar return; 170 ejected round capacity bin; 3/4-lb. capacity powder measure. Height above the bench, 34". Comes complete with factory adjusted carbide die set. From Dillon Precision Products, Inc.
Price: **$339.95**

DILLON XL 650

Frame: Aluminum alloy
Frame Type: NA
Die Thread: 7/8-14
Avg. Rounds Per Hour: 800-1000
Ram Stroke: 4-9/16"
Weight: 46 lbs.
Features: Five stations; auto indexing; auto case feed; removable tool head; auto prime system with 100-primer capacity; low primer supply alarm; auto powder measure; positive powder bar return; 220 ejected round capacity bin; 3/4-lb. capacity powder measure. 500-600 case feed capacity with optional auto case feed. Loads all pistol/rifle calibers less than 3-1/2" in length. Height above the bench, 44"; 3/4" bench overhang required. From Dillon Precision Products, Inc.
Price: Less dies **$504.95**

HORNADY Lock-N-Load AP

Frame: Die cast heat-treated aluminum alloy
Frame Type: O-frame
Die Thread: 7/8-14
Avg. Rounds Per Hour: NA
Ram Stroke: 3-3/4"
Weight: 26 lbs.
Features: Features Lock-N-Load bushing system that allows instant die changeovers; five-station die platform with option of seating and crimping separately or adding taper-crimp die; auto prime with large and small primer tubes with 100-primer capacity and protective housing; brass kicker to eject loaded rounds into 80-round capacity cartridge catcher; offset operating handle for leverage and unobstructed operation; 2" diameter ram driven by heavy-duty cast linkage arms rotating on steel pins. Comes with five Lock-N-Load die bushings, shellplate, deluxe powder measure, auto powder drop, and auto primer feed and shut-off, brass kicker and primer catcher. Lifetime warranty. From Hornady Mfg. Co.
Price: **$416.38**

Lee Load-Master

Frame: ASTM 380 aluminum
Frame Type: O-frame
Die Thread: 7/8-14
Avg. Rounds Per Hour: 600
Ram Stroke: 3¼"
Weight: 8 lbs., 4 oz.
Features: Available in kit form only. A 1¾" diameter hard chrome ram for handling largest magnum cases; loads rifle or pistol rounds; five station press to fac-tory crimp and post size; auto indexing with wedge lock mechanism to hold one ton; auto priming; removable turrets; four-tube case feeder with optional case collator and bullet feeder (late 1995); loaded round ejector with chute to optional loaded round catcher; quick change shellplate; primer catcher. Dies and shell-holder for one caliber included. From Lee Precision, Inc.
Price: Rifle **$320.00**
Price: Pistol **$330.00**
Price: Extra turret **$14.98**
Price: Adjustable charge bar **$9.98**

LEE Pro 1000

Frame: ASTM 380 aluminum and steel
Frame Type: O-frame
Die Thread: 7/8-14
Avg. Rounds Per Hour: 600
Ram Stroke: 3-1/4"
Weight: 8 lbs., 7 oz.
Features: Optional transparent large/small or rifle case feeder; deluxe auto-disk case-activated powder measure; case sensor for primer feed. Comes complete with carbide die set (steel dies for rifle) for one caliber. Optional accessories include: case feeder for large/small pistol cases or rifle cases; shell plate carrier with auto prime, case ejector, auto-index and spare parts; case collator for case feeder. From Lee Precision, Inc.
Price: **$225.98**

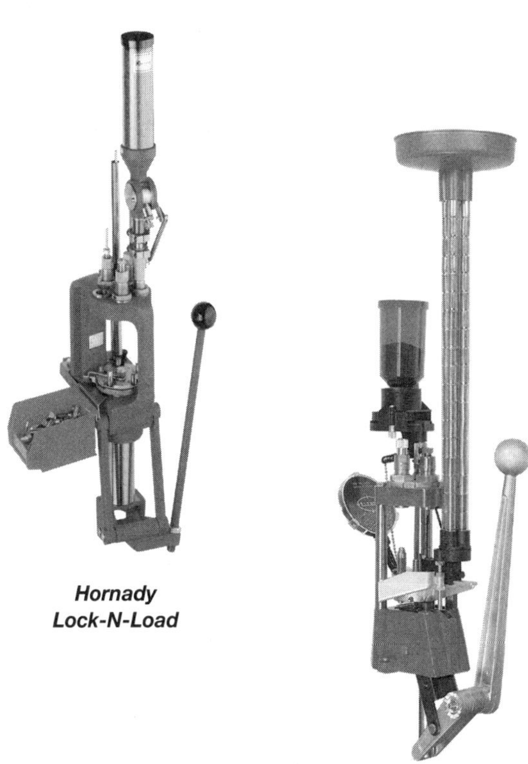

Hornady Lock-N-Load

Lee Load-Master

METALLIC CARTRIDGE PRESSES

PONSNESS/WARREN Metallic II
Frame: Die cast aluminum
Frame Type: H-frame
Die Thread: 7/8-14
Avg. Rounds Per Hour: 150+
Ram Stroke: NA
Weight: 32 lbs.
Features: Die head with five tapped 7/8-14 holes for dies, powder measure or other accessories; pivoting die arm moves case from station to station; depriming tube for removal of spent primers; auto primer feed; interchangeable die head. Optional accessories include additional die heads, powder measure extension tube to accommodate any standard powder measure, primer speed feeder to feed press primer tube without disassembly. Comes with small and large primer seating tools. Dies, powder measure and shellholder not included. From Ponsness/ Warren.
Price: **$375.00**
Price: Extra die head **$56.95**
Price: Primer speed feeder **$14.50**
Price: Powder measure extension **$29.95**
Price: Dust cover **$27.95**

RCBS Pro 2000™
Frame: Cast iron
Frame Type: H-Frame
Die Thread: 7/8-14
Avg. Rounds Per Hour: 500-600
Ram Stroke: NA
Weight: NA
Features: Five-station manual indexing; full-length sizing; removable die plate; fast caliber conversion. Uses APS Priming System. From RCBS.
Price: **$616.95**

RCBS Turret Press
Frame: Cast iron
Frame Type: NA
Die Thread: 7/8-14
Avg. Rounds Per Hour: 50 to 200
Ram Stroke: NA
Weight: NA
Features: Six-station turret head; positive alignment; on-press priming.
Price: **$243.95**

STAR Universal Pistol Press
Frame: Cast iron w/aluminum base
Frame Type: Unconventional
Die Thread: 11/16-24 or 7/8-14
Avg. Rounds Per Hour: 300
Ram Stroke: NA
Weight: 27 lbs.
Features: Four or five-station press depending on need to taper crimp; handles all popular handgun calibers from 32 Long to 45 Colt. Comes completely assembled and adjusted with carbide dies (except 30 Carbine) and shellholder to load one caliber. Prices slightly higher for 9mm and 30 Carbine. From Star Machine Works.
Price: With taper crimp **$1,055.00**
Price: Without taper crimp **$1,025.00**
Price: Extra tool head, taper crimp **$425.00**
Price: Extra tool head, w/o taper crimp **$395.00**

RCBS Pro 2000

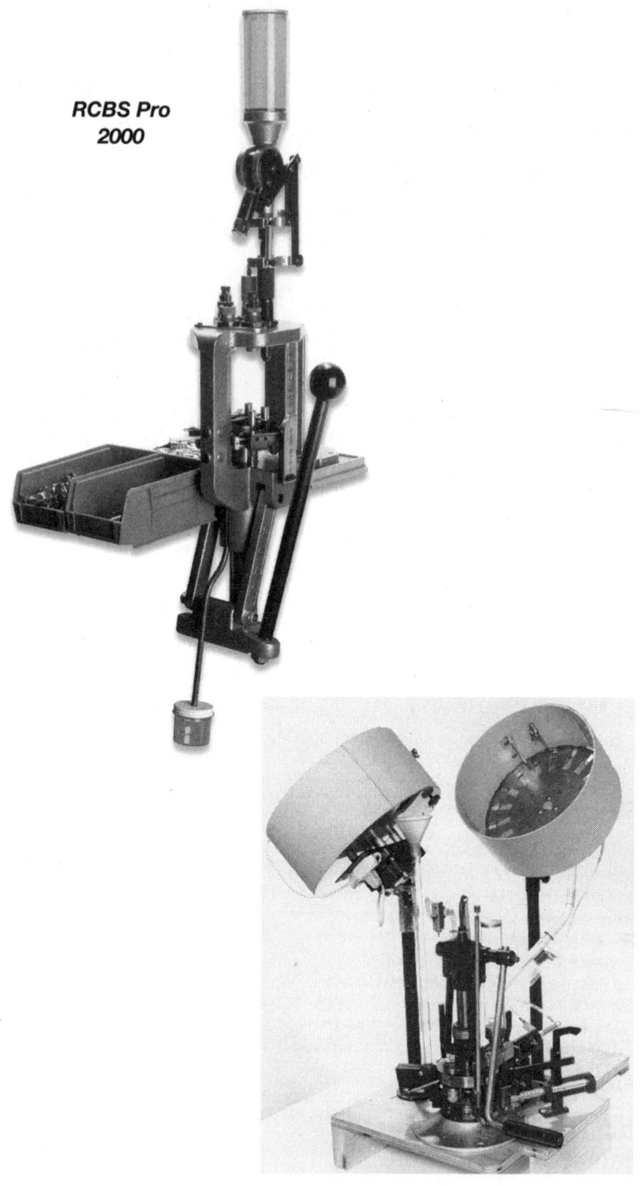

Fully-automated Star Universal

DILLON SL 900

Press Type: Progressive
Avg. Rounds Per Hour: 700-900
Weight: 51 lbs.
Features: 12-ga. only; factory adjusted to load AA hulls; extra large 25-pound capacity shot hopper; fully-adjustable case-activated shot system; hardened steel starter crimp die; dual-action final crimp and taper die; tilt-out wad guide; auto prime; auto index; strong mount machine stand. From Dillon Precision Products.
Price: $914.90

HOLLYWOOD Automatic Shotshell Press

Press Type: Progressive
Avg. Rounds Per Hour: 1,800
Weight: 100 lbs.
Features: Ductile iron frame; fully automated press with shell pickup and ejector; comes completely set up for one gauge; one starter crimp; one finish crimp; wad guide for plastic wads; decap and powder dispenser unit; one wrench for inside die lock screw; one medium and one large spanner wrench for spanner nuts; one shellholder; powder and shot measures. Available for 10, 12, 20, 28 or 410. From Hollywood Engineering.
Price: $5,000.00

HOLLYWOOD Senior Turret Press

Press Type: Turret
Avg. Rounds Per Hour: 200
Weight: 50 lbs.
Features: Multi-stage press constructed of ductile iron comes completely equipped to reload one gauge; one starter crimp; one finish crimp; wad guide for plastic wads; decap and powder dispenser unit; one wrench for inside die lock screw; one medium and one large spanner wrench for spanner nuts; one shellholder; powder and shot measures. Available for 10, 12, 16, 20, 28 or 410. From Hollywood Engineering.
Price: Press only $1,000.00
Price: Dies $200.00

HORNADY 366 Auto

Press Type: Progressive
Avg. Rounds Per Hour: NA
Weight: 25 lbs.
Features: Heavy-duty die cast and machined steel body and components; auto primer feed system; large capacity shot and powder tubes; adjustable for right- or left-hand use; automatic charge bar with shutoff; swing-out wad guide; primer catcher at base of press; interchangeable shot and powder bushings; life-time warranty. Available for 12, 20, 28 2-3/4" and 410 2-1/2". From Hornady Mfg. Co.
Price: $575.05
Price: Die set, 12, 20, 28 .... $202.77
Price: Magnum conversion dies, 12, 20 .... $43.25

LEE Load-All

Press Type: Single stage
Avg. Rounds Per Hour: 100
Weight: 3 lbs. 3 oz.
Features: Loads steel or lead shot; built-in primer catcher at base with door in front for emptying; recesses at each station for shell positioning; optional primer feed. Comes with safety charge bar with 24 shot and powder bushings. Available for 12-, 16-or 20-gauge. From Lee Precision, Inc.
Price: $57.98

MEC 600 Jr. Mark V

Press Type: Single stage
Avg. Rounds Per Hour: 150
Weight: 16 lbs.
Features: Spindex crimp starter for shell alignment during crimping; a cam-action crimp die; Pro-Check to keep charge bar properly positioned; adjustable for three shells. Available in 10, 12, 16, 20, 28 gauges and 410 bore. Die set not included. From Mayville Engineering Company, Inc.
Price: $145.58
Price: Die set $85.08

MEC 650N

Press Type: Progressive
Avg. Rounds Per Hour: 400
Weight: 19 lbs.
Features: Six-station press; does not resize except as separate operation; auto primer feed standard; three crimping stations for starting, closing

Dillon SL 900

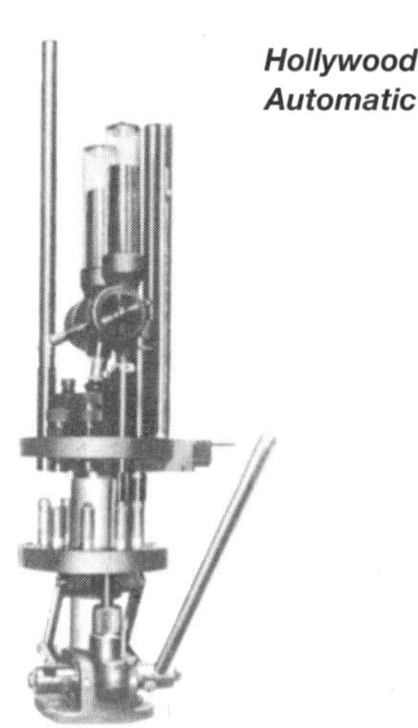

Hollywood Automatic

Hollywood Senior Turret Press

Hornady 366 Auto

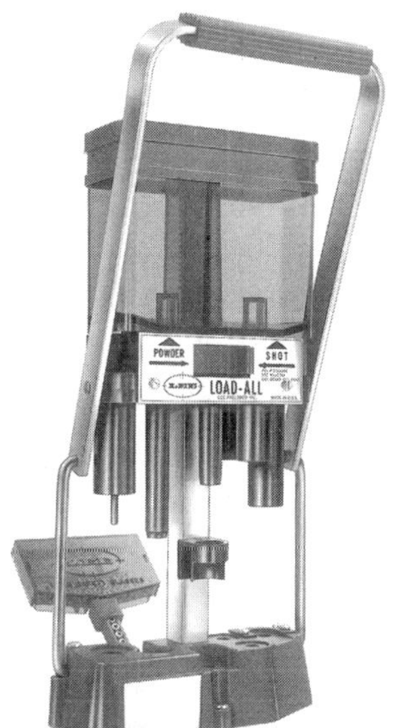

Lee Load-All

MEC 600 Jr. Mark V

MEC 650N

MEC 8567N Grabber

MEC 9000GN

MEC Steelmaster

MEC Sizemaster

and tapering crimp. Die sets not available. Available in 12, 16, 20, 28 and 410. From Mayville Engineering Company, Inc.

Price: **$290.40**

MEC 8567N Grabber

Press Type: Progressive
Avg. Rounds Per Hour: 400
Weight: 22 lbs.
Features: Six-station press; auto primer feed; auto-cycle charging; three-stage crimp; power ring resizer returns base to factory specs; resizes high and low base shells; optional kits to reload three shells and steel shot. Available in 12, 16, 20, 28 gauge and 410 bore. From Mayville Engineering Company, Inc.

Price: **$408.98**
Price: 3" kit, 12-ga. **$100.33**
Price: 3" kit, 20-ga. **$57.32**
Price: Steel shot kit **$50.15**

MEC 9000GN

Press Type: Progressive
Avg. Rounds Per Hour: 400
Weight: 27 lbs.
Features: All same features as the MEC Grabber but with auto-indexing and auto-eject. Finished shells automatically ejected from shell carrier to drop chute for boxing. Available in 12, 16, 20, 28 and 410. From Mayville Engineering Company, Inc.

Price: **$492.47**

MEC 9000HN

Press Type: Progressive
Avg. Rounds Per Hour: 400
Weight: 31 lbs.
Features: Same features as 9000GN with addition of foot pedal-operated hydraulic system for complete automation. Operates on standard 110V household current. Comes with bushing-type charge bar and three bushings. Available in 12, 16, 20, 28 gauge and 410 bore. From Mayville Engineering Company, Inc.

Price: **$1,005.90**

MEC 8120 Sizemaster

Press Type: Single stage
Avg. Rounds Per Hour: 150
Weight: 20 lbs.
Features: Power ring eight-fingered collet resizer returns base to factory specs; handles brass or steel, high or low base heads; auto primer feed; adjustable for three shells. Available in 10, 12, 16, 20, 28 gauges and 410 bore. From Mayville Engineering Company, Inc.

Price: **$220.42**
Price: Die set, 12, 16, 20, 28, 410 .... **$127.08**
Price: Die set, 10-ga. **$149.16**

MEC Steelmaster

Press Type: Single stage
Avg. Rounds Per Hour: 150
Weight: 20 lbs.
Features: Same features as Sizemaster except can load steel shot. Press is available for 3-1/2" 10-ga. and 12-ga. 2-3/4", 3" or 3-1/2". For loading lead shot, die sets available in 10, 12, 16, 20, 28 and 410. From Mayville Engineering Company, Inc.

Price: **$238.10**
Price: 12 ga. 3-1/2" **$266.69**

PONSNESS/WARREN Du-O-Matic 375C

Press Type: Progressive
Avg. Rounds Per Hour: NA
Weight: 31 lbs.
Features: Steel or lead shot reloader; large shot and powder reservoirs; bushing access plug for dropping in shot buffer or buckshot; positive lock charging ring to prevent accidental flow of powder; double-post construction for greater leverage; removable spent primer box; spring-loaded ball check for centering size die at each station; tip-out wad guide; two-gauge capacity tool head. Available in 10 (extra charge), 12, 16, 20, 28 and 410 with case lengths of 2-1/2", 2-3/4", 3" and 3-1/2". From Ponsness/ Warren.

Price: 12-, 20-, and 28-ga., 2-3/4" and 410, 2-1/2" **$289.00**
Price: 12-ga. 3-1/2"; 3" 12, 20, 410 .... **$305.00**
Price: 12, 20 2-3/4" **$383.95**
Price: 10-ga. press **$315.00**

PONSNESS/WARREN Hydro-Multispeed

Hydraulic system developed for Ponsness/Warren L/S-1000. Usable for the 950, 900 and 800 series presses. Three reloading speed settings operated with variable foot pedal control. Features stop/reverse at any station; automatic shutdown with pedal control release; fully adjustable hydraulic cylinder rod to prevent racking or bending of machine; quick disconnect hoses for ease of installation. Preassembled with step-by-step instructions. From Ponsness/Warren.

Price: **$879.00**
Price: Cylinder kit **$399.95**

PONSNESS/WARREN L/S-1000

Frame: Die cast aluminum
Avg. Rounds Per Hour: NA
Weight: 55 lbs.
Features: Fully progressive press to reload steel, bismuth or lead shot. Equipped with new Uni-Drop shot measuring and dispensing system which allows the use of all makes of shot in any size. Shells automatically resized and deprimed with new Auto-Size and De-Primer system. Loaded rounds drop out of shellholders when completed. Each shell pre-crimped and final crimped with Tru-Crimp system. Available in 10-gauge 3-1/2" or 12-gauge 2-3/4" and 3". 12-gauge 3-1/2" conversion kit also available. 20-gauge 2-3/4" and 3" special order only. From Ponsness/Warren.
Price: 12 ga. **$849.00**
Price: 10 ga. **$895.00**
Price: Conversion kit **$199.00**

PONSNESS/WARREN Size-O-Matic 900 Elite

Press Type: Progressive
Avg. Rounds Per Hour: 500-800
Weight: 49 lbs.
Features: Progressive eight-station press; frame of die-cast aluminum; center post design index system ensures positive indexing; timing factory set, drilled and pinned. Automatic features include index, deprime, reprime, powder and shot drop, crimp start, tapered final crimp, finished shell ejection. Available in 12, 20, 28 and 410. 16-ga. special order. Kit includes new shellholders, seating port, resize/primer knockout assembly, new crimp assembly. From Ponsness/Warren.
Price: **$749.00**
Price: Conversion tooling, 12, 20, 28, 410 . . . . **$189.00**

PONSNESS/WARREN Platinum 2000

Press Type: Progressive
Avg. Rounds Per Hour: 500-800
Weight: 52 lbs.
Features: Progressive eight-station press, similar to 900 and 950 except has die removal system that allows removal of any die component during reloading cycle. Comes standard with 25-lb. shot tube, 19" powder tube, brass adjustable priming feed allows adjustment of primer seating depth. From Ponsness/Warren.
Price: **$889.00**

RCBS The Grand

Press Type: Progressive
Avg. Rounds Per Hour: NA
Weight: NA
Features: Constructed from a high-grade aluminum casting, allows complete resizing of high and low base hulls. Available for 12 and 20 gauge.
Price: **$812.95**

RCBS Mini-Grand

Press Type: Progressive
Avg. Rounds Per Hour: 200
Weight: NA
Features: 7-station single-stage press, lead or steel reloading (with steel accessories). 12-gauge version loads 2-3/4" to 3-1/2" shells; 20-gauge product load 2-3/4" to 3" shotshells.
Price: **$147.95**

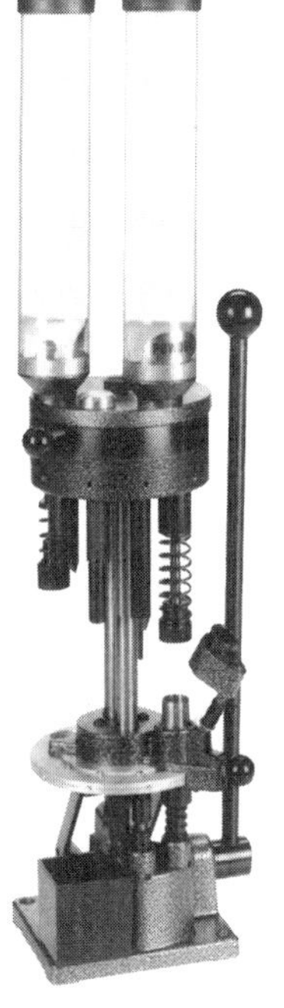

Ponsness/Warren Du-O-Matic 375C

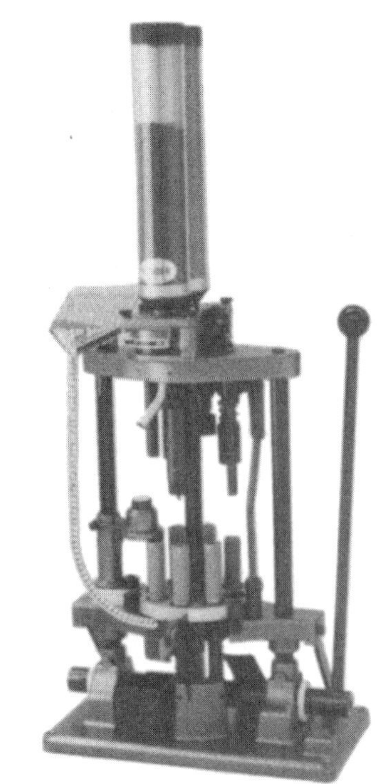

Ponsness/Warren Size-O-Matic 900 Elite

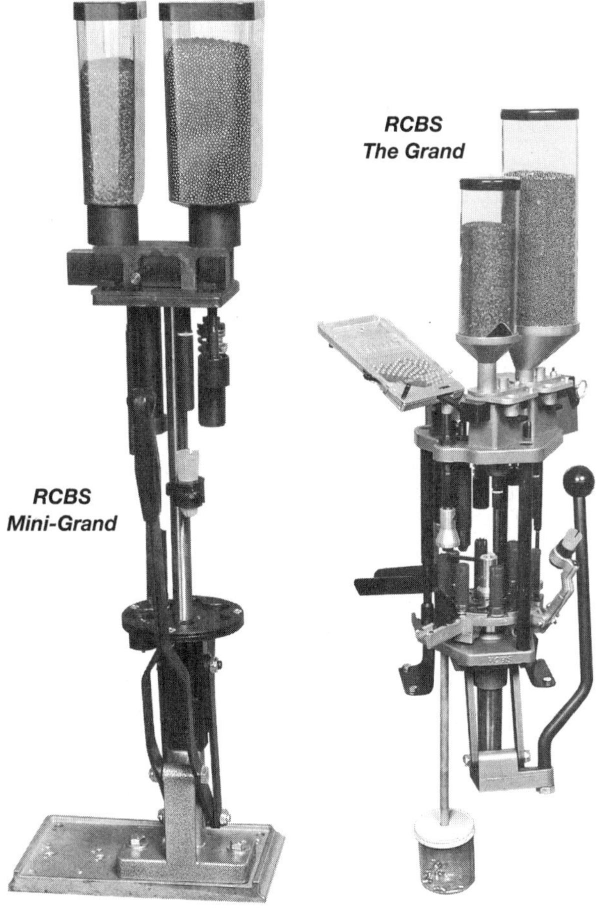

RCBS The Grand

RCBS Mini-Grand

Maker and Model	Magn.	Field at 100 Yds. (feet)	Eye Relief (in.)	Length (in.)	Tube Dia. (in.)	W & E Adjustments	Weight (ozs.)	Price	Other Data
ADCO									
Magnum 50mm[5]	0			4.1	45 mm	Int.	6.8	**$269.00**	[1]Multi-Color Dot system changes from red to green. [2]For airguns, paint ball, rimfires. Uses common lithium water battery. [3]Comes with standard dovetail mount. [4]10 MOA dot; black or nickel. [5]Square format; with mount battery. From ADCO Sales.
MIRAGE Ranger 1"	0			5.2	1	Int.	3.9	**159.00**	
MIRAGE Ranger 30mm	0			5.5	30mm	Int.	5	**159.00**	
MIRAGE Competitor	0			5.5	30mm	Int.	5.5	**229.00**	
IMP Sight[2]	0			4.5		Int.	1.3	**17.95**	
Square Shooter 2[3]	0			5		Int.	5	**99.00**	
MIRAGE Eclipse[1]	0			5.5	30mm	Int.	5.5	**229.00**	
Champ Red Dot	0			4.5		Int.	2	**33.95**	
Vantage 1"	0			3.9	1	Int.	3.9	**129.00**	
Vantage 30mm	0			4.2	30mm	Int.	4.9	**159.00**	
Vision 2000[6]	0	60		4.7		Int.	6.2	**79.00**	
e-dot ESB[1]	0			4.12	1	Int.	3.7	**139.00**	
e-dot E1B	0			4.12	1	Int.	3.7	**99.00**	
e-dot ECB	0			3.8	30mm	Int.	6.4	**99.00**	
e-dot E30B	0			4.3	30mm	Int.	4.6	**99.00**	
AIMPOINT									
Comp M2	0			5.1	30mm	Int.	7.8	**471.00**	Illuminates red dot in field of view. Noparallax (dot does not need to be centered). Unlimited field of view and eye relief. On/off, adj. intensity. Comp M2 Series: Standard CQB sight for Special Forces. CET technology. Rings-SRP-L and QRP fit Picatinny rails. QRW fits Weaver mount. QR = Quick Release. Comp M3 Series: Compact for bows, pistols. Black matte and silver metallic finishes (SM). Rings SRW-L, SRP-M, SRW-M. 9000 Series: Matte black and camo finishes. ACET technology. 30mm rings fit on Weaver rail, No 11286. [1]Comes with 30mm rings, battery, lense cloth. [2]Requires 1" rings. Black finish. AP Comp avail. in black, blue, SS, camo.
Comp ML2	0			5.1	30mm	Int.	7.8	**422.00**	
Comp ML2 2X	2			6.5	30mm	Int.	10.3	**551.00**	
Comp M3	0			5.1	30mm	Int.	7.8	**535.00**	
Comp ML3	0			5.1	30mm	Int.	7.8	**480.00**	
9000L	0			7.9	30mm	Int.	8.1	**370.00**	
9000L 2X	2			9.3	30mm	Int.	8.1	**470.00**	
9000SC	0			6.3	30mm	Int.	7.4	**370.00**	
9000SC Camo	0			6.3	30mm	Int.	7	**390.00**	
9000SC 2X	2			7.7	30mm	Int.	9.9	**470.00**	
Comp C3	0			4.9	30mm	Int.	7.1	**399.00**	
Comp C3 2X	2			6.1	30mm	Int.	9.5	**507.00**	
Comp SM	0			4.9	30mm	Int.	7.1	**372.00**	
Comp M[2]	0			5	30mm	Int.	6.1	**409.00**	
	0			6	30mm	Int.	6	**297.00**	
Series 3000 Universal[2]	0			6.25	1	Int.	6	**232.00**	
Series 5000/2x[1]	2			7	30mm	Int.	9	**388.00**	
APEX									
Model 4030		3-9x		40/14	42mm	Int.		**250.00**	
Model 4035		3.5-10x		28/10	50mm	Int.		**285.00**	
Model 4040		4-16x		23.6/6.2	50mm	Int.		**300.00**	
Model 4045		6-24x		15/4	50mm	Int.		**310.00**	
ARTEMIS 2000									
4x32	4	34.4	3.15	10.7	1	Int.	17.5	**215.00**	Click-stop windage and elevation adjustments; constantly centered reticle; rubber eyepiece ring; nitrogen filled. Imported from the Czech Republic by CZ-USA.
6x42	6	23	3.15	13.7	1	Int.	17.5	**317.00**	
7x50	7	18.7	3.15	13.9	1	Int.	17.5	**329.00**	
1.5-6x42	1.5-6	40-12.8	2.95	12.4	30mm	Int.	19.4	**522.00**	
2-8x42	2-8	31-9.5	2.95	13.1	30mm	Int.	21.1	**525.00**	
3-9x42	3-9	24.6-8.5	2.95	12.4	30mm	Int.	19.4	**466.00**	
3-12x50	3-12	20.6-6.2	2.95	14	30mm	Int.	22.9	**574.00**	
BEC									
EuroLux									
EL2510x56	2.5-10	39.4-11.5	3.25-2	15.1	30mm	Int.	25.4	**249.90**	Black matte finish. Multi-coated lenses; 1/4-MOA click adjustments (1/2-MOA on EL4x25, AR4x22WA); fog and water-proof. [1]For AR-15; bullet drop compensator; q.d. mount. [2]Rubber armored. Imported by BEC Inc. Partial listing shown. Contact BEC for complete details. [3]All Goldlabel scopes feature lighted reticles and finger-adjustable windage and elevation adjustments. [4]Bullet-drop compensator system for Mini-14 and AR-15 rifles.
EL39x42	3-9	34.1-13.2	3.5-3	12.3	30mm	Int.	17.7	**99.80**	
EL28x36	2-8	44.9-11.5	3.8-3	12.2	30mm	Int.	15.9	**149.50**	
ELA39x40RB[2]	3-9	39-13	3	12.7	30mm	Int.	14.3	**95.95**	
EL6x42	6	21	3	12.6	30mm	Int.	14.8	**69.00**	
EL4x42	4	29	3	12.6	30mm	Int.	14.8	**59.60**	
EL4x36	4	29	3	12	30mm	Int.	14	**49.90**	
EL4x25	4	26	3	7	30mm	Int.	7.6	**37.00**	
AR4x22WA[1]	4	24	3	7	34mm	Int.	13.6	**109.97**	
Goldlabel[3]									
GLI 624x50	6-24	16-4	3.5-3	15.3	1	Int.	22.5	**139.00**	
GLI 416x50	4-16	25-6	3.5-3	13.5	1	Int.	21.8	**135.00**	
GLI 39x40R[2]	3-9	39-13	3.5-3	12.7	28mm	Int.	18.5	**99.00**	
GLC 5x42BD[4]	5	24	3.5	8.7	1	Int.	16.5	**79.00**	

Maker and Model	Magn.	Field at 100 Yds. (feet)	Eye Relief (in.)	Length (in.)	Tube Dia. (in.)	W & E Adjustments	Weight (ozs.)	Price	Other Data
BEEMAN									
Rifle Scopes									
5045[1]	4-12	26.9-9	3	13.2	1	Int.	15	**275.00**	All scopes have 5 point reticle, all glass fully-coated lenses. [1]Parallel adjustable. Imported by Beeman.
5046[1]	6-24	18-4.5	3	16.9	1	Int.	20.2	**395.00**	
5050[1]	4	26	3.5	11.7	1	Int.	11	**80.00**	
5055[1]	3-9	38-13	3.5	10.75	1	Int.	11.2	**90.00**	
5060[1]	4-12	30-10	3	12.5	1	Int.	16.2	**210.00**	
5065[1]	6-18	17-6	3	14.7	1	Int.	17.3	**265.00**	
Pistol Scopes									
5021	2	19	10-24	9.1	1	Int.	7.4	**85.50**	
5020	1.5	14	11-16	8.3	.75	Int.	3.6	**NA**	
BSA									
Catseye[1]									
CE1545x32	1.5-4.5	78-23	4	11.25	1	Int.	12	**91.95**	[1]Waterproof, fogproof; multi-coated lenses; finger-adjustable knobs. [2]Waterproof, fogproof; matte black finish. [3]With 4" sunshade; target knobs; 1/8-MOA click adjustments. [4]Adjustable for parallax; with sun shades; target knobs, 1/8-MOA adjustments. Imported by BSA. [5]Red dot sights also available in 42mm and 50mm versions. [6]Includes Universal Bow Mount. [7]Five other models offered. From BSA.
CE310x44	3-10	39-12	3.25	12.75	1	Int.	16	**151.95**	
CE3510x50	3.5-10	30-10.5	3.25	13.25	1	Int.	17.25	**171.95**	
CE416x50	4-16	25-6	3	15.25	1	Int.	22	**191.95**	
CE624x50	6-24	16-3	3	16	1	Int.	23	**222.95**	
CE1545x32IR	1.5-4.5	78-23	5	11.25	1	Int.	12	**121.95**	
Deer Hunter[2]									
DH25x20	2.5	72	6	7.5	1	Int.	7.5	**59.95**	
DH4x32	4	32	3	12	1	Int.	12.5	**49.95**	
DH39x32	3-9	39-13	3	12	1	Int.	11	**69.95**	
DH39x40	3-9	39-13	3	13	1	Int.	12.1	**89.95**	
DH39x50	3-9	41-15	3	12.75	1	Int.	13	**109.95**	
DH2510x44	2.5-10	42-12	3	13	1	Int.	12.5	**99.95**	
DH1545x32	1.5-4.5	78-23	5	11.25	1	Int.	12	**79.95**	
Contender[3]									
CT24x40TS	24	6	3	15	1	Int.	18	**129.95**	
CT36x40TS	36	3	3	15.25	1	Int.	19	**139.95**	
CT312x40TS	3-12	28-7	3	13	1	Int.	17.5	**129.95**	
CT416x40TS	4-16	21-5	3	13.5	1	Int.	18	**131.95**	
CT624x40TS	6-24	16-4	3	15.5	1	Int.	20	**149.95**	
CT832x40TS	8-32	11-3	3	15.5	1	Int.	20	**171.95**	
CT312x50TS	3-12	28-7	3	13.75	1	Int.	21	**131.95**	
CT416x50TS	4-16	21-5	3	15.25	1	Int.	22	**151.95**	
CT624x50TS	6-24	16-4	3	16	1	Int.	23	**171.95**	
CT832x50TS	8-32	11-3	3	16.5	1	Int.	24	**191.95**	
Pistol									
P52x20	2	NA	NA	NA	NA	Int.	NA	**89.95**	
Platinum[4]									
PT24x44TS	24	4.5	3	16.25	1	Int.	17.9	**189.55**	
PT36x44TS	36	3	3	14.9	1	Int.	17.9	**199.95**	
PT624x44TS	6-24	15-4.5	3	15.25	1	Int.	18.5	**221.95**	
PT832x44TS	8-32	11-3.5	3	17.25	1	Int.	19.5	**229.95**	
.22 Special									
S39x32WR	3-9	37.7-14.1	3	12	1	Int.	12.3	**89.95**	
S4x32WR	4	26	3	10.75	1	Int.	9	**39.95-44.95**	
Air Rifle									
AR4x32	4	33	3	13	1	Int.	14	**69.95**	
AR27x32	2-7	48	3	12.25	1	Int.	14	**79.95**	
AR312x44	3-12	36	3	12.25	1	Int.	15	**109.95**	
Red Dot									
RD30[5]	0			3.8	30mm	Int.	5	**59.95**	
PB30[5]	0			3.8	30mm	Int.	4.5	**79.95**	
Bow30[6]	0			NA	30mm	Int.	5	**89.95**	
Big Cat									
BIgCat[7]	3.5-10	30-11	5	9.7	1	Int.	16.8	**219.95**	
BURRIS									
Mr. T Black Diamond Titanium									
2.5-10x50A	2.5-10	4.25-4.75		13.6			29	**1,518.00**	Available in Carbon Black, Titanium Gray and Autumn Gold finishes.
4-16x50	4-16	27-7.5	3.3-3.8	13.6	30mm	Int.	27	**1,594.00**	
Black Diamond									
3-12x50[3, 4, 6]	3.2-11.9	34-12	3.5-4	13.8	30mm	Int.	25	**974.00**	
6-24x50	6-24	18-6	3.5-4	16.2	30mm	Int.	25	**1,046.00**	
Fullfield II									
2.5x9	2.5	55	3.5-3.75	10.25	1	Int.	9	**307.00**	
1.75-5x[1, 2, 9, 10]	1.7-4.6	66-25	3.5-3.75	10.875	1	Int.	13	**400.00**	

Maker and Model	Magn.	Field at 100 Yds. (feet)	Eye Relief (in.)	Length (in.)	Tube Dia. (in.)	W & E Adjustments	Weight (ozs.)	Price
BURRIS *(cont.)*								
Fullfield II *(cont.)*								
3-9x40[1, 2, 3, 10]	3.3-8.7	38-15	3.5-3.75	12.625	1	Int.	15	**336.00**
3-9x50	3-9	35-15	3.5-3.75	13	1	Int.	18	**481.00**
3.5-10x50mm[3, 5, 10]	3.7-9.7	29.5-11	3.5-3.75	14	1	Int.	19	**542.00**
4.5-14x[1, 4, 8, 11]	4.4-11.8	27-10	3.5-3.75	15	1	Int.	18	**585.00**
6.5-20x[1, 3, 4, 6, 7, 8]	6.5-17.6	16.7	3.5-3.75	15.8	1	Int.	18.5	**656.00**
Compact Scopes								
1x XER[3]	1	51	4.5-20	8.8	1	Int.	7.9	**320.00**
4x[4, 5]	3.6	24	3.75-5	8.25	1	Int.	7.8	**397.00**
6x[1, 4]	5.5	17	3.75-5	9	1	Int.	8.2	**397.00**
6x HBR[1, 5, 8]	6	13	4.5	11.25	1	Int.	13	**415.00**
1-4x XER[3]	1-3.8	53-15	4.25-30	8.8	1	Int.	10.3	**467.00**
3-9x[4, 5]	3.6-8.8	25-11	3.75-5	12.625	1	Int.	11.5	**442.00**
4-12x[1, 4, 6]	4.5-11.6	19-8	3.75-4	15	1	Int.	15	**534.00**
Signature Series								
1.5-6x[2, 3, 5, 9, 10]	1.7-5.8	70-20	3.5-4	10.8	1	Int.	13	**601.00**
8x32[2, 5, 11]	2.1-7.7	53-17	3.5-4	11.75	1	Int.	14	**840.00**
3-10x[3, 5, 10, 13]	3.3-8.8	36-14	3.5-4	12.875	1	Int.	15.5	**665.00**
3-12x[3, 10]	3.3-11.7	34-9	3.5-4	14.25	1	Int.	21	**701.00**
4-16x[1, 3, 5, 6, 8, 10]	4.3-15.7	33-9	3.5-4	15.4	1	Int.	23.7	**760.00**
6-24x[1, 3, 5, 6, 8, 10, 13]	6.6-23.8	17-6	3.5-4	16	1	Int.	22.7	**787.00**
8-32x[8,10,12]	8.6-31.4	13-3.8	3.5-4	17	1	Int.	24	**840.00**
Speeddot 135[14]								
Red Dot	1			4.85	35mm	Int.	5	**291.00**
Handgun								
1.50-4x LER[1, 5, 10]	1.6-3	16-11	11-25	10.25	1	Int.	11	**411.00**
2-7x LER[3, 4, 5, 10]	2-6.5	21-7	7-27	9.5	1	Int.	12.6	**458.00**
2x LER[4, 5, 6]	1.7	21	10-24	8.75	1	Int.	6.8	**286.00**
4x LER[1, 4, 5, 6, 10]	3.7	11	10-22	9.625	1	Int.	9	**338.00**
3x12x LER[1, 4, 6]	9.5	4	8-12	13.5	1	Int.	14	**558.00**
Scout Scope								
1xXER[3,9]	1.5	32	4-24	9	1	Int.	7.0	**320.00**
2.75x[3,9]	2.7	15	7-14	9.375	1	Int.	7.0	**356.00**

Other Data

Black Diamond & Fullfield: All scopes avail. with Plex reticle. Steel-on-steel click adjustments. [1]Dot reticle on some models. [2]Post crosshair reticle extra. [3]Matte satin finish. [4]Available with parallax adjustment (standard on 10x, 12x, 4-12x, 6-12x, 6-18x, 6x HBR and 3-12x Signature). [5]Silver matte finish extra. [6]Target knobs extra, standard on silhouette models. LER and XER with P.A., 6x HBR. [7]Sunshade avail. [8]Avail. with Fine Plex reticle. [9]Available with Heavy Plex reticle. [10]Available with Posi-Lock. [11]Available with Peep Plex reticle. [12]Also avail. for rimfires, airguns. [13]Selected models available with camo finish.
Signature Series: LER=Long Eye Relief; IER=Intermediate Eye Relief; XER=Extra Eye Relief.
Speeddot 135: [14]Waterproof, fogproof, coated lenses, 11 bright ness set tings; 3-MOA or 11-MOA dot size; includes Weaver-style rings and battery. **Partial listing shown.** Contact Burris for complete details.

Plex — Fine Plex — Peep Plex

Target Dot — Heavy Plex & Electro-Dot Plex

Ballistic Mil-Dot — Mil-Dot

BUSHNELL (Bausch & Lomb Elite rifle scopes sold under Bushnell brand)

Maker and Model	Magn.	Field at 100 Yds. (feet)	Eye Relief (in.)	Length (in.)	Tube Dia. (in.)	W & E Adjustments	Weight (ozs.)	Price
Elite 4200 RainGuard								
426244M[1]	6-24	18-6	3	16.9	1	Int.	20.2	**696.95**
422104G[2]	2.5-10	41.5-10.8	3	13.5	1	Int.	16	**579.95**
422152	2.5-10	40.3-10.8	3.3	14.3	1	Int.	18	**766.95**
424164M	4-16	26-7	3.5	18.6	1	Int.	18.6	**614.95**
424165M	4-16	26-7	3	15.6	1	Int.	22	**794.95**
428324M	8-32	14-3.75	3.3	18	1	Int.	22	**766.95**
Elite 3200 RainGuard								
325155M	5-15	21-7	3	15.9	1	Int.	19	**486.95**
324124A[1]	4-12	26.9-9	3	13.2	1	Int.	15	**426.95**
321040M	10	11	3.5	11.7	1	Int.	15.5	**290.95**
323940G[2]	3-9	33.8-11.5	3	12.6	1	Int.	13	**279.95**
322732M	2-7	44.6-12.7	3	11.6	1	Int.	12	**276.95**
3239544G[3]	3-9	31.5-10.5	3	15.7	1	Int.	19	**348.95**
Elite 3200 Handgun RainGuard								
322632M7	2-6	10-4	20	9	1	Int.	10	**404.95**
322636	2-6	10-4	20	9	1	Int.	10	**448.95**
Holosight								
510021	1x	Unlimited	6"/10'	4.1	NA	Int.	6.4	**450.95**
530021	1x	Unlimited	Unlimited	6	NA	Int.	12	**350.95**
530027	1x	Unlimited	Unlimited	6	NA	Int.	12	**370.95**
Legend								
752732M	2-7	56-16	3.5	11.6	1	Int.	11.6	**194.95**
753940M	3-9	36-13	3.5	13.1	1	Int.	14.6	**215.95**
753950M	3-9	36-13	3.5	13.1	1	Int.	16	**236.95**
754124M	4-12	30.9-10.1	3.5	14.4	1	Int.	17.3	**275.95**
755154M	5-15	23.8	3.5	14.6	1	Int.	17.7	**287.95**
Trophy								
730134	1-2.8	68	Unlimited	5.5	1	Int.	6	**124.95**
731500[1]	1.75-5	68-23	3.5	10.8	1	Int.	12.3	**161.95**
734124[1]	4-12	32-11	3	12.5	1	Int.	16.1	**273.95**
733940[2]	3-9	42-14	3	11.7	1	Int.	13.2	**139.95**
736184	6-18	17.3-6	3	14.8	1	Int.	17.9	**343.95**

(Bushnell)
[1]Wide Angle. [2]Also silver finish.

(Bushnell Elite)
[1]Adj. objective, sunshade; with 1/4-MOA dot or Mil Dot reticle. [2]Also in matte and silver finish. [3]50mm objective; also in matte finish. [4]Also in silver finish. **Partial listings shown. Contact Bushnell Performance Optics for details.**

Maker and Model	Magn.	Field at 100 Yds. (feet)	Eye Relief (in.)	Length (in.)	Tube Dia. (in.)	W & E Adjustments	Weight (ozs.)	Price	Other Data
BUSHNELL *(cont.)*									
Turkey & Brush									
731421	1.75-4	73-30	3.5	10.8	32mm	Int.	10.9	**155.95**	
Trophy Handgun									Multi-X Circle-X
732632	2-6	21-7	9-26	9.1	1	Int.	10.9	**260.95**	
Banner									
711545	1.5-4.5	67-23	3.5	10.5	1	Int.	10.5	**105.95**	
713944	3-9	36-13	4	11.5	1	Int.	12.5	**113.95**	
713950	3-9	26-10	3	16	1	Int.	19	**169.95**	
714124	4-12	29-11	3	12	1	Int.	15	**142.95**	Mil-Dot 3-2-1 Low-Light
716185	6-18	17-6	3	16	1	Int.	18	**190.95**	
Sportsman									
720038	3-9	37-14	3.5	12	1	Int.	6	**92.95**	
720039	3-9	38-13	3.5	10.75	1	Int.	11.2	**105.95**	
720412[4]	4-12	27-9	3.2	13.1	1	Int.	14.6	**128.95**	
721393	3-9	35-12	3.5	11.75	1	Int.	10	**62.95**	
721548	1.5-4.5	71-25	3.5	10.4	1	Int.	11.8	**99.95**	¼ M.O.A. European
721403	4	29	4	11.75	1	Int.	9.2	**51.80**	
723940M	3-9	42-14	3	12.7	1	Int.	12.5	**86.95**	
22 Rimfire									
762239	3-9	40-13	3	11.75	1	Int.	11.2	**55.95**	
762243	4	30	3	11.5	1	Int.	10	**47.95**	
EUROPTIK SUPREME									
4x36K	4	39	3.5	11.6	26mm	Int.	14	**795.00**	[1]Military scope with adjustable parallax. Fixed powers have 26mm tubes, variables have 30mm tubes. Some models avail. with steel tubes. All lenses multi-coated. Dust and water tight. From Europtik.
6x42K	6	21	3.5	13	26mm	Int.	15	**875.00**	
8x56K	8	18	3.5	14.4	26mm	Int.	20	**925.00**	
1.5-6x42K	1.5-6	61.7-23	3.5	12.6	30mm	Int.	17	**1,095.00**	
2-8x42K	2-8	52-17	3.5	13.3	30mm	Int.	17	**1,150.00**	
2.5-10x56K	2.5-10	40-13.6	3.5	15	30mm	Int.	21	**1,295.00**	
3-12x56 Super	3-12	10.8-34.7	3.5-2.5	15.2	30mm	Int.	24	**1,495.00**	
4-16x56 Super	4-16	9.8-3.9	3.1	18	30mm	Int.	26	**1,575.00**	
3-9x40 Micro	3-9	3.2-12.1	2.7	13	1	Int.	14	**1,450.00**	
2.5-10x46 Micro	2.5-10	13.7-33.4	2.7	14	30mm	Int.	20	**1,395.00**	
4-16x56 EDP[1]	4-16	22.3-7.5	3.1	18	30mm	Int.	29	**1,995.00**	
7-12x50 Target	7-12	8.8-5.5	3.5	15	30mm	Int.	21	**1,495.00**	
JAEGER									
ST-10		10, 17	Varies	13	30mm, 35mm		34	**895.00**	All scopes available w/standard and extra-long eye relief eyepiece. Variable power military and police tactical scope systems are also available. Offers scope rings and bases. By U.S.O. Jaeger.
SN-1 Long Range		17, 22, 42	12.35 (10x)	Varies	30mm, 35mm, 40mm		36	**2,395.00**	
SN6 2d Perimeter		10, 17, 22	12.35 (10x)	Varies	30mm, 35mm, 40mm		34	**1,295.00**	
SN-9 Extreme Range		22, 42	6.2 (22x)	Varies			62.4	**2,600.00**	
SN-12 CQB		3, 4	38 (3x)	7.5	1		34	**865.00**	
USMC 10x Sniper		10	10.36	12.5	1		34	**2,500.00**	
USMC M40A3		10	10.36	12.5	1		34	**NA**	
JH-4 Safari		1-4	119-34	9.25	30mm		31	**1,195.00**	
JH-3 Denali		1.8-10x	48.7-12.35	13	30mm		32	**1,695.00**	
JH-3 Serengeti		3.2-17x		14.5	30mm		33	**1,895.00**	
JH-T-PAL Chucker		3.8-22x	30-6.2	17.5	30mm		34	**1,995.00**	
KAHLES									
C-1 Series									
C1-4	1-1.4	108-31.8	3.55	10.83	30mm	Int.	14.6	**943.33**	Aluminum tube. Multi-coated, waterproof. Imported from Austria by Swarovski Optik.
C5-6x42	1.5-6	72-21.3	3.55	12.01	30mm	Int.	16.4	**1,043.33**	
C2.5-10	2.5-10	43.5-12.9	3.55	12.8	30mm	Int.	17.3	**1,187.76**	
C3-12	3-12	37.5-10.8	3.55	13.98	30mm	Int.	19.4	**1,332.22**	
American Hunter Riflescopes									
2-7x36	2-7	48-27.3	3.35	11.06	1	Int.	12.2	**621.11**	
3-9	3-9	39-14.5	3.35	12.09	1	Int.	13.1	**732.22**	
Compact Fixed Power									
4x36	4	34.5	3.15	11.22	1	Int.	12.7	**665.56**	
6x42	6	23.4	3.15	12.4	1	Int.	14.5	**854.44**	
Compact 30mm Riflescopesw/Illuminated Reticle									
CSX 1-4x24	1.1-4	110.94-31.78	3.55	11.04	30mm	Int.	15.4	**1,630.00**	
CSX 1-6x42	1.5-6	74.96-21.29	3.55	12.2	30mm	Int.	17.15	**1,808.00**	
CSX 2.5-10x50	2.5-10	43.5-12.9	3.55	12.8	30mm	Int.	18.3	**1,963.00**	

Maker and Model	Magn.	Field at 100 Yds. (feet)	Eye Relief (in.)	Length (in.)	Tube Dia. (in.)	W & E Adjustments	Weight (ozs.)	Price	Other Data
KAHLES *(cont.)*									
Compact 30mm Riflescopes, Illuminated Reticle									
CBX 2.5-10x50	2.5-10'	43.5-12.9	3.55	12.8	30mm	Int.	17.3	**1,832.00**	
CBX 3-12x56	3-12	37.5-10.8	3.55	13.98	30mm	Int.	19.4	**1,921.00**	
CL 1" Riflescopes									
CL3-9x42	3-9	39-15	3.60	12.09	1	Int.	14.46	**887.78**	
CL3-10	3-10	34-12	3.60	12.59	1	Int.	16.4	**1,108.00**	
CL4-12	4-12	29-10	3.60	12.59	1	Int.	18.34	**1,153.29**	
CL 1" Riflescopes with Multizero									
CL3-9x42	3-9	39-15	3.60	12.09	1	Int.	14.99	**1,242.67**	
CL3-10x50	3-10	34-12	3.60	12.59	1	Int.	16.93	**1,275.00**	
CL4-12x52	4-12	29-10	3.60	12.59	1	Int.	18.87	**1,353.67**	
LEATHERWOOD									
Uni-Dial (1" & 30mm Main Tube)									
UD2510x44MD	2.5-10	47.2-11.9	3	13.2	1, 30mm	Int.	15.3	**299.00**	All air-glass surfaces are fully multi-coated to maximize light transmission.
UD312x50MD	3-12	40.3-10.2	3	13.6	1, 30mm	Int.	25.6	**367.00**	
UD416X50MD	4-16	24.1-6.3	3.25	14.1	1, 30mm	Int.	26.8	**385.00**	
UD730X50MD	7-30	10.6-3.5	3.3	17.2	1, 30mm	Int.	29.7	**475.00**	
UD2510X44MD	2.5-10	47.2-11.9	3	13.2	1, 30mm	Int.	15.3	**299.00**	
Top Angle Professional Series (30mm Main Tube)									
TP312X50MD	3-12	40.3-10.2	3	13.6	30mm	Int.	25.6	**299.00**	
TP416X50MD	4-16	24.1-6.3	3.25	14.1	30mm	Int.	26.5	**349.00**	
TP624X50MD	6-24	12-4	3.25	15.5	30mm	Int.	27	**399.00**	
TP730X50MD	7-30	10.6-3.5	3.3	17.2	30mm	Int.	29.8	**449.00**	
TP832X56MDIR	8-32	7.6-1.8	3.3	17.6	30mm	Int.	30.2	**549.00**	
Professional Series (30mm Main Tube)									
PR156X42	1.5-6	63.1-15.7	3	11.8	30mm	Int.	17.7	**199.00**	
PR2510X44MD	2.5-10	47.2-11.9	3	13.2	30mm	Int.	18.1	**239.00**	
PR312X44MD	3-12	40.3-10.2	3	13.6	30mm	Int.	25.6	**259.00**	
PR416X44MD	4-16	24.1-6.3	3.25	14.1	30mm	Int.	26.5	**319.00**	
Buck Country Series (1" Main Tube)									
BC156X42	1.5-6	63.1-15.7	3	11.8	1	Int.	14.5	**129.00**	
BC39X40IR	3-9	37.7-12.6	3.25	12.5	1	Int.	16.8	**149.00**	
BC39X50	3-9	38-12.7	3.25	12.7	1	Int.	17.3	**159.00**	
BC39X50IR	3-9	38-12.7	3.25	12.7	1	Int.	17.8	**169.00**	
Toby Bridges Expedition Muzzleloader Scope Series (1" Main Tube)									
TB-ML39X40	3-9	37.7-12.6	3.25	12.5	1	Int.	15.8	**179.00**	
Leatherwood Camputer A.R.T. Tactical Scope									
ART2510X44	2.5-10	47.2-11.9	3	13.2	1	Int.	25.2	**459.00**	
ART624X50	6-24	12-4	3.25	15.5	1	Int.	27	**599.00**	
Long Eye Relief Series (1" Main Tube)									
LER156X32	1.5-6	19.3-6.4	12.6-8.8	11.02	1	Int.	12.1	**185.00**	
LER27x32	2-7	18.8-6.3	13.2-8.7	10.9	1	Int.	12.3	**187.00**	
Red Dot Series									
ES1X25	1	40	Unlimited	4.49		Int.	3.6	**65.00**	
ES1X30TP	1	68	Unlimited	3.86		Int.	6.4	**78.00**	
ES1X50TP	1	88	Unlimited	3.86		Int.	8.5	**95.50**	
Wm. Malcolm Scope Series									
M634321	6X	10	4	30.5	¾	Int.	32.5	**439.00**	
M334151	3X	15	4.5	17	¾	Int.	17.5	**299.00**	
LEICA									
Ultravid 1.75-6x32	1.75-6	47-18	4.8-3.7	11.25	30mm	Int.	14	**749.00**	Aluminum tube with hard anodized matte black finish with titanium accents; finger-adjustable windage and elevation with 1/4-MOA clicks. Made in U.S. From Leica.
Ultravid 3.5-10x42	3.5-10	29.5-10.7	4.6-3.6	12.62	30mm	Int.	16	**849.00**	
Ultravid 4.5-14x42	4.5-14	20.5-7.4	5-3.7	12.28	30mm	Int.	18	**949.00**	

Leicaplex Standard — Leica Dot — Standard Dot — Crosshair — Euro — Post & Plex

Maker and Model	Magn.	Field at 100 Yds. (feet)	Eye Relief (in.)	Length (in.)	Tube Dia. (in.)	W & E Adjustments	Weight (ozs.)	Price	Other Data
LEUPOLD									
M8-3.5x10	3.2-9.5	29.9	4.7	13.5	30mm	Int.	19.5	**1,124.99**	Constantly centered reticles, choice of Duplex, tapered CPC, Leupold Dot, Crosshair and Dot. CPC and Dot reticles extra. [1]3x9 Compact, 6x Compact, 12x, 3x9, and 6.5x20 come with adjustable objective. Sunshade available for all adjustable objective scopes, **$23.20-$41.10.** Partial listing shown. **Contact Leupold for complete details.**
M8-2.7-28	2.66	41	3.8	9.9	1	Int.	8.2	**299.99**	
M8-4X Compact RF	3.6	25.5	4.5	9.2	1	Int.	7.5	**289.99**	
Vari-X 2-7x	2.5-6.5	41.7-17.3	4.2	10.8	1	Int.	10	**299.99**	
Vari-X 3-9x	3.3-8.5	32-13.1	4.2	12.2	1	Int.	12	**314.99**	
M8-4X	4	24	4	10.5	1	Int.	9.3	**249.99**	

Maker and Model	Magn.	Field at 100 Yds. (feet)	Eye Relief (in.)	Length (in.)	Tube Dia. (in.)	W & E Adjustments	Weight (ozs.)	Price	Other Data
LEUPOLD *(cont.)*									
M8-6x36mm	5.9	17.7	4.3	11.3	1	Int.	10	**469.99**	Duplex; CPC; Post & Duplex; Leupold Dot; Dot
M8-6x42mm	6	17	4.5	11.9	1	Int.	11.3	**424.99**	
M8-12x40	11.6	9.1	4.2	13	1	Int.	13.5	**474.99**	
Vari-X 3-9x	3.5-8.6	32.9-13.1	4-2	12.2	1	Int.	12	**454.99**	
Vari-X-III 1.5-5x20	1.5-4.5	65-17	4.4-3.6	9.4	1	Int.	9.7	**499.99**	
Vari-X-III 1.75-6x32	1.9-5.6	51	4.4-3.2	11.4	1	Int.	11.6	**499.99**	
Vari-X-III 2.5x8	2.6-7.8	37-13.5	4.4-3.5	11.4	1	Int.	11.6	**499.99**	
Vari-X-III 3.5-10x40	3.9-9.6	29.7-11	4.4-3.5	12.6	1	Int.	13	**549.99**	
Vari-X-III 3.5-10x50	3.3-9.5	29.8-11	4.4-3.5	12.2	1	Int.	15.1	**624.99**	
Vari-X-III 4.5-14x40	4.8-14.2	19.9	4.4-3.6	12.6	1	Int.	13.2	**699.99**	
Vari-X-III 4.5-14x50	4.9-14.4	19.1	4.4-3.6	12.6	1	Int.	16	**789.99**	
Vari-X III 4.5-14x50 LRT	4.9-14.3	19-6	5-3.7	12.1	30mm	Int.	17.5	**999.00**	
Vari-X-III 6.5-20 A.O.	6.5-19.2	14.3-5.6	5-3.6	14.3	1	Int.	16	**749.99**	
Vari-X III 6.5-20xLRT	6.5-19.2	14.3-5.5	4.4	14.2	1	Int.	21	**974.99**	
Vari-X III 8.5-25x40 LRT	8.3-24.3	11.3-4.3	5.2	14.3	1	Int.	21	**1,039.99**	
Vari-X III 8.5-25x 50 LRT	8.3-24.3	11.3-4.3	5.2-7	14.4	30mm	Int.	21	**1,149.99**	
Mark 4 M1-10x40	10	11.1	3.6	13.125	30mm	Int.	21	**1,124.99**	
Mark 4 M1-16x40	16	6.6	4.1	12.875	30mm	Int.	22	**1,509.99**	
Mark 4 M3-10x40LRT	10	13.1	3.4	13.125	30mm	Int.	21	**939.99**	
Mark 4 6.5x20[1]	6.5-19.5	14.3-5.5	5.5-3.8	11.2	30mm	Int.	16	**1,198.99**	
LPS 1.5-6x42	1.5-6	58.7-15.7	4	11.2	30mm	Int.	16	**1,198.99**	
LPS 2.5-10x45	2.6-9.8	37.2	4.5-3.8		1	Int.	17.2	**1,119.99**	
LPS 3.5-14x52	3.5-14	28-7.2	4	13.1	30mm	Int.	22	**1,249.99**	
Rimfire									
Vari-X 2-7x RF Special	3.6	25.5	4.5	9.2	1	Int.	7.5	**299.99**	
Shotgun									
M8 2.5x20	2.3	39.5	4.9	8.4	1	Int.	6	**249.99**	
LYMAN									
Super TargetSpot[1]	10, 12, 15, 20, 25, 30	5.5	2	24.3	.75	Int.	27.5	**685.00**	Made under license from Lyman to Lyman's orig. specs. Blue steel. Threepoint suspension rear mount with .25-min. click adj. Data listed for 20x model. [1]Price appx. Made in U.S. by Parsons Optical Mfg. Co.
McMILLAN									
Vision Master 2.5-10x	2.5-10	14.2-4.4	4.3-3.3	13.3	30mm	Int.	17	**1,250.00**	42mm obj. lens; .25-MOA clicks; nitrogen filled, fogproof, waterproof; etched duplex-type reticle. [1]Tactical Scope with external adj. knobs, military reticle; 60+ min. adj.
Vision Master Model 1[1]	2.5-10	14.2-4.4	4.3-3.3	13.3	30mm	Int.	17	**1,250.00**	
MEOPTA									
Artemis 2000 6x42	6	21	3.1	13.7	30mm	Int.	17.6	**NA**	Steel tubes are waterproof, dustproof, and shockproof; nitrogen filled. Anti-reflective coatings, protective rubber eye piece, clear caps. Made in Czech Replublic by Meopta.
R1 7x56RD	7	17.1	3.1	14.1	1	Int.	19/2	**NA**	
MEPROLIGHT									
Meprolight Reflex Sights 14-21 5.5 MOA 1x30[1]	1			4.4	30mm	Int.	5.2	**335.00**	[1]Also available with 4.2 MOA dot. Uses tritium and fiber-optics, no batteries required. From Hesco, Inc.
MILLETT									
Buck 3-9x44	3-9	38-14	3.25-4	13	1	Int.	16.2	**249.65**	13-MOA dot. 25-MOA dot. 33-, 5-, 8-, 10-MOA dots. 410-MOA dot. All have click adjustments; waterproof, shockproof; 11 dot intensity settings. All avail. in matte/black or silver finish. From Millett Sights.
Buck 3.5-10x50	3.5-10	NA	NA	NA	1	NA	NA	**270.65**	
Buck 3-12x44 A/O	3-12	NA	NA	NA	1	NA	NA	**270.65**	
Buck 4-16x44 A/O	4-16	NA	NA	NA	1	NA	NA	**290.00**	
Buck Varmint 4-16x56	4-16	NA	NA	NA	30mm	NA	NA	**380.00**	
Buck Varmint 6-25x56	6-25	NA	NA	NA	30mm	NA	NA	**405.00**	
Buck Varmint 6-25x56	6-25	NA	NA	NA	30mm	NA	NA	**431.00**	
Buck Lightning 1.5-6x44	1.5-6	NA	NA	NA	1	NA	NA	**323.00**	
Buck Lightning 3-9x44	3-9	NA	NA	NA	1	NA	NA	**323.00**	
Buck Silver 3-9x40	3-9	NA	NA	NA	1	NA	NA	**135.95**	
Buck Silver 4-12x40 A/O	4-12	NA	NA	NA	1	NA	NA	**170.00**	
Buck Silver 6-18x40 A/O	6-18	NA	NA	NA	1	NA	NA	**170.00**	
MultiDot SP[3]	1	50		4.8	30mm	Int.	5.3	**205.90**	
MIRADOR									
RXW 4x40[1]	4	37	3.8	12.4	1	Int.	12	**179.95**	[1]Wide angle scope. Multi-coated objective lens. Nitrogen filled; water proof; shockproof. From Mirador Optical Corp.
RXW 1.5-5x20[1]	1.5-5	46-17.4	4.3	11.1	1	Int.	10	**188.95**	
RXW 3-9x40	3-9	43-14.5	3.1	12.9	1	Int.	13.4	**251.95**	

Maker and Model	Magn.	Field at 100 Yds. (feet)	Eye Relief (in.)	Length (in.)	Tube Dia. (in.)	W & E Adjustments	Weight (ozs.)	Price	Other Data
NIGHTFORCE									
NXS 1-4X24	1.0-4	95-25	3.5	8.8	30mm		17	**1,215.00**	Lighted reticles with 11 intensity levels. Most scopes have choice of reticles. From Lightforce U.S.A. 11 custom reticles, illuminated reticles, 30mm tubes, Mil-Spec scratch resistant coatings. NXS models feature 1/4 MOA windage and elevation adjustments and incorporate a side focus/parallax adjustment except on the 1-4 and 2.5-10. Waterproof to 100 ft., function tested thermal stability from -80 F - +250 F. Recoil and impact tested at 1250 Gs for both positive and negative forces. BR models feature 1/8 MOA windage and elevation adjustment, adjustable objective for parallax correction.
NXS 2.5-10X24	2.5-10	44-11	3.7	9.9	30mm	Int.	17	**1,256.00**	
NXS 3.5-15X50	3.5-15	27.6-7.3	3.9	14.7	30mm	Int.	30	**1,411.00**	
NXS 3.5-15X56	3.5-15	27.6-7.3	3.8	14.8	30mm	Int.	31	**1,517.00**	
NXS 5.5-22X50	5.5-22	17.5-4.7	3.7	15.1	30mm	Int.	31	**1,528.00**	
NXS 5.5-22X56	5.5-22	17.5-4.7	3.9	15.2	30mm	Int.	32	**1,544.00**	
NXS 8-32X56	8.0-32	12.1-3.1	3.8	15.9	30mm	Int.	34	**1,675.00**	
NXS 12-42X56	12.0-42	8.2-2.4	3.8	16.1	30mm	Int.	34	**1,817.00**	
BR 8-32X56	8.0-32	9.4-3.1	2.9	16.6	30mm	Int.	36	**1,271.00**	
BR 12-42X56	12.0-42	6.7-2.3	2.9	17	30mm	Int.	36	**1,342.00**	
NIKON									
Buckmasters									
4x40	4	30.4	3.3	12.7	1	Int.	11.8	**159.95**	Super multi-coated lenses and blackening of all internal metal parts for maximum light gathering capability; positive .25-MOA; fogproof; waterproof; shockproof; luster and matte finish. [1]Also available in matte silver finish. [2]Available in silver matte finish. [3]Available with TurkeyPro or Nikoplex reticle. [4]Silver Shadow finish; black matte **$296.95**. Partial listing shown. From Nikon, Inc.
3-9x40[4]	3.3-8.6	33.8-11.3	3.5-3.4	12.7	1	Int.	13.4	**209.95**	
3-9x50	3.3-8.6	33.8-11.3	3.5-3.4	12.9	1	Int.	18.2	**299.95**	
4-12x50	4-12	24.3-8.0	3.7	13.9	1	Int.	20.6	**349.95**	
Monarch UCC									
4x40[2]	4	26.7	3.5	11.7	1	Int.	11.7	**229.95**	
1.5-4.5x20[3]	1.5-4.5	67.8-22.5	3.7-3.2	10.1	1	Int.	9.5	**239.95**	
2-7x32	2-7	46.7-13.7	3.9-3.3	11.3	1	Int.	11.3	**269.95**	
3-9x40[1]	3-9	33.8-11.3	3.6-3.2	12.5	1	Int.	12.5	**299.95**	
3.5-10x50	3.5-10	25.5-8.9	3.9-3.8	13.7	1	Int.	15.5	**439.95**	
4-12x40 A.O.	4-12	25.7-8.6	3.6-3.2	14	1	Int.	16.6	**369.95**	
6.5-20x44	6.5-19.4	16.2-5.4	3.5-3.1	14.8	1	Int.	19.6	**469.95**	
2x20 EER	2	22	26.4	8.1	1	Int.	6.3	**169.95**	
NORINCO									
N2520	2.5	44.1	4		1	Int.		**52.28**	Partial listing shown. Some with Ruby Lens coating, blue/black and matte finish. Imported by Nic Max, Inc.
N420	4	29.3	3.7		1	Int.		**52.70**	
N640	6	20	3.1		1	Int.		**67.88**	
N154520	1.5-4.5	63.9-23.6	4.1-3.2			Int.		**80.14**	
N251042	2.5-10	27-11	3.5-2.8		1	Int.		**206.60**	
N3956	3-9	35.1-6.3	3.7-2.6		1	Int.		**231.88**	
N31256	3-12	26-10	3.5-2.8		1	Int.		**290.92**	
NC2836M	2-8	50.8-14.8	3.6-2.7		1	Int.		**255.60**	
PARSONS									
Parsons Long Scope	6	10	2	28-34+	.75	Ext.	13	**475.00-525.00**	Adj. for parallax, focus. Micrometer rear mount with .25-min. click adjust ments. Price is approximate. Made in U.S. by Parsons Optical Mfg. Co.
PENTAX									
Lightseeker 1.75-6x[1]	1.75-6	71-20	3.5-4	10.8	1	Int.	13	**546.00**	[1]Glossy finish; Matte finish, Heavy Plex or Penta-Plex, **$546.00**. [2]Glossy finish; Matte finish, **$594.00**. [3]Glossy finish; Matte finish, **$628.00**; Heavy Plex, add **$20.00**. [4]Matte finish; Mil-Dot, **$798.00**. [5]Glossy finish; Matte finish, **$652.00**; Heavy Plex, add **$10.00**. [6]Glossy finish; Matte finish, **$816.00**; with Heavy Plex, **$830.00**; with Mil-Dot, **$978.00**. [7]Matte finish; with Mil-Dot, **$1,018.00**. [8]Matte finish, with Mil-Dot, **$1,098.00**. [9]Lightseeker II, Matte finish, **$844.00**. [10]Lightseeker II, Glossy finish, **$636.00**. [11]Lightseeker II, Matte finish, **$660.00**. [12]Lightseeker II, Matte finish, **$878.00**. [13]Matte finish; Advantage finish, Break-up Mossy Oak finish, Treestand Mossy Oak finish, **$364.00**. From Pentax Corp.
Lightseeker 2-8x[2]	2-8	53-17	3.5-4	11.7	1	Int.	14	**594.00**	
Lightseeker 3-9x[3, 4, 10, 11]	3-9	36-14	3.5-4	12.7	1	Int.	15	**594.00**	
Lightseeker 3.5-10x[5]	3.5-10	29.5-11	3.5-4	14	1	Int.	19.5	**630.00**	
Lightseeker 4-16x[6, 9]	4-16	33-9	3.5-4	15.4	1	Int.	22.7	**888.00**	
Lightseeker 6-24x[7, 12]	6-24	18-5.5	3.5-4	16	1	Int.	23.7	**1,028.00**	
Lightseeker 8.5-32x[8]	8.5-32	13-3.8	3.5-4	17.2	1	Int.	24	**968.00**	
Shotgun									
Lightseeker 2.5x[13]	2.5	55	3.5-4	10	1	Int.	9	**398.00**	
Lightseeker Zero-X SG Plus	0	51	4.5-15	8.9	1	Int.	7.9	**372.00**	
Lightseeker Zero-X/ V Still-Target	0-4	53.8-15	3.5-7	8.9	1	Int.	10.3	**476.00**	
Lightseeker Zero X/ V	0-4	53.8-15	3.5-7	8.9	1	Int.	10.3	**454.00**	

Heavy Plex **Fine Plex** **Penta-Plex** **Deepwoods Plex** **Comp-Plex** **Mil-dot**

Maker and Model	Magn.	Field at 100 Yds. (feet)	Eye Relief (in.)	Length (in.)	Tube Dia. (in.)	W & E Adjustments	Weight (ozs.)	Price	Other Data
RWS									
300	4	36	3.5	11.75	1	Int.	13.2	**170.00**	
450	3-9	43-14	3.5	12	1	Int.	14.3	**215.00**	

Maker and Model	Magn.	Field at 100 Yds. (feet)	Eye Relief (in.)	Length (in.)	Tube Dia. (in.)	W & E Adjustments	Weight (ozs.)	Price	Other Data
SCHMIDT & BENDER									All scopes have 30-yr. warranty, click adjustments, centered reticles, rotation indicators. [1]Glass reticle; aluminum. Available in aluminum with mounting rail. [2]Aluminum only. [3]Parallax adjustment in third turret; extremely fine crosshairs. [4]Available with illuminated reticle that glows red; third turret houses on/off switch, dimmer and battery. [5]4-16x50/Long Range. From Schmidt & Bender, Inc. Available with illuminated crosshairs and parallax adjustment.
Fixed									
4x36	4	30	3.25	11	1	Int.	14	**979.00**	
6x42	6	21	3.25	13	1	Int.	17	**1,069.00**	
8x56	8	16.5	3.25	14	1	Int.	22	**1,229.00**	
Variables									
2.5-10x56[1,4]	2.5-10	37.5-12	3.90	14	30mm	Int.	24.6	**1,659.00**	
3-12x42[2]	3-12	34.5-11.5	3.90	13.5	30mm	Int.	19	**2,059.00**	
3-12x50[1,4]	3-12	33.3-12.6	3.90	13.5	30mm	Int.	22.9	**2,059.00**	
4-16x50 Varmint[3,5]	4-16	22.5-7.5	3.90	14	30mm	Int.	26	**1,979.00**	
Police/Marksman II									
3-12x50LP	3-12	33.3-12.6	3.74	13.9	34mm	Int.	18.5	**2,849.00**	
SCHMIDT & BENDER ZENITH SERIES									
3-12x50	3-12	33.3-11.4	3.70	13.71	NA	NA	23.4	**1,795.00**	
2.5-10x56	2.5-10	39.6-12	3.70	14.81	NA	NA	24	**1,759.00**	
1.1-4x24	1.1-4	96/30	3.70	11.2	30mm	Int.	16	**1,439.00**	

No. 1 (fixed) **No. 1 variable** **No. 2** **No. 3** **No. 4** **No. 6** **No. 7** **No. 8** **No. 8 Dot** **No. 9**

Maker and Model	Magn.	Field at 100 Yds. (feet)	Eye Relief (in.)	Length (in.)	Tube Dia. (in.)	W & E Adjustments	Weight (ozs.)	Price	Other Data
SIGHTRON									
Variables									[1]Adjustable objective. [2]Satin black; also stainless. Electronic Red Dot scopes come with ring mount, front and rear extension tubes, polarizing filter, battery, haze filter caps, wrench. Rifle, pistol, shotgun scopes have aluminum tubes, Exac Trak adjustments. Lifetime warranty. From Sightron, Inc. [3]3" sun shade. [4]Mil-Dot or Plex reticle. [5]Dot or Plex reticle.
SII 1.56x42	1.5-6	50-15	3.8-4	11.69	1	Int.	15.35	**372.25**	
SII 2.58x42	2.5-8	36-12	3.6-4.2	11.89	1	Int.	12.82	**338.40**	
SII 39x42[2,4,5]	3-9	34-12	3.6-4.2	12.00	1	Int.	13.22	**356.22**	
SII 312x42[4]	3-12	32-9	3.6-4.2	11.89	1	Int.	12.99	**421.55**	
SII 3.510x42	3.5-10	32-11	3.6	11.89	1	Int.	13.16	**421.01**	
SII 4.514x42[1]	4.5-14	22-7.9	3.6	13.88	1	Int.	16.07	**481.14**	
Target									
SII 24x44	24	4.1	4.33	13.30	1	Int.	15.87	**441.82**	
SII 416x42[2,3,4,5]	4-16	26-7	3.6	13.62	1	Int.	16	**481.11**	
SII 624-42[2,3,5]	6-24	16-5	3.6	14.6	1	Int.	18.7	**562.96**	
Compact									
SII 4x32	4	25	4.5	9.69	1	Int.	9.34	**266.86**	
SII 2.5-10x32	2.5-10	41-10.5	3.75-3.5	10.9	1	Int.	10.39	**338.40**	
Shotgun									
SII 2.5x20SG	2.5	41	4.3	10.28	1	Int.	8.46	**266.88**	
Pistol									
SII 1x28P[4]	1	30	9-24	9.49	1	Int.	8.46	**314.79**	
SII 2x28P[4]	2	16-10	9-24	9.49	1	Int.	8.28	**314.79**	
SIMMONS									
22 Mag.									[1]Matte; also polished finish. [2]Silver; also black matte or polished. [3]Black matte finish. [4]Granite finish. [5]Camouflage. [6]Black polish. [7]With ring mounts. [8]Silver; black polish avail. [9]50mm obj.; black matte. [11]Black or silver matte. [10]75-yd. parallax; black or silver matte. [11]Octagon body; rings included; black matte or silver finish. [12]Black matte finish; also available in silver. [13]Smart reticle. [14]Target turrets. **Only selected models shown.** Contact Simmons Outdoor Corp. for complete details.
80102[2]	4	29.5	3	11.75			11	**49.99**	
80103[1]	4	23.5	3	7.25			8.25	**49.99**	
80103[7]	3-9	29.5	3.3	11.5			10	**59.99**	
Aetec									
2100[8]	2.8-10	44-14	5	11.9	1	Int.	15.5	**189.99**	
21041[6]	3.8-12	33-11	4	13.5	1	Int.	20	**199.99**	
44 Mag									
M-1044[3]	3-10	34-10.5	3	12.75	1	Int.	15.5	**149.99**	
M-1045[3]	4-12	29.5-9.5	3	13.2	1	Int.	18.25	**169.99**	
M-1047[3]	6.5-20	14-.5	2.6-3.4	12.8	1	Int.	19.5	**199.99**	
1048[3,14] (3)	6.5-20	16-5.5	2.6-3.4	14.5	1	Int.	20	**219.99**	
M-1050DM[3,13]	3.8-12	26-9	3	13.08	1	Int.	16.75	**189.99**	
8-Point									
4-12x40mm AO[3]	4-12	29-10	3-2 7/8	13.5	1	Int.	15.75	**99.99**	
4x32mm[3]	4	28.75	3	11.625	1	Int.	14.25	**34.99**	
3-9x32mm[3]	3-9	37.5-13	3-2 7/8	11.875	1	Int.	11.5	**39.99**	
3-9x40mm[12]	3-9	37-13	3-2 7/8	12.25	1	Int.	12.25	**49.99-79.99**	
3-9x50mm[3]	3-9	32-11.75	3-2 7/8	13	1	Int.	15.25	**79.99**	
Prohunter									
7700	2-7	53-16.25	3	11.5	1	Int.	12.5	**79.99**	
7710[2]	3-9	36-13	3	12.6	1	Int.	13.5	**89.99**	
7716	4-12	26-9	3	12.6	1	Int.	16.75	**129.99**	
7721	6-18	18.5-6	3	13.75	1	Int.	16	**144.99**	
7740[3]	6	21.75	3	12.5	1	Int.	12	**99.99**	

Maker and Model	Magn.	Field at 100 Yds. (feet)	Eye Relief (in.)	Length (in.)	Tube Dia. (in.)	W & E Adjustments	Weight (ozs.)	Price	Other Data
SIMMONS *(cont.)*									Truplex™ Smart ProDiamond® Crossbow
Prohunter Handgun									
7732[12]	2	22	9-17	8.75	1	Int.	7	**109.99**	
7738[12]	4	15	11.8-17.6	8.5	1	Int.	8	**129.99**	
82200	2-6							**159.99**	
Whitetail Classic									
WTC 11[4]	1.5-5	75-23	3.4-3.2	9.3	1	Int.	9.7	**184.99**	
WTC 12[4]	2.5-8	45-14	3.2-3	11.3	1	Int.	13	**199.99**	
WTC 13[4]	3.5-10	30-10.5	3.2-3	12.4	1	Int.	13.5	**209.99**	
WTC 15[4]	3.5-10	29.5-11.5	3.2	12.75	1	Int.	13.5	**289.99**	
WTC 45[4]	4.5-14	22.5-8.6	3.2	13.2	1	Int.	14	**265.99**	
Whitetail Expedition									
1.5-6x32mm[3]	1.5-6	72-19	3	11.16	1	Int.	15	**259.99**	
3-9x42mm[3]	3-9	40-13.5	3	13.2	1	Int.	17.5	**269.99**	
4-12x42mm[3]	4-12	29-9.6	3	13.46	1	Int.	21.25	**299.99**	
6-18x42mm[3]	6-18	18.3-6.5	3	15.35	1	Int.	22.5	**319.99**	
Pro50									
8800[9]	4-12	27-9	3.5	13.2	1	Int.	18.25	**179.99**	
8810[9]	6-18	17-5.8	3.6	13.2	1	Int.	18.25	**174.99**	
808825	3.5-10	32-8.75	3.5	3.25	1	Int.	14.5	**179.99**	
808830	2.5-10	39-12.2	2.75	12.75	1	Int.	15.9	**179.99**	
Shotgun									
2100[4]	4	16	5.5	8.8	1	Int.	9.1	**84.99**	
2100[5]	2.5	24	6	7.4	1	Int.	7	**59.99**	
7789D	2	31	5.5	8.8	1	Int.	8.75	**99.99**	
7790D	4	17	5.5	8.5	1	Int.	8.75	**114.99**	
7791D	1.5-5	76-23.5	3.4	9.5	1	Int.	10.75	**138.99**	
Blackpowder									
BP0420M[11]	4	19.5	4	7.5	1	Int.	8.3	**59.99**	
BP2732M[10]	2-7	57.7-16.6	3	11.6	1	Int.	12.4	**129.99**	
Red Dot									
5100421	1			4.8	30mm	Int.	4.7	**44.99**	
5111222	1			5.25	42mm	Int.	6	**49.99**	
Pro Air Gun									
21608 A.O.	4	25	3.5	12	1	Int.	11.3	**99.99**	
21613 A.O.	4-12	25-9	3.1-2.9	13.1	1	Int.	15.8	**179.99**	
21619 A.O.	6-18	18-7	2.9-2.7	13.8	1	Int.	18.2	**189.99**	
SPRINGFIELD ARMORY									
	6		3.5	13	1	Int.	14.7	**379.00**	[1]Range finding reticle with automatic bullet drop compensator for 223 match ammo to 700 yds. [2]Also avail. as 2nd Gen. with target knobs and adj. obj., **$549.00**; as 3rd Gen. with illuminated reticle, **$749.00**; as Mil-Dot model with illuminated Target Tracking reticle, target knobs, adj. obj., **$698.00**. [3]Unlimited range finding, target knobs, adj. obj., illuminated Target Tracking green reticle. All scopes have matte black finish, internal bubble level, 1/4-MOA clicks. From Springfield, Inc.
4-14x70 Tactical Government Model[1]	4-14		3.5	14.25	1	Int.	15.8	**395.00**	
4-14x56 1st Gen. Government Model[2]	4-14		3.5	14.75	30mm	Int.	23	**480.00**	
10x56 Mil-Dot Government Model[3]	10		3.5	14.75	30mm	Int.	28	**672.00**	
6-20x56 Mil-Dot Government Model	6-20		3.5	18.25	30mm	Int.	33	**899.00**	
SWAROVSKI OPTIK									TDS No. 4 No. 4A No. 7A Plex No. 24
PH Series									
1.25-4x24	1.25-4	98.4-31.2	3.15	10.63	30mm	Int.	16.2	**1,333.23**	
1.5-6x421	1.5-6	65.4-21	3.15	12.99	30mm	Int.	20.8	**1,483.34**	
2.5-10x42	2.5-10	39.6-12.6	3.15	13.23	30mm	Int.	19.8	**1,705.56**	
3-12x50	3-12	33-10.5	3.15	14.33	30mm	Int.	22.4	**1,727.78**	
4-16x50	4-16	30-8.5	3.15	14.22	30mm	Int.	22.3	**1,754.44**	
6-24x50	6-24	18.6-5.4	3.15	15.4	30mm	Int.	23.6	**1,976.67**	
AV Series									
3-9x36	3-9	39-13.5	3.35	11.8	1	Int.	11.7	**854.44**	
3-10x42AV	3-10	33-11.7	3.35	12.44	1	Int.	12.7	**943.33**	
4-12x50AV	4-12	29.1-9.9	3.35	13.5	1	Int.	13.9	**987.78**	
6-18x50	6-18	17.4-6.6	3.5	14.84	1	Int.	20.3	**1,065.56**	
SWIFT									
600 4x15	4	17	2.8	10.6	.75	Int.	3.5	**15.00**	All Swift scopes, with the exception of the 4x15, have Quadraplex reticles, are fogproof and waterproof. The 4x15 has crosshair reticle and is non-waterproof. [1]Available in regular matte black or silver finish. [2]Comes with ring mounts, wrench, lens caps, extension tubes, filter, battery. [3]Regular and matte black finish. [4]Speed Focus scopes. Partial listing shown. From Swift Instruments.
601 3-7x20	3-7	25-12	3-2.9	11	.75	Int.	5.6	**35.00**	
650 4x32	4	26	4	12	1	Int.	9.1	**75.00**	
653 4x40WA[1]	4	35	4	12.2	1	Int.	12.6	**125.00**	
654 3-9x32	3-9	35-12	3.4-2.9	12	1	Int.	9.8	**125.00**	
656 3-9x40WA[1]	3-9	40-14	3.4-2.8	12.6	1	Int.	12.3	**140.00**	

Maker and Model	Magn.	Field at 100 Yds. (feet)	Eye Relief (in.)	Length (in.)	Tube Dia. (in.)	W & E Adjustments	Weight (ozs.)	Price	Other Data
SWIFT *(cont.)*									
657 6x40	6	28	4	12.6	1	Int.	10.4	**125.00**	
658 2-7x40WA[3]	2-7	55-18	3.3-3	11.6	1	Int.	12.5	**160.00**	
659 3.5-10x44WA	3.5-10	34-12	3-2.8	12.8	1	Int.	13.5	**230.00**	
665 1.5-4.5x21	1.5-4.5	69-24.5	3.5-3	10.9	1	Int.	9.6	**125.00**	
665M 1.5-4.5x21	1.5-4.5	69-24.5	3.5-3	10.9	1	Int.	9.6	**125.00**	
666M Shotgun 1x20	1	113	3.2	7.5	1	Int.	9.6	**130.00**	
667 Fire-Fly[2]	1	40		5.4	30mm	Int.	5	**220.00**	
668M 4x32	4	25	4	10	1	Int.	8.9	**120.00**	
669M 6-18x44	6-18	18-6.5	2.8	14.5	1	Int.	17.6	**220.00**	
680M	3.9	43-14	4	18	40mm	Int.	17.5	**399.95**	
681M	1.5-6	56-13	4	11.8	40mm	Int.	17.5	**399.95**	
682M	4-12	33-11	4	15.4	50mm	Int.	21.7	**499.95**	
683M	2-7	55-17	3.3	11.6	32mm	Int.	10.6	**499.95**	
Premier Rifle Scopes									
648M[1] 1.5-4.5	32	71-25	3.05-3.27	10.41	1	Int.	12.7	**179.95**	
649R 4-12	50	29.5-9.5	3.3-3	13.8	1	Int.	15.8	**245.00**	
658M 2-7	40	55-18	3.3-3	11.6	1	Int.	12.5	**175.00**	
659S 3.5-10	44	34-12	3-2.8	12.8	1	Int.	13.5	**215.00**	
669M 6-18	44	18-6.5	2.8	14.5	1	Int.	17.6	**230.00**	
671M 3-9	50	35-25	3.24-3.12	15.5	1	Int.	18.2	**250.00**	
672M 6-18	50	19-6.7	3.25-3	15.8	1	Int.	20.9	**260.00**	
674M 3-9	40	40-14.2	3.6-2.9	12	1	Int.	13.1	**170.00**	
676S 4-12	40	29.3-10.5	3.15-2.9	12.4	1	Int.	15.4	**180.00**	
677M 6-24	50	18-5	3.1-3.2	15.9	1	Int.	20.8	**280.00**	
678M 8-32	50	13-3.5	3.13-2.94	16.9	1	Int.	21.5	**290.00**	
685M[3] 3-9	40	39-13.5	3.7-2.8	12.4	1	Int.	20.5	**189.95**	
686M[3] 6.5-20	44	19-6.5	2.7	15.6	1	Int.	23.6	**249.95**	
687M[2] 4.5-14	44	25.5-8.5	3.2	14.1	1	Int.	21.5	**220.00**	
688M[2] 6-18	44	19.597	2.8	15.4	1	Int.	22.6	**240.00**	
Standard Rifle Scopes									
587 4	32	25	3.1	11.7	1	Int.	13	**50.00**	
653M 4	40	35	4	12.2	1	Int.	12.6	**128.00**	
654M 3-9	32	35-12	3.4-2.9	12	1	Int.	9.8	**125.00**	
656 3-9	40	40-14	3.4-2.8	12.6	1	Int.	12.3	**140.00**	
657M 6	40	28	4	12.6	1	Int.	10.4	**125.00**	
660M[4] 2-6	32	14-4.5	20-12.6	5.5	1	Int.	10.6	**241.80**	
661M[4] 4	32	6.6	13.8	9.4	1	Int.	9.9	**130.00**	
663S[4] 4	32	9.8	7.3	7.2	1	Int.	8.5	**130.00**	
665M 1.5-4.5	21	69-24.5	3.5-3	10.8	1	Int.	9.6	**125.00**	
668M 4	32	25	4	10	1	Int.	8.9	**120.00**	
TASCO									
Target & Varmint									
VAR251042M	2.5-10	35.9	3	14	1	Int.	19.1	**89.95**	
MAG624X40	6-24	17-4	3	16	1	Int.	19.1	**113.95**	
VAR624X42M	6-24	13-3.7	7	16	1	Int.	19.6	**113.95**	
TG624X44DS	15-4.5	15-4.5	3	16.5	1	Int.	19.6	**199.95**	
World Class									
BA1545X32	1.5-4.5	77-23	4	11.25	1	Int.	12	**59.95**	
DWC39X40N	3-9	41-15	3.5	12.75	1	Int.	13	**73.95**	
WA39X40N	3-9	41-15	3.5	12.75	1	Int.	13	**73.95**	
WA39X40STN	3-9	41-15	3.5	12.75	1	Int.	13	**73.95**	
DWC39X50N	3-9	41-13	3	12.5	1	Int.	15.8	**87.95**	
DWC39X40M	3-9	41-15	3.5	12.75	1	Int.	13	**73.95**	
DWC416X40	4-16	22.5-5-9	3.7	14	1	Int.	16	**103.95**	
ProPoint									
PDP2	1	40	Un.	5	1	Int.	5.5	**117.95**	
PDP3	1	52	Un.	5	1	Int.	5.5	**137.95**	
PD3ST	1	52	Un.	5	1	Int.	5.5	**143.95**	
PDPRGD	1	60	Un.	5.4	1	Int.	5.7	**91.95**	
Golden Antler									
GA3940	3-9	41-15	3	12.75	1	Int.	13	**57.95**	
GA3932AGD	3-9	39	3	13.25	1	Int.	12	**43.95**	
Pronghhorn									
PH39X40D	3-9	39-13	3	13	1	Int.	12.1	**47.95**	
PH4X32D	4	32	3	12	1	Int.	11	**32.95**	
PH2533	2.5	43	3.2	11.4	1	Int.	10.1	**32.95**	
.22 Riflescopes									
MAG39X32D	3-9	17.75-6	3	12.75	1	Int.	11.3	**55.95**	

Maker and Model	Magn.	Field at 100 Yds. (feet)	Eye Relief (in.)	Length (in.)	Tube Dia. (in.)	W & E Adjustments	Weight (ozs.)	Price	Other Data
TASCO *(cont.)*									
Rimfire									
RF37X20D	3-7	24	2.5	11.5	1	Int.	5.7	**23.95**	
RF4X15D	4	20.5	2.5	11	1	Int.	3.8	**7.95**	
Red Dot									
BKR30	1	57	Un.	3.75	1	Int.	6	**45.95**	
BKR3022* (22 rimfire)	1	57	Un.	3.75	1	Int.	6	**45.95**	
BKR42	1	62	Un.	3.75	1	Int.	6.7	**57.95**	
THOMPSON/CENTER RECOIL PROOF SERIES									
Pistol Scopes									
8315[1]	2.5-7	15-5	8-21, 8-11	9.25	1	Int.	9.2	**364.00**	[1]Black; lighted reticle. From Thompson/Center Arms.
8326	2.5-7	15-5	8-21, 8-11	9.25	1	Int.	10.5	**432.00**	
Muzzleloader Scopes									
8658	1	60	3.8	9.125	1	Int.	10.2	**146.00**	
8662	4	16	3	8.8	1	Int.	9.1	**141.00**	
TRIJICON									
Reflex II 1x24	1			4.25		Int.	4.3	**400.00**	[1]Advanced Combat Optical Gunsight for AR-15, M16, with integral mount. Other mounts available. All models feature tritium and fiber optics dual-lighting system that requires no batteries. From Trijicon, Inc.
TA44 1.5x16[1]	1.5	39	2.4	5.34		Int.	5.31	**990.00**	
TA45 1.5x24[1]	1.5	25.6	3.6	5.76		Int.	5.92	**990.00**	
TA47 2x20[1]	2	29.5	2.1	5.3		Int.	5.82	**990.00**	
TA50 3x24[1]	3	25.6	1.4	5		Int.	5.89	**990.00**	
TA11 3.5x35[1]	3.5	28.9	2.4	8		Int.	14	**1,295.00**	
TA01 4x32[1]	4	36.8	1.5	5.8		Int.	9.9	**990.00**	
AccuPoint									
3-9x40 TR20	3-9	33.8-11.3	3.6-3.2	12.2	1	Int.	12.8	**750.00**	
1.25-4x24 TR21	1.25-4	61.6-20.5	4.8-3.4	10.2	1	Int.	11.4	**699.00**	
2.5-10x56 TR22	2.5-10	37.6-10.1	4.1-2.8	13.8	30mm	Int.	22.1	**950.00**	
ULTRA DOT									
Micro-Dot Scopes[1]									
1.5-4.5x20 Rifle	1.5-4.5	80-26	3	9.8	1	Int.	10.5	**297.00**	[1]Brightness-adjustable fiber optic red dot reticle. Waterproof, nitro gen-filled one-piece tube. Tinted see-through lens covers and battery included. [2]Parallax adjustable. [3]Ultra Dot sights include rings, battery, polarized filter, and 5-year warranty. All models available in black or satin finish. [4]Illuminated red dot has 11 brightness settings. Shock-proof aluminum tube. From Ultra Dot Distribution.
2-7x32	2-7	54-18	3	11	1	Int.	12.1	**308.00**	
3-9x40	3-9	40-14	3	12.2	1	Int.	13.3	**327.00**	
4x-12x56[2]	4-12	30-10	3	14.3	1	Int.	18.3	**417.00**	
Ultra-Dot Sights[3]									
Ultra-Dot 25[4]	1			5.1	1	Int.	3.9	**159.00**	
Ultra-Dot 30[4]	1			5.1	30mm	Int.	4	**179.00**	
UNERTL									
1" Target	6, 8, 10	16-10	2	21.5	.75	Ext.	21	**675.00**	[1]Dural .25-MOA click mounts. Hard coated lenses. Non-rotating objective lens focusing. [2].25-MOA click mounts. [3]With target mounts. [4]With calibrated head. [5]Same as 1" Target but without objective lens focusing. [6]Range focus unit near rear of tube. Price is with Posa or standard mounts. Magnum clamp. From Unertl.
10X	10	10.3	3	12.5	1	Ext.	35	**2,500.00**	
1.25" Target[1]	8, 10, 12, 14	12-16	2	25	.75	Ext.	21	**715.00**	
1.5" Target	10, 12, 14, 16, 18, 20	11.5-3.2	2.25	25.5	.75	Ext.	31	**753.50**	
2" Target[2]	10, 12, 14, 16, 18, 24, 30, 32, 36	8	2.25	26.25	1	Ext.	44	**918.50**	
Varmint, 1.25"[3] 3" Ultra Varmint, 2"[4]	15	12.6-7	2.25	24	1	Ext.	34	**918.50**	
Small Game[5]	3, 4, 6	25-17	2.25	18	.75	Ext.	16	**550.00**	
Programmer 200[6]	10, 12, 14, 16, 18, 20, 24, 30, 36	11.3-4		26.5	1	Ext.	45	**1,290.00**	
B8									
Tube Sight				17		Ext.		**420.00**	
U.S. OPTICS									
SN-3									
1.8-10x44mm	1.8-10	41.6-12.8	2.69	13.2	30mm	Int.	27.5	**1,545.00**	Prices shown are estimates; scopes built to order; choice of reticles; front focal plane (FFP); extra-heavy MIL-SPEC construction; individual W&E rebound springs; up to 80mm objective lenses; up to 40mm tube diameter; all lenses multi-coated. Modular components allow a variety of fixed or variable magnifications. Night Vision dealer. Made in U.S. by U.S. Optics.
3.2-17x44mm	3.2-17	25.3-8.3	2.66	15.7	30mm	Int.	31	**1,920.00**	
3.2-17x58mm	3.2-17	25.3-8.3	2.73	15.75	30mm	Int.	34	**1,920.00**	
3.8-22x44mm	3.8-22	21.6-6.6	2.69	17.9	30mm	Int.	36	**2,285.00**	
3.8x58mm	3.8-22	21.6-6.6	2.85	17.6	30mm	Int.	38	**2,285.00**	
SN-3 TPAL									
3.2-17x44mm	3.2-17	25.8-8.3	2.66	15.7	30mm	Int.	36	**2,120.00**	
5-25x58mm	56-25	16.6-5.3	2.68	17.9	30mm	Int.	40	**2,535.00**	
SN-4									
1-4x22mm	1-4	110-33	2.8	9.7	30mm	Int.	18	**1,115.00**	
1.5-6x28mm	1-4	64.6-25.3	2.82	10.7	30mm	Int.	20	**1,220.00**	

Maker and Model	Magn.	Field at 100 Yds. (feet)	Eye Relief (in.)	Length (in.)	Tube Dia. (in.)	W & E Adjustments	Weight (ozs.)	Price	Other Data
WEAVER									
Riflescopes									
K2.5[1]	2.5	35	3.7	9.5	1	Int.	7.3	**132.86**	[1]Gloss black. [2]Matte black. [3]Silver. [4]Satin. All scopes are shock-proof, waterproof, and fogproof. Dual-X reticle available in all except V24 which has a fine X-hair and dot; T-Series in which certain models are available in fine X-hair and dots; Qwik-Point red dot scopes which are available in fixed 4 or 12 MOA, or variable 4-8-12 MOA. V16 also available with fine X-hair, dot or Dual-X reticle. T-Series scopes have Micro-Trac® adjustments. From Weaver Products.
K4[1,2]	3.7	26.5	3.3	11.3	1	Int.	10	**149.99**	
K6[1]	5.7	18.5	3.3	11.4	1	Int.	10	**154.99**	
KT15[1]	14.6	7.5	3.2	12.9	1	Int.	14.7	**281.43**	
V3[1,2]	1.1-2.8	88-32	3.9-3.7	9.2	1	Int.	8.5	**189.99**	
V9[1,2]	2.8-8.7	33-11	3.5-3.4	12.1	1	Int.	11.1	**249.99-299.99**	
V9x50[1,2]	3-9	29.4-9.9	3.6-3	13.1	1	Int.	14.5	**239.99**	
V10[1-3]	2.2-9.6	38.5-9.5	3.4-3.3	12.2	1	Int.	11.2	**259.99-269.99**	
V10-50[1-3]	2.3-9.7	40.2-9.2	2.9-2.8	13.75	1	Int.	15.2	**279.99**	
V16 MDX[2,3]	3.8-15.5	26.8-6.8	3.1	13.9	1	Int.	16.5	**329.99**	
V16 MFC[2,3]	3.8-15.5	26.8-6.8	3.1	13.9	1	Int.	16.5	**329.99**	
V16 MDT[2,3]	3.8-15.5	26.8-6.8	3.1	13.9	1	Int.	16.5	**329.99**	
V24 Varmint[2]	6-24	15.3-4	3.15	14.3	1	Int.	17.5	**379.99-399.99**	
Handgun									
H2[1-3]	2	21	4-29	8.5	1	Int.	6.7	**161.43**	
H4[1-3]	4	18	11.5-18	8.5	1	Int.	6.7	**175.00**	
VH4[1-3]	1.5-4	13.6-5.8	11-17	8.6	1	Int.	8.1	**215.71**	
VH8[1-3]	2.5-8	8.5-3.7	12.16	9.3	1	Int.	8.3	**228.57**	
Rimfire									
RV7[2]	2.5-7	37-13	3.7-3.3	10.75	1	Int.	10.7	**148.57**	
Grand Slam									
6-20x40mm Varminter Reticle[2]	6-20X	16.5-5.25	2.75-3	14.48	1	Int.	17.75	**419.99**	
6-20x40mm Fine Crosshairs w/Dot[2]	6-20X	16.5-5.25	2.75-3	14.48	1	Int.	17.75	**419.99**	
1.5-5x32mm[2]	1.5-5X	71-21	3.25	10.5	1	Int.	10.5	**349.99**	
4.75x40mm[2]	4.75X	14.75	3.25	11	1	Int.	10.75	**299.99**	
3-10x40mm[2]	3-10X	35-11.33	3.5-3	12.08	1	Int.	12.08	**329.99**	
3.5-10x50mm[2]	3.5-10X	30.5-10.8	3.5-3	12.96	1	Int.	16.25	**389.99**	
4.5-14x40mm	4.5-14X	22.5-10.5	3.5-3	14.48	1	Int.	17.5	**399.99**	
T-Series									
T-64	614	14	3.58	12.75	1	Int.	14.9	**424.95**	
T-36[3-4]	36	3	3	15.1	1	Int.	16.7	**489.99**	
ZEISS									
ZM/Z									
6x42MC	6	22.9	3.2	12.7	1	Int.	13.4	**749.00**	**ZM/Z:** [1]Also avail. with illuminated reticle. All scopes have .25-min. click-stop adjustments. Choice of Z-Plex or fine crosshair reticles. Rubber armored objective bell, rubber eyepiece ring. Lenses have T-Star coating for highest light transmission. VM/V scopes avail. with rail mount. Partial listing shown. From Carl Zeiss Optical, Inc.
8x56MC	8	18	3.2	13.8	1	Int.	17.6	**829.00**	
1.25-4x24MC	1.25-4	105-33	3.2	11.46	30mm	Int.	17.3	**779.00**	
1.5-6x42MC	1.5-6	65.5-22.9	3.2	12.4	30mm	Int.	18.5	**899.00**	
2.5-10x48MC[1]	2.5-10	33-11.7	3.2	14.5	30mm	Int.	24	**1,029.00**	
3-12x56MC[1]	3-12	27.6-9.9	3.2	15.3	30mm	Int.	25.8	**1,099.00**	
Conquest									
3-9x40MC[3]	3-9	37.5	3.34	12.36	1	Int.	17.28	**499.99**	**Conquest:** [1]Stainless. [2]Turkey reticle. [3]Black matte finish. All scopes have .25-min. click-stop adjustments. Choice of Z-Plex, Turkey or fine crosshair reticles. Coated lenses for highest light transmission. Partial listing shown. From Carl Zeiss Optical, Inc.
3-9x40MC[1]	3-9	37.5	3.34	12.36	1	Int.	17.28	**529.99**	
3-9x40S[3]	3-9	37.5	3.34	12.36	1	Int.	17.28	**499.99**	
3-9x40S[2,3]	3-9	37.5	3.34	12.36	1	Int.	17.28	**529.99**	
3-12x56MC[3]	2.5-10	27.6	3.2	15.3	30mm	Int.	25.8	**1,049.00**	
3-12x56MC[1]	3-12	27.6	3.2	15.3	30mm	Int.	25.8	**1,079.00**	
VM/V									
1.1-4x24 VariPoint T	1.1-4	120-34	3.5	11.8	30mm	Int.	15.8	**1,699.00**	
1.5-6x42T	1.5-6	65.5-22.9	3.2	12.4	30mm	Int.	18.5	**1,299.00**	
2.5-10x50T	2.5-10	47.1-13	3.5	12.5	30mm	Int.	16.25	**1,499.00**	
3-12x56T	3-12	37.5-10.5	3.5	13.5	30mm	Int.	19.5	**1,499.00**	
3-9x42T	3-9	42-15	3.74	13.3	1	Int.	15.3	**1,999.00**	
5-15x42T	5-15	25.7-8.5	3.74	13.3	1	Int.	15.4	**1,399.00**	

Hunting scopes in general are furnished with a choice of reticlecrosshairs, post with crosshairs, tapered or blunt post, or dot crosshairs, etc. The great majority of target and varmint scopes have medium or fine crosshairs but post or dot reticles may be ordered. W=windage; E=Elevation; MOA=Minute of Angle or 1" (approx.) at 100 yards.

Kahles CSX1-1-4

Schmidt & Bender 3-12x50

Sightron SII 39x42

Alpec Mini Shot

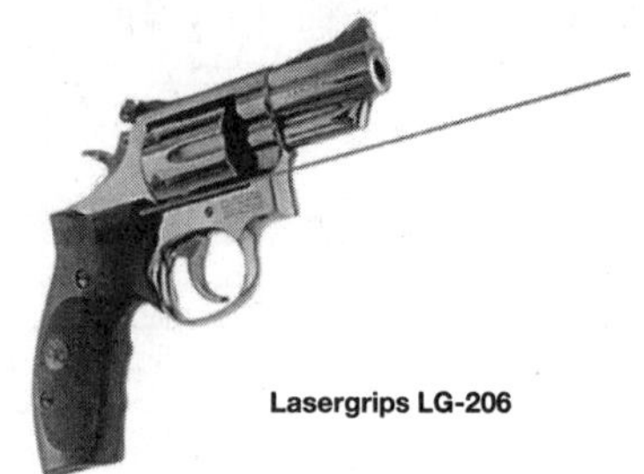
Lasergrips LG-206

Laser Devices ULS 2001 with TLS 8R light

Maker and Model	Wave length (nm)	Beam Color	Lens	Operating Temp. (degrees F.)	Weight (ozs.)	Price	Other Data
ALPEC							
Power Shot[1]	635	Red	Glass	NA	2.5	**$199.95**	[1]Range 1000 yards. [2]Range 300 yards. Mini Shot II range 500 yards, output 650mm, $129.95. [3]Range 300 yards; Laser Shot II 500 yards; Super Laser Shot 1000 yards. Black or stainless finish aluminum; removable pressure or push-button switch. Mounts for most hand guns, many rifles and shotguns. From Alpec Team, Inc.
Mini Shot[2]	670	Red	Glass	NA	2.5	**$99.95**	
Laser Shot[3]	670	Red	Glass	NA	3.0	**$99.95**	
BEAMSHOT							
GreenBeam 1000[1]	670	Green	Glass	NA	3.8	**$600.00**	[1]Black or silver finish; adj. for windage and elevation; 300-yd. range; also M1000/S (500-yd. range), M1000/u (800-yd.). From Quarton USA Co.
GreenBeam 2000	635/670	Red	Glass	NA	2.0	**$440.00**	
1001/u	635	Red	Glass	NA	3.8	**$110.00**	
780	780	Red	Glass	NA	3.8	**NA**	
BSA							
LS650[1]	N/A	Red	NA	NA	NA	**$49.95**	[1]Comes with mounts for 22/air rifle and Weaver-style bases.
LASERAIM							
LRS-0650-SSW	650	Red	Glass	NA	1.2	**$96.00**	[1]Laser projects 2" dot at 100 yds.: with rotary switch; with Hotdot **$237.00**; with Hotdot touch switch **$357.00**. [2]For Glock 17-27; G1 Hotdot **$299.00**; price installed. 10Fits std. Weaver base, no rings required; 6-MOA dot; seven brightness settings. All have W&E adj.; black or satin silver finish. From Laseraim Technologies, Inc.
LRS-0650-SCS	650	Red	Glass	NA	1.2	**$96.00**	
LRS-0650-CCW	650	Red	Glass	NA	1.2	**$96.00**	
LRS-0635-SSW	635	Red	Glass	NA	1.2	**$112.00**	
LRS-0635-SCS	635	Red	Glass	NA	1.2	**$112.00**	
LRS-0635-CCW	635	Red	Glass	NA	1.2	**$112.00**	
QDL-65GB-730	650	Red	Glass	NA	1.8	**$119.95**	
QDL-65SW-730	650	Red	Glass	NA	1.8	**$119.95**	
QDL-63GB-730	635	Red	Glass	NA	1.8	**$147.95**	
QDL-63SW-730	635	Red	Glass	NA	1.8	**$147.95**	
PLR-0006-140	650	Red	Glass	NA	1.8	**$78.95**	
PLW-0006-140	635	Red	Glass	NA	1.8	**$78.95**	
BLS-0650/0635-140	650/635	Red	Glass	NA	NA	**$78.95**	
Lasers							
MA-35RB Mini Aimer[1]				NA	1.0	**$129.00**	
G1 Laser[2]				NA	2.0	**$229.00**	
LASER DEVICES							
BA-1[1]	632	Red	Glass	NA	2.4	**$372.00**	[1]For S&W P99 semi-auto pistols; also BA-2, 5 oz., $339.00. [2]For revolvers. [3]For HK, Walther P99. [4]For semi-autos. [5]For rifles; also FA- 4/ULS, 2.5 oz. **$325.00**. [6]For HK sub guns. [7]For military rifles. [8]For shotguns. [9]For SIG-Pro pistol. [10]Universal, semi-autos. From Laser Devices, Inc.
BA-3[2]	632	Red	Glass	NA	3.3	**$332.50**	
BA-5[3]	632	Red	Glass	NA	3.2	**$372.00**	
Duty-Grade[4]	632	Red	Glass	NA	3.5	**$372.00**	
FA-4[5]	632	Red	Glass	NA	2.6	**$358.00**	
LasTac[1]	632	Red	Glass	NA	5.5	**$298.00 to 477.00**	
MP-5[6]	632	Red	Glass	NA	2.2	**$495.00**	
MR-2[7]	632	Red	Glass	NA	6.3	**$485.00**	
SA-2[8]	632	Red	Glass	NA	3.0	**$360.00**	
SIG-Pro[9]	632	Red	Glass	NA	2.6	**$372.00**	
ULS-2001[10]	632	Red	Glass	NA	4.5	**$210.95**	
Universal AR-2A	632	Red	Glass	NA	4.5	**$445.00**	
LASERGRIPS							
LG-301/401/401-P1[1]	633	Red-Orange	Glass	NA		**$299.00**	Replaces existing grips with built-in laser high in the right grip panel. Integrated pressure sensi tive pad in grip activates the laser. Also has master on/off switch. [1]For Colt 1911/Commander. [2]For all Glock models. Option on/off switch. Requires factory installation. [3]For S&W K, L, N frames, round or square butt (LG-207); [4]For Taurus small-frame revolvers. [5]For Ruger SP-101. [6]For SIG Sauer P226. From Crimson Trace Corp. [7]For Beretta 92/96. [8]For Ruger MK II. [9]For S&W J-frame. [10]For Sig Sauer P228/229. [11]For Colt 1911 full size, wraparound. [12]For Beretta 92/96, wraparound. [13]For Colt 1911 compact, wraparound. [14]For S&W J-frame, rubber.
LG-304/404/404-P1[2]	633	Red-Orange	Glass	NA		**$229.00**	
LG-302/312[3]	633	Red-Orange	Glass	NA		**$229.00**	
LG-617[4]	633	Red-Orange	Glass	NA		**$229.00**	
LG-619[5]	633	Red-Orange	Glass	NA		**$229.00**	
LG-626[6]	633	Red-Orange	Glass	NA		**$595.00**	

Lasermax Glock 23 Lasers

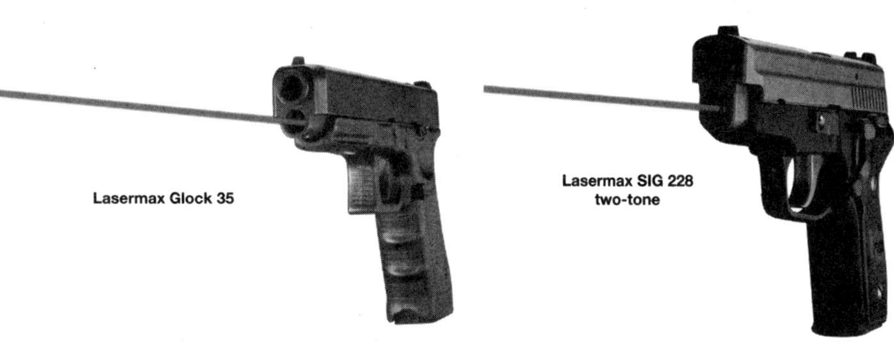

Lasermax Glock 35

Lasermax SIG 228 two-tone

Maker and Model	Wave length (nm)	Beam Color	Lens	Operating Temp. (degrees F.)	Weight (ozs.)	Price	Other Data
LG-629[7]	633	Red-Orange	Glass	NA		$299.00	
LG-203[8]	633	Red-Orange	Glass	NA		$299.00	
LG-389[9]	633	Red-Orange	Glass	NA		$299.00	
LG-320[10]	633	Red-Orange	Glass	NA		$299.00	
LG-326[11]	633	Red-Orange	Glass	NA		$329.00	
LG-329[12]	633	Red-Orange	Glass	NA		$329.00	
LG-359[13]	633	Red-Orange	Glass	NA		$329.00	
LG-101[14]	633	Red-Orange	Glass	NA		$299.00	
LASERLYTE							
LLX-0006-140/090[1]	635/645	Red		NA	1.4	$159.95	[1]Dot/circle or dot/crosshair projection; black or stainless. [2]Also 635/645mm model. From Tac Star Laserlyte. in grip activates the laser. Also has master on/off switch.
WPL-0004-140/090[2]	670	Red		NA	1.2	$109.95	
TPL-0004-140/090[2]	670	Red		NA	1.2	$109.95	
T7S-0004-140[2]	670	Red		NA	0.8	$109.95	
LASERMAX							
LMS-1131P[1]	635	Red-Orange	Glass	15° F - 120° F	.6	$339.00	Internal Laser Sights: Replace the recoil spring/guide rod assembly and include a customized takedown lever that serves as the laser on/off switch. For Glock, Sigarms, Beretta, Springfield and 1911 Gov't models and more. Easy installation - no gunsmithing necessary. Laser/Tactical Lights: LaserMax's distinctive pulsing beam combines with a 60 Lumen Tactical Light in the integrated LMS-1202 shotgun unit. Compatability: [1]Glock 19, 23, 32, 38 [2]Glock 17, 22, 31, 37 [3]Glock 34, 35, 17L, 24, 37L [4]Glock 20, 21 [5]Glock 20, 21 FG/R [6]Glock 26, 27, 33 [7]Glock 39 [8]Glock 36 [9]Glock 29, 30 [10]SIG P220, .45 ACP [11]SIG P225 [12]SIG P226, 9mm [13]SIG P226, 9mm* [14]SIG P226 .357/.40 [15]SIG P228 [16]SIG P229 [17]SIG P239, .357, .40 [18]SIG P245 [19]1911 Gov't, matte [20]1911 Gov't, stainless [21]1911 Gov't, blued [22]Para 1911, matte [23]Para 1911, stainless [24]Para 1911, blued [25]Springfield XD, 3" [26]Springfield XD, 4", 9mm, .357 [27]Springfield XD, 4", .40 [28]Springfield XD, 5" [29]Beretta 92/96 Centurion [30]Beretta 92/96 full-size [31]S&W 5906-type, stainless [32]S&W, full-size [33]Remington 870, 1100, 11-87; Benelli M1014 12-gauge semi-auto combat shotgun
LMS-1141P[2]	635	Red-Orange	Glass	15° F - 120° F	.6	$339.00	
LMS-1141LP[3]	635	Red-Orange	Glass	15° F - 120° F	.6	$339.00	
LMS-1151P[4]	635	Red-Orange	Glass	15° F - 120° F	.6	$339.00	
LMS-1151PFGR[5]	635	Red-Orange	Glass	15° F - 120° F	.6	$339.00	
LMS-1161[6]	635	Red-Orange	Glass	15° F - 120° F	.6	$339.00	
LMS-1171[7]	635	Red-Orange	Glass	15° F - 120° F	.6	$339.00	
LMS-1181[8]	635	Red-Orange	Glass	15° F - 120° F	.6	$339.00	
LMS-1191[9]	635	Red-Orange	Glass	15° F - 120° F	.6	$339.00	
LMS-2201[10]	635	Red-Orange	Glass	15° F - 120° F	.6	$399.00	
LMS-2251[11]	635	Red-Orange	Glass	15° F - 120° F	.6	$399.00	
LMS-2261[12]	635	Red-Orange	Glass	15° F - 120° F	.6	$399.00	
LMS-2261S[13]	635	Red-Orange	Glass	15° F - 120° F	.6	$399.00	
LMS-2263[14]	635	Red-Orange	Glass	15° F - 120° F	.6	$399.00	
LMS-2281[15]	635	Red-Orange	Glass	15° F - 120° F	.6	$399.00	
LMS-2291[16]	635	Red-Orange	Glass	15° F - 120° F	.6	$399.00	
LMS-2391[17]	635	Red-Orange	Glass	15° F - 120° F	.6	$399.00	
LMS-2451[18]	635	Red-Orange	Glass	15° F - 120° F	.6	$399.00	
LMS-1911M[19]	635	Red-Orange	Glass	15° F - 120° F	.6	$399.00	
LMS-1911S[20]	635	Red-Orange	Glass	15° F - 120° F	.6	$399.00	
LMS-1911B[21]	635	Red-Orange	Glass	15° F - 120° F	.6	$399.00	
LMS-PARA1911M[22]	635	Red-Orange	Glass	15° F - 120° F	.6	$399.00	
LMS-PARA1911S[23]	635	Red-Orange	Glass	15° F - 120° F	.6	$399.00	
LMS-PARA1911B[24]	635	Red-Orange	Glass	15° F - 120° F	.6	$399.00	
LMS-3XD[25]	635	Red-Orange	Glass	15° F - 120° F	.6	$399.00	
LMS-4XD9/357[26]	635	Red-Orange	Glass	15° F - 120° F	.6	$399.00	
LMS-4XD40[27]	635	Red-Orange	Glass	15° F - 120° F	.6	$399.00	
LMS-5XD[28]	635	Red-Orange	Glass	15° F - 120° F	.6	$399.00	
LMS-1431[29]	635	Red-Orange	Glass	15° F - 120° F	.6	$399.00	
LMS-1441[30]	635	Red-Orange	Glass	15° F - 120° F	.6	$399.00	
LMS-591S[31]	635	Red-Orange	Glass	15° F - 120° F	.6	$399.00	
LMS-591B[32]	635	Red-Orange	Glass	15° F - 120° F	.6	$399.00	
LMS-1202[33]	635	Red-Orange	Glass	15° F - 120° F	.6	$399.00	

Maker, Model, Type	Adjust.	Scopes	Price
ADCO			
Std. Black or nickel		1"	**$13.95**
Std. Black or nickel		30mm	**$13.95**
Rings Black or nickel		30mm with 3/8" grv.	**$13.95**
Rings Black or nickel		1" raised 3/8" grv.	**$13.95**
AIMTECH			
AMT Auto Mag II .22 Mag.	No	Weaver rail	**$56.99**
Beretta/Taurus 92/99	No	Weaver rail	**$63.25**
Browning Buckmark/Challenger II	No	Weaver rail	**$56.99**
Browning Hi-Power	No	Weaver rail	**$63.25**
Glock 17, 17L, 19, 23, 24 etc. no rail	No	Weaver rail	**$63.25**
Glock 20, 21 no rail	No	Weaver rail	**$63.25**
Glock 9mm and .40 with access. rail	No	Weaver rail	**$74.95**
Govt. 45 Auto/.38 Super	No	Weaver rail	**$63.25**
Hi-Standard (Mitchell version) 107	No	Weaver rail	**$63.25**
H&K USP 9mm/40 rail mount	No	Weaver rail	**$74.95**
Ruger Mk I, Mk II	No	Weaver rail	**$49.95**
Ruger P85/P89	No	Weaver rail	**$63.25**
S&W K, L, N frames	No	Weaver rail	**$63.25**
S&W K, L, N with tapped top strap*	No	Weaver rail	**$69.95**
S&W Model 41 Target 22	No	Weaver rail	**$63.25**
S&W Model 52 Target 38	No	Weaver rail	**$63.25**
S&W Model 99 Walther frame rail mount	No	Weaver rail	**$74.95**
S&W 2nd Gen. 59/459/659 etc.	No	Weaver rail	**$56.99**
S&W 3rd Gen. full size 5906 etc.	No	Weaver rail	**$69.95**
S&W 422, 622, 2206	No	Weaver rail	**$56.99**
S&W 645/745	No	Weaver rail	**$56.99**
S&W Sigma	No	Weaver rail	**$64.95**
Taurus PT908	No	Weaver rail	**$63.25**
Taurus 44 6.5" bbl.	No	Weaver rail	**$69.95**
Walther 99	No	Weaver rail	**$74.95**
Shotguns			
Benelli M-1 Super 90	No	Weaver rail	**$44.95**
Benelli Montefeltro	No	Weaver rail	**$44.95**
Benelli Nova	No	Weaver rail	**$69.95**
Benelli Super Black Eagle	No	Weaver rail	**$49.95**
Browning A-5 12-ga.	No	Weaver rail	**$40.95**
Browning BPS 12-ga.	No	Weaver rail	**$40.95**
Browning Gold Hunter 12-ga.	No	Weaver rail	**$44.95**
Browning Gold Hunter 20-ga.	No	Weaver rail	**$49.95**
Browning Gold Hunter 10-ga.	No	Weaver rail	**$49.95**
Beretta 303 12-ga.	No	Weaver rail	**$44.95**
Beretta 390 12-ga.	No	Weaver rail	**$44.95**
Beretta Pintail	No	Weaver rail	**$44.95**
H&K Fabarms Gold/Silver Lion	No	Weaver rail	**$49.95**
Ithaca 37/87 12-ga.	No	Weaver rail	**$40.95**
Ithaca 37/87 20-ga.	No	Weaver rail	**$40.95**
Mossberg 500/Maverick 12-ga.	No	Weaver rail	**$40.95**
Mossberg 500/Maverick 20-ga.	No	Weaver rail	**$40.95**
AIMTECH *(cont.)*			
Mossberg 835 3.5" Ulti-Mag	No	Weaver rail	**$40.95**
Mossberg 5500/9200	No	Weaver rail	**$40.95**
Remington 1100/1187 12-ga.	No	Weaver rail	**$42.80**
Remington 1100/1187 12-ga. LH	No	Weaver rail	**$42.80**
Remington 1100/1187 20-ga.	No	Weaver rail	**$40.95**
Remington 1100/1187 20-ga. LH	No	Weaver rail	**$40.95**
Remington 870 12-ga.	No	Weaver rail	**$40.95**
Remington 870 12-ga. LH	No	Weaver rail	**$40.95**
Remington 870 20-ga.	No	Weaver rail	**$42.80**
Remington 870 20-ga. LH	No	Weaver rail	**$42.80**
Remington 870 Express Magnum	No	Weaver rail	**$40.95**
Remington SP-10 10-ga.	No	Weaver rail	**$49.95**
Winchester 1300 12-ga.	No	Weaver rail	**$40.95**
Winchester 1400 12-ga.	No	Weaver rail	**$40.95**
Winchester Super X2	No	Weaver rail	**$44.95**
"Rib Rider" Ultra Low Profile Mounts Non See-Through 2-piece rib attached			
Mossberg 500/835/9200	No	Weaver rail	**$29.95**
Remington 1100/1187/870	No	Weaver rail	**$29.95**
Winchester 1300	No	Weaver rail	**$29.95**
1-Piece Rib Rider Low Rider Mounts			
Mossberg 500/835/9200	No	Weaver rail	**$29.95**
Remington 1100/1187/870	No	Weaver rail	**$29.95**
Winchester 1300	No	Weaver rail	**$29.95**
2-Piece Rib Rider See-Through			
Mossberg 500/835/9200	No	Weaver rail	**$29.95**
Remington 1100/1187/870	No	Weaver rail	**$29.95**
Winchester 1300	No	Weaver rail	**$29.95**
1-Piece Rib Rider See-Through			
Mossberg 500/835/9200	No	Weaver rail	**$29.95**
Remington 1100/1187/870	No	Weaver rail	**$29.95**
Winchester 1300	No	Weaver rail	**$29.95**
Rifles			
AR-15/M16	No	Weaver rail	**$21.95**
Browning A-Bolt	No	Weaver rail	**$21.95**
Browning BAR	No	Weaver rail	**$21.95**
Browning BLR	No	Weaver rail	**$21.95**
Marlin 336	No	Weaver rail	**$21.95**
Mauser Mark X	No	Weaver rail	**$21.95**
Remington 700 Short Action	No	Weaver rail	**$21.95**
Remington 700 Long Action	No	Weaver rail	**$21.95**
Remington 7400/7600	No	Weaver rail	**$21.95**
Ruger 10/22	No	Weaver rail	**$21.95**
Ruger Mini 14 Scout Rail**	No	Weaver rail	**$89.50**
Savage 110, 111, 113, 114, 115, 116	No	Weaver rail	**$21.95**
Winchester Model 70	No	Weaver rail	**$21.95**
Winchester 94 AE	No	Weaver rail	**$21.95**

All mounts no-gunsmithing, iron sight usable. Rifle mounts are solid see-through bases. All mounts accommodate standard Weaver-style rings of all makers. From Aimtech division, L&S Technologies, Inc. *3-blade sight mount combination. **Replacement handguard and mounting rail.

Maker, Model, Type	Adjust.	Scopes	Price
A.R.M.S.			
M16A1, A2, AR-15	No	Weaver rail	**$59.95**
Multibase	No	Weaver rail	**$59.95**
#19 ACOG Throw Lever Mt.	No	Weaver rail	**$160.00**
#19 Weaver/STANAG Throw Lever Rail	No	Weaver rail	**$150.00**
STANAG Rings	No	30mm	**$75.00**
Throw Lever Rings	No	Weaver rail	**$119.00**
Ring Inserts	No	1", 30mm	**$29.00**
#22M68 Aimpoint Comp Ring Throw Lever	No	Weaver rail	**$109.00**
#38 Std. Swan Sleeve[1]	No		**$180.00**
#39 A2 Plus Mod. Mt.	No	#39T rail	**$125.00**

[1]Avail. in three lengths. From A.R.M.S., Inc.

Maker, Model, Type	Adjust.	Scopes	Price
AO			
AO/Lever Scout Scope	No	Weaver rail	**$50.00**

No gunsmithing required for lever-action rifles with 8" Weaver-style rails; surrounds barrel shank; 6" long; low profile. AO Sight Systems Inc.

Maker, Model, Type	Adjust.	Scopes	Price
B-SQUARE			
Pistols (centerfire)			
Colt M1911	E only	Weaver rail	**$83.27**
H&K USP, 9mm and 40 S&W	No	Weaver rail	**$83.27**
Pistols (rimfire)			
Browning Buck Mark	No	Weaver rail	**$41.45**
Ruger Mk I/II, bull or taper	No	Weaver rail	**$47.23-67.46**
Revolvers			
Colt Anaconda/Python/Taurus 689	No	Weaver rail	**$70.49-79.44**
Ruger Single-Six	No	Weaver rail	**$70.49**
Ruger GP-100	No	Weaver rail	**$74.58-84.06**
Ruger Blackhawk, Super	No	Weaver rail	**$74.58-84.06**
Ruger Redhawk, Super	No	Weaver rail	**$74.58-84.06**
Smith & Wesson K, L, N	No	Weaver rail	**$74.58-84.06**
Taurus 66, 669, 607, 608	No	Weaver rail	**$70.49-79.44**
InterLock Rings (sporting rifles)			
1" Standard Dovetail (w/recoil blade)	No	Weaver rail	**$35.55-40.45**
30mm Stand. Dovetail (w/recoil blade)	No	Weaver rail	**$40.45**
1"x11mm Dovetail	No	Weaver rail	**$38.00**
1"x.22 Dovetail	No	Weaver rail	**$35.55**
InterLock Adjustable Rings (sporting rifles)			
1" Standard Dovetail (w/recoil blade)	Yes	Weaver rail	**$67.40**
30mm Stand. Dovetail (w/recoil blade)	Yes	Weaver rail	**$72.30**
1"x11mm Dovetail	Yes	Weaver rail	**$67.40**
1"x.22 Dovetail	Yes	Weaver rail	**$72.30**
InterLock One-Piece Bases			
Most models			**$6.93**
Modern Military (rings incl.)			
AK-47/MAC 90	No	Weaver rail	**$72.57**
Colt AR-15	No	Weaver rail	**$97.28**
FN/FAL/LAR (See-Thru rings)	No	Weaver rail	**$109.59**
B-SQUARE *(cont.)*			
Classic Military (rings incl.)			
H&K 91	No	Weaver rail	**$121.89**
Mauser 38, 94, 96, 98	E only	Weaver rail	**$88.26**
Mosin-Nagant (all)	E only	Weaver rail	**88.26**
Air Rifles			
RWS, Diana, BSA, Gamo	W&E	11mm rail	**$67.48**
Weihrauch, Anschutz, Beeman, Webley	W&E	11mm rail	**$72.21**
Shotgun Saddle Mounts			
Benelli Super 90 (See-Thru)	No	Weaver rail	**$68.85**
Browning BPS, A-5 9 (See-Thru)	No	Weaver rail	**$68.85**
Browning Gold 10/12/20-ga. (See-Thru)	No	Weaver rail	**$65.11-68.85**
Ithaca 37, 87	No	Weaver rail	**$68.85**
Mossberg 500/Mav. 88	No	Weaver rail	**$68.85**
Mossberg 835/Mav. 91	No	Weaver rail	**$68.85**
Remington 870/1100/11-87	No	Weaver rail	**$68.85**
Remington SP10	No	Weaver rail	**$68.85**
Winchester 1200-1500	No	Weaver rail	**$68.85**

Prices shown for anodized black finish; add **$10** for stainless finish. Partial listing of mounts shown here. Contact B-Square for complete listing and details.

Maker, Model, Type	Adjust.	Scopes	Price
BEEMAN			
Two-Piece, Med.	No	1"	**$36.65**
Deluxe Two-Piece, High	No	1"	**$38.00**
Deluxe Two-Piece	No	30mm	**$52.00**
Deluxe One-Piece	No	1"	**$69.35**
Dampa Mount	No	1"	**$153.35**

All grooved receivers and scope bases on all known air rifles and 22-cal. rimfire rifles (1/2" to 5/8" 6mm to 15mm).

Maker, Model, Type	Adjust.	Scopes	Price
BOCK			
Swing ALK[1]	W&E	1", 26mm, 30mm	**$349.00**
Safari KEMEL[2]	W&E	1", 26mm, 30mm	**$149.00**
Claw KEMKA[3]	W&E	1", 26mm, 30mm	**$224.00**
ProHunter Fixed[4]	No	1", 26mm, 30mm	**$95.00**

[1]Q.D.: pivots right for removal. For Steyr-Mannlicher, Win. 70, Rem. 700, Mauser 98, Dakota, Sako, Sauer 80, 90. Magnum has extra-wide rings, same price. [2]Heavy-duty claw-type reversible for front or rear removal. For Steyr-Mannlicher rifles. [3]True claw mount for bolt-action rifles. Also in extended model. For Steyr-Mannlicher, Win. 70, Rem. 700. Also avail. as Gunsmith Bases, not drilled or contoured same price. [4]Extra-wide rings. Imported from Germany by GSI, Inc.

Maker, Model, Type	Adjust.	Scopes	Price
BSA			
AA Airguns	Yes	Super Ten, 240 Magnum, Maxi gripped scope rail equipped air rifles	**$59.99 (adj). $29.99 (fixed)**
BURRIS			
Supreme (SU) One-Piece (T)[1]	W only	1" split rings, 3 heights	**1-piece base - $23.00-27.00**
Trumount (TU) Two-Piece (T)	W only	1" split rings, 3 heights	**2-piece base - $21.00-30.00**
Trumount (TU) Two-Piece Ext.	W only	1" split rings	**$26.00**
Browning 22-cal. Auto Mount[2]	No	1" split rings	**$20.00**

Maker, Model, Type	Adjust.	Scopes	Price
BURRIS *(cont.)*			
1" 22-cal. Ring Mounts[3]	No	1" split rings	**$24.00-41.00**
L.E.R. (LU) Mount Bases[4]	W only	1" split rings	**$24.00-52.00**
L.E.R. No Drill-No Tap Bases[4, 7, 8]	W only	1" split rings	**$48.00-52.00**
Extension Rings[5]	No	1" scopes	**$28.00-46.00**
Ruger Ring Mount[6, 9]	W only	1" split rings	**$50.00-68.00**
Std. 1" Rings[9]		Low, medium, high heights	**$29.00-43.00**
Zee Rings[9]		Fit Weaver bases; medium and high heights	**$29.00-44.00**
Signature Rings	No	30mm split rings	**$68.00**
Rimfire/Airgun Rings	W only	1" split rings, med. & high	**$24.00-41.00**
Double Dovetail (DD) Bases	No	30mm Signature	**$23.00-26.00**

[1]Most popular rifles. Universal rings, mounts fit Burris, Universal, Redfield, Leupold and Browning bases. Comparable prices. [2]Browning Standard 22 Auto rifle. [3]Grooved receivers. [4]Universal dovetail; accepts Burris, Universal, Redfield, Leupold rings. For Dan Wesson, S&W, Virginian, Ruger Blackhawk, Win. 94. [5]Medium standard front, extension rear, per pair. Low standard front, extension rear per pair. [6]Compact scopes, scopes with 2" bell for M77R. [7]Selected rings and bases available with matte Safari or silver finish. [8]For S&W K, L, N frames, Colt Python, Dan Wesson with 6" or longer barrels. [9]Also in 30mm.

Maker, Model, Type	Adjust.	Scopes	Price
BUSHNELL			
Centerfire rings, 2 piece, #763103	Integral 2 piece	1", matte black	**$15.95**
22 rings, 2 piece, #763022	Integral 2 piece	1", matte	**$6.95**
CATCO			
Enfield Drop-In	No	1"	**$39.95**

Uses Weaver-style rings (not incl.). No gunsmithing required. See-Thru design. From CATCO.

Maker, Model, Type	Adjust.	Scopes	Price
CLEAR VIEW			
Universal Rings, Mod. 101[1]	No	1" split rings	**$21.95**
Standard Model[2]	No	1" split rings	**$21.95**
Broad View[3]	No	1"	**$21.95**
22 Model[4]	No	3/4", 7/8", 1"	**$13.95**
SM-94 Winchester[5]	No	1" split rings	**$23.95**
94 EJ[6]	No	1" split rings	**$21.95**

[1]Most rifles by using Weaver-type base; allows use of iron sights. [2]Most popular rifles; allows use of iron sights. [3]Most popular rifles; low profile, wide field of view. [4]22 rifles with grooved receiver. [5]Side mount. [6]For Win. A.E. From Clear View Mfg.

Maker, Model, Type	Adjust.	Scopes	Price
CONETROL			
Huntur[1] (base & rings)	W only	1", split rings, 3 heights	**$119.88**
Gunnur[2] (base & rings)	W only	1", split rings, 3 heights	**$149.88**
Custum[3] (base & rings)	W only	1", split rings, 3 heights	**$179.88**
One-Piece Side Mount Base[4]	W only		
DapTar Bases[5]	W only		
Pistol Bases, 2- or 3-ring[6]	W only		
Fluted Bases[7]	W only		**$179.88**
Metric Rings[8]	W only	26mm, 26.5mm, 30mm	**$119.96-179.88**

CONETROL *(cont.)*

[1]All popular rifles, including metric-drilled foreign guns. Price shown for base, two rings. Matte finish. [2]Gunnur grade has mirror-finished rings to match scopes. Satin-finish base to match guns. Price shown for base, two rings. [3]Custom grade has mirror-finished rings and mirror-finished, streamlined base. Price shown for base, two rings. [4]Win. 94, Krag, older split-bridge Mannlicher-Schoenauer, Mini-14, etc. Prices same as above. [5]For all popular guns with integral mounting provision, including Sako, BSA Ithacagun, Ruger, Tikka, H&K, BRNO and many others. Also for grooved-receiver rimfires and air rifles. Prices same as above. [6]For XP-100, T/C Contender, Colt SAA, Ruger Blackhawk, S&W and others. [7]Sculptured two-piece bases as found on fine custom rifles. Price shown is for base alone. Also available unfinished **$119.88**, or finished but unblued **$149.88**. [8]26mm, 26.5mm, and 30mm rings made in projectionless style, in three heights. Three-ring mount for T/C Contender and other pistols in Conetrol's three grades. Any Conetrol mount available in stainless steel add 50 percent. Adjust-Quik-Detach (AQD) mounting is now available from Conetrol. Jam screws return the horizontal-split rings to zero. Adjustable for windage. AQD bases **$99.96**. AQD rings **$99.96**. (Total cost of complete setup, rings and two-piece base, is **$199.92**).

Maker, Model, Type	Adjust.	Scopes	Price
EAW			
Quick-Loc Mount	W&E	1", 26mm	**$345.00**
	W&E	30mm	**$360.00**
Magnum Fixed Mount	W&E	1", 26mm	**$305.00**
	W&E	30mm	**$320.00**

Fit most popular rifles. Available in 4 heights, 4 extensions. Reliable return to zero. Stress-free mounting. Imported by New England Custom Gun Svc.

Maker, Model, Type	Adjust.	Scopes	Price
GENTRY			
Feather-Light Rings and Bases	No	1", 30mm	**$90.00-125.00**

Bases for Rem. Seven, 700, Mauser 98, Browning A-Bolt, Weatherby Mk. V, Win. 70, HVA, Dakota. Two-piece base for Rem. Seven, chrome-moly or stainless. Rings in matte, regular blue, or stainless gray; four heights. From David Gentry.

Maker, Model, Type	Adjust.	Scopes	Price
GRIFFIN & HOWE			
Topmount[1]	No	1", 30mm	**$625.00**
Sidemount[2]	No	1", 30mm	**$255.00**
Garand Mount[3]	No	1"	**$255.00**

[1]Quick-detachable, double-lever mount with 1" rings, installed; with 30mm rings **$875.00**. [2]Quick-detachable, double-lever mount with 1" rings; with 30mm rings **$375.00**; installed, 1" rings. **$405.00**; installed, 30mm rings **$525.00**. [3]Price installed, with 1" rings **$405.00**. From Griffin & Howe.

Maker, Model, Type	Adjust.	Scopes	Price
G. G. & G.			
Remington 700 Rail	No	Weaver base	**$135.00**
Sniper Grade Rings	No	30mm	**$159.95**
M16/AR15 F.I.R.E. Std.[1]	No	Weaver rail	**$75.00**
M16/AR15 F.I.R.E. Scout	No	Weaver rail	**$82.95**
Aimpoint Standard Ring	No		**$164.95**
Aimpoint Cantilever Ring	No	Weaver rail	**$212.00**

[1]For M16/A3, AR15 flat top receivers; also in extended length. From G. G. & G.

Maker, Model, Type	Adjust.	Scopes	Price
IRONSIGHTER			
Ironsighter See-Through Mounts[1]	No	1" split rings	**$26.46**
Ironsighter S-94[4]	No	1" split rings	**$40.74**
Ironsighter AR-15/M-16[6]	No	1", 30mm	**$63.10**
Ironsighter 22-Cal.Rimfire[2]	No	1"	**$18.45**
Model #570[7]	No	1" split rings	**$26.46**
Model #573[7]	No	30mm split rings	**$40.74**
Model #727[3]	No	.875" split rings	**$16.60**
Blackpowder Mount[5]	No	1"	**$34.20-78.25**

Maker, Model, Type	Adjust.	Scopes	Price
IRONSIGHTER *(cont.)*			

[1]Most popular rifles. Rings have oval holes to permit use of iron sights. [2]For 1" dia. scopes. [3]For .875 dia. scopes. [4]For 1" dia. extended eye relief scopes. [5]Fits most popular blackpowder rifles; two-piece (CVA, Knight, Marlin and Austin & Halleck) and one-piece integral (T/C). [6]Model 716 with 1" #540 rings; fits Weaver-style bases. Some models in stainless finish. [7]New detachable Weaver-style rings fit all Weaver-style bases. Price: **$26.95**. From Ironsighter Co.

K MOUNT by KENPATABLE

Maker, Model, Type	Adjust.	Scopes	Price
Shotgun Mount	No	1", laser or red dot device	**$49.95**
SKS[1]	No	1"	**$39.95**

Wrap-around design; no gunsmithing required. Models for Browning BPS, A-5 12-ga., Sweet 16, 20, Rem. 870/1100 (LTW, and L.H.), S&W 916, Mossberg 500, Ithaca 37 & 51 12-ga., S&W 1000/3000, Win. 1400. [1]Requires simple modification to gun. From KenPatable Ent.

KRIS MOUNTS

Maker, Model, Type	Adjust.	Scopes	Price
Side-Saddle[1]	No	1", 26mm split rings	**$12.98**
Two-Piece (T)[2]	No	1", 26mm split rings	**$8.98**
One Piece (T)[3]	No	1", 26mm split rings	**$12.98**

[1]One-piece mount for Win. 94. [2]Most popular rifles and Ruger. [3]Blackhawk revolver. Mounts have oval hole to permit use of iron sights.

KWIK-SITE

Maker, Model, Type	Adjust.	Scopes	Price
Adapter	No	1"	**$13.50**
KS-W2[2]	No	1"	**$13.50**
KS-W94[3]	No	1"	**$38.64**
KS-WEV (Weaver-style rings)	No	1"	**$10.50**
KS-WEV-HIGH	No	1"	**$10.50**
KS-T22 1"[4]	No	1"	**$17.95**
KS-FL Flashlite[5]	No	Mini or C cell flash light	**$37.95**
KS-T88[6]	No	1"	**$11.84**
KS-T89	No	30mm	**$13.50**
KSN 22 See-Thru	No	1", 7/8"	**$17.95**
KSN-T22	No	1", 7/8"	**$17.95**
KSN-M-16 See-Thru (for M16 + AR-15)	No	1"	**$49.95**
KS-202[1]	No	1"	**$25.14**
KS-203	No	30mm	**$38.64**
KSBP[7]	No	Integral	**$76.95**
KSB Base Set			**$5.95**
Combo Bases & Rings	No	1"	**$19.84**

Bases interchangeable with Weaver bases. [1]Most rifles. Allows use of iron sights. [2]22-cal. rifles with grooved receivers. Allows use of iron sights. [3]Model 94, 94 Big Bore. No drilling or tapping. Also in adjustable model **$52.14**. [4]Non-See-Thru model for grooved receivers. [5]Allows C-cell or Mini Mag Lites to be mounted atop See-Thru mounts. [6]Fits any Redfield, Tasco, Weaver or Universal-style Kwik-Site dovetail base. [7]Blackpowder mount with integral rings and sights.

Maker, Model, Type	Adjust.	Scopes	Price
LASER AIM	No	Laser Aim	**$19.99-69.00**

Mounts Laser Aim above or below barrel. Available for most popular hand guns, rifles, shotguns, including militaries. From Laser Aim Technologies, Inc.

LEUPOLD

Maker, Model, Type	Adjust.	Scopes	Price
STD Bases[1]	W only	One- or two-piece bases	**$25.40**
STD Rings[2]		1" super low, low, medium, high	**$33.60**
DD RBH Handgun Mounts[2]	No		**$34.00**
Dual Dovetail Bases	No		**$25.40**
Dual Dovetail Rings[4]		1", low, med, high	**$33.60**
Ring Mounts	No	7/8", 1"	**$102.80**
22 Rimfire[4]	No	7/8", 1"	**$73.60**
Gunmaker Base[3]	W only	1"	**$73.60**
Quick Release Rings		1", low, med., high	**$43.00-81.00**
Quick Release Bases[5]	No	1", one- or two-piece	**$73.60**

[1]Base and two rings; Casull, Ruger, S&W, T/C; add **$5.00** for silver finish. [2]Rem. 700, Win. 70-type actions. For Ruger No. 1, 77, 77/22; interchangeable with Ruger units. For dovetailed rimfire rifles. Sako; high, medium, low. [3]Must be drilled, tapped for each action. [4]13mm dovetail receiver. [5]BSA Monarch, Rem. 40x, 700, 721, 725, Ruger M77, S&W 1500, Weatherby Mark V, Vanguard, Win. M70.

MARLIN

Maker, Model, Type	Adjust.	Scopes	Price
One-Piece QD (T)	No	1" split rings	**$10.10**

Most Marlin lever actions.

MILLETT RINGS

Maker, Model, Type	Adjust.	Scopes	Price
One-Piece Bases[6]	Yes	1"	**$26.41**
Universal Two-Piece Bases			
700 Series	W only	Two-piece bases	**$26.41**
FN Series	W only	Two-piece bases	**$26.41**
70 Series[1]	W only	1", two-piece bases	**$26.41**
Angle-Loc Rings[2]	W only	1", low, medium, high	**$35.49**
Ruger 77 Rings[3]		1"	**$38.14**
Shotgun Rings[4]		1"	**$32.55**
Handgun Bases, Rings[5]		1"	**$36.07-80.38**
30mm Rings[7]		30mm	**$20.95-41.63**
Extension Rings[8]		1"	**$40.43-56.44**
See-Thru Mounts[9]	No	1"	**$29.35-31.45**
Shotgun Mounts[10]	No	1"	**$52.45**
Timber Mount	No	1"	**$81.90**

BRNO, Rem. 40x, 700, 722, 725, 7400 Ruger 77 (round top), Marlin, Weatherby, FN Mauser, FN Brownings, Colt 57, Interarms Mark X, Parker-Hale, Savage 110, Sako (round receiver), many others. [1]Fits Win. M70 70XTR, 670, Browning BBR, BAR, BLR, A-Bolt, Rem. 7400/7600, Four, Six, Marlin 336, Win. 94 A. E., Sav. 110. [2]To fit Weaver-type bases. [3]Engraved. Smooth **$34.60**. [4]For Rem. 870, 1100; smooth. [5]Two- and three-ring sets for Colt Python, Trooper, Diamondback, Peacekeeper, Dan Wesson, Ruger Redhawk, Super Redhawk. [6]Turn-in bases and Weaver-style for most popular rifles and T/C Contender, XP100 pistols. [7]Both Weaver and turn-in styles; three heights. [8]Med. or high; ext. front std. rear, ext. rear std. front, ext. front ext. rear; **$40.90** for double extension. [9]Many popular rifles, Knight MK-85, T/C Hawken, Renegade, Mossberg 500 Slugster, 835 slug. [10]For Rem. 879/1100, Win. 1200, 1300/1400, 1500, Mossberg 500. Some models available in nickel at extra cost. New Angle-Loc two-piece bases fit all Weaver-style rings. In smooth, matte and nickel finishes, they are available for Browning A-Bolt, Browning BAR/BLR, Interarms MK X, FN, Mauser 98, CVA rifles with octagon barrels, CVA rifles with round receiver, Knight MK-85, Knight Wolverine, Remington 700, Sauer SHR 970, Savage 110, Winchester 70 **$24.95** to **$28.95**. From Millett Sights.

MMC

Maker, Model, Type	Adjust.	Scopes	Price
AK[1]	No		**$39.95**
FN FAL/LAR[2]	No		**$59.95**

[1]Fits all AK derivative receivers; Weaver-style base; low-profile scope position. [2]Fits all FAL versions; Weaver-style base. From MMC.

REDFIELD

Maker, Model, Type	Adjust.	Scopes	Price
JR-SR (T)[1]. One/two-piece bases.	W only	3/4", 1", 26mm, 30mm	**JR: $15.99-46.99 SR:15.99-33.49**
Ring (T)[2]	No	3/4" and 1"	**$27.95-29.95**

SCOPES / Hunting, Target & Varmint

Maker, Model, Type	Adjust.	Scopes	Price
REDFIELD *(cont.)*			
Widefield See-Thru Mounts	No	1"	**$15.95**
Ruger Rings[3]	No	1", med., high	**$30.49-36.49**
Ruger 30mm[4]	No	1"	**$37.99-40.99**

[1]Low, med. & high, split rings. Reversible extension front rings for 1". Two-piece bases for Sako. Colt Sauer bases **$39.95**. Med. Top Access JR rings nickel-plated **$28.95**. SR two-piece ABN mount nickel-plated **$22.95**. [2]Split rings for grooved 22s; 30mm, black matte **$42.95**. [3]For Ruger Model 77 rifles, medium and high; medium only for M77/22. [4]For Model 77. Also in matte finish **$45.95**. Scout mounts available for Mosin Nagant, Schmidt Rubin K-31, 98K Mauser, Husqvarna Mauser, Persian Mauser, Turkish Mauser.

Maker, Model, Type	Adjust.	Scopes	Price
S&K			
Insta-Mount (T) Bases and Rings[1]	W only	Weaver & S&K rings	**$55.10-160.00**
Insta-Mount (T) Scout Mounts[2]	W only	Weaver & S&K rings	**From $51.00**
Conventional Rings[3]	W only	1" horizontally split rings	**From $40.00**
Skulptured™ Bases, Rings[4]	W only	Uses only S&K rings	**From $46.00**
Smooth Kontoured™ Rings[5]	W only	1", 30mm vertically split	**From $58.00**

[1]1903, A3, M1 Carbine, #1 Lee Enfield. MkIII, #4, #5, M1917, M98 Mauser, AR-180, M-14, M-1, Mini-14, M1-A, Krag, Win. 94, SKS Type 56, Arasaka. [2]Mosin Nagant 91/30, 91/59 & M44, Schmidt Rubin K-31 &1911, M98 Mauser, Yugo 48, 24-47 & 48A, Carl Gustaf, Husqvarna, Persion, Turkish, Finnish, Czechslovakian 24 & 98/22, Chiliean, Arasaka. 3 horizontally split in low & high & supplied in matte & gloss. [4]For most popular rifles alredy drilled & tapped – also Sako, CZ, Tikka & 3/8 dovetail 22s in matte, gloss, mirror & stainless. Standard & extension bases available. Custom bases. [5]No projections; weigh 1/2 oz each; matte, gloss, mirror or stainless in low, med & high.

Maker, Model, Type	Adjust.	Scopes	Price
SAKO			
QD Dovetail	W only	1"	**$70.00-155.00**

Sako, or any rifle using Sako action, 3 heights available. Stoeger, importer.

Maker, Model, Type	Adjust.	Scopes	Price
SPRINGFIELD, INC.			
M1A Third Generation	No	1" or 30mm	**$123.00**
M1A Standard	No	1" or 30mm	**$77.00**
M6 Scout Mount	No		**$29.00**

Weaver-style bases. From Springfield, Inc.

Maker, Model, Type	Adjust.	Scopes	Price
TALBOT			
QD Bases	No		**$180.00-190.00**
Rings	No	1", 30mm	**$50.00-70.00**

Blue or stainless steel; standard or extended bases; rings in three heights. For most popular rifles. From Talbot QD Mounts.

Maker, Model, Type	Adjust.	Scopes	Price
TASCO			
Centerfire rings #791DSC	Integral	1", 30mm, matte black	**$5.95**
High centerfire rings #793DSC	Special high	1", matte black aluminum	**$5.95**
.22/airgun rings #797DSC	Yes	1", matte black aluminum	**$5.95**
.22/airgun "Quick Peep" rings #799DSC	Yes	1", matte black aluminum	**$5.95**

Maker, Model, Type	Adjust.	Scopes	Price
THOMPSON/CENTER			
Duo-Ring Mount[1]	No	1"	**$78.00**
Weaver-Style Bases	No		**$14.00-28.50**
Weaver-Style Rings[2]	No	1"	**$36.00**

[1]Attaches directly to T/C Contender bbl., no drilling/tapping; also for T/C M/L rifles, needs base adapter; blue or stainless. [2]Medium and high; blue or silver finish. From Thompson/Center.

Maker, Model, Type	Adjust.	Scopes	Price
UNERTL			
1/4 Click[1]	Yes	3/4", 1" target scopes	**Per set $285.00**

[1]Unertl target or varmint scopes. Posa or standard mounts, less bases. From Unertl.

Maker, Model, Type	Adjust.	Scopes	Price
WARNE			
Premier Series (all steel)			
T.P.A. (Permanently Attached)	No	1", 4 heights 30mm, 2 heights	**$87.75-98.55**
Premier Series Rings fit Premier Series Bases			
Premier Series (all-steel Q.D. rings)			
Premier Series (all steel) Quick detachable lever	No	1", 4 heights 26mm, 2 heights 30mm, 3 heights	**$129.95-131.25** **$142.00**
BRNO 19mm	No	1", 3 heights 30mm, 2 heights	**$125.00-136.70**
BRNO 16mm		1", 2 heights	**$125.00**
Ruger	No	1", 4 heights 30mm, 3 heights	**$125.00-136.70**
Ruger M77	No	1", 3 heights 30mm, 2 heights	**$125.00-136.70**
Sako Medium & Long Action	No	1", 4 heights 30mm, 3 heights	**$125.00-136.70**
Sako Short Action	No	1", 3 heights	**$125.00**
All-Steel One-Piece Base, ea.			**$38.50**
All-Steel Two-Piece Base, ea.			**$14.00**
Maxima Series (fits all Weaver-style bases)			
Permanently Attached[1]	No	1", 3 heights 30mm, 3 heights	**$25.50** **$36.00**
Adjustable Double Lever[2]	No	1", 3 heights 30mm, 3 heights	**$72.60** **$80.75**
Thumb Knob	No	1", 3 heights 30mm, 3 heights	**$59.95** **$68.25**
Stainless-Steel Two-Piece Base, ea.			**$15.25**

Vertically split rings with dovetail clamp, precise return to zero. Fit most popular rifles, handguns. Regular blue, matte blue, silver finish. [1]All-Steel, non-Q.D. rings. [2]All-steel, Q.D. rings. From Warne Mfg. Co.

Maker, Model, Type	Adjust.	Scopes	Price
WEAVER			
Top Mount	No	7/8", 1", 30mm, 33mm	**$24.95-38.95**
Side Mount	No	1", 1" long	**$14.95-34.95**
Tip-Off Rings	No	7/8", 1"	**$24.95-32.95**
Pivot Mounts	No	1"	**$38.95**
Complete Mount Systems			
Pistol	No	1"	**$75.00-105.00**
Rifle	No	1"	**$32.95**
SKS Mount System	No	1"	**$49.95**
Pro-View (no base required)	No	1"	**$13.95-15.95**
Converta-Mount, 12-ga. (Rem. 870, Moss. 500)	No	1", 30mm	**$74.95**
See-Thru Mounts			
Detachable	No	1"	**$27.00-32.00**
System (no base required)	No	1"	**$15.00-35.00**
Tip-Off	No	1"	**$15.00**

Maker, Model, Type	Adjust.	Scopes	Price
WEAVER *(cont.)*			

Nearly all modern rifles, pistols, and shotguns. Detachable rings in standard, See-Thru, and extension styles, in Low, Medium, High or X-High heights; gloss (blued), silver and matte finishes to match scopes. Extension rings are only available in 1" High style and See-Thru X-tensions only in gloss finish. Tip-Off rings only for 3/8" grooved receivers or 3/8" grooved adaptor bases; no base required. See-Thru & Pro-View mounts for most modern big bore rifles, some in silver. No Drill & Tap Pistol systems in gloss or silver for Colt Python, Trooper, 357, Officer's Model, Ruger Single-Six, Security-Six (gloss finish only), Blackhawk, Super Blackhawk, Blackhawk SRM 357, Redhawk, Mini-14 Series (not Ranch), Ruger 22 Auto Pistols, Mark II, Smith & Wesson I- and current K-frames with adj. rear sights. Converta-Mount Systems in Standard and See-Under for Mossberg 500 (12- and 20-ga.), Remington 870, 11-87 (12- and 20-ga. lightweight), Winchester 1200, 1300, 1400, 1500. Converta-Brackets, bases, rings also available for Beretta A303 and A390, Browning A-5, BPS Pump, Ithaca 37, 87. From Weaver.

Maker, Model, Type	Adjust.	Scopes	Price
WEIGAND			
Browning Buck Mark[1]	No		**$29.95**
Integra Mounts[2]	No		**$39.95-69.00**
S&W Revolver[3]	No		**$29.95**
Ruger 10/22[4]	No		**$14.95-39.95**
Ruger Revolver[5]	No		**$29.95**
Taurus Revolver[4]	No		**$29.95-65.00**
Lightweight Rings	No	1", 30mm	**$29.95-39.95**
1911			
SM3[6]	No	Weaver rail	**$99.95**
APCMNT[7]	No		**$69.95**

[1]No gunsmithing. [2]S&W K, L, N frames, Taurus vent rib models, Colt Anaconda/Python, Ruger Redhawk, Ruger 10/22. [3]K, L, N frames. [4]Three models. [5]Redhawk, Blackhawk, GP100. [6]3rd Gen., drill and tap, without slots **$59.95**. [7]For Aimpoint Comp. Red Dot scope, silver only. From Weigand Combat Handguns, Inc.

Maker, Model, Type	Adjust.	Scopes	Price
WIDEVIEW			
Premium 94 Angle Eject and side mount	No	1"	**$22.44**
Premium See-Thru	No	1"	**$22.44**
22 Premium See-Thru	No	3/4", 1"	**$16.47**
Universal Ring Angle Cut	No	1"	**$31.28**
Universal Ring Straight Cut	No	1"	**$18.70**
Solid Mounts			
Lo Ring Solid[1]	No	1"	**$22.44**
Hi Ring Solid[1]	No	1"	**$18.14**
SR Rings		1", 30mm	**$16.32**
22 Grooved Receiver	No	1"	**$16.32**
Blackpowder Mounts[2]	No	1"	**$22.44**
High, extra-high ring mounts with base	No	up to 60mm	**$30.16**
AR15 and M16	No		**$33.92**

[1]For Weaver-type base. Models for many popular rifles. Low ring, high ring and grooved receiver types. [2]No drilling, tapping, for T/C Renegade, Hawken, CVA, Knight Traditions guns. From Wideview Scope Mount Corp.

Maker, Model, Type	Adjust.	Scopes	Price
WILLIAMS			
Side Mount with HCO Rings[1]	No	1", split or extension rings	**$74.35**
Side Mount, Offset Rings[2]	No	Same	**$61.45**
Sight-Thru Mounts[3]	No	1", 7/8" sleeves	**$19.50**
Streamline Mounts	No	1" (bases form rings)	**$26.50**

[1]Most rifles, Br. S.M.L.E. (round rec.) $14.41 extra. [2]Most rifles including Win. 94 Big Bore. [3]Many modern rifles, including CVA Apollo, others with 1" octagon barrels.

Maker, Model, Type	Adjust.	Scopes	Price
YORK			
M-1 Garand	Yes	1"	**$39.95**

Centers scope over the action. No drilling, tapping or gunsmithing. Uses standard dovetail rings. From York M-1 Conversions.

NOTES

(S) Side Mount; (T) Top Mount; 22mm=.866"; 25.4mm=1.024"; 26.5mm=1.045"; 30mm=1.81".

Sporting Leaf and Open Sights

AUTOMATIC DRILLING REAR SIGHT Most German and Austrian drillings have this kind of rear sight. When rifle barrel is selected the rear sight automatically comes to the upright position. Base length 2.165", width .472", folding leaf height .315". From New England Custom Gun Service.
Price: .... $4[illegible].50

CLASSIC MARBLE/WILLIAMS STYLE FULLY ADJUSTABLE REAR SPORTING SIGHTS Screw-on attachment. Dovetailed graduated windage and elevation adjustment. Elevation and windage lock with set screws. Available in steel or lightweight alloy construction. From Sarco, Inc.
Price: .... $1[illegible].50

ERA MASTERPIECE ADJUSTABLE REAR SIGHTS Precision-machined, all-steel, polished and blued. Attaches with 8-36 socket head screw. Use small screwdriver to adjust windage and elevation. Available for various barrel widths. From New England Custom Gun Service.
Price: $99.00

ERA CLASSIC ADJUSTABLE REAR SIGHT Similar to the Masterpiece unit except windage is adjusted by pushing sight sideways, then locking it with a reliable clamp. Precision machined all steel construction, polished, with 6-48 fastening screw and Allen wrench. Shallow "V" and "U" notch. Length 2.170", width .550". From New England Custom Gun Service.
Price: $79.00

ERA EXPRESS SIGHTS A wide variety of open sights and bases for custom installation. Partial listing shown. From New England Custom Gun Service.
Price: One-leaf express $79.00
Price: Two-leaf express $89.00
Price: Three-leaf express $99.00
Price: Bases for above .... $48.00 to $53.00
Price: Standing rear sight, straight $19.00
Price: Base for above $30.00

ERA CLASSIC EXPRESS SIGHTS Standing or folding leaf sights are securely locked to the base with the ERA Magnum Clamp, but can be loosened for sighting in. Base can be attached with two socket-head cap screws or soldered. Finished and blued. Barrel diameters from .600" to .930". From New England Custom Gun Service.
Price: One-leaf express $125.00
Price: Two-leaf express $135.00
Price: Three-leaf express $145.00

ERA MASTERPIECE REAR SIGHT Adjustable for windage and elevation, and adjusted and locked with a small screwdriver. Comes with 8-36 socket- head cap screw and wrench. Barrel diameters from .600" to .930".
Price: $75.00

G.G. & G. SAME PLANE APERTURE M-16/AR-15 A2-style dual aperture rear sight with both large and small apertures centered on the same plane.
Price: $45.00

LYMAN No.16 Middle sight for barrel dovetail slot mounting. Folds flat when scope or peep sight is used. Sight notch plate adjustable for elevation. White triangle for quick aiming. Designed to fit 3/8" dovetail slots. Three heights: A-.400" to.500", B-.345" to .445", C-.500" to .600". A slot blank designed to fill dovetail notch when sight is removed is available.
Price: $5.00
Price: $13.25

MARBLE FALSE BASE #76, #77, #78 New screw-on base for most rifles replaces factory base. 3/8" dovetail slot permits installation of any folding rear sight. Can be had in sweat-on models also.
Price: $8.00

MARBLE FOLDING LEAF Flattop or semi-buckhorn style. Folds down when scope or peep sights are used. Reversible plate gives choice of "U" or "V" notch. Adjustable for elevation.
Price: $16.00
Price: Also available with both windage and elevation adjustment $18.00

MARBLE SPORTING REAR With white enamel diamond, gives choice of two "U" and two "V" notches or different sizes. Adjustment in height by means of double step elevator and sliding notch piece. For all rifles; screw or dovetail installation.
Price: .... $16.00 to $17.00

MARBLE #20 UNIVERSAL New screw or sweat-on base. Both have .100" elevation adjustment. In five base sizes. Three styles of U-notch, square notch, peep. Adjustable for windage and elevation.
Price: Screw-on.. $23.00
Price: Sweat-on $21.00

MILLETT SPORTING & BLACKPOWDER RIFLE Open click adjustable rear fits 3/8" dovetail cut in barrel. Choice of white outline, target black or open express V rear blades. Also available is a replacement screw-on sight with express V, .562" hole centers. Dovetail fronts in white or blaze orange in seven heights (.157"-.540").
Price: Dovetail or screw-on rear. $58.38
Price: Front sight $12.96

MILLETT SCOPE-SITE Open, adjustable or fixed rear sights dovetail into a base integral with the top scope-mounting ring. Blaze orange front ramp sight is integral with the front ring half. Rear sights have white outline aperture. Provides fast, short-radius, Patridge-type open sights on the top of the scope. Can be used with all Millett rings, Weaver-style bases, Ruger 77 (also fits Redhawk), Ruger Ranch Rifle, No. 1, No. 3, Rem. 870, 1100; Burris, Leupold and Redfield bases.
Price: Scope-Site top only, windage only. $31.15
Price: As above, fully adjustable $66.10
Price: Scope-Site Hi-Turret, fully adjustable, low, medium, high $66.10

WHITWORTH STYLE ENGLISH 3 LEAF EXPRESS SIGHTS Folding leafs marked in 100, 200 and 300 yard increments. Slide assembly is dovetailed in base. Available in four different styles: 3 folding leaves, flat bottom; 1 fixed, 2 folding leaves, flat bottom; 3 folding leaves, round bottom; 1 fixed, 2 folding leaves, round bottom. Available from Sarco, Inc.
Price: $49.95

WICHITA MULTI RANGE SIGHT SYSTEM Designed for silhouette shooting. System allows you to adjust the rear sight to four repeatable range settings, once it is pre-set. Sight clicks to any of the settings by turning a serrated wheel. Front sight is adjustable for weather and light conditions with one adjustment. Specify gun when ordering.
Price: Rear sight. $145.00
Price: Front sight $110.00

WILLIAMS DOVETAIL OPEN SIGHT (WDOS) Open rear sight with windage and elevation adjustment. Furnished "U" notch or choice of blades. Slips into dovetail and locks with gib lock. Heights from .281" to .531".
Price: With blade. $19.50
Price: Less blade $12.45
Price: Rear sight blades, each $7.05

WILLIAMS GUIDE OPEN SIGHT (WGOS) Open rear sight with windage and elevation adjustment. Bases to fit most military and commercial barrels. Choice of square "U" or "V" notch blade, 3/16", 1/4", 5/16", or 3/8" high.
Price: Less blade. $19.50
Price: Extra blades, each $7.05

WILLIAMS WGOS OCTAGON Open rear sight for 1" octagonal barrels. Installs with two 6-48 screws and uses same hole spacing as most T/C muzzleloading rifles. Four heights, choice of square, U, V, or B blade.
Price: $26.55

WILLIAMS WSKS, WAK47 Replaces original military-type rear sight. Adjustable for windage and elevation. No drilling or tapping. Peep

aperture or open. For SKS carbines, AK-47-style rifles.
Price: Aperture.. $25.95
Price: Open $24.95

WILLIAMS WM-96 Fits Mauser 96-type military rifles. Replaces original rear sight with open blade or aperture. Fully adjustable for windage and elevation. No drilling or tapping.
Price: Aperture.. $25.95
Price: Open $24.95

WILLIAMS FIRE RIFLE SETS Replacement front and rear fiber optic sights. Red bead front, two green elements in the fully-adjustable rear. Made of CNC-machined metal.
Price: For Ruger 10/22. $24.95
Price: For most Marlin and Win. (3/8" dovetail) $34.95
Price: For Remington (newer style sight base) $28.95

Aperture and Micrometer Receiver Sights

A2 REAR SIGHT KIT Featuring an exclusive numbered windage knob. For .223 AR-style rifles. From ArmaLite, Inc.
Price: $55.00

AO GHOST RING HUNTING SIGHT Fully adjustable for windage and elevation. Available for most rifles, including blackpowder guns. Minimum gunsmithing required for most installations; matches most mounting holes. From AO Sight Systems, Inc.
Price: $90.00

AO Ghost Ring

AO AR-15/M-16 APERTURE Drop-in replacement of factory sights. Both apertures are on the same plane. Large ghost ring has .230" inside diameter; small ghost ring has .100" inside diameter. From AO Sight Systems, Inc.
Price: $30.00

AO BACKUP GHOST RING SIGHTS Mounts to scope base and retains zero when reinstalled in the field. Affords same elevation/windage adjustability as AO Hunting Ghost Rings. Included are both .191" and .230" apertures and test posts. Available for Ruger, Sako, Remington 700 and other rifles. From AO Sight Systems, Inc.
Price: $65.00

AO TACTICAL SIGHTS For HK UMP/USC/G36/SL8/MP5. The Big Dot Tritium or standard dot tritium is mated with a large .300" diameter rear ghost ring. The "same plane" rear aperture flips from the .300" to a .230" diameter ghost ring. From AO Sight Systems, Inc.
Price: $90.00 to $120.00

BEEMAN/FEINWERKBAU 5454 MATCH APERTURE SIGHT Small size, new-design sight uses constant-pressure flat springs to eliminate point of impact shifts.
Price: $440.85

BEEMAN SPORT APERTURE SIGHT Positive click micrometer adjustments. Deluxe version has target knobs. For air rifles with grooved receivers.
Price: Deluxe $50.00

BUSHMASTER COMPETITION A2 REAR SIGHT ASSEMBLY Elevation and windage mechanism feature either 1/2 or 1/4 minute of adjustment. Long distance aperture allows screw-in installation of any of four interchangeable micro-apertures.
Price: 1/2 M.O.A. $109.95
Price: 1/4 M.O.A. $114.95

DPMS NATIONAL MATCH Replaces the standard A2 rear sight on M16/AR-15 rifles. Has 1/4-minute windage and 1/2-minute elevation adjustments. Includes both a .052" and .200" diameter aperture.
Price: $92.99

ENFIELD NO. 4 TARGET/MATCH SIGHT Originally manufactured by Parker-Hale, has adjustments up to 1,300 meters. Micrometer click adjustments for windage. Adjustable aperture disc has six different openings from .030" to .053". From Sarco, Inc.
Price: $49.95

EAW RECEIVER SIGHT A fully adjustable aperture sight that locks securely into the EAW quick-detachable scope mount rear base. Made by New England Custom Gun Service.
Price: $80.00

ERA SEE-THRU Contains fiber optic center dot. Fits standard 3/8" American dovetails. Locks in place with set screw. Ideal for use on moving targets. Width 19.5mm. Available in low (.346", medium .425" and high .504" models. From New England Custom Gun Service.
Price: $40.00

G. G.& G. MAD IRIS Multiple Aperture Device is a four sight, rotating aperture disk with small and large apertures on the same plane. Mounts on M-16/ AR-15 flattop receiver. Fully adjustable.
Price: $141.95
Price: A2 IRIS, two apertures, full windage adjustments ... $124.95

KNIGHT'S ARMAMENT 600 METER FOLDING REAR SIGHT Click adjustable from 200 to 600 meters with clearly visible range markings. Intermediate clicks allows for precise zero at known ranges. Allows use of optical scopes by folding don. Mounts on rear of upper receiver rail on SR-25 and similar rifles. From Knight's Armament Co.
Price: $181.00

KNIGHT'S ARMAMENT FOLDING 300M SIGHT Mounts on flat-top upper receivers on SR-25 and similar rifles. May be used as a back-up iron sight for a scoped rifle/carbine or a primary sight. Peep insert may be removed to expose the 5mm diameter ghost ring aperture. From Knight's Armament Co.
Price: $144.00

LYMAN No. 2 Tang Sight Designed for the Winchester Model 94. Has high index marks on aperture post; comes with both .093" quick sighting aperture, .040" large disk aperture, and replacement mounting screws.
Price: $76.00
Price: For Marlin lever actions $76.00

LYMAN No. 57 1/4-minute clicks. Stayset knobs. Quick-release slide, adjustable zero scales. Made for almost all modern rifles.
Price: $67.50
Price: No. 57SME, 57SMET (for White Systems Model 91 and Whitetail rifles) $62.50

LYMAN 57GPR Designed especially for the Lyman Great Plains Rifle. Mounts directly onto the tang of the rifle and has 1/4-minute micrometer click adjustments.
Price: $62.50

Lyman 57GPR

Lyman 66SKS

LYMAN No. 66 Fits close to the rear of flat-sided receivers, furnished with Stayset knobs. Quick-release slide, 1/4-min. adjustments. For most lever or slide action or flat-sided automatic rifles.
Price: $67.50
Price: No. 66MK (for all current versions of the Knight MK-85 in-line rifle with flat-sided receiver) $67.50
Price: No. 66SKS fits Russian and Chinese SKS rifles; large and small

apertures **$67.50**
Price: No. 66 WB for Model 1886 Winchester lever actions **$67.50**

LYMAN No. 66U Light weight, designed for most modern shotguns with a flat-sided, round-top receiver. 1/4-minute clicks. Requires drilling, tapping. Not for Browning A-5, Rem. M11.
Price: **$71.50**

LYMAN 90MJT RECEIVER SIGHT Mounts on standard Lyman and Williams FP bases. Has 1/4-minute audible micrometer click adjustments, target knobs with direction indicators. Adjustable zero scales, quick-release slide. Large 7/8" diameter aperture disk.
Price: Right- or left-hand **$74.95**

Lyman 90MJT

LYMAN RECEIVER SIGHT Audible-click adjustments for windage and elevation, coin-slotted "stayset" knobs and two interchangeable apertures. For Mauser, Springfield, Sako, T/C Hawken, Rem. 700, Win. 70, Savage 110, SKS, Win. 94, Marlin 336 and 1894.
Price: **$53.99**

LYMAN 1886 #2 TANG SIGHT Fits the Winchester 1886 lever action rifle and replicas thereof not containing a tang safety. Has height index marks on the aperture post and an .800" maximum elevation adjustment. Included is a .093" x 1/2" quick-sighting aperture and .040 x 5/8" target disk.
Price: **$76.00**

MARBLE PEEP TANG SIGHT All-steel construction. Micrometer-like click adjustments for windage and elevation. For most popular old and new lever- action rifles.
Price: **$125.00**

MILLETT PEEP RIFLE SIGHTS Fully adjustable, heat-treated nickel steel peep aperture receiver sight for the Mini-14. Has fine windage and elevation adjustments; replaces original.
Price: Rear sight, Mini-14 .... **$68.95**
Price: Front sight, Mini-14 .... **$37.95**
Price: Front and rear combo with hood **$89.95**

NATIONAL MATCH REAR SIGHT KIT For AR-15 style rifles. From Armalite, Inc.
Price: 1/2 W, 1/2E **$80.00**
Price: 1/4 W, 1/2 E **$80.00**

NECG PEEP SIGHT FOR WEAVER SCOPE MOUNT BASES Attaches to Weaver scope mount base. Windage adjusts with included Allen wrenches, elevation with a small screwdriver. Furnished with two apertures (.093" and .125" diameter hole) and two interchangeable elevation slides for high or low sight line. From New England Custom Gun Service.
Price: **$85.00**

NECG PEEP SIGHT FOR GROOVED MOUNT BASES Windage adjusts with included Allen wrenches, elevation with a small screwdriver. Furnished with two apertures (.093" and .125" diameter hole) and two interchangeable elevation slides for high or low sight line. From New England Custom Gun Service.
Price: **$85.00**

NECG RUGER PEEP SIGHT Made for Ruger M-77 and No. 1 rifles, it is furnished with .093" and .125" opening apertures. Can be installed on a standard Ruger rear mount base or quarter rib. Tightening the aperture disk will lock the elevation setting in place. From New England Custom Gun Service.
Price: **$85.00**

T/C HUNTING STYLE TANG PEEP SIGHT Compact, all steel construction, with locking windage and elevation adjustments. For use with "bead style" and fiber optic front sights. Models available to fit all traditional T/C muzzleloading rifles. From Thompson/Center Arms.
Price: **$58.00**

T/C CONTENDER CARBINE PEEP SIGHT All-steel, low profile, click-adjustable unit mounting on the pre-drilled tapped scope mount holes on the T/C Contender Carbine. From Thompson/Center Arms.
Price: **$56.00**

TRIJICON 3-DOT NIGHT SIGHTS Self-luminous and machined from steel. Available for the M16/AR-15, H&K rifles. Front and rear sets and front only.
Price: .... **$50.00 to $99.00**

WILLIAMS APERTURE SIGHT Made to fit SKS rifles.
Price: **$19.95**

WILLIAMS FIRE SIGHT PEEP SETS Combines the Fire Sight front bead with Williams fully adjustable metallic peep rear.
Price: For SKS **$39.95**
Price: For Ruger 10/22, 99/44, 96/22, 96/22 Mag. **$48.95**
Price: For Marlin or Winchester lever actions .... **$50.95 to $80.95**

WILLIAMS FP Internal click adjustments. Positive locks. For virtually all rifles, T/C Contender, Heckler & Koch HK-91, Ruger Mini-14, plus Win., Rem., and Ithaca shotguns.
Price: From **$70.95**
Price: With Target Knobs **$82.50**
Price: FP-GR (for dovetail-grooved receivers, .22s and air guns) **$70.95**

Williams Target FP

WILLIAMS TARGET FP Similar to the FP series but developed for most bolt-action rimfire rifles. Target FP High adjustable from 1.250" to 1.750" above centerline of bore; Target FP Low adjustable from .750" to 1.250". Attaching bases for Rem. 540X, 541-S, 580, 581, 582 (#540); Rem. 510, 511, 512, 513-T, 521-T (#510); Win. 75 (#75); Savage/ Anschutz 64 and Mark 12 (#64). Some rifles require drilling, tapping.
Price: High or Low **$78.95**
Price: Base only **$20.95**

WILLIAMS 5-D SIGHT Low cost sight for shotguns, 22s and the more popular big game rifles. Adjustment for windage and elevation. Fits most guns without drilling and tapping. Also for British SMLE, Winchester M94 Side Eject.
Price: From **$38.95**
Price: With Shotgun Aperture **$38.95**

WILLIAMS 5D RECEIVER SIGHT Alloy construction and similar design to the FP model except designed to fit Win. 94, Marlin 336, Marlin 1895, Mauser 98.
Price: **$34.50**

WILLIAMS GUIDE (WGRS) Receiver sight for 30 M1 Carbine, M1903A3 Springfield, Savage 24s, Savage-Anschutz and Weatherby XXII. Utilizes military dovetail; no drilling. Double-dovetail windage adjustment, sliding dovetail adjustment for elevation.
Price: .... **$36.95 to $49.95**

Vernier Tang Sights

BALLARD TANG SIGHTS Available in variety of models including short & long staff hunter, Pacific & Montana, custom units allowing windage & elevation adjustments. Uses 8x40 base screws with screw spacing of 1.120". From Axtell Rifle Co.
Price: .... **$175.00 to $325.00**

LYMAN TANG SIGHT Made for Win. 94, 1886, Marlin 30, 336 and 1895.
Price: .... **$59.99 to $64.99**

MARLIN TANG SIGHTS Available in short and long staff hunter models using 8x40 base screws and screw spacing of 1.120". From Axtell Rifle Co.
Price: . . . . **$170.00 to $180.00**

PEDERSOLI CREEDMORE Adjustable for windage and elevation, fits Traditions by Pedersoli rifles and other brands. From Dixie Gun Works.
Price: **$110.00**

REMINGTON TANG SIGHTS Available in short-range hunter and vernier, mid- and long-range vernier and custom models with windage and elevation adjustments. Uses 10x28 base screws, with screw spacing of 1.940". Eye disk has .052" hole with 10x40 thread. From Axtell Rifle Co.
Price: . . . . **$175.00 to $325.00**

SHARPS TANG SIGHTS Reproduction tang sights as manufactured for various Sharps rifles through the years 1859-1878. Wide variety of models available including Standard Issue Sporting Peep, Hartford Transition Mid and Long Range, and Custom Express Sights. From Axtell Rifle Co.
Price: . . . . **$150.00 to $340.00**

STEVENS CUSTOM Available in thin base short and long staff hunter, mid and long range sporting vernier, custom mid and long range (custom models allow windage and elevation adjustments) models. Uses 5x40 base screws with screw spacing of 1.485". From Axtell Rifle Co.
Price: . . . . **$170.00 to $325.00**

TAURUS TANG SIGHT Made of blue steel, available for Taurus Models 62, 72, 172, 63, 73 and 173. Folds down, aperture disk sight, height index marks on aperture post.
Price: **$77.00**

WINCHESTER & BROWNING TANG SIGHTS Available in variety of models, including thin & thick base short & long staff hunter, mid & long range sporting vernier and custom units. Screw spacing of 2.180" on all models. From Axtell Rifle Co.
Price: . . . . **$170.00 to $325.00**

Globe Target Front Sights

AXTELL CUSTOM GLOBE Designed similar to the original Winchester #35 sight, it contains five inserts. Also available with spirit level. From Axtell Rifle Co.
Price: . . . . **$125.00 to $175.00**

BALLARD FRONT SIGHTS Available in windgauge with spirit level, globe with clip, and globe with spirit level (all with five inserts) and beach combination with gold plated rocker models. Dovetail of .375" for all. From Axtell Rifle Co.
Price: . . . . **$125.00 to $240.00**

Lyman 20 LJT Globe Front

LYMAN 20 MJT TARGET FRONT Has 7/8" diameter, one-piece steel globe with 3/8" dovetail base. Height is .700" from bottom of dovetail to center of aperture; height on 20 LJT is .750". Comes with seven Anschutz-size steel inserts-two posts and five apertures .126" through .177".
Price: 20 MJT or 20 LJT **$33.75**

LYMAN NO. 17A TARGET Includes seven interchangeable inserts: four apertures, one transparent amber and two posts .50" and .100" in width.
Price: **$28.25**
Price: Insert set **$13.25**

LYMAN 17AEU Similar to the Lyman 17A except has a special dovetail design to mount easily onto European muzzleloaders such as CVA, Traditions and Investarm. All steel, comes with eight inserts.
Price: **$26.00**

LYMAN NO. 93 MATCH Has 7/8" diameter, fits any rifle with a standard dovetail mounting block. Comes with seven target inserts and accepts most Anschutz accessories. Hooked locking bolt and nut allows quick removal, installation. Base available in .860" (European) and .562" (American) hole spacing.
Price: **$45.00**

MAYNARD FRONT SIGHTS Custom globe with five inserts and clip. Also available with spirit level bracket and windgauge styles. From Axtell Rifle Co.
Price: . . . . **$125.00 to $240.00**

PEDERSOLI GLOBE A tunnel front sight with 12 interchangeable inserts for high precision target shooting. Fits Traditions by Pedersoli and other rifles.
Price: **$69.95**

REMINGTON FRONT SIGHTS Available in windgauge with spirit level, custom globe with clip and custom globe with spirit level (all with five inserts) and beach combination with gold plated rocker models. Dovetail .460". From Axtell Rifle Co.
Price: . . . . **$125.00 to $250.00**

SHARPS FRONT SIGHTS Original-style globe with non-moveable post and pinhead. Also available with windgauge and spirit level. From Axtell Rifle Co.
Price: . . . . **$100.00 to $265.00**

WILLIAMS TARGET GLOBE FRONT Adapts to many rifles. Mounts to the base with a knurled locking screw. Height is .545" from center, not including base. Comes with inserts.
Price: **$49.95**
Price: Dovetail base (low) .220" **$19.95**
Price: Dovetail base (high) .465" **$19.95**
Price: Screw-on base, .300" height, .300" radius **$19.95**
Price: Screw-on base, .450" height, .350" radius **$19.95**
Price: Screw-on base, .215" height, .400" radius **$19.95**

WINCHESTER & BROWNING FRONT SIGHTS Available in windgauge with spirit level, globe with clip, globe with spirit level (all with five inserts) and beach combination with gold plated rocker models. From Axtell Rifle Co.
Price: . . . . **$125.00 to $240.00**

Front Sights

AO TACTICAL SIGHTS Three types of drop-in replacement front posts–round top or square top night sight posts in standard and Big Dot sizes, or white stripe posts in .080 and .100 widths. For AR15 and M16 rifles. From AO Sight Systems, Inc.
Price: . . . . **$30.00 to $90.00**

AO RIFLE TEST POSTS Allows easy establishment of correct front post height. Provides dovetail post with .050" segments to allow shooter to "shoot-n-snip", watching point-of-impact walk into point of aim. Available for 3/8" standard dovetail, Ruger-style or Mauser. From AO Sight Systems, Inc.
Price: **$5.00**

AR-10 DETACHABLE FRONT SIGHT Allows use of the iron rear sight, but are removable for use of telescopic sights with no obstruction to the sight line, For AR-style rifles. From ArmaLite, Inc.
Price: . . . . **$50.00 to $70.00**
Price: Tritium Dot Express **$60.00**

BUSHMASTER FLIP-UP FRONT SIGHT Made for V Match AR-style rifles, this sight unit slips over milled front sight bases and clamps around barrel. Locks with the push of a button. For use with flip-up style rear sights or the A3 removable carry handle. From Bushmaster Firearms.
Price: **$99.95**

BUSHMASTER A2 COMPETITION FRONT SIGHT POST Surface ground on three sides for optimum visual clarity. Available in two widths: .052"; and .062". From Bushmaster Firearms.
Price: **$12.95**

CLASSIC STREAMLINED FRONT SPORTER RAMP SIGHT Comes with blade and sight cover. Serrated and contoured ramp. Screw-on attachment. Slide-on sight cover is easily detachable. Gold bead. From Sarco, inc.
Price: **$13.50**

ERA BEADS FOR RUGER RIFLES White bead and fiber optic front sights that replace the standard sights on M-77 and No. 1 Ruger rifles. Using 3/32" beads, they are available in heights of .330", .350", .375", .415" and .435". From New England Custom Gun Service.
Price: . . . . **$22.00 to $35.00**

ERA FRONT SIGHTS European-type front sights inserted from the front. Various heights available. From New England Custom Gun Service.
Price: 1/16" silver bead. **$18.00**
Price: 3/32" silver bead **$20.00**
Price: Sourdough bead **$20.00**
Price: Fiber optic **$35.00**
Price: Folding night sight with ivory bead **$49.00**

Knight's Armament

KNIGHT'S ARMAMENT FRONT STANDING/FOLDING SIGHT Mounts to the SR-25 rifle barrel gas block's MilStd top rail. Available in folding sight model. From Knight's Armament Co.
Price: . . . . **$145.00 to $175.00**

KNIGHT'S ARMAMENT CARRYING HANDLE SIGHT Rear sight and carry handle for the SR-25 rifle. Has fixed range and adjustable windage. From Knight's Armament Co.
Price: **$181.15**

KNIGHT'S ARMAMENT MK II FOLDING FRONT SIGHT For the SR-25 rifle. Requires modified handguard. From Knight's Armament Co.
Price: **$175.00**

KNIGHT'S ARMAMENT FOR FREE-FLOATING RAS Mounts to free-floating SR-25 and SR-15 RAS (rail adapter system) rifle forends. Adjustable for elevation. Made of aluminum. From Knight's Armament Co.
Price: **$155.25**

KNS PRECISION SYSTEMS SIGHT Screws into front base. Hooded for light consistency; precision machined with fine wire crosshairs measuring .010- inches thick. Aperture measures .240-inches diameter. Standard and duplex reticles. Available for AK-47, MAK-90, AR-15, M16, FN-FAL, H&K 91, 93, 94, MP5, SP89, L1A1, M1 Garand.
Price: **$25.99**

LYMAN HUNTING SIGHTS Made with gold or white beads 1/16" to 3/32" wide and in varying heights for most military and commercial rifles. Dovetail bases.
Price: **$8.95**

MARBLE STANDARD Ivory, red, or gold bead. For all American-made rifles, 1/16" wide bead with semi-flat face that does not reflect light. Specify type of rifle when ordering.
Price: **$10.00**

MARBLE CONTOURED Has 3/8" dovetail base, .090" deep, is 5/8" long. Uses standard 1/16" or 3/32" bead, ivory, red, or gold. Specify rifle type.
Price: **$11.50**

NATIONAL MATCH FRONT SIGHT POST Has .050" blade. For AR-style rifle. From ArmaLite, Inc.
Price: **$12.00**

T/C FIBER OPTIC FRONT MUZZLELOADER SIGHT Ramp-style steel with fiber optic bead for all tradition cap locks, both octagonal and round barrels with dovetail, and most T/C rifles. From Thompson/Center Arms.
Price: . . . . **$16.95 to $36.00**

TRIJICON NIGHT SIGHT Self-luminous tritium gas-filled front sight for the M16/AR-15 series.
Price: **$85.00**

WILLIAMS GOLD BEAD Available in .312", .343", and .406" high models all with 3/32" bead.
Price: **$11.95**

WILLIAMS RISER BLOCKS For adding .250" height to front sights when using a receiver sight. Two widths available: .250" for Williams Streamlined Ramp or .340" on all standard ramps having this base width. Uses standard 3/8" dovetail.
Price: **$7.95**

WILLIAMS AR-15 FIRESIGHT Fiber optic unit attaches to any standard AR-15-style front sight assembly. From Williams Gun Sight Co.
Price: **$45.95**

Ramp Sights

ERA MASTERPIECE Banded ramps; 21 sizes; hand-detachable beads and hood; beads inserted from the front. Various heights available. From New England Custom Gun Service.
Price: Banded ramp **$54.00**
Price: Hood **$10.50**
Price: 1/16" silver bead **$11.50**
Price: 3/32" silver bead **$16.00**
Price: Sourdough bead **$14.50**
Price: Fiber optic **$22.00**
Price: Folding night sight with ivory bead **$39.50**

HOLLAND & HOLLAND STYLE FRONT SIGHT RAMPS Banded and screw-on models in the Holland & Holland-style night sight. Flips forward to expose a .0781" silver bead. Flip back for use of the .150" diameter ivory bead for poor light or close-up hunting. Band thickness .040", overall length 3.350", band length 1.180". From New England Custom Gun Service.
Price: . . . . **$90.00 to $115.00**

LYMAN NO. 18 SCREW-ON RAMP Used with 8-40 screws but may also be brazed on. Heights from .10" to .350". Ramp without sight.
Price: **$13.75**

MARBLE FRONT RAMPS Available in polished or dull matte finish or serrated style. Standard 3/8x.090" dovetail slot. Made for MR-width (.340") front sights. Can be used as screw-on or sweat-on. Heights: .100", .150", .300".
Price: Polished or matte **$14.00**
Price: Serrated **$10.00**

NECG UNIVERSAL FRONT SIGHTS Available in five ramp heights and three front sight heights. Sights can be adjusted up or down .030" with an Allen wrench. Slips into place and then locks into position with a set screw. Six different front sight shapes are offered, including extra large and fiber optic. All hoods except the extra low ramp slide on from the rear and click in place. Extra low ramp has spring-loaded balls to lock hood. Choose from three hood sizes. From New England Custom Gun Service.
Price: **$34.00**

T/C TARGET SIGHT FOR OCTAGON BARREL MUZZLELOADERS A precision rear sight with click adjustments (via knurled knobs) for windage and elevation. Available for 15/16-inch and 1-inch octagon barrels with a screw hole spacing of .836-inch between centers. From Thompson/Center Arms.
Price: **$56.00**

T/C FIBER OPTIC MUZZLELOADER SIGHT Click adjustable for windage and elevation. Steel construction fitted with Tru-Glo™ fiber optics. Models available for most T/C muzzleloading rifles. Fits others with 1-inch and 15/16-inch octagon barrels with a hole spacing of .836-inch between screws. From Thompson/Center Arms.
Price: **$36.00**

WILLIAMS SHORTY RAMP Companion to "Streamlined" ramp, about 1/2" shorter. Screw-on or sweat-on. It is furnished in 1/8", 3/16", 9/32", and 3/8" heights without hood only. Also for shotguns.
Price: **$20.95**
Price: With dovetail lock **$21.95**

WILLIAMS STREAMLINED RAMP Available in screw-on or sweat-on models. Furnished in 9/16", 7/16", 3/8", 5/16", 3/16" heights.
Price: **$24.95**
Price: Sight hood **$4.95**

WILLIAMS STREAMLINED FRONT SIGHTS Narrow (.250" width) for Williams Streamlined ramps and others with 1/4" top width; medium (.340" width) for all standard factory ramps. Available with white, gold or fluorescent beads, 1/16" or 3/32".
Price: . . . . **$10.95 to $11.95**

Handgun Sights

AO EXPRESS SIGHTS Low-profile, snag-free express-type sights. Shallow V rear with white vertical line, white dot front. All-steel, matte black finish. Rear is available in different heights. Made for most pistols, many with double set-screws. From AO Sight Systems, Inc.
Price: Standard Set, front and rear **$60.00**
Price: Big Dot Set, front and rear **$60.00**
Price: Tritium Set, Standard or Big Dot **$90.00**
Price: 24/7 Pro Express, Std. or Big Dot Tritium **$120.00**

BO-MAR DELUXE BMCS Gives 3/8" windage and elevation adjustment at 50 yards on Colt Gov't 45; sight radius under 7". For GM and Commander models only. Uses existing dovetail slot. Has shield-type rear blade.
Price: **$65.95**
Price: BMCS-2 (for GM and 9mm) . . . **$68.95**
Price: Flat bottom **$65.95**
Price: BMGC (for Colt Gold Cup), angled serrated blade, rear **$68.95**
Price: BMGC front sight **$12.95**
Price: BMCZ-75 (for CZ-75,TZ-75, P-9 and most clones). Works with factory front **$68.95**

Bo-Mar BMGS

BO-MAR FRONT SIGHTS Dovetail style for S&W 4506, 4516, 1076; undercut style (.250", .280", 5/16" high); Fast Draw style (.210", .250", .230" high).
Price: **$12.95**

BO-MAR BMU XP-100/ T/C CONTENDER No gunsmithing required; has .080" notch.
Price: **$77.00**

Bo-Mar BMU XP-100

BO-MAR BMML For muzzleloaders; has .062" notch, flat bottom.
Price: **$65.95**
Price: With 3/8" dovetail **$65.95**

BO-MAR RUGER "P" ADJUSTABLE SIGHT Replaces factory front and rear sights.
Price: Rear sight **$65.95**
Price: Front sight **$12.00**

BO-MAR BMR Fully adjustable rear sight for Ruger MKI, MKII Bull barrel autos.
Price: Rear **$65.95**
Price: Undercut front sight **$12.00**

BO-MAR GLOCK Fully adjustable, all-steel replacement sights. Sight fits factory dovetail. Longer sight radius. Uses Novak Glock .275" high, .135" wide front, or similar.
Price: Rear sight **$68.95**
Price: Front sight **$20.95**

BO-MAR LOW PROFILE RIB & ACCURACY TUNER Streamlined rib with front and rear sights; 7 1/8" sight radius. Brings sight line closer to the bore than standard or extended sight and ramp. Weight 5 oz. Made for Colt Gov't 45, Super 38, and Gold Cup 45 and 38.
Price: **$140.00**

BO-MAR COMBAT RIB For S&W Model 19 revolver with 4" barrel. Sight radius 5 3/4", weight 5 1/2 oz.
Price: **$127.00**

BO-MAR WINGED RIB For S&W 4" and 6" length barrels-K-38, M10, HB 14 and 19. Weight for the 6" model is about 7 1/4 oz.
Price: **$140.00**

BO-MAR COVER-UP RIB Adjustable rear sight, winged front guards. Fits right over revolver's original front sight. For S&W 4" M-10HB, M-13, M-58, M- 64 & 65, Ruger 4" models SDA-34, SDA-84, SS-34, SS-84, GF-34, GF-84.
Price: **$130.00**

Chip McCormick "Drop-In"

CHIP MCCORMICK "DROP-IN" A low mount sight that fits any 1911-style slide with a standard military-type dovetail sight cut (60x.290"). Dovetail front sights also available. From Chip McCormick Corp.
Price: **$47.95**

CHIP MCCORMICK FIXED SIGHTS Same sight picture (.110" rear, 110" front) that's become the standard for pro combat shooters. Low mount design with rounded edges. For 1911-style pistols. May require slide machining for installation. From Chip McCormick Corp.
Price: **$24.95**

C-MORE SIGHTS Replacement front sight blades offered in two types and five styles. Made of Du Pont Acetal, they come in a set of five high-contrast colors: blue, green, pink, red and yellow. Easy to install. Patridge style for Colt Python (all barrels), Ruger Super Blackhawk (7 1/2"), Ruger Blackhawk (4 5/8"); ramp style for Python (all barrels), Blackhawk (4 5/8"), Super Blackhawk (7 1/2" and 10 1/2"). From C-More Systems.
Price: Per set **$19.95**

METALLIC SIGHTS

G.G. & G. GHOST RINGS Replaces the factory rear sight without gunsmithing. Black phosphate finish. Available for Colt M1911 and Commander, Beretta M92F, Glock, S&W, SIG Sauer.
Price: **$65.00**

Heinie Slant Pro

HEINIE SLANT PRO Made with a slight forward slant, the unique design of these rear sights is snag free for unimpeded draw from concealment. The combination of the slant and the rear serrations virtually eliminates glare. Made for most popular handguns. From Heinie Specialty Products.
Price: . . . . **$50.35 to $122.80**

HEINIE STRAIGHT EIGHT SIGHTS Consists of one tritium dot in the front sight and a slightly smaller Tritium dot in the rear sight. When aligned correctly, an elongated 'eight' is created. The Tritium dots are green in color. Designed with the belief that the human eye can correct vertical alignment faster than horizontal. Available for most popular handguns. From Heinie Specialty Products.
Price: . . . . **$104.95 to $122.80**

HEINIE CROSS DOVETAIL FRONT SIGHTS Made in a variety of heights, the standard dovetail is 60 degrees x .305" x .062" with a .002 taper. From Heinie Specialty Products.
Price: . . . . **$20.95 to $47.20**

JP GHOST RING Replacement bead front, ghost ring rear for Glock and M1911 pistols. From JP Enterprises.
Price: **$79.95**
Price: Bo-Mar replacement leaf with JP dovetail front bead . **$99.95**

LES BAER CUSTOM ADJUSTABLE LOW MOUNT REAR SIGHT Considered one of the top adjustable sights in the world for target shooting with 1911- style pistols. Available with Tritium inserts. From Les Baer Custom.
Price: . . . . **$49.00** (standard); **$99.00** (tritium)

LES BAER DELUXE FIXED COMBAT SIGHT A tactical-style sight with a very low profile. Incorporates a no-snag design and has serrations on sides. For 1911-style pistols. Available with Tritium inserts for night shooting. From Les Baer Custom.
Price: . . . . **$26.00 (standard); $67.00 (with Tritium)**

LES BAER DOVETAIL FRONT SIGHT Blank dovetail sight machined from bar stock. Can be contoured to many different configurations to meet user's needs. Available with Tritium insert. From Les Baer Custom.
Price: . . . . **$17.00** (standard); **$47.00** (with Tritium insert)

LES BAER FIBER OPTIC FRONT SIGHT Dovetail .330x65 degrees, .125" wide post, .185" high, .060" diameter. Red and green fiber optic. From Les Baer Custom.
Price: **$24.00**

LES BAER PPC-STYLE ADJUSTABLE REAR SIGHT Made for use with custom built 1911-style pistols, allows the user to preset three elevation adjustments for PPC-style shooting. Milling required for installation. Made from 4140 steel. From Les Baer Custom.
Price: . **$120.00**

Les Baer PPC-Style Adjustable Rear Sight

LES BAER DOVETAIL FRONT SIGHT WITH TRITIUM INSERT This fully contoured and finished front sight comes ready for gunsmith installation. From Les Baer Custom.
Price: **$47.00**

MMC TACTICAL GHOST RING SIGHT Click adjustable for elevation with 30 MOA total adjustment in 3 MOA increments. Click windage adjustment. Machined from solid steel and heat-treated. Front sights available in banded tactical or serrated ramp. Available with or without tritium and in three different finishes. Available for all shotgun makes and models.
Price:. . . . . **$24.95-$149.95**

MEPROLIGHT TRITIUM NIGHT SIGHTS Replacement sight assemblies for low-light conditions. Available for pistols (fixed and adj.), rifles, shotguns. 12- year warranty for useable illumination, while non-TRU-DOT have a 5-year warranty. Distributed in America by Kimber.
Price: Kahr K9, K40, fixed, TRU-DOT **$100.00**
Price: Ruger P85, P89, P94, adjustable, TRU-DOT **$156.00**
Price: Ruger Mini-14R sights **$140.00**
Price: SIG Sauer P220, P225, P226, P228, adjustable, TRU-DOT . **$156.00**
Price: Smith&Wesson autos, fixed or adjustable, TRU-DOT **$100.00**
Price: Taurus PT92, PT100, adjustable, TRU-DOT **$156.00**
Price: Walther P-99, fixed, TRU-DOT **$100.00**

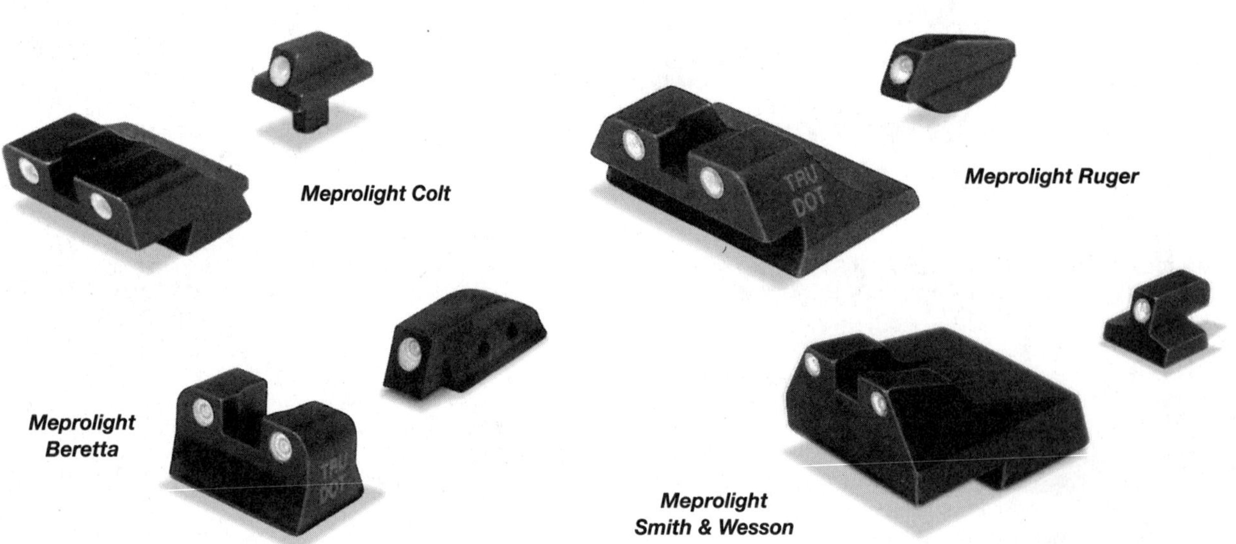

Meprolight Colt

Meprolight Ruger

Meprolight Beretta

Meprolight Smith & Wesson

METALLIC SIGHTS

Price: Shotgun bead **$32.00**
Price: Beretta M92, Cougar, Brigadier, fixed, TRU-DOT . . . **$100.00**
Price: Browning Hi-Power, adjustable, TRU-DOT **$156.00**
Price: Colt M1911 Govt., adjustable, TRU-DOT **$156.00**

MILLETT SERIES 100 REAR SIGHTS All-steel highly visible, click adjustable. Blades in white outline, target black, silhouette, 3-dot. Fit most popular revolvers and autos.
Price: . . . . **$54.95 to $88.95**

MILLETT BAR/DOT Made with orange or white bar or dot for increased visibility. Available for Beretta 84, 85, 92S, 92SB, Browning, Colt Python & Trooper, Ruger GP 100, P85, Redhawk, Security Six.
Price: . . . . **$14.99 to $24.99**

MILLETT 3-DOT SYSTEM SIGHTS The 3-Dot System sights use a single white dot on the front blade and two dots flanking the rear notch. Fronts available in Dual-Crimp and Wide Stake-On styles, as well as special applications. Adjustable rear sight available for most popular auto pistols and revolvers including Browning Hi-Power, Colt 1911 Government and Ruger P85.
Price: Front, from **$18.00**
Price: Adjustable rear **$63.95**

MILLETT REVOLVER FRONT SIGHTS All-steel replacement front sights with either white or orange bar. Easy to install. For Ruger GP-100, Redhawk, Security-Six, Police-Six, Speed-Six, Colt Trooper, Diamondback, King Cobra, Peacemaker, Python, Dan Wesson 22 and 15-2.
Price: . . . . **$15.20 to $18.00**

MILLETT DUAL-CRIMP FRONT SIGHT Replacement front sight for automatic pistols. Dual-Crimp uses an all-steel two-point hollow rivet system. Available in eight heights and four styles. Has a skirted base that covers the front sight pad. Easily installed with the Millett Installation Tool Set. Available in Blaze Orange Bar, White Bar, Serrated Ramp, Plain Post. Available in heights of .185", .200", .225", .275", .312", .340" and .410".
Price: **$18.00**

MILLETT STAKE-ON FRONT SIGHT Replacement front sight for automatic pistols. Stake-On sights have skirted base that covers the front sight pad. Easily installed with the Millet Installation Tool Set. Available in seven heights and four styles-Blaze Orange Bar, White Bar, Serrated Ramp, Plain Post. Available for Glock 17L and 24, others.
Price: **$18.00**

MILLETT ADJUSTABLE TARGET Positive light-deflection serration and slant to eliminate glare and sharp edge sight notch. Audible "click" adjustments. For AMT Hardballer, Beretta 84, 85, 92S, 92SB, Browning Hi-Power, Colt 1911 Government and Gold Cup, Colt revolvers, Dan Wesson 15, 41, 44, Ruger revolvers, Glock 17, 17L, 19, 20, 21, 22, 23.
Price: **$63.95**

MILLETT ADJUSTABLE WHITE OUTLINE Similar to the Target sight, except has a white outline on the blade to increase visibility. Available for the same handguns as the Target model, plus BRNO CZ-75/TZ-75/TA-90 without pin on front sight, and Ruger P85.
Price: **$63.95**

OMEGA OUTLINE SIGHT BLADES Replacement rear sight blades for Colt and Ruger single action guns and the Interarms Virginian Dragoon. Standard Outline available in gold or white notch outline on blue metal. From Omega Sales, Inc.
Price: **$10.00**

OMEGA MAVERICK SIGHT BLADES Replacement "peep-sight" blades for Colt, Ruger SAs, Virginian Dragoon. Three models available-No. 1, Plain; No. 2, Single Bar; No. 3, Double Bar Rangefinder. From Omega Sales, Inc.
Price: Each. **$10.00**

ONE RAGGED HOLE Replacement rear sight ghost ring sight for Ruger handguns. Fits Blackhawks, Redhawks, Super Blackhawks, GP series and Mk. II target pistols with adjustable sights. From One Ragged Hole, Tallahassee, Florida.

Price: **$24.95**
Price: Winchester Model 92s and Marlin 36/336/1894/ etc . . **$34.95**

PACHMAYR ACCU-SET Low-profile, fully adjustable rear sight to be used with existing front sight. Available with target, white outline or 3-dot blade. Blue finish. Uses factory dovetail and locking screw. For Browning, Colt, Glock, SIG Sauer, S&W and Ruger autos. From Pachmayr.

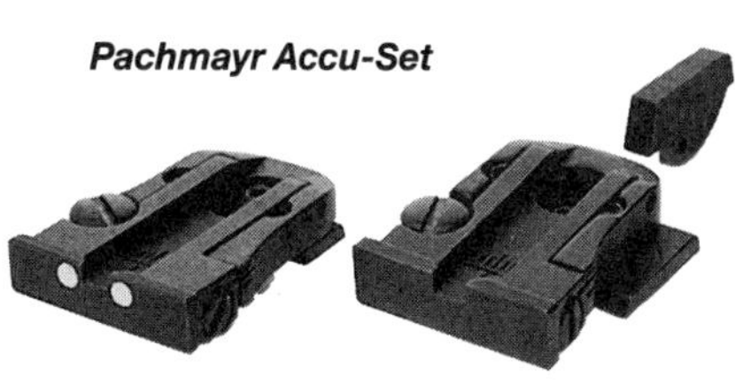
Pachmayr Accu-Set

Price: **$59.98**

P-T TRITIUM NIGHT SIGHTS Self-luminous tritium sights available for virtually all makes and models of handguns, shotguns and rifles. Ten different configurations. Sights have lifetime guarantee, including tritium replacement. From Miniature Machine Corp. (MMC).
Price: . . . . **$45.00-$89.00**

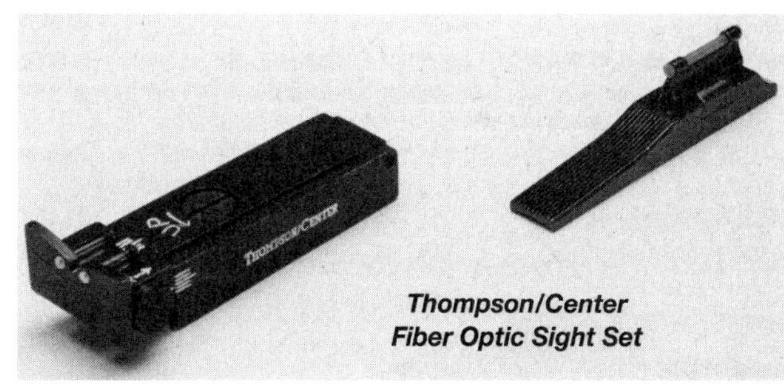
Thompson/Center Fiber Optic Sight Set

T/C ENCORE FIBER OPTIC SIGHT SETS Click adjustable, steel rear sight and ramp-style front sight, both fitted with Tru-GloTM fiber optics. Specifically- designed for the T/C Encore pistol series. From Thompson/Center Arms.
Price: **$49.35**

T/C ENCORE TARGET REAR SIGHT Precision, steel construction with click adjustments (via knurled knobs) for windage and elevation. Models available with low, medium and high blades. From Thompson/Center Arms.
Price: **$54.00**

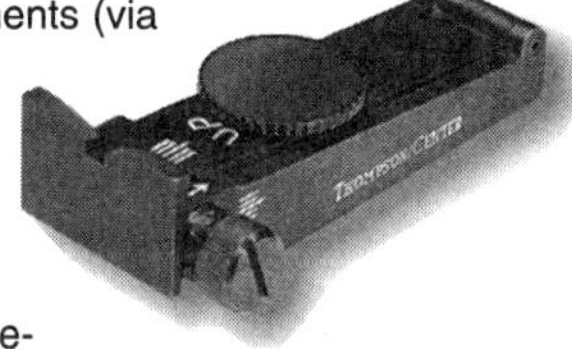
Thompson/Center Target Rear Sight

TRIJICON NIGHT SIGHTS Three-dot night sight system uses tritium lamps in the front and rear sights. Tritium "lamps" are mounted in silicone rubber inside a metal cylinder. A polished crystal sapphire provides protection and clarity. Inlaid white outlines provide 3-dot aiming in daylight also. Available for most popular handguns including Glock 17, 19, 20, 21, 23, 24, 25, 26,

Trijicon Night Sight

Wichita Series 70/80 Sight

29, 30, H&K USP, Ruger P94, SIG P220, P225, 226, Colt 1911. Front and rear sets available. From Trijicon, Inc.

Price: . . . . **$99.00-$175.00**

TRIJICON 3-DOT Self-luminous front iron night sight for the Ruger SP101.

Price: **$50.00**

WICHITA SERIES 70/80 SIGHT Provides click windage and elevation adjustments with precise repeatability of settings. Sight blade is grooved and angled back at the top to reduce glare. Available in Low Mount Combat or Low Mount Target styles for Colt 45s and their copies, S&W 645, Hi-Power, CZ 75 and others.

Price: Rear sight, target or combat **$80.70**

Price: Front sight, Patridge or ramp **$15.00**

WICHITA GRAND MASTER DELUXE RIBS Ventilated rib has wings machined into it for better sight acquisition and is relieved for Mag-Na-Porting. Milled to accept Weaver see-thru-style rings. Made of stainless; front and rear sights blued. Has Wichita Multi-Range rear sight system, adjustable front sight. Made for revolvers with 6" barrel.

Price: Model 301S, 301B (adj. sight K frames with custom bbl. of 1" to 1.032" dia. L and N frame with 1.062" to 1.100" dia. bbl.) **$265.00**

Price: Model 303S, 303B (adj. sight K, L, N frames with factory barrel) **$250.00**

WICHITA MULTI-RANGE QUICK CHANGE SIGHTING SYSTEM Multi-range rear sight can be pre-set to four positive repeatable range settings. Adjustable front sight allows compensation for changing lighting and weather conditions with just one front sight adjustment. Front sight comes with Lyman 17A Globe and set of apertures.

Price: Rear sight **$145.00**

Price: Front, sight **$110.00**

Williams Fire Sight Set

WILLIAMS FIRE SIGHT SETS Red fiber optic metallic sight replaces the original. Rear sight has two green fiber optic elements. Made of CNC-machined aluminum. Fits all Glocks, Ruger P-Series (except P-85), S&W 910, Colt Gov't. Model Series 80, Ruger GP 100 and Redhawk, and SIG Sauer (front only).

Price: Front and rear set **$46.95**

Price: SIG Sauer front **$23.95**

Price: Ruger P345/KP345 (2006) **$46.95**

Price: Taurus PT111, PT140, PT145, PT1232, PT138 . . . . . **$46.95**

WILSON ADJUSTABLE REAR SIGHTS Machined from steel, the click adjustment design requires simple cuts and no dovetails for installation. Available in several configurations: matte black standard blade with .128" notch; with .110" notch; with Tritium dots and .128" square or "U" shaped notch; and Combat Pyramid. From Wilson Combat.

Price: . . . . **$24.95 to $69.95**

WILSON NITE-EYES SIGHTS Low-profile, snag free design with green and yellow Tritium inserts. For 1911-style pistols. From Wilson Combat.

Price: **$119.95**

WILSON TACTICAL COMBAT SIGHTS Low-profile and snag-free in design, the sight employs the Combat Pyramid shape. For many 1911-style pistols and some Glock models. From Wilson Combat.

Price: **$139.95**

Shotgun Sights

AO SHOTGUN SIGHTS 24/7 Pro Express sights fit Remington rifle sighted barrels. Front sight divetails into existing ramp, rear installs on Remington rear ramp. Available in Big Dot Tritium or Standard Dot Tritium. Three other styles (for pedestal base, beaded, and ribbed barrels) provide a Big Dot Tritium front that epoxies over the existing bead front sight. From AO Sight Systems, Inc.

Price: 24/7 Tritium Sets. . . . . **$90.00 to $120.00**

Price: Big Dot Tritium (front only) **$60.00**

BRADLEY SHOTGUN SIGHTS Front beads available in sizes of 1/8" and 5/32" in thread sizes of #3-56, #6-48, and #8-40. From 100 Straight Products.

Price: **$5.00**

BRADLEY CENTER SIGHTS Available in 1/16" bead size and #3-56 thread or taper. Plain brass, bright silver and white finishes. From 100 Straight Products.

Price: . . . . **$2.50 to $6.00 each**

BRADLEY SHOTGUN SIGHT ASSORTMENT An assortment of the most frequently used sights including six each of 18-3, 18-6,532-3, 532-7, 532-9, MB-01 and MB-11. From 100 Straight Products.

Price: **$119.95**

CARLSON SHOTGUN SIGHT A brilliant orange bead securely held by two bands. Used for low light conditions. Bead size .150", thread size 6-48. From Carlson's and 100 Straight Products.

Price: **$7.50**

FIRE FLY EM-109 SL SHOTGUN SIGHT Made of aircraft-grade aluminum, this 1/4-oz. "channel" sight has a thick, sturdy hollowed post between the side rails to give a Patridge sight picture. All shooting is done with both eyes open, allowing the shooter to concentrate on the target, not the sights. The hole in the sight post gives reduced-light shooting capability and allows for fast, precise aiming. For sport or combat shooting. Model EM-109 fits all vent. rib and double barrel shotguns and muzzleloaders with octagon barrel. Model MOC-110 fits all plain barrel shotguns without screw-in chokes. From JAS, Inc.

Price: **$35.00**

LYMAN Three sights of over-sized ivory beads. No. 10 Front (press fit) for double barrel or ribbed single barrel guns **$4.50;** No. 10D Front (screw fit) for non-ribbed single barrel guns (comes with wrench) **$5.50;** No. 11 Middle (press fit) for double and ribbed single barrel guns.

Price: **$4.75**

MMC M&P COMBAT SHOTGUN SIGHT SET A durable, protected ghost ring aperture, combat sight made of steel. Fully adjustable for windage and elevation.

Price: M&P Sight Set (front and rear). **$73.45**

Price: As above, installed **$83.95**

MMC TACTICAL GHOST RING SIGHT Click adjustable for elevation with 30 MOA total adjustment in 3 MOA increments. Click windage adjustment. Machined from solid steel and heat-treated. Front sights available in banded tactical or serrated ramp. Available with or without tritium and in three different finishes. Available for all shotgun makes and models.

Price:. . . . . **$24.95-$149.95**

MARBLE SHOTGUN BEAD SIGHTS No. 214-Ivory front bead, 11/64", tapered shank **$4.40;** No. 223-Ivory rear bead, .080", tapered shank **$4.40;** No. 217-Ivory front bead, 11/64", threaded shank **$4.75;** No. 223-T-Ivory rear bead, .080, threaded shank **$5.95.** Reamers, taps and wrenches available from Marble Arms.

MEPROLIGHT Ghost ring sight set for Benelli tactical shotguns. From Meprolight, Inc.

Price: **$100.00**

MILLETT SHURSHOT SHOTGUN SIGHT A sight system for shotguns with ventilated rib. Rear sight attaches to the rib, front sight replaces the front bead. Front has an orange face, rear has two orange bars. For 870, 1100 or other models.

Price: Rear, fixed..... **$14.95**
Price: Adjustable front and rear set **$35.95**
Price: Front......... **$14.95**

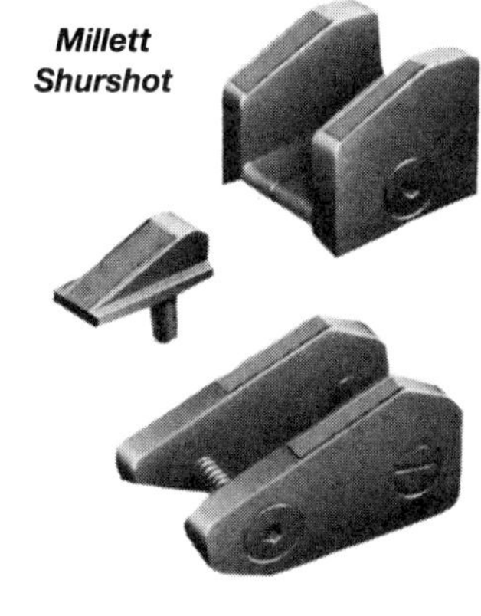

Millett Shurshot

NECG IVORY SHOTGUN BEAD Genuine ivory shotgun beads with 6-48 thread. Available in heights of .157" and .197". From New England Custom Gun Service.
Price: **$9.00**

POLY-CHOKE Replacement front shotgun sights in four styles-Xpert, Poly Bead, Xpert Mid Rib sights, and Bev-L-Block. Xpert Front available in 3x56, 6x48 thread, 3/32" or 5/32" shank length, gold, ivory **$4.70**; or Sun Spot orange bead $**5.95**; Poly Bead is standard replacement 1/8" bead, 6x48 **$2.95**; Xpert Mid Rib in tapered carrier (ivory only) **$5.95**, or 3x56 threaded shank (gold only) **$2.95**; Hi and Lo Blok sights with 6x48 thread, gold or ivory **$5.25**. From Marble Arms.

SLUG SIGHTS Made of non-marring black nylon, front and rear sights stretch over and lock onto barrel. Sights are low profile with blaze orange front blade. Adjustable for windage and elevation. For plain-barrel (non-ribbed) guns in 12-, 16- and 20-gauge, and for shotguns with 5/16" and 3/8" ventilated ribs. From Innovision Ent.
Price: **$11.95**

TRIJICON 3-DOT NIGHT SIGHTS Self-luminous and machined from steel. Available for Remington 870, 1100, 1187.
Price: .... **$75.00 to $175.00**

WILLIAMS GUIDE BEAD SIGHT Fits all shotguns, 1/8" ivory, red or gold bead. Screws into existing sight hole. Various thread sizes and shank lengths.
Price: **$8.50**

WILLIAMS UNIVERSAL SLUGGER shotgun fire sight set. Fiber optic, front and rear metallic sights attach to most vent ribs. Adjustable for windage and elevation. No gunsmithing required.
Price: **$39.95**

WILLIAMS FIRE SIGHTS Fiber optic light gathering front sights in red or yellow, glow with natural light. Fit 1/4", 5/16" or 3/8" vent. ribs, most popular shotguns.
Price: **$18.95**

Sight Attachments

MERIT ADJUSTABLE APERTURES Eleven clicks give 12 different apertures. No. 3 Disc and Master, primarily target types, 0.22" to .125"; No. 4, 1/2" dia. hunting type, .025" to .155". Available for all popular sights. The Master, with flexible rubber light shield, is particularly adapted to extension, scope height, and tang sights. All models have internal click springs; are hand fitted to minimum tolerance.
Price: No. 3 Master Disk............................ **$66.00**
Price: No. 3 Target Disc (Plain Face) **$56.00**
Price: No. 4 Hunting Disc **$48.00**

MERIT LENS DISC Similar to Merit Iris Shutter (Model 3 or Master) but incorporates provision for mounting prescription lens integrally. Lens may be obtained locally from your optician. Sight disc is 7/16" wide (Model 3), or 3/4" wide (Master).
Price: No. 3 Target Lens Disk........................ **$68.00**

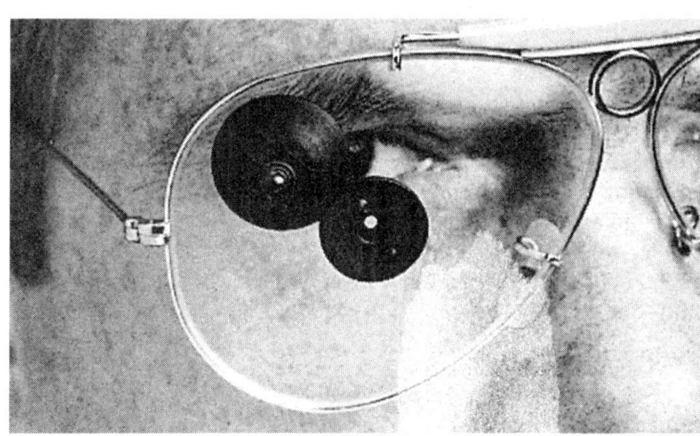

Merit Optical Attachment

Price: No. 3 Master Lens Disk **$78.00**

MERIT OPTICAL ATTACHMENT For iron sight shooting with handgun or rifle. Instantly attached by rubber suction cup to prescription or shooting glasses. Swings aside. Aperture adjustable from .020" to .156".
Price: **$65.00**

WILLIAMS APERTURES Standard thread, fit most sights. Regular series 3/8" to 1/2" O.D., .050" to .125" hole. "Twilight" series has white reflector ring.
Price: Regular series.................................. **$7.95**
Price: Twilight series **$9.95**
Price: Wide open 5/16" aperture for shotguns fits 5-D or Foolproof sights (specify model) **$10.95**

Simmons 1280

ALPEN MODEL 711 20x50 mini-scope, 20x, 50mm eyepiece, field of view at 1,000 yds. 147 ft., multi-coated lens, weighs 10 oz., waterproof.
Price: **$60.97**

ALPEN MODEL 722 12-36x compact, 50mm eyepiece, field of view at 1,000 yds: 115 ft. (12x); 59 ft. (36x); multi-coated lens, weighs 27 oz., waterproof.
Price: **$124.20**

ALPEN MODEL 725 and 728 Compact 15-45x60, 60mm obj., center focus, multi- coated lens, field of view at 1,000 yds: 136 ft. (15x); 107 ft. (45x); weighs 27 oz., waterproof.
Price: .... **$151.62 and $154.85**

ALPEN MODEL 730 15-30x50, 60mm obs., field of view at 1,000 yds: 136 ft. (15x); 99 ft. (50x); multi-coated lens, weighs 28 oz., waterproof.
Price: **$116.14**

ALPEN MODEL 788 20-60x80, 80mm obj., field of view at 1,000 yds: 93 ft. (20x); 47 ft. (60x); multi-coated lens, weighs 64 oz., waterproof.
Price: **$404.69**

BUSHNELL DISCOVERER, 15x to 60x zoom, 60mm objective. Constant focus throughout range. Field of view at 1,000 yds.: 38 ft. (60x), 150 ft. (15x). Comes with lens caps. Length: 17-1/2"; weighs 48.5 oz.
Price: **$342.95**

BUSHNELL ELITE 15x to 45x zoom, 60mm objective. Field of view at 1,000 yds.: 125 ft.@15X, 65 ft.@45X. Length: 12.2"; weighs 26.5 oz. Waterproof, armored. Tripod mount. Comes with black case and rainguard.
Price: **$586.95**

BUSHNELL ELITE ZOOM 20x-60x, 70mm objective. Roof prism. Field of view at 1,000 yds.: 90 ft.@20X, 50 ft.@60X. Length: 16"; weighs 40 oz. Waterproof, armored. Tripod mount. Comes with black case.
Price: **$806.95**

BUSHNELL 80MM ELITE 20x-60x zoom, 80mm objective. Field of view at 1,000 yds.: 98 ft.@20X, 50 ft.@60X. Weighs 53 oz. Length: 17". Interchangeable bayonet-style eyepieces. Built-in peep sight.
Price: With EDPrime Glass.......... **$1,173.95**

BUSHNELL TROPHY 65mm objective, 20x-60x zoom. Field of view at 1,000 yds. 90 ft. (20x), 45 ft. (60x). Length: 12.7"; weighs 20 oz. Black rubber armored, waterproof. Case included.
Price: **$297.95**

BUSHNELL COMPACT TROPHY 50mm objective, 20x-50x zoom. Field of view at 1,000 yds. 92 ft. (20x), 52 ft. (50x). Length: 12.2"; weighs 17 oz. Black rubber armored, waterproof. Case included.
Price:.......... **$257.95**

BUSHNELL COMPACT SENTRY 18-36x50mm objective. Field of view at 1,000 yds.: 15 ft.@18X, 75 ft.@36X. Length: 14.7", weighs 31 oz. With tripod and hard case. Waterproof.
Price:.......... **$157.95**

BUSHNELL SPACEMASTER 20x-45x zoom. Long eye relief. Rubber armored, prismatic. 60mm objective. Field of view at 1,000 yds.: 90 ft.@20X, 30 ft.@45X. Minimum focus 20 ft. Length: 12.7"; weighs 43 oz.
Price: With tripod, carrying case and 20x-45x LER eyepiece. **$502.95**

BUSHNELL SPACEMASTER COLLAPSIBLE 15-45x zoom, 50mm objective lens. Field of view at 1,000 yds., 113 ft. (15x), 52 ft. (45x). Length: 8". Weighs 22.8 oz. Comes with tripod, window mount and case.
Price:.......... **$209.95**

BUSHNELL SPORTVIEW 15x-45x zoom, 50mm objective. Field of view at 1,000 yds. 103 ft. (15x), 35 ft. (45x). Length: 17.4"; weighs 34.4 oz.
Price: With tripod and carrying case.......... **$91.95**

BUSHNELL LEGEND 20x-60x zoom, 60mm objective. Field of view at 1,000 yds. 138 ft. (20x), 68 ft. (60x). Length: 14.3"; weighs 34.3 oz.
Price: With carrying case **$398.95**

CELESTRON MINI 50MM ZOOM Offset 45° or straight body. Comes with 12x36x eyepiece. 50mm obj. Field of view at 1,000 yds. 160 (or 82), waterproof. Length: 8.5", weighs 1.4 lbs.
Price: .... **NA**

CELESTRON ULTIMA SERIES Offset 45° or straight body. 18x55, 20-60 zoom or 22- 60 zoom. Aperture: 65mm, 80mm or 100mm, field of view at 1,000 yds., 89' at 18x, 38' at 55x, 105' at 20x, 95' at 22x, 53' at 66x. Length: 13", 16" or 19". Weighs 2.3 to 4.5 lbs.
Price: Body.......... **NA**

HERMES 1 70mm objective, 16x, 25x, 40x. Field of view at 1,000 meters 160 ft. (16x), 75 ft. (40x). Length: 12.2"; weighs 33 oz. From CZ-USA.
Price: Body.......... **$359.00**
Price: 25x eyepiece **$86.00**
Price: 40x eyepiece **$128.00**

KOWA TS-500 SERIES Offset 45° or straight body. Comes with 20-40x zoom eyepiece or 20x fixed eyepiece. 50mm obj. Field of view at 1,000 yds.: 171 ft. (20x fixed), 132-74 ft. (20-40x zoom). Length: 8.9-10.4", weighs 13.4-14.8 oz.
Price: TS-501 (offset 45° body w/20x fixed eyepiece) **$258.00**
Price: TS-502 (straight body w/20x fixed eyepiece) **$231.00**
Price: TS-501Z (offset 45° body w/20-40x zoom eyepiece) . **$321.00**
Price: TS-502Z (straight body w/20-40x zoom eyepiece) ... **$290.00**

KOWA TS-660 SERIES Offset 45° or straight body. Fully waterproof. Available with ED lens. Sunshade and rotating tripod mount. 66mm obj. Field of view at 1,000 yds.: 177 ft. (20xW), 154 ft. (27xW), 131 ft. (30xW), 102 ft. (25x), 92 ft. (25xLER), 108-79 ft. (20-40x multi-coated zoom), 98-62 ft. (20-60x high grade zoom). Length: 12.3"; weighs 34.9-36.7 oz.
Price: TSN-662 body (straight).......... **$610.00**
Price: TSN-663 body (45 offset, ED lens) **$1,070.00**
Price: TSN-664 body (straight, ED lens) **$1,010.00**
Price: TSE-Z6 (20-40x multi-coatedzoom eyepiece) **$378.00**
Price: TSE-17HB (25x long eye relief eyepiece) **$240.00**
Price: TSE-14W (30x wide angle high-grade eyepiece) **$288.00**
Price: TSE-21WB (20x wide-angle eyepiece) **$230.00**
Price: TSE-15 WM (27x wide-angle eyepiece) **$182.00**
Price: TSE-16 PM (25x eyepiece) **$108.00**
Price: TSN-DA1 digital photo adapter **$105.00**
Price: DA1 adapter rings **$43.00**
Price: TSN-PA2 (800mm photo adapter) **$269.00**
Price: TSN-PA4 (1200mm photo adapter) **$330.00**
Price: Camera mounts (for use with photo adapter) **$30.00**
Price: Eyepieces for TSN 77mm series, TSN-660 series, 661 body (45° offset) **$660.00**

KOWA TSN-660 SERIES Offset 45° or straight body. Fully waterproof. Available with fluorite lens. Sunshade and rotating tripod mount. 66mm obj., field of view at 1,000 yds: 177 ft. (20x), 154 ft. (27xW), 131 ft. (30xW), 102 ft. (25x), 92 ft. (25xLER), 62 ft. (40x), 108-79 ft. (20-40x Multi-Coated Zoom), 102- 56 ft. (20-60x zoom), 98-62 ft. (20- 60x High Grade Zoom). Length: 12.3"; weighs 34.9-36.7 oz. Note: Eyepieces for TSN 77mm Series, TSN-660 Series, and TSN610 Series are interchangeable.

Price: TSN-661 body (45° offset) **$660.00**
Price: TSN-662 body (straight) **$610.00**
Price: TSN-663 body (45° offset, fluorite lens) **$1,070.00**
Price: TSN-664 body (straight, fluorite lens) **$1,010.00**
Price: TSE-Z4 (20-60x high-grade zoom eyepiece) **$378.00**
Price: TSE-Z6 (20-40x multi-coated zoom eyepiece) **$250.00**
Price: TSE-17HB (25x long eye relief eyepiece) **$240.00**
Price: TSE-14W (30x wide angle eyepiece) **$288.00**
Price: TSE-21WB (20x wide angle eyepiece) **$230.00**
Price: TSE-15PM (27x wide angle eyepiece) **$182.00**
Price: TSE-10PM (40x eyepiece) **$108.00**
Price: TSE-16PM (25x eyepiece) **$105.00**
Price: TSN-DA1 (digital photo adapter) **$105.00**
Price: Adapter rings for DA1 .... **$43.00**
Price: TSN-PA2 (800mm photo adapter) **$269.00**
Price: TSN-PA4 (1200mm photo adapter) **$330.00**
Price: Camera mounts (for use with photo adapter) **$30.00**

KOWA TSN-820M SERIES Offset 45° or straight body. Fully waterproof. Available with fluorite lens. Sunshade and rotating tripod mount. 82mm obj., field of view at 1,000 yds: 75 ft. (27xLER, 50xW), 126 ft. (32xW), 115-58 ft. (20-60xZoom). Length: 15"; weighs 49.4-52.2 oz.
Price: TSN-821M body (45° offset) **$850.00**
Price: TSN-822M body (straight) **$770.00**
Price: TSN-823M body (45° offset, fluorite lens) **$1,850.00**
Price: TSN-824M body (straight, fluorite lens) **$1,730.00**
Price: TSE-Z7 (20-60x zoom eyepiece) **$433.00**
Price: TSE-9W (50x wide angle eyepiece) **$345.00**
Price: TSE-14WB (32x wide angle eyepiece) **$366.00**
Price: TSE-17HC (27x long eye relief eyepiece) **$248.00**
Price: TSN-DA1 (digital photo adapter) **$105.00**
Price: Adapter rings for DA1 .... **$43.00**
Price: TSN-PA2C (850mm photo adapter) **$300.00**
Price: Camera mounts (for use with photo adapter) **$30.00**

LEUPOLD 10-20x40mm COMPACT 40mm objective, 10-20x. Field of view at 100 yds. 19.9-13.6 ft.; eye relief 18.5mm (10x). Overall length: 7.5", weighs 15.8 oz. Rubber armored.
Price:. **$439.95**

LEUPOLD 55-30x50 COMPACT 50mm objective, 15-30x. Field of view at 100 yds. 13.6 ft.; eye relief 17.5mm; Overall length: 11"; weighs 1.5 oz.
Price: **$564.99**

LEUPOLD Wind River Sequoia 15-30x60mm, 60mm objective, 15-30x. Field of view at 100 yds.: 13.1 ft.; eye relief: 16.5mm. Overall length: 13". Weighs 35.1 oz.
Price: **$294.99**

LEUPOLD Wind River Sequoia 15-45x60mm Angled. Armored, 15-45x. Field of view at 100 yds.: 13.1-6.3 ft.; eye relief: 16.5-13.0. Overall length: 12.5". Weighs 35.1 oz.
Price: **$309.99**

LEUPOLD Golden Ring 12-40x60mm; 12.7x38.1x. Field of view at 100 yds.: 16.8-5.2 ft.; eye relief: 30.0; Overall length: 12.4". Weighs 37.0 oz.
Price: **$1,124.99**

LEUPOLD Golden Ring 15-30x50mm Compact Armored; 15.2-30.4x; field of view at 100 yds.: 13.6-8.9 ft.; eye relief: 17.5-17.1; overall length: 11.0". Weighs 21.5 oz.
Price:. **$564.99**

MIRADOR TTB SERIES Draw tube armored spotting scopes. Available with 75mm or 80mm objective. Zoom model (28x-62x, 80mm) is 11-7/8" (closed), weighs 50 oz. Field of view at 1,000 yds. 70-42 ft. Comes with lens covers.
Price: 28-62x80mm. **$1,133.95**
Price: 32x80mm **$971.95**
Price: 26-58x75mm **$989.95**
Price: 30x75mm **$827.95**

MIRADOR SSD SPOTTING SCOPES 60mm objective, 15x, 20x, 22x, 25x, 40x, 60x, 20-60x; field of view at 1,000 yds. 37 ft.; length: 10 1/4"; weighs 33 oz.
Price: 25x **$575.95**
Price: 22x Wide Angle **$593.95**
Price: 20-60x Zoom **$746.95**
Price: As above, with tripod, case **$944.95**

MIRADOR SIA SPOTTING SCOPES Similar to the SSD scopes except with 45° eyepiece. Length: 12-1/4"; weighs 39 oz.
Price: 25x **$809.95**
Price: 22x Wide Angle **$827.95**
Price: 20-60x Zoom **$980.95**

MIRADOR SSR SPOTTING SCOPES 50mm or 60mm objective. Similar to SSD except rubber armored in black or camouflage. Length: 11-1/8"; weighs 31 oz.
Price: Black, 20x. **$521.95**
Price: Black, 18x Wide Angle **$539.95**
Price: Black, 16-48x Zoom **$692.95**
Price: Black, 20x, 60mm, EER **$692.95**
Price: Black, 22x Wide Angle, 60mm **$701.95**
Price: Black, 20-60x Zoom **$854.95**

MIRADOR SSF FIELD SCOPES Fixed or variable power, choice of 50mm, 60mm, 75mm objective lens. Length: 9-3/4"; weighs 20 oz. (15-32x50).
Price: 20x50mm **$359.95**
Price: 25x60mm **$440.95**
Price: 30x75mm **$584.95**
Price: 15-32x50mm Zoom **$548.95**
Price: 18-40x60mm Zoom **$629.95**
Price: 22-47x75mm Zoom **$773.95**

MIRADOR SRA MULTI ANGLE SCOPES Similar to SSF Series except eyepiece head rotates for viewing from any angle.
Price: 20x50mm **$503.95**
Price: 25x60mm **$647.95**
Price: 30x75mm **$764.95**
Price: 15-32x50mm Zoom **$692.95**
Price: 18-40x60mm Zoom **$836.95**
Price: 22-47x75mm Zoom **$953.95**

MIRADOR SIB FIELD SCOPES Short-tube, 45° scopes with porro prism design. 50mm and 60mm objective. Length: 10 1/4"; weighs 18.5 oz. (15- 32x50mm); field of view at 1,000 yds. 129-81 ft.
Price: 20x50mm **$386.95**
Price: 25x60mm **$449.95**
Price: 15-32x50mm Zoom **$575.95**
Price: 18-40x60mm Zoom **$638.95**

NIKON FIELDSCOPES 60mm and 78mm lens. Field of view at 1,000 yds. 105 ft. (60mm, 20x), 126 ft. (78mm, 25x). Length: 12.8" (straight 60mm), 12.6" (straight 78mm); weighs 34.5 to 47.5 oz. Eyepieces available separately.
Price: 60mm straight body **$499.99**
Price: 60mm angled body **$519.99**
Price: 60mm straight ED body **$779.99**
Price: 60mm angled ED body **$849.99**
Price: 78mm straight ED body **$899.99**
Price: 78mm angled ED body **$999.99**
Price: Eyepieces (15x to 60x) .... **$146.95 to $324.95**
Price: 20-45x eyepiece (25-56x for 78mm) **$320.55**

NIKON 60mm objective, 20x fixed power or 15-45x zoom. Field of view at 1,000 yds. 145 ft. (20x). Gray rubber armored. Straight or angled eyepiece. Weighs 44.2 oz., length: 12.1" (20x).
Price: 20x60 fixed (with eyepiece) **$290.95**
Price: 15-45x zoom (with case, tripod, eyepiece) **$578.95**

PENTAX PF-80ED 80mm objective lens available in 18x, 24x, 36x, 48x, 72x and 20- 60x. Length: 15.6", weighs 11.9 to 19.2 oz.
Price: **$1,320.00**

SIGHTRON SII836x50 Kit 50mm objective lens, 18x-36x zoom. Field of view at 1,000 yds 105 ft. (18x), 73.5 ft. (36x). Length: 10.4"; weighs 20.1 oz. Black rubber finish. Kit comes with aluminum case and table-top tripod.
Price:. **$235.28**

SIGHTRON SIIWP2050x65 65mm objective lens, 20x-50x zoom. Field of view at 1,000 yds 84 ft. (20x), 47 ft. (50x). Length: 13.4"; weighs 31.5 oz. Black rubber finish. Fanny-pack case. Also available in 80mm (13.8" length, 40.5 oz. weight).

Price: 65mm **$528.00**
Price: 80mm **$607.00**

SIGHTRON SIIWP2060x63 Multi-coated 63mm objective lens, 20x-60x and 25x wide-angle fully multi-coated eyepieces. Field of view at 1,000 yds 89 ft. (20x), 58 ft. (60x), 110 ft (25x). Length: 14.4"; weighs 32.7 oz. Black rubber finish. Custom Cordura Case.
Price: **$793.04**

SIMMONS 1280 50mm objective, 15-45x zoom. Black matte finish. Ocular focus. Peep finder sight. Waterproof. Field of view at 95-51 ft. 1,000 yds. Weights 33.5 oz., length: 12".
Price: With tripod **$189.99**

SIMMONS 1281 60mm objective, 20-60x zoom. Black matte finish. Ocular focus. Peep finder sight. Waterproof. Field of view at 78-43 ft. 1,000 yds. Weights 34.5 oz. Length: 12".
Price: With tripod **$209.99**

SIMMONS 77206 PROHUNTER 50mm objectives, 25x fixed power. Field of view at 1,000 yds. 113 ft.; length: 10.25"; weighs 33.25 oz. Black rubber armored.
Price: With tripod case **$160.60**

SIMMONS 41200 REDLINE 50mm objective, 15x-45x zoom. Field of view at 1,000 yds. 104-41 ft.; length: 16.75"; weighs 32.75 oz.
Price: With hard case and tripod..................................... **$74.99**
Price: 20-60x, 60mm objective **$99.99**

SWAROVSKI ATS-STS 65mm or 80mm objective, 20-60x zoom, or fixed 20x, 30x 45x eyepieces. Field of view at 1,000 yds. 180 ft. (20xSW), 126 ft. (30xSW), 84 ft. (45xSW), 108-60 ft. (20-60xS) for zoom. Length: 13.98" (ATS/STS 80), 12.8" (ATS/STS 65); weighs 45.93 oz. (ATS 80), 47.70 oz. (ATS 80HD), 45.23 oz. (STS 80), 46.91 oz. (STS 80 HD), 38.3 oz. (ATS 65), 39.9 oz. (ATS 65HD) 38.1 oz. (STS 65), 39.2 oz. (STS 65 HD).
Price: ATS 65 (angled eyepiece) **$1,254.45**
Price: STS 65 (straight eyepiece) **$1,254.45**
Price: ATS-80/STS 80 .... **$1,565.57**
Price: ATS/STS 80 (HD) **$2,110.01**
Price: 20xSW **$372.23**
Price: 30xSW **$388.90**
Price: 45xSW **$432.23**

SWIFT LYNX M836 15x-45x zoom, 60mm objective. Weighs 7 lbs., length: 14". Has 45° eyepiece, sunshade.
Price: **$315.00**

SWIFT NIGHTHAWK M849U 80mm objective, 20x-60x zoom, or fixed 19, 25x, 31x, 50x, 75x eyepieces. Has rubber armored body, 1.8x optical finder, retractable lens hood, 45° eyepiece. Field of view at 1,000 yds. 60 ft. (28x), 41 ft. (75x). Length: 13.4 oz.; weighs 39 oz.
Price: Body only **$870.00**
Price: 20-68x eyepiece **$370.00**
Price: Fixed eyepieces .... **$130.00 to $240.00**
Price: Model 849 (straight) body **$795.00**

SWIFT LYNX 60mm objective, 15-45x zoom, 45° inclined roof prism, magenta coated on all air-to-glass surfaces, rubber armored body, length: 14", weighs 30 oz. Equipped with sun shade, threaded dust covers and low level tripod.
Price: complete..................................... **$330.00**

SWIFT TELEMASTER M841 60mm objective. 15x to 60x variable power. Field of view at 1,000 yds. 160 feet (15x) to 40 feet (60x). Weighs 3.25 lbs.; length: 18" overall.
Price: **$399.50**

SWIFT PANTHER M844 15x-45x zoom or 22x WA, 15x, 20x, 40x. 60mm objective. Field of view at 1,000 yds. 141 ft. (15x), 68 ft. (40x), 95-58 ft. (20x-45x).
Price: Body only **$380.00**
Price: 15x-45x zoom eyepiece **$120.00**
Price: 20x-45x zoom (long eye relief) eyepiece **$140.00**
Price: 15x, 40x eyepiece **$65.00**
Price: 22x WA eyepiece **$80.00**

SWIFT M700T 12x-36x, 50mm objective. Field of view at 100 yds. 16 ft. (12x), 9 ft. (36x). Length: 14"; weighs 3.22 lbs. (with tripod).
Price: **$30.00**

TASCO 15-45x zoom, 50mm objective lens, Field of view at 1000 yds: 115 ft. (15x), Length: 132". Weighs 24 oz. Matte black finish.
Price: **$128.95**

TASCO 20-50x zoom, 50mm objective. Field of view at 1000 yds: 147 ft. (20x). Length: 7.5". Weighs 10.6 oz. Black finish.
Price: **$80.95**

TASCO 20-60x zoom, 60mm objective. Field of view at 1000 yds: 91 ft. (20x). Length: 13.8". Weighs 30 oz. Black finish.
Price: **$138.95**

TASCO 12-36x zoom 50mm objective. Field of view at 1000 yds. 144 ft. (12x). Length: 7.8". Weighs 17 oz. Black rubber armor. Includes carrying case.
Price: **$118.95**

UNERTL "FORTY-FIVE" 54mm objective. 20x (single fixed power). Field of view at 100 yds. 10',10"; eye relief 1"; focusing range infinity to 33 ft. Weighs about 32 oz.; overall length: 15-3/4". With lens covers.
Price: With mono-layer magnesium coating.............. **$810.00**

UNERTL STRAIGHT PRISMATIC 24x63. 63.5mm objective, 24x. Field of view at 100 yds., 7 ft. Relative brightness, 6.96. Eye relief 1/2". Weighs 40 oz.; length: closed 19". Push-pull and screw-focus eyepiece. 16x and 32x eyepieces $125.00 each.
Price:. **$786.00**

UNERTL 20x STRAIGHT PRISMATIC 54mm objective, 20x. Field of view at 100 yds. 8.5 ft. Relative brightness 6.1. Eye relief 1/2". Weighs 36 oz.; length: closed 13-1/2". Complete with lens covers.
Price:. **$695.00**

UNERTL TEAM SCOPE 100mm objective. 15x, 24x, 32x eyepieces. Field of view at 100 yds. 13 to 7.5 ft. Relative brightness, 39.06 to 9.79. Eye relief 2" to 1-1/2". Weighs 13 lbs.; length: 29-7/8" overall. Metal tripod, yoke and wood carrying case furnished (total weighs 80 lbs.).
Price:. **$3,624.50**

WEAVER 20x50 50mm objective. Field of view 124 ft. at 100 yds. Eye relief .85"; weighs 21 oz.; overall length: 10". Waterproof, armored.
Price:. **$249.99**

WEAVER 15-40x60 ZOOM 60mm objective. 15x-40x zoom. Field of view at 100 yds. 119 ft. (15x), 66 ft. (60x). Overall length: 12.5", weighs 26 oz. Waterproof, armored.
Price:. **$399.99**

BRILEY SCREW-IN CHOKES

Installation of these choke tubes requires that all traces of the original choking be removed, the barrel threaded internally with square threads and then the tubes are custom fitted to the specific barrel diameter. The tubes are thin and, therefore, made of stainless steel. Cost of installation for single-barrel guns (pumps, autos), lead shot, 12-gauge, **$179.00**, 20-gauge **$179.00**; steel shot **$209.00** and **$179.00**, all with three chokes; over/unders and side-by-sides, lead shot, 12-gauge, **$399.00**, 20-gauge **$399.00**; steel shot **$499.00** and **$499.00**, all with five chokes. For 10-gauge auto or pump with two steel shot chokes, **$209.00**; over/unders, side-by-sides with three steel shot chokes, **$299.00**. For 16-gauge auto or pump, three lead shot chokes, **$199.00**; over/unders, side-by-sides with five lead shot chokes, $**449.00**. The 28 and 410-bore run **$199.00** for autos and pumps with three lead shot chokes, **$449.00** for over/unders and side-by-sides with five lead shot chokes. Rifle muzzle brake, **$250.00**

CARLSON'S CHOKE TUBES

Manufactures choke tubes for Beretta, Benelli, Remington, Winchester, Browning Invector and Invector Plus, TruChokes, FranChokes, American Arms, Ruger and more. All choke tubes are manufactured from corrosion resistant stainless steel. Most tubes are compatible with lead, steel, Hevi-shot, etc. Available in flush mount, extended sporting clay and extended turkey designs, ported and non-ported. Also offers sights, rifled choke tubes and other accessories for most shotgun models. Prices range from **$16.95** to **$41.95**.

CUTTS COMPENSATOR

The Cutts Compensator is one of the oldest variable choke devices available. Manufactured by Lyman Gunsight Corporation, it is available with a steel body. A series of vents allows gas to escape upward and downward. For the 12-ga. Comp body, six fixed-choke tubes are available: the Spreader–popular with skeet shooters; Improved Cylinder; Modified; Full; Superfull, and Magnum Full. Full, Modified and Spreader tubes are available for 12 or 20. Cutts Compensator, complete with wrench, adaptor and any single tube **$87.50**. All single choke tubes **$26.00** each. No factory installation available.

DAYSON AUTOMATIC BRAKE SYSTEM

This system fits most single barrel shotguns threaded for choke tubes, and cuts away 30 grooves on the exterior of a standard one-piece wad as it exits the muzzle. This slows the wad, allowing shot and wad to separate faster, reducing shot distortion and tightening patterns. The A.B.S. choke tube is claimed to reduce recoil by about 25 percent, and with the muzzle brake up to 60 percent. Ventilated choke tubes available from .685" to .725", in .005" increments. Model I ventilated choke tube for use with A.B.S. muzzle brake, **$49.95**; for use without muzzle brake, **$52.95**; A.B.S. muzzle brake, from **$69.95**. Contact Dayson Arms for more data.

GENTRY QUIET MUZZLE BRAKE

Developed by gunmaker David Gentry, the "Quiet Muzzle Brake" is said to reduce recoil by up to 85 percent with no loss of accuracy or velocity. There is no increase in noise level because the noise and gases are directed away from the shooter. The barrel is threaded for installation and the unit is blued to match the barrel finish. Price, installed, is **$150.00**. Add **$15.00** for stainless steel, **$45.00** for knurled cap to protect threads. Shipping extra.

JP MUZZLE BRAKE

Designed for single shot handguns, AR-15, Ruger Mini-14, Ruger Mini Thirty and other sporting rifles, the JP muzzle brake redirects high pressure gases against a large frontal surface which applies forward thrust to the gun. All gases are directed up, rearward and to the sides. Priced at **$79.95** (AR-15 or sporting rifles), **$89.95** (bull barrel and SKS, AK models), **$89.95** (Ruger Minis), dual chamber model **$79.95**. From JP Enterprises, Inc.

KDF SLIM LINE MUZZLE BRAKE

This threaded muzzle brake has 30 pressure ports that direct combustion gases in all directions to reduce felt recoil up to a claimed 80 percent without affecting accuracy or ballistics. Reduces felt recoil of a 30-06 to that of a 243. Price, installed, is **$199.00**. From KDF, Inc.

KDF KICK ARRESTOR

This mercury-filled, inertia-type recoil reducer is installed in the butt of a wood or synthetic stock (rifle or shotgun) to reduce recoil up to 20 percent. Adds 16 oz. ot the weight of the gun Measures 6.25; L x .75" in diameter. Price, installed, is **$165.00**. From KDF, Inc.

LASERAIM

Simple, no-gunsmithing compensator reduces felt recoil and muzzle flip by up to 30 percent. Machined from single piece of stainless steel (Beretta/Taurus model made of aircraft aluminum). In black and polished finish. For Colt Government/ Commander and Beretta/Taurus full-size pistols. Weighs 1 ounce. **$49.00**. From Laseraim Arms Inc.

MAG-NA-PORT

Electrical Discharge Machining works on any firearm except those having non-conductive shrouded barrels. EDM is a metal erosion technique using carbon electrodes that control the area to be processed. The Mag-Na-Port venting process utilizes small trapezoidal openings to direct powder gases upward and outward to reduce recoil. No effect is had on bluing or nickeling outside the Mag-Na-Port area so no refinishing is needed. Rifle-style porting on single shot or large caliber handguns with barrels 7-1/2" or longer is **$115.00**; Dual Trapezoidal porting on most handguns with minimum barrel length of 3", **$115.00**; standard revolver porting, $**88.50**; Scandium/titanium-sleeved barrels **$139.50** (2 ports) or **$195.00** (4 ports); porting through the slide and barrel for semi-autos, **$129.50**; traditional rifle porting, **$135.00**. Prices do not include shipping, handling and insurance. From Mag-Na-Port International.

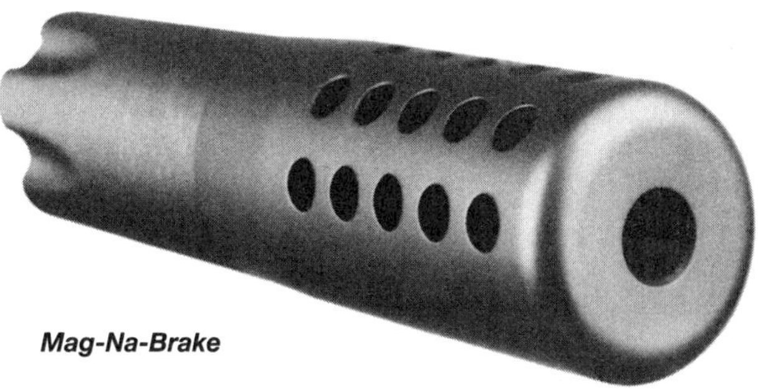

Mag-Na-Brake

MAG-NA-BRAKE

A screw-on brake under 2" long with progressive integrated exhaust chambers to neutralize expanding gases. Gases dissipate with an opposite twist to prevent the brake from unscrewing, and with a 5° forward angle to minimize sound pressure level. Available in blue, satin blue, bright or satin stainless. Standard and Light Contour installation cost **$195.00** for bolt-action rifles, many single action and single shot handguns. A knurled thread protector supplied at extra cost. Also available in Varmint-style with exhaust chambers covering 220° for prone-position shooters. From Mag-Na-Port International.

POLY-CHOKE

Marble Arms Corp., manufacturer of the Poly-Choke adjustable shotgun choke, now offers two models in 12-, 16-, 20-, and 28-gauge–the ventilated and standard-style chokes. Each provides nine choke settings including Xtra-Full and Slug. The ventilated model reduces 20 percent of a shotgun's recoil, the company claims, and is priced at **$135.00**. The standard model is **$125.00**. Postage not included. Contact Marble Arms for more data.

Pro-Port

PRO-PORT

A compound ellipsoid muzzle venting process similar to Mag-Na-Porting, only exclusively applied to shotguns. Like Mag-Na-Porting, this system reduces felt recoil, muzzle jump, and shooter fatigue. Pro-Port is a patented process and installation is available in both the U.S. and Canada. Cost for the Pro-Port process is **$139.00** for over/unders (both barrels); **$110.00** for only the top or bottom barrel; and **$88.50** for single-barrel shotguns. Optional pigeon porting costs **$25.00** extra per barrel. Prices do not include shipping and handling. From Mag-Na-Port International.

QUE INDUSTRIES ADJUSTABLE MUZZLE BRAKE

The Que Brake allows for fine-tuning of a rifle's accuracy by rotating the brake to one of 100 indexed stops. Mounts in minutes without barrel modification with heat-activated tensioning ring. The slotted exhaust ports reduce recoil by venting gases sideways, away from rifle. **$189.50**. From Que Industries.

SSK ARRESTOR BRAKE

This is a true muzzle brake with an expansion chamber. It takes up about 1" of barrel and reduces velocity accordingly. Some Arrestors are added to a barrel, increasing its length. Said to reduce the felt recoil of a 458 to that approaching a 30-06. Can be set up to give zero muzzle rise in any caliber, and can be added to most guns. For handgun or rifle. Prices start at **$95.00**. Contact SSK Industries for full data.

WEB DIRECTORY

THE 2009 GUN DIGEST WEB DIRECTORY

by Holt Bodinson

The GUN DIGEST Web Directory is now in its tenth year of publication and grows with every edition. The firearms industry is doing a remarkably good job of adapting to e-commerce. More and more firearm related businesses are striking out and creating their own discrete web pages because it's never been easier with the inexpensive software programs now available.

The Internet is a dynamic environment and since our last edition, there have been numerous changes. Companies have consolidated and adopted a new owner's web site address. New companies have appeared and old companies and discussion groups have disappeared. Search engines are now more powerful than ever and seem to root out even the most obscure reference to a product name or manufacturer.

The following index of web addresses is offered to our readers as a convenient jumping-off point. Half the fun is just exploring what's out there. Considering that most of the web pages have hot links to other firearm-related web pages, the Internet trail just goes on-and-on once you've taken the initial step to go online.

Here are a few pointers:

If the web site you desire is not listed, try using the full name of the company or product, typed without spaces, between www.-and-.com, for example, www.krause.com. Probably 95 percent of current Web sites are based on this simple, self-explanatory format.

Try a variety of search engines like Google, Microsoft Internet Explorer, Yahoo, Ask.com, Dogpile.com, Metacrawler, GoTo.com, HotBot, AltaVista, Lycos, Excite, InfoSeek, Looksmart, and WebCrawler while using key words such as gun, firearm, rifle, pistol, blackpowder, shooting, hunting—frankly, any word that relates to the sport. Each search engine combs through their indices in a different fashion and produces different results. Google is currently the dominant, general search engine with a penetration of 45 PERCENT. Accessing the various search engines is simple. Just type www.google.com for example, and you're on your way.

Welcome to the digital world of firearms. It's a wired world.

WEB DIRECTORY

AMMUNITION AND COMPONENTS

A-Square Co.: **: www.asquarecompany.com**
3-D Ammunition: **: www.3dammo.com**
Accurate Arms Co. Inc: **: www.accuratepowder.com**
ADCO/Nobel Sport Powder: **www.adcosales.com**
Aguila Ammunition: **www.aguilaammo.com**
Alexander Arms: **www.alexanderarms.com**
Alliant Powder: **www.alliantpowder.com**
American Ammunition: **www.a-merc.com**
American Derringer Co.: **www.amderringer.com**
American Pioneer Powder: **www.americanpioneerpowder.com**
Ammo Depot: **www.ammodepot.com**
Arizona Ammunition, Inc.: **www.arizonaammunition.com**
Ballistic Products,Inc.: **www.ballisticproducts.com**
Barnaul Cartridge Plant: **www.ab.ru/~stanok**
Barnes Bullets: **www.barnesbullets.com**
Baschieri & Pellagri: **www.baschieri-pellagri.com**
Beartooth Bullets: **www.beartoothbullets.com**
Bell Brass: **www.bellbrass.com**
Berger Bullets, Ltd.: **www.bergerbullets.com**
Berry's Mfg., Inc.: **www.berrysmfg.com**
Big Bore Bullets of Alaska: **www.awloo.com/bbb/index.htm**
Big Bore Express: **www.powerbeltbullets.com**
Bismuth Cartridge Co.: **www.bismuth-notox.com**
Black Dawge Cartridge: **www.blackdawgecartridge.com**
Black Hills Ammunition, Inc.: **www.black-hills.com**
Brenneke of America Ltd.: **www.brennekeusa.com**
Buffalo Arms: **www.buffaloarms.com**
Calhoon, James, Bullets: **www.jamescalhoon.com**
Cartuchos Saga: **www.saga.es**
Cast Performance Bullet: **www.castperformance.com**
CCI: **www.cci-ammunition.com**
Centurion Ordnance: **www.aguilaammo.com**
Century International Arms: **www.centuryarms.com**
Cheaper Than Dirt: **www.cheaperthandirt.com**
Cheddite France: **www.cheddite.com**
Claybuster Wads: **www.claybusterwads.com**
Clean Shot Powder: **www.cleanshot.com**
Cole Distributing: **www.cole-distributing.com**
Combined Tactical Systems: **www.less-lethal.com**
Cor-Bon/Glaser : **www.cor-bon.com**
Cowboy Bullets: **www.cowboybullets.com**
Defense Technology Corp.: **www.defense-technology.com**
Denver Bullet Co. denbullets@aol.com
Dillon Precision: **www.dillonprecision.com**
Dionisi Cartridge: **www.dionisi.com**
DKT, Inc.: **www.dktinc.com**
Down Range Mfg.: **www.downrangemfg.com**
Dynamit Nobel RWS Inc.: **www.dnrws.com**
Elephant/Swiss Black Powder: **www.elephantblackpowder.com**
Eley Ammunition: **www.eleyusa.com**
Eley Hawk Ltd.: **www.eleyhawk.com**
Environ-Metal: **www.hevishot.com**
Estate Cartridge: **www.estatecartridge.com**
Extreme Shock Munitions: **www.extremeshockusa.net**
Federal Cartridge Co.: **www.federalpremium.com**
Fiocchi of America: **www.fiocchiusa.com**
Fowler Bullets: **www.benchrest.com/fowler**
Gamebore Cartridge: **www.gamebore.com**
Garrett Cartridges: **www.garrettcartridges.com**
Gentner Bullets: **www.benchrest.com/gentner/**
Glaser Safety Slug, Inc.: **www.corbon.com**
GOEX Inc.: **www.goexpowder.com**
GPA: **www.cartouchegpa.com**
Graf & Sons: **www.grafs.com**
Hastings: **www.hastingsammunition.com**
Hawk Bullets: **www.hawkbullets.com**
Hevi.Shot: **www.hevishot.com**
Hi-Tech Ammunition: **www.iidbs.com/hitech**
Hodgdon Powder: **www.hodgdon.com**
Hornady: **www.hornady.com**
Hull Cartridge: **www.hullcartridge.com**
Huntington Reloading Products: **www.huntingtons.com**
Impact Bullets: **www.impactbullets.com**
IMR Smokeless Powders: **www.imrpowder.com**
International Cartridge Corp: **www.iccammo.com**
Israel Military Industries: **www.imisammo.co.il**
ITD Enterprise: **www.itdenterpriseinc.com**
Kent Cartridge America: **www.kentgamebore.com**
Knight Bullets: **www.benchrest.com/knight/**
Kynoch Ammunition: **www.kynochammunition.com**
Lapua: **www.lapua.com**
Lawrence Brand Shot: **www.metalico.com**
Lazzeroni Arms Co.: **www.lazzeroni.com**
Leadheads Bullets: **www.proshootpro.com**
Lightfield Ammunition Corp: **www.lightfieldslugs.com**
Lomont Precision Bullets: **www.klomont.com/kent**
Lost River Ballistic Technologies,Inc.: **www.lostriverballistic.com**
Lyman : **www.lymanproducts.com**
Magkor Industries.: **www.magkor.com**
Magnum Muzzleloading Products: **www.mmpsabots.com**
Magnus Bullets: **www.magnusbullets.com**
MagSafe Ammunition: **www.realpages.com/magsafeammo**
Magtech: **www.magtechammunition.com**
Masterclass Bullet Co.: **www.mastercast.com**
Meister Bullets: **www.meisterbullets.com**
Midway USA: **www.midwayusa.com**
Miltex,Inc.: **www.miltexusa.com**
Mitchell Mfg. Co.: **www.mitchellsales.com**
MK Ballistic Systems: **www.mkballistics.com**
Mullins Ammunition: **www.mullinsammunition.com**
National Bullet Co.: **www.nationalbullet.com**
Navy Arms: **www.navyarms.com**
Nobel Sport: **www.nobelsportammo.com**
Norma: **www.norma.cc**
North Fork Technologies: **www.northforkbullets.com**
Nosler Bullets,Inc.: **www.nosler.com**
Old Western Scrounger: **www.ows-ammunition.com**
Oregon Trail/Trueshot Bullets: **www.trueshotbullets.com**
Pattern Control: **www.patterncontrol.com**
PMC: **www.pmcammo.com**
Polywad: **www.polywad.com**
PowerBelt Bullets: **www.powerbeltbullets.com**
PR Bullets: **www.prbullet.com**
Precision Ammunition: **www.precisionammo.com**
Precision Reloading: **www.precisionreloading.com**
Pro Load Ammunition: **www.proload.com**
Quality Cartridge: **www.qual-cart.com**
Rainier Ballistics: **www.rainierballistics.com**
Ram Shot Powder: **www.ramshot.com**
Reloading Specialties Inc.: **www.reloadingspecialties.com**
Remington: **www.remington.com**
Rio Ammo: **www.rioammo.com**
Rocky Mountain Cartridge: **www.rockymountaincartridge.com**
RUAG Ammotec: **www.ruag.com**
Samco Global Arms: **www.samcoglobal.com**
Schuetzen Powder: **www.schuetzenpowder.com**
Sellier & Bellot USA inc.: **www.sb-usa.com**
Shilen: **www.shilen.com**
Sierra: **www.sierrabullets.com**
Simunition.: **www.simunition.com**
SinterFire, Inc.: **www.sinterfire.com**
Speer Bullets: **www.speer-bullets.com**
Sporting Supplies Int'l Inc.: **www.ssiintl.com**
Starline: **www.starlinebrass.com**
Swift Bullets Co.: **www.swiftbullet.com**
Ten-X Ammunition: **www.tenxammo.com**
Top Brass: **www.top-brass.com**
Triton Cartridge: **www.a-merc.com**
Trueshot Bullets: **www.trueshotbullets.com**

Tru-Tracer: **www.trutracer.com**
Ultramax Ammunition: **www.ultramaxammunition.com**
Vihtavuori Lapua: **www.vihtavuori-lapua.com**
Weatherby: **www.weatherby.com**
West Coast Bullets: **www.westcoastbullet.com**
Western Powders Inc.: **www.westernpowders.com**
Widener's Reloading & Shooters Supply: **www.wideners.com**
Winchester Ammunition: **www.winchester.com**
Windjammer Tournament Wads.: **www.windjammer-wads.com**
Wolf Ammunition: **www.wolfammo.com**
Woodleigh Bullets: **www.woodleighbullets.com.au**
Zanders Sporting Goods: **www.gzanders.com**

CASES, SAFES, GUN LOCKS, AND CABINETS

Ace Case Co.: **www.acecase.com**
AG English Sales Co.: **www.agenglish.com**
All Americas' Outdoors: **www.innernet.net/gunsafe**
Alpine Cases: **www.alpinecases.com**
Aluma Sport by Dee Zee: **www.deezee.com**
American Security Products: **www.amsecusa.com**
Americase: **www.americase.com**
Avery Outdoors, Inc.: **www.averyoutdoors.com**
Bear Track Cases: **www.beartrackcases.com**
Boyt Harness Co.: **www.boytharness.com**
Bulldog Gun Safe Co.: **www.gardall.com**
Cannon Safe Co.: **www.cannonsafe.com**
CCL Security Products: **www.cclsecurity.com**
Concept Development Corp.: **www.saf-t-blok.com**
Doskocil Mfg. Co.: **www.doskocilmfg.com**
Fort Knox Safes: **www.ftknox.com**
Franzen Security Products: **www.securecase.com**
Frontier Safe Co.: **www.frontiersafe.com**
Granite Security Products: **www.granitesafe.com**
Gunlocker Phoenix USA Inc.: **www.gunlocker.com**
GunVault: **www.gunvault.com**
Hakuba USA Inc.: **www.hakubausa.com**
Heritage Safe Co.: **www.heritagesafecompany.com**
Hide-A-Gun: **www.hide-a-gun.com**
Homak Safes: **www.homak.com**
Hunter Company: **www.huntercompany.com**
Kalispel Case Line: **www.kalispelcaseline.com**
Knouff & Knouff, Inc.: **www.kkair.com**
Knoxx Industries: **www.knoxx,com**
Kolpin Mfg. Co.: **www.kolpin.com**
Liberty Safe & Security: **www.libertysafe.com**
New Innovative Products: **www.starlightcases**
Noble Security Systems Inc.: **www.noble.co.ll**
Phoenix USA Inc.: **www.gunlocker.com**
Plano Molding Co.: **www.planomolding.com**
Rhino Gun Cases: **www.rhinoguns.com**
Rhino Safe: **www.rhinosafe.com**
Safe Tech, Inc.: **www.safrgun.com**
Saf-T-Hammer: **www.saf-t-hammer.com**
Saf-T-Lok Corp.: **www.saf-t-lok.com**
San Angelo All-Aluminum Products Inc.: **sasptuld@x.netcom.com**
Securecase: **www.securecase.com**
Shot Lock Corp.: **www.shotlock.com**
Smart Lock Technology Inc.: **www.smartlock.com**
Sportsmans Steel Safe Co.: **www.sportsmansteelsafes.com**
Stack-On Products Co.: **www.stack-on.com**
Starlight Cases: **www.starlightcases.com**
Sun Welding: **www.sunwelding.com**
T.Z. Case Int'l : **www.tzcase.com**
Versatile Rack Co.: **www.versatilegunrack.com**
V-Line Industries: **www.vlineind.com**
Winchester Safes: **www.fireking.com**
Ziegel Engineering: **www.ziegeleng.com**
Zonetti Armor: **www.zonettiarmor.com**

CHOKE DEVICES, RECOIL REDUCERS, SUPPRESSORS AND ACCURACY DEVICES

Advanced Armament Corp.: **www.advanced-armament.com**
100 Straight Products: **www.100straight.com**
Answer Products Co.: **www.answerrifles.com**
Briley Mfg: **www.briley.com**
Carlson's: **www.choketube.com**
Colonial Arms: **www.colonialarms.com**
Comp-N-Choke: **www.comp-n-choke.com**
Gemtech: **www.gem-tech.com**
Hastings: **www.hastingsbarrels.com**
Kick's Industries: **www.kicks-ind.com**
LimbSaver: **www.limbsaver.com**
Mag-Na-Port Int'l Inc.: **www.magnaport.com**
Metro Gun: **www.metrogun.com**
Patternmaster Chokes: **www.patternmaster.com**
Poly-Choke: **www.poly-choke.com**
Sims Vibration Laboratory: **www.limbsaver.com**
Teague Precision Chokes: **www.teague.ca**
Truglo: **www.truglo.com**

CHRONOGRAPHS AND BALLISTIC SOFTWARE

Barnes Ballistic Program: **www.barnesbullets.com**
Ballisticard Systems: **www.ballisticards.com**
Competition Electronics: **www.competitionelectronics.com**
Competitive Edge Dynamics: **www.cedhk.com**
Hodgdon Shotshell Program: **www.hodgdon.com**
Lee Shooter Program: **www.leeprecision.com**
Load From A Disk: **www.loadammo.com**
Oehler Research Inc.: **www.oehler-research.com**
PACT: **www.pact.com**
ProChrony: **www.competitionelectronics.com**
Quickload: **www.neconos.com**
RCBS Load: **www.rcbs.com**
Shooting Chrony Inc: **www.shootingchrony.com**
Sierra Infinity Ballistics Program: **www.sierrabullets.com**

CLEANING PRODUCTS

Accupro: **www.accupro.com**
Ballistol USA: **www.ballistol.com**
Battenfeld Technologies: **www.battenfeldtechnologies.com**
Birchwood Casey: **www.birchwoodcasey.com**
Blue Wonder: **www.bluewonder.com**
Bore Tech: **www.boretech.com**
Break-Free, Inc.: **www.break-free.com**
Bruno Shooters Supply: **www.brunoshooters.com**
Butch's Bore Shine: **www.lymanproducts.com**
C.J. Weapons Accessories: **www.cjweapons,com**
Clenzoil: **www.clenzoil.com**
Corrosion Technologies: **www.corrosionx.com**
Dewey Mfg.: **www.deweyrods.com**
Eezox Inc.: **www.xmission.com**
G 96: **www.g96.com**
Gunslick Gun Care: **www.gunslick.com**
Gunzilla: **www.topduckproducts.com**
Hollands Shooters Supply: **www.hollandgun.com**
Hoppes: **www.hoppes.com**
Hydrosorbent Products: **www.dehumidify.com**
Inhibitor VCI Products: **www.theinhibitor.com**
Iosso Products: **www.iosso.com**
KG Industries: **www.kgcoatings.com**
Kleen-Bore Inc.: **www.kleen-bore.com**
L&R Mfg.: **www.lrultrasonics.com**
Lyman: **www.lymanproducts.com**
Mil-Comm Products: **www.mil-comm.com**
Militec-1: **www.militec-1.com**
Mpro7 Gun Care: **www.mp7.com**
Otis Technology, Inc.: **www.otisgun.com**

Outers: **www.outers-guncare.com**
Ox-Yoke Originals Inc.: **www.oxyoke.com**
Parker-Hale Ltd.: **www.parker-hale.com**
Prolix Lubricant: **www.prolixlubricant.com**
ProShot Products: **www.proshotproducts.com**
ProTec Lubricants: **www.proteclubricants.com**
Rusteprufe Labs: **www.rusteprufe.com**
Sagebrush Products: **www.sagebrushproducts.com**
Sentry Solutions Ltd.: **www.sentrysolutions.com**
Shooters Choice Gun Care: **www.shooters-choice.com**
Silencio: **www.silencio.com**
Slip 2000: **www.slip2000.com**
Stony Point Products: **www.uncle-mikes.com**
Tetra Gun: **www.tetraproducts.com**
The TM Solution thetmsolution@comsast.net
Top Duck Products: **www.topduckproducts.com**
Ultra Bore Coat: **www.ultracoatingsinc.com**
World's Fastest Gun Bore Cleaner: **www.michaels-oregon.com**

FIREARM MANUFACTURERS AND IMPORTERS

AAR, Inc.: **www.iar-arms.com**
A-Square: **www.asquarecompany.com**
Accuracy Int'l North America: **www.accuracyinternational.org**
Accuracy Rifle Systems: **www.mini-14.net**
Ace Custom 45's: **www.acecustom45.com**
Advanced Weapons Technology: **www.AWT-Zastava.com**
AIM: **www.aimsurplus.com**
AirForce Airguns: **www.airforceairguns.com**
Air Gun, Inc.: **www.airrifle-china.com**
Airguns of Arizona: **www.airgunsofarizona.com**
Airgun Express: **www.airgunexpress.com**
Alchemy Arms: **www.alchemyltd.com**
Alexander Arms: **www.alexanderarms.com**
American Derringer Corp.: **www.amderringer.com**
American Spirit Arms Corp.: **www.gunkits.com**
American Western Arms: **www.awaguns.com**
Anics Corp.: **www.anics.com**
Anschutz: **www.anschutz-sporters.com**
Answer Products Co.: **www.answerrifles.com**
AR-7 Industries,LLC: **www.ar-7.com**
Ares Defense Systems: **www.aresdefense.com**
Armalite: **www.armalite.com**
Armi Sport: **www.armisport.com**
Armory USA: **www.globaltraders.com**
Armsco: **www.armsco.net**
Armscorp USA Inc.: **www.armscorpusa.com**
Arnold Arms: **www.arnoldarms.com**
Arsenal Inc.: **www.arsenalinc.com**
Arthur Brown Co.: **www.eabco.com**
Atlanta Cutlery Corp.: **www.atlantacutlery.com**
Auction Arms: **www.auctionarms.com**
Autauga Arms,Inc.: **www.autaugaarms.com**
Auto-Ordnance Corp.: **www.tommygun.com**
AWA Int'l: **www.awaguns.com**
Axtell Rifle Co.: **www.riflesmith.com**
Aya: **www.aya-fineguns.com**
Baikal: **www.baikalinc.ru/eng/**
Ballard Rifles,LLC: **www.ballardrifles.com**
Barrett Firearms Mfg.: **www.barrettrifles.com**
Beeman Precision Airguns: **www.beeman.com**
Benelli USA Corp.: **www.benelliusa.com**
Benjamin Sheridan: **www.crosman.com**
Beretta U.S.A. Corp.: **www.berettausa.com**
Bernardelli: **www.bernardelli.com**
Bersa: **www.bersa-llama.com**
Bill Hanus Birdguns: **www.billhanusbirdguns.com**
Blaser Jagdwaffen Gmbh: **www.blaser.de**
Bleiker: **www.bleiker.ch**
Bluegrass Armory: **www.bluegrassarmory.com**
Bond Arms: **www.bondarms.com**
Borden's Rifles, Inc.: **www.bordensrifles.com**
Boss & Co.: **www.bossguns.co.uk**
Bowen Classic Arms: **www.bowenclassicarms.com**
Briley Mfg: **www.briley.com**
BRNO Arms: **www.zbrojovka.com**
Brown, David McKay: **www.mckaybrown.com**
Brown, Ed Products: **www.brownprecision.com**
Browning: **www.browning.com**
BSA Guns: **www.bsaguns.com**
BUL Ltd.: **www.bultransmark.com**
Bushmaster Firearms/Quality Parts: **www.bushmaster.com**
BWE Firearms: **www.bwefirearms.com**
Caesar Guerini USA: **www.gueriniusa.com**
Cape Outfitters: **www.doublegun.com**
Carbon 15: **www.professional-ordnance.com**
Caspian Arms, Ltd.: **www.caspianarmsltd.8m.com**
Casull Arms Corp.: **www.casullarms.com**
Calvary Arms: **www.calvaryarms.com**
CDNN Investments, Inc.: **www.cdnninvestments.com**
Century Arms: **www.centuryarms.com**
Chadick's Ltd.: **www.chadicks-ltd.com**
Champlin Firearms: **www.champlinarms.com**
Chapuis Arms: **www.doubleguns.com/chapuis.htm**
Charles Daly: **www.charlesdaly.com**
Charter Arms: **www.charterfirearms.com**
CheyTac USA: **www.cheytac.com**
Christensen Arms: **www.christensenarms.com**
Cimarron Firearms Co.: **www.cimarron-firearms.com**
Clark Custom Guns: **www.clarkcustomguns.com**
Cobra Enterprises: **www.cobrapistols.com**
Cogswell & Harrison: **www.cogswell.co.uk/home.htm**
Colt's Mfg Co.: **www.colt.com**
Compasseco, Inc.: **www.compasseco.com**
Connecticut Valley Arms: **www.cva.com**
Cooper Firearms: **www.cooperfirearms.com**
Corner Shot: **www.cornershot.com**
Crosman: **www.crosman.com**
Crossfire, L.L.C.: **www.crossfirelle.com**
C.Sharp Arms Co.: **www.csharparms.com**
CVA: **www.cva.com**
CZ USA: **www.cz-usa.com**
Daisy Mfg Co.: **www.daisy.com**
Dakota Arms Inc.: **www.dakotaarms.com**
Dan Wesson Firearms: **www.danwessonfirearms.com**
Davis Industries: **www.davisindguns.com**
Detonics USA: **www.detonicsusa.com**
Diana: **www.diana-airguns.de**
Dixie Gun Works: **www.dixiegunworks.com**
Dlask Arms Corp.: **www.dlask.com**
D.P.M.S., Inc.: **www.dpmsinc.com**
D.S.A, Inc.: **www.dsarms.com**
Dumoulin: **www.dumoulin-herstal.com**
Dynamit Noble: **www.dnrws.com**
Eagle Imports,Inc.: **www.bersa-llama.com**
Ed Brown Products: **www.edbrown.com**
EDM Arms: **www.edmarms.com**
E.M.F. Co.: **www.emf-company.com**
Enterprise Arms: **www.enterprise.com**
E R Shaw: **www.ershawbarrels.com**
European American Armory Corp.: **www.eaacorp.com**
Evans, William: **www.williamevans.com**
Excel Arms: **www.excelarms.com**
Fabarm: **www.fabarm.com**
FAC-Guns-N-Stuff: **www.gunsnstuff.com**
Falcon Pneumatic Systems: **www.falcon-airguns.com**
Fausti Stefano: **www.faustistefanoarms.com**
Firestorm: **www.firestorm-sgs.com**
Flodman Guns: **www.flodman.com**
FN Herstal: **www.fnherstal.com**
FNH USA: **www.fnhusa.com**

WEB DIRECTORY

Franchi: **www.franchiusa.com**
Freedom Arms: **www.freedomarms.com**
Galazan: **www.connecticutshotgun.com**
Gambo Renato: **www.renatogamba.it**
Gamo: **www.gamo.com**
Gary Reeder Custom Guns: **www.reeder-customguns.com**
Gazelle Arms: **www.gazellearms.com**
German Sport Guns: **www.germansportguns.com**
Gibbs Rifle Company: **www.gibbsrifle.com**
Glock: **www.glock.com**
Griffin & Howe: **www.griffinhowe.com**
Grizzly Big Boar Rifle: **www.largrizzly.com**
GSI Inc.: **www.gsifirearms.com**
Guerini: **www.gueriniusa.com**
Gunbroker.Com: **www.gunbroker.com**
Hammerli: **www.carl-walther.com**
Hatfield Gun Co.: **www.hatfield-usa.com**
Hatsan Arms Co.: **www.hatsan.com.tr**
Heckler and Koch: **www.hk-usa.com**
Henry Repeating Arms Co.: **www.henryrepeating.com**
Heritage Mfg.: **www.heritagemfg.com**
Heym: **www.heym-waffenfabrik.de**
High Standard Mfg.: **www.highstandard.com**
Hi-Point Firearms: **www.hi-pointfirearms.com**
Holland & Holland: **www.hollandandholland.com**
H&R 1871 Firearms: **www.hr1871.com**
H-S Precision: **www.hsprecision.com**
Hunters Lodge Corp.: **www.hunterslodge.com**
IAR Inc.: **www.iar-arms.com**
Imperial Miniature Armory: **www.1800miniature.com**
Interarms: **www.interarms.com**
International Military Antiques, Inc.: **www.ima-usa.com**
Inter Ordnance: **www.interordnance.com**
Intrac Arms International LLC: **www.hsarms.com**
Israel Arms: **www.israelarms.com**
Iver Johnson Arms: **www.iverjohnsonarms.com**
Izhevsky Mekhanichesky Zavod: **www.baikalinc.ru**
Jarrett Rifles,Inc.: **www.jarrettrifles.com**
J&G Sales, Ltd.: **www.jgsales.com**
Johannsen Express Rifle: **www.johannsen-jagd.de**
Jonathan Arthur Ciener: **www.22lrconversions.com**
JP Enterprises, Inc.: **www.jprifles.com**
Kahr Arms/Auto-Ordnance: **www.kahr.com**
K.B.I.: **www.kbi-inc.com**
Kel-Tec CNC Ind., Inc.: **www.kel-tec.com**
Kifaru: **www.kifaru.net**
Kimber: **www.kimberamerica.com**
Knight's Mfg. Co.: **www.knightsarmco.com**
Knight Rifles: **www.knightrifles.com**
Korth: **www.korthwaffen.de**
Krieghoff GmbH: **www.krieghoff.de**
KY Imports, Inc.: **www.kyimports.com**
Krieghoff Int'l: **www.krieghoff.com**
L.A.R Mfg: **www.largrizzly.com**
Lazzeroni Arms Co.: **www.lazzeroni.com**
Legacy Sports International: **www.legacysports.com**
Les Baer Custom, Inc.: **www.lesbaer.com**
Lewis Machine & Tool Co.: **www.lewismachine.net**
Linebaugh Custom Sixguns: **www.sixgunner.com/linebaugh**
Ljutic: **www.ljuticgun.com**
Llama: **www.bersa-llama.com**
Lone Star Rifle Co.: **www.lonestarrifle.com**
Magnum Research: **www.magnumresearch.com**
Majestic Arms: **www.majesticarms.com**
Markesbery Muzzleloaders: **www.markesbery.com**
Marksman Products: **www.marksman.com**
Marlin: **www.marlinfirearms.com**
Mauser: **www.mauser.com**
McMillan Bros Rifle Co.: **www.mcfamily.com**
MDM: **www.mdm-muzzleloaders.com**
Meacham Rifles: **www.meachamrifles.com**
Merkel: **www.hk-usa.com**
Miller Arms: **www.millerarms.com**
Miltech: **www.miltecharms.com**
Miltex, Inc.: **www.miltexusa.com**
Mitchell's Mausers: **www.mitchellsales.com**
MK Ballistic Systems: **www.mkballistics.com**
M-Mag: **www.mmag.com**
Montana Rifle Co.: **www.montanarifleman.com**
Mossberg: **www.mossberg.com**
Navy Arms: **www.navyarms.com**
Nesika: **www.nesika.com**
New England Arms Corp.: **www.newenglandarms.com**
New England Custom Gun Svc, Ltd.: **www.newenglandcustom-gun.com**
New England Firearms: **www.hr1871.com**
New Ultra Light Arms: **www.newultralight.com**
North American Arms: **www.northamericanarms.com**
Nosler Bullets,Inc.: **www.nosler.com**
Nowlin Mfg. Inc.: **www.nowlinguns.com**
O.F. Mossberg & Sons: **www.mossberg.com**
Ohio Ordnance Works: **www.ohioordnanceworks.com**
Olympic Arms: **www.olyarms.com**
Panther Arms: **www.dpmsinc.com**
Para-Ordnance: **www.paraord.com**
Pedersoli Davide & Co.: **www.davide-pedersoli.com**
Perazzi: **www.perazzi.com**
Pietta: **www.pietta.it**
PKP Knife-Pistol: **www.sanjuanenterprise.com**
Power Custom: **www.powercustom.com**
Professional Arms: **www.professional-arms.com**
PTR 91,Inc.: **www.ptr91.com**
Purdey & Sons: **www.purdey.com**
Remington: **www.remington.com**
Republic Arms Inc.: **www.republicarmsinc.com**
Rhineland Arms, Inc.: **www.rhinelandarms.com**
Rigby: **www.johnrigbyandco.com**
Rizzini USA: **www.rizziniusa.com**
Robar Companies, Inc.: **www.robarguns.com**
Robinson Armament Co.: **www.robarm.com**
Rock River Arms, Inc.: **www.rockriverarms.com**
Rogue Rifle Co. Inc.: **www.chipmunkrifle.com**
Rohrbaugh Firearms: **www.rohrbaughfirearms.com**
Rossi Arms: **www.rossiusa.com**
RPM: **www.rpmxlpistols.com**
Russian American Armory: **www.raacfirearms.com**
RUAG Ammotec: **www.ruag.com**
Sabatti SPA: **www.sabatti.com**
Sabre Defense Industries: **www.sabredefense.com**
Saco Defense: **www.sacoinc.com**
Safari Arms: **www.olyarms.com**
Sako: **www.berettausa.com**
Samco Global Arms Inc.: **www.samcoglobal.com**
Sarco Inc.: **www.sarcoinc.com**
Savage Arms Inc.: **www.savagearms.com**
Scattergun Technologies Inc.: **www.wilsoncombat.com**
Searcy Enterprises: **www.searcyent.com**
Shiloh Rifle Mfg.: **www.shilohrifle.com**
SIGARMS,Inc.: **www.sigarms.com**
Simpson Ltd.: **www.simpsonltd.com**
SKB Shotguns: **www.skbshotguns.com**
Smith & Wesson: **www.smith-wesson.com**
SOG International, Inc.: **soginc@go-concepts.com**
Sphinx System: **www.sphinxarms.com**
Springfield Armory: **www.springfield-armory.com**
SSK Industries: **www.sskindustries.com**
Stag Arms: **www.stagarms.com**
Steyr Arms, Inc. : **www.steyrarms.com**
Stoeger Industries: **www.stoegerindustries.com**
Strayer-Voigt Inc.: **www.sviguns.com**

Sturm,Ruger & Company: **www.ruger-firearms.com**
Tactical Solutions: **www.tacticalsol.com**
Tar-Hunt Slug Guns, Inc.: **www.tar-hunt.com**
Taser Int'l: **www.taser.com**
Taurus: **www.taurususa.com**
Taylor's & Co., Inc.: **www.taylorsfirearms.com**
Tennessee Guns: **www.tennesseeguns.com**
The 1877 Sharps Co.: **www.1877sharps.com**
Thompson Center Arms: **www.tcarms.com**
Tikka: **www.berettausa.com**
TNW, Inc. tncorp@aol.com
Traditions: **www.traditionsfirearms.com**
Tristar Sporting Arms: **www.tristarsportingarms.com**
Uberti: **www.ubertireplicas.com**
Ultra Light Arms: **www.newultralight.com**
Umarex: **www.umarex.com**
U.S. Firearms Mfg. Co.: **www.usfirearms.com**
Valkyrie Arms: **www.valkyriearms.com**
Vektor Arms: **www.vektorarms.com**
Verney-Carron: **www.verney-carron.com**
Volquartsen Custom Ltd.: **www.volquartsen.com**
Vulcan Armament: **www.vulcanarmament.com**
Walther USA: **www.waltheramerica.com**
Weatherby: **www.weatherby.com**
Webley and Scott Ltd.: **www.webley.co.uk**
Westley Richards: **www.westleyrichards.com**
Widley: **www.widleyguns.com**
Wild West Guns: **www.wildwestguns.com**
William Larkin Moore & Co.: **www.doublegun.com**
Wilson Combat: **www.wilsoncombat.com**
Winchester Rifles and Shotguns: **www.winchesterguns.com**

GUN PARTS, BARRELS, AFTER-MARKET ACCESSORIES

300 Below: **www.300below.com**
Accuracy International of North America: **www.accuracyinternational.org**
Accuracy Speaks, Inc.: **www.accuracyspeaks.com**
Advanced Barrel Systems: **www.carbonbarrels.com**
Advantage Arms: **www.advantagearms.com**
Aim Surplus: **www.aimsurplus.com**
AK-USA: **www.ak-103.com**
American Spirit Arms Corp.: **www.gunkits.com**
AMT Gun Parts: **www.amt-gunparts.com**
Armatac Industries: **www.armatac.com**
Badger Barrels, Inc.: **www.badgerbarrels.com**
Bar-Sto Precision Machine: **www.barsto.com**
Battenfeld Technologies: **www.battenfeldtechnologies.com**
Bellm TC's: **www.bellmtcs.com**
Belt Mountain Enterprises: **www.beltmountain.com**
Bergara Barrels: **www.bergarabarrels.com**
Briley: **www.briley.com**
Brownells: **www.brownells.com**
B-Square: **www.b-square.com**
Buffer Technologies: **www.buffertech.com**
Bullberry Barrel Works: **www.bullberry.com**
Bulldog Barrels: **www.bulldogbarrels.com**
Bushmaster Firearms/Quality Parts: **www.bushmaster.com**
Butler Creek Corp: **www.butler-creek.com**
Cape Outfitters Inc.: **www.capeoutfitters.com**
Caspian Arms Ltd.: **www.caspianarms.com**
Cheaper Than Dirt: **www.cheaperthandirt.com**
Chesnut Ridge: **www.chestnutridge.com/**
Chip McCormick Corp: **www.chipmccormickcorp.com**
Choate Machine & Tool Co.: **www.riflestock.com**
Cierner, Jonathan Arthur: **www.22lrconversions.com**
CJ Weapons Accessories: **www.cjweapons.com**
Colonial Arms: **www.colonialarms.com**
Comp-N-Choke: **www.comp-n-choke.com**
Cylinder & Slide Shop: **www.cylinder-slide.com**
Dave Manson Precision Reamers.: **www.mansonreamers.com**
Digi-Twist: **www.fmtcorp.com**
Dixie Gun Works: **www.dixiegun.com**
Douglas Barrels: **www.benchrest.com/douglas/**
DPMS: **www.dpmsinc.com**
D.S.Arms,Inc.: **www.dsarms.com**
eBay: **www.ebay.com**
Ed Brown Products: **www.edbrown.com**
EFK Marketing/Fire Dragon Pistol Accessories: **www.flmfire.com**
E.R. Shaw: **www.ershawbarrels.com**
Forrest Inc.: **www.gunmags.com**
Fulton Armory: **www.fulton-armory.com**
Galazan: **www.connecticutshotgun.com**
Gemtech: **www.gem-tech.com**
Gentry, David: **www.gentrycustom.com**
GG&G: **www.gggaz.com**
Green Mountain Rifle Barrels: **www.gmriflebarrel.com**
Gun Parts Corp.: **www.e-gunparts.com**
Harris Engineering: **www.harrisbipods.com**
Hart Rifle Barrels: **www.hartbarrels.com**
Hastings Barrels: **www.hastingsbarrels.com**
Heinie Specialty Products: **www.heinie.com**
Holland Shooters Supply: **www.hollandgun.com**
H-S Precision: **www.hsprecision.com**
100 Straight Products: **www.100straight.com**
I.M.A.: **www.ima-usa.com**
Jack First Gun Shop: **www.jackfirstgun.com**
Jarvis, Inc.: **www.jarvis-custom.com**
J&T Distributing: **www.jtdistributing.com**
John's Guns: **www.johnsguns.com**
John Masen Co.: **www.johnmasen.com**
Jonathan Arthur Ciener, Inc.: **www.22lrconversions.com**
JP Enterprises: **www.jpar15.com**
Keng's Firearms Specialities: **www.versapod.com**
KG Industries: **www.kgcoatings.com**
Kick Eez: **www.kickeez.com**
Kidd Triggers: **www.coolguyguns.com**
King's Gunworks: **www.kingsgunworks.com**
Knoxx Industries: **www.knoxx.com**
Krieger Barrels: **www.kriegerbarrels.com**
K-VAR Corp.: **www.k-var.com**
Les Baer Custom, Inc.: **www.lesbaer.com**
Lilja Barrels: **www.riflebarrels.com**
Lone Star Rifle Co.: **www.lonestarrifles.com**
Lone Wolf Dist.: **www.lonewolfdist.com**
Lothar Walther Precision Tools Inc.: **www.lothar-walther.de**
M&A Parts, Inc.: **www.m-aparts.com**
MAB Barrels: **www.mab.com.au**
Majestic Arms: **www.majesticarms.com**
Marvel Products, Inc.: **www.marvelprod.com**
MEC-GAR SrL: **www.mec-gar.it**
Mesa Tactical: **www.mesatactical.com**
Michaels of Oregon Co.: **www.michaels-oregon.com**
North Mfg. Co.: **www.rifle-barrels.com**
Numrich Gun Parts Corp.: **www.e-gunparts.com**
Pachmayr: **www.pachmayr.com**
Pac-Nor Barrels: **www.pac-nor.com**
Para Ordinance Pro Shop: **www.ltms.com**
Point Tech Inc.: **pointec@ibm.net**
Promag Industries: **www.promagindustries.com**
Power Custom, Inc.: **www.powercustom.com**
Red Star Arms: **www.redstararms.com**
Rocky Mountain Arms: **www.rockymountainarms.com**
Royal Arms Int'l: **www.royalarms.com**
R.W. Hart: **www.rwhart.com**
Sarco Inc.: **www.sarcoinc.com**
Scattergun Technologies Inc.: **www.wilsoncombat.com**
Schuemann Barrels: **www.schuemann.com**
Seminole Gunworks Chamber Mates: **www.chambermates.com**
Shilen: **www.shilen.com**

Sims Vibration Laboratory: **www.limbsaver.com**
Smith & Alexander Inc.: **www.smithandalexander.com**
Speed Shooters Int'l: **www.shooternet.com/ssi**
Sprinco USA Inc.: **sprinco@primenet.com**
STI Int'l: **www.stiguns.com**
S&S Firearms: **www.ssfirearms.com**
SSK Industries: **www.sskindustries.com**
Sunny Hill Enterprises: **www.sunny-hill.com**
Tactical Innovations: **www.tacticalinc.com**
Tapco: **www.tapco.com**
Trapdoors Galore: **www.trapdoors.com**
Triple K Manufacturing Co. Inc.: **www.triplek.com**
U.S.A. Magazines Inc.: **www.usa-magazines.com**
Verney-Carron SA: **www.verney-carron.com**
Volquartsen Custom Ltd.: **www.volquartsen.com**
W.C. Wolff Co.: **www.gunsprings.com**
Waller & Son: **www.wallerandson.com**
Weigand Combat Handguns: **www.weigandcombat.com**
Western Gun Parts: **www.westerngunparts.com**
Wilson Arms: **www.wilsonarms.com**
Wilson Combat: **www.wilsoncombat.com**
Wisner's Inc.: **www.wisnerinc.com**
Z-M Weapons: **www.zmweapons.com/home.htm**

GUNSMITHING SUPPLIES AND INSTRUCTION

American Gunsmithing Institute: **www.americangunsmith.com**
Battenfeld Technologies: **www.battenfeldtechnologies.com**
Bellm TC's: **www.bellmtcs.com**
Brownells, Inc.: **www.brownells.com**
B-Square Co.: **www.b-square.com**
Clymer Mfg. Co.: **www.clymertool.com**
Craftguard Metal Finishing: **crftgrd@aol.com**
Dem-Bart: **www.dembartco.com**
Doug Turnbull Restoration: **www.turnbullrestoration,com**
Du-Lite Corp.: **www.dulite.com**
Dvorak Instruments: **www.dvorakinstruments.com**
Gradiant Lens Corp.: **www.gradientlens.com**
Grizzly Industrial: **www.grizzly.com**
Gunline Tools: **www.gunline.com**
Harbor Freight: **www.harborfreight.com**
JGS Precision Tool Mfg. LLC: **www.jgstools.com**
Mag-Na-Port International: **www.magnaport.com**
Manson Precision Reamers: **www.mansonreamers.com**
Midway: **www.midwayusa.com**
Murray State College: **www.mscok.edu**
Olympus America Inc.: **www.olympus.com**
Pacific Tool & Gauge: **www.pacifictoolandgauge.com**
Trinidad State Junior College: **www.trinidadstate.edu**

HANDGUN GRIPS

Ajax Custom Grips, Inc.: **www.ajaxgrips.com**
Altamont Co.: **www.altamontco.com**
Aluma Grips: **www.alumagrips.com**
Badger Grips: **www.pistolgrips.com**
Barami Corp.: **www.hipgrip.com**
Blu Magnum Grips: **www.blumagnum.com**
Buffalo Brothers: **www.buffalobrothers.com**
Crimson Trace Corp.: **www.crimsontrace.com**
Eagle Grips: **www.eaglegrips.com**
Falcon Industries: **www.ergogrips.net**
Herrett's Stocks: **www.herrettstocks.com**
Hogue Grips: **www.getgrip.com**
Kirk Ratajesak: **www.kgratajesak.com**
Lett Custom Grips: **www.lettgrips.com**
N.C. Ordnance: **www.gungrip.com**
Nill-Grips USA: **www.nill-grips.com**
Pachmayr: **www.pachmayr.com**
Pearce Grips: **www.pearcegrip.com**
Trausch Grips Int.Co.: **www.trausch.com**
Tyler-T Grips: **www.t-grips.com**
Uncle Mike's:: **www.uncle-mikes.com**

HOLSTERS AND LEATHER PRODUCTS

Akah: **www.akah.de**
Aker Leather Products: **www.akerleather.com**
Alessi Distributor R&F Inc.: **www.alessiholsters.com**
Alfonso's of Hollywood: **www.alfonsogunleather.com**
Armor Holdings: **www.holsters.com**
Bagmaster: **www.bagmaster.com**
Bianchi International: **www.bianchi-intl.com**
Blackhills Leather: **www.blackhillsleather.com**
BodyHugger Holsters: **www.nikolais.com**
Boyt Harness Co.: **www.boytharness.com**
Brigade Gun Leather: **www.brigadegunleather.com**
Chimere: **www.chimere.com**
Classic Old West Styles: **www.cows.com**
Conceal It: **www.conceal-it.com**
Concealment Shop Inc.: **www.theconcealmentshop.com**
Coronado Leather Co.: **www.coronadoleather.com**
Covert Carry: **www.covertcarry.com**
Creedmoor Sports, Inc.: **www.creedmoorsports.com**
Custom Leather Wear: **www.customleatherwear.com**
Defense Security Products: **www.thunderwear.com**
Dennis Yoder: **www.yodercustomleather.com**
DeSantis Holster: **www.desantisholster.com**
Dillon Precision: **www.dillonprecision.com**
Don Hume Leathergoods, Inc.: **www.donhume.com**
Ernie Hill International: **www.erniehill.com**
Fist: **www.fist-inc.com**
Fobus USA: **www.fobusholster.com**
Front Line Ltd. frontlin@internet-zahav.net
Galco: **www.usgalco.com**
Gilmore's Sports Concepts: **www.gilmoresports.com**
Gould & Goodrich: **www.gouldusa.com**
Gunmate Products: **www.gun-mate.com**
Hellweg Ltd.: **www.hellwegltd.com**
Hide-A-Gun: **www.hide-a-gun.com**
Holsters.Com: **www.holsters.com**
Horseshoe Leather Products: **www.horseshoe.co.uk**
Hunter Co.: **www.huntercompany.com**
Kirkpatrick Leather Company: **www.kirkpatrickleather.com**
KNJ: **www.knjmfg.com**
Kramer Leather: **www.kramerleather.com**
Law Concealment Systems: **www.handgunconcealment.com**
Levy's Leathers Ltd.: **www.levysleathers.com**
Michaels of Oregon Co.: **www.michaels-oregon.com**
Milt Sparks Leather: **www.miltsparks.com**
Mitch Rosen Extraordinary Gunleather: **www.mitchrosen.com**
Old World Leather: **www.gun-mate.com**
Pacific Canvas & Leather Co.: **paccanadleather@directway.com**
Pager Pal: **www.pagerpal.com**
Phalanx Corp.: **www.smartholster.com**
PWL: **www.pwlusa.com**
Rumanya Inc.: **www.rumanya.com**
S.A. Gunleather: **www.elpasoleather.com**
Safariland Ltd. Inc.: **www.safariland.com**
Shooting Systems Group Inc.: **www.shootingsystems.com**
Strictly Anything Inc.: **www.strictlyanything.com**
Strong Holster Co.: **www.strong-holster.com**
The Belt Co.: **www.conceal-it.com**
The Leather Factory Inc.: **lflandry@flash.net**
The Outdoor Connection: **www.outdoorconnection.com**
Top-Line USA inc.: **www.toplineusa.com**
Triple K Manufacturing Co.: **www.triplek.com**
Wilson Combat: **www.wilsoncombat.com**

MISCELLANEOUS SHOOTING PRODUCTS

10X Products Group: **www.10Xwear.com**

WEB DIRECTORY

Aero Peltor: **www.aearo.com**
American Body Armor: **www.americanbodyarmor.com**
Armor Holdings Products: **www.armorholdings.com**
Battenfeld Technologies: **www.battenfeldtechnologies.com**
Beamhit: **www.beamhit.com**
Beartooth: **www.beartoothproducts.com**
Bodyguard by S&W: **www.yourbodyguard.com**
Burnham Brothers: **www.burnhambrothers.com**
Collectors Armory: **www.collectorsarmory.com**
Dalloz Safety: **www.cdalloz.com**
Deben Group Industries Inc.: **www.deben.com**
Decot Hy-Wyd Sport Glasses: **www.sportyglasses.com**
E.A.R., Inc.: **www.earinc.com**
First Choice Armor: **www.firstchoicearmor.com**
Gunstands: **www.gunstands.com**
Howard Leight Hearing Protectors: **www.howardleight.com**
Hunters Specialities: **www.hunterspec.com**
Johnny Stewart Wildlife Calls: **www.hunterspec.com**
Merit Corporation: **www.meritcorporation.com**
Michaels of Oregon: **www.michaels-oregon.com**
MPI Outdoors: **www.mpioutdoors.com**
MTM Case-Gard: **www.mtmcase-gard.com**
North Safety Products: **www.northsafety-brea.com**
Plano Molding: **www.planomolding.com**
Pro-Ears: **www.pro-ears.com**
Second Chance Body Armor Inc.: **www.secondchance.com**
Silencio: **www.silencio.com**
Smart Lock Technologies: **www.smartlock.com**
Surefire: **www.surefire.com**
Taser Int'l: **www.taser.com**
Walker's Game Ear Inc.: **www.walkersgameear.com**

MUZZLELOADING FIREARMS AND PRODUCTS

American Pioneer Powder: **www.americanpioneerpowder.com**
Armi Sport: **www.armisport.com**
Barnes Bullets: **www.barnesbullets,com**
Black Powder Products: **www.bpiguns.com**
Buckeye Barrels: **www.buckeyebarrels.com**
CVA: **www.cva.com**
Davide Perdsoli & co.: **www.davide-pedersoli.com**
Dixie Gun Works, Inc.: **www.dixiegun.com**
Elephant/Swiss Black Powder: **www.elephantblackpowder.com**
Goex Black Powder: **www.goexpowder.com**
Green Mountain Rifle Barrel Co.: **www.gmriflebarrel.com**
Harvester Bullets: **www.harvesterbullets.com**
Hornady: **www.hornady.com**
Jedediah Starr Trading Co.: **www.jedediah-starr.com**
Jim Chambers Flintlocks: **www.flintlocks.com**
Kahnke Gunworks: **www.powderandbow.com/kahnke/**
Knight Rifles: **www.knightrifles.com**
L&R Lock Co.: **www.lr-rpl.com**
Log Cabin Shop: **www.logcabinshop.com**
Lyman: **www.lymanproducts.com**
Magkor Industries : **www.magkor.com**
MDM Muzzleloaders: **www.mdm-muzzleloaders.com**
Millennium Designed Muzzleloaders: **www.mdm-muzzleloaders.com**
MSM, Inc.: **www.msmfg.com**
Muzzleload Magnum Products: **www.mmpsabots.com**
Muzzleloading Technologies, Inc.: **www.mtimuzzleloading.com**
Navy Arms: **www.navyarms.com**
Northwest Trade Guns: **www.northstarwest.com**
Nosler, Inc.: **www.nosler.com**
October Country Muzzleloading: **www.oct-country.com**
Ox-Yoke Originals Inc.: **www.oxyoke.com**
Pacific Rifle Co.: **pacificrifle@aol.com**
Palmetto Arms: **www.palmetto.it**
Pietta: **www.pietta.it**
Powerbelt Bullets: **www.powerbeltbullets.com**
PR Bullets: **www.prbullets.com**
Precision Rifle Dead Center Bullets: **www.prbullet.com**
R.E. Davis CVo.: **www.redaviscompany.com**
Remington: **www.remington.com**
Rightnour Mfg. Co. Inc.: **www.rmcsports.com**
The Rifle Shop trshoppe@aol.com
Savage Arms, Inc.: **www.savagearms.com**
Schuetzen Powder: **www.schuetzenpowder.com**
TDC: **www.tdcmfg.com**
Thompson Center Arms: **www.tcarms.com**
Traditions Performance Muzzleloading: **www.traditionsfirearms.com**

PUBLICATIONS, VIDEOS, AND CD'S

A&J Arms Booksellers: **www.ajarmsbooksellers.com**
Airgun Letter: **www.airgunletter.com**
American Cop: **www.americancopmagazine.com**
American Firearms Industry: **www.amfire.com**
American Handgunner: **www.americanhandgunner.com**
American Hunter: **www.nrapublications.org**
American Rifleman: **www.nrapublications.org**
American Shooting Magazine: **www.americanshooting.com**
Blacksmith: **sales@blacksmithcorp.com**
Black Powder Cartridge News: **www.blackpowderspg.com**
Black Powder Guns & Hunting: **www.bpghmag.com**
Black Powder Journal: **www.blackpowderjournal.com**
Blue Book Publications: **www.bluebookinc.com**
Combat Handguns: **www.combathandguns.com**
Concealed Carry: **www.uscca.us**
Cornell Publications: **www.cornellpubs.com**
Countrywide Press: **www.countrysport.com**
DBI Books/Krause Publications: **www.krause.com**
Delta Force: **www.infogo.com/delta**
Gun List: **www.gunlist.com**
Gun Video: **www.gunvideo.com**
GUNS Magazine: **www.gunsmagazine.com**
Guns & Ammo: **www.gunsandammomag.com**
Gunweb Magazine: **www Links: www.imags.com**
Gun Week: **www.gunweek.com**
Gun World: **www.gunworld.com**
Harris Publications: **www.harrispublications.com**
Heritage Gun Books: **www.gunbooks.com**
Krause Publications: **www.krause.com**
Law and Order: **www.hendonpub.com**
Moose Lake Publishing: **MooselakeP@aol.com**
Munden Enterprises Inc.: **www.bob-munden.com**
Outdoor Videos: **www.outdoorvideos.com**
Precision Shooting: **www.precisionshooting.com**
Predator Extreme: **www.predatorextreme.com**
Predator & Prey: **www.predatorandpreymag.com**
Ray Riling Arms Books: **www.rayrilingarmsbooks.com**
Rifle and Handloader Magazines: **www.riflemagazine.com**
Safari Press Inc.: **www.safaripress.com**
Shoot! Magazine: **www.shootmagazine.com**
Shooters News: **www.shootersnews.com**
Shooting Illustrated: **www.nrapublications.org**
Shooting Industry: **www.shootingindustry.com**
Shooting Sports Retailer: **www.shootingsportsretailer.com**
Shooting Sports USA: **www.nrapublications.org**
Shotgun News: **www.shotgunnews.com**
Shotgun Report: **www.shotgunreport.com**
Shotgun Sports Magazine: **www.shotgun-sports.com**
Small Arms Review: **www.smallarmsreview.com**
Small Caliber News: **www.smallcaliber.com**
Sporting Clays Web Edition: **www.sportingclays.net**
Sports Afield: **www.sportsafield.com**
Sports Trend: **www.sportstrend.com**
Sportsmen on Film: **www.sportsmenonfilm.com**
SWAT Magazine: **www.swatmag.com**
The Gun Journal: **www.shooters.com**
The Shootin Iron: **www.off-road.com/4x4web/si/si.html**

WEB DIRECTORY

The Single Shot Exchange Magazine: **singleshot@earthlink.net**
The Sixgunner: **www.sskindustries.com**
Voyageur Press: **www.voyageurpress.com**
VSP Publications: **www.gunbooks.com**
Vulcan Outdoors Inc.: **www.vulcanpub.com**

RELOADING TOOLS

Ballisti-Cast Mfg.: **www.ballisti-cast.com**
Battenfeld Technologies: **www.battenfeldtechnologies.com**
Bruno Shooters Supply: **www.brunoshooters.com**
Camdex, Inc.: **www.camdexloader.com**
CH/4D Custom Die: **www.ch4d.com**
Colorado Shooters Supply: **www.hochmoulds.com**
Corbin Mfg & Supply Co.: **www.corbins.com**
Dillon Precision: **www.dillonprecision.com**
Forster Precision Products: **www.forsterproducts.com**
GSI International, Inc.: **www.gsiinternational.com**
Hanned Line: **www.hanned.com**
Harrell's Precision: **www.harrellsprec.com**
Holland's Shooting Supplies: **www.hollandgun.com**
Hornady: **www.hornady.com**
Huntington Reloading Products: **www.huntingtons.com**
J & J Products Co.: **www.jandjproducts.com**
Lead Bullet Technology: **LBTisaccuracy@lmbris.net**
Lee Precision,Inc.: **www.leeprecision.com**
Littleton Shotmaker: **www.leadshotmaker.com**
Load Data: **www.loaddata.com**
Lyman: **www.lymanproducts.com**
Magma Engineering: **www.magmaengr.com**
Mayville Engineering Co. (MEC): **www.mecreloaders.com**
Midway: **www.midwayusa.com**
Moly-Bore: **www.molybore.com**
MTM Case-Guard: **www.mtmcase-guard.com**
NECO: **www.neconos.com**
NEI : **www.neihandtools.com**
Neil Jones Custom Products: **www.neiljones.com**
Ponsness/Warren: **www.reloaders.com**
Ranger Products: **www.pages.prodigy.com/rangerproducts.home.htm**
Rapine Bullet Mold Mfg Co.: **www.bulletmoulds.com**
RCBS: **www.rcbs.com**
Redding Reloading Equipment: **www.redding-reloading.com**
Russ Haydon's Shooting Supplies: **www.shooters-supply.com**
Sinclair Int'l Inc.: **www.sinclairintl.com**
Stoney Point Products Inc: **www.stoneypoint.com**
Thompson Bullet Lube Co.: **www.thompsonbulletlube.com**
Vickerman Seating Die: **www.castingstuff.com**
Wilson(L.E. Wilson): **www.lewilson.com**

RESTS— BENCH, PORTABLE, ATTACHABLE

Battenfeld Technolgies: **www.battenfeldtechnologies.com**
Bench Master: **www.bench-master.com**
B-Square: **www.b-square.com**
Bullshooter: **www.bullshooterssightingin.com**
Desert Mountain Mfg.: **www.benchmasterusa.com**
Harris Engineering Inc.: **www.harrisbipods**
Kramer Designs: **www.snipepod.com**
L Thomas Rifle Support: **www.ltsupport.com**
Level-Lok: **www.levellok.com**
Midway: **www.midwayusa.com**
Predator Sniper Styx: **www.predatorsniperstyx.com**
Ransom International: **www.ransom-intl.com**
R.W. Hart: **www.rwhart.com**
Sinclair Intl, Inc.: **www.sinclairintl.com**
Stoney Point Products: **www.uncle-mikes.com**
Target Shooting: **www.targetshooting.com**
Varmint Masters: **www.varmintmasters.com**
Versa-Pod: **www.versa-pod.com**

SCOPES, SIGHTS, MOUNTS AND ACCESSORIES

Accumount: **www.accumounts.com**
Accusight: **www.accusight.com**
ADCO: **www.shooters.com/adco/index/htm**
Adirondack Opitcs: **www.adkoptics.com**
Advantage Tactical Sight: **www.advantagetactical.com**
Aimpoint: **www.aimpoint.com**
Aim Shot, Inc.: **www.miniosprey.com**
Aimtech Mount Systems: **www.aimtech-mounts.com**
Alpec Team, Inc.: **www.alpec.com**
Alpen Outdoor Corp.: **www.alpenoutdoor.com**
American Technologies Network, Corp.: **www.atncorp.com**
AmeriGlo, LLC: **www.ameriglo.net**
AO Sight Systems Inc.: **www.aosights.com**
Ashley Outdoors, Inc.: **www.ashleyoutdoors.com**
ATN: **www.atncorp.com**
Badger Ordnance: **www.badgerordnance.com**
Beamshot-Quarton: **www.beamshot.com**
BSA Optics: **www.bsaoptics.com**
B-Square Company, Inc.: **www.b-square.com**
Burris: **www.burrisoptics.com**
Bushnell Performance Optics: **www.bushnell.com**
Carl Zeiss Optical Inc.: **www.zeiss.com**
Carson Optical: **www.carson-optical.com**
CenterPoint Precision Optics: **www.centerpointoptics.com**
C-More Systems: **www.cmore.com**
Conetrol Scope Mounts: **www.conetrol.com**
Crimson Trace Corp.: **www.crimsontrace.com**
Crossfire L.L.C.: **www.amfire.com/hesco/html**
DCG Supply Inc.: **www.dcgsupply.com**
D&L Sports: **www.dlsports.com**
DuraSight Scope Mounting Systems: **www.durasight.com**
EasyHit, Inc.: **www.easyhit.com**
EAW: **www.eaw.de**
Elcan Optical Technologies: **www.armament.com,: www.elcan.com**
Electro-Optics Technologies: **www.eotechmdc.com/holosight**
Europtik Ltd.: **www.europtik.com**
Fujinon, Inc.: **www.fujinon.com**
Gilmore Sports: **www.gilmoresports.com**
Gradient Lens Corp.: **www.gradientlens.com**
Hakko Co. Ltd.: **www.hakko-japan.co.jp**
Hesco: **www.hescosights.com**
Hi-Lux Optics: **www.hi-luxoptics.com**
Hitek Industries: **www.nightsight.com**
HIVIZ: **www.hivizsights.com**
Hollands Shooters Supply: **www.hollandguns.com**
Horus Vision: **www.horusvision.com**
Hunter Co.: **www.huntercompany.com**
Innovative Weaponry,Inc.: **www.ptnightsights.com**
Ironsighter Co.: **www.ironsighter.com**
ITT Night Vision: **www.ittnightvision.com**
Kahles: **www.kahlesoptik.com**
Kowa Optimed Inc.: **www.kowascope.com**
Kwik-Site Co.: **www.kwiksitecorp.com**
L-3 Communications-Eotech: **www.l-3com.com**
Laser Bore Sight: **www.laserboresight.com**
Laser Devices Inc.: **www.laserdevices.com**
Lasergrips: **www.crimsontrace.com**
LaserLyte: **www.laserlytesights.com**
LaserMax Inc.: **www.lasermax.com**
Laser Products: **www.surefire.com**
Leapers, Inc.: **www.leapers.com**
Leatherwood: **www.hi-luxoptics.com**
Leica Camera Inc.: **www.leica-camera.com/usa**
Leupold: **www.leupold.com**
LightForce/NightForce USA: **www.nightforcescopes.com**
Lyman: **www.lymanproducts.com**
Lynx: **www.b-square.com**
Marble's Outdoors: **www.marblesoutdoors.com**

MDS,Inc.: **www.mdsincorporated.com**
Meopta: **www.meopta.com**
Meprolight: **www.kimberamerica.com**
Micro Sight Co.: **www.microsight.com**
Millett : **www.millettsights.com**
Miniature Machine Corp.: **www.mmcsight.com**
Montana Vintage Arms: **www.montanavintagearms.com**
Mounting Solutions Plus: **www.mountsplus.com**
NAIT: **www.nait.com**
Newcon International Ltd.: **newconsales@newcon-optik.com**
Night Force Optics: **www.nightforcescopes.com**
Night Optics USA, Inc.: **www.nightoptics.com**
Night Owl Optics: **www.nightowloptics.com**
Night Vision Systems: **www.nightvisionsystems.com**
Nikon Inc.: **www.nikonusa.com**
North American Integrated Technologies: **www.nait.com**
O.K. Weber, Inc.: **www.okweber.com**
Optolyth-Optic: **www.optolyth.de**
Pentax Corp.: **www.pentaxlightseeker.com**
Premier Reticles: **www.premierreticles.com**
Redfield: **www.redfieldoptics.com**
Rifle Electronics: **www.theriflecam.com**
R&R Int'l Trade: **www.nightoptic.com**
Schmidt & Bender: **www.schmidt-bender.com**
Scopecoat: **www.scopecoat.com**
Scopelevel: **www.scopelevel.com**
Segway Industries: **www.segway-industries.com**
Shepherd Scope Ltd.: **www.shepherdscopes.com**
Sightron: **www.sightron.com**
Simmons: **www.simmonsoptics.com**
S&K: **www.scopemounts.com**
Springfield Armory: **www.springfield-armory.com**
Sure-Fire: **www.surefire.com**
Swarovski/Kahles: **www.swarovskioptik.com**
Swift Optics: **www.swiftoptics.com**
Talley Mfg. Co.: **www.talleyrings.com**
Tasco: **www.tascosales.com**
Trijicon Inc.: **www.trijicon.com**
Truglo Inc.: **www.truglo.com**
UltraDot: **www.ultradotusa.com**
Unertl Optical Co.: **www.unertlopics.com**
US Night Vision: **www.usnightvision.com**
U.S. Optics Technologies Inc.: **www.usoptics.com**
Valdada-IOR Optics: **www.valdada.com**
Warne: **www.warnescopemounts.com**
Weaver Mounts: **www.weaver-mounts.com**
Weaver Scopes: **www.weaveroptics.com**
Wilcox Industries Corp: **www.wilcoxind.com**
Williams Gun Sight Co.: **www.williamsgunsight.com**
XS Sight Systems: **www.xssights.com**
Zeiss: **www.zeiss.com**

SHOOTING ORGANIZATIONS, SCHOOLS AND RANGES

Amateur Trapshooting Assoc.: **www.shootata.com**
American Custom Gunmakers Guild: **www.acgg.org**
American Gunsmithing Institute: **www.americangunsmith.com**
American Pistolsmiths Guild: **www.americanpistol.com**
American Shooting Sports Council: **www.assc.com**
American Single Shot Rifle Assoc.: **www.assra.com**
Antique Shooting Tool Collector's Assoc.: **www.oldshooting-tools.org**
Assoc. of Firearm & Tool Mark Examiners: **www.afte.org**
BATF: **www.atf.ustreas.gov**
Blackwater Lodge and Training Center: **www.blackwaterlodge.com**
Boone and Crockett Club: **www.boone-crockett.org**
Buckmasters, Ltd.: **www.buckmasters.com**
Cast Bullet Assoc.: **www.castbulletassoc.org**
Citizens Committee for the Right to Keep & Bear Arms: **www.ccrkba.org**
Civilian Marksmanship Program: **www.odcmp.com**
Colorado School of Trades: **www.gunsmith-school.com**
Ducks Unlimited: **www.ducks.org**
4-H Shooting Sports Program: **www.4-hshootingsports.org**
Fifty Caliber Institute: **www.fiftycal.org**
Fifty Caliber Shooters Assoc.: **www.fcsa.org**
Firearms Coalition: **www.nealknox.com**
Front Sight Firearms Training Institute: **www.frontsight.com**
German Gun Collectors Assoc.: **www.germanguns.com**
Gun Clubs: **www.associatedgunclubs.org**
Gun Owners' Action League: **www.goal.org**
Gun Owners of America: **www.gunowners.org**
Gun Trade Asssoc. Ltd.: **www.brucepub.com/gta**
Gunsite Training Center,Inc.: **www.gunsite.com**
Handgun Hunters International: **www.sskindustries.com**
Hunting and Shooting Sports Heritage Fund: **www.huntandshoot.org**
International Defense Pistol Assoc.: **www.idpa.com**
International Handgun Metallic Silhouette Assoc.: **www.ihmsa.org**
International Hunter Education Assoc.: **www.ihea.com**
International Single Shot Assoc.: **www.issa-schuetzen.org**
Jews for the Preservation of Firearms Ownership: **www.jpfo.org**
Mule Deer Foundation: **www.muledeer.org**
Muzzle Loaders Assoc. of Great Britain: **www.mlagb.com**
National 4-H Shooting Sports: **www.4-hshootingsports.org**
National Association of Sporting Goods Wholesalers: **www.nasgw.org**
National Benchrest Shooters Assoc.: **www.benchrest.com**
National Muzzle Loading Rifle Assoc.: **www.nmlra.org**
National Reloading Manufacturers Assoc: **www.reload-nrma.com**
National Rifle Assoc.: **www.nra.org**
National Rifle Assoc. ILA: **www.nraila.org**
National Shooting Sports Foundation: **www.nssf.org**
National Skeet Shooters Association: **www.nssa-nsca.com**
National Sporting Clays Assoc.: **www.nssa-nsca.com**
National Wild Turkey Federation: **www.nwtf.com**
NICS/FBI: **www.fbi.gov**
North American Hunting Club: **www.huntingclub.com**
Order of Edwardian Gunners (Vintagers): **www.vintagers.org**
Outdoor Industry Foundation: **www.outdoorindustryfoundation.org**
Pennsylvania Gunsmith School: **www.pagunsmith.com**
Quail Unlimited: **www.qu.org**
Right To Keep and Bear Arms: **www.rkba.org**
Rocky Mountain Elk Foundation: **www.rmef.org**
SAAMI: **www.saami.org**
Safari Club International: **www.scifirstforhunters.org**
Scholastic Clay Target Program: **www.nssf.org/sctp**
Second Amendment Foundation: **www.saf.org**
Second Amendment Sisters: **www.2asisters.org**
Shooting Ranges Int'l: **www.shootingranges.com**
Single Action Shooting Society: **www.sassnet.com**
Students for Second Amendment: **www.sf2a.org**
S&W Academy and Nat'l Firearms Trng. Center: **www.sw-academy.com**
Tactical Defense Institute: **www.tdiohio.com**
Ted Nugent United Sportsmen of America: **www.tnugent.com**
Thunder Ranch: **www.thunderranchinc.com**
Trapshooters Homepage: **www.trapshooters.com**
Trinidad State Junior College: **www.trinidadstate.edu**
U.S. Concealed Carry Association: **www.uscca.us**
U.S. Int'l Clay Target Assoc.: **www.usicta.com**
United States Fish and Wildlife Service: **www.fws.gov**
U.S. Practical Shooting Assoc.: **www.uspsa.org**
USA Shooting: **www.usashooting.com**
Varmint Hunters Assoc.: **www.varminthunter.org**
U.S. Sportsmen's Alliance: **www.ussportsmen.org**
Women Hunters: **www.womanhunters.com**
Women's Shooting Sports Foundation: **www.wssf.org**

WEB DIRECTORY

STOCKS

Advanced Technology: **www.atigunstocks.com**
Battenfeld Technologies: **www.battenfeldtechnologies.com**
Bell & Carlson, Inc.: **www.bellandcarlson.com**
Boyd's Gunstock Industries, Inc.: **www.boydgunstocks.com**
Butler Creek Corp: **www.butler-creek.com**
Calico Hardwoods, Inc.: **www.calicohardwoods.com**
Choate Machine: **www.riflestock.com**
Elk Ridge Stocks: **www.reamerrentals.com/elk_ridge.htm**
Fajen: **www.battenfeldtechnologies.com**
Great American Gunstocks: **www.gunstocks.com**
Herrett's Stocks: **www.herrettstocks.com**
High Tech Specialties: **www.bansnersrifle.com/hightech**
Holland's Shooting Supplies: **www.hollandgun.com**
Knoxx Industries: **www.blackhawk.com**
Lone Wolf: **www.lonewolfriflestocks.com**
McMillan Fiberglass Stocks: **www.mcmfamily.com**
MPI Stocks: **www.mpistocks.com**
Precision Gun Works: **www.precisiongunstocks.com**
Ram-Line: **www.outers-guncare.com**
Rimrock Rifle Stock: **www.rimrockstocks.com**
Royal Arms Gunstocks: **www.imt.net/~royalarms**
S&K Industries: **www.sandkgunstocks.com**
Speedfeed, Inc.: **www.speedfeedinc.com**
Tiger-Hunt Curly Maple Gunstocks: **www.gunstockwood.com**
Wenig Custom Gunstocks Inc.: **www.wenig.com**

TARGETS AND RANGE EQUIPMENT

Action Target Co.: **www.actiontarget.com**
Advanced Interactive Systems: **www.ais-sim.com**
Birchwood Casey: **www.birchwoodcasey.com**
Bullet Proof Electronics: **www.thesnipertarget.com**
Caswell Meggitt Defense Systems: **www.mds-caswell.com**
Champion Traps & Targets: **www.championtarget.com**
Handloader/Victory Targets: **www.targetshandloader.com**
Just Shoot Me Products: **www.ballistictec.com**
Laser Shot: **www.lasershot.com**
Mountain Plains Industries: **www.targetshandloader.com**
MTM Products: **www.mtmcase-gard.com**
Natiional Target Co.: **www.nationaltarget.com**
Newbold Target Systems: **www.newboldtargets.com**
Porta Target,Inc.: **www.portatarget.com**
Range Management Services Inc.: **www.casewellintl.com**
Range Systems: **www.shootingrangeproducts.com**
Reactive Target Systems Inc.: **chrts@primenet.com**
ShatterBlast Targets: **www.daisy.com**
Super Trap Bullet Containment Systems: **www.supertrap.com**
Thompson Target Technology: **www.thompsontarget.com**
Tombstone Tactical Targets: **www.tttargets.com**
Visible Impact Targets: **www.crosman.com**
White Flyer: **www.whiteflyer.com**

TRAP AND SKEET SHOOTING EQUIPMENT AND ACCESSORIES

Auto-Sporter Industries: **www.auto-sporter.com**
10X Products Group: **www.10Xwear.com**
Claymaster Traps: **www.claymaster.com**
Do-All Traps, Inc.: **www.doalloutdoors.com**
Laporte USA: **www.laporte-shooting.com**
Outers: **www.blount.com**
Trius Products Inc.: **www.triustraps.com**
White Flyer: **www.whiteflyer.com**

TRIGGERS

Brownells: **www.brownells.com**
Chip McCormick Corp.: **www.chipmccormickcorp.com**
Huber Concepts: **www.huberconcepts.com**
Kidd Triggers.: **www.coolguyguns.com**
Shilen: **www.shilen.com**
Timney Triggers: **www.timneytrigger.com**

MAJOR SHOOTING WEB SITES AND LINKS

24 Hour Campfire: **www.24hourcampfire.com**
Alphabetic Index of Links: **www.gunsgunsguns.com**
Ammo Guide: **www.ammoguide.com**
Auction Arms: **www.auctionarms.com**
Benchrest Central: **www.benchrest.com**
Big Game Hunt: **www.biggamehunt.net**
Bullseye Pistol: **www.bullseyepistol.com**
Firearms History: **www.researchpress.co.uk/firearms**
Gun Broker Auctions: **www.gunbroker.com**
Gun Index: **www.gunindex.com**
Gun Industry: **www.gunindustry.com**
Gun Blast: **www.gunblast.com**
Gun Boards: **www.gunboards.com**
GunsAmerica.com: **www.gunsamerica.com**
Guns Unified Nationally Endorsing Dignity: **www.guned.com**
Gun Shop Finder: **www.gunshopfinder.com**
Hunt and Shoot (NSSF): **www.huntandshoot.org**
Keep and Bear Arms: **www.keepandbeararms.com**
Leverguns: **www.leverguns.com**
Load Swap: **www.loadswap.com**
Outdoor Press Room: **www.outdoorpressroom.com**
Outdoor Yellow Pages: **www.outdoorsyp.com**
Real Guns: **www.realguns.com**
Shooters Forum: **www.shootersforum.com**
Shooter's Online Services: **www.shooters.com**
Shotgun Sports Resource Guide: **www.shotgunsports.com**
Sixgunner: **www.sixgunner.com**
Sniper's Hide: **www.snipershide.com**
Sportsman's Web: **www.sportsmansweb.com**
Surplus Rifles: **www.surplusrifle.com**
Wing Shooting USA: **www.wingshootingusa.org**

AAFTA News (M)
5911 Cherokee Ave., Tampa, FL 33604. Official newsletter of the American Airgun Field Target Assn.

Accurate Rifle, The
Precisions Shooting, Inc., 222 Mckee Street, Manchester CT 06040. $37/yr. Dedicated to the rifle accuracy enthusiast.

Action Pursuit Games Magazine (M)
CFW Enterprises, Inc., 4201 W. Vanowen Pl., Burbank, CA 91505 818-845-2656. $4.99 single copy U.S., $5.50 Canada. Editor: Dan Reeves. World's leading magazine of paintball sports.

Air Gunner Magazine
4 The Courtyard, Denmark St., Wokingham, Berkshire RG11 2AZ, England/011-44-734-771677. $U.S. $44/yr. Leading monthly airgun magazine in U.K.

Airgun Ads
Box 33, Hamilton, MT 59840/406-363-3805; Fax: 406-363-4117. $35/yr. (for first mailing; $20 for second mailing; $35 for Canada and foreign orders.) Monthly tabloid with extensive For Sale and Wanted airgun listings.

Airgun Letter, The
Gapp, Inc., 4614 Woodland Rd., Ellicott City, MD 21042-6329/410-730-5496; Fax: 410-730-9544; e-mail: staff@airgnltr.net; http://www.airgunletter.com. $21 U.S., $24 Canada, $27 Mexico and $33 other foreign orders, 1 yr. monthly newsletter for airgun users and collectors.

Airgun World
4 The Courtyard, Denmark St., Wokingham, Berkshire RG40 2AZ, England/011-44-734-771677. Call for subscription rates. Oldest monthly airgun magazine in U.K., sister publication to *Air Gunner*.

Alaska Magazine
Morris Communications, 735 Broad Street, Augusta, GA 30901/706-722-6060. Hunting, fishing and life on the Last Frontier articles of Alaska and western Canada.

American Firearms Industry
Nat'l. Assn. of Federally Licensed Firearms Dealers, 2455 E. Sunrise Blvd., Suite 916, Ft. Lauderdale, FL 33304. $35.00/yr. For firearms retailers, distributors and manufacturers.

American Guardian
NRA, 11250 Waples Mill Rd., Fairfax, VA 22030. Publications division. $15.00/yr. Magazine features personal protection; home-self-defense; family recreation shooting; women's issues; etc.

American Gunsmith
Belvoir Publications, Inc., 75 Holly Hill Lane, Greenwich, CT 06836-2626/203-661-6111. $49.00 (12 issues). Technical journal of firearms repair and maintenance.

American Handgunner*
Publisher's Development Corp., 12345 World Trade Drive, San Diego, CA 92128/800-537-3006 $16.95/yr. Articles for handgun enthusiasts, competitors, police and hunters.

American Hunter (M)
National Rifle Assn., 11250 Waples Mill Rd., Fairfax, VA 22030 (Same address for both.) Publications Div. $35.00/yr. Wide scope of hunting articles.

American Rifleman (M)
National Rifle Assn., 11250 Waples Mill Rd., Fairfax, VA 22030 (Same address for both). Publications Div. $35.00/yr. Firearms articles of all kinds.

American Survival Guide
McMullen Angus Publishing, Inc., 774 S. Placentia Ave., Placentia, CA 92670-6846. 12 issues $19.95/714-572-2255; FAX: 714-572-1864.

Armes & Tir*
c/o FABECO, 38, rue de Trévise 75009 Paris, France. Articles for hunters, collectors, and shooters. French text.

Arms Collecting (Q)
Museum Restoration Service, P.O. Box 70, Alexandria Bay, NY 13607-0070. $22.00/yr.; $62.00/3 yrs.; $112.00/5 yrs.

Australian Shooter (formerly Australian Shooters Journal)
Sporting Shooters' Assn. of Australia, Inc., P.O. Box 2066, Kent Town SA 5071, Australia. $60.00/yr. locally; $65.00/yr. overseas surface mail. Hunting and shooting articles.

Backwoodsman Magazine, The
P.O. Box 627, Westcliffe, CO 81252. $16.00/yr. 6 issues; $30.00/2 yrs.; sample copy $2.75. Subjects include muzzle-loading, woodslore, primitive survival, trapping, homesteading, blackpowder cartridge guns, 19th century how-to.

Black Powder Cartridge News (Q)
SPG, Inc., P.O. Box 761, Livingston, MT 59047/ Phone/Fax: 406-222-8416. $17/yr. (4 issues) ($6 extra 1st class mailing).

Blackpowder Hunting (M)
Intl. Blackpowder Hunting Assn., P.O. Box 1180Z, Glenrock, WY 82637/307-436-9817. $20.00/yr., $36.00/2 yrs. How-to and where-to features by experts on hunting; shooting; ballistics; traditional and modern blackpowder rifles, shotguns, pistols and cartridges.

Black Powder Times
P.O. Box 234, Lake Stevens, WA 98258. $20.00/yr.; add $5/year for Canada, $10/year other foreign. Tabloid newspaper for blackpowder activities; test reports.

Blade Magazine
Krause Publications, 700 East State St., Iola, WI 54990-0001. $25.98 for 12 issues. Foreign price (including Canada-Mexico) $50.00. A magazine for all fans of handmade, factory and antique knives.

Caliber
GFI-Verlag, Theodor-Heuss Ring 62, 50668 Koln, Germany. For hunters, target shooters and reloaders.

Caller, The (Q) (M)
National Wild Turkey Federation, P.O. Box 530, Edgefield, SC 29824. Tabloid newspaper; 4 issues/yr. (membership fee $25.00)

Cartridge Journal (M)
Robert Mellichamp, 907 Shirkmere, Houston, TX 77008/713-869-0558. Dues $12 for U.S. and Canadian members (includes the newsletter); 6 issues.

Cast Bullet, The*(M)
Official journal of The Cast Bullet Assn., Dir. of Membership, 203 E. 2nd St., Muscatine, IA 52761. Membership $14/year, incl. 6 issues.

Cibles
14, rue du Patronage-Laique, BP 2057, 52902 Chaumont, cedex 9, France. French-language magazine also carries small amount of arms-related and historical content. 12 issues/year. Tel/03-25-03-87-47/Email: cibeles@graphycom.com; Web: www.graphycom

COLTELLI, che Passione (Q)
Casella postale N.519, 20101 Milano, Italy/Fax: 02-48402857. $15/yr., $27/2 yrs. Covers all types of knives—collecting, combat, historical. Italian text.

Combat Handguns*
Harris Publications, Inc., 1115 Broadway, New York, NY 10010.

Deer & Deer Hunting Magazine
Krause Publications, 700 E. State St., Iola, WI 54990-0001. $19.95/yr. (9 issues). For the serious deer hunter. Web: www.krause.com

Derringer Peanut, The (M)
The National Association of Derringer Collectors, P.O. Box 20572, San Jose, CA 95160. A newsletter dedicated to developing the best derringer information. Write for details.

Deutsches Waffen Journal
Journal-Verlag Schwend GmbH, Postfach 100340, D-74503 Schwäbisch Hall, Germany/0791-404-500; FAX:0791-404-505 and 404-424. DM102/yr. (interior); DM125.30 (abroad), postage included. Antique and modern arms and equipment. German text.

Double Gun Journal
P.O. Box 550, East Jordan, MI 49727/800-447-1658. $35/4 issues.

Ducks Unlimited, Inc. (M)
1 Waterfowl Way, Memphis, TN 38120

Engraver, The (M) (Q)
P.O. Box 4365, Estes Park, CO 80517/970-586-2388; Fax: 970-586-0394. Mike Dubber, editor. The journal of firearms engraving.

Field, The
King's Reach Tower, Stamford St., London SE1 9LS England. £36.40 U.K./yr.; 49.90 (overseas, surface mail) yr.; £82.00 (overseas, air mail)/yr. Hunting and shooting articles, and all country sports.

Field & Stream
Time4 Media, Two Park Ave., New York, NY 10016/212-779-5000. 12 issues/$19.97. Monthly shooting column. Articles on hunting and fishing.

Field Tests
Belvoir Publications, Inc., 75 Holly Hill Lane; P.O. Box 2626, Greenwich, CT 06836-2626/203-661-6111; 800-829-3361 (subscription line). U.S. & Canada $29/yr., $58/2 yrs.; all other countries $45/yr., $90/2 yrs. (air).

Fur-Fish-Game
A.R. Harding Pub. Co., 2878 E. Main St., Columbus, OH 43209. $15.95/yr. Practical guidance for trapping, fishing and hunting.

Gottlieb-Tartaro Report, The
Second Amendment Foundation, James Madison Bldg., 12500 NE 10th Pl., Bellevue, WA 98005/206-454-7012; Fax:206-451-3959. $30/12 issues. An insider's guide for gun owners.

Gray's Sporting Journal
P.O. Box 1207, Augusta, GA 30903. $36.95/6 issues. Hunting and fishing. Expeditions and Guides Book (Annual Travel Guide).

Gun Digest, The Magazine (formerly Gun List)†
700 E. State St., Iola, WI 54990. $37.98/yr. (26 issues); $66.98 (52 issues). Indexed market publication for firearms collectors and active shooters; guns, supplies and services. Web: www.krause.com

Gun News Digest (Q)
Second Amendment Fdn., P.O. Box 488, Station C, Buffalo, NY 14209/716-885-6408; Fax:716-884-4471. $10 U.S.; $20 foreign.

Gun Report, The
World Wide Gun Report, Inc., Box 38, Aledo, IL 61231-0038. $33.00/yr. For the antique and collectable gun dealer and collector.

Gunmaker (M) (Q)
ACGG, P.O. Box 812, Burlington, IA 52601-0812. The journal of custom gunmaking.

* Published bi-monthly
† Published weekly
‡ Published three times per month
All others are published monthly
M Membership requirements; write for details
Q Published Quarterly

PERIODICAL PUBLICATIONS

Gunrunner, The
Div. of Kexco Publ. Co. Ltd., Box 565G, Lethbridge, Alb., Canada T1J 3Z4. $23.00/yr., sample $2.00. Monthly newspaper, listing everything from antiques to artillery.

Gun Show Calendar (Q)
700 E. State St., Iola, WI 54990. $14.95/yr. (4 issues). Gun shows listed; chronologically and by state. Web: www.krause.com

Gun Tests
11 Commerce Blvd., Palm Coast, FL 32142. The consumer resource for the serious shooter. Write for information.

Gun Trade News
Bruce Publishing Ltd., P.O. Box 82, Wantage, Ozon OX12 7A8, England/44-1-235-771770; Fax: 44-1-235-771848. Britain's only "trade only" magazine exclusive to the gun trade.

Gun Week†
Second Amendment Foundation, P.O. Box 488, Station C, Buffalo, NY 14209. $35.00/yr. U.S. and possessions; $45.00/yr. other countries. Tabloid paper on guns, hunting, shooting and collecting (36 issues).

Gun World
Y-Visionary Publishing, LP 265 South Anita Drive, Ste. 120, Orange, CA 92868. $21.97/yr.; $34.97/2 yrs. For the hunting, reloading and shooting enthusiast.

Guns & Ammo
Intermedia, 6420 Wilshire Blvd., Los Angeles, CA 90048/213-782-2780. $23.94/yr. Guns, shooting, and technical articles.

Guns
Publishers Development Corporation, 12345 World Trade Drive, San Diego, CA 92128/800-537-3006. $19.95/yr. In-depth articles on guns, shooting equipment and accessories for collectors, hunters and shooters.

Guns Review
Ravenhill Publishing Co. Ltd., Box 35, Standard House, Bonhill St., London EC 2A 4DA, England. £20.00 sterling (approx. U.S. $38 USA & Canada)/yr. For collectors and shooters.

H.A.C.S. Newsletter (M)
Harry Moon, Pres., P.O. Box 50117, South Slope RPO, Burnaby BC, V5J 5G3, Canada/604-438-0950; Fax:604-277-3646. $25/yr. U.S. and Canada. Official newsletter of The Historical Arms Collectors of B.C. (Canada).

Handgunner*
Richard A.J. Munday, Seychelles house, Brightlingsen, Essex CO7 ONN, England/012063-305201. £18.00 (sterling).

Handguns*
Intermedia, 6420 Wilshire Blvd., Los Angeles, CA 90048/323-782-2868. For the handgunning and shooting enthusiast.

Handloader*
Wolfe Publishing Co., 2626 Stearman Road, Ste. A, Prescott, AZ 86301/520-445-7810; Fax: 520-778-5124. $22.00/yr. The journal of ammunition reloading.

INSIGHTS*
NRA, 11250 Waples Mill Rd., Fairfax, VA 22030. $15.00/yr., includes NRA jr. membership; $10.00 adult subscriptions (12 issues). Details for the young hunter and target shooter; emphasizes gun safety, marksmanship training, hunting skills.

International Arms & Militaria Collector (Q)
Arms & Militaria Press, P.O. Box 80, Labrador, Qld. 4215, Australia. $39.50/yr. (U.S. & Canada), 2 yrs./$77.50; A$37.50 (others)/yr., 2 yrs./$73.50 air express mail; surface mail is less.

International Shooting Sport*/UIT Journal
International Shooting Union (UIT), Bavariaring 21, D-80336 Munich, Germany. Europe: (Deutsche Mark) DM44.00/yr., DM83.00/2 yrs.; outside Europe: DM50.00/yr., DM95.00/2 yrs. (air mail postage included.) For international sport shooting.

Internationales Waffen-Magazin
Habegger-Verlag Zürich, Postfach 9230, CH-8036 Zürich, Switzerland. SF 105.00 (U.S. $73.00) surface mail/10 issues. Modern and antique arms, self-defense. German text; English summary of contents.

Journal of the Arms & Armour Society, The (M)
A. Dove, P.O. Box 10232, London, SW19 2ZD England. £15.00 surface mail; £20.00 airmail sterling only yr. Articles for the historian and collector.

Journal of the Historical Breechloading Smallarms Assn.
Published annually. P.O. Box 12778, London, SE1 6XB, England. $21.00/yr. Articles for the collector plus mailings of short articles on specific arms, reprints, newsletters, etc.

Knife World
Knife World Publications, P.O. Box 3395, Knoxville, TN 37927. $15.00/yr.; $25.00/2 yrs. Published monthly for knife enthusiasts and collectors. Articles on custom and factory knives; other knife-related interests, monthly column on knife identification, military knives.

Man At Arms*
P.O. Box 460, Lincoln, RI 02865. $27.00/yr., $52.00 2 yrs. plus $8.00 for foreign subscribers. The N.R.A. magazine of arms collecting-investing, with articles for the collector of antique arms and militaria.

Mannlicher Collector, The (Q)(M)
Mannlicher Collectors Assn., Inc., P.O. Box 7144, Salem Oregon 97303. $20/yr. subscription included in membership.

MAGNUM
Rua Madre Rita Amada de Jesus, 182, Granja Julieta, Sao Paulo – SP – 04721-050 Brazil. No details.

MAN/MAGNUM
S.A. Man (Pty) Ltd., P.O. Box 35204, Northway, Durban 4065, Republic of South Africa. SA Rand 200.00 for 12 issues. Africa's only publication on hunting, shooting, firearms, bushcraft, knives, etc.

Marlin Collector, The (M)
R.W. Paterson, 407 Lincoln Bldg., 44 Main St., Champaign, IL 61820.

Muzzle Blasts (M)
National Muzzle Loading Rifle Assn., P.O. Box 67, Friendship, IN 47021/812-667-5131. $35.00/yr. membership. For the blackpowder shooter.

Muzzleloader Magazine*
Scurlock Publishing Co., Inc., Dept. Gun, Route 5, Box 347-M, Texarkana, TX 75501. $18.00 U.S.; $22.50 U.S./yr. for foreign subscribers. The publication for blackpowder shooters.

National Defense (M)*
American Defense Preparedness Assn., Two Colonial Place, Suite 400, 2101 Wilson Blvd., Arlington, VA 22201-3061/703-522-1820; FAX: 703-522-1885. $35.00/yr. Articles on both military and civil defense field, including weapons, materials technology, management.

National Knife Magazine (M)
Natl. Knife Coll. Assn., 7201 Shallowford Rd., P.O. Box 21070, Chattanooga, TN 37424-0070. Membership $35/yr.; $65/Int'l yr.

National Rifle Assn. Journal (British) (Q)
Natl. Rifle Assn. (BR.), Bisley Camp, Brookwood, Woking, Surrey, England. GU24, OPB. £24.00 Sterling including postage.

National Wildlife*
Natl. Wildlife Fed., 1400 16th St. NW, Washington, DC 20036, $16.00/yr. (6 issues); *International Wildlife*, 6 issues, $16.00/yr. Both, $22.00/yr., includes all membership benefits. Write attn.: Membership Services Dept., for more information.

New Zealand GUNS*
Waitekauri Publishing, P.O. 45, Waikino 3060, New Zealand. $NZ90.00 (6 issues)/yr. Hunting and firearms in New Zealand.

New Zealand Wildlife (Q)
New Zealand Deerstalkers Assoc., Inc., P.O. Box 6514, Wellington, N.Z. $30.00 (N.Z.). Hunting, shooting and firearms/game research articles.

North American Hunter* (M)
P.O. Box 3401, Minnetonka, MN 55343/612-936-9333; e-mail: huntingclub@pclink.com. $18.00/yr. (7 issues). Articles on all types of North American hunting.

Outdoor Life
Time4 Media, Two Park Ave., New York, NY 10016. $14.97/10 issues. Extensive coverage of hunting and shooting. Shooting column by Jim Carmichel.

La Passion des Courteaux (Q)
Phenix Editions, 25 rue Mademoiselle, 75015 Paris, France. French text.

Paintball Games International Magazine
Aceville Publications, Castle House, 97 High St., Colchester, Essex, England CO1 1TH/011-44-206-564840. Write for subscription rates. Leading magazine in the U.K. covering competitive paintball activities.

Paintball News
PBN Publishing, P.O. Box 1608, 24 Henniker St., Hillsboro, NH 03244/603-464-6080. $35 U.S./yr. Bi-weekly. Newspaper covering the sport of paintball, new product reviews and industry features.

Paintball Sports (Q)
Paintball Publications, Inc., 540 Main St., Mount Kisco, NY 10549/941-241-7400. $24.75 U.S./yr., $32.75 foreign. Covering the competitive paintball scene.

Performance Shooter
Belvoir Publications, Inc., 75 Holly Hill Lane, Greenwich, CT 06836-2626/203-661-6111. $45.00/yr. (12 issues). Techniques and technology for improved rifle and pistol accuracy.

Petersen's HUNTING Magazine
Primedia, 6420 Wilshire Blvd., Los Angeles, CA 90048. $19.94/yr.; Canada $29.34/yr.; foreign countries $29.94/yr. Hunting articles for all game; test reports.

P.I. Magazine
America's Private Investigation Journal, 755 Bronx Dr., Toledo, OH 43609. Chuck Klein, firearms editor with column about handguns.

Pirsch
BLV Verlagsgesellschaft GmbH, Postfach 400320, 80703 Munich, Germany/089-12704-0;Fax:089-12705-354. German text.

Point Blank
Citizens Committee for the Right to Keep and Bear Arms (sent to contributors), Liberty Park, 12500 NE 10th Pl., Bellevue, WA 98005

---

* Published bi-monthly
† Published weekly
‡ Published three times per month
All others are published monthly
M Membership requirements; write for details
Q Published Quarterly

PERIODICAL PUBLICATIONS

POINTBLANK (M)
Natl. Firearms Assn., Box 4384 Stn. C, Calgary, AB T2T 5N2, Canada. Official publication of the NFA.

Police Marksman, The*
6000 E. Shirley Lane, Montgomery, AL 36117. $17.95/yr. For law enforcement personnel.

Police Times (M)
3801 Biscayne Blvd., Miami, FL 33137/305-573-0070.

Popular Mechanics
Hearst Corp., 224 W. 57th St., New York, NY 10019. Firearms, camping, outdoor oriented articles.

Precision Shooting
Precision Shooting, Inc., 222 McKee St., Manchester, CT 06040. $37.00/yr. U.S. Journal of the International Benchrest Shooters, and target shooting. Considerable coverage of varmint shooting, big bore, small bore, schuetzen, lead bullet, wildcats and precision reloading.

Rifle*
Wolfe Publishing Co., 2626 Stearman Road, Ste. A, Prescott, AZ 86301/520-445-7810; Fax: 520-778-5124. $19.00/yr. The sporting firearms journal.

Rifle's Hunting Annual
Wolfe Publishing Co., 2626 Stearman Road, Ste. A, Prescott, AZ 86301/520-445-7810; Fax: 520-778-5124. $4.99/yr.. Dedicated to the finest pursuit of the hunt.

Rod & Rifle Magazine
Lithographic Serv. Ltd., P.O. Box 38-138, Wellington, New Zealand. $50.00/yr. (6 issues). Hunting, shooting and fishing articles.

Safari* (M)
Safari Magazine, 4800 W. Gates Pass Rd., Tucson, AZ 85745/602-620-1220. $55.00 (6 times). Journal of big game hunting, published by Safari Club International. Also publish *Safari Times*, a monthly newspaper, included in price of $55.00 national membership.

Second Amendment Reporter
Second Amendment Foundation, James Madison Bldg., 12500 NE 10th Pl., Bellevue, WA 98005. $15.00/yr. (non-contributors).

Shoot! Magazine*
Shoot! Magazine Corp., 1770 West State Stret PMB 340, Boise ID 83702/208-368-9920; Fax: 208-338-8428. Web: www.shootmagazine.com; $32.95 (6 times/yr.). Cowboy action shooting and the Western-era firearms and ammunition.

Shooter's News
23146 Lorain Rd., Box 349, North Olmsted, OH 44070/216-979-5258; Fax: 216-979-5259. $29 U.S./yr., $54/2 yrs.; $52 foreign surface. A journal dedicated to precision riflery.

Shooting Industry
Publisher's Dev. Corp., 12345 World Trade Drive, San Diego, CA 92128. $50.00/yr. To the trade. $25.00.

Shooting Sports USA
NRA of America, 11250 Waples Mill Road, Fairfax, VA 22030. Subscriptions for NRA members are $5/yr. for classified shooters and $10 for non-classified shooters. $15/non-NRA members. Covering events, techniques and personalities in competitive shooting.

Shooting Sportsman*
P.O. Box 11282, Des Moines, IA 50340/800-666-4955 (for subscriptions). Editorial: P.O. Box 1357, Camden, ME 04843. $19.95 for six issues. The magazine of wingshooting and fine guns.

Shooting Times & Country Magazine, The (England)†
IPC Magazines Ltd., King's Reach Tower, Stamford St, 1 London SE1 9LS, England/0171-261-6180; Fax: 0171-261-7179. £65 (approx. $98.00)/yr.; £79/yr. overseas (52 issues). Game shooting, wild fowling, hunting, game fishing and firearms articles. Britain's best selling field sports magazine.

Shooting Times
Intermedia, 2 News Plaza, P.O. Box 1790, Peoria, IL 61656/309-682-6626. $16.97/yr. Guns and shooting articles on every gun activity.

Shotgun News, The‡
Intermedia, 2 News Plaza, P.O. Box 1790, Peoria, IL 61656/800-495-8362. 36 issues/yr. @ $28.95; 12 issues/yr. @ $19.95. foreign subscription call for rates. Sample copy $4.00. Gun ads of all kinds.

SHOT Business
National Shooting Sports Foundation, Flintlock Ridge Office Center, 11 Mile Hill Rd., Newtown, CT 06470-2359/203-426-1320; FAX: 203-426-1087. For the shooting, hunting and outdoor trade retailer.

Shotgun Sports
PO Box 6810, Auburn, CA 95604/916-889-2220; FAX: 916-889-9106. $31.00/yr. Trapshooting how-to's, shotshell reloading, patterning, tests and evaluations, sporting clays action, waterfowl/upland hunting. Call 1-800-676-8920 for a free sample copy.

Single Shot Exhange Magazine, The
PO Box 1055, York SC 29745/803-628-5326. $31.50/yr., monthly. Articles for blackpowder shooters and antique arms collectors.

Single Shot Rifle Journal* (M)
Editor John Campbell, PO Box 595, Bloomfield Hills, MI 48303/248-458-8415. Email: jcampbel@dmbb.com Annual dues $35 for 6 issues. Journal of the American Single Shot Rifle Assn.

Sixgunner, The (M)
Handgun Hunters International, P.O. Box 357, MAG, Bloomingdale, OH 43910

Skeet Shooting Review, The
National Skeet Shooting Assn., 5931 Roft Rd., San Antonio, TX 78253. $20.00/yr. (Membership incl. mag.) Competition results, personality profiles of top shooters, how-to articles, technical, reloading information.

Soldier of Fortune
Subscription Dept., P.O. Box 348, Mt. Morris, IL 61054. $29.95/yr.; $39.95 Canada; $50.95 foreign.

Sporting Classics
Sporting Classics, Inc., P.O. Box 23707, Columbia, SC 29223/1-800-849-1004. 1 yr. 6 issues/$23.95; 2 yrs. 12 issues/$38.95; 3 yrs. 18 issues/$47.95. Firearms & outdoor articles and columns.

Sporting Clays Magazine
Patch Communications, 5211 South Washington Ave., Titusville, FL 32780/407-268-5010; FAX: 407-267-7216. $29.95/yr. (12 issues). Official publication of the National Sporting Clays Association.

Sporting Goods Business
Miller Freeman, Inc., One Penn Plaza, 10th Fl., New York, NY 10119-0004. Trade journal.

Sporting Goods Dealer
Two Park Ave., New York, NY 10016. $100.00/yr. Sporting goods trade journal.

Sporting Gun
Bretton Court, Bretton, Peterborough PE3 8DZ, England. £27.00 (U.S. $36.00), airmail £35.50/yr. For the game and clay enthusiasts.

Sports Afield
15621 Chemical Lane, Huntington Beach CA 92648. U.S./800-234-3537. International/714-894-9080. Web: www.sportsafield.com. $29.97/9 issues. America's oldest outdoor publication devoted to high-end sporting pursuits, especially in North America and Africa.

Squirrel Hunter, The
P.O. Box 368, Chireno, TX 75937. $14.00/yr.

Stott's Creek Calendar
Stott's Creek Printers, 2526 S 475 W, Morgantown, IN 46160/317-878-5489. (3 issues) $11.50/yr.; (6 issues) $20.00/2 yrs. Lists all gun shows everywhere in convenient calendar form.

Super Outdoors
2695 Aiken Road, Shelbyville, KY 40065/502-722-9463; 800-404-6064; Fax: 502-722-8093. Mark Edwards, publisher.

TACARMI
Via E. De Amicis, 25; 20123 Milano, Italy. $100.00/yr. approx. Antique and modern guns. (Italian text.)

Territorial Dispatch—1800s Historical Publication (M)
National Assn. of Buckskinners, 4701 Marion St., Suite 324, Livestock Exchange Bldg., Denver, CO 80216. Michael A. Nester & Barbara Wyckoff, editors. 303-297-9671.

Trap & Field
1000 Waterway Blvd., Indianapolis, IN 46202. $25.00/yr. Official publ. Amateur Trapshooting Assn. Scores, averages, articles.

Turkey Call* (M)
Natl. Wild Turkey Federation, Inc., P.O. Box 530, Edgefield, SC 29824. $25.00 with membership (6 issues/yr.)

Turkey & Turkey Hunting*
Krause Publications, 700 E. State St., Iola, WI 54990-0001. $13.95 (6 issue/yr.). Magazine with leading-edge articles on all aspects of wild turkey behavior, biology and successful ways to hunt better. Learn the proper techniques to calling, the right equipment, and more.

U.S. Handgunner, The* (M)
U.S. Revolver Assn., 40 Larchmont Ave., Taunton, MA 02780. $10.00/yr. General handgun and competition articles. Bi-monthly.

U.S. Airgun Magazine
P.O. Box 2021, Benton, AR 72018/800-247-4867; Fax: 501-316-8549. 10 issues/yr. Cover the sport from hunting, 10-meter, field target and collecting.

Varmint Hunter Magazine, The (Q)
The Varmint Hunters Assn., Box 759, Pierre, SD 57501/800-528-4868. $24.00/yr.

Waffenmarkt-Intern
GFI-Verlag, Theodor-Heuss Ring 62, 50668 K'ln, Germany. Only for gunsmiths, licensed firearms dealers and their suppliers in Germany, Austria and Switzerland.

Wild Sheep (M) (Q)
Foundation for North American Wild Sheep, 720 Allen Ave., Cody, WY 82414. Web: http://iigi.com/os/non/fnaws/fnaws.htm; e-mail: fnaws@wyoming.com. Official journal of the foundation.

Wisconsin Outdoor Journal
Krause Publications, 700 E. State St., Iola, WI 54990-0001. $17.97/yr. (8 issues). Web: www.krause.com. For Wisconsin's avid hunters and fishermen, with features from all over that state with regional reports, legislative updates, etc.

Women & Guns
P.O. Box 488, Sta. C, Buffalo, NY 14209. $24.00/yr. U.S.; $72.00 foreign (12 issues). Only magazine edited by and for women gun owners.

World War II*
Cowles History Group, 741 Miller Dr. SE, Suite D-2, Leesburg, VA 20175-8920. Annual subscriptions $19.95 U.S.; $25.95 Canada; 43.95 foreign. The title says it—WWII; good articles, ads, etc.

---

* Published bi-monthly
† Published weekly
‡ Published three times per month
All others are published monthly
M Membership requirements; write for details
Q Published Quarterly

FOR COLLECTOR ✻ HUNTER ✻ SHOOTER ✻ OUTDOORSMAN

IMPORTANT NOTICE TO BOOK BUYERS

Books listed here may be bought from Ray Riling Arms Books Co., 6844 Gorsten St., Philadelphia, PA 19119, Phone 215-438-2456; FAX: 215-438-5395. E-mail: sales@rayrilingarmsbooks.com. Larry Riling is the researcher and compiler of "The Arms Library" and a seller of gun books for over 65 years. The Riling stock includes books classic and modern, many hard-to-find items, and many not obtainable elsewhere. These pages list a portion of the current stock. They offer prompt, complete service, with delayed shipments occurring only on out-of-print or out-of-stock books.

Visit our Web site at www.rayrilingarmsbooks.com and order all of your favorite titles online from our secure site.

NOTICE FOR ALL CUSTOMERS: Remittance in U.S. funds must accompany all orders. For your convenience we accept VISA, MasterCard, Discover & American Express. For shipments in the U.S., add $7.00 for the 1st book and $2.00 for each additional book for postage and insurance. Minimum order $10.00. International Orders add $13.00 for the 1st book and $5.00 for each additional book. All International orders are shipped at the buyer's risk unless an additional $5 for insurance is included. USPS does not offer insurance to all countries unless shipped Air-Mail. Please e-mail or call for pricing.

Payments in excess of order or for "Backorders" are credited or fully refunded at request. Books "As-Ordered" are not returnable except by permission and a handling charge on these of 10% or $2.00 per book, whichever is greater, is deducted from refund or credit. Only Pennsylvania customers must include current sales tax.

A full variety of arms books also available from Rutgers Book Center, 127 Raritan Ave., Highland Park, NJ 08904/732-545-4344; FAX: 732-545-6686 or I.D.S.A. Books, 3220 E. Galbraith Rd., Cincinnati, OH 45236. Email IDSABooks@IDSABooks.com; www.IDSABooks.com.

BALLISTICS AND HANDLOADING

ABC's of Reloading, 7th Edition, by Bill Chevalier, Iola, WI, Krause Publications, 2005. 288 pp., illustrated with 550 b&w photos. Softcover. NEW. $21.95

American Cartridge, The, by Charles Suydam, Borden Publishing Co. Alhambra, CA, 1986. 184 pp., illus. Softcover $24.95

An illustrated study of the rimfire cartridge in the United States.

Ammo and Ballistics II, by Robert W. Forker, Safari Press, Inc., Huntington Beach, CA, 2002. 298 pp., illus. Paper covers. $19.95

Ballistic data on 125 calibers and 1,400 loads out to 500 yards.

Barnes Bullets Reloading Manual Number 3, Barnes Bullets, American Fork, UT, 2003. 668 pp., illus. $29.95

Features data and trajectories on the new weight X, XBT and Solids in calibers from .22 to .50 BMG.

Black Powder, Pig Lead and Steel Silhouettes, by Paul A. Matthews, Prescott, AZ, Wolfe Publishing, 2002. 132 pp., illustrated with b&w photographs and detailed drawings and diagrams. Softcover. NEW. $16.95

Cartridge Reloading Tools of the Past, by R.H. Chamberlain, and Tom Quigley, Castle Rock, WA, 1998. 167 pp., illus. Paper covers. $25.00

A detailed treatment of the extensive Winchester and ideal line of handloading tools and bullet molds, plus Remington, Marlin, Ballard, Browning, Maynard, and many others.

Cast Bullets for the Black Powder Rifle, by Paul A. Matthews, Wolfe Publishing Co., Prescott, AZ, 1996. 133 pp., illus. Paper covers. $22.50

The tools and techniques used to make your cast bullet shooting a success.

Complete Blackpowder Handbook, 5th Edition, by Sam Fadala, DBI Books, a division of Krause Publications, Iola, WI, 2006. 448 pages, with over 650 b&w photos. Paper covers. $26.95

More than 650 detailed photos illustrating new gear and demonstrating effective techniques. Written for every blackpowder enthusiast-hunters, war re-enactors, collectors, cowboy action shooters, target shooters and DIY blackpowder hobbyists.

Complete Reloading Manual, One Book / One Caliber, CA, Load Books USA, 2000. $7.95 each

Contains unabridged information from U.S. bullet and powder makers. With thousands of proven and tested loads, plus dozens of various bullet designs and different powders. Spiral bound. Available in all calibers.

Designing and Forming Custom Cartridges for Rifles and Handguns, by Ken Howell. Precision Shooting, Manchester, CT. 2002. 600 pp., illus. $59.95

The classic work in its field, out of print for the last few years and virtually unobtainable on the used book market, now returns in an exact reprint of the original. Full size (8½" x 11"), hardcovers. Dozens of cartridge drawings never published anywhere before–dozens you've never heard of (guaranteed!). Precisely drawn to the dimensions specified by the men who designed them, the factories that made them, and the authorities that set the standards. All drawn to the same format and scale (1.5x) for most, how to form them from brass. Other practical information included.

Early Gunpowder Artillery 1300-1600 by John Norris, London, The Crowood Press, 2003. 1st edition. 141 pp., with 160 b&w photos. Hardcover. New in new dust jacket. $34.95

Early Loading Tools & Bullet Molds, Pioneer Press, 1988. 88 pp., illus. Softcover. $7.50

Handbook for Shooters and Reloaders, by P.O. Ackley, Salt Lake City, UT, 1998, (Vol. I), 567 pp., illus. Includes a separate exterior ballistics chart. $24.95; (Vol. II), a new printing with specific new material. 495 pp., illus. $21.95

Handgun Stopping Power; The Definitive Study, by Marshall & Sandow. Boulder, CO, Paladin Press, 1992. 240 pp. $45.00

Offers accurate predictions of the stopping power of specific loads in calibers from 380 Auto to 45 ACP, as well as such specialty rounds as the Glaser Safety Slug, Federal Hydra-Shok, MagSafe, etc. This is the definitive methodology for predicting the stopping power of handgun loads, the first to take into account what really happens when a bullet meets a man.

Handloader's Digest: 18th Edition edited by Ken Ramage, Iola, WI, Krause Publications, 2003. 300 b&w photos, 256 pp. Softcover. NEW. $19.95

Handloader's Manual of Cartridge Conversions, Revised 3rd edition, by John Donnelly, and Bryce Towsley, Accokeek, MD, Stoeger Publications, 2004. 609pp, Hardcover. NEW $39.95

Over 900 cartridges described in detail, complete with dimensions, and accurate drawings. Includes case capacities and all physical data.

Hatcher's Notebook, by S. Julian Hatcher, Stackpole Books, Harrisburg, PA, 1992. 488 pp., illus. $39.95

A reference work for shooters, gunsmiths, ballisticians, historians, hunters and collectors.

Headstamped Cartridges and Their Variations; Volume 1, by Daniel L. Shuey, W.R.A. Co., Rockford, IL, WCF Publications, 2003. 351 pp. illustrated with b&w photos. Hardcover. NEW. $55.00

Headstamped Cartridges and Their Variations; Volume 2, by Daniel L. Shuey, W.R.A. Co., Rockford, IL, WCF Publications, 2003. 351 pp. illustrated with b&w photos. Hardcover. NEW. $55.00

History & Development of Small Arms Ammunition, Volume 1, Second Edition–With A Value Guide, Martial Long Arms, Flintlock through Rimfire, by George A. Hoyem, Missoula, MI, Armory Publications, 2005. Hardcover. New in new dust jacket. $60.00

Hornady Handbook of Cartridge Reloading, 7th Edition, edited by Larry Steadman, Hornady Mfg. Co., Grand Island, NE, 2007, 978 pages, illus. $44.95

This completely revised and updated manual contains load data for almost every cartridge available, including the latest developments like the 204 Ruger and 500 S&W. Includes tips on basic reloading, rifle and handgun load data and an illustrated glossary.

How-To's for the Black Powder Cartridge Rifle Shooter, by Paul A. Matthews, Wolfe Publishing Co., Prescott, AZ, 1995. 45 pp. Paper covers. $22.50

Covers lube recipes, good bore cleaners and over-powder wads. Tips include compressing powder charges, combating wind resistance, improving ignition and much more.

Loading the Black Powder Rifle Cartridge, by Paul A. Matthews, Wolfe Publishing Co., Prescott, AZ, 1993. 121 pp., illus. Paper covers. $22.50

Author Matthews brings the blackpowder cartridge shooter valuable information on the basics, including cartridge care, lubes and moulds, powder charges and developing and testing loads in his usual authoritative style.

Lyman 48th Reloading Handbook, No. 48. Connecticut, Lan Publishing Corporation, 2003. 48th edition. 480 pp. Softcover. NEW. $26.95

Lyman Cast Bullet Handbook, 3rd Edition, edited by C. Kenneth Ramage, Lyman Publications, Middlefield, CT, 1980. 416 pp., illus. Paper covers. $19.95

Information on more than 5000 tested cast bullet loads and 19 pages of trajectory and wind drift tables for cast bullets.

Lyman Black Powder Handbook, 2nd Edition, edited by Sam Fadala, Lyman Products for Shooters, Middlefield, CT, 2000. 239 pp., illus. Paper covers. $19.95

Comprehensive load information for the modern blackpowder shooter.

Lyman Shotshell Handbook, 5th Edition, edited by Edward A. Matunas, Lyman Products Co., Middlefield, CT, 2007. 330 pp., illus. Paper covers. $25.95

This new 5th edition covers cases, wads and primers currently offered by all leading manufacturers in all gauges from .410 to 10 gauge. In addition, the latest and also the most popular powders from Alliant, Hodgdon, Accurate, IMR, VihtaVuori, Ramshot, Winchester are included.

Make It Accurate-Get the Maximum Performance from Your Hunting Rifle, by Craig Boddington, Long Beach, CA, Safari Press, 1999. Hardcover. New in new dust jacket. $24.95

Metallic Cartridge Conversions: The History of the Guns and Modern Reproductions, by Dennis Adler, Foreword by R. L. Wilson, Iola, WI, Krause Publications, 2003. 1st edition. 208 pp. 250 color photos. Hardcover. New in new dust jacket. $39.95

Modern Exterior Ballistics, by Robert L. McCoy, Schiffer Publishing Co., Atglen, PA, 1999. 128 pp. $95.00

Advanced students of exterior ballistics and flight dynamics will find this comprehensive textbook on the subject a useful addition to their libraries.

Modern Reloading 2nd Edition, by Richard Lee, Inland Press, 2003. 623 pp., illus. $29.95

The how-to's of rifle, pistol and shotgun reloading plus load data for rifle and pistol calibers.

Mr. Single Shot's Cartridge Handbook, by Frank de Haas, Mark de Haas, Orange City, IA, 1996. 116 pp., illus. Paper covers. $22.50

This book covers most of the cartridges, both commercial and wildcat, that the author has known and used.

Norma Reloading Manual, by Norma Precision AB, 2004, 1st edition. Data for over 2,000 loads in 73 calibers. 432pp, hardcover, NEW. $34.95

Nosler Reloading Manual #5, edited by Gail Root, Nosler Bullets, Inc., Bend, OR, 2002. 516 pp., illus. $29.99

Combines information on their ballistic tip, partition and handgun bullets with traditional powders and new powders never before used, plus trajectory information from 100 to 500 yards.

Reloading for Shotgunners, 4th Edition, by Kurt D. Fackler, and M.L. McPherson, DBI Books, a division of Krause Publications, Iola, WI, 1997. 320 pp., illus. Paper covers. $19.95

Expanded reloading tables with over 11,000 loads. Bushing charts for every major press and component maker. All new presentation on all aspects of shotshell reloading by two of the top experts in the field.

Reloading Tools, Sights and Telescopes for S/S Rifles, by Gerald O. Kelver, Brighton, CO, 1982. 163 pp., illus. Softcover. $15.00

A listing of most of the famous makers of reloading tools, sights and telescopes with a brief description of the products they manufactured.

Rimfire Cartridge in the United States and Canada, Illustrated History of Rimfire Cartridges, Manufacturers, and the Products Made from 1857-1984, by John L. Barber, Thomas Publications, Gettysburg, PA 2000. 1st edition. Profusely illus. 221 pp. $50.00

The author has written an encyclopedia of rimfire cartridges from the 22 to the massive 1.00 in. Gatling. Fourteen chapters, six appendices and an excellent bibliography.

Round Ball to Rimfire: Civil War Small Arms Ammunition, Vol. 1, by Dean S. Thomas, Gettysburg, PA, Thomas Publications, 2003. 344 pp. Hardcover. $40.00

Federal Ordnance Dept., Arsenals, Smoothbores & Rifle Muskets. Detailed information on the Ordnance Department, Northern arsenals, patents, designers, & manufacturers of Federal musket ammunition.

Round Ball to Rimfire: Civil War Small Arms Ammunition, Vol. 2, by Dean S. Thomas, Gettysburg, PA, Thomas Publications, 2004. 528 pp. Hardcover. NEW. $49.95

Federal breechloading carbines and rifles. Federal carbine and rifle ammunition. Detailed information on patents, designers, & manufacturers of Federal breechloaders and their ammunition.

Round Ball to Rimfire: Civil War Small Arms Ammunition, Vol. 3, by Dean S. Thomas, Gettysburg, PA, Thomas Publications, 2005. 488 pp. Hardcover. $49.95

Federal pistols, revolvers and miscellaneous essays. Detailed information on patents, designers, & manufacturers. Miscellaneous essays wrap-up the Northern side of the story.

Shotshells & Ballistics, Safari Press, 2002. 275 pp., photos. Softcover, $19.95

Accentuated with photos from the field and the range, this is a reference book unlike any other.

Sierra Reloading Manual, 5th Edition: Rifle and Handgun Manual of Reloading Data. Sedalia, MO, Sierra Bullets, 2003. Hardcover. NEW. $39.95

Speer Reloading Manual No. 13, edited by members of the Speer research staff, Omark Industries, Lewiston, ID, 1999. 621 pp., illus. $29.95

With 13 new sections containing the latest technical information and reloading trends for both novice and expert in this latest edition. More than 9,300 loads are listed, including new propellant powders from Accurate Arms, Alliant, Hodgdon and Vihtavuori.

Stopping Power: A Practical Analysis of the Latest Handgun Ammunition, by Marshall & Sanow, Paladin Press, 2002. 600+ photos, 360 pp. Softcover. $49.95

Stopping Power bases its conclusions on real-world facts from real-world gunfights. It provides the latest street results of actual police and civilian shootings in all of the major handgun calibers, from 22 LR to 45 ACP, plus more than 30 chapters of vital interest to all gun owners.

Street Stoppers, The Latest Handgun Stopping Power Street Results, by Marshall & Lanow, Boulder, CO, Paladin Press, 1996. 374 pp., illus. Softcover. $42.95

Street Stoppers is the long-awaited sequel to ***Handgun Stopping Power***. It provides the latest results of real-life shootings in all of the major handgun calibers, plus more than 25 thought-provoking chapters that are vital to anyone interested in firearms, wound ballistics, and combat shooting. This book also covers the street results of the hottest new caliber to hit the shooting world in years, the 40 Smith & Wesson, plus updated street results of the latest exotic ammunition.

Understanding Firearm Ballistics, 6th Edition, by Robert A. Rinker, Mulberry House Corydon, IN, 2005. 437 pp., illus. Paper covers. New, revised and expanded. $24.95

Explains basic to advanced firearm ballistics in understandable terms.

Why Not Load Your Own?, by Col. T. Whelen, Gun Room Press, Highland Park, NJ 1996, 4th ed., rev. 237 pp., illus. $20.00

A basic reference on handloading, describing each step, materials and equipment. Includes loads for popular cartridges.

Wildcat Cartridges, "Reloader's Handbook of Wildcat Cartridge Design", by Fred Zeglin, privately printed, 2005. 1st edition. 287 Pages, Hard back book. Forward by Wayne van Zwoll. Pictorial Hardcover. NEW. $39.95

Twenty-two chapters cover wildcatting from every possible angle. History, dimensions, load data, and how to make or use reloading tool and reamers. If you're interested in reloading or wildcatting this is a must have book.

Wildcat Cartridges Volumes 1 & 2 Combination, by the editors of *Handloaders* magazine, Wolfe Publishing Co., Prescott, AZ, 1997. 350 pp., illus. Paper covers. $39.95

A profile of the most popular information on wildcat cartridges that appeared in the *Handloaders* magazine.

W.R.A. Co.; Headstamped Cartridges and their Variations; Volume 1, by Daniel Shuey, Rockford, IL, WCF Publications, 2001. 298pp illustrated with b&w photos, Hardcover, NEW. $55.00

W.R.A. Co.; Headstamped Cartridges and their Variations; Volume 2, by Daniel Shuey, Rockford, IL, WCF Publications, 2003. 351pp illustrated with b&w photos, Hardcover, NEW. $50.00

COLLECTORS

1 October 1934 SS Dienstalterliste, by the Ulric of England Research Unit San Jose, CA, R. James Bender Publishing, 1994. Reprint softcover. NEW. $29.95

10. Panzer Division: In Action in the East, West and North Africa 1939-1943, by Jean Resta and N. Moller, Canada, J.J. Fedorowicz Publishing Inc., 2003. 1st edition. Hardcover. NEW. $89.95

18th Century Weapons of the Royal Welsh Fuziliers from Flixton Hall, by Erik Goldstein, Thomas Publications, Gettysburg, PA, 2002. 1st edition. 126 pp., illustrated with b&w photos. Softcover. $19.95

.45-70 Springfield Book I, by Albert Frasca and Robert Hill, Frasca Publishing, 2000. Memorial edition. Hardback with gold embossed cover and spine. $95.00

The Memorial edition reprint of the .45-70 Springfield was done to honor Robert H. Hill who was an outstanding Springfield collector, historian, researcher, and gunsmith. Only 1,000 of these highly regarded books were printed, using the same binding and cover material as the original 1980 edition. The book is considered the bible for 45-70 Springfield Trapdoor collectors.

.45-70 Springfield Book II 1865-1893, by Albert Frasca, Frasca Publishing, Springfield, Ohio 1997, 400+ pp. and 400+ photographs which cover ALL the trapdoor Springfield models. Hardback with gold embossed cover and spine. A MUST for the trapdoor collector! $85.00

.45-70 Springfield 4th Ed. Revised & Expanded, The, by Joe Poyer and Craig Riesch, North Cape Publications, Tustin, CA, 2006. 274 pp., illus. Paper covers. $19.95

Every part and every change to that part made by the Ordnance Department is described in photos and drawings. Dimensions and finishes are listed for each part in both the text and tables.

'51 Colt Navies, by Nathan L. Swayze, The Gun Room Press, Highland Park, NJ, 1993. 243 pp., illus. $59.95

The Model 1851 Colt Navy, its variations and markings.

1862 U.S. Cavalry Tactics, by Philip St. George Cooke, Mechanicsburg, PA, Stackpole Books, 2004. 416 pp. Hardcover. New in new dust jacket. $19.89

A Collector's Guide to the '03 Springfield, by Bruce N. Canfield, Andrew Mowbray Inc., Lincoln, RI, 2004. 160 pp., illus. Paper covers. $22.00

A comprehensive guide follows the '03 through its unparalleled tenure of service. Covers all of the interesting variations, modifications and accessories of this highly collectible military rifle.

An Illustrated Guide To The '03 Springfield Service Rifle, by Bruce N. Canfield Andrew Mowbray, Inc., Pictorial Hardcover 2005. $49.95

Your ultimate guide to the military '03 Springfield! Three times as large as the author's previous best selling book on this topic. Covers all models, all manufacturers and all conflicts, including WWI, WWII and beyond. Heavily illustrated. Serial number tables, combat photos, sniper rifles and more! 240 pages, illustrated with over 450 photos.

Complete Guide To The United States Military Combat Shotguns, by Bruce N. Canfield Andrew Mowbray, Inc., 2007. 1st edition. 312 Pages. $49.95

From the famed Winchester M97 to the Mossberg and beyond! Expanded and updated covereage of American combat shotguns with three times the information found in the author's pervious best-selling book on this topic. Hundreds of detailed photographs show you the specific features that you need to recognize in order to identify fakes and assembled guns. Special, in-depth historical coverage of WWI, WWII, Korea, Vietnam and Iraq!

A Collector's Guide to United States Combat Shotguns, by Bruce N. Canfield, Andrew Mowbray Inc., Lincoln, RI, 1992. 184 pp., illus. Paper covers. $24.00

This book provides full coverage of combat shotguns, from the earliest examples right up to the Gulf War and beyond.

A Collector's Guide to Winchester in the Service, by Bruce N. Canfield, Andrew Mowbray, Inc., Lincoln, RI, 1991. 192 pp., illus. Paper covers. $24.00

The firearms produced by Winchester for the national defense. From Hotchkiss to the M14, each firearm is examined and illustrated.

A Concise Guide to the Artillery at Gettysburg, by Gregory Coco, Thomas Publications, Gettysburg, PA, 1998. 96 pp., illus. Paper covers. $10.00

Coco's book on Gettysburg is a beginner's guide to artillery and its use at the battle. It covers the artillery batteries, describing the types of cannons, shells, fuses, etc. using interesting narrative and human interest stories.

A Glossary of the Construction, Decoration and Use of Arms and Armor in All Countries and in All Times, by George Cameron Stone, Dover Publishing, New York 1999. Softcover. $39.95

An exhaustive study of arms and armor in all countries through recorded history-from the Stone Age up to WWII. With over 4,500 b&w illustrations, this Dover edition is an unabridged republication of the work originally published in 1934 by the Southworth Press, Portland, MA. A new Introduction has been specially prepared for this edition.

A Guide to American Trade Catalogs 1744-1900, by Lawrence B. Romaine, Dover Publications, New York, NY. 422 pp., illus. Paper covers. $12.95

A Guide to Ballard Breechloaders, by George J. Layman, Pioneer Press, Union City, TN, 1997. 261 pp., illus. Paper covers. $19.95

Documents the saga of this fine rifle from the first models made by Ball & Williams of Worchester, to its production by the Marlin Firearms Co., to the cessation of 19th century manufacture in 1891, and finally to the modern reproductions made in the 1990s.

A Guide to the Maynard Breechloader, by George J. Layman, George J. Layman, Ayer, MA, 1993. 125 pp., illus. Paper covers. $14.95

The first book dedicated entirely to the Maynard family of breech-loading firearms. Coverage of the arms is given from the 1850s through the 1880s.

A Guide to U.S. Army Dress Helmets 1872-1904, by Kasal and Moore, North Cape Publications, 2000. 88 pp., illus. Paper covers. $15.95

This thorough study provides a complete description of the Model 1872 and 1881 dress helmets worn by the U.S. Army.

A Study of Remington's Smoot Patent and Number Four Revolvers, by Parker Harry, Parker Ora Lee, and Joan Reisch, Foreword by Roy M. Marcot, Santa Ana, CA, Armslore Press, Graphic Publishers, 2003. 1st edition. 120 pp., profusely illus., plus 8-page color section. Softcover. $17.95

A detailed, pictorial essay on Remington's early metallic cartridge-era pocket revolvers: their design, development, patents, models, identification and variations. Includes the biography of arms inventor Wm. S. Smoot, as well as a mini-history of the Remington Arms Company.

Accoutrements of the United States Infantry, Riflemen, and Dragoons 1834-1839, by R.T. Huntington, Historical Arms Series No. 20. Canada, Museum Restoration. 58 pp. illus. Softcover. $8.95

Although the 1841 edition of the U.S. Ordnance Manual provides ample information on the equipment that was in use during the 1840s, it is evident that the patterns of equipment that it describes were not introduced until 1838 or 1839. This guide is intended to fill this gap in our knowledge by providing an overview of what we now know about the accoutrements that were issued to the regular infantryman, rifleman, and dragoon, in the 1830s with excursions into earlier and later years.

Ackermann Military Prints: Uniforms of the British and Indian Armies 1840-1855, by William Y. Carman with Robert W. Kenny Jr., Schiffer Publications, Atglen, PA, 2002. 1st edition. 176 pp., with over 160 color images. $69.95

Afrikakorps: Rommel's Tropical Army in Original Color, by Bernd Peitz, Gary Wilkins. Atglen, PA, Schiffer Publications, 2004. 1st edition. 192 pp., with over 200 color and b&w photographs. Hardcover. New in new dust jacket. $59.95

Air Guns, by Eldon G. Wolff, Duckett's Publishing Co., Tempe, AZ, 1997. 204 pp., illus. Paper covers. $35.00

Historical reference covering many makers, European and American guns, canes and more.

All About Southerners, by Lionel J. Bogut, White Star, Inc., 2002. A limited edition of 1,000 copies. Signed and numbered. 114 pp., including bibliography, and plenty of b&w photographs and detailed drawings. Hardcover. $29.95

Detailed look at the characteristics and design of the "Best Little Pistol in the World."

Allgemeine-SS The Commands, Units and Leaders of the General SS, by Mark C. Yerger, Atglen, PA, Schiffer Publications, 1997. 1st edition. Hardcover. New in new dust jacket. $49.95

Allied and Enemy Aircraft: May 1918; Not to be Taken from the Front Lines, Historical Arms Series No. 27. Canada, Museum Restoration. Softcover. $8.95

The basis for this title is a very rare identification manual published by the French government in 1918 that illustrated 60 aircraft with three or more views: French, English American, German, Italian, and Belgian, which might have been seen over the trenches of France. Each is described in a text translated from the original French. This is probably the most complete collection of illustrations of WWI aircraft that has survived.

American Beauty; The Prewar Colt National Match Government Model Pistol, by Timothy J. Mullin, Collector Grade Publications, Cobourg, Ontario, Canada. 72 pp., illus. $34.95

Includes over 150 serial numbers, and 20 spectacular color photos of factory engraved guns and other authenticated upgrades, including rare "double-carved" ivory grips.

American Civil War Artillery 1861-65: Field Artillery, by Philip Oxford Katcher, United Kingdom, Osprey Publishing, 2001. 1st edition. 48 pp. Softcover. $14.95

Perhaps the most influential arm of either army in the prosecution of the American Civil War, the artillery of both sides grew to be highly professional organizations. This book covers all the major artillery pieces employed, including the Napoleon, Parrott Rifle and Mountain Howitzer.

American Military and Naval Belts, 1812-1902, by R. Stephen Dorsey, Eugene, OR, Collectors Library, 2002. 1st edition. Hardcover. $80.00

With introduction by Norm Flayderman, this massive work is the NEW key reference on sword belts, waist belts, sabre belts, shoulder belts and cartridge belts (looped and non-looped). At over 460 pp., this 8½" x 11" book offers over 840 photos (primarily in color) and original period drawings. In addition, this work offers the first, comprehensive research on the Anson Mills woven cartridge belts, the belt-related patents and the government contracts from 1880 through 1902. This book is a "must" for all accoutrements collectors, military historians and museums.

American Military Headgear Insignia, by Michael J. O'Donnell and J. Duncan, Campbell, Alexandria, VA, O'Donnell Publishing, 2004. 1st edition. 311 pp., 703 photo figures, 4 sketches. Hardcover. New in new dust jacket. $89.95

American Military Saddle, 1776-1945, The, by R. Stephen Dorsey and Kenneth L. McPheeters, Collector's Library, Eugene, OR, 1999. 400 pp., illus. $67.00

The most complete coverage of the subject ever written on the American Military Saddle. Nearly 1,000 actual photos and official drawings, from the major public and private collections in the U.S. and Great Britain.

American Police Collectibles; Dark Lanterns and Other Curious Devices, by Matthew G. Forte, Turn of the Century Publishers, Upper Montclair, NJ, 1999. 248 pp., illus. $24.95

For collectors of police memorabilia (handcuffs, police dark lanterns, mechanical and chain nippers, rattles, billy clubs and nightsticks) and police historians.

American Thunder II: The Military Thompson Submachine Guns, by Frank Iannamico, Harmony, ME, Moose Lake Publishing, 2004, 2nd edition. Many great photographs that show detail markings and features of the various models, as well as vintage WW11 photographs showing the Thompson in action. 536 pages, Soft cover, NEW. $29.95

An Introduction to the Civil War Small Arms, by Earl J. Coates and Dean S. Thomas, Thomas Publishing Co., Gettysburg, PA, 1990. 96 pp., illus. Paper covers. $10.00

The small arms carried by the individual soldier during the Civil War.

Arming the Glorious Cause; Weapons of the Second War for Independence, by James B. Whisker, Daniel D. Hartzler and Larry W. Tantz, Old Bedford Village Press, Bedford, PA., 1998. 175 pp., illus. $45.00

A photographic study of Confederate weapons.

Arms & Accoutrements of the Mounted Police 1873-1973, by Roger F. Phillips, and Donald J. Klancher, Museum Restoration Service, Ont., Canada, 1982. 224 pp., illus. $49.95 Also, available in paperback, $29.95

A definitive history of the revolvers, rifles, machine guns, cannons, ammunition, swords, etc. used by the NWMP, the RNWMP and the RCMP during the first 100 years of the Force.

Arms and Armor in Colonial America 1526-1783, by Harold Peterson, Dover Publishing, New York, 2000. 350 pp. with over 300 illustrations, index, bibliography and appendix. Softcover. $34.95

Over 200 years of firearms, ammunition, equipment and edged weapons.

Arms and Armor in the Art Institute of Chicago, by Waltler J. Karcheski, Bulfinch, New York 1999. 128 pp., 103 color photos, 12 b&w illustrations. $50.00

The George F. Harding Collection of arms and armor is the most visited installation at the Art Institute of Chicago–a testament to the enduring appeal of swords, muskets and the other paraphernalia of medieval and early modern war. Organized both chronologically and by type of weapon, this book captures the best of this astonishing collection in 115 striking photographs-most in color–accompanied by illuminating text.

Arms Makers of Western Pennsylvania, by James B. Whisker, Old Bedford Village Press. 1st edition. Deluxe hardbound edition, 176 pp., $50.00

Printed on fine coated paper with many large photographs and detailed text describing the period, lives, tools, and artistry of the Arms Makers of Western Pennsylvania.

Arsenal of Freedom: The Springfield Armory 1890-1948, by Lt. Col. William Brophy, Andrew Mowbray, Inc., Lincoln, RI,1997. 20 pgs. of photos. 400 pp. As new, Softcover. $29.95

A year-by-year account drawn from offical records. Packed with reports, charts, tables and line drawings.

Art of Remington Arms, by Tom Davis, Sporting Classics, 2004, 1st edition. Large format book, featuring 200 paintings by Remington Arms over the years on it's calendars, posters, shell boxes, etc. 50 full-color by Bob Kuhn alone. Hardcover. NEW $54.95

Astra Automatic Pistols, by Leonardo M. Antaris, FIRAC Publishing Co., Sterling, CO, 1989. 248 pp., illus. $55.00

Charts, tables, serial ranges, etc. The definitive work on Astra pistols.

Ballard: The Great American Single Shot Rifle, by John T. Dutcher. Denver, CO, privately printed, 2002. 1st edition. 380 pp., illustrated with b&w photos, with 8-page color insert. Hardcover. New in new dust jacket. $79.95

Basic Documents on U.S. Martial Arms, commentary by Col. B.R. Lewis, reissue by Ray Riling, Phila., PA, 1956 and 1960. Rifle Musket Model 1855. Each $10.00

The first issue rifle of musket caliber, a muzzleloader equipped with the Maynard Primer, 32 pp. Rifle Musket Model 1863. The typical Union muzzleloader of the Civil War, 26 pp. Breech-Loading Rifle Musket Model 1866. The first of our 50-caliber breechloading rifles, 12 pp. Remington Navy Rifle Model 1870. A commercial type breech-loader made at Springfield, 16 pp. Lee Straight Pull Navy Rifle Model 1895. A magazine cartridge arm of 6mm caliber, 23 pp. Breech-Loading Arms (five models) 27 pp. Ward-Burton Rifle Musket 1871, 16 pp.

Battle Colors: Insignia and Aircraft Markings of the Eighth Air Force in World War II, by Robert A. Watkins, Atglen, PA, Schiffer Publications, 2004. Hardcover. $45.00

This book is an invaluable tool for anyone with an interest in the history of the U.S. Eighth Air Force in World War II. 128 pages, with over 500 color illustrations.

Battle Colors: Insignia and Aircraft Markings of the Eighth Air Force in World War II, Vol. 2, by Robert A. Watkins, Atglen, PA, Schiffer Publications, 2006. $45.00

This work includes diagrams showing approved specifications for the size and placement of all versions of the U.S. insignia as applied to USAAF P-38, P-47 and P-51 fighter aircraft. Also included are all unit airfield location maps and order-of-battle charts for all combat air elements assigned to the 8th AAF from June 1942 through June 1945. 144 pages, with over 600 color profiles, insignia, photographs, and maps. Hardcover

Battle Weapons of the American Revolution, by George C. Neuman, Scurlock Publishing Co., Texarkana, TX, 2001. 400 pp. Illus. Softcovers. $44.95

The most extensive photographic collection of Revolutionary War weapons ever in one volume. More than 1,600 photos of over 500 muskets, rifles, swords, bayonets, knives and other arms used by both sides in America's War for Independence.

Bedford County Rifle and Its Makers, by Calvin Hetrick, Introduction by George Shumway, George Shumway Pub., 1975. 40 pp. illus. Softcover. $10.00

The author's study of the graceful and distinctive muzzle-loading rifles made in Bedford County, Pennsylvania, stands as a milestone on the long path to the understanding of America's longrifles.

Belgian Rattlesnake; The Lewis Automatic Machine Gun, by William M. Easterly, Collector Grade Publications, Cobourg, Ontario, Canada, 1998. 584 pp., illus. $79.95

The most complete account ever published on the life and times of Colonel Isaac Newton Lewis and his crowning invention, the Lewis Automatic machine gun.

Best of Holland & Holland, England's Premier Gunmaker, by Michael McIntosh and Jan G. Roosenburg. Safari Press, Inc., Long Beach, CA, 2002. 1st edition. 298 pp. Profuse color illustrations. $69.95

Holland & Holland has had a long history of not only building London's "best" guns but also providing superior guns–the ultimate gun in finish, engraving, and embellishment.

Big Guns, Civil War Siege, Seacoast, and Naval Cannon, by Edwin Olmstead, Wayne E. Stark, and Spencer C. Tucker, Museum Restoration Service, Bloomfield, Ontario, Canada, 1997. 360 pp., illus. $80.00

This book is designed to identify and record the heavy guns available to both sides by the end of the Civil War.

Blue Book of Air Guns, 6th Edition, edited by S.P. Fjestad, Blue Book Publications, Inc. Minneapolis, MN 2007. $29.95

It contains most of the popular 2007 and vintage makes and models with detailed descriptions and up-to-date pricing! There are also hundreds of b&w images, and the Color Photo Grading System™ allows readers to stop guessing at airgun condition factors.

Blue Book of Gun Values, 28th Edition, edited by S.P. Fjestad, Blue Book Publications, Inc. Minneapolis, MN 2007. $39.95

This new edition simply contains more firearm values and information than any other single publication. Expanded to 2,080 pages featuring over 100,000 firearms prices, up-to-date pricing and information on thousands of firearms, including new 2007 makes/models. Completely revised 80 page color Photo Percentage Grading System.

Blue Book of Modern Black Powder Values, 4th Edtion, by Dennis Adler, Blue Book Publications, Inc. Minneapolis, MN 2005. 271 pp., illus. 41 color photos. $24.95

This new title contains more up-to-date blackpowder values and related information than any other single publication and will keep you up-to-date on modern blackpowder models and prices, including most makes and models introduced by 2005!

Blunderbuss 1500-1900, The, by James D. Forman, Historical Arms Series No. 32. Canada, Museum Restoration, 1994. 40 pp., illus. Softcover. $8.95

An excellent and authoritative booklet giving tons of information on the Blunderbuss, a very neglected subject.

Boarders Away Volume I: With Steel-Edged Weapons & Polearms, by William Gilkerson, Andrew Mowbray, Inc. Publishers, Lincoln, RI, 1993. 331 pp. $48.00

Contains the essential 24-page chapter "War at Sea" which sets the historical and practical context for the arms discussed. Includes chapters on Early Naval Weapons, Boarding Axes, Cutlasses, Officers Fighting Swords and Dirks, and weapons at hand of Random Mayhem.

ARMS LIBRARY

Boarders Away, Volume II: Firearms of the Age of Fighting Sail, by William Gilkerson, Andrew Mowbray, Inc. Publishers, Lincoln, RI, 1993. 331 pp., illus. $65.00

Covers the pistols, muskets, combustibles and small cannons used aboard American and European fighting ships, 1626-1826.

Boston's Gun Bible, by Boston T. Party, Ignacio, CO, Javelin Press, August 2000. Expanded edition. Softcover. $28.00

This mammoth guide for gun owners everywhere is a completely updated and expanded edition (more than 500 new pages!) of Boston T. Party's classic Boston on Guns and Courage. Boston gives new advice on which shoulder weapons and handguns to buy and why, before exploring such topics as why you should consider not getting a concealed carry permit, what guns and gear will likely be outlawed next and much more.

Bren Gun Saga, by Thomas B. Dugelby, Collector Grade Publications, Cobourg, Ontario, Canada, 1999, revised and expanded edition. 406 pp., illus. $65.95

A modern, definitive book on the Bren in this revised expanded edition, which in terms of numbers of pages and illustrations is nearly twice the size of the original.

British Board of Ordnance Small Arms Contractors 1689-1840, by De Witt Bailey, Rhyl, England, W. S. Curtis, 2000. 150 pp. $18.00

Thirty years of research in the Archives of the Ordnance Board in London has identified more than 600 of these suppliers. The names of many can be found marking the regulation firearms of the period. In the study, the contractors are identified both alphabetically and under a combination of their date period together with their specialist trade.

British Enfield Rifles, Volume 1, The SMLE MK I and MK III Rifles, by Charles R. Stratton, North Cape Pub., Tustin, CA, 1997. 150 pp., illus. Paper covers. $16.95

A systematic and thorough examination on a part-by-part basis of the famous British battle rifle that endured for nearly 70 years as the British Army's number one battle rifle.

British Enfield Rifles, Volume 2, No. 4 and No. 5 Rifles, by Charles R. Stratton, North Cape Publications, Tustin, CA, 1999. 150 pp., illus. Paper covers. $16.95

The historical background for the development of both rifles describing each variation and an explanation of all the marks, numbers and codes found on most parts.

British Enfield Rifles, Volume 4, The Pattern 1914 and U. S. Model 1917 Rifles, by Charles R. Stratton, North Cape Publications, Tustin, CA, 2000. Paper covers. $16.95

One of the least known American and British collectible military rifles is analyzed on a part by part basis. All markings and codes, refurbishment procedures and WWII upgrade are included as are the various sniper rifle versions.

British Falling Block Breechloading Rifle from 1865, by Jonathan Kirton, Tom Rowe Books, Maynardsville, TN, 2nd edition, 1997. 380 pp., illus. $70.00

Expanded edition of a comprehensive work on the British falling block rifle.

British Gun Engraving, by Douglas Tate, Safari Press, Inc., Huntington Beach, CA, 1999. 240 pp., illus. Limited, signed and numbered edition, in a slipcase. $80.00

A historic and photographic record of the last two centuries.

British Gunmakers: Volume One – London, by Nigel Brown, London, Quiller, 2004. 280 pp., 33 colour, 43 b&w photographs, line drawings. Hardcover. $99.95

British Gunmakers: Volume Two-Birmingham, Scotland, And the Regions, by Nigel Brown, London, Quiller, 2005. 1st edition. 439pp, hardcover. $99.95

With this book, read in conjunction with Volume One, the reader or scholar should be able to trace the history and likely age of any shotgun or rifle made in this region since 1800.

British Military Flintlock Rifles 1740-1840, With a Remarkable Wealth of Data about the Riflemen and Regiments that Carried These Weapons, by De Witt Bailey, Andrew Mowbray, Inc. Lincoln, RI, 2002. 1st edition. 264 pp. with over 320 photographs. Hardcover. $47.95

Pattern 1776 Rifles, the Ferguson Breechloader, the famous Baker Rifle, rifles of the Hessians and other German Mercenaries, American Loyalist rifles, rifles given to Indians, Cavalry rifles and rifled carbines, bayonets, accoutrements, ammunition and more.

British Service Rifles and Carbines 1888-1900, by Alan M. Petrillo, Excaliber Publications, Latham, NY, 1994. 72 pp., illus, Paper covers. $11.95

A complete review of the Lee-Metford and Lee-Enfield rifles and carbines.

British Single Shot Rifles, Volume 1, Alexander Henry, by Wal Winfer, Tom Rowe, Maynardsville, TN, 1998, 200 pp., illus. $50.00

Detailed study of the single shot rifles made by Henry. Illustrated with hundreds of photographs and drawings.

British Single Shot Rifles, Volume 3, Jeffery, by Wal Winfer, Rowe Publications, Rochester, N.Y., 1999. 260 pp., illus. $60.00

The Farquharsen as made by Jeffery and his competitors, Holland & Holland, Bland, Westley, Manton. Large section on the development of nitro cartridges including the 600.

British Single Shot Rifles, Volume 4; Westley Richards, by Wal Winfer, Rowe Publications, Rochester, N.Y., 2000. 265 pp., illus., photos. $60.00

In this 4th volume, Winfer covers a detailed study of the Westley Richards single shot rifles, including Monkey Tails, Improved Martini, 1872,1873, 1878,1881, 1897 Falling Blocks. He also covers Westley Richards cartridges, history and reloading information.

British Single Shot Rifles, Volume 5; Holland & Holland, by Winfer, Wal, Rochester, NY: Rowe Publications, 2004. 1st edition. ISBN: 097076085X. 218 pages. Hardcover. New in new dust jacket. (12063)

Volume 5 of the never ending study of the British single shot. One of the rarest and finest quality single shots made by any British firm is described. A large section is devoted to the cartridge developments carried on by Hollands with a large section on their Paradox cartridges.

Broad Arrow: British & Empire Factory Production, Proof, Inspection, Armourers, Unit & Issue Markings, by Ian Skennerton. Australia, Arms & Militaria Press, 2001. 140 pp., circa 80 illus. Stiff paper covers. $29.95

Thousands of service markings are illustrated and their applications described. Invaluable reference on units, also ideal for medal collectors.

Browning Dates of Manufacture, compiled by George Madis, Art and Reference House, Brownsboro, TX, 1989. 48 pp. $8.00

Gives the date codes and product codes for all models from 1824 to the present.

Browning Sporting Firearms: Dates of Manufacture, by D. R. Morse. Phoenix, AZ, Firing Pin Enterprizes, 2003. 37 pp. Softcover. New. $6.95

Covers their pistols, revolvers, rifles, shotguns and commemoratives, plus, models and serial numbers.

Browning Machine Gun Volume 1-Rifle Caliber Brownings in U.S. Service, by Dolf Goldsmith, Canada: Collector Grade Publications, 2005. 1st Edition, 552 pages, 568 illustrations. Hardcover. $79.95

This profusely illustrated history covers all models of the U.S. Browning, from the first "gas hammer" Model 1895 and the initial recoil-operated Models of 1901 and 1910, through the adoption and manufacture of the famous water-cooled heavy Model 1917 during World War I and the numerous Interwar experimental tank and aircraft guns, most of which were built up on surplus M1917 receivers.

Browning Machine Gun Volume 2-Rifle Caliber Brownings Abroad, by Dolf Goldsmith, Canada: Collector Grade Publications, 2006. 1st Edition, 392 pages, with over 486 illustrations. Hardcover, $69.95

This second volume of Dolf Goldsmith's series on Browning machine guns proves beyond doubt that the rifle-caliber Browning was simply the most popular and most-used machine gun ever designed. In some ways this book is even more engrossing than Volume I, as it describes and illustrates in considerable detail the many variations on the basic Browning which were manufactured and/or used by over twenty countries, in virtually every corner of the world, in both World Wars, in Korea and in Vietnam.

Browning–Sporting Arms of Distinction 1903-1992, by Matt Eastman, Long Beach, CA, Safari Press, 2004. 428 pp., profuse illus. Hardcover. $50.00

Bullard Firearms, by G. Scott Jamieson, Schiffer Publications, Atglen, PA 2002. 400 pp., with over 1100 color and b&w photos, charts, diagrams. Hardcover. $100.00

Bullard Firearms is the story of a mechanical genius whose rifles and cartridges were the equal of any made in America in the 1880s, yet little of substance had been written about James H. Bullard or his arms prior to 1988 when the first edition, called ***Bullard Arms***, was published. This greatly expanded volume, with over 1,000 b&w and 150 color plates, most not previously published, answers many of the questions posed in the first edition. The final chapter outlines, in chart form, almost 500 Bullard rifles by serial number, caliber and type. Quick and easy to use, this book is a real benefit for collectors and dealers alike.

Burning Powder, compiled by Major D.B. Wesson, Wolfe Publishing Company, Prescott, AZ, 1992. 110 pp. Soft cover. $10.95

A rare booklet from 1932 for Smith & Wesson collectors.

Burnside Breech Loading Carbines, The, by Edward A. Hull, Andrew Mowbray, Inc., Lincoln, RI, 1986. 95 pp., illus. $16.00

No. 1 in the "Man at Arms Monograph Series." A model-by-model historical/technical examination of one of the most widely used cavalry weapons of the American Civil War based upon important and previously unpublished research.

C.S. Armory Richmond: History of the Confederate States Armory, Richmond, VA and the Stock Shop at the C.S. Armory, Macon, GA., by Paul Davies, privately printed, 2000. 368 pp., illustrated with b&w photos. Hardcover. $75.00

The American Society of Arms Collectors is pleased to recommend C.S. Armory Richmond as a useful and valuable reference for collectors and scholars in the field of antique firearms. Gives fantastic explanations of machinery, stocks, barrels, and every facet of the production process during the timeframe covered in this book.

Cacciare A Palla: Uso E Tecnologia Dell'arma Rigata, by Marco E. Nobili, Italy, Il Volo Srl, 1994. 4th Edition-1st printing. 397 pp., illustrated with b&w photographs. Hardcover. New in new dust jacket. $75.00

Call of Duty; Military Awards and Decorations of the United States of America, by John E. Strandberg, LTC and Roger James Bender, San Jose, CA, R. James Bender Publishing, 2005. (New expanded edition). 559 pp. illustrated with 1,293 photos (most in color). Hardcover. NEW. $67.95

Camouflage Uniforms of European and NATO Armies; 1945 to the Present, by J. F. Borsarello, Atglen, PA, Schiffer Publications. Over 290 color and b&w photographs, 120 pp. Softcover. $29.95

This full-color book covers nearly all of the NATO, and other European armies' camouflaged uniforms, and not only shows and explains the many patterns, but also their efficacy of design. Described and illustrated are the variety of materials tested in over 40 different armies, and includes the history of obsolete trial tests from 1945 to the present time. This book provides a superb reference for the historian, reenactor, designer, and modeler.

Camouflage Uniforms of the Waffen-SS A Photographic Reference, by Michael Beaver, Schiffer Publishing, Atglen, PA. Over 1,000 color and b&w photographs and illustrations, 296 pp. $69.95

Finally a book that unveils the shroud of mystery surrounding Waffen-SS camouflage clothing. Illustrated here, both in full color and in contemporary b&w photographs, this unparalleled look at Waffen-SS combat troops and their camouflage clothing will benefit both the historian and collector.

Canadian Colts for the Boer War, by Col. Robert D. Whittington III. Hooks, TX, Brownlee Books, 2003. A limited edition of 1,000 copies. Numbered. 5 pp. Paper covers. New. $15.00

A study of Colt Revolvers issued to the First and Second Canadian Contingents Special Service Force.

Canadian Colts for the Boer War, Part 2, Col. Robert D. by Whittington III, Hooks, TX, Brownlee Books, 2005. A limited edition of 1,000 copies. Numbered. 5 pp. Paper covers, NEW. $5.00

Canadian Gunsmiths from 1608: A Checklist of Tradesmen, by John Belton, Historical Arms Series No. 29. Canada, Museum Restoration, 1992. 40 pp., 17 illustrations. Softcover. $8.95

This checklist is a greatly expanded version of HAS No. 14, listing the names, occupation, location, and dates of more than 1,500 men and women who worked as gunmakers, gunsmiths, armorers, gun merchants, gun patent holders, and a few other gun related trades.

Canadian Miliitaria Directory & Sourcebook Second Edition, by Clive M. Law, Ont. Canada, Service Publications, 1998. pp. 90. Softcover. NEW. $14.95

Cap Guns, by James Dundas, Schiffer Publishing, Atglen, PA, 1996. 160 pp., illus. Paper covers. $29.95

Over 600 full-color photos of cap guns and gun accessories with a current value guide.

Carbines of the Civil War, by John D. McAulay, Pioneer Press, Union City, TN, 1981. 123 pp., illus. Paper covers. $12.95

A guide for the student and collector of the colorful arms used by the Federal cavalry.

Carbines of the U.S. Cavalry 1861-1905, by John D. McAulay, Andrew Mowbray Publishers, Lincoln, RI, 1996. $35.00

Covers the crucial use of carbines from the beginning of the Civil War to the end of the cavalry carbine era in 1905.

Cartridge Carbines of the British Army, by Alan M. Petrillo, Excalibur Publications, Latham, NY, 1998. 72 pp., illus. Paper covers. $11.95

Begins with the Snider-Enfield which was the first regulation cartridge carbine introduced in 1866 and ends with the 303 caliber No.5, Mark 1 Enfield.

Cartridges for Collectors, by Fred Datig, Pioneer Press, Union City, TN, 1999. Three volumes of 176 pp. each. Vol. 1 (Centerfire); Vol. 2 (Rimfire and Misc.) types. Volume 1, softcover only, $19.95. Volumes 2 and 3, hardcover. $19.95

Vol. 3 (Additional Rimfire, Centerfire, and Plastic). All illustrations are shown in full-scale drawings.

Civil War Arms Makers and Their Contracts, edited by Stuart C. Mowbray and Jennifer Heroux, Andrew Mowbray Publishing, Lincoln, RI, 1998. 595 pp. $39.50

A facsimile reprint of the Report by the Commissioner of Ordnance and Ordnance Stores, 1862.

Civil War Arms Purchases and Deliveries, edited by Stuart C. Mowbray, Andrew Mowbray Publishing, Lincoln, RI, 1998. 300pp., illus. $39.50

A facsimile reprint of the master list of Civil War weapons purchases and deliveries including Small Arms, Cannon, Ordnance and Projectiles.

Civil War Cartridge Boxes of the Union Infantryman, by Paul Johnson, Andrew Mowbray, Inc., Lincoln, RI, 1998. 352 pp., illus. $45.00

There were four patterns of infantry cartridge boxes used by Union forces during the Civil War. The author describes the development and subsequent pattern changes to these cartridge boxes. All updated prices, scores of new listings, and hundreds of new pictures! It's the one reference work no collector should be without. An absolute must.

Civil War Collector's Price Guide; 11th Edition, Orange, VA, Publisher's Press, 2006. 300 pps., softbound, heavily illustrated, full color cover. $37.95

Our newly released 11th edition of the popular Civil War Collector's Price Guide! Expanded to include new images and new listings.

Civil War Commanders, by Dean Thomas, Thomas Publications, Gettysburg, PA. 1998. 72 pp., illus., photos. Paper covers. $9.95

138 photographs and capsule biographies of Union and Confederate officers. A convenient personalities reference guide.

Civil War Heavy Explosive Ordnance: A Guide to Large Artillery Projectiles, Torpedoes, and Mines, by Jack Bell, Denton, TX, University of North Texas Press, 2003. 1,016 b&w photos. 537 pp. Hardcover. New in new dust jacket. $50.00

Civil War Infantryman: In Camp, on the March, and in Battle, by Dean Thomas, Thomas Publications, Gettysburg, PA. 1998. 72 pp., illus. Softcovers. $12.95

Uses first-hand accounts to shed some light on the "common soldier" of the Civil War from enlistment to muster-out, including camp, marching, rations, equipment, fighting, and more.

Civil War Pistols, by John D. McAulay, Andrew Mowbray Inc., Lincoln, RI, 1992. 166 pp., illus. $38.50

A survey of the handguns used during the American Civil War.

Civil War Relic Hunting A to Z, by Robert Buttafuso, Sheridan Books, 2000. 1st edition. illus., 91 pp., b&w illustrations. Softcover. NEW. $21.95

Civil War Sharps Carbines and Rifles, by Earl J. Coates and John D. McAulay, Thomas Publications, Gettysburg, PA, 1996. 108 pp., illus. Paper covers. $12.95

Traces the history and development of the firearms including short histories of specific serial numbers and the soldiers who received them.

Civil War Small Arms of the U.S. Navy and Marine Corps, by John D. McAulay, Mowbray Publishing, Lincoln, RI, 1999. 186 pp., illus. $39.00

The first reliable and comprehensive guide to the firearms and edged weapons of the Civil War Navy and Marine Corps.

Collecting Military Headgear; A Guide to 5000 Years of Helmet History, by Robert Atglen Attard, PA, Schiffer Publications, 2004. 1st edition. Hardcover. New in new dust jacket. $69.95

Collecting Third Reich Recordings, by Stuart McKenzie, San Jose, CA, R. James Bender Publishing, 2001. 1st edition. Softcover. NEW. $29.95

Collector's Illustrated Encyclopedia of the American Revolution, by George C. Neumann and Frank J. Kravic, Rebel Publishing Co., Inc., Texarkana, TX, 1989. 286 pp., illus. $42.95

A showcase of more than 2,300 artifacts made, worn, and used by those who fought in the War for Independence.

Colonel Thomas Claiborne Jr. and the Colt Whitneyville-Walker Pistol, by Col. Robert D. Whittington III, Hooks, TX, Brownlee Books, 2005. A limited edition of 1,000 copies. Numbered. 8 pp. Paper covers, NEW. $7.50

Colonels in Blue: Union Army Colonels of the Civil War, by Roger Hunt, New York, Atglen, PA, Schiffer Publications, 2003. 1st edition. 288 pp., with over 640 b&w photographs. Hardcover. New in new dust jacket. $59.95

Colonial Frontier Guns, by T.M. Hamilton, Pioneer Press, Union City, TN, 1988. 176 pp., illus. Paper covers. $17.50

A complete study of early flint muskets of this country.

Colt 1909 Military Revolvers; The 1904 Thompson-Lagarde Report, and General John J. Pershing, by Col. Robert D. Whittington III. Hooks, TX, Brownlee Books, 2003. A limited edition of 1,000 copies. Numbered. 10 pp. Paper covers. New. $10.00

The 1904 Thompson-Lagarde Report, and General John J. Pershing.

Colt and Its Collectors Exhibition Catalog for Colt: The Legacy of A Legend, Buffalo Bill Historical Center, Cody, Wyoming. Colt Collectors Association, 2003. 1st edition. Hardcover. New in new dust jacket. $125.00

Colt and Its Collectors accompanies the upcoming special exhibition, Colt: The Legacy of a Legend, opening at the Buffalo Bill Historical Center in May 2003. Numerous essays, over 750 color photographs by Paul Goodwin.

Colt Armory, by Ellsworth Grant, Man-at-Arms Bookshelf, Lincoln, RI, 1996. 232 pp., illus. $35.00

A history of Colt's Manufacturing Company.

Colt Engraving Book, Volumes I & II, by R. L. Wilson. Privately printed, 2001. Each volume is appx. 500 pp., with 650 illustrations, most in color. $390.00

This third edition from the original texts of 1974 and 1982 has been fine-tuned and dramatically expanded, and is by far the most illuminating and complete. With over 1,200 illustrations, more than 2/3 of which are in color, this book joins the author's The Book of Colt Firearms, and Fine Colts as companion volumes. Approximately 1,000 pages in two volumes, each signed by the author, serial numbered, and strictly limited to 3000 copies. Volume I covers from the Paterson and pre-Paterson period through c.1921 (end of the Helfricht period). Volume II commences with Kornbrath, and Glahn, and covers Colt embellished arms from c.1919 through 2000.

Colt Model 1905 Automatic Pistol, by John Potocki, Andrew Mowbray Publishing, Lincoln, RI, 1998. 191 pp., illus. $28.00
Covers all aspects of the Colt Model 1905 Automatic Pistol, from its invention by the legendary John Browning to its numerous production variations.

Colt Peacemaker British Model, by Keith Cochran, Cochran Publishing Co., Rapid City, SD, 1989. 160 pp., illus. $35.00
Covers those revolvers Colt squeezed in while completing a large order of revolvers for the U.S. Cavalry in early 1874, to those magnificent cased target revolvers used in the pistol competitions at Bisley Commons in the 1890s.

Colt Peacemaker Encyclopedia, by Keith Cochran, Cochran Publishing Co., Rapid City, SD, 1986. 434 pp., illus. $60.00
A must-have book for the Peacemaker collector.

Colt Peacemaker Encyclopedia, Volume 2, by Keith Cochran, Cochran Publishing Co., SD, 1992. 416 pp., illus. $60.00
Included in this volume are extensive notes on engraved, inscribed, historical and noted revolvers, as well as those revolvers used by outlaws, lawmen, movie and television stars.

Colt Pistols, Texas, And The U.S. Army 1847-1861, by Col. Robert D. Whittington III. Hooks, TX, Brownlee Books, 2003. A limited edition of 1,000 copies. Numbered. 8 pp. Paper covers. New. $7.50
A study of the Colt pistols used in Texas by the U.S. Army between 1847-1861. A remarkable detailed report.

Colt Presentations: From the Factory Ledgers 1856-1869, by Herbert G. Houze. Lincoln, RI, Andrew Mowbray, Inc., 2003. 112 pp., 45 b&w photos. Softcover. $21.95
Samuel Colt was a generous man. He also used gifts to influence government decision makers. But after Congress investigated him in 1854, Colt needed to hide the gifts from prying eyes, which makes it very difficult for today's collectors to document the many revolvers presented by Colt and the factory. Using the original account journals of the Colt's Patent Fire Arms Manufacturing Co., renowned arms authority Herbert G. Houze finally gives us the full details behind hundreds of the most exciting Colts ever made.

Colt Single Action Army Revolver Study: New Discoveries, by Kenneth Moore, Lincoln, RI, Andrew Mowbray, Inc., 2003. 1st edition. 200 pp., with 77 photos and illustrations. Hardcover. New. $49.95
Twenty-five years after co-authoring the classic Study of the Colt Single Action Army Revolver, Ken fills in the gaps and sets the record straight. The serial number data alone will astound you. Includes, ejector models, special section on low serial numbers, U.S. Army testing data, new details about militia S.A.A.'s plus a true wealth of cartridge info.

Colt Single Action Army Revolvers: The Legend, the Romance and the Rivals, by "Doc" O'Meara, Krause Publications, Iola, WI, 2000. 160 pp., illustrated with 250 photos in b&w and a 16-page color section. $22.95
Production figures, serial numbers by year, and rarities.

Colt Single Action Army Revolvers and Alterations, by C. Kenneth Moore, Mowbray Publishers, Lincoln, RI, 1999. 112 pp., illus. $35.00
A comprehensive history of the revolvers that collectors call "Artillery Models." These are the most historical of all S.A.A. Colts, and this new book covers all the details.

Colt Single Action Army Revolvers and the London Agency, by C. Kenneth Moore, Andrew Mowbray Publishers, Lincoln, RI, 1990. 144 pp., illus. $35.00
Drawing on vast documentary sources, this work chronicles the relationship between the London Agency and the Hartford home office.

Colt Sporting Firearms: Dates of Manufacture, by D.R. Morse, Phoenix, AZ, Firing Pin Enterprizes, 2003. 82 pp. Softcover. New. $6.95
Covers their pistols, revolvers, rifles, shotguns and commemoratives, plus models and serial numbers.

Colt U.S. General Officers' Pistols, by Horace Greeley IV, Andrew Mowbray Inc., Lincoln, RI, 1990. 199 pp., illus. $38.00
These unique weapons, issued as a badge of rank to General Officers in the U.S. Army from WWII onward, remain highly personal artifacts of the military leaders who carried them. Includes serial numbers and dates of issue.

Colt Walker's, Walkers Controversy is Solved, by Col. Robert D. Whittington III. Hooks, TX, Brownlee Books, 2005. A limited edition of 1,000 copies. Numbered. 17 pp. Paper covers. New. $15.00
The truth about serial numbers on the Colt Whitneyville-Walker Pistols presented to Captain Samuel Hamilton Walker by Sam Colt and J. B. Colt on July 28th, 1847.

Colts from the William M. Locke Collection, by Frank Sellers, Andrew Mowbray Publishers, Lincoln, RI, 1996. 192 pp., illus. $55.00
This important book illustrates all of the famous Locke Colts, with captions by arms authority Frank Sellers.

Colt's Dates of Manufacture 1837-1978, by R.L. Wilson, published by Maurie Albert, Coburg, Australia; N.A. distributor Madis Books, TX, 1997. 61 pp. $8.50
An invaluable pocket guide to the dates of manufacture of Colt firearms up to 1978.

Colt's Pocket '49: Its Evolution Including the Baby Dragoon and Wells Fargo, by Robert Jordan and Darrow Watt, privately printed, Loma Mar, CA 2000. 304 pp., with 984 color photos, illus. Beautifully bound in a deep blue leather-like case. $125.00
Detailed information on all models and covers engaving, cases, accoutrements, holsters, fakes, and much more. Included is a summary booklet containing information such as serial numbers, production ranges and identifing photos. This book is a masterpiece on its subject.

Colt's SAA Post War Models, by George Garton, The Gun Room Press, Highland Park, NJ, 1995. 166 pp., illus. $39.95
Complete facts on the post-war Single Action Army revolvers. Information on calibers, production numbers and variations taken from factory records.

Combat Helmets of the Third Reich: A Study in Photographs, by Thomas Kibler, Pottsboro, TX, Reddick Enterprises, 2003. 1st edition. 96 pp., illustrated in full color. Pictorial softcover. NEW. $19.95

Combat Perspective The Thinking Man's Guide to Self-Defense, by Gabriel Suarez, Boulder, CO, Paladin Press, 2003. 1st edition. 112 pp. Softcover. NEW. $15.00

Complete Guide to United States Military Medals 1939 to Present, 6th Edition, by Colonel Frank C. Foster, Medals of America Press, Fountain Inn, SC, 2006. 168 pp., illus., photos. $29.95
Complete criteria for every Army, Navy, Marine, Air Force, Coast Guard, and Merchant Marine award since 1939. All decorations, service medals, and ribbons shown in full color and accompanied by dates and campaigns, as well as detailed descriptions on proper wear and display.

Complete Guide to the M1 Garand and the M1 Carbine, by Bruce N. Canfield, 2nd printing, Andrew Mowbray Inc., Lincoln, RI, 1999. 296 pp., illus. $39.50
Expanded and updated coverage of both the M1 Garand and the M1 Carbine, with more than twice as much information as the author's previous book on this topic.

Complete Guide to U.S. Infantry Weapons of the First War, by Bruce Canfield, Andrew Mowbray, Publisher, Lincoln, RI, 2000. 304 pp., illus. $39.95
The definitive study of the U.S. Infantry weapons used in WWI.

Complete Guide to U.S. Infantry Weapons of World War Two, by Bruce Canfield, Andrew Mowbray, Publisher, Lincoln, RI, 1995. 303 pp., illus. $39.95
A definitive work on the weapons used by the United States Armed Forces in WWII.

Confederate Belt Buckles & Plates, by Steve E. Mullinax, O'Donnell Publishing, Alexandria, VA, 1999. Expanded edition. 247 pp., illus. Hardcover. $34.00
Hundreds of crisp photographs augment this classic study of Confederate accoutrement plates.

Confederate Carbines & Musketoons Cavalry Small Arms Manufactured in and for the Southern Confederacy 1861-1865, by John M. Murphy, Santa Ana, CA, privately printed, 2002. Reprint. Hardcover. New in new dust jacket. $79.95

Confederate Rifles & Muskets: Infantry Small Arms Manufactured in the Southern Confederacy 1861-1865, by John M. Murphy. Santa Ana, CA, privately printed, 1996. Reprint. 768 pp., 8 pp. color plates, profusely illustrated. Hardcover. $119.95
The first in-depth and academic analysis and discussion of the "long" longarms produced in the South by and for the Confederacy during the American Civil War. The collection of Dr. Murphy is doubtless the largest and finest grouping of Confederate longarms in private hands today.

Confederate Saddles & Horse Equipment, by Ken R. Knopp, Orange, VA, Publisher's Press, 2002. 194 pps., illus. Hardcover. $39.95
A pioneer work on the subject. After 10 years of research Ken Knopp has compiled a thorough and fascinating study of the little-known field of Confederate saddlery and equipment. An indispensable source for collectors and historians.

Cooey Firearms, Made in Canada 1919-1979, by John A. Belton, Museum Restoration, Canada, 1998. 36pp., with 46 illus. Paper covers. $8.95
More than 6 million rifles and at least 67 models were made by this small Canadian riflemaker. They have been identified from the first 'Cooey Canuck' through the last variations made by the 'Winchester-Cooey'. Each is descibed and most are illustrated in this first book on the Cooey.

Cowboy and Gunfighter Collectible, by Bill Mackin, Mountain Press Publishing Co., Missoula, MT, 1995. 178 pp., illus. Paper covers. $25.00

A photographic encyclopedia with price guide and makers' index.

Cowboy Collectibles and Western Memorabilia, by Bob Bell and Edward Vebell, Schiffer Publishing, Atglen, PA, 1992. 160 pp., illus. Paper covers. $29.95

The exciting era of the cowboy and the wild west collectibles including rifles, pistols, gun rigs, etc.

Cowboy Culture: The Last Frontier of American Antiques, by Michael Friedman, Schiffer Publishing, Ltd., West Chester, PA, 2002. 300 pp., illus. $89.95

Covers the artful aspects of the old west, the antiques and collectibles. Illustrated with clear color plates of over 1,000 items such as spurs, boots, guns, saddles, etc.

Cowboys and the Trappings of the Old West, by William Manns and Elizabeth Clair Flood, Zon International Publishing Co., Santa Fe, NM, 1997, 1st edition. 224 pp., illus. $45.00

A pictorial celebration of the cowboy dress and trappings.

Custom Firearms Engraving, by Tom Turpin, Krause Publications, Iola, WI, 1999. 208 pp., illus. $49.95

Over 200 four-color photos with more than 75 master engravers profiled. Engravers directory with addresses in the U.S. and abroad.

Daisy Air Rifles & BB Guns: The First 100 Years, by Neal Punchard. St. Paul, MN, Motorbooks, 2002. 1st edition. 10" x 10", 156 pp., 300 color. Hardcover. $29.95

Flash back to the days of your youth and recall fond memories of your Daisy. Daisy Air Rifles and BB Guns looks back fondly on the first 100 years of Daisy BB rifles and pistols, toy and cork guns, accessories, packaging, period advertising and literature.

Death From Above: The German FG42 Paratrooper Rifle, New Expanded Edition, by Blake Stevens, Collector Grade Publications, Canada, 2007. 228 pages, 278 illustrations. $59.95

This book depicts and describes seven basic models of the FG42, from the earliest prototype (the Type 'A') through the first or 'early' production series (the Type 'E') with its distinctively swept-back handgrip and intricately machined receiver, then the initial Rheinmetall redesign utilizing a stamped receiver (the Type 'F'), followed by the ultimate if extremely short-lived final series-production model, the Type 'G'. Amazingly, virtually none of the Type 'G' components will interchange with their lookalike Type 'F' counterparts. This includes magazines.

Decorations, Medals, Ribbons, Badges and Insignia of the United States Navy; World War II to Present, by James G. Thompson, Medals of America Press, Fountain Inn, SC. 2005. 124 pp., illus. $29.95

The most complete guide to United States Army medals, ribbons, rank, insignia and patches from WWII to the present day. Each medal and insignia shown in full color. Includes listing of respective criteria and campaigns.

Defending the Dominion, Canadian Military Rifles, 1855-1955, by David Edgecombe. Service Publications, Ont., Canada, 2003. 168 pp., with 60+ illustrations. Hardcover. $39.95

This book contains much new information on the Canadian acquisition, use and disposal of military rifles during the most significant century in the development of small arms. In addition to the venerable Martini-Henry, there are chapters on the Winchester, Snider, Starr, Spencer, Peabody, Enfield rifles and others.

Derringer in America, Volume 1, The Percussion Period, by R.L. Wilson and L.D. Eberhart, Andrew Mowbray Inc., Lincoln, RI, 1985. 271 pp., illus. $48.00

A long awaited book on the American percussion derringer.

Derringer in America, Volume 2, the Cartridge Period, by L.D. Eberhart and R.L. Wilson, Andrew Mowbray Inc., Publishers, Lincoln, RI, 1993. 284 pp., illus. $65.00

Comprehensive coverage of cartridge derringers organized alphabetically by maker. Includes all types of derringers known by the authors to have been offered in the American market.

Devil's Paintbrush: Sir Hiram Maxim's Gun, by Dolf Goldsmith, 3rd Edition, expanded and revised, Collector Grade Publications, Toronto, Canada, 2002. 384 pp., illus. $79.95

The classic work on the world's first true automatic machine gun.

Dressed For Duty: America's Women in Uniform, 1898-1973 Volume I, by Jill Halcomb Smith, San Nose, CA, Bender Publishing, 2002. 1st edition. 480 pages-1,089 photos & illustrations (many in color), deluxe binding. Hardcover. NEW. $54.95

Dressed For Duty: America's Women in Uniform, 1898-1973 Volume II, by Jill Halcomb Smith, San Nose, CA, Bender Publishing, 2004. 1st edition. 544 pages-1,300 photos & illustrations (many in color), deluxe binding. Hardcover. NEW. $59.95

Dr. Josephus Requa Civil War Dentist and the Billinghurst-Requa Volley Gun, by John M. Hyson Jr., and Margaret Requa DeFrancisco, Museum Restoration Service, Bloomfield, Ont., Canada, 1999. 36 pp., illus. Paper covers. $8.95

The story of the inventor of the first practical rapid-fire gun to be used during the American Civil War.

Dutch Luger (Parabellum) A Complete History, by Bas J. Martens and Guus de Vries, Ironside International, Alexandria, VA, 1995. 268 pp., illus. $49.95

The history of the Luger in the Netherlands. An extensive description of the Dutch pistol and trials and the different models of the Luger in the Dutch service.

E.C. Prudhomme's Gun Engraving Review, by E. C. Prudhomme, R&R Books, Livonia, NY, 1994. 164 pp., illus. $60.00

As a source for engravers and collectors, this book is an indispensable guide to styles and techniques of the world's foremost engravers.

Eagle on U.S. Firearms, by John W. Jordan, Pioneer Press, Union City, TN, 1992. 140 pp., illus. Paper covers. $17.50

Stylized eagles have been stamped on government owned or manufactured firearms in the U.S. since the beginning of our country. This book lists and illustrates these various eagles in an informative and refreshing manner.

Emblems of Honor; Patches and Insignia of the U.S. Army from the Great War to the Early Cold War Vol. IV Armor-Cavalry-Tank Destroyer, by Kurt Keller, Constabulary, PA, privately printed, 2005. 1st edition, signed. 232 pp., with over 600 color photos. Hardcover. New in new dust jacket. $59.95

Emma Gees, by Capt. Herbert W. McBride, Mt. Ida, AR, Lancer Publishing, 2003. 224 pp., b&w photos. Softcover. NEW. $19.95

Encyclopedia of Rifles & Handguns; A Comprehensive Guide to Firearms, edited by Sean Connolly, Chartwell Books, Inc., Edison, NJ., 1996. 160 pp., illus. $26.00

Encyclopedia of United States Army Insignia and Uniforms, by William Emerson, OK, University of Oklahoma Press, 1996. Hardcover. NEW. $134.95

Enemies Foreign and Domestic, by Matthew Bracken, San Diego, CA, Steelcutter Publishing, 2003. Softcover. NEW. $19.89

Eprouvettes: A Comprehensive Study of Early Devices for the Testing of Gunpowder, by R.T.W. Kempers, Royal Armouries Museum, Leeds, England, 1999. 352 pp., illustrated with 240 b&w and 28 color plates. $125.00

Equipment of the WWII Tommy, by David Gordon, Missoula, MT, Pictorial Histories Publishing, 2004. 1st edition. Softcover. NEW. $24.95

Fifteen Years in the Hawken Lode, by John D. Baird, The Gun Room Press, Highland Park, NJ, 1976. 120 pp., illus. $24.95

A collection of thoughts and observations gained from many years of intensive study of the guns from the shop of the Hawken brothers.

Fighting Colors: The Creation of Military Aircraft Nose Art, by Gary Velasco, Paducah, KY, Turner Publishing, 2005. 1st edition. Hardcover. New in new dust jacket. $57.95

Fighting Iron, by Art Gogan, Andrew Mowbray, Inc., Lincoln, R.I., 2002. 176 pp., illus. $28.00

It doesn't matter whether you collect guns, swords, bayonets or accoutrement–sooner or later you realize that it all comes down to the metal. If you don't understand the metal, you don't understand your collection.

Fine Art of the West, by Byron Price, New York, Abbeville Press, 2004, 2nd revised edition. $75.00

A glossary and bibliography complete this first comprehensive look at one of America's most fascinating forms of artistic expression. 276 pages illustrated with color photos.

Firearm Suppressor Patents; Volume 1: United States Patents, by N.R. Parker, Foreword by Alan C. Paulson, Boulder, CO, Paladin Press, 2004. 392 pp., illus. Softcover. $45.00

Firearms from Europe, 2nd Edition, by David Noe, Larry W. Yantz, Dr. James B. Whisker, Rowe Publications, Rochester, N.Y., 2002. 192 pp., illus. $45.00

A history and description of firearms imported during the American Civil War by the United States of America and the Confederate States of America.

Firearms of the American West 1803-1865, Volume 1, by Louis A. Garavaglia and Charles Worman, University of Colorado Press, Niwot, CO, 1998. 402 pp., illus. $79.95

Traces the development and uses of firearms on the frontier during this period.

Firearms of the American West 1866-1894, Volume 2, by Louis A. Garavaglia and Charles G. Worman, University of Colorado Press, Niwot, CO, 1998. 416 pp., illus. $79.95

A monumental work that offers both technical information on all of the important firearms used in the West during this period and a highly entertaining history of how they were used, who used them, and why.

Firepower from Abroad, by Wiley Sword, Andrew Mowbray Publishing, Lincoln, R.I., 2000. 120 pp., illus. $23.00

The Confederate Enfield and the LeMat revolver and how they reached the Confederate market.

Flayderman's Guide to Antique American Firearms and Their Values, 8th Edition, edited by Norm Flayderman, Krause Publications, Iola, WI, 2001. 692 pp., illus. Paper covers. $34.95

A completely updated and new edition with more than 3,600 models and variants extensively described with all marks and specifications necessary for quick identification.

Flintlock Fowlers: The First Guns Made in America, by Tom Grinslade, Texarkana, TX: Scurlock Publishing Co., 2005. 1st edition. 248 pages. Hardcover. New in new dust jacket. $75.00 Paperback $38.00

The most complete compilation of fowlers ever in one book. Essential resource for collectors, builders and flintlock enthusiasts!

F.N. F.A.L. Assembly, Disassembly Manual 7.62mm, by Skennerton & Riling, Ray Riling Arms Books Co. Philadelphia, PA 2004. 36 pages, $5.00

Over 60 photos & line drawings. Ideal workshop reference for stripping & assembly with exploded parts drawings, specifications, service accessories, historical information and recommended reading references. Triple saddle-stitched binding with durable plastic laminated cover makes this an ideal workshop guide.

FN-FAL Rifle, et al, by Duncan Long, Paladin Press, Boulder, CO, 1999. 144 pp., illus. Paper covers. $18.95

Detailed descriptions of the basic models produced by Fabrique Nationale and the myriad variants that evolved as a result of the firearms' universal acceptance.

Freund & Bro. Pioneer Gunmakers to the West, by F.J. Pablo Balentine, Graphic Publishers, Newport Beach, CA, 1997. 380 pp., illus. $69.95

The story of Frank W. and George Freund, skilled German gunsmiths who plied their trade on the Western American frontier during the final three decades of the nineteenth century.

Full Circle: A Treatise On Roller Locking, by Blake Stevens, Collector Grade Publications, Toronto, Canada, 2006. 536 pages, with over 737 illustrations. $79.95

After the war the roller lock was taken from Germany first to France; then to Spain, and Switzerland; through Holland; and finally back "Full Circle" to Germany again, where it was used in the G3, the service rifle of the Bundeswehr, from 1959 through to the adoption of the 5.56mm G36 in 1995. The classic work on the world's first true automatic machine gun.

Fusil de Tulole in New France, 1691-1741, by Russel Bouchard, Museum Restorations Service, Bloomfield, Ontario, Canada, 1997. 36 pp., illus. Paper covers. $8.95

The development of the company and the identification of their arms.

Gas Trap Garand, by Billy Pyle, Collector Grade Publications, Cobourg, Ontario, Canada, 1999 316 pp., illus. $59.95

The in-depth story of the rarest Garands of them all, the initial 80 Model Shop rifles made under the personal supervision of John Garand himself in 1934 and 1935, and the first 50,000 plus production "gas trap" M1's manufactured at Springfield Armory between August, 1937 and August, 1940.

George Schreyer, Sr. and Jr., Gunmakers of Hanover, Pennsylvania, by George Shumway, George Shumway Publishers, York, PA, 1990. 160pp., illus. $50.00

This monograph is a detailed photographic study of almost all known surviving longrifles and smoothbore guns made by highly regarded gunsmiths George Schreyer, Sr. and George Schreyer Jr.

German and Austrian Gunmakers Trade Catalogs, by George Hoyem, Jaeger Press, 2002. This is a 252 page 11" x 8.5" case bound book with a four color dust jacket, compiled by Hans E. Pfingsten and George A. Hoyem, containing five illustrated gunmakers trade catalogues dating from 1914 to 1935, three of them export issues in German, English, French and Spanish. Hardcover. New in new dust jacket. $60.00

German Anti-Tank Weapons-Panzerbuchse, Panzerfaust and Panzerschrek: Propaganda Series Volume 5, by DeVries and Martens. Alexandria,VA, Ironside Intl., 2005. 1st edition. 152pp, illustrated with 200 high quality b&w photos, most never published before. Hardcover, NEW. $38.95

German Assault Rifle 1935-1945, The, by Peter R. Senich, Paladin Press, Boulder, CO, 1987. 328 pp., illus. $60.00

A complete review of machine carbines, machine pistols and assault rifles employed by Hitler's Wehrmacht during WWII.

German Belt Buckles 1845-1945: Buckles of the Enlisted Soldiers, by Peter Nash Atglen, PA, Schiffer Publications, 2003. 1st edition. Hardcover. New in new dust jacket. $59.95

German Camouflaged Helmets of the Second World War; Volume 1: Painted and Textured Camouflage, by Branislav Atglen Radovic, PA, Schiffer Publications, 2004. 1st edition. Hardcover. New in new dust jacket. $79.95

German Camouflaged Helmets of the Second World War; Volume 2: Wire, Netting, Covers, Straps, Interiors, Miscellaneous, by Branislav Atglen Radovic, PA, Schiffer Publications, 2004. 1st edition. Hardcover. New in new dust jacket. $79.95

German Cross in Gold-Holders of the SS and Police, by Mark Yerger, San Jose, CA, Bender Publishing, 2004. 1st edition. 432 pp., 295 photos and illustrations, deluxe binding. Hardcover. NEW. $44.95

German Cross in Gold-Holders of the SS and Police Volume 2-"Das Reich", by Mark Yerger, San Jose, CA, Bender Publishing, 2005. 1st edition. 432 pp., 295 photos and illustrations, deluxe binding. Hardcover. NEW. $44.95

German K98k Rifle, 1934-1945: The Backbone of the Wehrmacht, by Richard D. Law, Collector Grade Publications, Toronto, Canada, 1993. 336 pp., illus. $69.95

The most comprehensive study ever published on the 14,000,000 bolt-action K98k rifles produced in Germany between 1934 and 1945.

German Machine Guns, by Daniel D. Musgrave, revised edition, Ironside International Publishers, Inc. Alexandria, VA, 1992. 586 pp., 650 illus. $49.95

The most definitive book ever written on German machine guns. Covers the introduction and development of machine guns in Germany from 1899 to the rearmament period after WWII.

German Military Abbreviations, by Military Intelligence Service, Canada, Service Publications. 268 pp. Stiff paper covers. NEW. $16.95

German Paratroops: Uniforms, Insignia & Equipment of the Fallschirmjager in World War II, by Robert Atglen Kurtz, PA, Schiffer Publications, 2003. 1st edition. Hardcover. New in new dust jacket. $59.95

German Tanks of World War II in Color, by Michael Green; Thomas Anderson; Frank Schultz, St. Paul, MN, MBI Publishing Company, 2000. 1st edition. Softcover. NEW. $14.95

Government Issue: U.S. Army European Theater of Operations Collector Guide, by Henry-Paul Enjames, Philippe Charbonnier, France, Histoire & Collections, 2004. Hardcover, NEW. $49.89

Government Models, by William H.D. Goddard, Andrew Mowbray Publishing, Lincoln, RI, 1998. 296 pp., illus. $58.50

The most authoritative source on the development of the Colt model of 1911.

Grasshoppers and Butterflies, by Adrian B. Caruana, Museum Restoration Service, Alexandria Bay, N.Y., 1999. 32 pp., illus. Paper covers. $8.95

No.39 in the Historical Arms Series. The light 3 pounders of Pattison and Townsend.

Greenhill Dictionary of Guns and Gunmakers: From Colt's First Patent to the Present Day, 1836-2001, by John Walter, Greenhill Publishing, 2001, 1st edition, 576 pp., illustrated with 200 photos, 190 trademarks and 40 line drawings, Hardcover. $59.95

Covers military small arms, sporting guns and rifles, air and gas guns, designers, inventors, patentees, trademarks, brand names and monograms. A famed book of great value, truly encyclopedic in scope and sought after by firearms collectors.

Gun Powder Cans & Kegs, by Ted and David Bacyk and Tom Rowe, Rowe Publications, Rochester, NY, 1999. 150 pp., illus. $65.00

The first book devoted to powder tins and kegs. All cans and kegs in full color. With a price guide and rarity scale.

Gun Tools, Their History and Identification, by James B. Shaffer, Lee A. Rutledge and R. Stephen Dorsey, Collector's Library, Eugene, OR, 1992. 375 pp., illus. $30.00

Written history of foreign and domestic gun tools from the flintlock period to WWII.

Gun Tools, Their History and Identifications, Volume 2, by Stephen Dorsey and James B. Shaffer, Collectors' Library, OR, 1997. 396 pp., illus. Paper covers. $30.00

Gun tools from the Royal Armouries Museum in England, Pattern Room, Royal Ordnance Reference Collection in Nottingham and from major private collections.

Gunmakers of London 1350-1850 with Supplement, by Howard L. Blackmore, Museum Restoration Service, Alexandria Bay, NY, 1999. 222 pp., illus. Two volumes. Slipcased. $135.00

A listing of all the known workmen of gunmaking in the first 500 years, plus a history of the guilds, cutlers, armourers, founders, blacksmiths, etc. 260 gunmarks are illustrated. Supplement is 156 pages, and begins with an introductory chapter on "foreign" gunmakers followed by records of all the new information found about previously unidentified armourers, gunmakers and gunsmiths.

Guns of Dagenham: Lanchester, Patchett, Sterling, by Peter Laidler and David Howroyd, Collector Grade Publications, Inc., Canada, 1995. 310 pp. illus. $39.95
An in-depth history of small arms made by the Sterling Company of Dagenham, England, from 1940 until Sterling was purchased by British Aerospace in 1989 and closed.

Guns of Remington: Historic Firearms Spanning Two Centuries, compiled by Howard M. Madaus, Biplane Productions, Publisher, in cooperation with Buffalo Bill Historical Center, Cody, WY, 1998. 352 pp., illustrated with over 800 color photos. $79.95
A complete catalog of the firearms in the exhibition, "It Never Failed Me: The Arms & Art of Remington Arms Company" at the Buffalo Bill Historical Center, Cody, Wyoming.

Guns of the Third Reich, by John Walter, Pennsylvania, Stackpole Books, 2004. 1st edition. 256pp, 60 illust. Hardcover. $34.95
John Walter examines the full range of guns used by the Third Reich from the commercially successful Walter PP and PPK, to the double-action, personal defense pistols Mauser HSc and Sauer M38.

Guns of the Western Indian War, by R. Stephen Dorsey, Collector's Library, Eugene, OR, 1997. 220 pp., illus. Paper covers. $30.00
The full story of the guns and ammunition that made western history in the turbulent period of 1865-1890.

Gunsmiths of Illinois, by Curtis L. Johnson, George Shumway Publishers, York, PA, 1995. 160 pp., illus. $50.00
Genealogical information is provided for nearly 1,000 gunsmiths. Contains hundreds of illustrations of rifles and other guns, of handmade origin, from Illinois.

Gunsmiths of Manhattan, 1625-1900: A Checklist of Tradesmen, by Michael H. Lewis, Museum Restoration Service, Bloomfield, Ont., Canada, 1991. 40 pp., illus. Paper covers. $8.95
This listing of more than 700 men in the arms trade in New York City prior to about the end of the 19th century will provide a guide for identification and further research.

Gunsmiths of Maryland, by Daniel D. Hartzler and James B. Whisker, Old Bedford Village Press, Bedford, PA, 1998. 208 pp., illus. $45.00
Covers firelock Colonial period through the breech-loading patent models. Featuring longrifles.

Gunsmiths of Virginia, by Daniel D. Hartzler and James B. Whisker, Old Bedford Village Press, Bedford, PA, 1992. 206 pp., illus. $40.00
A photographic study of American longrifles.

Gunsmiths of West Virginia, by Daniel D. Hartzler and James B. Whisker, Old Bedford Village Press, Bedford, PA, 1998. 176 pp., illus. $40.00
A photographic study of American longrifles.

Gunsmiths of York County, Pennsylvania, by Daniel D. Hartzler and James B. Whisker, Old Bedford Village Press, Bedford, PA, 1998. 160 pp., illus. $40.00
Photographs and research notes on the longrifles and gunsmiths of York County, Pennsylvania.

Hand Forged for Texas Cowboys, by Kurt House, an Antonio, TX, Three Rivers Publishing, 2005. This beautifully illustrated book features color photos as well as b&w period photos, and will be a welcome addition to the library of any reader. 160 pages. Hardcover. New in new dust jacket. $69.95

Harrington & Richardson Sporting Firearms: Dates of Manufacture 1871-1991, by D.R. Morse. Phoenix, AZ, Firing Pin Enterprizes, 2003. 14 pp. Softcover. NEW. $6.95
Covers their pistols, revolvers, rifles, shotguns and commemoratives, plus models.

Hawken Rifle: Its Place in History, by Charles E. Hanson Jr., The Fur Press, Chadron, NE, 1979. 104 pp., illus. Paper covers. $15.00
A definitive work on this famous rifle.

Hi-Standard Sporting Firearms: Dates of Manufacture, by D.R. Morse. 1926-1992. Phoenix, AZ, Firing Pin Enterprizes, 2003. 22 pp. Softcover. New. $6.95
Covers their pistols, revolvers, rifles, shotguns and commemoratives, plus models and serial numbers.

High Standard: A Collector's Guide to the Hamden & Hartford Target Pistols, by Tom Dance, Andrew Mowbray, Inc., Lincoln, RI, 1991. 192 pp. Paper covers. $24.00
From Citation to Supermatic, all of the production models and specials made from 1951 to 1984 are covered according to model number or series.

History of Modern U.S. Military Small Arms Ammunition, Volume 1, 1880-1939, revised by F.W. Hackley, W.H. Woodin and E.L. Scranton, Thomas Publications, Gettysburg, PA, 1998. 328 pp., illus. $49.95
This revised edition incorporates all publicly available information concerning military small arms ammunition for the period 1880 through 1939 in a single volume.

History of Modern U.S. Military Small Arms Ammunition, Volume 2, 1940-1945, by F.W. Hackley, W.H. Woodin and E.L. Scranton, Gun Room Press, Highland Park, NJ, 1998. 297 pages, illustrated. $49.95
Based on decades of original research conducted at the National Archives, numerous military, public and private museums and libraries, as well as individual collections, this edition incorporates all publicly available information concerning military small arms ammunition for the period 1940 through 1945.

History of Smith & Wesson Firearms, by Dean Boorman, Lyons Press, New York, NY, 2002. 44 pp., illustrated in full color. Hardcover. $29.95
The definitive guide to one of the world's best-known firearms makers. Takes the story through the years of the Military and Police 38 and of the Magnum cartridge, to today's wide range of products for law-enforcement customers.

History of Winchester Rifles, by Dean Boorman, Lyons Press, New York, NY, 2001. 144 pp., illus. 150 full-color photos. $29.95
A captivating and wonderfully photographed history of one of the most legendary names in gun lore.

History of Colt Firearms, by Dean Boorman, Lyons Press, New York, NY, 2001. 144 pp., illus. $29.95
Discover the fascinating story of the world's most famous revolver, complete with more than 150 stunning full-color photographs.

Holsters and Shoulder Stocks of the World, by Anthony Vanderlinden, Greensboro, NC, Wet Dog Publications, 2005. 1st edition. Hardcover $45.95
About 500 holsters and shoulder-stocks will be documented in this first edition. Pistols are listed by make and model. The user guide references the countries that used the holsters so that collectors can instantly refer to either a pistol model or country or use. 204 pages, with over 1000 b& w photos.

Honour Bound: The Chauchat Machine Rifle, by Gerard Demaison and Yves Buffetaut, Collector Grade Publications, Inc., Cobourg, Ont., Canada, 1995. $39.95
The story of the CSRG (Chauchat) machine rifle, the most manufactured automatic weapon of WWI.

Hunting Weapons from the Middle Ages to the Twentieth Century, by Howard L. Blackmore, Dover Publications, Meneola, NY, 2000. 480 pp., illus. Paper covers. $16.95
Dealing mainly with the different classes of weapons used in sport: swords, spears, crossbows, guns, and rifles, from the Middle Ages until the present day.

Illustrations of United States Military Arms 1776-1903 and Their Inspector's Marks, compiled by Turner Kirkland, Pioneer Press, Union City, TN, 1988. 37 pp., illus. Paper covers. $7.00
Reprinted from the 1949 Bannerman catalog. Valuable information for both the advanced and beginning collector.

Imperial German Military Officers' Helmets and Headdress 1871-1918, by Thomas N.G. Stubbs, Atglen, PA, Schiffer Publications, 2003. 1st edition. Hardcover. New in new dust jacket. $79.95

Imperial Japanese Grenade Rifles and Launchers, by Gregory A. Babich and Thomas A. Keep Lemont, PA, Dutch Harlow Publishing, 2004. 1st edition. Hardcover. New in new dust jacket. $75.00

Indian Trade Relics, by Lar Hothem, Paducah, KY, Collector Books, 2003. 1st edition. 320pp. Pictorial Hardcover. NEW. $29.95

Indian War Cartridge Pouches, Boxes and Carbine Boots, by R. Stephen Dorsey, Collector's Library, Eugene, OR, 1993. 156 pp., illus. Paper covers. $20.00
The key reference work to the cartridge pouches, boxes, carbine sockets and boots of the Indian War period 1865-1890.

Individual Gear and Personal Items of the GI in Europe 1942-1945; From Pro-Kits to Pin-Up, by James Klokner, Atglen., PA, Schiffer Publications, 2005. 224 pages with over 470 color and b&w photographs. Hardcover. $59.95
This book is by far the best and most complete study available of personal items of the American soldier during World War II and truly an indispensable resource.

International Armament, with History, Data, Technical Information and Photographs of Over 800 Weapons, 2nd edition, new printing, by George B. Johnson, Alexandria, VA, Ironside International, 2002. Hardcover. New in new dust jacket. $59.95
The development and progression of modern military small arms. Over 800 photographs and illustrations with both historical and technical data. Two volumes are now bound into one book.

ARMS LIBRARY

Jaeger Rifles, collected articles published in Muzzle Blasts, by George Shumway, York PA, 2003. Reprint. 108 pp., illus. Stiff paper covers. New. $30.00

Thirty-six articles previously published in ***Muzzle Blasts*** are reproduced here.

Japanese Rifles of World War Two, by Duncan O. McCollum, Excalibur Publications, Latham, NY, 1996. 64 pp., illus. Paper covers. $18.95

A sweeping view of the rifles and carbines that made up Japan's arsenal during the conflict.

Kentucky Rifle, by Captain John G.W. Dillin, George Shumway Publisher, York, PA, 1993. 221 pp., illus. $50.00

This well-known book was the first attempt to tell the story of the American longrifle. This edition retains the original text and illustrations with supplemental footnotes provided by Dr. George Shumway.

Legends and Reality of the AK, by Val Shilin and Charlie Cutshaw, Paladen Press, Boulder, CO, 2000. 192 pp., illus. Paper covers. $35.00

A behind-the-scenes look at history, design and impact of the Kalashnikov family of weapons.

Light 6-Pounder Battalion Gun of 1776, by Adrian Caruana, Museum Restoration Service, Bloomfield, Ontario, Canada, 2001. 76 pp., illus. Paper covers. $8.95

London Gun Trade, 1850-1920, by Joyce E. Gooding, Museum Restoration Service, Bloomfield, Ontario, Canada, 2001. 48 pp., illus. Paper covers. $8.95

Names, dates and locations of London gunmakers working between 1850 and 1920 are listed. Compiled from the original Kelly's post office directories of the City of London.

London Gunmakers and the English Duelling Pistol, 1770-1830, by Keith R. Dill, Museum Restoration Service, Bloomfield, Ontario, Canada, 1997. 36 pp., illus. Paper covers. $8.95

Ten gunmakers made London one of the major gunmaking centers of the world. This book examines how the design and construction of their pistols contributed to that reputation and how these characteristics may be used to date flintlock arms.

Longrifles of Pennsylvania, Volume 1, Jefferson, Clarion & Elk Counties, by Russel H. Harringer, George Shumway Publisher, York, PA, 1984. 200 pp., illus. $50.00

First in series that will treat in great detail the longrifles and gunsmiths of Pennsylvania.

M1 Garand .30 Assembly, Disassembly Manual, by Skennerton & Riling, Ray Riling Arms Books Co. Philadelphia, PA 2004. 36 pages, $5.00

With over 60 photos & line drawings. Ideal workshop reference for stripping & assembly with exploded parts drawings, specifications, service accessories, historical information and recommended reading references.

M1 Carbine .30 M1, M1A1, M2 & M3 Assembly, Disassembly Manual, by Skennerton & Riling, Ray Riling Arms Books Co. Philadelphia, PA 2004. 36 pages, $5.00

With over 60 photos & line drawings. Ideal workshop reference for stripping & assembly with exploded parts drawings, specifications, service accessories, historical information and recommended reading references.

M1 Carbine: A Revolution in Gun-Stocking, by Grafton H. Cook II and Barbara W. Cook, Lincoln, RI, Andrew Mowbray, Inc., 2002. 1st edition. 208 pp., heavily illustrated with 157 rare photographs of the guns and the men and women who made them. Softcover. $29.95

Shows you, step by step, how M1 carbine stocks were made, right through to assembly with the hardware. Also contains lots of detailed information about other military weapons, like the M1A1, the M1 Garand, the M14 and much, much more.

M1 Carbine: Design, Development, and Production, by Larry Ruth, Gun Room Press, Highland Park, NJ, 1987. 291 pp., illus. Paper $19.95

The origin, development, manufacture and use of this famous carbine of WWII.

M1 Carbine Owner's Guide, by Larry Ruth and Scott A. Duff, Scott A. Duff Publications, Export, PA, 1997. 126 pp., illus. Paper covers. $21.95

This book answers the questions M1 owners most often ask concerning maintenance activities not encounted by military users.

M1 Garand: Owner's Guide, by Scott A. Duff, Scott A. Duff Publications, Export, PA, 1998. 132 pp., illus. Paper covers. $21.95

This book answers the questions M1 owners most often ask concerning maintenance activities not encounted by military users.

M1 Garand Complete Assembly Guide, Vol 2, by Scott A. Duff, Scott A. Duff Publications, Export, PA, 2006. 162 pp., illus. Paper covers. $20.95

This book goes beyond the military manuals in depth and scope, using words It won't make you an Garand armorer, but it will make you a more knowledgeable owner.

M1 Garand: Post World War, by Scott A. Duff, Scott A. Duff Publications, Export, PA, 1990. 139 pp., illus. Softcover. $21.95

A detailed account of the activities at Springfield Armory through this period. International Harvester, H&R, Korean War production and quantities delivered. Serial numbers.

M1 Garand: World War II, by Scott A. Duff, Scott A. Duff Publications, Export, PA, 2001. 210 pp., illus. Paper covers. $34.95

The most comprehensive study available to the collector and historian on the M1 Garand of WWII.

M1 Garand 1936 to 1957, 4th Edition, Revised & Expanded, by Joe Poyer and Craig Riesch, North Cape Publications, Tustin, CA, 2006. 232 pp., illus. PC. $19.95

Describes the entire range of M1 Garand production in text and quick-scan charts.

M1 Garand Serial Numbers and Data Sheets, by Scott A. Duff, Scott A. Duff Publications, Export, PA, 1995. 101 pp., illus. Paper covers. $11.95

Provides the reader with serial numbers related to dates of manufacture and a large sampling of data sheets to aid in identification or restoration.

Machine Guns, by Ian V. Hogg, Iola, WI, Krause Publications, 2002. 1st edition. 336 pp., illustrated with b&w photos with a 16-page color section. Softcover. $29.95

A detailed history of the rapid-fire gun, 14th Century to present. Covers the development, history and specifications.

Made in the C.S.A.: Saddle Makers of the Confederacy, by Ken R. Knopp, Hattiesburg, MS, privately printed, 2003. 1st edition signed. 205 pp., illus., signed by the author. Softcover. NEW. $30.00

Maine Made Guns and Their Makers, by Dwight B. Demeritt Jr., Maine State Museum, Augusta, ME, 1998. 209 pp., illus. $55.00

An authoritative, biographical study of Maine gunsmiths.

Marksmanship in the U.S. Army, by William Emerson, Oklahoma, Univ. of Oklahoma Press, 2004 256 pages Illustrated with b&w photos. Hardcover. NEW $64.95

Marlin Firearms: A History of the Guns and the Company That Made Them, by Lt. Col. William S. Brophy, USAR, Ret., Stackpole Books, Harrisburg, PA, 1989. 672 pp., illus. $89.95

The definitive book on the Marlin Firearms Co. and their products.

Martini-Henry .450 Rifles & Carbines, by Dennis Lewis, Excalibur Publications, Latham, NY, 1996. 72 pp., illus. Paper covers. $11.95

The stories of the rifles and carbines that were the mainstay of the British soldier through the Victorian wars.

Mauser Bolt Rifles, by Ludwig Olson, F. Brownell & Son, Inc., Montezuma, IA, 1999. 364 pp., illus. $64.95

The most complete, detailed, authoritative and comprehensive work ever done on Mauser bolt rifles. Completely revised deluxe 3rd edition.

Mauser Military Rifle Markings, by Terence W. Lapin, Arlington, VA, Hyrax Publishers, LLC, 2001. 167 pp., illus. 2nd edition. Revised and expanded. Softcover. $22.95

A general guide to reading and understanding the often mystifying markings found on military Mauser rifles. Includes German Regimental markings as well as German police markings and WWII German Mauser subcontractor codes. A handy reference to take to gun shows.

Military Holsters of World War II, by Eugene J. Bender, Rowe Publications, Rochester, NY, 1998. 200 pp., illus. $49.95

A revised edition with a new price guide of the most definitive book on this subject.

Military Remington Rolling Block Rifle, The, by George Layman, Pioneer Press, TN, 1998. 146 pp., illus. Paper covers. $24.95

A standard reference for those with an interest in the Remington rolling block family of firearms.

Mortimer, the Gunmakers, 1753-1923, by H. Lee Munson, Andrew Mowbray Inc., Lincoln, RI, 1992. 320 pp., illus. $65.00

Seen through a single, dominant, English gunmaking dynasty, this fascinating study provides a window into the classical era of firearms artistry.

Mossberg Sporting Firearms: Dates of Manufacture, by D.R. Morse, Phoenix, AZ, Firing Pin Enterprizes, 2003. Softcover. NEW. $6.95

Covers their pistols, revolvers, rifles, shotguns and commemoratives, plus models and serial numbers.

MP38, 40, 40/1 & 41 Submachine Gun, by de Vries & Martens. Propaganda Photo Series, Volume II. Alexandria, VA, Ironside International, 2001. 1st edition. 150 pp., illustrated with 200 high quality b&w photos. Hardcover. $34.95

Covers all essential information on history and development, ammunition and accessories, codes and markings, and contains photos of nearly every model and accessory. Includes a unique selection of original German WWII propaganda photos, most never published before.

Navy Luger, by Joachim Gortz and John Walter, Handgun Press, Glenview, IL, 1988. 128 pp., illus. $24.95

The 9mm Pistole 1904 and the Imperial German Navy. A concise illustrated history.

New World of Russian Small Arms and Ammunition, by Charlie Cutshaw, Paladin Press, Boulder, CO, 1998. 160 pp., illus. $42.95
Detailed descriptions, specifications and first-class illustrations of the AN-94, PSS silent pistol, Bizon SMG, Saifa-12 tactical shotgun, the GP-25 grenade launcher and more cutting edge Russian weapons.

Number 5 Jungle Carbine, by Alan M. Petrillo, Excalibur Publications, Latham, NY, 1994. 32 pp., illus. Paper covers. $7.95
A comprehensive treatment of the rifle that collectors have come to call the "Jungle Carbine"– the Lee-Enfield Number 5, Mark 1.

Observations on Colt's Second Contract, November 2, 1847, by G. Maxwell Longfield and David T. Basnett, Museum Restoration Service, Bloomfield, Ontario, Canada, 1997. 36 pp., illus. Paper covers. $6.95
This study traces the history and the construction of the Second Model Colt Dragoon supplied in 1848 to the U.S. Cavalry.

Official Soviet SVD Manual, The, by Major James F. Gebhardt (Ret.), Paladin Press, Boulder, CO, 1999. 112 pp., illus. Paper covers. $22.00
Operating instructions for the 7.62mm Dragunov, the first Russian rifle developed from scratch specifically for sniping.

Ordnance Tools, Accessories & Appendages of the M1 Rifle, by Billy Pyle. Houston, TX, privately printed, 2002. 2nd edition. 206 pp., illustrated with b&w photos. Softcover $40.00

OSS Special Weapons II, by John Brunner, Williamstown, NJ, Phillips Publications, 2005, 2nd edition. 276pp. profusely illustrated with photos, some in color. Hardcover, New in New DJ. $59.95

P-08 Parabellum Luger Automatic Pistol, The, edited by J. David McFarland, Desert Publications, Cornville, AZ, 1982. 20 pp., illus. Paper covers. $11.95
Covers every facet of the Luger, plus a listing of all known Luger models.

Packing Iron, by Richard C. Rattenbury, Zon International Publishing, Millwood, NY, 1993. 216 pp., illus. $45.00
The best book yet produced on pistol holsters and rifle scabbards. Over 300 variations of holster and scabbards are illustrated in large, clear plates.

Painted Steel, Steel Pots Volume 2, by Chris Armold, Bender Publishing, San Jose, CA, 2001. 384 pp.-1,053 photos, hundreds in color. $57.95
From the author of ***Steel Pots: The History of America's Steel Combat Helmets*** comes ***Painted Steel: Steel Pots, Vol. II.*** This companion volume features detailed chapters on painted and unit marked helmets of WWI and WWII, plus a variety of divisional, regimental and subordinate markings. Special full-color plates detail subordinate unit markings such as the tactical markings used by the U.S. 2nd Division in WWI.

Parker Gun Catalog 1900, by Parker Brothers, Davis, IL: Old Reliable Publishing, 1996. Reprint. One of the most attractive and sought-after of the Parker gun catalogs, this one shows the complete Parker line circa 1900. This is the only catalog which pictures EH and NH grades, and is the first to picture $50.00 VH grade. A deluxe reprint, 15pp., illustrated. Stiff Paper Covers. Fine. $10.00

Parker Gun Catalog 1910, by Parker Brothers, Davis, IL: Old Reliable Publishing, 1996. Reprint. One of the most attractive and sought-after of the Parker gun catalogs, this one shows the complete Parker line circa 1910. A deluxe reprint, 20pp., illustrated. Stiff Paper Covers. Fine. $10.00

Parker Gun Catalog 1913 (Flying Ducks), by Parker Brothers, Davis, IL: Old Reliable Publishing, 1996. 36pp., illustrated. Stiff Paper Covers. Fine. $20.00
One of the most attractive and sought-after of the Parker gun catalogs, this one shows the complete Parker line circa 1913. A deluxe reprint, it has the same embossed cover as the original "Flying Ducks" catalog.

Pattern Dates for British Ordnance Small Arms, 1718-1783, by DeWitt Bailey, Thomas Publications, Gettysburg, PA, 1997. 116 pp., illus. Paper covers. $20.00
The weapons discussed in this work are those carried by troops sent to North America between 1737 and 1783, or shipped to them as replacement arms while in America.

Percussion Ammunition Packets 1845-1888 Union, Confederate & European, by John J. Malloy, Dean S. Thomas and Terry A. White with Foreward by Norm Flayderman. Gettysburg, PA, Thomas Publications, 2003. 1st edition. 134 pp., illustrated with color photos. Hardcover. New. $75.00
Finally a means to recognize the untold variety of labeled types of ammunition box labels.

Peters & King, by Thomas D. Schiffer. Krause Publications, Iola, WI 2002. 1st edition. 256 pp., 200+ b&w photos with a 32-page color section. Hardcover. $44.95
Discover the history behind Peters Cartridge and King Powder and see how they shaped the arms industry into what it is today and why their products fetch hundreds, even thousands of dollars at auctions. Current values are provided for their highly collectible product packaging and promotional advertising premiums such as powder kegs, tins, cartridge boxes, and calendars.

Presentation and Commercial Colt Walker Pistols, by Col. Robert D. Whittington III. Hooks, TX, Brownlee Books, 2005. A limited edition of 1,000 copies. Numbered. 21 pp. Paper covers. New. $15.00
A study of events at the Whitneyville Armoury and Samuel Colt's Hartford Factory from 1 June 1847 to 29 November 1848.

Presentation and Commercial Colt Walker Pistols, 2nd Revision, by Col. Robert D. Whittington III. Hooks, TX, Brownlee Books, 2006. A limited edition of 1,000 copies. Numbered. 26 pp. Paper covers. New. $20.00
A study of events at the Whitneyville Armoury and Samuel Colt's Hartford Factory from 1 June 1847 to 29 November 1848. Updated.

Price Guide: Orders and Decorations Germany, 1871-1945, Second Edition, by Klaus Lubbe, Germany, Niemann,2004. 2nd edition. German and English text. 817 pages, over 2,000 photos. Hardcover. NEW. $104.95
It is a reference for prices as well as on the differences between the various orders, decorations, award documents, award cases of issue, and miniatures. No fantasy pieces are included, or projected orders which were never realized.

Proud Promise: French Autoloading Rifles, 1898-1979, by Jean Huon, Collector Grade Publications, Inc., Cobourg, Ont., Canada, 1995. 216 pp., illus. $39.95
The author has finally set the record straight about the importance of French contributions to modern arms design.

Purdey Gun and Rifle Makers: The Definitive History, by Donald Dallas, Quiller Press, London, 2000. 245 pp., illus. Color throughout. A limited edition of 3,000 copies. Signed and numbered. With a PURDEY book plate. $99.95

Queen Anne Pistol, 1660-1780: A History of the Turn-Off Pistol, by John W. Burgoyne, Bloomfield, Ont., Canada, Museum Restoration Service, 2002. 1st edition-Historical Arms New Series No. 1. 120 pp. Pictorial hardcover. $35.00
A detailed, fast moving, thoroughly researched text and almost 200 cross-referenced illustrations.

Recreating the 18th Century Powder Horn, by Scott and Cathy Sibley, Texarkana, TX, Scurlock Publishing, 2005. 1st edition. 91 pages. Softcover. NEW. $19.95
Scott and Cathy Sibley demonstrates every detail and secret of recreating an 18th century powder horn. New and experienced horn makers will enjoy this how-to book. Lavishly illustrated wtih full-color photos and step-by-step illustrations.

Red Shines The Sun: A Pictorial History of the Fallschirm-Infantrie, by Eric Queen. San Jose, CA, R. James Bender Publishing, 2003. 1st edition. Hardcover. $69.95
A culmination of 12 years of research, this reference work traces the history of the Army paratroopers of the Fallschirm-Infanterie from their origins in 1937, to the expansion to battalion strength in 1938, then on through operations at Wola Gulowska (Poland), and Moerdijk (Holland). This 240-page comprehensive look at their history is supported by 600 images, many of which are in full color, and nearly 90% are previously unpublished.

Reloading Tools, Sights and Telescopes for Single Shot Rifles, by Gerald O. Kelver, Brighton, CO, 1982. 163 pp., illus. Paper covers. $13.95
A listing of most of the famous makers of reloading tools, sights and telescopes with a brief description of the products they manufactured.

Remington-Lee Rifle, by Eugene F. Myszkowski, Excalibur Publications, Latham, NY, 1995. 100 pp., illus. Paper covers. $22.50
Features detailed descriptions, including serial number ranges, of each model from the first Lee magazine rifle produced for the U.S. Navy to the last Remington-Lee small bore shipped to the Cuban Rural Guard.

Remington 'America's Oldest Gunmaker', The Official Authorized History of the Remington Arms Company, by Roy Marcot. Madison, NC, Remington Arms Company, 1999. 1st edition. 312 pp., with 167 b&w illustrations, plus 291 color plates. $79.95
This is without a doubt the finest history of that firm ever to have been compiled. Based on firsthand research in the Remington company archives, it is extremely well written.

Remington Sporting Firearms: Dates of Manufacture, by D.R. Morse, Phoenix, AZ, Firing Pin Enterprizes, 2003. 43 pp. Softcover. New. $6.95
Covers their pistols, revolvers, rifles, shotguns and commemoratives, plus models and serial numbers.

Remington's Vest Pocket Pistols, by Robert E. Hatfield, Lincoln, RI, Andrew Mowbray, Inc., 2002. 117 pp. Hardcover. $29.95
While Remington Vest Pocket pistols have always been popular with collectors, very little solid information has been available about them. Inside you will find 100+ photographs, serial number data, exploded views of all four Remington Vest Pocket pistol sizes, component parts lists and a guide to disassembly and

reassembly. Also includes a discussion of Vest Pocket Wire-Stocked Buggy/Bicycle rifles, plus the documented serial number story.

Revolvers of the British Services 1854-1954, by W.H.J. Chamberlain and A.W.F. Taylerson, Museum Restoration Service, Ottawa, Canada, 1989. 80 pp., illus. $27.50

Covers the types issued among many of the United Kingdom's naval, land or air services.

Rifles of the U.S. Army 1861-1906, by John D. McAulay, Andrew Mowbray, Inc., Lincoln, RI, 2003. 1st edition. Over 40 rifles covered, 278 pp., illus. Hardcover. New. $47.95

This exciting new book by renowned authority John McAulay gives the reader detailed coverage of the issue and actual field service of America's fighting rifles, both in peacetime and in war, including their military service with the infantry, artillery, cavalry and engineers. One feature that all readers will value is the impressive number of historical photos, taken during the Civil War, the Mexican War, the Indian Wars, the Spanish-American War, the Philippine Insurrection and more. Procurement information, issue details and historical background.

Ruger and his Guns, by R.L. Wilson, Book Sales, New York, NY, 2006. 358 pp., illus. $24.95

A history of the man, the company and their firearms.

Running Recon: A photo Jorney with SOG Special Ops Along the Ho Chi Minh Trail, by Frank Grecco. Boulder, CO: Paladin Press, 2006. Softcover. NEW. $50.00

Running Recon is a combination of military memoir and combat photography book. It reflects both the author's experience in Kontum, Vietnam, from April 1969 to April 1970 as part of the top-secret Studies and Observation Group (SOG) and the collective experience of SOG veterans in general.

Russell M. Catron and His Pistols, by Warren H. Buxton, Ucross Books, Los Alamos, NM, 1998. 224 pp., illus. Paper covers. $49.50

An unknown American firearms inventor and manufacturer of the mid-twentieth century. Military, commerical, ammunition.

SAFN-49 and the FAL, by Joe Poyer and Dr. Richard Feirman, North Cape Publications, Tustin, CA, 1998. 160 pp., illus. Paper covers. $14.95

The first complete overview of the SAFN-49 battle rifle, from its pre-WWII beginnings to its military service in countries as diverse as the Belgian Congo and Argentina. The FAL was a "light" version of the SAFN-49 and it became the Free World's most adopted battle rifle.

Sash Hook Smith & Wesson Revolvers, The, by Col. Robert D. Whittington III. & and Kolman A. Gabel, Hooks, TX, Brownlee Books, 2003. A limited edition of 1,000 copies. Numbered. 10 pp. Paper covers. New. $10.00

The true story of the Sash Hook Smith & Wesson Revolvers and how they came to be.

Savage Sporting Firearms: Dates of Manufacture 1907-1997, by D.R. Morse. Phoenix, AZ, Firing Pin Enterprizes, 2003. 22 pp. Softcover. New. $6.95

Covers their pistols, revolvers, rifles, shotguns and commemoratives, plus models and serial numbers.

Scottish Firearms, by Claude Blair and Robert Woosnam-Savage, Museum Restoration Service, Bloomfield, Ont., Canada, 1995. 52 pp., illus. Paper covers. $8.95

This revision of the first book devoted entirely to Scottish firearms is supplemented by a register of surviving Scottish long guns.

Sharps Firearms, by Frank Seller, Denver, CO, 1998. 358 pp., illus. $65.00

Traces the development of Sharps firearms with full range of guns made including all martial variations.

Sight Book; Winchester, Lyman, Marble, and Other Companies, by George Madis, Borwsboro,TX, Art & Reference House, 2005. 1st edition. 183 pages, with over 350 illustrations. Hardcover. NEW. $26.95

Silk and Steel: Women at Arms, by R. L. Wilson, New York, Random House, 2003. 1st edition. 300+ Striking four-color images; 8½" x 11", 320 pgs. Hardcover. New in new dust jacket. (9775). $65.00

Beginning with Artemis and Diana, goddesses of hunting, evolving through modern times, here is the first comprehensive presentation on the subject of women and firearms. No object has had a greater impact on world history over the past 650 years than the firearm, and a surprising number of women have been keen on the subject, as shooters, hunters, collectors, engravers, and even gunmakers.

SKS Carbine, by Steve Kehaya and Joe Poyer, North Cape Publications, Tustin, CA, 1997. 150 pp., illus. Paper covers. $16.95

The first comprehensive examination of a major historical firearm used through the Vietnam conflict to the diamond fields of Angola.

SKS Type 45 Carbines, by Duncan Long, Desert Publications, El Dorado, AZ, 1992. 110 pp., illus. Paper covers. $19.95

Covers the history and practical aspects of operating, maintaining and modifying this abundantly available rifle.

Slave Badges and the Slave-Hire System in Charleston, South Carolina, 1783-1865, by Harlan Greene, Harry S. Hutchins Jr., Brian E. Hutchins. Jefferson, NC, McFarland & Company, 2004. 152 pp. Hardcover, NEW. $35.00

Smith & Wesson 1857-1945, by Robert J. Neal and Roy G. Jinks, R&R Books, Livonia, NY, 1996. 434 pp., illus. $50.00

The bible for all existing and aspiring Smith & Wesson collectors.

Smith & Wesson Sporting Firearms: Dates of Manufacture, by D.R. Morse, Phoenix, AZ, Firing Pin Enterprizes, 2003. 76 pp. Softcover. NEW. $6.95

Covers their pistols, revolvers, rifles, shotguns and commemoratives, plus models and serial numbers.

Sniper Variations of the German K98k Rifle, by Richard D. Law, Collector Grade Publications, Ontario, Canada, 1997. 240 pp., illus. $47.50

Volume 2 of "Backbone of the Wehrmacht" the author's in-depth study of the German K98k rifle. This volume concentrates on the telescopic-sighted rifle of choice for most German snipers during WWII.

Southern Derringers of the Mississippi Valley, by Turner Kirkland, Pioneer Press, Tenn., 1971. 80 pp., illus., paper covers. $10.00

A guide for the collector and a much-needed study.

Soviet Russian Tokarev "TT" Pistols and Cartridges 1929-1953, by Fred Datig, Graphic Publishers, Santa Ana, CA, 1993. 168 pp., illus. $39.95

Details of rare arms and their accessories are shown in hundreds of photos. It also contains a complete bibliography and index.

Spencer Repeating Firearms, by Roy M. Marcot, New York, Rowe Publications, 2002. 316 pp.; numerous b&w photos and illustrations. Hardcover. $65.00

Springfield 1903 Rifles, by Lt. Col. William S. Brophy, USAR, Ret., Stackpole Books Inc., Harrisburg, PA, 1985. 608 pp., illus. $75.00

The illustrated, documented story of the design, development, and production of all the models, appendages, and accessories.

SS Headgear, by Kit Wilson. Johnson Reference Books, Fredericksburg, VA. 72 pp., 15 full-color plates and over 70 b&w photos. $16.50

An excellent source of information concerning all types of SS headgear, to include Allgemeine-SS, Waffen-SS, visor caps, helmets, overseas caps, M-43's and miscellaneous headgear. Also includes a guide on the availability and current values of SS headgear. This guide was compiled from auction catalogs, dealer price lists, and input from advanced collectors in the field.

SS Helmets: A Collector's Guide, Vol 1, by Kelly Hicks, Johnson Reference Books, Fredericksburg, VA. 96 pp., illus. $17.50

Deals only with SS helmets and features some very nice color close-up shots of the different SS decals used. Over 85 photographs, 27 in color. The author has documented most of the known types of SS helmets, and describes in detail all of the vital things to look for in determining the originality, style type, and finish.

SS Helmets: A Collector's Guide, Vol 2, by Kelly Hicks. Johnson Reference Books, Fredericksburg, VA. 2000. 128 pp. 107 full-color photos, 14 period photos. $25.00

Volume II contains dozen of highly detailed, full-color photos of rare and original SS and Field Police helmets, featuring both sides as well as interior view. The outstanding decal section offers detailed close-ups of original SS and Police decals and, in conjunction with Volume I, completes the documentation of virtually all types of original decal variations used between 1934 and 1945.

SS Uniforms, Insignia and Accoutrements, by A. Hayes. Schiffer Publications, Atglen, PA. 1996. 248 pp., with over 800 color and b&w photographs. $69.95

This new work explores in detailed color the complex subject of Allgemeine and Waffen-SS uniforms, insignia, and accoutrements. Hundreds of authentic items are extensively photographed in close-up to enable the reader to examine and study.

Sturmgewehr! From Firepower to Striking Power, by Hans-Dieter Handrich. Canada, Collector Grade, 2004. 1st edition. 600pp., 392 illustrations. Hardcover $79.95

Hans-Dieter spent years researching original documentation held in the military archives of Germany and elsewhere to produce the entire technical and tactical history of the design, development and fielding of the world's first mass-produced assault rifle and the revolutionary 7.92x33mm Kurz cartridge.

Sturm Ruger Sporting Firearms: Dates of Manufacture, by D.R. Morse, Phoenix, AZ, Firing Pin Enterprizes, 2003. 22 pp. Softcover, NEW. $6.95

Covers their pistols, revolvers, rifles, shotguns and commemoratives, plus models and serial numbers.

Sumptuous Flaske, by Herbert G. Houze, Andrew Mowbray, Inc., Lincoln, RI, 1989. 158 pp., illus. Softcover. $35.00

Catalog of a recent show at the Buffalo Bill Historical Center bringing together some of the finest European and American powder flasks of the 16th to 19th centuries.

Swedish Mauser Rifles, The, by Steve Kehaya and Joe Poyer, North Cape Publications, Tustin, CA, 1999. 267 pp., illus. Paper covers. $19.95

Every known variation of the Swedish Mauser carbine and rifle is described, all match and target rifles and all sniper versions. Includes serial number and production data.

System Lefaucheaux: Continuing the Study of Pinfire Cartridge Arms Including Their Role in the American Civil War, by Chris C. Curtis, Foreword by Norm Flayderman, Armslore Press, 2002. 1st edition. 312 pp., heavily illustrated with b&w photos. Hardcover. New in new dust jacket. $44.95

Thoughts on the Kentucky Rifle in its Golden Age, by Joe K. Kindig, III. York, PA, George Shumway Publisher, 2002. Annotated second edition. 561 pp.; Illustrated. This scarce title, long out of print, is once again available. Hardcover. $85.00

The definitive book on the Kentucky Rifle, illustrating 266 of these guns in 856 detailed photographs.

Tin Lids–Canadian Combat Helmets, #2 in "Up Close" Series, by Roger V. Lucy, Ottawa, Ontario, Service Publications, 2000. 2nd edition. 48 pp. Softcover. NEW. $17.95

Toys That Shoot and Other Neat Stuff, by James Dundas, Schiffer Books, Atglen, PA, 1999. 112 pp., illus. Paper covers. $24.95

Shooting toys from the twentieth century, especially 1920s to 1960s, in over 420 color photographs of BB guns, cap shooters, marble shooters, squirt guns and more. Complete with a price guide.

Trade Guns of the Hudson's Bay Company 1670-1970, Historical Arms New Series No. 2, by S. James Gooding, Bloomfield, Ont. Canada, Museum Restoration Service, 2003. 1st edition. 158 pp., thoroughly researched text. Includes bibliographical references. Pictorial hardcover. NEW. $35.00

Trapdoor Springfield, by M.D. Waite and B.D. Ernst, The Gun Room Press, Highland Park, NJ, 1983. 250 pp., illus. $39.95

The first comprehensive book on the famous standard military rifle of the 1873-92 period.

Treasures of the Moscow Kremlin: Arsenal of the Russian Tsars, A Royal Armories and the Moscow Kremlin exhibition, HM Tower of London 13, June 1998 to 11 September, 1998, BAS Printers, Over Wallop, Hampshire, England. XXII plus 192 pp. over 180 color illustrations. Text in English and Russian. $65.00

For this exhibition catalog, each of the 94 objects on display are photographed and described in detail to provide the most informative record of this important exhibition.

U.S. Army Headgear 1812-1872, by John P. Langellier and C. Paul Loane. Atglen, PA, Schiffer Publications, 2002. 167 pp., with over 350 color and b&w photos. Hardcover. $69.95

This profusely illustrated volume represents more than three decades of research in public and private collections by military historian John P. Langellier and Civil War authority C. Paul Loane.

U.S. Army Rangers & Special Forces of World War II Their War in Photographs, by Robert Todd Ross, Atglen, PA, Schiffer Publications, 2002. 216 pp., over 250 b&w and color photographs. Hardcover. $59.95

Never before has such an expansive view of WWII elite forces been offered in one volume. An extensive search of public and private archives unearthed an astonishing number of rare and never before seen images, including color. Most notable are the nearly 20 exemplary photographs of Lieutenant Colonel William O. Darby's Ranger Force in Italy, taken by Robert Capa, considered by many to be the greatest combat photographer of all time.

U.S. Guns of World War II, by Paul Davies, Gettysburg, PA, Thomas Publications, 2004. 1st edition. A record of army ordnance research and the development of small arms. Hundreds of photos. 144pp, Softcover. NEW. $17.95

U.S. Handguns of World War II: The Secondary Pistols and Revolvers, by Charles W. Pate, Andrew Mowbray, Inc., Lincoln, RI, 1998. 515 pp., illus. $39.00

This indispensable new book covers all of the American military handguns of WWII except for the M1911A1 Colt automatic.

U.S. Martial Single Shot Pistols, by Daniel D. Hartzler and James B. Whisker, Old Bedford Village Press, Bedford, PA, 1998. 128 pp., illus. $45.00

A photographic chronicle of military and semi-martial pistols supplied to the U.S. Government and the several States.

U.S. Military Arms Dates of Manufacture from 1795, by George Madis, Dallas, TX, 1995. 64 pp. Softcover. $9.95

Lists all U.S. military arms of collector interest alphabetically, covering about 250 models.

U.S. Naval Handguns, 1808-1911, by Fredrick R. Winter, Andrew Mowbray Publishers, Lincoln, RI, 1990. 128 pp., illus. $26.00

The story of U.S. Naval handguns spans an entire century–included are sections on each of the important naval handguns within the period.

U.S. Silent Service-Dolphins & Combat Insignia 1924-1945, by David Jones. Bender Publishing, San Jose, CA, 2001. 224 pp., 532 photos (most in full color). $39.95

This beautiful full-color book chronicles, with period letters and sketches, the developmental history of U.S. submarine insignia prior to 1945. It also contains many rare and never before published photographs, plus interviews with WWII submarine veterans, from enlisted men to famous skippers. All known contractors are covered plus embroidered versions, mess dress variations, the Roll of Honor, submarine combat insignia, battleflags, launch memorabilia and related submarine collectibles (postal covers, match book covers, jewelry, posters, advertising art, postcards.

Uniform and Dress Army and Navy of the Confederate States of America (Official Regulations), by Confederate States of America, Ray Riling Arms Books, Philadelphia, PA, 1960. $20.00

A portfolio containing a complete set of nine color plates especially prepared for framing, reproduced in exactly 200 sets from the very rare Richmond, VA., 1861 regulations.

Uniforms & Equipment of the Austro-Hungarian Army in World War One, by Spencer A. Coil, Atglen, PA, Schiffer Publications, 2003. 1st edition. 352 pp., with over 550 b&w and color photographs. Hardcover. New in new dust jacket. $69.95

Uniforms and Insignia of the Cossacks in the German Wehrmacht in World War II, by Peter Schuster and Harald Tiede, Atglen, PA, Schiffer Publications, 2003. 1st edition. 160 pp., illustrated with over 420 b&w and color photographs. Hardcover. New in new dust jacket. $49.95

Uniforms & Equipment of the Imperial German Army 1900-1918: A Study in Period Photographs, by Charles Woolley, Schiffer Publications, Atglen, PA, 2000. 375 pp., over 500 b&w photographs and 50 color drawings. Fully illustrated. $69.95

Features formal studio portraits of pre-war dress and wartime uniforms of all arms. Includes a 60-page full-color uniform section reproduced from rare 1914 plates.

Uniforms of the Third Reich: A Study in Photographs, by Maguire Hayes, Schiffer Publications, Atglen, PA, 1997. 200 pp., with over 400 color photographs. $69.95

This new book takes a close look at a variety of authentic WWII era German uniforms including examples from the Army, Luftwaffe, Kriegsmarine, Waffen-SS, Allgemeine-SS, Hitler youth and political leaders. Various accoutrements worn with the uniforms are also included to aid the collector.

Uniforms of the United States Army, 1774-1889, by Henry Alexander Ogden, Dover Publishing, Mineola, NY. 1998. 48 pp. of text plus 44 color plates. Softcover. $9.95

A republication of the work published by the quarter-master general, United States army in 1890. A striking collection of lithographs and a marvelous archive of military, social, and costume history portraying the gamut of U.S. Army uniforms from fatigues to full dress, between 1774 and 1889.

Uniforms of the Waffen-SS; Black Service Uniform-LAH Guard Uniform-SS Earth-Grey Service Uniform-Model 1936 Field Service Uniform-1939-1940-1941 Volume 1, by Michael D. Beaver, Schiffer Publications, Atglen, PA, 2002. 272 pp., with 500 color, and b&w photos. $79.95

This spectacular work is a heavily documented record of all major clothing articles of the Waffen-SS. Hundreds of unpublished photographs were used in production. This book is indispensable and an absolute must-have for any serious historian of WWII German uniforms.

Uniforms of the Waffen-SS; Sports and Drill Uniforms-Black Panzer Uniform-Camouflage-Concentration Camp Personnel-SD-SS Female Auxiliaries, Volume 3, by Michael D. Beaver, Schiffer Publications, Atglen, PA, 2002. 272 pp., with 500 color, and b&w photos. $79.95

Uniforms of the Waffen-SS; 1942-1943-1944-1945-Ski Uniforms-Overcoats-White Service Uniforms-Tropical Clothing, Volume 2, by Michael D. Beaver, Schiffer Publications, Atglen, PA, 2002. 272 pp., with 500 color, and b&w photos. $79.95

Uniforms, Organization, and History of the German Police, Volume I, by John R. Angolia and Hugh Page Taylor, San Jose, CA, R. James Bender Publishing, 2004. 704 pp. illustrated with b&w and color photos. Hardcover. NEW. $59.95

United States Marine Corps Uniforms, Insignia, and Personal Items of World War II, by Harlan Glenn Atglen, PA: Schiffer Publications, 2005. 1st edition. 272pp. Hardcover. NEW $79.95

Covering in detail the combat and dress uniforms of the United States Marine in World War II, this new volume is destined to become the World War II Marine Corps collector's reference! Shown in detail are the herringbone utilities that Marines wore from Guadalcanal to Okinawa, as well as Summer Service, Winter Service and Dress (Blues) uniforms.

United States Martial Flintlocks, by Robert M. Reilly, Mowbray Publishing Co., Lincoln, RI, 1997. 264 pp., illus. $40.00
A comprehensive history of American flintlock longarms and handguns (mostly military) c. 1775 to c. 1840.

United States Submachine Guns: From the American 180 to the ZX-7, by Frank Iannamico, Harmony, ME, Moose Lake Publishing, 2004. 1st edition. This profusely illustrated new book covers the research and development of the submachine gun in the U.S. from World War I to the present. to1943. Many photos and charts, nearly 500 pages! Soft cover. NEW. $29.95

Variations of Colt's New Model Police and Pocket Breech Loading Pistols, by John D. Breslin, William Q. Pirie and David E. Price, Lincoln, RI, Andrew Mowbray Publishers, 2002. 1st edition. 158 pp., heavily illustrated with over 160 photographs and superb technical detailed drawings and diagrams. Pictorial hardcover. $37.95
A type-by-type guide to what collectors call small frame conversions.

Vietnam Order of Battle, by Shelby L. Stanton, William C. Westmoreland. Mechanicsburg, PA, Stackpole Books, 2003. 1st edition. 416 pp., 32 in full color, 101 pp. halftones. Hardcover. New in new dust jacket. $69.95

Visor Hats of the United States Armed Forces 1930-1950, by Joe Tonelli, Atglen, PA, Schiffer Publications, 2003. 1st edition. Hardcover. New in new dust jacket. $79.95

W.F. Cody Buffalo Bill Collector's Guide with Values, The, by James W. Wojtowicz, Collector Books, Paducah, KY, 1998. 271 pp., illus. $24.95
A profusion of colorful collectibles including lithographs, programs, photographs, books, medals, sheet music, guns, etc. and today's values.

Walther: A German Legend, by Manfred Kersten, Safari Press, Inc., Huntington Beach, CA, 2000. 400 pp., illus. $85.00
This comprehensive book covers, in rich detail, all aspects of the company and its guns, including an illustrious and rich history, the WWII years, all the pistols (models 1 through 9), the P-38, P-88, the long guns, 22 rifles, centerfires, Wehrmacht guns, and even a gun that could shoot around a corner.

Walther P-38 Pistol, by Maj. George Nonte, Desert Publications, Cornville, AZ, 1982. 100 pp., illus. Paper covers. $12.95
Complete volume on one of the most famous handguns to come out of WWII. All models covered.

Walther Pistols: Models 1 Through P99, Factory Variations and Copies, by Dieter H. Marschall, Ucross Books, Los Alamos, NM. 2000. 140 pp., with 140 b&w illustrations, index. Paper covers. $19.95
This is the English translation, revised and updated, of the highly successful and widely acclaimed German language edition. This book provides the collector with a reference guide and overview of the entire line of the Walther military, police, and self-defense pistols from the very first to the very latest. Models 1-9, PP, PPK, MP, AP, HP, P.38, P1, P4, P38K, P5, P88, P99 and the Manurhin models. Variations, where issued, serial ranges, calibers, marks, proofs, logos, and design aspects in an astonishing quantity and variety are crammed into this very well researched and highly regarded work.

Walther Models PP & PPK, 1929-1945 - Volume 1, by James L. Rankin, Coral Gables, FL, 1974. 142 pp., illus. $40.00
Complete coverage on the subject as to finish, proofmarks and Nazi Party inscriptions.

Walther Volume II, Engraved, Presentation and Standard Models, by James L. Rankin, J.L. Rankin, Coral Gables, FL, 1977. 112 pp., illus. $40.00
The new Walther book on embellished versions and standard models. Has 88 photographs, including many color plates.

Walther, Volume III, 1908-1980, by James L. Rankin, Coral Gables, FL, 1981. 226 pp., illus. $40.00
Covers all models of Walther handguns from 1908 to date, includes holsters, grips and magazines.

Winchester an American Legend, by R.L. Wilson, New York, Book Sales, 2004. Reprint. Hardcover. New in new dust jacket. $24.95

Winchester Bolt Action Military & Sporting Rifles 1877 to 1937, by Herbert G. Houze, Andrew Mowbray Publishing, Lincoln, RI, 1998. 295 pp., illus. $45.00
Winchester was the first American arms maker to commercially manufacture a bolt action repeating rifle, and this book tells the exciting story of these Winchester bolt actions.

Winchester Book, by George Madis, David Madis Gun Book Distributor, Dallas, TX, 2000. 650 pp., illus. $54.50
A new, revised 25th anniversary edition of this classic book on Winchester firearms. Complete serial ranges have been added.

Winchester Dates of Manufacture 1849-1984, by George Madis, Art & Reference House, Brownsboro, TX, 1984. 59 pp. $8.50
A most useful work, compiled from records of the Winchester factory.

Winchester Engraving, by R.L. Wilson, Beinfeld Books, Springs, CA, 1989. 500 pp., illus. $185.00
A classic reference work of value to all arms collectors.

Winchester Handbook, The, by George Madis, Art & Reference House, Lancaster, TX, 1982. 287 pp., illus. $26.95
The complete line of Winchester guns, with dates of manufacture, serial numbers, etc.

Winchester Lever Action Repeating Firearms, Vol. 1, The Models of 1866, 1873 and 1876, by Arthur Pirkle, North Cape Publications, Tustin, CA, 1995. 112 pp., illus. Paper covers. $19.95
Complete, part-by-part description, including dimensions, finishes, markings and variations throughout the production run of these fine, collectible guns.

Winchester Lever Action Repeating Rifles, Vol. 2, The Models of 1886 and 1892, by Arthur Pirkle, North Cape Publications, Tustin, CA, 1996. 150 pp., illus. Paper covers. $19.95
Describes each model on a part-by-part basis by serial number range complete with finishes, markings and changes.

Winchester Lever Action Repeating Rifles, Vol. 3, The Model of 1894, by Arthur Pirkle, North Cape Publications, Tustin, CA, 1998. 150 pp., illus. Paper covers. $19.95
The first book ever to provide a detailed description of the Model 1894 rifle and carbine.

Winchester Lever Legacy, The, by Clyde "Snooky" Williamson, Buffalo Press, Zachary, LA, 1988. 664 pp., illus. $75.00
A book on reloading for the different calibers of the Winchester lever action rifle.

Winchester Model 1876 "Centennial" Rifle, The, by Herbert G. Houze. Lincoln, RI, Andrew Mowbray, Inc., 2001. Illustrated with over 180 b&w photographs. 192 pp. Hardcover. $45.00
The first authoritative study of the Winchester Model 1876 written using the company's own records. This book dispels the myth that the Model 1876 was merely a larger version of the Winchester company's famous Model 1873 and instead traces its true origins to designs developed immediately after the American Civil War. For Winchester collectors, and those interested in the mechanics of the 19th-century arms industry, this book provides a wealth of previously unpublished information.

Winchester Pocket Guide: Identification & Pricing for 50 Collectible Rifles and Shotguns, by Ned Schwing, Iola, WI, Krause Publications, 2004. 1st edition. 224 pp., illus. Softcover. NEW. $12.95

Winchester Repeating Arms Company Its History & Development from 1865 to 1981, by Herbert G. Houze, Iola, WI, Krause Publications, 2004. 1st edition. Softcover. NEW. $34.98

Winchester Single-Shot, Volume 1; A History and Analysis, The, by John Campbell, Andrew Mowbray, Inc., Lincoln, RI, 1995. 272 pp., illus. $55.00
Covers every important aspect of this highly-collectible firearm.

Winchester Single-Shot, Volume 2; Old Secrets and New Discoveries, The, by John Campbell, Andrew Mowbray, Inc., Lincoln, RI, 2000. 280 pp., illus. $55.00
An exciting follow-up to the classic first volume.

Winchester Sporting Firearms: Dates of Manufacture, by D.R. Morse, Phoenix, AZ, Firing Pin Enterprizes, 2003. 45 pp. Softcover. NEW. $6.95
Covers their pistols, revolvers, rifles, shotguns and commemoratives, plus models and serial numbers.

Winchester-Lee Rifle, The, by Eugene Myszkowski, Excalibur Publications, Tucson, AZ 2000. 96 pp., illus. Paper covers. $22.95
The development of the Lee Straight Pull, the cartridge and the approval for military use. Covers details of the inventor and memorabilia of Winchester-Lee related material.

World War One Collectors Handbook Volumes 1 and 2, by Paul Schulz, Hayes Otoupalik and Dennis Gordon, Missoula, MT, privately printed, 2002. Two volumes in one edition. 110 pp., loaded with b&w photos. Softcover. NEW. $21.95
Covers, uniforms, insignia, equipment, weapons, souvenirs and miscellaneous. Includes price guide. For all of you Doughboy collectors, this is a must.

World War II German War Booty, A Study in Photographs, by Thomas M. Johnson, Atglen, PA, Schiffer Publications, 2003. 1st edition. 368 pp. Hardcover. New in new dust jacket. $79.95

Worldwide Webley and the Harrington and Richardson Connection, by Stephen Cuthbertson, Ballista Publishing and Distributing Ltd., Gabriola Island, Canada, 1999. 259 pp., illus. $50.00
A masterpiece of scholarship. Over 350 photographs plus 75 original documents, patent drawings, and advertisements accompany the text.

World's Great Handguns: From 1450 to the Present Day, The, by Roger Ford, Secaucus, NJ, Chartwell Books, Inc., 1997. 1st edition. 176 pp. Hardcover. New in new dust jacket. $19.95

Edged Weapons

A Photographic Supplement of Confederate Swords, with addendum, by William A. Albaugh III, Broadfoot Publishing, Wilmington, NC. 1999. 205 plus 54 pp. of the addendum, illustrated with b&w photos. $45.00

Advanced Bowie Techniques: The Finer Points of Fighting with a Large Knife, by Dwight McLemore, Boulder, CO, Paladin Press, 2005. 1st edition. 248 pp. Soft cover. NEW. $35.00

Progressive drills combine techniques into sequences designed to show you how to maximize time, distance and movement to create openings for attacking or defending yourself against one or more opponents.

Advertising Cutlery; With Values, by Richard White, Schiffer Publishing, Ltd., Atglen, PA, 176 pp., with over 400 color photos. Softcover. $29.95

Advertising Cutlery is the first-ever publication to deal exclusively with the subject of promotional knives. Containing over 400 detailed color photographs, this book explores over 100 years of advertisements stamped into the sides of knives.

Allied Military Fighting Knives; And the Men Who Made Them Famous, by Robert A. Buerlein, Paladin Press, Boulder, CO, 2001. 185 pp., illustrated with b&w photos. Softcover. $35.00

American Eagle Pommel Sword: The Early Years 1794-1830, The, by Andrew Mowbray, Manrat Arms Publications, Lincoln, RI, 1997. 244 pp., illus. $65.00

The standard guide to the most popular style of American sword.

American Military Bayonets of the 20th Century, by Gary M. Cunningham, Scott A. Duff Publications, Export, PA, 1997. 116 pp., illus. Paper covers. $21.95

A guide for collectors, including notes on makers, markings, finishes, variations, scabbards, and production data.

American Premium Guide To Knives & Razors; Identification and Value Guide 6th Edition, by Jim Sargent, Iola, WI, Krause Publications, 2004. 504 pp. plus 2,500 b&w photos. Softcover. NEW. $24.99

American Primitive Knives 1770-1870, by G.B. Minnes, Museum Restoration Service, Ottawa, Canada, 1983. 112 pp., illus. $24.95

Origins of the knives, outstanding specimens, structural details, etc.

American Socket Bayonets and Scabbards, by Robert M. Reilly, 2nd printing, Andrew Mowbray, Inc., Lincoln, RI, 1998. 208 pp., illus. $45.00

Full coverage of the socket bayonet in America, from Colonial times through the post-Civil War.

American Sword, 1775-1945, The, by Harold L. Peterson, Ray Riling Arms Books, Co., Phila., PA, 2001. 286 pp. plus 60 pp. of illus. $49.95

1977 reprint of a survey of swords worn by U.S. uniformed forces, plus the rare "American Silver Mounted Swords, (1700-1815)."

American Swords and Sword Makers, by Richard H. Bezdek, Paladin Press, Boulder, CO, 1994. 648 pp., illus. $79.95

The long-awaited definitive reference volume to American swords, sword makers and sword dealers from Colonial times to the present.

American Swords & Sword Makers Volume 2, by Richard H. Bezdek, Paladin Press, Boulder, CO, 1999. 376 pp., illus. $69.95

More than 400 stunning photographs of rare, unusual and one-of-a-kind swords from the top collections in the country.

American Swords from the Philip Medicus Collection, edited by Stuart C. Mowbray, with photographs and an introduction by Norm Flayderman, Andrew Mowbray Publishers, Lincoln, RI, 1998. 272 pp., with 604 swords illustrated. $55.00

Covers all areas of American sword collecting.

Ames Sword Company Catalog: An Exact Reprint of the Original 19th Century Military and Fraternal Sword Catalog, by Stuart C. Mowbray, Lincoln, RI, Andrew Mowbray, Inc., 2003. 1st edition. 200 pp., 541 swords illustrated with original prices and descriptions. Pictorial hardcover. $37.50

The level of detail in these original catalog images will surprise you. Dealers who sold Ames swords used this catalog in their stores, and every feature is clearly shown. Reproduced directly from the incredibly rare originals, military, fraternal and more! Shows the whole Ames line, including swords from the Civil War and even earlier. Lots of related military items like belts, bayonets, etc.

Ames Sword Company, 1829-1935, by John D. Hamilton, Andrew Mowbray Publisher, Lincoln, RI, 1995. 255 pp., illus. $45.00

An exhaustively researched and comprehensive history of America's foremost sword manufacturer and arms supplier during the Civil War.

Antique American Switchblades; Identification & Value Guide, by Mark Erickson, Iola, WI, Krause Publications, 2004. 1st edition. Softcover. NEW. $19.95

Antlers & Iron II, by Krause Publications, Iola, WI, 1999. 40 pp., illustrated with 100 photos. Paper cover. $12.00

Lays out actual plans so you can build your mountain man folding knife using ordinary hand tools. Step-by-step instructions, with photos, design, antler slotting and springs.

Art of Throwing Weapons, by James W. Madden, Paladin Press, Boulder, CO, 1993. 102 pp., illus. $14.00

This comprehensive manual covers everything from the history and development of the five most common throwing weapons–spears, knives, tomahawks, shurikens and boomerangs–to their selection or manufacture, grip, distances, throwing motions and advanced combat methods.

Arte of Defence an Introduction to the Use of the Rapier, by William E. Wilson, Union City, CA, Chivalry Bookshelf, 2002. 1st edition. 167 pp., illustrated with over 300 photographs. Softcover $24.95

Battle Blades: A Professional's Guide to Combat Fighting Knives, by Greg Walker; Foreword by Al Mar, Paladin Press, Boulder, CO, 1993. 168 pp., illus. $40.95

The author evaluates daggers, Bowies, switchblades and utility blades according to their design, performance, reliability and cost.

Bayonet in New France, 1665-1760, by Erik Goldstein, Museum Restoration Service, Bloomfield, Ontario, Canada, 1997. 36 pp., illus. Paper covers. $8.95

Traces bayonets from the recently developed plug bayonet, through the regulation socket bayonets, which saw service in North America.

Bayonets from Janzen's Notebook, by Jerry Jansen, Cedar Ridge Publications, Tulsa, OK, 2000. 6th printing. 258 pp., illus. Hardcover. $45.00

This collection of over 1,000 pieces is one of the largest in the U.S.

Bayonets: An Illustrated History, by Martin J. Brayley, Iola, WI, Krause Publications, 2004. 1st edition 256 pp., illus. Softcover. NEW. $29.95

Bayonets, Knives & Scabbards; United States Army Weapons Report 1917 Thru 1945, edited by Frank Trzaska, Knife Books, Deptford, NJ, 1999. 80 pp., illus. Paper covers. $15.95

Follows the United States edged weapons from the close of WWI through the end of WWII. Manufacturers involved, dates, numbers produced, problems encountered, and production data.

Best of U.S. Military Knives, Bayonets & Machetes, by M.H. Cole, edited by Michael W. Silvey. Privately printed, 2002. Hardcover. New in new dust jacket. $59.95

Blade's Guide to Making Knives, by Joe Kertzman, Iola,WI, Krause Publications,2005. 1st edition. Soft cover. $24.89

Techniques for everything from forging steel to making a tomahawk are covered for the diverse population of knife makers. 160 pages, 250 color illustrations demonstrate expert techniques.

Book of the Sword, The, by Richard F. Burton, Dover Publications, New York, NY, 1987. 199 pp., illus. Paper covers. $12.95

Traces the sword's origin from its birth as a charged and sharpened stick through diverse stages of development.

Borders Away, Volume 1: With Steel, by William Gilkerson, Andrew Mowbray, Inc., Lincoln, RI, 1991. 184 pp., illus. $48.00

A comprehensive study of naval armament under fighting sail. This first volume covers axes, pikes and fighting blades in use from 1626 to 1826.

Borders Away, Volume 2: Firearms of the Age of Fighting Sail, by William Gilkerson, Andrew Mowbray, Inc., Lincoln, RI, 1999. 331 pp., illus. with 200 photos, 16-color plates. $65.00

Completing a two-volume set, this impressive work covers the pistols, muskets, combustibles, and small cannons once employed aboard American and European fighting ships.

Bowie and Big-Knife Fighting System, by Dwight C. McLemore, Boulder, CO, Paladin Press, 2003. 240 pp., illus. Softcover. NEW. $35.00

Bowie Knife: Unsheathing an American Legend, by Norm Flayderman, Lincoln, RI, Andrew Mowbray, Inc., 2004. 1st edition. New in new dust jacket. $79.95

Bowie Knives and Bayonets of the Ben Palmer Collection, 2nd Edition, by Ben Palmer, Bill Moran and Jim Phillips. Williamstown, NJ, Phillips Publications, 2002. 224 pp. Illustrated with photos. Hardcover. $49.95

Vastly expanded with more than 300 makers, distributors and dealers added to the makers list; chapter on the Bowie knife photograph with 50 image photo gallery of knife holders from the Mexican War, Civil War, and the West; contains a chapter on Bowie Law; includes several unpublished Bowie documents, including the first account of the Alamo.

Bowies, Big Knives, and the Best of Battle Blades, by Bill Bagwell, Paladin Press, Boulder, CO. 2001. 184 pp., illus. Paper covers. $30.00
This book binds the timeless observations and invaluable advice of master bladesmith and blade combat expert Bill Bagwell under one cover for the first time. Here, you'll find all of Bagwell's classic SOF columns, plus all-new material linking his early insights with his latest conclusions.

British & Commonwealth Bayonets, by Ian D. Skennerton and Robert Richardson, I.D.S.A. Books, Piqua, OH, 1986. 404 pp., 1300 illus. $40.00

Case Cutler Dynasty, The, by Brad Lockwood, Paducah,KY, Collector Books, 2005. 1st edition. 320 pages. Pictorial hardcover. NEW. $19.95
The Case Cutlery Dynasty shows how history becomes mythology over time, money is sometimes thicker than blood, and how a single family from humble beginnings came to dominate an important American industry.

Civil War Cavalry & Artillery Sabers, 1833-1865, by John H. Thillmann, Andrew Mowbray, Inc. Lincoln, RI, 2002. 1st edition. 500+ pp., over 50 color photographs, 1,373 b&w illustrations, coated paper, dust jacket, premium hardcover binding. Hardcover. $79.95

Clandestine Edged Weapons, by William Windrum, Phillips Publications, Williamstown, NJ, 2001. 74 pp., illustrated with b&w photographs. Pictorial softcover. $9.95

Collecting the Edged Weapons of Imperial Germany, by Johnson & Wittmann, Johnson Reference Books, Fredericksburg, VA, 1989. 363 pp., illus. $39.50
An in-depth study of the many ornate military, civilian, and government daggers and swords of the Imperial era.

Collector's Guide to Ames U.S. Contract Military Edged Weapons: 1832-1906, by Ron G. Hickox, Pioneer Press, Union City, IN, 1993. 70 pp., illus. Paper covers. $17.50
While this book deals primarily with edged weapons made by the Ames Manufacturing Company, this guide refers to other manufacturers of United States swords.

Collector's Guide to E.C. Simmons Keen Kutter Cutlery Tools, by Jerry and Elaine Heuring, Paducah, KY, Collector Books, 2000. 1st edition. 192 pp. Softcover. $19.95

Collector's Guide to Switchblade Knives, an Illustrated Historical and Price Reference, by Richard V. Langston, Paladin Press, Boulder, CO. 2001. 224 pp., illus. $49.95
It has been more than 20 years since a major work on switchblades has been published, and never has one showcased as many different types as Rich Langston's new book. It contains a history of the early cutlery industry in America; the evolution of switchblades; and an illustrated reference section that helps collectors and novices alike identify all kinds of knives.

Complete Bladesmith: Forging Your Way to Perfection, by Jim Hrisoulas, Paladin Press, Boulder, CO, 1987. 192 pp., illus. $42.95
Novices as well as the experienced bladesmith will benefit from this definitive guide to smithing world-class blades.

Complete Book of Pocketknife Repair, by Ben Kelly Jr., Krause Publications, Iola, WI, 1995. 130 pp., illus. Paper covers. $10.95
Everything you need to know about repairing knives can be found in this step-by-step guide to knife repair.

Complete Enclyclopedia to Knives, by A.E. Hartink, NJ, Chartwell, 2005. More than 600 superb illustrations. 448 pages. Hardcover. New in new Dust Jacket. $19.95

Confederate Edged Weapons, by W.A. Albaugh, R&R Books, Lavonia, NY, 1994. 198 pp., illus. $40.00
The master reference to edged weapons of the Confederate forces. Features precise line drawings and an extensive text.

Connoisseur's Book of Japanese Swords, The, by Kodauska Nagayama, International, Tokyo, Japan, 1997. 348 pp., illus. $75.00
Translated by Kenji Mishina. A comprehensive guide to the appreciation and appraisal of the blades of Japanese swords. The most informative guide to the blades of Japanese swords ever to appear in English.

Counterfeiting Antique Cutlery, by Gerald Witcher, National Brokerage and Sales, Inc., Brentwood, TN. 1997. 512 pp., illustrated with 1,500-2,000 b&w photographs. $24.95

Cutting Edge: Japanese Swords in the British Museum, by Victor Harris, VT, Tuttle Publishing, 2005. 1st edition. It includes hundreds of photos, with 16 pages in full color. 160 pages, illustrated with 320 b&w photos; 34 color photos; and a 2-page spread of line art. Hardcover. New in new Dust Jacket. $40.00

Daggers and Fighting Knives of the Western World: From the Stone Age til 1900, by Harold Peterson, Dover Publishing, Mineola, NY, 2001. 96 pp., plus 32 pp. of matte stock. Over 100 illustrations. Softcover. $9.95
The only full-scale reference book devoted entirely to the subject of fighting knives, flint knives, daggers of all sorts, scramasaxes, hauswehren, dirks and more. 108 plates, bibliography and Index.

Earliest Commando Knives, by William Windrum. Phillips Publications, Williamstown, NJ. 2001. 74 pp., illus. Softcover. $9.95

Edged Weapon Accouterments of Germany 1800-1945, Kreutz, Hofmann, Johnson, Reddick, Pottsboro, TX, Reddick Enterprises, 2002. 1st edition. Hardcover. NEW. $49.00

Eickhorn Edged Weapons Exports, Vol. 1: Latin America, by A.M. de Quesada Jr. and Ron G. Hicock, Pioneer Press, Union City, TN, 1996. 120 pp., illus. Softcovers. $15.00
This research studies the various Eickhorn edged weapons and accessories manufactured for various countries outside of Germany.

Exploring the Dress Daggers and Swords of the SS, by Thomas T. Wittmann, Johnson Reference Books, Fredericksburg, VA, 2003. 1st edition. 750 pp., illustrated with nearly 1000 photographs, many in color. $150.00
Profusely illustrated with historically important period in-wear photographs. Most artifacts appearing for the first time in reference.

Exploring the Dress Daggers of the German Army, by Thomas T. Wittmann, Johnson Reference Books, Fredericksburg, VA, 1995. 350 pp., illus. $69.95
The first in-depth analysis of the dress daggers worn by the German Army.

Exploring the Dress Daggers of the German Luftwaffe, by Thomas T. Wittmann, Johnson Reference Books, Fredericksburg, VA, 1998. 350 pp., illus. $79.95
Examines the dress daggers and swords of the German Luftwaffe. The designs covered include the long DLV patterns, the Glider Pilot designs of the NSFK and DLV, 1st and 2nd model Luftwaffe patterns, the Luftwaffe sword and the General Officer Degen. Many are pictured for the first time in color.

Exploring The Dress Daggers of the German Navy, by Thomas T. Wittmann, Johnson Reference Books, Fredericksburg, VA, 2000. 560 pp., illus. $89.95
Explores the dress daggers and swords of the Imperial, Weimar, and Third Reich eras, from 1844-1945. Provides detailed information, as well as many superb b&w and color photographs of individual edged weapons. Many are pictured for the first time in full color.

Fighting Tomahawk: An Illustrated Guide to Using the Tomahawk and Long Knife as Weapons, by Dwight C. McLemore, Boulder, CO, Paladin Press, 2004. 1st edition. 296 pp. Softcover. NEW. $39.95

First Commando Knives, by Prof. Kelly Yeaton and Col. Rex Applegate, Phillips Publications, Williamstown, NJ, 1996. 115 pp., illus. Paper covers. $12.95
Here is the full story of the Shanghai origins of the world's best known dagger.

George Schrade and His Accomplishments, by George Schrade, privately printed, 2004. 84 pp. Softcover. NEW. $25.00

German Clamshells and Other Bayonets, by G. Walker and R.J. Weinard, Johnson Reference Books, Fredericksburg, VA, 1994. 157 pp., illus. $22.95
Includes unusual bayonets, many of which are shown for the first time. Current market values are listed.

German Etched Dress Bayonets (Extra-Seitengewehr) 1933-1945, by Wayne H. Techet. Printed by the author, Las Vegas, NV. 2002. Color section and value guide. 262 pp. Limited edition of 1,300 copies. Signed and numbered. $55.00
Photographs of over 200 obverse and reverse motifs. Rare SS and Panzer patterns pictured for the first time, with an extensive chapter on reproductions and Red Flags.

German Swords and Sword Makers: Edged Weapons Makers from the 14th to the 20th Centuries, by Richard H. Bezdek, Paladin Press, Boulder, CO, 2000. 248 pp., illus. Paper covers $40.00
This book contains the most information ever published on German swords and edged weapons makers from the Middle Ages to the present.

Halberd and other European Polearms 1300-1650, by George Snook, Museum Restoration Service, Bloomfield, Ontario, Canada, 1998. 40 pp., illus. Paper covers. $8.95
A comprehensive introduction to the history, use, and identification of the staff weapons of Europe.

Highland Swordsmanship: Techniques of the Scottish Swordmasters, edited by Mark Rector. Chivalry Bookshelf, Union City, CA, 2001. 208 pp., Includes more than 100 illustrative photographs. Softcover $29.95
Rector has done a superb job at bringing together two influential yet completely different 18th century fencing manuals from Scotland. Adding new interpretive plates, Mark offers new insights and clear presentations of many useful techniques.

How to Make a Tactical Folder, by Bob Tetzuola, Krause Publications, Iola, WI, 2000. 160 pp., illus. Paper covers. $16.95
Step-by-step instructions and outstanding photography guide the knifemaker from start to finish.

How to Make Folding Knives, by Ron Lake, Frank Centofante and Wayne Clay, Krause Publications, Iola, WI, 1995. 193 pp., illus. Paper covers. $13.95

With step-by-step instructions, learn how to make your own folding knife from three top custom makers.

How to Make Knives, by Richard W. Barney and Robert W. Loveless, Krause Publications, Iola, WI, 1995. 182 pp., illus. Paper covers. $13.95

Complete instructions from two premier knife makers on making high-quality, handmade knives.

How to Make Multi-Blade Folding Knives, by Eugene Shadley & Terry Davis, Krause Publications, Iola, WI, 1997. 192 pp., illus. Paper covers. $19.95

This step-by-step instructional guide teaches knifemakers how to craft these complex folding knives.

KA-BAR: The Next Generation of the Ultimate Fighting Knife, by Greg Walker, Paladin Press, Boulder, CO, 2001. 88 pp., illus. Softcover. $16.00

The KA-BAR fighting/utility knife is the most widely recognized and popular combat knife ever to be produced in the United States. Since its introduction on 23 November 1942, the KA-BAR has performed brilliantly on the battlefields of Europe, the South Pacific, Korea, Southeast Asia, Central America and the Middle East, earning its moniker as the "ultimate fighting knife."

Kalashnikov Bayonets: The Collector's Guide to Bayonets for the AK and its Variations, by Martin D. Ivie, Texas, Diamond Eye Publications, 2002. 1st edition. 220 pp., with over 250 color photos and illustrations. Hardcover. $59.95

Knife and Tomahawk Throwing: The Art of the Experts, by Harry K. McEvoy, Charles E. Tuttle, Rutland, VT, 1989. 150 pp., illus. Softcover. $8.95

The first book to employ side-by-side the fascinating art and science of knives and tomahawks.

Knife in Homespun America and Related Items: Its Construction and Material, as used by Woodsmen, Farmers, Soldiers, Indians and General Population, by Madison Grant, York, PA, privately printed, 1984. 1st edition. 187 pp., profusely illustrated. $45.00

Shows over 300 examples of knives and related items made and used by woodsmen, farmers, soldiers, Indians and the general frontier population.

Knife Talk, The Art and Science of Knifemaking, by Ed Fowler, Krause Publications, Iola, WI, 1998. 158 pp., illus. Paper covers. $14.95

Valuable how-to advice on knife design and construction plus 20 years of memorable articles from the pages of "*Blade*" Magazine.

Knifemakers of Old San Francisco, by Bernard Levine, 2nd edition, Paladin Press, Boulder, CO, 1998. 150 pp., illus. $39.95

The definitive history of the knives and knife-makers of 19th century San Francisco.

Knives 2007 27th Anniversary Edition, edited by Joe Kertzman, Iola, WI, Krause Publications, 2006. Softcover. NEW. $27.99

Knives of the United States Military-World War II, by Michael W. Silvey, privately printed, Sacramento, CA 1999. 250 pp., illustrated with full color photos. $60.00

240 full-page color plates depicting the knives of WWII displayed against a background of wartime accoutrements and memorabilia. The book focuses on knives and their background.

Knives of the United States Military in Vietnam: 1961-1975, by Michael W. Silvey, privately printed, Sacramento, CA., 139 pp. Hardcover. $45.00

A beautiful color celebration of the most interesting and rarest knives of the Vietnam War, emphasizing SOG knives, Randalls, Gerbers, Eks, and other knives of this era. Shown with these knives are the patches and berets of the elite units who used them.

Master Bladesmith: Advanced Studies in Steel, by Jim Hrisoulas, Paladin Press, Boulder, CO, 1990. 296 pp., illus. Paper Covers $46.00

The author reveals the forging secrets that for centuries have been protected by guilds.

Medieval Swordsmanship, Illustrated Methods and Techniques, by John Clements, Paladin Press, Boulder, CO, 1998. 344 pp., illus. $40.00

The most comprehensive and historically accurate view ever written of the lost fighting arts of Medieval knights.

Military Knife & Bayonet Book, by Homer Brett, World Photo Press, Japan. 2001. 392 pp., illus. $69.95

Professional studio color photographs with more than 1,000 military knives and knife-bayonets illustrated. Both the U.S. and foreign sections are extensive, and includes standard models, prototypes and experimental models. Many of the knives and bayonets photographed have never been previously illustrated in any other book. The U.S. section also includes the latest developments in military Special Operations designs. Written in Japanese and English.

Military Knives: A Reference Book, by Frank Trzaska (editor), Knife Books, Deptford, NJ, 2001. 255 pp., illus. Softcover. $17.95

A collection of your favorite Military Knife articles from the pages of *Knife World* magazine. 67 articles ranging from the Indian Wars to the present day modern military knives.

Modern Combat Blades, by Duncan Long, Paladin Press, Boulder, CO, 1993. 128 pp., illus. $30.00

Long discusses the pros and cons of bowies, bayonets, commando daggers, kukris, switchblades, butterfly knives, belt-buckle blades and many more.

Modern Fencing: A Comprehensive Manual for the Foil, The Epee, The Sabre, by Clovis Deladrier, Boulder, CO, Paladin Press, 2005. 312pp. Soft cover. NEW. $35.00

Though long out of print, Modern Fencing is still considered one of the best fencing manuals ever written and is often cited by modern fencing masters for its concise lessons and excellent photos.

Modern Swordsman, The, by Fred Hutchinson, Paladin Press, Boulder, CO, 1999. 80 pp., illus. Paper covers. $22.00

Realistic training for serious self-defense.

Moran, 50 Years Anniversary Knives: The Complete History of Their Making, by Dominique Beaucant, Privately Printed, 1998, Signed by the publisher. Soft cover, 108 pp. Soft cover. NEW. $20.00

Includes photos and descriptions of the 50 knives Moran made to celebrate his golden anniversary as a knife maker, and much more.

Officer Swords of the German Navy 1806-1945, by Claus P. Stefanski & Dirk, Schiffer Publications, Atglen, PA, 2002. 1st edition. 176 pp., with over 250 b&w and color photos. Hardcover. $59.95

Official Price Guide to Collector Knives; 14th Edition, by C. Houston Price, New York, House of Collectibles, 2004. 500 photos, 8 pp. in color. 497 pp. Softcover. NEW. $17.95

Official Scout Blades with Prices, by Ed Holbrook, privately printed, 2004. Softcover. NEW. $25.00

On Damascus Steel, by Dr. Leo S. Figiel, Atlantis Arts Press, Atlantis, FL, 1991. 145 pp., illus. $65.00

The historic, technical and artistic aspects of Oriental and mechanical Damascus. Persian and Indian sword blades, from 1600-1800, which have never been published, are illustrated.

Pattern-Welded Blade: Artistry in Iron, The, by Jim Hrisoulas, Paladin Press, Boulder, CO, 1994. 120 pp., illus. Paper Covers $30.00

Reveals the secrets of this craft–from the welding of the starting billet to the final assembly of the complete blade.

Pocket Knives of the United States Military, by Michael W. Silvey, Sacramento, CA, privately printed, 2002. 135 pp. Hardcover. $34.95

This beautiful new full color book is the definitive reference on U.S. military folders. Pocket Knives of the United States Military is organized into the following sections: Introduction, The First Folders, WWI, WWII, and Postwar (which covers knives up through the late 1980s). Essential reading for pocketknife and military knife collectors alike!

Randall Chronicles, The, by Pete Hamilton, privately printed, 2002. 160 pp., profusely illustrated in color. Hardcover in dust jacket. $79.95

Randall Fighting Knives In Wartime: WWII, Korea, and Vietnam, by Robert E. Hunt. Paducah, Ky, Turner Publishing Company, 2002. 192 pp. Hardcover. $44.95

While other books on Randall knives have been published, this new title is the first to focus specifically on Randalls with military ties. There are three main sections, containing more than 80 knives from the WWII, Korea, and Vietnam War periods. Each knife is featured in a high quality, full page, full color photograph, with the opposing page carrying a detailed description of the knife and its history or other related information.

Randall Made Knives, by Robert L. Gaddis, Paladin Press, Boulder, CO, 2000. 292 pp., illus. $59.95

Plots the designs of all 24 of Randall's unique knives. This step-by-step book, seven years in the making, is worth every penny and moment of your time.

Randall Made Knives-A Timeline, The Quick Reference Guide, by Edna and Sheldon Wickersham, privatey printed, 2005. $20.00

This 12" x 25" two-sided laminated reference sheet folds neatly into a back pants pocket, and allows you to date any given Randall knife with a good degree of confidence, wherever you need it. A great resource for all Randall fans! Stiff Paper Covers.

Randall Military Models; Fighters, Bowies and Tang Knives, by Robert E. Hunt, Paducah, Ky, Turner Publishing Company, 2004. 304 pages (including 150 full color photos) Hardcover. $74.95

This new volume provides a vast amount of material, carefully organized & presented to enable the reader to further his own research in the areas most interesting to him.

Randall Fighting Knives: Rare, Unique & Experimental Knives, by Robert E. Hunt, Paducah, Ky, Turner Publishing Company, 2006. 176 pages. Hardcover. $59.95

Many of the knives featured in this new compilation have been held in private collections and museums, and demonstrate the continuous design innovation that remains a hallmark of Randall Made Knives.

Remington Knives–Past & Present, by Ron Stewart and Roy Ritchie, Paducah, KY, Collector Books, 2005. 1st edition. 288 pp. Softcover. NEW. $16.95

Renaissance Swordsmanship, by John Clements, Paladin Press, Boulder, CO, 1997. 152 pp., illus. Paper covers. $25.00

The illustrated use of rapiers and cut-and-thrust swords.

Rice's Trowel Bayonet, reprinted by Ray Riling Arms Books Co., Philadelphia, PA, 1968. 8 pp., illus. Paper covers. $3.00

A facsimile reprint of a rare circular originally published by the U.S. government in 1875 for the information of U.S. troops.

Scottish Dirk, The, by James D. Forman, Museum Restoration Service, Bloomfield, Ont., Canada, 1991. 60 pp., illus. Paper covers. $8.95

More than 100 dirks are illustrated with a text that sets the dirk and Sgian Dubh in their socio-historic content following design changes through more than 300 years of evolution.

Seitengewehr: History of the German Bayonet, 1919-1945, by George T. Wheeler, Johnson Reference Books, Fredericksburg, VA, 2000. 320 pp., illus. $44.95

Provides complete information on Weimar and Third Reich bayonets, as well as their accompanying knots and frogs. Illustrates re-issued German and foreign bayonets utilized by both the Reichswehr and the Wehrmacht, and details the progression of newly manufactured bayonets produced after Hitler's rise to power. Book contains an up-to-date price guide including current valuations.

Silver Mounted Swords: The Lattimer Family Collection; Featuring Silver Hilts Through the Golden Age, by Daniel Hartzler, Rowe Publications, New York, 2000. 300 pp., with over 1,000 illustrations and 1,350 photos. Oversize 9" x12". $75.00

The world's largest Silver Hilt collection.

Small Arms Identification Series, No. 6. British Service Sword & Lance Patterns, by Ian Skennerton, I.D.S.A. Books, Piqua, OH, 1994. 48 pp. $12.50

Small Arms Series, No. 2. The British Spike Bayonet, by Ian Skennerton, I.D.S.A. Books, Piqua, OH, 1982. 32 pp., 30 illus. $9.95

Socket Bayonets of the Great Powers, by Robert W. Shuey, Excalibur Publications, Tucson, AZ, 2000 96 pp., illus. Paper covers $22.95

With 175 illustrations, the author brings together, in one place, many of the standard socket arrangements used by some of the " Great Powers." With an illustrated glossary of blade shape and socket design.

Socket in the British Army 1667-1783, The, by Erik Goldstein, Andrew Mowbray, Inc., Lincoln, RI, 2001. 136 pp., illus. $23.00

The spectacle of English "redcoats" on the attack, relentlessly descending upon enemy lines with fixed bayonets, is one of the most chilling images from European history and the American Revolution. Drawing upon new information from archaeological digs and archival records, the author explains how to identify each type of bayonet and shows which bayonets were used where and with which guns.

Switchblade: The Ace of Blades, Revised and Updated, by Ragnar Benson and edited by Michael D. Janich, Boulder, CO, Paladin Press, 2004. 104 pp. Softcover. $16.00

Switchblades of Italy, by Tim Zinser, Dan Fuller and Neal Punchard. Paducah, KY, Turner Publishing, 2002. 128 pp. Hardcover. New in new dust jacket. $44.95

The first ever comprehensive publication about Italian switchblade knives, featuring knives and history from the late 1700s to the 1970s.

Swords and Blades of the American Revolution, by George C. Neumann, Rebel Publishing Co., Inc., Texarkana, TX, 1991. 288 pp., illus. $36.95

The encyclopedia of bladed weapons–swords, bayonets, spontoons, halberds, pikes, knives, daggers, axes–used by both sides, on land and sea, in America's struggle for independence.

Swords and Sabers of the Armory at Springfield, by Burton A. Kellerstedt, New Britain, CT, 1998. 121 pp., illus. Softcover. $29.95

The basic and most important reference for its subject, and one that is unlikely to be surpassed for comprehensiveness and accuracy.

Swords and Sword Makers of England and Scotland, by Richard H. Bezdek, Boulder, CO, Paladin Press, 2003. 1st edition. 424 pp., illus. Hardcover. New in new dust jacket. $69.95

Covers English sword makers from the 14th century and Scottish makers from the 16th century all the way through the renowned Wilkinson Sword Company and other major sword manufacturers of today. Also, the important early English sword- and blade-making communities of Hounslow Heath and Shotley Bridge, and the influential Cutlers Company of London. Includes more than 450 spectacular photographs of English and Scottish swords of every type and era from some of the world's major collections.

Tactical Folding Knife; A Study of the Anatomy and Construction of the Liner-Locked Folder, by Bob Terzuola, Krause Publications, Iola, WI. 2000. 160 pp., 200 b&w photos, illus. Paper covers. $16.00

Step-by-step instructions and outstanding photography guide the knifemaker from start to finish. This book details everything from the basic definition of a tactical folder to the final polishing as the knife is finished.

Tactical Knives, by Dietmar Pohl, Iola, WI, Krause Publications, 2003. 191 Pages, illustrated with 170 color photos. Softcover. $24.95

Dozens of knife styles are identified and showcased, including survival knives, multi-tool, tantos, Bowie, machetes, and other trench, commando, boot, and neck knives. Special attention is given to knives that served troops in WWII and Vietnam, as well as those carried by today's Special Forces.

Travels for Daggers, Historic Edged Weaponry, by Eiler R. Cook, Hendersonville, NC, 2004. 1st edition. Hardcover. 288 illustrations $50.00

An indispensable guide for all collectors, historians, military members, travelers, and the intellectually curious interested in the edged weaponry of the world.

U.S. M-3 Trench Knife of World War Two, The, by Vincent J. Coniglio and Robert S. Laden. Matamoras, PA, privately printed, 2003. 2nd printing. Softcover. NEW. $18.00

U.S. Military Knives, Bayonets and Machetes Price Guide, 5th Edition, by Frank Trzaska (editor), Knife Books, Deptford, NJ, 2006. 80 pp., illus. Softcover. $9.95

This volume follows in the tradition of the previous three versions of using major works on the subject as a reference to keep the price low to you.

U.S. Naval Officers; Their Swords and Dirks Featuring the Collection of the United States Naval Academy Museum, by Peter Tuite, Lincoln, RI, Andrew Mowbray, Inc., 2005. 1st edition. 240 pp., illustrated with over 500 color photos. Pictorial hardcover. NEW. $75.00

Wayne Goddards $50 Knife Shop: Getting Started Without Investing a Fortune, by Wayne Goddard, Krause Publications, Iola, WI, 2006. 160 pp., illus. Softcover. $19.95

This book expands on information from Goddard's popular column in *Blade* magazine to show knifemakers of all skill levels how to create helpful gadgets and supply their shop on a shoestring. The easiest guide to making knives is Wayne Goddard's $50 Knife Shop, Revised. 200+ color photos demonstrate basic knife making techniques.

Wittmann German Dagger Price Guide for 2004, The, by David Hohaus and Thomas Wittmann, Moorestown, NJ, 2004. 1st edition. Stiff paper covers. NEW. $11.95

Wonder of Knifemaking, by Wayne Goddard, Krause Publications, Iola, WI. 2000. 160 pp., illustrated with 150 b&w photos and 16-page color section. Softcover. $19.95

Master bladesmith Wayne Goddard draws on his decades of experience to answer questions of knifemakers at all levels. As a columnist for *Blade* magazine, Goddard has been answering real questions from real knifemakers for the past eight years. Now, all the details are compiled in one place as a handy reference for every knifemaker, amateur or professional.

GENERAL

331+ Essential Tips and Tricks; A How-To Guide for the Gun Collector, by Stuart Mowbray, Lincoln, RI, 2006. 1st edition, photographs. Full color, 272 pp., 357 photographs. Soft cover. NEW. $35.99

Everything from gun photography to detecting refinishes can be found in this comprehensive new reference book.

A Rifleman Went to War, by H. W. McBride, Lancer Militaria, Mt. Ida, AR, 1987. 398 pp., illus. $29.95

The classic account of practical marksmanship on the battlefields of WWI.

Action Shooting: Cowboy Style, by John Taffin, Krause Publications, Iola, WI, 1999. 320 pp., illus. $39.95

Details on the guns and ammunition. Explanations of the rules used for many events.

Advanced Muzzleloader's Guide, by Toby Bridges, Stoeger Publishing Co., So. Hackensack, NJ, 1985. 256 pp., illus. Paper covers. $14.95

The complete guide to muzzle-loading rifles, pistols and shotguns–flintlock and percussion.

Aids to Musketry for Officers & NCOs, by Capt. B.J. Friend, Excalibur Publications, Latham, NY, 1996. 40 pp., illus. Paper covers. $7.95

A facsimile edition of a pre-WWI British manual filled with useful information for training the common soldier.

Airgun Odyssey, by Steve Hanson, Manchester, CT, Precision Shooting, Inc., 2004. 1st edition. 175 pp. Pictorial softcover. $27.95

America's Great Gunmakers, by Wayne van Zwoll, Stoeger Publishing Co., So. Hackensack, NJ, 1992. 288 pp., illus. Paper covers. $16.95

This book traces in great detail the evolution of guns and ammunition in America and the men who formed the companies that produced them.

ARMS LIBRARY

American Air Rifles, by James E. House, Krause Publications, Iola, WI, 2002. 1st edition. 208 pp., with 198 b&w photos. Softcover. $22.95
Air rifle ballistics, sights, pellets, games, and hunting caliber recommendations are thoroughly explained to help shooters get the most out of their American air rifles. Evaluation of more than a dozen American-made and American-imported air rifle models.

American and Imported Arms, Ammunition and Shooting Accessories, Catalog No. 18 of the Shooter's Bible, Stoeger, Inc., reprinted by Fayette Arsenal, Fayetteville, NC, 1988. 142 pp., illus. Paper covers. $10.95
A facsimile reprint of the 1932 Stoeger's Shooter's Bible.

American B.B. Gun: A Collector's Guide, by Arni T. Dunathan. A.S. Barnes and Co., Inc., South Brunswick, 2001. 154 pp., illustrated with nearly 200 photographs, drawings and detailed diagrams. Hardcover. $35.00

Annie Oakley of the Wild West, by Walter Havighurst, New York, Castle Books, 2000. 246 pp. Hardcover. New in new dust jacket. $10.00

Antique Guns; The Collector's Guide, by Steve Carpenteri, Accokeek, MD: Stoeger Publications, 2005. Revised edition. 260 pages, illus. plus a 32 page color section. Soft cover. New. $22.95
Covers a vast spectrum of pre-1900 firearms: those manufactured by U.S. gun makers as well as Canadian, French, German, Belgian, Spanish and other foreign firms.

Armed Response, by Massad Ayoob, and David Kenik, NY, Merril Press, 2005. 179 pages, with b&w photos. Foreword by Massad Ayoob. Soft cover. NEW. $19.95
These are valuable real-life lessons about preparing to face a lethal threat, winning a gunfight, and surviving the ensuing court battle that can not be found outside of expensive tactical schools.

Arming & Equipping the United States Cavalry 1865-1902, by Dusan Farrington, Lincoln, RI: Andrew Mowbray, Inc., 2005. 1st edition. $68.95
775 photos!!! Simply packed with serial numbers, issue information, reports from the field and more! Meticulously researched and absolutely up-to-date. A complete reference to all the arms and accoutrements. And at a bargain price to boot! Hardcover. New in new dust jacket. $68.95

Arming the Glorious Cause: Weapons of the Second War for Independence, by James B. Whisker, Daniel D. Hartzler and Larry W. Yantz, R & R Books, Livonia, NY, 1998. 175 pp., illus. $45.00
A photographic study of Confederate weapons.

Arms & Armor in the Art Institute of Chicago, by Walter J. Karcheski Jr., Bulfinch Press, Boston, MA, 1995. 128 pp., illus. $35.00
Now, for the first time, the Art Institute of Chicago's arms and armor collection is presented in the visual delight of 103 color illustrations.

Arms for the Nation: Springfield Longarms, edited by David C. Clark, Scott A. Duff, Export, PA, 1994. 73 pp., illus. Paper covers. $9.95
A brief history of the Springfield Armory and the arms made there.

Arrowmaker Frontier Series Volume 1, by Roy Chandler, Jacksonville, NC, Ron Brigade Armory, 2000. 390 pp. Hardcover. New in new dust jacket. $38.95

Arsenal of Freedom, The Springfield Armory, 1890-1948: A Year-by-Year Account Drawn from Official Records, compiled and edited by Lt. Col. William S. Brophy, USAR Ret., Andrew Mowbray, Inc., Lincoln, RI, 1991. 400 pp., illus. Softcover. $29.95
A "must buy" for all students of American military weapons, equipment and accoutrements.

Art of American Arms Makers Marketing Guns, Ammunition, and Western Adventure During the Golden Age of Illustration, by Richard C., Rattenbury, Oklahoma City, OK, National Cowboy Museum, 2004. 132 pp. of color photos. Softcover. NEW. $29.95

Art of American Game Calls, by Russell E. Lewis, Paducah, KY, Collector Books, 2005. 1st edition. 176 pp. Pictorial hardcover. NEW. $24.95

Art of Blacksmithing, by Alex W. Bealer, New York, Book Sales, 1996. Revised edition. 440 pp. Hardcover. New in new dust jacket. $10.00

Art of Remington Arms, Sporting Classics, 2004, by Tom Davis. 1st edition. Hardcover. NEW. $60.00

Battle of the Bulge: Hitler's Alternate Scenarios, by Peter Tsouras, Mechanicsburg, PA, Stackpole Books, 2004. 1st edition. 256 pp., 24 b&w photos, 10 maps. Hardcover. NEW. $34.95

Belgian Rattlesnake: The Lewis Automatic Machine Gun, The, by William M. Easterly, Collector Grade Publications, Inc., Cobourg, Ont. Canada, 1998. 542 pp., illus. $79.95
A social and technical biography of the Lewis automatic machine gun and its inventors.

Benchrest Shooting Primer, The, edited by Dave Brennan, Precision Shooting, Inc., Manchester, CT, 2000. 2nd edition. 420 pp., illustrated with b&w photographs, drawings and detailed diagrams. Pictorial softcover. $24.95
The very best articles on shooting and reloading for the most challenging of all the rifle accuracy disciplines...benchrest shooting.

Black Rifle Frontier Series Volume 2, The, by Roy Chandler, Jacksonville, NC, Iron Brigade Armory, 2002. 226 pp. Hardcover. New in new dust jacket. $42.95
In 1760, inexperienced Jack Elan settles in Sherman's Valley, suffers tragedy, is captured by hostiles, escapes, and fights on. This is the "2nd" book in the Frontier Series.

Blue Book of Airguns 6th Edition, by Robert Beeman and John Allen, Minneapolis, MN, Blue Book Publications, Inc., 2007. Softcover. NEW. $29.95

Blue Book of Gun Values, 28th Edition (2007 Edition), by S.P. Fjestad, Minneapolis, MN, Blue Book Publications, Inc., 2080 pp., illus. Paper covers. $39.95

Blue Book of Modern Black Powder Values, 4th Edition, by Dennis Adler, John Allen, Minneapolis, MN, Blue Book Publications, Inc., 2004. Softcover. NEW. $24.95

Bodyguard Manual, by Leroy Thompson, Mechanicsburg,PA. Greehnill Books, 2005. 208 pages, 16 pages of plates. Soft cover. NEW. $23.95
Bodyguard Manual details the steps a protective team takes to prevent attack as well as the tactics employed when it is necessary to counter one.

British Small Arms of World War II, by Ian D. Skennerton, Arms & Militaria Press, Australia, 1988. 110 pp., 37 illus. $25.00

C Stories, by Jeff Cooper, Sycamore Island Books, 2005. 1st edition. Quite simply, CStories is Jeff Cooper at his best. illus., 316 pp. Hardcover. New in new dust jacket. $49.95

Carbine and Shotgun Speed Shooting: How to Hit Hard and Fast in Combat, by Steve Moses. Paladin Press, Boulder, CO. 2002. 96 pp., illus. Softcover $18.00
In this groundbreaking book, he breaks down the mechanics of speed shooting these weapons, from stance and grip to sighting, trigger control and more, presenting them in a concise and easily understood manner.

Cavalry Raids of the Civil War, by Col. Robert W. Black, Mechanicsburg, PA, Stackpole Books, 2004. 1st edition. 288 pp., 30 b&w drawings. Softcover. NEW. $17.95

CO2 Pistols and Rifles, by James E. House, Iola, WI, Krause Publications, 2004. 1st edition 240 pp., with 198 b&w photos. Softcover. NEW. $24.95

Combatives FM-3-25.150, by U.S. Army, Boulder, CO, Paladin Press, 2004. Photos, illus., 272 pp. Soft cover. NEW. $19.95
This exact reprint of the U.S. Army's most current field manual on hand-to-hand combat (FM 3-25.150) reflects the first major revision to the Army's close-quarters combat program in a decade. This field manual shows them how.

Complete .50-caliber Sniper Course, The, by Dean Michaelis, Paladin Press, Boulder, CO, 2000. 576 pp., illus., $60.00
The history from German Mauser T-Gewehr of WWI to the Soviet PTRD and beyond. Includes the author's Program of Instruction for Special Opcrations Hard-Target Interdiction Course.

Complete Guide to Game Care and Cookery, 4th Edition, The, by Sam Fadala, Krause Publications, Iola, WI, 2003. 320 pp., illus. Paper covers. $21.95
Over 500 photos illustrating the care of wild game in the field and at home with a separate recipc section providing over 400 tested recipes.

Concealed Handgun Manual, 4th Edition, The, by Chris Bird, San Antonio, TX, Privateer Publications, 2004. 332 pp., illus. Softcover, NEW. $21.95

Cowboys & the Trappings of the Old West, by William Manns & Elizabeth Clair Flood, Santa Fe, NM, ZON International Publishing Company, 1997. 224 pp., 550 colorful photos. Foreword by Roy Rogers. Hardcover. $45.00
Big & beautiful book covering: Hats, boots, spurs, chaps, guns, holsters, saddles and more. It's really a pictorial cele bration of the old time buckaroo. This exceptional book presents all the accoutrements of the cowboy life in a comprehensive tribute to the makers. The history of the craftsmen and the evolution of the gear are lavishly illustrated.

Cowgirls, Revised and Expanded 2nd Edition Early Images and Collectibles Price Guide, by Judy Crandall, Atglen, PA, Schiffer Publications, 2005. 2nd edition. Soft cover. NEW. $24.95
The First Ladies from the Great American West live again in this comprehensive pictorial chronicle.

Cowgirls: Women of the Wild West, by Elizabeth Clair Flood and William Maims, edited by Helene Helene, Santa Fe, NM, ZON

International Publishing Company, 2000. 1st edition. Hardcover. New in new dust jacket. $45.00

Custom Firearms Engraving, by Tom Turpin, Krause Publications, Iola, WI, 1999. 208 pp., illus. $49.95

Provides a broad and comprehensive look at the world of firearms engraving. The exquisite styles of more than 75 master engravers are shown on beautiful examples of handguns, rifles, shotguns, and other firearms, as well as knives.

Custom Gunmakers of the 20th Century, by Michael Pretov, Manchester, CT, Precision Shooting, 2005. 168 pages, illustrated with Photos. Hardcover. $24.95 NEW.

Daisy Air Rifles & BB Guns: The First 100 Years, by Neal Punchard, St. Paul, MN, Motorbooks, 2002. 1st edition. Hardcover, 10" x 10", 156 pp., 300 color. Hardcover. $29.95

Dead On, by Tony Noblitt and Warren Gabrilska, Paladin Press, Boulder, CO, 1998. 176 pp., illus. Paper covers. $22.00

The long-range marksman's guide to extreme accuracy. *Defensive Use of Firearms*, by Stephen Wenger, Boulder,CO, Paladin Press, 2005. 5½" x 8½", soft cover, illus., 120 pp. Soft cover. NEW. $20.00

This concise and affordable handbook offers the reader a set of common-sense principles, tactics and techniques distilled from hundreds of hours of the author's training, which includes certification as a law-enforcement handgun, shotgun, patrol rifle and tactical shooting instructor.

Do or Die A Supplementary Manual on Individual Combat, by Lieut. Col. A.J. Drexel Biddle, U.S.M.C.R., Boulder, CO, Paladin Press, 2004. 80 pp., illus. Softcover, $15.00

Down to Earth: The 507th Parachute Infantry Regiment in Normandy: June 6-july 11 1944, by Martin Morgan ICA, Atglen, PA, Schiffer Publishing, 2004. 1st edition. 304 pp., color and b&w photos. Hardcover. New in new dust jacket. $69.95

Effective Defense: The Woman, the Plan, the Gun, by Gila Hayes, Onalaska, WA, Police Bookshelf, 2000. 2nd edition. Photos, 264 pp. Softcover. NEW. $16.95

Elmer Keith: The Other Side of a Western Legend, by Gene Brown, Precision Shooting, Inc., Manchester, CT 2002. 1st edition. 168 pp., illustrated with b&w photos. Softcover. $19.95

An updated and expanded edition of his original work, incorporating new tales and information that have come to light in the past six years. Gene Brown was a long time friend of Keith, and today is unquestionably the leading authority on Keith's books.

Encyclopedia of Native American Bows, Arrows and Quivers, by Steve Allely and Jim Hamm, The Lyons Press, N.Y., 1999. 160 pp., illus. $29.95

A landmark book for anyone interested in archery history, or Native Americans.

Exercise of Armes, The, by Jacob de Gheyn, Dover Publications, Inc., Mineola, NY, 1999. 144 pp., illus. Paper covers. $14.95

Republications of all 117 engravings from the 1607 classic military manual. A meticulously accurate portrait of uniforms and weapons of the 17th century Netherlands.

Fighting Iron: A Metals Handbook for Arms Collectors, by Art Gogan, Mowbray Publishers, Inc., Lincoln, RI, 2002. 176 pp., illus. $28.00

A guide that is easy to use, explains things in simple English and covers all of the different historical periods that we are interested in.

FBI Guide to Concealable Weapons, by the FBI, Boulder, Co, Paladin Press, 2005. As citizens responsible for our own safety, we must know everything possible about the dangers that face us, and awareness is the first, vital step in this direction. Photos, 88 pp. Soft cover. NEW. $15.00

Filipino Fighting Whip: Advanced Training Methods and Combat Applications, The, by Tom Meadows, Boulder, CO, Paladin Press, 2005. This book is a comprehensive guide for advanced training methods and combat applications as practiced and taught by the best fighters and whip practitioners in the world. 216 pp. Soft cover. NEW. $20.00

Fine Art of the West, by Byron B. Price and Christopher Lyon, New York, Abbeville Press, 2004. Hardcover. NEW. $75.00

Firearm Suppressor Patents, Volume One: United States Patents, by N.R. Parker, Boulder, CO, Paladin Press, 2004. 392 pages, illustrated. Soft cover. NEW. $45.00

This book provides never-before-published interviews with three of today's top designers as well as a special section on the evolution of cutting-edge silencer mounting systems.

Firearms Assembly Disassembly; Part 4: Centerfire Rifles (2nd Edition), by J. B. Wood, Iola, WI, Krause Publications, 2004. 2nd edition. 576 pp., 1,750 b&w photos. Softcover. NEW. $24.95

Fireworks: A Gunsight Anthology, by Jeff Cooper, Paladin Press, Boulder, CO, 1998. 192 pp., illus. Paper cover. $27.00

A collection of wild, hilarious, shocking and always meaningful tales from the remarkable life of an American firearms legend.

Force-On-Force Gunfight Training: The Interactive, Reality Based Solution, by Gabriel Suarez, Boulder,CO, Paladin Press, 2005. 105 pages, illustrated with photos. Soft cover. NEW. $15.00

Fort Robinson, Frontier Series, Volume 4, by Roy Chandler, Jacksonville, NC, Ron Brigade Armory, 2003. 1st edition. 560 pp. Hardcover. New in new dust jacket. $39.95

Frederic Remington: The Color of Night, by Nancy Anderson, Princeton University Press, 2003. 1st edition. 136 color illus, 24 halftones; 10" x 11", 208 pgs. Hardcover, New in new dust jacket. $49.95; UK $52.49

From a Stranger's Doorstep to the Kremlin Gate, by Mikhail Kalashnikov, Ironside International Publishers, Inc., Alexandria, VA, 1999. 460 pp., illus. $34.95

A biography of the most influential rifle designer of the 20th century. His AK-47 assault rifle has become the most widely used (and copied) assault rifle of this century.

Frontier Rifleman, The, by H.B. LaCrosse Jr., Pioneer Press, Union City, TN, 1989. 183 pp., illus. Softcover. $17.50

The Frontier rifleman's clothing and equipment during the era of the American Revolution, 1760-1800.

Galloping Thunder: The Stuart Horse Artillery Battalion, by Robert Trout, Mechanicsburg, PA, Stackpole Books, 2002. 1st edition. Hardcover, NEW. $39.95

Gatling Gun: 19th Century Machine Gun to 21st Century Vulcan, The, by Joseph Berk, Paladin Press, Boulder, CO, 1991. 136 pp., illus. $34.95

Here is the fascinating on-going story of a truly timeless weapon, from its beginnings during the Civil War to its current role as a state-of-the-art modern combat system.

German Artillery of World War Two, by Ian V. Hogg, Stackpole Books, Mechanicsburg, PA, 1997, 304 pp., illus. $44.95

Complete details of German artillery use in WWII.

Gone Diggin: Memoirs of a Civil War Relic Hunter, by Toby Law, Orange, VA, Publisher's Press, 2002. 1st edition signed. 151 pp., illustrated with b&w photos. $24.95

The true story of one relic hunter's life-The author kept exacting records of every relic hunt and every relic hunter he was with working with.

Gun Digest 2007, 61st Annual Edition, edited by Ken Ramage, Iola, WI, Krause Publications, 2006. Softcover. NEW. $27.95

This all new 61st edition continues the editorial excellence, quality, content and comprehensive cataloguing that firearms enthusiasts have come to know and expect. The most read gun book in the world for the last half century.

Gun Digest Book of Cowboy Action Shooting: Gear, Guns, Tactics, The, edited by Kevin Michalowski, Iola, WI, Krause Publications, 2005. Softcover. 288 pages, plus 200 b&w photos! $24.99

This one-of-a-kind guide offers complete coverage of the sport from the top experts and personalities in the field.

Gun Digest Book of Exploded Firearms Drawings: 975 Isometric Views, The, by Harold Murtz, Iola,WI, Krause Publications, 2005, 3rd edition. 1032pp, 975 photos. Soft cover. $34.95

This book is sure to become a must-have for gunsmiths, shooters and law enforcement officials!

Gun Digest Blackpowder Loading Manual New Expanded 4th Edition, by Sam Fadala, Iola, WI, Krause Publications, 2006. 352 pp., illus. Softcover. NEW. $27.95

All blackpowder rifle, pistol, and shotgun users should be equipped with the new information supplied in this seminal reference--complete with loading tutorial and instructive articles expertly written by author Sam Fadala. Loading techniques are covered for more than 250 different modern blackpowder firearms--the illustrations are clear and the text is expertly laid out--easily understandable to even the most novice shooter. Experts will also benefit from the tips and techniques of Sam Fadala. This is the must-have book blackpowder shooters have been craving.

Gun Digest Book of Deer Guns, The, edited by Dan Shideler, Iola, WI, Krause Publications, 2004. 1st edition Softcover, NEW. 160pp, 225 b&w photos. $14.99

An illustrated catalog section details deer rifles, shotguns, handguns and muzzleloaders, complete with current pricing information from "Modern Gun Values." A special reference section includes selected portions of the Arms Library, as well as a website directory of state game and fish departments. This practical guide is a must for any deer hunter!

Gun Digest Book of Guns for Personal Defense Arms & Accessories for Self-Defense, The, edited by Kevin Michalowski, Iola, WI, Krause Publications, 2004. 1st edition Softcover. NEW. 160pp plus 200 b&w photos! $14.99

Handgun enthusiasts or anyone looking to find out about handguns for personal defense will find everything they need to know in the pages of this comprehensive guide and reference. Readers will learn the basics of selection and use of handguns for personal defense. The book covers uses of revolvers, semi-automatic pistols, ammunition, holsters, firearms training options, buying a used gun and much more. A catalog section contains listings of currently available pistols and revolvers suitable for personal defense, complete with pricing for each.

Gun Digest Book of Sporting Clays, 3rd Edition, The, edited by Rick Sapp, Iola, WI, Krause Publications, 2005. 1st edition Softcover, NEW. 288 pages, illustrated. $19.95

New articles cover equipment selection, strategies, technical issues and more. Features a review of the 50 best clay ranges in the country -Includes a fully illustrated catalog of currently available sporting clays shotguns showing complete specifications and retail prices.

Gun Digest Book of Trap & Skeet Shooting, 4th Edition, The, edited by Rick Sapp, Iola, WI, Krause Publications, 2004. 1st edition Softcover, NEW. 256 pages, illustrated. $22.95

The book includes comprehensive coverage on choosing and fitting the right shotgun for each sport, explains the hows and whys of chokes in plain language, and provides an in-depth review of shells, loads and reloading. Valuable reference tools include the official rules for each game as well as a manufacturer's directory for guns, ammunition, clothing and accessories.

Gun Engraving, by C. Austyn, Safari Press Publication, Huntington Beach, CA, 1998. 128 pp., plus 24 pp. of color photos. $50.00

A well-illustrated book on fine English and European gun engravers. Includes a fantastic pictorial section that lists types of engravings and prices.

Gun Notes, Volume 1, by Elmer Keith, Safari Press, Huntington Beach, CA, 2002. 219 pp., illus. Softcover. $24.95

A collection of Elmer Keith's most interesting columns and feature stories that appeared in *"Guns & Ammo"* magazine from 1961 to the late 1970s.

Gun Notes, Volume 2, by Elmer Keith, Safari Press, Huntington Beach, CA, 2002. 292 pp., illus. Softcover. $24.95

Covers articles from Keith's monthly column in *"Guns & Ammo"* magazine during the period from 1971 through Keith's passing in 1982.

Guns & Shooting: A Selected Bibliography, by Ray Riling, Ray Riling Arms Books Co., Phila., PA, 1982. 434 pp., illus. Limited, numbered edition. $75.00

A limited edition of this superb bibliographical work, the only modern listing of books devoted to guns and shooting.

Guns Illustrated 2007: 39th Edition, edited by Ken Ramage, Iola, WI, Krause Publications, 2006. Softcover. NEW. $21.95

Highly informative, technical articles on a wide range of shooting topics by some of the top writers in the industry. A catalog section lists more than 3,000 firearms currently manufactured in or imported to the U.S.

Guns of the Gunfighters: Lawmen, Outlaws & TV Cowboys, by Doc O'Meara, Iola, WI, Krause Publications, 2003. 1st edition. 16-page color section, 225 b&w photos. Hardcover. $34.95

Explores the romance of the Old West, focusing on the guns that the good guys & bad guys, real & fictional characters, carried with them. Profiles of more than 50 gunslingers, half from the Old West and half from Hollywood, include a brief biography of each gunfighter, along with the guns they carried. Fascinating stories about the TV and movie celebrities of the 1950s and 1960s detail their guns and the skill–or lack thereof–they displayed.

Guns, Bullets, and Gunfighters, by Jim Cirillo, Paladin Press, Boulder, CO, 1996. 119 pp., illus. Paper covers. $16.00

Lessons and tales from a modern-day gunfighter.

Gunstock Carving: A Step-by-Step Guide to Engraving Rifles and Shotguns, by Bill Janney, East Pertsburg, PA, Fox Chapel Publishing, October 2002. 89 pp., illustrated in color. Softcover. $19.95

Learn gunstock carving from an expert. Includes step-by-step projects and instructions, patterns, tips and techniques.

Hands Off! Self Defense for Women, by Maj. Fairbairn, Boulder, CO: Paladin Press, 2004. 56 pages. Soft cover. NEW. $15.00

Paladin Press is proud to bring back a work by the inimitable self-defense master W.E. Fairbairn so that a new generation of Americans can enjoy his teachings.

Hand-To-Hand Combat: United States Naval Institute, by U.S. Navy, Boulder, CO, Paladin Press, 2003. 1st edition. 240 pp. Softcover. $25.00

Now you can own one of the classic publications in the history of U.S. military close-quarters combat training. In 11 photo-heavy chapters, Hand-to-Hand Combat covers training tips; vulnerable targets; the brutal fundamentals of close-in fighting; frontal and rear attacks; prisoner search and control techniques; disarming pistols, rifles, clubs and knives; offensive means of "liquidating an enemy"; and much more. After reading this book (originally published by the United States Naval Institute in 1943), you will see why it has long been sought by collectors and historians of hand-to-hand combat.

Hidden in Plain Sight, "A Practical Guide to Concealed Handgun Carry" (Revised 2nd Edition), by Trey Bloodworth and Mike Raley, Paladin Press, Boulder, CO, 1997, softcover, photos, 176 pp. $20.00

This invaluable guide offers the latest advice on what to look for when choosing a CCW, how to dress for comfortable, effective concealed carry, traditional and more unconventional carry modes, accessory holsters, customized clothing and accessories, accessibility data based on draw-time comparisons and new holsters on the market. Includes 40 new manufacturer listings.

HK Assault Rifle Systems, by Duncan Long, Paladin Press, Boulder, CO, 1995. 110 pp., illus. Paper covers. $27.95

The little known history behind this fascinating family of weapons tracing its beginnings from the ashes of WWII to the present time.

Holsters for Combat and Concealed Carry, by R.K. Campbell, Boulder, CO, Paladin Press, 2004. 1st edition. 144 pp. Softcover. NEW. $22.00

Hostage Rescue Manual; Tactics of the Counter-Terrorist Professionals, by Leroy Thompson, Mechanicsburg, PA. Greenhill Books, 2005. 208 pages, with 16 pages of photos. Soft cover. $23.95

Incorporating vivid photographs and diagrams of rescue units in action, the Hostage Rescue Manual is the complete reference work on counter-terrorist procedures all over the world.

Hunter's Guide to Accurate Shooting, by Wayne van Zwoll, Guilford, CT, Lyons Press, 2002. 1st edition. 288 pp. Hardcover. $29.95

Firearms expert van Zwoll explains exactly how to shoot the big-game rifle accurately. Taking into consideration every pertinent factor, he shows a step-by-step analysis of shooting and hunting with the big-game rifle.

Hunting Time: Adventures in Pursuit of North American Big Game: A Forty-Year Chronicle, The, by John E. Howard, Deforest, WI, Saint Huberts Press, 2002. 1st edition. 537 pp., illustrated with drawings. Hardcover. $29.95

From a novice's first hunt for whitetailed deer in his native Wisconsin, to a seasoned hunter's pursuit of a Boone and Crockett Club record book caribou in the northwest territories, the author carries the reader along on his forty year journey through the big game fields of North America.

Instinct Combat Shooting; Defensive Handgunning for Police, by Chuck Klein, Flushing, NY, Looseleaf Law, 2004. 54 pages. Soft cover. NEW. $22.95

Tactical tips for effective armed defense, helpful definitions and court-ready statements that help you clearly articulate and competently justify your deadly force decision-making.

Jack O'Connor Catalogue of Letters, by Ellen Enzler Herring, Agoura, CA, Trophy Room Books, 2002. 1st edition. Hardcover. NEW. 262 pages, 18 illustrations. $55.00

During a sixteen year period beginning in 1960, O'Connor exchanged many letters with his pal, John Jobson. Material from nearly three hundred of these has been assembled and edited by Ellen Enzler Herring and published in chronological order. A number of the letters have been reproduced in full or part. They offer considerable insight into the beloved gun editor and "Dean of Outdoor Writers"over and beyond what we know about him from his books.

Jane's Guns Recognition Guide: 4th Edition, by Ian Hogg, Terry Gander, NY, Harper Collins, 2005. 464 pages, illustrated. Soft cover. NEW. $24.95

This book will help you identify them all. Jane's, always known for meticulous detail in the information of military equipment, aircraft, ships and much more!

Kill or Get Killed, by Col. Rex Applegate, Paladin Press, Boulder, CO, 1996. 400 pp., illus. $49.95

The best and longest-selling book on close combat in history.

Living With Terrorism; Survival Lessons from the Streets of Jerusalem, by Howard Linett, Boulder, CO, Paladin Press, 2005. 277 pages, illustrated with photos. Soft cover. NEW. $20.00

Before these dangers become a reality in your life, read this book.

Lost Classics of Jack O'Connor, The, edited by Jim Casada, Columbia, SC, Live Oak Press, 2004. 1st edition. Hardcover. New in new dust jacket. 33 photos, 40 illus by Dan Burr; 376 pages, with illustrations and photos. $35.00

You'll find 40 of O'Connor's most fascinating stories in the Trade Edition of Lost Classics. Exciting tales with a twist of humor.

Manual for H&R Reising Submachine Gun and Semi-Auto Rifle, edited by George P. Dillman, Desert Publications, El Dorado, AZ, 1994. 81 pp., illus. Paper covers. $14.95

A reprint of the Harrington & Richardson 1943 factory manual and the rare military manual on the H&R submachine gun and semi-auto rifle.

Manufacture of Gunflints, The, by Sydney B.J. Skertchly, facsimile reprint with new introduction by Seymour de Lotbiniere, Museum Restoration Service, Ontario, Canada, 1984. 90 pp., illus. $24.50

Limited edition reprinting of the very scarce London edition of 1879.

Master Tips, by J. Winokur, Potshot Press, Pacific Palisades, CA, 1985. 96 pp., illus. Paper covers. $11.95

Basics of practical shooting.

Military and Police Sniper, The, by Mike R. Lau, Precision Shooting, Inc., Manchester, CT, 1998. 352 pp., illus. Paper covers. $34.95

Advanced precision shooting for combat and law enforcement.

ARMS LIBRARY

Military Small Arms of the 20th Century, 7th Edition, by Ian V. Hogg and John Weeks, DBI Books, a division of Krause Publications, Iola, WI, 2000. 416 pp., illus. Paper covers. Over 800 photographs and illustrations. $24.95

Covers small arms of 46 countries.

Modern Guns Identification and Values, 16th Edition, by Steve and Russell Quertermous, Paducah, KY, Collector's Books, 2006. 1800+ illus; 8.5"x11", 575 pgs. Soft cover. NEW. $18.95

Updated edition features current market values for over 2,500 models of rifles, shotguns, & handguns. Contains model name, gauge or caliber, action, finish or stock & forearm, barrel, cylinder or magazine, sights, weight & length, & comments.

Modern Gun Values: 13th Edition, edited by Dan Shideler, Krause Publications, Iola, WI, 2006. Softcover. NEW. 680 Pages, 3,000+ b&w photos. $24.95

This all-new expanded edition helps collectors identify the firearm, evaluate condition and determine value. Detailed specifications—and current values from specialized experts—are provided for domestic and imported handguns, rifles, shotguns and commemorative firearms. Heavily illustrated. Over 7,500 arms described and valued, in three grades of condition, according to the NRA's Modern standards.

Modern Law Enforcement Weapons & Tactics, 3rd edition, by Patrick Sweeney, Iola, WI, Krause Publications, 2004. Illustrated, b&w photos, 256 pages. $22.99

Sweeney walks you through the latest gear and tactics employed by American law enforcement officers.

Modern Sporting Guns, by Christopher Austyn, Safari Press, Huntington Beach, CA, 1994. 128 pp., illus. $40.00

A discussion of the "best" English guns; round action, over-and-under, boxlocks, hammer guns, bolt action and double rifles as well as accessories.

More Tactical Reality; Why There's No Such Thing as an Advanced Gunfight, by Louis Awerbuck, Boulder, CO, Paladin Press, 2004. 144 pp. Softcover. $25.00

MP-40 Machine Gun, The, Desert Publications, El Dorado, AZ, 1995. 32 pp., illus. Paper covers. $11.95

A reprint of the hard-to-find operating and maintenance manual for one of the most famous machine guns of WWII.

Naval Percussion Locks and Primers, by Lt. J. A. Dahlgren, Museum Restoration Service, Bloomfield, Canada, 1996. 140 pp., illus. $35.00

First published as an Ordnance Memoranda in 1853, this is the finest existing study of percussion locks and primers origin and development.

Official Soviet AKM Manual, translated by Maj. James F. Gebhardt (Ret.), Paladin Press, Boulder, CO, 1999. 120 pp., illus. Paper covers. $18.00

This official military manual, available in English for the first time, was originally published by the Soviet Ministry of Defence. Covers the history, function, maintenance, assembly and disassembly, etc. of the 7.62mm AKM assault rifle.

One-Round War: U.S.M.C. Scout-Snipers in Vietnam, by Peter Senich, Paladin Press, Boulder, CO, 1996. 384 pp., illus. Paper covers $59.95

Sniping in Vietnam focusing specifically on the Marine Corps program.

Optics Digest: Scopes, Binoculars, Rangefinders, and Spotting Scopes, by Clair Rees, Long Beach, CA, Safari Press, 2005. 189 pp. Softcover. NEW. $24.95

OSS Special Operations in China, by Col. F. Mills and John W. Brunner, Williamstown, NJ, Phillips Publications, 2003. 1st edition. 550 pp., illustrated with photos. Hardcover. New in new dust jacket. $34.95

Paintball Digest The Complete Guide to Games, Gear, and Tactics, by Richard Sapp, Iola, WI, Krause Publications, 2004. 1st edition. 272 pp. Softcover. NEW. $19.99

Paleo-Indian Artifacts: Identification & Value Guide, by Lar Hothem, Paducah, KY, Collector Books, 2005. 1st edition. 379 pp. Pictorial hardcover. NEW. $29.95

Panzer Aces German Tank Commanders of WWII, by Franz Kurowski, translated by David Johnston, Mechanicsburg, PA, Stackpole Books, 2004. 1st edition. 448 pp., 50 b&w photos Softcover. NEW. $19.95

Parker Brothers: Knight of the Trigger, by Ed Muderlak, Davis, IL, Old Reliable Publishing, 2002. 223 pp. $25.00

Knight of the Trigger tells the story of the Old West when Parker's most famous gun saleman traveled the country by rail, competing in the pigeon ring, hunting with the rich and famous, and selling the "Old Reliable" Parker shotgun. The life and times of Captain Arthur William du Bray, Parker Brothers' on-the-road sales agent from 1884 to 1926, is described in a novelized version of his interesting life.

Peril in the Powder Mills: Gunpowder & Its Men, by David McMahon & Anne Kelly Lane, West Conshohocken, PA, privately printed, 2004. 1st edition. 118 pp. Softcover. NEW. $18.95

Powder Horns and their Architecture; And Decoration as Used by the Soldier, Indian, Sailor and Traders of the Era, by Madison Grant, York, PA, privately printed, 1987. 165 pp., profusely illustrated. Hardcover. $45.00

Covers homemade pieces from the late eighteenth and early nineteenth centuries.

Practically Speaking: An Illustrated Guide-The Game, Guns and Gear of the International Defensive Pistol Association, by Walt Rauch, Lafayette Hills, PA, privately printed, 2002. 1st edition. 79 pp., illustrated with drawings and color photos. Softcover. $24.95

The game, guns and gear of the International Defensive Pistol Association with real-world applications.

Present Sabers: A Popular History of the U.S. Horse Cavalry, by Allan T. Heninger, Tucson, AZ, Excalibur Publications, 2002. 1st edition. 160 pp., with 148 photographs, 45 illustrations and 4 charts. Softcover. $24.95

An illustrated history of America's involvement with the horse cavalry, from its earliest beginnings during the Revolutionary War through its demise in WWII. The book also contains several appendices, as well as depictions of the regular insignia of all the U.S. Cavalry units.

Principles of Personal Defense, by Jeff Cooper, Paladin Press, Boulder, CO, 2006. 80 pp., illus. Paper covers. $14.00

This revised edition of Jeff Cooper's classic on personal defense offers great new illustrations and a new preface while retaining the theory of individual defense behavior presented in the original book.

Queen's Rook: A Soldier's Story, by Croft Barker, Flatonia,TX, Cistern Publishing, 2004. Limited edition of 500 copies. 177 pages, with 50 never before published photographs. Soft cover. NEW. $35.00

Men of the U.S. Army were assigned to South Vietnamese Infantry companies and platoons. Many of these men were lost in a war that is still misunderstood. This is their story, written in their own words. These Americans, and the units they lived with, engaged in savage fights against Viet Cong guerillas and North Vietnamese Army Regulars in the dark, deadly jungles north of Saigon.

Quotable Hunter, The, edited by Jay Cassell and Peter Fiduccia, The Lyons Press, N.Y., 1999. 224 pp., illus. $20.00

This collection of more than three hundred memorable quotes from hunters through the ages captures the essence of the sport, with all its joys idiosyncrasies, and challenges.

Real World Self-Defense by Jerry Vancook, Boulder, CO, Paladin Press, 1999. 224 pp. Soft cover. NEW. $20.00

Presenting tactics and techniques that are basic, easy to learn and proven effective under the stress of combat, he covers unarmed defense, improvised weapons, edged weapons, firearms and more, photos, illus.

Renaissance Drill Book, by Jacob de Gheyn, edited by David J. Blackmore, Mechanicsburg, PA, Greenhill Books, 2003. 1st edition. 248 pp., 117 illustrations. Hardcover. $24.95

Jacob de Gheyn's Exercise of Armes was an immense success when first published in 1607. It is a fascinating 17th-century military manual, designed to instruct contemporary soldiers how to handle arms effectively, and correctly, and it makes for a unique glimpse into warfare as waged in the Thirty Years War and the English Civil War. In addition, detailed illustrations show the various movements and postures to be adopted during use of the pike.

Running Recon, A Photo Journey with SOG Special Ops Along the Ho Chi Minh Trail, by Frank Greco, Boulder, CO, Paladin Press, 2004. Paper covers. $50.00

Running Recon is a combination of military memoir and combat photography book. It reflects both the author's experience in Kontum, Vietnam, from April 1969 to April 1970 as part of the top-secret Studies and Observation Group (SOG) and the collective experience of SOG veterans in general. What sets it apart from other Vietnam books is its wealth of more than 700 photographs, many never before published, from the author's personal collection and those of his fellow SOG veterans.

Sharpshooting for Sport and War, by W.W. Greener, Wolfe Publishing Co., Prescott, AZ, 1995. 192 pp., illus. $30.00

This classic reprint explores the *first* expanding bullet; service rifles; shooting positions; trajectories; recoil; external ballistics; and other valuable information.

Shooter's Bible 2007 No. 98, by Wayne Van Zwoll, Stoeger Publishing, 2006. 576 pages. Pictorial Soft cover. NEW. $24.95

New for this edition is a special Web Directory designed to complement the regular Reference section, including the popular Gun finder index.

Shooting Buffalo Rifles of the Old West, by Mike Venturino, MLV Enterprises, Livingston, MT, 2002. 278 pp., illustrated with b&w photos. Softcover. $30.00

This tome will take you through the history, the usage, the many models, and the actual shooting (and how to's) of the many guns that saw service on the Frontier and are lovingly called "Buffalo Rifles" today. If you love to shoot your Sharps, Ballards, Remingtons, or Springfield "Trapdoors" for hunting or competition, or simply love Old West history, your library WILL NOT be complete without this latest book from Mike Venturino!

Shooting Colt Single Actions, by Mike Venturino, MLV Enterprises, Livingston, MT, 1997. 205 pp., illus. Softcover. $25.00
A complete examination of the Colt Single Action including styles, calibers and generations, b&w photos throughout.

Shooting Lever Guns of the Old West, by Mike Venturino, MLV Enterprises, Livingston, MT, 1999. 300 pp., illus. Softcover. $27.95
Shooting the lever action type repeating rifles of our American West.

Shooting Sixguns of the Old West, by Mike Venturino, MLV Enterprises, Livingston, MT, 1997. 221 pp., illus. Paper covers. $26.50
A comprehensive look at the guns of the early West: Colts, Smith & Wesson and Remingtons, plus blackpowder and reloading specs.

Shooting to Live, by Capt. W.E. Fairbairn and Capt. E.A. Sykes, Paladin Press, Boulder, CO, 1997, 4½" x 7", soft cover, illus., 112 pp. $14.00
Shooting to Live is the product of Fairbairn's and Sykes' practical experience with the handgun. Hundreds of incidents provided the basis for the first true book on life-or-death shootouts with the pistol. Shooting to Live teaches all concepts, considerations and applications of combat pistol craft.

Small Arms of World War II, by Chris Chant, St. Paul, MN, MBI Publishing Company, 2001. 1st edition. 96 pp., single page on each weapon with photograph, description, and a specifications table. Hardcover. New. $13.95
Detailing the design and development of each weapon, this book covers the most important infantry weapons used by both Allied and Axis soldiers between 1939 and 1945. These include both standard infantry bolt-action rifles, such as the German Kar 98 and the British Lee-Enfield, plus the automatic rifles that entered service toward the end of the war, such as the Stg 43. As well as rifles, this book also features submachine guns, machine guns and handguns and a specifications table for each weapon.

Sniper Training, FM 23-10, Reprint of the U.S. Army field manual of August, 1994, Paladin Press, Boulder, CO, 1995. 352 pp., illus. Paper covers. $30.00
The most up-to-date U.S. military sniping information and doctrine.

Song of Blue Moccasin, by Roy Chandler, Jacksonville, NC, Ron Brigade Armory, 2004. 231 pp. Hardcover. New in new dust jacket. $45.00

Speak Like a Native; Professional Secrets for Mastering Foreign Languages, by Michael Janich, Boulder CO, Paladin Press, 2005. 136 pages. Soft cover. NEW. $19.00
No matter what language you wish to learn or the level of fluency you need to attain, this book can help you learn to speak like a native.

Special Operations: Weapons and Tactics, by Timothy Mullin, London, Greenhill Press, 2003. 1st edition. 176 pp., with 189 illustrations. $39.95
The tactics and equipment of Special Forces explained in full, Contains 200 images of weaponry and training. This highly illustrated guide covers the full experience of special operations training from every possible angle. There is also considerable information on nonfirearm usage, such as specialized armor and ammunition.

Standard Catalog of Firearms 2008, 18th Edition, by Dan Shideler, Iola, WI, Krause Publications, 2007. 1504 pages, 7,100+ b&w photos, plus a 16-page color section. Paper covers. $34.95
Now in its 18th year and completely updated for 2008, this edition of the world famous Standard Catalog of Firearms is bigger and better than ever. With entries for virtually all of the world's commercial firearms from the percussion era to the present day, Standard Catalog of Firearms is the only book you need to identify and price collectible rifles, handguns and shotguns. Features include "Sleepers": Collectible firearms that are outperforming the market. Value Trends: Real-Life auction reports showing value ranges. How to buy and sell on the Internet.

Standard Catalog of Military Firearms 3rd Edition: The Collector's Price & Reference Guide, by Ned Schwing, Iola, WI, Krause Publications, 2005. 480 pp. Softcover. $29.99
A companion volume to Standard Catalog of Firearms, this revised and expanded second edition comes complete with all the detailed information readers found useful and more. Listings beginning with the early cartridge models of the 1870s to the latest high-tech sniper rifles have been expanded to include more models, variations, historical information, and data, offering more detail for the military firearms collector, shooter, and history buff. Identification of specific firearms is easier with nearly 250 additional photographs. Plus, readers will enjoy "snap shots," small personal articles from experts relating real-life experiences with exclusive models. Revised to include every known military firearm available to the U.S. collector. Special feature articles on focused aspects of collecting and shooting.

Street Tough, Hard Core, Anything Goes, Street Fighting Fundamentals, by Phil Giles, Boulder, CO, Paladin Press, 2004. 176 pages. Soft cover. NEW. $25.00
A series of intense training drills performed at full power and full speed sets the Street Tough program apart from all other self-defense regimens.

Stress Fire, Vol. 1: Stress Fighting for Police, by Massad Ayoob, Police Bookshelf, Concord, NH, 1984. 149 pp., illus. Paper covers. $11.95
Gunfighting for police, advanced tactics and techniques.

Stress Fire Gunfighting for Police Vol. 2; Advanced Combat Shotgun, by Massad Ayoob, Police Bookshelf, Concord, NH, 1997. 212 pp., illus. Paper covers. $12.95
The long-awaited second volume in Massad Ayoob's series on Advanced Gunfighting for Police. Learn to control the 12-gauge shotgun in the most rapid fire, pain-rree aimed fire from the shoulder, Speed reloads that don't fail under stress, proven jam-response techniques, keys to selecting a good shotgun.

Tactical Advantage, The, by Gabriel Suarez, Paladin Press, Boulder, CO, 1998. 216 pp., illus. Paper covers. $22.00
Learn combat tactics that have been tested in the world's toughest schools.

Tactical Marksman, by Dave M. Lauch, Paladin Press, Boulder, CO, 1996. 165 pp., illus. Paper covers. $35.00
A complete training manual for police and practical shooters.

Tim Murphy Rifleman Frontier Series Volume 3, by Roy Chandler, Jacksonville, NC, Iron Brigade Armory, 2003. 1st edition. 396 pp. Hardcover. $39.95
Tim Murphy may be our young nation's earliest recognized hero. Murphy was seized by Seneca Tribesmen during his infancy. Traded to the Huron, he was renamed and educated by Sir William Johnson, a British colonial officer. Freed during the prisoner exchange of 1764, Murphy discovered his superior ability with a Pennsylvania longrifle. An early volunteer in the Pennsylvania militia, Tim Murphy served valiantly in rifle companies including the justly famed Daniel Morgan's Riflemen. This is Murphy's story.

To Ride, Shoot Straight, and Speak the Truth, by Jeff Cooper, Paladin Press, Boulder, CO, 1997, 5½" x 8½", soft-cover, illus., 384 pp. $32.00
Combat mind-set, proper sighting, tactical residential architecture, nuclear war-these are some of the many subjects explored by Jeff Cooper in this illustrated anthology. The author discusses various arms, fighting skills and the importance of knowing how to defend oneself, and one's honor, in our rapidly changing world.

Trailriders Guide to Cowboy Action Shooting, by James W. Barnard, Pioneer Press, Union City, TN, 1998. 134 pp., plus 91 photos, drawings and charts. Paper covers. $24.95
Covers the complete spectrum of this shooting discipline, from how to dress to authentic leather goods, which guns are legal, calibers, loads and ballistics.

Traveler's Guide to the Firearms Laws of the Fifty States, 2007 Edition, by Scott Kappas, KY, Traveler's Guide, 2007, 64pp,. Softcover. $12.95

U.S. Army Hand-to-Hand Combat: FM 21-150, 1954 Edition, Boulder,CO, Paladin Press, 2005. 192 pp. illus. Soft cover. $20.00

U.S. Infantry Weapons in Combat: Personal Experiences from World War II and Korea, by Mark Goodwin w/ forward by Scott Duff, Export, PA, Scott Duff Pub., 2005.
237pp, over 50 photos and drawings. Soft cover. $23.50
The stories about U.S. infantry weapons contained in this book are the real hands-on experiences of the men who actually used them for their intended purposes.

U.S. Marine Corp Rifle and Pistol Marksmanship, 1935, reprinting of a government publication, Lancer Militaria, Mt. Ida, AR, 1991. 99 pp., illus. Paper covers. $11.95
The old corps method of precision shooting.

U.S. Marine Corps Scout/Sniper Training Manual, Lancer Militaria, Mt. Ida, AR, 1989. Softcover. $27.95
Reprint of the original sniper training manual used by the Marksmanship Training Unit of the Marine Corps Development and Education Command in Quantico, Virginia.

U.S. Marine Corps Scout-Sniper, World War II and Korea, by Peter R. Senich, Paladin Press, Boulder, CO, 1994. 236 pp., illus. $44.95
The most thorough and accurate account ever printed on the training, equipment and combat experiences of the U.S. Marine Corps Scout-Snipers.

U.S. Marine Corps Sniping, Lancer Militaria, Mt. Ida, AR, 1989. Irregular pagination. Softcover. $18.95
A reprint of the official Marine Corps FMFM1-3B.

U.S. Marine Uniforms-1912-1940, by Jim Moran, Williamstown, NJ, Phillips Publications, 2001. 174 pp., illustrated with b&w photographs. Hardcover. $49.95

Ultimate Sniper: An Advanced Training Manual for Military and Police Snipers, Updated and Expanded Edition, by Major John L. Plaster, Paladin Press, Boulder, CO, 2006. 584 pp., illus. Paper covers. $49.95
Now this revolutionary book has been completely updated and expanded for the 21st century. Through revised text, new photos, specialized illustrations, updated charts and additional information sidebars, The Ultimate Sniper once again thoroughly details the three great skill areas of sniping – marksmanship, fieldcraft and tactics.

Uniforms And Equipment of the Imperial Japanese Army in World War II, by Mike Hewitt, Atglen, PA, Schiffer Publications, 2002. 176 pp., with over 520 color and b&w photos. Hardcover. $59.95

Unrepentant Sinner, by Col. Charles Askins, Paladin Press, Boulder, CO, 2000. 322 pp., illus. $29.95

The autobiography of Colonel Charles Askins.

Vietnam Order of Battle, by Shelby L. Stanton, William C. Westmoreland, Mechanicsburg, PA, Stackpole Books, 2003. 1st edition. 416 pp., 32 in full color, 101 halftones. Hardcover. $69.95

A monumental, encyclopedic work of immense detail concerning U.S. Army and allied forces that fought in the Vietnam War from 1962 through 1973. Extensive lists of units providing a record of every Army unit that served in Vietnam, down to and including separate companies, and also including U.S. Army aviation and riverine units. Shoulder patches and distinctive unit insignia of all divisions and battalions. Extensive maps portraying unit locations at each six-month interval. Photographs and descriptions of all major types of equipment employed in the conflict. Plus much more!

Warriors; On Living with Courage, Discipline, and Honor, by Loren Christensen, Boulder, CO, Paladin Press, 2004. 376 pages. Soft cover. NEW. $20.00

The writers who contributed to this work are a diverse mix, from soldiers, cops and SWAT officers to martial art masters to experts in the fields of workplace violence, theology and school safety. They are some of the finest warrior authors, warrior trainers and warrior scholars today. Many have faced death, survived and now teach others to do the same. Here they speak candidly on what it's like to sacrifice, to train, to protect.

"Walking Stick" Method of Self-Defence, The, by an officer of the Indian police, Boulder, CO: Paladin Press, 2004. 1st edition. 112 pages. Soft cover. NEW. $15.00

The entire range of defensive and offensive skills is discussed and demonstrated, including guards, strikes, combinations, counterattacks, feints and tricks, double-handed techniques and training drills.

Weapons of Delta Force, by Fred Pushies, St. Paul, MN, MBI Publishing Company, 2002. 1st edition. 128 pgs., 100 b&w and 100 color illustrated. Hardcover. $24.95

America's elite counter-terrorist organization, Delta Force, is a handpicked group of the U.S. Army's finest soldiers. Delta uses some of the most sophisticated weapons in the field today, and all are detailed in this book. Pistols, sniper rifles, special mission aircraft, fast attack vehicles, SCUBA and paratrooper gear, and more are presented in this fully illustrated account of our country's heroes and their tools of the trade.

Weapons of the Waffen-SS, by Bruce Quarrie, Sterling Publishing Co., Inc., 1991. 168 pp., illus. $24.95

An in-depth look at the weapons that made Hitler's Waffen-SS the fearsome fighting machine it was.

Weatherby: The Man, The Gun, The Legend, by Grits and Tom Gresham, Cane River Publishing Co., Natchitoches, LA, 1992. 290 pp., illus. $34.95

A fascinating look at the life of the man who changed the course of firearms development in America.

Winchester Era, The, by David Madis, Art & Reference House, Brownsville, TX, 1984. 100 pp., illus. $19.95

Story of the Winchester company, management, employees, etc.

Winchester Pocket Guide; Identification and Pricing for 50 Collectible Rifles and Shotguns, by Ned Schwing, Iola,WI, Krause Publications, 2004. 224 pages, illustrated. Soft cover. NEW. $12.95

The Winchester Pocket Guide also features advice on collecting, grading and pricing the collectible firearms.

With British Snipers to the Reich, by Capt. C. Shore, Lander Militaria, Mt. Ida, AR, 1988. 420 pp., illus. $29.95

One of the greatest books ever written on the art of combat sniping.

World's Machine Pistols and Submachine Guns-Vol. 2a 1964 to 1980, The, by Nelson & Musgrave, Ironside International, Alexandria, VA, 2000. 673 pp. $69.95

Containing data, history and photographs of over 200 weapons. With a special section covering shoulder stocked automatic pistols, 100 additional photos.

Wyatt Earp: A Biography of the Legend: Volume 1: The Cowtown Years, by Lee A. Silva, Santa Ana, CA, privately printed, 2002. 1st edition signed. Hardcover. New in new dust jacket. $86.95

GUNSMITHING

Accurizing the Factory Rifle, by M.L. McPhereson, Precision Shooting, Inc., Manchester, CT, 1999. 335 pp., illus. Paper covers. $44.95

A long-awaiting book, which bridges the gap between the rudimentary (mounting sling swivels, scope blocks and that general level of accomplishment) and the advanced (precision chambering, barrel fluting, and that general level of accomplishment) books that are currently available today.

Antique Firearms Assembly Disassembly: The Comprehensive Guide to Pistols, Rifles, & Shotguns, by David Chicoine, Iola, WI, Krause Publications, 2005. 528 pages, 600 b&w photos & illus. Soft cover. NEW. $29.95

Create a resource unequaled by any. Features over 600 photos of antique and rare firearms for quick identification.

Art of Engraving, The, by James B. Meek, F. Brownell & Son, Montezuma, IA, 1973. 196 pp., illus. $47.95

A complete, authoritative, imaginative and detailed study in training for gun engraving. The first book of its kind–and a great one.

Checkering and Carving of Gun Stocks, by Monte Kennedy, Stackpole Books, Harrisburg, PA, 1962. 175 pp., illus. $39.95

Revised, enlarged cloth-bound edition of a much sought-after, dependable work.

Firearms Assembly/Disassembly, Part I: Automatic Pistols, 2nd Revised Edition, The Gun Digest Book of, by J.B. Wood, DBI Books, a division of Krause Publications, Iola, WI, 1999. 480 pp., illus. Paper covers. $24.95

Covers 58 popular autoloading pistols plus nearly 200 variants of those models integrated into the text and completely cross-referenced in the index.

Firearms Assembly/Disassembly Part II: Revolvers, Revised Edition, The Gun Digest Book of, by J.B. Wood, DBI Books, a division of Krause Publications, Iola, WI, 1997. 480 pp., illus. Paper covers. $27.95

Covers 49 popular revolvers plus 130 variants. The most comprehensive and professional presentation available to either hobbyist or gunsmith.

Firearms Assembly/Disassembly Part III: Rimfire Rifles 3rd Edition, The Gun Digest Book of, by J. B. Wood, Krause Publications, Iola, WI, 2006. Softcover. 576 Pages, 1,590 b&w photos. $27.95

This redesigned volume provides comprehensive step-by-step disassembly instruction patterns for 74 rifles-nearly 200 firearms when combined with variations. All the hands-on information you need to increase accuracy and speed.

Firearms Assembly/Disassembly Part IV: Centerfire Rifles, 3rd Revised Edition, The Gun Digest Book of, by J.B. Wood, Krause Publications, Iola, WI, 2004. 480 pp., illus. Paper covers. $24.95

Covers 54 popular centerfire rifles plus 300 variants. The most comprehensive and professional presentation available to either hobbyist or gunsmith.

Firearms Assembly/Disassembly, Part V: Shotguns, Revised Edition, The Gun Digest Book of, by J.B. Wood, Krause Publications, Iola, WI, 2002. 480 pp., illus. Paper covers. $24.95

Covers 46 popular shotguns plus over 250 variants with step-by-step instructions on how to dismantle and reassemble each. The most comprehensive and professional presentation available to either hobbyist or gunsmith.

Firearms Assembly: The NRA Guide to Rifle and Shotguns, NRA Books, Wash., DC, 1980. 264 pp., illus. Paper covers. $14.95

Text and illustrations explaining the takedown of 125 rifles and shotguns, domestic and foreign.

Firearms Assembly: The NRA Guide to Pistols and Revolvers, NRA Books, Wash., DC, 1980. 253 pp., illus. Paper covers. $14.95

Text and illustrations explaining the takedown of 124 pistol and revolver models, domestic and foreign.

Firearms Bluing and Browning, by R.H. Angier, Stackpole Books, Harrisburg, PA. 151 pp., illus. $19.95

A world master gunsmith reveals his secrets of building, repairing and renewing a gun, quite literally, lock, stock and barrel. A useful, concise text on chemical coloring methods for the gunsmith and mechanic.

Guns and Gunmaking Tools of Southern Appalachia, by John Rice Irwin, Schiffer Publishing Ltd., 1983. 118 pp., illus. Paper covers. $9.95

The story of the Kentucky rifle.

Gunsmith Kinks, by F.R. (Bob) Brownell, F. Brownell & Son, Montezuma, IA, 1st ed., 1969. 496 pp., well illus. $22.98

A widely useful accumulation of shop kinks, short cuts, techniques and pertinent comments by practicing gunsmiths from all over the world.

Gunsmith Kinks 2, by Bob Brownell, F. Brownell & Son, Publishers, Montezuma, IA, 1983. 496 pp., illus. $22.95

A collection of gunsmithing knowledge, shop kinks, new and old techniques, shortcuts and general know-how straight from those who do them best–the gunsmiths.

Gunsmith Kinks 3, edited by Frank Brownell, Brownells Inc., Montezuma, IA, 1993. 504 pp., illus. $24.95

Tricks, knacks and "kinks" by professional gunsmiths and gun tinkerers. Hundreds of valuable ideas are given in this volume.

Gunsmith Kinks 4, edited by Frank Brownell, Brownells Inc., Montezuma, IA, 2001. 564 pp., illus. 332 detailed illustrations. 560+ pages with 706 separate subject headings and over 5000 cross-indexed entries. $27.75

An incredible gold mine of information.

Gunsmith Machinist, The, by Steve Acker, Village Press Publications Inc, Michigan. 2001. Hardcover, New in new dust jacket. $69.95

Gunsmith of Grenville County: Building the American Longrifle, The, by Peter Alexander, Texarkana, TX, Scurlock Publishing Co., 2002. 400 pp.in, with hundreds of illustrations, and six color photos of original rifles. Stiff paper covers. $45.00

The most extensive how-to book on building longrifles ever published. Takes you through every step of building your own longrifle, from shop set up and tools to engraving, carving and finishing.

Gunsmithing, by Roy F. Dunlap, Stackpole Books, Harrisburg, PA, 1990. 742 pp., illus. $44.95

A manual of firearm design, construction, alteration and remodeling. For amateur and professional gunsmiths and users of modern firearms.

Gunsmithing at Home: Lock, Stock and Barrel, by John Traister, Stoeger Publishing Co., Wayne, NJ, 1997. 320 pp., illus. Paper covers. $19.95

A complete step-by-step fully illustrated guide to the art of gunsmithing.

Gunsmithing Shotguns: The Complete Guide to Care & Repair, by David Henderson, New York, Globe Pequot, 2003. 1st edition. Hardcover. NEW. $24.95

Gunsmithing: Guns of the Old West: Expanded 2nd Edition, by David Chicoine, Iola, WI, Krause Publications, 2004. 446 pp.in, illus. Softcover. NEW. $29.95

This updated second edition guides collectors, cowboy action shooters, hobbyists and Old West re-enactors through repairing and improving Old West firearms. New additions include 125 high-resolution diagrams and illustrations, five new handgun models, four new long gun models, and an expanded and illustrated glossary. The book offers expanded coverage of the first edition's featured guns (over 40 original and replica models), as well as updated gunsmithing tips and advice. The step-by-step, detailed illustrations demonstrate to both amateur and advanced gunsmiths how to repair and upgrade Old West firearms.

Gunsmithing: Pistols & Revolvers: Expanded 2nd Edition, by Patrick Sweeney, Iola, WI, Krause Publications, 2004. 384 Pages, illustrated, 850 b&w photos. $24.99

Set up an efficient and organized workplace and learn what tools are needed. Then, tackle projects like installing new grips, adjusting trigger pull and sight replacement. Includes a troubleshooting guide, glossary terms and a directory of suppliers and services for most brands of handguns.

Gunsmithing: Rifles, by Patrick Sweeney, Krause Publications, Iola, WI, 1999. 352 pp., illus. Paper covers. $24.95

Tips for lever-action rifles. Building a custom Ruger 10/22. Building a better hunting rifle.

Home Gunsmithing the Colt Single Action Revolvers, by Loren W. Smith, Ray Riling Arms Books, Co., Phila., PA, 2001. 119 pp., illus. $24.95.

Affords the Colt Single Action owner detailed, pertinent information on the operating and servicing of this famous and historic handgun.

How to Convert Military Rifles, Williams Gun Sight Co., Davision, MI, new and enlarged seventh edition, 1997. 76 pp., illus. Paper covers. $13.95

This latest edition updated the changes that have occured over the past thirty years. Tips, instructions and illustratons on how to convert popular military rifles as the Enfield, Mauser 96 and SKS just to name a few are presented.

Mauser M98 & M96, by R.A. Walsh, Wolfe Publishing Co., Prescott, AR, 1998. 123 pp., illus. Paper covers. $32.50

How to build your own favorite custom Mauser rifle from two of the best bolt action rifle designs ever produced–the military Mauser Model 1898 and Model 1896 bolt rifles.

Mr. Single Shot's Gunsmithing-Idea-Book, by Frank de Haas, Mark de Haas, Orange City, IA, 1996. 168 pp., illus. Paper covers. $22.50

Offers easy to follow, step-by-step instructions for a wide variety of gunsmithing procedures all reinforced by plenty of photos.

Recreating the American Longrifle, by William Buchele, et al, George Shumway Publisher, York, Pa, 5th edition, 1999. 175 pp., illus. $40.00

Includes full size plans for building a Kentucky rifle.

Story of Pope's Barrels, The, by Ray M. Smith, R&R Books, Livonia, NY, 1993. 203 pp., illus. $39.00

A reissue of a 1960 book whose author knew Pope personally. It will be of special interest to Schuetzen rifle fans, since Pope's greatest days were at the height of the Schuetzen-era before WWI.

Survival Gunsmithing, by J.B. Wood, Desert Publications, Cornville, AZ, 1986. 92 pp., illus. Paper covers. $11.95

A guide to repair and maintenance of the most popular rifles, shotguns and handguns.

Tactical 1911, The, by Dave Lauck, Paladin Press, Boulder, CO, 1998. 137 pp., illus. Paper covers. $20.00

Here is the only book you will ever need to teach you how to select, modify, employ and maintain your Colt.

HANDGUNS

.22 Caliber Handguns; A Shooter's Guide, by D.F. Geiger, Lincoln, RI, Andrew Mowbray, Inc., 2003. 1st edition. Softcover. $21.95

.380 Enfield No. 2 Revolver, The, by Mark Stamps and Ian Skennerton, I.D.S.A. Books, Piqua, OH, 1993. 124 pp., 80 illus. Paper covers. $19.95

9mm Parabellum; The History & Development of the World's 9mm Pistols & Ammunition, by Klaus-Peter Konig and Martin Hugo, Schiffer Publishing Ltd., Atglen, PA, 1993. 304 pp., illus. $39.95

Detailed history of 9mm weapons from Belguim, Italy, Germany, Israel, France, U.S.A., Czechoslovakia, Hungary, Poland, Brazil, Finland and Spain.

A Study of Colt New Army and Navy Pattern Double action Revolvers 1889-1908, by Robert Best. Privately Printed, 2005, 2nd Printing. 276 pages. Hardcover $62.00

A Study…" is a detailed look into Colt's development and production of the Double Action Swing Out Cylinder New Army and Navy series revolvers. Civilian model production, U.S. Army and Navy models and contracts, and other Government organizations using these revolvers are all covered in this book. There are over 150 photographs with 24 pages of color photos to show specific markings and manufacturing changes. Fully documented.

Advanced Master Handgunning, by Charles Stephens, Paladin Press, Boulder, CO, 1994. 72 pp., illus. Paper covers. $14.00

Secrets and surefire techniques for winning handgun competitions.

Advanced Tactical Marksman More High Performance Techniques for Police, Military, and Practical Shooters, by Dave M. Lauck. Paladin Press, Boulder, CO, 2002. 1st edition. 232 pp., photos, illus. Softcover $35.00

Lauck, one of the most respected names in high-performance shooting and gunsmithing, refines and updates his 1st book. Dispensing with overcomplicated mil-dot formulas and minute-of-angle calculations, Lauck shows you how to achieve superior accuracy and figure out angle shots, train for real-world scenarios, choose optics and accessories.

American Beauty: The Prewar Colt National Match Government Model Pistol, by Timothy Mullin, Collector Grade Publications, Canada, 1999. 72 pp., 69 illus. $34.95

69 illustrations, 20 in full color photos of factory engraved guns and other authenticated upgrades, including rare 'double-carved' ivory grips.

Automatic Pistol, The, by J.B.L. Noel, Foreword by Timothy J. Mullin, Boulder, CO, Paladin Press, 2004. 128 pp., illus. Softcover. NEW. $14.00

Ayoob Files: The Book, The, by Massad Ayoob, Police Bookshelf, Concord, NH, 1995. 223 pp., illus. Paper covers. $14.95

The best of Massad Ayoob's acclaimed series in *American Handgunner* magazine.

Big Bore Handguns, by John Taffin, Krause Publications, Iola, WI, 2002. 1st edition. 352 pp., 320 b&w photos with a 16-page color section. Hardcover. $39.95

Gives honest reviews and an inside look at shooting, hunting, and competing with the biggest handguns around. Covers handguns from major gunmakers, as well as handgun customizing, accessories, reloading, and cowboy activities. Significant coverage is also given to handgun customizing, accessories, reloading, and popular shooting hobbies including hunting and cowboy activities.

Bill Ruger's .22 Pistol: A Photographic Essay of the Ruger Rimfire Pistol, by Don Findlay, New York, Simon & Schuster, 2000. 2nd printing. Limited edition of 100 copies, signed and numbered. Hardcover, NEW. $100.00

Browning High Power Automatic Pistol (Expanded Edition), by Blake R. Stevens, Collector Grade Publications, Canada, 1996. 310 pp., with 313 illus. $49.95

An in-depth chronicle of seventy years of High Power history, from John M. Browning's original 16-shot prototypes to the present. Profusely illustrated with rare original photos and drawings from the FN Archive to describe virtually every sporting and military version of the High Power. The Expanded Edition contains 30 new pages on the interesting Argentine full-auto High Power, the latest FN 'MK3' and BDA9 pistols, plus FN's revolutionary P90 5.7x28mm Personal Defense Weapon, and more!

Browning Hi-Power Assembly, Disassembly Manual 9mm, by Skennerton & Riling, Ray Riling Arms Books Co. Philadelphia, PA, 2005. 36 pages, illustrated. $5.00

Ideal workshop reference for stripping & assembly with exploded parts drawings, specifications, service accessories, historical information and recommended reading references. Ideal workbook for shooters and collectors alike. The binding is triple saddle-stitched with a durable plastic laminated cover.

Browning Hi-Power Pistols, Desert Publications, Cornville, AZ, 1982. 20 pp., illus. Paper covers. $13.95

Covers all facets of the various military and civilian models of the Browning Hi-Power pistol.

Canadian Military Handguns 1855-1985, by Clive M. Law, Museum Restoration Service, Bloomfield, Ont., Canada, 1994. 130pp., illus. $40.00

A long-awaited and important history for arms historians and pistol collectors.

Classic Handguns of the 20th Century, by David Arnold. Iola, WI, Krause Publications, 2004. 144 pages, color photos. Softcover. $24.99

You'll need this book to find out what qualities, contributions and characteristics made each of the twenty handguns found within a "classic" in the eyes of noted gun historian and author, David W. Arnold. Join him on this most fascinating visual walk through the most significant and prolific handguns of the 20th century. From the Colt Single-Action Army Revolver and the German P08 Luger to the Walther P-38 and Beretta Model 92.

Collecting U. S. Pistols & Revolvers, 1909-1945, by J. C. Harrison. The Arms Chest, Oklahoma City, OK, 1999. 2nd edition (revised). 185 pp., illus. Spiral bound. $35.00

Valuable and detailed reference book for the collector of U.S. pistols & revolvers. Identifies standard issue original military models of the M1911, M1911A1 and M1917 Cal .45 pistols and revolvers as produced by all manufacturers from 1911 through 1945. Plus .22 Ace models, National Match models, and similar foreign military models produced by Colt or manufactured under Colt license, plus arsenal repair, refinish and lend-lease models.

Colt .45 Pistol M1911A1 Assembly, Disassembly Manual, by Skennerton & Riling, Ray Riling Arms Books Co. Philadelphia, PA, 2005. 36 pages, illustrated. $5.00

Ideal workshop reference for stripping & assembly with exploded parts drawings, specifications, service accessories, historical information and recommended reading references. Ideal workbook for shooters and collectors alike. The binding is triple saddle-stitched with a durable plastic laminated cover.

Colt .45 Auto Pistol, compiled from U.S. War Dept. Technical Manuals, and reprinted by Desert Publications, Cornville, AZ, 1978. 80 pp., illus. Paper covers. $14.95

Covers every facet of this famous pistol from mechanical training, manual of arms, disassembly, repair and replacement of parts.

Colt Single Action Army Revolver Study: New Discoveries, by Kenneth Moore, Lincoln, RI, Andrew Mowbray, Inc., 2003. 1st edition. Hardcover. NEW. $47.95

Combat Perspective; The Thinking Man's Guide to Self-Defense, by Gabriel Suarez, Boulder, CO, Paladin Press, 2003. 1st edition. 112 pp. Softcover. $15.00

In the Combat Perspective, Suarez keys in on developing your knowledge about and properly organizing your mental attitude toward combat to improve your odds of winning – not just surviving – such a fight. In this book he examines each in a logical and scientific manner, demonstrating why, when it comes to defending your life, the mental edge is at least as critical to victory as the tactical advantage.

Complete Encyclopedia of Pistols & Revolvers, by A.E. Hartnik, Knickerbocker Press, New York, NY, 2003. 272 pp., illus. $19.95

A comprehensive encyclopedia specially written for collectors and owners of pistols and revolvers.

Concealable Pocket Pistols: How to Choose and Use Small-Caliber Handguns, by Terence McLeod, Paladin Press, 2001. 1st edition. 80 pp. Softcover. $14.00

Small-caliber handguns are often maligned as too puny for serious self-defense, but millions of Americans own and carry these guns and have used them successfully to stop violent assaults. Find out what millions of Americans already know about these practical self-defense tools.

Concelealed Handgun Manual, The, 4th Edition, by Chris Bird. San Antonio, Privateer Publications, 2004. 332 pages, illus. Softcover. NEW. $21.95

If you carry a gun for personal protection, or plan to, you need to read this book. You will learn whether carrying a gun is for you, what gun to choose and how to carry it, how to stay out of trouble, when to shoot and how to shoot, gunfighting tactics, what to expect after you have shot someone, and how to apply for a concealed-carry license in 30 states, plus never-before published details of actual shooting incidents.

Confederate Lemat Revolver; Secret Weapon of the Confederacy?, The, by Doug Adams, Lincoln, RI, Andrew Mowbray, Inc.,2005. 1st edition. Nearly 200 spectacular full-color illustrations and over 70 b&w period photos, illustrations and patent drawings. 112 pages. Softcover. NEW. $29.95

This exciting new book describes LeMat's wartime adventures aboard blockade runners and alongside the famous leaders of the Confederacy, as well as exploring, as never before, the unique revolvers that he manufactured for the Southern Cause.

Darling Pepperbox: The Story of Samuel Colt's Forgotten Competitors in Bellingham, The, Mass. and Woonsocket, RI, by Stuart C. Mowbray, Lincoln, RI, Andrew Mowbray, Inc., 2004. 1st edition. 104 pp. Softcover. NEW. $19.95

Developmental Cartridge Handguns of .22 Calibre, as Produced in the United States & Abroad from 1855 to 1875, by John S. Laidacker, Atglen, PA, Schiffer Publications, 2003. Reprint. 597 pp., with over 860 b&w photos, drawings, and charts. Hardcover. $100.00

This book is a reprint edition of the late John Laidacker's personal study of early .22 Cartridge Handguns from 1855-1875. Laidacker's primary aim was to offer a quick reference to the collector, and his commentary on the wide variety of types, variations and makers, as well as detailed photography, make this a superb addition to any firearm library.

Effective Handgun Defense, by Frank James, Iola, WI, Krause Publications, 2004. 1st edition. 223 pp, illustated, softcover. NEW $19.95

Effective Handgun Defense, it's readily apparent that he'd have had no problem making his way in an urban environment either. He has a keen mind for the requirements and nuances for "concealed carry" and personal defense, and a fluid style of presenting his material that is neither awkward nor "precious."

Engraved Handguns of .22 Calibre, by John S. Laidacker, Atglen, PA, Schiffer Publications, 2003. 1st edition. 192 pp., with over 400 color and b&w photos. $69.95

Essential Guide to Handguns: Firearms Instruction for Personal Defense and Protection, by Stephen Rementer and Brian Eimer, Phd., Flushing, NY, Looseleaf law Publications, 2005. 1st edition. Over 300 pages plus illustrations. Softcover. NEW. $24.89

Farnam Method of Defensive Handgunning, The, by John S. Farnam, Police Bookshelf, 1999. 191 pp., illus. Paper covers. $24.00

A book intended to not only educate the new shooter, but also to serve as a guide and textbook for his and his instructor's training courses.

Fast and Fancy Revolver Shooting, by Ed McGivern, Anniversary Edition, Winchester Press, Piscataway, NJ, 1984. 484 pp., illus. $19.95

A fascinating volume, packed with handgun lore and solid information by the acknowledged dean of revolver shooters.

French Service Handguns: 1858-2004, by Eugene Medlin & Jean Huon, Tommy Gun Publications, 2004. 1st edition. Over 200 pages and more than 125 photographs. Hardcover, NEW. $44.95

Over 10 years in the making, this long awaited volume on French handguns is finally here. this book offers in depth coverage on everything from the 11mm Pinfire to the 9mm Parabellum-including various Lefaucheux revolvers, MAB's, Spanish pistols, and revolvers used in WWI, Uniques, plus, many photos of one-of-a-kind prototypes of the French contract Browning, Model 1935s, and 35a pistols used in WWII.

German Handguns: The Complete Book of the Pistols and Revolvers of Germany, 1869 to the Present, by Ian Hogg, Greenhill Publishing, 2001. 320 pp., 270 illustrations. Hardcover. $49.95

Ian Hogg examines the full range of handguns produced in Germany from such classics as the Luger M1908, Mauser HsC and Walther PPK, to more unusual types such as the Reichsrevolver M1879 and the Dreyse 9mm. He presents the key data (length, weight, muzzle velocity, and range) for each weapon discussed and also gives its date of introduction and service record, evaluates and discusses peculiarities, and examines in detail particular strengths and weaknesses.

Glock in Competition, by Robin Taylor, Spokane, WA, Taylor Press, 2006, 2nd edition. 248pp, Softcover. NEW $19.95

Covered topics include reloading, trigger configurations, recalls, and refits, magazine problems, modifying the Glock, choosing factory ammo, and a host of others.

Glock: The New Wave in Combat Handguns, by Peter Alan Kasler, Paladin Press, Boulder, CO, 1993. 304 pp., illus. $27.00

Kasler debunks the myths that surround what is the most innovative handgun to be introduced in some time.

Glock's Handguns, by Duncan Long, Desert Publications, El Dorado, AR, 1996. 180 pp., illus. Paper covers. $19.95

An outstanding volume on one of the world's newest and most successful firearms of the century.

Gun Digest Book of Beretta Pistols, The, by Massad Ayoob, Iola, WI, Krause Publications, 2005. 288 pages, 300+ photos help with identification. Softcover. $27.99

This new release from the publishers of Gun Digest, readers get information including caliber,weight and barrel lengths for modern pistols. A review of the accuracy and function of all models of modern Beretta pistols give active shooters details needed to make the most of this popular firearm. More than 300 photographs, coupled with articles detailing the development of design and style of these handguns, create a comprehensive must-have resource.

Gun Digest Book of Combat Handgunnery 5th Edition, The, Complete Guide to Combat Shooting, by Massad Ayoob, Iola, WI, Krause Publications, 2002. $22.95

Tap into the knowledge of an international combat handgun expert for the latest in combat handgun designs, strengths and limitations; caliber, size, power and ability; training and technique; cover, concealment and hostage situations. Unparalleled!

Gun Digest Book of the 1911, The, by Patrick Sweeney, Krause Publications, Iola, WI, 2002. 336 pp., with 700 b&w photos. Softcover. $27.95

Complete guide of all models and variations of the Model 1911. The author also includes repair tips and information on buying a used 1911.

Gun Digest Book of the 1911 2nd Edition, The, by Patrick Sweeney, Krause Publications, Iola, WI, 2006. 336 pp., with 700 b&w photos. Softcover. $27.95

Complete guide of all models and variations of the Model 1911. The author also includes repair tips and information on buying a used 1911.

Gun Digest Book of the Glock; A Comprehensive Review, Design, History and Use, The, Iola, WI, Krause Publications, 2003. 303 pp., with 500 b&w photos. Softcover. 27.95

Examine the rich history and unique elements of the most important and influential firearms design of the past 50 years, the Glock autoloading pistol. This comprehensive review of the revolutionary pistol analyzes the performance of the various models and chamberings and features a complete guide to available accessories and little-known factory options. You'll see why it's the preferred pistol for law enforcement use and personal protection.

Gun Digest Book of the SIG-Sauer, The, by Massad Ayoob, Iola, WI, Krause Publications, 2005. 1st edition 304pp. Softcover. NEW. $27.99

Noted firearms training expert Massad Ayoob takes an in-depth look at some of the finest pistols on the market. If you own a SIG-Sauer pistol, have consdered buying one or just appreciate the fine quality of these pistols, this is the book for you. Ayoob takes a practical look at each of the SIG-Sauer pistols including handling characteristics, and design and performance. Each gun in every caliber is tested and evaluated, giving you all the details you need as you choose and use your SIG-Sauer pistol.

Gun Digest Book of Smith & Wesson, The, by Patrick Sweeney, Iola, WI, Krause Publications, 2005. 1st edition. Covers all categories of Smith & Wesson Guns in both competition and law enforcement. 312pp, 500 b&w photos. Softcover, NEW. $27.99

Hand Cannons: The World's Most Powerful Handguns, by Duncan Long, Paladin Press, Boulder, CO, 1995. 208 pp., illus. Paper covers. $22.00

Long describes and evaluates each powerful gun according to their features.

Handgun Combatives, by Dave Spaulding, Flushing, NY, Looseleaf Law Publications,2005. 212pp, with 60 plus photos, softcover. NEW $22.95

Handgun Stopping Power "The Definitive Study," by Evan P. Marshall & Edwin J. Sanow, Paladin Press, Boulder, CO, 1997. 240 pp. photos. Softcover. $45.00

Dramatic first-hand accounts of the results of handgun rounds fired into criminals by cops, storeowners, cabbies and others are the heart and soul of this long-awaited book. This is the definitive methodology for predicting the stopping power of handgun loads, the first to take into account what really happens when a bullet meets a man.

Handguns 2007, 19th Edition, Ken Ramage, Iola WI, Gun Digest Books, 2006, 320pp, 500 b&w photos, Softcover. NEW. $24.99

Target shooters, handgun hunters, collectors and those who rely upon handguns for self-defense will want to pack this value-loaded and entertaining volume in their home libraries. Shooters will find the latest pistol and revolver designs and accessories, plus test reports on several models. The handgun becomes an artist's canvas in a showcase of engraving talents. The catalog section–with comprehensive specs on every known handgun in production–includes a new display of semi-custom handguns, plus an expanded, illustrated section on the latest grips, sights, scopes and other aiming devices. Offer easy access to products, services and manufacturers.

Handguns of the Armed Organizations of the Soviet Occupation Zone and German Democratic Republic, by Dieter H. Marschall, Los Alamos, NM, Ucross Books, 2000. Softcover. NEW. $29.95

Translated from German this groundbreaking treatise covers the period from May 1945 through 1996. The organizations that used these pistols are described along with the guns and holsters. Included are the P08, P38, PP, PPK, P1001, PSM, Tokarev, Makarov, (including .22 LR, cutaway, silenced, Suhl marked), Stechlin, plus Hungarian, Romanian and Czech pistols.

Heckler & Koch's Handguns, by Duncan Long, Desert Publications, El Dorado, AR, 1996. 142 pp., illus. Paper covers. $19.95

Traces the history and the evolution of H&K's pistols from the company's beginning at the end of WWII to the present.

Hidden in Plain Sight, by Trey Bloodworth & Mike Raley, Paladin Press, Boulder, CO, 2003. Paper covers. $20.00

A practical guide to concealed handgun carry.

High Standard: A Collectors Guide to the Hamden & Hartford Target Pistols, by Tom Dance, Andrew Mowbray, Inc., Lincoln, RI, 1999. 192 pp., heavily illustrated with b&w photographs and technical drawings. $24.00

From Citation to Supermatic, all of the production models and specials made from 1951 to 1984 are covered according to model number or series, making it easy to understand the evolution to this favorite of shooters and collectors.

High Standard Automatic Pistols 1932-1950, by Charles E. Petty, The Gun Room Press, Highland Park, NJ, 1989. 124 pp., illus. $19.95

A definitive source of information for the collector of High Standard arms.

Hi-Standard Pistols and Revolvers, 1951-1984, by James Spacek, Chesire, CT, 1998. 128 pp., illus. Paper covers. $14.95

Technical details, marketing features and instruction/parts manual of every model High Standard pistol and revolver made between 1951 and 1984. Most accurate serial number information available.

History of Smith & Wesson Firearms, by Dean Boorman, New York, Lyons Press, 2002. 1st edition. 144 pp., illustrated in full color. Hardcover. $29.95

The definitive guide to one of the world's best-known firearms makers. Takes the story through the years of the Military & Police .38 & of the Magnum cartridge, to today's wide range of products for law-enforcement customers.

How to Become a Master Handgunner: The Mechanics of X-Count Shooting, by Charles Stephens, Paladin Press, Boulder, CO, 1993. 64 pp., illus. Paper covers. $14.00

Offers a simple formula for success to the handgunner who strives to master the technique of shooting accurately.

How to Customize Your Glock: Step-By-Step Modifications You Can Do at Little Cost, by Robert and Morgan Boatman, Paladin Press, Boulder, CO, 2005, 1st edition. 8½" x 11", photos, 72 pp. Softcover. NEW. $20.00

This mini-"Glocksmithing" course by Glock enthusiasts Robert and Morgan Boatman first explains why you would make a specific modification and what you gain in terms of improved performance. The workbook format makes the manual simple to follow as you work on your Glock, andhigh-resolution photos illustrate each part and step precisely. Make your Glock work even more effectively for you bythinking outside the box.

Inglis Diamond: The Canadian High Power Pistol, by Clive M. Law, Collector Grade Publications, Canada, 2001. 312 pp., illus. $49.95

This definitive work on Canada's first and indeed only mass produced handgun, in production for a very brief span of time and consequently made in relatively few numbers, the venerable Inglis-made Browning High Power covers the pistol's initial history, the story of Chinese and British adoption, use post-war by Holland, Australia, Greece, Belgium, New Zealand, Peru, Brasil and other countries. All new information on the famous light-weights and the Inglis Diamond variations. Completely researched through official archives in a dozen countries. Many of the bewildering variety of markings have never been satisfactorily explained until now

Japanese Military Cartridge Handguns 1893-1945, A Revised and Expanded Edition of Hand Cannons of Imperial Japan, by Harry L. Derby III and James D. Brown, Atglen, PA, Schiffer Publications, 2003. 1st edition. Hardcover. New in new dust jacket. $79.95

When originally published in 1981, *The Hand Cannons of Imperial Japan* was heralded as one of the most readable works on firearms ever produced. To arms collectors and scholars, it remains a prized source of information on Japanese handguns, their development, and their history. In this new revised and expanded edition, original author Harry Derby has teamed with Jim Brown to provide a thorough update reflecting twenty years of additional research. An appendix on valuation has also been added, using a relative scale that should remain relevant despite inflationary pressures. For the firearms collector, enthusiast, historian or dealer, this is the most complete and up-to-date work on Japanese military handguns ever written.

Living with Glocks: The Complete Guide to the New Standard in Combat Handguns, by Robert H. Boatman, Boulder, CO, Paladin Press, 2002. 1st edition. 184 pp., illus. Hardcover. $29.95

In addition to demystifying the enigmatic Glock trigger, Boatman describes and critiques each Glock model in production. Separate chapters on the G36, the enhanced G20 and the full-auto G18 emphasize the job-specific talents of these standout models for those seeking insight on which Glock pistol might best meet their needs. And for those interested in optimizing their Glock's capabilities, this book addresses all the peripherals–holsters, ammo, accessories, silencers, modifications and conversions, training programs and more.

Living With the 1911, by Robert Boatman, Boulder, CO, Paladin Press, 2005. 144pp, softcover. NEW $25.00

Luger P'08 Pistol, 9mm Assembly, Disassembly Manual, by Skennerton & Riling, Ray Riling Arms Books Co. Philadelphia, PA, 2005. 36 pages, illustrated. $5.00

Ideal workshop reference for stripping & assembly with exploded parts drawings, specifications, service accessories, historical information and recommended reading references. The binding is triple saddle-stitched with a durable plastic laminated cover.

Luger Handbook, by Aarron Davis, Krause Publications, Iola, WI, 1997. 112 pp., illus. Paper covers. $9.95

Now you can identify any of the legendary Luger variations using a simple decision tree. Each model and variation includes pricing information, proof marks and detailed attributes in a handy, user-friendly format. Plus, it's fully indexed. Instantly identify that Luger!

Lyman Pistol and Revolver Handbook, 3rd edition, by Lyman. Middletown, CT, Lyman Products Corp, 2005. 3rd edition. 272pp, Softcover. NEW $22.95

Makarov Pistol Assembly, Disassembly Manual 9mm, by Skennerton & Riling, Ray Riling Arms Books Co. Philadelphia, PA, 2005. 36 pages, illustrated. $5.00

Ideal workshop reference for stripping & assembly with exploded parts drawings, specifications, ervice accessories, historical information and recommended reading references. The binding is triple saddle-stitched with a durable plastic laminated cover.

Mauser Self-Loading Pistol, by Belford & Dunlap, Borden Publishing Co., Alhambra, CA. Over 200 pp., 300 illus., large format. $29.95

The long-awaited book on the "Broom Handles," covering their inception in 1894 to the end of production. Complete and in detail: pocket pistols, Chinese and Spanish copies.

Mauser Broomhandle Model 1896 Pistol Assembly, Disassembly Manual, by Skennerton & Riling, Ray Riling Arms Books Co. Philadelphia, PA, 2005. 36 pages, illustrated. $5.00

Ideal workshop reference for stripping & assembly with exploded parts drawings, specifications, service accessories, historical information and recommended reading references.

Mental Mechanics of Shooting: How to Stay Calm at the Center, by Vishnu Karmakar and Thomas Whitney, Littleton, CO, Center Vision, Inc., 2001. 144 pp. Softcover. $19.95

Not only will this book help you stay free of trigger jerk, it will help you in all areas of your shooting.

Model 35 Radom Pistol, The, by Terence Lapin, Hyrax Publishers, 2004. 95 pages with b&w photos, Stiff paper covers. NEW. $18.95

Model 1911 Automatic Pistol, by Robert Campbell, Accokeek, Maryland, Stoeger Publications, 2004. Hardcover. NEW. $24.95

Modern Law Enforcement Weapons & Tactics, 3rd Edition, by Patrick Sweeney, Iola, WI, Krause Publications, 2004. 256 pp. Softcover. NEW. $22.99

Official 9mm Markarov Pistol Manual, translated into English by Major James Gebhardt, U.S. Army (Ret.), Desert Publications, El Dorado, AR, 1996. 84 pp., illus. Paper covers. $14.95

The information found in this book will be of enormous benefit and interest to the owner or a prospective owner of one of these pistols.

Operator's Tactical Pistol Shooting Manual; A Practical Guide to Combat Marksmanship, by Erik Lawrence, Linesville, PA, Blackheart Publishing, 2003. 1st edition. 233 pp. Softcover. $24.50

This manual-type book begins with the basics of safety with a pistol and progresses into advanced pistol handling. A self-help guide for improving your capabilities with a pistol at your own pace.

P08 Luger Pistol, by de Vries & Martens, Alexandria, VA, Ironside International, 2002. 152 pp., illustrated with 200 high quality b&w photos. Hardcover. $34.95

Covers all essential information on history and development, ammunition and accessories, codes and markings, and contains photos of nearly every model and accessory. Includes a unique selection of original German WWll propaganda photos, most never published before.

P-08 Parabellum Luger Automatic Pistol, edited by J. David McFarland, Desert Publications, Cornville, AZ, 1982. 20 pp., illus. Paper covers. $14.95

Covers every facet of the Luger, plus a listing of all known Luger models.

P-38 Pistol: Postwar Distributions, 1945-1990, Volume 3, by Warren Buxton, Ucross Books, Los Alamos, MN 1999, plus an addendum to Volumes 1 & 2. 272 pp. with 342 illustrations. $75.00

P-38 Pistol: The Contract Pistols, 1940-1945, Volume 2, by Warren Buxton, Ucross Books, Los Alamos, MN 1999. 256 pp. with 237 illustrations. $75.00

P-38 Pistol: The Walther Pistols, 1930-1945, Volume 1, by Warren Buxton, Ucross Books, Los Alamos, MN 1999. 328 pp. with 160 illustrations. $75.00

A limited run reprint of this scarce and sought-after work on the P-38 Pistol.

Peacemakers: Arms and Adventure in the American West, by RL Wilson. New York, Book Sales, 2004, reprint. 392pp. colored endpapers, 320 full color illustrations. Hardcover in New DJ, NEW. $24.89

Percussion Pistols and Revolvers: History, Performance and Practical Use, by Mike Cumpston and Johnny Bates, Texas, Iunivers, Inc, 2005. 1st edition. 208 pages. Softcover. $19.95

With the advent of the revolving pistols came patents that created monopolies in revolver production and the through-bored cylinder necessary for self-contained metallic cartridges. The caplock revolvers took on a separate evolution and remained state of the art long after the widespread appearance of cartridge-firing rifles and shotguns.

Pistol as a Weapon of Defence in the House and on the Road, by Jeff Cooper, Boulder, CO, Paladin Press, 2004. 1st edition. 48pp. Softcover. NEW. $9.00

Penned in 1875 and recently discovered collecting dust on a library bookshelf, this primer for the pistol is remarkably timely in its insights and observations. From a historical perspective, it contains striking parallels to the thinking and controversy that swirl about the practical use of the pistol today.

Pistols of the World; Fully Revised, 4th Edition, Iola, WI, Krause Publications, 2005. 432pp, chronicles 2,500 handguns made from 1887-2004. Stiff paper covers, NEW. $22.95

More than 1,000 listings and 20 years of coverage were added since the previous edition.

Pistols of World War I, by Robert J. Adamek, Pittsburgh, Pentagon Press, 2001. 1st edition signed and numbered. 296 pp. with illustrations and photos. Softcover. $45.00

Over 90 pistols illustrated, technical data, designers, history, proof marks. Over 25 pistol magazines illustrated with dimensions, serial number ranges. Over 35 cartridges illustrated with dimensions, manufactures, year of introduction. Weapons from 16 countries involved in WWI, statistics, quantities made, identification.

Remington Large-Bore Conversion Revolvers, by R. Phillips. Canada, Prately printed, 2005. Limited printing of 250 signed and numbered copies in leather hardcover. 126pp, with 200 illustrations. NEW $55.00

Ruger .22 Automatic Pistol, Standard/Mark I/Mark II Series, by Duncan Long, Paladin Press, Boulder, CO, 1989. 168 pp., illus. Paper covers. $16.00

The definitive book about the pistol that has served more than 1 million owners so well.

Ruger .22 Automatic Pistols: The Complete Guide for all Models from 1947 to 2003, Grand Rapids, MI, The Ruger Store, 2004. 74 pp., 66 high-resolution grayscale images. Printed in the U.S.A. with card stock cover and bright white paper. Softcover. NEW. $12.95

Includes 'rare' complete serial numbers and manufacturing dates from 1949-2004.

Ruger "P" Family of Handguns, by Duncan Long, Desert Publications, El Dorado, AZ, 1993. 128 pp., illus. Paper covers. $14.95

A full-fledged documentary on a remarkable series of Sturm Ruger handguns.

Ruger Pistol Reference Booklet 1949-1982 (Pocket Guide to Ruger Rimfire Pistols Standard and Mark I), by Don Findlay. Lubbock Tx, 2005. Softcover. 24 pages, illustrated with b&w photos. $9.95

Designed for the professional un dealer as well as the collector. Complete list of serial numbers as well as production dates. Also, includes photos of the original boxes the guns came in.

Semi-automatic Pistols in Police Service and Self Defense, by Massad Ayoob, Police Bookshelf, Concord, NH, 1990. 25 pp., illus. Softcover. $11.95

First quantitative, documented look at actual police experience with 9mm and 45 police service automatics.

Shooting Colt Single Actions, by Mike Venturino, Livingston, MT, 1997. 205 pp., illus. Paper covers. $25.00

A definitive work on the famous Colt SAA and the ammunition it shoots.

SIG Handguns, by Duncan Long, Desert Publications, El Dorado, AZ, 1995. 150 pp., illus. Paper covers. $19.95

The history of SIG/Sauer handguns, including Sig, Sig-Hammerli and Sig/Sauer variants.

Smith & Wesson's Automatics, by Larry Combs, Desert Publications, El Dorado, AZ, 1994. 143 pp., illus. Paper covers. $19.95

A must for every S&W auto owner or prospective owner.

Smith & Wesson: Sixguns of the Old West, by David Chicoine. Lincoln, RI., Andrew Mowbray, Inc., 2004. 1st edition. 480 pages, countless photos and detailed technical drawings. Hardcover. New in new dust jacket. $69.49

The Schofields, The Americans, The Russians, The New Model #3s, and The DAs.

Smith & Wesson American Model; In U.S. And Foreign Service, by Charles W. Pate, Mowbray Publishers, Lincoln, RI, 2006. 408 pp., illus. $65.00

This new book is an awesome new collector's guide to the S&W American. A huge resource on the military and western use of this classic large frame revolver.

Spanish Handguns: The History of Spanish Pistols and Revolvers, by Gene Gangarosa Jr., Stoeger Publishing Co., Accokeek, MD, 2001. 320 pp., illustrated, b&w photos. Paper covers. $21.95

Standard Catalog Of Luger, by Aarron Davis, Gun Digest Books, Iola WI, 2006. 256 pages, illustrated with photos. Paper Covers $29.99

This comprehensive identification and price guide goes a long way to giving Luger enthusiasts information to enjoy and be successful in an extremely active collector market. With Standard Catalog of Luger, firearms enthusiasts receive an unrivaled reference that includes: Reproductions of symbols and makers' marks from every model of Luger for use in accurately identifying the hundreds of Luger variations, More than 1,000 detailed photos and line illustrations demonstrating design and performance of Luger pistols, Manufacturing data and model rarity information to aid collectors when buying

Lugers as an investment. Perfect for firearms collectors, gun shop owners, auction houses, museums, and appraisers.

Standard Catalog Of Smith & Wesson; 3rd Edition, by Jim Supica, & Richard Nahas, Gun Digest Books, Iola WI, 2006 384 pages, with photos, Hardcover. $39.99

Definitive Smith & Wesson identification and pricing reference, includes 350+ full-color photos for improved identification. Smith & Wesson is one of the hottest manufacturers of handguns, offering more new models than any other maker-39 new products in 2005 alone. Comprehensive coverage of Smith & Wesson firearm line including the only handgun in the world in continuous production since 1899. The 3rd Edition combines full color photos with details collectors need to identify and better appreciate all Smith & Wesson firearms.

Star Firearms, by Leonardo M. Antaris, Davenport, TA, Firac Publications Co., 2002. 1st edition. Hardcover. New in new dust jacket. $119.95

Tactical 1911, by Dave Lauck, Paladin Press, Boulder, CO, 1999. 152 pp., illus. Paper covers. $22.00

The cop's and SWAT operator's guide to employment and maintenance.

Tactical Pistol, by Gabriel Suarez, Foreword by Jeff Cooper, Paladin Press, Boulder, CO, 1996. 216 pp., illus. Paper covers. $25.00

Advanced gunfighting concepts and techniques.

Tactical Pistol Shooting; Your Guide to Tactics that Work, by Erik Lawrence. Iola, WI, Krause Publications, 2005. 1st edition. More than 250 step-by-step photos to illustrate techniques. 233pp, Softcover. NEW $18.95

Thompson/Center Contender Pistol, by Charles Tephens, Paladin Press, Boulder, CO, 1997. 58 pp., illus. Paper covers. $14.00

How to tune and time, load and shoot accurately with the Contender pistol.

U.S. Handguns of World War II, The Secondary Pistols and Revolvers, by Charles W. Pate, Mowbray Publishers, Lincoln, RI, 1997. 368 pp., illus. $39.00

This indispensable new book covers all of the American military handguns of WWII except for the M1911A1.

Walther P-38 Assembly, Disassembly Manual 9mm, by Skennerton & Riling, Ray Riling Arms Books Co. Philadelphia, PA, 2005. 36 pages, illustrated. $5.00

Ideal workshop reference for stripping & assembly with exploded parts drawings, specifications, service accessories, historical information and recommended reading references. The binding is triple saddle-stitched with a durable plastic laminated cover.

Walther Pistols: Models 1 Through P99, Factory Variations and Copies, by Dieter H. Marschall, Ucross Books, Los Alamos, NM. 2000. 140 pp., with 140 b&w illustrations, index. Paper covers. $21.95

This is the English translation, revised and updated, of the highly successful and widely acclaimed German language edition. This book provides the collector with a reference guide and overview of the entire line of the Walther military, police, and self-defense pistols from the very first to the very latest Variations, where issued, serial ranges, calibers, marks, proofs, logos, and design aspects in an astonishing quantity and variety are crammed into this very well researched and highly regarded work.

Hunting

NORTH AMERICA

A Varmint Hunter's Odyssey, by Steve Hanson with guest chapter by Mike Johnson, Precision Shooting, Inc. Manchester, CT, 1999. 279 pp., illus. Paper covers. $39.95

A new classic by a writer who eats, drinks and sleeps varmint hunting and varmint rifles.

Advanced Black Powder Hunting, by Toby Bridges, Stoeger Publishing Co., Wayne, NJ, 1998. 288 pp., illus. Paper covers. $21.95

The first modern day publication to be filled from cover to cover with guns, loads, projectiles, accessories and the techniques to get the most from today's front loading guns.

Adventures of an Alaskan-You Can Do, by Dennis W. Confer, Foreword by Craig Boddington. Anchorage, AK, Wiley Ventures, 2003. 1st edition. 279 pp., illus. Softcover. $24.95

This book is about 45% fishing, 45% hunting, & 10% related adventures; travel, camping and boating. It is written to stimulate, encourage and motivate readers to make happy memories that they can do on an average income and to entertain, educate and inform readers of outdoor opportunities.

Aggressive Whitetail Hunting, by Greg Miller, Krause Publications, Iola, WI, 1995. 208 pp., illus. Paper covers. $14.95

Learn how to hunt trophy bucks in public forests, private farmlands and exclusive hunting grounds from one of America's foremost hunters.

Alaska Safari, by Harold Schetzle & Sam Fadala, Anchorage, AK, Great Northwest Publishing, 2002. Revised 2nd edition. 366 pp., illus. with b&w photos. Softcover. $29.95

The author has brought a wealth of information to the hunter and anyone interested in Alaska. Harold Schetzle is a great guide and has also written another book of stories of Alaska hunting taken from many, many years of hunting and guiding. The most comprehensive guide to Alaska hunting.

Alaskan Adventures-Volume I-The Early Years, by Russell Annabel, Long Beach, CA, Safari Press,2005, 2nd printing. 453pp. illus. Hardcover. New in new dust jacket. $35.00

No other writer has ever been able to capture the spirit of adventure and hunting in Alaska like Russell Annabel.

Alaskan Yukon Trophies Won and Lost, by G.O. Young, Wolfe Publishing, Prescott, AZ, 2002. Softcover. $35.00

.A classic big game hunting tale with 273 pages b&w photographs and a five-page epilogue by the publisher.

American Duck Shooting, by George Bird Grinnell, Stackpole Books, Harrisburg, PA, 1991. 640 pp., illus. Paper covers. $19.95

First published in 1901 at the height of the author's career. Describes 50 species of waterfowl, and discusses hunting methods common at the turn of the century.

Bear Hunting in Alaska: How to Hunt Brown and Grizzly Bears, by Tony Russ, Northern Publishing, 2004. 116 b&w photos, illus. 256 pgs. Soft cover. Excellent. $22.95

Teaches every skill you will need to prepare for, scout, find, select, stalk, shoot and care for one of the most sought-after trophies on earth – the Alaskan brown bear and the Alaskan Grizzly.

Bears of Alaska, by Erwin Bauer, Sasquatch Books, 2002. Soft cover. Excellent. $15.95

Best of Babcock, The, by Havilah Babcock, Introduction by Hugh Grey, The Gunnerman Press, Auburn Hills, MI, 1985. 262 pp., illus. $19.95

A treasury of memorable pieces, 21 of which have never before appeared in book form.

Blacktail Trophy Tactics, by Boyd Iverson, Stoneydale Press, Stevensville, MI, 1992. 166 pp., illus. Paper covers. $14.95

A comprehensive analysis of blacktail deer habits, describing a deer's and man's use of scents, still hunting, tree techniques, etc.

Bowhunter's Handbook, Expert Strategies and Techniques, by M.R. James with Fred Asbell, Dave Holt, Dwight Schuh and Dave Samuel, DBI Books, a division of Krause Publications, Iola, WI, 1997. 256 pp., illus. Paper covers. $19.95

Tips from the top on taking your bowhunting skills to the next level.

Buffalo Harvest, The, by Frank Mayer as told to Charles Roth, Pioneer Press, Union City, TN, 1995. 96 pp., illus. Paper covers. $12.50

The story of a hide hunter during his buffalo hunting days on the plains.

Call of the Quail: A Tribute to the Gentleman Game Bird, by Michael McIntosh, et al., Countrysport Press, Traverse City, MI, 1990. 175 pp., illus. $35.00

A new anthology on quail hunting.

Calling All Elk, by Jim Zumbo, Cody, WY, 1989. 169 pp., illus. Paper covers. $14.95

The only book on the subject of elk hunting that covers every aspect of elk vocalization.

Complete Book of Grouse Hunting, The, by Frank Woolner, The Lyons Press, New York, NY, 2000. 192 pp., illus. Paper covers. $24.95

The history, habits, and habitat of one of America's great game birds–and the methods used to hunt it.

Complete Book of Mule Deer Hunting, The, by Walt Prothero, The Lyons Press, New York, NY, 2000. 192 pp., illus. Paper covers. $24.95

Field-tested practical advice on how to bag the trophy buck of a lifetime.

Complete Book of Wild Turkey Hunting, The, by John Trout Jr., The Lyons Press, New York, NY, 2000. 192 pp., illus. Paper covers. $24.95

An illustrated guide to hunting for one of America's most popular game birds.

Complete Book of Woodcock Hunting, The, by Frank Woolner, The Lyons Press, New York, NY, 2000. 192 pp., illus. Paper covers. $24.95

A thorough, practical guide to the American woodcock and to woodcock hunting.

Complete Guide To Hunting Wild Boar in California, The, by Gary Kramer, Safari Press, 2002. 1st edition. 127 pp., 37 photos. Softcover. $15.95

Gary Kramer takes the hunter all over California, from north to south and east to west. He discusses natural history, calibers, bullets, rifles, pistols, shotguns, black powder, and bow and arrows—even recipes.

Complete Venison Cookbook from Field to Table, The, by Jim & Ann Casada, Krause Publications, Iola, WI, 1996. 208 pp., Comb-bound. $12.95

More than 200 kitchen-tested recipes make this book the answer to a table full of hungry hunters or guests.

Cougar Attacks: Encounters of the Worst Kind, by Kathy Etling, NY, Lyons Press, 2004. 1st edition. 256 pages, illustrated with b&w photos. Soft cover. NEW. $14.95

Blood-curdling encounters between the big cats of North America and their most reluctant prey, humans.

Coyote Hunting, by Phil Simonski, Stoneydale Press, Stevensville, MT, 1994. 126 pp., illus. Paper covers. $12.95
Probably the most thorough "how-to-do-it" book on coyote hunting ever written.

Dabblers & Divers: A Duck Hunter's Book, compiled by the editors of *Ducks Unlimited* magazine, Willow Creek Press, Minocqua, WI, 1997. 160 pp., illus. $39.95
A word-and-photographic portrayal of waterfowl hunter's singular intimacy with, and passion for, watery haunts and wildfowl.

Deer & Deer Hunting, by Al Hofacker, Krause Publications, Iola, WI, 1993. 208 pp., illus. $34.95
Coffee-table volume packed full of how-to-information that will guide hunts for years to come.

Dreaming the Lion, by Thomas McIntyre, Countrysport Press, Traverse City, MI, 1994. 309 pp., illus. $35.00
Reflections on hunting, fishing and a search for the wild. Twenty-three stories by *Sports Afield* editor, Tom McIntyre.

Eastern Cougar: Historic Accounts, Scientific Investigations, and New Evidence, by Chris Bolgiano, Mechanicsburg,PA, Stackpole Books, 2005. Soft cover. NEW. $19.95
This fascinating anthology probes America's troubled history with large predators and makes a vital contribution to the wildlife management debates of today.

Elk and Elk Hunting, by Hart Wixom, Stackpole Books, Harrisburg, PA, 1986. 288 pp., illus. $34.95
Your practical guide to fundamentals and fine points of elk hunting.

Elk Hunting Guide: Skills, Gear, and Insight, by Tom Airhart, Stackpole Books,2005. 432pp, 71 b&w photos, 38 illus. $19.95
A thorough, informative guide to the growing sport of elk hunting with in-depth coverage of current equipment and gear, techniques for tracking elk and staying safe in the wilderness and advice on choosing guides and outfitters.

Elk Hunting in the Northern Rockies, by Ed Wolff, Stoneydale Press, Stevensville, MT, 1984. 162 pp., illus. $18.95
Helpful information about hunting the premier elk country of the northern Rocky Mountain states–Wyoming, Montana and Idaho.

Elk Hunting with the Experts, by Bob Robb, Stoneydale Press, Stevensville, MT, 1992. 176 pp., illus. Paper covers. $15.95
A complete guide to elk hunting in North America by America's top elk hunting expert.

Encyclopedia of Buffalo Hunters and Skinners Volume 1 A-D, by Gilbert Reminger, Pioneer Press, 2003. The first volume in the series. 286 pages, acknowledgements, introduction, preface, illustrated, maps, plates, portraits, appendices, bibliography, index. Hardcover. NEW. $35.00

Encyclopedia of Buffalo Hunters and Skinners Volume 2 E-K, by Gilbert Reminger, Pioneer Press, 2006. The 2nd volume in the series. 285 pages, 115 photos, 15 drawings/newspaper items, and 6 maps. Index, Bibliography. Hardcover. $35.00
Vol. II covers hunters and skinners, that have so far surfaced, with surnames that begin with E-K, beginning with skinner William Earl and runs through the Kuykendall brothers, Judge and John, who hunted late (1886-1888) in southeastern New Mexico.

Fair Chase in North America, by Craig Boddington, Long Beach, CA, Safari Press, 2004. 1st edition. Hardcover. New in new dust jacket. $39.95

Getting a Stand, by Miles Gilbert, Pioneer Press, Union City, TN, 1993. 204 pp., illus. Paper covers. $13.95
An anthology of 18 short personal experiences by buffalo hunters of the late 1800s, specifically from 1870-1882.

Greatest Elk; The Complete Historical and Illustrated Record of North America's Biggest Elk, by R. Selner, Safari Press, Huntington Beach, CA, 2000. 209 pp., profuse color illus. $39.95
Here is the book all elk hunters have been waiting for! This oversized book holds the stories and statistics of the biggest bulls ever killed in North America. Stunning, full-color photographs highlight over 40 world-class heads, including the old world records!

Grouse and Woodcock, A Gunner's Guide, by Don Johnson, Krause Publications, Iola, WI, 1995. 256 pp., illus. Paper covers. $14.95
Find out what you need in guns, ammo, equipment, dogs and terrain.

Gunning for Sea Ducks, by George Howard Gillelan, Tidewater Publishers, Centreville, MD, 1988. 144 pp., illus. $14.95
A book that introduces you to a practically untouched arena of waterfowling.

Head Fer the Hills-Volume VI (1934-1960), by Russell Annabel, Long Beach, CA, Safari Press, 2005, Deluxe, Limited, Signed edition. 312pp., photos, drawings. Hardcover in a Slipcase. NEW. $60.00
As Tex Cobb, Russell Annabel's famous mentor and eternal companion, was famous for saying, "Head fer the hills," which is exactly what Rusty did.

Heck with Moose Hunting, The, by Jim Zumbo, Wapiti Valley Publishing Co., Cody, WY, 1996. 199 pp., illus. $17.95
Jim's hunts around the continent including encounters with moose, caribou, sheep, antelope and mountain goats.

High Pressure Elk Hunting, by Mike Lapinski, Stoneydale Press Publishing Co., Stevensville, MT, 1996. 192 pp., illus. $19.95
The secrets of hunting educated elk revealed.

Horns in the High Country, by Andy Russell, Alfred A. Knopf, NY, 1973. 259 pp., illus. Paper covers. $12.95
A many-sided view of wild sheep and their natural world.

How to Hunt, by Dave Bowring, Winchester Press, Piscataway, NJ, 1982. 208 pp., illus. Hardcover $15.00
A basic guide to hunting big game, small game, upland birds, and waterfowl.

Hunt High for Rocky Mountain Goats, Bighorn Sheep, Chamois & Tahr, by Duncan Gilchrist, Stoneydale Press, Stevensville, MT, 1992. 192 pp., illus. Paper covers. $19.95
The source book for hunting mountain goats.

Hunter's Alaska, The, by Roy F. Chandler, Iron Brigade, 2005. Hardcover. NEW. $49.95
This is a book written by Roy F. Chandler (Rocky). Rocky's Alaskan travels span half a century. Hunters hoping to hunt the "Great Land" will read exactly how it is done and what they can hope for if they ever make it into the Alaskan wilderness. This is a new publication of 2500 signed and numbered copies. Previous books, written by Rocky, about hunting Alaska have become collectors items. This book has some information from the prior books and much more "added" information.

Hunting Adventure of Me and Joe, by Walt Prothero, Safari Press, Huntington Beach, CA, 1995. 220 pp., illus. $22.50
A collection of the author's best and favorite stories.

Hunting America's Wild Turkey, by Toby Bridges, Stoeger Publishing Company, Pocomoke, MD, 2001. 256 pp., illus. $16.95
The techniques and tactics of hunting North America's largest, and most popular, woodland game bird.

Hunting Hard in Alaska, by Marc Taylor, Anchorage, AK, Biblio Distribution, 2003 Softcover. $19.95

Hunting In Alaska: A Comprehensive Guide, by Christopher Batin, Alaska Angler Pubs., 2002. 430 pages. Soft cover. NEW. $29.95

Hunting the Land of the Midnight Sun, by Alaska Professional Hunters Assoc., Safari Press, 2005. Hardcover. New in new dust jacket. $29.95
Contains contributions by Rob Holt, Gary King, Gary LaRose, Garth Larsen, Jim Shockey, Jeff Davis, and many others.

Hunting Mature Bucks, by Larry L. Weishuhn, Krause Publications, Iola, WI, 1995. 256 pp., illus. Paper covers. $14.95
One of North America's top white-tailed deer authorities shares his expertise on hunting those big, smart and elusive bucks.

Hunting Open-Country Mule Deer, by Dwight Schuh, Sage Press, Nampa, ID, 1989. 180 pp., illus. $18.95
A guide taking Western bucks with rifle and bow.

Hunting the Rockies, Home of the Giants, by Kirk Darner, Marceline, MO, 1996. 291 pp., illus. $25.00
Understand how and where to hunt Western game in the Rockies.

Hunting Western Deer, by Jim and Wes Brown, Stoneydale Press, Stevensville, MT, 1994. 174 pp., illus. Paper covers. $14.95
A pair of expert Oregon hunters provide insight into hunting mule deer and blacktail deer in the western states.

Hunting Wild Turkeys in the West, by John Higley, Stoneydale Press, Stevensville, MT, 1992. 154 pp., illus. Paper covers. $12.95
Covers the basics of calling, locating and hunting turkeys in the western states.

Hunting with the Twenty-Two, by Charles Singer Landis, R&R Books, Livonia, NY, 1994. 429 pp., illus. $35.00
A miscellany of articles touching on the hunting and shooting of small game.

In Search of the Buffalo, by Charles G. Anderson, Pioneer Press, Union City, TN, 1996. 144 pp., illus. Paper covers. $13.95
The primary study of the life of J. Wright Mooar, one of the few hunters fortunate enough to kill a white buffalo.

In the Turkey Woods, by Jerome B. Robinson, The Lyons Press, N.Y., 1998. 207 pp., illus. $24.95
Practical expert advice on all aspects of turkey hunting–from calls to decoys to guns.

Kodiak Island and its Bears, by Harry Dodge, Anchorage, Great Northwest Publishing, 2004. 364 pages, carefully indexed, thoughtfully footnoted, and lavishly illustrated. $27.50
This is the most significant volume about Kodiak Island and its bears that has been published in at least 20 years. This book now stands to become a new classic for all time.

Lost Classics of Jack O'Connor, by Jim Casada, Live Oak Press, 2004. Exciting tales with a twist of humor. 33 photos, 40 illus. by Dan

Burr; 376 pages, with illustrations and photos. Hardcover. New in new dust jacket. $35.00

Montana-Land of Giant Rams, Volume 2, by Duncan Gilchrist, Outdoor Expeditions and Books, Corvallis, MT, 1992. 208 pp., illus. $34.95

The reader will find stories of how many of the top-scoring trophies were taken.

Montana-Land of Giant Rams, Volume 3, by Duncan Gilchrist, Outdoor Expeditions and Books, Corvallis, MT, 1999. 224 pp., illus. Paper covers. $19.95

All new sheep information including over 70 photos. Learn about how Montana became the "Land of Giant Rams" and what the prospects of the future are.

More Tracks: 78 Years of Mountains, People & Happiness, by Howard Copenhaver, Stoneydale Press, Stevensville, MT, 1992. 150 pp., illus. $18.95

A collection of stories by one of the back country's best storytellers about the people who shared with Howard his great adventure in the high places and wild Montana country.

Mostly Huntin', by Bill Jordan, Everett Publishing Co., Bossier City, LA, 1987. 254 pp., illus. $21.95

Jordan's hunting adventures in North America, Africa, Australia, South America and Mexico.

Mule Deer: Hunting Today's Trophies, by Tom Carpenter and Jim Van Norman, Krause Publications, Iola, WI, 1998. 256 pp., illus. Paper covers. $19.95

A tribute to both the deer and the people who hunt them. Includes info on where to look for big deer, prime mule deer habitat and effective weapons for the hunt.

Muzzleloading for Deer and Turkey, by Dave Ehrig, Stackpole Books,2005. 475 pages, 293 b&w photos. Hardcover. New in new dust jacket. $29.95

My Health is Better in November, by Havilah Babcock, University of S. Carolina Press, Columbia, SC, 1985. 284 pp., illus. $24.95

Adventures in the field set in the plantation country and backwater streams of SC.

North American Waterfowler, The, by Paul S. Bernsen, Superior Publ. Co., Seattle, WA, 1972. 206 pp. Paper covers. $9.95

The complete inside and outside story of duck and goose shooting. Big and colorful, illustrations by Les Kouba.

Old Man and the Boy, The, by Robert Ruark, Henry Holt & Co., New York, NY, 303 pp., illus. $24.95

A timeless classic, telling the story of a remarkable friendship between a young boy and his grandfather as they hunt and fish together.

Old Man's Boy Grows Older, The, by Robert Ruark, Henry Holt & Co., Inc., New York, NY, 1993. 300 pp., illus. $24.95

The heartwarming sequel to the best-selling *The Old Man and the Boy.*

One Man, One Rifle, One Land; Hunting all Species of Big Game in North America, by J.Y. Jones, Safari Press, Huntington Beach, CA, 2000. 400 pp., illus. $59.95

Journey with J.Y. Jones as he hunts each of the big-game animals of North America–from the polar bear of the high Arctic to the jaguar of the low-lands of Mexico–with just one rifle.

Outdoor Pastimes of an American Hunter, by Theodore Roosevelt, Stackpole Books, Mechanicsburg, PA, 1994. 480 pp., illus. Paper covers. $18.95

Stories of hunting big game in the West and notes about animals pursued and observed.

Outlaw Gunner, The, by Harry M. Walsh, Tidewater Publishers, Cambridge, MD, 1973. 178 pp., illus. $22.95

A colorful story of market gunning in both its legal and illegal phases.

Pheasant Days, by Chris Dorsey, Voyageur Press, Stillwater, MN, 1992. 233 pp., illus. $24.95

The definitive resource on ringnecks. Includes everything from basic hunting techniques to the life cycle of the bird.

Pheasant Hunter's Harvest, by Steve Grooms, Lyons & Burford Publishers, New York, NY, 1990. 180 pp. $22.95

A celebration of pheasant, pheasant dogs and pheasant hunting. Practical advice from a passionate hunter.

Pheasant Tales, by Gene Hill et al, Countrysport Press, Traverse City, MI, 1996. 202 pp., illus. $39.00

Charley Waterman, Michael McIntosh and Phil Bourjaily join the author to tell some of the stories that illustrate why the pheasant is America's favorite game bird.

Pheasants of the Mind, by Datus Proper, Wilderness Adventures Press, Bozeman, MT, 1994. 154 pp., illus. $25.00

No single title sums up the life of the solitary pheasant hunter like this masterful work.

Portraits of Elk Hunting, by Jim Zumbo, Safari Press, Huntington Beach, CA, 2001. 222 pp. illus. $39.95

Zumbo has captured in photos as well as in words the essence, charisma, and wonderful components of elk hunting: back-country wilderness camps, sweaty guides, happy hunters, favorite companions, elk woods, and, of course, the majestic elk. Join Zumbo in the uniqueness of the pursuit of the magnificent and noble elk.

Precision Bowhunting: A Year-Round approach to taking Mature Whitetails, by John and Chrs Eberhart, Stackpole Books, 2005. 214pp, b&w photos. Soft cover. NEW. $16.95

Packed with vital information and fresh insights, Precision Bow hunting belongs on the bookshelf of every serious bow hunter.

Proven Whitetail Tactics, by Greg Miller, Krause Publications, Iola, WI, 1997. 224 pp., illus. Paper covers. $19.95

Proven tactics for scouting, calling and still-hunting whitetail.

Quest for Dall Rams, by Duncan Gilchrist, Duncan Gilchrist Outdoor Expeditions and Books, Corvallis, MT, 1997. 224 pp., illus. Paper covers. $19.95

The most complete book of Dall sheep ever written. Covers information on Alaska and provinces with Dall sheep and explains hunting techniques, equipment, etc.

Quest for Giant Bighorns, by Duncan Gilchrist, Outdoor Expeditions and Books, Corvallis, MT, 1994. 224 pp., illus. Paper covers. $19.95

How some of the most successful sheep hunters hunt and how some of the best bighorns were taken.

Radical Elk Hunting Strategies, by Mike Lapinski, Stoneydale Press Publishing Co., Stevensville, MT, 1988. 161 pp., illus. $18.95

Secrets of calling elk in close.

Rattling, Calling & Decoying Whitetails, by Gary Clancy, edited by Patrick Durkin, Krause Publications, Iola, WI, 2000. 208 pp., illus. Paper covers. $19.95

How to consistently coax big bucks into range.

Records of North American Caribou and Moose, Craig Boddington et al, The Boone & Crockett Club, Missoula, MT, 1997. 250 pp., illus. $24.95

More than 1,800 caribou listings and more than 1,500 moose listings, organized by the state or Canadian province where they were taken.

Records of North American Elk and Mule Deer, 2nd Edition, edited by Jack and Susan Reneau, The Boone & Crockett Club, Missoula, MT, 1996. 360 pp., illus. Paper cover, $18.95; hardcover, $24.95

Updated and expanded edition featuring more than 150 trophy, field and historical photos of the finest elk and mule deer trophies ever recorded.

Records of North American Sheep, Rocky Mountain Goats and Pronghorn, edited by Jack and Susan Reneau, The Boone & Crockett Club, Missoula, MT, 1996. 400 pp., illus. Paper cover, $18.95; hardcover, $24.95

The first B&C Club records book featuring all 3941 accepted wild sheep, Rocky Mountain goats and pronghorn trophies.

Reflections on Snipe, by Worth Mathewson, illustrated by Eldridge Hardie, Camden, ME, Country Sport Press, 2003. Hardcover. 144 pp. $25.00

Reflections on Snipe is a delightful compendium of information on snipe behavior and habitats; gunning history; stories from the field; and the pleasures of hunting with good companions, whether human or canine.

Ringneck; A Tribute to Pheasants and Pheasant Hunting, by Steve Grooms, Russ Sewell and Dave Nomsen, The Lyons Press, New York, NY, 2000. 120 pp., illus. $40.00

A glorious full-color coffee-table tribute to the pheasant and those who hunt them.

Rooster! A Tribute to Pheasant Hunting, by Dale C. Spartas, Riverbend Publishing, 2003. 1st edition. 150+ glorious photos of pheasants, hunting dogs and hunting trips with family and friends. 128 pgs. Hardcover. $39.95

A very special, must-have book for the 2.3 million pheasant hunters across the country!

Rub-Line Secrets, by Greg Miller, edited by Patrick Durkin, Krause Publications, Iola, WI, 1999. 208 pp., illus. Paper covers. $19.95

Based on nearly 30 years' experience. Proven tactics for finding, analyzing and hunting big bucks' rub-lines.

Season, The, by Tom Kelly, Lyons & Burford, New York, NY, 1997. 160 pp., illus. $22.95

The delight and challenges of a turkey hunter's spring season.

Secret Strategies from North America's Top Whitetail Hunters, compiled by Nick Sisley, Krause Publications, Iola, WI, 1995. 256 pp., illus. Paper covers. $14.95

Bow and gun hunters share their success stories.

Sheep Hunting in Alaska–The Dall Sheep Hunter's Guide, by Tony Russ, Outdoor Expeditions and Books, Corvallis, MT, 1994. 160 pp., illus. Paper covers. $19.95

A how-to guide for the Dall sheep hunter.

Southern Deer & Deer Hunting, by Larry Weishuhn and Bill Bynum, Krause Publications, Iola, WI, 1995. 256 pp., illus. Paper covers. $14.95

Mount a trophy southern whitetail on your wall with this firsthand account of stalking big bucks below the Mason-Dixon line.

Spring Gobbler Fever, by Michael Hanback, Krause Publications, Iola, WI, 1996. 256 pp., illus. Paper covers. $15.95

Your complete guide to spring turkey hunting.

Stand Hunting for Whitetails, by Richard P. Smith, Krause Publications, Iola, WI, 1996. 256 pp., illus. Paper covers. $14.95

The author explains the tricks and strategies for successful stand hunting.

Successful Black Bear Hunting, by Bill Vaznis, Iola,WI, Krause Publications, 2004. 144 pages, illustrated with full color photographs and drawings. Pictorial Soft cover. $23.99

Sultan of Spring: A Hunter's Odyssey Through the World of the Wild Turkey, The, by Bob Saile, The Lyons Press, New York, NY, 1998. 176 pp., illus. $22.95

A literary salute to the magic and mysticism of spring turkey hunting.

Taking Big Bucks, by Ed Wolff, Stoneydale Press, Stevensville, MT, 1987. 169 pp., illus. $18.95

Solving the whitetail riddle.

Tales of Quails 'n Such, by Havilah Babcock, University of S. Carolina Press, Columbia, SC, 1985. 237 pp. $19.95

A group of hunting stories, told in informal style, on field experiences in the South in quest of small game.

They Left Their Tracks, by Howard Coperhaver, Stoneydale Press Publishing Co., Stevensville, MT, 1990. 190 pp., illus. $18.95

Recollections of 60 years as an outfitter in the Bob Marshall Wilderness.

To Heck with Moose Hunting, by Jim Zumbo, Wapiti Publishing Co., Cody, WY, 1996. 199 pp., illus. $17.95

Jim's hunts around the continent and even an African adventure.

Track Pack: Animal Tracks In Full Life Size, by Ed Gray, Mechanicsburg, PA, Stackpole Books, 2003. 1st edition. Spiral-bound, 34 pp. $7.95

An indispensable reference for hunters, trackers, and outdoor enthusiasts. This handy guide features the tracks of 38 common North American animals, from squirrels to grizzlies.

Trickiest Thing in Feathers, The, by Corey Ford, compiled and edited by Laurie Morrow, illustrated by Christopher Smith, Wilderness Adventures, Gallatin Gateway, MT, 1998. 208 pp., illus. $29.95

Here is a collection of Corey Ford's best wing-shooting stories, many of them previously unpublished.

Upland Equation: A Modern Bird-Hunter's Code, The, by Charles Fergus, Lyons & Burford Publishers, New York, NY, 1996. 86 pp. $18.00

A book that deserves space in every sportsman's library. Observations based on firsthand experience.

Upland Tales, edited by Worth Mathewson, Sand Lake Press, Amity, OR, 1996. 271 pp., illus. $29.95

A collection of articles on grouse, snipe and quail.

Waterfowler's World, by Bill Buckley, Ducks Unlimited, Inc., Memphis, TN, 1999. 192 pp., illustrated in color. $37.50

An unprecedented pictorial book on waterfowl and waterfowlers.

When the Duck Were Plenty, by Ed Muderlak, Safari Press, Inc., Huntington Beach, CA, 2000. 300 pp., illus. $29.95

The golden age of waterfowling and duck hunting from 1840 until 1920. An anthology.

Whitetail: Behavior Through the Seasons, by Charles J. Alsheimer, Krause Publications, Iola, WI, 1996. 208 pp., illus. $34.95

In-depth coverage of whitetail behavior presented through striking portraits of the whitetail in every season.

Whitetail: The Ultimate Challenge, by Charles J. Alsheimer, Krause Publications, Iola, WI, 1995. 228 pp., illus. Paper covers. $14.95

Learn deer hunting's most intriguing secrets–fooling deer using decoys, scents and calls–from America's premier authority.

Whitetails by the Moon, by Charles J. Alsheimer, edited by Patrick Durkin, Krause Publications, Iola, WI, 1999. 208 pp., illus. Paper covers. $19.95

Predict peak times to hunt whitetails. Learn what triggers the rut.

Wildfowler's Season, by Chris Dorsey, Lyons & Burford Publishers, New York, NY, 1998. 224 pp., illus. $37.95

Modern methods for a classic sport.

Wildfowling Tales, by William C. Hazelton, Wilderness Adventures Press, Belgrade, MT, 1999. 117 pp., illustrated with etchings by Brett Smith. In a slipcase. $50.00

Tales from the great ducking resorts of the continent.

Windward Crossings: A Treasury of Original Waterfowling Tales, by Chuck Petrie et al, Willow Creek Press, Minocqua, WI, 1999. 144 pp., 48 color art and etching reproductions. $35.00

An illustrated, modern anthology of previously unpublished waterfowl hunting (fiction and creative nonfiction) stories by America's finest outdoor journalists.

Wings of Thunder: New Grouse Hunting Revisited, by Steven Mulak, Countrysport Books, Selma, AL, 1998. 168 pp. illus. $30.00

The author examines every aspect of New England grouse hunting as it is today–the bird and its habits, the hunter and his dog, guns and loads, shooting and hunting techniques, practice on clay targets, clothing and equipment.

Woodchuck Hunter, The, by Paul C. Estey, R&R Books, Livonia, NY, 1994. 135 pp., illus. $25.00

This book contains information on woodchuck equipment, the rifle, telescopic sights and includes interesting stories.

AFRICA/ASIA/ELSEWHERE

A Bullet Well Placed; One Hunter's Adventures Around the World, by Johnny Chilton, Safari Press, 2004. 245 pages. Hardcover. New in new dust jacket. $34.95

Painting a picture of what it is actually like to be there and do it, this well-written book captures the excitement and emotions of each journey.

A Country Boy in Africa, by George Hoffman, Trophy Room Books, Agoura, CA, 1998. 267 pp., illustrated with over 100 photos. Limited, numbered edition signed by the author. $85.00

In addition to the author's long and successful hunting career, he is known for developing a most effective big game cartridge, the .416 Hoffman.

A Hunter's Africa, by Gordon Cundill, Trophy Room Books, Agoura, CA, 1998. 298 pp., over 125 photographic illustrations. Limited numbered edition signed by the author. $125.00

A good look by the author at the African safari experience-elephant, lion, spiral-horned antelope, firearms, people and events, as well as the clients that make it worthwhile.

A Hunter's Wanderings in Africa, by Frederick Courteney Selous, Alexanders Books, Alexander, NC, 2003. 504 pp., illus. $28.50

A reprinting of the 1920 London edition. A narrative of nine years spent amongst the game of the far interior of South Africa.

A Pioneering Hunter, by B Marsh, Safari Press, 2006. A limited edition of 1,000 copies. Signed and Numbered. 107. 247pp, color photos. Hardcover in a Slipcase. NEW. $65.00

Elephant cropping, buffalo tales, and colorful characters—this book has it all.

A Professional Hunter's Journey of Discovery, by Alec McCallum, Agoura, CA, Trophy Room Books, 2003. Limited edition of 1,000. Signed and numbered. 132 pp. Hardcover. New in new dust jacket. $125.00

A View From A Tall Hill: Robert Ruark in Africa, by Terry Wieland, Bristol, CT, Country Sport Press, 2004. Reprint. 432 pp., Hardcover New in new dust jacket $45.00

African Adventures and Misadventures: Escapades in East Africa with Mau Mau and Giant Forest Hogs, by William York, Long Beach, CA, Safari Press, 2003. A limited edition of 1,000 copies. Signed and numbered. 250 pp., color and b&w photos. Hardcover in a slipcase. $70.00

From his early days in Kenya when he and a companion trekked alone through the desert of the NFD and had to fend off marauding lions that ate his caravan ponies to encountering a Mau Mau terrorist who took potshots at his victims with a stolen elephant gun, the late Bill York gives an entertaining account of his life that will keep you turning the pages. As with York's previous book, the pages are loaded with interesting anecdotes, fascinating tales, and well-written prose that give insight into East Africa and its more famous characters.

African Game Trails, by Theodore Roosevelt, Peter Capstick, Series Editor, St. Martin's Press, New York, NY 1988. 583 pp., illus. $26.95

The famed safari of the noted sportsman, conservationist, and president.

African Hunter II, edited by Craig Boddington and Peter Flack, Foreword by Robin Hurt, Introduction by James Mellon, Long Beach, CA, Safari Press, 2004. 606 pp., profuse color and b&w photos. Hardcover. $135.00

James Mellon spent five years hunting in every African country open to hunting during the late 1960s and early 1970s, making him uniquely qualified to write a book of such scope and breadth. Because so much has changed in today's Africa, however, it was necessary to update the original. With over 500 full-color pages, hundreds of photographs, and updated tables on animals and where they are available, this is THE book to consult for the information on Africa today.

African Rifles & Cartridges, by John Taylor, The Gun Room Press, Highland Park, NJ, 1977. 431 pp., illus. $35.00

Experiences and opinions of a professional ivory hunter in Africa describing his knowledge of numerous arms and cartridges for big game. A reprint.

African Twilight, by Robert F. Jones, Wilderness Adventure Press, Bozeman, MT, 1994. 208 pp., illus. $36.00

Details the hunt, danger and changing face of Africa over a span of three decades.

Atkin, Grant & Lang: A Detailed History of Enduring Gunmakers (trade edition), by Don Masters, Safari Press, 2005. 316pp., color and b&w photos. Hardcover. New in new dust jacket. $69.89

The history of three makers and their several relatives making guns under their own names. In the pages of this book you can learn all the details of the gun makers: dates, premises, main employees, rises and declines in sales fortunes, as well as the many interesting historical anecdotes and insights we have come to expect from Don Masters.

Baron in Africa; The Remarkable Adventures of Werner von Alvensleben, by Brian Marsh, Foreword by Ian Player, Safari Press, Huntington Beach, CA, 2001. 288 pp., illus. $35.00

Follow his career as he hunts lion, goes after large kudu, kills a full-grown buffalo with a spear, and hunts for elephant and ivory in some of the densest brush in Africa. The adventure and the experience were what counted to this fascinating character, not the money or fame; indeed, in the end he left Mozambique with barely more than the clothes on his back. This is a must-read adventure story of one of the most interesting characters to have come out of Africa after WWII.

Buffalo!, by Craig Boddington, Safari Books, 2006. 256pp, color photos, Hardcover. NEW. $39.95

Craig tells his readers where to hunt, how and when to hunt, and what will happen when they do hunt. He describes what it means to rush the herd, one of his favorite methods of hunting these worthy opponents. He tells of the great bull in Masailand that he almost got, of the perfect hunt he had in Zambia, and of the charge he experienced in Tanzania.

Buffalo, Elephant, & Bongo (trade edition): Alone in the Savannas and Rain Forests of the Cameroon, by Reinald Von Meurers, Long Beach, CA, Safari Press, 2004. Hardcover. New in new dust jacket. $39.50

Cottar: The Exception was the Rule, by Pat Cottar, Trophy Room Books, Agoura, CA, 1999. 350 pp., illus. Limited, numbered and signed edition. $135.00

The remarkable big game hunting stories of one of Kenya's most remarkable pioneers.

Dangerous Game, True Stories of Dangerous Hunting on Three Continents, The, Safari Press, 2006. A limited edition of 500 copies. Signed and Numbered. 225pp, photos. Hardcover in a Slipcase. NEW. $70.00

Death and Double Rifles, by Mark Sullivan, Nitro Express Safaris, Phoenix, AZ, 2000. 295 pp., illus. $85.00

Sullivan has captured every thrilling detail of hunting dangerous game in this lavishly illustrated book. Full of color pictures of African hunts & rifles.

Death in a Lonely Land, by Peter Capstick, St. Martin's Press, New York, NY, 1990. 284 pp., illus. $22.95

Twenty-three stories of hunting as only the master can tell them.

Death in the Dark Continent, by Peter Capstick, St. Martin's Press, New York, NY, 1983. 238 pp., illus. $22.95

A book that brings to life the suspense, fear and exhilaration of stalking ferocious killers under primitive, savage conditions, with the ever present threat of death.

Death in the Long Grass, by Peter Hathaway Capstick, St. Martin's Press, New York, NY, 1977. 297 pp., illus. $22.95

A big game hunter's adventures in the African bush.

Death in the Silent Places, by Peter Capstick, St. Martin's Press, New York, NY, 1981. 243 pp., illus. $23.95

The author recalls the extraordinary careers of legendary hunters such as Corbett, Karamojo Bell, Stigand and others.

Elephant Hunters, Men of Legend, by Tony Sanchez-Arino, Safari Press, 2005. A limited edition of 1,000 copies. Signed and Numbered. 240 pages. Hardcover in a Slipcase. NEW. $100.00

This newest book from Tony Sanchez is the most interesting ever to emerge on that intrepid and now finished breed of man: Elephant Hunters, Men of Legend.

Encounters with Lions, by Jan Hemsing, Trophy Room Books, Agoura, CA, 1995. 302 pp., illus. $75.00

Some stories fierce, fatal, frightening and even humorous of when man and lion meet.

Fodor's African Safari, From Budget to Big Spending Where and How to Find the Best Big Game Adventure in Southern and Eastern Africa, by David Bristow, Julian Harrison, Chris Swiac, New York, Fodor's, 2004. 1st edition. 190 pp. Softcover. NEW. $9.95

Frederick Selous: A Hunting Legend-Recollections By and About the Great Hunter (trade edition), by F.C. Selous (edited by James Casada), Safari Press, 2005. 187pp., illus. Hardcover. $34.95

This second book on Selous, edited by Africana expert Dr. James Casada, completes the work on the lost writings by Selous begun in Africa's Greatest Hunter.

From Mt. Kenya to the Cape: Ten Years of African Hunting, by Craig Boddington, Long Beach, CA, Safari Press, 2005. Hardcover. New in new dust jacket. $39.95

This wealth of information makes not only great reading, but the appendixes also provide tips on rifles, cartridges, equipment, and how to plan a safari.

From Sailor to Professional Hunter: The Autobiography of John Northcote, Trophy Room Books, Agoura, CA, 1997. 400 pp., illus. Limited edition, signed and numbered. $125.00

Only a handful of men can boast of having a 50-year professional hunting career throughout Africa as John Northcote has had.

Gone are the Days; Jungle Hunting for Tiger and other Game in India and Nepal 1953-1969, by Peter Byrne, Safari Press, Inc., Huntington Beach, CA, 2001. 225 pp., illus. Limited signed, numbered, slipcased. $70.00

Great Hunters: Their Trophy Rooms and Collections, Volume 1, compiled and published by Safari Press, Inc., Huntington Beach, CA, 1997. 172 pp., illustrated in color. $60.00

A rare glimpse into the trophy rooms of top international hunters. A few of these trophy rooms are museums.

Great Hunters: Their Trophy Rooms & Collections, Volume 2, compiled and published by Safari Press, Inc., Huntington Beach, CA, 1998. 224 pp., illustrated with 260 full-color photographs. $60.00

Volume Two of the world's finest, best produced series of books on trophy rooms and game collections. 46 sportsmen sharing sights you'll never forget on this guided tour.

Great Hunters: Their Trophy Rooms & Collections, Volume 3, compiled and published by Safari Press, Inc., Huntington Beach, CA, 2000. 204 pp., illustrated with 260 full-color photographs. $60.00

At last, the long-awaited third volume in the best photographic series ever published of trophy room collections is finally available. As before, each trophy room is accompanied by an informative text explaining the collection and giving you insights into the hunters who went to such great efforts to create their trophy rooms. All professionally photographed in the highest quality possible.

Great Hunters: Their Trophy Rooms & Collections, Volume 4, compiled and published by Safari Press, Inc., Huntington Beach, CA, 2005. 204 pp., illustrated with 260 full-color photographs. $60.00

At last, the long-awaited fourth volume in the best photographic series ever published of trophy room collections is finally available. Each trophy room is accompanied by an informative text explaining the collection and giving you insights into the hunters who went to such great efforts to create their trophy rooms. All professionally photographed in the highest quality possible.

Heart of an African Hunter, by Peter Flack, Long Beach, CA, Safari Press, 2005. 266 pp. illustrated with b&w photos. Hardcover. NEW. $35.00

Hemingway in Africa: The Last Safari, by Christopher Ondaatje, Overlook Press, 2004. 1st edition. 240 pp. Hardcover. New in new dust jacket. $37.50

Horn of the Hunter, by Robert Ruark, Safari Press, Long Beach, CA, 1987. 315 pp., illus. $35.00

Ruark's most sought-after title on African hunting, here in reprint.

Hunter's Tracks, by J.A. Hunter, Safari Press Publications, Huntington Beach, CA, 1999. 240 pp., illus. $24.95

This is the exciting story of John Hunter's efforts to capture the shady head man of a gang of ivory poachers and smugglers. The story is interwoven with the tale of one of East Africa's most grandiose safaris taken with an Indian maharaja.

Hunting in Ethiopia, An Anthology, by Tony Sanchez-Arino, Safari Press, Huntington Beach, CA, 1996. 350 pp., illus. Limited, signed and numbered edition. $135.00

The finest selection of hunting stories ever compiled on hunting in this great game country.

Hunting in Kenya, by Tony Sanchez-Arino, Safari Press, Inc., Huntington Beach, CA, 2000. 350 pp., illus. Limited, signed and numbered edition in a slipcase. $135.00

The finest selection of hunting stories ever compiled on hunting in this great game country make up this anthology.

Hunting in the Sudan, An Anthology, compiled by Tony Sanchez-Arino, Safari Press, Huntington Beach, CA, 1992. 350 pp., illus. Limited, signed and numbered edition in a slipcase. $125.00

The finest selection of hunting stories ever compiled on hunting in this great game country.

Hunting Instinct, The, by Phillip D. Rowter, Safari Press, Inc., Huntington Beach, CA, 2005, trade edition. Hardcover. New in new dust jacket. $29.95

Safari chronicles from the Republic of South Africa and Namibia 1990-1998.

Hunting the Dangerous Game of Africa, by John Kingsley-Heath, Sycamore Island Books, Boulder, CO, 1998. 477 pp., illus. $95.00

Written by one of the most respected, successful, and ethical P.H.'s to trek the sunlit plains of Botswana, Kenya, Uganda, Tanganyika, Somaliland, Eritrea, Ethiopia, and Mozambique. Filled with some of the most gripping and terrifying tales ever to come out of Africa.

Hunting, Settling and Remembering, by Philip H. Percival, Trophy Room Books, Agoura, CA, 1997. 230 pp., illus. Limited, numbered and signed edition. $85.00

If Philip Percival is to come alive again, it will be through this, the first edition of his easy, intricate and magical book illustrated with some of the best historical big game hunting photos ever taken.

Hunting Trips in The Land of the Dragon; Anglo and American Sportsmen in Old China, 1870-1940, by Kenneth Czech, Safari Press, 2005. Hardcover. New in new dust jacket. $34.95

The first part of this anthology takes the reader after duck, pheasant, and other upland game while the second part focuses on the large game of China and the border regions. The latter includes hunts for Manchurian tiger, tufted deer, goral, wild goat, wild yak, antelope, takin, wild sheep in the Mongolian Altai, wapiti, blue sheep, ibex, Ovis poli of the Pamir, wild sheep of the Tian Shan, brown bear, and panda--all written by such famous names as Major General Kinloch, St. George Littledale, Kermit Roosevelt, and Roy Chapman Andrews.

In the Salt, by Lou Hallamore, Trophy Room Books, Agoura, CA, 1999. 227 pp., illustrated in b&w and full color. Limited, numbered and signed edition. $125.00

A book about people, animals and the big game hunt, about being outwitted and outmaneuvered. It is about knowing that sooner or later your luck will change and your trophy will be "in the salt."

International Hunter 1945-1999, Hunting's Greatest Era, by Bert Klineburger, Sportsmen on Film, Kerrville, TX, 1999. 400 pp., illus. A limited, numbered and signed edition. $125.00

The most important book of the greatest hunting era by the world's preeminent international hunter.

Jim Corbett Collection, by Jim Corbett, Safari Press, 2005. 1124 pages, illus, 5 volumes. Hardcover in a Slipcase. NEW. $100.00

The complete set of Jim Corbett's works, housed in a printed slipcase and feature the work of the internationally famous wildlife artist Guy Coheleach.

King of the Wa-Kikuyu, by John Boyes, St. Martin Press, New York, NY, 1993. 240 pp., illus. $19.95

In the 19th and 20th centuries, Africa drew to it a large number of great hunters, explorers, adventurers and rogues. Many have become legendary, but John Boyes (1874-1951) was the most legendary of them all.

Kwaheri! On the Spoor of Big Game in East Africa, by Robert von Reitnauer, Long beach, CA, Safari Press, 2005. A limited edition of 1,000 copies. Signed and Numbered. 285 pages, illustrated with photos. Hardcover in a Slipcase. NEW. $75.00

This is the story of an immense land in the days before the truly big tuskers all but disappeared. A very good read.

Last Horizons: Hunting, Fishing and Shooting on Five Continents, by Peter Capstick, St. Martin's Press, New York, NY, 1989. 288 pp., illus. $19.95

The first in a two-volume collection of hunting, fishing and shooting tales from the selected pages of *The American Hunter, Guns & Ammo* and *Outdoor Life.*

Last of the Ivory Hunters, by John Taylor, Safari Press, Long Beach, CA, 1990. 354 pp., illus. $29.95

Reprint of the classic book "Pondoro" by one of the most famous elephant hunters of all time.

Legends of the Field: More Early Hunters in Africa, by W.R. Foran, Trophy Room Press, Agoura, CA, 1997. 319 pp., illus. Limited edition. $100.00

This book contains the biographies of some very famous hunters: William Cotton Oswell, F.C. Selous, Sir Samuel Baker, Arthur Neumann, Jim Sutherland, W.D.M. Bell and others.

Lives of A Professional Hunting Family, by Gerard Agoura Miller, Trophy Room Books, 2003. A limited edition of 1,000 copies. Signed and numbered. 303 pp., 230 b&w photographic illustrations. Hardcover. $135.00

Lost Classics, by Robert Ruark, Safari Press, Huntington Beach, CA, 1996. 260 pp., illus. $35.00

The magazine stories that Ruark wrote in the 1950s and 1960s finally in print in book form.

Lost Wilderness; True Accounts of Hunters and Animals in East Africa, by Mohamed Ismail and Alice Pianfetti, Safari Press, Inc., Huntington Beach, CA, 2000. 216 pp., photos, illus. Limited edition signed, numbered and slipcased. $60.00

Mahonhboh, by Ron Thomson, Hartbeesport, South Africa, 1997. 312 pp., illus. Limited signed and numbered edition. $50.00

Elephants and elephant hunting in South Central Africa.

Man-Eaters of Tsavo, The, by Lt. Colonel J.H. Patterson, Peter Capstick, series editor, St. Martin's Press, New York, NY, 1986, 5th printing. 346 pp., illus. $22.95

Maneaters and Marauders, by John "Pondoro" Taylor, Long Beach, CA, Safari Press, 2005. 1st edition, Safari edition. Hardcover. New in new dust jacket. $29.95

McElroy Hunts Asia, by C.J. McElroy, Safari Press, Inc., Huntington Beach, CA, 1989. 272 pp., illus. $50.00

From the founder of SCI comes a book on hunting the great continent of Asia for big game: tiger, bear, sheep and ibex. Includes the story of the all-time record Altai Argali as well as several markhor hunts in Pakistan.

Memoirs of A Sheep Hunter, by Rashid Jamsheed, Safari Press, Inc., Huntington Beach, CA, 1996. 330 pp., illus. $70.00

The author reveals his exciting accounts of obtaining world-record heads from his native Iran, and his eventual move to the U.S. where he procured a grand-slam of North American sheep.

Memoirs of An African Hunter (Trade Edition), by Terry Irwin, Safari Press, 2005. 411pp, 95 color and 20 b&w photos, large format. Hardcover $70.00

Memories of Africa; Hunting in Zambia and Sudan, by W. Brach, Safari Press, 2005. 2005. A limited edition of 1,000 copies. Signed and Numbered. 285 pages, illustrated with photos. Hardcover in a Slipcase. NEW. $85.00

Written with an interesting flair and a true graphic perspective of the animals, people, and the hunt, this is a realistic portrayal, not Hollywood-style swaggering and gun-slinging, of hunting the magnificent wildlife of Zambia and Sudan over the last three decades.

Mundjamba: The Life Story of an African Hunter, by Hugo Seia, Trophy Room Books, Agoura, CA, 1996. 400 pp., illus. Limited, numbered and signed by the author. $125.00

An autobiography of one of the most respected and appreciated professional African hunters.

My Africa: A Professional Hunter's Journey of Discovery, by Alec McCallum, Trouphy Room Books, 2003. Limited Edition: 1000. Signed and numbered. hunting. 232pp. Hardcover. New in new dust jacket. $125.00

My Wanderings Though Africa: The Life and Times of a Professional Hunter, by Mike and James Cameron, Safari Press, 2004. Deluxe, Limited, Signed edition. 208pp, b&w photos. Hardcover in a Slipcase. NEW. $75.00

This is a book for readers whose imagination carries them into a world where reality means starry skies, the call of a jackal and the moan of a lion, the smell of gun oil, and smoke from a cooking fire rising into the African night.

On Target, by Christian Le Noel, Trophy Room Books, Agoura, CA, 1999. 275 pp., illus. Limited, numbered and signed edition. $85.00

History and hunting in Central Africa.

One Long Safari, by Peter Hay, Trophy Room Books, Agoura, CA, 1998. 350 pp., with over 200 photographic illustrations and 7 maps. Limited numbered edition signed by the author. $100.00

Contains hunts for leopards, sitatunga, hippo, rhino, snakes and, of course, the general African big game bag.

Optics for the Hunter, by John Barsness, Safari Press, Inc., Huntington Beach, CA, 1999. 236 pp., illus. $24.95

An evaluation of binoculars, scopes, range finders, spotting scopes for use in the field.

Out in the Midday Shade, by William York, Safari Press, Inc., Huntington Beach, CA, 2005. Trade Edition. Hardcover. New in new dust jacket. $35.00

Path of a Hunter, The, by Gilles Tre-Hardy, Trophy Room Books, Agoura, CA, 1997. 318 pp., illus. Limited Edition, signed and numbered. $85.00

A most unusual hunting autobiography with much about elephant hunting in Africa.

Perfect Shot: Mini Edition for Africa, The, by Kevin Robertson, Long Beach, CA, Safari Press, 2004. 2nd printing Softcover. NEW. $17.95

Perfect Shot: Shot Placement for African Big Game, The, by Kevin "Doctari" Robertson, Safari Press, Inc., Huntington Beach, CA, 1999. 230 pp., illus. $65.00

The most comprehensive work ever undertaken to show the anatomical features for all classes of African game. Includes caliber and bullet selection, rifle selection and trophy handling.

Peter Capstick's Africa: A Return to the Long Grass, by Peter Hathaway Capstick, St. Martin's Press, N. Y., NY, 1987. 213 pp., illus. $35.00

A first-person adventure in which the author returns to the long grass for his own dangerous and very personal excursion.

Pondoro, by John Taylor, Safari Press, Inc., Huntington Beach, CA, 1999. 354 pp., illus. $39.95

The author is considered one of the best storytellers in the hunting book world, and Pondoro is highly entertaining. A classic African big-game hunting title.

Quotable Hunter, The, by Jay Cassell and Peter Fiduccia, The Lyons Press, N.Y., 1999. 288 pp., illus. $20.00

This collection of more than three hundred quotes from hunters through the ages captures the essence of the sport, with all its joys, idosyncrasies, and challenges.

Return to Toonaklut-The Russell Annabel Story, by Jeff Davis, Long Beach, CA, Safari Press, 2002. 248 pp., photos, illus. $34.95

Those of us who grew up after WW II cannot imagine the Alaskan frontier that Rusty Annabel walked into early in the twentieth century. The hardships, the resourcefulness, the natural beauty, not knowing what lay beyond the next horizon, all were a part of his existence. This is the story of the man behind the legend, and it is as fascinating as any of the tales Rusty Annabel ever spun for the sporting magazines.

Rifles and Cartridges for Large Game-From Deer to Bear-Advice on the Choice of A Rifle, by Layne Simpson, Long Beach, CA, Safari Press, 2002. Illustrated with 100 color photos, oversize book. 225 pp., color illus. $39.95

Layne Simpson, who has been field editor for *Shooting Times* magazine for 20 years, draws from his hunting experiences on five continents to tell you what rifles, cartridges, bullets, loads, and scopes are best for various applications, and he explains why in plain English. Developer of the popular 7mm STW cartridge, Simpson has taken big game with rifle cartridges ranging in power from the .220 Swift to the .460 Weatherby Magnum, and he pulls no punches when describing their effectiveness in the field.

Rifles for Africa; Practical Advice on Rifles and Ammunition for an African Safari, by Gregor Woods, Long Beach, CA, Safari Press, 2002. 1st edition. 430 pp., illus., photos. $39.95

Invaluable to the person who seeks advice and information on what rifles, calibers, and bullets work on African big game, be they the largest land mammals on earth or an antelope barely weighing in at 20 lbs.!

Robert Ruark's Africa, by Robert Ruark, edited by Michael McIntosh, Countrysport Press, Selma, AL, 1999. 256 pp. illustrated with 19 original etchings by Bruce Langton. $32.00

These previously uncollected works of Robert Ruark make this a classic big-game hunting book.

Safari: The Last Adventure, by Peter Capstick, St. Martin's Press, New York, NY, 1984. 291 pp., illus. $22.95

A modern comprehensive guide to the African Safari.

Safari Rifles: Double, Magazine Rifles and Cartridges for African Hunting, by Craig Boddington, Safari Press, Huntington Beach, CA, 1990. 416 pp., illus. $37.50

A wealth of knowledge on the safari rifle. Historical and present double-rifle makers, ballistics for the large bores, and much, much more.

Sands of Silence, by Peter H. Capstick, Saint Martin's Press, New York, NY, 1991. 224 pp., illus. $35.00

Join the author on safari in Nambia for his latest big-game hunting adventures.

Song of the Summits-Hunting Sheep, Ibex, and Markhor in Asia, Europe, and North America, by Jesus Yurén, Long Beach, CA, Safari Press, 2003. Limited edition. Hardcover in a slipcase. NEW. $75.00

Sunset Tales of Safariland, by Stan Bleazard, Trophy Room Books, 2006. Deluxe, Limited, Signed edition. Large 8½" x11" format, bound in sumptuous forest green gilt stamped suede binding. 274 pages. 113 b&w photographic illustrations and index. NEW. $125.00

Sunset Tales of Safariland will be of considerable interest to anyone interested in big game hunting.

Tales of the African Frontier, by J.A. Hunter, Safari Press Publications, Huntington Beach, CA, 1999. 308 pp., illus. $24.95

The early days of East Africa is the subject of this powerful John Hunter book.

Tanzania Safari: Hei Safari, by Robert DePole, Trophy Room Books, 2004. Sumptuous Burgundy gilt stamped faux suede binding, 343 pages plus 12 page index of people and places. 32 pages of black & white photographic illustrations. Hardcover. NEW. $125.00

The reader will "see" the animals on the pages long enough to remember them forever.

To Heck With It-I'm Going Hunting-My First Eighteen Years as an International Big-Game Hunter-Limited Edition, by Arnold Alward with Bill Quimby, Long Beach, CA, Safari Press, 2003. Deluxe, 1st edition, limited to 1,000 signed copies. NEW. $80.00

Uganda Safaris, by Brian Herne, Winchester Press, Piscataway, NJ, 1979. 236 pp., illus. $24.95

The chronicle of a professional hunter's adventures in Africa.

Under the African Sun, by Dr. Frank Hibben, Safari Press, Inc., Huntington Beach, CA, 1999. Limited edition signed, numbered and in a slipcase. $85.00

Forty-eight years of hunting the African continent.

Under the African Sun, by Dr. Frank Hibben, Safari Press, Inc., Huntington Beach, CA, 2005. Trade edition. 305 pages illustrated with b&w and color photos. Hardcover. New in new dust jacket. $39.95

Under the Shadow of Man Eaters, by Jerry Jaleel, The Jim Corbett Foundation, Edmonton, Alberta, Canada, 1997. 152 pp., illus. A limited, numbered and signed edition. Paper covers. $35.00

The life and legend of Jim Corbett of Kumaon.

Use Enough Gun, by Robert Ruark, Safari Press, Huntington Beach, CA, 1997. 333 pp., illus. $35.00

Robert Ruark on big game hunting.

Warrior: The Legend of Col. Richard Meinertzhagen, by Peter H. Capstick, St. Martins Press, New York, NY, 1998. 320 pp., illus. $23.95

A stirring and vivid biography of the famous British colonial officer Richard Meinertzhagen, whose exploits earned him fame and notoriety as one of the most daring and ruthless men to serve during the glory days of the British Empire.

Waterfowler's World, The, by Bill Buckley, Willow Creek Press, Minocqua, WI, 1999. 176 pp., 225 color photographs. $37.50

Waterfowl hunting from Canadian prairies, across the U.S. heartland, to the wilds of Mexico, from the Atlantic to the Pacific coasts and the Gulf of Mexico.

Weatherby: Stories From the Premier Big-Game Hunters of the World, 1956-2002, The, edited by Nancy Vokins, Long Beach, CA, Safari Press, 2004. Deluxe, limited, signed edition. 434 pp., profuse color and b&w illus. Hardcover in a slipcase. $200.00

Wheel of Life-Bunny Allen, A Life of Safaris and Sex, The, by Bunny Allen, Long Beach, CA, Safari Press, 2004. 1st edition. 300 pp., illus, photos. Hardcover. $34.95

Wind, Dust & Snow-Great Rams of Asia, by Robert M. Anderson, Collectors Covey, 1997. Deluxe Limited edition of 500 copies. Signed and Numbered. 240pp profuse illus. More than 200 photos some on the greatest Asian rams ever taken by sportsmen. $150.00

A complete chronology of modern exploratory and pioneering Asian sheep-hunting expeditions from 1960 until 1996, with wonderful background history and previously untold stories.

With a Gun in Good Country, by Ian Manning, Trophy Room Books, Agoura, CA, 1996. Limited, numbered and signed by the author. $85.00

A book written about that splendid period before the poaching onslaught which almost closed Zambia and continues to the granting of her independence. It then goes on to recount Manning's experiences in Botswana, Congo, and briefly in South Africa.

Yoshi-The Life and Travels of an International Trophy Hunter, by W. Yoshimoto with Bill Quimby, Long Beach, CA, Safari Press, Inc., 2002. A limited edition of 1,000 copies, signed and numbered. 298 pp., color and b&w photos. Hardcover in a slipcase. $85.00

Watson T. Yoshimoto, a native Hawaiian, collected all 16 major varieties of the world's wild sheep and most of the many types of goats, ibex, bears, antelopes, and antlered game of Asia, Europe, North America, South America, and the South Pacific...as well as the African Big Five. Along the way he earned the respect of his peers and was awarded hunting's highest achievement, the coveted Weatherby Award.

RIFLES

'03 Springfield Rifles Era, by Clark S. Campbell, Richmond, VA, privately printed, 2003. 1st edition. 368 pp., 146 illustrations, drawn to scale by author. Hardcover. $58.00

A much-expanded version of this author's famous The '03 Springfield (1957) and The '03 Springfields (1971), representing 40 years of research into all things '03. Part I is a complete and verifiably correct study of all standardized and special-purpose models of the U.S. M1903 Springfield rifle, in both .22 and .30 calibers, including those prototypes which led to standard models, and also all standardized .30 caliber cartridges, including National and International Match, and caliber .22. Part II is the result of the author's five years as a Research and Development Engineer with Remington Arms Co., and will be of inestimable value to anyone planning a custom sporter, whether or not based on the '03.

.303 SMLE Rifle No. 1 Assembly, Disassembly Manual, by Skennerton & Riling, Ray Riling Arms Books Co. Philadelphia, PA 2004. 36 pages, $5.00

With over 60 photos & line drawings. Ideal workshop reference for stripping & assembly with exploded parts drawings, specifications, service accessories, historical information and recommended reading references.

.303 British Rifle No. 4 Assembly, Disassembly Manual, by Skennerton & Riling, Ray Riling Arms Books Co. Philadelphia, PA 2004. 36 pages, $5.00

With over 60 photos & line drawings. Ideal workshop reference for stripping & assembly with exploded parts drawings, specifications, service accessories, historical information and recommended reading references.

.577 Snider-Enfield Rifles & Carbines; British Service Longarms, by Ian Skennerton. 1866-C.1880. Australia, Arms & Militaria Press, 2003. 1st edition. 240 pp. plus 8 color plates, 100 illustrations. Marking Ribbon. Hardcover. $39.50

The definitive study of Britain's first breech-loading rifle, at first converted from Enfield muskets, then newly made with Mk III breech. The trials, development, rifle and carbine models are detailed; new information along with descriptions of the cartridges.

1903 Springfield Assembly, Disassembly Manual .30 Model, by Skennerton & Riling, Ray Riling Arms Books Co. Philadelphia, PA 2004. 36 pages, $5.00

With over 60 photos & line drawings. Ideal workshop reference for stripping & assembly with exploded parts drawings, specifications, service accessories, historical information and recommended reading references.

1903 Springfield Rifle and Its Variations, by Joe Poyer, Tustin, CA, North Cape Publications, 2004. 466 pages, illustrated with hundreds of color and b& drawings and photos. Soft cover. NEW. $22.95

It covers the entire spectrum of the Model 1903 rifle from the rod bayonet to the M1903A4 sniper rifle.

A Master Gunmaker's Guide to Building Bolt-Action Rifles, by Bill Holmes, Boulder, CO, Paladin Press, 2003. Photos, illus., 152 pp. Softcover. $25.00

Many people today call themselves gunmakers, but very few have actually made a gun. Most buy parts wherever available and simply assemble them. During the past 50 years Bill Holmes has built from scratch countless rifles, shotguns and pistols of amazing artistry, ranging in caliber from .17 to .50.

A Potpourri of Single Shot Rifles and Actions, by Frank de Haas and Mark de Haas, Ridgeway, MO, 1993. 153 pp., illus. Paper covers. $22.50

The author's 6th book on non-bolt-action single shots. Covers more than 40 single-shot rifles in historical and technical detail.

Accurizing & Shooting Lee-Enfields, by Ian Skennerton, Australia, Arms & Militaria Press, 2005. 35pp, saddle-stitched laminated covers. ALL color photos and illustrations. Stiff paper covers. NEW. $15.00

This new full color heavily illustrated work by Ian Skennerton answers all those questions regarding the use of the Lee Enfield Rifles. Packed with detailed information covering the guns, the armourer's tools, and the sighting options for this fascinating series.

AK-47 and AK-74 Kalashnikov Rifles and Their Variations, by Joe Poyer, Tustin, CA, North Cape Publications, 2004. 1st edition. Softcover, NEW. 188 pages, illustrated. $22.95

This is the newest book in the "Shooter's and Collector's Guide" series. Prepared with the help of members of the Kalashnikov Collectors Association, this 188 page book surveys every variation of the 7.62 AK-47 and the 5.45 AK-74 developed in the old Soviet Union on a part-to-part basis to permit easy identification of original rifles and those made from kits available from various manufacturers in different countries.

AK-47 Assembly, Disassembly Manual 7.62 X 39mm, by Skennerton & Riling, Ray Riling Arms Books Co. Philadelphia, PA 2004. 36 pages, $5.00

With over 60 photos & line drawings. Ideal workshop reference for stripping & assembly with exploded parts drawings, specifications, service accessories, historical information and recommended reading references. Ideal workbook for shooters and collectors alike. Triple saddle-stitched binding with durable plastic laminated cover makes this an ideal workshop guide.

AK-47 Assault Rifle, Desert Publications, Cornville, AZ, 1981. 150 pp., illus. Paper covers. $15.95

Complete and practical technical information on the only weapon in history to be produced in an estimated 30,000,000 units.

American Hunting Rifles: Their Application in the Field for Practical Shooting, by Craig Boddington, Safari Press, Huntington Beach, CA, 1996. 446 pp., illus. Second printing trade edition. Softcover $24.95

Covers all the hunting rifles and calibers that are needed for North America's diverse game.

American Krag Rifle and Carbine, by Joe Poyer, North Cape Publications, Tustin, CA, 2002. 1st edition. 317 pp., illustrated with hundreds of b&w drawings and photos. Softcover. $19.95

Provides the arms collector, historian and target shooter with a part by part analysis of what has been called the rifle with the smoothest bolt action ever designed. All changes to all parts are analyzed in detail and matched to serial number ranges. A monthly serial number chart by production year has been devised that will provide the collector with the year and month in which his gun was manufactured. A new and complete exploded view was produced for this book.

American Percussion Schuetzen Rifle, by J. Hamilton and T. Rowe, Rochester, NY, Rowe Publications, 2005. 1st edition. 388 pp. Hardcover. New in new dust jacket. $98.00

An Illustrated Guide to the '03 Springfield Service Rifle, by Bruce Canfield, Lincoln, RI, Andrew Mowbray, 2005. 240 pages, illustrated with over 450 photos. Pictorial Hardcover. NEW. $49.95

Your ultimate guide to the military '03 Springfield! Covers all models, all manufacturers and all conflicts, including WWI, WWII and beyond. Heavily illustrated with professional photography showing the details that separate a great collectible rifle from the rest. Serial number tables, combat photos, sniper rifles and more!

AR-15 & M-16 5.56mm Assembly, Disassembly Manual, by Skennerton & Riling, Ray Riling Arms Books Co. Philadelphia, PA 2004. 36 pages, $5.00

With over 60 photos & line drawings. Ideal workshop reference for stripping & assembly with exploded parts drawings, specifications, service accessories, historical information and recommended reading references.

AR-15 Complete Owner's Guide, Volume 1, 2nd Edition, by Walt Kuleck and Scott Duff, Export, PA, Scott A. Duff Publications, 2002. 224 pp., 164 photographs & line drawings. Softcover. $21.95

This book provides the prospective, new or experienced AR-15 owner with the in-depth knowledge he or she needs to select, configure, operate, maintain and troubleshoot his or her rifle. The Guide covers history, applications, details of components and subassemblies, operating, cleaning, maintenance, and future of perhaps the most versatile rifle system ever produced. A comprehensive Colt model number table and pre-/post-ban serial number information are included.

AR-15 Complete Assembly Guide, Volume 2, by Walt Kuleck and Clint McKee. Export, PA, Scott A. Duff Publications, 2002. 1st edition. 155 pp., 164 photographs & line drawings. Softcover. $19.95

This book goes beyond the military manuals in depth and scope, using words and pictures to clearly guide the reader through every operation required to assemble their AR-15-type rifle. You'll learn the best and easiest ways to build your rifle. It won't make you an AR-15 armorer, but it will make you a more knowledgeable owner. In short, if you build it, you'll know how to repair it.

AR-15/M16, A Practical Guide, by Duncan Long, Paladin Press, Boulder, CO, 1985. 168 pp., illus. Paper covers. $22.00

The definitive book on the rifle that has been the inspiration for so many modern assault rifles.

Argentine Mauser Rifles 1871-1959, by Colin Atglen, Webster, PA, Schiffer Publications, 2003. 1st edition. 304 pp., over 400 b&w and color photographs, drawings, and charts. Hardcover. $79.95

This is the complete story of Argentina's contract Mauser rifles from the purchase of their first Model 1871s to the disposal of the last shipment of surplus rifles received in the United States in May 2002. The Argentine Commission's relentless pursuit of tactical superiority resulted in a major contribution to the development of Mauser's now famous bolt-action system.

Art of Shooting with the Rifle, by Col. Sir H. St. John Halford, Excalibur Publications, Latham, NY, 1996. 96 pp., illus. Paper covers. $12.95

A facsimile edition of the 1888 book by a respected rifleman providing a wealth of detailed information.

Art of the Rifle, by Jeff Cooper, Paladin Press, Boulder, CO, 1997. 104 pp., illus. Paper covers $22.00

Everything you need to know about the rifle whether you use it for security, meat or target shooting.

Assault Rifle, by Maxim Popenker, and Anthony Williams, London, Crowood Press, 2005. 224 pages. Hardcover. New in new dust jacket. $34.95

Includes brief historical summary of the assault rifle, its origins and development; gun design including operating mechanisms and weapon configuration, and more. The second part includes: national military rifle programs since the end of WWII; history of developments in each country including experimental programs; and detailed descriptions of the principal service and experimental weapons.

Ballard: The Great American Single Shot Rifle, by John T. Dutcher, Denver, CO, privately printed, 2002. 1st edition. 380 pp., illustrated with b&w photos, with an 8-page color insert. Hardcover. $79.95

Benchrest Actions and Triggers, by Stuart Otteson. Rohnert Park, CA, Adams-Kane Press, July 2003. Limited edition. 64 pp. Softcover. $27.95

Stuart Otteson's *Benchrest Actions and Triggers* is truly a lost classic. Benchrest Actions and Triggers is a compilation of 17 articles Mr. Otteson wrote. The articles contained are of particular interest to the benchrest crowd. Reprinted by permission of Wolfe Publishing.

Black Magic: The Ultra Accurate AR-15, by John Feamster, Precision Shooting, Manchester, CT, 1998. 300 pp., illus. $29.95

The author has compiled his experiences pushing the accuracy envelope of the AR-15 to its maximum potential. A wealth of advice on AR-15 loads, modifications and accessories for everything from NRA Highpower and Service Rifle competitions to benchrest and varmint shooting.

Black Rifle, M16 Retrospective, by R. Blake Stevens and Edward C. Ezell, Collector Grade Publications, Toronto, Canada, 1987. 416 pp., 441 illustrations and photos. $59.95

At the time of this writing, the 5.56mm NATO M16A2 rifle is heir to world wide acceptance after a quarter-century of U.S. service, longer than any other U.S. rifle in this century except the 1903 bolt-action Springfield. Its history has been far from one of calm acceptance.

Black Rifle II: The M16 into the 21st Century, by Christopher R. Bartocci, Canada, Collector Grade Publications, 2004. 408 pages, 626 illustrations. $69.95

This book chronicles all the new third- and fourth-generation rifle and carbine models which have been introduced by Colt and Diemaco since ***The** Black Rifle* was originally published, and describes and depicts the myriad of enhanced sights and rails systems which help make the M16s of today the most versatile, modular and effective combat weapons in the world. Includes an in-depth reference compendium of all Colt military and civilian models and components.

Blitzkrieg!-The MP40 Maschinenpistole of WWII, by Frank Iannamico, Harmony, ME, Moose Lake Publishing, 2003. 1st edition. Over 275 pp., 280 photos and documents. Softcover. $29.95

It's back, now in a new larger 8"x11" format. Lots of new information and many unpublished photos. This book includes the history and development of the German machine pistol from the MP18.I to the MP40.

Bolt Action Rifles, Expanded 4th Edition, by Frank de Haas and Wayne van Zwoll, Krause Publications, Iola, WI 2003. 696 pp., illustrated with 615 b&w photos. Softcover. $29.95

British .22RF Training Rifles, by Dennis Lewis and Robert Washburn, Excaliber Publications, Latham, NY, 1993. 64 pp., illus. Paper covers. $10.95

The story of Britain's training rifles from the early Aiming Tube models to the post-WWII trainers.

Building Double Rifles on Shotgun Actions, by W. Ellis Brown, Ft. Collins, CO, Bunduki Publishing, 2001. 1st edition. 187 pp., including index and b&w photographs. Hardcover. $55.00

Carbine .30 M1, M1A1, M2 & M3 Assembly, Disassembly Manual, by Skennerton & Riling, Ray Riling Arms Books Co. Philadelphia, PA 2004. 36 pages, over 60 photos & line drawings. $5.00

Ideal workshop reference for stripping & assembly with exploded parts drawings, specifications, service accessories, historical information and recommended reading references.

Classic Sporting Rifles, by Christopher Austyn, Safari Press, Huntington Beach, CA, 1997. 128 pp., illus. $50.00

As the head of the gun department at Christie's Auction House the author examines the "best" rifles built over the last 150 years.

Collectable '03, by J.C. Harrison, The Arms Chest, Oklahoma City, OK. 1999. 2nd edition (revised). 234 pp., illustrated with drawings, Spiral bound. $35.00

Valuable and detailed reference book for the collector of the Model 1903 Springfield rifle.

Collecting Classic Bolt Action Military Rifles, by Paul S. Scarlata, Andrew Mowbray, Inc., Lincoln, RI, 2001. 280 pp., illus. $39.95

Over 400 large photographs detail key features you will need to recognize in order to identify guns for your collection. Learn the original military configurations of these service rifles so you can tell them apart from altered guns and bad restorations. The historical sections are particularly strong, giving readers a clear understanding of how and why these rifles were developed, and which troops used them.

Collecting the Garand, by J.C. Harrison, The Arms Chest, Oklahoma City, OK. 2001. 2nd edition (revised). 198 pp., illus. with pictures and drawings. Spiral bound. $35.00

Valuable and detailed reference book for the collector of the Garand.

Collecting the M1 Carbine, by J.C. Harrison, The Arms Chest, Oklahoma City, OK. 2000. 2nd edition (revised). 247 pp., illustrated with pictures and drawings. Spiral bound. $35.00

Valuable and detailed reference book for the collector of the M1 Carbine. Identifies standard issue original military models of M1 and M1A1 Models of 1942, '43, '44, and '45 carbines as produced by each manufacturer, plus arsenal repair, refinish and lend-lease.

Competitive AR15: The Mouse That Roared, by Glenn Zediker, Zediker Publishing, Oxford, MS, 1999. 286 pp., illus. Paper covers. $29.95

A thorough and detailed study of the newest precision rifle sensation.

Complete AR15/M16 Sourcebook, Revised and Updated Edition, by Duncan Long, Paladin Press, Boulder, CO, 2002. 336 pp., illus. Paper covers. $39.95

The latest development of the AR15/M16 and the many spin-offs now available, selective-fire conversion systems for the 1990s, the vast selection of new accessories.

Complete Book of the .22: A Guide to the World's Most Popular Guns, by Wayne van Zwoll, Lyons Press, 2004. 1st edition. 336 pgs. Hardcover. NEW. $26.95

Complete Guide to the M1 Garand and the M1 Carbine, by Bruce Canfield, Andrew Mowbray, Inc., Lincoln, RI, 1999. 296 pp., illus. $39.50

Covers all of the manufacturers of components, parts, variations and markings. The total story behind these guns, from their invention through WWII, Korea, Vietnam and beyond! 300+ photos show you features, markings, overall views and action shots. Thirty-three tables and charts give instant reference to serial numbers, markings, dates of issue and proper configurations. Special sections on sniper guns, National Match rifles, exotic variations, and more!

Complete M1 Garand, by Jim Thompson, Paladin Press, Boulder, CO, 1998. 160 pp., illus. Paper cover. $24.00

A guide for the shooter and collector, heavily illustrated.

Crown Jewels: The Mauser In Sweden; A Century of Accuracy and Precision, by Dana Jones, Canada, Collector Grade Publications, 2003. 1st edition. 312 pp., 691 illustrations. Hardcover. $49.95

Here is the first in-depth study of all the Swedish Mausers: the 6.5mm M/94 carbines, M/96 long rifles, M/38 short rifles, Swedish K98Ks (called the M/39 in 7.92x57mm, then, after rechambering to fire the 8x63mm machine un cartridge, the M/40); sniper rifles, and other military adaptations such as grenade launchers and artillery simulators. Also covers a wide variety of the micrometer-adjustment rear sight inserts and "diopter" receiver sights produced for the Swedish Mauser. Full chapters on bayonets and the many accessories, both military and civilian.

Defending the Dominion, Canadian Military Rifles, 1855-1955, by David Edgecombe, Ont. Canada, Service Publications, 2003. 1st edition. 168 pp., with 60+ illustrations. Hardcover. NEW. $39.95

Desperate Measures-The Last Ditch Weapons of the Nazi Voksstrurm, by Darrin Weaver, Canada, Collector Grade Publications, 2005. 424 pages, 558 illustrations. $69.50

All are covered in detail, and the book includes many previously unpublished photographs of original Volkssturm weapons, including prototypes and rare presentation examples.

F.N.-F.A.L. Auto Rifles, Desert Publications, Cornville, AZ, 1981. 130 pp., illus. Paper covers. $18.95

A definitive study of one of the free world's finest combat rifles.

FAL Rifle, by R. Blake Stevens and Jean van Rutten, Collector Grade Publications, Cobourg, Canada, 1993. 848 pp., illus. $129.95

Originally published in three volumes, this classic edition covers North American, UK and Commonwealth and the metric FAL's.

Fighting Rifle, by Chuck Taylor, Paladin Press, Boulder, CO, 1983. 184 pp., illus. Paper covers. $25.00

The difference between assault and battle rifles and auto and light machine guns.

FN-49; Last Elegant Old-World Military Rifle, by Wayne Johnson, Greensboro, NC, Wet Dog Pub. 2004. 200 pages with Over 300 quality b&w photographs. $45.95

The FN-49 The Last Elegant old World Military Rifle book contains both information on the SAFN as well as the AFN rifle.

FN-FAL Rifle, The, et al, by Duncan Long, Delta Press, El Dorado, AR, 1998. 148 pp., illus. Paper covers. $18.95

A comprehensive study of one of the classic assault weapons of all times. Detailed descriptions of the basic models plus the myriad of variants that evolved as a result of its universal acceptance.

Forty Years with the .45-70, 2nd Edition, Revised and Expanded, by Paul A. Matthews, Wolfe Publishing Co., Prescott, AZ, 1997. 184 pp., illus. Paper covers. $17.95

This book is pure gun lore of the .45-70. It not only contains a history of the cartridge, but also years of the author's personal experiences.

Garand .30 Assembly, Disassembly Manual, by Skennerton & Riling, Ray Riling Arms Books Co. Philadelphia, PA 2004. 36 pages, $5.00

With over 60 photos & line drawings. Ideal workshop reference for stripping & assembly with exploded parts drawings, specifications, service accessories, historical information and recommended reading references.

German Sniper 1914-1945, by Peter R. Senich, Paladin Press, Boulder, CO, 1997 8½" x 11", hardcover, photos, 468 pp. $79.95

The complete story of Germany's sniping arms development through both world wars. Presents more than 600 photos of Mauser 98's, Selbstladegewehr 41s and 43s, optical sights by Goerz, Zeiss, etc., plus German snipers in action. An exceptional hardcover collector's edition for serious military historians everywhere.

Great Remington 8 and Model 81 Autoloading Rifles, by John Henwood, Canada, Collector Grade Publications, 2003. 1st edition. 304 pp., 291 illustrations, 31 in color. Hardcover. $59.95

Gun Digest Book of the.22 Rimfire, by James House, Iola,WI, Krause Publications, 2005. 288 pgs. Soft cover. 250 b&w photos. NEW. $24.99

The most comprehensive guide to rimfire weapons & ammo. Info on current & vintage models. Covers the history, sights & sighting, techniques for testing accuracy, options for enhancing models, & more.

Gun-Guides, AK-47 AKM All Variants, Disassembly and Reassembly Guide, by Gun Guides, 2005. 16pp, illustrations, cardstock cover. Bright white paper. Soft cover. NEW. $6.99

The complete guide for ALL models.

Gun-Guides, Colt AR15 and All Variants, Disassembly and Reassembly Guide, by Gun Guides, 2005. 16pp, illustrations, cardstock cover. Bright white paper. Soft cover. NEW. $6.99

The complete guide for ALL models.

Gun-Guides, 1911 Pistols & All Variants-Disassembly & Reassembly, by Gun Guides, 2006. 16pp, illustrations, cardstock cover. Bright white paper. Soft cover. NEW. $6.99

The complete guide for ALL models.

ARMS LIBRARY

Gun-Guides, Glock, Disassembly and Reassembly for All Models, by Gun Guides, 2005. 16pp, illustrations, cardstock cover. Bright white paper. Soft cover. NEW. $6.99

The complete guide for ALL models.

Gun-Guides, Remington 1100, 11-87 Shotguns, Disassembly and Reassembly Guides, by Gun Guides, 2005. The complete guide for ALL models, 16pp, illustrations, Cardstock cover. Bright white paper. Soft cover. NEW. $6.99

Gun-Guides, Remington 870 Shotguns, Disassembly and Reassembly Guides, by Gun Guides, 2005. The complete guide for ALL models, 16pp, illustrations, Cardstock cover. Bright white paper. Soft cover. NEW. $6.99

Gun-Guides, Ruger .22 Automatic Pistols: The Complete Guide for All Models from 1947 to 2003, by Gun Guides, 2005. 74 pages, 66 high-resolution grayscale images. Cardstock cover. Bright white paper. $11.95

The complete guide for ALL models. Includes "rare" complete serial numbers and manufacturing dates from 1949-2004.

Gun-Guides, Ruger Single Action Revolvers, Blackhawk, Super Blackhawk, Vaquero and Bisley Models Disassembly and Reassembly Guide for All Models, 1955-2005, by Gun Guides, 2005. 16pp, illustrations, cardstock cover. Bright white paper. $6.99

The complete guide for ALL models.

Gun-Guides, Ruger 10/22 & 10/17 Carbines Complete Guide to All Models from 1964-2004, by Gun Guides, 2005. 55 pages & 66 high-resolution grayscale images. Bright white paper. Soft cover. NEW. $11.95

Easy to use: Comb binding lies open and flat on your work surface. Includes all serial numbers and manufacture dates for all models from 1964-2004!

Gun-Guides, Ruger Mini-14 Complete Guide to All Models from 1972-2003, by Gun Guides, 2005. 52pp, illustrations, cardstock cover. Bright white paper. Soft cover. NEW. $11.95

The complete guide for ALL models.

Gun-Guides, SKS Semi-Automatic Rifles, Disassembly and Reassembly Guide, by Gun Guides, 2005. 16pp, illustrations, cardstock cover. Bright white paper. Soft cover. NEW. $6.99

The complete guide for ALL models.

Handbook of Military Rifle Marks 1866-1950 (third edition), by Richard Hoffman, and Noel Schott, Maple leaf Militaria Publications, 2002. 66 pp, with illustrations, signed by the authors. Stiff paper covers. NEW. $20.00

An illustrated book of military rifles and marks. Officially being used as a reference tool by many law enforcement agencies including BATF, the St. Louis and Philadelphia Police Departments and the Illinois State Police.

High Performance Muzzle Loading Big Game Rifles, by Toby Bridges, Maryland, Stoeger Publications, 2004. 160 pages. Pictorial Hardcover. NEW. $24.95

Covers all aspects of in-lines including getting top performance, working up loads, choosing projectiles, scope selection, coping with muzzleloader trajectory, tips for maintaining accuracy, plus much, much more.

Historic Henry Rifle: Oliver Winchester's Famous Civil War Repeater, by Wiley Sword, Andrew Mowbray, Inc., Lincoln, RI. 2002. Softcover. $29.95

Tested and proved in the fiery crucible of the Civil War, the Henry Rifle became the forerunner of the famous line of Winchester Repeating Rifles that "Won the West." Here is the fascinating story from the frustrations of early sales efforts aimed at the government to the inspired purchase of the Henry Rifle by veteran soldiers who wanted the best weapon.

Hitler's Garands: German Self-Loading Rifles of World War II, by Darrin W. Weaver, Collector Grade Publications, Canada, 2001. 392 pp., 590 illustrations. $69.95

Hitler's Wehrmacht began WWII armed with the bolt-action K98k, a rifle only cosmetically different from that with which Imperial Germany had fought the Great War a quarter-century earlier. Then in 1940, the Heereswaffenamt (HWaA, the Army Weapons Office) issued a requirement for a new self-loading rifle.

How-To's for the Black Powder Cartridge Rifle Shooter, by Paul A. Matthews, Wolfe Publishing Co., Prescott, AZ, 1996. 136 pp., illus. Paper covers. $22.50

Practices and procedures used in the reloading and shooting of blackpowder cartridges.

Imperial Japanese Grenade Rifles and Launchers, by Greg Babisch and Thomas Keep, Lemont, PA, Dutch Harlow Publishing, 2004. 247 pages, illustrated with numerous b&w and color photos throughout. Hardcover. New in new dust jacket. $75.00

This book is a must for museums, military historians, and collectors of Imperial Japanese rifles, rifle cartridges, and ordnance.

Jaeger Rifles Collected Articles Published in Muzzle Blasts, by George Shumway, York, PA, George Shumway, 2003. 108 pp., illus. Stiff paper covers. NEW. $30.00

Johnson Rifles and Machine Guns: The Story of Melvin Maynard Johnson Jr. and his Guns, by Bruce N. Canfield, Lincoln, RI, Andrew Mowbray, Inc., 2002. 1st edition. 272 pp. with over 285 photographs. Hardcover. $49.95

The M1941 Johnson rifle is the hottest WWII rifle on the collector's market today. From invention and manufacture through issue to the troops, this book covers them all!

Kalashnikov: The Arms and the Man, A Revised and Expanded Edition of the AK47 Story, by Edward C. Ezell, Canada, Collector Grade Publications, 2002. 312 pp., 356 illustrations. Hardcover. $59.95

The original edition of The AK47 Story was published in 1986, and the events of the intervening fifteen years have provided much fresh new material. Beginning with an introduction by Dr. Kalashnikov himself, this is a most comprehensive study of the "life and times" of the AK, starting with the early history of small arms manufacture in Czarist Russia and then the Soviet Union.

Last Enfield: SA80–The Reluctant Rifle, by Steve Raw, Collector Grade Publications, Canada 2003. 1st edition. 360 pp., with 382 illustrations. Hardcover. $49.95

This book presents the entire, in-depth story of its subject firearm, in this case the controversial British SA80, right from the founding of what became the Royal Small Arms Factory (RSAF) Enfield in the early 1800s; briefly through two world wars with Enfield at the forefront of small arms production for British forces; and covering the adoption of the 7.62mm NATO cartridge in 1954 and the L1A1 rifle in 1957.

Last Steel Warrior: The U.S. M14 Rifle, by Frank Iannamico, Moose Lake Pub., 2006. With over 400 pages and 537 photos and illustrations. Soft cover. NEW. $29.95

Acclaimed gun author Frank Iannamico's latest book covers history, development and deployment of the influential M14 rifle.

Lee Enfield No. 1 Rifles, by Alan M. Petrillo, Excaliber Publications, Latham, NY, 1992. 64 pp., illus. Paper covers. $10.95

Highlights the SMLE rifles from the Mark 1-VI.

Lee Enfield Number 4 Rifles, by Alan M. Petrillo, Excalibur Publications, Latham, NY, 1992. 64 pp., illus. Paper covers. $10.95

A pocket-sized, bare-bones reference devoted entirely to the .303 WWII and Korean War vintage service rifle.

Legendary Sporting Rifles, by Sam Fadala, Stoeger Publishing Co., So. Hackensack, NJ, 1992. 288 pp., illus. Paper covers. $16.95

Covers a vast span of time and technology beginning with the Kentucky longrifle.

Li'l M1 .30 Cal. Carbine, by Duncan Long, Desert Publications, El Dorado, AZ, 1995. 203 pp., illus. Paper covers. $19.95

Traces the history of this little giant from its original creation.

Living With the Big .50, The Shooter's Guide to the World's Most Powerful Rifle, Robert Boatman, Boulder, CO, Paladin Press, 2004. 176 pp. Soft cover. NEW. $29.00

Living with the Big .50 is the most thorough book ever written on this powerhouse rifle.

M1 Carbine Owner's Manual, M1, M2 & M3 .30 Caliber Carbines, Firepower Publications, Cornville, AZ, 1984. 102 pp., illus. Paper covers. $9.95

The complete book for the owner of an M1 carbine.

M1 Carbine Owner's Guide, by Scott A. Duff, Export, PA, Scott Duff Publications, 2002. 144 pages, illustrated. $21.95

Tells you what to look for before you choose a Carbine for collecting or shooting. Identification guide with serial numbers by production quarter for approximate date of manufacture. Illustrated, complete guide to markings, nomenclature of parts, assembly, disassembly and special tools. History and identification guide with serial numbers by production quarter for approximate date of manufacture. Includes troubleshooting, maintenance, cleaning and lubrication guide.

M1 Garand .30 Assembly, Disassembly Manual, by Skennerton & Riling, Ray Riling Arms Books Co. Philadelphia, PA 2004. 36 pages, over 60 photos & line drawings. $5.00

Ideal workshop reference for stripping & assembly with exploded parts drawings, specifications, service accessories, historical information and recommended reading references.

M1 Garand Owners Guide, Vol 1, by Scott A. Duff, Export, PA, Scott Duff Publications, 2002. 126 pages, illustrated. $21.95

Makes shooting, disassembly and maintenance work easier. Contains a brief history as well as production dates and other information to help identify who made it and when. Line drawings identify the components and show their position and relationships plainly.

M1 Garand Complete Assembly Guide, Vol. 2, by Walt Kuleck, and Clint McKee, Export, PA, Scott Duff Publications, 2004. 162 pp. $21.95

You'll learn the best and easiest ways to build your rifle. It won't make you a Garand armorer, but it will make you a more knowledgeable owner. You'll be able to do more with (and to) your rifle.

M1 Garand Serial Numbers & Data Sheets, by Scott A. Duff, Scott A. Duff, Export, PA, 1995. 101 pp. Paper covers. $11.95
This pocket reference book includes serial number tables and data sheets on the Springfield Armory, gas trap rifles, gas port rifles, Winchester Repeating Arms, International Harvester and H&R Arms Co. and more.

M1 Garand: Post World War, by Scott A. Duff, Scott A. Duff Publications, Export, PA, 1990. 139 pp., illus. Softcover. $21.95
A detailed account of the activities at Springfield Armory through this period. International Harvester, H&R, Korean War production and quantities delivered. Serial numbers.

M1 Garand: World War 2, by Scott A. Duff, Scott A. Duff Publications, Export, PA, 1993. 210 pp., illus. Paper covers. $34.95
The most comprehensive study available to the collector and historian on the M1 Garand of WWII.

M14 Rifle Assembly, Disassembly Manual 7.62mm, by Skennerton & Riling, Ray Riling Arms Books Co. Philadelphia, PA 2004. 36 pages, over 60 photos & line drawings. $5.00
Ideal workshop reference for stripping & assembly with exploded parts drawings, specifications, service accessories, historical information and recommended reading references.

M14 Owner's Guide and Match Conditioning Instructions, by Scott A. Duff and John M. Miller, Duff Publications, Export, PA, 1996. 180 pp., illus. Paper covers. $19.95
Traces the history and development from the T44 through the adoption and production of the M14 rifle.

M14 Complete Assembly Guide; Vol. 2, by Walt Kuleck, and Clint McKee, Duff Publications, Export, PA, 1996. 180 pp., illus. Paper covers. $24.95
You'll learn the best and easiest ways to enhance, disassemble and assemble your rifle. It won't make you an M14/M1A armorer, but it will make you a knowledgeable owner. You'll be able to do more with (and to) your rifle.

M14 Rifle, facsimile reprint of FM 23-8, Desert Publications, Cornville, AZ, 50 pp., illus. Paper $11.95
Well illustrated and informative reprint covering the M-14 and M-14E2.

M14-Type Rifle: A Shooter's And Collector's Guide; 3rd Edition Revised and Expanded edition, by Joe Poyer, North Cape Publications, Tustin, CA, 2007. 104 pp., illus. Paper covers. $19.95
This new revised and expanded edition examines the M14 rifle and its two sniper variations on a part-by-part basis but surveys all current civilian semiautomatic M14-type rifles and components available today. It also provides as a guide for shooters who want to restore an M14 to original condition or build a superb match rifle. Included are the Chinese variations of the M14. The history of the development and use of the M14 in Vietnam, and now in Iraq and Afghanistan, is detailed. The book is fully illustrated with photos and drawings that clarify the text. Appendices provide up-to-date information on parts and supplies and gunsmithing services.

M14/M14A1 Rifles and Rifle Marksmanship, Desert Publications, El Dorado, AZ, 1995. 236 pp., illus. Paper covers. $19.95
Contains a detailed description of the M14 and M14A1 rifles and their general characteristics, procedures for disassembly & assembly, operating and functioning of the rifles.

M16/AR15 Rifle, by Joe Poyer, North Cape Publications, Tustin, CA, 1998. 150 pp., illus. Paper covers. $19.95
From its inception as the first American assault battle rifle to the firing lines of the National Matches, the M16/AR15 rifle in all its various models and guises has made a significant impact on the American rifleman.

Major Ned H. Roberts and the Schuetzen Rifle, edited by Gerald O. Kelver, Brighton, CO, 1998. 3rd edition. 122 pp., illus. $13.95
A compilation of the writings of Major Ned H. Roberts which appeared in various gun magazines.

Mannlicher Military Rifles: Straight Pull and Turn Bolt Designs, Paul Scarlata, Lincoln, RI, Andrew Mowbray, 2004. Hardcover, 168 pages 8.5 x 11, filled with black & white photos. Hardcover. NEW $32.49
Profusely illustrated with close-up photos, drawings and diagrams, this book is the most detailed examination of Mannlicher military rifles ever produced in the English language.

Mauser Military Rifles Of The World, 4th Edition, by Robert Ball, Iola, WI, Krause Publications, 2006. 448 pp., with historical data, coupled with detailed color photos. $49.95
The ultimate Mauser military rifle reference, this superior guide is packed with more models, all-color photos and Mauser history tailored to the interests and needs of firearms collectors. With more than 50 countries represented, 75 years of Mauser military rifle production is meticulously cataloged with descriptions, historical details, model specifications and markings, for easy identification by collectors.

Mauser Military Rifle Markings, 2nd Edition, Revised and Expanded, by Terence Lapin, Hyrax Publishers, Arlington, VA. 2005, 167 pages, illustrated. Softcover. $22.95
A general guide to reading and understanding the often mystifying markings found on military Mauser Rifles. Includes German Regimental markings as well as German police markings and W.W. 2 German Mauser subcontractor codes. A handy reference to take to gun shows.

Mauser Rifles & Carbines Assembly, Disassembly Manual, by Skennerton & Riling, Ray Riling Arms Books Co. Philadelphia, PA 2004. 36 pages, over 60 photos & line drawings. $5.00
Ideal workshop reference for stripping & assembly with exploded parts drawings, specifications, service accessories, historical information and recommended reading references.

Mauser Smallbore Sporting, Target and Training Rifles, by Jon Speed, Collector Grade Publications, Inc., Cobourg, Ont., Canada, 1998. 372 pp., illus. $67.50
The history of all the smallbore sporting, target and training rifles produced by the legendary Mauser-Werke of Obendorf am Neckar.

Mauser: Original-Oberndorf Sporting Rifles, by Jon Speed, Collector Grade Publications, Inc., Cobourg, Ont., Canada, 1997. 508 pp., illus. $89.95
The most exhaustive study ever published of the design origins and manufacturing history of the original Oberndorf Mauser Sporter.

MG34-MG42 German Universal Machineguns, by Folke Myrvang, Collector Grade Publications, Canada. 2002. 496 pp., 646 illustrations. $79.95
This is the first-ever COMPETE study of the MG34 & MG42. Here the author presents in-depth coverage of the historical development, fielding, tactical use of and modifications made to these remarkable guns and their myriad accessories and ancillaries, plus authoritative tips on troubleshooting.

Military Bolt Action Rifles, 1841-1918, by Donald B. Webster, Museum Restoration Service, Alexander Bay, NY, 1993. 150 pp., illus. $34.50
A photographic survey of the principal rifles and carbines of the European and Asiatic powers of the last half of the 19th century and the first years of the 20th century.

Military Rifles of Japan, 5th Edition, by F.L. Honeycutt, Julin Books, Lake Park, FL, 1999. 208 pp., illus. $42.00
A new revised and updated edition. Includes the early Murata-period markings, etc.

Mini-14, by Duncan Long, Paladin Press, Boulder, CO, 1987. 120 pp., illus. Paper covers. $17.00
History of the Mini-14, the factory-produced models, specifications, accessories, suppliers, and much more.

MKB 42, MP43, MP44 and the Sturmgewehr 44, by de Vries & Martens. Alexandria, VA, Ironside International, 2003. 1st edition. 152 pp., illustrated with 200 high quality b&w photos. Hardcover. $39.95
Covers all essential information on history and development, ammunition and accessories, codes and markings, and contains photos of nearly every model and accessory. Includes a unique selection of original German WWII propaganda photos, most never published before.

Modern Guns: Fred Adolph Genoa, by Fred Adolph, Oceanside, CA, Armory Publications, 2003. One of only a few catalogs that list 2, 3 and 4 barrel guns. 68 pages, illustrated. Stiff Paper Covers. New. $19.95

Modern Sniper Rifles, by Duncan Long, Paladin Press, Boulder, CO, 1997, 8½" x 11", soft cover, photos, illus., 120 pp. $20.00
Noted weapons expert Duncan Long describes the .22 LR, single-shot, bolt-action, semiautomatic and large-caliber rifles that can be used for sniping purposes, including the U.S. M21, Ruger Mini-14, AUG and HK-94SG1. These and other models are evaluated on the basis of their features, accuracy, reliability and handiness in the field. The author also looks at the best scopes, ammunition and accessories.

More Single Shot Rifles and Actions, by Frank de Haas and Mark de Haas, Orange City, IA, 1996. 146 pp., illus. Paper covers. $22.50
Covers 45 different single shot rifles. Includes the history plus photos, drawings and personal comments.

Mosin-Nagant Assembly, Disassembly Manual 7.62mmR, by Skennerton & Riling, Ray Riling Arms Books Co. Philadelphia, PA 2004. 36 pages, $5.00
With over 60 photos & line drawings. Ideal workshop reference for stripping & assembly with exploded parts drawings, specifications, service accessories, historical information and recommended reading references.

Mosin-Nagant Rifle, by Terence W. Lapin, North Cape Publications, Tustin, CA, 1998. 30 pp., illus. Paper covers. $19.95
The first ever complete book on the Mosin-Nagant rifle written in English. Covers every variation.

Mr. Single Shot's Book of Rifle Plans, by Frank de Haas and Mark de Haas, Orange City, IA, 1996. 85 pp., illus. Paper covers. $22.50
Contains complete and detailed drawings, plans and instructions on how to build four different and unique breech-loading single shot rifles of the author's own proven design.

Muskets of the Revolution and the French & Indian Wars; The Smoothbore Longarm in Early America, Including British, French, Dutch, German, Spanish, and American Weapons, by Bill Ahearn, Lincoln, RI, Andrew Mowbray, 2005. 248 pages, illustrated. Pictorial hardcover. NEW. $49.95

Not just a technical study of old firearms, this is a tribute to the bravery of the men who fought on both sides of that epic conflict and a celebration of the tools of freedom that have become so much a part of our national character. Includes many never-before published photos!

Neutrality Through Marksmanship: A Collector's and Shooter's Guide to Swedish Army Rifles 1867-1942, by Doug Bowser, Camellia City Military Publications, 1996. 1st edition. Stiff paper covers. NEW. $20.00

No. 4 (T) Sniper Rifle: An Armourer's Perspective, The, by Peter Laidler with Ian Skennerton, I.D.S.A. Books, Piqua, OH, 1993. 125 pp., 75 illus. Paper covers. $19.95

A reprint of the 1864 London edition. Captain Heaton was one of the great rifle shots from the earliest days of the Volunteer Movement.

Official SKS Manual, Translation by Major James F. Gebhardt (Ret.), Paladin Press, Boulder, CO, 1997. 96 pp., illus. Paper covers. $16.00

This Soviet military manual covering the widely distributed SKS is now available in English.

Official Soviet AK-47 Manual: Operating Instructions for the 5.45mm Kalashnikov Assault Rifle, and Kalashnikov Light Machine Gun, by James Gebhardt, Boulder, CO, Paladin Press, 2006. 8½" x 11", illus., 150 pp. Soft cover. NEW. $25.00

Written to teach Russian soldiers every detail of the operation and maintenance of the Kalashnikov Assault Rifle (AK-74) and Kalashnikov Light Machine Gun (RPK-74), this manual includes ballistic tables, zeroing information, combat firing instructions, data for the 5.45mm service cartridge and more.

Old German Target Arms: Alte Schiebenwaffen, by Jesse Thompson, C. Ron Dillon, Allen Hallock and Bill Loos, Rochester, NY, Tom Rowe Publications, 2003. 1st edition. 392 pp. Hardcover. $98.00

History of Schueten shooting from the middle ages through WWII. Hundreds of illustrations, most in color. History & memorabilia of the Bundesschiessen (State or National Shoots), bird target rifles, American shooters in Germany. Schutzen rifles such as matchlocks, wheellocks, flintlocks, percussion, bader, bornmuller, rifles by Buchel and more.

Old German Target Arms: Alte Schiebenwaffen Volume 2, by Jesse Thompson, C. Ron Dillon, Allen Hallock and Bill Loos, Rochester, NY, Tom Rowe Publications, 2004. 1st edition. 392 pp. Hardcover. $98.00

Old German Target Arms: Alte Schiebenwaffen Volume 3, by Jesse Thompson, C. Ron Dillon, Allen Hallock and Bill Loos, Rochester, NY, Tom Rowe Publications, 2005. 1st edition. 392 pp. Hardcover. $98.00

Ordnance Tools, Accessories & Appendages of the M1 Rifle, by Billy Pyle, Houston, TX, privately printed, 2002. 2nd edition. 206 pp., illustrated with b&w photos. Softcover. $40.00

This is the new updated second edition with over 350 pictures and drawings, of which 30 are new. Part I contains accessories, appendages, and equipment. Part II covers ammunition, grenades, and pyrotechnics. Part III shows the inspection gages. Part IV presents the ordnance tools, fixtures, and assemblies. Part V contains miscellaneous items related to the M1.

Police Rifles, by Richard Fairburn, Paladin Press, Boulder, CO, 1994. 248 pp., illus. Paper covers. $35.00

Selecting the right rifle for street patrol and special tactical situations.

Poor Man's Sniper Rifle, by D. Boone, Paladin Press, Boulder, CO, 1995. 152 pp., illus. Paper covers. $18.95

Here is a complete plan for converting readily available surplus military rifles to high-performance sniper weapons.

Precision Shooting with the M1 Garand, by Roy Baumgardner, Precision Shooting, Inc., Manchester, CT, 1999. 142 pp., illus. Paper covers. $12.95

Starts off with the ever popular ten-article series on accurizing the M1 that originally appeared in Precision Shooting in the 1993-95 era. There follows nine more Baumgardner-authored articles on the M1 Garand and finally a 1999 updating chapter.

Remington 700, by John F. Lacy, Taylor Publishing Co., Dallas, TX, 2002. 208 pp., illus. $54.95

Covers the different models, limited editions, chamberings, proofmarks, serial numbers, military models, and much more.

Remington Autoloading and Pump Action Rifles, by Eugene Myszkowski, Tucson, AZ, Excalibur Publications, 2002. 132 pp., with 162 photographs, 6 illustrations and 18 charts. Softcover. $20.95

An illustrated history of Remington's centerfire Models 760, 740, 742, 7400 and 7600. The book is thoroughly researched and features many previously unpublished photos of the rifles, their accessories and accoutrements. Also covers high grade, unusual and experimental rifles. Contains information on collecting, serial numbers and barrel codes.

Rifle Rules: Magic for the Ultimate Rifleman, by Don Paul, Kaua'i, HI, Pathfinder Publications, 2003. 1st edition. 116 pp., illus. Softcover. $14.95

A new method that shows you how to add hundreds of yards to your effective shooting ability. Ways for you to improve your rifle's accuracy which no factory can do. Illustrations & photos added to make new concepts easy.

Rifle Shooter, by G. David Tubb, Oxford, MS, Zediker Publishing, 2004. 1st edition. 416 pp softcover, 7" x 10" size, 400 photos and illustrations, very high quality printing. Softcover. $34.95

This is not just a revision of his landmark "Highpower Rifle" but an all-new, greatly expanded work that reveals David's thoughts and recommendations on all aspects of precision rifle shooting. Each shooting position and event is dissected and taken to extreme detail, as are the topics of ammunition, training, rifle design, event strategies, and wind shooting. You will learn the secrets of perhaps the greatest rifleman ever, and you'll learn how to put them to work for you!

Rifles of the U.S. Army 1861-1906, by John D. McAulay, Lincoln, RI, Andrew Mowbray, Inc., 2003. 1st edition. 278 pp., illus. Hardcover. NEW. $45.89

Rifles of the White Death (Valkoisen Kuoleman Kivaarit) A Collector's and Shooter's Guide to Finnish Military Rifles 1918-1944, by Doug Bowser, MS, Camellia City Military Publications, 1998. 1st edition. Stiff paper covers. NEW. $35.00

Rock In A Hard Place The Browning Automatic Rifle, by James L. Ballou. Collector Grade, Canada, 2004. 1st edition. 500 pages, with 751 illustrations. Hardcover $79.95

This first-ever in-depth study of the popular BAR includes clear photos of all U.S.-made military and commercial models, experimental models from Britain and France, plus offshore copies and clones from Belgium, Poland and Sweden.

Rock Island Rifle Model 1903, by C.S. Ferris, Export, PA, Scott A. Duff Publications, 2002. 177 pp., illustrated with b&w photographs. Foreword by Scott A. Duff. Softcover. $22.95

S.L.R.–Australia's F.N. F.A.L., by Ian Skennerton and David Balmer, Arms & Militaria Press, 1989. 124 pp., 100 illus. Paper covers. $24.50

Schuetzen Rifles, History and Loading, by Gerald O. Kelver, Pioneer Press, Union City, TN, 1998. 3rd edition. Illus. $13.95

Reference work on these rifles, their bullets, loading, telescopic sights, accuracy, etc. A limited, numbered ed.

Serbian and Yugoslav Mauser Rifles, by Banko Bogdanovich, Tustin, CA, North Cape Publications, 2005. 278pp. Soft cover. NEW. $19.95

In Serbian and Yugoslav Mauser Rifles, each model is discussed in its own chapter. All serial numbers are presented by year. All markings are presented and translated and all finishes and changes to all models are described in text and charts and well illustrated with both photographs and excellent drawings for clarity.

Shooting Lever Guns of the Old West, by Mike Venturino, MLV Enterprises, Livingston, MT, 1999. 300 pp., illus. Paper covers. $27.95

Shooting the lever action type repeating rifles of our American west.

Shooting the .43 Spanish Rolling Block, by Croft Barker, Flatonia, TX, Cistern Publishing, 2003. 1st edition. 137 pp. Softcover. $25.50

The source for information on .43 caliber rolling blocks. Lots of photos and text covering Remington & Oveido actions, antique cartridges, etc. Features smokless & black powder loads, rifle disassembly and maintenance, 11mm bullets. Required reading for the rolling block owner.

Shooting the Blackpowder Cartridge Rifle, by Paul A. Matthews, Wolfe Publishing Co., Prescott, AZ, 1994. 129 pp., illus. Paper covers. $22.50

A general discourse on shooting the blackpowder cartridge rifle and the procedure required to make a particular rifle perform.

Single Shot Military Rifle Handbook, by Croft Barker, Flatonia, TX, Cistern Publishing, 2005. Includes over 40 new high quality photos of vintage rifles, antique cartridges and related equipment. 130pp., many b&w photos. Soft cover. NEW. $25.50

Contains instruction on preparing authentic ammunition, shooting techniques, the uses of vintage military sights, rifle refurbishing, etc. Evolution of the single shot military rifle and the center fire cartridge is described.

Single Shot Rifles and Actions, by Frank de Haas, Orange City, IA, 1990. 352 pp., illus. Softcover. $27.00

The definitive book on over 60 single shot rifles and actions.

SKS Carbine 7.62 x 39mm Assembly, Disassembly Manual, by Skennerton & Riling, Ray Riling Arms Books Co. Philadelphia, PA 2004. 36 pages, over 60 photos & line drawings. $5.00

Ideal workshop reference for stripping & assembly with exploded parts drawings, specifications, service accessories, historical information and recommended reading references.

ARMS LIBRARY

Small Arms Identification Series, No. 1–.303 Rifle, No. 1 S.M.L.E. Marks III and III*, by Ian Skennerton, I.D.S.A. Books, Piqua, OH, 1981. 48 pp. $10.50

Small Arms Identification Series, No. 2–.303 Rifle, No. 4 Marks I, & I*, Marks 1/2, 1/3 & 2, by Ian Skennerton, I.D.S.A. Books, Piqua, OH, 1994. 48 pp. $10.50

Small Arms Identification Series, No. 3–9mm Austen Mk I & 9mm Owen Mk I Sub-Machine Guns, by Ian Skennerton, I.D.S.A. Books, Piqua, OH, 1994. 48 pp. $10.50

Small Arms Identification Series, No. 4–.303 Rifle, No. 5 Mk I, by Ian Skennerton, I.D.S.A. Books, Piqua, OH, 1994. 48 pp. $10.50

Small Arms Identification Series, No. 5–.303-in. Bren Light Machine Gun, by Ian Skennerton, I.D.S.A. Books, Piqua, OH, 1994. 48 pp. $10.50

Springfield Rifle M1903, M1903A1, M1903A3, M1903A4, Desert Publications, Cornville, AZ, 1982. 100 pp., illus. Paper covers. $14.95

Covers every aspect of disassembly and assembly, inspection, repair and maintenance.

Still More Single Shot Rifles, by James J. Grant, Pioneer Press, Union City, TN, 1995. 211 pp., illus. $29.95

This is Volume Four in a series of single-shot rifles by America's foremost authority. It gives more in-depth information on those single-shot rifles that were presented in the first three books.

Sturm, Ruger 10/22 Rifle and .44 Magnum Carbine, by Duncan Long, Paladin Press, Boulder, CO, 1988. 108 pp., illus. Paper covers. $15.00

An in-depth look at both weapons detailing the elegant simplicity of the Ruger design. Offers specifications, troubleshooting procedures and ammunition recommendations.

Swedish Mauser Rifles, by Steve Kehaya and Joe Poyer, Tustin, CA, North Cape Publications, 2004. 2nd edition, revised. 267 pp., illus. Softcover. $19.95

Every known variation of the Swedish Mauser carbine and rifle is described including all match and target rifles and all sniper versions. Includes serial number and production data.

Swiss Magazine Loading Rifles 1869 to 1958, by Joe Poyer, Tustin, CA, North Cape Publications, 2003. 1st edition. 317 pp., illustrated with hundreds of b&w drawings and photos. Softcover. $19.95

It covers the K-31 on a part-by-part basis, as well as its predecessor models of 1889 and 1911, and the first repeating magazine rifle ever adopted by a military, the Model 1869 Vetterli rifle and its successor models. Also includes a history of the development and use of these fine rifles. Details regarding their ammunition, complete assembly/disassembly instructions as well as sections on cleaning, maintenance and trouble shooting.

Tactical Rifle, by Gabriel Suarez, Paladin Press, Boulder, CO, 1999. 264 pp., illus. Paper covers. $25.00

The precision tool for urban police operations.

Target Rifle in Australia, by J.E. Corcoran, R&R, Livonia, NY, 1996. 160 pp., illus. $40.00

A most interesting study of the evolution of these rifles from 1860-1900. British rifles from the percussion period through the early smokeless era are discussed.

Total Airguns; The Complete Guide to Hunting with Air Rifles, by Peter Wadeson, London, Swan Hill Press, 2005. 300 pages, illustrated with b&w photos. Hardcover. NEW. $29.95

This book covers every aspect from choosing a rifle and scope to field craft and hunting techniques, camouflage, decoys, night shooting, and equipment maintenance. Extensive details on all air gun shooting techniques.

U.S. M1 Carbine: Wartime Production, 5th Edition, Revised and Expanded! by Craig Riesch, North Cape Publications, Tustin, CA 2007 237 pages. $19.95

The book contains 38 charts and 212 photographs, and 14 drawings. The book provides a history of the M1 Carbine's development, manufacture and use during World War II, as well as through the Korean War and the war in Vietnam. All variations of the M1 Carbine are discussed – M1, M1A1, and M2 – by manufacturer. Serial number ranges for original manufacture are included.

U.S. Rifle .30 Model 1917 and .303 British Pattern 1914 Assembly, Disassembly Manual, by Skennerton & Riling, Ray Riling Arms Books Co. Philadelphia, PA 2004. 36 pages, over 60 photos & line drawings. $5.00

Ideal workshop reference for stripping & assembly with exploded parts drawings, specifications, service accessories, historical information and recommended reading references. Ideal workbook for shooters and collectors alike. Triple saddle-stitched binding with durable plastic laminated cover makes this an ideal workshop guide.

U.S. Marine Corps AR15/M16 A2 Manual, reprinted by Desert Publications, El Dorado, AZ, 1993. 262 pp., illus. Paper covers. $16.95

A reprint of TM05538C-23&P/2, August, 1987. The A-2 manual for the Colt AR15/M16.

U.S. Marine Corps Rifle Marksmanship, by U.S. Marine Corps, Boulder, CO, Paladin Press, 2002. Photos, illus., 120 pp. Softcover. $20.00

This manual is the very latest Marine doctrine on the art and science of shooting effectively in battle. Its 10 chapters teach the versatility, flexibility and skills needed to deal with a situation at any level of intensity across the entire range of military operations. Topics covered include the proper combat mindset; cleaning your rifle under all weather conditions; rifle handling and marksmanship the Marine way; engaging targets from behind cover; obtaining a battlefield zero; engaging immediate threat, multiple and moving targets; shooting at night and at unknown distances; and much more.

U.S. Rifle M14–From John Garand to the M21, by R. Blake Stevens, Collector Grade Publications, Inc., Toronto, Canada, revised 2nd edition, 1991. 350 pp., illus. $49.50

A classic, in-depth examination of the development, manufacture and fielding of the last wood-and-metal ("lock, stock, and barrel") battle rifle to be issued to U.S. troops.

United States Rifle Model of 1917, by CS Ferris, Export, PA, Scott Duff Pubs., 2004. 213 pages, illustrated with b&w photographs. Foreword by Scott A. Duff. Soft cover. NEW. $23.95

If you are interested in the study of the United States Rifle Model of 1917 and have been disappointed by the lack of information available, then this book is for you!

Ultimate in Rifle Accuracy, by Glenn Newick, Stoeger Publishing Co., Wayne, NJ, 1999. 205 pp., illus. Paper covers. $11.95

This handbook contains the information you need to extract the best performance from your rifle.

War Baby! The U.S. Caliber 30 Carbine, Volume 1, by Larry Ruth, Collector Grade Publications, Toronto, Canada, 1992. 512 pp., illus. $69.95

Volume 1 of the in-depth story of the phenomenally popular U.S. caliber 30 carbine. Concentrates on design and production of the military 30 carbine during WWII.

War Baby Comes Home: The U.S. Caliber 30 Carbine, Volume 2, by Larry Ruth, Collector Grade Publications, Toronto, Canada, 1993. 386 pp., illus. $49.95

The triumphant completion of Larry Ruth's two-volume, in-depth series on the most popular U.S. military small arm in history.

Winchester: An American Legend, by R.L. Wilson, NY, Book Sales, 2004, reprint. 404 pages, illustrated with color and b&w photographs. Hardcover. New in new dust jacket. $29.95

Winchester Model 52: Perfection in Design, by Herbert Houze, Iola, WI, Krause Publications, 2006. Soft cover. NEW. $22.95

Herbert Houze unravels the mysteries surrounding the development of what many consider the most perfect rifle ever made. The book covers the rifle's improvements through five modifications. Users, collectors and marksmen will appreciate each variation's history, serial number sequences and authentic photos.

Winchester Model 61 Assembly, Disassembly Manual, by Skennerton & Riling, Ray Riling Arms Books Co. Philadelphia, PA 2004. 36 pages, over 60 photos & line drawings. $5.00

Ideal workshop reference for stripping & assembly with exploded parts drawings, specifications, service accessories, historical information and recommended reading references.

Winchester Model 70 Assembly, Disassembly Manual, by Skennerton & Riling, Ray Riling Arms Books Co. Philadelphia, PA 2004. 36 pages, over 60 photos & line drawings. $5.00

Ideal workshop reference for stripping & assembly with exploded parts drawings, specifications, service accessories, historical information and recommended reading references.

Winchester Model 94 Assembly, Disassembly Manual, by Skennerton & Riling, Ray Riling Arms Books Co. Philadelphia, PA 2004. 36 pages, over 60 photos & line drawings. $5.00

Ideal workshop reference for stripping & assembly with exploded parts drawings, specifications, service accessories, historical information and recommended reading references.

Winchester Slide-Action Rifles, Models 61, 62, 1890 & 1906, by Ned Schwing, Iola, WI, Krause Publications, 2004. 456 Pages, illustrated, 300 b&w photos. Soft cover. NEW. $39.95

Take a complete historical look at the favorite slide-action guns of America through Ned Schwing's eyes. Explore receivers, barrels, markings, stocks, stampings and engraving in complete detail.

Workbench AR-15 Project; A Step by Step Guide to Building Your Own Legal AR-15 Without Paperwork, The, by D.A. Hanks, Boulder, CO, Paladin Press, 2004. 80 pages, photos. Soft cover. NEW. $19.89

Hanks walks you through the entire process with clear text and detailed photos—staying legal, finishing the lower receiver, assembling all the parts and test-firing your completed rifle. For academic study only.

Shotguns

A Collector's Guide to United States Combat Shotguns, by Bruce N. Canfield, Andrew Mowbray Inc., Publishers, Lincoln, RI, 1993. 184 pp., illus. Paper covers. $24.00

Full coverage of the combat shotgun, from the earliest examples to the Gulf War and beyond.

A.H. Fox: "The Finest Gun in the World," revised and enlarged edition, by Michael McIntosh, Countrysport, Inc., New Albany, OH, 1995. 408 pp., illus. $60.00

The first detailed history of one of America's finest shotguns.

Advanced Combat Shotgun: Stress Fire 2, by Massad Ayoob, Police Bookshelf, Concord, NH, 1993. 197 pp., illus. Paper covers. $14.95

Advanced combat shotgun fighting for police.

Best Guns, by Michael McIntosh, Countrysport Press, Selma, AL, 1999, revised edition. 418 pp. $45.00

Combines the best shotguns ever made in America with information on British and Continental makers.

Best of Holland & Holland, England's Premier Gunmaker, by Michael McIntosh and Jan G. Roosenburg. Long Beach, CA, Safari Press, Inc., 2002. 1st edition. 298 pp., profuse color illustrations. Hardcover. $69.95

Holland & Holland has had a long history of not only building London's "best" guns but also providing superior guns–the ultimate gun in finish, engraving, and embellishment. From the days of old in which a maharaja would order 100 fancifully engraved H&H shotguns for his guests to use at his duck shoot to the recent elaborately decorated sets depicting the Apollo 11 moon landing or the history of the British Empire, all of these guns represent the zenith in the art and craft of gunmaking and engraving. Never before have so many superlative guns from H&H–or any other maker for that matter–been displayed in one book.

Better Shot, by Ken Davies, Quiller Press, London, England, 1992. 136 pp., illus. $39.95

Step-by-step shotgun techniques with Holland and Holland.

Black's Buyer's Directory 2007 Wing & Clay, by James Black, Grand View Media, 2006. Soft cover. NEW. $17.95

1,637 companies in 62 sections providing shotgun related products and services worldwide. Destinations: 1,412 hunting destinations, 1,279 sporting clays, trap and skeet clubs state by state.

Breaking Clays, by Chris Batha, Stackpole Books, Mechanicsburg, PA, 2005. Hardcover. $29.95

This clear and concise book offers a distillation of the best tips and techniques that really work to improve your scores and give you the knowledge to develop to your full shooting potential

Browning Auto-5 Shotguns: The Belgian FN Production, by H. M. Shirley Jr. and Anthony Vanderlinden, Geensboro, NC, Wet Dog Publications, 2003. Limited edition of 2,000 copies, signed by the author. 233 pp., plus index. Over 400 quality b&w photographs and 24 color photographs. Hardcover $59.95

This is the first book devoted to the history, model variations, accessories and production dates of this legendary gun. This publication is to date the only reference book on the Auto-5 (A-5) shotgun prepared entirely with the extensive cooperation and support of Browning, FN Herstal, the Browning Firearms Museum and the Liege Firearms Museum.

Browning-Sporting Arms of Distinction 1903-1992, by Matt Eastman, Safari Press, 2005. Hardcover. $50.00

Finally, the history of the Browning family, the inventions, the company, and Browning's association with Colt, Winchester, Savage, and others is detailed in this all-inclusive book, which is profusely illustrated with hundreds of pictures and charts.

Cogswell & Harrison; Two Centuries of Gunmaking, by G. Cooley and J. Newton, Safari Press, Long Beach, CA, 2000. 128 pp., 30 color photos, 100 b&w photos. $39.95

The authors have gathered a wealth of fascinating historical and technical material that will make the book indispensable, not only to many thousands of "Coggie" owners worldwide, but also to anyone interested in the general history of British gunmaking.

Defensive Shotgun, The, by Louis Awerbuck, S.W.A.T. Publications, Cornville, AZ, 1989. 77 pp., illus. Softcover. $14.95

Cuts through the myths concerning the shotgun and its attendant ballistic effects.

Ducks Unlimited Guide to Shotgunning, The, by Don Zutz, Willow Creek Press, Minocqua, WI, 2000. 166 pg. Illustrated. $24.50

This book covers everything from the grand old guns of yesterday to today's best shotguns and loads, from the basic shotgun fit and function to expert advice on ballistics, chocks, and shooting techniques.

Fine European Gunmakers: Best Continental European Gunmakers & Engravers, by M. Nobili, Long Beach, CA, Safari Press, 2002. 250 pp., illustated in color. $69.95

Many experts argue that Continental gunmakers produce guns equally as good or better than British makers. Marco Nobili's new work showcases the skills of the best craftsmen from continental Europe. The book covers the histories of the individual firms and looks at the guns they currently build, tracing the developments of their most influential models.

Firearms Assembly/Disassembly, Part V: Shotguns, 2nd Edition, The Gun Digest Book of, by J.B. Wood, Krause Publications, Iola, WI, 2002. 560 pp., illus. $24.95

Covers 54 popular shotguns plus over 250 variants. The most comprehensive and professional presentation available to either hobbyist or gunsmith.

Game Shooting, by Robert Churchill, Countrysport Press, Selma, AL, 1998. 258 pp., illus. $30.00

The basis for every shotgun instructional technique devised and the foundation for all wingshooting and the game of sporting clays.

Greatest Hammerless Repeating Shotgun Ever Built: The Model 12 Winchester 1912-1964 by David Riffle, 1995. Color illustrations. 195 large detailed b&w photos, 298 pgs. Pictorial hardcover. NEW. $54.95

This offers an extremely well written and detailed year-by-year study of the gun, its details, inventors, makers, engravers, and star shooters.

Greener Story, by Graham Greener, Safari Press, Long Beach, CA, 2000. 231 pp., color and b&w illustrations. $69.95

The history of the Greener gunmakers and their guns.

Gunsmithing Shotguns: The Complete Guide to Care & Repair, by David Henderson, New York, Globe Pequot, 2003. 1st edition, b&w photos & illus; 6" x 9", 256 pp., illus. Hardcover. $24.95

An overview designed to provide insight, ideas and techniques that will give the amateur gunsmith the confidence and skill to work on his own guns. General troubleshooting, common problems, stocks and woodworking, soldering and brazing, barrel work and more.

Heyday of the Shotgun, by David Baker, Safari Press, Inc., Huntington Beach, CA, 2000. 160 pp., illus. $39.95

The art of the gunmaker at the turn of the last century when British craftsmen brought forth the finest guns ever made.

Holland & Holland: The "Royal" Gunmaker, by Donald Dallas, London, Safari Press, 2004. 1st edition. 311 pp. Hardcover. $75.00

Donald Dallas tells the fascinating story of Holland & Holland from its very beginnings, and the history of the family is revealed for the first time. The terrific variety of the firm's guns and rifles is described in great detail and set within the historical context of their eras. The book is profusely illustrated with 112 color and 355 b&w photographs, mostly unpublished. In addition many rare guns and rifles are described and illustrated.

House of Churchill, by Don Masters, Safari Press, Long Beach, CA, 2002. 512 pp., profuse color and b&w illustrations. $79.95

This marvelous work on the house of Churchill contains serial numbers and dates of manufacture of its guns from 1891 forward, price lists from 1895 onward, a complete listing of all craftsmen employed at the company, as well as the prices realized at the famous Dallas auction where the "last" production guns were sold. It was written by Don Masters, a long-time Churchill employee, who is keeping the flame of Churchill alive.

Italian Gun, by Steve Smith and Laurie Morrow, Wilderness Adventures, Gallatin Gateway, MT, 1997. 325 pp., illus. $49.95

The first book ever written entirely in English for American enthusiasts who own, aspire to own, or simply admire Italian guns.

Ithaca Featherlight Repeater; The Best Gun Going, by Walter C. Snyder, Southern Pines, NC, 1998. 300 pp., illus. $89.95

Describes the complete history of each model of the legendary Ithaca Model 37 and Model 87 Repeaters from their conception in 1930 throught 1997.

Ithaca Gun Company from the Beginning, by Walter C. Snyder, Cook & Uline Publishing Co., Southern Pines, NC, 2nd edition, 1999. 384 pp., illustrated in color and b&w. $90.00

The entire family of Ithaca Gun Company products is described along with new historical information and the serial number/date of manufacturing listing has been improved.

Little Trapshooting Book, by Frank Little, Shotgun Sports Magazine, Auburn, CA, 1994. 168 pp., illus. Paper covers. $19.95

Packed with know-how from one of the greatest trapshooters of all time.

Mental Training for the Shotgun Sports, by Michael J. Keyes, Shotgun Sports, Auburn, CA, 1996. 160 pp., illus. Paper covers. $29.95

The most comprehensive book ever published on what it takes to shoot winning scores at trap, skeet and sporting clays.

More Shotguns and Shooting, by Michael McIntosh, Countrysport Books, Selma, AL, 1998. 256 pp., illus. $30.00

From specifics of shotguns to shooting your way out of a slump, it's McIntosh at his best.

Mossberg Shotguns, by Duncan Long, Delta Press, El Dorado, AR, 2000. 120 pp., illus. $24.95

This book contains a brief history of the company and its founder, full coverage of the pump and semiautomatic shotguns, rare products and a care and maintenance section.

Mysteries of Shotgun Patterns, by George G. Oberfell and Charles E. Thompson, Ray Riling Arms Books, Philadelphia, PA, 2005. 164 pp., illus. Paper covers. $25.00

Shotgun ballistics for the hunter in non-technical language.

Parker Gun, by Larry Baer, Gun Room Press, Highland Park, NJ, 1993. 195 pp., illustrated with b&w and color photos. $35.00

Covers in detail, production of all models on this classic gun. Many fine specimens from great collections are illustrated.

Parker Guns 'The Old Reliable'-A Concise History of the Famous American Shotgun Manufacturing Co., by Ed Muderlak, Long Beach, CA, Safari Press, 2004. results. A must-have for the American shotgun enthusiast. Hardcover. New in new dust jacket. $48.50

Parker Gun Identification & Serialization, by S.P. Fjestad, Minneapolis, MN, Blue Book Publications, 2002. 1st edition. Softcover. $34.95

This new 608-page publication is the only book that provides an easy reference for Parker shotguns manufactured between 1866-1942. Included is a comprehensive 46-page section on Parker identification, with over 100 detailed images depicting serialization location and explanation, various Parker grades, extra features, stock configurations, action types, and barrel identification.

Parker Story: Volumes 1 & 2, by Bill Mullins, "et al." The Double Gun Journal, East Jordan, MI, 2000. 1,025 pp. of text and 1,500 color and monochrome illustrations. Hardbound in a gold-embossed cover. $295.00

The most complete and attractive "last word" on America's preeminent double gun maker. Includes tables showing the number of guns made by gauge, barrel length and special features for each grade.

Pigeon Shooter: The Complete Guide to Modern Pigeon Shooting, by Jon Batley, London, Swan Hill press, 2005. Hardcover. NEW. $29.95

Covering everything from techniques to where and when to shoot. This updated edition contains all the latest information on decoys, hides, and the new pigeon magnets as well as details on the guns and equipment required and invaluable hands-on instruction.

Purdey Gun and Rifle Makers: The Definitive History, by Donald Dallas, Quiller Press, London 2000. 245 pp., illus. Signed and numbered. Limited edition of 3,000 copies. With a PURDEY bookplate. $100.00

Re-Creating the Double Barrel Muzzle Loading Shotgun, by William R. Brockway, York, PA, George Shumway, 2003. Revised 2nd edition. 175 pp., illus. Includes full size drawings. Softcover. $40.00

This popular book, first published in 1985 and out of print for over a decade, has been updated by the author. This book treats the making of double guns of classic style, and is profusely illustrated, showing how to do it all. Many photos of old and contemporary shotguns.

Reloading for Shotgunners, 4th Edition, by Kurt D. Fackler and M.L. McPherson, DBI Books, a division of Krause Publications, Iola, WI, 1997. 320 pp., illus. Paper covers. $19.95

Expanded reloading tables with over 11,000 loads. Bushing charts for every major press and component maker. All new presentation on all aspects of shotshell reloading by two of the top experts in the field.

Remington Double Shotguns, by Charles G. Semer, Denver, CO, 1997. 617 pp., illus. $60.00

This book deals with the entire production and all grades of double shotguns made by Remington during the period of their production 1873-1910.

Shotgun Encyclopedia, The, by John Taylor, Safari Press, Inc., Huntington Beach, CA, 2000. 260 pp., illus. $34.95

A comprehensive reference work on all aspects of shotguns and shotgun shooting.

Shotgun Technicana, by Michael McIntosh and David Trevallion, Camden, ME, Down East Books, 2002. 272 pp., with 100 illustrations. Hardcover $28.00

Everything you wanted to know about fine double shotguns by the nation's foremost experts.

Shotgun–A Shooting Instructor's Handbook, by Michael Yardley, Long Beach, CA, Safari Press, 2002. 272 pp., b&w photos, line drawings. Hardcover. $29.95

This is one of the very few books intended to be read by shooting instructors and other advanced shooters. There is practical advice on gun fit, and on gun and cartridge selection.

Shotgunning: The Art and the Science, by Bob Brister, Winchester Press, Piscataway, NJ, 1976. 321 pp., illus. $18.95

Hundreds of specific tips and truly novel techniques to improve the field and target shooting of every shotgunner.

Shotguns and Shooting, by Michael McIntosh, Countrysport Press, New Albany, OH, 1995. 258 pp., illus. $30.00

The art of guns and gunmaking, this book is a celebration no lover of fine doubles should miss.

Shotguns & Shotgunning, by Layne Simpson, Iola, WI, Krause Publications, 2003. 1st edition. High-quality color photography 224 pp., color illus. Hardcover. $36.95

This is the most comprehensive and valuable guide on the market devoted exclusively to shotguns. Part buyer's guide, part technical manual, and part loving tribute, shooters and hunters of all skill levels will enjoy this comprehensive reference tool.

Spanish Best: The Fine Shotguns of Spain, 2nd Edition, by Terry Wieland, Down East Books, Traverse City, MI, 2001. 364 pp., illus. $60.00

A practical source of information for owners of Spanish shotguns and a guide for those considering buying a used shotgun.

Streetsweepers: The Complete Book of Combat Shotguns, Revised and Updated Edition, by Duncan Long, Boulder Co, Paladin Press, 2004. illus., 224 pp. Soft cover. NEW. $35.00

Including how to choose the right gauge and shot, decipher the terminology and use special-purpose rounds such as flechettes and tear-gas projectiles; and gives expert instruction on customizing shotguns, telling you what you must know about the assault weapon ban before you choose or modify your gun.

Successful Shotgunning; How to Build Skill in the Field and Take More Birds in Competition, by Peter F. Blakeley, Mechanicsburg, PA, Stackpole Books, 2003. 1st edition. 305 pp., illustrated with 119 b&w photos & 4-page color section with 8 photos. Hardcover. $24.95

Successful Shotgunning focuses on wing-shooting and sporting clays techniques.

Tactical Shotgun, The, by Gabriel Suzrez, Paladin Press, Boulder, CO, 1996. 232 pp., illus. Paper covers. $25.00

The best techniques and tactics for employing the shotgun in personal combat.

Trapshooting is a Game of Opposites, by Dick Bennett, Shotgun Sports, Inc., Auburn, CA, 1996. 129 pp., illus. Paper covers. $19.95

Discover everything you need to know about shooting trap like the pros.

U.S. Winchester Trench and Riot Guns and Other U.S. Military Combat Shotguns, by Joe Poyer, North Cape Publications, Tustin, CA, 1992. 124 pp., illus. Paper covers. $15.95

A detailed history of the use of military shotguns, and the acquisition procedures used by the U.S. Army's Ordnance Department in both world wars.

Uncle Dan Lefever, Master Gunmaker: Guns of Lasting Fame, by Robert W. Elliott, privately printed, 2002. Profusely illustrated with b&w photos, with a 45-page color section. 239 pp. Handsomely bound, with gilt titled spine and top cover. Hardcover. $60.00

Winchester Model 12 Assembly, Disassembly Manual, by Skennerton & Riling, Ray Riling Arms Books Co. Philadelphia, PA 2004. 36 pages, over 60 photos & line drawings. $5.00

Ideal workshop reference for stripping & assembly with exploded parts drawings, specifications, service accessories, historical information and recommended reading references. Ideal workbook for shooters and collectors alike. Triple saddle-stitched binding with durable plastic laminated cover makes this an ideal workshop guide.

Winchester Model Twelve, by George Madis, Art and Reference House, Dallas, TX, 1982. 176 pp., illus. $26.95

A definitive work on this famous American shotgun.

Winchester Model 97 Assembly, Disassembly Manual, by Skennerton & Riling, Ray Riling Arms Books Co. Philadelphia, PA 2004. 36 pages, over 60 photos & line drawings. $5.00

Ideal workshop reference for stripping & assembly with exploded parts drawings, specifications, service accessories, historical information and recommended reading references. Ideal workbook for shooters and collectors alike. Triple saddle-stitched binding with durable plastic laminated cover makes this an ideal workshop guide.

World's Fighting Shotguns, by Thomas F. Swearengen, T.B.N. Enterprises, Alexandria, VA, 1998. 500 pp., illus. $59.95

The complete military and police reference work from the shotgun's inception to date, with up-to-date developments.

ARMS ASSOCIATIONS

UNITED STATES

ALABAMA

Alabama Gun Collectors Assn.
Secretary, P.O. Box 70965, Tuscaloosa, AL 35407

ALASKA

Alaska Gun Collectors Assn., Inc.
C.W. Floyd, Pres., 5240 Little Tree, Anchorage, AK 99507

ARIZONA

Arizona Arms Assn.
Don DeBusk, President, 4837 Bryce Ave., Glendale, AZ 85301

CALIFORNIA

California Cartridge Collectors Assn.
Rick Montgomery, 1729 Christina, Stockton, CA 95204 209-463-7216 eves.

California Waterfowl Assn.
4630 Northgate Blvd., #150, Sacramento, CA 95834

Greater Calif. Arms & Collectors Assn.
Donald L. Bullock, 8291 Carburton St., Long Beach, CA 90808-3302

Los Angeles Gun Ctg. Collectors Assn.
F.H. Ruffra, 20810 Amie Ave., Apt. #9, Torrance, CA 90503

Stock Gun Players Assn.
6038 Appian Way, Long Beach, CA, 90803

COLORADO

Colorado Gun Collectors Assn.
L.E.(Bud) Greenwald, 2553 S. Quitman St., Denver, CO 80219/303-935-3850

Rocky Mountain Cartridge Collectors Assn.
John Roth, P.O. Box 757, Conifer, CO 80433

CONNECTICUT

Ye Connecticut Gun Guild, Inc.
Dick Fraser, P.O. Box 425, Windsor, CT 06095

FLORIDA

Unified Sportsmen of Florida
P.O. Box 6565, Tallahassee, FL 32314

GEORGIA

Georgia Arms Collectors Assn., Inc.
Michael Kindberg, President, P.O. Box 277, Alpharetta, GA 30239-0277

ILLINOIS

Illinois State Rifle Assn.
P.O. Box 637, Chatsworth, IL 60921

Mississippi Valley Gun & Cartridge Coll. Assn.
Bob Filbert, P.O. Box 61, Port Byron, IL 61275/309-523-2593

Sauk Trail Gun Collectors
Gordell M. Matson, P.O. Box 1113, Milan, IL 61264

Wabash Valley Gun Collectors Assn., Inc.
Roger L. Dorsett, 2601 Willow Rd., Urbana, IL 61801 217-384-7302

INDIANA

Indiana State Rifle & Pistol Assn.
Thos. Glancy, P.O. Box 552, Chesterton, IN 46304

Southern Indiana Gun Collectors Assn., Inc.
Sheila McClary, 309 W. Monroe St., Boonville, IN 47601/812-897-3742

IOWA

Beaver Creek Plainsmen Inc.
Steve Murphy, Secy., P.O. Box 298, Bondurant, IA 50035

Central States Gun Collectors Assn.
Dennis Greischar, Box 841, Mason City, IA 50402-0841

KANSAS

Kansas Cartridge Collectors Assn.
Bob Linder, Box 84, Plainville, KS 67663

KENTUCKY

Kentuckiana Arms Collectors Assn.
Charles Billips, President, Box 1776, Louisville, KY 40201

Kentucky Gun Collectors Assn., Inc.
Ruth Johnson, Box 64, Owensboro, KY 42302/502-729-4197

LOUISIANA

Washitaw River Renegades
Sandra Rushing, P.O. Box 256, Main St., Grayson, LA 71435

MARYLAND

Baltimore Antique Arms Assn.
Mr. Cillo, 1034 Main St., Darlington, MD 21304

MASSACHUSETTS

Bay Colony Weapons Collectors, Inc.
John Brandt, Box 111, Hingham, MA 02043

Massachusetts Arms Collectors
Bruce E. Skinner, P.O. Box 31, No. Carver, MA 02355/508-866-5259

MICHIGAN

Association for the Study and Research of .22 Caliber Rimfire Cartridges
George Kass, 4512 Nakoma Dr., Okemos, MI 48864

MINNESOTA

Sioux Empire Cartridge Collectors Assn.
Bob Cameron, 14597 Glendale Ave. SE, Prior Lake, MN 55372

MISSISSIPPI

Mississippi Gun Collectors Assn.
Jack E. Swinney, P.O. Box 16323, Hattiesburg, MS 39402

MISSOURI

Greater St. Louis Cartridge Collectors Assn.
Don MacChesney, 634 Scottsdale Rd., Kirkwood, MO 63122-1109

Mineral Belt Gun Collectors Assn.
D.F. Saunders, 1110 Cleveland Ave., Monett, MO 65708

Missouri Valley Arms Collectors Assn., Inc.
L.P Brammer II, Membership Secy., P.O. Box 33033, Kansas City, MO 64114

MONTANA

Montana Arms Collectors Assn.
Dean E. Yearout, Sr., Exec. Secy., 1516 21st Ave. S., Great Falls, MT 59405

Weapons Collectors Society of Montana
R.G. Schipf, Ex. Secy., 3100 Bancroft St., Missoula, MT 59801 406-728-2995

NEBRASKA

Nebraska Cartridge Collectors Club
Gary Muckel, P.O. Box 84442, Lincoln, NE 68501

NEW HAMPSHIRE

New Hampshire Arms Collectors, Inc.
James Stamatelos, Secy., P.O. Box 5, Cambridge, MA 02139

NEW JERSEY

Englishtown Benchrest Shooters Assn.
Michael Toth, 64 Cooke Ave., Carteret, NJ 07008

Jersey Shore Antique Arms Collectors
Joe Sisia, P.O. Box 100, Bayville, NJ 08721-0100

New Jersey Arms Collectors Club, Inc.
Angus Laidlaw, Vice President, 230 Valley Rd., Montclair, NJ 07042/201-746-0939; e-mail: acclaidlaw@juno.com

NEW YORK

Iroquois Arms Collectors Assn.
Bonnie Robinson, Show Secy., P.O. Box 142, Ransomville, NY 14131/716-791-4096

Mid-State Arms Coll. & Shooters Club
Jack Ackerman, 24 S. Mountain Terr., Binghamton, NY 13903

NORTH CAROLINA

North Carolina Gun Collectors Assn.
Jerry Ledford, 3231-7th St. Dr. NE, Hickory, NC 28601

OHIO

Ohio Gun Collectors Assn.
P.O. Box 9007, Maumee, OH 43537-9007/419-897-0861; Fax: 419-897-0860

Shotshell Historical and Collectors Society
Madeline Bruemmer, 3886 Dawley Rd., Ravenna, OH 44266

The Stark Gun Collectors, Inc.
William I. Gann, 5666 Waynesburg Dr., Waynesburg, OH 44688

OREGON

Oregon Arms Collectors Assn., Inc.
Phil Bailey, P.O. Box 13000-A, Portland, OR 97213-0017 503-281-6864; off.: 503-281-0918

Oregon Cartridge Collectors Assn.
Boyd Northrup, P.O. Box 285, Rhododendron, OR 97049

PENNSYLVANIA

Presque Isle Gun Collectors Assn.
James Welch, 156 E. 37 St., Erie, PA 16504

SOUTH CAROLINA

Belton Gun Club, Inc.
Attn. Secretary, P.O. Box 126, Belton, SC 29627/864-369-6767

Gun Owners of South Carolina
Membership Div.: William Strozier, Secretary, P.O. Box 70, Johns Island, SC 29457-0070/803-762-3240; Fax: 803-795-0711; e-mail: 76053.222@compuserve. com

SOUTH DAKOTA

Dakota Territory Gun Coll. Assn., Inc.
Curt Carter, Castlewood, SD 57223

TENNESSEE

Smoky Mountain Gun Coll. Assn., Inc.
Hugh W. Yabro, President, P.O. Box 23225, Knoxville, TN 37933

Tennessee Gun Collectors Assn., Inc.
M.H. Parks, 3556 Pleasant Valley Rd., Nashville, TN 37204-3419

TEXAS

Houston Gun Collectors Assn., Inc.
P.O. Box 741429, Houston, TX 77274-1429

Texas Gun Collectors Assn.
Bob Eder, Pres., P.O. Box 12067, El Paso, TX 79913/915-584-8183

Texas State Rifle Assn.
1131 Rockingham Dr., Suite 101, Richardson, TX 75080-4326

VIRGINIA

Virginia Gun Collectors Assn., Inc.
Addison Hurst, Secy., 38802 Charlestown Height, Waterford, VA 20197/540-882-3543

WASHINGTON

Association of Cartridge Collectors on the Pacific Northwest
Robert Jardin, 14214 Meadowlark Drive KPN, Gig Harbor, WA 98329

Washington Arms Collectors, Inc.
Joyce Boss, P.O. Box 389, Renton, WA, 98057-0389/206-255-8410

WISCONSIN

Great Lakes Arms Collectors Assn., Inc.
Edward C. Warnke, 2913 Woodridge Lane, Waukesha, WI 53188

Wisconsin Gun Collectors Assn., Inc.
Lulita Zellmer, P.O. Box 181, Sussex, WI 53089

WYOMING

Wyoming Weapons Collectors
P.O. Box 284, Laramie, WY 82073/307-745-4652 or 745-9530

NATIONAL ORGANIZATIONS

Amateur Trapshooting Assn.
David D. Bopp, Exec. Director, 601 W. National Rd., Vandalia, OH 45377/937-898-4638; Fax: 937-898-5472

American Airgun Field Target Assn.
5911 Cherokee Ave., Tampa, FL 33604

American Coon Hunters Assn.
Opal Johnston, P.O. Cadet, Route 1, Box 492, Old Mines, MO 63630

American Custom Gunmakers Guild
Jan Billeb, Exec. Director, 22 Vista View Drive, Cody, WY 82414-9606 (307) 587-4297 (phone/fax) Email: acgg@acgg.org Web: www.acgg.org

American Defense Preparedness Assn.
Two Colonial Place, 2101 Wilson Blvd., Suite 400, Arlington, VA 22201-3061

American Paintball League
P.O. Box 3561, Johnson City, TN 37602/800-541-9169

American Pistolsmiths Guild
Alex B. Hamilton, Pres., 1449 Blue Crest Lane, San Antonio, TX 78232/210-494-3063

American Police Pistol & Rifle Assn.
3801 Biscayne Blvd., Miami, FL 33137

American Single Shot Rifle Assn.
Gary Staup, Secy., 709 Carolyn Dr., Delphos, OH 45833 419-692-3866. Web: www.assra.com

American Society of Arms Collectors
George E. Weatherly, P.O. Box 2567, Waxahachie, TX 75165

American Tactical Shooting Assn. (A.T.S.A.)
c/o Skip Gochenour, 2600 N. Third St., Harrisburg, PA 17110 717-233-0402; Fax: 717-233-5340

Association of Firearm and Tool Mark Examiners
Lannie G. Emanuel, Secy., Southwest Institute of Forensic Sciences, P.O. Box 35728, Dallas, TX 75235/214-920-5979;
Fax: 214-920-5928; Membership Secy., Ann D. Jones, VA Div. of Forensic Science, P.O. Box 999, Richmond, VA 23208 804-786-4706; Fax: 804-371-8328

Boone & Crockett Club
250 Station Dr., Missoula, MT 59801-2753

Browning Collectors Assn.
Secretary: Scherrie L. Brennac, 2749 Keith Dr., Villa Ridge, MO 63089/314-742-0571

The Cast Bullet Assn., Inc.
Ralland J. Fortier, Editor, 4103 Foxcraft Dr., Traverse City, MI 49684

Citizens Committee for the Right to Keep and Bear Arms
Natl. Hq., Liberty Park, 12500 NE Tenth Pl., Bellevue, WA 98005

Colt Collectors Assn.
25000 Highland Way, Los Gatos, CA 95030/408-353-2658

Contemporary Longrifle Association
P.O. Box 2097, Staunton, VA 24402/540-886-6189 Web: www.CLA@longrifle.ws

Ducks Unlimited, Inc.
Natl. Headquarters, One Waterfowl Way, Memphis, TN 38120 901-758-3937

Fifty Caliber Shooters Assn.
PO Box 111, Monroe UT 84754-0111

Firearms Coalition/Neal Knox Associates
Box 6537, Silver Spring, MD 20906 301-871-3006

Firearms Engravers Guild of America
Rex C. Pedersen, Secy., 511 N. Rath Ave., Lundington, MI 49431 616-845-7695 (Phone/Fax)

Foundation for North American Wild Sheep
720 Allen Ave., Cody, WY 82414-3402; web site: iigi.com/os/non/fnaws/fnaws.htm; e-mail: fnaws@wyoming.com

Freedom Arms Collectors Assn.
P.O. Box 160302, Miami, FL 33116-0302

Garand Collectors Assn.
P.O. Box 181, Richmond, KY 40475

Glock Collectors Association
P.O. Box 1063, Maryland Heights, MO 63043 314-878-2061 Phone/Fax

Glock Shooting Sports Foundation
BO Box 309, Smyrna GA 30081 770-432-1202; Web: www.gssfonline.com

Golden Eagle Collectors Assn. (G.E.C.A.)
Chris Showler, 11144 Slate Creek Rd., Grass Valley, CA 95945

Gun Owners of America
8001 Forbes Place, Suite 102, Springfield, VA 22151/703-321-8585

Handgun Hunters International
J.D. Jones, Director, P.O. Box 357 MAG, Bloomingdale, OH 43910

Harrington & Richardson Gun Coll. Assn.
George L. Cardet, 330 S.W. 27th Ave., Suite 603, Miami, FL 33135

High Standard Collectors' Assn.
John J. Stimson, Jr., Pres., 540 W. 92nd St., Indianapolis, IN 46260 Web: www.highstandard.org

Hopkins & Allen Arms & Memorabilia Society (HAAMS)
P.O. Box 187, 1309 Pamela Circle, Delphos, OH 45833

International Ammunition Association, Inc.
C.R. Punnett, Secy., 8 Hillock Lane, Chadds Ford, PA 19317 610-358-1285; Fax: 610-358-1560

International Benchrest Shooters
Joan Borden, RR1, Box 250BB, Springville, PA 18844 717-965-2366

International Blackpowder Hunting Assn.
P.O. Box 1180, Glenrock, WY 82637/307-436-9817

IHMSA (Intl. Handgun Metallic Silhouette Assn.)
PO Box 368, Burlington, IA 52601 Web: www.ihmsa.org

International Society of Mauser Arms Collectors
Michael Kindberg, Pres., P.O. Box 277, Alpharetta, GA 30239-0277

Jews for the Preservation of Firearms Ownership (JPFO) 501(c)(3)
2872 S. Wentworth Ave., Milwaukee, WI 53207 414-769-0760; Fax: 414-483-8435

The Mannlicher Collectors Assn.
Membership Office: P.O. Box 1249, The Dalles, Oregon 97058

Marlin Firearms Collectors Assn., Ltd.
Dick Paterson, Secy., 407 Lincoln Bldg., 44 Main St., Champaign, IL 61820

Merwin Hulbert Association,
2503 Kentwood Ct., High Point, NC 27265

Miniature Arms Collectors/Makers Society, Ltd.
Ralph Koebbeman, Pres., 4910 Kilburn Ave., Rockford, IL 61101 815-964-2569

M1 Carbine Collectors Assn. (M1-CCA)
623 Apaloosa Ln., Gardnerville, NV 89410-7840

National Association of Buckskinners (NAB)
Territorial Dispatch—1800s Historical Publication, 4701 Marion St., Suite 324, Livestock Exchange Bldg., Denver, CO 80216 303-297-9671

The National Association of Derringer Collectors
P.O. Box 20572, San Jose, CA 95160

National Assn. of Federally Licensed Firearms Dealers
Andrew Molchan, 2455 E. Sunrise, Ft. Lauderdale, FL 33304

National Association to Keep and Bear Arms
P.O. Box 78336, Seattle, WA 98178

National Automatic Pistol Collectors Assn.
Tom Knox, P.O. Box 15738, Tower Grove Station, St. Louis, MO 63163

National Bench Rest Shooters Assn., Inc.
Pat Ferrell, 2835 Guilford Lane, Oklahoma City, OK 73120-4404 405-842-9585; Fax: 405-842-9575

National Muzzle Loading Rifle Assn.
Box 67, Friendship, IN 47021 812-667-5131 Web: www.nmlra@nmlra.org

National Professional Paintball League (NPPL)
540 Main St., Mount Kisco, NY 10549/914-241-7400

National Reloading Manufacturers Assn.
One Centerpointe Dr., Suite 300, Lake Oswego, OR 97035

National Rifle Assn. of America
11250 Waples Mill Rd., Fairfax, VA 22030/703-267-1000 Web: www.nra.org

National Shooting Sports Foundation, Inc.
Doug Painter, President, Flintlock Ridge Office Center, 11 Mile Hill Rd., Newtown, CT 06470-2359 203-426-1320; Fax: 203-426-1087

National Skeet Shooting Assn.
Dan Snyuder, Director, 5931 Roft Road, San Antonio, TX 78253-9261/800-877-5338 Web: nssa-nsca.com

National Sporting Clays Assn.
Ann Myers, Director, 5931 Roft Road, San Antonio, TX 78253-9261/800-877-5338 Web: nssa-nsca.com

National Wild Turkey Federation, Inc.
P.O. Box 530, 770 Augusta Rd., Edgefield, SC 29824

North American Hunting Club
P.O. Box 3401, Minnetonka, MN 55343/612-936-9333; Fax: 612-936-9755

North American Paintball Referees Association (NAPRA)
584 Cestaric Dr., Milpitas, CA 95035

North-South Skirmish Assn., Inc.
Stevan F. Meserve, Exec. Secretary, 507 N. Brighton Court, Sterling, VA 20164-3919

Old West Shooter's Association
712 James Street, Hazel TX 76020 817-444-2049

Remington Society of America
Gordon Fosburg, Secretary, 11900 North Brinton Road, Lake, MI 48623

Rocky Mountain Elk Foundation
P.O. Box 8249, Missoula, MT 59807-8249/406-523-4500; Fax: 406-523-4581; Web: www.rmef.org

Ruger Collector's Assn., Inc.
P.O. Box 240, Greens Farms, CT 06436

Safari Club International
4800 W. Gates Pass Rd., Tucson, AZ 85745/520-620-1220

Sako Collectors Assn., Inc.
Jim Lutes, 202 N. Locust, Whitewater, KS 67154

Second Amendment Foundation
James Madison Building, 12500 NE 10th Pl., Bellevue, WA 98005

ARMS ASSOCIATIONS

Single Action Shooting Society (SASS)
23255-A La Palma Avenue, Yorba Linda, CA 92887/714-694-1800; Fax: 714-694-1815 email: sasseot@aol.com Web: www.sassnet.com

Smith & Wesson Collectors Assn.
Cally Pletl, Admin. Asst.,PO Box 444, Afton, NY 13730

The Society of American Bayonet Collectors
P.O. Box 234, East Islip, NY 11730-0234

Southern California Schuetzen Society
Dean Lillard, 34657 Ave. E., Yucaipa, CA 92399

Sporting Arms and Ammunition Manufacturers' Institute (SAAMI)
Flintlock Ridge Office Center, 11 Mile Hill Rd., Newtown, CT 06470-2359/203-426-4358; Fax: 203-426-1087

Sporting Clays of America (SCA)
Ron L. Blosser, Pres., 9257 Buckeye Rd., Sugar Grove, OH 43155-9632/614-746-8334; Fax: 614-746-8605

Steel Challenge
23234 Via Barra, Valencia CA 91355 Web: www.steelchallenge.com

The Thompson/Center Assn.
Joe Wright, President, Box 792, Northboro, MA 01532/508-845-6960

U.S. Practical Shooting Association/IPSC
Dave Thomas, P.O. Box 811, Sedro Woolley, WA 98284/360-855-2245 Web: www.uspsa.org

U.S. Revolver Assn.
Brian J. Barer, 40 Larchmont Ave., Taunton, MA 02780/508-824-4836

U.S.A. Shooting
U.S. Olympic Shooting Center, One Olympic Plaza, Colorado Springs, CO 80909/719-578-4670; Web: wwwusashooting.org

The Varmint Hunters Assn., Inc.
Box 759, Pierre, SD 57501 Member Services 800-528-4868

Weatherby Collectors Assn., Inc.
P.O. Box 478, Pacific, MO 63069 Web: www.weatherbycollectors.com Email: WCAsecretary@aol.com

The Wildcatters
P.O. Box 170, Greenville, WI 54942

Winchester Arms Collectors Assn.
P.O. Box 230, Brownsboro, TX 75756/903-852-4027

The Women's Shooting Sports Foundation (WSSF)
4620 Edison Avenue, Ste. C, Colorado Springs, CO 80915 719-638-1299; Fax: 719-638-1271 email: wssf@worldnet.att.net

ARGENTINA

Asociacion Argentina de Coleccionistas de Armes y Municiones
Castilla de Correos No. 28, Succursal I B, 1401 Buenos Aires, Republica Argentina

AUSTRALIA

Antique & Historical Arms Collectors of Australia
P.O. Box 5654, GCMC Queensland 9726, Australia

The Arms Collector's Guild of Queensland, Inc.
Ian Skennerton, P.O. Box 433, Ashmore City 4214, Queensland, Australia

Australian Cartridge Collectors Assn., Inc.
Bob Bennett, 126 Landscape Dr., E. Doncaster 3109, Victoria, Australia

Sporting Shooters Assn. of Australia, Inc.
P.O. Box 2066, Kent Town, SA 5071, Australia

BRAZIL

Associaçao de Armaria Coleçao e Tiro (ACOLTI)
Rua do Senado, 258 - 2 andar, Centro, Rio de Janeiro - RJ - 20231-002 Brazil / tel: 0055-21-31817989

CANADA

ALBERTA

Canadian Historical Arms Society
P.O. Box 901, Edmonton, Alb., Canada T5J 2L8

National Firearms Assn.
Natl. Hq: P.O. Box 1779, Edmonton, Alb., Canada T5J 2P1

BRITISH COLUMBIA

The Historical Arms Collectors of B.C. (Canada)
Harry Moon, Pres., P.O. Box 50117, South Slope RPO, Burnaby, BC V5J 5G3, Canada 604-438-0950; Fax: 604-277-3646

ONTARIO

Association of Canadian Cartridge Collectors
Monica Wright, RR 1, Millgrove, ON, LOR IVO, Canada

Tri-County Antique Arms Fair
P.O. Box 122, RR #1, North Lancaster, Ont., Canada K0C 1Z0

EUROPE

BELGIUM

European Cartridge Research Association
Graham Irving, 21 Rue Schaltin, 4900 Spa, Belgium 32.87.77.43.40; Fax: 32.87.77.27.51

CZECHOSLOVAKIA

Spolecnost Pro Studium Naboju (Czech Cartridge Research Association)
JUDr. Jaroslav Bubak, Pod Homolko 1439, 26601 Beroun 2, Czech Republic

DENMARK

Aquila Dansk Jagtpatron Historic Forening (Danish Historical Cartridge Collectors Club)
Steen Elgaard Møller, Ulriksdalsvej 7, 4840 Nr. Alslev, Denmark 10045-53846218; Fax: 00455384 6209

ENGLAND

Arms and Armour Society
Hon. Secretary A. Dove, P.O. Box 10232, London, 5W19 2ZD, England

Dutch Paintball Federation
Aceville Publ., Castle House 97 High Street, Colchester, Essex C01 1TH, England/011-44-206-564840

European Paintball Sports Foundation
c/o Aceville Publ., Castle House 97 High St., Colchester, Essex, C01 1TH, England

Historical Breechloading Smallarms Assn.
D.J. Penn M.A., Secy., P.O. Box 12778, London SE1 6BX, England

National Rifle Assn.
(Great Britain) Bisley Camp, Brookwood, Woking Surrey GU24 OPB, England/01483.797777; Fax: 014730686275

United Kingdom Cartridge Club
Ian Southgate, 20 Millfield, Elmley Castle, Nr. Pershore, Worcestershire, WR10 3HR, England

FRANCE

STAC-Western Co.
3 Ave. Paul Doumer (N.311); 78360 Montesson, France 01.30.53-43-65; Fax: 01.30.53.19.10

GERMANY

Bund Deutscher Sportschützen e.v. (BDS)
Borsigallee 10, 53125 Bonn 1, Germany

Deutscher Schützenbund
Lahnstrasse 120, 65195 Wiesbaden, Germany

NORWAY

Scandinavian Ammunition Research Association
c/o Morten Stoen, Annerudstubben 3, N-1383 Asker, Norway

NEW ZEALAND

New Zealand Cartridge Collectors Club
Terry Castle, 70 Tiraumea Dr., Pakuranga, Auckland, New Zealand

New Zealand Deerstalkers Association
P.O. Box 6514 TE ARO, Wellington, New Zealand

SOUTH AFRICA

Historical Firearms Soc. of South Africa
P.O. Box 145, 7725 Newlands, Republic of South Africa

Republic of South Africa Cartridge Collectors Assn.
Arno Klee, 20 Eugene St., Malanshof Randburg, Gauteng 2194, Republic of South Africa

S.A.A.C.A. (Southern Africa Arms and Ammunition Assn.)
Gauteng office: P.O. Box 7597, Weltevreden Park, 1715, Republic of South Africa/ 011-679-1151; Fax: 011-679-1131; e-mail: saaaca@iafrica.com
Kwa-Zulu Natal office: P.O. Box 4065, Northway, Kwazulu-Natal 4065, Republic of South Africa

SAGA (S.A. Gunowners' Assn.)
P.O. Box 35203, Northway, Kwazulu-Natal 4065, Republic of South Africa

SPAIN

Asociacion Espanola de Colleccionistas de Cartuchos (A.E.C.C.)
Secretary: Apdo. Correos No. 1086, 2880-Alcala de Henares (Madrid), Spain. President: Apdo. Correos No. 682, 50080 Zaragoza, Spain

2009
GUN DIGEST
DIRECTORY OF THE
ARMS TRADE

The Product Directory contains 84 product categories. The Manufacturer's Directory alphabetically lists the manufacturer's work with their addresses, phone numbers, FAX numbers and internet addresses, if available.

DIRECTORY OF THE ARMS TRADE INDEX

PRODUCT & SERVICE DIRECTORY

AMMUNITION COMPONENTS, SHOTSHELL

A.W. Peterson Gun Shop, Inc., The
Ballistic Products, Inc.
Blount, Inc., Sporting Equipment Div.
CCI/Speer Div of ATK
Cheddite, France S.A.
Dina Arms Corporation
Gentner Bullets
Guncrafter Industries
Magtech Ammunition Co. Inc.
National Gun, Inc.
Peterson Gun Shop, Inc., A.W.
Precision Reloading, Inc.
Ravell Ltd.
Tar-Hunt Custom Rifles, Inc.
Vitt/Boos

AMMUNITION COMPONENTS--BULLETS, POWDER, PRIMERS, CASES

A.W. Peterson Gun Shop, Inc., The
Acadian Ballistic Specialties
Accuracy Unlimited
Accurate Arms Co., Inc.
Action Bullets & Alloy Inc.
ADCO Sales, Inc.
Alaska Bullet Works, Inc.
Alex, Inc.
Alliant Techsystems, Smokeless Powder Group
Allred Bullet Co.
Alpha LaFranck Enterprises
American Products, Inc.
Armfield Custom Bullets
A-Square Co.
Austin Sheridan USA, Inc.
Baer's Hollows
Ballard Rifle & Cartridge Co., LLC
Barnes Bullets, Inc.
BC-Handmade Bullets
Beartooth Bullets
Bell Reloading, Inc.
Berger Bullets Ltd.
Berry's Mfg., Inc.
Big Bore Bullets of Alaska
Big Bore Express
Bitterroot Bullet Co.
Black Belt Bullets (See Big Bore Express)
Black Hills Shooters Supply
Black Powder Products
Blount, Inc., Sporting Equipment Div.
Blue Mountain Bullets
Brenneke GmbH
Briese Bullet Co., Inc.
BRP, Inc. High Performance Cast Bullets
Buck Stix-SOS Products Co.
Buckeye Custom Bullets
Buckskin Bullet Co.
Buffalo Arms Co.
Buffalo Bullet Co., Inc.
Buffalo Rock Shooters Supply
Bull-X, Inc.
Butler Enterprises
C. Sharps Arms Co. Inc./ Montana Armory
Cain's Outdoors, Inc.
Canyon Cartridge Corp.
Cast Performance Bullet Company
Casull Arms Corp.
CCI/Speer Div of ATK
Champion's Choice, Inc.
Cheddite, France S.A.
CheVron Bullets
Chuck's Gun Shop
Clean Shot Technologies
Competitor Corp., Inc.
Cook Engineering Service
Cummings Bullets
Curtis Cast Bullets
Curtis Gun Shop (See Curtis Cast Bullets)
Custom Bullets by Hoffman
D.L. Unmussig Bullets
Dakota Arms, Inc.
Davide Pedersoli and Co.
Dina Arms Corporation
DKT, Inc.
Dohring Bullets
Eichelberger Bullets, Wm.
Eley Ltd.
Federal Cartridge Co.
Fiocchi of America, Inc.
Firearm Brokers
Forkin Custom Classics
Fowler, Bob (See Black Powder Products)
Freedom Arms, Inc.
Gehmann, Walter (See Huntington Die Specialties)
GOEX, Inc.
Golden Bear Bullets
Gotz Bullets
Grayback Wildcats
Gun City
Gun Works, The
Harris Enterprises
Harrison Bullets
Hart & Son, Inc.
Hawk Laboratories, Inc. (See Hawk, Inc.)
Hawk, Inc.
Heidenstrom Bullets
Hercules, Inc. (See Alliant Techsystems Smokeless Powder Group)
Hi-Performance Ammunition Company
Hirtenberger AG
Hobson Precision Mfg. Co.
Hodgdon Powder Co.
Hornady Mfg. Co.
HT Bullets
Hunters Supply, Inc.
Huntington Die Specialties
Impact Case & Container, Inc.
Imperial Magnum Corp.
IMR Powder Co.
Intercontinental Distributors, Ltd.
J R Guns
J R Guns
J&D Components
J&L Superior Bullets (See Huntington Die Specialties)
J.R. Williams Bullet Co.
James Calhoon Mfg.
Jamison International
Jensen Bullets
Jensen's Firearms Academy
Jericho Tool & Die Co., Inc.
Jester Bullets
JLK Bullets
JRP Custom Bullets
Kaswer Custom, Inc.
Keith's Bullets
Ken's Kustom Kartridges
Knight Rifles
Knight Rifles (See Modern Muzzleloading, Inc.)
Lawrence Brand Shot (See Precision Reloading, Inc.)
Liberty Shooting Supplies
Lindsley Arms Cartridge Co.
Littleton, J. F.
Lomont Precision Bullets
Lyman Products Corp.
Magnus Bullets
MagSafe Ammo, Inc.
Magtech Ammunition Co. Inc.
Markesbery Muzzle Loaders, Inc.
McMurdo, Lynn
Meister Bullets (See Gander Mountain)
Men-Metallwerk Elisenhuette GmbH
Midway Arms, Inc.
MI-TE Bullets
Montana Precision Swaging
Mulhern, Rick
Nagel's Custom Bullets
Nammo Lapua Oy
National Bullet Co.
National Gun, Inc.
Naval Ordnance Works
North American Shooting Systems
North Devon Firearms Services
Northern Precision
Northwest Custom Projectile
Nosler, Inc.
OK Weber, Inc.
Oklahoma Ammunition Co.
Old Wagon Bullets
Old Western Scrounger LLC
Ordnance Works, The
Oregon Trail Bullet Company
Pacific Rifle Co.
Page Custom Bullets
Penn Bullets
Peterson Gun Shop, Inc., A.W.
Petro-Explo Inc.
Phillippi Custom Bullets, Justin
Pinetree Bullets
PMC Ammunition
Polywad, Inc.
Pony Express Reloaders
Power Plus Enterprises, Inc.
Precision Delta Corp.
Price Bullets, Patrick W.
PRL Bullets, c/o Blackburn Enterprises
Professional Hunter Supplies
Proofmark Corp.
PWM Sales Ltd.
Quality Cartridge
Quarton Beamshot
Rainier Ballistics
Ravell Ltd.
Redwood Bullet Works
Reloading Specialties, Inc.
Remington Arms Co., Inc.
Rhino
Robinson H.V. Bullets
Rubright Bullets
Russ Haydon's Shooters' Supply
SAECO (See Redding Reloading Equipment)
Scharch Mfg., Inc.-Top Brass
Schneider Bullets
Schroeder Bullets
Schumakers Gun Shop
Seebeck Assoc., R.E.
Shappy Bullets
Sharps Arms Co., Inc., C.
Shilen, Inc.
Sierra Bullets
SOS Products Co. (See Buck Stix-SOS Products Co.)
Southern Ammunition Co., Inc.
Specialty Gunsmithing
Speer Bullets
Spencer's Rifle Barrels, Inc.
SSK Industries
Star Ammunition, Inc.
Star Custom Bullets
Starke Bullet Company
Starline, Inc.
Stewart's Gunsmithing
Swift Bullet Co.
T.F.C. S.p.A.
Taracorp Industries, Inc.
Tar-Hunt Custom Rifles, Inc.
TCCI
TCSR
Thompson Bullet Lube Co.
Thompson Precision
Traditions Performance Firearms
True Flight Bullet Co.
Tucson Mold, Inc.
USAC
Vann Custom Bullets
Vihtavuori Oy/Kaltron-Pettibone
Vincent's Shop
Viper Bullet and Brass Works
Watson Bullets
Western Nevada West Coast Bullets
Widener's Reloading & Shooting Supply, Inc.
Wildey F. A., Inc.
Winchester Div. Olin Corp.
Woodleigh (See Huntington Die Specialties)
Wyant Bullets
Wyoming Custom Bullets
Zero Ammunition Co., Inc.

AMMUNITION, COMMERCIAL

3-Ten Corp.
A.W. Peterson Gun Shop, Inc., The
Ad Hominem
Air Arms
American Ammunition
Arms Corporation of the Philippines
A-Square Co.
Austin Sheridan USA, Inc.
Ballistic Products, Inc.
Benjamin/Sheridan Co., Crosman
Black Hills Ammunition, Inc.
Blount, Inc., Sporting Equipment Div.
Brenneke GmbH
Buchsenmachermeister
Buffalo Arms Co.
Buffalo Bullet Co., Inc.
Bull-X, Inc.
Cabela's
Casull Arms Corp.
CBC
CCI/Speer Div of ATK
Champion's Choice, Inc.
Cleland's Outdoor World, Inc.
Cor-Bon Inc./Glaser LLC
Crosman Airguns
Cubic Shot Shell Co., Inc.
Dan Wesson Firearms
Dead Eye's Sport Center
Delta Arms Ltd.
Effebi SNC-Dr. Franco Beretta
Eley Ltd.
Ellett Bros.
Estate Cartridge, Inc.
Federal Cartridge Co.
Fiocchi of America, Inc.
Firearm Brokers
Garrett Cartridges, Inc.
Garthwaite Pistolsmith, Inc., Jim
Gibbs Rifle Co., Inc.
Gil Hebard Guns, Inc.
Glaser LLC
Glaser Safety Slug, Inc. (see CorBon/Glaser
GOEX, Inc.
Goodwin's Guns
Grayback Wildcats
Gun City
Gun Room Press, The
Gun Works, The
Guncrafter Industries
Hansen & Co.
Hart & Son, Inc.
Hastings
Hi-Performance Ammunition Company
Hirtenberger AG
Hofer Jagdwaffen, P.
Hornady Mfg. Co.
Hunters Supply, Inc.
Intercontinental Distributors, Ltd.
Ion Industries, Inc.
Keng's Firearms Specialty, Inc.
Kent Cartridge America, Inc.
Knight Rifles
Lethal Force Institute (See Police Bookshelf)
Lock's Philadelphia Gun Exchange
Lomont Precision Bullets
Magnum Research, Inc.
MagSafe Ammo, Inc.
Magtech Ammunition Co. Inc.
Markell, Inc.
Men-Metallwerk Elisenhuette GmbH
Mullins Ammunition
Nammo Lapua Oy
National Gun, Inc.
New England Ammunition Co.
Oklahoma Ammunition Co.
Old Western Scrounger LLC
Outdoor Sports Headquarters, Inc.
P.S.M.G. Gun Co.
Paragon Sales & Services, Inc.
Parker & Sons Shooting Supply
Peterson Gun Shop, Inc., A.W.
PMC Ammunition
Police Bookshelf
Polywad, Inc.
Pony Express Reloaders
Precision Delta Corp.
Quality Cartridge
R.E.I.
Ravell Ltd.
Remington Arms Co., Inc.
Rucker Dist. Inc.
RWS (See U.S. Importer-Umarex-USA)
Sellier & Bellot, USA, Inc.
Southern Ammunition Co., Inc.
Speer Bullets
Starr Trading Co., Jedediah
TCCI
Thompson Bullet Lube Co.
Umarex USA
USAC
VAM Distribution Co. LLC
Vihtavuori Oy/Kaltron-Pettibone
Voere-KGH GmbH
Weatherby, Inc.
Westley Richards & Co. Ltd.
Whitestone Lumber Corp.
Widener's Reloading & Shooting Supply, Inc.
Wildey F. A., Inc.
William E. Phillips Firearms
Winchester Div. Olin Corp.
Zero Ammunition Co., Inc.

AMMUNITION, CUSTOM

3-Ten Corp.
A.W. Peterson Gun Shop, Inc., The
Accuracy Unlimited
AFSCO Ammunition
Allred Bullet Co.
American Derringer Corp.
American Products, Inc.
Arms Corporation of the Philippines
Ballard Rifle & Cartridge Co., LLC
Bear Arms
Berger Bullets Ltd.
Big Bore Bullets of Alaska

Black Hills Ammunition, Inc.
Blue Mountain Bullets
Brynin, Milton
Buckskin Bullet Co.
Buffalo Arms Co.
CBC
CFVentures
Champlin Firearms, Inc.
Country Armourer, The
Cubic Shot Shell Co., Inc.
Custom Tackle and Ammo
D.L. Unmussig Bullets
Dakota Arms, Inc.
Dead Eye's Sport Center
DKT, Inc.
Estate Cartridge, Inc.
GDL Enterprises
Gentner Bullets
GOEX, Inc.
Grayback Wildcats
Hawk, Inc.
Hirtenberger AG
Hobson Precision Mfg. Co.
Horizons Unlimited
Hornady Mfg. Co.
Hunters Supply, Inc.
J R Guns
Jensen Bullets
Jensen's Arizona Sportsman
Jensen's Firearms Academy
Kaswer Custom, Inc.
L. E. Jurras & Assoc.
L.A.R. Mfg., Inc.
Lethal Force Institute (See Police Bookshelf)
Lindsley Arms Cartridge Co.
Linebaugh Custom Sixguns
MagSafe Ammo, Inc.
Magtech Ammunition Co. Inc.
McMurdo, Lynn
Men-Metallwerk Elisenhuette GmbH
Mullins Ammunition
Oklahoma Ammunition Co.
P.S.M.G. Gun Co.
Peterson Gun Shop, Inc., A.W.
Phillippi Custom Bullets, Justin
Power Plus Enterprises, Inc.
Precision Delta Corp.
Professional Hunter Supplies
Quality Cartridge
R.E.I.
Sandia Die & Cartridge Co.
SOS Products Co. (See Buck Stix-SOS Products Co.)
Specialty Gunsmithing
Spencer's Rifle Barrels, Inc.
SSK Industries
Star Custom Bullets
Stewart's Gunsmithing
TCCI
Vitt/Boos
Watson Bullets
Zero Ammunition Co., Inc.

AMMUNITION, FOREIGN

A.W. Peterson Gun Shop, Inc., The
Ad Hominem
AFSCO Ammunition
Air Arms
Armscorp USA, Inc.
B&P America
Cape Outfitters
CBC
Cheddite, France S.A.
Cubic Shot Shell Co., Inc.
Dead Eye's Sport Center
DKT, Inc.
E. Arthur Brown Co. Inc.
Fiocchi of America, Inc.
Gamebore Division, Polywad, Inc.
Gibbs Rifle Co., Inc.
GOEX, Inc.
Gunsmithing, Inc.
Hansen & Co.
Heidenstrom Bullets
Hirtenberger AG
Hornady Mfg. Co.
International Shooters Service
Intrac Arms International
J R Guns
Jack First, Inc.
K.B.I. Inc.
MagSafe Ammo, Inc.
Magtech Ammunition Co. Inc.
Marksman Products
Mullins Ammunition
Oklahoma Ammunition Co.
P.S.M.G. Gun Co.
Paragon Sales & Services, Inc.
Paul Co., The
Peterson Gun Shop, Inc., A.W.
Petro-Explo Inc.
Precision Delta Corp.
R.E.T. Enterprises
RWS (See U.S. Importer-Umarex-USA)
Samco Global Arms, Inc.
Southern Ammunition Co., Inc.
Speer Bullets
Stratco, Inc.
T.F.C. S.p.A.
Umarex USA
Vector Arms, Inc.
Victory Ammunition
Vihtavuori Oy/Kaltron-Pettibone
Wolf Performance Ammunition

ANTIQUE ARMS DEALER

Ackerman & Co.
Ad Hominem
Antique American Firearms
Antique Arms Co.
Aplan Antiques & Art
Ballard Rifle & Cartridge Co., LLC
Bear Mountain Gun & Tool
Bob's Tactical Indoor Shooting Range & Gun Shop
Buffalo Arms Co.
C. Sharps Arms Co. Inc./ Montana Armory
Cape Outfitters
CBC-BRAZIL
Chadick's Ltd.
Chambers Flintlocks Ltd., Jim
Champlin Firearms, Inc.
Chuck's Gun Shop
Clements' Custom Leathercraft, Chas
Cousin Bob's Mountain Products
D&D Gunsmiths, Ltd.
David R. Chicoine
DBA Werth Services
Dixie Gun Works
Dixon Muzzleloading Shop, Inc.
Duffy, Charles E. (See Guns Antique & Modern DBA)
Ed's Gun House
Ed's Gun House
Enguix Import-Export
Fagan Arms
Flayderman & Co., Inc.
Getz Barrel Company
Glass, Herb
Goergen's Gun Shop, Inc.
Golden Age Arms Co.
Goodwin's Guns
Gun Hunter Books (See Gun Hunter Trading Co.)
Gun Hunter Trading Co.
Gun Room Press, The
Gun Room, The
Gun Works, The
Guns Antique & Modern DBA / Charles E. Duffy
Hallowell & Co.
Hammans, Charles E.
HandCrafts Unltd. (See Clements' Custom Leathercraft)
Handgun Press
Hansen & Co.
Imperial Miniature Armory
James Wayne Firearms for Collectors and Investors
Kelley's
Knight's Manufacturing Co.
Ledbetter Airguns, Riley
LeFever Arms Co., Inc.
Lever Arms Service Ltd.
Lock's Philadelphia Gun Exchange
Log Cabin Sport Shop
Logdewood Mfg.
Madis Books
Martin B. Retting Inc.
Martin's Gun Shop
Michael's Antiques
Mid-America Recreation, Inc.
Montana Outfitters, Lewis E. Yearout
Muzzleloaders Etcetera, Inc.
New England Arms Co.
Olathe Gun Shop
P.S.M.G. Gun Co.
Peter Dyson & Son Ltd.
Pony Express Sport Shop
Powder Horn Ltd.
Ravell Ltd.
Reno, Wayne
Retting, Inc., Martin B.
Robert Valade Engraving
Rutgers Book Center
Samco Global Arms, Inc.
Sarco, Inc.
Scott Fine Guns Inc., Thad
Shootin' Shack
Sportsmen's Exchange & Western Gun Traders, Inc.
State Line Gun Shop
Stott's Creek Armory, Inc.
Track of the Wolf, Inc.
Turnbull Restoration, Doug
Westley Richards & Co. Ltd.
Wild West Guns
Winchester Sutler, Inc., The
Yearout, Lewis E. (See Montana Outfitters)

APPRAISER - GUNS, ETC.

A.W. Peterson Gun Shop, Inc., The
Ackerman & Co.
Antique Arms Co.
Barta's Gunsmithing
Beitzinger, George
Blue Book Publications, Inc.
Bob's Tactical Indoor Shooting Range & Gun Shop
Bonham's & Butterfields
Cape Outfitters
Chadick's Ltd.
Champlin Firearms, Inc.
Christie's East
Clark Firearms Engraving
Cleland's Outdoor World, Inc.
Clements' Custom Leathercraft, Chas
Colonial Arms, Inc.
Colonial Repair
Corry, John
Custom Tackle and Ammo
D&D Gunsmiths, Ltd.
David R. Chicoine
DBA Werth Services
DGR Custom Rifles
Dietz Gun Shop & Range, Inc.
Dixie Gun Works
Dixon Muzzleloading Shop, Inc.
Duane's Gun Repair (See DGR Custom Rifles)
Ed's Gun House
Eversull Co., Inc.
Fagan Arms
Ferris Firearms
Firearm Brokers
Flayderman & Co., Inc.
Frontier Arms Co., Inc.
Gene's Custom Guns
Getz Barrel Company
Gillmann, Edwin
Goergen's Gun Shop, Inc.
Golden Age Arms Co.
Griffin & Howe, Inc.
Griffin & Howe, Inc.
Gun City
Gun Hunter Books (See Gun Hunter Trading Co.)
Gun Hunter Trading Co.
Gun Room Press, The
Gun Shop, The
Gun Works, The
Guncraft Books (See Guncraft Sports, Inc.)
Guncraft Sports, Inc.
Guncraft Sports, Inc.
Gunsmithing, Inc.
Hallowell & Co.
Hammans, Charles E.
HandCrafts Unltd. (See Clements' Custom Leathercraft)
Handgun Press
Hank's Gun Shop
Hansen & Co.
Irwin, Campbell H.
Ithaca Classic Doubles
J R Guns
J.W. Wasmundt-Gunsmith
Jackalope Gun Shop
James Wayne Firearms for Collectors and Investors
Jensen's Arizona Sportsman
JG Airguns, LLC
Kelley's
Ken Eyster Heritage Gunsmiths, Inc.
L.L. Bean, Inc.
Lampert, Ron
LaRocca Gun Works
Ledbetter Airguns, Riley
LeFever Arms Co., Inc.
Lock's Philadelphia Gun Exchange
Log Cabin Sport Shop
Logdewood Mfg.
Long, George F.
Madis Books
Martin B. Retting Inc.
Martin's Gun Shop
Mathews Gun Shop & Gunsmithing, Inc.
McCann Industries
Mercer Custom Guns
Montana Outfitters, Lewis E. Yearout
Muzzleloaders Etcetera, Inc.
New England Arms Co.
Nu Line Guns, Inc.
Olathe Gun Shop
Orvis Co., The
P&M Sales & Services, LLC
P.S.M.G. Gun Co.
Pasadena Gun Center
Pentheny de Pentheny
Perazone-Gunsmith, Brian
Peterson Gun Shop, Inc., A.W.
Pettinger Books, Gerald
Pony Express Sport Shop
Powder Horn Ltd.
R.A. Wells Custom Gunsmith
R.E.T. Enterprises
Retting, Inc., Martin B.
Robert Valade Engraving
Russ Haydon's Shooters' Supply
Rutgers Book Center
Scott Fine Guns Inc., Thad
Shootin' Shack
Sportsmen's Exchange & Western Gun Traders, Inc.
State Line Gun Shop
Steven Dodd Hughes
Stott's Creek Armory, Inc.
Stratco, Inc.
Swampfire Shop, The (See Peterson Gun Shop, Inc., A.W.)
Ten-Ring Precision, Inc.
Weber & Markin Custom Gunsmiths
Whitestone Lumber Corp.
Wild West Guns
Williams Shootin' Iron Service, The Lynx-Line
Winchester Sutler, Inc., The
Yearout, Lewis E. (See Montana Outfitters)

AUCTIONEER - GUNS, ETC.

"Little John's" Antique Arms
Bonham's & Butterfields
Buck Stix-SOS Products Co.
Christie's East
Fagan Arms
Pete de Coux Auction House
Sotheby's

BOOKS & MANUALS (PUBLISHERS & DEALERS)

A.W. Peterson Gun Shop, Inc., The
Alpha 1 Drop Zone
American Gunsmithing Institute
American Handgunner Magazine
Armory Publications
Arms & Armour Press
Austin Sheridan USA, Inc.
Ballistic Products, Inc.
Ballistic Products, Inc.
Barnes Bullets, Inc.
Beartooth Bullets
Beeman Precision Airguns
Blacksmith Corp.
Blacktail Mountain Books
Blue Book Publications, Inc.
Blue Ridge Machinery & Tools, Inc.
Boone's Custom Ivory Grips, Inc.
Brownells, Inc.
Buchsenmachermeister
C. Sharps Arms Co. Inc./ Montana Armory
Cain's Outdoors, Inc.
Cape Outfitters
Cheyenne Pioneer Products
Collector's Armoury, Ltd.
Colonial Repair
Crit' R Calls
David R. Chicoine
deHaas Barrels
Dixon Muzzleloading Shop, Inc.
Excalibur Publications
Executive Protection Institute
F+W Publications, Inc.
Fulton Armory
Galati International
GAR
Golden Age Arms Co.
Gun City
Gun Digest (See F+W Publications)
Gun Hunter Books (See Gun Hunter Trading Co.)
Gun Hunter Trading Co.
Gun Room Press, The
Gun Works, The
Guncraft Books (See Guncraft Sports, Inc.)

PRODUCT & SERVICE DIRECTORY

Guncraft Sports, Inc.
Gunnerman Books
GUNS Magazine
Gunsmithing, Inc.
H&P Publishing
Handgun Press
Harris Publications
Hawk Laboratories, Inc. (See Hawk, Inc.)
Hawk, Inc.
Heritage/VSP Gun Books
Hodgdon Powder Co.
Hofer Jagdwaffen, P.
Hornady Mfg. Co.
Huntington Die Specialties
I.D.S.A. Books
Info-Arm
InterMedia Outdoors, Inc.
Ironside International Publishers, Inc.
Jantz Supply, Inc.
Jeff's Outfitters
JG Airguns, LLC
Kelley's
King & Co.
Koval Knives
KP Books Division of F+W Publications
L.B.T.
Lebeau-Courally
Lethal Force Institute (See Police Bookshelf)
Log Cabin Sport Shop
Lyman Products Corp.
Machinist's Workshop-Village Press
Madis Books
Madis Books
Magma Engineering Co.
Montana Armory, Inc.
Montana Precision Swaging
Mulberry House Publishing
Nammo Lapua Oy
NgraveR Co., The
Numrich Gun Parts Corporation
OK Weber, Inc.
Outdoor Sports Headquarters, Inc.
Paintball Games International Magazine Aceville
Pansch, Robert F
Pejsa Ballistics
Pete Rickard Co.
Pettinger Books, Gerald
PFRB Co.
Police Bookshelf
Precision Reloading, Inc.
Precision Shooting, Inc.
Professional Hunter Supplies
Ravell Ltd.
Ray Riling Arms Books Co.
Remington Double Shotguns
Russ Haydon's Shooters' Supply
Rutgers Book Center
S&S Firearms
Safari Press, Inc.
Saunders Gun & Machine Shop
Scharch Mfg., Inc.-Top Brass
Scharch Mfg., Inc.-Top Brass
Semmer, Charles (See Remington Double Shotguns)
Sharps Arms Co., Inc., C.
Shotgun Sports Magazine, dba Shootin' Accessories Ltd.
Sierra Bullets
Speer Bullets
SPG, Inc.
Stackpole Books
Star Custom Bullets
Stoeger Industries
Stoeger Publishing Co. (See Stoeger Industries)
Swift Bullet Co.
The Midwest Shooting School
Thomas, Charles C.
Track of the Wolf, Inc.
Trafalgar Square
Trotman, Ken
Tru-Balance Knife Co.
Vega Tool Co.
VSP Publishers (See Heritage/ VSP Gun Books)
W.E. Brownell Checkering Tools
WAMCO-New Mexico
Wells Creek Knife & Gun Works
Wilderness Sound Products Ltd.
Williams Gun Sight Co.
Winfield Galleries LLC
Wolfe Publishing Co.

BULLET CASTING, ACCESSORIES

A.W. Peterson Gun Shop, Inc., The
Ballisti-Cast, Inc.
Buffalo Arms Co.
Bullet Metals
Cast Performance Bullet Company
CFVentures
Cooper-Woodward Perfect Lube
Davide Pedersoli and Co.
Ferguson, Bill
Fluoramics, Inc.
Hanned Line, The
Huntington Die Specialties
L.B.T.
Lee Precision, Inc.
Lithi Bee Bullet Lube
Lyman Products Corp.
MA Systems, Inc.
Magma Engineering Co.
NEI Handtools, Inc.
Rapine Bullet Mould Mfg. Co.
Redding Reloading Equipment
SPG, Inc.

BULLET CASTING, FURNACES & POTS

A.W. Peterson Gun Shop, Inc., The
Ballisti-Cast, Inc.
Buffalo Arms Co.
Bullet Metals
Ferguson, Bill
GAR
Gun Works, The
Lee Precision, Inc.
Lyman Products Corp.
Magma Engineering Co.
Rapine Bullet Mould Mfg. Co.
Thompson Bullet Lube Co.

BULLET CASTING, LEAD

A.W. Peterson Gun Shop, Inc., The
Action Bullets & Alloy Inc.
Ames Metal Products Co.
Buckskin Bullet Co.
Buffalo Arms Co.
Bullet Metals
Gun Works, The
Hunters Supply, Inc.
Jericho Tool & Die Co., Inc.
Lee Precision, Inc.
Lithi Bee Bullet Lube
Magma Engineering Co.
Montana Precision Swaging
Penn Bullets
Proofmark Corp.
SPG, Inc.
Splitfire Sporting Goods, L.L.C.
Walters Wads

BULLET PULLERS

A.W. Peterson Gun Shop, Inc., The
Battenfeld Technologies, Inc.
Davide Pedersoli and Co.
Gun Works, The
Howell Machine, Inc.
Huntington Die Specialties
Royal Arms Gunstocks

BULLET TOOLS

A.W. Peterson Gun Shop, Inc., The
Brynin, Milton
Camdex, Inc.
Corbin Mfg. & Supply, Inc.
Eagan Gunsmiths
Hanned Line, The
Lee Precision, Inc.
Niemi Engineering, W. B.
North Devon Firearms Services
Rorschach Precision Products
Sport Flite Manufacturing Co.
WTA Manufacturing

BULLET, CASE & DIE LUBRICANTS

Beartooth Bullets
Bonanza (See Forster Products)
Buckskin Bullet Co.
Buffalo Arms Co.
Camp-Cap Products
CFVentures
Cooper-Woodward Perfect Lube
CVA
Ferguson, Bill
Forster Products, Inc.
GAR
Guardsman Products
Hanned Line, The
Heidenstrom Bullets
Hornady Mfg. Co.
Javelina Lube Products
Knoell, Doug
L.B.T.
Lee Precision, Inc.
Lithi Bee Bullet Lube
MI-TE Bullets
RCBS Operations/ATK
Reardon Products
Rooster Laboratories
Shay's Gunsmithing
Uncle Mike's (See Michaels of Oregon, Co.)
Widener's Reloading & Shooting Supply, Inc.
Young Country Arms

CARTRIDGES FOR COLLECTORS

Ackerman & Co.
Ad Hominem
Armory Publications
Cameron's
Campbell, Dick
Colonial Repair
Country Armourer, The
Cubic Shot Shell Co., Inc.
Duane's Gun Repair (See DGR Custom Rifles)
Ed's Gun House
Ed's Gun House
Enguix Import-Export
Goergen's Gun Shop, Inc.
Gun City
Gun Hunter Books (See Gun Hunter Trading Co.)
Gun Hunter Trading Co.
Gun Room Press, The
Jack First, Inc.
Kelley's
Liberty Shooting Supplies
Madis Books
Michael's Antiques
Montana Outfitters, Lewis E. Yearout
Numrich Gun Parts Corporation
Pasadena Gun Center
Pete de Coux Auction House
Samco Global Arms, Inc.
SOS Products Co. (See Buck Stix-SOS Products Co.)
Stone Enterprises Ltd.
Ward & Van Valkenburg
Yearout, Lewis E. (See Montana Outfitters)

CASE & AMMUNITION PROCESSORS, INSPECTORS, BOXERS

A.W. Peterson Gun Shop, Inc., The
Ammo Load Worldwide, Inc.
Hafner World Wide, Inc.
Scharch Mfg., Inc.-Top Brass

CASE CLEANERS & POLISHING MEDIA

A.W. Peterson Gun Shop, Inc., The
Battenfeld Technologies, Inc.
Buffalo Arms Co.
G96 Products Co., Inc.
Gun Works, The
Huntington Die Specialties
Lee Precision, Inc.
Penn Bullets
Tru-Square Metal Products, Inc.
VibraShine, Inc.

CASE PREPARATION TOOLS

A.W. Peterson Gun Shop, Inc., The
Battenfeld Technologies, Inc.
Forster Products, Inc.
High Precision
Huntington Die Specialties
J. Dewey Mfg. Co., Inc.
K&M Services
Lee Precision, Inc.
Match Prep-Doyle Gracey
Plum City Ballistic Range
PWM Sales Ltd.
RCBS Operations/ATK
Redding Reloading Equipment
Russ Haydon's Shooters' Supply
Sinclair International, Inc.
Six Enterprises
Stoney Point Products, Inc.

CASE TRIMMERS, TRIM DIES & ACCESSORIES

A.W. Peterson Gun Shop, Inc., The
Buffalo Arms Co.
Creedmoor Sports, Inc.
Forster Products, Inc.
Fremont Tool Works
K&M Services
Lyman Products Corp.
Match Prep-Doyle Gracey
OK Weber, Inc.
PWM Sales Ltd.
Redding Reloading Equipment

CASE TUMBLERS, VIBRATORS, MEDIA & ACCESSORIES

A.W. Peterson Gun Shop, Inc., The
Battenfeld Technologies, Inc.
Berry's Mfg., Inc.
CH Tool & Die/4-D Custom Die Co.
Dillon Precision Products, Inc.
Penn Bullets
Raytech Div. of Lyman Products Corp.
Tru-Square Metal Products, Inc.
VibraShine, Inc.

CASES, CABINETS, RACKS & SAFES - GUN

All Rite Products, Inc.
Allen Co., Inc.
Alumna Sport by Dee Zee
American Display Co.
American Security Products Co.
Americase
Art Jewel Enterprises Ltd.
Bagmaster Mfg., Inc.
Barramundi Corp.
Berry's Mfg., Inc.
Big Spring Enterprises "Bore Stores"
Bison Studios
Black Sheep Brand
Brauer Bros.
Browning Arms Co.
Bushmaster Hunting & Fishing
Cannon Safe, Inc.
Chipmunk (See Oregon Arms, Inc.)
Connecticut Shotgun Mfg. Co.
D&L Industries (See D.J. Marketing)
D.J. Marketing
Dara-Nes, Inc. (See Nesci Enterprises, Inc.)
Deepeeka Exports Pvt. Ltd.
Doskocil Mfg. Co., Inc.
DTM International, Inc.
EMF Co. Inc.
English, Inc., A.G.
Enhanced Presentations, Inc.
Eversull Co., Inc.
Flambeau, Inc.
Fort Knox Security Products
Freedom Arms, Inc.
Galati International
GALCO International Ltd.
Gun-Ho Sports Cases
Hall Plastics, Inc., John
Homak
Hoppe's Div. Penguin Industries, Inc.
Hunter Co., Inc.
Hydrosorbent Dehumidifiers
Impact Case & Container, Inc.
Jeff's Outfitters
Johanssons Vapentillbehor, Bert
Kalispel Case Line
KK Air International (See Impact Case & Container Co., Inc.)
Knock on Wood Antiques
Kolpin Outdoors, Inc.
Lakewood Products Div of Midwest Textile
Liberty Safe
Marsh, Mike
McWelco Products
Morton Booth Co.
MPC
MTM Molded Products Co., Inc.
Nalpak
Necessary Concepts, Inc.
Nesci Enterprises Inc.
Oregon Arms, Inc. (See Rogue Rifle Co., Inc.)
Outa-Site Gun Carriers
Outdoor Connection, Inc., The

PRODUCT & SERVICE DIRECTORY

Pflumm Mfg. Co.
Poburka, Philip (See Bison Studios)
Powell & Son (Gunmakers) Ltd., William
Prototech Industries, Inc.
Rogue Rifle Co., Inc./Chipmunk Rifles
S.A.R.L. G. Granger
Schulz Industries
Silhouette Leathers
Southern Security
Sportsman's Communicators
Sun Welding Safe Co.
Tinks & Ben Lee Hunting Products (See Wellington Outdoors)
Trulock Tool
Universal Sports
W. Waller & Son, Inc.
Whitestone Lumber Corp.
Wilson Case, Inc.
Woodstream
Zanotti Armor, Inc.
Ziegel Engineering

CHOKE DEVICES, RECOIL ABSORBERS & RECOIL PADS

3-Ten Corp.
A.W. Peterson Gun Shop, Inc., The
Action Products, Inc.
Bansner's Ultimate Rifles, LLC
Bartlett Engineering
Battenfeld Technologies, Inc.
Bob Allen Sportswear
Briley Mfg. Inc.
Brooks Tactical Systems-Agrip
Brownells, Inc.
Buffer Technologies
Bull Mountain Rifle Co.
C&H Research
Cation
Chicasaw Gun Works
Clearview Products
Colonial Arms, Inc.
Connecticut Shotgun Mfg. Co.
CRR, Inc./Marble's Inc.
Danuser Machine Co.
Dina Arms Corporation
Gentry Custom LLC
Gruning Precision, Inc.
Harry Lawson LLC
Hastings
Haydel's Game Calls, Inc.
Hogue Grips
Holland's Shooters Supply, Inc.
I.N.C. Inc. (See Kickeez I.N.C., Inc.)
Jackalope Gun Shop
Jenkins Recoil Pads
JP Enterprises, Inc.
KDF, Inc.
Kickeez, I.N.C., Inc.
London Guns Ltd.
Lyman Products Corp.
Mag-Na-Port International, Inc.
Marble Arms (See CRR, Inc./ Marble's Inc.)
Middlebrooks Custom Shop
Mobile Area Networks, Inc.
Morrow, Bud
Nu Line Guns, Inc.
One Of A Kind
P.S.M.G. Gun Co.
Palsa Outdoor Products
Parker & Sons Shooting Supply
Precision Reloading, Inc.
Pro-Port Ltd.
Que Industries, Inc.
RPM
Shotguns Unlimited
Simmons Gun Repair, Inc.
Stan Baker Sports
Stone Enterprises Ltd.
Time Precision
Truglo, Inc.
Trulock Tool
Uncle Mike's (See Michaels of Oregon, Co.)
Universal Sports
Virgin Valley Custom Guns
Williams Gun Sight Co.
Wilsom Combat
Wise Guns, Dale

CHRONOGRAPHS & PRESSURE TOOLS

C.W. Erickson's Mfg., L.L.C.
Clearview Products
Competition Electronics, Inc.
Hege Jagd-u. Sporthandels GmbH
Mac-1 Airgun Distributors
Oehler Research, Inc.
PACT, Inc.
Romain's Custom Guns, Inc.
Savage Arms, Inc.
Stratco, Inc.
Tepeco

CLEANERS & DEGREASERS

A.W. Peterson Gun Shop, Inc., The
Barnes Bullets, Inc.
Camp-Cap Products
G96 Products Co., Inc.
Gun Works, The
Hafner World Wide, Inc.
Half Moon Rifle Shop
Kleen-Bore, Inc.
Modern Muzzleloading, Inc.
Northern Precision
Parker & Sons Shooting Supply
Parker Gun Finishes
PrOlix®lubricants
R&S Industries Corp.
Rusteprufe Laboratories
Sheffield Knifemakers Supply, Inc.
Shooter's Choice Gun Care
Sierra Specialty Prod. Co.
Spencer's Rifle Barrels, Inc.
United States Products Co.

CLEANING & REFINISHING SUPPLIES

A.W. Peterson Gun Shop, Inc., The
AC Dyna-tite Corp.
Alpha 1 Drop Zone
American Gas & Chemical Co., Ltd.
Armite Laboratories Inc.
Atlantic Mills, Inc.
Atsko/Sno-Seal, Inc.
Barnes Bullets, Inc.
Battenfeld Technologies, Inc.
Beeman Precision Airguns
Bill's Gun Repair
Birchwood Casey
Blount, Inc., Sporting Equipment Div.
Blount/Outers ATK
Blue and Gray Products Inc. (See Ox-Yoke Originals)
Break-Free, Inc.
Brownells, Inc.
C.S. Van Gorden & Son, Inc.
Cain's Outdoors, Inc.
Camp-Cap Products
CCI/Speer Div of ATK
Cleland's Outdoor World, Inc.
Connecticut Shotgun Mfg. Co.
Creedmoor Sports, Inc.
CRR, Inc./Marble's Inc.
Custom Products (See Jones Custom Products)
Cylinder & Slide, Inc., William R. Laughridge
Dara-Nes, Inc. (See Nesci Enterprises, Inc.)
Deepeeka Exports Pvt. Ltd.
Dem-Bart Checkering Tools, Inc.
Desert Mountain Mfg.
Du-Lite Corp.
Dykstra, Doug
E&L Mfg., Inc.
Effebi SNC-Dr. Franco Beretta
Faith Associates
Flitz International Ltd.
Fluoramics, Inc.
Frontier Products Co.
G96 Products Co., Inc.
Golden Age Arms Co.
Guardsman Products
Gunsmithing, Inc.
Hafner World Wide, Inc.
Half Moon Rifle Shop
Hammans, Charles E.
Hoppe's Div. Penguin Industries, Inc.
Hornady Mfg. Co.
Hydra-Tone Chemicals, Inc.
Hydrosorbent Dehumidifiers
Iosso Products
J. Dewey Mfg. Co., Inc.
Jantz Supply, Inc.
Jonad Corp.
K&M Industries, Inc.
Kellogg's Professional Products
Kesselring Gun Shop
Kleen-Bore, Inc.
Knight Rifles
Laurel Mountain Forge
Lee Supplies, Mark
Lewis Lead Remover, The (See Brownells, Inc.)
List Precision Engineering
LPS Laboratories, Inc.
Lyman Products Corp.
Mac-1 Airgun Distributors
Marble Arms (See CRR, Inc./ Marble's Inc.)
Mark Lee Supplies
Micro Sight Co.
MTM Molded Products Co., Inc.
Nesci Enterprises Inc.
Northern Precision
October Country Muzzleloading
Otis Technology, Inc.
Outers Laboratories Div. of ATK
Parker & Sons Shooting Supply
Parker Gun Finishes
Paul Co., The
Pete Rickard Co.
Precision Airgun Sales, Inc.
PrOlix®lubricants
Pro-Shot Products, Inc.
R&S Industries Corp.
Radiator Specialty Co.
Richards MicroFit Stocks, Inc.
Rooster Laboratories
Saunders Gun & Machine Shop
Schumakers Gun Shop
Shooter's Choice Gun Care
Shotgun Sports Magazine, dba Shootin' Accessories Ltd.
Silencio/Jackson Products, Inc.
Sinclair International, Inc.
Sno-Seal, Inc. (See Atsko/Sno-Seal, Inc.)
Southern Bloomer Mfg. Co.
Splitfire Sporting Goods, L.L.C.
Stoney Point Products, Inc.
Svon Corp.
T.F.C. S.p.A.
Tennessee Valley Mfg.
Tetra Gun Care
Texas Platers Supply Co.
Tru-Square Metal Products, Inc.
United States Products Co.
Van Gorden & Son Inc., C. S.
Venco Industries, Inc. (See Shooter's Choice Gun Care)
VibraShine, Inc.
Watson Bullets
WD-40 Co.
Wick, David E.
Willow Bend
Young Country Arms

COMPUTER SOFTWARE - BALLISTICS

Action Target, Inc.
AmBr Software Group Ltd.
Arms, Programming Solutions (See Arms Software)
Ballistic Program Co., Inc., The
Barnes Bullets, Inc.
Corbin Mfg. & Supply, Inc.
Country Armourer, The
Data Tech Software Systems
Gun Works, The
Hodgdon Powder Co.
Jensen Bullets
Oehler Research, Inc.
Outdoor Sports Headquarters, Inc.
PACT, Inc.
Pejsa Ballistics
Powley Computer (See Hutton Rifle Ranch)
RCBS Operations/ATK
Sierra Bullets
W. Square Enterprises

CUSTOM GUNSMITH

A&W Repair
A.A. Arms, Inc.
A.W. Peterson Gun Shop, Inc., The
Acadian Ballistic Specialties
Accuracy Unlimited
Acra-Bond Laminates
Actions by "T" Teddy Jacobson
Adair Custom Shop, Bill
Ahlman Guns
Aldis Gunsmithing & Shooting Supply
Alpha Precision, Inc.
Alpine Indoor Shooting Range
Amrine's Gun Shop
Antique Arms Co.
Armament Gunsmithing Co., Inc.
Arms Craft Gunsmithing
Armscorp USA, Inc.
Artistry in Wood
Art's Gun & Sport Shop, Inc.
Baelder, Harry
Bain & Davis, Inc.
Bansner's Ultimate Rifles, LLC
Barnes Bullets, Inc.
Baron Technology
Barrel & Gunworks
Barta's Gunsmithing
Bauska Barrels
Bear Arms
Bear Mountain Gun & Tool
Beitzinger, George
Bengtson Arms Co., L.
Bill Adair Custom Shop
Bill Wiseman and Co.
Billings Gunsmiths
BlackStar AccuMax Barrels
BlackStar Barrel Accurizing (See BlackStar AccuMax)
Bob Rogers Gunsmithing
Bond Custom Firearms
Borden Ridges Rimrock Stocks
Borovnik K.G., Ludwig
Bowen Classic Arms Corp.
Brace, Larry D.
Briese Bullet Co., Inc.
Briganti Custom Gunsmith
Briley Mfg. Inc.
Broad Creek Rifle Works, Ltd.
Brockman's Custom Gunsmithing
Broken Gun Ranch
Brown Precision, Inc.
Buchsenmachermeister
Buckhorn Gun Works
Buehler Custom Sporting Arms
Bull Mountain Rifle Co.
Bullberry Barrel Works, Ltd.
Burkhart Gunsmithing, Don
Campbell, Dick
Carolina Precision Rifles
Carter's Gun Shop
Caywood, Shane J.
CBC-BRAZIL
Chambers Flintlocks Ltd., Jim
Champlin Firearms, Inc.
Chicasaw Gun Works
Chuck's Gun Shop
Clark Custom Guns, Inc.
Clark Firearms Engraving
Classic Arms Company
Classic Arms Corp.
Clearview Products
Cleland's Outdoor World, Inc.
Coffin, Charles H.
Cogar's Gunsmithing
Colonial Arms, Inc.
Colonial Repair
Colorado Gunsmithing Academy
Colorado School of Trades
Colt's Mfg. Co., Inc.
Competitive Pistol Shop, The
Conrad, C. A.
Corkys Gun Clinic
Cullity Restoration
Custom Shop, The
Custom Single Shot Rifles
D&D Gunsmiths, Ltd.
D.L. Unmussig Bullets
Dangler's Custom Flint Rifles
D'Arcy Echols & Co.
Darlington Gun Works, Inc.
Dave's Gun Shop
David Miller Co.
David R. Chicoine
David W. Schwartz Custom Guns
Davis, Don
DBA Werth Services
Delorge, Ed
Del-Sports, Inc.
DGR Custom Rifles
DGS, Inc., Dale A. Storey
Dietz Gun Shop & Range, Inc.
Dilliott Gunsmithing, Inc.
Don Klein Custom Guns
Donnelly, C. P.
Duane A. Hobbie Gunsmithing
Duane's Gun Repair (See DGR Custom Rifles)
Duffy, Charles E. (See Guns Antique & Modern DBA)
Duncan's Gun Works, Inc.
E. Arthur Brown Co. Inc.
Ed Brown Products, Inc.
Ed Brown Products, Inc.
Eggleston, Jere D.
Entreprise Arms, Inc.
Erhardt, Dennis
Eversull Co., Inc.
Evolution Gun Works, Inc.
FERLIB
Ferris Firearms
Fisher, Jerry A.
Fisher Custom Firearms
Fleming Firearms
Flynn's Custom Guns
Forkin Custom Classics
Forster, Kathy (See Custom Checkering)

PRODUCT & SERVICE DIRECTORY

Forster, Larry L.
Forthofer's Gunsmithing & Knifemaking
Frontier Arms Co., Inc.
Fullmer, Geo. M.
Fulton Armory
G.G. & G.
Galaxy Imports Ltd., Inc.
Garthwaite Pistolsmith, Inc., Jim
Gary Reeder Custom Guns
Gator Guns & Repair
Genecco Gun Works
Gene's Custom Guns
Gentry Custom LLC
George Hoenig, Inc.
Gillmann, Edwin
Gilmore Sports Concepts, Inc.
Goens, Dale W.
Goodling's Gunsmithing
Grace, Charles E.
Greg Gunsmithing Repair
Gre-Tan Rifles
Griffin & Howe, Inc.
Griffin & Howe, Inc.
Gruning Precision, Inc.
Gun Doc, Inc.
Gun Shop, The
Gun Works, The
Guncraft Books (See Guncraft Sports, Inc.)
Guncraft Sports, Inc.
Guncraft Sports, Inc.
Guns Antique & Modern DBA / Charles E. Duffy
Gunsite Training Center
Gunsmithing Ltd.
Hamilton, Alex B. (See Ten-Ring Precision, Inc.)
Hammans, Charles E.
Hammerli Service-Precision Mac
Hammond Custom Guns Ltd.
Hank's Gun Shop
Hanson's Gun Center, Dick
Harry Lawson LLC
Hart & Son, Inc.
Hart Rifle Barrels, Inc.
Hartmann & Weiss GmbH
Hawken Shop, The (See Dayton Traister)
Hecht, Hubert J., Waffen-Hecht
Heilmann, Stephen
Heinie Specialty Products
Hensley, Gunmaker, Darwin
High Bridge Arms, Inc.
High Performance International
High Precision
High Standard Mfg. Co./F.I., Inc.
Hill, Loring F.
Hiptmayer, Armurier
Hiptmayer, Klaus
Hoag, James W.
Hodgson, Richard
Hoehn Sales, Inc.
Hofer Jagdwaffen, P.
Holland's Shooters Supply, Inc.
Holland's Shooters Supply, Inc.
Huebner, Corey O.
Imperial Magnum Corp.
Irwin, Campbell H.
Israel Arms Inc.
Ivanoff, Thomas G. (See Tom's Gun Repair)
J R Guns
J&S Heat Treat
J.J. Roberts / Engraver
J.W. Wasmundt-Gunsmith
Jack Dever Co.
Jackalope Gun Shop
James Calhoon Mfg.
Jamison's Forge Works
Jarrett Rifles, Inc.
Jarvis, Inc.
Jay McCament Custom Gunmaker
Jensen's Arizona Sportsman
Jim Norman Custom Gunstocks
Jim's Precision, Jim Ketchum
John Rigby & Co.
John's Custom Leather
Jones Custom Products, Neil A.
Juenke, Vern
K. Eversull Co., Inc.
KDF, Inc.
Keith's Custom Gunstocks
Ken Eyster Heritage Gunsmiths, Inc.
Ken Starnes Gunmaker
Ketchum, Jim (See Jim's Precision)
Kilham & Co.
King's Gun Works
Kleinendorst, K. W.
KOGOT
Korzinek Riflesmith, J.
L. E. Jurras & Assoc.
Lampert, Ron
LaRocca Gun Works
Larry Lyons Gunworks
Laughridge, William R. (See Cylinder & Slide, Inc.)
Lazzeroni Arms Co.
LeFever Arms Co., Inc.
Les Baer Custom, Inc.
Linebaugh Custom Sixguns
List Precision Engineering
Lock's Philadelphia Gun Exchange
Lone Star Rifle Company
Long, George F.
Mag-Na-Port International, Inc.
Mahovsky's Metalife
Makinson, Nicholas
Martini & Hagn, Ltd.
Martin's Gun Shop
Martz, John V.
Mathews Gun Shop & Gunsmithing, Inc.
Mazur Restoration, Pete
McCann, Tom
McCluskey Precision Rifles
McGowen Gunsmithing
McMillan Rifle Barrels
MCS, Inc.
Mercer Custom Guns
Michael's Antiques
Mid-America Recreation, Inc.
Middlebrooks Custom Shop
Miller Arms, Inc.
Miller Custom
Mills Jr., Hugh B.
Moeller, Steve
Monell Custom Guns
Morrison Custom Rifles, J. W.
Morrow, Bud
Mo's Competitor Supplies (See MCS, Inc.)
Mowrey's Guns & Gunsmithing
Mullis Guncraft
Muzzleloaders Etcetera, Inc.
NCP Products, Inc.
Neil A. Jones Custom Products
Nelson's Custom Guns, Inc.
Nettestad Gun Works
New England Arms Co.
New England Custom Gun Service
Newman Gunshop
Nicholson Custom
Nickels, Paul R.
North American Shooting Systems
Nowlin Guns, Inc.
Nu Line Guns, Inc.
October Country Muzzleloading
Olson, Vic
Orvis Co., The
Ottmar, Maurice
Ozark Gun Works
P&M Sales & Services, LLC
P.S.M.G. Gun Co.
PAC-NOR Barreling, Inc.
Pagel Gun Works, Inc.
Parker & Sons Shooting Supply
Parker Gun Finishes
Pasadena Gun Center
Paterson Gunsmithing
Paul and Sharon Dressel
Paulsen Gunstocks
Peacemaker Specialists
Pence Precision Barrels
Pennsylvania Gunsmith School
Penrod Precision
Pentheny de Pentheny
Perazone-Gunsmith, Brian
Performance Specialists
Pete Mazur Restoration
Peterson Gun Shop, Inc., A.W.
Piquette's Custom Engraving
Plum City Ballistic Range
Powell & Son (Gunmakers) Ltd., William
Power Custom, Inc.
Professional Hunter Supplies
Quality Custom Firearms
R&J Gun Shop
R.A. Wells Custom Gunsmith
Ray's Gunsmith Shop
Renfrew Guns & Supplies
Ridgetop Sporting Goods
Ries, Chuck
RMS Custom Gunsmithing
Robar Co., Inc., The
Robert Valade Engraving
Robinson, Don
Romain's Custom Guns, Inc.
Ron Frank Custom
Royal Arms Gunstocks
Ruger's Custom Guns
Rupert's Gun Shop
Savage Arms, Inc.
Schiffman, Mike
Schumakers Gun Shop
Score High Gunsmithing
Sharp Shooter Supply
Shaw, Inc., E. R. (See Small Arms Mfg. Co.)
Shay's Gunsmithing
Shooters Supply
Shootin' Shack
Shotguns Unlimited
Sig Sauer, Inc.
Silver Ridge Gun Shop (See Goodwin Guns)
Simmons Gun Repair, Inc.
Singletary, Kent
Siskiyou Gun Works (See Donnelly, C. P.)
Skeoch, Brian R.
Sklany's Machine Shop
Small Arms Mfg. Co.
Smith, Art
Snapp's Gunshop
Speiser, Fred D.
Spencer Reblue Service
Spencer's Rifle Barrels, Inc.
Splitfire Sporting Goods, L.L.C.
Sportsmen's Exchange & Western Gun Traders, Inc.
Spradlin's
Springfield Armory
Springfield, Inc.
SSK Industries
Star Custom Bullets
State Line Gun Shop
Steelman's Gun Shop
Steffens, Ron
Steven Dodd Hughes
Stiles Custom Guns
Stott's Creek Armory, Inc.
Sturgeon Valley Sporters
Sullivan, David S. (See Westwind Rifles, Inc.)
Swampfire Shop, The (See Peterson Gun Shop, Inc., A.W.)
Swann, D. J.
Swenson's 45 Shop, A. D.
Swift River Gunworks
Szweda, Robert (See RMS Custom Gunsmithing)
Taconic Firearms Ltd., Perry Lane
Tank's Rifle Shop
Tar-Hunt Custom Rifles, Inc.
Tarnhelm Supply Co., Inc.
Taylor & Robbins
Tennessee Valley Mfg.
Ten-Ring Precision, Inc.
Terry K. Kopp Professional Gunsmithing
Terry Theis-Engraver
Time Precision
Tom's Gun Repair, Thomas G. Ivanoff
Tom's Gunshop
Trevallion Gunstocks
Trulock Tool
Tucker, James C.
Turnbull Restoration, Doug
Upper Missouri Trading Co.
Van Horn, Gil
Van Patten, J. W.
Vest, John
Virgin Valley Custom Guns
Wardell Precision
Weatherby, Inc.
Weber & Markin Custom Gunsmiths
Wells Sport Store
Wells Sport Store
Wessinger Custom Guns & Engraving
Westley Richards & Co. Ltd.
Westwind Rifles, Inc., David S. Sullivan
White Barn Wor
Wichita Arms, Inc.
Wiebe, Duane
Wild West Guns
William E. Phillips Firearms
Williams Gun Sight Co.
Williams Shootin' Iron Service, The Lynx-Line
Williamson Precision Gunsmithing
Wilsom Combat
Winter, Robert M.
Wise Guns, Dale
Wright's Gunstock Blanks
Zeeryp, Russ

CUSTOM METALSMITH

A&W Repair
A.W. Peterson Gun Shop, Inc., The
Ackerman & Co.
Ahlman Guns
Alaskan Silversmith, The
Aldis Gunsmithing & Shooting Supply
Alpha Precision, Inc.
Amrine's Gun Shop
Antique Arms Co.
Artistry in Wood
Baron Technology
Barrel & Gunworks
Bauska Barrels
Bear Mountain Gun & Tool
Beitzinger, George
Bengtson Arms Co., L.
Bill Adair Custom Shop
Billings Gunsmiths
Billingsley & Brownell
Bob Rogers Gunsmithing
Bowen Classic Arms Corp.
Brace, Larry D.
Briganti Custom Gunsmith
Broad Creek Rifle Works, Ltd.
Brown Precision, Inc.
Buckhorn Gun Works
Buehler Custom Sporting Arms
Bull Mountain Rifle Co.
Bullberry Barrel Works, Ltd.
Campbell, Dick
Carter's Gun Shop
Caywood, Shane J.
Checkmate Refinishing
Colonial Repair
Colorado Gunsmithing Academy
Craftguard
Crandall Tool & Machine Co.
Cullity Restoration
Custom Shop, The
Custom Single Shot Rifles
D&D Gunsmiths, Ltd.
D'Arcy Echols & Co.
Dave's Gun Shop
DBA Werth Services
Delorge, Ed
DGS, Inc., Dale A. Storey
Dietz Gun Shop & Range, Inc.
Dilliott Gunsmithing, Inc.
Don Klein Custom Guns
Duane's Gun Repair (See DGR Custom Rifles)
Erhardt, Dennis
Eversull Co., Inc.
Ferris Firearms
Fisher, Jerry A.
Forster, Larry L.
Forthofer's Gunsmithing & Knifemaking
Fullmer, Geo. M.
Genecco Gun Works
Gentry Custom LLC
Grace, Charles E.
Gun Shop, The
Gunsmithing Ltd.
Hamilton, Alex B. (See Ten-Ring Precision, Inc.)
Harry Lawson LLC
Hartmann & Weiss GmbH
Hecht, Hubert J., Waffen-Hecht
Heilmann, Stephen
High Precision
Hiptmayer, Armurier
Hiptmayer, Klaus
Hoag, James W.
Holland's Shooters Supply, Inc.
Holland's Shooters Supply, Inc.
Ivanoff, Thomas G. (See Tom's Gun Repair)
J J Roberts Firearm Engraver
J&S Heat Treat
J.J. Roberts / Engraver
Jackalope Gun Shop
Jamison's Forge Works
Jay McCament Custom Gunmaker
KDF, Inc.
Ken Eyster Heritage Gunsmiths, Inc.
Ken Starnes Gunmaker
Kilham & Co.
Kleinendorst, K. W.
Lampert, Ron
LaRocca Gun Works
Larry Lyons Gunworks
Les Baer Custom, Inc.
List Precision Engineering
Lock's Philadelphia Gun Exchange
Mahovsky's Metalife
Makinson, Nicholas
Martini & Hagn, Ltd.
Mazur Restoration, Pete
McFarland, Stan
Mid-America Recreation, Inc.
Miller Arms, Inc.
Morrison Custom Rifles, J. W.
Morrow, Bud
Mullis Guncraft
Nelson's Custom Guns, Inc.
Nettestad Gun Works
New England Custom Gun Service
Nicholson Custom

DECOYS

DIE ACCESSORIES, METALLIC

DIES, METALLIC

DIES, SHOTSHELL

ENGRAVER, ENGRAVING TOOLS

GAME CALLS

GAUGES, CALIPERS & MICROMETERS

GUN PARTS, U.S. & FOREIGN

PRODUCT & SERVICE DIRECTORY

List Precision Engineering
Lodewick, Walter H.
Logdewood Mfg.
Lomont Precision Bullets
Long, George F.
Markell, Inc.
Martin's Gun Shop
Mid-America Recreation, Inc.
Mobile Area Networks, Inc.
Morrow, Bud
Mo's Competitor Supplies (See MCS, Inc.)
North Star West, Inc.
Nu Line Guns, Inc.
Numrich Gun Parts Corporation
Olathe Gun Shop
Olympic Arms Inc.
P.S.M.G. Gun Co.
Pacific Armament Corp
Peacemaker Specialists
Perazone-Gunsmith, Brian
Performance Specialists
Peter Dyson & Son Ltd.
Peterson Gun Shop, Inc., A.W.
Ranch Products
Randco UK
Ravell Ltd.
Retting, Inc., Martin B.
Romain's Custom Guns, Inc.
Ruger (See Sturm Ruger & Co., Inc.)
Rutgers Book Center
S&S Firearms
Sabatti SPA
Samco Global Arms, Inc.
Sarco, Inc.
Scherer Supplies, Inc.
Shootin' Shack
Silver Ridge Gun Shop (See Goodwin Guns)
Simmons Gun Repair, Inc.
Smires, C. L.
Smith & Wesson
Southern Ammunition Co., Inc.
Southern Armory, The
Sportsmen's Exchange & Western Gun Traders, Inc.
Springfield Sporters, Inc.
Springfield, Inc.
Steyr Mannlicher GmbH & Co. KG
STI International
Strayer-Voigt, Inc.
Sturm Ruger & Co. Inc.
Sunny Hill Enterprises, Inc.
Swampfire Shop, The (See Peterson Gun Shop, Inc., A.W.)
T&S Industries, Inc.
Tank's Rifle Shop
Tar-Hunt Custom Rifles, Inc.
Tarnhelm Supply Co., Inc.
Taylor's & Co., Inc.
Terry K. Kopp Professional Gunsmithing
Tom Forrest, Inc.
VAM Distribution Co. LLC
W. Waller & Son, Inc.
W.C. Wolff Co.
Wescombe, Bill (See North Star West)
Wild West Guns
Williams Mfg. of Oregon
Wilson Combat
Winchester Sutler, Inc., The
Wise Guns, Dale
Wisners, Inc.

GUNS & GUN PARTS, REPLICA & ANTIQUE

A.W. Peterson Gun Shop, Inc., The
Ackerman & Co.
Ahlman Guns
Armi San Paolo
Auto-Ordnance Corp.
Ballard Rifle & Cartridge Co., LLC
Bear Mountain Gun & Tool
Billings Gunsmiths
Bob's Gun Shop
Buffalo Arms Co.
Cash Mfg. Co./ TDC
CBC-BRAZIL
CCL Security Products
Chambers Flintlocks Ltd., Jim
Chicasaw Gun Works
Cimarron F.A. Co.
Cogar's Gunsmithing
Colonial Repair
Colt Blackpowder Arms Co.
Colt's Mfg. Co., Inc.
Custom Single Shot Rifles
Delhi Gun House
Delta Arms Ltd.
Dilliott Gunsmithing, Inc.
Dixie Gun Works
Dixon Muzzleloading Shop, Inc.
Duncan's Gun Works, Inc.
Ed's Gun House
Euroarms of America, Inc.
Flintlocks, Etc.
Getz Barrel Company
Golden Age Arms Co.
Gun Doc, Inc.
Gun Hunter Books (See Gun Hunter Trading Co.)
Gun Hunter Trading Co.
Gun Room Press, The
Gun Works, The
Hastings
Heidenstrom Bullets
IAR Inc.
Imperial Miniature Armory
Ithaca Classic Doubles
Jack First, Inc.
JG Airguns, LLC
Ken Starnes Gunmaker
L&R Lock Co.
List Precision Engineering
Lock's Philadelphia Gun Exchange
Log Cabin Sport Shop
Logdewood Mfg.
Lone Star Rifle Company
Martin's Gun Shop
Mathews Gun Shop & Gunsmithing, Inc.
McCann Industries
Mid-America Recreation, Inc.
Mowrey Gun Works
Navy Arms Company
North Star West, Inc.
Nu Line Guns, Inc.
Numrich Gun Parts Corporation
Olathe Gun Shop
Parker & Sons Shooting Supply
Pasadena Gun Center
Peacemaker Specialists
Peter Dyson & Son Ltd.
Pony Express Sport Shop
R.A. Wells Custom Gunsmith
Randco UK
Ravell Ltd.
Retting, Inc., Martin B.
Rutgers Book Center
S&S Firearms
Samco Global Arms, Inc.
Sarco, Inc.
Shootin' Shack
Silver Ridge Gun Shop (See Goodwin Guns)
Simmons Gun Repair, Inc.
Sklany's Machine Shop
Southern Ammunition Co., Inc.
Starr Trading Co., Jedediah
Stott's Creek Armory, Inc.
Taylor's & Co., Inc.
Tennessee Valley Mfg.
Tristar Sporting Arms, Ltd.
Turnbull Restoration, Doug
Upper Missouri Trading Co.
VTI Gun Parts
Weber & Markin Custom Gunsmiths
Wescombe, Bill (See North Star West)
Whitestone Lumber Corp.
Winchester Sutler, Inc., The

GUNS, AIR

A.W. Peterson Gun Shop, Inc., The
Air Arms
Air Venture Airguns
AirForce Airguns
Airrow
Allred Bullet Co.
Arms Corporation of the Philippines
BEC, Inc.
Beeman Precision Airguns
Benjamin/Sheridan Co., Crosman
Bryan & Assoc.
BSA Guns Ltd.
Compasseco, Ltd.
Component Concepts, Inc.
Crosman Airguns
Daisy Outdoor Products
Daystate Ltd.
Domino
Effebi SNC-Dr. Franco Beretta
European American Armory Corp. (See E.A.A. Corp.)
Feinwerkbau Westinger & Altenburger
Gamo USA, Inc.
Gun Room Press, The
Hammerli Service-Precision Mac
IAR Inc.
International Shooters Service
J.G. Anschutz GmbH & Co. KG
JG Airguns, LLC
Labanu Inc.
Leapers, Inc.
List Precision Engineering
Mac-1 Airgun Distributors
Marksman Products
Maryland Paintball Supply
Nationwide Airgun Repair
Olympic Arms Inc.
Pardini Armi Srl
Park Rifle Co., Ltd., The
Precision Airgun Sales, Inc.
Ripley Rifles
Robinson, Don
RWS (See U.S. Importer-Umarex-USA)
Safari Arms/Schuetzen Pistol Works
Savage Arms, Inc.
Sig Sauer, Inc.
Smith & Wesson
Steyr Mannlicher GmbH & Co. KG
Stone Enterprises Ltd.
Tippman Sports, LLC
Tristar Sporting Arms, Ltd.
Trooper Walsh
Umarex USA
Walther GmbH, Carl
Webley Limited
Weihrauch KG, Hermann

GUNS, FOREIGN MANUFACTURER U.S. IMPORTER

A.W. Peterson Gun Shop, Inc., The
Accuracy International Precision Rifles (See U.S.)
Accuracy Int'l. North America, Inc.
Ad Hominem
Air Arms
Armas Garbi, S.A.
Armas Kemen S. A. (See U.S. Importers)
Armi Perazzi S.P.A.
Armi San Marco (See Taylor's & Co.)
Armi Sport (See Cimarron Firearms, E.M.F., KBI & Taylor's & Co.)
Arms Corporation of the Philippines
Armscorp USA, Inc.
Arrieta S.L.
Astra Sport, S.A.
Atamec-Bretton
AYA (See U.S. Importer-New England Custom Gun Serv
B.A.C.
B.C. Outdoors
BEC, Inc.
Benelli Armi S.P.A.
Benelli USA Corp.
Beretta Pietro S.P.A.
Beretta U.S.A. Corp.
Bernardelli, Vincenzo
Bersa S.A.
Bertuzzi (See U.S. Importer-New England Arms Co.)
Bill Hanus Birdguns, LLC
Blaser Jagdwaffen GmbH
Borovnik K.G., Ludwig
Bosis (See U.S. Importer-New England Arms Co.)
Brenneke GmbH
Browning Arms Co.
Bryan & Assoc.
BSA Guns Ltd.
Buchsenmachermeister
Cabanas (See U.S. Importer-Mandall Shooting Supply
Cabela's
Cape Outfitters
CBC
Century International Arms, Inc.
Champlin Firearms, Inc.
Chapuis Armes
Churchill (See U.S. Importer-Ellett Bros.)
Collector's Armoury, Ltd.
Cosmi Americo & Figlio S.N.C.
Crucelegui, Hermanos (See U.S. Importer-Mandall)
Dakota (See U.S. Importer-EMF Co., Inc.)
Dakota Arms, Inc.
Daly, Charles/KBI
Davide Pedersoli and Co.
Domino
Dumoulin, Ernest
Eagle Imports, Inc.
EAW (See U.S. Importer-New England Custom Gun Serv
Ed's Gun House
Effebi SNC-Dr. Franco Beretta
EMF Co. Inc.
Euro-Imports
Eversull Co., Inc.
F.A.I.R., S.R.L.
Fabarm S.p.A.
FEG
Feinwerkbau Westinger & Altenburger
FERLIB
Fiocchi Munizioni S.A. (See U.S. Importer-Fiocch
Firearms Co. Ltd. / Alpine (See U.S. Importer-Mandall
Flintlocks, Etc.
Galaxy Imports Ltd., Inc.
Gamba Renato Bremec Srl
Gamo (See U.S. Importers-Arms United Corp., Daisy M
Gibbs Rifle Co., Inc.
Glock GmbH
Goergen's Gun Shop, Inc.
Griffin & Howe, Inc.
Griffin & Howe, Inc.
Grulla Armes
Hammerli AG
Hammerli USA
Hartford (See U.S. Importer-EMF Co. Inc.)
Hartmann & Weiss GmbH
Heckler & Koch, Inc.
Hege Jagd-u. Sporthandels GmbH
Helwan (See U.S. Importer-Interarms)
Hofer Jagdwaffen, P.
Holland & Holland Ltd.
Howa Machinery, Ltd.
I.A.B. (See U.S. Importer-Taylor's & Co., Inc.)
IAR Inc.
IGA (See U.S. Importer-Stoeger Industries)
Imperial Magnum Corp.
Imperial Miniature Armory
Inter Ordnance of America LP
International Shooters Service
Intrac Arms International
J.G. Anschutz GmbH & Co. KG
JSL Ltd. (See U.S. Importer-Specialty Shooters Supply)
K. Eversull Co., Inc.
Kimar (See U.S. Importer-IAR, Inc.)
Korth Germany GmbH
Krico Deutschland GmbH
Krieghoff Gun Co., H.
Lakefield Arms Ltd. (See Savage Arms, Inc.)
Laurona Armas Eibar, S.A.L.
Lebeau-Courally
Lever Arms Service Ltd.
Lomont Precision Bullets
London Guns Ltd.
Marocchi F.lli S.p.A
Mauser Werke Oberndorf Waffensysteme GmbH
McCann Industries
MEC-Gar S.R.L.
Merkel
Mitchell's Mauser
Morini (See U.S. Importers-Mandall Shooting Supplies, Inc.)
Nammo Lapua Oy
New England Custom Gun Service
New SKB Arms Co.
Norica, Avnda Otaola
Norinco
Norma Precision AB (See U.S. Importers-Dynamit)
OK Weber, Inc.
Para-Ordnance Mfg., Inc.
Pardini Armi Srl
Perugini Visini & Co. SAS
Peters Stahl GmbH
Pietta (See U.S. Importers-Navy Arms Co, Taylor's
Piotti (See U.S. Importer-Moore & Co., Wm. Larkin)
PMC Ammunition
Powell & Son (Gunmakers) Ltd., William
Prairie Gun Works
Rizzini F.lli (See U.S. Importers-Wm. Larkin Moore & Co., N.E. Arms Corp.)
Rizzini SNC
Robinson Armament Co.
Rossi Firearms
Rottweil Compe
Rutten (See U.S. Importer-Labanu Inc.)
RWS (See U.S. Importer-Umarex-USA)

PRODUCT & SERVICE DIRECTORY

S.A.R.L. G. Granger
S.I.A.C.E. (See U.S. Importer-IAR Inc.)
Sabatti SPA
Sako Ltd. (See U.S. Importer-Stoeger Industries)
San Marco (See U.S. Importers-Cape Outfitters-EMF Co., Inc.
Sarsilmaz Shotguns-Turkey (see B.C. Outdoors)
Sauer (See U.S. Importers-Paul Co., The Sigarms Inc.)
Savage Arms (Canada), Inc.
SGS Importer's International, Inc.
SIG
SIG-Sauer (See U.S. Importer-Sigarms, Inc.)
SKB Shotguns
Societa Armi Bresciane Srl (See U.S. Importer-Jeff's Outfitters)
Sphinx Systems Ltd.
Springfield Armory
Springfield, Inc.
State Line Gun Shop
Steyr Mannlicher GmbH & Co. KG
T.F.C. S.p.A.
Tanfoglio Fratelli S.r.l.
Tanner (See U.S. Importer-Mandall Shooting Supplies, Inc.)
Taurus International Firearms (See U.S. Importer Taurus Firearms, Inc.)
Taurus S.A. Forjas
Techno Arms (See U.S. Importer- Auto-Ordnance Corp.)
Tikka (See U.S. Importer-Stoeger Industries)
TOZ (See U.S. Importer-Nygord Precision Products, Inc.)
Ugartechea S. A., Ignacio
Ultralux (See U.S. Importer-Keng's Firearms Specialty, Inc.)
Valtro USA, Inc.
Verney-Carron
Voere-KGH GmbH
Walther GmbH, Carl
Webley Limited
Weihrauch KG, Hermann
Westley Richards & Co. Ltd.
Yankee Gunsmith "Just Glocks"
Zabala Hermanos S.A.

GUNS, FOREIGN-IMPORTER

A.W. Peterson Gun Shop, Inc., The
Accuracy International
AcuSport Corporation
Armscor Precision
Auto-Ordnance Corp.
B.A.C.
B.C. Outdoors
Bell's Legendary Country Wear
Benelli USA Corp.
Bill Hanus Birdguns, LLC
Bridgeman Products
British Sporting Arms
Browning Arms Co.
Caesar Guerini USA, Inc.
Cape Outfitters
Century International Arms, Inc.
Champion Shooters' Supply
Champion's Choice, Inc.
Cimarron F.A. Co.
CVA
CZ USA
Daly, Charles/KBI
Dixie Gun Works
E&L Mfg., Inc.
E.A.A. Corp.
Eagle Imports, Inc.
Ellett Bros.
EMF Co. Inc.
Euroarms of America, Inc.
Eversull Co., Inc.
Fiocchi of America, Inc.
Flintlocks, Etc.
Franzen International, Inc. (See U.S. Importer-Importer Co.)
G.U., Inc. (See U.S. Importer-New SKB Arms Co.)
Galaxy Imports Ltd., Inc.
Gamo USA, Inc.
Giacomo Sporting USA
Glock, Inc.
GSI, Inc.
Gun Shop, The
Guncraft Books (See Guncraft Sports, Inc.)
Guncraft Sports, Inc.
Gunsite Training Center
Hammerli USA
IAR Inc.
Imperial Magnum Corp.
Imperial Miniature Armory
Intrac Arms International
K. Eversull Co., Inc.
K.B.I. Inc.
Keng's Firearms Specialty, Inc.
Krieghoff International, Inc.
Labanu Inc.
Legacy Sports International
Lion Country Supply
London Guns Ltd.
Magnum Research, Inc.
Marlin Firearms Co.
Marx, Harry (See U.S. Importer for FERLIB)
MEC-Gar U.S.A., Inc.
Mitchell Mfg. Corp.
Navy Arms Company
New England Arms Co.
OK Weber, Inc.
Orvis Co., The
P.S.M.G. Gun Co.
Para-Ordnance, Inc.
Paul Co., The
Perazone-Gunsmith, Brian
Perazzi U.S.A. Inc.
Powell Agency, William
Quality Arms, Inc.
Rocky Mountain Armoury
S.D. Meacham
Safari Arms/Schuetzen Pistol Works
Samco Global Arms, Inc.
Savage Arms, Inc.
Scott Fine Guns Inc., Thad
SGS Importer's International, Inc.
SKB Shotguns
Southern Ammunition Co., Inc.
Specialty Shooters Supply, Inc.
Springfield, Inc.
State Line Gun Shop
Stoeger Industries
Stone Enterprises Ltd.
Swarovski Optik North America Ltd.
Taurus Firearms, Inc.
Taylor's & Co., Inc.
Track of the Wolf, Inc.
Traditions Performance Firearms
Tristar Sporting Arms, Ltd.
Trooper Walsh
U.S. Importer-Wm. Larkin Moore
Umarex USA
VAM Distribution Co. LLC
Vector Arms, Inc.
VTI Gun Parts
Westley Richards Agency USA (See U.S. Importer
Yankee Gunsmith "Just Glocks"

GUNS, SURPLUS, PARTS & AMMUNITION

A.W. Peterson Gun Shop, Inc., The
Ahlman Guns
Alpha 1 Drop Zone
Armscorp USA, Inc.
B.A.C.
Bob's Gun Shop
Century International Arms, Inc.
Delta Arms Ltd.
Duncan's Gun Works, Inc.
Ed's Gun House
Firearm Brokers
Fleming Firearms
Fulton Armory
Gun City
Gun Hunter Books (See Gun Hunter Trading Co.)
Gun Hunter Trading Co.
Gun Room Press, The
Hank's Gun Shop
Hege Jagd-u. Sporthandels GmbH
Ken Starnes Gunmaker
LaRocca Gun Works
Lever Arms Service Ltd.
Martin B. Retting Inc.
Martin's Gun Shop
National Gun, Inc.
Navy Arms Company
Numrich Gun Parts Corporation
Oil Rod and Gun Shop
Olathe Gun Shop
Paragon Sales & Services, Inc.
Pasadena Gun Center
Power Plus Enterprises, Inc.
Ravell Ltd.
Retting, Inc., Martin B.
Rutgers Book Center
Samco Global Arms, Inc.
Sarco, Inc.
Shootin' Shack
Silver Ridge Gun Shop (See Goodwin Guns)
Simmons Gun Repair, Inc.
Sportsmen's Exchange & Western Gun Traders, Inc.
Springfield Sporters, Inc.
T.F.C. S.p.A.
Tarnhelm Supply Co., Inc.
Taylor's & Co., Inc.
Whitestone Lumber Corp.
Williams Shootin' Iron Service, The Lynx-Line

GUNS, U.S. MADE

3-Ten Corp.
A.A. Arms, Inc.
A.W. Peterson Gun Shop, Inc., The
Accu-Tek
Acra-Bond Laminates
Ad Hominem
Airrow
Allred Bullet Co.
American Derringer Corp.
AR-7 Industries, LLC
ArmaLite, Inc.
Armscorp USA, Inc.
Arsenal, Inc.
A-Square Co.
Austin & Halleck, Inc.
Auto-Ordnance Corp.
Ballard Rifle & Cartridge Co., LLC
Barrett Firearms Manufacturer, Inc.
Bar-Sto Precision Machine
Benjamin/Sheridan Co., Crosman
Beretta Pietro S.P.A.
Beretta U.S.A. Corp.
Bill Hanus Birdguns, LLC
Bill Russ Trading Post
Bond Arms, Inc.
Borden Ridges Rimrock Stocks
Borden Rifles Inc.
Brockman's Custom Gunsmithing
Browning Arms Co.
Bryan & Assoc.
Bushmaster Firearms, Inc.
C. Sharps Arms Co. Inc./ Montana Armory
Cabela's
Cape Outfitters
Casull Arms Corp.
CCL Security Products
Century International Arms, Inc.
Champlin Firearms, Inc.
Charter 2000
Cleland's Outdoor World, Inc.
Cobra Enterprises, Inc.
Colt's Mfg. Co., Inc.
Competitor Corp., Inc.
Competitor Corp., Inc.
Conetrol Scope Mounts
Connecticut Shotgun Mfg. Co.
Connecticut Valley Classics (See CVC, BPI)
Cooper Arms
Crosman Airguns
CVA
CZ USA
Dakota Arms, Inc.
Dan Wesson Firearms
Dayton Traister
Detonics USA
Dixie Gun Works
Downsizer Corp.
DS Arms, Inc.
DunLyon R&D, Inc.
E&L Mfg., Inc.
E. Arthur Brown Co. Inc.
Eagle Arms, Inc. (See ArmaLite, Inc.)
Ed Brown Products, Inc.
Ed Brown Products, Inc.
Ellett Bros.
Emerging Technologies, Inc. (See Laseraim Technologies, Inc.)
Empire Rifles
Entreprise Arms, Inc.
Essex Arms
Excel Industries, Inc.
Firearm Brokers
Fletcher-Bidwell, LLC
FN Manufacturing
Freedom Arms, Inc.
Fulton Armory
Galena Industries AMT
Gary Reeder Custom Guns
Genecco Gun Works
Gentry Custom LLC
George Hoenig, Inc.
Gibbs Rifle Co., Inc.
Gil Hebard Guns, Inc.
Gilbert Equipment Co., Inc.
Goergen's Gun Shop, Inc.
Granite Mountain Arms, Inc.
Gun Room Press, The
Gun Works, The
Guncrafter Industries
H&R 1871, LLC
Hammans, Charles E.
Hammerli USA
Harrington & Richardson (See H&R 1871, Inc.)
Hart & Son, Inc.
Hatfield Gun
Hawken Shop, The (See Dayton Traister)
Heritage Firearms (See Heritage Mfg., Inc.)
Heritage Manufacturing, Inc.
High Precision
High Standard Mfg. Co./F.I., Inc.
Hi-Point Firearms/MKS Supply
HJS Arms, Inc.
Hoehn Sales, Inc.
H-S Precision, Inc.
IAR Inc.
Imperial Miniature Armory
Israel Arms Inc.
Ithaca Classic Doubles
Ithaca Guns, LLC
J R Guns
Jim Norman Custom Gunstocks
John Rigby & Co.
John's Custom Leather
JP Enterprises, Inc.
K.B.I. Inc.
Kahr Arms
Kehr, Roger
Kelbly, Inc.
Kel-Tec CNC Industries, Inc.
Keystone Sporting Arms, Inc. (Crickett Rifles)
Kimber of America, Inc.
Knight Rifles
Knight's Manufacturing Co.
Kolar
L.A.R. Mfg., Inc.
Lakefield Arms Ltd. (See Savage Arms, Inc.)
Laseraim Technologies, Inc.
Les Baer Custom, Inc.
Lever Arms Service Ltd.
Ljutic Industries, Inc.
Lock's Philadelphia Gun Exchange
Lomont Precision Bullets
Lone Star Rifle Company
Madis Books
Mag-Na-Port International, Inc.
Magnum Research, Inc.
Marlin Firearms Co.
Mathews Gun Shop & Gunsmithing, Inc.
Maverick Arms, Inc.
McCann Industries
Meacham Tool & Hardware Co., Inc.
Mid-America Recreation, Inc.
Miller Arms, Inc.
MKS Supply, Inc. (See Hi-Point Firearms)
MOA Corporation
Montana Armory, Inc.
MPI Stocks
National Gun, Inc.
Navy Arms Company
NCP Products, Inc.
New Ultra Light Arms, LLC
Noreen, Peter H.
North American Arms, Inc.
North Star West, Inc.
Nowlin Guns, Inc.
Olympic Arms Inc.
Oregon Arms, Inc. (See Rogue Rifle Co., Inc.)
P&M Sales & Services, LLC
Parker & Sons Shooting Supply
Parker Gun Finishes
Phoenix Arms
Police Bookshelf
Precision Small Arms Inc.
Rapine Bullet Mould Mfg. Co.
Remington Arms Co., Inc.
Rifles, Inc.
Robinson Armament Co.
Rock River Arms
Rogue Rifle Co., Inc./Chipmunk Rifles
Rogue River Rifleworks
Rohrbaugh

PRODUCT & SERVICE DIRECTORY

Romain's Custom Guns, Inc.
RPM
Ruger (See Sturm Ruger & Co., Inc.)
Safari Arms/Schuetzen Pistol Works
Savage Arms (Canada), Inc.
Schumakers Gun Shop
Searcy Enterprises
Sharps Arms Co., Inc., C.
Sig Sauer, Inc.
Sklany's Machine Shop
Smith & Wesson
Sound Tech
Spencer's Rifle Barrels, Inc.
Springfield Armory
Springfield, Inc.
SSK Industries
State Line Gun Shop
STI International
Stoeger Industries
Strayer-Voigt, Inc.
Sturm Ruger & Co. Inc.
Sunny Hill Enterprises, Inc.
T&S Industries, Inc.
Taconic Firearms Ltd., Perry Lane
Tank's Rifle Shop
Tar-Hunt Custom Rifles, Inc.
Taurus Firearms, Inc.
Taylor's & Co., Inc.
Texas Armory (See Bond Arms, Inc.)
Thompson/Center Arms
Tippman Sports, LLC
Tristar Sporting Arms, Ltd.
U.S. Repeating Arms Co., Inc.
Uselton/Arms, Inc.
Vector Arms, Inc.
Volquartsen Custom Ltd.
Weatherby, Inc.
Wescombe, Bill (See North Star West)
Wessinger Custom Guns & Engraving
Whitestone Lumber Corp.
Wichita Arms, Inc.
Wildey F. A., Inc.
Wilsom Combat
Z-M Weapons

GUNSMITH SCHOOL

American Gunsmithing Institute
Colorado Gunsmithing Academy
Colorado School of Trades
Cylinder & Slide, Inc., William R. Laughridge
Gun Doc, Inc.
Lassen Community College, Gunsmithing Dept.
Laughridge, William R. (See Cylinder & Slide, Inc.)
Modern Gun Repair School
Murray State College
North American Correspondence Schools, The Gun Pro
Nowlin Guns, Inc.
NRI Gunsmith School
Pennsylvania Gunsmith School
Piedmont Community College
Pine Technical College
Professional Gunsmiths of America
Smith & Wesson
Southeastern Community College
Spencer's Rifle Barrels, Inc.
Trinidad St. Jr. Col. Gunsmith Dept.
Wright's Gunstock Blanks
Yavapai College

GUNSMITH SUPPLIES, TOOLS & SERVICES

A.W. Peterson Gun Shop, Inc., The
Alaskan Silversmith, The
Aldis Gunsmithing & Shooting Supply
Alley Supply Co.
Allred Bullet Co.
Alpec Team, Inc.
American Gunsmithing Institute
Ballard Rifle & Cartridge Co., LLC
Bar-Sto Precision Machine
Battenfeld Technologies, Inc.
Bauska Barrels
Bear Mountain Gun & Tool
Bengtson Arms Co., L.
Bill's Gun Repair
Blue Ridge Machinery & Tools, Inc.
Boyds' Gunstock Industries, Inc.
Briley Mfg. Inc.
Brockman's Custom Gunsmithing
Brownells, Inc.
Bryan & Assoc.
B-Square Company, Inc.
Buffer Technologies
Bushmaster Firearms, Inc.
C.S. Van Gorden & Son, Inc.
Cain's Outdoors, Inc.
Carbide Checkering Tools (See J&R Engineering)
Caywood, Shane J.
CBC-BRAZIL
Chapman Manufacturing Co.
Chicasaw Gun Works
Chip McCormick Corp.
Choate Machine & Tool Co., Inc.
Colonial Arms, Inc.
Colorado School of Trades
Colt's Mfg. Co., Inc.
Conetrol Scope Mounts
Cousin Bob's Mountain Products
CRR, Inc./Marble's Inc.
Custom Checkering Service, Kathy Forster
Dan's Whetstone Co., Inc.
D'Arcy Echols & Co.
Dem-Bart Checkering Tools, Inc.
Dem-Bart Checkering Tools, Inc.
Dixie Gun Works
Dixie Gun Works
Dremel Mfg. Co.
Du-Lite Corp.
Ed Brown Products, Inc.
Entreprise Arms, Inc.
Evolution Gun Works, Inc.
Faith Associates
FERLIB
Fisher, Jerry A.
Forgreens Tool & Mfg., Inc.
Forster, Kathy (See Custom Checkering)
Forster Products, Inc.
Gentry Custom LLC
Gilmore Sports Concepts, Inc.
Grace Metal Products
Gre-Tan Rifles
Gruning Precision, Inc.
Gun Works, The
Gunline Tools
Half Moon Rifle Shop
Hammond Custom Guns Ltd.
Hastings
Henriksen Tool Co., Inc.
High Performance International
High Precision
Holland's Shooters Supply, Inc.
Ironsighter Co.
Israel Arms Inc.
Ivanoff, Thomas G. (See Tom's Gun Repair)
J&R Engineering
J&S Heat Treat
J. Dewey Mfg. Co., Inc.
Jack First, Inc.
Jantz Supply, Inc.
Jenkins Recoil Pads
JGS Precision Tool Mfg., LLC
Jonathan Arthur Ciener, Inc.
Jones Custom Products, Neil A.
Kailua Custom Guns Inc.
Kasenit Co., Inc.
Kleinendorst, K. W.
Korzinek Riflesmith, J.
L. E. Jurras & Assoc.
LaBounty Precision Reboring, Inc
Laurel Mountain Forge
Lee Supplies, Mark
List Precision Engineering
Lock's Philadelphia Gun Exchange
London Guns Ltd.
Mahovsky's Metalife
Marble Arms (See CRR, Inc./ Marble's Inc.)
Mark Lee Supplies
Marsh, Mike
Martin's Gun Shop
McFarland, Stan
Menck, Gunsmith Inc., T.W.
Metalife Industries (See Mahovsky's Metalife)
Micro Sight Co.
Midway Arms, Inc.
MMC
Mo's Competitor Supplies (See MCS, Inc.)
Mowrey's Guns & Gunsmithing
Neil A. Jones Custom Products
New England Custom Gun Service
NgraveR Co., The
Nowlin Guns, Inc.
Nu Line Guns, Inc.
Ole Frontier Gunsmith Shop
Olympic Arms Inc.
Parker & Sons Shooting Supply
Parker Gun Finishes
Parker Gun Finishes
Paulsen Gunstocks
Perazone-Gunsmith, Brian
Peter Dyson & Son Ltd.
Power Custom, Inc.
Practical Tools, Inc.
Precision Specialties
R.A. Wells Custom Gunsmith
Ranch Products
Ransom International Corp.
Reardon Products
Rice, Keith (See White Rock Tool & Die)
Richards MicroFit Stocks, Inc.
Robar Co., Inc., The
Romain's Custom Guns, Inc.
Royal Arms Gunstocks
Score High Gunsmithing
SGS Importer's International, Inc.
Sharp Shooter Supply
Shooter's Choice Gun Care
Simmons Gun Repair, Inc.
Smith Abrasives, Inc.
Southern Bloomer Mfg. Co.
Spencer's Rifle Barrels, Inc.
Spradlin's
Starrett Co., L. S.
Stiles Custom Guns
Stoney Point Products, Inc.
Sullivan, David S. (See Westwind Rifles, Inc.)
Sunny Hill Enterprises, Inc.
T&S Industries, Inc.
T.W. Mench Gunsmith, Inc.
Tank's Rifle Shop
Tar-Hunt Custom Rifles, Inc.
Terry Theis-Engraver
Texas Platers Supply Co.
Tiger-Hunt Longrifle Gunstocks
Tom's Gun Repair, Thomas G. Ivanoff
Track of the Wolf, Inc.
Trinidad St. Jr. Col. Gunsmith Dept.
Trulock Tool
Turnbull Restoration, Doug
United States Products Co.
Van Gorden & Son Inc., C. S.
Venco Industries, Inc. (See Shooter's Choice Gun Care)
Volquartsen Custom Ltd.
W.C. Wolff Co.
Washita Mountain Whetstone Co.
Weigand Combat Handguns, Inc.
Wessinger Custom Guns & Engraving
White Rock Tool & Die
Wilcox All-Pro Tools & Supply
Wild West Guns
Will-Burt Co.
Williams Gun Sight Co.
Williams Shootin' Iron Service, The Lynx-Line
Willow Bend
Windish, Jim
Wise Guns, Dale
Wright's Gunstock Blanks
Yavapai College
Ziegel Engineering

HANDGUN ACCESSORIES

A.A. Arms, Inc.
A.W. Peterson Gun Shop, Inc., The
Action Direct, Inc.
ADCO Sales, Inc.
Advantage Arms, Inc.
Aimtech Mount Systems
Ajax Custom Grips, Inc.
Alpha 1 Drop Zone
American Derringer Corp.
Arms Corporation of the Philippines
Astra Sport, S.A.
Bagmaster Mfg., Inc.
Bar-Sto Precision Machine
Berry's Mfg., Inc.
Blue and Gray Products Inc. (See Ox-Yoke Originals)
Bond Custom Firearms
Bowen Classic Arms Corp.
Bridgeman Products
Broken Gun Ranch
Brooks Tactical Systems-Agrip
Bushmaster Hunting & Fishing
Butler Creek Corp.
Cannon Safe, Inc.
Centaur Systems, Inc.
Central Specialties Ltd. (See Trigger Lock Division)
Charter 2000
Cheyenne Pioneer Products
Chicasaw Gun Works
Clark Custom Guns, Inc.
Classic Arms Company
Concealment Shop, Inc., The
Conetrol Scope Mounts
Crimson Trace Lasers
CRR, Inc./Marble's Inc.
Cylinder & Slide, Inc., William R. Laughridge
D&L Industries (See D.J. Marketing)
D.J. Marketing
Dan Wesson Firearms
Delhi Gun House
DeSantis Holster & Leather Goods, Inc.
Dina Arms Corporation
Dixie Gun Works
Don Hume Leathergoods
Doskocil Mfg. Co., Inc.
E&L Mfg., Inc.
E. Arthur Brown Co. Inc.
E.A.A. Corp.
Eagle Imports, Inc.
Ed Brown Products, Inc.
Ed Brown Products, Inc.
Essex Arms
European American Armory Corp. (See E.A.A. Corp.)
Evolution Gun Works, Inc.
Falcon Industries, Inc.
Feinwerkbau Westinger & Altenburger
Fisher Custom Firearms
Fleming Firearms
Freedom Arms, Inc.
G.G. & G.
Galati International
GALCO International Ltd.
Garthwaite Pistolsmith, Inc., Jim
Gil Hebard Guns, Inc.
Gilmore Sports Concepts, Inc.
Glock, Inc.
Gould & Goodrich Leather, Inc.
Gun Works, The
Gun-Alert
Gun-Ho Sports Cases
H.K.S. Products
Hafner World Wide, Inc.
Hammerli USA
Heinie Specialty Products
Henigson & Associates, Steve
High Standard Mfg. Co./F.I., Inc.
Hill Speed Leather, Ernie
HIP-GRIP Barami Corp.
Hi-Point Firearms/MKS Supply
Hobson Precision Mfg. Co.
Hoppe's Div. Penguin Industries, Inc.
H-S Precision, Inc.
Hunter Co., Inc.
Impact Case & Container, Inc.
Jarvis, Inc.
JB Custom
Jim Noble Co.
John's Custom Leather
Jonathan Arthur Ciener, Inc.
JP Enterprises, Inc.
Kalispel Case Line
KeeCo Impressions, Inc.
King's Gun Works
KK Air International (See Impact Case & Container Co., Inc.)
Kolpin Outdoors, Inc.
L&S Technologies Inc. (See Aimtech Mount Systems)
LaserMax
Les Baer Custom, Inc.
Lock's Philadelphia Gun Exchange
Lohman Mfg. Co., Inc.
Mag-Na-Port International, Inc.
Marble Arms (See CRR, Inc./ Marble's Inc.)
Markell, Inc.
MEC-Gar S.R.L.
Middlebrooks Custom Shop
Millett Sights
Mogul Co./Life Jacket
MTM Molded Products Co., Inc.
National Gun, Inc.
No-Sho Mfg. Co.
Numrich Gun Parts Corporation
Outdoor Sports Headquarters, Inc.
Pachmayr Div. Lyman Products

Pager Pal
Parker & Sons Shooting Supply
Pearce Grip, Inc.
Phoenix Arms
Police Bookshelf
Practical Tools, Inc.
Precision Small Arms Inc.
Protector Mfg. Co., Inc., The
Ram-Line ATK
Ranch Products
Ransom International Corp.
RPM
Scherer Supplies, Inc.
SGS Importer's International, Inc.
Sig Sauer, Inc.
Simmons Gun Repair, Inc.
Southern Bloomer Mfg. Co.
Springfield Armory
Springfield, Inc.
SSK Industries
Sturm Ruger & Co. Inc.
Sun Welding Safe Co.
T.F.C. S.p.A.
Tactical Defense Institute
Tanfoglio Fratelli S.r.l.
Thompson/Center Arms
Trigger Lock Division / Central Specialties Ltd.
Trijicon, Inc.
Triple-K Mfg. Co., Inc.
Truglo, Inc.
United States Products Co.
Universal Sports
Volquartsen Custom Ltd.
W. Waller & Son, Inc.
W.C. Wolff Co.
Weigand Combat Handguns, Inc.
Wessinger Custom Guns & Engraving
Whitestone Lumber Corp.
Wichita Arms, Inc.
Wild West Guns
Williams Gun Sight Co.
Wilsom Combat
Yankee Gunsmith "Just Glocks"
Ziegel Engineering

HANDGUN GRIPS

A.A. Arms, Inc.
A.W. Peterson Gun Shop, Inc., The
African Import Co.
Ahrends Grips
Ajax Custom Grips, Inc.
Altamont Co.
American Derringer Corp.
Arms Corporation of the Philippines
Art Jewel Enterprises Ltd.
Baelder, Harry
Bob's Gun Shop
Boone Trading Co., Inc.
Boone's Custom Ivory Grips, Inc.
Boyds' Gunstock Industries, Inc.
Brooks Tactical Systems-Agrip
Clark Custom Guns, Inc.
Claro Walnut Gunstock Co.
Cole-Grip
Colonial Repair
Crimson Trace Lasers
Cylinder & Slide, Inc., William R. Laughridge
Dan Wesson Firearms
Dixie Gun Works
Dolbare, Elizabeth
E.A.A. Corp.
Eagle Imports, Inc.
Ed Brown Products, Inc.
EMF Co. Inc.
Essex Arms
European American Armory Corp. (See E.A.A. Corp.)
Falcon Industries, Inc.
Feinwerkbau Westinger & Altenburger
Fisher Custom Firearms
Garthwaite Pistolsmith, Inc., Jim
Goodwin's Guns
Herrett's Stocks, Inc.
High Standard Mfg. Co./F.I., Inc.
HIP-GRIP Barami Corp.
Hogue Grips
H-S Precision, Inc.
Huebner, Corey O.
International Shooters Service
Israel Arms Inc.
John Masen Co. Inc.
KeeCo Impressions, Inc.
Keng's Firearms Specialty, Inc.
Korth Germany GmbH
Les Baer Custom, Inc.
Lett Custom Grips
Linebaugh Custom Sixguns
Lyman Products Corp.
Michaels of Oregon Co.
Mobile Area Networks, Inc.
N.C. Ordnance Co.
Newell, Robert H.
Northern Precision
Pachmayr Div. Lyman Products
Pardini Armi Srl
Parker & Sons Shooting Supply
Pearce Grip, Inc.
Precision Small Arms Inc.
Robinson, Don
Rosenberg & Son, Jack A.
Roy's Custom Grips
Spegel, Craig
Stoeger Industries
Sturm Ruger & Co. Inc.
Sunny Hill Enterprises, Inc.
Tactical Defense Institute
Taurus Firearms, Inc.
Tirelli
Tom Forrest, Inc.
Triple-K Mfg. Co., Inc.
Uncle Mike's (See Michaels of Oregon, Co.)
Volquartsen Custom Ltd.
Western Mfg. Co.
Whitestone Lumber Corp.
Wright's Gunstock Blanks

HEARING PROTECTORS

A.W. Peterson Gun Shop, Inc., The
Aero Peltor
Ajax Custom Grips, Inc.
Browning Arms Co.
Creedmoor Sports, Inc.
David Clark Co., Inc.
Dillon Precision Products, Inc.
Dixie Gun Works
E-A-R, Inc.
Electronic Shooters Protection, Inc.
Gentex Corp.
Gun Room Press, The
Gunsmithing, Inc.
Hoppe's Div. Penguin Industries, Inc.
Kesselring Gun Shop
Parker & Sons Shooting Supply
Paterson Gunsmithing
Peltor, Inc. (See Aero Peltor)
Police Bookshelf
R.E.T. Enterprises
Ridgeline, Inc.
Rucker Dist. Inc.
Silencio/Jackson Products, Inc.
Tactical Defense Institute
Triple-K Mfg. Co., Inc.
Watson Bullets
Whitestone Lumber Corp.

HOLSTERS & LEATHER GOODS

A.A. Arms, Inc.
A.W. Peterson Gun Shop, Inc., The
Action Direct, Inc.
Action Products, Inc.
Aker International, Inc.
AKJ Concealco
Alessi Holsters, Inc.
Arratoonian, Andy (See Horseshoe Leather Products)
Bagmaster Mfg., Inc.
Bang-Bang Boutique (See Holster Shop, The)
Beretta Pietro S.P.A.
Bianchi International, Inc.
Bond Arms, Inc.
Brooks Tactical Systems-Agrip
Browning Arms Co.
Bull-X, Inc.
Camp-Cap Products
Cape Outfitters
Cathey Enterprises, Inc.
Chace Leather Products
Churchill Glove Co., James
Cimarron F.A. Co.
Classic Old West Styles
Clements' Custom Leathercraft, Chas
Cobra Sport S.R.I.
Collector's Armoury, Ltd.
Colonial Repair
Counter Assault
Delhi Gun House
DeSantis Holster & Leather Goods, Inc.
Dillon Precision Products, Inc.
Dixie Gun Works
Don Hume Leathergoods
Eagle Imports, Inc.
El Paso Saddlery Co.
Ellett Bros.
EMF Co. Inc.
Faust Inc., T. G.
Freedom Arms, Inc.
Gage Manufacturing
GALCO International Ltd.
Gil Hebard Guns, Inc.
Gilmore Sports Concepts, Inc.
GML Products, Inc.
Gould & Goodrich Leather, Inc.
Gun Leather Limited
Gun Works, The
Hafner World Wide, Inc.
HandCrafts Unltd. (See Clements' Custom Leathercraft)
Hank's Gun Shop
Heinie Specialty Products
Henigson & Associates, Steve
Hill Speed Leather, Ernie
HIP-GRIP Barami Corp.
Hobson Precision Mfg. Co.
Hogue Grips
Horseshoe Leather Products
Hunter Co., Inc.
Jeff's Outfitters
Jim Noble Co.
John's Custom Leather
Kirkpatrick Leather Co.
Kolpin Outdoors, Inc.
Korth Germany GmbH
Kramer Handgun Leather
L.A.R. Mfg., Inc.
Lock's Philadelphia Gun Exchange
Lone Star Gunleather
Markell, Inc.
Marksman Products
Michaels of Oregon Co.
National Gun, Inc.
No-Sho Mfg. Co.
Null Holsters Ltd. K.L.
October Country Muzzleloading
Oklahoma Leather Products, Inc.
Old West Reproductions, Inc. R.M. Bachman
Outdoor Connection, Inc., The
Pager Pal
Parker & Sons Shooting Supply
Pathfinder Sports Leather
Police Bookshelf
Protektor Model
PWL Gunleather
Renegade
Ringler Custom Leather Co.
Rogue Rifle Co., Inc./Chipmunk Rifles
S&S Firearms
Safariland Ltd., Inc.
Scharch Mfg., Inc.-Top Brass
Schulz Industries
Second Chance Body Armor
SGS Importer's International, Inc.
Sig Sauer, Inc.
Silhouette Leathers
Smith Saddlery, Jesse W.
Sparks, Milt
Stalker, Inc.
Starr Trading Co., Jedediah
Strong Holster Co.
Stuart, V. Pat
Tabler Marketing
Tactical Defense Institute
Ted Blocker Holsters
Tex Shoemaker & Sons, Inc.
Thad Rybka Custom Leather Equipment
Torel, Inc./Tandy Brands Outdoors/AA & E
Triple-K Mfg. Co., Inc.
Tristar Sporting Arms, Ltd.
Uncle Mike's (See Michaels of Oregon, Co.)
Venus Industries
W. Waller & Son, Inc.
Walt's Custom Leather, Walt Whinnery
Watson Bullets
Westley Richards & Co. Ltd.
Whinnery, Walt (See Walt's Custom Leather)
Wild Bill's Originals
Wilsom Combat

HUNTING & CAMP GEAR, CLOTHING, ETC.

A.W. Peterson Gun Shop, Inc., The
Action Direct, Inc.
Action Products, Inc.
Adventure 16, Inc.
All Rite Products, Inc.
Alpha 1 Drop Zone
Armor (See Buck Stop Lure Co., Inc.)
Atlanta Cutlery Corp.
Atsko/Sno-Seal, Inc.
Bagmaster Mfg., Inc.
Barbour, Inc.
Bauer, Eddie
Bear Archery
Beaver Park Product, Inc.
Beretta Pietro S.P.A.
Better Concepts Co.
Bill Russ Trading Post
Bob Allen Sportswear
Boonie Packer Products
Boss Manufacturing Co.
Browning Arms Co.
Buck Stop Lure Co., Inc.
Bushmaster Hunting & Fishing
Camp-Cap Products
Carhartt, Inc.
Case & Sons Cutlery Co., W R
Churchill Glove Co., James
Clarkfield Enterprises, Inc.
Classic Old West Styles
Clements' Custom Leathercraft, Chas
Coghlan's Ltd.
Cold Steel Inc.
Coleman Co., Inc.
Coulston Products, Inc.
Counter Assault
Dakota Corp.
Danner Shoe Mfg. Co.
Deepeeka Exports Pvt. Ltd.
Dr. O's Products Ltd.
Duofold, Inc.
Dynalite Products, Inc.
E-A-R, Inc.
Flambeau, Inc.
Forrest Tool Co.
Fox River Mills, Inc.
Frontier
G&H Decoys, Inc.
Gerber Legendary Blades
Glacier Glove
Grand Slam Hunting Products
HandCrafts Unltd. (See Clements' Custom Leathercraft)
High North Products, Inc.
Hinman Outfitters, Bob
Hodgman, Inc.
Houtz & Barwick
Hunter's Specialties Inc.
James Churchill Glove Co.
John's Custom Leather
K&M Industries, Inc.
Kamik Outdoor Footwear
Kolpin Outdoors, Inc.
L.L. Bean, Inc.
LaCrosse Footwear, Inc.
Leapers, Inc.
MAG Instrument, Inc.
Mag-Na-Port International, Inc.
McCann Industries
Murphy, R.R. Co., Inc.
Original Deer Formula Co., The
Orvis Co., The
Palsa Outdoor Products
Partridge Sales Ltd., John
Pointing Dog Journal, Village Press Publications
Powell & Son (Gunmakers) Ltd., William
Pro-Mark Div. of Wells Lamont
Ringler Custom Leather Co.
Rocky Shoes & Boots
Scansport, Inc.
Sceery Game Calls
Schaefer Shooting Sports
Servus Footwear Co.
Simmons Outdoor Corp.
Sno-Seal, Inc. (See Atsko/Sno-Seal, Inc.)
TEN-X Products Group
Tink's Safariland Hunting Corp.
Torel, Inc./Tandy Brands Outdoors/AA & E
Triple-K Mfg. Co., Inc.
Tru-Nord Compass
United Cutlery Corp.
Venus Industries
Walls Industries, Inc.
Wideview Scope Mount Corp.
Wilderness Sound Products Ltd.
Winchester Sutler, Inc., The
Wolverine Footwear Group
Woolrich, Inc.
Wyoming Knife Corp.

KNIVES & KNIFEMAKER'S SUPPLIES

A.G. Russell Knives, Inc.
A.W. Peterson Gun Shop, Inc., The
Action Direct, Inc.

PRODUCT & SERVICE DIRECTORY

Adventure 16, Inc.
African Import Co.
Aitor-Berrizargo S.L.
American Target Knives
Art Jewel Enterprises Ltd.
Atlanta Cutlery Corp.
B&D Trading Co., Inc.
Barteaux Machete
Beitzinger, George
Benchmark Knives (See Gerber Legendary Blades)
Beretta Pietro S.P.A.
Beretta U.S.A. Corp.
Bill Russ Trading Post
Boker USA, Inc.
Boone Trading Co., Inc.
Boone's Custom Ivory Grips, Inc.
Bowen Knife Co., Inc.
Brooks Tactical Systems-Agrip
Browning Arms Co.
Buck Knives, Inc.
Buster's Custom Knives
Cain's Outdoors, Inc.
Camillus Cutlery Co.
Campbell, Dick
Case & Sons Cutlery Co., W R
Chicago Cutlery Co.
Claro Walnut Gunstock Co.
Clements' Custom Leathercraft, Chas
Cold Steel Inc.
Coleman Co., Inc.
Collector's Armoury, Ltd.
Compass Industries, Inc.
Creative Craftsman, Inc., The
Crosman Blades (See Coleman Co., Inc.)
CRR, Inc./Marble's Inc.
Cutco Cutlery
damascususa@inteliport.com
Dan's Whetstone Co., Inc.
Deepeeka Exports Pvt. Ltd.
Delhi Gun House
DeSantis Holster & Leather Goods, Inc.
Diamond Machining Technology Inc. (See DMT)
Dixie Gun Works
Dolbare, Elizabeth
EdgeCraft Corp., S. Weiner
Empire Cutlery Corp.
Eze-Lap Diamond Prods.
Flitz International Ltd.
Forrest Tool Co.
Forthofer's Gunsmithing & Knifemaking
Fortune Products, Inc.
Frank Knives
Frost Cutlery Co.
Galati International
George Ibberson (Sheffield) Ltd.
Gerber Legendary Blades
Glock, Inc.
Golden Age Arms Co.
Gun Room, The
Gun Works, The
H&B Forge Co.
Hafner World Wide, Inc.
Hammans, Charles E.
HandCrafts Unltd. (See Clements' Custom Leathercraft)
Harris Publications
High North Products, Inc.
Hoppe's Div. Penguin Industries, Inc.
Hunter Co., Inc.
J.A. Blades, Inc. (See Christopher Firearms Co.)
J.A. Henckels Zwillingswerk Inc.
Jantz Supply, Inc.
Jenco Sales, Inc.
Jim Blair Engraving
Johnson Wood Products
KA-BAR Knives
Kasenit Co., Inc.
Kershaw Knives
Knifeware, Inc.
Koval Knives
Lamson & Goodnow Mfg. Co.
Lansky Sharpeners
Leapers, Inc.
Leatherman Tool Group, Inc.
Lethal Force Institute (See Police Bookshelf)
Marble Arms (See CRR, Inc./ Marble's Inc.)
McCann Industries
Normark Corp.
North Star West, Inc.
October Country Muzzleloading
Outdoor Edge Cutlery Corp.
Plaza Cutlery, Inc.
Police Bookshelf
Queen Cutlery Co.
R&C Knives & Such
R. Murphy Co., Inc.
Randall-Made Knives
Robert Valade Engraving
Scansport, Inc.
Schiffman, Mike
Sheffield Knifemakers Supply, Inc.
Smith Saddlery, Jesse W.
Springfield Armory
Spyderco, Inc.
Starr Trading Co., Jedediah
T.F.C. S.p.A.
Terry Theis-Engraver
Traditions Performance Firearms
Traditions Performance Firearms
Tru-Balance Knife Co.
Tru-Nord Compass
United Cutlery Corp.
Utica Cutlery Co.
Venus Industries
W.R. Case & Sons Cutlery Co.
Washita Mountain Whetstone Co.
Wells Creek Knife & Gun Works
Wenger North America/Precise Int'l.
Western Cutlery (See Camillus Cutlery Co.)
Whinnery, Walt (See Walt's Custom Leather)
Wideview Scope Mount Corp.
Wyoming Knife Corp.

LABELS, BOXES & CARTRIDGE HOLDERS

Ballistic Products, Inc.
Berry's Mfg., Inc.
Cabinet Mtn. Outfitters Scents & Lures
Cheyenne Pioneer Products
Del Rey Products
DeSantis Holster & Leather Goods, Inc.
Flambeau, Inc.
Hafner World Wide, Inc.
J&J Products, Inc.
Kolpin Outdoors, Inc.
Liberty Shooting Supplies
Midway Arms, Inc.
MTM Molded Products Co., Inc.
Outdoor Connection, Inc., The
Walt's Custom Leather, Walt Whinnery
Ziegel Engineering

LEAD WIRES & WIRE CUTTERS

Ames Metal Products Co.
Big Bore Express
Bullet Swaging Supply, Inc.
Corbin Mfg. & Supply, Inc.
D.L. Unmussig Bullets
Liberty Mfg., Inc.
Montana Precision Swaging
Northern Precision
Sport Flite Manufacturing Co.
Star Ammunition, Inc.

LOAD TESTING & PRODUCT TESTING

Ballistic Research
Bridgeman Products
Briese Bullet Co., Inc.
Buckskin Bullet Co.
Clearview Products
Dead Eye's Sport Center
Defense Training International, Inc.
Duane's Gun Repair (See DGR Custom Rifles)
Gruning Precision, Inc.
H.P. White Laboratory, Inc.
Hank's Gun Shop
Henigson & Associates, Steve
J&J Sales
Jensen Bullets
Jonathan Arthur Ciener, Inc.
L. E. Jurras & Assoc.
L.B.T.
Liberty Shooting Supplies
Linebaugh Custom Sixguns
Lomont Precision Bullets
McMurdo, Lynn
Middlebrooks Custom Shop
Modern Gun Repair School
Multiplex International
Oil Rod and Gun Shop
Plum City Ballistic Range
Precision Reloading, Inc.
R.A. Wells Custom Gunsmith
Rupert's Gun Shop
SOS Products Co. (See Buck Stix-SOS Products Co.)
Spencer's Rifle Barrels, Inc.
Tar-Hunt Custom Rifles, Inc.
Trinidad St. Jr. Col. Gunsmith Dept.
W. Square Enterprises
X-Spand Target Systems

LOADING BLOCKS, METALLIC & SHOTSHELL

A.W. Peterson Gun Shop, Inc., The
Battenfeld Technologies, Inc.
Buffalo Arms Co.
Huntington Die Specialties
Jericho Tool & Die Co., Inc.
Sinclair International, Inc.

LUBRISIZERS, DIES & ACCESSORIES

A.W. Peterson Gun Shop, Inc., The
Ballisti-Cast, Inc.
Buffalo Arms Co.
Cast Performance Bullet Company
Cooper-Woodward Perfect Lube
Eagan Gunsmiths
GAR
Hart & Son, Inc.
Javelina Lube Products
Lee Precision, Inc.
Lithi Bee Bullet Lube
Lyman Products Corp.
Magma Engineering Co.
PWM Sales Ltd.
RCBS Operations/ATK
S&S Firearms
SPG, Inc.
Thompson Bullet Lube Co.
United States Products Co.
WTA Manufacturing

MOULDS & MOULD ACCESSORIES

A.W. Peterson Gun Shop, Inc., The
Ad Hominem
American Products, Inc.
Ballisti-Cast, Inc.
Buffalo Arms Co.
Bullet Swaging Supply, Inc.
Cast Performance Bullet Company
Davide Pedersoli and Co.
Eagan Gunsmiths
GAR
Gun Works, The
Huntington Die Specialties
L.B.T.
Lee Precision, Inc.
Lyman Products Corp.
Magma Engineering Co.
MEC-Gar S.R.L.
North Star West, Inc.
October Country Muzzleloading
Old West Bullet Moulds
Pacific Rifle Co.
Penn Bullets
Peter Dyson & Son Ltd.
Rapine Bullet Mould Mfg. Co.
RCBS Operations/ATK
S&S Firearms

MUZZLE-LOADING GUNS, BARRELS & EQUIPMENT

A.W. Peterson Gun Shop, Inc., The
Accuracy Unlimited
Ackerman & Co.
Allen Mfg.
Armi San Paolo
Austin & Halleck, Inc.
Bentley, John
Big Bore Express
Birdsong & Assoc., W. E.
Black Powder Products
Blount/Outers ATK
Blue and Gray Products Inc. (See Ox-Yoke Originals)
Buckskin Bullet Co.
Bullberry Barrel Works, Ltd.
Butler Creek Corp.
Cabela's
Cain's Outdoors, Inc.
California Sights (See Fautheree, Andy)
Cash Mfg. Co./ TDC
Caywood Gunmakers
CBC-BRAZIL
Chambers Flintlocks Ltd., Jim
Chicasaw Gun Works
Cimarron F.A. Co.
Cogar's Gunsmithing
Colonial Repair
Colt Blackpowder Arms Co.
Cousin Bob's Mountain Products
Curly Maple Stock Blanks (See Tiger-Hunt)
CVA
Dangler's Custom Flint Rifles
Davide Pedersoli and Co.
Dayton Traister
deHaas Barrels
Delhi Gun House
Dixie Gun Works
Dixie Gun Works
Dixon Muzzleloading Shop, Inc.
Dolbare, Elizabeth
Ellett Bros.
EMF Co. Inc.
Euroarms of America, Inc.
Flintlocks, Etc.
Fort Hill Gunstocks
Fowler, Bob (See Black Powder Products)
Frontier
Getz Barrel Company
Goergen's Gun Shop, Inc.
Golden Age Arms Co.
Green Mountain Rifle Barrel Co., Inc.
Gun Works, The
H&R 1871, LLC
Hastings
Hawken Shop, The
Hawken Shop, The (See Dayton Traister)
Hege Jagd-u. Sporthandels GmbH
Hodgdon Powder Co.
Hoppe's Div. Penguin Industries, Inc.
Hornady Mfg. Co.
House of Muskets, Inc., The
Hydra-Tone Chemicals, Inc.
IAR Inc.
Impact Case & Container, Inc.
Ironsighter Co.
J. Dewey Mfg. Co., Inc.
Jamison's Forge Works
K&M Industries, Inc.
Kalispel Case Line
Kennedy Firearms
Knight Rifles
Knight Rifles (See Modern Muzzleloading, Inc.)
Kolar
L&R Lock Co.
L&S Technologies Inc. (See Aimtech Mount Systems)
Lakewood Products Div of Midwest Textile
Lodgewood Mfg.
Log Cabin Sport Shop
Lothar Walther Precision Tool Inc.
Lyman Products Corp.
Markesbery Muzzle Loaders, Inc.
Mathews Gun Shop & Gunsmithing, Inc.
McCann, Tom
Michaels of Oregon Co.
Millennium Designed Muzzleloaders
Modern Muzzleloading, Inc.
Mowrey Gun Works
Navy Arms Company
Newman Gunshop
North Star West, Inc.
October Country Muzzleloading
Oklahoma Leather Products, Inc.
Olson, Myron
Pacific Rifle Co.
Parker & Sons Shooting Supply
Parker Gun Finishes
Pecatonica River Longrifle
Peter Dyson & Son Ltd.
Pioneer Arms Co.
Rossi Firearms
S&S Firearms
Selsi Co., Inc.
Simmons Gun Repair, Inc.
Sklany's Machine Shop
Smokey Valley Rifles
South Bend Replicas, Inc.
Southern Bloomer Mfg. Co.
Splitfire Sporting Goods, L.L.C.
Starr Trading Co., Jedediah
Stone Mountain Arms
Sturm Ruger & Co. Inc.
Taylor's & Co., Inc.
Tennessee Valley Mfg.
Thompson Bullet Lube Co.
Thompson/Center Arms
Tiger-Hunt Longrifle Gunstocks
Track of the Wolf, Inc.

PRODUCT & SERVICE DIRECTORY

Traditions Performance Firearms
Truglo, Inc.
Uncle Mike's (See Michaels of Oregon, Co.)
Universal Sports
Upper Missouri Trading Co.
Venco Industries, Inc. (See Shooter's Choice Gun Care)
Village Restorations & Consulting, Inc.
Virgin Valley Custom Guns
Voere-KGH GmbH
W.E. Birdsong & Assoc.
Wescombe, Bill (See North Star West)
William E. Phillips Firearms
Woodworker's Supply
Wright's Gunstock Blanks
Young Country Arms
Ziegel Engineering

PISTOLSMITH

A.W. Peterson Gun Shop, Inc., The
Acadian Ballistic Specialties
Accuracy Unlimited
Actions by "T" Teddy Jacobson
Adair Custom Shop, Bill
Ahlman Guns
Aldis Gunsmithing & Shooting Supply
Alpha Precision, Inc.
Alpine Indoor Shooting Range
Armament Gunsmithing Co., Inc.
Bain & Davis, Inc.
Bar-Sto Precision Machine
Bengtson Arms Co., L.
Bill Adair Custom Shop
Billings Gunsmiths
Bowen Classic Arms Corp.
Broken Gun Ranch
Caraville Manufacturing
Chicasaw Gun Works
Chip McCormick Corp.
Clark Custom Guns, Inc.
Colonial Repair
Colorado School of Trades
Colt's Mfg. Co., Inc.
Corkys Gun Clinic
Cylinder & Slide, Inc., William R. Laughridge
D&D Gunsmiths, Ltd.
D&L Sports
David R. Chicoine
Dayton Traister
Dilliott Gunsmithing, Inc.
Duncan's Gun Works, Inc.
Ellicott Arms, Inc. / Woods Pistolsmithing
Evolution Gun Works, Inc.
Ferris Firearms
Firearm Brokers
Fisher Custom Firearms
Forkin Custom Classics
G.G. & G.
Garthwaite Pistolsmith, Inc., Jim
Gary Reeder Custom Guns
Genecco Gun Works
Gentry Custom LLC
Greider Precision
Gun Doc, Inc.
Gun Works, The
Guncraft Sports, Inc.
Guncraft Sports, Inc.
Gunsite Training Center
Hamilton, Alex B. (See Ten-Ring Precision, Inc.)
Hammerli Service-Precision Mac
Hammond Custom Guns Ltd.
Hank's Gun Shop
Hanson's Gun Center, Dick
Hawken Shop, The (See Dayton Traister)
Heinie Specialty Products
High Bridge Arms, Inc.
High Standard Mfg. Co./F.I., Inc.
Hoag, James W.
Irwin, Campbell H.
Ivanoff, Thomas G. (See Tom's Gun Repair)
J R Guns
J&S Heat Treat
Jackalope Gun Shop
Jarvis, Inc.
Jensen's Arizona Sportsman
Jungkind, Reeves C.
Kaswer Custom, Inc.
Ken Starnes Gunmaker
Kilham & Co.
King's Gun Works
La Clinique du .45
LaRocca Gun Works
Lawson, John G. (See Sight Shop, The)
Leckie Professional Gunsmithing
Les Baer Custom, Inc.
Linebaugh Custom Sixguns
List Precision Engineering
Long, George F.
Mag-Na-Port International, Inc.
Mahovsky's Metalife
Marvel, Alan
Mathews Gun Shop & Gunsmithing, Inc.
McGowen Gunsmithing
MCS, Inc.
Middlebrooks Custom Shop
Miller Custom
Mitchell's Accuracy Shop
MJK Gunsmithing, Inc.
Modern Gun Repair School
Mo's Competitor Supplies (See MCS, Inc.)
Mowrey's Guns & Gunsmithing
Mullis Guncraft
NCP Products, Inc.
Novak's, Inc.
Nowlin Guns, Inc.
Nu Line Guns, Inc.
Olathe Gun Shop
Paris, Frank J.
Pasadena Gun Center
Peacemaker Specialists
Performance Specialists
Peterson Gun Shop, Inc., A.W.
Piquette's Custom Engraving
Power Custom, Inc.
Precision Specialties
Randco UK
Ries, Chuck
Rim Pac Sports, Inc.
Robar Co., Inc., The
RPM
Ruger's Custom Guns
Score High Gunsmithing
Shooters Supply
Shootin' Shack
Sight Shop, The
Singletary, Kent
Spradlin's
Springfield, Inc.
SSK Industries
State Line Gun Shop
Swenson's 45 Shop, A. D.
Swift River Gunworks
Ten-Ring Precision, Inc.
Terry K. Kopp Professional Gunsmithing
Time Precision
Tom's Gun Repair, Thomas G. Ivanoff
Turnbull Restoration, Doug
Volquartsen Custom Ltd.
Walters Industries
Wardell Precision
Wessinger Custom Guns & Engraving
White Barn Wor
Wichita Arms, Inc.
Wild West Guns
Williams Gun Sight Co.
Williamson Precision Gunsmithing
Wilsom Combat
Wright's Gunstock Blanks

POWDER MEASURES, SCALES, FUNNELS & ACCESSORIES

A.W. Peterson Gun Shop, Inc., The
Battenfeld Technologies, Inc.
Buffalo Arms Co.
Cain's Outdoors, Inc.
CH Tool & Die/4-D Custom Die Co.
Davide Pedersoli and Co.
Dillon Precision Products, Inc.
Fremont Tool Works
Frontier
GAR
High Precision
Hoehn Sales, Inc.
J R Guns
Jones Custom Products, Neil A.
Modern Muzzleloading, Inc.
Neil A. Jones Custom Products
Pacific Rifle Co.
Precision Reloading, Inc.
RCBS Operations/ATK
Redding Reloading Equipment
Saunders Gun & Machine Shop
Schumakers Gun Shop
Spencer's Rifle Barrels, Inc.
Vega Tool Co.
VibraShine, Inc.
VTI Gun Parts

PRESS ACCESSORIES, METALLIC

A.W. Peterson Gun Shop, Inc., The
Buffalo Arms Co.
Hollywood Engineering
Huntington Die Specialties
MA Systems, Inc.
R.E.I.
Redding Reloading Equipment
Thompson Tool Mount
Vega Tool Co.

PRESS ACCESSORIES, SHOTSHELL

A.W. Peterson Gun Shop, Inc., The
Hollywood Engineering
Lee Precision, Inc.
MEC, Inc.
R.E.I.

PRESSES, ARBOR

A.W. Peterson Gun Shop, Inc., The
Blue Ridge Machinery & Tools, Inc.
Hoehn Sales, Inc.
K&M Services
RCBS Operations/ATK
Spencer's Rifle Barrels, Inc.

PRESSES, METALLIC

A.W. Peterson Gun Shop, Inc., The
Austin Sheridan USA, Inc.
Battenfeld Technologies, Inc.
CH Tool & Die/4-D Custom Die Co.
Dillon Precision Products, Inc.
Fremont Tool Works
Hornady Mfg. Co.
Huntington Die Specialties
Lee Precision, Inc.
Meacham Tool & Hardware Co., Inc.
Midway Arms, Inc.
R.E.I.
RCBS Operations/ATK
Spencer's Rifle Barrels, Inc.

PRESSES, SHOTSHELL

A.W. Peterson Gun Shop, Inc., The
Ballistic Products, Inc.
Dillon Precision Products, Inc.
Hornady Mfg. Co.
MEC, Inc.
Spolar Power Load, Inc.

PRESSES, SWAGE

A.W. Peterson Gun Shop, Inc., The
Bullet Swaging Supply, Inc.
Corbin Mfg. & Supply, Inc.
Howell Machine, Inc.

PRIMING TOOLS & ACCESSORIES

A.W. Peterson Gun Shop, Inc., The
Bald Eagle Precision Machine Co.
GAR
Hart & Son, Inc.
Huntington Die Specialties
K&M Services
RCBS Operations/ATK
Simmons, Jerry
Sinclair International, Inc.

REBORING & RERIFLING

Ahlman Guns
Barrel & Gunworks
Bauska Barrels
BlackStar AccuMax Barrels
BlackStar Barrel Accurizing (See BlackStar AccuMax)
Buffalo Arms Co.
Champlin Firearms, Inc.
Ed's Gun House
Ivanoff, Thomas G. (See Tom's Gun Repair)
Jonathan Arthur Ciener, Inc.
LaBounty Precision Reboring, Inc
NCP Products, Inc.
Pence Precision Barrels
Redman's Rifling & Reboring
Rice, Keith (See White Rock Tool & Die)
Ridgetop Sporting Goods
Savage Arms, Inc.
Shaw, Inc., E. R. (See Small Arms Mfg. Co.)
Siegrist Gun Shop
Simmons Gun Repair, Inc.
Stratco, Inc.
Terry K. Kopp Professional Gunsmithing
Time Precision
Tom's Gun Repair, Thomas G. Ivanoff
Turnbull Restoration, Doug
Van Patten, J. W.
Wells Sport Store
White Rock Tool & Die

RELOADING TOOLS AND ACCESSORIES

Advance Car Mover Co., Rowell Div.
American Products, Inc.
Ammo Load Worldwide, Inc.
Armfield Custom Bullets
Armite Laboratories Inc.
Arms Corporation of the Philippines
Atsko/Sno-Seal, Inc.
Bald Eagle Precision Machine Co.
Ballistic Products, Inc.
BC-Handmade Bullets
Berger Bullets Ltd.
Berry's Mfg., Inc.
Blount, Inc., Sporting Equipment Div.
Blue Mountain Bullets
Blue Ridge Machinery & Tools, Inc.
Bonanza (See Forster Products)
BRP, Inc. High Performance Cast Bullets
Brynin, Milton
Buck Stix-SOS Products Co.
Buffalo Arms Co.
C&D Special Products (See Claybuster Wads & Harvester Bullets)
Camdex, Inc.
Canyon Cartridge Corp.
Case Sorting System
CCI/Speer Div of ATK
CH Tool & Die/4-D Custom Die Co.
CheVron Bullets
Cook Engineering Service
Curtis Cast Bullets
Custom Products (See Jones Custom Products)
CVA
D.C.C. Enterprises
Davide Pedersoli and Co.
Davis, Don
Davis Products, Mike
Denver Instrument Co.
Dillon Precision Products, Inc.
Dropkick
E&L Mfg., Inc.
Eagan Gunsmiths
Eichelberger Bullets, Wm.
Enguix Import-Export
Euroarms of America, Inc.
Federated-Fry (See Fry Metals)
Ferguson, Bill
Fisher Custom Firearms
Flambeau, Inc.
Flitz International Ltd.
Forster Products, Inc.
Fremont Tool Works
Fry Metals
Gehmann, Walter (See Huntington Die Specialties)
Graf & Sons
Graphics Direct
Graves Co.
Green, Arthur S.
Gun City
Hanned Line, The
Hanned Precision (See The Hanned Line)
Harrell's Precision
Harris Enterprises
Harrison Bullets
Heidenstrom Bullets
High Precision
Hirtenberger AG
Hodgdon Powder Co.
Holland's Shooters Supply, Inc.
Hornady Mfg. Co.
Howell Machine, Inc.
Hunters Supply, Inc.
Image Ind. Inc.
Imperial Magnum Corp.
INTEC International, Inc.
Iosso Products
J&L Superior Bullets (See Huntington Die Specialties)

PRODUCT & SERVICE DIRECTORY

Jack First, Inc.
Javelina Lube Products
JLK Bullets
Jonad Corp.
Jones Custom Products, Neil A.
Jones Moulds, Paul
K&M Services
Kapro Mfg. Co. Inc. (See R.E.I.)
Knoell, Doug
Korzinek Riflesmith, J.
L.A.R. Mfg., Inc.
L.E. Wilson, Inc.
Lee Precision, Inc.
Liberty Mfg., Inc.
Liberty Shooting Supplies
Lithi Bee Bullet Lube
Littleton, J. F.
Lock's Philadelphia Gun Exchange
Lyman Instant Targets, Inc. (See Lyman Products Corp.)
Lyman Products Corp.
MA Systems, Inc.
Magma Engineering Co.
Match Prep-Doyle Gracey
Mayville Engineering Co. (See MEC, Inc.)
MCS, Inc.
MEC, Inc.
Midway Arms, Inc.
MI-TE Bullets
Montana Armory, Inc.
Mo's Competitor Supplies (See MCS, Inc.)
MTM Molded Products Co., Inc.
MWG Co.
Nammo Lapua Oy
Newman Gunshop
North Devon Firearms Services
Old West Bullet Moulds
Outdoor Sports Headquarters, Inc.
Paragon Sales & Services, Inc.
Pinetree Bullets
Ponsness, Warren
Professional Hunter Supplies
Protector Mfg. Co., Inc., The
R.A. Wells Custom Gunsmith
R.E.I.
Rapine Bullet Mould Mfg. Co.
Redding Reloading Equipment
Reloading Specialties, Inc.
Rice, Keith (See White Rock Tool & Die)
Rochester Lead Works
Rooster Laboratories
Rorschach Precision Products
SAECO (See Redding Reloading Equipment)
Sandia Die & Cartridge Co.
Saunders Gun & Machine Shop
Saville Iron Co. (See Greenwood Precision)
Seebeck Assoc., R.E.
Sharp Shooter Supply
Sharps Arms Co., Inc., C.
Sierra Specialty Prod. Co.
Silver Eagle Machining
Skip's Machine
Sno-Seal, Inc. (See Atsko/Sno-Seal, Inc.)
SOS Products Co. (See Buck Stix-SOS Products Co.)
Spencer's Rifle Barrels, Inc.
SPG, Inc.
SSK Industries
Stalwart Corporation
Star Custom Bullets
Stoney Point Products, Inc.
Stratco, Inc.
Taracorp Industries, Inc.
TCCI
TCSR
Tetra Gun Care
Thompson/Center Arms
Vega Tool Co.
Venco Industries, Inc. (See Shooter's Choice Gun Care)
VibraShine, Inc.
Vibra-Tek Co.
Vihtavuori Oy/Kaltron-Pettibone
Vitt/Boos
W.B. Niemi Engineering
W.J. Riebe Co.
WD-40 Co.
Webster Scale Mfg. Co.
White Rock Tool & Die
Widener's Reloading & Shooting Supply, Inc.
Wise Custom Guns
Woodleigh (See Huntington Die Specialties)
Young Country Arms

RESTS BENCH, PORTABLE AND ACCESSORIES

A.W. Peterson Gun Shop, Inc., The
Adventure 16, Inc.
Armor Metal Products
B.M.F. Activator, Inc.
Bald Eagle Precision Machine Co.
Bald Eagle Precision Machine Co.
Bartlett Engineering
Battenfeld Technologies, Inc.
Blount/Outers ATK
Browning Arms Co.
B-Square Company, Inc.
Clift Mfg., L.R.
Desert Mountain Mfg.
Harris Engineering Inc.
Hart & Son, Inc.
Hidalgo, Tony
Hoehn Sales, Inc.
Hoppe's Div. Penguin Industries, Inc.
J&J Sales
Keng's Firearms Specialty, Inc.
Kolpin Outdoors, Inc.
Kramer Designs
Midway Arms, Inc.
Millett Sights
Outdoor Connection, Inc., The
Protektor Model
Ransom International Corp.
Russ Haydon's Shooters' Supply
Saville Iron Co. (See Greenwood Precision)
Sinclair International, Inc.
Six Enterprises
Stoney Point Products, Inc.
Tonoloway Tack Drives
Torel, Inc./Tandy Brands Outdoors/AA & E
Varmint Masters, LLC
Wichita Arms, Inc.
York M-1 Conversion
Zanotti Armor, Inc.
Ziegel Engineering

RIFLE BARREL MAKER

Airrow
American Safe Arms, Inc.
Barrel & Gunworks
Bauska Barrels
Bill Wiseman and Co.
BlackStar AccuMax Barrels
BlackStar Barrel Accurizing (See BlackStar AccuMax)
Border Barrels Ltd.
Buchsenmachermeister
Bullberry Barrel Works, Ltd.
Bushmaster Firearms, Inc.
Carter's Gun Shop
Christensen Arms
Cincinnati Swaging
D.L. Unmussig Bullets
deHaas Barrels
Dilliott Gunsmithing, Inc.
Dina Arms Corporation
DKT, Inc.
Donnelly, C. P.
Douglas Barrels, Inc.
Gaillard Barrels
Getz Barrel Company
Getz Barrel Company
Granite Mountain Arms, Inc.
Green Mountain Rifle Barrel Co., Inc.
Gruning Precision, Inc.
Gun Works, The
Half Moon Rifle Shop
Hart Rifle Barrels, Inc.
Hastings
Hofer Jagdwaffen, P.
H-S Precision, Inc.
Krieger Barrels, Inc.
Les Baer Custom, Inc.
Lilja Precision Rifle Barrels
Lothar Walther Precision Tool Inc.
Martini & Hagn, Ltd.
McGowen Gunsmithing
McMillan Rifle Barrels
Mid-America Recreation, Inc.
Modern Gun Repair School
Morrison Precision
Obermeyer Rifled Barrels
Olympic Arms Inc.
PAC-NOR Barreling, Inc.
Pence Precision Barrels
Perazone-Gunsmith, Brian
Rogue Rifle Co., Inc./Chipmunk Rifles
Sabatti SPA
Savage Arms, Inc.
Schneider Rifle Barrels, Inc.
Shaw, Inc., E. R. (See Small Arms Mfg. Co.)
Shilen, Inc.
Siskiyou Gun Works (See Donnelly, C. P.)
Small Arms Mfg. Co.
Specialty Shooters Supply, Inc.
Spencer's Rifle Barrels, Inc.
Steyr Mannlicher GmbH & Co. KG
Strutz Rifle Barrels, Inc., W. C.
Swift River Gunworks
Terry K. Kopp Professional Gunsmithing
Turnbull Restoration, Doug
Verney-Carron
Virgin Valley Custom Guns
Wells Sport Store
William E. Phillips Firearms
Wilson Arms Co., The

SCOPES, MOUNTS, ACCESSORIES, OPTICAL EQUIPMENT

A.R.M.S., Inc.
A.W. Peterson Gun Shop, Inc., The
Accu-Tek
Ackerman, Bill (See Optical Services Co.)
Action Direct, Inc.
ADCO Sales, Inc.
Aimpoint, Inc.
Aimtech Mount Systems
Air Venture Airguns
All Rite Products, Inc.
Alley Supply Co.
Alpec Team, Inc.
Apel GmbH, Ernst
ArmaLite, Inc.
B.A.C.
B.M.F. Activator, Inc.
Bansner's Ultimate Rifles, LLC
Barrett Firearms Manufacturer, Inc.
Beaver Park Product, Inc.
BEC, Inc.
Beeman Precision Airguns
Benjamin/Sheridan Co., Crosman
Bill Russ Trading Post
BKL Technologies
Blount, Inc., Sporting Equipment Div.
Blount/Outers ATK
Borden Rifles Inc.
Broad Creek Rifle Works, Ltd.
Brockman's Custom Gunsmithing
Brownells, Inc.
Brunton U.S.A.
BSA Optics
B-Square Company, Inc.
Bull Mountain Rifle Co.
Burris Co., Inc.
Bushmaster Firearms, Inc.
Bushnell Outdoor Products
Butler Creek Corp.
Cabela's
Carl Zeiss Inc.
Center Lock Scope Rings
Chuck's Gun Shop
Clark Custom Guns, Inc.
Clearview Mfg. Co., Inc.
Compass Industries, Inc.
Compasseco, Ltd.
Concept Development Corp.
Conetrol Scope Mounts
Creedmoor Sports, Inc.
Crimson Trace Lasers
Crosman Airguns
D.C. Engineering, Inc.
D.C.C. Enterprises
D.L. Unmussig Bullets
Daisy Outdoor Products
Del-Sports, Inc.
DHB Products
Dolbare, Elizabeth
E. Arthur Brown Co. Inc.
Eagle Imports, Inc.
Edmund Scientific Co.
Eggleston, Jere D.
Ellett Bros.
Emerging Technologies, Inc. (See Laseraim Technologies, Inc.)
Entreprise Arms, Inc.
Evolution Gun Works, Inc.
Excalibur Electro Optics, Inc.
Excel Industries, Inc.
Falcon Industries, Inc.
Farr Studio, Inc.
Freedom Arms, Inc.
Fujinon, Inc.
G.G. & G.
Galati International
Gentry Custom LLC
Gil Hebard Guns, Inc.
Gilmore Sports Concepts, Inc.
Goodwin's Guns
GSI, Inc.
Gun South, Inc. (See GSI, Inc.)
Gunsmithing, Inc.
Hammerli USA
Hart & Son, Inc.
Harvey, Frank
Highwood Special Products
Hiptmayer, Armurier
Hiptmayer, Klaus
Hoehn Sales, Inc.
Holland's Shooters Supply, Inc.
Hunter Co., Inc.
Impact Case & Container, Inc.
Ironsighter Co.
J R Guns
Jantz Supply, Inc.
Jena Eur
Jerry Phillips Optics
Jewell Triggers, Inc.
John Masen Co. Inc.
John's Custom Leather
Kahles A. Swarovski Company
Kalispel Case Line
KDF, Inc.
Keng's Firearms Specialty, Inc.
Kesselring Gun Shop
Kimber of America, Inc.
Knight's Manufacturing Co.
Koehler-Optics
Kowa Optimed, Inc.
KVH Industries, Inc.
Kwik-Site Co.
L&S Technologies Inc. (See Aimtech Mount Systems)
L.A.R. Mfg., Inc.
Laser Devices, Inc.
Laseraim Technologies, Inc.
LaserMax
Leapers, Inc.
Leica Sport Optics
Les Baer Custom, Inc.
Leupold & Stevens, Inc.
Lilja Precision Rifle Barrels
List Precision Engineering
Lohman Mfg. Co., Inc.
Lomont Precision Bullets
London Guns Ltd.
Mac-1 Airgun Distributors
Mag-Na-Port International, Inc.
Marksman Products
Maxi-Mount Inc.
McMillan Optical Gunsight Co.
MCS, Inc.
MDS
Meopta USA, LLC
Merit Corp.
Military Armament Corp.
Millett Sights
Mirador Optical Corp.
Mitchell Optics, Inc.
MMC
Monell Custom Guns
Mo's Competitor Supplies (See MCS, Inc.)
MWG Co.
New England Custom Gun Service
Nikon, Inc.
Norincoptics (See BEC, Inc.)
Olympic Optical Co.
Op-Tec
Optical Services Co.
Orchard Park Enterprise
Oregon Arms, Inc. (See Rogue Rifle Co., Inc.)
Outdoor Connection, Inc., The
Parker & Sons Shooting Supply
Parsons Optical Mfg. Co.
PECAR Herbert Schwarz GmbH
Pentax U.S.A., Inc.
PMC Ammunition
Precision Sport Optics
Quarton Beamshot
R.A. Wells Custom Gunsmith
Ram-Line ATK
Ranch Products
Randolph Engineering, Inc.
Rice, Keith (See White Rock Tool & Die)
Robinson Armament Co.
Rogue Rifle Co., Inc./Chipmunk Rifles
Romain's Custom Guns, Inc.
RPM
S&K Scope Mounts
Saunders Gun & Machine Shop
Schmidt & Bender, Inc.
Schumakers Gun Shop
Scope Control, Inc.
Score High Gunsmithing
Segway Industries
Selsi Co., Inc.
Sharp Shooter Supply
Shepherd Enterprises, Inc.
Sightron, Inc.
Simmons Outdoor Corp.

PRODUCT & SERVICE DIRECTORY

Six Enterprises
Southern Bloomer Mfg. Co.
Spencer's Rifle Barrels, Inc.
Splitfire Sporting Goods, L.L.C.
Sportsmatch U.K. Ltd.
Spradlin's
Springfield Armory
Springfield, Inc.
SSK Industries
Stiles Custom Guns
Stoeger Industries
Stoney Point Products, Inc.
Sturm Ruger & Co. Inc.
Sunny Hill Enterprises, Inc.
Swarovski Optik North America Ltd.
Swift Instruments
T.K. Lee Co.
Talley, Dave
Tasco Sales, Inc.
Thompson/Center Arms
Traditions Performance Firearms
Trijicon, Inc.
Truglo, Inc.
U.S. Optics, A Division of Zeitz Optics U.S.A.
Ultra Dot Distribution
Uncle Mike's (See Michaels of Oregon, Co.)
Unertl Ordance Co., Inc.
United Binocular Co.
Virgin Valley Custom Guns
Voere-KGH GmbH
Watson Bullets
Weaver Products ATK
Weaver Scope Repair Service
Webley Limited
Weigand Combat Handguns, Inc.
Wessinger Custom Guns & Engraving
Westley Richards & Co. Ltd.
White Rock Tool & Die
Whitestone Lumber Corp.
Wideview Scope Mount Corp.
Wilcox Industries Corp.
Wild West Guns
Williams Gun Sight Co.
York M-1 Conversion
Zanotti Armor, Inc.

SHELLHOLDERS

A.W. Peterson Gun Shop, Inc., The
CH Tool & Die/4-D Custom Die Co.
Fremont Tool Works
GAR
Hart & Son, Inc.
Huntington Die Specialties
K&M Services
King & Co.
Protektor Model
PWM Sales Ltd.
RCBS Operations/ATK
Redding Reloading Equipment
Vega Tool Co.

SHOOTING/TRAINING SCHOOL

Alpine Indoor Shooting Range
American Gunsmithing Institute
American Small Arms Academy
Auto Arms
Beretta U.S.A. Corp.
Bob's Tactical Indoor Shooting Range & Gun Shop
Bridgeman Products
Chapman Academy of Practical Shooting
Chelsea Gun Club of New York City, Inc.
CQB Training
Defense Training International, Inc.
Executive Protection Institute
Ferris Firearms
Front Sight Firearms Training Institute
Gene's Custom Guns
Gentner Bullets
Gilmore Sports Concepts, Inc.
Griffin & Howe, Inc.
Griffin & Howe, Inc.
Gun Doc, Inc.
Guncraft Books (See Guncraft Sports, Inc.)
Guncraft Sports, Inc.
Guncraft Sports, Inc.
Gunsite Training Center
Henigson & Associates, Steve
High North Products, Inc.
Jensen's Arizona Sportsman
Jensen's Firearms Academy
L.L. Bean, Inc.
Lethal Force Institute (See Police Bookshelf)
Long, George F.
McMurdo, Lynn
Mendez, John A.
Midwest Shooting School, The
NCP Products, Inc.
North American Shooting Systems
North Mountain Pine Training Center (See Executive Protection Institute)
Nowlin Guns, Inc.
Paxton Quigley's Personal Protection Strategies
Pentheny de Pentheny
Performance Specialists
Protektor Model
SAFE
Shoot Where You Look
Shooter's World
Shooters, Inc.
Smith & Wesson
Specialty Gunsmithing
Starlight Training Center, Inc.
Tactical Defense Institute
The Midwest Shooting School
Thunder Ranch
Western Missouri Shooters Alliance
Yankee Gunsmith "Just Glocks"
Yavapai Firearms Academy Ltd.

SHOTSHELL MISCELLANY

A.W. Peterson Gun Shop, Inc., The
American Products, Inc.
Ballistic Products, Inc.
Bridgeman Products
Gun Works, The
Lee Precision, Inc.
MEC, Inc.
R.E.I.
RCBS Operations/ATK
Shotgun Sports Magazine, dba Shootin' Accessories Ltd.
T&S Industries, Inc.
Vitt/Boos
Ziegel Engineering

SIGHTS, METALLIC

100 Straight Products, Inc.
A.W. Peterson Gun Shop, Inc., The
Accura-Site (See All's, The Jim Tembelis Co., Inc.)
Ad Hominem
Alley Supply Co.
Alpec Team, Inc.
Andela Tool & Machine, Inc.
AO Sight Systems
ArmaLite, Inc.
Aspen Outfitting Co.
Axtell Rifle Co.
B.A.C.
Ballard Rifle & Cartridge Co., LLC
BEC, Inc.
Bob's Gun Shop
Bo-Mar Tool & Mfg. Co.
Bond Custom Firearms
Bowen Classic Arms Corp.
Brockman's Custom Gunsmithing
Brooks Tactical Systems-Agrip
Brownells, Inc.
Buffalo Arms Co.
Bushmaster Firearms, Inc.
California Sights (See Fautheree, Andy)
Cape Outfitters
Cape Outfitters
Cash Mfg. Co./ TDC
Center Lock Scope Rings
Champion's Choice, Inc.
Chip McCormick Corp.
C-More Systems
Colonial Repair
CRR, Inc./Marble's Inc.
D.C. Engineering, Inc.
Davide Pedersoli and Co.
DHB Products
Dixie Gun Works
DPMS (Defense Procurement Manufacturing Services, Inc.)
Duffy, Charles E. (See Guns Antique & Modern DBA)
E. Arthur Brown Co. Inc.
Effebi SNC-Dr. Franco Beretta
Evolution Gun Works, Inc.
Farr Studio, Inc.
G.G. & G.
Garthwaite Pistolsmith, Inc., Jim
Goergen's Gun Shop, Inc.
Gun Doctor, The
Guns Antique & Modern DBA / Charles E. Duffy
Gunsmithing, Inc.
Hank's Gun Shop
Heidenstrom Bullets
Heinie Specialty Products
Hiptmayer, Armurier
Hiptmayer, Klaus
Innovative Weaponry Inc.
International Shooters Service
J.G. Anschutz GmbH & Co. KG
Jeff's Outfitters
JP Enterprises, Inc.
Keng's Firearms Specialty, Inc.
Knight Rifles
Knight's Manufacturing Co.
L.P.A. Inc.
Leapers, Inc.
Les Baer Custom, Inc.
List Precision Engineering
London Guns Ltd.
Lyman Instant Targets, Inc. (See Lyman Products Corp.)
Marble Arms (See CRR, Inc./ Marble's Inc.)
MCS, Inc.
MEC-Gar S.R.L.
Merit Corp.
Mid-America Recreation, Inc.
Middlebrooks Custom Shop
Millett Sights
MMC
Modern Muzzleloading, Inc.
Montana Armory, Inc.
Montana Vintage Arms
Mo's Competitor Supplies (See MCS, Inc.)
Navy Arms Company
New England Custom Gun Service
Newman Gunshop
Novak's, Inc.
OK Weber, Inc.
One Ragged Hole
Parker & Sons Shooting Supply
Perazone-Gunsmith, Brian
RPM
Sharps Arms Co., Inc., C.
Slug Site
STI International
T.F.C. S.p.A.
Talley, Dave
Tank's Rifle Shop
Trijicon, Inc.
Truglo, Inc.
U.S. Optics, A Division of Zeitz Optics U.S.A.
Weigand Combat Handguns, Inc.
Wichita Arms, Inc.
Wild West Guns
Williams Gun Sight Co.
Wilsom Combat
Wilsom Combat
XS Sight Systems

STOCK MAKER

Acra-Bond Laminates
Amrine's Gun Shop
Antique Arms Co.
Artistry in Wood
Aspen Outfitting Co.
Bain & Davis, Inc.
Bansner's Ultimate Rifles, LLC
Baron Technology
Billings Gunsmiths
Boltin, John M.
Borden Ridges Rimrock Stocks
Bowerly, Kent
Boyds' Gunstock Industries, Inc.
Brace, Larry D.
Briganti Custom Gunsmith
Broad Creek Rifle Works, Ltd.
Brown Precision, Inc.
Buehler Custom Sporting Arms
Bullberry Barrel Works, Ltd.
Burkhart Gunsmithing, Don
Campbell, Dick
Caywood, Shane J.
Chicasaw Gun Works
Chuck's Gun Shop
Claro Walnut Gunstock Co.
Coffin, Charles H.
Colorado Gunsmithing Academy
Custom Shop, The
Custom Single Shot Rifles
D&D Gunsmiths, Ltd.
Dangler's Custom Flint Rifles
D'Arcy Echols & Co.
David W. Schwartz Custom Guns
DBA Werth Services
DGR Custom Rifles
DGR Custom Rifles
DGS, Inc., Dale A. Storey
Don Klein Custom Guns
Duncan's Gun Works, Inc.
Erhardt, Dennis
Eversull Co., Inc.
Fieldsport Ltd.
Fisher, Jerry A.
Forster, Larry L.
Gary Goudy Classic Stocks
Genecco Gun Works
Gene's Custom Guns
Gillmann, Edwin
Grace, Charles E.
Great American Gunstock Co.
Gruning Precision, Inc.
Gunsmithing Ltd.
Hank's Gun Shop
Harry Lawson LLC
Heilmann, Stephen
Hensley, Gunmaker, Darwin
Heydenberk, Warren R.
High Tech Specialties, Inc.
Huebner, Corey O.
Jack Dever Co.
Jackalope Gun Shop
Jamison's Forge Works
Jay McCament Custom Gunmaker
Jim Norman Custom Gunstocks
John Rigby & Co.
K. Eversull Co., Inc.
Keith's Custom Gunstocks
Ken Eyster Heritage Gunsmiths, Inc.
Larry Lyons Gunworks
Martini & Hagn, Ltd.
Mathews Gun Shop & Gunsmithing, Inc.
McFarland, Stan
McGowen Gunsmithing
Mercer Custom Guns
Mid-America Recreation, Inc.
Mike Yee Custom Stocking
Mitchell, Jack
Mobile Area Networks, Inc.
Modern Gun Repair School
Morrow, Bud
Nelson's Custom Guns, Inc.
Nettestad Gun Works
Nickels, Paul R.
Paul and Sharon Dressel
Paulsen Gunstocks
Pawling Mountain Club
Pecatonica River Longrifle
Pentheny de Pentheny
Quality Custom Firearms
R&J Gun Shop
R.A. Wells Custom Gunsmith
Richards MicroFit Stocks, Inc.
RMS Custom Gunsmithing
Robinson, Don
Ron Frank Custom
Royal Arms Gunstocks
Ruger's Custom Guns
Skeoch, Brian R.
Smith, Art
Smith, Sharmon
Speiser, Fred D.
Steven Dodd Hughes
Stott's Creek Armory, Inc.
Sturgeon Valley Sporters
Taylor & Robbins
Tennessee Valley Mfg.
Tiger-Hunt Longrifle Gunstocks
Treebone Carving
Tucker, James C.
Turnbull Restoration, Doug
Vest, John
Weber & Markin Custom Gunsmiths
Wells Sport Store
Wenig Custom Gunstocks
Wiebe, Duane
Wild West Guns
Williamson Precision Gunsmithing
Winter, Robert M.

STOCKS (COMMERCIAL)

A.W. Peterson Gun Shop, Inc., The
Accuracy Unlimited
Acra-Bond Laminates
African Import Co.
Ahlman Guns
Aspen Outfitting Co.
B.A.C.
Baelder, Harry
Bansner's Ultimate Rifles, LLC
Barnes Bullets, Inc.
Battenfeld Technologies, Inc.
Beitzinger, George
Bell & Carlson, Inc.
Blount, Inc., Sporting Equipment Div.
Blount/Outers ATK
Bob's Gun Shop

PRODUCT & SERVICE DIRECTORY

Borden Ridges Rimrock Stocks
Borden Rifles Inc.
Bowerly, Kent
Boyds' Gunstock Industries, Inc.
Brockman's Custom Gunsmithing
Buckhorn Gun Works
Bull Mountain Rifle Co.
Butler Creek Corp.
Cali'co Hardwoods, Inc.
Cape Outfitters
Caywood, Shane J.
Chambers Flintlocks Ltd., Jim
Chicasaw Gun Works
Claro Walnut Gunstock Co.
Coffin, Charles H.
Colonial Repair
Colorado Gunsmithing Academy
Colorado School of Trades
Conrad, C. A.
Curly Maple Stock Blanks (See Tiger-Hunt)
Custom Checkering Service, Kathy Forster
D&D Gunsmiths, Ltd.
D&G Precision Duplicators (See Greenwood Precision)
D.C. Engineering, Inc.
Davide Pedersoli and Co.
DBA Werth Services
DGR Custom Rifles
Duane's Gun Repair (See DGR Custom Rifles)
Effebi SNC-Dr. Franco Beretta
Eggleston, Jere D.
Eversull Co., Inc.
Falcon Industries, Inc.
Falcon Industries, Inc.
Fieldsport Ltd.
Fisher, Jerry A.
Folks, Donald E.
Forster, Kathy (See Custom Checkering)
Forthofer's Gunsmithing & Knifemaking
Game Haven Gunstocks
George Hoenig, Inc.
Gervais, Mike
Gillmann, Edwin
Goens, Dale W.
Golden Age Arms Co.
Great American Gunstock Co.
Gun Shop, The
Hammerli USA
Hanson's Gun Center, Dick
Harry Lawson LLC
Hecht, Hubert J., Waffen-Hecht
Hensley, Gunmaker, Darwin
High Tech Specialties, Inc.
Hiptmayer, Armurier
Hiptmayer, Klaus
Hogue Grips
H-S Precision, Inc.
Huebner, Corey O.
Israel Arms Inc.
Ivanoff, Thomas G. (See Tom's Gun Repair)
Jarrett Rifles, Inc.
Jeff's Outfitters
Jim Norman Custom Gunstocks
John Masen Co. Inc.
Johnson Wood Products
KDF, Inc.
Keith's Custom Gunstocks
Kelbly, Inc.
Kilham & Co.
Klingler Woodcarving
McDonald, Dennis
McMillan Fiberglass Stocks, Inc.
Michaels of Oregon Co.
Mid-America Recreation, Inc.
Miller Arms, Inc.
Mitchell, Jack
Mobile Area Networks, Inc.
Morrison Custom Rifles, J. W.
MPI Stocks
MWG Co.
NCP Products, Inc.
Nelson's Custom Guns, Inc.
New England Arms Co.
New England Custom Gun Service
Newman Gunshop
Oil Rod and Gun Shop
One Of A Kind
Orvis Co., The
Ottmar, Maurice
Pagel Gun Works, Inc.
Paragon Sales & Services, Inc.
Parker & Sons Shooting Supply
Paul and Sharon Dressel
Paulsen Gunstocks
Pawling Mountain Club
Pecatonica River Longrifle
Perazone-Gunsmith, Brian
Powell & Son (Gunmakers) Ltd., William
Precision Gun Works
R&J Gun Shop
R.A. Wells Custom Gunsmith
Ram-Line ATK
Rampart International
Richards MicroFit Stocks, Inc.
RMS Custom Gunsmithing
Robinson, Don
Robinson Armament Co.
Robinson Firearms Mfg. Ltd.
Romain's Custom Guns, Inc.
Ron Frank Custom
Saville Iron Co. (See Greenwood Precision)
Schiffman, Mike
Score High Gunsmithing
Simmons Gun Repair, Inc.
Six Enterprises
Speiser, Fred D.
Stan De Treville & Co.
Stiles Custom Guns
Swann, D. J.
Swift River Gunworks
Szweda, Robert (See RMS Custom Gunsmithing)
T.F.C. S.p.A.
Tecnolegno S.p.A.
Tiger-Hunt Longrifle Gunstocks
Tirelli
Tom's Gun Repair, Thomas G. Ivanoff
Track of the Wolf, Inc.
Treebone Carving
Trevallion Gunstocks
Tuttle, Dale
Virgin Valley Custom Guns
Volquartsen Custom Ltd.
Weber & Markin Custom Gunsmiths
Wenig Custom Gunstocks
Western Mfg. Co.
Wild West Guns
Williams Gun Sight Co.
Windish, Jim
Wright's Gunstock Blanks
Zeeryp, Russ

STUCK CASE REMOVERS

A.W. Peterson Gun Shop, Inc., The
GAR
Huntington Die Specialties
Redding Reloading Equipment
Tom's Gun Repair, Thomas G. Ivanoff

TARGETS, BULLET & CLAYBIRD TRAPS

A.W. Peterson Gun Shop, Inc., The
Action Target, Inc.
Air Arms
American Target
Beeman Precision Airguns
Benjamin/Sheridan Co., Crosman
Birchwood Casey
Blount, Inc., Sporting Equipment Div.
Blount/Outers ATK
Blue and Gray Products Inc. (See Ox-Yoke Originals)
Brown Precision, Inc.
Bull-X, Inc.
Caswell Inc.
Champion Target Co.
Creedmoor Sports, Inc.
Crosman Airguns
D.C.C. Enterprises
Daisy Outdoor Products
Diamond Mfg. Co.
Federal Champion Target Co.
H-S Precision, Inc.
Hunterjohn
J.G. Dapkus Co., Inc.
Kennebec Journal
Kleen-Bore, Inc.
Lakefield Arms Ltd. (See Savage Arms, Inc.)
Leapers, Inc.
Lyman Instant Targets, Inc. (See Lyman Products Corp.)
Marksman Products
Mendez, John A.
Mountain Plains Industries
MSR Targets
National Target Co.
North American Shooting Systems
Outers Laboratories Div. of ATK
Palsa Outdoor Products
Passive Bullet Traps, Inc. (See Savage Range Systems, Inc.)
PlumFire Press, Inc.
Precision Airgun Sales, Inc.
Protektor Model
Quack Decoy & Sporting Clays
Remington Arms Co., Inc.
Rockwood Corp.
Rocky Mountain Target Co.
Savage Range Systems, Inc.
Schaefer Shooting Sports
Seligman Shooting Products
Shooters Supply
Shoot-N-C Targets (See Birchwood Casey)
SPG, Inc.
Sun Welding Safe Co.
Target Shooting, Inc.
Thompson Target Technology
Trius Traps, Inc.
Universal Sports
Watson Bullets
Woods Wise Products
World of Targets (See Birchwood Casey)
X-Spand Target Systems

TAXIDERMY

African Import Co.
Bill Russ Trading Post
Kulis Freeze Dry Taxidermy
World Trek, Inc.

TRAP & SKEET SHOOTER'S EQUIPMENT

American Products, Inc.
Bagmaster Mfg., Inc.
Ballistic Products, Inc.
Beretta Pietro S.P.A.
Blount/Outers ATK
Bob Allen Sportswear
Bridgeman Products
C&H Research
Campbell, Dick
Cape Outfitters
Danuser Machine Co.
Fiocchi of America, Inc.
Gun Works, The
Hoppe's Div. Penguin Industries, Inc.
Jamison's Forge Works
Jenkins Recoil Pads
Jim Noble Co.
Kalispel Case Line
Kolar
Lakewood Products Div of Midwest Textile
Ljutic Industries, Inc.
Mag-Na-Port International, Inc.
MEC, Inc.
Moneymaker Guncraft Corp.
MTM Molded Products Co., Inc.
NCP Products, Inc.
Pachmayr Div. Lyman Products
Palsa Outdoor Products
Pro-Port Ltd.
Protektor Model
Quack Decoy & Sporting Clays
Remington Arms Co., Inc.
Rhodeside, Inc.
Shotgun Sports Magazine, dba Shootin' Accessories Ltd.
Stan Baker Sports
T&S Industries, Inc.
TEN-X Products Group
Torel, Inc./Tandy Brands Outdoors/AA & E
Trius Traps, Inc.
Truglo, Inc.
Universal Sports
Weber & Markin Custom Gunsmiths
X-Spand Target Systems
Ziegel Engineering

TRIGGERS, RELATED EQUIPMENT

A.W. Peterson Gun Shop, Inc., The
B&D Trading Co., Inc.
B.M.F. Activator, Inc.
Bond Custom Firearms
Boyds' Gunstock Industries, Inc.
Broad Creek Rifle Works, Ltd.
Bull Mountain Rifle Co.
Chicasaw Gun Works
Dayton Traister
Dolbare, Elizabeth
Eversull Co., Inc.
Feinwerkbau Westinger & Altenburger
Gentry Custom LLC
Gun Works, The
Hart & Son, Inc.
Hastings
Hawken Shop, The (See Dayton Traister)
High Performance International
Holland's Shooters Supply, Inc.
Impact Case & Container, Inc.
Jewell Triggers, Inc.
John Masen Co. Inc.
Jones Custom Products, Neil A.
JP Enterprises, Inc.
K. Eversull Co., Inc.
Kelbly, Inc.
KK Air International (See Impact Case & Container Co., Inc.)
Knight's Manufacturing Co.
L&R Lock Co.
Les Baer Custom, Inc.
List Precision Engineering
London Guns Ltd.
M.H. Canjar Co.
Master Lock Co.
Miller Single Trigger Mfg. Co.
NCP Products, Inc.
Neil A. Jones Custom Products
Nowlin Guns, Inc.
Penrod Precision
Perazone-Gunsmith, Brian
Robinson Armament Co.
Sharp Shooter Supply
Shilen, Inc.
Simmons Gun Repair, Inc.
Spencer's Rifle Barrels, Inc.
Tank's Rifle Shop
Target Shooting, Inc.
Time Precision
Watson Bullets
York M-1 Conversion

MANUFACTURER'S DIRECTORY

A

A Zone Bullets, 2039 Walter Rd., Billings, MT 59105 / 800-252-3111; FAX: 406-248-1961

A&W Repair, 2930 Schneider Dr., Arnold, MO 63010 / 617-287-3725

A.A. Arms, Inc., 4811 Persimmont Ct., Monroe, NC 28110 / 704-289-5356 or 800-935-1119; FAX: 704-289-5859

A.B.S. III, 9238 St. Morritz Dr., Fern Creek, KY 40291

A.G. Russell Knives, Inc., 2900 S. 26th St., Rogers, AR 72758 / 800-255-9034; FAX: 479-636-8493 ag@agrussell.com agrussell.com

A.R.M.S., Inc., 230 W. Center St., West Bridgewater, MA 02379-1620 / 508-584-7816; FAX: 508-588-8045

A.W. Peterson Gun Shop, Inc., The, 4255 West Old U.S. 441, Mount Dora, FL 32757-3299 / 352-383-4258; FAX: 352-735-1001

AC Dyna-tite Corp., 155 Kelly St., P.O. Box 0984, Elk Grove Village, IL 60007 / 847-593-5566; FAX: 847-593-1304

Acadian Ballistic Specialties, P.O. Box 787, Folsom, LA 70437 / 504-796-0078 gunsmith@neasolft.com

Accuracy Den, The, 25 Bitterbrush Rd., Reno, NV 89523 / 702-345-0225

Accuracy International Precision Rifles (See U.S.)

Accuracy International, Foster, P.O. Box 111, Wilsall, MT 59086 / 406-587-7922; FAX: 406-585-9434

Accuracy Int'l. North America, Inc., P.O. Box 5267, Oak Ridge, TN 37831 / 423-482-0330; FAX: 423-482-0336

Accuracy Unlimited, 7479 S. DePew St., Littleton, CO 80123

Accuracy Unlimited, 16036 N. 49 Ave., Glendale, AZ 85306 / 602-978-9089; FAX: 602-978-9089 fglenn@cox.net www.glenncustom.com

Accura-Site (See All's, The Jim Tembelis Co., Inc.)

Accurate Arms Co., Inc., 5891 Hwy. 230 West, McEwen, TN 37101 / 931-729-4207; FAX: 931-729-4211 burrensburg@aac-ca.com www.accuratepowder.com

Accu-Tek, 4510 Carter Ct., Chino, CA 91710

Ackerman & Co., Box 133 U.S. Highway Rt. 7, Pownal, VT 05261 / 802-823-9874 muskets@togsther.net

Ackerman, Bill (See Optical Services Co.)

Acra-Bond Laminates, 134 Zimmerman Rd., Kalispell, MT 59901 / 406-257-9003; FAX: 406-257-9003 merlins@digisys.net www.acrabondlaminates.com

Action Bullets & Alloy Inc., RR 1, P.O. Box 189, Quinter, KS 67752 / 785-754-3609; FAX: 785-754-3629 bullets@ruraltel.net

Action Direct, Inc., 14285 SW 142nd St., Miami, FL 33186-6720 / 800-472-2388; FAX: 305-256-3541 info@action-direct.com www.action-direct.com

Action Products, Inc., 954 Sweeney Dr., Hagerstown, MD 21740 / 301-797-1414; FAX: 301-733-2073

Action Target, Inc., P.O. Box 636, Provo, UT 84603 / 801-377-8033; FAX: 801-377-8096 www.actiontarget.com

Actions by "T" Teddy Jacobson, 16315 Redwood Forest Ct., Sugar Land, TX 77478 / 281-565-6977 tjacobson@houston.rr.com www.actionsbyt.com

AcuSport Corporation, William L. Fraim, One Hunter Place, Bellefontaine, OH 43311-3001 / 937-593-7010; FAX: 937-592-5625 www.acusport.com

Ad Hominem, 3130 Gun Club Lane, RR #3, Orillia, ON L3V 6H3 CANADA / 705-689-5303; FAX: 705-689-5303

Adair Custom Shop, Bill, 2886 Westridge, Carrollton, TX 75006

ADCO Sales, Inc., 4 Draper St. #A, Woburn, MA 01801 / 781-935-1799; FAX: 781-935-1011

Advance Car Mover Co., Rowell Div., P.O. Box 1, 240 N. Depot St., Juneau, WI 53039 / 414-386-4464; FAX: 414-386-4416

Advantage Arms, Inc., 25163 W. Ave. Stanford, Valencia, CA 91355 / 661-257-2290

Adventure 16, Inc., 4620 Alvarado Canyon Rd., San Diego, CA 92120 / 619-283-6314

Aero Peltor, 90 Mechanic St., Southbridge, MA 01550 / 508-764-5500; FAX: 508-764-0188

African Import Co., 22 Goodwin Rd., Plymouth, MA 02360 / 508-746-8552; FAX: 508-746-0404 africanimport@aol.com

AFSCO Ammunition, 731 W. Third St., P.O. Box L, Owen, WI 54460 / 715-229-2516 sailers@webtv.net

Ahlman Guns, 9525 W. 230th St., Morristown, MN 55052 / 507-685-4243; FAX: 507-685-4280 www.ahlmans.com

Ahrends Grips, Box 203, Clarion, IA 50525 / 515-532-3449; FAX: 515-532-3926 ahrends@goldfieldaccess.net www.ahrendsgripsusa.com

Aimpoint, Inc., 14103 Mariah Ct., Chantilly, VA 20151-2113 / 877-246-7668; FAX: 703-263-9463 info@aimpoint.com www.aimpoint.com

Aimtech Mount Systems, P.O. Box 223, Thomasville, GA 31799 / 229-226-4313; FAX: 229-227-0222 mail@aimtech-mounts.com www.aimtech-mounts.com

Air Arms, Hailsham Industrial Park, Diplocks Way, Hailsham, E. Sussex, BN27 3JF ENGLAND / 011-0323-845853; FAX: 1323 440573 general.air-arms.co.uk. www.air-arms.co.uk.

Air Venture Airguns, 9752 E. Flower St., Bellflower, CA 90706 / 562-867-6355

AirForce Airguns, P.O. Box 2478, Fort Worth, TX 76113 / 817-451-8966; FAX: 817-451-1613 www.airforceairguns.com

Airrow, 11 Monitor Hill Rd., Newtown, CT 06470 / 203-270-6343

Aitor-Berrizargo S.L., Eitua 15 P.O. Box 26, 48240, Berriz (Viscaya), SPAIN / 43-17-08-50 info@aitor.com www.ailor.com

Ajax Custom Grips, Inc., 9130 Viscount Row, Dallas, TX 75247 / 214-630-8893; FAX: 214-630-4942

Aker International, Inc., 2248 Main St., Suite 6, Chula Vista, CA 91911 / 619-423-5182; FAX: 619-423-1363 aker@akerleather.com www.akerleather.com

AKJ Concealco, P.O. Box 871596, Vancouver, WA 98687-1596 / 360-891-8222; FAX: 360-891-8221 Concealco@aol.com www.greatholsters.com

Alana Cupp Custom Engraver, P.O. Box 207, Annabella, UT 84711 / 801-896-4834

Alaska Bullet Works, Inc., 9978 Crazy Horse Drive, Juneau, AK 99801 / 907-789-3834; FAX: 907-789-3433

Alaskan Silversmith, The, 2145 Wagner Hollow Rd., Fort Plain, NY 13339 / 518-993-3983 sidbell@capital.net www.sidbell.cizland.com

Aldis Gunsmithing & Shooting Supply, 502 S. Montezuma St., Prescott, AZ 86303 / 602-445-6723; FAX: 602-445-6763

Alessi Holsters, Inc., 2465 Niagara Falls Blvd., Amherst, NY 14228-3527 / 716-691-5615

Alex, Inc., 3420 Cameron Bridge Rd., Manhattan, MT 59741-8523 / 406-282-7396; FAX: 406-282-7396

All American Lead Shot Corp., P.O. Box 224566, Dallas, TX 75062

All Rite Products, Inc., 9554 Wells Circle, Suite D, West Jordan, UT 84088-6226 / 800-771-8471; FAX: 801-280-8302 info@allriteproducts.com www.allriteproducts.com

Allard, Gary/Creek Side Metal & Woodcrafters, Fishers Hill, VA 22626 / 540-465-3903

Allen Co., Inc., 525 Burbank St., Broomfield, CO 80020 / 303-469-1857 or 800-876-8600; FAX: 303-466-7437

Allen Firearm Engraving, P.O. Box 155, Camp Verde, AZ 86322 / 928-567-6711 rosebudmulgco@netzero.com rosebudmulgco@netzero.com

Allen Mfg., 2784 Highway 23, Brook Park, MN 55007

Alley Supply Co., P.O. Box 848, Gardnerville, NV 89410 / 775-782-3800; FAX: 775-782-3827 jetalley@aol.com www.alleysupplyco.com

Alliant Techsystems, Smokeless Powder Group, P.O. Box 6, Rt. 114, Bldg. 229, Radford, VA 24141-0096 www.alliantpowder.com

Allred Bullet Co., 932 Evergreen Drive, Logan, UT 84321 / 435-752-6983; FAX: 435-752-6983

Alpec Team, Inc., 1231 Midas Way, Sunnyvale, CA 94085 / 510-606-8245; FAX: 510-606-4279

Alpha 1 Drop Zone, 2121 N. Tyler, Wichita, KS 67212 / 316-729-0800; FAX: 316-729-4262 www.alpha1dropzone.com

Alpha LaFranck Enterprises, P.O. Box 81072, Lincoln, NE 68501 / 402-466-3193

Alpha Precision, Inc., 3238 Della Slaton Rd., Comer, GA 30629-2212 / 706-783-2131 jim@alphaprecisioninc.com www.alphaprecisioninc.com

Alpine Indoor Shooting Range, 2401 Government Way, Coeur d'Alene, ID 83814 / 208-676-8824; FAX: 208-676-8824

Altamont Co., 901 N. Church St., P.O. Box 309, Thomasboro, IL 61878 / 217-643-3125 or 800-626-5774; FAX: 217-643-7973

Alumna Sport by Dee Zee, 1572 NE 58th Ave., P.O. Box 3090, Des Moines, IA 50316 / 800-798-9899

Amadeo Rossi S.A., Rua: Amadeo Rossi, 143, Sao Leopoldo, RS 93030-220 BRAZIL / 051-592-5566 rossi.firearms@pnet.com.br

Amato, Jeff. See: J&M PRECISION MACHINING

AmBr Software Group Ltd., P.O. Box 301, Reisterstown, MD 21136-0301 / 800-888-1917; FAX: 410-526-7212

American Ammunition, 3545 NW 71st St., Miami, FL 33147 / 305-835-7400; FAX: 305-694-0037

American Derringer Corp., 127 N. Lacy Dr., Waco, TX 76705 / 800-642-7817 or 254-799-9111; FAX: 254-799-7935

American Display Co., 55 Cromwell St., Providence, RI 02907 / 401-331-2464; FAX: 401-421-1264

American Gas & Chemical Co., Ltd., 220 Pegasus Ave., Northvale, NJ 07647 / 201-767-7300

American Gunsmithing Institute, 1325 Imola Ave. #504, Napa, CA 94559 / 707-253-0462; FAX: 707-253-7149 www.americangunsmith.com

American Handgunner Magazine, 12345 World Trade Dr., San Diego, CA 92128 / 800-537-3006; FAX: 858-605-0204 www.americanhandgunner.com

American Pioneer Video, P.O. Box 50049, Bowling Green, KY 42102-2649 / 800-743-4675

American Products, Inc., 14729 Spring Valley Road, Morrison, IL 61270 / 815-772-3336; FAX: 815-772-8046

American Safe Arms, Inc., 1240 Riverview Dr., Garland, UT 84312 / 801-257-7472; FAX: 801-785-8156

American Security Products Co., 11925 Pacific Ave., Fontana, CA 92337 / 909-685-9680 or 800-421-6142; FAX: 909-685-9685

American Small Arms Academy, P.O. Box 12111, Prescott, AZ 86304 / 602-778-5623

American Target, 1328 S. Jason St., Denver, CO 80223 / 303-733-0433; FAX: 303-777-0311

American Target Knives, 1030 Brownwood NW, Grand Rapids, MI 49504 / 616-453-1998

Americase, P.O. Box 271, 1610 E. Main, Waxahachie, TX 75165 / 800-880-3629; FAX: 214-937-8373

Ames Metal Products Co., 4323 S. Western Blvd., Chicago, IL 60609 / 773-523-3230 or 800-255-6937; FAX: 773-523-3854 amesmetal@webtv.net

Amherst Arms, P.O. Box 1457, Englewood, FL 34295 / 941-475-2020; FAX: 941-473-1212

Ammo Load Worldwide, Inc., 815 D St., Lewiston, ID 83501 / 800-528-5610; FAX: 208-746-1730 info@ammoload.com www.ammoload.com

Amrine's Gun Shop, 937 La Luna, Ojai, CA 93023 / 805-646-2376

Amsec, 11925 Pacific Ave., Fontana, CA 92337

AMT/Crusader Arms, 5200 Mitchelldale, Ste. E17, Houston, TX 77092 / 800-272-7816 www.highstandard.com

Analog Devices, Box 9106, Norwood, MA 02062

Andela Tool & Machine, Inc., RD3, Box 246, Richfield Springs, NY 13439

Anderson Manufacturing Co., Inc., 22602 53rd Ave. SE, Bothell, WA 98021 / 206-481-1858; FAX: 206-481-7839

Andres & Dworsky KG, Bergstrasse 18, A-3822 Karlstein, Thaya, AUSTRIA / 0 28 44-285; FAX: 0 28 44-28619 andres.dnorsky@wvnet.as

Angelo & Little Custom Gun Stock Blanks, P.O. Box 240046, Dell, MT 59724-0046

Antique American Firearms, Douglas Carlson, P.O. Box 71035, Dept. GD, Des Moines, IA 50325 / 515-224-6552 drearlson@mailstation.com

Antique Arms Co., 1110 Cleveland Ave., Monett, MO 65708 / 417-235-6501

AO Sight Systems, 2401 Ludelle St., Fort Worth, TX 76105 / 888-744-4880; or 817-536-0136; FAX: 817-536-3517

Apel GmbH, Ernst, Am Kirschberg 3, D-97218, Gerbrunn, GERMANY / 0 (931) 707192 info@eaw.de www.eaw.de

Aplan Antiques & Art, James O., HC 80, Box 793-25, Piedmont, SD 57769 / 605-347-5016

AR-7 Industries, LLC, 998 N. Colony Rd., Meriden, CT 06450 / 203-630-3536; FAX: 203-630-3637

ArmaLite, Inc., P.O. Box 299, Geneseo, IL 61254 / 800-336-0184 or 309-944-6939; FAX: 309-944-6949

Armament Gunsmithing Co., Inc., 525 Rt. 22, Hillside, NJ 07205 / 908-686-0960; FAX: 718-738-5019 armamentgunsmithing@worldnet.att.net

Armas Garbi, S.A., 12-14 20.600 Urki, 12, Eibar (Guipuzcoa), SPAIN / 943 20 3873; FAX: 943 20 3873 armosgarbi@euskalnet.n

Armas Kemen S. A. (See U.S. Importers)

Armfield Custom Bullets, 10584 County Road 100, Carthage, MO 64836 / 417-359-8480; FAX: 417-359-8497

Armi Perazzi S.P.A., Via Fontanelle 1/3, 1-25080, Botticino Mattina, ITALY / 030-2692591; FAX: 030-2692594

Armi San Marco (See Taylor's & Co.)

Armi San Paolo, 172-A, I-25062, via Europa, ITALY / 030-2751725

Armi Sport (See Cimarron Firearms, E.M.F., KBI & Taylor's & Co.)

Armite Laboratories Inc., 1560 Superior Ave., Costa Mesa, CA 92627 / 949-646-9035; FAX: 949-646-8319 armite@pacbell.net www.armitelahs.com

Armoloy Co. of Ft. Worth, 204 E. Daggett St., Fort Worth, TX 76104 / 817-332-5604; FAX: 817-335-6517 info@armoloyftworth.com www.armoloyftworth.com

Armor (See Buck Stop Lure Co., Inc.)

Armor Metal Products, P.O. Box 4609, Helena, MT 59604 / 406-442-5560; FAX: 406-442-5650

Armory Publications, 2120 S. Reserve St., PMB 253, Missoula, MT 59801 / 406-549-7670; FAX: 406-728-0597 armorypub@aol.com www.armorypub.com

MANUFACTURER'S DIRECTORY

Arms & Armour Press, Wellington House, 125 Strand, London, WC2R 0BB ENGLAND / 0171-420-5555; FAX: 0171-240-7265
Arms Corporation of the Philippines, Armscor Ave. Brgy. Fortune, Marikina City, PHILIPPINES / 632-941-6243 or 632-941-6244; FAX: 632-942-0682 info@armscor.com.ph
Arms Craft Gunsmithing, 1106 Linda Dr., Arroyo Grande, CA 93420 / 805-481-2830
Arms, Programming Solutions (See Arms Software)
Armscor Precision, 5740 S. Arville St. #219, Las Vegas, NV 89118 / 702-362-7750
Armscorp USA, Inc., 4424 John Ave., Baltimore, MD 21227 / 301-775-8134 info@armscorpusa.com www.armscorpusa.com
Arratoonian, Andy (See Horseshoe Leather Products)
Arrieta S.L., Morkaiko 5, 20870, Elgoibar, SPAIN / 34-43-743150; FAX: 34-43-743154
Arsenal, Inc., 5015 W. Sahara Ave., Ste. 125, Las Vegas, NV 89146 / 888-539-2220; FAX: 702-643-2088 www.arsenalinc.com
Art Jewel Enterprises Ltd., Eagle Business Ctr., 460 Randy Rd., Carol Stream, IL 60188 / 708-260-0400
Artistry in Wood, 134 Zimmerman Rd., Kalispell, MT 59901 / 406-257-9003; FAX: 406-257-9167 merlins@digisys.net www.acrabondlaminates.com
Art's Gun & Sport Shop, Inc., 6008 Hwy. Y, Hillsboro, MO 63050
Aspen Outfitting Co., Jon Hollinger, 9 Dean St., Aspen, CO 81611 / 970-925-3406
A-Square Co., 205 Fairfield Ave., Jeffersonville, IN 47130 / 812-283-0577; FAX: 812-283-0375
Astra Sport, S.A., Apartado 3, 48300 Guernica, Espagne, SPAIN / 34-4-6250100; FAX: 34-4-6255186
Atamec-Bretton, 19 rue Victor Grignard, F-42026, St.-Etienne (Cedex 1, FRANCE / 33-77-93-54-69; FAX: 33-77-93-57-98
Atlanta Cutlery Corp., 2143 Gees Mill Rd., Box 839 CIS, Conyers, GA 30207 / 800-883-0300; FAX: 404-388-0246
Atlantic Mills, Inc., 1295 Towbin Ave., Lakewood, NJ 08701-5934 / 800-242-7374
Atsko/Sno-Seal, Inc., 2664 Russell St., Orangeburg, SC 29115 / 803-531-1820; FAX: 803-531-2139 info@atsko.com www.atsko.com
Austin & Halleck, Inc., 2150 South 950 East, Provo, UT 84606-6285 / 877-543-3256 or 801-374-9990; FAX: 801-374-9998 www.austinhallek.com
Austin Sheridan USA, Inc., 89 Broad St., Middlefield, CT 06455 / 860-346-2500; FAX: 860-346-2510 asusa@sbcglobal.net www.austinsheridanusa.com
Auto Arms, 738 Clearview, San Antonio, TX 78228 / 512-434-5450
Auto-Ordnance Corp., P.O. Box 220, Blauvelt, NY 10913 / 914-353-7770
Autumn Sales, Inc. (Blaser), 1320 Lake St., Fort Worth, TX 76102 / 817-335-1634; FAX: 817-338-0119
Avnda Otaola Norica, 16 Apartado 68, 20600, Eibar, SPAIN
AWC Systems Technology, P.O. Box 41938, Phoenix, AZ 85080-1938 / 623-780-1050; FAX: 623-780-2967 awc@awcsystech.com www.awcsystech.com
Axtell Rifle Co., 353 Mill Creek Road, Sheridan, MT 59749 / 406-842-5814
AYA (See U.S. Importer-New England Custom Gun Serv

B

B&D Trading Co., Inc., 3935 Fair Hill Rd., Fair Oaks, CA 95628 / 800-334-3790 or 916-967-9366; FAX: 916-967-4873
B&P America, 12321 Brittany Cir., Dallas, TX 75230 / 972-726-9069
B.A.C., 17101 Los Modelos St., Fountain Valley, CA 92708 / 435-586-3286
B.C. Outdoors, Larry McGhee, PO Box 61497, Boulder City, NV 89006 / 702-294-3056; FAX: 702-294-0413 jdalton@pmcammo.com www.pmcammo.com
B.M.F. Activator, Inc., 12145 Mill Creek Run, Plantersville, TX 77363 / 936-894-2397; FAX: 936-894-2397 bmf25years@aol.com
Baelder, Harry, Alte Goennebeker Strasse 5, 24635, Rickling, GERMANY / 04328-722732; FAX: 04328-722733
Baer's Hollows, P.O. Box 603, Taft, CA 93268 / 719-438-5718
Bagmaster Mfg., Inc., 2731 Sutton Ave., St. Louis, MO 63143 / 314-781-8002; FAX: 314-781-3363 sales@bagmaster.com www.bagmaster.com
Bain & Davis, Inc., 307 E. Valley Blvd., San Gabriel, CA 91776-3522 / 626-573-4241; FAX: 626-573-8102 baindavis@aol.com
Baker, Stan. See: STAN BAKER SPORTS
Bald Eagle Precision Machine Co., 101-A Allison St., Lock Haven, PA 17745 / 570-748-6772; FAX: 570-748-4443 bepmachine@aol.com baldeaglemachine.com
Ballard, Donald. See: BALLARD INDUSTRIES
Ballard Industries, Donald Ballard Sr., P.O. Box 2035, Arnold, CA 95223 / 408-996-0957; FAX: 408-257-6828
Ballard Rifle & Cartridge Co., LLC, 113 W. Yellowstone Ave., Cody, WY 82414 / 307-587-4914; FAX: 307-527-6097 ballard@wyoming.com www.ballardrifles.com
Ballistic Products, Inc., 20015 75th Ave. North, Corcoran, MN 55340-9456 / 763-494-9237; FAX: 763-494-9236 info@ballisticproducts.com www.ballisticproducts.com
Ballistic Program Co., Inc., The, 2417 N. Patterson St., Thomasville, GA 31792 / 912-228-5739 or 800-368-0835
Ballistic Research, 1108 W. May Ave., McHenry, IL 60050 / 815-385-0037
Ballisti-Cast, Inc., P.O. Box 1057, Minot, ND 58702-1057 / 701-497-3333; FAX: 701-497-3335
Bang-Bang Boutique (See Holster Shop, The)
Bansner's Ultimate Rifles, LLC, P.O. Box 839, 261 E. Main St., Adamstown, PA 19501 / 717-484-2370; FAX: 717-484-0523 bansner@aol.com www.bansnersrifle.com
Barbour, Inc., 55 Meadowbrook Dr., Milford, NH 03055 / 603-673-1313; FAX: 603-673-6510
Barnes Bullets, Inc., P.O. Box 215, American Fork, UT 84003 / 801-756-4222 or 800-574-9200; FAX: 801-756-2465 email@barnesbullets.com www.barnesbullets.com
Baron Technology, 62 Spring Hill Rd., Trumbull, CT 06611 / 203-452-0515; FAX: 203-452-0663 dbaron@baronengraving.com www.baronengraving.com
Barraclough, John K., 55 Merit Park Dr., Gardena, CA 90247 / 310-324-2574 jbarraclough@sbcglobal.net
Barramundi Corp., P.O. Drawer 4259, Homosassa Springs, FL 32687 / 904-628-0200
Barrel & Gunworks, 2601 Lake Valley Rd., Prescott Valley, AZ 86314 / 928-772-4060 www.cutrifle.com
Barrett Firearms Manufacturer, Inc., P.O. Box 1077, Murfreesboro, TN 37133 / 615-896-2938; FAX: 615-896-7313
Bar-Sto Precision Machine, 73377 Sullivan Rd., P.O. Box 1838, Twentynine Palms, CA 92277 / 760-367-2747; FAX: 760-367-2407 barsto@eee.org www.barsto.com
Barta's Gunsmithing, 10231 U.S. Hwy. 10, Cato, WI 54230 / 920-732-4472
Barteaux Machete, 1916 SE 50th Ave., Portland, OR 97215-3238 / 503-233-5880
Bartlett Engineering, 40 South 200 East, Smithfield, UT 84335-1645 / 801-563-5910
Bates Engraving, Billy, 2302 Winthrop Dr. SW, Decatur, AL 35603 / 256-355-3690 bbrn@aol.com www.angelfire.com/al/billybates
Battenfeld Technologies, Inc., 5885 W. Van Horn Tavern Rd., Columbia, MO 65203 / 573-445-9200; FAX: 573-447-4158 battenfeldtechnologies.com
Bauer, Eddie, 15010 NE 36th St., Redmond, WA 98052
Baumgartner Bullets, 3011 S. Alane St., W. Valley City, UT 84120
Bauska Barrels, 105 9th Ave. W., Kalispell, MT 59901 / 406-752-7706
BC-Handmade Bullets, 482 Comerwood Court, S. San Francisco, CA 94080 / 650-583-1550; FAX: 650-583-1550
Bear Archery, RR 4, 4600 Southwest 41st Blvd., Gainesville, FL 32601 / 904-376-2327
Bear Arms, 374-A Carson Rd., St. Mathews, SC 29135
Bear Mountain Gun & Tool, 120 N. Plymouth, New Plymouth, ID 83655 / 208-278-5221; FAX: 208-278-5221
Beartooth Bullets, P.O. Box 491, Dept. HLD, Dover, ID 83825-0491 / 208-448-1865 bullets@beartoothbullets.com beartoothbullets.com
Beaver Park Product, Inc., 840 J St., Penrose, CO 81240 / 719-372-6744
BEC, Inc., 1227 W. Valley Blvd., Suite 204, Alhambra, CA 91803 / 626-281-5751; FAX: 626-293-7073
Beeks, Mike. See: GRAYBACK WILDCATS
Beeman Precision Airguns, 5454 Argosy Dr., Huntington Beach, CA 92649 / 714-890-4808; FAX: 714-890-4808
Beitzinger, George, 116-20 Atlantic Ave., Richmond Hill, NY 11419 / 718-847-7661
Bell & Carlson, Inc., Dodge City Industrial Park, 101 Allen Rd., Dodge City, KS 67801 / 800-634-8586 or 620-225-6688; FAX: 620-225-6688 email@bellandcarlson.com
Bell Reloading, Inc., 1725 Harlin Lane Rd., Villa Rica, GA 30180
Bell's Gun & Sport Shop, 3309-19 Mannheim Rd., Franklin Park, IL 60131
Bell's Legendary Country Wear, 22 Circle Dr., Bellmore, NY 11710 / 516-679-1158
Benchmark Knives (See Gerber Legendary Blades)
Benelli Armi S.P.A., Via della Stazione, 61029, Urbino, ITALY / 39-722-307-1; FAX: 39-722-327427
Benelli USA Corp., 17603 Indian Head Hwy., Accokeek, MD 20607 / 301-283-6981; FAX: 301-283-6988 benelliusa.com
Bengtson Arms Co., L., 6345-B E. Akron St., Mesa, AZ 85205 / 602-981-6375
Benjamin/Sheridan Co., Crosman, Rts. 5 and 20, E. Bloomfield, NY 14443 / 716-657-6161; FAX: 716-657-5405 www.crosman.com
Bentley, John, 128-D Watson Dr., Turtle Creek, PA 15145
Beretta Pietro S.P.A., Via Beretta, 18, 25063, Gardone Valtrompia, ITALY / 39-30-8341-1 www.beretta.com
Beretta U.S.A. Corp., 17601 Beretta Dr., Accokeek, MD 20607 / 301-283-2191; FAX: 301-283-0435
Berger Bullets Ltd., 5443 W. Westwind Dr., Glendale, AZ 85310 / 602-842-4001; FAX: 602-934-9083
Bernardelli, Vincenzo, P.O. Box 460243, Houston, TX 77056-8243 www.bernardelli.com
Bernardelli, Vincenzo, Via Grande, 10, Sede Legale Torbole Casaglia, Brescia, ITALY / 39-30-8912851-2-3; FAX: 39-030-2150963 bernardelli@bernardelli.com www.bernardelli.com
Berry's Mfg., Inc., 401 North 3050 East St., St. George, UT 84770 / 435-634-1682; FAX: 435-634-1683 sales@berrysmfg.com www.berrysmfg.com
Bersa S.A., Benso Bonadimani, Magallanes 775 B1704 FLC, Ramos Mejia, ARGENTINA / 011-4656-2377; FAX: 011-4656-2093+ info@bersa-sa.com.ar www.bersa-sa.com.ar
Bert Johanssons Vapentillbehor, S-430 20 Veddige, SWEDEN,
Bertuzzi (See U.S. Importer-New England Arms Co.)
Better Concepts Co., 663 New Castle Rd., Butler, PA 16001 / 412-285-9000
Beverly, Mary, 3969 102nd Pl. N., Clearwater, FL 33762
Bianchi International, Inc., 27969 Jefferson Ave., Temecula, CA 92590 / 951-676-5621; FAX: 951-676-6777 www.customerservice@bianchi-intl.com www.bianchi- intl.com
Big Bore Bullets of Alaska, P.O. Box 521455, Big Lake, AK 99652 / 907-373-2673; FAX: 907-373-2673 doug@mtaonline.net ww.awloo.com/bbb/index.
Big Bore Express, 2316 E. Railroad St., Nampa, ID 83651 / 800-376-4010 FAX: 208-466-6927 info@powerbeltbullets.com bigbore.com
Big Spring Enterprises "Bore Stores", P.O. Box 1115, Big Spring Rd., Yellville, AR 72687 / 870-449-5297; FAX: 870-449-4446
Bilal, Mustafa. See: TURK'S HEAD PRODUCTIONS
Bilinski, Bryan. See: FIELDSPORT LTD.
Bill Adair Custom Shop, 2886 Westridge, Carrollton, TX 75006 / 972-418-0950
Bill Austin's Calls, Box 284, Kaycee, WY 82639 / 307-738-2552
Bill Hanus Birdguns, LLC, P.O. Box 533, Newport, OR 97365 / 541-265-7433; FAX: 541-265-7400 www.billhanusbirdguns.com
Bill Russ Trading Post, William A. Russ, 25 William St., Addison, NY 14801-1326 / 607-359-3896
Bill Wiseman and Co., 10456 State Highway 6 S, College Sta, TX 77845 / 979-690-3456
Billeb, Stephen. See: QUALITY CUSTOM FIREARMS
Billings Gunsmiths, 1841 Grand Ave., Billings, MT 59102 / 406-256-8390; FAX: 406-256-6530 blgsgunsmiths@msn.com
Billingsley & Brownell, P.O. Box 25, Dayton, WY 82836 / 307-655-9344
Bill's Gun Repair, 1007 Burlington St., Mendota, IL 61342 / 815-539-5786
Billy Bates Engraving, 2302 Winthrop Dr. SW, Decatur, AL 35603 / 256-355-3690 bbrn@aol.com www.angelfire.com/al/billybates
Birchwood Casey, 7900 Fuller Rd., Eden Prairie, MN 55344 / 800-328-6156 or 612-937-7933; FAX: 612-937-7979
Birdsong & Assoc., W. E., 1435 Monterey Rd., Florence, MS 39073-9748 / 601-366-8270
Bismuth Cartridge Co., 3500 Maple Ave., Suite 1650, Dallas, TX 75219 / 214-521-5880; FAX: 214-521-9035
Bison Studios, 1409 South Commerce St., Las Vegas, NV 89102 / 702-388-2891; FAX: 702-383-9967
Bitterroot Bullet Co., 2001 Cedar Ave., Lewiston, ID 83501-0412 / 208-743-5635 brootbil@lewiston.com
BKL Technologies, P.O. Box 5237, Brownsville, TX 78523
Black Belt Bullets (See Big Bore Express)
Black Hills Ammunition, Inc., P.O. Box 3090, Rapid City, SD 57709-3090 / 605-348-5150; FAX: 605-348-9827
Black Hills Shooters Supply, P.O. Box 4220, Rapid City, SD 57709 / 800-289-2506
Black Powder Products, 67 Township Rd. 1411, Chesapeake, OH 45619 / 614-867-8047
Black Sheep Brand, 3220 W. Gentry Pkwy., Tyler, TX 75702 / 903-592-3853; FAX: 903-592-0527

Blacksmith Corp., P.O. Box 280, North Hampton, OH 45349 / 937-969-8389; FAX: 937-969-8399 sales@blacksmithcorp.com www.blacksmithcorp.com
BlackStar AccuMax Barrels, 11501 Brittmoore Park Drive, Houston, TX 77041 / 281-721-6040; FAX: 281-721-6041
BlackStar Barrel Accurizing (See BlackStar AccuMax)
Blacktail Mountain Books, 42 First Ave. W., Kalispell, MT 59901 / 406-257-5573
Blaser Jagdwaffen GmbH, D-88316, Isny Im Allgau, GERMANY
Blount, Inc., Sporting Equipment Div., 2299 Snake River Ave., P.O. Box 856, Lewiston, ID 83501 / 800-627-3640 or 208-746-2351; FAX: 208-799-3904
Blount/Outers ATK, P.O. Box 39, Onalaska, WI 54650 / 608-781-5800; FAX: 608-781-0368
Blue and Gray Products Inc. (See Ox-Yoke Originals)
Blue Book Publications, Inc., 8009 34th Ave. S., Ste. 175, Minneapolis, MN 55425 / 952-854-5229; FAX: 952-853-1486 bluebook@bluebookinc.com www.bluebookinc.com
Blue Mountain Bullets, 64146 Quail Ln., Box 231, John Day, OR 97845 / 541-820-4594; FAX: 541-820-4594
Blue Ridge Machinery & Tools, Inc., P.O. Box 536-GD, Hurricane, WV 25526 / 800-872-6500; FAX: 304-562-5311 blueridgemachine@worldnet.att.net www.blueridgemachinery.com
BMC Supply, Inc., 26051 - 179th Ave. SE, Kent, WA 98042
Bob Allen Sportswear, One Bort Dr., Osceola, IA 50213 / 210-344-8531; FAX: 210-342-2703 sales@bob-allen.com www.bob-allen.com
Bob Rogers Gunsmithing, P.O. Box 305, 344 S. Walnut St., Franklin Grove, IL 61031 / 815-456-2685; FAX: 815-456-2685 3006bud@netscape.comm
Bob's Gun Shop, P.O. Box 200, Royal, AR 71968 / 501-767-1970; FAX: 501-767-1970 gunparts@hsnp.com www.gun-parts.com
Bob's Tactical Indoor Shooting Range & Gun Shop, 90 Lafayette Rd., Salisbury, MA 01952 / 508-465-5561
Boessler, Erich, Am Vogeltal 3, 97702, Munnerstadt, GERMANY
Boker USA, Inc., 1550 Balsam Street, Lakewood, CO 80214 / 303-462-0662; FAX: 303-462-0668 sales@bokerusa.com bokerusa.com
Boltin, John M., P.O. Box 644, Estill, SC 29918 / 803-625-2185
Bo-Mar Tool & Mfg. Co., 6136 State Hwy. 300, Longview, TX 75604 / 903-759-4784; FAX: 903-759-9141 marykor@earthlink.net bo-mar.com
Bonadimani, Benso. See: BERSA S.A.
Bonanza (See Forster Products), 310 E. Lanark Ave., Lanark, IL 61046 / 815-493-6360; FAX: 815-493-2371
Bond Arms, Inc., P.O. Box 1296, Granbury, TX 76048 / 817-573-4445; FAX: 817-573-5636 www.bondarms.com
Bond Custom Firearms, 8954 N. Lewis Ln., Bloomington, IN 47408 / 812-332-4519
Bonham's & Butterfields, 220 San Bruno Ave., San Francisco, CA 94103 / 415-861-7500; FAX: 415-861-0183 arms@butterfields.com www.butterfields.com
Boone Trading Co., Inc., P.O. Box 669, Brinnon, WA 98320 / 800-423-1945 or 360-796-4330; FAX: 360-796-4511 sales@boonetrading.com boonetrading.com
Boone's Custom Ivory Grips, Inc., 562 Coyote Rd., Brinnon, WA 98320 / 206-796-4330
Boonie Packer Products, P.O. Box 12517, Salem, OR 97309-0517 / 800-477-3244 or 503-581-3244; FAX: 503-581-3191 customerservice@booniepacker.com www.booniepacker.com
Borden Ridges Rimrock Stocks, RR 1 Box 250 BC, Springville, PA 18844 / 570-965-2505; FAX: 570-965-2328
Borden Rifles Inc., RD 1, Box 250 #BC, Springville, PA 18844 / 717-965-2505; FAX: 717-965-2328
Border Barrels Ltd., Riccarton Farm, Newcastleton, SCOTLAND UK
Borovnik K.G., Ludwig, 9170 Ferlach, Bahnhofstrasse 7, AUSTRIA / 042 27 24 42; FAX: 042 26 43 49
Bosis (See U.S. Importer-New England Arms Co.)
Boss Manufacturing Co., 221 W. First St., Kewanee, IL 61443 / 309-852-2131 or 800-447-4581; FAX: 309-852-0848
Bostick Wildlife Calls, Inc., P.O. Box 728, Estill, SC 29918 / 803-625-2210; or 803-625-4512
Bowen Classic Arms Corp., P.O. Box 67, Louisville, TN 37777 / 865-984-3583 bcacorp@aks.net www.bowenclassicarms.com
Bowen Knife Co., Inc., P.O. Box 802, Magnolia, AR 71754 / 800-397-4794; FAX: 870-234-9005 info@bowen.com www.bowenknife.com
Bowerly, Kent, 710 Golden Pheasant Dr., Redmond, OR 97756 / 541-923-3501 bowerly@bendbroadband.com
Boyds' Gunstock Industries, Inc., 25376 403 Rd. Ave., Mitchell, SD 57301 / 605-996-5011; FAX: 605-996-9878 www.boydsgunstocks.com
Brace, Larry D., 771 Blackfoot Ave., Eugene, OR 97404 / 541-688-1278; FAX: 541-607-5833
Brauer Bros., P.O. Box 2485, McKinney, TX 75070 / 976-548-8881; FAX: 972-548-8886 www.brauerbros.com
Break-Free, Inc., 13386 International Pkwy., Jacksonville, FL 32218 / 800-428-0588; FAX: 904-741-5407 contactus@armorholdings.com www.break-free.com
Brenneke GmbH, P.O. Box 1646, 30837, Langenhagen, GERMANY / +49-511-97262-0; FAX: +49-511-97262-62 info@brenneke.de brenneke.com
Bridgeman Products, Harry Jaffin, 153 B Cross Slope Ct., Englishtown, NJ 07726 / 732-536-3604; FAX: 732-972-1004
Briese Bullet Co., Inc., 3442 42nd Ave. SE, Tappen, ND 58487 / 701-327-4578; FAX: 701-327-4579
Brigade Quartermasters, 1025 Cobb International Blvd., Dept. VH, Kennesaw, GA 30144-4300 / 404-428-1248 or 800-241-3125; FAX: 404-426-7726
Briganti, A.J. See: BRIGANTI CUSTOM GUNSMITH
Briganti Custom Gunsmith, A.J. Briganti, 512 Rt. 32, Highland Mills, NY 10930 / 845-928-9573
Briley Mfg. Inc., 1230 Lumpkin, Houston, TX 77043 / 800-331-5718 or 713-932-6995; FAX: 713-932-1043
Brill, R. See: ROYAL ARMS INTERNATIONAL
British Sporting Arms, RR 1, Box 193A, Millbrook, NY 12545 / 845-677-8303; FAX: 845-677-5756 info@bsaltd.com www.bsaltd.com
Broad Creek Rifle Works, Ltd., 120 Horsey Ave., Laurel, DE 19956 / 302-875-5446; FAX: 302-875-1448 bcrw4guns@aol.com
Brockman's Custom Gunsmithing, 445 Idaho St., Gooding, ID 83330 / 208-934-5050 brockman@brockmansrifles.com www.brockmansrifles.com
Broken Gun Ranch, 10739 126 Rd., Spearville, KS 67876 / 316-385-2587; FAX: 316-385-2597 nbowlin@ucom.net www.brokengunranch
Brooker, Dennis, Rt. 1, Box 12A, Derby, IA 50068 / 515-533-2103
Brooks Tactical Systems-Agrip, 279-C Shorewood Ct., Fox Island, WA 98333 / 253-549-2866; FAX: 253-549-2703 brooks@brookstactical.com www.brookstactical.com
Brown Precision, Inc., 7786 Molinos Ave., Los Molinos, CA 96055 / 530-384-2506; FAX: 916-384-1638 www.brownprecision.com
Brownells, Inc., 200 S. Front St., Montezuma, IA 50171 / 800-741-0015; FAX: 800-264-3068 orderdesk@brownells.com www.brownells.com
Browning Arms Co., One Browning Place, Morgan, UT 84050 / 801-876-2711; FAX: 801-876-3331 www.browning.com
Browning Arms Co. (Parts & Service), 3005 Arnold Tenbrook Rd., Arnold, MO 63010 / 617-287-6800; FAX: 617-287-9751
BRP, Inc. High Performance Cast Bullets, 1210 Alexander Rd., Colorado Springs, CO 80909 / 719-633-0658
Brunton U.S.A., 2255 Brunton Ct., Riverton, WY 82501 info@brunton.com www.brunton.com
Bryan & Assoc., R. D. Sauls, P.O. Box 5772, Anderson, SC 29623-5772 / 864-261-6810 bryanandac@aol.com www.huntersweb.com/bryanandac
Brynin, Milton, P.O. Box 383, Yonkers, NY 10710 / 914-779-4333
BSA Guns Ltd., Armoury Rd. Small Heath, Birmingham B11 2PP, ENGLAND / 011-021-772-8543; FAX: 011-021-773-0845 sales@bsagun.com www.bsagun.com
BSA Optics, 3911 SW 47th Ave., Ste. 914, Ft. Lauderdale, FL 33314 / 954-581-2144; FAX: 954-581-3165 4info@basaoptics.com www.bsaoptics.com
B-Square Company, Inc., 8909 Forum Way, Ft. Worth, TX 76140 / 800-433-2909; FAX: 817-926-7012 bsquare@b-square.com www.b-square.com
Buchsenmachermeister, Peter Hofer Jagdwaffen, A-9170 Ferlach, Kirchgasse 24, Kirchgasse, AUSTRIA / 43 4227 3683; or 43 664 3200216; FAX: 43 4227 368330 peterhofer@hoferwaffen.com www.hoferwaffen.com
Buck Knives, Inc., 660 Lochsa St., Post Falls, ID 83854 / 208-262-0500; FAX: 800-326-2825 www.buckknives.com
Buck Stix-SOS Products Co., Box 3, Neenah, WI 54956
Buck Stop Lure Co., Inc., 3600 Grow Rd. NW, P.O. Box 636, Stanton, MI 48888 / 989-762-5091; FAX: 989-762-5124 buckstop@nethawk.com www.buckstopscents.com
Buckeye Custom Bullets, 6490 Stewart Rd., Elida, OH 45807 / 419-641-4463
Buckhorn Gun Works, 8109 Woodland Dr., Black Hawk, SD 57718 / 605-787-6472
Buckskin Bullet Co., P.O. Box 1893, Cedar City, UT 84721 / 435-586-3286
Budin, Dave. See: DEL-SPORTS, INC.
Buehler Custom Sporting Arms, P.O. Box 4096, Medford, OR 97501 / 541-664-9109 rbrifle@earthlink.net
Buenger Enterprises/Goldenrod Dehumidifier, 3600 S. Harbor Blvd., Oxnard, CA 93035 / 800-451-6797 or 805-985-5828; FAX: 805-985-1534
Buffalo Arms Co., 660 Vermeer Ct., Ponderay, ID 83852 / 208-263-6953; FAX: 208-265-2096 www.buffaloarms.com
Buffalo Bullet Co., Inc., 12637 Los Nietos Rd., Unit A, Santa Fe Springs, CA 90670 / 800-423-8069; FAX: 562-944-5054 rdanlitz@verizon.net
Buffalo Gun Center, 3385 Harlem Rd., Buffalo, NY 14225 / 716-833-2581; FAX: 716-833-2265 www.buffaloguncenter.com
Buffalo Rock Shooters Supply, R.R. 1, Ottawa, IL 61350 / 815-433-2471
Buffer Technologies, P.O. Box 105047, Jefferson City, MO 65110 / 573-634-8529; FAX: 573-634-8522 sales@buffertech.com buffertech.com
Bull Mountain Rifle Co., 6327 Golden West Terrace, Billings, MT 59106 / 406-656-0778
Bullberry Barrel Works, Ltd., 2430 W. Bullberry Ln., Hurricane, UT 84737 / 435-635-9866; FAX: 435-635-0348 fred@bullberry.com www.bullberry.com
Bullet Metals, Bill Ferguson, P.O. Box 1238, Sierra Vista, AZ 85636 / 520-458-5321; FAX: 520-458-1421 info@theantimonyman.com www.bullet-metals.com
Bullet Swaging Supply, Inc., P.O. Box 1056, 303 McMillan Rd., West Monroe, LA 71291 / 318-387-3266; FAX: 318-387-7779 leblackmon@colla.com
Bull-X, Inc., 411 E. Water St., Farmer City, IL 61842-1556 / 309-928-2574 or 800-248-3845; FAX: 309-928-2130
Burkhart Gunsmithing, Don, P.O. Box 852, Rawlins, WY 82301 / 307-324-6007
Burnham Bros., P.O. Box 1148, Menard, TX 78659 / 915-396-4572; FAX: 915-396-4574
Burris Co., Inc., P.O. Box 1747, 331 E. 8th St., Greeley, CO 80631 / 970-356-1670; FAX: 970-356-8702
Bushmaster Firearms, Inc., 999 Roosevelt Trail, Windham, ME 04062 / 800-998-7928; FAX: 207-892-8068 info@bushmaster.com www.bushmaster.com
Bushmaster Hunting & Fishing, 451 Alliance Ave., Toronto, ON M6N 2J1 CANADA / 416-763-4040; FAX: 416-763-0623
Bushnell Outdoor Products, 9200 Cody, Overland Park, KS 66214 / 913-752-3400 or 800-423-3537; FAX: 913-752-3550
Buster's Custom Knives, P.O. Box 214, Richfield, UT 84701 / 435-896-5319; FAX: 435-896-8333 www.warenskiknives.com
Butler Creek Corp., 9200 Cody St., Overland Park, KS 66214 / 800-845-2444 or 406-388-1356; FAX: 406-388-7204
Butler Enterprises, 834 Oberting Rd., Lawrenceburg, IN 47025 / 812-537-3584
Buzz Fletcher Custom Stockmaker, 117 Silver Road, P.O. Box 189, Taos, NM 87571 / 505-758-3486

C

C&D Special Products (See Claybuster Wads & Harvester Bullets)
C&H Research, 115 Sunnyside Dr., Box 351, Lewis, KS 67552 / 316-324-5445 or 888-324-5445; FAX: 620-324-5984 info@mercuryrecoil.com www.mercuryrecoil.com
C. Sharps Arms Co. Inc./Montana Armory, 100 Centennial Dr., P.O. Box 885, Big Timber, MT 59011 / 406-932-4353; FAX: 406-932-4443 www.csharpsarms.com
C.S. Van Gorden & Son, Inc., 1815 Main St., Bloomer, WI 54724 / 715-568-2612 vangorden@bloomer.net
C.W. Erickson's Mfg., L.L.C., P.O. Box 522, Buffalo, MN 55313 / 763-682-3665; FAX: 763-682-4328 cwerickson@archerhunter.com www.archerhunter.com
Cabanas (See U.S. Importer-Mandall Shooting Supply
Cabela's, One Cabela Drive, Sidney, NE 69160 / 308-254-5505; FAX: 308-254-8420
Cabinet Mtn. Outfitters Scents & Lures, P.O. Box 766, Plains, MT 59859 / 406-826-3970
Caesar Guerini USA, Inc., 700 Lake St., Cambridge, MD 21613 / 410-901-1131; FAX: 410-901-1137 info@gueriniusa.com www.gueriniusa.com
Cain's Outdoors, Inc., 1832 Williams Hwy., Williamstown, WV 26187 / 304-375-7842; FAX: 304-375-7842 muzzleloading@cainsoutdoor.com www.cainsoutdoor.com
Cali'co Hardwoods, Inc., 3580 Westwind Blvd., Santa Rosa, CA 95403 / 707-546-4045; FAX: 707-546-4027 calicohardwoods@msn.com

MANUFACTURER'S DIRECTORY

California Sights (See Fautheree, Andy)
Camdex, Inc., 2330 Alger, Troy, MI 48083 / 810-528-2300; FAX: 810-528-0989
Cameron's, 16690 W. 11th Ave., Golden, CO 80401 / 303-279-7365; FAX: 303-568-1009 ncnoremac@aol.com
Camillus Cutlery Co., 54 Main St., Camillus, NY 13031 / 315-672-8111; FAX: 315-672-8832
Campbell, Dick, 196 Garden Homes Dr., Colville, WA 99114 / 509-684-6080; FAX: 509-684-6080 dicksknives@aol.com
Camp-Cap Products, P.O. Box 3805, Chesterfield, MO 63006 / 866-212-4639; FAX: 636-536-6320 mandrytrc@sbcglobal.net www.langenberghats.com
Cannon Safe, Inc., 216 S. 2nd Ave. #BLD-932, San Bernardino, CA 92400 / 800-242-1055; FAX: 909-382-0707 info@cannonsafe.com www.cannonsafe.com
Canyon Cartridge Corp., P.O. Box 152, Albertson, NY 11507 FAX: 516-294-8946
Cape Outfitters, 599 County Rd. 206, Cape Girardeau, MO 63701 / 573-335-4103; FAX: 573-335-1555
Caraville Manufacturing, P.O. Box 4545, Thousand Oaks, CA 91359 / 805-499-1234
Carbide Checkering Tools (See J&R Engineering)
Carhartt, Inc., 5750 Mercury Dr., Dearborn, MI 48126 / 800-833-3118 www.carhartt.com
Carl Walther GmbH, B.P. 4325, D-89033, Ulm, GERMANY
Carl Zeiss Inc., 13005 N. Kingston Ave., Chester, VA 23836 / 800-441-3005; FAX: 804-530-8481
Carlson, Douglas. See: ANTIQUE AMERICAN FIREARMS
Carolina Precision Rifles, 1200 Old Jackson Hwy., Jackson, SC 29831 / 803-827-2069
Carrell, William. See: CARRELL'S PRECISION FIREARMS
Carrell's Precision Firearms, William Carrell, 1952 W. Silver Falls Ct., Meridian, ID 83642-3837
Carry-Lite, Inc., P.O. Box 1587, Fort Smith, AR 72902 / 479-782-8971; FAX: 479-783-0234
Carter's Gun Shop, 225 G St., Penrose, CO 81240 / 719-372-6240 rlewiscarter@msn.com
Case & Sons Cutlery Co., W R, Owens Way, Bradford, PA 16701 / 814-368-4123 or 800-523-6350; FAX: 814-768-5369 info@wrcase.com www.wrcase.com
Case Sorting System, 12695 Cobblestone Creek Rd., Poway, CA 92064 / 619-486-9340
Cash Mfg. Co./ TDC, P.O. Box 130, 201 S. Klein Dr., Waunakee, WI 53597-0130 / 608-849-5664; FAX: 608-849-5664 office@tdcmfg.com www.tdcmfg.com
Caspian Arms, Ltd., 14 North Main St., Hardwick, VT 05843 / 802-472-6454; FAX: 802-472-6709
Cast Bullet Association, The, 12857 S. Road, Hoyt, KS 66440-9116 cbamemdir@castbulletassoc.org www.castbulletassoc.org
Cast Performance Bullet Company, P.O. Box 1466, Rainier, OR 97048 / 503-556-3006; FAX: 503-556-8037 info@bornhunter.com www.bornhunter.com
Casull Arms Corp., P.O. Box 1629, Afton, WY 83110 / 307-886-0200
Caswell Inc., 2540 2nd St. NE, Minneapolis, MN 55410 / 847-639-7666; FAX: 847-639-7694 www.caswellintl.com
Cathey Enterprises, Inc., P.O. Box 2202, Brownwood, TX 76804 / 915-643-2553; FAX: 915-643-3653
Cation, 2341 Alger St., Troy, MI 48083 / 810-689-0658; FAX: 810-689-7558
Caywood, Shane J., P.O. Box 321, Minocqua, WI 54548 / 715-277-3866
Caywood Gunmakers, 18 Kings Hill Estates, Berryville, AR 72616 / 870-423-4741 www.caywoodguns.com
CBC, Avenida Humberto de Campos 3220, 09400-000, Ribeirao Pires, SP, BRAZIL / 55 11 4822 8378; FAX: 55 11 4822 8323 export@cbc.com.bc www.cbc.com.bc
CBC-BRAZIL, 3 Cuckoo Lane, Honley, Yorkshire HD7 2BR, ENGLAND / 44-1484-661062; FAX: 44-1484-663709
CCG Enterprises, 5217 E. Belknap St., Halton City, TX 76117 / 800-819-7464
CCI/Speer Div of ATK, P.O. Box 856, 2299 Snake River Ave., Lewiston, ID 83501 / 800-627-3640 or 208-746-2351
CCL Security Products, 199 Whiting St., New Britain, CT 06051 / 800-733-8588
Cedar Hill Game Calls, LLC, 238 Vic Allen Rd., Downsville, LA 71234 / 318-982-5632; FAX: 318-982-2031
Centaur Systems, Inc., 1602 Foothill Rd., Kalispell, MT 59901 / 406-755-8609; FAX: 406-755-8609
Center Lock Scope Rings, 9901 France Ct., Lakeville, MN 55044 / 952-461-2114; FAX: 952-461-2194 marklee55044@usfamily.net
Central Specialties Ltd. (See Trigger Lock Division)
Century International Arms, Inc., 430 S. Congress Ave. Ste. 1, Delray Beach, FL 33445-4701 / 800-527-1252; FAX: 561-265-4520 support@centuryarms.com www.centuryarms.com
CFVentures, 509 Harvey Dr., Bloomington, IN 47403-1715 paladinwilltravel@yahoo.com www.caversam16.freeserve.co.uk
CH Tool & Die/4-D Custom Die Co., 711 N. Sandusky St., P.O. Box 889, Mt. Vernon, OH 43050-0889 / 740-397-7214; FAX: 740-397-6600 info@ch4d.com ch4d.com
Chace Leather Products, 507 Alden St., Fall River, MA 02722 / 508-678-7556; FAX: 508-675-9666 chacelea@aol.com www.chaceleather.com
Chadick's Ltd., P.O. Box 100, Terrell, TX 75160 / 214-563-7577
Chambers Flintlocks Ltd., Jim, 116 Sams Branch Rd., Candler, NC 28715 / 828-667-8361; FAX: 828-665-0852 www.flintlocks.com
Champion Shooters' Supply, P.O. Box 303, New Albany, OH 43054 / 614-855-1603; FAX: 614-855-1209
Champion Target Co., 232 Industrial Parkway, Richmond, IN 47374 / 800-441-4971
Champion's Choice, Inc., 201 International Blvd., LaVergne, TN 37086 / 615-793-4066; FAX: 615-793-4070 champ.choice@earthlink.net www.champchoice.com
Champlin Firearms, Inc., P.O. Box 3191, Woodring Airport, Enid, OK 73701 / 580-237-7388; FAX: 580-242-6922 info@champlinarms.com www.champlinarms.com
Chapman Academy of Practical Shooting, 4350 Academy Rd., Hallsville, MO 65255 / 573-696-5544; FAX: 573-696-2266 hq@chapmanacademy.com chapmanacademy.com
Chapman, J. Ken. See: OLD WEST BULLET MOULDS
Chapman Manufacturing Co., 471 New Haven Rd., Durham, CT 06422 / 860-349-9228; FAX: 860-349-0084 sales@chapmanmfg.com www.chapmanmfg.com
Chapuis Armes, Z1 La Gravoux, BP15, 42380 P.O. Box 15, St. Bonnet-le-Chatea, FRANCE / (33)477.50.06.96; FAX: (33)477 50 10 70 info@chapuis.armes.com www.chapuis-
Charter 2000, 273 Canal St., Shelton, CT 06484 / 203-922-1652
Checkmate Refinishing, 370 Champion Dr., Brooksville, FL 34601 / 352-799-5774; FAX: 352-799-2986 checkmatecustom.com
Cheddite, France S.A., 99 Route de Lyon, F-26501, Bourg-les-Valence, FRANCE / 33-75-56-4545; FAX: 33-75-56-3587 info@cheddite.com www.cheddite.com
Chelsea Gun Club of New York City, Inc., 237 Ovington Ave., Apt. D53, Brooklyn, NY 11209 / 718-836-9422 or 718-833-2704
CheVron Bullets, RR1, Ottawa, IL 61350 / 815-433-2471
Cheyenne Pioneer Products, P.O. Box 28425, Kansas City, MO 64188 / 816-413-9196; FAX: 816-455-2859 cheyennepp@aol.com www.cartridgeboxes.com
Chicago Cutlery Co., 5500 N. Pearl St., Ste. 400, Rosemont, IL 60018 / 847-678-8600 www.chicagocutlery.com
Chicasaw Gun Works, 4 Mi. Mkr., 322 Willow Br. Pluto Rd., Shady Spring, WV 25918-0868 / 304-763-2848; FAX: 304-763-3725
Chip McCormick Corp., P.O. Box 694, Spicewood, TX 78669 / 800-328-2447; FAX: 830-693-4975 www.chipmccormickcorp.com
Chipmunk (See Oregon Arms, Inc.)
Choate Machine & Tool Co., Inc., P.O. Box 218, 116 Lovers Ln., Bald Knob, AR 72010 / 501-724-6193; or 800-972-6390; FAX: 501-724-5873
Christensen Arms, 192 East 100 North, Fayette, UT 84630 / 435-528-7999; FAX: 435-528-7494 www.christensenarms.com
Christie's East, 20 Rockefeller Plz., New York, NY 10020-1902 / 212-606-0406 christics.com
Chu Tani Ind., Inc., P.O. Box 2064, Cody, WY 82414-2064
Chuck's Gun Shop, P.O. Box 597, Waldo, FL 32694 / 904-468-2264
Churchill (See U.S. Importer-Ellett Bros.)
Churchill, Winston G., 2838 20 Mile Stream Rd., Proctorville, VT 05153 / 802-226-7772
Churchill Glove Co., James, P.O. Box 298, Centralia, WA 98531 / 360-736-2816; FAX: 360-330-0151
Cimarron F.A. Co., P.O. Box 906, Fredericksburg, TX 78624-0906 / 830-997-9090; FAX: 830-997-0802 cimgraph@koc.com www.cimarron-firearms.com
Cincinnati Swaging, 2605 Marlington Ave., Cincinnati, OH 45208
Clark Custom Guns, Inc., 336 Shootout Lane, Princeton, LA 71067 / 318-949-9884; FAX: 318-949-9829
Clark Firearms Engraving, 6347 Avon Ave., San Gabriel, CA 91775-1801 / 818-287-1652
Clarkfield Enterprises, Inc., 1032 10th Ave., Clarkfield, MN 56223 / 612-669-7140
Claro Walnut Gunstock Co., 1235 Stanley Ave., Chico, CA 95928 / 530-342-5188; FAX: 530-342-5199 wally@clarowalnutgunstocks.com www.clarowalnutgunstocks.com
Classic Arms Company, Rt 1 Box 120F, Burnet, TX 78611 / 512-756-4001
Classic Arms Corp., P.O. Box 106, Dunsmuir, CA 96025-0106 / 530-235-2000
Classic Old West Styles, 1060 Doniphan Park Circle C, El Paso, TX 79936 / 915-587-0684
Clean Shot Technologies, 21218 St. Andrews Blvd. Ste 504, Boca Raton, FL 33433 / 888-866-2532
Clearview Mfg. Co., Inc., 413 S. Oakley St., Fordyce, AR 71742 / 870-352-8557; FAX: 870-352-7120
Clearview Products, 3021 N. Portland, Oklahoma City, OK 73107
Cleland's Outdoor World, Inc., 10306 Airport Hwy., Swanton, OH 43558 / 419-865-4713; FAX: 419-865-5865 mail@clelands.com www.clelands.com
Clements' Custom Leathercraft, Chas, 1741 Dallas St., Aurora, CO 80010-2018 / 303-364-0403; FAX: 303-739-9824 gryphons@home.com kuntaoslcat.com
Clenzoil Worldwide Corp., Jack Fitzgerald, 25670 1st St., Westlake, OH 44145-1430 / 440-899-0482; FAX: 440-899-0483
Clift Mfg., L.R., 3821 Hammonton Rd., Marysville, CA 95901 / 916-755-3390; FAX: 916-755-3393
Clymer Mfg. Co., 1645 W. Hamlin Rd., Rochester Hills, MI 48309-3312 / 248-853-5555; FAX: 248-853-1530
C-More Systems, P.O. Box 1750, 7553 Gary Rd., Manassas, VA 20108 / 703-361-2663; FAX: 703-361-5881
Cobra Enterprises, Inc., 1960 S. Milestone Drive, Suite F, Salt Lake City, UT 84104 FAX: 801-908-8301 www.cobrapistols@networld.com
Cobra Sport S.R.l., Via Caduti Nei Lager No. 1, 56020 San Romano, Montopoli v/Arno Pi, ITALY / 0039-571-450490; FAX: 0039-571-450492
Coffin, Charles H., 3719 Scarlet Ave., Odessa, TX 79762 / 915-366-4729; FAX: 915-366-4729
Cogar's Gunsmithing, 206 Redwine Dr., Houghton Lake, MI 48629 / 517-422-4591 ecogar@peoplepc.com
Coghlan's Ltd., 121 Irene St., Winnipeg, MB R3T 4C7 CANADA / 204-284-9550; FAX: 204-475-4127
Cold Steel Inc., 3036 Seaborg Ave. Ste. A, Ventura, CA 93003 / 800-255-4716; or 800-624-2363; FAX: 805-642-9727
Cole-Grip, 16135 Cohasset St., Van Nuys, CA 91406 / 818-782-4424
Coleman Co., Inc., 3600 N. Hydraulic, Wichita, KS 67219 / 800-835-3278 www.coleman.com
Collector's Armoury, Ltd., Tom Nelson, 9404 Gunston Cove Rd., Lorton, VA 22079 / 703-493-9120; FAX: 703-493-9424 www.collectorsarmoury.com
Collings, Ronald, 1006 Cielta Linda, Vista, CA 92083
Colonial Arms, Inc., P.O. Box 636, Selma, AL 36702-0636 / 334-872-9455; FAX: 334-872-9540 colonialarms@mindspring.com www.colonialarms.com
Colonial Repair, 47 Navarre St., Roslindale, MA 02131-4725 / 617-469-4951
Colorado Gunsmithing Academy, RR 3 Box 79B, El Campo, TX 77437 / 719-336-4099 or 800-754-2046; FAX: 719-336-9642
Colorado School of Trades, 1575 Hoyt St., Lakewood, CO 80215 / 800-234-4594; FAX: 303-233-4723
Colt Blackpowder Arms Co., 110 8th Street, Brooklyn, NY 11215 / 718-499-4678; FAX: 718-768-8056
Colt's Mfg. Co., Inc., P.O. Box 1868, Hartford, CT 06144-1868 / 800-962-COLT or 860-236-6311; FAX: 860-244-1449
Compass Industries, Inc., 104 East 25th St., New York, NY 10010 / 212-473-2614 or 800-221-9904; FAX: 212-353-0826
Compasseco, Ltd., 151 Atkinson Hill Ave., Bardstown, KY 40004 / 502-349-0910
Competition Electronics, Inc., 3469 Precision Dr., Rockford, IL 61109 / 815-874-8001; FAX: 815-874-8181
Competitive Pistol Shop, The, 5233 Palmer Dr., Fort Worth, TX 76117-2433 / 817-834-8479
Competitor Corp., Inc., 26 Knight St. Unit 3, P.O. Box 352, Jaffrey, NH 03452 / 603-532-9483; FAX: 603-532-8209 competitorcorp@aol.com competitor-pistol.com
Component Concepts, Inc., 530 S. Springbrook Road, Newberg, OR 97132 / 503-554-8095; FAX: 503-554-9370 cci@cybcon.com www.phantomonline.com
Concealment Shop, Inc., The, 3550 E. Hwy. 80, Mesquite, TX 75149 / 972-289-8997 or 800-444-7090; FAX: 972-289-4410 theconcealmentshop@msn.com
Concept Development Corp., 16610 E. Laser Drive, Suite 5, Fountain Hills, AZ 85268-6644

Conetrol Scope Mounts, 10225 Hwy. 123 S., Seguin, TX 78155 / 830-379-3030 or 800-CONETROL; FAX: 830-379-3030 email@conetrol.com www.conetrol.com
Connecticut Shotgun Mfg. Co., P.O. Box 1692, 35 Woodland St., New Britain, CT 06051 / 860-225-6581; FAX: 860-832-8707
Connecticut Valley Classics (See CVC, BPI)
Conrad, C. A., 3964 Ebert St., Winston-Salem, NC 27127 / 919-788-5469
Cook Engineering Service, 891 Highbury Rd., Vict 3133, 3133 AUSTRALIA
Cooper Arms, P.O. Box 114, Stevensville, MT 59870 / 406-777-0373; FAX: 406-777-5228
Cooper-Woodward Perfect Lube, 4120 Oesterle Rd., Helena, MT 59602 / 406-459-2287 cwperfectlube@mt.net cwperfectlube.com
Corbin Mfg. & Supply, Inc., 600 Industrial Circle, P.O. Box 2659, White City, OR 97503 / 541-826-5211; FAX: 541-826-8669 sales@corbins.com www.corbins.com
Cor-Bon Inc./Glaser LLC, P.O. Box 173, 1311 Industry Rd., Sturgis, SD 57785 / 605-347-4544 or 800-221-3489; FAX: 605-347-5055 email@corbon.com www.corbon.com
Corkys Gun Clinic, 4401 Hot Springs Dr., Greeley, CO 80634-9226 / 970-330-0516
Corry, John, 861 Princeton Ct., Neshanic Station, NJ 08853 / 908-369-8019
Cosmi Americo & Figlio S.N.C., Via Flaminia 307, Ancona, ITALY / 071-888208; FAX: 39-071-887008
Coulston Products, Inc., P.O. Box 30, 201 Ferry St. Suite 212, Easton, PA 18044-0030 / 215-253-0167 or 800-445-9927; FAX: 215-252-1511
Counter Assault, 120 Industrial Court, Kalispell, MT 59901 / 406-257-4740; FAX: 406-257-6674
Country Armourer, The, P.O. Box 308, Ashby, MA 01431-0308 / 508-827-6797; FAX: 508-827-4845
Cousin Bob's Mountain Products, 7119 Ohio River Blvd., Ben Avon, PA 15202 / 412-766-5114; FAX: 412-766-9354
CP Bullets, 1310 Industrial Hwy #5-6, Southhampton, PA 18966 / 215-953-7264; FAX: 215-953-7275
CQB Training, P.O. Box 1739, Manchester, MO 63011
Craftguard, 3624 Logan Ave., Waterloo, IA 50703 / 319-232-2959; FAX: 319-234-0804
Crandall Tool & Machine Co., 19163 21 Mile Rd., Tustin, MI 49688 / 616-829-4430
Creative Craftsman, Inc., The, 95 Highway 29 N., P.O. Box 331, Lawrenceville, GA 30246 / 404-963-2112; FAX: 404-513-9488
Creedmoor Sports, Inc., 1405 South Coast Hwy., Oceanside, CA 92054 / 800-273-3366; FAX: 760-757-5558 shoot@creedmoorsports.com www.creedmoorsports.com
Creighton Audette, 19 Highland Circle, Springfield, VT 05156 / 802-885-2331
Crimson Trace Lasers, 8090 S.W. Cirrus Dr., Beverton, OR 97008 / 800-442-2406; FAX: 503-627-0166 travis@crimsontrace.com www.crimsontrace.com
Crit' R Calls, P.O. Box 999, La Porte, CO 80535 / 970-484-2768; FAX: 970-484-0807 critrcall@larinet.net www.critrcall.com
Crit'R Call (See Rocky Mountain Wildlife Products)
Crosman Airguns, Rts. 5 and 20, E. Bloomfield, NY 14443 / 716-657-6161; FAX: 716-657-5405
Crosman Blades (See Coleman Co., Inc.)
CRR, Inc./Marble's Inc., 420 Industrial Park, P.O. Box 111, Gladstone, MI 49837 / 906-428-3710; FAX: 906-428-3711
Crucelegui, Hermanos (See U.S. Importer-Mandall)
Cubic Shot Shell Co., Inc., 98 Fatima Dr., Campbell, OH 44405 / 330-755-0349
Cullity Restoration, 209 Old Country Rd., East Sandwich, MA 02537 / 508-888-1147
Cummings Bullets, 1417 Esperanza Way, Escondido, CA 92027
Cupp, Alana, Custom Engraver, P.O. Box 207, Annabella, UT 84711 / 801-896-4834
Curly Maple Stock Blanks (See Tiger-Hunt)
Curtis Cast Bullets, 527 W. Babcock St., Bozeman, MT 59715 / 406-587-8117; FAX: 406-587-8117
Curtis Gun Shop (See Curtis Cast Bullets)
Custom Bullets by Hoffman, 2604 Peconic Ave., Seaford, NY 11783
Custom Calls, 607 N. 5th St., Burlington, IA 52601 / 319-752-4465
Custom Checkering Service, Kathy Forster, 2124 S.E. Yamhill St., Portland, OR 97214 / 503-236-5874
Custom Products (See Jones Custom Products)
Custom Shop, The, 890 Cochrane Crescent, Peterborough, ON K9H 5N3 CANADA / 705-742-6693
Custom Single Shot Rifles, 9651 Meadows Lane, Guthrie, OK 73044 / 405-282-3634
Custom Tackle and Ammo, P.O. Box 1886, Farmington, NM 87499 / 505-632-3539
Cutco Cutlery, P.O. Box 810, Olean, NY 14760 / 716-372-3111
CVA, 5988 Peachtree Corners East, Norcross, GA 30071 / 770-449-4687; FAX: 770-242-8546 info@cva.com www.cva.com
Cylinder & Slide, Inc., William R. Laughridge, 245 E. 4th St., Fremont, NE 68025 / 402-721-4277; FAX: 402-721-0263 bill@cylinder-slide.com www.cylinder- slide.com
CZ USA, P.O. Box 171073, Kansas City, KS 66117 / 913-321-1811; FAX: 913-321-4901

D

D&D Gunsmiths, Ltd., 363 E. Elmwood, Troy, MI 48083 / 248-583-1512; FAX: 248-583-1524
D&G Precision Duplicators (See Greenwood Precision)
D&L Industries (See D.J. Marketing)
D&L Sports, P.O. Box 651, Gillette, WY 82717 / 307-686-4008
D.C. Engineering, Inc., 17195 Silver Parkway, Ste. 135, Fenton, MI 48430 / 248-382-1210 guns@rifletech.com www.rifletech.com
D.C.C. Enterprises, 259 Wynburn Ave., Athens, GA 30601
D.J. Marketing, 10602 Horton Ave., Downey, CA 90241 / 310-806-0891; FAX: 310-806-6231
D.L. Unmussig Bullets, 7862 Brentford Dr., Richmond, VA 23225 / 804-320-1165; FAX: 804-320-4587
Daisy Outdoor Products, P.O. Box 220, Rogers, AR 72757 / 479-636-1200; FAX: 479-636-0573 www.daisy.com
Dakota (See U.S. Importer-EMF Co., Inc.)
Dakota Arms, Inc., 130 Industry Road, Sturgis, SD 57785 / 605-347-4686; FAX: 605-347-4459 info@dakotaarms.com www.dakotaarms.com
Dakota Corp., 77 Wales St., P.O. Box 543, Rutland, VT 05701 / 802-775-6062 or 800-451-4167; FAX: 802-773-3919
Daly, Charles/KBI, P.O. Box 6625, Harrisburg, PA 17112 / 866-DALY GUN
Da-Mar Gunsmith's, Inc., 102 1st St., Solvay, NY 13209
damascususa@inteliport.com, 149 Deans Farm Rd., Tyner, NC 27980 / 252-221-2010 damascususa@inteliport.com www.damascususa.com
Dan Wesson Firearms, 5169 Rt. 12 South, Norwich, NY 13815 / 607-336-1174; FAX: 607-336-2730 dwservice@cz-usa.com dz-usa.com
Dangler, Homer. See: DANGLER'S CUSTOM FLINT RIFLES
Dangler's Custom Flint Rifles, Homer L. Dangler, 2870 Lee Marie Dr., Adrian, MI 49221 / 517-266-1997 homerdangler@yahoo.com
Danner Shoe Mfg. Co., 12722 N.E. Airport Way, Portland, OR 97230 / 503-251-1100 or 800-345-0430; FAX: 503-251-1119
Dan's Whetstone Co., Inc., 418 Hilltop Rd., Pearcy, AR 71964 / 501-767-1616; FAX: 501-767-9598 questions@danswhetstone.com www.danswhetstone.com
Danuser Machine Co., 550 E. Third St., P.O. Box 368, Fulton, MO 65251 / 573-642-2246; FAX: 573-642-2240 sales@danuser.com www.danuser.com
Dara-Nes, Inc. (See Nesci Enterprises, Inc.)
D'Arcy Echols & Co., P.O. Box 421, Millville, UT 84326 / 435-755-6842
Darlington Gun Works, Inc., P.O. Box 698, 516 S. 52 Bypass, Darlington, SC 29532 / 803-393-3931
Darwin Hensley Gunmaker, P.O. Box 329, Brightwood, OR 97011 / 503-622-5411
Data Tech Software Systems, 19312 East Eldorado Drive, Aurora, CO 80013
Dave Norin Schrank's Smoke & Gun, 2010 Washington St., Waukegan, IL 60085 / 708-662-4034
Dave's Gun Shop, P.O. Box 2824, Casper, WY 82602-2824 / 307-754-9724
David Clark Co., Inc., P.O. Box 15054, Worcester, MA 01615 / 508-756-6216; FAX: 508-753-5827 sales@davidclark.com www.davidclark.com
David Condon, Inc., 109 E. Washington St., Middleburg, VA 22117 / 703-687-5642
David Miller Co., 3131 E. Greenlee Rd., Tucson, AZ 85716 / 520-326-3117
David R. Chicoine, PO Box 635, Gastonia, NC 28053 / 704-853-0265 bnpress@quik.com www.oldwestgunsmith.com
David W. Schwartz Custom Guns, 2505 Waller St., Eau Claire, WI 54703 / 715-832-1735
Davide Pedersoli and Co., Via Artigiani 57, Gardone VT, Brescia 25063, ITALY / 030-8915000; FAX: 030-8911019 info@davidepedersoli.com www.davide_pedersoli.com
Davis, Don, 1619 Heights, Katy, TX 77493 / 713-391-3090
Davis Industries (See Cobra Enterprises, Inc.)
Davis Products, Mike, 643 Loop Dr., Moses Lake, WA 98837 / 509-765-6178 or 509-766-7281
Daystate Ltd., Birch House Lanee, Cotes Heath Staffs, ST15.022, ENGLAND / 01782-791755; FAX: 01782-791617
Dayton Traister, 4778 N. Monkey Hill Rd., P.O. Box 593, Oak Harbor, WA 98277 / 360-679-4657; FAX: 360-675-1114
DBA Werth Services, T. W. Werth, 1203 Woodlawn Rd., Lincoln, IL 62656 / 217-732-1300; FAX: 217-735-5106 twwerth@yahoo.com
D-Boone Ent., Inc., 5900 Colwyn Dr., Harrisburg, PA 17109
Dead Eye's Sport Center, 76 Baer Rd., Shickshinny, PA 18655 / 570-256-7432 deadeyeprizz@aol.com
Deepeeka Exports Pvt. Ltd., D-78, Saket, Meerut-250-006, INDIA / 011-91-121-640363 or ; FAX: 011-91-121-640988 deepeeka@poboxes.com www.deepeeka.com
Defense Training International, Inc., 749 S. Lemay, Ste. A3-337, Ft. Collins, CO 80524 / 303-482-2520; FAX: 303-482-0548 www.defense_training.com
deHaas Barrels, 20049 W. State Hwy. Z, Ridgeway, MO 64481 / 660-872-6308 dehaas@grm.net
Del Rey Products, P.O. Box 5134, Playa Del Rey, CA 90296-5134 / 213-823-0494
Delhi Gun House, 1374 Kashmere Gate, New Delhi 110 006, INDIA / 2940974 or 394-0974; FAX: 2917344 dgh@vsnl.com www.dgh@vsnl.com
Delorge, Ed, 6734 W. Main, Houma, LA 70360 / 985-223-0206 delorge@triparish.net www.eddelorge.com
Del-Sports, Inc., Dave Budin, P.O. Box 685, 817 Main St., Margaretville, NY 12455 / 845-586-4103; FAX: 845-586-4105
Delta Arms Ltd., P.O. Box 1000, Delta, VT 84624-1000
Delta Enterprises, 284 Hagemann Drive, Livermore, CA 94550
Dem-Bart Checkering Tools, Inc., 1825 Bickford Ave., Snohomish, WA 98290 / 360-568-7356 walt@dembartco.com www.dembartco.com
Denver Instrument Co., 6542 Fig St., Arvada, CO 80004 / 800-321-1135 or 303-431-7255; FAX: 303-423-4831
DeSantis Holster & Leather Goods, Inc., 431 Bayview Ave., Amityville, NY 11701 / 631-841-6300; FAX: 631-841-6320 www.desantisholster.com
Desert Mountain Mfg., P.O. Box 130184, Coram, MT 59913 / 800-477-0762 or 406-387-5361; FAX: 406-387-5361
Detonics USA, 53 Perimeter Center East #200, Atlanta, GA 30346 / 866-759-1169
DGR Custom Rifles, 4191 37th Ave. SE, Tappen, ND 58487 / 701-327-8135
DGS, Inc., Dale A. Storey, 1117 E. 12th, Casper, WY 82601 / 307-237-2414; FAX: 307-237-2414 dalest@trib.com www.dgsrifle.com
DHB Products, 336 River View Dr., Verona, VA 24482-2547 / 703-836-2648
Diamond Machining Technology Inc. (See DMT)
Diamond Mfg. Co., P.O. Box 174, Wyoming, PA 18644 / 800-233-9601
Dibble, Derek A., 555 John Downey Dr., New Britain, CT 06051 / 203-224-2630
Dietz Gun Shop & Range, Inc., 421 Range Rd., New Braunfels, TX 78132 / 830-885-4662
Dilliott Gunsmithing, Inc., 657 Scarlett Rd., Dandridge, TN 37725 / 865-397-9204 gunsmithd@aol.com dilliottgunsmithing.com
Dillon Precision Products, Inc., 8009 East Dillon's Way, Scottsdale, AZ 85260 / 480-948-8009 or 800-762-3845; FAX: 480-998-2786 sales@dillonprecision.com www.dillonprecision.com
Dina Arms Corporation, P.O. Box 46, Royersford, PA 19468 / 610-287-0266; FAX: 610-287-0266 dinaarms@erols.com www.users.erds.com/dinarms
Dixie Gun Works, P.O. Box 130, Union City, TN 38281 / 731-885-0700; FAX: 731-885-0440 info@dixiegunworks.com www.dixiegunworks.com
Dixon Muzzleloading Shop, Inc., 9952 Kunkels Mill Rd., Kempton, PA 19529 / 610-756-6271 dixonmuzzleloading.com
DJ Illinois River Valley Calls, Inc., P.O. Box 370, S. Pekin, IL 61564-0370 / 866-352-2557; FAX: 309-348-3987 djcalls@grics.net www.djcalls.com
DKT, Inc., 14623 Vera Dr., Union, MI 49130-9744 / 800-741-7083 orders; FAX: 616-641-2015
DLO Mfg., 10807 SE Foster Ave., Arcadia, FL 33821-7304
DMT-Diamond Machining Technology, Inc., 85 Hayes Memorial Dr., Marlborough, MA 01752 FAX: 508-485-3924
Dohring Bullets, 100 W. 8 Mile Rd., Ferndale, MI 48220
Dolbare, Elizabeth, P.O. Box 502, Dubois, WY 82513-0502 / 307-450-7500 edolbare@hotmail.com www.scrimshaw-engraving.com
Domino, P.O. Box 108, 20019 Settimo Milanese, Milano, ITALY / 1-39-2-33512040; FAX: 1-39-2-33511587

MANUFACTURER'S DIRECTORY

Don Hume Leathergoods, Don Hume, 500 26th Ave. NW, Miami, OK 74354 / 800-331-2686; FAX: 918-542-4340 info@donhume.com www.donhume.com
Don Klein Custom Guns, 433 Murray Park Dr., Ripon, WI 54971 / 920-748-2931 daklein@charter.net www.donkleincustomguns.com
Donnelly, C. P., 405 Kubli Rd., Grants Pass, OR 97527 / 541-846-6604
Doskocil Mfg. Co., Inc., P.O. Box 1246, 4209 Barnett, Arlington, TX 76017 / 817-467-5116; FAX: 817-472-9810
Douglas Barrels, Inc., 5504 Big Tyler Rd., Charleston, WV 25313-1398 / 304-776-1341; FAX: 304-776-8560 www.benchrest.com/douglas
Downsizer Corp., P.O. Box 710316, Santee, CA 92072-0316 / 619-448-5510 www.downsizer.com
DPMS (Defense Procurement Manufacturing Services, Inc.), 13983 Industry Ave., Becker, MN 55308 / 800-578-DPMS or 763-261-5600; FAX: 763-261-5599
Dr. O's Products Ltd., 1177 US Route SW, Selkirk, NY 12150
Dremel Mfg. Co., 4915-21st St., Racine, WI 53406
Dri-Slide, Inc., 411 N. Darling, Fremont, MI 49412 / 616-924-3950
Dropkick, 1460 Washington Blvd., Williamsport, PA 17701 / 717-326-6561; FAX: 717-326-4950
DS Arms, Inc., P.O. Box 370, 27 West 990 Industrial Ave., Barrington, IL 60010 / 847-277-7258; FAX: 847-277-7259 www.dsarms.com
DTM International, Inc., 40 Joslyn Rd., P.O. Box 5, Lake Orion, MI 48362 / 313-693-6670
Duane A. Hobbie Gunsmithing, 2412 Pattie Ave., Wichita, KS 67216 / 316-264-8266
Duane's Gun Repair (See DGR Custom Rifles)
Dubber, Michael W., P.O. Box 312, Evansville, IN 47702 / 812-424-9000; FAX: 812-424-6551
Duffy, Charles E. (See Guns Antique & Modern DBA), 224 Williams Ln., P.O. Box 2, West Hurley, NY 12491 / 845-679-2997 ceo1923@prodigy.net
Du-Lite Corp., 171 River Rd., Middletown, CT 06457 / 203-347-2505; FAX: 203-347-9404
Dumoulin, Ernest, Rue Florent Boclinville 8-10, 13-4041, Votten, BELGIUM / 41 27 78 92
Duncan's Gun Works, Inc., 1619 Grand Ave., San Marcos, CA 92078 / 760-727-0515; FAX: 760-591-9245
DunLyon R&D, Inc., 52151 E. U.S. Hwy. 60, Miami, AZ 85539 / 928-473-9027
Duofold, Inc., RD 3 Rt. 309, Valley Square Mall, Tamaqua, PA 18252 / 717-386-2666; FAX: 717-386-3652
Dybala Gun Shop, P.O. Box 1024, FM 3156, Bay City, TX 77414 / 409-245-0866
Dykstra, Doug, 411 N. Darling, Fremont, MI 49412 / 616-924-3950
Dynalite Products, Inc., 215 S. Washington St., Greenfield, OH 45123 / 513-981-2124

E

E&L Mfg., Inc., 4177 Riddle Bypass Rd., Riddle, OR 97469 / 541-874-2137; FAX: 541-874-3107
E. Arthur Brown Co. Inc., 650 County Road 40 NW, Garfield, MN 56332 / 320-762-8847; or 800-950-9088 FAX: 320-763-4310 sales@eabco.com www.eabco.com
E.A.A. Corp., P.O. Box 1299, Sharpes, FL 32959 / 407-639-4842 or 800-536-4442; FAX: 407-639-7006
Eagan, Donald. See: EAGAN GUNSMITHS
Eagan Gunsmiths, Donald V. Eagan, P.O. Box 196, Benton, PA 17814 / 570-925-6134
Eagle Arms, Inc. (See ArmaLite, Inc.)
Eagle Grips, Eagle Business Center, 460 Randy Rd., Carol Stream, IL 60188 / 800-323-6144 or 708-260-0400; FAX: 708-260-0486
Eagle Imports, Inc., 1750 Brielle Ave., Unit B1, Wanamassa, NJ 07712 / 732-493-0333; FAX: 732-493-0301 gsodini@aol.com www.bersafirearmsusa.com
E-A-R, Inc., Div. of Cabot Safety Corp., 5457 W. 79th St., Indianapolis, IN 46268 / 800-327-3431; FAX: 800-488-8007
EAW (See U.S. Importer-New England Custom Gun Serv
Ed Brown Products, Inc., P.O. Box 492, Perry, MO 63462 / 573-565-3261; FAX: 573-565-2791 edbrown@edbrown.com www.edbrown.com
Ed Brown Products, Inc., 43825 Muldrow Trl., P.O. Box 492, Perry, MO 63462 / 573-565-3261; FAX: 573-565-2791 edbrown@edbrown.com www.edbrown.com
Edenpine, Inc. c/o Six Enterprises, Inc., 320 D Turtle Creek Ct., San Jose, CA 95125 / 408-999-0201; FAX: 408-999-0216
EdgeCraft Corp., S. Weiner, 825 Southwood Rd., Avondale, PA 19311 / 610-268-0500 or 800-342-3255; FAX: 610-268-3545 www.edgecraft.com
Edmisten Co., P.O. Box 1293, Boone, NC 28607
Edmund Scientific Co., 101 E. Gloucester Pike, Barrington, NJ 08033 / 609-543-6250
Ed's Gun House, Rt. 1, Box 62, Minnesota City, MN 55959 / 507-689-2925
Ed's Gun House, Ed Kukowski, P.O. Box 62, Minnesota City, MN 55959 / 507-689-2925
Effebi SNC-Dr. Franco Beretta, via Rossa, 4, 25062, ITALY / 030-2751955; FAX: 030-2180414
Eggleston, Jere D., 400 Saluda Ave., Columbia, SC 29205 / 803-799-3402
Eichelberger Bullets, Wm., 158 Crossfield Rd., King Of Prussia, PA 19406
El Paso Saddlery Co., P.O. Box 27194, El Paso, TX 79926 / 915-544-2233; FAX: 915-544-2535 info@epsaddlery.com www.epsaddlery.com
Electro Prismatic Collimators, Inc., 1441 Manatt St., Lincoln, NE 68521
Electronic Shooters Protection, Inc., 15290 Gadsden Ct., Brighton, CO 80603 / 800-797-7791; FAX: 303-659-8668 esp@usa.net espamerica.com
Eley Ltd., Selco Way Minworth Industrial Estate, Minworth Sutton Coldfield, West Midlands, B76 1BA ENGLAND / 44 0 121-313-4567; FAX: 44 0 121-313-4568 www.eleyammunition.com
Ellett Bros., 267 Columbia Ave., P.O. Box 128, Chapin, SC 29036 / 803-345-3751 or 800-845-3711; FAX: 803-345-1820 www.ellettbrothers.com
Ellicott Arms, Inc. / Woods Pistolsmithing, 8390 Sunset Dr., Ellicott City, MD 21043 / 410-465-7979
EMAP USA, 6420 Wilshire Blvd., Los Angeles, CA 90048 / 213-782-2000; FAX: 213-782-2867
Emerging Technologies, Inc. (See Laseraim Technologies, Inc.)
EMF Co. Inc., 1900 E. Warner Ave., Suite 1-D, Santa Ana, CA 92705 / 949-261-6611; FAX: 949-756-0133
Empire Cutlery Corp., 12 Kruger Ct., Clifton, NJ 07013 / 201-472-5155; FAX: 201-779-0759
Empire Rifles, P.O. Box 406, Meriden, NH 03770 info@empirerifles.com www.empirerifles.com
English, Inc., A.G., 708 S. 12th St., Broken Arrow, OK 74012 / 918-251-3399 info@agenglish.com www.agenglish.com
Engraving Artistry, 36 Alto Rd., Burlington, CT 06013 / 860-673-6837
Enguix Import-Export, Alpujarras 58, Alzira, Valencia, SPAIN / (96) 241 43 95; FAX: (96) 241 43 95
Enhanced Presentations, Inc., 3504 Iris St., Wilmington, NC 28409 / 910-799-1622; FAX: 910-799-5004
Ensign-Bickford Co., The, 660 Hopmeadow St., Simsbury, CT 06070
Entreprise Arms, Inc., 5321 Irwindale Ave., Irwindale, CA 91706-2025 / 626-962-8712; FAX: 626-962-4692 www.entreprise.com
EPC, 1441 Manatt St., Lincoln, NE 68521 / 402-476-3946
Erhardt, Dennis, 4508 N. Montana Ave., Helena, MT 59602 / 406-442-4533
Essex Arms, P.O. Box 363, Island Pond, VT 05846 / 802-723-6203; FAX: 802-723-6203
Estate Cartridge, Inc., 900 Bob Ehlen Dr., Anoka, MN 55303-7502 / 409-856-7277; FAX: 409-856-5486
Euber Bullets, No. Orwell Rd., Orwell, VT 05760 / 802-948-2621
Euroarms of America, Inc., P.O. Box 3277, Winchester, VA 22604 / 540-662-1863; FAX: 540-662-4464 mail@euroarms.net www.euroarms.net
Euro-Imports, George Tripes, 412 Slayden St., Yoakum, TX 77995 / 361-293-9353; FAX: 361-293-9353 mrbrno@yahoo.com
European American Armory Corp. (See E.A.A. Corp.)
Eversull Co., Inc., 1 Tracemont, Boyce, LA 71409 / 318-793-8728; FAX: 318-793-5483 bestguns@aol.com
Evolution Gun Works, Inc., 48 Belmont Ave., Quakertown, PA 18951-1347 www.egw-guns.com
Excalibur Electro Optics, Inc., P.O. Box 400, Fogelsville, PA 18051-0400 / 610-391-9105; FAX: 610-391-9220
Excalibur Publications, P.O. Box 89667, Tucson, AZ 85752 / 520-575-9057 excalibureditor@earthlink.net
Excel Industries, Inc., 4510 Carter Ct., Chino, CA 91710 / 909-627-2404; FAX: 909-627-7817 www.excelarms.com or accu-tekfirearms.com
Executive Protection Institute, P.O. Box 802, Berryville, VA 22611 / 540-554-2540; FAX: 540-554-2558 ruk@crosslink.net www.personalprotecion.com
Eze-Lap Diamond Prods., P.O. Box 2229, 15164 W. State St., Westminster, CA 92683 / 714-847-1555; FAX: 714-897-0280

F

F.A.I.R., S.R.L., Via Gitti, 41, 25060 Marcheno (BS), 25060 Marcheno Bresc, ITALY / 030 861162-8610344; FAX: 030 8610179 info@fair.it www.fair.it
F+W Publications, Inc., 700 E. State St., Iola, WI 54990 / 715-445-2214; FAX: 715-445-4087
Fabarm S.p.A., Via Averolda 31, 25039 Travagliato, Brescia, ITALY / 030-6863629; FAX: 030-6863684 info@fabarm.com www.fabarm.com
Fagan Arms, 22952 15 Mile Rd., Clinton Township, MI 48035 / 810-465-4637; FAX: 810-792-6996
Faith Associates, P.O. Box 549, Flat Rock, NC 28731-0549 FAX: 828-697-6827
Falcon Industries, Inc., P.O. Box 1690, Edgewood, NM 87015 / 505-281-3783; FAX: 505-281-3991 shines@ergogrips.net www.ergogrips.net
Farm Form Decoys, Inc., 1602 Biovu, P.O. Box 748, Galveston, TX 77553 / 409-744-0762 or 409-765-6361; FAX: 409-765-8513
Farr Studio, Inc., 17149 Bournbrook Ln., Jeffersonton, VA 22724-1796 / 615-638-8825
Farrar Tool Co., Inc., 11855 Cog Hill Dr., Whittier, CA 90601-1902 / 310-863-4367; FAX: 310-863-5123
Faulhaber Wildlocker, Dipl.-Ing. Norbert Wittasek, Seilergasse 2, A-1010 Wien, AUSTRIA / 43-1-5137001; FAX: 43-1-5137001 faulhaber1@utanet.at
Faulk's Game Call Co., Inc., 616 18th St., Lake Charles, LA 70601 / 337-436-9726; FAX: 337-494-7205 www.faulkcalls.com
Faust Inc., T. G., 544 Minor St., Reading, PA 19602 / 610-375-8549; FAX: 610-375-4488
Fautheree, Andy, P.O. Box 4607, Pagosa Springs, CO 81157 / 970-731-5003; FAX: 970-731-5009
Feather, Flex Decoys, 4500 Doniphan Dr., Neosho, MO 64850 / 318-746-8596; FAX: 318-742-4815
Federal Cartridge Co., 900 Ehlen Dr., Anoka, MN 55303 / 612-323-2300; FAX: 612-323-2506
Federal Champion Target Co., 232 Industrial Pkwy., Richmond, IN 47374 / 800-441-4971; FAX: 317-966-7747
Federated-Fry (See Fry Metals)
FEG, Budapest, Soroksariut 158, H-1095, HUNGARY
Feinwerkbau Westinger & Altenburger, Neckarstrasse 43, 78727, Oberndorf a. N., GERMANY / 07423-814-0; FAX: 07423-814-200 info@feinwerkbau.de www.feinwerkbau.de
Ferguson, Bill, P.O. Box 1238, Sierra Vista, AZ 85636 / 520-458-5321; FAX: 520-458-9125
Ferguson, Bill. See: BULLET METALS
FERLIB, Via Parte 33 Marcheno/BS, Marcheno/BS, ITALY / 00390308610191; FAX: 00390308966882 info@ferlib.com www.ferlib.com
Ferris Firearms, 7110 F.M. 1863, Bulverde, TX 78163 / 210-980-4424
Fieldsport Ltd., Bryan Bilinski, 3313 W. South Airport Rd., Traverse City, MI 49684 / 616-933-0767
Fiocchi Munizioni S.A. (See U.S. Importer-Fiocch
Fiocchi of America, Inc., 5030 Fremont Rd., Ozark, MO 65721 / 417-725-4118 or 800-721-2666; FAX: 417-725-1039
Firearm Brokers, PO Box 91787, Louisville, KY 40291 firearmbrokers@aol.com www.firearmbrokers.com
Firearms Co. Ltd. / Alpine (See U.S. Importer-Mandall
Firearms Engraver's Guild of America, 3011 E. Pine Dr., Flagstaff, AZ 86004 / 928-527-8427 fegainfo@fega.com
Fisher, Jerry A., 631 Crane Mt. Rd., Big Fork, MT 59911 / 406-837-2722
Fisher Custom Firearms, 2199 S. Kittredge Way, Aurora, CO 80013 / 303-755-3710
Fitzgerald, Jack. See: CLENZOIL WORLDWIDE CORP.
Flambeau, Inc., 15981 Valplast Rd., Middlefield, OH 44062 / 216-632-1631; FAX: 216-632-1581 www.flambeau.com
Flayderman & Co., Inc., P.O. Box 2446, Fort Lauderdale, FL 33303 / 954-761-8855 www.flayderman.com
Fleming Firearms, 7720 E. 126th St. N., Collinsville, OK 74021-7016 / 918-665-3624
Fletcher-Bidwell, LLC, 305 E. Terhune St., Viroqua, WI 54665-1631 / 866-637-1860 fbguns@netscape.net
Flintlocks, Etc., 160 Rossiter Rd., P.O. Box 181, Richmond, MA 01254 / 413-698-3822; FAX: 413-698-3866 flintetc@berkshire.rr.com
Flitz International Ltd., 821 Mohr Ave., Waterford, WI 53185 / 414-534-5898; FAX: 414-534-2991
Fluoramics, Inc., 18 Industrial Ave., Mahwah, NJ 07430 / 800-922-0075; FAX: 201-825-7035 pdouglas@fluoramics.com www.tufoil.com
Flynn's Custom Guns, P.O. Box 7461, Alexandria, LA 71306 / 318-455-7130
FN Manufacturing, P.O. Box 24257, Columbia, SC 29224 / 803-736-0522

Folks, Donald E., 205 W. Lincoln St., Pontiac, IL 61764 / 815-844-7901
Foredom Electric Co., Rt. 6, 16 Stony Hill Rd., Bethel, CT 06801 / 203-792-8622
Forgreens Tool & Mfg., Inc., P.O. Box 955, Robert Lee, TX 76945 / 915-453-2800; FAX: 915-453-2460
Forkin Custom Classics, 205 10th Ave. S.W., White Sulphur Spring, MT 59645 / 406-547-2344
Forrest Tool Co., P.O. Box 768, 44380 Gordon Ln., Mendocino, CA 95460 / 707-937-2141; FAX: 717-937-1817
Forster, Kathy (See Custom Checkering)
Forster, Larry L., Box 212, 216 Hwy. 13 E., Gwinner, ND 58040-0212 / 701-678-2475
Forster Products, Inc., 310 E. Lanark Ave., Lanark, IL 61046 / 815-493-6360; FAX: 815-493-2371 info@forsterproducts.com www.forsterproducts.com
Fort Hill Gunstocks, 12807 Fort Hill Rd., Hillsboro, OH 45133 / 513-466-2763
Fort Knox Security Products, 1051 N. Industrial Park Rd., Orem, UT 84057 / 801-224-7233 or 800-821-5216; FAX: 801-226-5493
Forthofer's Gunsmithing & Knifemaking, 5535 U.S. Hwy. 93S, Whitefish, MT 59937-8411 / 406-862-2674
Fortune Products, Inc., 205 Hickory Creek Rd., Marble Falls, TX 78654 / 210-693-6111; FAX: 210-693-6394 randy@accusharp.com
Foster, . See: ACCURACY INTERNATIONAL
Fountain Products, 492 Prospect Ave., West Springfield, MA 01089 / 413-781-4651; FAX: 413-733-8217
Fowler, Bob (See Black Powder Products)
Fox River Mills, Inc., P.O. Box 298, 227 Poplar St., Osage, IA 50461 / 515-732-3798; FAX: 515-732-5128
Fraim, William. See: ACUSPORT CORPORATION
Frank Knives, 1147 SW Bryson St. 1, Dallas, OR 97338 / 503-831-1489; FAX: 541-563-3041
Frank Mittermeier, Inc., P.O. Box 1, Bronx, NY 10465
Franzen International, Inc. (See U.S. Importer-Importer Co.)
Freedom Arms, Inc., P.O. Box 150, Freedom, WY 83120 / 307-883-2468; FAX: 307-883-2005
Fremont Tool Works, 1214 Prairie, Ford, KS 67842 / 316-369-2327
Front Sight Firearms Training Institute, P.O. Box 2619, Aptos, CA 95001 / 800-987-7719; FAX: 408-684-2137
Frontier, 2910 San Bernardo, Laredo, TX 78040 / 956-723-5409; FAX: 956-723-1774
Frontier Arms Co., Inc., 401 W. Rio Santa Cruz, Green Valley, AZ 85614-3932
Frontier Products Co., 2401 Walker Rd., Roswell, NM 88201-8950 / 505-627-0763
Frost Cutlery Co., P.O. Box 22636, Chattanooga, TN 37422 / 615-894-6079; FAX: 615-894-9576
Fry Metals, 4100 6th Ave., Altoona, PA 16602 / 814-946-1611
Fujinon, Inc., 10 High Point Dr., Wayne, NJ 07470 / 201-633-5600; FAX: 201-633-5216
Fullmer, Geo. M., 2499 Mavis St., Oakland, CA 94601 / 510-533-4193
Fulton Armory, 8725 Bollman Place No. 1, Savage, MD 20763 / 301-490-9485; FAX: 301-490-9547 www.fulton-armory.com
Furr Arms, 91 N. 970 West, Orem, UT 84057 / 801-226-3877; FAX: 801-226-3877

G

G&H Decoys, Inc., P.O. Box 1208, Hwy. 75 North, Henryetta, OK 74437 / 918-652-3314; FAX: 918-652-3400
G.C. Bullet Co., Inc., 40 Mokelumne River Dr., Lodi, CA 95240
G.G. & G., 3602 E. 42nd Stravenue, Tucson, AZ 85713 / 520-748-7167; FAX: 520-748-7583 ggg&3@aol.com www.ggg&3.com
G.U., Inc. (See U.S. Importer-New SKB Arms Co.)
G96 Products Co., Inc., 85 5th Ave., Bldg. #6, Paterson, NJ 07544 / 973-684-4050; FAX: 973-684-3848 g96prod@aol
Gage Manufacturing, 20820 W. Kaibab Rd., Buckeye, AZ 85326 / 310-832-3546
Gaillard Barrels, Box 68, St. Brieux, SK S0K 3V0 CANADA / 306-752-3769; FAX: 306-752-5969
Galati International, P.O. Box 10, 616 Burley Ridge Rd., Wesco, MO 65586 / 636-584-0785; FAX: 573-775-4308 support@galatiinternational.com www.galatiinternational.com
Galaxy Imports Ltd., Inc., P.O. Box 3361, Victoria, TX 77903 / 361-573-4867 galaxy06@suddenlink.net
GALCO International Ltd., 2019 W. Quail Ave., Phoenix, AZ 85027 / 623-474-7070; FAX: 623-582-6854 customerservice@usgalco.com www.usgalco.com
Galena Industries AMT, 5463 Diaz St., Irwindale, CA 91706 / 626-856-8883; FAX: 626-856-8878
Gamba Renato Bremec Srl, Via Artigiani 93, 25063 Gardone V.T. BS, ITALY / 30-8910264-5; FAX: 30-8912180 infocomm@renatogamba.it www.renatogamba.it
Game Haven Gunstocks, 13750 Shire Rd., Wolverine, MI 49799 / 616-525-8257
Gamebore Division, Polywad, Inc., P.O. Box 7916, Macon, GA 31209 / 478-477-0669 or 800-998-0669
Gamo (See U.S. Importers-Arms United Corp., Daisy M
Gamo USA, Inc., 3911 SW 47th Ave., Suite 914, Fort Lauderdale, FL 33314 / 954-581-5822; FAX: 954-581-3165 gamousa@gate.net www.gamo.com
Gander Mountain, Inc., 12400 Fox River Rd., Wilmont, WI 53192 / 414-862-6848
GAR, 590 McBride Ave., West Paterson, NJ 07424 / 973-754-1114; FAX: 973-754-1114 garreloading@aol.com www.garreloading.com
Garrett Cartridges, Inc., P.O. Box 178, Chehalis, WA 98532 / 360-736-0702 www.garrettcartridges.com
Garthwaite Pistolsmith, Inc., Jim, 12130 State Route 405, Watsontown, PA 17777 / 570-538-1566 www.garthwaite.com
Gary Goudy Classic Stocks, 1512 S. 5th St., Dayton, WA 99328 / 509-382-2726 goudy@icehouse.net
Gary Reeder Custom Guns, 2601 7th Ave. E., Flagstaff, AZ 86004 / 928-526-3313; FAX: 928-527-0840 gary@reedercustomguns.com www.reedercustomguns.com
Gator Guns & Repair, 7952 Kenai Spur Hwy., Kenai, AK 99611-8311
GDL Enterprises, 409 Le Gardeur, Slidell, LA 70460 / 504-649-0693
Gehmann, Walter (See Huntington Die Specialties)
Genco, P.O. Box 5704, Asheville, NC 28803
Genecco Gun Works, 10512 Lower Sacramento Rd., Stockton, CA 95210 / 209-951-0706; FAX: 209-931-3872
Gene's Custom Guns, P.O. Box 10534, White Bear Lake, MN 55110 / 651-429-5105; FAX: 651-429-7365
Gentex Corp., 5 Tinkham Ave., Derry, NH 03038 / 603-434-0311; FAX: 603-434-3002 sales@derry.gentexcorp.com www.derry.gentexcorp.com
Gentner Bullets, 109 Woodlawn Ave., Upper Darby, PA 19082 / 610-352-9396 dongentner@rcn.com www.gentnerbullets.com
Gentry Custom LLC, 314 N. Hoffman, Belgrade, MT 59714 / 406-388-GUNS gentryshop@earthlink.net www.gentrycustom.com
George & Roy's, P.O. Box 2125, Sisters, OR 97759-2125 / 503-228-5424 or 800-553-3022; FAX: 503-225-9409
George Hoenig, Inc., 4357 Frozen Dog Rd., Emmett, ID 83617 / 208-365-7716; FAX: 208-365-3472 gnhoenig@msn.com
George Ibberson (Sheffield) Ltd., 25-31 Allen St., Sheffield, S3 7AW ENGLAND / 0114-2766123; FAX: 0114-2738465 sales@eggintongroup.co.uk www.eggintongroup.co.uk
Gerber Legendary Blades, 14200 SW 72nd Ave., Portland, OR 97223 / 503-639-6161 or 800-950-6161; FAX: 503-684-7008
Gervais, Mike, 3804 S. Cruise Dr., Salt Lake City, UT 84109 / 801-277-7729
Getz Barrel Company, P.O. Box 88, 426 E. Market St., Beavertown, PA 17813 / 570-658-7263; FAX: 570-658-4110 www.getzbrl.com
Giacomo Sporting USA, 6234 Stokes Lee Center Rd., Lee Center, NY 13363
Gibbs Rifle Co., Inc., 219 Lawn St., Martinsburg, WV 25401 / 304-262-1651; FAX: 304-262-1658 support@gibbsrifle.com www.gibbsrifle.com
Gil Hebard Guns, Inc., 125 Public Square, P.O. Box 3, Knoxville, IL 61448-0003 / 309-289-2700; FAX: 309-289-2233
Gilbert Equipment Co., Inc., 960 Downtowner Rd., Mobile, AL 36609 / 205-344-3322
Gillmann, Edwin, 33 Valley View Dr., Hanover, PA 17331 / 717-632-1662 gillmaned@superpa.net
Gilmore Sports Concepts, Inc., 5949 S. Garnett Rd., Tulsa, OK 74146 / 918-250-3810; FAX: 918-250-3845 info@gilmoresports.com www.gilmoresports.com
Glacier Glove, 4890 Aircenter Circle, Suite 210, Reno, NV 89502 / 702-825-8225; FAX: 702-825-6544
Glaser LLC, P.O. Box 173, Sturgis, SD 57785 / 605-347-4544 or 800-221-3489; FAX: 605-347-5055 email@corbon.com www.safetyslug.com
Glaser Safety Slug, Inc. (see CorBon/Glaser safetyslug.com
Glass, Herb, P.O. Box 25, Bullville, NY 10915 / 914-361-3021
Glimm, Jerome. See: GLIMM'S CUSTOM GUN ENGRAVING
Glimm's Custom Gun Engraving, Jerome C. Glimm, 19 S. Maryland, Conrad, MT 59425 / 406-278-3574 lag@mcn.net www.gunengraver.biz
Glock GmbH, P.O. Box 50, A-2232, Deutsch, Wagram, AUSTRIA
Glock, Inc., P.O. Box 369, Smyrna, GA 30081 / 770-432-1202; FAX: 770-433-8719
Glynn Scobey Duck & Goose Calls, Rt. 3, Box 37, Newbern, TN 38059 / 731-643-6128
GML Products, Inc., 394 Laredo Dr., Birmingham, AL 35226 / 205-979-4867
Goens, Dale W., P.O. Box 224, Cedar Crest, NM 87008 / 505-281-5419
Goergen's Gun Shop, Inc., 17985 538th Ave., Austin, MN 55912 / 507-433-9280; FAX: 507-433-9280 jim_debgoergen@msn.com
GOEX, Inc., P.O. Box 659, Doyline, LA 71023-0659 / 318-382-9300; FAX: 318-382-9303 mfahringer@goexpowder.com www.goexpowder.com
Golden Age Arms Co., 115 E. High St., Ashley, OH 43003 / 614-747-2488
Golden Bear Bullets, 3065 Fairfax Ave., San Jose, CA 95148 / 408-238-9515
Goodling's Gunsmithing, 1950 Stoverstown Rd., Spring Grove, PA 17362 / 717-225-3350
Goodwin, Fred. See: GOODWIN'S GUNS
Goodwin's Guns, Fred Goodwin, 1028 Silver Ridge Rd., Silver Ridge, ME 04776 / 207-365-4451
Gotz Bullets, 11426 Edgemere Ter., Roscoe, IL 61073-8232
Gould & Goodrich Leather, Inc., 709 E. McNeil St., Lillington, NC 27546 / 910-893-2071; FAX: 910-893-4742 info@gouldusa.com www.gouldusa.com
Gournet Artistic Engraving, Geoffroy Gournet, 820 Paxinosa Ave., Easton, PA 18042 / 610-559-0710 ggournet@yahoo.com www.gournetusa.com
Gournet, Geoffroy. See: GOURNET ARTISTIC ENGRAVING
Grace, Charles E., 718 E. 2nd, Trinidad, CO 81082 / 719-846-9435 riflemakerone@yahoo.com
Grace Metal Products, P.O. Box 67, Elk Rapids, MI 49629 / 616-264-8133
Graf & Sons, 4050 S. Clark St., Mexico, MO 65265 / 573-581-2266; FAX: 573-581-2875 customerservice@grafs.com www.grafs.com
Grand Slam Hunting Products, Box 121, 25454 Military Rd., Cascade, MD 21719 / 301-241-4900; FAX: 301-241-4900 rlj6call@aol.com
Granite Mountain Arms, Inc., 3145 W. Hidden Acres Trail, Prescott, AZ 86305 / 520-541-9758; FAX: 520-445-6826
Grant, Howard V., Hiawatha 15, Woodruff, WI 54568 / 715-356-7146
Graphics Direct, P.O. Box 372421, Reseda, CA 91337-2421 / 818-344-9002
Graves Co., 1800 Andrews Ave., Pompano Beach, FL 33069 / 800-327-9103; FAX: 305-960-0301
Grayback Wildcats, Mike Beeks, 5306 Bryant Ave., Klamath Falls, OR 97603 / 541-884-1072; FAX: 541-884-1072 graybackwildcats@aol.com
Great American Gunstock Co., 3420 Industrial Drive, Yuba City, CA 95993 / 800-784-4867; FAX: 530-671-3906 gunstox@hotmail.com www.gunstocks.com
Green, Arthur S., 485 S. Robertson Blvd., Beverly Hills, CA 90211 / 310-274-1283
Green Head Game Call Co., RR 1, Box 33, Lacon, IL 61540 / 309-246-2155
Green Mountain Rifle Barrel Co., Inc., P.O. Box 2670, 153 W. Main St., Conway, NH 03818 / 603-447-1095; FAX: 603-447-1099 info@gmriflebarrel.com www.gmriflebarrel.com
Greg Gunsmithing Repair, 3732 26th Ave. N., Robbinsdale, MN 55422 / 612-529-8103
Greg's Superior Products, P.O. Box 46219, Seattle, WA 98146
Greider Precision, 431 Santa Marina Ct., Escondido, CA 92029 / 760-480-8892; FAX: 760-480-9800 greider@msn.com
Gre-Tan Rifles, 29742 W.C.R. 50, Kersey, CO 80644 / 970-353-6176; FAX: 970-356-5940 www.gtrtooling.com
Griffin & Howe, Inc., 33 Claremont Rd., Bernardsville, NJ 07924 / 908-766-2287; FAX: 908-766-1068 info@griffinhowe.com www.griffinhowe.com
Griffin & Howe, Inc., 340 W. Putnam Ave., Greenwich, CT 06830 / 203-618-0270 info@griffinhowe.com www.griffinhowe.com
Groenewold, John. See: JG AIRGUNS, LLC
GRS/Glendo Corp., P.O. Box 1153, 900 Overlander St., Emporia, KS 66801 / 620-343-1084 or 800-836-3519; FAX: 620-343-9640 glendo@glendo.com www.glendo.com
Grulla Armes, Apartado 453, Avda Otaloa 12, Eiber, SPAIN

MANUFACTURER'S DIRECTORY

Gruning Precision, Inc., 7101 Jurupa Ave., No. 12, Riverside, CA 92504 / 909-289-4371; FAX: 909-689-7791 gruningprecision@earthlink.net www.gruningprecision.com
GSI, Inc., 7661 Commerce Ln., Trussville, AL 35173 / 205-655-8299
Guarasi, Robert. See: WILCOX INDUSTRIES CORP.
Guardsman Products, 411 N. Darling, Fremont, MI 49412 / 616-924-3950
Gun City, 212 W. Main Ave., Bismarck, ND 58501 / 701-223-2304
Gun Digest (See F+W Publications), 700 E. State St., Iola, WI 54990 / 715-445-2214; FAX: 715-445-4087 www.gundigestmagazine.com
Gun Doc, Inc., 5405 NW 82nd Ave., Miami, FL 33166 / 305-477-2777; FAX: 305-477-2778 www.gundoc.com
Gun Doctor, The, P.O. Box 72817, Roselle, IL 60172 / 708-894-0668
Gun Hunter Books (See Gun Hunter Trading Co.), 5075 Heisig St., Beaumont, TX 77705 / 409-835-3006; FAX: 409-838-2266 gunhuntertrading@hotmail.com
Gun Hunter Trading Co., 5075 Heisig St., Beaumont, TX 77705 / 409-835-3006; FAX: 409-838-2266 gunhuntertrading@hotmail.com
Gun Leather Limited, 116 Lipscomb, Fort Worth, TX 76104 / 817-334-0225; FAX: 800-247-0609
Gun Room Press, The, 127 Raritan Ave., Highland Park, NJ 08904 / 732-545-4344; FAX: 732-545-6686 gunbooks@rutgersgunbooks.com www.rutgersgunbooks.com
Gun Room, The, 1121 Burlington, Muncie, IN 47302 / 765-282-9073; FAX: 765-282-5270 bshstleguns@aol.com
Gun Shop, The, 5550 S. 900 East, Salt Lake City, UT 84117 / 801-263-3633
Gun South, Inc. (See GSI, Inc.)
Gun Vault, 7339 E. Acoma Dr., Ste. 7, Scottsdale, AZ 85260 / 602-951-6855
Gun Works, The, 247 S. 2nd St., Springfield, OR 97477 / 541-741-4118; FAX: 541-988-1097 info@thegunworks.com www.thegunworks.com
Gun-Alert, 1010 N. Maclay Ave., San Fernando, CA 91340 / 818-365-0864; FAX: 818-365-1308
Guncraft Books (See Guncraft Sports, Inc.), 10737 Dutchtown Rd., Knoxville, TN 37932 / 865-966-4545; FAX: 865-966-4500 findit@guncraft.com www.guncraft.com
Guncraft Sports, Inc., 10737 Dutchtown Rd., Knoxville, TN 37932 / 865-966-4545; FAX: 865-966-4500 findit@guncraft.com www.usit.net/guncraft
Guncraft Sports, Inc., Marie C. Wiest, 10737 Dutchtown Rd., Knoxville, TN 37932 / 865-966-4545; FAX: 865-966-4500 findit@guncraft.com www.guncraft.com
Guncrafter Industries, 171 Madison 1510, Huntsville, AR 72740 / 479-665-2466 www.guncrafterindustries.com
Gun-Ho Sports Cases, 110 E. 10th St., St. Paul, MN 55101 / 612-224-9491
Gunline Tools, 2950 Saturn St., "O", Brea, CA 92821 / 714-993-5100; FAX: 714-572-4128
Gunnerman Books, P.O. Box 81697, Rochester Hills, MI 48308 / 248-608-2856 gunnermanbks@att.net
Guns Antique & Modern DBA / Charles E. Duffy, 224 Williams Lane, P.O. Box 2, West Hurley, NY 12491 / 845-679-2997 ceo1923@prodigy.net
GUNS Magazine, 12345 World Trade Dr., San Diego, CA 92128-3743 / 619-297-5350; FAX: 619-297-5353
Gunsight, The, 5292 Kentwater Pl., Yorba Linda, CA 92886
Gunsite Training Center, P.O. Box 700, Paulden, AZ 86334 / 520-636-4565; FAX: 520-636-1236
Gunsmithing Ltd., 3 Lacey Place, 2530 Post Rd., Southport, CT 06890 / 203-254-0436; FAX: 203-254-1535
Gunsmithing, Inc., 30 W. Buchanan St., Colorado Springs, CO 80907 / 719-632-3795; FAX: 719-632-3493 www.nealsguns.com
Gurney, F. R., Box 13, Sooke, BC V0S 1N0 CANADA / 604-642-5282; FAX: 604-642-7859

H

H&B Forge Co., Rt. 2, Geisinger Rd., Shiloh, OH 44878 / 419-895-1856
H&P Publishing, 7174 Hoffman Rd., San Angelo, TX 76905 / 915-655-5953
H&R 1871, LLC, 60 Industrial Rowe, Gardner, MA 01440 / 508-632-9393; FAX: 508-632-2300 hr1871@hr1871.com www.hr1871.com
H. Krieghoff Gun Co., Boschstrasse 22, D-89079, Ulm, GERMANY / 731-401820; FAX: 731-4018270
H.K.S. Products, 7841 Founion Dr., Florence, KY 41042 / 606-342-7841 or 800-354-9814; FAX: 606-342-5865
H.P. White Laboratory, Inc., 3114 Scarboro Rd., Street, MD 21154 / 410-838-6550; FAX: 410-838-2802 info@hpwhite.com www.hpwhite.com
Hafner World Wide, Inc., P.O. Box 1987, Lake City, FL 32055 / 904-755-6481; FAX: 904-755-6595 hafner@isgroupe.net
Hagn Rifles & Actions, P.O. Box 444, Cranbrook, BC V1C 4H9 Canada / 250-489-4861
Half Moon Rifle Shop, 490 Halfmoon Rd., Columbia Falls, MT 59912 / 406-892-4409 halfmoonrs@centurytel.net
Hall Plastics, Inc., John, P.O. Box 1526, Alvin, TX 77512 / 713-489-8709
Hallowell & Co., P.O. Box 1445, Livingston, MT 59047 / 406-222-4770; FAX: 406-222-4792 morris@hallowellco.com www.hallowellco.com
Hally Caller, 443 Wells Rd., Doylestown, PA 18901 / 215-345-6354; FAX: 215-345-6354 info@hallycaller.com www.hallycaller.com
Hamilton, Alex B. (See Ten-Ring Precision, Inc.)
Hammans, Charles E., P.O. Box 788, 2022 McCracken, Stuttgart, AR 72160-0788 / 870-673-1388
Hammerli AG, Industrieplaz, a/Rheinpall, CH-8212 Neuhausen, SWITZERLAND info@hammerli.com www.haemmerliich.com
Hammerli Service-Precision Mac, Rudolf Marent, 9711 Tiltree St., Houston, TX 77075 / 713-946-7028 rmarent@webtv.net
Hammerli USA, 19296 Oak Grove Circle, Groveland, CA 95321 FAX: 209-962-5311
Hammond Custom Guns Ltd., 619 S. Pandora, Gilbert, AZ 85234 / 602-892-3437
HandCrafts Unltd. (See Clements' Custom Leathercraft), 1741 Dallas St., Aurora, CO 80010-2018 / 303-364-0403; FAX: 303-739-9824 gryphons@home.com kuntaoslcat.com
Handgun Press, P.O. Box 406, Glenview, IL 60025 / 847-657-6500; FAX: 847-724-8831 handgunpress@comcast.net
Hank's Gun Shop, Box 370, 50 W. 100 South, Monroe, UT 84754 / 435-527-4456 hanksgs@altazip.com
Hanned Line, The, 4463 Madoc Way, San Jose, CA 95130 smith@hanned.com www.hanned.com
Hanned Precision (See The Hanned Line)
Hansen & Co., 244-246 Old Post Rd., Southport, CT 06490 / 203-259-6222; FAX: 203-254-3832
Hanson's Gun Center, Dick, 233 Everett Dr., Colorado Springs, CO 80911
Harford (See U.S. Importer-EMF Co., Inc.)
Harrell's Precision, 5756 Hickory Dr., Salem, VA 24153 / 540-380-2683
Harrington & Richardson (See H&R 1871, Inc.)
Harris Engineering Inc., Dept. GD54, 999 Broadway, Barlow, KY 42024 / 270-334-3633; FAX: 270-334-3000
Harris Enterprises, P.O. Box 105, Bly, OR 97622 / 503-353-2625
Harris Hand Engraving, Paul A., 113 Rusty Ln., Boerne, TX 78006-5746 / 512-391-5121
Harris Publications, 1115 Broadway, New York, NY 10010 / 212-807-7100; FAX: 212-627-4678
Harrison Bullets, 6437 E. Hobart St., Mesa, AZ 85205
Harry Lawson LLC, 3328 N. Richey Blvd., Tucson, AZ 85716 / 520-326-1117; FAX: 520-326-1117
Hart & Son, Inc., Robert W., 401 Montgomery St., Nescopeck, PA 18635 / 717-752-3655; FAX: 717-752-1088
Hart Rifle Barrels, Inc., P.O. Box 182, 1690 Apulia Rd., Lafayette, NY 13084 / 315-677-9841; FAX: 315-677-9610 hartriflebarrels@sbcglobal.net hartbarrels.com
Hartford (See U.S. Importer-EMF Co. Inc.)
Hartmann & Weiss GmbH, Rahlstedter Bahnhofstr. 47, 22143, Hamburg, GERMANY / (40) 677 55 85; FAX: (40) 677 55 92 hartmannundweiss@t-online.de
Harvey, Frank, 218 Nightfall, Terrace, NV 89015 / 702-558-6998
Hastings, P.O. Box 135, Clay Center, KS 67432 / 785-632-3169; FAX: 785-632-6554
Hatfield Gun, 224 N. 4th St., St. Joseph, MO 64501
Hawk Laboratories, Inc. (See Hawk, Inc.), 849 Hawks Bridge Rd., Salem, NJ 08079 / 609-299-2700; FAX: 609-299-2800
Hawk, Inc., 849 Hawks Bridge Rd., Salem, NJ 08079 / 609-299-2700; FAX: 609-299-2800 info@hawkbullets.com www.hawkbullets.com
Hawken Shop, The, P.O. Box 593, Oak Harbor, WA 98277 / 206-679-4657; FAX: 206-675-1114
Hawken Shop, The (See Dayton Traister)
Haydel's Game Calls, Inc., 5018 Hazel Jones Rd., Bossier City, LA 71111 / 318-746-3586; FAX: 318-746-3711 www.haydels.com
Hecht, Hubert J., Waffen-Hecht, P.O. Box 2635, Fair Oaks, CA 95628 / 916-966-1020
Heckler & Koch GmbH, P.O. Box 1329, 78722 Oberndorf, Neckar, GERMANY / 49-7423179-0; FAX: 49-7423179-2406
Heckler & Koch, Inc., 21480 Pacific Blvd., Sterling, VA 20166-8900 / 703-450-1900; FAX: 703-450-8160 www.hecklerkoch-usa.com
Hege Jagd-u. Sporthandels GmbH, P.O. Box 101461, W-7770, Ueberlingen a. Boden, GERMANY
Heidenstrom Bullets, Dalghte 86-3660 Rjukan, 35091818, NORWAY, olau.joh@online.tuo
Heilmann, Stephen, P.O. Box 657, Grass Valley, CA 95945 / 530-272-8758; FAX: 530-274-0285 sheilmann@jps.net www.metalwood.com
Heinie Specialty Products, 301 Oak St., Quincy, IL 62301-2500 / 217-228-9500; FAX: 217-228-9502 rheinie@heinie.com www.heinie.com
Helwan (See U.S. Importer-Interarms)
Henigson & Associates, Steve, P.O. Box 2726, Culver City, CA 90231 / 310-305-8288; FAX: 310-305-1905
Henriksen Tool Co., Inc., 8515 Wagner Creek Rd., Talent, OR 97540 / 541-535-2309; FAX: 541-535-2309
Henry Repeating Arms Co., 110 8th St., Brooklyn, NY 11215 / 718-499-5600; FAX: 718-768-8056 info@henryrepeating.com www.henryrepeating.com
Hensley, Gunmaker, Darwin, P.O. Box 329, Brightwood, OR 97011 / 503-622-5411
Heppler, Keith. See: KEITH'S CUSTOM GUNSTOCKS
Hercules, Inc. (See Alliant Techsystems Smokeless Powder Group)
Heritage Firearms (See Heritage Mfg., Inc.)
Heritage Manufacturing, Inc., 4600 NW 135th St., Opa Locka, FL 33054 / 305-685-5966; FAX: 305-687-6721 infohmi@heritagemfg.com www.heritagemfg.com
Heritage/VSP Gun Books, P.O. Box 887, McCall, ID 83638 / 208-634-4104; FAX: 208-634-3101 heritage@gunbooks.com www.gunbooks.com
Herrett's Stocks, Inc., P.O. Box 741, Twin Falls, ID 83303 / 208-733-1498
Hesse Arms, Robert Hesse, 1126 70th St. E., Inver Grove Heights, MN 55077-2416 / 651-455-5760; FAX: 612-455-5760
Hesse, Robert. See: HESSE ARMS
Heydenberk, Warren R., 1059 W. Sawmill Rd., Quakertown, PA 18951 / 215-538-2682
Hidalgo, Tony, 12701 SW 9th Pl., Davie, FL 33325 / 954-476-7645
High Bridge Arms, Inc., 3185 Mission St., San Francisco, CA 94110 / 415-282-8358
High North Products, Inc., P.O. Box 2, Antigo, WI 54409 / 715-627-2331; FAX: 715-623-5451
High Performance International, 5734 W. Florist Ave., Milwaukee, WI 53218 / 414-466-9040; FAX: 414-466-7050 mike@hpirifles.com hpirifles.com
High Precision, Bud Welsh, 80 New Road, E. Amherst, NY 14051 / 716-688-6344; FAX: 716-688-0425 welsh5168@aol.com www.high-precision.com
High Standard Mfg. Co./F.I., Inc., 5200 Mitchelldale St., Ste. E17, Houston, TX 77092-7222 / 713-462-4200 or 800-272-7816; FAX: 713-681-5665 info@highstandard.com
High Tech Specialties, Inc., P.O. Box 839, 293 E Main St., Rear, Adamstown, PA 19501 / 717-484-0405; FAX: 717-484-0523 bansner@aol.com www.hightech- specialties.com
Highwood Special Products, 1531 E. Highwood, Pontiac, MI 48340
Hill, Loring F., 304 Cedar Rd., Elkins Park, PA 19027
Hill Speed Leather, Ernie, 4507 N 195th Ave., Litchfield Park, AZ 85340 / 602-853-9222; FAX: 602-853-9235
Hinman Outfitters, Bob, 107 N Sanderson Ave., Bartonville, IL 61607-1839 / 309-691-8132
Hi-Performance Ammunition Company, 5231 Greensburg Rd., Apollo, PA 15613 / 304-674-9000; FAX: 304-675-6700 gjrahiperwvo@yahoo.com
HIP-GRIP Barami Corp., P.O. Box 252224, West Bloomfield, MI 48325-2224 / 248-738-0462; FAX: 248-738-2542 hipgripja@aol.com www.hipgrip.com
Hi-Point Firearms/MKS Supply, 8611-A North Dixie Dr., Dayton, OH 45414 / 877-425-4867; FAX: 937-454-0503 www.hi-pointfirearms.com
Hiptmayer, Armurier, RR 112 750, P.O. Box 136, Eastman, PQ J0E 1P0 CANADA / 514-297-2492
Hiptmayer, Heidemarie, RR 112 750, P.O. Box 136, Eastman, PQ J0E 1P0 CANADA / 514-297-2492
Hiptmayer, Klaus, RR 112 750, P.O. Box 136, Eastman, PQ J0E 1P0 CANADA / 514-297-2492
Hirtenberger AG, Leobersdorferstrasse 31, A-2552, Hirtenberg, AUSTRIA / 43(0)2256 81184; FAX: 43(0)2256 81808 www.hirtenberger.ot

MANUFACTURER'S DIRECTORY

HJS Arms, Inc., P.O. Box 3711, Brownsville, TX 78523-3711 / 956-542-2767; FAX: 956-542-2767
Hoag, James W., 8523 Canoga Ave., Suite C, Canoga Park, CA 91304 / 818-998-1510
Hobson Precision Mfg. Co., 210 Big Oak Ln., Brent, AL 35034 / 205-926-4662; FAX: 205-926-3193 cahobbob@dbtech.net
Hodgdon Powder Co., 6231 Robinson, Shawnee Mission, KS 66202 / 913-362-9455; FAX: 913-362-1307
Hodgman, Inc., 1100 Stearns Dr., Sauk Rapids, MN 56379
Hodgson, Richard, 9081 Tahoe Lane, Boulder, CO 80301
Hoehn Sales, Inc., 2045 Kohn Road, Wright City, MO 63390 / 636-745-8144; FAX: 636-745-7868 ron@hoehnsales.com
Hofer Jagdwaffen, P., A9170 Ferlach, Kirchgasse 24, Kirchgasse, AUSTRIA / 43 4227 3683; FAX: 43 4227 368330 peterhofer@hoferwaffen.com www.hoferwaffen.com
Hoffman New Ideas, 821 Northmoor Rd., Lake Forest, IL 60045 / 312-234-4075
Hogue Grips, P.O. Box 1138, Paso Robles, CA 93447 / 800-438-4747 or 805-239-1440; FAX: 805-239-2553
Holland & Holland Ltd., 33 Bruton St., London, ENGLAND / 44-171-499-4411; FAX: 44-171-408-7962
Holland's Shooters Supply, Inc., P.O. Box 69, Powers, OR 97466 / 541-439-5155; FAX: 541-439-2105 bestrifles@aol.com www.hollandguns.com
Hollinger, Jon. See: ASPEN OUTFITTING CO.
Hollywood Engineering, 10642 Arminta St., Sun Valley, CA 91352 / 818-842-8376; FAX: 818-504-4168 cadqueenel1@aol.com
Homak, 350 N. La Salle Dr. Ste. 1100, Chicago, IL 60610-4731 / 312-523-3100; FAX: 312-523-9455
Hoppe's Div. Penguin Industries, Inc., 9200 Cody St., Overland Park, KS 66214 / 800-845-2444
Horizons Unlimited, P.O. Box 426, Warm Springs, GA 31830 / 706-655-3603; FAX: 706-655-3603
Hornady Mfg. Co., P.O. Box 1848, Grand Island, NE 68802 / 800-338-3220 or 308-382-1390; FAX: 308-382-5761
Horseshoe Leather Products, Andy Arratoonian, The Cottage Sharow, Ripon, ENGLAND U.K. / 44-1765-605858 andy@horseshoe.co.uk www.holsters.org
House of Muskets, Inc., The, PO Box 4640, Pagosa Springs, CO 81157 / 970-731-2295
Houtz & Barwick, P.O. Box 435, W. Church St., Elizabeth City, NC 27909 / 800-775-0337 or 919-335-4191; FAX: 919-335-1152
Howa Machinery, Ltd., 1900-1 Sukaguchi Kiyosu, Aichi 452-8601, JAPAN / 81-52-408-1231; FAX: 81-52-401-4999 howa@howa.co.jp http://www.howa.cojpl
Howell Machine, Inc., 815 D St., Lewiston, ID 83501 / 208-743-7418; FAX: 208-746-1703 ammoload@microwavedsl.com www.ammoload.com
H-S Precision, Inc., 1301 Turbine Dr., Rapid City, SD 57701 / 605-341-3006; FAX: 605-342-8964
HT Bullets, 244 Belleville Rd., New Bedford, MA 02745 / 508-999-3338
Hubert J. Hecht Waffen-Hecht, P.O. Box 2635, Fair Oaks, CA 95628 / 916-966-1020
Huebner, Corey O., P.O. Box 564, Frenchtown, MT 59834 / 406-721-7168 bugsboys@hotmail.com
Huey Gun Cases, 820 Indiana St., Lawrence, KS 66044-2645 / 785-842-0062; FAX: 785-842-0062 ketchsailor27@aol.com www.hueycases.com
Hume, Don. See: DON HUME LEATHERGOODS
Hunter Co., Inc., 3300 W. 71st Ave., Westminster, CO 80030 / 303-427-4626; FAX: 303-428-3980 debbiet@huntercompany.com www.huntercompany.com
Hunterjohn, P.O. Box 771457, St. Louis, MO 63177 / 314-531-7250 www.hunterjohn.com
Hunter's Specialties Inc., 6000 Huntington Ct. NE, Cedar Rapids, IA 52402-1268 / 319-395-0321; FAX: 319-395-0326
Hunters Supply, Inc., 1177 Hwy. 96, Regina, NM 87046 / 940-437-2458; FAX: 940-437-2228 hunterssupply@hotmail.com www.hunterssupply.net
Huntington Die Specialties, 601 Oro Dam Blvd., Oroville, CA 95965 / 530-534-1210 or 866-735-6237; FAX: 530-534-1212 buy@huntingtons.com www.huntingtons.com
Hydra-Tone Chemicals, Inc., 7065 Production Coast, Florence, KY 41042 / 859-534-5630; FAX: 859-594-3312 graff-off@hydra-tone.com www.hydra-tone.com
Hydrosorbent Dehumidifiers, P.O. Box 437, Ashley Falls, MA 01222 / 800-448-7903; FAX: 413-229-8743 orders@dehumidify.com www.dehumidify.com

I

I.A.B. (See U.S. Importer-Taylor's & Co., Inc.)
I.D.S.A. Books, 3220 E. Galbraith Rd., Cincinnati, OH 45236 / 513-985-9112; FAX: 513-985-9116 idsabooks@idsabooks.com www.idsabooks.com
I.N.C. Inc. (See Kickeez I.N.C., Inc.)
I.S.W., 106 E. Cairo Dr., Tempe, AZ 85282
IAR Inc., 33171 Camino Capistrano, San Juan Capistrano, CA 92675 / 949-443-3642; FAX: 949-443-3647 sales@iar-arms.com iar-arms.com
Ide, Ken. See: STURGEON VALLEY SPORTERS
IGA (See U.S. Importer-Stoeger Industries)
Image Ind. Inc., 11220 E. Main St., Huntley, IL 60142-7369 / 630-766-2402; FAX: 630-766-7373
Impact Case & Container, Inc., P.O. Box 1129, Rathdrum, ID 83858 / 877-687-2452; FAX: 208-687-0632 bradk@icc-case.com www.icc-case.com
Imperial Magnum Corp., P.O. Box 249, Oroville, WA 98844 / 604-495-3131; FAX: 604-495-2816
Imperial Miniature Armory, 1115 FM 359, Richland, TX 77449 / 800-646-4288; FAX: 832-595-8787 miniguns@houston.rr.com www.1800miniature.com
IMR Powder Co., 1080 Military Turnpike, Suite 2, Plattsburgh, NY 12901 / 518-563-2253; FAX: 518-563-6916
Info-Arm, P.O. Box 1262, Champlain, NY 12919 / 514-955-0355; FAX: 514-955-0357 infoarm@qc.aira.com
Innovative Weaponry Inc., 2513 E. Loop 820 N., Fort Worth, TX 76118 / 817-284-0099 or 800-334-3573
INTEC International, Inc., P.O. Box 5708, Scottsdale, AZ 85261 / 602-483-1708
Inter Ordnance of America LP, 3305 Westwood Industrial Dr., Monroe, NC 28110-5204 / 704-821-8337; FAX: 704-821-8523
Intercontinental Distributors, Ltd., P.O. Box 815, Beulah, ND 58523
InterMedia Outdoors, Inc., 6420 Wilshire Blvd., Los Angeles, CA 90048 / 213-782-2000; FAX: 213-782-2867
International Shooters Service, P.O. Box 185234, Ft. Worth, TX 76181 / 817-595-2090; FAX: 817-595-2090 is_s_@sbcglobal.net www.iss- internationalshootersservice.com
Intrac Arms International, 5005 Chapman Hwy., Knoxville, TN 37920
Ion Industries, Inc., 3508 E Allerton Ave., Cudahy, WI 53110 / 414-486-2007; FAX: 414-486-2017
Iosso Products, 1485 Lively Blvd., Elk Grove Village, IL 60007 / 847-437-8400; FAX: 847-437-8478
Iron Bench, 12619 Bailey Rd., Redding, CA 96003 / 916-241-4623
Ironside International Publishers, Inc., P.O. Box 1050, Lorton, VA 22199 / 703-493-9120; FAX: 703-493-9424
Ironsighter Co., P.O. Box 85070, Westland, MI 48185 / 734-326-8731; FAX: 734-326-3378 www.ironsighter.com
Irwin, Campbell H., 140 Hartland Blvd., East Hartland, CT 06027 / 203-653-3901
Israel Arms Inc., 5625 Star Ln. #B, Houston, TX 77057 / 713-789-0745; FAX: 713-914-9515 www.israelarms.com
Ithaca Classic Doubles, Stephen Lamboy, No. 5 Railroad St., Victor, NY 14564 / 716-924-2710; FAX: 716-924-2737 ithacadoubles.com
Ithaca Guns, LLC, 420 N. Walpole St., Upper Sandusky, OH 43351 / 419-294-4113; FAX: 419-294-9433 service@ithacaguns.com www.ithacaguns-usa.com
Ivanoff, Thomas G. (See Tom's Gun Repair)

J

J J Roberts Firearm Engraver, 7808 Lake Dr., Manassas, VA 20111 / 703-330-0448; FAX: 703-264-8600 james.roberts@angelfire.com www.angelfire.com/va2/ engraver
J R Guns, P.O. Box 370, Monticello, NY 12701 / 845-794-2510
J&D Components, 75 East 350 North, Orem, UT 84057-4719 / 801-225-7007 www.jdcomponents.com
J&J Products, Inc., 9240 Whitmore, El Monte, CA 91731 / 818-571-5228; FAX: 800-927-8361
J&J Sales, 1501 21st Ave. S., Great Falls, MT 59405 / 406-727-9789 mtshootingbench@yahoo.com www.j&jsales.us
J&L Superior Bullets (See Huntington Die Specialties)
J&M Precision Machining, Jeff Amato, RR 1 Box 91, Bloomfield, IN 47424
J&R Engineering, P.O. Box 77, 200 Lyons Hill Rd., Athol, MA 01331 / 508-249-9241
J&R Enterprises, 4550 Scotts Valley Rd., Lakeport, CA 95453
J&S Heat Treat, 803 S. 16th St., Blue Springs, MO 64015 / 816-229-2149; FAX: 816-228-1135
J. Dewey Mfg. Co., Inc., P.O. Box 2014, Southbury, CT 06488 / 203-264-3064; FAX: 203-262-6907 deweyrods@att.net www.deweyrods.com
J. Korzinek Riflesmith, RD 2, Box 73D, Canton, PA 17724 / 717-673-8512
J.A. Blades, Inc. (See Christopher Firearms Co.)
J.A. Henckels Zwillingswerk Inc., 9 Skyline Dr., Hawthorne, NY 10532 / 914-592-7370
J.G. Anschutz GmbH & Co. KG, Daimlerstr. 12, D-89079 Ulm, Ulm, GERMANY / 49 731 40120; FAX: 49 731 4012700 JGA-info@anschuetz-sport.com www.anschuetz-sport.com
J.G. Dapkus Co., Inc., Commerce Circle, P.O. Box 293, Durham, CT 06422 www.explodingtargets.com
J.J. Roberts / Engraver, 7808 Lake Dr., Manassas, VA 20111 / 703-330-0448 jjrengraver@aol.com www.angelfire.com/va2/engraver
J.R. Williams Bullet Co., 2008 Tucker Rd., Perry, GA 31069 / 912-987-0274
J.W. Morrison Custom Rifles, 4015 W. Sharon, Phoenix, AZ 85029 / 602-978-3754
J.W. Wasmundt-Gunsmith, Jim Wasmundt, P.O. Box 130, 140 Alder St., Powers, OR 97466-0130 / 541-439-2044 jwasm@juno.com
Jack A. Rosenberg & Sons, 12229 Cox Ln., Dallas, TX 75234 / 214-241-6302
Jack Dever Co., 8520 NW 90th St., Oklahoma City, OK 73132 / 405-721-6393 jbdever1@home.com
Jack First, Inc., 1201 Turbine Dr., Rapid City, SD 57703 / 605-343-9544; FAX: 605-343-9420
Jack Jonas Appraisals & Taki, 13952 E. Marina Dr., #604, Aurora, CO 80014
Jackalope Gun Shop, 1048 S. 5th St., Douglas, WY 82633 / 307-358-3441 wildcatoutfitters@msn.com www.jackalopegunshop.com
Jaffin, Harry. See: BRIDGEMAN PRODUCTS
Jagdwaffen, Peter. See: BUCHSENMACHERMEISTER
James Calhoon Mfg., 4343 U.S. Highway 87, Havre, MT 59501 / 406-395-4079 www.jamescalhoon.com
James Churchill Glove Co., PO Box 298, Centralia, WA 98531 / 360-736-2816; FAX: 360-330-0151 churchillglove@localaccess.com
James Wayne Firearms for Collectors and Investors, 2608 N. Laurent, Victoria, TX 77901 / 361-578-1258; FAX: 361-578-3559
Jamison International, Marc Jamison, 3551 Mayer Ave., Sturgis, SD 57785 / 605-347-5090; FAX: 605-347-4704 jbell2@masttechnology.com
Jamison, Marc. See: JAMISON INTERNATIONAL
Jamison's Forge Works, 4527 Rd. 6.5 NE, Moses Lake, WA 98837 / 509-762-2659
Jantz Supply, Inc., 309 West Main Dept HD, Davis, OK 73030-0584 / 580-369-2316; FAX: 580-369-3082 jantz@jantzusa.com www.knifemaking.com
Jarrett Rifles, Inc., 383 Brown Rd., Jackson, SC 29831 / 803-471-3616 www.jarrettrifles.com
Jarvis, Inc., 1123 Cherry Orchard Lane, Hamilton, MT 59840 / 406-961-4392
Javelina Lube Products, P.O. Box 337, San Bernardino, CA 92402 / 909-350-9556; FAX: 909-429-1211
Jay McCament Custom Gunmaker, Jay McCament, 1730-134th St. Ct. S., Tacoma, WA 98444 / 253-531-8832
JB Custom, P.O. Box 6912, Leawood, KS 66206 / 913-381-2329
Jeff Flannery Engraving, 11034 Riddles Run Rd., Union, KY 41091 / 859-384-3127; FAX: 859-384-2222 engraving@fuse.net www.flannerygunengraving.com
Jeff's Outfitters, 63F Sena Fawn, Cape Girardeau, MO 63701 / 573-651-3200; FAX: 573-651-3207 info@jeffsoutfitters.com www.jeffsoutfitters.com
Jena Eur, P.O. Box 319, Dunmore, PA 18512
Jenco Sales, Inc., P.O. Box 1000, Manchaca, TX 78652 / 800-531-5301; FAX: 800-266-2373 jencosales@sbcglobal.net
Jenkins Recoil Pads, 5438 E. Frontage Ln., Olney, IL 62450 / 618-395-3416
Jensen Bullets, RR 1 Box 187, Arco, ID 83213 / 208-785-5590
Jensen's Arizona Sportsman, 1325 W. Silverlake Rd. Unit 144, Tucson, AZ 85713 / 602-325-3346; FAX: 602-322-5704
Jensen's Firearms Academy, 3975 E. Dripping Springs Rd., Winkelman, AZ 85292 / 602-293-8516
Jericho Tool & Die Co., Inc., 121 W. Keech Rd., Bainbridge, NY 13733-3248 / 607-563-8222; FAX: 607-563-8560 jerichotool.com www.jerichotool.com
Jerry Phillips Optics, P.O. Box L632, Langhorne, PA 19047 / 215-757-5037; FAX: 215-757-7097
Jesse W. Smith Saddlery, 0499 County Road J, Pritchett, CO 81064 / 509-325-0622
Jester Bullets, Rt. 1 Box 27, Orienta, OK 73737
Jewell Triggers, Inc., 3620 Hwy. 123, San Marcos, TX 78666 / 512-353-2999; FAX: 512-392-0543

JG Airguns, LLC, John Groenewold, P.O. Box 830, Mundelein, IL 60060 / 847-566-2365; FAX: 847-566-4065 john@jgairguns.biz www.jgairguns.biz
JGS Precision Tool Mfg., LLC, 60819 Selander Rd., Coos Bay, OR 97420 / 541-267-4331; FAX: 541-267-5996 jgstools@harborside.com www.jgstools.com
Jim Blair Engraving, P.O. Box 64, Glenrock, WY 82637 / 307-436-8115 jblairengrav@msn.com
Jim Noble Co., 204 W. 5th St., Vancouver, WA 98660 / 360-695-1309; FAX: 360-695-6835 jnobleco@aol.com
Jim Norman Custom Gunstocks, 14281 Cane Rd., Valley Center, CA 92082 / 619-749-6252
Jim's Precision, Jim Ketchum, 1725 Moclips Dr., Petaluma, CA 94952 / 707-762-3014
JLK Bullets, 414 Turner Rd., Dover, AR 72837 / 501-331-4194
Johanssons Vapentillbehor, Bert, S-430 20, Veddige, SWEDEN
John Hall Plastics, Inc., P.O. Box 1526, Alvin, TX 77512 / 713-489-8709
John J. Adams & Son Engravers, 7040 VT Rt 113, Vershire, VT 05079 / 802-685-0019
John Masen Co. Inc., 1305 Jelmak, Grand Prairie, TX 75050 / 817-430-8732; FAX: 817-430-1715
John Partridge Sales Ltd., Trent Meadows Rugeley, Staffordshire, WS15 2HS ENGLAND
John Rigby & Co., 500 Linne Rd. Ste. D, Paso Robles, CA 93446 / 805-227-4236; FAX: 805-227-4723 jrigby@calinet www.johnrigbyandco.com
John's Custom Leather, 523 S. Liberty St., Blairsville, PA 15717 / 724-459-6802; FAX: 724-459-5996 john'scustoml eather@verizon.net www.jcleather.com
Johnson Wood Products, 34897 Crystal Road, Strawberry Point, IA 52076 / 563-933-6504 johnsonwoodproducts @yahoo.com
Jonad Corp., 2091 Lakeland Ave., Lakewood, OH 44107 / 216-226-3161
Jonathan Arthur Ciener, Inc., 8700 Commerce St., Cape Canaveral, FL 32920 / 321-868-2200; FAX: 321-868-2201 www.22lrconversions.com
Jones Custom Products, Neil A., 17217 Brookhouser Rd., Saegertown, PA 16433 / 814-763-2769; FAX: 814-763-4228 njones@mdvl.net neiljones.com
Jones, J. See: SSK INDUSTRIES
Jones Moulds, Paul, 4901 Telegraph Rd., Los Angeles, CA 90022 / 213-262-1510
JP Enterprises, Inc., P.O. Box 378, Hugo, MN 55038 / 651-426-9196; FAX: 651-426-2472 www.jprifles.com
JP Sales, Box 307, Anderson, TX 77830
JRP Custom Bullets, RR2 2233 Carlton Rd., Whitehall, NY 12887 / 518-282-0084 or 802-438-5548
JSL Ltd. (See U.S. Importer-Specialty Shooters Supply)
Juenke, Vern, 25 Bitterbush Rd., Reno, NV 89523 / 702-345-0225
Jungkind, Reeves C., 509 E. Granite St., Llano, TX 78643-3055 / 325-247-1151
Jurras, L. See: L. E. JURRAS & ASSOC.
Justin Phillippi Custom Bullets, P.O. Box 773, Ligonier, PA 15658 / 412-238-9671

K

K&M Industries, Inc., Box 66, 510 S. Main, Troy, ID 83871 / 208-835-2281; FAX: 208-835-5211
K&M Services, 5430 Salmon Run Rd., Dover, PA 17315 / 717-292-3175; FAX: 717-292-3175
K. Eversull Co., Inc., 1 Tracemont, Boyce, LA 71409 / 318-793-8728; FAX: 318-793-5483 bestguns@aol.com
K.B.I. Inc., P.O. Box 6625, Harrisburg, PA 17112 / 717-540-8518; FAX: 717-540-8567
KA-BAR Knives, 200 Homer St., Olean, NY 14760 / 800-282-0130; FAX: 716-790-7188 info@ka-bar.com www.ka-bar.com
Kahles A. Swarovski Company, 2 Slater Rd., Cranston, RI 02920 / 401-946-2220; FAX: 401-946-2587
Kahr Arms, P.O. Box 220, 630 Route 303, Blauvelt, NY 10913 / 845-353-7770; FAX: 845-353-7833 www.kahr.com
Kailua Custom Guns Inc., 51 N. Dean Street, Coquille, OR 97423 / 541-396-5413 kailuacustom@aol.com www.kailuacustom.com
Kalispel Case Line, P.O. Box 267, Cusick, WA 99119 / 509-445-1121
Kamik Outdoor Footwear, 554 Montee de Liesse, Montreal, PQ H4T 1P1 CANADA / 514-341-3950; FAX: 514-341-1861
Kapro Mfg. Co. Inc. (See R.E.I.)
Kasenit Co., Inc., 39 Park Ave., Highland Mills, NY 10930 / 845-928-9595; FAX: 845-986-8038
Kaswer Custom, Inc., 13 Surrey Drive, Brookfield, CT 06804 / 203-775-0564; FAX: 203-775-6872
KDF, Inc., 2485 Hwy. 46 N., Seguin, TX 78155 / 830-379-8141; FAX: 830-379-5420
KeeCo Impressions, Inc., 346 Wood Ave., North Brunswick, NJ 08902 / 800-468-0546
Kehr, Roger, 2131 Agate Ct. SE, Lacy, WA 98503 / 360-491-0691
Keith's Bullets, 942 Twisted Oak, Algonquin, IL 60102 / 708-658-3520
Keith's Custom Gunstocks, Keith M. Heppler, 540 Banyan Circle, Walnut Creek, CA 94598 / 925-934-3509; FAX: 925-934-3143 kmheppler@hotmail.com
Kelbly, Inc., 7222 Dalton Fox Lake Rd., North Lawrence, OH 44666 / 216-683-4674; FAX: 216-683-7349
Kelley's, P.O. Box 125, Woburn, MA 01801-0125 / 800-879-7273; FAX: 781-272-7077 kels@star.net www.kelsmilitary.com
Kellogg's Professional Products, 325 Pearl St., Sandusky, OH 44870 / 419-625-6551; FAX: 419-625-6167 skwigton@sbcglobal.net
Kelly, Lance, 1723 Willow Oak Dr., Edgewater, FL 32132 / 904-423-4933
Kel-Tec CNC Industries, Inc., P.O. Box 236009, Cocoa, FL 32923 / 321-631-0068; FAX: 321-631-1169 www.kel-tec.com
Ken Eyster Heritage Gunsmiths, Inc., 6441 Bisop Rd., Centerburg, OH 43011 / 740-625-6131; FAX: 740-625-7811
Ken Starnes Gunmaker, 15617 NE 324th Circle, Battle Ground, WA 98604 / 360-666-5025; FAX: 360-666-5024 kstarnes@kdsa.com
Keng's Firearms Specialty, Inc., 875 Wharton Dr., P.O. Box 44405, Atlanta, GA 30336-1405 / 404-691-7611; FAX: 404-505-8445 kfs@bellsouth.net www.versa- pod.com
Kennebec Journal, 274 Western Ave., Augusta, ME 04330 / 207-622-6288
Kennedy Firearms, 10 N. Market St., Muncy, PA 17756 / 717-546-6695
Kenneth W. Warren Engraver, P.O. Box 2842, Wenatchee, WA 98807 / 509-663-6123; FAX: 509-665-6123
Ken's Kustom Kartridges, 331 Jacobs Rd., Hubbard, OH 44425 / 216-534-4595
Kent Cartridge America, Inc., P.O. Box 849, 1000 Zigor Rd., Kearneysville, WV 25430
Keowee Game Calls, 608 Hwy. 25 North, Travelers Rest, SC 29690 / 864-834-7204; FAX: 864-834-7831
Kershaw Knives, 18600 SW Teton Ave., Tualatin, OR 97062 / 503-682-1966 or 800-325-2891; FAX: 503-682-7168
Kesselring Gun Shop, 4024 Old Hwy. 99N, Burlington, WA 98233 / 360-724-3113; FAX: 360-724-7003 info@kesselrings.com www.kesselrings.com
Ketchum, Jim (See Jim's Precision)
Keystone Sporting Arms, Inc. (Crickett Rifles), 8920 State Route 405, Milton, PA 17847 / 800-742-2777; FAX: 570-742-1455
Kickeez, I.N.C., Inc., 13715 NE 384th St., La Center, WA 98629 / 877-542-5339; FAX: 954-656-4527 info@kickeezproducts www.kickeez.products.com
Kilham & Co., Main St., P.O. Box 37, Lyme, NH 03768 / 603-795-4112
Kimar (See U.S. Importer-IAR, Inc.)
Kimber of America, Inc., 1 Lawton St., Yonkers, NY 10705 / 800-880-2418; FAX: 914-964-9340
King & Co., P.O. Box 1242, Bloomington, IL 61702 / 309-473-3964 or 800-914-5464; FAX: 309-473-2161
King's Gun Works, 1837 W. Glenoaks Blvd., Glendale, CA 91201 / 818-956-6010; FAX: 818-548-8606
Kirkpatrick Leather Co., P.O. Box 677, Laredo, TX 78040 / 956-723-6631; FAX: 956-725-0672 mike@kirkpatrickleather.com www.kirkpatrickleather.com
KK Air International (See Impact Case & Container Co., Inc.)
Kleen-Bore, Inc., 8909 Forum Way, Ft. Worth, TX 76140 / 413-527-0300; FAX: 817-926-7012 info@kleen-bore.com www.kleen-bore.com
Kleinendorst, K. W., RR 1, Box 1500, Hop Bottom, PA 18824 / 570-289-4687; FAX: 570-289-8673
Klingler Woodcarving, P.O. Box 141, Thistle Hill, Cabot, VT 05647 / 802-426-3811 www.vermartcrafts.com
Knifeware, Inc., P.O. Box 3, Greenville, WV 24945 / 304-832-6878
Knight Rifles, 21852 Hwy. J46, P.O. Box 130, Centerville, IA 52544 / 515-856-2626; FAX: 515-856-2628 www.knightrifles.com
Knight Rifles (See Modern Muzzleloading, Inc.)
Knight's Manufacturing Co., 701 Columbia Blvd., Titusville, FL 32780 / 321-607-9900; FAX: 321-268-1498 civiliansale s@knightarmco.com www.knightarmco.com
Knock on Wood Antiques, 355 Post Rd., Darien, CT 06820 / 203-655-9031
Knoell, Doug, 9737 McCardle Way, Santee, CA 92071 / 619-449-5189
Knopp, Gary. See: SUPER 6 LLC
Koehler-Optics, 630 E. Rockland Rd., P.O. Box 6313, Libertyville, IL 60048 / 847-362-7757; FAX: 847-362-7757
Koevenig's Engraving Service, Box 55 Rabbit Gulch, Hill City, SD 57745 / 605-574-2239 ekoevenig@msn.com
KOGOT, 410 College, Trinidad, CO 81082 / 719-846-9406; FAX: 719-846-9406
Kolar, 1925 Roosevelt Ave., Racine, WI 53406 / 414-554-0800; FAX: 414-554-9093
Kolpin Outdoors, Inc., P.O. Box 107, 205 Depot St., Fox Lake, WI 53933 / 414-928-3118; FAX: 414-928-3687 cdutton@kolpin.com www.kolpin.com
Korth Germany GmbH, Robert Bosch Strasse, 11, D-23909, 23909 Ratzeburg, GERMANY / 4541-84 03 63; FAX: 4541-84 05 35 info@korthwaffen.de www.korthwaffen.com
Korth USA, 437R Chandler St., Tewksbury, MA 01876 / 978-851-8656; FAX: 978-851-9462 info@kortusa.com www.korthusa.com
Korzinek Riflesmith, J., RD 2 Box 73D, Canton, PA 17724 / 717-673-8512
Koval Knives, 5819 Zarley St., Suite A, New Albany, OH 43054 / 614-855-0777; FAX: 614-855-0945 koval@kovalknives.com www.kovalknives.com
Kowa Optimed, Inc., 20001 S. Vermont Ave., Torrance, CA 90502 / 310-327-1913; FAX: 310-327-4177 scopekowa@kowa.com www.kowascope.com
KP Books Division of F+W Publications, 700 E. State St., Iola, WI 54990-0001 / 715-445-2214
Kramer Designs, P.O. Box 129, Clancy, MT 59634 / 406-933-8658; FAX: 406-933-8658
Kramer Handgun Leather, P.O. Box 112154, Tacoma, WA 98411 / 800-510-2666; FAX: 253-564-1214 www.kramerleather.com
Krico Deutschland GmbH, Nurnbergerstrasse 6, D-90602, Pyrbaum, GERMANY / 09180-2780; FAX: 09180-2661
Krieger Barrels, Inc., 2024 Mayfield Rd, Richfield, WI 53076 / 262-628-8558; FAX: 262-628-8748
Krieghoff Gun Co., H., Boschstrasse 22, D-89079 Elm, GERMANY / 731-4018270
Krieghoff International, Inc., 7528 Easton Rd., Ottsville, PA 18942 / 610-847-5173; FAX: 610-847-8691 info@krieghoff.com www.krieghoff.com
Kukowski, Ed. See: ED'S GUN HOUSE
Kulis Freeze Dry Taxidermy, 725 Broadway Ave., Bedford, OH 44146 / 440-232-8352; FAX: 440-232-7305 jkulis@kastaway.com kastaway.com
KVH Industries, Inc., 110 Enterprise Center, Middletown, RI 02842 / 401-847-3327; FAX: 401-849-0045
Kwik-Site Co., 5555 Treadwell St., Wayne, MI 48184 / 734-326-1500; FAX: 734-326-4120 kwiksitecorp@aol.com www.kwiksiteco@aol.com

L

L&R Lock Co., 2328 Cains Mill Rd., Sumter, SC 29154 / 803-481-5790; FAX: 803-481-5795
L&S Technologies Inc. (See Aimtech Mount Systems)
L. Bengtson Arms Co., 6345-B E. Akron St., Mesa, AZ 85205 / 602-981-6375
L. E. Jurras & Assoc., L. E. Jurras, P.O. Box 680, Washington, IN 47501 / 812-254-6170; FAX: 812-254-6170 jurras@sbcglobal.net www.leejurras.com
L.A.R. Mfg., Inc., 4133 W. Farm Rd., West Jordan, UT 84088 / 801-280-3505; FAX: 801-280-1972
L.B.T., Judy Smith, HCR 62, Box 145, Moyie Springs, ID 83845 / 208-267-3588 lbtisaccuracy@imbris.net
L.E. Wilson, Inc., Box 324, 404 Pioneer Ave., Cashmere, WA 98815 / 509-782-1328; FAX: 509-782-7200
L.L. Bean, Inc., Freeport, ME 04032 / 207-865-4761; FAX: 207-552-2802
L.P.A. Inc., Via Alfieri 26, Gardone V.T., Brescia, ITALY / 30-891-14-81; FAX: 30-891-09-51
L.R. Clift Mfg., 3821 Hammonton Rd., Marysville, CA 95901 / 916-755-3390; FAX: 916-755-3393
La Clinique du .45, 1432 Rougemont, Chambly, PQ J3L 2L8 CANADA / 514-658-1144
Labanu Inc., 2201-F Fifth Ave., Ronkonkoma, NY 11779 / 516-467-6197; FAX: 516-981-4112
LaBoone, Pat. See: MIDWEST SHOOTING SCHOOL, THE
LaBounty Precision Reboring, Inc, 7968 Silver Lake Rd., PO Box 186, Maple Falls, WA 98266 / 360-599-2047; FAX: 360-599-3018
LaCrosse Footwear, Inc., 18550 NE Riverside Parkway, Portland, OR 97230 / 503-766-1010 or 800-323-2668;

FAX: 503-766-1015 customerservice@lacrossfootwear.com www.lacrossefootwear.com
Lake Center Marina, P.O. Box 670, St. Charles, MO 63302 / 314-946-7500
Lakefield Arms Ltd. (See Savage Arms, Inc.)
Lakewood Products Div of Midwest Textile, PO Box 342, Suamico, WI 54173 / 800-872-8458; FAX: 877-676-3559 info@lakewoodproduct.com www.lakewoodproducts.com
Lamboy, Stephen. See: ITHACA CLASSIC DOUBLES
Lampert, Ron, Rt. 1, 44857 Schoolcraft Trl., Laporte, MN 56461 / 218-854-7345
Lamson & Goodnow Mfg. Co., 15 Greenfield St., Greenfield, MA 01301 / 800-872-6564; FAX: 413-774-7776 info@lamsonsharp.com www.lamsonsharp.com
Lansky Levine, Arthur. See: LANSKY SHARPENERS
Lansky Sharpeners, Arthur Lansky Levine, P.O. Box 50830, Las Vegas, NV 89016 / 702-361-7511; FAX: 702-896-9511
LaPrade, P.O. Box 250, Ewing, VA 24248 / 423-733-2615
LaRocca Gun Works, 51 Union Place, Worcester, MA 01608 / 508-754-2887; FAX: 508-754-2887 www.laroccagunworks.com
Larry Lyons Gunworks, 29994 M 62 W., Dowagiac, MI 49047 / 616-782-9478
Laser Devices, Inc., 2 Harris Ct. A-4, Monterey, CA 93940 / 831-373-0701; FAX: 831-373-0903 sales@laserdevices.com www.laserdevices.com
Laseraim Technologies, Inc., P.O. Box 3548, Little Rock, AR 72203 / 501-375-2227
Laserlyte, 2201 Amapola Ct., Torrance, CA 90501
LaserMax, 3495 Winton Place, Rochester, NY 14623-2807 / 800-527-3703; FAX: 585-272-5427 customerservice@lasermax-inc.com www.lasermax.com
Lassen Community College, Gunsmithing Dept., P.O. Box 3000, Hwy. 139, Susanville, CA 96130 / 916-251-8800; FAX: 916-251-8838 staylor@lassencollege.edu www.lassencommunitycollege.edu
Laughridge, William R. (See Cylinder & Slide, Inc.)
Laurel Mountain Forge, P.O. Box 52, Crown Point, IN 46308 / 219-548-2950; FAX: 219-548-2950
Laurona Armas Eibar, S.A.L., Avenida de Otaola 25, P.O. Box 260, Eibar 20600, SPAIN / 34-43-700600; FAX: 34-43-700616
Lawrence Brand Shot (See Precision Reloading, Inc.)
Lawson, John. See: SIGHT SHOP, THE
Lawson, John G. (See Sight Shop, The)
Lazzeroni Arms Co., P.O. Box 26696, Tucson, AZ 85726 / 888-492-7247; FAX: 520-624-4250
Leapers, Inc., 7675 Five Mile Rd., Northville, MI 48167 / 248-486-1231; FAX: 248-486-1430
Leatherman Tool Group, Inc., 12106 NE Ainsworth Cir., P.O. Box 20595, Portland, OR 97294 / 503-253-7826; FAX: 503-253-7830
Lebeau-Courally, Rue St. Gilles, 386 4000, Liege, BELGIUM / 042-52-48-43; FAX: 32-4-252-2008 info@lebeau-courally.com www.lebeau-courally.com
Leckie Professional Gunsmithing, 546 Quarry Rd., Ottsville, PA 18942 / 215-847-8594
Ledbetter Airguns, Riley, 1804 E Sprague St., Winston Salem, NC 27107-3521 / 919-784-0676
Lee Precision, Inc., 4275 Hwy. U, Hartford, WI 53027 / 262-673-3075; FAX: 262-673-9273 info@leeprecision.com www.leeprecision.com
Lee Supplies, Mark, 9901 France Ct., Lakeville, MN 55044 / 612-461-2114 marklee55044@usfamily.net
LeFever Arms Co., Inc., 6234 Stokes, Lee Center Rd., Lee Center, NY 13363 / 315-337-6722; FAX: 315-337-1543
Legacy Sports International, 206 S. Union St., Alexandria, VA 22314 / 703-548-4837 www.legacysports.com
Leica Sport Optics, 1 Pearl Ct., Ste. A, Allendale, NJ 07401 / 201-995-1686 www.leica-camera.com/usa
Les Baer Custom, Inc., 29601 34th Ave., Hillsdale, IL 61257 / 309-658-2716; FAX: 309-658-2610 www.lesbaer.com
LesMerises, Felix. See: ROCKY MOUNTAIN ARMOURY
Lethal Force Institute (See Police Bookshelf), P.O. Box 122, Concord, NH 03301 / 603-224-6814; FAX: 603-226-3554 ayoob@attglobal.net www.ayoob.com
Lett Custom Grips, 672 Currier Rd., Hopkinton, NH 03229-2652 / 800-421-5388; FAX: 603-226-4580 info@lettgrips.com www.lettgrips.com
Leupold & Stevens, Inc., 14400 NW Greenbrier Pky., Beaverton, OR 97006 / 503-646-9171; FAX: 503-526-1455
Lever Arms Service Ltd., 2131 Burrard St., Vancouver, BC V6J 3H7 CANADA / 604-736-2711; FAX: 604-738-3503 leverarms@leverarms.com www.leverarms.com
Lew Horton Dist. Co., Inc., 15 Walkup Dr., Westboro, MA 01581 / 508-366-7400; FAX: 508-366-5332
Lewis Lead Remover, The (See Brownells, Inc.)
Liberty Mfg., Inc., 2233 East 16th St., Los Angeles, CA 90021 / 323-581-9171; FAX: 323-581-9351 libertymfginc@aol.com
Liberty Safe, 999 W. Utah Ave., Payson, UT 84651-1744 / 800-247-5625; FAX: 801-489-6409
Liberty Shooting Supplies, P.O. Box 357, Hillsboro, OR 97123 / 503-640-5518; FAX: 503-640-5518 info@libertyshootingsupplies.com www.libertyshootingsupplies.com
Lilja Precision Rifle Barrels, P.O. Box 372, Plains, MT 59859 / 406-826-3084; FAX: 406-826-3083 lilja@riflebarrels.com www.riflebarrels.com
Lincoln, Dean, Box 1886, Farmington, NM 87401
Lindsay Engraving & Tools, Steve Lindsay, 3714 W. Cedar Hills, Kearney, NE 68845 / 308-236-7885 steve@lindsayengraving.com www.handgravers.com
Lindsay, Steve. See: LINDSAY ENGRAVING & TOOLS
Lindsley Arms Cartridge Co., P.O. Box 2024, 772 River Rd., Henniker, NH 03242 / 603-995-1267
Linebaugh Custom Sixguns, P.O. Box 455, Cody, WY 82414 / 307-645-3332 www.customsixguns.com
Lion Country Supply, P.O. Box 480, Port Matilda, PA 16870
List Precision Engineering, Unit 1 Ingley Works, 13 River Road, Barking, ENGLAND / 011-081-594-1686
Lithi Bee Bullet Lube, 1728 Carr Rd., Muskegon, MI 49442 / 616-788-4479 lithibee@att.net
"Little John's" Antique Arms, 1740 W. Laveta, Orange, CA 92668
Littleton, J. F., 275 Pinedale Ave., Oroville, CA 95966 / 916-533-6084
Ljutic Industries, Inc., 2402 W J St., Yakima, WA 98902 / 509-248-0476; FAX: 509-576-8233 ljuticgun@earthlink.net www.ljuticgun.com
Lock's Philadelphia Gun Exchange, 6700 Rowland Ave., Philadelphia, PA 19149 / 215-332-6225; FAX: 215-332-4800 locks.gunshop@verizon.net
Lodewick, Walter H., 2816 NE Halsey St., Portland, OR 97232 / 503-284-2554 wlodewick@aol.com
Lodgewood Mfg., P.O. Box 611, Whitewater, WI 53190 / 262-473-5444; FAX: 262-473-6448 lodgewd@idcnet.com lodgewood.com
Log Cabin Sport Shop, 8010 Lafayette Rd., Lodi, OH 44254 / 330-948-1082; FAX: 330-948-4307 logcabin@logcabinshop.com www.logcabinshop.com
Logdewood Mfg., P.O. Box 611, Whitewater, WI 53190 / 262-473-5444; FAX: 262-473-6448 lodgewd@idcnet.com www.lodgewood.com
Lohman Mfg. Co., Inc., 4500 Doniphan Dr., P.O. Box 220, Neosho, MO 64850 / 417-451-4438; FAX: 417-451-2576
Lomont Precision Bullets, 278 Sandy Creek Rd., Salmon, ID 83467 / 208-756-6819; FAX: 208-756-6824 www.klomont.com
London Guns Ltd., Box 3750, Santa Barbara, CA 93130 / 805-683-4141; FAX: 805-683-1712
Lone Star Gunleather, 1301 Brushy Bend Dr., Round Rock, TX 78681 / 512-255-1805
Lone Star Rifle Company, 11231 Rose Road, Conroe, TX 77303 / 936-856-3363; FAX: 936-856-3363 dave@lonestar.com
Long, George F., 1402 Kokanee Ln., Grants Pass, OR 97527 / 541-476-0836
Lothar Walther Precision Tool Inc., 3425 Hutchinson Rd., Cumming, GA 30040 / 770-889-9998; FAX: 770-889-4919 lotharwalther@mindspring.com www.lothar- walther.com
LPS Laboratories, Inc., 4647 Hugh Howell Rd., P.O. Box 3050, Tucker, GA 30084 / 404-934-7800
Lupton, Keith. See: PAWLING MOUNTAIN CLUB
Lyman Instant Targets, Inc. (See Lyman Products Corp.)
Lyman Products Corp., 475 Smith St., Middletown, CT 06457-1541 / 800-423-9704; FAX: 860-632-1699 lymansales@cshore.com www.lymanproducts.com

M

M.H. Canjar Co., 6510 Raleigh St., Arvada, CO 80003 / 303-295-2638; FAX: 303-295-2638
MA Systems, Inc., P.O. Box 894, Pryor, OK 74362-0894 / 918-824-3705; FAX: 918-824-3710
Mac-1 Airgun Distributors, 13974 Van Ness Ave., Gardena, CA 90249-2900 / 310-327-3581; FAX: 310-327-0238 mac1@maclairgun.com www.mac1airgun.com
Machinist's Workshop-Village Press, P.O. Box 629, Traverse City, MI 49685 / 800-447-7367; FAX: 231-946-6180
Madis Books, P.O. Box 545, Brownsboro, TX 75756 / 903-852-6480; FAX: 903-852-5486 madisbooks@earthlink.net www.madisbooks.com
Madis Books, 2453 West Five Mile Pkwy., Dallas, TX 75233 / 214-330-7168
MAG Instrument, Inc., 1635 S. Sacramento Ave., Ontario, CA 91761 / 909-947-1006; FAX: 909-947-3116
Magma Engineering Co., P.O. Box 161, 20955 E. Ocotillo Rd., Queen Creek, AZ 85242 / 602-987-9008; FAX: 602-987-0148
Mag-Na-Port International, Inc., 41302 Executive Dr., Harrison Twp., MI 48045-1306 / 586-469-6727; FAX: 586-469-0425 email@magnaport.com www.magnaport.com
Magnum Power Products, Inc., P.O. Box 17768, Fountain Hills, AZ 85268
Magnum Research, Inc., 7110 University Ave. NE, Minneapolis, MN 55432 / 800-772-6168 or 763-574-1868; FAX: 763-574-0109 info@magnumresearch.com
Magnus Bullets, P.O. Box 239, Toney, AL 35773 / 256-420-8359; FAX: 256-420-8360 bulletman@mchsi.com www.magnusbullets.com
MagSafe Ammo, Inc., 4700 S. US Highway 17/92, Casselberry, FL 32707-3814 / 407-834-9966; FAX: 407-834-8185 www.magsafeammo.com
Magtech Ammunition Co. Inc., 248 Apollo Dr. Ste. 180, Linolakes, MN 55014 / 800-466-7191; FAX: 763-235-4004 www.magtechammunition.com
Mahovsky's Metalife, R.D. 1, Box 149a Eureka Road, Grand Valley, PA 16420 / 814-436-7747
Makinson, Nicholas, RR 3, Komoka, ON N0L 1R0 CANADA / 519-471-5462
Mallardtone Game Calls, 10406 96th St., Court West, Taylor Ridge, IL 61284 / 309-798-2481; FAX: 309-798-2501
Marble Arms (See CRR, Inc./Marble's Inc.)
Marent, Rudolf. See: HAMMERLI SERVICE-PRECISION MAC
Mark Lee Supplies, 9901 France Ct., Lakeville, MN 55044 / 952-461-2114; FAX: 952-461-2194 marklee55044@usfamily.net
Markell, Inc., 422 Larkfield Center 235, Santa Rosa, CA 95403 / 707-573-0792; FAX: 707-573-9867
Markesbery Muzzle Loaders, Inc., 7065 Production Ct., Florence, KY 41042 / 859-342-5553; FAX: 859-342-2380 www.markesbery.com
Marksman Products, 5482 Argosy Dr., Huntington Beach, CA 92649 / 714-898-7535 or 800-822-8005; FAX: 714-891-0782
Marlin Firearms Co., 100 Kenna Dr., North Haven, CT 06473 / 203-239-5621; FAX: 203-234-7991 www.marlinfirearms.com
Marocchi F.lli S.p.A, Via Galileo Galilei 8, I-25068 Zanano, ITALY
Marsh, Mike, Croft Cottage, Main St., Derbyshire, DE4 2BY ENGLAND / 01629 650 669
Marshall Enterprises, 792 Canyon Rd., Redwood City, CA 94062
Martin B. Retting Inc., 11029 Washington, Culver City, CA 90232 / 213-837-2412 retting@retting.com
Martini & Hagn, Ltd., 1264 Jimsmith Lake Rd., Cranbrook, BC V1C 6V6 CANADA / 250-417-2926; FAX: 250-417-2928 martini-hagn@shaw.ca www.martiniandhagngunmakers.com
Martin's Gun Shop, 937 S. Sheridan Blvd., Lakewood, CO 80226 / 303-922-2180 rdrnnr74479@peoplepc.com
Martz, John V., 8060 Lakeview Lane, Lincoln, CA 95648 FAX: 916-645-3815
Marvel, Alan, 3922 Madonna Rd., Jarretsville, MD 21084 / 301-557-6545
Marx, Harry (See U.S. Importer for FERLIB)
Maryland Paintball Supply, 8507 Harford Rd., Parkville, MD 21234 / 410-882-5607
Master Lock Co., 2600 N. 32nd St., Milwaukee, WI 53245 / 414-444-2800
Match Prep-Doyle Gracey, P.O. Box 155, Tehachapi, CA 93581 / 661-822-5383; FAX: 661-823-8680 gracenotes@as.net www.matchprep.com
Mathews Gun Shop & Gunsmithing, Inc., 2791 S. Gaffey St., San Pedro, CA 90731-6515 / 562-928-2129; FAX: 562-928-8629
Mauser Werke Oberndorf Waffensysteme GmbH, Postfach 1349, 78722, Oberndorf/N., GERMANY
Maverick Arms, Inc., 7 Grasso Ave., P.O. Box 497, North Haven, CT 06473 / 203-230-5300; FAX: 203-230-5420
Maxi-Mount Inc., P.O. Box 291, Willoughby Hills, OH 44096-0291 / 440-944-9456; FAX: 440-944-9456 maximount454@yahoo.com
Mayville Engineering Co. (See MEC, Inc.)
Mazur Restoration, Pete, 13083 Drummer Way, Grass Valley, CA 95949 / 530-268-2412
McCament, Jay. See: JAY MCCAMENT CUSTOM GUNMAKER
McCann, Tom, 14 Walton Dr., New Hope, PA 18938 / 215-862-2728
McCann Industries, P.O. Box 641, Spanaway, WA 98387 / 253-537-6919; FAX: 253-537-6919 mccann.machine@worldnet.att.net www.mccannindustries.com
McCluskey Precision Rifles, 10502 14th Ave. NW, Seattle, WA 98177 / 206-781-2776

MANUFACTURER'S DIRECTORY

McCombs, Leo, 1862 White Cemetery Rd., Patriot, OH 45658 / 740-256-1714
McDonald, Dennis, 8359 Brady St., Peosta, IA 52068 / 319-556-7940
McFarland, Stan, 2221 Idella Ct., Grand Junction, CO 81505 / 970-243-4704
McGhee, Larry. See: B.C. OUTDOORS
McGowen Gunsmithing, 5961 Spruce Lane, St. Anne, IL 60964 / 815-937-9816; FAX: 815-937-4024
Mchalik, Gary. See: ROSSI FIREARMS
McKenzie, Lynton, 6940 N. Alvernon Way, Tucson, AZ 85718 / 520-299-5090
McMillan Fiberglass Stocks, Inc., 1638 W. Knudsen Dr. #101, Phoenix, AZ 85027 / 623-582-9635; FAX: 623-581-3825 mfsinc@mcmfamily.com www.mcmfamily.com
McMillan Optical Gunsight Co., 28638 N. 42nd St., Cave Creek, AZ 85331 / 602-585-7868; FAX: 602-585-7872
McMillan Rifle Barrels, 10456 State Highway 6 S, College Sta, TX 77845 / 979-690-3456
McMurdo, Lynn, P.O. Box 404, Afton, WY 83110 / 307-886-5535
MCS, Inc., 166 Pocono Rd., Brookfield, CT 06804-2023 / 203-775-1013; FAX: 203-775-9462
McWelco Products, 6730 Santa Fe Ave., Hesperia, CA 92345 / 619-244-8876; FAX: 760-244-9398 help@mcwelco.com www.mcwelco.com
MDS, P.O. Box 1441, Brandon, FL 33509-1441 / 813-653-1180; FAX: 813-684-5953
Meacham Tool & Hardware Co., Inc., 37052 Eberhardt Rd., Peck, ID 83545 / 208-486-7171 smeacham@clearwater.net www.meachamrifles.com
Measures, Leon. See: SHOOT WHERE YOU LOOK
MEC, Inc., 715 South St., Mayville, WI 53050 reloaders@mayvl.com www.mecreloaders.com
MEC-Gar S.R.L., Via Madonnina 64, Gardone V.T. Brescia, ITALY / 39-030-3733668; FAX: 39-030-3733687 info@mec-gar.it www.mec-gar.it
MEC-Gar U.S.A., Inc., Hurley Farms Industr. Park, 905 Middle St., Middletown, CT 06457 / 203-262-1525; FAX: 203-262-1719 mecgar@aol.com www.mec- gar.com
Mech-Tech Systems, Inc., 1602 Foothill Rd., Kalispell, MT 59901 / 406-755-8055
Meister Bullets (See Gander Mountain)
Mele, Frank, 201 S. Wellow Ave., Cookeville, TN 38501 / 615-526-4860
Menck, Gunsmith Inc., T.W., 5703 S 77th St., Ralston, NE 68127
Mendez, John A., 1309 Continental Dr., Daytona Beach, FL 32117-3807 / 407-344-2791
Men-Metallwerk Elisenhuette GmbH, P.O. Box 1263, Nassau/Lahn, D-56372 GERMANY / 2604-7819
Meopta USA, LLC, 50 Davids Dr., Hauppauge, NY 11788 / 631-436-5900 ussales@meopta.com www.meopta.com
Mercer Custom Guns, 216 S. Whitewater Ave., Jefferson, WI 53549 / 920-674-3839
Merit Corp., P.O. Box 9044, Schenectady, NY 12309 / 518-346-1420 sales@meritcorporation.com www.meritcorporation.com
Merkel, Schutzenstrasse 26, D-98527 Suhl, Suhl, GERMANY FAX: 011-49-3681-854-203 www.merkel-waffen.de
Metal Merchants, P.O. Box 186, Walled Lake, MI 48390-0186
Metalife Industries (See Mahovsky's Metalife)
Michael's Antiques, Box 203, East Schodack, NY 12063
Michaels of Oregon Co., 9200 Cody St., Overland Park, KS 66214 / 800-845-2444 www.michaels-oregon.com
Micro Sight Co., 502 May St., Arroyo Grande, CA 93420-2832
Microfusion Alfa S.A., Paseo San Andres N8, P.O. Box 271, Eibar 20600, 20600 SPAIN / 34-43-11-89-16; FAX: 34-43-11-40-38
Mid-America Recreation, Inc., 1328 5th Ave., Moline, IL 61265 / 309-764-5089; FAX: 309-764-5089 fmilcusguns@aol.com www.midamericarecreation.com
Middlebrooks Custom Shop, 7366 Colonial Trail East, Surry, VA 23883 / 757-357-0881; FAX: 757-365-0442
Midway Arms, Inc., 5875 W. Van Horn Tavern Rd., Columbia, MO 65203 / 800-243-3220; FAX: 800-992-8312 www.midwayusa.com
Midwest Gun Sport, 1108 Herbert Dr., Zebulon, NC 27597 / 919-269-5570
Midwest Shooting School, The, Pat LaBoone, 2550 Hwy. 23, Wrenshall, MN 55797 / 218-384-3670 shootingschool@starband.net
Midwest Sport Distributors, Box 129, Fayette, MO 65248
Mike Davis Products, 643 Loop Dr., Moses Lake, WA 98837 / 509-765-6178; or 509-766-7281
Mike Yee Custom Stocking, 29927 56 Pl. S., Auburn, WA 98001 / 253-839-3991 miknadyee@comcast.net
Military Armament Corp., P.O. Box 120, Mt. Zion Rd., Lingleville, TX 76461 / 817-965-3253
Millennium Designed Muzzleloaders, P.O. Box 536, Routes 11 & 25, Limington, ME 04049 / 207-637-2316
Miller Arms, Inc., 1310 Industry Rd., Sturgis, SD 57785-9129 / 605-642-5160; FAX: 605-642-5160
Miller Custom, 210 E. Julia, Clinton, IL 61727 / 217-935-9362
Miller Single Trigger Mfg. Co., 6680 Rt. 5-20, P.O. Box 471, Bloomfield, NY 14469 / 585-657-6338; FAX: 585-657-7743 info@turnbullrestoration.com turnbullrestoration.com
Millett Sights, 16131 Gothard St., Huntington Beach, CA 92647 / 714-842-5575 or 800-645-5388; FAX: 714-843-5707 sales@millettsights.com www.millettsights.com
Mills Jr., Hugh B., 3615 Canterbury Rd., New Bern, NC 28560 / 919-637-4631
Mirador Optical Corp., P.O. Box 11614, Marina Del Rey, CA 90295-7614 / 310-821-5587; FAX: 310-305-0386
Mitchell, Jack, c/o Geoff Gaebe, Addieville East Farm, 200 Pheasant Dr., Mapleville, RI 02839 / 401-568-3185
Mitchell Mfg. Corp., P.O. Box 9295, Fountain Valley, CA 92728 / 714-444-2220
Mitchell Optics, Inc., 2072 CR 1100 N, Sidney, IL 61877 / 217-688-2219 or 217-621-3018; FAX: 217-688-2505 mitchell@attglobal.net
Mitchell's Accuracy Shop, 68 Greenridge Dr., Stafford, VA 22554 / 703-659-0165
Mitchell's Mauser, P.O. Box 9295, Fountain Valley, CA 92728 / 714-979-7663; FAX: 714-899-3660
MI-TE Bullets, 1396 Ave. K, Ellsworth, KS 67439 / 785-472-4575; FAX: 785-472-5579
MJK Gunsmithing, Inc., 417 N. Huber Ct., E. Wenatchee, WA 98802 / 509-884-7683
MKS Supply, Inc. (See Hi-Point Firearms)
MMC, 4430 Mitchell St., North Las Vegas, NV 89081 / 800-998-7483; FAX: 702-267-9463 info@mmcsight.com www.mmcsight.com
MOA Corporation, 285 Government Valley Rd., Sundance, WY 82729 / 307-283-3030 www.moaguns.com
Mobile Area Networks, Inc., 2772 Depot St., Sanford, FL 32773 / 407-333-2350; FAX: 407-333-9903 georgew@mobilan.com www.mobilan.com
Modern Gun Repair School, P.O. Box 846, Saint Albans, VT 05478 / 802-524-2223; FAX: 802-524-2053 jfwp@dlilearn.com www.mgsinfoadlifearn.com
Modern Muzzleloading, Inc., P.O. Box 130, Centerville, IA 52544 / 515-856-2626
Moeller, Steve, 1213 4th St., Fulton, IL 61252 / 815-589-2300
Mogul Co./Life Jacket, 500 N. Kimball Rd., Ste. 109, South Lake, TX 76092
Monell Custom Guns, 228 Red Mills Rd., Pine Bush, NY 12566 / 845-744-3021
Moneymaker Guncraft Corp., 1420 Military Ave., Omaha, NE 68131 / 402-556-0226
Montana Armory, Inc., 100 Centennial Dr., P.O. Box 885, Big Timber, MT 59011 / 406-932-4353; FAX: 406-932-4443
Montana Outfitters, Lewis E. Yearout, 308 Riverview Dr. E., Great Falls, MT 59404 / 406-761-0859; or 406-727-4560
Montana Precision Swaging, P.O. Box 4746, Butte, MT 59702 / 406-494-0600; FAX: 406-494-0600
Montana Rifleman, Inc., 2593A Hwy. 2 East, Kalispell, MT 59901 / 406-755-4867
Montana Vintage Arms, 2354 Bear Canyon Rd., Bozeman, MT 59715
Morini (See U.S. Importers-Mandall Shooting Supplies, Inc.)
Morrison Custom Rifles, J. W., 4015 W Sharon, Phoenix, AZ 85029 / 602-978-3754
Morrison Precision, 6719 Calle Mango, Hereford, AZ 85615 / 520-378-6207 morprec@c2i2.com
Morrow, Bud, 11 Hillside Lane, Sheridan, WY 82801-9729 / 307-674-8360
Morton Booth Co., P.O. Box 123, Joplin, MO 64802 / 417-673-1962; FAX: 417-673-3642
Mo's Competitor Supplies (See MCS, Inc.)
Moss Double Tone, Inc., P.O. Box 1112, 2101 S. Kentucky, Sedalia, MO 65301 / 816-827-0827
Mountain Plains Industries, 3720 Otter Place, Lynchburg, VA 24503 / 800-687-3000; FAX: 434-386-6217 MPI_targets@com.cast www.targetshandloader.com
Mowrey Gun Works, P.O. Box 246, Waldron, IN 46182 / 317-525-6181; FAX: 317-525-9595
Mowrey's Guns & Gunsmithing, 119 Fredericks St., Canajoharie, NY 13317 / 518-673-3483
MPC, P.O. Box 450, McMinnville, TN 37110-0450 / 615-473-5513; FAX: 615-473-5516 thebox@blomand.net www.mpc-thebox.com
MPI Stocks, P.O. Box 83266, Portland, OR 97283 / 503-226-1215; FAX: 503-226-2661
MSR Targets, P.O. Box 1042, West Covina, CA 91793 / 818-331-7840
MTM Molded Products Co., Inc., 3370 Obco Ct., Dayton, OH 45414 / 937-890-7461; FAX: 937-890-1747
Mulberry House Publishing, P.O. Box 2180, Apache Junction, AZ 85217 / 888-738-1567; FAX: 480-671-1015
Mulhern, Rick, Rt. 5, Box 152, Rayville, LA 71269 / 318-728-2688
Mullins Ammunition, Rt. 2 Box 304N, Clintwood, VA 24228 / 276-926-6772; FAX: 276-926-6092 mammo@extremeshockusa.com www.extremeshockusa.com
Mullis Guncraft, 3523 Lawyers Road E., Monroe, NC 28110 / 704-283-6683
Multiplex International, 26 S. Main St., Concord, NH 03301 FAX: 603-796-2223
Multipropulseurs, La Bertrandiere, 42580, FRANCE / 77 74 01 30; FAX: 77 93 19 34
Mundy, Thomas A., 69 Robbins Road, Somerville, NJ 08876 / 201-722-2199
Murphy, R.R. Murphy Co., Inc. See: MURPHY, R.R. CO., INC.
Murphy, R.R. Co., Inc., R.R. Murphy Co., Inc. Murphy, P.O. Box 102, Ripley, TN 38063 / 901-635-4003; FAX: 901-635-2320
Murray State College, 1 Murray Campus St., Tishomingo, OK 73460 / 508-371-2371 darnold@mscol.edu
Muzzleloaders Etcetera, Inc., 9901 Lyndale Ave. S., Bloomington, MN 55420 / 952-884-1161 www.muzzleloaders-etcetera.com
MWG Co., P.O. Box 971202, Miami, FL 33197 / 800-428-9394 or 305-253-8393; FAX: 305-232-1247

N

N.C. Ordnance Co., P.O. Box 3254, Wilson, NC 27895 / 919-237-2440; FAX: 919-243-9845 bharvey@nc.rr.com www.gungrip.com
Nagel's Custom Bullets, 100 Scott St., Baytown, TX 77520-2849
Nalpak, 1267 Vernon Way, El Cajon, CA 92020
Nammo Lapua Oy, P.O. Box 5, Lapua, FINLAND / 358-6-4310111; FAX: 358-6-4310317 info@nammo.ti www.lapua.com
Nastoff, Steve. See: NASTOFFS 45 SHOP, INC.
Nastoffs 45 Shop, Inc., Steve Nastoff, 1057 Laverne Dr., Youngstown, OH 44511
National Bullet Co., 1585 E. 361 St., Eastlake, OH 44095 / 216-951-1854; FAX: 216-951-7761
National Gun, Inc., 3709 W. Flagler St., Coral Gables, FL 33134 / 305-642-2355
National Target Co., 3958-D Dartmouth Ct., Frederick, MD 21703 / 800-827-7060; FAX: 301-874-4764 www.nationaltarget.com
Nationwide Airgun Repair, 2310 Windsor Forest Dr., Louisville, KY 40272 / 502-937-2614 shortshoestring@insightbb.com
Naval Ordnance Works, 467 Knott Rd., Sheperdstown, WV 25443 / 304-876-0998; FAX: 304-876-0998 nvordfdy@earthlink.net
Navy Arms Company, 219 Lawn St., Martinsburg, WV 25405 / 304-262-9870; FAX: 304-262-1658 info@navyarms.com www.navyarms.com
NCP Products, Inc., 3500 12th St. N.W., Canton, OH 44708 / 330-456-5130; FAX: 330-456-5234
Necessary Concepts, Inc., P.O. Box 571, Deer Park, NY 11729 / 516-667-8509; FAX: 516-667-8588
NEI Handtools, Inc., P.O. Box 370356, El Paso, TX 79937-0356 / 915-772-0259 neihandtools@hotmail.com www.neihandtools.com
Neil A. Jones Custom Products, 17217 Brookhouser Road, Saegertown, PA 16433 / 814-763-2769; FAX: 814-763-4228
Nelson, Gary K., 975 Terrace Dr., Oakdale, CA 95361 / 209-847-4590
Nelson, Stephen. See: NELSON'S CUSTOM GUNS, INC.
Nelson's Custom Guns, Inc., Stephen Nelson, 7430 Valley View Dr. N.W., Corvallis, OR 97330 / 541-745-5232 nelsons-custom@attbi.com
Nesci Enterprises Inc., P.O. Box 119, Summit St., East Hampton, CT 06424 / 203-267-2588
Nesika Bay Precision, 22239 Big Valley Rd., Poulsbo, WA 98370 / 206-697-3830

Nettestad Gun Works, 38962 160th Avenue, Pelican Rapids, MN 56572 / 218-863-1338
New England Ammunition Co., 1771 Post Rd. East, Suite 223, Westport, CT 06880 / 203-254-8048
New England Arms Co., Box 278, Lawrence Lane, Kittery Point, ME 03905 / 207-439-0593; FAX: 207-439-0525 info@newenglandarms.com www.newenglandarms.com
New England Custom Gun Service, 438 Willow Brook Rd., Plainfield, NH 03781 / 603-469-3450; FAX: 603-469-3471 bestguns@comcast.net www.newenglandcustom.com
New Orleans Jewelers Supply Co., 206 Charters St., New Orleans, LA 70130 / 504-523-3839; FAX: 504-523-3836
New SKB Arms Co., C.P.O. Box 1401, Tokyo, JAPAN / 81-3-3943-9550; FAX: 81-3-3943-0695
New Ultra Light Arms, LLC, P.O. Box 340, Granville, WV 26534 / 304-292-0600 newultralight@cs.com
Newark Electronics, 4801 N. Ravenswood Ave., Chicago, IL 60640
Newell, Robert H., 55 Coyote, Los Alamos, NM 87544 / 505-662-7135
Newman Gunshop, 2035 Chester Ave. #411, Ottumwa, IA 52501-3715 / 515-937-5775
NgraveR Co., The, 67 Wawecus Hill Rd., Bozrah, CT 06334 / 860-823-1533; FAX: 860-887-6252 ngraver98@aol.com www.ngraver.com
Nicholson Custom, 17285 Thornlay Road, Hughesville, MO 65334 / 816-826-8746
Nickels, Paul R., 2216 Jacob Dr., Santa Clara, UT 84765-5399 / 435-652-1959
Niemi Engineering, W. B., Box 126 Center Rd., Greensboro, VT 05841 / 802-533-7180; FAX: 802-533-7141
Nighthawk Custom, 1306 W. Trimble, Berryville, AR 72616 / 877-268-GUNS; (4867) or 870-423-GUNS; FAX: 870-423-4230 www.nighthawkcustom.com
Nikon, Inc., 1300 Walt Whitman Rd., Melville, NY 11747 / 516-547-8623; FAX: 516-547-0309
Noreen, Peter H., 5075 Buena Vista Dr., Belgrade, MT 59714 / 406-586-7383
Norica, Avnda Otaola, 16 Apartado 68, Eibar, SPAIN
Norinco, 7A Yun Tan N, Beijing, CHINA
Norincoptics (See BEC, Inc.)
Norma Precision AB (See U.S. Importers-Dynamit)
Normark Corp., 10395 Yellow Circle Dr., Minnetonka, MN 55343-9101 / 612-933-7060; FAX: 612-933-0046
North American Arms, Inc., 2150 South 950 East, Provo, UT 84606-6285 / 800-821-5783 or 801-374-9990; FAX: 801-374-9998
North American Correspondence Schools, The Gun Pro, Oak & Pawney St., Scranton, PA 18515 / 717-342-7701
North American Shooting Systems, P.O. Box 306, Osoyoos, BC V0H 1V0 CANADA / 250-495-3131; FAX: 250-495-3131 rifle@cablerocket.com
North Devon Firearms Services, 3 North St., Braunton, EX33 1AJ ENGLAND / 01271 813624; FAX: 01271 813624
North Mountain Pine Training Center (See Executive Protection Institute)
North Star West, Inc., P.O. Box 487, 57 Terrace Ct., Superior, MT 59872 / 406-822-8778 laffindog@msn.com www.northstarwest.com
Northern Precision, 329 S. James St., Carthage, NY 13619 / 315-493-1711
Northside Gun Shop, 2725 NW 109th, Oklahoma City, OK 73120 / 405-840-2353
Northwest Custom Projectile, P.O. Box 127, Butte, MT 59703-0127 www.customprojectile.com
No-Sho Mfg. Co., 10727 Glenfield Ct., Houston, TX 77096 / 713-723-5332
Nosler, Inc., P.O. Box 671, Bend, OR 97709 / 800-285-3701 or 541-382-3921; FAX: 541-388-4667 www.nosler.com
Novak's, Inc., 1206 1/2 30th St., P.O. Box 4045, Parkersburg, WV 26101 / 304-485-9295; FAX: 304-428-6722 www.novaksights.com
Nowlin Guns, Inc., 20622 S 4092 Rd., Unit B, Claremore, OK 74017 / 918-342-0689; FAX: 918-342-0624 nowlinguns@msn.com nowlinguns.com
NRI Gunsmith School, P.O. Box 182968, Columbus, OH 43218-2968
Nu Line Guns, Inc., 8150 CR 4055, Rhineland, MO 65069 / 573-676-5500; FAX: 573-676-3400 nlg@ktis.net www.nulineguns
Null Holsters Ltd. K.L., 161 School St. N.W., Resaca, GA 30735 / 706-625-5643; FAX: 706-625-9392 ken12@mindspring.com www.klnullholsters.com
Numrich Gun Parts Corporation, 226 Williams Lane, P.O. Box 299, West Hurley, NY 12491 / 866-686-7424; FAX: 877-GUNPART info@gunpartscorp.com www.@e-gunparts.com

O

O.F. Mossberg & Sons, Inc., 7 Grasso Ave., North Haven, CT 06473 / 203-230-5300; FAX: 203-230-5420
Oakman Turkey Calls, RD 1, Box 825, Harrisonville, PA 17228 / 717-485-4620
Obermeyer Rifled Barrels, 23122 60th St., Bristol, WI 53104 / 262-843-3537; FAX: 262-843-2129 www.obermeyerbarrels.com
October Country Muzzleloading, P.O. Box 969, Dept. GD, Hayden, ID 83835 / 208-772-2068; FAX: 208-772-9230 dawn@octobercountry.com www.octobercountry.com
Oehler Research, Inc., P.O. Box 9135, Austin, TX 78766 / 512-327-6900 or 800-531-5125; FAX: 512-327-6903 www.oehler-research.com
Oil Rod and Gun Shop, 69 Oak St., East Douglas, MA 01516 / 508-476-3687
OK Weber, Inc., P.O. Box 7485, Eugene, OR 97401 / 541-747-0458; FAX: 541-747-5927 okweber@pacinfo www.okweber.com
Oker's Engraving, P.O. Box 126, Shawnee, CO 80475 / 303-838-6042 engraver@netscape.com
Oklahoma Ammunition Co., 3701A S. Harvard Ave., No. 367, Tulsa, OK 74135-2265 / 918-396-3187; FAX: 918-396-4270
Oklahoma Leather Products, Inc., 500 26th NW, Miami, OK 74354 / 918-542-6651; FAX: 918-542-6653
Olathe Gun Shop, 716-A South Rogers Road, Olathe, KS 66062 / 913-782-6900; FAX: 913-782-6902 info@olathegunshop.com www.olathegunshop.com
Old Wagon Bullets, 32 Old Wagon Rd., Wilton, CT 06897
Old West Bullet Moulds, J. Ken Chapman, P.O. Box 519, Flora Vista, NM 87415 / 505-334-6970
Old West Reproductions, Inc. R.M. Bachman, 446 Florence S. Loop, Florence, MT 59833 / 406-273-2615; FAX: 406-273-2615 rick@oldwestreproductions.com www.oldwestreproductions.com
Old Western Scrounger LLC, 219 Lawn St., Martinsburg, NV 25401 / 304-262-9870; FAX: 304-262-1658 www.ows-ammo.com
Ole Frontier Gunsmith Shop, 2617 Hwy. 29 S., Cantonment, FL 32533 / 904-477-8074
Olson, Myron, 989 W. Kemp, Watertown, SD 57201 / 605-886-9787
Olson, Vic, 5002 Countryside Dr., Imperial, MO 63052 / 314-296-8086
Olympic Arms Inc., 620-626 Old Pacific Hwy. SE, Olympia, WA 98513 / 360-456-3471; FAX: 360-491-3447 info@olyarms.com www.olyarms.com
Olympic Optical Co., 5801 Safety Dr. NE, Belmont, MI 49306-0032 / 901-794-3890 or 800-238-7120; FAX: 901-794-0676
One Of A Kind, 15610 Purple Sage, San Antonio, TX 78255 / 512-695-3364
One Ragged Hole, P.O. Box 13624, Tallahassee, FL 32317-3624
Op-Tec, P.O. Box L632, Langhorn, PA 19047 / 215-757-5037; FAX: 215-757-7097
Optical Services Co., P.O. Box 1174, Santa Teresa, NM 88008-1174 / 505-589-3833
Orchard Park Enterprise, P.O. Box 563, Orchard Park, NY 14127 / 616-656-0356
Ordnance Works, The, 2969 Pigeon Point Rd., Eureka, CA 95501 / 707-443-3252
Oregon Arms, Inc. (See Rogue Rifle Co., Inc.)
Oregon Trail Bullet Company, P.O. Box 529, Dept. P, Baker City, OR 97814 / 800-811-0548; FAX: 514-523-1803
Original Deer Formula Co., The, P.O. Box 1705, Dickson, TN 37056 / 800-874-6965; FAX: 615-446-0646 deerformula1@aol.com www.deerformula.com
Orvis Co., The, Rt. 7, Manchester, VT 05254 / 802-362-3622; FAX: 802-362-3525
Otis Technology, Inc., RR 1 Box 84, Boonville, NY 13309 / 315-942-3320
Ottmar, Maurice, 920 Timber Trl, Cedar Park, TX 78613
Outa-Site Gun Carriers, 219 Market St., Laredo, TX 78040 / 210-722-4678 or 800-880-9715; FAX: 210-726-4858
Outdoor Connection, Inc., The, 7901 Panther Way, Waco, TX 76712-6556 / 800-533-6076; FAX: 254-776-3553 info@outdoorconnection.com www.outdoorconnection.com
Outdoor Edge Cutlery Corp., 4699 Nautilus Ct. S. Ste. 503, Boulder, CO 80301-5310 / 303-530-7667; FAX: 303-530-7020 www.outdooredge.com
Outdoor Enthusiast, 3784 W. Woodland, Springfield, MO 65807 / 417-883-9841
Outdoor Sports Headquarters, Inc., 967 Watertower Ln., West Carrollton, OH 45449 / 513-865-5855; FAX: 513-865-5962
Outers Laboratories Div. of ATK, Route 2, P.O. Box 39, Onalaska, WI 54650 / 608-781-5800; FAX: 608-781-0368
Ozark Gun Works, 11830 Cemetery Rd., Rogers, AR 72756 / 479-631-1024; FAX: 479-631-1024 ozarkgunworks@cox.net www.geocities.com

P

P&M Sales & Services, LLC, 4697 Tote Rd. Bldg. H-B, Comins, MI 48619 / 989-848-8364; FAX: 989-848-8364 info@pmsales-online.com
P.S.M.G. Gun Co., 10 Park Ave., Arlington, MA 02174 / 781-646-1699; FAX: 781-643-7212 psmg2@aol.com
Pachmayr Div. Lyman Products, 475 Smith St., Middletown, CT 06457 / 860-632-2020 or 800-225-9626; FAX: 860-632-1699 lymansales@cshore.com www.pachmayr.com
Pacific Armament Corp, 4813 Enterprise Way, Unit K, Modesto, CA 95356 / 209-545-2800 gunsparts@att.net
Pacific Rifle Co., P.O. Box 841, Carlton, OR 97111 / 503-852-6276 pacificrifle@aol.com
PAC-NOR Barreling, Inc., 99299 Overlook Rd., P.O. Box 6188, Brookings, OR 97415 / 541-469-7330; FAX: 541-469-7331 chris@pac-nor.com www.pac-nor.com
PACT, Inc., P.O. Box 535025, Grand Prairie, TX 75053 / 972-641-0049; FAX: 972-641-2641
Page Custom Bullets, P.O. Box 25, Port Moresby, NEW GUINEA
Pagel Gun Works, Inc., 2 SE 1st St., Grand Rapids, MN 55744
Pager Pal, P.O. Box 700695, Dallas, TX 75370 info@concealcity.com www.pagerpal.com
Paintball Games International Magazine Aceville, Castle House 97 High St., Essex, ENGLAND / 011-44-206-564840
Palsa Outdoor Products, P.O. Box 81336, Lincoln, NE 68501 / 402-488-5288; FAX: 402-488-2321
Pansch, Robert F, 1004 Main St. #10, Neenah, WI 54956 / 920-725-8175
Paragon Sales & Services, Inc., 2501 Theodore St., Crest Hill, IL 60435-1613 / 815-725-9212; FAX: 815-725-8974
Para-Ordnance Mfg., Inc., 980 Tapscott Rd., Scarborough, ON M1X 1E7 CANADA / 416-297-7855; FAX: 416-297-1289
Para-Ordnance, Inc., 1919 NE 45th St., Ste 215, Ft. Lauderdale, FL 33308 / 416-297-7855; FAX: 416-297-1289 info@paraord.com www.paraord.com
Pardini Armi Srl, Via Italica 154, 55043, Lido Di Camaiore Lu, ITALY / 584-90121; FAX: 584-90122
Paris, Frank J., 17417 Pershing St., Livonia, MI 48152-3822
Park Rifle Co., Ltd., The, Unit 6a Dartford Trade Park, Power Mill Lane, Dartford DA7 7NX, ENGLAND / 011-0322-222512
Parker & Sons Shooting Supply, 9337 Smoky Row Road, Strawberry Plains, TN 37871 / 865-933-3286; FAX: 865-932-8586
Parker Gun Finishes, 9337 Smokey Row Rd., Strawberry Plains, TN 37871 / 865-933-3286; FAX: 865-932-8586 parcraft7838@netzero.com
Parsons Optical Mfg. Co., PO Box 192, Ross, OH 45061 / 513-867-0820; FAX: 513-867-8380 psscopes@concentric.net
Partridge Sales Ltd., John, Trent Meadows, Rugeley, ENGLAND
Pasadena Gun Center, 206 E. Shaw, Pasadena, TX 77506 / 713-472-0417; FAX: 713-472-1322
Passive Bullet Traps, Inc. (See Savage Range Systems, Inc.)
Paterson Gunsmithing, 438 Main St., Paterson, NJ 07502 / 201-345-4100
Pathfinder Sports Leather, 2920 E. Chambers St., Phoenix, AZ 85040 / 602-276-0016
Patrick W. Price Bullets, 16520 Worthley Drive, San Lorenzo, CA 94580 / 510-278-1547
Pattern Control, 114 N. Third St., P.O. Box 462105, Garland, TX 75046 / 214-494-3551; FAX: 214-272-8447
Paul A. Harris Hand Engraving, 113 Rusty Lane, Boerne, TX 78006-5746 / 512-391-5121
Paul and Sharon Dressel, 209 N. 92nd Ave., Yakima, WA 98908 / 509-966-9233; FAX: 509-966-3365 dressels@nwinfo.net www.dressels.com
Paul Co., The, 27385 Pressonville Rd., Wellsville, KS 66092 / 785-883-4444; FAX: 785-883-2525
Paul Jones Moulds, 4901 Telegraph Rd., Los Angeles, CA 90022 / 213-262-1510
Paulsen Gunstocks, Rt. 71, Box 11, Chinook, MT 59523 / 406-357-3403
Pawling Mountain Club, Keith Lupton, P.O. Box 573, Pawling, NY 12564 / 914-855-3825
Paxton Quigley's Personal Protection Strategies, 9903 Santa Monica Blvd., 300, Beverly Hills, CA 90212 / 310-281-1762 www.defend-net.com/paxton

MANUFACTURER'S DIRECTORY

Payne Photography, Robert, Robert, P.O. Box 141471, Austin, TX 78714 / 512-272-4554
Peacemaker Specialists, 144 Via Fuchsia, Paso Robles, CA 93446 / 805-238-9100; FAX: 805-238-9100 www.peacemakerspecialists.com
Pearce Grip, Inc., P.O. Box 40367, Fort Worth, TX 76140 / 817-568-9704; FAX: 817-568-9707 info@pearcegrip.com www.pearcegrip.com
PECAR Herbert Schwarz GmbH, Kreuzbergstrasse 6, 10965, Berlin, GERMANY / 004930-785-7383; FAX: 004930-785-1934 michael.schwarz@pecar-berlin.de www.pecar-berlin.de
Pecatonica River Longrifle, 5205 Nottingham Dr., Rockford, IL 61111 / 815-968-1995; FAX: 815-968-1996
Pedersen, C. R., 2717 S. Pere Marquette Hwy., Ludington, MI 49431 / 231-843-2061; FAX: 231-845-7695 fega@fega.com
Pedersen, Rex C., 2717 S. Pere Marquette Hwy., Ludington, MI 49431 / 231-843-2061; FAX: 231-845-7695 fega@fega.com
Peifer Rifle Co., P.O. Box 220, Nokomis, IL 62075
Pejsa Ballistics, 1314 Marquette Ave., Apt 906, Minneapolis, MN 55403 / 612-332-5073; FAX: 612-332-5204 pejsa@sprintmail.com pejsa.com
Peltor, Inc. (See Aero Peltor)
Pence Precision Barrels, 7567 E. 900 S., S. Whitley, IN 46787 / 219-839-4745
Pendleton Woolen Mills, P.O. Box 3030, 220 N.W. Broadway, Portland, OR 97208 / 503-226-4801
Penn Bullets, P.O. Box 756, Indianola, PA 15051
Pennsylvania Gun Parts Inc., RR 7 Box 150, Mount Pleasant, PA 15666
Pennsylvania Gunsmith School, 812 Ohio River Blvd., Avalon, Pittsburgh, PA 15202 / 412-766-1812; FAX: 412-766-0855 pgs@pagunsmith.edu www.pagunsmith.edu
Penrod, Mark. See: PENROD PRECISION
Penrod Precision, Mark Penrod, 312 College Ave., P.O. Box 307, N. Manchester, IN 46962 / 260-982-8385 markpenrod@kconline.com
Pentax U.S.A., Inc., 600 12th St. Ste. 300, Golden, CO 80401 / 303-799-8000; FAX: 303-460-1628 www.pentaxlightseeker.com
Pentheny de Pentheny, c/o H.P. Okelly, 321 S. Main St., Sebastopol, CA 95472 / 707-824-1637; FAX: 707-824-1637
Perazone-Gunsmith, Brian, Cold Spring Rd., Roxbury, NY 12474 / 607-326-4088; FAX: 607-326-3140 bpgunsmith@catskill.net www.bpgunsmith@catskill.net
Perazzi U.S.A. Inc., 1010 West Tenth, Azusa, CA 91702 / 626-334-1234; FAX: 626-334-0344 perazziusa@aol.com
Performance Specialists, 308 Eanes School Rd., Austin, TX 78746 / 512-327-0119
Perugini Visini & Co. SAS, Via Camprelle, 126, 25080 Nuvolera, ITALY / 30-6897535; FAX: 30-6897821 info@peruvisi@visini.com
Pete de Coux Auction House, 14940 Brenda Dr., Prescott, AZ 86305-7447 / 928-776-8285; FAX: 928-776-8276 pdbullets@commspeed.net
Pete Mazur Restoration, 13083 Drummer Way, Grass Valley, CA 95949 / 530-268-2412; FAX: 530-268-2412
Pete Rickard Co., 115 Roy Walsh Rd., Cobleskill, NY 12043 / 518-234-2731; FAX: 518-234-2454 rickard@telenet.net www.peterickard.com
Peter Dyson & Son Ltd., 3 Cuckoo Lane, Honley, Holmfirth, West Yorkshire, HD9 6AS ENGLAND / 44-1484-661062; FAX: 44-1484-663709 peter@peterdyson.co.uk
Peter Hale/Engraver, 997 Maple Dr., Spanish Fork, UT 84660-2524 / 801-798-8215
Peters Stahl GmbH, Stettiner Strasse 42, D-33106, Paderborn, GERMANY / 05251-750025; FAX: 05251-75611 info@peters-stahl.com www.peters-stahl.com
Peterson Gun Shop, Inc., A.W., 4255 W. Old U.S. 441, Mt. Dora, FL 32757-3299 / 352-383-4258; FAX: 352-735-1001
Petro-Explo Inc., 7650 U.S. Hwy. 287, Suite 100, Arlington, TX 76017 / 817-478-8888
Pettinger Books, Gerald, 47827 300th Ave., Russell, IA 50238 / 641-535-2239 gpettinger@lisco.com
Pflumm Mfg. Co., 10662 Widmer Rd., Lenexa, KS 66215 / 800-888-4867; FAX: 913-451-7857
PFRB Co., P.O. Box 1242, Bloomington, IL 61702 / 800-914-5464; FAX: 888-554-8369
Phillippi Custom Bullets, Justin, P.O. Box 773, Ligonier, PA 15658 / 724-238-2962; FAX: 724-238-9671 jrp@wpa.net http://www.wpa.net~jrphil
Phoenix Arms, 4231 Brickell St., Ontario, CA 91761 / 909-937-6900; FAX: 909-937-0060
Piedmont Community College, P.O. Box 1197, Roxboro, NC 27573 / 336-599-1181; FAX: 336-597-3817 www.piedmont.cc.nc.us
Pietta (See U.S. Importers-Navy Arms Co, Taylor's
Pine Technical College, 1100 4th St., Pine City, MN 55063 / 800-521-7463; FAX: 612-629-6766
Pinetree Bullets, 133 Skeena St., Kitimat, BC V8C 1Z1 CANADA / 604-632-3768; FAX: 604-632-3768
Pioneer Arms Co., 355 Lawrence Rd., Broomall, PA 19008 / 215-356-5203
Piotti (See U.S. Importer-Moore & Co., Wm. Larkin)
Piquette, Paul. See: PIQUETTE'S CUSTOM ENGRAVING
Piquette's Custom Engraving, Paul R. Piquette, 309 North St., Feeding Hills, MA 01030 / 413-789-4582 ppiquette@comcast.net www.pistoldynamics.com
Plaza Cutlery, Inc., 3333 Bristol, 161 South Coast Plaza, Costa Mesa, CA 92626 / 714-549-3932
Plum City Ballistic Range, N2162 80th St., Plum City, WI 54761 / 715-647-2539
PlumFire Press, Inc., 30-A Grove Ave., Patchogue, NY 11772-4112 / 800-695-7246; FAX: 516-758-4071
PMC Ammunition, P.O. Box 940878, Houston, TX 77094-7878 / 281-759-9020; FAX: 281-759-0784 kbauer@pmcammo.com www.pmcammo.com
Poburka, Philip (See Bison Studios)
Pointing Dog Journal, Village Press Publications, P.O. Box 968, Dept. PGD, Traverse City, MI 49685 / 800-272-3246; FAX: 616-946-3289
Police Bookshelf, P.O. Box 122, Concord, NH 03301 / 603-224-6814; FAX: 603-226-3554 ayoob@attglobal.net www.ayoob.com
Polywad, Inc., P.O. Box 396, Roberta, GA 31078 / 478-836-4932; or 800-998-0669 FAX: 478-836-4937 welcome@polywad.com www.polywad.com
Ponsness, Warren, 7634 W. Ohio St., Rathdrum, ID 83858 / 800-732-0706; FAX: 208-687-2233 www.reloaders.com
Pony Express Reloaders, 608 E. Co. Rd. D, Suite 3, St. Paul, MN 55117 / 612-483-9406; FAX: 612-483-9884
Pony Express Sport Shop, 23404 Lyons Ave., PMB 448, Newhall, CA 91321-2511 / 818-895-1231
Powder Horn Ltd., P.O. Box 565, Glenview, IL 60025 / 305-565-6060
Powell & Son (Gunmakers) Ltd., William, 35-37 Carrs Lane, Birmingham, B4 7SX ENGLAND / 121-643-0689; FAX: 121-631-3504 sales@william-powell.co.uk www.william-powell.co.uk
Powell Agency, William, 22 Circle Dr., Bellmore, NY 11710 / 516-679-1158
Power Custom, Inc., 29739 Hwy. J, Gravois Mills, MO 65037 / 573-372-5684; FAX: 573-372-5799 rwpowers@laurie.net www.powercustom.com
Power Plus Enterprises, Inc., P.O. Box 38, Warm Springs, GA 31830 / 706-655-2132
Powley Computer (See Hutton Rifle Ranch)
Practical Tools, Inc., 7067 Easton Rd., P.O. Box 133, Pipersville, PA 18947 / 215-766-7301; FAX: 215-766-8681
Prairie Gun Works, 1-761 Marion St., Winnipeg, MB R2J 0K6 CANADA / 204-231-2976; FAX: 204-231-8566
Pranger, Ed G., 1414 7th St., Anacortes, WA 98221 / 206-293-3488
Precision Airgun Sales, Inc., 5247 Warrensville Ctr. Rd., Maple Hts., OH 44137 / 216-587-5005; FAX: 216-587-5005
Precision Cast Bullets, 101 Mud Creek Lane, Ronan, MT 59864 / 406-676-5135
Precision Delta Corp., P.O. Box 128, Ruleville, MS 38771 / 662-756-2810; FAX: 662-756-2590
Precision Firearm Finishing, 25 N.W. 44th Avenue, Des Moines, IA 50313 / 515-288-8680; FAX: 515-244-3925
Precision Gun Works, 104 Sierra Rd., Dept. GD, Kerrville, TX 78028 / 830-367-4587
Precision Reloading, 124 S. Main St., Mitchell, SD 57301 / 605-996-9984
Precision Reloading, Inc., 124 S. Main St., Mitchell, SD 57301 / 800-223-0900; FAX: 605-996-9987 info@precisionreloading.com www.precisionreloading.com
Precision Shooting, Inc., 222 McKee St., Manchester, CT 06040 / 860-645-8776; FAX: 860-643-8215 www.precisionshooting.com
Precision Small Arms Inc., 9272 Jeronimo Rd., Ste. 121, Irvine, CA 92618 / 800-554-5515 or 949-768-3530; FAX: 949-768-4808 www.tcbebe.com
Precision Specialties, 131 Hendom Dr., Feeding Hills, MA 01030 / 413-786-3365; FAX: 413-786-3365
Precision Sport Optics, 15571 Producer Lane, Unit G, Huntington Beach, CA 92649 / 714-891-1309; FAX: 714-892-6920
Preslik's Gunstocks, 4245 Keith Ln., Chico, CA 95926 / 916-891-8236
Price Bullets, Patrick W., 16520 Worthley Dr., San Lorenzo, CA 94580 / 510-278-1547
Primos Hunting Calls, 604 First St., Flora, MS 39071 / 601-879-9323; FAX: 601-879-9324 www.primos.com
PRL Bullets, c/o Blackburn Enterprises, 114 Stuart Rd., Ste. 110, Cleveland, TN 37312 / 423-559-0340
Professional Gunsmiths of America, 1209 South 13 Hwy., Lexington, MO 64067 / 816-529-1337
Professional Hunter Supplies, P.O. Box 608, 468 Main St., Ferndale, CA 95536 / 707-786-9140; FAX: 707-786-9117 wmebride@humboldt.com
PrOlix®lubricants, P.O. Box 1466, West Jordan, UT 84084-8466 / 801-569-2763; FAX: 801-569-8225 prolix@prolixlubricant.com www.prolixlubricant.com
Pro-Mark Div. of Wells Lamont, 6640 W. Touhy, Chicago, IL 60648 / 312-647-8200
Proofmark Corp., P.O. Box 357, Burgess, VA 22432 / 804-453-4337; FAX: 804-453-4337 proofmark@direcway.com www.proofmarkbullets.com
Pro-Port Ltd., 41302 Executive Dr., Harrison Twp., MI 48045-1306 / 586-469-6727; FAX: 586-469-0425 e-mail@magnaport.com www.magnaport.com
Pro-Shot Products, Inc., P.O. Box 763, Taylorville, IL 62568 / 217-824-9133; FAX: 217-824-8861 www.proshotproducts.com
Protector Mfg. Co., Inc., The, 443 Ashwood Pl., Boca Raton, FL 33431 / 407-394-6011
Protektor Model, 1-11 Bridge St., Galeton, PA 16922 / 814-435-2442 mail@protektormodel.com www.protektormodel.com
Prototech Industries, Inc., 10532 E Road, Delia, KS 66418 / 785-771-3571 prototec@grapevine.net
PWL Gunleather, P.O. Box 450432, Atlanta, GA 31145 / 800-960-4072 covert@pwlusa.com www.pwlusa.com
PWM Sales Ltd., N.D.F.S., Gowdall Lane, Pollington DN14 0AU, ENGLAND / 01405862688; FAX: 01405862622 Paulwelburn9@aol.com
Pyramyd Stone Inter. Corp., 2447 Suffolk Lane, Pepper Pike, OH 44124-4540

Q

Quack Decoy & Sporting Clays, 4 Ann & Hope Way, P.O. Box 98, Cumberland, RI 02864 / 401-723-8202; FAX: 401-722-5910
Quaker Boy, Inc., 5455 Webster Rd., Orchard Parks, NY 14127 / 716-662-3979; FAX: 716-662-9426
Quality Arms, Inc., Box 19477, Dept. GD, Houston, TX 77224 / 281-870-8377 arrieta2@excite.com www.arrieta.com
Quality Cartridge, P.O. Box 445, Hollywood, MD 20636 / 301-373-3719 www.qual-cart.com
Quality Custom Firearms, Stephen Billeb, 22 Vista View Dr., Cody, WY 82414 / 307-587-4278; FAX: 307-587-4297 stevebilleb@wyoming.com
Quarton Beamshot, 4538 Centerview Dr., Ste. 149, San Antonio, TX 78228 / 800-520-8435; FAX: 210-735-1326 www.beamshot.com
Que Industries, Inc., P.O. Box 2471, Everett, WA 98203 / 425-303-9088; FAX: 206-514-3266 queinfo@queindustries.com
Queen Cutlery Co., P.O. Box 500, Franklinville, NY 14737 / 800-222-5233; FAX: 800-299-2618

R

R&C Knives & Such, 2136 Candy Cane Walk, Manteca, CA 95336-9501 / 209-239-3722; FAX: 209-825-6947
R&D Gun Repair, Kenny Howell, RR1 Box 283, Beloit, WI 53511
R&J Gun Shop, 337 S. Humbolt St., Canyon City, OR 97820 / 541-575-2130 rjent@centurytel.net
R&S Industries Corp., 8255 Brentwood Industrial Dr., St. Louis, MO 63144 / 314-781-5169 ron@miraclepolishingcloth.com www.miraclepolishingcloth.com
R. Murphy Co., Inc., 13 Groton-Harvard Rd., P.O. Box 376, Ayer, MA 01432 / 617-772-3481 www.r.murphyknives.com
R.A. Wells Custom Gunsmith, 3452 1st Ave., Racine, WI 53402 / 414-639-5223
R.E. Seebeck Assoc., P.O. Box 59752, Dallas, TX 75229
R.E.I., P.O. Box 88, Tallevast, FL 34270 / 813-755-0085
R.E.T. Enterprises, 2608 S. Chestnut, Broken Arrow, OK 74012 / 918-251-GUNS; (4867) FAX: 918-251-0587
R.T. Eastman Products, P.O. Box 1531, Jackson, WY 83001 / 307-733-3217; or 800-624-4311
Rabeno, Martin, 530 The Eagle Pass, Durango, CO 81301 / 970-382-0353 fancygun@aol.com

MANUFACTURER'S DIRECTORY

Radiator Specialty Co., 1900 Wilkinson Blvd., P.O. Box 34689, Charlotte, NC 28234 / 800-438-6947; FAX: 800-421-9525 tkrossell@gunk.com www.gunk.com
Rainier Ballistics, 4500 15th St. East, Tacoma, WA 98424 / 800-638-8722; FAX: 253-922-7854 sales@rainierballistics.com www.rainierballistics.com
Ram-Line ATK, P.O. Box 39, Onalaska, WI 54650
Rampart International, 2781 W. MacArthur Blvd., B-283, Santa Ana, CA 92704 / 800-976-7240 or 714-557-6405
Ranch Products, P.O. Box 145, Malinta, OH 43535 / 313-277-3118; FAX: 313-565-8536 stevenacrawford@msn.com ranchproducts.com
Randall-Made Knives, P.O. Box 1988, Orlando, FL 32802 / 407-855-8075
Randco UK, 286 Gipsy Rd., Welling, DA16 1JJ ENGLAND / 44 81 303 4118
Randolph Engineering, Inc., Ranger Shooting Glasses, 26 Thomas Patten Dr., Randolph, MA 02368 / 800-541-1405; FAX: 781-986-0337 sales@randolphusa.com www.randolphusa.com
Range Brass Products Company, P.O. Box 218, Rockport, TX 78381
Ransom International Corp., P.O. Box 3845, Prescott, AZ 86302 / 928-778-7899; FAX: 928-778-7993 ransom@cableone.net www.ransomrest.com
Rapine Bullet Mould Mfg. Co., 9503 Landis Lane, East Greenville, PA 18041 / 215-679-5413; FAX: 215-679-9795
Ravell Ltd., 289 Diputacion St., 08009, Barcelona, SPAIN / 34(3) 4874486; FAX: 34(3) 4881394
Ray Riling Arms Books Co., 6844 Gorsten St., Philadelphia, PA 19119 / 215-438-2456; FAX: 215-438-5395 sales@rayrilingarmsbooks.com www.rayrilingarmsbooks.com
Ray's Gunsmith Shop, 3199 Elm Ave., Grand Junction, CO 81504 / 970-434-6162; FAX: 970-434-3452
Raytech Div. of Lyman Products Corp., 475 Smith Street, Middletown, CT 06457-1541 / 860-632-2020 or 800-225-9626; FAX: 860-632-1699 raysales@cshore.com www.raytech-
RCBS Operations/ATK, 605 Oro Dam Blvd., Oroville, CA 95965 / 800-533-5000; FAX: 530-533-1647 www.rcbs.com
Reardon Products, P.O. Box 126, Morrison, IL 61270 / 815-772-3155
Recoilless Technologies, Inc. (RTI), RTI/High-Low, 2141 E. Cedar #2, Tempe, AZ 85281 / 480-966-7051
Red Diamond Dist. Co., 1304 Snowdon Dr., Knoxville, TN 37912
Redding Reloading Equipment, 1089 Starr Rd., Cortland, NY 13045 / 607-753-3331; FAX: 607-756-8445 techline@redding-reloading.com www.redding- reloading.com
Redfield Media Resource Center, 4607 N.E. Cedar Creek Rd., Woodland, WA 98674 / 360-225-5000; FAX: 360-225-7616
Redman's Rifling & Reboring, 189 Nichols Rd., Omak, WA 98841 / 509-826-5512
Redwood Bullet Works, 3559 Bay Rd., Redwood City, CA 94063 / 415-367-6741
Reed, Dave, Rt. 1, Box 374, Minnesota City, MN 55959 / 507-689-2944
Reimer Johannsen, Inc., 438 Willow Brook Rd., Plainfield, NH 03781 / 603-469-3450; FAX: 603-469-3471
Reloaders Equipment Co., 4680 High St., Ecorse, MI 48229
Reloading Specialties, Inc., Box 1130, Pine Island, MN 55463 / 507-356-8500; FAX: 507-356-8800
Remington Arms Co., Inc., 870 Remington Drive, P.O. Box 700, Madison, NC 27025-0700 / 800-243-9700; FAX: 336-548-8700 info@remington.com www.remington.com
Remington Double Shotguns, 7885 Cyd Dr., Denver, CO 80221 / 303-429-6947
Renegade, P.O. Box 31546, Phoenix, AZ 85046 / 602-482-6777; FAX: 602-482-1952
Renfrew Guns & Supplies, R.R. 4, Renfrew, ON K7V 3Z7 CANADA / 613-432-7080
Reno, Wayne, 2808 Stagestop Road, Jefferson, CO 80456
Republic Arms, Inc. (See Cobra Enterprises, Inc.)
Retting, Inc., Martin B., 11029 Washington, Culver City, CA 90232 / 213-837-2412
RG-G, Inc., P.O. Box 935, Trinidad, CO 81082 / 719-845-1436
RH Machine & Consulting Inc., P.O. Box 394, Pacific, MO 63069 / 314-271-8465
Rhino, P.O. Box 787, Locust, NC 28097 / 704-753-2198
Rhodeside, Inc., 1704 Commerce Dr., Piqua, OH 45356 / 513-773-5781
Rice, Keith (See White Rock Tool & Die)
Richards MicroFit Stocks, Inc., P.O. Box 1066, Sun Valley, CA 91352 / 800-895-7420; FAX: 818-771-1242 sales@rifle-stocks.com www.rifle-stocks.com
Ridgeline, Inc., Bruce Sheldon, P.O. Box 930, Dewey, AZ 86327-0930 / 800-632-5900; FAX: 520-632-5900
Ridgetop Sporting Goods, P.O. Box 306, 42907 Hilligoss Ln. East, Eatonville, WA 98328 / 360-832-6422; FAX: 360-832-6422
Ries, Chuck, 415 Ridgecrest Dr., Grants Pass, OR 97527 / 503-476-5623
Rifles, Inc., 3580 Leal Rd., Pleasanton, TX 78064 / 830-569-2055; FAX: 830-569-2297
Riggs, Jim, 206 Azalea, Boerne, TX 78006 / 210-249-8567
Riley Ledbetter Airguns, 1804 E. Sprague St., Winston Salem, NC 27107-3521 / 919-784-0676
Rim Pac Sports, Inc., 1034 N. Soldano Ave., Azusa, CA 91702-2135
Ringler Custom Leather Co., 31 Shining Mtn. Rd., Powell, WY 82435 / 307-645-3255
Ripley Rifles, 42 Fletcher Street, Ripley, Derbyshire, DE5 3LP ENGLAND / 011-0773-748353
Rizzini F.lli (See U.S. Importers-Wm. Larkin Moore & Co., N.E. Arms Corp.)
Rizzini SNC, Via 2 Giugno, 7/7Bis-25060, Marcheno (Brescia), ITALY
RMS Custom Gunsmithing, 4120 N. Bitterwell, Prescott Valley, AZ 86314 / 520-772-7626 www.customstockmaker.com
Robar Co., Inc., The, 21438 N. 7th Ave., Suite B, Phoenix, AZ 85027 / 623-581-2648; FAX: 623-582-0059 info@robarguns.com www.robarguns.com
Robert Evans Engraving, 332 Vine St., Oregon City, OR 97045 / 503-656-5693
Robert Valade Engraving, 931 3rd Ave., Seaside, OR 97138 / 503-738-7672
Robinett, R. G., P.O. Box 72, Madrid, IA 50156 / 515-795-2906
Robinson, Don, Pennsylvania Hse, 36 Fairfax Crescent, W Yorkshire, ENGLAND / 01484-421-362 donrobinsonuk@yahoo.co.uk www.guns4u2.co.uk
Robinson Armament Co., P.O. Box 16776, Salt Lake City, UT 84116 / 801-355-0401; FAX: 801-355-0402 zdf@robarm.com www.robarm.com
Robinson Firearms Mfg. Ltd., 1699 Blondeaux Crescent, Kelowna, BC V1Y 4J8 CANADA / 604-868-9596
Robinson H.V. Bullets, 3145 Church St., Zachary, LA 70791 / 504-654-4029
Rochester Lead Works, 76 Anderson Ave., Rochester, NY 14607 / 716-442-8500; FAX: 716-442-4712
Rock River Arms, 101 Noble St., Cleveland, IL 61241
Rockwood Corp., Speedwell Division, 136 Lincoln Blvd., Middlesex, NJ 08846 / 800-243-8274; FAX: 980-560-7475
Rocky Mountain Armoury, Mr. Felix LesMerises, 610 Main Street, P.O. Box 691, Frisco, CO 80443-0691 / 970-668-0136; FAX: 970-668-4484 felix@rockymountainarmoury.com
Rocky Mountain Target Co., 3 Aloe Way, Leesburg, FL 34788 / 352-365-9598
Rocky Shoes & Boots, 294 Harper St., Nelsonville, OH 45764 / 800-848-9452 or 614-753-1951; FAX: 614-753-4024
Rogue Rifle Co., Inc./Chipmunk Rifles, 1140 36th St. N., Ste. B, Lewiston, ID 83501 / 208-743-4355; FAX: 208-743-4163 customerservice@roguerifle.com www.roguerifle.com
Rogue River Rifleworks, 500 Linne Road #D, Paso Robles, CA 93446 / 805-227-4706; FAX: 805-227-4723 rrrifles@calinet.com
Rohner, Hans, 1148 Twin Sisters Ranch Rd., Nederland, CO 80466-9600
Rohner, John, 186 Virginia Ave., Asheville, NC 28806 / 828-281-3704
Rohrbaugh, P.O. Box 785, Bayport, NY 11705 / 631-363-2843; FAX: 631-363-2681 API380@aol.com
Romain's Custom Guns, Inc., RD 1, Whetstone Rd., Brockport, PA 15823 / 814-265-1948 romwhetstone@penn.com
Ron Frank Custom, 7131 Richland Rd., Ft. Worth, TX 76118 / 817-284-9300; FAX: 817-284-9300 rfrank3974@aol.com
Rooster Laboratories, P.O. Box 414605, Kansas City, MO 64141 / 816-474-1622; FAX: 816-474-7622
Rorschach Precision Products, 417 Keats Cir., Irving, TX 75061 / 214-790-3487
Rosenberg & Son, Jack A., 12229 Cox Ln., Dallas, TX 75234 / 214-241-6302
Ross, Don, 12813 West 83 Terrace, Lenexa, KS 66215 / 913-492-6982
Rosser, Bob, 2809 Crescent Ave., Suite 20, Homewood, AL 35209 / 205-870-4422; FAX: 205-877-4525 www.hand-engravers.com
Rossi Firearms, Gary Mchalik, 16175 NW 49th Ave., Miami, FL 33014-6314 / 305-474-0401; FAX: 305-623-7506
Rottweil Compe, 1330 Glassell, Orange, CA 92667
Royal Arms Gunstocks, 919 8th Ave. NW, Great Falls, MT 59404 / 406-453-1149; FAX: 406-453-1149 royalarms@bresnar.net www.lmt.net/~royalarms
Royal Arms International, R J Brill, P.O. Box 6083, Woodland Hills, CA 91365 / 818-704-5110; FAX: 818-887-2059 royalarms.com
Roy's Custom Grips, 793 Mt. Olivet Church Rd., Lynchburg, VA 24504 / 434-993-3470
RPM, 15481 N. Twin Lakes Dr., Tucson, AZ 85739 / 520-825-1233; FAX: 520-825-3333
Rubright Bullets, 1008 S. Quince Rd., Walnutport, PA 18088 / 215-767-1339
Rucker Dist. Inc., P.O. Box 479, Terrell, TX 75160 / 214-563-2094
Ruger (See Sturm Ruger & Co., Inc.)
Ruger, Chris. See: RUGER'S CUSTOM GUNS
Ruger's Custom Guns, Chris Ruger, 1050 Morton Blvd., Kingston, NY 12401 / 845-336-7106; FAX: 845-336-7106 rugerscustom@outdrs.net rugergunsmith.com
Rundell's Gun Shop, 6198 Frances Rd., Clio, MI 48420 / 313-687-0559
Rupert's Gun Shop, 2202 Dick Rd., Suite B, Fenwick, MI 48834 / 517-248-3252 17rupert@pathwaynet.com
Russ Haydon's Shooters' Supply, 15018 Goodrich Dr. NW, Gig Harbor, WA 98329 / 877-663-6249; FAX: 253-857-7884 info@shooters-supply.com www.shooters- supply.com
Russ, William. See: BILL RUSS TRADING POST
Rusteprufe Laboratories, 1319 Jefferson Ave., Sparta, WI 54656 / 608-269-4144; FAX: 608-366-1972 rusteprufe@centurytel.net www.rusteprufe.com
Rutgers Book Center, 127 Raritan Ave., Highland Park, NJ 08904 / 732-545-4344; FAX: 732-545-6686 gunbooks@rutgersgunbooks.com www.rutgersgunbooks.com
Rutten (See U.S. Importer-Labanu Inc.)
RWS (See U.S. Importer-Umarex-USA), 6007 S. 29th St., Fort Smith, AR 72908

S

S&K Scope Mounts, RD 2 Box 21C, Sugar Grove, PA 16350 / 814-489-3091 or 800-578-9862; FAX: 814-489-5466 comments@scopemounts.com www.scopemounts.com
S&S Firearms, 74-11 Myrtle Ave., Glendale, NY 11385 / 718-497-1100; FAX: 718-497-1105 info@ssfirearms.com ssfirearms.com
S.A.R.L. G. Granger, 66 Cours Fauriel, 42100, Saint Etienne, FRANCE / 04 77 25 14 73; FAX: 04 77 38 66 99
S.D. Meacham, 1070 Angel Ridge, Peck, ID 83545
S.I.A.C.E. (See U.S. Importer-IAR Inc.)
Sabatti SPA, Via A Volta 90, 25063 Gandome V.T.(BS), Brescia, ITALY / 030-8912207-831312; FAX: 030-8912059 info@sabatti.it www.sabatti.com
SAECO (See Redding Reloading Equipment)
Safari Arms/Schuetzen Pistol Works, 620-626 Old Pacific Hwy. SE, Olympia, WA 98513 / 360-459-3471; FAX: 360-491-3447 info@olyarms.com www.olyarms.com
Safari Press, Inc., 15621 Chemical Lane B, Huntington Beach, CA 92649 / 714-894-9080; FAX: 714-894-4949 info@safaripress.com www.safaripress.com
Safariland Ltd., Inc., 3120 E. Mission Blvd., P.O. Box 51478, Ontario, CA 91761 / 909-923-7300; FAX: 909-923-7400
SAFE, P.O. Box 864, Post Falls, ID 83877 / 208-773-3624; FAX: 208-773-6819 staysafe@safe-llc.com www.safe-llc.com
Sako Ltd. (See U.S. Importer-Stoeger Industries)
Sam Welch Gun Engraving, Sam Welch, HC 64 Box 2110, Moab, UT 84532 / 435-259-8131
Samco Global Arms, Inc., 6995 NW 43rd St., Miami, FL 33166 / 305-593-9782; FAX: 305-593-1014 samco@samcoglobal.com www.samcoglobal.com
Sampson, Roger, 2316 Mahogany St., Mora, MN 55051 / 320-679-4868
San Marco (See U.S. Importers-Cape Outfitters-EMF Co., Inc.
Sandia Die & Cartridge Co., 37 Atancacio Rd. NE, Albuquerque, NM 87123 / 505-298-5729
Sarco, Inc., 323 Union St., Stirling, NJ 07980 / 908-647-3800; FAX: 908-647-9413
Sarsilmaz Shotguns-Turkey (see B.C. Outdoors)
Sauer (See U.S. Importers-Paul Co., The Sigarms Inc.)
Sauls, R. See: BRYAN & ASSOC.

MANUFACTURER'S DIRECTORY

Saunders Gun & Machine Shop, 145 Delhi Rd., Manchester, IA 52057 / 563-927-4026
Savage Arms (Canada), Inc., 248 Water St., P.O. Box 1240, Lakefield, ON K0L 2H0 CANADA / 705-652-8000; FAX: 705-652-8431 www.savagearms.com
Savage Arms, Inc., 100 Springdale Rd., Westfield, MA 01085 / 413-568-7001; FAX: 413-562-7764
Savage Range Systems, Inc., 100 Springdale Rd., Westfield, MA 01085 / 413-568-7001; FAX: 413-562-1152 snailtraps@savagearms.com www.snailtraps.com
Saville Iron Co. (See Greenwood Precision)
Scansport, Inc., P.O. Box 700, Enfield, NH 03748 / 603-632-7654
Sceery Game Calls, P.O. Box 6520, Sante Fe, NM 87502 / 505-471-9110; FAX: 505-471-3476
Schaefer Shooting Sports, P.O. Box 1515, Melville, NY 11747-0515 / 516-643-5466; FAX: 516-643-2426 robert@robertschaefer.com www.schaefershooting.com
Scharch Mfg., Inc.-Top Brass, 10325 Co. Rd. 120, Salida, CO 81201 / 800-836-4683; FAX: 719-539-3021 topbrass@scharch.com www.handgun-brass.com
Scherer, Liz. See: SCHERER SUPPLIES, INC.
Scherer Supplies, Inc., Liz Scherer, Box 250, Ewing, VA 24248 FAX: 423-733-2073
Schiffman, Mike, 8233 S. Crystal Springs, McCammon, ID 83250 / 208-254-9114
Schmidt & Bender, Inc., P.O. Box 134, Meriden, NH 03770 / 603-469-3565; FAX: 603-469-3471 info@schmidtbender.com www.schmidtbender.com
Schneider Bullets, 3655 West 214th St., Fairview Park, OH 44126
Schneider Rifle Barrels, Inc., 1403 W. Red Baron Rd., Payson, AZ 85541 / 602-948-2525
School of Gunsmithing, The, 430 Technology Parkway, Norcross, GA 30092 / 800-223-4542 www.ashworthuniveristy.edu
Schroeder Bullets, 1421 Thermal Ave., San Diego, CA 92154 / 619-423-3523; FAX: 619-423-8124
Schulz Industries, 16247 Minnesota Ave., Paramount, CA 90723 / 213-439-5903
Schumakers Gun Shop, 512 Prouty Corner Lp. A, Colville, WA 99114 / 509-684-4848
Scope Control, Inc., 5775 Co. Rd. 23 SE, Alexandria, MN 56308 / 612-762-7295
Score High Gunsmithing, 9812-A, Cochiti SE, Albuquerque, NM 87123 / 800-326-5632 or 505-292-5532; FAX: 505-292-2592 scorehi@scorehi.com www.probed2000.com
Scott Fine Guns Inc., Thad, P.O. Box 412, Indianola, MS 38751 / 601-887-5929
Searcy Enterprises, P.O. Box 584, Boron, CA 93596 / 760-762-6771; FAX: 760-762-0191
Second Chance Body Armor, P.O. Box 578, Central Lake, MI 49622 / 616-544-5721; FAX: 616-544-9824
Seebeck Assoc., R.E., P.O. Box 59752, Dallas, TX 75229
Segway Industries, P.O. Box 783, Suffern, NY 10901-0783 / 914-357-5510
Seligman Shooting Products, Box 133, Seligman, AZ 86337 / 602-422-3607 shootssp@yahoo.com
Sellier & Bellot, USA, Inc., P.O. Box 27006, Shawnee Mission, KS 66225 / 913-685-0916; FAX: 913-685-0917
Selsi Co., Inc., P.O. Box 10, Midland Park, NJ 07432-0010 / 201-935-0388; FAX: 201-935-5851
Semmer, Charles (See Remington Double Shotguns), 7885 Cyd Dr., Denver, CO 80221 / 303-429-6947
Servus Footwear Co., 1136 2nd St., Rock Island, IL 61204 / 309-786-7741; FAX: 309-786-9808
SGS Importer's International, Inc., 1750 Brielle Ave., Unit B1, Wanamassa, NJ 07712 / 732-493-0302; FAX: 732-493-0301 gsodini@aol.com www.firestorm- sgs.com
Shappy Bullets, 76 Milldale Ave., Plantsville, CT 06479 / 203-621-3704
Sharp Shooter Supply, 4970 Lehman Road, Delphos, OH 45833 / 419-695-3179
Sharps Arms Co., Inc., C., 100 Centennial, Box 885, Big Timber, MT 59011 / 406-932-4353
Shaw, Inc., E. R. (See Small Arms Mfg. Co.)
Shay's Gunsmithing, 931 Marvin Ave., Lebanon, PA 17042
Sheffield Knifemakers Supply, Inc., P.O. Box 741107, Orange City, FL 32774-1107 / 386-775-6453; FAX: 386-774-5754 email@sheffieldsupply.com www.sheffieldsupply.com
Sheldon, Bruce. See: RIDGELINE, INC.
Shepherd Enterprises, Inc., Box 189, Waterloo, NE 68069 / 402-779-2424; FAX: 402-779-4010 sshepherd@shepherdscopes.com www.shepherdscopes.com
Sherwood, George, 46 N. River Dr., Roseburg, OR 97470 / 541-672-3159
Shilen, Inc., 205 Metro Park Blvd., Ennis, TX 75119 / 972-875-5318; FAX: 972-875-5402
Shiloh Rifle Mfg., P.O. Box 279, Big Timber, MT 59011
Shoot Where You Look, Leon Measures, Dept GD, 408 Fair, Livingston, TX 77351
Shooters Arms Manufacturing, Inc., Rivergate Mall, Gen. Maxilom Ave., Cebu City 6000, PHILIPPINES / 6332-254-8478 www.shootersarms.com.ph
Shooter's Choice Gun Care, 15050 Berkshire Ind. Pkwy., Middlefield, OH 44062 / 440-834-8888; FAX: 440-834-3388 www.shooterschoice.com
Shooter's Edge Inc., 3313 Creekstone Dr., Fort Collins, CO 80525
Shooters Supply, 153 Childs Rd., Trout Creek, MT 59874 / 509-452-1181
Shooter's World, 3828 N. 28th Ave., Phoenix, AZ 85017 / 602-266-0170
Shooters, Inc., 5139 Stanart St., Norfolk, VA 23502 / 757-461-9152; FAX: 757-461-9155 gflocker@aol.com
Shootin' Shack, 357 Cypress Drive, No. 10, Tequesta, FL 33469 / 561-746-2731; FAX: 772-545-4861 ckeays@comcast.net
Shoot-N-C Targets (See Birchwood Casey)
Shotgun Sports, P.O. Box 6810, Auburn, CA 95604 / 530-889-2220; FAX: 530-889-9106 custsrv@shotgunsportsmagazine.com shotgunsportsmagazine.com
Shotgun Sports Magazine, dba Shootin' Accessories Ltd., P.O. Box 6810, Auburn, CA 95604 / 530-889-2220; FAX: 530-889-9106 custsrv@shotgunsportsmagazine.com
Shotguns Unlimited, 2307 Fon Du Lac Rd., Richmond, VA 23229 / 804-752-7115
Siegrist Gun Shop, 8752 Turtle Road, Whittemore, MI 48770 / 989-873-3929
Sierra Bullets, 1400 W. Henry St., Sedalia, MO 65301 / 816-827-6300; FAX: 816-827-6300 www.sierrabullets.com
Sierra Specialty Prod. Co., 1344 Oakhurst Ave., Los Altos, CA 94024 FAX: 415-965-1536
SIG, CH-8212 Neuhausen, SWITZERLAND
Sig Sauer, Inc., 18 Industrial Dr., Exeter, NH 03833 / 603-772-2302; FAX: 603-772-9082 siginfo@sigsauer.com www.sigsauer.com
Sight Shop, The, John G. Lawson, 1802 E. Columbia Ave., Tacoma, WA 98404 / 253-474-5465 parabellum9@aol.com www.thesightshop.org
Sightron, Inc., 1672B Hwy. 96, Franklinton, NC 27525 / 919-528-8783; FAX: 919-528-0995 info@sightron.com www.sightron.com
SIG-Sauer (See U.S. Importer-Sigarms, Inc.)
Silencio/Jackson Products, Inc., 1859 Bowles Ave., Ste. 200, Fenton, MO 63026 / 636-717-6600; FAX: 636-717-6800
Silhouette Leathers, 8598 Hwy. 51 N. #4, Millington, TN 38053 silhouetteleathers@yahoo.com silhouetteleathers.com
Silver Eagle Machining, 18007 N. 69th Ave., Glendale, AZ 85308
Silver Ridge Gun Shop (See Goodwin Guns)
Simmons, Jerry, 715 Middlebury St., Goshen, IN 46528-2717 / 574-533-8546
Simmons Gun Repair, Inc., 700 S. Rogers Rd., Olathe, KS 66062 / 913-782-3131; FAX: 913-782-4189
Simmons Outdoor Corp., 6001 Oak Canyon, Irvine, CA 92618 / 949-451-1450; FAX: 949-451-1460 www.meade.com
Sinclair International, Inc., 2330 Wayne Haven St., Fort Wayne, IN 46803 / 260-493-1858 or 800-717-8211; FAX: 260-493-2530 sales@sinclairintl.com www.sinclairintl.com
Singletary, Kent, 4538 W. Carol Ave., Glendale, AZ 85302 / 602-526-6836 kent@kscustom www.kscustom.com
Siskiyou Gun Works (See Donnelly, C. P.)
Six Enterprises, 320-D Turtle Creek Ct., San Jose, CA 95125 / 408-999-0201; FAX: 408-999-0216
SKB Shotguns, 4441 S. 134th St., Omaha, NE 68137 / 800-752-2767; FAX: 402-330-8040 skb@skbshotguns.com www.skbshotguns.com
Skeoch, Brian R., P.O. Box 279, Glenrock, WY 82637 / 307-436-9655 skeochbrian@netzero.com
Skip's Machine, 364 29 Road, Grand Junction, CO 81501 / 303-245-5417
Sklany's Machine Shop, 566 Birch Grove Dr., Kalispell, MT 59901 / 406-755-4257
Slug Site, 21300 Hwy. 5, Versailles, MO 65084 / 573-378-6430 clancy@localnet.com
Small Arms Mfg. Co., 5312 Thoms Run Rd., Bridgeville, PA 15017 / 412-221-4343; FAX: 412-221-4303 www.ershawbarrels.com
Smires, C. L., 5222 Windmill Lane, Columbia, MD 21044-1328
Smith & Wesson, 2100 Roosevelt Ave., Springfield, MA 01104 / 413-781-8300; FAX: 413-731-8980 qa@smith-wesson.com www.smith-wesson.com
Smith, Art, P.O. Box 645, Park Rapids, MN 56470 / 218-732-5333
Smith, Mark A., P.O. Box 182, Sinclair, WY 82334 / 307-324-7929
Smith, Michael, 2612 Ashmore Ave., Red Bank, TN 37415 / 615-267-8341
Smith, Ron, 5869 Straley, Fort Worth, TX 76114 / 817-732-6768
Smith, Sharmon, 4545 Speas Rd., Fruitland, ID 83619 / 208-452-6329 sharmon@fmtc.com
Smith Abrasives, Inc., 1700 Sleepy Valley Rd., Hot Springs, AR 71902-5095 / 501-321-2244; FAX: 501-321-9232 www.smithabrasives.com
Smith, Judy. See: L.B.T.
Smith Saddlery, Jesse W., 0499 County Road J, Pritchett, CO 81064 / 509-325-0622
Smokey Valley Rifles, E1976 Smokey Valley Rd., Scandinavia, WI 54977 / 715-467-2674
Snapp's Gunshop, 6911 E. Washington Rd., Clare, MI 48617 / 989-386-9226 snapp@glccomputers.com
Sno-Seal, Inc. (See Atsko/Sno-Seal, Inc.)
Societa Armi Bresciane Srl (See U.S. Importer-Jeff's Outfitters)
SOS Products Co. (See Buck Stix-SOS Products Co.), Box 3, Neenah, WI 54956
Sotheby's, 1334 York Ave. at 72nd St., New York, NY 10021 / 212-606-7260
Sound Tech, Box 738, Logan, NM 88426 / 205-999-0416; or 505-487-2277 silenceio@wmconnect.com www.soundtechsilencers.com
South Bend Replicas, Inc., 61650 Oak Rd., South Bend, IN 46614 / 574-289-4500
Southeastern Community College, 1015 S. Gear Ave., West Burlington, IA 52655 / 319-752-2731
Southern Ammunition Co., Inc., 4232 Meadow St., Loris, SC 29569-3124 / 803-756-3262; FAX: 803-756-3583
Southern Armory, The, 25 Millstone Rd., Woodlawn, VA 24381 / 703-238-1343; FAX: 703-238-1453
Southern Bloomer Mfg. Co., P.O. Box 1621, Bristol, TN 37620 / 423-878-6660; FAX: 423-878-8761 southernbloomer@earthlink.net www.southernbloomer.com
Southern Security, 1700 Oak Hills Dr., Kingston, TN 37763 / 423-376-6297; FAX: 800-251-9992
Sparks, Milt, 605 E. 44th St. No. 2, Boise, ID 83714-4800
Spartan-Realtree Products, Inc., 1390 Box Circle, Columbus, GA 31907 / 706-569-9101; FAX: 706-569-0042
Specialty Gunsmithing, Lynn McMurdo, P.O. Box 404, Afton, WY 83110 / 307-886-5535
Specialty Shooters Supply, Inc., 3325 Griffin Rd., Suite 9mm, Fort Lauderdale, FL 33317
Speer Bullets, P.O. Box 856, Lewiston, ID 83501 / 208-746-2351 www.speer-bullets.com
Spegel, Craig, P.O. Box 387, Nehalem, OR 97131 / 503-368-5653
Speiser, Fred D., 2229 Dearborn, Missoula, MT 59801 / 406-549-8133
Spencer Reblue Service, 1820 Tupelo Trail, Holt, MI 48842 / 517-694-7474
Spencer's Rifle Barrels, Inc., 4107 Jacobs Creek Dr., Scottsville, VA 24590 / 804-293-6836; FAX: 804-293-6836 www.spencersriflebarrels.com
SPG, Inc., P.O. Box 1625, Cody, WY 82414 / 307-587-7621; FAX: 307-587-7695 spg@cody.wtp.net www.blackpowderspg.com
Sphinx Systems Ltd., Gesteigtstrasse 12, CH-3800, Matten, BRNE, SWITZERLAND
Splitfire Sporting Goods, L.L.C., P.O. Box 1044, Orem, UT 84059-1044 / 801-932-7950; FAX: 801-932-7959 www.splitfireguns.com
Spolar Power Load, Inc., 17376 Filbert, Fontana, CA 92335 / 800-227-9667
Sport Flite Manufacturing Co., 637 Kingsley Trl., Bloomfield Hills, MI 48304-2320 / 248-647-3747
Sporting Clays Of America, 9257 Buckeye Rd., Sugar Grove, OH 43155-9632 / 740-746-8334 FAX: 740-746-8605
Sports Afield Magazine, 15621 Chemical Lane B, Huntington Beach, CA 92649 / 714-894-9080; FAX: 714-894-4949 info@sportsafield.com www.sportsafield.com
Sportsman Safe Mfg. Co., 6309-6311 Paramount Blvd., Long Beach, CA 90805 / 800-266-7150; or 310-984-5445
Sportsman's Communicators, 588 Radcliffe Ave., Pacific Palisades, CA 90272 / 800-538-3752
Sportsmatch U.K. Ltd., 16 Summer St. Leighton,, Buzzard Beds, Bedfordshire, LU7 1HT ENGLAND / 4401525-381638; FAX: 4401525-851236 info@sportsmatch-uk.com www.sportsmatch-
Sportsmen's Exchange & Western Gun Traders, Inc., 813 Doris Ave., Oxnard, CA 93030 / 805-483-1917

Spradlin's, 457 Shannon Rd., Texas Creek Cotopaxi, CO 81223 / 719-275-7105; FAX: 719-275-3852 spradlins@prodigy.net www.spradlins.net
Springfield Armory, 420 W. Main St., Geneseo, IL 61254 / 309-944-5631; FAX: 309-944-3676 sales@springfield-armory.com www.springfieldarmory.com
Springfield Sporters, Inc., RD 1, Penn Run, PA 15765 / 412-254-2626; FAX: 412-254-9173
Springfield, Inc., 420 W. Main St., Geneseo, IL 61254 / 309-944-5631; FAX: 309-944-3676
Spyderco, Inc., 820 Spyderco Way, Golden, CO 80403 / 800-525-7770; FAX: 303-278-2229 sales@spyderco.com www.spyderco.com
SSK Industries, J. D. Jones, 590 Woodvue Lane, Wintersville, OH 43953 / 740-264-0176; FAX: 740-264-2257 www.sskindustries.com
Stackpole Books, 5067 Ritter Rd., Mechanicsburg, PA 17055-6921 / 717-796-0411 FAX: 717-796-0412 tmanney@stackpolebooks.com www.stackpolebooks.com
Stalker, Inc., P.O. Box 21, Fishermans Wharf Rd., Malakoff, TX 75148 / 903-489-1010
Stalwart Corporation, P.O. Box 46, Evanston, WY 82931 / 307-789-7687; FAX: 307-789-7688
Stan Baker Sports, Stan Baker, 10000 Lake City Way, Seattle, WA 98125 / 206-522-4575
Stan De Treville & Co., 4129 Normal St., San Diego, CA 92103 / 619-298-3393
Star Ammunition, Inc., 5520 Rock Hampton Ct., Indianapolis, IN 46268 / 800-221-5927; FAX: 317-872-5847
Star Custom Bullets, P.O. Box 608, 468 Main St., Ferndale, CA 95536 / 707-786-9140; FAX: 707-786-9117 wmebridge@humboldt.com
Star Machine Works, P.O. Box 1872, Pioneer, CA 95666 / 209-295-5000
Starke Bullet Company, P.O. Box 400, 605 6th St. NW, Cooperstown, ND 58425 / 888-797-3431
Starkey Labs, 6700 Washington Ave. S., Eden Prairie, MN 55344
Starkey's Gun Shop, 9430 McCombs, El Paso, TX 79924 / 915-751-3030
Starlight Training Center, Inc., Rt. 1, P.O. Box 88, Bronaugh, MO 64728 / 417-843-3555
Starline, Inc., 1300 W. Henry St., Sedalia, MO 65301 / 660-827-6640; FAX: 660-827-6650 info@starlinebrass.com http://www.starlinebrass.com
Starr Trading Co., Jedediah, P.O. Box 2007, Farmington Hills, MI 48333 / 877-857-8277; FAX: 248-683-3282 mtman1849@aol.com www.jedediah-starr.com
Starrett Co., L. S., 121 Crescent St., Athol, MA 01331 / 978-249-3551; FAX: 978-249-8495
State Line Gun Shop, 443 Firchburg Rd., Mason, NH 03048 / 603-878-2854; FAX: 603-878-3905 miniguns@empire.net www.statelinegunshop.com
Steelman's Gun Shop, 10465 Beers Rd., Swartz Creek, MI 48473 / 810-735-4884
Steffens, Ron, 18396 Mariposa Creek Rd., Willits, CA 95490 / 707-485-0873
Stegall, James B., 26 Forest Rd., Wallkill, NY 12589
Steve Henigson & Associates, P.O. Box 2726, Culver City, CA 90231 / 310-305-8288; FAX: 310-305-1905
Steve Kamyk Engraver, 9 Grandview Dr., Westfield, MA 01085-1810 / 413-568-0457 stevek201@comcast.net
Steven Dodd Hughes, P.O. Box 545, Livingston, MT 59047 / 406-222-9377; FAX: 406-222-9377
Stewart's Gunsmithing, P.O. Box 5854, Pietersburg North 0750, Transvaal, SOUTH AFRICA / 01521-89401
Steyr Arms, P.O. Box 2609, Cumming, GA 30028 / 770-888-4201 www.steyrarms.com
Steyr Mannlicher GmbH & Co. KG, Ramingtal 46, A-4442 Kleinraming, Steyr, AUSTRIA / 0043-7252-896-0; FAX: 0043-7252-78620 office@steyr- mannlicher.com www.steyr-mannlicher.com
STI International, 114 Halmar Cove, Georgetown, TX 78628 / 800-959-8201; FAX: 512-819-0465 www.stiguns.com
Stiles Custom Guns, 76 Cherry Run Rd., Box 1605, Homer City, PA 15748 / 712-479-9945 glstiles@yourinter.net www.yourinter.net/glstiles
Stoeger Industries, 17603 Indian Head Hwy., Suite 200, Accokeek, MD 20607-2501 / 301-283-6300; FAX: 301-283-6986 www.stoegerindustries.com
Stoeger Publishing Co. (See Stoeger Industries)
Stone Enterprises Ltd., 426 Harveys Neck Rd., P.O. Box 335, Wicomico Church, VA 22579 / 804-580-5114; FAX: 804-580-8421
Stone Mountain Arms, 5988 Peachtree Corners E., Norcross, GA 30071 / 800-251-9412
Stoney Point Products, Inc., 9200 Cody St., Overland Park, KS 66214 / 800-845-2444; FAX: 507-354-7236 stoney@newulmtel.net www.stoneypoint.com
Storm, Gary, P.O. Box 5211, Richardson, TX 75083 / 214-385-0862
Stott's Creek Armory, Inc., 2526 S. 475W, Morgantown, IN 46160 / 317-878-5489 stottscrk@aol.com www.Sccalendar.aol.com
Stratco, Inc., P.O. Box 2270, Kalispell, MT 59901 / 406-755-1221; FAX: 406-755-1226
Strayer, Sandy. See: STRAYER-VOIGT, INC.
Strayer-Voigt, Inc., Sandy Strayer, 3435 Ray Orr Blvd., Grand Prairie, TX 75050 / 972-513-0575
Strong Holster Co., 39 Grove St., Gloucester, MA 01930 / 508-281-3300; FAX: 508-281-6321
Strutz Rifle Barrels, Inc., W. C., P.O. Box 611, Eagle River, WI 54521 / 715-479-4766
Stuart, V. Pat, 279 Pilson, Greenville, VA 24440 / 540-377-6187
Sturgeon Valley Sporters, Ken Ide, P.O. Box 283, Vanderbilt, MI 49795 / 989-983-4338 k.ide@mail.com
Sturm Ruger & Co. Inc., 200 Ruger Rd., Prescott, AZ 86301 / 928-541-8820; FAX: 520-541-8850 www.ruger.com
"Su-Press-On", Inc., P.O. Box 09161, Detroit, MI 48209 / 313-842-4222
Sullivan, David S. (See Westwind Rifles, Inc.)
Sun Welding Safe Co., 290 Easy St. No. 3, Simi Valley, CA 93065 / 805-584-6678; or 800-729-SAFE; (7233) FAX: 805-584-6169 sun_welding@sbcglobal.net www.sunweldingsafes.com
Sunny Hill Enterprises, Inc., W1790 Cty. HHH, Malone, WI 53049 / 920-418-3906; FAX: 920-795-4822 triggerguard@sunny-hill.com www.sunny-hill.com
Super 6 LLC, Gary Knopp, 3806 W. Lisbon Ave., Milwaukee, WI 53208 / 414-344-3343; FAX: 414-344-0304
Sure-Shot Game Calls, Inc., P.O. Box 816, 6835 Capitol, Groves, TX 77619 / 409-962-1636; FAX: 409-962-5465
Svon Corp., 2107 W. Blue Heron Blvd., Riviera Beach, FL 33404 / 508-881-8852
Swampfire Shop, The (See Peterson Gun Shop, Inc., A.W.)
Swann, D. J., 5 Orsova Close, Eltham North Vic., 3095 AUSTRALIA / 03-431-0323
Swanson, Mark, 975 Heap Avenue, Prescott, AZ 86301 / 928-778-4423
Swarovski Optik North America Ltd., 2 Slater Rd., Cranston, RI 02920 / 401-946-2220 or 800-426-3089; FAX: 401-946-2587
Swenson's 45 Shop, A. D., 3839 Ladera Vista Rd., Fallbrook, CA 92028-9431
Swift Bullet Co., P.O. Box 27, 201 Main St., Quinter, KS 67752 / 913-754-3959; FAX: 913-754-2359
Swift Instruments, 12105 W. Cedar Dr., Lakewood, CO 80228 / 877-697-9438; FAX: 800-382-6789 www.swift-sportoptics.com
Swift River Gunworks, 450 State St., Belchertown, MA 01007 / 413-323-4052
Szweda, Robert (See RMS Custom Gunsmithing)

T

T&S Industries, Inc., 1027 Skyview Dr., W. Carrollton, OH 45449 / 513-859-8414; FAX: 937-859-8404 keith.tomlinson@tandsshellcatcher.com www.tandsshellcatcher.com
T.F.C. S.p.A., Via G. Marconi 118, B, Villa Carcina 25069, ITALY / 030-881271; FAX: 030-881826
T.G. Faust, Inc., 544 Minor St., Reading, PA 19602 / 610-375-8549; FAX: 610-375-4488
T.K. Lee Co., 1282 Branchwater Ln., Birmingham, AL 35216 / 205-913-5222 odonmich@aol.com www.scopedot.com
T.W. Mench Gunsmith, Inc., 5703 S. 77th St., Ralston, NE 68127 guntools@cox.net http://llwww.members.cox.net/guntools
Tabler Marketing, 2554 Lincoln Blvd., Suite 555, Marina Del Rey, CA 90291 / 818-386-0373; FAX: 818-386-0373
Taconic Firearms Ltd., Perry Lane, P.O. Box 553, Cambridge, NY 12816 / 518-677-2704; FAX: 518-677-5974
Tactical Defense Institute, 2174 Bethany Ridges, West Union, OH 45693 / 937-544-7228; FAX: 937-544-2887 tdiohio@dragonbbs.com www.tdiohio.com
Talley, Dave, P.O. Box 369, Santee, SC 29142 / 803-854-5700 or 307-436-9315; FAX: 803-854-9315 talley@diretway www.talleyrings.com
Talon Industries Inc. (See Cobra Enterprises, Inc.)
Tanfoglio Fratelli S.r.l., via Valtrompia 39, 41, Brescia, ITALY / 011-39-030-8910361; FAX: 011-39-030-8910183 info@tanfoglio.it www.tanfoglio.it
Tanglefree Industries, 1261 Heavenly Dr., Martinez, CA 94553 / 800-982-4868; FAX: 510-825-3874
Tank's Rifle Shop, P.O. Box 474, Fremont, NE 68026-0474 / 402-727-1317; FAX: 402-721-9045 jtank@tanksrifleshop.com www.tanksrifleshop.com
Tanner (See U.S. Importer-Mandall Shooting Supplies, Inc.)
Taracorp Industries, Inc., 1200 Sixteenth St., Granite City, IL 62040 / 618-451-4400
Target Shooting, Inc., P.O. Box 773, Watertown, SD 57201 / 605-882-6955; FAX: 605-882-8840
Tar-Hunt Custom Rifles, Inc., 101 Dogtown Rd., Bloomsburg, PA 17815 / 570-784-6368; FAX: 570-389-9150 rfritz@tarhunt.com www.tar-hunt.com
Tarnhelm Supply Co., Inc., 431 High St., Boscawen, NH 03303 / 603-796-2551; FAX: 603-796-2918 info@tarnhelm.com www.tarnhelm.com
Tasco Sales, Inc., 2889 Commerce Pkwy., Miramar, FL 33025
Taurus Firearms, Inc., 16175 NW 49th Ave., Miami, FL 33014 / 305-624-1115; FAX: 305-623-7506
Taurus International Firearms (See U.S. Importer Taurus Firearms, Inc.)
Taurus S.A. Forjas, Avenida Do Forte 511, Porto Alegre, RS BRAZIL 91360 / 55-51-347-4050; FAX: 55-51-347-3065
Taylor & Robbins, P.O. Box 164, Rixford, PA 16745 / 814-966-3233
Taylor's & Co., Inc., 304 Lenoir Dr., Winchester, VA 22603 / 540-722-2017; FAX: 540-722-2018 info@taylorsfirearms.com www.taylorsfirearms.com
TCCI, P.O. Box 302, Phoenix, AZ 85001 / 602-237-3823; FAX: 602-237-3858
TCSR, 3998 Hoffman Rd., White Bear Lake, MN 55110-4626 / 800-328-5323; FAX: 612-429-0526
Techno Arms (See U.S. Importer- Auto-Ordnance Corp.)
Tecnolegno S.p.A., Via A. Locatelli, 6 10, 24019 Zogno, ITALY / 0345-55111; FAX: 0345-55155
Ted Blocker Holsters, 9438 SW Tigard St., Tigard, OR 97223 / 800-650-9742; FAX: 503-670-9692 www.tedblockerholsters.com
Tennessee Valley Mfg., 14 County Road 521, Corinth, MS 38834 / 601-286-5014 tvm@avsia.com www.avsia.com/tvm
Ten-Ring Precision, Inc., Alex B. Hamilton, 1449 Blue Crest Lane, San Antonio, TX 78232 / 210-494-3063; FAX: 210-494-3066
TEN-X Products Group, 1905 N. Main St., Suite 133, Cleburne, TX 76031-1305 / 972-243-4016 or 800-433-2225; FAX: 972-243-4112
Tepeco, P.O. Box 342, Friendswood, TX 77546 / 713-482-2702
Terry K. Kopp Professional Gunsmithing, 1209 South 13 Hwy., Lexington, MO 64067 / 816-529-1337 tkkopp@earthlink.net
Terry Theis-Engraver, Terry Theis, 21452 FM 2093, Harper, TX 78631 / 830-864-4438
Testing Systems, Inc., 220 Pegasus Ave., Northvale, NJ 07647
Tetra Gun Care, 8 Vreeland Rd., Florham Park, NJ 07932 / 973-443-0004; FAX: 973-443-0263
Tex Shoemaker & Sons, Inc., 714 W. Cienega Ave., San Dimas, CA 91773 / 909-592-2071; FAX: 909-592-2378 texshoemaker@texshoemaker.com www.texshoemaker.com
Texas Armory (See Bond Arms, Inc.)
Texas Platers Supply Co., 2453 W. Five Mile Parkway, Dallas, TX 75233 / 214-330-7168
Thad Rybka Custom Leather Equipment, 2050 Canoe Creek Rd., Springvale, AL 35146-6709
Thad Scott Fine Guns, Inc., P.O. Box 412, Indianola, MS 38751 / 601-887-5929
The Midwest Shooting School, 2550 Hwy. 23, Wrenshall, MN 55797 / 218-384-3670 patrick@midwestshootingschool.com www.midwestshootingschool.com
Theis, Terry. See: TERRY THEIS-ENGRAVER
Thiewes, George W., 14329 W. Parada Dr., Sun City West, AZ 85375
Things Unlimited, 235 N. Kimbau, Casper, WY 82601 / 307-234-5277
Thirion Gun Engraving, Denise, P.O. Box 408, Graton, CA 95444 / 707-829-1876
Thomas, Charles C., 2600 S. First St., Springfield, IL 62704 / 217-789-8980; FAX: 217-789-9130 books@ccthomas.com ccthomas.com
Thompson Bullet Lube Co., 6341 FM 2965, Wills Point, TX 75169 / 866-476-1500; FAX: 866-476-1500 thompsonbulletlube.com www.thompsonbulletlube.com
Thompson Precision, 110 Mary St., P.O. Box 251, Warren, IL 61087 / 815-745-3625
Thompson Target Technology, 4804 Sherman Church Ave. S.W., Canton, OH 44710 / 330-484-6480; FAX: 330-491-1087 www.thompsontarget.com
Thompson Tool Mount, 1550 Solomon Rd., Santa Maria, CA 93455 / 805-934-1281 ttm@pronet.net www.thompsontoolmount.com

MANUFACTURER'S DIRECTORY

Thompson/Center Arms, P.O. Box 5002, Rochester, NH 03866 / 603-332-2394; FAX: 603-332-5133 tech@tcarms.com www.tcarms.com
Thunder Ranch, 96747 Hwy. 140 East, Lakeview, OR 97630 / 541-947-4104; FAX: 541-947-4105 troregon@centurytel.net www.thunderranchinc.com
Tiger-Hunt Longrifle Gunstocks, Box 379, Beaverdale, PA 15921 / 814-472-5161 tigerhunt4@aol.com www.gunstockwood.com
Tikka (See U.S. Importer-Stoeger Industries)
Time Precision, 4 Nicholas Sq., New Milford, CT 06776-3506 / 860-350-8343; FAX: 860-350-6343 timeprecision@aol.com www.benchrest.com/timeprecision
Tinks & Ben Lee Hunting Products (See Wellington Outdoors)
Tink's Safariland Hunting Corp., P.O. Box 244, 1140 Monticello Rd., Madison, GA 30650 / 706-342-4915; FAX: 706-342-7568
Tippman Sports, LLC, 2955 Adams Center Rd., Fort Wayne, IN 46803 / 260-749-6022; FAX: 260-441-8504 www.tippmann.com
Tirelli, Snc Di Tirelli Primo E.C., Via Matteotti No. 359, Gardone V.T. Brescia, ITALY / 0039-030-8912819; FAX: 0039-030-832240 tirelli@tirelli.it www.tirelli.it
TM Stockworks, 6355 Maplecrest Rd., Fort Wayne, IN 46835 / 219-485-5389
Tom Forrest, Inc., P.O. Box 326, Lakeside, CA 92040 / 619-561-5800; FAX: 888-GUN-CLIP info@gunmag.com www.gunmags.com
Tombstone Smoken' Deals, 4038 E. Taro Ln., Phoenix, AZ 85050
Tom's Gun Repair, Thomas G. Ivanoff, 76-6 Rt. Southfork Rd., Cody, WY 82414 / 307-587-6949
Tom's Gunshop, 3601 Central Ave., Hot Springs, AR 71913 / 501-624-3856
Tonoloway Tack Drives, HCR 81, Box 100, Needmore, PA 17238
Torel, Inc./Tandy Brands Outdoors/AA & E, 208 Industrial Loop, Yoakum, TX 77995 / 361-293-6366; FAX: 361-293-9127
TOZ (See U.S. Importer-Nygord Precision Products, Inc.)
Track of the Wolf, Inc., 18308 Joplin St. NW, Elk River, MN 55330-1773 / 763-633-2500; FAX: 763-633-2550 sales@trackofthewolf.com www.trackofthewolf.com
Traditions Performance Firearms, P.O. Box 776, 1375 Boston Post Rd., Old Saybrook, CT 06475 / 860-388-4656; FAX: 860-388-4657 info@traditionsfirearms.com www.traditionsfirearms.com
Trafalgar Square, P.O. Box 257, N. Pomfret, VT 05053 / 802-457-1911
Trail Visions, 5800 N. Ames Terrace, Glendale, WI 53209 / 414-228-1328
Treebone Carving, P.O. Box 551, Cimarron, NJ 87714 / 505-376-2145 treebonecarving.com
Treemaster, P.O. Box 247, Guntersville, AL 35976 / 205-878-3597
Trevallion Gunstocks, 9 Old Mountain Rd., Cape Neddick, ME 03902 / 207-361-1130
Trigger Lock Division / Central Specialties Ltd., 220-D Exchange Dr., Crystal Lake, IL 60014 / 847-639-3900; FAX: 847-639-3972
Trijicon, Inc., 49385 Shafer Ave., P.O. Box 930059, Wixom, MI 48393-0059 / 248-960-7700; or 800-338-0563; FAX: 248-960-7725 info@trijicon.com www.trijicon.com
Trilby Sport Shop, 1623 Hagley Rd., Toledo, OH 43612-2024 / 419-472-6222
Trilux, Inc., P.O. Box 24608, Winston-Salem, NC 27114 / 910-659-9438; FAX: 910-768-7720
Trinidad St. Jr. Col. Gunsmith Dept., 600 Prospect St., Trinidad, CO 81082 / 719-846-5631; FAX: 719-846-5667
Tripes, George. See: EURO-IMPORTS
Triple-K Mfg. Co., Inc., 2222 Commercial St., San Diego, CA 92113 / 619-232-2066; FAX: 619-232-7675 sales@triplek.com www.triplek.com
Tristar Sporting Arms, Ltd., 1816 Linn St. #16, N. Kansas City, MO 64116-3627 / 816-421-1400; FAX: 816-421-4182 tristarsporting@sbcglobal.net www.tristarsportingarms
Trius Traps, Inc., P.O. Box 25, 221 S. Miami Ave., Cleves, OH 45002 / 513-941-5682; FAX: 513-941-7970 triustraps@fuse.net www.triustraps.com
Trooper Walsh, 2393 N. Edgewood St., Arlington, VA 22207
Trotman, Ken, P. O. Box 505, Huntingdon, PE 29 2XW ENGLAND / 01480 454292; FAX: 01480 384651 enquiries@kentrotman.com www.kentrotman.com
Tru-Balance Knife Co., P.O. Box 140555, Grand Rapids, MI 49514 / 616-647-1215
True Flight Bullet Co., 5581 Roosevelt St., Whitehall, PA 18052 / 610-262-7630; FAX: 610-262-7806
Truglo, Inc., P.O. Box 1612, McKinna, TX 75070 / 972-774-0300; FAX: 972-774-0323 www.truglosights.com
Trulock Tool, P.O. Box 530, Whigham, GA 31797 / 229-762-4678; FAX: 229-762-4050 trulockchokes@hotmail.com trulockchokes.com
Tru-Nord Compass, 1504 Erick Lane, Brainerd, MN 56401 / 218-829-2870; FAX: 218-829-2870 www.trunord.com
Tru-Square Metal Products, Inc., 640 First St. SW, P.O. Box 585, Auburn, WA 98071 / 253-833-2310 or 800-225-1017; FAX: 253-833-2349 t-tumbler@qwest.net
Tucker, James C., P.O. Box 366, Medford, OR 97501 / 541-664-9160 jctstocker@yahoo.com
Tucson Mold, Inc., 930 S. Plumer Ave., Tucson, AZ 85719 / 520-792-1075; FAX: 520-792-1075
Turk's Head Productions, Mustafa Bilal, 13545 Erickson Pl. NE, Seattle, WA 98125-3794 / 206-782-4164; FAX: 206-783-5677 info@turkshead.com www.turkshead.com
Turnbull Restoration, Doug, 6680 Rts. 5 & 20, P.O. Box 471, Bloomfield, NY 14469 / 585-657-6338; FAX: 585-657-7743 info@turnbullrestoration.com www.turnbullrestoration.com
Tuttle, Dale, 4046 Russell Rd., Muskegon, MI 49445 / 616-766-2250

U

U.S. Importer-Wm. Larkin Moore, 8430 E. Raintree Ste. B-7, Scottsdale, AZ 85260
U.S. Optics, A Division of Zeitz Optics U.S.A., 5900 Dale St., Buena Park, CA 90621 / 714-994-4901; FAX: 714-994-4904 www.usoptics.com
U.S. Repeating Arms Co., Inc., 275 Winchester Ave., Morgan, UT 84050-9333 / 801-876-3440; FAX: 801-876-3737 www.winchester-guns.com
U.S. Tactical Systems (See Keng's Firearms Specialty, Inc.)
Ugartechea S. A., Ignacio, Chonta 26, Eibar, SPAIN / 43-121257; FAX: 43-121669
Ultra Dot Distribution, P.O. Box 362, 6304 Riverside Dr., Yankeetown, FL 34498 / 352-447-2255; FAX: 352-447-2266
Ultralux (See U.S. Importer-Keng's Firearms Specialty, Inc.)
Umarex USA, 6007 S. 29th St., Fort Smith, AR 72908 / 479-646-4210; FAX: 479-646-4206 info@umarexusa.com www.umarexusa.com
Uncle Bud's, HCR 81, Box 100, Needmore, PA 17238 / 717-294-6000; FAX: 717-294-6005
Uncle Mike's (See Michaels of Oregon, Co.)
Unertl Ordance Co., Inc., 2900 S. Highland Dr., Bldg. 19, Unit B, Las Vegas, NV 89109 / 702-369-4092; FAX: 702-369-4571 info@unertloptics.com www.unertloptics.com
UniTec, 1250 Bedford SW, Canton, OH 44710 / 216-452-4017
United Binocular Co., 9043 S. Western Ave., Chicago, IL 60620
United Cutlery Corp., 1425 United Blvd., Sevierville, TN 37876 / 865-428-2532 or 800-548-0835; FAX: 865-428-2267 www.unitedcutlery.com
United States Products Co., 518 Melwood Ave., Pittsburgh, PA 15213-1136 / 412-621-2130; FAX: 412-621-8740 sales@uspborepaste.com www.uspborepaste.com
Universal Sports, P.O. Box 532, Vincennes, IN 47591 / 812-882-8680; FAX: 812-882-8680
Upper Missouri Trading Co., P.O. Box 100, 304 Harold St., Crofton, NE 68730-0100 / 402-388-4844 www.uppermotradingco.com
USAC, 4500-15th St. East, Tacoma, WA 98424 / 206-922-7589
Uselton/Arms, Inc., 842 Conference Dr., Goodlettsville, TN 37072 / 615-851-4919
Utica Cutlery Co., 820 Noyes St., Utica, NY 13503 / 315-733-4663; FAX: 315-733-6602

V

V. H. Blackinton & Co., Inc., 221 John L. Dietsch, Attleboro Falls, MA 02763-0300 / 508-699-4436; FAX: 508-695-5349
Valdada Enterprises, P.O. Box 773122, 31733 County Road 35, Steamboat Springs, CO 80477 / 970-879-2983; FAX: 970-879-0851 www.valdada.com
Valtro USA, Inc., 1281 Andersen Dr., San Rafael, CA 94901 / 415-256-2575; FAX: 415-256-2576
VAM Distribution Co. LLC, 1141-B Mechanicsburg Rd., Wooster, OH 44691 www.rex10.com
Van Gorden & Son Inc., C. S., 1815 Main St., Bloomer, WI 54724 / 715-568-2612
Van Horn, Gil, P.O. Box 207, Llano, CA 93544
Van Patten, J. W., 214 Christian Hill Rd., Milford, PA 18337 / 717-296-7069
Vann Custom Bullets, 2766 N. Willowside Way, Meridian, ID 83642
Varmint Masters, LLC, Rick Vecqueray, P.O. Box 6724, Bend, OR 97708 / 541-318-7306; FAX: 541-318-7306 varmintmasters@bendcable.com www.varmintmasters.net
Vecqueray, Rick. See: VARMINT MASTERS, LLC
Vector Arms, Inc., 270 W. 500 N., North Salt Lake, UT 84054 / 801-295-1917; FAX: 801-295-9316 vectorarms@bbscmail.com www.vectorarms.com
Vega Tool Co., c/o T. R. Ross, 4865 Tanglewood Ct., Boulder, CO 80301 / 303-530-0174 clanlaird@aol.com www.vegatool.com
Venco Industries, Inc. (See Shooter's Choice Gun Care)
Venus Industries, P.O. Box 246, Sialkot-1, PAKISTAN FAX: 92 432 85579
Verney-Carron, 54 Boulevard Thiers-B.P. 72, 42002 St. Etienne Cedex 1, St. Etienne Cedex 1, FRANCE / 33-477791500; FAX: 33-477790702 email@verney- carron.com www.verney-carron.com
Vest, John, 1923 NE 7th St., Redmond, OR 97756 / 541-923-8898
VibraShine, Inc., P.O. Box 577, Taylorsville, MS 39168 / 601-785-9854; FAX: 601-785-9874 rdbeke@vibrashine.com www.vibrashine.com
Vibra-Tek Co., 1844 Arroya Rd., Colorado Springs, CO 80906 / 719-634-8611; FAX: 719-634-6886
Victory Ammunition, P.O. Box 1022, Milford, PA 18337 / 717-296-5768; FAX: 717-296-9298
Vihtavuori Oy, FIN-41330 Vihtavuori, FINLAND, / 358-41-3779211; FAX: 358-41-3771643
Vihtavuori Oy/Kaltron-Pettibone, 1241 Ellis St., Bensenville, IL 60106 / 708-350-1116; FAX: 708-350-1606
Village Restorations & Consulting, Inc., P.O. Box 569, Claysburg, PA 16625 / 814-239-8200; FAX: 814-239-2165 www.villagerestoration@yahoo.com
Vincent's Shop, 210 Antoinette, Fairbanks, AK 99701
Viper Bullet and Brass Works, 11 Brock St., Box 582, Norwich, ON N0J 1P0 CANADA
Viramontez Engraving, Ray Viramontez, 601 Springfield Dr., Albany, GA 31721 / 229-432-9683 sgtvira@aol.com
Viramontez, Ray. See: VIRAMONTEZ ENGRAVING
Virgin Valley Custom Guns, 450 E 800 N. #20, Hurricane, UT 84737 / 435-635-8941; FAX: 435-635-8943 vvcguns@infowest.com www.virginvalleyguns.com
Vitt/Boos, 1195 Buck Hill Rd., Townshend, VT 05353 / 802-365-9232
Voere-KGH GmbH, Untere Sparchen 56, A-6330 Kufstein, Tirol, AUSTRIA / 0043-5372-62547; FAX: 0043-5372-65752 voere@aon.com www.voere.com
Volquartsen Custom Ltd., 24276 240th Street, P.O. Box 397, Carroll, IA 51401 / 712-792-4238; FAX: 712-792-2542 info@volquartsen.com www.volquartsen.com
Vorhes, David, 3042 Beecham St., Napa, CA 94558 / 707-226-9116; FAX: 707-253-7334
VSP Publishers (See Heritage/VSP Gun Books), P.O. Box 887, McCall, ID 83638 / 208-634-4104; FAX: 208-634-3101 heritage@gunbooks.com www.gunbooks.com
VTI Gun Parts, P.O. Box 509, Lakeville, CT 06039 / 860-435-8068; FAX: 860-435-8146 mail@vtigunparts.com www.vtigunparts.com

W

W. Square Enterprises, 9826 Sagedale Dr., Houston, TX 77089 / 281-484-0935; FAX: 281-464-9940 lfdw@pdq.net www.loadammo.com
W. Waller & Son, Inc., 52 Coventry Dr., Sunapee, NH 03782 / 603-763-3320 or 800-874-2247 FAX: 603-763-3225; waller@wallerandson.com www.wallerandson.com
W.B. Niemi Engineering, Box 126 Center Road, Greensboro, VT 05841 / 802-533-7180 or 802-533-7141
W.C. Wolff Co., P.O. Box 458, Newtown Square, PA 19073 / 610-359-9600 or 800-545-0077 mail@gunsprings.com www.gunsprings.com
W.E. Birdsong & Assoc., 1435 Monterey Rd., Florence, MS 39073-9748 / 601-366-8270
W.E. Brownell Checkering Tools, 9390 Twin Mountain Cir., San Diego, CA 92126 / 858-695-2479; FAX: 858-695-2479
W.J. Riebe Co., 3434 Tucker Rd., Boise, ID 83703
W.R. Case & Sons Cutlery Co., Owens Way, Bradford, PA 16701 / 814-368-4123 or 800-523-6350; FAX: 814-368-1736 jsullivan@wrcase.com www.wrcase.com
Wagoner, Vernon G., 2325 E. Encanto St., Mesa, AZ 85213-5917 / 480-835-1307
Waldron, Herman, Box 475, 80 N. 17th St., Pomeroy, WA 99347 / 509-843-1404
Walls Industries, Inc., P.O. Box 98, 1905 N. Main, Cleburne, TX 76033 / 817-645-4366; FAX: 817-645-7946 www.wallsoutdoors.com
Walters Industries, 6226 Park Lane, Dallas, TX 75225 / 214-691-6973

MANUFACTURER'S DIRECTORY

Walters, John. See: WALTERS WADS
Walters Wads, John Walters, 500 N. Avery Dr., Moore, OK 73160 / 405-799-0376; FAX: 405-799-7727 www.tinwadman@cs.com
Walther America, P.O. Box 22, Springfield, MA 01102 / 413-747-3443 www.walther-usa.com
Walther GmbH, Carl, B.P. 4325, D-89033 Ulm, GERMANY
Walt's Custom Leather, Walt Whinnery, 1947 Meadow Creek Dr., Louisville, KY 40218 / 502-458-4361
WAMCO-New Mexico, P.O. Box 205, Peralta, NM 87042-0205 / 505-869-0826
Ward & Van Valkenburg, 114 32nd Ave. N., Fargo, ND 58102 / 701-232-2351
Ward Machine, 5620 Lexington Rd., Corpus Christi, TX 78412 / 512-992-1221
Wardell Precision, P.O. Box 391, Clyde, TX 79510-0391 / 325-893-3763 fwardell@valornet.com
Washita Mountain Whetstone Co., 418 Hilltop Rd., Pearcy, AR 71964 / 501-767-1616; FAX: 501-767-9598 www.@hsnp.com
Wasmundt, Jim. See: J.W. WASMUNDT-GUNSMITH
Watson Bros., 39 Redcross Way, London Bridge SE1 1H6, London, ENGLAND FAX: 44-171-403-336
Watson Bullets, 231 Allies Pass, Frostproof, FL 33843 / 863-635-7948 cbestbullet@aol.com
Wayne Specialty Services, 260 Waterford Drive, Florissant, MO 63033 / 413-831-7083
WD-40 Co., 1061 Cudahy Pl., San Diego, CA 92110 / 619-275-1400; FAX: 619-275-5823
Weatherby, Inc., 1605 Commerce Way, Paso Robles, CA 93446 / 805-227-2600; FAX: 805-237-0427 www.weatherby.com
Weaver Products ATK, P.O. Box 39, Onalaska, WI 54650 / 800-648-9624 or 608-781-5800; FAX: 608-781-0368
Weaver Scope Repair Service, 1121 Larry Mahan Dr., Suite B, El Paso, TX 79925 / 915-593-1005 frank@weaver-scope-repair.com www.weaver-scope-repair.com
Webb, Bill, 6504 North Bellefontaine, Kansas City, MO 64119 / 816-453-7431
Weber & Markin Custom Gunsmiths, 4-1691 Powick Rd., Kelowna, BC V1X 4L1 CANADA / 250-762-7575; FAX: 250-861-3655 www.weberandmarkinguns.com
Webley Limited, Universe House Planetary Rd., Key Industrial Park, Willenhall, WV13 3YA ENGLAND / 011-01902-722144; FAX: 011-1902-722880 sales@webley.co.uk
Webster Scale Mfg. Co., P.O. Box 188, Sebring, FL 33870 / 813-385-6362
Weigand Combat Handguns, Inc., 1057 South Main Rd., Mountain Top, PA 18707 / 570-868-8358; FAX: 570-868-5218 sales@jackweigand.com www.jackweigand.com
Weihrauch KG, Hermann, Industriestrasse 11, 8744 Mellrichstadt, Mellrichstadt, GERMANY
Welch, Sam. See: SAM WELCH GUN ENGRAVING
Wellington Outdoors, P.O. Box 244, 1140 Monticello Rd., Madison, GA 30650 / 706-342-4915; FAX: 706-342-7568
Wells Creek Knife & Gun Works, 32956 State Hwy. 38, Scottsburg, OR 97473 / 541-587-4202; FAX: 541-587-4223
Wells, Margaret. See: WELLS SPORT STORE
Wells, Rachel. See: WELLS SPORT STORE
Wells Sport Store, Margaret R Wells, 110 N. Summit St., Prescott, AZ 86301 / 928-445-3655 www.wellssportstore@cableone.net
Wells Sport Store, Rachel Wells, 110 N. Summit St., Prescott, AZ 86301 / 928-445-3655 rachelwells@cableone.net www.cableone.net
Welsh, Bud. See: HIGH PRECISION
Wenger North America/Precise Int'l., 15 Corporate Dr., Orangeburg, NY 10962 / 800-431-2996; FAX: 914-425-4700
Wenig Custom Gunstocks, 103 N. Market St., P.O. Box 249, Lincoln, MO 65338 / 660-547-3334; FAX: 660-547-2881 gustock@wenig.com www.wenig.com
Werth, T. See: DBA WERTH SERVICES
Wescombe, Bill (See North Star West)
Wessinger Custom Guns & Engraving, 268 Limestone Rd., Chapin, SC 29036 / 803-345-5677
West, Jack L., 1220 W. Fifth, P.O. Box 427, Arlington, OR 97812
Western Cutlery (See Camillus Cutlery Co.)
Western Mfg. Co., 550 Valencia School Rd., Aptos, CA 95003 / 831-688-5884 lotsabears@eathlink.net
Western Missouri Shooters Alliance, P.O. Box 11144, Kansas City, MO 64119 / 816-597-3950; FAX: 816-229-7350
Western Nevada West Coast Bullets, P.O. Box 2270, Dayton, NV 89403-2270 / 702-246-3941; FAX: 702-246-0836
Westley Richards & Co. Ltd., 40 Grange Rd., Birmingham, ENGLAND / 010-214722953; FAX: 010-214141138 sales@westleyrichards.com www.westleyrichards.com
Westley Richards Agency USA (See U.S. Importer
Westwind Rifles, Inc., David S. Sullivan, P.O. Box 261, 640 Briggs St., Erie, CO 80516 / 303-828-3823 westwindrifles@comcast.net
Weyer International, 2740 Nebraska Ave., Toledo, OH 43607 / 419-534-2020; FAX: 419-534-2697
Whinnery, Walt (See Walt's Custom Leather)
White Barn Wor, 431 County Road, Broadlands, IL 61816
White Pine Photographic Services, Hwy. 60, General Delivery, Wilno, ON K0J 2N0 CANADA / 613-756-3452
White Rock Tool & Die, 6400 N. Brighton Ave., Kansas City, MO 64119 / 816-454-0478
Whitestone Lumber Corp., 148-02 14th Ave., Whitestone, NY 11357 / 718-746-4400; FAX: 718-767-1748 whstco@aol.com
Wichita Arms, Inc., 923 E. Gilbert, Wichita, KS 67211 / 316-265-0661; FAX: 316-265-0760 sales@wichitaarms.com www.wichitaarms.com
Wick, David E., 1504 Michigan Ave., Columbus, IN 47201 / 812-376-6960
Widener's Reloading & Shooting Supply, Inc., P.O. Box 3009 CRS, Johnson City, TN 37602 / 615-282-6786; FAX: 615-282-6651
Wideview Scope Mount Corp., 13535 S. Hwy. 16, Rapid City, SD 57702 / 605-341-3220; FAX: 605-341-9142 wvdon@rapidnet.com www.wideviewscopemount.com
Wiebe, Duane, 1111 157th St. Ct. E., Tacoma, WA 98445 / 253-535-0066; FAX: 253-535-0066 duane@directcom.net
Wiest, Marie. See: GUNCRAFT SPORTS, INC.
Wilcox All-Pro Tools & Supply, 4880 147th St., Montezuma, IA 50171 / 515-623-3138; FAX: 515-623-3104
Wilcox Industries Corp., Robert F. Guarasi, 53 Durham St., Portsmouth, NH 03801 / 603-431-1331; FAX: 603-431-1221
Wild Bill's Originals, P.O. Box 13037, Burton, WA 98013 / 206-463-5738; FAX: 206-465-5925 billcleaver@centurytel.net billcleaver@centurytel.net
Wild West Guns, 7100 Homer Dr., Anchorage, AK 99518 / 800-992-4570 or 907-344-4500; FAX: 907-344-4005 wwguns@ak.net www.wildwestguns.alaska.net
Wilderness Sound Products Ltd., 4015 Main St. A, Springfield, OR 97478
Wildey F. A., Inc., 45 Angevin Rd., Warren, CT 06754-1818 / 860-355-9000; FAX: 860-354-7759 wildeyfa@optonline.net www.wildeyguns.com
Will-Burt Co., 169 S. Main, Orrville, OH 44667
William E. Phillips Firearms, 38 Avondale Rd., Wigston, Leicester, ENGLAND / 0116 2886334; FAX: 0116 2810644 william.phillips2@tesco.net
William Powell Agency, 22 Circle Dr., Bellmore, NY 11710 / 516-679-1158
Williams Gun Sight Co., 7389 Lapeer Rd., Box 329, Davison, MI 48423 / 810-653-2131 or 800-530-9028; FAX: 810-658-2140 williamsgunsight.com
Williams Mfg. of Oregon, 110 East B St., Drain, OR 97435 / 503-836-7461; FAX: 503-836-7245
Williams Shootin' Iron Service, The Lynx-Line, Rt. 2 Box 223A, Mountain Grove, MO 65711 / 417-948-0902; FAX: 417-948-0902
Williamson Precision Gunsmithing, 117 W. Pipeline, Hurst, TX 76053 / 817-285-0064; FAX: 817-280-0044
Willow Bend, P.O. Box 203, Chelmsford, MA 01824 / 978-256-8508; FAX: 978-256-8508
Wilsom Combat, 2234 CR 719, Berryville, AR 72616-4573 / 800-955-4856; FAX: 870-545-3310 info@wilsoncombat.com www.wilsoncombat.com
Wilson Arms Co., The, 63 Leetes Island Rd., Branford, CT 06405 / 203-488-7297; FAX: 203-488-0135
Wilson Case, Inc., P.O. Box 1106, Hastings, NE 68902-1106 / 800-322-5493; FAX: 402-463-5276 sales@wilsoncase.com www.wilsoncase.com
Wilson Combat, 2234 CR 719, Berryville, AR 72616-4573 / 800-955-4856
Winchester Div. Olin Corp., 427 N. Shamrock, E. Alton, IL 62024 / 618-258-3566; FAX: 618-258-3599
Winchester Sutler, Inc., The, 270 Shadow Brook Lane, Winchester, VA 22603 / 540-888-3595; FAX: 540-888-4632
Windish, Jim, 2510 Dawn Dr., Alexandria, VA 22306 / 703-765-1994
Winfield Galleries LLC, 748 Hanley Industrial Ct., St. Louis, MO 63144 / 314-645-7636; FAX: 314-781-0224 info@winfieldgalleries.com www.winfieldgalleries.com
Winter, Robert M., P.O. Box 484, 42975-287th St., Menno, SD 57045 / 605-387-5322
Wise Custom Guns, 1402 Blanco Rd., San Antonio, TX 78212-2716 / 210-828-3388
Wise Guns, Dale, 1402 Blanco Rd., San Antonio, TX 78212 / 210-734-9999
Wisners, Inc., P.O. Box 58, Adna, WA 98522 / 360-748-4590; FAX: 360-748-6028 parts@wisnersinc.com www.wisnersinc.com
Wolf Performance Ammunition, 2201 E. Winston Rd., Ste. K, Anaheim, CA 92806-5537 / 702-837-8506; FAX: 702-837-9250
Wolfe Publishing Co., 2625 Stearman Rd., Ste. A, Prescott, AZ 86301 / 928-445-7810 or 800-899-7810; FAX: 928-778-5124 wolfepub@riflemag.com www.riflemagazine.com
Wolverine Footwear Group, 9341 Courtland Dr. NE, Rockford, MI 49351 / 616-866-5500; FAX: 616-866-5658
Woodleigh (See Huntington Die Specialties)
Woods Wise Products, P.O. Box 681552, Franklin, TN 37068 / 800-735-8182; FAX: 615-726-2637
Woodstream, P.O. Box 327, Lititz, PA 17543 / 717-626-2125; FAX: 717-626-1912
Woodworker's Supply, 1108 North Glenn Rd., Casper, WY 82601 / 307-237-5354
Woolrich, Inc., Mill St., Woolrich, PA 17701 / 800-995-1299; FAX: 717-769-6234/6259
World of Targets (See Birchwood Casey)
World Trek, Inc., 7170 Turkey Creek Rd., Pueblo, CO 81007-1046 / 719-546-2121; FAX: 719-543-6886
Wright's Gunstock Blanks, 8540 SE Kane Rd., Gresham, OR 97080 / 503-666-1705 doyal@wrightsguns.com www.wrightsguns.com
WTA Manufacturing, P.O. Box 164, Kit Carson, CO 80825 / 719-962-3570 or 719-962-3570 wta@rebeltec.net http://www.members.aol.com/ductman249/wta.html
Wyant Bullets, Gen. Del., Swan Lake, MT 59911
Wyoming Custom Bullets, 1626 21st St., Cody, WY 82414
Wyoming Knife Corp., 101 Commerce Dr., Fort Collins, CO 80524 / 303-224-3454

X

XS Sight Systems, 2401 Ludelle St., Fort Worth, TX 76105 / 888-744-4880; FAX: 800-734-7939
X-Spand Target Systems, 26-10th St. SE, Medicine Hat, AB T1A 1P7 CANADA / 403-526-7997; FAX: 403-528-2362

Y

Yankee Gunsmith "Just Glocks", 2901 Deer Flat Dr., Copperas Cove, TX 76522 / 817-547-8433; FAX: 254-547-8887 ed@justglocks.com www.justglocks.com
Yavapai College, 1100 E. Sheldon St., Prescott, AZ 86301 / 520-776-2353; FAX: 520-776-2355
Yavapai Firearms Academy Ltd., P.O. Box 27290, Prescott Valley, AZ 86312 / 928-772-8262; FAX: 928-772-0062 info@yfainc.com www.yfainc.com
Yearout, Lewis E. (See Montana Outfitters)
York M-1 Conversion, 12145 Mill Creek Run, Plantersville, TX 77363 / 936-894-2397; FAX: 936-894-2397 bmf25years@aol.com
Young Country Arms, William, 1409 Kuehner Dr. #13, Simi Valley, CA 93063-4478

Z

Zabala Hermanos S.A., P.O. Box 97, Elbar Lasao, 6, Elgueta, Guipuzcoa, 20600 SPAIN / 34-943-768076; FAX: 34-943-768201 imanol@zabalahermanos.com www.zabalabermanos.com
Zander's Sporting Goods, 7525 Hwy. 154 West, Baldwin, IL 62217-9706 / 800-851-4373; FAX: 618-785-2320
Zanotti Armor, Inc., 123 W. Lone Tree Rd., Cedar Falls, IA 50613 / 319-232-9650 www.zanottiarmor.com
Zeeryp, Russ, 1601 Foard Dr., Lynn Ross Manor, Morristown, TN 37814 / 615-586-2357
Zero Ammunition Co., Inc., 1601 22nd St. SE, P.O. Box 1188, Cullman, AL 35056-1188 / 800-545-9376; FAX: 205-739-4683 zerobulletco@aoz.com www.zerobullets.com
Ziegel Engineering, 1390 E. Bunnett St. "F", Signal Hill, CA 90755 / 562-596-9481; FAX: 562-598-4734 ziegel@aol.com www.ziegeleng.com
Zim's, Inc., 4370 S. 3rd West, Salt Lake City, UT 84107 / 801-268-2505
Z-M Weapons, 203 South St., Bernardston, MA 01337 / 413-648-9501; FAX: 413-648-0219

NUMBERS

100 Straight Products, Inc., P.O. Box 6148, Omaha, NE 68106 / 402-556-1055; FAX: 402-556-1055
3-Ten Corp., P.O. Box 269, Feeding Hills, MA 01030 / 413-789-2086; FAX: 413-789-1549 www.3-ten.com